COPINGER AND SKONE JAMES

on

COPYRIGHT

21 Jan 1999

From BBC Scotland

to

The Law Workshop Library.

Hoping you understand this
letter than I did.

Alistair G Bonnington
SOLICITOR
BBC SCOTLAND.

AUSTRALIA
The Law Book Company Ltd.
Sydney : Brisbane : Melbourne : Perth

CANADA
The Carswell Company Ltd.
Agincourt, Ontario

INDIA
N.M. Tripathi Private Ltd.
Calcutta and Delhi

M.P.P. House
Bangalore
and
Universal Book Traders
New Delhi

ISRAEL
Steimatzky's Agency Ltd.
Jerusalem : Tel Aviv : Haifa

PAKISTAN
Pakistan Law House
Karachi

COPINGER AND SKONE JAMES

ON

COPYRIGHT

INCLUDING

INTERNATIONAL COPYRIGHT

WITH THE STATUTES, ORDERS

CONVENTIONS AND AGREEMENTS THERETO RELATING

AND

PRECEDENTS AND COURT FORMS

ALSO RELATED FORMS OF PROTECTION

THIRTEENTH EDITION

BY

E. P. SKONE JAMES, M.A.
Bencher of the Middle Temple

SIR JOHN MUMMERY, M.A., B.C.L.
One of Her Majesty's Judges of the High Court
Bencher of Gray's Inn
An Honorary Fellow of Pembroke College, Oxford

J. E. RAYNER JAMES, M.A., LL.B.
One of Her Majesty's Counsel

K. M. GARNETT, M.A.
One of Her Majesty's Counsel

Copyright Law of the U.S.A.
DAVID NIMMER, A.B. (STANFORD), J.D. (YALE)
Of Counsel
Irell & Manella, Los Angeles, California

Taxation
STEPHEN SILMAN, M.A.
of the Middle Temple, Barrister

Industrial Designs
ROBERT SKONE JAMES, M.A.
Chartered Patent Agent
Gill Jennings & Every, London

LONDON
Sweet & Maxwell
1991

First edition by W.A. Copinger 1870
Second edition by W.A. Copinger 1881
Third edition by W.A. Copinger 1893
Fourth edition by J.M. Easton 1904
Fifth edition by J.M. Easton 1915
Sixth edition by F.E. Skone James 1927
Seventh edition by F.E. Skone James 1936
Eighth edition by F.E. Skone James 1948
Ninth edition by F.E. & E.P. Skone James 1958
Tenth edition by E.P. Skone James 1965
Eleventh edition by E.P. Skone James 1971
Second edition by E.P. Skone James 1977
Twelfth edition by E.P. Skone James, John F. Mummery
    and J.E. Rayner James 1980
Thirteenth edition by E.P. Skone James, John F. Mummer,
    J.E. Rayner James and K.M. Garnett 1991

Published in 1991 by
Sweet & Maxwell Limited of
South Quay Plaza, 183 Marsh Wall, London E14 9FT
Computerset by Promenade Graphics Ltd., Cheltenham
and printed in Great Britain by
The Bath Press,
Bath, Avon

British Library Cataloguing in Publication Data
Copinger, W.A. (Walter Arthur)
Copinger and Skone James on copyright.–13th ed.
1. Great Britain. Copyright. Law
I. Title II. Skone, James E.P. (Edward Purcell)
344.106482

ISBN 0–421–39200–2

Acknowledgment:
statutory material used
in this publication is
Crown copyright

PREFACE

When the Twelfth Edition of this book was published, in 1980, it was mentioned, in the Preface, that the preparation of that edition had been delayed following the publication, in March 1977, of the Report of the Committee to consider the Law on Copyright and Designs under the chairmanship of the Honourable Mr Justice Whitford, in anticipation that new legislation might follow fairly promptly thereafter. In fact this did not happen, and it was not until the 15 November 1988 that the Copyright, Designs and Patents Act 1988 received the Royal Assent. Even then its copyright provisions were not brought into force until August 1, 1989 and the remaining provisions have been brought into force from time to time thereafter.

The 1988 Act repealed the whole of the Copyright Act 1956 and of the Copyright (Computer Software) Amendment Act 1985, but did not repeal section 15 of the Copyright Act 1911. It also repealed the whole of the Performers' Protection Acts 1958, 1963 and 1972. The 1988 Act, as its name suggests, deals with a large number of other matters, one of the most important, in the copyright field, being the introduction of a design right. Further, since the 1988 Act has preserved protection under the Registered Designs Act 1949 (notwithstanding the recommendation of the Whitford Committee that it should be repealed), there are now three possible types of protection available in this field, namely copyright, design right and registered designs. Indeed, the 1988 Act also provides for certain persons, who may not be copyright owners, to have the same rights and remedies as copyright owners, in certain circumstances: sections 296 and 298. Other matters of importance in this field are the abolition, by the 1988 Act, of the compulsory licence to make records of music (section 8, 1956 Act), the non-expert test in relation to artistic infringement (section 9 (8), 1956 Act) and conversion damages (section 18, 1956 Act). Further, almost all perpetual copyrights have been abolished by the 1988 Act, as have those of the universities and colleges. Notwithstanding this, the 1988 Act has created a new perpetual non-copyright right for the Hospital for Sick Children, Great Ormond Street, to receive royalties in respect of the exploitation of the play "Peter Pan" by Sir James Matthew Barrie, the copyright in which expired on 31 December 1987.

Related matters dealt with by the 1988 Act are performers' rights and persons having recording rights, and moral rights. Article 6 bis, imposing an obligation to provide a paternity right and an integrity right, was introduced into the Berne Convention by the Rome revision (1928). But, although before the 1988 Act there might have been some protection at common law and under section 43 of the 1956 Act, it has taken this country some 60 years to provide for moral rights by statute.

Although the 1988 Act to a large extent repeats and expands the effect of the 1956 Act, it does not repeat the format of that Act. That is to say, whereas under the 1956 Act separate sections dealt with individual works or subject matters, the 1988 Act starts by classing them all as works and then, in separate sections, deals with individual matters such as authorship, ownership, duration and so on. As a result, the structure of this book has had to be completely reorganised and, in large parts, rewritten to conform with the structure of the 1988 Act. Because of this, and to assist the reader, we have provided mini indices at the start of each Chapter and Appendix. There are now Chapters dealing with moral rights, performers' rights and persons having recording rights, and design right, and Precedents and Court Forms have been included in a separate Appendix. Many of the provisions of the 1988 Act require the making of Orders in Council, and all Orders in Council that have been made at the time of writing have been referred to. The relevant parts of the 1988 Act and most of such Orders in Council are printed in this book, as are the 1956 Act and the 1911 Act, with Comparative Tables. Finally, apart from the 1988 Act, this book has been revised throughout to take into account other statutes passed, and cases decided, since the last edition. Indeed, the Chapter relating to Civil Remedies has been considerably expanded and re-written because of the large number of decisions relating thereto.

In the international field, the passing of the 1988 Act has enabled this country to ratify the Paris Act of the Berne Convention on September 29, 1989. But perhaps of more importance, America is now a party to the Berne Convention having acceded to the Paris Act with effect from March 1, 1989. As a result, steps have been taken which substantially increase the protection given to American works in the United Kingdom.

Because of the advent of the 1988 Act, the task of preparing a new edition of this book has been vastly increased and we are therefore glad to welcome Kevin Garnett as an additional member of the editorial team on this occasion. We are again indebted to Stephen Silman who, on this occasion, has re-written the Chapter on income tax, capital gains tax, inheritance tax and stamp duty. Sadly Professor Alan Latman, who revised the Chapter on American law in the last edition, died in 1984. Happily his place has been taken by David Nimmer (the son of the late Professor Melville Nimmer) to whom we are also indebted. We are also indebted to Robert Skone James who has written the Chapter on Industrial Designs, dealing, in particular, with the new design right. We would also like to thank Nigel Cooper for his help in researching and updating the Chapter on Community Law.

We would also like to thank Julia Clark for her assistance in researching the overseas case law, and for preparing the Contents list. Our thanks are also due to Simon Barker and other members of Chambers at 5 New Square, who have done invaluable work in proof reading the Appendices. We would also like to thank the Publishers for preparing the Tables and Index.

In conclusion it is, perhaps, unfortunate that a branch of the law, which was already complex enough, will now, with the coming into force of the 1988 Act, become even more complex. Apart from the size of the Act, its change of format and its new provisions, it does not help that some comparatively simple matters have been made more difficult. A further complication has been caused by the substantial amendment of the 1988 Act by the Broadcasting Act 1990, and publication has been delayed to enable these amendments to be dealt with in this book. The 1988 Act, as amended, may, therefore, well prove to be a nightmare for copyright users and a minefield for copyright practitioners.

Lincoln's Inn,	E. P. Skone James	J. E. Rayner James
January 1991	John F. Mummery	K. M. Garnett

CONTENTS

CHAPTER 1
NATURE AND HISTORY OF COPYRIGHT

CHAPTER 2
SUBJECT MATTER OF COPYRIGHT PROTECTION

CHAPTER 3
CONDITIONS FOR SUBSISTENCE OF COPYRIGHT

CHAPTER 8

INFRINGEMENT OF COPYRIGHT: PRIMARY INFRINGEMENT

CHAPTER 9

SECONDARY OR INDIRECT INFRINGEMENT OF COPYRIGHT

CHAPTER 10

PERMITTED ACTS

CHAPTER 11
CIVIL REMEDIES

CHAPTER 12
LIBRARIES

CHAPTER 13
CROWN AND PARLIAMENTARY RIGHTS.
UNIVERSITIES' AND COLLEGES' RIGHTS

TABLE OF STATUTES

xv

1

TABLE OF STATUTORY INSTRUMENTS
AND STATUTORY RULES AND ORDERS

CONVENTIONS

AGREEMENTS

TREATIES

COMMUNITY SECONDARY LEGISLATION

TABLE OF UNITED STATES LEGISLATION

TABLE OF CASES

Table of Cases

Table of Cases

NATURE AND HISTORY OF COPYRIGHT

Contents   *Para.*

1. Nature of Copyright

Distinction between copyright and other similar rights: no copy-   1–1
right in ideas. Copyright law is concerned, in essence, with the negative
right of preventing the copying of physical material.[1] It is not concerned
with the reproduction of ideas, but with the reproduction of the form in
which ideas are expressed.[2] Originally copyright law was concerned with
the field of literature and the arts but, in seeking, in particular, to keep up
with advances in technology, the protection given by copyright law has
been considerably expanded over the years. Thus, today, not only is protection given to literary, dramatic, musical and artistic works (with, for
instance, computer programs being protected as literary works[3]), but also
to sound recordings, films, broadcasts, cable programmes and the typographical arrangement of published editions.[4] Copyright is a property
right,[5] but one result of this expansion in protection is that, whereas this
branch of the law used to be described by all as "intellectual property," it
is now described, by some, as "industrial property."

Copyright is not a monopoly, unlike patents and registered designs,
which are.[6] Thus, if it can be shown that two precisely similar works were
in fact produced wholly independently of one another, there can be no
infringement of copyright by one of the other.[7]

---

[1] *George Hensher Ltd.* v. *Restawhile Upholstery (Lancs.) Ltd.* [1976] A.C. 64 at 98; *Fraser* v. *Thames Television Ltd.* [1984] Q.B. 44 at 60; *Performing Right Society Ltd.* v. *Rangers F.C. Supporters Club* [1975] R.P.C. 626 at 633; *British Leyland Motor Corporation* v. *Armstrong Patents Co. Ltd.* [1986] R.P.C. 279 at 302.

[2] See *Jefferys (C.)* v. *Boosey (T.)* (1855) 4 H.L.C. 815; *Donoghue* v. *Allied Newspapers Ltd.* [1938] Ch. 106 at 109 and 110; *Gleeson* v. *H. R. Denne Ltd.* [1975] R.P.C. 471; *Gomme (E.) Ltd.* v. *Relaxateze Upholstery Ltd.* [1976] R.P.C. 377; *Catnic Components Ltd.* v. *Hill & Smith Ltd.* [1978] F.S.R. 405; *L.B. (Plastics) Ltd.* v. *Swish Products Ltd.* [1979] R.P.C. 551 (H.L.); *L. A. Randall Pty. Ltd.* v. *Millman Services Pty. Ltd.* [1977–78] 17 A.L.R. 140; *Kleeneze Ltd.* v. *D.R.G. (U.K.) Ltd.* [1984] F.S.R. 399; *George Ward (Moxley) Ltd.* v. *Richard Sankey Ltd.* [1988] F.S.R. 66. *Green* v. *Broadcasting Corp. of New Zealand* [1989] R.P.C. 700. And see Copyright, Designs and Patents Act 1988 ("C.D.P.A. 1988"), s.3(2).

[3] C.D.P.A. 1988, s.3.

[4] See Chap. 2, *post.*

[5] C.D.P.A. 1988, ss.1(1), 90(1) and 96(2); compare Copyright Act 1956, s.36(1), and Copyright Act 1842, s.25.

[6] *British Leyland, supra,* at 361; *L.B. (Plastics) Ltd., supra,* at 570.

[7] *Corelli* v. *Gray* (1913) 29 T.L.R. 570; *Rees* v. *Melville* [1911–16] Mac. C.C. 96 at 168; *Hollinrake* v. *Truswell* [1894] 3 Ch. 420; *Libraco Ltd.* v. *Shaw Walker Ltd.* (1913) 30 T.L.R. 22; *Wesman* v. *McNamara* [1923–28] Mac. C.C. 121; *Francis Day & Hunter Ltd.* v. *Bron* [1963] Ch. 567; and see § 8–9 *et seq post.*

1–2 **Whether copyright protection should be unlimited in time?** Since copyright law does not create a monopoly, it has been argued that the basic protection which the law of copyright affords, namely that of preventing unlawful reproduction, should extend without limit of time. Prior to the 1911 Act unpublished literary works had a perpetual right at common law. But such right ended on publication, after which an author had to base his claim for protection upon his statutory right, if any.[8] However, common law copyright was abolished by the 1911 Act, which provided that no person should be entitled to copyright or any similar right otherwise than under and in accordance with the provisions of that Act, or of any other statutory enactment for the time being in force.[9] The 1956 Act[10] and the 1988 Act,[11] contain similar provisions. Nevertheless, an unlimited statutory term for unpublished literary (and other) works was created by the 1911 Act,[12] and continued by the 1956 Act,[13] but not by the 1988 Act, except in the case of works of unknown authorship.[14] The 1988 Act also ended[15] the perpetual copyrights granted to universities and colleges by the Copyright Act 1775,[16] preserved by the 1911 Act,[17] and by the 1956 Act.[18] Having regard to this it is, perhaps, surprising that the 1988 Act has created a new perpetual non-copyright right. Such right is a right for the Hospital for Sick Children, Great Ormond Street, to receive royalties in respect of certain acts of exploitation of the play *Peter Pan* by Sir James Matthew Barrie, notwithstanding that the copyright in such work expired on December 31, 1987.[19]

1–3 **Development of law of copyright.** The law of copyright was first concerned only with preventing the unlawful reproduction of copies of books, since when it has developed in two directions. First, it has extended the subject-matter of protection by including dramatic, musical and artistic works and later gramophone records, then films, sound and television broadcasts and published editions, and now cable programmes and computer programs. Secondly, it has extended the classes of acts which constitute infringement.

1–4 **Definitions of copyright.** The expression "copyright" has developed its meaning in a corresponding manner. Before the 1911 Act it seems that the expression "copyright" was confined to the right of multiplying copies and did not include the performing right in dramatic or musical works,[20] and it is a matter of some doubt whether the expression "copyright" was

---

[8] *Donaldson* v. *Beckett* (1774) 4 Burr. 2408; as to other works, see *Albert* (*Prince*) v. *Strange* (1849) 1 M. & G. 25. See also § 1–43, *post.*
[9] Copyright Act 1911, s.31.
[10] Copyright Act 1956, s.46(5).
[11] C.D.P.A. 1988, s.171(2).
[12] Copyright Act 1911, s.17(1).
[13] Copyright Act 1956, ss.2(3), 3(4).
[14] C.D.P.A. 1988, ss.9(4), (5), 12 and Sched. 1, para. 12. See §§ 6–5, 6–8 and 6–10 *post.*
[15] C.D.P.A. 1988, Sched. 1, para. 13.
[16] 15 Geo. 3, c.53.
[17] Copyright Act 1911, s.33.
[18] Copyright Act 1956, s.46(1), and see Chap. 13, *post.*
[19] C.D.P.A. 1988, ss.149 and 301 and Sched. 6, and see Chap. 6, *post.*
[20] See Pollock C.B., *Chappell* v. *Purday* (1845) 14 M. & W. 303.

before that date used only in relation to the right to restrain publication of published works, or so as to include also the right of an author to restrain publication of his unpublished works.[21]

After the 1911 Act the expression "copyright" in this country came to be used as meaning all the rights conferred by the 1911 Act upon authors, composers and artists in respect of their literary, dramatic, musical and artistic works.[22] But, as has been seen, copyright does not essentially mean a right to do something, but a right to restrict the doing of acts by others,[23] and, when copyright is referred to as "an exclusive right" the emphasis is on the word "exclusive." The 1956 Act accordingly defined "copyright" as meaning the exclusive right to do and to authorise other persons to do the acts restricted under that Act by the copyright in a work of that description,[24] and that copyright was infringed by a person who, without the licence of the copyright owner, did, or authorised another person to do, any of such acts.[25] That Act then proceeded, in the sections dealing with the various classes of works, to state what were the acts restricted by the copyright in those works.[26] Although the format of the 1988 Act differs from that of the 1956 Act, the result is the same. Thus the 1988 Act, whilst not defining "copyright" otherwise than as a property right,[27] provides that the owner of the copyright in a work has the exclusive right to do the acts restricted by the copyright in a work of that description specified in that Act,[28] and that copyright is infringed by a person who, without the licence of the copyright owner, does, or authorises another to do, any of the restricted acts[29] set out in various sections of that Act.[30]

2. History of Copyright

Early control of printing. It was only after the introduction of printing   **1-21** that any serious question as to the copyright in literary works could be expected to arise. An early statute of Richard III in 1483[31] encouraged the printing of books, and permitted their importation, but this statute was repealed 50 years later on protectionist grounds, it being alleged, in the preamble of the repealing statute in 1533[32] that such a "marvellous number of printed books" were imported into the realm to the prejudice of the "King's natural subjects," who "have given themselves so diligently to learn and exercise the said craft of printing, that at this day there be within this realm a great number cunning and expert in the said science or

---

[21] *Re Dickens* [1935] Ch. 267.
[22] See Copyright Act 1911, s.1(2).
[23] See § 1–1 *ante*.
[24] Copyright Act 1956, s.1(1).
[25] *Ibid.* s.1(2).
[26] For instance, *ibid.* ss.2(5), 3(5).
[27] C.D.P.A. 1988, s.1(1).
[28] *Ibid.* ss.2(1) and 16(1).
[29] *Ibid.* s.16(2).
[30] *Ibid.* ss.17–21.
[31] 1 Ric. 3, c. 9.
[32] 25 Hen. 8, c. 15.

craft of printing as able to exercise the said craft in all points as any stranger in any other realm or country." A similar plea is urged on behalf of the bookbinders, who, "having no other faculty wherewith to get their living, be destitute of work and likely to be undone, except some reformation herein be had."[33]

As the number of printers increased in England, the King assumed a prerogative of granting printing privileges, and the earliest copyright protection took the form of printers' licences, and became a source of considerable profit to the King and his favourites.

1–22 **Original charter of the Stationers' Company.** In the year 1556 the original charter of the Stationers' Company was granted by Philip and Mary. It was the declared object of the Crown at that time to prevent the propagation of the reformed religion, and it seems to have been thought that this could most effectually be brought about by imposing the severest restrictions on the press. About this period there were several decrees and ordinances of the Star Chamber regulating the manner of printing, the number of presses throughout the kingdom, and prohibiting all printing against the force and meaning of any of the statutes or laws of the realm. Until the year 1640 the Crown, through the instrumentality of the Star Chamber, exercised this restrictive jurisdiction without limit, enforcing, by the summary powers of search, confiscation and imprisonment, its decrees, without the least obstruction from Westminster Hall or Parliament in any instance.

1–23 **Decrees of Star Chamber.** In 1556, by a decree of the Star Chamber, it was forbidden, amongst other things, to print contrary to any ordinance, prohibition, or commandment in any of the statutes or laws of the realm, or any injunction, letters patent, or ordinances set forth, or to be set forth, by the Queen's grant, commission or authority.

By another decree, dated June 23, 1585, every book was required to be licensed, and all persons were prohibited from printing "any book, work, or copy against the form or meaning of any restraint contained in any statute or laws of this realm, or in any injunction made by Her Majesty, or her Privy Council; or against the true intent and meaning of any letters patent, commissions, or prohibitions under the great seal, or contrary to any allowed ordinance set down for the good government of the Stationers' Company."

In 1623, a proclamation was issued to enforce this decree; reciting that it had been evaded, amongst other ways "by printing beyond the sea such allowed books, works, or writings, as have been imprinted within the realm, by such to whom the sole printing thereof by letters patent or lawful ordinance or authority doth appertain."

In 1637, the Star Chamber again decreed that "no person is to print or import (if printed abroad) any book or copy which the Company of Stationers, or any person, hath or shall, by any letters patent, order or

---

[33] We recognise in this statute the prototype of the American "manufacturing clause," see §§ 18–16 and 18–46, *post*.

entrance in their register book, or otherwise, have the right, privilege, authority, or allowance, soleley to print."[34]

First Licensing Act. In 1640, however, the Star Chamber was abolished;   **1-24** the King's authority was set at naught; all the regulations of the press, and restraints previously imposed upon unlicensed printers by proclamations, decrees of the Star Chamber and charter powers given to the Stationers' Company, were deemed and certainly were illegal. The licentiousness of libels induced Parliament to make an ordinance which prohibited printing, unless the book was first licensed. The ordinance prohibited printing without the consent of the owner, or importing (if printed abroad), upon pain of forfeiting the same to the *owner or owners of the copies* of the said books, etc. The provision necessarily presupposed the property to exist; it would have been nugatory if there had been no admitted owner. An owner could not at that time have existed otherwise than by common law. In 1649 the Long Parliament made another ordinance; and in 1662 the Licensing Act was passed[35] which interdicted the printing of any book unless first licensed and entered in the register of the Stationers' Company. It ordered that no person should presume to print "any heretical, seditious, schismatical, or offensive books or pamphlets, wherein any doctrine or opinion shall be asserted or maintained which is contrary to the Christian faith, or the doctrine or discipline of the Church of England, or which shall, or may, tend to be to the scandal of religion or the church, or the government or governors of the church, state, or commonwealth, or of any corporation or particular person or persons whatever." It further prohibited the publication of unlicensed books, prescribed regulations as to printing and empowered the King's messengers, and the master and wardens of the Stationers' Company, to seize books suspected of containing matters hostile to the Church or Government. It was necessary to print in the beginning of every licensed book the certificate of the licenser to the effect that the books contained nothing "contrary to the Christian faith, or the doctrine or discipline of the Church of England, or against the state and government of this realm, or contrary to good life or good manners, or otherwise, as the nature and subject of the work shall require." To prevent fraudulent changes in a book after it had been licensed, a copy was required to be deposited with the licenser when application was made for a licence.

The Act further prohibited any person from printing or importing with-   **1-25** out the consent of the owner, any book which any person had the sole right to print by virtue of letters patent, or "by force or virtue of any entry or entries thereof duly made or to be made, in the register book of the said Company of Stationers, or in the register book of either of the universities." The penalty of piracy was forfeiture of the books and six shillings and eightpence for each copy, half to go to the King, and half to the owner.

The sole property of the owner is here acknowledged in express terms as a common law right; and the legislature which passed that Act could

---

[34] 4 Burr. 2312.
[35] 13 & 14 Car. 2, c. 33.

never have entertained the most distant idea "that the productions of the brain were not a subject-matter of property." To support an action on this statute, ownership had to be proved or the plaintiff could not have recovered, because the action was to be brought by the owner who was to have a moiety of the penalty. The various provisions of this Act effectually prevented piracies, without actions at law or Bills in equity. But cases arose of disputed property. Some of them were between different patentees of the Crown; in some the point was whether the property belonged "to the author, from his invention and labour, or the King, from the subject-matter."

1–26   The ordinance of 1643 prohibited the printing or importing of any book that had been lawfully licensed and entered in the register of the Stationers' Company, "for any particular member thereof, without the licence and consent of the owner." The penalty prescribed was forfeiture of the book to the owner, "and such further punishment as shall be thought fit." This clause was repeated in the ordinances of 1647, 1649, and 1652.

It has been questioned whether these clauses were applicable to any other than members of the Stationers' Company—in fact, whether they were more than by-laws for the regulation of the members *inter se*, but it is doubtful whether any such restriction can be put upon their scope.

1–27   The Licensing Act 1662 was continued by several Acts of Parliament, but expired May, 1679, soon after which there is a case in Lilly's *Entries of Hilary Term*.[36] In this case an action was brought for printing 4,000 copies of the *Pilgrim's Progress*, of which the plaintiff was the true proprietor, whereby he lost the profit and benefit of his copy. There is no account, however, of the case having been proceeded with.

1–28   **Ordinances of the Stationers' Company.** In 1681, all legislative protection having ceased, the Stationers' Company adopted an ordinance, or by-law, which recited that several members of the company had *great part of their estates in copies*, that by ancient usage of the company, when any book or copy was duly entered in their register to any member, such person had always been reputed and taken to be the proprietor of such book or copy, and ought to have the sole printing thereof. The ordinance further recited that this privilege and interest had of late been often violated and abused; and it then provided a penalty against such violation by any member or members of the company, where the copy had been duly entered in their register. The true view of this ordinance would seem to be, that the members of the Stationers' Company, finding their estates in copies, which belonged to them by the common law, no longer under the protection of the Licensing Act (the repeal of which had incidentally withdrawn the protection that had always been inserted in it, though it had necessarily no connection with the system of licensing), undertook to provide for the failure of legislation, as far as they could, by an ordinance applicable, of course, to their own members only. The ordinance however, only shows,

---

[36] 31 Car. 2, B.R.. *Ponder* v. *Bradyl*, Lilly's *Entries*, 67; see Carter, 89; 4 Burr. 2317; Skinner 234; 1 Mod. 257.

in connection with other historical proof, what the common law right was then supposed to be. It was much the same as if an association of persons were to agree that any one of their number should pay a penalty for violating the acknowledged rights of property of any other person in the association, provided such rights were duly entered in their common records. It would not be an attempt to create the right, but it would justly be regarded as acknowledgment of the existence of such a right.[37]

In another by-law, passed in 1694, it was stated that copies were constantly bargained and sold amongst the members of the company as their property, and devised to their children and others for legacies and to their widows for maintenance; and it was ordained that if any member should, without the consent of the member by whom the entry was made, print or sell the same, he should forfeit for every copy 12 pence.

New legislation sought. For many years successively, attempts were **1–29** made to obtain a new Licensing Act. Such a Bill once passed the Upper House, but the attempt miscarried upon constitutional objections to a licence. Proprietors of copyright had so long been protected by summary measures that they regarded an action at law as an inadequate remedy. A Bill in equity was never even thought of: no hope of its success appears at the time to have been entertained.

In one of the petitions presented to the House in support of applications to Parliament in 1709, for a Bill to protect copyright, the last clause or paragraph was as follows: "The liberty now set on foot of breaking through this ancient and reasonable usage is no way to be effectually restrained but by an Act of Parliament. For by common law, a bookseller, can recover no more costs than he can prove damage, but it is impossible for him to prove the tenth, nay, perhaps, the hundreth part of the damage he suffers; because a thousand counterfeit copies may be dispersed into as many hands over the kingdom, and he not be able to prove the sale of them. Besides, the defendant is always a pauper, and so the plaintiff must lose his costs of suit. (No man of substance has been known to offend in this particular, nor will any ever appear in it.) Therefore, the only remedy by the common law is to confine a beggar to the rules of the King's Bench or Fleet, and there he will continue the evil practice with impunity. We therefore pray that confiscation of counterfeit copies be one of the penalties to be inflicted on offenders."[38]

The Statute of Anne 1709.[39] In response to these applications, in the **1–30** year 1709 the first Copyright Act was passed. This Act gave authors of books then printed the sole right and liberty of printing them for a term of 21 years from April 10, 1710, and of books not then printed the sole right of printing for 14 years, with a proviso that, after the expiration of the said term of 14 years, the sole right of printing or disposing of copies should return to the authors thereof, if they were then living, for another term of 14 years. The titles to books had be registered in the register book of the Stationers' Company, and 9 copies had to be delivered to certain libraries.

---

[37] *Curtis on Copyright*, p. 38.
[38] 4 Burr. 2318.
[39] 8 Anne, c. 19.

This statute, passed with a view to giving a greater protection to copyright, had the unexpected result of curtailing it; for, in the case of *Donaldson* v. *Beckett*,[40] the House of Lords finally decided that the effect of the statute was to extinguish the common law copyright in published works, though leaving the common law copyright in unpublished works unaffected. Common law copyright was abolished by the 1911 Act.[41]

The universities and colleges, alarmed at the consequence of this decision, applied for and, in 1775, obtained an Act of Parliament[42] establishing in perpetuity their right to all the copies given or bequeathed to them or which might thereafter be given to or acquired by them theretofore. Such rights have now been ended by the 1988 Act.[43]

1–31 **Copyright Act 1814.**[44] The period for which copyright was capable of existing was somewhat varied by section 4 of this Act, which enacted that, instead of enduring for 14 years, and contingently for 14 more, authors should have the sole liberty of printing and reprinting their works for the term of 28 years, to commence from the day of the first publication of the same; and, further, if the author should be living at the expiration of that period, for the residue of his natural life.

1–32 **Copyright Act 1842.**[45] The 1709 and 1814 Acts were repealed by the Copyright Act 1842. To Mr. Serjeant Talfourd was due the honour of obtaining this piece of legislative justice. From 1837 to 1842, in spite of the opposition of Macaulay, he used his best endeavours and expended his most eloquent strains to accomplish its passing. In contending for an extension of the period during which protection was afforded to literary works, he burst forth: "There is something peculiarly unjust in bounding the term of an author's property by his natural life, if he should survive so short a period as 28 years. It denies to age and experience the probable reward it permits to youth—to youth, sufficiently full of hope and joys to slight its promises. It gives a bounty to haste, and informs the laborious student, who would wear away his strength to complete some work which 'the world will not willingly let die,' that the more of his life he devotes to its perfection, the more limited shall be his interests in its fruits. It stops the progress of remuneration at the moment it is most needed; and when the benignity of nature would extract from her last calamity a means of support and comfort to the survivors—at the moment when his name is invested with the solemn interest of the grave—when his eccentricities or frailties excite a smile or a shrug no longer—when the last seal is set upon his earthly course, and his works assume their place among the classics of his country—your law declares that his works shall become your property, and you requite him by seizing the patrimony of his children."

The 1842 Act extended the period of copyright to the life of the author and 7 years after his death, or a term of 42 years from publication, which-

---

[40] (1774) 4 Burr. 2408.
[41] See § 1–2, *ante*.
[42] 15 Geo. 3, c. 53: and see Copyright Act 1801 (41 Geo. 3, c. 107).
[43] See § 1–2 *ante*.
[44] 54 Geo. 3, c. 156.
[45] 5 & 6 Vict. c. 45.

ever should be the longer, or 42 years from publication if published after the author's death. The 1842 Act contained provisions for registration at Stationers' Hall. This was not compulsory, but had to be effected before any action could be brought against infringers. In spite of its defects, both in substance and in draftsmanship, the 1842 Act remained the governing statute as to literary copyright until it was repealed by the 1911 Act.[46]

Engraving copyright. In the realm of artistic copyright, engravings were the first subjects to receive legislative protection. In 1734 the Engraving Copyright Act[47] was passed, conferring copyright upon these for a term of 14 years.   1–33

No provision was made in this Act for the protection of any work of which the engraver was not also the designer; and this has been accounted for by the fact that Hogarth, by whose influence the Act was introduced, was invariably the designer as well as the engraver of his celebrated works.

The Engraving Copyright Act of 1766[48] was passed to remedy this oversight, and extended protection to any person making an engraving from the original work of another. It also enlarged the period of protection to 28 years from the date of first publication. A further Act, the Prints Copyright Act of 1777,[49] enlarged the remedies for piracy; the Prints Copyright Act of 1836[50] extended the provisions of the Engravings Acts to Ireland, and the International Copyright Act of 1852[51] to prints taken by lithography or other mechanical process.

Sculpture copyright. Works of sculpture were the next in order to be protected, by the Sculpture Copyright Act 1814,[52] the term of protection being 14 years from first publication, with a further reversionary term of 14 years to the author if then living and he had not divested himself of the copyright.   1–34

Musical and dramatic copyright. Musical and dramatic compositions were held to be "books" within the meaning of the Copyright Acts relating to literary works[53]; but the performing right was not statutorily protected until the year 1833, when the Dramatic Copyright Act, commonly known as Bulwer Lytton's Act,[54] conferred an exclusive right of public performance for 28 years, with a reversionary period to the author for the residue of his life, provided the work was printed and published; if the work was not printed or published the term of protection was uncertain.   1–35

Bulwer Lytton's Act only referred to dramatic pieces, but section 20 of

---

[46] 1 & 2 Geo. 5, c. 46.
[47] 8 Geo. 2, c. 13.
[48] 6 Geo. 3, c. 38.
[49] 17 Geo. 3, c. 57.
[50] 6 & 7 Will. 4, c. 59.
[51] 15 & 16 Vict. c. 12, s.14.
[52] 54 Geo. 3, c. 56.
[53] *Bach* v. *Longman* (1777) 2 Cowp: 623, *Storace* v. *Longman* (1809) 2 Camp. 26, note; and see § 1–32, *ante*.
[54] 3 & 4 Will. 4, c. 15.

the Literary Copyright Act 1842[55] dealt with the performing rights both in musical and dramatic pieces, and extended protection to the performing rights in both classes of works for a similar period to that provided for the duration of copyright in books, namely, a period of 42 years from first public representation or performance, or the life of the author and 7 years after, whichever should be the longer: and 42 years from first public representation or performance for posthumous pieces.

1–36   Certain abuses arose with respect to the performing rights in musical works. In particular, a man named Wall gained considerable notoriety by purchasing performing rights and enforcing payment of penalties—which penalties were fixed at 40s. a performance by Bulwer Lytton's Act—from innocent infringers. This led to the passing of the Copyright (Musical Compositions) Acts of 1882 and 1888,[56] which required that notice of reservation of rights of public performance of any musical composition should be printed on every published copy thereof and left the question of payment of costs and amount of penalties to the discretion of the court.

1–37   Owing to the injury caused to proprietors of the copyright in musical compositions by the practice of selling pirated copies of songs and music through the medium of street hawkers, and the difficulty of ascertaining any substantial person to proceed against for infringement, the Musical (Summary Proceedings) Act 1902, and the Musical Copyright Act 1906,[57] were passed providing summary methods of procedure against infringers of musical copyright. Both these last-mentioned Acts remained unrepealed by the 1911 Act, but were repealed by the 1956 Act.

1–38   **Painting, drawing and photographic copyright.** The last class of works to receive statutory protection were paintings, drawings and photographs, which were, for the first time, protected by the Fine Arts Copyright Act, 1862.[58] This Act purported to protect paintings, drawings and photographs for the term of the life of the author and 7 years after his death, but to obtain the full benefit of the Act, registration at Stationers' Hall was necessary. However, the wording of the Act was such as to produce the somewhat remarkable result that, unless the work was executed upon commission, so as to vest the copyright initially in the person commissioning the work, the copyright was lost altogether upon the first sale of the work unless, on that occasion, there was some written instrument signed by the artist dealing with the copyright, either by way of express assignment to the purchaser, or by way of express retention by the artist.[59] It should be observed that this requirement probably also applied to works of foreign origin, the copyright wherein in this country was secured by Convention or Order in Council, though it seems unlikely that foreign artists would have been aware of this peculiar provision of English law on a first sale to a dealer in their own country.

[55] 5 & 6 Vict. c. 45. Lectures were protected by the Lectures Copyright Act 1835 (5 & 6 Will. 4, c. 65).
[56] 45 & 46 Vict. c. 40; 51 and 52 Vict. c. 17.
[57] 2 Edw. 7, c. 15; 6 Edw. 7, c. 36.
[58] 25 & 26 Vict. c. 68.
[59] *Copinger* (4th ed.), pp. 366, 367.

Royal Commission of 1875. Having regard to the number of Acts in   **1–39**
force dealing with different branches of the law of copyright, a consolidating statute was urgently required. In 1875 a Royal Commission was
appointed to inquire into the working of the Copyright Acts, and the
Commissioners presented their Report in 1878. In this Report they
stated[60]: "The first observation which a study of the existing law suggests
is that its form, as distinguished from its substance, seems to us bad. The
law is wholly destitute of any sort of arrangement, incomplete, often
obscure, and, even when it is intelligible upon long study, it is in many
parts so ill-expressed that no one who does not give such study to it can
expect to understand it. The common law principles, which lie at the root
of the law, have never been settled. The well-known cases of *Millar* v. *Taylor, Donaldson* v. *Beckett*, and *Jefferys* v. *Boosey* ended in a difference of
opinion amongst many of the most eminent judges who have ever sat upon
the Bench. The 14 Acts of Parliament which deal with the subject were
passed at different times between 1735 and 1875.[61] They are drawn in different styles, and some are drawn so as to be hardly intelligible. Obscurity
of style, however, is only one of the defects of these Acts. Their arrangement is often worse than their style. Of this the Copyright Act of 1842 is a
conspicuous instance."

The Berne Convention. In spite, however, of the recommendations of   **1–40**
the Commissioners, no consolidating statute was passed—difficulties with
the colonies particularly standing in the way of any settlement which
should include any alterations in the existing law. In the year 1885, Great
Britain was represented at the Conference of Powers held at Berne, which
resulted in the framing of the Berne Convention, to which Great Britain
adhered. Previously to doing so the International Copyright Act, 1886[62]
was passed, making the necessary alterations and additions to the International Copyright Act 1844[63] to enable Great Britain to give the required
protection to foreign authors.
    In the year 1908 the considerable modifications of the original Berne
Convention, which were carried at the Conference of the Powers held at
Berlin, rendered it imperative that Great Britain should amend her copyright laws, if she was to fall into line with the other Powers, and be in a
position to give to foreigners the protection required by the Revised Convention.

Committee of 1909. In 1909 a Committee was appointed "to examine   **1–41**
the various points in which the revised International Copyright Convention, signed at Berlin on November 13, 1908, is not in accordance with the
law of the United Kingdom, including those points which are expressly
left to the internal legislation of each country, and to consider in each case
whether that law should be altered so as to enable His Majesty's Government to give effect to the Revised Convention." This Committee, after

---

[60] paras, 7, 8, 9.
[61] Several more were added between 1875 and 1910.
[62] 49 & 50 Vict. c. 33.
[63] 7 & 8 Vict. c. 12.

hearing evidence, reported to Parliament[64] generally approving the provisions of the Revised Convention, and recommending the passing of a consolidating and amending Act.

1–42   **Copyright Act 1911.** In the year 1910 a Bill to give effect to these recommendations was drafted and introduced into the House of Commons, but was dropped for that Session. In 1911, however, another Bill was introduced which, after being modified in several respects during its passage through Parliament, was at length passed by both Houses, and received the Royal Assent on December 16, 1911.[65] This Act repealed all previous statutes on the subject of literary and artistic copyright, with the exception of the Musical (Summary Proceedings) Copyright Act of 1902 and the Musical Copyright Act of 1906,[66] and one section of the Fine Arts Copyright Act of 1862.[67] The 1911 Act came into force on July 1, 1912.[68]

1–43   **Abolition of common law copyright.** The 1911 Act also abolished common law copyright.[69] Except in the cases of paintings, drawings and photographs,[70] unpublished works received no statutory protection prior to the commencement of the 1911 Act,[71] but were protected, if at all, under the common law.[72] This was a perpetual right for unpublished works which ceased on publication, after which an author had to base his claim for protection upon his statutory right, if any. The nature of this common law protection was fully discussed in *Re Dickens*,[73] in which a question at issue was whether the common law right in an unpublished manuscript passed under a bequest, taking effect before the passing of the 1911 Act, of "all my private papers," and the Court of Appeal held that the right was an incorporeal right existing independently of the property in the manuscript and one which did not pass to a legatee or donee on a bequest or gift of the manuscript itself.

1–44   **Committee of 1951.** The Berne Convention was further revised at Rome in 1928 and at Brussels in 1948, and, in 1951, a further Committee was appointed "to consider and report whether any, and, if so, what changes are desirable in the law relating to copyright in literary, dramatic, musical and artistic works with particular regard to technical developments and to the revised international convention for the protection of literary and

---

[64] Report of the Committee on the Law of Copyright, Cd. 4976 (1909).
[65] 1 & 2 Geo. 5, c. 46. For a survey of the law of copyright immediately prior to the Copyright Act 1911, see Copinger (12th ed.) §§ 1105–1333, and see Chap. 5 *post*.
[66] *Ante*, § 1–37.
[67] *Ante* § 1–38.
[68] Copyright Act 1911, s.37(2)(a).
[69] See § 1–2 *ante*.
[70] *Tuck & Sons* v. *Priester* (1887) 19 Q.B.D. 48; Fine Arts Copyright Act 1862 (25 & 26 Vict. c. 68), s.1.
[71] See n. 68 *ante*.
[72] *Donaldson* v. *Beckett* (1774) 4 Burr. 2408; *Millar* v. *Taylor* (1769) 4 Burr. 2303; *Jefferys* v. *Boosey* (1855) 4 H.L.C. 815; *Beckford* v. *Hood* (1798) 7 T.R. 620; *Mayall* v. *Higbey* (1862) 1 H. & C. 148; *Macmillan & Co.* v. *Dent* [1907] 1 Ch. 107; *Mansell* v. *Valley Printing Co.* [1908] 2 Ch. 441; *Bowden Bros.* v. *Amalgamated Pictorials Ltd.* [1911] 1 Ch. 386; *Albert (Prince)* v. *Strange* (1849) 1 M. & G. 25.
[73] [1935] Ch. 267.

artistic works signed at Brussels in June 1948 and to consider and report on related matters." The Committee also took into consideration the Universal Copyright Convention which was subsequently signed at Geneva in 1952 under the auspices of UNESCO.[74] This Committee, after hearing evidence, reported to Parliament[75] recommending that Her Majesty's Government should accede to the Convention as revised at Brussels in 1948, and proposing a number of changes in the law.

Copyright Act 1956. In 1955 a Bill to give effect to these recommendations was introduced into the House of Lords and, after a number of modifications introduced in both Houses, received the Royal Assent on November 5, 1956.[76] This Act repealed the 1911 Act (except ss.15, 34 and 37[77]), the Musical (Summary Proceedings) Copyright Act of 1902 and the Musical Copyright Act of 1906 and the outstanding section of the Fine Arts Copyright Act of 1862. It came into force on June 1, 1957,[78] and was amended by the Design Copyright Act 1968. **1–45**

Committee of 1973. In 1973 another Committee was appointed to consider and report whether any, and if so what, changes were desirable in the law relating to copyright as provided in particular by the 1956 Act and the 1968 Act, including the desirability of retaining the system of protection of industrial designs by the Registered Designs Act 1949. However, there was expressly excluded from the terms of reference any consideration of the merits of lending to the public as one of the acts restricted by copyright in a work and, in fact, a public lending right has now been established by the Public Lending Right Act 1979.[79] **1–46**

The Committee, after receiving written and oral evidence, reported to Parliament.[80] The report contained a large number of recommendations. Apart from recommending the repeal of registered design monopoly protection as now provided by the Registered Designs Act 1949, other major recommendations were made to take account of the problems raised by developments or improvements since the 1951 Committee in the techniques by which documents can be reproduced, in the techniques for recording sounds and sequences of visual images and in computer technology. The report also contained recommendations in relation to the United Kingdom's obligations under various international conventions having regard, in particular, to the revision of the Berne Convention at Stockholm in 1967 and at Paris in 1971, and of the Universal Convention also at Paris in 1971.

---

[74] As a result this Convention is variously referred to as the Universal, Geneva or UNESCO Convention.
[75] Report of the Committee on the Law of Copyright, Cmd. 8662 (1952).
[76] 4 & 5 Eliz. 2, c. 74.
[77] ss.34 and 37(2) were repealed by the Statute Law (Repeals) Act 1986 (c. 12).
[78] S.I. 1957 No. 863 *Copinger* (12th ed.), § 1735.
[79] c. 10 *post* §§ 12–12 and A–647.
[80] Report of the Committee to consider the Law on Copyright and Designs, Cmnd. 6732 (1977).

1–47 **Semiconductor Products.** By the Semiconductor Products (Protection of Topography) Regulations 1987[81] a topography right, similar to copyright, was given to the designs of semiconductor products. These regulations were made on August 20, 1987, and came into force on November 7, 1987.

1–48 **Copyright, Designs and Patents Act 1988.** The 1956 Act was further amended, in particular by the Copyright Act 1956 (Amendment) Act 1982, the Copyright (Amendment) Act 1983, the Cable and Broadcasting Act 1984 and the Copyright (Computer Software) Amendment Act 1985. In October 1987 a Bill was introduced into the House of Lords which, as its title suggests, was not limited to copyright. In fact it contained 7 Parts, only one of which was concerned with copyright and new statutory moral rights, the others being concerned with such matters as new statutory performers' rights, a new design right and amendments to the Registered Designs Act 1949. Other provisions were concerned with patents and Patent Agents and Trade Mark Agents. As a result, the Bill comprised, altogether, some 277 sections and some 7 Schedules. The Bill had a rough ride through both Houses of Parliament both as to content and drafting but, by the time the Bill received the Royal Assent on November 15, 1988,[82] the number of sections had risen to 306 and the number of Schedules to 8. One section and one Schedule created a new perpetual non-copyright right in favour of the Hospital for Sick Children, Great Ormond Street. By comparison, the 1956 Act had only 51 sections with 9 Schedules, and the 1911 Act had only 37 sections and 2 Schedules.

For an Act which may well survive into the next century, it is, perhaps, unfortunate that an opportunity has been missed to simplify what was already a complex branch of the law. Thus, although the 1973 Committee recommended that the structure of the 1956 Act should be revised in order that the law should be placed on a plain and uniform basis, and that there should be one comprehensive definition section at the beginning of the Act,[83] this has not happened. For instance, Part I of the 1988 Act, dealing with copyright, has eight interpretation sections at the end of that Part, and countless definitions in the earlier sections. Thus, for example, whereas under the 1956 Act only one section was needed to deal with ownership of copyright by reason of employment under a contract of service or apprenticeship (section 4), under the 1988 Act two sections are needed (sections 11 and 178). Further, whereas it might have been thought that the logical place to find provisions dealing with subsistence of copyright would be immediately after the provisions dealing with protected works, in the 1988 Act the provisions as to subsistence are to be found almost at the end of the Part of the Act dealing with copyright, after the provisions dealing with the Copyright Tribunal. All this notwithstanding that the Explanatory and Financial Memorandum to the Bill stated that the copyright Part thereof replaced the 1956 Act with a fresh statement of the law on a more logical and consistent basis, taking into account the technological changes of the last 30 years and making various reforms.

---

[81] S.I. 1987 No. 1497: see § A–565 and Chap. 20, *post.*
[82] c. 48: see § A–3, *post.*
[83] Cmnd. 6732 para. 43.

The 1988 Act, *inter alia*, repealed the whole of the 1956 Act, and of the Copyright (Computer Software) Amendment Act 1985, and of the Performers' Protection Acts 1958, 1963 and 1972, but did not repeal section 15 of the 1911 Act which was left unrepealed by the 1956 Act and the Statute Law (Repeals) Act 1986.[84]

The 1988 Act is being brought into force in stages. Thus, certain matters relating to patents, and the provisions for the benefit of the Hospital for Sick Children, Great Ormond Street, were brought into force when the 1988 Act received the Royal Assent on November 15, 1988.[85] Certain other provisions relating to patents were brought into force on January 15, 1989.[86] The rest of the 1988 Act was to be brought into force on such day or days as might be appointed by statutory instrument.[87]

Thus the copyright provisions, and certain other major provisions, of the 1988 Act, were brought into force on August 1, 1989, from which date the 1956 Act and other relevant Acts were repealed.[88] For the purpose only of enabling the subordinate legislation thereunder to be made to come into force on August 1, 1989, some provisions of the 1988 Act were brought into force earlier.[89] Further parts of the 1988 Act were brought into force on August 13, 1990.[90] The final parts of the 1988 Act were brought into force on January 1, 1991.[91]

Semiconductor Products. There have also been new Regulations concerned with the design of semiconductor products[92] which revoked the earlier Regulations.[93] **1–49**

The future. The 1988 Act and statutory instruments thereunder have already been dogged by misfortune. Thus, no less than 9 statutory instruments thereunder have had to be revoked for a variety of reasons.[94] Further, Scott J., in the first reported decision on the 1988 Act,[95] concerned with the new section 298 of that Act, struck out the statement of claim as disclosing no cause of action. Although this decision was reversed by the Court of Appeal,[96] which held that section 298 itself created both the right and the remedy, it demonstrates that judicial interpretation of at least the newest provisions of the 1988 Act may well be necessary. Finally, notwithstanding that the copyright provisions of the 1988 Act only came **1–50**

---

[84] c. 12.
[85] s.305.
[86] See n. 85 *ante*.
[87] See n. 85 *ante*.
[88] S.I. 1989 No. 816: see § B–5 *post*. However, by amendment of this Order by S.I. 1989 No. 1303, s. 304(4) and (6) were brought into force on July 28, 1989: see § B–12 *post*.
[89] S.I. 1989 No. 955 which, because of a defect, was amended by S.I. 1989 No. 1032: see § B–8 *post*.
[90] S.I. 1990 No. 1400: see § B–243 *post*.
[91] S.I. 1990 No. 2168 § B–247 *post*.
[92] S.I. 1989 No. 1100 as amended by S.I. 1989 No. 2147 and S.I. 1990 No. 1003.
[93] S.I. 1987 No. 1497 § 1–47 *ante*: and see Chap. 20, *post*.
[94] S.I.s 1989 No. 981 by No. 1292, 1989 No. 988 by No. 1293, 1989 No. 990 by No. 1294, 1989 No. 991 by No. 1296, 1989 No. 1007 by No. 1067, 1989 No. 1008 by No. 1068, 1989 Nos. 1009 and 1069 by No. 1212 and 1989 No. 1010 by No. 1070.
[95] *BBC Enterprises Ltd.* v. *Hi-Tech Xtravision Ltd.* [1990] F.S.R. 217.
[96] [1990] Ch. 609.

into force on August 1, 1989, substantial amendments have now been made by the Broadcasting Act 1990,[97] including the creation of two new forms of compulsory licence concerned with the inclusion of sound recordings (but not the music on the sound recordings) in broadcasts and cable programmes, and the provision of information about broadcast programmes.[98] Altogether an unfortunate beginning for an Act no doubt intended to operate in this field of law until at least the beginning of the next century.

---

[97] c. 42. The provisions of this Act are to come into force on various dates: see the Broadcasting Act 1990 (Commencement No. 1 and Transitional Provisions) Order 1990 (S.I. 1990 No. 2347 (c. 61)), § B–254 *post.*
[98] *Ibid.* ss. 175 and 176.

SUBJECT MATTER OF COPYRIGHT PROTECTION

1. Introduction

Copyright works. The works in which copyright can subsist under the **2–1**
1988 Act, subject to the conditions for subsistence being met,[1] are described in section 1(1) of the 1988 Act as follows:

(a) original literary, dramatic, musical or artistic works,

(b) sound recordings, films, broadcasts or cable programmes,

and

(c) the typographical arrangement of published editions.

Works of these descriptions in which copyright subsists are referred to in the 1988 Act as "copyright works."[2] Each of these categories of works will be discussed in turn in this Chapter.

2. Literary Works

Statutory definition. By section 3(1) of the 1988 Act, "literary work" **2–2**
means any work, other than a dramatic or musical work, which is written, spoken or sung, and includes a table or compilation and a computer program. The express inclusion of a table or compilation repeats, in substance, section 48(1) of the 1956 Act.[3] The express inclusion of a computer

---

[1] C.D.P.A. 1988, ss.1(3) and 153; see Chap. 3, *post.*
[2] C.D.P.A. 1988, s.1(2).
[3] With the substitution of "a" for "any," which, though introduced into the definition in the Copyright Act 1956, was not considered to add anything to the definition; *per* Upjohn J. *Football League Ltd.* v. *Littlewoods Pools Ltd.* [1959] Ch. 637 at 650.

program follows the position adopted by the Copyright (Computer Software) Amendment Act 1985,[4] section 1(1) of which provided that such a program was to be treated as a literary work under the 1956 Act. In other respects, however, the definition of a literary work in the 1988 Act introduces new elements.

2–3 **Dramatic and musical works cannot be literary works.** The definition now expressly excludes dramatic and musical works from also being literary works. Whilst it had been recognised in the case of songs under the 1956 Act that the words and music were the subject of separate copyrights as literary and musical works respectively, and to that extent the categories were mutually exclusive,[5] it was not necessarily so as between dramatic and literary works. Under the present definition, if the work is properly a dramatic work, then it would appear that by that fact alone it cannot also be a literary work.[6]

2–4 **Written, spoken or sung.** The definition now expressly refers to one form which a literary work can take as being written. "Writing" is defined in section 178 of the 1988 Act as including any form of notation or code, whether by hand or otherwise and regardless of the method by which, or medium in or on which, it is recorded, and "written" is to be construed accordingly. This definition repeats, in substance but with enlargement,[7] the definition of "writing" in section 48(1) of the 1956 Act. However, the definition of a literary work expressly also envisages that the work may comprise words which are spoken or sung but are not written. It had been suggested that under the 1956 Act a literary work required to be expressed in some form of notation, before it could qualify as a literary work (irrespective of the requirements for copyright subsisting in such work),[8] but that is not so under the present definition, which clearly includes an extempore speech, lecture or judgment as capable of being a literary work.[9]

2–5 **The work must take some permanent form.** Copyright protection is not given to ideas or information, however novel or valuable, unless reduced into some form which can be characterised as a literary work,[10] and whilst such work may comprise ideas or information in the form they

---

[4] 1985 c. 41 (repealed by the 1988 Act).

[5] *Redwood Music Ltd.* v. *B. Feldman & Co. Ltd.* [1979] R.P.C. 385.

[6] Compare the definition of "musical work" which states that it is "exclusive of any words or action intended to be sung, spoken or performed with the music" and which therefore allows the same "work" to be both a musical work (as to the musical elements) and a dramatic work (as to the dramatic elements); see § 2–17, *post*.

[7] The reference to "code" is new, and the description of the manner and method of notation has been deliberately enlarged.

[8] See *Copinger* (12th ed.), §§ 53 and 85.

[9] Following the recommendation of the 1977 Copyright Committee, Cmnd. 6732, para. 609 (viii).

[10] There is no copyright in news, as such, but only in the literary form given to news: *per* North J., *Walter* v. *Steinkopff* [1892] 3 Ch. 489; *Wilson* v. *Lukepy* [1875] 1 V.L.R. 127; and see *Football League Ltd.* v. *Littlewoods Pools Ltd.* [1959] Ch. 637 at 651; *Independent Television Publications Ltd. and The British Broadcasting Corporation* v. *Time Out Ltd.* [1984] F.S.R. 64 at 68–72.

are spoken or sung, it must be borne in mind that a literary work is not entitled to copyright protection unless and until it takes on a more permanent form by being recorded, whether in writing or otherwise.[11] Human readability is not a requirement as to the form of the recording. Thus an original extempore speech, lecture or judgment would now be capable of being protected as a literary work once delivered, provided that some record of it, whether in shorthand or by mechanical means such as a tape recorder, was made when it was delivered.[12] Similarly, the lyrics of a song, even though not previously written down, would be capable of being protected as a literary work once sung, provided that the singing was recorded, as will often be the case when such performance is given as part of a recording session in a studio.

By whom noted. It is immaterial by whom the literary work is in fact **2–6** recorded.[13] Thus, if an author dictates to a stenographer, he will acquire copyright in his material as a literary work at the moment it is recorded in the notation of shorthand. This is on the basis that the person dictating the material is in fact the author of it, and it would be immaterial that the shorthand writer was not an employee.[14] Similarly, in the case of an original extempore speech, lecture or judgment which is recorded by another either by shorthand or on a tape recorder, it would appear that the person delivering the same would now be entitled to copyright in the speech, lecture or judgment,[15] whilst the person recording the same would be entitled to a separate (but necessarily dependent) copyright in the record, as a literary work if in shorthand, or as a sound recording if on tape. Again, the pop musician who performs a song comprising lyrics composed in his head creates a literary work when he sings such lyrics in a recording studio and they are recorded, and it is immaterial that the sound recording is made by the recording studio or the record company. In such cases there will be separate copyrights, often in separate ownership, in the literary work and the recording.

"Literary work." Whilst a work which is intended to afford another **2–7** pleasure in the form of literary enjoyment is one of the most obvious types of work qualifying as a "literary work," it has long been recognised that the word "literary" in the context of Copyright Acts does not import any requirement of literary style or merit. This was confirmed by the Court of Appeal in *Exxon Corporation* v. *Exxon Insurance Consultants International Ltd.*,[16] in which the Court held that it is sufficient for a work to be a literary work

---

[11] C.D.P.A. 1988, s.3(2).

[12] Compare under the old law, *Walter* v. *Lane* [1900] A.C. 539 and the discussion at § 4–6, *post.* As to filming of a dramatic work being the reduction of the work to a material form for the purposes of the equivalent provision to s.49 (4) of the 1956 Act, see *Green* v. *Broadcasting Corporation of New Zealand* [1982] R.P.C. 417 at 477 (Court of Appeal of New Zealand).

[13] C.D.P.A. 1988, s.3(3), following the recommendation of the 1977 Copyright Committee, Cmnd. 6732, para. 609 (viii). See further, § 3–49, *post.*

[14] See *Donoghue* v. *Allied Newspapers Ltd.* [1938] Ch. 106, and § 4–6, *post.*

[15] See § 2–5, *ante.*

[16] [1982] R.P.C. 69.

if it was intended to afford information and instruction.[17] Thus newspapers,[18] letters,[19] business letters,[20] and examination papers[21] have qualified for protection as literary works. Indeed, the work need not express a meaning in ordinary language, and thus there may be copyright in a list of words used as a telegraph code,[22] or in a catalogue of type,[23] or in a system of shorthand.[24] Again, so long as there is a sufficient amount of skill and labour in constructing or selecting the material,[25] no particular skill in the literary form itself is needed. Thus, copyright has been conferred in respect of newspaper telegrams,[26] in the rules of a game,[27] in the rules and coupon for a football competition,[28] in tallies for bridge parties[29] and in tables comprising grids of five-letter sequences for a monthly newspaper competition.[30]

2–8 **Compilations.** Notwithstanding the inclusion in the definition of "literary work" of compilations, it is assumed this relates not only to compilations of literary material, but also to compilations of literary and artistic material and even of artistic material alone. Protection has been given to such compilations as an arrangement of broadcasting programmes,[31] school textbooks,[32] a book of receipts,[33] a book of scientific questions and

---

[17] Approving the definition of a literary work given by Davey L.J. in *Hollinrake* v. *Truswell* [1884] 3 Ch. 420 at 427–8 as one which "is intended to afford either information and instruction or pleasure in the form of literary enjoyment"; *c.f. International Business Machines Corporation* v. *Spirales Computers Inc.* (1984) 12 D.L.R. (4th) 351, in which the Federal Court of Canada, in holding that a computer program was the subject of copyright, rejected this definition, stating that all that was required for a literary work was an expression of ideas in composition or language.

[18] *Cox* v. *Land and Water Journal Co.* (1869) L.R. 9. Eq. 324; *Walter* v. *Steinkopff* [1892] 3 Ch. 489; *Johnson* v. *George Newnes Ltd.* [1894] 3 Ch. 633; *Walter* v. *Lane* [1900] A.C. 539; there is no copyright in news as such, see n. 10, *ante*.

[19] *Walter* v. *Lane* [1900] A.C. 539; *Donoghue* v. *Allied Newspapers Ltd.* [1938] Ch. 106. See also "Copyright in Letters" printed as an addendum in [1905–10] Mac. C.C.

[20] *Tett Bros. Ltd.* v. *Drake & Gorham Ltd.* [1928–35] Mac.C.C. 492. *British Oxygen Co. Ltd.* v. *Liquid Air Ltd.* [1925] Ch. 383; there is no copyright in news as such, see n. 10, *ante*.

[21] *University of London Press Ltd.* v. *University Tutorial Press Ltd.* [1916] 2 Ch. 601; for a discussion of the meaning of "literary" in the Copyright Act 1911 see *ibid.* at 608 *per* Petersen J.

[22] *Anderson (D. P.) & Co. Ltd.* v. *The Lieber Code Co.* [1917] 2 K.B. 469; *Ager* v. *P. & O. Steam Navigation Co.* (1884) 26 Ch.D. 637; *Ager* v. *Collingridge* (1886) 2 T.L.R. 291.

[23] *Masson, Seeley & Co. Ltd.* v. *Embosotype Manufacturing Co.* (1924) 41 R.P.C. 160.

[24] *Pitman* v. *Hine* (1884) 1 T.L.R. 39; but see *Fournet* v. *Pearson Ltd.* (1897) 14 T.L.R. 82.

[25] See as to the requirements for subsistence of copyright in literary works, § 3–25 *et seq., post*.

[26] *Walter* v. *Steinkopff* [1892] 3 Ch. 489; *Exchange Telegraph Co. Ltd.* v. *Central News Ltd.* [1897] 2 Ch. 48.

[27] *Caley (A. J.) & Son Ltd.* v. *Garnett (G.) & Sons Ltd.* [1936–45] Mac.C.C. 99; but see *Cable* v. *Marks* (1882) 52 L.J. Ch. 107.

[28] *Ladbroke (Football) Ltd.* v. *William Hill (Football) Ltd.* [1964] 1 W.L.R. 273.

[29] *Stevenson (A.)* v. *Crook (H. F.)* [1938] Ex. (Can.) 299.

[30] *Express Newspapers* v. *Liverpool Daily Post* [1985] F.S.R. 306; [1985] 1 W.L.R. 1089.

[31] *British Broadcasting Co.* v. *Wireless League Gazette Publishing Co.* [1926] Ch. 433; *Independent Television Publications Ltd. and The British Broadcasting Corporation* v. *Time Out Ltd.* [1984] F.S.R. 64.

[32] *Educational Co. of Ireland Ltd.* v. *Fallon Bros. Ltd.* [1919] 1 I.R. 62; *Ghafur* v. *Jwala* [1921] A.I.R. All. 95; *Leanie* v. *Pillans* [1843] 5 Dunl. (Ct. of Sess.) 416.

[33] *Matthewson* v. *Stockdale* (1806) 12 Ves. 270; *Church* v. *Linton* (1894) 250 O.R. 131.

answers,[34] a directory,[35] a trade advertisement,[36] a mining report,[37] a list of registered bills of sale and deeds of arrangement extracted from official sources,[38] a list of foxhounds and hunting days,[39] a list of Stock Exchange prices,[40] biographical notes of prominent golfers published in a golf annual,[41] a list of brood mares with their sires and a list of stallions with daughters at the stud,[42] a list of weights and acceptances for horse racing,[43] a list of books,[44] a list of characteristics of racehorses,[45] a manual of classified information for the use of motor car insurers,[46] an alphabetical list of railway stations contained in *Bradshaw's Railway Guide*,[47] chronological fixture lists of football clubs,[48] football pool coupons,[49] columns of birth and death announcements in a newspaper,[50] contract forms,[51] sheets of election results,[52] and business literature.[53] Trade catalogues are generally compilations, and as such are capable of protection as literary works.[54] On similar principles, a computer database, stored on tape, disk or by other electronic means, would also generally be a compilation and capable of protection as a literary work. Whether a particular work of any of the descriptions mentioned above is in fact protected, depends, *inter alia*, on whether it satisfies the requirement of originality.[55]

---

[34] *Jarrold* v. *Houlston* (1857) 3 K. & J. 708.

[35] *Kelly* v. *Morris* (1866) L.R. 1 Eq. 697; *Morris* v. *Ashbee* (1868) L.R. 7 Eq. 34; *Morris* v. *Wright* (1870) 5 Ch. 279.

[36] *Maple & Co.* v. *Junior Army and Navy Stores* (1882) 21 Ch.D. 369.

[37] *Kenrick* v. *Danube Collieries, etc., Co. Ltd.* (1891) 39 W.R. 473.

[38] *Trade Auxiliary Co.* v. *Middlesbrough, etc. Association* (1889) 40 Ch.D. 425; *Cate* v. *Devon, etc. Newspaper Co.* (1889) 40 Ch.D. 500.

[39] *Cox* v. *Land and Water Journal Co.* (1869) L.R. 9 Eq. 324.

[40] *Exchange Telegraph Co. Ltd.* v. *Gregory & Co.* [1896] 1 Q.B. 147; *Stevens & Sons* v. *Waterlow & Sons Ltd.* [1877] 41 J.P. 37.

[41] *Nisbet (J.) & Co. Ltd.* v. *The Golf Agency* (1907) 23 T.L.R. 370.

[42] *Weatherby & Sons* v. *International Horse Agency and Exchange Ltd.* [1910] 2 Ch. 297.

[43] *Winterbottom* v. *Wintle* (1947) 50 W.A.L.R. 58; *T.M. Hall & Co.* v. *Whittington & Co.* [1892] 18 V.L.R. 525.

[44] *J. Whitaker & Sons Ltd.* v. *Publishers' Circular Ltd.* [1946–47] Mac.C.C. 10.

[45] *Portway Press Ltd.* v. *Hague* (1957) R.P.C. 426; and see *Canterbury Park Race Course Co. Ltd.* v. *Hopkins* (1932) 49 W.N. (N.S.W.) 27; *Demerara Turf Club* v. *Phang* (1963) 6 W.I.R. 177 and *Ascot Jockey Club Ltd.* v. *Simons* (1968) 64 W.W.R. 411.

[46] *Underwriters Survey Bureau Ltd.* v. *Amer. Home Fire Ass. Co.* (1939) 4 D.L.R. 89.

[47] *Blacklock (H.) & Co. Ltd.* v. *Arthur Pearson (C.) Ltd.* [1915] 2 Ch. 376; *c.f. Leslie* v. *Young (J.) & Sons Ltd.* [1894] A.C. 335.

[48] *Football League Ltd.* v. *Littlewoods Pools Ltd.* [1959] Ch. 637.

[49] *Ladbroke (Football) Ltd.* v. *William Hill (Football) Ltd.* [1964] 1 W.L.R. 273.

[50] *John Fairfax & Sons Pty. Ltd.* v. *Australian Consolidated Press Ltd.* [1960] S.R. (N.S.W.) 413.

[51] *Capital Finance Co.* v. *Bowmaker (Commercial) Ltd.* [1964] R.P.C. 463 and *Capital Finance Co.* v. *Lombank Ltd.* [1964] R.P.C. 467; see also *Alexander (W.)* v. *Mackenzie (R.)* (1846) 9 Sess.-Cas.D. 748; *Real Estate Institute of N.S.W.* v. *Wood* (1923) 23 S.R. (N.S.W.) 349.

[52] *Press Association Ltd.* v. *Northern and Midland Reporting Agency* [1905–10] Mac.C.C. 306.

[53] *Coral Index Ltd.* v. *Regent Index Ltd.* [1970] R.P.C. 147; *Van Oppen & Co. Ltd.* v. *Leonard Van Oppen* (1903) 20 R.P.C. 617; *Masson, Seeley & Co. Ltd.* v. *Embosotype Manufacturing Co.* (1924) 41 R.P.C. 160; *Warran* v. *Foster Brothers Clothing Co. Ltd.* [1906] 51 S.J. 145; *Southern* v. *Bailes* [1894] 38 S.J. 681; *Co-operative Union Ltd.* v. *Kilmore, etc. Ltd.* [1912] 47 I.L.T. 7; *Elanco Products Ltd.* v. *Mandops (Agrochemical Specialists) Ltd.* [1979] F.S.R. 46.

[54] *Hotten* v. *Arthur* (1863) 1 H. & M. 603; *Grace* v. *Newman* (1875) L.R. 19 Eq. 623; *Maple & Co.* v. *Junior Army and Navy Stores* (1882) 21 Ch.D. 369 (overruling *Cobbett* v. *Woodward* (1872) L.R. 14 Eq. 407 to the contrary); *Davis* v. *Benjamin* [1906] 2 Ch. 491.

[55] As to which, see § 3–35, *et seq., post.*

2–9 **Computer programs.** As already stated, the express inclusion of computer programs as literary works follows the position under the previous law, after the Copyright (Computer Software) Amendment Act 1985.[56] This Act adopted the recommendation of the 1977 Copyright Committee[57] that all computer programs and other items of computer software which have involved a sufficient degree of skill and/or labour in their creation to be considered as works in the normal copyright sense, and which have been reduced to writing or some other material form from which they can be reproduced, should be clearly protected under copyright law. Within that formulation clearly fall the more obvious form for "literary" works, such as a print out of a computer program, but it would include other forms of storing a computer program, such as punched cards, punched tapes, magnetic tapes, magnetic cores, disks and micro-chips. The 1988 Act contains no definition of a computer program, but it seems that it will include any program which has the effect of controlling a computer to operate in a particular way. No doubt a computer program must still possess the general characteristics, discussed above,[58] required for something to qualify as a literary work, but this would usually be the case.[59]

2–10 **Works refused protection as literary works.** A single invented word, even though original, has been held not to qualify as a literary work[60] and titles of books and magazines, at least so far as short titles of unoriginal character are concerned, do not qualify as literary works.[61] Whilst written advertisements are clearly capable of copyright protection as literary

---

[56] 1985 c. 41 (repealed by the 1988 Act). The Act was retrospective and applied to computer programs made before the Commencement of the Act as well as afterwards: *Milltronics Ltd. v. Hycontrol Ltd.* [1990] F.S.R. 273. It had already been held that an assembly code program for a computer was capable of protection as a literary work under the 1956 Act (*per* Goulding J. in *Sega Enterprises Ltd. v. Richards* [1983] F.S.R. 73) and that computer programs generally were capable of protection as literary works (*per* Megarry V-C. in *Thrustcode Ltd. v. W. W. Computing Ltd.* [1983] F.S.R. 502); see also *Gates v. Swift* [1982] R.P.C. 339 (Anton Piller order granted by Graham J. in respect of alleged piracy of computer programs). The same approach had been adopted in America (*Whelan Associates Inc. v. Jaslow Dental Laboratory Inc.* [1987] F.S.R. 1) and in South Africa (*Northern Office Micro Computers (Pty.) Ltd. v. Rosenstein* [1982] F.S.R. 124).

[57] Cmnd. 6732, para. 520 (i).

[58] See § 2–7, *ante.*

[59] See *Computer Edge Pty. Ltd. v. Apple Computer Inc.* [1986] F.S.R. 537, in the High Court of Australia at Canberra, in which the majority, ruling on the Australian Copyright Act 1968, prior to its amendment by the Australian Copyright Amendment Act 1984 (which gave a degree of protection to computer programs), applied these requirements and distinguished between the source code of each program, which did qualify as a literary work, and the object code of each program stored as electrical impulses in a silicon chip, which they held did not qualify as a literary work.

[60] *Exxon Corporation v. Exxon Insurance Consultants International Ltd.* [1982] R.P.C. 69. It has been held in other cases that English law recognises no property or monopoly in a name *per se*, see *Taverner Rutledge Ltd. v. Trexapalm Ltd.* [1975] F.S.R. 479 *per* Walton J. at p. 483; *Kean v. McGivan* [1982] F.S.R. 119 ("Social Democratic Party").

[61] See §§ 21–29 to 21–31, *post.* See also *Rose v. Information Services Ltd.* [1987] F.S.R. 254 and Graham J. in *Exxon Corporation v. Exxon Insurance Consultants International Ltd.* [1982] R.P.C. 69 at 79. As to the right to the title of a newspaper, see *Licensed Victuallers' Newspaper Co. v. Bingham* (1888) 38 Ch.D. 449. See generally, as to titles, § 21–29, *et seq., post.*

works,[62] it has been held, on the grounds of triviality, that there is no copyright in the advertisement slogan, "youthful appearances are social necessities, not luxuries,"[63] nor in the stringing together, for advertisement purposes, of a number of commonplace sentences.[64] The court declined, under the old law, to hold that there was copyright in respect of a cardboard pattern sleeve containing upon it scales, figures and descriptive words for adapting it to sleeves of any dimensions,[65] a list of sporting selections,[66] a scoring sheet used for cricket,[67] or an album for holding photographs,[68] and, under the later law, in respect of a card containing spaces and certain directions for filing particulars under the National Health Insurance Act 1911,[69] a race card containing the names of competitors in a race in the order in which they were drawn,[70] a selection of tables for use in a diary,[71] and headings and explanatory notes for football pools coupons.[72]

3. Dramatic Works

Statutory definition. By section 3(1) of the 1988 Act, "dramatic work" is **2–11** defined as including a work of dance[73] or mime. This definition is in substance the same as that under the 1956 Act,[74] which referred to a choreographic work or entertainment in dumb show. However, the definition in the 1956 Act also required a dramatic work to be "reduced to writing in the form in which the work or entertainment is to be presented."[75] It was thought that this had introduced a change from the position under the 1911 Act, which had required the form of the work "to be fixed in writing

---

[62] Some doubt had been expressed on the point under the law prior to 1911: *Lamb* v. *Evans* [1892] 3 Ch. 462; on appeal [1893] 1 Ch. 218; see now *Machinery Market Ltd.* v. *Sheen Publishing Ltd.* [1983] F.S.R. 431.

[63] *Sinanide* v. *La Maison Kosmeo* (1928) 139 L.T. 365.

[64] *Kirk* v. *Fleming (J. & R.) Ltd.* [1928–35] Mac.C.C. 44.

[65] *Hollinrake* v. *Truswell* [1894] Ch. 420; followed in *Boosey* v. *Wright* [1900] 1 Ch. 122; but see Whitford J. in *Express Newspapers plc* v. *Liverpool Daily Post & Echo plc* [1985] F.S.R. 306 at 310.

[66] *Chilton* v. *Progress Printing, etc., Co.* [1895] 2 Ch. 29; *Fournet* v. *Pearson Ltd.* (1897) 14 T.L.R. 82; *Smith's Newspapers Ltd.* v. *The Labour Daily* (1925) 25 S.R. (N.S.W.) 593.

[67] *Page* v. *Wisden* (1869) 20 L.T. 435; and see *Griffen* v. *Kingston, etc., Co.* (1889) 17 O.R. 660 (railway ticket).

[68] *Schove* v. *Schmincke* (1886) 33 Ch.D. 546.

[69] *Libraco Ltd.* v. *Shaw Walker Ltd.* (1913) 30 T.L.R. 22.

[70] *Greyhound Racing Association Ltd.* v. *Shallis* [1923–28] Mac.C.C. 370; but see *Canterbury Park Race Course Co. Ltd.* v. *Hopkins* (1932) 49 W.N. (N.S.W.) 27; *Odhams Press Ltd.* v. *London and Provincial Sporting News Agency, etc., Ltd.* [1936] Ch. 357; *Demerara Turf Club* v. *Phang* (1963) 6 W.I.R. 177 and *Ascot Jockey Club Ltd.* v. *Simons* (1968) 64 W.W.R. 411.

[71] *G. A. Cramp & Sons Ltd.* v. *Frank Smythson Ltd.* [1944] A.C. 329; and see *Cartwright* v. *Wharton* [1912] 25 O.L.R. 357 (system of indexing) and *Thomas Forman & Sons Ltd.* v. *Balding & Mansell* [1928–35] Mac.C.C. 501 (calendar).

[72] *William Hill (Football) Ltd.* v. *Ladbroke (Football) Ltd.* [1980] R.P.C. 539 (Court of Appeal).

[73] Under the law prior to 1911, it was held that there could be no copyright in a dance: *Bishop* v. *Viviana & Co.* [1905–10] Mac.C.C. 211.

[74] Copyright Act 1956 s.48(1).

[75] *Ibid.*

or otherwise."[76] The reinstatement, in the present definition,[77] of the words "in writing or otherwise" ensures that the position is as it was thought to be under the 1911 Act, namely that a sketch or dramatic work which is not otherwise written down or the subject of any form of notation, may acquire copyright protection if recorded, for example, on film, at the moment of performance.[78]

2–12   **Dramatic and musical works.** Whilst a dramatic work cannot, by definition,[79] also be a literary work, the same is not the case as between a dramatic and a musical work. If a dramatic work includes music, the musical elements are capable of copyright protection as a musical work, but it would seem that the work as a whole is still capable of protection as a dramatic work.[79a]

2–13   **Importance of distinction between literary and dramatic and musical works.** The distinction between a dramatic work or musical work and a literary work, already much less important under the 1956 Act than it had been under the law prior to 1911, ceases to be of any importance under the 1988 Act, which seeks to apply the same rules uniformly to each work, with the exception of the infringement of making an adaptation of the work, where it is only in the case of a dramatic work that it is an infringement to make an adaptation of it by converting it into a non-dramatic work.[80]

2–14   **What constitutes a dramatic work.** Under the law prior to 1911, because of the definitions contained in the Dramatic Copyright Act 1833[81] and the Literary Copyright Act 1842,[82] the courts held that the words "dramatic entertainment" should be construed in such a way that they required a dramatic work to be capable of being printed and published, in order for it to be the subject of copyright protection.[83] It was no doubt for this reason that it was considered that neither a pantomime nor a choreographic work was entitled to copyright protection.[84] The need for the existence of some work capable of being printed and published disappeared under the 1911 Act, and therefore such old cases are of limited help in

---

[76] See *Copinger* (12th ed.), § 164; the 1911 Act adopted the words of Article 2 of the Berne Convention, repeated in the Brussels Convention, but not in the Stockholm or Paris Conventions which left any requirement for fixation to domestic legislation.

[77] C.D.P.A. 1988, s.3(2), and see § 2–5, *ante*.

[78] See, for example, *Green* v. *Broadcasting Corporation of New Zealand* [1982] R.P.C. 417 at 477 (New Zealand Court of Appeal).

[79] C.D.P.A. 1988, s.3(1); and see § 2–3, *ante*.

[79a] *Ibid.* n. 79

[80] C.D.P.A. 1988, s.21(3)(ii), and see § 8–31, *post*.

[81] Giving to authors of "any tragedy, comedy, play, opera, farce or other dramatic piece of entertainment" the sole liberty of performing it: Dramatic Copyright Act 1833 (3 & 4 Will. 4, c. 15).

[82] Declaring that "the words 'dramatic piece' shall be construed to mean and include every tragedy, comedy, play, opera, farce or other scenic, musical, or dramatic entertainment": Literary Copyright Act 1842 (5 & 6 Vict. c. 45).

[83] *Tate* v. *Fullbrook* [1908] 1 K.B. 821; *Tree* v. *Bowkett* (1896) 74 L.T. 77; *Beere* v. *Ellis* (1889) 5 T.L.R. 330.

[84] *Karno* v. *Pathé Frères Ltd.* (1909) 100 L.T. 260. In *Lee* v. *Simpson* (1847) 3 C.B. 871 the written introduction to a pantomime was protected, but it is not clear that the protection extended to the pantomime itself.

establishing what does constitute a dramatic work. Under the present definition, essentially the same as that in the 1911 and 1956 Acts, a work must be a dramatic work, pure and simple, or a work of dance or a mime. A dramatic work implies a work that is capable of being performed.[85] Further, it is thought that the performance must be one which involves action. Works of dance and mime clearly predicate action, but a work consisting of words to be spoken or sung, would not, it is suggested, be a dramatic work unless the performance of the words is to be accompanied by action. Thus, a singer who sings in character costume but without action would not, it is thought, be performing a dramatic work.[86]

Scenic effects. The words "scenic arrangement," which had appeared in **2–15** the definition of dramatic work in the 1911 Act,[87] were dropped from the definition of dramatic work in the 1956 Act. This was taken to limit the scope of the definition, and to confine protection to something which has dramatic action without regard to any elements of background or production. It had already been held under the 1911 Act, in *Tate* v. *Fullbrook*,[88] that mere scenic effects, taken by themselves and apart from the words and incidents of the piece, were not protected by copyright, but as was admitted by the Lords Justices in that case once there is dialogue, scenic effects become accessory to the dramatic work, and the whole becomes the subject of copyright, in the sense that they are the background of the dramatic action and are therefore part of it. If the scenic effects are fitted to a totally different dialogue, that may not be an infringement; but if the dialogue is not dissimilar, the fact that the scenic effects also correspond with those found in the earlier work may be evidence of plagiarism. Nowadays, scenic effects will most often be the subject of prior drawings, which will be capable of protection as artistic works.[89]

Characters, make-up, incidents, "gags." Equally, in *Tate* v. *Fullbrook*[90] **2–16** it was held that the plaintiff could have no copyright in the incidents, the make-up or the "gag" in his sketch which comprised comic dialogue grounded on very slight dramatic action. Such aspects of a dramatic performance are not themselves the subjects of protection, apart from either

---

[85] The features claimed as constituting the format of a television show, being unrelated to each other except as accessories to be used in the presentation of some other dramatic or musical performance, lacked the essential characteristic of sufficient unity to be capable of performance: *Green* v. *Broadcasting Corporation of New Zealand* [1989] R.P.C. 700 (P.C.).

[86] *Tate* v. *Fullbrook* [1908] 1 K.B. 821 at 832, *per* Farwell L.J.

[87] Dramatic work was defined as including "any piece for recitation, choreographic work or entertainment in dumb show, the scenic arrangement or acting form of which is fixed in writing or otherwise": Copyright Act 1911, s.35.

[88] [1908] 1 K.B. 821; contrary to the dictum of Brett J. in *Chatterton* v. *Cave* (1876) as reported in 33 L.T. 255.

[89] This is possibly the explanation of the decision in *Perkin* v. *Ray Bros.* [1911–16] Mac.C.C. 288, where copyright was held to subsist in the *mise en scene* of a revue. The use of scenic effects coupled with the use of a name may also give rise to a passing-off action; see § 21–28, *et seq.*, *post*.

[90] [1908] 1 K.B. 821.

words or defined movements.[91] The basis for the "gag" being held not to be the subject of copyright was that, generally speaking, the author of the "gag" is not the writer of the play, but the actor who speaks the words, and that, even if the writer of the play and the speaker of the "gag" should happen to be the same person, the "gag" is not a permanent part of the play, but is intended to be changed from time to time. There must be some certainty in the subject matter of copyright.[92] But if such certainty is attained, there seems no reason why the author of the "gag" should not have copyright in it.

4. Musical Works

2–17 **Statutory definition.** The 1988 Act defines "musical work" as a work consisting of music, exclusive of any words or action intended to be sung, spoken or performed with the music.[93] "Music" is defined in the *Shorter Oxford English Dictionary* as sounds in melodic or harmonic combination, whether produced by voice or instruments.[94] There is no requirement in the statutory definition of a musical work that the music must be in writing or other notation. However, as with a literary and a dramatic work, for music to be the subject matter of copyright it must first be recorded, in writing or otherwise.[95] Again, it is immaterial how or by whom it is so recorded.[96] This is of particular importance in relation to much of the modern "pop" type of music, which is played straight onto tapes without having first been written down. So, as with the lyrics,[97] the pop musician who performs a song comprising music composed in his head creates a musical work when he plays such music in a recording studio and it is recorded, and it is immaterial that the sound recording is made by the recording studio or the record company. In such cases there will be separate copyrights, often in separate ownership, in the musical work and in the recording.

2–18 **Consequences of requirement of being recorded.** It follows from the combination of sections 3(1) and 3(2) of the 1988 Act that if A improvises a tune in B's presence, then A has created a musical work. However, at

---

[91] But see as to protection given to situations and incidents in a play, *Rees* v. *Melville* [1911–1916] Mac.C.C. 96 and 168 and § 8–48, *et seq., post.*

[92] *Tate* v. *Thomas* [1921] 1 Ch. 503; and see *Green* v. *Broadcasting Corporation of New Zealand,* [1989] R.P.C. 700 (P.C.) (required certainty lacking in "dramatic format" claimed in respect of television show).

[93] s.3(1); there was no definition of musical work in the Copyright Act 1911 or in the Copyright Act 1956.

[94] An identical definition was given in the now repealed Musical (Summary Proceedings) Copyright Act 1902 (2 Edw. 7, c. 15, s.3) but which continued by requiring the music to be "printed, reduced to writing or otherwise graphically produced or reproduced."

[95] s.3(2).

[96] s.3(3) but see § 3–49, *post.*

[97] See § 2–6, *ante.*

that point the tune is not protected by copyright, as it is neither written down nor otherwise recorded. If B carries the tune away in his head and subsequently records it, then by such act by B the tune may become protected by copyright.[98] However, B is not the author of the tune, as he is not the person who created it.[99] Although it is B's act in recording the tune which caused the tune to be the subject of copyright, upon such recording taking place it would seem clear that A is the owner of any copyright thereby subsisting in the tune and could therefore sue B for infringing his copyright.[1]

Musical work also a dramatic work. The definition of a musical work **2–19** makes it clear that it does not include words intended to be sung or spoken with the music. It is presumed, firstly, that the intention being referred to is the intention of the author of the music and, secondly, that the material time for establishing the intention is the time he creates the music. Any such words, if they constitute a literary work,[2] are treated as a separate work, entitled to a separate copyright, and the mutually exclusive nature of the two types of works is strictly maintained. However, as already pointed out,[3] a dramatic work may include music, and in a number of cases the question arose whether a particular work was a dramatic piece as well as a musical work.[4] The position under the 1988 Act seems clear: in such a case the music will be entitled to a separate copyright, notwithstanding that the music also forms an integral part of the dramatic work, as in the case of a work of dance written to music, or an opera. This question is now less important, since the owner of copyright in a dramatic work has the same rights as those enjoyed by the owner of copyright in a musical work.[5]

5. Artistic Works

Statutory definition. By section 4(1) of the 1988 Act, "artistic work" **2–20** means:

(a) a graphic work, photograph, sculpture or collage, irrespective of artistic quality;
(b) a work of architecture being a building or a model for a building; or
(c) a work of artistic craftsmanship.

---

[98] Depending on the point discussed at § 3–49, *post.*
[99] See s.9(1) and § 4–5, *et seq. post.*
[1] Subject to the not inconsiderable evidential difficulty A would face of proving that he was in fact the author of the tune published by B.
[2] See § 2–7, *ante.*
[3] See § 2–12, *ante.*
[4] *Russell* v. *Smith* (1848) 12 Q.B. 217; *Clark* v. *Bishop* (1872) 25 L.T. 908; *Roberts* v. *Bignell* (1887) 3 T.L.R. 552; *Fuller* v. *The Blackpool Winter Gardens, etc., Co. Ltd.* [1895] 2 Q.B. 429.
[5] But see § 2–13, *ante.*

2–21   **Graphic works, etc.** The term "graphic work" is new in the 1988 Act, and is defined to include any painting,[6] drawing, diagram, map, chart or plan,[7] engraving,[8] etching, lithograph, woodcut or similar work.[9] "Photograph" is defined to mean a recording of light or other radiation on any medium on which an image is produced or from which an image may by any means be produced, and which is not part of a film.[10] Save for the last clause, this definition is new and is so worded to ensure that such modern inventions as holograms are capable of protection as artistic works by being photographs. The last clause of the definition, which in this respect follows the definition in the 1956 Act,[11] excludes a single frame of a film from being capable of protection as a photograph. A single frame of a film is, however, protectable as part of a film.[12]

"Sculpture" is defined in the 1988 Act to include a cast or model made for purposes of sculpture,[13] but the 1988 Act does not otherwise define what is a sculpture.[14] Whilst a carved wooden model produced as a step in the process of manufacturing Frisbees has been held to qualify as a sculpture,[15] it has been held that models or casts fashioned in plasticine or some other suitable modelling material which were no more than steps in the production first of prototypes and later in the manufacturing of tooling and were not intended to have any permanent existence did not fall within the definition of sculpture.[16] A collage is now specifically included as an artistic work.[17]

---

[6] "Painting" is not defined, but is a word in the ordinary usage of English language, and must be on a surface; it does not embrace facial make-up (of Adam Ant): *Merchandising Corporation of America Inc.* v. *Harpbond Ltd.* [1983] F.S.R. 32.

[7] As to protection of maps and plans of imaginary things, see *Braithwaite Burn & Co.* v. *Trustees of the Port of Madras* (1956) 2 Mad. L.J. 486.

[8] Rubber stereos used for printing onto transfer paper were held to be engravings under the 1956 Act: *James Arnold and Co. Ltd.* v. *Miafern Ltd.* [1980] R.P.C. 397. Similarly, dies and moulds were held in New Zealand to be engravings: *Wham-O Manufacturing Co.* v. *Lincoln Industries Ltd.* [1985] R.P.C. 130.

[9] C.D.P.A. 1988, s.4(2); embracing the previous definition found in s.3(1) and those of "drawing" and "engraving" (with the immaterial omission of "print") in s.48(1) of the 1956 Act.

[10] C.D.P.A. 1988, s.4(2).

[11] Compare the definition in the Copyright Act 1956, s.48(1): "any product of photography or any process akin to photography, other than a part of a cinematograph film."

[12] Being a recording on any medium from which a moving image may by any means be produced; see *Spelling Goldberg Productions Inc.* v. *B.P.C. Publishing* [1981] R.P.C. 283, and § 2–30, *post.*

[13] C.D.P.A. 1988, s.4(2), repeating the definition in s.48(1) of the Copyright Act 1956.

[14] The *Oxford English Dictionary* defines the art of sculpture as the art of forming representations of objects or abstract designs in the round or in relief by chiselling stone, carving wood, modelling clay, casting metal or similar processes.

[15] See *Wham-O Manufacturing Co.* v. *Lincoln Industries Ltd.* [1985] R.P.C. 130 (New Zealand Court of Appeal), in which wooden models from which dies and moulds were made were held to be sculptures, but not the moulded discs themselves.

[16] *Davis (J & S) (Holdings) Ltd.* v. *Wright Health Group Ltd.* [1988] R.P.C. 403.

[17] There was some doubt as to whether a collage fell within the definition of an artistic work under the 1956 Act.

Artistic quality. In the case of artistic works described under sub- **2–22**
paragraph (*a*), the words "irrespective of artistic quality" occur.[18] The
definition of "artistic work" under the 1911 Act did not contain such
words,[19] but it was generally considered that the word "artistic" was
merely used as a generic term to include the different processes of creating
works set out in the definition section and that, provided that a work was
produced by one of such processes, and that its creation involved some
skill or labour on the part of the artist, it was protected.[20] The use of the
word "artistic" was thought to be equivalent to that of the word "literary," which, as already pointed out,[21] was held to refer only to the nature
of the material being written or printed and not to its literary quality.

This contrasts with the position in the case of artistic works falling
within sub-paragraphs (*b*) and (*c*), where such words do not occur.[22]

Protected works. Simplicity is not enough to prevent copyright subsist- **2–23**
ing in an artistic work, and drawings for rivets and the like have been held
protectable.[23] On the other hand, it has been held that settings or arrangements of furniture are not protectable works.[24] Protection has been
accorded to the artistic part of a trade mark,[25] designs for labels,[26] and to
a signature and Union emblem.[27] Drawings for standard parts for vehicles
such as engines and gear boxes[28] and exhausts,[29] and engineering drawings generally,[29a] have been held capable of protection as artistic works.

Point patterns for knitted fabrics,[30] and drawings for clerical shirts[31]
have been protected as artistic works. In cases concerned with dress
designs infringement is often alleged, where applicable, in the design

---

[18] As under the Copyright Act 1956, s.3(1)(*a*).
[19] Copyright Act 1911, s.35(1).
[20] Thus merely commercial designs were protected under the Copyright Act 1911: *Waters* v. *Huygen (M.A.) & Co.* [1923–28] Mac.C.C. 17; *Purefoy Engineering Co. Ltd.* v. *Sykes, Boxall & Co. Ltd.* (1955) 72 R.P.C. 89.
[21] See § 2–5, *ante*.
[22] See §§ 2–27 and 2–28, *post*.
[23] *British Northrop Ltd.* v. *Texteam Blackburn Ltd.* [1974] R.P.C. 57. See also *Ogden Industries Pty. Ltd.* v. *Kis (Australia) Ltd.* [1983] F.S.R. 619 (New South Wales Supreme Court: drawings of key-profiles held subject of copyright protection); but even if simple, such drawings must be original, see further § 3–25, *et seq.*, *post*.
[24] *Jarman & Platt Ltd.* v. *I. Barget Ltd.* [1977] F.S.R. 260.
[25] *Karo Step Trade Mark* [1977] R.P.C. 255.
[26] *Charles Walker & Co. Ltd.* v. *The British Picker Co. Ltd.* [1961] R.P.C. 57; *Taverner Rutledge Ltd.* v. *Specters, Ltd.* [1959] R.P.C. 83.
[27] In March 1977 (the *Daily Telegraph*, March 1, 1977) Mr. Clive Jenkins and his Union were awarded damages for infringement of copyright by the use of the facsimile of his signature and the Union's emblem. In *News Group Newspapers Ltd.* v. *Minor Group Newspapers (1986) Ltd.* [1989] F.S.R. 126, it was assumed that the masthead of The Sun was capable of being protected as an artistic work, subject to its originality.
[28] *Nichols Advanced Vehicle Systems Inc.* v. *Rees* [1979] R.P.C. 127.
[29] *L.B. (Plastics) Ltd.* v. *Swish Products Ltd.* [1979] R.P.C. 551; *Kwik Lok Corporation* v. *W.B.W. Engineers Ltd.* [1975] F.S.R. 237; *British Leyland Motor Corporation* v. *T. I. Silencers Ltd.* [1981] F.S.R. 213; *British Leyland Motor Corporation* v. *Armstrong Patents Co. Ltd.* [1972] F.S.R. 481. In *The Times*, November 12, 1975 it was reported that an undertaking had been given in respect of alleged infringement of designs for micro-circuits.
[29a] *Supra*, n. 29.
[30] As drawings: *Lerose Ltd.* v. *Hawick Jersey International Ltd.* [1973] F.S.R. 15.
[31] *Gleeson* v. *H. R. Denne Ltd.* [1975] R.P.C. 471.

sketch, cutting patterns and prototype garment.[32] The sketch is undoubt-edly a work capable of protection.[33] It is less clearly established which categories of work the patterns and prototype garment must fall into in order to be protected. It has been suggested, with some judicial appro-val,[34] that the patterns are protected as drawings, and they have been so treated in two subsequent cases.[35] It has also been suggested, with some judicial approval,[36] that the prototype garment is protected as a work of artistic craftsmanship.[37]

Typeface designs were considered capable of protection under the 1956 Act as artistic works, at least as to designs of individual letters, although doubt was expressed as to whether designs for founts (*i.e.* complete sets of lettering) qualified as artistic works.[38] The 1988 Act proceeds on the assumption that designs for typefaces qualify for protection as artistic works (without making any distinction between individual letters and sets).[39]

2–24 Drawings not ideas protected. Ideas, however original, are not pro-tected by copyright. Consequently, where a very simple diagram embodies an original idea, it is the diagram and not the idea which is pro-tected. In such a case the protection afforded by copyright is relatively weak, as exemplified by the case of *Kenrick & Co. v. Lawrence & Co.*[40] In that case the plaintiff conceived the idea of printing and publishing cards bearing a representation of a hand holding a pencil in the act of complet-ing a cross within a square, with a view to such cards being used at elec-tions by illiterate voters. The plaintiff procured an artist to make, under his directions, a drawing of the representation. Subsequently the defend-ants published similar cards with a hand holding a pencil, but the hand in the defendants' cards was in a slightly different position, though the idea was clearly taken from the plaintiff's cards. It was held that the defend-ants had not infringed the plaintiff's copyright. There was no copyright in the idea; the defendants' work was not an exact reproduction of the plain-tiff's, and the plaintiff was not entitled to prevent anyone from producing such a simple design as a hand in a square in any form.[41]

---

[32] *Radley Gowns Ltd.* v. *Costas Spyrou* [1975] F.S.R. 455.

[33] See *J. Bernstein Ltd.* v. *Sidney Murray Ltd.* [1981] R.P.C. 303.

[34] See n. 32, *ante.*

[35] *Merlet* v. *Mothercare plc* [1984] F.S.R. 358. The point was conceded in *House of Spring Gardens Ltd.* v. *Point Blank Ltd.* [1983] F.S.R. 213 (High Court of Ireland).

[36] See n. 32, *ante.*

[37] See § 2–27, *post.*

[38] See the 1977 Copyright Committee, Cmnd. 6732, paras. 524 and 529. The Committee recommended (*ibid.* para. 538) that the United Kingdom should ratify the Vienna Agree-ment on the Protection of Typefaces (signed by the United Kingdom on June 12, 1973) (Cmnd. 5754, set out in *Copinger* (12th ed.), App. C, § 2011), but to date the United King-dom has not done so.

[39] C.D.P.A. 1988, s.178 defines "typeface" as including an ornamental motif used in print-ing, and see ss.54 and 55 and § 10–60, *et seq., post.*

[40] (1890) 25 Q.B.D. 99. *c.f. Nottage* v. *Jackson* (1883) 11 Q.B.D. 627; and *Commercial Signs* v. *General Motors Products of Canada, Ltd.* (1937) 2 D.L.R. 310.

[41] See also *George Ward (Moxley) Ltd.* v. *Richard Sankey Ltd.* [1988] F.S.R. 66, where Whitford J. adopted a similar approach to the copying of an idea for the design of flower pots.

Works of architecture. Works of architecture, as distinct from the plans, **2–25**
drawings and sketches of such works,[42] were first made capable of being
the subject of copyright protection under the 1911 Act.[43]

A work of architecture is defined by the 1988 Act as being a building or
a model for a building,[44] and "building" is defined by such Act as including any fixed structure, and a part of a building or fixed structure.[45] Apart
from this statutory definition, no general definition of "building" can be
given,[46] although it has been said that, prima facie, a "building" means
"a block of brick or stone work covered in by a roof."[47] The term must be
construed reasonably, having regard to the object of the statute.[48] Upon
this principle, it is thought that the building or structure must be of such a
character as is usually erected upon, or constructed under, the ground and
that in each case it involves something of substance, with an element of
permanence. If a building or structure has these characteristics, then it
will be entitled to protection, not only as a whole, but in individual architectural features, including internal features of design.[49] On this basis a
chimney-piece might, it is thought, be entitled to copyright. It has been
held that a garden, consisting of a layout including steps, walls, ponds and
other structures in stone, was capable of protection as "a structure."[50]

In view of the foregoing, it is questionable whether the introduction in
the 1988 Act of the qualification "fixed" to the term "structure" is helpful.
Presumably "fixed" means fixed to the ground, and is intended to denote
a degree of permanence, but the term may itself introduce argument as to
the degree and duration of fixation which is envisaged and could result in
some arbitrary distinctions between works capable of protection as architectural works and others which are not. For example, a construction such
as a summer house, which rests by its own weight on the ground but is not
otherwise fixed to the ground, would seem by this requirement to be
excluded from being a work of architecture, but would be capable of being
a work of architecture if fixed to the ground in any way (even if such fixing
was intended to be only temporary).

---

[42] All protected as artistic works since the Copyright Act 1956, whereas under the Copyright
Act 1911 sketches and plans were protected as literary works by reason of the definition in
s.35(1).

[43] Copyright Act 1911, s.35(1). The contention that there could not be a separate copyright
in a building, as distinct from in the plans on which the building was based, was rejected
in *Meikle* v. *Maufe* [1941] 3 All E.R. 144. For a fuller discussion of the development of the
law in relation to architectural works see *Copinger* (12th ed.), §§ 251–252.

[44] C.D.P.A. 1988, s.4(1)(*b*), in identical terms to the definition in s.3(1)(*b*) of the Copyright
Act 1956.

[45] C.D.P.A. 1988, s.4(2), in identical terms to the definition in s.48(1) of the Copyright Act
1956, except for the introduction of the word "fixed."

[46] *Per* Byles J., *Stevens* v. *Gourley* (1860) 7 C.B. (N.S.) 99.

[47] *Moir* v. *Williams* [1892] 1 Q.B. 264. See also *Waite's Exors.* v. *Commissioners of Inland Revenue*
[1914] 3 K.B. 196.

[48] *Per* Lindley L.J. *Lavy* v. *London County Council* [1895] 2 Q.B. 577, 582. *British Transport Docks
Board* v. *Williams* [1970] 1 W.L.R. 652. It is suggested, therefore, that cases decided under
other Acts, *e.g.* the London Building Acts, have little or no application. As to erections
that have been held to be "buildings or structures" see 4 Halsbury's *Laws of England* (4th
ed.), para. 1144. Se also *H. E. Dibble Ltd.* v. *Moore* [1970] 2 Q.B. 181.

[49] *Vincent* v. *Universal Housing Co. Ltd.* [1928–35] Mac.C.C. 275.

[50] *Meikle* v. *Maufe* [1941] 3 All E.R. 144.

2–26   **Artistic character or design of architectural work.** Under the 1911
Act the definition of a work of architecture required that it should have
"an artistic character or design" and expressly provided that the protection given was to be confined to the artistic character and design and
should not extend to processes or methods of construction.[51] The reference
to artistic character or design and the proviso were both omitted in the
definition under the 1956 Act,[52] and this is followed in the 1988 Act. However, it is thought that the omission of such words in the 1956 Act did not
produce any substantial alteration in the law. While drawings and plans
are protected "irrespective of artistic quality,"[53] the omission of these
words in respect of architectural works maintains, in effect, the requirement under the 1911 Act that such works, in order to be architectural
works, must have some artistic character or design.

2–27   **Works of artistic craftsmanship.** Prior to the decision in *George Hensher
Ltd.* v. *Restawile Upholstery (Lancs) Ltd.*[54] below, the only decision in this
country as to the meaning of works of artistic craftsmanship was that in
Burke etc. Ltd. v. *Spicers Dress Designs*,[55] a decision under the 1911 Act
which, like the 1956 Act, also protected such works.[56]

In *Burke etc. Ltd.* v. *Spicers Dress Designs*,[57] Clauson J. was clearly doubtful whether a lady's dress was capable of enjoying copyright protection as
a work of artistic craftsmanship,[58] citing definitions of "artistic" and
"artist" in the *Oxford English Dictionary* as showing that the proper question was whether a designer who designs and makes frocks was thereby
cultivating "one of the fine arts in which the object is mainly to gratify the
aesthetic emotions by perfection of execution whether in creation or representation."[59]

In two cases, one in Australia, *Cuisenaire* v. *Reed*,[60] and the other in
Canada, *Cuisenaire* v. *South West Imports Ltd.*,[61] it was held that a set of rods,
specifically designed for teaching mathematics, was not a work of artistic
craftsmanship. There was no craftsmanship in the making of the rods as
no skill was involved in cutting or colouring them. Nor were they artistic.

The case of *George Hensher Ltd.* v. *Restawile Upholstery (Lancs) Ltd.*,[62]
which went to the House of Lords, concerned the prototype of a piece of
furniture. The plaintiffs, at the trial, relied also on drawings, but, having

---

[51] Copyright Act 1911, s.35(1).
[52] Copyright Act 1956, s.3(1)(*b*).
[53] See § 2–22, *ante*.
[54] [1975] R.P.C. 31; [1976] A.C. 64.
[55] [1936] Ch. 400.
[56] Copyright Act 1911, ss.1 and 35(1); Copyright Act 1956, s.3(1).
[57] See n. 55, *ante*.
[58] The actual decision was that there was no copyright vested in the firm which executed the
design because the firm's servants, who made the dress from a third party's design, did
not originate any artistic element which might subsist.
[59] The point was left open in *Radley Gowns Ltd.* v. *Costas Spyrou* [1975] F.S.R. 455 at 466; and
see *George Hensher Ltd.* v. *Restawile Upholstery (Lancs) Ltd.* [1975] R.P.C. 31 at 49.
[60] [1963] V.R. 719; see especially Pape J., at p. 730. See also *Komesaroff* v. *Mickle* [1988]
R.P.C. 204 in which the Supreme Court of Victoria held that a product called "moving
sand pictures" was not a work of artistic craftsmanship.
[61] [1968] 1 Ex.C.R. 493; 37 Fox's C.P.C. 81.
[62] See n. 54, *ante*.

lost this claim at trial, it was not pursued further on appeal. The defendants conceded at first instance that the prototype was a work of "craftsmanship,"[63] but not that it was "artistic," and denied subsistence of copyright. A remarkable feature of the case, as was pointed out by Lord Kilbrandon,[64] is that the House of Lords rejected definitions of "artistic" framed by the trial judge, the Court of Appeal, counsel for the plaintiffs and two by counsel for the defendants; further, each member of the House of Lords hearing the appeal provided a definition of his own. The decision of the House of Lords was that the prototype was not a "work of artistic craftsmanship," being a matter to be determined in the light of the evidence and that, in that case, the evidence was wholly inadequate to establish that the furniture in question merited the epithet "artistic."

However, whereas some members of the House of Lords thought the intention of the author was paramount in deciding whether the work was artistic or not, others thought it only important. In *Merlet* v. *Mothercare plc*,[65] Walton J., adopting the former approach as being the one he considered favoured by the majority of the House of Lords, held that the prototype of a cape for a mother and child was not a work of art, but a basic commodity, and was therefore not entitled to copyright as a work of artistic craftsmanship, even if its creation had involved sufficient craftsmanship.

6. Sound Recordings

Statutory definition. The 1988 Act follows the position adopted under the 1956 Act,[66] and confers a separate copyright on sound recordings. "Sound recording" is defined as meaning: **2–28**

(a) a recording of sounds, from which the sounds may be reproduced, or

(b) a recording of the whole or any part of a literary, dramatic or musical work, from which sounds reproducing the work or part may be produced,

regardless of the medium on which the recording is made or the method by which the sounds are reproduced or produced.[67]

The omission in this definition of the exclusion of sound tracks, contained in the definition in the 1956 Act,[68] clearly introduces a change of

---

[63] Probably wrongly, in the view of each of the members of the House of Lords.

[64] [1976] A.C. 64 at 98.

[65] [1984] F.S.R. 358. The Judge also pointed out that, in accordance with the judgments in *Hensher*, it was not for the court, at least in the first instance, to make a value judgment.

[66] Copyright Act 1956, s.12(1) and (2). This had not been the position under the 1911 Act, which first conferred copyright on records, perforated rolls and other contrivances for the mechanical reproduction of sounds "in like manner as if such contrivances were musical works": s.19(1). For a fuller discussion of the development of the law in relation to sound recordings generally, see *Copinger* (12th ed.), §§ 811–816.

[67] C.D.P.A., s.5(1).

[68] Copyright Act 1956, s.12(9), which defined a sound recording as meaning the aggregate of the sounds embodied in and capable of being reproduced by means of a record of any description, other than a sound track associated with a cinematograph film.

substance.[69] Apart from this difference in relation to sound tracks, the definition differs generally in form from that contained in the 1956 Act[70] and, in particular, introduces two sub-paragraphs into the definition. Clearly the first sub-paragraph is intended to cover a recording where there is no underlying work, such as a recording of people talking, or of other sounds such as the sounds of wildlife, whereas the second sub-paragraph is intended to cover the recording of the performance of works which may themselves be the subject of separate copyrights. However, given that the definition in the 1956 Act was equally apt to cover both sorts of recordings, it is not clear why it was thought necessary to change the definition from the somewhat shorter and simpler one used in the 1956 Act.

2–29 **Sound tracks of films.** As indicated above,[71] the 1988 Act has introduced a change in the treatment of sound tracks of films. Under the 1956 Act, sound tracks were expressly excluded from the definition of sound recordings,[72] and the definition of a cinematograph film included sounds embodied in any sound track associated with the film.[73] These provisions are not repeated in the 1988 Act, and the sound track of a film, including a sound track existing at the date of commencement of the 1988 Act,[74] is now accordingly entitled to copyright protection as a sound recording.[75]

7. Films

2–30 **Statutory definition.** The 1988 Act follows the position adopted under the 1956 Act,[76] and confers a separate copyright on a film.[77] Under the 1988 Act a film is defined as a recording on any medium from which a moving image may by any means be produced.[78] This definition retains the essential element of a moving image,[79] found in the definition of "cinematograph film" contained in the 1956 Act,[80] but is otherwise in a much

---

[69] See § 2–29, *post.*

[70] See n. 68, *ante.*

[71] See § 2–28, *ante.*

[72] Copyright Act 1956, s.12(9).

[73] Copyright Act 1956, s.13(9).

[74] C.D.P.A. 1988, Sched. 1 para. 8(1); subject to the provisions of para. 8(2).

[75] This reverts to the position under the 1911 Act, under which the sound track of a film was separately protected as a contrivance by means of which sounds might be mechanically reproduced; see § 2–28, n. 63, *ante.*

[76] Copyright Act 1956, s.13(1) and (2).

[77] This had not been the position under the Copyright Act 1911, which treated a film as a series of photographs, each of which was protected as an artistic work: see *Pathé Pictures Ltd.* v. *Bancroft* [1928–35] Mac.C.C. 403; *Barker, etc., Ltd.* v. *Hulton (E.) & Co. Ltd.* (1912) 28 T.L.R. 496; *Nordisk Films Co. Ltd.* v. *Onda* [1917–23] Mac.C.C. 337.

[78] C.D.P.A. 1988, s.5(1).

[79] A single frame of a film could not therefore itself constitute a film, nor would it be protectable as a photograph (see § 2–21, *ante*) although it would be protectable as part of a film: see *Spelling Goldberg Productions Inc.* v. *B.P.C. Publishing* [1981] R.P.C. 283.

[80] "Any sequence of visual images recorded on material of any description (whether translucent or not) so as to be capable, by the use of that material, either of being shown as a moving picture, or of being recorded on other material (whether translucent or not) by the use of which it can be so shown": Copyright Act 1956, s.13(10).

simplified form which removes any doubt that may have existed as to whether the definition under the 1956 Act covered video recordings.[81] Film sound tracks, protected under the 1956 Act as part of the film,[82] are now entitled to copyright separately as sound recordings.[83]

8. Broadcasts

Statutory definition. By section 6(1) of the 1988 Act a broadcast is **2–31** defined as meaning a transmission by wireless telegraphy of visual images, sounds or other information which—

(a) is capable of being lawfully received by members of the public, or

(b) is transmitted for presentation to members of the public.

The essential element of this definition, that copyright is conferred in respect of visual images and sounds which are broadcast, remains the same as under the definition in the 1956 Act,[84] although the distinction, maintained in the 1956 Act, between television broadcasts[85] and sound broadcasts[86] is abandoned and a single composite definition is provided. Further, under the 1956 Act[87] only broadcasts made by the British Broadcasting Corporation and the Independent Broadcasting Authority[88] were entitled to copyright, whereas no such restriction is contained in sections 1(*b*) and 6(1) of the 1988 Act.

Broadcasting. The definition of broadcasting as the transmission by **2–32** wireless telegraphy substantially repeats the position under the 1956 Act, in slightly simpler terms.[89]

Reception by the public. Whilst the expression "broadcast" was not **2–33** defined under the 1956 Act in such a way as to distinguish it from other forms of wireless communication, it was assumed[90] that the expression

---

[81] Following the recommendation of the 1977 Copyright Committee, Cmnd. 6732, paras. 889 and 916, that this should be made clear, notwithstanding their view that video recordings were within the definition in the 1956 Act.

[82] Copyright Act 1956, s.13(9).

[83] See § 2–29, *ante*.

[84] Copyright Act 1956 s.14(1) and (10). For a fuller discussion of the development of the law relating to copyright protection for broadcasts, see *Copinger* (12th ed.) §§ 881–883.

[85] "Television broadcast" being defined as meaning visual images broadcast by way of television together with any sounds broadcast for reception along with those images: Copyright Act 1956, s.14(10).

[86] "Sound broadcast" being defined as meaning sounds broadcast otherwise than as part of a television broadcast: Copyright Act 1956, s.14(10).

[87] s.14(1)(*a*) and (*b*).

[88] Formerly the Independent Television Authority; Sound Broadcasting Act 1972 (c. 31), s.1, repealed and replaced by Independent Broadcasting Authority Act 1973 (c. 19) ss. 1, 38 and 39; repealed and replaced by the Broadcasting Act 1981 (c. 68), ss.1 and 65(3), (4) and Sched. 8, para. 7 and Sched. 9 (since repealed by the Broadcasting Act 1990, c. 42).

[89] Copyright Act 1956, s.48(2) defined broadcasting (by reference to the same expression in the Wireless Telegraphy Act 1949) as, in substance, meaning the emission of messages by electromagnetic energy otherwise than over wires.

[90] See *Copinger* (12th ed.), § 886.

necessarily involved the messages being received, or being capable of being received, by a large public. The present definition, by referring to the public in sub-paragraphs (*a*) and (*b*), makes this requirement clear.

The present definition introduces, however, a new qualification, in that if the broadcast is not transmitted for presentation to members of the public (and therefore does not fall within sub-paragraph (*b*) of the definition) it is only a broadcast for the purposes of the 1988 Act if it is capable of being *lawfully* received by members of the public. In the case of an encrypted transmission, for example by satellite, it is to be regarded as capable of being lawfully received by members of the public only if decoding equipment has been made available to members of the public by or with the authority of the person making the transmission or the person providing the contents of the transmission.[91]

9. Cable Programmes

2–34   **Statutory definition.** "Cable programme" is defined by the 1988 Act as meaning any item included in a cable programme service.[92] "Cable programme service" is in turn defined as meaning a service consisting wholly or mainly in sending visual images, sounds or other information by means of a telecommunications system,[93] that is by electronic means.[94] The definition of cable programme service excludes a transmission by wireless telegraphy, ensuring that a transmission cannot qualify for copyright protection both as a broadcast and as a cable programme. As in the case of a broadcast,[95] in order to be capable of being the subject of copyright, the cable programme service must be aimed at the public, in that it must be sent for reception either for presentation to members of the public, or at two or more places (whether simultaneously or not).[96]

2–35   **Excepted services.** There are a number of services which are excepted from the definition of a cable programme service,[97] principally, it would seem, because they are not really services which are aimed at the public. Those excepted include: a service which has as an essential feature not only the transmission of visual images, sounds or other information to the recipient but also the reception from the recipient of information (other than signals sent for the operation or control of the service)[98]; services run for the purposes of a business, or by an individual for domestic purposes, and which are entirely within the control of such business or individual

---

[91] C.D.P.A. 1988, s.6(2).
[92] C.D.P.A. 1988, s.7(1); this was the position under s.14A of the 1956 Act, introduced by s.22 of the Cable and Broadcasting Act 1984 (c. 46) (since repealed by the Broadcasting Act 1990, c. 42).
[93] *Ibid.*; following closely the definition in s.2 of the Cable and Broadcasting Act 1984 (since repealed by the Broadcasting Act 1990), previously applying to s.14A of the 1956 Act by s.14A(11).
[94] C.D.P.A. 1988, s.178.
[95] See § 2–33 *ante*.
[96] See n. 92, *ante*.
[97] C.D.P.A. 1988, s.7(2)
[98] *Ibid.*, s.7(2)(*a*).

and are not connected to any other telecommunications system[99]; a service operating in or connecting premises in single occupation (except where the services form part of the amenities provided for residents or inmates of premises run as a business) and not connected to any other telecommunications system[1]; and services run for persons providing broadcasting or cable programme services or programmes for such services.[2] There is provision for the Secretary of State by order to add or remove exceptions.[3]

10. Typographical Arrangements of Published Editions

Protection for typographical arrangements. Evidence was given before the 1952 Copyright Committee that protection was required for typographical arrangements. A publisher who had gone to considerable trouble and expense in setting up in type a new edition of a non-copyright work appeared to have no remedy under the 1911 Act if another publisher, having purchased a copy of the edition, proceeded to reproduce copies thereof by photographic process. The Copyright Committee therefore recommended that protection should be given in such circumstances,[4] and this was achieved by section 15(1) of the 1956 Act, which accorded copyright protection to typographical arrangements of published editions of one or more literary, dramatic or musical works. **2–36**

Statutory definition. Typographical arrangements of published editions are now protected under section 1(1)(c) of the 1988 Act. For the purposes of that provision, "published edition" means a published edition of the whole or any part of one or more literary, dramatic or musical works.[5] It is to be noted that there is no requirement that the work itself should still be, or indeed should ever have been, the subject of copyright, although it must qualify under the Act as a literary, dramatic or musical work.[6] **2–37**

11. Subject Matter Not Protected on Grounds of Public Policy

Copyright is a creature of statute. The 1988 Act accords copyright to the works described in section 1(1) which meet the requirements for subsistence of copyright set out in section 153 and Chapter IX of the Act. Nowhere in the 1988 Act is that right qualified by considerations of public policy, and indeed this has been so in successive earlier copyright enact- **2–38**

---

[99] *Ibid.*, s.7(2)(*b*) and (*c*).
[1] *Ibid.*, s.7(2)(*d*).
[2] *Ibid.*, s.7(2)(*e*).
[3] *Ibid.*, s.7(3).
[4] Cmnd. 8662, paras. 308 and 310.
[5] C.D.P.A. 1988, s.8(1), in the same terms as s.15(1) of the 1956 Act.
[6] See *Machinery Market Ltd.* v. *Sheen Publishing Ltd.* [1983] F.S.R. 431. See further § 3–54, *post*, for conditions as to subsistence of copyright in typographical arrangements of published editions.

ments.[7] However, there are a variety of cases where a claim of copyright in a work has not been enforced because the court has considered the work to be libellous, immoral, obscene, scandalous or irreligious,[8] or to involve deception of the public.[9]

2–39 **Basis for courts' refusal to protect subject matter.** In an early case,[10] the courts' refusal to protect such subject matter was put on the ground that in order to establish such a claim the author must, in the first place, show a right to sell, which in such a case he could not do and so could not acquire a property in the work. It is probably more accurate to say that the ground for refusal by the courts to intervene is that it is against public policy to protect rights of publication and sale of works, where publication and sale would themselves be against the public interest.[11] It is not that there is no copyright in such a work, but rather that the courts will not enforce such copyright.[12]

Similarly, it would appear that if the infringing work is of a nature which the court would not protect, a plaintiff, although his work is unobjectionable, cannot succeed insofar as his claim is that the infringing work is to be treated as his own, as is the case with a claim for delivery up, an account of profits or, under the former law, conversion damages. In such a case his proper remedy would be to disaffirm the work and claim infringement damages and an injunction.[13]

Where a defendant succeeds in a proceeding on the ground that the work infringed will not be protected owing to its objectionable character, the defendant will not recover costs.[14]

2–40 **Libellous, immoral, obscene, scandalous or irreligious works.** There are a number of cases where works considered by the courts to fall into these descriptions have been refused protection,[15] although the argument

---

[7] Similar considerations apply in relation to the subsistence of copyright under the Copyright Acts in works which themselves infringe copyright: see *per* Goff J., in *Redwood Music Ltd. v. Chappell & Co. Ltd.*, [1982] R.P.C. 109 at 120 and § 3–44 *et seq., post.*

[8] See § 2–40, *post.*

[9] See § 2–41, *post.*

[10] *Stockdale v. Onwhyn* (1826) 5 B. & C. 173.

[11] See *Pastickniak v. Dojacek* [1923–28] Mac.C.C. 423; *Glyn v. Weston Feature Film Co.* [1916] 1 Ch. 261; *British Oxygen Co. Ltd. v. Liquid Air Ltd.* [1925] Ch. 383; *Massie & Renwick Ltd. v. Underwriters' Survey Ltd.* [1940] S.C.R. 218; *A.G. v. Guardian Newspapers Ltd. (No.2)* [1988] 3 All E.R. 545 at 645b, 654 g/h, 668d (H.L.). In some cases a defence of "fair dealing" may be available; see *Hubbard v. Vosper* [1972] 2 Q.B. 84.

[12] *A.G. v. Guardian Newspapers Ltd. (No. 2), supra.*

[13] *Glyn v. Weston Feature Film Co. Ltd.* [1916] 1 Ch. 261 at 270.

[14] *Glyn v. Weston Feature Film Co. Ltd.* [1916] 1 Ch. 261; *Baschet v. London Illustrated Standard Co.* [1900] 1 Ch. 73.

[15] *Stockdale v. Onwhyn* (1826) 5 B. & C. 173; *Hime v. Dale* (1809) 2 Camp, 27n; *Walcot v. Walker* (1802) 7 Ves. 1; *Poplett v. Stockdale* (1825) 1 Ry. & M. 337; *Gee (A.P.) v. Pritchard (W.)* (1818) 2 Swans, 402; *Southey v. Sherwood* (1817) 2 Mer. 435; *Murray v. Benbow* (1822) Jac. 474n; *Lawrence v. Smith* (1822) Jac. 471; *Fores v. Johnes* (1802) 4 Esp. 95; *Gale v. Leckie* (1817) 2 Stark. N.P. 107; *Baschet v. London Illustrated Standard Co.* [1900] 1 Ch. 73; *Glyn v. Weston Feature Film Co. Ltd.* [1916] 1 Ch. 261; *Pastickniak v. Dojacek* [1923–28] Mac.C.C. 423; and *A. Bloom & Sons Ltd. v. Black* [1936–45] Mac.C.C. 274 (injunction refused in respect of a vulgar and indecent will); *A.G. v. Guardian Newspapers Ltd. (No. 2),* n. 11, *ante.*

that protection of the work would be against public policy on such grounds has not always succeeded.[16] The doctrine has, on occasion, been carried very far, particularly in relation to works considered to be of an irreligious tendency,[17] or to be immoral.[18] Such readiness on the part of the judges to apply their own views in deciding what works should be refused protection as being immoral, obscene, scandalous or irreligious, gave rise to criticism.[19] In the present day, in which the public perception of such matters is different, the courts can be expected to reflect this difference and to take an attitude which is far less protective of the public. Thus, for example in relation to religious matters, it is generally considered permissible to attack the Christian religion so long as it is not done in an offensive manner,[20] and the same may be so in relation to the religious beliefs of any body of persons.[21] Similarly, whereas in the past protection has been refused to works which were considered immoral or indecent,[22] in the present day, at least in relation to sexual conduct, protection would only be refused under this principle to a work considered as having a grossly immoral tendency.[23] Equally, no doubt the principle

---

[16] *Barnard* v. *White & Co.* [1923–28] Mac.C.C. 218 (form for credit betting on football matches not against public policy); see also *Sitwell* v. *Sun Engraving Co. Ltd.* [1936–45] Mac.C.C. 137 (poem alleged to be libellous). In *Hime* v. *Dale* (1809) 2 Camp, 27n Lord Ellenborough accepted the principle that if a work appeared so gross a libel as to affect public morals then it would not be protected, but did not consider the work in question of such a nature. See also *Goeie Hoop Vitgewers (Eieodoms) B.P.K.* v. *Central News Agency* (1935) (2) S.A. 843.

[17] See, for example, *Lawrence* v. *Smith* (1822) Jac. 471 (injunction refused by Lord Eldon in respect of a work which contradicted Scripture); *Murray* v. *Benbow* (1822) Jac. 474 (injunction refused by Lord Eldon in respect of Lord Byron's poem "Cain").

[18] *Murray* v. *Benbow* (1822) Jac. 474n (injunction refused by Leach V.-C. in respect of Lord Byron's work "Don Juan"); *Stockdale* v. *Onwhyn* (1826) 5 B. & C. 173 (Abbott C.J. directed a non-suit at trial of an action to compensate for infringement of the copyright in a book of memoirs of Harriette Wilson, a courtesan, containing matter in some parts which was highly indecent and in other parts slanderous). In *Poplett* v. *Stockdale* (1825) 1 Ry. & M. 337 Best C.J. refused to allow the printer of the work in *Stockdale* v. *Onwhyn* to maintain an action for his bill against the publisher who employed him, on the basis that although the defendant was equally guilty with the plaintiff, he would not, as Lord Kenyon once said, sit to take an account between two robbers on Hounslow Heath.

[19] Story J., in referring to Lord Eldon's decision in the above cases, said (2 Story's Eq. Jur., p. 938) "If a court of equity, under colour of its general authority, is to enter upon all the moral, theological, metaphysical, and political inquiries, . . . and if it is to decide dogmatically upon the character and bearing of such discussions, and the rights of authors growing out of them, it is obvious that absolute power is conferred over the subject of literary property, which may sap the very foundations on which it rests, and retard, if not entirely suppress, the means of arriving at physical as well as at metaphysical truth."

[20] See *R.* v. *Lemon* [1979] A.C. 617, involving an alleged blasphemous libel concerning the Christian religion published in the magazine *Gay News*. See also *Chaplin* v. *Leslie Frewin (Publishers) Ltd.* [1966] Ch. 71, where, although both Danckwerts and Winn L.JJ. considered the book in question to contain blasphemous passages, the point was not taken as to whether this affected the subsistence of copyright in the book, or the court's willingness to intervene to protect such copyright.

[21] See *R.* v. *Lemon* [1979] A.C. 617.

[22] Compare the works refused protection in *A. Bloom & Sons Ltd.* v. *Black* [1936–45] Mac.C.C. 274; *Stockdale* v. *Onwhyn* (1826) 5 B. & C. 173; *Murray* v. *Benbow* (1822) Jac. 474n.

[23] This was the view adopted by Browne-Wilkinson V.-C. in *Stephens* v. *Avery* [1988] Ch. 449.

could still effectively be invoked to refuse protection in relation to a work which was considered to be no more than pornography.[24]

2–41   **Works involving deception of the public.** In an early case,[25] a plaintiff failed in an action against the defendant for pirating a work of a devotional character, on the ground that the plaintiff's work falsely professed to be a translation from the German of an author who had a high reputation for writings of this kind, and that this had been done to deceive purchasers and to give the work a value which it would not otherwise have had.

Subsequently, this principle was applied where the plaintiff published an illustrated catalogue of trucks, trolleys and barrows made by him which contained pages headed "Inventor, patentee, and sole maker" and "Slingsby's Patents," despite the plaintiff having no English patent for the various articles represented.[26] The catalogue also contained pictures of buildings on which the plaintiff's name was written in large letters, although the plaintiff did not occupy the whole of them. The defendant had copied the plaintiff's catalogue, but the plaintiff was refused an injunction on the ground that the catalogue was calculated to deceive the public (as to the plaintiff having patents and as to its building), and that the plaintiff was attempting to obtain trade regardless of the manner in which it was obtained.

---

[24] Although the question as to what is pornographic according to the moral code of the day could still present the court with a problem, where art and pornography may overlap.

[25] *Wright* v. *Tallis* (1845) 1 C.B. 893.

[26] *Slingsby* v. *Bradford Patent Truck, etc., Co.* [1905] W.N. 122; [1906] W.N. 51; see also *Hayward Bros.* v. *Lely & Co.* (1887) 56 L.T. 418 and see *A.G.* v. *Guardian Newspapers Ltd. (No. 2)*, n. 11, *ante.*

Conditions for Subsistence of Copyright

1. Introduction

The scheme of the 1988 Act compared to that of the 1956 Act. Under   **3–1** the 1956 Act, the requirements for copyright to subsist in each type of work were to be found included among the provisions dealing with that particular description of work.[1] The scheme of the 1988 Act is different, and section 1, after enumerating the descriptions of works in which copyright may subsist under that Act,[2] provides, in relation to all such works, that copyright does not subsist in such works unless the requirements set out in Chapter IX of the Act with respect to qualification for copyright

---

[1] Copyright Act 1956, ss.2(1) and (2), 3(2) and (3), 12(1) and (2), 13(1) and (2), 14(1) and 15(1).

[2] C.D.P.A. 1988, s.1(1); and see Chap. 2, § 2–1, *ante.*

protection are met.[3] Chapter IX contains a common set of provisions for the subsistence of copyright in published and unpublished works of all descriptions,[4] with special provision being made in the case of broadcasts and cable programmes.[5]

3–2 **Qualification for copyright protection.** Copyright does not subsist in a work unless the qualification requirements of Chapter IX of the Act are met.[6] For all descriptions of works, the 1988 Act provides two bases on which copyright protection may be obtained. The first is by reason of the requirements as to the author being met, irrespective of whether the work has been published or not.[7] The second, which applies to works which have been published, is by reason of the requirements as to the country in which the work was first published being met.[8] In the case of broadcasts and cable programmes, the 1988 Act replaces the concept of publication with that of transmission, and the second basis for qualification for such works is by reason of the requirements being met as to the country from which the broadcast or cable programme emanated.[9] The two bases are entirely independent of each other, and all that is necessary for copyright to subsist in a work is that the requirements relating to one basis should be satisfied. Special provisions apply to such works where the copyright belongs to the Crown, to Parliament or to certain international organisations.[10]

3–3 **Time at which qualification requirements must be met.** The qualification requirements themselves all relate to a situation at a specific time (generally when the work was made or first published, as the case may be), from which it would follow that, if those requirements are met at the required time, later events (for example, the author ceasing to be a qualifying person or the country of first publication ceasing to be one to which the 1988 Act extends) are irrelevant to the continued subsistence of copyright. That this is the case is made clear, in that the 1988 Act specifically provides that it is sufficient for copyright to subsist in a work if the qualification requirements are once satisfied in respect of that work, and that copyright does not cease to subsist in that work by reason of any subsequent event.[11]

---

[3] *Ibid.*, s.1(3).
[4] *Ibid.*, ss.154 and 155; see *post.*
[5] *Ibid.*, s.156; see § 3–52, *post.*
[6] *Ibid.*, s.153(1).
[7] *Ibid.*, s.154; and see § 3–4, *et seq., post.*
[8] *Ibid.*, s.155; and see § 3–10, *et seq., post.*
[9] *Ibid.*, s.153(1)(*c*) and 156; and see § 3–52, *post.*
[10] *Ibid.*, s.153(2); and see §§ 3–56, 3–57, *post.*
[11] *Ibid.*, s.153(3). This was not so under the 1956 Act, since a work entitled to copyright by reason of the nationality of its author would subsequently have lost protection by first publication in a country to which the 1956 Act was not extended or applied; see *Copex Establishment* v. *Flegon, The Times*, August 18, 1967, and *Bodley Head* v. *Flegon* [1972] R.P.C. 587.

2. Qualifying Conditions for All Works

A. *By reference to the author*

Qualifying person. A work[12] qualifies for copyright protection if the   **3–4**
author was at the material time a qualifying person.[13] A qualifying person
is defined as the following classes of persons, namely: a British citizen,
a British Dependent Territories citizen, a British National (Overseas), a
British Overseas citizen, a British subject, a British protected person, a
person domiciled or resident in the United Kingdom or another country
to which the relevant provisions of the 1988 Act extend, and a body corporate incorporated under the laws of the United Kingdom or of another
country to which the relevant provisions of that Act extend.[14]

British citizen, etc. The terms British citizen, British Dependent Terri-   **3–5**
tories citizen, British National (Overseas), British Overseas citizen,
British subject and British protected person are all defined in the British
Nationality Act 1981.[15] The status of British citizenship is principally
acquired through birth in the United Kingdom to a parent who is a
British citizen or who is settled, that is ordinarily resident, in the United
Kingdom; other methods of acquisition include by descent, that is birth
outside the United Kingdom to a person who is a British citizen, by adoption, by naturalisation or, in appropriate circumstances, by registration.[16]
British Dependent Territories citizenship is conferred on citizens of a
number of specified countries.[17] British National (Overseas) means a person who is so defined under the Hong Kong (British Nationality) Order
1986.[18] British Overseas citizenship is a residual category for citizens of
the United Kingdom and Colonies who do not acquire, under the 1981
Act, British citizenship or British Dependent Territories citizenship.[19]
British subjects under the 1981 Act[20] are those who immediately before

---

[12] These provisions apply to all descriptions of works; broadcasts could not qualify for protection under the 1956 Act by their author being a qualified person; see further § 3–52,
post.

[13] The term used in the 1956 Act was "qualified person," (see Copyright Act 1956, ss.2(1),
3(2), 12(1) and 13(1)) but the concept remains the same (see Copyright Act 1956, s.1(5)).

[14] C.P.D.A. 1988, s.154(1). The 1956 Act adopted the same test for corporate bodies being
qualified persons, but the 1911 Act had referred to such bodies "having an established
place of business." This remains the test in relation to certain existing works: see § 3–21,
post.

[15] 1981 c. 61 (as amended); the Act came into force on January 1, 1983 and repeals the definitions of British subject and Commonwealth citizen formerly contained in the Interpretation Act 1978 (c. 30), Sched. 1.

[16] British Nationality Act 1981, ss.1–14 and see the British Nationality (Hong Kong) Act
1990 (c. 34).

[17] *Ibid.* ss.16–25; the countries are those specified in Sched. 6 as: Anguilla, Bermuda, British
Antartic Territory, British Indian Ocean Territory, Cayman Islands, Falkland Islands
and Dependencies, Gibralter, Hong Kong, Montserrat, Pitcairn, Henderson, Ducie and
Oeno Islands, St. Christopher and Nevis, St Helena and Dependencies, Sovereign Base
Areas of Akrotiri and Dhekelia, Turks and Caicos Islands and Virgin Islands.

[18] S.I. 1986 No. 948.

[19] *Ibid.* ss.26–29; as to the status of citizenship of the United Kingdom and Colonies, see the
British Nationality Act 1948 (11 & 12 Geo. 6, c. 56) now almost entirely repealed by the
British Nationality Act 1981.

[20] *Ibid.* ss.30–35.

that Act came into force were British subjects without citizenship or were British subjects by virtue of being former citizens of Eire, under the British Nationality Act 1948[21] or were British subjects by registration under the British Nationality Act 1965.[22] British protected persons are those persons declared to be such by an Order in Council made in relation to any territory which was a former protectorate, protected state or United Kingdom trust territory within the meaning of those terms under the British Nationality Act 1948[23] and who are not citizens of certain specified territories mentioned in Schedule 3 to the British Nationality Act 1981.[24]

3–6 **Domicile.** No attempt is made, in the 1988 Act, to define domicile, the meaning of which is therefore left to the general law to determine.[25] Domicile may be obtained either by birth, operation of law,[26] or by choice. Domicile of origin prevails in the absence of a domicile of choice, that is if a domicile of choice has never been acquired or, if once acquired, has been abandoned. Further, a domicile of choice is acquired when a man fixes voluntarily his sole or chief residence in a particular place with an intention of continuing to reside there for an unlimited time.[27] A domicile of choice may be abandoned when, after a departure from a country, a man no longer has an intention to return there.[28]

3–7 **Residence.** As with the concept of domicile, the 1988 Act does not attempt to define residence, and the meaning of residence in the 1988 Act is therefore left to the general law. Where there is nothing to show that the term residence is used in a more extensive sense, it denotes the place where an individual eats, drinks and sleeps, or where his family or his servants eat, drink and sleep.[29] It seems clear that it implies something more permanent than a visit, but the degree of permanence is hard to define.[30] It is suggested that it will be sufficient to show that the author, at the time

---

[21] British Nationality Act 1948 ss.2, 13 and 16, now repealed by the British Nationality Act 1981.

[22] 1965 c. 34, repealed by the British Nationality Act 1981.

[23] British Nationality Act 1948 ss.30 and 32, now repealed (save as to s.32(3)) by the British Nationality Act 1981.

[24] British Nationality Act 1981, s.38; the territories mentioned are: Antigua and Barbuda, Australia, The Bahamas, Bangladesh, Barbados, Belize, Botswana, Canada, Republic of Cyprus, Dominica, Fiji, The Gambia, Grenada, Guyana, India, Jamaica, Kenya, Kiribati, Lesotho, Malawi, Malaysia, Malta, Mauritius, Nauru, New Zealand, Nigeria, Papua New Guinea, Saint Lucia, Saint Vincent and the Grenadines, Seychelles, Sierra Leone, Singapore, Solomon Islands, Sri Lanka, Swaziland, Tanzania, Tonga, Trinidad and Tobago, Tuvalu, Uganda, Vanuatu, Western Samoa, Zambia, Zimbabwe. Under the British Nationality Act 1981, s.37, citizens of these territories are Commonwealth citizens and will not, as from the commencement of that Act, by the fact of their citizenship of that country be British subjects (as they were under s.1(3) of the British Nationality Act 1948).

[25] Other statutory definitions for particular purposes (see for example, Civil Jurisdiction and Judgments Act 1982 (c. 27) ss.41–46 defining domicile for the purposes of that Act) may not therefore be of much assistance.

[26] See Domicile and Matrimonial Proceedings Act 1973 (c. 45).

[27] *In the Estate of Fuld, decd.* (No. 3) [1968] P. 675; *Plummer* v. *I.R.C.* [1988] 1 W.L.R. 292.

[28] See *Buswell* v. *I.R.C.* [1974] 1 W.L.R. 1631; *Re Flynn* [1968] 1 W.L.R. 103; and *I.R.C.* v. *Bullock* [1976] 1 W.L.R. 1178.

[29] *R.* v. *The Overseers of Norwood* (1866) L.R. 2 Q.B. 457; *Sinclair* v. *Sinclair* [1968] P. 189; *R.* v. *Barnet L.B.C. Ex p. Shah* [1983] 2 A.C. 309 (H.L.).

[30] Se *MacRae* v. *MacRae* [1949] P. 397 and *Stransky* v. *Stransky* [1954] P. 428.

the work was made, was living at a place within the country in question as his home.[31]

Material time. The material time for the purposes of satisfying the test as to the author of a literary, dramatic, musical or artistic work being a qualifying person is, in the case of an unpublished work, when the work was made, or if the making of the work extended over a period, a substantial part of that period,[32] and, in the case of a published work, when the work was first published, or, if the author had died before first publication, immediately before his death.[33] A literary, dramatic or musical work is made when it is recorded in writing or otherwise[34]; there is no equivalent definition as to when an artistic work is made.[35] The material time for the purposes of satisfying the test as to the author of sound recordings, films and broadcasts being a qualifying person is also when they were made,[36] but, as with artistic works, there is no definition of when such works are made,[37] nor is there any specific provision, such as in the case of literary, dramatic, musical and artistic works,[38] to deal with the situation (which is likely to be the case for most films) where the making extends over a period of time. In relation to cable programmes, the material time is when the programme is included in a cable programme service,[39] and, in relation to typographical arrangements of a published edition, it is when the edition was first published.[40] Where the work is a work of joint authorship,[41] the work qualifies for copyright protection if at the material time any of the authors satisfies the above requirements, but only those authors who satisfy such requirements are taken into account when determining ownership and duration of the copyright so subsisting.[42]

---

[31] For cases on residence decided under the Income Taxes Acts, see: *Lloyd (T.)* v. *S.I.R.* (1883) 11 Sess.Cas. (4th Ser.) 687; *Levene* v. *C.I.R.* [1928] A.C. 217; *C.I.R.* v. *Lysaght* [1928] A.C. 234; and *Reed* v. *Clark* [1986] Ch. 1; and see *Cicutti* v. *Suffolk* [1981] 1 W.L.R. 558 (a case under the Education Act) and *R.* v. *Sec. State Ex p. Margueritte* [1983] 1 Q.B. 180 (a case under the British Nationality Act); and see § 16–14, *post*.

[32] CDPA 1988, s.154(4)(a). As to who is the author of such works, see *ibid.* s.9(1) and § 4–5, *et seq., post*.

[33] *Ibid.*, s.154(4)(b).

[34] *Ibid.*, s.3(2), re-enacting s.49(4) of the 1956 Act; writing includes any form of notation or code, whether by hand or otherwise: *ibid.* s.178. Making is not therefore the same as the first creation of the work: *e.g.* music may be composed, and even performed, before it is "made" for the purposes of the 1988 Act.

[35] Nor was there under the 1956 Act.

[36] C.D.P.A. 1988, s.154(5)(a) and (b). As to who is the author of such works, see *ibid.* s.9(2) and § 4–49, *et seq., post*.

[37] *cf.* Copyright Act 1956, s.12(8), which provided that a sound recording was made when the first record embodying the recording was produced.

[38] See n. 33, *ante*.

[39] C.D.P.A. 1988, s.154(5)(c). As to who is the author of such works, see *ibid* s.9(2) and § 4–61, *et seq., post*.

[40] *Ibid.*, s.154(5)(d). As to who is the author of such works, see *ibid* s.9(2) and § 4–64, *et seq., post*.

[41] As to which see Chap. 7, *post*.

[42] C.D.P.A. 1988, s.154(3); and also for the purpose of determining whether the work is anonymous or pseudonymous under s.57.

3–9 **Foreign works.** The reference in the definition of qualifying person to a country to which the provisions extend is to the extension of Part I of the 1988 Act by Order in Council under section 157 to any of the Channel Islands, the Isle of Man or any colony.[43] An author who is a citizen or subject of, or domiciled or resident in or, in the case of a corporate body, is incorporated under the law of a country to which that Act does not extend, but to which its provisions have been applied by an Order under section 159,[44] is not by such fact brought within the definition of a qualifying person (although he may be a qualifying person if he otherwise satisfies the requirements of that definition). The works of such authors qualify independently for copyright protection by virtue of the author being, at the material time,[45] a citizen or subject of, or domiciled or resident in or, in the case of a corporate body, incorporated under the law of such country.[46]

B. *By reference to the place of first publication*

3–10 **Qualification by reference to country of first publication.** Under the 1911 Act, the subsistence of copyright in a published work depended solely on the place of first publication and consequently copyright could often be lost or gained by publication. This was so, in particular, in relation to works emanating from the United States of America, since, by Order in Council, copyright was extended to the unpublished works of subjects or residents of the United States, but not to works first published there.[47] The position was different under the 1956 Act, and subsistence of copyright in published works depended, not only upon the place of first publication but also, whatever that place, on whether the author was a qualified person when the work was first published or, if he died before publication, on whether he was a qualified person immediately before his death.[48] The position remains the same under the 1988 Act as it was under the 1956 Act, in that a literary, dramatic, musical or artistic work, typographical arrangement of a published edition, a sound recording or a film qualifies for copyright protection if it is first published in the United Kingdom, or in another country to which the relevant provisions of the 1988 Act extend.[49] These provisions do not therefore apply to cable programmes and broadcasts, to which the special provisions of section 156 of the 1988 Act apply.[50]

3–11 **Importance of determining when a work is published: existing works.** The new provisions of the 1956 Act, referred to in paragraph 3–10 above, did not apply to works which were first published before the commencement of the 1956 Act.[51] Consequently, it remained, under the 1956

---

[43] As to which see Chap. 17, *post.*
[44] See n. 44. *ante.*
[45] See § 3–8, *ante.*
[46] Under C.D.P.A. 1988, s.154(2).
[47] S.R. & O. 1915 No. 130.
[48] Copyright Act 1956, ss.2(2), 3(3).
[49] C.D.P.A. 1988, s.155(1). See § 3–2, *ante.*
[50] *Ibid.*, s.156; see § 3–52, *post.*
[51] *I.e.* June 1, 1957; Copyright Act 1956, Sched. 7, para. 1.

Act, of substantial importance to determine whether or not a work was published. Even in the case of an existing work published after the commencement of the 1956 Act the date for determining whether or not the author was a qualified person was different, so that, if the work was not first published in the United Kingdom or in another country to which the relevant provisions of the 1988 Act extended, it was necessary to ascertain different information about the author to that which was relevant while the work remained unpublished. Moreover, the term of copyright in certain cases ran from first publication.[52] While the term of copyright in relation to photographs taken after the commencement of the 1988 Act now does not run from first publication,[53] and the position is now different in relation to works first published in the United States of America, following that country becoming a signatory to the Berne Convention,[54] whether a work was published, and if so when and where, are questions which remain important under the 1988 Act in many cases in respect of works in existence before the commencement of that Act, particularly in relation to the term of copyright in such works.[55]

Publication: generally. Publication, in relation to a work, means the issue of copies of the work to the public.[56] This definition is given in respect of all works in which copyright may subsist under the 1988 Act. It follows that a work cannot be orally published,[57] and that there can be no publication of a work of which there exists only a single example.[58] Indeed, the issue of copies must be such that it is intended to satisfy the reasonable requirements of the public and not be merely colourable, or else it does not constitute publication.[59] The term "copy" must be construed in accordance with the provisions contained in section 17 of the 1988 Act defining copying and copies.[60] For the issue of copies to constitute publication, it must have been done by or with the licence of the copyright owner.[61]   **3–12**

Publication: literary, dramatic, musical and artistic works and typographical arrangements of published editions. In addition to the general definition of publication,[62] the 1988 Act provides that in the case of a literary, dramatic, musical or artistic work, publication includes making such a work available to the public by means of an electronic   **3–13**

---

[52] *e.g.* published photographs and sound recordings.
[53] See § 6–8, *post*.
[54] See § 3–23, *post*.
[55] C.D.P.A. 1988, Sched. 1, para. 5(1) and para. 12, and see Chap. 6, *post*.
[56] *Ibid.*, s.175(1).
[57] Thus delivery of a lecture from notes does not constitute publication of the notes: see § 3–13, *post*. Public performance of a dramatic work had been held to be publication of the work, prior to the 1911 Act changing the law in this respect: see § 3–13, n. 69, *post*.
[58] Save, now, in the case of a work of architecture: C.D.P.A. 1988, s.175(3); see § 3–13, *post*. A writer of a private letter does not publish the letter by sending it to his correspondent, although by sending it to a newspaper for publication he would be licensing its publication by the newspaper.
[59] C.D.P.A. 1988, s.175(5), re-enacting s.49(2)(*b*) of the 1956 Act; see further, § 3–17, *post*.
[60] *Ibid.*, s.17(1); see further § 3–13, *post*.
[61] *Ibid.*, ss.175(6) and 178.
[62] *Ibid.*, s.175(1); see § 3–12, *ante*.

retrieval system.[63] In relation to literary, dramatic, musical and artistic works, a copy means a reproduction of the work in any material form, including one stored electronically.[64] Reproduction for these purposes does not include, as it does for the purposes of an infringement,[65] a reproduction of a substantial part of the work.[66]

The performance, broadcasting or inclusion in a cable programme service[67] of a literary, dramatic or musical work does not constitute publication,[68] but the issue of records embodying such a work is not now excluded, as it was under the 1956 Act,[69] from constituting publication. Where lectures, addresses, speeches and sermons have been recorded in writing or some other form, and are thus capable of being protected as literary works,[70] they do not become published by being delivered in public, since such delivery falls within the definition of performance of such works,[71] and is therefore excluded from constituting publication.[72] Such works may be published by the issue of reports, or even of copies of notes, with the acquiescence of the author. A lecturer would probably be held to license publication if he delivered his lectures knowing reporters were present, subject to any express or implied obligation on the part of those hearing the lecture to the contrary.[73]

Although, in relation to two-dimensional artistic works, "copy" includes a copy in three dimensions and in relation to three-dimensional artistic works includes a copy in two dimensions,[74] an artistic work is not published by being exhibited,[75] and a work of architecture in the form of a building, a sculpture or a work of artistic craftsmanship is not published

---

[63] *Ibid.*, s.175(1).

[64] *Ibid.*, s.17(1), (2).

[65] See *Ibid.*, s.16(3)(a).

[66] The position is therefore the same as under the Copyright Act 1956, s.49(2).

[67] Otherwise than for the purposes of an electronic retrieval system: s.175(4)(a)(ii).

[68] C.D.P.A. 1988, s.175(4)(a); this follows the position under the 1956, and 1911, Acts. The 1911 Act effected a change in this respect, in that public performance of a dramatic work had previously been held to constitute publication: *Boucicault* v. *Delafield* (1863) 1 H. & M. 597; *Boucicault* v. *Chatterton* (1877) 5 Ch.D. 267; *Caird* v. *Sime* (1887) 12 App.Cas. 326. *Walter* v. *Lane* [1900] A.C. 539; *Falcon* v. *The Famous Players Film Co. Ltd.* [1926] 2 K.B. 747 (C.A.).

[69] Copyright Act 1956, s.49(2)(a).

[70] *University of London Press Ltd.* v. *University Tutorial Press Ltd.* [1916] 2 Ch. 601; and see §§ 2-4, 2-5, *ante*.

[71] C.D.P.A. 1988, s.19(2); re-enacting the previous position in relation to such works, under the Copyright Act 1956, ss.49(2)(a) and s.48(1), and, before that, the Copyright Act 1911, s.1(3).

[72] C.D.P.A. 1988, s.175(4)(a)(i).

[73] See *Nicols* v. *Pitman* (1884) 26 Ch.D. 374; *Caird* v. *Sime* (1887) 12 App.Cas. 326) and, now, C.D.P.A. 1988, s.58. In an American case, *Keene (L.)* v. *Kimball (M.)* (1860) 16 Gray (82 Mass.) 545, Hoar J. said: "The student who attends a medical lecture may have a perfect right to remember as much as he can, and afterwards to use the information thus acquired in his own medical practice, or to communicate it to students or classes of his own, without involving the right to commit the lecture to writing, for the purpose of subsequent publication in print or by oral delivery."

[74] C.D.P.A. 1988, s.17(3); as under the 1956 Act, s.48(1).

[75] C.D.P.A. 1988, s.175(4)(b)(i). This was not so under the 1956 Act, see s.49(2)(a). It was held, prior to 1911, that exhibition of a painting in a public gallery, the rules of which forbade the public to copy, was not a publication of the work: *Turner* v. *Robinson* (1860) 10 Ir.Ch. 121, 510.

by the issue to the public of copies of a graphic work representing, or photographs of, such work.[76] Having regard to these provisions, therefore, a three-dimensional artistic work, or work of artistic craftsmanship, can only be published by the issue of three-dimensional copies of such work; for example, in the case of a work of sculpture, by copies cast from the original work. A work of architecture in the form of a building, or an artistic work incorporated into a building, was not published under the 1956 Act by being constructed,[77] but under the 1988 Act is treated as published when constructed.[78] The issue to the public of copies of a film including an artistic work,[79] and the inclusion of such a work in a broadcast or a cable programme service, do not constitute publication of the artistic work.[80]

In relation to typographical arrangements of published editions, copy is defined as meaning a facsimile copy of the arrangement,[81] which is further defined as including a copy which is reduced or enlarged in scale.[82] From this it necessarily follows that the copy will be identical (save for any enlargement or reduction) to the original typographical arrangement, but, again, if the copies only relate to part of the typographical arrangement and not the whole, their issue will not constitute publication of the typographical arrangement.[83]

What is a reproduction. Although, therefore, the 1988 Act refers, for the purposes of publication of a literary, dramatic, musical or artistic work, to the issue of copies,[84] because of the terms of section 17 of that Act which define copying and copies in relation to such works by reference to reproduction,[85] it remains necessary to consider, for the purposes of publication of such works, what is a reproduction. Since it was considered necessary to provide specifically that the issue of copies of graphic works representing, and of photographs of, works of architecture, sculptures and works of artistic craftsmanship should not constitute publication,[86] it appears to have been considered by the legislature that such graphic works and photographs would have been copies, and therefore reproductions, for the purposes of publication. Thus, the issue to the public of authorised graphic works or photographs of a painting, which, it would follow, are   **3-14**

---

[76] C.D.P.A. 1988, s.175(4)(b)(ii). As to the meaning of graphic work, see s.4(2) and § 2-21, *ante*.

[77] Copyright Act 1956, s.49(2)(a). It was doubted whether such a work could ever be published under the 1956 Act, save possibly by the issue to the public of paintings or drawings of the work: see *Copinger* (12th ed.), §§ 265 and 266.

[78] C.D.P.A. 1988, s.175(3).

[79] *Ibid.* 1988, s.175(4)(iii); "inclusion" is not defined, but this is not intended to cover the situation where the film is properly a reproduction of the work, for example a cartoon film which reproduces each of the artistic works comprising the drawings for the film; such drawings are published by the issue of copies of the film in which they are reproduced: *Warner Bros. Inc.* v. *The Roadrunner Ltd.* [1988] F.S.R. 292.

[80] C.D.P.A. 1988, s.175(4)(b)(iv).

[81] *Ibid.*, s.17(5).

[82] *Ibid.*, s.178.

[83] See *Ibid.*, s.16(3)(a) and nn. 66, 67 *ante*; *sed quaere* whether such issue would constitute publication of that part to which the copies relate.

[84] *Ibid.*, s.175(1)(a); *cf.* Copyright Act 1956, s.49(2)(c). See § 3-13, *ante*.

[85] *Ibid.*, s.17(2).

[86] *Ibid.*, s.175(4)(b)(ii); re-enacting, as regards works of architecture and sculptures, the former provisions of the 1911 Act (s.1(3)) and of the 1956 Act (s.49(2)(a)).

reproductions for these purposes, would constitute publication of such painting. Similarly, by excluding publication by the issue to the public of copies of a film in which the artistic work is included,[87] it appears to have been considered that such inclusion would have constituted reproduction for the purposes of publication.[88] This approach to "reproduction" for the purposes of publication is in accordance with the decision under the 1956 Act in *Merchant Adventurers Ltd.* v. *M. Grew & Co. Ltd.*,[89] that drawings for light-fittings were published by the sale to the public of the three-dimensional fittings made from the drawings on the basis that "reproduction", of the 1956 Act in section 49(2) (*c*) should not have been given a more restricted meaning than "reproduction" in section 48(1) of that Act where it was defined as including three-dimensional reproductions of two-dimensional artistic works. Nevertheless, questions may arise in relation to other works. For instance, if A were to translate his manuscript work and publish the translation before the original, would that be a publication of the original? It is suggested that it would not, and that the proper view of the matter is that where what is published so differs from the original that it is capable of existing as a separate copyright work, it is this separate copyright work which is published, not the original. This reasoning would apply to a dramatisation of an unpublished novel as well as to a translation. Thus, it is suggested that the publication of a pianoforte arrangement of an opera, or that of a few of the orchestral parts, would not be a publication of the opera itself.[90] These views are confirmed by the fact that the making of an adaptation of a work is treated as distinct from reproduction.[91]

3–15 **Publication: sound recordings and films.** Copy is not further defined in the 1988 Act in relation to sound recordings. Nor does the 1988 Act further positively define publication in relation to sound recordings, and the definition given in the 1956 Act, as the issue to the public of records embodying the recording or any part of it,[92] is not repeated in the 1988 Act. Although the issue of records reproducing the whole sound recording clearly remains the issue of copies of the recording, and therefore publication of the sound recording under the 1988 Act, it is less clear whether, under the 1988 Act, the issue of records which reproduce part only of a sound recording is a publication of the whole sound recording, as it was under the 1956 Act.[93]

---

[87] C.D.P.A. 1988, s.175(4)(*b*)(iii).

[88] This would remain so, however, in the case of a cartoon film, which in the true sense is a copy of the drawings produced for the film; such drawings would be published by the issue of copies of the film to the public: see *Warner Bros. Inc.* v. *The Roadrunner Ltd.* [1988] F.S.R. 292.

[89] [1972] Ch. 242; and see *Sifam Electrical Instruments Co. Ltd.* v. *Sangamo Weston Ltd.* [1971] F.S.R. 337 and *British Northrop Ltd.* v. *Texteam Blackburn Ltd.* [1974] R.P.C. 57.

[90] *Boosey* v. *Fairlie* (1877) 7 Ch.D. 301.

[91] C.D.P.A. 1988, ss.17(1) and 21(1).

[92] Copyright Act 1956, s.12(9).

[93] By virtue of the words "or any part thereof" included in the definition in s.12(9) of the 1956 Act; *cf.* C.D.P.A. 1988, s.172—is the omission of these words in the 1988 Act "merely a change of expresson"? Contrast the position in relation to literary, dramatic, musical and artistic works and typographical arrangements, discussed at § 3–13, nn. 66, 67, and 77, *ante*.

Similarly, the 1988 Act contains no definition of publication specifically in relation to films other than the general definition of issue of copies to the public. The definition given in the 1956 Act as the sale, letting on hire, or offer for sale or hire, of copies of the film to the public,[94] is not repeated in the 1988 Act. This definition was wider than the ordinary definition of publication (issue of copies to the public), but still gave rise to the question whether letting on hire of copies merely to exhibitors, rather than to the general public, constituted publication. The absence, now, of any specific definition of publication in relation to films would appear to resurrect all the problems previously thought to exist under the 1911 Act,[95] as to what constitutes publication of a film, since, in particular, the first issue of copies to the public is usually the letting of copies on hire to exhibitors. In relation to a film, a copy includes a photograph of the whole or a substantial part of any image forming part of such work.[96] Playing or showing a sound recording or film in public does not constitute publication, nor does broadcasting it or including it in a cable programme service.[97]

When copies of a work are issued to the public. In order for a work to   **3–16** be published, not only must the copies of the work be made, but they must be issued to the public. Issue for the purposes of sale is not essential,[98] although, if copies are issued for such a purpose, that would amount to publication.[99] A presentation of copies on the part of the author to individuals, or to a limited class,[1] or even the sending of advance copies to the press for review, would not, it is thought, be publication, but gratuitous circulation generally would seem to be so.[2] Thus, in *Prince Albert* v. *Strange*,[3] it appeared that her Majesty Queen Victoria and the Prince Consort had given to their close friends lithographic copies of drawings and etchings which they had made for their own amusement. This was not a publication. In *Infabrics Ltd.* v. *Jaytex Shirt Co. Ltd.*[4] the Court of Appeal thought that an offer or exposure for sale would not be publication but

---

[94] Copyright Act 1956, s.13(10).

[95] Prior to the 1956 Act enlarging the definition of publication in relation to films, films had been regarded as unpublished works, because of the definition of publication in the 1911 Act (s.1(3)) as issue of copies to the public.

[96] C.D.P.A. 1988, s.17(4); it was open to question under the 1956 Act whether a single frame could be a copy of a film for the purposes of publication (see *Spelling Goldberg Productions Inc.* v. *B.P.C. Publishing* [1981] R.P.C. 283); if the present definition applies equally for the purpose of subsistence as for infringement, then this question would seem to be answered, *sed quare*, and *cf.* the position in relation to sound recordings discussed n. 94, *ante*.

[97] C.D.P.A. 1988, s.175(4)(c).

[98] See *British Northrop Ltd.* v. *Texteam Blackburn Ltd.* [1974] R.P.C. 57.

[99] *White* v. *Geroch* (1819) 2 B. & Ald. 298; *Blanchett* v. *Ingram* (1887) 3 T.L.R. 687.

[1] For example, the issue of copies of the Oscar statuette to Acadamy Award winners was held not to be publication: *Oscar Trade Mark* [1980] F.S.R. 429.

[2] *Novello* v. *Sudlow* (1852) 12 C.B. 177; subject to the requirement that the issue of copies must be intended to satisfy the reasonable requirements of the public and not be merely colourable, as to which see § 3–17, *post*.

[3] (1849) 1 M. & G. 25.

[4] [1980] Ch. 282, *per* Buckley L.J. at p. 292 (expressing the same view as to a sale by private treaty); reversed on appeal as to the meaning of publication for the purposes of infringement: [1982] A.C. 1 (H.L.).

that any consequent sale which resulted in the issue of reproductions of the work to the public would constitute publication.[5]

3–17 **Colourable publication.** For the issue of copies of the work to the public to constitute publication it must be intended to satisfy the reasonable requirements of the public and not be merely colourable.[6] The question as to what is a merely colourable publication arose in the case of *Francis, Day & Hunter* v. *Feldman & Co.*,[7] in which the plaintiffs were the owners of the copyright in a song called "You made me love you (I didn't want to do it)". The author of the song was an American author who assigned his copyright in it to a firm in New York. This firm published the song simultaneously in New York and Canada on May 5, 1913.[8] In April 1913 they sent 12 copies of the song to the plaintiffs with instructions to copyright the song in the United Kingdom on May 5, 1913. On that day the plaintiffs sent one copy to the British Museum and filed one copy at their London office. They also sent four copies to the agent for receiving copies for the university libraries, and the remaining six copies they exposed for sale on the counter in the retail department of their business premises in London. They did not advertise the song, and there was no immediate demand for it, but subsequently it became a great success and was the subject of large sales. The plaintiffs acquired the copyright in the song for the United Kingdom. It was held that the publication in England, on May 5, 1913, was not "colourable only," and that it was sufficient to show that there was an intention to satisfy the demands of the public if such demand should arise.

In *Copex Establishment* v. *Flegon*,[9] on an application for interlocutory relief to restrain the publication of a book, the question whether copyright subsisted in the book depended solely on whether it had been published in the United Kingdom. The plaintiff's evidence was to the effect that 169 copies of the book in the Russian language had been placed on sale at more than 50 booksellers. On the first occasion of sale the demand did not exceed the supply, but, since the publicity given to the case, there had been extra demand which had exceeded the supply and it was intended to satisfy that demand. The defendant argued that this was not publication in that it was not intended to satisfy the reasonable requirements of the public, and that there had been deliberate under-supplying of the work in Russia to protect the forthcoming publications of the book in volume form and serial form in English. No decision was reached on the issue so raised, as undertakings were given until the trial of the action[10]

In *Bodley Head* v. *Flegon*,[11] it was held that, since there was no evidence of any clandestine publication (*samizdat*) of the novel in Russia before its

[5] But see *British Northrop Ltd.* v. *Texteam Blackburn Ltd.* [1974] R.P.C. 57.
[6] C.D.P.A. 1988, s.175(5), re-enacting Copyright Act 1956, s.49(2)(*b*) and Copyright Act 1911, s.35(3).
[7] [1914] 2 Ch. 728.
[8] Canada was not at that date part of His Majesty's dominions to which the 1911 Act extended.
[9] *The Times*, August 18, 1967.
[10] See, as to sufficiency of evidence of publication, *Warner Bros. Inc.* v. *The Roadrunner Ltd.* [1988] F.S.R. 292.
[11] [1972] R.P.C. 587.

publication in France, it was unnecessary to decide whether *samizdat* publication could in any event be treated as publication within the meaning of the 1956 Act. The learned Judge however doubted whether *samizdat* circulation could possibly be regarded as an effort to satisfy the reasonable requirements of the Russian public. By its nature it was a clandestine circulation which intentionally disregarded the requirements of the Russian public, because such requirements could not lawfully either be voiced by potential readers or satisfied by the author.

Place of publication. In cases where the place of first publication is   **3–18** material, it would appear that it is the place where copies are first put on offer to the public.[12] In the Canadian case of *Grossman* v. *Canada Cycle Co.*[13] the posting of copies of a newspaper to subscribers in the United Kingdom was held not to amount to publication in the United Kingdom; further, that even delivery in the United Kingdom of such copies would probably not be a sufficient publication as it was not making the paper available to the general public.

First publication: simultaneous publication. As discussed above,[14] a   **3–19** literary, dramatic, musical or artistic work, typographical arrangement of a published edition, sound recording or film is entitled to copyright if first published in the United Kingdom or a country to which the relevant provisions extend, or if the author was a qualified person at the time when the work was first published, or at his death if this occurred before first publication.[15] The reference to a country to which the provisions extend is to the extension of Part I of the 1988 Act by Order in Council under section 157 of that Act to any of the Channel Islands, the Isle of Man or any colony.[16] Such works also qualify for copyright protection where they are first published in a country to which the Act does not extend, but to which its provisions have been applied by an Order under section 159.[17] In all these cases, therefore, it is essential to determine what is meant by "first" publication. The 1988 Act provides, as did the 1956 Act,[18] that publication in one country shall not be regarded as other than than the first publication by reason of simultaneous publication elsewhere, and for this purpose publication elsewhere within the previous 30 days shall be treated as simultaneous.[19] What is frequently in copyright law described as simultaneous publication therefore means any two or more publications which take place within a period of 30 days. Under the 1911 Act the relevant provision provided a period of 14 days only.[20] This period continued to

---

[12] *British Northrop Ltd.* v. *Texteam Blackburn Ltd.* [1974] R.P.C. 57. As to publication in parts, see *Low* v. *Ward* (1868) L.R. 6 Eq. 415. The Court of Appeal in *Infabrics Ltd.* v. *Jaytex Shirt Co. Ltd.* [1980] Ch. 282, *per* Buckley L.J. at p. 292, expressed the view that offer for sale would not be publication.
[13] [1901–04] Mac.C.C. 36.
[14] See § 3–10, *ante*.
[15] C.D.P.A. 1988, s.155(1).
[16] As to which see Chap. 17, *post*.
[17] Under C.D.P.A. 1988, s.155(2); see Chap. 17, *post*.
[18] Copyright Act 1956, s.49(2)(*d*).
[19] C.D.P.A. 1988, s.155(3).
[20] Copyright Act 1911, s.35(3).

apply under the 1956 Act,[21] in the case of a publication taking place before June 1, 1957, and, by virtue of the transitional provisions in the 1988 Act,[22] this period still remains applicable in relation to existing works published before such date.

C. *Existing works*

3–20   **Existing works.** An existing work, for the purposes of the 1988 Act, is a work the making of which was both begun and completed before August 1, 1989.[23] Unlike the definition of material time for the purposes of satisfying the test as to the requirements for subsistence of copyright by reference to a work's author,[24] in the case of a work the making of which extended over a period of time, it is the time of completion of the making of the work alone which governs whether the new provisions of the 1988 Act as to subsistence apply to the work. Nevertheless, where the making of the work was begun before, but completed after, August 1, 1988, it may still be necessary to consider the position during the making of the work prior to such date in order to determine whether copyright subsists in the work by reference to the requirements as to authorship being satisfied.[25]

3–21   **Subsistence of copyright in existing works.** The 1988 Act provides that copyright subsists in an existing work after August 1, 1989 only if it subsisted immediately before such date, or if it is published after such date in accordance with the requirements as to first publication contained in section 154 of that Act.[26] The new provisions as to the subsistence of copyright introduced by the 1988 Act are, therefore, not to apply to events which occurred before August 1, 1989.[27] For example, if copyright did not subsist under the 1956 Act in a musical work, but records reproducing that work had been released in the United Kingdom prior to August 1, 1989,[28] such release does not operate to confer copyright on the work after commencement. Similarly, copyright will not subsist by virtue of publication under the 1988 Act in a work of architecture in the form of a building which was constructed prior to commencement.[29] On the other hand, if copyright did subsist in an existing work under the 1956 Act, then copyright continues to subsist under the 1988 Act, irrespective of whether the requirements for subsistence set out in the 1988 Act are in fact satisfied in relation to such work.[30] This approach to existing works in effect preserves the importance of the previous law under the 1956 Act in relation to such works. Thus, in relation to photographs taken, and sound recordings

---

[21] Copyright Act 1956, Sched. 7, para. 33(1).
[22] C.D.P.A. 1988, Sched. 1, para. 5(1) and para. 35.
[23] *Ibid.*, Sched. 1, para. 2.
[24] See § 3–8, *ante.*
[25] See n. 25. *ante.*
[26] C.D.P.A. 1988, Sched. 1, para. 5(1) and (2)(*a*); but see, as to foreign works, § 3–23, *post.*
[27] Save in respect of works which are not existing works, because although their making began before commencement it was completed after such date: see § 3–20, *ante.*
[28] An act which did not constitute publication of the musical work under the Copyright Act 1956, (s.49(2)(*a*)) but which does under the 1988 Act; see § 3–13, *ante.*
[29] C.D.P.A. 1988, 175(3); and see § 3–13, *ante.*
[30] *Ibid.*, Sched. 1, para. 35.

made, before June 1, 1957 the requirement as to qualification by reference to the author where it is a corporate body being incorporated under the laws of a country, continues to mean, under the 1988 Act, in relation to such works, a reference to such body having its established place of business in such country.[31]

Existing works: special provisions. The general approach of the 1988 **3–22** Act to existing works, discussed above,[32] is supplemented by specific transitional provisions to ensure that copyright is not conferred on certain existing works which did not enjoy copyright protection under the Copyright Act 1956.

Thus, copyright does not subsist under the 1988 Act in an artistic work made before June 1, 1957, which at the time it was made constituted a design capable of registration under the Registered Designs Act 1949 and was used, or intended to be used, as a model or pattern to be multiplied by industrial process.[33]

The same approach of maintaining the existing law is taken in relation to certain existing films, film sound-tracks, broadcasts and cable programmes. Thus no copyright subsists under the 1988 Act in films as such made before June 1, 1957, but provision is made for preserving the dramatic and artistic copyright in such films corresponding to the rights so subsisting by virtue of the 1911 Act.[34] Film sound-tracks made before August 1, 1989 are now treated as sound recordings, not, as previously, as part of the film. However, for certain purposes, including subsistence of copyright, they continue to be treated as if they were part of the film.[35] Broadcasts made before June 1, 1957 and cable programmes included in a cable programme service before January 1, 1985 are not entitled to copyright protection.[36]

Foreign existing works. The only exception to the principle that events **3–23** occurring before August 1, 1989 cannot entitle existing works to copyright protection if they did not enjoy such protection under the 1956 Act,[37] is in relation to existing foreign works, which may qualify for copyright protection after commencement by virtue of an Order made under section 159 of the 1988 Act applying Part I of that Act to a country to which those provisions do not extend.[38]

The point is of most significance in relation to existing American works made before June 1, 1957, in particular old American films, and which did not qualify for copyright protection under the 1956 Act until the adher-

---

[31] This being the definition of qualified persons which were corporate bodies under the 1911 Act, as preserved under the Copyright Act 1956, Sched. 7, para. 39(4).
[32] See § 3–21, *ante.*
[33] C.D.P.A. 1988, Sched. 1, para. 6; this maintains the position as it was under the Copyright Act 1956, Sched. 7, para. 8 and Sched. 8, para. 2.
[34] C.D.P.A. 1988, Sched. 1, para. 7; this maintains the position as it was under the Copyright Act 1956, Sched. 7, paras. 14, 15 and 16.
[35] C.D.P.A. 1988, Sched. 1, para. 8; see further, §§ 2–29 and 2–30, *ante.*
[36] C.D.P.A. 1988, Sched. 1, para. 9; this maintains the position as it was under the Copyright Act 1956, Sched. 7, para. 17 and s.14A (added, with effect from January 1, 1985, by the Cable and Broadcasting Act 1984, ss.22 to 24 (now repealed)).
[37] *I.e.* the principle underlying C.D.P.A. 1988, Sched. 1, para. 5(1) discussed at § 3–21, *ante.*
[38] C.D.P.A. 1988, Sched. 1, para. 5(2); and see Chap. 17, *post.*

ence of the United States of America to the Berne Convention led to the inclusion of that country in Schedule 1 of the Order applying the 1956 Act to such works.[39] The wording of that Order made it clear that such previously unprotected works could qualify for copyright protection under the 1956 Act either by virtue of a publication which took place in the United States of America before June 1, 1957, or by reason of the author being a citizen, resident or subject of such country.[40] This alteration in protection afforded to foreign existing works has greatly diminished the importance previously attributed to the question whether it was possible to publish old American films, a question upon which the copyright protection in the United Kingdom of such films in turn depended.[41]

The position under the 1988 Act is the same, by virtue of the provisions of an Order made under Section 159 of that Act.[42] Such Order contains its own "transitional" provisions intended to deal with the situation where, prior to such work becoming protected in the United Kingdom, a person has committed himself to investment with a view to exploitation of the work in a way which would, after the work has become protected, be an infringement of copyright.[43]

3–24 **Unprotected work qualifying for protection.** Although the Orders in Council made under the Copyright Acts to comply with the Berne Convention and Universal Copyright Convention must make the event more unusual than in the past,[44] circumstances may still occur in which an unpublished work was unprotected in the United Kingdom, but subsequently became protected by reason of its publication here.[45] For instance, apart from international arrangements, a foreign artist does not, by exhibiting his painting in the United Kingdom, become entitled to copyright here. Until he has issued copies to the public, any person is at liberty (unless acting in breach of confidence or contract) to photograph, engrave, or otherwise copy the original work and to sell those copies in the United Kingdom. This, again, being done without the licence of the artist, does not constitute publication of the work,[46] and therefore, if the artist himself subsequently issues reproductions to the public in the United Kingdom (or another country to which the 1988 Act is applied or to which its provisions are extended), he thereby gains copyright in the United Kingdom in his original. What then is the position of the first copyist? Clearly, he cannot be sued for piracy merely because he has in his possession copies of the work, for those copies were lawfully made and the

---

[39] The Copyright (International Conventions) Order 1979, S.I. 1979 No. 1715 as amended with effect from March 8, 1989 by The Copyright (International Conventions) (Amendment) Order 1989, S.I. 1989 No. 157, § D–5, *post.*

[40] *Ibid.* para. 6.

[41] See *Copinger* (12th ed), § 797.

[42] The Copyright (Application to Other Countries) (No. 2) Order 1989 (S.I. 1989 No. 1293), paras. 2(1) and (2). See D–22, *post.*

[43] *Ibid.* para. 7(1) and (2).

[44] But, as to the particular problem caused in relation to existing works by the retrospective effect given under the Order in Council to the United States of America becoming a signatory to the Berne Convention, see § 3–23, *ante.*

[45] See *Copex Establishment* v. *Flegon, The Times,* August 18, 1967, where the authoress was Mrs. Svetlana Alliluyeva, Stalin's daughter; and see *Bodley Head* v. *Flegon* [1972] R.P.C. 587.

[46] C.D.P.A. 1988, ss.175(6) and 178.

subsequent acquisition of copyright by the author cannot, prima facie, have a retrospective effect so as to render an act unlawful which was perfectly lawful at the time it was committed.[47] It is equally clear that the copyist cannot make or print any further copies (even from the copies he has already made). However, it is not so clear whether he can dispose of copies which he has on hand at the date when the artist acquired his copyright. Under the 1956 Act, it was suggested that the test remained whether copies were lawfully made when made, and, if so, their subsequent sale could not give rise to an infringement.[48] The case was considered to be analogous to that of a person who has assigned his copyright, or granted a licence to publish for a term which has expired. It was held, under the old law, that an assignor could dispose of copies manufactured before the date of his assignment, and that a licensee could do the same with regard to copies manufactured before his licence ran out.[49] The position would appear to be different under the 1988 Act, in that the putting into circulation of copies not previously put into circulation now constitutes an infringement, if done without the copyright owner's licence, irrespective of whether the copies were infringing copies when made.[50]

3. Literary, Dramatic, Musical and Artistic Works: Originality

A. *Introduction*

Statutory provision. By section 1(1)(*a*) of the 1988 Act copyright sub-   **3–25**
sists, subject to the qualifying conditions for subsistence being met,[51] in original literary, dramatic, musical and artistic works. There is no difference between this provision and the equivalent provisions of the 1956 Act,[52] or of the 1911 Act,[53] so far as concerns the requirement of originality, and decisions on the point under the earlier Acts remain valid.

Relevance of pre-1911 decisions. Before the commencement of the   **3–26**
1911 Act, there was no general statutory requirement of originality for copyright works. Neither the Literary Copyright Act 1842,[54] nor the Engravings Copyright Act 1766,[55] used the expression "original", whilst

---

[47] This is the approach taken under the various Orders in Council in relation to acts which were lawful when done, where previously unprotected works become protected in the United Kingdom; see § 3–23, *ante*.

[48] See Copyright Act 1956, s.5(3).

[49] *Taylor* v. *Pillow* (1869) L.R. 7 Eq. 418 (a case of assignment); *Howitt* v. *Hall* (1862) 6 L.T. 348 (a case of licence); *cf.* the dicta to the contrary with regard to gramophone records under the Copyright Act 1911, s.2(2): *Monckton* v. *Pathé Frères Ltd.* [1914] 1 K.B. 395; see § 15–37, *post*.

[50] C.D.P.A. 1988, s.18 and see § 8–92 *et seq. post*.

[51] See § 3–2 and § 3–4, *et seq.*, *ante*.

[52] Copyright Act 1956, ss.2(1) and (2), and 3(2) and (3).

[53] Copyright Act 1911, s.1(1).

[54] 5 & 6 Vict. c. 45.

[55] 7 Geo. 3, c. 38.

the Sculpture Copyright Act 1814,[56] and the Fine Arts Copyright Act 1862,[57] referred respectively to "original sculptures" and "original paintings."

The leading case on the law prior to the 1911 Act was *Walter v. Lane*,[58] in which the House of Lords decided that a reporter was entitled to copyright under the Literary Copyright Act 1842 in his verbatim report of a public speech of Lord Rosebery. The report appeared in *The Times* and had been copied by the defendant in a book produced by the defendant of Lord Rosebery's speeches. However, Lord Halsbury L.C. specifically referred as a basis for his decision to the absence of "original" in the statute[59] and Davey L.J. considered that the fact no originality or literary skill was required for the report had less to do with it than the principle that a person should not avail himself of another's skill, labour and expense, by copying his work.[60]

It had been thought that that the insertion of the word "original" in the Act of 1911 did not, having regard to the limited meaning attached to such term in decisions after such date, alter the law.[61] But Cross J., in *Roberton v. Lewis*,[62] said that while it was not necessary for him to decide the point, in view of the change in the law brought about by the introduction of the word "original" into the 1911 and 1956 Acts, it was at least arguable that *Walter v. Lane*[63] was no longer good law. However, this argument was raised in *Express Newspapers plc v. News (U.K) Ltd*,[64] and was rejected by Browne-Wilkinson V.C., who held that *Walter v. Lane* is still good law.

B. *Originality of expression, not of content*

3–27 **Expression, not content.** Copyright protection is given to literary, dramatic, musical and artistic works and not to ideas,[65] and therefore it is original skill or labour in execution of the work, and not originality of thought, which is required.[66] The word "original" does not, in this connection, mean that the work must be the expression of original or inventive thought; the originality required relates to the expression of the

---

[56] 54 Geo. 3, c. 56.
[57] 25 & 26 Vict. c. 68.
[58] [1900] A.C. 539.
[59] *Ibid.* p. 549.
[60] *Ibid.* p. 552; as to which see: *Collis v. Cater Ltd.* (1898) 78 L.T. 613; *Jarrold v. Houlston* (1857) 3 K. & J. 708.
[61] See earlier editions of *Copinger*.
[62] [1976] R.P.C. 169 (decided in 1960); *Sifam Electrical Instrument Co. Ltd. v. Sangamo Weston Ltd.* [1973] R.P.C. 899 and *L.B. (Plastics) Ltd. v. Swish Products Ltd.* [1979] R.P.C. 551.
[63] See n. 59 *ante*.
[64] [1990] F.S.R 359, following the decision of the High Court of Australia in *Sands McDougall Proprietary Ltd. v. Robinson.* 23 C.L.R. 89.
[65] See the discussion in *Plix Products Ltd. v. Frank M. Winstone (Merchants)* [1986] F.S.R. 63 at p. 92–93; and see §1–1, text and n. 2, *ante*.
[66] See *Kilvington Bros. Ltd. v. Goldberg* (1957) 8 D.L.R. (2d) 768 (copyright in a tombstone) and *Martin v. Polyplas Manufacturers Ltd.* [1969] N.Z.L.R. 1046 (copyright in three-dimensional engravings of two-dimensional designs for coins).

thought.[67] The position in this respect under the Copyright Acts may be contrasted with the standard required for registered designs under the Registered Designs Act 1949. The requirement for registration under that Act is of novelty, so that, if a design in fact resembles an existing design, it may not be registered, even though the designer of the second design arrived at this design entirely independently of the first design.

Meaning of "original": expenditure of independent skill or labour. **3–28**
What the Copyright Acts require is that the work should originate from the author; it must not be copied from another work, for a mere copyist does not obtain copyright in his copy.[68] This is the true meaning of "original." A work may be "original" in this sense, even though the author has drawn on knowledge common to himself and others,[69] or has used already existing material.[70]

Mere copy. Despite the fact that the copying, even in the same medium, **3–29**
of an artistic work, requires a higher degree of skill and judgment than the mere reproduction of a literary work, it has been stated that skill, labour and judgment merely in the process of copying cannot confer originality and the mere copyist cannot have protection for his copy.[71] Particularly, therefore, where the reproduction is in the same medium as the original, there must be more than an exact reproduction to secure copyright; there must be some element of material alteration or embellishment which suffices to make the totality of the work an original work.[72] If the original, in the case of a painting, is used merely as a model to give the idea of the new work or, in the case of a photograph, merely as a basis to be worked up by photographic process to something different, then the new work may be entitled to protection; but, if the result is simply a slavish copy, it will not be protected.[73] Thus, where the work was traced from an existing shape, that was held not to involve sufficient skill and labour to create an original artistic work.[74]

---

[67] *Per* Petersen J. in *University of London Press Ltd.* v. *University Tutorial Press Ltd.* [1916] 2 Ch. 601 at 608; cited with approval: *Macmillan & Co. Ltd.* v. *Cooper (K. & J.)* (1923) 40 T.L.R. 186 at 190; *British Broadcasting Co.* v. *Wireless League Gazette Publishing Co.* [1926] Ch. 433 at 440; *Ladbroke (Football) Ltd.* v. *William Hill (Football) Ltd.* [1964] 1 W.L.R. 273 at 277; *L.B. (Plastics) Ltd.* v. *Swish Products Ltd.* [1977] F.S.R. 87; [1979] F.S.R. 145; and see *Ascot Jockey Club Ltd.* v. *Simons* (1968) 64 W.W.R. 411.

[68] See *per* Lord James in *Walter* v. *Lane* [1900] A.C. 539 at 554; *Barfield* v. *Nicholson* (1824) 2 Sim.St. 1; *Leslie* v. *Young (J.) & Sons* [1894] A.C. 335 and § 3–30, *post*.

[69] *Per* Petersen J. in *University of London Press Ltd.* v. *University Tutorial Press Ltd.* [1916] 2 Ch. 601 at 608; and see *Macmillan & Co. Ltd.* v. *Cooper (K. & J.)* (1923) 40 T.L.R. 186 (selection or abridgment of a non-copyright work), in which Lord Atkinson cited with approval *Emerson* v. *Davies*, Storey's U.S. Rep. 768 (1845). And see *Dutt (S.K.)* v. *Law Book Co.* [1954] A.L.J. 125; *Gouindan* v. *Gopalakrishna Kone* (1955) Mad.W.N. 369.

[70] See further § 3–32, *et seq.*, *post*.

[71] *Per* Lord Oliver in *Interlego A.G.* v. *Tyco Industries Inc.* [1989] A.C. 217 at 262H–263A.

[72] See n. 72 *ante*.

[73] *cf. Re Martin (T.J.)* (1884) 10 V.L.R. 196; see § 3–28, *ante*; see also *Wham-O Manufacturing Co.* v. *Lincoln Industries Ltd.* [1982] R.P.C. 281 at 291 (High Court of New Zealand).

[74] *J. & S. Davis (Holding) Ltd.* v. *Wright Heath Group Ltd.* [1988] R.P.C. 403, at 412.

3–30 Examples of these principles. In accordance with the principles discussed above, such works as mathematical tables have been held to be protected, if their author has worked them out for himself, even though identical tables have previously been published.[75] Although the idea or information embodied in the tables is not novel, the result of the author's labour of compilation is a set of tables upon which the author has done original work. Similarly, it has been held in a Scottish case[76] that the author of a collection of precedents or "styles" constructed by following the directions of a statute was entitled to copyright protection, although any two persons with a knowledge of the subject would be bound to arrive at a similar result.[77]

3–31 Photographs. Again, while it may be that there is no copyright in a photograph of an existing photograph,[78] it is thaought that, if a person takes a photograph of a scene in nature which is identical with a former photograph of the same scene, he will have copyright in his photograph although the idea of taking the photograph was derived from his having seen the first photograph.

3–32 Degree of independent skill or labour required. It is clear that the standard of originality required by the Copyright Acts is a low one,[79] but it is almost impossible to define in any precise terms the amount of knowledge, labour, judgment or literary skill or taste which the author of a work must bestow on its composition in order for it to acquire copyright.[80] It is here that the real difficulty lies. There is no guiding principle as to the quantum of skill or judgment required.[81] Simplicity, as such, is not enough to prevent copyright subsisting unless extreme, such as a straight line,[82] or a circle.[83] In the absence of any clear guidance on the question, all that is left is to examine the decisions on the point as indicative of the degree of skill and labour which the courts have considered requisite in various sets of circumstances.[84]

---

[75] *Bailey* v. *Taylor* (1830) 1 Russ. & My. 73; see also *Stevenson (A.)* v. *Crook (H.F.)* [1938] Ex.(Can.) 299.

[76] *Alexander (W.)* v. *Mackenzie (R.)* (1846) 9 Sc.Sess.Cass. (2nd Ser.) 748; see also *Real Estate Institute of N.S.W.* v. *Wood* (1923) 23 S.R. (N.S.W.) 349; *Capital Finance Co. Ltd.* v. *Bowmaker (Commercial) Ltd.* [1964] R.P.C. 463; and *Capital Finance Co. Ltd.* v. *Lombank Ltd.* [1964] R.P.C. 467.

[77] As, for example, where two persons produce separate, but strikingly similar, pictures to illustrate the same text of a story: see *Blackwell* v. *Harper* (1740) 2 Atk. 92.

[78] See § 3–34, *post.* As to what is protected by the copyright in a photograph, see *Bauman* v. *Fussell* [1978] R.P.C. 485 (decided in 1953).

[79] See *Jagdish Prasad Gupta* v. *Parmeshwar Prasad Singh* [1966] A.I.R. Patna 33.

[80] See, *per* Lord Atkinson in *Macmillan & Co. Ltd.* v. *Cooper (K. & J.)* (1923) 40 T.L.R. 186; this statement was approved by the House of Lords in *G.A. Cramp & Sons Ltd.* v. *Frank Smythson Ltd.* [1944] A.C. 329; see also *Ladbroke (Football) Ltd.* v. *William Hill (Football) Ltd.* [1964] 1 W.L.R. 273.

[81] As was pointed out by Maugham J., in *Cambridge University Press* v. *University Tutorial Press Ltd.* (1928) 45 R.P.C. 335.

[82] *British Northrop Ltd.* v. *Texteam Blackburn Ltd.* [1974] R.P.C. 537.

[83] *Karo Step Trade Mark* [1977] R.P.C. 255; *Gleeson* v. *H.R. Denne Ltd.* [1975] R.P.C. 471; but see *Solar Thomson Engineering Co. Ltd.* v. *Barton* [1977] R.P.C. 537; see also *Duriron Inc.* v. *Hugh Jennings Ltd.* [1984] F.S.R. 1.

[84] See, in relation to literary and artistic works respectively, the cases cited in §§ 2–10 and 2–23, *ante.*

C. *Kinds of skill and labour*

Use of existing subject-matter. As has been seen,[85] where the author   **3–33**
has produced his result without reference to any pre-existing subject-
matter, it is immaterial that the result is not novel, or that anyone else
could have produced the same result, or that the idea or scheme from
which the result has been produced is open to the public. But where the
author has made use of existing subject-matter, more difficulty arises, and
it has to be determined whether he has expended sufficient independent
skill and labour to justify copyright protection for his result.[86]

It is suggested that, in determining whether the work is original and
entitled to copyright the work must be looked at as a whole and if, notwithstanding that the author has used existing subject-matters, he has
expended sufficient independent skill and labour, he will be entitled to
copyright protection for his work.[87] This difficulty frequently arises in
relation to revisions of engineering drawings and the question whether it is
only the revision, rather than the whole of the revised drawing, which may
be entitled to copyright. However, in *L.B. (Plastics) Ltd.* v. *Swish Products
Ltd.*,[88] it was held that where there has been a previous drawing or a
model from which a new drawing is prepared, or some sketches have been
made which are in part redrawn, the new drawing may be entitled to
copyright as a whole because of the amount of skill and labour involved in
producing it.[89] Whether it is so entitled to copyright depends on whether
there has been the addition of some element of material alteration or
embellishment which suffices to make the totality of the work an original
work.[90] This is a matter of fact and degree; even an alteration or addition
which is quantitatively small may, if material, suffice to create an original
work.[91] Even if such a revised or updated drawing is entitled to copyright,
there may be problems in establishing infringement of such a work in that
the courts, in considering whether a substantial part has been taken, may
disregard the parts which have been taken without alteration from the
pre-existing works.[92]

The kinds of skill or labour which are commonly employed to make a
copyright work from existing subject-matter are change of medium, selection and arrangement, and abridgment; these will be considered in turn.

---

[85] See § 3–28, *ante*.

[86] *Martin* v. *Polyplas Manufacturers Ltd.* [1969] N.Z.L.R. 1046; see also *Ashmore* v. *Douglas-Home* [1987] F.S.R. 553.

[87] See *Ladbroke (Football) Ltd.* v. *William Hill (Football) Ltd.* [19641] 1 W.L.R. 273; *Redwood Music Ltd.* v. *Chappell & Co. Ltd.* [1982] R.P.C. 109.

[88] [1979] R.P.C. 551. And see *Temple Instruments Ltd.* v. *Hollis Heels Ltd.* [1971] F.S.R. 634; *Radley Gowns Ltd.* v. *Costas Spyrou* [1975] F.S.R. 455; and *Interfirm Comparison (Australia) Pty. Ltd.* v. *Law Society of New South Wales* [1977] R.P.C. 137.

[89] See also: *Allibert S.A.* v. *O'Connor* [1981] F.S.R. 613; *Politechnika* v. *Dallas Print Transfers Ltd.* [1982] F.S.R. 529 at 539; *Rexnold Inc.* v. *Ancon Ltd.* [1983] F.S.R. 662; *Wham-O Manufactur-ing Co.* v. *Lincoln Industries Ltd.* [1985] R.P.C. 127 (Court of Appeal of New Zealand); *Inter-lego A.G.* v. *Tyco Inc.* [1989] A.C. 217.

[90] *Per* Lord Oliver in *Interlego A.G.* v. *Tyco Industries Inc.* [1989] A.C. 217 at 263C.

[91] See n. 86. *ante*.

[92] See *Warwick Film Productions Ltd.* v. *Eisinger* [1969] Ch. 508 and see § 3–46, *post*.

(i) Change of medium

3–34   **Change of medium.** The work of a reporter in reporting a speech delivered orally is an example of the expenditure of skill and labour in connection with a change of medium.[93] Another example is the work of a translator, which has always been entitled to protection.[94]

In relation to artistic works, a change of medium will often entitle a reproduction of an existing artistic work to independent protection. For example, it was held, under the Fine Arts Copyright Act 1862,[95] that a photograph of an engraving was entitled to protection.[96]

Again, an engraver is almost invariably a copyist, but his work may still be original in the sense that he has employed skill and judgment in its production. An engraver produces the resemblance he wishes by means which are very different from those employed by the painter or draughtsman from whom he copies; means which require a high degree of skill and labour.[97] The engraver produces his effect by the management of light and shade, or, as the term of his art expresses it, the *chiaroscuro*. The required degree of light and shade are produced by different lines and dots; the engraver must decide on the choice of the different lines or dots for himself, and on his choice depends the success of his print.[98]

(ii) Selection and arrangement

3–35   **Compilations.** The labour and skill employed in selecting and arranging existing subject-matter may give copyright protection to the resulting work.[99] This was recognised by the inclusion in the definitions of "literary work" in the 1911 and 1956 Acts of "compilations."[1] Section 3(1) of the 1988 Act defines literary work as including "a table or compilation." Protection has been given under this head to a wide variety of works,[2] but where the labour of selection is negligible, copyright protection has been refused.[3]

---

[93] See *Walter* v. *Lane* [1900] A.C. 539.

[94] *Byrne* v. *Statist Co.* [1914] 1 K.B. 622; *Wyatt* v. *Barnard* (1814) 3 V. & B. 77.

[95] 25 & 26 Vict. c. 68.

[96] *Graves' Case* (1869) L.R. 4 Q.B. 715.

[97] *Martin* v. *Polyplas Manufacturers Ltd.* [1969] N.Z.L.R. 1046 (copyright in three-dimensional engravings of two-dimensional designs for coins).

[98] *Newton* v. *Cowie* (1827) 4 Bing. 234; *Martin* v. *Wright* (1833) 6 Sim. 297.

[99] *Moffatt and Paige Ltd.* v. *Gill (G) & Sons Ltd.* (1902) 86 L.T. 465

[1] Copyright Act 1911, s.35; Copyright Act 1956, s.48(1).

[2] For a list of cases, see § 2–8, *ante.* See also *MacMillan & Co.* v. *Suresh Chunder Deb* (1890) 17 I.L.R. (Calcutta) 951, where an infringement of the "Golden Treasury" was restrained; *Black (A. and C.) Ltd.* v. *Munay (A) & Son* (1870) 9 Sc. Sess. Cas. (3 Ser). 341; *Harman Pictures N.V.* v. *Osborne* [1967] 1 W.L.R. 723; *Ravenscroft* v. *Herbert & Anor.* [1980] R.P.C. 193, (selection of incidents from real life); and *Fernald* v. *Jay Lewis Productions Ltd.* [1975] F.S.R. 499.

[3] *e.g. G.A. Cramp & Sons Ltd.* v. *Frank Smythson Ltd.* [1944] A.C. 329 (mere selection of various common tables for insertion in pocket diary); *Greyhound Racing Association Ltd.* v. *Shallis* [1923–28] Mac.C.C. 370.

Trade catalogues; football pools. It is clear that trade catalogues can be   **3–36**
the subject-matter of copyright as compilations.[4] It is, of course, always
open to question whether the component parts of the catalogue are original or merely taken from a common source,[5] but a catalogue is generally
a compilation upon which the compiler has exercised skill and judgment.[6]
It has been argued that skill and labour employed merely in selecting suitable parts to include in the catalogue is irrelevant to the creation of a
copyright compilation.[7] This argument has been used with regard to the
compilation of the Football League fixture list, on the basis that the selection of appropriate dates upon which the teams should meet was for the
purposes of the League activities and not for the compilation of its fixture
list. But Upjohn J.[8] held that copyright subsisted in the list, and that part
of the skill and labour involved in its preparation was that of working out
the appropriate dates of matches. This view has been upheld in the House
of Lords in connection with the copyright in a compilation of football
pools coupons.[9]

Selections. Selections of poems or prose compositions may also be pro-   **3–37**
tected,[10] as may selections of incidents from real life,[11] and arrangements
of private letters. Thus, in *Parry* v. *Moring*,[12] the plaintiff had had copied
the private letters of Sir William Temple and had then translated them
into modern English and arranged them in the order in which he considered that they had been written, and published them with notes. The
view was expressed in the course of the interlocutory application that such
an arrangement of private letters was entitled to copyright; the defendant
submitted to an injunction and an inquiry as to damages, agreeing to treat
the motion as the trial of the action.

---

[4] *Hotten* v. *Arthur* (1863) 1 H. & M. 603; *Grace* v. *Newman* (1875) L.R. 19 Eq. 623; *Maple &
Co.* v. *Junior Army and Navy Stores* (1882) 21 Ch.D. 369 (overruling *Cobbett* v. *Woodward*
(1872) L.R. 14 Eq. 407, to the contrary). Illustrations in trade catalogues are protected as
artistic works, although text and illustrations together may be protected as a compilation.
[5] *Collis* v. *Cater Ltd.* (1898) 78 L.T. 613; *Harpers Ltd.* v. *Barry, Henry & Co. Ltd.* (1892) 20
Sess.Cas. (4th Ser.) 133; *cf. Cooper* v. *Stephens* [1895] 1 Ch. 567; *Marshall (W.) & Co. Ltd.* v.
Bull (A.H.) Ltd. (1901) 85 L.T. 77.
[6] *Lamb* v. *Evans* [1893] 1 Ch. 218; *Collis* v. *Cater Ltd.* (1898) 78 L.T. 613; *Kelly* v. *Morris*
(1886) L.R. 1 Eq. 697; *Morris* v. *Ashbee* (1868) L.R. 7 Eq. 34; and see *Slumber-Magic Adjustable Bed Co. Ltd.* v. *Sleep-King Adjustable Bed Co. Ltd.* [1985] 1 W.W.R. 112 (Supreme Court
of British Columbia).
[7] And see *Purefoy Engineering Company Ltd.* v. *Sykes, Boxall & Co. Ltd.* (1955) 72 R.P.C. 89,
where the Court of Appeal held that the copyright existed in the arrangement of the catalogue (which had involved a sufficient amount of labour and skill), and not in the selection
of the parts embodied in the catalogue.
[8] *Football League Ltd.* v. *Littlewoods Pools Ltd.* [1959] Ch. 637; and see *J. & C. Moores* v. *Customs and Excise Commissioners* [1963] 1 W.L.R. 817.
[9] *Ladbroke (Football) Ltd.* v. *William Hill (Football) Ltd.* [1964] 1 W.L.R. 273; distinguishing
Purefoy Engineering Company Ltd. v. *Sykes, Boxall & Co. Ltd.* (1955) 72 R.P.C. 89, n. 8, *ante*.
And see *Warwick Film Productions Ltd.* v. *Eisinger* [1969] Ch. 508 and *Industrial Furnaces Ltd.*
v. *Reeves* [1970] R.P.C. 605.
[10] *Macmillan & Co.* v. *Suresh Chunder Deb* (1890) 17 Indian L.R. (Calcutta) 951.
[11] See *Harman Pictures N.V.* v. *Osborne* [1967] 1 W.L.R. 723; *Poznanski* v. *London Film Production
Ltd.* [1936–45] Mac.C.C. 107; *MacGregor* v. *Powell* [1936–45] Mac.C.C. 233; and *Ravenscroft* v. *Herbert & Anor.* [1980] R.P.C. 193.
[12] *The Times*, April 13 and 14, 1903, Farwell J.

3–38 **Adaptation of old play.** Copyright may be secured in the adaptation of a play which is itself common property. Thus, in *Hatton* v. *Keane*,[13] where it appeared that the defendant had designed a dramatic representation, consisting of one of Shakespeare's plays, with certain alterations in the text, original music, scenic effects, and other accessories, the court did not doubt that the production, as a whole, was a proper subject of copyright, although the play itself was, in its original form, common property.[14]

3–39 **New arrangement of music.** So, in the case of musical compositions, not only an original composition but any substantially new arrangement or adaptation of an old piece of music is a proper subject of copyright; and the person who makes the new arrangement or adaptation is the "author" of it and entitled to the copyright in it.[15] If A makes a pianoforte score of the music of B's opera,[16] or if he writes words and accompaniments to an old non-copyright melody,[17] A is, in either case, properly described as the author of the new composition.

(iii) Abridgment

3–40 **Abridgments.** Copyright may similarly exist in a genuine abridgment.[18] To constitute a genuine abridgment, the sense and meaning of the entire work must be preserved, and then the act of abridgment is the product of the understanding, employed in moulding and reducing a large work into a small one. Independent labour must be apparent and the reduction of the size of a work merely by copying some of its parts and omitting others confers no copyright.[19] To abridge in the legal sense of the word is to preserve the substance, the essence of the work, in language suited to such a purpose, language substantially different from that of the original. To make such an abridgment requires the exercise of mind, labour, skill and judgment, and the result is not merely copying.[20]

3–41 **Headnotes.** The digest of a law report, usually included in and known as the headnote, is a species of abridgment. In *Sweet* v. *Benning*,[21] Crowder J. expressed the view that the headnote, or the side or marginal note of a

[13] (1859) 7 C.B. 268.

[14] But see *Ashmore* v. *Douglas-Home* [1987] F.S.R. 553, where it was held that there had been insufficient alterations to create an original work out of a play which was in the public domain.

[15] *Redwood Music Ltd.* v. *Chappell & Co. Ltd.* [1982] R.P.C. 109.

[16] *Wood* v. *Boosey* (1867) L.R. 3 Q.B. 223; (1866) L.R. 2 Q.B. 340; and *Boosey* v. *Fairlie* (1877) 7 Ch.D. 301.

[17] *Leader* v. *Purday* (1848) 7 C.B. 4; *Austin* v. *Columbia Gramophone Co. Ltd.* [1971–23] Mac.C.C. 398; *Lover* v. *Davidson* (1856) 1 C.B.(N.S.) 182. But see, as to the need for original additions or arrangements: *Roberton* v. *Lewis* [1976] R.P.C. 169 (decided in 1960).

[18] *Gyles* v. *Wilcox* (1740) 2 Atk. 141; *Ganga'vishnu Shrikisanda's* v. *Moreshuar Ba'Puj Hegishte* [1889] I.L.R. 13 Bom. 358.

[19] As was found to be the case in *Macmillan & Co. Ltd.* v. *Cooper (K. & J.)* (1923) 40 T.L.R. 186.

[20] An equivalent passage, appearing in former editions of this work, was cited with approval in *Macmillan & Co. Ltd.* v. *Cooper (K. & J.)* (1923) 40 T.L.R. 186 at 187.

[21] (1855) 16 C.B. 459 at 491. See *D'Almaine* v. *Boosey* (1835) 1 Y. & C. Ex. 288 at 301; *Ragunthan* v. *All India Reporter Ltd.* [1971] 4 A.I.R. Bom. 48; and *Jogesh Chandra Chaudhuri* v. *Mohim Chandra Rai* [1914] C.W.N. 1078.

report, was something upon which much skill and exercise of thought is required, to express in clear and concise language the principle of law to be deduced from the decision, or the facts and circumstances, which bring the case within some principle or rule of law or of practice. Whether viewed as a separate brief report or as an independent deduction from the report, there is clearly sufficient exertion of skill and labour to render it the subject of copyright. It is interesting to note that the 1988 Act, in the defence provided in relation to copying abstracts of articles on scientific or technical subjects,[22] recognises that an abstract of an article can be entitled to its own copyright.

D. *New editions*

Old cases. It is thought that the position with regard to new editions of   **3–42** existing works differed after the commencement of the 1911 Act from that which existed before that Act. Under the Literary Copyright Act 1842,[23] no action could be brought in respect of infringement of copyright in a book unless the book was duly registered at Stationers' Hall. Consequently, if a new edition were registered, and the date of publication entered as the date of publication of the new edition, the question was whether the new edition, regarded as a whole, was a new book or not. If it were, the registration was correct, and an action for infringement of the book could be brought; if it were not, and the new edition were merely the old book with slight variations, then the registration was invalid.[24]

Present position. The distinction drawn in the cases on the law before   **3–43** 1911 is not now relevant. What is important is any original work done by the editor. Such work may consist of additions to, or alterations of, the text which, if they are not merely trivial, but are material so as to make the totality of the work original, will be protected in the same way as any original literary work, whether they form a substantial part of the complete work or not.[25] Alternatively, such work may consist of new arrangement of the existing subject-matter.[26] For instance, in *Blacklock (H.) & Co. Ltd.* v. *Arthur Pearson (C.) Ltd.*,[27] it was held that the index to a new edition of Bradshaw was an original work. Joyce J. expressed the view that a book which consists of a specification of the conditions at a given moment of a constantly changing subject-matter is a new work even though some of the particulars given may not have altered.

---

[22] C.D.P.A. 1988, s.60 and see § 10–82, *post.*

[23] 5 & 6 Vict. c. 45, s.24.

[24] *Thomas* v. *Turner* (1886) 33 Ch.D. 292; *Black (A. & C.) Ltd.* v. *Murray (A.) & Son* (1870) 9 Sc.Sess.Cas. (3rd Ser.) 341; *Hedderwick* v. *Griffin* (1841) 3 Dunl. (Ct of Sess.) 383.

[25] *Interlego A.G.* v. *Tyco Industries Inc.* [1990] A.C. 217 (P.C.) *per* Lord Oliver at 263C and see *Black* v. *Murray* (1870) 9 Macph. 341.

[26] See § 3–35, *ante.*

[27] [1915] 2 Ch. 376 at 384.

It follows, therefore, that where a work not out of copyright is edited, there may be two copyrights, that in the original text and that in the new edition.

E. *Works infringing copyright in other works*

3–44 **Subsistence of copyright in an infringing work: the question of principle.** There is nothing, either in principle or in the Copyright Acts, to suggest that copyright cannot subsist in a work which is a piracy of another copyright work, where the pirated work is not a slavish copy, but is one involving the expenditure by its originator of time, skill and labour.[28] A particular example of such a pirated work is an unauthorised translation of a copyright work, where the translator may have expended considerable time, skill and labour in producing the translation, and there would seem no reason why such a work, even if unauthorised, should not be entitled to its own copyright.

3–45 **Cases in which question has been raised.** Nevertheless, the argument that copyright cannot subsist in a pirated work has been raised in a number of cases. Thus, in an early case, *Cary* v. *Faden*,[29] . . . Lord Loughborough, in refusing an injunction to restrain an infringement of the copyright in a road book, appears to have been influenced by the fact that the plaintiff's work was an infringement of the copyright in an earlier work. But this decision went only to relief and not the question of subsistence. However, in *Wood* v. *Boosey*,[30] a case concerned with an arrangement of the score of an opera, Kelly C.B. decided that, although the work of the arranger, if published without the authority of the composer of the original opera, would be a piracy of that work, nevertheless was a new and substantive work in itself which was the subject of copyright.[31] It would appear from this decision that copyright can subsist in a piracy, the preparation of which involved the expenditure of time, skill and labour by its originator. On the other hand, in *Gramophone Co. Ltd.* v. *Stephen Cawardine & Co.*,[32] Maugham J., in considering the nature of the protection afforded to gramophone records under section 19 of the 1911 Act, proceeded on the stated assumption that the section gave the protection only in respect of records lawfully made, which was the case before him.[33]

---

[28] See *University of London Press Ltd.* v. *University Tutorial Press Ltd.* [1916] 2 Ch. 601 at 608; s.1(1) of the 1988 Act provides that copyright subsists in every original literary, dramatic, musical and artistic work, without qualification in respect of plagiarised works.

[29] (1799) 5 Ves.23, and see *Edward Thompson & Co.* v. *American Law Book Co.* [1905–10] Mac.C.C. 16.

[30] (1866) L.R. 2 Q.B. 340; (1867) L.R. 3 Q.B. 223; and see *Sailendra Nath De* v. *Chayanika Chire Mandir* (1950) 55 Cal.W.N. 713; *Gouindan.* v. *Gopalakrishna Kone* [1955] Mad.W.N. 369 and *Walter* v. *Lane* [1900] A.C. 539 at 558.

[31] (1867) L.R. 3 Q.B. at 229; and see *Leader* v. *Purday* (1884) 7 C.B. 4.

[32] [1934] Ch. 450.

[33] *Ibid.* at 457. But see *Ashmore* v. *Douglas-Home* [1987] F.S.R. 553; *cf.* C.D.P.A. 1988, s.5(2).

Question of principle decided: present law. More recently, in *Redwood*   **3—46**
Music Ltd. v. *Chappell & Co. Ltd.*[34] Goff J., referring to *Wood* v. *Boosey*,
supra, firmly rejected the argument that copyright could not subsist under
the 1956 Act in an infringing work. The present position is thus that copyright can, as a matter of principle, subsist in an infringing work. Whether
it does so or not will depend on whether the pirated work has involved the
expenditure by its author of time, skill and labour, and it is suggested that
this is so whether the entire work is pirated, or merely part of it, provided
that its originator has expended time, skill and labour on the material pirated.

Extent of protection afforded to work infringing copyright. Never-   **3—47**
theless, the question remains as to the extent of protection afforded by
such copyright in a pirated work. In *Warwick Film Productions Ltd.* v. *Eisinger*,[35] the plaintiffs alleged infringement of copyright in two books, one
entitled *The Trials of Oscar Wilde* edited by Mr. Montgomery Hyde, and
the other entitled *Oscar Wilde: Three Times Tried* written anonymously.
Plowman J. held that both books were entitled to copyright, but that the
plaintiffs had not established any title to the copyright in *Three Times Tried*.
It appeared that part of the Hyde book consisted of trial scenes taken from
Three Times Tried, without any proper authority. The defendants argued
that since, when Mr Hyde wrote his book, he had no permission from
anyone who had been proved to be the owner of the copyright in *Three
Times Tried* to use that book, his accounts of the trials must be regarded as
piratical and that no copyright subsisted in a pirated book or, at any rate,
in so much of it as was pirated. In the alternative, the defendants argued
that, as a matter of law, copyright can subsist in some parts of a literary
work without subsisting in those parts which consist of copied raw
material on which no labour and skill have been expended. Plowman J., in
dealing with these arguments, referred to the different approach to the
problem propounded in *Ladbroke (Football) Ltd.* v. *William Hill (Football)
Ltd.*,[36] which he said arose where a literary work includes unoriginal or
pirated material.[37]

In accordance with this approach, Plowman J. held that Mr. Hyde's
copying from *Three Times Tried* was of two kinds, namely edited copying
and unedited copying. As regards the edited copying, this had been copied
by the defendant Eisinger only to a limited extent which, by itself, did not
constitute a substantial part of the Hyde book. As to Mr. Hyde's unedited
copying, it had no originality and attracted copyright, as part of the whole
book, only by reason of its collocation. When robbed of that collocation it
did not represent a substantial part and so did not involve an infringement
of it. In the result he held that there had been no reproduction of a substantial part of the Hyde book and no infringement of copyright.[38]

---

[34] [1982] R.P.C. 109 at 120.
[35] [1969] Ch. 508.
[36] [1964] 1 W.L.R. 273; and see *Industrial Furnaces Ltd.* v. *Reaves* [1970] R.P.C. 605 at 624.
[37] [1969] Ch. at 530.
[38] See *Industrial Furnaces Ltd.* v. *Reaves* [1970] R.P.C. 605 at 624.

3–48   It would therefore appear, from such decisions, that first, where pirated material is joined with original material, the whole may be entitled to copyright, and secondly, if no work has been done on the pirated material, if that is copied, it will not be considered a substantial part for the purposes of infringement, but thirdly, if work has been done on the pirated material it may be considered a substantial part for such purposes. The question remains whether the courts will grant relief in the case of a work which consists in part of pirated material, on which time, skill and labour has been expended and where the part copied, unlike in the *Warwick Film* case, is a substantial part of the whole work, but consists entirely of pirated material. It is suggested that the courts might well be unwilling to grant relief in such a case, on the grounds of public policy, and certainly where the relief is sought against the original copyright owner, unless, perhaps, he had later given permission.[39]

4. Particular Requirements as to Form: Various Works

A. *Literary, dramatic and musical works*

3–49   **Recording in writing or otherwise.** Copyright does not subsist in a literary, dramatic or musical work unless and until it is recorded in writing or otherwise.[40] Writing includes any form of notation or code, whether by hand or otherwise and regardless of the method by which, or medium in or on which, it is recorded.[41] It is immaterial whether the work is recorded by or with the permission of the author.[42] One possible interpretation of these words leaves open the question whether, when the recording is not made by the author, his permission for such recording to be made is necessary in order for the work thereby to qualify for subsistence of copyright. No doubt such permission would readily be implied in many circumstances, but it is suggested that the alternative interpretation is to be preferred, whereby it is relevant whether the author did or did not consent.[43] This would avoid the result which would otherwise follow, for example, where a qualifying person composes a musical work in his head, and plays it on an instrument to someone else, who records it on a tape recorder in circumstances where no permission can be implied for him to do so, that such other person would be free to copy the musical work and

---

[39] *Glyn* v. *Weston Feature Film Co.* [1916] 1 Ch. 261 at 269 and see § 2–38, *et seq., ante*. See also *Slingsby* v. *Bradford Patent Truck, etc., Co.* [1905] W.N. 122, [1906] W.N. 51; *Cary* v. *Faden* (1799) 5 Ves. 23; *Edward Thompson & Co.* v. *American Law Book Co.* [1905–10] Mac.C.C. 16 and *Sweet* v. *G.W. Bromley & Co.* [1905–10] Mac.C.C. 203.

[40] C.D.P.A. 1988, s.3(2).

[41] *Ibid.*, s.178.

[42] *Ibid.*, s.3(3).

[43] The recommendation of the 1977 Copyright Committee, Cmnd. 6732, para. 609(viii), on this aspect was that consent should be irrelevant.

exploit it without the permission of the author, on the basis that no copyright subsisted in the musical work at that time.

B. *Sound recordings and films*

Sound recordings and films. Copyright in an unpublished sound   **3–50**
recording or film depended, under the 1956 Act, on the maker being a
qualified person at the time the recording was made.[44] The maker was
defined differently in respect of sound recordings and films. In respect of
the former, the maker was the person who owned the first recording embodying the recording at the time when that recording was made,[45] and in
respect of the latter, the maker was the person by whom the arrangements
necessary for the making of the film were undertaken.[46] Under the 1988
Act, copyright in an unpublished sound recording or film depends on the
qualification of the author,[47] and the author is defined in relation to both
works as the person by whom the arrangements necessary for the making
of the recording or film are undertaken.[48]

Sound recordings and films: copies of previous sound recordings or   **3–51**
films. Originality, as such, is not a requirement for the subsistence of
copyright in sound recordings and films, but the 1988 Act provides that
copyright does not subsist in a sound recording or film which is, or to the
extent that it is, a copy taken from a previous sound recording or film.[49]
This applies whether such copy was authorised or not. Under the 1956
Act there was no requirement of originality and no such provision.

C. *Broadcasts and cable programmes*

Broadcasts and cable programmes. The general qualifying conditions   **3–52**
otherwise applicable to all works by reference to the author[50] are applicable to broadcasts and cable programmes.[51] Copyright also subsists in
such works by reference to the place of transmission. Thus, copyright subsists in a broadcast or cable programme if it is sent from a place which is
either in the United Kingdom, or in a country to which the relevant provisions of the 1988 Act extend,[52] or in a country to which that Act does not

---

[44] Copyright Act 1956, ss.12(1) and 13(1).
[45] *Ibid.*, s.12(8).
[46] Copyright Act 1956, s.13(10).
[47] C.D.P.A. 1988, s.153(1).
[48] *Ibid.*, s.9(2)(*a*).
[49] *Ibid.*, s.5(2).
[50] *Ibid.*, s.155.
[51] This was not so under the 1956 Act, since only the BBC and IBA could obtain copyright protection for broadcasts; see § 2–31, *ante.*
[52] C.D.P.A. 1988, s.156(2); as to the extension of the provisions of the 1988 Act, see s.157 and Chap. 17, *post.*

extend but to which its provisions have been applied by under section 159[53] by virtue of an Order made under that section.[54]

3–53 Repeat broadcasts and cable programmes. The qualification provisions for copyright protection in respect of broadcasts and cable programmes under the 1988 Act do not refer to the first transmission of the broadcast or cable programme, and that Act does not disqualify from copyright protection a broadcast or cable programme which is an authorised repeat of an earlier broadcast, or of a cable programme previously included in a cable programme service.[55] Such authorised repeat broadcasts and cable programmes are therefore entitled to their own copyright, but it is provided that such copyright expires at the same time as that in the original broadcast or cable programme.[56] Presumably, where the broadcast or cable programme repeats an earlier broadcast or programme but contains new material, the subsequent broadcast or cable programme will be protected as such for its own full term of copyright, as to that part containing the new material.[57] However, copyright does not subsist in a broadcast or cable programme which infringes, or to the extent that it infringes, the copyright in, in each case, either another broadcast or cable programme.[58] In addition, copyright does not subsist in a cable programme if it is included in a cable programme service by reception and immediate re-transmission of a broadcast.[59]

---

[53] C.D.P.A. 1988, s.156(2); as to *ibid.* s.159 and Orders made thereunder, see Chap. 17, *post.*

[54] The Copyright (Application to Other Countries) (No. 2) Order 1989, S.I. 1989 No. 1293, § D–22, *post.* As to the position under the 1956 Act, see *Copinger*, 12th ed., § 885. See the International Convention for the Protection of Performers, Producers of Phonograms and Broadcasting Organisations, Cmnd. 2425, ratified by the United Kingdom on October 30, 1963 and entered into force on May 18, 1964, see text § C–121, *post*; The European Agreement on the Protection of Television Broadcasts, concluded on June 22, 1960, Cmnd. 1508. See text § C–81, *post,* ratified by the United Kingdom on October 30, 1963 and entered into force on May 18, 1964. A Protocol to such Agreement was concluded on January 22, 1965, and entered into force on March 24, 1965; Cmnd. 2744. It was signed without reservation in respect of ratification by the United Kingdom on February 23, 1965. See text, §C–96, *post.* A second Protocol to such Agreement was concluded on January 14, 1974, and entered into force on December 31, 1974; Cmnd. 5954. It was signed without reservation in respect of ratification by the United Kingdom on March 15, 1974. See text, §C–102, *post,* and see Report of 1977 Copyright Committee, Cmnd. 6732, para. 87. A third Protocol to such agreement was concluded on March 21, 1983, and entered into force on January 1, 1985; see text, § C–107, *post.* See also European Agreement concerning Programme Exchanges by means of Television Films concluded on December 15, 1958 Cmnd. 1509, see text, § C–108 *post,* signed by the United Kingdom on December 15, 1958 and entered into force on July 1, 1961. Also, Convention Relating to the Distribution of Programme-carrying Signals Transmitted by Satellite, concluded on May 21, 1974, see text, § C–192, *post.* The United Kingdom is not a signatory; see Report of 1977 Copyright Committee, Cmnd. 6732, paras. 86 and 88.

[55] Compare the approach adopted in the case of sound recordings, films and typographical arrangements under C.D.P.A. 1988, ss.5(2) and 8(2).

[56] C.D.P.A. 1988, s.14(2) and (3); see § 6–20, *post.*

[57] This would appear to follow from general principles, although s. 14(3) of the 1988 Act does not use the phrase "or to the extent that it is a repeat."

[58] C.D.P.A. 1988, s.6(6) and s.7(6)(*b*).

[59] *Ibid.*, s.7(6)(*a*).

D. *Typographical Arrangements*

Typographical arrangements. Copyright subsists, subject to the **3–54** requirements being met as to qualification for copyright protection,[60] in a typographical arrangement of a published edition.[61] "Published edition" means a published edition of the whole or any part of one or more literary, dramatic or musical works.[62] Although the work of which the typographical arrangement is made must therefore qualify as one or more of literary, dramatic and musical work as defined by the 1988 Act,[63] there is no requirement that such work should itself have qualified for copyright protection at any time. The reference to the edition having been published must be construed in accordance with the definition of publication in the Act.[64]

Copies of previous typographical arrangements. Under section 8(2) **3–55** of the 1988 Act, copyright does not subsist in the typographical arrangement of a published edition if, or to the extent that, it reproduces the typographical arrangement of a previous edition.[65] Reproduction is not now a defined term under the 1988 Act,[66] and, strictly, the reference should have been to copying not reproducing, since copying is defined, in relation to typographical arrangements, as meaning making a facsimile copy of the arrangement.[67] In the context, this is clearly what was intended, and no doubt "reproduces" in section 8(2) will be so construed.

5. Copyrights Belonging to the Crown, Parliament and Certain International Organisations

Subsistence of Crown and Parliamentary copyright. The general **3–56** qualifying conditions contained in Chapter IX of the 1988 Act applicable by section 153(1) of that Act to all works, do not apply in relation to Crown copyright, Parliamentary copyright and copyright belonging to certain international organisations.[68] This is because the provisions contained in that Act dealing with each of these types of works contain their own provisions as to the subsistence of copyright in such works. Thus, where work is made by Her Majesty or by an officer or servant of the Crown in the course of his duties,[69] or is made by or under the direction or control of the House of Commons or the House of Lords,[70] then the work qualifies for copyright protection whether (as would no doubt usually be

---

[60] See §§ 3–4, *et seq., ante.*
[61] C.D.P.A. 1988, s.1(1)(*c*); see § 2–37, *ante.*
[62] *Ibid.*, s.8(1)(*c*).
[63] *Ibid.*, s.3(1).
[64] *Ibid.*, s.175; see § 3–12, *et seq., ante.*
[65] *Ibid.*, s.8(2); re-enacting Copyright Act 1956, s.15(1), proviso.
[66] As it was under the 1956 Act (s.48(1)).
[67] C.D.P.A. 1988, s.17(5); facsimile is defined as including a copy which is reduced or enlarged in scale (s.178).
[68] *Ibid.*, s.153(2).
[69] *Ibid.*, s.163(1)(*a*).
[70] *Ibid.*, s.165(1)(*a*); and see s.165(4) as to what works fall within this provision.

the case) or not the general qualifying conditions by reference to the author,[71] the place of first publication[72] or, in the case of broadcasts and cable programmes, the place of transmission,[73] are satisfied.

3–57 **Copyright vesting in certain international organisations.** Where an original literary, dramatic, musical or artistic work is made by an officer or employee of, or is published by, one of a number of international organisations designated by Order in Council,[74] and such work does not otherwise qualify for copyright protection under the 1988 Act by reference to its author or the place of first publication,[75] then copyright nevertheless subsists in that work.[76] The approach to works, the copyright in which belongs to such international organisations, is therefore different to that adopted towards Crown and Parliamentary copyright in two respects: this provision only applies to original literary, dramatic, musical and artistic works, and not to all works, and it only applies if the work does not otherwise qualify for copyright protection.

---

[71] *Ibid.*, s.154.
[72] *Ibid.*, s.155.
[73] *Ibid.*, s.156.
[74] Under *Ibid.*, s.168(2); see further §§ 17–88, *et seq.*, and 17–110, *post.*
[75] *I.e.* under *ibid.*, ss.154 or 155.
[76] C.D.P.A. 1988, s.168(1)(*a*) and (*b*). This re-enacts, in a simpler form, the former provision contained in s.33(2) and (3) of the 1956 Act. See §§ 17–88, *et seq.*, and 17–110, *post.*

THE FIRST OWNER OF COPYRIGHT

1. Introduction

Author is the first owner. With exceptions, which will be considered **4–1**
later in this chapter, the "author" of a work is taken to be the first owner
of the copyright in the work.[1]

The 1988 Act provides that the law in force at the time when a work was **4–2**
made must be applied to determine who was the "author" of the work and
who was the first owner of copyright.[2] In relation to works made before
August 1, 1989 (defined by the 1988 Act as "existing works"[3]), therefore,
the provisions of the 1956, 1911 or the even earlier Acts need to be
applied, as appropriate. For this purpose, where the making of a work
extended over a period, the work is to be taken as having been made when
its making was completed.[4] Various statutory presumptions may apply, in
proceedings, to determine who is the author of a work. These are considered elsewhere.[5]

---

[1] C.D.P.A. 1988, s.11(1), Copyright Act 1956, s.4(1), Copyright Act 1911, s.5(1).
[2] C.D.P.A. 1988, Sched. 1, paras. 10, 11(1).
[3] *Ibid*, para. 1(3).
[4] *Ibid*.
[5] See § 11–86, *et seq., post*.

4-3 **The 1988 Act: meaning of "author".** The 1988 Act defines "author" as meaning the person who creates the work.[6] In relation to various categories of work, namely sound recordings, films, broadcasts, cable programmes and typographical arrangements of published editions, this expression is further defined.[7]

4-4 **The earlier Acts compared.** Under the 1956, 1911 and earlier Acts, the author of the copyright in a literary, dramatic, musical or artistic work was, with exceptions, to be the first owner of the copyright.[8] With the exception of photographs under the 1911 and 1956 Acts, the expression "author" was not further defined. In relation to the other categories of works in which copyright subsisted under the 1956 Act, namely sound recordings, cinematograph films, broadcasts, cable programmes and published editions of works, the expression "author" was not used and the Act contained separate provisions as to first ownership. Under the 1911 Act contrivances for the mechanical reproduction of sounds were equated with musical works and that Act contained a separate definition of "author" in relation to such works.[9]

2. Literary, Dramatic, Musical and Artistic Works

A. *Authorship*

4-5 **Pre- and post-1988 Act works.** As has already been noted,[10] in relation to works made before August 1, 1989, the provisions of the 1956, 1911 or the even earlier Acts must be applied, as the case may be. As to the 1956, 1911 and earlier Acts, these merely provided that, with exceptions, "the author" should be entitled to the copyright in these categories of works.[11] Except in the case of photographs in the 1956 and 1911 Acts,[12] this expression was not further defined although it was the subject of a number of decisions.[13] Under the 1988 Act, the expression "author" is defined for

---

[6] C.D.P.A. 1988, s.9(1).

[7] See § 4–49, *et seq., post.*

[8] Copyright Act 1956, s.4(1); Copyright Act 1911, s.5(1); Literary Copyright Act 1842 ("books", musical and dramatic works; except that where publication of a book was posthumous the copyright belonged to the proprietor of the manuscript from which the work was published); Lectures Copyright Act 1835 (lectures); Dramatic Copyright Act 1833 (dramatic works); Engravings Copyright Acts 1734, 1766, Prints Copyright Act 1777 and International Copyright Act 1852 (engravings, etchings, prints, etc.: right to belong to inventor, designer, etc.); Sculpture Copyright Act 1814 (sculptures: right to belong to the maker); Fine Arts Copyright Act 1862 (paintings, drawings and photographs).

[9] Copyright Act 1911, s.19(1). See § 4–54, *post.*

[10] § 4–2, *supra.*

[11] Copyright Act 1956, s.4(1), Copyright Act 1911, s.5(1); and see n. 8, *supra.*

[12] See further §§ 4–12, 4–13 *post.*

[13] See § 4–6 *et seq., post.*

the first time to mean the person who created the work.[14] However, it is not thought that this new definition has altered the law in relation to the categories of works under consideration, so that the earlier decisions on authorship will still be good authority for the purposes of the 1988 Act.[15]

Meaning of author. Normally it will not be hard to determine who is the   **4–6** person who was the author of or who created a work falling into one of the categories under consideration, but cases of difficulty may arise. Thus it is clear that a person who merely suggests the plot of a novel or a play to the writer, or the subject of a picture to an artist, is not the author of the novel, play or picture.[16] It is equally clear that an amanuensis is not an author.[17] In considering this question it is necessary to see in what it is that copyright subsists.[18] Thus there is no copyright in ideas and, consequently, if a person who has an idea for a story, picture, or play, communicates it to another,[19] the production which is the result of the communication of the idea is the copyright of the person who has clothed the idea in form. The copyright in reminiscences, for instance, which are "ghost written", therefore belongs to the "ghost writer" and not to the person who relates the reminiscences to the "ghost writer."[20] On the other hand, if an author employs a shorthand writer to take down a story word for word in shorthand, the author is the owner of the copyright and not the shorthand writer. Again, the writer of a letter is clearly the author unless he is merely an amanuensis.[21] And where A extemporises, and B reduces the results to some permanent form, either simultaneously or, relying on his memory, later, it is thought that A will be regarded as the author of the work which is thus created.[22] But between these two extremes there may be gradations. It is suggested, however, that prima facie the author of a literary work is the person who originates the language used, and the author of an artistic work is the person who actually executes the design. If A's manuscript is corrected and improved by B it will probably be a question of the

---

[14] C.D.P.A. 1988, s.9(1).

[15] Support is given to this view by the general provisions as to construction contained in s.172 of the 1988 Act.

[16] *Shepherd* v. *Conquest* (1856) 17 C.B. 427; *Tate* v. *Thomas* [1921] 1 Ch. 503.

[17] *Walter* v. *Lane* [1900] A.C. 539. In the curious case of *Cummins* v. *Bond* [1927] 1 Ch. 167, it was held that a spiritualist medium was the owner of the copyright in a script which she believed to be dictated to her by a spirit. It would appear that this was clearly right, since, even admitting the hypothesis that a spirit supplied the ideas, the form of words in which copyright subsists came from the medium's brain; and see *Leah* v. *Two Worlds Publishing Co. Ltd.* [1951] Ch. 393.

[18] *Donoghue* v. *Allied Newspapers Ltd.* [1938] Ch. 106.

[19] The person who had the idea may be able to prevent its use by the person to whom he communicated it, on the grounds of breach of confidence; see *Gilbert* v. *The Star Newspaper Co. Ltd.* (1894) 11 T.L.R. 4; *Moore* v. *Edwardes* [1901–04] Mac.C.C. 44 and *Fraser* v. *Edwards* [1904–10] Mac.C.C. 10 and Chap. 21 *post.*

[20] See *Donoghue* v. *Allied Newspapers Ltd., supra; Housden* v. *Marshall* [1959] 1 W.L.R. 1; and *Chaplin* v. *Leslie Frewin (Publishers) Ltd.* [1966] Ch. 71; *Thrustcode Ltd.* v. *W.W. Computing Ltd.* [1985] F.S.R. 582.

[21] See *e.g. British Oxygen Co. Ltd.* v. *Liquid Air Ltd.* [1925] Ch. 383.

[22] See § 2–6, *ante.* It may well be that the record of the work created by B will be a separate copyright work, of which B is the author.

amount and value of the corrections and improvements as to whether the author is A or B, or whether they are joint authors.[23]

4–7 **"Author" of collective or composite work.** In the case of collective or composite works, such as encyclopedias, there will be distinct copyrights, namely, the copyright in the entire work and the copyright in the various separate contributions. The person who gathers together and arranges the entire work will generally be the author of the whole work, considered as a compilation.[24] As to the separate contributions, the author of these will be the person who wrote them. Thus where a person has written the entries in a work such as a directory using information supplied by others he will be the author of those entries, certainly where he has done more than simply copy such information verbatim.[25]

4–8 **"Author" of plot.** Where a person contributes suggestions for the plot and arrangement of a musical play of which others are the authors of the music and lyrics, that person is not a joint author with them, and has no copyright therein.[26] Again, where persons have provided incidents from their own lives as the basis of articles or stories in which these incidents have been written up by others, the person providing the incidents is not the author of the written matter since he did not take any part in producing the express matter which is the original literary work, and which is the subject-matter of copyright.[27]

4–9 **"Author" of artistic works.** In the case of artistic works, other than photographs, it is normally the person whose hands fix the picture upon the canvas, paper, stone, copperplate or wood who is the author. Thus where one person conceives of an idea for an artistic work but, being unable to draw, employs another, under his direction, to execute the idea,

---

[23] See Chap. 7, *post*, and *Springfield* v. *Thame* (1903) 89 L.T. 242, where the plaintiff had sent an account of an incident he had witnessed to a newspaper, and the account was so altered by the sub-editor of the paper that the latter was held to be the "author" of the newspaper paragraph. *cf. Samuelson* v. *Producer's Distributing Co. Ltd.* (1932) 48 R.P.C. 580, where it was held that the writer of an original version of a dramatic sketch was the sole author, notwithstanding that another person had revised and altered it for performance. For a case where the work was held to be one of joint authorship, see *Heptulla* v. *Orient Longman Ltd.* [1989] F.S.R. 598 (Delhi High Court) and § 7–2, *post*.

[24] In *Waterlow Publishers Ltd.* v. *Rose, The Times*, December 12, 1989, the Court of Appeal expressed no view as to the correctness of the definition, in *Laddie Prescott and Vitoria, The Modern Law of Copyright* (1980), of the author of a compilation as being "the person who gathers or organises the collection of material and who selects, orders and arranges it." The Court of Appeal also considered that there might be cases in which there was no indentifiable author of a compilation, in which case the statutory presumptions in s.20 of the 1956 Act (see now s.104 of the 1988 Act) would apply. *Sed quaere.*

[25] *James Nisbet & Co. Ltd.* v. *The Golf Agency* (1907) 23 T.L.R. 370. It has been held that even where the information provided by a third party for such entries has been used verbatim, the author of each contribution is the compiler of the directory who has asked for the information and not the third party: *Black (A. and C.) Ltd.* v. *Claude Stacey Ltd.* [1929] 1 Ch. 177. *Sed quaere.*

[26] *Tate* v. *Thomas* [1921] 1 Ch. 503.

[27] *Donoghue* v. *Allied Newspapers Ltd.* [1938] Ch. 106; *Evans* v. *E. Hulton & Co. Ltd.* [1923–28] Mac.C.C. 51; *Housden* v. *Marshall* [1959] 1 W.L.R. 1.

the former is not "the author" of the work.[28] Even in the case of lithographs it is submitted that the author is the person who does the drawing upon the stone. Although it is usual to employ a special lithographic designer to draw the design for the express purpose of having the same lithographed, the latter is not, it is thought, the author of the lithograph.

Works of architecture. As to works of architecture, the "author" of a **4–10** building might be either the architect or the builder. Under the 1911 Act, it was held that it was the architect, being the author of the plans used to construct the building.[29] This was on the basis that under the 1911 Act the protection was limited to the artistic character or design embodied in the building, in which the builder had played no part. It is thought that the position was the same under the 1956 Act, and is now the same under the 1988 Act, in a case where the builder simply builds from another's plans. Where, however, the builder uses his own plans or simply builds without reference to plans, presumably he will be the author.

"Author" of photographs: the 1988 Act. The 1988 Act contains no **4–11** special provisions as to authorship of photographs so that in relation to such works made after August 1, 1989[30] the general principle applies, namely, that the author of a photograph is the person who creates it.[31] This will almost invariably be the photographer.

"Author" of photographs: the 1956 Act. In accordance with the **4–12** general principle stated earlier,[32] in relation to photographs taken between June 1, 1957, and August 1, 1989, the 1956 Act must be applied to determine the questions of authorship and first ownership. Although the 1956 Act contained no general definition of "author," in relation to a photograph the author was defined to be the person who, at the time when the photograph was taken, was the owner of the material upon which it was taken.[33] This sometimes led to difficulties, for example where a press photographer used film stock belonging to a newspaper proprietor.[34]

"Author" of photographs: the 1911 Act. Again, in relation to photo- **4–13** graphs taken between July 1, 1912, and June 1, 1957, the 1911 Act must be applied to determine the question of authorship. The provisions of section 21 of the 1911 Act were to the same effect as those of the 1956 Act,

---

[28] *Kenrick & Co.* v. *Lawrence & Co.* (1890) 25 Q.B.D. 99, decided under the Fine Arts Copyright Act 1862. The possibility of the two being joint authors was left open. See also *Nottage* v. *Jackson* 11 Q.B.D. 627 at 631, 635. *Stannard* v. *Harrison* (1871) 19 W.R. 811, is distinguishable on the grounds that it was decided under the different wording of the Engraving Acts, 8 Geo. 2, c. 13; 7 Geo. 3, c. 38.

[29] *Meikle* v. *Maufe* [1941] 3 All E.R. 144. But *cf. Jackson* v. *Jones* (1934), unreported, where Farwell J. held that the author was the builder and not the architect.

[30] See § 4–2, *ante*.

[31] C.D.P.A. 1988, s.9(1).

[32] § 4–2, *supra*.

[33] Copyright Act 1956, s.48(1). The "author" of a photograph could therefore have been a company.

[34] This led the 1977 Copyright Committee to recommend that the author of a photograph should be the person responsible for its composition (Cmnd. 6732, paras. 587 and 609 (vii)), a proposal which is achieved by s.9(1) of the 1988 Act.

namely that the person who was the owner of the original negative at the time when such negative was made was to be deemed to be the author of the work. This express provision solved the difficulty which had previously existed in determining who was the "author" of a photograph.[35]

4–14   **"Author" of computer programs and computer-generated works: the 1988 Act.** Where a computer program is created by an individual, the person who is the author of such a work is to be established in accordance with the ordinary principles set out above.[36] Where, however, after August 1, 1989, a literary, dramatic, musical or artistic work is generated by computer in circumstances such that there is no human author of the work, the 1988 Act provides that the author shall be taken to be the person by whom the arrangements necessary for the creation of the work are undertaken.[37] This provision is new. It will clearly be important to distinguish cases in which there is and in which there is not a human author in this sense, since not only does this affect the question of ownership but also, for example, the period of copyright.[38] Whether or not there is a human author in cases where a computer is involved in the production of a work may be difficult to decide. In a case under the 1956 Act it was held on the particular facts that the computer and the computer programs used to produce a work were to be regarded simply as the tools of the person controlling them, just as is an author's pen.[39] Thus, where a person sits at a keyboard and himself creates a work, and the computer and associated computer programs merely assist him in the work of creation, it is thought proper to regard the work as having a human author. On the other hand, where, for example, a computer is employed to convert a program from one language to another, such as from assembly code to machine code, and no creative input is required from any human agency and nothing is required to be done other than to load the necessary programs and give the required commands, it is thought that the program thereby generated is properly to be regarded as having had no human author. In such cases, the "author" is to be regarded as the person who made the arrangements necessary for the creation of the work. This expression is similar to that used in the provisions of the 1988 Act relating to the authorship of sound recordings and films and is considered further below.[40]

4–15   **Computer-generated works: the 1956 Act.** The 1956 Act contained no such provision relating to cases where there was no human author. In cases where there was truly no human person who could be identified as the author of the work, even though human beings were involved in the creation of the work, it seems that there was no copyright in the work.

---

[35] See *Nottage* v. *Jackson* (1883) 11 Q.B.D. 627 and *Melville* v. *Mirror of Life Co.* [1895] 2 Ch. 531. The copyright in all pre-1911 Act photographs will by now have expired.

[36] § 4–6, *ante.*

[37] C.D.P.A. 1988, ss. 9(3), 178.

[38] The period of copyright in such computer-generated works is only 50 years from the end of the calendar year in which the work was made. See s.12(3) of the 1988 Act and § 6–11, *post.*

[39] *Express Newspapers plc* v. *Liverpool Daily Post & Echo plc* [1985] F.S.R. 306.

[40] See § 4–55 *post.*

B. *Commissioned Artistic Works*

The 1988 Act contains no special provisions relating to the ownership of **4–16** copyright in works which have been commissioned. In relation to new works, therefore, the general rule applies, namely that subject to the usual exceptions the first owner of copyright will be the person who creates it.[41] However, the earlier Acts contained important provisions relating to the commissioning of certain categories of works, and these still continue to apply in relation to works made before August 1, 1989, and also to works made after August 1, 1989, but whose making was commissioned before that date.[42] Those relating to artistic works are considered here.[43] In addition, the 1988 Act confers a new moral right entitling a person to a right of privacy in respect of photographs which were commissioned for private and domestic purposes.[44] The ownership of the new design right may also be affected where the design was commissioned.[44a] Previous decisions as to what amounts to commissioning may therefore also be useful in construing these provisions.

Commissioned artistic works under the 1956 Act. The provisions of **4–17** the 1956 Act apply to determine questions of first ownership of copyright in works made between June 1, 1957 and August 1, 1989,[45] and to works made after the latter date but which were commissioned before that date.[46] Where, however, a work was made after June 1, 1957, but pursuant to a contract made before that date, the provisions of the 1911 Act apply.[47] By section 4(3) of the 1956 Act it was provided that, where a person commissioned the taking of a photograph or the painting or drawing of a portrait or the making of an engraving, and paid or agreed to pay for it in money or money's worth, and the work was made in pursuance of that commission, the person who so commissioned the work should be entitled to any copyright subsisting under that Act. This provision was expressed to be subject to sub-section 4(2) of the 1956 Act, relating to the works of employees of newspaper proprietors and the like.[48] It was also subject to any agreement excluding the operation of the section and to Part VI of the Act, relating to assignments.[49] "Engraving" was defined as including any etching, lithograph, woodcut, print, or similar work, not being a photograph, and "photograph" was defined as any product of photography or any process akin to photography, other than part of a cinematograph film.[50] It would seem that the commissioner was entitled

---

[41] C.D.P.A. 1988, s.9(1). The question of ownership may of course still be affected by the terms of any contract or obligation pursuant to which the work was commissioned. See § 4–67 *post.*

[42] *Ibid*, Sched. 1, para. 11(2).

[43] As to commissioned sound recordings, see § 4–52, *post.*

[44] C.D.P.A. 1988, s.85(1). See § 22–57, *et seq., post.*

[44a] See § 20–104, *post.*

[45] See § 4–2 *ante.*

[46] See n. 42, *supra.*

[47] C.D.P.A. 1988, Sched. 1, para. 11(2) and Copyright Act 1956, Sched. 7, para. 3.

[48] See § 4–28 *et seq., post.*

[49] Copyright Act 1956, ss.4(5),(6).

[50] Copyright Act 1956, s.48(1).

to the copyright whether or not the work was completed.[51] It has been held that where a person ordered a design to be made by another, who then subcontracted necessary engraving work, the person ordering the design was entitled to the copyright in the engraving[52] This was on the basis that the person ordering the design commissioned all necessary articles to be made even though unaware of the need for them.

4–18   **Commissioned artistic works under the 1911 Act.** The provisions of the 1911 Act apply to determine questions of first ownership of copyright in works made between July 1, 1912, and June 1, 1957[53] and to works made after the latter date but which were commissioned by a contract made before June 1, 1957.[54] The 1911 Act provided[55] that where, in the case of an engraving, photograph or portrait, the plate or other original was ordered by some other person, and was made for valuable consideration in pursuance of that order, then, in the absence of any agreement to the contrary, the person by whom such plate or other original was ordered should be the first owner of the copyright. Again, the provision applied in the absence of any agreement to the contrary.[56] The Copyright Act 1911[57] contained very similar definitions of "engraving" and "photograph" to those in the 1956 Act, save that the words "other than a part of a cinematograph film" did not occur in the definition of photograph, since, under the 1911 Act, a film was protected as a photographic work.

4–19   **Pre-1911 Act commissioned works.** There was a similar provision in the Fine Arts Copyright Act 1862[58] to the effect that, where a painting, drawing or the negative of any photograph should be "made or executed for or on behalf of any person for a good or a valuable consideration," the copyright should belong to "the person for or on whose behalf the same shall be so made or executed."[59] Under this Act it was necessary, if the commissioned author wished to retain the copyright, for him to do so in writing.

4–20   **The Acts compared.** The differences between the 1911 Act and the 1862 Act were (1) that under the 1911 Act writing was not required if the artist desired to retain his copyright; the proviso only said "in the absence of any agreement to the contrary"; (2) that the 1862 Act referred to a work "made" for another, and the 1911 Act spoke of a plate or original "ordered" by some other person; (3) that the 1862 Act used the expression "a good or a valuable consideration," whereas the 1911 Act only had the words "valuable consideration."[60]

---

[51] *Art Direction Ltd.* v. *U.S.P. Needham (N.Z.) Ltd.* [1977] 2 N.Z.L.R. 12, decided under a similar provision of the New Zealand Act.

[52] *James Arnold and Co. Ltd.* v. *Miafern Ltd.* [1980] R.P.C. 397.

[53] See § 4–2, *ante.*

[54] See n. 47, *supra.*

[55] Copyright Act 1911, s.5(1)(*a*).

[56] *Ibid.*

[57] *Ibid*, s.35(1).

[58] 25 & 26 Vict. c. 68.

[59] *Petty* v. *Taylor* [1897] 1 Ch. 465; *Boucas* v. *Cooke* [1903] 2 K.B. 227.

[60] As to whether there may be any difference between the two expressions, see *Stackemann* v. *Paton* [1906] 1 Ch. 774.

The Copyright Act 1956, though expressed in different words, seems to have had the same meaning, in this respect, as the 1911 Act. It is possible that "money or money's worth" may have a narrower construction than "valuable consideration."[61]

Commissioned photographs. In *Stackemann v. Paton*[62] the plaintiffs were   **4–21** photographers who were in the habit of taking photographs of schools and the pupils attending them. This they did as a speculation. Their practice was to seek permission from the principals to take the photographs, it being clearly understood that no one was to be compelled to purchase copies, although, no doubt, the photographers had reasonable expectations of being able to effect sales amongst the pupils and others. The plaintiffs had obtained permission from the principal, who had gone to some trouble in showing the photographer over the interior of the school buildings, in gathering the pupils and grouping them for the purpose of being photographed. A certain number of copies were sold to pupils and others. The defendants were publishers of a book, the purpose of which was to advertise schools, and the proprietors of the school in question had supplied them with a block made from the plaintiffs' photographs to be used for advertising the school in the defendants' publication.

It was held that the copyright in the photographs was vested in the proprietors of the school, and that, therefore, the plaintiffs had no right to complain of their reproduction in the defendants' publication. The ground for this decision was that the school proprietors had given "good" consideration by reason of their permitting the photographer to have access to private buildings.[63]

It is not easy to reconcile this decision with the cases of *Ellis v. Marshall*   **4–22** *(H.) & Son*[64] and *Melville v. Mirror of Life Co.*,[65] in both of which it was held that celebrities who were requested by photographers to give sittings, without any charge being made for the taking of the photographs, did not acquire the copyright in the photographs, notwithstanding that they subsequently purchased some copies. These cases were distinguished in *Stackemann v. Paton* on the ground that the only possible consideration given by the celebrities was that they took the trouble to walk up to the photographer's room and to sit in his chair. But, even if quantity of consideration is a matter which ought to be considered at all, the consideration given by the principal who permitted access to his buildings seems, at least, no greater than that given by a celebrity who sacrifices his time to attend a photographer's studio. But whether or not *Stackemann v. Paton* was rightly decided under the law prior to 1911, it is thought that, if similar facts were to have recurred, the decision would not be the same under the 1911 or 1956 Acts.

---

[61] But see the definitions in the Law of Property Act, 1925, s.205(1)(xxi) and *Midland Bank Trust Co. Ltd. v. Green* [1981] A.C. 513.

[62] [1906] 1 Ch. 774.

[63] See, as to the granting of exclusive photographic rights at shows, and so on, *Sports and General Press Agency Ltd. v. "Our Dogs" Publishing Co. Ltd.* [1916] 2 K.B. 880; aff. [1917] 2 K.B. 125.

[64] (1895) 64 L.J.Q.B. 757.

[65] [1895] 2 Ch. 531.

4–23   As pointed out in *Sasha Ltd.* v. *Stoenesco*,[66] the question at issue in such cases under the 1911 Act was whether, in the hypothetical circumstances that the sitter declined to buy any copies of the photograph, the photographer would, in the circumstances of the case, be entitled to sue the sitter for work and labour done in the preparation of the negative. No express agreement about this would normally have been made in practice, so that it is a matter of implication from the circumstances. Where the sitter approached the photographer, without any kind of prior invitation, the implication would be that the sitter would have had to pay for the negative if he did not pay for it indirectly by buying copies, and the copyright would belong to the sitter.[67] But, if the sitter was the kind of person whom photographers were normally willing to photograph without payment, the fact that, in the particular instance, the approach was made by the sitter and not the photographer, does not give rise to an implication that the sitter had to pay, and therefore copyright rested with the photographer.[68] Commissioning involves both ordering work to be done and coming under an obligation to pay for that work, irrespective of whether any product of that work is purchased[69]

4–24   Commissioned engravings. Under section 5(1)(*a*) of the 1911 Act, it was held that, where the plaintiff submitted to the defendants a sketch, which was intended to be reproduced by lithographic process for advertisement purposes, and where the defendants asked him to submit a second sketch in different colours, the second sketch was the "original" of the lithograph within the meaning of that section, and was ordered for valuable consideration.[70]

4–25   Limits as to commissioning. It must not, however, be forgotten that it was only in the case of engravings and photographs *of any subject* that copyright could, under the 1911 or 1956 Acts, vest in the first instance in the person ordering, or commissioning, the engraving or photograph. There was no such provision in the case of any other artistic work, unless that work fell under the description of a "portrait." Consequently, in the case of drawings, not being portraits, even if commissioned, the copyright remained with the artist, unless expressly assigned. This often produced unexpected severances of copyright in the case of commercial art. Consider, for example, the case of an advertiser who placed an order for an

---

[66] (1929) 45 T.L.R. 350. And see *Hartnett* v. *Pinkett* (1953) 103 L.J. 204.

[67] *Boucas* v. *Cooke* [1903] 2 K.B. 227.

[68] Of course the copyright in a "snapshot" would have belonged to the owner of the negative, for it would not have been ordered, nor would consideration have been given, and there seems to be no legal ground, unless it be "breach of confidence," upon which a person who has been "snapshotted" can object to publication of the "snapshot"; it must be considered one of the risks of the highway. As to the right of privacy in photographs commissioned for private and domestic purposes, see now C.D.P.A. 1988, s.85(1), § 22–57, *et seq., post.*

[69] *Plix Products Ltd.* v. *Frank M. Winstone (Merchants)* [1986] F.S.R. 63.

[70] *Con Planck Ltd.* v. *Kolynos Inc.* [1925] 2 K.B. 804; compare s.4(3) of the Copyright Act 1956. *Cf. Nicol* v. *Barranger* [1917–23] Mac.C.C. 219. But a sketch which was never in fact used as an original for an engraving, though intended for that purpose, has been held, in Canada, not to fall within the similar provisions of the Canadian Act: *Toronto Carton Co.* v. *Manchester McGregor Ltd.* [1935] 2 D.L.R. 94.

advertisement. He was the owner of the final engraving or photograph comprising the advertisement, having commissioned it. But the advertisement probably started as a sketch or drawing, unaffected by this subsection, so that there is an outstanding copyright in the sketch or drawing which will not have vested in the advertiser as a result of the commission and which may cause trouble if the advertiser wishes to repeat the main design in a new advertisement.[71]

Commissioned portraits. There was no definition of a "portrait" in the 1911 or 1956 Acts. The dictionary definition of the word is "a representation or delineation of a person especially of the face, made from life by drawing, painting, photograph, engraving etc."[72]   **4–26**

In *Duke of Leeds* v. *Earl Amherst*[73] the question arose, upon the construction of a will, whether a picture of the Duke of Schomberg sitting, clad in armour, upon horseback, a battle scene forming the background of the picture, passed under a bequest of "portraits"; and it was held that it did. Whether a picture is a portrait or not seems to depend upon what is the main purpose of the picture. If the main object is the likeness of a person, it is not the less a portrait because of the presence of subordinate accessories in the picture. It is fairly clear that a "portrait" might include the likeness of more than one individual, but that, on the other hand, the mere fact that real persons happen to be delineated in a picture does not necessarily make that picture a "portrait."

In *Leah* v. *Two Worlds Publishing Co. Ltd.*[74] it was decided that a picture, painted by a spiritualist medium, of a dead person whom he had not seen, was a "portrait" for the purposes of section 5 of the 1911 Act. This was because it was intended to represent the deceased person as that person was when living, and that it was nonetheless a "portrait" because the materials that the artist used were entirely subjective.[75]   **4–27**

C. *The work of employees*

There are two other special classes of case in which the author of a literary, dramatic, musical or artistic work may not be the first owner of the copyright. The first is concerned with the work of employees of proprietors of newspapers, magazines and similar periodicals and the second with the work of employees generally.   **4–28**

---

[71] See, for example, the comments in *Plix Products Ltd.* v. *Frank M. Winstone (Merchants)* [1986] F.S.R. 63. The equitable title to the copyright in the sketch or drawing may nevertheless have vested in the advertiser. See § 4–67 *post.*

[72] *New English Dictionary.*

[73] (1845) 14 L.J. Ch. 73.

[74] [1951] Ch. 393.

[75] As, however, the father of the dead man only agreed to pay for the portrait after he had seen it, it was held that it was not "ordered" within the meaning of the section.

(i) Works made for publication in a newspaper, magazine or similar periodical

4–29 The 1988 Act makes no special provision for this category of work, so that the general provisions relating to works of employees[76] apply to such works made after August 1, 1989. In relation to such works made before this date, however, both the 1956, 1911 and earlier Acts made special provision. The absence of such a provision in the 1988 Act has effected a substantial change in the law in this area.

4–30 The 1956 Act. The provisions of this Act must be applied in relation to all such works made between June 1, 1957, and August 1, 1989.[77] Section 4(2) of the 1956 Act provided that where a literary, dramatic or artistic work was made by the author in the course of the author's employment by the proprietor of a newspaper, magazine or similar periodical under a contract of service or apprenticeship, and was so made for the purpose of publication in a newspaper, magazine or similar periodical, the proprietor should be entitled to the copyright in the work in so far as the copyright related to publication of the work in any newspaper, magazine or similar periodical, or to reproduction of the work for the purpose of its being so published; but in all other respects the author should be entitled to any copyright subsisting in the work by virtue of that Act. The subsection had effect subject to any agreement excluding its operation and to Part VI of the Act, relating to assignments.[78] What was meant by "contract of service or apprenticeship" is discussed below, but it should be noted that this provision did not apply in the case of musical works, and, in respect of works to which it did apply, only to such works if made for the purpose of publication "in" a newspaper, magazine or similar periodical. It would seem therefore that this provision did not apply to the separate copyright in the newspaper, magazine or periodical as such.

4–31 It was not provided that either the contract for the making of the work, or the agreement excluding the operation of the section, needed to be in writing, and presumably the latter might have been implied, either from the terms of a particular contract or from the circumstances of the particular case. While, however, the operation of the sub-section might have been excluded by agreement, it does not appear that it could have been extended by an agreement not amounting to an assignment. Thus the proprietor could not, merely by oral agreement, acquire the legal title to more than the newspaper right in the work. Where the work was not made by an employee under a contract of service, but by a paid independent contributor, it is thought that the equitable right to the entire copyright[79] ought not to have vested in the proprietor, unless there was something more than mere engagement and payment from which a contract to that effect could be inferred. Otherwise such a contributor would have been in a worse position than one who was employed under a contract of service, for

---

[76] See § 4–35 *et seq.*, *post.*
[77] See § 4–2 *ante.*
[78] Copyright Act 1956, ss.4(5), (6).
[79] As to equitable rights, see § 4–67 *et seq.*, *post.*

the latter was deemed to have the general rights of publication reserved to him.

What is meant by a contract of service or apprenticeship is discussed in **4–32** detail below. Where, however, a person was a director of a company and was also appointed "dress editress" at a fixed salary per annum, her duties occupying practically the whole of her time, she was held to be a clerk or servant of the company within the meaning of section 209 of the Companies (Consolidation) Act 1908. The position was held to be otherwise in the case of a person who was employed by the company at a fixed salary per annum to supply "fashion drawings" for the periodical, where although the company had first call on her services and her work occupied most of her time, she occasionally did work for other publishers. Nor was a person who was employed at a fixed salary per annum to supply weekly articles and other information for the periodical, but who also wrote for other publishers, a clerk or servant of the company.[80] Of course, even though a person might have been on the regular staff of a paper and under a contract of service, he would have retained the copyright in work done by him in his working time and outside the scope of his employment.[81] It is thought that even in the case of work done in his working time, but outside the scope of his employment, he would still have retained the legal title to the copyright in the work, although he might have been in breach of his contract with his employer and perhaps held the copyright upon trust for him.

The 1911 Act. The provisions of this Act must be applied in relation to **4–33** all such works made on or after July 1, 1912, but before June 1, 1957.[82] This Act contained a similar provision to that in the 1956 Act limiting the vesting of copyright in the case of employees, namely, that where the work made by the employee was an article or other contribution to a newspaper, magazine or similar periodical, there was to be deemed to be reserved to the author a right to restrain the publication of the work otherwise than as part of a newspaper, magazine of similar periodical.[83] It was doubted whether, under that Act, this provision gave to the employee anything except a bare statutory right to restrain publication by others.[84] It is not thought that the employee or any licensee from him gained any right to publish, since this would be an infringement of the copyright vested in the employer.

Pre-1911 Act works. The Literary Copyright Act 1842 contained an ill- **4–34** drafted section[85] under which the copyright in an "encyclopaedia, review, magazine, periodical work, or work published in a series of books or parts, or any book whatsoever" vested in the proprietor in certain cases. The

---

[80] *Re Beeton & Co. Ltd.* [1913] 2 Ch. 279; and see as to a newspaper's political and lobby correspondent, *Beloff* v. *Pressdram Ltd.* [1973] R.P.C. 765, *infra*.
[81] *Byrne* v. *Statist. Co.* [1914] 1 K.B. 622.
[82] See § 4–2, *ante*.
[83] Copyright Act 1911, s.5(1)(*b*).
[84] *Sun Newpapers Ltd.* v. *Whippie* (1928) 28 S.R. (N.S.W.) 473.
[85] Literary Copyright Act 1842, s.18.

proprietor had to prove that (i) he employed the writer to compose the articles; (ii) that the articles were composed on terms that the copyright should belong to the proprietor; and (iii) the articles were paid for by him.[86] The general opinion was that this section applied only to works of the character of encyclopedias, magazines and periodicals.[87] Whether the section applied where the terms were not express depended upon the inferences of fact to be drawn from the nature of the contract and all the circumstances.[88] It was held unreasonable to suppose that a person paid for the right to publish another's contributions in an encyclopedia leaving it open to the other to publish his contributions the next day in a separate form.[89] The section also provided that the author was to be at liberty, after a lapse of 28 years from the date of publication, to publish his articles in a separate form. The 1988 Act accordingly provides that where a work made before July 1, 1912, consists of an essay, article or portion forming part of and first published in a review, magazine or other periodical or work of a like nature, the copyright is subject to any right of publishing the essay, article or portion in a separate form to which the author was entitled at the commencement of the 1911 Act, or would, if that Act had not been passed, have become entitled under section 18 of the 1842 Act.[90]

(ii) Works made by employees generally

4–35 The 1988 Act. In relation to works made on or after August 1, 1989, section 11(2) of the 1988 Act provides that where a literary, dramatic, musical or artistic work is made by an employee in the course of his employment, his employer is the first owner of any copyright in the work, subject to any agreement to the contrary. The expressions "employee," "employment" and "employer" all refer to employment under a contract of service or of apprenticeship.[91]

4–36 Works made by employees: the 1956 Act. In relation to works made between June 1, 1957, and August 1, 1989, the provisions of the 1956 Act must be applied to determine the question of first ownership of copyright.[92] In fact the provisions of that Act were to precisely the same effect as those of the 1988 Act. Thus it was provided by section 4(4) of the 1956 Act that where a work was made in the course of an author's employment by another person under a contract of service or apprenticeship, that other person was entitled to any copyright subsisting in the work. This pro-

---

[86] Actual payment was necessary: *Richardson* v. *Gilbert* (1851) 1 Sim. (N.S.) 336; *Brown* v. *Cooke* [1874] 16 L.J. Ch. 140; *Collingridge* v. *Emmott* [1887] 57 L.T. 864.

[87] *cf. Ward, Lock & Co. Ltd.* v. *Long* [1906] 2 Ch. 550, where the view was expressed that the section extended to books generally.

[88] *Lawrence, etc., Ltd.* v. *Aflalo* [1904] A.C. 17; *Sweet* v. *Benning* (1855) 16 C.B. 459; *Lamb* v. *Evans* [1893] 1 Ch. 218; *Chantrey, etc., Co.* v. *Dey (T.H.)* (1912) 28 T.L.R. 499. *cf. Bishop of Hereford* v. *Griffin* (1848) 16 Sim. 190; *Walter* v. *Howe* (1881) 17 Ch.D. 708.

[89] *Lawrence, etc., Ltd.* v. *Aflalo, supra.*

[90] C.D.P.A. 1988, Sched. 1, para. 18. See also Copyright Act 1956, Sched. 7, para. 37 and Copyright Act 1911, Sched 1.

[91] *Ibid,* s.178.

[92] See § 4–2, *ante.*

vision only applied where the provisions regarding works of employees of newspaper proprietors[93] and commissioned works[94] did not apply, and also only had effect subject to any agreement excluding its operation and to Part VI of the Act, relating to assignments and the rights of government departments.[95]

Works made by employees: the 1911 Act. The provisions of this Act   **4–37** must be applied to works made on or after July 1, 1912, and before June 1, 1957. The provisions of this Act were substantially the same as those of 1956 Act. Thus section 5(1)(*b*) of the 1911 Act provided that where the author was in the employment of some other person under a contract of service or apprenticeship and the work was made in the course of his employment by that person, the person by whom the author was employed should, in the absence of any agreement to the contrary, be the first owner of any copyright in the work. This provision was subject to the further exception made in the case of contributions to newspapers.[96]

Pre-1911 Act works. Prior to the 1911 Act no general provision was   **4–38** made with respect to the works of employees. The provisions of section 18 of the Literary Copyright Act 1842 relating to certain works have already been considered.[97]

What is a "contract of service"? Whether a person is engaged under a   **4–39** "contract of service" or not is a question of law depending upon the facts,[98] the distinction being between a 'contract of service" and a "contract for services."

Apart from the difficulties which the use of this expression creates in   **4–40** relation to determining ownership of copyright mentioned below, in many cases there may be other difficulties, for example, even if the author was employed under a contract of service, was he employed to produce works of the kind in question; if he was, then was the particular work produced in the course of such employment[99]; finally, was there any agreement to the contrary?[1] Thus frequently works are produced by directors who have no contract of service with their companies or, if they have, it is not part of their duties thereunder to produce the works in question.[2]

---

[93] See § 4–30 *et seq., ante.*
[94] See § 4–16 *et seq., ante.*
[95] Copyright Act 1956, ss.4(5), (6).
[96] See § 4–33, *ante.*
[97] § 4–34 *ante.*
[98] *O'Kelly* v. *Trusthouse Forte plc* [1984] Q.B. 90. But an appellate court should only interfere with the trial court's finding of fact if there was no evidence to support the finding: *Lee Ting Sang* v. *Chung Chi-Keung* [1990] 2 A.C. 374 (P.C.).
[99] See § 4–45, *post.*
[1] See § 4–48, *post.*
[2] See *Antocks Lairn Ltd.* v. *I. Bloohn Ltd.* [1971] F.S.R. 490; *Parsons* v. *Albert J. Parsons & Sons Ltd.* [1979] F.S.R. 254. *cf. Gordex Ltd.* v. *Sorata Ltd.* [1986] R.P.C. 623.

4–41   There have been many suggested tests of "contract of service" in the decided cases,[3] though few of them in the field of copyright. Many of the older cases were cases under the Workman's Compensation Acts and the tests which evolved from these placed considerable emphasis on the amount of control of employer over employee: the more control, the more likely a contract of service.[4] No doubt in cases of a similar kind the amount of control is still an important factor.[5] The element of control was

---

[3] As examples, the following have been held not to be under a contract of service: clergy and ministers (*Re National Insurance Act* 1911 [1912] 2 Ch. 563; *Re National Insurance Act* 1911 (1912) 107 L.T. 143; *President of the Methodist Conference* v. *Parfitt* [1984] Q.B. 368.); doctors, surgeons and anaesthetists employed at a hospital (*Scottish Insurance Commissioners (The)* v. *The Royal Infirmary of Edinburgh*, 1913 S.C. 751; but see *Gold* v. *Essex County Council* [1942] 2 K.B. 293 and *Cassidy* v. *Ministry of Health* [1915] 2 K.B. 343 as to permanent hospital staff); a lecturer employed to explain the merits of an airship to persons attending an exhibition (*Waites* v. *The Franco-British Exhibition Inc.* (1909) 25 T.L.R. 441); a police cadet (*Wiltshire Police Authority* v. *Wynn* [1981] Q.B. 95); a sporting representative of a newspaper (*Re Ashley and Smith Ltd.* [1917–23] Mac.C.C. 54); a University examiner (*University of London Press Ltd.* v. *University Tutorial Pres Ltd.* [1916] 2 Ch. 601); a music-hall artiste (*Gould* v. *Minister of National Insurance* [1951] 1 K.B. 731); a member of what was in effect a co-operative of musicians forming an orchestra (*Winfield* v. *London Philharmonic Orchestra Ltd.* [1979] I.C.R. 726) and a freelance musician engaged by such an orchestra (*Addison* v. *London Philharmonic Orchestra Ltd.* [1981] I.C.R. 261); a concrete carrier (*Ready Mixed Concrete (South East) Ltd.* v. *Minister of Pensions and National Insurance* [1968] 2 Q.B. 497); a part-time teacher (*Argent* v. *Minister of Social Security* [1968] 1 W.L.R. 1749); (compare *Market Investigations Ltd.* v. *Minister of Social Security* [1969] 2 Q.B. 173 where a part-time interviewer was held to be under a contract of service); a screenplay writer (*Hexagon Pty. Ltd.* v. *Australian Broadcasting Commission* [1976] R.P.C. 628); a director of a family company (*Parsons* v. *Albert J. Parsons & Sons Ltd.* [1979] F.S.R. 254); a manager of an insurance company branch office (*Massey* v. *Crown Life Insurance Co.* [1978] 1 W.L.R. 676). On the other hand, a cartoonist (*Sun Newspapers Ltd.* v. *Whippie* (1928) 28 S.R. (N.S.W.) 473), a pupil teacher (*Re National Insurance Act 1911* [1913] 1 Ir.R. 219), and a professional footballer (*Walker* v. *The Crystal Palace Football Club Ltd.* [1910] 1 K.B. 87), have been held to be engaged under contracts of service; in the last case it was held sufficient that the footballer was bound to follow the general instructions of his employers. In *Amalgamated Engineering Union* v. *Minister of Pensions and National Insurance* [1963] 1 W.L.R. 441 the shop steward of the branch of the trade union of which he was a member was held to be under a contract of service; see also *Unsworth* v. *Pease, etc., Ltd.* [1937] 2 K.B. 504. In *Binding* v. *Great Yarmouth, etc., Commissioners* (1923) 16 B.W.C.C. 28, a salvage contractor was held to be under a contract of service, as was a resident-engineer in *Morren* v. *Swinton and Pendlebury Borough Council* [1965] 1 W.L.R. 576, a trapeze artiste in *Whittaker* v. *Ministry of Pensions and National Insurance* [1967] 1 Q.B. 156, a part-time interviewer in *Market Investigations Ltd.* v. *Minister of Social Security, supra*, a designer of cars in *Nichols Advanced Vehicle Systems Inc.* v. *Rees* [1979] R.P.C. 127, the political and lobby correspondent of a newspaper in *Beloff* v. *Pressdram Ltd.* [1973] R.P.C. 765, a driver of earth-moving machines in *Global Plant Ltd.* v. *Secretary of State for Social Services* [1972] 1 Q.B. 139, a professional dancer in *Fall* v. *Hitchen* [1973] 1 W.L.R. 286 and a building workman in *Ferguson* v. *John Dawson & Partners (Contractors) Ltd.* [1976] 1 W.L.R. 1213. In the case of *Re National Insurance Act* 1911 (1913) 108 L.T. 894, the contract of service was admitted, and the only question was as to whether they were manual labourers. In *Re Beeton & Co.* ([1913] 2 Ch. 279), the question was as to whether persons employed regularly to contribute articles to a magazine were "clerks or servants" within the meaning of the Companies (Consolidation) Act 1908, s.209). See also examples mentioned in *Stevenson, Jordan & Harrison Ltd.* v. *Macdonald & Evans* [1952] 1 T.L.R. 101.

[4] See *Short* v. *J. & W. Henderson Ltd.* (1946) 39 B.W.C.C. 62; *Simmons* v. *Heath Laundry Co.* [1910] 1 K.B. 543; In *Re Ashley & Smith Ltd.* [1917–23] Mac.C.C. 54.

[5] See *Gould* v. *Minister of National Insurance* [1951] 1 K.B. 731; *Ready Mixed Concrete (South East) Ltd.* v. *Minister of Pensions and National Insurance* [1968] 2 Q.B. 497; *National Federation of Sub-Postmasters* v. *Minister of Health* (1939) 161 L.T. 337.

considered important in *University of London Press Limited* v. *University Tutorial Press Limited*[6] in deciding whether or not the author of certain examination papers was employed under a contract of service for the purposes of the equivalent section of the 1911 Act. However, more recently, it has been recognised that degree of control is not always so important, particularly in the case of professional people who may be employed under contracts of service.[7]

The two expressions indicate the distinction between, for example, the   **4–42** case of a man engaged to do some specific work under a considerable measure of control, extending not only to the work which he does but also to the way in which he does it, on the one hand, and that of a man engaged more in the capacity of an independent contractor, for example, a man engaged professionally, on the other.[8] One feature of the difference is that under a contract of service, a man is employed as part of the business, and his work is done as an integral part of the business, whereas under a contract for services, his work, although done for the business, is not integrated into it, but is only an accessory to it.[9] The fundamental test has been said to be whether the person who performs the services is performing them in business on his own account. If so, the contract is one for services; if not, it is a contract of service.[10] Probably, however, no exhaustive list can be compiled of the considerations which are relevant in determining the question; control is no doubt an important factor but can no longer be regarded as the determining one.[11] Although parties cannot alter the nature of their relationship by putting a new label on it, where the situation is in doubt or ambiguous, so that it can be brought under one relationship or the other, it is open to the parties, by agreement, to stipulate what the legal situation between them should be.[12]

In the most recent copyright case in which the question has been con-   **4–43** sidered in detail,[13] it was said that the greater the skill required for an employee's work, the less significant was control in determining whether the employee was under a contract of service; control was just one of many factors whose influence varies according to the circumstances. The test which emerged from the authorities was whether, on the one hand, the employee is employed as part of the business and his work is an integral part of the business (contract of service), or whether, on the other, his work is not integrated into the business but is only accessory to it or the

---

[6] [1916] 2 Ch. 601.
[7] See *Morren* v. *Swinton and Pendlebury Borough Council* [1965] 1 W.L.R. 576; *Whittaker* v. *Minister of Pensions and National Insurance* [1967] 1 Q.B. 156.
[8] *Stevenson Jordan & Harrison Ltd.* v. *Macdonald & Evans* [1952] 1 T.L.R. 101, per Evershed M.R.
[9] *Ibid, per* Denning L.J.
[10] *Market Investigations Ltd.* v. *Minister of Social Security* [1969] 2 Q.B. 173.
[11] *Ibid.*
[12] *Massey* v. *Crown Life Insurance Co.* [1978] 1 W.L.R. 676.
[13] *Beloff* v. *Pressdram Ltd.* [1973] R.P.C. 765. For other copyright cases where the employment details are mentioned, see *University of London Press Ltd.* v. *University Tutorial Press Ltd.* [1916] 2 Ch. 601; *Hexagon Pty. Ltd.* v. *Australian Broadcasting Commission* [1976] R.P.C. 628; *Nichols Advanced Vehicle Systems Inc.* v. *Rees* [1979] R.P.C. 127.

work is done by him in business on his own account (contract for services).

4–44   The practical application of these principles to the facts of a particular case is often extremely difficult. Thus a prospective plaintiff, particularly one contemplating seeking interlocutory relief, is often faced with the difficult task of trying to decide conclusively whether he owns the copyright in the work in question prepared for him by someone who was employed by him to produce the work under a contract which may or may not be one of service. Further, since the final arbiters of the facts are the courts, the prospective plaintiff is faced with three possibilities. First, to take the risk that the contract is one of service so that he owns the copyright; or, secondly, to obtain an assignment from the employee of copyright and of accrued causes of action before issuing the writ; or, thirdly, to join the employee as co-plaintiff with him. The prudent course will always be to take either the second or third course.

4–45   **Course of employment.** In order that the copyright may vest in an employer it is not sufficient that the work is made by his employee. It must also be made "in the course of his employment." Thus where a translation was made by a person on the regular staff of a newspaper, but during his spare time, the copyright did not vest in his employers, but remained in the translator.[14] Again, where an accountant prepared and wrote lectures for delivery to universities and societies dealing with the business in which he was employed, it was held that this was not done in the course of his employment.[15] This was so notwithstanding that the giving of lectures was helpful to the company in that it served as an advertisement and, on that account, he was paid the expenses he incurred. On the other hand, where the work is done outside office hours, but is the type of work which the employee might be expected to undertake for his employer, and the results of which might later be used in competition, the employee may be in breach of his fiduciary duty by not disclosing the work to his employer. It is thought that the consequence of this would be that either the copyright would be held on constructive trust for the employer, or the employee would not be allowed to set up the claim that the work was not done in the course of his employment.[16]

4–46   One difficulty in determining whether or not the work was prepared in the course of the author's employment is the extent of the author's employment. That is to say, it may be difficult to determine what are his hours of employment and what is his "spare time." This question often arises in respect of school-teachers and the like who may well spend part of their "spare time" after school hours in preparing lessons, marking homework and so on. In relation to copyright the sort of problem which

---

[14] *Byrne* v. *Statist Co.* [1914] 1 K.B. 622.
[15] *Stevenson, Jordan & Harrison Ltd.* v. *Macdonald & Evans* [1952] 1 T.L.R. 101, Evershed M.R. citing the prima facie view that a university lecturer would be entitled to the copyright in his lectures in the absence of clear agreement to the contrary.
[16] See *Missing Link Software* v. *Magee* [1989] F.S.R. 361, where the cases referred to in nn. 14 and 15, *ante*, do not appear to have been cited.

can arise is where, for instance, a school-teacher, out of school hours, writes a play for the purposes of performance at his school which turns out to be so successful that it is worth exploiting commercially. But who owns the copyright in the play? Each case must, of course, depend on its own facts. However, in one unreported case[17] it was held, by the Court of Appeal, that, on the facts of that case, a part-time teacher's "homework," preparing lessons and marking books outside the classroom, was not required by her employment contract. The teacher's contract stipulated a particular number of hours per week, and the Court of Appeal said that difficulties would be posed if she was required to work outside the hours stipulated in her contract; she might be expected to do so and would probably have to do so, but there was nothing to suggest she was required to do this extra work.

Apprenticeship. As to apprenticeship, "an apprentice is a person bound **4–47** to another for the purpose of learning his trade or calling, the contract being of that nature that the master teaches and the other serves the master with the intention of learning."[18] Its purpose is to learn a craft or a trade or a profession such that when the apprenticeship is completed the apprentice becomes qualified in that trade or profession.[19]

Agreement to the contrary. Section 11(2) of the 1988 Act provides, as **4–48** did section 4(5) of the 1956 Act and section 5(1) of the 1911 Act, that these employment provisions are subject to agreement to the contrary. Such agreement may, it is assumed, be oral or be implied from conduct or circumstances.[20]

Under the 1911 Act, it was not possible, in a case not within the provisions, to agree to an initial vesting of copyright in someone other than the author. If any such agreement were made, the author nevertheless became the first owner of copyright in law and the person entitled to copyright became the owner in equity only and took subject to the rights of a purchaser for value without notice. This still continues to be the case if the agreement was made before June 1, 1957.[21] But, in the case of an agreement signed by or on behalf of a prospective owner of copyright after that date, copyright may now vest initially in the assignee as soon as the work is made.[22] In the case of an oral or implied agreement, however, the copyright will still vest in the author, subject to a right in equity of the person with whom the agreement is made to have an assignment in his favour. Where an author is engaged by a publisher to write a book or an article for

---

[17] *The Daily Telegraph*, April 7, 1979; see also *Current Law Year Book* (1977), para. 2855.
[18] *Per* Cockburn C.J., *Clapham* v. *St. Pancras* (1860) 6 Jur.(N.S.) 700; see *Fraser* v. *Minister of National Insurance* (1947) Sess.Cas. 594, *Horan* v. *Hayhoe* [1904] 1 K.B. 288, *Re Marryat* [1948] Ch. 298 and *Dunk* v. *George Waller & Son Ltd.* [1970] 2 Q.B. 163.
[19] *Wiltshire Police Authority* v. *Wynn* [1981] Q.B. 95.
[20] See *Massine* v. *De Basil* [1936–45] Mac.C.C. 223, in which the court implied such an agreement in the case of the author of the choreography of a ballet; see *Christopher Bede Studios Ltd.* v. *United Portraits Ltd.* [1958] N.Z.L.R. 250, where agreement to contrary was in writing and for valuable consideration.
[21] C.D.P.A. 1988, Sched. 1, para. 26(1). As to equitable ownership, see § 4–67, *post*.
[22] C.D.P.A. 1988, s.91(1); Copyright Act 1956, s. 37(1).

a capital sum, the law will generally presume that it was the intention of the parties that the copyright should belong to the publisher.[23]

3. First Owner in Relation to Other Works

4–49 The 1988 Act, as did the 1956 Act, makes further express provision as to who is to be the first owner of copyright in the remaining categories of works. These are now considered in turn. As already noted,[24] the 1988 Act uses the expression "author" in relation to all categories of works, although it is further defined in relation to the works now under consideration. The 1956 Act used different terminology.

A. *Sound recordings*

4–50 **The 1988 Act.** With one exception,[25] in relation to sound recordings made after August 1, 1989, the 1988 Act provides that the person who creates the work, and who is thus the "author" of it, is to be taken to be the person by whom the arrangements necessary for the making of the recording are undertaken.[26] This is the same form of wording as is used in the provisions of the 1956 and 1988 Acts dealing with ownership of the copyright in films.[27]

4–51 **Sound recordings under the 1956 Act.** The provisions of the 1956 Act apply in relation to sound recordings made before August 1, 1989, but after June 1, 1957,[28] and in relation to sound recordings made after August 1, 1989, but whose making was commissioned before that date.[29] This Act provided that, except for commissioned works, the "maker" of a sound recording was to be entitled to the copyright,[30] and the "maker" was defined to be the person who owned the first record embodying the sound recording at the time when the recording was made.[31]

4–52 **Commissioned sound recordings under the 1956 Act.** The 1956 Act further provided that where a person commissioned the making of a sound recording, and paid or agreed to pay for it in money or money's worth, and the recording was made in pursuance of that commission, that person, in the absence of any agreement to the contrary, was to be entitled to the copyright.[32] The position in relation to such recordings is thus similar to that existing under the 1956 Act with regard to commissioned artistic

---

[23] *Sweet* v. *Benning* (1855) 16 C.B. 459; *Lawrence, etc. Ltd.* v. *Aflalo* [1904] A.C. 17; *Lamb* v. *Evans* [1893] 1 Ch.D. 218; and see *Chantrey, etc., Co.* v. *Dey (T.H.)* (1912) 28 T.L.R. 499.
[24] See § 4–3, *ante.*
[25] See § 4–51.
[26] C.D.P.A. 1988, s.9(2)(a).
[27] See §§ 4–55, 4–56, *post.*
[28] See § 4–2, *ante.*
[29] C.D.P.A. 1988, Sched. 1, para. 11(2).
[30] Copyright Act 1956, s.12(4).
[31] *Ibid*, s.12(8).
[32] *Ibid*, s.12(4). See *Silly Wizard Ltd.* v. *Shaughnessy* [1984] F.S.R. 163 (Ct. of Sess.) for an example of a decision as to who, on the facts, owned the record.

works.[33] These provisions were also stated to be subject to the provisions of Part VI of the Act,[34] presumably referring to assignments of copyright and to the rights of government departments.

Film Sound-tracks: the 1956 Act. Under the 1956 Act the sounds   **4–53** embodied in any sound-track associated with a cinematograph film were to be taken to be included in the film.[35] Copyright therefore subsisted in such a sound-track as part of the copyright in the cinematograph film and not as a separate sound recording. Under the 1988 Act, however, copyright subsists in a sound-track as a sound recording in its own right and not as part of the copyright in the film.[36] The 1988 Act further provides that film sound-tracks to which the 1956 Act applied are now to be treated as sound recordings and not as part of the film.[37] This might have created difficulties concerning the ownership of the copyright in such sound recordings but the 1988 Act provides that the "author" and first owner of the copyright in such a film is to be treated as having been the "author" and first owner of the copyright in the sound recording.[38] Thus, whoever was the first owner of the copyright in the cinematograph film will be treated as having been the first owner of the copyright in the sound-track which is now to be regarded as a sound recording.

Sound recordings under the 1911 Act. In relation to sound recordings   **4–54** made before June 1, 1957, but after July 1, 1912, the provisions of the 1911 Act apply.[39] This Act provided that copyright was to subsist in records, perforated rolls, and other contrivances by means of which sounds might be mechanically reproduced, as if such contrivances were musical works, and the person who was the owner of the original plate at the time when it was made should be deemed to be the author of the work[40] and thus the first owner of the copyright in it.[41]

B. *Films*

The 1988 Act. In relation to films made after August 1, 1989, the 1988   **4–55** Act provides that the person who creates a film, and who is thus the "author" of it, is to be taken to be the person by whom the arrangements necessary for the making of the film are undertaken.[42] This will normally be the producer of the film and not, for example, the camera operator.[43]

---

[33] See §§ 4–16, *et seq., ante.*
[34] Copyright Act 1956, s.12(4).
[35] *Ibid*, s.13(9); see § 2–30, *ante.*
[36] C.D.P.A. 1988, s.5; see § 2–28, *ante.*
[37] *Ibid*, Sched. 1, para. 8(1).
[38] *Ibid*, Sched. 1, para. 8(2). The use of the expression "author" in relation to such 1956 Act works appears to be inappropriate.
[39] See § 4–2, *ante.*
[40] Copyright Act 1911, s.19(1).
[41] *Ibid*, s.5(1). "Plate" was defined by s.35(1) of the Act as including any matrix or other appliance by which records, perforated rolls or other contrivances for the acoustic representation of the work were or were intended to be made.
[42] C.D.P.A. 1988, s.9(2)(*a*).
[43] *Adventure Film Productions Ltd.* v. *Tulley, The Times*, October 14, 1982.

The word "undertaken" implies that it is the person responsible for such arrangements, particularly in the financial sense, who is the "author" of a film.[44] Thus where a shell company acted purely as a nominee and agent for another company, which was in reality providing the finance and control, the shell company was not the first owner of the copyright.[45] If the overall agreement between two persons is that one of them is to be the producer of a film, the fact that the other makes the arrangements for one particular location will not make the two of them joint authors in this sense.[46]

4–56 **The 1956 Act.** The provisions of the 1956 Act, which apply to all films made between June 1, 1957 and August 1, 1989,[47] were to the same effect. Thus the Act provided that the "maker" of a cinematograph film was to be entitled to any copyright subsisting in the film,[48] and the "maker" was the person by whom the arrangements necessary for the making of the film were undertaken.[49] This provision was stated to be subject to the provisions of Part VI of the Act,[50] again presumably referring to assignments of copyright and to the rights of government departments. As already noted,[51] a sound-track associated with a film to which the 1956 Act applied is no longer to be treated as included in the film, but as a separate sound recording, although the first owner of the copyright in the film is to be treated as the first owner of the copyright in the sound recording.

4–57 **Pre-1956 Act films.** There is no copyright in cinematograph films as such made before June 1, 1957.[52]

C. Broadcasts

4–58 **The 1988 Act.** In relation to broadcasts made after August 1, 1989, the 1988 Act provides that the person who creates the work, and who is thus the "author" of it, is to be taken to be the person making the broadcast or, in the case of a broadcast which relays another broadcast by reception and immediate re-transmission, the person making that other broadcast.[53] The 1988 Act further provides that references to the person making the broadcast are to the person transmitting the programme if he has responsibility to any extent for its contents, and to any person providing the programme who makes with the person transmitting it the arrangements necessary for its transmission.[54] In this context, the reference to a "programme" is to any item included in a broadcast. Where more than one person is to be taken as making the broadcast in accordance with the

---

[44] *Re F.G. (Films), Ltd.* [1953] 1 W.L.R. 483.
[45] *Ibid.*
[46] See n. 43.
[47] See § 4–2, *ante.*
[48] Copyright Act 1956, s.13(4).
[49] *Ibid*, s.13(10).
[50] *Ibid*, s.13(4).
[51] § 4–53, *ante.*
[52] C.D.P.A. 1988, Sched. 1, para. 7(1).
[53] C.D.P.A. 1988, s.9(2)(*b*).
[54] *Ibid*, s.6(3).

above definition, then the broadcast is to be treated as a work of joint authorship.[55]

The 1956 Act. In relation to broadcasts made before August 1, 1989, the **4–59** provisions of the 1956 Act apply to determine the question of first ownership.[56] This Act provided that the BBC or the IBA, as the case might be, was to be entitled to any copyright subsisting in a television or sound broadcast made by them.[57] A broadcast was to be taken to be made by the body by whom the visual images or sounds in question, or both, as the case might be, were broadcast.[58]

Pre-1956 Act broadcasts. There is no copyright in broadcasts made **4–60** before June 1, 1957.[59]

D. *Cable programmes*

The 1988 Act. In relation to cable programmes made after August 1, **4–61** 1989, the person who created the work, and who is thus the "author" of it, is taken to be the person providing the cable programme service in which the programme is included.[60]

The 1956 Act. In relation to cable programmes made before August 1, **4–62** 1989, the 1956 Act, as amended, similarly provided that the person providing the cable programme service in which a cable programme was included should be entitled to the copyright in such a work.[61]

Pre-1985 cable programmes. There is no copyright in cable pro- **4–63** grammes included in a cable programme service before January 1, 1985.[62]

E. *Typographical arrangements*

The 1988 Act. In relation to a typographical arrangement of a published **4–64** edition made after August 1, 1989, the person who created the work, and who is thus the "author" of it, is to be taken to be the publisher of it.[63]

The 1956 Act. The provisions of the 1956 Act, which apply to typogra- **4–65** phical arrangements made before August 1, 1989,[64] were to the same effect. Thus the publisher was to be entitled to the copyright subsisting in a published edition under that Act.[65]

---

[55] *Ibid*, s.10(2).

[56] See § 4–2, *ante*.

[57] Copyright Act 1956, s.14(2). The IBA is now to be dissolved and its assets divided: see the Broadcasting Act 1990, s.127.

[58] *Ibid*, s.14(10), unchanged by the amendment made to the Act by the Cable and Broadcasting Act 1984.

[59] C.D.P.A. 1988, Sched. 1, para. 9(*a*).

[60] C.D.P.A. 1988, s.9(2)(*c*).

[61] Copyright Act 1956, s.14A(3), as inserted by the Cable and Broadcasting Act 1984.

[62] Copyright Act 1956, s.14A(11), as inserted by the Cable and Broadcasting Act 1984; C.D.P.A. 1988, Sched. 1, para. 9(*b*).

[63] C.D.P.A. 1988, s.9(2)(*d*). As to the meaning of "publisher," see s.175(1).

[64] See § 4–2, *ante*.

[65] Copyright Act 1956, s.15(2).

4–66 Pre-1956 published editions. It appears that the 1956 Act applied to pre-1956 Act published editions, since that Act contained no relevant transitional provisions. Again, therefore, the publisher was entitled to the copyright in these works, although the 25 year term[66] will by now have expired in all such works.

4. Ownership in Other Circumstances

A. *Equitable ownership*

4–67 Since an equitable owner may commence proceedings alone and seek interlocutory relief,[67] it is often important to determine whether a prospective plaintiff is at least an equitable owner of the copyright in question.

There are no set rules for determining equitable ownership and, therefore, the most that can be done is to examine certain of the cases where equitable ownership has been held to subsist. Generally, it would appear that writing is not necessary to create an equitable interest, whether created by trust or otherwise, although it is necessary for the purpose of assigning such interest.[68] It seems that an equitable interest may be created, in the sense of holding the copyright on trust for another, where, for instance, drawings are prepared by a managing director of a company to whom the general employment provisions of the Copyright Acts do not apply. Thus, in *Antocks Lairn Ltd.* v. *I. Bloohn Ltd.*,[69] it was held that the managing director would hold the drawings he made in trust for his company and would have to assign the copyright in them to his company if and when called upon to do so. In *Massine* v. *De Basil*,[70] it was said that, even if the plaintiff, a dancer and choreographer, was not employed by the defendant under a contract of service, it was an implied term of his contract of employment that the defendant would be entitled to the rights in the plaintiff's work even if the plaintiff was an independent contractor; it was a necessary implication from all the facts of the case that such rights should, in equity, belong to the defendant and that the defendant should be entitled to have the rights assigned to him. In a case under the 1956 Act, *Merchant Adventurers Ltd.* v. *M. Grew & Co. Ltd.*,[71] where the draughtsman of a drawing was an "outside" designer to whom section 4(4) of the 1956 Act did not apply, it was held that the fact that he had been paid to make the drawing for the plaintiffs, that he claimed no ownership in its

---

[66] Copyright Act 1956, s.15(2).

[67] The legal owner must be joined before the action proceeds to trial. See generally, § 11–06 *post*, and *Performing Right Society Ltd.* v. *London Theatre of Varieties Ltd.* [1924] A.C. 1; *Merchant Adventurers Ltd.* v. *M. Grew & Co. Ltd.* [1972] Ch. 242.

[68] See, s.53 of the Law of Property Act 1925 and § 5–08, *post*; *Roban Jig & Tool Co. Ltd.* v. *Taylor* [1979] F.S.R. 130; *Wah Sang Industrial Co.* v. *Tackmay Industrial Co. Ltd.* [1980] F.S.R. 303 (Court of Appeal, Hong Kong).

[69] [1971] F.S.R. 490. Where a work is made by a director in the course of his employment under a contract of service the copyright will, of course, subject to any agreement to the contrary, belong to the company. See §§ 4–35 *et seq.*, *ante* and *Gardex Ltd.* v. *Sorata Ltd.* [1986] R.P.C. 623.

[70] [1936–45] Mac.C.C. 223.

[71] [1973] R.P.C. 1.

copyright and that the plaintiffs would be entitled to call for an assignment of such copyright to them, made the plaintiffs the owners in equity of
such copyright. The issue in such cases will usually be whether, on the
facts, the agreement to be implied is one whereby the author has sold his
copyright or merely granted some form of licence.[72] Again, where a work
is made by an employee outside office hours, but in breach of his fiduciary
duty to his employer, the employer may be entitled to the copyright in
equity.[73]

Another example of where an equitable interest was held to have been
created is *Performing Right Society* v. *London Theatre of Varieties Ltd.*[74] Prior to
the 1956 Act it was not possible to effect a legal assignment of the copyright in a future work, that is, in a work not yet written.[75] However, in that
case it was held that a written assignment of the performing rights in a
work not then in existence made the assignee the equitable owner of the
performing rights in the work after it had come into existence. Again, an
oral promise to assign an existing or future copyright given for consideration will normally be enforced by a decree of specific performance, so
that it will vest in the promisee an equitable title in the copyright, even
where the consideration has not been executed.[76]

But there may be circumstances which do not give rise to the creation of
an equitable interest, for instance where a copyright work is prepared by
A for B, or is given or sold by A to B, in either case for a particular purpose. Subject to the precise facts, the result of the transaction may simply
be that B becomes entitled to the property in the original work itself and to
a licence to use it for the particular purpose, but does not become equitable owner of the copyright therein.[77] One of the commonest cases where
this sort of situation arises is where an architect prepares plans for a
client.[78]

B. *Ownership by partnership*

Where a work is made by one partner in the ordinary course of the part-   **4–68**
nership business and for the purposes of the partnership, the copyright in
the work will become partnership property.[79] In the absence of a written
assignment, however, the legal title will remain with the author and will

---

[72] See *e.g. Ironside* v. *H.M. Attorney General* [1988] R.P.C. 197. As to a licence, see § 8–144 *et
seq., post.*

[73] See *Missing Link Software* v. *Magee* [1989] F.S.R. 361, and § 4–45, *ante.* As to the possibility
of the Crown being entitled in equity to the copyright in a former servant's work, see
Attorney-General v. *Guardian Newspapers Ltd. (No. 2)* [1990] A.C. 109, at 263A, and § 13–10,
post.

[74] [1924] A.C. 1.

[75] § 5–36, *post.*

[76] See *Western Front Ltd.* v. *Vestron Inc.* [1987] F.S.R. 66; *University of London Press Ltd.* v. *University Tutorial Press Ltd.* [1916] 2 Ch. 601; *Hexagon Pty. Ltd.* v. *Australian Broadcasting Commission* [1976] R.P.C. 628.

[77] See *Nicol* v. *Barranger* [1917–23] Mac.C.C. 219; *Cooper* v. *Stephens* [1895] 1 Ch. 567.

[78] See § 8–153 *et seq., post.*

[79] *Meikle* v. *Mauffe* [1941] 3 All E.R. 144; *Roban Jig & Tool Co. Ltd.* v. *Taylor* [1979] F.S.R.
130; *Murray* v. *King* [1986] F.S.R. 116 (Fed. Ct. Aus.); *cf. Coffey's Registered Designs* [1982]
F.S.R. 227, where the partnership business was not concerned with producing designs.

not devolve upon the partners; the partners' right is to have the copyright applied for the benefit of the partnership.[80]

C. *Ownership by unincorporated body*

4–69   The question of the vesting of copyright in an unincorporated body of persons has been discussed in a Canadian case.[81] It was held that, in the circumstances of that case, certain of the copyrights in question vested in the members as tenants in common so that any one or more of them could sue for infringement. In general, no doubt, the question of ownership will be determined in accordance with any rules of the association.

5. Ownership of Copyright and Physical Materials

4–70   It may be important to distinguish between the first owner of the copyright in a work and the owner of the physical material on which the work is first recorded. As has been seen,[82] for the purposes of the 1956 and 1911 Acts the question of authorship of a photograph was determined by the ownership of the material on which the photograph was taken. Again, under the 1956 Act, the question of who was the maker of a sound recording was determined by who was the owner of the first record embodying the recording.[83] Otherwise, however, the issues are not necessarily connected.

4–71   **Letters.** Thus, in the case of a letter which is entitled to copyright, the author is prima facie the first owner of the copyright in it. The position of the receiver of a letter is that, in the absence of some limitation imposed, either by the subject matter of the letter, or the circumstances under which it is sent, he has an unqualified title to the material upon which it is written,[84] and he can deal with it as absolute owner, subject only to the right retained by the author and his representatives to restrain publication in breach of confidence[85] and to restrain reproduction in infringement of copyright. The receiver is under no obligation to preserve the letter for the benefit of the writer: he is at liberty to destroy it, or to sell it for waste paper, or for the value of the autograph signature, or for any other purpose, if he pleases.[86]

4–72   **Letters, etc., sent to newspapers.** Letters and other manuscripts sent to the editor of a newspaper, as agent for the proprietor, are the property of the latter, and if the editor, after ceasing to be editor, attempts to use them

---

[80] *O'Brien* v. *Komersaroff* (1982) 56 A.L.J.R. 681.
[81] *Massie & Renwick Ltd.* v. *Underwriters' Survey Bureau Ltd.* [1940] S.C.R. 218.
[82] §§ 4–12, 4–13, *ante.*
[83] § 4–51, *ante.*
[84] *Thurston* v. *Charles* (1904) 21 T.L.R. 659; *Howard* v. *Harris* (1884) Cab. & El. 253.
[85] *Pope* v. *Curl* (1741) 2 Atk. 341; *Oliver* v. *Oliver* (1861) 11 C.B.(n.s.) *139*; *Howard* v. *Gunn* (1863) 32 Beav. 462; *Labouchere* v. *Hess* (1898) 77 L.T. 559; *Macmillan & Co.* v. *Dent* [1907] 1 Ch. 107; *Philip* v. *Pennell* [1907] 2 Ch. 577 and see *post*, § 21–10.
[86] *Baker* v. *Libbie* (1912) 210 Mass. 599, an American case. See also the discussion "Copyright in Letters", printed as an addendum to [1905–10] Mac.C.C.

for his own purposes, he will be restrained on the application of the proprietor, and be compelled to hand over such letters or other manuscripts.[87] The normal custom in such matters recognises no obligation on
the part of the proprietor of a newspaper to insure, or to preserve, any
manuscript sent to him uninvited, and if the manuscript is lost or destroyed, the author cannot recover for its value.[88] Of course, if an editor or
proprietor undertook to return unaccepted communications the case
would be different. The licence to be implied as to the use to which such
letters may be put is considered elsewhere.[89]

Power of governments to publish or withhold letters. It would appear **4–73**
that governments have a right, upon grounds of public policy, to publish
or to withhold all letters addressed to the public offices.[90] This exception
in favour of the government is not supposed to make such communications common property, to be published by any person who may see fit,
without the sanction of the government, nor to take away the property of
the writers or their representatives.

Architects' plans. The prima facie rule is that architects' plans them- **4–74**
selves become the property of the client.[91] But this rule does not mean
more than that the sheets of paper, with the plans drawn upon them,
belong to the client; it does not imply that the client is, without more, the
owner of the copyright in them and certainly it does not mean that the
client is the "author" of them.

---

[87] *Hogg* v. *Kirby* (1803) 8 Ves. 215; see as to gift of a manuscript *Thomas* v. *Times Book Company Ltd.* [1966] 1 W.L.R. 911.
[88] But see *Stone* v. *Long* [1901–04] Mac.C.C. 66.
[89] § 8–158, *post.*
[90] *Curtis on Copyright* (Amer.) 98; *Folsom* v. *Marsh* (1841) 2 Story (Amer.) 100. See also § 21–13, *post*, as to publication of state and government secrets in breach of confidence.
[91] *Gibbon* v. *Pease* [1905] 1 K.B. 810; *Ebdy* v. *M'Gowan* (1870); Hudson's Building and Engin-eering Contracts (10th ed.), p. 189; *Inala Industries Pty. Ltd.* v. *Associated Enterprises Pty. Ltd.* [1960] Q.S.R. 562. Although where the property in the completed plans passes to the client, the property in all notes, sketches and other material used by the architect in prep-aration of the plans probably remains with the architect: *Leicestershire County Council* v. *M. Faraday & Partners Ltd.* [1941] 2 K.B. 205; *Chantrey Martin* v. *Martin* [1953] 2 Q.B. 286.

TRANSMISSION OF AND DEALINGS IN COPYRIGHT

1. Introduction

Distinction between title to copyright and to physical material. The   **5–1**
ownership of copyright in a work is distinct from the ownership of the
physical material in which the copyright work is embodied. The transfer
of title to the physical material does not necessarily transfer the title to the
copyright, any more than the assignment of the copyright necessarily
transfers the title to the physical material.[1] The purchaser of a book, for

---

[1] See § 4–70 *et seq., ante.*

example, becomes the owner of the book, but he does not thereby become the owner of any part of the copyright in the literary work reproduced in the book. The copyright in the literary work remains with the copyright owner who enjoys and is entitled to enforce all the exclusive rights of copying, publication, adaptation, sale and so on conferred on him by copyright law. The sale of a book does not necessarily confer on the purchaser any right, either by way of assignment or licence, to exercise any of those exclusive rights.[2] No purchaser of a book would suppose that he, by his purchase, acquired the right to multiply copies of it. It is quite possible, however, that the purchaser of an artistic work, such as a picture, may be surprised to find that his purchase does not include the right to make copies of it by such means as engravings and photographs, nor even the right to prevent the artist or anyone else from making copies unless it amounted to a breach of contract, confidence or trust.[3] It is, nevertheless, the fact that such a purchaser can only obtain the right to make copies of the work he has purchased by entering into a licence or assignment of copyright.[4] For example, in *Cooper* v. *Stephens*,[5] the plaintiffs sold electro blocks for the purpose of printing certain drawings. The purchasers lent these blocks to the defendants in order that they, in turn, might print from them. Romer J. held that the plaintiffs were entitled to restrain the defendants from doing so, even though the defendants had the permission of the purchasers. "The sale of the blocks could not have had the effect of an assignment of copyright."[6] The Courts will not imply a licence to reproduce a work for commercial purposes simply from the sale of articles without express restriction on the use of copyright.[7] At the same time the Courts consider that the retention of the copyright by the vendor of a picture involves an "unnatural dissociation of two kinds of property," and, consequently, they will lean towards construing a document given at the time of the sale as an assignment of copyright.[8] An assignment of copyright is not effective unless it is in writing signed by or on behalf of the assignor.[9] There are circumstances in which the Courts will hold that the vendor of an article may not derogate from his grant by asserting his copyright against a purchaser in order to prevent him from exercising his right to repair the article.[10]

---

[2] *Time Life International (Nederlands) B.V.* v. *Interstate Parcel Express Co. Pty. Ltd.* [1978] F.S.R. 251 (High Court of Australia).

[3] *Post,* §§ 21–1 *et seq.*

[4] C.D.P.A. 1988, s.90. An equitable title may, however, arise from an implied agreement, see §§ 4–67, *ante.*

[5] [1895] 1 Ch. 567, followed by the C.A. in *Marshall (W.) & Co. Ltd.* v. *Bull (A.H.) Ltd.* (1901) 85 L.T. 77.

[6] *Ibid.* at 571; *Roberts* v. *Candiware Ltd.* [1980] F.S.R. 352.

[7] *Roberts* v. *Candiware Ltd.* (*supra*) (sale of knitting pattern book).

[8] *London Printing, etc., Alliance Ltd.* v. *Cox* [1891] 3 Ch. 291 at 304.

[9] C.D.P.A. 1988, s.90(3).

[10] *British Leyland Motor Corp. Ltd.* v. *Armstrong Patents Co. Ltd.* [1986] A.C. 577 (spare parts for cars). See §8–160, 161 *post.*

2. Transmission by Operation of Law

A. *Death*

Section 90(1) of the 1988 Act provides that copyright is transmissible by **5–2** assignment, by testamentary disposition or by operation of law, as personal or moveable property.[11] Therefore, upon the death of the original owner, it will pass by operation of law to his personal representatives[12] for the benefit of the person to whom he has bequeathed it, or, if the copyright owner has died intestate, for the benefit of his next-of-kin.[13]

Foreign owners. In the case of *Novello & Co. Ltd.* v. *Hinrichsen Edition* **5–3** *Ltd.*,[14] questions arose whether certain copyrights had been owned by enemies during a period after September 3, 1939. Wynn-Parry J. held that, on the death of a foreign owner of English copyrights, the copyrights in question vested in the President of the Probate, Divorce and Admiralty Division (now the President of the Family Division)[15] or in the Crown, and were liable to be divested on an administrator of the estate being appointed in England. It seems to follow from this decision that, in the case of an intestacy, title cannot be made to English copyrights except through an administrator appointed by the English court.

In the absence of evidence that the law of a foreign country is different from English law, the copyright vested in a foreign domiciled testator will vest on his death in the executor or executors appointed in his will.[16] It is then necessary for a grant of probate or grant of letters of administration with the will annexed to be obtained in England in order to prove the will, because only by virtue of such a grant can the will be proved in a court of law. The grant does not, however, confer title on the executor; it proves the document from which he derives title. It follows that, even if a grant of probate is not obtained by a plaintiff or a person from whom he has derived title to the copyright of the deceased testator until after the date of commencement of proceedings, he can still prove his title as at that date. As the executor's title is derived from the will, not from the grant, it makes no difference that the proof of title came into existence at a later date. The position is different in the case of an administrator who derives his title from the grant. The property of the deceased vests in him only from the date of the grant. If, before the date of the grant, he commences proceedings in respect of the deceased's copyright he will be unable to prove any

---

[11] It was expressly so provided by the Literary Copyright Act 1842, s.25 and s.36(1) of the 1956 Act. There was no express provision to that effect in the 1911 Act.

[12] *Re Dickens* [1935] Ch. 267.

[13] *Thompson (C.)* v. *Stanhope (E.)* (1774) 2 Amb. 737; *Burnett* v. *Chetwood* (1817) 2 Mer. 441; *Latour* v. *Bland* (1818) 2 Stark. 382. As to rights to royalties as between tenant for life and remainderman, see *Re Sullivan* [1930] 1 Ch. 84; *Davidson's Trustees* v. *Ogilvie* (1910) S.C. 294; and as between trustee in bankruptcy and equitable assignee, see *Re Trytel* [1952] W.N. 355.

[14] [1951] Ch. 595; see also *Novello & Co. Ltd.* v. *Eulenburg (E.) Ltd.* [1950] 1 All E.R. 44 (C.A.).

[15] Administration of Justice Act 1970, (c. 31) s.1.

[16] *Redwood Music Ltd.* v. *B. Feldman & Co. Ltd.* [1979] R.P.C. 1; *cf. Mackay* v. *Mackay* [1912] 2 S.L.T. 445.

title to that copyright as at the date of the commencement of the proceedings.[17]

B. *Bequest of an unpublished work*

5–4   The provisions of the 1988 Act on this point are a little more elaborate than section 38 of the 1956 Act, which provided that a bequest of an unpublished manuscript of a literary, dramatic, or musical work should, in the absence of a contrary intention, be construed as including the copyright therein owned by the testator before his death.

Section 93 of the 1988 Act supplies a rule of construction to the effect that copyright is to pass under a will with the unpublished work. The statutory rule is that certain bequests are to be construed as including the copyright in the relevant work in so far as the testator was the owner of the copyright immediately before his death. That rule is subject to a contrary intention indicated in the testator's will or a codicil to it. The bequests affected by the rule are those under which a person is entitled to original, material things recording or embodying copyright works, *i.e.* an original document or other material thing recording or embodying a literary, dramatic, musical or artisitic work which was not published before the death of the testator,[18] or an original material thing containing a sound recording or film which was not published before the death of the testator.[19] The rule applies whether the bequest is specific or general and whether the person is entitled under the bequest either beneficially or otherwise, *e.g.* to trustees on trust. These provisions do not apply where the testator died before the June 1, 1957.[20] Where the testator died on or after June 1, 1957, the provisions only apply in relation to an original document embodying a work.[21] In the case of an author who died before June 1, 1957, the ownership after his death of a manuscript of his, where such ownership has been acquired under a testamentary disposition made by him and the manuscript is of a work which has not been published or performed in public, is prima facie proof of the copyright being with the owner of the manuscript.[22]

C. *Bankruptcy*

5–5   The copyright in a published work passes to the trustee in bankruptcy of the copyright owner by operation of law without any assignment in writing.[23] As regards unpublished literary, dramatic or musical works, copyright is conferred upon an author as soon as his work is recorded in writing or otherwise and therefore the copyright in such works also passes

---

[17] See n. 16 *supra*.
[18] C.D.P.A. 1988 s.93(*a*).
[19] *Ibid.* s.93(*b*).
[20] *Ibid.* Para. 30(1)(*a*) of Sched. 1; s.17(2) of 1911 Act; *Re Dickens* [1935] Ch. 267.
[21] *Ibid.* Para. 30(1)(*b*) of Sched. 1: s.38 of 1956 Act.
[22] *Ibid.* Para. 30(2), Sched. 1.
[23] *Mawman* v. *Tegg* (1826) 2 Russ. 385; *Re Curry (W.), etc., & Co.* (1849) 12 Ir. Eq.R. 382; *Re Grant Richards* [1907] 2 K.B. 33. But not a personal right to publish: *Lucas* v. *Moncrieff* (1905) 21 T.L.R. 683.

to the trustee, though the trustee could not compel the author either to finish his manuscript, or to see the work through the press or otherwise through to completion.[24]

D. *Execution*

There is no process whereby copyright can be taken in execution by a judgment creditor of the proprietor,[25] although, of course, royalties due to the judgment debtor might be attached by garnishee proceedings or other process of execution, such as the appointment of a receiver.

5–6

3. Assignments

A. *General*

The main provisions of the 1988 Act, dealing with transfer of title, are contained in sections 90 and 91. In substance they differ little from the provisions of sections 36 and 37 of the 1956 Act.

5–7

B. *Varieties of assignments*

By section 90(3) of the 1988 Act it is provided that an assignment of copyright is not effective unless it is in writing signed by or on behalf of the assignor. The combined effect of section 90 of the 1988 Act and section 53(1)(*c*) of the Law of Property Act 1925 is that any assignment of copyright, whether it be of the legal or equitable interest, must be in writing.[26] Further, if the assignment is signed on behalf of the assignor, the person so signing must have the authority of the assignor.[27] A receiver appointed by the court over assets, which included copyright, has been held to have effectively signed an assignment of the copyright "on behalf of the assignor."[28] It should be borne in mind, having regard to the comparative youth of many composers of "pop" music, for instance, that infants[29] can own and dispose of copyrights in the same way as adults, but subject to the usual rules as to infants' contracts.[30] "Writing" includes any form of notation or code, whether by hand or otherwise and regardless of the method by which, or medium in, or on which, it is recorded[31] In the case of a body corporate the requirement that the assignment should be signed by or on behalf of any person is satisfied by the affixing of its seal.[32] This is a new provision.

5–8

---

[24] C.D.P.A. 1988 s.3(2). *Gibson* v. *Carruthers* (1842) 8 M. & W. 343.

[25] *Edwards & Co.* v. *Picard* (1909) 78 L.J.K.B. 1108.

[26] *Roban Jig & Tool Co. Ltd. & Anor.* v. *Taylor & Ors.* [1979] F.S.R. 130 at 143; see *Performing Right Society Ltd.* v. *London Theatre of Varieties Ltd.* [1924] A.C. 1 at 18; *Wah Sang Industrial Co.* v. *Takmay Industrial Co. Ltd.* [1980] F.S.R. 303 at 309 (Court of Appeal of Hong Kong).

[27] *Beloff* v. *Pressdram Ltd. & Anor.* [1973] 1 All E.R. 241; *Heptulla* v. *Orient Longman Ltd.* [1989] F.S.R. 598 at 610.

[28] *Murray* v. *King* [1986] F.S.R. 116 (Federal Court of Australia).

[29] See Family Law Reform Act 1969 (c. 46).

[30] *Chaplin* v. *Leslie Frewin (Publishers) Ltd.* [1966] Ch. 71.

[31] C.D.P.A. 1988 s.178.

[32] *Ibid.* s.176(1); and see Law of Property (Miscellaneous Provisions) Act 1989 (c. 34) s.1; Companies Act 1989 (c. 40) s.130.

5–9 **Partial assignment.** Section 90(2) of the 1988 Act deals with a "partial assignment." An assignment or other transmission of copyright may be limited so as to apply to one or more, but not all, of the things the copyright owner has the exclusive right to do; and to part, but not the whole, of the period for which copyright is to subsist.[33] It is important to determine, in any given situation, who is, at the relevant time, the owner of the particular right comprised in the copyright in a certain work.[34] Where different persons are in consequence of partial assignment or otherwise entitled to different aspects of copyright in a work, the "copyright owner" is the person who is entitled to the aspect of the copyright relevant for the purpose of the Act.[35] Copyright generally is also capable of being dealt with separately as to territory. It is increasingly common for copyright owners such as publishers and recording companies to operate through a system of assignments or exclusive licences of the copyright in favour of different companies in different territories.[36] This practice has important consequences in relation to those provisions of the 1988 Act concerning the importation or proposed importation into the United Kingdom of copyright works lawfully made abroad, but the making of which in the United Kingdom would have constituted an infringement of copyright of the work in question or a breach of an exclusive licence agreement relating to that work.[37]

5–10 **What words will effect an assignment.** The 1988 Act, as in the case of the 1911 and 1956 Acts, does not state that the assignment of copyright shall be in any special form, beyond that it shall be in writing,[38] signed by or on behalf of the assignor.[39] An agreement may constitute an assignment of copyright, even though the word "copyright" is not used in the document,[40] *e.g.* the copyright may be carried by a general expression such as "the assets of the business" if it formed part of those assets. The scope and effect of an assignment depends upon the true construction of the document or documents which have been signed. For example, an assignment

---

[33] C.D.P.A. 1988, s.90(2).

[34] *J. Albert & Sons Pty. Ltd. & Ors.* v. *Fletcher Construction Co. Ltd.* [1976] R.P.C. 615 (Supreme Court of New Zealand).

[35] C.D.P.A. 1988 s.173(1).

[36] See, *e.g. Polydor Ltd.* v. *Harlequin Record Shop Ltd. & Anor.* [1980] 1 C.M.L.R. 669; *CBS United Kingdom Ltd.* v. *Charmdale Record Distributors Ltd.* [1980] F.S.R. 289; *The Who Group Ltd.* v. *Stage One (Records) Ltd.* [1980] F.S.R. 268.

[37] C.D.P.A. 1988 ss.22, 24 and 27(3). See § 9–5 *et seq., post.*

[38] See n. 31 *ante.*

[39] *Ibid.* s.90(3). Under the law prior to 1911 an assignment of the copyright in a literary work was required to be in writing: *Leyland* v. *Stewart* (1876) 4 Ch.D. 419. The assignment of the copyright in an engraving had to be in writing, attested by two witnesses (Engraving Copyright Act 1734 (8 Geo. 2, c. 13), s.1); in a work of sculpture, by deed, attested by two witnesses (Sculpture Copyright Act 1814 (54 Geo. 3, c. 56), s.4); and in a painting, drawing, or photograph, in writing, signed by the proprietor of the copyright or his agent (Fine Arts Copyright Act 1862 (25 & 26 Vict. c. 68), s.3). It was generally considered that an assignment of literary copyright did not require to be attested, and the 1911 and 1956 Acts do not appear to require any attestation (*Cumberland* v. *Copeland* (1862) 1 Hurl. & C. 194; but see 8 Jur.(N.S.), Part II, p. 148). As to an assignment by a foreigner, see *Jefferys (C.)* v. *Boosey (T.)* (1855) 4 H.L.C. 815. See § G–1, *post,* for a precedent of an assignment of copyright.

[40] *Murray* v. *King* [1986] F.S.R. 116 (Federal Court of Australia).

of "the whole of the property, copyright and interest, present or future, vested or contingent" is wide enough to include future property or rights in the work in question.[41] A purported assignment made orally, or implied from conduct or circumstances would, no doubt, avail to protect the assignee against an action for infringement by the assignor, because it would have the effect of a licence of the owner, which is not required to be in writing, and which is a defence to claim for infringement.[42] The doctrine of non-derogation from grant may also be invoked to provide an alternative defence to implied licence.[43] An oral or implied assignment of copyright might even, if the consideration was executed, (*e.g.* payment of an outright fee for the work), be treated as an equitable assignment.[44] A mere receipt for the purchase-money may, under some circumstances, amount to an assignment of the copyright.[45] Since no particular form of words is required to constitute an assignment it has frequently been a matter of difficulty to determine, upon the construction of a particular document, whether it is an assignment, or bare licence.[46] It is, however, necessary to distinguish a legal assignment from an agreement to assign which gives only equitable rights liable to be defeated by a bona fide purchaser for value without notice of the equitable rights.[47]

Examples. In *London Printing, etc., Alliance Ltd.* v. *Cox*[48] the words on an **5–11** invoice, "For pastel picture and entire copyright, 'On the Threshold,' £52 10s.," and in *Savory (E.W.) Ltd.* v. *The World of Golf Ltd.*[49] the words on a receipt, "Received of Messrs. E.W.S., Ltd., the sum of £2 6s. 6d. for five original card designs, inclusive of all copyrights. Subjects: Four Golfing subjects; one Teddy Bear painting," were held to be sufficient assignments in writing of the copyright. In the latter case, oral evidence was admitted to identify the golfing subjects.

In both these cases, however, the property in the pictures themselves passed to the purchasers. In such cases the courts strive to hold that the copyright is not severed from the picture.[50] In *Lacy* v. *Toole*[51] it was held

---

[41] *Redwood Music Ltd.* v. *B. Feldman & Co. Ltd. & Ors.* [1979] R.P.C. 385 at 394.

[42] C.D.P.A. 1988, s.16(2); *Ironside* v. *H.M. Attorney-General* [1988] R.P.C. 197. See §8–144 *et seq., post.*

[43] *British Leyland Motor Corp. Ltd.* v. *Armstrong Patents Co. Ltd.* [1986] A.C. 577. See §8–160 *et seq., post.*

[44] *Wah Sang Industrial Co.* v. *Takmay Industrial Co. Ltd.* [1980] F.S.R. 303 (Court of Appeal of Hong Kong); *Ironside* v. *H.M. Attorney-General* [1988] R.P.C. 197.

[45] *Jefferys (C.)* v. *Kyle (M.)* (1855) 18 Sess.Cas. (2nd Ser.) 906; *Howitt* v. *Hall* (1862) 6 L.T. 348; *Levy* v. *Rutley* (1871) L.R. 6 C.P. 523; *Colburn* v. *Duncombe* (1838) 9 Sim. 151; *Ornamin (U.K.) Ltd.* v. *Bacsa Ltd.* [1964] R.P.C. 293.

[46] *British Actors Film Co. Ltd.* v. *Glover* [1918] 1 K.B. 299; *Macdonald (E.) Ltd.* v. *Eyles* [1921] 1 Ch. 631; *Barstow* v. *Terry* [1924] 2 Ch. 316; *Re "Clinical Obstetrics"* [1905–10] Mac.C.C. 176; *Neilson* v. *Horniman* [1905–10] Mac.C.C. 234; *Booth* v. *Richards* [1905–10] Mac.C.C. 284; *Chaplin* v. *Leslie Frewin (Publishers) Ltd.* [1966] Ch. 71; *Frisby* v. *British Broadcasting Corporation* [1967] Ch. 932. See *post*, §§ 15–14 *et seq.*

[47] *Ward, Lock & Co. Ltd.* v. *Long* [1906] 2 Ch. 550; *London Printing, etc., Alliance Ltd.* v. *Cox* [1891] 3 Ch. 291.

[48] [1891] 3 Ch. 291.

[49] [1914] 2 Ch. 566; *Murray* v. *King* [1986] F.S.R. 116 (Federal Court of Australia).

[50] *Ante*, § 5–1.

[51] (1867) 15 L.T. 512.

that an agreement to "let A have" a certain work in discharge of a debt owing to A, was sufficient to pass the copyright in the work to A. The intention of the parties must, however, always be regarded. In the case of an agreement with publishers whereby the publishers agreed to pay to an author a royalty of sixpence per copy on every copy of the work sold "in consideration of Mr. W. St. J. (author) giving Mr. W. C. N. (publishers) the sole and exclusive right of printing and publishing the series of 'Music and Higher Life,' and issuing the same in volume form," it was held that the agreement was a publishing licence only and not an assignment of copyright.[52] In *Ironside* v. *H.M. Attorney General*[53] the Court implied an equitable assignment or, alternatively, a full licence from the Royal Mint from the designer of the reverse face of coins who had been paid an outright lump sum fee for the designs. The implied rights extended to proof sets of coins as well as to circulating currency.

5–12 **Assignor may not reproduce the work.** An author who has assigned the copyright in his work may, like any other person, be restrained by the assignee from reproducing or authorising others to reproduce the work[54] except to the extent permitted by section 64 of the 1988 Act,[55] which is limited to the case of an artistic work. Thus, where the author of an artistic work is not the copyright owner, he does not infringe the copyright by copying the work in making another artistic work, provided he does not repeat or imitate the main design of the earlier work. It may be a matter of difficulty to prove infringement by an author of his own work, because mere similarity is not, in itself, an infringement, without proof of copying. When the works are by the same author, such similarity is natural and does not raise any necessary inference of improper use of former works.[56] An artist who assigns copyright in a work does not thereby assign his style or method of portraying similar subjects.[57] A composer who has assigned all the performing rights in his works is not entitled to license performances of his works. There is no implied reservation of such a right in the assignment, unless it can be shown that, in the circumstances of the case, it is necessary to imply a reservation to give business efficacy to the transaction.[58]

5–13 **Derivative works.** Where an author has created a second work by using material from an earlier work, questions may arise as to whether there are separate copyrights capable of being vested by assignment in different persons. In *Metzler & Co. (1920) Ltd.* v. *Curwen (J.) & Sons Ltd.*[59] it was held that an assignee of the copyright in a second work incorporating matter of a first work could maintain an action for infringement against a

---

[52] *Re Jude's Musical Compositions* [1907] 1 Ch. 651; *cf. Edwardes* v. *Cotton* (1903) 19 T.L.R. 34.
[53] [1988] R.P.C. 197.
[54] *Rooney* v. *Kelly* (1861) 14 Ir.Com.Law Rep. 158; *Colburn* v. *Simms* (1843) 2 Ha. 543; *Educational Co. of Ireland Ltd. (The)* v. *Fallon Brothers Ltd.* [1919] 1 I.R. 62.
[55] See § 10–91 *et seq., post.*
[56] But see *Francis Day & Hunter Ltd.* v. *Bron* [1963] Ch. 587 and *Industrial Furnaces Ltd.* v. *Reaves* [1970] R.P.C. 605 at 624.
[57] *Preston* v. *Raphael Tuck, etc., Ltd.* [1926] Ch. 667.
[58] *Performing Right Society Ltd.* v. *Harlequin Record Shops Ltd.* [1979] F.S.R. 233 at 241.
[59] [1928–35] Mac.C.C. 127.

person using the first work under a subsequent assignment from the author. This decision appears to have rested upon the construction of the assignment in that case. It is suggested that, if the derivative work is a work involving such skill and labour as to constitute it a new original work, the copyright in the first work and the derivative work respectively are capable of being separately assigned so that neither of the respective assignees should have any right of complaint against the other by reason of any exercise of the respective rights assigned to each.[60] The position is probably the same if the copyright in the first work was assigned by the author before he created and assigned the copyright in the second work, though the assignee might have contractual claims against the author.

Divisibility of copyright. As has been seen,[61] the 1988 Act expressly contemplates partial assignments limited as to time and as to means of reproduction. **5–14**

Time. Copyright could be assigned for a limited time under the law prior to 1911. It was decided that, in the absence of a special contract to the contrary, the assignor of a copyright was entitled, after the assignment, to continue selling copies of the work printed by him before the assignment and remaining in his possession.[62] Such copies had been lawfully made by him while he was the copyright owner. **5–15**

Example. In *Howitt* v. *Hall*[63] the defendants bought the copyright for four years in a book of which the plaintiff was the author. They continued for several years after the end of that term to sell copies which they had printed during the four years. The court refused an injunction to restrain such sales and held that the purchase of the copyright carried the right of printing; and that, while this right reverted to the author at the end of four years, the publishers were entitled to sell, after the expiration of that term, all copies which had been printed in good faith during the term. "The Copyright Acts," said Wood V.-C., "were directed against unlawful printing . . . ; and when, as in this case, the defendant had acquired the right of lawfully printing the work, he was at liberty to sell at any time what he had so printed."[64] **5–16**

Territory. It is not clear whether, under the law prior to 1911, copyright was divisible as to territory. The balance of authority was in favour of so holding.[65] The 1911 Act,[66] since it used the words "either generally or **5–17**

---

[60] See *Redwood Music Ltd.* v. *Chappell & Co. Ltd.* [1982] R.P.C. 109. See §3–44 *et seq., ante,* §5–12 *ante.*

[61] C.D.P.A. 1988 s.90(2). See § 5–9 *et seq., ante.*

[62] *Taylor* v. *Pillow* (1869) L.R. 7 Eq. 418; see *Tuck & Sons* v. *Priester* (1887) 19 Q.B.D. 48; *Tuck* v. *The Continental Printing Co.* (1887) 3 T.L.R. 150, 661, 826; *Troitzsch* v. *Rees* (1887) 3 T.L.R. 773.

[63] (1862) 6 L.T. 348. See, however, C.D.P.A. 1988, s.16(1)(*b*), s.18 as to issue of copies of work to the public as a restricted act.

[64] *Ibid.* at 350. But see n. 50, § 3–24 *ante.*

[65] *Jefferys (C.)* v. *Boosey (T.)* (1855) 4 H.L.C. 815; *Pitt Pitts* v. *George & Co.* [1896] 2 Ch. 866. As to the meaning of "London Right" in the case of a partial assignment of dramatic rights, *cf. Taylor* v. *Neville* (1878) L.J.Q.B. 254.

[66] Copyright Act 1911, s.5(2). See §5–9 *ante.*

subject to limitations to the United Kingdom or any self-governing Dominion or other part of His Majesty's Dominions to which this Act extends," clearly contemplated divisibility as to territory, but it appeared that the assignment must be in respect of a separate country.[67] This was confirmed by the 1956 Act, section 36(2)(*b*), which provided that an assignment of copyright might be limited so as to apply to any one or more, but not all, of the countries in relation to which the owner of the copyright had, by virtue of that Act, an exclusive right. The 1988 Act does not contain a similar express provision to that effect and it is submitted that the position as to territory has been changed as regards the territorial divisibility of copyright within the United Kingdom. It is not thought that reliance can be placed on section 172(2) of the 1988 Act to argue that the position remains unchanged. That enacts that a provision of Part I of the 1988 Act which corresponds to a provision of the previous law shall not be construed as departing from the previous law merely because of a change of expression. In the case of the provisions relating to partial assignment there has been more than a "change of expression." The position as to copyright generally in other territories remains the same. The owner of the copyright in, for example, a book or a sound recording, may make territorial arrangements for the distribution of copies and, in this way, prevent the importation for sale into one country of copies of the book or sound recording which have been lawfully made and sold by a different assignee or licensee of the copyright in another country.[68] This practice of territorial assignments and licences has important consequences in relation to the importation provisions of the 1988 Act[69] and is of particular significance in relation to the territories of the European Economic Community.[70]

5–18   **Mode of reproduction.** There is yet a third manner in which copyright may be divided. That is as to the mode of reproduction. Divisibility of mode of reproduction existed under the 1911 Act where the words were very wide, permitting as assignment of the copyright "wholly or partially." Thus, the performing rights, the translation rights, the gramophone rights, the photographic rights, the engraving rights, and so forth, were all capable of separate assignment. It followed, from section 5(3) of the 1911 Act, that the assignee of these separate rights could sue for the infringement of his own particular right without making the assignor a party to his action.

5–19   **Particular purpose.** While, however, the author could, under the 1911 Act, assign separately any one or more of the rights conferred upon him by that Act, it is suggested that a separate assignment of one of these rights, limited to a particular purpose, was not effective to vest title for that particular purpose, though it would have contractual effect. For example, it is

---

[67] See *Holt* v. *Woods* (1896) 17 N.S.W.R. 36; *Pitt Pitts* v. *George & Co.* [1896] 2 Ch. 866.

[68] C.D.P.A. 1988 s.22; *Time-Life International (Nederlands) B.V.* v. *Interstate Parcel Express Co. Pty. Ltd.* [1978] F.S.R. 251 at 274 (High Court of Australia). And see *post*, Chap. 14, *Polydor Ltd.* v. *Harlequin Record Shop Ltd. & Anor.* [1980] 1 C.M.L.R. 669; *CBS United Kingdom Ltd.* v. *Charmdale Record Distributors Ltd.* [1980] F.S.R 289; *The Who Group Ltd.* v. *Stage One (Records) Ltd.* [1980] F.S.R. 268.

[69] See § 9–16, *post*.

[70] See Chap. 14, *post*.

suggested that an assigment of "serial rights" in a work was ineffective to vest a title to "serial rights." The infringement is committed once and for all when the work is printed and, at that stage, it is impossible to know for certain whether printed sheets will be bound up for a single separate publication or for publication in parts over a period. If a grant of "serial rights" were to vest the legal title in the assignee, it would be impossible to know who was the proper plaintiff in an action for infringement by printing. It is suggested that the only effect of a grant of "serial rights," under the 1911 Act, was to give to the grantee a licence to print so long as the printed matter was published in serial form, but to leave the legal title in the copyright vested in the assignor. The same was true, it is suggested, of any other grant of rights limited, not as to mode of reproduction, but as to the purpose for which the material reproduced could be used.

Nevertheless, in the case of *Jonathan Cape Ltd.* v. *Consolidated Press Ltd.*[71] a **5–20** person to whom there had been granted the right to print in "volume form" was held entitled to sue in his own name as assignee. This case principally turned upon the construction of the document there in question. The point of a particular purpose does not seem to have been argued.

The 1988 Act, in dealing with partial assignments of this character, provides that an assignment or other transmission of copyright may be "limited so as to apply to one or more, but not all, of the things the copyright owned has the exclusive right to do."[72] Section 173 of the 1988 Act provides that, where different persons are (whether in consequence of a partial assignment or otherwise) entitled to different aspects of copyright in a work, the copyright owner for any purpose of Part I of the 1988 Act is the person who is entitled to the aspect of copyright relevant for that purpose. This provision is similar in effect to section 49(5) of the 1956 Act. It is likely, in the light of those provisions, that, so far as concerns documents executed after the commencement of the 1956 Act (June 1, 1957), the Court would recognise the right of the grantee of serial or volume rights to be treated as the copyright owner in respect of that right vested in him for that designated purpose and to sue alone. "Serial rights" and "volume rights" are "aspects" of the copyright.

Separate owners of separate rights. The 1988 Act makes it clear, as did **5–21** the 1956 Act,[73] that there will be separate and independent owners of the copyright in respect of the doing of different acts, or different classes of acts, and at different times. Rights of this character can be divided up horizontally and vertically so that different people can own different rights in different countries.[74] Each owner can only sue in respect of those acts which he himself is entitled to control, even though the infringement of some other part of the copyright might commercially damage the owner of the right under the partial assignment. Thus, in *Dicks* v. *Brooks*[75] it was held that the proprietor of the engraving rights in a picture called "The

---

[71] [1954] 1 W.L.R. 1313 and see § 15–17, *post.*
[72] C.D.P.A. 1988, s.90(2)(a).
[73] Copyright Act 1956, s.49(5).
[74] *CBS United Kingdom Ltd.* v. *Charmdale Record Distributors Ltd.* [1980] F.S.R. 289.
[75] (1880) 15 Ch.D. 22.

Huguenot" had no right to bring an action against a defendant who had published a chromo-printed pattern for woolwork copied from the original picture. The assignee of the performing rights in an opera was held not to be entitled to sue in respect of an infringement of the cinematograph rights.[76]

5–22 **Assignment of "copyright."** Having regard to the various derivative rights which flow from ownership of copyright, an assignor of copyright should always take care that the assignment is drawn in such a way as not to carry rights in excess of those intended to be assigned. In the Literary Copyright Act 1842,[77] there were express provisions dealing with this point. It was provided in section 22 that no assignment of any book, consisting of or containing a dramatic piece or musical composition, should, prima facie, be taken to convey to the assignee the performing rights. There were, and are, no similar provisions in the 1911, 1956 or 1988 Acts. An assignment of "copyright" would operate, in the absence of contrary intention, to convey to the assignee all the rights which go to make up copyright.[78]

C. *Reversionary rights*

5–23 Under the 1911 Act, there was a limitation on the power of an author to assign his copyright for longer than 25 years after his death. The limitation applied both to assignments of the whole copyright in a work and also to partial assignments of copyright.[79] The object of this limitation was to protect authors and their heirs from the consequences of an imprudent disposition of their special talent and originality.[80] This limitation, forming the proviso to section 5(2) of the 1911 Act, provided that, where the author was the first owner of the copyright, no assignment of the copyright or grant of any interest therein made by him (otherwise than by will) should be operative to vest in the assignee or grantee any rights with respect to the copyright in the work beyond the expiration of 25 years from the death of the author, and the reversionary interest in the copyright expectant on the determination of that period should, on the death of the author, notwithstanding any agreement to the contrary, devolve on his legal personal representatives as part of his estate, and that any agreement entered into by him as to the disposition of such reversionary interest should be null and void; but that nothing in the proviso should be construed as applying to the assignment of the copyright in a collective work, or to a licence to publish a work or part of a work as part of a collective work.

The proviso was repealed by the 1956 Act, but by paragraph 28(3) of Schedule 7 to the 1956 Act, it was provided that this proviso, as re-enacted

---

[76] *British Actors Film Co. Ltd.* v. *Glover* [1918] 1 K.B. 299.
[77] 5 & 6 Vict. c. 45.
[78] C.D.P.A. 1988, ss.1(1), 2(1); *Cumberland* v. *Planché* (1834) 1 A. & E. 580; *cf. Ex p. Hutchins & Romer* (1879) 4 Q.B.D. 483. See § G–1, *post.*
[79] *Redwood Music Ltd.* v. *Francis Day & Hunter Ltd.* [1978] R.P.C. 429 at 449.
[80] *Redwood Music Ltd.* v. *B. Feldman & Co. Ltd. & Ors.* [1979] R.P.C. 385 at 402; *Chappell & Co. Ltd.* v. *Redwood Music Ltd.* [1981] R.P.C. 337.

in Schedule 8 to that Act, was to apply to assignments and licences having effect with regard to copyright under that Act by the operation of any document made before the commencement of that Act. The position is now governed by paragraph 27 of Schedule 1 to the 1988 Act, which re-enacts the proviso to section 5(2) of the 1911 Act in respect of assignments of the copyright and grants of interests in it made by the author, being the first owner of the copyright, after the passing of the 1911 Act and before June 1, 1957. This means that, unless some further assignment has been made since the commencement of the 1956 Act (June 1, 1957), any relevant assignments or licences made before the commencement of that Act will only operate until the end of the 25 year period. Consequently, while the proviso does not affect post-1957 transactions, even in regard to pre-1957 copyrights, it will continue for many years to affect titles to pre-1957 copyrights which have been the subject of pre-1957 transactions.

Unaffected assignments. It is expressly provided by way of clarification **5–24** in the 1988 Act that nothing in paragraph 27 of Schedule 1 thereto affects three kinds of assignment relating to reversionary interests, namely:

    (a) an assignment of the reversionary interest by a person to whom it has been assigned;

    (b) an assignment of the reversionary interest after the death of the author by his personal representatives or any person becoming entitled to it; or

    (c) any assignment of the copyright after the reversionary interest has fallen in.[81]

It is also provided that the reversionary interest in the copyright expectant on the termination of the 25 year period may, after the commencement of the 1988 Act, be assigned by the author during his life. In the absence of any assignment the reversionary interest devolves on his death on his legal personal representatives as part of his estate.[82]

Proviso only applied if the author was the first owner of the copyright. **5–25** The proviso only applied in a case where the author was the first owner of the copyright. In the case, therefore, of an engraving, photograph, or portrait, where the plate or other original was ordered by some other person and was made for valuable consideration, or in the case of a work made by an author in the employment of some other person under a contract of service or apprenticeship, the proprietor of the copyright was at liberty to assign it for the full term. In neither of these cases did the copyright vest in the author in the first instance.[83]

Arrangements and adaptations. After the copyright in the work had **5–26** been assigned by the first owner, original arrangements or adaptations of the work may have been made by or with the licence of the assignee and given rise to fresh and independent copyrights in the arrangements or

---

[81] C.D.P.A. 1988, Sched. 1, para. 27(3).
[82] *Ibid.* Sched. 1, para. 27(2).
[83] Copyright Act 1911, s.5(1)(a) and (b).

adaptations. These copyrights will be vested in the person who made the arrangements or adaptations or in his employer or assignee. At the end of the 25 year period they do not revert to the author of the original work from which the arrangements or adaptations were made because he was not the first owner of the copyright in them. All that reverts to him is the copyright in the underlying work of which he was the author and first owner. This is the case even with arrangements and adaptations which were made without the licence of the author and first owner after the reversion has taken place. If the author and first owner has accepted royalties earned in respect of the exploitation of the arrangements or adaptations after the reversion has taken place, he will be taken to have impliedly licensed their exploitation and cannot sue for infringement of the copyright which has reverted to him until after he has revoked the licence and even then can only sue for acts which have been committed without his express or implied licence.[84]

5–27 **Proviso did not apply to collective works.** The proviso did not apply "to the *assignment* of the copyright in a collective work or a *licence* to publish a work or part of a work as part of a collective work."[85] In a collective work there may be several distinct copyrights—that is, the copyright in the complete work, considered as a whole, in addition to the various copyrights in the distinct contributions to the work. In the case of a song, there is no copyright in it as an entity; the words and the music each attract separate copyrights. On the other hand, an anthology enjoys a copyright of its own, as a compilation arising out of the original literary effort and judgment involved in the selection and arrangement of the subject-matter of the compilation. The copyright in the compilation is additional to and independent of and different from whatever copyright or copyrights may subsist in the component parts of the compilation. Dispositions of the copyright in the compilation, as distinct from the disposition of copyright in the separate parts, were excepted from the application of the proviso to section 5(2).[86] An "assignment" of the copyright in the compilation could have been made for the full period of copyright, and a "licence" to publish a contribution as part of the collective work could also have been granted for the like full period. But an "assignment" of the copyright in the contribution could not have been made for the period commencing 25 years after the author's death. The expression "the copyright in a collective work" refers only to that "compilation copyright" which exists, if at all, in addition to and apart from any separate copyright which may exist in the constituent parts of the collective work; it does not refer to the copyright in the separate constituent parts. Thus, in the case of a song, assignments of the distinct copyrights in the words and music written by different persons

---

[84] *Redwood Music Ltd.* v. *Chappell & Co. Ltd.* [1982] R.P.C. 109.

[85] A "collective work" meant (a) an encyclopedia, dictionary, year-book, or similar work; (b) a newspaper, review, magazine, or similar periodical; and (c) any work written in distinct parts by different authors, or in which works or parts of works of different authors are incorporated (Copyright Act 1911, s.35(1)). See para. 27(4) and (5) of the 1st Sched. to C.D.P.A. 1988.

[86] *Chappell & Co. Ltd.* v. *Redwood Music Ltd.* [1981] R.P.C. 337; *Redwood Music Ltd.* v. *B. Feldman & Co. Ltd.* [1979] R.P.C. 385; *Redwood Music Ltd.* v. *Chappell & Co. Ltd.* [1982] R.P.C. 109.

were not effective beyond the expiration of 25 years after the death of the respective authors. There is no independent copyright attributable to a song as a compilation and, therefore, nothing to fall within the exception to the proviso. What purports, however, to be an assignment of copyright in a work for use only as part of a collective work might amount to no more than a licence for that purpose and fall within the second half of the exception.[87]

Posthumous works. Inasmuch as it is only the author himself who was   **5–28** prohibited from assigning the entire copyright, the proviso could not apply to works posthumously published if the author was not the assignor, but it could if he was the assignor. Such works were entitled to protection until publication and for a period of 50 years thereafter.[88]

Proviso did apply to existing works, but not to existing assignments.   **5–29** While the proviso applied to works in existence prior to the 1911 Act, it did not apply to assignments made before the date of the passing of that Act (December 16, 1911), or between that date and the date of the commencement of that Act (July 1, 1912).[89] Those assignments were governed by the provisions of section 24 of the 1911 Act. The proviso to section 5(2) of that Act applied, however, to an assignment made by the author after the commencement of that Act in respect of the new copyright conferred by that Act on existing works.[90]

Quaere, as to photographs and mechanical instruments. It is uncer-   **5–30** tain whether the proviso against assignment applied to photographs and mechanical instruments, the copyright in both of which was for a period of 50 years from the date of the making of the negative or plate as the case may be, and vested in the owner of the negative or plate, who was to be "deemed to be the author of the work."[91] The proviso did not form part of the Bill as it was originally laid before the House of Commons, but was drafted and added to the Bill during its passage through the Committee stage. It would almost seem as though the draftsman of the proviso had overlooked the fact that, in the case of some works, the period of copyright protection bore no relation to the lives of their authors. Although the words of the proviso, at first sight, seem wide enough to cover photographs and records, it is suggested that the court is likely to exclude its application to such works. One reason, no doubt, for fixing the period of 25 years from the death of an author as the limit of the assignability of copyright was because, at that date, a work ceased to have exclusive copyright, and any person—including, of course, the assignee of the copyright, who then ceased to have the benefit of his assignment—could have published the work upon a royalty basis.[92] It is, however, doubtful whether a

---

[87] See n. 86 *supra*.
[88] Copyright Act 1911, s.17.
[89] *Coleridge-Taylor* v. *Novello & Co. Ltd.* [1938] Ch. 850.
[90] See n. 86 *supra*.
[91] Copyright Act 1911, ss.19 and 21.
[92] *Ibid.* s.3, proviso, see §§ 296 *et seq.*, *Copinger* (12th ed.). In the case, however, of works existing prior to the 1911 Act, this right did not arise until after 30 years from the death of the author (Copyright Act 1911, s.3). There was thus left a hiatus of five years.

photograph or a record could have been published upon this basis.[93] The assignee of the copyright in a photograph or record, whose author died shortly after the making of the negative or plate, would, therefore, be in an unfair position as compared with an assignee of, say, literary copyright. Another reason for excluding photographs and records from the proviso against assignment is that a corporation could have been deemed to be the "author" of either of these works, and, in such a case, the proviso could have had no possible application. Again, the proviso referred to the interest of the author after the termination of the period of his assignment as "the reversionary interest in the copyright expectant on the termination of that period." If works, as to which the existence of any reversionary period was problematical (for the author of a photograph might live for 25 years after the making of the photograph) were intended to be included, it would have been more in accordance with the rules of good draftsmanship to have added, after the words "reversionary interest," the words "if any."

5-31 **Illusory nature of the benefits conferred by the proviso.** The proviso to section 5(2) of the 1911 Act was inserted in the interest of an author's family, to prevent, if possible, a successful author from making improvident contracts of the fruits of his talent and originality to the detriment of his dependants.[94] In practice the benefits to the author's family or dependants have been somewhat illusory. The proviso rendered null and void any attempt by a living author to dispose of the reversionary interest in his copyright, and declared that this reversionary interest should "on the death of the author," devolve on his legal personal representatives "as part of his estate." This reversionary interest, unassignable during the author's lifetime,[95] therefore became an asset of the author's estate and assignable immediately upon his death by his personal representatives or by a beneficiary after assent.[96] It was consequently liable to be sold by his executors for the payment of his debts, and, even if not required for that purpose, it was frequently the duty of the executors to realise the interest for the purpose of winding up the author's estate.[97] Supposing the author made a specific bequest of his reversionary interest in his copyright, the specific legatee would probably be ready to sell that interest forthwith, rather than wait for a chance of income 25 years later. The only possible purchaser, at any rate in the case of a literary work, would, save in exceptional cases, be the author's publisher, and the amount which he would be prepared to give for a reversionary interest in a copyright falling into possession 25 years later would not be likely to be very large, particularly having regard to the fact that, even if he declined to purchase the reversion, he would be entitled to continue to publish the work, if he thought it

---

[93] See §303 *Copinger* (12th ed.).

[94] *Redwood Music Ltd.* v. *B. Feldman & Co. Ltd. & Ors.* [1979] R.P.C. 385 at 402; *Chappell & Co. Ltd.* v. *Redwood Music Ltd.* [1981] R.P.C. 337 at 344.

[95] It is now assignable, after commencement of the 1988 Act, by the author during his life: para. 27(2) of Sched. 1.

[96] *Chappell & Co. Ltd.* v. *Redwood Music Ltd.* [1981] R.P.C. 337 at 344.

[97] For instance, the rule well known to equity lawyers as the rule in *Howe* v. *Lord Dartmouth* (1802) 7 Ves. 137 a would apply. *cf. Pickering* v. *Evans* [1921] 2 Ch. 309.

worth while to do so, upon payment of a royalty to the owner of the copyright, and that, if he did purchase, he could not acquire an exclusive copyright.[98] Further, in the case of works originating in the United States of America, the descendants of the deceased author often executed assignments in favour of publishers with the primary purpose of transferring to the publishers the renewal rights in the works arising under American law at the expiration of 28 years from the date of first publication. Such agreements may, on their true construction according to the proper law of the agreements, be effective to transfer to the publishers the reversionary copyright arising under English law though there is no necessary implication that they do so when they are executed in the context of American renewal rights.[99]

Recommendation of 1952 Copyright Committee. The 1952 Copyright   **5–32**
Committee recommended that this proviso should not be continued on the ground that they were recommending the omission of the proviso to section 3 of the 1911 Act, which entitled anyone to publish works on compulsory royalty terms at the end of the 25 year period, and considered that the proviso to section 5(2) of that Act must also go, since it would seem to have been inserted so as to give the royalty, under section 3 of that Act, to the personal representatives of the author.[1] These recommendations were carried into effect by the 1956 Act as continued in force and clarified by the 1988 Act.

Summary of law affecting transfers of title. It may be convenient to   **5–33**
summarise the legal effect of documents in the classes of complete assignments and partial assignments.

(1) The transferee under a full or partial assignment can sue for infringement in his own name without adding any other party.
(2) So far as assignments are concerned, the transferee, whether for value or not, acquires a good title as against a later transferee, whether or not the latter had notice of the previous transfer.
(3) However where

    (a) any of the transactions are carried out orally,[2] or
    (b) in the case of an assignment of an existing copyright, the document executed is not in terms a transfer of copyright, but only an agreement to transfer;

the transferee can only proceed to trial if he takes a written assignment of copyright from the legal owner or, in the absence of such an assignment, joins the legal owner of the copyright, either as

---

[98] Copyright Act 1911, s.3.
[99] *Redwood Music Ltd.* v. *B. Feldman & Co. Ltd. & Ors.* [1979] R.P.C. 385 at 403; *Chappell & Co. Ltd.* v. *Redwood Music Ltd.* [1981] R.P.C. 337 at 350.
[1] Cmd. 8662, para. 23.
[2] *e.g. Cooper* v. *Stephens* [1895] 1 Ch. 567; *Dennison* v. *Ashdown* (1897) 13 T.L.R. 226; *Boucas* v. *Cooke* [1903] 2 K.B. 227, 236; *Drabble (Harold) Ltd.* v. *The Hycolite Manufacturing Co.* (1928) 44 T.L.R. 265; *Wah Sang Industrial Co.* v. *Takmay Industrial Co. Ltd.* [1980] F.S.R 303.

plaintiff or defendant,[3] and his title as equitable owner is not binding on an assignee without notice.

D. *Assignment of copyright not bona fide*

5–34   The court will always look behind the legal form to the reality of the transaction. The court will regard an assignment as bogus if, though in proper legal form, it was intended to take effect otherwise than as an assignment in substance and reality.[4] The court will, however, give effect to an assignment which is intended to be in all respects an out and out assignment, even though it was contemplated at the time of the assignment that the assignee would thereby be assisted or enabled to bring proceedings for infringement of the copyright against a third party.[5] If so expressed,[6] an assignment of copyright is effective to transfer to the assignee rights of action accrued to and vested in the assignor in respect of infringements of copyright which have occurred prior to the date of the assignment,[7] but it may be necessary, having regard to section 136 of the Law of Property Act 1925, to give notice of such assignment to the prospective defendant prior to the issue of proceedings.[8]

The question as to the rights of an assignee of copyright to make alterations in the work is treated in another place.[9] Television and broadcasting rights are also dealt with elsewhere.[10]

E. *Transfer of future copyright*

5–35   The 1988 Act contains provisions under which an agreement may be made before a work is created which will have the effect of vesting the copyright initially in the person with whom the agreement is made as soon as the work is created.[11] The provisions are similar in effect to those contained in section 37 of the 1956 Act. They deal only with assignments of future copyright by written agreement, and leave oral assignments of future copyright to be dealt with by applicable rules of equity.[12]

5–36   **Position under the 1911 Act.** The Copyright Act 1911 provided, in section 5(2) and (3), that the owner of the copyright might assign the right, either wholly or partially, and either generally or subject to limitations to

---

[3] *Neilson* v. *Horniman* (1909) 26 T.L.R. 188; *cf. Heap* v. *Hartley* (1889) 42 Ch.D. 461; *Woolley* v. *Broad* [1892] 1 Q.B. 806; *Macmillan & Co. Ltd.* v. *Dent* [1907] 1 Ch. 107; *Marshall (W.) & Co. Ltd.* v. *Bull (A.H.) Ltd.* (1901) 85 L.T. 77. And see §§ 4–67 *ante*, and 11–6 *et seq.*, *post*.
[4] *Landeker & Brown* v. *Woolff (L.)* (1907) 52 S.J. 45.
[5] *Beloff* v. *Pressdram Ltd. & Anor.* [1973] R.P.C. 765.
[6] See n. 5, *ante*.
[7] *In fabrics Ltd. & Ors.* v. *Jaytex Shirt Co. Ltd.* [1978] F.S.R. 451 at 461; *Form Tubes Ltd.* v. *Guinness Bros. plc* [1989] F.S.R. 41 at 43.
[8] *Beloff* v. *Pressdram Ltd. & Anor.*, *supra*; and see *Warner Bros. Records Inc.* v. *Rollgreen Ltd.* [1976] Q.B. 430.
[9] See § 15–6 *post* and Chap. 15, *post*, generally upon the subject of assignment.
[10] See §2–31 *et seq.*, *ante*. §4–58 *et seq.*, *ante*.
[11] *C.D.P.A.* 1988, s.91. See § G–2, *post*, for a precedent for an assignment of future copyright.
[12] *Wah Sang Industrial Co.* v. *Takmay Industrial Co. Ltd.* [1980] F.S.R. 303 (Court of Appeal of Hong Kong).

the United Kingdom or to one of His Majesty's Dominions, and either for the whole term or any part thereof, and might grant an interest in the right by licence; and that, under a partial assignment of copyright, the assignee should be treated for the purposes of that Act as the owner of the copyright in respect of the rights so assigned. Any assignment had to be in writing signed by the owner of the right or his duly authorised agent.

This section had no application to a document purporting to assign the **5–37** copyright in a non-existent work, since a document could not be signed by the owner of the right, and the author became the first owner of the copyright in such a work. Thus, although such a document might be enforced as an equitable assignment,[13] it would not entitle the assignee to sue for final judgment for infringement without joining the author as legal owner.[14] An equitable assignee of copyright is, however, entitled to apply for interlocutory relief without joining the legal owner as a party[15] The equitable assignee would be entitled to call upon the assignor to execute a legal assignment of the copyright to him and would be entitled to enforce his rights to a legal assignment against the assignor.[16] It was suggested, however, that the section might apply to the assignment of equitable rights in existing works.[17] An assignment of the copyright in all works then or thereafter belonging to the assignor was held to be a valid legal assignment in respect of all works of which the copyright was vested in the assignor at the date of the assignment.[18]

In the case of *Macdonald (E.) Ltd.* v. *Eyles*,[19] Petersen J. held that pub- **5–38** lishers who had an option to publish the next three future works of an author upon terms that would have made them owners in equity of the copyrights in the works upon their exercising their option, had a sufficient interest, after the author had written another work, but before they exercised their option, to restrain another publisher, who was aware of all the circumstances, from publishing the new work. The legal owner was a party to the action though a defendant, so that the court was in a position to enforce an equitable title without prejudice to the legal owner.

Position uncertain before the 1911 Act. There is some authority for the **5–39** view that, prior to 1911, there could not be a legal assignment of a work not in existence at the date of the alleged assignment.[20] However, in the case of *Ward, Lock & Co. Ltd.* v. *Long*[21] Kekewich J. held the contrary. In

---

[13] *Leader* v. *Purday* (1848) 7 C.B. 4; *Simms* v. *Marryat* (1851) 17 Q.B. 281; *Tailby (E.)* v. *The Official Receiver* (1888) 13 App. Cas. 523; *Wah Sang Industrial Co.* v. *Takmay Industrial Co. Ltd.* [1980] F.S.R. 303.

[14] *Performing Right Society Ltd.* v. *London Theatre of Varieties Ltd.* [1924] A.C. 1.

[15] *Merchant Adventurers Ltd.* v. *Grew & Co.* [1972] Ch. 242; *Roban Jig & Tool Co. Ltd.* v. *Taylor* [1979] F.S.R. 130 at 135; *Wah Sang Industrial Co.* v. *Takmay Industrial Co. Ltd.* (*supra*).

[16] *Hexagon Pty. Ltd.* v. *Australian Broadcasting Commission* [1976] R.P.C. 628 (Supreme Court of New South Wales).

[17] See n. 14 *ante*.

[18] *Canadian Performing Right Society* v. *Famous Players Canadian Corporation Ltd.* (1927) 60 O.L.R. 280 and 614.

[19] [1921] 1 Ch. 631.

[20] *Colburn* v. *Duncombe* (1838) 9 Sim. 151; *Sweet* v. *Shaw* (1839) 3 Jur. 217.

[21] [1906] 2 Ch. 550.

that case the plaintiffs offered to an author "£200 for the complete copy-right of a story containing not less than 80,000 words," on the lines of a synopsis which had been submitted by the author to the plaintiffs, and this offer was accepted. The story, when written, consisted of only about 70,000 words, and the plaintiffs paid the author the sum of £160, and declined to make any further payment. The author then purported to assign his copyright in the story to the defendants, who published it in ignorance of the author's contract with the plaintiffs. Kekewich J. granted an injunction against the infringement of the plaintiffs' copyright. The decision is unsatisfactory. The Judge seems to have hesitated to say that the letters which had passed between the author and the plaintiffs amounted to an assignment, but "an agreement to assign in matters of this kind is quite as good as a direct assignment in words, is enforceable in equity, and as between businessmen is complete."[22] It is suggested that there is a great deal of difference between a legal and an equitable assign-ment, for the one is enforceable, and the other is not enforceable, against a purchaser for value without notice. If the assignment to the plaintiffs in that case was an equitable assignment only, it is suggested that it was a departure from principle to hold that it held good against the innocent defendants, who appear to have had a legal assignment. The decision was based in some respects, upon the wording of sections 2 and 3 of the Liter-ary Copyright Act 1842,[23] which differs from that contained in the 1911 Act.

5–40 **Transfer of prospective copyright under the 1988 Act.** The 1988 Act, like the 1956 Act before it, contains a method of assigning rights before they come into existence.[24] The 1988 Act defines in section 91(2) "future copyright" as copyright which will or may come into existence in respect of any future work or class of works or on the occurrence of a future event, and provides that "prospective owner" is to be construed accordingly and includes a person who is prospectively entitled to copyright by virtue of such an agreement as is mentioned in section 91(1). That Act then pro-vides, in section 91(1), that where, by an agreement made in relation to any future copyright, and signed by or on behalf of the prospective owner of copyright, the prospective owner purports to assign the future copyright (wholly or partially) to another person, then if, on the copyright coming into existence, the assignee or another person claiming under him would be entitled as against all other persons to require the copyright to be vested in him, the copyright shall vest in the assignee or his successor in title by virtue of the subsection. The expression "entitled as against all other persons" presumably refers to the rules of priority which would have applied apart from that Act, if the prospective owner were claiming in a court of equity specific performance of an agreement to assign the future copyright to him. It may be that, in order to be specifically performable, an assignment of future copyright should always be supported by valuable consideration, even when the assignment is made under seal.[25]

---

[22] *Ibid.*. 557.
[23] 5 & 6 Vict. c. 45.
[24] C.D.P.A. 1988 s.91(1) & (2).Copyright Act 1956 s.37(1).
[25] See *post*, § 16–28. See s.176(1) C.D.P.A. 1988 and n. 53, *post*.

These provisions as to assignment of future copyright do not apply in relation to assignments made before June 1, 1957.[26]

Subsection (2) of section 37 of the 1956 Act dealt with the case where the person who would have been entitled to the copyright had died before the copyright came into existence and provided that the copyright should then devolve as if it had subsisted immediately before his death and he had then been the owner of the copyright. This provision has been repealed, but its repeal does not affect its operation in relation to an agreement made before commencement of the 1988 Act on August 1 1989.[27]

Not limited to one agreement. Section 91 of the 1988 Act contemplates, **5–41** not only a simple agreement between the author and one individual or company, as a result of which the copyright, when it comes into existence, will vest in such individual or company, but also a chain of assignments before the copyright comes into existence. In the latter case the copyright, when it comes into existence, will vest in the person or persons who, as a result of such documents, will then be the person or persons entitled thereto.[28] This result follows from subsection (2) of section 91, which defines "prospective owner" as including a person who is prospectively entitled to copyright by virtue of such an agreement as is mentioned in subsection (1) of that section.

These provisions do not apply in relation to foreign copyrights, so that a confirmatory assignment made after the foreign copyright comes into existence may well be necessary by the law of the country concerned. Therefore such an assignment should include a covenant for further assurance. The general effect on the title to works of transactions effected before the 1988 Act will be more fully considered later in this chapter.[29]

4. Licences

A. *General*

Licences are referred to in various sections of the 1988 Act. By section **5–42** 16(2) of that Act it is provided that copyright is infringed by a person who without the licence of the copyright owner, does or authorises another to do any of the acts restricted by such copyright. Section 90(4) of that Act states on whom licences are binding by providing that a licence granted by the copyright owner is binding on every successor in title to his interest in the copyright, except a purchaser in good faith for valuable consideration and without notice (actual or constructive)[30] of the licence, or a person deriving title from such a purchaser. Section 90(4) continues that references in that Act, to doing anything with, or without, the licence of the copyright owner shall be construed accordingly. By section 91(3) of

---

[26] C.D.P.A. 1988 Para. 26, Sched. 1.
[27] See n. 26.
[28] See *Chaplin* v. *Leslie Frewin (Publishers) Ltd.* [1966] Ch. 71.
[29] *Post,* §5–54 *et seq.*
[30] Law of Property Act 1925 (15 Geo 5. c. 20), s.199.

that Act it is provided that a licence granted by a prospective owner of copyright is binding on every successor in title to his interest (or prospective interest) in the right, except a purchaser in good faith for valuable consideration and without notice (actual or constructive) of the licence or a person deriving title from such a purchaser. References to doing anything with, or without, the licence of the copyright owner are to be construed accordingly.

5–43 **Position of licensee.** The licensee of copyright, or of prospective copyright, therefore, to the extent of the licence, can do acts restricted by the copyright as against the owner and anyone claiming through him, except a purchaser for value without notice. Except in connection with exclusive licences, there is no requirement that a licence shall be in writing. It can, therefore, be either oral, or implied from conduct, such as the payment and acceptance of royalties or other sums in respect of the exploitation of the copyright,[31] or from trade practice or custom.[32] A licence will not be implied merely because it would be reasonable between the parties: the test is whether it is necessary to give effect to the intention of the parties and to give business efficacy to their relationships.[33] The test of an implied licence is an objective one.[34] For example, if the owner of a building plot employs an architect to prepare plans for a house on that site, there might be an implied promise by the architect that, in return for his fee, he will grant a licence to the owner to use the plans for the building on that site. The implied licence may extend so as to enable a builder or another architect, employed by the owner, to make copies of the plans and to use them for that very building on that site, but for no other purpose. The implied licence may also extend to the purchaser of the site.[35] But a licence which amounts merely to a consent does not confer any interest in the right.[36] As it was put by Tindal C.J. in *Muskett* v. *Hill*[37] a dispensation or licence properly passes no interest, but only makes an action lawful which, without it, would have been unlawful."[38] Clearly, a licence which is not sole and exclusive cannot pass any interest in the right, since if it did, nothing

---

[31] *Redwood Music Ltd.* v. *Francis Day & Hunter Ltd.* [1978] R.P.C. 429; *Redwood Music Ltd.* v. *Chappell & Co. Ltd.* [1982] R.P.C. 109, *Time-Life International (Nederlands) B.V.* v. *Interstate Parcel Express Co. Pty. Ltd.* [1978] F.S.R. 251 at 270 (High Court of Australia): *Catnic Components & Anor.* v. *Hill and Smith Ltd.* [1978] F.S.R. 405; on appeal [1979] F.S.R. 619 (implied licence covering use made on expiry of patent of drawings forming part of specification); *Solar Thomson Engineering Co. Ltd.* v. *Barton* [1977] R.P.C. 537 (patent—implied licence to repair); *British Leyland Motor Corp. Ltd.* v. *Armstrong Patents Co. Ltd.* [1986] A.C. 577 at 623 (spare parts for car repairs); *Ironside* v. *H.M. Attorney-General* [1988] R.P.C. 197 (licence implied from payment of fee by Royal Mint for design of coin); *Heptulla* v. *Orient Longman Ltd.* [1989] F.S.R. 598 at 612 (High Court of Delhi): *Bailey* v. *Boccaccio* [1986] 4 NSWLR 701 (Artistic work for trade mark) see also § 8–147 *et seq., post*.

[32] *Express Newspapers plc* v. *News (U.K.) Ltd.* [1990] F.S.R. 359 at 368.

[33] *Shell U.K. Ltd.* v. *Lostock Garage Ltd.* [1976] 1 W.L.R. 1187 at 1197, 1200; *Sport International Bossum B.V.* v. *Hi-.Tec Sports Ltd.* [1988] R.P.C. 329.

[34] *Redwood Music Ltd.* v. *Chappell & Co. Ltd.* [1982] R.P.C. 109 at 128.

[35] *Blair* v. *Osborne & Tomkins* [1971] 2 Q.B. 78 at 85; *cf. Stovin Bradford* v. *Volpoint Properties Ltd.* [1971] Ch. 1007.

[36] See *Neilson* v. *Horniman* [1905–10] Mac.C.C. 234.

[37] (1840) 5 Bing.N.C. 694.

[38] See *Frisby* v. *B.B.C.* [1967] Ch. 932 at 948; *Street* v. *Mountford* [1985] A.C. 809 at 816.

would remain in the grantor out of which to grant subsequent licences,[39] A licence may be personal to the licensee, unless the circumstances of the granting of the licence and the terms of the licence justify the conclusion that it was intended to be assignable. A licence is not assignable where it appears that the licence was granted to the licensee because of his personal reputation.[40] A licence, if coupled with an interest in the right, would seem to be irrevocable.[41] A revocable licence may be revoked in accordance with its express terms, or, in the absence of an express term, on reasonable notice. The notice must purport to revoke the licence and not, for example, simply propose terms for its continuance.[42] If the licensor purports to revoke a revocable licence, but gives no notice or insufficient notice of revocation, the licensee cannot ignore the revocation and treat the licence as subsisting. On the other hand, the licensee cannot be treated as a wrongdoer for continuing to do what the licence permitted him to do until the expiry of the period which would have constituted reasonable notice.[43] A letter which is in fact a repudiation of a licence agreement does not constitute a notice to terminate the agreement pursuant to an express or implied term of the agreement.[44] Where there is a dispute as to title, the person revoking the licence should be in a position to produce proof of his title to the copyright before he can effectively revoke the licence.[45]

B. *Exclusive licences*

Right of exclusive licensee to sue under the 1911 Act. Before 1956, **5–44** the position of an exclusive licensee was somewhat doubtful as it had never been clearly decided whether or not he could sue in his own name. Having regard to the provisions of paragraph 25 of Schedule 1 to the 1988 Act, the operation of documents made before the commencement of the 1988 Act is still material. It may therefore still be necessary to consider the meaning of the expression "grant of any interest" in section 5(2) of the 1911 Act. One view of the matter was that these words conferred a legal interest in the right which would give the licensee an indefeasible title and enable him to sue in respect of infringements in his own name. The point was left open in the case of *British Actors Film Co. Ltd.* v. *Glover*[46] and in the case of *Jonathan Cape Ltd.* v. *Consolidated Press Ltd.*,[47] and has been debated since the 1911 Act was passed.

---

[39] *Warne* v. *Routledge* (1874) L.R. 18 Eq. 497; *Rundell* v. *Murray* (1821) Jac. 311; *Chaplin* v. *Leslie Frewin (Publishers) Ltd.* [1966] Ch. 71.
[40] *Dorling* v. *Honnor Marine Ltd.* [1964] Ch. 560 at 568. See § 15–10 *et seq., post.*
[41] *Hurst* v. *Picture Theatres Ltd.* [1915] 1 K.B. 1; *British Actors Film Co. Ltd.* v. *Glover* [1918] 1 K.B. 299; *Hart* v. *Hayman, etc., Ltd.* [1911–16] Mac.C.C.301; *Williams* v. *Feldman* [1911–16] Mac.C.C. 98; *Chaplin* v. *Leslie Frewin (Publishers) Ltd.* [1966] Ch. 71. See as to irrevocability of licences not coupled with an interest, *Hounslow London Borough Council* v. *Twickenham Garden Developments Ltd.* [1971] Ch. 233.
[42] *Redwood Music Ltd.* v. *Chappell & Co. Ltd.* [1982] R.P.C. 109.
[43] *Dorling* v. *Honnor Marine Ltd.* [1964] Ch. 560 at 567; *Martin-Baker Aircraft Co. Ltd.* v. *Canadian Flight Equipment Ltd.* [1955] 2 Q.B. 556.
[44] *Decro-Wall S.A.* v. *Marketing Ltd.* [1971] 1 W.L.R. 361 at 382.
[45] *Redwood Music Ltd.* v. *Chappell & Co. Ltd.* [1982] R.P.C. 109.
[46] [1918] 1 K.B. 299.
[47] [1954] 1 W.L.R. 1313; but see *Kinekor Film (Pty.) Ltd.* v. *Movie Time* [1976] I.S.A. 649.

As an argument against the grantee being able to sue, it is to be noted that, while there was an express provision that the assignee under a partial assignment was to be treated as the owner of such part, there was no similar provision with regard to a grantee by way of licence. It is thought, however, that the legislature inserted the provision with regard to a grantee by way of licence to cover the case of a transfer which was, in substance, a partial assignment, but, in form, was expressed as a licence, and might be difficult to construe as an assignment,[48] and that the real effect of this provision was to make it easier to construe a document as a partial assignment though, in form, expressed as a licence,[49] while leaving unaffected the law relating to documents which were, of necessity, licences only in the narrower sense, because they were not exclusive, or purported to deal with rights which were not susceptible of separate assignment.[50]

5-45   **And under the 1956 Act.** Section 19 of the 1956 Act, however, gave an exclusive licensee, as defined in that section, the right to sue in his own name.[51] This was only a right as against persons claiming no title through the copyright owner, and did not put an exclusive licensee in any stronger position than any other licensee as against persons claiming through the legal owner of the copyright. This followed from section 19(4) of the 1956 Act, which provided that, in any action brought by the exclusive licensee, any defence which would have been available to a defendant in the action if that section had not been enacted and the action had been brought by the owner of the copyright, should be available to that defendant as against the exclusive licensee. The rights of the exclusive licensee are contractual and not proprietary. The provisions of section 19 were purely procedural, entitling the exclusive licensee to enforce the proprietary rights of the copyright owner. The exclusive licensee was not, however, himself the owner of the copyright, was not treated as such owner (otherwise than for procedural purposes) and was not entitled to the copyright.[52] It would appear, therefore, that if the owner of the copyright granted a later licence in breach of his obligations to the exclusive licensee, the later licensee would have been protected in proceedings for infringement of copyright by anybody, since he could have relied upon his licence in an action brought by the owner of the copyright. In such a case the remedy of the exclusive licensee would appear to have been in damages only against the owner of the copyright, and possibly an injunction to restrain him granting further licences.

5-46   **Under the 1988 Act.** "Exclusive licence" is defined by section 92(1) of the 1988 Act as a licence in writing, signed by or on behalf of the copyright owner authorising the licensee to the exclusion of all other persons, including the person granting the licence, to exercise a right which would other-

---

[48] *e.g. Re Jude's Musical Compositions* [1907] 1 Ch. 651; see also *Withers* v. *Nethersole* [1946] 1 All E.R. 711; [1948] 1 All E.R. 400.

[49] *Messager* v. *British Broadcasting Co. Ltd.* [1929] A.C. 151.

[50] See *ante*, § 5–17.

[51] The section did not apply to a licence granted before the commencement of the 1956 Act (Copyright Act 1956, Sched. 7, para. 22).

[52] *CBS United Kingdom Ltd.* v. *Charmdale Record Distributors Ltd.* [1980] F.S.R. 289.

wise be exercisable exclusively by the copyright owner. The licensee under an exclusive licence has the same rights as against a sucessor in title, who is bound by the licence as he has against the person granting the licence.[53]

Rights of exclusive licensee. The main operative part of section 101(1)   **5–47**
of the 1988 Act provides that the exclusive licensee has, except against the copyright owner, the same rights and remedies in respect of matters occurring after the grant of the licence as if the licence had been an assignment. Such rights and remedies are concurrent with the rights and remedies of the copyright owner, and references to the copyright owner are to be construed accordingly.[54] The rights of the exclusive licensee against the owner of the copyright lie in contract only and may, of course, be defeated by a purchaser for value of the copyright without notice.[55]

Where necessary to join owner of copyright as party. It is further pro-   **5–48**
vided by the 1988 Act that, where an action for infringement of copyright brought by the copyright owner or an exclusive licensee relates to an infringement in respect of which they have concurrent rights of action, the copyright owner or, as the case may be, the exclusive licensee may not, without the leave of the court, proceed with the action unless the other is either joined as a plaintiff or added as a defendant.[56] The importance of this provision is that the exclusive licensee may proceed in the absence of the owner of the copyright with the leave of the court, and this may be a great convenience where the owner of the copyright is dead and no grant has been taken to his estate or he cannot be found or is otherwise unavailable.[57] The 1988 Act further provides that, the copyright owner or exclusive licensee who is added as a defendant, is not liable for any costs in the action, unless he takes part in the proceedings,[58] It is further provided that these provisions do not affect the granting of interlocutory relief on an application by a copyright owner or exclusive licensee alone.[59]

Special provisions as to damages, and account of profits. Special pro-   **5–49**
vision is made for the assessment of damages and account of profits in cases where an action for infringement of copyright is brought which relates (wholly or partly) to an infringement in respect of which the copyright owner and an exclusive licensee have or had concurrent rights of action. These provisions apply whether or not the copyright owner and the exclusive licensee are both parties to the action.

(1) *Damages.* In such cases the court, in assessing damages, must take into

---

[53] C.D.P.A. 1988, s.92(2) and see s.176(1) C.D.P.A. 1988 and n. 25, *ante.*
[54] *Ibid.* s.101(2).
[55] *Ibid.* s.90(4).
[56] *Ibid..* s.102(1); see *Warwick Film Productions Ltd.* v. *Eisinger* [1963] 1 W.L.R. 756. R.S.C., Order 52, r. 19, which dealt specifically with applications, under s.19(3) of the 1956 Act, for leave to proceed with an action without joining the other party as a plaintiff or adding him as a defendant, has not been repeated in the revised Rules. However, no doubt the procedure under the old Order 52, r. 19, namely, by summons in the action, will still be the appropriate method of making such an application.
[57] *Bodley Head Ltd.* v. *Flegon* [1972] R.P.C. 587.
[58] C.D.P.A. 1988, s.102(2).
[59] *Ibid.*, s.102(3).

account the terms of the licensee and any pecuniary remedy already awarded or available to either the copyright owner or the exclusive licensee in respect of the infringement.

(2) *Account of profits.* No account of profits shall be directed if an award of damages has been made, or an account of profits has been directed, in favour of the other of them in respect of the infringement.

If an account of profits is directed the court must apportion the profits between the copyright owner and the exclusive licensee as the court considers just, subject to any agreement between them.

(3) *Delivery up and right of seizure.* Special provision is also made for applying for delivery up orders and for the exercise of the right of seizure of infringing copies. The copyright owner is under an obligation to notify any exclusive licensee having concurrent rights before applying for a delivery up order or exercising the right of seizure of infringing copies. The court may on the application of the licensee make such order for delivery up or, as the case may be, prohibiting or permitting the exercise by the copyright owner of the right of seizure, as it thinks fit having regard to the terms of the licence.

C. *Construction of licences*

5–50 **Whether assignable.** A licence may be assignable, save where the licensee was chosen on account of his personal skill or reputation.[60]

5–51 **Sound films and television.** Questions may arise on the construction of the rights licensed where, after the date of the licence, there have been technological developments in modes of reproduction and exploitation which were not known to the parties at the time of the license. It was held in *Pathé Pictures Ltd.* v. *Bancroft,*[61] that a licence to produce a work " in moving picture films" does not authorise the production of a sound film of the work, but it was stated by Swift J., in the same case, that "cinematograph films" would include sound films, and "cinematograph rights" would include the right to reproduce by means of a sound film.

5–52 A similar question arose in the Australian case of *Williamson (J. C.) Ltd.* v. *M.G.M. Theatres Ltd.,*[62] and it was decided that a reservation of motion picture rights included sound films, on the ground that, at the date of agreement, the use of sound films commercially was "threatened," so that the parties must have contracted with this in view. It is thought, however, that in documents executed before the commercial use of sound films was contemplated, "cinematograph" or "moving picture" rights must be taken to be confined to the right to make contrivances for the visual per-

---

[60] *Re Jude's Musical Compositions* [1907] 1 Ch. 651; *Stevens* v. *Benning* (1855) 1 K. & J. 168; *Hole* v. *Bradbury* (1879) 12 Ch.D. 886; *Griffith* v. *Tower Publishing Co. Ltd.* [1897] 1 Ch. 21. See *Messager* v. *British Broadcasting Co. Ltd.* [1927] 2 K.B. 543, reversed on other grounds [1929] A.C. 151; *Dorling* v. *Honnor Marine Ltd.* [1964] Ch. 560 at 568. See §§ 15–10 *et seq., post.*
[61] [1928–35] Mac.C.C. 403.
[62] [1937] V.L.R. 140; (1937) 56 C.L.R. 567.

formance of the work, and not to comprise the quite distinct right to make contrivances for the audible performance thereof.

Support for this view is to be found in the decision of Buckley J. in *Hospital for Sick Children* v. *Walt Disney Productions Inc.*,[63] when he held that the grant, by Sir James Barrie, in an agreement made in 1919, of a licence to produce all his literary and dramatic works, for the term of their respective copyrights, "in cinematograph or moving picture films" was only effective to grant silent film rights and not sound film rights also. It was held that the proper construction of the relevant agreement depended upon what was then properly to be regarded as being in the contemplation of the parties. No help was to be gained from the use of the words "cinematograph" as well as "moving pictures" for if, at the date such agreement was entered into, the only kind of cinematograph or moving picture films that were known as being commercial propositions, or likely to become commercial propositions, within the period contemplated by the agreement, were silent films, it was impossible to conclude that, by using the word "cinematograph," the parties intended to refer to something other than the production of silent films.

However, in a limited appeal from the decision of Buckley J.,[64] Lord Denning M. R. said that the decisions in *L. C. Page & Co.* v. *Fox Film Corporation*[65] and *Williamson (J. C.) Ltd.* v. *M.G.M. Theatres Ltd.*[66] showed that, even before sound films were a commercial proposition, a grant of moving picture film rights was capable of carrying the right to make, not only a silent film, but also a sound film. The provisions of the 1919 agreement did not, however, comprehend sound films. That agreement was made in 1919 when sound films were very remote. Neither of the parties had them in mind. Harman L.J. considered that, to construe a document rightly, the court must seek, not merely what it thinks to be the intention of the parties; it must seek that intention in the words the parties have used. The words used in the 1919 Agreement were wide enough to cover talking films with living actors and, without coming to a concluded opinion, Harman L.J. thought that Buckley J. took too narrow a view, and that the better opinion would accord with the decision in the case of *Williamson* v. *M.G.M. Theatres.*[67] Salmon L.J. considered that the words of the 1919 Agreement were capable of passing, and would normally pass, the talking picture rights, even though commercial talking pictures were not in existence, and therefore not in the minds of the parties to the contract, at the time it was written. However, he went on to say that, although the words of the 1919 Agreement themselves were wide enough to cover sound films, taking the Agreement as a whole they applied only to silent films, he preferred to express no concluded opinion on this question.

A similar question could arise as to whether a licence to broadcast

---

[63] [1966] 1 W.L.R. 1055; and see *Serra* v. *Famous-Lasky Film Service Ltd.* (1922) 127 L.T. 109; *Messager* v. *British Broadcasting Co.* [1927] 2 K.B. 543; *Ricordi* v. *Paramount Pictures Inc.* (1950) 92 Fed.Supp. 537; *Rosenberg and Lesser* v. *Wright* (1934) 20 Copyright Decisions 599; *Murphy* v. *Warner Bros. Theatres* (1940) 112 Fed.Rep. 2d 634.

[64] [1968] Ch. 52.

[65] (1936) 83 Fed.Rep. 2d 196.

[66] See n. 62, *ante.*

[67] See n. 62 *ante.*

included a right to broadcast by television and as to whether a licence in respect of films made before the invention of video tapes, included the video rights.

Distinction between assignment and licence

5–53 The differences between assignments and licences are discussed at greater length elsewhere in this work.[68]

5. Transitional Provisions

A. *General principles*

5–54 Dealings in copyright are affected by provisions for securing the continuity of the law so far as the new copyright provisions (*i.e.* the provisions of the 1988 Act relating to copyright)[69] re-enact (with or without modification) earlier provisions. The following general principles are laid down:

(1) A reference in an enactment, instrument or other document to copyright, or to a work or other subject matter in which copyright subsists, which apart from the 1988 Act would be construed as referring to copyright under the 1956 Act, is to be construed, so far as may be required for continuing its effect, as being, or as the case may require, including, a reference to copyright under the 1988 Act or to works in which copyright subsists under that Act.[70]

(2) Anything done, or having effect as done, under or for the purposes of a provision repealed by the 1988 Act has effect as if done under or for the purposes of the corresponding provision of the new copyright provisions.[71]

(3) References (expressed or implied) in the 1988 Act or any other enactment, instrument or document to any of the new copyright provisions is, so far as the context permits, to be construed as including, in relation to times, circumstances and purposes before commencement, a reference to corresponding earlier provisions.[72]

(4) A reference (express or implied) in an enactment, instrument or other document to a provision repealed by the 1988 Act is to be construed, so far as may be required for continuing its effect, as a reference to the corresponding provision of that Act.[73]

There general principles have effect subject to any specific transitional provision or saving and to any express amendment made by the 1988 Act.[74]

---

[68] See §15–4 *et seq., post.*
[69] C.D.P.A. 1988 Sched. 1. para. 1(1).
[70] *Ibid.* Sched. 1, para. 4(2).
[71] *Ibid.* Sched. 1, para. 4(3).
[72] *Ibid.* Sched. 1, para. 4(4).
[73] *Ibid.* Sched. 1, para. 4(5).
[74] *Ibid.* Sched. 1, para. 4(6).

B. *Assignments and licences*

Title to existing works is governed by a number of specific provisions.

(i) Operation of pre-commencement documents and events

Any document made or event occurring before commencement which had   **5–55**
any operation affecting the ownership of the copyright in an existing work
or creating, transferring or terminating an interest, right or licence in
respect of the copyright in an existing work, has the corresponding operation in relation to copyright in the work under the 1988 Act.[75]

(ii) Construction of pre-commencement documents

Expressions used in such documents are to be construed in accordance   **5–56**
with their effect immediately before commencement.[76]
 The general effect of these provisions is that one should first construe
any assignment or licence effected before the commencement of the 1988
Act. Having done that, the title to the copyright conferred by the 1988 Act
will vest as it would have vested had the 1956 Act continued in force.

C. *Special cases*

Although the provisions of Schedule 1 to the 1988 Act apply in general to   **5–57**
all existing works (*i.e.* works made before commencement of the 1988 Act)
including works in existence at the commencement of the 1911 Act or the
1956 Act, there are modifications in special cases in the application of certain provisions of the 1988 Act to title to existing works.

(i) Assignment of future copyright

Section 91(1) of the 1988 Act, dealing with the assignment of future copy-   **5–58**
right and the statutory vesting of the legal interest on the copyright coming into existence, does not apply in relation to an agreement made before
June 1, 1957.[77] Further, the repeal by the 1988 Act of section 37(2) of
the 1956 Act, dealing with the devolution of future copyright where the
assignee dies before copyright comes into existence, does not affect the
operation of that provision in relation to an agreement made before commencement (August 1, 1989).[78]

(ii) Reversionary rights

The position in relation to reversionary rights has already been dis-   **5–59**
cussed.[79]

---

[75] *Ibid.* Sched. 1, para. 25(1).
[76] *Ibid.* Sched. 1, para. 25(2).
[77] *Ibid.* Sched. 1, para. 26(1): see §5–35 *et seq., ante.*
[78] *Ibid.* Sched. 1, para. 26(2).
[79] *Ibid.* Sched. 1, para. 27; See §5–23 *et seq., ante.*

(iii) Rights of exclusive licensees

5–60   Section 92(2) of the 1988 Act, dealing with the rights of an exclusive licensee against successors in title of a person granting the licence, does not apply in relation to an exclusive licence granted before commencement.[80]

(iv) Bequests

5–61   The position in relation to bequests of manuscripts and other material things embodying an unpublished work in cases where the testator died before June 1, 1957, or after that date and before commencement of the 1988 Act, has already been discussed.[81]

(v) Section 24 of the 1911 Act

5–62   Special provision is made for the case of assignments or grants of copyright by the author before the commencement of the 1911 Act.[82]

5–63   The term of copyright under the 1911 Act was, in general, longer than that subsisting under the pre-existing law. The 1911 Act accordingly, contained provisions under which assignments or licences subsisting at the commencement of that Act should determine when the old period of copyright ran out, and the 1911 copyright thereafter revested in the author or his personal representatives. The assignee or licensee was given certain options to be exercised when the old term of copyright expired.[83] The 1956 Act sought, in a series of complicated provisions, to maintain the respective rights of interested parties. It is necessary, first, to examine the nature of the provisions in this respect of section 24 of the 1911 Act and then to inquire how far these were affected by the 1956 Act and how far the position is changed by the 1988 Act.

5–64   **The revesting proviso.** Proviso (*a*) to section 24(1) of the 1911 Act was as follows: "if the author of any work in which any such right as is specified in the first column of Schedule 1 to this Act subsists at the commencement of this Act has, before that date, assigned the right or granted any interest therein for the whole term of the right, then at the date when, but for the passing of this Act, the right would have expired the substituted right conferred by this section shall, in the absence of express agreement, pass to the author of the work, and any interest therein created before the commencement of this Act and then subsisting shall determine; . . ."

5–65   **Express agreement.** This proviso provided for old copyright which had been assigned before the commencement of the 1911 Act (July 1, 1912), for the whole term and which was still owned by the assignee at that date because the term of copyright had not yet expired. At the date when the

---

[80] *Ibid.* Sched. 1, para. 29; See §5–46, *ante.*
[81] *Ibid.* Sched. 1, para. 30; See §5–4 *ante.*
[82] *Ibid.* Sched. 1, para. 28.
[83] Copyright Act 1911, s.24.

old copyright would have expired the extended period of copyright conferred by the 1911 Act was not to benefit the assignee, but to pass, "in the absence of express agreement," to the author who had assigned it or to his legal personal representatives subject to certain options exercisable by the assignee. The intention was to preserve the extended copyright for the authors of existing works. The words "in the absence of express agreement" mean "in the absence of an agreement expressly referring to the substituted right indentified as such."[84] It follows that these words cannot refer to an agreement made before the passing of the 1911 Act, however widely such an agreement was drawn in its references to copyright, "present or future, vested or contingent." The substituted right must be identified as the subject of the agreement, in terms clearly naming the right. The agreement must therefore be one made, either between the passing of the 1911 Act and the commencement of that Act, or after the commencement of that Act.

Partial assignment. The above provision only applied to the case of an **5–66**
assignment or grant of an interest covering the whole term of copyright. If the author had parted with his copyright for a period less than the whole original term, he would have a reversionary interest which would automatically confer upon him, by virtue of the earlier provisions of the section, the substituted right, which would become exercisable by him upon the falling in of his reversion. If, however, the author had granted a licence to one person for a portion of the old term, and then to another for the residue of that term, it is conceived that he would have granted an "interest" in his copyright "for the whole term" within the meaning of the proviso.

Assignment by a person other than the author. It is, however, import- **5–67**
ant to observe that the proviso only applied to a case where the assignment or licence has been made or granted by "the author" of the work. If, in any case, the copyright vested in the first instance in any person other than the author,[85] then an assignment or licence by such person prima facie passed to the assignee or licensee the benefit of the extended term conferred by the 1911 Act.

Rights of assignee notwithstanding revesting. Although the benefit of **5–68**
any extended term of copyright conferred by the 1911 Act prima facie vested in the original author of the work, and not in his assignee or licensee, it would have been unfair to deprive the assignee or licensee of the right to reap any advantage from the market which he had created. It often happens that the publisher, to whom the copyright belonged during the period of its existence, still retains an advantage over his trade competitors after the period of copyright protection has ceased. The 1911 Act recognised this by providing[86] that the person who, immediately before the date when the copyright would have expired under the repealed stat-

---

[84] *Chappell & Co. Ltd.* v. *Redwood Music Ltd.* [1981] R.P.C. 337.
[85] For example, in the case of collective works (*ante*, §5–27 *et seq*). In the case of collective works, the right of the author to publish his article separately after 28 years (Copyright Act 1842 (5 & 6 Vict. c. 45) was expressly reserved by the note to Sched. 1 to the 1911 Act.
[86] s.24 Copyright Act 1911.

utes, was the owner of any right or interest in the copyright, is to be entitled at his option either:

"(i) on giving such notice as hereinafter mentioned, to an assignment of the right or the grant of a similar interest therein for the remainder of the term of the right for such consideration as, failing agreement, may be determined by arbitration; or

(ii) without any such assignment or grant, to continue to reproduce or perform the work in like manner as theretofore subject to the payment, if demanded by the author within three years after the date at which the right would have so expired, of such royalties to the author as, failing agreement, may be determined by arbitration, or, where the work is incorporated in a collective work and the owner of the right or interest is the proprietor of that collective work, without any such payment."

The notice referred to had to be given not more than one year, nor less than six months, before the date at which the right would have so expired, and to be sent by registered post to the "author,"[87] or, if he could not with reasonable diligence be found, advertised in the *London Gazette* and in two London newspapers.[88]

5–69   **First option.** It is submitted that the true construction of the first option given was that a person, who had obtained an assignment of the old term copyright, was entitled to an assignment of the right, but not to the grant of a licence, and, vice versa, that a person who had obtained a licence for the whole of the old term, was entitled to a "similar" licence for the residue of the new term, but not to an assignment of the right.

5–70   **Second option.** If the assignee elected to adopt the second option given him by the proviso, he was not required to give any notice to the proprietor of the copyright, who forfeited any right to royalties if he failed to demand them within three years after the date when the old copyright would have expired. It was held, by the Court of Appeal,[89] that the effect of the second option was to give to the former assignee a non-exclusive licence to continue to exercise the same rights as he had previously enjoyed exclusively.

5–71   **Sale of stock on hand.** The point arises as to whether, if the assignee elects to take neither of the options conferred upon him by proviso (*a*), he is at liberty to sell any stock remaining on hand without any payment to the author or his personal representatives. It would seem that he can, since it is thought that there are no provisions under which a sale of copies, lawfully made, constitutes an infringement, except, possibly, the provisions relating to the publishing of the work.[90]

---

[87] This expression includes his personal representatives; Copyright Act 1911, s.24(2).

[88] The giving of this notice presumably bound the person giving it to purchase the right or interest. It is not clear how the assignment or grant, as the case may be, was to be obtained if the author or his personal representatives could not be found. The person giving the notice, however, would obtain an equitable title.

[89] *Loew's Inc.* v. *Littler* [1958] Ch. 650.

[90] *Infrabics Ltd.* v. *Jaytex Ltd.* [1982] A.C. 1. §8–92 and *post*, §15–37 *post*.

Collective works. It was provided by proviso (*a*)(ii) to section 24(1) of **5–72** the 1911 Act, that where a work, the copyright in which was assigned before the commencement of that Act was incorporated in a collective work, and the owner of the assigned right or interest was the proprietor of that collective work, such proprietor was to be entitled, during the extended term of copyright, to continue to reproduce the work without any payment to the author or his personal representatives. He could, however, only reproduce "in like manner as theretofore," so that he could not reproduce, without payment, an article contributed to the collective work, except as part of that collective work. Under section 18 of the Literary Copyright Act 1842[91] it often happened that the copyright of an article contributed to a collective work vested, *ab initio*, in the proprietor of the work.[92] In that case there would have been no assignment by "the author," and therefore proviso (*a*), to section 24(1), had no application. The extended term of copyright would belong to the proprietor of the collective work, subject to the concurrent right of the author, if the collective work was of a periodical nature—not otherwise—to publish his article in "separate form" when 28 years had elapsed since the original publication.[93] If however, either because the author expressly reserved the copyright in his article, or for any other reason, the copyright did not originally vest in the proprietor of the collective work, but became the property of the author, then, notwithstanding any subsequent assignment or grant of a licence to publish during the whole period of the old copyright made or given by him, the benefit of the extended term would belong to the author or his personal representatives, but the proprietor of the collective work would have the right, as against the author or his representatives, to continue to publish the article "in like manner as theretofore" without payment.

Provisions of the 1956 Act. As from the commencement of the 1956 Act, **5–73** two classes of cases had to be considered, namely (a) cases in which the pre-1911 copyright had already expired, and, (b) cases in which the pre-1911 copyright had not expired. It may be pointed out that, while the period of 42 years from first publication must have already expired in the case of works published before 1911, the alternative period of 7 years from the death of the author might well subsist in some cases.

Where the pre-1911 copyright term had already expired. Dealing **5–74** first with cases in which the pre-1911 copyright term had already expired before the commencement of the 1956 Act, it was provided in paragraph 38(2) of Schedule 7 to that Act that, if before its commencement, any event had occurred or notice had been given which in accordance with paragraph (*a*) of the proviso to subsection (1) of section 24 of the 1911 Act had had any operation affecting the ownership of the right conferred by the 1911 Act in relation to the work, or creating, transferring or terminating an interest, right or licence in respect of that right, that event or notice

---

[91] *Ante*, §5–27 *et seq.* As to collective works, see *Chappell & Co. Ltd.* v. *Redwood Music Ltd.* [1981] R.P.C. 337.
[92] *Lawrence, etc., Ltd.* v. *Aflalo* [1904] A.C. 17.
[93] See note to Sched. 1 to the 1911 Act.

was to have the corresponding operation in relation to the copyright in the work under the 1956 Act. Under that provision, therefore, where the copyright under the 1911 Act had revested in the author or his personal representatives under the proviso, the copyright under the 1956 Act revested also, and the operation of any notice given under the first option was also preserved. It was further provided that any right which, at a time after the commencement of the 1956 Act, would, by virtue of paragraph (*a*) of the said proviso to section 24 of the 1911 Act, have been exercisable in relation to the work or to the right conferred by the 1911 Act, if the 1956 Act had not been passed, should be exercisable in relation to the work, or to the copyright therein under the 1956 Act, as the case might be.[94] This would appear to have preserved the right conferred upon the assignee under the second option.

5–75   **Where the pre-1911 copyright term had not expired.** As to the case in which the old term did not expire until after the commencement of the 1956 Act, it was provided that if, in accordance with paragraph (*a*) of the said proviso, the right conferred by the 1911 Act would have reverted to the author or his personal representatives on the date referred to in that paragraph, and the said date fell after the commencement of the 1956 Act, then on that date (a) the copyright in the work under the 1956 Act was to revert to the author or his personal representatives as the case might be and, (b) any interest of any other person in that copyright which subsisted on that date, by virtue of any document made before the commencement of the 1911 Act, was thereupon to determine.[95] It will be observed that this provision did not deal with the options given to the prior assignee. It is thought, however, that the provision above-mentioned, under which any right which after the commencement of the 1956 Act would have been exercisable if the 1956 Act had not been passed, was to be exercisable in relation to the copyright under the 1956 Act, was wide enough, not only to include the second option in respect of works which had reverted before the commencement of the 1956 Act, but also the rights conferred by both options, upon the original assignee, where the pre-1911 term expired after the commencement of the 1956 Act.

5–76   **Provisions of the 1988 Act.** The 1988 Act makes provision for the case where copyright subsists in a literary, dramatic, musical or artistic work made before July 1, 1912 and where the author, in relation to that copyright, had, before the commencement of the 1911 Act, made such an assignment or grant as was mentioned paragraph (*a*) of the proviso to section 24(1) of the 1911 Act.[96]

It is provided that if, before commencement of the 1988 Act, any event has occurred or notice has been given which, by virtue of paragraph 38 of Schedule 7 to the 1956 Act, had any operation in relation to copyright in the work under that Act, the event or notice has the corresponding operation in relation to copyright under the 1988 Act.[97]

---

[94] Copyright Act 1956, Sched. 7, para. 38(3).
[95] Sched. 7, para. 38(4).
[96] C.D.P.A. 1988, Sched. 1. para 28(1).
[97] *Ibid.* Sched. 1, para. 28(2).

Further, any right, which immediately before commencement of the 1988 Act, would by virtue of paragraph 38(3) of Schedule 7 to the 1956 Act have been exercisable in relation to the work or copyright in it, is exercisable in relation to the work or copyright in it under the 1988 Act.[98]

Finally, if in accordance with paragraph 38(4) of Schedule 7 of the 1956 Act, copyright would, on a date after the commencement of the 1956 Act, have reverted to the author or his personal representatives and that date falls after the commencement of the new copyright provisions of the 1988 Act, the copyright in the work is to revert to the author or his personal representatives, as the case may be, and any interest of any other person in the copyright which subsists on that date, by virtue of any document made before the commencement of the 1911 Act, is to thereupon determine.[99]

---

[98] *Ibid.* Sched. 1, para. 28(3).
[99] *Ibid.* Sched. 1, para. 28(4).

CHAPTER 6

DURATION OF COPYRIGHT

1. Introduction

What is a fair term for copyright? Since literary works were first **6–1**
accorded copyright under statute,[1] there have been differing views as to
what should be the proper period of protection, some contending, in the
interests of literature, for a very short period and others, in the same interests, for perpetuity.

Those who argue in favour of a restricted period for copyright speak of
it as a monopoly[2]; whilst upholders of copyright in perpetuity speak of the
author's right to prevent others multiplying copies of his work as a right of
property. The issue of what is a fair term of copyright cannot be decided
by such attempts to categorise copyright, but by a consideration of what
protection an author of a copyright work can reasonably demand to
ensure an adequate return for his labours. A principal factor in such consideration is the nature of the copyright work and whether its creation
involves an element of industrial enterprise, as distinct from individual
literary, musical or artistic creativity.

In relation to literary works, it is generally accepted that literature cannot, in these days, be expected to flourish in a country possessing lax, or
insufficient copyright laws, and it is doubted whether the contrary argument that the existence of copyright laws militates against cheap literature
is sound. Indeed a publisher may think it worth while to bring out a cheap
edition of a work of which his monopoly in the market is secure for some
considerable period, but could not afford to do so if he ran the risk of other
cheap editions of the same work being brought out by other publishers.

At the same time, clearly some limit must be set on copyright protection. The longer the period of protection, the greater the practical difficulty of tracing title to a kind of property of which there can be no physical

---

[1] See Chap. 1, § 1–21, *et seq., ante.*
[2] As to how far this is correct, see §§ 1–1 and 1–2, *ante.*

possession. Also, at least as regards published works, it is unreasonable to give to the remote successors of the author, long after his death, a monopoly in what has in fact been made public by exploitation. That is particularly so in relation to works which by their nature involve an element of industrial, as distinct from literary, musical or artistic, creativity, and the tendency has been to accord such works a shorter, usually fixed, period of protection.

6–2 **The present period of protection.** At the Conference of the Powers held at Berlin in 1908 for the purpose of considering what modifications ought to be made to the Berne Convention,[3] it was decided that the minimum period of protection accorded to an author of a literary or artistic work[4] should be during his life and for a period of 50 years after his death.[5] This was accordingly adopted by the British Copyright Act 1911, for all literary, dramatic, musical and artistic works, with certain minor exceptions.[6] This position had the very considerable advantage over the position under the law prior to 1911, that the date of publication no longer had any bearing on the determination of copyright protection, save in certain excepted cases. Under the law prior to 1911, which gave an alternative period of copyright for literary works, either for the life of the author and 7 years after his death or a gross period of 42 years from the date of publication, whichever should be the longer,[7] the works of the same author were liable to fall into the public domain at different times. The change introduced by the 1911 Act has been followed in subsequent Copyright Acts, so that since 1911 all the works of the same author will, save in certain excepted cases,[8] fall into the public domain at the same time, namely 50 years after his death. Furthermore, since such date the term has depended on proof of the date of death, which is generally much easier to secure than proof of date of first publication.

6–3 **Brussels Convention.** The Brussels Convention (1948), while maintaining the standard period of 50 years from the death of the author, proposed (with the object of removing any uncertainty which might otherwise arise through difficulty in determining the precise date of death or other event) that the term of protection should always be deemed to begin on January 1, of the year following the event.[9] The Stockholm (1967) and Paris (1971) Conventions follow the Brussels Convention on the matter and this was adopted in the 1956 Act, and remains the position under the 1988 Act.

---

[3] See Chap. 17, "International Copyright," *post.*

[4] Such expression in the Convention encompasses every production in the literary, scientific and artistic domain, including dramatic and musical works: Art. 2.

[5] This was therefore the period provided for in the Berlin Convention (1908).

[6] Copyright Act 1911, s.3; photographs and sound contrivances were entitled to a straight term of 50 years from their making (*ibid.*, ss.21 and 19 respectively) and literary, dramatic and musical works first published after the death of the author were entitled to a term of 50 years from publication (*ibid.*, s.17).

[7] See § 1–32, *ante.*

[8] See n. 6, *ante.*

[9] Art. 7; and see Chap. 17, "International Copyright," *post.*

Universal Copyright Convention. The Universal Copyright Conven-   **6–4**
tion of 1952, provided, as does the Paris revision of 1971 of the Berne Convention, that the Convention States should give to works of Convention
nationals, or works first published in Convention States, protection for the
period given to their own nationals, but in any event a minimum of 25
years.[10] As this minimum was less than that required by the Brussels Convention (1948) (and, subsequently, the Paris Convention (1971)), this
country, in formulating the term of protection under the 1956 and 1988
Acts in relation to such works, has had regard to the Berne Convention as
so revised.

The 1988 Act. The 1988 Act provides two basic periods for protection for   **6–5**
works in which copyright subsists under the Act, reflecting the distinction,
refered to above,[11] as to whether the creation of the work involved an
element of industrial enterprise, as distinct from individual literary, musical or artistic creativity. Thus, the 1988 Act provides for all[12] literary, dramatic, musical and artistic works a period of protection lasting until the
end of the period of 50 years from the end of the calendar year in which the
author died,[13] and for sound recordings, films, broadcasts and cable programmes a period of protection lasting until the end of the period of 50
years from the making of such work.[14] Solely in relation to typographical
arrangements of published editions, the 1988 Act provides a period of 25
years from the end of the year in which the edition was first published.[15]

2. Literary, Dramatic, Musical and Artistic Works

General position: new works. By section 12(1) of the 1988 Act the nor-   **6–6**
mal period of protection for literary, dramatic, musical and artistic works
coming into existence after commencement[16] lasts until the end of the
period of 50 years from the end of the calendar year in which the author
died.[17] This is the same period of protection as applied generally to such
works under the 1956 Act,[18] but is now applied to all such works[19] and
remains the same for all such works whether or not at the author's death
such works have been published or otherwise publicly exploited.[20]

---

[10] See Chap. 17, "International Copyright," *post.*

[11] See § 6–1. *ante.*

[12] Following the recommendation of the 1977 Copyright Committee, Cmnd. 6732,
para. 656, that such period should be the maximum period of protection for all such
works; see further § 6–6, *post,* and see also as to existing works § 6–7, *post.*

[13] See § 6–6 *et seq., post*; where such works are computer-generated, then a straight 50 year
period is given and see, in the case of works of unknown authorship, §6–10, *post.*

[14] See § 6–12 *et seq., post* (sound recordings and films) and § 6–19 *et seq., post* (broadcasts and
cable programmes).

[15] See § 6–21, *post.*

[16] August 1, 1989.

[17] In the case of a work of joint authorship, this means the death of the last of the authors to
die: C.D.P.A. 1988, s.12(4)(*a*), and see generally § 7–10 *et seq., post.*

[18] As had also been the position under the 1911 Act.

[19] Under the 1956 Act this period did not apply to photographs or engravings; see as to
photographs, § 6–8, *post.*

[20] Under the 1956 Act the period was different depending on whether or not publication or
other public exploitation had taken place before the author's death; see § 6–9, *post.*

The general rule is subject to special provisions applying to works of unknown authorship,[21] computer-generated works[22] and works the copyright in which belongs to the Crown,[23] to the Houses of Parliament,[24] or to certain international organisations.[25]

6–7   General position: existing works. The general approach of the 1988 Act is that its provisions apply in relation to things existing at commencement[26] as they apply in relation to things coming into existence after commencement, subject to any express provision to the contrary.[27] However, as the 1988 Act has, with exceptions,[28] abolished the perpetual copyright previously possible for unpublished literary, dramatic, musical works and engravings and photographs,[29] certain transitional provisions were required to bring existing works into line with this new approach, and these are to be found in paragraph 12 of Schedule 1 to the 1988 Act.

Thus, existing literary, dramatic and musical works and engravings, whose author died before commencement, and photographs taken on or after June 1, 1957, which remained unpublished[30] at commencement, are all now given a further fixed period of protection of 50 years from January 1, 1990.[31] Where such works have been published[32] before commencement, then the term to be applied to them is the term which would have applied under the 1956 Act.[33] There are further provisions dealing with existing anonymous and pseudonymous works.[34]

Also following the recommendation of the 1977 Copyright Committee,[35] the 1988 Act has abolished the perpetual copyrights which were enjoyed by universities and colleges, originally under the Copyright Act 1775,[36] in respect of certain works. Such rights will now continue to subsist until December 31, 2039 and will then expire.[37] On the other hand, a new exception is made in the 1988 Act in relation to the play "Peter Pan" by Sir James Barrie, the copyright in which expired on December 31, 1987. Section 301, and Schedule 6, of the 1988 Act give to the trustees of The Hospital for Sick Children, Great Ormond Street, London a right to receive a royalty in respect of the public performance and certain other

---

[21] C.D.P.A. 1988, s.12(2); and see § 6–10, *post.*

[22] *Ibid.*, s.12(3); and see § 6–11, *post.*

[23] *Ibid.*, s.12(5); and see § 6–22, *et seq., post.*

[24] *Ibid.*, s.12(5); and see § 6–26, *post.*

[25] *Ibid.*, s.12(5); and see § 6–27, *post.*

[26] August 1, 1989.

[27] C.D.P.A. 1988, Sched. 1, para. 3.

[28] *I.e.* works of unknown authorship, see §6–10, *post.*

[29] Under ss.2(3) and 3(4) of the 1956 Act; following the recommendation of the 1977 Copyright Committee, Cmnd. 6732, para. 656; and see § 6–6, *ante.*

[30] Or, in the case of literary, dramatic and musical works, had not been performed in public, offered for sale to the public on records, broadcast or included in a cable programme.

[31] C.D.P.A. 1988, Sched. 1, para. 12(4), and see further as to photographs, §6–8, *post.*

[32] See n. 31, *ante.*

[33] C.D.P.A. 1988, Sched. 1, para. 12(2)(a), (b) and (c), and see further as to photographs, Sched. 1, §6–8, *post,* and as to posthumous works, §6–9, *post.*

[34] *Ibid.*, Sched. 1, para. 12(3), and see § 6–10, *post.*

[35] Cmnd. 6732, para. 656(iii).

[36] 15 Geo. 3, c. 53; and see further §13–47, *et seq., post.*

[37] C.D.P.A. 1988, Sched. 1, para. 13.

forms of exploitation[38] of such work, without limit in time, so long as the Hospital continues to have a separate identity and have purposes which include the care of sick children.[39]

Photographs. As indicated above, photographs taken after commence- **6–8**
ment[40] are now entitled to the full term of copyright, being 50 years from the end of the calendar year in which the author dies,[41] but are no longer entitled to the indefinite protection which they enjoyed under the 1956 Act whilst they remained unpublished.[42]

The term of copyright for photographs taken before commencement, if published before such date, or, if they were taken before June 1, 1957,[43] whether so published or not, continues until the date on which it would have expired under the 1956 Act;[44] that is, as regards photographs taken after June 1, 1957, until the end of the period of 50 years from the end of the calendar year in which the photograph is first published,[45] and as regards photographs taken before June 1, 1957, until the end of the period of 50 years from the end of the calendar year in which the photograph was taken.[46]

Photographs taken on or after June 1, 1957 and before commencement, but which remained unpublished at commencement, are given a further fixed period of protection of 50 years from January 1, 1990.[47]

Posthumous works. Under the 1956 Act literary, dramatic and musical **6–9**
works which at the author's death had not been published, performed in public, offered for sale to the public on records, broadcast or included in a cable programme, continued to enjoy copyright protection until the end of the period of 50 years from the end of the calendar year in which they were first published or otherwise publicly exploited in any of those ways.[48] Similarly, engravings which at the author's death had not been published continued to enjoy copyright protection until the end of the period of 50 years from the end of the calendar year in which they were first published.[49] These provisions appeared to apply to such works in existence

---

[38] *I.e.* commercial publication, broadcasting or inclusion in a cable programme service: *ibid.*, Sched. 6, para. 2(1).
[39] C.D.P.A. 1988, Sched. 6, para. 7(2).
[40] August 1, 1989.
[41] C.D.P.A. 1988, s.12(1), following the recommendation of the 1977 Copyright Committee, Cmnd. 6732, para. 656.
[42] Copyright Act 1956, s.3(4)(*b*), and see § 6–6, *ante*.
[43] Under the 1911 Act photographs were protected for a period of 50 years from the making of the original negative from which the photograph was directly or indirectly derived: Copyright Act 1911, s.21. The 1956 Act in substance maintained that period for photographs taken before June 1, 1957: Copyright Act 1956, Sched. 7, para. 2.
[44] C.D.P.A. 1988, Sched. 1, para. 12(2)(*c*).
[45] Copyright Act 1956, s.3(4)(*b*).
[46] *Ibid.*, Sched. 7, para. 2.
[47] C.D.P.A. 1988, Sched. 1, para. 12(4)(*c*).
[48] By the proviso to s.2(3) of the 1956 Act (as amended); by s.2(4) of the 1956 Act, references in s.2(3) to such acts included doing such acts in relation to an adaptation of the work.
[49] By sub-para. (*a*) of the proviso to s.3(4) of the 1956 Act, which only applied to engravings, not to all artistic works.

before June 1, 1957, as the 1956 Act contained no relevant transitional provisions.[50]

As indicated above,[51] these special rules have not been continued in the 1988 Act in relation to works coming into existence after commencement. In relation to existing works, where the period of 50 years has begun to run, then the period of copyright continues to be the same as it would have been under the 1956 Act,[52] but where such period has not begun to run, then a fixed further period of protection of 50 years from January 1, 1990 is given.[53]

6–10   **Works of unknown authorship.** Since the term of copyright in respect of literary, dramatic, musical and artistic works is normally fixed by reference to the date of death of the author, the provisions of Article 15 of the Brussels Convention,[54] which are directed at securing that an author can, if he desires it, preserve his anonymity, create a practical difficulty.[55] Provisions in relation to works published anonymously and pseudonymously were accordingly introduced by Schedule 2 to the 1956 Act.[56] The effect of these provisions was that where first publication of such works (other than photographs, to which the provisions did not apply[57]) was anonymous or pseudonymous, the term of copyright was for a period of 50 years from the end of the calendar year in which the work was first published. The provisions did not apply, however, where, at any time before the end of that period, it was possible for a person, without previous knowledge of the facts, to ascertain the identity of the author by reasonable enquiry.[58] A work was published anonymously or pseudonymously where no name or other indication of authorship, such as initials, was given on the work sufficient for a reasonable person to identify the author.

In relation to anonymous and pseudonymous literary, dramatic, musical and artistic[59] works coming into existence after commencement,[60] the 1988 Act confers the same term of copyright as previously conferred under the 1956 Act, of a period of 50 years, but now expressed to run from the end of the calendar year in which the work is first made available to the public.[61] The phrase "first made available to the public" clearly covers publication, that is the issue of copies to the public, but is wider in that it also expressly includes public performance of a literary, dramatic or musi-

---

[50] These provisions were substantially to the same effect as s.17(1) of the 1911 Act, save that the issue of records of a work may not have constituted publication of the work under that Act.

[51] See § 6–6, *ante.*

[52] C.D.P.A. 1988, Sched. 1, para. 12(2)(*a*) and (*b*).

[53] *Ibid.,* Sched. 1, para. 12(4)(*a*) and (*b*).

[54] 1948; see Art. 15 of the Paris Convention (1971).

[55] See § 17–21, *post.*

[56] The 1911 Act contained no equivalent provisions; and since the 1956 Act contained no relevant transitional provisions, it appeared that these provisions applied to all such works, whether published before or after June 1, 1957.

[57] Copyright Act 1956, Sched. 2, para. 1.

[58] *Ibid.,* Sched. 2, para. 2.

[59] Photographs are now no longer excepted from these provisions as they were under the 1956 Act; see n. 57, *ante.*

[60] August 1, 1989.

[61] C.D.P.A. 1988, s. 12(2).

cal work, public exhibition of an artistic work or of a film in which it is included, and broadcast or inclusion in a broadcast or in a cable programme service, provided in each case that no account is to be taken of any unauthorised act.[62] The provision applies "if the work is of unknown authorship", and this is to be regarded as so if it is not possible for a person to ascertain the identity of the author by reasonable inquiry. Further, if the identity of the author is once known, it shall not subsequently be regarded as unknown,[63] so that if at any time during the 50 year period of the term the identity of the author becomes known then the normal term of copyright will apply under section 12(1) of the 1988 Act. However, if the identity of the author becomes known after the end of that period, copyright in the work will already have expired and will not then revive to continue until 50 years after the death of the author.[64] In the case of works of joint authorship, they are only to be treated as works of unknown authorship if all their authors are unknown; if the identity of any one or more authors is known, then the term is determined by applying the normal rule under section 12(1) of the 1988 Act to that author or authors.[65]

Transitional provisions relating to anonymous and pseudonymous literary, dramatic, musical and artistic works existing at commencement are contained in paragraph 12 of Schedule 2 to the 1988 Act. Where such works[66] have been published[67] prior to commencement, then their term continues until the date it would have expired under the 1956 Act.[68] Where such works[69] remain unpublished[70] at commencement, then they are given a further period of 50 years from January 1, 1990, or, if made available to the public[71] during that period, from such date, unless in any case, the identity of the author becomes known during such period, in which case the normal term as provided in section 12(1) (the life of the author plus 50 years) applies.[72]

Computer-generated works. Computer-generated literary, dramatic, musical and artistic works, that is works generated by a computer in circumstances such that there is no human author of the work,[73] are subject to a special rule, reflecting the fact that they do not have a human author,[74] and are entitled only to a fixed period of 50 years from the end of the year in which the work was made.[75]   **6–11**

---

[62] *Ibid.* and compare the concept of "release" introduced in s.13(2) and discussed in § 6–13, *post.* For the full meaning of unauthorised, see *ibid.*, s.178.

[63] C.D.P.A. s.9(5), to the same effect as Sched. 2, para. 2 to the 1956 Act.

[64] *Ibid.*, s.12(2); this provision is new, but was probably implied by Sched. 2, para. 2, to the 1956 Act.

[65] C.D.P.A. 1988, s.12(4)(*a*)(ii) and (*b*); and see §§ 7–11, 7–12, *post.*

[66] Which for these purposes exclude photographs.

[67] That is applying the previous narrow criterion, not the new wider criterion of being made available to the public.

[68] C.D.P.A. 1988, Sched. 1, para. 12(3)(*a*).

[69] See n. 65, *ante.*

[70] See n. 66, *ante.*

[71] That is applying the new wider criterion of s.12(2).

[72] C.D.P.A. 1988, Sched. 1, para. 12(3)(*b*).

[73] *Ibid.*, s.178.

[74] But see s.9(3) of the 1988 Act.

[75] C.D.P.A. 1988, s.12(3).

3. Sound Recordings and Films

6-12　　**General position: new works.** In relation to a sound recording or film made after commencement,[76] copyright expires at the end of the period of 50 years from the end of the calendar year in which it is made,[77] or, if released before the end of that period, 50 years from the end of the calendar year in which it is released.[78] The 1988 Act has here introduced two changes into the position as it was under the 1956 Act, the first in the new concept of "release,"[79] and the second in setting a limit on the term of copyright in respect of unreleased sound recordings and films.[80]

6-13　　**"Release."** The 1988 Act introduces in relation to sound recordings and films a new concept of release, upon which the determination of the length of the term of copyright depends. Under the 1956 Act, the distinction turned on publication, which in the case of sound recordings and films did not occur when the sound recording or film was played or shown in public, or was broadcast or included in a cable programme service.[81] That is still the position, as regards publication, under the 1988 Act.[82] The new concept of "release" includes, but is wider than, publication and a sound recording or film is released not only when it is first published, but also when it is broadcast or included in a cable programme service or, in the case of a film or film sound-track,[83] when the film is first shown in public,[84] provided that in each case no account is to be taken of any unauthorised act.[85]

6-14　　**Limit imposed on term.** The second difference introduced by the 1988 Act is that, whilst under the 1956 Act copyright in unpublished sound recordings and films continued without limit in time until they were first published, and then expired at the end of 50 years from first publication,[86] the 1988 Act sets a limit on the term for unreleased sound recordings and films of 50 years from the end of the calendar year in which they are made.[87] It is only if a sound recording or film is released within such period that it will then enjoy copyright protection for a further period of 50 years from the end of the calendar year in which it was released.[88] The

---

[76] August 1, 1989.
[77] C.D.P.A. 1988, s.13(1)(*a*); contrast the position under s.12(1) and (2) of the 1956 Act.
[78] *Ibid.*, s.13(1)(*b*).
[79] See further § 6–13, *post.*
[80] See further § 6–14, *post.*
[81] Copyright Act 1956, ss.12(9) and 13(10).
[82] C.D.P.A. 1988, s.175(4)(*c*).
[83] A film sound track is now treated as a sound recording; see § 2–31, *ante.*
[84] C.D.P.A. 1988, s.13(2).
[85] For the full meaning of unauthorised in s.13(2), see s.178.
[86] Copyright Act 1956, ss.12(1) and (3), and 13(1) and (3) (although a limit of 50 years after registration was set in respect of films required to be registered under certain enactments: *ibid.* s.13(3)(*a*), as amended by the Films Act 1985 (c. 21) s.7(2))
[87] Following the recommendation of the 1977 Copyright Committee, Cmnd. 6732, para. 656(ii).
[88] C.D.P.A. 1988, s.13(2).

maximum possible period of copyright protection for a new sound recording or film is therefore 102 years.[89]

Existing works. In relation to sound recordings and films in existence at commencement,[90] the general approach of the 1988 Act in treating existing works in the same way as new works[91] is modified by the provisions of paragraph 12 of Schedule 1 to that Act, which preserve in relation to such works the former distinction based on publication,[92] so that the wider concept of release does not therefore apply to such works.   **6–15**

Existing published sound recordings. Thus, the term of copyright for a sound recording which, prior to commencement, has been published,[93] or, in the case of a sound recording made before June 1, 1957,[94] whether published or not, continues until the date on which it would have expired under the 1956 Act;[95] that is, as regards a sound recording made after June 1, 1957, until the end of 50 years from the end of the calendar year in which it was so published or registered,[96] and, as regards a sound recording made before that date, until the end of 50 years from the end of the year in which it was made.[97]   **6–16**

Existing published films. Similarly, in relation to existing films which, prior to commencement, have been published[98] or registered under former enactments relating to the registration of films,[99] the term of copyright protection continues until the date on which it would have expired under the 1956 Act;[1] that is until the end of 50 years from the end of the calendar year in which it was so published or registered.[2]   **6–17**

Existing unpublished works. Existing sound recordings and films which, at commencement,[3] remained unpublished,[4] or in the case of films, were not registrable under former enactments relating to registration of films,[5] are given a further period of protection of 50 years from January 1,   **6–18**

---

[89] Taking an extreme example of a sound recording or film made on January 1 in one year and not released until some time in the 51st year after that year; for example: made January 1, 1990, released January 1, 2041, copyright expires December 31, 2092.

[90] August 1, 1989.

[91] C.D.P.A. 1988, Sched. 1, para. 3.

[92] But as to registerable unpublished films, see § 6–18, *post.*

[93] As to what is publication in relation to a sound recording, see § 6–13 *ante.*

[94] Under the 1911 Act, sound recordings were protected for a period of 50 years from the end of the year in which they were made: Copyright Act 1911, s.19(1). The 1956 Act maintained that period for sound recordings made before June 1, 1957: Copyright Act 1956, Sched. 7, para. 11.

[95] C.D.P.A. 1988, Sched. 1, para. 12(2)(*d*).

[96] See Copyright Act 1956, s.12(3).

[97] See *Ibid.,* s.12(3) and Sched. 7, para. 11.

[98] As to what is publication in relation to a film, see §§ 6–13, *ante.*

[99] See Copyright Act 1956, s.13(3)(*a*), (as amended by the Films Act 1985, s.7(2)) and the Films Act 1985 (c. 21) which repealed the Films Act 1960 (8 & 9 Eliz. 2, c. 57).

[1] C.D.P.A. 1988, Sched. 1, para. 12(2)(*e*).

[2] See Copyright Act 1956, s.13(3).

[3] August 1, 1989.

[4] The criterion remains that of publication, not release; see § 6–13, *ante.*

[5] See Copyright Act 1956, s.13(3)(*a*) (as amended), and the Films Act 1985.

1990, regardless, therefore, of how long ago they were made.[6] At the end of that period the term of copyright expires, unless publication takes place during that period, when protection continues for a further period of 50 years after the calendar year in which publication took place.[7]

4. Broadcasts and Cable Programmes

6–19 **General position.** Copyright in a broadcast or cable programme expires at the end of the period of 50 years from the end of the calendar year in which the broadcast was made or the programme was included in a cable programme service.[8] The same provision applies to broadcasts and cable programmes made before commencement.[9]

6–20 **Repeat broadcasts and cable programmes.** Section 14(2) of the 1988 Act provides that copyright in a repeat broadcast or cable programme expires at the same time as the copyright in the original broadcast or cable programme.[10] A repeat broadcast or cable programme is one which is a repeat either of a broadcast previously made (but disregarding any broadcast, whether sound or television, made before June 1, 1957)[11] or of a cable programme previously included in a cable programme service.[12] This means, in effect, that no addition to the term of copyright can be acquired by virtue of a repetition of a broadcast or cable programme. However, if a repetition involves any substantial alteration of the material, then presumably the broadcast or cable programme will be a new broadcast or cable programme, and, at least as regards the additional material, will be entitled to a new copyright having its own term of 50 years from broadcast or inclusion in a cable programme service.[13]

5. Typographical Arrangements of Published Editions

6–21 **Typographical arrangements.** Copyright in the typographical arrangement of a published edition expires at the end of the period of 25 years from the end of the calendar year in which the edition was first published.[14] The same provision applies to typographical arrangements of an edition published before commencement.[15]

---

[6] C.D.P.A. 1988, Sched. 1, para. 12(5).
[7] *Ibid.*
[8] C.D.P.A., 1988, s.14(1); to the same effect as ss.14(2) and 14A(3) of the 1956 Act.
[9] C.D.P.A. 1988, Sched. 1, para. 12(6).
[10] To the same effect as ss.14(3) and 14A(4) of the 1956 Act.
[11] See C.D.P.A. 1988, Sched. 1, para. 9, preserving the effect of Sched. 7, para. 18 of the 1956 Act.
[12] C.D.P.A. 1988, s.14(3).
[13] See further § 3–53, *ante.*
[14] C.D.P.A. 1988, s.15; in the same terms as s.15(2) of the 1956 Act.
[15] C.D.P.A. 1988, Sched. 1, para. 12(6) and see §4–66, *ante.*

6. Crown Copyright

Former law. Under the 1956 Act, literary, dramatic and musical works **6–22** and engravings and photographs, the copyright in which vested in the Crown,[16] enjoyed perpetual copyright until publication, and once published continued to enjoy copyright protection for a period of 50 years from the end of the calendar year in which the work was first published.[17] Artistic works, other than engravings and photographs,[18] the copyright in which vested in the Crown,[19] enjoyed copyright protection for a period of 50 years from the end of the calendar year in which the work was made, irrespective of whether the work had been published or not.[20] Sound recordings and films, the copyright in which vested in the Crown,[21] enjoyed the same period of copyright protection as other sound recordings and films.[22]

The 1988 Act. The 1988 Act has introduced an important change, in that **6–23** the perpetual copyright in unpublished literary, dramatic and musical works and in unpublished engravings and photographs, the copyright in which vests in the Crown,[23] has been abolished.[24] The Act now provides a maximum period of copyright protection for all literary, dramatic, musical and artistic Crown copyright works, if they remain unpublished, of 125 years from the end of the calendar year in which they were made.[25] In the case of any such works which are published commercially[26] before the end of the period of 75 years from the end of the calendar year in which they were made, then such works continue to enjoy copyright protection for a further period of 50 years from the end of the year in which they are first published.[27] All other Crown copyright works enjoy the ordinary period of protection provided in relation to such works which are not Crown copyright.[28] In relation to literary, dramatic, musical and artistic Crown copyright works where the Crown is a joint owner of copyright in the work, the extended term only applies to the Crown's copyright, so that this may expire at a different time from the copyright not owned by the Crown attributable to the contribution of the other author or authors.[29]

---

[16] Under s.39(1) and (2) of the Copyright Act 1956 and see further as to Crown copyright Chap. 13, *post.*

[17] Copyright Act 1956, s.39(3) and s.39(4), proviso.

[18] In respect of which the period of 50 years ran from the end of that year in which such works were first published, see §13–11, *post.*

[19] See n.17, *ante.*

[20] Copyright Act 1956, s.39(4).

[21] Under s.39(5) of the Copyright Act 1956.

[22] Copyright Act 1956, s.39(5)(*b*).

[23] Under s.163 of the 1988 Act; and see further, Chap. 13 as to Crown copyright, *post.*

[24] Although the Act has not adopted the recommendation of the 1977 Copyright Committee that all the existing Crown copyright provisions should be abolished: Cmnd. 6732, para. 609(ix).

[25] C.D.P.A. 1988, s.163(3)(*a*).

[26] See *ibid.* s.175(2).

[27] *Ibid.* s.163(3)(*b*).

[28] *Ibid.* s.163(5).

[29] *Ibid.* s.163(4).

6–24 **Existing works.** Paragraph 41 of Schedule 1 to the 1988 Act contains transitional provisions in relation to the duration of certain Crown copyright works existing at the date of commencement.[30] Thus, in the case of Crown copyright literary, dramatic, musical, and artistic works, and sound recordings and films, which have been published[31] before commencement, copyright continues to subsist in such works until the date it would have expired under the 1956 Act.[32] The same applies to unpublished artistic works other than engravings and photographs,[33] and photographs taken and sound recordings made before June 1, 1957, whether published or not.[34] In relation to other works unpublished at the date of commencement, the new provisions are made to apply with some modification. Thus, Crown copyright literary, dramatic and musical works unpublished at commencement will now enjoy the same period of copyright protection as existing works,[35] subject to a minimum period of 50 years from January 1, 1990.[36] Crown copyright engravings and photographs taken on or after June 1, 1957, and which are unpublished at commencement, will enjoy copyright protection only for a period of 50 years from January 1, 1990.[37] Crown copyright films and (if made on or after June 1, 1957) sound recordings, which remained unpublished at commencement will enjoy copyright protection for a period of 50 years from January 1, 1990 unless published within that period, when copyright will continue to subsist until the end of the period of 50 years from the end of the calendar year in which publication took place.[38]

6–25 **Acts and Measures.** Crown copyright subsisting in every Act of Parliament or Measure of the General Synod of the Church of England[39] continues to subsist from Royal Assent until the end of the period of 50 years from the end of the calendar year in which Royal Assent was given.[40]

7. Copyright Vesting in Parliament and in Certain International Organisations

6–26 **Parliamentary copyright.** Parliamentary copyright in a literary, dramatic, musical or artistic work,[41] that is copyright subsisting in such a work made by or under the direction or control of the House of Commons

---

[30] August 1, 1989.
[31] Which term is to be construed as under the 1956 Act: C.D.P.A. 1988, Sched. 1, para. 41(1).
[32] C.D.P.A. 1988, Sched. 1, para. 41(2); and see § 6–1 *ante*.
[33] *Ibid.*, Sched. 1, para. 41(2)(*b*); such works were already subject to a fixed term of 50 years from the end of the year in which they were made: see § 6–1 *ante*.
[34] Such works enjoyed a fixed period of 50 years from the end of the calendar year in which they were made: Copyright Act 1956, Sched. 1, paras. 30 and 31.
[35] *I.e.* under C.D.P.A. 1988, s.163(3).
[36] *Ibid.*, Sched. 1, para. 41(3).
[37] *Ibid.*, Sched. 1, para. 41(4).
[38] *Ibid.*, Sched. 1, para. 41(5).
[39] Under s.164(1) of the 1988 Act; and see § 13–27, *et seq., post.*
[40] C.D.P.A. 1988, s.164(2).
[41] Which includes such works existing at commencement, if then unpublished: C.D.P.A. 1988, Sched. 1 para. 43(1).

or the House of Lords,[42] continues to subsist until the end of the period of 50 years from the end of the calendar year in which it was made.[43] Where copyright vests in Parliament in any other type of work made after commencement, then such copyright subsists for the ordinary period applicable to such work.[44] In the case of a work of joint authorship, where one or more but not all of the authors are acting under the direction or control of the House of Commons or the House of Lords, then the provisions of section 165 apply only to those authors and the copyright subsisting by virtue of their contribution to the work,[45] so that in the case of a literary, dramatic, musical or artistic work falling within such provision, the Parliamentary copyright may expire at a different time from the copyright attributable to the contribution of the other author or authors. Copyright in Parliamentary Bills ceases on Royal Assent, or the withdrawal or rejection of the Bill or end of the Session.[46]

Copyright of international organisations. Where a designated international organisation[47] is the first owner of copyright subsisting in a literary, dramatic, musical or artistic work,[48] then such copyright subsists until the end of the period of 50 years from the end of the year in which the work was made.[49] In the case of such works made but unpublished, before August 1, 1989, copyright subsists until the date it would have expired under the 1956 Act,[50] or the end of the period of 50 years from January 1, 1990, whichever is the earlier.[51] **6–27**

8. Abandonment of Copyright

Abandonment of copyright. It has been said that an author may by his conduct, or by his express desire, abandon his copyright, and give to the public a right to publish his work before the time when his copyright would expire.[52] There is no direct authority on the point,[53] and it is difficult to say what amount of evidence the courts would require as to the fact of a dedication of a copyright to the public. Clearly mere non-exploitation **6–28**

---

[42] C.D.P.A. 1988, s.165(1); and see § 13–33, *et seq.*, *post.*

[43] *Ibid.* s.165(3).

[44] *Ibid.* s.165(6) and Sched. 1, para. 43(1).

[45] *Ibid.* s.165(5).

[46] *Ibid.* s.166(5); the time from when such copyright begins to subsist depends on whether the Bill is a public, private or personal Bill: see *ibid.* s.166(2), (3) and (4).

[47] *I.e.* an organisation, the members of which include one or more states (C.D.P.A. 1988, s.178), which has been named in an Order in Council as one to which s.168 applies: s.168(2); see further §17–110, *post.*

[48] By virtue of s.168(1) of the 1988 Act.

[49] C.D.P.A. 1988, s.168(3); subject to any longer period specified by Order in Council for the purpose of the United Kingdom complying with its international obligations.

[50] *I.e.* indefinitely whilst the work remained unpublished and then for 50 years from the end of the year of publication: Copyright Act 1956, s.33(2) and (3) and §17–110, *post.*

[51] C.D.P.A. 1988, Sched. 1, para. 44(2).

[52] In *Millar* v. *Taylor* (1769) 4 Burr. 2303 at 2346; *Platt* v. *Button* (1813) 19 Ves. 447; *Rundell* v. *Murray* (1821) Jac. 311 at 316.

[53] See *Mellor* v. *Australian Broadcasting Commission* [1940] A.C. 491; *Romesh Chowdhry* v. *Kh. Ali Mohamad Nowsheri* [1965] A.I.R. Jammu and Kashmir 101.

by the copyright proprietor of his rights will not give grounds for such a plea of abandonment.[54] The argument that British Leyland had abandoned its copyright in its drawings of exhaust pipes was advanced in *British Leyland Motor Corporation* v. *Armstrong Patents Co. Ltd.*, but was rejected by Foster J. who considered that it was extremely difficult to divest oneself of a legal right.[55] A similar argument that the plaintiff's predecessor in title had released its copyright to the public domain, or had licensed the world to make copies, was rejected by the High Court of New Zealand in *Plix Products Ltd.* v. *Frank M. Winstone (Merchants)*.[56]

The question of abandonment of copyright has recently come before the courts as a result of the view expressed by Whitford J. in *Catnic Components Ltd.* v. *Hill & Smith Ltd.*[57] to the effect that a patentee, by applying for a patent must be deemed, upon publication, to have abandoned his copyright in drawings the equivalent of the patent drawings. The basis for this view was that a patentee in applying for a patent necessarily makes an election accepting that, in return for a potential monopoly, the material disclosed by him in the specification must, upon publication, be deemed to be open to be used by the public, subject only to such monopoly rights as he may acquire on his application for the patent and during the period for which his monopoly remains in force, whatever be the reason for the determination of the monopoly rights. This view was, however, obiter to the actual decision in the case and the Court of Appeal, whilst upholding the learned Judge's finding of non-infringement, declined to comment on the question of abandonment.[58] The view expressed by Whitford J. has not subsequently been the subject of a decision in the English courts,[59] although in cases in various other jurisdictions, where it has been referred to in support of the argument of abandonment, the courts have rejected the argument,[60] pointing out that in *Werner Motors Ltd.* v. *A.W. Gamage*

---

[54] See *Weldon* v. *Dicks* (1878) 10 Ch.D.247, in which the argument that the proprietor of the copyright in a book had lost his copyright by non-publication for a period of 12 years, during which the book had been allowed to remain out of print, was rejected.

[55] *British Leyland Motor Corporation* v. *Armstrong Patents Co. Ltd.* [1982] F.S.R. 481 at 492; although it would appear that the cases referred to in n. 52 *ante*, were not cited to the Judge. See also C.D.P.A. 1988, s.153(3) which, in the context of qualification for copyright protection, provides that, once the qualification requirements are satisfied, copyright does not cease to subsist by reason of any subsequent event.

[56] [1986] F.S.R. 63 at 87–88; affirmed on appeal (but this point not being the subject of the appeal): [1986] F.S.R. 608. See also § 8–148, text and n. 78, *post*.

[57] [1978] F.S.R. 405. The 1977 Copyright Committee, Cmnd. 6732, para. 915, recommended that any copyright in drawings reproduced in a patent specification should cease when the patent ceases to be in force.

[58] [1979] F.S.R. 619, C.A.

[59] The point was treated as arguable by Slade J. in *General Electric Co.* v. *Turbine Blading Ltd.* [1980] F.S.R. 510, on an application in a copyright action for discovery of patent drawings, and Falconer J. distinguished *Catnic* on its facts, without deciding its correctness on this point, in *Gardex Ltd.* v. *Serata Ltd.* [1986] R.P.C. 623. See also Whitford J., in *Rose Plastics GmbH* v. *William Beckett & Co. (Plastics) Ltd.* [1989] F.S.R. 113 at 123–4.

[60] *House of Spring Gardens Ltd.* v. *Point Blank Ltd.* [1983] F.S.R. 213 at p. 269 (High Court of Ireland, affirmed on appeal: [1985] F.S.R. 327); *Ogden Industries Pty Ltd.* v. *Kis (Australia) Ltd.* [1983] F.S.R. 619 (Supreme Court of New South Wales); *Wham-O Manufacturing Co.* v. *Lincoln Industries Ltd.* [1982] R.P.C. 281 at p. 297 (High Court of New Zealand); and in particular *Interlego AG.* v. *Tyco Industries Inc.* [1987] F.S.R. 409 where the point was fully discussed at 455 (Court of Appeal of Hong Kong).

Ltd.[61] (which was not referred to in *Catnic*), the Court of Appeal had held that there was no basis for putting an applicant to an election between a patent for an article and registration of a design for shape of a similar article.

---

[61] (1904) 21 R.P.C. 621.

WORKS OF JOINT AUTHORSHIP AND OWNERSHIP

1. Definition

For the purposes of the 1988 Act, a work of joint authorship means "a **7–1** work produced by the collaboration of two or more authors in which the contribution of each author is not distinct from that of the other author or authors."[1] The definition in the 1956 Act[2] was the same except that the word "separate" was used in the place of "distinct." It does not appear that this change in wording has effected any change in the law.[3] It was implicit that the express provisions of the 1911 and 1956 Acts relating to joint authorship related only to literary, dramatic, musical and artistic works since it was only in relation to such works that the expression "author" could be applied.[4] It is unclear whether works in which copyright could subsist under the 1956 Act, but in relation to which the expression "author" could not be applied, for example, cinematograph films, could be jointly owned by reason of joint collaboration in their cre-

---

[1] C.D.P.A. 1988, s.10(1).
[2] Copyright Act 1956, s.11(3); and see *Taylor (R.A.R.)* v. *Prior (L.)* (1957) *The Author*, LXVII, No. 3 at 60.
[3] The word "distinct" was in fact used in the equivalent provision of the 1911 Act (s.16(3)). The dictionary definition of "distinct" is "separate," and see also C.D.P.A. 1988, s.172(2). *cf.* the expression "collective work" in Copyright Act 1911, s.35(1), and C.D.P.A. 1988, ss.79(6), 81(4), 116(4)(*a*) and 178.
[4] See, *e.g. Fax Directory* v. *SA Fax Listings* [1990] 2 S.A. 164.

ation.[5] No such difficulty arises under the 1988 Act. The 1988 Act makes special provision in relation to broadcasts.[6]

7–2   As to what is a work of joint authorship, all the collaborators must answer the description of "authors," and, therefore, if one person is merely the medium for transmitting to paper, canvas, etc., the original work of another, that is not a joint work.[7] A person who merely suggests the idea, without contributing anything to the literary, dramatic or other form in which copyright subsists, is not a joint author,[8] nor is a person who revises and makes minor additions to an existing work,[9] unless it has been agreed that he should be treated as a joint author,[10] or unless both parties have made a contribution in furtherance of a common design.[11]

2. Rights of Co-Authors *inter se*

7–3   Co-authors will usually hold the copyright as tenants in common rather than as joint tenants,[12] although the circumstances may indicate otherwise. Thus there may be a strong inference that the property of husband and wife was intended to be owned as joint tenants.[13] In the absence of agreement to the contrary the shares of tenants in common will usually be equal[14] but, again, circumstances may indicate otherwise, as where a publishing agreement provides for payment of differing proportions of royalties to the joint authors.[15] Upon the death of one joint tenant his interest in the copyright will pass to his co-owners by survivorship.[16] Upon the

---

[5] See *Adventure Film Productions Ltd.* v. *Tulley, The Times,* October 14, 1982, which suggests that they could be, although the point was not argued. Against this it could be said that s.6(*c*) of the Interpretation Act 1978, which provides that in any Act, unless the contrary intention appears, words in the singular include the plural, should not have been applied since the fact that s.11 of the Copyright Act 1956 was restricted to works of which there were authors, does indicate a contrary intention. See also the 1977 Copyright Committee, Cmnd. 6732, para. 584. Such works could certainly be jointly owned as a result of a transmission of the copyright.

[6] C.D.P.A. 1988 s.10(2), §4–58, *ante.*

[7] *Ante,* § 4–6, but see *Kenrick & Co.* v. *Laurence & Co.* (1890) 25 Q.B.D. 99 at 106; *cf. George Hensher Ltd.* v. *Restawile Upholstery (Lancs.) Ltd.* [1976] A.C. 64; [1975] R.P.C. 31 at 40 and 41 (collaboration between employees in conception and design of chairs for employers).

[8] *Tate* v. *Thomas* [1921] 1 Ch. 503; *Evans* v. *E. Hulton & Co. Ltd.* [1924] W.N. 130; *Wiseman* v. *Weidenfeld & Nicholson Ltd.* [1985] F.S.R. 525.

[9] *Samuelson* v. *Producers Distributing Co. Ltd.* (1932) 48 R.P.C. 580; *Levy* v. *Rutley* (1871) L.R. 6 C.P. 523; *Tree* v. *Bowkett* (1896) 74 L.T. (N.S.) 77.

[10] *Prior* v. *Landsdowne Press Pty. Ltd.* [1977] R.P.C. 511 (Supreme Court of Victoria).

[11] *Levy* v. *Rutley, ante; Heptulla* v. *Orient Longman Ltd.* [1989] F.S.R. 598 (Delhi High Court).

[12] *Lauri* v. *Renad* [1892] 3 Ch. 402. It is true that the authority of this decision is diminished by the fact that Kekewich J. considered that *Powell* v. *Head* (1879) 12 Ch.D. 686, was conclusive on the point, whereas no such point was involved in that decision, for the persons there held to be tenants in common were each assignees of a moiety of the copyright from the author. It is, nevertheless, suggested that it is reasonably clear that the statement in the text is correct. See, however, *Marzials* v. *Gibbons* (1874) L.R. 9 Ch. 518.

[13] *Mail Newspapers plc* v. *Express Newspapers plc* [1987] F.S.R. 90, where the subject matter was the copyright in wedding photographs.

[14] See *Acorn Computers Ltd.* v. *MCS Microcomputer Systems Pty. Ltd* (1985) 57 A.L.R. 389; *Redwood Music Ltd.* v. *B. Feldman & Co. Ltd.* [1979] R.P.C. 1 at 4.

[15] See n.10.

[16] See n.13.

death of one tenant in common his interest passes to his personal representatives as part of his estate. The title to the undivided share of the deceased tenant in common vests on his death in the executors appointed in his will or, in the case of an intestacy, in the President of the Family Division until a grant of letters of administration has been made. No grant of probate or grant of letters of administration with the will annexed is required to confer title on the personal representatives, though it is necessary to prove the will, from which title is derived, by obtaining a grant.[17]

One of several owners cannot grant a licence to publish which will be **7–4** binding upon the others[18]; nor can he grant to a third party an exclusive licence within the meaning of the Copyright Acts since he cannot prevent his co-owners from doing any of the acts restricted by the copyright.[19] On the other hand, one of the joint owners can sue in respect of an infringement and obtain an injunction and his share of damages[20] without joining the other owners as plaintiffs, and an owner can obtain an injunction to restrain a joint owner from publishing the joint work without his consent.[21]

3. Co-Author an Employee

The position as to first ownership where one of the authors is acting in the **7–5** course of his employment under a contract of service and the other is not, or is employed by a different employer, is unclear. Arguably the provisions of the Copyright Acts making the employer the first owner of the copyright[22] do not apply since the reference to the author of a work is to be taken to be a reference to all authors in the case of a work of joint authorship.[23] Whatever the position as to the legal title in such circumstances, however, the employer will almost inevitably be entitled in equity to the employee's interest in the work.

4. Subsistence of Copyright in Joint Works

If the subsistence of copyright in a work depends upon the author satisfy- **7–6** ing the qualifying provisions of the 1988 Act, then if any one of the authors satisfies those requirements the work will qualify for copyright protection.[24] Where, however, a work of joint authorship qualifies for protection

---

[17] *Redwood Music Ltd.* v. *B. Feldman & Co. Ltd.*, *ante*, at pp. 6 and 7.

[18] C.D.P.A. 1988, s.173(2). The 1956 Act did not make such an express provision but this was in fact thought to be the position. See *Copinger*, (12th ed.), § 372, *Powell* v. *Head*, *supra* and Copyright Act 1956, Sched. 3, para. 6.

[19] *Mail Newspapers Plc* v. *Express Newspapers Plc* [1987] F.S.R. 90.

[20] *Lauri* v. *Renad*, *supra*; *Prior* v. *Landsdowne Press Pty. Ltd.*, *supra*; *Acorn Computers Ltd.* v. *MCS Microcomputer Systems Pty. Ltd.*, *supra*; *Waterlow Publishers Ltd.* v. *Rose (The Times)* December 12, 1989. *Quaere*, whether he could not recover the full amount of damages, subject to a liability to account to his co-authors.

[21] *Cescinsky* v. *George Routledge & Sons Ltd.* [1916] 2 K.B. 325.

[22] C.D.P.A. 1988, s.11(2); Copyright Act 1956, ss.4(2), (4).

[23] C.D.P.A. 1988, s.10(3); Copyright Act 1956, Sched. 3, para. 6.

[24] C.D.P.A. 1988, s.154(3). See Copyright Act 1956, Sched. 3, paras. 1, 4 for the corresponding provisions of the 1956 Act.

under this provision, only those authors who satisfy such requirements are to be taken into account in deciding who is the first owner of the copyright, determining the duration of copyright and whether the provisions of section 57 of the 1988 Act apply.[25]

7–7   Thus, suppose that A and B jointly produce a work, A being a British citizen, and B a foreigner not resident in the United Kingdom at the time when the work was made, nor entitled to protection under the international provisions of the 1988 Act.[26] In such a case B would not, while the work is unpublished, be entitled to any protection if he were the sole author,[27] and consequently A is to be treated, for the purposes of the Act, as if he were the sole author. Again, the duration of copyright would be determined by reference to A's life.

Although A is to be treated as the sole author for ascertaining legal ownership of copyright under the 1988 Act, it does not, of course, follow that B, in such circumstances, has no rights as against A. A is no doubt considered to be the legal owner of the entire copyright, and he—and he alone—could bring an action for infringement, but he may have contractual obligations towards B, and, in the absence of agreement to the contrary, he would probably be regarded as trustee of the copyright for himself and B in equal shares.

But A, apparently, could, while the work remained unpublished, alone grant licences in respect of the work.[28]

7–8   If, however, the work is first published in the United Kingdom, all the authors become legally entitled to the copyright.[29] What, then, is the position, supposing the author who, prior to publication, was considered as the sole author, granted a licence to publish contrary to the wishes of his co-author? It is thought that the publisher is not exposed to an action for infringement at the instance of the latter, but that he can rely upon the licence obtained from the author who, at the time when the licence was given, had the legal right to grant it.

5. Publication of Joint Works

7–9   The 1988 Act provides that for the purposes of determining whether a work has been published, no account shall be taken of any unauthorised act.[30] Where copyright does not subsist in the work, "unauthorised" means done otherwise than by or with the licence of the author, or, where section 11(2) of the 1988 Act would have applied,[31] his employer, or in either case persons claiming under him.[32] Since references to the author of

---

[25] *Ibid.* Section 57 of the Act contains a defence in the case of anonymous or pseudonymous works; see § 10–69, *post.*

[26] ss. 159, 154(2).

[27] See *ante,* § 3–4.

[28] *Lauri* v. *Renad* [1892] 3 Ch. 402; *Powell* v. *Head* (1879) 12 Ch.D. 686; *Trade Auxiliary Co.* v. *Middlesbrough, etc., Association* (1889) 40 Ch.D. 425.

[29] § 3–10 *et seq., ante.*

[30] C.D.P.A. 1988, s.175(6).

[31] See § 4–35, *ante.*

[32] C.D.P.A. 1988, s.178.

a work of joint authorship are to be construed as references to all the authors of the work,[33] the consent of all the authors (or their employers or persons claiming under them) must be obtained for the publication to be authorised.

6. Term of Copyright in Joint Works

There was no definite decision as to the term of copyright in a joint work **7–10** under the law before 1911, but probably a literary work was entitled to protection during the life of the longest liver of the co-authors and for a period of seven years from his death or for a period of 42 years from first publication, whichever period was the longer.[34]

The 1911 Act provided that, in the case of a work of joint authorship, copyright was to subsist during the life of the author who first died and for a term of 50 years after his death, or during the life of the author who died last, whichever period was the longer.[35]

The 1956 Act altered the law again in favour of the longer period and provided that the duration of copyright in a work of joint authorship was to be determined by reference to the date of death of the author who died last.[36] The position under the 1988 Act is the same.[37] But where the copyright in a work of joint authorship had expired before the commencement of the 1956 Act in accordance with the provisions of the 1911 Act, the extended term conferred by the 1956 Act did not apply to the work.[38] Under the 1988 Act, where copyright subsists only because one or more of the joint authors satisfy the qualifying provisions of the Act, then only those authors are to be taken into account in determining the duration of the copyright[39] The position was different under the 1911 Act, which expressly provided that for this purpose regard should be had to all the authors.[40] The 1956 Act made no such express provision, but the position is thought to have been the same as under the 1911 Act, and that the word "author" in paragraph 2 of Schedule 3 of the 1956 Act was used in its normal and natural meaning.

7. Term of Copyright: Identity of Authors Unknown or Only Partly Known

In relation to a literary, dramatic, musical or artistic work of joint author- **7–11** ship, if the identity of one or more of the authors is known and the identity of one or more of the others is not, copyright under the 1988 Act will expire at the end of the period of 50 years from the end of the calendar year in which the last of the authors whose identity is known dies.[41] For

---

[33] *Ibid.* s.10(3).
[34] *Nottage* v. *Jackson* (1883) 11 Q.B.D. 627, 637.
[35] Copyright Act 1911, s.16(1).
[36] Copyright Act 1956, Sched. 3, para. 2.
[37] C.D.P.A. 1988, s.12(4).
[38] Copyright Act 1956, Sched. 7, para. 10.
[39] C.D.P.A. 1988, s.154(3).
[40] Copyright Act 1911, s.16(2), proviso.
[41] C.D.P.A. 1988, ss.12(1), (4).

this purpose the identity of an author is to be regarded as unknown if it is not possible for a person to ascertain his identity by reasonable inquiry, although if his identity once becomes known it is not to be subsequently regarded as being unknown.[42] The 1956 Act was broadly to the same effect in that it provided that where a joint work was published under a pseudonym or pseudonyms, but one or more of the authors' true names was disclosed, then the authors or author whose name was known were, or was, to be treated as the sole authors, or author, for the purpose of ascertaining the term of copyright in the work by reference to a period from their deaths, or death.[43] There was no similar provision relating to anonymous, as opposed to pseudonymous, works of joint authorship, but it is thought that if an author admitted that his work was a joint work in collaboration with a person whose name was not to be disclosed, the term of copyright would in fact have been reckoned by reference to the date of death of the known author.

7-12   Where the identity of none of the authors of a literary, dramatic, musical or artistic work is known, then, in accordance with the usual principles, copyright will expire under the 1988 Act at the end of the period of 50 years from the end of the calendar year in which it is first made available to the public.[44] Where, however, the identity of one or more of the authors becomes known before the end of this period the above provision will apparently apply, that is, copyright will expire at the end of the period of 50 years from the end of the calendar year in which the last of the authors whose identity is known dies. The 1956 Act was again broadly to the same effect in that it provided that where a joint work, other than a photograph, was published, and the names of all the authors were pseudonyms, and the identity of the authors was not known and could not be ascertained by reasonable inquiry, copyright continued to subsist until the end of the period of 50 years from the end of the calendar year in which the work was first published and then expired.[45] Where, however, one or more of the authors' true names became known or were capable of being ascertained by reasonable inquiry within that 50 year period, then the authors or author whose name was known or could be so ascertained was to be treated as the sole authors, or author, for the purpose of ascertaining the term of copyright in the work by reference to a period from their deaths, or death.[46]

8. Statutory Presumptions and Joint Works

7-13   It is expressly provided by the 1988 Act[47] that, in the case of a work alleged to be a work of joint authorship, the presumption that a person named as author on published copies or on the work when made is the

---

[42] *Ibid.* s.9(5).
[43] Copyright Act, 1956, Sch. 3, para. 3.
[44] C.D.P.A. 1988, s.12(2); § 6–10, *ante.*
[45] Copyright Act 1956, Sched. 2, paras. 1, 2, 3.
[46] *Ibid.* paras. 3(2), (3).
[47] C.D.P.A. 1988, s.104(3).

author, and did not make the work in circumstances vesting the copyright in the work in someone else, is to apply in relation to each person alleged to be one of the authors. The 1956 Act made provision to similar effect.[48]

9. Application of 25-year period

It will be remembered that section 5(2) of the 1911 Act provided that an **7–14** author who was the first owner of the copyright in a work could not assign the copyright for any period extending beyond 25 years after his death except by will.[49] In effect this provision continues to apply to assignments made before June 1, 1957.[50] This provision applies to joint works,[51] but not to collective works.[52] This reverter provision has to be construed in the light of section 16 of the 1911 Act, which provided that "references in this Act to the period after the expiration of any specified number of years from the death of the author shall be construed as references to the period after the expiration of the like number of years from the death of the author who dies first or after the death of the author who dies last, whichever period may be the shorter." This provision was not, perhaps, a model of clear draftsmanship, but, in applying it to the reverter provision, its effect would appear to be that, where the reversion takes place, it takes place in respect of the shares of both joint authors at the same time. The date of reversion is ascertained by substituting, for the period after the expiration of 25 years from the death of the author referred to in the reverter provision, either the period after the expiration of 25 years from the death of the author who dies first, or the period after the death of the author who dies last, whichever period may be the shorter. The operation of the provision in the case of published joint works is illustrated in the following two examples in which A and B are joint authors of the relevant work:

(a) A dies first. B dies five years later. The period of copyright remaining after B's death was 45 years, whereas the period remaining after the expiration of 25 years from the death of A will be only 25 years and will therefore be the shorter period. Reversion will therefore take place 25 years after the death of A.

(b) A dies first. B does not die until 30 years later. In this case the shorter remaining period of copyright is the period of 20 years after the death of B. Reversion will therefore take place on the death of B.

It follows from these examples that it is impossible to know at the time of A's death when the reversion will occur, or, indeed, if it will occur at all. This can only be known on the death of B, the author who dies last.

---

[48] Copyright Act 1956, s.20(3).
[49] *Ante*, § 5–23.
[50] C.D.P.A. 1988, Sched. 1, para. 27.
[51] *Redwood Music Ltd.* v. *B. Feldman & Co. Ltd.* [1979] R.P.C. 1, and [1979] R.P.C. 385, 406.
[52] C.D.P.A. 1988, Sched. 1, para. 27(4). For the definition of a collective work for this purpose, which differs from the principal definition contained in the Act (s.178), see Sched. 1, para. 27(5).

The 1988 Act provides that any document made before August 1, 1989, which had any operation affecting the ownership of the copyright in an existing work or creating, transferring or terminating any interest, right or licence in respect of the copyright in an existing work, has the corresponding operation in relation to copyright in the work under the 1988 Act.[53] The position was the same under the 1956 Act.[54] Thus an assignment of a share in the copyright in a work of joint authorship to which the reverter provision applied, operates, in relation to the copyright subsisting under the 1988 Act, as it would have done in relation to the copyright subsisting under the 1911 Act.[55] The position under the 1956 Act was the same. It would also appear that, where an assignment was made in respect of a work of joint authorship before 1956, and the copyright was still subsisting at the commencement of the 1956 Act, then the work enjoyed the extended term, ascertained by reference to the author who died last.

10. Permitted Acts

7–15 As has been seen,[56] in general, references to the author of a work are to be construed in relation to a work of joint authorship as references to all the authors of the work.[57] In relation to the categories of acts permitted under the 1956 and 1988 Acts certain modifications are made in relation to works of joint authorship. These are considered elsewhere.[58]

---

[53] C.D.P.A. 1988, Sched. 1, para. 25(1).
[54] Copyright Act 1956, Sched. 7, para. 28.
[55] *Redwood Music Ltd.* v. *B. Feldman & Co. Ltd.*, [1979] R.P.C. 1 and [1979] R.P.C. 385 at 406.
[56] § 7–9, *ante.*
[57] C.D.P.A. 1988, s.10(3).
[58] Chap. 10, *post.*

CHAPTER 8

INFRINGEMENT OF COPYRIGHT: PRIMARY INFRINGEMENT

1. Introduction

Infringements of copyright may be divided into primary, or direct **8–1**
infringements, which consist of the unauthorised exercise by persons (not
being the copyright owners) of rights restricted by the Copyright Acts,
and secondary, or indirect infringements, which consist mainly of unauthorised dealings with articles which were made in infringement of copyright, together with various other acts. A basic distinction between the
two is that secondary infringement requires the defendant to have some
degree of knowledge that what is being done is an infringement, whereas
in the case of primary infringement any such knowledge is not an ingredient of the cause of action. In this chapter the subject of primary infringement is dealt with. Secondary infringements are dealt with in the
following chapter.[1]

---

[1] Chap. 9, *post.*

8–2 Relationship between the 1956 Act and the 1988 Act. In relation to acts done before August 1, 1989, the provisions of the 1956 Act will continue to apply. The provisions of the 1988 Act relating to infringement only apply to acts done after that date.[2] The provisions of the 1956 Act relating to infringement will therefore continue to be of importance for some time.

8–3 The 1988 Act. So far as concerns primary infringements, the 1988 Act provides that copyright in a work is infringed by a person who, without the licence of the copyright owner, does, or authorises another to do,[3] any of the acts which are designated as being "acts restricted by the copyright."[4] Such acts, which are the acts which the owner of the copyright has the exclusive right to do in the United Kingdom,[5] are as follows:

(a) In relation to all categories of works, to copy the work[6];

(b) In relation to all categories of works, to issue copies of the work to the public[7];

(c) In relation to literary, dramatic and musical works, to perform the work in public, and, in relation to sound recordings, films, broadcasts and cable programmes, to play or show the work in public[8];

(d) In relation to literary, dramatic, musical and artistic works, sound recordings, films, broadcasts and cable programmes, to broadcast the work or include it in a cable programme service[9];

(e) In relation to literary, dramatic and musical works, to make an adaptation of the work, or to do any of the acts specified in the previous paragraphs in relation to an adaptation of the work.[10]

Further, the 1988 Act specifically provides that the doing of any such act is a restricted act whether done in relation to the work as a whole or a substantial part of it[11] or whether done directly or indirectly.[12] In the latter case, it is also immaterial whether any intervening acts themselves infringe copyright.[13]

8–4 The 1956 Act. Under the Copyright Act 1956, the copyright in a work was infringed by any person who, not being the owner of the copyright, did, or authorised another person to do, in the United Kingdom, any of the acts which were designated by the Act as being the acts restricted by the copyright in a work of that description.[14] The acts designated as the

---

[2] C.D.P.A. 1988, Sched. 1, para. 14(1).
[3] As to authorisation, see § 8–134, *et seq., post.*
[4] C.D.P.A. 1988, s.16(2).
[5] *Ibid.* s.16(1).
[6] *Ibid.* s.16(1)(*a*), s.17.
[7] *Ibid.* s.16(1)(*b*), s.18.
[8] *Ibid.* s.16(1)(*c*), s.19.
[9] *Ibid.* s.16(1)(*d*), s.20.
[10] *Ibid.* s.16(1)(*e*), s.21.
[11] *Ibid.* s.16(3)(*a*); see further § 8–20, *et seq., post.*
[12] *Ibid.* s.16(3)(*b*); see further, § 8–14, *post.*
[13] *Ibid.* s.16(3), and see further, § 8–10, *post.*
[14] Copyright Act 1956, ss. 1(1),(2).

acts restricted by the copyright in the various descriptions of work were as follows:

(1) (a) in relation to literary, dramatic, musical and artistic works, reproducing the work in any material form[15];

   (b) in relation to a sound recording, making a record embodying the recording[16];

   (c) in relation to a cinematograph film, making a copy of the film[17];

   (d) in relation to a television broadcast or a cable programme in so far as it consisted of visual images, making, otherwise than for private purposes, a cinematograph film of it or a copy of such a film[18];

   (e) in relation to a sound broadcast, or in relation to a television broadcast or cable programme in so far as it consisted of sounds, making, otherwise than for private purposes, a sound recording of it or a record embodying such a recording[19];

   (f) in relation to a published edition, the making, by any photographic or similar process, of a reproduction of the typographical arrangement of the edition.[20]

(2) In relation to a literary, dramatic, musical or artistic work, publishing the work.[21]

(3) (a) In relation to a literary, dramatic or musical work, performing the work in public[22];

   (b) In relation to a sound recording, causing the recording to be heard in public[23];

   (c) In relation to a cinematograph film, causing the film, in so far as it consisted of visual images, to be seen in public, or, in so far as it consisted of sounds, to be heard in public[24];

   (d) In relation to a television broadcast or cable programme, causing it, in so far as it consisted of visual images, to be seen in public, or, in so far as it consisted of sounds, to be heard in public, if it was seen or heard by a paying audience.[25]

(4) (a) In relation to a literary, dramatic or musical work, or a sound

---

[15] *Ibid.* ss.2(5)(*a*), 3(5)(*a*).
[16] *Ibid.* s.12(5)(*a*).
[17] *Ibid.* s.13(5)(*a*).
[18] *Ibid.* ss.14(4)(*a*), 14A(5)(*a*). The Copyright Act 1956 was amended by the Cable and Broadcasting Act 1984 to make provision for cable programme services.
[19] *Ibid.* ss.14(4)(*b*), 14A(5)(*b*).
[20] *Ibid.* s.15(3).
[21] *Ibid.* ss.2(5)(*b*), 3(5)(*b*).
[22] *Ibid.* s.2(5)(*c*).
[23] *Ibid.* s.12(5)(*b*).
[24] *Ibid.* s.13(5)(*b*).
[25] *Ibid.* ss.14(4)(*c*), 14A(5)(*c*).

recording, cinematograph film or cable programme, broadcasting the work or, in the case of a television broadcast or a sound broadcast, rebroadcasting the work[26];

(b) in relation to an artistic work, including the work in a television broadcast.[27]

(5) In relation to all descriptions of works except published editions, including the work in a cable programme.[28]

(6) In relation to a literary, dramatic or musical work, making an adaptation of the work[29] or doing any of the acts restricted by the copyright in such works, as above, in relation to such an adaptation.[30]

8–5 Summary. The doing of any of these acts by a person other than the copyright owner, and without his licence,[31] is, therefore, an infringement of copyright, unless such exercise falls within one of the statutory exceptions,[32] or is otherwise excusable.[33] The exercise by an unauthorised person of each of such sole rights constitutes a separate tort.[34] On the other hand, any dealing with the work of the copyright owner which does not involve an exercise of one of these rights is not a direct infringement. Thus to make use of a book is not a piracy, if copies are not multiplied. To take a familiar instance, it is the custom for many Law Societies to print general conditions relating to the sale of real estate. A and B enter into a contract for sale and incorporate by reference into their agreement "the Conditions of Sale of the X Y Law Society." Assuming these conditions to be the subject of copyright, A and B are not infringing that copyright if they confine themselves to a reference and do not copy the conditions into their agreement.[34]

8–6 Licence and consent; permitted acts. What constitutes sufficient licence such that a person does not infringe the copyright of another is considered elsewhere.[35] The 1988 Act also contains a large number of provisions, as did the 1956 Act, by virtue of which certain acts which would otherwise be infringements are permitted. These are considered in a separate chapter.[36]

---

[26] *Ibid.* ss.2(5)(*d*), 12(5)(*c*), 13(5)(*c*), 14A(5)(*d*), 14(4)(*d*).

[27] *Ibid.* s.3(5)(*c*).

[28] *Ibid.* ss.2(5)(*e*), 3(5)(*d*), 12(5)(*c*), 13(5)(*d*), 14(4)(*d*), as amended by the Cable and Broadcasting Act 1984.

[29] *Ibid.* s.2(5)(*f*).

[30] *Ibid.* s.2(5)(*g*).

[31] See § 8–144, *et seq., post.*

[32] See Chap. 10, *post.*

[33] See § 11–30.

[34] *Ash* v. *Hutchinson & Co. (Publishers) Ltd.* [1936] Ch. 489.

[35] See § 8–144, *et seq., post.*

[36] See Chap. 10, *post.*

2. Infringement by Copying

A. *Copying in relation to all works*

(i) General principles

Introduction. Many of the cases cited in this chapter in regard to what   **8–7** constitutes infringement of copyright are decisions on the law as it existed before the commencement of the 1911 Act, or are decisions under that Act. While the basic nature of infringement of copyright has not changed, it may be helpful, in order to appreciate the decisions under the 1911 Act, to set out here the primary provisions of the Act as to infringement. The 1911 Act provided that copyright should be deemed to be infringed by any person who, without the consent of the owner of the copyright, did anything the sole right to do which was by that Act conferred on the owner of the copyright.[37] The primary right so conferred was "the sole right to produce or reproduce the work or any substantial part thereof in any material form whatsoever."[38] So far as decisions on the law before 1911 are concerned, it must be kept in mind that the language of the earlier statutes giving copyright protection differed substantially from that used in the later Acts and that, prior to the 1911 Act, there were a number of different statutes giving protection in different language to different classes of works.

Form, not idea, protected. A further preliminary observation is that it is   **8–8** essential to have in mind, in approaching any question of infringement, the nature of the thing protected by copyright law. What is protected is not original thought or information, but the original expression of thought or information in some concrete form.[39] Consequently, it is only an infringement if the defendant has made an unlawful use of the form in which the thought or information is expressed. The defendant must, to be liable, have made a substantial use of this form; he is not liable if he has taken from the work the essential idea, however original, and expressed the idea in his own form, or used the idea for his own purposes.[40] Protection of this kind can only be given, if at all, under the patent law, or by invoking the principles applicable to confidential information,[41] or passing-off,[42] for instance.

---

[37] Copyright Act 1911, s.2(1). Note that in rare cases it will still be necessary to refer to the infringement provisions of the 1911 Act in order to determine whether an article is an "infringing copy". See C.P.D.A. 1988, Sched.1, para 14(3) and § 9–6, *post.*

[38] s.1(2).

[39] See Chap. 1, *ante.*

[40] *Hollinrake* v. *Truswell* [1894] 3 Ch. 420; *McCrum* v. *Eisner* (1918) 87 L.J.Ch. 99; *Wilmer* v. *Hutchinson & Co., etc., Ltd.* [1936–45] Mac.C.C. 13; and see § 1–1, *ante.*

[41] *Corelli* v. *Gray* (1913) 29 T.L.R. 570. See Chap. 21, *post.*

[42] Chap. 21, *post.*

8–9   **Infringement involves copying.** There can be no infringement unless use has been made, directly or indirectly, of the plaintiff's work.[43] Under the 1988 Act, it is a restricted act "to copy" a work, although in relation to literary, dramatic, musical or artistic works, "copying" is further defined to mean "reproducing the work in any material form".[44] "Reproduce", rather than "copy", was also the expression used in the 1911 and 1956 Acts in this context. Broadly, to reproduce a work means to copy or represent it.[45] Under the earlier Copyright Acts the word copyright itself indicated that the right given was confined to copying in some form the work to which copyright protection was afforded and did not extend to an independent production of the original,[46] There must therefore be a causal connection between the copyright work and the infringing work.[47] Thus two photographs of the same scene or person, for example, may be almost identical, and so may two mathematical tables or two directories, but in every case each may have been made without reference to the other. There can be no doubt that, in all such cases, where neither work has been taken from the other, there is no infringement, however great the similarity, although, in one sense, it may be said that the later work "reproduces" the earlier.[48] One instance of this is where the authors of two books have used a common source. Their works may well be similar, but neither will be an infringement of the other.[49] But the fact that there is what would be a common source is no excuse if the author of one book does not use that source but uses the other author's book derived from that source.[50] There will be no infringement even if the defendant is proved to have obtained his idea from the earlier work, provided that he took his photograph or prepared his table or his directory independently. It has been pointed out[51] that the moral basis upon which the protective provisions of the Copyright Acts rest is the Eighth Commandment: "Thou shalt not steal." This, then, is a second way in which copyright protection differs from that afforded to patents. In the case of the latter, any person who produces the patented invention infringes the patent though he has arrived at his result by independent investigation.

---

[43] See § 1–1, *ante*; *L.B. (Plastics) Ltd.* v. *Swish Products Ltd.* [1979] R.P.C. 611 (H.L.); *Francis Day & Hunter Ltd.* v. *Bron* [1963] Ch. 587 at 611; *Kwik Lok Corporation* v. *W.B.W. Engineers Ltd.* [1975] F.S.R. 237; *Thomas Forman & Sons Ltd.* v. *Balding & Mansell* [1928–35] Mac.C.C. 501; *Wesman* v. *McNamara* [1923–28] Mac.C.C. 121; see also *Catnic Components Ltd.* v. *Hill & Smith Ltd.* [1979] F.S.R. 619 at 625 (C.A.).

[44] C.D.P.A. 1988, s.17(1).

[45] *Ladbroke (Football) Ltd.* v. *William Hill (Football) Ltd.* [1964] 1 W.L.R. 273, 276.

[46] *British Leyland Motor Corpn. Ltd.* v. *Armstrong Patents Co. Ltd.* [1986] A.C. 577, *per* Lord Griffiths; *Francis Day & Hunter Ltd.* v. *Bron* [1963] Ch. 587; *Brigid Foley Ltd.* v. *Ellott* [1982] R.P.C. 433.

[47] See n. 46 *ante*.

[48] *Corelli* v. *Gray, supra.*

[49] *Toole* v. *Young* [1873] 9 Q.B. 523; *Robl* v. *Palace Theatre (Limited)* [1911] 28 T.L.R. 69; *Schlesinger* v. *Bedford* [1890] 63 L.T. 762; *Corelli* v. *Gray* [1913] 29 T.L.R. 570; *Harman Pictures N.V.* v. *Osborne* [1967] 1 W.L.R. 723; *Krisarts S.A.* v. *Briar Fine Ltd.* [1977] F.S.R. 557.

[50] See *Elanco Products Ltd.* v. *Mandops (Agrochemicals Specialists) Ltd.* [1979] F.S.R. 46.

[51] *Macmillan & Co. Ltd.* v. *Cooper (K. & J.)* (1923) 40 T.L.R. 186, but *cf. C.B.S. Songs Ltd.* v. *Amstrad plc* [1988] A.C. 1013, *per* Lord Templeman, at p. 1057.

The concept of reproduction therefore consists of two elements, neither **8–10** element alone being sufficient. First, there must be a sufficient resemblance between the copyright work and the alleged infringement. Second, there must be a causal connection between the two.[52] In any case of infringement the plaintiff therefore has to establish, not only that the work in respect of which complaint is made in fact so nearly resembles his as to be capable of being an infringement, but also that it has in fact been produced by the use of those features of his work which, by reason of the knowledge, skill and labour employed in their production, constitute it an original copyright work.[53] Such use, however, may consist, not of a direct use of the plaintiff's work, but of the use of some other work derived from the plaintiff's work and being itself either an infringement or a licensed production.[54] The foregoing may be summarised by saying that there is no infringement unless it is established that the defendant has produced a work which both closely resembles the plaintiff's work and also has been produced by a direct or indirect use of those features of the plaintiff's work in which copyright subsists.

The defendant's work must in some real sense represent the plaintiff's. **8–11** Thus a literary work consisting of instructions will not be infringed by the making of an article according to those instructions.[55] It follows that the copyright in a book which describes a method of teaching mathematics is not infringed by making a series of coloured rods which demonstrate that method,[56] the copyright in the words and numerals in knitting guides is not infringed by making garments to those instructions,[57] and the copyright in a book of recipes is not infringed by making a dish following one of the recipes.[58] In accordance with these principles it is also submitted that a literary work in the form of a computer program, which contains data consisting of coordinates representing an object's shape, is not infringed by making an object to those coordinates.[59]

Proof of copying. In most cases copying can only be deduced by infer- **8–12** ence from all the surrounding circumstances[60] because normally there will be no evidence from anyone "being present and looking over the defend-

---

[52] *Billhöfer Maschinenfabrik GmbH* v. *Dixon & Co. Ltd.* [1990] F.S.R. 105.

[53] *McCrum* v. *Eisner* (1918) 87 L.J. Ch. 99 at p. 102; *De Manduit* v. *Gaumont, etc., Corp. Ltd.* [1936–45] Mac.C.C. 292, applied in *Allibert S.A.* v. *O'Connor* [1981] F.S.R. 613.

[54] See § 8–14 *post.*

[55] *Interlego A.G.* v. *Tyco Industries Inc.* [1989] A.C. 217; *Cuisenaire* v. *Reed* [1963] V.R. 719 and *Cuisenaire* v. *South West Imports Ltd.* [1968] 1 Ex.C.R. 493; *Lerose Ltd.* v. *Hawick Jersey International Ltd.* [1973] F.S.R. 15, applied in *Allibert S.A.* v. *O'Connor, supra.* See also *Davis (J. & S.) Holdings) Ltd.* v. *Wright Health Group Ltd.* [1988] R.P.C. 403, 414. For a case concerning musical works decided before the 1911 Act was passed, see *Boosey* v. *Whight* [1899] 1 Ch. 836; [1900] 1 Ch. 122.

[56] *Cuisenaire* v. *Reed, supra; Cuisenaire* v. *South West Imports Ltd., supra.*

[57] *Brigid Foley Ltd.* v. *Ellott* [1982] R.P.C. 433.

[58] *J & S Davis (Holdings) Ltd.* v. *Wright Health Group Ltd.* [1988] R.P.C. 403, at 414; *Computer Edge Pty. Ltd.* v. *Apple Computer Inc.* (1986) 65 A.L.R. 33, at 61.

[59] Although certain provisions of the 1988 Act appear to proceed on the basis that the position may be otherwise. See C.D.P.A. 1988, s.51, § 20–56, *post.* Note, however, that s.28(3) of the 1988 Act provides that no inference is to be drawn from such a section as to the scope of the acts restricted by copyright.

[60] *Antocks Lairn Ltd.* v. *I. Bloohn Ltd.* [1971] F.S.R. 490.

ants' shoulder" at the time they designed or made their work.[61] With regard to literary infringements, the occurrence in both the plaintiff's and defendant's works of the same errors,[62] or idiosyncrasies in style,[63] or redundancies,[64] is some indication of copying. Thus, similar language, order of describing a scheme and format of documents has been held to indicate copying of business literature.[65] Similarities in dimensions of engineering drawings may be explicable on the basis that they are for standard parts,[66] or are standard dimensions laid down by some authority, rather than that there has been copying. Dissimilarities, which may assist in establishing that a substantial part has not been copied, may also assist in showing that there has been no copying in fact.[67] Thus, although an alleged infringing article and a copyright drawing may appear similar when viewed from one angle, when viewed from another they may appear so dissimilar that any inference of copying is dispelled.[68]

8–13   The proper test, in all cases, probably involves four propositions: (1) In order to constitute reproduction within the meaning of the Act there must be (a) a sufficient degree of objective similarity between the two works, and (b) some causal connection.[69] (2) It is quite irrelevant to inquire whether the defendant was or was not consciously aware of such causal connection. (3) Where there is a substantial degree of objective similarity, this, of itself, will afford prima facie evidence to show that there is a causal connection between the plaintiff's and the defendant's work; at least it is a circumstance from which the inference may be drawn. (4) The fact that the defendant denies that he consciously copied affords some evidence to rebut the inference of causal connection arising from the objective similarity, but is in no way conclusive.[70] Thus if there is a sufficient similarity between the plaintiff's work and the defendant's,[71] and the defendant has had an opportunity to copy the plaintiff's work directly or indirectly, this will establish a prima facie case of copying which the defendant has to answer. This may be done by bringing forward some alternative explanation of the similarities, and the judge's task will then be, on the evidence as a whole, to decide whether there has been copying or not. The fact that the judge disbelieves a witness who denies copying does not necessarily

---

[61] *Sifam Electrical Instrument Co. Ltd.* v. *Sangamo Weston Ltd.* [1973] R.P.C. 899. *L.B. (Plastics) Ltd.* v. *Swish Products Ltd.* [1977] F.S.R. 87; [1979] F.S.R. 145; [1979] R.P.C. 551.

[62] *Deeks* v. *Wells* [1928–35] Mac.C.C. 353.

[63] See *Ravenscroft* v. *Herbert & Anor.* [1980] R.P.C. 193.

[64] *Billhöfer Maschinenfabrik GmbH* v. *Dixon & Co Ltd* [1990] F.S.R. 105.

[65] *Coral Index Ltd.* v. *Regent Index Ltd.* [1970] R.P.C. 147; *Ladbroke (Football) Ltd.* v. *William Hill (Football) Ltd.* [1964] 1 W.L.R. 273.

[66] *Kwik Lok Corporation* v. *W.B.W. Engineers Ltd.* [1975] F.S.R. 237.

[67] See *Gleeson* v. *H.R. Denne Ltd.* [1975] R.P.C. 471; *L.B. (Plastics) Ltd.* v. *Swish Products Ltd.*, *supra.*

[68] *Gomme Ltd.* v. *Relaxateze Upholstery Ltd.* [1976] R.P.C. 377.

[69] As to this limb of the test, see *Billhöfer Maschinenfabrik GmbH* v. *Dixon & Co. Ltd* [1990] F.S.R. 105, at 107.

[70] This test was thought probably correct by Willmer L.J. in *Francis Day & Hunter Ltd.* v. *Bron, supra,* and was found to be "helpful" by Whitford J. in *L.B. (Plastics) Ltd.* v. *Swish* [1977] F.S.R. 87.

[71] For a case in which the plaintiff failed to establish this, see *Rose* v. *Information Services Ltd.* [1987] F.S.R. 254.

prove the contrary, that is, copying.[72] Thus it would appear that similarity coupled with proof of access to the plaintiff's productions gives rise to an inference of copying and leads to a shift in the evidential burden from the plaintiff to the defendant to refute copying.[73]

Indirect Copying. Copyright may be infringed by copying something **8–14** which is itself a copy of the plaintiff's work, and the 1988 Act now expressly provides that references to the doing of an act restricted by the copyright in a work are to the doing of it either directly or indirectly.[74] The position was the same under the 1956 and 1911 Acts.[75] Indeed, in most cases of alleged infringement the copying is done indirectly, the plagiarist never having seen the original manuscript, engineering drawing, dress designer's sketch and so on, only the published work, piece of furniture, dress, or whatever, derived from the original work.[76] However if, notwithstanding that there is a "chain" from the defendant's work indirectly back to the plaintiff's work, all that is copied is the idea of the plaintiff's work, then there is no infringement.[77] But if the original work has been reproduced, it is no answer to say that it has been copied from a work which was itself, whether licensed or unlicensed, a copy of the original.[78] So, for example, where a plaintiff's plans are reproduced in three dimensions, and the results photographed without permission, the taking of the photograph will infringe any copyright in the plans if a substantial part is thereby reproduced.[79] This is so, even if the intervening work is of a nature not capable of being an infringement of copyright or enjoying copyright,[80] or even if there is no intervening work, the link being an aural description.[81] The latter point underlines the risk that, even if an independent designer is employed in an attempt to avoid infringement, it may be necessary to give him so much information that the work he produces is still an infringement.[82] It may even not be possible for a defendant to

---

[72] *Johnstone Safety Ltd.* v. *Peter Cook (International) Plc* [1990] F.S.R. 161, at 175.

[73] *L.B. (Plastics) Ltd.* v. *Swish Products Ltd.* (H.L.) [1979] R.P.C. 611; *Oscar Trade Mark* [1980] F.S.R. 429. See also *Sifam Electrical Instrument Co. Ltd.* v. *Sangamo Weston Ltd.* [1973] R.P.C. 899.

[74] s.16(3)(*b*).

[75] See *British Leyland Motor Corpn. Ltd.* v. *Armstrong Patents Co. Ltd.* [1986] A.C. 577, and the cases reviewed there.

[76] See cases in n. 79, *post*.

[77] *Gleeson* v. *H.R. Denne Ltd.* [1975] R.P.C. 471.

[78] C.D.P.A. 1988, s.16(3)(B); and see *Hanfstaengl* v. *Empire Palace* [1894] 3 Ch. 109; [1895] A.C. 20; *King Features Syndicate* v. *O. & M. Kleeman Ltd.* [1941] A.C. 417; *Cate* v. *Devon, etc., Newspaper Co.* [1889] 40 Ch.D. 500; *Ex p. Beal* [1868] L.R. 3 Q.B. 387; *Reade* v. *Lacy* [1861] 1 J. & H. 524; *Murray* v. *Bogue* [1853] 1 Drew. 353; *Fairlie* v. *Boosey* [1878] 4 App.Cas. 711.

[79] *Dorling* v. *Honnor Marine Ltd.* [1965] Ch. 1; and see *Merchant Adventurers Ltd.* v. *M. Grew & Co. Ltd.* [1971] F.S.R. 233; *Sifam Electrical Instrument Co. Ltd.* v. *Sangamo Weston Ltd.* [1971] F.S.R. 337; *Antocks Lairn Ltd.* v. *I. Bloohn Ltd.* [1971] F.S.R. 490; *Temple Instruments Ltd.* v. *Hollis Heels Ltd.* [1971] F.S.R. 634; *Lerose Ltd.* v. *Hawick Jersey International Ltd.* [1973] F.S.R. 15; *British Northrop Ltd.* v. *Texteam Blackburn Ltd.* [1973] F.S.R. 241; *L.B. (Plastics) Ltd.* v. *Swish Products Ltd.* [1977] F.S.R. 87, [1979] R.P.C. 611 (H.L.); *Catnic Components Ltd.* v. *Hill & Smith Ltd.* [1975] F.S.R. 529.

[80] See n. 78 *ante*.

[81] *Gleeson* v. *H.R. Denne Ltd.*, *supra*; *Solar Thomson Engineering Co. Ltd.* v. *Barton* [1977] R.P.C. 537; *Plix Products Ltd.* v. *Frank M. Winstone (Merchants) Ltd.* [1986] F.S.R. 63, 608 (Ct. of Appeal, New Zealand).

[82] *Solar Thomson Engineering Co. Ltd.* v. *Barton*, *supra*.

escape a charge of infringement by giving a designer very loose instructions and then prompting him to produce, for example by trial and error, a result which resembles the copyright work.[83] Where the plaintiff is the owner of the right to reproduce the work in a particular form only, for example as an engraving, he must show that the work of which he complains was copied from his work, and not from the original.[84] Again, if for instance, what is copied is a machine part, it must be shown that the part was made from the copyright drawing, not from a part made before the drawing was made.[85] Where it is alleged that the original copyright work has been copied via some intervening work, care must be taken when comparing the alleged infringing work with the intervening work, since the vital comparison is between the alleged infringement and the original work.[86]

The "intermediate" stage must, however, in some real and intelligible sense be a copy or representation of the work in which copyright subsists. Thus where a defendant compiled a catalogue from a plaintiffs' machinery parts, thereby bringing into being a catalogue substantially similar to the plaintiff's, the copyright in the plaintiff's catalogue was not infringed. This was because the machinery parts offered by the plaintiff did not represent in any physical form the descriptions of those parts in the catalogue.[87]

8–15   Ignorance no excuse. If, however, the defendant has in fact derived his work, either directly or indirectly, from the plaintiff's, the fact that the defendant was unaware that the work he has copied existed (for instance where what he copied, such as a dress, was made from a sketch of which he had no knowledge), or was the plaintiff's, or was the subject of copyright, affords no defence to the action,[88] although, it may affect the remedy.[89] Copyright being a proprietary right, ignorance is no excuse for infringement.[90] Similarly, it is no defence to infringement that the defendant has relied upon a licence or assignment, which he believed to have been granted by the owner of the copyright, if this is not the case, although, under the 1956 Act, this might have affected the remedy.[91]

8–16   Infringement actionable without damage. Nor is it a defence to infringement that the infringement has caused the plaintiff no damage. The right of the owner of copyright is not determined or measured by the amount of actual damage to him by reason of the infringement. Copyright

---

[83] *House of Spring Gardens Ltd.* v. *Point Blank Ltd.* [1983] F.S.R. 213.

[84] *Lucas* v. *Cooke* [1880] 13 Ch.D. 872.

[85] See *British Northrop Ltd.* v. *Texteam Blackburn Ltd., supra.,* and see *L.B. (Plastics) Ltd.* v. *Swish Products Ltd.* [1977] F.S.R. 87; *Billhöfer Maschinenfabrik GmbH* v. *Dixon & Co. Ltd.* [1990] F.S.R. 105.

[86] See, for example, *Johnstone Safety plc.* v. *Peter Cook (International) plc.* [1990] F.S.R. 161. Similarities between the alleged infringement and the intervening work may of course be evidence that copying of some kind has taken place.

[87] *Purefoy Engineering Co. Ltd.* v. *Sykes Boxall Co. Ltd.* [1954] 71 R.P.C. 227; [1955] 72 R.P.C. 89.

[88] In the case of secondary infringements, knowledge is material; see Chap. 9, *post.*

[89] C.D.P.A. 1988, s.97(1); Copyright Act 1956, s.17(2). See Chap. 11, *post.*

[90] *Mansell* v. *Valley Printing Co.* [1908] 2 Ch. 441; *Lee* v. *Simpson* (1847) 3 C.B. 871; *Wittman* v. *Oppenheim* (1884) 27 Ch.D. 260; *Byrne* v. *Statist Co.* [1914] 1 K.B. 622.

[91] Copyright Act 1956, s.18(2).

is a right of property, and he is entitled to come to court for the protection of that property, even though he does not show or prove actual damage.[92]

Subconscious copying. It is undecided whether there can be "subcon-   **8–17**
scious copying," that is, whether there can be infringement where the defendant honestly states that he was unaware that his work was a copy of the plaintiff's, even if the court is satisfied that he must have made subconscious use of it from memory, rather than conscious use by deliberate copying. Such a possibility has been discussed, particularly in relation to musical copyright cases,[93] and there is some judicial support for the view that if the work has in fact been copied it is irrelevant whether the defendant was or was not consciously aware that there was a causal connection between the plaintiff's work and his own.[94] A particularly difficult situation may arise where the defendant is accused of copying an earlier work of his own which he no longer has the right to reproduce, since it may be very hard for him to put out of his mind completely the earlier work.[95]

Reproduction "in any material form." In the case of a literary, dra-   **8–18**
matic, musical or artistic work, the 1988 Act provides,[96] as did the 1956 Act,[97] that it is an infringement to reproduce the work "in any material form." In general, therefore, a change of medium will not prevent there being an infringement. The 1956 Act provided that "reproduction" in the case of a literary, dramatic or musical work included the reproduction of the work in the form of a record[98] or a cinematograph film[99] but, with the exceptions discussed below,[1] the word "reproduce" is not further defined in the 1988 Act. It is not, however, thought that the general position has been altered.[2] Thus, for example, it is thought there is little doubt that the reproduction of these types of work in the form of records or tape recordings will amount to an infringement under the 1988 Act. The 1988 Act contains, as did the 1956 Act, further provision as to copying or reproduction in relation to artistic works, and this is considered separately.[3]

---

[92] *Per* Parkes J. in *Weatherby & Sons* v. *International Horse Agency and Exchange Ltd.* [1910] 2 Ch. 297, approved in *Hawkes & Son (London) Ltd.* v. *Paramount Film Service Ltd.* [1934] Ch. 593.

[93] *Ricordi (G.) & Co., etc., Ltd.* v. *Clayton & Waller Ltd.* [1928–35] Mac. C.C. 154 and *Francis Day & Hunter Ltd.* v. *Bron* [1963] Ch. 587 in which latter case U.S.A. decisions were cited in which such a claim had succeeded. See also *Rees* v. *Melville* [1911–16] Mac.C.C. 168; *Sinanide* v. *La Maison Kosmeo* (1927) 44 T.L.R. 371 and *Seager* v. *Copydex Ltd.* [1967] 1 W.L.R. 923 at 931.

[94] *Francis Day & Hunter Ltd.* v. *Bron* [1963] Ch. 587, *per* Willmer L.J. at p. 614. Upjohn L.J. declined to express a decided view and Diplock L.J. felt unable to deal with the matter without evidence of the nature of the mental processes involved.

[95] See, *e.g. Industrial Furnaces Ltd.* v. *Reaves* [1970] R.P.C. 605 at 623; *Galago Publishers (Pty.) Ltd.* v. *Erasmus* [1989] 1 S.A. 276, at 293. A limited defence may be available in the case of artistic works: see C.D.P.A. 1988, s.64, § 10–91 *et seq., post.*

[96] C.D.P.A. 1988, s.17(2).

[97] Copyright Act 1956, s.2(5)(*a*), 3(5)(*a*).

[98] See n.99 and, *e.g. Compo Co. Ltd.* v. *Blue Crest Music Inc.* (1980) 105 D.L.R. (3rd) 249.

[99] Copyright Act 1956, s.48(1) which also defined "record" to mean any disc, tape, perforated roll or other device in which sounds are embodied so as to be capable (with or without the aid of some other instrument) of being automatically reproduced therefrom. "Cinematograph film" was defined in s.13(10) of the Act.

[1] See § 8–19, *post.*

[2] See, *e.g.* the general interpretation provisions of s.172 of the Act.

[3] See § 8–52 *et seq., post.*

8–19 Reproduction in computers and in other transient forms. It is thought that under the 1956 Act as enacted it was an infringement of the copyright in a literary, dramatic, musical or artistic work to reproduce the work in computer-readable form, such as on magnetic tape or in a magnetic core.[4] This is on the basis that to do so would have been to reproduce the work in a material form. To an extent this was made explicit by the Copyright (Computer Software) Amendment Act 1985 which provided that, with effect from September 16, 1985, references in the 1956 Act to the reproduction of any work in a material form should include references to the storage of that work in a computer.[5] The 1988 Act has broadened this definition by providing that in relation to the above categories of work, copying includes storing the work in any medium by electronic means.[6] This very wide definition makes it reasonably clear that, in relation to acts done after August 1, 1989, virtually any form of storage by modern technological means will amount to copying. The 1988 Act goes further in that it provides that in relation to all categories of work the making of copies which are transient or incidental to some other use of the work will also amount to copying.[7] Thus the transient reproduction of any work, for example, on a blackboard or a computer screen or in a computer's memory, will amount to copying. It follows that in relation to computer programs their use will at some stage almost inevitably involve their being copied in this sense, so that, unless licensed, such use will be an infringement. It may of course be difficult to prove that such transient copying has taken place.

(ii) Colourable imitation and substantial part

8–20 Introduction. It is unusual for an infringement to consist of an exact copy or use of the whole of the plaintiff's work. In some cases, the defendant's work may to a greater or lesser degree resemble the whole of the plaintiff's work, in which case the question is whether the defendant's work is a colourable imitation.[8] Alternatively, the defendant's work may have been taken from part only of the plaintiff's work. Here, the defendant's work may be an exact reproduction of that part of the plaintiff's work or it may only to a greater or lesser degree resemble that part. In this alternative class of case, the first step is to identify the part of the plaintiff's work which is alleged to have been reproduced and then decide whether it constitutes a substantial part of the plaintiff's work. If it does, but it is not an exact copy of that part, it must then be decided whether it is a reproduction or colourable imitation of that part of the plaintiff's work.[9]

---

[4] See, e.g., *Apple Computer Inc.* v. *Mackintosh Computers Ltd.* (1988) 44 D.L.R. (4th) 74; *International Business Machines Corp.* v. *Computer Imports Ltd.* [1989] 2 N.Z.L.R. 395.

[5] Copyright (Computer Software) Amendment Act 1985, s.2. However, this section was not to affect the determination of whether anything done before September 16, 1985, was an infringement of copyright. See s.4(4)(*a*) of that Act.

[6] C.D.P.A. 1988, s.17(2). "Electronic" is defined to mean actuated by electric, magnetic, electro-magnetic, electro-chemical or electro-mechanical energy. See s.178.

[7] *Ibid.* s.17(6).

[8] *Sillitoe* v. *McGraw-Hill Book Co. (U.K.) Ltd.* [1983] F.S.R. 545.

[9] *Spectravest Inc.* v. *Aperknit Ltd.* [1988] F.S.R. 161.

Colourable imitation or copy. Where the alleged infringement **8–21** resembles either the whole or a substantial part of the plaintiff's work to a greater or lesser degree, and assuming that the defendant's work has in fact been taken from the plaintiff's, the Court has never allowed a defendant to evade the provisions of the Copyright Acts by merely altering the form of the original work. But the 1988 Act, as was the case with the 1956 Act, does not contain any direct statement that an imitation is to be treated as a reproduction. "Adaptation," in section 2(5)(*f*) of the 1956 Act, had a special and restricted meaning, as it does in section 16(1)(*e*) of the 1988 Act,[10] but this did not limit the generality of the word "reproduction" under the 1956 Act[11] and presumably the position is the same under the 1988 Act. The expression "colourable imitation" was used in the 1911 Act in defining the word "infringing" when used in relation to a copy,[12] but this expression does not appear in either of the two later Acts.[13] The question therefore appears to turn solely on the interpretation of the expression "reproduction," and the further definitions of this word in section 17 of the 1988 Act and section 48(1) of the 1956 Act are of limited assistance,[14] as these definitions merely include certain special forms of reproduction. It is thought, however, that the word "reproduction" in the 1988 and 1956 Acts has the same sense as the word "copy" has acquired in copyright law.[15]

Suggested test of "copy." Various definitions of "copy" have been sug- **8–22** gested,[16] but it is submitted that the true view of the matter is that, where the court is satisfied that a defendant has, in producing the alleged infringement, made a substantial use of those features of the plaintiff's work in which copyright subsists, an infringement will be held to have been committed; if he has made such use, he has exercised unlawfully the sole right which is conferred upon the plaintiff.[17]

Substantial part. Where part only of a plaintiff's work has been taken, **8–23** difficult questions arise as to the amount of copying or use necessary to constitute infringement. It has already been seen[18] that the 1988 Act provides that references to the doing of an act in relation to a work include the doing of that act in relation to either the whole of the work or any substantial part of it. The question of "substantial part" is of relevance in relation to all acts of infringement and all categories of works in which copyright may subsist but arises most often in relation to the issue of reproduction.

---

[10] See Copyright Act 1956, s.2(6) and C.D.P.A. 1988, s.21.

[11] *Francis Day & Hunter Ltd.* v. *Bron* [1963] Ch. 587.

[12] s.35(1).

[13] In *Sillitoe* v. *McGraw-Hill Book Co. (U.K.) Ltd.*, *supra*, however, it was accepted that the expression "reproduction" embraced a colourable imitation.

[14] See *Merchant Adventurers Ltd.* v. *M. Grew & Co. Ltd.* [1973] R.P.C. 1; [1972] Ch. 242, construing the provisions of the 1956 Act.

[15] See *Daily Calendar Supplying Bureau* v. *United Concern* [1967] A.I.R. Madras 381.

[16] *King Features Syndicate* v. *O. & M. Kleeman Ltd.* [1941] A.C. 417; *McCrum* v. *Eisner* (1918) 87 L.J.Ch. 99 at 102; *Hanfstaengl* v. *W.H. Smith & Sons* [1905] 1 Ch. 519 at 524; *West* v. *Francis* (1822) 5 B. & Ald. 737 at 743.

[17] *Krisarts S.A.* v. *Briarfine Ltd.* [1977] F.S.R. 557: and see *L.B. (Plastics) Ltd.* v. *Swish Products Ltd.* [1979] R.P.C. 611.

[18] See § 8–3, *supra*.

It is therefore proposed to deal with the general principles involved here. Further consideration is given to the topic later in this chapter in relation to particular categories of works.

8–24   **The 1988 and 1956 Acts compared.** The 1988 Act, which in relation to infringement applies to acts done after August 1, 1989,[19] provides that references to the doing of an act restricted by the copyright in a work are to the doing of it in relation to the work as a whole or any substantial part of it.[20] The 1956 Act provided that any reference in the Act to the doing of an act in relation to a work or other subject-matter should be taken to include a reference to the doing of that act in relation to a substantial part of the work or other subject matter, and any reference to a reproduction, adaptation or copy of a work should be taken to include a reference to a reproduction, adaptation or copy of a substantial part of the work.[21] Under the 1956 Act there was doubt, because of the wording of section 49(2), whether this "substantial part" provision applied to infringement by publication.[22] It is now clear, however, that the provision did apply.[23] No such difficulty applies in relation to the 1988 Act.[24] It does not appear, therefore, that the position under the 1988 Act is any different from that under the 1956 Act.

8–25   **Old law.** Historically, copyright law was first directed to the prevention of reprints, and extended to prevent the evasion of its provisions by the publication of parts of books, or the publication of imitations. Even under the Literary Copyright Act of 1842 there was no general statutory prohibition of the multiplication of parts of books, except in the single instance of "parts of a volume."

At an early date, however, it was established that the copying of a part of the work might be restrained.[25] Fair quotation was permitted and although this might have been difficult to define, it did not permit a defendant, under the pretence of quotation, to publish the whole or part of another's book.[26] It became established, before the 1911 Act, that any "unfair use" of another's work could be restrained.[27] The 1911 Act introduced the expression "substantial part" in defining the sole right to reproduce, perform and publish,[28] and the same expression was to be implied in connection with the other sole rights, that is, to dramatise, and so on.[29] Although the expression "substantial" was not defined, it seems reasonable to assume that it was used in the 1911 Act with a view to giving effect to the decisions under the law prior to 1911, and that these decisions, and

---

[19] C.P.D.A. 1988, Sched. 1, para. 14(1).
[20] s.16(3)(a).
[21] s.49(1).
[22] *Copinger* (12th ed.), § 465, and see § 8–93, *post.*
[23] *Infabrics Ltd.* v. *Jaytex Ltd.* [1982] A.C. 1.
[24] See § 8–92 *et seq., post.*
[25] *Mawman* v. *Tegg* (1826) 2 Russ. 385.
[26] *Wilkins* v. *Aiken* (1810) 17 Ves. 422.
[27] *Weatherby & Sons* v. *International Horse Agency and Exchange Ltd.* [1910] 2 Ch. 297.
[28] s.1(2).
[29] *Corelli* v. *Gray* (1913) 30 T.L.R. 116.

those under the 1911 Act, will be followed in interpreting the 1956 and 1988 Acts, which again do not define "substantial".

Quality not quantity taken the test. It has repeatedly been held that **8–26**
"substantial" in this connection relates much more to the quality of what has been taken than to the quantity.[30] The quality, or importance,[31] of the part taken is frequently more significant than the proportion which the borrowed part bears to the whole work.[32] Thus if so much is taken that the value of the original is sensibly diminished, or that the labours of the original author are substantially, and to an injurious extent, appropriated by another, that is sufficient, in law, to constitute a piracy *pro tanto*.

In deciding questions of this sort, regard must be had to the nature and **8–27**
objects of the selection made, the quantity and value of the materials used, and the degree to which the use may prejudice the sale, or diminish the profits, direct or indirect, or supersede the objects of the original work.[33] It may be relevant to consider whether there has been an *animus furandi* on the part of the defendant in the sense of an intention on the part of the defendant to take for the purpose of saving himself labour.[34] Many mixed ingredients enter into the consideration of such questions. In short, the question of substantiality is a matter of degree in each case and will be considered having regard to all the circumstances.[35] Generally, it is not useful to refer to particular decisions as to the quantity taken.[36]

Thus even a few bars of music may be a substantial part of a musical **8–28**
work if they constitute a recognisable reproduction of an essential part of the melody.[37] It is often said that "what is worth copying is prima facie

---

[30] See, for example, *Ladbroke (Football) Ltd.* v. *William Hill (Football) Ltd.* [1964] 1 W.L.R. 273, *per* Lord Reid at 276; see also *Industrial Furnaces Ltd.* v. *Reaves* [1970] R.P.C. 605 at 623; *Antocks Lairn Ltd.* v. *I. Bloohn Ltd.* [1971] F.S.R. 490; *George Hensher Ltd.* v. *Restawile (Upholstery) Lancs. Ltd.* [1975] R.P.C. 31.

[31] *Catnic Components Ltd.* v. *Hill & Smith Ltd.* [1982] R.P.C. 183, 223.

[32] This was the position even before the 1911 Act. See *Tinsley* v. *Lacey* (1863) 1 H. & M. 747; *Warne & Co.* v. *Seebohm* (1888) 39 Ch.D. 73; *Kelly* v. *Hooper* (1840) 4 Jur. 21; and see *Trade Auxiliary Co.* v. *Middlesborough, etc., Association* (1889) 40 Ch.D. 425.

[33] *Bramwell* v. *Halcomb* (1836) 3 My. & Cr. 737; *Saunders* v. *Smith* (1838) 3 My. & Cr. 711; *Neale* v. *Harmer* (1897) 13 T.L.R. 209; *Campbell* v. *Scott* (1842) 11 Sim. 31; see also *Chatterton* v. *Cave* (1878) 3 App.Cas. 483; *Ravenscroft* v. *Herbert & Anor.* [1980] R.P.C. 193. It is thought that little weight would today be attached to the argument that the infringing article is not likely to compete in the market place with the original. See, *e.g. Weatherby & Sons* v. *International Horse Agency and Exchange Ltd.* [1910] 2 Ch. 297.

[34] *Leco Instruments (U.K.) Ltd.* v. *Land Pyrometers Ltd.* [1982] R.P.C. 133, where summary judgment on the issue of substantiality was refused.

[35] *Ravenscroft* v. *Herbert & Anor., supra.*

[36] *Bramwell* v. *Halcomb, supra.*

[37] *Hawkes & Son (London) Ltd.* v. *Paramount Film Service Ltd.* [1934] Ch. 593; in *Ricordi (G.) & Co., etc., Ltd.* v. *Clayton and Waller Ltd.* [1928–35] Mac.C.C. 154, it was indicated that even eight bars of an air might constitute a substantial part of the air; see also *Kipling* v. *Genatosan Ltd.* [1917–23] Mac.C.C. 203; *Canadian Performing Right Society* v. *Canadian National Exhibition Association* [1934] 4 D.L.R. 154; *Chappell & Co. Ltd.* v. *Thomson (D.C.) & Co. Ltd.* [1928–35] Mac.C.C. 467; *Frankenburg* v. *Gibbens* (1952) *The Author*, LXIII, No. 2, at 36; *Fernald* v. *Jay Lewis Productions Ltd.* [1975] F.S.R. 499; *Pitman and Turner* v. *Fletcher and Macdonald* (1953) *The Author*, LXIV, No. 1, at 13; *Hubbard* v. *Vosper* [1972] 2 Q.B. 84; *L.B. (Plastics) Ltd.* v. *Swish Products Ltd.* [1979] R.P.C. 611 (H.L.); *Catnic Components Ltd.* v. *Hill & Smith Ltd.* [1975] F.S.R. 529; [1979] F.S.R. 619 (C.A.) (as to artistic works).

worth protecting."[38] But the plaintiff must be able to identify the substantial part which he alleges has been copied.[39] Further, where the plaintiff has himself copied from another's work, then if what has been copied has been taken without alteration, it may be disregarded in deciding whether what the defendant has copied is a substantial part of the plaintiff's work on the basis that, on its own, that part lacks originality.[40] Thus it may be easier to defend an action on the basis that what has been taken was not original, rather than attempting to establish that the plaintiff's work as a whole lacks originality, and is thus not entitled to copyright.

8–29   The test may, however, vary depending upon the type of work in question. Thus it may be one of the purposes of the author of a work such as a historical work to add to the knowledge of the reader and thus the sum total of human experience and understanding. If so, the author may have attributed to him an intention that the information in the work, if it is not to become sterile, may be used by the reader and thus the law will allow wider use of such a work.[41]

B. *Copying in relation to literary works*

8–30 **Introduction.** The general principles in relation to such works have already been considered.[42] More detailed consideration is now given to copying in relation to literary works. Difficulties most frequently arise in relation to what constitutes a substantial part of the plaintiff's work.

8–31 **Copying of compilations.** In the case of compilations, such as dictionaries, gazetteers, grammars, maps, arithmetical tables, almanacs, encyclopaedias and guide-books, new publications dealing with a similar subject-matter must, of necessity, resemble existing publications, and the defence of "common source" is frequently made where the new publication is alleged to constitute an infringement of an earlier one.[43]

This defence may merely consist in pointing out that the defendant's work might have been taken from earlier matter, and that its similarity to the plaintiff's does not create any necessary inference that it has been copied from the plaintiff's, rather than from other similar works. But a bare assertion that the plaintiff's work was not copied, without any explanation by the defendant as to how or when he worked or how long it took him, may well not be enough to rebut the inference of copying.[44] Whereas, with a strictly original work, any identity of phrase is sufficient evidence of copying, with many compilations it is only from external evidence, or from

---

[38] *Per* Petersen J. in *University of London Press Ltd.* v. *University Tutorial Press Ltd.* [1916] 2 Ch. 601 at 610, approved by both Lord Reid and Lord Pearce in *Ladbrook (Football) Ltd.* v. *William Hill (Football) Ltd.* [1964] 1 W.L.R. 273 at pp. 279 and 293.

[39] *Gomme Ltd.* v. *Relaxateze Upholstery Ltd.* [1976] R.P.C. 377.

[40] *Warwick Film Productions Ltd.* v. *Eisinger* [1969] Ch. 508.

[41] *Ravenscroft* v. *Herbert & anor., supra; Galago Publishers (Pty.) Ltd.* v. *Erasmus* [1989] 1 S.A. 276, at 293.

[42] See § 8–7 *et seq., ante.*

[43] See § 8–9, *ante.*

[44] *Harman Pictures N.V.* v. *Osborne* [1967] 1 W.L.R. 723.

a minute examination of textual errors, that an infringement can be established.[45]

Alternatively, the defence may be that the plaintiff has no copyright in **8–32**
his work, because it is not original, but a mere reproduction of earlier
matter.[46] But it must not be forgotten that, though a plaintiff has no copyright in the words, he may have copyright in the arrangement as a compilation.[47] Thus, for example, the work involved in the arrangement of a list
of football fixtures in chronological order may be sufficient to make the
work original, so that the systematic copying of the chronological list will
be an infringement.[48] The position where the list has been scrambled by
the defendant is uncertain.[49] It is submitted that it will depend upon
whether the assembly of the items in the first place itself involved sufficient effort, skill and labour to justify copyright protection.[50]

Lawful use of existing publications. But there is a large class of cases **8–33**
which present a further difficulty. While, as has been pointed out above,[51]
there is no monopoly in a copyright work, yet, with strictly original works,
any user of the earlier work to produce a similar result is an infringement.
Published compilations, however, are intended, not merely to be read, but
to be used, and the question arises how far they may be used in the preparation of a subsequent compilation.

It is no doubt true that the publication of certain books of this character
implies a licence to reproduce their contents.[52] Thus, clearly, a book of
legal precedents is intended to be used by practitioners, unless otherwise
stated, and it is submitted that a writer is entitled to use prior compilations on a similar subject in order to ascertain where he must go for his
material. It is thought, however, that the limits upon this implied licence
from publication are fairly clear, and in no case authorise the use of the
copyright material in the first work for the purpose of producing a second
work of a similar nature.[53] Thus the author of the precedent book authorises the use of his forms for use in practice, unless otherwise stated, but not
in a competing book of precedents. And the compiler of a directory may
use a prior directory in the same way as any other member of the public as

---

[45] *Kelly* v. *Morris* (1866) L.R. 1 Eq. 697; *Pike* v. *Nicholas* (1870) L.R. 5 Ch. 251; *Cox* v. *Land and
Water Journal Co.* (1869) L.R. 9 Eq. 324; *Jarrold* v. *Heywood* (1870) 18 W.R. 279; *Cadieux* v.
Beauchimin [1901–04] Mac.C.C. 4; *Mathieson* v. *Universal Stock Exchange* [1901–04]
Mac.C.C. 80; *Murray* v. *Bogue* (1853) 1 Drew. 353; *Emmett* v. *Meigs* [1921] 56 D.L.R. 63;
Deeks v. *Wells* [1928–35] Mac.C.C. 353.
[46] See § 3–33 *et seq., ante*, especially § 3–35.
[47] See, as to format, *Coral Index Ltd.* v. *Regent Index Ltd.* [1970] R.P.C. 147 and *Ladbroke (Football) Ltd.* v. *William Hill (Football) Ltd.* [1964] 1 W.L.R. 273.
[48] *Football League Ltd.* v. *Littlewoods Pools Ltd.* [1959] Ch. 637.
[49] This question was left open in *Football League Ltd.* v. *Littlewoods Pools Ltd., supra.* In *Demerara Turf Club* v. *Phang* (1963) W.I.R. 177, it was held that the publication in the defendant's coupon of a list of names of all horses in a race, taken from the plaintiff's programme
and coupon, but in a scrambled form, was an infringement.
[50] See, *e.g. Independent Television Publications Ltd.* v. *Time Out Ltd.* [1984] F.S.R. 64; *British Columbia Jockey Club* v. *Standen* (1986) 22 D.L.R. (4th) 467.
[51] § 8–9, *ante*.
[52] As to implied licences generally, see § 8–147 *et seq., post*.
[53] This passage was cited with approval in *Waterlow Publishers Ltd.* v. *Rose, The Independent,*
November 10, 1989.

a guide to what streets he must go to for his information, but he may not copy the information from the prior guide into a competing work. The point is illustrated by the following decisions.

8–34 **Statistics.** Where a plaintiff had produced statistical returns of coal imported into London, the defendant, in giving statistics for the whole of the United Kingdom, had copied the whole of the plaintiff's work, which then comprised one-third of his own work. The defendant acknowledged the source of his information. Having regard to the quantity and nature of the information which had been republished without the exercise of any independent thought and labour, and the prejudice to the plaintiff in having the sale of his work superseded by this republication, the defendant's work was held to be an infringement.[54] If the defendant, after collecting the information for himself, had checked his results by a comparison with the plaintiff's tables, that would have been a quite different thing from the wholesale extraction of the vital part of his work. No man is entitled to avail himself of the previous labours of another for the purpose of conveying to the public the same information, even though he adds additional information to that already published.

8–35 **Directories.** This is consistent with the law as laid down in *Kelly* v. *Morris*,[55] which was in the following terms: "In the case of a dictionary, map, guidebook, or directory, where there are certain common objects of information which must, if described correctly, be described in the same words, a subsequent compiler is bound to set about doing for himself that which the first compiler has done. In the case of a road-book, he must count the milestones for himself, . . . and the only use that he can legitimately make of a previous publication is to verify his own calculations and results when obtained."

8–36 It is not to be inferred from this, however, that in compiling a directory the compiler may not look into the previous directory of another for the purpose of ascertaining where a particular person lives and whether or not it is worth his while to call upon that person.[56] Nothing further is implied than that he may not take a passage from the directory, and go and see whether it happens to be accurate and, if it be accurate, bodily copy it into his directory.

8–37 Thus where a defendant copied the entries from the plaintiff's directory and then sent out canvassers to private residences to see if the information was correct, subsequently reprinting the information bodily in his own

---

[54] *Scott* v. *Stanford* (1867) L.R. 3 Eq. 718; *Morris* v. *Ashbee* (1868) L.R. 7 Eq. 34; *Mawman* v. *Tegg* (1826) 2 Russ. 385; *Jarrold* v. *Houlston* (1857) 3 K. & J. 708; *Cox* v. *Land and Water Journal Co.* (1869) L.R. 9 Eq. 324; *Trade Auxiliary Co.* v. *Middlesbrough, etc., Association* (1889) 40 Ch.D. 425; *Cate* v. *Devon, etc., Newspaper Co.* (1889) 40 Ch.D. 500.
[55] (1866) L.R. 1 Eq. 697.
[56] *Morris* v. *Wright* (1870) L.R. 5 Ch. 279; *Scott* v. *Stanford* (1867) L.R. 3 Eq. 718; *Cox* v. *Land and Water Journal Co.* (1869) L.R. 9 Eq. 324; *Pike* v. *Nicholas* (1870) L.R. 5 Ch. 251; *Hogg* v. *Scott* (1874) L.R. 18 Eq. 444; *Lamb* v. *Evans* [1893] 1 Ch. 218; *Kelly's Directories Ltd.* v. *Gavin* [1902] 1 Ch. 631; *Kemps' Commercial Guides Ltd.* v. *Fashion Publications Ltd.* (1955) *The Author*, LXV, No. 4, at 88.

work even where he had been unable to obtain confirmation that it was correct, the plaintiff's copyright was infringed.[57] The position is no different if each entry is verified and permission is received from the person canvassed for the insertion of the entry relating to him,[58] or if a defendant sends blank enquiry forms to persons, having found their names and addresses from the plaintiff's directory.[59] But it is perfectly legitimate for a defendant to refer to the plaintiff's work as a guide, leading him to various authorities or sources, and then to compile his own book from these authorities or sources.[60] The principle is that the defendant is not at liberty to use or avail himself of the labour which the plaintiff has been to for the purpose of producing his work; for that is merely to take away the result of another man's labour, or in other words, his property.[61]

Other compilations. Again, the principle is that if one person has, with **8–38** considerable labour, compiled a work from various sources which he has digested and arranged, then a defendant who instead of taking the pains of researching the common sources and obtaining his subject-matter from them, simply makes use of the other's labour and adopts his arrangement, perhaps with only slight variations, thus saving himself the pains and labour which the other used, this will be an illegitimate use.[62]

So, in the case of an original descriptive catalogue, for example, of fruit **8–39** and trees, a defendant may not copy the descriptions from it even though he verifies and corrects them from specimens in front of him. Although the defendant may quite properly get much help in the way of information, suggestions and so on from the earlier work, he must write his own descriptions from the actual specimens or common sources of information.[63]

How far originality of result relevant. In certain cases before 1911 it **8–40** appears to have been suggested that one test of whether or not an infringement had been committed, in respect of works of this character, was whether the efforts of the defendant had been such as to produce "an original work."[64] If this test means that a compiler may use earlier copyright material to any extent, provided that he adds sufficient labour of his own to produce something original, it is not a true test—at any rate at the present day. In order to judge an infringement one has to ascertain whether or

---

[57] *Kelly* v. *Morris* (1866) L.R. 1 Eq. 697.
[58] *Morris* v. *Ashbee* (1868) L.R. 7 Eq. 34. *Waterlow Publishers Ltd.* v. *Rose, The Times,* December 12, 1989.
[59] *Waterlow Directories Ltd.* v. *Reed Information Services Ltd., The Times,* October 11, 1990.
[60] *Morris* v. *Wright* (1870) L.R. 5 Ch.App. 279; *Pike* v. *Nicholas* (1870) L.R. 5 Ch.App. 251.
[61] *Hogg* v. *Scott* (1874) L.R. 18 Eq. 444.
[62] *Jarrold* v. *Houlston* (1857) 3 K. & J. 708.
[63] *Hogg* v. *Scott* (1874) L.R. 18 Eq. 444; *Cary* v. *Kearsley* (1802) 4 Esp. 167; *Matthewson* v. *Stockdale* (1806) 12 Ves. 270; *Longman (T.N.).* v. *Winchester* (1809) 16 Ves. 269; *Baily* v. *Taylor* (1830), 1 Russ. & My. 73; *Bramwell* v. *Halcomb* (1836) 3 My. & Cr. 737; *Kelly* v. *Hooper* (1840) 4 Jur. 21; *Murray* v. *Bogue* (1853) 1 Drew. 353.
[64] *Spiers* v. *Brown* (1858) 6 W.R. 352; *Reade* v. *Lacy* (1861) 1 J. & H. 524; and, in the case of a catalogue, *Hotten* v. *Arthur* (1863) 1 H. & M. 603; *vide, Wilkins* v. *Aitkin* (1810) 17 Ves. 422; *Bramwell* v. *Halcomb* (1836) 3 My. & Cr. 737; *Cornish* v. *Upton* (1861) 4 L.T. 862.

not the defendant has copied the plaintiff's material; the originality of the result may be evidence that he has not copied, but is not a final test.[65]

8–41 Compilations involving selection. While, as has been seen, the compiler of certain kinds of works may lawfully use prior compilations for the purpose of ascertaining the sources available, the position is not the same in regard to those compilations in which part of the merit lies in selection of what is compiled. Thus, for example, in cases involving a selection of quotations, a defendant is not at liberty to use another's anthology of quotations in the sense of going to the sources to see if they are correctly quoted and, if so, introducing them into his own work. This is because the whole merit in such a work is the appropriateness of the quotation, its adaptability to a particular end or its illustration of a particular characteristic. The choice of one quotation as opposed to another is one which may involve gifts both of knowledge and intelligence. Its aptness does not depend on the particular place where it may be found. One person may therefore not imitate and adopt the quotations selected and arranged by another.[66]

8–42   This principle applies to any selection or compilation which involves skill or judgment or some sort of discrimination in the elimination of the things or articles not needed for that sole purpose.[67] So, in the case of trade literature, a defendant is fully entitled to make use of any information, of a technical or any other kind, which is available to him in the public domain, for the purpose of compiling his labels and his trade literature, but he is not entitled to copy the plaintiff's labels or trade literature thereby making use of the plaintiff's skill and judgment and saving himself the trouble, and very possibly the cost, of assembling his own information, either from his own researches or from sources available in documents in the public domain, and thereby making his own selection of material to put into that literature and producing his own labels and trade literature.[68]

8–43 Abridgments. It is thought that the question whether abridgments, précis, synopses and similar works infringe copyright will depend upon whether the production has involved a substantial use of copyright material, or only of ideas and information. Any work which consists of extracts from the original, either verbatim, or with merely colourable alterations of language, would constitute an infringement. On the other

---

[65] See § 8–45, *post.*

[66] *Moffatt and Paige Ltd.* v. *Gill (G.) & Sons Ltd.* (1902) 86 L.T. 465, at 471; *cf. Macmillan & Co.* v. *Suresh Chunder Deb* (1890) 17 I.L.R. (Calcutta) 951, where an infringement of the "Golden Treasury" was restrained; *Black (A. and C.), Ltd.* v. *Murray (A.) & Son* (1870) 9 Sc.Sess.Cas. (3 Ser.) 341. See also *Harman Pictures N.V.* v. *Osborne* [1967] 1 W.L.R. 723 and *Ravenscroft* v. *Herbert & Anor.* [1980] R.P.C. 193, selection of incidents from real life; and see *Fernald* v. *Jay Lewis Productions Ltd.* [1975] F.S.R. 499.

[67] *Cambridge University Press* v. *University Tutorial Press Ltd.* [1923–28] Mac.C.C. 349. *cf. Blackie & Sons Ltd.* v. *The Lothian Book Publishing Co., etc., Ltd.* (1921) 29 C.L.R. 396; and *Graves* v. *Pocket Publications Ltd.* (1938) 54 T.L.R. 952 (infringement of a compilation in narrative form by a list setting out a series of figures derived from the narrative).

[68] *Elanco Products Ltd.* v. *Mandrops (Agrochemical Specialists) Ltd.* [1980] R.P.C. 213.

hand a mere epitome of the plot of a novel, or of the general development of a learned work, would not.

Some of the earlier authorities suggest a greater licence to abridgers **8–44** than this. Thus relief has been refused on the ground that in the particular circumstances the plaintiff's work could not be prejudiced by the defendant's work,[69] or that the defendant's work has involved judgment and learning in its production, and may be extremely useful,[70] even though prejudicial to the plaintiff.[71] It is thought that such cases would not be decided on these principles today.[72] Even so, the courts have never allowed an abridgment where the plaintiff's work is colourably shortened only,[73] for example where the facts and the *terms* in which the facts are related are the same in both works,[74] or if it contains whole chapters of the plaintiff's work[75] or simply extracts, consisting of passages either copied verbatim or rendered into *oratio obliqua*.[76] Again, a defendant will not be permitted to reproduce law reports verbatim, leaving out only the arguments of counsel,[77] nor to take verbatim the headnotes from law reports and arrange them in a different manner.[78]

Parodies and burlesques. Similar questions may arise as to whether a **8–45** parody or burlesque can be an infringement. In all cases the test is the same, namely whether the defendant's work reproduces the plaintiff's work or a substantial part of it.[79] The fact that the defendant has attempted to parody the plaintiff's work is not of itself a relevant consideration. Thus in the case of a literary or dramatic work, if the parody does not make substantial use of the language or incidents in the plaintiff's work there will be no infringement.[80] The substantial part test applies also in relation to parodies of musical[81] and artistic[82] works. The fact that sufficient skill and labour may have been expended on the parody to make it

---

[69] *Dodsley* v. *Kinnersley* (1737) 1 Amb. 402; *Gyles* v. *Wilcox* (1740) 2 Atk. 141.

[70] *Hodges (J.)* v. *Welsh (T.)* (1840) 2 Ir.Eq.Rep. 266.

[71] *Gyles* v. *Wilcox, supra*; *Hawkesworth* v. *Newbery* (1776) Lofft. 755.

[72] For a different approach, see *Dickens* v. *Lee* (1844) 8 Jur. 183; *Tinsley* v. *Lacy* (1863) 1 H. & M. 747. Some of these earlier cases seem to confuse the distinct questions (a) whether an abridgment is an original work entitled itself to copyright, and (b) whether the abridgment is a piracy of the abridged work. There is little doubt that an abridgment is, subject to the rights of the proprietor of the copyright in the original, itself capable of acquiring copyright: see § 3–40, *ante*.

[73] *Gyles* v. *Wilcox, supra*.

[74] *Bell* v. *Walker* (1784) 1 Bro.C.C. 450; *Story* v. *Holcombe*, 4 McLean 306 (Amer.) (1847).

[75] *D'Almaine* v. *Boosey* (1835) 1 Y. & C.Ex. 288.

[76] *Sillitoe* v. *McGraw-Hill Book Co. Ltd.* [1983] F.S.R. 545.

[77] *Butterworth* v. *Robinson* (1801) 5 Ves. 709.

[78] *Sweet* v. *Benning* (1855) 16 C.B. 459.

[79] *Schweppes Ltd.* v. *Wellingtons Ltd.* [1984] F.S.R. 210; *Williamson Music Ltd.* v. *Pearson Partnership* [1987] F.S.R. 97.

[80] *Glyn* v. *Weston Feature Film Co.* [1916] 1 Ch. 261; *Carlton* v. *Mortimer* [1917–23] Mac.C.C. 194.

[81] *Francis Day & Hunter Ltd.* v. *Feldman & Co.* [1914] 2 Ch. 728; *Williamson Music Ltd.* v. *Pearson Partnership* [1987] F.S.R. 97.

[82] *Twentieth Century Fox Film Corporation* v. *Anglo Amalgamated Film Distributors Ltd., The Times*, January 22, 1965; *Schweppes Ltd.* v. *Wellingtons Ltd.* [1984] F.S.R. 210.

an original work is not sufficient to prevent the parody being an infringement.[83]

8–46   Computer programs. The general issue of reproduction in computers has already been considered.[84] As to reproduction of a computer program itself, in the usual way, where it is alleged that the plaintiff's computer program has been reproduced, what has to be compared is the actual program in which copyright is claimed to subsist and the work which is alleged to reproduce it.[85] The plaintiff's program may have been written in a "high level" language, such as Basic, or Fortran, or alternatively in a lower level assembly language or source code. Usually the program will also exist in the lowest form of language of all, that is object or machine readable code, which is the form which can be read by the computer, and which will usually be in binary or hexadecimal form. The transfer of the program from assembly language to machine code will usually be a task carried out by machine.[86] The defendant's program may be written in the same language as the plaintiff's, in which case the two can be compared directly, or the defendant's program may be written in a different language or code, in which case the question will be whether the defendant's program is an adaption or translation of the plaintiff's program.[87] The fact that the defendant's work is stored in a medium by electronic means, for example in a chip, will not prevent it from being a copy,[88] nor will the fact that the production of copies is transient, for example on a visual display unit.[89] The making of "back-up" copies will also be an infringement, unless this has been licensed by the copyright owner.

8–47   The fact that two programs perform the same functions or produce the same displays on a screen will not by itself mean that there has been copying,[90] although, of course, this may give rise to an inference that this is what has happened.[91] Copying may take the form of copying of lines of instruction, either verbatim or only colourably imitated, or the structure of the plaintiff's program may have been reproduced, in whole or in part.[92] It is suggested that the usual principles[93] will apply in determining whether, if it is established that part of the plaintiff's program has been

---

[83] The suggestion in *Glyn* v. *Weston Feature Film Co.*, [1916] 1 Ch. 261 and in the headnote to *Joy Music Ltd.* v. *Sunday Pictorial Newspapers (1920) Ltd.* [1960] 2 Q.B. 60 that this may be material is incorrect. See *Schweppes Ltd.* v. *Wellingtons Ltd., supra*, followed in *Williamson Music Ltd.* v. *Pearson Partnership, supra*.

[84] § 8–19, *ante*

[85] *Thrustcode Ltd.* v. *W.W. Computing Ltd.* [1983] F.S.R. 502; *Apple Computers Inc.* v. *Mackintosh Computers Ltd.* (1988) 44 D.L.R. (4th) 74 (Fed. Ct. of Appeal. Can.).

[86] It may therefore be a "computer-generated" work; see C.D.P.A. 1988, s.9(3) and § 4–14, *ante*.

[87] See C.D.P.A. 1988, s.21(4), § 8–129, *post*.

[88] *Ibid.* s.17(2). It is thought the position was the same under the 1956 Act, as amended by the Copyright (Computer Software) Amendment Act 1985. See § 8–19, *ante*.

[89] *Ibid.* s.17(6).

[90] *Thrustcode Ltd.* v. *W.W. Computing Ltd., ante*.

[91] See, *e.g. Whelan Associates Inc.* v. *Jaslow Dental Laboratory Inc.* [1987] F.S.R. 1 (U.S. Ct. of Appeals).

[92] As to copying of the structure of a program, see *Whelan Associates Inc.* v. *Jaslow Dental Laboratory Inc.* [1987] F.S.R. 1.

[93] See § 8–20, *et seq., ante*.

taken, this amounts to a substantial part. Idiosyncrasies or mistakes in the plaintiff's program will support an inference of copying but the fact that both programs contain command sequences that are common in the industry will not by itself do so. Whether a defendant who has observed the results of the plaintiff's program in operation, but who has had no access to the plaintiff's program in any form, will infringe copyright if by a process of "reverse programming" he produces a program which is substantially similar to the plaintiff's, is an open question.[94] It is suggested that if the defendant has merely taken the idea of the plaintiff's program, as exemplified by it in operation, and has then by his own efforts created a work which resembles the plaintiff's, he will not have infringed, since he will not have taken any unfair advantage of the labour, skill and effort which went into the creation of the plaintiff's work. The position would, it is thought, be different if the defendant, in addition to merely reproducing the results of the plaintiff's program in operation, had observed and reproduced the routines by which these were achieved.

C. *Copying in relation to dramatic works*

Where the language of a dramatic work has been copied, no special con- **8–48**
siderations apply. However, a basic distinction between literary works and dramatic works is that, in the case of the latter, the choice of dramatic incident and the arrangement of situation may constitute, to a far greater extent, the real value of the work.[95] This section of the chapter is primarily concerned with whether infringement of a dramatic work can occur where only situations and plot, but not language, have been reproduced. Cases of infringement by turning a dramatic work into a non-dramatic work, and vice versa, are considered elsewhere.[96]

Old law. Under the law prior to 1911 there was some doubt whether the **8–49**
copyright in a dramatic work could be infringed unless actual words and phrases were used or colourably imitated. If scenes or points of drama were taken[97] or (in the case of a musical drama) words of some of the songs,[98] but not the embodiment of the plot in words to any substantial extent, there was no infringement.[99]

Present law. Since the passing of the 1911 Act, however, it has been **8–50**
established that a dramatic work may be infringed by a second dramatisation which reproduces dramatic incidents without using or imitating language. It is not necessary that the words in the dialogue should be the same, for the situations and incidents, and the mode in which the ideas are worked out and presented, may constitute a material portion of the whole

---

[94] See, *e.g.* the allegation of infringement in *Atari Inc.* v. *Philips Electronics & Associated Industries Ltd.* [1988] F.S.R. 416.

[95] See § 2–14 *et seq., ante*

[96] See §§ 8–130, 8–131, *post.*

[97] *Chatterton* v. *Cave* (1878) 3 App.Cas. 483.

[98] *Planché* v. *Braham* (1838) 4 Bing.N.C. 17.

[99] *Schlotz* v. *Amasis Ltd. & Fenn* [1905–10] Mac.C.C. 216; but see *Nethersole* v. *Bell* [1901–04] Mac.C.C. 64.

work. The court will have regard to the dramatic value and importance of what has been taken, even though the portion may in fact be small and the actual language not copied. On the other hand the fundamental idea of two plays may be the same, but if worked out separately and on independent lines they may be so different as to bear no real resemblance to one another.[1] In the same way, the incidents in common between the two works may be drawn from common stock and common knowledge. This may explain the similarities between the two works, so that a defence that there was no copying succeeds, or, even if there was copying, there may be no infringement since there was no originality in the part copied.[2] On the other hand, the fact that a dramatic work prepared for performance in one medium is performed in another should make no difference to the issue of infringement. The question remains whether a substantial use has been made of the series of dramatic incidents in which copyright subsists.

D. *Copying in relation to musical works*

8–51 The primary question in such cases remains whether the alleged infringement has made use of a substantial part of the skill and labour of the original composer.[3] Whether this has been done or not does not depend upon a note for note comparison but falls to be determined by the ear as well as by the eye.[4] Thus the most uneducated in music can recognise that an altered work of music is, in effect, the same as the original work.[5] If the appropriated music can still be recognised by the ear, the adding of variations will make no difference.[6] Notwithstanding this, it is, in fact, the common practice to call expert evidence to assist the court in recognising the similarities or differences which may exist between two musical works. Evidence has been given that a musical work can be copied without taking a single note directly from the original.[7] Where the plaintiff's work has been arranged or transcribed without licence this will constitute an infringement by making an adaptation of it. This is considered later.[8] Where part only of the plaintiff's work has been taken, it is appropriate to

---

[1] *Rees* v. *Melville* [1911–16] Mac.C.C. 96 and 168. See also *Sutton Vane* v. *Famous Players Film Co. Ltd.* [1928–35] Mac.C.C. 6; *Bolton* v. *British International Pictures Ltd.* [1936–45] Mac.C.C. 20; *Poznanski* v. *London Film Production Ltd.* [1936–45] Mac.C.C. 107; *Ashmore* v. *Douglas-Home* [1987] F.S.R. 553.

[2] *Robl* v. *Palace Theatre* (1911) 28 T.L.R. 69; *Bagge* v. *Millar* [1917–23] Mac.C.C. 179; *Dagnall* v. *British and Dominion Film Corporation Ltd.* [1928–35] Mac.C.C. 391.

[3] *Francis Day & Hunter Ltd.* v. *Bron* [1963] Ch. 587. See also the cases cited at § 8–28 *ante*, n. 37.

[4] *Austin* v. *Columbia Gramophone Co. Ltd* [1917–23] Mac.C.C. 398; *Francis Day & Hunter Ltd.* v. *Bron* [1963] Ch.587.

[5] *D'Almaine* v. *Boosey* (1835) 1 Y. & C.Ex. 288; *Francis Day & Hunter Ltd.* v. *Bron, supra.*

[6] *Boosey* v. *Fairlie* (1877) 7 Ch.D. 301; on appeal (1879) 4 App.Cas.711; see also *Leader* v. *Purday* (1848) 7 C.B.4; *Wood* v. *Boosey* (1867) L.R. 2 Q.B. 340; L.R. 3 Q.B. 223.

[7] *Austin* v. *Columbia Gramaphone Co. Ltd., supra.*

[8] See § 8–133 *post.*

ask whether the amount taken is so slender that it would be impossible to recognise it.[9]

Difficult cases have arisen where the work alleged to have been infringed consisted of an arrangement of non-copyright tunes,[10] or where the infringing work was produced by using an intervening work. In all such cases the question is one of fact whether the plaintiff's skill and labour has been appropriated, and similar musical errors may be evidence of such appropriation. Thus, a defendant cannot escape a charge of infringement of copyright in an operatic score by the argument that all he has done is to restore a piano arrangement of an operatic work back to an operatic score.[11]

E. *Copying in relation to artistic works*

As has been seen,[12] under the 1988 Act, as was the case under the 1956 **8–52** Act, the copyright in an artistic work is infringed by the reproduction of it, or any substantial part of it, in any material form without consent. It is further provided that in relation to artistic works, this includes the making of a three-dimensional copy of a two-dimensional work and the making of a two-dimensional copy of a three-dimensional work.[13] Section 9(8) of the 1956 Act, however, contained a defence in the case of a three-dimensional copy which did not appear to a non-expert to be a reproduction of the two-dimensional work alleged to have been infringed. This has not been repeated in the 1988 Act although the defence continues to apply in relation to acts done before August 1, 1989.[14] In relation to works made after this date, the 1988 Act provides a defence in the case of use of "design documents and models" and, subject to transitional provisions, earlier works of this description. A further defence is provided in cases where artistic works have been industrially exploited. These important provisions of the 1988 Act are considered elsewhere.[15]

Old law. Before proceeding to consider the principles involved it may be **8–53** helpful to point out the differences in language employed in earlier Copyright Acts.

The Fine Arts Copyright Act 1862,[16] provided, by section 1, that the copyright in a picture, drawing, or photograph should confer "the sole and exclusive right of copying, engraving, reproducing, and multiplying such painting or drawing, and the design thereof, or such photographs, and the negative thereof, by any means and of any size"; and, by section 6

---

[9] *Hawkes and Son (London) Ltd.* v. *Paramount Film Service Ltd.* [1934] Ch. 593. In that case the amount taken (28 bars) from the march "Colonel Bogey" was such it "would be recognised by any person," and was thus a substantial part. See also *Ricordi (G.) & Co., etc., Ltd.* v. *Clayton and Waller Ltd.* [1928–35] Mac.C.C. 154, where it was indicated that even eight bars of an air might constitute a substantial part of the air.

[10] *Ante*, §§ 3–32 and 3–39.

[11] *Boosey* v. *Fairlie* (1877) 7 Ch.D. 307.

[12] § 8–3, 8–4 *ante.*

[13] C.D.P.A. 1988, s.17(3); and see Copyright Act 1956, s.48(1). See § 8–65 *et seq., post.*

[14] See § 8–70 *et seq., post.*

[15] See Chap. 20 *post.*

[16] 25 & 26 Vict. c. 68.

of the same statute, penalties were imposed upon any person who, without the consent of the proprietor of the copyright, should "repeat, copy, colourably imitate, or otherwise multiply . . . any such work or the design thereof." In the case of engravings, copyright was infringed by any person who "shall copy in the whole, or in part, by varying, adding to, or diminishing from the main design"[17]; and, in the case of works of sculpture, by any person who should make or import "any pirated copy or pirated cast" of the original sculpture.[18]

Under the 1911 Act, the proprietor of the copyright in an artistic work had the sole right to produce or reproduce his work or any substantial part thereof in any material form whatever,[19] and his copyright was infringed by any person who invaded this right without his consent.[20] There was no reference in this Act to the "design" of the artistic work, except in section 22(1), which did not deal with infringement.

8–54 **General principles.** The general principles, which have already been discussed,[21] are equally applicable in cases of infringement of artistic copyright. Thus there is no copyright in an idea as such, so that if all the defendant has copied is the plaintiff's idea, and he has not appropriated the plaintiff's labour in putting that idea into practice, there will be no infringement.[22] In the same way, the fact that the plaintiff's work may have been the inspiration for the defendant's will not of itself make the defendant's work an infringement,[23] although if the "feeling and character" of the plaintiff's work has been taken this will be a relevant, but not conclusive, consideration.[24] It has to be determined whether the defendant has used a substantial part of those features of the plaintiff's work upon the preparation of which skill and labour has been employed. Once it is established that there has been such a use of the plaintiff's work, there will be an infringement, whether or not the defendant has used a different medium, and whether or not the infringing work has been derived directly from the plaintiff's. It is equally an infringement of copyright whether the size of the copy has been increased or reduced,[25] or the dimensions altered.[26]

8–55   With regard to truly original artistic works, the question whether the defendant has made such a use of the plaintiff's work can generally be answered merely by a comparison of the two works. Here a useful test of a

---

[17] Printers Copyright Act 1777, 17 Geo. 3, c. 57.

[18] Sculpture Copyright Act 1814 (54 Geo. 3, c. 56), s.3.

[19] Copyright Act 1911, s.1(2).

[20] s.2(1).

[21] § 8–7 *et seq.*, *ante*.

[22] *L.B. (Plastics) Ltd.* v. *Swish Products Ltd.* [1979] R.P.C. 611; *Kleeneze Ltd.* v. *D.R.G. (U.K.) Ltd.* [1984] F.S.R. 399; *George Ward (Moxley) Ltd.* v. *Richard Sankey Ltd.* [1988] F.S.R. 66.

[23] *Baumann* v. *Fussell* [1978] R.P.C. 485.

[24] *Ibid.*; *Brooks* v. *Religious Tract Society* (1897) 45 W.R. 476.

[25] *Hanfstaengl Art Publishing Co. (The)* v. *Holloway* [1893] 2 Q.B. 1; *cf. Gambart* v. *Ball* (1863) 14 C.B.(N.S.) 306; *Cooper* v. *Stephens* [1895] 1 Ch. 567; *Marshall (W.) & Co. Ltd.* v. *Bull (A.H.) Ltd.* (1901) 85 L.T. 77; *Johnstone Safety Ltd.* v. *Peter Cook (Int.) plc.* [1990] F.S.R. 161, at 174.

[26] *Wham-O Manufacturing Co.* v. *Lincoln Industries Ltd.* [1985] R.P.C. 127 (Ct. of Appeal of New Zealand); *Johnstone Safety Ltd.* v. *Peter Cook (Int.) plc.*, *ante*.

copy is that which comes so near to the original as to give every person seeing it the idea created by the original[27] or, alternatively, that which comes so near to the original as to suggest that original to the mind of every person seeing it.[28] Whether or not there has been an infringement must be a matter of degree and, in the case of an artistic work, the degree of resemblance is to be judged by the eye. But in the case of commercial designs, general resemblance is not so good a test, since resemblance may be due to common subject-matter or stock designs, and it is necessary to make a close examination of detail to see whether there has been infringement.[29] In addition, if the drawings are very rudimentary there may well be no infringement unless there is an almost exact reproduction of the drawings.[30]

Infringement by reproduction. The work must be actually reproduced **8-56** without the consent of the copyright owner in order to constitute an infringement by reproduction. However, if copies lawfully produced are issued to the public this may constitute a separate act of infringement of copyright under the 1988 Act.[31]

Where the defendant's work resembles the plaintiff's, the issue whether **8-57** the defendant's work amounts to a reproduction (assuming that a causal connection between the two is established) will in each case be a question of fact, to be determined by the trial judge,[32] and is largely a matter of impression.[33] Expert evidence may be called to point out similarities or coincidences, to support the contention of copying, although the expert must stop short of giving his opinion as to whether the defendant's work is in fact a copy: this is a question for the court.[34] In order to see whether an artistic work has been reproduced it is permissible to examine a greatly magnified form of the alleged infringing article.[35] Again, where the plaintiff's copyright drawing is a sectional representation of a three dimensional object, a sectioned version of the alleged infringement may be[36] used for

---

[27] *West* v. *Francis* (1822) 5 B. & Ald. 737 at 743; cited with approval in the House of Lords in *King Features Syndicate* v. *O. & M. Kleeman Ltd.* [1941] A.C. 417. But this form of definition is not complete, and does not take into account the necessity of proving actual copying. See *Merchant Adventurers Ltd.* v. *M. Grew & Co. Ltd.* [1971] F.S.R. 233 at 237.

[28] *Hanfstaengl* v. *W.H. Smith & Sons* [1905] 1 Ch. 519 at 524; see *Catnic Components Ltd.* v. *Hill & Smith Ltd.* [1975] F.S.R. 529; [1979] F.S.R. 619 (C.A.); *Lerose Ltd* v. *Hawick Jersey International Ltd.* [1973] F.S.R. 15; *Antocks Lairn Ltd.* v. *I. Bloohn Ltd.* [1971] F.S.R. 490; and see *Twentieth Century Fox Film Corp.* v. *Anglo Amalgamated Film Distributers Ltd.*, *The Times*, January 22, 1965.

[29] *Kenrick & Co.* v. *Lawrence & Co.* (1890) 25 Q.B.D. 99; *Nicol* v. *Barranger (C.A.)* [1917–23] Mac.C.C. 219; *Hanfstaengl* v. *Baines & Co. Ltd.* [1895] A.C. 20.

[30] *Politechnika Ipari Szovetkezet* v. *Dallas Print Transfers Ltd.* [1982] F.S.R. 529.

[31] See § 8–92 *et seq., ante.*

[32] *Baumann* v. *Fussell* [1978] R.P.C. 485. The actual decision in this case may have been surprising on its facts but the Court of Appeal, having come to the conclusion that the County Court Judge had correctly approached the issue as one of fact, was not prepared to interfere with his finding.

[33] *Merchandising Corporation of America* v. *Harpbond* [1983] F.S.R. 32.

[34] See n. 32, *ante.*

[35] *Guilford Kapwood Ltd.* v. *Embsay Fabrics Ltd.* [1983] F.S.R. 567, where the Court compared a greatly magnified version of the defendant's garment with the plaintiff's lapping diagram, used in a particular knitting process.

[36] *Johnstone Safety Ltd.* v. *Peter Cook (International) plc.* [1990] F.S.R. 161.

the purposes of comparison. Any dimensions and writing on the drawing may be looked at to interpret the drawing, and the artistic copyright in the drawing is the copyright as so interpreted.[37] But this does not mean that where all that the defendant has used are the dimensions and writing the artistic copyright will be infringed: There is no artistic copyright in such matters,[38] and a reproduction must in some way be a copy or representation of the original.[39] As has been seen,[40] the test of infringement is not affected by the fact that the defendant's work may be a parody of the plaintiff's.[41]

8–58   Copying is normally proved by establishing similarity combined with proof of access to the plaintiff's drawings or products. If this is done the burden then shifts to the defendant to show that there was independent creation.[42]

8–59   **Reproduction by a different process or in a different form.** The 1988 Act, as was the case with the 1956 Act, is not directed to the means of reproduction, but to the result. Thus if a manufactured article in fact reproduces the details which go to make up the copyright in the artistic work, the method of reproduction is immaterial. Similarly, the fact that the defendant's work is reproduced in a different form from the plaintiff's will not prevent it from being an infringement. Under the 1988 Act, as was the case under the 1956 Act, it is an infringement to reproduce an artistic work "in any material form."[43]

8–60   **Substantial part.** In the case of an artistic work, whether the part reproduced is substantial may depend upon how important that part is to the recognition and appreciation of the plaintiff's work.[44] Where the purpose of the artistic work is to convey information the importance of the part reproduced may fall to be judged by how far it contributes to the conveying of that information (but not how important the information is),[45] for the essence of an artistic work is that which is visually significant.[46] In this context "visually significant" means visually significant to the person to whom the information conveyed would normally be addressed, for

---

[37] *The Duriron Company Incorporated* v. *Hugh Jennings & Co. Ltd.* [1984] F.S.R. 1. See also *Catnic Components Ltd.* v. *Hill & Smith Ltd.* [1982] R.P.C. 183, at 223, approved in *Interlego Industries A.G.* v. *Tyco Industries Inc.* [1989] A.C. 217.

[38] *Ibid.*

[39] *Brigid Foley Ltd.* v. *Ellott* [1982] R.P.C. 433; *Davis (J & S) (Holdings) Ltd.* v. *Wright Health Group Ltd.* [1988] R.P.C. 403, 414; and see § 8–11, *ante.*

[40] § 8–45 *ante.*

[41] *Twentieth Century Fox Film Corporation* v. *Anglo Amalgamated Film Distributors Ltd.*, *The Times*, January 22, 1965.

[42] *L.B. (Plastics) Ltd.* v. *Swish Products Ltd.* [1979] R.P.C. 611; *King Features Syndicate Inc.* v. *O. & M. Kleeman Ltd.* [1941] A.C. 417; and see § 8–13 *ante.*

[43] C.D.P.A. 1988, s.17(2); Copyright Act 1956, s.3(5)(a).

[44] *Catnic Components Ltd.* v. *Hill & Smith Ltd.* [1982] R.P.C. 183, at p. 223, approved in *Interlego Industries A.G.* v. *Tyco Industries Inc.* [1989] A.C. 217. See also *Johnstone Safety Ltd.* v. *Peter Cook (International) plc.* [1990] F.S.R. 161.

[45] *Ibid.*

[46] *Rose Plastics GmbH* v. *William Beckett & Co. (Plastics) Ltd.* [1989] F.S.R. 114, adopted in *Interlego Industries A.G.* v. *Tyco Industries Inc., supra.*

example, in the case of an engineering drawing, an engineer and not an ordinary member of the public.[47] In accordance with general principles, where part only of the defendant's work appears similar to the plaintiff's, the whole of the plaintiff's work must be looked at to determine whether a substantial part has been reproduced. A plaintiff is not entitled to select parts only of his work, claiming copyright in those, so as to establish infringement by reproduction of just those parts.[48] The inquiry should be directed to what has been reproduced rather than what has not.[49] A sensible approach is to start by identifying that part of the plaintiff's work which is alleged to have been reproduced and deciding first whether that part constitutes a substantial part of the plaintiff's work, applying the usual qualitative test.[50] Again, if the defendant has merely reproduced a part of the plaintiff's work in which no copyright subsists, for example because it has no originality, there will be no infringement.[51]

8–61 Thus a copy of another's work will not escape infringement merely by the omission or substitution by the defendant of features in the plaintiff's work,[52] or by combining part of the plaintiff's work with his own or another's in producing the final result.[53] Minor or trivial differences will not prevent one work from being a reproduction of another.[54]

8–62 **Reproduction of photographs.** Cases where it is alleged that a photograph has been reproduced by a drawing or painting sometimes cause difficulties. The purpose of the Copyright Acts is to protect the photographer's work. Thus where a photographer takes a photograph of some scene, a defendant who uses the photograph to obtain an accurate impression of the relative positions of the individuals or objects in the scene, but otherwise recreates the scene in his own style, may well not infringe. This is because the relative positions of the individuals or objects are not the work of the photographer.[55] This may even be the case where the scene is not commonplace and the photograph may have been the inspiration for the defendant's work.[56] But where the defendant has in addition recreated the feeling and artistic character of the plaintiff's work this may be sufficient to amount to an infringement if a substantial portion of the plaintiff's work has thereby been taken.[57] The position may also be different if the photographer has arranged the subject-matter of the photo-

---

[47] *Billhöfer Maschinenfabrik GmbH* v. *T.H.Dixon & Co. Ltd.* [1990] F.S.R. 105.
[48] *Merchandising Corporation of America Inc.* v. *Harpbond Ltd.* [1983] F.S.R. 32.
[49] *Baumann* v. *Fussell* [1978] R.P.C. 485.
[50] *Spectravest Inc.* v. *Aperknit Ltd.* [1988] F.S.R. 161, citing *Baumann* v. *Fussell, supra,* and see § 8–20 *ante.*
[51] *Ibid.* n. 48.
[52] *Brooks* v. *Religious Tract Society* (1897) 45 W.R. 476.
[53] *London Stereoscopic, etc., Co. Ltd. (The)* v. *Kelly* (1888) 5 T.L.R. 169; *Weldons Ltd* v. *United Press Ltd.* [1905–10] Mac.C.C. 293.
[54] *British Northrop Ltd.* v. *Texteam Blackburn Ltd.* [1974] R.P.C. 57; *S.W. Hart & Co. Pty. Ltd.* v. *Edwards Hot Water Systems* [1986] F.S.R. 575; *Interlego A.G.* v. *Tyco Industries Inc.* [1987] F.S.R. 409.
[55] *Baumann* v. *Fussell* [1978] R.P.C. 485.
[56] *Ibid.*
[57] *Brooks* v. *Religious Tract Society* (1897) 45 W.R. 476; *Baumann* v. *Fussell, supra.*

graph to create some harmonious design[58] or has composed his photograph to include a particular selection of features which the defendant has copied.[59] In each case it is a matter of degree.

8–63 **Reproduction of scenes.** The same kind of problem may arise where the plaintiff's work is a painting or drawing of a scene. Even if the scene is a well-known one, the artist may well have made an original contribution to his picture by his choice of viewpoint, the balance of features in the foreground, middle ground and background, and the other details. A defendant who makes a substantial use of these features will infringe.[60]

8–64 **Maps.** In the case of maps, copyright will subsist not only in the outlines of the various features but also in the selection, arrangement and presentation of the various parts, such as towns, lakes, rivers, etc. If the defendant has copied the plaintiff's selection, amounting to a substantial part, he will have infringed.[61]

8–65 **Reproduction of artistic work in a different dimension.** As was the position under the 1956 Act,[62] it is expressly provided by the 1988 Act that it is an infringement to make a copy of a two dimensional artistic work in three dimensions and to make a copy of a three dimensional artistic work in two dimensions.[63] There was some doubt about this prior to 1911[64] but this was established to be the position under the 1911 Act.[65]

8–66   The change of medium or dimension may make proof of infringement more difficult but this is only a question of degree.[66] Thus an object, such as a dress, may not, when spread out on a table or held up to view, in fact reproduce a perspective drawing of someone wearing the garment, although when worn it may resemble it.[67] In each case, however, this is a question of fact and degree and there is no reason in principle why a three-dimensional object such as a dress may not infringe the copyright in a sketch for such an article.[68] Associated drawings may be looked at together to see if there has been an infringement,[69] but where it is alleged

---

[58] See n. 55, *ante*.

[59] *Krisarts S.A.* v. *Briarfine Ltd.* [1977] F.S.R. 557; and see § 8–63, *post*.

[60] *Krisarts S.A.* v. *Briarfine Ltd., supra.*

[61] *Geographia Ltd.* v. *Penguin Books Ltd.* [1985] F.S.R. 208; see also *General Drafting Co. Inc.* v. *Andrews* 37 F. 2d 54.

[62] Copyright Act 1956, s.48(1).

[63] C.D.P.A. 1988, s.17(3).

[64] *Hanfstaengl* v. *Empire Palace* [1894] 2 Ch. 1, where it was held on the facts of that case that *tableaux vivants* were not infringements of copyright in pictures, although the House of Lords considered that as a matter of law this was possible. See [1895] A.C. 20.

[65] *Bradbury, Agnew & Co.* v. *Day* (1916) 32 T.L.R. 349 and *King Features Syndicate* v. *O. & M. Kleeman Ltd.* [1941] A.C. 417, followed in *Walt Disney Productions* v. *H. John Edwards Publishing Co. Pty. Ltd.* (1954) 71 W.N. (N.S.W.) 150.

[66] *King Features Syndicate* v. *O. & M. Kleeman Ltd.* [1940] Ch. 523 (at first instance).

[67] *Burke, etc. Ltd.* v. *Spicers Dress Designs* [1936] Ch. 400, a case decided very much on its own facts: See the cases cited in the following footnote.

[68] *Gleeson* v. *H.R. Denne Ltd.* [1975] R.P.C. 471; *Radley Gowns Ltd.* v. *Coftas Spyrou* [1975] F.S.R. 455; *J. Bernstein Ltd.* v. *Sidney Murray Ltd.* [1981] R.P.C. 303.

[69] *Rose Plastics GmbH* v. *William Beckett & Co. (Plastics) Ltd.* [1989] F.S.R. 113, relying on *Solar Thomson Engineering Co.* v. *Barton* [1977] R.P.C. 537. See § 8–71, *post*.

that the copyright in two separate drawings has been infringed by one composite work, each drawing must be considered separately.[70] Written instructions and other material may be referred to in considering whether there is any causal link between the three-dimensional work and the drawing.[71]

Functional objects. A common situation arises where it is alleged that   **8–67**
the defendant has infringed by manufacturing a functional article which the plaintiff alleges reproduces a design or manufacturing drawing in which he owns the copyright. As already noted,[72] substantial changes in the law relating to designs and related works have been introduced by the 1988 Act, which are considered elsewhere,[73] but it still remains necessary to consider the general question of what amounts to reproduction of an artistic work in such cases.

Usually the defendant will not have had access to the drawing itself but   **8–68**
will have made his article by copying the article which the plaintiff has himself manufactured from the drawing.[74] Indirect copying in this way will still amount to "reproduction" of the plaintiff's work.[75] As has been seen, in judging whether a substantial part has been taken of a work of this kind, the importance of the part taken may fall to be judged by how far it contributes to the conveying of information about the article in question.[76] What is protected is the skill and labour devoted to making the artistic work, not the skill and labour devoted to developing the idea or invention communicated.[77] On the other hand, while it is the object of copyright in cases of this kind to ensure that the skill and effort of the draughtsman are rewarded,[78] the drawing in which copyright is claimed must, as in all cases, be considered as a whole. It is not correct to attempt to separate the skills of the draughtsman into those which were purely "artistic" and those which were directed to giving the article its operational efficiency, perhaps at the direction of an engineer, and thus argue that if no use has been made of the former skills there will have been no infringement.[79]

---

[70] *UPL Group Ltd.* v. *Dux Engineers Ltd.* [1989] 3 N.Z.L.R. 135, at 143.

[71] *British Leyland Motor Corporation* v. *Armstrong Patents* [1984] F.S.R. 591 (C.A.); *Interlego A.G.* v. *Tyco Industries Inc.* [1987] F.S.R. 409 (C.A., Hong Kong) and [1989] A.C. 217, 265 (P.C.). The point often arose in relation to s.9(8) of the 1956 Act; see § 8–71, *post.*

[72] § 8–52 *ante.*

[73] Chap. 20, *post.*

[74] *I.e.* by reverse engineering.

[75] *British Leyland Motor Corpn. Ltd.* v. *Armstrong Patents Co. Ltd.* [1986] A.C. 577. It has been said that where plaintiff's design has been indirectly copied but only to the extent of features that are purely functional, there should be no infringement: See *George Ward (Moxley) Ltd.* v. *Richard Sankey Ltd.* [1988] F.S.R. 66, *per* Whitford J., citing the dissenting judgment of Lord Griffiths in *British Leyland Motor Corp.* v. *Armstrong Patents Co. Ltd., supra. Sed Quaere.*

[76] See § 8–60 *ante.*

[77] *Catnic Components Ltd.* v. *Hill & Smith Ltd.* [1982] R.P.C. 183, at page 223, approved in *Interlego Industries A.G.* v. *Tyco Industries Inc.* [1989] A.C. 217.

[78] *British Leyland Motor Corpn. Ltd.* v. *Armstrong Patents Co. Ltd.* [1983] F.S.R. 50 (at first instance).

[79] *Ibid.* [1986] A.C. 577, 621 (H.L.).

8–69   This is not to say that it may not be relevant to analyse the drawing in which copyright is claimed to see which parts of the drawing were original to the draughtsman and which were not. Thus if the plaintiff's drawing is based partly upon an earlier drawing and all that the defendant has appropriated is the work of the earlier draughtsman, there will be no infringement of the drawing in which the plaintiff claims copyright.[80] It will of course also be the case that if the plaintiff's drawing is based wholly upon an earlier drawing, such that there is no copyright in the plaintiff's drawing at all, there can be no infringement.[81]

8–70   **The 1956 Act: section 9(8) defence.** Although the 1956 Act provided that it might be an infringement to convert an artistic work in two dimensions into a three-dimensional form,[82] section 9(8) of the 1956 Act further provided as follows: "The making of an object of any description which is in three dimensions shall not be taken to infringe the copyright in an artistic work in two dimensions, if the object would not appear, to persons who are not experts in relation to objects of that description, to be a reproduction of the artistic work." This provision caused considerable difficulties of interpretation and has not been repeated in the 1988 Act. Nevertheless, the 1956 Act will continue to apply in relation to acts done before August 1, 1989,[83] and the section 9(8) defence will therefore continue to be of relevance for some time to come.

8–71   In the circumstances, it may be of assistance to set out certain principles which appear from the subsection itself and the cases in which it was considered:

(i)   The subsection is a defence and only arises after the plaintiff has established that there has been what would otherwise be an infringement.[84] However, in practice, where the judge has found the substantial part test satisfied, it is unlikely he will find the section 9(8) test not satisfied[85]; see point (vii) below.

(ii)   As it is a defence, it must be pleaded by the defendant, on whom rests the onus of establishing it,[86] and it is a question of fact,[87] and impression, and thus normally will not be interfered with on appeal.[88]

(iii)   It only applies directly to infringement by reproduction, and of artistic works. However, it may be relevant also to the indirect infringements which are concerned with the sale and so on of articles the making of which did or would have constituted an infringement of the copyright in an artistic work.[89]

---

[80] See § 8–60 *ante.*
[81] As in *Interlego Industries A.G.* v. *Tyco Industries Inc.* [1989] A.C. 217; and see § 3–33, *ante.*
[82] s.48(1).
[83] C.D.P.A. 1988, Sched. 1, para. 14(1).
[84] *L.B. (Plastics) Ltd.* v. *Swish Products Ltd.* [1979] R.P.C. 551.
[85] *Ibid.*
[86] *Ibid.*, but in a criminal case the onus may be on the prosecution to show that the provision does not apply. See *R.* v. *Lee* [1980] F.S.R. 314.
[87] See n. 84, *ante.*
[88] *S.W. Hart & Co. Pty. Ltd.* v. *Edwards Hot Water Systems* [1986] F.S.R. 575.
[89] See § 9–3 *et seq., post.*

(iv)   Although it may be more convenient to compare the defendant's three-dimensional object with the plaintiff's three-dimensional object made from the plaintiff's original two-dimensional work, strictly the first should be compared with the last,[90] and it is the plaintiff's drawing taken as a whole which should be studied.[91]

(v)   Although it appears that the judge may be assisted by experts in deciding whether or not there has been copying, he may not have the assistance of experts in applying this test.[92] In virtually all the reported cases where the test has been relevant it has been the judge who has acted as the non-expert[93] although, in some cases, the judge may not in fact be entirely non-expert,[94] at least as to the interpretation of such matters as design drawings.[95] The desirability of calling non-expert evidence was raised in some of the earlier cases,[96] although the view was expressed that non-expert evidence was probably only necessary where the matter was in some doubt.[97] Indeed, in the only reported case where non-expert evidence was called, it was rejected.[98] In fact it has been doubted whether such evidence could be called and what its value would be if called.[99]

(vi)   The test is one of appearance[1] and it is, therefore, a little difficult to see why it was necessary to have this statutory test at all, having regard to the generally accepted tests from the cases still applicable to two-dimensional infringements[2] from which it would seem that, even in those cases, a copy will not be an infringement unless it satisfies an appearance test to the non-expert.

(vii)   It is suggested that, perhaps in an effort to avoid findings adverse to plaintiffs where copying has been established, various findings have been made with regard to section 9(8) which are, perhaps, a little surprising. Thus it is now accepted that it is proper to take into account any written matter on, say, the copyright drawing,[3] notwithstanding that what is in issue is artistic, not literary, infringement and the test is one of appearance. What if the writing is inaccurate? What if the writing is an extremely comprehensive explanation written by an expert? Again, where two or more contemporaneous, interrelated drawings are relied upon, whether sectional or plan, the Court may look at all of them for this purpose,

---

[90] See. n. 84. *ante*; *Johnstone Safety Ltd.* v. *Peter Cook (International) Plc.* [1990] F.S.R. 161.

[91] *Guilford Kapwood Ltd.* v. *Embsay Fabrics Ltd.* [1983] F.S.R. 567.

[92] See n. 84, *ante*.

[93] See *Dorling* v. *Honnor Marine Ltd.* [1965] Ch. 1; *I.M.I. Developments Ltd.* v. *F.C. Harrison Ltd.* [1970] R.P.C. 299; see also *British Northrop Ltd.* v. *Texteam Blackburn Ltd.* [1974] R.P.C. 57; *Sifam Electrical Instrument Co. Ltd.* v. *Sangamo Weston Ltd.* [1971] F.S.R. 337; *Antocks Lairn Ltd.* v. *I. Bloohn Ltd.* [1971] F.S.R. 490; *Catnic Components Ltd.* v. *Hill & Smith Ltd.* [1978] F.S.R. 405; *Nichols Advanced Vehicle Systems Inc.* v. *Rees* [1979] R.P.C. 127.

[94] *Ibid.*

[95] See n. 84, *ante*.

[96] See n. 93, *ante*.

[97] *Ibid.*

[98] *Lerose Ltd.* v. *Hawick Jersey International Ltd.* [1974] R.P.C. 42; See also *S.W. Hart & Co. Pty. Ltd.* v. *Edwards Hot Water Systems* [1986] F.S.R. 575.

[99] See n. 84, *ante*.

[1] *Ibid.*

[2] § 8–54, *ante*.

[3] *L.B. (Plastics) Ltd.* v. *Swish Products Ltd.*, *supra*; *Allibert S.A.* v. *O'Connor* [1981] F.S.R. 613.

together with any writing on them. The Court is not compelled to look at each drawing in isolation.[4] The position is otherwise if the drawings are not associated in the above sense,[5] or were not contemporaneous,[6] when each drawing must be examined in turn, and alone.[7] It is a matter of degree whether the copyright in sectional drawings can be infringed by a complete three dimensional object constructed from those drawings.[8] Some drawings, whether sectional or not, may be so simple that any reasonably intelligent person could visualise what they represented in three dimensions. Others may be extremely difficult to understand so that many non-experts would get little or nothing out of them.[9] In deciding whether a sectional drawing is infringed by a three dimensional article, the Court may compare a sectioned article with the drawing.[10] Where the drawings are sectional drawings, the notional unskilled observer should be treated as having the equivalent sectional piece before him for the purposes of comparison. In making the comparison he will be entitled to interpret the sectional drawing in the light of any contemporary associated drawings. If then an unskilled but reasonably intelligent observer would be able to recognise the section or piece to be an accurate or substantially accurate reproduction in three dimensional form of what is represented in two dimensions by the sectional drawing, the article will be an infringement. This is so even if the unsectioned article might not appear to him to be a three dimensional reproduction of the sectioned drawing.[11] But it has been held that this principle does not permit the notional observer to dissect the three dimensional object into its constituent parts to make the comparison.[12]

(viii)   It has been said[13] that it would be a wrong approach in deciding a question under section 9(8) to enumerate dissimilarities which are really there and which a non-expert would have recognised as dissimilarities, or points of identity which were not really there which a non-expert would have mistakenly thought he saw as points of identity. The defence under section 9(8) is concerned with points of resemblance or identity which are really there, but which the non-expert would have failed to recognise as points of resemblance or identity in the three-dimensional form, with the

---

[4] *Temple Instruments Ltd.* v. *Hollis Heels* [1971] F.S.R. 634; *Solar Thompson Engineering Co. Ltd.* v. *Barton* [1977] R.P.C. 537; *Rose Plastics GmbH* v. *William Beckett & Co. (Plastics) Ltd.* [1989] F.S.R. 113.

[5] *Interlego A.G.* v. *Tyco Industries Inc.* [1987] F.S.R. 409 (C.A., Hong Kong).

[6] *Merlet* v. *Mothercare plc* [1986] R.P.C. 115, 134.

[7] See n. 4 *ante*, and also *UPL Group Ltd.* v. *Dux Engineers Ltd.* [1989] 3 N.Z.L.R. 135, at 143.

[8] *Merchant Adventurers Ltd.* v. *M. Grew & Co. Ltd.* [1972] Ch. 242; and see *Ogden Industries Pty. Ltd.* v. *Kis (Australia) Ltd.* [1983] F.S.R. 619, where the copyright in cross-sectional drawings of key blanks was held to be infringed by the making of keys.

[9] *Ibid.*; *S.W. Hart & Co. Pty. Ltd.* v. *Edwards Hot Water Systems* [1986] F.S.R. 575.

[10] *Solar Thompson Engineering Co. Ltd.* v. *Barton* [1977] R.P.C. 537; *Brady* v. *Chemical Process Equipments Pte. Ltd.* [1988] F.S.R. 457; *Leco Instruments (U.K.) Ltd.* v. *Land Pyrometers Ltd.* [1982] R.P.C. 133; *Johnstone Safety Ltd.* v. *Peter Cook (International) Plc.* [1990] F.S.R. 161.

[11] *Ibid.*.

[12] *Merlet* v. *Mothercare plc, supra*, where, at first instance, the judge declined to dissect a garment into its constituent parts for the purpose of comparing it with cutting patterns. Perhaps the position would be different if the various panels of the defendant's garment could be unstitched and produced in evidence as the infringing articles.

[13] See n. 84, *ante*.

result that it would not have appeared to him that there had been the reproduction of any substantial part of the original artistic work. If it requires "detective work" to see that the three-dimensional object reproduces the plaintiff's drawing, the defence will probably be made out.[14] Differences in the function of the respective articles are irrelevant.[15]

Architects plans and works of architecture. It has already been seen **8-72** that copyright may subsist in both architects' plans and in the works of architecture themselves.[16] Architects are therefore concerned with infringements of their rights in three different forms. These are the copying of plans in the form of other plans,[17] the copying of plans in the form of buildings, and the copying of a building by another building.[18] The copying of a building by a two dimensional representation, such as a photograph or drawing, is not an infringement.[19]

Infringement of plan by plan. Where plans are alleged to be infringed **8-73** by other plans or sketches, the question to be decided is similar to that arising in connection with other artistic works.[20]

Infringement of plan by building. As an example of the second type of **8-74** infringement, it has been held[21] that an architect's elevation representing a shop front was infringed by the erection of an actual shop incorporating the elevation, on the ground that the same was a reproduction of the elevation "in a material form." It is submitted that this decision is confined to cases in which the appearance of the complete building appeals to the eye as being a reproduction of what appears on the architect's plan or elevation, and that it would not be an infringement of the copyright in a plan, such as a ground plan, to erect a building based thereon, if the resulting erection bore no resemblance to the plan except when dissected and measured.[22] But if a completed structure appears to the eye to be a reproduction of what appears in a floor plan then it will be an infringement.[23]

Infringement of building by building. The third form of infringement **8-75** is confined to copying that in which copyright subsists, namely the features of the building having artistic quality. Copyright is infringed by something which, to the eye, is a copy of the original,[24] and the use of pro-

---

[14] *Rose Plastics GmbH* v. *William Beckett (Plastics) Ltd.* [1989] F.S.R. 113.

[15] *Brady* v. *Chemical Process Equipments Pte. Ltd.* [1988] F.S.R. 457.

[16] See § 2–25, *ante*.

[17] See *Czezowski* v. *George W. Warr & King* (1959) 173 *Estates Gazette* 735, which was also concerned with the question of publication of plans; and *Ancher Mortlock Murray and Wooley Pty. Ltd and Others* v. *Hooker Homes Pty. Ltd.* [1971] 2 N.S.W.L.R. 278.

[18] See *Hay and Hay Construction Co. Ltd.* v. *Sloan* (1958) 12 D.L.R. (2d) 397; *Hay* v. *Saunders & Saunders* (1959) 17 D.L.R. (2d) 352 and *Ancher Mortlock Murray and Wooley Pty. Ltd. and Others* v. *Hooker Homes Pty. Ltd.*, *supra*.

[19] C.D.P.A. 1988, s.62. See § 10–87, *post*.

[20] See § 8–54 *et seq. ante*.

[21] *Chabot* v. *Davies* (1936) 155 L.T. 525; [1936] 3 All E.R. 221.

[22] See, *e.g. Burke, etc., Ltd.* v. *Spicers Dress Designs* [1936] Ch. 400.

[23] *Lend Lease Homes Pty. Ltd.* v. *Warrigal Homes Pty. Ltd.* [1970] 3 N.S.W.R. 265, where *Burke, etc. Ltd.* v. *Spicers Dress Designs*, *supra*, was distinguished.

[24] As in *Meikle* v. *Maufe* [1941] 3 All E.R. 144.

cesses or methods of construction would not, it is thought, constitute an infringement. Naturally it will be more difficult to prove infringement of copyright in an ordinary building than in one showing marked originality. An architect, who has erected a façade showing six windows and a door, clearly could not complain of another building showing the like number of windows and doors, for each architect may have drawn from common sources. But if his ordinary building has been slavishly copied down to the smallest detail, there seems no good reason for depriving him of the right to complain. Slight differences between buildings of no marked originality will prevent them from being held to be copies of each other, which would not be the case if the buildings were of an original character.

F. Copying in relation to other works

(i) Sound recordings

8–76   **The 1988 Act.** There is no further definition in the 1988 Act of "to copy" in relation to sound recordings. It is therefore an infringement of the copyright in a sound recording to copy it[25] or a substantial part of it,[26] either directly or indirectly.[27]

8–77   **The 1956 Act.** In relation to acts of infringement done before August 1, 1989, the 1956 Act continues to apply,[28] and by section 12(5)(a) of that Act it was an infringement of the copyright in a sound recording to make a record embodying the recording or a substantial part of it,[29] whether the record embodying the original recording was utilised directly or indirectly in so doing.[30] "Record" was defined as meaning any disc, tape, perforated roll or other device in which sounds are embodied so as to be capable (with or without the aid of some other instrument) of being automatically reproduced therefrom.[31]

8–78   **The Acts compared.** Under the 1956 Act it was clearly an infringement of the copyright in a sound recording to make any kind of device whereby the same sounds might be automatically reproduced. Thus it is suggested that in addition to the obvious ways in which the copyright in a sound recording might be so infringed, it would have been an infringement to store the recording digitally in a computer, if the sounds embodied in the recording were then capable of being reproduced automatically from the computer.[32] However, it was not an infringement of that copyright to reproduce the recorded material in musical notation or other written form, or to produce another record with, say, different musicians playing

---

[25] C.D.P.A. 1988, ss.16(1)(a), 17(1).
[26] *Ibid.* s.16(3)(a).
[27] *Ibid.* s.16(3)(b).
[28] *Ibid.* Sched. 1, para. 14(1).
[29] *Ibid.* s.49(1).
[30] *Ibid.* s.13(5).
[31] *Ibid.* s.48(1).
[32] Compare s.2 of the Copyright (Computer Software) Amendment Act 1985, which did not, however, deal with this issue.

the same music.[33] The 1988 Act is not so explicit but it is suggested that it is to the same effect.[34]

The 1956 Act: sound-tracks not "records." The definition of a sound **8–79** recording in the 1956 Act excluded "a sound-track associated with a cinematograph film," and this phrase was defined in section 13(10) of the 1956 Act as meaning any record of sounds which was incorporated in any print, negative, tape or other article on which the film or part of it, in so far as it consisted of visual images, was recorded, or which was issued by the maker of the film for use in conjunction with such an article. Such a sound recording was protected as part of the cinematograph film and not as a sound recording. It was provided, in section 13(9) of the 1956 Act that, where the sounds embodied in any sound-track were also embodied in a record other than such a sound-track or a record derived (directly or indirectly) from such a sound-track, copyright in the film was not infringed by any use made of the record, but this was a limitation upon the copyright in the sound-track of films, not upon the copyright in sound recordings existing apart from, though associated with, such sound-track. It would appear, therefore, that if the sounds embodied in a sound-track were also embodied in some other form of record, then copyright would have subsisted in such sound recording under section 12 of the 1956 Act. This might have happened if a live performance was recorded on a record other than a sound-track at the same time as it was recorded on a sound-track, or if a record other than the sound-track was made from the sound-track. Under the 1988 Act copyright subsists in the sound-track of a film as a sound recording.[35] A film sound-track which was to be taken to be included in a cinematograph film under the 1956 Act is now to be treated as a sound recording and not as part of the film.[36]

(ii) Films

The 1988 Act. Under the 1988 Act it is an infringement of the copyright **8–80** in a film to make a copy of it,[37] or a substantial part of it,[38] whether directly or indirectly.[39] This includes making a photograph of the whole or any substantial part of any image forming part of the film.[40]

The 1956 Act. Under the 1956 Act, which in relation to acts of infringe- **8–81** ment still applies to acts done before August 1, 1989,[41] it was an infringement of the copyright in a cinematograph film to make a copy of the film.[42] "Copy," in relation to a cinematograph film, was defined as any

---

[33] *CBS Records Australia Ltd.* v. *Telmak Teleproducts (Aust.) Pty. Ltd.* (1988) 79 A.L.R. 604.
[34] See C.D.P.A. 1988, s.172(2). But note that s.17(2) of the Act, which provides that copying includes storing a work in any medium by electronic means, only applies in relation to literary, dramatic, musical and artistic works. See § 8–19, *ante*.
[35] See § 2–29 *ante*.
[36] *Ibid.* C.D.P.A. 1988, Sched. 1, § 8(1).
[37] C.D.P.A. 1988, ss.16(1)(*a*), 17(1).
[38] *Ibid.* s.16(3)(*a*).
[39] *Ibid.* s.16(3)(*b*).
[40] *Ibid.* s.17(4).
[41] *Ibid.* Sched. 1, para. 14(1).
[42] Copyright Act 1956, s.13(5)(*a*).

print, negative, tape or other article on which the film or part of it was recorded.[43] Having regard to this definition, the "substantial part" test in the 1956 Act was held not to apply to infringement by making a copy of a film. It was therefore an infringement to make a copy of a single frame from a film since this constituted a "part" of the film.[44] It appears that it would also have been an infringement to make a copy of part of a single frame, provided that what was copied was a substantial part of that frame.[45]

8–82   **The Acts compared.** It would thus appear that the further statutory definition of copying in relation to a film in the 1988 Act has confirmed the judicial interpretation of the equivalent provision in the 1956 Act, and that therefore no substantive change has been effected. For there to be copying of a film under the 1956 Act it was clear that the actual sounds and visual images had to be reproduced, and that it was not sufficient if merely the sequence of events and location were re-created.[46] It is thought that this is also the position under the 1988 Act.

8–83   **The 1956 Act: sound-tracks.** Under the 1956 Act a cinematograph film was to be taken to include the sounds embodied in any sound-track associated with it.[47] But where the sounds embodied in the sound-track of a film were also embodied in a record, other than a sound-track or a record derived (directly or indirectly) from such a sound-track, the copyright in the film was not infringed by any use made of that record.[48] This provision was presumably required because it might otherwise have been argued that the copyright in a film (including sounds) could have been infringed by performing or broadcasting recorded words or music subsequently incorporated in the film. A film sound-track which was to be taken to be included in a cinematograph film under the 1956 Act is now to be treated as a sound recording and not as part of the film.[49]

(iii) Broadcasts

8–84   **The 1988 Act.** No further definition of "copying" in relation to a broadcast is given in the 1988 Act other than that it includes making a photograph of the whole or any substantial part of any image forming part of the broadcast.[50] In the usual way it will also be an infringement to copy the whole or any substantial part of the broadcast,[51] whether directly or indirectly.[52]

---

[43] *Ibid.* s.13(10).
[44] *Spelling Goldberg Productions Inc.* v. *B.P.C. Publishing Ltd.* [1981] R.P.C. 283.
[45] *Ibid.* p. 299.
[46] Although in such a case the copyright in the film-script or other underlying works might be infringed. See § 8–122 *et seq., post.* See also *Zeccola* v. *Universal City Studios Inc.* (1982) 46 A.L.R. 189 and *Telmak Teleproducts Australia Pty. Ltd.* v. *Bond International Pty. Ltd.* (1986) 65 A.L.R. 319, where the question was left open.
[47] See § 2–30 *ante.*
[48] Copyright Act 1956, s.13(9) proviso.
[49] See § 2–30 *ante,* and C.D.P.A. 1988, Sched. 1, § 8(1).
[50] C.D.P.A. 1988, s.17(4). But see s.71 of that Act, § 10–119, *post.*
[51] *Ibid.* s.16(3)(*a*).
[52] *Ibid.* s.16(3)(*b*).

The 1956 Act. The 1956 Act provided that, in the case of a television   **8–85**
broadcast, in so far as it consisted of visual images, the making, otherwise
than for private purposes, of a cinematograph film of it, or of a copy of
such a film, was a restricted act.[53] In the case of a sound broadcast or of a
television broadcast in so far as it consisted of sounds, the making, otherwise than for private purposes, of a sound recording of it, or of a record
embodying such a recording, was a restricted act.[54] The reference to
sounds included references to signals serving for the impartation of matter
otherwise than in the form of sounds or visual images.[55] In the case of a
television or sound broadcast made by the BBC or by the IBA, these
restrictions were to apply whether the act was done by the reception of the
broadcast or by making use of any record, print, negative, tape or other
article on which the broadcast had been recorded.[56]

The 1956 Act: Infringement of television broadcasts consisting of   **8–86**
visual images. So far as concerned television broadcasts consisting of
visual images, it was provided that the restrictions imposed were to apply
to any sequence of images sufficient to be seen as a moving picture, and
that, for the purpose of establishing an infringement of such copyright, it
was not necessary to prove that the acts in question extended to more than
such a sequence of images.[57] It appears, however, to be implied by this
provision that the reproduction of a single picture, or series of separate
pictures, which could not be used as a moving picture, would not have
constituted an infringement.

The 1956 Act: "Otherwise than for private purposes." The making of   **8–87**
films or records of broadcasts was only an infringement of the broadcasting rights if made "otherwise than for private purposes." It was provided
that a film or record should be taken to be made "otherwise than for private purposes" if it was made for the purposes of sale or letting for hire of
any copy of the film or record, broadcasting the film or record or including
it in a cable programme, or causing the film or record to be seen or heard
in public.[58] It would seem therefore, that if, for instance, only one cinematograph film was made of a television broadcast and this was made for the
purposes of selling such film (not a copy of it), this did not amount to
"otherwise than for private purposes." This may have had the surprising
result that, for instance, a person who made "one-off" video tapes of television broadcasts and sold them for exhibition abroad, did not thereby
infringe the copyright in the television broadcast. It should be observed
that the expression here was "in public" and not "by a paying audience"
and may, therefore, have had more extensive operation. As will be seen,[59]
it may not have been an infringement of the broadcasting rights to cause
television programmes to be seen by certain clubs or associations, but it

---

[53] Copyright Act 1956, s.14(4)(*a*).
[54] *Ibid.* s.14(4)(*b*).
[55] *Ibid.* s.14(11), as inserted by the Cable and Broadcasting Act 1984, Sched. 5, para. 6(8).
[56] *Ibid.* s.14(5). As to the definition of "reception" in this context, so as to cover simultaneous
transmissions, see s.48(4).
[57] Copyright Act 1956, s.14(6).
[58] s.14(7) as amended by the Cable and Broadcasting Act 1984, s.23(1).
[59] § 10–122, *post.*

may well have been an infringement of the recording rights for such associations to record performances for future exhibition to their members.

(iv) Cable programmes

8–88   **The 1988 Act.** No further definition of "to copy" in relation to a cable programme is given in the 1988 Act other than it includes making a photograph of the whole or any substantial part of any image forming part of the cable programme.[60]

8–89   **The 1956 Act.** The 1956 Act provided that it was an infringement of the copyright in a cable programme, in so far as it consisted of visual images, to make, otherwise than for private purposes, a cinematograph film of it or a copy of such a film or, in so far as it consisted of sounds, to make, otherwise than for private purposes, a sound recording of it or a record embodying such a recording.[61] The Act contained equivalent provisions to those relating to broadcasts in relation to indirect infringement[62] (save that they applied to any cable programme), the extent of the restricted acts[63] and the definition of making "for private purposes."[64]

(v) Typographical arrangements

8–90   **The 1988 Act.** The 1988 Act provides that in relation to the typographical arrangement of a published edition, copying means making a facsimile copy of the arrangement.[65] "Facsimile copy" is defined as including a copy which is reduced or enlarged in scale.[66]

8–91   **The 1956 Act.** The 1956 Act provided that the copyright in a published edition of a work was infringed by the making, by any photographic or similar process, of a reproduction of the typographical arrangement of the edition.[67]

3. Infringement by the Issue of Copies to the Public

8–92   **The 1988 Act.** As has been seen, one of the acts restricted by the copyright in all works is the issue of copies of the work to the public.[68] With certain exceptions, the expression "the issue to the public of copies of a

---

[60] C.D.P.A. 1988, s.17(4).
[61] Copyright Act 1956, s.14A(5), as inserted by the Cable and Broadcasting Act 1984.
[62] *Ibid.* s.14A(6), § 8–85 *ante.*
[63] *Ibid.* s.14A(7), § 8–86 *ante.*
[64] *Ibid.* s.14A(8), § 8–87 *ante.*
[65] C.D.P.A. 1988, s.17(5).
[66] *Ibid.* s.178.
[67] Copyright Act 1956, s.15(3). In *Machinery Market Ltd.* v. *Sheen Publishing Ltd.* [1983] F.S.R. 431, the defendants were held liable although it was their printers who had made the reproductions. It is not clear whether the printers were treated simply as the defendants' agents, although no doubt the defendants were liable for having authorised the infringement.
[68] C.D.P.A. 1988, ss.16(1)(*b*), 18(1), *ante*, § 8–3.

work" in this context means the act of putting into circulation copies not previously put into circulation, whether in the United Kingdom or elsewhere.[69] It is further provided that any subsequent distribution, sale, hiring or loan of those copies, or any subsequent importation of those copies into the United Kingdom, will not amount to an infringement under this class of restricted act.[70] Exceptions to this last provision are made in the case of sound recordings, films and computer programs, where any rental of copies to the public will amount to an infringement for this purpose.[71] "Rental" means any arrangement under which a copy of a work is made available (a) for payment (in money or money's worth) or (b) in the course of a business, as part of services or amenities for which payment is made, in either case on terms that it will or may be returned.[72] The full effect of these provisions is not clear. As will be seen, they appear to differ from the equivalent provisions of the 1956 Act.

The 1956 Act. The 1956 Act, which still continues to apply in relation to   **8–93**
acts done before August 1, 1989,[73] provided that in relation to literary, dramatic, musical and artistic works it was a restricted act to publish the work.[74] Although section 49(2)(c) of that Act provided that any such work should only be taken to have been published if reproductions of the work had been issued to the public, it was held[75] that this was not a definition of "publishing" for the purposes of that Act but related solely to the words used in sections 2(2) and 3(3) (which laid down conditions for subsistence of copyright in such works).[76] The expression "publishing" in the context of infringement therefore did not simply mean the issuing of works to the public, for otherwise an innocent retailer might have been liable for infringement.[77] Nor did it mean that which is done by a publisher.[78] Rather, it meant making public what had previously not been made public in the United Kingdom.[79] A defendant could therefore only be liable under this head if copies of the work had never before been issued to the public in the United Kingdom. The burden of proof is on the plaintiff to establish that the copyright work was previously unpublished in this sense.[80] Further, where the publication was, for example, by way of sale, it seems that only a few sales would have constituted publication in this sense,[81] presumably because after the first few sales the work would have

---

[69] *Ibid.* s.18(2).
[70] *Ibid.* ss.18(2)(*a*), (*b*).
[71] *Ibid.* s.18(2).
[72] *Ibid.* s.178.
[73] *Ibid.* Sched. 1, para. 14(1).
[74] Copyright Act 1956, ss.2(5)(*b*), 3(5)(*b*).
[75] *Infabrics Ltd.* v. *Jaytex Ltd.* [1982] A.C. 1.
[76] § 3–12, *et seq.*, *ante*.
[77] *Infabrics Ltd.* v. *Jaytex Ltd.*, *supra*, pp. 15, 17.
[78] *Ibid.* p. 16.
[79] *Ibid.*, p.17; *Wham-O Manufacturing Co.* v. *Lincoln Industries Ltd.* [1982] R.P.C. 281, 306. Under s.1(2) of the Copyright Act 1911 this was made express.
[80] See n. 74, p. 21.
[81] *Ibid.* p. 25.

been made public.[82] It is uncertain whether for the present purpose a work was published simply by the offer or exposure of copies to the public[83] or whether the public had actually to be issued with copies.[84] It is suggested that the former view is to be preferred. In accordance with the usual rule, the copyright in a work was infringed if a substantial part of it was published.[85] The place of publication was the place where copies were put on sale to the public.[86]

8–94   The 1956 Act did not require that for the purposes of infringement by publication the copies of the work so published should themselves have been unauthorised reproductions. Thus, for example, in the case of a work previously unpublished in the United Kingdom, it is thought it would have been an infringement of copyright to issue to the public in the United Kingdom imported copies of the work lawfully made in another territory.[87]

8–95   **The 1988 and 1956 Acts compared.** Under the 1988 Act the scope of this class of infringing act has been widened in that it now applies in the case of all descriptions of copyright works. More significantly, where particular copies of a work have not yet been put into circulation, it seems clear that the 1988 Act, unlike the 1956 Act, makes it an infringement to put *those* copies into circulation. This will be so notwithstanding the fact that the work has already been published in the sense that other copies of the work have already been put into circulation by the plaintiff in the United Kingdom. The 1988 Act therefore appears to be different from the 1956 Act in this respect. As under the 1956 Act, it will not matter whether the copies put into circulation were made with the consent of the copyright owner or are in fact infringing copies. The expression "in the United Kingdom or elsewhere" in section 18(2) of the 1988 Act apparently refers back to the expression "copies not previously put into circulation"[88]; thus if those copies have previously been put into circulation in, for example, the United States of America, it will not be an infringement under this section to put those copies into circulation in the United Kingdom.

It is less clear what the expression "the act of putting into circulation

---

[82] See also s.49(2)(*b*) of the Copyright Act 1956, which indicated that in regard to infringement, a merely colourable publication, not intended to satisfy the reasonable requirements of the public, should not be disregarded.

[83] *British Northrop Ltd.* v. *Texteam Blackburn Ltd.* [1974] R.P.C. 57 relying on *Francis, Day & Hunter* v. *Feldman & Co.* [1914] 2 Ch. 728. See also *Television Broadcasts Ltd.* v. *Mandarin Video Holdings Sdn. Bhd.* [1984] F.S.R. 111. These cases, however, were concerned with what constituted publication for the purposes of subsistence of copyright.

[84] *Infabrics Ltd.* v. *Jaytex Ltd.* [1980] Ch. 282 (C.A.), *per* Buckley L.J. at p. 291, *obiter,* although taking a mistaken view overall as to the meaning of publication. See [1982] A.C. 1 (H.L.).

[85] Copyright Act 1956, s.49(1), *Infabrics Ltd.* v. *Jaytex Ltd.* at [1982] A.C. p. 15. As to the doubt which existed previously, see Copinger (12th ed.), § 495.

[86] *British Northrop Ltd.* v. *Texteam Blackburn Ltd.* [1974] R.P.C. 57 (dealing with "publication" for the purposes of subsistence of copyright); and see *MacMillan* v. *Khan, etc., Zaka* [1895] I.L.R. 19 Bom. 557.

[87] But see Chap. 14, *post.*

[88] Presumably it cannot refer back to the words "the act of putting into circulation" since under s.16 the exclusive right is given to do this act "in the United Kingdom."

copies" itself means. In the common type of case the chain of distribution will start with the producer of the goods, which are then sent to a wholesaler, who in turn distributes them to retailers, who then make them available to the public. The producer at the head of the chain no doubt is the principal cause of the goods being put into eventual circulation and perhaps it is the intention of the Act to make this person liable for the primary infringement of issuing copies of the work to the public. This is given some support by the express provision that any subsequent distribution, sale, hiring or loan of those copies does not amount to an infringement, indicating perhaps that it is only the person at the head of the distribution chain who is liable under this section.[89]

8–96 The use of the word "subsequent" in subsections 18(2)(*a*) and (*b*) of the 1988 Act to qualify the acts specified there of distribution, sale, hiring, loan and importation indicates that any such act, if not subsequent to an earlier act of putting copies into circulation, will amount to an infringement under this section. As will be seen,[90] in general the acts of importation, distribution, sale and hiring amount to separate acts of infringement, but only if infringing copies are dealt with and only if the defendant has a sufficient degree of guilty knowledge. Under the present section, however, whoever puts into circulation copies of a work will be liable, notwithstanding his lack of knowledge, unless there has been some preceding act of putting those copies into circulation. The use of the expression "putting into circulation copies" appears to indicate that the offer or exposure of copies to the public will not by itself be sufficient to constitute an infringement.

8–97 If it is correct that the mere importation of copies of a work not previously in circulation amounts to an infringement under this section, the result appears to be anomalous and unduly harsh. Thus, as has already been noted, even the act of secondary infringement by importation of infringing copies is only committed if the defendant has sufficient knowledge that they are infringing copies. The word "subsequent" was only introduced into subsection (2)(*b*) at a late stage in the passage of the Bill; as the Bill previously stood it was clear that no importation of copies of a work could amount to an infringement under this section. The position may be that if goods are being imported there will always be someone higher up the distribution chain who has put those copies into circulation, even if it is only by the act of exportation from a place abroad. The difficulty with this view is that, if correct, it would mean that no act of importation would ever amount to an infringement under this section, and therefore it is difficult to see why subsection (2)(*b*) was enacted at all or why the word "subsequent" was introduced into what was previously a clear provision.

8–98 **The "rental" right.** The 1988 Act makes the rental of copies of certain works an act of primary infringement for the first time. The principal intention appears to have been to enable the owners of the copyright in

---

[89] *cf.* the definition of "publication" in the 1988 Act, s.175(1)(*a*).
[90] See § 9–3 *et seq., post.*

such works to prevent legitimate copies of the works being rented out and then duplicated in circumstances beyond the owner's control. Thus, as has already been seen, in the case of sound recordings, films and computer programs the restricted act of issuing copies to the public is to include "any" rental of copies to the public.[91] This appears to mean that any rental of such articles will amount to an infringement if done without the licence of the copyright owner, whether or not the articles are infringing copies and whether or not those articles have already been put into circulation. Again, in contrast to the act of secondary infringement by the letting for hire of infringing copies, no degree of guilty knowledge is required as an ingredient of the tort. In cases of this kind there will therefore usually be at least two separate instances of infringement under this section, first, the act of putting copies into circulation by the person at the head of the distribution chain (if done in the United Kingdom), second, the successive rental of those copies to the public by the person at the end of the chain. This provision does not, however, apply in relation to a copy of a sound recording, film or computer program acquired by any person before August 1, 1989 for the purpose of renting it to the public.[92] Nor does it apply to works other than those specified. Thus no such right is conferred on the owners of literary, dramatic or musical works which may be embodied in the rented work. The definition of "rental" has already been referred to,[93] and includes any arrangement under which a copy of a work is made available in the course of a business, as part of services or amenities for which payment is made. The provision of video cassette recordings of films by hotels to guests will therefore amount to "rental." Where a licensing scheme is in operation relating to such rentals this may be subject to a reference to the Copyright Tribunal.[94] Where there is no certified licensing scheme in operation, the Secretary of State may nevertheless provide for the rental of such copies to be treated as licensed subject to payment of a royalty.[95] This is dealt with elsewhere.[96]

4. Infringement by Performance, Showing or Playing of the Work in Public

8–99   **The 1988 Act.** Under the 1988 Act it is an act restricted by the copyright in a literary, dramatic or musical work to perform the work in public.[97] For this purpose, "performance" is defined to include delivery in the case of lectures, addresses, speeches and sermons[98] and, in general, includes any mode of visual or acoustic presentation, including presentation by means of a sound recording, film, broadcast or cable programme of the

---

[91] C.P.D.A. 1988, s.18(2).
[92] *Ibid.* Sched. 1, para. 14(2).
[93] § 8–92, *ante.*
[94] See C.D.P.A. 1988, s.117(c); § 15–65 *et seq., post,* and, in particular, § 15–90, *post.*
[95] *Ibid.* s.66.
[96] *Post,* § 10–100.
[97] C.D.P.A. 1988, s.19(1).
[98] *Ibid.* s.19(2)(a).

work.[99] These latter expressions are all further defined.[1] Thus, in addition to the obvious ways in which such works may be performed, a musical work embodied in a sound recording may be performed by its being played on a gramophone. In relation to a dramatic work, it is thought that if the incidents of the plot are visually presented this will amount to an infringement, even though the same language is not used.[2]

In relation to a sound recording, film, broadcast or cable programme   **8–100**
the playing or showing of the work in public is a restricted act.[3] Thus, for example, the playing of a sound recording in public by means of a record player or juke box would amount to a public performance not only of the literary or musical works embodied in it, but also of the sound recording itself.

In the usual way it is not only an infringement to do such acts in rela-   **8–101**
tion to the work as a whole but also in relation to any substantial part of it.[4] Again, it is a separate infringement to authorise such acts.[5]

Broadcasting and performance. It seems clear that under the 1988 Act   **8–102**
the expressions "performance," "playing" and "showing" used in the above senses include the doing of such acts by means of apparatus for receiving visual images or sounds conveyed by electronic means.[6] Thus, for example, the playing of a radio or television in public will amount to a public performance of works of the above descriptions embodied in the broadcast, and of the broadcast itself.[7] There was some doubt whether under the 1911 Act broadcasting itself constituted a public performance of the works embodied in it.[8] As will be seen, under the 1956 Act such an act was expressly excluded from the definition of performance and was a separate act of infringement.[9] This appears to be the position under the 1988 Act as well, in that the broadcasting of a work or its inclusion in a cable programme service is a separate act of infringement[10] and the Act expressly provides that in the case of infringement by the performance, playing or showing of a work in public by means of apparatus for receiving visual images or sounds conveyed by electronic means, the person by whom the visual images or sounds are sent is not to be regarded as respon-

---

[99] *Ibid.* s.19(2)(*b*).
[1] "Sound recording," "film": s.5(1); "broadcast": s.6(1); "cable programme": s.7(1).
[2] See § 8–50, *ante.*
[3] C.D.P.A. 1988, s.19(3).
[4] *Ibid.* s.16(3)(*a*).
[5] *Ibid.* s.16(2).
[6] See the wording of s.19(4). See s.178 for the definition of "electronic."
[7] See the various cases referred to in § 8–109 *et seq., post,* and *Australasian Performing Right Association Ltd.* v. *Tolbush Pty. Ltd.* (1986) 62 A.L.R. 521 (Sup. Ct. Queensland).
[8] See *Messager* v. *British Broadcasting Co. Ltd.* [1927] 2 K.B. 543; *Performing Right Society Ltd.* v. *Hammond's Bradford Brewery Co. Ltd.* [1934] Ch. 121. *cf. Mellor* v. *Australian Broadcasting Commission* [1940] A.C. 491. See also *Canadian Admiral Corporation Ltd.* v. *Rediffusion Inc.* (1954) Ex C R. 382; *Chappell & Co. Ltd.* v. *Associated Radio Co. of Australia Ltd.* [1925] V.L.R. 350; *Remick (J.H.) & Co.* v. *American Auto-Accessories Co.* [1923–1928] Mac.C.C. 173.
[9] See § 8–106 *post.*
[10] C.D.P.A. 1988, s.20. See § 8–118, *et seq., post.*

sible for the infringement.[11] The Act also provides that where a "performance" is performed, played or shown in public by such means, the performers themselves are not to be regarded as responsible for such an infringement.[12]

8–103 **The person liable for the infringement.** In the case of a public performance through the human agency of actors, singers, etc., there will usually be no difficulty in determining who is the performer. Difficulties may arise, however, in the case of performances, etc., through such means as radios, televisions or juke boxes. Under the 1956 Act, prima facie the person operating the apparatus was liable for the infringement, except in certain circumstances where the occupier of the relevant premises was made liable.[13] These provisions have not been repeated in the 1988 Act. Although the 1988 Act does contain provisions making certain persons liable who provide premises or apparatus for such performances, such acts are classed as secondary infringements and are dependent upon there being some person liable for the primary infringement. These secondary acts of infringement are considered in the next chapter.[14] In general, it is thought that the person liable for the primary act of infringement by performance, etc., in such cases will be the person who actually operates the apparatus by means of which the sounds or images are produced.[15] Other persons may of course be liable for having auhorised such an act.

8–104 **The 1956 Act.** Under the 1956 Act, which still applies in relation to acts done before August 1, 1989[16] it was an infringement of the copyright in a literary, dramatic or musical work to perform the work in public. The Act defined "performance" as including delivery, in relation to lectures, addresses, speeches and sermons, and in general as including any mode of visual or acoustic presentation, including any such presentation by the operation of wireless telegraphy apparatus, or by the exhibition of a cinematograph film, or by the use of a record, or by any other means.[17] Again, these latter expressions were further defined.[18]

8–105 The 1956 Act further provided that it was an act restricted by the copyright in a sound recording to cause it to be heard in public.[19] It was an act restricted by the copyright in a cinematograph film, a television broadcast and a cable programme to cause the work, in so far as it consisted of visual images, to be seen in public, or, in so far as it consisted of sounds, to be

---

[11] *Ibid.* s.19(4).
[12] *Ibid.*
[13] §§ 8–107, 8–108, *post.*
[14] § 9–26, *et seq., post.*
[15] See, *e.g. Performing Right Society Ltd.* v. *Hammond's Bradford Brewery Co. Ltd.* [1934] Ch. 121.
[16] C.D.P.A. 1988, Sched. 1, para. 14(1).
[17] Copyright Act 1956, s.48(1).
[18] "Wireless telegraphy apparatus," "record": s.48(1); "cinematograph film": s.13(10).
[19] Copyright Act 1956, s.12(5)(*b*).

heard in public.[20] In the case of a television broadcast or a cable pro-gramme, however, the copyright was infringed in this way only if it was seen or heard by a paying audience.[21] The Act contained no equivalent restriction in respect of sound broadcasts.

Again, therefore, the above works were in general infringed by anyone   **8–106** who operated a television or radio set in public by means of which such works were seen or shown. However, section 48(5) of the Act[22] provided that broadcasting, or including a work or other subject-matter in a cable programme, should not be taken to constitute performance, or to consti-tute causing visual images or sounds to be seen or heard.

Further, the 1956 Act provided that where visual images or sounds were   **8–107** displayed or emitted by any receiving apparatus, to which they were con-veyed by the transmission of electromagnetic signals (whether over paths provided by a material substance or not), the operation of any apparatus whereby the signals were transmitted, directly or indirectly, to the receiv-ing apparatus should not be taken to constitute performance or to consti-tute causing the visual images or sounds to have been seen or heard.[23] In such circumstances, however, in so far as the display or emission of the images or sounds constituted a performance, or caused them to be seen or heard, the performance, or the causing of the images or sounds to be seen or heard, as the case might have been, should be taken to have been effected by the operation of the receiving apparatus.[24]

Without prejudice to the effect of these last two paragraphs, the 1956   **8–108** Act further provided that where a work or an adaptation of a work was performed, or visual images or sounds were caused to be seen or heard, by the operation of certain apparatus provided by or with the consent of the occupier of the premises where the apparatus was situated, the occupier of those premises was, for the purposes of the 1956 Act, be taken to be the person giving the performance, or causing the images or sounds to be seen or heard, whether he was the person operating the apparatus or not.[25] This provision only applied to receiving apparatus to which sounds or images were conveyed by electromagnetic signals and to apparatus for reproducing sounds by the use of a record.[26] The person who supplied the apparatus might, however, subject to the particular facts of the case, have been liable for authorising the infringement.[27]

---

[20] *Ibid.* ss.13(5)(*b*), 14(4)(*c*), 14A(5)(*c*).

[21] *Ibid.* ss.14(4)(*c*), 14A(5)(*c*). As to the meaning of "paying audience," see § 8–116, *post.*

[22] As amended by the Cable and Broadcasting Act 1984.

[23] Copyright Act 1956, s.48(5)(*a*).

[24] *Ibid.* s.48(5)(*b*).

[25] *Ibid.* s.48(6). See also the dicta on the equivalent provisions of the New Zealand Act in *Phonographic Performances (N.Z.) Ltd.* v. *Lion Breweries Ltd.* [1980] F.S.R. 1.

[26] *Ibid.*.

[27] See § 8–140, *et seq., post.*

8–109 **"In public."** The expression "in public", used in the 1988, 1956 and 1911 Acts, has been the subject of a number of decisions.[28] Whether a particular performance takes place in public or not is in one sense a question of law in that the true meaning of the words "in public" is a matter of law, but in every case it is obviously a question of fact whether the facts of that case do or do not fall within that meaning.[29] The chief guide in answering the question should be the guide of common sense.[30]

8–110 The distinction is between performances which are public and those which are domestic or quasi domestic in character, that is, those in which the audience are present in their capacity as members of the particular home circle.[31] In drawing this distinction it is the character of the audience which is crucial[32] and in particular it is the relationship of the audience to the owner of copyright which is important rather than its relationship to the performer.[33] If it can be said that the audience is one which the owner of the copyright might fairly consider as part of his public then this indicates that the performance was "in public,"[34] particularly where the members of the audience are enjoying the work under conditions where they would normally pay for the privilege in one form or another.[35] It has been said that the key to the construction of these words is that what is intended to be protected is the value of the author's invention.[36] Consistently with this, it has also been said that it is the duty of the Court to protect the rights of persons such as authors and composers, according to a fair construction of the Act, so that it is important to bear in mind whether the public's demand for their works may be affected by such performances.[37]

8–111 Bearing in mind that it is the character of the audience and its relationship to the copyright owner which is crucially important, various other tests have been discussed in the decided cases. Thus, clearly, if the public at large is freely admitted the performance will almost certainly be in public, but the performance may also be in public if only a limited portion of the public is allowed to attend, for example the members of a club and their guests.[38] On the other hand the mere fact that guests are present at what would otherwise be a private performance will not make it public.[39]

---

[28] Under the law prior to 1911 the performance, to be an infringement of copyright, had to be presented at a place of dramatic entertainment. But it was held that this condition was fulfilled if the performance was at any place in public, since to hold otherwise would have deprived an author of his right to the profits of his work (*Russell* v. *Smith* (1848) 12 Q.B. 217). The 1911 Act gave effect to the decisions under the earlier law. See, for example *Glenville* v. *Selig Polyscope Co.* (1911) 27 T.L.R 554.

[29] *Jennings* v. *Stephens* [1936] Ch. 469; *Harms (Inc.) Ltd.* v. *Martins Club Ltd.* [1927] 1 Ch. 526.

[30] *Ernest Turner, etc., Ltd.* v. *Performing Right Society Ltd.* [1943] Ch. 167.

[31] *Duck* v. *Bates* (1884) 13 Q.B.D. 843; *Jennings* v. *Stephens* [1936] Ch. 469.

[32] *Jennings* v. *Stephens, supra.*

[33] *Jennings* v. *Stephens, supra*; *Ernest Turner, etc., Ltd.* v. *Performing Right Society Ltd.* [1943] Ch. 167; *Performing Right Society Ltd.* v. *Rangers F.C. Supporters Club* [1975] R.P.C. 626.

[34] See n. 32, *ante.*

[35] *Performing Right Society Ltd.* v. *Rangers F.C. Supporters Club, supra.*

[36] *Duck* v. *Bates, supra.*

[37] See n. 32, *ante.*

[38] *Harms (Inc.) Ltd.* v. *Martans Club Ltd.* [1927] 1 Ch. 526.

[39] See n. 32, *ante.*

The number of persons present is a relevant consideration, but nevertheless a performance may be in public even though the audience is very small.[40] Whether the performance is given with a view to monetary profit may be relevant,[41] but it is of very limited importance whether the actual performers are paid. Thus performers often give their services to the public free, whereas they are often paid when the occasion is undoubtedly private.[42] The fact that no charge is made for admission is of itself also of little importance.[43] The kind of place at which the performance occurs may be an indication of the type of performance, but clearly a private performance may be given in what is normally a public room, and a public performance given in a private house.[44] As already noted, it is important to consider whether the performance is likely to injure the owner of the copyright in the sense that some of the audience might be willing to pay to see or hear such a performance,[45] or whether the demand for the author's work might otherwise be diminished.[46] Thus if the person responsible for the performance would be likely to pay for a licence rather than have such performance stopped, then clearly the copyright owner will suffer by an unlicensed performance,[47] although obviously it is not in every such case that the performance will be in public.

While bearing in mind that each case must be considered separately on **8–112** its own facts, the following are examples of cases in which performances have been regarded as having taken place in public: the putting on of a drama by an amateur company for a charitable object, the public being admitted upon payment of money or by the issue of tickets generally[48]; the performance of music by a dance band at a proprietary dinner and dance club at which members and their guests were present, the membership being selective and by election but being drawn by invitation to the public[49]; a dramatic performance given at a village Women's Institute, even though the performers were all members of a neighbouring Institute, no one was present except members and no charge was made (all the adult female members of the village were, however, in practice eligible to join the Institute)[50]; the playing of gramophone records and the radio over loudspeakers to workers at a factory during working hours[51]; the performance of orchestral music in the lounge of a hotel, the audience consisting of residents of the hotel and members of the public who had dined there[52]; the playing of a radio in a public house's private room, but which the pub-

---

[40] *Ibid.*
[41] See n. 38, *ante.*
[42] See n. 32, *ante.*
[43] See n. 38, *ante*
[44] See n. 32, *ante.*
[45] See n. 38, *ante.*
[46] See n. 32, *ante.*
[47] *Performing Right Society Ltd.* v. *Harlequin Record Shops Ltd.* [1979] 1 W.L.R. 851.
[48] Given as an example in *Duck* v. *Bates* (1884) 13 G.B.D. 843.
[49] See n. 15, *ante.*
[50] See n. 9, *ante.*
[51] *Ernest Turner, etc., Ltd.* v. *Performing Right Society Ltd.* [1943] Ch. 167. This case is reported jointly with *Performing Right Society Ltd.* v. *Gillette Industries Ltd.*, a case in which the facts were very similar.
[52] *Performing Right Society Ltd.* v. *Hawthornes Hotel (Bournmouth) Ltd.* [1933] Ch. 855.

lic was freely able to use as a saloon bar[53]; the playing of a radio in a private room of a public house, but which could be heard in the adjoining public bar[54]; the playing of a radio in a private room adjoining a restaurant, but which could be heard in the restaurant, the principle being that the performance took place wherever it could be heard[55]; the performance of music to an audience consisting of members of a social club and their guests[56]; the playing of records in record shops to which the public was encouraged to enter without payment or invitation, the purpose and effect being to increase the sale of records, the evidence being that most record shop proprietors would pay for the necessary licence rather than be prevented from playing such records.[57]

8–113   On the other hand the putting on of a play by children or adults at home would obviously not be in public, being domestic and private.[58] The same would apply to a play put on for friends in a house hired for the occasion.[59] A performance given by an amateur dramatic club to nurses, attendants and others connected with a hospital, to which admission was free, the expenses being born by the governors of the hospital, was held not to be in public.[60]

8–114   An unresolved question is whether, for example, where music or television is relayed to hotel bedrooms, in which the music or television is then listened to or watched by the occupants, this amounts to a public performance. It has been decided in the Exchequer Court of Canada[61] that the performance of material by way of television in private homes, the material having been received by subscribers to a cable service, did not amount to public performance on the grounds that the character of the audience was purely domestic and even a large number of "private" performances could not be in public. It might therefore be argued that the character of the audience in separate hotel bedrooms is similar, each hotel bedroom being the occupant's "home" for the night and each performance being "private".[62] In a decision of the Supreme Court of New

---

[53] *Performing Right Society Ltd.* v. *George* (unreported but referred to in *Performing Right Society Ltd.* v. *Camelo* [1936] 3 All E.R. 557).

[54] *Performing Right Society Ltd.* v. *George, supra,* obiter but relied on in *Performing Right Society Ltd.* v. *Camelo, supra;* and see *Australian Performing Right Association Ltd.* v. *Canterbury-Bankstown League Club Ltd.* [1964–65] N.S.W.R. 138.

[55] *Performing Right Society Ltd.* v. *Camelo, supra.*

[56] *Performing Right Society Ltd.* v. *Rangers F.C. Supporters Club* [1975] R.P.C. 626.

[57] *Performing Right Society Ltd.* v. *Harlequin Record Shops Ltd.* [1979] 1 W.L.R. 851; *Australasian Performing Right Association Ltd.* v. *Tolbush Pty. Ltd.* (1986) 62 A.L.R. 521; and see *South African, etc., Ltd.* v. *Trust Butchers (Pty.) Ltd.* [1978] 1 S.A.L.R. 1052.

[58] Given as an example in *Duck* v. *Bates* (1884) 13 G.B.D. 843.

[59] *Ibid.*

[60] *Duck* v. *Bates, supra,* described there by Brett M.R. as a border-line and extreme case; see also the comments on this decision in *Jennings* v. *Stephens* [1936] Ch. 469 and *Harms (Inc.) Ltd.* v. *Martans Club Ltd.* [1927] 1 Ch. 526.

[61] *Canadian Admiral Corporation Ltd.* v. *Rediffusion Inc.* [1954] Ex.C.R. 382.

[62] See, *e.g. Mellor* v. *Australian Broadcasting Commission* [1940] A.C. 491 at p. 500; but *cf. Messager* v. *British Broadcasting Co. Ltd.* [1927] 2 K.B. 543.

South Wales,[63] however, the issue arose whether the watching of television sets by the occupants of motel rooms, to which films were relayed by means of a video cassette recorder and cables, amounted to public performance. The plaintiff's case was argued primarily on the basis that the presentation of a film in a single room, even to only one person, amounted to public performance. It was held that such presentation was in fact in public since the character of the audience was as guests of the motel and not as individuals in a private or domestic situation. In that capacity the guests were paying for the accommodation and the benefits which went with it. It is thought that for the same reasons the performance of works to inmates of prisons is "in public."

Exemptions. There are important exemptions relating to the public performance of sound recordings, broadcasts and cable programmes, which are considered elsewhere.[64]   **8–115**

The 1956 Act: "Paying audience". As has been seen,[65] under the 1956 Act it was an infringement of the copyright in a television broadcast or cable programme to cause it to be seen or heard in public, but only if it was so seen or heard by a "paying audience."[66] It was provided that such works were to be taken to be seen or heard by a paying audience if they were seen or heard by persons who had been admitted for payment to the place where the broadcast or programme was to be seen or heard, or had been admitted for payment to a place of which that place formed part.[67] Such works were also to be taken as having been seen or heard by a paying audience if the persons had been admitted to the place where the work was to be seen or heard in circumstances where goods or services were supplied there at prices which exceeded the prices usually charged at that place, and were partly attributable to the facilities afforded for seeing or hearing the works.[68] No account, however, was to be taken of persons admitted to the place in question as residents or inmates therein, or of persons admitted to that place as members of a club or society, where the payment was only for membership of the club or society, and the provision of facilities for seeing or hearing the works was only incidental to the main purposes of the club or society.[69]   **8–116**

These provisions can be compared with the exempting provisions of the 1956 Act, relating to the performance of records where persons resided or slept, or as part of the activities of a club or organisation.[70]   **8–117**

---

[63] *Rank Film Production Ltd.* v. *Dodds* [1983] 2 N.S.W.L.R. 553; see also *Hotel Mornington AB* v. *Foreningen Svenska Tonsattares Internationella Musikbyra (STIM)* [1982] E.C.C. 171 (Swedish Supreme Court); *Garware Plastics and Polyester Ltd.* v. *M/s Telelink* [1989] A.I.R. (Bombay) 331 (as to the meaning of "communication to the public" in the Indian Copyright Act).

[64] See Ch. 10, *post*, § 10–102 *et seq.*, § 10–121 *et seq.*

[65] § 8–105, *ante*.

[66] Copyright Act 1956, ss.14(4)(c), 14A(5)(c).

[67] *Ibid.* ss.14(8)(a), 14A(9)(a).

[68] *Ibid.* ss.14(8)(b), 14(A)(9)(b).

[69] *Ibid.* ss.14(8), 14(A)(9), provisos.

[70] *Ibid.* s.12(7), §10–103 *post.*

5. Infringement by Broadcasting or Inclusion in Cable Programme Service

8–118   **The 1988 Act.** As has been seen,[71] the sending of a broadcast or the inclusion of a work in a cable programme service will not itself amount to a public performance of any work, and the separate provision which is made for these acts is now considered. Thus the 1988 Act provides that the broadcasting of a work or its inclusion in a cable programme service in the United Kingdom is an act restricted by the copyright in a literary, dramatic, musical or artistic work, in a sound recording or film, and in a broadcast or cable programme.[72] "Broadcasting" means the transmission by wireless telegraphy of visual images, sounds or other information which is either capable of being lawfully received by members of the public or is transmitted for presentation to members of the public.[73] "Wireless telegraphy" is itself defined as the sending of electro-magnetic energy over paths not provided by a material substance constructed or arranged for that purpose.[74] The person broadcasting the work is to be taken to be the person transmitting the "programme" (being any item included in the broadcast) if that person has responsibility to any extent for its contents.[75] In addition to that person, where any other person provides the programme and makes the arrangements necessary for its transmission with the person transmitting it, that other person will also be taken to have broadcast the work.[76] In the ordinary case, therefore, it seems that the programme contractor will be liable if he includes one of the above works in an item contained in the broadcast. In the case of a satellite transmission, the place from which a transmission is made is the place from which the signals carrying the broadcast are transmitted to the satellite (the so-called "up-leg" part of the transmission).[77] The expression "cable programme service" has been considered elsewhere.[78] A work is included in a cable programme service if it is transmitted as part of the service.[79] The person who includes a work in a cable programme service is the person who provides the service.[80]

8–119   **The 1956 Act.** Again, as has been seen,[81] the 1956 Act, which still applies to acts done before August 1, 1989,[82] provided that broadcasting or including a work in a cable programme did not amount to public performance of a work. These acts were treated as separate categories of infringing acts. Thus it was an act restricted by the copyright in literary,

---

[71] See § 8–102, *ante.*
[72] C.D.P.A. 1988, s.20.
[73] *Ibid.* s.6(1).
[74] *Ibid.* s.178.
[75] *Ibid.* s.6(3).
[76] *Ibid.*
[77] *Ibid.* s.6(4).
[78] See § 2–34, *ante.*
[79] C.D.P.A. 1988, s.7(5).
[80] *Ibid.*
[81] See § 8–106, *ante.*
[82] C.D.P.A. 1988, Sched. 1, para. 14(1).

dramatic and musical works[83] and in sound recordings[84] and films[85] to broadcast the work or include it in a cable programme.[86] Further, the inclusion of an artistic work in a television broadcast or cable programme was an act restricted by the copyright in an artistic work.[87] In the case of a television broadcast or a sound broadcast it was a restricted act to rebroadcast the work or include it in a cable programme.[88] In the case of a cable programme, it was a restricted act to broadcast it or include it in a cable programme service.[89] In the case of broadcasts made by the BBC or the IBA, or in the case of cable programmes, these restrictions applied whether the act in question was done by the reception of the broadcast or programme or by making use of any record, print, negative, tape or other article on which the broadcast or programme had been recorded.[90] The Act contained an extended definition of "reception of a television broadcast or sound broadcast" to cover simultaneous transmissions, other than by way of broadcasting, and retransmissions.[91] However, the copyright in a television or sound broadcast was not infringed by any person who, by the reception and immediate re-transmission of the broadcast, included a programme in a cable programme service as a requirement imposed under section 13 of the Cable and Broadcasting Act 1984 or where it was made for reception in the area in which the cable service was provided, the broadcast not being a direct broadcast satellite service or an additional teletext service.[92] In relation to television broadcasts and cable programmes, in so far as they consisted of visual images, these restrictions applied to any sequence of visual images sufficient to be seen as a moving picture.[93]

The 1956 Act: Broadcasting. It would seem that the word "broadcast"   **8–120**
in the 1956 Act must have referred to the act of transmitting waves at large, so that the place where the broadcast was made was at the transmitter, and not the studio or other place where the television camera or microphone was situated. The expression "broadcasting" referred to broadcasting by "wireless telegraphy,"[94] which itself had the elaborate definition contained in the Wireless Telegraphy Act 1949.[95] It was, however, held that the expression included not only transmitting by wireless telegraphy but was broad enough to include anyone participating in the

---

[83] Copyright Act 1956, ss.2(5)(*d*), (*e*).

[84] *Ibid.* s.12(5)(*c*), except in the case of sound recordings originating in certain foreign countries. See The Copyright (International Conventions) Order 1979, *Copinger* (12th ed.), § 2140. There was also no infringement if records had been issued to the public not bearing a sufficient label: See s.12(6), and § 10–106, *post.*

[85] *Ibid.* s.13(5)(*c*), (*d*).

[86] See, *e.g. Performing Right Society Ltd.* v. *Marlin Communal Aerials Ltd.* [1982] E.C.C. 477.

[87] Copyright Act 1956. ss.3(5)(*c*), (*d*).

[88] *Ibid.* s.14(4)(*d*).

[89] *Ibid.* s.14A(5)(*d*).

[90] *Ibid.* ss.14(5), 14A(6).

[91] *Ibid.* s.48(4).

[92] *Ibid.* s.14(8A). See § 10–123, *post.*

[93] *Ibid.* ss.14(6), 14A(7).

[94] *Ibid.* s.48(2).

[95] *Ibid.*

broadcast, for example, the programme contractors and even the performers.[96]

8–121 **The 1956 Act: Inclusion in a cable programme.** The meaning of "cable programme" has been considered elsewhere.[97] The person providing the cable programme service was to be taken to be the person including the programme in the cable programme.[98]

6. Infringement by Making an Adaptation

8–122 **The 1988 Act.** Under the 1988 Act one of the acts restricted by the copyright in any literary, dramatic or musical work is to make an adaptation of the work.[99] Further consideration is given below to what amounts to an adaptation, but the Act provides that in general an adaptation is made when it is recorded, in writing or otherwise.[1] For this purpose, writing includes any form of notation or code, whether by hand or otherwise and regardless of the method by which, or medium in or on which, it is recorded.[2]

8–123 In addition, in relation to any adaptation of such a work, it is an act restricted by the copyright in the work to reproduce the adaptation in any material form, issue copies of it to the public, perform it in public or broadcast it or include it in a cable programme service.[3] For this purpose it is immaterial whether the adaptation itself has been recorded in the above sense when any such further act is done.[4] This provision makes it clear, for example, that copyright in a musical work may be infringed by performing an adaptation of it on stage, even though the adaptation itself has never been recorded.

8–124 In the usual way, it is a restricted act not only to do any of the above acts in relation to the work as a whole but also in relation to any substantial part of it.[5] Further, copyright is infringed not only by anyone who does one of these restricted acts without the licence of the copyright owner, but also by anyone who authorises the doing of such an act without licence.[6]

8–125 **The 1956 Act.** The 1956 Act, which for the purposes of infringement still applies to acts done before August 1, 1989,[7] also provided that it was an act restricted by the copyright in a literary, dramatic or musical work to

---

[96] *Independent Television Companies Association Ltd.* v. *Performing Right Society Ltd.*, The Times, February 23, 1982; *The Association of Independent Radio Contractors Ltd.* v. *Phonographic Performance Ltd.* (1980) (unreported).

[97] See § 2–34, *ante*.

[98] Copyright Act 1956, s.48(3).

[99] C.D.P.A. 1988, ss.16(1)(*e*), 21(1).

[1] *Ibid.*, s.21(1).

[2] *Ibid.* s.178.

[3] *Ibid.* s.21(2).

[4] *Ibid.*

[5] *Ibid.* s.16(3)(*a*).

[6] *Ibid.* s.16(2).

[7] *Ibid.* Sched. 1, para. 14(1).

make an adaptation of the work,[8] to reproduce such an adaptation in any material form, publish it, perform it in public, broadcast it or include it in a cable programme.[9]

Meaning of adaptation. The expression "adaptation" is defined in the 1988 Act, as it was in the 1956 Act, by reference to particular categories of work. Thus in relation to a literary or dramatic work the 1988 Act defines "adaptation" to mean (i) a translation of the work; (ii) a version of a dramatic work in which it is converted into a non-dramatic work or, as the case may be, a version of a non-dramatic work in which it is converted into a dramatic work; (iii) a version of the work in which the story or action is conveyed wholly or mainly by means of pictures in a form suitable for reproduction in a book, or in a newspaper, magazine or similar periodical.[10]   **8–126**

The definition of adaptation in the 1956 Act in relation to these works was identical,[11] except that in the case of conversion of a dramatic work into a non-dramatic work, or vice versa, the 1956 Act provided that the restricted act applied not only to the work in its original "language" but also in a different "language."[12] Since there was a separate provision relating to translations,[13] it is assumed that the word "language" here referred to a different expression, in the same tongue, of the plot or story. This provision has not been repeated in the 1988 Act. The 1988 Act also differs from the 1956 Act in that under the 1956 Act the definition of a dramatic work excluded a cinematograph film, as distinct from a scenario or script for a film.[14] On the other hand, the term "reproduction" in the case of a literary, dramatic or musical work was defined to include reproduction in the form of a cinematograph film.[15] With this exception, the 1988 Act appears not to have changed the existing law.   **8–127**

Translation. While there may have been some doubt, prior to the 1911 Act, whether copyright in a work could be infringed by making a translation of it,[16] since the 1911 Act it has been clear that it can be. "Translation" in this sense probably means the turning of the work from one human language into another, so that the conversion of a work into Morse code or Braille would not be a translation, but a reproduction of the work.[17] It should be noted that two separate rights may exist where there has been a translation, namely the right of the author of the original work to restrain reproduction, etc., of the original or any translated form and the right of the author of the translation to restrain reproduction of his   **8–128**

---

[8] Copyright Act 1956, s.2(5)(*f*).

[9] *Ibid.* s.2(5)(*g*).

[10] C.D.P.A. 1988, s.21(3)(*a*).

[11] Copyright Act 1956, s.2(6)(*a*).

[12] *Ibid.* ss.2(6)(*a*)(i), (ii).

[13] *Ibid.* s.2(6)(*a*)(iii).

[14] *Ibid.* s.48(1).

[15] *Ibid.*

[16] *Burnett* v. *Chetwood* (1817) 2 Mer. 441; *cf. Cate* v. *Devon, etc., Newspaper Co.* (1889) 40 Ch.D. 500.

[17] *Apple Computer, Inc.* v. *Mackintosh Computers Ltd.* (1988) 44 D.L.R. (4th) 74.

translation. Anyone wishing to reproduce a particular translation should therefore obtain a licence from the owner of the copyright in both the original and the translation. In the same way, if A's work is with permission translated by B, and C without permission retranslates from B's translation into the original language, C infringes A's and B's copyrights.[18] The position will be the same even where B's translation was unauthorised since, although an infringement, it will be entitled to copyright.[19]

8–129 **"Translation" of a computer program.** As noted above,[20] the expression "translation" normally envisages the conversion of a work from one language into another, in particular one human language into another. Whatever doubts there may originally have been as to whether a computer program converted from one language or code into another constituted an adaptation,[21] the 1988 Act provides that in relation to a computer program a "translation" includes a version of the program in which it is converted into or out of a computer language or code or into a different computer language or code, otherwise than incidentally in the course of running the program.[22] The effect of 1956 Act, taken with the Copyright (Computer Software) Amendment Act 1985, was precisely the same.[23]

8–130 **Dramatisation of non-dramatic works.**[24] Infringements of this kind may occur when the plaintiff's novel is turned into a play or a screenplay for a film.[25] In such cases there may of course be sufficient copying of language for the defendant's dramatic work to be a reproduction of the plaintiff's work, so that the defendant will have infringed simply by copying.[26] However, even where there is no language copying but, for example, the defendant has to a substantial extent taken the incidents and plot from the plaintiff's novel and turned them into a dramatic work, this will amount to an infringement.[27] The question is whether the situations or plot have been copied from the novel and then represented in dramatic

---

[18] *Murray* v. *Bogue* (1853) 1 Drew. 353 at 368.

[19] *Redwood Music Ltd.* v. *Chappell & Co. Ltd.* [1982] R.P.C. 109 and see § 3–44, *et seq., ante.*

[20] § 8–128, *ante.*

[21] See, *e.g. Computer Edge Pty. Ltd.* v. *Apple Computer Inc.* [1986] F.S.R. 537 (High Ct. of Aus.); *Sega Enterprises Ltd.* v. *Richards* [1983] F.S.R. 73; *Apple Computer, Inc.* v. *Mackintosh Computers Ltd., supra*; *International Business Machines Corporation* v. *Computer Imports Ltd.* [1989] 2 N.Z.L.R. 395.

[22] C.D.P.A. 1988, s.21(4).

[23] As already noted, in relation to infringements, the 1956 Act continues to apply in relation to acts done before August 1, 1989. Nothing in the 1985 Act was to affect the question whether anything done before September 16, 1985, amounted to an infringement: see s.4(4)(a) of that Act. The only difference in the wording between the 1988 Act and the equivalent provisions of the 1985 Act is that such a version of a computer program as an "adaptation" rather than a "translation."

[24] As to the position before the passing of the 1911 Act, and that Act's effect, see *Copinger,* (12th ed.), § 501.

[25] Under the 1956 Act, to turn a novel into a film would have been to reproduce the novel, not to have made an adaptation of it. See § 8–127, *ante.*

[26] Where there is a compilation copyright, this too may be infringed without actual language copying. See § 8–30, *et seq., ante.*

[27] *Corelli* v. *Gray* (1913) 30 T.L.R. 116.

form.[28] This is not to say that mere ideas or a character can be protected in this way, certainly if the character or ideas are not novel,[29] but if the combination of events which has been taken is not merely trivial, but amounts to a substantial part, there will be an infringement.[30] Thus, for example, copyright may be infringed by dramatising a novel in the form of a play, a sketch,[31] a script for a film or a film itself,[32] or a short story in the form of a ballet.[33] In the case of a historical work, which the plaintiff has compiled from various sources, it will in the usual way be necessary to examine whether the incidents in common between the two works which the defendant has dramatised have been taken by him from the plaintiff's work or from those other sources.[34]

Conversion of dramatic into non-dramatic work. As in the case of **8–131** non-dramatic works, a dramatic work may be infringed simply by its language being reproduced to a substantial extent. Even where there has not been such copying, however, the copyright in a dramatic work may be infringed if it is converted into a non-dramatic form. Thus, for example, short synopses of operas may not be infringements of the operatic works if the operas are simply described shortly and in very bare outline.[35] The position would presumably be different if numerous incidents were reproduced. Thus where the events and conversations in a play were described in detail, scene by scene, constituting more than just a synopsis, this was held to be an adaptation.[36] It made no difference that the descriptions formed part of a larger work and there were interspersed commentaries and other writings.

Strip cartoon may infringe. As has been seen,[37] in relation to a literary **8–132** or dramatic work, "adaptation" includes a version of the work in which the story or action is conveyed wholly or mainly by means of pictures in a form suitable for reproduction in a book, or in a newspaper, magazine or similar periodical.[38] A pictorial representation of the plot of a book or a play will therefore constitute infringement even though no words are used in the representation.

---

[28] *Kelly* v. *Cinema Houses Ltd.* [1928–35] Mac.C.C. 362.

[29] *Kelly* v. *Cinema Houses Ltd., supra; Dagnall* v. *British and Dominion Film Corporation Ltd.* [1928–35] Mac.C.C. 391 (a case of infringement of a dramatic work by reproduction); *Harman Pictures N.V.* v. *Osborne* [1967] 1 W.L.R. 723.

[30] *Kelly* v. *Cinema Houses Ltd., supra; Fernald* v. *Jay Lewis Productions Ltd.* [1975] F.S.R. 499; *cf. MacGregor* v. *Powell* [1936–45] Mac.C.C. 233; *De Mandnit* v. *Gaumont British Picture Corporation Ltd.* [1936–45] Mac.C.C. 292.

[31] *Corelli* v. *Gray, supra.*

[32] *Fernald* v. *Jay Lewis Productions Ltd., supra; Zeccola* v. *Universal City Studios Inc.* (1982) 46 A.L.R. 189; and see n. 25, *supra.*

[33] *Holland* v. *Vivian Van Damm Productions Ltd.* [1936–45] Mac.C.C. 69.

[34] *Harman Pictures N.V.* v. *Osborne* [1967] 1 W.L.R. 723.

[35] *Valcarenghi* v. *The Gramophone Co. Ltd.* [1928–35] Mac.C.C. 301, where it was found that the defendants had not infringed, not having transposed the work into a novel or short story.

[36] *Sillitoe* v. *McGraw-Hill Book Co. (U.K.) Ltd.* [1983] F.S.R. 545.

[37] § 8–126, *ante.*

[38] C.D.P.A. 1988, s.21(3)(*a*)(iii); Copyright Act 1956, s.2(6)(*a*)(iv).

8–133 **Musical works.** In relation to musical works, the 1988 Act defines adaptation to mean an arrangement or transcription of the work.[39] The 1956 Act contained precisely the same definition.[40]

7. Infringement by Authorisation

8–134 As already noted, under the 1988 Act copyright is infringed not only where a person not having the licence of the copyright owner does an act restricted by the copyright in a work, but also where he authorises the doing of such an act.[41] The position was the same under the 1956 and 1911 Acts.[42] "Authorisation" is a separate act of infringement from the act which is itself authorised.[43] Apart from questions of authorisation, a person may be liable with another as a joint infringer or for having procured the infringing act.[44] "Authorisation" does not apply to indirect acts of infringement.[45]

8–135 It has been doubted whether the word "authorise" added anything to the law when first introduced in the 1911 Act.[46] But it had been held prior to the passing of that Act that a person was only liable for infringements committed by his servants or agents[47] and the effect of the 1911 Act was to overrule this.[48] Thus a man will be liable for any infringement committed by his servant in the course of his employment,[49] but, if the infringer is not the servant of the defendant, he will only be liable if he authorised the particular act complained of,[50] and it must be a question of fact in each case whether he has given such authority—a question which has given rise to the real difficulty in most of the decided cases.[51]

8–136 **Meaning of "authorise."** Authorisation means the grant or purported grant, which may be express or implied, of the right to do the act complained of, whether the intention is that the grantee should do the act on his own account, or only on account of the grantor.[52]

---

[39] C.D.P.A. 1988, s.21(3)(*b*).
[40] Copyright Act 1956, s.2(6)(*b*).
[41] C.D.P.A. 1988, s.16(2).
[42] Copyright Act 1956, s.1(1); Copyright Act 1911, s.1(2).
[43] *Ash* v. *Hutchinson and Co. (Publishers) Ltd.* [1936] Ch. 489.
[44] As to which, see *Belegging-En, etc.* v. *Witten Industrial Diamonds Ltd.* [1979] F.S.R. 59, and *C.B.S. Songs Ltd.* v. *Amstrad plc.* [1988] A.C. 1013 (H.L.); *Amstrad Consumer Electronics plc.* v. *British Phonographic Industry Ltd.* [1986] F.S.R. 159 (C.A.) *Grower* v. *British Broadcasting Corporation* [1990] F.S.R. 595 and §11–12 *post.*
[45] The 1977 Copyright Committee, Cmnd. 6732, para. 749(iii), recommended that it should.
[46] See, *e.g. Performing Right Society* v. *Ciryl Theatrical Syndicate Ltd.* [1924] 1 K.B. 1.
[47] *Karno* v. *Pathé Frères Ltd.* (1909) 100 L.T. 260.
[48] *Falcon* v. *Famous Players Film Co.* [1926] 2 K.B. 474. See also *Fiel* v. *Lemaire* (1939) 4 D.L.R. (Can.) 561.
[49] *Performing Right Society Ltd.* v. *Mitchell and Booker, etc., Ltd.* [1924] 1 K.B. 762; *Canadian Performing Right Society* v. *Canadian National Exhibition Association* [1934] 4 D.L.R. 154.
[50] See *Australasian Performing Right Association Ltd.* v. *Miles* [1962] N.S.W.R. 405.
[51] See *Australasian Performing Right Association Ltd.* v. *Koolman* [1969] N.Z.L.R. 273.
[52] *C.B.S. Songs Ltd.* v. *Amstrad plc.* [1988] A.C. 1013 (H.L.) citing, with apparent approval, Atkin L.J.'s statement in *Falcon* v. *Famous Players Film Co.* [1926] 2 K.B. 474, at 499.

An expression which has often been used as equivalent to the word "authorise" is "sanction, approve or countenance."[53] But this must be treated with caution, particularly in so far as the word "countenance" is equivalent to the word "condone."[54] Thus in general an authorisation "can only come from someone having or purporting to have authority, and . . . an act is not authorised by someone who merely enables or possibly assists or even encourages another to do that act, but does not purport to have any authority which he can grant to justify the doing of the act."[55]

Clearly a person will have authorised an act if he gives permission for it **8–137** to be done, or grants the right to do the act in contemplation that it will in fact be done.[56] Likewise, a person who asks another to do an act, the former having the power to give or refuse permission to do that act, will be taken to have authorised it.[57] Cases where a person simply puts the means of doing the infringing act into another's hands are more difficult.[58] A person does not necessarily authorise an act to be done merely because he intentionally puts into another's hands the means by which the infringing act can be done if those means can also be used for a perfectly legitimate purpose,[59] even where it is known they will in fact inevitably be used for an infringing purpose.[60] This will be so particularly if the supplier has no control over how the means will be used,[61] since it is the essence of a grant or purported grant that the grantor has some degree of actual or apparent right to control the relevant actions of the grantee.[62] But where he retains control over the means in question the facts may warrant a finding of implicit authorisation.[63]

---

[53] *Falcon* v. *Famous Players Film Co., supra, per* Bankes L.J., following *Monckton* v. *Pathé Frères Pathephone Ltd.* [1914] 1 K.B. 395 and *Evans* v. *E. Hulton & Co. Ltd.* (1924) 131 L.T. 534.

[54] *Amstrad Consumer Electronics plc.* v. *British Phonographic Industry Ltd.* [1986] F.S.R. 159 (C.A.), *per* Lawton L.J. at 207, approved in *C.B.S. Songs Ltd.* v. *Amstrad plc.* [1988] A.C. 1013 at 1055.

[55] *Per* Whitford J. in *C.B.S. Inc.* v. *Ames Records & Tapes Ltd.* [1982] Ch. 91, at 106, approved in *Amstrad Consumer Electronics plc.* v. *British Phonographic Industry Ltd.* [1986] F.S.R. 159 (C.A.) at 211 and in *C.B.S. Songs Ltd.* v. *Amstrad plc.* [1988] A.C. (H.L.) at 1055.

[56] *Evans* v. *E. Hulton & Co. Ltd.* (1924) 131 L.T. 534.

[57] *Standen Engineering Ltd.* v. *A. Spalding & Sons Ltd.* [1984] F.S.R. 554.

[58] Whether or not the supply of equipment amounts to authorisation, such acts may well amount to secondary infringement. This is considered elsewhere; see § 9–23, *et seq., post.*

[59] See the cases cited in the examples given below.

[60] *Amstrad Consumer Electronics plc.* v. *British Phonographic Industry Ltd.* [1986] F.S.R. 159 (C.A.) at 211, and *C.B.S. Songs Ltd.* v. *Amstrad plc.* [1988] A.C. 1013 (H.L.), disapproving *RCA Corporation* v. *John Fairfax & Sons Ltd.* [1982] R.P.C. 91 (Supreme Ct. of New South Wales).

[61] *Vigneux* v. *Canadian Performing Right Society Ltd.* [1945] A.C. 108, cited with approval by Lawton and Glidewell LL.J. in the Court of Appeal in *Amstrad Consumer Electronics plc.* v. *British Phonographic Industry Ltd. supra*, whose judgments were themselves approved by the House of Lords, in *C.B.S. Songs Ltd.* v. *Amstrad plc., supra.*

[62] *Per* Slade L.J. in *Amstrad Consumer Electronics plc.* v. *British Phonographic Industry Ltd., supra*, whose judgment was approved by the House of Lords, in *C.B.S. Songs Ltd.* v. *Amstrad plc., supra.* See also *RCA Corporation* v. *John Fairfax & Sons Ltd., supra.*

[63] *Moorhouse* v. *University of New South Wales* [1976] R.P.C. 15, and *Amstrad Consumer Electronics plc.* v. *British Phonographic Industry Ltd.* [1986] F.S.R. 159, 211.

8–138   Authorisation may be inferred from acts which fall short of being positive and direct, and even indifference may be sufficient.[64] In each case it is a question of fact as to the true inference to be drawn from the conduct of the defendant.[65] Whether what the defendant has done amounts to an authorisation will often be a matter of impression,[66] particularly in the case of advertisements which appear to encourage a particular activity.[67] Ignorance of the fact that what will be done will be an infringement does not affect the question of liability.[68]

8–139   **Examples of "authorisation."** Where a person engages a band of musicians to perform in a theatre, but in his absence and without his knowledge and without him suspecting, the band performs works in infringement of copyright, he is not liable for authorising, even though he has the power to direct the band what to play and to dismiss them if they refuse.[69] But the position may well be different if that person does not care whether the performance is an infringement or not and is present when it is given.[70] Certainly, where a person engages a band to perform, and then approves a list of proposed titles which the band submits, this will amount to authorisation.[71] It has been said that a broadcaster who knows that his broadcast will be performed in public at hotels and other public places authorises such public performance, but it is doubted whether this is correct.[72]

8–140   As already indicated, cases in which the defendant provides the means by which the infringement is committed sometimes cause difficulties. Thus where a person places an order for the manufacture of an article upon another, the former having the power to prevent such manufacture, and an example of the article being available to copy, this amounts to authorisation.[73] Again, where a person sells the rights in a manuscript with a view to its publication, such publication being bound to infringe, this will amount to authorisation.[74] It has been said that the seller of a record authorises its use,[75] but whether the seller authorises its infringing use is, it is submitted, a different question, since the record may be used

---

[64] *Performing Right Society v. Ciryl Theatrical Syndicate Ltd.* [1924] 1 K.B. 1.
[65] *Ibid.*
[66] *RCA Corporation v. John Fairfax & Sons Ltd., supra.*
[67] *WEA International Inc. v. Hanimex Corporation Ltd.* (1987) 77 A.L.R. 456.
[68] *Performing Right Society Ltd. v. Bray U.D.C.* [1930] A.C. 377 (P.C.).
[69] *Ibid.* n. 63.
[70] *Monaghan v. Taylor* (1885) 2 T.L.R. 685, a case decided before the 1911 Act, where the issue was whether the defendant had caused or permitted a place to be used for public entertainment. See also *Bolton v. London Exhibitions Ltd.* (1898) 14 T.L.R. 550; *Green v. Irish Independent Co. Ltd.* [1899] 1 I.R. 386; *Colburn v. Simms* (1843) 2 Ha. 543 at 547.
[71] *Performing Right Society Ltd. v. Bray U.D.C.* [1930] A.C. 377 (P.C.). See also *Australasian Performing Right Association Ltd. v. Canterbury-Bankstown Leagues Club Ltd.* [1964–65] N.S.W.R. 138; and *Australasian Performing Right Association Ltd. v. Koolman* [1969] N.Z.L.R. 273.
[72] *Per* Viscount Maugham in *Mellor v. Australian Broadcasting Commission* [1940] A.C. 491. The point was not argued.
[73] *Standen Engineering Ltd. v. A. Spalding & Sons Ltd.* [1984] F.S.R. 554.
[74] *Evans v. E. Hulton & Co. Ltd.* (1924) 131 L.T. 534.
[75] *Monckton v. Pathé Frères Pathephone Ltd.* [1914] 1 K.B. 395.

for non-infringing purposes, for example, performance in private.[76] It is doubted whether the mere sale of a record would today be held to be an authorisation of the public performance of the musical work embodied in it. Thus where a record library lent out records and simultaneously offered blank tapes for sale at a discount, it was held that no authorisation of home taping had occurred.[77] Where defendants hired out to a cinema proprietor a film whose exhibition was bound to be an infringement, they were held to have authorised that act.[78]

Where the defendant sold hi-fi systems which included the facility for the high speed duplication of cassette tapes, this did not amount to authorisation even though the almost inevitable consequence would be that purchasers would use such equipment to make infringing copies.[79] In one Canadian case, the Privy Council stated that where a firm supplied a coin-operated juke box on hire for a fixed rent to a restaurant, and supplied the records for use in it, the firm was not, on these facts, to be taken to have authorised a public performance, having no control over the use of the machine or as to whether it was available to customers.[80] But a case on similar facts was distinguished in a later Australian decision, where it was held that the fact that the defendant supplied the records for use in the juke box gave the defendant sufficient control over its use to amount to authorisation.[81] In another Australian case, where a university provided copying machines close to its library, retaining control over them and over the books which were copied using the machines, and having reasonable grounds to suspect that infringements might occur if no adequate precautions to prevent this happening were taken, this was held to amount to authorisation.[82] How an English Court would decide cases on these facts

---

[76] The proposition quoted in the text was cited with apparent approval by the House of Lords in *C.B.S. Songs Ltd.* v. *Amstrad plc* [1988] A.C. 1013, on the basis that in the *Monckton* case "a performance of the muscial work by the use of the record was bound to be an infringing use and the record was sold for that purpose." *Sed quaere.*

[77] *C.B.S. Inc.* v. *Ames Records & Tapes Ltd.* [1982] Ch. 91. See also *A. & M. Records Inc.* v. *Audio Magnetics Incorporated (U.K.) Ltd.* [1979] F.S.R. 1; *Paterson Zochonis Ltd.* v. *Merfarken Packaging Ltd.* [1983] F.S.R. 273.

[78] *Falcon* v. *Famous Players Film Co.* [1926] 2 K.B. 474; *Fenning Film Service Ltd.* v. *Wolverhampton, etc., Cinemas Ltd.* [1914] 3 K.B. 1171; compare—prior to the 1911 Act—*Glenville* v. *Selig Polyscope Co.* (1911) 27 T.L.R. 554; see also *Karno* v. *Pathé Frères Ltd.* (1909) 100 L.T. 260. In America the contrary has been held: *Kalem Co.* v. *Harper Bros.* (1911) 222 U.S.R. 55.

[79] *C.B.S. Songs Ltd.* v. *Amstrad plc* [1988] A.C. 1013.

[80] *Vigneux* v. *Canadian Performing Right Society Ltd.* [1945] A.C. 108. The case was decided under the special provisions of the Canadian Act and the decision on "authorisation" was strictly obiter. See also the next footnote.

[81] *Winstone* v. *Wurlitzer, etc.* [1946] V.L.R. 338. However in *Vigneux* the defendant also supplied the records for use in the juke box and to this extent the case seems hard to distinguish on the facts, although this was not a matter which was commented on by the Court. See also the comments of Whitford J. in *C.B.S. Inc. Ames Records & Tapes Ltd.* [1982] Ch. 91. Vigneux was also distinguished in *Winstone* on the ground that in *Winstone* the juke-box was provided on a profit sharing arrangement rather than a fixed fee so that the arrangement was a joint venture for which the defendant was liable.

[82] *Moorhouse* v. *University of New South Wales* [1976] R.P.C. 151 (High Ct. of Aus.). There are extensive provisions in the 1988 Act regulating the extent of copying permitted by libraries. See § 10–30, *et seq., post.*

today is uncertain[83] but it is submitted that it is the degree of control which is crucial in such cases. Thus if the defendant retains control over the means by which the infringements can take place and knows or has reasonable grounds to suspect that infringements will occur but does nothing to prevent them, this will justify a finding of implicit authorisation. The 1988 Act has now widened the categories of secondary infringements to include the provision of apparatus, with knowledge, for the purpose of an infringing performance. These provisions are considered elsewhere.[84]

8–142   **Other matters.** There was some authority for the proposition that the word "authorise," in the 1911 Act, made it an infringement to authorise the commission of an infringement, whether the actual infringing act was done or not.[85] This view, however, has been doubted.[86] and it seems improbable that a mere instruction, which might be revoked before it caused damage, could, of itself, be an actionable wrong, though if the defendant, after request, refused to revoke the authority, a case for a *quia timet* injunction might, it is thought, be made out.[87]

Although the infringing act must be done in the United Kingdom or in a country to which the 1988 Act has been extended, it is not clear from the terms of the Act where the act of authorisation has to take place.[88] If place of authorisation is relevant, difficult questions may arise as to where the authority is given if given by telephone, letter or telex.[89] As has been noted,[90] a person who authorises the doing of a tortious act may be liable as a joint tortfeasor with the person who actually does the act, or for procuring the infringing act.[91]

---

[83] Dicta from *Vigneux* were cited in the Court of Appeal and the House of Lords in the *Amstrad* decisions but the decision on the facts was not commented upon. *Winstone* was cited to the House of Lords in *C.B.S. Songs Ltd.* v. *Amstrad* but not commented upon. *Moorhouse* appears to have been regarded in *Amstrad Consumer Electronics plc.* v. *British Phonographic Industry Ltd.* as correct on its own facts, which justified a finding of implicit authorisation; see [1986] F.S.R. 211.

[84] § 9–31 *et seq., post.*

[85] *Fenning Film Service Ltd.* v. *Wolverhampton, etc., Cinemas Ltd.* [1914] 3 K.B. 1171.

[86] *Performing Right Society Ltd.* v. *Mitchell and Booker, etc., Ltd.* [1924] 1 K.B. 762 at 773; *Moorhouse* v. *University of New South Wales* [1975] R.P.C. 454 at 467; *R.C.A. Corporation* v. *John Fairfax & Son Ltd.* [1982] R.P.C. 91; *Copyright Agency Ltd.* v. *Haines* [1982] F.S.R. 331; *W.E.A. International Inc.* v. *Hanimex Corp. Ltd.* (1987) 77 A.L.R. 456.

[87] *R.C.A. Corporation* v. *John Fairfax & Son Ltd., supra* (*quia timet* injunction refused); *W.E.A. International Inc.* v. *Hanimex Corp. Ltd., supra.*

[88] In *Rexnord Inc.* v. *Rollerchain Distributors Ltd.* [1979] F.S.R. 119, the German manufacturers of alleged infringing conveyor chains were with their consent joined as defendants in an action against the sole importers and distributors in the United Kingdom of such chains on the application of the defendants. As to infringement abroad, see § 11–31, *post.*

[89] See *Diamond* v. *Bank of London and Montreal Ltd.* [1979] Q.B. 333; *Brinkibon Ltd.* v. *Stahag, etc.* [1983] 2 A.C. 34.

[90] § 8–134, *ante.*

[91] *P.R.S. Ltd.* v. *Mitchell and Booker, etc., Ltd.* [1924] 1 K.B. 762; *Ash* v. *Hutchinson and Co. (Publishers) Ltd.* [1936] Ch. 489; *Morton-Norwich Products Inc.* v. *Intercen Ltd.* [1978] R.P.C. 501; *Ravenscroft* v. *Herbert & Anor.* [1980] R.P.C. 193.

It has been said, too, that it is necessary to plead some specific authoris-   **8–143**
ation of an actual breach of copyright affecting a particular plaintiff, and
that it is not sufficient to plead authorisation at large.[92] However, it is submitted that there is no reason in principle why a sufficiently clear act of
authorisation should not amount to an infringement even though not
addressed to a specific person.

8. Licence and Non-derogation from Grant

Introduction. The 1988 Act provides,[93] as did the 1956 Act,[94] that copy-   **8–144**
right is infringed by any person who does or authorises another person to
do any of the acts restricted by the copyright "without the licence" of the
copyright owner. The expression "without the licence" is to the same
effect, it is thought, as the expression "without the consent" which was
used in the 1911 Act.[95]

Successors in title. The 1988 Act provides, as did the 1956 Act, that a   **8–145**
licence granted by a copyright owner is binding on every successor in title
to his interest in the copyright, except a purchaser in good faith for valuable consideration and without notice (actual or constructive) of the
licence or a person deriving title from such a purchaser, and that references to doing anything with or without the licence of the copyright owner
are to be construed accordingly.[96] The licensee of copyright, to the extent
of the licence, can therefore do acts restricted by the copyright as against
the owner and anyone claiming through him, except a purchaser for value
without notice. The 1988 Act goes on to provide, again as did the 1956
Act, that a licence granted by the prospective owner of copyright is similarly binding upon every successor in title to his interest (or prospective
interest) in the right.[97] The 1956 Act made further express provision relating to sub-licences, which has not been repeated in the 1988 Act, such that
where the doing of anything was authorised by the grantee of a licence, or
a person deriving title from the grantee, and it was within the terms
(including any implied terms) of the licence for him to authorise it, it
should for the purposes of that Act be taken to be done with the licence of
the grantor and of every other person (if any) upon whom the licence was
binding.[98] So far as the position under the 1988 Act is concerned, where it
is within the terms of a licence to authorise others to do anything, presum-

---

[92] *A. & M. Records Inc.* v. *Audio Magnetics Incorporated (U.K.) Ltd.* [1979] F.S.R. 1.
[93] C.D.P.A. 1988, s.16(2).
[94] Copyright Act 1956, s.1(2).
[95] s.2(1). See also *Computermate Products (Aust) (Pty.) Ltd.* v. *Ozi-Soft Pty. Ltd.* (1988) 83 A.L.R.
492. Under the 1911 Act an interest in the copyright might be granted by a licence, provided that it was in writing. See s.5(2). The use of the word "consent" in s.2(1) may therefore have been used deliberately to indicate that such formality was not required for the
purposes of s.2. See *Mellor* v. *Australian Broadcasting Commission* [1940] A.C. 491; *Harold
Drabble Ltd.* v. *The Hycolite Manufacturing Company* [1923–28] Mac.C.C. 322; *Allen* v. *Lyon*
[1884] 5 O.R. 615; *Time-Life International (Nederlands) B.V.* v. *Interstate Parcel Express Co. Pty.
Ltd.* [1978] F.S.R. 251; compare *P.R.S.* v. *Coates* [1923–28] Mac.C.C. 103.
[96] C.D.P.A. 1988, s.90(4), Copyright Act 1956, s.36(4).
[97] C.D.P.A. 1988, s.91(3), Copyright Act 1956, s.37(3).
[98] Copyright Act 1956, s.49(7).

ably a person so authorised would always be able to say that the thing done was with the licence of the copyright owner. The 1988 Act provides that any document made or event occurring before August 1, 1989 which had any operation creating, transferring or terminating any licence in respect of the copyright in any work made before that date will have the corresponding operation in relation to the work under the 1988 Act.[99]

8–146 **Formalities.** Except in the case of an exclusive licence, there is no requirement that the licence be in writing. Although, therefore, a licence can be the result of a formal written agreement it can also be oral or implied from conduct, for example the payment and acceptance of royalties or other sums in respect of the exploitation of the copyright.[1] In the case of an implied licence, the test is an objective one, namely whether, viewing the facts objectively, the words and conduct of the alleged licensor, as made known to the alleged licensee, in fact indicated that the licensor consented to what the licensee was doing.[2]

8–147 **Implied licences.** Implied licences frequently cause difficulties. Since it will be the defendant who will have raised the issue of licence as a defence, no doubt the onus will be upon him to establish its terms.[3] In cases where a work is made by an independent contractor to be used by another for certain purposes, in circumstances such that the copyright is retained by the author,[4] some licence to use the work must be implied in favour of the latter if the contract is otherwise silent on the point. In such cases the principle to be applied is that "the engagement for reward of a person to produce material of a nature which is capable of being the subject of copyright implies a permission, or consent, or licence in the person giving the engagement to use the material in the manner and for the purpose in which and for which it was contemplated between the parties that it would be used at the time of the engagement."[5] It is suggested that the implied licence extends no further than to that which is necessary to give business efficacy to the contract,[6] and thus to allow use of the work for the purposes which were in the contemplation of both parties at the time the contract was made, but no further. It is thought that the same principle applies where the licence is gratuitous, for example in cases where the work is supplied knowing that it will be used for a particular purpose. As with all licences, the important questions to decide are the extent of permitted use, the persons entitled to benefit and the duration of the licence.

---

[99] C.D.P.A. 1988, Sched. 1, para. 25(1).

[1] *Redwood Music Ltd.* v. *Francis Day & Hunter Ltd.* [1978] R.P.C. 429; *Redwood Music Ltd.* v. *Chappell & Co. Ltd.* [1982] R.P.C. 109.

[2] *Redwood Music Ltd.* v. *Chappell & Co. Ltd., supra.*

[3] Technically, however, it will be for the Plaintiff to establish his cause of action by proving that the acts in question were done without licence. See *Computermate Products (Aust) Pty. Ltd.* v. *Ozi-Soft Pty. Ltd.* (1988) 83 A.L.R. 492.

[4] For example, because the contract expressly so provides or where it is not a term of the contract (express or implied) that the copyright should belong to the other.

[5] *Beck* v. *Montana Constructions Pty. Ltd.* [1964–65] N.S.W.R. 229, approved by the Court of Appeal in *Blair* v. *Osborne & Tomkins* [1971] 2 Q.B. 78. See also, *e.g. Ironside* v. *H.M. Attorney General* [1988] R.P.C. 197.

[6] *Stovin-Bradford* v. *Volpoint Ltd.* [1971] Ch. 1007; *R. & A. Bailey & Co. Ltd.* v. *Boccaccio Pty. Ltd.* (1988) 77 A.L.R. 177.

The licensee. A licence may be assignable or the circumstances of the   **8–148**
granting of the licence and its terms may justify the conclusion that it was
intended to be personal to the licensee. Thus a licence will not be assignable where it appears that the licence was granted to the licensee because
of his personal skill or reputation.[7] Alternatively, the licence as originally
granted may have extended in scope beyond the actual grantee, for
example, also to his workmen or professional advisers.[8] A licence may be
so expressed as to extend to the world at large.[9]

Other terms of the licence. Other questions which may arise in connec-   **8–149**
tion with licences are the circumstances in which the licence can be
revoked and the extent of the licence, for example, whether the licence
extends to exploitation by a technology not in existence when the right
was granted. These are matters which are considered elsewhere.[10]

Alterations. Where a party is not the copyright owner but has only a   **8–150**
licence to reproduce a work, whether he is entitled to make alterations to it
will in part depend upon the terms of the licence. Regard must now also
be had to an author's right not to have his work subjected to derogatory
treatment, a topic which is considered elsewhere.[11] As to the terms of the
licence, the licence may expressly or impliedly require that publication be
in an unaltered form or that no substantial alteration be made, but in the
absence of such a prohibition the licensee may make alterations, even substantial ones.[12] The court will, however, readily imply a term into any
contract limiting the right to make alterations,[13] particularly it is thought,
in cases where matters of artistic judgment are involved. In cases of a
more commercial character it is thought that the right to make at least
insubstantial alterations and additions will be more easily implied.

Thus the alteration of even one line in a play may be beyond the scope   **8–151**
of a production company's licence,[14] but insubstantial changes to an
architect's plans may be permitted.[15] A contributor to a newspaper who
has only granted a licence for the reproduction of his article will, in the
absence of any special contract, probably be taken to have accepted the
ordinary custom that editors may make alterations to unsigned articles,
but the court will readily imply a term that no substantial alteration may

---

[7] *Re Jude's Musical Compositions* [1907] 1 Ch. 651; *Stevens v. Benning* (1855) 1 K. & J. 168; *Hole v. Bradbury* (1879) 12 Ch.D. 886. *Griffith v. Tower Publishing Co. Ltd.* [1897] 1 Ch. 21. See *Messager v. British Broadcasting Co. Ltd.* [1927] 2 K.B. 543, reversed on other grounds [1929] A.C. 151; *Dorling v. Honnor Marine Ltd.* [1964] Ch. 560 at 568.
[8] *Blair v. Osborne & Tomkins, supra.*
[9] *Mellor v. Australian Broadcasting Commission* [1940] A.C. 491; *Computermate Products (Aust) Pty. Ltd. v. Ozi-Soft Pty. Ltd.* (1988) 83 A.L.R. 492; *cf. Plix Products Ltd. v. Frank M. Winstone (Merchants)* [1986] F.S.R. 63.
[10] See § 5–50, *ante.*
[11] See § 22–35, *et seq., post.*
[12] *Frisby v. British Broadcasting Corporation* [1967] Ch. 932.
[13] *Ibid.*
[14] *Frisby v. British Broadcasting Corporation, supra.* But the line was considered by the author to be the key line of the play.
[15] See the cases discussed below in relation to architects' plans, § 8–153 *et seq.*

be made to a signed article without the author's consent.[16] In the case of a letter to a newspaper written for publication, the newspaper not only has the implied right to publish it but also, by customary implication, the right to alter it, so long as the alterations are not of a nature to affect the credit or literary reputation of the writer.

8–152 **Terms for exercise of licence.** A licence will usually contain terms, express or implied, relating to its exercise, for example, that agreed fees be paid or that no alterations be made. The question then often arises as to the position of a licensee who does not observe such terms. If he simply does something for which he does not have permission, he will be acting beyond the terms of the licence and thus infringing.[17] Thus a person may have a licence to use another's work but not to claim it as his own,[18] nor to make alterations,[19] with the result that if he does so this is an infringement. Alternatively, the term may amount to a condition precedent to the exercise of the licence so that failure to comply with the term will again mean that what is done is an infringement. Thus it may be a condition precedent for the right to use a song in a film that the composer be credited, or at least that someone else should not be credited.[20] On the other hand, if the licence is given in return for a promise by the licensee, the licensor's only remedy will be in damages. This will often be the position where the promise in question is to pay the licensee.[21] Whether or not in any case such a term is a condition precedent, or a term whose breach will allow the licensor to revoke the licence, will depend upon the proper construction of the licence agreement.[22]

8–153 **Architects' plans and works of architecture.** Many of the problems connected with licences are illustrated by cases concerning architects' plans. As has been pointed out elsewhere,[23] although the actual plans prepared by an architect for a client usually belong to the client, the architect will in general be the first owner of the copyright in them.[24] The architect may also of course own the copyright in models for the building, or the building itself, as works of architecture,[25] and unless the client has acquired the copyright in such works he may not copy them unless he has some licence to do so. Thus, without a sufficient licence, even to make an extension to a building will be an infringement if the extension reproduces the design of the original building,[26] although the 1988 Act does provide a defence, as did the 1956 Act, in the case where such works are reproduced

---

[16] *Joseph* v. *National Magazine Co. Ltd.* [1959] Ch. 14, approved in *Frisby* v. *British Broadcasting Corporation, supra.*

[17] As, for example, in *Dunlop Pneumatic Tyre Co. Ltd.* v. *Buckingham, etc., Co. Ltd.* (1901) 18 R.P.C. 423 (a patent case).

[18] *Blair* v. *Osborne & Tomkins, supra.*

[19] *Frisby* v. *British Broadcasting Corportion, supra.*

[20] *Miller* v. *Cecil Film Ltd.* [1937] 2 All E.R. 464.

[21] *Ng* v. *Clyde Securities Ltd.* [1976] N.S.W.L.R. 443.

[22] *Ibid.*

[23] See § 4–74, *ante.*

[24] The normal term of the R.I.B.A. conditions is that the architect retains the copyright in his plans.

[25] See § 2–25, *ante.*

[26] *Meikle* v. *Maufe* [1941] 3 All E.R. 144.

for the purpose of reconstructing a building.[27] Often, however, it is clear that some licence to use the plans must be implied but, first, what is the extent of the use covered by the licence? For example, is it limited to an application for planning permission alone, or does it extend to obtaining planning permission and thereafter for use in constructing and repairing the building in accordance with the plans, perhaps as modified? Second, who is entitled to the benefit of the licence? Is it the original client, or the original client and anyone to whom he sells the site with the benefit of the planning permission, for instance, and in either case is the licence dependent upon the architect having been paid his fee?

The extent of the implied licence has been considered in a number of **8–154** cases. In one case[28] a plaintiff had prepared plans for the client for the purpose of obtaining full planning permission to build two houses on a site and had been paid the full scale fee under the R.I.B.A. conditions for that work. The site was sold after planning permission was obtained and the plans were then used by another firm in erecting houses on the site. It was held that in the circumstances the plaintiff had impliedly licensed the use of the plans for all purposes connected with the erection of that building on that site in substantial accordance with them, whether by the client or by the purchasers of the plot, and by their surveyors or workmen, and such that they might make copies of the plans for that purpose. This conclusion was reached on a consideration of the then R.I.B.A. Conditions under which the architect was paid for his work in stages and which envisaged that the architect's engagement might not run its full course, so that it would be wrong in principle for the architect to be able to hold the client to ransom such that the client would almost inevitably have to retain him, particularly where the scale fees fully compensated the architect for the work actually done.[29] The principle applied was that "the payment for sketch plans includes a permission or consent to use those sketch plans for the purpose for which they were brought into existence, namely, for the purpose of building a building in substantial accordance with them and for the purpose of preparing any necessary drawings as part of the task of building the building.[30] But where an architect charged a nominal amount purely for the purposes of preparing plans for a planning application, the amount being much less than the appropriate scale fee, no licence was implied further than one enabling the plans to be used for that purpose.[31] The reason why a nominal fee will be charged in many such cases is that if the planning application is refused the money spent by the client will be thrown away, whereas if it is granted the architect may expect to be engaged under the building contract and earn substantial

---

[27] See § 10–94, *post*. On the other hand, where the architect has himself parted with the copyright it will not be an infringement for him to copy the work in question provided he does not repeat or imitate the main design of the work: see § 10–91 *et seq., post*.

[28] *Blair* v. *Osborne & Tomkins* [1971] 2 Q.B. 78.

[29] See the analysis in *Stovin-Bradford* v. *Volpoint Ltd.* [1971] Ch. 1007.

[30] The Court of Appeal citing with approval this passage from *Beck* v. *Montana Constructions Pty. Ltd.* [1964–65] N.S.W.R. 229.

[31] *Stovin-Bradford* v. *Volpoint* [1971] Ch. 1007.

fees,[32] or at least to be further compensated.[33] Every case will, however, depend upon its own facts[34] and it may be that a licence would be implied even if the architect had not been paid full scale fees for the work done up to a particular stage, but had been asked to remain as architect for the project but had refused or demanded unreasonable terms for doing so.[35]

8–155   Where the architect has retained the copyright there will often be sound reasons for this. Thus he may thereby be able to prevent the plans being used for purposes other than the specific building contemplated.[36] But where a licence can be implied for all purposes connected with the erection of buildings in accordance with plans, the licence will usually extend to making changes to them which are not substantial or to adding detail to them, for example for the purpose of obtaining building regulation approval.[37] The licence will usually extend to successors in title to the property,[38] or the assignees from the original client,[39] and will extend to reproducing the plans in a leaflet intended to be shown to prospective purchasers of the building.[40] It will usually enable the owner and his successors in title and contractors to repair or renovate the building, particularly where this has become necessary because of the architect's own fault.[41] It will not, however, extend to permit someone to remove the architect's name from the plans and put them forward as his own, although in such cases the damage resulting may be small.[42]

8–156   Whether the architect may stop the use of the plans where he is unpaid will depend upon whether payment was a condition precedent, or on whether non-payment can be treated as a repudiatory act allowing the architect to terminate any licence. It has been said that one of the purposes for the architect retaining copyright is to enable him to prevent the use of his work by others who have paid him no fee,[43] but in the usual type of case, particularly where payment is not expected to be made at the outset, it is thought that the correct analysis will be that the licence is given in return for a debt, recoverable by action.[44] Where the original client has become insolvent, and the site has passed into another's hands, this rem-

---

[32] *Ibid. per* Salmon L.J., at p. 1019.

[33] *Ibid. per* Megaw L.J., at p. 1022.

[34] *Ibid.*

[35] *Ibid. per* Megaw L.J., at p. 1022, and *per* Salmon L.J., at p. 1019, citing the example of an architect of wide renown; and see also *Beck* v. *Montana Constructions Pty. Ltd., supra.*

[36] *Blair* v. *Osborne & Tomkins, supra, per* Widgery L.J. at p. 86.

[37] *Blair* v. *Osborne & Tomkins, supra;* see also *Barnett* v. *Cape Town Foreshaw Board* [1978] F.S.R. 176 (Cape Div. Ct.) but *cf. Netupsky* v. *Dominion Bridge Co. Ltd.* (1969) 68 W.W.R. 529. The point was left open in *Hunter* v. *Fitzroy Robinson and Partners* [1978] F.S.R. 167.

[38] *Blair* v. *Osborne & Tomkins, supra.*

[39] *Hunter* v. *Fitzroy Robinson and Partners, supra.*

[40] *Robert Allan & Partners* v. *Scottish Ideal Homes* (1972) S.L.T. (Shire Court Reports) 32. The use of drawings or photographs of buildings in such circumstances may now also be permissible by virtue of s.63 of the 1988 Act. See § 10–89, *post.*

[41] *ADI Ltd.* v. *Destein* (1983) 141 D.L.R. (3d) 370.

[42] *Blair* v. *Osborne & Tomkins, supra,* where the plaintiff was awarded £2.

[43] *Blair* v. *Osborne & Tomkins, supra, per* Widgery L.J. at p. 86.

[44] *Ng* v. *Clyde Securities Ltd.* [1976] N.S.W.L.R. 443.

edy may of course be worthless.[45] Where, however, the architect's consent has been given gratuitously, he may later withdraw it.[46]

Express terms of architect's appointment. The terms on which a client **8–157** may use an architect's plans may of course be regulated by the express terms of his appointment. The current (1982) edition of the R.I.B.A. standard conditions of appointment makes more detailed provision than the conditions considered in the earlier cases. Thus they provide that in certain defined circumstances the client may proceed to execute the project, or repair, maintain or renew the works, and so reproduce the architect's designs. The circumstances are that the architect has completed work to the planning application stage and that the client has paid or tendered any fees due to the architect. Where these conditions apply, therefore, the unpaid architect appears to have a valuable remedy against his client or against any third party who wishes to proceed with the project. The conditions also provide that the client's right to proceed is limited to the site or part of the site to which the design relates. Where the architect has reached a less advanced stage, the client may in general only proceed with the project if he obtains the architect's consent (not to be unreasonably withheld) and pays an additional fee.

Other examples of implied licences. The nature of the agreement to be **8–158** implied when an author submits an article or other manuscript for publication is considered elsewhere.[47] When a letter is written to a newspaper with a view to publication, since the copyright remains with the writer,[48] a licence to publish it is clearly implied. The extent to which alterations may be impliedly licensed in either of these circumstances has already been discussed.[49] As to other letters, whether the recipient of a letter has a licence to reproduce and publish it will obviously depend upon the circumstances, and although a licence to publish commercial letters may be more easily implied than in the case of private correspondence, publication in either case is likely to be an infringement.[50] Under the old law letters might be published to vindicate the character of the receiver[51] but it is thought that no such defence could now be relied upon in an action for infringement of copyright.[52] Commonly photographic agencies will submit prints or transparencies to newspapers on the understanding that the paper is at liberty to use them, whereupon a recognised fee will be paid. The legal effect of this arrangement will usually be that the agency makes an offer to permit the newspaper to use the photograph in return for a fee,

---

[45] As in *Ng* v. *Clyde Securities Ltd.*, *supra*.
[46] *Katz* v. *Cytrynbaum* (1984) 2 D.L.R. (4th) 52, following *Hart* v. *Hayman, Christy & Lilly Ltd.* [1911–16] Mac.C.C. 301.
[47] See § 15–2, *post*.
[48] See § 4–71, *ante*.
[49] § 8–150, *ante*.
[50] See, *e.g. Perceval (Lord and Lady)* v. *Phipps* (1813) 2 V. & B. (private letters); *Tett Bros. Ltd.* v. *Drake & Goreham Ltd.* [1928–35] Mac.C.C. 492 and *British Oxygen Co. Ltd.* v. *Liquid Air Ltd.* [1925] Ch. 383, (commercial correspondence).
[51] *Lytton (Earl of)* v. *Devy* (1884) 52 L.T. 121; *Labouchere* v. *Hess* (1898) 77 L.T. 559; *Folsom* v. *Marsh* (1841) 2 Story (Amer.) 100; *Howard* v. *Gunn* (1863) 32 Beav. 462. *cf. Palin* v. *Gathercole* (1844) 1 Col.C.C. 565.
[52] See *British Oxygen Co. Ltd.* v. *Liquid Air Ltd.*, *supra*; and see *Copinger* (12th ed.), § 80.

which offer is accepted by publication.[53] Like all offers made without consideration, however, it may be revoked by notice, and thereafter the newspaper has no right to publish photographs which have already been
submitted.[54] There may be a custom in the Press that one newspaper may
copy from another the quoted words of a third party,[55] but otherwise a
licence will not be implied from the fact that copying, for example by one
newspaper of another, is habitually carried on.[56] Clearly the forms in a
book of legal precedents are intended to be copied by practitioners, unless
otherwise stated, but a licence would not be implied to enable a purchaser
to write a second, competing work. Again, the retail sale of knitting patterns, even without any reservation, will not usually carry with it any
implied licence that the patterns may be reproduced for commercial purposes in unlimited quantities.[57]

8–159 **Implied licence: The right to repair.** Before the decision of the House
of Lords in *British Leyland Motor Corporation Ltd.* v. *Armstrong Patents Co.
Ltd.*[58] there were a number of decisions to the effect that a purchaser of an
article was entitled, by virtue of an implied licence from the vendor, to
reproduce a copyright work if this was done in the course of repair of the
article. Such decisions were reached by analogy with patent cases where
the form of the letters patent[59] forced the Court to imply some licence to
enable the purchaser of a patented article to use it and thus repair it. The
licence in such cases extends no further than enabling the purchaser to
prolong the life of the article by repair but not to make a new article under
the cover of repair.[60] The cases decided in relation to copyright established that such a licence extended to enable the purchaser to make spare
parts himself and to have such parts made for him,[61] and probably to have
two or more made at the same time against the future breakdown of the
article.[62] The licence did not, however, extend to the world at large so as
to enable a manufacturer to make spare parts in anticipation of future
orders,[63] nor to enable the manufacturer to copy any plans to which he
might have had access, as opposed to working backwards from the part
which he was going to replace.[64]

---

[53] *Bowden Bros* v. *Amalgamated Pictorials Ltd.* [1911] 1 Ch. 396.
[54] See n. 51.
[55] *Express Newspapers plc.* v. *News (U.K.) Ltd.* [1990] F.S.R. 359, where, on an application for
judgment under R.S.C. Order 14, the point was treated as being arguable.
[56] *Walter* v. *Steinkopff* [1892] 3 Ch. 489.
[57] *Roberts* v. *Candiware Ltd.* [1980] F.S.R. 352.
[58] [1986] A.C. 577.
[59] "To make, use, exercise and vend" the invention.
[60] *Dunlop Pneumatic Tyre Co.* v. *Neal* [1899] 1 Ch. 807; *Sirdar Rubber Co. Ltd.* v. *Wallington Weston & Co.* (1907) 24 R.P.C. 539.
[61] *Solar Thomson Engineering Co. Ltd.* v. *Barton* [1977] R.P.C. 537; *Gardner & Sons Ltd.* v. *Paul
Sykes Organisation Ltd.* [1981] F.S.R. 281, and *Weir Pumps Ltd.* v. *C.M.L. Pumps Ltd.* [1984]
F.S.R. 33.
[62] *British Leyland Motor Corporation Ltd.* v. *Armstrong Patents Co. Ltd.* [1984] F.S.R. 591; *Hoover
plc* v. *George Hulme Ltd.* [1982] F.S.R. 565.
[63] *Ibid.*
[64] *I.e.* by reverse engineering. See *Weir Pumps Ltd.* v. *C.M.L. Pumps Ltd., supra.*

Non-derogation from grant: the right to repair. The use by the courts   **8–160**
of an implied licence theory was artificial and gave rise to obvious difficulties, for example, where there was no privity of contract between the
manufacturer of the original article and its owner or the spare part manufacturer. The principle was largely abandoned by the House of Lords in
the *British Leyland* case, where the question arose whether an independent
manufacturer of replacement car exhaust systems could be stopped by the
owner of the copyright in the manufacturing drawings for such systems.
Starting from the premise that the purchaser of an article such as a car has
an inherent right to repair it, it was held, by an extension of the principle
of non-derogation from grant, that the common law would not allow a
copyright owner to assert a monopoly right to detract from the rights of
ownership, thereby affecting the value and use of the article sold. The
principle applied was that a grantor would not be allowed to derogate
from his grant by using intellectual property retained in such a way as to
render property granted by him unfit or materially unfit for the purpose
for which the grant was made.[65]

The extent of this doctrine as newly applied to the field of copyright has   **8–161**
yet to be worked out. The House of Lords recognised[66] that it was a novel
application of the principle of non-derogation from grant to prevent a
party exercising a statutory right. There is nothing in the 1988 Act which
apparently affects its general application.[67] Certain principles may, however, be tentatively stated:–

   (a) In a case where a question of patent protection simultaneously
      arises,[68] the principles relating to implied licences in such cases
      will still apply and the principle of non-derogation from grant
      need not and perhaps should not, be invoked.[69]

   (b) None of the "repair" cases[70] decided under the implied licence
      principle were disapproved on their facts and the result in each
      case would presumably be the same today.

   (c) The newly applied principle enables the owner of an article to have
      a replacement part made either by himself or by another, as before,
      but also enables a supplier to manufacture such stock in advance of
      anticipated orders.[71]

   (d) The principle appears to go further than the implied licence prin-
      ciple when applied in relation to patent cases in that the copyright

---

[65] [1986] A.C. 577 at p. 641, relying on *Browne* v. *Flower* [1911] 1 Ch. 219.
[66] At p. 627.
[67] And see, *e.g.* C.D.P.A. 1988, s.172(3).
[68] As it did in the *Solar Thomson* case, *supra*.
[69] *Per* Lord Bridge at p. 625. Lord Templeman, who gave the other leading speech, did not
expressly deal with the point. See also *Dellareed Ltd.* v. *Delkim Developments* [1988] F.S.R.
329.
[70] See n. 60, *supra*.
[71] *British Leyland Motor Corporation Ltd.* v. *Armstrong Patents Co. Ltd.* [1986] A.C. 577, 625.

owner is not entitled to complain of the manufacture of an entirely new part as opposed to simply the repair of an existing one.[72]

(e) The distinction between the two principles is further emphasised by the fact that the right to repair and thus reproduce copyright works cannot apparently be withheld even by the express terms of the contract of purchase.[73]

(f) A subcontractor who designs a part for a manufacturer, knowing the purpose for which it is to be used, cannot assert his copyright against the purchaser.[74]

(g) The right does not permit a defendant to take copies of the plaintiff's drawings directly[75] or, presumably, to make articles from such copies.

---

[72] As in the *British Leyland* case itself. This also appears to have been the position established under the implied licence cases. See *Gardner & Sons Ltd.* v. *Paul Sykes Organisation Ltd.* and *Weir Pumps Ltd.* v. *C.M.L. Pumps Ltd., supra.*
[73] *British Leyland Motor Corporation Ltd.* v. *Armstrong Patents Co. Ltd., supra,* at p. 643.
[74] *Ibid.*
[75] *Warman International Ltd.* v. *Envirotech Australia Pty. Ltd.* (1986) 67 A.L.R. 253 (Fed. Ct. Austr.).

Contents

1. Introduction

The 1988 Act provides, as did the 1956 Act, for secondary or indirect **9–1** classes of infringement, the principal characteristic of which is that it is a necessary ingredient of the tort that the defendant has a degree of "guilty knowledge." The 1988 Act has widened the scope of the secondary acts of infringement but only applies to acts done after August 1, 1989; the 1956 Act will continue to apply in relation to all acts done before that date.[1] As was the case under the 1956 Act, the 1988 Act does not provide that a person who authorises a secondary act of infringement is liable, although a person may nevertheless be liable for such an act under the common law, for example as a joint tortfeasor.[2]

The 1988 Act provides for three broad classes of secondary infringe- **9–2** ment. The first consists of various dealings with infringing copies, the second of providing the means for making infringing copies and the third of permitting or providing the means enabling infringing performances to take place. The three classes will be considered in turn, together with the equivalent provisions of the 1956 Act, where appropriate.

---

[1] C.D.P.A. 1988, Sched. 1, para. 14(1).

[2] See § 8–134, *ante* and § 11–12 *post*. The 1977 Copyright Committee, Cmmd. 6732, para. 749(iii), recommended that persons authorising indirect infringements should be liable.

2. Dealings in Infringing Copies

A. Introduction

9–3 **The 1988 Act.** The principal provisions of the 1988 Act apply to acts done in relation to infringing copies. Thus under the 1988 Act the copyright in a work is infringed by any person who, without the licence of the copyright owner:

(a) possesses in the course of a business,

(b) sells or lets for hire, or offers or exposes for sale or hire,

(c) in the course of a business exhibits in public or distributes, or

(d) distributes otherwise than in the course of a business to such an extent as to affect prejudicially the owner of the copyright,

an article which is, and which he knows or has reason to believe is, an infringing copy of the work.[3]

The copyright in a work is also infringed by any person who, without the licence of the copyright owner, imports into the United Kingdom, otherwise than for his private and domestic use, an article which is, and which he knows or has reason to believe is, an infringing copy of the work.[4] These provisions are no doubt principally directed, as were the equivalent provisions of the 1956 Act, to the position, not of manufacturers, but of third parties who may deal in infringing articles supplied to them.[5]

B. Infringing copy

9–4 An article is an infringing copy if its making constituted an infringement of the copyright in the work in question.[6] An article is also an infringing copy if:

(a) it has been or is proposed to be imported into the United Kingdom, and

(b) its making in the United Kingdom would have constituted an infringement of the copyright in the work in question, or a breach of an exclusive licence agreement relating to that work.[7]

This last provision relating to an exclusive licence agreement no doubt refers to the making of an article in the United Kingdom by the exclusive licensor, which by implication would be a breach of the exclusive licence. There are also a number of provisions in the 1988 Act whereby copies of works whose making did not constitute an infringement of copyright,

---

[3] C.D.P.A. 1988, s.23.
[4] *Ibid.* s.22.
[5] *Paterson Zochonis Ltd.* v. *Merfarken Packaging Ltd.* [1983] F.S.R. 273. But see § 8–92, *et seq., ante.*
[6] C.D.P.A. 1988, s.27(2).
[7] *Ibid.* s.27(3). As to the definition of an exclusive licence, see s.92(1) and § 5–46, *ante.*

because statutory exemptions applied, are nevertheless to be treated as infringing copies in certain subsequent events.[8] These provisions are dealt with elsewhere.[9] Where in any proceedings it is proved that an article of a copy of a work, and that copyright subsists or has at any time subsisted in the work, then for the purposes of deciding whether the article is an infringing copy is to be presumed until the contrary is proved that the article was made at a time when copyright subsisted in the work.[10]

Imported copies. As has been seen,[11] in the case of an article which has **9–5** been imported or which is proposed to be imported, the article will be an infringing copy if its making in the United Kingdom would have constituted an infringement of copyright or a breach of an exclusive licence agreement relating to that work. Thus the owner of the United Kingdom copyright or the United Kingdom exclusive licensee can object to the importation of and subsequent dealings in copies made abroad without his licence.[12] This is so even though the articles made abroad were legitimately purchased there on the open market, for the sale of articles in the ordinary course of business in one territory without restriction on resale does not carry with it any implied licence to import and sell those articles in another territory. The purchaser obtains the same rights as the purchaser of any other chattel, and the rights which flow from acquisition and ownership do not involve any such implied licence.[13] The definition of infringing copy in the case of an imported article involves making an assumption as to the circumstances in which the article was made. It was established under the equivalent provisions of the 1956 Act that the only assumption which had to be made for this purpose was that the article was made in the United Kingdom by the person who actually made it abroad.[14] The provision of the 1988 Act relating to an exclusive licence agreement means that a person who has such an agreement covering the United Kingdom may object to the importation of and dealings in articles even where they were made abroad by the owner of the United Kingdom copyright. In this respect the position under the 1956 Act was different.[15]

Infringing copies: Transitional provisions. Although for the purposes **9–6** of infringement, the 1988 Act only applies in relation to acts done after August 1, 1989, the article dealt in may of course have been made before this date. The 1988 Act provides that for the purposes of determining whether an article is an infringing copy, the 1956 Act is to be applied in relation to an article made after June 1, 1957 and before August 1, 1989, and the 1911 Act is to be applied to an article made before June 1, 1957.[16]

---

[8] *Ibid.* s.27(6).
[9] See §§ 10–21, 10–27, 10–29, 10–32, 10–67, 10–89, 10–113, 15–108, *post.*
[10] C.D.P.A. 1988, s. 28(4).
[11] § 9–4, *ante.*
[12] Subject to E.E.C. Law. See § 9–7, *post.*
[13] *Time-Life International (Nederlands) N.V.* v. *Interstate Parcel Express Co. Pty. Ltd.* [1978] F.S.R. 251; *Polydor Ltd.* v. *Harlequin Record Shops* [1980] F.S.R. 362; *Penguin Books Ltd.* v. *India Book Distributors* [1985] F.S.R. 120; *R. & A. Bailey & Co Ltd.* v. *Boccaccio Pty. Ltd.* (1988) 77 A.L.R. 177; *Computermate Products (Aus) Pty. Ltd.* v. *Ozi–Soft Pty. Ltd.* (1988) 83 A.L.R. 492.
[14] See § 9–11, *post.*
[15] *Ibid.*
[16] C.D.P.A. 1988, Sched. 1, para. 14(3).

In relation to articles made on or after August 1, 1989, the 1988 Act is to be applied.

9–7 The European Communities Act 1972. The 1988 Act expressly provides that nothing in these provisions of the 1988 Act shall be construed as applying to an article which may be lawfully imported into the United Kingdom by virtue of any enforceable Community right within the meaning of section 2(1) of the European Communities Act 1972.[17] Thus if an article is in free circulation within the European Economic Community it will not be an infringing copy for any purpose.[18]

C. Territorial extent

9–8 The 1988 Act's territorial extent. One possible difficulty with these provisions is that, unlike the case of primary acts of infringement,[19] and the equivalent provisions of the 1956 Act,[20] the acts of secondary infringement, apart from importation, are not restricted in express terms in the 1988 Act to acts done in the United Kingdom.[21] However, this Part of the Act is extended in the first place only to England and Wales, Scotland and Northern Ireland,[22] and the general principle of statutory construction is that unless the contrary is expressly enacted, English legislation does not extend to acts of foreigners who have never come into the jurisdiction.[23] Thus if an article whose making in the United Kingdom constituted an infringement of copyright, and which was thus an infringing copy, came into the hands of someone in a foreign jurisdiction, it would be surprising if the legislature intended that that person should become liable under the 1988 Act for selling the article in the foreign jurisdiction even where he had the necessary knowledge.

9–9   It might be argued, however, that the provision that an "infringing copy" may include one which is "proposed" to be imported into the United Kingdom indicates a contrary intention. Thus it might be said that the 1988 Act apparently expressly contemplates a situation in which the infringing article is not yet in the United Kingdom, and since possession of the infringing copy, its exposure for sale, exhibition in public and distribution with knowledge are all acts of infringement, it follows that the 1988 Act also contemplates that acts done outside the United Kingdom may be infringements. Purpose can still be given to this provision, however, consistent with infringement only occurring within the United Kingdom, if it is remembered that for the purposes of the Act an act can be done in the United Kingdom in relation to an article even

---

[17] *Ibid.* s.27(5).

[18] As to the effects of Community Law generally, see Chap. 14, *post*.

[19] See C.D.P.A. 1988, s.16(1).

[20] Copyright Act 1956, ss.5(2), (3), 16(2), (3). See also *Def Lepp Music* v. *Stuart-Brown* [1986] R.P.C. 271, confirming that the provisions of the 1956 Act were expressly confined to acts done in the UK or other countries to which the Act extended.

[21] C.D.P.A. 1988, ss.22, 23.

[22] *Ibid.* s.157(1).

[23] See *ex parte Blain* (1879) 12 Ch.D. 522; *Clark* v. *Oceanic Contractors Inc.* [1983] 2 A.C. 130.

though it has not been imported. Thus, first, although to "import" is not defined in the 1988 Act, it probably means to bring an article from abroad into port, such that the carriage is ended or its continuity is in some way broken.[24] Secondly, an act done on a British ship, aircraft or hovercraft will be treated as being done in the United Kingdom[25] and, in addition, the territorial waters of the United Kingdom are to be treated as part of the United Kingdom.[26] It follows that acts can be done in what is the United Kingdom for the purposes of the Act, for example on board a British ship, in relation to articles which are "proposed to be imported into the United Kingdom." If this is correct, then it would be an infringement of copyright to possess, with knowledge, a piratical article on board a British ship if it was proposed to import it into the United Kingdom, but it would not be an infringement to possess such an article on board a British ship if the article was neither made in the United Kingdom nor had ever been imported into the United Kingdom and it was not proposed to import it. It is therefore thought that the acts of secondary infringement are restricted to acts done in the United Kingdom.

D. The 1956 Act

Under the 1956 Act the copyright in a work was infringed by any person who, in the United Kingdom, and without the licence of the owner of the copyright: **9–10**

(a) sold, let for hire, or by way of trade offered or exposed for sale or hire any article, or

(b) by way of trade exhibited any article in public, or

(c) distributed any articles either for purposes of trade, or for other purposes, but to such an extent as to affect prejudicially the owner of the copyright in question,

if to his knowledge the making of the article constituted an infringement of that copyright or (in the case of an imported article) would have constituted an infringement of that copyright if the article had been made in the United Kingdom.[27]

The copyright in a work was also infringed by any person who, without the licence of the owner of the copyright, imported an article (otherwise than for his private and domestic use) into the United Kingdom, if to his knowledge the making of that article constituted an infringement of that copyright, or would have constituted such an infringement if the article had been made in the United Kingdom.[28]

The 1956 Act: Imported copies. The question arose under these pro-   **9–11**
visions relating to imported copies as to the hypothetical circumstances in which the articles were to be considered as having been made in the

---

[24] See § 9–16, *post.*
[25] C.D.P.A. 1988, s.162.
[26] *Ibid.* s.161.
[27] Copyright Act 1956, ss.5(3),(4), 16(3),(4).
[28] *Ibid.* ss.5(2), 16(2).

United Kingdom. For example, in a case where the article had been made abroad by the United Kingdom copyright owner, could an exclusive licensee in the United Kingdom complain about the importation of such articles? The answer to this question depended upon who was to be considered to have been the hypothetical maker of the articles in the United Kingdom. It was established that this person was the actual maker of the articles[29] so that in the example given above, the United Kingdom exclusive licensee would have had no cause of action against the importer for infringement of copyright since it would not have been an infringement of copyright for the actual copyright owner to have made the article in the United Kingdom, but only a breach of the exclusive licence. As already seen, the position has been altered under the 1988 Act.[30]

E. Infringement by possession

9–12   As has been seen,[31] under the 1988 Act copyright in a work is infringed by any person who, without the licence of the copyright owner, and with knowledge, possesses an infringing copy in the course of a business.[32] This provision is new, although the Literary Copyright Act 1842 did make it an infringement of copyright for anyone knowingly "to have in his possession for sale or hire" an imported book which infringed copyright.[33] "Business" is defined as including a trade or profession.[34] It would seem that the business in question must be that of the possessor, and not that of some other person who sold it to him.[35]

F. Infringment by sale

9–13   **Infringement by sale, etc: The two Acts compared.** As has been seen,[36] the 1988 Act provides that it is an infringement to offer or expose for sale or hire an infringing copy, whereas the 1956 Act only made such acts infringements if done by way of trade. Otherwise the provisions under both Acts appear to be the same. Under the 1988 Act the exhibition of an infringing article in public is only an infringement if done in the course of a business (which includes a trade or profession),[37] whereas under the 1956 Act such an act was an infringement if done "by way of trade," but there does not appear to be any difference in substance between the two provisions.

---

[29] *C.B.S. Ltd.* v. *Charmdale Record Distributors Ltd.* [1981] Ch. 91; *Polydor Ltd.* v. *Harlequin Record Shop* [1980] F.S.R. 194 and 362 (C.A.); *The Who Group* v. *Stage One (Records) Ltd.* [1980] F.S.R. 268. *cf. J. Albert & Sons Pty. Ltd.* v. *Fletcher Construction Ltd.* [1976] R.P.C. 615; *Barson Computers (N.Z.) Ltd.* v. *John Gilbert & Co. Ltd.* [1985] F.S.R. 489.

[30] See § 9–5, *ante*.

[31] § 9–3, *ante*.

[32] C.D.P.A. 1988, s.23(*a*).

[33] 5 & 6 Vict. c. 45, s.17. The 1977 Copyright Committee, Cmmd. 6732, para 749(ii), recommended that possession in the course of trade of imported articles only should be an infringement.

[34] C.D.P.A. 1988, s.178.

[35] See *Reid* v. *Kennett* (1986) Crim.L.R. 456, decided under s.21(4A), Copyright Act 1956.

[36] §9–3, *ante*.

[37] See n. 34, *ante*.

It is not an infringement under these provisions to invite offers for sale, **9–14**
for example by sending out a price list.[38] Nor does a person infringe copyright who merely attempts to effect a sale but who does not in the course of
doing so commit one of the specific acts of infringement.[39] Whether a sale
has taken place will be judged on the normal objective basis, and the fact
that one party had no subjective intention to enter into a contract or legal
relationship, for example on a trap purchase, will be irrelevant.[40] Where a
defendant has delivered copies of a work on a "sale or return basis" he is
not liable for any subsequent sale because he cannot demand the return of
the copies.[41] Nor is it an infringment under these provisions to sell a work
which has been lawfully made in the United Kingdom, although if copies
have not previously been put into circulation there may be an act of
infringement under the 1988 Act by the issuing of copies to the public.[42]

G. Infringement by distribution

The provisions of the 1988 and 1956 Acts appear to be identical in effect. **9–15**
To be an infringement the distribution must either be in the course of a
business (which includes a trade or profession)[43] or to such an extent as to
affect prejudicially the owner of the copyright. It is not, however, easy to
imagine a case in which distribution is neither in the course of a trade or
business nor prejudicial to the owner of the copyright.

H. Infringement by importation

No definition of what amounts to importation is contained in the 1988 or **9–16**
1956 Acts. It is thought that an article is imported when it is brought from
abroad into port or, in the case of carriage by aircraft, landed.[44] It is
thought that the carriage must be ended or its continuity in some way
broken,[45] so that an article is not imported if the vessel in which it is carried merely enters a port of call on its way to its final destination.[46] Nor is
an article imported if the vessel carrying it merely enters the territorial
waters of the United Kingdom.[47] But an article will be imported even
though it is landed only with the purpose of transporting it across the territory to another state.[48]

---

[38] *Norgren Co.* v. *Technomarking, The Times*, March 3, 1983.
[39] *Wolff* v. *Wood, The Times*, October 31, 1903; *Britain* v. *Kennedy* (1903) 19 T.L.R. 122.
[40] *Phillips* v. *Holmes* [1988] R.P.C. 613, decided under Copyright Act 1956, s.21(1).
[41] *Schofield & Sims Ltd.* v. *Gibson (R.) & Sons Ltd.* [1928–35] Mac.C.C. 64; but *cf. Savory (E.W.) Ltd.* v. *The World of Golf Ltd.* [1911–16] Mac.C.C. 149.
[42] See § 8–92 *et seq., ante.*
[43] See n. 34, *ante.*
[44] See, *e.g. Wilson* v. *Chambers & Co. Pty. Ltd.* (1926) 38 C.L.R. 138. For a definition of when an article is imported for Customs and Excise purposes see the Customs and Excise Management Act 1979, s.5.
[45] *Wilson* v. *Chambers & Co. Pty. Ltd., supra.*
[46] *Canada Sugar Refining Co.* v. *R.* [1898] A.C. 735.
[47] *R.* v. *Bull* (1974) 48 A.L.J.R. 232.
[48] *Grammophone Company of India Ltd.* v. *Pandey* [1985] F.S.R. 136.

9–17   Under the 1988 Act, as under the 1956 Act, the onus is on the importer to show, if he can, that the article was only imported for private or domestic use. Provision is also made for the owner of the copyright to restrict unlawful importation by giving notice to the Commissioners of Customs and Excise. The matter is dealt with elsewhere.[49]

I. Knowledge

9–18   Necessity to prove knowledge. As has been seen,[50] in relation to secondary infringements under the 1988 Act, it is necessary to prove that the defendant knew or had reason to believe he was dealing with an article which was an infringing copy of the work.[51] For the purposes of the 1956 Act the plaintiff must prove that the defendant knew that the making of the article constituted or (in the case of an imported article) would have constituted an infringement of copyright.[52] The introduction of the words "had reason to believe" in the 1988 Act might suggest that it will be easier for a plaintiff to prove "knowledge" under the 1988 Act than under the previous Acts. In the light of the interpretation given to the provisions of the 1956 Act, however, it is not clear that the 1988 Act has made any material change in the law in this respect, except perhaps to render liable a defendant who has negligently failed to make inquiry.

9–19   The decisions under the earlier Acts established that knowledge in this sense means actual and not constructive knowledge.[53] In every case it will be a question of fact whether the defendant had this requisite knowledge. It has been said that knowledge in this context means notice of facts such as would suggest to a reasonable man that a breach of the copyright law was being committed, or which would at least put him on inquiry.[54] Probably this means no more than where it is necessary to draw inferences the court is entitled to infer knowledge on the part of a particular person on the assumption that that person had the ordinary understanding expected of persons in his line of business.[55] Plainly it is likely that persons who deal every day with transactions involving copyright will be familiar with its incidents; others may be wholly ignorant. The defendant's own statements or gestures may of course be sufficient to establish knowledge, in which case questions as to what is to be inferred will not arise. But a person who deliberately refrains from inquiry and shuts his eyes to that which

---

[49] See § 19–18 *et seq.*, *post.*
[50] § 9–3 *ante.*
[51] C.D.P.A. 1988, ss.22, 23.
[52] Copyright Act 1956, ss.5(2), (3), 16(2), (3).
[53] *R.C.A. Corporation* v. *Custom Cleared Sales Pty. Ltd.* [1978] F.S.R. 576; applied in *Politechnika* v. *Dallas Print Transfers Ltd.* [1982] F.S.R. 529; *Hoover plc* v. *George Hulme Ltd.* [1982] F.S.R. 565 and *Hooi* v. *Brophy* (1984) 52 A.L.R. 710. See also *International Business Machines Corp.* v. *Computer Imports Ltd.* [1989] 2 N.Z.L.R. 395.
[54] *Albert* v. *Hoffnung & Co. Ltd.* [1921] 22 S.R.(N.S.W.) 75, followed in *Infabrics Ltd.* v. *Jaytex Shirt Co. Ltd.* [1978] F.S.R. 451 (at first instance). See also *Gramophone Co. Ltd.* v. *Music Machine (Pty.) Ltd.* [1973] 3 S.A.L.R. 188.
[55] See *R.C.A. Corporation* v. *Custom Cleared Sales Pty. Ltd., supra.*

is obvious cannot be heard to say that he lacks the requisite knowledge.[56] The provisions, however, contemplate specific knowledge about the circumstances in which a specific article was made and it may be that a defendant's general knowledge that an article may be an infringing copy will not be sufficient to fix him with knowledge.[57] The burden of proof is on the plaintiff and has been described as a heavy one.[58] Probably the knowledge of an agent would be imputed to his principal.[59]

It has been said, in a different context, that where a trader goes into the **9–20** market and finds what appears to be a novel product, it is not incumbent upon him, in the absence of some special circumstance, to enquire of the person offering the product whether there are any copyright complications involved in dealing with the product. He is entitled to assume that the vendor is in a position to sell what he offers to sell.[60]

If the defendant has knowledge of the relevant facts that is all that is **9–21** necessary.[61] Thus it is no defence for a defendant to say that although he knew the facts he nevertheless believed that as a matter of law no infringement would be committed, even if this was on the basis of legal advice.[62]

Where it is thought likely that a person may not be aware that he is **9–22** dealing in infringing goods, it is usually necessary to give him notice of the facts, commonly by letter, before it can safely be said that further dealings by him will amount to infringement.[63] Questions then arise as to the type of information which must be given and the period of notice allowed. On the above principles, sufficient information must be given to suggest to the recipient that an infringement will be committed if he continues to deal in the articles in question. The information must not be of such a general nature that the recipient can form no proper view as to what is being alleged.[64] Thus usually it will be necessary to identify the copyright work in question, and if a copy is not supplied then at least facilities should be offered for its inspection. As to the period of notice, a person is not fixed with knowledge at the instant he receives notice of a claim.[65] A period must be allowed sufficient to give him a reasonable opportunity to make

---

[56] *Columbia Picture Industries* v. *Robinson* [1987] Ch. 38.

[57] *Ibid.*

[58] *Infabrics Ltd.* v. *Jaytex Shirt Co. Ltd.* (at first instance), *supra*; *Sillitoe* v. *McGraw-Hill Book Co.* [1983] F.S.R. 545.

[59] *R.C.A. Corporation* v. *Custom Cleared Sales Pty. Ltd.*, *supra*.

[60] *Quaker Oats Co. Ltd.* v. *Alltrades Distributors Ltd.* [1981] F.S.R. 9. The context was a consideration of factors relevant to the grant of interlocutory relief. As to the effect of a copyright notice on imported goods, see *Clarke, Irwin & Co.* v. *C. Cole & Co.* (1960) 22 D.L.R. (2d) 183; and also *Godfrey, etc., Ltd.* v. *Coles Book Stores Ltd.* [1974] 40 D.L.R. (3d) 346 and *Simon & Schuster Inc.* v. *Coles Book Stores Ltd.* [1976] 61 D.L.R. (3d) 590.

[61] *Sillitoe* v. *McGraw-Hill Book Co.*, *supra*; *International Business Machines Corp.* v. *Computer Imports Ltd.* [1989] 2 N.Z.L.R. 395, at 418.

[62] *Ibid.*

[63] See, *e.g. Cooper* v. *Whittingham* (1880) 15 Ch.D. 501.

[64] *Hoover plc* v. *George Hulme Ltd.*, *supra*.

[65] *Van Dusen* v. *Kritz* [1936] 2 K.B. 176.

inquiries, obtain legal advice and make up his mind.[66] A period of 14 days is often taken as sufficient[67] but in each case it will be a question of fact.[68]

3. Providing the Means of Making Infringing Copies

9–23 The 1988 Act contains new provisions making persons liable who knowingly possess or provide the means for making infringing copies. Whether or not such acts may also amount to the separate tort of authorising an infringement is dealt with elsewhere.[69]

9–24 Thus the 1988 Act provides that the copyright in a work is infringed by a person who, without the licence of the copyright owner:

(a) makes,

(b) imports into the United Kingdom,

(c) possesses in the course of a business, or

(d) sells or lets for hire, or offers or exposes for sale or hire,

an article specifically designed or adapted for making copies of that work, knowing or having reason to believe that it is to be used to make infringing copies.[70]

Again, a "business" is defined as including a trade or profession.[71] The reference to an article "specifically designed or adapted for making copies of *that* work" seems to make it clear that dealing in an article which is generally designed for making copies, such as a photocopier or tape-recorder, will not fall within this provision. The provision appears to be directed to dealings in articles such as photographs, moulds, master recordings and the like which may be used to make copies of specific works. The article does not itself have to be an infringing copy.

9–25 The copyright in a work is also infringed by a person who, without the licence of the copyright owner, transmits the work by means of a telecommunications system (otherwise than by broadcasting or inclusion in a cable programme service), knowing or having reason to believe that infringing copies of the work will be made by means of the reception of the transmission in the United Kingdom or elsewhere.[72] "Telecommunications system" is defined as meaning a system for conveying visual images, sounds or other information by electronic means.[73] This provision is new and will make it an infringement, for example, to transmit a work down a

---

[66] *R.C.A. Corporation* v. *Custom Cleared Sales Pty. Ltd.* [1978] F.S.R. 576.
[67] See, *e.g. Infabrics Ltd.* v. *Jaytex Ltd.* (at first instance) [1978] F.S.R. 451.
[68] See, *e.g. Sillitoe* v. *McGraw-Hill Book Co.*, [1983] F.S.R. 545. In *Rexnold Inc.* v. *Ancon Ltd.* [1983] F.S.R. 662, nine days was held insufficient where the defendant had to make inquiries of manufacturers abroad.
[69] See § 8–140, *et seq.*, *ante.*
[70] C.D.P.A. 1988, s.24(1).
[71] *Ibid.* s.178.
[72] *Ibid.* s.24(2).
[73] *Ibid.* s.178, where "electronic" is also defined.

telephone line knowing that infringing copies will then be made. In such a case the person transmitting the work will often also have infringed by copying the work before, or in the course of, transmission. Where the transmission is by way of a broadcast or inclusion in a cable programme service an act of primary infringement will of course occur.[74] The provision that an infringement will occur under the present section if the sender knows or has reason to believe that infringing copies will then be made in the United Kingdom "or elsewhere" appears to be designed to prevent works being "exported" for copying overseas. The provision appears to be of limited application, however, since the definition of "infringing copy" is generally limited to copies either made in the United Kingdom or which have been or are intended to be imported into the United Kingdom.[75]

4. Permitting or Enabling Public Performance

A. Introduction

As has been seen,[76] the performance, playing and showing of various works in public are acts restricted by the copyright in such works. In addition to the general liability of persons who authorise such infringements, the 1988 Act also makes provision for secondary acts of infringement in cases where the defendant gave permission for premises to be used for performances or supplied the means by which such works were seen or heard in public. The wording of the 1988 Act, however, makes it clear that a person can only be liable under these provisions where there is already some other person liable for the primary infringement. The 1956 Act, which applies to acts done before August 1, 1989,[77] contained substantially more limited provisions.   **9–26**

B. Permitting use of premises

The 1988 Act provides that where the copyright in a literary, dramatic or musical work is infringed by a performance at a place of public entertainment, any person who gave permission for that place to be used for the performance is also liable for the infringement, unless when he gave permission he believed on reasonable grounds that the performance would not infringe copyright.[78] For this purpose, "place of public entertainment" includes premises which are occupied mainly for other purposes but are from time to time made available for hire for the purposes of public entertainment.[79]   **9–27**

---

[74] See § 8–118 *et seq., ante.*
[75] § 9–4, *ante.*
[76] See § 8–99 *et seq., ante.*
[77] C.D.P.A. 1988, Sched. 1, § 14(1).
[78] *Ibid.* s.25(1).
[79] *Ibid.* s.25(2).

9–28 **The 1956 Act.** The 1956 Act provided that the copyright in a literary, dramatic, or musical work was infringed by any person who permitted a place of public entertainment to be used for a performance in public of the work, where the performance constituted an infringement of the copyright in the work.[80] However, this provision did not apply in a case where the person permitting the place to be so used:

> (a) was not aware, and had no reasonable grounds for suspecting, that the performance would be an infringement of the copyright, or
>
> (b) gave the permission gratuitously, or for a consideration which was only nominal or (if more than nominal) did not exceed a reasonable estimate of the expenses to be incurred by him in consequence of the use of the place for the performance.[81]

"Place of public entertainment" was defined to include any premises which were occupied mainly for other purposes, but were from time to time made available for hire to such persons as might desire to hire them for purposes of public entertainment.[82]

9–29 **The Acts compared.** Whereas the 1956 Act created a separate tort of permitting a place to be used for a performance, the effect of the 1988 Act appears to be to make the defendant liable for the actual act of infringement by performance, presumably jointly with whoever is liable for that infringement.[83] On the other hand, no change in substance appears to have been effected by the alteration of the expression "any person who permits a place . . . to be used" to "any person who gave permission for [a] place to be used." The effect of the change in wording relating to the question of knowledge appears to be to increase the burden of proof on the defendant, in that under the 1988 Act he will have to show that he had reasonable grounds for his belief, whereas, under the 1956 Act, he merely had to show that he had no reasonable grounds for suspicion. The slight change in the definition of "place of public entertainment" does not appear to be of any significance. Finally, the 1988 Act has, of course, removed altogether the defence relating to the consideration given for the use of the premises.

9–30 **Permission.** Under both Acts, therefore, one of the crucial questions is whether permission was given for the use of the premises for the performance. The question whether the defendant committed the separate tort of authorising the performance will often arise at the same time.[84] As to permission, the giving of permission for use of the premises generally is not sufficient since the permission must be for the premises to be used for the performance complained of. Under the equivalent provisions of the 1911 Act it was said that a person does not permit what he cannot control, and does not permit the use of a place for the performance of a work if he

---

[80] Copyright Act 1956, s.5(5).

[81] *Ibid.* s.5(5), proviso.

[82] *Ibid.* s.5(6).

[83] As to which, see § 8–103 *ante.*

[84] As to authorisation, see § 8–134 *et seq., ante.*

does not know that the work is going to be performed.[85] Thus where a person permits premises to be used knowing which works will be performed, this will be sufficient to establish "permission," but not if the music to be performed is left to the performers and the defendant has no knowledge of what in fact will be performed.[86] Permission may be inferred from acts which fall short of being direct and positive, and may be inferred from indifference, but permission will not be inferred from a mere general authority to use a theatre for the performance of musical or dramatic works.[87] In an Australian case, it has been held that the owners of a hall who, under the terms of their contract of letting, cannot prevent the performance of which complaint is made, do not "permit" the performance.[88]

C. Provision of apparatus, etc

9–31

The 1988 Act makes further provision for secondary infringement where the copyright in a work is infringed by the public performance of a work or by the playing or showing of it in public. Thus various categories of person may also be liable where such infringement has occurred by means of apparatus for playing sound recordings, showing films or receiving visual images or sounds conveyed by electronic means.[89] Again, the wording of the 1988 Act makes it clear that a person can only be liable under these provisions where there is already some other person liable for the primary infringement.

9–32

First, a person who supplied the apparatus, or any substantial part of it, is liable for the infringement if, when he supplied the apparatus or part:

(a) he knew or had reason to believe that the apparatus was likely to be so used as to infringe copyright, or

(b) in the case of apparatus whose normal use involves a public performance, playing or showing, he did not believe on reasonable grounds that it would not be so used as to infringe copyright.[90]

Presumably, an infringement in the first case would occur where, for example, a person supplied a television for use in public, such as in a public house, knowing that no sufficient licence had been obtained. The second kind of case might arise where, for example, a juke box was supplied for use in public, or specialised equipment for use in a discotheque. Although the burden of proof as to the requisite degree of knowledge appears still to rest with the plaintiff, the intention in this latter kind of case appears to make that burden easier to discharge. In the ordinary type

---

[85] *Performing Right Society Ltd.* v. *Ciryl Theatrical Syndicate Ltd.* [1924] 1 K.B. 1.
[86] *Monaghan* v. *Taylor* 2 T.L.R. 685, cited in *Performing Right Society* v. *Ciryl Theatrical Syndicate Ltd., supra.*
[87] *Performing Right Society Ltd.* v. *Ciryl Theatrical Syndicate Ltd., supra.*
[88] *Australian Performing Right Association Ltd.* v. *Adelaide Corporation* (1928) 40 C.L.R. 481; see also *Canadian Performing Right Society* v. *Canadian National Exhibition Association* (1934) 4 D.L.R. 154; but *cf. Australian Performing Right Association* v. *Turner (J.) & Son* (1927) 27 S.R.(N.S.W.) 344.
[89] C.D.P.A. 1988, s.26(1).
[90] *Ibid.* s.26(2).

of case it will no doubt be sufficient to prove that the supply of apparatus has continued after a warning letter has been received.

9–33   Second, an occupier of premises who gave permission for the apparatus to be brought onto the premises is also liable for the infringement if, when he gave permission, he knew or had reason to believe that the apparatus was likely to be so used as to infringe copyright.[91] Again, this kind of case might arise where the occupier of a public house or discotheque allows equipment to be brought onto the premises knowing that no sufficient licence had been obtained.

9–34   Third, a person who supplied a copy of the sound recording or film used to infringe copyright is also liable for the infringement if when, he supplied it, he knew or had reason to believe that what he supplied, or a copy made directly or indirectly from it, was likely to be so used as to infringe copyright.[92] Persons who knowingly supply records for use in juke boxes are therefore likely to be caught by this provision.

9–35   **The 1956 Act.** The 1956 Act contained no equivalent categories of secondary infringement, although there were provisions which applied where apparatus was supplied by or with the consent of the occupier of premises, such that the occupier was to be taken to be the person liable for the infringement.[93] These have already been considered.[94]

---

[91] *Ibid.* s.26(3).
[92] *Ibid.* s.26(4).
[93] Copyright Act 1956, s.48(6).
[94] § 8–108, *ante.*

CHAPTER 10

PERMITTED ACTS

Contents   *Para.*

1. Introduction

10–1 Forty-nine sections[1] of the 1988 Act are devoted to the permitting of various acts which would otherwise amount to infringements of copyright. The 1956 Act also contained provisions of this kind but the 1988 Act has

---

[1] C.D.P.A. 1988, ss.28–76. Also considered in this chapter are the compulsory licences introduced by the Broadcasting Act 1990.

considerably altered their extent. The provisions of the 1956 Act still apply in relation to acts done before August 1, 1989.[2]

The permitted acts under the 1988 Act are grouped together into vari- **10–2** ous categories, namely, general,[3] education,[4] libraries and archives,[5] public administration,[6] designs,[7] typefaces,[8] works in electronic form,[9] miscellaneous provisions relating to literary, dramatic, musical and artistic works,[10] miscellaneous provisions relating to sound recordings, films and computer programs,[11] and miscellaneous provisions relating to broadcasts and cable programmes.[12] Except for the provisions for designs, which are considered elsewhere,[13] these are considered in turn in this chapter, together with the equivalent and other provisions of the 1956 Act, where appropriate. The 1988 Act expressly provides that each such provision is to be construed independently of each other, so that the fact that an act does not fall within one provision does not mean that it is not covered by another provision.[14] Again, the fact that an act may be done without infringing copyright by virtue of these provisions is not to mean that such an act may not be a breach of some other right or obligation,[15] for example, an express contractual term. Finally the Act provides that any act which may be done without infringing copyright in a literary, dramatic or musical work does not, where that work is an adaptation, infringe any copyright in the work from which the adaptation was made.[16] Since the provisions only apply once infringement is established, the onus will be on the defendant to establish that one of the defences applies,[17] and no doubt the provisions will be applied strictly against the defendant.[18] For convenience, there are also considered in this chapter other provisions of the Copyright Acts whereby statutory licences are conferred.

Non-statutory defences; public interest. Whether and to what extent **10–3** the defence of public interest may be established in an action for infringement of copyright is considered elsewhere.[19]

---

[2] *Ibid.* Sched. 1, para. 14(1).
[3] *Ibid.* ss.29–31, § 10–4 *et seq., post.*
[4] *Ibid.* ss.32–36, § 10–19 *et seq., post.*
[5] *Ibid.* ss.37–44, § 10–31 *et seq., post.*
[6] *Ibid.* ss.45–50, § 10–48 *et seq., post.*
[7] *Ibid.* ss.51–53, Chap. 20, *post.*
[8] *Ibid.* ss.54, 55, § 10–60 *et seq., post.*
[9] *Ibid.* s.56, § 10–65 *et seq., post.*
[10] *Ibid.* ss.57–65, § 10–69 *et seq., post.*
[11] *Ibid.* ss.66, 67, § 10–100 *et seq., post.*
[12] *Ibid.* ss.68–75, § 10–112 *et seq., post.*
[13] Chap. 20, *post.* See also, as to the defence provided by s.9(8) of the 1956 Act, § 8–70 *et seq., post.*
[14] C.D.P.A. 1988, s.28(4).
[15] *Ibid.* s.28(1).
[16] *Ibid.* s.76.
[17] *Sillitoe* v. *McGraw Hill Book Co.* [1983] F.S.R. 545 at 558.
[18] See *Beloff* v. *Presdram Ltd.* [1973] R.P.C. 765 and *Distillers Co. (Biochemicals) Ltd.* v. *Times Newspapers Ltd.* [1975] Q.B. 613.
[19] See § 11–30 *post.*

2. General Provisions

A. *Research and private study*

10–4 **The 1988 Act.** The 1988 Act provides that fair dealing with a literary, dramatic, musical or artistic work for the purposes of research or private study does not infringe any copyright in the work, or in the case of a published edition, in the typographical arrangement.[20] In addition, fair dealing with the typographical arrangement of a published edition for any of these purposes does not infringe any copyright in the arrangement.[21]

10–5 **The 1956 Act.** The 1956 Act also provided that no fair dealing with a literary, dramatic, musical or artistic work for the purposes of research or private study should constitute an infringement of the copyright in the work.[22] No equivalent provisions were made for published editions.[23]

10–6 **"Fair Dealing."** No doubt the expression "fair dealing" in the 1988 Act will be construed in the same way as it was under the 1956 Act and under the equivalent provisions of the 1911 Act.[24] The question of what amounted to "fair dealing" frequently arose under the law prior to 1911 in determining whether the use which had been made of the plaintiff's work was sufficient to constitute infringement.[25] Since the 1911 Act, however, the question of whether a substantial part has been taken is quite distinct from whether there has been a fair dealing. It is only when the court has determined that a substantial part has been taken that any question of fair dealing arises.[26] It has been said that once it is established that a substantial part has been taken no defence of fair dealing will be likely to succeed,[27] but it is doubted whether this can be correct as a matter of principle.[28]

10–7   What amounts to "fair dealing" most frequently arises in the context of what constitutes fair dealing for the purpose of criticism or review, a subject which is dealt with below.[29] In the present context, however, the mere fact that a work is reproduced for the purposes of private study will not, by itself, mean that such use amounts to a fair dealing.[30] Under the 1956 Act,

---

[20] C.D.P.A. 1988, s.29(1).

[21] *Ibid.* s.29(2).

[22] Copyright Act 1956, ss.6(1), 9(1).

[23] Indeed the 1956 Act contained no defences applicable to published editions, except in the case of libraries. This was often a trap.

[24] Copyright Act 1911, s.2(1)(i).

[25] *Bradbury v. Hotten* (1872) L.R. 8 Ex. 1; *cf. Leslie v. Young (J.) & Sons* [1894] A.C. 335; *Smith v. Chatto* (1874) 31 L.T. 775; *Cambridge University Press v. University Tutorial Press Ltd.* [1923–28] Mac.C.C. 349.

[26] *Johnstone v. Bernard Jones Publications Ltd.* [1938] Ch. 599; and see *Hawkes & Son (London) Ltd. v. Paramount Film Services Ltd.* [1934] Ch. 593; *Hubbard v. Vosper* [1972] 2 Q.B. 84; *Beloff v. Pressdram Ltd.*, *ante*; *Distillers Co. (Biochemicals) Ltd. v. Times Newspapers Ltd.*, *ante* and *L.B. (Plastics) Ltd. v. Swish Products Ltd.* [1979] F.S.R. 145; compare *Fraser v. Evans* [1969] 1 Q.B. 349.

[27] *Independent Television Publications Ltd. v. Time Out Ltd.* [1984] F.S.R. 64, at 75.

[28] See, for example, *Jonhstone v. Bernard Jones Publications Ltd.* [1938] Ch. 599, at 603.

[29] See § 10–10, *post.*

[30] *University of London Press Ltd. v. University Tutorial Press Ltd.* [1916] 2 Ch. 601.

it was held that to take advantage of this defence, the defendant himself must be engaged in the private study or research, so that it was no defence to reproduce a work in the form of study notes to be used by examination students.[31] The 1988 Act, as did the 1956 Act, makes further extensive provision as to the circumstances in which copies may be made by libraries for the purposes of research or private study by others[32] and the 1988 Act expressly provides that copying by a person other than the researcher or student himself is not fair dealing if the librarian or his agent goes beyond what is permissible under those provisions.[33] In addition, however, the 1988 Act expressly provides that copying by a person other than the researcher or student himself is also not fair dealing if, in any other case, the person doing the copying knows or has reason to believe that it will result in copies of substantially the same material being provided to more than one person at substantially the same time and for substantially the same purpose.[34] The 1988 Act therefore provides only a limited defence in the case of any copying being done by a person other than the person actually engaged in the research or private study. Thus it appears clear that there is no defence under this section if a teacher makes multiple copies of a work for use by a class of students.[35] On the other hand it seems that a student or researcher may ask another to make a copy of a work provided that the section is otherwise satisfied.

B. *Criticism, review and news reporting*

The 1988 Act. The 1988 Act provides that fair dealing with a work for the purpose of criticism or review, of that or another work or of a performance of a work, does not infringe any copyright in the work provided that it is accompanied by a sufficient acknowledgment.[36] In addition the 1988 Act provides that fair dealing with a work (other than a photograph) for the purpose of reporting current events does not infringe any copyright in the work provided that it is accompanied by a sufficient acknowledgment,[37] except that in connection with the reporting of current events by means of a sound recording, film, broadcast, or cable programme no such acknowledgment is required.[38] **10–8**

The 1956 Act. The 1956 Act provided that no fair dealing with a literary, dramatic, musical or artistic work should constitute an infringement of the copyright in that work if it was for the purposes of criticism or review, whether of that work or of another work, and was accompanied by a sufficient acknowledgment.[39] In addition, no fair dealing with a literary, dramatic or musical work (but not, surprisingly, an artistic work) constituted an infringement of copyright in that work if it was for the purposes of **10–9**

---

[31] *Sillitoe* v. *McGraw-Hill Book Co., ante.*
[32] C.D.P.A. 1988, ss.38–40; Copyright Act 1956, s.7. See § 10–34 *et seq., post.*
[33] C.D.P.A. 1988, s.29(3)(*a*).
[34] *Ibid.* s.29(3)(*b*).
[35] No doubt the position under the 1956 Act was the same. But see § 10–19 *et seq., post.*
[36] C.D.P.A. 1988, s.30(1). This provision applies to all categories of work. See s.28(2).
[37] *Ibid.* s.30(2).
[38] *Ibid.* s.30(3).
[39] Copyright Act 1956, ss.6(2), 9(2).

reporting current events (a) in a newspaper, magazine or similar periodical, or (b) by means of broadcasting, inclusion in a cable programme service, or in a cinematograph film, and, in the former category of cases, if it was accompanied by a sufficient acknowledgment.[40]

10–10   **"Fair dealing."** The meaning of this expression has already been considered in the context of research and private study.[41] What amounts to fair dealing will depend in each case upon its own facts, and what may be fair in one case will not necessarily be fair in another. In every case it will be a question of fact and impression.[42] The real objective of these provisions is to protect a reviewer or commentator who may want to use extracts from a work to illustrate his review, criticism or comment, and it is therefore important to look at the defendant's real objective in using the plaintiff's work.[43] Thus, as between trade rivals, it will not be fair for one to take the other's material and use it for his own benefit[44] so as to attract customers.[45] Factors which the courts may take into consideration include the number and extent of extracts taken and their proportion to any comments.[46] In the case of a very short work, however, it may, in the circumstances, be fair to quote every word of it.[47] Again, it may be relevant to consider whether the use which has been made of the extracts is directed solely to criticism or review, or whether there are other purposes,[48] for example, education.[49] It may also be material that the number of extracts taken would enable someone to do without the plaintiff's work altogether.[50] The fact that the work is unpublished will not by itself mean that the defence cannot apply[51] but it will be highly relevant that the work was in fact unpublished and never intended to be published, particularly where the document has been "leaked."[52] It may be relevant to consider the trade practice, in the sense of what publishers generally consider to be an acceptable amount to borrow from a work.[53] Finally it may be material that the defendant stands to enrich himself substantially by such use.[54]

---

[40] *Ibid.* s.6(3); although the giving of an acknowledgment in the latter category of cases may be relevant to the consideration of whether the dealing is fair.

[41] See § 10–7, *ante.*

[42] *Beloff* v. *Pressdram Ltd., ante; Hubbard* v. *Vosper, ante; Distillers Co. (Biochemicals) Ltd.* v. *Times Newspapers Ltd., ante; Sillitoe* v. *McGraw-Hill Book Co., ante; B.B.C.* v. *British Sky Broadcasting Ltd., The Times,* January 22, 1991.

[43] *Independent Television Publications Ltd.* v. *Time Out Ltd.* [1984] F.S.R. 64.

[44] *Hubbard* v. *Vosper* [1972] 2 Q.B. 84, 93; *Walter* v. *Steinkopff* [1892] 3 Ch. 489.

[45] *Associated Newspapers Group plc.* v. *News Group Newspapers Ltd.* [1986] R.P.C. 515; but see *B.B.C.* v. *British Sky Broadcasting Ltd., ante,* where trade rivalry did not prevent the use being held fair.

[46] *Hubbard* v. *Vosper, ante.*

[47] *Ibid. per* Megaw L.J. at p. 98, citing the example of an epitaph on a tombstone consisting of a dozen or 20 words.

[48] See n. 61, *ante.*

[49] *Sillitoe* v. *McGraw-Hill Book Co., ante.*

[50] *Ibid.*

[51] *Hubbard* v. *Vosper, ante; Beloff* v. *Pressdram, ante,* not following *British Oxygen Co. Ltd.* v. *Liquid Air Ltd.* [1925] Ch. 383. Note that the definition of "sufficient acknowledgement" in the 1988 Act specifically contemplates that the work may be unpublished. See § 10–14, *post.*

[52] *Beloff* v. *Pressdram Ltd., ante.*

[53] *See* n. 49, *ante.*

[54] *See* n. 49, *ante.*

"Criticism or review." The criticism or review need not be confined to the literary style of the plaintiff's work but may extend to the thoughts underlying it, for example the doctrine or philosophy[55] or ideas and events[56] expounded in the work. The copying of reported cases by the writers of legal textbooks has to be considered in the light of this provision. The matter was left in some doubt under the law prior to 1911,[57] but it is thought that the proper approach is to consider whether the matter is one of bona fide criticism of cases, or whether, under the guise of criticism, the textbook is really a collection of reports intended to be used as such. Similar considerations are no doubt involved in the case of reviews[58] and newspaper summaries.[59] In the case of examination papers it was held that their publication with a few lines of criticism for the use of students could not be justified under the equivalent provision of the 1911 Act.[60] The fact that there is another purpose, such as education, as well as the purpose of criticism or review, will not prevent the defence applying[61] although, as has been seen,[62] this may affect the question of "fair dealing."

10–11

Work reproduced need not be work criticised. Under both the 1956 and 1988 Acts the defence is available whether the work reproduced is that criticised or not.[63] Thus in criticising one work, it is permissible to quote from other comparable works for the purpose of exemplifying the criticism. Again, in criticising a work in a foreign language, it is permissible to quote from an English translation, although there is no criticism of the translation as such. Nevertheless, under the 1956 Act the criticism or review had to be of a "work," and since a performance was itself probably not a "work" within the meaning of that Act, it followed that the defence probably could not have been relied upon when, for example, quoting passages from a play in reviewing a performance of it. Under the 1988 Act the defence will now be available in such circumstances.[64]

10–12

Reporting current events. The events reported must obviously be current and not matters of history, but the work reproduced need not itself be "current" provided that it is used to report properly current events.[65] In deciding whether the work is being used for this purpose, a useful test may be whether it is reasonably necessary to refer to the work in order to deal

10–13

---

[55] *See* n. 46, *ante*.
[56] *Distillers Co. (Biochemicals) Ltd.* v. *Times Newspapers Ltd.*, *ante*.
[57] *Saunders* v. *Smith* (1838) 3 My. & Cr. 711; *Butterworth* v. *Kelly* (1888) 4 T.L.R. 430; *Hodges (J.)* v. *Welsh (T.)* (1840) 2 Ir.Eq.R. 266.
[58] *Harper & Bros.* v. *Biggs & Sons* [1905–10] Mac.C.C. 89.
[59] *Whittingham (C.)* v. *Wooler (T.J.)* (1818) 2 Swan. 428; *Bell* v. *Whitehead* (1839) 8 L.J.Ch. 141; *Maxwell* v. *Somerton* (1874) 30 L.T. 11; *Weatherby & Sons* v. *International Horse Agency and Exchange Ltd.* [1910] 2 Ch. 297.
[60] *University of London Press Ltd.* v. *University Tutorial Press Ltd.* [1916] 2 Ch. 601.
[61] *See* n. 49, *ante*.
[62] See § 10–10, *ante*.
[63] C.D.P.A. 1988, s.30(1); Copyright Act 1956, s.6(2).
[64] C.D.P.A. 1988, s.30(1).
[65] *Associated Newspapers Group plc* v. *News Group Newspapers Ltd.* [1986] R.P.C. 515. See, as to a case involving the use of excerpts of copyright broadcasts for the purposes of reporting current events (the 1990 World Cup), *B.B.C.* v. *British Sky Broadcasting Ltd.*, *ante*.

with the current events in question.[66] The work must be used for "reporting" current events and not for editorial or other purposes. The fact that a work has recently been published will not of itself mean that it is fair to reproduce it for the purpose of commenting on or reporting that fact.[67] The exclusion of photographs from this provision means that it is clear that a newspaper would not be able to make use of another's photograph without consent when reporting current events. It is thought that in any event such use is unlikely to be "fair."

10–14 **Sufficient acknowledgment.** The 1988 Act defines "sufficient acknowledgement" to mean an acknowledgment identifying the work in question by its title or other description, and identifying the author unless (a) in the case of a published work, it is published anonymously or (b) in the case of an unpublished work, it is not possible for a person to ascertain the identity of the author by reasonable inquiry.[68] The definition of this expression in the 1956 Act was broadly similar, namely an acknowledgement identifying the work in question by its title or other description and, unless the work was anonymous or the author had previously agreed or required that no acknowledgment of his name should be made, also identifying the author.[69] Thus under both Acts the acknowledgment must identify the work itself, although the circumstances in which it is not necessary to identify the author have been altered under the 1988 Act. For these purposes the "acknowledgement" must in some sense recognise the position or claims of the author. It is not sufficient that it is in fact apparent what the title of the work reproduced is, and who is its author, if it is treated as a non-copyright work.[70] Again, the acknowledgment must identify the author, not the copyright owner, of the other work.[71] It seems that if the part of the work which is used itself reproduces an underlying work, the underlying work should also be acknowledged. This may be a trap.

10–15 **The Acts compared.** These defences in the 1988 Act apply to works of all descriptions,[72] except that no fair dealing with a photograph for the purpose of reporting current events is permissible. The exemptions in the 1956 Act applied to a more limited range of works. Thus under the 1988 Act, for example, fair dealing with a film for the purposes of criticism, review or reporting current events is now permissible. As has been seen,[73] criticism or review of a performance, as well as a "work," is now expressly permitted under the 1988 Act. Under the 1956 Act the range of media used when relying on this defence was limited, but the 1988 Act is unlimited in this respect.

---

[66] *Ibid.*
[67] *Ibid.*
[68] C.D.P.A. 1988, s.178.
[69] Copyright Act 1956, s.6(10).
[70] *See* n. 49, *ante.*
[71] *Express Newspapers plc.* v. *News (U.K.) Ltd.* [1990] F.S.R. 359.
[72] C.D.P.A. 1988, s.28(2).
[73] § 10–12, *ante.*

C. *Incidental Inclusion of Copyright Material*

The 1988 Act. The 1988 Act provides that copyright in a work is not **10–16** infringed by its incidental inclusion in an artistic work, sound recording, film, broadcast or cable programme.[74] However, a musical work, words spoken or sung with music, or so much of a sound recording, broadcast or cable programme as includes a musical work or such words, is not to be regarded as incidentally included in another work if it is deliberately included.[75] This provision appears to prevent a defendant from arguing that, for example, the inclusion of the usual kind of background music in a film or television programme is not an infringement. Further, where by virtue of this provision the making of anything was not an infringement of copyright in a work, then the issue to the public of copies, or the playing, showing, broadcasting or inclusion in a cable programme service of that thing will not infringe the copyright in such a work either.[76] As to this, in relation to anything made before August 1, 1989, it is to be assumed that these provisions were in force at all material times.[77]

The 1956 Act. The 1956 Act provided that the copyright in an artistic **10–17** work was not infringed by its inclusion in a cinematograph film or a television broadcast, if its inclusion was only by way of background or was otherwise only incidental to the principal matters represented in the film or broadcast.[78] Further, where, by virtue of this provision, the making of a painting, drawing, engraving, photograph or film did not constitute an infringement of the copyright in an artistic work, then that copyright was not infringed by the publication of that painting, drawing, engraving, photograph or cinematograph film either.[79]

The Acts compared. The 1988 Act applies to all classes of works,[80] **10–18** whereas the 1956 Act was restricted in this respect to artistic works. Further, the categories of media in which such works may be included have also been widened. The limitation of the defence under the 1988 Act in cases of certain works deliberately included in other works,[81] even though this may have only been by way of background, appears to have made the defence under the 1988 Act more restrictive.

3. Education

A. *Education: things done for the purposes of instruction or examination*

The 1988 Act. The 1988 Act provides that the copyright in a literary, **10–19** dramatic, musical or artistic work is not infringed by its being copied in the course of instruction or of preparation for instruction, provided the

---

[74] C.D.P.A. 1988, s.31(1).
[75] *Ibid.* s.31(3).
[76] *Ibid.* s.31(2).
[77] *Ibid.* Sched. 1, para. 14(4).
[78] Copyright Act 1956, s.9(5).
[79] *Ibid.* s.9(6).
[80] C.D.P.A. 1988, s.28(2).
[81] *Ibid.*, s.31(3); §10–16 *ante.*

copying (a) is done by a person giving or receiving instruction, and (b) is not by means of a reprographic process.[82] "Reprographic process" is defined by the Act as meaning a process (a) for making facsimile copies, or (b) involving the use of an appliance for making multiple copies, and includes, in relation to a work held in electronic form, any copying by electronic means, but does not include the making of a film or sound recording.[83] Thus, for example, it seems that a teacher may copy on to a blackboard a substantial part of a literary work, and his pupils may copy it down. A teacher may also perform and make his own recording of a musical work, and use this for purpose of instruction. He may not, however, photocopy sheet music for use by the school choir.

In relation to a sound recording, film, broadcast or cable programme, copyright is not infringed by its being copied by making a film or film sound-track[84] in the course of instruction, or of preparation for instruction, in the making of films or film sound-tracks, provided the copying is done by a person giving or receiving instruction.[85]

10–20   The 1988 Act also provides that copyright is not infringed by anything done for the purposes of an examination by way of setting the questions, communicating the questions to the candidates or answering the questions.[86] However, this provision does not extend to the making of a reprographic copy of a musical work for use by an examination candidate in performing the work.[87] "Reprographic copy" refers to copying by a reprographic process.[88] Thus it will not be permissible to make a copy of sheet music for examination candidates instead of buying or hiring the sheet music itself.

10–21   If by virtue of these provisions the making of a copy of a work is not an infringement of copyright, but such copy is subsequently sold, let for hire, offered or exposed for sale or hire, then it is to be treated as an infringing copy for the purpose of that dealing.[89] Thus, if the person so dealing with that copy knows or has reason to believe it is an infringing copy, that dealing will amount to a secondary infringement under section 23 of the Act.[90] Once such an infringement has occurred, the copy will be treated as an infringing copy for all subsequent purposes, and not just for the purpose of that dealing or other dealings of that description.[91] Thus, for example, possession in the course of a business, with the requisite degree of knowledge, subsequent to such a dealing, will also amount to an infringement.[92] The purpose of these particular provisions appears to be to

---

[82] *Ibid.*, s.32(1). As to the limited exceptions provided for reprographic copying, see C.D.P.A. 1988, s.36, §10–29, *post.*
[83] *Ibid.* s.178, where "facsimile copy" and "electronic" are also defined.
[84] Film sound-tracks are now to be regarded as sound recordings and not part of the film. See § 2–30, *ante.*
[85] C.D.P.A. 1988 s.32(2).
[86] *Ibid.* s.32(3).
[87] *Ibid.* s.32(4).
[88] *Ibid.* s.178.
[89] *Ibid.* ss.32(5), 27(6).
[90] See Chap. 9, *ante.*
[91] C.D.P.A. 1988, s.32(5).
[92] *Ibid.* s.23(*a*).

prevent the commercial exploitation of copies made for educational purposes. As to the knowledge required to make such a dealing an infringement, in accordance with the usual principles, it will apparently be sufficient if the defendant has knowledge of the relevant facts, and his ignorance of these particular provisions, being matters of law, will be irrelevant.[93]

The 1956 Act. The 1956 Act made more limited provision in that it provided that the copyright in a literary, dramatic, musical or artistic work was not to be taken to be infringed by reason only that the work was reproduced, or an adaptation of the work was made or reproduced, (a) in the course of instruction, whether at a school or elsewhere, where the reproduction or adaptation was made by a teacher or pupil otherwise than by the use of a duplicating process, or (b) as part of the questions to be answered in an examination, or in an answer to such a question.[94] "School" and "duplicating process" were further defined.[95] This provision did not, however, apply to the publication of such a work or of an adaptation of it.[96] The 1956 Act also provided that dealings in such copies, in the knowledge that the making of them would have constituted an infringement but for these provisions, amounted to an infringement.[97] **10–22**

B. *Anthologies for educational use*

The 1988 Act. The 1988 Act provides that the inclusion of a short passage from a published literary or dramatic work in a collection which (a) is intended for use in educational establishments and is so described in its title, and in any advertisements issued by or on behalf of the publisher, and (b) consists mainly of material in which no copyright subsists, does not infringe the copyright in the work if the work itself is not intended for use in such establishments and the inclusion is accompanied by a sufficient acknowledgment.[98] This provision does not, however, authorise the inclusion of more than two excerpts from copyright works by the same author in collections published by the same publisher over any period of five years.[99] Further, in relation to any given passage, this reference to excerpts from works by the same author (a) is to be taken to include excepts from works by him in collaboration with another, and (b) if the passage in question is from such a work, is to be taken to include excerpts from works by any of the authors, whether alone or in collaboration with another.[1] The definition of "sufficient acknowledgement" has already been referred to.[2] "Educational establishment" is given an extended defi- **10–23**

---

[93] See § 9–18 *et seq., ante.*
[94] Copyright Act 1956, s.41(1).
[95] *Ibid.* s.41(7).
[96] *Ibid.* s.41(2).
[97] *Ibid.*
[98] C.D.P.A. 1988, s.33(1).
[99] *Ibid.* s.33(2).
[1] *Ibid.* s.33(3).
[2] See § 10–14, *ante.*

nition by the Act, and includes any school, which is itself defined.[3] References in these provisions to the use in an educational establishment are to any use for the educational purposes of such an establishment.[4]

10–24 **The 1956 Act.** The 1956 Act contained a very similar provision.[5]

C. Performing, etc., a work in course of activities of educational establishments

10–25 **The 1988 Act.** The 1988 Act provides that the performance of a literary, dramatic or musical work before an audience consisting of teachers and pupils at an educational establishment and other persons directly connected with the activities of the establishment (a) by a teacher or pupil in the course of the activities of the establishment, or (b) at the establishment by any person for the purposes of instruction, is not a public performance for the purposes of infringement of copyright.[6] In addition, the playing or showing of a sound recording, film, broadcast or cable programme before such an audience at an educational establishment for the purposes of instruction is not a playing or showing of the work in public for the purposes of infringement of copyright.[7] Reference has already been made to the definition of an "educational establishment."[8] "Teacher" and "pupil" are defined to mean any person who gives and any person who receives instruction, respectively.[9] As to the persons who may be "directly connected with the activities" of such an establishment, the Act provides that a person is not for this purpose directly connected with the activities of the educational establishment simply because he is the parent of a pupil at the establishment.[10] Thus a performance at which parents are present may, notwithstanding this provision, constitute a public performance for this purpose.[11] The matter would presumably depend upon whether parents were present merely as an audience, or because of some special relationship to the particular performance.

10–26 **The 1956 Act.** The 1956 Act contained broadly similar provisions. Thus it was provided that, for the avoidance of doubt, a performance of a literary, dramatic or musical work in the course of the activities of a school, by a person who was a teacher in or a pupil in attendance at the school, was not to be a performance in public, if the audience was limited to persons who were teachers in or pupils in attendance at the school, or were otherwise directly connected with the activities of the school, whether the performance was in class or otherwise in the presence of an audience.[12] A

---

[3] C.D.P.A. 1988, s.174. "Educational establishment," apart from any school, means any other educational establishment specified by the Secretary of State under his powers under s.174(1)(*b*) of the 1988 Act, as to which, see The Copyright (Educational Establishments) (No.2) Order 1989 (S.I. 1989 No.1068), §B–32, *post.*

[4] *Ibid.* s.33(4).

[5] Copyright Act 1956, s.6(6).

[6] C.D.P.A. 1988, s.34(1).

[7] *Ibid.* s.34(2).

[8] See §10–23 *ante.*

[9] C.D.P.A. 1988, s.174(5).

[10] *Ibid.* s.34(3).

[11] But see *Duck* v. *Bates* (1884) 13 Q.B.D. 843.

[12] Copyright Act 1956, s.41(3).

person was not, however, to be taken to be directly connected with the activities of a school by reason only that he was a parent or guardian of a pupil in attendance at the school.[13] These provisions also applied to causing the sounds or visual images of sound recordings, cinematograph films, television broadcasts and cable programmes to be heard or seen.[14] It is unclear whether the change in wording, from "*limited* to persons who are teachers in, or pupils in attendance at, the school" in the 1956 Act, to "*consisting of* teachers and pupils at an educational establishment" in the 1988 Act, has effected any substantive change in the law.

D. *Education: recording of broadcasts and cable programmes*

The 1988 Act. The 1988 Act provides that a recording of a broadcast or cable programme, or a copy of such a recording, may be made by or on behalf of an educational establishment for the educational purposes of that establishment without thereby infringing the copyright in the broadcast or cable programme, or in any work included in it.[15] However this provision does not apply if or to the extent that there is a licensing scheme certified for the purposes of the section under section 143 of the Act providing for the grant of licences.[16] The definition of "educational establishment" has already been referred to.[17] The section contains provisions of the kind already discussed making it an infringement to deal in copies made with the protection of this section.[18]   **10–27**

The 1956 Act. The 1956 Act contained no equivalent provisions.   **10–28**

E. *Education: reprographic copying*

The 1988 Act. The 1988 Act provides that the making of reprographic copies of passages from published literary, dramatic or musical works by or on behalf of an educational establishment for the purposes of instruction will not, in defined circumstances, be an infringement of copyright in the work or in the typographical arrangement.[19] Reference has already been made to the definition of "educational establishment."[20] Copies will be made "on behalf of" such an establishment if they are made for the purposes of that establishment by any person.[21] The circumstances in   **10–29**

---

[13] *Ibid.* s.41(4).

[14] *Ibid.* s.41(5).

[15] C.D.P.A. 1988, s.35(1).

[16] *Ibid.* s.35(2), and see, as to licensing schemes, Chap. 15, *post* and in particular, as to certification, and the licensing schemes so far certified, §15–109 and n. 97.

[17] See §10–23, *ante.* This provision also applies in relation to teachers who are employed by a local authority to give instruction elsewhere to pupils who are unable to attend an educational establishment. See The Copyright (Application of Provisions relating to Educational Establishments to Teachers) (No.2) Order 1989 (S.I. 1989 No. 1067), §B–28 *post*, made under s.174(2) of the 1988 Act.

[18] s.35(3), and see § 10–21, *ante.*

[19] s.36(1).

[20] See §10–23 *ante.* Again, this provision is extended to local authority teachers giving instruction elsewhere. See n. 17, *ante.*

[21] C.D.P.A. 1988, s.174(6).

which such copying will not amount to an infringement are that not more than 1 per cent. of any work may be copied by or on behalf of an establishment in any quarter, that is, in any period January 1 to March 31, April 1 to June 30, July 1 to September 30 or October 1 to December 31.[22] However, copying is not authorised by this section if, or to the extent that, licences are available authorising the copying in question and the person making the copies knew or ought to have been aware of that fact.[23] But where the terms of such a licence purport to restrict the proportion of a work which may be copied to less than the above percentage, then such terms are to that extent of no effect.[24] This will be so whether or not the licence imposes terms for payment.[25] It seems that in such a case copying will only be authorised if the terms of the licence are otherwise observed. The section contains provisions of the kind already discussed making it an infringement to deal in copies made with the protection of this section.[26]

10–30 **The 1956 Act.** The 1956 Act contained no equivalent provisions.

4. Libraries and Archives

A. *Introduction*

10–31 Demands are frequently made upon public libraries for photocopies of articles or parts of periodicals and books in their possession by students and research workers. The fair dealing provisions for purposes of research or private study will often not sufficiently cover this type of situation and in particular may not protect the librarian. The 1956 Act introduced provisions dealing with this problem, which in general terms are reproduced in the 1988 Act. The 1988 Act also makes new provision dealing with other situations faced by librarians and archivists.

10–32 **The 1988 Act.** The 1988 Act makes a number of provisions dealing with circumstances in which copying by librarians and archivists is permitted.[27] These provisions of the 1988 Act apply to libraries and archives of descriptions and in conditions prescribed by regulations made by the Secretary of State.[28] A number of the provisions require the librarian or archi-

---

[22] *Ibid.* s.36(2).
[23] *Ibid.* s.36(3). See also, as to the control over such licensing, §15–107 *et seq., post.*
[24] *Ibid.* s.36(4).
[25] See n. 24.
[26] C.D.P.A. 1988, s.36(5); § 10–21, *ante.*
[27] *Ibid.* 1988, ss.37–44.
[28] The Copyright (Librarians and Archivists) (Copying of Copyright Material) Regulations 1989 (S.I. 1989 No.1212), §B–181, *post,* made under ss.37, and 38 to 43, of the 1988 Act, the enabling provisions of which were themselves brought into force on June 9, 1989 by The Copyright, Designs and Patents Act 1988 (Commencement No. 2) Order 1989 (S.I. 1989 No. 955), §B–8 *post,* as amended by The Copyright, Designs and Patents Act 1988 (Commencement No. 3) Order 1989 (S.I. 1989 No. 1032), See §B–8 *post.* In this section of the work these regulations will simply be referred to as "the Regulations." In relation to different provisions of the 1988 Act, different classes of library are prescribed by the Regulations. These are dealt with in turn, *post.*

vist to be "satisfied" of certain matters, and in such cases regulations provide for cases in which the librarian or archivist may rely on or must require a signed declaration as to those matters.[29] If a person makes such a declaration which is false in a material particular and is then supplied with what, but for the exempting provisions, would be an infringing copy if made by him, then that copy will be treated as an infringing copy and that person will be liable for infringement as if he had made it himself.[30] In such circumstances it seems clear that the librarian or archivist will not himself be liable for any infringement. In these provisions, references to a librarian or archivist include a person acting on his behalf.[31]

The 1956 Act. The 1956 Act, which continues to apply in relation to acts done before August 1, 1989,[32] made similar but more limited provisions in relation to librarians of prescribed classes.[33] Regulations also prescribed the conditions relating to such provisions.[34]   **10–33**

B. *Articles in periodicals*

The 1988 Act. Under the 1988 Act, provided certain prescribed conditions are complied with, a librarian of a prescribed library may make and supply a copy of an article in a periodical without infringing any copyright in the text, in any illustrations accompanying the text or in the typographical arrangement.[35] For this purpose "article" includes an item of any description in the periodical.[36] The prescribed conditions include conditions (a) that copies are supplied only to persons satisfying the librarian that they require them for purposes of research or private study, and will not use them for any other purpose; (b) that no person is furnished with more than one copy of the same article or with copies of more than one article contained in the same issue of a periodical; and (c) that persons to whom copies are supplied are required to pay for them a sum not less than the cost (including a contribution to the general expenses of the library) attributable to their production.[37] The production of multiple copies of the same material under this exemption is further restricted by a provision to the effect that a copy shall be supplied only to a person satisfying the librarian that his requirement is not related to any similar requirement of another person.[38] For this purpose the regulations provide that a person's requirements are to be regarded as similar to those of   **10–34**

---

[29] C.D.P.A. 1988, s.37(2) and paras. 4(3) and 7(3) of the Regulations.

[30] *Ibid.* s.37(3).

[31] *Ibid.* s.37(6).

[32] *Ibid.* Sched. 1, para. 14(1).

[33] Copyright Act 1956, s.7.

[34] Copyright (Libraries) Regulations 1957 (S.I. 1957 No. 868). See *Copinger* (12th ed.), §§ 927, 1743.

[35] C.D.P.A. 1988 s.38(1). The prescribed libraries are those specified in Part A, Sched. 1 to the Regulations, except those conducted for profit. See Regulation 3(1). "Conducted for profit" in this context means a library which is established or conducted for profit or which forms part of, or is administered by, a body established or conducted for profit.

[36] *Ibid.* s.178.

[37] *Ibid.* s.38(2) and Regulation 4(2).

[38] *Ibid.* s.40(1) and Regulation 4(2).

another person if the requirements are for copies of substantially the same material at substantially the same time and for substantially the same purpose, and that persons' requirements shall be regarded as related if they receive instructions to which the material is relevant at the same time and place.[39]

10–35 **The 1956 Act.** The provisions of the 1956 Act were broadly similar. Thus the librarian of a prescribed library, or someone acting on his behalf, was entitled to make or supply a copy of an article contained in a periodical publication, subject to regulations made by the Board of Trade as the section provided.[40] "Article" was defined as including an item of any description[41] and, where the article was accompanied by one of more artistic works provided for explaining or illustrating it, such illustration might also be copied.[42]

10–36 The regulations prescribed the class of library to be entitled to the privilege and, in particular, that they were not to be established or conducted for profit.[43] They also made provision to secure that the copies were supplied only to persons satisfying the librarian, or a person acting on his behalf, that they required them for purposes of research or private study and would not use them for any other purpose, that no person was furnished with two or more copies of the same article, that no copy extended to more than one article in any one publication, and that the persons to whom copies were supplied were required to pay for them a sum not less than the cost attributable to their production, including a contribution to the general expenses of the library.[44] The copying of the typographical arrangement of a published edition was permitted by separate provision, considered below.[45]

C. Copying parts of published works

10–37 **The 1988 Act.** The 1988 Act provides that, if prescribed conditions are complied with, the librarian of a prescribed library may make and supply from a published edition a copy of part of a literary, dramatic or musical work (other than an article in a periodical) without infringing any copyright in the work, in any illustrations accompanying the work or in the typographical arrangement.[46] The prescribed conditions include restrictions similar in effect to those required for copying of articles in periodicals, referred to above,[47] save that no person is to be furnished with more than one copy of the same material or with a copy of more than a reasonable proportion of any work. What amounts to a reasonable proportion is

---

[39] *Ibid.* s.40(2) and Regulation 4(2)(*b*).
[40] Copyright Act 1956, s.7(1).
[41] *Ibid.* s.7(10).
[42] *Ibid.* s.7(9).
[43] *Ibid.* s.7(1), (2); and see the Regulations, n. 34, *supra.*
[44] *Ibid.* s.7(2).
[45] §10–38.
[46] C.D.P.A. 1988, s.39(1).
[47] *Ibid.* s.39(2) and Regulation 4.

not further defined. Again, similar further restrictions are imposed on the production of multiple copies of the same material as in the case of articles in periodicals.[48]

The 1956 Act. The 1956 Act was broadly to the same effect. Thus pre-   **10–38**
scribed libraries were also entitled to make and supply a copy of a part of a published literary, dramatic or musical work including, any accompanying illustrations, other than an article contained in a periodical publication.[49] Again safeguards were prescribed by regulations.[50] Furthermore this privilege was only to be exercised if the name and address of a person entitled to authorise the making of the copy was not known to the librarian and could not be ascertained by him by reasonable inquiry.[51] In connection with the copying of parts of published works, regulations were made securing that no copy to which the regulations applied extended to more than a reasonable proportion of the work in question.[52] The reproduction of the typographical arrangement of a published edition in such circumstances was the subject of separate provision.[53]

D. *Supply of copies to other libraries*

The 1988 Act. The 1988 Act provides that, if prescribed conditions are   **10–39**
complied with, the librarian of a prescribed library may make and supply to another prescribed library a copy of (a) an article in a periodical, or (b) the whole or part of a published edition of a literary, dramatic or musical work without infringing any copyright in the text of the article or, as the case may be, in the work, in any illustrations accompanying it or in the typographical arrangement.[54] This latter exemption (b), however, does not apply if at the time the copy is made the librarian making it knows, or could by reasonable inquiry ascertain, the name and address of a person entitled to authorise the making of the copy.[55] The prescribed conditions are that (a) not more than one copy is furnished; (b) in certain cases the other library furnishes a written statement that it does not know and could not by inquiry ascertain the person entitled to authorise the making of a copy; and (c) the other library pays a sum not less than the cost of producing the copy.[56]

The 1956 Act. The provisions of the 1956 Act were to the same effect,   **10–40**
except that they did not apply to typographical arrangements of published editions.[57]

---

[48] *Ibid.* s.40(1) and Regulation 4(2)(*b*).
[49] Copyright Act 1956, ss.7(3), (9).
[50] *Ibid.* s.7(3); and see the Regulations, n. 34, *supra.*
[51] *Ibid.* s.7(3) proviso.
[52] *Ibid.* ss.7(2), (4), and the Regulations, n. 34, *supra.*
[53] *Ibid.* s.15(4) and the Regulations, n. 34, *supra.*
[54] C.D.P.A. 1988, s.41(1).
[55] *Ibid.* s.41(2).
[56] Regulation 5.
[57] Copyright Act 1956, s.7(5).

E. *Replacement Copies of Works*

10–41 **The 1988 Act.** The 1988 Act provides that, if prescribed conditions[58] are complied with, the librarian or archivist of a prescribed library or archive may make a copy from any item in the permanent collection of the library or archive (a) in order to preserve or replace that item by placing the copy in its permanent collection in addition to or in place of it, or (b) in order to replace in the permanent collection of another prescribed library or archive an item which has been lost, destroyed or damaged. In these circumstances the librarian or archivist will not thereby infringe the copyright in any literary, dramatic or musical work, in any illustrations accompanying such a work or, in the case of a published edition, in the typographical arrangement.[59] The prescribed conditions are, however, to include provision for restricting the making of copies to cases where it is not reasonably practicable to purchase a copy of the item in question to fulfil that purpose.[60]

The 1956 Act contained no equivalent provisions.

F. *Copying of unpublished works*

10–42 **Introduction.** In many cases unpublished letters and manuscripts of historical or literary interest have been deposited with libraries or other institutions, and it may be in the general public interest that they should eventually be published. Under the 1956 Act the copyright in such unpublished works might have been perpetual[61] and it was often impractical for anyone desiring to publish the material to find out with certainty in whom the copyright was vested. On the other hand it might often have been difficult to find a publisher prepared to take the risk of publishing when a person might come forward able to prove a good title to the copyright. The 1956 Act therefore made provision dealing with the position.[62] The 1988 Act has altered the position relating to the period of copyright in unpublished works such that it is now only in relation to works of unknown authorship that there may be a perpetual copyright.[63] The provisions in the 1956 Act dealing with this problem have therefore not been repeated. In the light of the transitional provisions dealing with the period of copyright in such works,[64] however, the 1988 Act also contains transitional provisions such that the provisions of the 1956 Act in modified form continue to apply to "existing works."

10–43 **The 1988 Act.** The relevant provisions of the 1988 Act only apply to works made on or after August 1, 1989.[65] As to such works, the 1988 Act provides that, if prescribed conditions are complied with, the librarian or

---

[58] See Regulation 5.
[59] C.D.P.A. 1988, s.42(1).
[60] *Ibid.* s.42(2).
[61] Copyright Act 1956, s.2(3) proviso.
[62] § 10–44, *post.*
[63] C.D.P.A. 1988, s.12; § 6–10, *ante.*
[64] *Ibid.* Sched. 1, para. 12; and see § 6–10, *ante.*
[65] *Ibid.* Sched. 1, para. 16.

archivist of a prescribed library or achive may make and supply a copy of the whole or part of a literary, dramatic or musical work from a document in the library or archive without infringing any copyright in the work or any illustrations accompanying it.[66] This exemption does not apply, however, if at the time the copy is made the librarian or archivist making it is, or ought to be, aware of the fact that (a) the work had been published before the document was deposited in the library or archive, or (b) the copyright owner has prohibited copying of the work.[67] The prescribed conditions contain similar provisions, (a) restricting supply for purposes of research or private study only, (b) limiting the furnishing of multiple copies and (c) providing for payment, as in the case of published works.[68]

The 1956 Act: things done before August 1, 1989. In relation to acts **10–44** of infringement, the 1956 Act continues to apply to acts done before August 1, 1989.[69] Section 7(6) of the 1956 Act provided that, where the manuscript or a copy of an unpublished literary, dramatic or musical work was kept in a library, museum or other institution at which it was open to public inspection, and more than 50 years had elapsed from the end of the calendar year in which the author died, and more than 100 years had elapsed after the making of the work, then the work might be reproduced for purposes of research or private study, or with a view to publication. Further provision was then made dealing with the publication of a literary, dramatic or musical work ("the new work") incorporating the whole or part of a work to which the above provisions of section 7(6) applied ("the old work"). Thus section 7(7) permitted the new work to be lawfully published provided that, before publication, such notice of intended publication was given as was prescribed by regulations made by the Board of Trade, and provided that the identity of the owner of the copyright in the old work was not known to the publisher of the new work. It was contemplated, therefore, that the proposed publication incorporating the manuscript work should be advertised and if no one came forward establishing a valid title, then the work might be safely published. It was further provided that any subsequent publication of the new work, either in the same or in an altered form, should not be treated as an infringement of the copyright in the old work, except that, if the subsequent publication incorporated a part of the old work which was not included in the new work as originally published, then a fresh notice would have to be given, and it would again have to be established that the owner of the old work was not known at the date of the subsequent publication.[70] Although these provisions primarily applied only to literary, dramatic or musical works they might, as in the cases above referred to, also have applied in respect of artistic works provided for explaining or illustrating the work.[71] Where a work was lawfully published under these provisions it might also law-

---

[66] *Ibid.* s.43(1).
[67] *Ibid.* s.43(2).
[68] *Ibid.* s.43(3); Regulation 7.
[69] *Ibid.* Sched. 1, para. 14(1).
[70] Copyright Act 1956, s.7(7).
[71] *Ibid.* s.7(9).

fully be broadcast, included in a cable programme, performed in public or recorded.[72]

10–45   The regulations[73] prescribed by the Board of Trade provided for two notices, one not less than three months and the other not less than two months before the intended date of publication, with not less than one month between them. The notices were to be in a daily or Sunday newspaper with a national circulation in the United Kingdom. The particulars to be given in the notices were set out in the regulations.

10–46   **Existing works: things done on or after August 1, 1989.** As already noted,[74] even in the case of acts done after August 1, 1989, the provisions of the 1956 Act continue to apply in relation to existing works, although in modified form. "Existing works" are those works made before August 1, 1989,[75] and for this purpose where the making of a work extended over a period it is to be taken as having been made when its making was completed.[76] In relation to these works, the above provisions of the 1956 Act continue to apply in relation to acts done after August 1, 1989, save that there is no duty to give notice of intended publication.[77]

G. Copies required as condition of export

10–47   The 1988 Act provides that where an article of cultural or historical importance or interest cannot lawfully be exported from the United Kingdom unless a copy of it is made and deposited in an appropriate library or archive, it is not an infringement of copyright to make that copy.[78] The provision is new.[79]

5. Public Administration

A. Parliamentary and judicial proceedings

10–48   **The 1988 Act.** The 1988 Act provides that the copyright in any work is not infringed by anything done for the purposes of parliamentary or judicial proceedings.[80] "Parliamentary proceedings" are defined as including proceedings of the Northern Ireland Assembly or of the European Parliament.[81] "Judicial proceedings" are defined as including proceedings before any court, tribunal or person having authority to decide

---

[72] *Ibid.* s.7(8).
[73] The Copyright (Notice of Publication) Regulations 1957 (S.I. 1957 No. 865). See *Copinger* (12th ed.), § 1736.
[74] § 10–42, *ante*.
[75] C.D.P.A. 1988, Sched. 1, para. 1(3).
[76] *Ibid.*
[77] *Ibid.* Sched. 1, para. 16.
[78] *Ibid.* s.44.
[79] As to the background to its introduction, see *Copinger* (12th ed.), n. 79, p. 204.
[80] C.D.P.A. 1988 s.45(1).
[81] *Ibid.* s.178.

any matter affecting a person's legal rights or liabilities.[82] This would cover the Copyright Tribunal. It was held that the equivalent provisions of the New Zealand Act applied only to specific proceedings existing at the time the reproduction was made.[83] In addition, copyright is not infringed by anything done for the purposes of reporting such proceedings, but this is not to be construed as authorising the copying of a work which is itself a published report of the proceedings.[84]

The 1956 Act. The 1956 Act was more limited in extent. Thus the copy- **10–49** right in a literary, dramatic or musical or artistic work was not infringed by reproducing it for the purposes of a judicial proceeding or for the purposes of a report of a judicial proceeding.[85] The copyright in a cinematograph film was not infringed by making a copy of it for the purposes of a judicial proceeding or causing it to be seen or heard in public for the purposes of such a proceeding[86] and the copyright in a television broadcast, sound broadcast or cable programme was not infringed by anything done in relation to such work for the purposes of a judicial proceeding.[87] No such defence applied in the case of sound recordings or published editions of works, and the copyright in such works was often in fact infringed in the course of such proceedings, for example, by the photocopying of the typographical arrangement of law reports. "Judicial proceeding" was defined as meaning a proceeding before any court, tribunal or person having by law the power to hear, receive and examine evidence on oath.[88]

B. *Royal Commissions and statutory inquiries*

The 1988 Act. The 1988 Act provides that the copyright in any work is **10–50** not infringed by anything done for the purposes of the proceedings of a Royal Commission or statutory inquiry.[89] For this purpose, "Royal Commission" includes a Commission appointed for Northern Ireland by the Secretary of State in pursuance of the prerogative powers of Her Majesty delegated to him under section 7(2) of the Northern Ireland Constitution Act 1973.[90] "Statutory inquiry" means an inquiry held or investigation conducted in pursuance of a duty imposed or power conferred by or under an enactment.[91] Nor is the copyright in any work infringed by anything done for the purposes of reporting any such proceedings held in public, but this is not to be construed as authorising the copying of a work which is itself a published report of the proceedings.[92] Where a work, or material from it, is contained in a report of a Royal Commission or a statutory

---

[82] *Ibid.*
[83] *Auckland Medical Aid Trust* v. *Commissioner of Police* [1976] 1 N.Z.L.R. 485.
[84] C.D.P.A. 1988, s.45(2).
[85] Copyright Act 1956, ss.6(4), 9(7).
[86] *Ibid.* s.13(6).
[87] *Ibid.* ss.14(9), 14(A)(10).
[88] *Ibid.* s.48(1).
[89] C.D.P.A. 1988, s.46(1).
[90] *Ibid.* s.46(4).
[91] *Ibid.*
[92] *Ibid.* s.46(2).

inquiry, the copyright in the work is not infringed by issuing copies of the report to the public.[93]

10–51 **The 1956 Act.** The 1956 Act had no equivalent provisions but, as has been seen,[94] the 1956 Act contained limited defences in the case of a judicial proceeding, which was defined to mean any proceeding before any court, tribunal or person having by law power to hear, receive and examine evidence on oath.[95]

C. Material open to public inspection or on official register

10–52 **The 1988 Act.** The 1988 Act makes new provision in this respect. Thus under the 1988 Act where material is open to public inspection pursuant to a statutory requirement, or is on a statutory register, any copyright in the material as a literary work is not infringed by the copying of so much of the material as contains factual information of any description, by or with the authority of the appropriate person, for a purpose which does not involve the issuing of copies to the public.[96] For these purposes "statutory requirement" means a requirement imposed by provision made by or under an enactment, "statutory register" means a register maintained in pursuance of a statutory requirement, and the "appropriate person" is the person required to make the material open to public inspection or, as the case may be, the person maintaining the register.[97] This provision will, for example, enable a copy of a planning application to be taken, although only to the extent that it contains factual information. The 1988 Act further provides that the copyright in any work is also not infringed by the copying or issuing to the public of copies of material open to public inspection pursuant to such a statutory requirement and made with such authority if this is for the purpose of enabling the material to be inspected at a more convenient time or place or otherwise facilitating the exercise of any right for the purpose of which the requirement is imposed.[98] This provision would presumably, for example, enable copies to be made of records kept for public inspection by the Registrar of Companies.[99] Further, when material which is open to public inspection pursuant to a statutory requirement, or which is on a statutory register, contains information about matters of general scientific, technical, commercial or economic interest, copyright is not infringed by the copying or issuing to the public of copies of such material made with authority where this is for the purpose of disseminating that information.[1] The Secretary of State may

---

[93] *Ibid.* s.46(3).
[94] § 10–49, *ante.*
[95] Copyright Act 1956, s.48(1).
[96] C.D.P.A. 1988, s.47(1).
[97] *Ibid.* s.47(6).
[98] *Ibid.* s.47(2).
[99] The Registrar of Companies has in fact issued blanket licences giving authority to all persons to make copies under ss.47(1), (2) and (3).
[1] C.D.P.A. 1988 s.47(3).

provide that these provisions are only to apply to marked copies,[2] and may extend the provisions to material made open to public inspection by international organisations or under international agreements.[3]

The 1956 Act. The 1956 Act did not contain any equivalent provisions. **10–53**

D. *Material communicated to the Crown*

The 1988 Act. The 1988 Act makes new provision in a case where a liter- **10–54**
ary, dramatic, musical or artistic work has in the course of public business been communicated to the Crown for any purpose, by or with the licence of the copyright owner and a document or other material thing recording or embodying the work is owned by or in the custody or control of the Crown.[4] For this purpose "public business" includes any activity carried on by the Crown.[5] In such cases the Crown may, for the purpose for which the work was communicated to it, or any related purpose which could reasonably have been anticipated by the copyright owner, and subject to any agreement to the contrary,[6] copy the work and issue copies of the work to the public without infringing any copyright in the work.[7] The Crown may not, however, copy a work, or issue copies of a work to the public, by virtue of this section if the work has previously been published otherwise than by virtue of this section.[8]

The 1956 Act. The 1956 Act contained no equivalent provisions. **10–55**

E. *Public records*

The 1988 Act. The 1988 Act provides that material which is comprised in **10–56**
public records within the meaning of the Public Records Act 1958, the Public Records (Scotland) Act 1937 or the Public Records Act (Northern Ireland) 1923, which are open to public inspection in pursuance of any of those Acts, may be copied, and a copy may be supplied to any person, by or with the authority of any officer appointed under those Acts, without infringement of copyright.[9]

The 1956 Act. The 1956 Act contained a similar provision.[10] **10–57**

---

[2] *Ibid.* s.47(4). And see The Copyright (Material Open to Public Inspection) (Marking of Copies of Maps) Order 1989 (S.I. 1989 No.1099), §B–46 *post*, which prescribes the marking to be applied to maps, and The Copyright (Material Open to Public Inspection) (Marking of Copies of Plans and Drawings) Order 1990 (S.I. 1990 No. 1427), §B.–230 *post*, which prescribes the marking to be applied to plans or drawings copied under s.47(2).

[3] *Ibid.* s.47(5). As to the definition of "international organisation," see s.178. And see The Copyright (Material Open to Public Inspection) (International Organisations) Order 1989 (S.I. No. 1098), §B–42 *post*, which extends the provisions to the European Patent Office and the World Intellectual Property Organisation.

[4] *Ibid.* s.48(1). For the definition of "the Crown," see s.178.

[5] *Ibid.* s.48(4). New subs. (6) added by 1990 (c.19) Sched. 8.

[6] *Ibid.* s.48(5).

[7] *Ibid.* s.48(2).

[8] *Ibid.* s.48(3).

[9] *Ibid.* s.49.

[10] Copyright Act 1956, s.42, as amended by the Public Records Act 1958. As to the difficulties raised by this amendment, see *Copinger* (12th ed.), § 932.

F. *Acts Done under Statutory Authority*

10–58   **The 1988 Act.** The 1988 Act provides that where the doing of a particular act is specifically authorised by an Act of Parliament, whenever passed, then, unless the Act provides otherwise, the doing of that act does not infringe copyright.[11] This provision applies in relation to an enactment contained in Northern Ireland legislation as it applies in relation to an Act of Parliament.[12] However, this provision is not to be construed as excluding any defence of statutory authority otherwise available under or by virtue of any enactment.[13]

10–59   **The 1956 Act.** The 1956 Act contained no equivalent provision although it is thought that it would always have been a defence that a particular act was authorised by statute.

6. Typefaces

A. *Typefaces used in the ordinary course of printing*

10–60   **The 1988 Act.** Usually the design of a typeface will be an artistic work in which copyright subsists, and the use of such a typeface in, for example, a typewriter, will involve repeated reproduction of the artistic work. Often such use will be the subject of an implied licence or the principle of non-derogation from grant[14] permitting its use, but the 1988 Act makes express and wider provision dealing with the matter.[15] Thus the Act provides that it is not an infringement of copyright in an artistic work consisting of the design of a typeface (a) to use the typeface in the ordinary course of typing, composing text, typesetting or printing, (b) to possess an article for the purpose of such use, or (c) to do anything in relation to material produced by such use.[16] "Typeface" is defined as including an ornamental motif used in printing.[17]

10–61   This provision applies notwithstanding the fact that the article which is used, for example the typewriter key, is an infringing copy of the artistic work.[18] Thus, for example, a person who possesses or uses a typewriter key which is an infringing copy will not be liable for infringement in the above situations. However, any person who makes, imports or deals with articles such as these, being articles specifically designed or adapted for producing material in a particular typeface, or who possesses such articles

---

[11] C.D.P.A. 1988, s.50(1). An example is the requirement in s.19 of the Companies Act 1985 requiring a company to provide a copy of its memorandum and articles to a member on request.

[12] *Ibid.* s.50(2).

[13] *Ibid.* s.50(3).

[14] See § 8–144 *et seq., ante.*

[15] The provision was enacted to give effect to the 1973 Vienna Agreement for the protection of typefaces (Cmnd. 5754), *Copinger* (12th ed.), § 2011.

[16] C.D.P.A. 1988, s.54(1).

[17] *Ibid.* s.178.

[18] *Ibid.* s.54(1).

for the purposes of dealing with them, may nevertheless still be liable[19] for secondary infringement under section 24 of the Act,[20] or to be liable to deliver up such articles or have them seized,[21] or to the corresponding criminal sanctions.[22] For this purpose "dealing with" means selling, letting for hire, or offering or exposing for sale or hire, exhibiting in public or distributing.[23]

The 1956 Act. The 1956 Act contained no equivalent provisions but, as already noted,[24] the ordinary use of an article such as a typewriter key which was not an infringing copy would presumably have been permissible by virtue of an implied licence or the principle of non-derogation from grant.[25] **10–62**

B. *Articles for producing material in particular typeface*

The 1988 Act. The 1988 Act makes provision for cases where articles specifically designed or adapted for producing material in a particular typeface have been marketed by or with the licence of the copyright owner. Thus, after 25 years from the end of the calendar year in which the first such articles are marketed, the artistic work consisting of the design for that typeface may be copied by making further such articles or doing anything for this purpose.[26] In this context, "marketed" means sold, let for hire or offered or exposed for sale or hire whether in the United Kingdom or elsewhere.[27] In addition it will not be an infringement of copyright to do anything in relation to such articles.[28] It follows, for example, that after the 25-year period it would be permissible for anyone to make and sell replacement typewriter keys which reproduce the typeface used on the original typewriter. Where, however, such articles have been marketed before August 1, 1989, the 25-year period only runs from December 31, 1989.[29] **10–63**

The 1956 Act. The 1956 Act contained no equivalent provision, although to some extent no doubt it would have been possible to claim the benefit of an implied licence or to rely on the principle of non-derogation from grant in such circumstances, for example, where a typewriter key needed to be replaced, having worn out.[30] **10–64**

---

[19] *Ibid.* s.54(2).
[20] § 9–3 *et seq., ante.*
[21] C.D.P.A. 1988, ss.99, 100; § 11–17, § 11–8, *post.*
[22] *Ibid.* ss.107(2), 108; *post,* §§ 19–3, 19–9.
[23] *Ibid.* s.54(3).
[24] § 10–60, *ante.*
[25] See n. 14, *ante.*
[26] C.D.P.A. 1988, s.55(2).
[27] *Ibid.* s.55(3).
[28] *Ibid.* s.55(2).
[29] *Ibid.* Sched. 1, para. 14(5).
[30] See § 8–159 *et seq., ante.*

7. Works in Electronic Form

10–65 **The 1988 Act.** The 1988 Act makes new provision for the case where a work in electronic form, for example a computer program, is passed on by the first purchaser, to permit the transferee to use the work without infringing copyright. Thus the provision applies where a copy of such a work has been purchased on terms which expressly, impliedly or by virtue of any rule of law allow the purchaser to copy the work or to adapt it or make copies of an adaptation[31] of it, in connection with the purchaser's use of it.[32] Presumably "any rule of law" includes the principle of non-derogation from grant.[33] The provision applies to all works in "electronic form," which means a form usable only by electronic means, and "electronic" itself is defined to mean actuated by electric, magnetic, electro-magnetic, electro-chemical or electro-mechanical energy.[34]

10–66 In such cases, if there are no express terms (a) prohibiting the transfer of the copy by the purchaser, imposing obligations which continue after a transfer, prohibiting the assignment of any licence or terminating any licence on a transfer, or (b) providing for the terms on which a transferee may do the things which the purchaser was permitted to do, then anything which the purchaser was allowed to do may also be done without infringement of copyright by a transferee.[35] These provisions do not, however, apply in relation to a copy purchased before August 1, 1989.[36]

10–67 The 1988 Act goes on to provide that where the purchaser does not also transfer any copy, adaptation or copy of an adaptation made by him before the transfer, then such an article is to be treated for all purposes as an infringing copy, as from the time of the transfer,[37] so that he may become liable for secondary infringement of copyright.[38] Since possession of such an article in the course of business with the requisite degree of knowledge is one such act,[39] presumably such a person will almost invariably become liable, since he will usually have knowledge of the relevant facts.[40] Generally, these provisions also apply where the original purchased copy is no longer usable and a further copy used in its place is transferred.[41] Finally, they apply not only on the first transfer, but also on any subsequent transfer.[42]

---

[31] As to the meaning of adaptation see § 8–126, *ante*, and in particular as to computer programs, § 8–129, *ante*.
[32] C.D.P.A. 1988, s.56(1).
[33] See § 8–160, *ante*.
[34] C.D.P.A. 1988, s.178. No doubt a work stored on a compact disc is " a work in electronic form."
[35] *Ibid.* s.56(2).
[36] *Ibid.* Sched. 1, para. 14(6).
[37] *Ibid.* s.56(2).
[38] See § 9–3 *et seq.*, *ante*.
[39] C.D.P.A. 1988, s.23(*a*).
[40] See § 9–19, *ante*.
[41] C.D.P.A. 1988, s.56(3).
[42] *Ibid.* s.56(4).

The 1956 Act. The 1956 Act contained no equivalent provisions, **10–68** although no doubt a purchaser in appropriate circumstances would have been able to claim the benefit of an implied licence or rely on the principle of non-derogation from grant.[43]

8. Miscellaneous Provisions: Literary, Dramatic, Musical and Artistic Works

A. *Anonymous or pseudonymous works; assumptions as to expiry of copyright or death of the author*

The 1988 Act. The 1988 Act provides that the copyright in a literary, **10–69** dramatic, musical or artistic work is not infringed by an act done at a time when, or in pursuance of arrangements made at a time when

(a) it is not possible by reasonable inquiry to ascertain the identity of the author, and

(b) it is reasonable to assume
  (i) that copyright has expired, or
  (ii) that the author died 50 years or more before the beginning of the calendar year in which the act is done or the arrangements are made.[44]

However, this last provision, (ii), does not apply in relation to (a) a work in which Crown copyright subsists, or (b) a work in which copyright originally vested in an international organisation in respect of which a copyright period longer than 50 years has been specified.[45] In relation to "existing works" the Act contains further, transitional, provisions. "Existing works" are defined as works made before August 1, 1989.[46] In relation to such works the above assumption (b)(i) does not apply in relation either to photographs or rights conferred on universities and colleges by virtue of the Copyright Act 1775.[47] Further, the above assumption, (b)(ii), applies only in two alternative circumstances: (a) where the work is unpublished, so that the period of copyright is subject to the transitional provisions of the 1988 Act[48] only after the end of the period of 50 years from December 31, 1989[49]; or (b) in cases where paragraph 12(6) of Schedule 1 of the 1988 Act applies, that is, where the duration of copyright is the same under the amending or repealing provision of the 1988 Act as it was under the previous law.[50] In relation to works of joint authorship, these provisions apply only when it has not been possible to ascertain the

---

[43] See § 8–144 *et seq., ante.*
[44] C.D.P.A. 1988, s.57(1).
[45] *Ibid.* s.57(2). As to copyright vested in an international organisation, and the relevant period of copyright, see s.168 and §§ 3–57, 6–27, *ante.*
[46] *Ibid.* Sched. 1, para. 1(3).
[47] *Ibid.* Sched. 1, para. 15(2). As to the rights conferred by the 1775 Act, see § 13–47, *post.*
[48] *Ibid.* Sched. 1, para. 12(3)(*b*). See § 6–10, *ante.*
[49] *Ibid.* Sched. 1, para. 15(3)(*a*).
[50] *Ibid.* Sched. 1, para. 15(3)(*b*). As to the duration of copyright in such circumstances, see § 6–10, *ante.*

identity of any of the authors,[51] and the reference to "the author" having died is to be construed as a reference to all the authors having died.[52]

10–70 **The 1956 Act.** There were no equivalent provisions under the 1956 Act.

B. *Notes or recordings of spoken words*

10–71 **The 1988 Act.** The 1988 Act makes new provision such that where a person's spoken words are recorded, the subsequent use of that record cannot, in defined circumstances, be prevented by relying on any copyright "in the words as a literary work." Thus, subject to certain conditions, the 1988 Act provides that where a record of spoken words is made, in writing[53] or otherwise, for the purpose (a) of reporting current events, or (b) of broadcasting or including in a cable programme service the whole or part of the work, then it is not an infringement of any copyright in the words as a literary work to use the record or material taken from it (or to copy the record, or any such material, and use the copy) for that purpose.[54]

10–72 The conditions which must be complied with are that:

(a) the record is a direct record of the spoken words and is not taken from a previous record or from a broadcast or cable programme;

(b) the making of the record was not prohibited by the speaker and, where copyright already subsisted in the work, did not infringe copyright;

(c) the use made of the record or material taken from it is not of a kind prohibited by or on behalf of the speaker or copyright owner before the record was made; and

(d) the use is by or with the authority of a person who is lawfully in possession of the record.[55]

10–73 **The 1956 Act.** The 1956 Act contained no equivalent provision.

10–74 **Comment.** This section of the 1988 Act should be compared with that providing for fair dealing in works for the purpose of reporting current events[56] and that for enabling published works to be read in public and then recorded or broadcast.[57] The section presents a number of difficulties of interpretation.

10–75 **The copyright work.** The first is to identify the copyright work which is not infringed by virtue of the section. The section states that it is not an infringement "of any copyright in the words as a literary work" to use the

---

[51] *Ibid.* s.57(3)(a).
[52] *Ibid.* s.57(3)(b).
[53] Writing is defined as including any form of notation or code, whether by hand or otherwise and regardless of the method by which or medium in or on which it is recorded. See s.178 of the 1988 Act.
[54] C.D.P.A. 1988, s.58(1).
[55] *Ibid.* s.58(2).
[56] *Ibid.* s.30(2), § 10–8 *et seq., ante.*
[57] *Ibid.* s.59, § 10–80 *et seq., post.*

record or material taken from it.[58] At first sight this provision may seem curiously worded since no copyright can subsist in words as such, but only in the literary work which comes into existence once the words have been recorded, in writing or otherwise.[59] Presumably, however, the intention is that the provision should apply in the case where a person makes an *ex tempore* speech which is recorded by another. In such circumstances two copyright works may come into existence at the same time. The first is the literary work consisting of the speaker's words which are recorded, the copyright in which will normally be owned by the speaker.[60] The exempting provision no doubt applies to this work. The second work is the record itself which, if it is in writing, will be a literary work, or, if it is recorded on tape, will be a sound recording. The copyright in this will not normally be owned by the speaker.[61] It is less clear whether the exempting provision applies to this work, where it is a literary work. It is thought that it does not, so that the licence of the copyright owner will be required for its use, since the underlying purpose of the section appears to be limited to preventing the speaker stopping a report of his words being used by asserting copyright. There would also otherwise be created an arbitrary distinction between cases where the spoken words are recorded in writing and where they are recorded on tape.

There are, however, other works to which the provision applies. Thus it **10–76** is clear that the provision also applies where copyright subsisted in "the words as a literary work" already, that is, before the words were spoken.[62] An example of this is the case where the speaker writes his speech beforehand, and then delivers it from memory or his prepared text. The speaker will usually be the owner of the copyright in his prepared text. Another example is where the speaker recites an extract from some other copyright literary work. The copyright in this work may belong to the speaker or to some third party, whose licence to such use may or may not have been obtained. Where the licence of the third party was not obtained for the making of the record, then the section will not apply, since the making of the record will have infringed copyright.[63]

The position of the speaker. It is clear that the section applies whether **10–77** the words were spoken in public or in private. It is also clear that the section will apply unless the making of the record was expressly prohibited by the speaker, so that it appears that the onus will be on the speaker to prohibit such acts and not upon the maker of the record to seek permission. Nor does it appear that it is necessary that the speaker should even be aware that his words were being recorded. Thus, it is only in the case where he is coincidentally the owner of the copyright in an existing work from which his words are derived that his consent must be sought

---

[58] *Ibid.* s.58(1).
[59] See C.D.P.A. 1988, s.3 and §2–5 *et seq.*, *ante*.
[60] See §§2–6 and 4–6, *ante*.
[61] See §2–6 *ante* and C.D.P.A. 1988 s.3(3). As to the ownership of copyright in literary works and sound recordings, see §4–5 *et seq.*, and §4–50 *et seq.*, *ante*, respectively.
[62] See the wording of s.58(2)(*b*).
[63] Unless reliance can be placed on another of the defences provided by the 1988 Act, for example s.59, §10–80, *post*.

and obtained. Even if the speaker was aware that his words were being recorded, it does not appear that it is necessary that he knew the use which would be made of the record. This raises the possibility of the speaker being deceived as to the purposes for which the record will be used, although in a case where, for example, a politician makes a statement "off the record" there would no doubt be a strong implication that publication of its contents was prohibited within the meaning of section 58(2)(c). If the making of the record or its use is to be prohibited by the speaker, this must be done before the record is made and any attempt to do so afterwards will apparently be of no effect.

10–78   **The permitted uses.** The purposes for which the record was made may either be for the reporting of current events or for broadcasting the whole or part of the work or including it in a cable programme service. The meaning of "reporting current events" has already been considered in the context of the defence of fair dealing.[64] The only advantage of the present defence in this context appears to be that it can be relied upon if the dealing is neither fair nor accompanied by a sufficient acknowledgement. As to broadcasting the work or including it in a cable programme service, presumably the words "the whole or part of the work" in subsection 58(1)(b) must refer to the work whose use is permitted by the section. It is not necessary that there be any element of reporting current events under this limb, and it will apply, for example, to the recording and broadcasting of a work of poetry. The expression "for that purpose" in the concluding words of subsection (1) appear to indicate that if the record is made for one of the defined purposes it may not be used for the other. Yet it may not always be easy to tell for which purpose the record was made and in many cases it will be made for both purposes, for example the broadcasting of a current affairs programme. In such a case it would appear permissible then to use the record for the purpose of reporting current events in a newspaper.

10–79   The use may be of the record itself or of material taken from it, or a copy of the record. Thus where the record was in the form of a tape recording it appears permissible to transcribe it and print the transcript in a newspaper provided that this is for the purpose of reporting current events. Where the record was in writing it appears permissible to record that material on tape and broadcast the contents of the tape recording. The original "record" must, however, itself be a direct record of the spoken words and not taken, for example, from a broadcast of the spoken words. The express reference to it being permissible to copy the record, and to use the copy, raises the doubt, which might otherwise not have arisen, whether the making of third, fourth and later generation copies is permissible. Were it not for these words it would probably be implicit that the making of such further copies is permissible if for the defined purposes. In many cases a record of an interview will go through several generations of copies before it is printed or broadcast and it would clearly be highly inconvenient if such copying were restricted to the original record and

---

[64] § 10–13, *ante.*

only copies made directly from it. It is thought this cannot have been the intention of the legislature.

C. *Public reading or recitation*

The 1988 Act. The 1988 Act provides that the reading or recitation in public by one person of a reasonable extract from a published literary or dramatic work does not infringe any copyright in the work if it is accompanied by a sufficient acknowledgement.[65] The definition of "sufficient acknowledgement" has already been referred to.[66] In addition, copyright in a work is not infringed by the making of a sound recording, or the broadcasting or inclusion in a cable programme service, of a reading or recitation which by virtue of this provision does not infringe copyright in the work, provided that the recording, broadcast or cable programme consists mainly of material in relation to which it is not necessary to rely on that provision.[67] This latter provision will, for example, enable the televising of such events as Eisteddfods.   **10–80**

The 1956 Act. The provisions of the 1956 Act were more limited, in that although the reading or recitation in public by one person of any reasonable extract from a published literary or dramatic work was not to constitute an infringement if accompanied by a sufficient acknowledgement,[68] this did not apply to anything done for the purposes of broadcasting.[69]   **10–81**

D. *Abstracts of scientific or technical articles*

The 1988 Act. The 1988 Act makes new provision in this area. Thus where an article on a scientific or technical subject is published in a periodical accompanied by an abstract indicating the contents of the article, it is not an infringement of copyright in the abstract, or in the article, to copy the abstract or issue copies of it to the public.[70] For this purpose "article" includes an item of any description.[71] This provision does not, however, apply if or to the extent that there is a relevant licensing scheme certified under section 143 of the Act.[72] The provision will permit what was hitherto a widespread, but unauthorised activity within the scientific and technical communities.   **10–82**

The 1956 Act. The 1956 Act contained no equivalent provision.   **10–83**

---

[65] C.D.P.A. 1988, s.59(1).
[66] See § 10–14, *ante.*
[67] C.D.P.A. 1988, s.59(2).
[68] Copyright Act 1956, s.6(5).
[69] *Ibid.* proviso.
[70] C.D.P.A. 1988, s.60(1).
[71] *Ibid.* s.178.
[72] *Ibid.* s.60(2). As to such licensing schemes, see Chap. 15 and in particular, as to certification, §15–109, *post.*

E. *Recordings of Folksongs*

10–84 **Introduction.** The 1988 Act contains new provisions relating to the recording of folksongs for archival purposes, and the supply of copies of such recordings for the purposes of research or private study. The 1956 Act contained no equivalent provisions. The 1988 Act also contains, as did the 1956 Act, a defence in the case of fair dealing with literary or musical works for the purposes of private study. This has already been considered.[73]

10–85 **Making recordings.** The Act provides that so long as certain conditions are met, a sound recording[74] of a performance of a song may be made for the purpose of including it in an archive maintained by a "designated body" without infringing any copyright in the words as a literary work or in the accompanying musical work.[75] For this purpose a designated body is one designated by order of the Secretary of State by way of statutory instrument.[76] The Secretary of State is not to designate such a body unless satisfied that it is not established or conducted for profit.[76] There are three conditions to be met.

(1) The words of the song must be unpublished and of unknown authorship at the time when the recording is made.[77] For a literary work to be unpublished in this context, copies[78] of the work must not have been issued to the public or made available by means of an electronic retrieval system,[79] but a work will not have been published by its being performed, broadcast or included in a cable programme service.[80] Neither will colourable publication, not intended to satisfy the reasonable requirements of the public, amount to publication,[81] nor will any unauthorised publication.[82] For the words to be of "unknown authorship" the identity of the author, or in the case of works of joint authorship,[83] all the authors, must be unknown,[84] and the identity of an author will be regarded as unknown if it is not possible for a person to ascertain his identity by reasonable inquiry, although if his identity is once known it is not to be regarded subsequently as unknown.[85]

(2) The making of the recording does not infringe any other copyright. It follows that, particularly in relation to the music, the period of copyright must either have expired, or the licence of the copyright

---

[73] § 10–4 *et seq., ante.*
[74] For the definition of sound recording, see C.D.P.A. 1988 s.5(1).
[75] C.D.P.A. 1988 s.61(1).
[76] *Ibid.*, ss.61(5)(a), (6). As to such designated bodies, see The Copyright (Recordings of Folksongs for Archives) (Designated Bodies) Order 1989 (S.I. 1989 No.1012), §B–20 *post.*
[77] *Ibid.* s.61(2)(a).
[78] For the definition of copies, see *Ibid.* ss. 178, 17.
[79] *Ibid.* s.175(1).
[80] *Ibid.* s.175(4)(a).
[81] *Ibid.* s.174(5).
[82] *Ibid.* s.174(6). For the definition of "unauthorised," see *Ibid.* s.178.
[83] For the definition of a work of "joint authorship," see *Ibid.* s.10(1) and §7–1 *et seq., ante.*
[84] *Ibid.* s.9(4).
[85] *Ibid.* s.9(5).

owner must have been given or some other defence must be available, for example, that provided by section 57 of the 1988 Act.[86]

(3) The making of the recording is not prohibited by any performer.[87]

It will be noted that the exemption is not restricted to "folksongs" as such, this term only being used in the sideheading to the section.

Supply of copies. Once such a recording has been included in a relevant **10–86** archive, the Act provides that, subject to prescribed conditions, the archivist, or a person acting on his behalf,[88] may make and supply copies without infringing copyright in either the recording or the works included in it.[89] The conditions, prescribed by the Secretary of State,[90] include conditions (a) that copies are only supplied to persons satisfying the archivist that they require them for purposes of research or private study and will not use them for any other purpose, and (b) that no person is furnished with more than one copy of the same recording.[91]

F. *Representation of certain artistic works on display*

The 1988 Act. The 1988 Act, as did the 1956 Act, makes provision **10–87** enabling certain works on public display to be represented without infringing copyright. The provisions of the 1988 Act apply to (a) buildings, and (b) sculptures, models for buildings and works of artistic craftsmanship, if permanently situated in a public place[92] or in premises open to the public.[93] As to these works, copyright is not infringed by (a) making a graphic work representing it, (b) making a photograph or film of it, or (c) broadcasting or including in a cable programme service a visual image of it.[94] Further, copyright is not infringed by the issue to the public of copies, or the broadcasting or inclusion in a cable programme service, of anything whose making was, by virtue of this provision, not an infringement of copyright,[95] and in relation to anything made before August 1, 1989, it is to be assumed that these provisions were in force at all material times.[96] The expression "open to the public" presumably extends the section to premises to which the public are admitted only on licence or on payment and, if so, there would seem to be nothing to prevent the owner

---

[86] See § 10–69, *ante*.
[87] C.D.P.A. 1988, s.61(2)(*c*). As to performers' rights generally, see Chap. 23, *post*. As to a similar defence in respect of performers' rights, see C.D.P.A. 1988, Sched. 2, para. 14, and § 23–79, *post*.
[88] C.D.P.A. 1988, s.61(5)(*c*).
[89] *Ibid.* s.61(3).
[90] *Ibid.* s.61(5)(*b*).
[91] *Ibid.* s.61(4), and see S.I. 1989 No.1012, §B–20 *post*.
[92] See *Cawley* v. *Frost* [1976] 1 W.L.R. 1207.
[93] C.D.P.A. 1988, s.62(1). As to the definition and meaning of "buildings," "sculptures," "works of artistic craftsmanship," see s.4 and § 2–21 *et seq.*, *ante*.
[94] *Ibid.* s.62(2). As to the definitions and meaning of: "graphic work" and "photograph," see s.4(2) and § 2–21 *et seq.*, *ante*; "film," see s.5(1) and § 2–30, *ante*.
[95] *Ibid.* s.62(3).
[96] *Ibid.* Sched. 1, para. 14(4).

of the premises imposing conditions restricting the copying of the material exhibited.[97]

10–88 **The 1956 Act.** The 1956 Act contained a number of similar provisions. Thus the copyright in works of sculpture and works of artistic craftsmanship which were permanently situated in a public place, or in premises open to the public, were not infringed by the making of a painting, drawing, engraving or photograph of the work, or their inclusion in a cinematograph film or in a television broadcast.[98] Neither was the copyright in a work of architecture infringed by such acts.[99] Where, by virtue of these provisions, the making of any such work did not infringe copyright, then neither did the publication of the work infringe.[1]

G. Advertisement of sale of artistic works

10–89 **The 1988 Act.** The 1988 Act makes new provision enabling copies of artistic works to be dealt in for the purposes of advertising their sale. Thus the Act provides that it is not an infringement of copyright in an artistic work to copy it, or to issue copies of it to the public, for the purpose of advertising the sale of the work.[2] Thus, for example, it is now permissible in the course of selling a painting to make and publish copies of it in a catalogue. In relation to such copies, however, if they are subsequently dealt with, they are to be treated as infringing copies for the purposes of that dealing and, if that dealing infringes copyright, for all subsequent purposes.[3] Someone who so deals in such copies, and who has the requisite degree of knowledge, will therefore be liable for secondary infringement of copyright.[4]

10–90 **The 1956 Act.** The 1956 Act contained no equivalent provision, although obviously where the artistic work was being sold with the consent of the copyright owner a licence to make and publish copies in the above way could no doubt have been implied. In many cases, however, the owner of the picture would not have been the owner of the copyright in it.

H. Making of subsequent works by same author

10–91 **The 1988 Act.** The 1988 Act provides that where the author of an artistic work is not the copyright owner, he does not infringe the copyright by copying the work in making another artistic work, provided he does not repeat or imitate the main design of the earlier work.[5]

---

[97] See s.28(1) and also *Sports and General Press Agency Ltd.* v. *"Our Dogs" Publishing Co. Ltd.* [1916] 2 K.B. 880; [1917] 2 K.B. 125.

[98] Copyright Act 1956, s.9(3).

[99] *Ibid.* s.9(4).

[1] *Ibid.* s.9(6).

[2] C.D.P.A. 1988, s.63(1).

[3] *Ibid.* s.63(2). A copy is "dealt with" if it is sold, or let for hire, offered or exported for sale or hire, exhibited in public or distributed: *ibid.*

[4] See § 9–3 *et seq., ante,* and s.27(6).

[5] C.D.P.A. 1988, s.64.

The 1956 Act. The equivalent provision of the 1956 Act was in similar   **10–92**
terms, namely, that it was not an infringement of copyright in an artistic
work for the same author to make a subsequent artistic work not repeating
or imitating the main design of the earlier work, notwithstanding that part
of the earlier work was reproduced in the subsequent work, and was so
reproduced by the use of a mould, cast, sketch, plan, model or study made
for the purposes of the earlier work.[6]

Comment. It does not appear that the 1988 Act has substantially altered   **10–93**
the law. The various articles referred to in the 1956 Act, such as moulds,
etc., are all prima facie artistic works and the use of them is permitted
within the terms of the 1988 Act just as it was under the 1956 Act. As to
"design," it has been said, in a different context, that the design of a work
"means nothing more than the particular forms and arrangements
(whether of lines or colouring) which the copyright author has selected as
the vehicle for conveying his idea to those who see his work."[7] Thus it is
thought that if a picture consists of a group of persons or things, each the
subject of a separate study, the artist will be at liberty to make replicas of
the separate studies, but not to group them in such a way as to give the
general impression of the completed work for which the studies were originally made.

I. *Reconstruction of buildings*

The 1988 Act. The 1988 Act virtually repeats the provisions of the 1956   **10–94**
Act relating to reconstruction of buildings. Thus any copyright in a building, or in any drawings or plans in accordance with which the building
was constructed, by or with the licence of the copyright owner, is not
infringed by anything done for the purposes of reconstructing the building.[8] For this purpose, in relation to buildings constructed before August
1, 1989, the reference to the owner of the copyright in any drawings or
plans is to the person who at the time of construction was the owner of the
copyright in the drawings or plans under the 1956 or 1911 Acts, or earlier
legislation, as the case might be.[9]

The 1956 Act. The equivalent provisions of the 1956 Act appear to have   **10–95**
been to precisely the same effect.[10]

J. *Musical works: the statutory recording licence*

Under both the 1911 and 1956 Acts manufacturers were entitled to make   **10–96**
records of musical works which had previously been recorded with the
consent of the copyright owner, upon terms that they paid a statutory

---

[6] Copyright Act 1956, s.9(9).
[7] *Hansfstaengl (F.)* v. *Barnes (H.R.) & Co. Ltd.* [1895] A.C. 20 at 27, *per* Lord Watson, considering the provisions of the Fine Arts Copyright Act 1862. See also *Preston* v. *Raphael
Tuck, etc., Ltd.* [1926] Ch. 667.
[8] C.D.P.A. 1988, s.65.
[9] *Ibid.* Sched. 1, para. 14(7).
[10] Copyright Act 1956, s.9(10).

royalty. The provisions of the 1956 Act have been repealed by the 1988 Act and have not been repeated in the 1988 Act. The statutory recording licence has thus been abolished. The 1988 Act contains transitional provisions continuing the effect of the 1956 Act for a limited period.

10–97 **The 1956 Act.** In outline,[11] section 8 of the 1956 Act provided that where records of a musical work had previously been made in or imported into the United Kingdom with due authority for the purposes of retail sale, then the copyright in the musical work was not infringed by the making of records of the work for the purposes of retail sale provided the manufacturer gave the copyright owner notice of his intention to do so and paid a statutory royalty.[12] Provision was made such that the words previously associated with such a recording might also be reproduced.[13] The royalty payable was to be an amount equal to $6\frac{1}{4}$ per cent. of the ordinary retail selling price of the record,[14] although this might be altered following a public inquiry.[15] Regulations were prescribed setting out the particulars to be given by the manufacturer, including the estimated number of records intended to be sold or supplied.[16]

10–98 **Transitional provisions.** As already stated, the 1988 Act repeals these provisions of the 1956 Act[17] and no equivalent scheme is substituted by the 1988 Act. The provisions of the 1956 Act, however, continue to apply where the prescribed notice was given by the manufacturer before August 1, 1989, but only in respect of the making of records within one year of that date and up to the number of records stated in the notice as intended to be sold.[18]

K. The 1911 Act: compulsory licence to reproduce

10–99 **Compulsory right to reproduce on payment of royalties.** The proviso to section 3 of the 1911 Act gave a compulsory licence to reproduce for sale, on royalty terms, any work after the expiration of 25 (or, in the case of pre-1911 works, 30) years from the date of death of the author.[19] The 1956 Act repealed section 3 of the 1911 Act but maintained the effect of the proviso as a defence after 1956 to infringement in relation to reproductions of pre-1957 works in respect of which the requisite notice had been given.[20] As there was no limit set on the time before which the requisite notice could be given, it is conceivable that a notice could have been given before June 1, 1957 in respect of a work the copyright in which had then more than 25 years still to run. In such a case the defence could still be

---

[11] For a detailed discussion of the provisions, see *Copinger*, (12th ed.)., § 827 *et seq.* See also *Discount Inter-Shopping Co. Ltd.* v. *Micrometre Ltd.* [1984] Ch. 369.
[12] Copyright Act 1956, s.8(1).
[13] *Ibid.* s.8(5).
[14] *Ibid.* s.8(2).
[15] *Ibid.* s.8(3). An inquiry was held in 1977, but no change in the rate resulted.
[16] See *Copinger* (12th ed.), § 1737.
[17] C.D.P.A. 1988, 303(2).
[18] *Ibid.* Sched. 1, para. 21.
[19] See *Copinger* (8th ed.), pp. 87–92.
[20] C.D.P.A. 1988, Sched. 7, para. 9.

available today, despite the repeal of Schedule 7 of the 1956 Act, since the general words of paragraph 25(1) of Schedule 1 to the 1988 Act would appear sufficient to preserve such a defence. In practice, however, it is considered extremely unlikely that the proviso to section 3 of the 1911 Act continues to have any application.

9. Miscellaneous Provisions: Sound Recordings, Films and Computer Programs

A. *Rental of sound recordings, films and computer programs*

As has already be seen,[21] any rental of copies of sound recordings, films **10–100** and computer programs is an act restricted by the copyright in such works, and thus an infringement of copyright unless the licence of the copyright owner has been obtained. At the same time, however, the 1988 Act also provides, in cases to be specified by the Secretary of State, and where there is no licensing scheme in operation,[22] that such rental is to be treated as licensed subject only to payment of a reasonable royalty or other payment.[23] The Secretary of State may by order make different provisions for different cases and may further specify cases by reference to any factor relating to the work, the copies rented, the renter or the circumstances of the rental.[24] It is not clear between whom the royalty or other payment needs to be agreed for this purpose. In principle it would seem appropriate that the agreement should be reached at least with the copyright owner. Yet in most cases where the copyright owner has agreed a payment for the rental of his works such rentals would in fact then be licensed and there would be no need for any provision treating the rental as licensed. This provision does not affect the liability of any person who lets for hire or distributes an article which is and which he knows or has reason to believe is an infringing copy[25] and who is therefore liable for secondary infringement of copyright.

Computer programs. The 1988 Act further provides that the copyright **10–101** in a computer program is not infringed by the rental of copies to the public after the end of the period of 50 years from the end of the calendar year in which copies of it were first issued to the public in electronic form.[26] Again, the liability of any person who with knowledge deals in infringing copies is not affected.[27]

---

[21] § 8–98, *ante.*
[22] C.D.P.A. 1988, s.66(2). See, as to licensing schemes, Chap. 15, *post*, and, in particular as to certification, §15–109.
[23] *Ibid.* s.66(1).
[24] *Ibid.* s.66(3).
[25] *Ibid.* s.66(6), and see § 9–3 *et seq., ante.*
[26] *Ibid.* s.66(5).
[27] *Ibid.* s.66(6).

B. *Playing of Sound Recordings for Purposes of Clubs, etc.*

10–102   **The 1988 Act.** The 1988 Act continues the exemption contained in the 1956 Act relating to the playing of sound recordings in organisations such as clubs. The exemptions contained in the 1956 Act relating to the playing of sound recordings where persons reside or sleep has not been continued. The exemption in the 1988 Act relates, as did the wider exemption in the 1956 Act, only to sound recordings and not to any musical or literary works embodied in them. Thus the 1988 Act provides that if certain conditions are met, it is not an infringement of the copyright in a sound recording to play it as part of the activities of, or for the benefit of, a club, society or other organisation.[28] The conditions to be met are (a) that the organisation is not established or conducted for profit and its main objects are charitable or are otherwise concerned with the advancement of religion, education or social welfare, and (b) that the proceeds of any charge for admission to the place where the recording is to be heard are applied solely for the purposes of the organisation.[29]

10–103   **The 1956 Act.** The 1956 Act contained a provision to precisely the same effect.[30] Further provision was also made, however, to the effect that it was not an infringement of copyright in the sound recording to cause it to be heard in public at any premises where persons reside or sleep, as part of the amenities provided exclusively or mainly for residents or inmates therein, provided no special charge was made for admission.[31]

10–104   **Decisions under the Rating, etc., Act 1955.** The words "the organisation is not established or conducted for profit and its main objects are charitable or are otherwise concerned with the advancement of religion, education or social welfare," are similar to those which appeared in section 8 of the Rating and Valuation (Miscellaneous Provisions) Act 1955.[32] Whether the objects of an organisation are charitable or not is a question of the general law of charity upon which there is a great mass of authority. Legal charities have to fall into one of four classes, namely, the relief of poverty, the advancement of education, the advancement of religion, and other purposes beneficial to the community.[33] But, in addition to this, there must be an element of public benefit, so that a trust for the education of employees of a particular company is not a valid legal charity.[34] The expression "social welfare" in the Rating Act was the subject of a number of decisions. It was held that the expression meant the well-being (whether in the physical, mental or material sense) of individuals as mem-

---

[28] *Ibid.* s.67(1).

[29] *Ibid.* s.67(2).

[30] Copyright Act 1956, s.12(7)(*b*).

[31] *Ibid.* As to the interpretation of this provision see *Phonographic Performance Ltd.* v. *Pontins Ltd.* [1968] Ch. 290 and *Copinger* (12th ed.), § 856.

[32] 4 Eliz. 2, c. 9. See also the Miners' Welfare Act 1952 (15 & 16 Geo. 6 & 1 Eliz. 2, c. 23), s.16; and the Recreational Charities Act 1958 (6 & 7 Eliz. 2, c. 17), s.1; *I.R.C.* v. *McMullen* [1981] A.C. 1.

[33] *Income Tax Commissioners* v. *Pemsel* [1891] A.C. 531.

[34] *Oppenheim* v. *Tabacco Securities Trust Co. Ltd.* [1951] A.C. 297.

bers of society,[35] and that the words "concerned with the advancement of" require that the organisation does more than enable individuals to advance their own welfare,[36] and that such advancement must be a direct object of the organisation.[37] But it seems doubtful whether the element of public benefit necessary for a charity need subsist.[38] There have also been decisions upon the words "religion"[39] and "education."[40]

It will be noted that, where such an organisation is held to exist, the   **10–105** exception applies whether the record is performed as part of the activities of the organisation, which would presumably mean for the entertainment of those whose education or whose social welfare is being advanced, or it is performed for the benefit of the organisation, which would include a performance given to outsiders where the proceeds of the performance are applied solely for the purposes of the organisation.

10. Miscellaneous Provisions of the 1956 Act

A. *The 1956 Act: unmarked sound recordings*

The 1956 Act contained special provisions designed to secure that records   **10–106** should be labelled with the year of first publication so that it might be known when the copyright expired.[41] Thus, it was provided that the copyright in a sound recording was not infringed by a person who did an act which would otherwise have been an infringement, if records embodying that recording, or the part of the recording used, had previously been issued to the public in the United Kingdom and, at the time when those records were so issued, they did not bear a label or other mark indicating the year in which the recording was first published. It was, however, provided that this exemption would not apply if it was shown that the records in question were not issued by or with the licence of the owner of the copyright, or that the owner of the copyright had taken all reasonable steps for securing that records embodying the recording, or the part in question, would not be issued to the public in the United Kingdom without such a label or mark, either on the records themselves, or on their containers. Furthermore, these provisions did not apply to a sound recording made before June 1, 1957.[42] While obligations were thus imposed on record

---

[35] *National Deposit Friendly Society (Trustees)* v. *Skegness U.D.C.* [1959] A.C. 293; *Berry* v. *St. Marylebone B.C.* [1958] Ch. 406.

[36] *National Deposit Friendly Society (Trustees)* v. *Skegness U.D.C., supra; Independent Order of Oddfellows, etc.* v. *Manchester Corporation* [1957] 1 W.L.R. 1059.

[37] *General Nursing Council, etc.* v. *St. Marylebone B.C.* [1957] 1 W.L.R. 941; [1958] Ch. 921; but compare *Royal College of Nursing* v. *St. Marylebone B.C.* [1958] 1 W.L.R. 95.

[38] *Berry* v. *St. Marylebone B.C., supra; National Deposit Friendly Society (Trustees)* v. *Skegness U.D.C., supra,* but compare *Derbyshire Miners' Welfare Committee* v. *Skegness U.D.C.* [1957] 1 W.L.R. 764; [1958] 1 Q.B. 298.

[39] *United Grand Lodge, etc.* v. *Holborn B.C.* [1957] 1 W.L.R. 1080; *Berry* v. *St. Marylebone B.C., supra; In re South Place Ethical Society* [1980] 1 W.L.R. 1565.

[40] *Chartered Insurance Institute* v. *London Corporation* [1957] 1 W.L.R. 867; *I.R.C.* v. *McMullen* [1981] A.C. 1.

[41] Copyright Act 1956, s.12(6).

[42] *Ibid.* Sched. 7, para. 12.

manufacturers with regard to labelling, such labelling also helped to establish the title to the copyright in view of the presumptions established in section 20(7) of the Act.[43] These provisions of section 12 have not been repeated in the 1988 Act.

B. *1956 Act: where the copyright in a film had expired*

10–107   The 1956 Act provided that where the copyright in a film had expired, copyright in any literary, dramatic, musical or artistic work embodied therein was not infringed by the public showing of the film.[44] Presumably, however, it would still have been an infringement of any subsisting literary, or other copyright, to have made further copies of the film, since this would have involved a further infringement by reproduction. The provision is not repeated in the 1988 Act and seemingly will never have been of any effect, since at the time of its repeal no films would have been old enough for the copyright in them under the 1956 Act to have expired.

C. *1956 Act: provision to prevent overlapping of remedies*

10–108   Until the copyright in a film expires it is additional to and independent of the copyright in any material embodied in the film, and the rights of the owners of such copyrights, except in so far as covered by licences granted to the maker of the film, continue to operate and be enforceable in respect, for example, of public performances of the film. It was, indeed, expressly provided by the 1956 Act that all the different copyrights subsisting under the Act were to be independent of one another.[45] In order to prevent this operating with undue harshness, special provisions were contained in section 40 of the 1956 Act. While broadcasting a film or including it in a cable programme were not to constitute causing it to be seen or heard,[46] it might have been caused to be seen or heard by the operation of receiving apparatus,[47] whereupon, if this was in public, the occupier of the premises might have been liable.[48] Further, the owner of the copyright in the film was given separate sound broadcasting and television rights.[49] Provision was therefore made to meet the case of cinematograph films which were the subject of a television or sound broadcast, so as to prevent the result that their public performance might have been an infringement both of the broadcast right and of the cinematograph right. Thus where a film was broadcast and it was an authorised broadcast, that is to say, it was made by or with the licence of the owner of the copyright in the film, a person who caused the film to be seen or heard in public by the reception of the broadcast did not infringe the copyright in the film.[50] If, however, the

---

[43] See *Copinger* (12th ed.), § 665 and, as to the presumptions under the 1988 Act, § 11–89, *post*; see also §§ C–132, C–183, as to Convention provisions as to labelling.
[44] Copyright Act 1956, s.13(7).
[45] *Ibid.*, ss.16(6), (7).
[46] *Ibid.* s.48(5).
[47] *Ibid.* s.48(5)(*b*).
[48] *Ibid.* s.48(6).
[49] *Ibid.* s.13(5).
[50] *Ibid.* ss.40(2), (4).

broadcast was not an authorised broadcast, the owner of the copyright in the film was nevertheless not entitled to take proceedings against a person who caused the film to be seen or heard by the reception of the broadcast, but any damage resulting thereby was to be taken into account in assessing damages in any proceedings against the BBC or the IBA in respect of the copyright in the film.[51] These provisions, however, only protected a person who performed a film by the reception of a broadcast received, either directly, or by means of a relay or rebroadcast, and did not protect a person who performed a film made from a broadcast. Nor did they protect a person who made a film from a broadcast. These provisions are not repeated in the 1988 Act.

D. *The 1956 Act: inclusion of works in cable programme service*

The 1956 Act gave additional protection to a person operating a cable   **10–109** programme service where material included in the cable programme service was the subject of a broadcast by the British Broadcasting Corporation or the Independent Broadcasting Authority. Thus if the broadcast was made by or with the licence of the owner of the copyright in the work broadcast, any person who by the reception and immediate retransmission of the broadcast included a programme in a cable programme service, being a programme comprising a literary, dramatic or musical work, or an adaptation of such a work, or an artistic work, or a sound recording or cinematograph film, was to be in a like position in any proceedings for infringement of copyright, as if he had been the holder of a licence granted by the owner of the copyright in the relevant work to include it in the service.[52] If, on the other hand, the copyright owner had not authorised the broadcast, no proceedings were to be brought against the person including such a work in a cable programme service but, in assessing damages in any proceedings against the Corporation or Authority, there is to be taken into account any further infringement involved as a result of the inclusion of the work in the cable programme service.[53] The liability of the Corporation or the Authority as the case may be would appear to be unaffected by the fact that they may not have known of the transmission. These provisions only applied if either the programme was included in the service in pursuance of a requirement imposed under section 13(1) of the Cable and Broadcasting Act 1984 for the transmission of broadcasts, or if and to the extent that the broadcast was made for reception in the area in which the service was provided.[54] These provisions have not been repeated in the 1988 Act.

E. *The 1956 Act: duplication of licensing*

The 1956 Act contained provisions the effect of which was that a person   **10–110** who caused a sound recording to be heard in public as part of a broadcast or cable programme by the operation of a television or radio set had only

---

[51] *Ibid.*
[52] *Ibid.* s.40(3), as amended by the Cable and Broadcasting Act 1984.
[53] *Ibid.* s.40(4).
[54] *Ibid.* s.40(3A).

to obtain a licence from the broadcasting authority concerned or the owner of the cable programme rights, in respect of the broadcast or cable programme itself, and a licence from the owner of any musical, dramatic or literary copyright involved, but was not concerned with the sound recording right, as the case might have been. Thus where a sound or television broadcast was made by the British Broadcasting Corporation or the Independent Broadcasting Authority, and a person, by the reception of that broadcast, caused a sound recording to be heard in public, he did not thereby infringe the copyright in the sound recording.[55] Similar provisions applied in relation to cable programmes.[56]

10–111   The provisions relating to cinematograph films were more elaborate. In the case of an authorised broadcast, a person who caused a cinematograph film transmitted in the broadcast to be seen or heard in public was to be treated as if he held a licence from the owner of the copyright in the film.[57] Where the broadcast of the film was not authorised, however, the owner of the copyright in the film might sue the broadcasting authority, but not the person operating the receiving set, although the infringements at the receiving end might be taken into account in assessing damages.[58] Again, similar provisions applied in the case of cable programmes.[59] These provisions have not been repeated in the 1988 Act.

11. Miscellaneous Provisions: Broadcasting and Cable Programmes

A. *Incidental recording for purposes of broadcasting, etc.*

10–112 The 1988 Act makes provision, as did the 1956 Act, enabling a person who is entitled to broadcast a work or include it in a cable programme service to make a copy of it in some form for that purpose.[60] It is thought that often the person having the right to broadcast a work or include it in a cable programme service will also by implication have the right to make any copies of the work which are necessary for that purpose.

10–113   The provision applies in cases where by virtue of a licence or assignment of copyright a person is authorised to broadcast or include in a cable programme service (a) a literary, dramatic or musical work, or an adaptation of such a work, (b) an artistic work, or (c) a sound recording or film.[61] In such cases that person is, subject to conditions, to be treated as licensed by the owner of the copyright in the work to do or authorise certain further acts for the purposes of the broadcast or cable programme.

---

[55] *Ibid.*, s.40(1).
[56] *Ibid.* s.40A(1).
[57] *Ibid.* s.40(2).
[58] *Ibid.* s.40(4).
[59] *Ibid.* s.40A(2), (3).
[60] The provision was originally introduced into the 1956 Act to give effect to Article AII *bis* (3) of the Brussels Convention.
[61] C.D.P.A. 1988, s.68(1).

Thus in the case of a literary, dramatic or musical work, or an adaptation of such a work, the further acts are the making of a sound recording or film of the work or adaptation.[62] In the case of an artistic work the acts are the taking of a photograph or the making of a film of the work.[63] In the case of a sound recording or film, the acts are the making of a copy of it.[64] The licence is, however, subject to two conditions, namely that the recording, film, photograph or copy in question (a) shall not be used for any other purpose, and (b) shall be destroyed within 28 days of being first used for broadcasting the work or, as the case may be, including it in a cable programme service.[65] Where a recording, film, photograph or copy is made pursuant to the licence conferred by this section, but is then used for some purpose other than the broadcast or cable programme in question, then when used for that other purpose, that article is to be treated as an infringing copy.[66] Similarly any such article which is not destroyed within the specified 28-day period is also to be treated as an infringing copy for all purposes thereafter.[67] Any person who then deals with such an article with the requisite degree of knowledge will be liable for secondary infringement.[68]

The 1956 Act. The 1956 Act contained similar, but more limited provisions. Thus a person entitled to broadcast a literary, dramatic or musical work under an assignment or licence[69] was entitled to make a reproduction of the work solely for the purpose of broadcasting it, provided that the reproduction was not used for making any further reproductions from it, or for any other purpose except that of broadcasting in accordance with that assignment or licence, and that the reproduction was destroyed before the end of a period of 28 days beginning with the day on which it was first used for broadcasting the work in pursuance of the licence, or such extended period as might be agreed.[70] **10–114**

B. *Recording for Purposes of Supervision of Broadcasts, etc.*

The 1988 Act makes a provision enabling broadcast programmes to be recorded for the purposes of supervision and control of such programmes. Thus the copyright in a work is not infringed by the making or use by the B.B.C., for the purpose of maintaining supervision and control over programmes broadcast by them, of recordings of those programmes.[71] With the changes introduced by the Broadcasting Act 1990, the original provisions of the 1988 Copyright Act relating to the control by the I.B.A. and the Cable Authority have had to be amended. The 1988 Act now provides **10–115**

---

[62] *Ibid.* s.68(2)(*a*).
[63] *Ibid.* s.68(2)(*b*).
[64] *Ibid.* s.68(2)(*c*).
[65] *Ibid.* s.68(3).
[66] *Ibid.* s.68(4)(*a*).
[67] *Ibid.* s.68(4)(*b*).
[68] *Ibid.* s.27(6) and § 9–3, *ante.*
[69] If made or granted after June 1, 1957 (Copyright Act 1956, Sched. 7, para. 5).
[70] Copyright Act 1956, s.6(7). The provisions of this section also applied in relation to adaptations and inclusions of a work in a cable programme service. See ss.6(8), (9).
[71] C.D.P.A. 1988, s.69(1).

that the copyright in a work is not infringed by anything done in pursuance of:

(a) the powers of the new Independent Television Commission and Radio Authority to make and use recordings for the purpose of maintaining supervision over programmes included in licensed services;

(b) the complaints procedures operated by the new Broadcasting Complaints Commission and Broadcasting Standards Council;

(c) the powers of a justice of the peace to require production and copying of visual or sound recordings if he is satisfied that an offence under section 2 of the Obscene Publications Act 1959 or section 22 of the Public Order Act 1986 may have been committed;

(d) a condition included as part of a licensed service requiring the licence holder to produce material to the Independent Television Commission or the Radio Authority in exercise of their powers to supervise programmes;

(e) the Radio Authority's powers to require copies of scripts and any pre-recorded matter in advance of broadcasts[72]

Neither is the copyright in a work infringed by any use made by the Independent Television Commission, the Radio Authority, the Brodcasting Complaints Commission or the Broadcasting Standards Council of materials provided to them pursuant to their powers under the Broadcasting Act.[73]

10–116   **The 1956 Act.** Similar exemptions were given in the case of the Independent Broadcasting Authority, by the Broadcasting Act 1981,[74] and in the case of the Cable Authority's functions, by the Cable and Broadcasting Act 1984.[75]

C. *Recording for purposes of time-shifting for private purposes*

10–117   The 1988 Act makes new provision enabling broadcasts or cable programmes to be recorded, for example by means of a tape-recorder or video-cassette recorder, to enable them to be heard or seen at a later date. Thus the 1988 Act provides that it is not an infringement of the copyright in a broadcast or cable programme or any work included in it to make a recording for private or domestic use if it is solely for the purpose of enabling it to be viewed or listened to at a more convenient time.[76] It appears that when recorded in this way the copy is not an infringing copy for any purpose.[77] Thus, for example, films which are broadcast may be

---

[72] *Ibid.*, s.69(2), as substituted by the Broadcasting Act 1990, Sched. 20, para. 50(1). As to the provisions of C.D.P.A. 1988, s.69(2), as originally enacted, see § A–72, *post.*

[73] *Ibid.*, s.69(3), as substituted by the Broadcasting Act 1990, Sched. 20, para. 50(1). As to the provisions of C.D.P.A. 1988, s.69(3), as originally enacted, see § A–72, *post.*

[74] Broadcasting Act 1981, s.4(7).

[75] Cable and Broadcasting Act 1984, s.16(4).

[76] C.D.P.A. 1988, s.70.

[77] Compare, for example, the type of provision contained in s.68(4) of the Act.

copied for this purpose and then kept and viewed in private for an unlimited period. There is therefore nothing to stop private individuals building their own "film library" of such films, or even selling such original copies, provided they were not made for this purpose and provided also that copies of the films are not thereby put into circulation.[78]

The 1956 Act. Although under the 1956 Act it was not an infringement of **10–118** the copyright in a broadcast or cable programme to make a sound recording or cinematograph film of it for private purposes,[79] it would have been an infringement of the copyright in, for example, a cinematograph film or sound recording comprised in the broadcast.[80] Nevertheless such copying was widespread, although in practical terms it could not be prevented because of the difficulties of obtaining evidence.

D. *Photographs of television broadcasts or cable programmes*

The 1988 Act. As has been seen, the 1988 Act provides that in relation to **10–119** a film, television broadcast or cable programme, copying includes making a photograph of any image forming part of such a work.[81] At the same time however the 1988 Act makes provision relating to the taking of photographs of television broadcasts or cable programmes for private and domestic purposes. Thus under the 1988 Act the making for private and domestic use of a photograph[82] of the whole or any part of an image forming part of a television broadcast or cable programme, or a copy of such a photograph, does not infringe any copyright in the broadcast or cable programme or in any film included in it.[83] It will, however, be an infringement to take a photograph of an artistic work included within such a broadcast or cable programme.

The 1956 Act. Under the 1956 Act it was not an infringement of the **10–120** copyright in a television broadcast or a cable programme to make for private purposes a cinematograph film of such a work.[84] A single photograph was not, however, capable of being a "cinematograph film."[85]

E. *Free public showing or playing of broadcasts or cable programmes*

The 1988 Act. The 1988 Act contains provisions, as did the 1956 Act, **10–121** such that the showing or playing of broadcasts or cable programmes in public does not amount to an infringement if it is not to a paying audience. Thus under the 1988 Act the showing or playing in public of a broadcast or cable programme to an audience who have not paid for admission to the place where the broadcast or programme is to be seen or heard does

---

[78] See s.18 and §8–92, *ante.*
[79] Copyright Act 1956, ss.14(4)(*a*), (*b*), 14A(5)(*a*), (*b*). See §§ 8–87, 8–89, *ante.*
[80] *Ibid.* ss.13(5)(*a*), 12(5)(*a*).
[81] C.D.P.A. 1988, s.17(4). See §§ 8–80, 8–84, 8–88, *ante.*
[82] For the definition of "photograph," see C.D.P.A. 1988, s.4(2).
[83] C.D.P.A. 1988, s.71.
[84] Copyright Act 1956, ss.14(4)(*a*), 14A(5)(*a*).
[85] *Ibid.* s.13(10); and see § 8–81, *ante.*

not infringe any copyright in (a) the broadcast or cable programme, or (b) any sound recording or film included in it.[86] Such acts may still, however, amount to an infringement of the copyright in, for example, musical works comprised in the broadcast or cable programme if no licence has been obtained. The 1988 Act contains further provision as to the circumstances in which persons are to be treated or are not to be treated as having paid for admission. Thus the Act rather cumbersomely provides that an audience is to be treated as having paid for admission to a place if they have paid for admission to a place of which that place forms part.[87] They are also to be treated as having paid for admission to a place if goods or services are supplied at that place (or a place of which it forms part) (a) at prices which are substantially attributable to the facilities afforded for seeing or hearing the broadcast or programme, or (b) at prices exceeding those usually charged there and which are partly attributable to those facilities.[88] On the other hand persons admitted as residents or inmates of a place are not, for this purpose, to be regarded as having paid for admission to that place,[89] nor are persons admitted as members of a club or society where the payment is only for membership of the club or society and the provision of facilities for seeing or hearing broadcasts or programmes is only incidental to the main purposes of the club or society.[90] Where, however, the making of the broadcast or inclusion of the programme in a cable programme service was an infringement of the copyright in a sound recording or film, the fact that it was heard or seen in public by the reception of the broadcast or programme is to be taken into account in assessing the damages for that infringement.[91]

10–122 **The 1956 Act.** The 1956 Act contained a similar provision. Thus liability for causing a television broadcast or cable programme to be seen or heard in public was limited to performances before a paying audience.[92] The provisions as to what amounted to a paying audience were similar. Thus a television broadcast or cable programme was to be taken to be seen or heard by a paying audience if it was seen or heard by persons who either (a) had been admitted for payment to the place where the broadcast or programme was to be seen or heard or had been admitted for payment to a place of which that place formed part, or (b) had been admitted to the place where the broadcast or programme was to be seen or heard in circumstances where goods or services were supplied there at prices which exceeded the prices usually charged at that place and were partly attributable to the facilities afforded for seeing or hearing the broadcast or programme.[93] Where, however, persons were admitted for payment, no account was to be taken (a) of persons admitted to the place in question as residents or inmates therein, or (b) of persons admitted to that place as

---

[86] C.D.P.A. 1988, s.72(1).
[87] *Ibid.* s.72(2)(a).
[88] *Ibid.* s.72(2)(b).
[89] *Ibid.* s.72(3)(a).
[90] *Ibid.* s.72(3)(b).
[91] *Ibid.* s.72(4).
[92] Copyright Act 1956, ss.14(4)(c), 14A(5)(c). It was not an infringement of the copyright in a sound broadcast to cause it to be heard in public. See § 8–105, *ante*.
[93] *Ibid.* ss.14(8), 14A(9).

members of a club or society, where the payment was only for membership of the club or society and the provision of facilities for seeing or hearing television broadcasts or cable programmes was only incidental to the main purposes of the club or society.[94] It will be noted that whereas under the 1988 Act the copyright in any film or sound recording included in the broadcast or cable programme is not infringed in this type of situation, this was not the position under the 1956 Act.

F. *Reception and retransmission of broadcast in cable programme service*

The 1988 Act. The 1988 Act makes provision for cases where a broadcast   **10–123**
is made from a place in the United Kingdom and is, by reception and immediate retransmission, included in a cable programme service.[95] In such circumstances the copyright in the broadcast is not infringed if and to the extent that the broadcast is made for reception in the area in which the cable programme service is provided and is not a satellite transmission or an encrypted transmission.[96] Neither is the copyright in any work infringed if and to the extent that the broadcast is made for reception in the area in which the cable programme service is provided.[97] In such a case, however, where the making of the broadcast was an infringement of the copyright in the work, the fact that the broadcast was retransmitted as a programme in a cable programme service is to be taken into account in assessing the damages for that infringement.[98]

The 1956 Act. The 1956 Act contained broadly similar provisions.[99]   **10–124**

G. *Provision of sub-titled copies*

The 1988 Act makes new provision for the supply of sub-titled copies of   **10–125**
broadcasts and cable programmes. Thus a designated body may, for the purpose of providing people who are deaf or hard of hearing, or physically or mentally handicapped in other ways, with copies which are sub-titled or otherwise modified for their special needs, make copies of television broadcasts or cable programmes and issue copies to the public, without infringing any copyright in the broadcasts or cable programmes or works included in them.[1] For this purpose "designated body" means a body designated by Order of the Secretary of State, who is not to designate a body unless satisfied that it is not established or conducted for profit.[2] The provision does not apply if, or to the extent that, there is a licensing

---

[94] *Ibid.* ss.14(8), 14A(9) provisos.
[95] C.D.P.A. 1988, s.73(1).
[96] *Ibid.* s.73(2), as amended by the Broadcasting Act 1990, Sched. 21.
[97] *Ibid.* s.73(3), as amended by the Broadcasting Act 1990, Sched. 21.
[98] *Ibid.* n 97.
[99] Copyright Act 1956, s.14(8A). See § 8–119, *ante.*
[1] C.D.P.A. 1988, s.74(1).
[2] *Ibid.* s.74(2). The National Subtitling Library for Deaf People has been designated for this purpose. See The Copyright (Sub-titling of Broadcasts and Cable Programmes) (Designated Body) Order 1989 (S.I. 1989 No. 1013), §B–25 *ante.*

scheme in operation providing for the grant of licences.[3] The 1956 Act contained no equivalent provision.

H. *Recording for Archival Purposes*

10–126 The 1988 Act makes new provision enabling broadcasts and cable programmes to be recorded for archival purposes. Thus a recording of a broadcast or cable programme of a designated class, or a copy of such a recording, may be made for the purpose of being placed in an archive maintained by a designated body without thereby infringing any copyright in the broadcast or cable programme or in any work included in it.[4] "Designated" means designated by Order of the Secretary of State, and a body is not to be designated unless it is not established or conducted for profit.[5] The 1956 Act contained no equivalent provision.

I. *Information about Programmes*

10–127 The effective monopoly which the proprietors of the Radio Times and the TV Times had in the listings of future television and radio programmes[6] was the subject of some criticism,[6a] and with the United Kingdom's ratification of the Paris revision of the Berne Convention with effect from January 2, 1990,[7] it became possible for the United Kingdom, consistent with its Convention obligations, to make changes in this area. Accordingly, the Broadcasting Act 1990 has introduced further provisions into the 1988 Copyright Act entitling publishers, provided certain conditions are satisfied, to reproduce information about programmes which are to be broadcast.[8] Although this right takes effect by way of a compulsory licence,[9] the scheme of the Broadcasting Act is that these provisions are to take effect as if they were included in Chapter III of Part I of the 1988 Copyright Act,[10] the Chapter presently under consideration. The provisions apply not only to existing works, but also to future works and future copyright.[11]

---

[3] *Ibid.* s.74(4). As to such licensing schemes, see Chap. 15 and, in particular, as to certification, §15–109, *post*.

[4] *Ibid.* s.75(1).

[5] *Ibid.* s.75(2). All broadcasts other than encrypted transmissions and all cable programmes have been designated for this purpose. See The Copyright (Recording for Archives of Designated Class of Broadcasts and Cable Programmes) (Designated Bodies) (No.2) Order 1989 (S.I. 1989 No.2510), §B–208 *post*, which also designates four bodies.

[6] See, for example, *Independent Television Publications Ltd.* v. *Time Out Ltd.* [1984] F.S.R. 64; *British Broadcasting Corporation* v. *Wireless League Gazette Publishing Co.* [1926] Ch. 433.

[6a] See, *e.g.*, *Magill TV Guide/ITP, BBC and RTE* O.V. 1989 L78/43 (on appeal Cases T–69, T–70 and T–76), and §14–122, *post*.

[7] See § 17–9, *post*, and, in particular, Article 9(2) of Paris revision of the Berne Convention, § C–13, *post*.

[8] These provisions of the Broadcasting Act came into force on March 1, 1991, except that for the purpose of enabling publication of information about programmes intended to be included in a programme service after this date, the provisions came into force on January 1, 1991. See the Broadcasting Act 1990 (Commencement No. 1 and Transitional Provisions) Order 1990 (S.I. 1990 No. 2347), § B–254, *post*.

[9] Broadcasting Act 1990, Sched. 17, para. 4(1).

[10] *Ibid.* Sched. 17, para. 7(1).

[11] *Ibid.* Sched. 17, para. 7(3).

Provision of information. The Broadcasting Act first requires that a **10–128** person providing a programme service must make available information about future programmes to any one who wishes to publish such information in the United Kingdom.[12] The persons who are the providers of the programme services are defined,[13] and broadly constitute the B.B.C. or the persons licensed by the relevant authority to provide such services, as the case may be. The information which is to be provided consists of the titles of the programmes and the time of their proposed inclusion in a programme service,[14] but need not include information about any advertisement.[15] The obligation to provide this information is not satisfied if terms are imposed, other than as to copyright, prohibiting or restricting publication in the United Kingdom by the publisher.[16] The effect of these provisions is apparently to create a statutory duty.

The licensor. The Broadcasting Act then enables such information to be **10–129** reproduced and published, by providing for a compulsory licence scheme, the provisions of which are set out in Schedule 17 to that Act and are to have effect as if the Schedule was included in Chapter III of Part I of the 1988 Copyright Act.[17] For this purpose, the Broadcasting Act proceeds on the basis that the provider of the programme service is or was the owner of the copyright in the work containing the information, or at least has the right to grant licences. Thus the person to be approached for the licence is the programme service provider, and even where the provider of the programme service has assigned the copyright in the works containing the information, he, and not the assignee, is still to be treated as the copyright owner for this purpose.[18] An exception is provided in the case where such assignment took place before September 29, 1989, when the assignee is the person to be approached for the licence.[19] Where the copyright in the relevant work is not and has never been owned by the programme service provider, and he has no right to grant licences to a publisher, these provisions are seemingly of no application.[20]

Obtaining the licence. Where the programme service provider refuses **10–130** within a reasonable time to grant the publisher a licence on terms as to duration and payment which are acceptable to the publisher,[21] the publisher must first give notice of his intention to exercise the right to the programme service provider, asking him to propose terms of payment. After receipt of any such proposal (presuming that it is unacceptable) or after

---

[12] *Ibid.* s.176(1).
[13] *Ibid.* s.176(7).
[14] *Ibid.* s.176(2).
[15] *Ibid.* s.176(8).
[16] *Ibid.* s.176(5).
[17] *Ibid.* Sched. 17, para. 7(1).
[18] *Ibid.* Sched. 17, para. 1(2).
[19] *Ibid.* Sched. 17, para. 1(3). This paragraph also provides that in such circumstances the references elsewhere in the Schedule to the person providing the programme service are references to the assignee, and this approach is adopted in this discussion also.
[20] This appears to be the effect of the provisions of the Schedule, especially paras. 2(1)(*a*) and 4(1).
[21] Broadcasting Act 1990, Sched. 17. paras. 2(1), (2).

the expiry of a reasonable time, the publisher must then give the programme service provider reasonable notice of the date on which he proposes to begin exercising the right and the terms of payment which he proposes.[22] Then he must give reasonable notice to the Copyright Tribunal[23] of his intention to exercise the right and of the date on which he proposes to do so, and also apply to the Tribunal to settle terms of payment.[24]

10–131 **The licence.** Paragraph 4 of Schedule 17 of the Broadcasting Act then provides that once he has done all these things, and whether or not the Tribunal has yet settled terms of payment, the publisher, after the date specified in his notice to the programme service provider, and if he makes the required payments, shall be in the same position as if he held a licence. Thus the paragraph provides that where the publisher "does any act in circumstances in which the paragraph applies," he shall be in the same position as regards infringement of copyright as if he had at all material times been the holder of a licence to do so granted by the programme service provider.[25] This licence covers anything done on his behalf.[26] Paragraph 4 applies to any act restricted by the copyright in works containing the information.[27] Thus where, for example, the information is contained in a literary work, it apparently follows that the licence will extend to any act restricted by the copyright in such work. The publisher may therefore reproduce and publish the information in a newspaper or magazine, or broadcast it.

10–132 **Payment.** The required payments, which are to be made at not less than quarterly intervals,[28] are those determined by the Copyright Tribunal or, if no such determination has been made, those proposed by the programme service provider in response to the request from the publisher or, if no such proposal has been made or is considered by the publisher to be unreasonably high, those proposed by the publisher in his notice to the programme service provider.[29] Where an application is made to the Copyright Tribunal[30] to settle terms of payment, the Tribunal may make such order as it may determine to be reasonable in the circumstances.[31] The order will have effect from the date the publisher begins to exercise the right, so that any necessary adjustments in the amounts which have fallen

---

[22] *Ibid.* Sched. 17, para. 3(1)(*b*).

[23] As to the Copyright Tribunal and its procedure, see § 15–55 *et seq.*, and § 15–94 *et seq.*, *post.*

[24] Broadcasting Act 1990, Sched. 17, para. 3(2).

[25] *Cf.* the similar provisions of C.D.P.A. 1988, ss.123(2), 128.

[26] Broadcasting Act 1990, Sched. 17, para. 7(2).

[27] *Ibid.* Sched. 17, para. 2(1).

[28] *Ibid.* Sched. 17, para. 4(2).

[29] *Ibid.* Sched. 17, para. 4(3).

[30] See n.23, *ante.*

[31] Broadcasting Act 1990, Sched. 17, para. 5(1). Although s.129 of the 1988 Act specifies matters to which the Tribunal shall have regard in determining what is reasonable (see § 15–60, *post*), it is not clear that this section applies in the present case since the section only applies on a reference or application under Chapter VII of the 1988 Act.

due must be made.[32] An application may subsequently be made to review the order.[33] The provisions relating to such application are analogous to those relating to the Tribunal's jurisdiction over licensing schemes, which are dealt with elsewhere.[34] On such an application, the Tribunal shall consider the matter and confirm or vary the original order as it may determine to be reasonable in the circumstances.[35] The order made on such an application is to have effect from the date on which it is made or such later date as may be specified by the Tribunal.[36]

J. *Use as right of sound recordings in broadcasts and cable programme services.*

Under the Copyright Act 1956, it was an infringement of the copyright in **10–133** a record ("sound recording") to broadcast it or to include it in a cable programme. Similarly for any music recorded on such record. The 1988 Copyright Act contains similar provisions, save that the relevant acts are now broadcasting and inclusion in a cable programme service. A broadcaster, for instance, therefore requires two licences, one in respect of the record and one in respect of the music on the record. However, under the 1988 Act, as under the 1956 Act, such licences are subject to the jurisdiction of the Copyright Tribunal,[37] which has replaced the Performing Right Tribunal (the "PRT").

In 1980 the PRT gave its Decision on a reference to the PRT under section **10–134** 25 of the 1956 Act by The Association of Independent Radio Contractors ("AIRC") on behalf of the independent radio companies of Phonographic Performance Limited's ("PPL") Licence Scheme for the licensing of Programme Contractors, being members of AIRC, to broadcast PPL records. The Decision related, in the main, to the royalties payable, and the Order consequent upon such Decision varied the Licence Scheme. Following the judgment of the High Court on a case stated by the PRT at the request of AIRC, in 1986 the PRT modified its 1980 Order. In 1988 the Monopolies and Mergers Commission was requested to report on practices relating to the collective licensing of sound recordings for broadcasting and public performance. In its Report[38] the Commission, whilst concluding that collective licensing bodies were the best available mechanism for licensing sound recordings provided they could be restrained from using their monopoly unfairly, made a number of recommendations. These included an obligation on PPL to permit the use of its repertoire in return for equitable remuneration, a statutory licence for users, initially on the basis of self-assessed royalties, pending a Copyright Tribunal order on equitable remuneration, and abandonment of PPL's needletime constraints. The Commission stated in the Report that, of all the collective licensing bodies

---

[32] *Ibid.* Sched.17, para. 5(2).
[33] *Ibid.* Sched. 17, para. 6.
[34] § 15–75, *post.*
[35] Broadcasting Act 1990, Sched. 17, para. 6(3).
[36] *Ibid.* Sched. 17, para. 6(4).
[37] See § 15–65, *et seq., post.*
[38] Cm. 530.

dealing with sound recordings, only PPL came within the Commission's terms of reference.[39]

10–135   **The 1988 Act amended.** A statutory licence of the kind proposed, with unlimited needletime, has now been incorporated into the 1988 Copyright Act.[40] Thus with effect from February 1, 1991, the Broadcasting Act 1990 has amended the 1988 Copyright Act by introducing into it seven new sections, sections 135A to 135G, which provide for a statutory right to include sound recordings[41] in broadcasts and cable programme services.[42] The provisions do not confer any right to so include musical or associated lyrics embodied in the record, which must therefore be the subject of a separate agreement with the owner of these rights,[43] this not withstanding that broadcasting a sound recording will also involve broadcasting the music on the sound recordings. The scheme of the new provisions follows that of the provisions, also introduced into the 1988 Copyright Act by the Broadcasting Act 1990, dealing with the right to use information about programmes.[44] These have already been considered.[45]

10–136   **Necessary conditions.** The provisions proceed on the basis that there is a licensing body[46] which is capable of granting the necessary licence or procuring such a licence.[47] A person who wishes to include sound recordings in a broadcast or cable programme must then show that one of two conditions is satisfied:

(1) Either he does not already hold a licence,[48] and the licensing body refuses within a reasonable time[49] to grant or procure the grant of a licence allowing unlimited needletime[50] or such needletime as he has demanded, and whose terms of payment[51] are acceptable or which comply with an order of the Copyright Tribunal[52] relating to such a licence or any scheme under which it would be granted.

(2) Or, if he already holds a licence, the terms of the licence limit need-

---

[39] Paras. 3.6—3.8 and 7.6.

[40] See the report of the debate in the House of Lords, *Hansard*, H.L. vol. 522, col. 839 *et seq.*

[41] "Sound recording" in this context does not include a film sound track when accompanying a film: C.D.P.A. 1988, s.135A(5).

[42] It is, perhaps, a little strange that the licence is expressed to relate to "inclusion in a broadcast or cable programme service" of sound recordings, when the relevant infringing acts are "broadcasting" (not "inclusion in a broadcast") and "inclusion in a cable programme service."

[43] Usually, the Performing Right Society Ltd.

[44] Broadcasting Act 1990, s.176 and Sched. 17.

[45] § 10–127 *et seq., ante.*

[46] As to the definition of a licensing body, see C.D.P.A. 1988, s.116(2), and § 15–67, *post.*

[47] C.D.P.A. 1988, s.135A(1)(*a*). At present this body is Phonographic Performance Ltd.

[48] *I.e.*, a licence to include the recordings in a broadcast or cable programme service; but see n. 42, *ante.*

[49] C.D.P.A. 1988, s.135A(4).

[50] "Needletime" means the time in any period (whether determined as a number of hours in the period or a proportion of the period, or otherwise) in which any recordings may be included in a broadcast or cable programme service: C.D.P.A. 1988, s.135A(5).

[51] *I.e.*, terms as to payment for including sound recordings in a broadcast or cable programme service: C.D.P.A. 1988, s.135A(6).

[52] *I.e.*, made under s.135D. See § 10–139, *post.*

letime and the licensing body refuses within a reasonable time[53] to substitute or procure the substitution of terms allowing unlimited needletime or such needletime as he has demanded, or refuses to do so on terms as to payment referred to in (1), above.[54]

Proposal of terms. He must then give notice to the licensing body of his **10–137** intention to exercise the right, asking it to propose terms of payment.[55] After receiving such proposal (presuming that it is unacceptable), or after the expiry of a reasonable time, he must then give reasonable notice to the licensing body of the date on which he proposes to begin exercising the right, and the terms of payment which he proposes.[56] Where he already has a licence, the date specified in his notice must not be sooner than the date of expiry of the licence, except in a case referred to in paragraph (2), above.[57] Next he must give reasonable notice to the Copyright Tribunal of his intention to exercise the right, and of the date on which he proposes to begin to do so, and also apply to the Tribunal to settle the terms of payment.[58]

The Licence. Once all these conditions are satisfied, then, after the date **10–138** which was specified in his notice, if he includes in a broadcast or cable programme service any sound recordings, he is to be in the same position as regards infringement of copyright as if he had at all material times been the holder of a licence granted by the owner of the copyright, provided three further conditions are satisfied[59]:

(1) He complies with any reasonable condition, notice of which has been given to him by the licensing body, as to the inclusion of those recordings[60];

(2) He provides the licensing body with such information about their inclusion in the broadcast or cable service as it may reasonably require[61]; and

(3) Makes payments, not less than quarterly in arrears,[62] in the amount determined in accordance with any order of the Copyright Tribunal,[63] or, if no such order has been made, in accordance with the proposal of the licensing body in response to his earlier request

---

[53] C.D.P.A. 1988, s.135A(4).
[54] *Ibid.* s.135A(3).
[55] *Ibid.* s.135B(1)(*a*).
[56] *Ibid.* s.135B(1)(*b*).
[57] *Ibid.* s.135B(2).
[58] *Ibid.* s.135B(3).
[59] *Ibid.* s.135C(1).
[60] For example, perhaps, restricting the frequency with which a record is played. Although the Copyright Tribunal has jurisdiction to rule on the question of what is reasonable (see § 10–139, *post*), a person who is not prepared to wait for a decision from the Tribunal can still proceed. Obviously, if he does so, he takes the risk that it will eventually be decided that the condition was reasonable, in which case he will have infringed.
[61] Again, the Copyright Tribunal has jurisdiction to rule on the question of reasonableness: see § 10–139, *post*.
[62] C.D.P.A. 1988, s.135C(2).
[63] I.e. under C.D.P.A. 1988, s.135D. See § 10–139, *post*.

or, if no such proposal was made or is considered unreasonably high, in accordance with his proposal to the licensing body.

10–139   **The Copyright Tribunal.**[64] Once a person is treated as being the holder of a licence in accordance with these provisions, any existing licence is replaced.[65] The provisions relating to the application to the Copyright Tribunal to settle the terms of payment,[66] and the right to apply for review of any order,[67] follow the same form as those which relate to the right to use information about programmes.[68] In addition, however, a person exercising the right may also refer to the Tribunal any question whether a condition as to the inclusion of the sound recordings which was notified to him by the licensing body[69] was reasonable.[70] He may also refer to the Tribunal any question whether information required by the licensing body about sound recordings to be included[71] is information which can reasonably be required of him.[72] In either case, the Tribunal shall consider the matter and make such order as it may determine to be reasonable in the circumstances. In considering what is reasonable on any such application, or on an application to settle or review the terms of payment, the Tribunal is expressly required[73]:

(1) To have regard to the terms of any orders which it has made in the case of persons in similar circumstances exercising the right conferred by these provisions[74];

(2) To exercise its powers so as to secure that there is no unreasonable discrimination between persons exercising that right against the same licensing body.[75]

(3) Not to be guided, when settling terms of payment, by any order it has made under any enactment other than section 135D.[76]

---

[64] As to the Copyright Tribunal and its procedure, see § 15–55 *et seq.*, and § 19–94, *et seq.*, *post.*
[65] C.D.P.A. 1988, s.135C(4).
[66] *Ibid.* s.135D.
[67] *Ibid.* s.135F.
[68] Broadcasting Act 1990, s.176 and Sched. 17. See § 10–132 *et seq.*, *ante.*
[69] *I.e.*, under C.D.P.A. 1988, s.135C(1)(a). See § 10–138, *ante.*
[70] C.D.P.A. 1988, s.135E(1)(a).
[71] *I.e.* under C.D.P.A. 1988, s.135C(1)(b). See § 10–138, *ante.*
[72] C.D.P.A. 1988, s.135E(1)(b).
[73] As to other factors which may be taken into account, see C.D.P.A. 1988, s.129 and § 15–60, *post.*
[74] *Ibid.* s.135G(1)(a).
[75] *Ibid.* s.135G(1)(b).
[76] *Ibid.* s.135G(2). This requirement seems remarkable. Not only will it prevent the Tribunal having regard to orders made by the Performing Right Tribunal under the Copyright Act 1956, but also it will, for example, apparently prevent the Tribunal from having regard to any order it has made settling terms on which payment should be made in respect of musical or literary works included in broadcasts or cable programme services under the other provisions of the 1988 Act (see § 10–135, *ante*). Where, however, such terms have been agreed, it seems that the Tribunal may have regard to them.

(4) To take into account those factors which under section 134 of the 1988 Act are relevant on references or applications relating to licences in respect of works included in retransmissions.[77]

---

[77] *Ibid.* s.135G(3). As to these factors, see § 15–64, *post.*

CHAPTER 11

CIVIL REMEDIES

Contents

1. Introduction

11–1 The remedies given by the 1988 Act for infringement of copyright are of two classes, civil and criminal. As to the civil remedies, section 96 of the 1988 Act provides that an infringement of copyright is actionable by the copyright owner. In an action for such an infringement all such relief, by way of damages, injunctions, accounts or otherwise, is available to the plaintiff as is available in respect of the infringement of any other proprietary right. Precedents for court forms (*e.g.* writ, statements of claim and orders) are to be found in Appendix G. G–7 *et seq., post.*

11–2 **Changes.** The main changes in civil proceedings made by the 1988 Act may be summarised as follows:–

    (1) Damages for conversion of infringing copies recoverable under section 18 of the 1956 Act have been abolished for all proceedings for infringement of copyright, except for those instituted before the commencement of the 1988 Act (August 1, 1989);

    (2) The power of the court to award additional damages for infringement of copyright has been enlarged;

    (3) A restriction has been placed on the availability of remedies for infringement in proceedings where a defendant undertakes to take a licence of right where one is available;

    (4) The court has been given statutory power to make orders for the delivery up of infringing copies and for the forfeiture, destruction or other disposal of infringing copies or other articles;

    (5) The copyright owner, or a person authorised by him, may, subject to certain conditions, seize and detain infringing copies which are found exposed or otherwise immediately available for sale without the need for a court order;

    (6) Amendments are made to the rights and remedies of an exclusive licensee;

    (7) Amendments are also made to the presumptions which apply to proceedings for infringement of copyright;

(8) There are transitional provisions governing the extent to which the remedies and procedure under the 1956 Act continue to apply, and the extent to which the new copyright provisions apply to acts and things done before the commencement of the 1988 Act.

2. Who May Sue

A. *Copyright owner*

The remedies are given to the "copyright owner," that is to say, the orig- **11–3** inal owner, or a person deriving title under him by a valid assignment or otherwise. Where different persons are (whether in consequence of a partial assignment or otherwise) entitled to different aspects of copyright in a work, the copyright owner is the person who is entitled to the aspect of copyright relevant for the particular purpose of Part 1 of the 1988 Act.[1]

B. *Prospective owner*

Under the 1911 Act, in the case of an assignment of an interest in copy- **11–4** right not in existence at the time of the assignment, the assignee had no right to sue in his own name for infringements of copyright.[2] The older cases in which courts of equity had enforced the rights of equitable assignees[3] were cases of interim injunction only, and, unless the legal owner was a party to the proceedings, either as joint plaintiff or as a defendant,[4] a perpetual injunction could only be granted under very special circumstances.

Under the 1956 Act, however, provision was made for an assignment by a prospective owner of copyright so that, on the coming into existence of the copyright, the assignee, or a person claiming under him, acquired the legal title forthwith and, consequently, was entitled to sue and obtain all remedies open to an owner of copyright.[5] Similar provision is made for prospective ownership of copyright by the 1988 Act.[6]

C. *Relevant date of title*

It is essential that, at the date of the issue of the writ, the plaintiff has a **11–5** legal or equitable title to the copyright, for title is an essential ingredient of the cause of action for infringement and, without any title, the plaintiff has

---

[1] C.D.P.A. 1988, s.173(1).
[2] *Performing Right Society Ltd.* v. *London Theatre of Varieties Ltd.* [1922] 2 K.B. 433; [1924] A.C. 1.
[3] *Sweet* v. *Cater* (1841) 11 Sim. 572; *Hodges* (*J.*) v. *Welsh* (*T.*) (1840) 2 Ir.Eq.R. 266; *Simms* v. *Marryat* (1851) 17 Q.B. 281; *Hazlitt* v. *Templeman* (1866) 13 L.T. 593; *Grace* v. *Newman* (1875) L.R. 19 Eq. 623; *Bohn* v. *Bogue* (1846) 10 Jur. 420.
[4] *Performing Right Society Ltd.* v. *London Theatre of Varieties, supra*; *Macdonald* (*F.*) *Ltd.* v. *Eyles* [1921] 1 Ch. 631; *University of London Press Ltd.* v. *University Tutorial Press* [1916] 2 Ch. 601; *Nicol* v. *Barranger* [1917–23] Mac.C.C. 219; *Photocrom Co. Ltd.* (*The*) v. *Nelson* (*H. & W.*) *Ltd.* [1923–28] Mac.C.C. 293; *Antocks Lairn* v. *Bloohn* (*I.*) [1971] F.S.R. 490 at 493.
[5] Copyright Act 1956, s.37(1).
[6] C.D.P.A. 1988, s.91; see §§5–35 *et seq., ante.*

no cause of action.[7] A cause of action must exist at the date of the issue of the writ.[8] The plaintiff may commence the proceedings relying on the equitable title to the copyright and get in the legal title afterwards or join the legal owner; but a plaintiff with no title to the copyright cannot sue, acquire a title to the copyright by written assignment subsequently and then obtain the leave of the court to amend so as to validate the writ *ex post facto*.[9] A writ which is issued before the plaintiff has acquired any title to the copyright and before, therefore, the plaintiff has any cause of action, is incurably bad.[10] The plaintiff's proper course in such a case is to issue a new writ founded on his new cause of action.[11]

D. *Equitable owner*

11–6 It is also clear that a person who is entitled to call for an assignment of the copyright to him is the owner of the copyright in equity and is entitled to obtain an interlocutory injunction.[12]

E. *Licensees and agents*

11–7 An exclusive licence has, except against the copyright owner, the same rights and remedies in respect of matters occurring after the grant of the licence as if the licence had been an assignment. The rights and remedies are concurrent with those of the copyright owner.[13]

On the other hand, a mere agent to sell has not such an interest in the work as to entitle him to claim relief.[14] For example, the Mechanical Copyright Protection Society (M.C.P.S.), unlike the Performing Right Society (PRS) and the Phonographic Performance Ltd (PPI.), does not take assignments of copyright from its members and cannot, therefore, bring proceedings in its own name for infringement of its members' rights. It acts as agent for its members. A simple licensee is not the owner of the copyright or any interest in it, and cannot bring an action.[15] The essence of a licence is a contractual or personal relationship whereby the licensee is permitted to do an act or acts which would, but for the licence, be an infringement. It has been held that the licensee under a "sole licence"

---

[7] *Beloff* v. *Pressdram Ltd.* [1973] 1 All E.R. 241; [1973] R.P.C. 765.

[8] *Arrowin Ltd.* v. *Trimguard (U.K.) Ltd.* [1984] R.P.C. 581.

[9] *Roban Jig & Tool Co. Ltd. & Elkadart Ltd.* v. *Taylor & Ors.* [1979] F.S.R. 130; *Acorn Computers* v. *MCS Micro Computer Systems* (1984–85) 57 A.L.R. 389; see also *Nicol* v. *Barranger* [1912–23] Mac.C.C. 219.

[10] *Belegging-en Eploitatiensatschapig Lavender BV* v. *Witten Industrial Diamonds Ltd.* [1979] F.S.R. 59.

[11] *Form Tubes Ltd.* v. *Guinness Bros. plc* [1989] F.S.R. 41.

[12] *Merchant Adventurers Ltd.* v. *Grew & Co. Ltd.* [1972] Ch. 242 at 252; *Performing Right Society Ltd.* v. *London Theatre of Varieties Ltd.* (*supra.*) at 14, 15 and 35; *Ward Lock & Co. Ltd.* v. *Long* [1906] 2 Ch. 550; *University of London Press Ltd.* v. *University Tutorial* [1916] 2 Ch. 601; *Hexagon Pty. Ltd.* v. *Australian Broadcasting Commission* [1976] R.P.C. 628. *Roban Jig & Tool Co. Ltd.* v. *Taylor* [1979] F.S.R. 130 at 135; *Wah Sang Industrial Co.* v. *Takmay Industrial Co. Ltd.* [1980] F.S.R. 303.

[13] C.D.P.A. 1988, s.101(1), (2); see §§5–44 *et seq.*, *ante*; §11–9, *post*.

[14] *Nicol* v. *Stockdale* (1818) 3 Swans. 687; *Petty* v. *Taylor* [1897] 1 Ch. 465.

[15] *Nicol* v. *Barranger* [1917–23] Mac.C.C. 219.

could bring an action for infringement in his own name, but had to join the proprietor of the copyright, either as co-plaintiff with himself, or as defendant.[16]

F. *Joint owners*

Where copyright (or any aspect of copyright) is owned by more than one **11–8** person jointly, references to the copyright owner are to all the owners. In particular, any requirement of the licence of the copyright owner requires the licence of all of them.[17] Where a plaintiff has an assignment from some only of several part-owners, he may be entitled to sue to prevent a stranger from interfering with his rights,[18] or even a co-owner from doing so.[19]

G. *Exclusive licensee*

Section 101 of the 1988 Act provides that an exclusive licensee has the **11–9** same rights and remedies, except against the copyright owner, in respect of matters occurring after the grant of the licence as if the licence had been an assignment.[20] His rights and remedies are concurrent with those of the copyright owner and references in Part I of the 1988 Act to the copyright owner are to be construed accordingly.[21] In an action brought by an exclusive licensee, a defendant may avail himself of any defence which would have been available to him if the action had been brought by the copyright owner.[22] The court may give the plaintiff leave to proceed with his action without the joinder of the copyright owner as a plaintiff or his addition as a defendant.[23]

3. Who May Be Sued

A. *Primary infringers*

The persons who are primarily liable to be sued are individuals and com- **11–10** panies who, without the licence of the copyright owner, do, or authorise other persons to do, in relation to that work in the United Kingdom any one or more of the separate and distinct acts which are restricted by the copyright in the work.[24] Thus, in relation to a published book which is

---

[16] *Neilson v. Horniman* (1909) 26 T.L.R. 188; see, however, §5–44, *ante*; *Young & Anor.* v. *Odeon Music House Pty Ltd.* [1978] R.P.C. 621 at 630 (Supreme Court of New South Wales).

[17] C.D.P.A. 1988, s.173(2)

[18] *Lauri* v. *Renard* [1892] 3 Ch. 402; *Mail Newspapers plc* v. *Express Newspapers plc* [1987] F.S.R. 90. (Exclusive licence granted by one owner without consent of the other owner.)

[19] *Cescinsky* v. *George Routledge and Sons Ltd.* [1916] 2 K.B. 325.

[20] s.101(1).

[21] s.101(2).

[22] s.101(3). See §§5–44 *et seq.*, *ante*.

[23] s.102(1) C.D.P.A. 1988 *Bodley Head Ltd.* v. *Flegon* [1972] R.P.C. 587; and see §5–48 *ante*.

[24] C.D.P.A. 1988, s.16(1) and (2); doing and authorising the doing are separate acts of infringement; *Ash* v. *Hutchinson* [1936] Ch. 489. A plaintiff must plead specific authoris-ation of an actual breach of copyright affecting him: *A. & M. Records Inc. & Ors.* v. *Audio Magnets Incorporated (U.K.) Ltd.* [1979] F.S.R. 1. See §8–3, 8–134 *et seq.*, *ante*.

alleged to infringe copyright, the author, printers, publisher and whole-sale and retail sellers are all liable to be sued for infringement of copy-right.[25] A person who has personally committed primary infringements of copyright cannot escape personal liability simply because he has commit-ted them in the course of carrying out his duties as an employee or agent or as the director of a company.[26]

B. *Secondary infringers*

11–11 Persons may also be liable for secondary infringement such as importation and sale.[27] Although "authorising" does not apply to such an act a person authorising such an act may be liable as a joint tortfeasor.[28] There is no liability for facilitating an infringement of copyright by another, in the sense of conferring on another person a power to copy as distinct from granting him the right to copy. There is no general duty on a person under the 1988 Act, or at common law, actionable by the copyright owner to pre-vent or discourage or warn others against infringement, giving rise to an action in negligence for failing to do so.[29] Liability depends on proof of knowledge. Thus, in order to establish that a retailer of books or records is liable for infringement of copyright by selling or offering for sale books and records, it must be proved that the retailer knew at the relevant time or had reason to believe that the book or record was an infringing copy of the work.[30] The most common way of fixing the retailer with the requisite knowledge is by giving him express notice by letter of the plaintiff's alle-gation of infringement.[31] It was held that section 18 of the 1956 Act con-ferred on a plaintiff owner of copyright an independent and separate cause of action for conversion and that knowledge of the infringement on the part of the defendant retailer was not an ingredient of that cause of action. There might, therefore, be a cause of action in conversion against a defendant who, by reason of his innocence of the infringement, had not committed any infringement of copyright.[32] On this view, all that was necessary was that there had been an infringement with resulting infring-ing copies which the defendant possessed and had converted or was threa-tening to convert to his own use. In other words, the remedy in conversion was not confined to those cases where the defendant was an infringer, though it must, of course, be remembered that an innocent defendant had a defence to any pecuniary remedy for conversion of infringing copies.[33]

---

[25] C.D.P.A. 1988, s.17, 18 & 23.

[26] *C. Evans & Sons Ltd.* v. *Spritebrand Ltd.* [1985] F.S.R. 267 at 271.

[27] C.D.P.A. 1988, ss.22–26.

[28] See §11–12 *et seq., post.*

[29] *CBS Songs Ltd.* v. *Amstrad Comsumer Electronics plc* [1988] A.C. 1013; *Paterson Zochonis Ltd.* v. *Merfarken Packaging* [1983] F.S.R. 273.

[30] C.D.P.A. 1988, s.23.

[31] *Infabrics Ltd.* v. *Jaytex Shirt Co. Ltd.* [1980] F.S.R. 161; [1978] F.S.R. 451 at 467. See §9–18 *et seq., ante.*

[32] *W.E.A. Records Ltd.* v. *Benson King Ltd.* [1975] 1 W.L.R. 44; *Sutherland Publishing Co. Ltd.* v. *Caxton Publishing Ltd.* [1938] Ch. 174.

[33] Copyright Act, 1956 Act, s.18(2). See § 11–75, *post.*

The remedy of conversion is now only available where proceedings were begun before the commencement of the 1988 Act on August 1, 1989.[34]

C. *Joint tortfeasors*

In certain circumstances a person may be liable for infringement of copy-   **11–12**
right by reason of having been a joint tortfeasor. For example, if there is a concerted design by two persons to sell goods which infringe copyright, then the parties, who have such a design and execute it, are joint tort-feasors and are both liable for infringement.[35] This is so even if the under-lying agreement between the parties had been made abroad and one of the parties had done nothing within the jurisdiction. Provided that an act of infringement is in fact committed in the United Kingdom and it is proved that the defendants had a common design to commit that act, it does not matter whether the agreement which is the basis of such design was made within or outside the jurisdiction, nor does it matter that the defendant himself has not done any act within the jurisdiction which, taken by itself, could be said to amount to a several infringement.[36] It is a case of one tort committed by one of them on behalf and in concert with the other.

A person who procures a particular infringement of copyright by inducement, incitement or persuasion of an identifiable individual, is jointly and severally liable with the infringer for the damage suffered by the copyright owner. A person who sells and advertises to the public a product, such as a tape recorder, which might be used for either lawful or unlawful purposes, does not procure a breach of copyright by the pur-chaser or user who makes the decision as to use.[37] He may persuade the person to purchase the product, but does not procure him to use it to infringe copyright. Each must act with the other in the commission of the tort: for example, where two or more persons are closely involved in the design, production and manufacture of the infringing article. There is no common design and therefore no joint liability between a manufacturer and purchaser of recording equipment capable of being used to make infringing tapes. The manufacturer has no control over or interest in the equipment after sale.[38]

D. *Conspiracy*

Parties to a conspiracy to infringe copyright or related rights are also   **11–13**
liable to be sued. A conspiracy to injure may be established in cases where there is an agreement between two or more persons to effect by unlawful

---

[34] C.D.P.A. 1988, Sched. 1, para. 31(2).
[35] *Morton-Norwich Products Inc.* v. *Intercen Ltd.* [1978] R.P.C. 501; *Ash* v. *Hutchinson* [1936] Ch. 489; *P.R.S. Ltd.* v. *Mitchell, etc., Ltd.* [1924] 1 K.B. 762; *Ravenscroft* v. *Herbert & Anor.* [1980] R.P.C. 193; *Cadbury Ltd.* v. *Ulmer G.m.b.H.* [1988] F.S.R. 385; *Crystal Glass Industries Ltd.* v. *Alwince Products Ltd.* [1986] R.P.C. 259 (Court of Appeal of New Zealand); *CBS Songs Ltd.* v. *Amstrad Consumer Electronics plc* [1988] A.C. 1013; *Grower* v. *B.B.C.* [1990] F.S.R. 595 at 607–612.
[36] See, n. 35, *ante.*
[37] *CBS Songs Ltd.* v. *Amstrad Consumer Electronics plc* [1988] A.C. 1013.
[38] *Ibid.*, n. 37.

means an unlawful purpose for the predominant purpose of injuring the plaintiff.[39] In the case of a conspiracy to injure, the distinction between lawful and unlawful purpose depends upon the actual state of mind of the persons who combined together. In its simplest form the contrast is between the deliberate purpose of inflicting injury or causing damage, and the purpose of pursuing a legitimate end, knowing that the result will, in fact, cause injury or damage. Thus, if the predominant purpose or object which the persons combining together have in view is the promotion of their own interests, no action will lie. If they are shown to have no real or substantial interests to pursue and that they have vindictive feelings towards the plaintiff, it will be much easier to infer that their true and deliberate purpose is to inflict injury or damage on the other party.[40]

E. *Contribution*

11–14   A defendant who is liable in respect of any damage suffered by the plaintiff may recover contribution from any other person liable in respect of the same damage, whether jointly with him or otherwise.[41] In any proceedings for contribution, the amount of contribution recoverable from any person is to be such as may be found by the court to be just and equitable having regard to the extent of that person's responsibility for the damage in question.[42]

F. *Directors of companies*

11–15   If a company has committed one or more of the acts restricted by the copyright in a work, the directors may in certain circumstances be liable for having personally authorised the company to commit acts of infringement. Prima facie directors of a company are not liable simply because they are directors,[43] nor for infringements committed by servants of the company.[44] The position is different, however, if the directors ordered or procured the infringing acts to be done. If the directors themselves directed or procured the commission of the infringing acts they are liable in whatever sense they did so.[45] It is necessary to examine with care what part the director played personally in regard to the acts complained of; for

---

[39] *Sorrell* v. *Smith* [1925] A.C. 700; *Crofter Hand Woven Harris Tweed Co.* v. *Veitch* [1942] AC. 435; *Lonrho* v. *Shell Petroleum Co. Ltd.* (No. 2) [1982] A.C. 173; *Metall und Rohstoff A. & G.* v. *Donaldson Lufkin & Jenrette Inc.* [1990] 1 Q.B. 391; *Derby & Co. & Weldon* (No. 5) [1989] 1 W.L.R. 1244.

[40] *Jarman & Platt Ltd.* v. *Barget Ltd.* [1977] F.S.R. 260; See *Valor International Ltd.* v. *Application des Gaz & Anor.* [1979] R.P.C. 218, for pleading conspiracy.

[41] Civil Liability (Contribution) Act 1978, c.47 s.1.

[42] *Ibid.*, s.2(1).

[43] *Cropper, etc., Ltd.* v. *Cropper* (1906) 23 R.P.C. 388; *Rainham Chemical Works* v. *Belvedere Fish Guano Co. Ltd.* [1921] 2 A.C. 465 at 488; *Prichard & Constance (Wholesale) Co. Ltd.* v. *Amata Ltd.* (1924) 42 R.P.C. 63; *Evans & Sons Ltd.* v. *Spritebrand Ltd.* [1985] F.S.R. 267.

[44] *Performing Right Society Ltd.* v. *Ciryl Theatrical Syndicate Ltd.* [1924] 1 K.B. 1.

[45] *Performing Right Society Ltd.* v. *Ciryl Theatrical Syndicate Ltd.* [1924] 1 K.B. 1; *British Thomson-Houston Co. Ltd.* v. *Sterling Accessories Ltd.* [1924] 2 Ch. 33; *Betts* v. *De Vitre* 3 Ch. App. 441; *Mentmore Manufacturing Co. Ltd.* v. *National Merchandising Manufacturing Co. Inc.* (1978) 89 D.L.R. (3d) 195 (Can.).

example, to see whether he has ordered or procured tortious acts. It is not essential, however, to establish a knowing, deliberate, wilful participation in the alleged tort. Each case depends on its own particular facts.[46] Further, if a company is formed for the express purpose of committing infringing acts, the individuals promoting the company will be personally responsible for the consequences.[47]

G. *Other parties*

At any stage of the proceedings in any cause or matter the court may on **11–16** such terms as it thinks just, and either of its own motion or on application, order that there should be added as a party any person who ought to have been joined as a party or whose presence before the court is necessary to ensure that all issues in dispute in the cause or matter may be effectually and completely determined and adjudicated upon. The court may also order to be added any person between whom and any party to the cause or matter there may exist a question or issue arising out of, relating to or connected with any relief or remedy claimed in the cause or matter which in the opinion of the court it would be just and convenient to determine as between him and that party as well as between the parties to the cause or matter.[48] Thus in an action against an importer, a foreign supplier may be joined or, in a case against a retailer of allegedly infringing articles, the importer may be joined.[49]

4. Rights Against Persons in Possession

The court has power to make an order, on application by the owner of the **11–17** copyright in the work or the exclusive licensee, that an infringing copy or article be delivered up to him or to such other person as the court may direct.[50] This power does not affect any other power of the court;[51] for example, its equitable jurisdiction. The power is not available where a defendant in infringement proceedings undertakes to take a licence of right where such a licence is available.[52]

Application may be made for such an order where a person has an infringing copy of a work[53] in his possession, custody or control in the course of a business. Application may also be made where a person has in his possession, custody or control an article specifically designed or adapted for making copies of a particular copyright work, knowing or hav-

---

[46] *Evans & Sons Ltd.* v. *Spritebrand Ltd.* [1985] F.S.R. 267; *White Horse Distillers Ltd.* v. *Gregson Associates Ltd.* [1984] R.P.C. 61 at 90, 91; *A.P. Besson Ltd.* v. *Fulleon Ltd.* [1986] F.S.R. 319.

[47] *Rainham Chemical Works* v. *Belvedere Fish Guano Co.* [1921] 2 A.C. 465 at 475; *P.S. Johnson & Associates Ltd.* v. *Bucko Enterprises Ltd.* [1975] 1 N.Z.L.R. 311; *Prichard, etc., Ltd.* v. *Amata Ltd.* (1925) 42 R.P.C. 63.

[48] R.S.C., Ord. 15, r. 6.

[49] *Tetra Molectric Ltd.* v. *Japan Imports Ltd.* [1976] F.S.R. 238; *Rexnard Inc.* v. *Rollerchain Distributors Ltd.* [1979] F.S.R.1 19.

[50] C.D.P.A. 1988, s.99.

[51] *Ibid.* s.99(4). See §11–80, *post*

[52] *Ibid.* s.98. See §15–91, *post*.

[53] *Ibid.* See s.27.

ing reason to believe that it has been or is to be used to make infringing copies,[54] *e.g.* moulds used for mass produced articles. The requirement of knowledge only applies to such an article and does not apply to delivery up of infringing copies.[55]

A person to whom an infringing copy or other article is delivered in pursuance of an order must retain it pending the making of an order, or the decision not to make an order, as to the disposal of the infringing copy or other article under section 114 of the 1988 Act.[56]

An order for delivery up must not be made unless the court also makes, or it appears to the court that there are grounds for making, an order for the disposal of the infringing copy or other article under section 114 of that Act.[57]

In general, an application for an order for delivery up may not be made after the end of the period of six years from the date on which the infringing copy or article in question was made.[58]

An order may be made by the High Court, and also by the county court in cases where the value of the articles in question does not exceed the county court limit for actions in tort.[59]

5. Right of seizure without court order

11–18 The 1988 Act confers on copyright owners (including exclusive licensees) the right to seize infringing copies and other articles without the need for a court order,[60] such as an Anton Piller order. Because of the restricted circumstances in which and the stringent conditions under which the right may be exercised, the Anton Piller orders will continue to be an important judicial remedy.

11–19 The copyright owner, or a person authorised by him, may seize and detain an infringing copy of a work in specified circumstances. An article is an infringing copy if its making constituted an infringement of the copyright in the work in question.[61] An article is also an infringing copy if it has been, or is proposed to be, imported into the United Kingdom and its making in the United Kingdom would have constituted an infringement of the copyright in the work in question, or a breach of an exclusive licence agreement relating to that work.[62] Such an article is not, however, an infringing copy if it may be lawfully imported into the United Kingdom by virtue of any enforceable community right within the meaning of section 2(1) of the European Communities Act 1972.[63]

The expression "infringing copy" also includes a copy falling to be

---

[54] C.D.P.A. 1988, s.99(1).
[55] See n. 54 *ante.*
[56] C.D.P.A. 1988, S.99(3).
[57] *Ibid.* s.99(2).
[58] *Ibid.* s.99(2); s.113(1).
[59] *Ibid.* s.115.
[60] *Ibid.* s.100.
[61] *Ibid.* s.27(2).
[62] *Ibid.* s.27(3).
[63] *Ibid.* s.27(5); see §9–7, *ante* and §14–36, *post.*

treated as an infringing copy by virtue of various other provisions of the 1988 Act.[64]

11–20 The right to seize and detain is exercisable in the following circumstances:—

(1) The infringing copy of the work must be found exposed or otherwise immediately available for sale or hire.[65] The power is primarily for use against retailers of infringing material operating from time to time from stalls and street sites.

(2) The infringing copy must be one in respect of which the copyright owner would be entitled to apply for an order for delivery up,[66] *i.e.* where a person has an infringing copy of a work in his possession, custody or control in the course of a business.[67]

The power is not, therefore, exercisable in respect of material possessed by a person in a private or domestic capacity. In general, a copyright owner is not entitled to make application for a delivery up order after the end of the period of six years from the date on which the infringing copy or article in question was made.[68]

11–21 The right to seize and detain is exercisable subject to certain conditions:—

(1) Before anything is seized, notice of the time and place of the proposed seizure must be given to a local police station.[69]

(2) Although a person may, for the purpose of exercising the right, enter premises to which the public have access, he may not seize anything in the possession, custody or control of a person at a permanent or regular place of business of his.[70] "Premises" includes land, buildings, moveable structures, vehicles, vessels, aircraft and hovercraft.[71] This is an important condition which precludes "self help" seizure of goods from shops, offices, warehouses and other business premises.

(3) A person exercising the right may not use any force.[72] Like the requirement of prior notification to a local police station, this requirement has been imposed in the interests of maintaining public order.

(4) At the time when anything is seized there must be left at the place where it was seized a notice in the prescribed form containing the prescribed particulars as to the person by whom or on whose auth-

---

[64] C.D.P.A. 1988, s.27(6): See also ss.32(5), 35(3), 36(5), 37(3)(*b*), s.56(2), 63(2) and 68(4). See Ch. 10 *ante*, §10–2 *et passim.*

[65] *Ibid.* s.100(1).

[66] *Ibid.* Under s.99.

[67] *Ibid.* s.99(1).

[68] *Ibid.* s.99(3), s.113.

[69] *Ibid.* s.100(2).

[70] *Ibid.* s.100(3).

[71] *Ibid.* s.100(5).

[72] *Ibid.* s.100(3).

ority the seizure is made and the grounds on which it is made.[73] The forms and particulars are prescribed by order of the Secretary of State made by statutory instrument subject to annulment in pursuance of a resolution of either House of Parliament.[74]

(5) The exercise of the right to seize and detain is subject to any decision of the court in the exercise of its jurisdiction to make an order as to the disposal of an infringing copy or other article.[75] On application the court may make an order that infringing copies or other articles seized or detained shall be forfeited to the copyright owner or destroyed or otherwise dealt with as the court may think fit.[76]

6. Defences

11-22 It is, of course, always answer to a claim of infringement that the plaintiff has failed to establish an essential ingredient of his cause of action. In addition there are several points worth noting relevant to defences.

A. *Licence and permitted acts*

11-23 Copyright is not infringed if the person who does, or authorises another to do, acts restricted by the copyright has the licence of the copyright owner to do the act in question.[77] There are also many acts which may be done without the licence of the copyright owner and without infringing his rights. They are dealt with in Chapter III of the 1988 Act and are described as "Acts Permitted in relation to Copyright Works."[78]

B. *Ignorance not a defence*

11-24 As copyright is a proprietary right, ignorance is no excuse for primary infringement.[79] If the defendant has in fact derived his work, either directly or indirectly, from the plaintiff, the fact that the defendant was unaware that the work he has used existed (for instance, where what he copied was a dress made from a sketch of which he had no knowledge), or was the plaintiff's, or was the subject of copyright, affords no defence to the action for primary infringement, although it may affect the remedy. Similarly, it is no defence to liability for primary infringement that the defendant has relied upon a licence or assignment, which he believed had been granted by the owner of the copyright, if this is not the case; though, again, it may affect the remedy.

---

[73] C.D.P.A. 1988, s.100(4).

[74] *Ibid.* s.100(5), (6). See S.I. 1989 No. 1006, § B–16, *post.*

[75] *Ibid.* s.100(1).

[76] *Ibid.* s.114; see §§11–77 *et seq., post.*

[77] *Ibid.* s.16(2). See §8–144 *et seq., ante.*

[78] *Ibid.* ss.28–76: See Chap. 10, *ante.*

[79] *Mansell* v. *Valley Printing Co.* [1908] 2 Ch. 441; *Lee* v. *Simpson* (1847) 3 C.B. 871; *Wittman* v. *Oppenheim* (1884) 27 Ch.D. 260; *Byrne* v. *Statist Co.* [1914] 1 K.B. 622.

Liability for secondary infringement, such as by importation and sale or by providing means for making copies, is dependent on proof that the defendant knew or had reason to believe that he was dealing in infringing copies.[80]

C. *Defence to damages claim*

It is provided, in section 97(1) of the 1988 Act, that a plaintiff is not **11-25** entitled to damages in respect of an infringement, if it is shown that, at the time of the infringement, the defendant did not know, and had no reason to believe, that copyright subsisted in the work to which the action relates. The onus is on the defendant to establish these matters by evidence.[81] This defence to damages is, however, without prejudice to any other remedy. This provision is differently worded from the corresponding provision in the 1956 Act (s.17(2)) which provided that a plaintiff should not be entitled to damages in respect of an infringement, if it was proved or admitted that, at the time of the infringement, the defendant was not aware, and had no reasonable ground for suspecting, that copying subsisted in the work. It is not thought, however, that the change in language reflects any change in the law.[82]

Old law. The only corresponding provision of the 1911 Act was contained **11-26** in section 8, which provided that, where proceedings were taken in respect of the infringement of the copyright in any work, and the defendant in his defence alleged that he was not aware of the existence of the copyright in the work, the plaintiff was not to be entitled to any remedy other than an injunction or interdict in respect of the infringement if the defendant proved that, at the date of the infringement, he was not aware, and had no reasonable ground for suspecting, that copyright subsisted in the work.[83]

The discussion of the section in the case of *Byrne* v. *Statist Co.*[84] is still **11-27** relevant. There the plaintiff was employed by the proprietors of a newspaper to translate and summarise, in his spare time, a speech of the Governor of the State of Bahia, Brazil, reported in a foreign language, for the purpose of publication as an advertisement in their paper. The summarised translation was duly published in this way with the words "translated from the Portuguese language by F. D. Byrne" at the end. The defendants saw this advertisement, obtained permission from the Governor to publish it as an advertisement in their papers, for which they duly paid, and reproduced the plaintiff's translation verbatim. In an action for infringement of copyright the defendants unsuccessfully pleaded section 8 of the 1911 Act. Dealing with this plea, Bailhache J. remarked: "The defendants

---

[80] C.D.P.A. 1988, ss.22, 23 and 24.
[81] *James Arnold & Co. Ltd.* v. *Miafern Ltd.* [1980] R.P.C. 397 at 410.
[82] See C.D.P.A. 1988, s.172(2).
[83] Compare with s.9 of the Registered Designs Act 1949 (12, 13 & 14 Geo. 6, c. 88) before and after amendment by the 1988 Act and s.62 of the Patents Act 1977 (replacing s.59 of the Patents Act 1949).
[84] [1914] 1 K.B. 622. See also *Gribble* v. *Manitoba Free Press Ltd.* [1932] 1 D.L.R. 169; *John Lane The Bodley Head Ltd.* v. *Associated Newspapers Ltd.* [1936] 1 K.B. 715.

suggested that they had no reasonable ground to suspect that there was any copyright in the advertisement at all; but the advertisement contained upon its face an intimation that it was translated by the plaintiff. The defendants' witnesses admitted that that was an unusual and unprecedented fact, but stated that it was one to which they, as men of experience, attached no importance. In that I think they were wrong, and I find as a fact that there was reasonable ground to suspect that there was copyright in the plaintiff's translation. The position of the defendants in fact was not so much that they did not suspect copyright, as that they supposed the copyright was in the Governor of Bahia, whose instructions for its reproduction they had obtained. This merely amounts to saying that they supposed themselves to have the authority of the owner of the copyright, a very different thing from alleging and proving that they did not suspect that any copyright existed. It is this latter state of mind that section 8 requires to be proved, and section 8 is no protection to a person who, knowing or suspecting that copyright exists, makes a mistake as to the owner of the copyright, and under that mistake obtains authority to publish from a person who is not in fact the owner." The plaintiff was awarded £150 damages. It would appear that this decision is equally applicable to section 97(1) of the 1988 Act.

Section 97(1) of the 1988 Act thus affords no defence in a class of case that frequently arises where the defendant believed that the copyright belonged to some one other than the plaintiff and that he had that third person's permission to do the infringing act.[85] For example, a photograph is submitted to a newspaper for publication. The proprietors of the newspaper accordingly publish the same and pay for it, upon receiving an assurance that the copyright belongs to the person who submitted the photograph to them. They only become aware of the fact that they have been misinformed when a claim is made for damages for infringement of copyright. The newspaper proprietors cannot argue that they had no reason to believe that copyright existed. They were only deceived as to the person in whom the copyright was vested and so they have no defence upon the ground of ignorance under section 97(1).[86]

11–28   **To what cases section 97(1) might apply.** In what cases, then, can this section apply? When can a direct infringer have no reason to believe that copyright subsisted in the work which he copies? It is submitted that the proper attitude of mind of an infringer towards a work that he copies is that copyright in the latter subsists unless he has evidence to the contrary.[87] He can only have no reason to believe[88] that copyright subsists if he has grounds for thinking that (a) the period of copyright protection has run out; or (b) the work is of such a character that it ought not to be a subject of copyright; or (c) possibly, because the work is a foreign work.

If an infringer were to ascertain that the author of the original work was born 130 years ago, or that the work was published 100 years ago but,

---

[85] *James Arnold & Co. Ltd.* v. *Miafern Ltd.* [1980] R.P.C. 397.
[86] But see § 11–75, *post. The Lady Anne Tennant* v. *Associated Newspapers Group Ltd.* [1979] F.S.R. 298.
[87] n. 84.
[88] *A.P. Besson Ltd.* v. *Fulleon Ltd.* [1986] F.S.R. 319 at 321.

after due inquiry, he could not discover the date of the author's death, he might to have reason to believe that the copyright had run out. Or, again, if a work bearing no author's or publisher's name, is pronounced by experts to be the work of A, who died 60 years ago, whereas it, in fact, is the work of B, who died only 40 years ago, this, perhaps is another case in which this section might be successfully pleaded.[89] But it is suggested that no person has a right to assume, without inquiry, that a work published anonymously is not the subject of copyright. Nor, it is suggested, is ignorance of the existence of the copyright work (in a case of indirect copying),[90] a good basis for alleging ignorance that copyright subsisted in the work.

In deciding whether a defendant did not know and had no reason to believe that copyright subsisted in a work, the court will take into account all the relevant circumstances: for example, the nature of the plaintiff's work, the fact that the plaintiff's name was or was not printed on it, the fact that the work bore or did not bear a claim to copyright in it[91] and the fact that there may have been a long-standing practice of copying works of the character of the plaintiff's work without complaint. A general practice of copying would not, however, provide a defence to liability,[92] as distinct from a defence to damages.

If it is hard to imagine a case in which the section will be of any avail to a primary infringer, it is still harder to imagine a case in which a person deriving title under the original infringer could plead the section. As mentioned above, this section does not apply if the defendant publishes a work under a wrong impression as to who is the copyright owner. To take another example; a publisher publishes the work of X which, unknown to the publisher, contains large extracts from the work of Y. Y is a living person well known to the publisher. He cannot, it is thought, plead, successfully, that he did not know and had no reason to believe copyright did not subsist in Y's work. All he could urge is that he did not believe that X had copied from Y's work, and that, apparently, would not bring him within this section. Further, if the defendant pleads that he did not think the pirated work was of a character which ought to be entitled to copyright protection, upon the court holding the contrary, the defendant may have some difficulty in convincing the court that he had no reason for anticipating the court's decision.[93] Of course, it might be different if the defendant's belief was based upon a decision of the courts which was subsequently overruled.

Finally, if the work was a foreign work, it probably would be entitled to protection in this country, either because the Acts of 1956 and of 1988 had

---

[89] See *J. Whitaker & Sons Ltd.* v. *Publishers' Circular Ltd.* [1946–47] Mac.C.C. 10.

[90] See §8–14 *et seq.*, *ante*.

[91] *Swinstead* v. *R. Underwood & Sons* [1923–28] Mac.C.C. 39 (copyright in a tombstone. Defendant not liable for infringement damages).

[92] *Walter* v. *Steinkopff* [1892] 3 Ch. 489.

[93] See *Pytram Ltd.* v. *Models, etc., Ltd.* [1930] 1 Ch. 639, where a mistaken view of the construction of s.22 of the 1911 Act was stated by Clauson J. not to afford a defence under s.8 of that Act; he later held that, in fact, the view was not mistaken so that it was unnecessary to rely upon s.8 of that Act. See also *Field* v. *Lemaire* (1939) 4 D.L.R. 561. In *Cramp (G.A.) & Sons Ltd.* v. *Frank Smythson Ltd.* [1944] A.C. 329, Lord Macmillan reserved his opinion on the application of s.8.

been extended or applied to the works of such countries by Order in Council, or because the work was simultaneously published in this country. It is thought that, while a defendant would not be allowed to plead ignorance of an Order in Council, he might be able to say that he was unaware of simultaneous publication.

D. *Absence of damage not a defence*

11–29 The fact that the infringement has not caused the plaintiff copyright owner any damage is irrelevant to liability for infringement. Copyright is a right of property and the infringement of that right is actionable without proof of damage. A copyright owner is entitled to take legal proceedings for the protection of that property, even though he has not suffered or can not prove actual loss or damage.[94]

E. *Public interest*

11–30 The court may refuse to enforce copyright on the grounds of public interest, even though there is no reference to that defence in any of the Copyright Acts The defence of public interest has been successfully raised in cases in which the object of a copyright claim, coupled with a claim for breach of confidence, has been to prevent, or recover damages for, disclosure of information of a private or confidential character.[95]

7. Remedies and Procedure

A. *Introduction*

There are certain limitations on the remedies available, both jurisdictional and statutory.

11–31 **Jurisdiction.** Various provisions of the 1988 Act make it clear that that Act has no application outside the United Kingdom or the other countries to which it extends. Copyright conferred by that Act is defined in territorial terms, *i.e.* the exclusive right to do the restricted acts "in the United Kingdom."

A claim that acts done outside the United Kingdom constitute an infringement of United Kingdom copyright is not maintainable because only acts done in the United Kingdom constitute infringement direct or indirect of such copyright.[96] A claim that acts done outside the United Kingdom constitute an infringement of the copyright law of a foreign

---

[94] *Weatherby & Sons* v. *International Horse Agency and Exchange Ltd.* [1910] 2 Ch. 297; *Hawkes & Son (London) Ltd.* v. *Paramount Film Service Ltd.* [1934] Ch. 593.

[95] *Beloff* v. *Pressdram Ltd.* [1973] 1 All E.R. 241; *Lion Laboratories Ltd.* v. *Evans* [1985] Q.B. 527: see *Cambridge Nutrition Ltd.* v. *B.B.C.* [1990] 3 All E.R. 523 (Public interest as a factor indiscretion to grant or refuse injunction) see §2–38 *et seq., ante* and §21–20, *post.*

[96] *Def Lepp Music* v. *Stuart-Brown* [1986] R.P.C. 273; *Jonathan Cape Ltd.* v. *Consolidated Press Ltd.* [1954] 1 W.L.R. 1313.

country is not justiciable in the English courts. An infringement of foreign copyright is not a tort under English law. The English courts will not even entertain a claim to title to rights accruing under foreign copyright laws.[97] Actions relating to the validity or infringement of copyright are, like patent and trade mark 7actions, of a local nature.[98] The position is different with a passing off action based as it is on misrepresentation.[99]

The English courts are also reluctant to grant an injunction which will   **11–32** take effect in relation to the defendant's activities in countries outside the jurisdiction.[1] The fact, however, that the defendant is incorporated abroad is not a good ground for refusing an injunction, as the injunction could be enforced by sequestration of assets within the jurisdiction and it is for the defendant company to show that it has no assets within the jurisdiction.[2] Even if the company owns no assets within the jurisdiction at the date of the grant of the injunction it may have assets in the jurisdiction in the future.

With regard to an infringement of copyright committed on a British ship on the high seas, the matter was unclear under the 1956 Act. The courts have jurisdiction over torts committed on such ships[3] and statutes normally extend thereto.[4] By reason of section 162, Part I of the 1988 Act applies to things done on a British ship, aircraft or hovercraft as it applies to things done in the United Kingdom. Section 157 of the 1988 Act provides that Part I of that Act, which is concerned with copyright, extends to England and Wales, Scotland and Northern Ireland. It may be extended by Order in Council to any of the Channel Islands, the Isle of Man or any colony.[5] The territorial waters of the United Kingdom are treated as part of the United Kingdom.[6] Part I of the 1988 Act applies to things done in the United Kingdom sector of the continental shelf on a structure or vessel which is present there for purposes directly connected with the exploration of the sea bed or subsoil or the exploitation of their natural resources as it applies to things done in the United Kingdom.[7]

Undertaking to take licence of right in infringement proceedings.   **11–33** The 1988 Act imposes restrictions on the availability of certain remedies in cases where an undertaking is given by a defendant to infringement proceedings to take a licence of right.[8]

---

[97] *Tyburn Productions Ltd.* v. *Conan Doyle* [1990] 1 All E.R. 909. *Cf.* *"Morocco Bound" Syndicate Ltd.* v. *Harris* [1895] 1 Ch. 534; *Potter* v. *Broken Hill Pty Co. Ltd.* (1906) 3 C.L.R. 479 at 494, 496–7, 510; *Steinhardt & Son Ltd.* v. *Meth* (1961) 105 C.L.R. 440 at 443.

[98] See n. 97, *ante.*

[99] See, for example, *Alfred Dunhill Ltd.* v. *Sunoptic S.A.* [1979] F.S.R. 337; *Intercontex* v. *Schmidt* [1988] F.S.R. 575 at 578; *Chaplin* v. *Boys* [1971] A.C. 356.

[1] *Alfred Dunhill Ltd. & Anor.* v. *Sunoptic S.A. & Anor.* [1979] F.S.R. 337.

[2] *Hospital for Sick Children (Board of Governors)* v. *Walt Disney Productions Inc.* [1968] Ch. 52 at 69 and 71.

[3] *Lloyd* v. *Guibert* (1865) L.R. 1 Q.B. 115; *Davidson* v. *Hill* [1901] 2 K.B. 606.

[4] *Schwartz* v. *The India Rubber etc. Co. Ltd.* [1912] 2 K.B. 299.

[5] C.D.P.A. 1988, s.157(2).

[6] *Ibid.* s.161(1).

[7] *Ibid.* s.161(2).

[8] *Ibid.* s.98.

The restrictions apply in the following circumstances:–[9]

(1) There are in existence proceedings for infringement of copyright.

(2) In respect of that copyright a licence is available as of right under section 144 of that Act.

(3) The defendant to the proceedings undertakes to take a licence on such terms as may be agreed or, in default of agreement, settled by the Copyright Tribunal under that section. Section 144 of the 1988 Act provides for certain powers to be exercisable under the Fair Trading Act 1973 in consequence of a report of the Monopolies and Mergers Commission. Those powers include the provision that licences in respect of the copyright shall be available as of right.[10]

11–34 The defendant may give the undertaking at any time before final order in the proceedings and he may give it without any admission of liability.[11] The defendant is therefore entitled to continue to contest the action both on grounds of liability for infringement and quantum. The effect of the defendant giving the undertaking is that:–

(1) no injunction shall be granted against him[12]

(2) no order for delivery up shall be made[13] under section 99 of the 1988 Act; and

(3) the amount recoverable against him by way of damages or on an account of profits shall not exceed double the amount which would have been payable by him as licensee if such a licence on those terms had been granted before the earliest infringement.[14] The giving of the undertaking thus operates to provide a ceiling to the amount of payment which the defendant is liable to make to the plaintiff for infringement of copyright.

B. *Interlocutory relief*

(i) Injunction

11–35 The most important remedy for infringement of copyright and related forms of protection is an injunction. An injunction may be either interlocutory, that is one granted prior to the trial and only until after judgment or further order, or it may be final and permanent. The court has no jurisdiction to grant an interlocutory or a final injunction against the

---

[9] C.D.P.A. 1988, s.98(1).
[10] *Ibid.* s.144(1).
[11] *Ibid.* s.98(2).
[12] *Ibid.* s.98(1)(*a*).
[13] *Ibid.* s.98(1)(*b*).
[14] *Ibid.* s.98(1)(*c*).

Crown.[15] Most injunctions sought are of a negative or prohibitory nature. Different principles govern the court's discretion to grant interlocutory mandatory injunctions which are more drastic in their effects. Thus, the case must be unusually strong and clear. There must be a higher degree of assurance that at trial it will appear that the injunction has been rightly granted.[16] Regard will be had to the practical realities of the situation.[17]

Applications for interlocutory injunctions are frequently made in actions for infringement of copyright and related rights, since damages are rarely an adequate remedy for the injury suffered by the plaintiff.[18] The object of an interim injunction is to give to the plaintiff temporary protection against injury by the continuing violation of his rights for which he cannot be adequately compensated in damages in the action. This need to protect the plaintiff must be weighed against the corresponding need of the defendant to be protected against injury resulting from his being prevented from exercising his legal rights and for which injury he could not be adequately compensated under the plaintiff's cross undertaking in damages.[19] An interlocutory injunction is thus a temporary, discretionary remedy. It is available before the rights of the parties have been finally determined and, in the case of an *ex parte* injunction, even before the court has been appraised of the nature of the defendant's case.[20] It is not part of the court's function at this early stage in the litigation to try to resolve conflicts of evidence on affidavit as to the facts on which the claims of either party may ultimately depend. The evidence is incomplete because it is not until the trial that it is tested by oral cross-examination. Perfect justice cannot be achieved since the court is acting on imperfect information. It is not, therefore, appropriate for the court to decide conflicting questions of fact or difficult questions of law which call for detailed argument and mature consideration. These are matters to be dealt with at the trial.[21] In

11–36

---

[15] C.D.P.A. 1988, s.21 Crown Proceedings Act 1947; *R.* v. *Secretary of State for Transport Ex. p. Factortame Ltd.* [1989] 2 W.L.R. 997; *British Medical Association* v. *Greater Glasgow Health Board* [1989] A.C. 1211; but see *R.* v. *Secretary of State for Transport, Ex P. Factortame Ltd.* (No. 2) [1990] 3 W.L.R. 818 as to the effect of Community Law on interim injunctions against the Crown.

[16] *Leisure Data* v. *Bell* [1988] F.S.R. 367. *Films Rover International Ltd* v. *Cannon Film Sales Ltd.* [1987] 1 W.L.R. 670.

[17] See n.16, *ante*.

[18] *Coral Index Ltd.* v. *Regent Index Ltd.* [1970] R.P.C. 147; *Annabel's (Berkeley Square) Ltd.* v. *G. Schock* [1972] R.P.C. 838 at 845; *Slick Brands (Clothing) Ltd.* v. *Jollybird Ltd.* [1975] F.S.R. 470; *Foseco International Ltd.* v. *Fordath Ltd.* [1975] F.S.R. 507; *Combe International Ltd.* v. *Scholl (U.K.) Ltd.* [1980] R.P.C. 1; *Monet of London Ltd.* v. *Sybil Richards Ltd.* [1978] F.S.R. 368 at 375; *cf. Aljose Fashions Ltd.* v. *Alfred Young & Co. Ltd.* [1978] F.S.R. 364; *Foster* v. *Mountford and Rigby Ltd.* [1978] F.S.R. 582 (breach of confidence—Supreme Court of Northern Territory, Australia).

[19] See *Spottiswood* v. *Clark* (1846) 2 Ph. 154, (defendant to keep an account rather than granting an injunction).

[20] *Hoffmann-La Roche & Co. A.G.* v. *Secretary of State for Trade and Industry* [1975] A.C. 295; *American Cyanamid Co.* v. *Ethicon Ltd.* [1975] A.C. 396; *Morning Star Co-operative Society Ltd.* v. *Express Newspapers Ltd.* [1979] F.S.R. 113.

[21] *American Cyanamid Co.* v. *Ethicon Ltd.* [1975] A.C. 396; *Hubbard* v. *Pitt* [1976] Q.B. 142; *Fellowes & Son* v. *Fisher* [1976] Q.B. 122; *Netlon* v. *Bridport-Gundry Ltd.* [1979] F.S.R. 530; *John Hayter Motor Underwriting Agencies Ltd.* v. *R.B.H.S. Agencies Ltd.* [1977] F.S.R. 285 at 299; *cf.* the earlier practice: see *Fraser* v. *Evans* [1969] 1 Q.B. 349; *Donmar Productions Ltd.* v. *Bart* [1967] 1 W.L.R. 740; *Harman Pictures N.V.* v. *Osborne* [1967] 1 W.L.R. 723.

brief, at the interlocutory stage the court has to make a decision when the existence of the right or the violation of it or both is uncertain and will remain uncertain until final judgment is given in the action. The Court seeks to achieve a balance of justice, rather than of convenience. While the Court disregards fanciful claims, it must contemplate that either party may succeed and do its best to ensure that nothing occurs pending trial which will prejudice their rights. This is difficult because both parties are often asserting wholly inconsistent claims[22] Nevertheless the Court should attempt to hold the ring until a just decision on the validity of the claim can be made.[23]

11–37 **Arguable case.** At the hearing of the application for an interlocutory injunction the court must first be satisfied that the plaintiff has a real prospect of succeeding in his claim for a permanent injunction at the trial.[24] If the court is of the view that the claim is frivolous or vexatious an injunction will not be granted. The words "frivolous" and "vexatious" in this context are understood in a somewhat different sense than the same words are when used on an application to strike out a statement of claim or a defence as being frivolous or vexatious.[25] What the affidavit evidence must disclose is that there is a serious question to be tried and that the plaintiff has prospects of success which exist in substance and reality.[26] The plaintiff does not, as was formerly thought, have to establish that he has a strong prime facie case or a prima facie case or even a probability that he will succeed at the trial. The burden on the plaintiff is the lesser one of showing an arguable case to be tried.

It is not, however, sufficient for the plaintiff to establish that he has an honest, though virtually hopeless, claim.[27] It is clear that the Court has no power to grant an interlocutory injunction, except in protection or assertion of some legal or equitable right which it has jurisdiction to enforce by final judgment.[28] The injunction sought in the action must be part of the substantive relief to which the plaintiff's cause of action entitles him.

11–38 **Decision on motion.** Although the decision in the *American Cyanamid*[29] case had, as one of its objects, the shortening of applications for interlocutory injunctions, there may still be cases, particularly in the area of copyright and related rights, which are in effect decided on motion and where it is, accordingly, appropriate to hear full argument and give a decision on

---

[22] *Francome* v. *Mirror Group Newspaprs Ltd.* [1984] 1 W.L.R. 892.

[23] *Att.-Gen.* v. *Guardian Newspapers Ltd.* [1987] 1 W.L.R. 1248.

[24] See n. 21, *ante*.

[25] *Mothercare Ltd.* v. *Robson Books Ltd.* [1979] F.S.R. 466; *Mothercare U.K. Ltd.* v. *Penguin Books Ltd.* [1988] R.P.C. 113; *Grundy Television Pty Ltd.* v. *Startrain Ltd.* [1988] F.S.R. 581; *Scott Ltd.* v. *Nice-Pak Products Ltd.* [1988] F.S.R. 125; *cf. John Walker & Sons* v. *Rothmans International Ltd.* [1978] F.S.R. 357.

[26] See n. 25, *ante*.

[27] See n. 25, *ante*.

[28] *Siskina* v. *Distos Compania Naviera S.A.* [1979] A.C. 210 at 256.

[29] See n. 21, *ante*.

the merits.[30] There is nothing in the decision in *American Cyanamid*[31] to suggest that, in considering whether or not to grant an interlocutory injunction, the judge ought not to give full weight to the practical realities of the situation to which the injunction will apply.[32] On the facts, the House of Lords in *American Cyanamid*[33] was not dealing with a case in which the grant or refusal of an injunction at that stage would, in effect, dispose of the action finally in favour of whichever party was successful in the application, because there would be nothing left on which it was in the interests of the unsuccessful party to proceed to trial. Where the grant or refusal of the interlocutory injunction will have the practical effect of putting an end to the action because the harm that will have already been caused to a losing party by its grant or refusal is complete and of a kind for which money cannot constitute any worthwhile recompense, the degree of likelihood that the plaintiff would have succeeded in establishing his right to an injunction, if the action had gone to trial, is a factor to be brought into the balance by the judge in weighing the risks that injustice may result from his deciding the application one way rather than the other.[34]

Furthermore, in a substantial number of cases of infringement of copyright and related rights, there is no substantial dispute on the facts. All the essential facts are ascertained at the hearing of the motion, and, in those circumstances, it is permissible for the court to see whether the plaintiff has a strong prima facie case and whether there is a reasonably good answer. Many cases of this kind are, in effect, decided on motion because the grant or refusal of the injunction is decisive of the action and disposes of the dispute.[35]

Adequacy of Damages. If the court is satisfied that the plaintiff's claim   **11–39**
raises a serious question to be tried, it then goes on to consider whether its decision should be in favour of granting or refusing the injunction sought.

The governing principle is that the Court should first consider whether, if the plaintiff were to succeed in his claim for a permanent injunction at the trial, he would be adequately compensated by an award of damages

---

[30] *Thomas Marshall (Exports) Ltd.* v. *Guinle* [1979] Ch. 227; *Dunford* v. *Elliott Ltd.* v. *Johnston & Firth Brown Ltd.* [1978] F.S.R. 143 (breach of confidence); *Newsweek Inc.* v. *B.B.C.* [1979] R.P.C. 441 (passing off); *Office Overload Ltd.* v. *Gunn* [1977] F.S.R. 39 (restrictive convenant prima facie valid—injunction granted): *Revlon Inc. & Ors.* v. *Cripps & Lee Ltd.* [1980] F.S.R. 85 (passing off—no plausible cause of action—injunction refused); *Tetrosyle Ltd.* v. *Silver Paint & Lacquer Co. Ltd.* [1980] F.S.R. 68. *cf. Alfred Dunhill Ltd.* v. *Sunoptic S.A.* [1979] F.S.R. 337; *Lawrence David Ltd.* v. *Ashton* [1989] F.S.R. 87; *B.B.C.* v. *Talbot Motor Co. Ltd.* [1981] F.S.R. 228; *Biba Group Ltd.* v. *Biba Boutique* [1980] R.P.C. 413; *Rizla Ltd.* v. *Bryant & May Ltd.* [1986] R.P.C. 389; *Elan Digital Systems Ltd.* v. *Elan Computers Ltd.* [1984] F.S.R. 373; *CPC (United Kingdom) Ltd.* v. *Keenan* [1986] F.S.R. 527 at 530; *Nationwide Building Society* v. *Nationwide Estate Agents Ltd.* [1987] F.S.R. 579 at 585; *The Duriron Co. Inc.* v. *Hugh Jennings & Co. Ltd.* [1984] F.S.R. 1; *Associated Newspaper Group plc* v. *News Group Newspapers Ltd.* [1986] R.P.C. 515; *Marcus Publishing plc* v. *Hutton-Wild Communications Ltd.* [1990] R.P.C. 576.
[31] See n. 21, *ante*.
[32] *N.W.L. Ltd.* v. *Woods* [1979] 1 W.L.R. 1294; *Eng Mee Yong* v. *V. Letchumanan* [1980] A.C. 331; *Lawrence David Ltd.* v. *Ashton* [1989] F.S.R. 87; *Cambridge Nutrition Ltd.* v. *B.B.C.* [1990] 3 All E.R. 523.
[33] See n. 21, *ante*.
[34] See n. 32, *ante*.
[35] See n. 30 and 32, *ante*.

for the loss he would have sustained before the trial as a result of the continuing acts of the defendant. If damages in the measure recoverable at common law, including additional damages,[36] would be an adequate remedy and the defendant would be in a financial position to pay them, or if there is no substantial risk of damage to the plaintiff at all, the Court will normally refuse to grant an interim injunction, however strong the plaintiff's claim appeared then to be.[37] The mere fact that damages may be unquantifiable is not of itself a reason for granting an injunction.[38] The Court asks itself "what good will be done to the plaintiff by the grant of the injunction?"[39]

If, damages would not provide an adequate remedy for the plaintiff in the event of his succeeding at the trial, the Court then goes on to consider whether the defendant, if he were to succeed at the trial, would be adequately compensated under the plaintiff's cross undertaking in damages for the loss which the defendant would have sustained before the trial by being prevented from doing the acts sought to be restrained. If damages in the measure recoverable under the undertaking would be an adequate remedy and the plaintiff would be in a financial position to pay them, there would be no reason upon that ground for refusing an interlocutory injunction.[40]

It may be observed, at this point, that in actions for infringement of copyright and related rights, damages are often not an adequate remedy since there are difficulties both in ascertaining and in quantifying such damage as injury to the plaintiff's property, business, commercial opportunity, reputation and goodwill.[41]

11–40 **Balance of convenience.** If the Court is in doubt as to the adequacy of the respective remedies in damages available to either the plaintiff or the defendant or both, the question of the balance of convenience arises. The expression "balance of convenience" may be an unfortunate one and "balance of justice" a better one because the Courts' business is "justice, not convenience."[42] The Court considers the potential injustice to the plaintiff if the injunction is withheld and the potential injustice to the defendant if the injunction is granted. The course to be taken is that which would involve the least risk of ultimate injustice, having regard to the actual and potential rights and liabilities of the parties on both sides.[43] In *American Cyanamid*[44] the House of Lords laid down certain guidelines for

---

[36] *Mondaress Ltd.* v. *Bourne & Hollingsworth Ltd.* [1981] F.S.R. 118.

[37] *American Cyanamid Co.* v. *Ethicon Ltd.* [1975] A.C. 396; *British Association of Aesthetic Plastic Surgeons* v. *Cambright Ltd.* [1987] R.P.C. 549.

[38] *The Boots Co. Ltd.* v. *Approved Prescription Services Ltd.* [1988] F.S.R. 45

[39] *Hadmor Productions Ltd.* v. *Hamilton* [1983] 1 A.C. 191 at 224.

[40] See n. 37, *ante.*

[41] *Elanco Products Ltd.* v. *Mandops (Agrochemical Specialists) Ltd.* [1979] F.S.R. 46; *Mothercare Ltd.* v. *Robson Books Ltd.* [1979] F.S.R. 446; *Rolls Royce Motors Ltd. & Anor.* v. *Zanelli & Ors.* [1979] R.P.C. 148; *cf. Roussel Uclaf* v. *G. D. Searle & Co. Ltd.* [1977] F.S.R. 125; *News Group Newspapers Ltd.* v. *The Rocket Record Co. Ltd.* [1981] F.S.R. 89 at 106.

[42] *Francome* v. *Mirror Group Newspapers Ltd.* [1984] 1 W.L.R. 892 at 899.

[43] *Fleming Fabrications Ltd.* v. *Albion Cylinders Ltd.* [1989] R.P.C. 47; *Mail Newspapers plc* v. *Express Newspapers plc* [1987] F.S.R. 90.

[44] [1975] A.C. 396.

the exercise of the court's discretion. These guidelines should not be regarded as rigid rules.[45] There are in fact many matters to be taken into consideration in deciding where the balance of convenience lies. The various factors and the relative weight to be attached to them will vary from case to case. The decision to grant or to refuse an interlocutory injunction will often cause, to whichever party is unsuccessful on the application, some disadvantages which his ultimate success at the trial may show he ought to have been spared and damages may not be sufficient to compensate him fully for all those disadvantages.[46] In assessing where the balance of convenience lies, one significant factor is the extent to which the disadvantages of each party would be incapable of being compensated in damages. If, for example, the extent of uncompensatable damage to each party would not differ widely, the Court may take into account the relative strength of each party's case as revealed by the affidavit evidence adduced on the hearing of the application.[47] This is, however, the last and not the first factor to be taken into consideration. It is only at this stage that the Court is entitled to consider whether there is a substantial disparity on the merits and which party is more likely to succeed. The Court is not justified, even at this stage, in embarking on anything resembling a preliminary trial of the action upon conflicting affidavits in order to evaluate the strength of each party's case. There may be cases in which it is apparent on the evidence that there is no credible dispute that the strength of one party's case is disproportionate to that of the other party. Generally, however, the procedure on interlocutory applications is not appropriate to an inquiry into disputed facts.[48]

Status quo. Where other factors appear to be evenly balanced, the court **11–41** will usually take such measures as are calculated to preserve the status quo. If, on the one hand, the defendant is enjoined temporarily from doing something which he has not done before, the only effect of the interlocutory injunction in the event of his succeeding at the trial is to postpone the date at which he is able to embark on a course of action which he has not previously found it necessary to undertake. If, on the other hand, the defendant is interrupted in the conduct of an established enterprise, the injunction would cause much greater inconvenience to him since he would have to start again to establish it in the event of his succeeding at the trial.[49]

The preservation of the status quo particularly favours the grant of an injunction in those cases where the defendant has only just begun to do the act complained of and where he has no established business or his

---

[45] *Fellowes & Son* v. *Fisher* [1976] Q.B. 122; *Alfred Dunhill Ltd.* v. *Sunoptic S.A.* [1979] F.S.R. 337.
[46] *American Cyanamid Co.* v. *Ethicon Ltd.* [1975] A.C. 396.
[47] *Constable & Anor.* v. *Clarkson & Anor.* [1980] F.S.R. 123 at 126, 128; *The Quaker Oats Company* v. *Alltrades Distributors Ltd.* [1981] F.S.R. 9; *Cambridge Nutrition Ltd.* v. *B.B.C.* [1990] 3 All E.R. 523.
[48] *Ibid.* n.47.
[49] *American Cyanamid Co.* v. *Ethicon Ltd.*, *supra*.

sales and capital investment have been small, while the plaintiff has an established business.[50] In such cases it is often easier to calculate the damage which the defendant will suffer by reason of the injunction than it is to calculate the damage which will be done to the plaintiff if the defendant is not restrained. For example, it may be easier to calculate the expenditure thrown away by a defendant in printing and promoting a book, the publication of which is restrained by injunction, than it is to calculate the injury which will be done to the sales and goodwill of the plaintiff's existing book if publication by the defendant is not restrained.[51] The courts will generally, as a temporary measure, protect a long-established business against the activities of an interloper.[52]

The grant of an interim injunction will often be appropriate in a case of breach of confidence where, for example, a defendant raises a public interest defence which can only be determined at trial. If the information is published pending trial, the fair trial of the plaintiff's claim will be damaged because he will have lost irrevocably the right to have a confidence protected and damages are rarely an adequate remedy for the destruction of confidence. The effect of an interim injunction will simply be to postpone the time of publication without prejudicing the position of the defendant.[53]

There are, however, some cases in which the Courts will take the view that the damage to the plaintiff can be readily calculated by reference to the sales made by the defendant and that the damage which would be done to the defendant by preventing him from getting a foot in the market as soon as possible is not easily quantifiable.[54] The defendant may undertake to keep an account of his sales.[55] Where there is only a risk of unquantifiable damage to the plaintiff and a certainty of unquantifiable damage to the defendant the Court will often refuse to maintain the status

---

[50] *Elanco Products Ltd.* v. *Mandops (Agrochemical Specialists) Ltd.* [1979] F.S.R. 46; *Polydor Ltd.* v. *Harlequin Record Shop Ltd.* [1980] 1 C.M.L.R. 669 at 676; *Sodastream Ltd.* v. *Thorn Cascade Co. Ltd.* [1982] R.P.C. 459; *Biba Group Ltd.* v. *Biba Boutique* [1980] R.P.C. 413; *Esanda Ltd.* v. *Esanda Finance Ltd.* [1984] F.S.R. 96 (High Court of New Zealand); *Mail Newspapers plc* v. *Insert Media Ltd.* [1987] R.P.C. 521; *Fleming Fabrications Ltd.* v. *Albion Cylinders Ltd.* [1989] R.P.C. 47; *Missing Link Software* v. *Magee* [1989] F.S.R. 361 at 368; *Alfa Laval Cheese Systems Ltd.* v. *Wincanton Engineering Ltd.* [1990] F.S.R. 583 at 594.

[51] *Mothercare Ltd.* v. *Robson Books Ltd.* [1979] F.S.R. 466.

[52] *Chill Foods (Scotland) Ltd.* v. *Cool Foods Ltd.* [1977] R.P.C. 522.

[53] *Francome* v. *Mirror Group Newspapers Ltd.* [1984] 1 W.L.R. 892; *Lion Laboratories Ltd.* v. *Evans* [1985] Q.B. 527 at 551; *Att.-Gen.* v. *Guardian Newspapers Ltd.* [1987] 1 W.L.R. 1248; *cf. Cambridge Nutrition Ltd.* v. *B.B.C.* [1990] 3 All E.R. 523.

[54] *Catnic Components Ltd.* v. *Stressline Ltd.* [1976] F.S.R. 157; *Kwik Lok Corporation* v. *W.B.W. Engineers Ltd.* [1975] F.S.R. 237; *Belfast Ropework Co. Ltd.* v. *Pixdane Ltd.* [1976] F.S.R. 337; *Temple Instruments Ltd.* v. *Hollis Heels Ltd.* [1973] R.P.C. 15; *Polaroid Corpn.* v. *Eastman Kodak Co.* [1976] F.S.R. 530; [1977] F.S.R. 25 (C.A.); *Netlon* v. *Bridport-Gundry* [1979] F.S.R. 530; *Hunter* v. *Fitzroy Robinson & Partners* [1978] F.S.R 167; *Potters-Ballotini Ltd.* v. *Weston Baker* [1977] R.P.C. 202; *Corruplast Ltd.* v. *George Harrison (Agencies) Ltd.* [1978] R.P.C. 761; *Taverner Rutledge Ltd.* v. *Trexapalm Ltd.* [1977] R.P.C. 275; *The Boots Co. Ltd.* v. *Approved Prescription Services Ltd.* [1988] F.S.R. 45; *John Wyeth & Bro. Ltd.* v. *M. & A. Pharmachem* [1988] F.S.R. 26.

[55] *Catnic Compenents Ltd.* v. *Stressline Ltd.* [1976] F.S.R. 157 at 160, 163; *Concrete Systems* v. *Devon Symonds Holdings* [1978] S.A.S.R. 79.

quo and dismiss a claim for an injunction.[56] One course taken by the Court in such cases is to grant or refuse an injunction and order a speedy trial of the action.[57]

The time factor. One problem which has arisen in determining the status **11–42** quo is the fixing of the relevant time. It appears that this may well vary in different cases. It has been suggested[58] that the relevant date for determining the status quo may variously be the date on which the defendant first did the offending act, or the date on which the plaintiff first learned of that act, or the date on which the plaintiff first ought to have been aware of the defendant's act, or the date when the plaintiff first complained to the defendant, or the date when the plaintiff sent his letter before action or the date when the plaintiff issued his writ. There is much to be said in favour of the view that the status quo to be preserved by an injunction is that state of affairs which existed before the defendant first began to do the act which the plaintiff seeks to restrain by injunction.[59]

Ability to pay damages. The Court will take into account the fact that **11–43** the defendant might not be in a financial position to meet a claim for substantial damages against him and that the plaintiff is likely to suffer damage in excess of what the defendant can pay him.[60] Conversely, the Court will take into account the ability or otherwise of the plaintiff to compensate the defendant on the cross undertaking in damages.[61] The mere fact that a party is of slender means is not, however, conclusive of the grant or refusal of an injunction.[62] The Court will be particularly careful to consider these matters where the parties are limited companies and where the plaintiff is an individual normally resident outside the jurisdiction. In appropriate cases the Court may order the plaintiff's cross undertaking in damages to be fortified by security such as the deposit of a stipulated sum in court or the provision of a bond or bank guarantee from a substantial person or company with assets in the jurisdiction[63] or payment into a joint account.[64]

---

[56] *John Walker & Sons Ltd.* v. *Rothmans International Ltd.* [1978] F.S.R. 357; *Unidoor Ltd.* v. *Marks & Spencer plc* [1988] R.P.C. 275.

[57] *Lawrence David Ltd.* v. *Ashton* [1989] F.S.R. 87; *Johnson & Bloy (Holdings) Ltd.* v. *Wolstenholme Rink plc* [1989] F.S.R. 135. (both cases where an injunction was granted to enforce a restrictive covenant or obligation of confidence by ex-employees, pending a speedy trial); *Alfa Laval Cheese Systems Ltd.* v. *Wincanton Engineering Ltd.* [1990] F.S.R. 583 at 594.

[58] *Alfred Dunhill Ltd.* v. *Sunoptic S.A.* [1979] F.S.R. 337; see *Alfa Laval Cheese Systems Ltd.* v. *Wincanton Engineering Ltd., supra,* at 594.

[59] *Metric Resources Corpn.* v. *Leasemetric Ltd.* [1979] F.S.R. 571; *John Walker & Sons Ltd.* v. *Rothmans International Ltd.* [1978] F.S.R. 357; *Consorzio del Prosciutto di Parma* v. *Marks & Spencer plc* [1990] F.S.R. 530 at 541.

[60] *Missing Link Software* v. *Magee* [1989] F.S.R. 361 at 368.

[61] *Morning Star Co-operative Society Ltd.* v. *Express Newspapers Ltd.* [1979] F.S.R. 113.

[62] *Apple Corps Ltd.* v. *Lingasong Ltd.* [1977] F.S.R. 345.

[63] *Anton Piller K.G.* v. *Manufacturing Processes Ltd.* [1976] R.P.C. 719; *J. C. Penney Co. Inc.* v. *Penneys Ltd.* [1975] R.P.C. 367; *Harman Pictures N.V.* v. *Osborne* [1967] 1 W.L.R. 723; *Globelgance B.V.* v. *Sarkissian* [1974] R.P.C. 603.

[64] *Vernon & Co. (Pulp Products) Ltd.* v. *Universal Pulp Containers Ltd.* [1980] F.S.R. 179 at 191; *CPC (United Kingdom) Inc.* v. *Keenan* [1986] F.S.R. 527 at 536; *Brupat Ltd.* v. *Sandford Marine Products Ltd.* [1983] R.P.C. 61 at 67.

11–44 **Other relevant considerations.** None of the above-mentioned are rigid rules for the exercise of what is essentially a flexible discretionary jurisdiction.[65] The application of the above principles does present certain difficulties to the Courts, particularly the requirement that the prospects of success in the action have apparently to be disregarded except as a last resort when the balance of convenience is otherwise even. In many classes of case, particularly infringement of copyright and related rights, the judge is able to make a realistic assessment of the prospects of success and, indeed, the judge's decision is often taken by the parties as a sufficient indication of the probable outcome of the action. In some cases it is necessary for the Court to make an estimate of the relative strength of each party's case and *American Cyanamid* [66] permits the Court to do this in those cases where there are no essential facts in dispute or where the decision on the application will in fact be decisive of the action.[67]

It must further be borne in mind that there are many other factors varying from case to case which will influence the Court's decision to grant or withhold an interlocutory injunction. For example, in some cases the Court has held it against a defendant, in granting an injunction, that the defendant has walked into an existing situation with his eyes open and has taken a calculated risk. The Court has also held it against such a defendant that there has been no conduct by a plaintiff leading the defendant to suppose that his acts would be tolerated and that the defendant could have readily anticipated that the plaintiff would object.[68] The Court will discount obligations incurred by the plaintiff with a view to bolstering up his case on the balance of convenience.[69] On the other hand, it has been held against a plaintiff, where the court has refused to grant an injunction, that the effect of the injunction would be disastrous to the defendant and disrupt his business,[70] even though it appears that the defendant has acted in a surreptitious way in the manner that he has gone about establishing his business.[71] The fact that an interim injunction might drive a defendant into liquidation may be irrelevant if all the other matters to which attention is directed in *American Cyanamid (supra)* are satisfied.[72] The 1988 Act repeals section 17(4) of the 1956 Act which provided that, in an action for

---

[65] *Fellowes & Son* v. *Fisher* [1976] Q.B. 122; *Alfred Dunhill Ltd.* v. *Sunoptic S.A.* [1979] F.S.R. 337.

[66] [1975] A.C. 396.

[67] *Thomas Marshall (Exports) Ltd.* v. *Guinle* [1979] Ch. 227; *Dunford & Elliott Ltd.* v. *Johnston & Firth Brown Ltd.* [1978] F.S.R. 143; *Newsweek Inc.* v. *B.B.C.* [1979] R.P.C. 441; *Office Overload Ltd.* v. *Gunn* [1977] F.S.R. 39; *cf. Alfred Dunhill Ltd.* v. *Sunoptic S.A.* [1979] F.S.R. 337; *Cambridge Nutrition Ltd.* v. *B.B.C.* [1990] 3 All E.R. 523. See n.30 *supra.*

[68] *Hymac* v. *Priestman Bros. Ltd.* [1978] R.P.C. 495; *Netlon* v. *Bridport* [1979] F.S.R. 530; *News Group Newspapers Ltd.* v. *The Rocket Record Co. Ltd.* [1981] F.S.R. 89 at 107; *B.B.C.* v. *Talbot Motor Co. Ltd.* [1981] F.S.R. 228; *Elida Gibbs Ltd.* v. *Colgate-Palmolive Ltd.* [1983] F.S.R. 95; *Elan Digital Systems Ltd.* v. *Elan Computers Ltd.* [1984] F.S.R. 373; *Reckitt & Colman Products Inc.* v. *Borden Inc.* [1987] F.S.R. 228 at 240; *Consorzio del Prosciutto di Parma* v. *Marks & Spencer* p.l.c. [1990] F.S.R. 530 at 541.

[69] *Raindrop Data Systems Ltd.* v. *Systemics Ltd.* [1988] F.S.R. 354.

[70] *Fison Ltd.* v. *E. J. Godwin (Peat) Industries Ltd.* [1976] R.P.C. 653; *Baskin Robbins Ice Cream Co.* v. *Gutman* [1976] F.S.R. 545.

[71] *Potters-Ballotini* v. *Weston Baker* [1977] R.P.C. 202.

[72] *Roger Bullivant Ltd.* v. *Ellis* [1987] F.S.R. 172. *cf. Raindrop Data Systems Ltd.* v. *Systemics Ltd.* [1988] F.S.R. 354.

infringement of copyright in respect of the construction of a building, no injunction should be made after construction of the building had begun so as to prevent it from being completed, or so as to require the building, in so far as it had been constructed, to be demolished.[73]

The Court's discretion may also be affected by well settled rules of practice. For example, the court will not grant an injunction to restrain publication of statements alleged to be untrue, but which the defendant intends to justify at trial.[74] The interests of the public in general may also be taken into account in the exercise of the Court's discretion.[75]

Cross undertaking in damages. At the time of the application for an   **11–45** interlocutory injunction it is not possible for the Court to be absolutely certain that the plaintiff will succeed at the trial in establishing his legal right to restrain the defendant from doing what he is threatening to do or has started to do. If he should fail to do so, the defendant may have suffered loss as a result of having been prevented from doing what he was entitled to do while the interlocutory injunction was in force. The Courts have therefore established a means of providing the defendant with compensation for his loss in order to mitigate the injustice that may be done to him. It is in order to mitigate the risk of this loss that the Court will normally refuse to grant an interlocutory injunction unless the plaintiff is willing to furnish an undertaking by himself or by some other willing and responsible person "to abide by any order the court may make as to damages in case the court shall hereafter be of opinion that the defendant shall have sustained any damages by reason of this order which the plaintiff ought to pay."[76] The same is true on *ex parte* applications.[77] A plaintiff should specifically depose in his affidavit to information relevant to his ability to meet his liability on the cross undertaking.[78]

The court has no power to compel an applicant for an interlocutory injunction to furnish an undertaking as to damages. All that the court can do is to refuse the application if the plaintiff declines to do so. The undertaking is not given to the defendant, but is given to the court itself which exacts the undertaking for the defendant's benefit. The cross undertaking is not a matter of contract between the parties and an award of damages on such undertaking is not a tort or a breach of contract.[79] The Court retains a discretion not to enforce the undertaking if it considers that the conduct of the plaintiff in relation to the obtaining or continuing of the injunction or the enforcement of the undertaking makes it inequitable to do so. If the undertaking is enforced, the measure of damages payable under it is not discretionary. It is assessed as on an inquiry as to damages

---

[73] See *Hunter* v. *Fitzroy Robinson & Partners and Others* [1978] F.S.R. 167.

[74] *Sim* v. *Heinz (H.J.) Co. Ltd.* [1959] 1 W.L.R. 313; *Bestobell Paints Ltd.* v. *Biggs* [1975] F.S.R. 421; *Lord Brabourne* v. *Hough* [1981] F.S.R. 79; *Western Front Ltd.* v. *Vestron Inc.* [1987] F.S.R. 66; *Consorzio del Prosciutto di Parma* v. *Marks & Spencer p.l.c.* [1990] F.S.R. 530 at 536; see §21–23 n.61, *post*.

[75] *R.* v. *Secretary of State for Transport, Ex p. Factortame Ltd (No. 2)* [1990] 3 W.L.R. 818; *Cambridge Nutrition Ltd.* v. *B.B.C.* [1990] 3 All E.R. 523.

[76] *Hoffmann-La Roche & Co. A.G.* v. *Secretary of State for Trade and Industry* [1975] A.C. 295.

[77] *Vapormatic Co. Ltd.* v. *Sparex Ltd.* [1976] 1 W.L.R. 939.

[78] *Brigid Foley Ltd.* v. *Elliott* [1982] R.P.C. 433.

[79] *Fletcher Sutcliffe Wild Ltd.* v. *Burch* [1982] F.S.R. 64.

upon the same basis as that upon which damages for breach of contract would be assessed if the undertaking had been a contract between the plaintiff and the defendant that the plaintiff would not prevent the defendant from doing that which he was restrained from doing by the terms of the injunction.[80] If the injunction is discharged, an immediate inquiry on the cross undertaking may be ordered.[81] A claim for damages in respect of the cross undertaking should not be pleaded by way of counterclaim before the Court has decided whether or not the interim injunction should continue permanently and, if not, whether damages should be ordered to be paid on the cross undertaking.[82]

The cross undertaking is automatically implied, both in cases of the grant of an injunction and also on the giving of an undertaking to the court by the defendant.[83]

Where the Crown is seeking an interim injunction to enforce what is prima facie the law of the land, as opposed to its private proprietary rights, the persons against whom the Crown seeks the injunction are required to show good reason why the Crown should be required to give the undertaking as a condition of being granted the interlocutory injunction.[84]

11–46 **Procedure.** An interlocutory injunction is usually granted upon application by motion in the Chancery Division[85] or by summons to the Judge in Chambers in the Queen's Bench Division. Actions for infringement of copyright and related rights ought usually to be brought in the Chancery Division.[86] The evidence is given by affidavit. The Court does not demand perfection as to the evidence on interlocutory applications.[87] The plaintiff must show that the case is of some urgency, particularly where the application is for *ex parte* relief.[88] The applicant may seek *quia timet* relief, for example, in cases where publication of an infringing work is threatened. The affidavit evidence should deal with questions as to what damage the plaintiff would suffer if the injunction is refused and what damage the defendant will suffer if the injunction is granted and it is now common for evidence to be filed as to the respective financial means of the plaintiff and the defendant.[89] On an *ex parte* application it is now usual for the defendant to be informally notified of the application, to be present at the hear-

---

[80] *Hoffmann-La Roche & Co. A.G.* v. *Secretary of State for Trade and Industry* [1975] A.C. 295; *Novello* v. *James* (1854) 24 L.J. Ch. 111.

[81] *Lock International plc* v. *Beswick* [1989] 1 W.L.R. 1268.

[82] See n. 79, *ante*.

[83] *Catnic Components Ltd.* v. *Bainbridge Bros. (Engineers) Ltd.* [1976] F.S.R. 112.

[84] *Hoffman-La Roche & Co. A.G.* v. *Secretary of State for Trade and Industry, supra.*

[85] For a form of Notice of Motion, see § G–12, *post*.

[86] *Swedac Ltd.* v. *Magnet & Southerns plc* [1989] F.S.R. 243; *McCain International Ltd.* v. *Country Fair Foods Ltd.* [1981] R.P.C. 69 at 82, 83; and see Supreme Court Act 1981 (c.54) Sched. 1, as amended by C.D.P.A. 1988, Sched. 7 para. 28

[87] *British Northrop Ltd.* v. *Texteam Blackburn Ltd.* [1974] R.P.C. 57 at 71; *Merchant Adventurers Ltd.* v. *M. Grew & Co. Ltd.* [1973] R.P.C. 1 at 10; *Cavendish House (Cheltenham) Ltd.* v. *Cavendish Woodhouse Ltd.* [1970] R.P.C. 234. As to what constitutes "without prejudice" evidence see *Chocoladefabriken Lindt & Sprungli A.G.* v. *The Nestle Co. Ltd.* [1978] R.P.C. 287.

[88] For a form of *ex parte* Order, see § G–13, *post*.

[89] *Standex International Ltd.* v. *C.B. Blades* [1976] F.S.R. 114.

ing and to take part in it in order to assist the court,[90] although by taking part he runs the risk of being made liable for costs. On an *ex parte* application, the applicant is under a duty to make full and frank disclosure of all relevant facts.[91] This includes facts which the applicant would have known if he had made proper inquiries before making the application. The extent of the inquiries depends on the nature of the case, the order sought, the probable effect of the order on the defendant, the time available and all other circumstances. If full disclosure is not made, any injunction granted *ex parte* will be discharged so as to deprive the plaintiff of any advantage obtained by breach of duty and to deter others from acting in breach of duty though, in cases where the failure to disclose was innocent, that does not prevent the applicant from making a further application with full disclosure on notice to the other side.[92] The existence of a motion for an interim injunction does not excuse the plaintiff from serving a statement of claim in the usual way.[93]

On appeal from a judge's grant of refusal of an interlocutory injunction the function of the appellate court is not to exercise an independent discretion of its own. It must not interfere with the judge's exercise of his discretion merely on the ground that its members would have exercised the discretion differently. Before the judge's exercise of his discretion is set aside it must be shown that it was based on a misunderstanding of the law or evidence, or that it was so aberrant that no reasonable judge could have reached that conclusion, or that there has been a subsequent change of circumstances.[94]

Where the injunction granted restrains the defendant from infringing the "plaintiff's copyright," subsistence and ownership of the copyright claimed by the plaintiff are assumed.[95]

Costs of motions. The costs of any motion or summons for an interlocutory injunction are in the discretion of the court.[96] If an injunction is granted the court may order costs to be costs in the cause,[97] though the more usual order is for plaintiff's costs in the cause. Similarly, where an injunction is refused, the court will usually order the costs to be defendant's costs in the cause, though it may order costs in the cause where it **11–47**

---

[90] *Pickwick International Inc. (G.B.) Ltd.* v. *Multiple Sound Distributors Ltd.* [1972] 1 W.L.R. 1213; *Hunter Partners* v. *Wellings Partners* [1987] F.S.R. 83.

[91] *R.* v. *Kensington Income Tax Commissioners, Ex. parte Princess Edmond de Polignac* [1917] 1 Q.B. 486, 509; *Brink's Mat Ltd.* v. *Elcombe* [1988] 1 W.L.R. 1350.

[92] See *Polydor Ltd. & Anor.* v. *Harlequin Record Shops Ltd. & Anor.* [1980] F.S.R. 26 at 31; *Yardley & Co. Ltd.* v. *Higson* [1984] F.S.R. 304; *Bank Mallat* v. *Nikpour* [1985] F.S.R. 87; *Lloyds Bowmaker Ltd.* v. *Britannia Arrow Holdings PLC* [1988] 1 W.L.R. 1337; *Dormeuil Frères S.A.* v. *Nicolian International (Textiles) Ltd.* [1988] 1 W.L.R. 1362; *Ali and Fahd Shobokshi Group Ltd.* v. *Moneim* [1989] 1 W.L.R. 710; *Manor Electronics Ltd.* v. *Dickson* [1988] R.P.C. 618.

[93] *Hytrac Conveyors Ltd.* v. *Conveyors International Ltd.* [1983] F.S.R. 63; but see *Greek City Co. Ltd.* v. *Demetriou* [1983] F.S.R. 442.

[94] *Hadmor Productions Ltd.* v. *Hamilton* [1983] 1 A.C. 191.

[95] *Spectravest Inc.* v. *Aperknit Ltd.* [1988] F.S.R. 165; *Video Arts Ltd.* v. *Paget Industries Ltd.* [1988] F.S.R. 501, *cf. Staver Co. Inc.* v. *Digitext Display Ltd.* [1985] F.S.R. 512. See §G–12 *post* n. 66.

[96] See *Woodcock* v. *Denton Tackle Co. Ltd. & Marlow* [1978] F.S.R. 548 and see R.S.C. O.62 r. 3; *Kickers International S.A.* v. *Paul Kettle Agencies Ltd.* [1990] F.S.R. 436.

[97] *Steepleglade* v. *Stratford Investments Ltd.* [1976] F.S.R. 3.

considers the matter to be finely balanced.[98] If an injunction is refused after an "opposed" *ex parte* hearing the court may order the plaintiff to pay the costs.[99] In those cases where a motion is stood over to the trial on the application of the plaintiff before he has opened his motion, the court will usually reserve the costs to the trial judge.[1] Where, however, the plaintiff has opened his motion, he must either continue to move it and take the consequences or, if he does not wish to continue to move it, he must abandon it and pay the costs.[2] It appears that on the plaintiff's application to stand over a motion to the trial of the action the court has a discretion, though it has been held, in some cases, that the plaintiff is entitled to have his motion stood over to the trial as a matter of right, provided that he makes the application before he has begun to open his motion.[3] The plaintiff may also elect to save his motion.[4]

(ii) Anton Piller Orders[5]

11–48 In certain cases the High Court has an inherent jurisdiction, on an application made to the court by a plaintiff *ex parte* and *in camera*, to make a mandatory order requiring a defendant to permit or allow the plaintiff and his representatives to enter the defendant's premises, as specified in the order, so as to inspect articles and documents relevant to the proceedings and to remove them or take copies of them[6] and even to take the proceeds of infringing articles.[7] The person against whom the order is made must be a party to the proceedings.[8] The order does not authorise the plaintiff or his solicitors or anyone else to enter the premises unlawfully against the will of the defendant. It is not a search warrant; the order only authorises entry and inspection by permission of the defendant. The defendant therefore has the safeguard that the plaintiff or his agents must get his permission before entry onto the premises. Entry without his permission would be a trespass. The defendant is, however, ordered by the Court *in*

---

[98] *Cornelis Mania Franciscan Kenolis* v. *Tetro Style Ltd.* [1976] F.S.R. 3.

[99] *Pickwick International Inc. G.B. Ltd.* v. *Multiple Sound Distributors Ltd.* [1972] 1 W.L.R. 1213.

[1] *Simon Jeffrey Ltd.* v. *Shelana Fashions Ltd* [1977] R.P.C. 103; *Société Francaise D'Applications Commerciale et Industrielle SARL* v. *Electronic Concepts Ltd.* [1977] R.P.C. 106; *John Lang & Co. Ltd.* v. *Gold Star Publications Ltd.* [1967] F.S.R. 75; *Woodcock* v. *Denton Tackle Co. Ltd.* [1978] F.S.R. 548; *Gloverall Ltd.* v. *Durworth Ltd.* [1976] F.S.R. 543; see also *Simons Records Ltd.* v. *WEA Records Ltd.* [1980] F.S.R. 35; *Kickers International S.A.* v. *Paul Kettle Agencies Ltd.* (*supra*) at 438.

[2] *Pictograph Ltd.* v. *Lee Smith* [1964] R.P.C. 371; see also *Kickers International S.A.* v. *Paul Kettle Agencies Ltd.* [1990] F.S.R. 436 (where the costs of an abandoned motion were ordered to be paid by the plaintiff in any event and to be taxed forthwith).

[3] See n. 87 *ante*.

[4] *Max Factor Co.* v. *M.G.M.* [1983] F.S.R. 577.

[5] For a form of Order, see § G–14, *post*.

[6] *Anton Piller K.G.* v. *Manufacturing Processes Ltd. & ors.* [1976] Ch. 55; *E.M.I. Ltd.* v. *Pandit* [1976] R.P.C. 333; *Pall Europe Ltd.* v. *Microfiltrex Ltd.* [1976] R.P.C. 326; *Rank Film Distributors Ltd. & Ors.* v. *Video Information Centre & Ors.*, [1982] A.C. 380 *International Electronics Ltd.* v. *Weigh Data Ltd.*, *The Times*, March 13, 1980; *Gates* v. *Swift* [1981] F.S.R. 57; *Booker McConnell plc* v. *Plascow* [1985] R.P.C. 425; *Columbia Picture Industries Inc.* v. *Robinson* [1987] Ch. 38; *Manor Electronics Ltd.* v. *Dickson* [1988] R.P.C. 618; *Swedac Ltd.* v. *Magnet & Southerns plc* [1989] F.S.R. 243.

[7] *CBS United Kingdom Ltd.* v. *Lambert* [1983] Ch. 37.

[8] *AB* v. *CDE* [1982] R.P.C. 509; *EMI Records Ltd.* v. *Kudhail* [1985] F.S.R. 36.

personam to give his permission with the result that, if he does not do so, he is in contempt of court, but the plaintiff is still not entitled to enter in the absence of permission.

As part of the inspection order the court may also direct that there is no notification or publication of the judgment of the court until after service of the order and may direct that the defendant is not to disclose the subject -matter of the action or the plaintiff's interest therein, save for the purpose of obtaining legal advice. This direction is intended to prevent a defendant from alerting those suppliers from whom he has acquired infringing articles, or those customers to whom he has supplied infringing articles, as to what is happening.[9] The order of the Court normally contains an express provision that the defendant is entitled to apply to discharge the order although, with leave, he is also entitled to appeal against the order without first availing himself of the liberty to discharge it and even though the order has in fact been executed.[10] At the time of making the inspection order the court may also make an *ex parte* injunction in the usual form restraining the defendant from committing the alleged infringing acts. In an appropriate case the court may order the defendant to hand over to the plaintiff for safekeeping articles and documents. Any such articles and documents handed over should be retained by the plaintiff's solicitor in his safe custody.[11] The order thus operates as an order for discovery in advance of pleadings.[12]

Conditions for making order. An Anton Piller order is only made in the **11–49** most extreme circumstances, for the form of the order is drastic and its effects are far reaching. It involves serious inroads on principles of personal freedom, such as the presumption of innocence, the right not to be condemned unheard, protection against arbitrary searches and seizures and the privacy of the home. It is "at the extremity of the court's powers."[13] It is frequently accompanied by a Mareva injunction.[14] The combination of the two could have the effect of destroying a defendant's business without the defendant being in a position to set the order aside before it is executed.[15] This form of order has, in many copyright, confidence and passing off cases, proved to be one of great efficacy, because the defendant is taken completely by surprise before he is able to deal further with the documents and articles relating to the offending acts. The defendant knows nothing of the proceedings until he is required by the order to admit the plaintiff and his representatives to the premises. So effective have these orders been that the jurisdiction is now frequently exercised in cases of infringement of copyright,[16] passing off, infringement of patent,

---

[9] *Chanel Ltd.* v. *3 Pears Wholesale Cash & Carry Co.* [1979] F.S.R. 393.
[10] *Bestworth Ltd.* v. *Wearwell Ltd.* [1979] F.S.R. 320.
[11] *Universal City Studios Inc.* v. *Mukhler & Sons Ltd.* [1976] F.S.R. 252.
[12] *Crest Homes PLC* v. *Marks* [1987] A.C. 829 at 853.
[13] *Columbia Picture Industries Inc.* v. *Robinson* [1987] Ch 38; *Lock International plc* v. *Beswick* [1989] 1 W.L.R. 1268, at 1279; *Chappell* v. *United Kingdom* [1989] F.S.R. 617 (European Court of Human Rights—Anton Piller order not in breach of European Convention of Human Rights).
[14] See n. 46, *post.*
[15] See n. 13, *ante.*
[16] *Universal City Studies Inc.* v. *Mukhler, supra; Columbia Pictures Inc.* v. *Robinson* [1987] Ch. 38.

breach of confidence[17] and interference with business by unlawful means.[18] They have become "established weapons to combat copyright piracy."[19]

The justification for the exercise of this exceptional jurisdiction is that, on the facts of the particular case, it is essential that the plaintiff should have inspection, so that justice can be done between the parties where there is a grave danger that, if an unscrupulous defendant is forewarned, evidence of vital importance in the litigation will be destroyed or concealed from the court and from the plaintiff, or lost, or taken out of the jurisdiction, so that the plaintiff will be deprived of his remedy and the ends of justice thus defeated.[20] The fact that there is overwhelming evidence that a defendant has behaved wrongly does not justify an Anton Piller order. The making of an intrusive order *ex parte* even against a guilty defendant is contrary to normal principles of justice and can only be done where there is a paramount need to prevent a denial of justice to the plaintiff. "There must be proportionality between the perceived threat to the plaintiff's rights, and the remedy granted."[21] It must not be used as a means of finding out what claims can be made.[22]

Great care should be taken in the exercise of the jurisdiction and in the framing of the precise terms of the order to safeguard the defendant so as to ensure that no real harm is done to him and that his rights are respected. At one time the practice of the court allowed the balance to swing too far in favour of plaintiffs and Anton Piller orders were granted too readily with insufficient safeguards for defendants. This balance has now been corrected.[23] The order should be drawn so as to extend no further than the minimum extent necessary to achieve preservation of documents and articles which might otherwise be destroyed.[24]

Three conditions must be satisfied before the court will make an order: first, the plaintiff must show that he has an extremely strong prime facie case; secondly, the plaintiff must show that he has suffered, or is likely to suffer, very serious and irreparable damage if an order is not made; and, thirdly, there must be clear evidence that the defendant has in his possession incriminating documents or things and that there is a real possibility that he may destroy such material before any *inter partes* application can be made on notice.[25] The court proceeds on the basis that the overwhelming majority of people will comply with the court's orders as to pro-

---

[17] *Vapormatic Company Ltd.* v. *Sparex Ltd.* [1976] 1 W.L.R. 939; *Optical Coatings Ltd & Anor.* v. *Dan Fox & Ors.* (1980) C.A. (unreported); *Lock International plc* v. *Beswick* [1989] 1 W.L.R. 1268.

[18] *Carlin Music Corpn.* v. *Collins* [1979] F.S.R. 548; *Ex p. Island Records Ltd.* [1978] Ch. 122 at 145.

[19] *Columbia Picture Industries Inc.* v. *Robinson* [1987] Ch. 38; see, for example, *AB* v. *CDE* [1982] R.P.C. 509; *Wardle Fabrics Ltd.* v. *Myristis* [1984] F.S.R. 263.

[20] See n. 5, *ante*.

[21] *Lock International plc* v. *Beswick* [1989] 1 W.L.R.; *Columbia Picture Industries Inc.* v. *Robinson* [1987] Ch. 38, *cf. Booker McConnell plc* v. *Plascow* [1985] R.P.C. 425; *Dormeuil Frères S.A.* v. *Nicolian International (Textiles) Ltd.* [1988] 1 W.L.R. 1362; *Swedac Ltd.* v. *Magnet & Southerns plc* [1989] F.S.R. 243.

[22] *Hytrac Conveyors Ltd.* v. *Conveyors International Ltd.* [1983] F.S.R. 63.

[23] See n. 13, *ante*.

[24] See n. 13, *ante*.

[25] See n. 6, *ante*.

duction and delivery up of documents and will not make an order based on the "extravagent fears" of a person complaining of breach of copyright or confidence or passing off.[26]

In order to safeguard the defendant, the order expressly limits the persons who are entitled to inspect, defines the premises which can be inspected and specifies the purposes for which inspection is allowed. For example, the order normally requires that, on service of the order, the plaintiff's solicitor, who is an officer of the court, should be in attendance to explain the terms of the order to the defendant[27] and inform the defendant of his right to apply to have the order discharged. The solicitor who executes the order should make a detailed record of material removed before it is removed. No material should be taken unless it is clearly covered by the order. It is the solicitor's duty to ensure that the order is carried out with meticulous care and that he can give reliable evidence of what happens on execution of the order. He should identify the other representatives of the plaintiff to the defendant and must give the defendant an opportunity of considering the order and consulting his own solicitor. The evidence on which the order was obtained should be served with the order.[28] If the defendant wishes to apply to the Court to discharge the order as having been improperly obtained, he must be allowed to do so. The order should contain an express liberty to apply to vary or discharge the order on short notice. If the defendant refuses permission to enter the premises or to inspect documents and articles therein, the plaintiff and his agents must not force their way into the premises. They must accept the defendant's refusal and bring it to the notice of the court afterwards, if need be on application to commit the defendant. Further, the order will only normally be made in respect of precisely defined premises.[29] Only in special circumstances will a Court make an order describing the premises to be entered in general terms such as "any other premises under the control of the defendant" thus enabling the plaintiff to go and search anywhere that the defendant may have his premises. In the exercise of its discretion, the Court may decline to make such orders in respect of premises outside the jurisdiction, for example, in Scotland.[30]

Before making the order the Court should be satisfied, by specific evidence, that the plaintiff is good for any damages that might be ultimately awarded against him on the cross-undertaking in damages.[31] If an applicant fails to make full and frank disclosure of his financial position in connection with the cross-undertaking in damages, and other material matters, the defendant is entitled to have the order discharged even though it has been executed, subject to the court's discretion to maintain it, to claim damages on the cross-undertaking and for an order to return

---

[26] *Booker McConnell plc* v. *Plascow* [1985] R.P.C. 425 at 441.

[27] *VDU Installations Ltd.* v. *Integrated Computer Systems* [1989] F.S.R. 378.

[28] *International Electronics Ltd.* v. *Weigh Data Ltd., The Times,* March 13, 1980.

[29] *Protector Alarms Ltd.* v. *Maxim Alarms Ltd.* [1978] F.S.R. 442; *Cook Industries Inc.* v. *Galliher* [1979] Ch. 439; *Universal City Studios Inc.* v. *Mukhtar & Sons Ltd.* [1976] 2 All E.R. 330.

[30] See n. 29, *ante.*

[31] See n. 17, *ante.*

the material seized.[32] In deciding whether the defendant has suffered injustice as a result of the order, the Court takes into account the evidence brought to light by the order itself,[33] but failure to disclose relevant facts cannot be justified *ex post facto* by reference to material obtained on execution of the order showing impropriety on the part of the defendant.[34] In appropriate cases the court can require the cross-undertaking to be fortified by security in the form of deposited moneys in court, or the provision of a bank guarantee or bond in a stipulated sum.

As a matter of practice it is now usual for counsel for the plaintiff to put before the judge draft minutes of order which contain proper safeguards for the defendant. The applicant is under a duty to make full disclosure to the Court and to act in the utmost good faith.[35]

11–51 **Breach of order.** Whilst the order stands, the party who refuses access to his premises is in default of the order and he runs the risk of committal to prison even if his reason for refusal of consent is his intention to apply to have the order discharged.[36] However, if that party were to succeed in getting the order discharged, it is unlikely that he would be liable for any penalties for any breach of the order of which he may have been guilty while it subsisted.[37] There is no good ground for an immediate application for discharge if the only reason is to enforce the cross-undertaking in damages. That should be left to the trial.[38]

(iii) Identity of infringers

11–52 In an action for infringement of copyright or related rights, the court now frequently exercises its jurisdiction, on an application by motion or summons at an interlocutory stage in the action, to make an order requiring a defendant to make an affidavit setting out the names and addresses of the suppliers and purchasers of infringing material and articles known to him. He is also required to state in the affidavit the dates and quantities supplied, and to exhibit documents relating to supplies and purchases.[39] This is a valuable form of order because it enables the plaintiff in a copyright action, for example, to obtain from retailers of infringing goods details as to the wholesale or manufacturing sources of supply. The basis of the jurisdiction is that a person, whether he is himself an infringer, or has

---

[32] See n. 21, *ante.*

[33] *WEA Records Ltd.* v. *Visions Channel 4 Ltd.* [1983] 1 W.L.R. 721.

[34] *Manor Electronics Ltd.* v. *Dickson* [1988] R.P.C. 618.

[35] *Booker McConnell plc* v. *Plascow* [1985] R.P.C. 425; see also *Dormeuil Frères S.A.* v. *Nicolian International (Textiles) Ltd.* [1989] F.S.R. 255.

[36] See n. 7, *ante.*

[37] *Hallmark Cards Inc.* v. *Image Arts Ltd.* [1977] F.S.R. 150; *D. B. Baverstock* v. *Haycock* [1986] 1 NZLR 342; *Anvil Jewellery* v. *Riva Ridge Holdings* [1987] 1 NZLR 35. See as to penalties where there has been a breach, *Chanel Ltd.* v. *3 Pears Wholesale Cash & Carry Co.* [1979] F.S.R. 393.

[38] See n. 35, *ante.*

[39] *Radio Corporation of America* v. *Reddington's Rare Records* [1974] 1 W.L.R. 1445; *Harry Freedman* v. *Hillingdon Shirts Co. Ltd.* [1975] F.S.R. 449; *E.M.I. Ltd. & Anor.* v. *Sarwar* [1977] F.S.R. 146; *Loose* v. *Williamson* [1978] 1 W.L.R. 639; *E.M.I. Ltd. & Ors.* v. *Pandit* [1976] R.P.C. 333; *cf. Landi den Hartog B.V.* v. *Stoppe* [1976] F.S.R. 497 and *Terrell on Patents* (13th ed.), paras. 14.114 and 14.115.

become innocently involved without personal liability in the tortious acts of others, is under a duty to assist those injured by those acts to give full information by way of discovery and disclosure of the identity of the wrongdoers.[40] The application should be made promptly.[41] In appropriate cases, the disclosure of names of the defendant's customers may be limited to the plaintiff's advisers so as to protect the defendant from approaches to his customers by the plaintiff which would damage his goodwill or might amount to a misuse of confidential information.[42] Further, the defendant, if not a company, was entitled to claim privilege from giving discovery relating to the supply and sale of infringing copies on the ground that, by reason of the criminal offences in the 1956 Act he would tend to incriminate himself. Where the defendant was in genuine danger of self incrimination the court might abstain from making any order *ex parte* requiring immediate answers to questions or disclosure of documents.[43]

The frequent use of Anton Piller orders in proceedings for infringement   **11–53** of copyright coupled with orders to give discovery of names and addresses of suppliers and related documents gave rise to problems with the privilege against self incrimination. The circumstances in which infringement takes place frequently involves the commission of criminal offences or subjects the defendant to penalties. They may even involve a criminal conspiracy to defraud. In such cases, the defendant was able to claim the privilege against self incrimination to set aside an order for discovery or production of documents or information.[44]

In order to meet that situation the position as to the privilege against   **11–54** self incrimination was altered by the provisions of section 72 of the Supreme Court Act 1981 (as amended by Schedule 7 of the 1988 Act). The privilege has been withdrawn from a party and his or her spouse in the proceedings and circumstances specified in section 72. A person is not excused from answering questions put to him or from complying with an order by reason that to do so would tend to expose him or his or her spouse to proceedings for a related offence or the recovery of a related penalty. The withdrawal of the privilege applies to civil proceedings in the High Court for infringement of rights pertaining to any "intellectual property"—*i.e.* "patent, trademark, copyright, design right, registered design, technical or commercial information or other intellectual property"—or for passing off. It also applies to proceedings to obtain disclosure of information relating to the infringement of such a right.

---

[40] *Norwich Pharmacal Co.* v. *Customs and Excise Commissioners* [1974] A.C. 133; *British Steel Corp.* v. *Granada Television Ltd.* [1981] A.C. 1096; *X. Ltd* v. *Morgan-Grampian plc* [1990] 2 W.L.R. 1000.

[41] *Wilmot Breeden Ltd.* v. *Woodcock Ltd.* [1981] F.S.R. 15.

[42] *Kentron Properties Pty. Ltd.* v. *Jimmy's Co. Ltd.* [1979] F.S.R. 86 at 96.

[43] *Rank Film Distributors Ltd. & Ors.* v. *Video Information Centre & Ors.* [1982] A.C. 380; *International Electronics Ltd.* v. *Weigh Data Ltd.* (*supra*); *cf. Optical Coatings Ltd. & Anor.* v. *Dan Fox & Ors.* (1980) C.A. (unreported); *Lincoln International Ltd.* v. *Eagleton Direct Exports Ltd.* [1982] F.S.R. 161 (High Court of Hong Kong); *Snugkoat Ltd.* v. *Chaudhry* [1980] F.S.R. 286; *OCLI Optical Coatings Ltd.* v. *Spectron Optical Coatings Ltd.* [1980] F.S.R. 227. *cf. British Steel Corp.* v. *Granada Television Ltd.* (*supra*).

[44] *Rank Film Distributors Ltd.* v. *Video Information Centre* [1982] A.C. 380.

11–55   The defendant is, however, given the safeguard that no statement or admission by a person in answering a question or complying with an order is, in proceedings for a related offence, admissible against the person or his spouse. It is admissible in proceedings for perjury or contempt of court. A "related offence" is one which is committed by or in the course of the infringement or passing off to which the proceedings relate or "any offence" revealed by the facts on which the plaintiff relies in the proceedings. The effect of the definition of "related offence" is that it is only where there is a risk of further damage to the plaintiff that the defendant is denied the right to claim the privilege in respect of self incrimination for offences not committed by or in connection with the alleged infringement. The "related offence" is defined in different and much wider terms in the case of proceedings to prevent future torts than in the case of proceedings for past or present infringements.[45]

It is uncertain whether documents seized in execution of an Anton Piller order should be ordered to be returned to the defendant if he is entitled to rely on the privilege against self incrimination.

(iv) Mareva injunctions

11–56   The court also has a wide discretionary jurisdiction to make "Mareva" restraint and disclosure orders in respect of a defendant's assets both in and outside England and Wales and both before and after judgment, in order to prevent a defendant from taking action, such as disposal of assets, designed to frustrate subsequent orders of the court in favour of a plaintiff.[46]

C. Final relief

(i) Declaratory judgment

11–57   The Court will not make a declaratory order to the effect that copyright will subsist in documents not yet in existence, but which it is anticipated will be brought into existence. There must be before the court specific documents, the character of which can be established.[47] The Court will not make declarations of right amounting to conclusions of fact from hypothetical or assumed states of fact. There must be put before the Court evidence of an actual or intended infringement of copyright and the Court will not attempt an exhaustive enunciation of the factual circumstances in which infringement has or has not occurred.[48] The court will not normally grant on application for summary judgment a declaration that the plain-

---

[45] *Universal City Studios Inc.* v. *Hubbard* [1984] Ch. 225.
[46] s.37(1)–(3), Supreme Court Act 1981 (c.54); Supreme Court Practice Vol. 1. Notes to RSC Ord. 29, r. 1; *Siskina* v. *Distos Compania Naviera S.A.* [1979] A.C. 210; *Z Ltd.* v. *A-Z* [1982] Q.B. 558; *CBS U.K. Ltd.* v. *Lambert* [1983] Ch. 37; *Derby & Co. Ltd.* v. *Weldon* [1990] Ch. 48, 65. *Republic of Haiti* v. *Duvalier* [1990] Q.B. 202; *Brink's Mat Ltd.* v. *Elcombe* [1988] 1 W.L.R. 1350 (effect of non-disclosure on injunction). Form of order § G–15 *post.*
[47] *Odhams Press Ltd.* v. *London and Provincial Sporting News Agency, etc., Ltd.* [1936] Ch. 357.
[48] *Moorehouse & Angus Robertson (Publishers) Pty. Ltd.* v. *University of New South Wales* [1976] R.P.C. 51.

tiff's work does not infringe the defendant's work. A declaration as to non infringement is, like other forms of declaration, discretionary.[49]

(ii) Permanent injunction

If the plaintiff succeeds at the trial in establishing infringement of copy- **11–58** right, he will normally be entitled to a permanent injunction to restrain future infringements.[50] The question whether an injunction ought to be granted permanently is one which is determined by reference to the circumstances and state of the law existing at the date when the question falls to be determined and the court's consideration is not confined to those circumstances existing at the date of the writ.

Delay in taking proceedings. Delay,[51] unless explained, in making or **11–59** pursuing an application for an interlocutory injunction[52] is generally fatal, though the courts will balance the question of delay against the likelihood of the plaintiff ultimately succeeding in the action,[53] and will take into account whether or not the defendant has been led into expense, or lulled into security, or misled by the inaction of the plaintiff.[54] The question is whether the delay is culpable or unreasonable so as to make it unjust to grant the injunction sought. Delay is not prejudicial, for example, if it is explicable by attempts to settle the dispute.[55] A plaintiff is not precluded from asserting his rights, even by way of interlocutory injunction, merely because he has tolerated some acts which have infringed his rights.[56] The tendency of the Court is not to refuse an injunction at the hearing of the

---

[49] *Dellareed Ltd.* v. *Delkim Developments* [1988] F.S.R. 329.

[50] *P.R.S.* v. *Mitchell* [1924] 1 K.B. 762 at 774, *P.R.S.* v. *Berman* [1975] F.S.R. 400; *I.T.P. Ltd.* v. *Time Out* [1984] F.S.R. 64 at 75: See s.50 Supreme Court Act 1981; for form of order see § G–16, *post*.

[51] *Nichols Advanced Vehicle Systems Inc. & Ors.* v. *Rees, Oliver & Ors.* [1979] R.P.C. 127; *Park Court Hotel Ltd.* v. *Trans-World Hotels Ltd.* [1970] F.S.R. 89.

[52] *Southey* v. *Sherwood* (1817) 2 Mer. 435; *Mawman* v. *Tegg* (1826) 2 Russ. 385, 393; *Lewis* v. *Chapman* (1840) 3 Beav. 133; *Kenitex Chemicals Inc.* v. *Kenitex Textured Coating Ltd.* [1965] 2 F.S.R. 109 (3 months' delay—no injunction); *Bravington Ltd.* v. *Barrington Tennant* [1957] R.P.C. 183 (3 months' unexplained delay); *Celanese Corporation* v. *Akzo Chemie U.K. Ltd.* [1976] F.S.R. 273 (no injunction—6 months' delay between launching of motion and hearing of motion); *Radley Gowns Ltd.* v. *Costas Spyrou* [1975] F.S.R. 445; *Russel-Uclaf* v. *G. P. Searle & Co. Ltd.* [1977] F.S.R. 125; *Foseco Inernational Ltd.* v. *Fordath Ltd.* [1975] F.S.R. 507; *My Kinda Town* v. *Soll* [1983] R.P.C. 407 at 418; *Century Electronics Ltd.* v. *CVS Enterprises Ltd.* [1983] F.S.R. 1 (4 months delay after becoming aware of defendant's activities); *The Quaker Oats Company* v. *Alltrades Distributors Ltd.* [1981] F.S.R. 9 (2 months delay after learning of imports of infringing goods); *Hoover plc* v. *George Hulme Ltd.* [1982] F.S.R. 565 at 587, 588.

[53] *Cavendish House (Cheltenham) Ltd.* v. *Cavendish-Woodhouse Ltd.* [1968] R.P.C. 448; [1970] R.P.C. 234 (C.A.); *Effluent Disposal Ltd.* v. *Midlands Effluent Disposal Ltd.* [1970] R.P.C. 238; *The Great American Success Co. Ltd.* v. *Katteineh* [1976] F.S.R. 554.

[54] See n. 52, *ante*.

[55] *CPC (United Kingdom) Ltd.* v. *Keenan* [1986] F.S.R. 527.

[56] *News Group Newspapers Ltd.* v. *The Mirror Group Newspapers (1986) Ltd.* [1989] F.S.R. 126; *Raychem Corp.* v. *Thermon (U.K.) Ltd.* [1989] R.P.C. 423.

action merely on account of delay in instituting proceedings,[57] subject to
the provisions of the Limitation Act 1980. Under certain circumstances
delay might be held to amount to a tacit permission to reproduce the
work.[58]

11–60 **Actual damage need not be proved.** If the plaintiff proves that his copyright has been infringed, the court will grant an injunction without proof
of actual damage.[59] But he must show that there is a probability of
damage,[60] that the defendant is likely to continue his infringement, and
that this is not simply trivial.[61] In *Performing Right Society Ltd.* v. *Berman*[62] it
was held[63] that the plaintiff must show positively that the defendant is
likely to continue his infringement in cases where the prima facie position
was that the infringement had occurred once and for all and was finished
and done with. If, in addition, the defendant had given a bona fide undertaking not to repeat the infringement, that is an important factor which
would influence the court in refusing an injunction. In the majority of
cases, it would be very difficult for a plaintiff, whose rights had been
infringed, to prove positively a definite likelihood of a repetition of the
infringement. In that case infringement was alleged by the playing by a
band of music at a club operated by the defendants. No undertaking had
been given not to repeat the infringement. An injunction was granted notwithstanding that the club had subsequently closed down.

Moreover, an injunction will not be granted to restrain infringements of
future numbers of a periodical, although the defendants have systematic-
ally copied from numbers already published.[64] Upjohn J., in *Football
League Ltd.* v. *Littlewoods Pools Ltd.*,[65] declined, on this basis, to grant an
injunction in respect of the next season's fixture list. It is submitted, however, that in an appropriate case, in which the subject-matter of the
injunction can be clearly defined, an injunction may be granted in respect
of infringement of future copyright material on the footing that the cir-

---

[57] *Hogg* v. *Scott* (1874) L.R. 18 Eq. 444; *Morris* v. *Ashbee* (1868) L.R. 7 Eq. 34; *Fullwood* v. *Fullwood* (1878) 9 Ch.D. 176; *Reliance Rubber Co. Ltd.* v. *Reliance Tyre Co. Ltd.* (1925) 42 R.P.C.
91; *Aktiebologet Manus* v. *R. J. Fullwood & Bland Ltd.* (1948) 65 R.P.C. 329; *William C. Parker
Ltd.* v. *F. J. Ham & Son Ltd.* [1972] 1 W.L.R. 1583; *Birkett* v. *James* [1978] A.C. 297. As to
acquiescence and delay see *H. P. Bulmer Ltd.* v. *J. Bollinger S.A.* [1978] R.P.C. 79; *Nichols
Advanced Vehicle Systems Inc. & Ors.* v. *Rees, Oliver & Ors.* [1979] R.P.C. 127.

[58] *Rundell* v. *Murray* (1821) Jac. 311; *Saunders* v. *Smith* (1838) 3 My. & Cr. 711.

[59] *Weatherby & Sons* v. *Internatonal Horse Agency and Exchange Ltd.* [1910] 2 Ch. 297 at 305; *Smith*
v. *Johnson* (1863) 33 L.J.Ch. 137; *Hawkes and Son (London) Ltd.* v. *Paramount Film Service Ltd.*
[1934] Ch. 593 at 608; *Campbell* v. *Scott* (1842) 11 Sim. 31.

[60] *Borthwick* v. *The Evening Post* (1888) 37 Ch.D. 449 at 462.

[61] *Whittingham (C.)* v. *Wooler (T.J.)* (1818) 2 Swans. 428; *Baily* v. *Taylor* (1830) 1 Russ. & My.
73; *Cox* v. *Land & Water Journal Co.* (1869) L.R. 9 Eq. 324; *Lewis* v. *Fullarton* (1839) 2 Beav.
6 at 11.

[62] [1975] F.S.R. 400 (High Court of Rhodesia); *P.R.S. Ltd.* v. *Butcher* [1975] F.S.R. 405
(High Court of Rhodesia).

[63] See n. 62, *ante*.

[64] *Cate* v. *Devon, etc., Newspaper Co.* (1889) 40 Ch.D. 500 at 507; *Sweet* v. *G. W. Bromley & Co.*
[1905–10] Mac.C.C. 203; but see *Bradbury* v. *Sharp* [1891] W.N. 132 and *T. M. Hall & Co.*
v. *Whittington & Co.* [1892] 18 V.L.R. 525.

[65] [1959] Ch. 637.

cumstances justify *quia timet* relief.[66] An injunction may be refused on the grounds of public policy.[67]

Where portion only of the work is copied. Where only part of a work **11–61** has been copied, and the part which has been copied from the plaintiff's work can be separated from that which has not been copied, an injunction will be granted only against the objectionable part or parts.[68] But even where a very large proportion of a work of a piratical nature is unquestionably original, if the parts which have been copied cannot be separated from those which are original without destroying the use and value of the original matter, he who has made an improper use of that which did not belong to him must suffer the consequences of so doing, and an injunction will be granted against the whole.[69] He has only himself to blame for the consequences of mixing another person's work with his own in such a way that they cannot be separated.

Where the court, upon the evidence, was led to conclude that, if the **11–62** parts affected with the character of piracy were taken away, there would be left an imperfect work which could not, to any useful extent, serve the purpose intended by the publication, the injunction to restrain the publication of any parts pirated from the plaintiff's work was granted, without waiting till all the parts pirated could be distinctly marked.[70]

Form of Injunction. The injunction is usually directed to restraining the **11–63** commission of the act by servants and agents of the defendant as well as by the defendant himself. Farwell L.J., in referring to this practice, said[71]:

> "It is true that persons who are not parties to an action, and are therefore not bound by the injunction so as to be committed for a breach of it, may yet be amenable to the jurisdiction of the court if the injunction be negative, *i.e.* forbids something to be done, but it can only be on the ground of contempt in obstructing the course of justice by aiding and abetting in breach of an injunction of the court; and this is the ground on which 'servants and agents' are rendered liable for contempt whether they are mentioned in the order or not. The practice of mentioning them probably arose in order to give them warning."

The terms of the injunction must be clear, otherwise the court will not

---

[66] See *Phonographic Performance Ltd.* v. *Amusement Caterers (Peckham) Ltd.* [1963] 3 All E.R. 493; *Independent Television Publications Ltd.* v. *Time Out Ltd.* [1984] F.S.R. 64.

[67] *Massie & Renwick Ltd.* v. *Underwriters' Survey Bureau Ltd.* [1940] S.C.R. 218; and see §11–30 *ante* and § 21–20 *et seq., post.*

[68] *Jarrold* v. *Houlston* (1857) 3 K. & J. 708; *Lamb* v. *Evans* [1892] 3 Ch. 462.

[69] *Millar* v. *Taylor* (1769) 4 Burr. 2303; *Carey* v. *Longman* (1801) 1 East 1358; *Trusler* v. *Murray* (1801) 1 East 363n.; *Mawman* v. *Tegg* (1826) 2 Russ 385 at 391; *Finn* v. *Pugliese* (1918) 18 S.R.(N.S.W.) 530 (films); *Trengrouse* v. *"Sol" Syndicate* [1901–04] Mac.C.C. 13 and *Nichols Advanced Vehicle Systems Inc. & Ors.* v. *Rees, Oliver & Ors.* [1979] R.P.C. 127 at 141.

[70] *Lewis* v. *Fullarton* (1839) 2 Beav. 6; *Kelly* v. *Morris* (1866) L.R. 1 Eq. 697.

[71] *Brydges* v. *Brydges* [1909] P. 187 at 191; the present form was approved by the House of Lords in *Marengo* v. *Daily Sketch, etc., Ltd.* (1948) 65 R.P.C. 242; for form of order see §G–16 *post.*

grant it.[72] The defendant is entitled to know precisely what acts he is prohibited from committing.[73]

11–64 **Enforcement of injunctions.** Injunctions may be enforced against a defendant who is an individual by committal and sequestration; and against a defendant who is a body corporate, by sequestration; and also by committal and sequestration against its directors and other officers.[74] In less serious cases the court may, instead of these penalties, impose a fine and payment of costs,[75] or merely the payment of costs.[76] Breach of an undertaking to the court is punishable in the same way as breach of an injunction.[77] To establish contempt of court it is sufficient to prove that the defendant's conduct was intentional and that he knew all the facts which made it a breach of the order. It is not necessary to prove that the defendant knew it was a breach. The Court has to decide what the defendant has done, even if that involves deciding issues in the action.[78] If there is a dispute as to whether the defendant's conduct is a breach of an order or undertaking the defendant can apply to the court for guidance.[79] The Court has a discretion to decline to hear a litigant's appeal where he has wilfully and contumaciously failed to comply with an order of the Court.[80] Where, on a motion to commit for contempt of court, the court is satisfied that the breach of the undertaking to the court is also a breach of contract by the contemnor, in respect of which there is no defence to a claim for damages, the court may make a summary award of damages in addition to an order for costs on an indemnity basis.[81]

(iii) Damages

11–65 The next remedy is damages. Under section 96(2) of the 1988 Act a successful plaintiff is entitled to recover damages for the infringement of his right. This is the same position as under section 17 of the 1956 Act which

---

[72] See *Wilson & Whitworth Ltd.* v. *Express & Independent Newspapers Ltd.* [1969] R.P.C. 165; *Potters Ballotini Ltd.* v. *Weston-Baker* [1977] R.P.C. 202; *Aljose Fashions Ltd.* v. *Alfred Young and Co. Ltd.* [1978] F.R.S. 364; *British Northrop Ltd.* v. *Texteam Blackburn Ltd.* [1974] R.P.C. 57; [1976] R.P.C. 344; *see Landi Den Hartog B.V.* v. *Stopps* [1976] F.S.R. 497, injunction to restrain the copying of parts but not followed on other occasions; *The Staver Co. Inc.* v. *Digitext Display Ltd.* [1985] F.S.R. 512 at 518; *Video Arts Ltd.* v. *Paget Industries Ltd.* [1988] F.S.R. 501.

[73] See n.72, *ante.*

[74] R.S.C., Ord. 45, r. 5; Ord. 46, rr. 5 and Ord. 52. *Att.-General of Tuvala* v. *Philatelic Distribution Corporation Ltd.* [1990] 1 W.L.R. 926.

[75] R.S.C., Ord. 52, r. 9; *Phonographic Performance Ltd.* v. *Amusement Caterers (Peckham) Ltd.* [1964] Ch. 195; *Steiner Products Ltd.* v. *Willy Steiner Ltd.* [1966] 1 W.L.R. 986; *Ronson Products Ltd.* v. *Ronson Furniture Ltd.* [1966] R.P.C. 497; *Re Mileage Conference Group, etc. Ltd.'s Agreement* [1966] 1 W.L.R. 1137; *Re W. (B.) (An Infant)* [1969] 2 Ch. 50; *G.C.T. (Management) Ltd.* v. *The Laurie Marsh Group Ltd.* [1973] R.P.C. 432; *in Re Grantham Wholesale, etc., Ltd.* [1972] 1 W.L.R. 559; *Jennison* v. *Baker* [1972] 2 Q.B. 52.

[76] *Ronson Products Ltd.* v. *Ronson Furniture Ltd., supra.* In contempt proceedings costs are usually awarded on an indemnity basis.

[77] *Re Mileage Conference Group, etc., Ltd.'s Agreement, supra; Biba Ltd.* v. *Stratford Investments Ltd.* [1973] R.P.C. 799.

[78] *Spectravest Inc.* v. *Aperknit Ltd.* [1988] F.S.R. 161.

[79] See n. 78 a, *supra.*

[80] *X Ltd.* v. *Morgan Grampian Ltd.* [1990] 2 W.L.R. 1000.

[81] *Midland Marts Ltd.* v. *Hobday* [1989] 1 W.L.R. 1143.

continues to apply to pre-commencement proceedings. The measure of damage is the depreciation caused by the infringement to the value of the copyright as a chose in action.[82] Thus if the defendant has dealt with the plaintiff's copyright work as if he had a licence, the defendant ought to pay as damages an amount equivalent to the fair fee or royalty which he would have had to pay for a licence to do the acts which he has done.[83] In the case of industrial designs this might be a relatively small sum. There will also be taken into account any loss which the copyright owner has suffered by reason of the diminution of the sales of his work, or the loss of profit which he might otherwise have made,[84] but there will not be taken into account under this head any benefit which may have accrued to the defendant by the use of his work.[85] The fact that the pirated work may have injured the reputation of and vulgarised the original is also a fact that may be taken into consideration in assessing the amount of damages,[86] and generally the damages may be said to be at large.[87] The damages will not, however, include loss suffered because of the commission by a third party of another tort, such as passing off,[88] which has been facilitated by the defendant's infringement of copyright. The burden is on the plaintiff to prove damage, but not to a degree of certainty. Some loss of sales will be assumed.[89] Damages are usually assessed on an inquiry before the Master after liability for infringement has been established at the trial of the action, with costs of the inquiry reserved. It does not follow automatically that, because a plaintiff has obtained an injunction, he should be entitled to an inquiry as to damages. The court has a

---

[82] *Per* Lord Wright M.R., *Sutherland Publishing Co. Ltd.* v. *Caxton Publishing Co. Ltd.* [1936] Ch. 323 at 336; *Prior* v. *Landsdowne Press Pty. Ltd.* [1977] R.P.C. 511 (Supreme Court of Victoria); *Interfirm Comparison (Australia) Pty. Ltd.* v. *Law Society of New South Wales* [1977] R.P.C. 137; *Infabrics Ltd.* v. *Jaytex Shirt Co. Ltd.* [1984] R.P.C. 405 at 457; *Paterson Zochonis Ltd.* v. *Merfarken Packaging Ltd.* [1983] F.S.R. 273 at 281, 287, 294.

[83] *Stovin-Bradford* v. *Volpoint Ltd.* [1971] Ch. 1007 at 1016 and 1020; *Hunter* v. *Fitzroy Robinson & Partners* [1978] F.S.R. 167; *General Tire and Rubber Co.* v. *Firestone Tyre, etc., Ltd.* [1975] F.S.R. 273; *Lewis Trusts* v. *Bambers Stores Ltd.* [1983] F.S.R. 453 at 469. *Charles Church Developments plc* v. *Cronin* [1990] F.S.R. 1.

[84] *Birn Bros. Ltd.* v. *Keene & Co. Ltd.* [1918] 2 Ch. 281; *Fenning Film Service Ltd.* v. *Wolverhampton, etc., Cinemas Ltd.* [1914] 3 K.B. 1171. *Columbia Pictures Industries* v. *Robinson* [1988] F.S.R. 531 (Inquiry as to damages conducted by judge); *Allibert S.A.* v. *O'Connor* [1982] F.S.R. 317.

[85] *Prior* v. *Landsdowne Press Pty. Ltd.*, *supra* at p. 513.

[86] *Hanfstaengl* v. *W. H. Smith & Sons* [1905] 1 Ch. 519. In *Mansell (V.) & Co. Ltd.* v. *Wesley (H.) Ltd.* [1936–45] Mac.C.C. 288, it was held that the plaintiff was justified in withdrawing his stock, the design of which had been vulgarised, and adding to his claim for damages the loss so suffered. *Lewis Trusts* v. *Bambers Stores Ltd.* [1983] F.S.R. 453 at 469; *cf. Allibert S.A.* v. *O'Connor* [1982] F.S.R. 317 (High Court of Ireland).

[87] *Fenning Film Service Ltd.* v. *Wolverhampton, etc., Ltd.* [1914] 3 K.B. 1171. See as to damages for performing musical works in public, *Performing Right Society Ltd.* v. *Bradford Corporation* [1917–23] Mac.C.C. 309; *Performing Right Society Ltd.* v. *Berman* [1975] F.S.R. 400; *Performing Right Society, Ltd.* v. *Thompson* (1917) 34 T.L.R. 351; *Performing Right Society Ltd.* v. *Ciryl Theatrical Syndicate Ltd.* [1923] 2 K.B. 146; *Performing Right Society Ltd.* v. *Mitchell and Booker, etc., Ltd.* [1924] 1 K.B. 762 and *Performing Right Society Ltd.* v. *Camelo* [1936] 3 All E.R. 557. See also as to the possibility of recovering as damages the costs of employing inquiry agents, *British Motor Trade Association* v. *Salvadori* [1949] Ch. 556; *South African Music Rights Organisation Ltd.* v. *Trust Butchers (Pty.) Ltd.* (1978) 1 S.A.L.R. 1052 (a copyright case).

[88] *Paterson Zochonis Ltd.* v. *Merfarken Packaging Ltd.* [1983] F.S.R. 273.

[89] *Columbia Pictures Industries* v. *Robinson* (*supra*).

discretion to refuse an inquiry if satisfied, for example, that the inquiry would be fruitless because the amount recoverable would be slight.[90] An application to dismiss an inquiry as to damages for want of prosecution is not governed by the same considerations as on an application to strike out proceedings before an order has been made.[91]

(iv) Additional damages

11–66   The 1988 Act provides for the award of additional damages in suitable circumstances.[92] The court has power, having regard to all the circumstances, and in particular to the flagrancy of the infringement and any benefit accruing to the defendant by reason of the infringement, to award such additional damages as the justice of the case may require. The provisions of the 1988 Act are wider than section 17(3) of the 1956 Act which continues to apply to pre-commencement proceedings and which was expressly directed to providing effective relief for the plaintiff. If, for example, effective relief was available to the plaintiff in respect of another cause of action, such as libel or breach of confidence, or because conversion damages, as well as infringement damages, were available, relief might not be given by an award of additional damages for infringement of copyright.[93] This requirement no longer applies to proceedings instituted after the commencement of the 1988 Act on August 1, 1989. It is thought that additional damages might be appropriate where a defendant adopts a policy of continual infringement, but an injunction is not an appropriate remedy because the defendant reproduces different material on each occasion. Additional damages may also be awarded where the conduct of the defendant has been deceitful and treacherous, thereby obtaining benefits for himself and inflicting on the plaintiff humiliation for which it is difficult to compensate.[94] Flagrancy implies scandalous conduct, deceit including deliberate and calculated infringement where a defendant reaps a pecuniary advantage in excess of the damages he would otherwise have to pay.[95] Other relevant considerations are the defendant's general conduct with regard to the infringement and his motives for it, the plaintiff's corresponding behaviour, the injury to the plaintiff's feelings and the indignities and distress he has suffered and the defendant's lack of regret for the hurt and humiliation he has inflicted on the plaintiff.[96] The power to award additional damages does not relieve the court of the burden of assessing compensation where there is difficulty in quantifying harm suf-

---

[90] *McDonald's Hamburgers Ltd.* v. *Burger King (U.K.) Ltd.* [1987] F.S.R. 112; for form of order see §G–16, *post.*

[91] *Nichols Advanced Vehicle Systems Inc.* v. *Rees, Oliver & Ors (No. 2)* [1985] R.P.C. 445.

[92] C.D.P.A. 1988, s.97(2), and see *Rookes* v. *Barnard* [1964] A.C. 1129 at 1225; *South African Music Rights Organisation Ltd.* v. *Trust Butcher (Pty.) Ltd.* [1978] 1 S.A.L.R. 1052; for form of order see §G–16, *post.*

[93] *Nora Beloff* v. *Pressdram Ltd. & Anor.* [1973] R.P.C. 765; *Prior* v. *Landsdowne Press (Pty.) Ltd.* [1977] R.P.C. 511; *Ravenscroft* v. *Herbert & Anor.* [1980] R.P.C. 193.

[94] *Nichols Advanced Vehicle Systems Inc. & Ors.* v. *Rees Oliver & Ors.* [1979] R.P.C. 127; *Nichols Advanced Vehicle Systems Inc.* v. *Rees (No. 3)* [1988] R.P.C. 71 (£2000 additional damages awarded); *Besson Ltd.* v. *Fulleon Ltd.* [1986] F.S.R. 319.

[95] *Ravenscroft* v. *Herbert & Anor.* [1980] R.P.C. 193 at 206.

[96] See n. 93, *ante.*

fered by a party: it does not enable the court to compensate an injured party who has suffered irreparable harm. It is used to make awards where compensatory damages would not be recoverable under the usual rules relating to proof of damage and remoteness.[97] It seems that a claim for such additional damages should be specially pleaded.[98] The subsection is a comprehensive code for additional damages and there is no place for the award of aggravated, exemplary or punitive damages outside that subsection.[99]

In *Williams* v. *Settle*,[1] the Court of Appeal affirmed an order of a county **11–67** court judge awarding £1,000 damages against a photographer, who sold to the Press photographs taken by him for a client in circumstances in which the copyright vested in the client. Sellers L.J. referred to the flagrancy of the infringement, saying it was in total disregard, not only of the legal rights of the plaintiff regarding copyright, but of his feelings. Additional damages will not be awarded, however, where the defendant has, in good faith, formed the view that the plaintiff's material was only a colourable imitation or adaptation of existing material and when the defendant has not achieved any enhanced goodwill or trading advantage by use of the infringing material.[2]

The assessment of additional damages will usually be made by the Master in the course of the conduct of the inquiry as to damages for infringement of copyright,[3] though the trial judge may indicate in his judgment that additional damages should be awarded and the considerations which are relevant to the assessment of the additional damages.[4]

(v) Damages for conversion

Under section 18(1) of the 1956 Act the plaintiff could make a claim for **11–68** conversion damages. This provision has now been repealed, but continues to apply for the purposes of proceedings begun before commencement.[5] An account of the position under the 1956 Act is therefore necessary. By section 18(1) of that Act (as amended) it was provided that "the owner of any copyright shall be entitled to all such rights and remedies, in respect of the conversion or detention by any person of any infringing copy, or of any plate used or intended to be used for making infringing copies, as he would be entitled to if he were the owner of every such copy or plate and had been the owner thereof since the time when it was made." "Infringing copy" was defined, in relation to a literary, dramatic, musical or artistic work, as an article the making of which constitued an infringement of the

---

[97] *Mondaress Ltd.* v. *Bourne & Hollingsworth Ltd.* [1981] F.S.R. 118.
[98] See *Broome* v. *Cassell & Co. Ltd.* [1972] A.C. 1027 at 1083 and *Halsbury's Laws of England* (4th ed.), Vol. 36, para 26 *cf.* R.S.C. Ord. 18, r. 8(3).
[99] See n. 93, *ante.*
[1] [1960] 1 W.L.R. 1072. *Wellington Newpapers* v. *Dealers Guide* [1984] 2 NZLR 66; *cf. Pro Arts Inc.* v. *Campus Crafts Ltd.* (1980) 110 D.L.R. (3rd) 366.
[2] *International Credit Control Ltd. & Anor.* v. *Axelion & Anor.* [1974] 1 N.Z.L.R. 695 (Supreme Court of New Zealand).
[3] *The Lady Anne Tennant* v. *Associated Newspapers Group Ltd.* [1979] F.S.R. 298.
[4] See n. 73, *ante.*
[5] C.D.P.A. 1988, para. 31(2) Sched. 1.

copyright in the work, or in the case of an imported article, would have constituted an infringement of that copyright if the article had been made in the place into which it was imported.[6] The article in question might be any kind of reproduction which would constitute an infringement, including a record and, in the case of an artistic work, a version in different dimensions. However, it expressly did not include a reproduction in the form of a cinematograph film of a literary, dramatic, musical or artistic work, or of a published edition.[7] Further, since the making of an adaptation of a literary, dramatic or musical work was, under the 1956 Act, a separate infringement from the reproduction of the work,[8] it was arguable that such an adaptation was not an infringing copy. "Infringing copy" was further defined, in relation to a sound recording, as a record embodying the recording; in relation to a cinematograph film, as a copy of the film; in relation to a television broadcast or a sound broadcast or a cable programme as a copy of a cinematograph film of it, or a record embodying a sound recording of it; and, in relation to a published edition, as a reproduction of it not being a film.[9] "Plate" was defined as including any stereotype, stone, block, mould, matrix, transfer, negative or other appliance.[10] The right to conversion damages thus arose out of the statutory fiction of the notional attribution of ownership in the substrate upon which the infringing work was reproduced and not one of actual ownership of the article alleged to be converted. The right arose solely out of the infringement. Copyright was the only field of intellectual property in which a claim for conversion could be made and it was recognised that the remedy might work considerable hardship, particularly in the case of mass produced products where the substrate was of much greater value than the design imposed on or embodied in the article.[11] In the case of three dimensional articles made of metal the damages would depend on whether the article was made of some base or noble metal. The damages recoverable for conversion related, not only to the skill and labour of the copyright owner in the making of his drawings or other work, but also to the skills and expression involved in the production of the three dimensional article to which the copyright owner had contributed nothing. Damages on that scale could have operated as a deterrent to future infringement but were not a fair or just measure of damage suffered by the plaintiff or profit made by the defendant. Conversion damages, though excessive, were not regarded as a "penalty," for the purposes of resisting discovery.[12]

The burden of proof in the case of conversion damages was higher than

---

[6] Copyright Act 1956, s.18(3); see also § 9–4 *et seq.*, *ante*; and as to infringement in relation to works of architecture, see § 8–72 *et seq.*, *ante*.

[7] *Ibid.* s.18(3)(a).

[8] *Ibid.* s.2(5).

[9] *Ibid* s.18(3).

[10] *Ibid.* and see *R.* v. *Baldoli* [1911–16] Mac.C.C. 105 (positive copy of a film a "plate" if used for producing other copies).

[11] *Infabrics Ltd. & Ors.* v. *Jaytex Shirt Co. Ltd.* [1984] R.P.C. 405. For amendments to substantive and procedural aspects of the general law relating to conversion and detinue see Torts (Interference with Goods) Act 1977 (c. 32). *Nichols Advanced Vehicle Systems Inc.* v. *Rees* (*No.* 3) [1988] R.P.C. 71.

[12] *Richmark Camera Services Inc.* v. *Neilson-Hordell Ltd.* [1981] F.S.R. 413.

in the case of infringement damages. The evidence of the allegedly converted article had to be established "with some fair degree of certainty," to a standard of certainty or near certainty. The process of reasoning and inference appropriate to quantifying infringement damages was not necessarily sufficient to establish the number of infringing copies on which a conversion claim could be based.[13]

Once it had been proved that the articles were infringing copies it was not necessary, in a claim for damages for conversion, to prove that the defendant knew that he was dealing in or disposing of articles made in infringement of copyright and that he had therefore committed an act of infringement, although it would have been a defence if the defendant established that he believed, and had reasonable grounds for believing, that the articles converted were not infringing copies.[14]

Articles made or imported before the commencement of the 1956 Act. In the case of articles made or imported before the commencement of the 1956 Act, the foregoing provisions did not apply, but proceedings might have been brought or continued in respect of such articles in accordance with the corresponding provisions of section 7 of the 1911 Act.[15] These provisions are no longer of any practical importance. **11–69**

Damages for conversion and infringement cumulative. A question of difficulty arose whether damages for infringement under section 6 of the 1911 Act, and damages for conversion under section 7 of that Act, were alternative or cumulative. It was finally determined by the House of Lords that they were cumulative. This decision was equally applicable to the provisions of the 1956 Act.[16] But, though the two sets of damages were cumulative, they could not overlap.[17] For example, if there was an award of infringement damages by way of royalty in respect of infringing articles, the plaintiffs were not entitled to have damages for conversion in respect of the same articles without there being an allowance for overlap. Damages for conversion were liable to be reduced by the amount awarded for infringement.[18] The principle was more difficult to apply where the defendant's work had been sold at a different price than the plaintiff's, or contained additional subject-matter, or was in a form which vulgarised the plaintiff's work. In such cases the court presumably estimated, on the facts available, how far any overlap was involved and made provision accordingly.[19] **11–70**

---

[13] *Columbia Pictures Industries* v. *Robinson* [1988] F.S.R. 531 at 537.

[14] Copyright Act s.18(2); *Young & Anor. c. Odeon Music Home Pty Ltd. & Ors.* [1978] R.P.C. 621 (Supreme Court of New South Wales); but see *Infabrics Ltd. & Ors.* v. *Jaytex Shirt Co. Ltd., supra.*

[15] Copyright Act 1956, Sched. 7, para. 21.

[16] *Infabrics Ltd.* v. *Jaytex Shirt Co. Ltd.* [1982] A.C. 1; [1985] F.S.R. 75; *Lewis Trusts* v. *Bambers Stores Ltd.* [1983] F.S.R. 453.

[17] *Sutherland Publishing Co. Ltd.* v. *Caxton Publishing Co. Ltd.* [1936] Ch. 323 at 342; the judgment of the Court of Appeal was affirmed by the House of Lords on this point.

[18] *Lewis Trusts* v. *Bambers Stores Ltd.* [1983] F.S.R. 453 *cf. Allibert S.A.* v. *O'Connor* [1982] F.S.R. 317 (High Court of Ireland) (only infringement damages awarded).

[19] See *per* Lord Wright M.R. in *Sutherland Publishing Co. Ltd.* v. *Caxton Publishing Co. Ltd.* [1936] Ch. 323 at 327; *Infabrics Ltd.* v. *Jaytex Ltd, supra.*

11–71 **Measure of damages for conversion.** The measure of damages for conversion was the value of the article converted at the date of the conversion.[20] That date will usually be the date of the sale on the market to the
retailers, not the date of manufacture of the articles.[21] The damages may
include added costs increasing the value of the infringing article between
the date of manufacture and the date of sale.[22] The question of how that
value was to be assessed has been discussed in many cases. Lord Porter[23]
said; "I do not accept the view that an article has no value or a diminished
value to its owner because he has no machinery for selling it," and "The
value is not necessarily the price for which the owner could sell the article.
Is a publisher who infringes an author's copyright to make a large profit
out of an unexpectedly successful book because he could have bought the
copyright cheaply if before the publication he had approached the author
and paid his price?" and "It is the value known or unknown, which has to
be paid, and that value is not necessarily the price which the owner could
have obtained or would have taken. It may have to be ascertained by finding out what price for the infringing matter, in the form in which it is
offered, the public or some individual is prepared to pay, or in some other
way in the light of after events." Lord Roche said[24]: "It is true enough to
say that the value is the value to the owner; but it is wrong to say this if
you mean what the owner will make out of the thing in money if it is not
taken away from him." Where infringing copies were in fact sold by the
defendant, the value was usually assessed by reference to the sale price,
but allowing to the defendant all expenses which he proved to have been
properly and necessarily incurred by him after the conversion in effecting
the sale insofar as these expenses would not have been incurred but for the
sale; such expenses might be the cost of binding, and the cost of collection
and delivery, and the expense of advertising and selling. In a case where it
was held that the defendants had infringed the plaintiff's design, reproduced on a textile which was made up into shirts, the shirts were "infringing copies." The measure of damages for conversion was the value of the
shirts, not just the increase in the value of the shirts through the addition
of the design or the value of the shirts less the cost of the substrate or the
work put into the making of the shirts.[25] Where there was no market for

---

[20] *Birn Bros. Ltd.* v. *Keene & Co. Ltd., supra; Caxton Publishing Co. Ltd.* v. *Sutherland Publishing Co. Ltd.* [1939] A.C. 178 at 192; *Infabrics Ltd.* v. *Jaytex Ltd., supra; Wham-O Manufacturing Co.* v. *Lincoln Industries Ltd.* [1985] R.P.C. 127 (Court of Appeal of New Zealand). Normally the value would be ascertained at the date of the first act of conversion and subsequent changes of value will not affect the matter (see Salmond & Heuston, *Torts,* (19th ed.), pp. 627–628) *cf. Lewis Trusts* v. *Bambers Stores Ltd. (supra)* The question whether a subsequent rise in value not due to any act of the defendant can be taken into account (see *Greening* v. *Wilkinson* (1825) 1 C. & P. 625) was expressly reserved in *Sutherland Publishing Co. Ltd.* v. *Caxton Publishing Co. Ltd., supra.* but see now Salmond & Heuston, *Torts* (19th ed.), pp. 627–628; *Columbia Pictures Industries* v. *Robinson* [1988] F.S.R. 531 at 536.

[21] See n. 18 *ante.*

[22] *Wham-O Manufacturing Co.* v. *Lincoln Industries Ltd. (supra)* at 180.

[23] *Caxton Publishing Co. Ltd. Sutherland Publishing Co. Ltd.* [1939] A.C. 178 at 203, *Nichols Advanced Vehicle System Inc.* v. *Rees (No. 3)* [1988] R.P.C. 71.

[24] *Ibid.* at 192.

[25] *Lewis Trusts* v. *Bambers Stores Ltd.* [1983] F.S.R. 453. *Infabrics Ltd.* v. *Jaytex Shirt Co. Ltd.* [1984] R.P.C 405; *Fablaine Ltd.* v. *Leygill Ltd.* [1981] F.S.R. 597; *W.H. Brine Co.* v. *Whitton* (1981) 37 A.L.R. 190 (Federal Court of Australia).

the articles in question and therefore no sale price, the correct approach was to take the cost of the articles or their value to the owner of the copyright.[26]

The relevant act for calculating damages. The relevant act of conversion was also discussed. Lord Porter said[27]: "Conversion was defined by Atkin J. as he then was, in *Lancashire & Yorkshire Ry.* v. *MacNicoll.*[28] 'Dealing,' he said, 'with goods in a manner inconsistent with the right of the true owner amounts to a conversion, provided that it is also established that there is also an intention on the part of the defendant in so doing to deny the owner's right or to assert a right which is inconsistent with the owner's right.' Atkin J. goes on to point out that, where the act done is necessarily a denial of the owner's right or an assertion of a right inconsistent therewith, intention does not matter. Another way of reaching the same conclusion would be to say that conversion consists in an act intentionally done inconsistent with the owner's right though the doer may not know of or intend to challenge the property or possession of the true owner." The decision was that, where the infringement complained of consisted of a work which incorporated the plaintiff's material with non-infringing material, the binding together of sheets constituted a conversion. Until that stage was reached, the infringing matter could still have been delivered up to the plaintiff. Neither the act of producing the infringing material nor the mere possession of it amounts to a "dealing" or conversion.[29] But, once the infringing material was incorporated with the defendant's own property into a composite article, it was considered that the defendant had unequivocally dealt with this material as his own. It would seem that, where the infringing work was wholly the plaintiff's, so that no question of incorporation arose, the position might be different and the first act of conversion might be sale or the delivery of copies to a purchaser.[30] The exact moment at which the act of conversion was committed might be material, either by reason of the fact that time began to run from that date for the purposes of the statutory period of limitation,[31] or because variations of value after the date of conversion were not in general to be taken into account.[32] **11–72**

Where part only infringed. A difficult question arose where the work produced by the defendant consisted in part of infringing matter and in part of innocent matter. For example, the infringing article might have been packaged for sale in non-infringing packaging and an identifiable element on the sale price might be attributable to the packaging.[33] It was **11–73**

---

[26] *Nichols Advanced Vehicle Systems Inc.* v. *Rees (No. 3)* [1988] R.P.C. 71.

[27] *Caxton Publishing Co. Ltd.* v. *Sutherland Publishing Co. Ltd.* [1939] A.C. 178 at 201. *Crystal Glass Industry Ltd.* v. *Alwinco Products Ltd.* [1986] R.P.C. 259 (Court of Appeal of New Zealand).

[28] (1919) 88 L.J.K.B. 601 at 605.

[29] *Wham-O Manufacturing Co.* v. *Lincoln Industries Ltd.* [1985] R.P.C. 127.

[30] *Caxton Publishing Co. Ltd.* v. *Sutherland Publishing Co. Ltd.* [1939] A.C. 178; *Lewis Trusts* v. *Bambers Stores Ltd.* [1983] F.S.R. 433 and see *J. Whitaker & Sons Ltd.* v. *Publishers' Circular Ltd.* [1946–47] Mac.C.C. 10.

[31] § 11–96, *post.*

[32] § 11–72, n. 20, *ante.*

[33] *Wham-O Manufacturing Co.* v. *Lincoln Industries Ltd.* [1985] R.P.C. 127 at 181.

decided[34] that, in such a case, the value of the whole work had first to be assessed as though the whole work had been converted.[35] It was then necessary to ascertain the proportion of this sum which was properly attributable to the infringing material; this proportion represented the damage recoverable.[36] No exact method of calculation was prescribed. Clearly the respective amounts of infringing and non-infringing articles could not be conclusive, since it was the value, and not the amount of the material, which had to be taken into account.[37] The court, by what has been called *rusticum judicium*, had to determine, on the materials before it, the value of the plaintiff's part of the composite work at the date of conversion.[38]

11–74 **Successive conversions.** In the case of successive conversions each person committing an act of conversion was liable, unless innocent, to pay damages in full for the act of conversion committed by him. There might thus be successive and independent conversions, innocent or otherwise, by a series of sales and the true owner might claim against each person selling. The title of the goods was, however, extinguished by the satisfaction of a money judgment or payment in settlement of a claim. The plaintiff could not therefore recover any further damages once he had received full satisfaction as against any particular converter. Where damages for conversion or other wrongful interference were, or would have fallen to be, assessed on the footing that the claimant was being compensated for the whole of his interest in the goods (subject to any reduction for contributory negligence) payment of the assessed damages under all heads of settlement of a claim for damages for the wrong extinguished the claimant's title to that interest.[39]

11–75 **Defences under section 18(2).** The 1956 Act gave a defendant a measure of protection where damages were claimed on the conversion basis. It was sufficient for him to establish that he believed, and had reasonable grounds for believing, that the copies converted were not infringing copies.[40] The burden of proof was on the defendant.[41] This defence as to damages was not applicable to a defendant who had himself

---

[34] *John Lane, etc., Ltd.* v. *Associated Newspapers Ltd.* [1936] 1 K.B. 715; *Ash* v. *Dickie* [1936] Ch. 655; *Caxton Publishing Co. Ltd.* v. *Sutherland Publishing Co. Ltd.* [1939] A.C. 178.

[35] See § 11–72, *ante*.

[36] *Crystal Glass Industries Ltd.* v. *Alwinco Products Ltd.* [1986] R.P.C. 259 (Court of Appeal of New Zealand).

[37] See cases in n. 34, *ante*, and *Mansell (V.) & Co. Ltd.* v. *Wesley (H.) Ltd.* [1936–45] Mac.C.C. 288.

[38] § 11–71 *ante* n. 20, *ante*; *Ravenscroft* v. *Herbert & Anor.* [1980] R.P.C. 193 at 210.

[39] Torts (Interference with Goods) Act 1977 (c.32) s.5. *Infabrics Ltd.* v. *Jaytex Shirt Co. Ltd.* [1978] F.S.R. 451 at 470 and 471. See also *Ash* v. *Hutchinson & Co. (Publishers) Ltd.* [1936] Ch. 489; *Ash* v. *Dickie* [1936] Ch. 655; *Caxton Publishing Co. Ltd.* v. *Sutherland Publishing Co.* [1939] A.C. 178 at 198.

[40] Copyright Act 1956, s.18(2)(*b*). There were other defences under s.18(2)(*a*) and (*c*).

[41] *Infabrics Ltd.* v. *Jaytex Ltd.* [1984] R.P.C. 405; *James Arnold & Co. Ltd.* v. *Miafern Ltd.* [1980] R.P.C. 397. *Gardex Ltd.* v. *Sorata Ltd.* [1986] R.P.C. 623; *Wham-O Manufacturing Co.* v. *Lincoln Industries Ltd.* [1985] R.P.C. 127 (Court of Appeal of New Zealand).

originated the infringing work from which copies were made.[42] There was also no scope for the operation of section 18(2) where there was conscious copying by the defendant's own employee whose acts and knowledge were imputed to the defendant's employer.[43] It was primarily intended to apply to a defendant who was handling innocently, the infringing copies made from the infringing work; for example, the printer, who was generally not in a position to know whether material which he was asked to print was, or was not, an infringement of copyright. Unless what he was given to reproduce was obviously matter obtained from an existing work, it is thought that, under section 18(2) of the 1956 Act, he was generally protected, if he was acting on the instructions of a person whose good faith he had no reason to doubt. But it would seem that this provision also protected a publisher who had acquired a right to reproduce a work, which he believed to be the original material of the author with whom he had made a publishing agreement, or in respect of which he believed he had obtained a valid licence from the owner of the copyright.[44] This provision might not, however, have protected the publisher who published material which he had obtained from a person in possession of that material who simply asserted that, although a third person was the author of the material, he was entitled to deal with it. The onus was on the publisher, in such circumstances, to inquire as to how that person was entitled to deal with the copyright in question. The publisher was not entitled to rely on this provision where he had made no inquiry and where there was "no more than an unverified, unexplained and untested assertion of an unknown man, given under the temptation of a large sum of money, in suspicious circumstances."[45] Or where he took a deliberate risk as to whether what he was doing was wrong in law.[46] It was not enough for the defendant to "hope" that the copies were not infringing copies; he must have believed that they were not and have had reasonable grounds for that belief.[47] It was difficult for a defendant to establish that if he had not made any inquiry.[48]

In deciding whether a publisher had acted innocently within the meaning of section 18(2), the court investigated such matters as the steps taken by the publisher to obtain the material, the payments made for the use of the material, the source of the material and the general reputation of the publisher.[49] If a publisher had investigated the question of copyright and was justified in believing that he had been authorised to use the material, section 18(2) could be relied on.[50] A publisher was not entitled to rely on this provision where he had made no inquiry about the copyright position. It was incumbent on a person, who proposed to make use of a copyright work in a manner which might infringe copyright, to make such inquiries

---

[42] *James Arnold & Co. Ltd.* v. *Miafern Ltd.* [1980] R.P.C. 397.
[43] *J. Bernstein Ltd.* v. *Sydney Murray Ltd.* [1981] R.P.C. 303 at 335.
[44] See *Smith* v. *Daily News Ltd.* [1905–10] Mac.C.C. 302.
[45] *The Lady Anne Tennant* v. *Associated Newspapers Group Ltd.* [1979] F.S.R. 298 at 305.
[46] *Sillitoe* v. *McGraw-Hill Book Co.* [1983] F.S.R. 545.
[47] *Nichols Advanced Vehicle Systems Inc. & Ors.* v. *Rees, Oliver & Ors.* [1979] R.P.C. 127.
[48] *Wham-O Manufacturing Co.* v. *Lincoln Industries Ltd.* [1985] R.P.C. 127.
[49] *Spelling Goldberg Productions Inc.* v. *B.P.C. Publishing* [1979] F.S.R. 494 at 502.
[50] *Spelling Goldberg Productions Inc.* v. *B.P.C. Publishing Ltd.* [1981] R.P.C. 283 (C.A.).

and investigations as he reasonably could to satisfy himself that the work was free of copyright. If a person knew that a copy would, or might be an infringing copy, because, for example, he had been told that there was a copyright difficulty, forgetfulness, however genuine, could not give him reasonable grounds for believing it was not an infringing copy.[51] Further, a publisher had no defence under this provision in respect of any acts of conversion committed by him after receiving a letter before action from the plaintiff,[52] unless, possibly, he continued to act on legal advice that there had been no infringement. A publisher failed to establish this defence in a case where it had previously published works of the author (whose latest work was held to infringe the plaintiff's copyright) without complaint of infringement. The author had claimed that he had done more research in the writing of that book than for his previous books and that the nature of the work was such (historical fiction) that it was common for ideas to be derived from existing works without complaint of copyright infringement.[53] Further, there was no evidence in that case that the publisher had taken any steps to check that there was no infringement so far as the plaintiff's work was concerned. If a person consciously copied an article, such as a garment, made from drawings and was held liable for infringement of copyright in the drawings, he could not rely on the fact that he had not seen or was not aware of the drawings to establish a defence under section 18(2).[54] The Court also had regard to the plaintiff's conduct and awareness of the defendant's activities.[55]

(vi) Account of profits

11–76   Another remedy is an account of profits, which is an equitable remedy incidental to the right to an injunction.[56] The account is of net profits[57]; for example, the sale price of the infringing article, less manufacturing and delivery costs.[58] But a plaintiff cannot obtain both an account of profits and damages either for infringement or conversion, since a claim for an account condones the infringement.[59] A plaintiff is entitled to opt for damages or for an account of profits[60]; he is not entitled to be paid twice in

---

[51] See n. 50, *ante*.

[52] *Infrabrics Ltd.* v. *Jaytex Ltd.*, *supra*.

[53] *Ravenscroft* v. *Herbert & Anor.* [1980] R.P.C. 193 at 209.

[54] *J. Bernstein Ltd.* v. *Sydney Murray Ltd.* [1981] R.P.C. 303.

[55] *Smith* v. *Greenfield* [1985] F.S.R. 9 (High Court of Northern Ireland).

[56] C.D.P.A. 1988, s. 96(2); *Hogg* v. *Kirby* (1803) 8 Ves. 215; *Grimson* v. *Eyre* (1804) 9 Ves. 341 at 346; *Baily* v. *Taylor* (1830) 1 Russ. & My. 73; *Sheriff* v. *Coates* (1830) 1 R. & M. 159; *Kelly* v. *Hooper* (1840) 4 Jur. 21.

[57] *Delfe* v. *Delamotte* (1857) 3 K. & J. 581; *cf. Pike* v. *Nicholas* (1869) L.R. 5 Ch. 251.

[58] *My Kinda Town* v. *Soll* [1983] R.P.C. 15 at 49. *House of Spring Gardens Ltd.* v. *Point Blank Ltd.* [1985] F.S.R. 327 (Supreme Court of Ireland); *Potton Ltd.* v. *Yorkclose Ltd.* [1990] F.S.R. 11: *Van Camp Chocolates Ltd* v. *Milsbrooks Ltd* [1984] 1 NZLR 354.

[59] *Caxton Publishing Co. Ltd.* v. *Sutherland Publishing Co. Ltd.* [1939] A.C. 178 at 198; *De Vitre (J. D.)* v. *Betts (W.)* (1873) L.R. 6 H.L. 319.

[60] See n. 58, *ante*

respect of the same infringements. The principles upon which such an account is granted were thus stated by Wigram V.-C. in *Colburn v. Simms*.[61] "It is true," he said, "that the court does not, by an account, accurately measure the damage sustained by the proprietor of an expensive work from the invasion of his copyright by the publication of a cheaper book. It is impossible to know how many copies of the dearer book are excluded from sale by the interposition of the cheaper one. The court, by the account, as the nearest approximation which it can make to justice, takes from the wrongdoer all the profits he has made by his piracy, and gives them to the party who has been wronged. In doing this the court may often give the injured party more, in fact, than he is entitled to, for *non constat* that a single additional copy of the more expensive book would have been sold, if the injury by the sale of the cheaper book had not been committed. The court of equity, however, does not give anything beyond the account." The basis on which an account is ordered is that there should not be any unjust enrichment on the part of the defendant, and that the defendant should be deprived of any profit (even including an unrealised profit) attributable to wrongful acts committed in breach of the plaintiff's rights.[62] It is not the purpose of an account to inflict punishment on the defendant. While an account of profits may be a useful remedy in a simple case, it is very difficult to take where part only of the infringing material infringes the plaintiff's copyright. In such a case an attempt must be made to apportion profits according to the relative value of the infringing and non-infringing material.[63] For example, in a case of infringement of copyright in architectural drawings by the construction of houses, there would be excluded from the account profits attributable to the purchase, landscaping and sale of the land on which the houses were built, any increase in the value of the houses during the interval between the completion of the houses and sale, and profits attributable to the advertising, marketing and selling of the houses.[64]

A plaintiff is entitled to discovery for the purposes of the account, which is normally taken by the Master. The defendant must give full particulars, upon oath, of the number of copies printed and sold, and the cost of publication and distribution, verified by the production of all proper vouchers and receipts.[65] An account will be refused if it is clear that there are no profits.[66] In such a case the plaintiff may elect to claim damages and an inquiry as to the same,[67] and the plaintiff is bound by an election once made. No interest can be awarded on the sums to be paid until the amount of the profit has been ascertained.

---

[61] (1843) 2 Ha. 543, 560; see *Pike* v. *Nicholas* (1870) L.R. 5 Ch. 251 and *International Credit Control Ltd.* v. *Axelion* [1974] 1 N.Z.L.R. 695.
[62] See n. 58, *ante*
[63] See n. 58, *ante*
[64] *Potton Ltd.* v. *Yorkclose Ltd.* [1990] F.S.R. 11.
[65] *Stevens* v. *Brett* (1863) 12 W.R. 572.
[66] *Lee* v. *Alston* (1789) 1 Ves. 78; *Colburn* v. *Simms* (1843) 2 Ha. 543; *Powell* v. *Aiken* (1857) 4 K. & J. 343.
[67] *Mawman* v. *Tegg* (1826) 2 Russ. 385 at 400. *Thonton Hall Mnfg.* v. *Shanton Apparel* [1989] 3 NZLR 304.

(vii) Forfeiture

11–77   The court has power to make orders as to the disposal of infringing copies and other articles[68] which have been delivered up in pursuance of an order,[69] or which have been seized or detained by the copyright owner or a person authorised by him.[70] Such orders may be made by a county court where the value of the infringing copies and other articles in question does not exceed the county court limit for actions in tort.[71] The High Court also has jurisdiction to make such orders on application by originating summons or by summons or notice in a pending action[72]

An application may be made to the court for an order than an infringing copy or other article shall be–[73]

(1) forfeited to the copyright owner, or

(2) destroyed, or

(3) otherwise dealt with as the court may think fit.

An application may also be made (for example, by a defendant) for a decision that no such order should be made.[74] If the court decides that no order should be made, the person in whose possession, custody or control the copy or other article was before being delivered up or seized is entitled to its return.[75]

11–78   In considering what order (if any) should be made, the court is to consider whether other remedies available in an action for infringement of copyright would be adequate to compensate the copyright owner and to protect his interests.[76] Provision is made for the protection of the interests of third parties. The procedure for making an order includes service of notice on persons having an interest in the copies or other articles.[77] Any such person is entitled to appear in proceedings for such an order, whether or not he was served with notice, and to appeal against any order made, whether or not he appeared.[78] An order is not to take effect until the end of the period within which notice of an appeal may be given or, if before the end of that period, notice of appeal is duly given, until the final determination or abandonment of the proceedings on the appeal.[79]

---

[68] C.D.P.A. 1988, s.114. See S.I. 1990 No. 380 as to proceedings in Scotland; for form of order see §G–16, *post*.

[69] *Ibid.* ss.99 and 108.

[70] *Ibid.* s.100.

[71] *Ibid.* s.115(1); and by a Sheriff Court in Scotland: *ibid* s.115(2).

[72] *Ibid* s.115(3); and by the Court of Session in Scotland. As to procedure see R.S.C. Ord. 93 r. 24.

[73] *Ibid.* s.114(1)(*a*), (*b*).

[74] *Ibid.* s.114(1).

[75] *Ibid.* s.114(5).

[76] *Ibid.* s.114(2).

[77] *Ibid.* s.114(3); see R.S.C. Ord. 93; r. 24 and for Scotland S.I. 1990 No. 380 (s.37) §B–214, *post*.

[78] See n. 77, *ante*

[79] See n. 77, *ante*.

Where there is more than one person interested in a copy or other **11–79**
article, the court is to make such order as it thinks just and may, in particular, direct that the article be sold, or otherwise dealt with, and the proceeds divided.[80] A person has an interest in a copy or other article for the
purposes of these provisions if an order could be made in his favour in
respect of it under certain other provisions.[81] Apart from that express provision, the 1988 Act does not define what is meant by "an interest" or a
"person interested." The expressions would obviously embrace a person
who has a legal or equitable title to or interest in the copies or articles, or
to rights in them or an exclusive licence but are not necessarily so confined
and may extend to persons who have "commercial interests" which would
be damaged or prejudiced by orders for forfeiture, destruction or disposal.

(viii) Delivery up

The court now has a statutory power to make an order for delivery up of **11–80**
an infringing copy or article to the copyright owner, or to the exclusive
licensee, or to such other person as the court may direct.[82] The power to
order delivery up of infringing copies by virtue of their notional ownership
and detention or conversion under section 18 of the 1956 Act is no longer
available, except for proceedings instituted before the commencement of
the 1988 Act.[83]

The Court still has an inherent jurisdiction to order delivery up of
articles which have been created in violation of a plaintiffs right, but only
for the purposes of destruction.[84] The jurisdiction extends to articles
which are not in themselves infringing copies, if they were brought into
being as the result of the use of infringing copies.[85]

Where a defendant has mixed the plaintiff's work with work of his own,
then, if it is physically possible to sever one from the other, the order for
delivery up will apply only to the infringing material,[86] but where the
parts are physically inseparable the order for delivery up may extend to
the whole of the article.[87]

The exercise of the jurisdiction to make an order for delivery up, particularly at the interlocutory stage, may be affected by the provisions of

---

[80] *Ibid.* s.114(4).

[81] *Ibid.* s.114(6); see ss.204 and 231; and also s.58C of the Trade Marks Act, 1938.

[82] *Ibid.* s.99; see § 11–17 *ante.* For form of order see §G–16, *post.*

[83] *Ibid.* para 31(2) Sched 1 s.18; Copyright Act 1956; Torts (Interference with Goods) Act
1977 s.1; *Boosey* v. *Wright (No. 2)* (1900) 81 L.T. 265; *Sutherland Publishing Co. Ltd.* v. *Caxton
Publishing Co. Ltd.* [1936] Ch. 323 at 338; *Whiteley Ltd.* v. *Hilt* [1918] 2 K.B. 808; *Netupsky* v.
Dominion Bridge Co. Ltd. [1969] 70 W.W.R. 241.

[84] *Hole* v. *Bradbury* (1887) 12 Ch.D. 886; *cf. Delfe* v. *Delamotte* (1857) 3 K. & J. 581; *Stannard* v.
Harrison (1871) 11 W.R. 811.

[85] *Chappell & Co. Ltd.* v. *Columbia Gramophone Co.* [1914] 2 Ch. 124.

[86] *Werne & Co.* v. *Seebohm* (1888) 39 Ch.D. 73; *Nichols Advanced Vehicle Systems Inc.* v. *Rees*
[1979] R.P.C. 127.

[87] *Stevens* v. *Wildy* (1850) 11 L.J. Ch. 190; *Secretary of State for Defence* v. *Guardian Newspapers*
[1985] A.C. 339.

the Contempt of Court Act 1981 relating to disclosure of sources of information.[88]

(ix) Points as to Costs

11–81 Any discussion on the question of costs in civil proceedings must be in the context of the discretion of the Court which has full power to determine by whom and to what extent the costs of and incidental to proceedings are to be paid.[89] A person whose copyright has been infringed may not be bound to rest satisfied with the promise of the defendant not to commit any further infringement, and may press for an injunction or an undertaking to the court, and be entitled to the costs of such injunction or undertaking, even if damages awarded do not exceed a payment in.[90] It is not sufficient to entitle the defendant to escape being ordered to pay the plaintiff's costs of obtaining an injunction that he has, before issue of the writ, offered the plaintiff all that he was entitled to. But if, having made such an offer prior to action brought, the defendant were later to repeat the offer, enlarging it by including the costs of the action up to date, the costs of persisting in his action from the time of an offer to submit to an order, might be ordered against the plaintiff.[91] This may be the only way in which, where a wrong has been done, the defendant can escape from the liability of having the infringed rights asserted in court pronounced upon, and vindicated and a proper order obtained.[92] Moreover, cases of infringement of copyright should be heard in open court, and, therefore, even if the defendant admits liability, and consents to the requisite order being made in chambers, the plaintiff may be entitled to the costs of a motion for judgment in court.[93] In the Chancery Division a Master has power to make a consent order for an injunction, but only if the parties are unwilling to consent to an undertaking in lieu of an injunction.[94] It has been held that, where a plaintiff claims damages for infringement, detinue and conversion, the defendant may be given leave, under the old Rules of the Supreme Court, to pay into court one sum of money in respect of the whole action. Although the separate claims represent separate causes of action, the possibility of overlapping of damages[95] may embarrass the

---

[88] S.10; Contempt of Court Act 1981 (c. 49); *Secretary of State for Defence* v. *Guardian Newspapers Ltd.* [1985] A.C. 339.

[89] S.51 Supreme Court Act 1981; R.S.C. Ord. 62, r. 62, r. 2(4), r. 3.

[90] *Geary* v. *Norton* (1846) 1 De G. & Sm. 9; *Savory (E. W.) Ltd.* v. *The World of Golf Ltd.* [1914] 2 Ch. 566; *Performing Right Society Ltd.* v. *Ciryl Theatrical Syndicate Ltd.* [1923] 2 K.B. 146; *Samuelson* v. *Producers' Distributing Co. Ltd.* (1932) 48 R.P.C. 580; *Hall-Brown* v. *Iliffe & Sons Ltd.* [1928–35] Mac.C.C. 88; *Colgate Palmolive Ltd.* v. *Markwell Finance Ltd.* [1990] R.P.C. 197 at 200.

[91] *Jenkins* v. *Hope* [1896] 1 Ch. 278: see also R.S.C. Ord. 22 r. 14 on written offers without prejudice save as to costs; see *Colgate Palmolive Ltd.* v. *Markwell Finance Ltd.*, *supra* at 200, 201 (the offer there was held to be inadequate).

[92] *Per* Neville J. in *Savory (E. W.) Ltd.* v. *The World of Golf Ltd.*, *supra*. See *Mate & Son* v. *Samuel Stephen Ltd.* [1928–35] Mac.C.C. 257; *Oliver* v. *Dickin* [1936] 2 All E.R. 1004.

[93] *Smith (J. T.) and James (J. E.) Ltd.* v. *Service, Reeve & Co.* [1914] 2 Ch. 576; but see *Hanfstaengl* v. *Lewis* [1901–04] Mac.C.C. 68.

[94] Practice Direction [1975] 1 W.L.R. 129.

[95] See § 11–70, *ante*.

defendant unless he is allowed to pay in a single sum.[96] Under the present Rules, Ord. 22, r. 1(1) and (4), leave is not necessary.

The plaintiff, if he is successful, is usually entitled to his costs, although **11–82** there are occasions on which a plaintiff can be deprived of his costs for reasons short of misconduct.[97] The Rules provide that, if the court in the exercise of its discretion sees fit to make any order as to the costs of the proceedings, the court shall order the costs to follow the event, except when it appears to the court that in the circumstances of the case some other order should be made as to the whole or any part of the costs.[98] Where a plaintiff does not send a letter before action and the defendant, on receipt of the writ, offers to cease the activity complained of, the court may, in its discretion, dismiss with costs an application by the plaintiff for an interlocutory injunction.[99] In *Cooper v. Whittingham*,[1] Jessel J. thought that where a plaintiff came to enforce a legal right, and there had been no misconduct on his part, the court had no discretion, and could not take away his right to costs; and Chitty J. took the same view in *Upmann v. Forester*.[2] But in *Walter v. Steinkopff*,[3] North J. said that he could not understand that view—it was in the teeth of the Orders and Act, which say the judge has a discretion which he is to exercise; and, in the case of *American Tobacco Co. v. Guest*,[4] Stirling J. was of the same opinion. North J. considered that, in the case in question, the defendants had been hardly dealt with by being pulled up all at once without notice for doing what they had been doing for 12 years past and decided that the defendants should pay all the costs of the action down to a certain day, and also such further costs as would have been properly incurred by the plaintiffs in proceedings upon a motion, unopposed by the defendants, to make the interlocutory order perpetual, leaving all other costs to be borne by the parties who incurred them. But the mere fact that the damages are trifling is not sufficient reason for depriving the plaintiff of his costs.[5] If the defendant is successful he may, nevertheless, be deprived of his costs if the court thinks that he has conducted his case improperly, or his conduct prior to action has been, in the opinion of the court, unfair.[6] A defendant has been allowed costs, incurred before any statement of claim was delivered, in investigating common sources in order to show that his work was not derived from the plaintiffs, although such material was not required in the

---

[96] *Tallent v. Coldwell* [1938] Ch. 653; *Robertson v. Aberdeen Journals Ltd.* [1954] 1 W.L.R. 1084.
[97] R.S.C. Ord. 62, r. 3(3).
[98] For instances in the law of trade marks and passing off see *Kerly's Law of Trade Marks and Trade Names* (12th ed.) §§15–90 *et seq.*
[99] *Deane v. Schofield* [1962] R.P.C. 179.
[1] (1880) 15 Ch.D. 501; and see *Customagic Manufacturing Co. Ltd. v. Headquarters & General Supplies Ltd.* [1968] F.S.R. 150.
[2] (1883) 24 Ch.D. 231.
[3] [1892] 3 Ch. 489.
[4] [1892] 1 Ch. 630.
[5] *Hanfstaengl v. W. H. Smith & Sons* [1905] 1 Ch. 519.
[6] *Cobbett v. Woodward* (1872) L.R. 14 Eq. 407; *Pike v. Nicholas* (1870) L.R. 5 Ch. 251; *Kelly's Directories Ltd. v. Gavin* [1901] 1 Ch. 374; *cf. Liverpool, etc., Association Ltd. v. Commercial Press, etc., Ltd.* [1897] 2 Q.B. 1; *Corlton v. Mortimer* [1917–23] Mac.C.C. 194; *Bolton v. London Exhibitions Ltd.* (1898) 14 T.L.R. 550.

court because the plaintiff did not proceed with the action.[7] The amount of his costs which any party is entitled to receive is the amount allowed after taxation on the standard basis, unless it appears to the court to be appropriate to order costs to be taxed on the indemnity basis.[8]

8. Procedural and Related Matters

A. *Infringement of each right a separate tort*

11–83   It was held that the various rights conferred upon an author by section 1(2) of the 1911 Act, including the right "to authorise any such acts as aforesaid," were separate and distinct rights, and the infringement of each was a distinct and separate tort. Consequently judgment against the author of an infringing work for having authorised its printing was no bar to an action against the printer, though it was a bar to an action against the publisher for also authorising the printing.[9] Although the 1956 Act was differently framed, the same result followed, since section 1(2) of that Act treated the doing and the authorising of the doing of restricted acts as separate infringements. The position is the same under section 16(2) of the 1988 Act which also provides that the copyright in a work is infringed by a person who, without the licence of the copyright owner does, or authorises another to do, any of the acts restricted by the copyright.

B. *Form of defence*

11–84   The defendant to an action for infringement of copyright should, if he desires to dispute the subsistence of copyright in the work or the plaintiff's title to such copyright or both, specifically raise the point in his pleading. Also any plea of innocence, or any other specific defence should be pleaded with supporting facts.[10] He is not required (as he was under section 16 of the Literary Copyright Act 1842) to state in his defence the person he alleges to be the author or the proprietor of the copyright, though, in a proper case, the defendant might be ordered to answer interrogatories on the point.

C. *Summary judgment and striking out*

11–85   In cases where the defendant has no defence, or no plausible defence, to a claim for infringement of copyright the plaintiff may, by summons returnable before the Judge or by motion,[11] apply for summary judgment.[12]

---

[7] *Scheff* v. *Columbia Picture Corporation Ltd.* [1936–45] Mac.C.C. 254.

[8] R.S.C. Ord. 62, r. 3(4); *Berkeley Administration Inc.* v. *McClelland & Ors.* [1990] F.S.R. 565.

[9] *Ash* v. *Hutchinson & Co. (Publishers) Ltd.* [1936] Ch. 489.

[10] As to pleading of "Euro defences" see *Ransburg-Gema A.G.* v. *Electrostatic Plant Systems Ltd.* [1990] F.S.R. 287.

[11] *Sony Corporation* v. *Anand* [1982] F.S.R. 200.

[12] *Schweppes Ltd.* v. *Wellingtons Ltd.* [1984] F.S.R. 210; *Warner Brothers Inc.* v. *The Road Runner Ltd.* [1988] F.S.R. 292; *A. P. Besson Ltd.* v. *Fulleon Ltd.* [1986] F.S.R. 319.

Where a plaintiff has successfully obtained summary judgment against a defendant on the ground that he has no arguable defence, he cannot resist a "mirror image" counterclaim by the defendant on indistinguishable facts. This is so, even if he can demonstrate that there is an arguable defence: "it is not permissible to blow hot and cold."[13] The court will not, in the absence of changed circumstances, entertain an application for summary judgment where the application is inconsistent with an earlier consent order containing a direction for a speedy trial.[14] The judgment may contain a permanent injunction and an order for an inquiry as to damages, including, if appropriate, additional damages. The inquiry will normally be conducted before a Master.[15] Judgment may also be obtained on admissions made in a pleading, affidavit or otherwise[16]

In cases where the plaintiff's pleading or part of it has disclosed no reasonable cause of action at the date of the issue of the writ, the defendant may apply to the court for the pleading to be struck out and for the action to be dismissed in whole or in part.[17] The court may, on such an application, give leave to the plaintiff to amend his pleadings so as to disclose a cause of action.[18] The court will not strike out an action as an abuse of the process of the court on the ground that there is an existing action between the same parties and concerned with the same subject matter, where the second action is based on a different assignment of rights to the plaintiff and relies on different acts of infringement by the defendant.[19]

A copyright claim may also be struck out for want of prosecution if there has been inordinate and inexcusable delay carrying with it a risk that there could not be a fair trial and the same action could not be started again because the acts of infringement are statute barred.[20]

D. *Presumptions*

The 1988 Act contains a series of presumptions designed to assist a plaintiff in a copyright action whether on an application for interlocutory relief, or at the trial.[21] The presumptions as to subsistence and ownership in sec- **11–86**

---

[13] *Express Newspapers plc* v. *News (U.K.) Ltd.* [1990] F.S.R. 359.
[14] *Pierre Fabre S.A.* v. *Ronco Teleproducts Inc.* [1984] F.S.R. 148.
[15] *The Lady Anne Tennant* v. *Associated Newspapers Group Ltd.* [1979] F.S.R. 298.
[16] *Phonographic Performance Ltd.* v. *Grosvenor Leisure* [1984] F.S.R. 24; *Potton Ltd.* v. *Yorkclose Ltd.* [1990] F.S.R. 11; R.S.C. Ord. 27, r. 3.
[17] *Roban Jig & Tool Co. Ltd.* v. *Taylor* [1979] F.S.R. 130 (striking out—no title shown); *A. & M. Records Inc.* v. *Audio Magnetics Incorporated (U.K.) Ltd.* [1979] F.S.R. 1 (striking out—no reasonable cause of action); *cf. Gleeson* v. *J. Wippell & Co. Ltd.* [1979] F.S.R. 301 (res judicata—no striking out). *British Leyland Motor Corp. Ltd. & Ors.* v. *T. I. Silencers Ltd.* [1979] F.S.R. 591 (striking out defence on EEC point—see Chap. 14, *post*), *Valor International Ltd.* v. *Application Des Gaz and E. P. I. Leisure* [1979] R.P.C. 281 (pleading breaches of Treaty of Rome—see Chap. 14 § 14–135 *post*). *Paterson Zochonis Ltd.* v. *Merfarken Packaging Ltd.* [1983] F.S.R. 273; *Arrowin Ltd.* v. *Trimguard (U.K.) Ltd* [1984] R.P.C. 581; *My Kinda Bones Ltd.* v. *Dr. Pepper's Store Co. Ltd.* [1984] F.S.R. 289; *CBS Songs* v. *Amstrad Consumer Electronics plc* [1988] A.C. 1013; *Charles Church Developments plc* v. *Cronin* [1990] F.S.R. 1; *Grower* v. *B.B.C.* [1990] F.S.R. 595.
[18] See n. 17, *ante*.
[19] *Form Tubes Ltd.* v. *Guinness Brothers plc* [1989] F.S.R. 41.
[20] *Bestworth Ltd.* v. *Wearwell Ltd.* [1986] R.P.C. 527.
[21] C.D.P.A. 1988, ss.104–106. See also s.27(4) for presumption as to infringing copy.

tion 20 of the 1956 Act, which are not repeated in the 1988 Act, remain relevant for proceedings commenced before August 1, 1989.[22]

(i) Literary, dramatic, musical and artistic works

Where a name purporting to be that of the author appeared on copies of a literary, dramatic, musical or artistic work as published or, appeared on the work when it was made, the person whose name so appeared is to be presumed, until the contrary is proved, to be the author of the work.[23] If, however, the name purports to be that of an "arranger," the only presumption is that the "name" in question did some work of arrangement.[24] It is further to be presumed, until the contrary is proved, that the work was made in circumstances not falling within the provisions relating to works produced in the course of employment, or the provisions relating to Crown copyright, Parliamentary copyright or copyright of certain international organisations.[25] The name may be either the true name of the author, or a name by which he was commonly known.[26] The effect of this provision is that, where an author's name appears in the circumstances indicated, it will not be necessary for the plaintiff to prove that the person so named as author actually wrote, composed or created the work. It will be sufficient for the plaintiff to establish a documentary title commencing from such author. Where the work is alleged to be a work of joint authorship, a similar presumption is made in relation to each person alleged to be one of the authors of the work.[27]

11–87   Where the foregoing provision does not apply, that is to say, where an author's name does not appear on the work, but the work qualifies for copyright protection by virtue of first publication in the United Kingdom, or in another country to which the relevant provision of the 1988 Act extends, and a name purporting to be that of the publisher appeared on copies of the work as first published, the person whose name so appeared is presumed to have been the owner of the copyright at the time of publication.[28] This presumption applies until the contrary is proved.[29]

     If the publisher is to be presumed to have been the owner of the copyright at the time of publication, it follows that it is to be presumed that the author did not own the copyright at that time. The onus is on the person challenging the publisher's presumed ownership of the copyright to prove affirmatively that the person named as publisher did not own the copyright when the book was published.[30]

---

[22] C.D.P.A. 1988, Sched. 1 para 31(4) see §11–98, *post.*

[23] *Ibid.* s.104(2).

[24] *Per* Cross J. in *Roberton* v. *Lewis,* [1976] R.P.C. 169.

[25] *Ibid.* s.104(2)(*b*).

[26] See n. 23, *ante.*

[27] C.D.P.A. 1988, s.104(3).

[28] *Ibid.* s.104(4).

[29] See n. 28, *ante.*

[30] *Warwick Film Productions Ltd.* v. *Eisinger,* [1969] 1 Ch. 508; see §3–46, *ante.*

Deceased or anonymous authors. In the case of a literary, dramatic, **11–88** musical or artistic work, if the author of the work is dead, or the identity of the author cannot be ascertained by reasonable inquiry, the work is to be presumed to be an original work in the absence of evidence to the contrary.[31] Furthermore, in the like cases, it is to be presumed, in the absence of evidence to the contrary, that the plaintiff's allegations as to what was the first publication of the work and as to the country of first publication are correct.[32]

(ii) Presumptions regarding sound recordings

There are further presumptions which can be relied upon in any action **11–89** brought with respect to the copyright in a sound recording.[33] Where copies of the recording as issued to the public bear a label or other mark stating—(a) that a named person was the owner of copyright in the recording at the date of issue of the copies; or (b) that the recording was first published in a specified year or in a specified country—that label or mark shall be admissible as evidence of the facts so stated and shall be presumed to be correct until the contrary is proved.

(iii) Presumptions regarding other works

In proceedings brought with respect to a film, where copies of the film as **11–90** issued to the public bear a statement containing specified facts, that statement is admissible as evidence of the facts stated and is presumed to be correct until the contrary is proved.[34] The facts in question are, first, that a named person was the author or director of the film[35]; secondly, that a named person was the owner of the copyright in the film at the date of issue of the copies,[36] or thirdly, that the film was first published in a specified year or in a specified country.[37]

A presumption also applies to proceedings, with respect to a film where the film as shown in public, broadcast or included in a cable programme service bears a statement that a named person was the author or director of the film, or that a named person was the owner of the copyright in the film immediately after it was made.[38]

The presumption equally applies in proceedings relating to an infringement alleged to have occurred before the date on which copies were issued to the public or, as the case may be, before the film was shown in public, broadcast or included in a cable programme service.[39]

A similar provision applies in the case of a computer program where copies of the program are issued to the public in electronic form bearing a

---

[31] *Ibid.* s.104(5)(a).
[32] *Ibid.* s.104(5)(b).
[33] *Ibid.* s.105(1).
[34] *Ibid.* s.105(2).
[35] *Ibid.* s.105(2)(a).
[36] *Ibid.* s.105(2)(b).
[37] *Ibid.* s.105(2)(c).
[38] *Ibid.* s.105(5).
[39] See n. 38, *ante.*

statement that a named person was the owner of the copyright in the program at the date of issue of the copies or that the program was first published in a specified country or that copies of it were first issued to the public in electronic form in a specified year.[40]

(iv) Crown Copyright

11–91 Special provision is made for presumptions relating to works subject to Crown copyright. In proceedings brought with respect to a literary, dramatic or musical work in which Crown copyright subsists, where there appears on printed copies of the work a statement of the year in which the work was first published commercially, that statement shall be admissible in evidence of the fact stated and shall be presumed to be correct in the absence of evidence to the contrary.[41]

E. *Proof of copying*

11–92 Whether copying has occurred or not is a matter of fact. Direct evidence of copying is rarely available and reliance frequently has to be placed on inference drawn from circumstantial evidence. The basis of secondary proof of copying normally lies in the establishment of similarities between the plaintiff's work and the defendant's work, combined with proof of access by the author of the defendant's work to the plaintiff's work. It is good practice for the plaintiff to particularise at an early stage in an action the alleged points of similarity between his work and the defendant's work.[42] The existence of a striking general similarity coupled with evidence of the opportunity to copy will establish a prima facie case of copying which the defendant then has to answer. The evidential burden shifts to the defendant who then may seek to adduce evidence of some alternative explanation of the similarities between the two works, for example, evidence of independent creation or common source. The Court has declined to order interrogatories seeking evidence of the detailed history of the defendant's development of their copyright work on the grounds that they were "fishing" for information which would be the subject of evidence at the trial.[43] The task of the judge is then to consider the evidence as a whole and decide whether there has been copying or not.[44] An appellate court will not normally interfere with the judge's findings of fact.[45]

11–93 **Similar fact evidence.** The general rule in civil cases is that the court will admit evidence of similar facts if it is logically probative, that is, if it is logically relevant in determining the matter which is in issue, provided

---

[40] C.D.P.A. 1988, s.105(3).

[41] *Ibid.* s.106.

[42] *N. P. Windows Ltd.* v. *Cego Ltd.* [1989] F.S.R. 56.

[43] *Rockwell International Corp.* v. *Serck Industries Ltd.* [1988] F.S.R. 187.

[44] *L. B. (Plastics) Ltd.* v. *Swish Products Ltd.* [1979] R.P.C. 551 H.L.; *Antocks Lairn Ltd.* v. *I. Bloohn Ltd.* [1971] F.S.R. 490 at 493; *Catnic Components Ltd. & Anor.* v. *Hill and Smith Ltd.* [1979] F.S.R. 619 at 626; *The Duriron Co. Inc.* v. *Hugh Jennings & Co. Ltd.* [1984] F.S.R. 1; *Wham-O Manufacturing Co.* v. *Lincoln Industries Ltd.* [1985] R.P.C. 127 (Court of Appeal of New Zealand); and see *Francis Day & Hunter Ltd.* v. *Bron* [1963] Ch. 587 (proof of copying from memory).

[45] *L.B. (Plastics) Ltd.* v. *Swish Products Ltd.* (*supra*).

that it is not oppressive or unfair to the other side, and provided that the other side has fair notice of it and is able to deal with it.[46] Thus, where the issue in a copyright case is whether the similarity between the plaintiff's work and the defendant's work is due to copying or is a coincidence, it is relevant to know that the defendant has produced works which bear a close resemblance to works other than the plaintiff's works which are the subject of copyright. Whereas similarity between two works might be mere coincidence in one case, it is unlikely that there could be coincidental similarity in, say, four cases. The probative force of several resemblances together is much better than one alone. Although similar fact evidence is admissible to establish the possibility or probability of infringement, the court will not, in the absence of an allegation that the defendant has made a practice of copying others' work, order discovery of documents which are directed solely towards the credit of the defendant.[47]

Expert evidence. Expert evidence may be called to point out coinci- **11–94** dences, similarities or identical omissions with a view to establishing copying,[48] but it is not proper for an expert witness to state, as a matter of opinion, that the work was copied from another.[49] That is a question for the judge.

Expert witnesses may be called to give evidence on the question whether a particular work is a work of artistic craftmanship. The experts should be persons with special capabilities and qualifications for forming an opinion on the matter in question, although it will still be a question for the decision of the judge at the end of the day.[50]

As in the case of a witness of fact, there is no property in an expert witness so that one side cannot prohibit the other side from seeing a witness or calling him to give evidence or issuing him with a *subpoena*. Such a witness could not, however, give evidence as to communications, arising in the course of his being instructed by one party, which were protected by legal professional privilege.[51]

F. *Discovery and inspection*

Discovery and inspection of documents extends to all matters which are in **11–95** issue in the action and to any documents which contain information which might enable the party requiring discovery, either to advance his own case, or to damage the case of his adversary, but not so as to be oppressive to the party giving discovery. Discovery does not, however, extend to

---

[46] *Mood Music Publishing Co. Ltd.* v. *De Wolfe Ltd.* [1976] Ch. 119, *R.* v. *Scarrott* [1978] Q.B. 1016; *Omega* v. *Africio Textile* [1982] 1 S.A.L.R. 951; *Berger* v. *Raymond Sun Ltd.* [1984] 1 W.L.R. 625.
[47] *E. G. Music & Anor.* v. *S. F. (Films) Distributors Ltd. & Anor.* [1978] F.S.R. 121.
[48] *L. B. (Plastics) Ltd.* v. *Swish Products Ltd., supra,* at p. 619; *Billhöfer Maschinen Fabrik G.m.b.h.* v. *Dixon & Co. Ltd.* [1990] F.S.R. 105. The question of expert evidence should be raised on the Summons for Directions, R.S.C. Ord. 38, r. 36.
[49] *Deeks* v. *Wells* [1928–35] Mac.C.C. 353 (P.C.); *Bauman* v. *Fussell* [1978] R.P.C. 485.
[50] *George Hensher Ltd.* v. *Restawile Upholstery (Lancs.) Ltd.* [1976] A.C. 64 at 82.
[51] *Harmony Shipping Co. S.A.* v. *Saudi Europe Line Ltd.* [1979] 1 W.L.R. 1380.

matters which relate solely to the credit of a party.[52] The court has jurisdiction to order discovery even prior to service of the statement of claim,
but the power is rarely exercised.[53] If, as is common, there is a split trial as
to liability and quantum of damages, the Court will not normally require
discovery of documents relating only to quantum before his liability has
been established. If confidential documents are relevant the court may, in
its discretion, require the defendant to give an undertaking not to make
use of the information disclosed thereby and limit the right to take away
documents or make copies of them.[54] Inspection of documents relating to
trade secrets may be ordered subject to safeguards as to where and by
whom the documents may be inspected. A fair balance has to be struck
between the natural wish of a party to have his confidential documents
adequately protected and the natural wish of the other party to see any
documents which may support his case.[55] A defendant who was not a
company, was entitled to claim privilege from giving discovery of certain
documents relating to the supply and sale of infringing copies on the
ground that, by reason of the criminal offences in the 1956 Act, he would
tend to incriminate himself. This privilege was withdrawn in certain proceedings and circumstances specified in section 72 of the Supreme Court
Act 1981, as amended.[56]

Although a party to an action has prima facie an unrestricted right to
inspect the other party's documents, that right is only for the purposes of
the action and where there is a real risk that a party will use matters disclosed on inspection for a collateral purpose, the court can, under its
inherent jurisiction, prevent an abuse of the process of the court.[57] There
is an implied undertaking to the court by a solicitor, who has obtained
copies of documents belonging to his client's adversary, not to use the
copies or allow them to be used for any purpose other than the proper conduct of the action on behalf of his client. Breach of that undertaking,
which is exacted in the interests of justice, is a contempt of court.[58] The
implied undertaking prevents the use of the documents and of the information contained in them for collateral purposes, such as in a fresh action,
without the leave of the court. The court can also restrain the use of documents which have been obtained from the other party by stealth or by a

---

[52] *George Ballantine & Sons Ltd.* v. *F.E.R. Dixon & Son Ltd.* [1975] R.P.C. 111; R.S.C. Ord. 24,
E.G. Music v. *S.F. (Film) Distributors Ltd.* [1978] F.S.R. 121; *British Leyland Motor Corp. &
Ors.* v. *Wyatt Interpart Co. Ltd.* [1979] F.S.R. 39 and 583 (EEC point).

[53] *R.H.M. Foods Ltd.* v. *Bovril Ltd.* [1983] R.P.C. 275.

[54] *Centri-Spray* v. *Cera International Ltd. & Others* [1979] F.S.R. 175; see also on confidentiality
R. v. *N.S.P.C.C.* [1978] A.C. 171; *Science Research Council* v. *Nasse* [1980] A.C. 1028. See §
21–27, *post.*

[55] *Format Communications Mfg. Ltd.* v. *ITT (U.K.) Ltd.* [1983] F.S.R. 473; *Roussel Uclaf* v. *ICI*
[1989] R.P.C. 59; *Atari* v. *Philips Electronics and Associated Industries Ltd.* [1988] 5 F.S.R. 416;
Roussel Uclaf v. *I.C.I.* (No. 2) [1990] R.P.C. 45.

[56] Rank Film Distributors Ltd. & Ors. v. *Video Information Centre & Ors.*, [1982] A.C. 380 *cf.
Optical Coatings Ltd. & Anor.* v. *Dan Fox & Ors.* (1980) unreported; and *British Steel Corporation* v. *Granada Television Ltd.*, [1981] A.C. 1096. See §11–52 *et seq., ante.*

[57] *Church of Scientology of California* v. *Department of Health & Social Security* [1979] 1 W.L.R.
723.

[58] *Home Office* v. *Harman* [1983] 1 A.C. 280; *Sybron Corpn.* v. *Barclays Bank plc* [1985] Ch. 299.

trick or a mistake and refuse to admit them in evidence.[59] The restraint may extend to information derived from the documents so obtained. An application may be made to the court for permission for documents disclosed in one action to be used in another action. Leave is only granted in special circumstances and not as a general rule. Leave would not be granted to allow documents disclosed in one action to be used in other proceedings having no connection with the original cause of action.[60] The fact that the relevant material could be found in court transcripts of what was said in open court was not a good reason for granting leave.[61] The general policy of the Courts is to preserve the integrity of undertakings given to it not to use discovered material for any purpose other than the proper conduct of the action. Leave may be granted for the use of documents in proceedings for contempt of court if no injustice would be done in the circumstances of the case,[62] even though those documents were obtained on execution of an Anton Piller order. For the purposes of discovery of documents, the essential feature of a document is that it should convey information and, accordingly, a tape on which information is recorded is a document.[63] Inspection of a tape is given by the party giving discovery playing the tape to the party to whom discovery is given, who makes his own recording as it is played.[64] A film is also probably a document.[65]

The Vice-Chancellor, in *Sweet* v. *Maugham*,[66] said: "It has always been considered sufficient to allege, generally, that the defendant's work contains several passages which have been pirated from the plaintiff's work. Then, when the injunction has been moved for, the two works have been brought into court, and the counsel have pointed out to the court the passages which they rely upon as showing the piracy." This, however, is not the modern practice. A plaintiff, whether on motion for interlocutory relief, or in an action, is expected to indicate, in an exhibit to an affidavit or in particulars to a statement of claim, by reference to parallel passages or otherwise, the parts he mainly relies upon as constituting an infringement, although he may well reserve the right, at the trial, to rely upon general similarities as further evidence of piracy. If a plaintiff brings an action to protect a work, being only entitled to copyright in a small part of such work, he ought to tell the defendant, in his claim, what that part is, otherwise costs unnecessarily incurred must be borne by the plaintiff.[67]

In an action for infringement of copyright in a picture it is not necessary

---

[59] *ITC Film Distributors Ltd.* v. *Video Exchange Ltd.* [1982] Ch. 431; *English & American Insurance Co. Ltd.* v. *Herbert Smith* [1988] F.S.R. 232.

[60] *Commissioners of Customs & Excise* v. *Hamlin Slowe* [1986] F.S.R. 346.

[61] *CBS Songs Ltd.* v. *Amstrad Consumer Electronics plc* [1987] R.P.C. 417; see, however, R.S.C. O. 24, r. 14A, which came into force on October 1, 1987.

[62] *Crest Homes plc* v. *Marks* [1987] A.C. 829.

[63] *Grant* v. *South Western and County Properties Ltd.* [1975] Ch. 185.

[64] See n. 63, *ante.*

[65] *Senior* v. *Holdsworth* [1976] Q.B. 23.

[66] (1840) 11 Sim. 51; *Hotten* v. *Arthur* (1863) 1 H. & M. 603. As to points arising upon the form of the statement of claim in particular cases, see *Oliver* v. *Dickin* [1936] 2 All E.R. 1004; *Ash* v. *Hutchinson & Co. (Publishers) Ltd.* [1936] Ch. 489.

[67] *Page* v. *Wisden* (1869) 17 W.R. 483; and generally a defendant can obtain an order for particulars.

to produce the original from which the alleged copy has been made[68] if it can be proved by other satisfactory evidence.[69] Indeed, in many cases, the original work has disappeared or been destroyed before the action is commenced or comes to trial[70]

A plaintiff may confine his claim in copyright to part of an unpublished work and, in that case, he will not be required, on discovery, to disclose the remainder.[71]

G. Period of limitation

11–96 The 1988 Act, like the 1956 Act, provides no special limitation period, so that the 6-year period provided in the Limitation Act 1980[72] for actions for tort operates in respect of actions for infringement. The limitation period in respect of an action for conversion under the 1956 Act ran from the date of the conversion, and not from the date of the infringement since conversion was a separate tort. It was expressly provided that if, by virtue of section 3(2) of the Limitation Act 1939, the title of the owner of the copyright to an infringing copy would, if he had been the owner of such copy, have been extinguished at the end of the period mentioned in that subsection, he was not to be entitled to any rights and remedies, under section 18 of the 1956 Act, in respect of anything done in relation to that copy after the end of the period.[73] The effect of section 3(2) of the Limitation Act 1939, was that, where a cause of action for conversion or detention had accrued, and the period of six years had elapsed, and the owner had not recovered possession, the title of the owner of the chattel was extinguished.

It is important to note that each act of infringement is a separate tort. The fact that the plaintiff's remedy for one act of infringement is barred does not extinguish the plaintiff's copyright: he may sue for subsequent or continuing infringements committed within the limitation period.

9. Transitional Provisions

11–97 The commencement date of the copyright provisions of the 1988 Act was August 1, 1989. Transitional provisions regulate the extent to which the provisions of the 1956 Act continue to apply to infringements committed and other acts done before commencement and the applicability of the new remedies for infringement to pre-commencement acts and things.[74]

11–98 The general principles are that:

(1) the new copyright provisions of Part I of the 1988 Act apply in relation to things existing at commencement as they apply in relation

---

[68] *Lucas* v. *Williams & Sons* [1892] 2 Q.B. 113.
[69] *Wham-O Manufacturing Co.* v. *Lincoln Industries Ltd.* [1985] R.P.C. 127.
[70] *George Hensher Ltd.* v. *Restawile Upholstery (Lancs) Ltd.* [1976] A.C. 64 at 79H; *James Arnold & Co. Ltd.* v. *Miafern Ltd.* [1980] R.P.C. 397 at 402; *Allibert S.A.* v. *O'Connor* [1981] F.S.R. 613 at 621; *Wham-O Manufacturing Co.* v. *Lincoln Industries Ltd.* [1985] R.P.C. 127 at 142; *Plix Products Ltd.* v. *Frank M. Winstone (Merchants) Ltd.* [1986] F.S.R. 608.
[71] *Sitwell* v. *Sun Engraving Co. Ltd.* (1938) 107 L.J. Ch. 68.
[72] c. 58, s.2 (replacing the Limitation Act 1939) (2 & 3 Geo. 6, c. 21). §A–653, *post.*
[73] S.18(1), Copyright Act 1956. Now s.3(2) Limitation Act 1980. See §A–654, *post.*
[74] C.D.P.A. 1988, s.170 and Schedule 1, paras. 31–33.

to things coming into existence after commencement, subject to any express provision to the contrary[75]

(2) The whole of the 1956 Act has been repealed.[76]

The particular transitional provision affecting remedies for infringement are as follows:

(1) The remedies for infringement in sections 96 and 97, including the provision for additional damages, apply only in relation to an infringement of copyright committed after commencement. It is expressly provided that, in relation to infringements committed before commencement, section 17 of the 1956 Act continues to apply,[77] *e.g.* in relation to claims for infringement damages and additional damages.

(2) The remedy of conversion damages available under section 7 of the 1911 Act and section 18 of the 1956 Act does not apply after commencement except for purposes of proceedings begun before commencement.[78]

(3) The new statutory remedies of delivery up by court order (section 99) and seizure of infringing copies without court order (section 100) apply to infringing copies and other articles made before or after commencement.[79]

(4) Where section 17 or 18 of the 1956 Act applies, section 19 of that Act dealing with the rights and remedies of an exclusive licensee continues to apply. The provisions in the 1988 Act dealing with the rights and remedies of the exclusive licensee (sections 101–102) apply where sections 96 to 100 of the 1988 Act apply[80] and they do not apply to a licence granted before June 1, 1957 (the commencement date of the 1956 Act).

(5) The presumptions contained in section 20 of the 1956 Act continue to apply in proceedings brought by virtue of that Act. The presumptions in the 1988 Act, contained in sections 104 to 106, apply only in proceedings brought by virtue of the 1988 Act.[81]

---

[75] *Ibid.* Sched. 1, para. 3.
[76] *Ibid.* s.303(2), Schedule 8.
[77] *Ibid.* Sched. 1, para. 31(1). See §11–65 *et seq., ante.*
[78] *Ibid.* Sched. 1, para. 31(2). See §11–68 *et seq., ante.*
[79] *Ibid.* Sched. 1, para. 31(2). See §11–17 *and* 11–18, *ante.*
[80] *Ibid.* Sched. 1, para. 31(3). See §11–9, *ante.*
[81] *Ibid.* Sched. 1, para. 31(4). See §11–86 *et seq., ante.*

CHAPTER 12

LIBRARIES

Contents

1. Permitted acts in respect of Libraries and Archives

In relation to libraries and archives the 1988 Act, like the 1956 Act, contains provisions dealing with certain acts which do not constitute infringement of copyright. These provisions are dealt with elsewhere in this book.[1]   **12–1**

2. Deposit of Books

History of the privilege. The 1911 Act, in obedience to Article 4 of the   **12–2** Revised Convention of Berne, which provided that the enjoyment and exercise of the rights conferred by the Convention should not be subject to the performance of any formality, abolished all necessity for registration of copyright, but substantially re-enacted sections 6 to 9 of the Copyright Act 1842[2] relating to the deposit of published books at the British Museum and other libraries.[3] A strong protest was made by the publishing trade during the passage of the 1911 Act through Parliament with a view to getting these provisions, which were alleged to be an undue tax upon the trade, modified in favour of the publishers. But these efforts failed, and, in fact, the old law was slightly extended by the 1911 Act inasmuch as the National Library of Wales was added to the list of libraries which can, under certain circumstances, demand delivery of a copy of a published book.

Certain representations were made to the 1952 Copyright Committee that the delivery of copies of books to the libraries free of charge was unfair to publishers, but the Committee recommended that the privilege of the libraries of deposit to receive copies of published works should not be discontinued.[4] The 1956 Act in fact left unrepealed section 15 of the 1911 Act under which this privilege was conferred.[5]

---

[1] See Chap. 10, and, in particular, § 10–31 *et seq., ante.*
[2] 5 & 6 Vict. c. 45.
[3] Copright Act 1911, s.15.
[4] Cmd. 8662, para. 58.
[5] Copyright Act 1956, s.50(2) and Sched. 9, both repealed by the Statute Law (Repeals) Act 1974 (c. 22).

Although the 1977 Copyright Committee received evidence on a number of topics relating to libraries of deposit, it considered that, since the link between the legal recognition of property rights in published literary matter and its deposit in one or more designated libraries ceased to exist at a date now remote, there was no reason why the law of copyright should any longer concern itself with the subject of legal deposit. The Committee therefore made no formal recommendations on the subject although the Report set out the Committee's views on certain matters,[6] for instance that all deposit libraries should be on the same footing. The 1988 Act also left unrepealed section 15 of the 1911 Act.[7]

12–3 **The libraries entitled to the privilege.** Section 15(1) of the 1911 Act requires the publisher of every book published[8] in the United Kingdom to deliver, at his own expense, one copy of the book, within one month after publication, to the Trustees of the British Museum, who are to give a receipt for the same. But, by the Copyright (British Museum) Act 1915,[9] power was given to the Board of Trade, on application of the Trustees of the British Museum, to exempt from the obligations of this section trade publications unless copies thereof are demanded by the Trustees, and this power was exercised, in the cases of certain classes of trade publications, by a regulation of August 9, 1915.[10] By the British Museum Act 1932[11] it was provided that works of the classes mentioned in the Schedule (*i.e.* trade publications, timetables, tests and similar works) need not be supplied to the Trustees unless demanded, if such classes were prescribed by regulations made by the Trustees, and regulations were made by the Trustees on October 12, 1932.[12] It is understood that, although registers of voters are listed in these regulations, these are now regularly demanded. The 1915 Act was repealed by the 1932 Act, but, by section 2 of the 1932 Act, regulations made under the 1915 Act are to be deemed to have been made by the Trustees under the 1932 Act. This is unaffected by the 1956 and 1988 Acts. The British Library Act 1972,[13] which established the British Library and provided for the transfer of certain articles, the property of the Trustees of the British Museum, to the British Library Board, contained amendments affecting the above provisions.[14] Thus, as from July 1, 1973,[15] references in section 15(1), (3) and (6) to the Trustees of the British Museum are to have effect as if they were references to the Board. Therefore delivery is now required to the Board and not to the Trustees. The 1972 Act also provided for corresponding amendments in section 1(1) of the 1932 Act and provided that the power to make regulations under section 1(2) of the 1932 Act should be exercisable by the

---

[6] Cmnd. 6732, paras. 833 and 834.

[7] C.D.P.A. 1988 s.303 and Sched. 8.

[8] Presumably "publication" now has to be construed by reference to the definition in s.175 C.D.P.A. 1988: see Sched. 1, paras. 3 and 4 of that Act.

[9] 5 & 6 Geo. 5, c. 38.

[10] S.R. & O. 1915 No. 773, § B–1, *post.*

[11] 22 & 23 Geo. 5, c. 34, § A–618, *post.*

[12] S.R. & O. 1935 No. 278, § B–2. *post.*

[13] c. 54.

[14] *Ibid.* ss.1, 3 and 4.

[15] *Ibid.* s.3(2) and the British Library Act (Appointed Day) Order 1973 (No. 1125 (c. 27)).

Board, not by the Trustees. Finally, the 1972 Act provided that any regulations of the Trustees under that section which were in force immediately before July 1, 1973, should continue in force as if made by the Board thereunder with the substitution for references in the regulations to the Trustees, of references to the Board. This will therefore apply to the regulations made under the 1915 Act and under the 1932 Act.

Copies are likewise to be delivered for the benefit of the Bodleian Library, Oxford, the University Library, Cambridge, the Library of the Faculty of Advocates at Edinburgh,[16] the Library of Trinity College, Dublin and the National Library of Wales, at any time within a month after a written demand made within 12 months after publication or within one month after publication if demand is made before publication.[17] In the case of an encyclopedia, newspaper, review, magazine, or work published in a series of numbers or parts, the written demand may include all numbers or parts of the work which may be subsequently published.[17]

National Library of Wales. Originally the National Library of Wales   **12–4** was at a disadvantage as section 15(5) of the 1911 Act provides that the books of which copies are to be delivered to that library should not include books of such classes as might be specified in Board of Trade regulations, and the Board did issue regulations whereby copies could not be demanded of certain classes of books.[18] However such regulations have been revoked,[19] so that the National Library of Wales is now on the same footing as the other libraries.

Meaning of "book." For the purposes of section 15 of the 1911 Act, the   **12–5** expression "book" includes every part or division of a book, pamphlet, sheet of letterpress, sheet of music, map, plan, chart or table separately published, but does not include any second or subsequent edition of a book, unless such edition contains additions or alterations either in the letterpress or in the maps, prints, or other engravings belonging thereto.[20]

What copies are to be delivered. The copy to be delivered to the British   **12–6** Library Board must be one of the best copies published,[21] but the copy for each of the other libraries is to be one of the copies of which the largest number is printed for sale.[22]

---

[16] It is provided by the National Library of Scotland Act 1925 (15 & 16 Geo. 5, c.73) that the privileges enjoyed by this body shall thereafter be transferred to the National Library of Scotland.

[17] Copyright Act 1911, s.15(2).

[18] The National Library of Wales (Delivery of Books) Regulations 1924, as amended in 1956. *Copinger* (12th ed.), §1732.

[19] The National Library of Wales (Delivery of Books) (Amendment) Order 1987 (1987 S.I. No. 698), made by the Lord President of the Council substituted in s.15(5) of the 1911 Act for the Board of Trade by the Transfer of Functions (Arts, Libraries and National Heritage) Order 1986 (S.I. 1986 No. 600).

[20] Copyright Act 1911, s.15(7).

[21] *Ibid.* s.15(3).

[22] *Ibid.* s.15(4).

12–7 **Effect of failure to delivery copies.** Section 15 of the 1911 Act does not make delivery of the copies a condition of copyright. The only effect of non-compliance with the requirements of the section is to expose the publisher, upon whom the duty is imposed of delivering the requisite copies of the work, to a fine, not exceeding £5 and the value of the book, upon summary conviction.[23] That is to say, he is liable to a separate fine for each library in respect of which default is made.

12–8 **Foreign books published in England.** Section 29 of the 1911 Act provided that, where the Act was applied by Order in Council to works first published in a foreign country, the provisions of that Act as to the delivery of copies of books should not apply to works first published in such country except so far as was provided by the Order.[24] This provision is not repeated in the 1956 and 1988 Acts. Moreover, it must be pointed out that section 15 of the 1911 Act deals with all books published in the United Kingdom, irrespective of whether they are entitled to copyright protection or not, and does not use the expression "first published." It is understood that, while the libraries of deposit do not claim that every book, copies of which are issued to the public in the United Kingdom, falls within the section, they do make this claim where copies are so issued of a book upon which the imprint of a London publisher appears, whether alone or jointly with a foreign publisher, whether or not the work has been first published in another country.[25]

3. Deposit of Scripts

12–9 **Deposit of scripts of new plays.** Quite apart from the Copyright Acts, the Theatres Act 1968[26] requires delivery of copies of scripts of plays to the Trustees of the British Museum. Since the British Library Act 1972[27] makes no reference to the 1968 Act, presumably delivery has still to be made to the Trustees and not to the Board. Thus, the 1968 Act provides that,[28] with certain limited exceptions,[29] where there is given in Great Britain a public performance of a new play, being a performance based on a script, a copy of the actual script on which that performance was based must be delivered to the Trustees of the British Museum free of charge within the period of one month beginning with the date of the performance; the Trustees are required to give a written receipt for every script so delivered.

12–10 **Definitions.** The 1968 Act contains definitions of "script," "play," "public performance" and "public performance of a new play." Thus, "script" is defined as the text of the play (whether expressed in words or in musical

---

[23] Copyright Act 1911, s.15(6); and see Criminal Law Act 1977 (c. 45) s.31(5), (6) and Criminal Justice Act 1982 (c. 48) s.46.
[24] *Ibid.* s.29(1), proviso (iii).
[25] See discussion in Report of 1952 Copyright Committee, Cmd. 8662, paras. 60–65.
[26] c. 54.
[27] c. 54.
[28] Theatres Act 1968, s.11(1).
[29] *Ibid.* s.11(4).

or other notation) together with any stage or other directions for its perfor-mance, whether contained in a single document or not.[30] "Play" is defined as (a) any dramatic piece, whether involving improvisation or not, which is given wholly or in part by one or more persons actually present and per-forming and in which the whole or a major proportion of what is done by the person or persons performing, whether by way of speech, singing or action, involves the playing of a role, and (b) any ballet given wholly or in part by one or more persons actually present and performing, whether or not it falls within paragraph (a) of this definition.[31] "Public performance" is defined as including any performance in a public place within the mean-ing of the Public Order Act 1936,[32] and any performance which the public or any section thereof are permitted to attend, whether on payment or otherwise.[33] Finally "public performance of a new play" is defined as a public performance of a play of which no previous public performance has ever been given in Great Britain, but does not include a public perfor-mance of a play which either is based on a script substantially the same as that on which a previous public performance of a play given there was based, or is based substantially on a text of the play which has been pub-lished in the United Kingdom.[34]

Effect of failure to deliver copies. If the above-mentioned require-ments as to delivery are not complied with, then any person who pre-sented the relevant performance is liable, on summary conviction, to a fine not exceeding £5.[35] However, it is provided that a person is not to be treated as presenting a performance of a play by reason only of his taking part therein as a performer.[36] **12–11**

4. Public Lending Right

A. *Public Lending Right Act 1979*

Public lending right. After a long and chequered career a public lending right Bill became law in 1979. The Public Lending Right Act 1979[37] is, however, something of a misnomer. That is to say, although the object of the Act is to provide payments to authors out of a central fund, the "right" is not part of the author's copyright and is only conferred on authors if their books are lent to the public by local library authorities in the United Kingdom.[38] Books which are not lent do not, therefore, qualify; this will, **12–12**

---

[30] Theatres Act 1968, s.9(2).
[31] *Ibid.* s.18(1).
[32] 1 Edw. 8 & 1 Geo. 6, s.9; see now Criminal Justice Act 1972 (c. 71), s.33 and Roads (Scot-land) Act 1984 (c. 54), Sched. 9.
[33] See n. 31, *supra.*
[34] Theatres Act 1968, s.11(3).
[35] *Ibid.* s.11(2); and see Criminal Justice Act 1982 (c. 48) s.46.
[36] *Ibid.* s.18(2).
[37] c. 10, § A–647, *post.* The Act extends to Northern Ireland and came into force on March 1, 1980; S.I. 1980 No. 83 (c. 5); and see the Transfer of Functions (Acts, Libraries and National Heritage) Order 1986, (S.I. 1986 No. 600).
[38] Public Lending Right Act 1979, s.1(1).

no doubt, be the case for many books of reference. Moreover, to become eligible for a payment, the book must be registered.[39] It is only when the Registrar of Public Lending Right has determined, in accordance with a scheme, the sum (if any) due by way of public lending right in the case of any registered book, that the author obtains any effective "right" since only then is he able to recover such sums from the Registrar as a debt due.[40] Since the basic fund was initially £2 million for each financial year, from which administration expenses and so on are to be paid,[41] the annual sum received by any one author is likely to be small, as has proved to be the case. Further, as such sums are to be dependent upon the number of times a book is lent,[42] popular authors could benefit more than the less popular, as has also proved to be the case. Another factor which could reduce the sum per author is the fact that the Act applies to all authors, not just United Kingdom authors, so that foreign authors will also be entitled to benefit under the Act unless excluded by the scheme. Subject to any provision of the scheme, the "right," such as it is, is to last from the date of the book's first publication (or, if later, the beginning of the year in which application is made for it to be registered) until 50 years have elapsed since the end of the year in which the author died.[43]

12–13   **Administration of public lending right.** Most of the important matters relating to the administration of public lending right are not contained in the 1979 Act but are to be provided for by a scheme[44] which may be varied from time to time.[45]

Matters to be covered by the scheme are:

(a) Classes, descriptions and categories of books in respect of which public lending right subsists.[46]

(b) Scales of payments to be made from the central fund in respect of public lending right.[46]

(c) The establishment and maintenance of a register of books in respect of which public lending right subsists and the persons entitled to the right in respect of any registered book, the register to be conclusive as to subsistence of and entitlement to public lending right.[47]

(d) The making and amendment of entries in the register.[48]

(e) Public lending right:
  (i) to be established by registration,

---

[39] Public Lending Right Act 1979, s.1(7) and s.4.
[40] *Ibid.* s.1(5).
[41] *Ibid.* s.2: increased to £2.75 million by The Public Lending Right (Increase of Limit) Order 1985, (S.I. 1985 No. 201) and to £3.5 million by The Public Lending Right (Increase of Limit) Order 1988, (S.I. 1988 No. 609).
[42] *Ibid.* s.3(3).
[43] *Ibid.* s.1(6): and see § 12–24 *post*.
[44] *Ibid.* s.3(1).
[45] *Ibid.* s.3(7).
[46] *Ibid.* s.1(2).
[47] *Ibid.* s.1(4) and s.4(3).
[48] *Ibid.* s.4(4).

(ii) to be transmissible by assignment or assignation, by testamentary disposition or by operation of law, as personal or movable property.

(iii) to be claimed by or on behalf of the person for the time being entitled, and

(iv) to be renounced (either in whole or in part, and either temporarily or for all time) on notice being given to the Registrar of Public Lending Right to that effect.[49]

(f) Public lending right to be dependent on, and its extent ascertainable by reference to, the number of occasions on which books are lent out from particular libraries, to be specified by the scheme or identified in accordance with provision made by it.[50]

(g) Local library authorities to be required:
(i) to give information as to loans made by them to the public of books in respect of which public lending right subsists, or of other books, and

(ii) to arrange for books to be numbered, or otherwise marked or coded, with a view to facilitating the maintenance of the register and the ascertainment and administration of public lending right.[51]

(h) Local authorities will be reimbursed their expenses in giving effect to the scheme. The amount of such expenditure to be ascertained in accordance with such calculations as the scheme may prescribe.[52]

The register. Only books which fall within a class, description or **12–14** category of books prescribed by the scheme as one in respect of which public lending right subsists can be registered.[53] An entry on the register is conclusive both as to subsistence of and entitlement to public lending right.[54] Entries on the register are to be made or amended on application made in the manner prescribed by the scheme and supported by particulars so prescribed (verified as so prescribed) so as to indicate, in the case of any book, who (if anyone) is for the time being entitled to public lending right in respect of it.[55] The Registrar of Public Lending Right may direct the removal from the register of every entry relating to a book in whose case no sum has become due by way of public lending right for a period of at least 10 years, but without prejudice to a subsequent application for the entries to be restored to the register.[56] The Registrar may require the payment of fees, according to scales and rates prescribed by the scheme, for supplying copies of entries in the register; and the copy of an entry, certified under the hand of the Registrar or an officer of his with authority in

---

[49] Public Lending Right Act 1979, s.1(7).
[50] *Ibid.* s.3(3).
[51] *Ibid.* s.3(5).
[52] *Ibid.* s.3(6).
[53] *Ibid.* s.4(2).
[54] *Ibid.* s.4(3).
[55] *Ibid.* s.4(4).
[56] *Ibid.* s.4(5).

that behalf (which authority it is not necessary to prove) is to be admissible in evidence in all legal proceedings as of equal validity with the original.[57]

12-15 **Registrar of Public Lending Right.** Public lending right is to be administered by the Registrar of Public Lending Right and his staff,[58] the Registrar being under a duty to establish and maintain the register in accordance with the scheme and to determine the sums due by way of public lending right.[59] The central fund out of which sums will be paid in respect of public lending right will be under the control of the Registrar.[60]

12-16 **Offences.** The 1979 Act makes it an offence for any person, in connection with the entry of any matter whatsoever in the register, to make any statement which he knows to be false in a material particular or recklessly to make any statement which is false in a material particular. A person who commits such an offence is liable on summary conviction to a fine of not more than £1,000.[61]

Where such an offence has been committed by a body corporate is proved to have been committed with the consent or connivance of, or to be attributable to any neglect on the part of, a director, manager, secretary or other similar officer of the body corporate, or any person who was purporting to act in such capacity, he (as well as the body corporate) will be guilty of that offence and be liable to be proceeded against accordingly. Where the affairs of a body corporate are managed by its members, this provision applies in relation to the acts and defaults of a member in connection with his functions of management as if he were a director of the body corporate.[62]

B. The scheme

12-17 **History of the Scheme.** Some two years after the 1979 Act came into force,[63] a Scheme was promulgated as an Appendix to The Public Lending Right Scheme 1982 (Commencement) Order 1982,[64] since when it has been subjected to considerable amendment.[65]

12-18 **Registration required: eligible books and posthumously eligible books.** To be eligible for public lending right a book must be registered after application therefor.[66] But not all books are registrable.[67] Thus, for

---

[57] Public Lending Right Act 1979, s.4(6).
[58] *Ibid.* s.1(3).
[59] *Ibid.* s.1(4), (5).
[60] *Ibid.* s.2.
[61] *Ibid.* s.4(7): and see Criminal Justice Act 1982 (c. 48) s.46.
[62] *Ibid.* s.4(8).
[63] See n. 37, *supra.*
[64] S.I. 1982 No. 719.
[65] Currently the amending Statutory Instruments are, 1983 No. 480, 1983 No. 1688, 1984 No. 1847, 1985 No. 1581, 1986 No. 2103, 1987 No. 1908, 1988 No. 2070, 1989 No.2188 and 1990 No. 2360. The Scheme, as amended up to and including the 1990 Order, is set out in Appendix 2 of that Order; § A–657, *post.*
[66] Scheme Arts. 9, 10, 14, 14A, 17 and 17B, and Sched. 1.
[67] *Ibid.* Arts. 6 and 6A.

instance, books with more than four authors do not qualify except in special circumstances. Nor do serial publications such as newspapers, magazines, journals and periodicals. Further, if an application for first registration of public lending right in respect of a book has not been made before June 30, 1991, then such a book does not qualify unless it has an International Standard Book Number. Again, to qualify, the author, or at least one of the authors, must be an eligible person, or a posthumously eligible person.[68]

Eligible persons and posthumously eligible persons. An eligible person must be an author of the book who at the date of the application has his only or principal home in the United Kingdom or the Federal Republic of Germany, or, if he has no home, has been present in one of those countries for not less than 12 months out of the preceeding 24 months.[68] Thus, at the moment, the rights of foreign authors are limited, those from the Federal Republic of Germany benefiting, presumably, because British authors benefit from that country's system. Since the Scheme can be varied,[69] no doubt it could be further amended to include other foreign authors.   **12–19**

Under Article 5A of the Scheme, in relation to an application relating to a posthumously eligible book, an author who is dead is a posthumously eligible person if, had he been an applicant for first registration of public lending right in relation to that book at the date of his death, he would have been an eligible person in accordance with Article 5 of the Scheme.

Authors. Authors are also defined by the Scheme and include writers, translators, editors and compilers in certain circumstances, and illustrators.[70] As a result of the amendments in 1988 applications after an author's death are now possible.[71] Further, although a book has to be a printed and bound publication, books published up to 10 years after the author's death are included.[72]   **12–20**

The register. The register has to contain particulars of the title of the book, the name or names of the persons appearing on the title page as the authors thereof, the true identity of an author if different from such name, the number given to the book by the Registrar, the name and address of each person entitled to the right in respect of the book and, if more than one, the share of each such person in such right.[73] It would seem that, where a book has two or more authors, including any who are not eligible persons, the share of any non-eligible person will not be registered until he becomes and remains an eligible person and makes an application for registration.[74] Only registered owners are entitled to payment.[75]   **12–21**

---

[68] Scheme Arts. 5 and 5A: see Art. 5 (which defines "principal home") and Sched. 5.
[69] Public Lending Right Act 1979, s.3(7).
[70] Scheme Art. 4(1), but subject to Art. 4(2).
[71] *Ibid.* Arts. 5A, 6A, 14A and 17B.
[72] *Ibid.* Arts. 6 and 6A.
[73] *Ibid.* Arts. 7 and 8: and see Art. 9A. The register may be amended: *ibid.* Arts. 12 and 13.
[74] *Ibid.* Arts. 2(1) "eligible author", 9(2), (3), 9A, 14 and 17: as to posthumously eligible persons see *ibid.* Arts. 9(4), 9A, 14A and 17B.
[75] *Ibid.* Art. 47.

12–22 **Inspection of the register.** Since the right depends on registration,[76] and since the register is conclusive as to whether public lending right subsists in a particular book and also as to the persons (if any) who are for the time being entitled to the right,[77] it is, perhaps, surprising that the Scheme gives no automatic right for the public to inspect the register.[78] Indeed, the Scheme goes the other way in that it is provided[79] that the Registrar shall not supply a copy of any entry in the register otherwise than to a registered owner, as regards any entry which relates to his registered interest, or, such other person as the registered owner may direct, but if the entry also relates to other registered owners, only with the consent of all such owners. A fee is payable for a copy entry. But, without being able to inspect the register, how does a member of the public know whom to approach? What if a registered owner refuses to so direct? Why, indeed, is the consent of a registered owner necessary?

12–23 **Procedure for registration.** The Scheme sets out the procedures to be followed for registration of public lending right, or of an eligible author's share of the right, or of a posthumously eligible person's share of the right, for the transfer of a registered interest and for the renunciation of a registered interest.[80] The Registrar may require evidence to be submitted to satisfy him that a book is an eligible book, that a person applying as author for the first registration of public lending right, or the registration of a share of the right, is in fact the author of that book and is an eligible person, that any co-author who is not a party to an application for first registration of public lending right is dead or cannot be traced despite all reasonable steps having been taken to do so, and (where an application under Article 17(1)(c)(iv) has been made) that there is such an agreement or arrangement as is mentioned therein and that the share of public lending right of the person making the application is as specified in that agreement or arrangement.[81] For these purposes the Registrar may require a statutory declaration to be made.[81] The Registrar has power to treat applications as abandoned when information requested has not been given.[82] Also, under section 4(5) of the 1979 Act, the Registrar has power to remove entries from the register where no sum has become due by way of public lending right for a period of at least 10 years, although application for restoration to the register can be made subsequently.[83]

12–24 **Transmission and duration of public lending right.** The Scheme provides that a registered interest is transmissible by assignment or assignation, by testamentary disposition or by operation of law, as personal or movable property, so long, as regards a particular book, as the right in respect of that book is capable of subsisting.[84] Under the Scheme the

---

[76] Scheme Art. 10: see *ibid.* Art. 2(1) as to "registered interest."
[77] *Ibid.* Art. 11.
[78] See Public Lending Right Act 1979, s.4(3), (6).
[79] Scheme Art. 35.
[80] *Ibid.* Arts. 3, 14, 14A, 15, 16, 17, 17A and 17B and Sched. 1.
[81] *Ibid.* Art. 18.
[82] *Ibid.* Art. 33.
[83] *Ibid.* Art. 34.
[84] *Ibid.* Art. 19.

duration of public lending right in respect of a book and the period during which there may be dealings therein is from the date of the book's first publication (or, if later, the beginning of the sampling year in which application is made for it to be registered) until 50 years have elapsed since the end of the sampling year in which the author died, or, if the book is registered as the work of more than one author, as regards dealings in the share of the right attributable to that author, the end of the year in which that author died.[85] "Sampling year" means the period of 12 months ending on June 30.[86]

The procedure for transfer is dealt with in the Scheme,[87] and for the transfer to an author on attaining full age, since only adults can be registered.[88] Procedure following death is also dealt with by the Scheme.[89] The Scheme also deals with transfer on bankruptcy, liquidation or sequestration.[90] Finally, the Scheme provides for the procedure to be followed for renunciation of a registered interest.[91]

Calculation of public lending right. Public lending right is calculated **12–25** by means of two complex formulae set out in the Scheme.[92] The first formula determines the number of notional loans of a book in each sampling year. The second formula is used to calculate the sum due by way of public lending right using the number of notional loans. The basic element of the first formula in respect of any book is the number of loans of that book recorded during the sampling year at the operative sampling points in the various groups of service points. Service points which are to be operative sampling points or which are to be included in operative sampling points are designated yearly for the prescribed period by the Registrar from lists of service points (libraries and mobile libraries) supplied to the Registrar by local library authorities, with power for the Registrar to discontinue designation and designate a new sampling point. No operative sampling point is to remain an operative sampling point for more than four years. Loans are defined as loans whereby books are lent out from a service point to individual borrowers, and includes loans of books not normally held at that service point.[93] It would seem, therefore, that a book available in some libraries, but which might not be held at any of the current operative sampling points, would not qualify for public lending right. Further that, even if a book was available in an operative sampling point and was used, but was not lent, such as a reference book, it would not qualify for public lending right.

---

[85] Scheme Art. 20.
[86] *Ibid.* Art. 36.
[87] *Ibid.* Arts. 14, 21, 22, 23 and 24 and Sched. 1.
[88] *Ibid.* Arts. 14, 17(3) and 25 and Sched. 1.
[89] *Ibid.* Arts. 26 and 27.
[90] *Ibid.* Arts. 28, 29, 30 and 31.
[91] *Ibid.* Arts. 14 and 32 and Sched. 1.
[92] *Ibid.* Arts. 36–44 and 46 and Sched. 2.
[93] *Ibid.* Art. 36: and see Art. 42(3)(c) as to loans of an unregistered book where an International Standard Book Number is not specified in respect of that book in the report of a local library authority.

12–26 **Payment in respect of public lending right.** Any sum due in respect of
public lending right is to be paid without interest to the relevant registered
owner as at June 30 in any financial year, and will be paid on the last day
of that year unless paid earlier.[94] However, payment will not be made
unless the right has been claimed by or on behalf of the person for the time
being entitled, as to which the Registrar may require evidence.[95] At the
end of each financial year the Registrar is to give notice to every registered
owner, to whom a sum is payable by way of public lending right in respect
of that year, of the notional number of lendings for that year of each book
in respect of which he is a registered owner and the amount of such sum.
Where no sum is payable, notice will not be given of the number of
notional loans unless requested by the registered owner not later than six
months after the end of the relevant financial year.[96]

---

[94] Scheme Arts. 47, 49 and 51 and Sched. 4.
[95] *Ibid.* Arts. 48 and 50.
[96] *Ibid.* Art. 49(3), (5).

CHAPTER 13

CROWN AND PARLIAMENTARY RIGHTS. UNIVERSITIES' AND COLLEGES' RIGHTS.

Contents

1. Crown Rights

A. *Crown prerogative*

Extent of Crown prerogative. It has already been noticed that printing, **13–1** on its first introduction, was considered in England, as in other countries, to be a matter of State, and that the Crown claimed the right to authorise all species of publication whatsoever.[1] When the Crown lost this prerogative, it still claimed the exclusive right to print certain works. The claim has been made in respect of the Authorised Version of the Bible,[2] the Books of Common Prayer, Acts of Parliament[3] and other government publications, law books,[4] and even almanacks.[5]

---

[1] *Ante,* § 1–21.

[2] *Universities of Oxford and Cambridge (The)* v. *Richardson* (1802) 6 Ves. 689; *Manners* v. *Blair (D.H.)* (1828) 3 Bli. 391; *Re "Red Letter New Testament (Authorised Version) (The)"* (1900) 17 T.L.R. 1.

[3] *Basket* v. *University of Cambridge (The)* (1758) 1 W. Blackstone 105.

[4] *Roper* v. *Streater* (1685) (cited in *Stationers' Company* v. *Parker,* Skinner 233 at 234); *Millar* v. *Taylor* (1769) 4 Burr. 2303.

[5] *Stationers (The Co. of)* v. *Partridge* (1725) 10 Mod. 105; see *Gurney* v. *Longman* (1806) 13 Ves. 493.

13–2   **Bibles and Prayer Books.** The Queen's Printer and the Universities of Oxford and Cambridge hold patents from the Crown for the printing of Bibles and Prayer Books, and their right to prevent others from printing these works is well established.[6] Various reasons have been given for the existence of this prerogative of the Crown. Some have given it as their opinion that it is founded on the circumstances of the authorised translation of the Bible having been actually paid for by King James, and its having thus become the property of the Crown. But there seems little justification for this view. The better opinion would appear to be that the prerogative is to be referred to another consideration, namely, to the character of the duty imposed upon the chief executive officers of the Government to superintend the publication of the Acts of legislature and Acts of state of that description; and also of those works upon which the established doctrines of our religion are founded, that it is a duty imposed upon the first executive magistrate, carrying with it a corresponding prerogative. That was the opinion of Lord Camden, as expressed in the case of *Donaldson (A.) v. Beckett (T.)*,[7] and of Skinner C.B. in *Eyre and Strahan v. Carnan*.[8]

13–3   The authorities on this subject were reviewed in a full and exhaustive manner by the Supreme Court of New South Wales,[9] and the conclusion was reached that the right of the Crown in connection with such works is a proprietary right entitling the Crown, either to issue patents conferring upon the patentee the exclusive right of printing, or to enforce such right directly against an infringer. It was also considered that the Crown's prerogative rights in this respect could not be lost by non-user.

13–4   In *Universities of Oxford and Cambridge v. Eyre & Spottiswoode Ltd.*[10] the plaintiffs, as owners of the copyright in a new translation of the New Testament, sued the defendants for infringements of copyright for having printed and published a copy of part of the new translation without licence. The defendants contended that they were entitled to do so as holders of a patent from the Crown giving them the exclusive right to print books including New Testaments. They could not prevent the plaintiffs from publishing the new work because they also enjoyed a patent from the Crown, but the defendants, as Queen's printers, claimed an equal right. Arguments in the case covered the whole ground of the nature and extent of the prerogative and of the patents thereunder, but Plowman J. decided the case in favour of the plaintiffs on the ground that the royal prerogative did not include a right to infringe a modern copyright and could not, therefore, have conferred such a right by patent. The savings of the prerogative, contained in section 18 of the 1911 Act and section 46(2) of the 1956 Act, were intended to preserve the Crown rights to prevent the publication of material covered by the prerogative, but not to override the

---

[6] See cases cited above in n. 2.

[7] (1774) 4 Burr. 2408.

[8] (1781) 6 Bac.Ab. (7th ed.) 509.

[9] *Att.-Gen. for New South Wales (The) v. Butterworth & Co. (Australia) Ltd.* (1938) 38 S.R.(N.S.W.) 195.

[10] [1964] Ch. 736.

rights of others created by these Acts. The 1988 Act has similar but more restricted provisions preserving the prerogative.[11]

In fact prior to this case no attempt had been made to interfere with **13–5** modern translations of the Bible, and no attempt has ever been made to prevent any person from publishing a translation of one Book, or of a part of the Bible, from the original text, and enjoying a copyright in his production.

B. *Crown Copyright*

(i) Position before the 1911 Act

Government publications prior to 1911. With regard to other works **13–6** prepared and published by or on behalf of the Government, such as ordnance maps, blue books and so on, there appear to have been no decisions under the law before 1911, but it would seem that the Crown could only have been entitled to copyright therein under the general provisions of the Copyright Act, which primarily gave the copyright to the author.[12]

(ii) Position under the 1911 Act

Provisions of the 1911 Act. The 1911 Act provided[13] that, without **13–7** prejudice to any rights or privileges of the Crown, where any work was, whether before or after the commencement of that Act,[14] prepared or published by or under the direction or control of His Majesty or any government department, the copyright in the work was, subject to any agreement with the author, to belong to His Majesty, and in such case was to continue for a period of 50 years from the date of the first publication of the work. Thus the 1911 Act preserved the Crown prerogative.

(iii) Position under the 1956 Act

(a) *Generally*

Provisions of the 1956 Act. The 1956 Act dealt with the matter in a **13–8** more elaborate manner. In the first place, it was provided, in section 46(2) thereof, that nothing in that Act was to affect any right or privilege of the Crown subsisting otherwise than by virtue of an enactment, and that nothing in that Act was to affect any right or privilege of the Crown, or of any other person, under any enactment (including any enactment of the Parliament of Northern Ireland), except in so far as that enactment was expressly repealed, amended or modified by that Act. Thus the 1956 Act preserved the Crown prerogative.

---

[11] C.D.P.A. 1988, s.171(1), (5).
[12] *Ante*, § 4–1 *et seq*. This is subject to s.18 of the Literary Copyright Act 1842, *ante*, § 4–34.
[13] Copyright Act 1911, s.18.
[14] *I.e.* July 1, 1912; see Copyright Act 1911, s.37.

(b) *Works*

13–9   Subsistence of copyright in works not otherwise protected. The 1956 Act then provided that, where an original literary, dramatic, musical or artistic work was made by or under the direction or control of Her Majesty or a Government department,[15] copyright was to subsist therein if, apart from that provision, copyright would not subsist therein.[16] In other words, in the case of an unpublished work of which the author was not a qualified person, and which, accordingly, would not otherwise be protected, copyright was conferred if the work was made by or under such direction or control as aforesaid.

13–10   Ownership of copyright in works. Furthermore, subject to agreement, as described below, the copyright in every unpublished work, made by or under such direction or control, in which copyright subsisted, either under that section or the general provisions of the Act, was to vest in the Crown.[17] In the case of a published literary, dramatic, musical or artistic work, which was first published in the United Kingdom or in another country to which the 1956 Act extended, and which was published by or under the direction or control of Her Majesty or a Government department, the copyright was to vest in the Crown.[18] Presumably if the work, while unpublished, had obtained copyright and vested in the Crown under the preceding provision while unpublished, it would have continued to be protected, and to be so vested, even though first published out of the United Kingdom or any such other country as aforesaid. But, in any other case, if a work was first published out of the United Kingdom, and any such other country as aforesaid, no special protection was acquired, notwithstanding that the publication might have been by or under the direction or control of Her Majesty or a Government department. It will be observed that "direction or control" is a much wider expression than "contract of service," and works which had been commissioned by the Crown, from authors who were not under a contract of service, might well have vested in the Crown under this section. It was, however, expressly provided that these provisions were to have effect subject to any agreement made by or on behalf of Her Majesty or a Government department with the author of the work whereby it was agreed that the copyright in the work should vest in the author or in another person designated in the agreement in that behalf.[19] A work published under licence from the

---

[15] As defined in Copyright Act 1956, s.39(9).

[16] *Ibid.* s.39(1)(*a*).

[17] *Ibid.* s.39(1)(*b*): *Secretary of State for Defence* v. *Guardian Newspapers Ltd.* [1984] Ch. 156 (C.A.), [1985] A.C. 339 (H.L.) and see *Commonwealth* v. *John Fairfax & Sons Ltd.* (1980) 55 A.L.J.R. 45; *Director-General of Education* v. *Public Service Association of New South Wales* (1985) 41 P.R. 552.

[18] *Ibid.* s.39(2). In *Catnic Components Ltd.* v. *Hill & Smith Ltd.* [1978] F.S.R. 405 it was held that drawings in a patent, but not other drawings, were Crown copyright presumably because of this provision; see n. 37, *post.* In *Ironside* v. *H.M. Attorney-General* [1988] R.P.C. 197 it was held that the designs for decimal coinage were Crown copyright having been first published under the direction and control of a Government department.

[19] Copyright Act 1956, s.39(6): and see *ibid.* s.4(1).

Crown is not to be treated as being published under the direction or control of a Government department.[20]

In the "Spycatcher" case, a case concerned with the publication of a book written by a former employee of the counter-espionage branch of the British Security Service in association with a third party, it was suggested, by some of the Judges, that, in the circumstances of that case, the Crown might be the owner in equity of the copyright in the book, although no such claim had been made by the Crown.[21]

Term of copyright in works. It was further provided that the copyright **13–11** in a literary, dramatic or musical work which vested in the Crown in accordance with either of the preceding provisions should, in the case of an unpublished work, continue to subsist so long as the work remained unpublished and, in the case of a published work, should subsist (or continue to subsist), until the end of the period of 50 years from the end of the calendar year in which the work was first published.[22] In the case of an artistic work, which vested in the Crown, as aforesaid, copyright was to continue to subsist until the end of the period of 50 years from the end of the calendar year in which the work was made, except that, in the case of an engraving or a photograph, the copyright was to continue to subsist until the end of the period of 50 years from the end of the calendar year in which the engraving or photograph was first published.[23] It would appear, however, that if, by agreement, the copyright in a work commissioned by the Crown was to vest, not in the Crown, but in the author, then the normal term of copyright, in accordance with section 2 or section 3 of the 1956 Act would have applied.

(c) Records and films

Subsistence of copyright in records and films not otherwise pro- **13–12** **tected.** The 1956 Act further provided that, where a sound recording or cinematograph film was made by or under the direction or control of Her Majesty or a Government department, then, if apart from section 39 of that Act, copyright would not subsist in the recording or film, copyright was to subsist therein.[24]

Ownership and term of copyright in records and films. Furthermore, **13–13** the copyright in a sound recording or cinematograph film so made was, in any case, subject to agreement to the contrary with the maker of the sound recording or cinematograph film,[25] to vest in the Crown.[26] Such copyright was to subsist for the same period as was provided in section 12 or section 13, as the case may be, of the 1956 Act.[26]

---

[20] *British Broadcasting Company* v. *Wireless League Gazette Publishing Co.* [1926] Ch. 433; *Att.-Gen. for New South Wales (The)* v. *Butterworth & Co. (Australia) Ltd.* (1938) 38 S.R.(N.S.W.) 195.

[21] *A.G.* v. *Guardian Newspapers Ltd. (No. 2)* [1990] A.C. 109.

[22] Copyright Act 1956, s.39(3).

[23] *Ibid.* s.39(4).

[24] *Ibid.* s.39(5)(*a*).

[25] *Ibid.* s.39(6).

[26] *Ibid.* s.39(5)(*b*).

(d) *Old photographs, records and films*

13–14 **Term and subsistence.** In relation to photographs made before the commencement of the 1956 Act, copyright was to subsist for the period of 50
years from the end of the calendar year in which the photograph was
made[27] and, in the case of sound recordings made before the commencement of that Act, copyright was to subsist for the period of 50 years from
the end of the calendar year in which the recording was made.[28] In the
case of cinematograph films made before the commencement of the 1956
Act, copyright did not subsist therein as a cinematograph film, but, in so
far as it was an original dramatic work as defined in the 1911 Act, copyright would have subsisted therein as if it were a dramatic work for the
purposes of the 1956 Act.[29] Furthermore, in so far as such a cinematograph film was made up of photographs, these would have been protected
in the same way as other Crown photographs were protected under the
1956 Act.[30]

(e) *Other provisions of the 1956 Act*

13–15 **Application to Crown works, records and films.** It was provided, in
section 39(7) of the 1956 Act, that, except for the provisions relating to
subsistence or ownership or, in the case of literary, dramatic, musical or
artistic works, also relating to duration of copyright, the provisions of Part
I and Part II of that Act were respectively to apply in respect of works
made or published by or under the direction or control of Her Majesty or
a Government department and to records and films made by or under
such direction or control. Thus, the ordinary provisions as regards the
nature of infringement of copyright and the acts which would not constitute an infringement applied.[31]

(f) *Proceedings for infringement against Crown*

13–16 **Crown Proceedings Act 1947.** It was expressly provided, by section
39(8) of the 1956 Act, that, for the avoidance of doubt, the provisions of
section 3 of the Crown Proceedings Act 1947,[32] relating to infringements
of industrial property by servants or agents of the Crown, were to apply to
copyright under that Act.[33] Section 3 provided that, where any servant or
agent of the Crown infringed any copyright and the infringement was
committed with the authority of the Crown, then, subject to the provisions
of that Act, civil proceedings in respect of the infringement should lie

---

[27] Copyright Act 1956, Sched. 7. para. 30.
[28] *Ibid.* Sched. 7, para. 31(1).
[29] *Ibid.* Sched. 7, para. 31(2)(a) and (b).
[30] *Ibid.* Sched. 7, para. 31(2)(c).
[31] See as to photographic copies of birth certificates, etc., for purposes of judicial proceedings
or reports thereof: (1960) 57 L.S.Gaz 126.
[32] 10 & 11 Geo. 6, c. 44.
[33] But see Defence Contracts Act 1958 (6 & 7 Eliz. 2, c. 38) and Atomic Energy Authority
Act 1986 (c. 3), s.8(2). See also *The Semiconductor (Protection of Topography) Regulations* 1987
(S.I. 1987 No.1497), Sched. 2, *post.* §A–577, revoked and replaced by S.I. 1989 No.1100
amended by S.I. 1989 No.2147 and S.I. 1990 No.1003 *post.* § A–577A.

against the Crown, but, save as so expressly provided, no proceedings should lie against the Crown in respect of the infringement of any copyright.[34] A new and similar section 3 was substituted by the 1988 Act.[35] "Agent" is defined in section 38(2) of that Act as including an independent contractor employed by the Crown.

(g) *Proceedings to protect Crown copyright*

General Notice of 1975. Proceedings for protection of Crown copyright **13–17** were governed by the procedure indicated in the same Act.[36] But not all Crown copyrights under the 1956 Act were enforced. The practice with regard to such copyrights was indicated in a General Notice dated August 12, 1975,[37] which divided Government publications into the following classes:

(i) Bills and Acts of Parliament, Statutory Rules and Orders and Statutory Instruments.

(ii) Other Parliamentary papers, including reports of Select Committees of both Houses and papers laid before Parliament by Statute and by Command.

(iii) The Official Report of the House of Lords and House of Commons debates (*Hansard*).

(iv) Non-Parliamentary publications, comprising all papers of Government Departments not contained in the first three classes.

(v) Charts published by the Ministry of Defence (Navy Department) and maps and other publications published by the Ordnance Survey.

Such Notice provided that, since it was in the public interest that the information contained in publications falling in the first three classes should be diffused as widely as possible, the legal rights of the Crown in respect of copyright in them would not normally have been enforced.[38] But all Crown rights in respect of them were reserved and would have been asserted in cases considered by the Controller of HMSO as exceptional, for instance reproduction of any part of any such publication in

---

[34] It is provided by the State Immunity Act 1978 (c. 33), s.1(1) that a State is immune from the jurisdiction of the U.K. courts except as provided by that Act, and s.7 provides that a State is not immune as respects proceedings relating to an alleged infringement by the State in the U.K. of any copyright. "State" is defined by s.14 of that Act.

[35] C.D.P.A. 1988, s.303(1) and Sched. 7, para. 4. See The Semiconductor Products (Protection of Topography) Regulations 1987, Sched. 2 (S.I. 1987 No. 1497), *post.* § A–577, revoked and replaced by S.I. 1989 No.1100 amended by S.I. 1989 No.2147 and S.I. 1990 No.1003 *post.* §A–577A.

[36] Crown Proceedings Act 1947, s.13. The Queen in her personal capacity has the same rights as the subject: *Prince Albert v. Strange* (1849) H. & T. 1.

[37] Copinger (12th ed.) § 1813. This superseded Treasury Circular of 1958 as amended in 1965 which superseded Treasury Minutes of 1887 and 1912. By a Press Notice, dated June 25, 1969, the Controller of H.M. Stationery Office gave notice that, in future, under normal circumstances, no action would be taken to enforce the Crown's rights in patent specifications published in the United Kingdom by H.M. Stationery Office: see n. 18, *ante.*

[38] See *Bhagga (J.N.) v. State* [1959] 3 All I.R. 492.

undesirable contexts, or of the whole or a substantial part of any such publication, either as a separate document or as a major part of another work, in such a way as to result in a significant loss to public funds. Copies of documents within class (i) (Acts of Parliament, etc.), other than those reproduced by or by the order of HMSO, were not to purport to be published by authority. Reproductions from *Hansard* in connection with advertising were not permitted. And there was a warning as to privilege. The rights of the Crown with regard to works in class (iv) would normally have been enforced. Accordingly, acknowledgement of source and of the permission of the Controller of HMSO would have been required and suitable fees imposed for reproduction, which could have been waived or reduced in respect of publications where the commercial aspect was relatively unimportant. As to the documents in class (v), these were subject to appropriate arrangements for delegation between the Controller of HMSO and the Ministry of Defence (Navy Department) and Ordnance Survey.[39]

(iv) Position under the 1988 Act

(a) *Generally*

13–18 **Provisions of the 1988 Act.** It is provided, by section 171(1) of the 1988 Act, that nothing in the copyright Part of that Act is to affect, first, any right or privilege of any person under any enactment (except where the enactment is expressly repealed, amended or modified by that Act) and, secondly, any right or privilege of the Crown subsisting otherwise than under an enactment. These savings are, however, subject to sections 164(4) and 166(7) of the 1988 Act excluding other rights in the nature of copyright in respect of Acts, Measures and Bills.[40] Thus, subject to this limitation, the 1988 Act preserves the Crown prerogative. Section 163(6) of the 1988 Act provides that that section (concerned with Crown Copyright) does not apply to a work if, or to the extent that, Parliamentary copyright subsists in the work under sections 165 and 166 of the 1988 Act.[41]

(b) *New works*

13–19 **Works protected.** Works under the 1988 Act include, not only literary, dramatic, musical and artistic works, but also sound recordings, films, broadcasts, cable programmes and the typographical arrangement of published editions.[42]

---

[39] On October 23, 1913, a person was convicted at the Guildhall of piracy of the four mile Ordnance survey map and order to pay a fine of 40s., with 15 guineas costs, and also to give up or destroy all remaining copies (*R.* v. *Mutch, The Times*, October 24, 1913).
[40] C.D.P.A. 1988, s.171(5) and see *post* §§ 13–27 and 13–42.
[41] *Post*, § 13–33.
[42] C.D.P.A. 1988, s.1: compare Copyright Act 1956, s.39(1) and (5) *ante*, §§ 13–9 and 13–12.

Subsistence of copyright in works not otherwise protected. Section   **13–20**
163(1) of the 1988 Act provides that, where a work is made by Her Majesty or by an officer or servant of the Crown in the course of his duties, the work is to qualify for copyright protection notwithstanding section 153(1) of the 1988 Act. The latter section is the section which deals with qualification for copyright protection generally so that, even if a work would not qualify for protection under section 153(1), the effect of section 163(1) is that it will qualify for protection if made in accordance with that section. It is, however, provided, by section 163(4) of the 1988 Act that, in the case of a work of joint authorship where one or more but not all of the authors are persons falling within section 163(1), section 163 applies only in relation to those authors and the copyright subsisting by virtue of their contribution to the work. The Crown is defined, in section 178 of the 1988 Act, as including the Crown in right of Her Majesty's Government in Northern Ireland or in any country outside the United Kingdom to which the copyright Part of the 1988 Act extends. The requirement that the work should have been made by Her Majesty or by an officer or servant of the Crown in the course of his duties appears to go further than the equivalent requirement of the 1956 Act that the work, recording or film should have been made by or under the direction or control of Her Majesty or a Government department.[43]

Ownership of copyright in works. Her Majesty is to be the first owner   **13–21**
of any copyright in works made by Her Majesty or by an officer or servant of the Crown in the course of his duties.[44] Such copyright is referred to in the copyright Part of the 1988 Act as "Crown copyright", and that is so notwithstanding that it may be, or have been, assigned to another person.[45] The 1988 Act does not, like the 1956 Act,[46] have provisions making ownership of copyright by Her Majesty subject to any agreement as to the vesting thereof in another person. However, the vesting provision of the 1988 Act[47] takes effect subject to any such agreement entered into before commencement of the copyright provisions of the 1988 Act.[48] Under the 1956 Act[49] Her Majesty was entitled to the copyright in works first published by or under the direction or control of Her Majesty or a Government department. The 1988 Act contains no equivalent provision. However, provided the work was a work made by Her Majesty or by an officer or servant of the Crown in the course of his duties, then it would appear that, when and wherever published, copyright will subsist therein and Her Majesty will own such copyright by virtue of section 163(1), since section 153(1), referred to in section 163(1)(a), deals with all qualifications for copyright protection, including place of first publication.[50]

---

[43] Copyright Act 1956, s.39(1) and (5).
[44] C.D.P.A. 1988, s.163(1)(*b*), and see s.11(3). See s. 163(4) as to works of joint authorship.
[45] *Ibid.* s.163(2). "Crown copyright" in s.163 does not include copyright in Acts and Measures under s.164 of the 1988 Act.
[46] Copyright Act 1956, s.39(1), (2), (5) and (6): and see §§ 13–10 and 13–13, *ante.*
[47] See n. 44, *ante.*
[48] C.D.P.A. 1988, Sched. 1, para. 40(2): and see para. 10 as to who is the author of an existing work.
[49] Copyright Act 1956, s.39(2): and see § 13–10, *ante.*
[50] See C.D.P.A. 1988, s.153(2) and (3): see also s.158(2)(*b*).

13–22 **Term of copyright.** It is provided by the 1988 Act, section 163(3),[51] that Crown copyright in a literary, dramatic, musical or artistic work is to subsist until the end of the period of 125 years from the end of the calendar year in which the work was made.[52] But, if the work is published commercially[53] before the end of the period of 75 years from the end of the calendar year in which it was made, then such copyright is to subsist until the end of the period of 50 years from the end of the calendar year in which it was first so published.[54] Since no other special terms of copyright are provided for by section 163, and in view of section 163(5), the terms of Crown copyright for other works will be the normal terms provided by sections 13, 14 and 15 of the 1988 Act.

(c) *Old works*

13–23 **Subsistence, ownership and term.** In respect of works made before the commencement of the copyright provisions of the 1988 Act, (August 1, 1989), copyright will subsist therein after such commencement only if copyright subsisted in it immediately before such commencement.[55] Further, every work in which copyright subsisted under the 1956 Act immediately before such commencement is to be deemed to satisfy the requirements of the copyright Part of the 1988 Act as to qualification for copyright protection.[56] The first owner of the copyright in such a work is to be determined in accordance with the law in force at the time the work was made.[57] Finally it is provided that section 163 of the 1988 Act, dealing with Crown copyright, is to apply to an existing work if section 39 of the 1956 Act applied to the work immediately before such commencement and the work is not one to which section 164, 165 or 166 applies.[58]

The various terms of copyright in existing works to which section 163 of the 1988 Act applies are dealt with in paragraph 41 of Schedule 1 to that Act.[59] It is first provided that the question which provision applies to a work is to be determined by reference to the facts immediately before such commencement. Secondly, that expressions used in that paragraph, which are defined for the purposes of the 1956 Act, are to have the same meaning as in that Act. In relation to published literary, dramatic or musical works, artistic works other than engravings or photographs, published engravings, published photographs and photographs taken before June 1, 1957, published sound recordings and sound recordings made before June 1, 1957 and published films and films falling within section 13(3)(a) of the 1956 Act, copyright is to continue to subsist until the date on which it would have expired in accordance with the 1956 Act. June 1, 1957, was the date the 1956 Act came into force.

In relation to unpublished literary, dramatic or musical works, copy-

---

[51] See C.D.P.A. 1988, s.12(5). See s.163(4) as to works of joint authorship.
[52] *Ibid.* s.3(2).
[53] *Ibid.* s.175(2).
[54] See *ibid.* s.12(5).
[55] *Ibid.* Sched. 1, paras. 1, 2 and 5(1), but see para. 5(2).
[56] *Ibid.* Sched. 1, para. 35.
[57] *Ibid.* Sched. 1, para. 11(1), but see para. 11(2).
[58] *Ibid.* Sched. 1, para. 40(1): and see §§ 13–28, 13–33 and 13–42, *post.*.
[59] See *ibid.* Sched. 1, para. 12(7): and see §§ 13–11, 13–14 and 13–15, *ante.*

right is to continue to subsist until the date on which copyright expires in accordance with section 163(3) of the 1988 Act or the end of the period of 50 years from the end of the calendar year in which the copyright provisions of the 1988 Act come into force, whichever is the later. The term of copyright provided by section 163(3) is the end of the period of 125 years from the end of the calendar year in which the work was made or, if the work is published commercially before the end of the period of 75 years from the end of the calendar year in which it was made, the end of the period of 50 years from the end of the calendar year in which it was first so published.[60]

In relation to unpublished engravings and unpublished photographs taken on or after June 1, 1957, copyright is to continue to subsist until the end of the period of 50 years from the end of the calendar year in which the copyright provisions of the 1988 Act come into force.

Finally, in relation to films or sound recordings not dealt with above, copyright continues to subsist until the end of the period of 50 years from the end of the calendar year in which the copyright provisions of the 1988 Act come into force, unless the film or recording is published before the end of that period, in which case copyright expires 50 years from the end of the calendar year in which it is published.

(d) *Other provisions of the 1988 Act*

Application to Crown works. It is provided, by section 163(5) of the   **13-24**
1988 Act that, except as mentioned in that section, and subject to any express exclusion elsewhere in the copyright Part of that Act,[61] the provisions of that Part are to apply in relation to Crown copyright as to other copyright. Thus, as under the 1956 Act, prima facie the ordinary provisions as regards the nature of infringement of copyright and the acts which will not constitute an infringement apply.[62] However, in relation to the latter, there is an exception in relation to Crown copyright, namely assumption of death of author.[63]

(e) *Proceedings for infringement against Crown*

Crown Proceedings Act 1947. The 1988 Act has no provision equiva-   **13-25**
lent to section 39(8) of the 1956 Act which provided that, for the avoidance of doubt, section 3 of the Crown Proceedings Act 1947 should apply to copyright under the 1956 Act. However, since the 1988 Act itself substituted a new and similar section 3,[64] presumably the position will be the same after as before the 1988 Act.[65] There is, however, a new provision of the 1988 Act exempting the Crown from infringement in respect of material communicated to the Crown in the course of public business.[66]

---

[60] See § 13–22, *ante*.
[61] See, for instance, C.D.P.A. 1988, ss.11(3), 12(5) and 153(2).
[62] See Chaps. 8, 9 and 10, *ante*.
[63] C.D.P.A. 1988, s.57(2)(*a*) and (3).
[64] *Ibid.* Sched. 7, para. 4.
[65] See § 13–16, *ante*.
[66] C.D.P.A. 1988, s.48: and see as to "unauthorised" s.178 and para. 46, Sched. 1. See Chap. 10, *ante*.

(f) Proceedings to protect Crown copyright

13–26   **General Notice of 1990.** No doubt the position will be the same as when the 1956 Act was in force, namely that proceedings for protection of Crown copyright will be governed by the procedure indicated in the Crown Proceedings Act 1947.[67] In respect of literary, dramatic and musical works in which Crown copyright subsists, the 1988 Act contains a new presumption namely that, where there appears on printed copies of the work a statement of the year in which the work was first published commercially, that statement is to be admissible as evidence of the fact stated and is to be presumed to be correct in the absence of evidence to the contrary.[68] Such presumption does not apply to proceedings under section 107 of the 1988 Act.[69] Further, by reason of Schedule 1, paragraph 31(4) of the 1988 Act, the presumptions in the 1988 Act only apply to proceedings brought by virtue of that Act, and section 20 of the 1956 Act continues to apply in proceedings brought by virtue of that Act.

However, not all Crown copyrights under the 1988 Act will be strictly enforced. Thus, as with Crown copyright under the 1956 Act,[70] the practice with regard to such copyrights is indicated in a General Notice dated June 25, 1990.[71] This Notice also deals with the practice relating to Parliamentary copyright in Parliamentary items published by HMSO and administered by the Controller of HMSO.[72] For copyright purposes this Notice divides official material into six categories:

   (i) Statutory material, including Bills and Acts of Parliament, Statutory Rules and Orders, and Statutory Instruments;

  (ii) The Official Report of the House of Lords and House of Commons Debates (Hansard), Lords' Minutes, the Vote Bundle, Commons Order-books and Commons Statutory Instrument Lists;

 (iii) Other Parliamentary papers published by HMSO, including Reports of Select Committees of both Houses;

 (iv) Other Parliamentary material not published by HMSO;

  (v) Non-Parliamentiary material comprising all papers of Government Departments and Crown bodies—both published and unpublished—not contained in other classes;

 (vi) Charts and Navigational material published by the Ministry of Defence (Hydrographic Department) and maps and other items in all media published by Ordnance Survey.

Such Notice provides that considerable freedom is allowed in the reproduction of material in the first three categories within the guidelines prescribed by HMSO. Nevertheless all Crown rights in respect of this material are reserved and will be asserted in cases such as those where the material would be reproduced in an undesirable context or where the

---

[67] See § 13–17, *ante.*
[68] C.D.P.A. 1988, s.106, and see Chap. 11, *ante.* As to what is "commercial publication", see s.175(2), and see s.104(2)(*b*) and (3).
[69] *Ibid.* s.107(6), and see s.104(2)(*b*) and (3).
[70] See §13–17 *ante.*
[71] § B–219 *post.* This supersedes the General Notice of 1975: *Copinger* (12th ed.), § 1813.
[72] See § 13–38 *post.*

reproduction of the whole or part of the material falls outside the conditions specified in such guidelines, or where its reproduction could result in a significant loss of sales of official publications. Copies of Acts of Parliament, Statutory Rules and Orders and Statutory Instruments, other than those reproduced by the order of HMSO, do not have the legal standing of officially published versions produced by HMSO. Reproducing all or part of the Official Report for advertising purposes is not permitted. And there is a warning as to privilege. Applications for reproduction of material in the fourth category must be referred to the officials of the relevant House of Parliament. As to material in the fifth category, the rights of the Crown will normally be enforced and therefore acknowledgment of source and of the permission of the Controller of HMSO is required and suitable fees will be levied for reproduction. Fees will be waived or reduced in respect of use for professional, technical or scientific purposes where profit is not a primary purpose of reproduction. Fees may be reduced or waived for other specified purposes. As to material in the sixth category, this is subject to appropriate arrangements for delegation between the Controller of HMSO and the Ministry of Defence (Hydrographic Department) and Ordnance Survey.

(v) Crown Copyright in Acts and Measures

Generally. Apart from the general provisions of the 1988 Act relating to   **13–27**
Crown Copyright,[73] the 1988 Act, for the first time, introduces statutory provisions dealing expressly with copyright in Acts of Parliament and Measures of the General Synod of the Church of England. It also introduces statutory provisions dealing expressly with copyright in Parliamentary Bills.[74] The reasons for doing so are not entirely clear, but may be because, whereas previously copyright in Bills and Acts of Parliament may well have been Crown copyright,[75] under the 1988 Act copyright in Bills is to belong to one or both Houses of Parliament. A further reason may be the differing terms of copyright now to apply to Bills, Acts and Measures and Crown works generally. In respect of some of the other works previously considered to be Crown copyright,[75] it may be necessary, in the future, to consider whether the provisions of the 1988 Act dealing with Parliamentary copyright apply,[76] rather than the provisions of that Act dealing with Crown copyright.[77]

Acts and Measures protected. Section 164 of the 1988 Act deals with   **13–28**
copyright in Acts of Parliament and Measures of the General Synod of the Church of England, the latter including Church Assembly Measures.[78]

---

[73] C.D.P.A. 1988, s.163, and see § 13–18 *et seq., ante.*
[74] See § 13–43, *post.*
[75] See § 13–17, *ante.*
[76] C.D.P.A. 1988, ss.165 to 167.
[77] *Ibid.* ss.163 and 164, in particular s.163(6).
[78] *Ibid.* Sched. 1, para. 42(2).

Further, the provisions of section 164 apply to existing, as well as future, Acts and Measures.[79]

13-29 **Subsistence, ownership and duration of copyright.** The general provisions of the 1988 Act relating to subsistence,[80] ownership[81] and duration of copyright[82] do not apply to Crown copyright and, although copyright in Acts and Measures is to be considered Crown copyright, the general provisions of the 1988 Act relating to Crown copyright under section 163 thereof do not apply thereto.[83] Therefore, it would seem that subsistence, ownership and duration of copyright in Acts and Measures depend simply on section 164 of the 1988 Act.

Section 164(1) provides that Her Majesty is entitled to copyright in every Act of Parliament or Measure of the General Synod of the Church of England.[84] No other copyright, or right in the nature of copyright, is to subsist in an Act or Measure.[85]

Section 164(2) of the 1988 Act provides that copyright in Acts and Measures subsists from Royal Assent until the end of the period of 50 years from the end of the calendar year in which Royal Assent was given.

13-30 **Other provisions of the 1988 Act.** It is provided, by section 164(3) of the 1988 Act, that, except as mentioned in that section, the provisions of the copyright Part of the 1988 Act are to apply in relation to copyright under that section as to other Crown Copyright.[86]

C. Moral rights

13-31 **Exemption of Crown Works.** The 1988 Act contains new provisions establishing moral rights.[87] These include the right to be identified as author or director,[88] and the right to object to derogatory treatment of a work.[89] However, the right to be identified as author or director does not apply to works in which Crown copyright subsists.[90] Further the right to object to derogatory treatment of a work does not apply to works in which Crown copyright subsists, if what was done to such a work was done by or with the authority of the copyright owner unless the author or director is identified at the time of the relevant act or has previously been identified in or on published copies of the work. Further, where in such a case the right does apply, it is not infringed if there is a sufficient disclaimer.[91]

---

[79] C.D.P.A. 1988, Sched. 1, para. 42(1).
[80] *Ibid.* s.153(2).
[81] *Ibid.* s.11(3).
[82] *Ibid.* s.12(5).
[83] *Ibid.* s.164(3).
[84] Including Church Assembly Measures: *ibid.* Sched. 1, para. 42(2).
[85] *Ibid.* s.164(4).
[86] See § 13–24, *ante.*
[87] Chap. 22, *post.*
[88] C.D.P.A. 1988, ss.77–79.
[89] *Ibid.* ss.80–83.
[90] *Ibid.* s.79(7)(*a*).
[91] *Ibid.* s.82: as to what is a "sufficient disclaimer", see *ibid.* s.178.

D. *Design Right*

Crown a qualifying person. The 1988 Act creates a new right, design   **13–32**
right, separate from copyright.[92] Design right is a property right which
subsists in original designs,[93] and designs qualify for protection, inter alia,
if the designer is a qualifying person, or created in pursuance of a commission from, or in the course of employment with, a qualifying person, or
if the first marketing of articles made to the design is by a qualifying person.[94] Qualifying person includes the Crown and the government of any
other qualifying country.[95] The 1988 Act contains special provisions relating to Crown use of designs.[96]

2. Parliamentary Rights

A. *Parliamentary copyright*

(i) Provisions of the 1988 Act

Creation of Parliamentary copyright. The 1988 Act creates a new Par-   **13–33**
liamentary copyright[97] in respect of future works and existing unpublished literary, dramatic, musical and artistic works only.[98] However,
section 171(1) of the 1988 Act provides that nothing in the copyright Part
of that Act is to affect any right or privilege of either House of Parliament.
Parliamentary copyright bears some similarities to Crown copyright,[99]
but Crown copyright does not apply to a work if, or to the extent that, Parliamentary copyright applies.[1]

Works protected. Parliamentary copyright can apply to all classes of   **13–34**
works made by or under the direction or control of either House of Parliament, that is to say, not just literary, dramatic, musical and artistic works,
but also sound recordings, films, broadcasts, cable programmes and the
typographical arrangement of published editions.[2] Parliamentary copyright can also apply to works made by or under the direction or control of

---

[92] Chap. 20, *post.*
[93] C.D.P.A. 1988, s.213(1).
[94] *Ibid.* ss.218–220.
[95] *Ibid.* s.217(2) and (3): as to "country" and "the Crown" see *ibid.* s.263(1). And see The
Design Right (Semiconductor Topographies) Regulations 1989 (S.I. 1989 No.1100) as
amended by The Design Right (Semiconductor Topographies) (Amendment) Regulations 1989 and 1990 (S.I. 1989 No.2147 and S.I. 1990 No.1003), *post* §A–577A.
[96] *Ibid.* ss.240–244, 252 and 263(1) "government department"; see also Crown Proceedings
Act 1947 (10 & 11 Geo. 6, c. 44), s.3 as substituted by C.D.P.A. 1988, Sched. 7, para. 4,
and Atomic Energy Authority Act 1986 (c. 3), s.8(2) as amended by C.D.P.A. 1988,
Sched. 7, para. 33.
[97] C.D.P.A. 1988, s.165.
[98] *Ibid.* Sched. 1, para. 43(1).
[99] § 13–18 *et seq., ante.*
[1] C.D.P.A. 1988, s.163(6).
[2] *Ibid.* 1988, s.165.

any other legislative body of a country to which the provisions of the copyright Part of the 1988 Act have been extended.[3]

13–35 **Subsistence of copyright in works not otherwise protected.** Section 165(1) of the 1988 Act provides that, where a work is made by or under the direction or control of the House of Commons or the House of Lords, the work is to qualify for protection notwithstanding section 153(1) of the 1988 Act. Section 153 is the section which deals with qualification for copyright protection generally so that, even if a work would not qualify for protection under section 153(1), the effect of section 165(1) is that it will qualify for protection if made in accordance with that section.[4] It will be observed that the requirement for qualification is that the work is made "by or under the direction or control of" either House, which is similar to the requirement in section 39(1) and (5) of the 1956 Act relating to Crown copyright, but different from that under section 163(1) of the 1988 Act relating to Crown copyright.[5] However, section 161(5) of the 1988 Act provides that, in the case of a work of joint authorship where one or more but not all of the authors are acting on behalf of, or under the direction or control of, the House of Commons or the House of Lords, section 165 applies only in relation to those authors and the copyright subsisting by virtue of their contribution to the work. To assist in determining whether a work is made by or under the direction or control of either House, section 165(4) of the 1988 Act provides that such works include any work made by an officer or employee of the House concerned in the course of his duties and any sound recording, film, live broadcast or live cable programme of the proceedings of the House concerned. On the other hand, a work is not to be regarded as made by or under the direction or control of either House by reason only of its being commissioned by or on behalf of the House concerned.

13–36 **Ownership of copyright in works.** The House by whom, or under whose direction or control, the work is made is to be the first owner of any copyright in the work made by or under such direction or control, and if the work is made by or under the direction or control of both Houses, the two Houses are to be joint first owners of copyright.[6] Such copyright is referred to in the copyright Part of the 1988 Act as "Parliamentary copyright", and this is so, notwithstanding that it may be, or have been, assigned to another person.[7] Section 153(1) of the 1988 Act, referred to in section 165(1)(a) of that Act, deals with all qualifications for copyright protection including place of first publication[8] and, therefore, provided a work is made by or under the direction or control of either House,[9] it would seem that, when and wherever published, copyright will subsist therein and the relevant House, or both Houses, own such copyright by virtue of section 165(1).

---

[3] C.D.P.A. 1988, s.165(7) and (8). "Country" includes any territory; *ibid.* s.178.
[4] See *ibid.* ss.153(2) and (3) and 158(2)(*b*).
[5] §§ 13–9, 13–12 and 13–19, *ante.*
[6] C.D.P.A. 1988, s.165(1)(*b*). See s.165(5) as to works of joint authorship.
[7] *Ibid.* s.165(2).
[8] See *ibid.*, s.153(2) and (3): see also s.158(2).(b).
[9] *Ibid.* s.165(1).

Term of copyright. Section 165(3) of the 1988 Act provides[10] that Parliamentary copyright in a literary, dramatic, musical or artistic work is to subsist until the end of the period of 50 years from the end of the calendar year in which the work was made. No other special terms of copyright are provided for by section 165 and, therefore, in view of section 165(6), the terms of Parliamentary copyright for other works will be the normal terms provided by sections 13, 14 and 15 of the 1988 Act. However, for existing unpublished literary, dramatic, musical and artistic works which are also entitled to Parliamentary copyright,[11] presumably the term of copyright will be that provided in section 165(3) of the 1988 Act since paragraph 12, Schedule 1 and section 12 of the 1988 Act do not apply thereto.[12]   **13–37**

(ii) Other provisions of the 1988 Act

Application to Parliamentary works. Section 165(6) of the 1988 Act provides that, except as mentioned in that section, and subject to any express exclusion elsewhere in the copyright Part of the Act,[13] the provisions of that Part are to apply in relation to Parliamentary copyright as to other copyright. Thus the ordinary provisions as regards the nature of infringement of copyright and the acts which will not constitute an infringement apply.[14] A General Notice,[15] issued in June 1990, deals with the practice to be followed with regard to Parliamentary, as well as to Crown, copyright. This Notice provides that, for those Parliamentary items which HMSO publishes, the Controller of HMSO administers Parliamentary copyright. The conditions relating to the reproduction of this Parliamentary copyright material will be similar to those for Crown copyright. As to Parliamentary material not published by HMSO, applications for reproduction must be referred to the officials of the relevant House of Parliament. It is to be noted that copyright is not infringed by anything done for the purposes of Parliamentary proceedings or for the purposes of reporting such proceedings other than copying a published report of such proceedings.[16]   **13–38**

(iii) Status of Houses of Parliament

Ownership and legal proceedings. For the purposes of holding, dealing with and enforcing copyright, and in connection with all legal proceedings relating to copyright, each House of Parliament is to be treated as having the legal capacities of a body corporate, which will not be affected by a prorogation or dissolution.[17]   **13–39**

---

[10] And see C.D.P.A. 1988, s.12(5). See s.165(5) as to works of joint authorship.

[11] *Ibid.* para. 43(1), Sched. 1.

[12] *Ibid.* para. 12(7), Sched. 1 and s.12(5).

[13] See, for instance, C.D.P.A. 1988, ss.11(3), 12(5) and 153(2).

[14] See Chaps. 8, 9 and 10, *ante*. As to presumptions, see C.D.P.A. 1988, ss.104(2)(*b*) and (3) and 107(6), and Sched. 1, para. 31(4).

[15] See § 13–26, *ante* and §B–219 *post*.

[16] C.D.P.A. 1988, s.45. "Parliamentary proceedings" includes proceedings of the Northern Ireland Assembly or of the European Parliament: *ibid.* s.178.

[17] C.D.P.A. 1988, s.167(1).

13–40 **House of Commons.** The functions of the House of Commons as owner of copyright are to be exercised by the Speaker on behalf of the House. If so authorised by the Speaker, or in the case of a vacancy in the office of Speaker, those functions may be discharged by the Chairman of Ways and Means or a Deputy Chairman.[18] A person who on the dissolution of Parliament was Speaker of the House of Commons, Chairman of Ways and Means or a Deputy Chairman may continue to act until the corresponding appointment is made in the next Session of Parliament.[19] Legal proceedings relating to copyright are to be brought by or against the House of Commons in the name of "The Speaker of the House of Commons".[20]

13–41 **House of Lords.** The functions of the House of Lords as owner of copyright are to be exercised by the Clerk of the Parliaments on behalf of the House. If so authorised by him, or in the case of a vacancy in the office of Clerk of the Parliaments, those functions may be discharged by the Clerk Assistant or the Reading Clerk.[21] Legal proceedings relating to copyright are to be brought by or against the House of Lords in the name of "The Clerk of the Parliaments".[22]

(iv) Parliamentary copyright in bills

13–42 **Generally.** As well as the new provisions of the 1988 Act creating Parliamentary copyright,[23] the 1988 Act also includes new provisions dealing expressly with the copyright in Bills.[24]

13–43 **Bills protected.** Copyright is given to every Bill introduced into Parliament, including public Bills, private Bills and personal Bills.[25] However, not every such Bill is entitled to such copyright. Thus, there are excluded public Bills introduced into Parliament and published before the date on which the copyright provisions of the 1988 Act came into force, (August 1, 1989), private Bills of which a copy was deposited in either House before such date and personal Bills which were given a First Reading in the House of Lords before such date.[26]

13–44 **Subsistence, ownership and duration of copyright.** The general provisions of the 1988 Act relating to subsistence,[27] ownership,[28] and duration,[29] of copyright do not apply to Parliamentary copyright and, although copyright in Bills is to be considered Parliamentary copyright,

---

[18] C.D.P.A. 1988, s.167(2).
[19] *Ibid.* s.167(3).
[20] *Ibid.* s.167(5)(*a*).
[21] *Ibid.* s.167(4).
[22] *Ibid.* s.167(5)(*b*).
[23] *Ibid.* s.165 and see § 13–33 *et seq., ante.*
[24] See § 13–28, *ante.*
[25] C.D.P.A. 1988, s.166(1)–(4).
[26] C.D.P.A. 1988, Sched. 1, para. 43(2). As to old Bills, see *ibid.* para. 40(1), Sched. 1 and § 13–17, *ante.*
[27] *Ibid.* s.153(2).
[28] *Ibid.* s.11(3).
[29] *Ibid.* s.12(5).

the provisions of the 1988 Act relating to Parliamentary copyright under section 165 thereof do not apply thereto.[30] Thus, it would seem that subsistence, ownership and duration of copyright in Bills depend solely on section 166 of the 1988 Act.

Section 166(1) provides that copyright in every Bill introduced into Parliament belongs to one or both Houses of Parliament in accordance with the subsequent provisions of that section. It is further provided that no other copyright, or right in the nature of copyright, is to subsist in a Bill after copyright has once subsisted under section 166, but without prejudice to the subsequent operation of that section in relation to a Bill which, not having passed in one Session, is reintroduced in a subsequent Session.[31]

Ownership of copyright in a Bill depends upon whether it is a public Bill, a private Bill or a personal Bill. The copyright in a public Bill belongs in the first instance to the House into which the Bill is introduced, and after the Bill has been carried to the second House to both Houses jointly.[32] In the case of a private Bill, the copyright belongs to both Houses jointly.[33] Finally, in the case of a personal Bill, the copyright belongs in the first instance to the House of Lords, and after the Bill has been carried to the House of Commons to both Houses jointly.[34]

Although the term of copyright in a Bill of whatever nature ends at the same moment of time, the commencement date depends on whether the Bill is a public Bill, a private Bill or a personal Bill. Thus, in the case of a public Bill, the term commences from the time when the text of the Bill is handed in to the House in which it is introduced.[35] In the case of a private Bill, the term commences from the time when a copy of the Bill is first deposited in either House.[36] Finally, in the case of a personal Bill, the term commences from the time when it is given a First Reading in the House of Lords.[37] In all cases copyright ends on Royal Assent or, if the Bill does not receive Royal Assent, on the withdrawal or rejection of the Bill or the end of the Session.[38] However, copyright in a Bill continues to subsist notwithstanding its rejection in any Session by the House of Lords if, by virtue of the Parliament Acts 1911 and 1949,[39] it remains possible for it to be presented for Royal Assent in that Session.[40]

Other provisions of the 1988 Act. Section 166(6) of the 1988 Act provides that, except as mentioned in that section, the provisions of the copyright Part of the 1988 Act are to apply in relation to copyright under that section as to other Parliamentary copyright. **13–45**

---

[30] C.D.P.A. 1988, s.166(6).
[31] *Ibid.* s.166(7).
[32] *Ibid.* s.166(2).
[33] *Ibid.* s.166(3).
[34] *Ibid.* s.166(4).
[35] See n. 32, *ante.*
[36] See n. 33, *ante.*
[37] See n. 34, *ante.*
[38] *Ibid.*, s.166(5).
[39] 1 & 2 Geo. 5 c. 13 and 12, 13 & 14 Geo. 6 c. 103.
[40] See n. 38, *ante.*

B. *Moral rights*

13–46 **Exemption of Parliamentary works: Parliamentary proceedings.** As
has been mentioned,[41] the 1988 Act contains new provisions establishing
moral rights.[42] These include the right to be identified as author or director,[43] the right to object to derogatory treatment of a work[44] and the right
to privacy of certain photographs and films.[45] But the right to be identified
as author or director does not apply to works in which Parliamentary
copyright subsists.[46] Again, the right to object to derogatory treatment of
a work does not apply to works in which Parliamentary copyright subsists,
if what was done in relation to such a work was done by or with the authority of the copyright owner unless the author or director is identified at
the time of the relevant act or has previously been identified in or on published copies of the work. Further, where in such a case the right does
apply, it is not infringed if there is a sufficient disclaimer.[47] Finally, the
right to be identified and the right to privacy of certain photographs and
films are not infringed if the act in question would not infringe the
copyright in the work, inter alia because it is done for the purposes of Parliamentary proceedings or reporting Parliamentary proceedings in
accordance with section 45 of the 1988 Act.[48]

3. Universities' and Colleges' Rights

13–47 **Oxford and Cambridge Universities.** In 1534, Henry VIII granted
letters patent to the University of Cambridge empowering the Chancellor,
Masters and Scholars of that University to appoint University printers
although, apparently, no printing actually took place until 50 years thereafter. Similar letters patent were granted to the University of Oxford by
Charles I in 1632, although Oxford University had, it seems, begun printing in 1585. The granting by the Crown to the Universities of Oxford and
Cambridge of patents to print Bibles and Prayer Books has been dealt
with earlier in this Chapter.[49]

13–48 **Copyright Acts 1775 and 1801.** Immediately after, and in consequence
of, the decision in *Donaldson (A.)* v. *Beckett (T.)*,[50] the universities hastened
to Parliament, and, in 1775, obtained an Act[51] for enabling the two universities in England, the four universities in Scotland, and the several colleges of Eton, Westminster, and Winchester, to hold in perpetuity their
copyright in books given or bequeathed to them for the advancement of
useful learning and other purposes of education.

---

[41] § 13–31, *ante.*
[42] Chap. 22, *post.*
[43] C.D.P.A. 1988, ss.77–79.
[44] *Ibid.* ss.80–83.
[45] *Ibid.* s.85.
[46] *Ibid.* s.79(7)(a).
[47] *Ibid.* s.82: as to what is a "sufficient disclaimer" see *ibid.* s.178.
[48] *Ibid.* ss.79(4), 85(2).
[49] § 13–2, *ante.*
[50] (1774) 4 Burr. 2408.
[51] Copyright Act 1775 (15 Geo. 3, c. 53).

The right was to exist in all such books as had been before 1775, or should thereafter be, given or bequeathed by the authors of the same, or their representatives, to or in trust for those universities, or any college or house of learning within them, or to or in trust for the colleges of Eton, Westminster, and Winchester, or any of them, for the beneficial purpose of education within them or any of them.

The exception in favour of the universities and colleges was to extend only to their own books, so long as they were printed at the college press and for their sole benefit; and any delegation of the right was to work a forfeiture, and the privilege become of no effect.

A power was given, by the Act, to the universities, to sell or dispose of the copyright given or bequeathed to them, but if they should delegate, grant, lease, or sell the copyright of any book, or allow any person to print it, their privilege was to cease to exist. The copyright of any work presented to the universities was required to be registered at Stationers' Hall within two months after any such gift should come to the knowledge of the officers of the universities. Special penalties were imposed for any infringement of copyright. By another Act,[52] in 1801, a similar copyright was given to Trinity College, Dublin.

Literary Copyright Act 1842. The 1842 Act[53] repealed the 1801 Act, but not the 1775 Act. Nevertheless, by section 27 of the 1842 Act, the rights of the Universities (including Trinity College, Dublin) and of the colleges were saved from the operation of that Act. **13–49**

Copyright Act 1911. The 1775 Act and the 1842 Act were repealed by the 1911 Act, but section 33 of the 1911 Act provided that nothing in that Act should deprive any of the universities and colleges mentioned in the 1775 Act, of any copyright they already possessed under that Act, but the remedies and penalties for infringement of any such copyright should be under the 1911 Act and not under the 1775 Act. Otherwise, by reason of section 31 of the 1911 Act, no person was to be entitled to copyright or any similar right otherwise than under and in accordance with the provisions of the 1911 Act, or of any other statutory enactment for the time being in force. Therefore, in so far as any rights of Trinity College, Dublin, were saved by the 1842 Act, they appear to have been lost altogether as a result of the 1911 Act. **13–50**

Copyright Act 1956. The 1956 Act repealed virtually the whole of the 1911 Act, but section 46(1) of the 1956 Act provided that any rights conferred on universities and colleges by the 1775 Act, which continued to subsist in accordance with section 33 of the 1911 Act, notwithstanding the repeal of the 1775 Act, should continue to subsist in accordance with the 1775 Act notwithstanding any repeal effected by the 1956 Act. It was, however, also provided by section 46(1) of the 1956 Act that no proceedings should be brought under the 1775 Act, but that the provisions of Part III of the 1956 Act should apply for the enforcement of those rights as if they were copyright subsisting by virtue of the 1956 Act. It was further **13–51**

---

[52] Copyright Act 1801 (41 Geo. 3, c. 107).
[53] 5 & 6 Vict. c. 45.

provided, by section 46(5) of the 1956 Act, that no copyright, or right in the nature of copyright, should subsist otherwise than by virtue of that Act or of some other enactment in that behalf.

13–52 **Copyright, Designs and Patents Act 1988.** The remaining perpetual copyrights of the universities and colleges were brought to an end by the 1988 Act. Thus the 1988 Act, which repealed the 1956 Act, does not, by section 171(1), save such rights. Indeed such Act provides, in section 171(2) that, subject to the savings in section 171(1), no copyright or right in the nature of copyright should subsist otherwise than by virtue of the copyright Part of that Act or some other enactment in that behalf. Nonetheless these copyrights are preserved, for a limited time, by reason of paragraph 13 of Schedule 1, to the 1988 Act. This provides that the rights conferred on universities and colleges by the 1775 Act are to continue to subsist until the end of the period of 50 years from the end of the calendar year in which the copyright provisions of the 1988 Act come into force. They came into force on August 1, 1989. Since such rights are preserved for a limited time, such paragraph applies certain items from the copyright Part of the 1988 Act to those rights as they apply in relation to copyright under that Act. Such items are: Chapter III (acts permitted in relation to copyright works), Chapter VI (remedies for infringement), Chapter VII (provisions with respect to copyright licensing) and Chapter VIII (the Copyright Tribunal). Further, in relation to the permitted acts in section 57 of the 1988 Act it is provided, by paragraph 15(2) of Schedule 1 to that Act, that the assumption in section 57(1)(b)(i) of that Act as to expiry of copyright is not to apply in relation to such rights.

CHAPTER 14

COMMUNITY LAW

Contents

"In future, in transactions which cross the frontiers, we must no longer speak or think of English law as something on its own. We must speak and think of Community Law, of Community rights and obligations and we must give effect to them."[1]

1. Introduction

14–1 **Creation and enlargement of the EEC.** The European Community was created by the Treaty of Rome of March 25, 1957.[2] Together with the Treaties creating the European Coal and Steel Community and the European Atomic Energy Community, the Treaty set up a framework for economic and political co-operation among the original six founder Member States,[3] leading to the development of a Common Market. The United Kingdom of Great Britain and Northern Ireland, Denmark and the Republic of Ireland acceded to the European Communities on January 1, 1973.[4] Subsequently, membership of the Communities has expanded to 12 with the accession of Greece in 1981 and of Spain and Portugal in 1986.[5] The expansion of the Communities has not been merely geographic; the balance between the competence of the institutions of the Communities in the areas of economic, political and social policy and the sovereignty of the individual Member States has also been constantly shifting in favour of the former. The most recent developments extend and amend the areas of policy outlined in the Treaty and set out the programme for the achievement of a single market, free of internal frontiers, by January 1, 1993.[6]

14–2 **Scope of Chapter.** It is the object of this chapter to consider the effect of the accession of the United Kingdom to the Treaty, in the light of subsequent development of Community law, on the various rights enjoyed under the Copyright, Designs and Patents Act 1988 by the owner of copyright subsisting under that Act. Although it is beyond the scope of this chapter to describe in any detail the functions and workings of the Community and its institutions, or its aims or the principles on which it is based, for which purpose reference should be made to works devoted to these subjects,[7] it is considered necessary to an understanding of the problems caused in the field of copyright by accession to the Community, to give a brief description of the Community, its legal order, the integration

---

[1] *Per* Lord Denning M.R. in *H.P. Bulmer Ltd.* v. *J. Bollinger S.A.* [1974] Ch. 401 at 419B; [1974] 2 C.M.L.R. 91 at 111 [17].
[2] The Treaty of Rome is referred to in this chapter simply as "the Treaty," and references to an Article are to the Article in that Treaty unless otherwise specified.
[3] Belgium, the Federal Republic of Germany, France, Italy, Luxembourg and the Netherlands.
[4] By the Treaty of Accession of January 22, 1972.
[5] By the Treaties of Accession of May 28, 1979 and June 12, 1985, respectively.
[6] See the Single European Act which came into force on July 1, 1987 and amends and supplements the Treaty; see also the White Paper of the European Commission: "Completing the Internal Market" COM (85) 310.
[7] See, for example, *Halsbury's Laws of England,* (4th ed.), Vol. 52; Hartley, *The Foundations of European Community Law* Clarendon, (2nd ed., 1988); Kapteyn and Verloren van Themaat, *Introduction to the Law of the European Communities* (2nd ed., 1989); Wyatt and Dashwood, *The Substantive Law of the EEC* (Sweet & Maxwell, 2nd ed., 1987).

of this legal order into the laws of the United Kingdom and the principal aims of the Community.

2. The EEC: Its Institutions and Law

The EEC as a separate legal order. The Treaty is far more than a multi- **14–3** lateral agreement between states creating only mutual obligations between the contracting parties as a matter of international law.[8] By adopting the Treaty, the signatories have created a Community with its own legal order, integrated into the national order of the Member States, but having its own institutions, personality, capacity in law and its own independent powers.[9] These powers are exercised in accordance with the division of powers allocated in the Treaty, by the four institutions of the Community, the Parliament,[10] the Council of Ministers, the Commission[11] and the Court of Justice.[12]

The Treaty as a framework. Another important feature of the Treaty is **14–4** that it lays down general principles, and expresses aims and purposes. These are not circumscribed by the precise language of an English statute, and there are undoubted lacunae in the provisions of the Treaty. It is left to the institutions of the Community to provide the detailed provisions necessary to apply the principles and to achieve the declared purposes.

Community instruments. The more important of the instruments used **14–5** for this purpose are regulations, directives and decisions, which may be made, issued or taken by the Council or the Commission, under Article 189, and under the provisions of the Treaty dealing with the powers of each institution,[13] and dealing with the specific subject-matter of the instrument in question. By Article 189 regulations have general application and are binding in their entirety and directly applicable in all Member States. Directives are addressed to Member States and are binding as to the result to be achieved. Decisions, which may be addressed to Member States, or to individuals, as the case may require, are binding in their entirety upon those to whom they are addressed.

The development of Community law: the role of the Court of Jus- **14–6** **tice.** The most important role in the development and application of Community law is given to the Court of Justice, which has the ultimate

---

[8] Case 26/62 *Van Gend en Loos* v. *Nederlandse Administratie der Belastingen* [1963] E.C.R. 1; [1963] C.M.L.R. 105 at 129.

[9] Case 6/64 *Costa* v. *ENEL* [1964] E.C.R. 585; [1964] C.M.L.R. 425 at 455; Case 14/68 *Wilhelm, Walt* v. *Bundeskartellamt* [1969] E.C.R. 1; [1969] C.M.L.R. 100 at 119 [6].

[10] The Parliament and the Court of Justice became the same institutions for all three of the European Communities as a result of the Convention on Certain Institutions Common to the European Communities of March 25, 1957. The Assembly has, since 1962, generally been referred to as the European Parliament, and the Single European Act, Art. 3 has introduced the term "Parliament" into the Treaties where it has amended them. Regarding the new Court of First Instance, see § 14–9, *post*.

[11] The Commission and the Council are now the same institutions for all three of the European Communities, as a result of the Treaty of Merger of April 8, 1965.

[12] See n. 10, *ante*.

[13] Art. 145 for the Council; Art. 155 for the Commission.

responsibility under Article 164 for ensuring that in the interpretation and application of the Treaty the law is observed.[14] In carrying out this important role over the years since the Community was first established, the Court has produced a considerable body of case law, which accordingly forms part of Community law.[15]

14–7   The Court's role to date has principally been one of an appellate court, exercising one of the five jurisdictions set out in the Treaty, namely: actions for failure by a Member State to fulfil an obligation imposed on it under the Treaty (Articles 169 and 170); actions for annulment of an act of a Community institution (Article 173); actions for failure of a Community institution to act (Article 175); actions for damages in respect of the non-contractual liability of the Community (Articles 178 and 215); and requests for a preliminary ruling (Article 177).

14–8   The principal methods by which an individual may invoke the assistance of the Court are the action for annulment under Article 173 and the request for a preliminary ruling.[16] The action for annulment extends to all acts intended to have legal consequences, not just regulations, decisions and directives as defined by Article 189,[17] and extends to the acts of the European Parliament.[18] However, before an individual can attack the substance of an act, he must first show that his action is admissible by reason of the act being a decision addressed to him, or being a decision which, although in the form of a regulation or a decision addressed to another person, is of direct and individual concern to him.[19]

14–9   The Court also now has a role as a court of first instance. Following the amendment of the Treaties by the Single European Act, the Council was empowered to attach to the Court a Court of First Instance.[20] The Council exercised this power by its decision taken on October 24, 1988,[21] and the Court of First Instance assumed the exercise of its jurisdiction on October 31, 1989.[22] Initially the Court has jurisdiction at first instance in

---

[14] The Court has its own statutes, annexed as a Protocol to the Treaty, and its own rules of procedure. See, *e.g.* as to the role of the Court, Van Gerven (1974) C.M.L.Rev. 38; Brown and Jacobs, *The Court of Justice of the European Communities* (3rd ed., 1989); K. P. E. Lasok, *The European Court of Justice—Practice and Procedure* (Butterworths, 1984); J. Usher, *European Court Practice*, Oceana, 1983.

[15] To be found in the official Reports of Cases before the Court (E.C.R.) and also in the Common Market Law Reports (C.M.L.R.).

[16] See further § 14–18 *et seq., post.*

[17] Case 22/70 *Commission* v. *Council (ERTA)* [1971] E.C.R. 263; [1971] C.M.L.R. 335.

[18] Case 294/83 *Les Verts, Partie Ecologiste* v. *European Parliament* [1986] E.C.R. 1339; [1987] 2 C.M.L.R. 343.

[19] See Wyatt and Dashwood, *The Substantive Law of the EEC* (Sweet & Maxwell, 1987), pp. 75–76 and cases there cited. See also Kapteyn and Verloren van Themaat, *Introduction to the Law of the European Communities*, (1989), pp. 297–301.

[20] See Art. 32(d) ECSC Treaty, Art. 168A EEC Treaty and Art. 140A EAEC Treaty.

[21] Council Decision 88/591/ECSC, EEC, EURATOM of October 24, 1988; O.J. 1988 L319/1 (25.11.88); for the amended text see O.J. 1989 C215/1 and [1989] 3 C.M.L.R. 458. See also T. Millett, "The New European Court of First Instance" (1989) 38 I.C.L.Q. 811.

[22] Upon the President of the Court ruling that it has been properly constituted: *ibid.* Art. 13 and O.J. 1989, L317/48. Draft Rules of Procedure of the Court of First Instance have been published: O.J. 1990, C136/1 (5.6.90); [1990] 2 C.M.L.R. 420.

disputes between the Communities and their servants,[23] in actions by undertakings or associations of undertakings concerning individual acts (including omissions) of the Commission under the ECSC Treaty relating to levies on the production of coal and steel, control of production, pricing and competition policy, and in actions against a Community institution by a natural or legal person pursuant to Article 173(2) or Article 175(3) of the Treaty, concerning the implementation of the competition rules.[24] Possible future developments will include the extension of the Court's jurisdiction to include anti-dumping matters.[25] An appeal lies from the Court of First Instance to the full Court on points of law, or on grounds of lack of jurisdiction or breach of procedure.[26]

Interpretation of the Treaty and its implementing measures. The **14–10** Court of Justice has repeatedly emphasised the need to resort to the wording and spirit of the Treaty in order to deduce the meaning of Community rules.[27] By this approach the Court has even been able to fill in gaps in the Treaty.[28] This approach is very different from that of an English court in interpreting a statute, but is necessary, if the objects of the Treaty are to be achieved, because of the Treaty being no more than a framework. Uniformity in the interpretation and application of Community law throughout the Community requires that English courts adapt to this approach, when faced with the application or interpretation of provisions of the Treaty or its implementing measures.[29]

Direct applicability and effect of certain provisions of the Treaty **14–11** **and its implementing measures.** The direct applicability of regulations made under the Treaty has already been referred to.[30] The concept of direct applicability requires that immediate effect is given to the measure in question within the legal system of the Member States without further national legislation being required, or, indeed, permitted, except in limited circumstances.[31] Alongside the concept of direct applicability, the Court has developed the doctrine of direct effect. Under this doctrine

---

[23] *I.e.* under Art. 179 of the Treaty.

[24] Council Decision 88/591, *supra*, Art. 3(1).

[25] *Ibid.* Art. 3(3).

[26] See the new Art. 51 to the Protocol on the Statute of the Court of Justice of the EEC added by Art. 7 of the said Council Decision.

[27] Cases 28–30/62 *Da Costa en Schaake* v. *Nederlandse Administratie der Belastingen* [1963] E.C.R. 31; [1963] C.M.L.R. 224 at 237; Case 6/72 *Europemballage Corporation and Continental Can Co. Inc.* v. *Commission* [1973] E.C.R. 215; [1973] C.M.L.R. 199 at 223 [22].

[28] See, for possibly an extreme example, *Europemballage Corporation and Continental Can Co. Inc.* v. *Commission, supra.* See also the decision of the Hamburg Finanzgericht: *Re Tax on Imported Lemons* [1968] C.M.L.R. 1 at 2–3; Cases 142 & 156/84 *British American Tobacco Company Ltd.* v. *Commission* [1987] E.C.R. 4487, [1988] 4 C.M.L.R. 24.

[29] *H.P. Bulmer Ltd.* v. *J. Bollinger S.A.* [1974] Ch. 401; [1974] 2 C.M.L.R. 91 at 118–119 [38] and [42]. See also *R.* v. *Henn and Darby* (H.L.) [1981] A.C. 850 at 902 *et seq.*, *per* Lord Diplock.

[30] See § 14–5, *ante.*

[31] For the general rule see Case 39/72 *Commission* v. *Italy* [1973] E.C.R. 101. As to where a regulation positively requires further enactment in national legislation, see Case 128/78 *Re Tachographs: E.C. Commission* v. *United Kingdom* [1979] E.C.R. 419; [1979] 2 C.M.L.R. 45.

Community legislation may create in favour of an individual directly enforceable rights which a national court must recognise.[32]

14–12 Thus, the Court has held that not only regulations, but also Treaty Articles and directives, are capable of creating rights and obligations for the individual citizens of the Member States, such that they may invoke them before the national courts.[33] This is provided that the measure is clear and unambiguous, does not require any further action to be taken by the Community or by the national authorities and is unconditional.[34] Special problems arise in the case of directives, which should be implemented through appropriate national measures. However, the Court will not allow a Member State to profit from its own failure to implement Community law. Consequently, once time for implementation is past, the Court will allow an individual to rely on a directive, which meets the requirements for direct effect set out above, as against the organs of government of the Member State. As directives are addressed to the Member State, they do not create obligations on the individual and cannot therefore be relied upon under the doctrine of direct effect in proceedings between individuals.[35]

14–13 The Court has even extended the doctrine of direct effect to the principle of free movement of goods,[36] a principle which, though fundamental to the Treaty, was not then expressly referred to in a single Article.[37]

14–14 **Primacy of Community law.** A problem which has often arisen as a consequence of the creation of the separate legal order of the Community and its integration into the national order of Member States, and in particular

---

[32] On the contrast between the concepts of direct applicability and direct effect, see J. A. Winter, "Direct applicability and direct effect: two distinct and different concepts in Community law" (1972) 9 C.M.L.Rev. 425; Dashwood, "The principle of Direct Effect in European Community Law" (1978) 16 J.C.M.S. 229 at 231 *et seq.*

[33] See, *e.g.* Case 33/70 *SACE* v. *Italian Ministry of Finance* [1970] E.C.R. 1213; [1971] C.M.L.R. 123; Case 9/70 *Franz Grad* v. *Finanzamt Traunstein* [1970] E.C.R. 825; [1971] C.M.L.R. 1; Case 41/74 *Van Duyn* v. *Home Office* [1974] E.C.R. 1337; [1975] 1 C.M.L.R. 1; Case 43/75 *Defrenne* v. *Sabena* [1976] E.C.R. 455; [1976] 2 C.M.L.R. 98; Case 31/78 *Francesco Bussone* v. *Ministro Dell'Agricoltura e Foreste* [1978] E.C.R. 2429; [1979] 3 C.M.L.R. 18; Case 8/81 *Becker* v. *Finanzamt Munster-Innenstadt* [1982] E.C.R. 53; [1982] 1 C.M.L.R. 499; Case 104/81 *Hauptzollamt Mainz* v. *Kupferberg* [1982] E.C.R. 3641; [1983] 1 C.M.L.R. 1; Case 152/84 *Marshall* v. *Southampton & S.W. Hampshire Area Health Authority* [1986] E.C.R. 723; [1986] 1 C.M.L.R. 688; Case C–213/89 *R.* v. *Secretary of State for Transport ex p. Factortame Ltd.* [1990] 3 W.L.R. 818; [1990] 3 C.M.L.R. 1; Case C–188/89 *Foster* v. *British Gas plc.* [1990] 2 C.M.L.R. 833. For the views of national courts see, *e.g.*: *Garden Cottage Foods Ltd.* v. *Milk Marketing Bord* [1984] A.C. 130; [1983] 3 C.M.L.R. 43; *Bourgoin S.A.* v. *The Ministry of Agriculture, Fisheries & Food* [1986] 1 C.M.L.R. 267; *Pickstone* v. *Freemans* [1989] A.C. 66 and *R.* v. *Secretary of State for Transport, ex p. Factortame Ltd.* [1990] 3 C.M.L.R. 375; [1989] 2 C.M.L.R. 353 (Div.Ct.); [1989] 3 C.M.L.R. 1 (H.L.).

[34] See the cases cited in n. 33, *ante*, and see generally T. C. Hartley, *The Foundations of European Community Law*, (2nd ed., 1988), pp. 183 *et seq.*

[35] See Case 152/84 *Marshall* v. *Southampton & S.W. Hampshire Area Health Authority* [1986] E.C.R. 723; [1986] 1 C.M.L.R. 688 Case C–188/89 *Foster* v. *British Gas plc.* [1990] 2 C.M.L.R. 833.

[36] See § 14–24, *et seq., post.*

[37] The principle of free movement of goods is now expressly referred to in Art. 8A, following amendment of the Treaty by the Single European Act.

as a consequence of the direct applicability of some provision of Community law, is that of a conflict between a rule of Community law and a provision of the national legislation of a Member State. On each occasion when such a problem has been referred to it, the Court of Justice has taken the opportunity to pronounce firmly in favour of the primacy of the rule of Community law over the conflicting national provision, such that the general primacy of Community law over conflicting national law is now an established principle of Community law.[38]

3. Incorporation of Community Law into the Laws of the United Kingdom

Incorporation of the Treaty and implementing measures. This was **14–15** effected by section 2(1) of the European Communities Act 1972,[39] which provided, in terms which have been judicially described as "forthright, absolute and all-embracing,"[40] that all rights and obligations created by or arising under the Treaty which are, in accordance with the Treaty, to be given legal effect in the United Kingdom, shall be available in law and enforced accordingly. Such rights, referred to in the section as "enforceable Community rights," are more generally known as directly applicable and directly effective provisions.[41] It is further provided, by section 2(4) of the European Communities Act 1972, that any Act of Parliament, whether passed before or after that Act, shall be construed and have effect subject to section 2(1).[42]

Incorporation of the case law of the Court of Justice. This was **14–16** effected by section 3(1) of the European Communities Act 1972,[43] which provided that a question as to the meaning and effect of the Treaties or of any Community Instrument,[44] shall be a question of law, to be determined as such in accordance with the principles laid down by the Court of Justice.

Interpretation and application of Community law by the United **14–17** **Kingdom.** The combined effect of sections 2(1) and 3(1) of the European Communities Act 1972 is, therefore, that Community law, as a body of provisions of the Treaty and its implementing measures and judicial

---

[38] Case 6/64 *Costa* v. *ENEL* [1964] E.C.R. 585; [1964] C.M.L.R. 425 at 426; Case 14/68 *Wilhelm, Walt* v. *Bundeskartellamt* [1969] E.C.R. 1; [1969] C.M.L.R. 100 at 118–119 [6]; Case 106/77 *Amministrazione delle Finanze dello Stato* v. *Simmenthal SpA (No. 2)* [1978] E.C.R. 629; [1978] 3 C.M.L.R. 263. See also *Macarthys Ltd.* v. *Smith* (C.A.) [1980] 2 C.M.L.R. 217; *R.* v. *Secretary of State for Transport, ex p. Factortame Ltd.* [1989] 3 C.M.L.R. 1 (H.L.), and the ruling of the Court of Justice in that case: Case C–213/89, [1990] 3 C.M.L.R. 1; [1990] 3 W.L.R. 818.
[39] 1972 c. 68.
[40] *Per* Lord Denning M.R. in *H.P. Bulmer Ltd.* v. *J. Bollinger S.A.* [1974] Ch. 401 at 419A; [1974] 2 C.M.L.R. 91 at 111 [17].
[41] See § 14–11, *et seq., ante.*
[42] See *R.* v. *Secretary of State for Transport, ex p. Factortame Ltd.* [1989] 3 C.M.L.R. 1 (H.L.) and Case C–213/89 [1990] 3 C.M.L.R. 1; [1990] 3 W.L.R. 818.
[43] 1972 c. 68.
[44] As defined in Pt. II of Sched. 1 to the Act.

decisions interpreting and applying those provisions, is fully integrated into the laws of the United Kingdom, and, since January 1, 1973, has formed part of those laws, to be applied by the courts as part of our national legal order. This was expressly recognised in the judgments of the Court of Appeal in the first case to reach that court in which issues of Community law were raised.[45] Whilst the task of applying Community law in the United Kingdom falls on its courts, which alone are empowered to decide the case which is before them,[46] such courts are not the final courts for interpreting Community law. This task, as has already been stated,[47] falls to the Court of Justice.

14–18 **Reference to the Court of Justice.** Under Article 177,[48] where a question as to the interpretation of the Treaty or interpretation or validity of an act of a Community institution is raised before a national court, that court may, and where the decision of that court is final under national law must, request the Court of Justice to give a ruling on such question if it considers that a decision on the question is necessary to enable it to give its judgment. The Article provides for a clear separation between the roles of the national court and the Court of Justice.[49] The decision whether to refer a question or not is for the national court alone,[50] as is the formulation of the question, and the Court of Justice will not enter into a consideration of the correctness of the decision.[51] Nor will the Court of Justice reformulate the question, but it will seek to extract from the wording of the question, in the light of the facts found by the national court,[52] the question that relates to the interpretation of the Treaty.[53]

14–19 In the United Kingdom, therefore, all courts except the House of Lords have a complete discretion as to whether to refer a question to the Court of Justice, unless exercising a final jurisdiction. Provision is made, in the case

---

[45] *Application des Gaz S.A.* v. *Falks Veritas Ltd.* [1974] Ch. 381; [1974] 2 C.M.L.R. 75.

[46] Cases 28–30/62 *Da Costa en Schaake* v. *Nederlandse Administratie der Belastingen* [1963] E.C.R. 31; [1963] C.M.L.R. 224 at 237; *H.P. Bulmer Ltd.* v. *J. Bollinger S.A.* [1974] Ch. 401 at 419; [1974] 2 C.M.L.R. 91 at 112.

[47] *Ante,* § 14–6.

[48] For the text, see § F–10, *post.*

[49] See, *e.g.* Case 106/77 *Amministrazione delle Stato* v. *Simmenthal SpA (No. 2)* [1978] E.C.R. 629; [1978] 3 C.M.L.R. 263; Case 93/78 *Mattheus* v. *Doego Fruchtimport und Tiefkühlkost* [1978] E.C.R. 2203; [1979] 1 C.M.L.R. 551.

[50] Case 70/77 *Amministrazione delle Stato* v. *Simmenthal SpA (No. 3)* [1978] E.C.R. 1453; [1978] 3 C.M.L.R. 670. The decision is not one for the parties themselves: *Heinz-Wohrmann* v. *Commission* [1962] E.C.R. 501; [1963] C.M.L.R. 152. Case 93/78 *Mattheus* v. *Doego Fruchtimport und Tiefkühlkost, supra.*

[51] Case 13/68 *Salgoil* v. *Italian Ministry of Foreign Trade* [1968] E.C.R. 453; [1969] C.M.L.R. 181.

[52] The Court of Justice cannot itself enter into a preliminary investigation as to what such facts are: Case 13/61 *Robert Bosch GmbH* v. *Kleding-Verkoopbedrijf de Geus en Uitdenbogerd* [1962] E.C.R. 45; [1962] C.M.L.R. 1.

[53] Case 40/70 *Sirena S.R.L.* v. *Eda S.R.L.* [1971] E.C.R. 69; [1971] C.M.L.R. 260 at 272 [3]. Case 78/70 *Deutsche Grammophon GmbH* v. *Metro-SB-Grossmärkte GmbH & Co. K.G.* [1971] E.C.R. 487; [1971] C.M.L.R. 631 at 656 [3]; although the Court cannot do so when the information before it is not precise enough: Case 222/78 *ICAP* v. *Beneventi* [1979] E.C.R. 1163; [1979] 3 C.M.L.R. 475.

of the English High Court and the Court of Appeal, for the exercise of this power in the Rules of the Supreme Court, under Order 114.

Reference to the Court of Justice: guiding principles as to when   **14–20**
reference should be made. The principles governing the exercise of this power by the English courts were fully discussed by the Court of Appeal in *H.P. Bulmer Ltd.* v. *Bollinger S.A.*,[54] and may be summarised as follows.

The decision on the question of Community law must be necessary to enable the court to give its judgment; in other words, whichever way the question is decided it must be conclusive of the case before the court.[55] Where the party requesting the court to make a reference to the Court of Justice has obtained the relief it sought in the proceedings, on the basis of national law, the court may refuse to make a reference on the ground that it is unnecessary.[56] In considering whether a decision on the question is necessary, the fact that the Court of Justice has already given a ruling on the question in another case does not prevent a further reference being made.[57] If the court considers that, in the light of a previous ruling, or in its view, the point is reasonably clear and free from doubt, it may proceed to apply Community law, without making a reference.[58] The fact that a superior national court has already pronounced on a point of Community law cannot, of itself, take away the power of an inferior national court to refer the point to the Court of Justice under Article 177.[59] Before a refer-

---

[54] [1974] Ch. 401; [1974] 2 C.M.L.R. 91. The formulation of such principles by the Court of Appeal should not be taken to fetter the discretion of an inferior court under Art. 177: Cases 166/73, 146/73 *Firma Rheinmuhlen-Dusseldorf* v. *Einfuhr- und Vorratsstelle für Getreide und Futtermittel* [1974] E.C.R. 33; [1974] 1 C.M.L.R. 523. The formulation has been the subject of criticism; see Brown and Jacobs, *The Court of Justice of the European Communities* (1983) at p. 170; Wyatt and Dashwood, *The Substantive Law of the EEC* (Sweet & Maxwell, 1987), p. 79.

[55] See *Van Duyn* v. *Home Office* [1974] 1 W.L.R. 1107; [1974] 1 C.M.L.R. 347. But see, as to criticism of this statement of principle, Collins, *European Community Law in the United Kingdom* (Butterworths, 3rd ed., 1984), p. 136 and compare Cases 36 and 71/80 *Irish Creamery Milk Suppliers Association* v. *Ireland* [1981] E.C.R. 735, at 747–748; [1981] 2 C.M.L.R. 455.

[56] *H.P. Bulmer Ltd.* v. *J. Bollinger S.A.* (Whitford J.) [1975] 2 C.M.L.R. 479.

[57] Cases 28–30/62 *Da Costa en Schaake* v. *Nederlandse Administratie der Belastingen* [1963] E.C.R. 31; [1963] C.M.L.R. 224; Cases 166/73, 146/73 *Firma Rheinmühlen-Düsseldorf* v. *Einfuhr- und Vorratsstelle für Getreide und Futtermittel* [1974] E.C.R. 33; [1974] 1 C.M.L.R. 523; although the Court of Justice may answer the question by referring to an earlier ruling: Case 222/78 *ICAP* v. *Beneventi* [1979] E.C.R. 1163; [1979] 3 C.M.L.R. 475.

[58] Under the "acte claire" doctrine, see also Cases 28–30/62 *Da Costa en Schaake* v. *Nederlandse Administratie der Belastingen* [1963] E.C.R. 31; [1963] C.M.L.R. 224 at 237; Case 41/74 *Van Duyn* v. *Home Office* [1974] 1 W.L.R. 1107; [1974] 1 C.M.L.R. 347 at 359 [26]. For an example of its application see *R.* v. *Henn and Darby* (C.A.) [1978] 2 C.M.L.R. 688 at 692. However, the House of Lords, on appeal, made a reference under Art. 177 ([1981] A.C. 850 at 867; [1979] 2 C.M.L.R. 495 and see the judgment of the Court of Justice: Case 34/79 *R.* v. *Henn and Darby* [1981] A.C. 850; [1980] 1 C.M.L.R. 246) and in applying the answers to the case before it pointed out the dangers of the approach adopted by the Court of Appeal: [1981] A.C. 850, at 906C, *per* Lord Diplock. See also Collins, *op. cit.*, pp. 136 *et seq.*

[59] Cases 166/73, 146/73 *Firma Rheinmühlen-Düsseldorf* v. *Einfuhr- und Vorratsstelle für Getreide und Futtermittel* [1974] E.C.R. 33; [1974] 1 C.M.L.R. 523.

ence is to be made, the court should generally first ascertain the facts, since until this is done it is not usually possible to determine whether it is necessary to decide the question of Community law. It follows that although the court has power to make a reference at an interlocutory stage in the proceedings,[60] it will not be usual for it do so,[61] except in special cases, where, for example, no further facts are required to be found,[62] or there is no substantial issue of fact and no issue of law.[63] When a decision is taken to refer a question to the Court of Justice, the proceedings must then be stayed, unless the court otherwise orders,[64] until the Court of Justice has ruled on the question referred to it. The decision to refer a question to the Court of Justice, and the consequent stay of proceedings, do not affect the court's power to grant an interlocutory injunction in the meantime, in accordance with the ordinary principles governing the grant of such relief as laid down in *American Cyanamid Co.* v. *Ethicon Ltd.*[65] Where the court considers that a decision on a question of Community law is necessary to the determination of the case before it, and that court has a discretion whether to refer the question to the Court of Justice under Article 177(2), or not, then in exercising its discretion the court should take account of the following factors: the length of time taken to obtain a ruling of the Court of Justice,[66] the expense of doing so,[67] the wishes of the

---

[60] Recognised by the Court of Justice in Case 107/76 *Hoffmann-La Roche A.G.* v. *Centrafarm* [1977] E.C.R. 957; [1977] 2 C.M.L.R. 334 and stated *per* Graham J. in *Löwenbrau München* v. *Grünhalle Lager International Ltd.* [1974] F.S.R. 1; [1974] 1 C.M.L.R. 1. See also Cases 35–36/82 *Morson* and *Jhanjan* v. *The State of the Netherlands* [1982] E.C.R. 3723; [1983] 2 C.M.L.R. 221. The Court of Justice has even recognised the power of a national court to refer a question in *ex parte* proceedings: Case 70/77 *Amministrazione delle Stato* v. *Simmenthal SpA (No. 3)* [1978] E.C.R. 1453; [1978] 3 C.M.L.R. 670, although indicating that it may, in some cases, be in the interests of proper administration of justice that a reference be made only after both parties have been heard.

[61] *Löwenbräu München* v. *Grünhalle Lager International Ltd.* [1974] F.S.R. 1 at 9 [24]; *Polydor Ltd.* and *R.S.O. Records Inc.* v. *Harlequin Record Shop Ltd. and Simons Records Ltd.* [1980] 1 C.M.L.R. 669; on appeal the Court of Appeal reversed the first instance decision and made a preliminary reference, although Templeman L.J. stated that it would not be usual to make a reference at the interlocutory stage: [1980] 2 C.M.L.R. 413 at 426 [60] (before the Court of Justice: [1982] 2 E.C.R. 329; [1982] 1 C.M.L.R. 677); *D.D.S.A. Pharmaceuticals Ltd.* v. *Farbwerke Hoechst A.G.* [1975] 2 C.M.L.R. 50; [1975] F.S.R. 443.

[62] Case 51/75 *E.M.I. Records Ltd.* v. *CBS United Kingdom Ltd.* [1975] 1 C.M.L.R. 285; [1976] R.P.C. 1.

[63] Case 41/74 *Van Duyn* v. *Home Office* [1974] 1 W.L.R. 1107; [1974] 1 C.M.L.R. 347.

[64] Under Ord. 114, r. 4.

[65] [1975] A.C. 396; see § 11–30, *et seq., ante.* For example, an injunction was granted in *E.M.I. Records Ltd.* v. *CBS United Kingdom Ltd.* [1975] 1 C.M.L.R. 285; [1976] R.P.C. 1. The existence of a prima facie defence under Community law may, of course, be an important factor to consider leading to the refusal of an injunction: *per* Graham J. in *Löwenbräu München* v. *Grünhalle Lager International Ltd.* [1974] C.M.L.R. 1 at 7 [13]. See, however, where a Community right is asserted against an Act of Parliament, *R.* v. *Secretary of State for Transport, ex p. Factortame Ltd.* [1989] 3 C.M.L.R. 1 (H.L.) and the decision of the Court of Justice in Case C–213/89, [1990] 3 W.L.R. 818; [1990] 3 C.M.L.R. 1.

[66] This could easily take up to two years.

[67] The cost of a reference will usually be left by the Court of Justice to be dealt with by the national court; questions concerning the enforcement of such costs are not matters for the Court of Justice: Case 4/73 *J. Nold* v. *Ruhrkohle A.G.* [1977] E.C.R. 1; [1978] 2 C.M.L.R. 183.

parties,[68] the difficulty and importance of the question of interpretation,[69] and whether parallel proceedings are pending in other Member States.[70]

Formulation of the reference. In *Gerrit Holdijk*[71] the Court of Justice **14–21** summed up its case law as to the formulation of the reference in order to give guidance to the national courts in formulating the questions. If the grounds on which the court considers an answer to its questions to be necessary for judgment in the national proceedings are not clear from the file, the court should explain them. At the same time, the interpretation requested should be set in its legal context, and if the circumstances permit, the facts of the case and questions of national law should be settled at the time of reference to the Court of Justice. Information included in a reference not only enables the Court of Justice to give helpful answers, but it also allows the governments of the Member States and other interested parties to submit observations, and it is the Court's duty to ensure that the opportunity to submit observations is safeguarded.[72]

4. Principal Aims of the EEC

Realisation of a Common Market. In the original text of the Treaty, the **14–22** principal task of the Community is expressed in Article 2 as being the promotion throughout the Community of a harmonious development of economic activities, which is to be achieved by the establishment of a Common Market and the progressive approximation of the economic policies of Member States. The establishment of a common market is therefore expressed as a means to an end, rather than an end in itself, but it is this preliminary aim which implies before all else the removal of all obstacles to the free movement of goods, persons, services and capital within the territory of the Common Market, and therefore across the boundaries of the Member States.

Since July 1, 1987, the realisation of the Common Market has been sup- **14–23** plemented by the aim of achieving within the Community by December 31, 1992, an internal market, being an area without internal frontiers in which the free movement of goods, persons, services and capital is ensured according to the Treaty provisions.[73] This aim was inserted in the Treaty

---

[68] Although not a factor which may weigh heavily with the court: *H.P. Bulmer Ltd.* v. *J. Bollinger S.A.* [1974] Ch. 401 at 425; [1974] 2 C.M.L.R. 91 at 118 [36].

[69] In cases of lesser importance or difficulty, the court should consider deciding the question itself, in the interests of saving the expense and delay of a reference, and also of not overburdening the Court of Justice.

[70] In which case a reference may be more desirable, in order to avoid possible conflicting national decisions: *per* Graham J. in *E.M.I. Records Ltd.* v. *CBS United Kingdom Ltd.* [1975] 1 C.M.L.R. 285 at 297 [33]; [1976] R.P.C. 1; even where the point is not one of undue difficulty: *per* Whitford J., *obiter* in *H.P. Bulmer Ltd.* v. *J. Bollinger S.A.* [1975] 2 C.M.L.R. 479 at 489 [216].

[71] Cases 141–143/81, [1982] E.C.R. 1299; [1983] 2 C.M.L.R. 635.

[72] For further guidance as to the formulation of the reference by the national court, see the notes to Ord. 114 in the Rules of the Supreme Court. As to the practice and procedure for a reference to the Court of Justice, see Atkin, *Court Forms*, Vol. 17 (1985), pp. 153 *et seq.*

[73] Art. 8A; for the text, see § F–4, *post.*

by the Single European Act, an instrument that supplemented and amended the Treaty to expand the Community's competences and to facilitate the decision-making process among the Community Institutions. The actual substantive measures to be taken by the Community to achieve the internal market are set out in a separate document from the Commission, namely its White Paper entitled "Completing the Internal Market."[74] Primarily introduced as a series of economic measures needed to revitalise the Community, the completion of the Internal Market will further the development of the Community's competence for the political and social affairs of its Member States.

14–24 **Free movement of goods.** This objective is the subject of Articles 9 to 37 of the Treaty, forming the title *Free Movement of Goods*, which is the first title of Part Two of the Treaty, devoted to the foundations of the Community. The position of this title reflects the fundamental importance attributed to this objective in the framework of the Treaty, although the objective of free movement of goods was not itself expressed as a principle in any Article of the Treaty in its original form. The principle is now expressly referred to in Article 8A of the Treaty.[75] Nevertheless, well before this amendment to the Treaty, the Court of Justice, in its judgments in cases which came before it raising the issue of free movement of goods, stressed the importance of this principle which was to be deduced from the wording, spirit and structure of this title, and by such case law the Court established this principle as a rule of Community law as firmly as if it had from the beginning been expressly set out as such in an Article of the Treaty. Moreover, the effect of the Court's judgments is that the principle of free movement of goods enjoys the status of direct effect, with the consequences discussed above.[76]

14–25 Obstacles to the free movement of goods between Member States may be found in a variety of measures adopted by national governments, for example in customs duties, import quotas and subsidies for a particular national industry; they may also be found in practices adopted by individuals trading within the Common Market, which are aimed at restricting competition and isolating national markets. It is with these obstacles in mind that Article 3 describes the activities to be undertaken by the Community as including:

(a) the elimination, as between Member States, of customs duties and of quantitative restrictions on the import and export of goods, and of all other measures of equivalent effect; . . .

(f) the institution of a system ensuring that competition in the Common Market is not distorted.

---

[74] COM Doc. 85 (310) final. For a detailed commentary on the progress towards completion of the Internal Market, see Brealey and Quigley, *Completing the Internal Market, 1992 Handbook and 1992 Legislation* (Graham & Trotman, 2nd ed., 1990).
[75] Introduced by the Single European Act as of July 1, 1987.
[76] See § 14–11, *et seq., ante.*

Both these objectives find more detailed expression in later parts of the Treaty.[77]

Free movement of services. The general provisions governing the freedom to provide services are contained in Articles 59 to 66.[78] Where, however, the free movement of services touches on the field of transport or the liberalisation of banking and insurance services, the general provisions are subject to the particular provisions of the titles governing transport and the free movement of capital respectively.[79] The principle of free movement of goods was not expressly contained in the original Treaty, and yet has been the area in which the Community has experienced the fastest development. In contrast, the principle of free movement of services is contained in Article 3, but it is only in recent years that the Community has begun to focus its attention on the development of an effective regime for the free movement of services, in particular in relation to economic rather than professional services. **14–26**

In essence, the framework of the provisions on services requires the abolition of restrictions imposed on nationals established in one Member State who provide services to persons established in another Member State. The basic principles are set out in Articles 59 and 60,[80] both of which are directly effective Treaty provisions.[81] Article 60(2) defines services as including, in particular, activities of an industrial or commercial character, and activities of craftsmen and of the professions. The Court of Justice has further stated that the restrictions to be abolished pursuant to Articles 59 and 60 include all requirements imposed on the person providing the service by reason in particular of his nationality or the fact that he does not habitually reside in the state where the service is provided, which do not apply to persons established within the national territory or which may prevent or otherwise obstruct the activities of the person providing the service.[82] **14–27**

Rules on competition. The objective set out in Article 3(*f*) of the Treaty is the subject of Articles 85 to 94, *Rules on Competition*, which form the first chapter of Part Three of the Treaty, which is the part devoted to the policy of the Community. Of this chapter, Articles 85 and 86 are the most important Articles for present purposes. Article 85(1) prohibits agreements and concerted practices between undertakings which have as their object or effect the restriction of competition within the Common Market, **14–28**

---

[77] For the text of Arts. 2 and 3 see §§ F–1, F–2, *post*.

[78] For a general discussion of the freedom to provide services and the overlap with the right of establishment, see Kapteyn and Verloren van Themaat, *Introduction to the Laws of the European Communities*, (1989), pp. 427–452.

[79] Art. 61; see also Title III of the General Programme for the Abolition of Restrictions to Provide Services, which provides that the elimination of restrictions to provide services is subject (in addition to Art. 61) to Arts. 55 and 56, as well as to the provisions governing the free movement of goods, capital and persons and those concerning taxation: O.J. 1974 Sp.Ed. p. 3; Rudden and Wyatt, *Basic Community Laws*, (Clarendon Press, 1986).

[80] For the text of both Articles see §§ F–8, F–9, *post*.

[81] Case 33/74 *Van Binsbergen* v. *Bedrijfsvereniging Metaalnijverheid* [1974] E.C.R. 1299; [1975] 1 C.M.L.R. 298; see further § 14–11, *et seq. ante*.

[82] *Ibid.* [1974] E.C.R. at 1309 [10]; [1975] 1 C.M.L.R. 298 at 312 [10].

and which may affect trade between Member States. Article 85(2) provides for the effect of the prohibition on such agreements, and Article 85(3) provides for exemption from the prohibition in certain circumstances. Article 86 prohibits actions by undertakings in a dominant position within the Common Market which are an abuse of such position and which may affect trade between Member States. It will be noted, therefore, that the prohibitions of both Articles 85(1) and 86 are aimed at practices which may affect trade between Member States.

14–29   Both Articles 85(1) and 86 are directly applicable Treaty provisions,[83] and are therefore enforceable in proceedings in the national courts. In addition, the Commission is entrusted with the enforcement of the competition rules under Regulation 17,[84] adopted by the Council of Ministers in 1962 under Article 87 of the Treaty. The powers exercised by the Commission in this respect include the power to investigate the activities of undertakings and to issue decisions in respect of the practices investigated declaring that the prohibitions of Articles 85(1) and 86 do not apply, or applying the exemption in Article 85(3), or applying the prohibitions of Articles 85(1) and 86, in which case the Commission also has the power to impose fines on the undertakings concerned.[85]

5. The Exercise of Industrial and Commercial Property Rights and the Free Movement of Goods and Services

A. *Conflict between copyright and the aims of the EEC*

14–30   **Copyright as an industrial property right.** The term copyright is nowhere mentioned in the Treaty. Mention is made, however, in Article 36, of the term "industrial and commercial property rights", and also in Article 4(2)(*b*) of Regulation 17,[86] where the term is followed by the description "in particular patents, utility models, designs or trade marks." Despite the absence in such provisions of an express reference to copyright, there was little doubt that copyright was to be considered as an industrial property right for the purposes of the Treaty and its implementing measures.[87] This was confirmed by the Court of Justice in the case of *Musik-Vertrieb Membran* v. *GEMA*,[88] in which the Court rejected the argu-

---

[83] See Reg. 17 1962 O.J. 13/204 Art. 1 Case 13/61 *Robert Bosch GmbH* v. *Kleding-Verkoopbedrijf de Geus en Uitdenbogerd* [1962] E.C.R. 45; [1962] C.M.L.R. 1 (Art. 85(1)) and Case 127/73 *Belgische Radio en Televisie* v. *SABAM* [1974] E.C.R. 313; [1974] 2 C.M.L.R. 238 (Art. 86). See § 14–11, *et seq.*, *ante*. The text of Articles 85 and 86 is set out §§ F–6, F–9, *post*. See further *The Exercise of Industrial Property Rights and Rules on Competition*, § 14–96, *et seq.*, *post*.

[84] February 6, 1962; O.J. 1962 13/204.

[85] See further § 14–139, *post*.

[86] February 6, 1962; O.J. 1962 13/204.

[87] See the discussion in Adolf Dietz, *Copyright Law in the European Community*, p. 13, paras. 27–31. See also the submissions of Advocate-General Roemer in Case 78/70 *Deutsche Grammophon GmbH* v. *Metro-SB-Grossmärkte GmbH & Co. K.G.* [1971] E.C.R. 487; [1971] C.M.L.R. 631 at 646–647; Lord Denning M.R. in *Application des Gaz S.A.* v. *Falks Veritas Ltd.* [1974] Ch. 381; [1974] 2 C.M.L.R. 75 at 82 [23] *Yale Security Products Ltd.* v. *Newman* [1990] F.S.R. 320.

[88] Cases 55 & 57/80, [1981] E.C.R. 147; [1981] 2 C.M.L.R. 44; see also Case 402/85 *Basset* v. *SACEM* [1987] E.C.R. 1747 [11]; [1987] 3 C.M.L.R. 173 [11].

ment that its case law on industrial and commercial property rights could not extend to copyright because copyright was aimed at protecting the author's moral rights as much as his economic rights. The Court, while recognising the presence of both economic and moral rights behind the protection of copyright in national legislation, stated that the questions before it concerned the economic aspect of copyright and that the commercial exploitation of copyright raised the same issue as any other form of industrial and commercial property right in relation to the control of markets by the author and those acting under him. It is not surprising, therefore, that in a more recent Regulation dealing with block exemption under Article 85(3) for categories of franchise agreements,[89] the term "franchise" is defined as a package of industrial or intellectual property rights amongst which copyright is expressly included.

As between the different industrial property rights it has been pointed out that copyright is closer in nature to a patent than a trade mark.[90] It has been suggested that as between patents and trade marks, the underlying justification for the protection is stronger in the case of the former than the latter, and to the extent that this is correct, the same may apply to copyright.[91] However, one important difference between patents and copyright is that whereas the exercise of a patent right will necessarily involve the creation of a material object either itself the subject of the patent, or made by a process the subject of the patent, the exercise of copyright will not always do so, since copyright gives not only the right to control the production of products reproducing the copyright work, but also, for instance, the right to control performance of the copyright work. Unlike the right to control production, which is exhausted once a product is produced, the right to control performance is not exhausted upon the occasion of the first performance of the work. It is a right that will accrue in respect of each performance of the work, allowing an author to exercise a continuing control over the performance of his work.[92]   **14–31**

However, it is a common characteristic of all industrial and commercial property rights that they confer some degree of monopoly or exclusivity, and that the extent in content, time and territory of that monopoly or exclusivity is in the first instance a matter for the national law of the state granting the right in question.[93]

Territoriality. The fact that an industrial property right is the creature of the national laws of the state granting the right necessarily places limits on the territory within which such right is effective. This has been referred to   **14–32**

---

[89] Commission Regulation 4087/88, Art. 1(3) O.J. 1988 L 359/46.

[90] Advocate-General Roemer in Case 78/70 *Deutsche Grammophon GmbH* v. *Metro-SB-Grossmärkte GmbH & Co. K.G.* [1971] E.C.R. 487; [1971] C.M.L.R. 631 at 649. See also Case 40/70 *Sirena S.R.L.* v. *Eda S.R.L.* [1971] E.C.R. 69; [1971] C.M.L.R. 260 at 273 [7].

[91] See the views expressed by Advocate-General Dutheillet de Lamothe in *Sirena S.R.L.* v. *Eda S.R.L.*, [1971] E.C.R. 69 at 87; [1971] C.M.L.R. 260 at 264–265.

[92] See further, as to the importance of this distinction, § 14–60, *et seq., post.*

[93] See Case 144/81 *Keurkoop B.V.* v. *Nancy Kean Gifts B.V.* [1982] E.C.R. 2853; [1983] 2 C.M.L.R. 47; Case 341/87 *E.M.I. Electrola GmbH* v. *Patricia Im- und Export Verwaltungsgesellschaft GmbH* [1989] E.C.R. 79; [1989] 2 C.M.L.R. 413; Case 53/87 *Maxicar* v. *Renault* [1988] E.C.R. 6039; [1990] 4 C.M.L.R. 265.

as the "territoriality principle" of industrial property rights,[94] but it is really no more than a necessary reflection of the territorial limit to the sovereignty of the state concerned. In the present context an English court will not entertain an action under the Copyright, Designs and Patents Act 1988 by a plaintiff who is the author of a work entitled to copyright under that Act in respect of acts complained of as being committed in France, even if being committed by a defendant who is within the jurisdiction of the English court.[95] Such acts are not infringements of any rights granted to the plaintiff under the 1988 Act, and even if the plaintiff can establish that they are infringements of rights granted to him under French copyright law, they will not be justiciable in England,[96] on the basis that the plaintiff establishes the infringement of such rights as may be granted to him under French law.

International conventions in the field of copyright have helped to increase the protection available for the foreign copyright owner in the states adhering to such conventions, but this is achieved by each state according copyright to the works of foreign authors under its own national laws.[97] It is not the aim (or effect) of such conventions to create a unitary right recognised throughout the combined territories of the signatories.

14–33 **Monopoly or exclusivity.** Whilst international conventions have achieved a measure of harmonisation in certain aspects of the extent of the exclusivity granted by the laws of each state to the owner of copyright, notably in the duration of such exclusivity, the extent, particularly of the content, of such exclusivity remains a matter for the laws of each state. In the present context the exclusive rights granted to the owner of copyright under the Copyright, Designs and Patents Act 1988 generally include the right to reproduce, publish, broadcast and perform the work the subject of copyright in the manner and forms appropriate to the type of work in question, and also the right to authorise others to exercise such rights, or any one or more of the acts which the copyright owner has the exclusive right to do, and for part or all of the life of the copyright.

14–34 **Justification for monopoly or exclusivity: "exhaustion of rights."** The justification for the monopoly or exclusivity accorded to the owner of an industrial property right is that it gives him the protection necessary to allow him to obtain just recompense for his expenditure of time, effort and money in the creation or invention of the matter the subject of the right. Thus, where the exercise of the right can result in the production of a material object which will then be the subject of commerce, as is the case with a patent and, to a large extent with copyright, the owner of the right is able, in the territory of the state according such right, to control the production of such material objects, either by producing them himself, or by

---

[94] Advocate-General Roemer in Case 78/70 *Deutsche Grammophon GmbH* v. *Metro-SB-Gross-märkte GmbH & Co. K.G.* [1971] E.C.R. 487; C.M.L.R. 631 at 647–648.

[95] C.D.P.A. 1988, s.157(1); and see *"Morocco Bound" Syndicate, Ltd.* v. *Harris* [1898] 1 Ch. 534; *Def Lepp Music* v. *Stuart-Browne* [1986] R.P.C. 273; and see § 11–26, *ante.*

[96] See *Tyburn Productions Ltd.* v. *Conan Doyle* [1990] 1 All E.R. 909; [1990] 3 W.L.R. 167, and §11–26, *ante.*

[97] See Chap. 17, *post.*

licensing another to do so, and in either case he is able to extract his recompense on the occasion of the first sale of such products in that territory.
Thereafter such products can be freely sold by way of trade within the territory of that state (apart from any enforceable contractual terms preventing such resale) and the owner of the right cannot assert his monopoly or
exclusivity to prevent such resale. This is a characteristic common to all
industrial property rights. In terminology developed in continental jurisdictions the owner of the right has "exhausted his rights" by such authorised first sale.

Territorial monopoly or exclusivity and the prevention of imports.   **14-35**
The right of first sale accorded to the owner of an industrial property right
under the national laws of state A usually carries with it the right to prevent the importation into the territory of state A of products protected in
state A by the right in question, which have been manufactured in state B
without the authority of the owner of the right in state A. Without this
additional protection the monopoly or exclusivity could be rendered
valueless as a result of such international trade, and the whole purpose of
the monopoly or exclusivity would be defeated.

  Whether this protection for the owner's home market in state A can also
be invoked against imports of products in respect of the manufacture of
which in state B the owner could not complain, either because they were
manufactured by him under an equivalent right accorded to him by the
laws of state B, or by someone deriving title to such equivalent right from
him, or by a licensee under such right, either of himself or of his successor
in title, is a question which depends on the industrial property right concerned and on the national laws of state A under which such right is
enforced. The question may be put in continental terms as whether such a
sale, or disposition of the right of sale, abroad can properly be said to
exhaust the owner's rights under the laws of the home market. In England
the question turns, apart from considerations of Community law, entirely
on the precise terms in which the right to prevent imports is given by the
relevant statute to the owner of the industrial property right.

Imports into the United Kingdom. Under the Copyright Act 1956,[98]   **14-36**
the position appeared to turn on the answer to the hypothetical question
whether the product being imported was manufactured in the foreign
country by a person who, had he manufactured the product in the United
Kingdom, would not thereby have infringed copyright. If this question
was answered affirmatively, then importation of the product could not be
prevented, but if this question was answered in the negative, then importation could be prevented, even though the manufacture was in fact not an
infringement of copyright under the copyright laws of the country where
the product was actually manufactured.[99]

---

[98] Copyright Act 1956, ss.5(2) and 16(2).
[99] *Polydor Ltd. and R.S.O. Records Inc. v. Harlequin Record Shop Ltd. and Simons Records Ltd.* [1980]
    2 C.M.L.R. 413 (C.A.); [1980] F.S.R. 194; (for the decision of the ECJ on the effect of
    Community law, see [1982] E.C.R. 329; [1982] 1 C.M.L.R. 677; [1982] F.S.R. 358); *CBS
    United Kingdom Ltd. v. Charmdale Record Distributors Ltd.* [1981] Ch. 91; [1980] 2 All E.R.
    807; *The Who Group Ltd. and Polydor Ltd. v. Stage One (Records) Ltd.* [1980] 2 C.M.L.R. 429;
    [1980] F.S.R. 268.

14-37   The Copyright, Designs and Patents Act 1988 has maintained and tightened this rule.[1] Under the 1956 Act, the contractual nature of an exclusive licence prevented an exclusive licensee of the copyright in the United Kingdom from restraining the importation into the United Kingdom of products manufactured abroad by the copyright owner or by anyone under licence from him or his successor in title.[2] Importation of such products into the United Kingdom might have rendered the copyright owner in breach of his contract with the licensee, but it was not an infringement of the copyright, and consequently the restrictions on importation under the 1956 Act did not apply. Now, the 1988 Act has amended this prohibition on importation to include, in its definition of an infringing copy of a work, imported products the manufacture of which in the United Kingdom would have been a breach of an exclusive licence agreement in relation to that work.[3]

However, the 1988 Act also makes express provision for imports which are subject to Community law.[4] The definition of an infringing copy of a work in section 27(3) of the Act is not to be construed as applying to an article which may be lawfully imported into the United Kingdom by virtue of any enforceable Community right.[5]

14-38   The prevention of imports: conflict with the aims of the Community. The exercise of copyright, and other industrial property rights, to prevent imports into a state has so far been considered only in a national context, where the boundaries of the state define the limits for the purposes both of the enforcement of the right in question and of the state's control of its trade with other countries. In the context of the Community, copyright continues to be accorded by the separate national laws of each of the 12 Member States, with the consequence that national boundaries continue to determine the limits to the enforcement of each of these copyrights, but, as has been explained above,[6] the national boundaries are no longer allowed to present an obstacle to the free movement of goods and services within the Community. However, it should readily be appreciated, from the discussion above, that nationally-held industrial property rights such as copyright, by the very combination of their twin characteristics of territoriality and exclusivity, are capable of being used to prevent imports into one Member State of copies of a work lawfully on the market in another Member State, and thus constituting in themselves an obstacle to the free movement of goods and services within the Community.[7]

---

[1] C.D.P.A. 1988, ss.22, 27(1) and 27(3).
[2] Copyright Act 1956, s.19(4).
[3] C.D.P.A. 1988, s.27(3)(*b*).
[4] *Ibid.* s.27(5).
[5] As defined by s.2(1) of the European Communities Act 1972 (1972 c. 68); and see § 14–15, *ante.*
[6] See § 14–22, *ante.*
[7] As was stated in relation to patents by the Court of Justice in Case 24/67 *Parke, Davis* v. *Probel* [1968] E.C.R. 55; [1968] C.M.L.R. 47 at 58 [2]; and in relation to copyright in Cases 55 & 57/80 *Musik-Vertrieb Membran* v. *GEMA* [1981] E.C.R. 147 [13]; [1981] 2 C.M.L.R. 44.

Furthermore, the owner of the several copyrights accorded under the laws of each of the Member States may seek by agreement with others to divide up the exploitation of those rights by reference to the still-existing territorial boundaries of each of the Member States. By the terms of such agreements the owner of such rights may seek to protect the exclusivity of each of his licensees in their respective territories, with the result that the terms of the agreements may themselves constitute obstacles to free movement within the Community, thus preventing competition, and may therefore fall within the prohibition of the rules on competition. Either method of exercising his rights under the Copyright, Designs and Patents Act 1988, that is by asserting those rights by national proceedings, or by exploiting them through agreements with others, may therefore bring the owner of such rights into conflict with the provisions of the Treaty and of Community law.   **14–39**

B. *Resolution of the conflict between industrial property rights and the aims of the EEC*

(i) Creation of community industrial property rights

Creation of unitary rights. One solution to the problem of ensuring that industrial property rights do not present an obstacle to the realisation of the Common Market is to create a unitary right covering the combined territories of the 12 Member States, the content of which is determined by Community law, not by the national laws of the separate Member States, and to which effect is given in identical manner in the national courts of each Member State.   **14–40**

Community Patent Convention. Such was the objective of the Community Patent Convention, signed by the then nine Member States of the Community on December 15, 1975.[8] The Convention applies, by Articles 32 and 81, the principle of exhaustion of rights to patents, in that neither a national patent,[9] nor a Community patent, may be asserted to prevent the importation into one Member State of a product marketed in another Member State by the patentee or with his express consent or, in the case of a national patent, by a person with whom he has economic connections.[10]   **14–41**

Proposed Community Trade Mark. The development by the Community of a Community trade mark is currently in the process of negotiation. A proposed Regulation on a Community Trade Mark was put forward in 1980 and amended in 1984.[11] Once registered, the trade mark will be valid for the entire Community. If the proprietor of the Community trade mark is also the proprietor of an identical or similar national trade mark for the identical or similar goods or services, the effects of the national trade mark will be suspended for the period of validity of the   **14–42**

---

[8] O.J. 1976 L17/1.
[9] See, in the case of U.K. patents, the Patents Act 1977, ss.60(4) and 86.
[10] As defined in Art. 81(2), Community Patent Convention.
[11] O.J. 1980 C351/1; O.J. 1984 C230/1; [1981] 1 C.M.L.R. 365 (original text).

Community trade mark. However, any action for infringement of the Community trade mark will be heard by the courts of whichever Member State is determined to be the appropriate forum by the rules contained in the proposed Regulation.[12]

14-43 **Copyright.** So far as copyright is concerned, there have been no proposals for a Community copyright. Moreover, this industrial property right enjoys the special position that no registration system is required in any of the laws of the Member States for the subsistence of copyright under those laws, and also that a certain degree of harmonisation as to the content of the right in the Member States has already been achieved as a result of a succession of international conventions. It has been argued that there is therefore no need for a special agreement between Member States (such as the Community Patent Convention) but that further harmonisation necessary to allow for the realisation of the Common Market can be achieved by appropriate directives issued by the Council.[13]

(ii) Harmonisation of national industrial property rights

14-44 **Harmonisation of national laws.** Another solution which may be used to resolve Community problems, caused by differences in the national laws of the Member States, is for the Community institutions to seek harmonisation of the national laws concerned. This may be achieved by the Council, acting on a proposal from the Commission, issuing a directive under Articles 100 and, now, 100A of the Treaty.

Concurrently with the proposals for a Community trade mark, the Council has adopted such a directive requiring Member States to harmonise their national legislation on trade marks. The Directive will become effective in December 1991 and seeks to ensure the uniform protection of registered trade marks throughout the legal systems of Member States.[14]

14-45 **Commission Green Paper on Copyright.** Nevertheless, with the growing importance of high technology and the service industries in the economies of the industrialised Member States, the Community is increasingly concerned to ensure that there is available through the copyright laws of the Member States effective and uniform legal protection to prevent the misappropriation of copyright works through unauthorised copying. Consequently, the Commission published a consultative document, the Green Paper on Copyright and the Challenge of Technology.[15]

The Green Paper recognises that since all Member States are members of the Berne Convention and the Universal Copyright Convention, many areas of their copyright laws have already reached a fundamental level of convergence, such that any Community approach should only address

---

[12] Arts. 12 and 74 of the proposed Regulation.

[13] See § 14–44, *post*, and see generally, Adolf Dietz, *Copyright in the European Community*, pp. 243–244, paras. 650–655. See also the 1977 Copyright Committee, Cmnd. 6732, para. 125.

[14] O.J. 1989 L40/1; [1981] 1 C.M.L.R. 357 (original text); see generally on the current developments for the Community Trade Mark, Mark Brealey and Quigley, *Completing the Internal Market, 1992 Handbook and 1992 Legislation* (Graham & Trotman, 2nd. ed., 1990).

[15] Com. (88) 172 final, Bull. E.C. 6–1988, points 1.2.1 *et seq.*

Community problems.[16] These problems are considered by the Commission to be most urgent in six fields: piracy; home copying of sound and audio-visual material; distribution rights, exhaustion and rental rights for particular classes of works, especially sound and video recordings; the protection of computer programs; the protection of data bases; and the role of the Community in multilateral and bilateral external relations affecting these matters. Of particular interest in the present context are the general comments of the Commission, in the introduction to the Green Paper, as to the overall objectives which the Community should be looking to achieve in its development of copyright protection. These are described as fourfold.[17] First, the Community has to ensure the proper functioning of the Common Market, so that creators and providers of copyright goods and services are able to treat the Community as a single market. Secondly, the Community has to develop its policies so that the economy of the Community remains competitive with that of its trading partners. Thirdly, the Community has to guard against misappropriation by others outside its external frontiers of intellectual property that has required considerable investment in terms of finance and effort.[18] Fourthly, the Commission is concerned to ensure that copyright protection is not used to create monopolies of undue scope and duration, so that any copyright protection must take into account not only the interests of the right holder, but also those of third parties and the public at large. The central theme of these concerns, that of using copyright to create a favourable environment to stimulate and protect the creativity and investment of individuals for the benefit of the economy of the Community, balanced against the potential danger inherent in copyright of creating anti-competitive monopolies, is one that mirrors the conflicts which the Court of Justice has been faced with in developing its jurisprudence in the field of industrial property rights.

Community harmonisation measures with regard to copyright. The   **14–46** first copyright legislation resulting from the debate stimulated by the Green Paper to have reached the stage of a concrete proposal is a draft directive on the legal protection of computer programmes as literary works, for a period of 50 years from the date of creation.[19] This has been adopted by the Commission for transmission to the Council and the Parliament. In a separate, but related field, the Council has also adopted a Directive on the legal protection of topographies of semi-conductor products.[20] The regime set up under this Directive, which is without preju-

---

[16] *Ibid.* para. 1.4.9.

[17] *Ibid.* paras. 1.3.1–1.3.6.

[18] See, in respect of one possible method of challenging misappropriation of intellectual property by others outside the Community: *Re Unauthorised Reproduction of Sound Recordings in Indonesia* [1988] 1 C.M.L.R. 387, concerning the use of the New Commercial Policy Instrument, Council Regulation 2641/84 (O.J. 1984 L252/1), against illicit commercial practices.

[19] O.J. 1989 C91/4 [1989] 2 C.M.L.R. 180; amended proposal O.J. 1990 C–320/22.

[20] Council Directive 87/54 of December 16, 1986 on the legal protection of topographies of semi-conductor products (O.J. 1987 L24/36) extended by Council Decision 88/311 of May 31, 1988 in respect of persons from certain countries and territories (O.J. 1988 L140/13). See, as to the position in the United Kingdom, § 20–208 *et seq., post.*

dice to patent rights, copyright, and rights in respect of utility models conferred under international agreements, aims to protect the topographies of semi-conductors in so far as they are the result of the creator's own intellectual effort and are not commonplace in the semi-conductor industry. The rights created by the Directive are an independent form of intellectual property, but bear some similarity to the rights protected by copyright.

(iii) Resolution of the conflict by the Court of Justice

14–47 **Role of the Court of Justice.** In the absence of a unitary system of industrial property rights, it has been left to the Court of Justice to resolve the conflict between the national industrial property rights and the aims of the EEC. The Court's solution had to take account of the protection afforded to national property rights, in particular to industrial and commercial property rights, under Articles 222 and 36 of the Treaty.

14–48 **Article 222 of the Treaty.** Article 222, which is found in Part Six of the Treaty, devoted to general and final provisions, provides that the Treaty shall in no way prejudice the rules in Member States governing the system of property ownership.[21] However, the object of this Article is to guarantee, in a general manner, the freedom of the Member States to organise their own systems of property, but not to guarantee that the Community institutions may not intervene in the subjective right of property, as was affirmed by the Court of Justice by its judgment in *Consten & Grundig* v. *E.C. Commission.*[22]

14–49 **Article 36 of the Treaty.** Article 36 allows for exceptions to the principle of free movement of goods, in that the provisions of Articles 30 to 34 are not to preclude prohibitions on imports and exports justified on specified grounds which include the protection of industrial and commercial property, provided that such measures do not constitute a means of arbitrary discrimination or a disguised restriction on trade between Member States.[23] The Court of Justice has stated that, in so far as Article 36 provides exceptions to the fundamental rule of free movement of goods between Member States, the exceptions are to be interpreted strictly.[24]

14–50 **Distinction between the existence or substance of industrial property rights and their exercise.** The solution adopted by the Court of Justice has been to draw from the interpretation of these Articles a distinction between the existence of nationally-held industrial property rights

---

[21] For the text of Art. 222, see § F–11, *post.*
[22] Cases 56 & 58/64 *Consten & Grundig* v. *E.C. Commission* [1966] E.C.R. 299; [1966] C.M.L.R. 418; and see the Opinion of Advocate-General Roemer at [1966] C.M.L.R. 443.
[23] For the text of Art. 36, see § F–5, *post.*
[24] Case 7/68 *Re Export Tax on Art Treasures* [1968] E.C.R. 423; [1969] C.M.L.R. 1; Case 35/76 *Simmenthal SpA* v. *Amministrazione delle Finanze dello Stato* [1976] E.C.R. 1871; [1977] 2 C.M.L.R. 1; Case 113/80 *Commission* v. *Ireland* [1981] E.C.R. 1625; [1982] 1 C.M.L.R. 706; Case 95/81 *Commission* v. *Italy* [1982] E.C.R. 2187.

and their exercise. This distinction was first drawn by the Court in *Consten & Grundig v. E.C. Commission,*[25] in which the Court was considering an appeal against a decision of the Commission which prohibited, under Article 85(1), an agreement relating to the exercise of trade marks. The distinction has been developed in a number of cases since, in relation to trade marks,[26] copyright,[27] and similar rights of protection under German law,[28] design rights,[29] and patents.[30] The essence of the distinction is that Community law does not affect the grant, substance or existence of such rights, which remain a matter for the respective national laws of the Member States. However, Community law may interfere with the exercise of such rights to the extent that such exercise is contrary to a fundamental rule of Community law.

Development of distinction into principle of Community law. So far, **14–51** the distinction has been drawn in applications concerning the free movement of goods and services as well as the rules of competition. Although the distinction has primarily been developed by reference to Article 36 and the derogation in that Article for the protection of industrial and commercial property, the extension of the distinction to the free movement of services and to the application of competition policy has required the Court to develop the doctrine as a principle of Community law, of which Article 36 is an express example relating to the free movement of goods.

This is a progression from *Consten & Grundig v. E.C. Commission,*[31] where **14–52** the Court of Justice pointed out that Article 36 had, by its very terms and position in the Treaty, no application to the rules on competition.[32] The foundation for this extension by the Court of Justice of the distinction between the exercise of the rights of commercial and industrial property to fields beyond the free movement of goods is not fully explained in its

---

[25] Cases 56 & 58/64, [1966] E.C.R. 299; [1966] C.M.L.R. 418. For a commentary on the more recent developments, see Georges Friden, "Recent Developments in EEC Intellectual Property Law: The distinction between Existence and Exercise revisited." [1989] C.M.L.Rev. 193.

[26] Case 40/70 *Sirena S.R.L. v. Eda S.R.L.* [1971] E.C.R. 69; [1971] C.M.L.R. 260; Case 16/74 *Centrafarm B.V. v. Winthrop B.V.* [1974] E.C.R. 1183; [1974] 2 C.M.L.R. 480; Case 51/75 *E.M.I. Records Ltd. v. CBS United Kingdom Ltd.* [1976] E.C.R. 811; [1976] 2 C.M.L.R. 235; Case 58/80 *Dansk Supermarked A/S v. A/S Imerco* [1981] E.C.R. 181; [1981] 3 C.M.L.R. 590; Case C–10/89 *S.A. CNL–Sucal NV v. Hag GF AG.* [1990] 3 C.M.L.R. 571.

[27] Case 62/79 *Coditel S.A. v. Cine Vog Films S.A.* [1980] E.C.R. 881; [1981] 2 C.M.L.R. 362; Case 262/81 *Coditel S.A. v. Cine Vog Films S.A. (No. 2)* [1982] E.C.R. 3381; [1983] 1 C.M.L.R. 49; Case 270/80 *Polydor Ltd. and R.S.O. Records Inc. v. Harlequin Record Shop Ltd. and Simons Records Ltd.* [1982] E.C.R. 329; [1982] 1 C.M.L.R. 677; Case 58/80 *Dansk Supermarked A/S v. A/S Imerco* [1981] E.C.R. 181; [1981] 3 C.M.L.R. 590.

[28] *Deutsche Grammophon GmbH v. Metro-SB-Grossmärkte GmbH & Co. K.G.* [1971] E.C.R. 487; [1971] C.M.L.R. 631.

[29] Case 144/81 *Keurkoop B.V. v. Nancy Kean Gifts B.V.* [1982] E.C.R. 2853; [1983] 2 C.M.L.R. 47.

[30] Case 24/67 *Parke, Davis v. Probel* [1968] E.C.R. 55; [1968] C.M.L.R. 47; Cases 15 & 16/74 *Centrafarm B.V. v. Sterling Drug Inc.* [1974] E.C.R. 1147, 1183; [1974] 2 C.M.L.R. 480; Case 35/87 *Thetford Corporation v. Fiamma SpA* [1988] E.C.R. 3585; [1988] 3 C.M.L.R. 549.

[31] See n. 25, *ante.*

[32] Cases 56 & 58/64, [1966] E.C.R. 299; [1966] C.M.L.R. 418 at 476.

reasoning,[33] nor are there parallel exceptions in the chapters of the Treaty on the freedom to provide services or the application of competition rules. Nevertheless, in *Coditel S.A.* v. *Cine Vog Films S.A.*[34] the Court of Justice stated that whilst Article 59 prohibits restrictions upon the freedom to provide services, it does not thereby mean restrictions upon the exercise of certain economic activities which have their origin in the application of national legislation for the protection of intellectual property, save where such application constitutes a means of arbitrary discrimination or disguised restriction on trade between Member States. Possibly the method of explaining this teleological interpretation of the Treaty is to return to the willingness of the Court of Justice to develop principles for the application of Community law to ensure uniformity in its sectors of influence.[35] Moreover, the Court of Justice has stressed repeatedly that the goal of the Treaty is a single market. To the extent that the Court of Justice develops limits on the ability of national intellectual property laws to derogate from that goal, it would be illogical for the Court to apply different rules in respect of the market in goods to those applied in respect of the market in services.

14–53 **Development of concept of the specific object of an industrial property right.** The case law of the Court of Justice has made it clear that the existence of industrial and commercial property rights is not affected by the Treaty. Only the exercise of those rights requires justification as a derogation from the principle of free movement of goods or services, in that such derogation must not constitute a means of arbitrary discrimination or a disguised restriction on trade between Member States. In *Deutsche Grammophon GmbH* v. *Metro-SB-Grossmärkte GmbH & Co. K.G.*[36] the Court gave detailed consideration to the terms of Article 36 and held that the Article only permits restrictions on the freedom of trade to the extent that they are justified for *the protection of the rights that form the specific object of that property*.[37] The Court thereby further developed the concept of the distinction between the existence or substance and the exercise of the right, by introducing the concept of the specific object of the industrial property right. The specific object of the right is a matter of its substance, and the exercise by the owner of the right of what is no more than the specific object of the right will be protected by the derogation from the principle of free movement in Article 36. Anything further done by the owner of the right which restricts the free movement of goods or services between Member States will be struck down as incompatible with Community law.

Since its judgment in the *Deutsche Grammophon* case,[38] the Court has affirmed the concept of the specific object of the industrial property right

---

[33] See, *e.g.* Case 40/70 *Sirena S.R.L.* v. *Eda S.R.L.* [1971] E.C.R. 69; [1971] C.M.L.R. 260 at 273 [5].

[34] Case 62/79 [1980] E.C.R. 881 [15]; [1981] 2 C.M.L.R. 362 at 400 [15]; see also Case 262/81 *Coditel S.A.* v. *Cine Vog Films S.A. (No. 2)* [1982] E.C.R. 3381; [1983] 1 C.M.L.R. 49.

[35] See § 14–10, *ante*.

[36] [1971] E.C.R. 487; [1971] C.M.L.R. 631.

[37] *Ibid.* at 657 [11]; repeated by the Court in a later trade mark case: Case 119/75 *Terrapin (Overseas) Ltd.* v. *Terranova Industrie* [1976] E.C.R. 1039; [1976] 2 C.M.L.R. 482 at 505 [5].

[38] *Ante*, n. 36.

as governing the limits of the exceptions in Article 36 in favour of industrial property rights, in relation to patents,[39] trade marks,[40] copyright,[41] and registered designs.[42]

(iv) Specific object of Patents, Trade Marks and Copyright

(a) *Patents*

Specific object of patents. In relation to patents, the Court defined the **14–54** specific object as being to ensure that the creative effort of the inventor is rewarded by the grant of the exclusive right to use an invention for the purpose of making and effecting a first sale of industrial products, either directly or by the grant of licences, and to oppose any infringement.[43] In *Merck & Co. Inc.* v. *Stephar B.V.*[44] the Court reaffirmed this definition, but in so doing qualified the extent to which the patentee may rely on his patent rights to prevent the import and sale of the patented product coming from other Member States. Merck manufactured and marketed in all the Member States a drug known as "Moduretic." It held the patent for the drug in the majority of the Member States, including Holland. In Italy no patent protection was available for medicinal products. Merck sought to prevent the import for sale on the Dutch market of the drug from Italy. The Court of Justice acknowledged that had the drug been manufactured for sale or sold on the Italian market without the consent of Merck, Merck could have prevented its import into the Dutch market. However, the Court said that Merck had exhausted its rights when it elected to market its product in a country where no patent protection existed. In so deciding, the Court of Justice stated that the substance of a patent right lies in according the inventor an exclusive right of first placing the product on the market, by which he may obtain his reward for his creative effort. That right did not, however, guarantee the inventor such a reward in all circumstances, and it was for the inventor to decide under what conditions he will market his product. If the inventor decides to mar-

---

[39] Case 15/74 *Centrafarm B.V.* v. *Sterling Drug Inc.* [1974] E.C.R. 1147, 1183; [1974] 2 C.M.L.R. 480; Case 187/80 *Merck & Co. Inc.* v. *Stephar B.V.* [1981] E.C.R. 2063; [1981] 3 C.M.L.R. 463; Case 19/84 *Pharmon B.V.* v. *Hoechst AG* [1985] E.C.R. 2281; [1985] 3 C.M.L.R. 775; Case 193/83 *Windsurfing International Inc.* v. *E.C. Commission* [1986] E.C.R. 611, [1986] 3 C.M.L.R. 489.

[40] Case 16/74 *Centrafarm B.V.* v. *Winthrop B.V.* [1974] E.C.R. 1183; [1974] 2 C.M.L.R. 480; Case 3/78 *Centrafarm B.V.* v. *American Home Products Inc.* [1978] E.C.R. 1823; [1979] 1 C.M.L.R. 326; Case C–10/89 *S.A. CNL–Sucal NV* v. *Hag GF AG.* [1990] 3 C.M.L.R. 571.

[41] Case 62/79 *Coditel S.A.* v. *Cine Vog Films S.A.* [1980] E.C.R. 881; [1981] 2 C.M.L.R. 362; Cases 55 & 57/80 *Musik-Vertrieb Membran GmbH* v. *GEMA* [1981] E.C.R. 146; [1981] 2 C.M.L.R. 44; Case 262/81 *Coditel S.A.* v. *Cine Vog Films S.A. (No. 2)* [1982] E.C.R. 3381; [1983] 1 C.M.L.R. 49; Case 402/85 *Basset* v. *SACEM* [1987] E.C.R. 1747; [1987] 3 C.M.L.R. 173; see also the Opinion of Advocate-General Jacobs in Case 395/87 *Ministère Public* v. *Tournier* (unreported) and Cases 110/88, 241/88 and 242/88 *SACEM* v. *Lucazeau*, *SACEM* v. *Debelle and SACEM* v. *Soumagnac* (unreported), at paras. 22–26.

[42] Case 144/81 *Keurkoop B.V.* v. *Nancy Kean Gifts B.V.* [1982] E.C.R. 2853; [1983] 2 C.M.L.R. 47; Case 238/87 *Volvo AB* v. *Eric Veng (U.K.) Ltd.* [1988] E.C.R. 6211 [1989] 4 C.M.L.R. 122.

[43] Case 15/74 *Centrafarm B.V.* v. *Sterling Drug Inc.* [1974] E.C.R. 1147, 1183; [1974] 2 C.M.L.R. 480 at 503 [9].

[44] Case 187/80, [1981] E.C.R. 2063; [1981] 3 C.M.L.R. 463.

ket the product in a Member State which does not provide patent protection for the product, then he must accept the consequences of his choice as regards the free movement of goods within the Common Market.[45]

(b) *Trade Marks*

14–55 **Specific object of trade marks.** In relation to trade marks, the Court has defined the specific object as being the exclusive right to use the trade mark for the purpose of effecting the first sale of a product, thus protecting the owner of the trade mark against competitors who would take advantage of the status and reputation of the trade mark by selling goods improperly bearing the mark.[46] Both in relation to patents and trade marks, the Court went on to hold that the existence in national laws of provisions whereby the rights of the owner of the industrial property right in the Member State are not exhausted by the marketing of the protected product in another Member State constitutes an unjustified obstacle to the free movement of goods between Member States, where such marketing was lawfully effected in the second state by or with the consent of the owner of the industrial property right in the first state or by a person connected with him by ties of legal or economic dependence.[47]

(c) *Copyright*

14–56 **The Deutshe Grammophon Case.** Whilst the position was therefore quickly clarified in relation to patents and trade marks, the Court of Justice was not so clear, in its earlier judgment in the *Deutsche Grammophon* case, in relation to a right under German law similar to copyright. The Court merely stated that it conflicted with the provisions regarding the free movement of goods in the Common Market if a manufacturer of recordings so exercises the exclusive right granted to him by the legislation of a Member State to market protected articles as to prohibit the marketing in that Member State of products that have been sold by himself or with his consent in another Member State, solely because this marketing has not occurred in the territory of the first Member State.[48] The Court did not take the opportunity of defining in more precise terms the specific object of copyright,[49] yet clearly accepted that in the case before it

---

[45] *Ibid.* [9]–[11]; but compare the position concerning compulsory licences in Case 19/84 *Pharmon B.V.* v. *Hoechst AG* [1985] E.C.R. 2281; [1985] 3 C.M.L.R. 775.

[46] Case 16/74 *Centrafarm B.V.* v. *Winthrop B.V.* [1974] E.C.R. 1183; [1974] 2 C.M.L.R. 480 at 508 [8]. See also Case 102/77 *Hoffmann-La Roche AG* v. *Centrafarm* [1978] E.C.R. 1139; [1978] 3 C.M.L.R. 217 at 241 [7]; Case 3/78 *Centrafarm B.V.* v. *American Home Products Inc.* [1978] E.C.R. 1823; [1979] 1 C.M.L.R. 326; Case C–10/89 *S.A. CNL–Sucal NV.* v. *Hag GF AG.* [1990] 3 C.M.L.R. 571 at 608 [14], and articles on these cases by Martin van Empel, "Centrafarm Revisited: a few comments on cases 102/77 and 3/78," (1979) 16 C.M.L.Rev. 251 and Bryan Harris, "The 'exhaustion principle' and the Centrafarm cases" (1979) 4 E.L.Rev. 379; Case 1/81 *Pfizer Inc.* v. *Eurim-Pharm GmbH* [1981] E.C.R. 2913; [1982] 1 C.M.L.R. 406.

[47] Case 15/74 *Centrafarm B.V.* v. *Sterling Drug Inc.* [1974] E.C.R. 1147, 1183; [1974] 2 C.M.L.R. 480 at 503, 504 [10] and [11], and Case 16/74 *Centrafarm B.V.* v. *Winthrop B.V.* [1974] E.C.R. 1183; [1974] 2 C.M.L.R. 480 at 508, 509 [9] and [10].

[48] Case 78/70 *Deutsche Grammophon GmbH* v. *Metro-SB-Grossmärkte GmbH & Co. K.G.* [1971] E.C.R. 487; [1971] C.M.L.R. 631.

[49] *Ibid.* [1971] C.M.L.R. 631 at 657–658 [13].

the attempt by Deutsche Grammophon to prevent the reimportation of the products into Germany went beyond the specific object of the right in question.

When the case came back before the German court, issues arose on the **14–57** facts as to whether there had been a marketing of the records in France by Polydor S.A. (a wholly-owned subsidiary of Deutsche Grammophon) and as to whether Deutsche Grammophon was responsible for, and had therefore consented to, that marketing. The German court decided against Deutsche Grammophon on these issues, and applied the ruling of the Court of Justice to prevent Deutsche Grammophon from asserting its exclusive distribution rights in Germany, under the German Copyright Act, to prevent the reimportation of the records in question from France.[50]

Subsequent development by national courts. After the *Deutsche Gram-* **14–58** *mophon* case,[51] it was left to the national courts to define what they considered to be the specific object of copyright under their laws, guided by the rulings of the Court of Justice in that case and the *Centrafarm/Sterling*[52] and *Centrafarm/Winthrop*[53] cases. In *Time Limit S.A.* v. *SABAM*,[54] the Belgian Court of Appeal was called on to consider the validity of certain royalties levied by the Belgian performing right society SABAM. Following the guidance laid down by the Court of Justice in the above cases, the Belgian court defined the specific object of copyright in a musical work as including the right of reproduction, but not the rights to lay down the territorial limits within which the product embodying the reproduction may be marketed.

Further development by the Court of Justice. The first case concern- **14–59** ing reproduction rights and the exercise of copyright to come before the Court of Justice after the *Deutsche Grammophon* case was *Musik-Vertrieb Membran* v. *GEMA*.[55] This case raised the question of the compatibility with Community law of the practice of the German collecting society of collecting the difference between the royalty fees paid in the exporting Member State and the royalty fees payable in Germany when records were imported into Germany from another Member State. The Court, after rejecting the argument that the moral rights aspect of copyright required it to be treated differently to other industrial property rights, stated that the right involved in the case was the right to exploit commercially the marketing of the protected work, particularly in the form of licences granted in return for payment of royalties. In respect of the exercise of such an economic right, the Court reaffirmed, in accordance with its development of the doctrine of exhaustion of rights for other forms of industrial property and without therefore needing to define further the

---

[50] See also the Opinion of Advocate-General Roemer, *ibid.* at 647–648.
[51] *Deutsche Grammophon GmbH* v. *Metro-SB-Grossmärkte GmbH & Co. K.G.* [1972] C.M.L.R. 107.
[52] Case 15/74 *Centrafarm B.V.* v. *Sterling Drug Inc.* [1974] E.C.R. 1147, 1183; [1974] 2 C.M.L.R. 480.
[53] Case 16/74 *Centrafarm B.V.* v. *Winthrop B.V.* [1974] E.C.R. 1183; [1974] 2 C.M.L.R. 480.
[54] [1979] 2 C.M.L.R. 578 at 582 [9].
[55] Cases 55 & 57/80, [1981] E.C.R. 147; [1981] 2 C.M.L.R. 44.

specific object of copyright, that the copyright owner could not rely on the exclusive exploitation right conferred by copyright to restrict the importation of the sound recordings which had been lawfully marketed in another Member State by the copyright owner or with his consent.

14–60 **Divisibility of copyright: reproduction right and performance right.** As has already been stated,[56] copyright, unlike other forms of industrial property, is a divisible right, in that copyright in a work gives separate rights to control the reproduction and performance of the work. The Court of Justice has acknowledged that these two separate rights form divisible elements of the specific subject-matter of copyright, and that exhaustion of the right to control reproduction will not necessarily exhaust the right to control performance.[57] The two *Coditel* cases[58] raised the question of whether the owner of a copyright work could rely on that copyright to prevent the transmission in one Member State of the work lawfully broadcast in another Member State. In the first *Coditel* case, the Court was asked to consider the question in relation to Articles 30 and 36, and 59 and 60. The Court held that films differ from those literary and artistic works for which the placing of the work at the disposal of the public is inseparable from the circulation of the material object in which the work is reproduced, such as a book or a record. Rather, films belong to that category of literary and artistic works which are made available to the public by performance which can be infinitely repeated. The commercial exploitation of such works falls within the domain of movement of services. In these circumstances, the Court held that it is part of the essential function of copyright that the owner of the copyright in a film and his assigns may require fees for any showing of that film.[59] Consequently, the Court decided that the provisions of the Treaty relating to the freedom to provide services would not prevent the assignee of the performing right in a film from exercising his right to prohibit exhibition of the film in a Member State without his authority, if the film was picked up and transmitted after being broadcast in another Member State by a third party with the consent of the original owner.[60]

14–61 **Distinction applied to records and video cassettes**. Since the *Coditel* cases, the Court of Justice has further considered the specific subject-matter of copyright in the context of performances of sound recordings on records and of films on video cassettes. Both records and video cassettes are media where the commercial exploitation of the performance right in

---

[56] See § 14–31, *ante.*

[57] Case 62/79 *Coditel S.A.* v. *Cine Vog Films S.A.* [1980] E.C.R. 881; [1981] 2 C.M.L.R. 362; Case 262/81 *Coditel S.A.* v. *Cine Vog Films S.A. (No. 2)* [1982] E.C.R. 3381; [1983] 1 C.M.L.R. 49; Case 402/85 *Basset* v. *SACEM* [1987] E.C.R. 1747; [1987] 3 C.M.L.R. 173; Case 158/86 *Warner Brothers Inc.* v. *Erik Christiansen* [1988] E.C.R. 2605; [1990] 3 C.M.L.R. 684; Case 395/87 *Ministère Public* v. *Tournier* (unreported).

[58] Case 62/79 *Coditel S.A.* v. *Cine Vog Films S.A.* [1980] E.C.R. 881; [1981] 2 C.M.L.R. 362; Case 262/81 *Coditel S.A.* v. *Cine Vog Films S.A. (No. 2)* [1982] E.C.R. 3381; [1983] 1 C.M.L.R. 49.

[59] Case 62/79 *Coditel S.A.* v. *Cine Vog Films S.A.* [1980] E.C.R. 881; [1981] 2 C.M.L.R. 362 at 400 [14].

[60] *Ibid.* at [18].

the copyright work cannot be separated from the distribution of the material product subject to the right of reproduction. For both forms of reproduction of the copyright work the Court has upheld the right of the copyright owner to continue to exploit the commercial performance of his work despite the exhaustion of the right of reproduction in the material form of the copyright work.[61]

In *Ministère Public* v. *Tournier*,[62] the Court of Justice held that national   **14–62** copyright legislation which prevented the public performance of sound recordings from records, without the payment of royalties in respect of such performance, even when royalties have already been paid for the reproduction of the work in the form of such records in another Member State, is not incompatible with Articles 30 and 59.

The Court of Justice adopted a similar approach in *Warner Brothers Inc.*   **14–63** v. *Erik Christiansen*[63] to Danish legislation which allowed the owner of the Danish copyright to prevent the rental on the Danish market, without his consent, of video cassettes purchased in another Member State, where there was no legislation governing the exercise of copyright upon the rental of the cassettes and where they had been marketed with the consent of the owner of the copyright in that Member State. The Danish legislation was not, the Court held, incompatible with Articles 30 and 36.

Nevertheless this case provides greater difficulty in defining the border   **14–64** between the continuous right of exploitation in the performance of a work and the right of reproduction and first distribution of a work. In reaching its decision in *Warner Brothers Inc.* v. *Erik Christiansen*,[64] the Court avoided expressly classifying the protection of the rental right under Danish law as falling either under the continuing right of exploitation in the performance of the copyright work, or as being a departure from the principle that the right of reproduction and first marketing of a work is exhausted with respect to a product reproducing that work following the first placing of that product on the market by or with the consent of the copyright owner. Nevertheless, it is suggested that the Court's logic in reaching its decision closely follows its reasoning for the continuing protection of the copyright owner's right to exploit public performances of his work.

Thus, while the first marketing of a copyright work in a material form   **14–65** by or with the consent of the copyright owner within the Community will exhaust, in relation to that product, the right of exploitation in the reproduction of the copyright work, the right of exploitation in relation to the

---

[61] Case 402/85 *Basset* v. *SACEM* [1987] E.C.R. 1747; [1987] 3 C.M.L.R. 173 at [11]–[16], and *per* Advocate-General Lenz at p. 180 para. 26; Case 158/86 *Warner Brothers Inc.* v. *Erik Christiansen* [1988] E.C.R. 2605 at [13] and [18]; [1990] 3 C.M.L.R. 684; see also paras. 24 and 25 of the Opinion of Advocate-General Jacobs in Case 395/87 *Ministère Public* v. *Tournier* (unreported) and Cases 110/88, 241/88 and 242/88 *SACEM* v. *Lucazeau*, *SACEM* v, *Debelle* and *SACEM* v. *Soumagnac* (unreported).

[62] Case 395/87 (unreported) at para. 15. Contrast the Court's decision in Cases 55 & 57/80 *Musik-Vertrieb Membran* v. *GEMA* [1981] E.C.R. 147; [1981] 2 C.M.L.R. 44.

[63] Case 158/86 [1988] E.C.R. 2605; [1990] 3 C.M.L.R. 684.

[64] See n. 63, *ante*.

performance of the work thereby remains unaffected, even in respect of performance by means of that product.

C. *Limits on the application of the principles of free movement of goods and services and exhaustion of rights to the exercise of industrial property rights*

(i) Goods originating outside the EEC

14–66 **Goods originating outside the EEC.** An important limitation on the application of the principles of free movement of goods to restrain the exercise of an industrial property right arises from the case of *E.M.I. Records Ltd.* v. *CBS United Kingdom Ltd.*,[65] in which the Court of Justice held that such principle had no application to goods originating from outside the Community.[66] The Court explained this limitation on the principle on the ground that it is the free movement of goods *within* the Community which is the aim of the Common Market, and the exercise of industrial property rights to prevent the importation into a Member State of goods manufactured outside the Community in no way jeopardises the unity of the Common Market which Articles 30 to 37 and the principle embodied in them are intended to ensure.[67]

14–67 In the *E.M.I.* case, above, the Court of Justice had to consider the further problem of the exercise of an industrial property right in Member State A, against the importation into that state of goods from Member State B but which had been manufactured outside the Community. It was argued that the combined effect of Articles 9(2) and 10(1) of the Treaty was to place such goods for all purposes on an equal footing with goods manufactured in Member State B. Article 9(2) provides that the provisions, *inter alia*, of Articles 30 to 37 shall apply to products originating from non-Member States which are in free circulation in Member States. Article 10(1) provides that products originating from a non-Member State shall be considered in free circulation in a Member State if all import formalities and customs duties have been complied with and paid. The Court of Justice held, however, that neither the rules of the Treaty on the free movement of goods, nor those on the putting into free circulation of products from third countries, nor the principles governing the common commercial policy,[68] prohibit the proprietor of a mark in all Member States of the Community from exercising his right in order to prevent the importation of similar products bearing the same mark and coming from a non-Member State.[69]

---

[65] Case 51/75 [1976] E.C.R. 811; [1976] 2 C.M.L.R. 235.
[66] The territory of the Community comprises the national territories of the 12 Member States: Art. 227(1) and (2). However, problems may arise as to the precise extent of these territories for the purposes under discussion, for example in the case of the U.K., with the Channel Islands and the Isle of Man, and Gibraltar: see L. Gorley, *Prohibiting Restrictions on Trade within the EEC* (1985) p. 192.
[67] [1976] 2 C.M.L.R. 235 at 265 [11].
[68] Found in Arts. 110–116 of the Treaty, under which agreements have been concluded between the Community and certain third countries; see further § 14–69, *et seq.*, *post.*
[69] [1976] 2 C.M.L.R. 235 at 266 [21].

Applying this decision by analogy to copyright, therefore, the owner of   **14–68**
copyright in the United Kingdom may exercise his right under the Copyright, Designs and Patents Act 1988 to prevent the unlicensed importation
into the United Kingdom of products manufactured in the United States
of America, where such manufacture may have been lawful, but was not
by or with the consent of such owner of the United Kingdom copyright
within the meaning of the relevant provisions of the 1988 Act,[70] even if
importation was being effected via another Member State, at least where
the rights in that other Member State are owned by the same person.[71]

(ii) Goods originating in the territory of states associated with the EEC.

Agreements between initial countries and the EEC. The Community   **14–69**
has entered into agreements with a number of third countries, in some
cases with a view to such third countries becoming members of the Community,[72] in other cases with a view to developing trade and other links
between the Community and such third countries.[73] The form of such
agreements varies depending on the closeness of the commercial, political
and economic links which the agreement is intended to create between the
Community and the third country in question. However, nearly all such
agreements seek to improve the flow of trade between the Community and
such third country, and to this end include provisions similar to those in
Articles 30 to 37 of the Treaty.[74]

The question therefore arises in the case of each third country which   **14–70**
has entered into such an agreement with the Community, whether the
provisions of the agreement in question are such as to give rise to a principle of free movement of goods between the Community and such third
country which can be invoked as being of directly applicable effect to prevent the exercise of industrial property rights affecting that trade, in the
same way as the principle has been applied to trade between Member
States of the Community, as discussed above.[75]

---

[70] See §§ 14–36, 37, *ante.*

[71] As to the position where this is not so, see § 14–93, *et seq., post.*

[72] As in the case of the original treaties with Greece and Turkey, of July 9, 1961 and September 12, 1963, respectively.

[73] For example, the Treaties concluded with the EFTA countries, setting up a free trade area
between the Community and those countries: Austria, Iceland, Sweden, Switzerland, all
of July 22, 1972; Norway, May 14, 1973; and Finland, October 5, 1973. Others include:
Malta, December 5, 1970; Egypt, January 18, 1977; Lebanese Republic, May 3, 1977;
Cyprus, December 19, 1972; Israel, May 11, 1975; Mexico, July 15, 1975; and Lome Convention, December 15, 1989.

[74] See generally, *Encyclopaedia of European Community Law*, Vol. B, Part 12, and Vol. C, Part
C7.

[75] *Ante,* §§ 14–24 and see Bellamy and Child, *Common Market Law of Competition* (Sweet &
Maxwell, 1987), paras. 2–135, 2–136. See also articles: "Enforceability of the EEC-EFTA
Free Trade Agreements" N. March Hunnings, (1977) 2 E.L.Rev. 163; "A Reply," M.
Waelbrook, (1978) 3 E.L.Rev. 27 and "A Rejoinder," N. March Hunnings, (1978) 3
E.L.Rev. 278.

14–71 **Association Agreement between Portugal and the EEC.** This question came before the Court of Justice in *Polydor Ltd.* v. *Harlequin Record Shop Ltd.*,[76] on a request by the Court of Appeal for a preliminary ruling as to the interpretation and effect of the Agreement of July 22, 1972 between Portugal (at the time not a Member of the Community) and the Community. Article 14(2) of the Agreement, which came into force on January 1, 1973, provided for the abolition of measures having an effect on imports equivalent to quantitative restrictions by January 1, 1975. Article 23 of the Agreement provided in terms identical to Article 36 of the Treaty that the Agreement should not preclude prohibitions or restrictions on imports or exports justified on grounds of the protection of industrial property.

14–72 The plaintiffs, who were the owners of the exclusive right to manufacture records of certain sound recordings in the United Kingdom, sought to prevent the importation into the United Kingdom by the defendants of records embodying such sound recordings manufactured lawfully in Portugal under licence from a company associated with the plaintiffs, which was the holder of the exclusive right to manufacture records of the sound recordings in Portugal. It was argued, on an application for interlocutory relief, that Article 14(2) of the Agreement provided the defendants with a complete defence to the action. Reversing the decision at first instance, the Court of Appeal refused the grant of an interlocutory injunction and referred the issues of interpretation and effect of Articles 14(2) and 23 of the Agreement to the Court of Justices.

14–73 To reach its decision, the Court of Justice returned to first principles and examined the objectives of the Agreement of July 22, 1972, in comparison with the Treaty of Rome. The Court noted that the Agreement with Portugal was a Free Trade Agreement, the aims of which were different to those of the Treaty, which were to unite the national markets into a single market reproducing the conditions of a domestic market by establishing a Common Market and progressively approximating the economic policies of the Member States. The Court held that in the circumstances of the Agreement of July 22, 1972 restrictions on trade in goods might be justifiable on the grounds of protection of industrial and commercial property within the Community. Consequently in the framework of the free trade arrangement, a prohibition on the importation into the Community of products from a non-Member State based on copyright could be justified. Article 14(2) of the Agreement could not therefore be relied on to prohibit the enforcement of that right as a restriction on trade.

14–74 **Direct effect of such agreements.** Although the Court of Justice did not consider the question of direct effect in this case, the Court has subsequently held in relation to other treaties, for example Article 2(1) of the

---

[76] Case 270/80 *Polydor Ltd. and R.S.O. Ltd.* v. *Harlequin Record Shop Ltd. and Simons Records Ltd.* [1982] E.C.R. 329; [1982] 1 C.M.L.R. 677; and see *Adams* v. *Public Prosecutor, Canton Basle* [1978] 3 C.M.L.R. 480 in which the Swiss Supreme Court decided that Art. 23 of the EEC-Switzerland Treaty (in terms similar to Art. 85 of the EEC Treaty) does not create any right of action for private persons in the Swiss courts; see also, in respect of the EEC-Austria Treaty, *Austro-Mechana Gesellschaft* v. *Gramola Winter & Co.* [1984] 2 C.M.L.R. 626 (decision of the Austrian Supreme Court).

Yaounde Convention of 1963, that directly effective rights may arise within the Member States from a treaty with associated states.[77] The Court of Justice has made it clear that all agreements with third countries may be capable of giving rise to directly effective provisions. Further, the Court has rejected the argument that the question of direct effect is linked to the question of reciprocity. Failure by a third state to accord direct effect to the provisions of an agreement will not prevent those provisions having direct effect within the Community.[78]

(iii) Spurious goods

Right to oppose infringement part of substance of industrial prop- **14–75**
erty right. The limits introduced to the exercise on industrial property rights by the principle of free movement of goods, as set by the test of exhaustion of rights, have no application to the exercise of an industrial property right by the owner of that right against merely spurious goods, and this is so whatever the country of origin of such spurious goods. The reason for this is that it is part of the substance, or specific object, of an industrial property right to be able to prevent others making unauthorised use of the subject-matter protected by the industrial property right, in a manner which directly usurps the primary exclusive rights granted to the owner of the industrial property right. This was expressly confirmed by the Court of Justice in the *Centrafarm/Sterling* and *Centrafarm/Winthrop* cases,[79] in which it stated that the right to oppose infringement was part of the specific object of patents[80] and the right to prevent others taking advantage of a mark by selling goods improperly bearing the mark was part of the specific object of trade marks.[81] There has been no case before the Court of Justice expressly raising the protection of copyright works against spurious infringement. However, presumably a similar protection will be afforded to copyright works where the rights sought to be asserted against the spurious goods are part of the specific subject of copyright, whether relating to the right of reproduction or the right of performance.

Imported spurious goods. This right of protection arises both when the **14–76**
owner of an industrial property right in Member State A seeks to assert that right in state A against goods produced in state A, and when he seeks to assert that right in state A against goods manufactured in state B being imported into state A. In the latter case it does not matter whether state B is a Member State of the Community or not. So long as the goods have not been brought into existence with the consent of the owner in state A of the industrial property right, he has not, in connection with the creation of the

---

[77] Case 87/75 *Conceria Daniele Bresciani* v. *Amministrazione delle Finanze* [1976] E.C.R. 129; [1976] 2 C.M.L.R. 62; *cf.* Cases 518, 86/75 *E.M.I. Records Ltd.* v. *CBS United Kingdom Ltd.* and *E.M.I. Records Ltd.* v. *CBS Grammofon A/s*, [1976] E.C.R. 811 at 871; [1976] 2 C.M.L.R. 235 at 265–266 [17], [18] and [19].
[78] Case 104/81 *Hauptzollamt Mainz* v. *Kupferberg* [1982] E.C.R. 3641; [1983] 1 C.M.L.R. 1.
[79] Cases 15 & 16/74 1974 E.C.R. 1147, 1183; [1974] 2 C.M.L.R. 480.
[80] Case 15/74 [1974] 2 C.M.L.R. 508 [9].
[81] Case 16/74 [1974] 2 C.M.L.R. 508 [8]; see also *Centrafarm* v. *American Home Products Corporation* [1978] E.C.R. 1823; [1979] 1 C.M.L.R. 326.

goods, exercised that industrial property right, or any equivalent industrial property right he may enjoy in state B, so that the question of having exhausted either right cannot arise.[82] Thus, the owner of copyright under the Copyright, Designs and Patents Act 1988 may still assert his rights under that Act to prevent the importation into the United Kingdom of goods which reproduce his copyright work and which have been manufactured without his consent abroad, whether in the territory of a Member State of the Community or not.[83]

(iv) Exhaustion of rights: associated problems

14–77   **The principle of exhaustion of rights, consent and associated problems.** For copyright works legitimately marketed within the Community the essential problem remains the determination of the degree of connection required between the marketing of the work in Member State B and the person who seeks to exercise an industrial property right in Member State A to prevent the importation of that work before the principle of the exhaustion of rights applies to preclude him from doing so. In its development of the theory of the specific object of the various industrial property rights,[84] the Court has emphasised that the owner of such a right will be considered to have exhausted his rights when they have been exercised within the Community by the owner himself or with his consent, or by a person connected with him by ties of legal or economic dependence. Nevertheless the use of the notion of consent to determine the exhaustion of the rights by their owner does not provide a clear solution to all the problems that arise in seeking to resolve the conflict between the principles of free movement and the territorial nature of national industrial property regimes. In connection with copyright, three particular problems may be mentioned:

(a) where copyright protection afforded by the various national laws of the Member States differs in some material respect[85];

(b) where the owner of exclusive rights held in each Member State has dealt with them in some states so as to lose his exclusivity in those states[86]; and

(c) where the exclusive rights in different Member States are held by different persons, but were once held by the same person.[87]

(a) *Differing protection among Member States*

14–78   **Differing protection among Member States.** The absence of harmonisation among the Member States in the field of industrial and commercial property rights causes some uncertainty as to the position of the owner of

---

[82] See § 14–77, *et seq., post.*
[83] Principally under ss.22 and 27; previously under ss.5(2) and 16(2) of the 1956 Act.
[84] See § 14–53, *et seq., ante.*
[85] See § 14–78, *et seq., post.*
[86] See § 14–91, *et seq., post.*
[87] See § 14–93, *et seq., post.*

a right in one Member State seeking to prevent the import of the protected work from another Member State which provides for a lesser degree of protection for that right. Initially the question arose in connection with attempts to prevent the import of products from countries which either provided no equivalent industrial or commercial property right[88] or provided for such a right but subject to a system of compulsory licensing.[89] More recently the division of the specific object of copyright into two elements, the right of reproduction and the right of performance, has generated further complexities that must be resolved.

The importance of the notion of consent in addressing the dilemma of **14–79** differing levels of protection appeared early in the Court's jurisprudence. In *Parke, Davis & Co. v. Probel*,[90] the Court of Justice was asked for its preliminary ruling on a number of questions concerning the proposed exercise by the patentee in Holland of his patent rights in that country to prevent the import into and sale in Holland of medicine manufactured in Italy. At that time no patent protection was available in Italy in respect of the medicine. The Dutch patentee had no connection with and had not consented to the manufacture of the medicine in Italy. The answer given by the Court of Justice was that the principle of free movement of goods had no application to such a case, and the Dutch patentee was not prohibited by such principle from exercising his patent rights in Holland to prevent the import and sale of such medicine.

More recently, in *Merck & Co. Inc. v. Stephar B.V.*,[91] the Court of Justice **14–80** considered the position where a Dutch patentee was seeking to prevent the import into and sale in Holland by an importer of pharmaceutical products which the Dutch patentee had himself marketed in Italy. The Court of Justice, reaffirming its previous definition of the specific object of a patent right, refused to allow the principle of free movement of goods to be restricted so as to uphold the prohibition under national law of the importation of the goods. The crucial factor was that the patentee had chosen to market the product on the Italian market. Once he had made this choice, he had exhausted his patent rights in all territories of the Community in respect of those products so marketed. The Court stated that it is for the proprietor of the patent to decide, in the light of all the circumstances, which include the absence of patent protection in a given Member State, under what conditions he will market his product. If he chooses to do so in a Member State which does not provide patent protection, then he must accept the consequences of his choice as regards the free movement of those goods within the Common Market.[92] The Court of Justice viewed this as the logical extension of the principle established through its developing case law that the proprietor of an industrial or

---

[88] Such as in *Parke, Davis & Co. v. Probel*, n. 90, *post*.
[89] Such as in *Musik-Vertrieb Membran GmbH v. GEMA*, n. 94, *post* and *Pharmon B.V. v. Hoechst A.G.*, n. 97, *post*. and see also *Ramsberg-Gema A.G. v. Electrostatic Plant Systems Ltd.* 1990 F.S.R. 287.
[90] Case 24/67, [1968] E.C.R. 55; [1968] C.M.L.R. 47.
[91] Case 187/80. [1981] E.C.R. 2063; [1981] 3 C.M.L.R. 463; and see § 14–54, *ante*.
[92] *Ibid.* at 2081 [9] and [10].

commercial property right protected by a national law cannot rely on that law to protect the importation of a product which has been lawfully marketed in another Member State by the proprietor himself or with his consent.[93]

14–81   Part of the developing case law to which the Court was referring is the case of *Musik-Vertrieb Membran GmbH* v. *GEMA*.[94] GEMA, a German management collecting society, had brought separate actions in the German courts against Membran and against K-Tel International on the grounds that they had infringed the distribution rights of the authors represented by GEMA by importing into Germany sound recordings of musical works protected under German copyright. The sound recordings were already in free circulation in other Member States, *inter alia* in the United Kingdom, but GEMA claimed damages equivalent to the difference between the licence fees already paid in another Member State and the royalty in force in Germany. On a request by the German Federal Court of Justice for a preliminary ruling, the Court of Justice ruled that Articles 30 and 36 of the Treaty precluded the exercise of rights granted under national legislation which enabled a copyright management society, empowered to exercise the copyright of composers of musical works reproduced on sound recordings in other Member States, to invoke those rights on the distribution of the sound recordings in the national market following their circulation in that other Member State by or with the consent of the owners of those copyrights, in order to claim the payment of a fee equal to the royalties ordinarily paid for the marketing on the national market less the lower royalties already paid in the Member State of manufacture.[95]

14–82   It is to be noted that part of the factual background in the *Musik-Vertrieb* case, *supra*, was that the United Kingdom legislation enforced a statutory licensing scheme, taking effect after records of the work had been made with a view to sale by or with the licence of the author. This scheme included a fixed rate of royalty payment as a consequence of which contractual royalties tended to be agreed at the same level as the statutory rate. The Court of Justice refused to allow this statutory restriction on the freedom of the copyright owner to affect its decision. The Court's reasoning for this was twofold. First, the existence of a disparity between national laws which is capable of distorting competition between Member States cannot justify a Member State giving legal protection to practices of a private body which are incompatible with the rules concerning the free movement of goods. Secondly, within the Common Market an author has the right to choose the place in which, in the light of all the circumstances, he wishes to put the work in circulation. In making that choice the author looks to his best interests which may include not only the level of remuneration but other factors such as opportunities for distributing his work and the marketing facilities.[96]

---

[93] *Ibid.* at 2082 [11] and [12].
[94] Cases 55 & 57/80, [1981] E.C.R. 146; [1981] 2 C.M.L.R. 44.
[95] *Ibid.* at 166 [27].
[96] *Ibid.* at 165 [24] and [25].

In both the *Merck* and *Musik-Vertrieb* cases, *supra*, the Court refused to allow the exercise of national legislation to protect the owner of a right in one Member State from the effects of differing levels of protection under the laws of another Member State because the circulation of that work in that other Member State had been by, or with the consent of, the owner of the right. The importance of the existence of such consent is reinforced by the decision of the Court of Justice in *Pharmon B.V.* v. *Hoechst A.G.*[97] Under the United Kingdom patent legislation the holder of the patent for the drug "frusemide" was required to grant a compulsory licence for the manufacture, importation and sale of "frusemide" within the territory of the United Kingdom to a local undertaking. The licence contained a prohibition upon the exportation of the drugs manufactured under the licence. The licensee sold the drug to a Dutch undertaking which sought to market the drug in Holland in response to which the patent holder, Hoechst, instituted proceedings for an injunction. The Court of Justice, on a request for a preliminary ruling as to the compatibility of the Dutch patent legislation with Articles 30 and 36, upheld the right of the patent holder on the ground that, when a patent holder is required by the legislation of a Member State to grant a compulsory licence for the manufacture and marketing of the patented product, the patentee cannot be deemed to have consented to the operation of that third party, as he has been deprived of the right freely to determine the conditions under which he markets his products. Only in this way did the Court feel that the patent holder would be able to protect the substance of his exclusive rights under the patent. **14–83**

The Court of Justice returned to the doctrine of consent in the more recent case of *E.M.I. Electrola GmbH* v. *Patricia Im- und Export Verwaltungsgesellschaft GmbH.*[98] At issue was whether E.M.I. Electrola, the copyright holder in Germany for a particular sound recording still protected by German copyright, could prevent the import of copies of the sound recording marketed in Denmark. Although the copies of the sound recording had been marketed in Denmark without the consent of the holder of the Danish rights of reproduction and distribution for the sound recording, the marketing was lawful as the period of copyright protection in Denmark had expired. The defendants argued that since the works were lawfully marketed in Denmark, they were entitled to export them to Germany. In this instance the Court upheld the right of E.M.I. Electrola to rely on their exclusive rights of reproduction and distribution of the work in Germany. The expiry of the copyright protection in Denmark did not alter the absence of consent by the German right holder to the marketing of the work in another Member State. **14–84**

It would therefore seem that disparities between national legal systems for the protection of industrial and commercial property will not affect the Court's decision that the primary factor for deciding whether the principles of free movement override national protection for copyright works is

---

[97] Case 19/84, [1985] E.C.R. 2281; [1985] 3 C.M.L.R. 775.
[98] Case 341/87, [1989] E.C.R. 79; [1989] 2 C.M.L.R. 413.

the absence or presence of the consent of the right holder to the marketing of the work in the other Member State.[99]

14-85   Nevertheless, the application of the test of consent can be complicated. As the Court of Justice observed in *E.M.I. Electrola GmbH* v. *Patricia Im- und Export Verwaltungsgesellschaft GmbH*,[1] the present state of Community law is characterised by a lack of harmonisation or approximation of legislation on the protection of literary and artistic property. It is for the national legislatures to specify the conditions and rules of that protection.

Leaving the determination of conditions and rules of protection to the national legislatures raises two separate problems. Apart from differing periods of protection, differences in the nature of that protection lead to a variance between the rights that are protected in the different Member States.[2] Secondly, it may not be straightforward to determine whether the right being invoked is part of the existence and exercise of the right of reproduction in a copyright work, or whether the right is part of the existence and exercise of the right of performance in a copyright work. If it is the latter, the right may not be exhausted by a single exercise, but would appear to be capable of repeated exploitation.[3]

14-86   The present state of the jurisprudence of the Court of Justice suggests that not only will consent be the dominant factor in determining whether the holder of copyright has exhausted his rights, but also that the copyright owner will remain free to decide when to exercise that consent. The proviso to this remains the second sentence of Article 36, namely: the prohibitions or restrictions allowed or imposed by the national legislation must not be such as to constitute a means of arbitrary discrimination or a disguised measure for restricting trade between Member States.

14-87   So far, the Court of Justice has not been asked to consider the situation where the proprietor of an industrial property right in one Member State, either by deliberate choice or otherwise, has not obtained equivalent protection in other Member States where such rights are available. In such a case would the principles of free movement permit the owner of the right to prevent the import of products marketed by another, when it was his failure to obtain equivalent right protection which allowed that other to market the products in another Member State? Applying the test of consent as developed in the Court of Justice's case law discussed above, this question would be answered in the negative. But, in the case of patents, if the failure to obtain such a parallel patent were due to a deliberate choice, then could it be said that the exercise of the rights under the patent laws of one Member State where patent protectors had been obtained amounted, in the circumstances, to an arbitrary discrimination or a disguised restriction on trade between Member States?

---

[99] See the Opinion of Advocate General Darmon, *ibid.* at 418 *et seq.*

[1] Case 341/87, [1989] E.C.R. 79; [1989] 2 C.M.L.R. 413 at 423 [11].

[2] See, for example, the decision of the Court in Case 158/86 *Warner Brothers Inc.* v. *Erik Christiansen* ([1988] E.C.R. 2605; [1990] 3 C.M.L.R. 684), which leaves unclear the nature of the right protected by the Danish copyright laws relating to the rental of video-cassettes, referred to at § 14–63, *ante.*

[3] See § 14–60, *et seq.*, *ante.*

Similarly, if the holder of copyright in, say Holland, does not act to **14–88**
assert his rights against manufacture and sale of goods in Holland known
to him to be taking place in infringement of his rights, it cannot be said
that he has consented in a positive sense to such manufacture and sale,
but can it be said that in such circumstances the exercise of his rights
under the Copyright, Designs and Patents Act 1988 to prevent importation of those goods into the United Kingdom amounts to arbitrary discrimination or disguised restriction on such trade?[4]

Whether the proviso to Article 36 is satisfied, in any case, is, it is sug- **14–89**
gested, a matter for the consideration of the national court which is asked
to enforce the industrial property right in question.[5] There may be sound
commercial reasons why, in the first example, the owner of the patent
right in Holland does not wish to take out patent protection in a particular
country, and, in the second example, the owner of the copyright in the
United Kingdom does not wish to exercise his parallel rights in Holland to
prevent the infringement at source. If so, then it is difficult to see how such
action could be found to be arbitary or, indeed, to be aimed at trade
between Member States at all.[6]

Although no direct answer to these problems has been given by the **14–90**
Court of Justice, recent developments, as discussed above, would suggest
that, in such a situation, the Court would uphold the prohibition on the
imports. The Court of Justice has repeatedly stressed, that in the absence
of harmonisation, it will not interfere with the existence or structure of
national industrial property rights. Thus, in *Keurkoop B.V.* v. *Nancy Kean
Gifts B.V.*,[7] the Court of Justice was asked to pronounce on the compatibility of Dutch design rights with Articles 30 to 36. The design rights in
question could be acquired by the first person to register them, without
inquiry as to whether that person was also the author of the design or a
person claiming title under the author. The only right of challenge to that
registration vested in the author of the design or the person commissioning the design from the author. No creative or artistic activity was therefore required as a condition for a person to register a design. The question
was raised for the Court of Justice's preliminary ruling by the Dutch
Regional Court of Appeal, in proceedings in the Dutch courts in which the
proprietor of the Dutch design right sought to prevent the importation
into Holland of products manufactured in another Member State lawfully
but without his authority and which were identical to the registered

---

[4] See the arguments raised in *British Leyland Motor Corporation Ltd.* v. *Wyatt Interpart Company
Ltd.* [1979] F.S.R. 39; [1979] 1 C.M.L.R. 395; and [1979] F.S.R. 583; [1979] 3 C.M.L.R.
79 (C.A.); see also Case 53/87 *Maxicar* v. *Renault* [1988] E.C.R. 6039; [1990] 4 C.M.L.R.
265 at [12].

[5] As was confirmed by the Court of Justice in Case 3/78 *Centrafarm B.V.* v. *American Home
Products Corporation* [1978] E.C.R. 1823; [1979] 1 C.M.L.R. 326 at 343 [23]. See also *British
Leyland Motor Corporation Ltd.* v. *T.I. Silencers Ltd.* [1979] F.S.R. 591.

[6] See: *Lerose Ltd.* v. *Hawick Jersey International Ltd.* [1973] F.S.R. 15; [1973] C.M.L.R. 83;
Löwenbräu München v. *Grünhalle Lager International Ltd.* [1974] F.S.R. 1; [1974] C.M.L.R. 1
at 12 [32].

[7] Case 144/81, [1982] E.C.R. 2853; [1983] 2 C.M.L.R. 47; see also Case 53/87 *Maxicar* v.
Renault [1988] E.C.R. 6039; [1990] 4 C.M.L.R. 265.

design. The Court of Justice held that the design legislation in issue fell within the scope of the provisions of Article 36 on the protection of industrial and commercial property, and that the proprietor of the Dutch design right could prevent the importation into Holland from another Member State of products identical in appearance to the protected design, provided that they had not been marketed by him or with his consent and that the rights of the respective proprietors of the designs had been created independently of one another.

(b) *Loss of exclusivity in some Member States*

14–91 **Loss of exclusivity in some Member States.** It has not been unusual for the owner of copyright in a work in those countries of the world recognising his right, to divide the world into primary and secondary markets. Such has often been the case, for example, with literary works where language has a greater importance in determining markets than national boundaries. Thus an English author, or more usually the British publisher who has acquired his rights, might exploit his copyright by licensing the exclusive right of publication in the English language in North America to a North American publisher, reserving to himself the exclusive right of publication in the English language in the United Kingdom, whilst allowing either party to sell their copies of the work in the English language in other secondary markets such as the rest of Europe. What if the North American publisher, or someone else, then imports into Holland a large quantity of copies of the work in the English language, which were lawfully produced in North America, and someone then seeks to import these into the United Kingdom? Is the British publisher entitled to assert his exclusive rights against such imports? It may be that the copies in question were first sold in North America, in which case the British publisher would have received royalties calculated on the higher rate appropriate to a primary, exclusive, market, but even so, on the principle in *E.M.I. Records Ltd.* v. *CBS United Kingdom Ltd.*,[8] why should a first sale in a non-Member State have any effect on exclusive rights enjoyed in a Member State? On the other hand, the copies in question may have been the subject of a first sale by the North American publisher in Holland, from which the British publisher would have received royalties calculated on the lower rate appropriate to a secondary, non-exclusive, market. In such a case the first marketing of the works in Holland took place with the consent of the British publisher, and applying the test of consent, as currently developed, he would be considered to have exhausted his exclusive rights within the Community by such first marketing, notwithstanding that he received only the lower royalty.[9] Should this be the correct analysis of the application of the principle of the exhaustion of rights and the notion of consent to the division between primary and secondary markets, the distinction between markets, when both are within the Common Market,

---

[8] Case 51/75 [1976] E.C.R. 811; [1976] 2 C.M.L.R. 235.
[9] Cases 55 & 57/80, *Musik-Vertrieb Membran GmbH* v. *GEMA* [1981] E.C.R. 146; [1981] 2 C.M.L.R. 44; Case 58/80 *Dansk Supermarked A/S* v. *Imerco A/S* [1981] E.C.R. 181; [1981] 3 C.M.L.R. 590; Case 187/80 *Merck & Co. Inc.* v. *Stephar B.V.* [1981] E.C.R. 2063; [1981] 3 C.M.L.R. 463.

becomes one that is difficult, if not impossible, to protect through the use of exclusive national copyright.

The case law of the Court of Justice shows a growing awareness of the   **14–92** commercial difficulties inherent in the use of the notion of consent within a market which lacks harmonisation. However, the concept of exhaustion of rights, in its present state of development does, not provide ready answers to the problems which may arise from the complex manner in which copyright is capable of exploitation in different countries, for what, in the past, have been considered justifiable commercial reasons,[10] and the concept requires a good deal more definition before these questions can be answered with any confidence.[11]

(c) *Common origin of rights*

Common origin of rights. The divisibility of copyright geographically   **14–93** by reference to national boundaries, or even in areas which cut across national boundaries, allows the owner of copyrights in various Member States to dispose of his rights in relation to particular territories to different persons by way of outright assignments or by licences. Once this has occurred, does EEC law prevent the assignee or licensee of the owner of the copyright under the Copyright, Designs and Patents Act 1988 from asserting his right to prevent imports into the United Kingdom of products made in France by the assignee or licensee from the same person of the French copyright?[12]

The position is far from clear. It may be that a distinction has to be   **14–94** drawn between direct sales by the assignee or licensee in Member State A into Member State B, where the rights are held by a different assignee or licensee, and sales into Member State B by another who has purchased the goods in Member State A from the assignee or licensee there. The principle of exhaustion of rights may only apply where there has been a first marketing by the holder of the right, or with his consent. This produces the anomalous result that the assignee or licensee in Member State B could assert his rights against direct sales into his territory by the assignee or licensee in Member State A, but could not assert his rights against an indirect sale into Member State B following a first sale in Member State A.[13] The position would appear to be the same under the Com-

---

[10] See, for example, the concern expressed in relation to these problems by the 1977 Copyright Committee, Cmnd. 6732, paras. 83–84.

[11] See, for example, the discussion on Distribution Right, Exhaustion and Rental Right, in Chapter 4 of the Commission's Green Paper on Copyright and the Challenge of Technology, Commission (COM (88) 172 final).

[12] *I.e.* under C.D.P.A. 1988, s. 27(5).

[13] See Cases 55 & 57/80, *Musik-Vertrieb Membran GmbH* v. *GEMA* [1981] E.C.R. 146; [1981] 2 C.M.L.R. 44 at [15]; Case 341/87 *E.M.I. Electrola GmbH* v. *Patricia Im- und Export Verwaltungsgesellschaft GmbH* [1989] E.C.R. 79; [1989] 2 C.M.L.R. 413 at 422 [4] and the Opinion of Advocate General Darmon, at 419–420. For the contrary position with regard to the rights of an assignee of the rights of performance in a cinematograph film in his territory, by or through the means of the assignee in another Member State, see Case 62/79 *Coditel S.A.* v. *Cine Vog Films S.A.* [1980] E.C.R. 881; [1981] 2 C.M.L.R. 362; Bellamy and Child, *op. cit.*, paras. 7–046 and 7–048.

munity Patent Convention,[14] where the principle depends on a previous marketing and the issue is whether such marketing was by the patentee, or with his consent.[15]

14–95   In relation to trade marks, the "common origin" principle was developed early in the case law of the Community.[16] No distinction was made between direct and indirect sales, nor did the application of the principle depend on a previous marketing. It was sufficient in the case of trade marks for the principle of free movement of goods within the Community to apply in order to prevent the exercise of a trade mark in Member State A against goods bearing that mark and lawfully originating in Member State B, that the two marks should have had a common origin. This left it unclear how far this principle extended to other industrial property rights. The Court of Justice's decision that the principle did not apply to patents granted under compulsory licence,[17] allowed the premise that by analogy it did not apply to other industrial property rights such as copyright and designs.[18] The Court of Justice has now clarified the position and reconsidered the "common origin" principle. The principle no longer has a role to play in the resolution of the conflict between the free movement of goods and national intellectual property rights. In its ruling in *S.A. CNL—Sucal N.V.* v. *Hag GF A.G.*,[19] the Court rejected the principle of common origin, and confirmed its doctrine that exceptions to the principle of free movement of goods in the Common Market will be allowed only in so far as the exceptions are justified for safe-guarding rights which are the specific subject matter of that property.[20] This ruling does not resolve all the unanswered problems raised by the Court's notion of exhaustion of rights, but it does remove the uncertainty that was caused by the parallel existence of the independent doctrine of common origin.

---

[14] See § 14–41, *ante*, and Bellamy and Child, *op. cit.* paras. 7–019–7–021.

[15] See n. 14, *ante*.

[16] Case 40/70 *Sirena S.R.L.* v. *Eda S.R.L.* [1971] E.C.R. 69; [1971] C.M.L.R. 260; Case 192/73 *Van Zuylen Freres* v. *Hag* [1974] E.C.R. 731; [1974] 2 C.M.L.R. 127; Case 119/75 *Terrapin (Overseas) Ltd.* v. *Terranova Industrie* [1976] E.C.R. 1039; [1976] 2 C.M.L.R. 482 at 506 [6]. See also *Re the Persil Trade Mark* [1978] F.S.R. 348; [1978] 1 C.M.L.R. 395; Case 3/78 *Centrafarm B.V.* v. *American Home Products Corporation* [1978] E.C.R. 1823; [1979] 1 C.M.L.R. 326. See also Bellamy and Child, *op. cit.*, paras. 7–027–7–035.

[17] See Bellamy and Child, *op. cit.*, paras. 7–019 and 7–029; Case 19/84 *Pharmon B.V.* v. *Hoechst A.G.* [1985] E.C.R. 2281; [1985] 3 C.M.L.R. 775.

[18] In Case 119/75 *Terrapin (Overseas) Ltd.* v. *Terranova Industrie* [1976] E.C.R. 1039; [1976] 2 C.M.L.R. 482 the Court of Justice justified the application of the common origin doctrine to trade marks on the ground that the basic function of a trade mark, that is to guarantee to consumers that the product has the same origin, is already undermined where the original right has been subdivided; (at 506 [6]). Such reasoning would not appear to be applicable to the subdivision of copyrights or patents. See also the remarks of Advocate General Roemer, Case 78/70 *Deutsche Grammophon GmbH* v. *Metro-SB-Grossmärkte GmbH & Co. K.G.* [1971] E.C.R. 487; [1971] C.M.L.R. 631 at 649, to the effect that copyright is more closely related to patent rights than to the trade mark right. This was later reaffirmed by Advocate General Darmon in Case 341/87 *E.M.I. Electrola GmbH* v. *Patricia Im- und Export Verwaltungsgesellschaft GmbH* [1989] E.C.R. 79; [1989] 2 C.M.L.R. 413 at 417.

[19] Case C–10/89, [1990] 3 C.M.L.R. 571.

[20] *Ibid.* at 607 [12].

6. The Exercise of Industrial Property Rights and the Rules on Competition

A. *Introduction*

What has so far been said has concentrated on one particular method of **14–96** exercising industrial property rights, and in particular copyright, namely by asserting the exclusivity or monopoly the subject of such rights in proceedings in national courts brought against goods in commercial circulation. It has been explained how such an exercise of rights by their owner can in certain circumstances bring the owner of the rights into conflict with the aims of the Community.

Whilst it is not necessary for there to be any agreement behind the exercise of the industrial property right in question for the principles of free movement to be invoked against such exercise, it will have become apparent, from the examples used in the discussion above, that the background to such exercise often includes one or more agreements, in the nature of assignments or licences. Because of the very nature of the exclusivity or monopoly afforded by industrial property rights, the background to their exercise may also reveal that the owner of such rights has, by virtue of his exclusivity or monopoly, a position of commercial power on the market such that he is immune from the effects of competition. It now falls to consider the application of the Rules on Competition contained in the Treaty to such agreements relating to industrial property rights (Article 85) and to such dominant position acquired by virtue of industrial property rights (Article 86). It should be noted that, where the Rules on Competition do apply to an agreement relating to the exploitation of an industrial property right, or to the use made of a dominant position enjoyed because of an industrial property right, their application is entirely independent of any application which the principles of free movement may also have to the exercise of the industrial property right in question. However, as has already been pointed out,[21] both the Rules on Competition and the principles of free movement of goods and services are provisions of the Treaty which are designed to achieve the same aim, namely the unity of the Common Market, through the removal of obstacles to trade between Member States.

Although the distinction between the existence and the exercise of an **14–97** industrial property right has been drawn most often in cases involving the principle of free movement of goods and Article 36 of the Treaty, it has already been pointed out that this distinction was first drawn by the Court of Justice in *Consten & Grundig v. E.C. Commission*,[22] a case involving the application of Article 85(1). The Commission, in applying Article 85(1) to an exclusive distribution agreement between Grundig (the German manufacturer) and Consten (the French distributor), enjoined the parties not to use national laws relating to trade marks to obstruct parallel imports.[23] The Court of Justice held that such an injunction did not touch

---

[21] See § 14–22, *et seq., ante.*
[22] Cases 56 & 58/64, [1966] E.C.R. 299; [1966] C.M.L.R. 418.
[23] *Re Grundig's Agreement*, O.J. 1964, 161/2545; [1964] C.M.L.R. 489.

the grant of those rights under the national laws concerned, but merely limited their exercise to the extent necessary for the attainment of the prohibition of Article 85(1). Thus, although Article 36 itself has no application to the competition rules,[24] it stems from a principle,[25] namely the distinction between the existence and exercise of industrial property rights, which is as relevant to the application of Article 85(1), and, as will be seen below,[26] Article 86 of the competition rules, as to the application of the principles of free movement discussed above.

B. *Article 85(1)*

14–98 **General.** Article 85 comprises three paragraphs, the first of which prohibits certain restrictive agreements, the second of which declares prohibited agreements to be void,[27] and the third of which provides for exemption in certain cases of individual agreements or types of agreements prohibited by Article 85(1).[28]

The agreements, decisions and concerted practices between undertakings[29] which are prohibited by Article 85(1) are those which satisfy the two requirements of:

(i) being capable of appreciably affecting trade between Member States and

(ii) having as their object or effect the perceptible restriction of competition within the Common Market.

Examples of the types of restrictions which fall within Article 85(1) are given in sub-paragraphs (*a*) to (*e*) of the Article, and can be broadly summarised as terms fixing selling prices or conditions, limiting or controlling production, sharing markets, applying dissimilar conditions to equivalent transactions and tying the other party to extraneous obligations. It is beyond the scope of this chapter to examine in detail what is meant by the concepts expressed in Article 85(1) of "agreements," "concerted practices" and "undertakings," and what is necessary for the two requirements of applicability to be met, and reference should be made to works devoted to the EEC competition rules.[30] However, in the context of industrial property rights generally and copyright in particular, a number of points can be made as to the implications of the terms "agreements," and

---

[24] Cases 56 & 58/64, [1966] E.C.R. 299; [1966] C.M.L.R. 418 at 476.
[25] As was recognised by the Court of Justice in Case 40/70 *Sirena S.R.L.* v. *Eda S.R.L.* [1971] E.C.R. 69; [1971] C.M.L.R. 260 at 273.
[26] See § 14–122, *post.*
[27] See § 14–130, *post.*
[28] See § 14–103, *post.* For the text of Art. 85, see § F–8, *post.*
[29] Which term includes individuals such as authors, artists, artistes, inventors and plant breeders: *Re Unitel*, O.J. 1978, L157/39; [1978] 3 C.M.L.R. 306; *A.O.I.P.* v. *Beyrard* O.J. 1976, L6/8; [1976] 1 C.M.L.R. D14 (for subsequent developments see the 12th Report on Competition Policy (1983) point 90); *H. Vaessen B.V.* v. *Alex Morris* O.J. 1979, L19/32; [1979] 1 C.M.L.R. 511; Case 258/78 *Nungesser* v. *Commission* [1982] E.C.R. 2015; [1983] 1 C.M.L.R. 278.
[30] See Bellamy and Child, *Common Market Laws of Competition*; Nicholas Green, *Commercial Agreements and Competition Law, Practice and Procedure in the U.K. and EEC*; Graham & Trotman, (1986); Richard Whish, *Competition Law* (Butterworths, 2nd ed., 1989).

"trade," before dealing with the problem of licensing agreements generally.

Agreement. For Article 85(1) to apply, there must be an agreement, **14–99** decision or concerted practice between undertakings. An agreement may be oral.[31] It may also exist, for the purposes of Article 85(1), in the terms of a compromise of legal proceedings brought by the owner of an industrial property right for the enforcement of such right.[32] The first owner of an industrial property right enjoys the right as a result of a legal status granted by a state to his invention, product or work, and such ownership itself has nothing to do with the elements of agreement, decision or concerted practice mentioned in Article 85(1).[33] However, the Court of Justice has made it clear that Article 85(1) will apply when there is an agreement for the exercise of that ownership or even its creation, and that, although the industrial property right, as a legal entity, will not fall within the class of agreements, decisions or concerted practices prohibited by Article 85(1), the exercise of that right may be subject to the prohibitions in the Treaty when it is the purpose, the means or the result of an agreement, decision or concerted practice.[34] If the Commission finds that such an agreement, decision or concerted practice is in existence, and that there is an infringement of Article 85(1), it can require those undertakings concerned to bring the infringement to an end,[35] adopting the course it considers most suitable to end the anti-competitive practice.[36]

Assignment of rights as the agreement. Where an industrial property **14–100** right is involved, an agreement will most commonly be found, for the purposes of Article 85(1), in a licence, whereby the owner of the right licenses a particular form of its exploitation to another.[37] However, the Court of

---

[31] Case 28/77 *Tepea* v. *Commission* [1978] E.C.R. 1391; [1978] 3 C.M.L.R. 392.

[32] *Re the Eisele-INRA Agreement* O.J 1978, L286/23; [1978] 3 C.M.L.R. 434; Case 258/78 *Nungesser* v. *Commission* [1982] E.C.R. 2015 at 2074–2076; [1983] 1 C.M.L.R. 278; Case 35/83 *BAT Cigaretten-Fabriken GmbH* v. *Commission* [1985] E.C.R. 363; [1985] 2 C.M.L.R. 470 Case 65/86 *Bayer A.G.* v. *Süllhöfer* [1988] E.C.R. 5249; [1990] 4 C.M.L.R. 182; and see also *Sport International Bussum B.V.* v. *Hi-Tec Sports Ltd.* [1990] F.S.R. 312.

[33] Case 24/67 *Parke, Davis & Co.* v. *Probel* [1968] E.C.R. 55; [1968] C.M.L.R. 47 at 59. Case 51/75 *E.M.I. Records Ltd.* v. *CBS United Kingdom Ltd.* [1976] E.C.R. 811; [1976] 2 C.M.L.R. 235 at 266 [26]; Case 258/78 *Nungesser* v. *Commission* [1982] E.C.R. 2015; [1983] 1 C.M.L.R. 278 [28]; Case 144/81 *Keurkoop B.V.* v. *Nancy Kean Gifts B.V.* [1982] E.C.R. 2853 at 2873; [1983] 2 C.M.L.R. 47.

[34] Case 144/81 *Keurkoop B.V.* v. *Nancy Kean Gifts B.V.* [1982] E.C.R. 2853 at 2873 [27]; [1983] 2 C.M.L.R. 47. See also Case 15/74 *Centrafarm B.V.* v. *Sterling Drug Inc.* [1974] E.C.R. 1147; [974] 2 C.M.L.R. 480.

[35] Art. 3 of Reg. 17, O.J. 1962, 13/204; Bellamy and Child, *op. cit.*, Appendix 21.

[36] For example, the Commission may order the owner of the right to cease preventing parallel imports: *Re Grundig's Agreement*, O.J. 1964. 161/2545; [1964] C.M.L.R. 489. See also, in relation to Art. 86 *Magill TV Guide/ITP, BBC & RTE*, O.J. 1989 L78/43, ([1989] 4 C.M.L.R. 757 (now under appeal)) where the Commission ordered ITP, BBC and RTE to make available to each other and third parties their individual advance weekly programme listings and to allow reproduction of those listings. For a case where the basis on which such an order was made is open to criticism, see *Re Advocaat Zwarte Kip*, O.J. 1974, L237/12; [1975] F.S.R. 27; [1974] 2 C.M.L.R. D79 and Bellamy and Child, *op. cit.*, § 7–052.

[37] For example, *U.I.P.*, O.J. 1989 L226/25; [1990] 4 C.M.L.R. 749.

Justice in *Sirena S.R.L.* v. *Eda S.R.L.*,[38] held that the exercise of trade mark rights may come within the prohibition of Article 85(1) if it is "the object, means or consequence of an agreement," and that the agreement for these purposes could comprise an assignment. The Court held that the simultaneous assignment to several concessionaires of national trade mark rights for the same product may prejudice trade between Member States and distort competition in the Common Market, if this has the effect of re-establishing rigid frontiers between Member States.

14–101   Assignment of rights: continuing effects. However, the Court of Justice went on in *Sirena*,[39] to state that it was sufficient for Article 85(1) to apply, in that case to an agreement concluded before the date the Treaty took effect, if the effects of the agreement continued after that date.[40]

The judgment in *Sirena* left it unclear when an agreement such as an assignment could be considered as continuing to have its effects. What if the assignment were a bare assignment containing no other terms as to the future exercise of the right by the assignee, or if any such terms as it may have contained had become spent by the passing of time? In *E.M.I. Records Ltd.* v. *CBS United Kingdom Ltd.*[41] the Court of Justice repeated the principle that the exercise of a trade mark may fall within the prohibition of Article 85(1) if it were to manifest itself as the subject, means or consequence of a restrictive agreement.[42] The Court then stated that an agreement could continue to produce its effects after it had formally ceased to be in force, but should only be regarded as doing so if, from the behaviour of the persons concerned, there may be inferred the existence of elements of concerted practice peculiar to the agreement and producing the same result as that envisaged by the agreement. The Court added that such an inference should not be drawn when the effects do not exceed those flowing from the mere exercise of the national trade mark rights.[43]

14–102   Trade between Member States. Before the prohibition of Article 85(1) can apply to an agreement, decision or concerted practice, it must be such that it may affect trade between Member States. For this purpose it is sufficient, unless the *de minimis* exception applies,[44] that the agreement, decision or concerted practice is capable of having an actual or potential effect on the pattern of trade between Member States.[45]

---

[38] Case 40/70, [1971] E.C.R. 69; [1971] C.M.L.R. 260. For patents, see Case 15/74 *Centrafarm B.V.* v. *Sterling Drug Inc.* [1974] E.C.R. 1147 and for rights in registered designs, see Case 144/81 *Keurkoop B.V.* v. *Nancy Kean Gifts B.V.* [1982] E.C.R. 2853 at 2873 [27]; [1983] 2 C.M.L.R. 47.

[39] Case 40/70, [1971] E.C.R. 69; [1971] C.M.L.R. 260.

[40] *Ibid.* [1971] C.M.L.R. 260 at 274 [12].

[41] Case 51/75, [1976] E.C.R. 811; [1976] 2 C.M.L.R. 235.

[42] [1976] 2 C.M.L.R. 235 at 266–267 [27], [28].

[43] *Ibid.* at 267 [30]–[32]. See generally Bellamy and Child, *op. cit.*, §§ 7–052 and 7–053.

[44] See Bellamy and Child, *op. cit.*, § 2–119; Case 193/83 *Windsurfing International* v. *Commission* [1986] E.C.R. 611; [1986] 3 C.M.L.R. 489 at 540.

[45] See Bellamy and Child, *op. cit.*, § 2–113 *et seq.* and Case 27/87 *La SPRL Louis Erauw-Jacquery* v. *La Société cooperative la Hesbignonne* [1988] E.C.R. 1919 at [14].

The term "trade" for the purposes of Articles 85 and 86, means trade both in goods and in services.[46] Thus, in *Re GEMA (No. 1)*,[47] a case under Article 86 involving the German performing right society, the Commission held that the society had abused its dominant position in a number of respects, and that such practices were capable of affecting trade between Member States, *inter alia*, by providing an obstacle to the establishment of a single market in the supply of services of publishers of musical works.[48] Also, in *State* v. *Sacchi*[49] the Court of Justice, while holding that the provision of television broadcasts fell within the rules relating to the supply of services (Articles 59–66) rather than free movement of goods, clearly considered that Article 86 could apply to the provision of such services.[50]

Article 85(3): exemption from Article 85(1). In certain circumstances   **14–103** the Commission has the power, under Article 85(3) of the Treaty, to declare the provisions of Article 85(1) inapplicable to an agreement, decision or concerted practice. It is only the Commission that has this power, subject to review as to its exercise by the Court of Justice. Thus, while a national court may find an agreement to be contrary to Article 85(1),[51] such court has no power to grant an exemption under Article 85(3).

Essentially, the power of exemption provided for in Article 85(3) is intended for those agreements, decisions and concerted practices which contribute to improving the production or distribution of goods or promoting technical or economic progress. However, it is a condition, for eligibility for exemption, that a fair share of the resulting benefit must pass to the consumer. Further, any restrictions imposed on the undertakings concerned must be indispensable to the attainment of those objectives and those undertakings must not thereby be afforded the possibility of eliminating competition in respect of a substantial part of the market for the products in question.[52]

The powers granted to the Commission under Article 85(3) are exercisable in relation to an individual agreement, decision or practice. Alternatively, the Commission has the power to issue block exemptions for certain

---

[46] Case 22/79 *Greenwich Film Productions, Paris* v. *SACEM*, [1979] E.C.R. 3275; [1980] 1 C.M.L.R. 629 at 644 [11]; Case 7/82 *GVL* v. *Commission* [1983] E.C.R. 483 at 504; [1983] 3 C.M.L.R. 645.

[47] O.J. 1971, L134/15; [1971] C.M.L.R. D35.

[48] *Ibid.* at D56.

[49] Case 155/73, [1974] E.C.R. 409; [1974] 2 C.M.L.R. 177.

[50] [1974] 2 C.M.L.R. 177 at 204 [17]. See also as to cable diffusion of television: Case 52/79 *Procureur du Roi* v. *Debauve* and Case 62/79 *Coditel S.A.* v. *Cine Vog Films S.A.* [1980] E.C.R. 833 and 881; [1981] 2 C.M.L.R. 362; Case 262/81 *Coditel S.A.* v. *Cine Vog Films S.A. (No. 2)* [1982] E.C.R. 3381; [1983] 1 C.M.L.R. 49. See also *Re Unitel*, O.J. 1978, L157/39; [1978] 3 C.M.L.R. 306 where the Commission was of the view that "trade" covered the commercial exploitation of an artiste's services.

[51] See § 14–131, *post.*

[52] For the text of Art. 85(3), see *post* § F–8. See also *Elopak* v. *Tetra Pak* O.J. 1988 L272/27; [1990] 4 C.M.L.R. 47, at 74–76; U.I.P. O.J. 1989 L226/25; [1990] 4 C.M.L.R. 749.

categories of agreement, including agreements imposing restrictions relating to the acquisition or use of industrial property rights, or the rights arising out of contracts for the assignment of, or the right to use, a method of manufacture or knowledge relating to the use or application of industrial processes.[53]

Drawing from its experience, gained over several years of applying the criteria for exempting agreements dealing with industrial property rights by individual decision pursuant to Article 85(3), the Commission has now adopted three Regulations granting block exemptions to such categories of agreements. The first was the exemption for patent licensing agreements[54] and more recently there have been the exemptions for franchising agreements[55] and for know-how licensing agreements.[56] These exemptions govern agreements between no more than two undertakings; if there are more parties, then individual exemption must be sought. All three Regulations follow a pattern, and they form useful guidance as to the types of clauses which the Commission considers fall within Article 85(3), as well as those clauses which the Commission considers fall within Article 85(1) but do not merit exemption. While not binding on the Commission, the recitals to the Regulations are of value in setting out the current policy of the Commission with regard to agreements dealing with industrial property rights.

14–104 **Copyright licensing agreements.** A licence for the exploitation of an industrial property right usually contains many detailed terms intended to govern each party's position with regard to the other, and to the subject-matter of the agreement, for the duration of the licence. Several of those terms will seek to restrict one party's freedom of action in respect of the other party or the subject-matter of the agreement, and will therefore constitute a restriction on that party's competitive position, thus bringing the agreement within Article 85(1) if such restriction amounts to a perceptible restriction on competition within the Common Market and if it is capable of affecting appreciably trade between Member States. It will be appreciated, from the examples given in sub-paragraphs (a) to (e) of Article 85(1) of the types of restrictions which fall within the prohibition of Article 85(1),[57] that many of the usual restrictions contained in a licence for the exploitation of an industrial property right fall within these examples, thus bringing the agreement within Article 85(1) and raising again the conflict between the exercise of industrial property rights and the provisions of the Treaty.

---

[53] By Art. 1 of Council Regulation 19/65, O.J. 1965, 36/533. See also Bellamy and Child, *op. cit.*, Appendix 6.

[54] Reg. 2349/84, O.J. 1984, L219/15, reprinted as amended, O.J. 1985, L113/34. For general comment, see Valentine Korah, *Patent Licensing and EEC Competition Rules, Regulation 2349/84*, (ESC Publishing Ltd., 1985).

[55] Reg. 4087/88, O.J. 1988, L359/46; Valentine Korah, *Franchising and the EEC Competition Rules, Regulation 4087/88* (ESC Publishing Ltd., 1989).

[56] Reg. 556/89, O.J. 1989, L61/1; Valentine Korah, *Know-how Licensing Agreements and the EEC Competition Rules, Regulation 556/89* (ESC Publishing Ltd., 1989).

[57] See § 14–99, *ante*.

Commission's approach to licensing agreements. The solution to this **14–105** conflict which has found most favour with the Commission in its decisions on patent and know-how licensing agreements is to apply the principle of the distinction between the existence or substance of the industrial property right and its exercise, already discussed above. Thus, restrictions imposed on a licensee, which are co-extensive with the specific object of the licensor's right, are not within Article 85(1). But restrictions which go beyond the specific object of the licensor's right, and seek to obtain for the licensor or licensee an additional advantage or protection, are within Article 85(1).

An instance of this approach is the current stance of the Commission **14–106** and the Court of Justice with regard to exclusive licences. The Commission's present position is that it acknowledges that an exclusive licensing agreement (that is an agreement in which the licensor undertakes not to exploit the "licensed invention," be it a product or technology, in the licensed territory himself, and not to grant further licences there), may not itself be incompatible with Article 85(1), when it is concerned with the introduction and protection of new technology in the licensed territory, depending on the scale of research involved and the size of the risk in manufacturing and marketing a product which is unfamiliar to users in the licensed territory at the time the agreement is made.[58]

This approach by the Commission represents a restrictive interpret- **14–107** ation of the decision of the Court of Justice in *Nungesser* v. *Commission*.[59] In that case Nungesser was assigned the breeding rights in West Germany for four varieties of maize seed by a French organisation and was also given exclusive propagating and selling rights for those seeds in that territory. The case came before the Court of Justice on Nungesser's appeal against the decision of the Commission, which had found these arrangements to be contrary to Article 85(1) and ineligible for exemption under Article 85(3). In a judgment which partially allowed Nungesser's appeal, the Court distinguished between the so-called open exclusivity of a licence where the exclusivity relates solely to the contractual relationship between the owner of the right and the licensee, with the owner merely undertaking not to grant other licences for the same territory and not to compete with the licensee in that territory, and a licence where the exclusivity is buttressed by contractual terms which are aimed at eliminating competition in the products and territory in question from third parties, such as parallel importers or licensees for other territories. In the particular case before it, the Court held that, having regard to the specific nature of the product in question, the grant of an open exclusive licence, which did not

---

[58] See recital (11) to the Registration granting block exemption in respect of patent licensing agreements and recital (6) to the Registration granting block exemption in respect of know-how licensing agreements nn. 52, 54 *ante*. See, however, *Elopak* v. *Tetra Pak* O.J. 1988 L272/27; [1990] 4 C.M.L.R. 47, on appeal Case T–51/89 *Tetra Park Rausing S.A.* v. *Commission*, judgment of the Court of First Instance 10.7.90 (unreported).

[59] Case 258/78, [1982] E.C.R. 2015; [1983] 1 C.M.L.R. 278. See, for comment, Bellamy and Child, *op. cit.*, § 7–065 *et seq.*

affect the position of such third parties, was not in itself incompatible with Article 85(1).[60]

14–108 The Commission has in the past adopted an approach towards licensing agreements based on a different principle, that of the limited licence.[61] Under this principle, when the restriction on the licensee is a result of the partial retention by the licensor of the rights under the industrial property right, then the restriction should not fall within Article 85(1), as the restriction does no more than express the fact that the licence is a permission to do an act which would otherwise be an infringement of the licensor's exclusive right. Thus, if any such particular act falls outside the terms of the licence, then the licensee is no more entitled to do the act than any third party.[62] The Commission later withdrew the Notice,[63] and seems subsequently to have rejected this principle in its Regulations granting block exemption for patent licensing agreements,[64] and for franchise agreements.[65] The Court of Justice also appears to have supported the rejection of this principle.[66]

14–109 **Licensing agreements: particular clauses.** The identification of the particular clauses that fall within the restrictions imposed by Article 85(1) and the determination of whether exemption under Article 85(3) will be available, is becoming an increasingly difficult task as the Commission seeks that fine line between the protection of new technology and the encouragement of investment on the one hand, and the need to prevent practices that restrict or distort the pattern of competition within the Community on the other hand. Guidance as to the stance of the Commission and the attitude of the Court of Justice can be gathered from indi-

---

[60] Case 258/78, [1982] E.C.R. 2015; [1983] 1 C.M.L.R. 278 [53] and [58]; *c.f. Elopak* v. *Tetra Pak*, n. 56, *ante*; and for the views of the Commission regarding exclusive licences for the broadcasting of films, see *U.I.P.* O.J. 1989 L226/25; [1990] 4 C.M.L.R. 749, and *Film Purchases by German Television Stations*, O.J. 1989 L284/36; [1990] 4 C.M.L.R. 841 (on appeal Case T-157/89 *Nefico B.V.* v. *Commission* and Case T-168/89 *MGM/UA* v. *Commission*).

[61] See the Commission's Notice on Patent Licensing Agreements of December 24, 1962, which was withdrawn in 1984, O.J. 1984, C220/14.

[62] See, for an example of this approach, Buckley L.J. in *Chemidus Warvin Ltd.* v. *Soc. pour la Transformation* [1977] F.S.R. 181; [1978] 3 C.M.L.R. 514 at 520 [19].

[63] In 1984; O.J. 1984, C220/14.

[64] Under Art. 3(5) of Reg. 2349/84 granting block exemption in respect of patent licensing agreements, O.J. 1984, L219/15 (amended O.J. 1985, L113/34), a limitation on the quantity of products to be manufactured by the licensee is a "restriction" under Art. 85(1).

[65] Under Art. 3(1)(e) of Reg. 4087/88 granting block exemption in respect of franchise agreements, O.J. 1988, L359/46, the franchisee may be placed under an obligation not to engage directly or indirectly in any similar business in a territory where it would compete with a member of the franchised network, including the franchisor, and the franchisee may be held to this obligation after termination of the agreement, for a reasonable period not exceeding one year, in the territory where it has exploited the franchise.

[66] In Case 193/83 *Windsurfing International* v. *Commission* [1986] E.C.R. 611; [1986] 3 C.M.L.R. 489 at [45 & 46] the Court rejected the view that quality control formed part of the specific subject-matter of the patent *per se.* Such controls as are exercisable must be exercised according to quality and safety criteria agreed on in advance and which must be objectively verifiable. See further Bellamy and Child, *op. cit.*, § 7–059.

vidual decisions and block exemption Regulations of the Commission, as well as the case law of the Court of Justice.[67]

In *Windsurfing International* v. *Commission*,[68] the Court of Justice was **14–110** asked to review the Commission's decision[69] that the licensing agreements the applicant had concluded with certain of its European licensees were contrary to Article 85(1). The applicant was the United States patent owner for sailboards, an apparatus comprising the board and the rig. The applicant had sought to protect the patents for sailboards in the United Kingdom and the Federal Republic of Germany. The agreements under challenge were concluded in relation to the German patents. The scope of the patent was one of the issues before the Court. The applicant contended it applied to the whole sailboard, that is the board and the rig. The Commission, later upheld by the Court, considered it only applied to the rig. From this starting point, the Commission considered the following clauses to be contrary to Article 85(1):

(a) the obligation on the licensees:
   (i) to exploit the licensed patents only for sailboards that had Windsurfing International's prior approval;
   (ii) not to supply rigs manufactured under the German patent separately and without the boards approved by Windsurfing International;
   (iii) to pay royalties on the rigs manufactured under the patent on the basis of the net selling price of a complete board;
   (iv) to fix on the boards a notice giving details of the licensor;
   (v) to acknowledge both the word marks and the design marks of the licensor;
   (vi) (in two of the agreements) not to challenge the licensed patents;[70] and

(b) the rights of the licensor in relation to some of the licensees to terminate the agreements should the licensees start production in a territory not covered by the patents.

---

[67] *Re Burroughs/Delplanque* O.J. 1972 L13/50; [1972] C.M.L.R. D72; *Re Burroughs/Delplanque* O.J. 1972 L13/53; [1972] C.M.L.R. D67; *Re Davidson Rubber* O.J. 1972 L143/31; [1972] C.M.L.R. D52; *Re Raymond/Nagoya* O.J. 1972 L143/39; [1972] C.M.L.R. D45; *Re Kabelmetal* O.J. 1975 L222/34; [1975] 2 C.M.L.R. D40; *Re Bronbemaling* O.J. 1975 L249/27; [1975] 2 C.M.L.R. D67; *A.O.I.P./Beyrard* O.J. 1976 L6/8; [1976] 1 C.M.L.R. D14; *Breeders Rights—Maize Seed* O.J. 1978 L286/23; [1978] 3 C.M.L.R. 434 on appeal Case 258/78 *Nungesser* v. *Commission* [1982] E.C.R. 2015; [1983] 1 C.M.L.R. 278; *H. Vaessen B.V.* v. *Alex Morris* O.J. 1979 L19/32; [1979] 1 C.M.L.R. 511; *Windsurfing International* O.J. 1983 L229/1; [1984] 1 C.M.L.R. 1; on appeal: Case 193/83 *Windsurfing International* v. *Commission* [1986] E.C.R. 611; [1986] 3 C.M.L.R. 489; *Velcro/Aplix* O.J. 1985 L233/22; *Boussois/Interpaine* O.J. 1987 L50/30; *Rich Products/Jus Rol* O.J. 1988 L69/21; Case 65/86 *Bayer A.G.* v. *Süllhöfer* [1988] E.C.R. 5249; [1990] 4 C.M.L.R. 182; Case 27/87 *la SPRL Louis Erauw-Jacquery* v. *La Hesbignonne* [1988] E.C.R. 1919; Case 320/87 *Ottung* v. *Weilbach and Schmidt* [1990] 4 C.M.L.R. 915; *U.I.P.* O.J. 1989 L226/25; [1990] 4 C.M.L.R. 749; *Film Purchases by German Television Stations* O.J. 1989 L284/36; [1990] 4 C.M.L.R. 841; (on appeal Case T-157/89 *Nefico B.V.* v. *Commission* and Case T-168/89 *MGM/UA* v. *Commission*).
[68] Case 193/83 [1986] E.C.R. 611; [1986] 3 C.M.L.R. 489.
[69] O.J. 1983 L229/1; [1984] 1 C.M.L.R. 1.
[70] As to no-challenge clauses, see further *Bayer A.G.* v. *Süllhöfer*, n. 67, *ante* and *Sport International Bussum B.V.* v. *Hi-Tec Sports Ltd.* [1990] F.S.R. 312.

14–111   The Court upheld these findings by the Commission, except as regards the obligation to pay royalties on the rigs manufactured under the patents on the basis of a net selling price of a complete board. The Court considered this obligation did not infringe Article 85(1), since, if, as under new agreements, royalties were charged on the price of the rig alone, it would be equitable to calculate a higher rate of royalties for the licensor.

14–112   The two most recent block exemption Regulations issued by the Commission, relating to franchise agreements and know-how licensing agreements,[71] are instructive as to the Commission's approach regarding industrial property rights for technical information which is not patentable.[72] The exemption for franchise agreements is the first expressly to refer to copyright as being among the rights protected.[73] Both exemption Regulations refer to clauses that generally do not fall within the scope of Article 85(1). At the same time, the importance of the economic and legal circumstances surrounding an agreement is emphasised, since both Regulations make it clear that it is the surrounding circumstances that may alter the status of the clauses and bring them within the scope of Article 85(1).[74]

14–113   The clauses that would not normally fall within Article 85(1) concern:
    (a) under the block exemption for franchise agreements[75]:
        (i) non-disclosure to third parties of the know-how provided by the franchisor even after termination of the agreement;
        (ii) communication to the franchisor of experience gained in exploiting the franchise and the obligation to grant the franchisor and other franchisees a non-exclusive licence to use such information;
        (iii) an obligation to inform the franchisor of infringements of the industrial property rights and either assist in or take legal action to protect them;
        (iv) an obligation to use the know-how only for the purpose of the franchise, both during and after termination of the franchise agreement;
        (v) an obligation to attend or have its staff attend training courses arranged by the franchisor;
        (vi) an obligation to apply the franchisor's commercial methods including modifications and to use the licensed industrial property rights;
        (vii) an obligation to comply with the franchisor's standards for equipment, presentation of the premises and/or means of transport;
        (viii) a right of inspection for the franchisor over the premises and/

---

[71] Commission Reg. 4087/88, O.J. 1988 L359/46 and Commission Reg. 556/89, O.J. 1989 L61/1.

[72] See also Art. 2(1) of Reg. 2349/84, granting block exemption for patent licensing agreements.

[73] Reg. 4087/88, Art. 1(3)(1).

[74] Reg. 4087/88, recital (11) and Reg. 556/89, recital (10).

[75] Reg. 4087/88, Art. 3.

or means of transport, including the goods sold or the services provided, as well as over the inventory and accounts of the franchisee;

(ix) a ban on the franchisee changing the contract premises without the consent of the franchisor;

(x) a ban on the franchisee assigning the rights and obligations under the agreement without the franchisor's consent; and

(b) under the block exemption for know-how licensing agreements[76]:

(i) an obligation on the licensee not to divulge the know-how communicated by the licensor, both during and after termination of the agreement;

(ii) an obligation on the licensee not to grant sub-licences or assign the licence;

(iii) an obligation on the licensee not to exploit the know-how after the termination of the agreement if it is still secret;

(iv) a limited obligation on the licensee to disclose experience gained in exploiting the licensed technology to the licensor and to grant to him a non-exclusive licence for any improvements to, or new application of, the technology.[77]

(v) the imposition of minimum quality standards, or an obligation to obtain supplies or services from the licensor, or an undertaking designated by him, in so far as this is necessary for:

(1) technically satisfactory exploitation of the licensed technology;

(2) ensuring uniform quality standards among the licensor's licensees,

as well as allowing the licensor to carry out necessary checks.

(vi) an obligation on the licensee to aid the licensor in protecting the licensed patents, provided this does not fetter the licensee's right to challenge the patents or contest the secrecy of the know-how unless the licensee has been involved in its disclosure.

(vii) an obligation on the licensee to continue paying royalties until the end of the contract term even though the know-how has become public knowledge.

(viii) an obligation on the licensee to restrict his exploitation of the licensed technology to one or more technical fields covered by the technology or one or more product markets.

(ix) minimum royalty payments, or minimum production targets or operation exploiting the technology.

(x) an obligation on the licensor to grant the licensee any more favourable terms that he might subsequently grant to another undertaking.

(xi) an obligation to mark the licensed product with the licensor's name.

---

[76] Reg. 556/89, Art. 2.

[77] By Art. 2(4)(*a*) and (*b*), the licensor can only impose this obligation if certain conditions are met.

(xii) an obligation on the licensee not to use the licensor's know-how to construct facilities for third parties.

14–114 Copyright licensing agreements: decisions of the Court and the Commission. Copyright licences have so far received little formal attention from either the Court of Justice or the Commission. However, it is suggested that the approach adopted by the Commission and the Court in the cases concerning know-how licensing and patent licensing agreements is applicable to copyright licensing agreements where many of the same considerations apply.[78]

14–115   Decisions by the Court regarding copyright agreements have mainly required interpretation of Articles 30, 36, 59 and 86. However, in *Coditel (No. 2)*[79] the Court discussed the application of Article 85 to an agreement between a film producer and a film distribution company. The producer granted the distribution company, Cine Vog, exclusive rights of distribution in Belgium for a film. Coditel, a cable television diffusion service company, broadcast the film in Belgium after picking up a transmission of the film in West Germany. Consequently, Cine Vog brought an action for breach of its distribution rights. In its defence, Coditel maintained that a contract concerning an exclusive licence or assignment of copyright could amount to an agreement, decision or concerted practice under Article 85. In its judgment, the Court acknowledged that the exercise of copyright in a film may come within the prohibition of Article 85(1), but only where there are "economic or legal circumstances, the effect of which is to restrict film distribution to an appreciable degree or to distort competition on the cinematographic market, regard being had to the specific characteristics of that market."[80] The Court left the determination of the answer to this question to the national court.

14–116   In the more recent decisions of *Ministère Public* v. *Tournier* and *Lucazeau* v. *SACEM, SACEM* v. *Debelle, SACEM* v. *Soumagnac*[81] the Court of Justice was asked to examine the effect of Article 85(1) on the contractual and *de facto* relationships that exist between the copyright societies within the Community. As to the reciprocal contracts between the societies, the Court pointed to their double aim: the establishment of identical conditions of use for the consumers in a Member State, whatever the origin of

---

[78] Thus in its investigations concerning an exclusive licence covering certain industrial property rights relating to "design" furniture, the Commission applied the principles laid down by the Court in Case 258/78 *Nungesser* v. *Commission*; see *Knoll/Hille-Form*, 13th Report on Competition Policy, 1983 at point 142.

[79] Case 262/81 *Coditel S.A.* v. *Cine Vog Films S.A.* [1982] E.C.R. 3381; [1983] 1 C.M.L.R. 49 at 278.

[80] *Ibid.* at [17]. For the application for the decision of *Coditel* (No. 2) to the field of television rights in films and the limitations imposed on the relevant licensing agreements, see the Commission Decision, *Film Purchases by German Television Stations* O.J. 1989 L284/36; [1990] 4 C.M.L.R. 841 (on appeal Case T-157/89 *Nefico B.V.* v. *Commission* and Case T-168/89 *MGM/UA* v. *Commission*). The Commission also considered the application of Arts. 85(1) and 85(3) to a structure of agreements governing the production and distribution of feature motion pictures: *U.I.P.* O.J. 1989 L226/25; [1990] 4 C.M.L.R. 749.

[81] Case 395/87, judgment of July 13, 1989 (unreported), paras. 16–26; Cases 110/88, 241/88 & 242/88, judgment of July 13, 1989 (unreported), paras. 10–20.

the protected work; and the ability of the original copyright society to rely on the protection system put in place by the society in the other Member State without having to put into place their own network of contracts and controls with the consumers in that Member State. To this extent the contracts themselves were not restrictive of competition and do not fall within Article 85(1). The Court stressed that the decision would have been different had the contracts included a clause forbidding the societies to offer direct access to their repertoire to consumers established abroad.[82] Further, the Court went on to add that, if this refusal of access was achieved through a concerted practice, this would also fall within Article 85(1). The decision as to the existence of a concerted practice was one for the referring national court, but the Court of Justice did add that a concerted practice should not be presumed if the parallelism of behaviour could be explained otherwise, for example by the need of foreign copyright societies to establish their own system of administration and control in other Member States.

The final question posed to the Court under Article 85 in *Ministère Public*   **14–117** v. *Tournier*[83] related to the refusal of SACEM to allow the French discotheques access to only part of the repertoire under its control, namely the English and American collections. The Court's answer to this problem was that a refusal of access to only part of the foreign repertoires does not have the object or effect of restricting competition within the Common Market if access to only a part of the repertoire still allowed the full protection of the interests of the authors, composers and publishers of the music without increasing the charges incurred for the administration of the contracts and for the control of the use of the protected musical works. The determination of the answer to this test is one for the national court.

In a number of earlier cases the Commission has intervened to condemn   **14–118** practices aimed at partitioning the Common Market by means of copyright licensing agreements and, as a result of such intervention, the practice complained of in each case was terminated. Thus, in *Re BBC*[84] the Commission asserted that the BBC, which enjoyed a licence to broadcast and otherwise exploit a particular children's programme from a Dutch company, and which sub-licensed under that licence the right to manufacture toys and other products associated with the characters in the programme, was impeding its sub-licensee, by the terms of the sub-licence, from exporting such toys and other products to the Netherlands. In response to the Commission's complaint, the BBC agreed not to impede such exports. In *Re Dutch Books*[85] the Commission intervened to obtain the alteration of terms of sale practised by publishers belonging to the Dutch publishers' association, which prevented exports and imports of

---

[82] The original clause in these contracts providing for such a refusal of access was removed at the request of the Commission.

[83] Case 395/87, judgment of July 13, 1989 (unreported), paras. 27–33.

[84] [1976] 1 C.M.L.R. D89. See also *Re STEMRA*, 11th Report on Competition Policy, 1981 at point 98. An export ban was considered not to be justified by the fact that the royalties payable in the exporting country are different from those in the country of destination.

[85] [1976] 1 C.M.L.R. D2.

books between Holland and Belgium. In *Re Old Man of the Sea*[86] one publisher held the licence for the whole of the Community for *The Old Man of the Sea* and sub-licensed its rights in respect of all Member States except the United Kingdom and Eire, but itself failed to provide copies of the book for sale in Eire. The Commission's intervention secured the appointment by the publisher of a sub-licensee for Eire. In *Re Ernest Benn Ltd.*[87] the Commission applied the principle discussed above[88] of free movement of goods within the Community in relation to books which had been sold with the consent of the copyright owner in the United Kingdom; the latter was not then permitted to seek to control the ultimate destination of the books, and, in particular, to prevent their being resold in the territory of his German exclusive licensee.

14–119   In *RAI/Unitel*,[89] the German company Unitel was forced to amend its exclusive contracts with four opera singers. The contracts included a non-competition clause for a considerable period. Following discussions with the Commission, Unitel undertook to ensure that the making of a film was not delayed unnecessarily, so that the non-competition clause was not overly extended. Unitel also agreed to waive its exclusive rights for important cultural events. In these circumstances the Commission felt the exclusive contract for one form of exploitation only and one work would not normally be caught by Article 85. The Commission also pointed out to Unitel's competitor, the complainant RAI, that attempts to organise a boycott of Unitel's productions might also be conduct caught by Articles 85 and 86, or, in RAI's case, Article 90.

14–120   In *Knoll/Hille-Form*,[90] a licensing agreement between Knoll and Hille-Form granted Hille-Form exclusive manufacturing and distribution rights for the United Kingdom and Eire for various furniture designs. The Commission considered the agreement did not meet the conditions for an exclusive licence set out in *Nungesser* v. *Commission*.[91] In particular, no exemption would be available under Article 85(3) since both groups had significant market positions and there was, in fact, no independent intra-Community trade. The two parties agreed to consider the export ban void and allow direct sales in each other's territory. In *BIEM-IFPI*,[92] the performing right society agreed to end any geographical restrictions on the exportation of sound recordings and to calculate royalties on the basis of the manufacturers' published selling price to retailers. In *Re GEMA*,[93] the German copyright protection society agreed to drop its proposals to levy royalties on all custom pressing work done in West Germany. Custom pressing is the manufacture of records by an independent company on behalf of a sound recording supplier. Normally the supplier obtains a licence from one of the copyright licensing societies in the Community,

---

[86] [1977] 1 C.M.L.R. D121.
[87] [1979] 3 C.M.L.R. D636.
[88] See § 14–30 *et seq.*, *ante.*
[89] 12th Report on Competition Policy, 1982 at point 90.
[90] 13th Report on Competition Policy, 1983 at point 142.
[91] Case 258/78, [1982] E.C.R. 2015; [1983] 1 C.M.L.R. 278.
[92] 13th Report on Competition Policy, 1983 at point 147.
[93] 15th Report on Competition Policy, 1985 at point 81.

but manufacture does not necessarily take place in the Member State where the licence for reproduction was obtained. GEMA sought to levy royalties on all custom pressing when the supplier obtained the reproduction licence in a Member State other than Germany. The Commission considered that this amounted to the resurrection of national barriers by contractual means. After GEMA dropped its proposals, the Commission discontinued its proceedings. But the Commission did uphold GEMA's right to check custom pressers to verify whether the supplier had a valid licence and, if not, to bring an action for infringement against the custom presser. GEMA's rights were also confirmed to the extent that it might take measures to safeguard the copyright claims of the copyright protection society that granted the licence.

C. *Article 86*

General. Article 86 prohibits any abuse by one or more undertakings[94] of **14–121** a dominant position within the Common Market, or in a substantial part of it, in so far as it may affect trade between Member States.[95]

The prohibition is followed by a list of examples of prohibited practices in sub-paragraphs (a) to (d) in similar terms to those which follow the prohibition in Article 85(1),[96] taking into account the difference that Article 85(1) is aimed at agreements and concerted practices between undertakings.

This chapter is concerned only with the application of Article 86 to the existence and exercise of industrial property rights in general, and copyright in particular, and reference should be made to other works for a discussion of what is involved in the concept of market dominance and what is the relevant market by which dominance must be judged.[97]

Article 86 and industrial property rights. The question of industrial **14–122** property rights and Article 86 first arose in the *Parke, Davis* case,[98] where the Court of Justice held that the ownership and exercise of a patent right does not by itself give its holder a dominant position for the purpose of Article 86. This has been repeated in the *Sirena*[99] and *E.M.I.* v. *CBS*[1] cases in relation to trade marks, and in the *Deutsche Grammophon* case[2] in relation to the right analogous to copyright there in issue. This is not to say that the owner of an industrial property right may not, in fact, have a dominant position which he seeks to maintain by the use of his industrial property right, but such dominance must be established by reference to his position in the relevant market in the same way as for any other undertak-

---

[94] See § 14–98, n. 29, *ante.*
[95] See § 14–102, *ante.*
[96] See § 14–98, *ante.*
[97] See Bellamy and Child, *op. cit.*, Chap. 8 and in particular paras. 8–061 *et. seq.*
[98] Case 24/67 *Parke, Davis & Co.* v. *Probel* [1968] E.C.R. 55; [1968] C.M.L.R. 47.
[99] Case 40/70 *Sirena S.R.L.* v. *Eda S.R.L.* [1971] E.C.R. 69; [1971] C.M.L.R. 260.
[1] Case 51/75 *E.M.I. Records Ltd.* v. *CBS United Kingdom Ltd.* [1976] E.C.R. 811; [1976] 2 C.M.L.R. 235.
[2] Case 78/70 *Deutsche Grammophon GmbH* v. *Metro-SB-Grossmärkte GmbH & Co.* [1971] E.C.R. 487; [1971] C.M.L.R. 631.

ing,[3] for example in the case of copyright in certain sound recordings by considering whether the artistes in the recording are exclusively bound to such undertaking, what is the popularity of such artistes with the public, the duration and extent of the obligations undertaken by them towards such undertakings, the opportunities for other manufacturers of recordings to obtain artistes for comparable performances, and the market strength of the undertaking in the relevant market.[4] Where the owner of an industrial property right does have a dominant position within the meaning of Article 86, then the cases referred to establish that the mere exercise of the industrial property right does not constitute an abuse of such dominance,[5] even if the owner of the right is able to charge a higher price for his products because of the exclusivity or monopoly conferred by the right. However, for the owner of an industrial property right in a dominant position to charge a price which is so high as to be incapable of being objectively justified, may amount to an abuse of such dominance, and any exercise of the industrial property right aimed at maintaining such dominance might then fall within the prohibition of Article 86.[6]

14–123   Thus, in *Basset* v. *SACEM*[7] the Court of Justice upheld the right of a copyright management society to charge a supplementary mechanical reproduction royalty on top of the performance royalty for the public performance of sound recordings as this was a power granted to it by national legislation, even though that right is not provided for by the Member State where the recordings were lawfully placed on the market. But the Court added that it was possible for the level of royalties to be such that Article 86 might be invoked. Since the national court had found that SACEM had a dominant position, it followed that its conduct would be contrary to Article 86 if anything it did amounted to an abuse, particularly by imposing unreasonable conditions.[8]

14–124   Another example of an abusive exercise of industrial property is where a number of undertakings owning similar industrial property rights, and together enjoying a dominant position, commence several infringement actions against a competitor, which are then stayed on condition that the competitor enter into an agreement with such undertakings.[9] Further, it can amount to an abuse within Article 86 for an undertaking which occu-

---

[3] See § 14–98, n. 29, *ante*.

[4] Case 78/70 *Deutsche Grammophon GmbH* v. *Metro-SB-Grossmärkte GmbH & Co.* [1971] C.M.L.R. 631 at 658 [18]; Case 7/82 *GVL* v. *Commission* [1983] E.C.R. 483; [1983] 3 C.M.L.R. 645 at [44]; and see, in the case of trade marks, Case 51/75 *E.M.I. Records Ltd.* v. *CBS United Kingdom Ltd.* [1976] 2 C.M.L.R. 235 at 267 [36].

[5] Case 40/70 *Sirena S.R.L.* v. *Eda S.R.L.* [1971] E.C.R. 69; [1971] C.M.L.R. 260 at 275 [17]; Case 78/80 *Deutsche Grammophon GmbH* v. *Metro-SB-Grossmärkte GmbH & Co.* [1971] C.M.L.R. 631 at 658 [19]. See also Case 238/87 *A.B. Volvo* v. *Erik Veng (U.K.) Ltd.* [1988] E.C.R. 6211; [1989] 4 C.M.L.R. 122.

[6] See n. 5, *ante*; for the particular application of Art. 86 to copyright licensing, see *Magill TV Guide/ITP, BBC and RTE* O.J. 1989 L78/43 (on appeal Cases T–69, T–70 and T–76).

[7] [1987] E.C.R. 1747; [1987] 3 C.M.L.R. 173.

[8] *Ibid.*, at [18], [19]; see further Case 395/87 *Ministère Public* v. *Tournier* (unreported) judgment para. 38; Cases 110/88, 241/88 & 242/88 *Lucazeau* v. *SACEM; SACEM* v. *Debelle; SACEM* v. *Soumagnac* (unreported), para. 25.

[9] See *Re Y.K.K.'s Complaint* [1978] 3 C.M.L.R. 44.

pies a dominant position in spare parts for its products to refuse to supply such spare parts.[10] Spare parts for industrial machines are often the subject of copyright drawings, and such copyright may be exercised in such a way as to seek to maintain a dominant position enjoyed in respect of the spare parts; such exercise may, in certain circumstances, amount to an abuse of the dominant position, and be prohibited by Article 86.[11]

However, in *Volvo AB.* v. *Erik Veng (U.K.) Ltd.*,[12] the Court of Justice **14–125** had to consider the question of a refusal to licence the manufacture of spare body panels for cars in connection with registered design rights. Volvo, the registered proprietor in the United Kingdom for the design of the body panels, sought to prevent Veng importing into the United Kingdom Volvo body panels manufactured without authority from Volvo. The Court of Justice in a brief judgment, answering only one of the three questions referred to it, stated that in the absence of harmonised laws within the Community, the individual is entitled to the protection of the subject-matter of his rights to the extent determined by the national legislature. In this case the right of a proprietor of a registered design included, as part of the subject-matter of his exclusive right, the right to prevent third parties manufacturing and selling, or importing, products identical to the design. Thus, forcing a proprietor to grant a licence, even in return for a reasonable royalty, would deprive the proprietor of the substance of his rights. A refusal to grant a licence cannot, therefore, be an abuse of a dominant position.[13] However, the Court added that the exercise of an exclusive right by the proprietor of a registered design in respect of car body panels may be prohibited by Article 86 if it involves on the part of an undertaking holding a dominant position, certain abusive conduct, such as the arbitrary refusal to supply spare parts to independent repairers, the fixing of prices for spare parts at an unfair level or a decision no longer to produce spare parts for a particular model even though many cars of that model

---

[10] *Liptons Cash Registers* v. *Hugin* O.J. 1978 L122/23; [1978] 1 C.M.L.R. D19. On appeal Case 22/78 *Hugin* v. *Commission* [1979] E.C.R. 1869; [1979] 3 C.M.L.R. 345. As to refusal by a dominant undertaking to supply generally amounting to an abuse of such dominance, see *Zoya* v. *Commercial Solvents Corpn.* O.J. 1972 L299/51 [1973] C.M.L.R. D50; on appeal Cases 6–7/73 *Istituto Chemioterapicao Italiano Spa and Commercial Solvents Corpn.* v. *Commission* [1974] E.C.R. 223; [1974] 1 C.M.L.R. 309. As to the position regarding computers and interface information, see for guidance the IBM settlement, [1984] 3 C.M.L.R. 147, 14th Report on Competition Policy, point 94, *et seq.*

[11] Such an argument has been advanced as a defence to an action for infringement of copyright in parts for motor vehicles; see *British Leyland Motor Corporation Ltd.* v. *Wyatt Interpart Company Ltd.* [1979] F.S.R. 39; [1979] 1 C.M.L.R. 395 and subsequently at [1979] F.S.R. 583; [1979] 3 C.M.L.R. 79. See also the 15th Report on Competition Policy 1985, point 49—Ford Body Panels. The Commission opened proceedings following complaints that Ford was claiming copyright protection for body panels and refusing to grant licences on reasonable terms. Ford offered to grant licences to competitors in the U.K. for the manufacture and sale of such body panels and also offered to settle the infringement proceedings against those competitors in the English courts; but see text to n. 10, *post.*

[12] Case 238/87, [1988] E.C.R. 6211; [1989] 4 C.M.L.R. 122; Case 53/87 *Maxicar* v. *Renault* [1988] E.C.R. 6039; [1990] 4 C.M.L.R. 265.

[13] And see *Yale Security Products Ltd.* v. *Newman* [1990] F.S.R. 320; *Ransburge-Gema A.G.* v. *Electrostatic Plant Systems Ltd.* [1990] F.S.R. 287.

are still in circulation, provided such conduct is liable to affect trade between Member States.[14]

14–126   This decision seems to strike a balance between the right of an industrial property right owner to exercise those rights given to him by the national legislature and the need to prevent the abuse of a dominant position by a refusal to supply. Volvo may still exercise its rights under the registered design legislation to prevent the importation of unlawfully manufactured copies, yet its market behaviour in supplying legitimate spares will be controlled.[15]

14–127   **Authors' rights societies.** Authors' rights societies have come under particular scrutiny under Article 86.[16] In *Re GEMA*[17] the Commission held that the German performing right society had a dominant position within the meaning of Article 86, and had abused that position by the following practices: discriminating against authors from other Member States; binding its members to unjustified obligations, such as the assignment by the author of all his rights to GEMA; preventing foreign publishers from becoming ordinary members of GEMA; extending copyright through contractual means to non-copyright works; discriminating against

(i)   independent importers of gramophone records as compared with manufacturers of records and

(ii) importers of tape and optical sound recorders as compared with German manufacturers of such recorders.

In *Belgische Radio & Televisie* v. *SABAM*[18] the Court of Justice had to consider questions referred to it raising the validity under Article 86 of practices carried out by the Belgian association of authors, composers and publishers, SABAM. The Court held that in determining whether a national copyright society is imposing unfair conditions on its members or on third parties, account is to be taken of all relevant interests so as to ensure a balance between the needs of the members for freedom from restraint, and for effective management of their rights.[19] The Court went on to hold that for the society to require a compulsory assignment by an author to it of all his copyrights, present and future, may amount to an

---

[14] Case 238/87 *AB Volvo* v. *Erik Veng (U.K.) Ltd.* [1988] E.C.R. 2605; [1989] 4 C.M.L.R. 122 at [9] and Case 53/87 *Maxicar* v. *Renault* [1988] E.C.R. 6039; [1990] 4 C.M.L.R. 265 at [16].

[15] The *Volvo* decision appears to be in conflict with the approach of the Commission in Ford Body Panels (see n. 11, *ante*), although the lack of information as to the latter decision makes it difficult to assess the degree of any such conflict.

[16] See further as to the application of the Rules on Competition to performing right societies: Ernst-Joachim Mestmacker, *Journal of World Trade Law 1976* Special Supplement No. 3, Chap. IV.

[17] O.J. 1971 L134; 15; [1971] C.M.L.R. D35; see also *Re Gema (No. 2)* O.J. 1972 L166/22; [1972] C.M.L.R. D115.

[18] Case 127/73 [1974] E.C.R. 313; [1974] 2 C.M.L.R. 238.

[19] [1974] 2 C.M.L.R. 238 at 283 [8].

unfair condition, especially if the assignment is to remain effective for a considerable time after the author has left the society.[20]

In *GVL* v. *Commission*[21] the Court was asked to overturn the Com- **14–128** mission's decision[22] that the German collecting society GVL had abused a dominant position by refusing to conclude management contracts or otherwise manage the performer's rights for artistes of other Member States not resident in Germany. Upholding the Commission's decision and finding that GVL had a monopoly on the relevant market for the secondary exploitation of copyright, the Court held that a refusal by a *de facto* monopoly to provide its services to all who might be in need of them, but who are not in a category defined by that undertaking by nationality or residence, is an abuse of a dominant position. Thus GVL could not refuse its services to foreign artistes not resident in Germany; they may also wish to assert rights of secondary exploitation. GVL knew it was preventing those artistes from being paid the royalties they were entitled to. More recently in *Basset* v. *SACEM*,[23] the Court held that a copyright management society would not be infringing Article 86 by exercising the powers granted to it by national legislation. However, it is possible that the level of royalty or combined royalties charged by the society might be such as to bring Article 86 into operation. The French court had already found that the royalties charged by SACEM were not unreasonable, so the Court of Justice made no further comment in this particular case.

The practices of the French copyright society SACEM received further **14–129** attention from the Court of Justice in a series of cases[24] challenging the restrictions it imposed on discotheques using the repertoire of authors registered with SACEM and collecting societies in other Member States having reciprocal agreements with SACEM. The challenge under Article 86 was to the level of royalties charged by SACEM to discotheques for the performance of the protected works in comparison with copyright societies in other Member States. In the judgment of the Court, if those rates were significantly higher than those charged by the other copyright societies, when compared on an equal basis, the difference would be an indication of abuse. It is then for the society in question to justify the difference objectively.[25] An attempt by SACEM to justify the difference on the basis of its greater administrative zeal was rejected by the Court as also being capable of explanation by the lack of competition on the market, allowing SACEM to develop an unnecessarily burdensome administration. In *Ministère Public* v. *Tournier*[26] the Court went slightly further than in the

---

[20] *Ibid.*, at 283 [12]; see also *Greenwich Films S.A.* v. *SACEM* [1979] 2 C.M.L.R. 535 and Case 22/79, [1979] E.C.R. 3275; [1980] 1 C.M.L.R. 629.

[21] Case 7/82, [1983] E.C.R. 483; [1983] 3 C.M.L.R. 645.

[22] O.J. 1981 L370/49; [1982] 1 C.M.L.R. 221.

[23] [1987] E.C.R. 1717; [1987] 3 C.M.L.R. 173.

[24] Case 395/87 *Ministère Public* v. *Tournier*, judgment 13/7/89 (unreported); Cases 110/88, 241/88 & 242/88 *Lucazeau* v. *SACEM*; *SACEM* v. *Debelle*; *SACEM* v. *Sougmagnac* (unreported).

[25] *Ibid.* paras. 38 and 25 of the respective judgments.

[26] *Ibid.* para. 34 of the judgment.

other cases by adding that the imposition of any inequitable contractual term by a dominant undertaking is an abuse of Article 86.

D. *Direct effect of prohibition in Articles 85 and 86*

14–130 **General.** As has been stated above, Articles 85(1) and 86 are directly applicable Treaty provisions and are enforceable as such in proceedings in the national courts.[27] The operation of the prohibition is not, however, retroactive in English law, and does not affect the lawfulness of agreements or practices prior to the accession of the United Kingdom to the Community.[28] In the case of the prohibition in Article 85(1), Article 85(2) expressly provides that agreements or decisions prohibited pursuant to Article 85(1) shall be automatically void. It has been established by the Court of Justice that it is only those clauses which actually infringe Article 85(1) which are void, and not the whole of the agreement, providing that the infringing clauses can be severed.[29] Whether severance is possible is a matter for the national law governing the agreement and depends on its rules on such matters as consideration and fundamental change. The Court of Appeal has confirmed that this is the position so far as English law is concerned.[30] In *Société de Vente de Ciements et Betons*,[31] the Court of Justice affirmed its decision in *Technique Minière* v. *Maschinenbau Ulm*[32] and stated that the issue of the consequences of nullity of the prohibited clauses is one for the national courts.

14–131 **Provisional validity: prohibited agreements.** The operation of the prohibition of Article 85(1) has been qualified, so far as proceedings in the national courts are concerned, by the concept introduced by the Court of Justice of provisional validity of agreements entered into before the prohibition became directly applicable, (which, for undertakings in the six founder Member States, was March 13, 1962, the date when Regulation 17 came into force applying the prohibition of Article 85(1)) and which had been duly notified to the Commission, or were non-notifiable agreements.[33] The same qualification has been argued to apply to agreements which did not fall within Article 85(1) prior to the accession of the United Kingdom to the community on January 1, 1973, but did so thereafter, and

---

[27] See §§ 14–29 and 14–18, *ante*.

[28] *Application des Gaz S.A.* v. *Falks Veritas Ltd.* (C.A.) [1978] 1 C.M.L.R. 383; *Valor International Ltd.* v. *Application des Gaz S.A.* (Whitford J.) [1978] 2 C.M.L.R. 296; (C.A.) [1978] 3 C.M.L.R. 87; [1979] R.P.C. 281.

[29] Case 56/65 *La Technique Minière* v. *Maschinenbau Ulm GmbH* [1966] E.C.R. 235; [1966] C.M.L.R. 357 at 376; Cases 56 & 68/64 *Consten & Grundig Verkaufs-GmbH* v. *Commission* [1966] E.C.R. 299; [1966] C.M.L.R. 418 at 474–475.

[30] *Chemidus Wavin Ltd.* v. *Soc. pour la Transformation* (C.A.) [1977] F.S.R. 181; [1978] 3 C.M.L.R. 514. See also the judgment of Walton J. at [1977] F.S.R. 19; [1976] 2 C.M.L.R. 387.

[31] Case 319/82 *Société de Vente de Ciments et Betons* v. *Kerpen & Kerpen* [1983] E.C.R. 4173 at 4184–4185; [1985] 1 C.M.L.R. 511 [11], [12].

[32] Case 56/65 *La Technique Minière* v. *Maschinenbau Ulm GmbH* [1966] E.C.R. 235; [1986] C.M.L.R. 357.

[33] See § 14–137, *post*.

which were likewise duly notified to the Commission, or were non-notifiable agreements.[34]

Article 86: prohibited practices. Since the prohibition in Article 86 is **14–132** directed at unilateral practices of undertakings, there is no need for any declaration of nullity corresponding to that found in Article 85(2). However, the abuse of a dominant position may well involve acts recognised as having legal consequences under the national law concerned, for example contracts, as in the case of contracts between authors and their performing right society, and in such a case it is for the national court to determine the effect of Article 86 on such acts.[35]

Effect of prohibitions in English law: procedure. In general, it may **14–133** be said that the prohibitions of Articles 85(1) and 86 are to be applied in proceedings before the English courts in the same way as any other rules of English law. However, the nature of the investigation required for the determination of their applicability presents problems of particularity in pleading,[36] and when summary judgment under Order 14 is sought.[37]

A particular problem can arise due to the fact that the Commission has **14–134** an independent jurisdiction, under Regulation 17, to investigate agreements, decisions and practices which it considers fall within Articles 85 and 86 and to issue a decision to the party or parties concerned prohibiting such agreements, decisions and practices and imposing fines.[38] The Court of Justice has ruled that, even when the Commission has initiated a procedure under Articles 2, 3 or 6 of Regulation 17,[39] the national court still has jurisdiction to apply Article 85(1),[40] although it may choose to stay the proceedings. The approach adopted by the English courts when the question of the validity of an agreement, decision or practice under Article 85 or 86 has been raised both before it and with the Commission, has been to allow a stay of the English proceedings, pending the Com-

---

[34] See Bellamy and Child, *op. cit.*, § 10–008 and §§ 11–046 *et seq.*; Kerse, *EEC Anti-Trust Procedure*, (2nd ed., 1988), pp. 308 *et seq.*, where the problems caused by the concept of provisional validity are discussed generally. See also *De Vereniging ter Bevordering van de Belangen des Boekhandels* v. *Eldi Records B.V.* [1980] 1 C.M.L.R. 584 (District Court of Amsterdam) and Court of Justice, Case 106/79 [1980] E.C.R. 1137; [1980] 3 C.M.L.R. 719.

[35] Case 127/73 *Belgische Radio & Televisie* v. *SABAM* [1974] E.C.R. 313; [1974] 2 C.M.L.R. 238 at 284 [14]; Case 22/79 *Greenwich Film Productions* v. *SACEM* [1979] E.C.R. 3275 [10]; [1980] 1 C.M.L.R. 629.

[36] See Rules of the Supreme Court, para. 18/12/3 and *British Leyland Motor Corporation Ltd.* v. *Wyatt Interpart Ltd.* [1979] F.S.R. 39; [1979] 1 C.M.L.R. 395; *Valor International Ltd.* v. *Application des Gaz S.A.* (Whitford J.) [1978] 1 C.M.L.R. 30; [1979] R.P.C. 281; *British Leyland Motor Corporation Ltd.* v. *T.I. Silencers Ltd.* [1979] F.S.R. 591 and subsequently at [1980] 2 C.M.L.R. 133; *Potato Marketing Board* v. *Drysdale* [1986] 3 C.M.L.R. 331 (C.A.); *Ransburg-GEMA A.G.* v. *Electrostatic Plant Systems* [1989] 2 C.M.L.R. 712; 1990 F.S.R. 287; *Yale Products Ltd* v. *Newman* [1990] F.S.R. 320.

[37] See *Dymond* v. *G.B. Briton (Holdings) Ltd.* [1976] 1 C.M.L.R. 133; see generally § [11–80], *ante*.

[38] See § 14–136, *post*.

[39] See § 14–136, *post*.

[40] Case 127/73 *Belgische Radio & Televisie* v. *SABAM* [1974] E.C.R. 313; [1974] 2 C.M.L.R. 238.

mission adopting a decision in the matter.[41] Furthermore, where the defendant, in proceedings before the English court, raises the defence that the plaintiff is acting in breach of Article 85 or 86, and the plaintiff claims privilege against discovery of the documents relevant to the determination of the issue,[42] then the English court may stay the proceedings until the Commission has given a decision on the matter.[43]

14–135 Prohibitions giving rise to cause of action in tort. The discussion above concerns proceedings in which the effect of the prohibitions of Articles 85 and 86 is raised as a defence. The question also arises whether the infringement of such prohibitions gives rise to a cause of action for the recovery of damages at the instance of a party alleging that he has been injured by such infringements. Articles 85 and 86 have been described as creating "new torts,"[44] but this has subsequently been qualified.[45] More recently, the House of Lords and the Court of Appeal have acknowledged that a right to damages will arise from breach of Article 86 on the basis of breach of statutory duty.[46] The position is presumably the same, therefore, in respect of breach of Article 85(1).

E. Enforcement of the rules on competition by the Commission[47]

14–136 Powers of the Commission. As has already been stated, under Regulation 17, adopted by the Council on February 6, 1962 under Article 87 of the Treaty, the enforcement of the Rules on Competition is entrusted to the Commission. This jurisdiction is in many respects co-extensive with the jurisdiction of the national courts to apply the prohibitions of Articles 85(1) and 86 in civil proceedings before them.[48] However, the Commission has sole power (subject to review by the Court of Justice): (i) to declare Article 85(1) inapplicable to individual agreements, pursuant to Article 85(3)[49]; (ii) to issue negative clearance, that is a certificate that, on the facts disclosed to it, there are not grounds for the Commission to take any action under Article 85(1) or 86 in respect of a particular agreement,

---

[41] *Aero Zipp Fasteners Ltd.* v. *Y.K.K. Fasteners (U.K.) Ltd.* [1978] F.S.R. 301; [1978] 2 C.M.L.R. 88. Whitford J. at 98 [32] pointed out that the decision of the Commission would not necessarily dispose of all the issues in the national proceedings; see Bellamy and Child, *op. cit.*, § 10–005.

[42] On the basis of *Rio Tinto Zinc Corporation* v. *Westinghouse Electric Corporation (No. 2)* [1978] A.C. 547; [1978] 1 C.M.L.R. 100.

[43] *British Leyland Motor Corporation Ltd.* v. *Wyatt Interpart Ltd.* [1979] F.S.R. 583; [1979] 3 C.M.L.R. 79; and see as to the conditions upon which the stay was granted: [1980] F.S.R. 18.

[44] *Application des Gaz S.A.* v. *Falks Veritas Ltd.* (C.A.) [1974] Ch. 381; [1974] 2 C.M.L.R. 75, *per* Lord Denning M.R. at 84 [27] and [28].

[45] *Valor International Ltd.* v. *Application des Gaz S.A.* [1978] 3 C.M.L.R. 87; [1979] R.P.C. 281, *per* Roskill L.J. at 99 [43].

[46] *Garden Cottage Foods* v. *Milk Marketing Board* [1984] A.C. 130; [1983] 3 C.M.L.R. 43; *Bourgoin* v. *Ministry of Agriculture* [1986] Q.B. 716; [1986] 1 C.M.L.R. 267; see also *Cutsforth* v. *Mansfield Inns* [1986] 1 W.L.R. 588.

[47] See generally Kerse, *EEC Anti-Trust Procedure* (2nd ed., 1988) and Bellamy and Child, *op. cit.*

[48] Art. 9(1), Reg. 17.

[49] See § 14–137, *post.*

decision or practice[50]; and (iii) to impose fines on the undertakings found by it to have infringed Article 85(1) or 86.[51]

Notification of agreements. Where block exemption is not available for any reason,[52] an agreement may still be exempted under Article 85(3), by individual decision of the Commission, but, for this purpose, the parties must notify the agreement to the Commission,[53] unless the agreement is one not requiring notification.[54] Notification for the purposes of individual exemption is usually made at the same time as applying for negative clearance.[55]   **14–137**

The agreements which do not require to be notified to the Commission include bipartite agreements which only impose restrictions on the exercise of the rights of the assignee or user of industrial property rights.[56] Caution is necessary, however, in relying on this exemption from notification. In *Re Advocaat*[57] the Commission held that a licence to use a trade mark was outside the exemption because restrictions were accepted by the licensor; this will always be so, for example, where the licence is exclusive. Further, in *H. Vaessen B.V.* v. *Alex Moris*,[58] a patent licensing agreement contained a no-challenge clause and a clause imposing an exclusive purchasing obligation relating to products not covered by the patent. The Commission held that these restrictions went beyond those referred to in Article 4(2)(*b*), and that the agreement was not exempt from notification. The parties to an agreement which is exempt from notification may, nevertheless, notify it to the Commission.[59]   **14–138**

Investigation by the Commission. Once an application has been made for negative clearance and/or notification for exemption under Article 85(3), the Commission will, of course, have become aware of the existence of the agreement. In addition many agreements or practices suspected of infringing Article 85 or 86 are brought to the attention of the Commission by complaints made by third parties whose interests are adversely affected by the agreement or practice. In whatever way the existence of the agreement, decision or practice comes to the attention of the Commission,[60] it is then able to require the undertakings concerned to provide it with infor-   **14–139**

---

[50] Art. 2, Reg. 17.
[51] Art. 15, Reg. 17.
[52] As to block exemption, see § 14–102, *ante*.
[53] Arts. 4(1) and 5(1), Reg. 17.
[54] Under Arts. 4(2) and 5(2), Reg. 17.
[55] See Bellamy and Child, *op. cit.* Chap. 11, and in particular § 11–006.
[56] Art. 4(2)(2)(*b*), Reg. 17.
[57] O.J. 1974 L237/12; [1974] 2 C.M.L.R. D79; see also *Toltecs/Dorcet* O.J. 1982 L379/19; [1983] 1 C.M.L.R. 412; on appeal Case 35/83 *BAT* v. *Commission* [1985] E.C.R. 363; [1985] 2 C.M.L.R. 470.
[58] O.J. 1979 L19/32; [1979] 1 C.M.L.R. 511; see also *Windsurfing International* O.J. 1983 L229/1; [1984] 1 C.M.L.R. 1; on appeal Case 193/83 *Windsurfing International* v. *Commission* [1986] E.C.R. 611; [1986] 3 C.M.L.R. 489.
[59] Arts. 4(2) and 5(2), Reg. 17. For the effect and advantages of notification generally, see Bellamy and Child, *op. cit.*, § 11–023.
[60] And this may be as a result of its own investigations, for example in carrying out a sectoral inquiry under Art. 12, Reg. 17.

mation,[61] and to use its extensive powers of investigation.[62] In the course of such investigations, undertakings often alter the terms of their agreements, or cease practices complained of by the Commission, without the need for the Commission to proceed to a formal decision. However, if the undertakings persist in their agreements, decisions or practices complained of, or if the Commission considers the infringement has been deliberate or serious, the Commission will then initiate the decision-making process, which is an administrative, not judicial, procedure, by addressing a document, called a Statement of Objections, to the undertakings concerned, in which the matters complained of must be sufficiently clearly set out.[63] The undertakings then have the opportunity to make their submissions to the Commission in a document called a Reply,[64] and then at an oral hearing, if they wish.[65] The result of the administrative procedure is that the Commission, after taking the opinion of the Advisory Committee on Restrictive Practices and Monopolies,[66] adopts a decision to the effect, either that the prohibitions of Articles 85 and 86 do not, or do, apply, and, if the latter, granting or refusing exemption under Article 85(3), if applicable. If the decision is to the effect that Article 85(1) applies and Article 85(3) does not, or that Article 86 applies, the Commission may order the undertakings concerned to desist from carrying out the offending agreements, decisions or practices, and may impose fines in respect of any past infringement which it finds to have been either intentional or negligent of an amount from 1,000 to 1,000,000 European units of account (the ECU) (or a greater sum not exceeding 10 per cent. of the turnover in the preceding business year of each of the undertakings participating in the infringement).[67] In fixing the amount of any fine, the Commission is to have regard to the gravity and the duration of the infringement.[68] The undertakings to whom a decision is addressed by the Commission may appeal the whole or part of the decision to the Court of Justice under Article 173 of the treaty.[69]

---

[61] Under Art. 11, Reg. 17; fines may be imposed for failure to supply the required information: Art. 15(1)(b), Reg. 17.

[62] Under Art. 14, Reg. 17, which gives the authorised officials of the Commission power to examine and take copies of an undertaking's books and records, to ask for oral explanations on the spot and to enter the undertaking's premises.

[63] Art. 2(1), Reg. 99/63, O.J. 1963 127/2268; see Bellamy and Child, *op. cit.*, Appendix 23.

[64] Arts. 2(4) and (3), Reg. 17; Art. 3, Reg. 99/63.

[65] Art. 19(1), Reg. 17; Art. 7(1), Reg. 99/63.

[66] Arts. 10(3), 15(7) and 16(3), Reg. 17.

[67] Art. 15(2), Reg. 17.

[68] *Ibid.*

[69] See generally Kerse, *EEC Anti-Trust Procedure* (2nd ed., 1988), Chap. 7.

ARRANGEMENTS BETWEEN COPYRIGHT OWNERS AND
LICENSEES

1. Publishing Agreements

A. *Formalities of publishing arrangements*

No formalities required. Contracts between authors and publishers are   **15–1**
not, as in some countries, regulated by any special law, but their validity,
construction and enforcement depend upon the ordinary rules of law
governing contracts relating to dealings with personal property. Such contracts do not even have to be in writing, unless they are to effect an assignment of copyright or are to constitute an exclusive licence (with the
licensee being able to sue in his own name), when in each case writing is
required.[1] In practice, such arrangements vary, through many gradations
of formality, from an oral or implied licence to publish a single article
(which provides a good defence to an action for infringement),[2] to a full-

---

[1] C.D.P.A. 1988, ss.90(3) and 92(1).
[2] See § 8–44 *et seq., ante.*

length publishing agreement. It is the informal agreement, leaving many essential terms to implication, that most often renders difficult the determination of the respective rights of the parties.

15–2   Informal agreement: dispatch of manuscript. The simplest form of contract is where a manuscript is sent to a publisher without anything being said about terms. It seems probable that, in the case of an article sent to the editor or publishers of a newspaper or journal, the sending of the manuscript would by custom, or necessary implication, be treated as an offer of a licence to publish in consideration of payment on the usual terms for such a publication, and that such offer can at once be accepted by the editor or publisher without further communication.[3] If, however, before publication, there are detailed discussions about the form of publication and these never fructify, no licence to publish will be implied.[4] Where the matter is left to implication, the normal custom in such matters recognises no obligation on the part of the proprietor of the newspaper to insure, or to preserve, any manuscript sent to him uninvited, and if the manuscript is lost or destroyed, the author cannot recover for its value.[5] The position would be different if an editor or proprietor undertook to return unaccepted communications.

15–3   On the other hand, in the case of a larger work, it would seem that the sending of the manuscript is merely an offer to enter into negotiations and does not constitute an offer capable of immediate acceptance so as to form a binding contract. What, short of actual publication, amounts to an acceptance of an author's manuscript will depend upon the circumstances of the case, but if the publisher retains the article and has it put into type and a proof sent for revision to the writer, the latter may generally treat this as an acceptance of his manuscript and sue the publisher for the price, though the article is never, in fact, published.[6] Whether the manuscript itself becomes the property of the publisher must depend on the nature of the work and the circumstances surrounding the submission of the manuscript to the publisher, including the terms of any contract between the publisher and the author.[7]

B. Distinction between assignment and licence

15–4   Formal agreement: assignment or licence. In the case of more formal publishing agreements, the most important point to determine is whether an outright disposal of any copyright is intended, by vesting the same in

---

[3] See *Hall-Brown* v. *Iliffe & Sons Ltd.* [1928–35] Mac.C.C. 88, where, on the particular facts, it was held that there was no licence. See also *Malcolm* v. *Chancellor, Masters and Scholars of the University of Oxford* (C.A.) *The Times*, December 19, 1990.

[4] *Hall-Brown* v. *Iliffe & Sons Ltd., supra.*

[5] But see *Stone* v. *Long* [1901–04] Mac.C.C. 66.

[6] *Macdonald* v. *National Review*, Westminster County Court, May 16, 1893; *Pall Mall Gazette*, May 17, 1893. See *Malcolm* v. *Chancellor, Masters and Scholars of the University of Oxford, supra.*

[7] See *Hogg* v. *Kirby* (1803) 8 Ves. 215; *Howard* v. *Harris* (1884) Cababé & Ellis 253; *Stone* v. *Long* [1901–04] Mac.C.C. 66; *Thomas* v. *Times Book Co. Ltd.* [1966] 1 W.L.R. 911 *Moorhouse* v. *Angus & Robertson (No. 1) Pty.* [1980] F.S.R. 231 (Supreme Court New South Wales); and see also *Copyright*, No. 5, May 1966, p. 144; as to letters, see § 8–158, *ante.*

the publisher, or whether a licence only is intended. A number of distinctions between the rights of the parties, according to whether an assignment or licence has been executed, arise with regard to the right to sue in respect of infringement,[8] the right to make alterations to the work,[9] the liability of an assign of the publisher for royalties payable to the author,[10] the position consequent on the bankruptcy or insolvency of the publisher,[11] and the assignability of the benefit of the agreement by the publisher.[12]

Right to sue for infringement. Where the right to publish has been disposed of by way of an assignment, the publisher will enjoy the full legal title to the copyright and will alone be entitled to enforce the right against third parties. In the case of a licence, which, in a publishing agreement, will normally be an exclusive licence, an exclusive licensee may sue for infringement of copyright but must (where the exclusive licensee and copyright owner have concurrent rights of action) join his licensor as a party to the action, except where an interlocutory injunction is sought.[13] However, it is provided that any defence which would have been available to a defendant in the action, if the action had been brought by the owner of the copyright, shall be available to that defendant as against the exclusive licensee,[14] so that where a defendant has been licensed by the copyright owner, the exclusive licensee's only remedy is against the copyright owner, for breach of contract. Furthermore, an exclusive licensee remains liable to have the value of his licence prejudiced by a later assignment of copyright by the author to an assignee taking without notice of the licence.[15]   **15–5**

Right to alter. So far as copyright alone is concerned,[16] a publisher, who is by assignment the absolute owner of the copyright in a work, may, without the consent of the author, publish successive editions of the work and in doing so may make additions, corrections, omissions and other changes in the original work.[17] Whereas, where the publisher has only a licence to publish, the licence may expressly, or by implication, only extend to publication in unaltered form, so that the publisher, if he publishes in an altered form, may thereby commit an act of infringement of copyright.[18] This passage was approved by Goff J. in *Frisby* v. *British Broadcasting Cor-*   **15–6**

---

[8] See § 15–5, *post.*
[9] See § 15–6, *post.*
[10] See § 15–7, *post.*
[11] See § 15–8, *post.*
[12] See § 15–10, *post.*
[13] C.D.P.A. 1988, ss.101 and 102.
[14] *Ibid.* s.101(3), re-enacting a similar provision introduced by s.19(4) of the 1956 Act, but which was not thought to have changed the previously existing law.
[15] See C.D.P.A. 1988, s.90(4).
[16] See text and nn. 22 & 23, *post*, as to other causes of action which may be invoked by the author and see, as to the author's right to object to derogatory treatment of his work, Chap. 23, *post.*
[17] See *Lee* v. *Gibbings* (1892) L.T. 263, where the court declined to interfere in a case in which a purchaser of a stock of books rebound them in a mutilated form and see, now, n. 16, *ante.*
[18] See *Joseph* v. *National Magazine Co. Ltd.* [1959] Ch. 14: see also §§ 8–150 and 8–151, *ante.*

poration[19] who held that, in the absence of a prohibition against publication in an altered form, the licensee had a right to make alterations, even substantial ones; but the court would readily imply a term limiting the right to make alterations.

However, even where the copyright in the work has been assigned by the author, the author may remain entitled to assert his right under the 1988 Act to object to any addition to or deletion from or alteration to or adaptation of his work, unless he has in the assignment waived such right.[20] Even apart from any application of the author's moral rights,[21] publication of the work in an altered form, when the alteration has been done by another, cannot lawfully be represented as having been done by the author of the original, if the public are induced to believe that it is the work of the author, and the author is thereby damaged or deprived of sales.[22] Further, the publication under an author's name of a work not his own and without his consent in circumstances that would injure his character or reputation may constitute actionable defamation.[23]

15–7   **Right to royalties.** The position of an author who assigns his copyright and stipulates for payment on royalty terms may be a difficult one. If the publisher assigns the copyright to a third party, the author cannot sue the third party for his royalties because no privity of contract exists between them,[24] and the original publisher may become insolvent. The rights of an author who had assigned his copyright on royalty terms and then sought to sue a purchaser from the assignee for royalties, were fully considered in the case of *Barker* v. *Stickney*[25] by the Court of Appeal. The claim was put on three grounds, namely, for a vendor's lien, for a charge on the copyright assigned, and on the basis of a covenant the burden of which ran with the copyright.[26] The court held that, so far as a claim based on lien was concerned, this failed since the vendor had accepted the purchaser's covenant to pay royalties in satisfaction of his claim for the price, and, therefore, was not an unpaid vendor. A charge could only arise if it was clearly and expressly created by the document and this was not the case. So far as the burden running with the copyright, the court held that it was

---

[19] [1967] Ch. 932; and see *Cox* v. *Cox* (1853) 11 Hare 118; *Crookes* v. *Petter* (1860) 6 Jur.(N.S.) 1131; *Booth* v. *Edward Lloyd Ltd.* (1909) 26 T.L.R. 549; *Gilbert* v. *Workman* [1905–10] Mac.C.C. 235.

[20] C.D.P.A. 1988, ss.80 and 87(1) and see Chap. 23, *post.*

[21] See Chap. 23, *post.*

[22] *Ridge* v. *The English Illustrated Magazine Ltd.* [1911–16] Mac.C.C. 91; *Springfield* v. *Thame* (1903) 89 L.T. 242; and C.D.P.A. 1988, s.84, (in relation to literary, dramatic, musical and artistic works).

[23] *Ridge* v. *The English Illustrated Magazine Ltd.* [1911–16] Mac.C.C. 91; *Lee* v. *Gibbings* (1892) L.T. 263; *Mosely* v. *Stanley Paul & Co.* [1917–23] Mac.C.C. 341; *Glyn* v. *Weston Feature Film Co.* [1916] 1 Ch. 261; *Archbold* v. *Sweet* (1832) 1 Moo. & Rob. 162; *Humphreys* v. *Thomson & Co. Ltd.* [1905–10] Mac.C.C. 148; and see Chap. 23, *post.*

[24] *Bagot Pneumatic Tyre Co.* v. *Clipper Pneumatic Tyre Co.* [1902] 1 Ch. 146 and see *Beswick* v. *Beswick* [1968] A.C. 58.

[25] [1919] 1 K.B. 121.

[26] Based on the general principle stated by Knight-Bruce L.J. in *De Mattos* v. *Gibson* (1859) 4 De G. & J. 276.

settled law[27] that the purchaser of a chattel is not bound by mere notice of stipulations made by his vendor unless he was himself a party to the contract in which the stipulations were made, and that, since there was nothing to distinguish a chose in action such as copyright from chattels or land, a person acquiring a chose in action is not bound by mere notice of a personal covenant by his predecessor in title. Whether this last point should be reconsidered in the light of the decision in *Lord Strathcona Steamship Co. Ltd. v. Dominion Coal Co. Ltd.*[28] where the principle of *De Mattos v. Gibson*[29] was applied in the case of a ship, remains undecided.[30] It seems fairly clear, however, that as the law now stands, an author who has entered into a publishing agreement in which the copyright is assigned to the publisher on royalty terms, has no right of action for the royalties against an assign of the publisher. In *Barker v. Stickney, supra*, Scrutton L.J. suggested that authors might seek protection against assignees who publish without paying the royalties by keeping the copyright themselves and assigning no more than a right to publish conditional upon royalties being paid and only assignable if they are provided for.[31] It is suggested that the authors' interests would be still better protected by ensuring that they grant only a non-assignable licence to publish, conditional on royalties being paid, although such an arrangement as suggested by Scrutton L.J. might in any case be more readily construed as a licence rather than an assignment.[32]

Insolvency of publisher. The subsequent insolvency of the publisher **15–8** affords a further example of the importance of the distinction between a licence and an assignment. In the case of *Re Grant Richards*,[33] it was held that, where an author had assigned his copyright in consideration of the payment of royalties, and, upon the bankruptcy of the publisher, his trustee continued the publisher's business for some time, the author had no right to claim payment of the royalties in full, but could only prove in the bankruptcy for damages. On the other hand, in a case where there was an agreement by the publisher to pay a share of profits to the author, and the copyright still remained vested in him, it was held that the agreement was terminated by the bankruptcy of the publisher, whose trustee in bankruptcy was restrained from reprinting or republishing the book, even on

---

[27] Applying *Taddy & Co. v. Sterious & Co.* [1904] 1 Ch. 354; *McCruther v. Pitcher* [1904] 2 Ch. 306; and *Dunlop Tyre Co. Ltd. v. Selfridge & Co. Ltd.* [1915] A.C. 847.

[28] [1926] A.C. 108.

[29] *Supra.*

[30] In *Port Line Ltd. v. Ben Line Steamers Ltd.* [1958] 2 Q.B. 146, Diplock J. decided that the *Strathcona* case was wrongly decided but, even if it was rightly decided, the defendants did not come within its principles. See also *Tito and Ors. v. Waddell and Ors.* (No. 2) [1977] Ch. 106 at 300E, where Megarry V.-C. treated *Barker v. Stickney, supra,* as being decided as a matter of construction, and commented that it left open the question whether an author might successfully sue an assignee for royalties in an appropriate case under "the pure benefit and burden principle," discussed in that case, *ibid.* at 290 *et seq.* See also *Swiss Bank v. Lloyds Bank* [1979] 1 Ch. 548 (Browne-Wilkinson J.) and on appeal [1982] A.C. 584.

[31] *Barker v. Stickney* [1919] 1 K.B. 121 at 133, 134.

[32] See § 15–15, *post.*

[33] [1907] 2 K.B. 33.

the terms of continuing to pay the author his share of profits, but without prejudice to the right of the trustee to dispose of stock.[34]

15–9   The effect of the decision of *Re Grant Richards*[35] was altered as regards the bankruptcy of a publisher by section 60 of the Bankruptcy Act 1914,[36] which prevented the publisher's trustee in bankruptcy from selling or authorising the sale of copies of the work or dealing with his interest in the copyright except upon terms which ensured that the author would receive such royalties as would have been payable by the bankrupt.[37] This provision, which did not apply where the insolvent publisher was a company,[38] was repealed by the Insolvency Act 1985,[39] as replaced by the Insolvency Act 1986,[40] but continues to have effect in relation to any transaction entered into before the commencement of the Insolvency Act 1986.[41]

15–10   Right to assign. Again, the distinction between a licence and an assignment is important in connection with the question of the assignability by the publisher of the benefit of a publishing agreement. Where the publisher takes an assignment of copyright, he has a right which he can transfer at will and, in default of an express agreement not to assign, he cannot be deprived of that right. Further, even if there is such an express agreement against assignment, it would seem to be ineffective as against a subsequent assignee without notice. Moreover, the mere fact that the publisher is to pay royalties or a share of profits to the author will not give rise to any implication of an agreement not to assign.[42] On the other hand, a licence can expressly be made personal and terminable upon any purported assignment of its benefit and, even without such express provision, will, in general, be read as containing an implied provision to this effect.

15–11   In such cases the question whether the benefit of a publishing agreement is assignable by the publisher turns upon whether the agreement ought to be regarded as of a personal nature or not. Contracts of a personal character are not assignable,[43] and wherever the author is to be remunerated either by a share of profits or by royalties, prima facie the

---

[34] *Lucas* v. *Moncrieff* (1905) 21 T.L.R. 683.

[35] [1907] 2 K.B. 33.

[36] 4 & 5 Geo. 5, c. 59; s.102 of the Bankruptcy (Scotland) Act 1913 (3 & 4 Geo. 5, c. 20), was to the same effect.

[37] As to whether the provision was applicable where the publisher had a mere licence, see *Henham* v. *Alston Rivers Ltd.* [1911–16] Mac.C.C. 330, and *Copinger* (12th ed.) § 1162.

[38] *Re Health Promotion Ltd.* [1932] 1 Ch. 65.

[39] c. 65.

[40] c. 45.

[41] Sched. 11, para. 15.

[42] *Simms* v. *Marryat* (1851) 17 Q.B. 281.

[43] See *Booth* v. *Richards* [1905–10] Mac.C.C. 284. Such contracts would also be brought to an end by the death of one of the parties; see McCardie J. in *Messager* v. *British Broadcasting Co. Ltd.* [1927] 2 K.B. 543 at 554, to the effect that a licence to a theatrical producer terminated with the death of the producer. The decision was overruled by the House of Lords [1929] A.C. 151, on the ground that the document in issue was an assignment and not a licence. See *Hales* v. *T. Fisher Unwin Ltd.* [1923–28] Mac.C.C. 31 for an application of this principle where the publishers were a limited company.

contract is of a personal nature. Thus, where a publishing agreement provided that the publishers should incur the expenses of publication, were to fix the price and decide on how the book should be published, and had the right to call on the author to prepare a new edition, with the author being entitled to a share of the profits after repayment of the expenses of publication, the Court held that such an agreement was a personal contract with the author, not an assignment of the copyright, and that consequently the benefit of such agreement could not be assigned by the publishers.[44]

Assignability where publishers a limited company. The same principles have been held to apply in a case where the publishers were a limited company, and the proposed assignment was to be made by a receiver and manager of the company appointed in a debenture-holder's action. The court declined to accede to the view that a distinction ought to be drawn between a limited company and an individual publisher, and considered that an author might repose confidence in a company, notwithstanding that the constitution of the company might alter and its officers might be changed at any time.[45]   **15–12**

Assignability where publishers to pay a fixed sum. If, on the other hand, the publisher is under an obligation to pay to the author a definite sum of money for the privilege of publishing his work, it seems probable that the publisher would have the right, in the absence of express provision, to assign the benefit of the agreement, though the literary interests of the author might possibly be affected to some extent, yet the change of publisher could not, at least directly, cause him any pecuniary injury.   **15–13**

How to distinguish assignment and licence as a matter of construction. It will have been seen, from the foregoing, that it is of great importance to distinguish between an assignment and a licence. But it is often not easy to make this distinction, as a matter of construction of the words used in agreements between authors and publishers.[46] Thus, in the case of *Sweet* v. *Cater*,[47] the agreement, after reciting that the author had prepared a tenth edition of his work, which the publisher desired to purchase, and that it had been agreed that a certain printer should print a given number of copies, and the publisher should pay to the author for the said 10th edition a certain sum, went on to direct that the work should be in a given number of volumes, and should be sold to the public for a given price. It   **15–14**

---

[44] *Stevens* v. *Benning* (1855) 1 K. & J. 168, see in particular *per* Wood V.-C. at 174; affirmed 6 D.M. & G. 223; *Reade* v. *Bentley* (1858) 3 K. & J. 271; *Hole* v. *Bradbury* (1879) 12 Ch.D. 886.

[45] *Griffith* v. *Tower Publishing Co. Ltd.* [1897] 1 Ch. 21; *Hales* v. *T. Fisher Unwin Ltd.* [1923–28] Mac.C.C. 31. See also, where the publishers were a partnership, *Hole* v. *Bradbury* (1879) 12 Ch.D. 886; and *Sampson Low, Marston & Co. Ltd.* v. *Duckworth & Co.* [1923–28] Mac.C.C. 205, in which Russell J. held that the benefit of an exclusive publishing licence extended to the partnership as it existed from time to time during the term of the copyright, but not to a limited company in which the partnership assets became vested, but which otherwise had nothing to do with the former partnership.

[46] See, for example, *Western Front Ltd.* v. *Vestron Inc.* [1987] F.S.R. 66 at 75–76; and see § 5–10 *et seq.*, *ante*.

[47] (1841) 11 Sim. 572

was objected that the plaintiff, the publisher, was not, under this agreement, the proprietor of the copyright within the meaning of section 4 of the Copyright Act 1814,[48] but a mere licensee to sell a given number of copies. The Court overruled the objection, holding that the copyright was equitably vested in the purchaser until the whole edition referred to in the contract was sold, on the ground that the contract was obligatory on both parties, that the plaintiff was bound to sell, and, therefore, the author was bound to abstain from doing anything which would interfere with the sale. The Court, moreover, was of the opinion that the equitable right to the copyright endured until the number of copies fixed by the terms of the agreement had been exhausted.

15–15   **Presumption against assignment.** But wherever there are continuing obligations on the part of the publisher—for instance, the payment of royalties to the author—the tendency of the courts is to construe the agreement as conferring upon the publisher a conditional licence to publish, rather than as giving him an equitable title to the copyright. Thus, in *Re Jude's Musical Compositions*,[49] the plaintiff was a proprietor of the copyright in a series of musical compositions called "Music and the Higher Life." In the year 1900 the defendant company, through their managing director, agreed, in consideration of the plaintiff giving to the company "the sole and exclusive right of printing and publishing" this series in volume form, first, to bear the whole cost of printing and issuing the volume, secondly, to pay the plaintiff 6d. on every copy sold, and thirdly, to supply the plaintiff with such copies as he should require at 1s. 6d. per copy, such copies not to be liable to the royalty of 6d. It was held by the Court of Appeal, affirming Kekewich J.,[50] that this was a mere publishing agreement and not an assignment of copyright. The Court of Appeal based their decision largely upon the fact that the defendants were only to be at liberty to publish the musical compositions in "volume form," but Kekewich J. appears to have thought that the fact that the defendants were to be under continuing obligations to the plaintiff was evidence of an intention not to assign the copyright. This view was supported by the case of *Stevens* v. *Benning*,[51] where Page Wood V.-C. accepted that an agreement whereby the publishers had the right of printing and publishing the author's work, so long as they performed certain conditions, was very different from one whereby an author agreed that certain persons should have the sole power of printing and publishing his work for all time, and considered that the latter would, but the former would not, be a disposal of the copyright. There may, however, be other indications in the publishing agreement which suggest that an assignment of copyright is intended, for example, where it provides that the publishers are to sue in respect of infringements of copyright of the published work.[52]

---

[48] 54 Geo. 3, c. 156.
[49] [1907] 1 Ch. 651.
[50] [1906] 2 Ch. 595.
[51] (1855) 1 K. & J. 168, aff. 6 D.M. & G. 223; see also *Sampson Low, Marston & Co. Ltd.* v. *Duckworth & Co.* [1923–28] Mac.C.C. 205.
[52] See *Macdonald (E.) Ltd.* v. *Eyles* [1921] 1 Ch. 631, where such a term was included in the agreement giving an option to publish being considered by the court.

The distinction between an assignment and a licence was further con- **15–16**
sidered by the House of Lords in the case of *Messager* v. *British Broadcasting
Co. Ltd.*[53] in connection with an agreement regarding dramatic rights. In
that case clause 1 of the agreement provided: "The licensors hereby grant
to the licensee the sole and exclusive right of representing or performing
the play in the United Kingdom." This was held to be in plain terms an
assignment of the performing right the effect of which was not curtailed
merely because of the use of the words "licensors" and "licensee" or
because payment was to be made on a royalty basis. In arriving at this
decision weight was given to the fact that the document contained a provision that in certain events the rights should "revert to and become again
the absolute property of the licensors." In *Chaplin* v. *Leslie Frewin (Publishers) Ltd.*[54] the Court of Appeal held that the words "the publishers shall
during the legal term of the copyright have the exclusive right of producing, publishing and selling the said work," constituted an assignment.
Danckwerts L.J. said[55] that the use of the word "assigns" in other clauses
and the absence of an express provision for reverter did not affect the
matter. It would, he thought, be reasonable to imply a reverter where
necessary. He also said that, even if the words "grant" or "assign" were
not used, the intention to assign might appear from the context.

Again, in *Barstow* v. *Terry*[56] a provision that, on certain conditions, "the **15–17**
entire rights for the United Kingdom, etc., in the play become theirs
inalienably and they shall present it when and where they will within the
countries aforesaid paying fees on the following scale," was held an
assignment of the entire performing rights in the play. In *Jonathan Cape
Ltd.* v. *Consolidated Press Ltd.*[57] an agreement whereby the author granted
to publishers, their successors and assigns the exclusive right to print and
publish an original work or any part or abridgment thereof, in volume
form, during the legal term of unrestricted copyright in the English
language, throughout the British Commonwealth, on royalty terms, was
held to be an assignment of part of the copyright in the work to the publishers. It was also held in this case that it was an infringement of that part
of the copyright consisting of the right to publish in volume form to publish substantially the whole of the work in a single issue of a magazine, and
that it was immaterial that it was not published in the form of an object
with thick cardboard sides and back and merely had a paper cover.[58]
It seems to follow, from these decisions, that the only safe course to
adopt, where a licence only is intended, is to say expressly "by way of

---

[53] [1929] A.C. 151; see also *Canadian Performing Right Society* v. *Famous Players Canadian Corpn.
Ltd.* (1927) 60 Ont.L.R. 280, 614; [1929] A.C. 456.
[54] [1966] Ch. 71; compare *Frisby* v. *British Broadcasting Corporation* [1967] Ch. 932 where the
agreement was held to be a licence: see also *Re "Clinical Obstetrics"* [1905–10] Mac.C.C.
176; *Neilson* v. *Horniman* [1905–10] Mac.C.C. 234; *Booth* v. *Richards* [1905–10] Mac.C.C.
284 and *C.I.R.* v. *Longmans Green & Co. Ltd.* [1928–35] Mac.C.C. 345.
[55] [1966] Ch. at 94.
[56] [1924] 2 Ch. 316.
[57] [1954] 1 W.L.R. 1313.
[58] The meaning of the expressions "volume form" and "serial form" were considered in this
case; see *Heinemann* v. *Smart Set Publishing Co.* [1905–10] Mac.C.C. 221 as to the meaning of
"serial rights" and "magazine rights."

licence only" or to use words to that effect. Such words may not be conclusive in themselves as to the nature of the agreement made between the parties, if the other terms as a whole indicate that the reality is otherwise.[59] The terminology used by the parties is, however, one factor which the court could not properly ignore in construing the agreement.[60]

C. *Common forms of formal publishing agreements*

15–18   Formal agreement: common forms of publishing arrangements. Agreements between authors and publishers fall commonly into four classes:

> (i)   outright disposals of copyright, whether for a fixed sum or on royalty terms[61];
>
> (ii) licences for a period on royalty terms[62];
>
> (iii) profit-sharing agreements[63]; and
>
> (iv) publication on commission.[64]

15–19   Agreements for outright disposal of copyright. The consequences for the author of making an outright disposal of his copyright in consideration of a receiving royalties have been discussed above.[65] Where copyright is sold for a single payment, the matter is relatively simple because the rights of the parties are concluded at once.

If the terms of the arrangement between the author and the publisher are that the copyright in the work is to belong to the publisher (whether upon payment of a fixed sum or royalties) an assignment in writing of the copyright by the author to the publisher should be made, even though the work has been written to the order of the publisher, since unless the relationship of employer and employee exists between the publisher and the author, the copyright will vest, in the first instance, in the author.[66]

It should be remembered that under the 1988 Act,[67] an assignment in writing of the copyright in a work not yet created will operate to vest the copyright in the work in the assignee as soon as the work comes into existence and without further assurance. However, this provision only operates if, on the coming into existence of the copyright, the assignee would

---

[59] See for example on the employee/self-employed subcontractor question, *Ferguson* v. *Dawson & Partners* [1976] 1 W.L.R. 1213 (C.A.).

[60] See for example on the lease/licence question, *Street* v. *Mountford* [1985] A.C. 809 and *A.G. Securities* v. *Vaughan* [1990] 1 A.C. 417 (in particular *per* Ld. Templeman at 463H); and see *Massey* v. *Crown Life Insurance Co.* [1978] 1 W.L.R. 676 (C.A.) as to the ability of the parties to stipulate what the legal situation between them shall be.

[61] See § 15–19, *post.*

[62] See § 15–20, *post.*

[63] See § 15–21 *et seq., post.*

[64] See § 15–24, *post.*

[65] See § 15–4, *et seq., ante.*

[66] C.D.P.A. 1988, ss.11(1) and (2) and see Chap. 4, *ante.* As to what would amount to an assignment, see § 5–10 *ante.* If no assignment has been executed, however, the publisher may have equitable rights, see § 4–67, *ante.*

[67] C.D.P.A. 1988, s.91, re-enacting in similar terms the provision to such effect first introduced in s.37 of the 1956 Act.

be entitled as against all other persons to require the copyright to be vested in him.[68] Consequently, if an author has made an agreement with one publisher to assign the copyright in his next book to that publisher, and subsequently, when about to write that book, he agrees to assign the copyright in it to a second publisher, the copyright will, upon the book being written, vest in the first publisher and not in the second publisher. Both agreements will operate as agreements only until the work is in fact created, so that their priority will depend merely upon the dates of the respective agreements and be unaffected by any question of notice.[69]

If an author is employed to write for a fixed payment, the employer may not be entitled to complain because the result is unsatisfactory where he has agreed to accept the product of the skill and taste of the author.[70]

After an author has parted with the copyright in a book he is not at liberty to reproduce substantially the same matter in another work. In the absence of any special agreement, the second publication would be an infringement of the copyright in the first.[71]

An outright disposal of copyright by an author to a publisher places the publisher under no obligation, in the absence of express agreement, to publish the work, notwithstanding that the author may thereby fail to acquire additional reputation.[72]

Agreements conferring licences. The advisability in the case of a   **15–20** royalty agreement, from the point of view of the author, of securing that a licence only is granted has already been discussed.[73]

If the royalty payable to the author is a certain proportion of the price of the work, the agreement should fix a minimum price at which the work is to be sold,[74] which may be a "long" price, enabling a discount to be allowed to the general public, or a "net" price, allowing no such discount. The royalty payable to the author will, generally, be calculated upon the retail price at which copies of the work are supplied to the "trade."[75]

Profit-sharing agreement. An agreement between author and publisher   **15–21** to the effect that the former shall contribute the manuscript, and the latter shall, in the first place, defray the cost of the bringing out of the work, and repay himself out of the proceeds of the sale, and that the net profits shall be divided, generally creates a profit-sharing agreement in the nature of a partnership in the sale of the work, though not in the copyright. It is prob-

---

[68] The words "apart from this sub-section" previously contained in s.37(1) of the 1956 Act have been omitted in s.91(1) of the 1988 Act, but, it is thought, without altering the effect of the sub-section.

[69] See also, as to the position under an option to publish an author's next work, *Macdonald (E.) Ltd.* v. *Eyles* [1921] 1 Ch. 631.

[70] *Ellis* v. *British Filmcraft Productions Ltd.* [1928–35] Mac.C.C. 51.

[71] *Colburn* v. *Simms* (1843) 2 Hare 543; see as to artistic works C.D.P.A. 1988, s.64.

[72] See *Nichols* v. *The Amalgamated Press* [1905–10] Mac.C.C. 166; and *Hole* v. *Bradbury* [1879] 12 Ch.D. 886 at 895.

[73] See § 15–4, *ante*.

[74] As to price maintenance agreements and fixing of minimum prices by suppliers, see § 15–47, *post*.

[75] If the book is published in different bindings this must be taken into consideration in the agreement. Royalties are not usually paid on press or other free copies. As to an author's right to royalties on remainder sales see *Farmer* v. *Grant Richards* [1901–04] Mac.C.C. 78.

able, however, that the author would not be liable for paper and printing supplied where the entire risk is taken by the publisher, and no credit is given to the author.[76]

15–22   **Whether a joint venture is terminable by notice.** The true relationship between author and publisher under a profit-sharing agreement was discussed in *Reade* v. *Bentley*,[77] in which it was held that the relationship was in the nature of a joint venture, and was more than one of simple agency, since a mere agent does not share in the risk of an undertaking, whereas the publisher under such an arrangement undertook the whole expense and risk of publishing the work. In considering whether such a joint venture could be terminated, Wood V.-C., commenting that the only obligation on the publisher was to publish a single edition, held that it was terminable by the author on reasonable notice, that is as to future editions which the publisher had not yet commenced publishing and in respect of which the publisher had incurred no expense.[78]

15–23   **Profit-sharing creates a fiduciary relationship.** A profit-sharing agreement between an author and a publisher establishes a fiduciary relationship between the parties, and the author is entitled to an account from the publisher.[79] For this purpose the publisher must produce all books and documents necessary for the proper vouching of the accounts; he is not entitled to charge the author at a higher rate for the expenses of printing, paper, etc., than he himself actually pays, and must give the author the benefit of all trade commissions and discounts.[80] Where the author may terminate the contract at the end of each edition the damages recoverable by an author against a publisher are limited to the profits which he would have received from one reasonable edition.[81]

15–24   **Works published on commission.** Where an author is prepared to run the entire risk of the publication of a work, he usually employs a publisher to publish and sell the work on his behalf at a fixed commission.[82] In this case the publisher is simply agent for the author, and the entire liability for the expenses of printing and publishing the work falls upon the latter; but he receives the gross proceeds of sales, less the publisher's commission. It is, however, a well-known practice of publishers, in accounting for sales, to reckon "thirteen copies as twelve" or "twenty-five copies as twenty-four," and it should be made clear in the agreement whether this practice is intended to apply as between the parties. It should further be made clear whether the particular publisher is to have the exclusive right

---

[76] See *Gardiner* v. *Childs* (1837) 8 C. & P. 345.

[77] (1858) 4 K. & J. 656.

[78] *Ibid.* at 664 to 669. *cf. Holland* v. *Methuen & Co. Ltd.* [1928–35] Mac.C.C. 247, where in a case of a royalty agreement and not a profit-sharing agreement, it was held that there was no right to determine.

[79] *Barry* v. *Stevens* (1862) 31 Beav. 258.

[80] Such was the opinion of counsel in the year 1893, instructed on behalf of the Society of Authors.

[81] *Abrahams* v. *Reiach Ltd.* [1922] 1 K.B. 477.

[82] See *Colles* v. *Maugham* [1905–10] Mac.C.C. 267 as to a literary agent's entitlement to commission.

of publication, or whether the author is to be at liberty to make similar contracts with other publishers.[83]

D. *Matters to be considered in drafting publishing agreements*

Drafting of publishing agreements. Every well-drafted agreement   **15–25**
between an author and a publisher should clearly state what are the precise rights which the publisher is to acquire. As has been seen,[84] copyright under the 1988 Act is divisible as to time and classes of acts. Is the agreement to include all translation rights, abridgment rights, selection rights, dramatisation rights, film rights, television rights, and so on, or are these to be reserved to the author? Is the publisher to have foreign rights as well as United Kingdom rights? In the case of musical and dramatic works, is the publisher to have the performing right and the right to authorise reproduction by records or other mechanical instruments? Has the Performing Right Society Limited any rights? Does the author retain film rights? In the case of music a distinction may be made between use of the music as background or incidental music for a film and use as an essential part of a dramatico-musical work. In the case of novels intended to be published in "serial form" in magazines, is the right of publication in "volume form" included, or is the author to be left free to arrange for "volume form" publication independently?[85] The serial publisher may require the right to serialise before any "volume form" publication, but in such case some time limit should be required. In the case of pictures, is the publisher to have the right of reproduction by all processes, or only by photography, engraving, lithography, or some other process, and is the original to become the property of the publisher or to be returnable within any, and, if so, what, time to the artist? In whom is the secondary copyright in the negative or plate to be vested? All these are points which should be made clear upon the face of the agreement. If, again, the publisher is to have the right to publish only a single edition of a work, this should be stated, and the number of copies of which the edition is to consist should be declared, for otherwise a publisher might, if so disposed, print 20,000 as one edition.[86]

Construction of the word "edition." The meaning of the word "edi-   **15–26**
tion," and the construction to be placed upon it, were fully discussed in *Reade* v. *Bentley*.[87] It was argued that where a work has once been stereotyped, the term "edition" was no longer applicable; and that when a work is published in what are called "thousands," 20,000 or 30,000 being circulated, each 1,000 could not properly be called an "edition." Wood V.-C., however, thought that not merely in point of etymology, but having

---

[83] *Abrahams* v. *Reiach Ltd.*, *supra.*

[84] *Ante*, § 5–14 *et seq.*

[85] The meaning of the expressions "volume form" and "serial form" was considered in *Jonathan Cape Ltd.* v. *Consolidated Press Ltd.* [1954] 1 W.L.R. 1313; see *Heineman* v. *Smart Set Publishing Co.* [1905–10] Mac.C.C. 221 as to the meaning of "serial rights" and "magazine rights."

[86] *Per* Wood V.-C. in *Reade* v. *Bentley* (1858) 4 K. & J. 656 at 667; *Sweet* v. *Cater* (1841) 11 Sim. 572; *Stevens* v. *Benning* (1855) 1 K. & J. 168; *Benning* v. *Dove* (1831) 5 C. & P. 427.

[87] (1858) 4 K. & J. 656.

regard to what actually takes place in the publication of any work, an "edition" of a work was the putting of it forth before the public, and if this were done in batches at successive periods, each successive batch was a new edition; and the question whether the individual copies had been printed by means of movable type or by stereotype did not seem to him to be material. If movable type were used, the type having been broken up, the new edition was prepared by setting up the type afresh, printing afresh, advertising afresh, and repeating all the other necessary steps to obtain a new circulation of the work. In that case the contemplated break between the two editions was more complete, because, until the type was again set up, nothing further could be done. It made no substantial difference as regards the meaning of the term "edition," whether the new "thousand" had been printed by a resetting of movable type, or by stereotype, or whether they had been printed at the same time with the former thousand or subsequently. A new "edition" is published whenever, having in his storehouse a certain number of copies, the publisher issues a fresh batch of them to the public. This, according to the practice of the trade, is done, as is well known, periodically. And if, after printing 20,000 copies, a publisher should think it expedient, for the purpose of keeping up the price of the work, to issue them in batches of a thousand at a time, keeping the rest under lock and key, each successive issue would be a new "edition" in every sense of the word.[88]

15–27 **Terms as to number of copies.** Where the agreement is for the exclusive publication of a specified number of copies, that number only can be printed and sold, and, until their sale, the author cannot revoke the authority given to the publishers, or himself publish the work.[89]

A term that the publishers shall publish a second edition, if demanded by the public, and print as many copies as they can sell, gives the publishers the right, when such demand arises, to publish and sell as many copies as can properly be considered to belong to that edition, and to prevent the author, or any other person, from publishing until such copies have been sold.[90]

If the agreement is silent as to the number of copies to be published, the publisher must publish such a number as is reasonable in all the circumstances.[91]

15–28 **Terms as to style of publication.** The publisher is bound to observe the terms of the contract between himself and the author as to the manner and style of the publication,[92] and the price at which it shall be issued to the

---

[88] *Per* Wood V.-C., in *Reade* v. *Bentley* (1858) 4 K. & J. 656 at 666, 667. See *Blackwood (R.)* v. *Brewster (D).* (1860) 23 Sess.Cas. (2nd Ser.) 142. In this case it was held that an editor, under an agreement that he should prepare every new edition of a work, and should receive a certain sum for his services, is not entitled to superintend, or to claim payment for, the reprinting of a part of the work to replace copies destroyed by fire. The copies reprinted under such circumstances do not form a new edition, but go to replace the part of the edition destroyed.

[89] *Reade* v. *Bentley* (1858) 3 K. & J. 271; (1858) 4 K. & J. 656.

[90] *Pulte* v. *Derby* (1852) 20 Fed.Cas. 51.

[91] *Abrahams* v. *Reiach Ltd.* [1922] 1 K.B. 477.

[92] *Benning* v. *Dove* (1831) 5 C. & P. 427.

public, but if the price at which the work is to be sold is not fixed by the agreement, or otherwise arranged by the author and publisher, the latter is the proper person to determine the same.[93] At the same time, he would not be permitted to fix upon a style, or sell at a price, which would be clearly injurious, either to the literary reputation, or the pecuniary interests of the author, without his consent. The writer of a signed article is entitled to complain of alteration in the text made without his consent.[94]

Implication as to the number of editions. When neither the time during which the publication is to last, nor the number of editions or copies to be published, is specified, the publisher is not bound to publish more than the first edition; and the author, by giving proper notice, may end the contract and prevent the publication of any further editions.[95] But the publisher is at liberty to continue publishing successive editions on the terms of the contract until the receipt of such notice; and the author is not entitled to restrain the publication or sale of any edition on which the publisher has incurred expenses before receiving notice to end the agreement.[96]　　**15–29**

Warranty on sale of copyright. Where the executor and son of the deceased author, in reply to an offer from a publishing house relating to one of his father's works, replied that he would be happy to treat with them "respecting the copyright" in it; and, in another letter, said he had accepted their offer "for the exclusive right of publishing it," and gave a receipt for the money paid "for permission to publish the work so long as the copyright may endure; that right to be exclusively their own for ten years from this date," it was held that this amounted to an express warranty of title, and an equitable assignment of the copyright having, unknown to the executor, been previously made to another publisher, the executor was held liable to an action for breach of the warranty.[97]　　**15–30**

Assignment comprising world rights. In *Campbell Connelly & Co. Ltd.* v. *Noble*[98] Wilberforce J. had to consider the American law of renewal copyright. He was required to construe a purely English contract assigning the full copyright for all countries for the period of copyright as far as it was assignable by law, together with all rights therein which the author then had or might thereafter become entitled to. Notwithstanding American authorities to the effect that American renewal copyright did not pass unless expressly mentioned the learned judge held that the assignee under the English contract had become entitled to the renewal right. The Ameri-　　**15–31**

---

[93] *Benning* v. *Dove*, *supra*; *Abrahams* v. *Reiach Ltd.* [1922] 1 K.B. 477.
[94] *Joseph* v. *National Magazine Co. Ltd.* [1959] Ch. 14.
[95] *Reade* v. *Bentley* (1858) 3 K. & J. 271; 4 K. & J. 656; *Warne* v. *Routledge* (1874) L.R. 18 Eq. 497. In this last case it was held that no agreement could be implied on the part of the author not to bring out a second edition until all the first edition was sold. See, however, *Holland* v. *Methuen & Co. Ltd.* [1928–35] Mac.C.C. 247.
[96] *Reade* v. *Bentley*, *supra*.
[97] *Simms* v. *Marryat* (1851) 17 Q.B. 281.
[98] [1963] 1 W.L.R. 252. For the converse case see *Redwood Music Ltd.* v. *Francis, Day & Hunter Ltd.* [1978] R.P.C. 429 at 458; [1979] R.P.C. 385 at 403 (C.A.). See also *Western Front Ltd.* v. *Vestron Inc.* [1987] F.S.R. 66, at 75–76.

can decisions were decisions as to the construction and effect of American contracts. He was entitled to look at American law to ascertain the nature of the renewal right, but not to enable him to construe the assignment, which was a matter of English law.

15–32 **Screen credit.** Where a licence is granted to use a work as part of a film, there is an implied term that credit for the work will not be given to some other person in presenting and advertising the film and to do so is an infringement of copyright in the work entitling the author to recover damages.[99] Indeed, an author's remedy in such a case will usually be confined to damages after the event, unless he is in a position to seek an interlocutory injunction against distribution and exhibition of the film in which he alleges his work is wrongly credited at an early enough stage in the film's production for the principles governing the grant of interlocutory injunctions[1] to be in his favour.[2]

15–33 **Failure to supply work.** If an author agrees in writing to supply a bookseller or publisher with a manuscript of a work to be printed by the latter, an action for damages can be maintained for refusing to furnish the same,[3] and the publisher can recover as damages any outlay made in reliance on the contract and the estimated loss of profit,[4] provided the work is not one which, if published, would be libellous,[5] or would subject the author to punishment.[6]

If an author undertakes to compose a work and dies before completing it, his executors or administrators are discharged from the contract, for the undertaking was merely personal in its nature, and, by the intervention of the contractor's death, has become impossible to be performed.[7] And if an author becomes bankrupt his trustee has no power to compel him to complete the work.[8]

Where a work called the "Elements of Mechanical Philosophy" was published in parts, the agreement between the author and publisher being that each part should be paid for when issued, and after the publication of a complete part the progress of the work was interrupted by the death of the author, it was held that the representatives of the deceased author were entitled to payment of the stipulated price of the published part.[9]

---

[99] *Miller* v. *Cecil Film Ltd.* (1937) 53 T.L.R. 544; [1937] 2 All E.R. 464; and see § 15–35 and § 8–152, *ante, post* and *Tolnay* v. *Criterion Film Productions Ltd.* [1936] 2 All E.R. 1625.

[1] As to which see § 11–30 *et seq., ante.*

[2] See as to a case where an artiste unsuccessfully sought to prevent the distribution and exhibition of a film in which she alleged she was entitled to a particular screen credit in respect of the title song: *S.V.B. Ltd.* v. *Eon Productions Ltd., The Times,* November 22, 1965. See now, as to the right to be identified, § 22–8, *post.*

[3] *Gale* v. *Leckie* (1817) 2 Stark.N.P. 107. The Court of Chancery, however, could not compel him to write; see § 15–34, *post.*

[4] *Clarke* v. *Price* (1819) Wils.C.R. 157.

[5] *Lyne* v. *Sampson, Low, The Times,* February 17, 1873.

[6] *Gale* v. *Leckie, supra.*

[7] *Marshall* v. *Broadhurst* (1831) 1 Tyrwh. 348 at 350; *Cooke* v. *Colcraft* (1773) 2 W. Blackstone 856. But it may be that nonetheless, if the author has assigned the copyright in the work, the copyright in the completed part may pass to the publisher.

[8] *Gibson* v. *Carruthers* (1842) 8 M. & W. 343.

[9] *Constable (A.) & Co.* v. *Robison's Trustees* (1808) 14 Fac.Dec. 166.

Specific performance. A court of equity will not decree specific perfor- **15–34** mance of an agreement to write a book. It has no power to go so far, and were it capable of making such an order, there would be no means of enforcing it.[10]

On the other hand, while a publishing agreement remains completely unperformed, it may be impracticable for the court to decree specific performance by the publisher of his agreement to publish, yet, in a case where the order could be enforced without practical difficulty, such a decree may be made. Thus, in the case of *Barrow* v. *Chappell & Co. Ltd.*[11] where the plaintiff claimed specific performance of an oral contract made with the defendant company, that the defendant company should publish in a certain journal a musical work composed by the plaintiff, Danckwerts J. felt able to make an order for specific performance against the publishers on the basis that the plaintiff had fully performed everything required on his part, and damages for failure to publish would be difficult to assess and not an adequate remedy. In *Joseph* v. *National Magazine Co. Ltd.*[12] Harman J. distinguished the former case. He said the court could not order specific performance of an agreement to publish where the exact terms of the subject-matter to be published had never been agreed.

Damages for failure to publish by agreed date. In the *Barrow* case, **15–35** *supra*, the Judge made an order for payment by the publishers of damages in respect of delay in publication, having found as a fact that the contract was a contract to publish in November 1949, or within a reasonable time thereafter, and that this contract had been broken.[13] In another case[14] the Court of Appeal awarded to an author damages against a publisher for failure to publish by an agreed date. The damages were based upon an estimate of what the plaintiff would have got if the defendants had carried out their bargain and the court left open the question whether, in an appropriate case, the plaintiff might also have recovered some damages for loss of publicity. In *Joseph* v. *National Magazine Co. Ltd.*,[15] damages were assessed on the loss to the plaintiff as an expert in jade of the enhancement of his reputation which would have resulted from the publication.

---

[10] *Clarke* v. *Price* (1819) Wils.C.R. 157: see *Page One Records Ltd.* v. *Britton* [1968] 1 W.L.R. 157 and *Denmark Productions* v. *Boscobel Productions Ltd.* [1969] 1 Q.B. 699. But specific performance of an agreement to assign a copyright may be decreed: *Thombleson* v. *Black* (1837) 1 Jur. 198; and see *Macdonald (E.) Ltd.* v. *Eyles* [1921] 1 Ch. 631 at 638 where Peterson J. construed the author's agreement in that case, not as a contract of personal service, but as a contract to sell the products of the author's labour or industry, of which specific performance could be awarded in the form of an injunction to prevent the author disposing of the work in breach of that agreement; see also *Transatlantic Records Ltd.* v. *Bulltown Ltd.* [1980] C.A. Transcript 164; *cf. Warren* v. *Mendy* [1989] 1 W.L.R. 853.
[11] [1976] R.P.C. 355 (decided in 1951).
[12] [1959] Ch. 14.
[13] See *White* v. *Constable & Co.* [1901–04] Mac.C.C. 2; and see *Planché* v. *Colburn* (1831) 8 Bing. 14 as to an author's right to claim *quantum meruit* for work done when publication is abandoned.
[14] *Goffin* v. *Staples & Staples Ltd.* [1946–47] Mac.C.C. 1. See also *Abrahams* v. *Reiach Ltd.* [1922] 1 K.B. 477.
[15] [1959] 1 Ch. 14; and see *Tolnay* v. *Criterion Film Productions Ltd.* [1936] 2 All E.R. 1625, as to damages being awarded for deprivation of a screen credit.

15–36 **Purchaser of copyright not bound to publish.** As stated above,[16] where the copyright in a work is sold outright, and there is no express agreement to publish the same, the proprietor may decline to publish, so that an author should expressly make the publication by the purchaser part of the agreement. But where there is an agreement to publish, without stating any date of publication, an undertaking to publish within a reasonable time will be implied.[17]

15–37 **Stock in hand.** The transfer of the material object does not, even in the case of a picture, prima facie operate to transfer the copyright.[18] On the other hand the right of selling the material object is not part of the copyright conferred upon an author by the 1988 Act. Copyright is infringed by reproduction of a work, not by sale of it unless such sale amounts to putting into circulation copies not previously put into circulation.[19] It is true that a person who sells a work, which to his knowledge infringes copyright, is, by section 22 of the 1988 Act, exposed to an action for infringement of copyright. But no person can, it is thought, be sued for selling a work which has been lawfully made, save only in the case of a work lawfully made in another country, but improperly imported into this country,[20] or for putting into circulation copies not previously put into circulation.[21] Prima facie, therefore, any owner of a work which is the subject of copyright may sell it to any person, and at any price that he pleases, but may not make copies of it, or authorise the making of copies of it, unless he owns the copyright in it, or is given permission by the copyright owner.

It follows that, if a publisher is given a right to publish a copyright work for a limited period, which has expired, he is entitled to sell stock which he has on hand, provided he has not manufactured in excess of the numbers permitted by his contract. Thus, in the case of *Howitt* v. *Hall*,[22] the defendants paid to the plaintiff, the author of a work entitled "A Boy's Adventures in Australia," the sum of £250, "being the purchase-money, as agreed, for the copyright and sole right of sale for four years" of that work. At the expiration of the term of four years the defendants still had a number of unsold copies of the work in stock, and these the court held they were entitled to dispose of as they pleased.[23]

On the same principles, it has been held that the assignor of the copyright in a work is equally at liberty to sell any copies of the work manufactured prior to the date of the assignment,[24] and the trustee in bankruptcy

---

[16] See § 15–19, *ante*.
[17] *Crane* v. *C. Arthur Pearson Ltd.* [1936–45] Mac.C.C. 125.
[18] See § 5–1, *ante*.
[19] C.D.P.A. 1988, ss.17, 18.
[20] *Ibid.* ss.22, 27. But see *Monckton* v. *Pathé Films Ltd.* [1914] 1 K.B. 395.
[21] C.D.P.A. 1988, s.18.
[22] (1862) 6 L.T. 348; see, in particular Wood V.-C. at 350. This could now amount to an infringement under s.18 of the 1988 Act, but it is thought that permission to sell off such stock would readily be implied.
[23] Consequently, it is usual in publishing agreements, which are liable to determination, to provide that, upon such determination, the author is to be at liberty to purchase stock undisposed of at cost price.
[24] *Taylor* v. *Pillow* (1869) L.R. 7 Eq. 418; but see the comment at n. 22, *ante*.

or liquidator of a publisher, whose publishing agreement is terminated by the bankruptcy or insolvency, can also dispose of stock.[25]

E. *Restrictions undertaken by authors*

Contractual restrictions placed on authors: early decisions. In *Morris* **15–38**
v. *Colman,*[26] where the defendant had contracted with the proprietors of the Haymarket Theatre not to write dramatic pieces for any other theatre, the Lord Chancellor maintained that such a contract was not unreasonable upon either construction, whether it was that the defendant should not write for any other theatre without the licence of the proprietors of the Haymarket Theatre, or whether it gave to those proprietors merely a right of pre-emption. And in *Macdonald (E.) Ltd.* v. *Eyles,*[27] an authoress who had agreed that a publisher should have an option to acquire the copyright in her next three books was restrained from publishing them with another publisher; and the second publisher, who had purchased the copyright in her next work with knowledge of the agreement, was also restrained.

However in *Brooke* v. *Chitty,*[28] where the defendant had undertaken not to write or edit any work upon the criminal law, except a work of which the plaintiff had purchased the copyright, and an advertisement of an edition of Burn's "Justice of the Peace," by the defendant, had appeared, Lord Brougham refused to grant an injunction, observing that the defendant was at liberty to write in his closet what he pleased, and that the court would not interfere until there was a violation of the alleged undertaking by actual printing and publication.[29]

The Schroeder case. The authority of these decisions now requires to be **15–39**
reconsidered in the light of the case of *Macaulay* v. *Schroeder Music Publishing Co. Ltd.,*[30] which finally dispelled whatever doubts may previously have existed as to the applicability of the principles established in cases on agreements in restraint of trade[31] to agreements for the exclusive provision of services for a definite period. Such agreements may also now have to be considered in the light of Article 85 of the Treaty of Rome.[32]

In *Macaulay* v. *Schroeder, supra,* the House of Lords, affirming the Court of Appeal and Plowman J., held that an agreement between a songwriter and music publishers, whereby the publishers engaged the songwriter's exclusive services for the term of the agreement was, having regard to all its terms, unduly restrictive and in unreasonable restraint of trade and

---

[25] *Lucas* v. *Moncrieff* (1905) 21 T.L.R. 683; *Re Curry (W.), etc., Co.* (1849) 12 Ir.Eq.R. 382; but see s.60 of the Bankruptcy Act 1914, (repealed) and §§ 15–8, 15–9, *ante* and see the comment at n. 22, *ante.*
[26] (1812) 18 Ves. 437.
[27] [1921] 1 Ch. 631; but any time-limit in such an option will be construed strictly: *Martin Hopkinson Ltd.* v. *Muspratt* [1928–35] Mac.C.C. 334.
[28] (1847) 2 Coop.C.C. 216; *cf. Brook* v. *Wentworth* (1795) 3 Anst. 881.
[29] But see *Barfield* v. *Nicholson* (1824) 2 Sim. & St. 1; *Sweet* v. *Archbold* (1833) 10 Bing. 133.
[30] [1974] 1 W.L.R. 1308 (H.L.). See also *Clifford Davis Management Ltd.* v. *W.E.A. Records Ltd.* [1975] 1 W.L.R. 61 (C.A.).
[31] See in particular *Esso Petroleum Co. Ltd.* v. *Harper's Garage (Stourport) Ltd.* [1968] A.C. 269.
[32] See § 14–39 *et seq., ante,* and, for example, *Re Unitel* [1978] 3 C.M.L.R. 306.

was therefore contrary to public policy and unenforceable, and that this was so, notwithstanding that the agreement was in the publishers' standard form, which was a form in common use between music publishers and songwriters.

15–40 Whilst the agreement in *Macaulay* v. *Schroeder, supra*, was in form an agreement for exclusive services, which contained an express restriction on the songwriter's ability to work for any other music publishers, with an assignment of the product of the writer's talent created during the period of the agreement,[33] it was the restriction inherent in this assignment of future works which was throughout seen as the restriction which brought the agreement within the principles applicable to agreements in restraint of trade. It follows, therefore, that these principles are equally applicable to an agreement which in form is simply an assignment of present and future works, or even of future works only, to be composed during the period of the agreement, and which contains no express restrictions on the songwriter's ability to pursue his profession, but only terms directly connected with the assignment, such as for the payment by the publishers of royalties on works published under the agreement. All such agreements and assignments have therefore to be considered in the light of the decision in *Macaulay* v. *Schroeder, supra*, What is required is a consideration of the agreement as a whole, and an assessment of the cumulative effect of the restrictions in it, whether such restrictions are expressed, or merely follow, by necessary implication, from the very fact of an assignment of future works.

15–41 It is clear that, for the purposes of deciding whether an agreement is in unreasonable restraint of trade or unduly restrictive, the agreement must be considered as at the date it is entered into.[34] The court is not therefore entitled to have regard to how the agreement has in practice been operated, nor to the motives of the party under the restraint who now wishes to be free of his bargain.[34]

15–42 In *Macaulay* v. *Schroeder, supra*, certain terms were singled out as pointing to a conclusion that the agreement in that case was unduly restrictive, and they are mentioned here, for the guidance of those seeking to avoid entering into a publishing agreement which may subsequently be found to be unduly restrictive. Of particular importance is the duration of the term of the agreement,[35] and this will include any possible extension, whether automatic in certain events, or at the option of the publishers. Then the exclusivity of the services and the extent of the works covered by the agreement must be considered. Are all outlets for the writer's creative talents covered, or only those in certain fields, leaving him free to exploit his talents in other fields? Are all the writer's past and future works

---

[33] The material terms of the agreement are set out in Lord Reid's speech: [1974] 1 W.L.R. at 1310.

[34] *Per* Lord Reid, *ibid.* at 1309H.

[35] *Per* Lord Reid, *ibid.* at 1312G. The term under consideration was for five years, extendable for a further five years on royalties payable in the first five years exceeding a stated amount.

created during the term of the agreement covered? Clearly the narrower the scope of the restriction in these two respects, the less likely that it would be found unreasonable. The right to assign the benefit of the agreement may be a relevant consideration; an unqualified right in this respect on the part of the publishers,[36] coupled with a qualified right or an express prohibition against such assignment on the part of the writer may well be unreasonable. Are the publishers under any meaningful obligation to publish and exploit any of the writer's works? If it is not practicable to provide for such an obligation,[37] it may be advisable to give the writer a right to terminate the agreement, and to call for re-assignment of the copyright in unpublished works, if the publishers do not publish his works.[38]

Looked at as a whole can it be said that the agreement could, whether **15–43** by deliberate manipulation or not, result in the sterilisation of the earning output of the writer for a considerable time?[39] If so, it will be for the party imposing the restrictions to show that they are both reasonably necessary for the protection of that party's legitimate interests, and commensurate with the benefits secured to the party restricted. This brings the test applicable to such agreements closer to the approach of Lord Diplock in *Macaulay* v. *Schroeder, supra*, who agreed with Lord Reid's analysis of the restrictive effect of the terms of the agreement, and stated that the question to be asked was the same as in all cases where the court was faced with a bargain that on its face appeared unconscionable, by reason of the unequal bargaining power of the parties, that is, "was the bargain fair?"[40] Whichever formulation was adopted, the publishers in *Macaulay* v. *Schroeder, supra*, were held not to have discharged the onus on them in the light of the restrictive nature of the agreement, to justify its restrictions, or to show that the agreement as a whole was fair. Lord Reid summarised the position as follows: "Any contract by which a person engages to give his exclusive services to another for a period necessarily involves extensive restriction during that period of the common law right to exercise any lawful activity he chooses in such manner as he thinks best. Normally the doctrine of restraint of trade has no application to such restrictions: they require no justification. But if contractual restrictions appear to be unnecessary or to be reasonably capable of enforcement in an oppressive manner, then they must be justified before they can be enforced. In the present case the respondent assigned to the appellants 'the full copyright

---

[36] As to the particular effect of such a right, see Lord Reid, *ibid*. at 1313B.

[37] As to which see Lord Reid, *ibid*. at 1313H; as to the meaning of an undertaking to use "best endeavours," see *IBM United Kingdom Ltd*. v. *Rockware Glass Ltd*. [1980] F.S.R. 335 and *Imasa Ltd*. v. *Technic Incorporated* [1981] F.S.R. 534.

[38] Such a provision would considerably mitigate the otherwise restrictive effect of the agreement: *per* Lord Reid, *ibid*. at 1314A/B; see, for a case where the reassignment provisions failed to save the agreement, *Zang Tumb Tuum Records Ltd*. v. *Johnson* [1990] 5 EIPR 175.

[39] See, for a case where this was held to be so, applying *Schroeder*, *Zang Tumb Tuum Records Ltd* v. *Johnson, supra*.

[40] *Ibid*. at 1315H–1316A. And see further as to the court's jurisdiction to refuse to enforce such bargains, *Lloyds Bank* v. *Bundy* [1975] Q.B. 326 (C.A.) and *Clifford Davis Management Ltd* v. *W.E.A. Records Ltd*. [1975] 1 W.L.R. 61; but see *National Westminster Bank plc* v. *Morgan* [1985] A.C. 686 (H.L.) disapproving Lord Denning M.R. in *Bundy, ibid*. at 339, to the effect that English courts will grant relief where there has been "inequality of bargaining power."

for the whole world' in every musical composition 'composed, created or conceived' by him alone or in collaboration with any other person during a period of five or it might be 10 years. He received no payment (apart from an initial £50) unless his work was published and the appellants need not publish unless they chose to do so. And if they did not publish he had no right to terminate the agreement or to have copyrights re-assigned to him. I need not consider whether in any circumstances it would be possible to justify such a one-sided agreement. It is sufficient to say that such evidence as there is falls far short of justification. It must therefore follow that the agreement, so far as unperformed, is unenforceable."[41]

15–44   The declaration granted in *Macaulay v. Schroeder, supra*, was that the agreement was contrary to public policy and void. However, agreements found to be in restraint of trade are usually voidable, not void and it may be that such an agreement is better described as unenforceable.[42] Clearly the writer is not bound by the agreement from the moment it is held to be in restraint of trade, and it would follow that any assignment in the agreement of the copyright in future works would not be effective to vest in the publishers the copyright in works brought into existence after the agreement is held to be in restraint of trade. What the position is regarding copyrights in works already brought into existence at that date is far from clear.[43] If such an agreement were truly void, it would follow that no assignment of such copyright would have taken place but if, as it is thought, such an agreement is merely voidable as to the future, then the position may be that the legal title to such works in existence before the agreement is avoided is effectively assigned to the assignee at law by such agreement, and notwithstanding the subsequent avoidance of the agreement remains vested in the assignee, subject to the Court ordering, in the exercise of its equitable jurisdiction, re-assignment of the copyright in such works. This question will be particularly important in the case of any such works which the publishers have already at that date exploited, either themselves, or by granting rights to others. A further unanswered problem arises in connection with any separate assignment of copyright in particular works which a songwriter engaged under such an agreement is asked by the publishers to execute. Such assignments are often taken, for no further consideration than the publishers' promise to pay royalties on the work being published, usually in the same terms as in the principal agreement. In themselves such individual assignments are clearly not within the principles applied in *Macaulay v. Schroeder, supra*, but, in that the only reason for their execution is the pre-existing obligation under the

---

[41] [1974] 1 W.L.R. 1314H.
[42] See Lord Reid, *ibid.* at 1315A/B; see also *Clifford Davis Management Ltd.* v. *W.E.A. Records Ltd.* [1975] 1 W.L.R 61 and *Zang Tumb Tuum Records Ltd. v. Johnson, supra.*
[43] The judgment of the Court of Appeal in *Schroeder*, delivered by Russell L.J. ([1974] 1 All E.R. 171 at 181f), confirmed that the assignment was ineffective as to the copyright in works not in existence at the time the agreement was avoided, but the statement that the assignment of copyright in works already brought into existence at that time remained effective (*per* Russell L.J. [1974] 1 All E.R. 171 at 181e/f) was based on a concession made to such effect by counsel for the plaintiffs. Compare the position where the agreement is set aside in equity for undue influence and breach of fiduciary duty: *O'Sullivan* v. *Management Agency and Music Ltd.* [1985] Q.B. 428 at 459 C/D.

principal agreement, if this latter agreement is subsequently found to be unenforceable, should not the same apply to any such individual assignments?[44]

Author at liberty to publish a continuation of his work. But where no such restrictions had been undertaken by the author, and the publisher had agreed with the author for an edition of a history to be written by the latter, in four volumes, and had obtained subscriptions for all that could fall within his edition, the court held that the author was at liberty to publish a continuation of the history which embraced part of the period and also much of the matter contained in the last of the four volumes.[45] **15–45**

Agreement to employ author on similar terms. An author and publisher entered into an agreement under which the author was to edit the whole of the plays of Shakespeare (to be called the *Temple Shakespeare*), and was to write an introduction, notes, and glossary for each play. The publisher was to pay the author a royalty, and the copyright was vested in the publisher. One of the clauses of the agreement was that, in the event of a cheaper or other form of edition of any of the plays being thought advisable by the publisher, it should form the subject of an agreement with the author on similar *pro rata* terms to those embodied in that agreement. Subsequently, the publisher produced a *Temple Shakespeare* for schools, with notes, introduction, and glossary written by a person other than the author. The Court held this to be breach of the publishing agreement and, on the author bringing his action, whilst refusing an injunction restraining the publication of the school edition, ordered a reference to chambers to assess the damages the plaintiff had suffered.[46] **15–46**

F. Resale Price Maintenance and EEC rules on competition

Price maintenance agreements: former law. Questions regarding price maintenance agreements in regard to the selling price of books have been raised from time to time, and, until legislation was introduced in 1956[47] which affected such price maintenance agreements, the position seems to have been as follows. The 1956 Act did not, and the 1988 Act does not, include amongst the monopolies conferred upon the copyright owner the exclusive right of selling the work,[48] and, therefore, the patent cases in which it has been held that the purchaser of a patented article is bound by any restrictions imposed by the owner of the patent with regard to user of the patented article, provided there is knowledge of the contract between **15–47**

---

[44] This was the Court's approach in *O'Sullivan* v. *Management Agency and Music Ltd., supra* at 459 C/D.

[45] *Blackie, etc., & Co.* v. *Aikman (J.)* (1827) 5 Sess.Cas. 719. As to the respective rights of a writer and publisher of a periodical to continue to publish the periodical in the old name after termination of their agreement, see *Ingram* v. *Stiff* (1859) 5 Jur. 947; *Clowes* v. *Hogg* [1870] W.N. 268; *Constable (A.) & Co.* v. *Brewster* (1825) 3 Sess.Cas. 215.

[46] *Gollancz* v. *Dent* (1903) 88 L.T. 358.

[47] Restrictive Trade Practices Act 1956, 4 & 5 Eliz. 2, c. 68.

[48] See § 15–37, *ante.*

his immediate vendor and the patent owner at the time of the purchase,[49] have no application to copyright works. The owner of a copyright work was not bound by any restrictions in regard to the use or sale of the work, unless he had contracted to observe such restrictions. If a copyright owner sold to a purchaser upon the footing that the work was not to be sold at less than a certain price, and the purchaser did so, he was liable, not for infringement of copyright, but for breach of contract.[50] Such contract, however, did not, under the ordinary law, run with the work, so that a sub-purchaser was not liable to the copyright owner for selling under the stipulated price, even though he had full knowledge of the contract between his immediate vendor and the copyright owner, unless such sub-purchaser had himself contracted to observe the stipulations as to price, because of lack of privity of contract.[51] Sometimes, as affording some additional protection to the copyright owner, an agreement was entered into by the purchaser, not only that he would not himself sell under a certain stipulated price, but that he would, on the occasion of any sub-sale, procure that the sub-purchaser should enter into a similar agreement. Such agreement was not in restraint of trade, so that an action would lie if the purchaser failed to obtain any such agreement from the sub-purchaser.[52] Even if the sub-purchaser did enter into such a contract, there would generally be no privity of contract between the copyright owner and the sub-purchaser, so that the former would have no direct right of action against the sub-purchaser for breach of the latter's contract.[53]

15–48 **Price maintenance agreements: present law.** This position was altered by the Restrictive Trade Practices Act 1956,[54] and later by the Resale Prices Act 1964.[55] The relevant provisions of these Acts are now to be found substantially re-enacted in the Restrictive Trade Practices Act 1976,[56] and the Resale Prices Act 1976.[57]

The Restrictive Trade Practices Act 1976, prohibits any collective agreement between suppliers as to the prices and conditions on which they will supply goods which is declared by the Restrictive Practices

---

[49] See *National Phonograph, etc., Ltd.* v. *Menck* [1911] A.C. 336, and the cases there cited; the position in relation to patents depends on the particular statutory rights given to the patentee, as to which see now Patents Act 1977, s.44. In America it has been held that, notwithstanding that, under the American Act, the copyright owner is given the exclusive right of vending the work, a sale in breach of a notice not to sell at less than a stated price is not an infringement of copyright: *Bobbs-Merrill Co.* v. *Straus* (1908) 210 U.S.R. 339.

[50] *Benning* v. *Dove* (1833) 5 C. & P. 427.

[51] *Taddy & Co.* v. *Sterious & Co.* [1904] 1 Ch. 354; *McGruther* v. *Pitcher* [1904] 2 Ch. 306; *Dunlop Pneumatic Tyre Co. Ltd* v. *Selfridge & Co. Ltd.* [1915] A.C. 847; *Barker* v. *Stickney* [1919] 1 K.B. 121; *cf. Lord Strathcona Steamship Co. Ltd* v. *Dominion Coal Co. Ltd.* [1926] A.C. 108, but see *Port Line Ltd.* v. *Ben Line Steamers Ltd.* [1958] 2 Q.B. 146; *Swiss Bank* v. *Lloyds Bank* [1979] Ch. 548 and *Tito* v. *Waddell* (No. 2) 1977 Ch. 106 and see §15–7, *ante*.

[52] *Elliman Sons & Co.* v. *Carrington & Sons Ltd.* [1901] 2 Ch. 275. As to agreements between manufacturers to keep up prices, see *Urmston* v. *Whitelegg Bros.* (1890) 63 L.T. 455.

[53] *Dunlop Pneumatic Tyre Co. Ltd.* v. *Selfridge & Co. Ltd.*, *supra.*

[54] 4 & 5 Eliz. 2, c. 68; as amended by the Restrictive Trade Practices Act 1968 (c. 66) and the Fair Trading Act 1973.

[55] c. 58.

[56] c. 34.

[57] c. 53.

Court to be contrary to the public interest.[58] This provision replaces the previously existing provision of the Restrictive Trade Practices Act 1956, to similar effect,[59] which had led to the Publishers' Association of the United Kingdom seeking and obtaining the declaration of the Restrictive Practices Court that the Net Book Agreement 1957, being the agreement under which most British publishers agreed to adopt certain standard sets of conditions of sale for their books to retailers, including terms as to minimum resale price, was not contrary to public policy, and that the restrictions contained in such Agreement were not therefore void under that Act.[60] This decision continues to have effect for the purposes of the Restrictive Trade Practices Act 1976.[61] Agreements for the collective enforcement of conditions as to resale prices (for example, by the refusal to supply) are, however, absolutely prohibited.[62]

The Resale Prices Act 1976 further prohibits the fixing of minimum resale prices by suppliers in their contracts with dealers,[63] except in relation to classes of goods exempted by the Court.[64] An application was successfully made under the previously existing provisions of the Resale Prices Act 1964,[65] to include books among the classes of goods so exempted.[66] This exemption continues to have effect for the purposes of the Resale Prices Act 1976.[67] The present position is therefore that an individual publisher may enforce certain conditions as to minimum prices against any retailer, including one not a party to the original sale, who acquired the books with notice of the conditions, despite the lack of privity of contract.[68] Moreover, such conditions may be enforced by an injunction restraining the defendant from reselling in breach of any such condition goods thereafter to be sold by the plaintiff, whether of the same description as the goods proved to have been resold in breach of the condition, or of any other description.[69] This seems to provide for a much wider form of injunction than would normally be granted by the court, which will usually limit the injunction to any repetition of the precise acts of which complaint has been made and proved.

EEC Rules on Competition. Terms relating to resale prices and other **15–49** terms contained in publishing agreements which are restrictions of one party's trading position, may fall within the prohibition of Article 85(1) of the Treaty of Rome, where the restriction is capable of affecting trade between Member States of the European Economic Community, and reference should be made to the discussion of the effect of the Rules on

---

[58] s.2(1)–(4).
[59] Restrictive Trade Practices Act 1956, s.20(3).
[60] *Re Net Book Agreement* 1957 [1962] 1 W.L.R. 1347.
[61] Restrictive Trade Practices Act 1976, Sched. 4.
[62] Resale Prices Act 1976, s.1(1), (2) (replacing Restrictive Trade Practices Act 1956, s.24).
[63] s.9(1).
[64] ss.14, 19.
[65] ss.1(1), 5.
[66] See *Re Net Book Reference, The Times*, March 2, 1968 and *Board of Trade Journal* May 10, 1968.
[67] Resale Prices Act 1976, Sched. 2.
[68] *Ibid.* s.26(2) (replacing Restrictive Trade Practices Act 1956, s.25(1)).
[69] *Ibid.* s.26(5) (replacing Restrictive Trade Practices Act 1956, s.25(4)).

Competition in such Treaty on the exercise of industrial property rights in Chapter 14, *ante*.[70]

2. Control of Licences by the Copyright Tribunal

A. *Introduction*

15–50   **Organisations controlling the exercise of copyright.** In most countries a development in the field of copyright has been the creation of organisations to control the exercise of copyright and in particular performing and recording rights. Such organisations either acquire copyrights from their members, or act as agents on behalf of their members to enforce copyrights. They issue licences in respect of their members' works and, in the last resort, enforce the rights of their members by legal action. From the point of view of composers of music and owners of musical copyright the system has great advantages, in that no individual composer or copyright owner can, in practice, secure adequate protection for his work, or deal with the very large number of persons and bodies wishing to exploit such works. The system also has considerable advantages, from the point of view those wishing to exploit such works, in that licences can be obtained from a single organisation, whereas, without such a system, it would be necessary to obtain individual licences from a large number of owners of copyright, and the delay and inconvenience, and the risk of exploiting such works without having obtained a licence from the person entitled to give one, would greatly add to the difficulty and expense of exploiting such works.[71] Among the principal organisations which have been established in the United Kingdom are Performing Right Society Limited (PRS), Mechanical Copyright Protection Society Limited (MCPS) and Phonographic Performance Limited (PPL). There are also equivalent organisations established in most other European countries.

15–51   **Public interest and need for public control.** The existence of such organisations is therefore to the advantage of the public in facilitating wider access by the public to such works, but it has also given rise to complaints of the abuse of what have become monopoly rights, since virtually all popular music is now controlled by such organisations. It therefore came to be felt, in a number of countries, that some measure of public control over the activities of such organisations was necessary in the public interest.[72]

15–52   **Copyright Committee 1952.** At the Brussels Copyright Conference, the United Kingdom delegation, in accepting the provisions of Article 11 of the proposed Convention, declared that H.M. Government remained free to enact such legislation as it might consider necessary in the public interest to prevent or deal with any abuse of the monopoly rights conferred

---

[70] § 14–38 *et seq., ante.*
[71] See the 1977 Copyright Committee, Cmnd. 6732, para. 390.
[72] See, as to the position of such organisations under Article 86 of the Treaty of Rome, § 14–51, *ante.*

upon owners of copyright by the law of the United Kingdom.[73] In view of this declaration it was open to the 1952 Copyright Committee, notwithstanding that it was recommending adherence to the Brussels Convention, to make proposals for the compulsory adjustment of tariffs charged by such copyright organisations. One method suggested was that of compulsory arbitration, but this did not seem wholly satisfactory, in that it was necessary to envisage not only disputes between a collecting organisation and an organisation of performers, but also cases where individual persons were aggrieved, and moreover, what was really required was some method of arriving at tariffs which would be binding not only between the parties to the reference, but also in respect of any other persons wishing to exercise similar rights. The Committee therefore proposed that a standing tribunal should be established to decide disputes between collecting organisations and would-be users of controlled works.[74] This proposal was accepted by the legislature and was embodied in sections 23 to 30 of the 1956 Act.

Performing Right Tribunal. Section 23 of the 1956 Act established the   **15–53** Performing Right Tribunal (PRT) with the jurisdiction conferred by the provisions of the 1956 Act.[75] The PRT had two principal functions.[76] The first was to confirm or vary licence schemes put into operation by organisations under which licences were to be granted to the public in certain classes of cases.[77] The second was to deal with applications by individuals who were aggrieved, either because an organisation operating a licence scheme refused to grant the individual a licence in accordance with the scheme, or because the individual claimed that there was no applicable licence scheme and the organisation refused to grant him a licence.[78] The PRT was concerned with licences dealing with only three types of right. First, the right to perform in public, broadcast or diffuse, a literary dramatic or musical work or an adaptation thereof.[79] Secondly, the right to cause a sound recording to be heard in public or to be broadcast.[80] Thirdly, the right to cause a television broadcast to be seen or heard in public.[81] The rights, therefore, covered in effect, the whole of the performing and broadcasting rights conferred by the 1956 Act, other than the right to include an artistic work in a television broadcast, the right to cause a film to be seen or heard in public or to be broadcast, and the right to re-broadcast a sound or television broadcast.

Proposals for reform. The functions of the PRT were considered by the   **15–54** 1977 Copyright Committee, which recommended that it should be given jurisdiction over a wider range of matters, including reprographic

---

[73] See *Copinger* (11th ed.), App. C §§ 1696, 1706.
[74] Cmnd. 8662, para. 210.
[75] Copyright Act 1956, ss.24 to 27A.
[76] *Ibid.* s.24(1).
[77] *Ibid.* ss.25 and 26.
[78] *Ibid.* ss.27(1) and (2) and 27A.
[79] *Ibid.* s.24(2)(*a*); a right (as to musical works and associated works) usually controlled by PRS.
[80] *Ibid.* s.24(2)(*b*); a right usually controlled by PPL.
[81] *Ibid.* s.24(2)(*c*); a right controlled by the BBC or the IBA.

licences, video recording, licences to use music on film sound-tracks, and copyright clearances where the copyright owner cannot be traced.[82] The Committee also proposed that the tribunal's name should be changed to the Copyright Tribunal, in view of the recommended increase in its jurisdiction. The White Paper generally followed these recommendations in relation to the change and name of the tribunal and the extension of its functions,[83] and also made recommendations as to the introduction of more specific criteria for the tribunal to base its decision on, and for improvements in the procedure before the tribunal. These recommendations were enacted in the 1988 Act, Chapter VIII of which establishes the Copyright Tribunal as the successor to the PRT.

B. *The Copyright Tribunal*

15–55   **The Copyright Tribunal.** Section 145 of the 1988 Act enacts that the Tribunal established under section 23 of the 1956 Act is renamed the Copyright Tribunal.[84] The Tribunal's membership has been enlarged in view of its increased jurisdiction, and is now to consist of a chairman and two deputy chairmen appointed by the Lord Chancellor, each being a barrister, advocate or solicitor of not less than seven years standing or a person who has held judicial office, and not less than two and not more than eight ordinary members appointed by the Secretary of State.[85]

15–56   **Constitution of the Copyright Tribunal.** For the purposes of any proceedings the Copyright Tribunal shall consist of a chairman (who shall be either the chairman or a deputy chairman of the Tribunal) and two or more ordinary members.[86] Decisions are arrived at by majority, with the chairman exercising a casting vote.[87] There are provisions ensuring that the Tribunal remains duly constituted where a member is unable to continue after proceedings are part heard,[88] and for the appointment of one of the ordinary members to act as chairman together with a suitably qualified person to advise on law, where it is the chairman who is unable to continue.[89]

15–57   **Jurisdiction of the Copyright Tribunal.** Following the proposals for reform discussed above,[90] the Copyright Tribunal has been given an extended jurisdiction, covering not only the functions previously carried

---

[82] Cmnd. 6732, paras. 788–790; the Committee also recommended that the Tribunal should have jurisdiction in respect of royalties payable under s.8 of the 1956 Act (assuming the statutory licence was to be retained) and over the amount of the levy on blank tape (assuming such levy was to be introduced).

[83] Cmnd. 9712 (1986) Ch. 18, broadly following proposals set out in the 1981 Green Paper, Cmnd. 8302.

[84] Proceedings pending before the PRT before August 1, 1989 will now be heard by the Copyright Tribunal, and are now subject to The Copyright Tribunal Rules 1989: see r. 55 made pursuant to C.D.P.A. 1988, Sched. 1, para. 34 § B–105, *post*.

[85] C.D.P.A. 1988, ss.145(2), (3).

[86] *Ibid.* s.148(1), derived from Copyright Act 1956, Sched. 4, para. 3.

[87] *Ibid.* s.148(2), derived from Copyright Act 1956, Sched. 4, para. 4.

[88] *Ibid.* s.148(3).

[89] *Ibid.* s.148(4) and (5).

[90] § 15–54, *ante*.

out by the PRT in relation to licence schemes and licences by licensing bodies (but now in relation to a wider variety of copyright licences), but also five further specific functions introduced by the 1988 Act and two further specific functions subsequently introduced into the 1988 Act by the Broadcasting Act 1990. The Copyright Tribunal therefore now has jurisdiction to hear and determine:

(a) references of proposed or existing licensing schemes[91];

(b) applications with respect to entitlement to a licence under a licensing scheme[92];

(c) references or applications with respect to licensing by a licensing body[93];

(d) appeals against an order by the Secretary of State as to the coverage of a licensing scheme or licence in respect of reprographic copying by an educational establishment[94];

(e) applications to settle a royalty or other sum payable for rental of a sound recording, film or computer program[95];

(f) applications to settle the terms of a copyright licence available as of right consequent on a report of the Monopolies and Mergers Commission[96];

(g) applications to give consent to the making of a recording from a previous recording of a performance on behalf of a performer who cannot be traced or who unreasonably withholds his consent[97];

(h) applications to determine the royalty or other remuneration payable to the trustees for the Hospital for Sick Children in respect of the use of the play "Peter Pan" by Sir James Matthew Barrie.[98]

(i) applications to settle the terms of payment under a compulsory licence in respect of information about a programme service[99];

(j) applications to settle the terms of payment or as to the reasonableness of any condition in relation to the use as of right of sound recordings in broadcasts or cable programme services[1];

---

[91] C.D.P.A. 1988, ss.118, 119 and 120; and see further § 15–68, *et seq., post.*

[92] *Ibid.* ss.121 and 122; and see further § 15–76, *et seq., post.*

[93] *Ibid.* ss.125, 126 and 127; and see further § 15–79, *et seq., post.*

[94] *Ibid.* s.139; and see further § 15–89, *post.*

[95] *Ibid.* s.142; and see further § 15–90, *post.*

[96] *Ibid.* s.144(4); and see further § 15–91, *post.*

[97] *Ibid.* s.190; and see further § 15–93, *post.*

[98] *Ibid.* Sch. 6, para. 5; and see further § 15–92, *post.*

[99] Broadcasting Act 1990, Sched. 17, paras. 5 and 6, introduced into Chapter III of Part I, and s.149, of the 1988 Act by the Broadcasting Act 1990, Sched. 17, para. 7(1); see further § 10–127, *et seq., ante.*

[1] C.D.P.A. 1988, ss.135D, 135E and 135F, introduced into the 1988 Act and into s.149 of the 1988 Act by amendment by the Broadcasting Act 1990, s.175(1) and (2); see further § 10–133, *et seq., ante.*

15–58   Procedure before the Copyright Tribunal. The Lord Chancellor, in the exercise of powers conferred under the 1988 Act,[2] has made certain rules regulating the procedure to be followed in respect of proceedings before the Copyright Tribunal.[3] The Chairman has also issued a Practice Direction, giving guidance on a number of procedural matters.[4] The principal aspects of the procedure before the Copyright Tribunal are discussed further below.[5] The Copyright Tribunal has statutory power to order any party to proceedings before it to pay the costs of any other party.[6]

15–59   Appeal to the Court on point of law. Under the 1956 Act[7] any question of law arising in the course of proceedings before the PRT could be referred by the PRT, at the request of any party, to the High Court[8] for decision, whether before or after the PRT gave its decision in the proceedings. The procedure was by way of case stated.[9] The legislature did not adopt this approach in the 1988 Act,[10] which makes provision for an appeal to the High Court on any point of law arising from a decision of the Copyright Tribunal.[11] Such an appeal can therefore be made only after the Copyright Tribunal has made a decision, and the Court has no power to refuse to entertain the appeal.[12] Provision is made for such appeal under The Copyright Tribunal Rules, and for suspension of the Copyright Tribunal's order pending the outcome of the appeal.[13]

15–60   Factors the Copyright Tribunal is required to take into account in all proceedings. Under the 1956 Act the PRT was required to make such orders as were reasonable in all the circumstances,[14] but the 1956 Act set out no guidance as to what was reasonable. The general requirement under the 1988 Act remains that the Copyright Tribunal should make such orders as are reasonable in all the circumstances.[15] However, the 1988 Act, whilst providing that the Copyright Tribunal has a general obli-

---

[2] C.D.P.A. 1988, s.150, derived partly from Copyright Act 1956, Sched. 4, para. 6.

[3] The Copyright Tribunal Rules 1989, S.I. 1989 No. 1129; see § B–49, *et seq., post*, based, to a large extent, on The Performing Right Tribunal Rules (as amended), made under the Copyright Act 1956; and see the Copyright Tribunal (Amendment) Rules 1991, S.I. 1991 No. 201, § B–265, *et seq., post*, amending the Rules to deal with applications to the Tribunal in relation to information about television programmes and use as of right of sound recordings in broadcasts and cable programme services.

[4] See § B–127 *et seq., post*.

[5] See § 15–94, *et seq., post*.

[6] C.D.P.A. 1988, s.151; and see r. 48 § B–98, *post*. The PRT had a similar power, rarely exercised, under Copyright Act 1956, Sched. 4, para. 5 and r. 24 of The Performing Right Tribunal Rules 1965; see *Copinger* (12th ed.), § 1781.

[7] Copyright Act 1956, s.30.

[8] In Scotland, the Court of Session.

[9] Copyright Act 1956, s.30(5), and see rr. 19 to 21 of The Performing Right Tribunal Rules 1965 (as amended), Copinger (12th ed.), §§ 1775–1778.

[10] In the light of representations made by the Council on Tribunals.

[11] C.D.P.A. 1988, s.152. There is no restriction on further appeal from the decision of the Court. A decision for these purposes includes, it would seem, an interlocutory decision.

[12] Under the 1956 Act, a case could be stated on a point of law at any time in the proceedings, and the Court could refuse to entertain the reference where the PRT refused to state a case (but see *AIRC Ltd.* v. *Phonographic Performance Ltd.* [1983] F.S.R. 637).

[13] rr. 42 to 45, The Copyright Tribunal Rules 1989, §§ B–92 to B–95, *post*.

[14] Copyright Act 1956, ss.25(6), 26(4), 27(5) and 27A(4).

[15] ss.118(3), 119(3), 120(4), 121(4), 122(3), 125(3), 126(4), 127(3), 142(2) and Sch. 6, para. 5(1).

gation in any case to have regard to all relevant considerations,[16] gives further guidance, applicable to all proceedings, as to what is reasonable by providing that the Copyright Tribunal shall, in determining what is reasonable, have regard to the availability and the terms of other schemes or licences to other persons in similar circumstances, and shall exercise its powers so as to secure that there is no unreasonable discrimination between the actual or prospective licensees making the application and licensees under alternative schemes or licences being operated or granted by the same person.[17]

Particular factors the Copyright Tribunal is required to take into account in certain proceedings. The 1988 Act also sets out a number of other particular factors, in addition to the general requirements discussed above,[18] which the Copyright Tribunal is required to take into account in proceedings dealing with specific matters.[19] In all cases the aim of the 1988 Act is to seek to maintain a fair balance between the interests of those seeking licences under licence schemes and from licensing bodies, and those whose rights in the copyright works or other subject-matter involved are affected. The relevant provisions of the 1988 Act, which are contained in sections 130 to 134, fall into three types of case: the first two are each individual situations which are singled out for special consideration, and the third comprises a number of situations each involving a subsequent copyright work which includes in it other copyright works where the licence in respect of the subsequent copyright work has been obtained (or is not required) but the licence in respect of the underlying works is itself the subject of the proceedings. **15–61**

Particular factors: **15–62**
(i) Licences for reprographic copying. Proceedings relating to the licensing for reprographic copying of published literary, dramatic, musical or artistic works or of the typographical arrangement of published editions may come before the Copyright Tribunal either under the general provisions relating to licensing schemes or to licences granted by licensing bodies,[20] or, where the party seeking the licence is an educational establishment, under the specific provisions relating to such copying by educational establishments.[21] In all such proceedings the Copyright Tribunal shall have regard to the extent of the availability of other published editions of the work, the proportion of the work to be copied and the nature of the use to which the copies are likely to be put.[22] These factors are clearly of importance not only to whether it is reasonable that a licence is not available (*e.g.* because too large a part of the work is to be photocopied

---

[16] *Ibid.* s.135.
[17] *Ibid.* s.129.
[18] See § 15–60, *ante.*
[19] The particular factors required to be taken into account by C.D.P.A. 1988, s.135G, in relation to applications in respect of the use as of right of sound recordings in broadcasts and cable programme services are discussed at § 10–139, *ante.*
[20] *Ibid.* ss.116–128; see § 15–65 *et seq., post.*
[21] *Ibid.* s.139; see § 15–89 and § 15–107, *et seq., post.*
[22] *Ibid.* s.130.

and published editions are available, or because the use to which the photocopies are to be put is damaging to the copyright owner's own commercial exploitation of his copyright), but also to what is a reasonable fee for the licence sought. This provision provides the means for the Copyright Tribunal to ensure that excessive photocopying does not become a substitute for the normal access to such works through the purchase of published editions.

15–63   Particular factors:

(ii) Licences in respect of recordings, broadcasts or cable programmes including an entertainment or event. In proceedings relating to licences for sound recordings, films, broadcasts or cable programmes which include any entertainment or other event,[23] the Copyright Tribunal shall have regard to any conditions imposed by the promoter of the entertainment or other event (other than conditions which seek to regulate the charges to be imposed in respect of licences or which relate to payment for the grant of facilities to make the recording, etc.[24]), and shall not regard the refusal or failure to grant a licence as unreasonable if it could not have been granted consistently with those conditions.[25] The situation envisaged here is analogous to those discussed under (iii) below, except that there may be no underlying work by means of the copyright in which the promoter can control the subsequent exploitation of his entertainment or event, and his only opportunity to do so is through the contract with the maker of the recording. The aim of the 1988 Act is, therefore, to ensure that the reasonable rights of the promoter of the entertainment or event to control the making of a recording of his entertainment or event and its further use, by means of contractual terms imposed on the maker of the recording, are not circumvented by the possibility of others being entitled to obtain licences from the maker to exploit the recording under the general provisions of the 1988 Act in relation to licensing schemes and licences granted by licensing bodies. Unless promoters of such entertainments and events can be assured that such conditions will be respected, they might well be unwilling to permit the recording to be made and exploited at all.

15–64   Particular factors:

(iii) Licences in respect of underlying copyright works. In these cases the aim of the 1988 Act is to ensure that any consideration already received or stipulated for by the owner of the copyright in the underlying work at the time he authorises the making and showing of the subsequent copyright work, or which he may otherwise be entitled to obtain in respect of any further use by others of that subsequent copyright work, is taken

---

[23] *I.e.* proceedings brought under the general provisions applying to licensing schemes and licences granted by licensing bodies, see § 15–65 *et seq., post.*

[24] C.D.P.A. 1988, s.132(3).

[25] *Ibid.* s.132(2); this provision is based on s.29(4) of the 1956 Act which applied to television broadcasts, and is now extended to cover sound recordings, films, cable programmes and sound broadcasts.

into account, so as to ensure, in effect, that his overall remuneration from the licensing of his work, both directly by himself and indirectly by the owner of the subsequent copyright work, is neither unreasonably high (because he is paid in respect of some uses twice), or unreasonably low (because he is not paid at all in respect of some uses).

This principle applies to proceedings relating to licences for educational establishments for the recording by them or on their behalf of broadcasts or cable programmes which include copyright works, or for the making of copies of such recordings, for educational purposes[26]; proceedings relating to licences in respect of the rental to the public of sound recordings, films or computer programs[27]; proceedings relating to licences in respect of the copyright in sound recordings, films, broadcasts or cable programmes[28]; and proceedings relating to licences in respect of works to be included in immediate re-transmissions of broadcasts or cable programmes.[29]

In the last mentioned case, there are further special provisions which apply, depending on whether the re-transmission is to be in the same area as that of the original transmission, or partly or wholly in an area outside that of the original transmission. Where the re-transmission is to be the same area as the original transmission, the Copyright Tribunal, in considering what charges, if any, should be made in respect of either transmission, must take into account any charges the copyright owner is entitled to receive in respect of the other transmission, thus preventing the copyright owner obtaining remuneration twice over in respect of the same area.[30] Where the re-transmission is to an area wholly outside the area of the original transmission, then the Copyright Tribunal must leave the further transmission out of account in considering what charges, if any, should be paid in respect of the first transmission, thus leaving the copyright owner to make his own terms with the party making the re-transmission.[31] Where there is partial overlap in the areas of the original transmission and the re-transmission, and the re-transmission occurs as a result of the statutory obligation imposed under the Cable and Broadcasting Act 1984,[32] then the Copyright Tribunal is required to ensure that the

---

[26] C.D.P.A. 1988, s.131(1) and (2); such proceedings would be brought under the general provisions applying to licensing schemes and licences granted by licensing bodies, see § 15–65 *et seq., post* and § 15–109, n. 32, *post.*

[27] C.D.P.A. 1988, s.133(1); and see further § 15–90, *post.*

[28] *Ibid.* s.133(2); such proceedings would be brought under the general provisions applying to licensing schemes and licences granted by licensing bodies, see § 15–65 *et seq., post.* Foreign broadcasts and cable transmissions may therefore be relevant where charges under U.K. licences or foreign licences have been negotiated to take account of foreign re-transmission (see as to the former position under s.28 of the 1956 Act: *Copinger* (12th ed.), § 1271).

[29] C.D.P.A. 1988, s.134; such proceedings would be brought under the general provisions applying to licensing schemes and licences granted by licensing bodies, see § 15–65 *et seq., post.* Reception and re-transmission may be a permitted act, see C.D.P.A. 1988, s.73 and § 10–122, *ante.*

[30] C.D.P.A. 1988, s.134(2).

[31] *Ibid.* s.134(3).

[32] c. 46; s.13(1).

charges payable by the party making the first transmission adequately reflect that fact.[33]

C. Control by the Copyright Tribunal of licensing schemes and licensing bodies

15–65 Introduction. The aim of the provisions establishing control by the Copyright Tribunal over licensing schemes and licences by licensing bodies is to prevent copyright owners abusing what has come to be recognised as a monopoly or near monopoly power in their dealings with those wishing to be licensed to exploit their copyright works. However, this control is only exerciseable (apart from certain other situations discussed below[34]) in a situation involving either a licensing scheme or a licensing body, as these terms are defined.[35] A copyright owner is not obliged to operate or join a licensing scheme,[36] or to agree to a licensing body exercising or administering his copyright, and in general, if he does neither and refuses to grant a licence, then such refusal is not subject to the overriding jurisdiction of the Copyright Tribunal. It is only, therefore, when a copyright owner himself chooses to operate a tariff for licences of his works, or agrees to his works being owned or administered by a collecting society acting on his behalf, that the grant and the terms of a licence affecting his works may be referred to the Copyright Tribunal.

15–66 Licensing scheme. "Licensing Scheme" is defined[37] as a scheme setting out the classes of cases in which the operator of the scheme, or the person on whose behalf he acts, is willing to grant copyright licences and the terms on which licences would be granted in those classes of cases. The term "scheme" is to include anything in the nature of a scheme, whether described as such, or as a tariff, or by any other name.[38] A "copyright licence" is a licence to do, or to authorise the doing of,[39] any of the acts restricted by copyright.[40]

---

[33] C.D.P.A. 1988, s.134(4).

[34] See § 15–88, *post.*

[35] See §§ 15–66, 15–67, *post.*

[36] But, in relation to educational recording of broadcasts and cable programmes, the copying of abstracts of scientific or technical articles, the rental of sound recordings, films and computer programs and adding sub-titles to broadcasts and cable programmes for the hard of hearing, certain acts are deemed not to be infringements if there is no licensing scheme in existence under which royalties are payable: C.D.P.A. 1988, ss.35, 60, 66 and 74; see §§ 10–27, 10–82, 10–99 and 10–124, *ante* and § 15–109, *post.*

[37] C.D.P.A. 1988, s.116(1); derived from Copyright Act 1956, s.24(4) where the term defined was "licence scheme."

[38] *Ibid.*

[39] The express inclusion of these words reverses the decision of Whitford J. on the different wording of s.24(2) of the 1956 Act to the effect that the PRT's jurisdiction was limited to the right itself and not the right to authorise as well: *Reditune Ltd.* v. *PRS* [1981] F.S.R. 165.

[40] C.D.P.A. 1988, s.116(3); compare the much narrower definition under the 1956 Act in s.24(2), and see § 15–53, *ante*; but see the further definitions in ss.117 and 124 which limit the schemes and licences which fall within the jurisdiction of the Copyright Tribunal, §§ 15–69 and 15–79, *post.*

Licensing body. "Licensing body" is defined[41] as meaning a society or **15–67** other organisation which has as its main object, or one of its main objects, the negotiation of granting of copyright licences,[42] either as owner or prospective owner of copyright, or as agent for the owner or prospective owner of copyright, and whose main objects include the granting of licences covering works of more than one author. Collective works[43] are not "works of more than one author" for these purposes, nor are works made by employees of one person, firm, company or group of companies.[44] The definition is therefore intended to cover collective licensing societies and agencies rather than individual publishers or authors, whose activities fall within the jurisdiction of the Copyright Tribunal only if they operate a licensing scheme.

(i) References and applications with respect to licensing schemes

References and applications involving licensing schemes. The dis- **15–68** tinction, introduced in the 1956 Act, between references and applications relating to general tariffs and those relating to individual complaints, is maintained in the 1988 Act. Under sections 118, 119 and 120 of the 1988 Act the subject of the reference is the scheme itself whereas under sections 121 and 122 of that Act the subject of the application is the availability of an individual licence to a person claiming to be covered by the scheme.

Jurisdiction over licensing schemes. The jurisdiction of the Copyright **15–69** Tribunal over licensing schemes depends both on the nature of the right and the work the subject of the licensing scheme, and also on the identity of the party operating the licensing scheme. Thus, a distinction is made between, on the one hand, licensing schemes dealing with licences to copy, to perform, play or show in public, to broadcast or to include in a cable programme literary, dramatic, musical or artistic works or films,[45] and, on the other hand, licensing schemes dealing with licences to do any restricted act in relation to any sound recordings, broadcasts, cable programmes and typographical arrangements of published editions and those dealing with licences for the rental of copies to the public of sound recordings, films and computer programs. In the former case the Copyright Tribunal only has jurisdiction over the scheme if it is operated by a licensing

---

[41] C.D.P.A. 1988, s.116(2); derived from Copyright Act 1956, s.24(3), but without drawing the distinctions previously made as between the different forms of licences set out in s.24(2) of that Act.

[42] That is a licence to do, or to authorise the doing of, any of the acts restricted by copyright: *Ibid.* s.116(3); compare the much narrower definition under the 1956 Act in s.24(2), and see § 15–53 and § 15–66, *ante.*

[43] That is a single work of more than one author, or a number of such works where the authors are the same.

[44] C.D.P.A. 1988, s.116(4).

[45] For these purposes a film sound track, when accompanying a film, is a film.

body; in the latter cases, the jurisdiction exists whether the operator of the scheme is a licensing body or not.[46]

15–70   **Reference of a proposed scheme.** Under the 1956 Act, a licence scheme could be referred to the PRT at any time whilst in operation.[47] The 1988 Act, whilst retaining this jurisdiction,[48] has, in section 118, introduced the possibility of referring a proposed licensing scheme to the Copyright Tribunal before it has begun to be operated.[49] A proposed scheme may be referred to the Copyright Tribunal by an organisation claiming to be representative of persons claiming that they require licences in cases of a description to which the scheme would apply.[50] The validity of such an organisation's claim to be representative of such class of persons is a matter which the Copyright Tribunal will decide.[51] The Copyright Tribunal must first consider whether the reference is premature, in which case it will refuse to entertain it.[52]

15–71   **Reference of an existing scheme.** In the case of an existing scheme, where a dispute arises with respect to the scheme between the licensing body operating it and any person claiming that he requires a licence in cases of a description to which the scheme applies, or an organisation claiming to be representative of persons requiring such licences, the scheme may be referred to the Copyright Tribunal either by such person or by such organisation.[53] An existing scheme which has been referred to the Copyright Tribunal remains in operation until the reference has been determined.[54]

15–72   **Order confirming or varying the scheme.** Where an existing or proposed licensing scheme is referred under section 118 or 119 of the 1988 Act, the Copyright Tribunal is empowered to make such order, either confirming or varying the scheme, in so far as it relates to cases of the description to which the reference relates, or, in the case of a proposed scheme, generally, as the Tribunal may determine to be reasonable in the circumstances.[55] The Copyright Tribunal's order may be either for an indefinite period, or for such period as the Tribunal may determine.[56]

---

[46] C.D.P.A. 1988, s.117; the narrower jurisdiction over the former works reflects the fact that they are subject to the Berne Convention, whereas the latter works are not.

[47] Copyright Act 1956, s.25(1); and see *Performing Right Society Ltd.* v. *Working Men's Club and Institute Ltd.* [1988] F.S.R. 586.

[48] C.D.P.A. 1988, s.119; see § 15–71, *post.*

[49] *Ibid.* s.118.

[50] *Ibid.* s.118(1); by Form 1: r. 3(1), The Copyright Tribunal Rules 1989, §§ B–53 and B–109, *post.*

[51] See as to "credentials," rr. 2(1) and 6, The Copyright Tribunal Rules 1989, §§ B–52 and B–56, *post.*

[52] C.D.P.A. 1988, s.118(2) and r. 3(3) § B–53, *post.* The Tribunal will normally consider the matter on the basis of written submissions only (Practice Direction, para. 3, § B–129, *post*).

[53] C.D.P.A. 1988, s.119(1); by Form 1: r. 3(1), The Copyright Tribunal Rules 1989 §§ B–53 and B–109, *post.*

[54] C.D.P.A. 1988, s.119(2).

[55] *Ibid.* ss.118(3), 119(3); as to reasonableness, see s.129 and § 15–60, *ante* and as to other factors to be considered, see §§ 15–61 to 15–64, *ante.*

[56] C.D.P.A. 1988, ss.118(4), 119(4).

Effect of order. A licensing scheme confirmed or varied by the Copyright **15–73** Tribunal remains in operation (or in the case of a proposed scheme comes into and remains in force) for so long as the Tribunal's order remains in force.[57] The effect of an order of the Copyright Tribunal with respect to a licensing scheme is that if, during the continuance of the order, a person has complied with the terms and conditions which, in accordance with the licensing scheme as confirmed or varied by the order, would be applicable to a licence granted in accordance with the scheme, and has paid any charges payable in respect of such licence (or, if the amount payable could not be ascertained, has given an undertaking to pay such charges) then he is to be in the same position as if he had at all material times been the holder of a licence granted by the owner of the copyright in question in accordance with the scheme.[58] The exact effect of these provisions will therefore depend on the precise form of any scheme as varied or confirmed by the Tribunal. It would seem, however, that once a licensing scheme has been confirmed or varied by the Tribunal, as covering a particular description of cases, it will not be necessary for an actual licence to be issued to a person wishing to carry out activities falling within the scheme with regard to a case covered by that description, since it will be sufficient if he complies with the terms and conditions of the licensing scheme and pays fees as required under it. If, however, a licence is actually issued, the parties are bound by the terms of the licence and the protection of the order is irrelevant.

Date from which order takes effect. Under the 1956 Act the PRT had **15–74** no power to backdate its order, which took effect on the scheme from the date the order was made.[59] The 1988 Act has introduced a limited ability for the Copyright Tribunal to backdate the effect of its order on the scheme referred to it. Thus, where the order of the Tribunal varies the amount of charges payable under a licensing scheme, the Tribunal may direct that the order has such effect from a date earlier than that on which the order is made, but not earlier than the date on which the reference was made or, if later, on which the scheme came into operation.[60] Any necessary repayments, or further payments, in respect of charges already paid must then be made.[61]

Further reference. Where the Copyright Tribunal has made an order **15–75** with respect to a licensing scheme,[62] the scheme may be referred again to the Tribunal in relation to cases of the description to which the order

---

[57] *Ibid.* s.123(1).

[58] *Ibid.* s.123(2); presumably protecting such person both from proceedings for infringement of copyright and from prosecution for offences under *ibid.* s.107.

[59] See *Performing Right Society Ltd.* v. *Working Men's Club and Institute Ltd.* [1988] F.S.R. 586; *The British Broadcasting Corporation* v. *Performing Right Society Ltd.* (1967) PRT 22/67 (unreported).

[60] C.D.P.A. 1988, s.123(3); as a matter of construction of s.123 it would appear that this provision does not apply to an application under s.121.

[61] *Ibid.*

[62] *I.e.* under any of ss.118, 119 or 120 of the 1988 Act.

applies.[63] On the second and any subsequent reference, application may be made not only by such an organisation or person as may initiate a first reference, but also by the licensing body operating the scheme.[64] In order, however, to avoid constant references with regard to the same description of cases, a licensing scheme may not, without the special leave of the Copyright Tribunal, be referred back to the Tribunal within 12 months from the date of the order on the previous reference, or, if the previous order was made so as to be in force for 15 months or less, until the last three months before expiry of the order.[65] An application for special leave must be made to the Copyright Tribunal on the appropriate form together with a statement of the grounds for the application.[66] A licensing scheme which is made the subject of a further reference remains in operation until the reference is determined.[67] On a further reference, the Copyright Tribunal has the same powers with regard to the order it can make as in the case of an initial reference.[68]

15–76   Application for individual licence where scheme exists. Under the 1956 Act, an application for an individual licence in relation to a scheme could only be made where the scheme applied, but the licensing body operating the scheme would not grant a licence to the applicant in accordance with the scheme.[69] Thus, no application could be made in relation to the scheme where it contained terms or conditions, other than relating to the amount of a charge for a licence, which excluded from the scheme the class of case in respect of which the applicant sought a licence.[70] Under the 1988 Act, however, an applicant may make an application to the Copyright Tribunal for an individual licence where a licensing scheme exists in two situations, depending, again, whether the licence sought is or is not covered by the scheme. The first, which re-enacts the position under the 1956 Act, is where the applicant claims, in a case covered by the scheme, that the operator has refused or failed within a reasonable time to grant to him, or to procure the grant to him of, a licence in accordance with the scheme.[71] The second, which is new, is where the applicant seeks a licence in respect of a case which is excluded from the scheme and claims

---

[63] C.D.P.A. 1988, s.120(1); by Form 1: r. 3(1) The Copyright Tribunal Rules 1989, §§ B–53 and B–109, *post*. This statutory provision deals with subsequent referral of a scheme in relation to the same description of classes previously the subject of the order; the same scheme may be referred any number of times to the Tribunal under s.119, quite apart from this provision, if the reference is in relation each time to a description of classes within the scheme but not the subject of a previous order (*cf.* s.26(7) of the 1956 Act, not specifically re-enacted).

[64] C.D.P.A. 1988, s.120(1); this allows the operator of the scheme to seek to have the terms as to payment, or other terms, varied.

[65] *Ibid.* s.120(2); and see n. 91, *ante*.

[66] By Form 3: r. 4(1), The Copyright Tribunal Rules 1989, §§ B–54 and B–110, *post*; such grounds might consist of a material change of circumstances, or new arguments raised by another applicant.

[67] C.D.P.A. 1988, s.120(3).

[68] *Ibid.* s.120(4) and (5); see § 15–72, *ante*.

[69] Copyright Act 1956, s.27(2).

[70] This being the effect of *ibid.* ss.24(5) and 27(1).

[71] C.D.P.A. 1988, s.121(1); by Form 2: r. 3(1), The Copyright Tribunal Rules 1989, §§ B–53 and B–110, *post*.

that the operator of the scheme either has refused to grant a licence, and that in the circumstances it is unreasonable that a licence should not be granted, or has proposed terms for a licence which are unreasonable.[72] A case is treated as excluded from a licensing scheme for this purpose if either the case falls within exceptions provided for in the scheme or is so similar to a case in which a licence is granted under the scheme that it is unreasonable that it should not be dealt with in the same way.[73] On an application under section 121 of the 1988 Act, the Copyright Tribunal, if satisfied that the claim is well-founded, must make an order declaring that, in respect of the matters specified in the order, the applicant is entitled to a licence on such terms and conditions as the Tribunal may determine to be applicable in accordance with the scheme, or, as the case may be, reasonable in the circumstances.[74] The order may be made either for an indefinite period, or for such period as the Tribunal may determine.[75]

Effect of order. Where the Copyright Tribunal has made an order under section 121, and, during the continuance of the order, the person in whose favour the order is made pays out charges payable in accordance with the order (or, if the amount payable cannot be ascertained, gives an undertaking to pay such charges) and complies with the other terms of the order, then such person is to be in the same position as if he had at all material times been the holder of a licence granted by the owner of the copyright in question.[76]   **15–77**

Further reference. Where the Copyright Tribunal has made an order under section 121 of the 1988 Act that a person is entitled to a licence under a licensing scheme, the operator of the scheme or the original applicant may apply to the Tribunal for a review of its order.[77] As with other provisions in the 1988 Act dealing with subsequent references,[78] such an application may not be made, without the special leave of the Copyright Tribunal, within 12 months from the date of the order on the previous reference, or, if the previous order was made so as to be in force for 15 months or less, until the last three months before expiry of the order.[79] An application for special leave must be made to the Copyright Tribunal on the appropriate form together with a statement of the grounds for the   **15–78**

---

[72] *Ibid.* s.121(2); by Form 2: r. 3(1), The Copyright Tribunal Rules 1989.
[73] *Ibid.* s.121(3).
[74] C.D.P.A. 1988, s.121(4); as to reasonableness, see s.129 and § 15–60, *ante* and as to other factors to be considered, see §§ 15–61 to 15–64, *ante*.
[75] *Ibid.* s.121(5).
[76] *Ibid.* s.123(5); presumably protecting such person both from proceedings for infringement of copyright and from prosecution for offences under *ibid.* s.107; and see s.123(2), § 15–73, *ante*. As a matter of construction of s.123 it would appear that subs. (3) does not apply to an application under s.121, so that there is no ability to backdate the effect of the order as to the amount payable.
[77] C.D.P.A. 1988, s.122(1); by Form 2: r. 3(1) The Copyright Tribunal Rules 1989, §§ B–53 and B–110, *post*. This allows the operator of the scheme to seek to have the terms as to payment, or other terms, varied.
[78] See § 15–75, *ante*, and § 15–85, *post*.
[79] C.D.P.A. 1988, s.122(2).

application.[80] On a further reference, the Copyright Tribunal has the same powers with regard to the order it can make as in the case of an initial reference.[81]

(ii) References and applications with respect to licensing bodies

15–79 **Jurisdiction over licences by licensing bodies.** Where no licensing scheme exists or is proposed, the Copyright Tribunal has jurisdiction in relation to the granting and terms of licences only when the party from whom the licence is sought is a licensing body.[82] The jurisdiction of the Tribunal then depends, as in the case of licensing schemes,[83] on the nature of the right and the work the subject of the licence. Thus, in relation to literary, dramatic, musical or artistic works or films,[84] the Copyright Tribunal has jurisdiction over licences to copy, to perform, play or show in public, to broadcast or to include in a cable programme any such works.[85] In relation to sound recordings,[86] broadcasts, cable programmes and typographical arrangements of published editions, the Tribunal has jurisdiction over licences to do any restricted act in relation to such works,[87] and in relation to sound recordings, films and computer programs the Tribunal has jurisdiction over licences for the rental of copies of such works to the public.[88]

15–80 **Reference of a proposed licence.** A person seeking a licence[89] from a licensing body may refer the terms of the proposed licence to the Copyright Tribunal under section 125(1) of the 1988 Act.[90] As with a reference of a proposed licensing scheme,[91] the Tribunal must first decide whether the reference is premature, in which case it will refuse to entertain it.[92] If the Tribunal does entertain the reference, it may make such order, either confirming or varying the terms of the proposed licence, as the Tribunal may determine to be reasonable in the circumstances.[93] The Copyright Tribunal's order may be either for an indefinite period or for such period as the tribunal may determine.[94]

---

[80] By Form 3: r. 4(1), The Copyright Tribunal Rules 1989, §§ B–54 and B–111, *post*; such grounds might consist of a material change of circumstances, or new arguments raised by another applicant.

[81] C.D.P.A. 1988, s.120(4) and (5); see § 15–72, *ante*.

[82] *Ibid.* s.124.

[83] See § 15–69, *ante*.

[84] For these purposes a film sound track, when accompanying a film, is a film.

[85] C.D.P.A. 1988, s.124(*a*); the narrower jurisdiction over these works reflects the fact that they are subject to the Berne Convention, whereas the other works are not.

[86] See n. 80, *ante*.

[87] C.D.P.A. 1988, s.124(*b*).

[88] *Ibid.* s.124(*c*).

[89] *I.e.* one falling within the jurisdiction of the Tribunal; see § 15–79, *ante*.

[90] By Form 7: r. 20(1), The Copyright Tribunal Rules 1989, §§ B–70 and B–115, *post*.

[91] See § 15–66, *ante*.

[92] C.D.P.A. 1988, s.125(2); and r. 20(3), The Copyright Tribunal Rules 1989, § B–70, *post*. The Tribunal will normally consider the matter on the basis of written submissions only (Practice Direction, para. 3, § B–129, *post*).

[93] C.D.P.A. 1988, s.125(3); as to reasonableness, see s.129 and § 15–60, *ante*, and as to other factors to be considered, see §§ 15–61 to 15–64, *ante*.

[94] *Ibid.* s.125(4).

Reference of an expiring licence. A licensee under a licence[95] which is   **15–81**
due to expire, whether by effluxion of time or as a result of notice given by
the licensing body, may apply under section 126(1) of the 1988 Act to the
Copyright Tribunal within the last three months before the licence is due
to expire,[96] on the ground that it is unreasonable in the circumstances that
the licence should cease to be in force.[97] The effect of such an application
is to continue the licence in force until the application as been determined.[98] On such an application the Copyright Tribunal may make such
order, either confirming or varying the terms of the proposed licence, as
the Tribunal may determine to be reasonable in the circumstances.[99] The
Copyright Tribunal's order may be either for an indefinite period or for
such period as the Tribunal may determine.[1]

Effect of order. Where the Copyright Tribunal has made an order under   **15–82**
section 125 or section 126 of the 1988 Act, and, during the continuance of
the order, the person entitled to the benefit of the order pays any charges
payable in accordance with the order (or, if the amount payable cannot be
ascertained, gives an undertaking to pay such charges) and complies with
the other terms of the order, then such person is to be in the same position
as if he had at all material times been the holder of a licence granted by
the owner of the copyright in question.[2]

Date from which order takes effect. As in the case of orders relating to   **15–83**
licensing schemes,[3] the 1988 Act has introduced a limited ability for the
Copyright Tribunal to backdate the effect of its order under section 125 or
section 126 of the 1988 Act with regard to the charges payable.[4] Thus, the
Tribunal may direct that the order has effect with regard to the charges
payable from a date earlier than that on which the order is made, but not
earlier than the date on which the reference was made or, if later, on
which the licence was granted or, as the case may be, was due to expire.[5]
Any necessary repayments, or further payments, in respect of charges
already paid must then be made.[6]

Transfer of benefit of order. The benefit of an order made by the Copy-   **15–84**
right Tribunal under section 125 or section 126 of the 1988 Act may be
assigned, provided such assignment was not prohibited under the terms of
the order, or the original licence, as the case may be.[7]

---

[95] *I.e.* one falling within the jurisdiction of the tribunal; see § 15–79, *ante*.
[96] C.D.P.A. 1988, s.126(2).
[97] By Form 7: r. 20(1), The Copyright Tribunal Rules 1989, §§ B–70 and B–115, *post*.
[98] C.D.P.A. 1988, s.126(3).
[99] *Ibid.* s.126(3); as to reasonableness, see s.129 and § 15–60, *ante*, and as to other factors to
  be considered, see §§ 15–61 to 15–64, *ante*.
[1] *Ibid.* 1988, s.126(4).
[2] *Ibid.* s.128(1); presumably protecting such person both from proceedings for infringement
  of copyright and from prosecution for offences under *ibid.* s.107; and see s.123(2), § 15–73,
  ante.
[3] See § 15–74, *ante*.
[4] C.D.P.A. 1988, s.128(3).
[5] *Ibid.*
[6] *Ibid.*
[7] C.D.P.A. 1988, s.128(2).

15–85   **Further reference.** Where the Copyright Tribunal has made an order with respect to a licence,[8] the licence may be referred back to the Tribunal for review.[9] On the second and any subsequent reference, application may be made not only by the licensee who initiated the initial reference (or by a person subsequently becoming entitled to the benefit of the order),[10] but also by the licensing body.[11] In order, however, to avoid constant references, a licence may not, without the special leave of the Copyright Tribunal, be referred back to the Tribunal within 12 months from the date of the order on the previous reference, or, if the previous order was made so as to be in force for 15 months or less, until the last three months before expiry of the order.[12] An application for special leave must be made to the Copyright Tribunal on the appropriate form together with a statement of the grounds for the application.[13] On a further reference, the Copyright Tribunal has the same powers with regard to the order it can make as in the case of an initial reference.[14]

(iii) Implied indemnity in certain licensing schemes and licences

15–86   **Implied indemnity.** In the case both of licensing schemes and licences granted by licensing bodies which license the reprographic copying[15] of published literary, dramatic, musical or artistic works, or the typographical arrangement of published editions, there is implied into the scheme or the licence an undertaking by the operator of the scheme, or the licensing body granting the licence, as the case may be, to indemnify the licensee against any liability, including as to costs,[16] which he may incur by infringing copyright by making or authorising the making of reprographic copies of a work within the apparent scope of his licence.[17]

15–87   **Conditions for availability of indemnity.** A licensee is taken to act within the scope of his licence in respect of a work which is not in fact within the licence where it is not apparent, from an inspection both of the licence and of the work, that the work does not fall within the description of works to which the licence applies.[18] It is to be noted that, whilst it is

---

[8] *I.e.* under s.125, 126 or 127.

[9] C.D.P.A. 1988, s.127; by Form 8: r. 20(1), The Copyright Tribunal Rules 1989, §§ B–70 and B–116, *post.*

[10] See § 15–83, *ante.*

[11] C.D.P.A. 1988, s.127(1); this allows the licensing body to seek to have the terms as to payment, or other terms, varied.

[12] C.D.P.A. 1988, s.127(2).

[13] By Form 3: r. 21, The Copyright Tribunal Rules 1989, §§ B–71 and B–111, *post;* such grounds might consist of a material change of circumstances, or new arguments raised by another applicant.

[14] C.D.P.A. 1988, s.127(3); see § 15–81, *ante.*

[15] As defined in C.D.P.A. 1988, s.178.

[16] Which include those reasonably incurred in relation to actual or contemplated proceedings: C.D.P.A. 1988, s.136(4).

[17] *Ibid.* s.136(1) and (2). This provision is new, and gives statutory force to the scheme previously operated voluntarily by the Copyright Licensing Agency (an association of publishers and authors); see the White Paper, Cmnd. 9712, para. 8.7.

[18] C.D.P.A. 1988, s.136(3)(*a*). Given the terms of this sub-paragraph, it is not clear what sub-paragraph (*b*) adds.

not a condition of availability of the indemnity that the licensee should in fact have checked the terms both of the licence and the work, he would in all cases be wise to do so. The scheme or licence may also contain provisions, provided they are reasonable,[19] regulating the manner in which and the time within which the licensee may make a claim under the indemnity,[20] and for the operator of the scheme or the licensing body to take over the conduct of the licensee's defence in any proceedings affecting the amount of the liability under the indemnity.[21]

D. *Control by the Copyright Tribunal of other licensing*

Other controls exercised by the Copyright Tribunal. In addition to its general jurisdiction in respect of licensing schemes and licences granted by licensing bodies, discussed above,[22] the Copyright Tribunal exercises control over licensing of copyright works in a number of other areas by reason of various provisions in the 1988 Act, dealing with schemes for reprographic copying by educational establishments,[23] the rental right in respect of sound recordings, films and computer programs,[24] licences of right available consequent on a report of the Monopolies and Mergers Commission[25] and the determination of a royalty payable to the trustees of the Hospital for Sick Children in respect of the play "Peter Pan"[26], compulsory licences in respect of information about a progamme service[27] and in respect of use as of right of sound recordings in broadcasts or cable programme services.[28] In one further case relating to the rights in performances given under Part II of the 1988 Act,[29] the Copyright Tribunal exercises a control over the consent of a performer to the making of a recording of a previous recording of his performance.[30] **15–88**

Power to extend coverage of scheme or licence for reprographic copying. The 1988 Act establishes a system of control by the Secretary of State over licensing schemes and licences granted by a licensing body which license educational establishments to make reprographic copies of published literary, dramatic, musical or artistic works or of the typographical arrangements of published editions.[31] The Copyright Tribunal is **15–89**

---

[19] *Ibid.* s.136(5); presumably a court would refuse to give effect to any conditions which it considered unreasonable.

[20] *Ibid.* s.136(5)(*a*).

[21] *Ibid.*

[22] See § 15–65 *et seq., ante.*

[23] C.D.P.A. 1988, s.139; see § 15–89, *post.*

[24] *Ibid.* s.142; see § 15–90, *post.*

[25] *Ibid.* s.144(4); see § 15–91, *post.*

[26] *Ibid.* sched. 6, para. 5; see § 15–92, *post.*

[27] Broadcasting Act 1990, Sched. 17, paras. 5 and 6, introduced into Chapter III of Part I, and s.149, of the 1988 Act by the Broadcasting Act 1990, Sched. 17, para. 7(1); see further § 10–127, *et seq., ante.*

[28] C.D.P.A. 1988, ss.135D, 135E and 135F, introduced into the 1988 Act and into s.149 of the 1988 Act by amendment by the Broadcasting Act 1990, s.175(1) and (2); see further § 10–133, *et seq., ante.*

[29] See Chap. 23, *post.*

[30] *Ibid.* s.190; see § 15–93, *post.*

[31] C.D.P.A. 1988, ss.137–141; see §§ 15–107 and 15–109, *post.*

given jurisdiction to hear appeals from orders made by the Secretary of State in the exercise of this control.[32] Thus, where the Secretary of State has made an order extending the coverage of a scheme or licence[33] or an order confirming, varying or discharging any previous such order,[34] the owner of the copyright in a work the subject of the order and, in the case of a subsequent order, any organisation representative of educational establishments which was given notice of the initial application for the order and made representations in respect of it, may appeal to the Tribunal.[35] The appeal must be brought within six weeks of the making of the order (which does not take effect for such period).[36] Although the Tribunal has power to entertain an appeal brought after such period, its decision will not then affect the validity of anything done in reliance on the order before the decision of the Tribunal takes effect.[37] In deciding the appeal the Tribunal is required to have regard, in addition to all other relevant circumstances,[38] to the extent to which published editions of the works in question are otherwise available, to the proportion of the work to be copied and to the nature of the use to which the copies are likely to be put.[39]

15–90 **Settling royalty in respect of rental right.** The 1988 Act in certain cases provides that certain acts are deemed not to be infringements of copyright if there is no licensing scheme in existence under which royalties are payable.[40] In such cases, where no scheme exists, the acts may be carried out without any payment being required to be made to the copyright owner, except in the case of the rental right, where reasonable royalties are to be so paid.[41] In default of agreement between the copyright owner and the person claiming to be treated as being licensed by him under section 66(1) of the 1988 Act, either of them may apply to the Copyright Tribunal to determine the royalty or other sum to be paid to the copyright owner.[42] Upon such an application, the Tribunal shall make such order as it may determine to be reasonable in all the circumstances,[43] and such order takes effect from the date on which it was made, or such later date as the Tribunal shall specify.[44] Either party may subsequently apply to the Tri-

---

[32] C.D.P.A. 1988, s.139(1) and (2).

[33] Under C.D.P.A. 1988, s.137.

[34] Under C.D.P.A. 1988, s.138.

[35] C.D.P.A. 1988, s.139(1) and (2); by Form 9 or 10, r. 24 The Copyright Tribunal Rules 1989, §§ B–74, B–117 and B–118, *post.*

[36] *Ibid.* s.139(3) and (4).

[37] *Ibid.* s.139(5).

[38] *Ibid.* s.135; see § 15–60, *ante.*

[39] *Ibid.* s.130; see § 15–62, *ante* and, as to considering other relevant circumstances, see *ibid.* s.135 and § 15–60, *ante.*

[40] See § 15–65, n. 38, *ante.*

[41] C.D.P.A. 1988, s.66(1); see § 10–99, *ante.*

[42] *Ibid.* s.142(1); by Form 11, r. 27, The Copyright Tribunal Rules 1989, §§ B–77 and B–119, *post.*

[43] C.D.P.A. 1988, s.142(2); as to reasonableness, see s.135 and § 15–60, *ante,* and as to other factors to be considered, see s.133(1) and § 15–64, *ante.*

[44] *Ibid.* s.142(5).

bunal to vary its order,[45] but not, without the special leave of the Tribunal, within 12 months of the original order or previous application. An application for special leave must be made to the Tribunal on the appropriate form together with a statement of the grounds for the application.[46] On a further application the Copyright Tribunal has the same powers with regard to the order it can make as in the case of an initial application.[47]

Settling terms of licence available as of right consequent on a report **15–91** **of the Monopolies and Mergers Commission.** Section 144 of the 1988 Act supplements, with reference to copyright, the general controls under United Kingdom legislation[48] over anti-competitive or monopolistic practices under the Fair Trading Act 1973[49] and the Competition Act 1980.[50] This provision was introduced as a result of the comments by the Monopolies and Mergers Commission in its report into the licensing of copyright in respect of spare body panels for cars by the Ford Motor Company Limited.[51] The Commission concluded that Ford's practices were anti-competitive and contrary to the public interest, but that there was no remedy against such practices under existing legislation. Now, under section 144 of the 1988 Act,[52] where the Commission has specified in its report[53] matters which in its opinion operate, or may be expected to operate, or have operated against the public interest and which include either conditions in licences granted by a copyright owner restricting the use by the licensee of the copyright work or preventing the copyright owner granting other licences, or a refusal of a copyright owner to grant licences of reasonable terms, then the powers conferred on the Secretary of State under the Fair Trading Act 1973[54] include the power to cancel or modify those conditions as well as the power to provide (in addition or instead) that licences in respect of the copyright shall be available as of right.[55] The Secretary of State may only exercise such powers if he is satisfied that to do so will not contravene any Convention relating to copyright to which the United Kingdom is a party.[56] If the terms of a licence available under this section cannot be agreed, then the person requiring the licence may

---

[45] *Ibid.* s.142(3) and (4); by Form 12, r. 27, The Copyright Tribunal Rules 1989, §§ B–77 and B–120, *post.*

[46] By Form 3: r. 28, The Copyright Tribunal Rules 1989, §§ B–78 and B–111, *post*; such grounds might consist of a material change of circumstances, or new arguments raised by another applicant.

[47] C.D.P.A. 1988, s.142(3).

[48] As to the possible application of EEC law, see Chap. 14 and in particular § 14–38, *et seq., ante.*

[49] 1973 c. 41.

[50] 1980 c. 21.

[51] *Ford Motor Co. Ltd.* (1985) Cmnd. 9437.

[52] A provision which is closely modelled on s.53 of the Patents Act 1977 (c. 37).

[53] Which may be as a result of a reference made to it under either the Fair Trading Act 1973 or the Competition Act 1980.

[54] Under Pt. I of Sched. 8 thereto.

[55] C.D.P.A. 1988, s.144(1).

[56] *Ibid.* s.144(3); the exercise of such powers in respect of the exercise of copyright may be inconsistent with the Berne Convention: see Greaves [1987] 1 E.I.P.R. 3, 5.

apply to the Copyright Tribunal to settle the terms,[57] and the licence, as so settled, takes effect from the date of application to the Tribunal.[58]

15–92   **Settling the royalty or other remuneration payable to the trustees for the Hospital for Sick Children in respect of the use of the play "Peter Pan."** The Copyright Tribunal has a similar jurisdiction, to that discussed above in relation to the rental right, to settle the royalty or other remuneration payable to the trustees of The Hospital for Sick Children, Great Ormond Street, London in respect of the public performance, commercial publication, broadcasting or inclusion in a cable programme service of the play "Peter Pan" written by Sir James Barrie, under the right conferred by the 1988 Act on the trustees.[59] In default of agreement as to the amount to be paid to the trustees, an application may be made to the Copyright Tribunal to determine the royalty or other remuneration to be paid,[60] and the Tribunal shall make such order as it considers reasonable in all the circumstances.[61] Application may be made to the Tribunal subsequently to vary its order,[62] but not, without the special leave of the Tribunal, within 12 months from the original order or application. An application for special leave must be made to the Tribunal on the appropriate form together with a statement of the grounds for the application.[63] On a further application the Copyright Tribunal has the same powers with regard to the order it can make as in the case of an initial application,[64] and any variation made by the Tribunal has effect from the date when made or such later date specified by the Tribunal.[65]

15–93   **Granting consent on behalf of a performer to the making of a recording from a previous recording of a performance.** The Copyright Tribunal has been given the power to grant consent on behalf of a performer to the making of a recording from a previous recording of a performance, where either the identity or whereabouts of the performer cannot be ascertained by reasonable inquiry, or where the performer unreasonably withholds his consent.[66] The Tribunal shall not give consent where the basis of the application is that the identity or whereabouts of the performer cannot be ascertained except after the service or publication of such notices as are required by The Copyright Tribunal Rules or by direction of the Tribunal.[67] Before giving consent on behalf of a per-

---

[57] *Ibid.* s.144(4); by Form 13, r. 31, The Copyright Tribunal Rules 1989, §§ B–81 and B–121, *post*. As to the factors to be considered by the Tribunal, see §§ 15–60 to 15–64, *ante*.

[58] C.D.P.A. 1988, s.144(5).

[59] *Ibid.* s.301 and Sched. 6, para. 2(1); see § 6–7, *ante*.

[60] *Ibid.* Sched. 6, para. 5(1); by Form 15, r. 38, The Copyright Tribunal Rules 1989, §§ B–88 and B–123, *post*.

[61] C.D.P.A. 1988, Sched. 6, para. 5(1); as to reasonableness, see s.135 and § 15–60, *ante*.

[62] By Form 16, r. 38, The Copyright Tribunal Rules 1989, §§ B–88 and B–124, *post*.

[63] By Form 3: r. 39, The Copyright Tribunal Rules 1989, §§ B–89 and B–111, *post*; such grounds might consist of a material change of circumstances, or new arguments raised by another applicant.

[64] C.D.P.A. 1988, Sched. 6, para. 5(2).

[65] *Ibid.* Sched. 6, para. 5(4).

[66] *Ibid.* s.190; see §§ 23–53 and 23–54, *post*. The application is made by Form 14: r. 34, The Copyright Tribunal Rules 1989, §§ B–84 and B–122, *post*.

[67] *Ibid.* s.190(3); and see r. 35, The Copyright Tribunal Rules 1989, § B–85, *post*.

former whose identity and whereabouts are known, but who has refused his consent, the Tribunal must be satisfied that the reasons for withholding consent do not include the protection of any legitimate interest of the performer.[68] The onus is on the performer to show what his reasons are for withholding his consent, and, in the absence of evidence as to his reasons, the Tribunal may draw its own conclusions.[69] In deciding whether to grant consent on behalf of the performer, the Tribunal is bound to take into account two factors, namely whether the original recording was made with his consent and is lawfully in the possession or control of the person wishing to make the further recording, and whether the making of the further recording is consistent with the obligations of the parties to the arrangements under which the original recording was made.[70] Where the Tribunal gives consent on behalf of a performer, it may attach such conditions as it considers appropriate,[71] and, in default of agreement between the applicant and the performer, the Tribunal shall also determine what payment is to be made to the performer.[72]

E. *Procedure before the Copyright Tribunal*

Provisions governing procedure. The procedure before the Tribunal is   **15–94**
governed by The Copyright Tribunal Rules,[73] made by the Lord Chancellor in the exercise of powers conferred under the 1988 Act.[74] Subject to the provisions of the Act and of the Rules, the Tribunal has power to regulate its own procedure,[75] and in exercise of this power the Chairman has issued a Practice Direction giving further guidance as to the procedure which will be followed by the Tribunal.[76] In addition, certain provisions of the Arbitration Act 1950[77] dealing with the examination of parties and witnesses on oath, the power of the High Court to issue subpoenas and make orders, *inter alia*, as to security for costs, discovery and interrogatories, and the power of the arbitrator to make interim awards and correct slips in any award, are made applicable to proceedings before the Tribunal.[78] So far as the Rules themselves are concerned, these first set out the full procedure on references and applications with respect to licensing schemes[79]; this follows largely, but with some modifications, the procedure set out in the former Performing Right Tribunal Rules made under the 1956 Act. It

---

[68] *Ibid.* s.190(4).
[69] *Ibid.* the performer will usually set out his reasons in his answer to the application: see r. 36(1), The Copyright Tribunal Rules 1989, § B–86, *post.*
[70] *Ibid.* s.190(5).
[71] *Ibid.* s.190(2).
[72] *Ibid.* s.190(6).
[73] S.I. 1989 No. 1129; see § B–46, *et seq., post,* as amended by the Copyright Tribunal (Amendment) Rules 1991, S.I. 1991 No. 201, § B–265 *et seq., post.*
[74] C.D.P.A. 1988, s.150.
[75] r. 54.
[76] The procedure set out in the Practice Direction is stated (para. 1) to be compulsory, subject to a direction of the Tribunal to the contrary. See § B–127, *et seq., post.*
[77] 1950 c. 27, ss.12, 14, 17 and 26 (and, in relation to proceedings before the Tribunal in Northern Ireland, the equivalent sections of the Arbitration Act (Northern Ireland) 1937 (c. 8(N.I.)).
[78] C.D.P.A. 1988, s.150(2) and r. 46 and Sched. 2, §§ B–96 and B–107, *post.*
[79] rr. 3 to 19. Based on the former Performing Right Tribunal Rules (1965) under the 1956 Act, for which see *Copinger* (12th ed.), § 1758 *et seq.*

is this procedure which is, in general, described below. The Rules then deal separately with each of the other jurisdictions now exercised by the Tribunal,[80] setting out the procedure for commencing such proceedings and providing for any specific matters relevant to that jurisdiction,[81] and then applying such of the rules relating to references and applications with respect to licensing schemes as are appropriate to the particular jurisdiction. The final provisions of the Rules contain provisions of general application as to appeal, costs, and other procedural matters.

15–95   **Secretary and service of documents.** The Tribunal has an office,[82] and its business is administered by the Secretary. Under the Rules a variety of documents are required to be served, sometimes directly by a party on another party or person. Where direct service is required, the document may be sent by pre-paid post to the person (or to his solicitor or agent[83]) at his address for service, or, where no such address has been given, at his registered office, principal place of business of last known address.[84] In other cases service must be effected on the Secretary, by pre-paid post at his office,[85] and the Secretary then has to serve copies on others. In the latter case, the Secretary will stipulate the number of copies required.[86]

15–96   **Commencement and withdrawal of proceedings.** All types of proceedings are to be commenced by notice in one of the prescribed forms served on the Secretary.[87] In each case the applicant has to serve with the form a statement of his case.[88] The Secretary then, as soon as is practicable, serves copies on the appropriate persons, being, in the case of a reference or application with respect to a licensing scheme, the operator of the licensing scheme named in the application, or, where the application is for review of a previous order, every person who was a party to the proceedings when the previous order was made.[89] Where the application relates to

---

[80] For the different jurisdictions of the Tribunal, see § 15–57, *ante.*

[81] For example, in the case of proceedings under s.190(1)(*a*) (application for Tribunal's consent on behalf of a performer whose identity and whereabouts are unknown), the inquiries which the Tribunal makes to establish that the identity and whereabouts cannot be ascertained.

[82] The address is: Room 1509 State House, 66–71 High Holborn, London WC1R 4TP. The office is open from 10.00 to 16.00 each weekday except Good Friday, Christmas Day and Bank Holidays (r. 52, § B–102, *post*).

[83] r. 50(5), § B–100, *post*; *i.e.* a solicitor or agent appointed to act in the proceedings by notice in writing to the Secretary in accordance with r. 15.

[84] r. 50(1), § B–100, *post.*

[85] *Ibid.*

[86] Practice Direction, para. 2, § B–128, *post.*

[87] rr. 3, 20, 24, 26A, 27, 31, 34, 38 and 41A. In each case a fee is payable in accordance with r. 49 and Sched. 1, § B–106, *post.*

[88] Under the former rules governing the procedure of the PRT (r. 3(2), The Performing Right Tribunal Rules 1965, *Copinger* (12th ed.) § 1760), the applicant also had to serve with his application a list of relevant documents in his possession. This burdensome requirement has been dropped, and indeed there is no automatic discovery at any stage under the new Rules or the standard form of directions, although a party can seek such a direction where appropriate.

[89] r. 3(2), § B–53, *post.*

a proposed scheme,[90] the Tribunal will first consider whether the reference is premature.[91] For this purpose the respondent will be invited to comment in writing and the Tribunal will normally reach a decision without hearing oral submissions.[92] A reference or application may be withdrawn by the applicant at any time before it has been finally disposed of, by notice in writing served on the Secretary and on every other party to the proceedings.[93] Such withdrawal does not prevent the Tribunal making an order as to the payment of costs incurred up to the time such notice is served,[94] or from proceeding to determine the reference or application if it decides to do so on the application of any other party to the proceedings.[95]

Advertisement of proceedings. Except where the Tribunal has declined   **15–97**
to entertain a reference on the grounds that it is premature,[96] or the Chairman in any other case otherwise directs, the application or reference is then advertised.[97] The advertisement gives details of the application or reference, and the names and addresses of the applicant and any other organisation or person served with notice of the proceedings.[98] The advertisement states the time within which any objection to the applicant's credentials must be received,[99] and within which any other organisation or person may apply to intervene in the proceedings.[1]

Intervention in the proceedings. Any organisation or person may apply   **15–98**
to be made a party to the proceedings by serving a notice on the Secretary in the prescribed form within the time stated in the advertisement.[2] On being served with such notice the Secretary must, as soon as practicable, serve copies of the notice on every other party to the proceedings and must serve on the intervener a copy of the applicant's reference or application and statement of case and any other notice of intervention.[3] These provisions are substantially repeated (taking account of the difference that there is no advertisement, and therefore no time within which the intervention must be made) in relation to references and applications with respect to licensing bodies,[4] and in that form they are applied to intervention in each of the other types of proceedings before the Tribunal by any

---

[90] Under C.D.P.A. 1988, s.118; the same applies in the case of an application with respect to a licence proposed to be granted by a licensing body, under C.D.P.A. 1988, s.125. See § 15–70 and § 15–80, *ante.*

[91] Pursuant to C.D.P.A. 1988, s.118(2) and r. 4 (or s.125(2) and r. 20(3)).

[92] Practice Direction, para. 3, § B–129, *post.*

[93] r. 16(1), § B–66 *post.*

[94] *Ibid.* as to costs, see § 15–105, *post.*

[95] r. 16(2), § B–66, *post.*

[96] See § 15–96, *ante.*

[97] r. 5(1), § B–55, *post*; advertisement is only required for an application or reference relating to a licensing scheme, but may be directed under r. 35 in respect of an application under s.190 of the 1988 Act for the Tribunal's consent on behalf of a performer.

[98] r. 5(2), § B–55, *post.*

[99] See § 15–99, *post.*

[1] See § 15–98, *post.*

[2] r. 7(1) and Form 5, §§ B–57 and B–115, *post*; such notice may be served after the expiry of such time with the leave of the Chairman or the Tribunal. See also, as to intervening in other proceedings, rr. 23, 26, 26D, 30, 33, 37, 41, 41D and 44.

[3] r. 7(2), § B–57, *post.*

[4] r. 23, § B–73, *post.*

organisation or person claiming to have a substantial interest in those proceedings.[5]

15–99   **Objections to applicant's credentials.** A licensing scheme may be referred to the Tribunal by an organisation claiming to be representative of persons claiming that they require licences in cases of a description to which a licensing scheme applies or, in the case of a proposed scheme, would apply.[6] The organisation's credentials, that is the validity of its claim to be representative of a class of persons,[7] may be challenged by any other organisation or person, within the time stipulated in the advertisement of the proceedings,[8] by serving on the Secretary a notice, or by the Tribunal of its own motion.[9] The Secretary must then serve notice of the objections on every party to the proceedings and the proceedings are automatically stayed from that moment until further order.[10] The Chairman then gives directions for the parties to make written representations on the issue of the validity of the credentials.[11] The Tribunal may decide the issue on the basis of the written submissions, or may give any objector and any other party the opportunity of making oral representations at a hearing.[12] If, after considering the objections, the Tribunal is not satisfied as to the credentials, it will direct that no further proceedings are to be taken on the reference or application, except in relation to any order for costs which the Tribunal may make.[13] If, on the other hand, the Tribunal is satisfied as to the credentials, it will direct that the reference or application shall proceed, and the Tribunal may give such consequential directions as are appropriate.[14]

15–100   **Objections to intervener's credentials.** Objections may also be made to an intervener's credentials, that is, the possession by the intervener of a sufficient interest in the matter in dispute.[15] In relation to proceedings with respect to licensing schemes, the party intending to object to an intervener's credentials must serve notice in the prescribed form on the Secretary, who will then serve copies on every other party.[16] The Tribunal may of its own motion object to an intervener's credentials, in which case the Secretary must serve notice of such objection, together with a statement of the reasons for it, on every other party.[17] Unless the Chairman

---

[5] rr. 26, 30, 33, 37, 41 and, in respect of an application under r. 43 (for suspension of Tribunal's order pending appeal), r. 44.

[6] C.D.P.A. 1988, ss.118(1), 119(1) and 120(1); only such an organisation may refer a proposed scheme.

[7] r. 2(1), § B–52, *post.*

[8] See § 15–97, *ante;* such time may be extended by the Tribunal or Chairman: r. 6(1), § B–56, *post.*

[9] In Form 4: r. 6(1), §§ B–56 and B–112, *post.*

[10] r. 6(2).

[11] r. 6(3).

[12] r. 6(3).

[13] r. 6(4) and r. 48.

[14] r. 6(5).

[15] r. 2(1).

[16] In Form 6: rr. 8(1) and (2), §§ B–58 and B–14, *post.*

[17] r. 8(3).

makes such a direction on the hearing for directions,[18] an objection to an intervener's credentials does not operate as a stay of the proceedings, and is considered by the Tribunal at the same time as the reference or application in question.[19] These provisions also apply to objecting to the credentials of an organisation or person seeking to intervene in each of the other types of proceedings before the Tribunal.[20]

Completion of written cases. In the case of proceedings with respect to   **15–101**
a licensing scheme, the operator of the scheme must, within 28 days of being served with the applicant's statement of case, serve on the Secretary a written answer to the applicant's case.[21] An intervener has 21 days from the time limited in the advertisement[22] within which to serve on the Secretary a statement of the case he intends to make.[23] The Secretary must then serve copies of such answer and case on every other party.[24] This completes the written pleadings in the proceedings, save that a party may, without leave, amend his statement of case or answer at any time prior to the date fixed by the Chairman on the hearing for directions, after which leave is required.[25] The amendment is made by serving a copy on the Secretary, who must, as soon as practicable, serve a copy on every other party.[26] In the case of other types of proceedings before the Tribunal, the respondent has 21 days after service on him of the applicant's statement of case within which to serve his written answer on the Secretary,[27] who must then serve a copy of the same on every other party.

Directions. Upon the expiry of the time limited by the Rules for the ser-   **15–102**
vice of a statement of case by an intervener or of the answer by the respondent, the Chairman is to appoint a date and place for the attendance of the parties for the purpose of his giving directions as to the further conduct of the proceedings.[28] The Secretary is to give every party and every intervener 21 days' notice of such hearing.[29] In a two-party case, the applicant must, not less than 14 days before the hearing, send to the respondent and to the Secretary his written proposals for directions, and the respondent must reply to the applicant stating whether he agrees the directions, and if not what directions he counter-proposes.[30] A draft of the directions normally to be made in a two-party case is scheduled to the Practice Direc-

---

[18] See § 15–102, *post.*
[19] r. 8(4); *cf.* the position in relation to an applicant's credentials, § 15–99, *ante.*
[20] See rr. 23, 26, 26D, 30, 33, 37, 41, 41D and 44.
[21] r. 9(1), § B–59, *post.* Time may be extended by consent or by the Tribunal or the Chairman: r. 51, § B–101, *post.*
[22] See § 15–97, *ante.*
[23] r. 9(2).
[24] r. 9(3).
[25] r. 10(1) and (3), § B–60, *post*; as to the hearing for directions, see § 15–102, *post.*
[26] r. 10(2).
[27] See rr. 22(1), 25(1), 26C(1), 29(1), 32(1), 36(1), 40(1) and 41C(1). Time may be extended by consent or by the Tribunal or the Chairman: r. 51, § B–101, *post.*
[28] r. 11(1). These provisions are applied to all types of proceedings before the Tribunal: rr. 22(2), 25(2), 26C(2), 29(2), 32(2), 36(2), 40(2) and 41C(2).
[29] *Ibid.*
[30] Practice Direction, para. 4(*b*), § B–130, *post.*

tion.[31] Where there are more than two parties, each party should send its written proposals to the other parties and to the Secretary not less than 10 days before the hearing.[32] The parties may agree the directions to be made, in which case the Chairman may make an order accordingly.[33] Where the directions are not agreed in advance, and the hearing for directions proceeds, the Chairman shall give every party attending an opportunity to be heard and shall consider the oral and written representations, and shall make such directions as will lead to the just, expeditious and economical disposal of the proceedings.[34] The Chairman may give directions as to the date and place of the substantive hearing, if one is requested by any party,[35] the procedure to be followed in regard to the submission and exchange of written arguments,[36] the date after which no amended statement of case or answer is to be served without leave,[37] the preparation and delivery by the applicant of an agreed schedule setting out the issues to be determined and the contentions of each party in relation thereto,[38] the admission of facts and documents and the discovery and inspection of documents,[39] the giving of evidence on affidavit[40] and the consideration by the Tribunal of any objection made to an intervener's credentials.[41] Although not mentioned specifically in Rule 11, an important alteration in the procedure to be adopted by the Copyright Tribunal is the introduction of the exchange between the parties and service on the Tribunal of written evidence prior to the hearing, in the form of witness statements.[42] It was envisaged that this would shorten the length of the hearing, and go some way to meeting the criticism made in the past that hearings before the PRT were too long and costly.[43] Further directions may be given at a later date.[44] Failure to comply with a direction may result in the party concerned being debarred from taking any further part in the proceedings without the leave of the Tribunal.[45] Core bundles and

---

[31] Practice Direction, para. 4(*a*), § B–130, *post*.

[32] Practice Direction, para. 4(*c*), § B–130, *post*.

[33] Practice Direction, para. 4(*e*), § B–130, *post*.

[34] r. 11(2).

[35] r. 11(2)(i). Any party requesting a date to be set should make inquiries of the other parties as to suitable dates, and should provide an estimate of the likely length of the hearing: Practice Direction, para. 4(*d*).

[36] r. 11(2)(ii).

[37] r. 11(2)(iii).

[38] r. 11(2)(iv) and Practice Direction, para. 6, §§ B–61 and B–131, *post*. Under the PRT Rules there was a similar provision rarely used in recent years, as it had been found time-consuming and of little use. Skeleton arguments including references to the evidence and authorities relied upon must also be served on the Secretary and on each other party not less than 14 days before the hearing date, and failure to do so may result in an adverse costs order: Practice Direction, paras. 7 and 8, § B–131, *post*.

[39] r. 11(2)(v); the draft order does not include any specific order as to discovery.

[40] r. 11(2)(vi).

[41] r. 11(2)(vii).

[42] There is provision in the draft order (see § B–137, *post*,) for the preparation and exchange of evidence in the form of witness statements and see Practice Direction para. 5.

[43] See the 1986 White Paper, Cmnd. 9712, para. 18.19.

[44] r. 11(3).

[45] r. 11(4).

bundles of copies of authorities should also be lodged with the Secretary at least seven days before the hearing date.[46]

The substantive hearing. The hearing is to be in public, unless the Tribunal or the Chairman otherwise orders.[47] Every party (which includes an intervener whose application is pending) to a reference or application which is considered at an oral hearing before the Tribunal is entitled to attend the hearing and to address the Tribunal and to give evidence and call witnesses.[48] Any party may authorise some other person (who may be a solicitor) to act for him in the proceedings[49] and may be represented at the hearing by solicitor or counsel or any other person allowed by the Tribunal or the Chairman to appear on his behalf, or, except in the case of a corporation or unincorporated body, may appear in person.[50] Evidence is to be given orally or, if agreed, or the Tribunal or the Chairman so orders, by affidavit, but the Tribunal may at any stage of the proceedings require the attendance of any deponent for examination and cross-examination.[51] Criticism has, in the past, been made of the length of proceedings before the PRT.[52] On the basis that the Tribunal will have read in advance the pleadings, written evidence and the skeleton arguments,[53] substantial opening speeches are not required, and each party would normally be allowed no more than one-and-a-half hours for its opening speech.[54] Lengthy closing speeches are discouraged, and each party is encouraged to provide at the beginning of its closing speech a written summary of the main points to be made.[55] Lengthy cross-examination is also discouraged, and an order may be obtained to the effect that a witness need not be cross-examined merely for the purpose of challenging his evidence.[56] The draft order for directions contains an order that a party wishing to cross-examine another party's witness must give prior notice to that effect.[57]

The decision. The Copyright Tribunal is to give its decision in writing, **15–104** including a statement of its reasons, and, where on a reference the Tribunal has varied the scheme, a copy of the scheme so varied is to be annexed to the decision.[58] Unless the operation of the decision is suspended,[59] the Secretary is to send a copy of the decision to every party[60] and is to make a copy available for inspection at the office.[61] Short par-

[46] Practice Direction, paras. 9 and 10, §§ B–131, 132, *post.*
[47] r. 14(2), § B–64, *post.*
[48] r. 14(1).
[49] r. 15(1), § B–65, *post;* such agent must be appointed by notice in writing to the Secretary: r. 15(2).
[50] r. 15(5).
[51] r. 14(3).
[52] See § 15–102, n. 67, *ante.*
[53] See § 15–102, *ante.*
[54] Practice Direction, para. 11, § B–133, *post.*
[55] Practice Direction, para. 13, § B–135, *post.*
[56] Practice Direction, para. 12, § B–134, *post.*
[57] Para. 8 of the draft; see § B–137, *post.*
[58] r. 17, § B–67, *post.*
[59] Under r. 42 or 43; see § 15–106, *post.*
[60] r. 17; § B–67, *post.*
[61] r. 18; as to the office, see § 15–95, *ante.* Members of the public may obtain copies of decisions on request from the office.

ticulars of the decision may be advertised if the Chairman so directs.[62] Except where the operation of the order is suspended,[63] the Tribunal's order takes effect from such date and shall remain in force for such period as shall be specified in the order.[64]

15–105   **Costs.** The costs of and incidental to any proceedings are in the discretion of the Copyright Tribunal which may make any order for the payment of costs by one party to another in respect of the whole or part of the proceedings.[65] Such an order may be for payment of a lump sum by way of costs or such proportion of the costs as may be just, and, in the latter case, the Copyright Tribunal may direct that the amount be assessed by the Chairman or be taxed by a taxing officer.[66] Orders for the payment of costs by one party to another were rarely made by the PRT. The Copyright Tribunal has given warning that it will consider exercising this power against any party which it considers responsible for undue prolixity in its evidence at the hearing, and that, whilst it is not the Copyright Tribunal's practice that in all cases costs will follow the event, the fact that a party's case may have been unreasonably maintained will be an important factor in considering the exercise of its discretion as to costs.[67] The practice developed in civil litigation of making offers "without prejudice as to costs"[68] is also available in proceedings before the Copyright Tribunal.[69]

15–106   **Appeal.** The substantive provisions which now provide for an appeal on a point of law from the Copyright Tribunal to the High Court, rather than the procedure formally applicable of referring proceedings before the PRT to the High Court by way of case stated, have been discussed above.[70] Such appeal is to be brought within 28 days of the date of the decision of the Tribunal.[71] The appeal is brought by service on the Secretary and on every other party of a notice of appeal in the prescribed form.[72] On receipt of the notice of appeal the Tribunal may, of its own motion, suspend the operation of its order,[73] and any party to the proceedings may apply to the Tribunal for it to do so.[74] A copy of such application must be served on every other party by the Secretary, and objections to a suspension may be lodged by any other party within 14 days of his being served with such notice.[75] The procedure for determining such an application is then the

---

[62] r. 18, § B–68, *post*.
[63] See n. 83, *ante*.
[64] r. 19, § B–69, *post*; subject to the statutory provisions which govern the earliest date from which the order may take effect (see § 15–74, *ante*).
[65] r. 48(1), § B–78, *post*.
[66] r. 48(2).
[67] Practice Direction, para. 14, § B–136, *post*.
[68] So called "Calderbank" letters, following the procedure commended by the Court of Appeal in *Calderbank* v. *Calderbank* [1976] Fam. 93.
[69] Practice Direction, para. 15, § B–136, *post*.
[70] See § 15–59, *ante*.
[71] r. 42(1), § B–92, *post*; the court (but not the Tribunal: r. 51) has power to extend time.
[72] In Form 17; r. 42(2), §§ B–92 and B–125, *post*.
[73] r. 42(4).
[74] By Form 18; r. 43(1), §§ B–93 and B–126, *post*.
[75] r. 43(2).

same as set out above, including the possibility for intervention by a person or organisation not previously a party to the proceedings.[76] If the Tribunal refuses the application, it must give reasons for its decision.[77] If the Tribunal does suspend its order, then sections 123 and 128 of the 1988 Act do not have effect for the duration of the suspension.[78]

F. *Other controls over copyright licensing*

Reprographic copying by educational establishments. The 1988 Act   **15–107** provides a special regime in sections 137 to 141 in respect of reprographic copying;[79] of published literary, dramatic, musical or artistic works or of typographical arrangements of published editions by educational establishments.[80] Where a licensing scheme, to which sections 118 to 123 of the 1988 Act apply,[81] or a licence, to which sections 125 to 128 of that Act apply,[82] exists and provides for the licensing of reprographic copying of such works by educational establishments, then the Secretary of State has power to extend the coverage of such scheme or licence to works of a description similar to those covered but unreasonably excluded from it, provided that to do so would not conflict with the normal exploitation of the works or unreasonably prejudice the legitimate interests of the copyright owners.[83] Where the Secretary of State proposes to make such an order, he must give notice to the copyright owners, the licensing body in question and appropriate persons or organisations representative of educational establishments.[84] Such notice must inform the persons of their right to make written or oral representations to the Secretary of State within six months of the notice, and if any person wishes to make oral representations, the Secretary of State will appoint a person to hear them.[85] The Secretary of State, in making his decision, must take into account representations made to him and all other matters as appear to him to be relevant.[86] There is provision for the variation or discharge by the Secretary of State of any order previously made by him under section 137 of the 1988 Act on the application of the copyright owner.[87] Such variation cannot be made within two years of the original order or of a previous application seeking to vary it, unless the Secretary of State is satisfied that the circumstances are exceptional.[88] The Secretary of State may proceed to confirm

---

[76] rr. 43(3) and 44.

[77] r. 43(4).

[78] See §§ 15–73, 15–77 and 15–82, *ante.*

[79] Reprographic copying means copying by a process for making facsimile copies or involving the use of an appliance for making multiple copies, or, in the case of a work held in electronic form, copying by electronic means: C.D.P.A. 1988, s.178.

[80] Educational establishment means any school (as further defined) and other description of educational establishment specified for such purpose by an order of the Secretary of State: C.D.P.A. 1988, s.174.

[81] See § 15–69, *ante.*

[82] See § 15–79, *ante.*

[83] C.D.P.A. 1988, s.137(1) and (2).

[84] *Ibid.* s.137(3).

[85] *Ibid.* s.137(4).

[86] *Ibid.* s.137(5).

[87] *Ibid.* s.138(1).

[88] *Ibid.* s.138(2).

the previous order on considering the grounds for the application without further representations,[89] but if he does not, the procedure to be followed is the same as that described above for the making of a decision under section 137 of the 1988 Act.[90] The Secretary of State's decision under each of these sections is subject to a right of appeal to the Copyright Tribunal.[91]

15–108   **Inquiry whether scheme or licence required.** The Secretary of State may appoint a person to inquire into whether new provision is required, by way of a licensing scheme or general licence, to authorise the making by or on behalf of educational establishments of reprographic copies of published literary, dramatic, musical or artistic works or of the typographical arrangements of published editions.[92] The procedure to be followed on such an inquiry is to be laid down by regulation by statutory instrument.[93] The person holding the inquiry is not to recommend the making of new provision unless he is satisfied that it would be to the advantage of educational establishments and that to do so would neither conflict with the normal exploitation of the works nor unreasonably prejudice the legitimate interests of the copyright owners.[94] A recommendation for new provision shall also specify any terms, other than terms as to charges payable, on which authorisation under the new provision should be available.[95] Where provision has not been made in accordance with such a recommendation within one year,[96] the Secretary of State has power to order that the making of reprographic copies of the works to which the recommendation relates by educational establishments for the purposes of instruction shall be treated as if licensed by the owners of the copyrights in the works.[97] The order is to be made by statutory instrument, and shall not come into force until at least six months after it is made.[98] The order may provide that any existing more restrictive licence shall cease to have effect, and shall provide for the terms of the licence, which shall be royalty-free.[99] The order may also provide that copies made pursuant to the order (and, therefore, when made not infringing copies[1]) are to be treated as infringing copies if sold, let for hire, offered or exposed for sale or hire or exhibited in public.[2]

15–109   **Certification of licensing schemes.** The Secretary of State is given power to certify a licensing scheme on the application of the person operating or proposing to operate it for the purposes of displacing other pro-

---

[89] *Ibid.* s.138(3).

[90] *Ibid.* s.138(4).

[91] *Ibid.* s.139; see, as to the procedure, § 15–94, *et seq., ante.*

[92] *Ibid.* s.140; as to the meaning of reprographic copying and educational establishments, see § 15–107, *ante.*

[93] *Ibid.* s.140(2), (3) and (6).

[94] *Ibid.* s.140(4).

[95] *Ibid.* s.140(5).

[96] *I.e.* no licensing scheme or licence complying with the recommendation has been established or granted: C.D.P.A. 1988, s.141(2).

[97] C.D.P.A. 1988, s.141(1).

[98] *Ibid.* s.141(7) and (8).

[99] *Ibid.* s.141(3) and (4).

[1] *Ibid.* s.27; and see § 9–4, *ante.*

[2] *Ibid.* s.141(5).

visions of the 1988 Act which permit certain acts in relation to the works the subject of the scheme.[3] The sections affected are: section 35 (educational recording of broadcasts or cable programmes),[4] section 60 (copying or issuing to the public copies of abstracts of scientific or technical articles),[5] section 66 (rental of sound recordings, films and computer programs),[6] section 74 (sub-titled copies of broadcasts or cable programmes for people who are deaf or hard of hearing)[7] and section 141 (reprographic copying of published works by educational establishments).[8] The scheme may be certified if the Secretary of State is satisfied that it enables the works to which it relates to be identified with sufficient certainty by persons likely to require licences and sets out clearly the charges, if any, payable and other terms on which licences will be granted.[9] The order is made by statutory instrument and the scheme is to be scheduled to the order; the order is not to not take effect before eight weeks after it is made.[10] A certified scheme may not be effectively varied unless a corresponding amendment is made to the order; the Secretary of State must make such an amendment where the scheme has been varied by the Copyright Tribunal.[11] The Secretary of State may revoke an order if it appears to him that the scheme has ceased to be operated, or is no longer being operated according to its terms.[12]

---

[3] *Ibid.* s.143(1).

[4] s.35(2); and see § 10–27, *ante.* Schemes so far certified under this provision include schemes operated by Guild Sound and Vision Limited (but subsequently withdrawn), Educational Recording Agency Limited and Open University Educational Enterprises Limited; see The Copyright (Certification of Licensing Scheme for Educational Recording of Broadcasts) (Guild Sound and Vision Limited) Order 1990, (S.I. 1990 No. 878) but revoked by The Copyright (Certification of Licensing Scheme for Educational Recording of Broadcasts) (Guild Sound and Vision Limited) Order 1990, (S.I. 1990 No. 2007) and The Copyright (Certification of Licensing Scheme for Educational Recording of Broadcasts) (Educational Recording Agency Limited) Order 1990, (S.I. 1990 No. 879) and The Copyright (Certification of Licensing Scheme for Educational Recording of Broadcasts) (Open University Educational Enterprises Limited) Order 1990, (S.I. 1990 No. 2008).

[5] s.60(2); and see § 10–82, *ante.*

[6] s.66(2); and see § 10–99, *ante.*

[7] s.74(4); and see § 10–124, *ante.*

[8] See § 10–29, and § 15–107, *ante.*

[9] C.D.P.A. 1988, s.143(2).

[10] *Ibid.* s.143(3).

[11] *Ibid.* s.143(4).

[12] *Ibid.* s.143(5).

INCOME TAX, CAPITAL GAINS TAX, INHERITANCE TAX AND STAMP DUTY

1. Preliminary

The text of this chapter has been written with particular reference to **16–1** authors and to literary copyright, because so many of the decided tax cases are concerned with this particular topic. Nonetheless, the principles governing the taxation of authors apply equally to any other individual who makes his living from a profession which involves the exploitation of copyright, and this chapter should be read accordingly. Similarly the principles governing the taxation of copyright will extend, not only to copyright in all forms of work, but also to design right. Accordingly, unless otherwise stated, references in this chapter to copyright should be read so as to include design right.

2. Income Tax

A. Introduction. How the fruits of authorship are taxed depends upon **16–2** the manner in which a number of factors are combined. At the outset it may be helpful to summarise the most important of these factors:

(a) the identity of the recipient (whether the author or a third party);

(b) the nature of the receipt (whether a royalty or a lump sum);

(c) the date of the receipt (whether before or after the author ceases to practise his profession);

(d) the status of the recipient (whether or not resident or domiciled in the United Kingdom);

(e) the location of the profession (whether or not practised in the United Kingdom).

It is convenient to treat the identity of the recipient as the primary classifi- **16–3** cation and to consider the other factors as each of the two classes of recipient are dealt with. Authors are dealt with in paragraphs 16–4 to 16–14, *post* and third parties in paragraphs 16–15 to 16–19, *post*. In what follows, references to a person being "taxable" or to "taxation" are references to income tax unless otherwise stated.

16–4　**B. Sums received by an author.** An author who is resident in the United Kingdom and who is carrying on his profession here[1] is taxable upon any royalties he receives whether or not they are received in the United Kingdom.[2] He is similarly taxable upon any lump sums received on the grant of a licence to use a copyright or the total or partial assignment of a copyright,[3] or as compensation or damages for infringement of a copyright.[4]

16–5　The fact that a person produces copyright by an isolated piece of writing rather than in the course of a profession does not mean, of itself, that any profit escapes tax.[5] Where, for example, an independent individual collaborates with a journalist to produce a series of articles, the individual is taxable upon sums received from the transaction unless the individual is being paid mainly for publication rights, any services that he renders being incidental.[6]

16–6　**C. Basis of taxation.** An author carrying on a profession in the United Kingdom is taxable on the preceding year basis except where the special commencement or discontinuance rules apply.[7] The amount of his profit for any year is determined by reference to sums actually received less expenditure actually incurred in the basis period (the so-called "cash basis"). Copyrights are not stock-in-trade or work in progress and do not require to be brought into account for tax purposes.

16–7　**D. Gifts.** Where a trader disposes of an item of trading stock otherwise than in the course of his trade (for example by giving an item away otherwise than to forward the interest of the trade), he is treated for tax purposes as if he had earned, as a trading receipt, an amount equal to the market value of the item at the time of the disposal.[8] It has been held, however, that this rule does not apply to persons carrying on a profession and accordingly an author who gives away his copyright is not treated as if he had received as income an amount equal to the market value of the

---

[1] Where a U.K. resident author carries on his profession wholly abroad see § 16–13, *post*.

[2] Under Case II of Sched. D: Income and Corporation Taxes Act 1988 ("I.C.T.A. 1988") s.18(3).

[3] *Glasson* v. *Rougier* [1944] 1 All E.R. 535; 26 T.C. 86; *Howson* v. *Monsell* [1950] 2 All E.R. 1239; 31 T.C. 529. The principle underlying these decisions is that a professional receipt is incapable of being capital for tax purposes. See also *Billam* v. *Griffith* [1941] 23 T.C. 752; *McKenzie* v. *Arnold* [1952] 33 T.C. 363.

[4] Because any sum which a professional man derives from the carrying on of his profession is income. *cf. Rolfe* v. *Nagel* [1982] S.T.C. 53. As to copyright damages generally see §§ 16–16 and 16–30, *post*.

[5] But the appropriate case of Sched. D would be VI rather than II: I.C.T.A. 1988, s.18(3).

[6] Compare *Hobbs* v. *Hussey* [1942] 1 K.B. 491 with *Housden* v. *Marshall* [1958] 38 T.C. 233. See also *Alloway* v. *Phillips* [1980] 1 W.L.R. 888.

[7] ss.60–63 of I.C.T.A. 1988.

[8] *Sharkey* v. *Wernher* [1956] A.C. 58; 36 T.C. 275.

copyright at the date of the gift.[9] However, such a transaction may result in a charge to capital gains tax upon the author.[10]

E. Top-slicing relief: Lump sum on sale of copyright after 10 years **16–8** **or more.** If more than 10 years after the first publication of a work the copyright[11] is assigned in whole or in part, or licensed[12] by the author[13] and the duration of the assignment or licence is not less than two years, any lump sum[14] receivable for such an assignment or licence is taxable as if it were receivable over more than one year. If the duration of the assignment or licence exceeds six years, the sum is treated as if it were receivable in six equal instalments at yearly intervals, the first of which becomes due in the year in which the sum actually becomes receivable.[15] If the duration is less than six years the sum is similarly spread over a period corresponding to the actual duration.[16] If the author dies during the period over which the sum is to be spread, subject to an election that can be made by his personal representatives, any instalments which are notionally outstanding at the death are treated as having become receivable on the date when the last instalment before the death became receivable.[17] The election that the personal representatives may make is that the tax payable on the instalments notionally outstanding at the date of death is not to exceed the tax that would have been payable on all the instalments had they been spread over the period from the date of the assignment or licence to the date of death.[18] A corresponding rule (which is subject to a corresponding election to be made by the author) applies where instalments are notionally outstanding at the retirement of the author.[19] A claim for the relief at present under consideration cannot be made in respect of a payment if a prior claim for relief has been made under the provisions considered below.[20]

F. Top-slicing: Other circumstances. If no prior claim has been made **16–9** for the relief considered above,[21] where an author grants a licence[22] to use, or totally or partially assign, a copyright[23] that has taken him more than 12 months to create his taxability for certain sums receivable by reason of

---

[9] *Mason* v. *Innes* [1967] Ch. 1079.
[10] See § 16–27, *post.*
[11] The section also applies to public lending right: I.C.T.A. 1988, s.537. There is no corresponding provision in relation to design right.
[12] Both ss.534 and 535 of I.C.T.A. 1988 use the expression "grant any interest in the copyright by licence." A similar provision is to be found in section 5(2) of the Copyright Act 1911, which is not repeated by subsequent Copyright Acts, and which has never been satisfactorily construed: see *Copinger* 12th ed. § 431.
[13] Including a joint author: *ibid.* s.535(11).
[14] Including an advance on account of royalties that is not returnable: *ibid.*
[15] *Ibid.* s.535(1) and (2).
[16] *Ibid.* s.535(1) and (3).
[17] *Ibid.* s.535(4).
[18] *Ibid.* s.535(5).
[19] *Ibid.* s.535(6).
[20] *Ibid.* s.535(9).
[21] *Ibid.* s.534(6).
[22] See n. 12, *ante.*
[23] The section also applies to public lending right: *ibid.* s.537. Corresponding provisions apply to design right: *ibid.* s.537[A] inserted by C.D.P.A. 1988, Sched. 7 para. 36(6).

the grant or assignment is computed as if the sums had become receivable over a period of more than one year.[24] The sums to which this relief applies are:

(a) lump sums, including an advance on account of royalties which is not returnable, at any time after the first publication of the work, and

(b) royalties receivable within two years of the first publication of the work.[25]

If the author spent between one and two years in producing the copyright, half the receipt is taxed as income of the year in which it became receivable and half as income of the preceding year.[26] If the time exceeded two years, one-third of the receipt is taxed as income of the year in which it became receivable, one-third as the income of the preceding year and the final third as the income of the year before that.[27]

16–10   **G. Post-cessation receipts.** As a matter of general Revenue law an author is not taxable on:

(a) lump sums received on the sale of a book *after* the discontinuance of his profession,[28] or

(b) lump sums or royalties received after the discontinuance of his profession from contracts made *before* the discontinuance of his profession.[29]

Sums falling within (b) above are, however, taxable under the "post-cessation receipts" rules[30] which apply to " . . . sums arising from the carrying on of the trade, profession or vocation during any period before the discontinuance (not being sums otherwise chargeable to tax)." Although the view is widely held that sums falling within (a) above are also caught, it is far from clear that this is correct. The authors incline to the view that such sums "arise" from the sale of copyright after discontinuance—not from the carrying on of the profession before the discontinuance—and thus fall outside the "post-cessation receipts" rules. However, so long as significant sales continue to take place, it may be difficult for the author to establish that a discontinuance has occurred.[31]

As will have been inferred from their exclusion from (b) above, royalties

---

[24] I.C.T.A. 1988, s.534(1).

[25] *Ibid.* s.534(4).

[26] *Ibid.* s.534(2).

[27] *Ibid.* s.534(3).

[28] After the permanent discontinuance of his profession an author is in the same position as a third party: see § 16–16, *post.*

[29] *Stainers Executors* v. *Purchase* [1952] A.C. 280; 32 T.C. 367; *Carson* v. *Cheyney's Executor* [1959] A.C. 412; 38 T.C. 240.

[30] I.C.T.A. 1988, ss.103 and 104.

[31] Because it is just as much part of an author's profession to turn his copyright to account as it is to write the books in which the copyright subsisted: see *Carson* v. *Cheyney's Executors, ante.*

paid under a royalty contract formed *after* the discontinuance of an author's profession are taxable on general principles.[32]

H. The foreign element. If an author is not resident in the United Kingdom, but is carrying on his profession of author here, receipts from his United Kingdom writings are prima facie liable to United Kingdom taxation[33] and will probably also be liable to taxation in the country where he is resident. Provided that the country of his residence has a double-tax treaty with the United Kingdom, the author will normally be exempted from United Kingdom taxation by the treaty.

16–11

In any year in which an author is not resident and in which he does not practise his profession in the United Kingdom his professional income is not subject to United Kingdom taxation.[34] However, the profits earned in that year may form the basis of an assessment to tax for the following year of assessment if the author is then resident and domiciled in the United Kingdom provided that he is still carrying on his profession abroad.[35]

16–12

An author who is resident and domiciled in the United Kingdom, but who is practising his profession wholly abroad, is liable to tax on all his receipts.[36] An author who is resident but not domiciled here,[37] and who practises his profession wholly abroad, is liable to tax only on the receipts that he enjoys in the United Kingdom as cash, either by bringing the receipts in as cash, or by reconverting them in the United Kingdom to cash from any form in which they had been converted abroad (the "remittance basis" of taxation).[38] Moreover, an author who is resident but not domiciled here and who carries on his profession wholly abroad is not liable to tax on sums remitted to the United Kingdom in a year after that

16–13

---

[32] See § 16–15 and n. 45, *post*.

[33] s.18(1) of I.C.T.A. 1988. Note that copyright royalties paid to a non-resident author are not subject to deduction of tax at source under s.536 of I.C.T.A. 1988: see H.C. Written Answer, November 10, 1969, Vol. 791, col. 31.

[34] Even if he previously carried on his profession here, he is not subject to the post-cessation receipts rules because there will have been no discontinuance. As to the position when an author permanently discontinues a profession carried on wholly abroad see n. 36, *post*. But a retired author who is not resident in the U.K. is subject to the post-cessation receipts rules if he was carrying on his profession in the U.K. up to the date of his discontinuance, save that he will not be so chargeable on receipts which represent income arising outside the U.K. (ss.103(3) and 104(3) of I.C.T.A. 1988).

[35] *Elmhirst* v. *I.R.C.* 21 T.C. 381. In the case of an author who becomes resident but not domiciled here, such royalties, if remitted, would form the basis of an assessment to tax for the following year.

[36] Under Case V of Sched. D which applies to income arising from possessions out of the U.K. Such an author will not be taxable on sums that arise after he discontinues his profession because the "post-cessation" receipts rules apply only to professions taxable under Case II of Sched. D: *ibid*. ss.103 and 104.

[37] Or, being a Commonwealth citizen or a citizen of the Republic of Ireland, is not ordinarily resident in the U.K.

[38] I.C.T.A. 1988, s.65(5). There is also a deemed remittance where money borrowed in the U.K. is repaid abroad out of unremitted income: *ibid*. s.65(6) to (9).

in which he ceases to practise his profession even though they arose before the cessation.[39]

16–14 **I. Residence.** Historically it has always been a feature of United Kingdom tax law that there is no statutory test of residence, and that the term "resident" must be given its ordinary meaning.[40] Accordingly, the question of whether a person is resident or not is generally determined by reference to such factors as the regularity, purpose and duration of his visits to the United Kingdom, and the existence of a home in the United Kingdom. A comprehensive survey of the meaning of residence is beyond the scope of this chapter, but attention is drawn to the following points:

(a) any person who is present in the United Kingdom in any financial year for periods exceeding six months is resident in that year[41];

(b) any person conducting a profession in the United Kingdom who maintains a home here in any year is resident for any such year in which he visits the United Kingdom[42];

(c) it is the Revenue's view that a person who visits the United Kingdom for periods averaging at least three months per year becomes resident after four years of such visits, unless his arrangements indicated from the start that regular visits of such duration were to be made, in which case he would be resident from the first year[43];

(d) if a British subject who has hitherto been resident leaves the United Kingdom for some temporary purpose only, he does not thereby cease to be resident.[44]

16–15 **J. Royalties received by third parties and personal representatives.** As a matter of general revenue law a third party or a personal representative is taxable[45] only upon royalties derived from a royalty contract made either by himself or another third party at any time, or by the author after his retirement. Accordingly, as a matter of general revenue law, royalties

---

[39] Because the post-cessation receipts rules apply only to professions taxable under Case II of Sched. D: see n. 36, *ante*.

[40] In July 1988 the Revenue produced a consultative document entitled "Residence in the United Kingdom: The Scope of U.K. Taxation for Individuals" which proposed the introduction of a statutory test of residence based on days of presence in the U.K. The proposals were subsequently shelved.

[41] s.336(2) of I.C.T.A. 1988.

[42] *Lowenstein* v. *De Salis*, 10 T.C. 424.

[43] See Revenue Booklet IR20 "Residence and Non-residence: Liability to Tax in the United Kingdom" 1986, paras. 20–30. See also *I.R.C.* v. *Lysaght* [1928] A.C. 234; 13 T.C. 511.

[44] s. 334 of I.C.T.A. 1988. See *Reed* v. *Clark* [1985] S.T.C. 323, where a musician who settled in Los Angeles on April 3, 1978, and returned to the U.K. on May 2, 1979, was held not to have gone abroad for a temporary purpose.

[45] Generally under Case III of Sched. D: see *Asher* v. *London Film Productions Ltd.* [1944] K.B. 133; *Hume* v. *Asquith* [1969] 2 Ch. 58. There may, however, be cases where royalties are not pure income profit in the hands of the recipient in which case Case VI applies: *Curtis Brown Ltd.* v. *Jarvis*, 14 T.C. 744; *Lawrence* v. *I.R.C.* [1940] 23 T.C. 333. See also the dictum of Pennycuick J. in *Noddy Subsidiary Rights Co. Ltd.* v. *I.R.C.* [1966] 3 All E.R. 458.

paid under a contract made by the author in the course of his profession and later assigned to a third party, or which later vest in personal representatives, escape the charge to income tax,[46] unless caught by the provisions considered in paragraphs 16–17 to 16–19, *post*.

K. Lump sums. A lump sum received by a third party (other than a **16–16** dealer in copyright)[47] or personal representative on the assignment or partial assignment of copyright is capital,[48] and is not generally subject to income tax. On the other hand, a lump sum received on the grant of a copyright licence may be either capital or income depending on the true character of the transaction.[49] Thus a lump sum has been held to be capital where the grant of the licence substantially diminished the capital value of the copyright.[50] But a lump sum which is calculated by reference to some anticipated quantum of user[51] or is on account of royalties[52] will normally be income.

Damages for infringement of copyright may also be taxable as income, if they represent compensation for the unauthorised use of copyright rather than the diminution of its capital value.[53]

L. Anti-avoidance provisions. If a royalty or lump sum, which is not **16–17** chargeable to income tax in the hands of a third party, comes into his hands as a result of arrangements which are designed to exploit the earning capacity of an author and which have as their main object, or one of their main objects, the avoidance or reduction of liability to income tax, then the *author* is chargeable to income tax on the receipt, although he is entitled to recover the tax from the third party.[54] Further, there are a number of other provisions which may have the result that sums received by third parties are treated as income of the author. Thus, where an author makes a settlement of copyright or of a contractual right to royalties, any income which arises under the settlement will, if the author has retained any interest under the settlement, continue to be treated as his income.[55] An author who transfers copyright to a non-resident will be subject to tax on income which the non-resident receives as a result of the

---

[46] *Hume* v. *Asquith, ante.*

[47] *cf. Shiner* v. *Lindblom* [1960] 39 T.C. 367.

[48] *Withers* v. *Nethersole* [1948] 1 All E.R. 400; 28 T.C. 501, a case of the partial assignment of copyright.

[49] *Withers* v. *Nethersole, ante.* The principle is the same as that which applies to patent licences: compare *Rustproof Metal Window Co. Ltd.* v. *I.R.C.* [1947] 2 All E.R. 454; 29 T.C. 243 with *Murray* v. *I.C.I. Ltd.* [1967] Ch. 1038; 44 T.C. 175.

[50] *Haig's Trustees* v. *I.R.C.* [1939] S.C. 676; 22 T.C. 725.

[51] *Withers* v. *Nethersole, ante.*

[52] Compare *I.R.C.* v. *Longmans Green & Co. Ltd.* [1932] 17 T.C. 272 with *Beare* v. *Carter* [1940] 2 K.B.187; 23 T.C. 353.

[53] *Raja's Commercial College* v. *Glan Singh* [1977] A.C. 312; [1976] S.T.C. 282. What matters is the character of the payment and not the authority under which it is paid.

[54] I.C.T.A. 1988, s.775.

[55] Under the "settlement" provisions in Part XV of I.C.T.A. 1988. Similar rules apply to dispositions of income which cannot exceed six years: I.C.T.A. 1980, s.660.

transfer, if the author has power to enjoy that income and a purpose of the transfer was the avoidance of tax.[56]

16–18   Further, the "post-cessation receipt" provisions discussed at paragraph 16–10 *ante* apply to lump sums and royalties received by third parties as well as by the author himself. Accordingly lump sums or royalties received by third parties or personal representatives under contracts made by the author before he discontinued his profession are chargeable to income tax if received after the discontinuance.[57] Conversely, since the provisions only apply to sums received after a profession has been discontinued, royalties received by a third party under a royalty contract assigned to him by the author are not caught *so long as the author continues to practise his profession.*

16–19   It is considered that lump sums received by third parties or personal representatives on the sale by them of copyright fall outside the post-cessation receipts provisions altogether.[58] In the case of lump sums paid to the personal representatives of the author of a literary, dramatic, musical or artistic work as consideration for the assignment by them, wholly or partially, of the copyright on the work, it is expressly provided that the post-cessation receipts provisions are not to apply.[59] In the authors' view this is a declaratory provision, intended for the avoidance of doubt,[60] and does not imply that such sums would be caught if received by the author or by a third party other than the author's personal representatives.[61]

16–20 **M. The payer.** A royalty paid by a trader will be deductible in computing the profits of his trade if the royalty is a trading expense, that is to say expenditure which is neither capital[62] nor disallowed by I.C.T.A. 1988, s.74.[63] The same principle applies to a lump sum paid by a trader for the grant of a licence over copyright, which may be either revenue or capital depending on the circumstances of the case, in particular the nature and duration of the rights granted by the licence and the purpose for which they have been acquired.[64] Damages paid by a trader for infringement of

---

[56] I.C.T.A. 1988, s.739.

[57] There is an automatic discontinuance on death.

[58] Post-discontinuance sales by an author are discussed at § 16–10 *ante*. The position of third parties is *a fortiori*.

[59] I.C.T.A. 1988, ss.103(3)(*b*) and 104(3). There is a corresponding provision relating to assignments of design right: *ibid.* s.103(3)(*bb*) inserted by C.D.P.A. 1988, Sched. 7, para. 36(3).

[60] *cf.* the dictum of Lord Herschell in *West Derby Union* v. *Metropolitan Life Assurance Society* [1897] A.C. at p. 656.

[61] For example a legatee of copyright.

[62] On ordinary principles of commercial accounting it will generally be proper for a trader to charge royalties against income even if the royalties are consideration for the acquisition of a capital asset in the form of copyright. *cf. C.I.R.* v. *Land Securities Investment Trust* [1969] 2 All E.R. 430; 45 T.C. 495 where rentcharges were disallowed as capital because it was not proper to debit them against income.

[63] A royalty which is an annual payment in the hands of the recipient will not be disallowed under I.C.T.A. 1988, s.74(m) if it is a trading expense: *Paterson Engineering Co. Ltd.* v. *Duff*, 24 T.C. 43.

[64] For a full treatment of the distinction between capital and revenue expenditure see *Whiteman on Income Tax* paras. 7–02–7–11.

copyright will normally be deductible in computing the profits of his trade if the infringement was incidental to the carrying on of the trade.[65]

A copyright royalty paid by a non-trader or which, if paid by a trader, is **16–21** not a trading expense, is not allowable for income tax purposes, even if it is an annual payment in the hands of the recipient.[66] Further, it must be paid gross, unless the recipient is normally resident abroad,[67] in which case the payer is obliged to deduct tax at the basic rate from the payment and account to the Revenue for the tax.[68] It is then up to the non-resident, if entitled to do so, to claim the tax so deducted from the Revenue. Where any royalty payment is made through the hands of an agent resident in the United Kingdom, and the agent is entitled as against the author to deduct commission from the payment, the sum from which he must deduct tax at the basic rate is the residue of the royalty payment after the deduction of the commission.[69] If the amount of the commission is not ascertained at the time of the payment, tax is deductible from the gross amount of the payment, but when the amount of commission becomes ascertained, the agent may reclaim from the Revenue an amount equal to tax at the basic rate on the commission.[70]

There are corresponding provisions for royalties paid to non-resident owners of design right.[71]

Every person carrying on a trade or business may be required by notice **16–22** to make a return of periodical or lump sum payments made in respect of any copyright, public lending right or design right. The same applies to any body of persons carrying on activities which do not constitute a trade or business.[72]

N. Films, tapes or discs. Where any person carries on a trade or business **16–23** which includes the exploitation[73] of a film, tape or disc, any expenditure on the production or acquisition of a film, tape or disc is regarded as expenditure of a revenue nature,[74] notwithstanding that it would be capi-

---

[65] See *Herald and Weekly Times Ltd.* v. *Federal Commissioner of Taxation* [1932] 48 C.L.R. 113 (concerning the deductibility of libel damages by a newspaper).

[66] I.C.T.A. 1988, s.125 (ousting the general rule that annual payments are deductible in computing the total income of an individual, or are a charge on income in the case of a company).

[67] I.C.T.A. 1988, s.536 (which also applies to public lending right: *ibid.* s.537). The section does not apply to non-resident professional authors: see n. 33, *ante*. Nor does it apply to payments in respect of copyright in a cinematographic film or video recording, or the sound-track of such a film or recording, so far as it is not generally exploited: *ibid.* s.536(2) as substituted by C.D.P.A. 1988, Sched. 7, para. 36(5).

[68] I.C.T.A. 1988, s.536(1); unless the royalties are from exported copies of a work: *ibid.* and unless the Revenue has agreed that tax need not be deducted. It has been held that a lump sum may be a royalty for the purpose of this provision; *I.R.C.* v. *Longmans Green*, 17 T.C. 272, *ante*.

[69] *Ibid.* s.536(3).

[70] *Ibid.* s.536(4).

[71] *Ibid.* s.537B (inserted by C.D.P.A. 1988, Sched. 7, para. 36(6)).

[72] Taxes Management Act 1970, s.16 (as amended by C.D.P.A. 1988, Sched. 7 para. 13).

[73] The exploitation of an asset is not precluded from being a trade because the exploitation takes the form of granting licences; *Noddy Subsidiary Rights Co. Ltd.* v. *I.R.C.* [1966] 3 All E.R. 459; 43 T.C. 458.

[74] Finance Act 1982, s.72(3). The expenditure is allocated to "relevant periods" as defined.

tal under general revenue law,[75] and any sum received from the disposal of any interest in or right in or over the film, tape or disc is regarded as a receipt of a revenue nature.[76]

3. Capital Gains Tax

16–24 **A. Introduction.** A person who is resident or ordinarily resident[77] in the United Kingdom is chargeable to capital gains tax on the disposal[78] of copyright[79] wherever it is situate,[80] save that an individual who, whilst being resident or ordinarily resident in the United Kingdom is not domiciled here, is taxable only on a remittance basis[81] in respect of gains arising on the disposal of copyright situate abroad.[82]

16–25 Although a person who disposes of copyright is prima facie liable to capital gains tax, there are special rules to ensure that sums taken into account for income tax purposes are left out of account for capital gains tax.[83] Thus an author who disposes of copyright will not be subject to capital gains tax if the consideration is taken into account for income tax purposes as a professional receipt.[84]

16–26 **B. Sales.** Unless the consideration is chargeable to income tax, an arm's length sale of copyright to an unconnected person will bring about a charge to capital gains tax on the difference between the consideration received and the acquisition cost[85] of the copyright plus the appropriate indexation allowance. Notwithstanding the general rule referred to above, that sums taken into account for income tax purposes are left out of

---

[75] Unless they are trading stock, the original master print of a film and the copyright in it are capital assets of the trade of film production or distribution and the Revenue accept that they are plant. Before the introduction of F.A. 1982, s.72 this meant that expenditure on the production of the master print qualified for capital allowances, and any profit on disposal was a capital receipt. This treatment still applies to certain films, tapes and discs certified by the Secretary of State.

[76] F.A. 1982, s.72(6).

[77] "Resident" and "ordinarily resident" have the same meanings for the purposes of capital gains tax as they have for income tax: *ibid.* s.18(1). See § 16–14, *ante*. It is arguable that a person cannot be ordinarily resident in the U.K. unless he is resident here but the Revenue do not share this view.

[78] Which includes a part disposal: Capital Gains Tax Act ("C.G.T.A.") 1979, s.19(2).

[79] Incorporeal property is an "asset" for capital gains tax purposes: *ibid.* s.19(1). As to design right see § 16–1, *ante*. Where a third party disposes of the benefit of a royalty contract he will generally be subject to capital gains tax. *cf.* C.G.T.A. 1979, s.144(c) and *Rank Xerox* v. *Lane* [1981] A.C. 629; S.T.C. 740; [1980] R.P.C. 385. But an author who commutes royalties for a lump sum is liable to income tax: *Glasson* v. *Rougier* [1944] 1 All E.R. 535; 26 T.C. 86.

[80] *Ibid.* s.2(1).

[81] *Ibid.* s.14(1), and see *ibid.* s.14(2) for the definition of remittance for these purposes.

[82] Copyright, design right and franchises, and rights or licenses to use any copyright work or design in which design right subsists, are situated in the U.K. if they or any right derived from them, are exercisable in the U.K.: *ibid.* s.18(4)(hb) as substituted by C.D.P.A. 1988, Sched. 7, para. 26. And see *Redwood Music Ltd.* v. *B. Feldman & Co. Ltd.* [1979] R.P.C. 1.

[83] *Ibid.* s.31(1).

[84] See § 16–4, *ante*.

[85] See § 16–29, *post*.

account for capital gains tax, the Revenue are not precluded from taking into account as consideration the capitalised value of any right to receive royalties[86] and, if such right is incapable of valuation, the consideration for the sale is market value.[87] Further, where there is a sale of copyright otherwise than by way of bargain at arm's length or to a connected person, market value is automatically substituted for the actual consideration.[88]

C. Gifts A gift of copyright, being a disposal otherwise than by way of **16–27** bargain at arm's length, is treated as a disposal at market value and will bring about a charge to capital gains tax on the difference between the market value of the copyright at the date of gift and the acquisition cost of the copyright plus the appropriate indexation allowance. However, hold-over relief will sometimes be available, in particular where the donor is an individual and either (a) the gift is a chargeable transfer for inheritance tax purposes, or (b) the copyright satisfies the requirement that it is an asset used for the purpose of a trade or profession carried on by the donor.[89] The effect of hold-over relief is that the gain realised on the gift is not brought into charge for capital gains tax purposes until the copyright is disposed of by the donee.[90]

It is considered that a gift[91] of future copyright (that is for instance **16–28** copyright not yet in existence)[92] has no capital gains tax consequences, because no asset is disposed of either at the date of assignment or when the copyright comes into existence.[93] At the date of assignment there is no asset in existence, and when the copyright does come into existence it automatically vests in the assignee without ever having vested in the author.[94]

D. Acquisition cost. Where there is a disposal of copyright by a person **16–29** who owned it on March 31, 1982, his acquisition cost will be the market value of the copyright on that date.[95] Otherwise the acquisition cost of

---

[86] C.G.T.A. 1979, s.31(3). Thus, where copyright is assigned in return for royalties, the assignor (whether author or third party) is exposed to the risk of double taxation, namely CGT on the capitalised value of the royalties and income tax on the royalties as they come in. The authors know of no case in practice where the Revenue have invoked this subsection in the context of copyright royalties, and it may be that the Revenue view the rather odd words "are not precluded" as being permissive. In the authors' view, however, the provision is declaratory and confers no such discretion on the Revenue.

[87] *Ibid.* s.29A(1)(*b*).

[88] *Ibid.* ss.29A(1)(*a*) and 62.

[89] *Ibid.* ss.126 and 147A. The donee must generally be a U.K. resident.

[90] Or the donee emigrates: Finance Act 1981, s.79.

[91] It is understood that the Revenue take the point (which is probably right) that a gratuitous assignment of future copyright is ineffective even under seal. Accordingly, to ensure that an assignment of future copyright is effective it should be supported by consideration however nominal.

[92] See C.D.P.A. 1988, s.91(2).

[93] See *Whiteman on Capital Gains Tax* (4th ed., 1988) para. 7.07: "the word disposal involves there being some proprietary or beneficial right in the disposer at the time".

[94] C.D.P.A. 1988, s.91, provides that the assignment takes effect by way of an agreement: *ibid.* s.91(1).

[95] Finance Act 1988, s.87.

copyright in the hands of a third party will be the consideration which he gave for it,[96] unless the acquisition was otherwise than by bargain at arm's length or from a connected person, in which case it will be market value.[97] So far as the author is concerned, his acquisition cost will consist of any allowable expenditure incurred in creating the copyright[98]; but if, as will normally be the case, the expenditure has already been allowed in an income tax computation, it will not be allowable expenditure for the purposes of capital gains tax.[99] Personal representatives are treated as having acquired assets from the deceased at their market value at the date of death.[1]

Where there is a disposal of copyright which at the date of disposal has less than 50 years to run, the acquisition cost of the person making the disposal is written off on a straight-line basis from the date of acquisition to the date on which the copyright will expire.[2]

16–30   **E. Capital sums derived from assets.** There is a disposal for capital gains tax purposes whenever a capital sum is derived from copyright.[3] Thus, unless it is taxable as income, any sum received on the grant of, or under the terms of, a licence to exploit copyright, or as damages for infringement of copyright, will be subject to capital gains tax.[4]

Although moral rights[5] are not assignable,[6] this does not prevent them being "assets" for capital gains tax purposes because they can be waived[7] and thus turned to account.[8] It follows that, unless it is taxable as income,[9] any sum which a person obtains in return for waiving moral rights is subject to capital gains tax as a capital sum derived from assets.[10] On the other hand, where an infringement of moral rights has occurred, it is thought that any sum which an individual receives by way of compensation or damages will not be a chargeable gain.[11]

---

[96] C.G.T.A. 1979, s.32(1)(a).

[97] See n. 88, *ante.*

[98] C.G.T.A. 1979, s.32(1)(a).

[99] *Ibid.* s.33(1).

[1] *Ibid.* s.49(1)(a). Where the value of any assets has been ascertained for the purpose of inheritance tax (see §§ 16–31 and 16–32, *post*) that value is taken to be market value at the date of death for CGT purposes.: *ibid.* s.153.

[2] *Ibid.* s.38.

[3] *Ibid.* s.20.

[4] Such damages will not qualify for concessionary treatment because there is an underlying asset: see Extra Statutory Concession D33 "Capital gains tax on compensation and damages."

[5] See Chap. 22, *post.*

[6] C.D.P.A. 1988, s.94.

[7] *Ibid.* s.87.

[8] See *O'Brien* v. *Benson's Hosiery* [1979] 53 T.C. 241.

[9] Either as a professional receipt or under Case VI of Sched. D.

[10] The sums will not fall within C.G.T.A. 1979, s.19(5) because there will be no infringement in these circumstances (C.D.P.A. 1988, s.87).

[11] C.G.T.A. 1979, s.19(5), which applies to compensation or damages for any wrong or injury suffered by an individual in his person or profession. C.D.P.A. 1988, s.103(1) states that infringement is actionable as a breach of statutory duty, and the Revenue accept that damages in tort are covered by s.19(5): see the Extra Statutory Concession referred to at n. 4, *ante.*

4. Inheritance Tax

A. Death. On the death of an author inheritance tax is payable on the   **16–31**
value of any copyrights and, in so far as he has assigned his copyrights on
royalty terms, on the value of any publishing agreements which at the
time of death were either vested in him or comprised in a settlement in
which he had an interest in possession or were property subject to a reservation.[12] The basis of valuation of the property for the purposes of inheritance tax is that established in section 160 of the Inheritance Tax Act
1984, namely the price which the property might reasonably be expected
to fetch if sold in the open market immediately before the death.[13] A valuation by a publisher or literary agent is evidence[14] of open market value,
although the Capital Taxes Office (which has its own experts on copyright
valuation) is not bound to accept it.

B. Gifts or settlements of copyrights. It is not uncommon for authors to   **16–32**
make *inter vivos* gifts or settlements of their copyrights. Where the gift is to
an individual or the settlement is either (a) a settlement in which an individual has an interest in possession, or (b) an accumulation and maintenance settlement, the gift or settlement will be a "potentially exempt
transfer" and will not be subject to inheritance tax unless the author dies
within seven years.[15] In that event the "potentially exempt transfer" will
be converted into a "chargeable transfer" and inheritance tax will become
payable on the value of the copyrights at the time of the gift or settlement
(less the value of any consideration received by the author). However, the
rate at which inheritance tax is payable is the rate in force at the time of
death,[16] and tapering relief is available if the death occurs more than three
years after the date of the gift or settlement.[17] A gift or settlement which
does not fall into any of the categories mentioned above will be a chargeable transfer[18] at the time when it is made, and inheritance tax will be
payable at the lifetime rates[19] on the value of the copyrights comprised in
the gift or settlement. If the author dies within seven years the tax payable
on the chargeable transfer is recomputed at the full death rates in force at

---

[12] Inheritance Tax Act ("I.H.T.A.") 1984, ss.4(1), 5 and 49(1); Finance Act 1986, s.102(3).
There are important exemptions for property passing to the surviving spouse and for gifts
to charity: *ibid.* ss.18 and 23. The Inheritance Tax Act 1984 is the re-named Capital
Transfer Act 1984: see s.100(1)(*a*) Finance Act 1986.

[13] If the death of the author affects the value, the change is taken into account as though it
had occurred immediately before the death: *ibid.* s.171.

[14] It is admissible as expert evidence.

[15] I.H.T.A. 1984, s.3A.

[16] *Ibid.* Sched. 2, para. 1A.

[17] *Ibid.* s.7(4).

[18] A chargeable transfer is a transfer of value made by an individual other than an exempt
transfer (*ibid.* s.2). A transfer of value is any disposition which reduces the value of the
transferor's estate. Apart from the exemptions mentioned in n. 12, *ante*, there is also an
important exemption for transfers not exceeding £3,000 in any one year: *ibid.* s.19.

[19] Lifetime transfers are charged at one-half of the death rates: *ibid.* s.7(2).

the time of death and, if this results in a higher amount of tax, the balance becomes payable.[20]

Where there is an effective assignment of future copyright it is apprehended that the Revenue may invoke the so-called "associated operations" provisions[21] if (as will usually be the case) it can be said that the assignment and the creation of the copyright were effected with reference to one another. If so, the assignment will be treated as having taken place at the time when the copyright comes into existence.

A sale of copyright (whether existing or future) at arm's length will not attract inheritance tax even if the consideration received by the author subsequently proves to be inadequate.[22]

16–33 **C. Business property relief.** In the absence of any authority on the point it is unclear whether copyright comprised in the estate of an author at the time of his death qualifies for business property relief.[23] In practice, however, the authors understand that the Revenue do afford business property relief on the death of an author who was carrying on his profession at the time of death, or at least until shortly before his death. Although the Revenue regard this treatment as concessionary, in the opinion of the authors there are persuasive arguments in favour of the view that, on the death of a professional author, the copyrights comprised in his estate qualify for business property relief as a matter of law.[24] On the other hand, where an author makes an *inter vivos* gift or settlement of copyright, it is difficult to see how business property relief can ever be available because there is no transfer of a business—only a transfer of individual business assets.[25]

16–34 **D. Author domiciled out of the United Kingdom.** If an author is domiciled[26] out of the United Kingdom, inheritance tax is payable only in respect of his copyrights situate in the United Kingdom.[27] As in respect of any particular work separate copyrights subsist in different parts of the world under the laws of different countries, it is apprehended that copyright in a particular work only subsists in the United Kingdom in so far as it is protected by the Copyright, Designs and Patents Act 1988, and that the copyright in the work which is protected in other countries by other laws is situate in those countries and not in the United Kingdom.[28]

---

[20] Lifetime transfers are charged at one-half of the death rates: s.7(5). Because of tapering relief tax at the death rates may be lower, but there is no refund in that event: *ibid.* s.7(5).

[21] I.H.T.A. 1984, s.268.

[22] *Ibid.* s.10.

[23] *Ibid.* ss.103 *et seq.*

[24] See Dymond *Capital Taxes* paras. 24.710–711.

[25] *cf.* the capital gains tax cases of *McGregor* v. *Adcock* [1977] 3 All E.R. 65; 51 T.C. 692; and *Mannion* v. *Johnston* [1988] S.T.C. 758.

[26] For inheritance tax purposes the meaning of domicile in general law is extended by I.H.T.A. 1984, s.267.

[27] *Ibid.* s.6(1).

[28] For inheritance tax purposes there is no "situs" code comparable to C.G.T.A. 1979, s.18: see n. 82, *ante.*

5. Stamp Duty

A. Sales of copyright. An assignment or partial assignment of copyright   **16–35**
for a monetary consideration[29] is liable to stamp duty as a conveyance on
sale assessed *ad valorem* upon the amount or value of the consideration.[30]
Any other instrument, such as a declaration of trust, is similarly dutiable
if it operates as a conveyance on sale. If the consideration for the sale is, or
includes, a royalty of wholly uncertain amount, such as a royalty per copy
sold, no *ad valorem* duty is imposed on the royalty consideration; but, if
there is a sum which can be calculated at the time of sale, such as a minimum or maximum royalty, *ad valorem* duty is payable on the fixed sum
even though the royalty is of a fluctuating amount.[31] Although, as a
general rule, duty is payable on the full amount of the consideration
regardless of how far in the future it is payable,[32] where the consideration
consists of periodical payments such as royalties, duty is restricted to sums
payable during the period of 20 years from the date of the instrument.[33]

B. Agreements and licences. An agreement for the sale of copyright or   **16–36**
of any interest in copyright is subject to the same *ad valorem* duty as a conveyance on sale.[34] Any subsequent conveyance in conformity with the
agreement is not subject to further duty but, where the subsequent conveyance takes place within six months from the date of the agreement and
is duly stamped, the agreement need not itself be stamped. An exclusive
licence over copyright is "property" for stamp duty purposes,[35] and the
grant of an exclusive licence is stampable as a conveyance on sale even
though the instrument operates by way of grant rather than transfer.[36] On
the other hand, a non-exclusive licence is not subject to *ad valorem* duty
because it is neither a sale nor a transfer of property.

C. Gifts. A gift or other voluntary disposition of copyright is no longer   **16–37**
subject to *ad valorem* stamp duty. Further, an instrument which effects a
gift or other voluntary disposition no longer needs to be presented to the
Stamp Office for adjudication if it falls within the categories listed in the

---

[29] Or consideration consisting of stock or marketable securities: see *John Foster and Sons Ltd.* v.
I.R.C. [1894] 1 K.B. 516 at 528.

[30] F.A. 1984, s.109. See also Stamp Act 1891, s.6(1).

[31] *Underground Electric Rwys.* v. *I.R.C.* [1906] A.C. 21; *Underground Electric Rwys. and Glyn Mills*
v. *I.R.C.* [1916] 1 K.B. 306; *Independent Television Authority* v. *I.R.C.* [1961] A.C. 427. The
principle that duty is charged on the maximum consideration that may become payable
under the sale agreement is known as the contingency principle and is considered to apply
generally for stamp duty purposes even though it derives from cases concerned with the
obsolete bond covenant duty.

[32] *Blendett* v. *I.R.C.* [1984] S.T.C. 95.

[33] Stamp Act 1891, s.56.

[34] *Ibid.* s.59. Where there is an agreement for the sale of copyright and manuscript, the consideration has to be apportioned since the manuscript is "goods" and is not dutiable
under s.59. In *Re Dickens* [1935] Ch. 267 consideration was apportioned equally between
the copyright and the manuscript.

[35] *cf. Smelting Corporation of Australia* v. *I.R.C.* [1897] 1 Q.B. 175 (a patent case). There is no
decided case on copyright.

[36] *cf. George Wimpey & Co. Ltd.* v. *I.R.C.* [1975] 1 W.L.R. 995.

Schedule to the Stamp Duties (Exempt Instruments) Regulations and includes the appropriate certificate.[37]

16–38   **D. Foreign copyright.** An agreement for the sale of foreign copyright is not subject to *ad valorem* duty,[38] nor is an assignment of foreign copyright unless it is either executed in the United Kingdom or relates to anything done or to be done in the United Kingdom.[39]

---

[37] S.I. 1987 No. 516.

[38] Stamp Act 1891, s.59(1).

[39] *Ibid.* s.14(4). Where there is a sale of both U.K. and foreign copyright, duty may be saved by having two separate instruments.

INTERNATIONAL COPYRIGHT AND THE PROTECTION OF
WORKS ORIGINATING OUTSIDE THE UNITED KINGDOM

1. International Copyright

A. *Scope of international copyright*

Relationship between international conventions, treaties and agree-   **17–1**
ments, and domestic law. International copyright is concerned with
treaties, conventions or agreements between nations requiring their signa-

tories to respect, in their own countries, the copyright of nationals of other signatories. There is no general principle of international law requiring such protection[1] and, before the making of international agreements regarding the matter, a book written by a foreigner and published abroad could obtain no protection in this country.[2]

In some countries such conventions, treaties or agreements are regarded by the courts as part of the law of the land but, in the United Kingdom, since 1911, this is not the case. The courts, except in very limited circumstances,[3] are not concerned to interpret such treaties, conventions or agreements, but only Acts of Parliament and Orders in Council made for the purpose of giving effect thereto.[4]

It becomes necessary, therefore, in considering copyright from the international aspect, to deal, first, with the general body of conventions, treaties and agreements regulating the copyright relations between different countries, and, secondly,[5] with the protection actually afforded to foreign works by the law of this country.

Because of their importance, the two major Conventions, the Berne Convention and the Universal Copyright Convention, are dealt with in detail in this part of this Chapter. Other Conventions and Agreements to which this country is a party are dealt with, where necessary, in the relevant parts of this book.

B. *The Berne Convention and its Revisions*

(i) History

17–2   **Early treaties.** Prior to 1886, international copyright was regulated by treaties between a number of European nations. In England the Crown was authorised, by the International Copyright Act 1844,[6] and various amending Acts,[7] by Order in Council, to direct that foreign works should be entitled to copyright in the United Kingdom, and pursuant to these Acts a large number of Orders in Council were promulgated to give effect to these treaties. The general purport of these treaties was to give the authors of works first published in one of the federated States the same privileges in the other States as would have been enjoyed if the work had been first published there.

17–3   **Berne Convention.** A complicated state of circumstances arose, for the rights of an author in foreign countries varied according to the particular treaty or Order in Council, and, in 1885, an attempt was made by several

---

[1] Curtis, *Copyright*, p. 22; see *Def Lepp Music* v. *Stuart-Brown* [1986] R.P.C. 273.

[2] *Guichard* v. *Mori* (1831) 9 L.J.Ch. 227. The question of how far under the Acts of Anne and of 1842 an alien could obtain copyright at all in England (apart from the International Copyright Acts) was discussed in *Jefferys (C.)* v. *Boosey (T.)* (1855) 4 H.L.C. 815, and *Routledge* v. *Low* (1868) L.R. 3 H.L. 100.

[3] *Post*, § 17–81. See, however, as to the Treaty of Rome 1957, Chap. 14, *ante*.

[4] *The Jade* [1976] 1 W.L.R. 430. See also *Smith etc. Ltd.* v. *R.D. Harbottle (Mercantile) Ltd.* [1980] R.P.C. 363 and *E's Applications* [1983] R.P.C. 231.

[5] See n. 3, *ante*.

[6] 7 & 8 Vict. c. 12.

[7] 15 & 16 Vict. c. 12; 25 & 26 Vict. c. 68; 38 & 39 Vict. c. 12.

of the great Powers meeting in Conference to secure uniformity throughout their dominions. Great Britain was a party to this Conference, which resulted in the framing of a Convention, known as the Berne Convention, whereby the contracting States were "constituted into a Union for the protection of the rights of authors over their literary and artistic works."[8] To enable Great Britain to give effect to this Convention by Orders in Council, the International Copyright Act 1886[9] was passed.

Additional Act of Paris 1896. In the year 1896 another Conference of the Powers was held in Paris to consider certain modifications of the original Convention which experience had shown to be necessary or expedient. This Conference resulted in what was called the "Additional Act of Paris 1896." This was adopted by Great Britain on March 7, 1898, but Great Britain was then unable to accept an "Interpretative Clause" that was agreed to by the other Powers. **17–4**

The Revised Berne Convention of Berlin 1908. In the year 1908 a further Conference of the Powers was held in Berlin, the object of which was "to secure, if possible, a general agreement to such a revision of the Berne Convention and the Additional Act of Paris as would enable the contracting States to sign a single new instrument containing stipulations of a more complete and simple character, with a view, not only to affording a more effectual protection to the author, but also to removing the more salient difficulties which had been encountered in the working of the existing arrangements."[10] The result of the Conference was the Revised Berne or Berlin Convention 1908, which replaced the original Convention of 1887, and the Additional Act of Paris 1896, except that States who were signatories to the original Convention and the Additional Act of Paris could still elect to be bound by the provisions of these Conventions in preference to those of the Revised Convention.[11] An additional Protocol was agreed to on March 20, 1914. **17–5**

Rome and Brussels Conventions. The Berne Convention was revised at Rome in 1928 and again at Brussels in 1948. The latter revision involved alterations to which effect could only be given in the United Kingdom by new legislation and one of the reasons for the passing of the 1956 Act was to enable the United Kingdom to ratify the Brussels Convention.[12] **17–6**

Stockholm Convention. The Berne Convention was again revised at Stockholm in 1967.[13] This introduced the controversial Protocol Regarding Developing Countries[14] designed to meet the wishes of certain devel- **17–7**

---

[8] Berne Convention 1887, Art. 1. Great Britain adhered to this Convention on November 28, 1887.
[9] 49 & 50 Vict. c. 33.
[10] Report of British Commissioners, Blue Book 1909, Miscellaneous (No. 2) Cd. 4467, p. 5.
[11] Revised Convention Art. 27.
[12] For text see § 1681 *et seq.* of *Copinger* (10th ed.).
[13] Cmnd. 4412. For text see § 1681 *et seq.* of *Copinger* (11th ed.). See "Analysis of the Protocol Regarding Developing Countries" by Dorothy M. Schrader, *Bulletin of the Copyright Society of the U.S.A.*, February 1970, Vol. 17, No. 3, p. 160.
[14] See *Protocol Regarding the Developing Countries* by R.F. Whale.

oping countries who considered the extent of protection provided by the Berne Convention too great in the light of the particular domestic circumstances of such countries. The Protocol therefore provided that any such country which ratified or acceded to the Convention may make reservations in respect of certain matters which would have the effect of giving less protection in that country than is afforded in other countries of the Berne Union.

17–8   The adoption of the Protocol, despite opposition, led to a serious situation in the international copyright field. Thus, although Article 21 of the Stockholm Convention made the Protocol an integral part of the Convention, Article 28 provided that any country ratifying or acceding to the Convention may declare that its ratification or accession is not to apply to the substantive provisions of the Convention and the Protocol. As a result, by 1970, none of the major developed countries had ratified or acceded to the substantive provisions thereof; this country, for instance, acceded only to the administrative provisions and final clauses thereof, namely Articles 22 to 38.

17–9   **Paris Act.** This situation was particularly unfortunate since it had been hoped that one of the results of the Stockholm revision would have been that the United States of America would eventually join the Berne Union after revising its domestic law. However, such hopes faded as a result of what transpired at Stockholm. Serious attempts were therefore made, following Stockholm, to try and resolve this situation, including proposals to revise the Universal Copyright Convention and to revise further the Berne Convention. In fact both Conventions were revised in Paris in 1971, Articles 22 and 23 of the Paris revision of Berne being amended in October 1979. The main change, in 1971, as regards the Berne Convention, was the dropping of Article 21 relating to the Protocol Regarding Developing Countries and the Protocol itself and, instead, to provide acceptable special provisions in favour of developing countries in Article 21 and an Appendix in the Paris revision of Berne. As a result many countries, including some of the major countries, including this country, have now adhered to the Paris Act. So far as the United States of America is concerned, that country has now acceded to the Paris Act with effect from March 1, 1989. Because of some of the alterations in the Paris Act, there would have to have been amendments of the 1956 Act before this country could have adhered to such provisions: Article 36.[15] However, it would seem that the 1988 Act (the copyright provisions of which came into force on August 1, 1989) contained sufficient amendments to the law to enable this country to ratify the Paris Act, which it did on September 29, 1989, with effect from January 2, 1990. What follows, therefore, is concerned mainly with an examination of the substantive provisions of the Paris Act, which are basically the same as those of the Stockholm Convention.[16]

---

[15] See Report of the 1977 Copyright Commmittee, Cmnd. 6732, paras. 50–60 and 85 and Intellectual Property and Innovation (White Paper) 1986 Cmnd. 9712.

[16] For text see § C–1 *et seq. post.* For an examination of the equivalent provisions of the Brussels Convention, see *Copinger* (10th ed.), Chap. 24 and of the Stockholm Convention see *Copinger* (10th ed.), Chap. 24.

(ii) Substantive provisions of Paris Act

Principles underlying the Convention. Two systems are possible for **17–10** an international copyright convention. The theoretically most satisfactory system would be a complete copyright code to be applied in each country of the Union both for nationals and subjects of other countries of the Union.[17] A less satisfactory system is one which merely requires each Member State to give to the nationals of other Member States the same protection as it gives to its own members, with the result that the measure of protection will vary from state to state. The system in fact adopted in the Berne Convention represented a compromise of the two systems and the revisions of the Convention alluded to above have tended to extend the principle of the common code. In fact the Paris Act embodies a reasonably complete code but, as will be seen, specifically reserves to members the right to deal with certain matters by their own legislation.

Eligibility for protection. Articles 4, 5 and 6 of the Berlin, Rome and **17–11** Brussels Conventions contained the fundamental dual principle of mutual protection and code protection. Articles 4, 5 and 6(1) of the Brussels Convention have been redrafted and rearranged to form Articles 3, 4 and 5 of the Paris Act.

Article 3 contains the general criteria for eligibility for protection and provides as follows:

"(1) The protection of this Convention shall apply to:
  (*a*) Authors who are nationals of one of the countries of the Union, for their works, whether published or not;
  (*b*) Authors who are not nationals of one of the countries of the Union, for their works first published in one of those countries, or simultaneously in a country outside the Union and in a country of the Union.

(2) Authors who are not nationals of one of the countries of the Union but who have their habitual residence in one of them shall, for the purposes of this Convention, be assimilated to nationals of that country."

This Article is broader in scope than the Brussels Convention, since works of nationals of Union countries are to be protected, even if first publication takes place in a non-Union country. The previous position was that first publication in a non-Union country would have meant loss of protection: Article 4 of Brussels. Further, protection is to be afforded to nationals of non-Union countries habitually resident in a Union country.[18] It is to be noted that the Paris Act provides, in a similar way to the Brussels Convention, that it is open to any country of the Union to restrict protection of works whose authors are nationals of a non-Union country which does not give reciprocal rights and are not habitually resident in a country of the Union: Article 6.

---

[17] See § 14–25, *ante.*
[18] See C.D.P.A. 1988, s.154.

The Paris Act (Article 4) contains special criteria of eligibility for protection in respect of cinematographic works and works of architecture (new in Stockholm). This Article provides:

"The protection of this Convention shall apply, even if the conditions of Article 3 are not fulfilled, to:

(a) Authors of cinematographic works the maker of which has his headquarters or habitual residence in one of the countries of the Union;

(b) Authors of works of architecture erected in a country of the Union or of other artistic works incorporated in a building or other structure located in a country of the Union."

17–12   What is "publication"? As has been seen, under Article 3 of the Paris Act protection, in the case of authors who are not nationals of one of the countries of the Union, depends upon first publication of the work in a Union country, or simultaneously in a non-Union country and in a Union country. Article 3(3) provides that the expression "published works" is to mean works published with the consent of their authors, whatever may be the means of manufacture of the copies, provided that the availability of such copies has been such as to satisfy the reasonable requirements of the public, having regard to the nature of the work. The performance of a dramatic, dramatico-musical, cinematographic or musical work, the public recitation of a literary work, the communication by wire or the broadcasting of literary or artistic works, the exhibition of a work of art and the construction of a work of architecture is not to constitute publication.

This definition has been changed in certain respects from that in Article 4(4) of the Brussels Convention. Thus the present definition is to apply generally whereas, under Article 4(4), the definition was only to apply for the purposes of Articles 4, 5 and 6 of the Brussels Convention. Again, whereas previously it had been understood that there could be no publication unless it was authorised, the new definition expressly limits publication to works published with the consent of the authors. Finally, the language used is now more suitable to cover various kinds of works, in that publication depends, to some extent, on the nature of the work. The concept of publication in the Paris Act is, therefore, similar to that adopted by the 1988 Act,[19] and all that is required to constitute publication in a particular country is that copies should be made available for sale in that country, with the consent of the copyright owner, sufficient to satisfy the reasonable requirements of the public there, having regard to the nature of the work.

17–13   It will have been noted that, under the Paris Act, the construction of a work of architecture does not constitute publication. However, the 1988 Act provides that the construction of a work of architecture in the form of a building is to be the equivalent of publication of the work.[20]

---

[19] See C.D.P.A. 1988, s.175.
[20] Compare *ibid.* s.175(3) and Copyright Act, 1956, s.49(2)(a). See § 3–13, *ante.*

Simultaneous publication. The alternative to first publication in a **17–14**
Union country, to entitle authors who are nationals of non-Union countries to the protection of the Paris Act, is simultaneous publication in a
non-Union country and in a Union country: Article 3. Prior to the Brussels Convention the only provision dealing with "simultaneous publication" was Article 4 in connection with country of origin. As there was no
definition of this term, "simultaneous" prima facie appeared to involve
publication on the same day. However, Article 4(3) of the Brussels Convention added a definition which is substantially repeated in Article 3(4)
of the Paris Act. That is that a work is to be considered as having been
published simultaneously in several countries if it has been published in
two or more countries within 30 days of its first publication.[21]

Extent of protection. The extent of protection is dealt with in Article 5 of **17–15**
the Paris Act which provides as follows:

> "(1) Authors shall enjoy, in respect of works for which they are pro-
> tected under this Convention, in countries of the Union other than the
> country of origin, the rights which their respective laws do now or
> may hereafter grant to their nationals, as well as the rights specially
> granted by this Convention. . . .

> (3) Protection in the country of origin is governed by domestic law.
> However, when the author is not a national of the country of origin of
> the work for which he is protected under this Convention, he shall
> enjoy in that country the same rights as national authors."

A distinction is made between the extent of protection in the country of
origin and in other countries of the Union, since protection in the country
of origin is governed by the domestic law but, in countries other than the
country of origin, the author is given, not only the rights which are given
under their domestic laws, but also the rights granted by the Convention.
In theory, therefore, an author can be worse off in the country of origin
than in other countries of the Union.

Country of origin. It will be noted that, under Article 5 of the Paris Act, **17–16**
authors are protected in countries other than the country of origin, and
that a distinction is made as to the type of protection afforded in the
country of origin and in other countries. Country of origin is defined in
Article 5(4) as follows:

> "The country of origin shall be considered to be:
> (*a*) in the case of works first published in a country of the Union, that
> country; in the case of works published simultaneously in several
> countries of the Union which grant different terms of protection,
> the country whose legislation grants the shortest term of protec-
> tion;
> (*b*) in the case of works published simultaneously in a country out-
> side the Union and in a country of the Union, the latter country;

---

[21] See C.D.P.A. 1988, s.155(3).

(*c*) in the case of unpublished works or of works first published in a country outside the Union, without simultaneous publication in a country of the Union, the country of the Union of which the author is a national provided that:

(i) when these are cinematographic works the maker of which has his headquarters or his habitual residence in a country of the Union, the country of origin shall be that country, and

(ii) when these are works of architecture erected in a country of the Union or other artistic works incorporated in a building or other structure located in a country of the Union, the country of origin shall be that country.''

17–17 **Rights of nationals of a Union country.** The result of the above Articles is that nationals of a Union country are to be accorded protection in every Union country for (a) unpublished works, (b) works published in the Union country in which protection is sought, (c) works published in another Union country, and (d) works published in a non-Union country. This last is a change from the Brussels Convention under which, subject to simultaneous publication, protection was lost if a work was first published in a non-Union country: Article 4(1) of Brussels. Thus, a British subject can claim in, say, France, national treatment both for his unpublished works and for his published works wherever published.

It has been mentioned above (§17–11) that nationals of non-Union countries, but habitually resident in one of them, are to be assimilated to nationals of that country (Article 3(2) of Paris); also that cinematographic works and works of architecture may be protected in certain circumstances irrespective of the nationality of their authors.

17–18 **Rights of nationals of a non-Union country.** Nationals of a non-Union country, other than those habitually resident in a Union country, are to be accorded protection for their works first published in a Union country, or simultaneously published in a non-Union country and in a Union country. No protection is, therefore, given to unpublished works of nationals of non-Union countries unless they are habitually resident in a Union country.[22] This means that an author, being a national of a non-Union country, habitually resident in, say, France is protected in France under the Convention for his unpublished works, which would not be the case if he was habitually resident in his own country. However, it has been mentioned above (§ 17–16) that cinematographic works and works of architecture may be protected, in certain circumstances, irrespective of the nationality of their authors.

17–19 **No formalities.** It was provided by Article 2 of the original Berne Convention that enjoyment of the rights conferred by the Convention should be "subject to the accomplishment of the conditions and formalities prescribed by the law of the country of origin of the work," and, in order to make it clear that the formalities of the country in which protection was sought need not be complied with, the Interpretative Declaration of Paris

---

[22] See C.D.P.A. 1988, ss.154 and 155. As to the meaning of "publication," and "simultaneous publication," see §§ 17–12 and 17–14, *ante.*

provided that the copyright should depend upon these conditions and formalities "solely." It followed from these provisions that it was always necessary, where a foreigner sought protection in a country other than that in which he first published his work, to inquire as to what formalities were prescribed by the country of origin of the work, and, moreover, the question was raised whether, if a work was totally unprotected in its country of origin, it could claim any protection in other Union countries. Obviously, such a question might involve inquiries into difficult points of foreign law upon which the local tribunal might find it hard to pronounce a correct decision.[23] The Berlin Convention, however, marked a considerable advance in principle by providing, in Article 4,[24] that "the enjoyment and exercise of" copyright in the various countries "shall not be subject to the performance of any formality," and that "such enjoyment and such exercise are independent of the existence of protection in the country of origin of the work"—that is to say, there are not to be any formalities precedent to obtaining copyright, for instance, reservation of copyright, nor any formalities precedent to the bringing of an action for infringement, such as the registration which was necessary under the repealed English legislation—prior to the commencement of proceedings to enforce copyright in a literary work. "Consequently"—as the paragraph proceeded— "apart from the express stipulations of the present Convention, the extent of protection, as well as the means of redress secured to the author to safeguard his rights, shall be governed exclusively by the laws of the country where protection is claimed."

However, it is to be noted that this paragraph, now Article 5(2) of Paris, only applies to the rights conferred in Article 5(1) of Paris, that is to say, to the rights enjoyed in countries other than the country of origin of the work. The equivalent Article 4(2) of the Brussels Convention only applied to the rights in Article 4(1) of that Convention which was concerned with the rights of nationals of a Union country. Article 5(1) of the Paris Act, however, applies both to the rights of nationals of non-Union countries as well as to the rights of nationals of Union countries.

The term of protection. By Article 2, paragraph (2), of the original Convention it was provided that copyright "must not exceed, in the other countries, the duration of the protection granted in the said country of origin." At the meeting of the representatives of the Powers at Berlin in 1908, an effort was made to induce the Powers to agree to a uniform term of protection as a condition of membership of the Union. This effort did not, **17–20**

---

[23] For instance, the point was raised in the German courts as to whether Oscar Wilde's work, *Salome*, would have been debarred from copyright in England upon the ground that the work was blasphemous. In England it was provided by s.2(3) of the International Copyright Act 1886 (now repealed), that "the International Copyright Acts and an Order made thereunder shall not confer on any person *any greater right* or longer term of coyright in any work than that enjoyed in the foreign country in which such work was first published." As to the difficulties that arose upon the words "any greater right," see *Hanfstaengl* v. *Empire Palace* [1894] 3 Ch. 109; and as to compliance with the conditions of the country of origin, *Sarpy* v. *Holland* [1908] 2 Ch. 198.

[24] Equivalent provisions are contained in the Rome, Brussels, Stockholm and Paris Conventions.

however, entirely succeed, and Article 7 (revised in the Brussels Convention) of the Berlin Convention was agreed to as a compromise.

17–21   Article 7 was again revised in the Stockholm Convention, repeated in the Paris Act, and contains some new provisions. The basic term of protection is still to be the life of the author and 50 years after his death: Article 7(1). However, unlike the Brussels Convention, minimum terms of protection have now been laid down for cinematographic works, photographic works and works of applied art. Thus, in the case of cinematographic works, the countries of the Union may provide that the term of protection is to expire 50 years after the work has been made available to the public with the consent of the author,[25] or, failing such an event within 50 years from the making of such a work, 50 years after the making: Article 7(2).[26] In the case of photographic works and works of applied art in so far as they are protected as artistic works, it is to be a matter for legislation in the countries of the Union to determine the term of protection thereof; however, this term is to last at least until the end of a period of 25 years from the making of such a work: Article 7(4). In the case of anonymous or pseudonymous works where the identity of the author remains undisclosed, the period is 50 years after the work has been lawfully made available to the public: Article 7(3). Article 7(4) of the Brussels Convention referred to 50 years from the date of publication. However, the Paris Act (like Stockholm) now provides that countries of the Union are not required to protect anonymous or pseudonymous works in respect of which it is reasonable to presume that their author has been dead for 50 years: Article 7(3).[27]

Article 7(5) of the Paris Act provides that the term of protection subsequent to the death of the author and the terms provided by paragraphs (2) (cinematographic works), (3) (anonymous and pseudonymous works), and (4) (photographic works and works of applied art) are to run from the date of death or of the event referred to in those paragraphs, but such terms are to be deemed to begin on January 1 of the year following the death or such event.

17–22   The Brussels Convention omitted the provisions of Article 7(2) of the Rome Convention which entitled countries of the Union to provide a shorter period of protection than those laid down in Article 7, and this necessitated the abolition, by the 1956 Act, of the proviso to section 3 of the 1911 Act allowing works to be published under a compulsory licence at the expiration of 25 years from the death of the author. On the other hand, a provision of the Paris Act (new in Stockholm) permits those countries of the Union bound by the Rome Act of the Convention which grant in their domestic legislation shorter terms of protection than those in Article 7, to maintain such terms when ratifying or acceding to the Paris Act: Article 7(7).

---

[25] See § 17–12, *ante*.
[26] See C.D.P.A. 1988, s.13.
[27] See *ibid.* ss.9(4) and 12(2).

The Paris Act further provides that the countries of the Union may grant a term of protection in excess of those provided by Article 7: Article 7(6). Again, the Paris Act provides that in any case the term is to be governed by the legislation of the country where protection is claimed, but unless the legislation of that country otherwise provides, the term is not to exceed the term fixed in the country of origin of the work: Article 7(8). **17–23**

It will be noticed that the Paris Act does not, in respect of the basic term of protection, draw any distinction between published and unpublished works. **17–24**

The Rome Convention added, for the first time, provisions with regard to the minimum term of copyright in works of joint authorship, namely one expiring with the death of the author who dies last. However, the Brussels Convention dropped this provision and, instead, provided that, in the case of a work of joint authorship, the term of protection was to be calculated from the date of the death of the last surviving author: Article 7 *bis*. As a result, the maximum term of 50 years from the death of the last surviving author became obligatory and this again resulted in an alteration in English law under the provisions of the 1956 Act, continued by the 1988 Act. The Paris Act contains an equivalent provision: Article 7 *bis*. **17–25**

Protected works. What are the works which must be protected? Article 1 of the Paris Act states that the countries to which the Convention applies are constituted into a Union for the protection of the rights of authors in their "literary and artistic works." Article 2(1) then provides that the expression "literary and artistic works" shall include every production in the literary, scientific, and artistic domain, whatever may be the mode or form of its expression, such as books, pamphlets, and other writings; lectures, addresses, sermons and other works of the same nature; dramatic or dramatico-musical works, choreographic works and entertainments in dumb show, musical compositions with or without words; cinematographic works to which are assimilated works expressed by a process analogous to cinematography; works of drawing, painting, architecture, sculpture, engraving and lithography; photographic works to which are assimilated works expressed by a process analogous to photography; works of applied art, illustrations; maps, plans, sketches, and three-dimensional works relative to geography, topography, architecture or science. **17–26**

This definition presents something of a trap to the English lawyer accustomed to the general words "literary, dramatic, musical and artistic works" in the English Copyright Acts who may therefore think that the words "literary and artistic works" appearing in the Convention do not include dramatic or musical works. Prior to the Revised Convention, there was no obligation to protect choreographic works or works of architecture, but, in countries where such works received protection, the other Union countries were entitled to the benefit of such protection. Photographic and cinematographic works were included in the definition of "literary and artistic works" for the first time by the Brussels Convention. Photographic works were previously protected under Article 3 which was not repeated

in the Brussels Convention. Prior to the Brussels Convention cinematographic productions were protected under Article 14, but only as literary
or artistic works if the author had given the work an original character: in
the absence of such an original character they were protected as photographic works. This qualification on their protection was adopted in the
1911 Act, and the change brought about by the Brussels Convention was
followed in the 1956 Act by the introduction of a special section dealing
with the copyright in cinematograph films.[28] This definition has slight
changes from that in the Brussels Convention, in particular the deletion of
the words "the acting form of which is fixed in writing or otherwise" after
the reference to "entertainments in dumb show." This is because Article
2(2) of Paris provides that it shall be a matter for legislation in the countries of the Union to prescribe that works in general, or any specified categories of works, shall not be protected unless they have been fixed in some
material form.[29]

The Paris Act expressly provides, however, that the protection of the
Convention is not to apply to news of the day, nor to miscellaneous facts
having the character of mere items of press information: Article 2(8).
Article 9(3) of the Brussels Convention was slightly differently worded in
that it provided that the protection of the Convention was not to apply to
news of the day nor to miscellaneous information having the character of
mere items of news. Thus, no copyright protection is afforded by the Convention to news or facts constituting press information. There are no
equivalent provisions of English law, and material published in the press
is afforded the same protection as other literary material, subject only to
the qualification that information is not protected as such by copyright
law, but only the form in which the information is expressed.

17–27   **Translations, adaptations and arrangements, collections, works of
applied art.** Article 2(3) of the Paris Act then goes on to provide that
"Translations, adaptations, arrangements of music and other alterations
of a literary or artistic work shall be protected as original works without
prejudice to the copyright in the original work." The countries of the
Union are therefore bound to make provision for the protection of the
above-mentioned works and also for collections such as encyclopedias and
anthologies: Article 2(5). On the other hand, it is a matter for legislation
in the countries of the Union to determine the protection to be granted to
official texts of a legislative, administrative and legal nature, and to official
translations of such texts: Article 2(4).

The provisions of Article 2 as to adaptations must be read in conjunction with Article 12, which declares that authors of literary or artistic
works are to enjoy the exclusive right of authorising adaptations, arrangements and other alterations of their works. It is a matter of domestic legislation as to how far works of applied art and industrial designs and models
are protected, subject to Article 7(4): Article 2(7). Article 7(4) provides
for a minimum term of protection of 25 years from the making of a work of
applied art.[30]

---

[28] Copyright Act 1956, s.13: and see C.D.P.A. 1988, s.1(1)*(b)*.
[29] See C.D.P.A. 1988, s.3(2) and (3).
[30] See § 17–21, *ante*.

Speeches. Lectures and speeches first received protection, as such, under **17–28** the Rome Convention; previously, unless constituting literary works, they would not have been within the provisions of the existing Conventions. As a consequence it is provided (Article 2 *bis*) that the domestic legislation of any country may limit protection in respect of political or legal speeches and may determine the conditions under which lectures and addresses delivered in public may be reproduced by the press, broadcast, communicated to the public by wire and made the subject of public communication as envisaged in Article 11 *bis* (1),[31] when such use is justified by the informatory purpose. Article 2 *bis* of the Brussels Convention was limited to reproduction by the press. On the other hand, such Article was not restricted to public lectures and addresses, nor did it contain a reference to the use being justified by the informatory purpose.

Translation rights. It will be noticed that translations are to be pro- **17–29** tected, and this, apparently, whether the same are authorised or not, subject to the rights of the author of the original work: Article 2(3). Article 8 deals with the rights of the author of the original work, stipulating that:

"Authors of literary and artistic works protected by this Convention shall enjoy the exclusive right of making and of authorising the translation of their works throughout the term of protection of their rights in the original works."

The question of translations is of prime importance from the international point of view, for it is only by means of translations that an author of a literary or scientific work can practically make his work known in a country speaking another language than his own. Complete rights in respect of authorising translations were only gained for the first time under the Berlin Convention. The original Convention only gave the exclusive right of translation for a period of 10 years from publication of the original work, and this only to authors who were subjects of a Union country. The Additional Act of Paris gave to such authors the exclusive right of translation during the whole period of copyright in the original article, subject, however, to the condition that an authorised translation, in the language for which protection was claimed, should be published in a Union country within 10 years from the first publication of the original work. Under the Berlin, Rome, Brussels, Stockholm and Paris Conventions authors—whether citizens of a Union country or not—who first published in a Union country, enjoy the exclusive right of authorising a translation during the entire period of copyright in the original work, free from any such conditions as to publication of an authorised translation. Under the Stockholm, and now Paris, Conventions authors of a Union country would enjoy this right even if they had published in a non-Union country. However, a number of countries have declined to adopt these provisions.[32] Citizens of non-Union countries, however, have no right to protection against translations of their unpublished works.

---

[31] See § 17–36, *post* and §10–71 *et seq., ante.*
[32] See § 17–52, *post.*

17–30 **Reproduction rights.** Prior to Stockholm the Convention did not contain a provision expressly recognising a right of reproduction, notwithstanding that such a right was commonplace in the legislation of many countries of the Union. To correct this anomaly the Stockholm Convention provided, and Paris now provides, that authors of literary and artistic works protected by the Convention are to have the exclusive right of authorising the reproduction of these works in any manner or form: Article 9(1). Further, that any sound or visual recording is to be considered as a reproduction for the purposes of the Convention: Article 9(3). However, both Conventions go on to provide that the countries of the Union may permit the reproduction of such works in special cases, provided that such reproduction does not conflict with a normal exploitation of the work and does not unreasonably prejudice the legitimate interests of the author: Article 9(2).[33] Because of the introduction of Article 9 it has not been necessary to repeat Article 13(1) of Brussels giving authors of musical works the right to authorise the recording of such works.

17–31 **Exceptions**
(a) Quotations. The Paris Act contains, in Articles 10 and 10 *bis*, provisions relating to exceptions from the rights granted by the Convention. Thus, Article 10(1) provides that it is to be permissible to make quotations from published works, provided that their making is compatible with fair practice and their extent does not exceed that justified by the purpose, including quotations from newspaper articles and periodicals in the form of press summaries. This is wider than Article 10(1) of the Brussels Convention, which was new and only permitted quotations from newspaper articles and periodicals, and "short" quotations at that. However, when a work is quoted, the source and name of the author, if given, must be mentioned: Article 10(3).[34] Again, Article 10(2), which revises Article 10(2) of the Brussels Convention, provides that it is to be a matter for legislation in the countries of the Union and for special agreements existing or to be concluded between them, to permit the utilisation, to the extent justified by the purpose, of literary or artistic works by way of illustration in publications, broadcasts or sound or visual recordings for teaching, provided such utilisation is compatible with fair practice. Again this is subject to mention being made of the source and name of the author, if given: Article 10(3).[35]

17–32 **(b) Reporting current events.** Article 10 *bis* (1) provides that it is to be a matter for the legislation in the countries of the Union to permit the reproduction by the press, the broadcasting or the communication to the public by wire of articles published in newspapers or periodicals on current economic, political or religious topics, and of broadcast works of the same character, in cases in which the reproduction, broadcasting or such communication thereof is not expressly reserved, providing the source is indicated. The legal consequences of a breach of this obligation are to be determined by the legislation of the country where protection is claimed.

---

[33] See C.D.P.A. 1988, ss.28–76.
[34] See *ibid.* ss.29 and 30.
[35] See *ibid.* ss.32–36.

Article 9(2) of the Brussels Convention contained a similar provision except that it was confined to reproduction by the press. Article 10 *bis* (2) provides further that it is also to be a matter for such legislation to determine the conditions under which, for the purpose of reporting current events by means of photography, cinematography, broadcasting or communication to the public by wire, literary or artistic works seen or heard in the course of the event may, to the extent justified by the informatory purpose, be reproduced and made available to the public. This provision is wider than Article 10 *bis* of the Brussels Convention, which was new and which it replaces, and, in particular, is no longer limited to "short extracts" from literary and artistic works. However, the use is limited to the extent justified by the informatory purpose and the works must have been seen or heard in the course of the event.[36]

(c) Compulsory licences to record. Article 13(1) of the Brussels Convention, which provided that the authors of musical works were to have the exclusive rights of recording such works and the public performance by means of mechanical instruments of the work thus recorded, was not repeated in the Stockholm Convention as the first right was covered by Article 9 of the Stockholm Convention, repeated in Paris, and the second right by Article 11 of the Stockholm Convention, repeated in Paris. However, the Stockholm Convention, like the Brussels Convention, contained provisions, repeated in Paris, permitting the countries of the Union to impose reservations and conditions on the rights of authors of musical works to record their works, so as to permit compulsory licences to record such music: Art. 13(1). However, such Article makes clear that compulsory licences may also extend to words accompanying the music, whereas, under Article 13 of the Brussels Convention, this was not clear. But such reservations and conditions are not to be prejudicial to the rights of the authors of the music and words to obtain equitable remuneration. The 1911 Act gave the right to record on royalty terms in respect of any work which had previously been recorded, and this right was repeated in the 1956 Act, but abolished by the 1988 Act.[37] **17–33**

Performing rights and recitation rights. The performing rights of authors of dramatic, dramatico-musical and musical works are required to be protected by Article 11 of the Paris Act. Under the original Convention these rights had to be specially reserved by notice on the title page, if the work was published, but the Berlin, Rome and Brussels Conventions provided that authors, to enjoy protection, should not be bound to forbid the public presentation or performance thereof. This provision was deleted in the Stockholm Convention as being superfluous and is not repeated in the Paris Act. The Stockholm Convention, and now the Paris Act, makes clear that the public performance of a work by gramophone records is included so that that part of Article 13(1) of the Brussels Convention relating thereto was not repeated in the Stockholm Convention, nor is it repeated in the Paris Act. Apart from public performance the Article also covers any communication to the public of the performance of **17–34**

---

[36] See C.D.P.A. 1988, s.30: and see § 10–8 *et seq.*, *ante.*
[37] See *ibid.* Sched. 1, para. 21.

such works. By the same Article, authors of dramatic or dramatico-musical works are required to be protected, during the existence of their rights in the original works, against the unauthorised public performance or communication of translations of their works.

Rights relating to the recitation of literary works were given to the authors thereof by Article 11 *ter* of the Stockholm Convention, repeated in Paris, which expanded Article 11 *ter* of the Brussels Convention to equate recitation rights to performing rights under Article 11. Thus Article 11 *ter* covers the public recitation of literary works and also any communication to the public of the recitation of such works. Also, by the same Article, authors of literary works are required to be protected, during the existence of their rights in the original works, against the unauthorised public recitation or communication of translations of their works.

17–35 **Copyright Tribunal.** In connection with Article 11 of the Brussels Convention the United Kingdom delegation at Brussels declared that they accepted the provisions of Article 11 on the understanding that H.M. Government remained free to enact such legislation as they might consider necessary, in the public interest, to prevent or deal with any abuse of the monopoly rights conferred upon owners of copyright by the law of the United Kingdom. It was in reliance upon this declaration that the 1956 Act introduced a Performing Right Tribunal with powers to modify and enforce licences granted by licensing bodies for the public performance of works controlled by such bodies.[38] This declaration was not repeated at Stockholm (or Paris), but it was agreed that countries were free to enact measures to restrict possible abuses of monopoly. The Performing Right Tribunal has now been renamed as the Copyright Tribunal with a much wider jurisdiction.[39]

17–36 **Broadcasting rights.** The Rome Convention first introduced provisions with regard to radio communication, but these were substantially amplified by the Brussels Convention and repeated in the Stockholm and Paris Conventions. By Article 11 *bis* of the Paris Act it is provided that authors of literary and artistic works are to have the exclusive right of authorising the communication of their works to the public by wireless, the communication of their works to the public by wire or by rebroadcasting of the broadcast of the work when the communication is made by an organisation other than the original one, and the communication of their works to the public by loudspeaker or other instrument transmitting the broadcast of the work. The conditions for the exercise of these rights are left to the legislation of individual countries, provided that such legislation does not affect the right of the author to obtain equitable remuneration.

---

[38] Copyright Act 1956, ss.23–30.
[39] C.D.P.A. 1988, ss.116–152: and see Chap. 15, *ante*. This jurisdiction now covers the compulsory licence to include sound recordings (but not the music on the sound recordings) in broadcasts and cable programme services created by an amendment of the 1988 Act introduced by s.175 of the Broadcasting Act 1990 (c.42), and the compulsory licence to provide information about broadcast programmes introduced by s.176 of and Sched. 17 to the 1990 Act. As to the coming into force of these provisions, see the Broadcasting Act 1990 (Commencement No. 1 and Transitional Provisions) Order 1990 (S.I. 1990 No. 2347), § B–254 *post*.

The Paris Act, therefore, confers upon authors three distinct rights in respect of broadcast performances of their works: namely, first, the right to restrict the original broadcast, secondly, the right to restrict any diffusion of the broadcast by an independent receiving authority, and thirdly, the right to restrict the public performance of the broadcast at the receiving end. The first two rights were clearly conferred by the 1956 Act,[40] but, after much discussion during the passing of that Act, the right to restrict the operation of a diffusion service was considerably qualified by section 40(3) of that Act.[41]

Records of broadcasts. It is further provided, by Article 11 *bis* (3) of the Paris Act, that a permission to broadcast is not to imply permission to record the broadcast. But there then follows a somewhat ambiguous paragraph as follows: **17–37**

> "It shall, however, be a matter for legislation in the countries of the Union to determine the regulations for ephemeral recordings made by a broadcasting organisation by means of its own facilities and used for its own broadcasts. The preservation of these recordings in official archives may, on the ground of their exceptional documentary character, be authorised by such legislation."

Section 6(7) of the 1956 Act was designed to give effect to the provisions of the Article as to ephemeral recordings, but there was no provision for the preservation of recordings in official archives.[42]

Cinematograph rights. As has already been pointed out,[43] cinematographic works are now treated as of the class of literary and artistic works receiving general protection under Article 2 of the Paris Act. But the rights of authors of literary or artistic works, whose material may be included in a cinematograph film, are dealt with in Article 14 of the Paris Act, and it is expressly stated, by Article 14 *bis* (1) thereof, previously Article 14(2) of the Brussels Convention, that the protection of a cinematographic work as an original work is without prejudice to the rights of the author of the work adapted or reproduced. The author is required to be given the exclusive right of authorising, first, the cinematographic adaptation and reproduction of his works, and the distribution of the works thus adapted or reproduced and, secondly, the right of public performance and communication to the public by wire of the works thus adapted or reproduced. The latter right was new in the Stockholm Convention. Article 14 further provides that the adaptation into any other artistic form of a cinematographic production derived from literary or artistic works is, without prejudice to the authorisation of the author of the cinematographic production, to remain subject to the authorisation of the   **17–38**

---

[40] Copyright Act 1956, ss.2(5)(*d*) and (*e*) and 3(5)(*c*) and (*d*).

[41] ss.2, 3 and 40, Copyright Act 1956, were amended by the Cable and Broadcasting Act 1984 (c. 46). See now C.D.P.A. 1988, ss.16(1), 72 and 73.

[42] See now C.D.P.A. 1988, ss.68 and 75, which latter section provides for recording for archival purposes. See § 10–111 *et seq.* and § 10–128, *ante*.

[43] *Ante*, § 17–26.

authors of the original works. Section 13(7) of the 1956 Act provided that where the copyright in a cinematograph film had expired, a person who caused the film to be seen, or to be seen and heard, in public did not thereby infringe any copyright subsisting in any literary, dramatic, musical or artistic work. Since the film copyright may well have expired before that in the works included in them, it is difficult to see how this provision accorded with Article 14 of the Paris Act. The 1988 Act contains no such provision.

17–39   **Sound-tracks of films.** Article 14(3) of the Paris Act provides that the provisions of Article 13(1) are not to apply, and Article 13(1) thereof entitles member countries to impose reservations and conditions upon the right of authors of musical works and associated words to restrict the recording of their works. Article 14(3), therefore, seems designed to prevent countries restricting in any manner the rights of authors of musical works to have these works included in the sound-tracks of cinematograph films. While there was some doubt whether, under section 19(2) of the 1911 Act, the compulsory licence provisions thereby enacted could be utilised for the purpose of cinematograph films, it is clear that the similar provisions of section 8 of the 1956 Act did not apply, since they applied only where a manufacturer intended to sell a record by retail. Section 8 of the 1956 Act has been repealed by the 1988 Act, which contains no equivalent provision.

17–40   **Cinematograph films.** It has been mentioned above[44] that cinematographic works are included in the class of works protected under Article 2, and that Article 14 *bis* (1) provides that such protection is without prejudice to the copyright in any work adapted or reproduced. Article 14 *bis* (1) goes on to make clear what was previously understood to be the position, namely that the owner of the copyright in a cinematographic work is to have the same rights as the author of an original work, including the rights under Article 14.[45]

Article 14 *bis* (2)(*a*), which was new to Stockholm, leaves the question of ownership of the copyright in a cinematographic work to the legislation of the country where protection is claimed. However, the rest of Article 14 *bis* (2) and Article 14 *bis* (3), which also were new to Stockholm, contain provisions dealing with the rights of authors of contributions to a cinematographic work in countries where they are included among the owners of the copyright in such a work. Section 13(4) and (10) of the 1956 Act, however, provided that the maker of a cinematograph film, that is the person by whom the arrangements necessary for the making of the film are undertaken, was the initial owner of the copyright in the film, and sections 9(2) and 11 of the 1988 Act provide that such owner is the author of the film, being the person by whom such arrangements are undertaken.

17–41   **"Droit moral."** The Rome Convention, for the first time, introduced provisions intended to extend an author's rights beyond those generally understood to be included in the term "copyright." These provisions

---

[44] *Ante,* §§ 17–26 and 17–38.
[45] *Ante,* §§ 17–38 and 17–39.

cover what is known on the Continent as the author's "droit moral." These provisions were extended by the Brussels Convention, Article 6 *bis*, and provided, first, that even after the assignment of his copyright, the author should have the right during his lifetime to claim authorship of the work, and to object to any "distortion, mutilation or other alteration thereof or any other action in relation to the said work which would be prejudicial to his honour or reputation." Secondly, it was provided that the rights granted to the author as aforesaid should, after his death, be maintained at least until the expiry of the copyright. Thirdly, the means of redress was left to the national law. These provisions were, with amendments, repeated in the Stockholm and Paris Conventions.

Thus, the Stockholm Convention, in Article 6 *bis*, whilst preserving the author's right to claim authorship of the work (the paternity right), has made slight changes in the wording, repeated in the Paris Act, of the right to object to mutilation (the integrity right) which now covers the right of the author to object to any "distortion, mutilation or other modification of, or other derogatory action in relation to, the said work, which would be prejudicial to his honour or reputation." A further amendment, introduced by Article 6 *bis* of the Stockholm Convention and repeated in the Paris Act, is to make the grant of such rights compulsory at least until the expiration of the copyright, rather than during the author's lifetime and optional thereafter until the expiration of copyright as under Article 6 *bis* of the Brussels Convention.

It will be observed, first, that the Brussels, Stockholm and Paris Conventions make the grant of such rights compulsory for the period prescribed and, secondly, that such Conventions require the rights to be safeguarded by the legislation of the country where protection is claimed. It would seem to follow from this that, not only are countries of the Union bound to grant such rights, but that they must be granted by statute law. So far as this country is concerned, prior to the 1988 Act the only statute law at all concerned with either of these rights was section 43 of the 1956 Act. But even this section, whilst going some way to grant an integrity right, only did so in respect of artistic works. Further, not only did such section not grant a paternity right to authors but, instead, made it an offence to ascribe paternity to a non-author. Other than this, and actions for passing off, defamation and slander of goods, English law did not, before the 1988 Act, afford protection for the rights provided for in Article 6 *bis*.[46] **17-42**

It would appear, therefore, that, prior to the 1988 Act, this country had not complied with the obligations of Article 6 *bis*, and it is interesting to note, in this regard, that the 1952 Copyright Committee stated that, in the 20 years since the Rome Convention was accepted, no other Union country had complained that this country had failed to discharge its obligations under Article 6 *bis*.[47] However the 1977 Copyright Committee, after having considered the matter in detail, in particular the question whether this country had failed to discharge such obligations,[48] recom-

[46] See Chap. 22, *post.*
[47] Cmnd. 8662, para. 220.
[48] Cmnd. 6732, paras. 50–57.

mended that the Copyright Act should be amended to make proper provision for moral rights under copyright law.[49] It is to be noted that Article 36 of the Paris Convention provides that it is understood that, at the time a country becomes bound by that Convention, it will be in a position, under its domestic law, to give effect to the provisions of that Convention, and the 1988 Act now, for the first time in this country, provides statutory protection for moral rights, by granting a paternity right, an integrity right and a right to privacy of certain photographs and films, as well as providing for false attribution of authorship.[50] This was done as from August 1, 1989, just before the United Kingdom deposited its instrument of ratification of the Paris Convention on September 29, 1989, with effect from January 2, 1990.

17-43   **"Droit de suite."** A further new right, which was introduced for the first time in the Brussels Convention, deals with what is known, on the Continent, as the "droit de suite." Article 14 *ter* of the Stockholm Convention, replacing Article 14 *bis* of the Brussels Convention, provided, and now Article 14 *ter* of the Paris Act provides, that the author or, after his death, the persons or institutions authorised by national legislation are, with respect to original works of art and original manuscripts, to enjoy the inalienable right to an interest in any sale of the work subsequent to the first transfer thereof by the author thereof. This matter, however, is left to the legislation of individual members[51] and cannot be claimed in any country introducing such legislation by an author belonging to a country which does not have such legislation. The 1977 Copyright Committee recommended that "droit de suite" should not be introduced in the United Kingdom,[52] and the 1988 Act makes no provision for such a right.

17-44   **Protection of rights.** The remedy of a person whose work has been pirated is to be governed by the local law. Article 4(2) of Brussels, replaced by Article 5(2) of Stockholm, and now by Article 5(2) of Paris provides that, "apart from the provisions of this Convention, the extent of protection, as well as the means of redress afforded to the author to protect his rights, shall be governed exclusively by the laws of the country where protection is claimed."[53]

However, seizure of the pirated copies is a remedy which ought to be

---

[49] Cmnd. 6732, para. 85(vi).
[50] C.D.P.A. 1988, ss.2(2), 77–89, 94, 95, 103, and Sched. 1, paras. 22, 23 and 24; and see Chap. 22, *post.*
[51] See as to "droit de suite" in France and certain other countries, "The 'droit de suite' " by Robert Plaisant, *Copyright,* August 1969, No. 8, p. 157; in Germany, *Copyright,* February 1980, p. 85, letter from the Federal Republic of Germany by Adolf Dietz.
[52] Cmnd. 6732, para. 805.
[53] An important and instructive case came before the Paris Court of Appeal which, affirming the decision of the Seine Civil Tribunal, held that the manager of the Paris branch and representative in Paris of an Argentine newspaper was liable in damages for putting on sale in France copies of the newspaper printed in Buenos Aires, and containing pirated portions of a novel written by a French author. This liability, the court stated, would exist "even if the legislation of the country of publication accorded no protection to copyright": *Foley* v. *Cazaux, Le Droit d'Auteur* (1913) p. 100.

secured to authors by the legislation of every Union country, for Article 16[54] provides as follows:

> "(1) Infringing copies of a work shall be liable to seizure in any country of the Union where the work enjoys legal protection.
>
> (2) The provisions of the preceding paragraph shall also apply to reproductions coming from a country where the work is not protected, or has ceased to be protected.
>
> (3) The seizure shall take place in accordance with the legislation of each country."

Notwithstanding the provisions of the Convention, each Union country is to be at liberty "to permit, to control, or to prohibit, by legislation or regulation, the circulation, presentation, or exhibition of any work or production in regard to which the competent authority may find it necessary to exercise that right"; Article 17 of the Paris Act.

Presumptions. Article 15 of the Paris Act, as did Article 15 of the Brussels Convention and Article 15 of the Stockholm Convention, provides for certain presumptions.[55] Thus, Article 15(1) provides that, in order that the author of a literary or artistic work protected by the Convention shall, in the absence of proof to the contrary, be regarded as such and consequently entitled to institute infringement proceedings in the countries of the Union, it is to be sufficient for his name to appear on the work in the usual manner.   **17-45**

Article 15(1) is to be applicable even if the name is a pseudonym, where the pseudonym adopted by the author leaves no doubt as to his identity. Article 15(3), however, provides that, in the case of anonymous and pseudonymous works, other than those referred to in Article 15(1), the publisher whose name appears on the work, in the absence of proof to the contrary, is to be deemed to represent the author, and in that capacity he is to be entitled to protect and enforce the author's rights. These provisions are to cease to apply when the author reveals his identity and establishes his claim to authorship of the work.

Article 15 of the Stockholm Convention, now Article 15 of the Paris Act, also contained certain new provisions. Thus, Article 15(2) provides that the person or body corporate whose name appears on a cinematographic work "in the usual manner" shall, in the absence of proof to the contrary, be presumed to be the maker of such work.[56]

Again, Article 15(4) provides that, in the case of unpublished works where the identity of the author is unknown, but where there is every ground to presume that he is a national of a country of the Union, it is to be a matter for legislation in that country to designate the competent authority who shall represent the author and shall be entitled to protect and enforce his rights in the countries of the Union.[57]

---

[54] See also Art. 13(3) as to seizure of recordings: and see C.D.P.A. 1988, ss.100 and 114.
[55] See C.D.P.A. 1988, ss.104–106.
[56] See *ibid.* s.105.
[57] See *ibid.* s.169.

17–46 **Retrospective effect.** An alteration was made as regards retrospective effect in the Berlin Convention, and is repeated in the Rome, Brussels, Stockholm and Paris Conventions. Under the original Convention it was provided that its provisions should apply to all works which, at the time of its coming into force, had "not yet fallen into the public domain in their country of origin." The Berlin, Rome, Brussels, Stockholm and Paris Conventions (Article 18(1)) only except works which have, at the moment of their coming into force, fallen into the public domain in their country of origin "through the expiry of the term of protection." Works, therefore, which have, in the country of their origin, lost their protection owing to failure to comply with formalities, such as registration and so forth, are intended to be protected under the Conventions, as also, apparently, are works which were previously entitled to no protection whatsoever, for instance (in some countries), works of architecture and photographs.[58] On the other hand, Article 18(2) provides that if, through the expiry of the term of protection which was previously granted, a work has fallen into the public domain of the country where protection is claimed, that work is not to be protected anew. These provisions are to apply also in the case of new accessions to the Union, and to cases in which protection is extended by the application of Article 7 or by the abandonment of reservations: Articles 18(4).

Article 18(3), however, provides that the application of the principle laid down in Article 18(1) and (2) is to take effect subject to any provisions contained in special conventions to that effect existing or to be concluded between countries of the Union, and that, in the absence of such provisions, the respective countries are to determine, so far as they are respectively concerned, the conditions of application of such principle.

17–47 **Convention not to limit wider protection.** Article 19 of the Paris Act expressly states that the Convention is not to preclude authors from the benefit of any greater protection granted by the local law, and Article 20 thereof preserves the right of member countries to make special agreements with other member countries giving greater protection to their respective nationals than is required under the Convention.

(iii) Administrative provisions and final clauses of Paris Act

17–48 **Administrative provisions and final clauses.** Articles 22 to 26 of the Stockholm Convention, now Articles 22 to 26 of the Paris Act, contain the administrative provisions, and Articles 27 to 38, the final clauses of both Conventions, contain certain general provisions. Articles 22 and 23 of the Paris Act were amended in October 1979. Article 24 of the Paris Act provides that the administrative tasks with respect to the Union are to be performed by the International Bureau, being the International Bureau of

---

[58] The 1911 Act did not comply with the provisions as to retrospective effect and, in adhering to the Revised Convention, Great Britain made a reservation upon the point. This reservation was not maintained when Great Britain ratified the Rome Convention, presumably on the ground that it was not necessary to do so in view of the fact that the Convention did not make necessary any alteration of English law previously in force. The Acts of 1956 and 1988 appear, in substance, to comply with this Article.

Intellectual Property referred to in the Convention establishing the World Intellectual Property Organisation[59]: Article 22(2)(ii).

This latter Convention was framed at Stockholm in 1967 and was signed by this country on July 14, 1967. The objects of the Organisation established by such Convention are stated to be to promote the protection of intellectual property throughout the world through co-operation among States and, where appropriate, in collaboration with any other international organisation, and to ensure administrative co-operation among the various Unions, including the Berne Union: Article 3. Article 12(1) of this Convention provides that the Organisation is to enjoy on the territory of each Member State, in conformity with the laws of that State, such legal capacity as may be necessary for the fulfilment of the Organisation's objectives and for the exercise of its functions. Accordingly this country has provided by statutory instrument,[60] which comes into operation on the date on which the Convention enters into force with respect to this country, that the Organisation is to have the legal capacities of a body corporate. The Convention was ratified by this country on February 26, 1969, and entered into force on April 26, 1970.

(iv) Protocol regarding developing countries of Stockholm Convention

Protocol. As has been mentioned,[61] the Stockholm revision of the Berne Convention introduced the controversial Protocol Regarding Developing Countries which provided that any developing country which ratified or acceded to the Convention may make reservations in respect of certain matters, which would have the effect of giving less protection in that country than is afforded in other countries of the Union. Because of this controversy, however, although Article 21 of Stockholm made the Protocol an integral part of the Convention, this was subject to the provisions of Article 28 of Stockholm which enabled any country ratifying or acceding to the Convention to declare that its ratification or accession was not to apply to the substantive provisions of the Convention and the Protocol. Since the previous Conventions remain in force in relations with countries of the Union which do not ratify or accede to the Paris Act (Article 32(1)), although no other countries may ratify or accede to earlier Conventions or make a declaration under Article 5 of the Protocol, once Articles 1 to 21 and the Appendix to the Paris Act have entered into force (Article 34), as they did on October 10, 1974, it is still necessary to consider the Protocol. **17–49**

Mode of operation of Protocol. Article 1 of the Protocol provides that any country regarded as a developing country in conformity with the established practice of the General Assembly of the United Nations which ratifies or accedes to the Stockholm Convention, and which, having regard to its economic situation and its social or cultural needs, does not consider itself immediately in a position to make provision for the protec- **17–50**

---

[59] For text see § C–156 *et seq., post.*
[60] The World Intellectual Property Organisation (Immunities and Privileges) Order 1968 (S.I. 1968 No. 890).
[61] § 17–7, *ante.*

tion of all the rights provided for by the Convention, may declare that it will, for a period of the first 10 years during which it is a party thereto, avail itself of any or all of the stipulated reservations.

However, where a country no longer needs to maintain any or all of such reservations, it can withdraw such reservation or reservations: Article 2. On the other hand, any country which has made such reservations and which, at the end of the prescribed period of 10 years, having regard to its economic situation and its social or cultural needs, still does not consider itself in a position to withdraw such reservations, may continue to maintain any or all of the reservations until it ratifies or accedes to the next revision of the Convention: Article 3. Further, Article 4 provides that, if a country ceases to be regarded as a developing country, it shall no longer have the right to maintain any of such reservations six years after the prescribed notification of such cessation.

17–51 **Reservations.**
(a) Term.[62] The first reservation enables a developing country to substitute for the term of 50 years in Article 7(1), (2) and (3) of Stockholm a different term, provided it is not less than 25 years. Article 7(1) of Stockholm prescribes the basic term of protection, Article 7(2) thereof the term for cinematographic works and Article 7(3) thereof the term for anonymous and pseudonymous works. Such reservation also enables a developing country to substitute for the term of 25 years in Article 7(4) of Stockholm in respect of photographic works and works of applied art, a different term, provided it is not less than 10 years.

17–52 **(b) Translation rights.**[63] The second reservation permits the substitution for Article 8 of Stockholm, which gives to authors the exclusive right to make and authorise the translation of their works during the term of protection of their rights in the original works, of provisions cutting down the author's translation rights in certain circumstances. Thus, the exclusive right of translation is to cease if the author has not availed himself of it, within 10 years from the date of first publication of the original work, by publishing or causing to be published, in one of the countries of the Union, a translation in the language for which protection is to be claimed.

Further, in certain circumstances, compulsory licences to publish translations may be obtained. Thus, if after the expiration of three years from the date of first publication of the work, or of any longer period determined by national legislation of the developing country concerned, a translation of the work has not been published in that country into the national, or official, or regional language or languages of that country by or with the authority of the owner of the translation rights, any "national" of such country may obtain a non-exclusive licence of a limited kind from the "competent authority" to translate the work and publish the translation in any of such languages in which it has not been published. A licence may also be granted if all previous editions of a particular translation in that country are out of print. But such a licence is not to be granted when the author has withdrawn from circulation all copies of the work.

---

[62] See § 17–20, *et seq., ante.*
[63] See § 17–29, *ante.*

However, the "national" must either have requested and been denied permission to make and publish a translation, or been unable to find the owner of the translation rights and made applications for a licence to the persons prescribed by the Protocol. Further, the owner of the translation rights must be compensated for the prescribed period, the translation must be a correct translation and the original title and name of the author of the work must be printed on all copies of the published translation. Finally, the Protocol provides for termination of the licence if, during the term of 10 years from the date of first publication, the author publishes or causes to be published a translation in the country where the licence has been granted.

(c) Reproduction rights.[64] The third reservation introduces compulsory licences in respect of reproduction rights by allowing the application of Article 9(1) of Stockholm, which gives authors the exclusive right of authorising the reproduction of their works in any manner or form, subject to certain compulsory licence provisions. These provisions are similar to those mentioned above in respect of translation rights, though such licences are limited to reproduction and publication of the work for educational or cultural purposes. Further, the licence will terminate if the author publishes or causes to be published his work in the country where the licence has been granted.   **17–53**

(d) Broadcasting rights.[65] The fourth reservation permits the substitution for Article 11 *bis* (1) and (2) of Stockholm of certain provisions which have the effect of cutting down an author's broadcasting rights. Thus, under the Protocol, authors are only to have the exclusive right of authorising the broadcasting of their works and the communication to the public of such broadcasts, and then only if such communication is made for profit-making purposes.   **17–54**

(e) General. The fifth reservation is of a general nature and permits the restriction, exclusively for teaching, study and research in all fields of education, of the protection of works, subject to the authors being compensated in conformity with standards of payment made to national authors.   **17–55**

(v) Appendix to Paris Act

Appendix. As has been mentioned,[66] the Paris Act has dropped Article 21 relating to the Protocol Regarding Developing Countries and the Protocol itself, and substituted another Article 21 and an Appendix containing provisions dealing with developing countries, such Article providing that the Appendix forms an integral part of the Paris Act. However, this is subject to Article 28 under which any country may declare that its ratification or accession shall not apply to the substantive provisions of the Paris Act and the Appendix.   **17–56**

---

[64] See § 17–30, *ante.*
[65] See § 17–36, *ante.*
[66] See § 17–9, *ante.*

17–57 **Mode of operation of Appendix.** Article 1 of the Appendix provides that any country regarded as a developing country in conformity with the established practice of the General Assembly of the United Nations which ratifies or accedes to the Paris Act and which, having regard to its economic situation and its social or cultural needs, does not consider itself immediately in a position to make provision for the protection of all the rights as provided for in the Paris Act, may declare that it avails itself of one or both faculties in Articles 2 and 3; or instead of availing itself of the faculty in Article 2 may make a declaration according to Article 5(1)(*a*) relating to Article 30. Any such declaration notified before the expiration of the first 10 years from the entry into force of the substantive provisions of the Paris Act and the Appendix lasts until the expiration of such period. Any notification after the expiration of that period lasts for 10 years. Any such declarations may be renewed in whole or in part for further periods of 10 years.

Any country which has ceased to be regarded as a developing country cannot renew its declaration and, whether or not it withdraws its declaration, it is precluded from availing itself of such faculties after the expiration of the 10 year period then running, or from the expiration of a period of three years after it has ceased to be regarded as a developing country, whichever period expires later. Notwithstanding a declaration ceases to be effective, copies in stock made under a licence granted by virtue of the Appendix may be disposed of. Further, where a country avails itself of any of such faculties, no country may give less protection to works originating in the former country than it is obliged to give under the substantive provisions of the Paris Act.

17–58 **The faculty under Article 2; Translation rights.**[67] This enables a developing country, in relation to works published in printed or analogous form of reproduction, to substitute for the exclusive right of translation provided for in Article 8 of the Paris Act, a system of non-exclusive and non-transferable licences, granted by the competent authority, subject to certain conditions and the provisions of Article 4. As the latter largely apply also to Article 3 licences they are dealt with below after the faculty under Article 3.

The first condition is one of time. Thus, if after the expiration of a period of three years, or any longer period determined by the national legislation of such country, commencing on the date of first publication of the work, a translation of the work has not been published in a language in general use in that country by the owner of the translation rights, or with his authorisation, any national of such country may obtain a licence to make a translation of the work in the said language and publish the translation in printed or analogous forms of reproduction. Alternatively a licence may be granted if all the editions of the translation published in the language concerned are out of print. A further alternative arises in the case of translations into a language which is not in general use in one or more developed countries who are Union members; in which case one year is to be substituted for the period of three years above mentioned. But

---

[67] See § 17–29, *ante.*

any developing country availing itself of this faculty may, with the unanimous agreement of the developed countries which are Union members and in which the same language is in general use, substitute, in the case of translations into that language for the said period of three years an agreed shorter period of not less than one year; this provision will not apply where the language in question is English, French or Spanish. However, these time limits only bring the faculty into operation. That is to say, no licence obtainable after a three year period is to be granted until a further period of six months has elapsed or nine months in the case of a one year period, in each case from the date the applicant complies with the requirements of Article 4(1), or, where the identity or address of the owner of the translation rights is unknown, from the date on which the applicant sends copies of his application submitted to the competent authority as provided by Article 4(2).

Apart from the condition as to time, Article 2 imposes other conditions. Thus, if during such six or nine months period a translation in the language in respect of which the application was made is published by the owner of the translation rights or with his authorisation, no licence can be granted. Any licence in fact granted can only be for the purpose of teaching, scholarship or research. If a licence is granted, but a translation of the work is published by the owner of the translation rights or with his authorisation at a price reasonably related to that normally charged in the country for comparable works, the licence will terminate if such translation is in the same language and with substantially the same content as the translation published under the licence. However, existing stocks may be disposed of. No licence may be granted when the author has withdrawn all copies of the work from circulation.

Article 2 also contains provisions dealing with licences in respect of works with illustrations as well as text, and translations for the purposes of use in broadcasts.

The faculty under Article 3; Reproduction rights.[68] This enables a   **17–59** developing country to substitute for the exclusive right of reproduction provided for in Article 9 of the Paris Act a system of non-exclusive and non-transferable licences, granted by the competent authority, subject to certain conditions and the provisions of Article 4 dealt with below. The works to which this faculty applies are works published in printed or analogous forms of reproduction and to the reproduction in audio-visual form of certain lawfully made audio-visual fixations and to the translation of any incorporated text.

As with Article 2, the first condition is one of time. Thus, a licence may be obtained by a national of such country to reproduce and publish a particular edition of a work at a price reasonably related to that normally charged in the country for comparable works or a lower price for use in connection with systematic instructional activities if, after the expiration of the prescribed period, copies of such edition have not been distributed in that country to the general public or in connection with systematic instructional activities, by the owner of the reproduction rights or with his

---

[68] See § 17–30, *ante*.

authorisation, at such first mentioned price. A licence may also be obtained to reproduce and publish an edition of the work which has been so distributed if, after the expiration of the applicable period, no authorised copies of the edition have been on sale for a period of six months in such country to the general public or in connection with systematic instructional activities at a price reasonably related to that normally charged in that country for comparable works.

The commencing date for the various prescribed periods is the date of first publication of the edition in question and the periods are, subject to any longer periods determined by the legislation of the country in question: for works of the natural and physical sciences, including mathematics, and of technology, three years; for works of fiction, poetry, drama and music, and for art books, seven years; for all other works, five years. Again, these periods only bring the faculty into operation. Thus no licence obtainable after a three year period is to be granted until six months from the date the applicant complies with the requirements of Article 4(1) or, where the identity or the address of the owner of the reproduction rights is unknown, from the date on which the applicant sends, as provided by Article 4(2), copies of his application submitted to the competent authority. In respect of other periods there appears to be no extra time factor unless the owner of the rights cannot be found and Article 4(2) applies. In which case no licence is to be granted until three months from the date of the dispatch of the copies of the application.

Article 3 imposes other conditions apart from time. Thus, if during the extra periods of six or three months above mentioned a distribution of copies of the edition in question has taken place in the country of the kind mentioned above, no licence is to be granted. Further, no licence is to be granted if the author has withdrawn from circulation all copies of the edition in question. Again, a licence to reproduce and publish a translation of a work is not to be granted if, either the translation was not published by the owner of the translation rights or with his authorisation, or the translation is not in a language in general use in the country concerned. Also if a distribution of copies of the edition in question has taken place in the country of the kind mentioned above, any licence granted is to terminate if such edition is in the same language and with substantially the same content as the edition which was published under the licence. However, existing stocks may be disposed of.

17–60   **The provisions of Article 4.** The provisions of Articles 2 and 3 are subject to Article 4 which contains certain provisions relating to procedural matters and licence terms.

As to procedure, Article 4 provides that a licence under Articles 2 or 3 may only be granted if the applicant, in accordance with the procedure of the country concerned, establishes, either that he has requested, and been denied, the necessary authorisation by the owner of the relevant rights, or that, after due diligence, he was unable to find such owner. He must also, when making his request, inform any designated national or international information centre. If the owner cannot be found, then Article 4 requires the applicant to send copies of his application to the competent authority for a licence to various persons.

As to licence terms, Article 4 contains certain provisions which, it would seem, would have to be contained in a licence or, at least, taken into account when the licence is granted. Thus, it is provided that the name of the author is to be indicated in all copies of the translation or reproduction published under the licence. The title of the work and, in the case of a translation, the original title of the work is to appear on all such copies. Further, licences to export are not permitted and all such copies are to bear a notice in the appropriate language stating that the copies are available for distribution only in the country or territory to which the licence applies. Also, the licence must provide for just compensation of the owner of the relevant rights and for payment and transmittal of such compensation. Finally, national legislation must ensure a correct translation of the work, or an accurate reproduction of the particular edition, as the case may be.

(vi) Entry into force of Stockholm Convention

Ratification or accession. Because of the controversy over the introduction into the Stockholm revision of the Berne Convention of the Protocol Regarding Developing Countries,[69] which was made an integral part of the Stockholm Convention (Article 21), such Convention permitted any country of the Union ratifying or acceding to the Convention to declare that its ratification or accession was not to apply to the substantive provisions of the Convention (Articles 1 to 21) and the Protocol: Article 21(1)(*b*)(i). Alternatively such a country might declare that its ratification or accession was not to apply to the administrative provisions of the Convention (Articles 22 to 26): Article 28(1)(*b*)(ii). Ratification or accession in either way carried with it the final clauses of the Stockholm Convention (Articles 27 to 38): Article 28(3). There were, therefore, two distinct ways in which a country of the Union might have become a party to the Stockholm Convention but, as a result, none of the major developed countries ratified or acceded to the substantive provisions of the Stockholm Convention. **17-61**

The substantive provisions and the Protocol of Stockholm. Articles 1 to 21 and the Protocol were to come into force with respect to the first five countries which had ratified or acceded without declaring that their ratification or accession should not apply to such Articles and Protocol, and without making the declaration permitted by paragraph (1)(*b*)(i) of the Protocol, three months after the deposit of the fifth instrument of ratification or accession: Article 28(2)(*a*). As Articles 1 to 21 and the Appendix to the Paris Act came into force on October 10, 1974, no country may now ratify or accede to Stockholm; Article 34(1) Paris. However, the previous Conventions remain in force in relations with countries of the Union which do not ratify or accede to the Paris Act; Article 32(1) Paris. **17-62**

The Protocol. However, the Protocol could be applied before the entry into force of the Stockholm Convention (Article 28(2)(*d*)) and, therefore, Article 28(2)(*a*) was made subject to the provisions of Article 5 of the Pro- **17-63**

---

[69] See § 17-7, *ante.*

tocol. Article 5 provided that any country of the Union might declare, at any time before becoming bound by Articles 1 to 21 and the Protocol, either (a) in the case of a developing country, that it intended to apply the provisions of the Protocol to works whose country of origin is a country of the Union which admits the application of the reservations under the Protocol, or (b) that it admitted the application of the provisions of the Protocol to works of which it is the country of origin by countries which, on becoming bound by Articles 1 to 21 and by the Protocol, or on making a declaration of application of the Protocol by virtue of the provision of (a), have made reservations permitted by the Protocol. If a country had already separately accepted the Protocol in accordance with Article 5 thereof, its declaration under Article 28(1)(*b*)(i) might only relate to Articles 1 to 20; Article 28(1)(*c*).

17–64   **The administrative provisions.** The administrative provisions of the Stockholm Convention, Articles 22 to 26, were to come into force with respect to the first seven countries which had ratified or acceded without declaring that their ratification or accession did not apply to such Articles, three months after the deposit of the seventh instrument of ratification or accession: Article 28(2)(*b*).

17–65   **Declarations and notifications.** The Stockholm Convention provided for various declarations or notifications. For instance, Article 7(7) provided that any country of the Union bound by the Rome Convention, which grants shorter terms of protection than those provided for in Article 7 of the Stockholm Convention, might maintain such terms when ratifying or acceding to the Stockholm Convention. Again, Article 33, which provided, in paragraph (1), for the settling of disputes about the interpretation or application of the Stockholm Convention, provided, in paragraph (2), that a country, when ratifying or acceding to the Stockholm Convention, might declare that it did not consider itself bound by paragraph (1). Further, Article 38(2) provided that countries of the Union not bound by Articles 22 to 26 (the administrative provisions of the Stockholm Convention) might, until five years after the entry into force of the Convention establishing the World Intellectual Property Organisation[70] exercise, if they so desired, the rights provided under such Articles as if they were bound by such Articles, by giving written notification thereof as prescribed by Article 38(2).

17–66   **State of ratifications or accessions.** The only countries which have adhered to the substantive provisions of the Stockholm Convention and the Protocol are Chad, Germany (Democratic Republic), Mauritania, Pakistan, Rumania and Senegal. Notwithstanding that this is more than five countries, it seems the substantive provisions are not in force in view of the declarations made by Pakistan and Mauritania.[71]

On the other hand, the administrative provisions of the Stockholm Convention did come into force, the following countries having adhered thereto: Australia, Austria, Belgium, Canada, Chad, Denmark, Fiji, Finland,

---

[70] See § 17–48, *ante.*
[71] See § 17–62, *ante.*

Germany (Democratic Republic), Germany (Federal Republic), Ireland, Israel, Liechtenstein, Morocco, Pakistan, Rumania, Senegal, Spain, Sweden, Switzerland and the United Kingdom. The United Kingdom has now ratified the Paris Convention with effect from January 2, 1990.

The validity of the instrument of accession deposited by the German Democratic Republic was disputed. Rumania's ratification was accompanied by declarations under Articles 7(7) and 33(2). Pakistan and Senegal made declarations under Article 5(1)(*a*) of the Protocol. Buglaria and Sweden made declarations under Article 5(1)(*b*) of the Protocol. Pakistan's accession was accompanied by a declaration that Pakistan availed itself of the reservations in Article 1 of the Protocol other than that in Article 1 (*a*): Mauritania's accession was accompanied by a declaration that Mauritania availed itself of the reservations in Article 1 of the Protocol. Finally, the following countries availed themselves of the provisions of Article 38(2): Argentina, Belgium, Brazil, Bulgaria, Cameroon, Chile, Czechoslovakia, Dahomey, France, Gabon, Greece, Holy See, Hungary, Italy, Ivory Coast, Japan, Luxembourg, Malta, Monaco, Netherlands, Niger, Norway, Portugal, South Africa, Tunisia, Turkey and Yugoslavia.

(vii) Entry into force of Paris Act

Ratification or accession. The method of entry into force of the Paris Act **17–67** is complicated. Thus, under Article 28(2), Articles 1 to 21 (the substantive provisions) and the Appendix are to come into force three months after both the following conditions are fulfilled. First, at least five countries of the Union have ratified or acceded to the Paris Act without making a declaration under paragraph (1)(*b*) of Article 28. Secondly, France, Spain, the United Kingdom and the United States of America have become bound by the Paris revision of the Universal Copyright Convention. Such entry into force applies to those countries of the Union which, at least three months before the coming into force, have deposited instruments of ratification or accession not containing a declaration under paragraph (1)(*b*) of Article 28. With regard to any other Union country which ratifies of accedes to the Paris Act without making such a declaration, Articles 1 to 21 and the Appendix are to come into force three months after the date on which the Director General has notified the deposit of the relevant instrument of ratification or accession, unless a subsequent date has been indicated in the instrument deposited, in which case entry into force takes place on the date indicated.

The declaration under Article 28(1)(*b*) is to the effect that the ratification or accession of the country concerned is not to apply to Articles 1 to 21 and the Appendix. However, if such country has previously made a declaration under Article 6(1) of the Appendix, then it may declare only that its ratification or accession is not to apply to Articles 1 to 20. Any country which has made such a declaration may at a later time declare that it extends the effects of its ratification or accession to those provisions.

So far as Articles 22 to 38 (the administrative and final provisions) are concerned, Article 28(3) provides that, as regards any country which ratifies or accedes to the Paris Act with or without a declaration under Article 28(1)(*d*), Articles 22 to 38 are to come into force three months after the date on which the Director General has notified the deposit of the relevant instrument of ratification or accession, unless a subsequent date has been indicated in the instrument deposited, in which case entry into force takes place on the date indicated.

Articles 29 and 30(2)(*b*) contain provisions for accession by non-Union countries.

Article 29 *bis* provides that the ratification or accession to the Paris Act by any country not bound by Articles 22 to 38 of the Stockholm Convention is, for the sole purposes of Article 14(2) of the Convention establishing the World Intellectual Property Organisation,[72] to amount to ratification of or accession to the Stockholm Convention with the limitation set forth in Article 28(1)(*b*)(i) thereof.

Article 30(2)(*a*) enables any country ratifying or acceding to the Paris Act, subject to Article 5(2) of the Appendix, to retain the benefit of the reservations it has previously formulated.

Finally, Article 6(1) of the Appendix (relating to developing countries) provides that any Union country may declare, as from the date of the Paris Act, and at any time before becoming bound by Articles 1 to 21 and the Appendix, as follows: (i) if it is a country which, were it bound by Articles 1 to 21 and the Appendix, would be entitled to avail itself of the faculties referred to in Article 1(1) of the Appendix, that it will apply the provisions of Article 2 or of Article 3 of the Appendix or of both to works whose country of origin is a country which, pursuant to (ii), admits the application of those Articles to such works, or which is bound by Articles 1 to 21 and this Appendix; such declaration may, instead of referring to Article 2, refer to Article 5 of the Appendix; (ii) that it admits the application of the Appendix to works of which it is the country of origin by countries which have made a declaration under (i) or a notification under Article 1 of the Appendix.

Articles 1 to 21 and the Appendix entered into force on October 10, 1974, by which time the requirements of Article 28(2)(*a*) had been complied with. Articles 22 to 38 are also now in force.

The following countries have now ratified or acceded to the whole of the Paris Act including the Appendix: Australia, Austria, Barbados, Benin (Dahomey), Brazil, Bulgaria, Burkina Faso (Upper Volta), Cameroon, Central African Republic, Chile, Columbia, Congo, Costa Rica, Cyprus, Czechoslovakia, Denmark, Egypt, Finland, France, Gabon, German Democratic Republic, German Federal Republic, Greece, Guinea, Holy See, Honduras, Hungary, India, Italy, Ivory Coast, Japan, Lesotho, Liberia, Libya, Luxembourg, Malaysia, Mali, Mauritania, Mauritius, Mexico, Monaco, Morocco, Netherlands, Niger, Peru, Portugal, Rwanda, Senegal, Spain, Surinam, Sweden, Togo, Trinidad and Tobago, Tunisia, United Kingdom, United States of America, Uruguay, Venezuela, Yugoslavia and Zaire.

The following countries have now ratified or acceded to the Paris Act, other than Articles 1 to 21 and the Appendix, by reason of having made a declaration under Article 28(1)(*b*): Argentina, Bahamas, Iceland, Malta,

---

[72] § C–156, *post.*

Norway, Philippines, Poland, South Africa, Sri Lanka (Ceylon), Thailand and Zimbabwe.

Egypt, Bulgaria, India, South Africa, Liberia, Libya, Bahamas, Malta, German Democratic Republic, Czechoslovakia, Lesotho, Mauritius, Thailand and Venezuela have made a declaration as to not being bound by Article 33(1). Tunisia has made a declaration as to Article 33(1). Cameroon, Congo, Mexico, India and Uruguay have made a notification under Article 38(1) of the Paris Act. However, Cameroon, Congo, India, Mexico and Uruguay later ratified the Paris Act. Japan, Thailand and Yugoslavia have made a declaration under Article 30(2)(*a*) of the Paris Act as to retaining the benefit of previous reservations. Portugal has made a declaration under Article 14 *bis* (2)(*c*). India has made a declaration under Article 14 *bis* (3).

The United Kingdom, German Federal Republic and Norway have made a declaration under Article 6(1)(ii) of the Appendix. The United Kingdom and the German Federal Republic later ratified the Paris Act. Egypt, Guinea, India, Lesotho, Liberia, Malaysia, Mauritius, Mexico, Niger, Tunisia and Surinam have availed themselves of the faculties in Articles 2 and 3 of the Appendix. Cyprus has made a declaration under Article 5 (1)(a)(ii) of the Appendix.

(viii) Present members of the Copyright Union

Countries forming the Copyright Union.[73] At the moment of writing **17–68** the following countries form the Copyright Union: Argentina, Australia, Austria, Bahamas, Barbados, Belgium, Benin (Dahomey), Brazil, Bulgaria, Burkina Faso (Upper Volta), Cameroon, Canada, Central African Republic, Chad, Chile, Columbia, Congo, Costa Rica, Cyprus, Czechoslovakia, Denmark, Egypt, Fiji, Finland, France (including overseas departments and territories), Gabon, German Democratic Republic (and Berlin (East))[73], German Federal Republic (and Berlin (West))[73], Great Britain (including her colonies and possessions), Greece, Guinea, Holy See, Honduras, Hungary, Iceland, India, Irish Republic, Israel, Italy, Ivory Coast, Japan, Lebanon, Lesotho, Liberia, Libya, Liechtenstein, Luxembourg, Madagascar (Malagasy Republic), Malaysia, Mali, Malta, Mauritania, Mauritius, Mexico, Monaco, Morocco, Netherlands (and her colonies), New Zealand, Niger, Norway, Pakistan, Peru, Philippines, Poland, Portugal (and Portuguese overseas provinces), Rumania, Rwanda, Senegal, Spain, Sri Lanka (Ceylon), Surinam, Sweden, Switzerland, Thailand, Togo, Trinidad and Tobago, Tunisia, Turkey, Union of South Africa, United States of America, Uruguay, Venezuela, Yugoslavia, Zaire and Zimbabwe.

---

[73] The situation is constantly changing and the current position can be obtained by consulting *Copyright*, a monthly review published by the World Intellectual Property Organisation. For instance it is understood that, as a result of the unification of West and East Germany on October 3, 1990, the national and international copyright position in respect of the unified country is as it was for West Germany before unification. See *Copyright*, January, 1991, pp. 6, 12 and 16.

C. *The Universal Copyright Convention and its Revision*

(i) History

17–69 **Object of Convention.** Largely with the object of creating a bridge between the Berne Convention countries on the one hand and the Pan-American Convention countries on the other hand,[74] and particularly in the hope that the United States might be persuaded to enter into copyright relations with the Berne Union countries, a draft International Convention was prepared under the auspices of UNESCO, which resulted in the Universal Copyright Convention, signed at Geneva on September 6, 1952.[75] Recommendations were made for the holding of a revision Conference in mid-1971 for the purpose of revising this Convention in an attempt to resolve the unfortunate situation which had arisen over the Protocol Regarding Developing Countries to the Stockholm revision of the Berne Convention, and in fact the Universal Copyright Convention, like the Berne Convention, was revised in Paris in 1971.

(ii) Substantive provisions

17–70 **Main provisions.** Basically, the effect of the revised Universal Copyright Convention[76] is that each contracting State undertakes to give to the unpublished works of the nationals of all other contracting States the same protection as it gives to the unpublished works of its own nationals as well as the protection specially granted by the Convention, and further undertakes to give to the published works of nationals of the other contracting States wherever first published, and to published works of the nationals of any country if first published in one of the other contracting States, the same rights as it gives to works first published in its own territory as well as the protection specially granted by the Convention. Furthermore, such published works, if first published outside the territory of the contracting State in question and not being the work of a national author, are to enjoy such protection without formality, such as registration or the deposit of copies, provided only that from the time of first publication all copies published bear the symbol © accompanied by the name of the copyright proprietor and the year of first publication, placed in such manner and location as to give reasonable notice of claim of copyright.[77] The Convention is not to apply to works which, at the effective date of the Convention in a contracting State where protection is claimed, are permanently in the public domain in that State.

17–71 **Term of copyright.** The Convention provides for a minimum term of protection, namely, the life of the author and 25 years after his death. It is, however, provided that any contracting State which, upon the effective

---

[74] *Post,* § 17–76.

[75] As a result the Convention is variously referred to as the Universal, Geneva or UNESCO Convention. The United States acceded to the Paris Act of Berne with effect from March 1, 1989.

[76] For texts see § C–50 *et seq. post.*

[77] The positioning of such notice on various types of works is considered in the UNESCO Copyright Bulletin, 1957, Vol. X, No. 2 at pp. 225 and 247.

date of the Convention in that State, does not compute the term of protection upon the basis of the life of the author, shall be entitled to compute the term of protection from the date of first publication of the work or from its registration prior to publication, provided that the term of protection is not to be less than 25 years from the date of first publication or registration. "Publication" is defined in the Convention as meaning the reproduction in tangible form and the general distribution to the public of copies of a work from which it can be read or otherwise visually perceived.

Minimum protection required. As to the nature of the protection to be **17–72** afforded, the Convention provides that each contracting State shall give adequate and effective protection to the rights of authors and other copyright proprietors in literary, scientific and artistic works, including writings, musical, dramatic and cinematographic works, and paintings, engravings and sculpture. It is further provided that these rights are to include the basic rights ensuring the author's economic interests, including the exclusive right to authorise reproduction by any means, public performance and broadcasting, and are to extend to the work either in its original form or in any form recognisably derived from the original. Any contracting State may make exceptions that do not conflict with the spirit and provisions of the Convention, to such rights, but shall nevertheless accord a reasonable degree of effective protection to each of the rights to which exception has been made. It is also provided that such rights include the exclusive right to make, publish and authorise the making and publication of translations of works, but the contracting State may make provision for compulsory licences to translate if, after the expiration of a period of seven years from the date of first publication, a translation has not been published in a language in general use in that State.

While promising protection on the general lines above indicated, this **17–73** Convention does not describe the details of protection which are to be afforded by the contracting States and substantially leaves the mode and extent of protection to the separate legislation of each State. It only extended further than the Berne Convention in requiring protection to be given to published works, not only if first published in a contracting State, but if first published anywhere, if the author is a national of a contracting State.[78] To meet this requirement of the Convention, and in order to enable the United Kingdom to ratify the Convention, the 1956 Act altered the law of the United Kingdom so as to protect the published works of nationals of contracting States although first published outside the United Kingdom and the Convention area.[79] The most important amendment in the Paris revision of this Convention was to provide for various forms of compulsory licence in favour of developing countries similar to those in the Appendix to the Paris revision of the Berne Convention.[80] This did not call for any revision of this country's law and this country has, in fact, ratified the Paris revision of this Convention.

Countries, may ratify, accept or accede to this Convention which comes

---

[78] But see now Art. 3(1) of the Paris Act of Berne, § 17–11, *ante.*
[79] Copyright Act 1956, ss.2(2) and 3(3) and see C.D.P.A. 1988, ss.154 and 155.
[80] See § 17–57, *ante.*

into force three months after the deposit of 12 instruments of ratification, acceptance or accession. Subsequently it will come into force in respect of any State three months after that State has deposited its instrument of ratification, acceptance or accession.

(iii) Entry into force of 1971 Convention

17–74 **Ratification or accession.** Accession to the 1971 Convention by a State not party to the 1952 Convention is also to constitute accession to that Convention; but if its instrument of accession is deposited before the 1971 Convention comes into force, such State may make its accession to the 1952 Convention conditional upon the coming into force of the 1971 Convention. After the coming into force of the 1971 Convention, no State may accede solely to the 1952 Convention. Relations between States party to the 1971 Convention and States that are party only to the 1952 Convention, are to be governed by the 1952 Convention. However, any State party only to the 1952 Convention may, by a notification deposited with the Director General, declare that it will admit the application of the 1971 Convention to works of its nationals or works first published in its territory by all States party to the 1971 Convention.

The 1971 Convention in fact came into force on July 10, 1974, three months after the deposit of 12 instruments of ratification, acceptance or accession.

The following countries have now ratified or acceded to the 1971 Convention: Algeria, Australia, Bahamas, Bangladesh, Barbados, Brazil, Bulgaria, Cameroon, Colombia, Costa Rica, Czechoslovakia, Denmark, Dominican Republic, El Salvador, Finland, France, German Democratic Republic (and Berlin (East)), German Federal Republic (and (Berlin (West)), Guinea, Holy See, Hungary, India, Italy, Japan, Kenya, Korea (Republic of), Mexico, Monaco, Morocco, Netherlands, Niger, Norway, Panama, Peru, Poland, Portugal, Rwanda, Saint Vincent and the Grenadines, Senegal, Spain, Sri Lanka (Ceylon), Sweden, Trindad and Tobago, Tunisia, United Kingdom, United States of America and Yugoslavia.

The following countries have availed themselves of the exceptions in favour of developing countries: Algeria, Bangladesh, Korea (Republic of), Mexico and Tunisia.

(iv) Parties to the Universal Copyright Convention

17–75 **Convention countries.**[81] At the moment of writing the following countries are parties to the Universal Copyright Convention: Algeria, Andorra, Argentina, Australia, Austria, Bahamas, Bangladesh, Barbados, Belgium, Belize, Brazil, Bulgaria, Cambodia (Kampuchea), Cameroon, Canada, Chile, Colombia, Costa Rica, Cuba, Czechoslovakia, Denmark, Dominican Republic, Ecuador, El Salvador, Fiji, Finland, France, German Democratic Republic (and Berlin (East))[81], German Federal Republic (and Berlin (West))[81], Ghana, Great Britain,[82] Greece,

---

[81] See n. 73, § 17–68, *ante*.
[82] The effective date for Great Britain was September 27, 1957, and, as regards the 1971 Convention, was July 10, 1974.

Guatemala, Guinea, Haiti, Holy See, Hungary, Iceland, India, Irish Republic, Israel, Italy, Japan, Kenya, Korea (Republic of), Lao People's Democratic Republic (Laos), Lebanon, Liberia, Liechtenstein, Luxembourg, Malawi, Malta, Mauritius, Mexico, Monaco, Morocco, Netherlands, New Zealand, Nicaragua, Niger, Nigeria, Norway, Pakistan, Panama, Paraguay, Peru, Philippines, Poland, Portugal, Rwanda, Saint Vincent and the Grenadines, Senegal, Spain, Sri Lanka (Ceylon), Sweden, Switzerland, Trinidad and Tobago, Tunisia, Union of Soviet Socialist Republics, United States of America, Venezuela, Yugoslavia and Zambia.

D. *Pan-American Conventions*

There are certain American Conventions—the Montevideo Convention **17–76** and the various Pan-American Conventions,[83] to none of which is Great Britain a party. The Montevideo Convention (January 11, 1889) adopts a wholly different principle to that of the Berne Convention, conferring upon an author belonging to one country of the Union in the other countries of the Union the rights which he enjoys in the country where he first publishes, not the rights which authors enjoy in the country where the infringement takes place, so that, under this Convention, the law of the country of origin follows the work into the other countries of the Union. It appears that the Montevideo Convention applies as between Argentina on the one hand and Austria, Belgium, France, German Federal Republic, Hungary, Italy and Spain on the other; between Bolivia on the one hand and Austria, German Federal Republic and Hungary on the other; and between Paraguay on the one hand and Austria, Belgium, France, German Federal Republic, Hungary, Italy and Spain on the other.

The Pan-American Conventions are those of Mexico City (1902), Rio de Janeiro (1906), Buenos Aires (1910) and Havana (1928). The later of these Conventions are both modifications of the original Convention of 1902, and all adopt the Berne principle of according national protection to works published in any of the countries of the Union. But under the Convention of 1902, in order to obtain copyright in another country, it was an "indispensable" condition that the author or his representatives should address a petition to the official department of each government, claiming the recognition of the right. This was modified by the later Conventions, and, under the Convention of 1910, it simply provided that "the acknowledgment of a copyright obtained in one State, in conformity with its laws, shall produce its effects of conferring full right in all the other States without the necessity of complying with any other formality, provided always there shall appear in the work a statement that indicates the reservation of the property right." The Convention of 1902 was ratified by Guatemala (1902), El Salvador (1902), Costa Rica (1903), Honduras (1904), Nicaragua (1904), Dominica (1907), and the United States (1908). The Convention of 1906 was ratified by Guatemala (1909), Honduras (1908), El Salvador (1910), Nicaragua (1909), Costa Rica (1908), Ecuador (1909),

---

[83] The full text of these Conventions will be found in "Copyright Laws and Treaties of the World," prepared by UNESCO.

Chile (1910), Panama (1911) and Brazil (1911). The Convention of 1910 has been ratified by the United States, Dominica, Guatemala, Honduras, Panama, Nicaragua, Ecuador, Brazil, Costa Rica, Uruguay, Peru, Paraguay, Haiti, Colombia, Argentina, Bolivia, Chile and Mexico. The Convention of 1928 has been ratified by Costa Rica, Ecuador, Guatemala, Nicaragua and Panama. An agreement was concluded in Caracas in 1911 which has been ratified by Bolivia, Ecuador, Peru and Venezuela. A further Pan-American Convention was concluded at Washington in 1946 under the terms of which rights of copyright set out in some detail are to be conferred as between the signatory countries without formality or restriction. This Convention has been ratified by Argentina, Bolivia, Brazil, Chile, Columbia, Costa Rica, Cuba, Dominica, Ecuador, Guatemala, Haiti, Honduras, Mexico, Nicaragua and Paraguay.

2. Protection of Works of Foreign Origin: Application of Act

A. *General*

(i) Position before the 1911 Act

17–81   Implementation of treaties, conventions and agreements. It is clear that the parties to treaties, conventions and agreements can give effect to them, either by making the treaty, for instance, which they have ratified, part of the municipal law of the country, or by making separate legislation to carry its provisions into effect. This country, prior to the 1911 Act, had adopted the first alternative in respect of copyright since, by Orders in Council made under the International Copyright Acts of 1844 and 1866, the original Berne Convention and the Act of Paris were given full effect in this country and were interpreted by the courts.[84] These Acts, however, were repealed by the 1911 Act in the dominions to which that Act applied, and the scheme of the 1911 Act, the 1956 Act and the 1988 Act is to give to British works rights as large as those required by the Convention and, by Orders in Council, to give these rights to foreign works.[85]

The method of giving such rights to foreign works by Order in Council is to apply the provisions of the relevant Act to such works, thereby giving such works equivalent protection in this country to British works. This is to be distinguished from extending the provisions of the relevant Act to a country by Order in Council, thereby making that Act the law of that country. Extension is dealt with in Part 3 of this Chapter. Foreign works can, however, obtain protection in this country by other routes than the Orders in Council, for instance by simultaneous publication.

---

[84] *E.g.* in *Hanfstaengl* v. *Empire Palace* [1894] 3 Ch. 109.
[85] See § 17–1, *ante*; in case of ambiguity see *Hogg* v. *Toye and Co. Ltd.* [1935] Ch. 497 at 520 and *Warwick Film Productions Ltd.* v. *Eisinger* [1969] 1 Ch. 508 at 521; see also *Cheney* v. *Conn* [1968] 1 W.L.R. 242 and *Monte Ulia (Owners)* v. *Banco (Owners)* [1971] P. 137. See, however, as to the Treaty of Rome 1957, Chap. 14, *ante*.

(ii) Position under the 1911 Act

Orders in Council under the 1911 Act. A general Order in Council was   **17–82**
made on June 24, 1912[86] for the purpose of applying the 1911 Act, in
accordance with section 29, to works originating in countries of the Copyright Union, and subsequent Orders were made, as necessity arose, by
reason of countries joining the Union or altering their reservations to the
Convention. By an Order in Council[87] dated March 16, 1933, all previous
Orders were revoked, but without prejudice to existing rights, and the
provisions of section 29 of the Act were applied to all countries of the
Copyright Union. Under this Order, as under previous Orders, the term
of protection was limited to that conferred by the law of the country of origin of the work, and limitations were imposed in respect of those countries
which had made reservations to the Convention. In respect of existing
works, it was provided that rights extinguished by virtue of section 5 of the
International Copyright Act 1886, that is by virtue of non-publication in
the English language within 10 years, should not be revived by the Order,
and that the copyright in musical works should include mechanical rights
where no contrivances had been made or sold in His Majesty's dominions
before the dates mentioned in the Schedule.

Preservation of Orders in Council made under the 1911 Act. In   **17–83**
order to prevent Orders in Council made under the 1911 Act lapsing
immediately upon the commencement of the 1956 Act and its repeal of the
1911 Act, it was provided, in paragraph 40 of Schedule 7 to the 1956
Act,[88] that such Orders, and all the provisions of the 1911 Act required for
the purposes of any proceedings arising out of the operation of such continuance, were to continue in force until the occurrence of whichever of the
following events first occurred, that was to say:

(a) the revocation of the Order under the 1911 Act;

(b) the coming into operation of an Order under the 1956 Act in the
case of the foreign country in question; and

(c) the expiration of the period of 2 years from the repeal of the 1911
Act.

(iii) Position under the 1956 Act

Power to apply the 1956 Act to other countries. By section 32 of the   **17–84**
1956 Act, Her Majesty[89] was authorised, by Order in Council, to make
provision for applying any of the provisions of that Act, in the case of a
country to which those provisions did not extend, so as to secure that
those provisions:

(a) applied in relation to literary, dramatic, musical or artistic works,

---

[86] S.R. & O. 1912 No. 913.
[87] S.R. & O. 1933 No. 253; *Copinger* (8th ed.), p. 459.
[88] Para. 40, Sched. 7, Copyright Act 1956, was repealed by Statute Law (Repeals) Act 1986
(c. 12).
[89] See, as to the extension of s.32, Copyright Act 1956 to Hong Kong, §17–161 *post.*

sound recordings, cinematograph films or editions first published in that country as they applied to such works first published in the United Kingdom;

(b) applied in relation to persons who, at a material time, were citizens or subjects of that country as they applied in relation to British subjects;

(c) applied in relation to persons who, at a material time, were domiciled or resident in that country as they applied in relation to persons domiciled or resident in the United Kingdom;

(d) applied in relation to bodies incorporated under the laws of that country as they applied in relation to bodies incorporated under the laws of any part of the United Kingdom;

(e) applied in relation to television broadcasts and sound broadcasts made from places in that country by one or more organisations constituted in or under the laws of that country as they applied in relation to television broadcasts and sound broadcasts made by the British Broadcasting Corporation or the Independent Broadcasting Authority[90]; and

(f) applied in relation to cable programmes sent from places in that country as they applied in relation to cable programmes sent from places in the United Kingdom.[91]

Any such Order in Council could have been made subject to exceptions and modifications, and could have applied either generally or in relation to specified classes of works or classes of cases.

17–85 **Limitation on power to apply the 1956 Act.** The power to make such Orders was, however, limited, in that an Order was not to be made applying any of the provisions of the 1956 Act in the case of a country, other than a country which was a party to a Convention relating to copyright to which the United Kingdom was also a party; "unless Her Majesty is satisfied that, in respect of the class of works or other subject-matter to which those provisions relate, provision has been or will be made under the laws of that country whereby adequate protection will be given to owners of copyright under this Act." This limitation was in slightly different language from that contained in the similar provisions in section 29 of the 1911 Act, which stated that, before making an Order: "His Majesty shall be satisfied that that foreign country has made, or has undertaken to make, such provisions, if any, as it appears to His Majesty expedient to require for the protection of works entitled to copyright under this Act."

17–86 **Self-governing dominions.** It is further to be observed that, whilst section 29 of the 1911 Act enabled Orders in Council to be made in respect of works originating in "a foreign country," section 32 of the 1956 Act

---

[90] See Independent Broadcasting Authority Act 1973 (c. 19), ss.1, 38 and 39; repealed by Broadcasting Act 1981 (c. 68), s.65(4) and Sched. 9, but 1973 Act amendment preserved by 1981 Act para. 7, Sched. 8.

[91] Sub-para. (*f*) was added by the Cable and Broadcasting Act 1984 (c. 46).

applied to works originating in any country. This is because the 1911 Act extended, or was capable of being extended, throughout the British Empire, including the self-governing dominions, whereas the 1956 Act was only capable of being extended to the Isle of Man, the Channel Islands and any colony.[92] Consequently, protection of works originating in a self-governing dominion or member of the Commonwealth had to be provided by Order in Council in the same way as in the case of a foreign country.

Power to curtail protection. The 1956 Act gave[93] power to deprive citizens or subjects of countries not giving adequate protection to British works, of copyright under that Act. That power arose if the laws of a country failed to give adequate protection to British works, or to one or more classes of such works. A "British work," for this purpose, meant a work of which the author, at the time when the work was made, was a qualified person.[94] Where the circumstances contemplated arose, an Order in Council could have been made providing that copyright under the 1956 Act should not subsist in works, or classes of works, first published after a date specified in the Order, if at the time of their first publication the authors were citizens or subjects of the country designated by the Order, and not at that time persons domiciled or resident in the United Kingdom, or in another country to which that Act extended, or were bodies incorporated under the laws of the country designated by the Order. Such an Order could have been made in respect of literary, dramatic, musical and artistic works, sound recordings and cinematograph films. However, no such Order was ever made. The section only applied to published works because the unpublished works of foreign authors could, in any case, only have obtained protection by an Order in Council under section 32 of the 1956 Act, and could have been penalised merely by revoking or varying such an Order. What this section contemplated was the exclusion from copyright protection of works first published in the United Kingdom which would otherwise have obtained automatic protection under the main provisions of the 1956 Act. **17–87**

International organisations. Section 33 of the 1956 Act also provided for the conferring of copyright by Order in Council upon original literary, dramatic, musical or artistic works made by or under the direction or control of an international organisation, and whether or not such organisation had the legal capacity of a body corporate.[95] The section also applied where such a work was first published by or under the direction or control of such an organisation. Such section also dealt with duration and ownership of such copyright. **17–88**

---

[92] Copyright Act 1956, s.31, and see § 17–130, *post.*
[93] Copyright Act 1956, s.35.
[94] *Ibid.* s.35(5).
[95] This did not apply to works made or published before the commencement of the 1956 Act (Sched. 7, para. 27). See Copyright (International Organisations) Order 1957 (1957 S.I. No. 1524) *Copinger* (12th ed.) § 2116.

17–89 **Orders in Council under section 32 of the 1956 Act.**
(i) Countries other than Taiwan, Singapore and Indonesia. By an
Order in Council made under section 32 of the 1956 Act, and coming into
operation on September 27, 1957,[96] the 1956 Act was applied to works
originating in the countries specified in Schedule 1 to that Order, being
countries which had adhered to the Berne or Universal Copyright Conventions, in relation to all classes of works then covered by that Act other
than television broadcasts and sound broadcasts. This Order was
amended by further Orders. Another Order made in 1964,[97] which came
into operation on May 21, 1964, replaced these Orders, and was itself
amended by further Orders. Another Order made in 1972,[98] which came
into operation on May 31, 1972, replaced the 1964 Order and amending
Orders, and was itself amended by further Orders. Another Order made
in 1979[99] which came into operation on January 24, 1980, replaced the
1972 Order and amending Orders, and was itself amended by further
Orders. Dealing first with works, including for this purpose sound recordings, cinematograph films and published editions, the 1956 Act was
applied in relation to such works first published in such countries, and in
relation to the citizens or subjects of such countries, and to persons domiciled or resident in such countries, and in relation to bodies incorporated
under the laws of such countries.[1] The general effect of the Order, therefore, was that all such works were to be treated as if they had been first
published in the United Kingdom, or had been made by British subjects,
persons domiciled or resident in the United Kingdom, or United Kingdom companies. It will be recalled that, under sections 2(2) and 3(3) of
the 1956 Act, a published work could have enjoyed copyright protection,
not only by reason of the place of publication, but also because the author
was a qualified person when the work was first published, and similar provision was made in regard to sound recordings, cinematograph films and
published editions.[2] Consequently, under the Order, copyright could have
been enjoyed in the United Kingdom in respect of published works, not
only because they had been first published in a country to which the
Order applied, but also, if not so published, because the author, maker or
publisher fell within the provisions of the Order.

17–90 **Works made after Order.** So far as concerns works or subject-matters
made after the commencement of the 1957 Order there were only two
respects in which the copyright in such works differed from that in a work
of United Kingdom origin. The first concerned the term of such copyright

---

[96] S.I. 1957 No. 1523. *Copinger* (12th ed.) § 2105. The date is the date at which the Universal
Copyright Convention took effect so far as Great Britain is concerned, § 17–75 n. 82, *ante*.
[97] The Copyright (International Conventions) Order 1964 (S.I. 1964 No. 690). *Copinger*
(12th ed.) § 2117.
[98] The Copyright (International Conventions) Order 1972 (S.I. 1972 No. 673). *Copinger*
(12th ed.) § 2128.
[99] The Copyright (International Conventions) Order 1979 (S.I. 1979 No. 1715), *post*, § D–5:
and see *Milltronics Ltd.* v. *Hycontrol Ltd.* [1990] F.S.R. 273.
[1] Certain countries adhered to Conventions subsequent to the 1957 Order and accordingly
the 1964 Order, the 1972 Order and the 1979 Order applied to them as from later dates.
[2] Copyright Act 1956, ss.12(1), 13(1) and 15(1).

and was general, and the second was of a limited character in respect of the copyright in sound recordings.

(a) Term of copyright. It was provided, in the 1957 Order, that the term **17–91** of copyright in a work protected under the provisions of that Order was not to exceed that granted by the country of origin of the work without formality, other than that specified in the Universal Copyright Convention, to a British work of the same class. "British work" meant a work made by a British subject resident in the United Kingdom, or by a company incorporated under the laws of the United Kingdom, and which, if published, was first published in the United Kingdom.

However, this provision was cancelled by an Order[3] coming into operation on August 11, 1958, so that the normal term under the 1956 Act was applicable to all such works. But this amending Order was not to revive copyrights, so that it may still be necessary to consider the provisions of the original Order if, under such provisions, the term would have expired between September 27, 1957, and August 11, 1958. This will involve knowledge of the relevant foreign law, and of the meaning of "country of origin" in the Order. It is assumed that the revocation of the 1957 and 1958 Orders by the 1964 Order, and of the 1964 Order by the 1972 Order, and of the 1972 Order by the 1979 Order, did not revive copyrights.[4]

Meaning of "country of origin." Owing to the requirements of the vari- **17–92** ous Conventions and the complications ensuing as a result of the simultaneous publication of works in a number of countries, the expression "country of origin" received a complicated definition in the 1957 Order which may be shortly summarised as follows:

In the case of a work which was published in a country belonging to either of the Conventions it meant, if first published in such a country and not simultaneously published elsewhere, that country.

In the case of simultaneous publication, which meant, in the case of publications occurring before the commencement of that Order, publications within 14 days of one another, and, in any other case, within a period of 30 days of one another, there were four classes of case. If a work was simultaneously published in a Berne country and a non-Berne country, the country of origin was the Berne country. If the work was simultaneously published in a Universal Copyright Convention country and a country which was not a member of either Convention, the country of origin was the Universal Copyright Convention country. If a work was simultaneously published in several Berne countries, the country of origin was the country giving the shortest term of protection. If a work was simultaneously published in a number of Universal Copyright Convention countries and not in a Berne country, the country of origin was the country giving the shortest term of protection.

In the case of a work which was unpublished or first published in a country which did not belong to either Convention, the country of origin

---

[3] The Copyright (International Conventions) (Amendment) Order 1958 (S.I. 1958 No. 1254).

[4] See Art. 11, 1964 Order and Art. 2(2) 1972 Order and Interpretation Act 1889, s.38 (52 & 53 Vict. c. 63) and Interpretation Act 1978 (c. 30), ss.16, 21, 23. And see § 17–112 (g) *post*.

was the country whose laws gave the longest term of protection to such a work of the following, namely, the country of which the author was a subject or citizen, the country in which the author was domiciled, the country in which the author was resident or, where the author or maker was a body corporate, the country in which such body was incorporated.

17–93   **(b) Sound recordings.** The provision about sound recordings was that, in relation to any country other than Australia, Austria, Barbados, Brazil, Burkina, Chile, Colombia, Congo (People's Republic), Costa Rica, Cyprus, Czechoslovakia, Denmark, Dominican Republic, Ecuador, El Salvador, Federal Republic of Germany (and Berlin (West)), Fiji, Finland, France, Guatemala, India, Republic of Ireland, Israel, Italy, Luxembourg, Mexico, Monaco, New Zealand, Niger, Nigeria, Norway, Pakistan, Panama, Paraguay, Peru, Philippines, Spain, Sri Lanka (Ceylon), Sweden, Switzerland and Uruguay, the acts restricted by the copyright in a sound recording were not to include causing the recording to be heard in public or broadcasting the recording.[5]

17–94   **Existing works.** The provisions of the 1979 Order applied to works existing at the commencement of the 1957 Order, subject as aforesaid and to certain further qualifications:

17–95   (a) In the first place, copyright was not to subsist by virtue of the 1979 Order in any work by reason only of its publication before a specified date in a country which was a party to the Universal Copyright Convention, but which was not a country of the Berne Copyright Union.[6] This, combined with the operation of paragraph 1 of Schedule 7 to the 1956 Act, Article 4 and Schedule 2 to the 1972 Order, Article 2 and Schedule 2 to the 1964 Order and paragraph 5 of Schedule 4 to the 1957 Order, had the effect that works first published in a Universal Copyright Convention country, not being a Berne Convention country, before the specified date, would not have enjoyed United Kingdom copyright, notwithstanding that their authors may have been subjects of a country to which the 1957, 1964, 1972 and 1979 Orders applied at the date of publication.

17–96   (b) There was an exception to this in the case of works first published in the United States during the periods of the two wars which already enjoyed copyright in the United Kingdom by virtue of the Wartime Orders hereafter mentioned.[7] Such works would also have enjoyed the full term of United Kingdom copyright, notwith-

---

[5] Copyright (International Conventions) Order 1979 (S.I. 1979 No. 1715), Art. 5 and Sched. 3 as amended, *post,* § D–5; and see Copyright (International Conventions) Order 1972 (S.I. 1972 No. 673) Art. 5 and Sched. 3 as amended, Copyright (International Conventions) Order 1964 (S.I. 1964 No. 690), Art. 3 and Sched. 3 as amended, and Copyright (International Conventions) Order 1957 (S.I. 1957 No. 1523) Art. 1 proviso (iii) as amended.

[6] *Ibid.* Art. 4(1) and (2) and Sched. 2.

[7] *Ibid.* Art. 4(3)(*b*), *post,* §§ 17–114 and 17–115.

standing the provisions about the term of copyright hereinbefore mentioned.[8]

(c) There was also an exception in respect of Bahamas, Barbados, Belize, Cyprus, Fiji, Ghana, Kenya, Malawi, Malta, Mauritius, Nigeria, Trinidad and Tobago, St. Vincent and the Grenadines, Zambia and Zimbabwe.[9]

Provisions relating to translations and broadcasts.   **17-97**
(a) Translations. It was provided by the 1979 Order[10] that nothing in the 1956 Act, as applied by that Order, was to be construed as reviving any right to make, or restrain the making of, or any right in respect of, translations, if such right had ceased before the commencement of that Order. This referred, in particular, to certain provisions of the Order in Council (Copyright (Rome Convention) Order, 1933) made under the 1911 Act restricting the translation rights in works originating in certain countries because these countries also restricted translation rights.[11]

(b) Broadcasts. The 1979 Order provided[12] that the provisions of section   **17-98**
14 of the 1956 Act, so far as they related to sound broadcasts, were to apply in relation to sound broadcasts made from places in a number of named countries by any organisation constituted under the laws of such countries. It also provided[13] that the provisions of section 14 of the 1956 Act, so far as they related to television broadcasts, were to apply in relation to television broadcasts made from places in another series of countries by any organisation constituted under the laws of such countries.

1956 Act was to apply as if references to commencement of Act were   **17-99**
references to specified date. There was a general provision in the 1979 Order,[14] as in the 1972 Order,[15] as in the 1964 Order[16] that, in Schedule 7 to the 1956 Act, references to the commencement of that Act, or to the repeal of any provision of the 1911 Act were to be treated, in relation to any work or other subject-matter in which copyright subsisted by virtue of the 1979 Order, as references to the dates specified.

---

[8] § 17–91, *ante.*

[9] 1979 No. 1715 Art. 4(3)(*a*) as amended.

[10] 1979 No. 1715 Art. 7; see also Art. 1 proviso (v), Copyright (International Conventions) Order 1957 (S.I. 1957 No. 1523), Art. 6, Copyright (International Conventions) Order 1964 (S.I. 1964 No. 690) and Art. 7, Copyright (International Conventions) Order 1972 (S.I. 1972 No. 673).

[11] S.R. & O. 1933, No. 253 Art. 2, proviso (ii); see also proviso (vi).

[12] Copyright (International Conventions) Order 1979 (S.I. 1979 No. 1715), Art. 8 and Sched. 4, and see Copyright (International Conventions) Order 1972 (S.I. 1972 No. 673), Art. 8 and Sched. 4 and Copyright (International Conventions) Order 1964 (S.I. 1964 No. 690), Art. 8 and Sched. 5.

[13] *Ibid.* Art. 9 and Sched. 5; and see 1972 Order, Art. 9 and Sched. 5 and 1964 Order, Art. 9 and Sched. 6.

[14] Copyright (International Conventions) Order 1979 (S.I. 1979 No. 1715), Art. 4 and Sched. 2.

[15] Copyright (International Conventions) Order 1972 (S.I. 1972 No. 673), Art. 4 and Sched. 2.

[16] Copyright (International Conventions) Order 1964 (S.I. 1964 No. 690), Art. 2 and Sched. 2.

17–100 **Preservation of existing rights.** Finally, the 1957, 1964, 1972 and 1979 Orders contained general provisions preserving existing rights of persons who, before the commencement of each Order, had incurred expenditure or liability in connection with the reproduction or performance of any work or other subject-matter.[17]

17–101 **Unrepeated provisions of 1957 Order.**
(a) As to royalty terms for recorded music. The 1957 Order contained provisions[18] affecting the right to record music on royalty terms, which had the effect that, in the case of works published before certain dates set out in a Table to the Order, such works might be recorded on royalty terms, notwithstanding that they had not been previously recorded in the United Kingdom. Furthermore, in the case of such works which had been recorded and records sold in the United Kingdom before the relevant date, such works should be freely recorded. Where copyright was conferred by the Order for the first time on a musical work, then, for the purposes of the last-mentioned provision, the date of the Order was to be the relevant date. This provision was not repeated in the 1964, 1972 and 1979 Orders.

17–102 **(b) As to copyright in sound recordings.** There was also in the 1957 Order a provision[18] about the copyright in sound recordings. This referred back, through paragraph 13 of Schedule 7 to the 1956 Act, to section 19(8) of the 1911 Act which gave copyright under the 1911 Act, in respect of existing sound recordings, provided that the making thereof would not have infringed copyright in some other sound recording if that Act had been in force at the time of the making thereof. This provision of the 1957 Order seemed intended to apply the dates mentioned in Schedule 4 thereto, or the date of the commencement of that Order, as the case might be, for the date of the commencement of the 1911 Act in paragraph 13 of Schedule 7 to the 1956 Act. This provision also was not repeated in the 1964, 1972 and 1979 Orders.

17–103 **(c) As to revocation of previous Orders.** The 1957 Order[19] revoked all the previous Orders in Council relating to works of foreign origin, but it was provided that where, by virtue of any of such Orders, copyright subsisted in a work immediately before the commencement of the 1957 Order and copyright did not subsist therein by the 1957 Order, it should continue to subsist as if such Order had not been revoked. The effect of this provision was not altogether clear. The intention clearly was to keep alive copyright in works of foreign origin in which copyright subsisted at the commencement of the 1957 Order, but which would not acquire copyright under the 1956 Act by virtue of the prior provisions of that Order. It seems that the only effect of this provision was to preserve the copyright in such works during the 2 years mentioned in paragraph 40(2)(c) of Sched-

---

[17] 1979 Order Art. 6, 1972 Order, Art. 6, 1964 Order, Arts. 4 and 10 and 1957 Order, Art. 2.
[18] Copyright (International Conventions) Order 1957 (S.I. 1957 No. 1523), Art. 1, proviso (iv) and Sched. 4.
[19] *Ibid.* Art. 3.

ule 7 to the 1956 Act.[20] It, also, was not repeated in the 1964, 1972 and 1979 Orders.

(ii) Taiwan. By an Order in Council made under section 32 of the 1956   **17–104**
Act, and coming into operation on December 17, 1985,[21] the 1956 Act was applied to works originating in Taiwan in relation to all classes of works covered by that Act, other than television broadcasts, sound broadcasts and cable programmes. As to works, including for this purpose sound recordings, cinematograph films and published editions, the 1956 Act was applied in relation to such works first published in Taiwan, and in relation to citizens or subjects of China, being citizens or subjects who were resident or domiciled in Taiwan, and in relation to bodies incorporated under the laws of Taiwan. The general effect of this Order was that all such works were to be treated as if they had been first published in the United Kingdom, or had been made by British subjects or companies. This Order contained no restriction on the copyright in sound recordings,[22] but it did contain a provision excluding from section 2(5)(*f*) of the 1956 Act the right to make a translation of the work. The Order contained a provision that, in Schedule 7 to the 1956 Act, for references to the commencement of that Act there were substituted references to July 10, 1985, and that copyright was not to subsist by virtue of such Order in any work or other subject matter by reason only of its publication in Taiwan before that date. Finally such Order contained a general provision preserving existing rights of persons who, before the commencement of such Order, had incurred expenditure or liability in connection with the reproduction or performance of any work or other subject matter.

(iii) Singapore. By another Order in Council made under section 32 of   **17–105**
the 1956 Act, and coming into force on June 18, 1987,[23] the 1956 Act was apparently, applied in relation to all classes of works and subject-matters covered by that Act originating in Singapore. It would appear that television broadcasts, sound broadcasts and cable programmes were to be included since these were not expressly excluded although, if included, the Order did not make clear how the provisions as to broadcasts, for instance, were to be applied, and from when.[24] As to works, including for this purpose sound recordings, cinematograph films and published editions, the 1956 Act was applied in relation to such works first published in Singapore, and in relation to residents in Singapore, and in relation to bodies incorporated under the laws of Singapore. The general effect of this Order was that all such works were to be treated as if they had been first published in the United Kingdom, or had been made by British residents or companies. Citizens of Singapore were not referred to as they were qualified persons.[25] This Order contained a restriction on the copyright in

---

[20] Para. 40 Sched. 7, Copyright Act 1956 was repealed by the Statute Law (Repeals) Act 1986 (c. 12).
[21] S.I. 1985, No. 1777, § D–18, *post.*
[22] See § 17–93, *ante.*
[23] S.I. 1987 No. 940, § D–19, *post.*
[24] See § 17–98, *ante.*
[25] Copyright Act 1956, s.1(5).

sound recordings, namely that the acts restricted by the copyright in a sound recording were not to include causing the recording to be heard in public, broadcasting the recording or including it in a cable programme.[26] Finally such Order contained a general provision preserving existing rights of persons who, before the commencement of such Order, had incurred expenditure or liability in connection with the reproduction or performance of any work or other subject matter.

17–106   **(iv) Indonesia.** By another Order in Council made under section 32 of the 1956 Act, and coming into force on May 26, 1988,[27] the provisions of section 12 of the 1956 Act (copyright in sound recordings) and all the other provisions of that Act relevant to that section were applied to give protection to sound recordings originating in Indonesia. Thus these provisions were applied in relation to sound recordings first published in Indonesia, and in relation to makers of sound recordings who were citizens or subjects of or resident in Indonesia, or bodies incorporated under the laws of Indonesia. The general effect of this Order was that all such sound recordings were to be treated as if they had been first published in the United Kingdom, or had been made by British subjects, or United Kingdom residents or companies. Sound recordings protected under this Order were entitled to full sound recording copyright. Finally, such Order contained a general provision preserving existing rights of persons who, before the commencement of the Order, had incurred expenditure or liability in connection with the making of a record embodying a sound recording, or causing a sound recording to be heard in public, or the broadcasting of a sound recording or its inclusion in a cable programme.

D. *Position under the 1988 Act*

17–107   **Power to apply the 1988 Act to other countries.** By section 159 of the 1988 Act Her Majesty is authorised, by Order in Council, to make provision for applying any of the provisions of Part I of the Act dealing with copyright, in the case of a country[28] to which such Part does not extend, so as to secure that those provisions:

(a) apply in relation to persons who are citizens or subjects of that country or are domiciled or resident there, as they apply to persons who are British citizens or are domiciled or resident in the United Kingdom, or

(b) apply in relation to bodies incorporated under the law of that country as they apply in relation to bodies incorporated under the law of a part of the United Kingdom, or

(c) apply in relation to works first published in that country as they apply in relation to works first published in the United Kingdom, or

(d) apply in relation to broadcasts made from or cable programmes

---

[26] See n. 22, *ante.*
[27] S.I. 1988 No. 797, § D–20, *post.*
[28] "Country" includes any territory: C.D.P.A. 1988, s.178.

sent from that country as they apply in relation to broadcasts made from or cable programmes sent from the United Kingdom.

Any such Order can be made subject to exceptions and modifications, and may apply either generally or in relation to specified classes of works or classes of cases. A statutory instrument containing an Order in Council under section 159 is subject to annulment in pursuance of a resolution of either House of Parliament.

These provisions correspond to those of section 32 of the 1956 Act as amended.[29] Further, the provisions of the 1988 Act dealing with qualification for copyright protection expressly provide for cases where an Order has been made under section 159.[30]

Limitation on power to apply the 1988 Act. The power to make such **17–108** Orders is, as under section 32 of the 1956 Act,[31] limited in that an Order is not to be made in relation to a country,[32] other than a Convention country or another member State of the European Economic Community, unless Her Majesty is satisfied that provision has been or will be made under the law of that country, in respect of the class of works to which the Order relates, giving adequate protection to the owners of copyright under Part I of the 1988 Act. A Convention country is a country which is a party to a Convention relating to copyright to which the United Kingdom is also a party.[33]

Power to curtail protection. Section 160 of the 1988 Act, like section 35 **17–109** of the 1956 Act,[34] gives power to deprive citizens or subjects of countries not giving adequate protection to British works, of copyright under the 1988 Act. This power arises if the laws of a country[35] fail to give adequate protection to British works, or to one or more classes of such works. A British work is a work of which the author was a qualifying person at the material time within the meaning of section 154 of the 1988 Act.[36] In the given circumstances, an Order in Council can be made providing, either generally or in respect of specified classes of cases, that works first published after a date specified in the Order do not qualify for copyright protection by virtue of such publication if at the time of their first publication the authors are citizens or subjects of the country designated by the Order and not domiciled or resident in the United Kingdom or another country to which the relevant provisions of Part I of the 1988 extend,[37] or are bodies incorporated under the laws of the designated country. Such an Order may be made in respect of literary, dramatic, musical and artistic works, sound recordings and films. No such Order has yet been made. A statutory instrument containing an Order in Council under section 160 of

---

[29] *Ante*, § 17–84.

[30] C.D.P.A. 1988, ss.154(2) and (3), 155(2) and 156(2). As to existing works, see Sched. 1, para. 5, in particular para. 5(2)(*b*), and para. 35.

[31] *Ante*, § 17–85.

[32] See n. 28, *ante*.

[33] C.D.P.A. 1988, s.159(3) and (4).

[34] *Ante*, § 17–87.

[35] See n. 28, *ante*.

[36] *Ante*, Chap. 3.

[37] See, as to countries ceasing to be colonies, C.D.P.A. 1988, s.158(2)(*a*).

the 1988 Act is subject to annulment in pursuance of a resolution of either House of Parliament.

17–110 **International Organisations.** Section 168 of the 1988 Act[38] contains provisions for conferring copyright on original literary, dramatic, musical and artistic works made by officers or employees of, or published by an international organisation and which do not qualify for copyright protection under sections 154 or 155 of the 1988 Act.[39] In such circumstances the organisation is to be the first owner of such copyright.[40] Such copyright subsists until the end of the period of 50 years from the end of the calendar year in which the work was made or such longer period as may be specified by Order in Council for the purpose of complying with the international obligations of the United Kingdom.[41] Any work in which copyright subsisted by virtue of section 33 of the 1956 Act immediately before commencement of the copyright provisions of the 1988 Act is to be deemed to satisfy the requirements of section 168(1) of the 1988 Act, but otherwise section 168 does not apply to works made or, as the case may be, published before such commencement. Copyright in any such work which is unpublished continues to subsist until the date on which it would have expired in accordance with the 1956 Act, or the end of the period of 50 years from the end of the calendar year in which the copyright provisions of the 1988 Act come into force, whichever is the earlier.[42]

An international organisation means an organisation the members of which include one or more states,[43] and the international organisations to which section 168 of the 1988 Act applies are those to which Her Majesty has by Order in Council declared that it is expedient that such section should apply.[44] Such an organisation is to be deemed to have, and to have had at all material times, the legal capacities of a body corporate for the purpose of holding, dealing with and enforcing copyright and in connection with all legal proceedings relating to copyright.[45] A statutory instrument containing an Order in Council under section 168 of the 1988 Act is subject to annulment in pursuance of a resolution of either House of Parliament.[46]

The 1988 Act also contains provisions relating to moral rights and works in which copyright originally vested in an international organisation.[47]

---

[38] For the corresponding provision of the Copyright Act 1956, s.33, see § 17–88, *ante*.
[39] See C.D.P.A. 1988, s.153(2) and (3).
[40] *Ibid.* s.168(1), and see s.11(3).
[41] *Ibid.* s.168(3), and see s.12(5).
[42] *Ibid.* Sched. 1, para. 44.
[43] *Ibid.* s.178.
[44] *Ibid.* s.168(2). By The Copyright (International Organisations) Order 1989 (S.I. 1989 No. 989), *ibid.* s.168 was applied to the United Nations, the Specialised Agencies of the United Nations and the Organisation of American States; see § D–21, *post*. And see *ibid.* s.302 as to the giving of financial assistance to international organisations.
[45] *Ibid.* s.168(4). See, as to presumptions, C.D.P.A. 1988, ss.104(2)(*b*) and (3) and 107(6), and Chap. 11, *ante*. See, as to exceptions from infringement, s.57(2)(*b*) and Chap. 10, *ante*.
[46] *Ibid.* s.168(5).
[47] *Ibid.* ss.79(7)(*b*) and 82(1)(*c*) and (2): "sufficient disclaimer" s.178.

Anonymous unpublished works: folklore. Section 169 of the 1988 Act   **17–111**
contains new provisions conferring copyright, in certain circumstances, on
unpublished literary, dramatic, musical or artistic works of unknown
authorship[48] where there is evidence that the author (or, in the case of a
joint work, any of the authors) was a qualifying individual by connection
with a country outside the United Kingdom. A qualifying individual is a
person who at the material time (within the meaning of section 154 of the
1988 Act[49]) was a person whose works qualified under that section for
copyright protection.[50] Section 169(2) of the 1988 Act further provides
that if under the law of that country a body is appointed to protect and
enforce copyright in such works, Her Majesty may by Order in Council
designate that body for the purposes of that section. No such Order has
yet been made. Such a designated body is to be recognised in the United
Kingdom as having authority to do in place of the copyright owner anything, other than assign copyright, which it is empowered to do under the
law of that country, in particular bringing proceedings in its own name.[51]
Section 169 of the 1988 Act does not apply if there has been an assignment
of copyright in the work by the author of which notice has been given to
the designated body, and nothing in that section is to affect the validity of
an assignment of copyright made, or licence granted, by the author or a
person lawfully claiming under him.[52] A statutory instrument containing
an Order in Council under section 169 of the 1988 Act is subject to annulment in pursuance of a resolution of either House of Parliament.[53]

Order in Council under section 159 of the 1988 Act   **17–112**
(a) Generally. By an Order in Council made under section 159 of the
1988 Act, and coming into force on August 1, 1989,[54] various provisions of
the 1988 Act were applied in various ways, to various works originating in
various foreign countries, including Taiwan, Singapore and, for certain
purposes, Indonesia. This Order, though similar to, is more complicated
than, the Orders made under section 32 of the 1956 Act,[55] and it is important, at the outset, to bear in mind two matters. The first is that Article 6 of
the Order provides that nothing in the Order is to be taken as derogating
from the effect of paragraph 35, Schedule 1 to the 1988 Act, and paragraph 35 provides that every work in which copyright subsisted under the
1956 Act immediately before August 1, 1989 is to be deemed to satisfy the
requirements of Part I of the 1988 Act as to qualification for copyright
protection. Part I includes sections 153–156 dealing with qualification for

---

[48] As to "unknown authorship," see *ibid.* s.9(4) and (5). "Folklore" is not referred to in *ibid.*
s.169, only in the side note thereto.
[49] *Ante* Chap. 3.
[50] C.D.P.A. 1988, s.169(5).
[51] *Ibid.* s.169(3).
[52] *Ibid.* s.169(6).
[53] *Ibid.* s.169(4).
[54] The Copyright (Application to Other Countries) (No. 2) Order 1989 (S.I. 1989
No. 1293), as amended by The Copyright (Application to Other Countries) (No. 2)
(Amendment) Order 1989 (S.I. 1989 No. 2415) and The Copyright (Application to Other
Countries) (No. 2) (Amendment) Order 1990 (S.I. 1990 No. 2153); § D–22, *post.* See as to
the unification of Germany n. 73 § 17–68 *ante.*
[55] See § 17–89 *et seq., ante.*

copyright protection. The second is that the Articles of the Order granting protection (Articles 2, 3 and 4) are made subject to Article 7. Article 7 contains a provision, applicable where copyright subsists in a work by virtue of the Order, but did not subsist prior thereto, which provision deems certain acts not to be infringements which are not or were not infringements at the relevant time, unless the owner of the copyright or his exclusive licensee (if any) pays such compensation as, failing agreement, may be determined by arbitration.

(b) Works. The 1988 Act, section 1, protects, as works, literary, dramatic, musical and artistic works, sound recordings, films, broadcasts, cable programmes and the typographical arrangement of published editions, film sound-tracks being protected as sound recordings, not as part of a film as under the 1956 Act. The Order gives protection to all such works, other than cable programmes, except in the case of Singapore.

(c) Literary, dramatic, musical and artistic works, films and the typographical arrangements of published editions. The Order, Article 2(1), provides that sections 153, 154 and 155 of the 1988 Act are to apply in relation to:

(i) persons who are citizens or subjects of a country specified in Schedule 1 to the Order or are domiciled or resident there as they apply to persons who are British citizens or are domiciled or resident in the United Kingdom;

(ii) bodies incorporated under the law of such a country as they apply in relation to bodies incorporated under the law of a part of the United Kingdom; and

(iii) works first published in such a country as they apply in relation to works first published in the United Kingdom.

"First published" includes simultaneous publication under section 155(3) of the 1988 Act. This prima facie entitlement to copyright is then withdrawn, by Article 2(2), in respect of certain works because of circumstances relating to their first publication. Where copyright does subsist in a work by virtue of Article 2(1), then Article 2(3) provides that the whole of Part I of the 1988 Act including Schedule 1 thereto apply in relation to the work, save in the case of designs of typefaces, as to which there are limitations. Schedule 1 to the Order includes Singapore and Taiwan, but not Indonesia. There are special modifications to Article 2 in Schedule 4 to the Order in respect of Singapore and Taiwan.

(d) Sound recordings. By Article 3 of the Order, foreign sound recordings are to be protected in the same way as foreign films are protected under Article 2 thereof, subject to certain modifications. These have the effect of excluding from infringement of the copyright in a sound recording, playing in public, broadcasting, inclusion in a cable programme, secondary infringement under section 26 of the 1988 Act and the summary offences under section 107(3) of that Act, unless either at least one of the countries relevant to the work for the purposes of Article 2(1) is specified in Schedule 2 to the Order, or the sound recording in question is a film sound-track accompanying a film. No doubt the latter is occasioned by reason of the fact that film sound-tracks are now protected under the 1988 Act as sound recordings. A further modification is that Article 2(1), as modified by Schedule 4 to the Order, is to apply as if Indonesia was specified in Schedule 1 to the Order. Indonesia and Taiwan are included in Schedule 2 to the Order, but not Singapore.

(e) Broadcasts. Article 4(1) of the Order provides that, in relation to broadcasts, sections 153, 154 and 156 of the 1988 Act apply in relation to:

  (i) persons who are citizens or subjects of a country specified in Schedule 3 to the Order or are domiciled or resident there as they apply to persons who are British citizens or are domiciled or resident in the United Kingdom;

  (ii) bodies incorporated under the law of such a country as they apply in relation to bodies incorporated under the law of a part of the United Kingdom; and

  (iii) broadcasts made from such a country as they apply to broadcasts made from the United Kingdom.

If the words "TV only" appear by the country in Schedule 3 to the Order, only TV broadcasts are protected: Article 4(2). Further, if a broadcast was made before the "relevant date," as defined by Article 4(5), copyright will not subsist therein: Article 4(3). Where copyright does subsist in a broadcast by virtue of Article 4(1), then Article 4(4) and (5) provide that the whole of Part I of the 1988 Act including Schedule 1 thereto apply in relation to the broadcast, subject to provisions dealing with the duration of copyright in repeats under section 14(2) of the 1988 Act. Singapore is included in Schedule 3 to the Order, and Article 4 applies to Singaporian broadcasts with the modifications in Schedule 4 to the Order.

(f) Cable programmes. Singaporian cable programmes are protected under Article 4 of the Order in the same way as broadcasts by reason of Article 4(6), subject to modifications in Schedule 4 to the Order.

(g) Revocation of previous Orders. The Order, by Article 8 and Schedule 5, revoked the existing Orders under section 32 of the 1956 Act insofar as they formed part of the law of the United Kingdom, and also an abortive Order under section 159 of the 1988 Act.

B. *United States*

Position under old law. There was no treaty between Great Britain and   **17–113** the United States on the subject of copyright, and it was not until 1891, after the passage of the Act commonly called the "Chace Act," that British authors could obtain any effective protection for their works in that country. The Chace Act was repealed by the Copyright Act 1909, under which British authors could obtain a certain measure of protection for their works, by virtue of a proclamation by the President of the United

States to the effect that the British law grants to citizens of the United States the benefit of copyright on substantially the same basis as its own citizens.[56] American citizens were in fact able to obtain copyright in their works by first publishing them in England, or simultaneously[57] in England or a Convention country and America; and they could, no doubt, sue in England in respect of any publication in breach of trust or confidence.[58] Further, by an Order in Council dated February 3, 1915,[59] made under section 29 of the 1911 Act, the protection of that Act was extended to works of classes (*b*) and (*c*) of that section, that is, unpublished works.[60] But works first published in America had no protection in this country.

17–114 **Wartime legislation.** By an Order in Council dated February 9, 1920,[61] the 1911 Act was applied to works first published in the United States between August 1, 1914 and the termination of the war, which had not been republished in the British Empire (except the self-governing dominions[62]) prior to February 2, 1920, provided the work was published in such area not later than 6 months after the termination of the war. It would appear that, if an authorised publication was made in the area in question after the 14 days allowed by the 1911 Act, but before February 2, 1920, advantage could not be taken of this Order. By an Order in Council[63] dated August 6, 1942, as amended by an Order in Council[63] dated October 9, 1950, the 1911 Act was applied to works first published in the United States between September 3, 1939, and December 29, 1950, which had not been published in the same area[64] within 14 days of the publication in the United States. In order to take advantage of this Order publication must have been made not later than December 28, 1950.[65] The 1942 Order came into operation on the date of its publication in the *London Gazette*, March 10, 1944. While persons taking action before the commencement of the 1942 Order, on the assumption that no copyright existed, are given certain protection for accrued rights and interests, it remained obscure whether, if an authorised publication was in fact made, the owner thereof had a title by relation back.

17–115 **Present position of United States works.** Copyright under the 1956 Act was originally conferred in respect of works of United States origin by reason of that country's adherence to the Universal Copyright Convention, but the provisions of the Orders conferring this right were not retro-

---

[56] See *post*, § 18–23.
[57] As to the meaning of this expression, see *ante*, Chap. 3. The time for publication was extended during the war by an Order of February 9, 1920, § D–2, *post*.
[58] *Post*, Chap. 21.
[59] S.R. & O. 1915 No. 130. See *Copinger* (8th ed.), p. 468.
[60] *OSCAR Trade Mark* [1979] R.P.C. 173, on appeal to the Court from the Registrar [1980] F.S.R. 429.
[61] S.R. & 0. 1920 No. 257, *post*, § D–2.
[62] In *Warner Brothers Inc.* v. *The Roadrunner Ltd.* [1988] F.S.R. 292, it was held that, under the 1942 Order, this area did include the self-governing dominions: but see Copyright Act 1911, ss.25 and 29, and § 17–117, *post*.
[63] S.R. & 0. 1942 No. 1579; S.I. 1950 No. 1641, *post*, § D–4. The four Orders were repealed by the 1957 Order, but see *ante*, § 17–94 and *post*, § 17–115.
[64] See n. 62, *ante*.
[65] See *Plantation Wood (Lancing) Ltd.'s Applications for a Trade Mark* [1958] R.P.C. 400.

spective in relation to published works except in so far as such works had already acquired copyright under these wartime Orders. However, this position changed after the United States acceded to the Paris Act of the Berne Convention with effect from March 1, 1989. This was because the most recent Order concerned with conferring copyright under the 1956 Act on works of United States origin was amended, as from March 8, 1989, in such a way as to remove United States works from the qualification on protection in such Order of works first published in America before September 27, 1957,[66] other than in accordance with the wartime Orders. As this amendment would appear to grant copyright to works not previously entitled thereto, the amending Order contained a general provision preserving existing rights of persons who, before the commencement of such Order, had incurred expenditure or liability in connection with the reproduction or performance of any work or other subject-matter. Further, this amendment would appear to make reliance on the wartime Orders of less importance. Of course many existing works would have obtained United Kingdom protection, under the 1956 Act, by having been simultaneously published in the United Kingdom or a Berne Convention country, without the necessity of reliance upon such Orders in Council. An Order in Council has now been made under section 159 of the 1988 Act applying the copyright provisions of the 1988 Act to works originating in various foreign countries including the United States.[67]

C. *Works of enemy origin*

1914–1918 War legislation. Prior to the commencement of the   **17–116** 1914–1918 War, Germany, as a member of the Berne Convention, and Austria-Hungary by a special copyright treaty,[68] had been given, by Orders in Council, rights in this country in respect of works published in those countries, or whose authors were subjects of or residents in those countries. Where works were made or published before the outbreak of the war, the copyright in this country, if the property of an enemy, became liable, under the Trading with the Enemy Acts 1914 to 1918, to be vested in the Public Trustee as the Custodian of Enemy Property.[69] With regard to works made or published in an enemy country after the outbreak of the war, it was doubted whether any copyright in this country was acquired, though the Orders in Council creating such copyright do not appear to have been revoked. To remove these doubts it was provided, by the Trading with the Enemy (Copyright) Act 1916,[70] that the copyright created by the aforesaid Orders in Council in enemy works should subsist and should be vested in the Custodian of Enemy Property. A large number of enemy copyrights were vested in the Custodian in the course of the war, and

---

[66] The Copyright (International Conventions) Order 1979 (S.I. 1979 No. 1715), as amended by The Copyright (International Conventions) (Amendment) Order 1989 (S.I. 1989 No. 157), § D–5, *post*; and see §§ 17–94 and 17–95, *ante*.

[67] *Ante*, § 17–112.

[68] This treaty, and the Order in Council made in conformity with it, will be found set out in full in *Copinger* (5th ed.).

[69] 4 & 5 Geo. 5, c. 87, s.4(1); 8 & 9 Geo. 5, c. 31, s.8.

[70] 6 & 7 Geo. 5, c. 32: and see § 17–82 *et seq.*, *ante*.

licences were granted in respect of the publication of such works in this country. The Treaties of Peace provided for the revesting of such copyrights, but subject to severe disabilities. The terms upon which the revesting took place are set out, as regards Germany and Austria, in an Order in Council of November 9, 1920,[71] made under the powers conferred by the Trading with the Enemy Act 1914, and the Treaty of Peace Orders 1919 and 1920, and, as regards Hungary, in an Order in similar terms dated August 16, 1921. These Orders reserved power to the Board of Trade to grant licences, but the provisions of these Orders were revoked in 1930,[72] so that, subject to any licences which may have been granted, it appears that the owner of the work is now again beneficially entitled to it. In order, however, to follow the title to such works, it may still be necessary to consider the effect of this legislation upon German, Austrian and Hungarian works made or published before the termination of the war, that is, in the case of Germany, before January 10, 1920,[73] in the case of Austria, July 16, 1920,[74] and, in the case of Hungary, August 31, 1921,[75] since such works, if vested in the Custodian at any time, became revested, subject to the disabilities and restrictions created by the Peace Treaties and set out in the Orders in Council above referred to.

17–117   **1939–1945 War legislation.** By section 5 of the Patents, Designs, Copyright and Trade Marks (Emergency) Act 1939,[76] provision is made for the preservation of enemy copyrights and the continuing in force of Orders in Council made under the Copyright Act in relation to enemy countries. The result is that the war did not affect the creation or continuance of British copyrights in works originating in enemy countries. The 1939 Act[77] also continued in force licences granted by enemies to persons resident in the United Kingdom, subject to control. The 1939 Act[78] also gave power to the comptroller to grant licences in respect of enemy copyrights, and to vary existing licences.[79] In consequence of these provisions few copyrights were vested in the Custodian under the ordinary trading with the enemy legislation, matters being dealt with by leaving the copyrights vested in enemies and granting licences as required. Certain German copyrights might however have been affected by virtue of the Enemy Property Act 1953,[80] in consequence of the exercise by, or on behalf of, the Crown of the rights thereby conferred.

---

[71] S.R. & O. 1920 (No. 2119).

[72] Order in Council May 17, 1930 (S.R. & O. 1930 (No. 341)).

[73] By Order in Council of February 9, 1920, made under the Termination of the Present War (Definition) Act 1918 (8 & 9 Geo. 5, c. 59).

[74] By Order in Council July 22, 1920, made under that Act.

[75] By Order in Council August 10, 1921, made under that Act.

[76] (2 & 3 Geo. 6, c. 107). The 1939 Act was amended by the C.D.P.A. 1988 (s. 303(1) and (2) and Scheds. 7 and 8) to take account of design right: and see Copyright Act 1956, Sched. 7, para. 44(*b*), C.D.P.A. 1988, Sched. 1, para. 4(2). See also § 17–82 *et seq.*, *ante*.

[77] *Ibid.* s.1.

[78] *Ibid.* ss.1 and 2.

[79] The nature and effect of these powers was discussed in *Novello & Co. Ltd.* v. *Eulenburg (E.) Ltd.* [1950] 1 All E.R. 44 and *Novello & Co. Ltd.* v. *Hinrichsen Edition Ltd.* [1951] Ch. 595, 1026.

[80] (1 & 2 Eliz. 2, c. 52), most of which was repealed by the Statute Law (Repeals) Act 1976 (c. 16).

3. Protection of Works Originating in the British Commonwealth: Extension of Act

A. *Position before the 1911 Act*

Colonial Conference 1910. In the year 1910, during the presence of rep-   **17–118**
resentatives of the British colonies and dependencies in England, a conference of those representatives was held upon the subject-matter of
copyright in the British dominions. Mr. Sydney Buxton, the then President of the Board of Trade, urged upon the representatives the extreme
desirability of obtaining a uniform code of copyright laws which should
apply throughout the King's dominions. At this conference certain resolu-
tions were passed, generally recognising this desirability but insisting, at
the same time, that, at any rate, self-governing colonies ought not to be
bound by any Imperial Copyright Act, or be made party to any convention or treaty entered into by the home government, without the assent of
those colonies, and that all colonies ought to have the right to make local
modifications in the law.[81] Accordingly, the 1911 Act was extended in
general terms throughout H.M. dominions, but the self-governing dominions were given rights to decide whether or not it should operate within
their territories. In fact, as hereinafter appears, they all adopted the 1911
Act and, in consequence, the 1911 Act operated throughout the British
Commonwealth. The 1956 Act, however, was framed so that it could only
extend to the United Kingdom, the Isle of Man, the Channel Islands, colonies and protected territories. The 1988 Act can only extend to the
United Kingdom (including United Kingdom territorial waters and
British ships, aircraft and hovercraft), the Channel Islands, the Isle of
Man and colonies.

Law prior to 1911 Act. Having regard to questions of title affecting older   **17–119**
works, it is still necessary to understand the law as it existed prior to the
1911 Act. The Literary Copyright Act 1842 expressly extended copyright
to every part of the British dominions,[82] but none of the Acts relating to
artistic or dramatic copyright contained any similar provision. The Fine
Arts Copyright Act 1862 did refer to the British dominions, giving copyright in all works made in the British dominions or elsewhere,[83] but it was
held that there was nothing in that Act to extend the copyright throughout
the British dominions, the provisions of sections 8 and 10 providing for the
recovery of the penalties in England, Scotland and Ireland, and forbidding the importation into the United Kingdom of copies made in any part
of the British dominions indicating a contrary intention.[84]

Whilst, therefore, a British author publishing a literary work in the
United Kingdom obtained, under the Literary Copyright Act 1842, an
imperial copyright, extending throughout the British dominions, and was
thus enabled to prevent piracies in any colony, a British artist, first pub-

---

[81] Report of Colonial Conference 1910 (Cd. 5272).
[82] (5 & 6 Vict. c.45) s.29.
[83] (25 & 26 Vict. c.68) s.1.
[84] *Graves (Henry) & Co. Ltd. v. Gorrie* [1903] A.C. 496.

lishing in the United Kingdom, obtained no imperial copyright, but, if he desired to prevent infringements in a colony, needed to acquire local copyright according to the laws of the particular colony.

17–120 **Rights of colonial authors in United Kingdom.** Conversely, it was held that the Literary Copyright Act 1842 did not confer copyright in the United Kingdom on works first published in the colonies.[85] This grievance was, however, removed by the International Copyright Act 1886, which, by section 8, provided that the Copyright Acts should, subject to the provisions of the Act of 1886, apply to a literary or artistic work first produced in a *British possession* in like manner as they applied to a work first produced in the United Kingdom: provided (a) that the enactments respecting the registry of the copyright in such work should not apply if the law of such possession provided for the registration of such copyright; and (b) that where such work was a book, the delivery to any persons or body of persons of a copy of any such work should not be required. If, therefore, in the particular colony there was no provision for registration, then the registration needed to be effected in this country.

The result, therefore, was that any work produced in the colonies became entitled to the same copyright as it would have obtained if it had been first produced in the United Kingdom, but that, although literary works published in the United Kingdom obtained copyright throughout the dominions, this was not the case with regard to artistic works.

17–121 **Foreign reprints.** By section 17 of the Literary Copyright Act 1842 all persons, other than the proprietor of the copyright or persons authorised by him, were forbidden to import into any part of the British dominions, for sale or hire, any printed book first composed or written or printed and published within the United Kingdom, wherein there should be copyright, and reprinted in any country or place out of the British dominions, under penalty of £10, and double the value of the books.[86] Complaints arose, especially from Canada, with regard to this prohibition. It was contended that, in the sparsely populated colonies, where the circulating library system did not prevail, the price of English books was practically prohibitive, whilst English publishers feared to issue special cheap colonial editions, because they would not be able to prevent their re-importation into Great Britain. With a view to remedying these grievances, in 1847 there was passed an Act, commonly known as the Foreign Reprints Act,[87] enabling the Crown, by Order in Council, to suspend the prohibition against importation into the colonies of English copyright works, subject to their making suitable provisions for the protection of British authors. Under this Act numerous Orders in Council were issued by virtue of which cheap foreign reprints of copyright works were permitted to be imported into various colonies.

---

[85] *Routledge* v. *Low* (1868) L.R. 3 H.L. 100.
[86] And see the Customs Consolidation Act 1876 (39 & 40 Vict. c. 36), ss.151 and 152; and *Black* v. *Imperial Book Co. Ltd.* (1903) 5 Ontario L.R. 184; (1905) 21 T.L.R. 540.
[87] Its official title is the Colonial Copyright Act 1847 (10 & 11 Vict. c. 95).

B. *Position under the 1911 Act*

Provisions of the 1911 Act. The provisions of the 1911 Act relating to   **17–122**
the British possessions were contained in sections 25 to 28. The countries
subject to the Crown were divided into three classes: (a) dominions of the
Crown, other than self-governing colonies; (b) self-governing colonies,
meaning thereby the Dominion of Canada, the Commonwealth of Australia, the Dominion of New Zealand, the Union of South Africa, and Newfoundland[88]; and (c) protectorates and Cyprus.

Non self-governing colonies and protectorates. The provisions of the   **17–123**
1911 Act relating to the colonies, other than the self-governing dominions,
and to the protectorates and Cyprus, were comparatively simple. Section
25(1) enacted that that Act, "except such of the provisions thereof as are
expressly restricted to the United Kingdom,[89] shall extend throughout
His Majesty's dominions," subject to a saving in respect of a self-governing dominion. Section 28 enabled His Majesty by Order in Council to
extend the 1911 Act to any territories under his protection, and to Cyprus,
"and, on the making of any such Order, this Act shall, subject to the provisions of the Order, have effect as if the territories to which it applies or
Cyprus were part of His Majesty's dominions to which this Act extends."
The legislature of any British possession to which the 1911 Act extended
had, however, power to modify, or add to, any of the provisions of that Act
in its application to the possession.[90]
  Thus, for the purposes of copyright, the colonies, other than the self-
governing colonies, were treated as parts of the United Kingdom, and
British copyright extended to all such colonies, and, vice versa, colonial
copyright extended to the United Kingdom, except those modifications
and additions to the British Act which the legislature of any colony should
make, those only applying locally. Similarly, the following protectorates,
to which by an Order in Council[91] dated June 24, 1912, the British Act
was extended, were equally considered for copyright purposes to be part
of the United Kingdom, namely, Cyprus, the Bechuanaland Protectorate,
East Africa Protectorate, Gambia Protectorate, Gilbert and Ellice Islands
Protectorate, Northern Nigeria Protectorate, Northern Territories of the
Gold Coast, Nyasaland Protectorate, Northern Rhodesia, Southern Rhodesia, Sierra Leone Protectorate, Somaliland Protectorate, Southern
Nigeria Protectorate, Solomon Islands Protectorate, Swaziland and
Uganda Protectorate. Further, the British Act was extended to Palestine
by an Order in Council of March 21, 1924, to Tanganyika by an Order
in Council of April 16, 1924, to the Federated Malay States by Order in
Council[92] of February 12, 1931, and to British Cameroons by Order
in Council of March 16, 1933. Most of such colonies and protectorates
passed local laws regarding the seizure by the customs of infringing copies

---

[88] Copyright Act 1911, s.35(1).
[89] *I.e.*, Copyright Act 1911, ss.11 and 12, relating to summary remedies.
[90] Copyright Act 1911, s.27: and see *Rediffusion (Hong Kong) Ltd.* v. *Att.-Gen. of Hong Kong*
  [1970] A.C. 1136, and *Butterworth and Co. (Publishers) Ltd.* v. *Ng Sui Nam* [1987] R.P.C. 485.
[91] See § D–1, *post*.
[92] See § D–3, *post*.

and introducing penal provisions similar to those contained in section 11 of the 1911 Act, such laws being authorised by section 27 of that Act.

The 1911 Act came into force in the above-mentioned possessions (including the Channel Islands other than Jersey) on July 1, 1912, except that it came into force in the Isle of Man on July 5, 1912, in India on October 30, 1912, in Papua on February 1, 1913, and in Jersey on March 8, 1913. The 1911 Act came into force in the above-mentioned protectorates at the dates referred to in the respective Orders.

17–124   **Self-governing dominions.** The self-governing dominions all became dominions to which the 1911 Act extended.[93] Section 25(1) of the 1911 Act provided that that Act should not extend to the self-governing dominions unless declared by the legislature of any dominion so to apply, either without modifications, or with modifications relating exclusively to procedure and remedies, or necessary for its application to the dominion. Newfoundland adopted the 1911 Act without modifications. The Commonwealth of Australia and the Union of South Africa made certain modifications.

17–125   Canada and New Zealand did not adopt this procedure, but passed independent Acts on similar lines to the 1911 Act. By section 25(2) of the 1911 Act it was provided that, if the Secretary of State certified, by notice published in the *London Gazette*, that any self-governing dominion had passed legislation under which works, the authors whereof were, at the date of the making of the works, British subjects resident elsewhere than in the dominion or (not being British subjects) were resident in the parts of His Majesty's dominions to which that Act extended, enjoyed within the dominion rights substantially identical with those conferred by that Act, then, whilst such legislation continued in force, the dominion should, for the purposes of the rights conferred by that Act, be treated as if it were a dominion to which that Act extended.

The Canadian Act of 1921 complied with the provisions of this section in its terms, and the New Zealand Act of 1913 also complied with them when coupled with an Order of the Executive Council made thereunder of March 27, 1914. The Secretary of State in fact certified, in respect of both dominions, under section 25(2), in 1923 as to Canada and in 1914 as to New Zealand.[94]

17–126   **The Republic of Ireland.** By an Order in Council dated October 27, 1930, made in pursuance of the Irish Free State (Consequential Provisions) Act 1922,[95] the Irish Free State was deemed to be a self-governing dominion for the purposes of the 1911 Act, and, by a further Order in Council dated October 27, 1930, made in pursuance of section 26(3) of the 1911 Act, the 1911 Act was declared to apply to works first published in the Irish Free State and to works of which the authors were, at the time of making the work, resident in the Irish Free State, provided that there was to be no right to prevent the translation into English of literary or dra-

---

[93] As regards the Republic of Ireland, see § 17–126, *post.*
[94] See *Mansell* v. *Star Printing, etc., Ltd.* [1937] A.C. 872 and *Walt Disney Productions* v. *(H.) John Edwards Publishing Co. Pty. Ltd.* (1954) 71 W.N.(N.S.W.) 150.
[95] (13 Geo. 5, c. 2).

matic works in Irish if an authorised translation was not made within 10 years from publication. This Order in Council was preserved by the provisions of paragraph 40(4) of Schedule 7 to the 1956 Act,[96] but was repealed by the Copyright (International Conventions) Order 1957[97] which applied the 1956 Act to the Republic of Ireland as a Berne Convention country.

The 1911 Act was repealed in the Irish Free State by an Irish Free State Act[98] passed in 1927 but, since this was thought to create doubts as to subsisting copyrights,[99] a further Act was passed in 1929[1] declaring that, so far as was necessary for the subsistence in the Irish Free State of copyrights, the 1911 Act and every Order made thereunder should be deemed to continue to have full force and effect in the Irish Free State. A new Copyright Act was passed on April 8, 1963, to replace the existing law[2]; it has considerable resemblances to the 1956 Act.

International arrangements with dominions. With regard to any international arrangements which were made by the United Kingdom, it was provided that any Order in Council made under section 29 of the 1911 Act[3] was to apply to all His Majesty's dominions, except the self-governing dominions and any other possession specified in the Order.[4] Accordingly, the various Orders in Council which were made under that section applied the Order to all the dominions, colonies and possessions of the Crown, with the exception of the self-governing dominions, and also to Cyprus and the protectorates to which the Copyright Act was by Order in Council extended.[5] With regard to the self-governing dominions the 1911 Act authorised the Governor in Council of any such dominion to which that Act extended to make, as respects that dominion, the like Orders as the Crown in Council was, under sections 29 and 30 of that Act, authorised to make with regard to dominions other than self-governing dominions, and the provisions of those sections were, with the necessary modifications, to apply accordingly.[6] Orders in Council were, under this power, or a similar power in their own Acts, made by Australia, New Zealand, Newfoundland and the Union of South Africa, while the same effect was produced by the terms of the Canadian Act itself. **17–127**

Repeal by dominions of pre-1911 legislation. It is to be noted that section 26(1) of the 1911 Act gave to the legislature of any self-governing dominion power to repeal any enactment relating to copyright, including **17–128**

---

[96] Repealed by Statute Law (Repeals) Act 1986 (c. 12), but see s.2 thereof.
[97] § 2105 *Copinger* (12th ed.): see Copyright (International Conventions) Order 1979, as amended, *post*, § D–5.
[98] Industrial and Commercial Property (Protection) Act 1927, No. 16 of 1927. See *Copinger* (9th ed.), App. E.
[99] *Performing Right Society Ltd.* v. *Bray U.D.C.* [1930] A.C. 377.
[1] Copyright (Preservation) Act 1929, No. 25 of 1929. See *Copinger* (9th ed.), App. E.
[2] Copyright Act (No. 10 of 1963).
[3] See *ante* § 17–82.
[4] Copyright Act 1911, s.30(1) and (3).
[5] See § 17–123, *ante* and § D–1, *post*.
[6] Copyright Act 1911, s.30(2).

the 1911 Act. All the dominions repealed the legislation prior to the 1911 Act which applied to them.[7]

C. *Position Under the 1956 Act*

17–129   **Repeal of the 1911 Act in the United Kingdom.** Paragraph 41 of Schedule 7 to the 1956 Act provided that, in so far as the 1911 Act, or any Order in Council made thereunder, formed part of the law of any country other than the United Kingdom at a time after that Act had been wholly or partly repealed in the law of the United Kingdom, it should, so long as it formed part of the law of that country, be construed and have effect as if that Act had not been so repealed.[8] The repeal of the 1911 Act in the United Kingdom, therefore, did not affect its operation, either in colonial territories, or in the self-governing dominions.

17–130   **Extension of the 1956 Act to other countries.** Power was given, by section 31 of the 1956 Act, to extend that Act and Orders in Council made under that Act, by Order in Council, to the Isle of Man, any of the Channel Islands, any colony,[9] any country outside H.M. dominions in which for the time being Her Majesty had jurisdiction, and any country consisting partly of one or more colonies and partly of one or more such countries as are last mentioned. Such Orders in Council could have extended the 1956 Act subject to exceptions and modifications. By extending provisions of the Act they become the law of the country to which they have been extended. This is to be contrasted with applying provisions of the Act to foreign works whereby they are given equivalent protection in this country to British works, which is dealt with in Part 2 of this Chapter. No Order in Council was made extending the main provisions of the 1956 Act to the Channel Islands[10] and so the 1911 Act remained in force there.[11]

17–131   **Extension Orders Under the 1956 Act.**

(**i**) Orders in Council under the 1956 Act were extended to various countries, either by the Orders in Council themselves,[12] or by other Orders in Council.[13] The 1956 Act and various Orders in Council thereunder were extended, by Orders in Council, to the following countries: the

---

[7] And see § 17–139, *post* as to repeal of the Copyright Act 1911.

[8] See, as to repeal of the 1911 Act as part of the law of any country in the Commonwealth, the Copyright Act 1956 (Transitional Extension) Order 1959 (S.I. 1959 No. 103).

[9] See *Rediffusion (Hong Kong) Ltd.* v. *Att.-Gen. of Hong Kong* [1970] A.C. 1136.

[10] See n. 8, *ante*.

[11] Copyright Act 1911, ss.25(1) and 37(2)(*c*). The date the Act of 1911 came into operation in the Channel Islands was July 1, 1912, except for Jersey when the date was March 8, 1913. S.37(2) was repealed by Statute Law (Repeals) Act 1986 (c. 12).

[12] See, for instance, The Copyright (International Conventions) Order 1979 (S.I. 1979 No. 1715) as amended § D–5 *post*, and The Copyright (Singapore) Order 1987 (S.I. 1987 No. 940) § D–19 *post*; and see Pt. 2 of this Chap.

[13] See, for instance, The Copyright (Singapore) (Amendment) Order 1987 (S.I. 1987 No. 1030), The Copyright (Taiwan) (Extension to Territories) Order 1987 (S.I. 1987 No. 1826), The Copyright (Taiwan Order) (Isle of Man Extension) Order 1987 (S.I. 1987 No. 1833) and The Copyright (Singapore) (Amendment) Order 1988 (S.I. 1988 No. 1297); and see Pt. 2 of this Chap.

Isle of Man as from May 31, 1959,[14] Sarawak as from January 1, 1960,[15] Gibraltar as from June 1, 1960,[16] Fiji as from February 1, 1961,[17] Uganda as from January 1, 1962,[18] Zanzibar as from January 1, 1962,[19] Bermuda as from August 6, 1962,[20] North Borneo as from August 6, 1962,[21] the Bahamas as from October 11, 1962,[22] the Virgin Islands as from October 11, 1962,[23] the Falkland Islands as from June 10, 1963,[24] St. Helena and dependencies as from June 10, 1963,[25] Seychelles as from June 10, 1963,[26] Kenya as from July 4, 1963,[27] Mauritius as from May 21, 1964,[28] Montserrat as from November 5, 1965,[29] St. Lucia as from November 5, 1965,[30] Bechuanaland as from December 4, 1965,[31] Cayman Islands as from December 4, 1965,[32] Grenada as from January 1, 1966,[33] British Guiana as from February 5, 1966,[34] British Honduras as from June 16, 1966,[35] Saint Vincent as from July 5, 1967,[36] Hong Kong as from December 12, 1972[37] and the British Indian Ocean Territory as from May 14, 1984.[38] Each Order contains exceptions and modifications which vary according to local circumstances.

(**ii**) The Copyright (Computer Software) Amendment Act 1985[39] was to be construed as one with the 1956 Act[40] so that the provisions thereof

---

[14] The Copyright (Isle of Man) Order 1959 (S.I. 1959 No. 861), The Copyright (Isle of Man) Order 1970 (S.I. 1970 No. 1437) and the Copyright (Isle of Man) Order 1971 (S.I. 1971 No. 1848): these three Orders were revoked and repealed by The Copyright (Isle of Man) Order 1986 (S.I. 1986 No. 1299). See also The Copyright Act 1956 (Transitional Extension) Order 1959 (S.I. 1959 No. 103).

[15] The Copyright (Sarawak) Order 1959 (S.I. 1959 No. 2215).

[16] The Copyright (Gibraltar) Order 1960 (S.I. 1960 No. 847), as amended by The Copyright (Gibraltar) (Amendment) Order 1985 (S.I. 1985 No. 1986).

[17] The Copyright (Fiji) Order 1961 (S.I. 1961 No. 60).

[18] The Copyright (Uganda) Order 1961 (S.I. 1961 No. 2462).

[19] The Copyright (Zanzibar) Order 1961 (S.I. 1961 No. 2463), as amended by The Copyright (Zanzibar) (Amendment) Order 1962 (S.I. 1962 No. 629).

[20] The Copyright (Bermuda) Order 1962 (S.I. 1962 No. 1642), as amended by The Copyright (Bermuda) (Amendment) Order 1985 (S.I. 1985 No. 1985).

[21] The Copyright (North Borneo) Order 1962 (S.I. 1962 No. 1643).

[22] The Copyright (Bahamas) Order 1962, (S.I. 1962 No. 2184).

[23] The Copyright (Virgin Islands) Order 1962 (S.I. 1962 No. 2185), as amended by The Copyright (Virgin Islands) (Amendment) Order 1985 (S.I. 1985 No. 1988).

[24] The Copyright (Falkland Islands) Order 1963 (S.I. 1963 No. 1037).

[25] The Copyright (St. Helena) Order 1963 (S.I. 1963 No. 1038).

[26] The Copyright (Seychelles) Order 1963 (S.I. 1963 No. 1039).

[27] The Copyright (Kenya) Order 1963 (S.I. 1963 No. 1147).

[28] The Copyright (Mauritius) Order 1964 (S.I. 1964 No. 689).

[29] The Copyright (Montserrat) Order 1965 (S.I. 1965 No. 1858), as amended by The Copyright (Montserrat) (Amendment) Order 1985 (S.I. 1985 No. 1987).

[30] The Copyright (St. Lucia) Order 1965 (S.I. 1965 No. 1859).

[31] The Copyright (Bechuanaland) Order 1965 (S.I. 1965 No. 2009).

[32] The Copyright (Cayman Islands) Order 1965 (S.I. 1965 No. 2010).

[33] The Copyright (Grenada) Order 1965 (S.I. 1965 No. 2158).

[34] The Copyright (British Guiana) Order 1966 (S.I. 1966 No. 79).

[35] The Copyright (British Honduras) Order 1966 (S.I. 1966 No. 685).

[36] The Copyright (St. Vincent) Order 1967 (S.I. 1967 No. 974).

[37] The Copyright (Hong Kong) Order 1972 (S.I. 1972 No. 1724), as amended by The Copyright (Hong Kong) (Amendment) Order 1979 (S.I. 1979 No. 910) and The Copyright (Hong Kong) (Amendment) Order 1990 (S.I. 1990 No. 588).

[38] The Copyright (British Indian Ocean Territory) Order 1984 (S.I. 1984 No. 541).

[39] c. 41.

[40] *Ibid.* s.4(2).

could be extended to other countries like the provisions of the 1956 Act. The provisions of the 1985 Act were accordingly extended to the Isle of Man[41] and to a number of other countries.[42]

17–132 **Effect where the 1956 Act was so extended.** Copyright was defined, in section 1(1) of the 1956 Act, as the exclusive right to do and authorise others to do certain acts in the United Kingdom or in any other country to which the provisions of that Act extended, and, to the extent that the 1956 Act and Orders in Council thereunder had been so extended, common conditions for obtaining copyright protection existed throughout the area to which that Act and Orders in Council were so extended. Thus, the definition of "qualified person," in section 1(5) of the 1956 Act, included a person domiciled or resident in the United Kingdom or in another country to which any provision of that Act extended, and a body incorporated under the laws of any such country. Further, "first publication," in sections 2(2) and 3(3) of that Act, included first publication in the United Kingdom or in another country to which the section extended. Similar provisions occurred in sections 12(2), 13(2) and 15(1) of the 1956 Act. Also as to infringement, in sections 1(2), 5 and 16. Further, by section 36(2)(*b*) of the 1956 Act, an assignment of copyright could be limited so as to apply to any one or more, but not all, of the countries in relation to which the owner of the copyright had by virtue of that Act the exclusive right to do certain acts.

The advantages of having such common conditions for obtaining and enforcing copyright throughout that area were, however, diminished by reason of some countries in that area becoming independent and in some cases enacting their own copyright legislation.[43] A further consequence of independence was that many such countries became countries to which the provisions of the 1956 Act were applied,[44] rather than extended.

17–133 **Power of such other countries to modify the 1956 Act.** While the legislature of any country to which any provisions of the 1956 Act had been extended, as aforesaid, could have modified or added to those provisions in their operation as part of the law of that country, no such modifications or additions, except in so far as they related to procedure and remedies, were to be made so as to apply to any work or other subject-matter unless the qualification of authorship or publication arose with reference to that other country.[45] In fact numerous modifications of a minor character were embodied in the Orders in Council above referred to.

---

[41] The Copyright (Isle of Man) Order 1986 (S.I. 1986 No. 1299).
[42] The Copyright (Computer Software) (Extension to Territories) Order 1987 (S.I. 1987 No. 2200).
[43] See § 17–139 *post* and Pt. 2 of Chap. 18, *post.*
[44] See The Copyright (International Conventions) Order 1979 (S.I. 1979 No. 1715), as amended, § D–5 *post*, and Pt. 2 of this Chap.
[45] Copyright Act 1956, s.31(3): and see *Rediffusion (Hong Kong) Ltd.* v. *Att.-Gen of Hong Kong* [1970] A.C. 1136.

Proceedings in the United Kingdom. It was further provided[46] that, for the purposes of any proceedings under the 1956 Act in the United Kingdom, where the proceedings related to an act done in a country to which any provisions of that Act extended subject to exceptions, modifications or additions, the procedure and remedies were to be in accordance with that Act in its operation as part of the law of the United Kingdom; but, if the act did not constitute an infringement of copyright in its operation as part of the law of the country where the act was done, it was not to be treated as constituting an infringement of copyright under that Act in its operation as part of the law of the United Kingdom. Presumably the usual conditions would have applied in respect of service out of the jurisdiction but, subject to this, it appears that a defendant could have been sued in the United Kingdom in respect of an infringement in a colony, provided that the act of infringement would have been an infringement by the law of the colony if the proceedings had been brought there, but the procedure and remedies would have been those of the United Kingdom. **17–134**

Position as to colonial territories and self-governing dominions distinguished. So far as the colonial territories are concerned, the making of the necessary Orders in Council created a similar situation to that existing under the 1911 Act. But, so far as concerns the self-governing dominions, these were outside the operation of the 1956 Act, and works originating in their territory were only protected in the United Kingdom in the same manner as works originating in foreign countries were protected, that is to say, by Order in Council under section 32 of the 1956 Act, applying the provisions of the 1956 Act to works originating in such countries.[47] **17–135**

Position in period before Orders in Council made. To provide for the interim period after the commencement of the 1956 Act, and before Orders were made extending or applying that Act to colonial and self-governing territories, provision was made in paragraph 39 of Schedule 7 to that Act. The effect of this paragraph appeared to be that, until any such Order was made, for the purposes of construing any reference in any provision of that Act to countries to which that provision extended, such provision was treated as extending to the territory in question whether it was a self-governing territory or not. The Copyright (International Conventions) Order 1957, which came into operation on September 27, 1957,[48] applied the Act of 1956 in respect of works originating in the self-governing dominions, that position being continued by the Copyright (International Conventions) Order 1964,[49] then by the Copyright (International Conventions) Order 1972[50] and then by the Copyright (International Conventions) Order 1979.[51] Works originating in other Commonwealth territories would have remained protected by virtue of **17–136**

[46] Copyright Act 1986, s.31(4).
[47] See § 17–89, *ante.*
[48] S.I. 1957 No. 1523.
[49] S.I. 1964 No. 690.
[50] S.I. 1972 No. 673.
[51] S.I. 1979 No. 1715, § D–5, *post.*

paragraph 39 until the making of Orders in Council extending the 1956 Act thereto.

17–137 **The Republic of Ireland.** As stated above,[52] the Republic of Ireland was treated as a self-governing dominion to which the 1911 Act did not extend and copyright protection was afforded to works originating in that country by an Order in Council made under section 26(3) of the 1911 Act. After the commencement of the 1956 Act, therefore, paragraph 40(4) of Schedule 7 to that Act[53] applied in relation to the Irish Republic, and it was accordingly treated as a foreign country in respect of which an Order in Council under section 29 of the 1911 Act had been made. But the Republic of Ireland was one of the countries in respect of which protection was given by virtue of the Copyright (International Conventions) Order 1957,[54] then by the Copyright (International Conventions) Order 1964,[55] then by the Copyright (International Conventions) Order 1972[56] and then by the Copyright (International Conventions) Order 1979.[57] The 1956 Act itself, in defining "qualified person," included an individual who was a citizen of the Republic of Ireland, but not a body corporate incorporated under the laws of the Republic, and the Republic of Ireland was not a country to which that Act extended for the purpose of the provisions regarding first publication.

17–138 **International arrangements with dominions.** As the 1956 Act could not have been extended to the self-governing dominions, international protection therein depended upon the 1911 Act, and Orders in Council made thereunder so long as that Act was in force therein. In so far as the self-governing dominions have passed new Copyright Acts of their own, the nature of international protection therein will fall to be determined according to the provisions of those Acts.

17–139 **Repeal of Imperial Acts and enactment of local Copyright Acts.**[58] The following countries have now passed their own Copyright Acts, repealing the 1911 Act, or its equivalent: India in 1957, Ghana in 1961, Bangladesh in 1962, Pakistan in 1962, New Zealand in 1962, Sierra Leone in 1965, Zambia in 1965, Malawi in 1965, South Africa in 1965, Tanzania in 1966, Malta in 1967, Australia in 1968, Nigeria in 1970, Cyprus in 1976, Sri Lanka in 1979, Barbados in 1981, Trinidad and Tobago in 1985 and Singapore in 1987. Uganda, Kenya and Mauritius have passed their own Copyright Acts repealing the 1956 Act in 1964, 1966 and 1986 respectively. Malaysia has passed its own Copyright Act, repealing the 1911 and 1956 Acts, in 1969.

---

[52] § 17–126, *ante.*

[53] Repealed by Statute Law (Repeals) Act 1986 (c. 12), but see s.2 thereof.

[54] See n. 48, *ante.*

[55] See n. 48, *ante.*

[56] See n. 50, *ante.*

[57] See n. 51, *ante.*

[58] See also Pt. 2 of Chap. 18, *post* as to these countries' most recent Acts. See also The Copyright (Status of Former Dependent Territories) Order 1990 (S.I. 1990 No. 1512), § D–44 *post.*

D. *Position under 1988 Act*

Extension of the 1988 Act to other countries. Power is given, by section 157 of the 1988 Act,[59] to extend the copyright provisions of the 1988 Act and Orders in Council made thereunder, by Order in Council to any of the Channel Islands, the Isle of Man or any colony.[60] The extending Orders in Council can extend such provisions and Orders in Council subject to exceptions and modifications.[60]   **17–140**

Power of such other countries to modify the 1988 Act. The legislature of any country to which the copyright provisions of the 1988 Act have been extended may, under section 157 of the 1988 Act, as under section 31 of the 1956 Act,[61] modify or add to such provisions in their operation as part of the law of that country. But such modifications or additions are limited to adapting such provisions to the circumstances of the country concerned as regards procedure and remedies or as regards works qualifying for copyright protection by virtue of a connection with that country.[62]   **17–141**

Effect where the 1988 Act is so extended. As has been seen,[63] where the 1956 Act and Orders in Council thereunder had been extended, common conditions for obtaining copyright protection existed throughout the area to which that Act and Orders in Council were so extended, with the advantages resulting therefrom.   **17–142**

However, the situation does not appear to have been continued in its entirety by the 1988 Act. Thus, by section 157(1) of the 1988 Act, that Act is to extend to England and Wales, Scotland and Northern Ireland,[64] and the countries to which the 1988 Act can be extended are more limited than under the 1956 Act.[65] Further, copyright under the 1988 Act does not, as under the 1956 Act, appear to cover the right to do and restrain the doing of certain acts in countries to which the Act has been extended as well as in the United Kingdom. Thus, by section 2 of the 1988 Act, the copyright owner is given the exclusive right to do the restricted acts specified in Chapter II of that Act, and the various sections in Chapter II, which also cover infringement, appear to be limited to the doing of certain acts in the United Kingdom.[66] Again, section 90(2) of the 1988 Act does not, like section 36(2)(b) of the 1956 Act, contain a provision for partial assignments as to one or more countries. Finally, the 1988 Act contains no provision similar to section 31(4) of the 1956 Act[67] under which proceedings could

---

[59] This power is more limited than that under Copyright Act 1956, s.31, § 17–143, *ante*. See also C.D.P.A. 1988, s.304(3), (4) and (5).
[60] C.D.P.A. 1988, s.157(2) and (3): and see s.304(6).
[61] See § 17–133, *ante*.
[62] C.D.P.A. 1988, s.157(4).
[63] § 17–132, *ante*.
[64] See C.D.P.A. 1988, s.161 and para. 38, Sched. 1 as to the territorial waters of the U.K. and the U.K. sector of the continental shelf. See also *ibid.* s.162 and para. 39, Sched. 1 as to British ships, aircraft and hovercraft.
[65] See n. 59, *ante*: and see §§ 17–130 and 17–140, *ante*.
[66] See C.D.P.A. 1988, ss.16–27, in particular ss.16, 18, 22, 24 and 27, and compare Copyright Act 1956, ss.1(1) and (2), 5 and 16.
[67] See § 17–134, *ante*.

be brought in the United Kingdom in respect of an act done in a country to which the 1988 Act has been extended.

On the other hand, certain of the conditions for qualifying for copyright protection under the 1988 Act are similar to those under the 1956 Act[68] in that, for instance, by section 154(1) of the 1988 Act, individuals domiciled or resident in a country to which the copyright provisions of the 1988 Act have been extended and bodies incorporated under the law of such a country are included. Also included, by section 155(1) of the 1988 Act, are works first published in such a country as are, by section 156(1) of that Act, broadcasts made from and cable programmes sent from a place in such a country.

The result of the foregoing would appear to be that, although the relevant provisions of the 1988 Act can be extended to another country, as could the provisions of the 1956 Act, and although, as under the 1956 Act, a person resident in a country to which the 1988 Act has been extended, for instance, may get copyright under the 1988 Act, nonetheless whereas, under the 1956 Act, an act done in a country to which the 1956 Act had been extended could be an infringement of copyright under the 1956 Act as well as of copyright under the 1956 Act as extended to that country, it will not now be an infringement of copyright under the 1988 Act to do an act in a country to which the 1988 Act has been extended. This will, if at all, only be an infringment of that country's law, that is the 1988 Act as extended to that country.

17–143 **Countries ceasing to be colonies.** Section 158 of the 1988 Act contains certain provisions applicable where the country to which the copyright provisions of that Act have been extended ceases to be a colony of the United Kingdom.[69] If that happens, such a country is, as from the date on which it ceases to be a colony, not to be treated as a country to which such copyright provisions extend for the purposes of section 160(2)(a) thereof[70] and of sections 163 and 165 thereof.[71] Nonetheless it is to continue to be treated as a country to which such copyright provisions extend for the purposes of qualification for copyright protection[72] until an Order in Council is made in respect of that country under section 159 of the 1988 Act[73] or an Order in Council is made declaring that it shall cease to be so treated by reason of the fact that such copyright provisions as part of the law of that country have been repealed or amended.[74] A statutory instrument containing such a declaratory Order in Council is subject to annulment in pursuance of a resolution of either House of Parliament.[75]

---

[68] See, for instance, Copyright Act 1956, ss.1(5), 2(1) and (2), 3(2) and (3), 12(1) and (2), 13(1) and (2) and 15(1).

[69] C.D.P.A. 1988, s.158(1) and (2).

[70] § 17–109, *ante.*

[71] §§ 13–18, 13–33, *ante.*

[72] C.D.P.A. 1988, ss.154–156.

[73] § 17–107, *ante.*

[74] C.D.P.A. 1988, s.158(3). As to countries in which the 1911 Act or the 1956 Act is in force ceasing to be a colony, see *ibid.* Sched. 1, para. 36(5).

[75] *Ibid.* s.158(4).

Self-governing dominions and the Republic of Ireland. Self-govern-   **17–144**
ing dominions do not fall within the extending provisions of the 1988 Act.
The position was the same under the 1956 Act.[76] Protection of works originating in the self-governing dominions will, therefore, depend on an
Order in Council being made under section 159 of the 1988 Act applying
the copyright provisions of that Act to such works.[77]

The 1988 Act, s.154(1), does not, as did the 1956 Act in the definition of
"qualified person,"[78] include citizens of the Republic of Ireland in the
definition of "qualifying person," nor does the 1988 Act, s.157(2), include
the Republic of Ireland as a country to which the 1988 Act can be
extended for the purposes of qualification by place of first publication, for
instance.[79] Therefore, protection of works originating in the Republic of
Ireland will also depend on such an Order in Council being made.

Dependent territories.   **17–145**
(i) General. As has been seen, the 1956 Act was extended to the Isle of
Man and a number of other countries,[80] but not, except to a limited
extent, to the Channel Islands, where the 1911 Act remained in force.[81]
The 1988 Act, para. 36, Sched. 1, contains provisions dealing with what
are defined as dependent territories, that is any of the Channel Islands,
the Isle of Man or any colony.[82]

(ii) Channel Islands. Paragraph 36(1), Schedule 1, to the 1988 Act, pro-   **17–146**
vides that the 1911 Act is to remain in force as part of the law of any
dependent territory in which it was in force immediately before the commencement of the copyright provisions of the 1988 Act, such as the Channel Islands, until such provisions come into force in that territory by
virtue of an Order under section 157 of the 1988 Act (extension),[83] or in
the case of the Channel Islands, the 1911 Act is repealed by Order under
paragraph 36(3). Certain provisions of the 1956 Act were, in fact,
extended to the Channel Islands, (as well as to the Isle of Man and certain
other countries), by Order in Council,[84] and paragraph 36(2), of Schedule
1, to the 1988 Act provides that an Order in Council in force immediately
before such commencement which extends to any dependent territory any
provisions of the 1956 Act shall remain in force as part of the law of that
territory until the copyright provisions of the 1988 Act come into force in
that territory by virtue of an Order under section 157 of the 1988 Act
(extension), and while it remains in force such an Order may be varied
under the provisions of the 1956 Act under which it was made. It would

---

[76] §§ 17–127, 17–135, 17–138, *ante.*
[77] §§ 17–89, 17–107, *ante.*
[78] Copyright Act 1956, s.1(5) and see § 3–5 and § 17–137, *ante.*
[79] C.D.P.A. 1988, ss.155 and 156.
[80] § 17–131, *ante.*
[81] § 17–130, *ante.*
[82] C.D.P.A. 1988, Sched. 1, para. 36(6).
[83] *Ante,* § 17–140: and see *ibid.* s.157(5). Certain non-copyright provisions of the 1988 Act
    have been extended to Guernsey under *ibid.* s.304(5) by The Copyright, Designs and
    Patents Act 1988 (Guernsey) Order 1989 (S.I. 1989 No.1997): § 24–6 *et seq. post,* and
    § B–201, *post.*
[84] The Copyright Act 1956 (Transitional Extension) Order 1959 (S.I. 1959 No. 103).

appear, therefore, that, until an Order is made under the 1988 Act, the position in the Channel Islands remains the same. At the moment no such Orders have been made.

As to the future, presumably the Order in Council extending certain provisions of the 1956 Act to the Channel Islands[84] will go if, and when, an Order is made in respect of the Channel Islands under section 157 of the 1988 Act. So far as the 1911 Act is concerned, this will remain in force in the Channel Islands until an Order is made under section 157 or the Act is repealed by an Order under paragraph 36(3). Paragraph 36(3) provides that, if it appears to Her Majesty that provision with respect to copyright has been made in the law of any of the Channel Islands otherwise than by extending the copyright provisions of the 1988 Act, Her Majesty may by Order in Council repeal the 1911 Act as it has effect as part of the law of that territory. However, if such an Order is made, it will be made, apparently, in a situation where the copyright provisions of the 1988 Act have not been extended to the Channel Islands. If that be so, it is unclear what is to happen to the Order extending certain provisions of the 1956 Act to the Channel Islands,[84] since, although paragraph 36(3) also refers to revoking an Order extending the 1956 Act, this appears, when taken with paragraph 36(2)(*b*), only to relate to the Isle of Man.[85]

Finally, paragraph 36(4) provides that a dependent territory in which the 1911 or 1956 Act remains in force is to be treated, in the law of the countries to which the copyright provisions of the 1988 Act extend, as a country to which such provisions extend. Further, that those countries are to be treated in the law of such a territory as countries to which the 1911 Act or, as the case may be, the 1956 Act extends. The Channel Islands are dependent territories but, again, this is not entirely clear since certain provisions of the 1956 Act have been extended to the Channel Islands.[86]

17–147   **(iii) Isle of Man.** Paragraph 36(2), Schedule 1, to the 1988 Act, provides that an Order in Council in force immediately before the commencement of the copyright provisions of the 1988 Act which extends to any dependent territory, such as the Isle of Man, any of the provisions of the 1956 Act is to remain in force as part of the law of that territory until such provisions come into force in that territory by virtue of an Order under section 157 of the 1988 Act (extension),[87] or in the case of the Isle of Man, the Order is revoked by Order under paragraph 36(3), and while it remains in force such an Order may be varied under the provisions of the 1956 Act under which it was made.

Thus it would appear that the position in the Isle of Man will remain the same until an Order is made under the 1988 Act, either under section 157, or under paragraph 36(3). No such Orders have yet been made.

---

[85] §§ 17–130, 17–131, *ante.*

[86] See n. 84, *ante.*

[87] *Ante,* § 17–130; and see C.D.P.A. 1988 s.157(5). Certain non-copyright provisions of the 1988 Act have been extended to the Isle of Man under *ibid.* s.304(4) and (6) by The Copyright, Designs and Patents Act 1988 (Isle of Man) (No. 2) Order 1989 (S.I. 1989 No.1292); § B–195, *post*, by the C.D.P.A. 1988 (Isle of Man) Order 1990 (S.I. 1990 No. 1505); § B–238 *post* and by C.D.P.A. 1988 (Isle of Man) (No. 2) Order 1990 (S.I. 1990 No. 2293); § B–251 *post.*

Paragraph 36(3) provides that, if it appears to Her Majesty that provision with respect to copyright has been made in the law of the Isle of Man otherwise than by extending the copyright provisions of the 1988 Act, Her Majesty may by Order in Council revoke the Order extending the 1956 Act there. Whilst the 1956 Act remains in force in the Isle of Man, by reason of paragraph 36(4) the Isle of Man is to be treated, in the laws of the countries to which the copyright provisions of the 1988 Act extend, as a country to which such provisions extend. Further, those countries are to be treated in the law of the Isle of Man, as countries to which the 1956 Act extends.

(iv) Hong Kong and other dependent territories. By reason of para- **17–148**
graph 36(1)(*a*) and (2)(*a*), of Schedule 1, to the 1988 Act, the position will remain the same until an Order is made under section 157 of the 1988 Act extending the copyright provisions of the 1988 Act and Orders in Council made thereunder to such territories. No such Orders have yet been made. Indeed, as to Hong Kong, it seems possible that no such Order will be made. Thus, certain provisions of the 1956 Act, not including section 32 of that Act, were extended to Hong Kong by Orders in Council.[88] Further, paragraph 36(2), of Schedule 1, to the 1988 Act, which provides that such Orders in Council are to remain in force until an Order is made under section 157 of the 1988 Act, also provides that, while they remain in force, they may be varied under the provisions of the 1956 Act under which they were made. Such a variation has now been made by a further Order in Council with effect from April 12, 1990.[89] The effect of this further Order in Council is to extend to Hong Kong section 32 of the 1956 Act suitably amended. Section 32 of the 1956 Act enabled Her Majesty, by Order in Council, to apply the provisions of the 1956 Act to countries to which they did not extend,[90] and the amended section 32 extended to Hong Kong will enable the Governor of Hong Kong by Order to apply provisions of the 1956 Act to such countries. Further, whereas certain Orders in Council applying provisions of the 1956 Act were extended to Hong Kong,[91] the only Order in Council so far made applying provisions of the 1988 Act[92] has not been extended to Hong Kong.[93] Paragraph 36(4) deals with the relationship between a dependent territory and other countries whilst the 1911 or 1956 Act remains in force in such territory.

Non-dependent territories. Under section 31(1) of the 1956 Act, that **17–149**
Act could be, and was, extended to certain countries.[94] Also, by virtue of paragraph 39(2), of Schedule 7, to the 1956 Act, certain countries were to

---

[88] The Copyright (Hong Kong) Order 1972 (1972 S.I. No. 1724) and The Copyright (Hong Kong) (Amendment) Order 1979 (1979 S.I. No. 910); § 17–131, *ante*.

[89] The Copyright (Hong Kong) (Amendment) Order 1990 (1990 S.I. No. 588).

[90] See § 17–84 *et seq., ante.*

[91] See, for instance, The Copyright (International Conventions) Order 1979 (1979 S.I. No. 1715) as amended, § D–5, *post* and The Copyright (Singapore) Order 1987 (1987 S.I. No. 940), § D–19, *post.*

[92] The Copyright (Application to Other Countries) (No. 2) Order 1989 (1989 S.I. No. 1293) as amended, § D–22, *post.*

[93] See § 17–112, *ante.*

[94] See n. 85, *ante.*

be treated as countries to which the 1956 Act extended.[95] Paragraph 37, of Schedule 1, to the 1988 Act contains provisions dealing with such of those countries which were not immediately before the commencement of the copyright provisions of the 1988 Act dependent territories. Dependent territory means any of the Channel Islands, the Isle of Man or any colony,[96] and paragraph 37(1) provides that Her Majesty may by Order in Council conclusively declare for the purposes of paragraph 37 whether a country[97] was a country to which the 1956 Act extended or was treated as such a country.[98]

Paragraph 37(2) provides that a country to which paragraph 37 applies is to be treated as a country to which the copyright provisions of the 1988 Act extend for the purposes of sections 154 to 156 of the 1988 Act (qualification for copyright protection) until an Order in Council is made in respect of that country under section 159 of the 1988 Act (application),[99] or an Order in Council is made declaring that it shall cease to be so treated by reason of the fact that the provisions of the 1956 Act or, as the case may be, the 1911 Act, which extended there as part of the law of that country have been repealed or amended.[1] A statutory instrument containing an Order in Council under paragraph 37 is subject to annulment in pursuance of a resolution of either House of Parliament.[2]

---

[95] § 17–136, *ante.*

[96] C.D.P.A. 1988, Sched. 1, para. 36(6), and see § 17–145, *ante.*

[97] "Country" includes any territory: *ibid.* s.178.

[98] See The Copyright (Status of Former Dependent Territories) Order 1990 (S.I. 1990 No. 1512), § D–44 *post.*

[99] § 17–107, *ante.*

[1] *Ibid.* n. 99.

[2] C.D.P.A. 1988, Sched. 1, para. 37(3).

COPYRIGHT LAW OF THE UNITED STATES OF AMERICA AND GENERAL TABLE OF COPYRIGHT LAWS OF COMMONWEALTH AND FOREIGN COUNTRIES

Contents

I. Copyright Law of the United States of America

A. *General*

In the United States, copyright in a published work depends entirely upon **18–1** the legislation of Congress, but unpublished works were, until a decade ago, protected by the common law, as in England prior to the United Kingdom Copyright Act of 1911. The Constitution of March 4, 1789, authorised Congress "to promote the progress of science and useful arts by securing for limited times to authors and inventors the exclusive right to their respective writings and discoveries," and this provision is the source of the federal legislative power in matters of copyright. The first copyright statute was passed in 1790, with general revisions taking place approximately every 40 years through to 1909. An important intermediate development was the Chace Act of 1891 which first recognised copyright in works by foreign authors.

Copyright Act of 1909. In the year 1909 Congress passed "an Act to **18–2** amend and consolidate the Acts respecting copyright," which repealed all laws or parts of laws in conflict with its provisions.[1] This Act was amended several times and the copyright law of the United States was then codified in an Act of March 4, 1947, which has been amended on a number of occasions, most recently in 1976 in its entirety.[2]

---

[1] s.63.

[2] Title 17, U.S. Code in post-1978 form § E-1 *et seq. post.* For pre-1978 form, see *Nimmer on Copyright*, App. 6 and *Copinger* (12th ed.) § 2161 *et seq.*

B. *Law before 1978*

(i) Domestic works

18–3 **Subjects of copyright.** The subjects of copyright under the Act were: (a) books, (b) periodicals, (c) lectures, sermons and addresses, (d) dramatic and dramatico-musical compositions, (e) musical compositions, (f) maps, (g) works of art, (h) reproductions of works of art, (i) drawings or plastic works of a scientific or technical character, (j) photographs, (k) prints and pictorial illustrations, (l) motion picture photo-plays, (m) motion pictures other than photo-plays, (n) sound recordings.[3]

18–4 **Industrial designs.** There has been considerable discussion of the qualification of ornamental designs for industrial articles to be registered. The leading case, *Mazer* v. *Stein*,[4] decided that a statuette, which had been registered as a work of art, did not lose copyright protection by being used as a lamp base. Since this decision many works of art have been registered, notwithstanding that they have been embodied in articles of an industrial character. On the other hand, objects of simple utility will not be so registered unless they can be justified as works of art.

18–5 **Sound recordings.** For many years, gramophone records were not registrable for statutory protection. Therefore neither the copying of actual records, nor the performance in public of the music embodied therein, was an infringement of statutory copyright in the records. Of course such acts might have infringed the statutory rights of the copyright owner of the music, but neither the gramophone manufacturers, nor the performing artists had any remedy, though it is understood that in some states the copying of records was regarded as a common law wrong. All of this was changed in 1971, when the Sound Recording Amendment, P.L. 92–140, granted protection against reproduction (but not imitation or performance) to sounds fixed after February 15, 1972, on a phonorecord through the contributions of performers and recording organisations. State remedies for unauthorised reproductions of earlier recordings were deemed preserved.[5]

18–6 **Unpublished works.** Common law copyright was expressly preserved,[6] but statutory copyright might instead have been obtained in certain categories of unpublished works, "of which copies are not reproduced for sale."[7]

18–7 **Persons entitled to copyright.** The persons entitled by the Act to copyright protection for their works were the author or proprietor, or his executors, administrators or assigns.[8] But, except on the conditions dis-

---

[3] s.5.
[4] (1954) 347 U.S. 201.
[5] *Goldstein* v. *California* (1973) 412 U.S. 546.
[6] s.2.
[7] s.12.
[8] s.9.

cussed below, copyright was not extended to the work of an author or proprietor who was a citizen or subject of a foreign state or nation. Moreover, except on such conditions, the text of any book in the English language had to be printed from type set in the U.S.A. In case of a work produced "for hire," the employer was treated as the author.[9]

Term of copyright. The term of copyright in the United States was an   **18–8** original term of 28 years from the date of first publication,[10] with a right of renewal for a second period of 28 years. In the course of proposals for a general extension of the renewal term as part of an overall revision of Title 17, U.S. Code, an interim series of Acts[11] was passed beginning in 1962, extending until December 31, 1976, all renewal copyrights which would have expired between September 19, 1962, and December 31, 1976. As ultimately enacted on October 19, 1976, the general revision further extended these renewal terms.[12]

This right of renewal belonged, in the case of a work made for hire, a posthumous or a composite work, such as a periodical or encyclopedia, to the proprietor of the work, and, in other cases, to (a) the author, if still living; (b) the widow, widower, or children[13] of the author, if the author was not living; (c) the author's executor, if such widow, widower, or children were not living; (d) if the author, widow, widower, and children were all dead, and the author left no will, his next-of-kin. Application for renewal had to be made and registered within one year prior to the expiration of the first term.[14] But, in the case of works of United Kingdom authorship falling for renewal on or after September 3, 1939, the period was extended.[15] The assign of the author was not able to claim this renewal, but could have enforced against the author an agreement to assign the renewal copyright. If the author did not survive so as to be entitled to renew, such an agreement would not have been enforceable against the other statutory beneficiaries, including even the author's executor.[16] Several United States decisions had decided that an assignment of copyright should not generally be construed as being intended to pass the renewal right unless such right was specifically mentioned, but it has been held that these decisions were inapplicable to an English contract, which must be construed in accordance with English rules of construction.[17]

---

[9] s.26.

[10] In the case of copyrights registered for unpublished works discussed above, the 28 years were computed from the date of such registration: *Marx v. United States*, (1938) 96 F. (2d) 204.

[11] P.L. 87–668, 89–142, 90–416, 91–147, 91–555, 92–170, 92–566 and 93–573.

[12] s.304(*b*) and Transitional and Supplementary, s.102, 90 Stat. 2598–2599. See *post*, § 18–42. The discussion of the 1976 Act in general is found at *post*, § 18–38 *et seq.*

[13] If a widow and child both survived the author, they shared in the renewal; *De Sylva v. Ballentine* (1956) 351 U.S. 570.

[14] s.24.

[15] See amending Act of 1941 and Presidential Proclamation of March 10, 1944. *Copinger* (12th ed.) § 2296.

[16] *Miller Music Corp.* v. *Charles N. Daniels, Inc.* (1960) 362 U.S. 373.

[17] *Campbell Connelly & Co. Ltd.* v. *Noble* [1963] 1 W.L.R. 252 and see Chap. 15, *ante.*

18–9   **Assignment of copyright.** Copyright is distinct from the property in the material object copyrighted; and, without more, a transfer of the material object did not transfer the copyright.[18] Copyright had to be assigned by an instrument in writing signed by the proprietor of the copyright;[19] if executed in a foreign country, a copyright assignment had to be acknowledged by the assignor before a consular officer or secretary of legation of the United States authorised by law to administer oaths or perform notarial acts in order to benefit from a prima facie presumption of execution.[20] All assignments had to be recorded to afford protection against a purchaser for value without notice but non-recordation was no defence to an action for infringement. It was the theory of United States transfer law that copyright is indivisible.[21]

18–10   **Publication.** The Act contained no precise definition of "publication," but, by section 26, "the date of publication" was, in the case of a work of which copies were reproduced for sale or distribution, to be "the earliest date when copies of the first authorized edition were placed on sale, sold, or publicly distributed by the proprietor of the copyright or under his authority." Publication, therefore, only took place with the concurrence of the proprietor of the copyright, and it would seem that, for books at least, there must have been an issue of copies. Representation on the stage of a play was not a publication of it, nor was the public performance of a musical composition publication. It is not very clear whether the public exhibition of a work of art was a publication—it would seem to have depended upon the circumstances. In the case of *American Tobacco Co.* v. *Werckmeister*,[22] it was held that public exhibition, in a place where copying was forbidden, did not amount to publication, but the court added "we do not mean to say that the public exhibition of a painting or statue where all might see and freely copy it, might not amount to publication within the statute, regardless of the artist's purpose or notice of reservation of rights which he takes no measure to protect."[23] Some believe that the issue of records of a musical work did not amount to publication of it, although the opposite result was more often reached.[24] It results from the foregoing that many works might have been publicly disseminated, by various forms of performance or exhibition (or even, arguably, issue of records), without losing perpetual protection at common law.

---

[18] s.27.

[19] s.28.

[20] s.29.

[21] Under this theory, there could only have been one owner of copyright and in the absence of its assignment, book rights, dramatic rights and motion picture rights could have been transferred separately only by "licenses." This theory often resulted in copyright forfeiture under the 1909 Act. See 3 *Nimmer on Copyright* §§ 10.01–10.02. On that basis, the 1976 Act discarded the indivisibility doctrine. See *post*, § 18–43.

[22] (1907) 207 U.S. 284.

[23] *cf. Letter Edged in Black Press, Inc.* v. *Public Building Commission of Chicago* (1970) 320 F.Supp. 1303.

[24] Compare *Rosette* v. *Rainbo Record Mfg. Corpn.* (1976) 546 F. 2d 461 with *McIntyre* v. *Double A Music Corp.* (1958) 166 F.Supp. 681; *Shapiro, Bernstein & Co.* v. *Miracle Record Co.* (1950) 91 F.Supp. 473.

Copyright notice. Copyright was obtained by publication "with the   **18–11**
notice of copyright required by this title," such notice being expressly
required for all copies published in the United States.[25] By section 19 it
was provided that this copyright notice "shall consist either of the word
'Copyright', the abbreviation 'Copr.,' or the symbol ©, accompanied by
the name of the copyright proprietor, and if the work be a printed literary,
musical, or dramatic work, the notice shall include also the year in which
the copyright was secured by publication." In the case of copies of works
mentioned in section 5(*f*) to (*k*),[26] the notice might have consisted of the
letter C enclosed with a circle, thus ©, accompanied by the initials, monogram, mark or symbol of the copyright proprietor, provided that on some
accessible portion of such copies, or of the margin, back, permanent base,
or pedestal, or of the substance on which such copies were mounted, his
name appeared. In the case of books or other printed publications, the
notice should have been upon the title page or the page immediately following; in the case of a periodical, either upon the title page or upon the
first page of text of each separate number, or under the title heading; or, in
the case of a musical work, either upon its title page or the first page of
music; provided that one notice of copyright in each volume, or in each
number of a newspaper or periodical published, would have been sufficient.[27]

Effect of omission of copyright notice. Accidental omission of the   **18–12**
copyright notice from a few copies did not invalidate the copyright, but
damages were not in that case recoverable against an innocent infringer,
and an injunction might have been refused, except on the terms of reimbursing the expenses of an innocent infringer.[28] On the other hand, often
no relief seemed possible if the copyright notice was in the wrong place or
a wrong form.[29]

Registration and deposit. The next step was to register the copyright,   **18–13**
which was effected by deposit at the Copyright Office of two complete
copies of the best edition of the work,[30] with a proper application for registration and a money order for the amount of registration fee. A partnership might have registered.[31] The Act required this deposit to be made
"promptly," but this has not been enforced at all rigidly.[32]

Failure to make deposit. The effect of a failure to deposit the necessary   **18–14**
copies and to register the copyright was not to invalidate the copyright in
the first instance, but only to prevent any action for infringement being

---

[25] s.10. The notice might have been omitted in the case of foreign made copies not offered for
sale in the United States, though it has been thought that the notice should appear on the
work when first published, wherever such publication takes place.
[26] *Ante*, § 18–3.
[27] s.20.
[28] s.12.
[29] *Freeman v. Trade Register* (1909) 173 Fed.Rep. 419; *Bowker on Copyright* (Amer.), p. 131. As
to false copyright notices, see ss.105 and 106.
[30] s.13 and see s.12. As to foreign works, see *post*, §§ 18–28, 18–29.
[31] *Campbell v. Wireback* (1920) 269 Fed.Rep. 372.
[32] *Washingtonian Publishing Co. v. Pearson* (1939) 306 U.S. 30.

brought until such deposit and registration had been effected.[33] But notice might have been given by the Register of Copyrights requiring the deposit to be made, and, upon failure to comply with this notice within three months—or six months in the case of a foreign country—the proprietor of the copyright would have been liable to a fine, and the copyright would have become void.[34] This provision has not resulted in many forfeitures.

18–15 **Deposit in case of unpublished work.** In the case of unpublished works, statutory copyright might have been obtained by deposit of one complete copy, in the case of a lecture, sermon, address, dramatic or musical work; a positive print, in the case of a photograph; a photographic reproduction, in the case of works of art, etc.[35] If, however, the work was afterwards published, deposit had to be made in the ordinary way.[36]

18–16 **The "manufacturing provisions."** In addition to the above formalities, printed "books," except the original text[37] of a book of foreign origin in a language other than English, except where the provisions of the Universal Copyright Convention apply, had to comply with the "manufacturing provisions" of the Act. That is to say, they had to be "printed from type set within the limits of the United States, either by hand or by the aid of any kind of typesetting machine, or from plates made within the limits of the United States from type set therein, or, if the text be reproduced by lithographic process, or photo-engraving process, then by a process wholly performed within the limits of the United States, and the printing of the text and binding of the said book shall be performed within the limits of the United States."[38] These requirements also extended to the illustrations of the book, and to separate lithographs or photo-engraving except when, in either case, the subjects represented were located in a foreign country and illustrated a scientific work or reproduced a work of art. An affidavit to this effect had to be made at the time of depositing the necessary copies,[39] and failure to comply with the manufacturing provisions has been said to suspend the enforceability of the copyright.[40]

18–17 **Rights of owner of copyright.** The proprietor of the copyright had the exclusive right (a) to print, reprint, publish, copy, and vend the work; (b) to translate, dramatise, arrange, or adapt the work; (c) to deliver in public for profit a lecture, sermon, or address; (d) publicly to perform certain works and publicly to perform *for profit* certain other works.[41]

---

[33] s.13.

[34] s.14.

[35] s.12.

[36] See n. 35, *supra*.

[37] It is to be noted that the exemption only applied to the "original text." It has been suggested that the French translation of a German book, for instance, had to comply with the manufacturing provisions. Bowker, p. 155.

[38] s.16.

[39] s.17.

[40] However, it can be maintained that, following the expiration of the manufacturing clause on July 1, 1986, works previously published in contravention of the now-defunct clause have the disability removed from their copyright status, and are now fully enforceable. See 2 *Nimmer on Copyright* § 7.23[E] (1989 ed.).

[41] s.1.

Reproduction by records, etc. Authors of works published after July 1, **18–18**
1909, were also given the sole right to authorise the reproduction of their
works by means of mechanical instruments,[42] but subject to the condition,
as regards musical works, that once the owner of the copyright had permitted such reproduction, any other person might have made similar use
of the copyrighted work upon payment of a fixed royalty of two cents on
every record. The records themselves were not entitled to copyright by
reason of this provision.[43]

For profit. There was, as indicated, a distinction regarding the perform- **18–19**
ing right, namely that, in the case of a musical work, performance was
only an infringement if "for profit." This included playing music at hotels
and restaurants, but not charitable performances, even for raising funds.
There was a special exemption for "juke-boxes," although, clearly, coin-
operated record players are normally operated "for profit."[44]

Fair use. The owner's rights were limited in a series of judicial decisions **18–20**
on the principle of "fair use."[45] Such exceptions might fall under the headings of quotation for review or criticism, quotation for illustration in scientific works, parody, news summary, reproduction for study, reproduction
for purposes of legal proceedings, fortuitous reproduction in newsreels,
etc.

Damages. Section 101 of the Act was directed to damages. In view of the **18–21**
obvious difficulty, in copyright cases, of proving the actual damage suffered this section provided a minimum penalty of $250 which might have
been recovered without legal proof of damage.

Prohibition against importation. The provisions of the Act as regards **18–22**
importation of copyright works were somewhat unusual, inasmuch as they
expressly prohibited the importation of copyright books under certain circumstances. Section 107 provided, generally, against the importation of
"piratical copies," and even of copies authorised to be imported by the
owner of the copyright which had not been produced in accordance with
the manufacturing provisions of the Act. But, except as regards piratical
copies, the prohibition was not applied to (a) works in raised characters
for the use of the blind; (b) foreign-made periodicals containing authorised copyright matter; (c) authorised editions of works in foreign
languages of which only an English translation had been copyrighted in
the United States; (d) authorised copies published abroad when imported
under special circumstances. This permitted the importation of authorised copies for individual use and not for sale, provided not more than one
copy was imported at one time; by or for the United States, or by or for
certain educational authorities, including free libraries, not more than one
copy at a time; or when parts of libraries or collections were purchased

---

[42] s.1(*e*). As to foreign works, see *post*, § 18–25.
[43] See *ante*, § 18–5.
[44] s.1(*e*).
[45] See, *e.g. Williams & Wilkins Co.* v. *U.S.* (1973) 487 F.2d 1345, aff'd by an equally divided
Court (1975) 420 U.S. 376.

and imported *en bloc* for the use of such authorities as before mentioned, or formed parts of personal baggage belonging to persons or families arriving from foreign countries, and were not intended for sale.

(ii) Works of foreign origin

18–23   **The Chace Act of 1891.** As noted above, it was not until 1891 that a foreign author or publisher had rights as against an American publisher who reprinted or issued in America an infringing work. Common law protection for unpublished works had always been available to authors of any nationality. The first Copyright Act of 1790 was expressly applicable only to citizens of the United States or persons resident there, and this provision was maintained in all subsequent amendments of the law until the Chace Act of 1891. Under that Act, foreigners could obtain American copyright, provided they were citizens or subjects of a foreign State or nation which permitted to Americans "the benefit of copyright on substantially the same basis as its own citizens," or of a State or nation which was "a party to an international agreement which provides for reciprocity in the granting of copyright by the terms of which agreement the United States of America may, at its pleasure, become a party to such an agreement."

18–24   **Law prior to 1978.** First, aliens who were domiciled in the United States could have acquired statutory protection for their works in the same way as American citizens.[46] Secondly, by Presidential proclamation pursuant to section 9(*b*) of the Act, the citizens or subjects of a number of foreign countries giving reciprocal protection to United States works might also have acquired statutory protection for their works in the same way as American citizens. Thirdly and more recently, since the United States adhered to the Universal Copyright Convention, a more complex series of provisions applied.[47] Basically authorship by a Convention national or first publication in a Convention country would have sufficed.

18–25   **Gramophone records.** With regard to the exclusive right to make contrivances by which a musical work may be mechanically produced, it was provided[48] that, as regards musical works, this right shall not apply to the "works of a foreign author or composer unless the foreign state or nation of which such author or composer is a citizen or subject grants, either by treaty, convention, agreement, or law, to citizens of the United States similar rights."

18–26   **Proclamations.** Presidential proclamations have been issued according the right to acquire general copyright in the United States to citizens of a number of countries including Great Britain and her possessions and colonies, including the self-governing dominions, and the following other countries—Argentina, Austria, Belgium, Brazil, Chile, Costa Rica, Cuba,

---

[46] s.9(*a*).
[47] *Post*, § 18–33.
[48] s.1(*e*).

Czechoslovakia, Denmark, Finland, France, Germany, Greece, Israel, Italy, Irish Republic, Luxembourg, Mexico, Monaco, The Netherlands and her possessions, Norway, Philippines, Poland, Portugal, Rumania, South Africa, Spain, Sweden, Switzerland and Tunis. The right to obtain gramophone and similar rights was also accorded to the citizens of the same countries.

Special wartime provisions. An amending Act of 1919 added a provision to section 9 to enable authors who, owing to war conditions, had been unable to register their copyright in the United States before first publication abroad to obtain copyright by so doing within 15 months of the declaration of peace, provided that it was proclaimed that they were nationals of a country which extended reciprocal rights to citizens of the United States. Proclamations were made that such rights had been extended to citizens of the United States by Great Britain (apart from the self-governing dominions), Denmark, Germany, Austria, Hungary, Italy and New Zealand. A further amendment to the said section was made by an Act of 1941 enabling a proclamation to be made extending, for the benefit of nationals of a country affording reciprocal rights, the time for performance of all formalities required by the law of the United States for such a period as the President should consider proper. A proclamation was issued in March, 1944,[49] giving the benefit of this amendment to residents in Great Britain and in a number of British possessions, and extending the time until further proclamation. In July 1967 a proclamation was made in favour of German citizens.   **18–27**

Formalities to be observed. But, so far as concerns all the foregoing provisions, foreign authors were required to observe all the formalities to which United States authors were subject.   **18–28**

Therefore, as a condition to copyright protection, foreign works had to be registered for renewal at the Copyright Office in Washington at the expiration of the initial 28-year term, and immediately upon publication every copy had to bear the necessary copyright notice.[50] There were, however, two modifications of the law in favour of foreigners, first, in respect of deposit of copies[51] and, secondly, as regards the manufacturing provisions.[52]

Deposit of one copy sufficient. We have seen that the United States author had to deposit two complete copies of the best edition of his work. Section 13 provided that, if the work was by an author who was a citizen or subject of a foreign state or nation, and had been published in a foreign country, only *one* complete copy of the best edition then published in such foreign country needed to be deposited.   **18–29**

Manufacturing provisions. As has been pointed out, all books, except the original text of books of foreign origin written in a language *other than English*, were required to comply with the "manufacturing provisions" of   **18–30**

[49] *Copinger* (12th ed.) § 2296.
[50] *Ante,* § 18–11.
[51] *Ante,* § 18–13.
[52] *Ante,* § 18–16.

the Act.[53] Thus, a book published by a British, or other foreign author, in the English language, had to have been printed from type set within the United States, and the printing and binding must also have been performed within the limits of that country. This was a particularly onerous condition of copyright, and accounted for the fact that the great majority of English books were, prior to the alteration of the law produced by United States adherence to the Universal Copyright Convention, entirely unprotected in America.[54]

18–31   **Ad interim protection.** Section 22 of the Act, as amended in 1949,[55] afforded a substantial concession by enabling authors to obtain an *ad interim* protection for their works published abroad in the English language prior to the date of their publication in the United States. In order to obtain this *ad interim* protection, which was to have all the force and effect of copyright under the Act, deposit had to have been made at the Copyright Office, not later than six months after the publication of the work abroad, of a complete copy of the foreign edition,[56] with a request for the reservation of the copyright. The protection continued for five years after first publication abroad.[57] This provisional copyright became permanent when, within the period of provisional protection, an authorised edition of the book was published within the United States complying with the manufacturing provisions of the Act.[58] Thus, books in the English language could have obtained *ad interim* protection for a period of five years from first publication abroad. Of course, if an American edition with notice of copyright was published simultaneously with the English edition, there would have been no necessity to apply for *ad interim* protection, and this was the course which was adopted by many of the larger publishing firms having offices in both countries.

18–32   **Manufacturing provisions did not apply to artistic, dramatic, or musical works.** It must further be remembered that the manufacturing provisions only applied to "books," and, moreover, to "the printed book or periodical specified in section 5, subsections (*a*) and (*b*)," and to lithographs and photo-engravings[59] so that, not only were other types of artistic works exempted from those provisions, but also dramatic and musical compositions, which were specified in subsections (*d*) and (*e*) of section 5, notwithstanding that such works had been printed in book form.[60] The proprietors of the copyright in such works could, therefore, have obtained copyright for their foreign editions upon complying with the general formalities of the Act, without having them manufactured in the United States. First publication upon American soil was not expressly stated to be

---

[53] *Ante*, § 18–16.
[54] But see *ante*, § 18–16 n. 40.
[55] The amendment altered the periods of deposit and protection from 60 days to six months and from four months to five years.
[56] It was not necessary that this copy should have had the copyright notice required by s.9.
[57] s.22.
[58] s.23.
[59] *Ante*, § 18–16.
[60] *Ditson (O.)* v. *Littleton* (1895) 67 Fed.Rep. 905; *Hervieu* v. *Ogilvie (J. S.) Pub. Co.* (1909) 169 Fed.Rep. 978.

essential, provided the work had the requisite copyright notice and deposit of one copy with the requisite copyright notice had been made "promptly" at the Copyright Office in America.[61]

Universal Copyright Convention. The position, however, of the protec-   **18–33**
tion afforded by the United States to works originating abroad was completely altered as a result of United States accession to the Universal Copyright Convention which was, in fact, ratified by the United States on September 16, 1955. This required adherent countries to give protection without formality other than as specified. Accordingly, by an amendment to section 9 of the Act, made by an amending Act of August 1954, a third case in which copyright under the Act might have extended to the work of an author or proprietor who was a citizen or subject of a foreign state or nation was introduced. The amendment, subsection (*c*), provided that, when the Convention was in force between the United States and the foreign state or nation of which such author was a citizen or subject, or in which the work was first published, any work to which copyright was extended pursuant to that subsection was to be exempt from (1) the requirement that a foreign state or nation must grant to United States citizens mechanical reproduction rights similar to those specified therein; (2) the obligatory deposit requirements of the Act; (3) the manufacturing provisions; (4) the import prohibitions to the extent that they were related to the manufacturing provisions; and (5) the requirements of sections 19 and 20 of the Act relating to the copyright notice. Where this subsection applied, the only formality required, in order that a work might have obtained copyright in the United States, was that "from the time of first publication all the copies of the work published with the authority of the author or other copyright proprietor shall bear the symbol © accompanied by the name of the copyright proprietor and the year of first publication placed in such manner and location as to give reasonable notice of claim of copyright." It would appear clear that this requirement involved the application of the symbol upon all copies wherever published. It is to be observed that the details of the notice required under the Act itself, in sections 19 and 20, were not made applicable to the notice under this section, though they might have afforded some indication of what is a "manner and location" such as to give reasonable notice of claim. Unpublished works were protected without formality. The revision of the Convention adopted in Paris in 1971 has been adhered to by the United States.

Effect on works having ad interim copyright. It was further provided,   **18–34**
by section 9, subsection (*c*) that, upon the coming into force of the Convention in a foreign state or nation, every book or periodical of a citizen or subject thereof, in which *ad interim* copyright was subsisting at the effective date of the said coming into force, was to have copyright for 28 years from the date of first publication abroad without the necessity of complying with the further formalities specified in section 23 of the Act. This referred to the manufacturing provisions. Presumably, where this provision applied the provisions of the Act itself about copyright notice, and not

---

[61] *Ante,* § 18–13.

those of the amending subsection, were the relevant ones. As this provision was made with regard to works in existence at the date of the coming into force of the Convention, it would seem that the remaining provisions of the subsection were not intended to be retrospective, or to apply to works first published anywhere before the coming into force of the Convention, but this would have been a matter for decision by the United States courts.

18–35   **Works to which new provisions were not applicable.** It was further provided, by section 9, subsection (*c*), that the provisions of such subsection were not to extend to works of an author who was a citizen of, or domiciled in, the United States of America, regardless of place of first publication, or to works first published in the United States. This suggested that works of non-American authors should not have been first published in the United States, if Convention protection in the United States was desired.

18–36   **When Convention came into force.** As provided by Article 9 (ix) of the Convention, the Convention came into force between the United States and the United Kingdom, on September 27, 1957, that is three months after the United Kingdom deposited its instrument of ratification.

18–37   **Treaties and Conventions.** America is only recently party to the Berne Convention,[62] but has long adhered to the Pan-American Convention of 1902, including the modifications made to that Convention at Buenos Aires in 1910.[63] She also has bilateral copyright agreements with several dozen nations.[64]

It would appear that enemy subjects did not lose their rights during the 1914–1918 war, though a law of October 6, 1917, imposed compulsory licences,[65] and it is apprehended that a similar situation arose in the 1939–1945 war.[66]

C. *Law after 1978*

(i) Copyright Act of 1976

18–38   **The programme for revision.** The efforts producing the current United States copyright statute commenced with a programme of studies in 1955 and culminated in enactment on October 19, 1976.[67] For most purposes, the statute became effective on January 1, 1978. Its earliest legislative predecessor was introduced into Congress in 1964[68] and, after extensive hear-

---

[62] *Post,* § 18–47 *et seq.*
[63] *Ante,* § 17–76.
[64] Copyright Office Circular No. 38a.
[65] See an article in the *Droit d'Auteur,* April 15, 1925.
[66] See § 18–27, *ante,* and *Copyright,* No. 10, October 1967, p. 249.
[67] Title 17 U.S.C., 90 Stat. 2541 *et seq.,* Public Law 94–553.
[68] H.R. 11947 and S. 3008, 88th Cong., 2d Sess.

ings,[69] one version passed the House of Representatives,[70] but not the Senate, in 1967. The following decade of technological developments and controversy were tracked by further hearings and capped by definitive Senate[71] and House[72] reports furnishing the background for passage.

Relevance of prior law. The new law does not cleanly sweep away the old law. In many respects the post-1978 United States copyright law remains a blend of the 1909 and 1976 Statutes as well as case law and administrative regulations thereunder. For example: **18–39**

(1) Causes of action arising before January 1, 1978, are governed by then existing law.[73] Since the statutes of limitations under both laws are three years, such claims were litigated through December 31, 1980 and, in the case of tolling of the statute of limitations or through other exceptional means, occasionally beyond that date.[74]

(2) Since works in the public domain on January 1, 1978, were not revived,[75] one must apply old law to all pre-1978 works to test whether indeed they had such public domain status on such date.[76]

(3) Certain 1976 Act provisions expressly provide that the law in a particular respect shall be what it was on December 31, 1977.[77]

(4) Other provisions, notably the renewal section,[78] adopt, in substantially *haec verba*, 1909 Act language, thereby calling up old judicial precedents.

(5) Still other provisions, such as those dealing with copyrightability[79] and fair use[80] contain new language, but arrive with a legislative gloss expressing an intent to leave precedents unchanged.[81]

(6) Finally, as with all new statutes, certain interstices in the new Act will undoubtedly be filled with old law precedents, at least by way of analogy.

---

[69] See, *e.g. Copyright Law Revision, Hearings before Subcommittee No. 3 of the Committee on the Judiciary, House of Representatives, 89th Cong., 1st Sess. on H.R.* 4347, *H.R.* 5680, *H.R.* 6831 *and H.R.* 6835 (1965).

[70] H.R. 2512, passed on April 11, 1967.

[71] S.Rep. No. 94–473, 94th Cong., 1st Sess. (1975).

[72] H.R.Rep. No. 94–1476, 94th Cong., 2d Sess. (1976). A Conference Report, H.R.Rep. No. 94–1733, 94th Cong., 2d Sess. (1976), sets forth the resolution of specific differences between the Senate and House versions of the bill prior to final floor debate and passage.

[73] Trans. & Suppl. s.112, 90 Stat. 2600.

[74] *e.g. Kamar International* v. *Russ Berrie & Co.* (1987) 829 F.2d 783.

[75] Trans. & Suppl. s.103, 90 Stat. 2599. See *post*, § 18–42.

[76] Moreover, Trans. & Suppl. s.108, 90 Stat. 2600, permits pre-1978 works to carry a notice complying with either statute in distributions on or after January 1, 1978.

[77] ss.113(*b*), 118(*b*)(4). In addition, s.117 was to the same effect until its amendment on December 12, 1980, by Public Law 96–517, 94 Stat. 3015.

[78] s.304(*a*). See *ante*, § 18–8.

[79] s.102(*a*).

[80] s.107.

[81] H.R.Rep. No. 94–1476 at 51, 66 and S.Rep. No. 94–473 at 50, 62.

18–40 **Single Federal system.** The 1976 Act establishes a single Federal régime of copyright protection for intellectual works, in fixed form, whether published or unpublished.[82] The statute pre-empts any rights which the States might recognise in such subject-matter if they are "equivalent to . . . rights within the general scope of copyright . . . "[83] Protection commences without formality upon "creation," *i.e.* when the work is first fixed in a tangible medium of expression.[84] Conditions subsequent such as notice, registration of claims to copyright and recordation of transfers are imposed in connection with preservation and full exercise of rights.

18–41 **Subjects of copyright.** Copyright is available for "original works of authorship fixed in any tangible medium of expression, now known or later developed from which they can be perceived, reproduced or otherwise communicated, either directly or with the aid of a machine or device."[85] The statute lists as non-exhaustive examples of such works, literary,[86] musical, dramatic, choreographic, pictorial, graphic and sculptural works[87] as well as sound recordings, pantomimes and motion pictures and other audio-visual works. Congress intended to impart into this potentially broad range of subject-matter pre-existing judicial standards of "originality" and also, to permit future expansion of protected subject-matter under its Constitutional power to protect the "writings" of "authors."[88]

Works created by United States Government employees as part of official duties are expressly excluded from protection.[89] On that basis, federal statutes and judicial opinions are in the public domain. Long custom also dictates that state statutes and judicial opinions are likewise unprotected by U.S. copyright. Congress added explicit protection for mask works of semiconductor chips under the Semiconductor Chip Protection Act of 1984.[90] Although codified adjacent to the Copyright Act of

---

[82] s.301(*a*). This is to be contrasted with the prior dual system under which unpublished works were generally protected by State common law. See *ante*, § 18–1.

[83] *Ibid.*

[84] See definition of "created" in s.101.

[85] s.102(*a*).

[86] The statutory language, fortified by the legislative history, establishes the copyrightability of computer programs, data bases and machine-readable material, under the general rubric of "literary works." This result, confirming prior administrative practice of The Copyright Office, has been supported, though not unanimously, by a Presidential Commission considering this matter. See National Commission on New Technological Uses of Copyrighted Works ("CONTU") Final Report (July 31, 1978). Acting on the CONTU majority opinion, Congress dispelled any lingering doubt as to the copyrightability of computer programs by the Computer Software Copyright Act of 1980, Public Law 96–517, 94 Stat. 3015.

[87] *cf. Esquire* v. *Ringer* (1978) 591 F.2d 796. For the current attempt to distinguish between copyrightable pictorial, graphic and sculptural works and non-copyrightable industrial designs, see the definition of the former term and of "useful article" in s.101, the provisions of s.113 and the discussion in H.R.Rep. No. 94–1476 at 54–55 and 105–06 (1976).

[88] S.Rep. No. 94–473, 94th Cong., 1st Sess. 50–51 (1975); H.R.Rep. No. 94–1476, 94th Cong., 2d Sess. 51–52 (1976).

[89] s.105. See *Schnapper* v. *Foley* (1979) 471 F.Supp. 426. This provision is inapplicable to works of foreign governments, although foreign statutes, judicial opinions, etc., may be deemed non-copyrightable by reason of public policy.

[90] Public Law 98–620, 98 Stat. 3347. As to the position in the United Kingdom see Chap. 20 *post*.

1976,[91] the 1984 Act actually creates a new and *sui generis* form of intellectual property; accordingly, the discussion herein of duration, formalities and other aspects of copyright protection should not be considered applicable to such mask works.[92] In the six years since the 1984 Act has been on the books, it has generated but one published judicial opinion.

Term of copyright and termination of grants. The new statute does   **18–42**
not protect any work in the public domain prior to January 1, 1978.[93]
With respect to the duration of protection for works created on and after January 1, 1978, United States law takes a significant step toward the law of the United Kingdom as well as those of most other countries. Such works are generally protected for the lifetime of the author (or the survivor of joint authors)[94] plus 50 years after his or her death.[95] In the case of anonymous and pseudonymous works and works made for hire, *i.e.* those created in the course of employment or certain specially-commissioned categories of works expressly so designated, the term endures for 75 years after publication or 100 years after creation, whichever period is shorter.[96]

Works which were unpublished as of January 1, 1978 and not protected by statutory copyright are assimilated for durational purposes to works created thereon or thereafter, but with certain minimum periods of protection, *i.e.* through December 31, 2002, or if published before then, until December 31, 2027.[97]

Copyrights in their first term of statutory protection on January 1, 1978, require special attention, because they involve a renewal procedure which must be followed in order to prevent their falling into the public domain after 28 years. This procedure requires the timely filing of a renewal application by the proper claimant as determined by the intricate scheme long in United States law.[98] The application must be filed during the last year of the original term and the statute makes all terms end at the end of the calendar year.[99] Accordingly, a renewal application must be filed during the calendar year containing the 28th anniversary of the commencement of protection. Upon following such procedure, the claimant will enjoy an additional 47 years of protection for total copyright protection of 75 years. It must be reiterated that nothing in the "life plus 50" philosophy reflected in other portions of the statute will save works in their original term of statutory copyright from entering the public domain in the absence of renewal.

---

[91] See s.901 *et seq.* § E–86 *post.*
[92] H.R.Rep. No. 98–781, 98th Cong., 2d Sess. (1984), at 5.
[93] Trans. & Suppl. s.103, 90 Stat. 2599. This is but one of the many reasons the 1909 Statute and case law thereunder remain relevant, since determination of pre-January 1, 1978, public domain status depends on such earlier jurisprudence.
[94] s.302(*b*).
[95] s.302(*a*).
[96] s.302(*c*).
[97] s.303.
[98] s.304(*a*); *cf.* s.24 of the 1909 law and *ante*, § 18–8. Although, in other particulars, the Berne Convention Implementation Act of 1988 eliminates copyright formalities, *post*, § 18–48, the requirement of renewal of pre-1978 works continues to apply upon expiration of the initial 28-year term, even with respect to Berne Convention claimants.
[99] s.305. Under the 1909 law, protection commenced on publication or where applicable on registration *prior* to publication under s.12. See *ante*, § 18–8.

Works in their renewal term of statutory copyright are subject to still another durational scheme.[1] Terms of copyright in such works are automatically extended so as to endure for 75 years from the date protection commenced. This provision does not add 19 years in every case to the former 56 years of original terms because certain works began enjoying extended protection, *i.e.* beyond 56 years, even before the general effective date of the new statute by reason of the interim extensions already mentioned.[2] These are works, the renewal copyright terms of which would have expired between September 19, 1962 and December 31, 1977, but for the interim extensions.[3]

As to copyright protection extended beyond 56 years, the statute grants authors and their specified beneficiaries a right to recapture rights previously granted.[4] This is accomplished by way of an option to terminate transfers and licences, which may be exercised upon 2–10 years' notice and is subject to a number of other conditions and exceptions. For example, works made for hire are excluded from the scope of termination and the grantee's right to utilise derivative works made under authority of the grant is preserved from the effect of termination.

18–43   **Ownership and assignment.** Initial ownership of copyright is vested in the author or authors of a work,[5] but an employer or other person for whom a "work made for hire"[6] is prepared is considered the "author" of the work for copyright purposes.[7] Exclusive rights may be transferred and enjoyed separately, but all exclusive transfers (though not non-exclusive licenses) must be evidenced by a writing signed by the grantor.[8] A system of recordation of transfers is provided in order to resolve questions of priority between conflicting transfers and licenses.[9] Recordation can potentially afford constructive notice and protect an owner against the consequences of the placement of someone else's name in the copyright notice. It is also a prerequisite to an infringement action by a transferee.

Although the 1976 Act facilitates fragmented transfers by discarding the old United States notion of the indivisibility of copyright,[10] it introduces two new express limitations on transfers. First, transferability does not include Government seizure or expropriation from an unwilling author.[11] This limitation was introduced in response to fears that the adherence to the Universal Copyright Convention by the U.S.S.R. might permit the use of copyright (expropriated and thus "owned" by the

---

[1] s.304(*b*).

[2] See *ante*, § 18–8. The statute immediately upon enactment (October 19, 1976), extended otherwise expiring renewal terms to December 31, 1977.

[3] It may also be convenient to identify these as works originally copyrighted between September 19, 1906, and December 31, 1921, and duly renewed.

[4] s.304(*c*).

[5] s.201(*a*).

[6] See definition of "work made for hire" in s.101 and *ante*, § 18–42.

[7] s.201(*b*).

[8] s.204.

[9] s.205.

[10] See *ante*, § 18–9 and n. 21.

[11] s.201(*e*).

Government) as a means of suppressing dissident views in nations owing Convention obligations to enforce copyrights.[12]

The other limitation is a right to terminate transfers made by authors after January 1, 1978.[13] This right has a number of significant differences, as well as similarities,[14] to the option to recapture rights for the extended renewal term previously mentioned. It is also exercisable on 2–10 years' notice, but is not generally effective until 35 years after the grant.[15]

Notice and registration. The 1976 law carried forward a "general **18–44** requirement" of a copyright notice on visually perceptible published copies[16] and a parallel requirement on published "phonorecords."[17] However, a later section will show that these notice requirements persisted only until 1989.[18] The changes introduced add a greater measure of flexibility as to the position and, to some extent, the form of such notice, as well as curative provisions covering omissions and defects.[19] Thus, whenever a work is published anywhere in the world, the statute provides that the familiar claim symbol ©, "Copyright" or "Copr." (or simply ℗ in the case of phonorecords embodying sound recordings); the year of first publication; and the name or generally recognisable alternative designation of the owner of copyright shall be affixed "in such manner and location as to give reasonable notice of the claim to copyright." The Register of Copyrights has promulgated regulations furnishing non-exhaustive examples of what is reasonable in this regard.[20] The year date may be the date of publication of a derivative work incorporating previously published material and may, in certain cases, be omitted altogether.

Omission of notice from a relatively small number of copies or phonorecords will not invalidate copyright; nor will omission in violation of an express writing conditioning authorisation to distribute upon use of a notice. Moreover, any omission, arguably even if deliberate, will not be fatal if registration is made within five years and a reasonable effort is made to add notice to copies or phonorecords later distributed in the United States.

Registration, while theoretically optional, seems to be even more important under the new statute. In addition to its role in curing omission of notice and protecting the actual owner where the wrong owner is named in the notice, registration is important in the event of litigation,

---

[12] 119 Cong.Rec. S.9387 (March 26, 1973).
[13] s.203.
[14] For example, works made for hire are not subject to termination.
[15] The two rights to terminate grants in the 1976 U.S. Copyright Act may be compared and contrasted with the automatic reversion of granted rights found in the proviso to s.5(2) of the U.K. Copyright Act 1911. See *Redwood Music Limited* v. *B. Feldman & Co. Ltd.* [1979] R.P.C. 385.
[16] s.401. See definition of "published" in s.101.
[17] s.402. S.101 divides material objects embodying copyrighted works into "copies" and "phonorecords," the latter constituting the only objects capable of embodying purely aural works, *i.e.* "sound recordings."
[18] *Post*, § 18–48. The discussion in the text above should be considered applicable only to the decennial period from January 1, 1978 until March 1, 1989.
[19] s.405.
[20] See 42 Fed.Reg. 64374 (December 23, 1977).

and in fact is generally a prerequisite to suit.[21] Moreover, early registration will insure prima facie proof of validity and the potential availability of statutory damages and attorney's fees.[22]

18–45 **Rights.** It is in the area of rights that one finds the controversies that delayed revision for at least a decade. The resulting compromises have produced a number of detailed exemptions and limitations. The basic rights are those of reproduction, adaptation (*i.e.* the preparation of derivative works), distribution, public performance and public display. For the first time, unauthorised importation also constitutes infringement and this covers not only piratical copies, but also genuine ones imported in violation of a contractual restriction.[23]

The exemptions include the first statutory recognition of fair use, together with an indication of some of the purposes and criteria for determining application of the exemption.[24] Under detailed conditions, special exemptions as to reproduction and distribution of single copies are provided for libraries and archives[25] and as to public performance and display for certain educational, religious, charitable and other purposes.[26] In addition, circumscribed "ephemeral recording" privileges[27] are accorded to broadcasters and other "transmitting organisations."[28]

Over and above the foregoing exemptions, limitations on exclusive rights are imposed through the medium of five so-called compulsory licenses. One carries forward the 1909 provision covering phonorecords embodying non-dramatic musical compositions, with certain modifications including an increase in statutory rate.[29] A second replaces the well-known "juke-box exemption"[30] and a third, the judicial exemption previously accorded re-transmission by cable of copyrighted broadcast material.[31] The fourth compulsory license permits public broadcasting to record, perform and display published non-dramatic musical, pictorial, graphic and sculptural works, upon payment of fees either voluntarily negotiated or determined by the newly-created Copyright Royalty Tribunal.[32] This body also reviews, at specified intervals, the statutory rates initially set for the other three compulsory licenses and supervises distribution of juke-box and cable royalties.[33] Finally, Congress added a fifth

---

[21] s.411.

[22] s.412.

[23] s.602. Administrative exclusion by the U.S. Customs Service is limited to piratical copies. S.602(*b*).

[24] s.107.

[25] s.108.

[26] s.110.

[27] s.112.

[28] To "transmit" a performance or display is, according to s.101, "to communicate it by any device or process whereby images or sounds are received beyond the place from which they are sent."

[29] s.115. The fee is 2.75 cents per work or 0.5 cent per minute of playing time thereof, whichever is larger.

[30] s.116. See *ante*, § 18–19.

[31] s.111. See *Teleprompter Corp.* v. *CBS* (1974) 415 U.S. 394.

[32] s.118.

[33] See s.801 *et seq.*

compulsory license, via the Satellite Home Viewer Act of 1988.[34] This law, which became effective on January 1, 1989, provides that satellite carriers may engage in secondary transmissions of signals emanating from super stations and television networks, provided that the satellite carriers pay a set monthly fee per home to the Copyright Royalty Tribunal for distribution to affected copyright owners.[35] This fifth compulsory license is an interim measure designed to protect a nascent industry; it expires on December 31, 1994.[36]

The "manufacturing clause." The 1976 Act loosened the manufactur-   **18–46**
ing clause in several particulars.[37] Most importantly, failure to comply with its provisions no longer suspends enforceability of the subject work's copyright, although it does serve as a defence in certain situations. Among the partial and total exemptions in the new manufacturing clause, perhaps most important are those extending permissible manufacture to Canada, exempting certain personal, governmental and educational importations, as well as importations up to 2,000 copies, and automatically conferring full-term protection on works covered by the predecessor provision in the 1909 Act providing for five-year *ad interim* copyrights.[38] The 1976 Act also continues the ban on importation into the United States of works contravening the manufacturing clause, enforced by the United States Customs Service.

Of greater importance than the differing contours of the manufacturing clause under the 1976 Act from its 1909 Act precursor is the fact that it has expired as of July 1, 1986. Therefore, as to newly-created works, this parochial feature of U.S. law can be entirely ignored.[39]

(ii) The Berne Convention Implementation Act of 1988

U.S. Accession to the Berne Convention. In October, 1988, the Con-   **18–47**
gress amended the 1976 Act in several particulars to eliminate some obstacles to United States adherence to the Berne Convention. In particular, the Berne Convention Implementation Act of 1988[40] refined the protection accorded to architectural works and revised the juke-box compulsory licence.[41] Most importantly, the 1988 amendment eliminated some of the more onerous copyright formalities that had long set the U.S. apart from most of the world copyright community.[42] These changes took effect on March 1, 1989; on that same day, the United States finally acceded to the world's foremost multilateral copyright convention, over a century after the Berne Convention was promulgated.

The governing copyright law in the United States after March 1, 1989 is

---

[34] Act of November 16, 1988, Pub. L. 100–667, 102 Stat. 3935.
[35] s.119.
[36] Act of November 16, 1988, s.207.
[37] s.601.
[38] Tran. & Suppl. s.107, 90 Stat. 2600: and see §18–31 *ante*.
[39] A question remains as to the impact of the manufacturing clause as to pre-1978 works in violation of its terms. See *ante*, § 18–16, n. 40.
[40] Public Law 100–568, 102 Stat. 2853.
[41] *Ante*, § 18–45.
[42] *Post*, § 18–48.

somewhat complex. The 1976 Act continues to provide overarching structure—in its unamended form it applies to suits alleging infringement occurring prior to March 1, 1989, and, subject to the alterations worked by the Berne Convention Implementation Act of 1988, it also applies to infringement actions for conduct occurring after March 1, 1989. In addition, however, it has already been noted that the 1976 Act preserved in several respects features of its predecessor, the 1909 Act.[43] Even during the 1990's and beyond, it may therefore be anticipated that reference will be necessary to the 1909 Act, for example to determine whether a given copyright notice sufficed to protect a work published in 1950.[44]

18–48 **Revisions to formalities.** The most important change made by the Berne Convention Implementation Act of 1988 was to eliminate the talismanic significance of copyright notice. After March 1, 1989, no longer does lack of notice threaten copyright subsistence, as it did immediately upon unnoticed publication under the 1909 Act, and five years after unnoticed publication with no intervening copyright registration under the 1976 Act. Although still advisable to affix copyright notice to published works in order to take advantage of the remedy of precluding a defence of innocent infringement in mitigation of damages, no penalty attaches to absence of notice (apart from ineligibility for the foregoing remedy).[45] Nonetheless, works published through February 28, 1989, are still governed by the original provisions of the 1976 Act. Therefore, even in a suit adjudicated in 1992, *i.e.* during the Berne era, the failure to affix notice to a work published (in the United States or abroad) in 1985 and never registered with the United States Copyright Office[46] will prove fatal to the plaintiff's claim.[47]

In addition to notice, the Berne Convention Implementation Act of 1988 modified the registration requirement.[48] During the Berne era, registration continues to afford a prima facie presumption of copyright validity and to make potentially available the remedies of statutory damages and attorney's fees.[49] However, as to unnoticed publications following March 1, 1989, given that notice is prospectively no longer required, registration cannot serve the purpose of curing omission of notice.[50] Finally, although registration continues to be a prerequisite for an American copyright proprietor to file suit, it is waived with respect to "Berne Convention works whose country of origin is not the United States."[51]

---

[43] *Ante,* § 18–39.
[44] See 2 *Nimmer on Copyright* § 7.02[C][3] (1989 edition).
[45] ss.401(*d*), 402(*d*) (added in 1989).
[46] Such registration must have taken place within five years after publication, *i.e.* no later than 1990. See s.405(*a*)(2). Thus, even though the text below explains that registration is nominally voluntary after March 1, 1989, the instant hypothetical reveals the necessity to register under certain circumstances even after that date.
[47] See 2 *Nimmer on Copyright* § 7.02[C] (1989 ed.).
[48] *Ante,* § 18–44.
[49] *Ibid.*
[50] *Ibid.* Note, however, that as to a work published without copyright notice *before* March 1, 1989, registration could continue to be required. See n. 46 *supra.*
[51] s.411(*a*). Lengthy definitions of "Berne Convention works" and "country of origin" have been added to the statute to give content to the instant exemption from registration. See s.101.

Last, the 1988 amendment eliminates the prerequisite of recordation of transfer formerly placed on copyright transferees.[52] Other copyright formalities are left unchanged, inasmuch as the manufacturing clause had already expired *ex proprio vigore* by the time of U.S. accession to the Berne Convention,[53] and the requirements of deposit of published works do not affect copyright subsistence.[54]

International provisions. Compared to the 1909 Act, the 1976 Act, particularly as augmented by the Berne Convention Implementation Act of 1988, affords greater international protection. First, as to unpublished works, the 1976 Act accords protection independent of the nationality of the author.[55] As to published works, the scope of potential coverage is expanded, but nationality can still be a factor. A work is protected if its author is, at the time of publication, a citizen or domiciliary of the United States or of another nation covered by a copyright treaty with the United States.[56] Even if this nationality requirement is not met, the work may be protected if first published in the United States, or in a country adhering either to the Berne Convention or the Universal Copyright Convention, or if the work comes within the scope of a Presidential proclamation. **18–49**

Thus, works in which publishers or others in the United Kingdom are interested can qualify for protection in the United States on a number of bases, including *any* of the following:

(1) authorship by a national or domiciliary of: (a) the United Kingdom, (b) the United States or (c) any other of the more than 80 countries with which the United States has copyright treaty relations.

(2) first publication in: (a) the United Kingdom, (b) the United States or (c) any of the member countries of the Berne Convention or Universal Copyright Convention.[57]

Retroactivity and moral rights. Article 18 of the Berne Convention nominally requires newly-adhering states to afford copyright protection to works still protected in their Berne countries of origin, even if those works previously had been considered in the newly-adhering state's public domain (other than through expiry of term).[58] Article 18 is subject to some leeway in terms of implementation; the United States has deliber- **18–50**

---

[52] *Ante*, § 18–43.

[53] *Ante*, § 18–46.

[54] *Ante*, § 18–13. Note in addition the requirement for renewal registration also persists after March 1, 1989, even with respect to Berne Convention works. *Ante*, § 18–42, n. 98.

[55] s.104(*a*).

[56] s.104(*b*). Also protected are works authored by a stateless person or foreign sovereign or published by the United Nations or the Organisation of American States.

[57] Such first publication must occur at a time when both the United States and the country of publication adhere to the subject Convention. Thus, publication in a Berne Convention country can secure U.S. copyright protection only after March 1, 1989, the date of American adherence. By like measure, publication in South Korea can secure U.S. copyright protection only following October 1, 1987, the date of Korean accession to the Universal Copyright Convention.

[58] S. Ricketson, *The Berne Convention for the Protection of Literary and Artistic Works: 1886–1986* 666 (1987) ("to exclude retroactivity altogether will work harshly against the foreign author, and deprive the new convention of much of its *raison d'être*").

ately chosen[59] a very broad policy of implementation, effectively granting no resurrection of works in the United States public domain as of February 28, 1989.[60]

Congress also chose, again quite consciously, not to alter U.S. law to comply with the moral rights provision of the Berne Convention, Article 6 *bis*. The 1988 amendment explicitly states that "The provisions of the Berne Convention, the adherence of the United States thereto, and satisfaction of United States obligations thereunder, do not expand or reduce any right of an author of a work" to claim a paternity or integrity right therein.[61] A fierce debate continues to rage over whether U.S. law, independent of Berne accession, accords sufficient recognition to the paternity and integrity rights to comply with Article 6 *bis*.[62] In any event, American membership in the Berne Union may hasten the growth of moral rights jurisprudence in the United States,[63] somewhat telescoping the British experience since Great Britain, who joined the Berne Convention (1887), took sixty years after the introduction of moral rights in the Rome version (1928), before legislating strong moral rights provisions (1988). Until then the only protection available was at common law and under section 43 of the United Kingdom Copyright Act of 1956.[64]

---

[59] H.R.Rep. No. 100–609, 100th Cong., 2d Sess. (1988), at 51–52.

[60] See Public Law 100–568, s.12.

[61] Public Law 100–568, s.3(*b*).

[62] Compare *Final Report of Ad Hoc Working Group on U.S. Adherence to the Berne Convention*, 10 Colum.-VLA J. L. & Arts 513, 547–57 (1986) *with* Damich, *Moral Rights in the United States and Article 6bis of the Berne Convention*, 10 Colum.-VLA J. L. & Arts 655, (1986).

[63] See 2 *Nimmer on Copyright* § 8.21[A][2][*b*] (1989 ed.).

[64] See Chap. 22 *post*.

2. General Table of Copyright Laws of Commonwealth and Foreign Countries[65]

Country	Date of Principal Law	Period of Protection	Convention or other protection for United Kingdom works		
			Berne [66] [67]	UNESCO [68]	Other
Afghanistan	1950	20 years from registration			None—local registration
Albania	1947	Life of the author and limited rights thereafter			None
Algeria	1973	25 years from beginning of calendar year following author's death		Paris*	
Andorra	None	Radio-Andorra regulated by private agreements		Geneva	
Argentina	1933	50 years from death of author	Paris B Brussels	Geneva	
Australia	1968	50 years from end of calendar year in which author died	Paris A	Paris	
Austria	1936	70 years from death of author	Paris A	Paris	
Bahamas	1956	50 years from end of calendar year in which author died	Paris B Brussels	Paris	

[65] In many cases the principal law has been amended or additional laws have been passed. Some countries have different terms for different works and different terms for foreign works. In some cases the period of protection has been extended. This Table is intended, therefore, as a general guide only and more detailed information can be obtained from *Copyright Laws and Treaties of the World*, published by UNESCO.

[66] For the purposes of this Table, countries which have ratified or acceded to the entire Paris revision of the Berne Convention, including the Appendix, are indicated thus "Paris A." Those countries which have declared that their ratification or accession does not apply to Arts. 1–21 and such Appendix are indicated thus "Paris B." Those countries which have given notification under Art. 38(1) are indicated thus "Paris C": unless they have later ratified the Paris Act. Those countries which have made a declaration under Art. 6(1)(ii) of such Appendix are indicated thus "Paris D." Countries which have availed themselves of the faculties in Arts. 2 and 3 of such Appendix are indicated thus "Paris E." Those countries which have made a declaration under Art. 5 of such Appendix are indicated thus "Paris F." Those countries which have made a declaration under Art. 14 *bis*(3) are indicated thus "Paris G." Those countries which have made a declaration under Art. 14 *bis*(2)(*c*) are indicated thus "Paris H."

[67] The substantive provisions of the Stockholm revision did not and cannot now come into force. However, previous conventions remain in force in relations with countries of the Union which do not ratify or accede to the Paris Act. In the case of countries who have ratified or acceded to the whole of the Paris Act and the Appendix, no reference is made to Stockholm or earlier revisions. Those countries which declared that their ratification or accession did not apply to Arts. 1–21 of the Stockholm revision and the Protocol Regarding Developing Countries, or ratified or acceded to the entire Stockholm revision, the substantive provisions of which have not come into force, are indicated thus "Stockholm B." Countries, other than those indicated as Paris A or Paris B, which have given notification under Art. 38(2) of the Stockholm revision are indicated thus "Stockholm C." For the position as to declarations as to the Protocol and other declarations see §§ 17–65, 17–66 and 17–67 *ante*.

[68] Countries which have ratified or acceded to the 1971 Convention are indicated thus "Paris"; others thus "Geneva." Countries which have availed themselves of the exceptions in favour of developing countries are indicated thus "Paris*."

Country	Date of Principal Law	Period of Protection	Convention or other protection for United Kingdom works		
			Berne [66] [67]	UNESCO [68]	Other
Bangladesh	1962	50 years from January 1, following the death of the author		Paris*	
Barbados	1981	Life of the author and 50 calendar years immediately following year of his death	Paris A	Paris	
Belgium	1886	50 years from death of author	Stockholm B, C, Brussels	Geneva	
Belize (British Honduras)	Uncertain	Uncertain		Geneva	
Benin (Dahomey)	1984	50 calendar years after end of year of author's death	Paris A		
Bolivia	1909	30 years from death of author			None—local registration and deposit
Brazil	1973	60 years from January 1 of year following death of author	Paris A	Paris	
Bulgaria	1951	50 years from January 1, following death of author	Paris A	Paris	
Burkina Faso (Upper Volta)	1983	50 years from end of calendar year in which author died	Paris A		
Burundi	1978	50 years from end of calendar year in which author died			Uncertain
Cambodia (Kampuchea)	1934	Uncertain		Geneva	
Cameroon	1982	50 years from end of calendar year in which author died	Paris A	Paris	
Canada	1952	50 years from death of author	Stockholm B Rome	Geneva	
Central African Republic (Empire)	1985	50 calendar years after end of year of author's death	Paris A		
Chad	Uncertain	Uncertain	Stockholm B Brussels		
Chile	1970	30 years from death of author	Paris A	Geneva	Local registration required
China	1990	December 31st of 50th year after author's death.			
Colombia	1982	80 years from death of author	Paris A	Paris	
Congo (People's Republic)	1982	50 years from December 31 of the year of the author's death	Paris A		
Costa Rica	1982	50 years from December 31 of year of author's death	Paris A	Paris	
Cuba	1977	25 years from January 1, of year following author's death		Geneva	

638

Country	Date of Principal Law	Period of Protection	Convention or other protection for United Kingdom works		
			Berne [66] [67]	UNESCO [68]	Other
Cyprus	1976	50 years from December 31, of the year of the author's death	Paris A, F		
Czechoslovakia	1965	50 years from December 31 of the year of the author's death	Paris A	Paris	
Denmark	1961	50 years from end of calendar year in which author died	Paris A	Paris	
Dominican Republic	1986	50 years from death of author		Paris	
Ecuador	1976	50 years from death of author		Geneva	
Egypt	1954	50 years from death of author	Paris A, E		
El Salvador	1963	50 years from death of author		Paris	
Ethiopia	1960	The life of the author and limited rights thereafter			None
Fiji	Uncertain	Uncertain	Stockholm B Brussels	Geneva	
Finland	1961	50 years from end of year in which author died	Paris A	Paris	
France	1957	50 (70 for musical works) years from December 31 of the year of the author's death	Paris A	Paris	
Gabon	1987	50 years from end of calendar year in which author died	Paris A		
German Democratic Republic (and Berlin (East)) [69]	1965	50 years from December 31 of year of author's death	Paris A	Paris	
German Federal Republic (and Berlin (West)) [70]	1965	70 years from end of calendar year in which author died	Paris A, D	Paris	
Ghana	1985	50 years from death of author		Geneva	
Greece	1920	50 years from December 31, of the year of the author's death	Paris A	Geneva	
Guatemala	1954	50 years from death of author		Geneva	
Guinea	1980	80 calendar years from end of year of author's death and thereafter domain public payant	Paris A, E	Paris	
Haiti	1968	Life of author and 25 years		Geneva	
Holy See	1960	The end of the 50th calendar year from the death of the author	Paris A	Paris	

Country	Date of Principal Law	Period of Protection	Convention or other protection for United Kingdom works		
			Berne [66] [67]	UNESCO [68]	Other
Honduras	1919	10, 15 or 20 years from issue of patent according to importance of work	Paris A		
Hungary	1969	50 years from death of author	Paris A	Paris	
Iceland	1972	50 years after year of author's death	Rome, Paris B	Geneva	
India	1957	50 years from January 1, following death of author	Paris A, C, E, G	Paris	
Indonesia	1982	50 years from death of author			Protection under local law
Iran	1970	30 years from death of author			Uncertain
Iraq	1971	25 years from death of author or 50 years from publication whichever is longer			Protection under local law
Ireland, Republic of	1963	50 years from December 31, of year of the author's death	Stockholm B Brussels	Geneva	
Israel	1911	70 years from January 1, following the death of the author or publication	Stockholm B Brussels	Geneva	
Italy	1941	The end of the 50th calendar year from the death of the author	Paris A	Paris	
Ivory Coast	1978	99 years from end of calendar year in which author died	Paris A		
Japan	1970	50 years from end of year of author's death	Paris A	Paris	
Jordan	1912	30 years from death of author			None
Kenya	1966	25 years from end of year in which author dies		Paris	
Korea (Republic of)	1986	50 years from January 1, following death of author		Paris*	
Lao People's Democratic Republic (Laos)	Uncertain	Uncertain		Geneva	
Lebanon	1924	50 years from death of author	Rome	Geneva	
Lesotho	1989	50 years after end of year in which author dies	Paris A, E		
Liberia	1972	25 years after death of author	Paris A, E	Geneva	
Libya	1968	25 years from death of author or 50 years from first publication whichever is the longer	Paris A		
Liechtenstein	1928	50 years from death of author	Stockholm B Brussels	Geneva	

Country	Date of Principal Law	Period of Protection	Convention or other protection for United Kingdom works		
			Berne [66] [67]	UNESCO [68]	Other
Luxembourg	1972	50 years from January 1, following the death of author	Paris A	Geneva	
Madagascar (Malagasy Republic)	1957	50 years from end of year in which author died	Brussels		
Malawi	1989	End of 50th calendar year after year in which author died		Geneva	
Malaysia	1987	50 years from death of author	Paris A, E		Protection under local law
Mali	1977	50 years from death of author	Paris A		
Malta	1967	25 years after end of year in which author dies	Paris B, Rome	Geneva	
Mauritania	Uncertain	Uncertain	Paris A		
Mauritius	1986	50 years after end of year in which author dies	Paris A, E	Geneva	
Mexico	1956	50 years from death of author	Paris A, E	Paris*	
Monaco	1948	50 years from death of author	Paris A	Paris	
Morocco	1970	50 years from the end of the year in which author died	Paris A	Paris	
Nepal	1966	50 years from death of author			None—local registration
Netherlands	1912	50 years from January 1, of year after death of author	Paris A	Paris	
New Zealand	1962	50 years from the end of calendar year in which author died	Rome	Geneva	
Nicaragua	1904	Life of the author with limited rights thereafter		Geneva	
Niger	Uncertain	Uncertain	Paris A, E	Paris	
Nigeria	1988	70 years from the end of the calendar year in which author died		Geneva	
Norway	1961	50 years from end of the year of death of author	Paris B, D Brussels	Paris	
Pakistan	1962	50 years from January 1, following the death of the author	Stockholm B Rome	Geneva	
Panama	1916	80 years from death of author		Paris	
Paraguay	1985	50 years from death of author		Geneva	
Peru	1961	50 years from January 1, following the death of the author	Paris A	Paris	
Philippines	1972	50 years from January 1, following the death of author	Paris B Brussels	Geneva	
Poland	1952	25 years from death of author	Paris B	Paris	

Country	Date of Principal Law	Period of Protection	Convention or other protection for United Kingdom works		
			Berne [66] [67]	UNESCO [68]	Other
Portugal	1985	January 1 next after 50 years from death of author	Paris A, H	Paris	
Rumania	1956	The life of the author and limited rights thereafter	Stockholm B Rome		
Rwanda	1983	50 years from the death of the author	Paris A	Paris	
Saint Vincent and the Grenadines	Uncertain	Uncertain		Paris .	
Saudi Arabia	1989	50 years from death of author			Protection under local law
Senegal	1973	50 calendar years from end of year of author's death	Paris A	Paris	
Sierra Leone	1965	50 years from the end of the calendar year in which the author died			Protection under local law
Singapore	1987	50 years after expiration of calendar year in which author died			Uncertain
South Africa	1978	50 years from the end of the year in which the author died	Paris B, Brussels		
Spain	1987	60 years from January 1, following the death of the author	Paris A	Paris	
Sri Lanka (Ceylon)	1979	50 years from end of calender year in which author died	Paris B Rome	Paris	
Sudan	1974	25 years from death of author			Uncertain
Surinam	Uncertain	Uncertain	Paris A, E		
Sweden	1960	End of 50th year after year in which author died	Paris A	Paris	
Switzerland	1922	50 years from death of author	Stockholm B Brussels	Geneva	
Syria	1924	50 years from death of author			None—local deposit
Tanzania	1966	25 years from death of author			Protection under local law
Thailand	1978	50 years from end of calendar year in which author died	Paris B Berlin		
Togo	Uncertain	Uncertain	Paris A		
Tonga	1985	50 years from end of calendar year in which author died			Protection under local law
Trinidad and Tobago	1985	50 years following calendar year of author's death	Paris A	Paris	
Tunisia	1966	50 years from death of author	Paris A, E	Paris*	
Turkey	1951	50 years from death of author	Brussels		

Country	Date of Principal Law	Period of Protection	Convention or other protection for United Kingdom works		
			Berne [66] [67]	UNESCO [68]	Other Protection under local law
Uganda	1964	50 years from end of year in which author dies			
United States of America	1976	For works created on or after January 1, 1978, life of the author and 50 years expiring at end of calendar year[71]	Paris A	Paris	
U.S.S.R.	1964	25 years from January 1, of year after death of author		Geneva	
Uruguay	1937	40 years from death of author	Paris A		
Venezuela	1962	50 years from January 1, of year after death of author	Paris A	Geneva	
Yugoslavia	1978	50 years from January 1 following death of author	Paris A	Paris	
Zaire (Congo (Kinshasa))	1986	50 calendar years following year of author's death	Paris A		
Zambia	1965	25 years from death of author		Geneva	
Zimbabwe	Uncertain	Uncertain	Paris B Rome		

[69] See n.73 § 17–68 *ante* as to the copyright position as a result of the unification of West and East Germany on October 3, 1990.

[70] *Ibid*. n.66.

[71] See §§ 18–8 and 18–24 *ante*.

CRIMINAL PROCEEDINGS

Contents

1. Criminal Proceedings for Infringement of Copyright

A. Old law

19–1 The 1911 Act imposed certain summary remedies for infringement of copyright and also maintained unrepealed certain earlier Acts imposing summary remedies in respect of dealings with musical works. These Acts were repealed by the 1956 Act. The only summary proceedings in respect of infringement were those contained in section 21 of the 1956 Act. That section was subsequently amended by the Copyright Act 1956 (Amendment) Act 1982 and the Copyright (Amendment) Act 1983. That section is now repealed and replaced by section 107 of the 1988 Act. Section 21 of the 1956 Act, as amended, continues to apply in relation to acts done before commencement. The provisions of section 107 apply only in relation to acts done after commencement.[1]

B. *Section 107 of the 1988 Act*

(i) Prohibited acts

19–2   A person commits an offence who, without the licence of the copyright owner,[2] does various acts in relation to an article which is, and which he knows or has reason to believe is, an infringing copy[3] of a copyright work. The prohibited acts are making for sale or hire[4]; importing into the United Kingdom otherwise than for his private and domestic use[5]; possessing in the course of a business with a view to committing any act infringing the copyright[6]; in the course of a business selling or letting for hire, offering or exposing for sale or hire, exhibiting in public or distributing[7]; distributing otherwise than in the course of a business to such an extent as to affect prejudicially the owner of the copyright.[8] A sale is made when there is an offer, an acceptance and an agreed price. The court examines objectively what passed between the parties, not their subjective intentions.[9]

19–3   Other offences are committed by a person who knows or has reason to believe that an article is to be used to make infringing copies for sale or hire or for use in the course of a business. Those offences are committed by a person who makes an article specifically designed or adapted for making copies of a particular copyright work[10] or has such an article in his possession.[11]

19–4   Criminal offences may also be committed in relation to the public performance of works. Where copyright is infringed (otherwise than by reception of a broadcast or cable programme) by the public performance of a literary, dramatic or musical work or by the playing or showing in public of a sound recording or film, any person who caused the work to be so performed, played or shown is guilty of an offence if he knew, or had reason to believe, that copyright would be infringed.[12] This appears to be directed against the person responsible for the performance and not against the actual performer.

---

[1] C.D.P.A. 1988, Sched. 1 para. 33(1).
[2] C.D.P.A. 1988, ss.173 and 101(2).
[3] See § 19–5 *et seq., post.*
[4] C.D.P.A. 1988, s.107(1)(*a*).
[5] *Ibid.* s.107(1)(*b*).
[6] *Ibid.* s.107(1)(*c*).
[7] *Ibid.* s.107(1)(*d*)(i)–(iv).
[8] *Ibid.* s.107(1)(*e*).
[9] *Phillips* v. *Holmes* [1988] R.P.C. 613. (A decision on s.21(1)(*b*), of the 1956 Act.)
[10] C.D.P.A. 1988, s.107(2)(*a*).
[11] *Ibid.* s.107(2)(*b*).
[12] *Ibid.* s.107(3)(*a*), (*b*).

(ii) The meaning of "infringing copy"

For the purposes of these provisions, an article is an infringing copy if its **19–5** making constituted an infringement of the copyright in the work in question.[13] An article is also an infringing copy if it has been or is proposed to be imported into the United Kingdom and its making in the United Kingdom would have constituted an infringement of the copyright in the work in question, or a breach of an exclusive licence agreement[14] relating to that work.[15] This is not so, however, in the case of an article which may lawfully be imported into the United Kingdom by virtue of any enforceable Community right within the meaning of section 2(1) of the European Communities Act 1972.[16]

Infringing copy also includes a copy falling to be treated as an infring- **19–6** ing copy by virtue of other provisions relating to copies[17] made for purposes of instruction or examination[18]; recordings made by educational establishments for purposes of instruction[19]; reprographic copying by educational establishments for purposes of instruction[20]; copies made by a librarian or archivist in reliance on a false declaration[21]; further copies and adaptations of a work in electronic form retained on transfer of the principal copy[22]; copies made for the purpose of advertising artistic works for sale[23]; copies made for purpose of broadcast or cable programme[24] and provision for a statutory licence for certain reprographic copying by educational establishments.[25]

(iii) Proof

Certain presumptions assist proof in criminal proceedings. Where in any **19–7** proceedings (civil or criminal) the question arises whether an article is an infringing copy and it is shown, first, that the article is a copy of the work and, secondly, that copyright subsists in the work or has subsisted at any time, it is presumed, until the contrary is proved, that the article was made at a time when copyright subsisted in the work.[26]

The presumptions as to various matters connected with copyright contained in sections 104 to 106[27] of the 1988 Act do not, however, apply to proceedings for an offence under section 107 of that Act.[28] They do, how-

---

[13] C.D.P.A. 1988, s.27(1), (2).
[14] *Ibid.* s.92(1).
[15] *Ibid.* s.27(3)(a), (b). See § 5–44 *et seq., ante.*
[16] *Ibid.* s.27(5).
[17] *Ibid.* s.27(6).
[18] *Ibid.* s.32(5).
[19] *Ibid.* s.35(3).
[20] *Ibid.* s.36(5).
[21] *Ibid.* s.37(3)(b).
[22] *Ibid.* s.56(2).
[23] *Ibid.* s.63(2).
[24] *Ibid.* s.68(4).
[25] *Ibid.* s.141.
[26] *Ibid.* s.27(4).
[27] See § 11–86 *et seq., ante.*
[28] C.D.P.A. 1988, s.107(6).

ever, apply to proceedings for an order for delivery up in criminal proceedings made under section 108.[29]

(iv) Penalties

19–8 A person guilty of the offence of making articles for sale or hire, or importing them into the United Kingdom otherwise than for his private and domestic use or distributing them in the course of a business or otherwise to such an extent as to affect prejudicially the owner of the copyright, is liable to substantial penalties. On summary conviction such a person is liable to imprisonment for a term not exceeding six months or a fine not exceeding the statutory maximum or both.[30] On conviction on indictment he is liable to a fine or imprisonment for a term not exceeding two years or both. A person guilty of any other offence under section 107 of the 1988 Act is liable on summary conviction to imprisonment for a term not exceeding six months or a fine not exceeding level five on the standard scale or both.[31]

(v) Order for delivery up

19–9 The Court before which proceedings are brought against a person for an offence under section 107 of the 1988 Act may order that the infringing copy or article be delivered up to the copyright owner or to such other person as the Court may direct.[32]

19–10 Before this jurisdiction can be exercised the Court must first be satisfied that at the time of his arrest or charge the person had in his possession, custody or control in the course of a business an infringing copy of a copyright work or[33] that he had in his possession, custody or control an article specifically designed or adapted for making copies of a particular copyright work.[34] In the latter case the Court must also be satisfied that the person knew or had reason to believe that the article had been or was to be used to make infringing copies.[35]

A person is treated as charged with an offence when he is orally charged or is served with a summons or indictment.[36]

An order may be made by the Court of its own motion or on the application of the prosecutor.[37] An order may also be made whether or not the person is convicted of the offence.[38]

---

[29] See § 19–28 *et seq., post.*
[30] C.D.P.A. 1988, s.107(4).
[31] *Ibid.* s.107(5); s.37 Criminal Justice Act 1982 (c.48).
[32] *Ibid.* s.108(1).
[33] *Ibid.* s.108(1)(a).
[34] *Ibid.* s.108(1)(b).
[35] See n. 34, *ante.*
[36] C.D.P.A. 1988, s.108(2)(a); if in Scotland, when he is cautioned, charged or served with a complaint or indictment.
[37] *Ibid.* s.108(3); or in Scotland, on the application of the Lord Advocate or procurator fiscal.
[38] *Ibid.* s.108(3).

There are, however, restrictions on the Court's powers to make a   **19–11**
delivery up order. First, the Court cannot make an order after the end of
the period of six years from the date on which the infringing copy or article
in question was made. This is subject to extension of the period in cases of
disability or concealed fraud.[39] Secondly, the Court cannot make an order
if it appears to the Court unlikely that any order will be made as to disposal of the infringing copy or other article.[40]

If a delivery up order is made and complied with, the person to whom   **19–12**
the infringing copy or other article is delivered up in pursuance of the
order must retain it pending the making of a disposal order, or the
decision not to make a disposal order.[41]
 An appeal lies to the Crown Court from a delivery up order made by a
magistrates' court.[42]
 The powers conferred to order delivery up are additional to other statutory powers of the Court as to forfeiture in criminal proceedings.[43]

(vi) Search warrants

Search warrants may be issued authorising a constable to enter and   **19–13**
search premises, using such reasonable force as is necessary.[44] The warrant may authorise persons to accompany any constable executing the
warrant.[45] It remains in force for 28 days from the date of its issue.[46]

A warrant is issued by a justice of the peace on information on oath   **19–14**
given by a constable.[47] The information must satisfy him that there are
reasonable grounds for believing that an offence has been committed
under the provisions relating to the sale, hire, importation or distribution
of infringing copies or is about to be committed in any premises.[48] He
must also be satisfied that evidence that such an offence has been or is
about to be committed is in those premises.[49]
 "Premises" includes land, buildings, moveable structures, vehicles, aircraft and hovercraft.[50]

---

[39] C.D.P.A. 1988, s.108(3)(a). The period is that specified in s.113.
[40] *Ibid.* s.108(3)(b). Disposal orders are made under s.114: see § 11–77 *et seq.*, *ante*.
[41] *Ibid.* s.108(5).
[42] *Ibid.* s.108(4)(a). In Northern Ireland an appeal lies to the county court and in Scotland
   appeal may be made in the same manner as against sentence.
[43] *Ibid.* s.108(6). Other powers are conferred on the Court by s.43 of the Powers of Criminal
   Courts Act, 1973; ss.223 and 436 of the Criminal Procedure (Scotland) Act 1975; and
   Article 7 of the Criminal Justice (Northern Ireland) Order, 1980.
[44] *Ibid.* s.109(1).
[45] *Ibid.* s.109(3)(a).
[46] *Ibid.* s.109(3)(b).
[47] *Ibid.* s.109(1).
[48] *Ibid.* s.109(1)(a).
[49] *Ibid.* s.109(1)(b).
[50] *Ibid.* s.109(5).

19–15   The power to issue a search warrant does not extend to authorising a search for certain classes of personal or confidential material.[51] In executing a warrant a constable may seize an article if he reasonably believes that it is evidence that any offence has been or is about to be committed under section 107(1) of the 1988 Act.[52] These provisions apply in relation to offences committed before commencement (1st August 1989) in relation to which section 21A or 21B of the 1956 Act applied. The latter provisions continue to apply, however, in relation to warrants issued before commencement.[53]

(vii) Liability of officers of body corporate

19–16   Where an offence under section 107 of the 1988 Act committed by a body corporate is proved to have been committed with the consent or connivance of a director, manager, secretary or other similar officer of the body, or a person purporting to act in any such capacity, he as well as the body corporate is guilty of the offence.[54] He is liable to be proceeded against and punished. In relation to a body corporate whose affairs are managed by its members "director" means a member of the body corporate.[55]

C. Other offences

19–17   Apart from the offences created by section 107 of the 1988 Act, it is also possible to prosecute offenders for a statutory conspiracy. If a person agrees with any other person that a course of conduct shall be pursued which will necessarily involve the commission of any offence by one or more of the parties to the agreement if the agreement is carried out in accordance with their intention, he is guilty of conspiring to commit the offence in question.[56] Whenever a conspiracy, if carried into execution, would involve the commission of a substantive offence (for example, under section 107 of the 1988 Act) the offence committed is a statutory conspiracy and should be indicted as such rather than as a common law conspiracy to defraud.[57] In those circumstances it is improper to pursue a common law conspiracy to defraud, even if the offence involves an element of fraud[58] and a fortiori where there is no necessary connotation of fraud. Thus, it was held that where there was a conspiracy under which a cinema projectionist temporarily removed feature films from a cinema to lend to others to make master video tape copies of them and then returned them, it was not indictable as a common law conspiracy to defraud since the conspiracy, if carried into execution, involved the commission of a substantive offence under section 21 of the 1956 Act.[59] It was also held that

---

[51] C.D.P.A. 1988, s.109(2) The material is of the kinds mentioned in s.9(2) of the Police and Criminal Evidence Act 1984.

[52] *Ibid.* s.109(4).

[53] *Ibid.* Sched. 1, para. 33(2).

[54] *Ibid.* s.110(1).

[55] *Ibid.* s.110(2).

[56] s.1(1) of the Criminal Law Act 1977.

[57] *R. v. Lloyd* [1985] Q.B. 829 at 838.

[58] *R. v. Ayres* [1984] A.C. 447 at 455.

[59] *R. v. Lloyd (supra).*

there was no statutory conspiracy to steal the films in question because the intention was to deprive the owners of the films temporarily and not permanently.[60]

2. Seizure of Imported Copies

A. Notice procedure

Section 111 of the 1988 Act gives to the owner of the copyright in any pub-   **19–18**
lished literary, dramatic or musical work, the right to give notice to the Commissioners of Customs and Excise requesting them to treat as prohibited goods printed copies of the work which are infringing copies.[61] The notice must state that he is the owner of the copyright in the work and specify the period during which the goods are to be treated as prohibited. The period must not exceed five years, and shall not extend beyond the period for which the copyright is to subsist.[62] The owner of the copyright in a sound recording or film may also give a notice in writing to the Commissioners with a view to preventing importation of infringing copies. The notice must state these matters: first, that the person giving the notice is the owner of the copyright in the work; secondly, that infringing copies of the work are expected to arrive in the United Kingdom at a time and a place specified in the notice, and thirdly, that he requests the Commissioners to treat the copies as prohibited goods.[63] An article is an infringing copy if its making constituted an infringement of copyright or, in the case of articles imported or proposed to be imported into the United Kingdom, its making in the United Kingdom would have constituted an infringement of copyright or breach of an exclusive licence agreement.[64]

When a notice under section 111 of the 1988 Act is in force, the importation of goods to which the notice relates is prohibited. The prohibition does not, however, render a person liable to any penalty other than forfeiture of the goods.[65] The restriction on importation is not to apply to the importation of any article by a person for his private and domestic use.[66]

B. Power of Commissioners to make regulations

The Commissioners are empowered to make regulations prescribing the   **19–19**
form in which notice is to be given and requiring a person giving notice, either at the time of giving the notice, or at the time when the goods are

---

[60] *R.* v. *Lloyd* (*supra*): s.1(1) of the Theft Act 1968. As to alleged tortious conspiracy to injure see *Jarman & Platt Ltd.* v. *I. Barget Ltd.* [1977] F.S.R. 260. *Lonrho* v. *Shell Petroleum Co. Ltd. (No. 2)* [1982] A.C. 173; *Metall und Rohstoff A.G.* v. *Donaldson Lufkin & Jenrette Inc.* [1990] 1 Q.B. 391; *Derby & Co.* v. *Weldon (No. 5)* [1989] 1 W.L.R. 1244. As to criminal conspiracy see also *R.* v. *Willetts* (1906) 70 J.P. 127; *R.* v. *Bokenham, The Times,* July 22, 1910.
[61] C.D.P.A. 1988, s.111(1).
[62] *Ibid.* s.111(2).
[63] *Ibid.* s.111(3).
[64] *Ibid.* s.27(1), (2), (3). See s.27(5) as to importation from EEC countries.
[65] *Ibid.* s.111(4).
[66] See n. 65, *ante.*

imported, or at both those times, to furnish the Commissioners with such evidence, and to comply with such other conditions (if any), as may be specified in the regulations.[67] It is further provided that the regulations may provide for the payment of fees or the giving of security to the Commissioners in respect of any liability or expense which they may incur in consequence of the detention and for keeping the Commissioners, whether security is given or not, indemnified against any such liability or expense.[68] The regulations, made by statutory instrument subject to annulment in pursuance of a resolution of either House of Parliament, may make different provision as respects different classes of case to which they apply. Regulations have been made and are now in force.[69] They include such incidental and supplementary provisions as the Commissioners consider expedient.[70]

19–20 **Importance of this remedy.** In view of the fact that, under the 1956 and 1988 Acts, an imported copy of a work, which would have infringed copyright if made in the United Kingdom, is an infringing copy, without the necessity of proving that the importer knew that it would be an infringement,[71] this method of restricting importation of infringing material is probably of less importance than it was prior to the commencement of the 1956 Act. It affords, however, a simple method of enabling an English publisher or record or film producer to prevent the flooding of his market with cheap foreign copies. Such copies may well have been made under licence for sale abroad, but they can still be restricted under these provisions, if imported, provided that the licence did not cover manufacture or sale in England.[72]

C. Action for discovery

19–21 An action for discovery for the purpose of obtaining the names and addresses of importers of infringing copies can be brought against the Commissioners of Customs and Excise even though there is no cause of action for infringement against the Commissioners themselves. The jurisdiction of the court to order the disclosure of the identity of infringers is based on the general principle that a person, albeit innocently and without incurring personal liability, is under a duty, if involved in the tortious acts of others, to assist the person injured by giving him full information by way of discovery and disclosing the identity of wrongdoers. This duty exists even though the Commissioners' involvement is in consequence of the performance of a statutory duty.[73]

---

[67] C.D.P.A. 1988, s.112(1).
[68] *Ibid.* s.112(2).
[69] *Ibid.* s.112(3), (4); see the Copyright (Customs) Regulations S.I. 1989, No. 1178. See § B–168, *post.*
[70] See n. 69, *ante.*
[71] s.27(3): see s.27(5) and Ch. 14, § 14–36 *et seq., post* on imports from EEC countries. See also *C.B.S. United Kingdom Ltd.* v. *Charmdale Record Distributors Ltd.* [1980] F.S.R. 289.
[72] See n. 71, *ante.*
[73] *Norwich Pharmacal* v. *Customs and Excise Commissioners* [1974] A.C. 133; *British Steel Corporation* v. *Granada Television Ltd.* [1981] A.C. 1096. See also § 11–52 *et seq., ante.*

3. Infringement of Performers' Rights

A. General

The 1988 Act also imposes criminal liability for making, dealing with or **19–22**
using illicit recordings in relation to performances and empowers the
Court in criminal proceedings to make delivery up and disposal orders.[74]
These provisions replace the Performers' Protection Acts 1958–1972
which have been repealed.[75]

B. Criminal liability

(i) Prohibited acts

A person commits an offence who, without sufficient consent, does a pro- **19–23**
hibited act in relation to a recording which is, and which he knows or has
reason to believe is, an illicit recording.[76] Thus, a person commits an
offence if he does any of the following acts in those circumstances:

(1) makes for sale or hire; or

(2) imports into the United Kingdom otherwise than for his private
and domestic use; or

(3) possesses in the course of a business with a view to committing any
act infringing the rights conferred by Part II; or

(4) in the course of a business sells or lets for hire, or offers or exposes
for sale or hire, or distributes an illicit recording.[77]

A person also commits an offence who causes a recording of a perfor- **19–24**
mance made without sufficient consent to be shown or played in public or
broadcast or included in a cable programme service, thereby infringing
any of the rights conferred by Part II of the 1988 Act, if he knows or has
reason to know that those rights are thereby infringed.[78] A person guilty of
an offence of making for sale or hire, or importation or distribution of an
illicit recording is liable on summary conviction to imprisonment for a
term not exceeding six months or to a fine not exceeding the statutory
maximum, or both. He is liable on conviction on indictment to a fine or
imprisonment for a term not exceeding two years or both.[79] A person
guilty of any other offence is liable on summary conviction to a fine not
exceeding level five on the standard scale or imprisonment for a term not
exceeding six months, or both.[80]

---

[74] C.D.P.A. 1988, ss.198–205; see Ch. 23 on Performers' rights and recording rights generally.
[75] *Ibid.* s.303(2), Sched. 8.
[76] *Ibid.* s.198(1): see s.197(1) for meaning of illicit recording and §23–41 *post.*
[77] *Ibid.* s.198(1)(*a*)–(*d*).
[78] *Ibid.* s.198(2).
[79] *Ibid.* s.198(5).
[80] *Ibid.* s.198(6).

(ii) Permitted acts

19–25 No offence is committed by the commission of an act which, by virtue of any provision of Schedule 2 of the 1988 Act, may be done without infringing the rights conferred by Part II of that Act.[81]

(iii) Sufficient consent

19–26 No offence is committed if the person has "sufficient consent." This is to be compared and contrasted with the consent required in order to avoid civil liability for infringement of performers' rights.[82]

19–27 "Sufficient consent" in the case of a qualifying performance means the consent of the performer.[83] In the case of a non-qualifying performance subject to an exclusive recording contract, a distinction is drawn between the making of the recording, for which the consent of the performer or the person having the recording right is sufficient consent,[84] and dealing with or using the recording, in which case the consent of the person having recording rights is sufficient.[85]

The relevant person having recording rights is the person having those rights at the time the consent is given or, if there is more than one such person, all of them.[86]

An exclusive recording contract may cover non-qualifying as well as qualifying performances. The definition is such that it relates simply to the performances of performers.[87]

(iv) Order for delivery up

19–28 The Court may in appropriate circumstances make an order for the delivery up of an illicit recording. This does not affect the powers of the Court under other legislation for the forfeiture of property in criminal proceedings.[88]

19–29 The order may be made by the Court before which proceedings are brought against a person for an offence under section 198 of the 1988 Act. If satisfied that, at the time of his arrest or charge, that person had in his possession, custody or control in the course of a business an illicit recording of a performance, the Court may order that the illicit recording be delivered up to a person having performers' rights or recording rights in relation to the performance or to such other person as the Court may

---

[81] C.D.P.A. 1988, s.198(4). See §23–64 *et seq., post.*
[82] See *ibid.* s.182(1), s.183(1), s.184(1), s.186(1), s.187(1), s.188(1).
[83] *Ibid.* s.198(3)(*a*).
[84] *Ibid.* s.198(3)(*b*)(i).
[85] *Ibid.* s.198(3)(*b*)(ii).
[86] *Ibid.* s.198(3).
[87] *Ibid.* s.185(1).
[88] *Ibid.* s.199(6). See s.43 of the Power of Criminal Courts Act, 1973; ss.223 and 436 of the Criminal Procedure (Scotland) Act, 1975; Article 7 of the Criminal Justice (Northern Ireland) Order, 1980.

direct.[89] The person to whom an illicit recording is delivered up by such an order must retain it pending the making of the disposal order or,[90] the decision not to make such an order.[91]

A person is treated as charged with an offence if he is orally charged or is served with a summons or indictment.[92]

There is a limitation period. An order for delivery up shall not be made **19–30** in any case after the end of the period of six years from the date on which the illicit recording in question was made.[93]

A delivery up order may be made by the Court of its own motion. It **19–31** may also be made on the application of the prosecutor.[94] The order may be made whether or not the person is convicted of the offence.[95] A delivery up order shall not be made, however, in two cases: first, after the end of the six-year limitation period for the remedy of delivery up[96]; secondly, it shall not be made if it appears to the Court unlikely that any disposal order will be made.[97]

An appeal lies from a delivery up order made by a Magistrates' Court to the Crown Court.[98]

(v) Disposal orders

The Court may make disposal orders in respect of illicit recordings **19–32** delivered up in pursuance of a delivery up order made in criminal proceedings.[99]

(vi) Search warrants

A search warrant may be issued by a Justice of the Peace (or, in Scotland, **19–33** a Sheriff or a Justice of the Peace), authorising a constable to enter and search premises, using such reasonable force as is necessary.[1] The warrant remains in force for 28 days from the date of its issue.[2] Before the warrant is issued the Justice of the Peace must be satisfied that there are reasonable grounds for belief as to two matters: first, that an offence of making, importing or distributing illicit recordings has been, or is about to be, committed in any premises; and, secondly, that evidence that such an

---

[89] C.D.P.A. 1988, s.199(1).

[90] Under *ibid.* s.204.

[91] *Ibid.* s.199(5).

[92] *Ibid.* s.199(2); or, in Scotland when he is cautioned, charged or served with a complaint or indictment: s.199(2)(*b*).

[93] *Ibid.* s.203(4).

[94] *Ibid.* s.199(3); or in Scotland on the application of the Lord Advocate or procurator-fiscal.

[95] *Ibid.* s.199(3).

[96] *Ibid.* s.199(3)(*a*): see s.203.

[97] *Ibid.* s.199(3)(*b*): see s.204.

[98] *Ibid.* s.199(4); or, in Northern Ireland, in the county court; or in Scotland in the same manner as appeal against sentence.

[99] *Ibid.* s.204(1) see § 23–97 *et seq., post.*

[1] *Ibid.* s.200(1).

[2] *Ibid.* s.200(3)(*b*).

offence has been or is about to be committed is in the premises.[3] "Premises" includes land, buildings, fixed or moveable structures, vehicles, vessels, aircraft and hovercraft.[4] The warrant may authorise persons to accompany the constable executing the warrant.[5] The power does not extend to authorising a search for certain classes of personal or confidential material.[6]

(vii) False representation of authority

19–34   It is also an offence for a person to represent falsely that he is authorised by any person to give consent for the purposes of Part II of the 1988 Act in relation to a performance. No offence is committed if the person making the representation believed on reasonable grounds that he was so authorised.[7]

A person guilty of this offence is liable on summary conviction to imprisonment for a term not exceeding six months or a fine not exceeding level five on the standard scale or both.[8]

(viii) Liability of officers for offences committed by bodies corporate

19–35   Where an offence is committed by a body corporate and it is proved to have been committed with the consent or connivance of a director, manager, secretary, or other similar officer of the body, or a person purporting to act in any such capacity, he, as well as the body corporate, is guilty of the offence and liable to be proceeded against and punished accordingly.[9] In relation to a body corporate whose affairs are managed by its members, "director" means a member of the body corporate.[10]

(ix) Courts

19–36   In England, Wales and Northern Ireland a County Court may entertain proceedings for a delivery up order and a disposal order where the value of the illicit recordings in question does not exceed the County Court limit for actions in tort.[11] In Scotland proceedings for a delivery up order or a disposal order may be brought in the Sheriffs Court.[12] These provisions do not effect the jurisdiction of the High Court or, in Scotland, the Court of Session.[13]

---

[3] C.D.P.A. 1988, s.200(1)(*a*), (*b*).
[4] *Ibid.* s.200(4).
[5] *Ibid.* s.200(3)(*a*).
[6] *Ibid.* s.200(2): see s.9(2) of the Police and Criminal Evidence Act 1984.
[7] *Ibid.* s.201(1).
[8] *Ibid.* s.201(2).
[9] *Ibid.* s.202(1).
[10] *Ibid.* s.202(2).
[11] *Ibid.* s.205(1).
[12] *Ibid.* s.205(2).
[13] *Ibid.* s.205(3).

RELATED FORMS OF PROTECTION—1
INDUSTRIAL DESIGNS

1. Interrelation of Copyright, Registered Design and Design Right protection

A. *Position before the 1988 Act*

20–1   The 1911 and 1956 Acts. As it had generally been considered that it was not within the proper field of artistic copyright to protect purely industrial designs, measures were taken, both under the 1911 Act and the 1956 Act, to limit artistic copyright in this respect and to secure that works of this class should receive protection under the Designs Acts.[1] Under the latter Acts, protection is only afforded to works in respect of which a design is registered and the term of protection is much shorter. On the other hand, registration under the Designs Acts gives an exclusive right to make use of the registered design and not merely, as under the Copyright Acts, a right to prevent copying. The method adopted in the two Copyright Acts of limiting artistic copyright in this connection was, however, entirely different. Under the 1911 Act, works were excluded altogether from artistic copyright, if capable of registration under the Designs Acts and if intended for use as a model or pattern for industrial production.[2] However, the 1956 Act adopted a different approach[3] and, whilst permitting full artistic copyright to subsist in works, put limits upon the acts which could constitute an infringement of that copyright where a corresponding design was registered, or the design was applied industrially and no design was registered. Subject to these limits, full copyright protection was retained. But, since the copyright protection was only qualified from the date of use (or registration), it was necessary to amend the Registered Designs Act 1949 so that prior publication as a purely artistic work should not prevent registration as a design when such use was first contemplated.[4]

20–2   Design Copyright Act 1968. Notwithstanding the Report of the Designs Committee 1962,[5] which, by a majority, favoured the continuation of the 1956 Act system of cutting down artistic copyright where a design was used for industrial purposes with the consent of the copyright owner, in October 1968 the Design Copyright Act 1968[6] was enacted, which radically changed the position of industrial designs under the 1956 Act. Thus, instead of cutting down the artistic copyright in designs actually used for industrial purposes, or in respect of which a design had been registered, the 1968 Act amended section 10 of the 1956 Act in such a way that the 1956 Act allowed full artistic copyright to such designs for a limited time,

---

[1] For an examination of the interrelation of copyright and registered designs, see *British Leyland Motor Corp.* v. *Armstrong Patents Co. Ltd.* [1986] R.P.C. 279 (H.L.).
[2] Copyright Act 1911, s.22(1).
[3] Copyright Act 1956, s.10, before amendment.
[4] *Ibid.* s.44.
[5] Cmnd. 808.
[6] c. 68.

even if used for industrial purposes and even if a design was registered. However, the 1968 Act did not contain any transitional provisions and, therefore, the scope of its operation was not clear.[7]

B. *Position after the 1988 Act*

Report of Copyright and Designs Committee 1977. The terms of reference of this committee were to consider and report whether any, and if so what, changes were desirable in the law relating to copyright as provided in particular by the 1956 Act and the 1968 Act, including the desirability of retaining the system of protection of industrial designs provided by the Registered Designs Act 1949. The basic and unanimous recommendation in its Report[8] was that registered design monopoly protection, as provided by the Registered Designs Act 1949, should be repealed. However, the 1986 White Paper[9] not only proposed retention of registered design protection, although limited to genuinely aesthetic designs, but also the introduction of a new unregistered design right.   **20–3**

The 1988 Act. The 1988 Act follows the White Paper proposals and, as a result, there now exist, side by side, three possible forms of protection, namely copyright, registered design and unregistered design right.[10] Further, artistic copyright, except in respect of old designs, is no longer concerned with any considerations involving the registration of designs, although the 1988 Act does contain certain general limitations on the copyright in new designs.[11] However, design right only subsists where a design has been recorded in a design document or an article has been made to the design after the commencement of the 1988 Act (August 1, 1989),[12] and where copyright subsists in a work which consists of or includes a design in which design right subsists, it is not an infringement of design right in the design to do anything which is an infringement of the copyright in that work.[13]   **20–4**

Transitional provisions. Although, as has been mentioned, for the future, copyright is no longer limited by any considerations involving the registration of designs, the pre-1988 Act position has been preserved by the 1988 Act in respect of artistic works created before June 1, 1957 and, to a limited extent, the pre-1988 Act position is still relevant to works created after June 1, 1957 and before August 1, 1989. It is therefore still necessary to consider, in some detail, what was the position in respect of works created before August 1, 1989.   **20–5**

---

[7] See § 20–35, *post.*
[8] Cmnd. 6732, paras. 200–202 and 751.
[9] Cmnd. 9712, para. 3.17 *et seq.*
[10] See § 20–60 *et seq., post.*
[11] C.D.P.A. 1988, ss.51–53 and Sched. 1, paras. 19 and 20; and see § 20–41, *post.*
[12] *Ibid.* s.213(6), (7).
[13] *Ibid.* s.236.

2. Artistic Works Created before August 1, 1989

A. *Artistic works created before June 1, 1957*

(i) Position under the 1911 Act

20–6   Section 22 of the 1911 Act. Subsection (1) of this section provided that:

> "This Act shall not apply to designs capable of being registered under the Patents and Designs Act, 1907, except designs which, though capable of being so registered, are not used or intended to be used as models or patterns to be multiplied by any industrial process."

Subsection (2) of this section dealt with rules under the 1907 Act for determining the conditions under which a design was to be deemed to be used for such purposes as aforesaid. Therefore, any designs to which this section applied were deprived of their full Copyright Act copyright.

(ii) Position under the 1956 Act

20–7   Paragraph 8, Schedule 7, to the 1956 Act. This position was maintained by the 1956 Act which provided, in Schedule 7, paragraph 8(1), that section 10 of the 1956 Act was not to apply to artistic works made before the commencement of that section (June 1, 1957). Paragraph 8(2) then provided that:

> "Copyright shall not subsist by virtue of this Act in any artistic work made before the commencement of section 10 which, at the time when the work was made, constituted a design capable of registration under the Registered Designs Act, 1949, or under the enactments repealed by that Act, and was used, or intended to be used, as a model or pattern to be multiplied by any industrial process."

Paragraph 8(3) brought in the Rules by which a design was to be deemed to be used as a model or pattern to be multiplied by any industrial process.[14]

Apart from, in effect, bringing section 22 of the 1911 Act up to date by referring to the 1949 Act as well as to enactments repealed by that Act, the 1956 Act provision eradicated two difficulties of interpretation in respect of section 22 of the 1911 Act, namely the double negative and the time when protection was excluded.[15] As to the latter, unless it can be said that, at the time when the work was made, it was used, or intended to be used by the artist, as a model or pattern to be multiplied by an industrial process, it would enjoy protection under the Copyright Act, notwithstanding that it was afterwards used for such a purpose.[16]

---

[14] Copyright Act 1956, Sched. 8, para. 2.
[15] See *King Features Syndicate* v. *O. & M. Kleeman Ltd.* [1941] A.C. 417 at 427: but see Lord Bridge in *British Leyland Motor Corp.* v. *Armstrong Patents Co. Ltd.* [1986] R.P.C. 279 at 355 and *Warner Brothers Inc.* v. *The Roadrunner Ltd.* [1988] F.S.R. 292.
[16] *King Features Syndicate* v. *O. & M. Kleeman Ltd.* [1941] A.C. 417; *Ware* v. *Anglo-Italian, etc., Agency Ltd. (No. 1)* [1917–23] Mac.C.C. 346.

(iii) Designs capable of being registered

Definitions of designs. Both section 22 of the 1911 Act and Schedule 7,   **20–8**
paragraph 8 of the 1956 Act refer to designs capable of being registered,
section 22 referring to the Patents and Designs Act 1907, and paragraph 8
referring to the Registered Designs Act 1949 or enactments repealed by
that Act. Section 93 of the 1907 Act, as amended by section 19 of the
Patents and Designs Act 1919, contained a definition of a "design,"[17] and
these sections were repealed by the 1949 Act. Section 1(3) of the 1949 Act,
prior to amendment by the 1988 Act, contained a definition of a
"design."[18] Further, section 1(4) of the 1949 Act, prior to such amendment, provided for Rules to be made for excluding from registration under
the 1949 Act designs for articles primarily literary or artistic in character.
Rules were made[19] excluding from registration under the 1949 Act:

(1) works of sculpture[20] other than casts or models used or intended to
be used as models or patterns to be multiplied by any industrial
process.
(2) wall plaques[21] and medals.[22]
(3) printed matter primarily of a literary or artistic character, including book jackets, calendars, certificates, coupons, dressmaking patterns, greetings cards, leaflets, maps, plans, postcards, stamps,
trade advertisements, trade forms, and cards, transfers, and the
like.[23]

However, where the design was subsequently produced in artistic form,
for instance by a photograph of the industrial object, the subsequent work,
though embodying the design, was not excluded from copyright protection.[24]

---

[17] It was held by Clauson J., in *Pytram Ltd.* v. *Models, etc., Ltd.* [1930] 1 Ch. 639, that the
amending provisions of the 1919 Act had to be regarded although this Act was not passed
at the date of the 1911 Act. See *Weir Pumps Ltd.* v. *CML Pumps Ltd.* [1984] F.S.R. 33.
[18] See as to "article," Registered Designs Act 1949, s.44(1). See generally as to definitions of
"designs," *Interlego A.G.* v. *Tyco Industries Inc.* [1988] R.P.C. 343.
[19] Rule 26, Designs Rules, 1949 (S.I. 1949 No. 2368) (Copinger 12th ed.) § 1734. Such Rules
were revoked and replaced by the Design Rules 1984 (S.I. 1984 No. 1989) which contained a similar Rule 26: § B–3, *post.* The 1984 Rules were revoked and replaced by The
Registered Designs Rules 1989 (S.I. 1989 No. 1105) which contain a Rule 26 similar to
Rule 26 of the 1984 Rules: § B–4, *post.* However, the 1989 Rules came into force on August
1, 1989, the date the 1988 Act copyright provisions came into force.
[20] *Pytram Ltd.* v. *Models, etc. Ltd.* [1930] 1 Ch. 639.
[21] *Usher* v. *Barlow* [1952] 69 R.P.C. 27: and see *Interlego A.G.* v. *Tyco Industries Inc.* [1988]
R.P.C. 343 at 360, 361.
[22] *Reliance (Nameplates) Ltd.* v. *Art Jewels Ltd.* [1953] 1 W.L.R. 530.
[23] As to difficulties in construing this Rule, see *Klarmann (H.) Ltd.* v. *Henshaw Linen Supplies*
[1960] R.P.C. 150.
[24] *Ware* v. *Anglo-Italian, etc., Agency Ltd. (No. 2)* [1917–23] Mac.C.C. 371. In the Australian
case of *Buzacott & Co. Ltd.* v. *Dutch* (1929) 30 S.R.(N.S.W.) 22, however, it was held that
representations in a catalogue of designs for articles are not protected under the Copyright
Act if the designs are capable of registration under the Designs Act, but the correctness of
this decision must be doubted.

20–9   **"Capable of registration."** This still left the question whether the designs were capable of registration, the main problem being whether "capable of registration" referred only to capacity as a possible subject-matter for registration, or also included the requirement of novelty.[25] It was held, under the 1911 Act,[26] that a work which existed before the commencement of that Act, if it had not been registered under the Patents and Designs Act 1907, was entitled to copyright under the 1911 Act because, at the commencement of that Act, it was not capable of registration as a design for lack of novelty.[27] The strange result of this decision was pointed out, by the Privy Council, in *Interlego A.G.* v. *Tyco Industries Inc.*,[28] and the contrary conclusion was reached in a Canadian case[29] and by Whitford J. in *Interlego A.G.* v. *Alex Folley, etc. Ltd.*.[30] Indeed, the Privy Council, in *Interlego A.G.*, *supra*, affirming the decision on this point of the Hong Kong Court of Appeal,[31] held that the words "constituted a design capable of being registered" refer to designs possessing, when they were made, those essential characteristics which qualify them as "designs" and rejected any requirement of novelty. Otherwise, as was pointed out by Lord Oliver, there did not appear to be any logic in according copyright to works possessing all the relevant features for registration but which were denied protection for want of novelty or originality and, at the same time, denying it to works possessing those same features but which the author does not choose to register.

(iv) Position under the 1988 Act

20–10   **Repeal of the 1956 Act.** The 1988 Act repealed the whole of the 1956 Act, including Schedules 7 and 8 thereto, as of August 1, 1989, when the copyright provisions of the 1988 Act came into force. However, the existing situation with regard to artistic works created before June 1, 1957 was continued by paragraph 6, Schedule 1 to the 1988 Act. Thus, paragraph 6(1) provides that:

> "Copyright shall not subsist by virtue of this Act in an artistic work made before 1st June 1957 which at the time the work was made constituted a design capable of registration under the Registered Designs Act 1949 or under the enactments repealed by that Act, and was used, or intended to be used, as a model or pattern to be multiplied by an industrial process."

This, therefore, made similar provision for such works as under the 1956 Act, paragraph 8(2), Schedule 7, but in relation to 1988 Act copyright, rather than 1956 Act copyright. Further, paragraph 6(1) of the 1988 Act

---

[25] See, for instance, s.1(2) Registered Designs Act 1949, before amendment by the 1988 Act.

[26] *Stevenson Blake* v. *Grant, Legros Ltd.* (1916) 33 R.P.C. 406.

[27] *Stenor Ltd.* v. *Whitesides (Clitheroe) Ltd.* [1948] A.C. 107: and see *Inerlego A.G.* v. *Tyco Industries Inc. supra.*

[28] [1988] R.P.C. 343 at 359, 360, 362, 364.

[29] *Bayliner Marine Corp.* v. *Doral Boats Ltd.* [1987] F.S.R. 497.

[30] [1987] F.S.R. 283: and see *Con Plank Ltd.* v. *Kolynos Inc.* [1925] 2 K.B. 804.

[31] [1987] F.S.R. 409.

will, no doubt, be construed in the same way as paragraph 8(2) of the 1956 Act.[32] Also, paragraph 6(2), Schedule 1 to the 1988 Act, contains a similar provision defining when a design is to be deemed to be used as a model or pattern to be multiplied by an industrial process to that in paragraph 2, Schedule 8 to the 1956 Act. "Article" and "Set of articles" are defined in the same terms by section 44(1) of the Registered Designs Act 1949 before and after amendment by the 1988 Act.

B. *Artistic works created after June 1, 1957 and before October 25, 1968*

(i) Position under the 1956 Act

General. Section 10 of the 1956 Act, before its amendment by the Design   **20–11** Copyright Act 1968, adopted a different approach to the matter to that adopted by section 22 of the 1911 Act. Thus, under the 1956 Act, full artistic copyright could subsist in works but, where a corresponding design was registered under the Registered Designs Act 1949, or the design was applied industrially and no design was registered, section 10 provided that certain acts were not to be infringements of that copyright. Subject to these limitations, full copyright protection was retained. It is therefore necessary to consider separately the two sets of circumstances giving rise to these limitations.

(ii) Corresponding design registered

"Corresponding design." The first set of circumstances envisaged by   **20–12** section 10 of the 1956 Act, before amendment by the 1968 Act, was where an artistic copyright subsisted and a corresponding design was registered under the Registered Designs Act 1949. "Corresponding design" was defined, in section 10(7) of the 1956 Act, as meaning a design which, when applied to an article, resulted in a reproduction of that work. "Reproduction" was defined in section 48(1) of the 1956 Act as including, in the case of an artistic work, a version produced by converting the work into a three-dimensional form, or, if it was in three dimensions, by converting it into a two-dimensional form. In section 9(8) of the 1956 Act it was provided that the making of an object of any description which was in three dimensions was not to be taken to infringe the copyright in an artistic work in two dimensions, if the object would not appear, to persons who were not experts in relation to objects of that description, to be a reproduction of the artistic work. Though this provision did not in terms qualify reproduction, but rather infringement, it did, in effect, amount to a limit upon what was meant by "reproduction," and it is suggested that anything which was not a reproduction in this sense was not a corresponding design because it would have been unnecessary to apply section 10 of the 1956 Act to a case where, as a result of section 9(8) of that Act, the industrial article would not infringe copyright in the artistic work. "Design" was not defined by the 1956 Act, but presumably, in this section, had the

---

[32] C.D.P.A. 1988, s.172.

same meaning as in the Registered Designs Act 1949, prior to amendment by the 1988 Act.[33]

20–13 **Corresponding design registered without the knowledge of the copyright owner.** Normally a corresponding design would have been registered by the owner of the copyright in the artistic work. To safeguard the copyright owner, where this was not the case, provision was made in Schedule 1 to the 1956 Act.[34] Thus, where copyright subsisted in an artistic work and proceedings were brought under the 1956 Act, and a corresponding design had been registered, but it was proved or admitted that the person registered was not the proprietor thereof for the purposes of the 1949 Act and was registered without the knowledge of the owner of the copyright in the artistic work, then, for the purposes of the copyright proceedings, the registration was to be treated as never having been effected: accordingly, in relation to that registration, section 10(1) of the 1956 Act was not to apply and nothing in section 7 of the 1949 Act was to provide any defence. If, however, the act of infringement alleged was done in pursuance of an assignment or licence from the registered proprietor in good faith in reliance upon the registration, and without notice of any proceedings for cancellation or rectification, then section 10(1) of the 1956 Act would have applied. Section 10(1) (including the reference to Schedule 1[35]) was deleted by the Design Copyright Act 1968, which Act also amended Schedule 1 to the 1956 Act to accord.[36] It is, however, difficult to see how, in view of the deletion of section 10(1), Schedule 1 had any application to artistic works made after the commencement of section 10 since the 1968 Act had no transitional provisions.[37]

20–14 **Design "proprietor" and copyright "owner" not necessarily the same.** By section 2 of the Registered Designs Act 1949, before amendment by the 1988 Act, it was provided that the author of a design should be treated as the proprietor of the design provided that, where the design was executed by the author for another person for good consideration, that other person was to be treated, for the purposes of that Act, as the proprietor; and where a design, or the right to apply a design to any article, became vested, whether by assignment, transmission or operation of law, in any person other than the original proprietor, either alone or jointly with the original proprietor, that other person, or, as the case may be, the original proprietor and that other person, was or were to be treated for the purposes of that Act as the proprietor of the design or as the proprietor of the design in relation to that article. It follows that the proprietor of the design under the 1949 Act might not have been the same person as the owner of the artistic copyright under the 1956 Act. For example, under section 4 of the 1956 Act, it was only in the case of a photograph, portrait or engraving that the copyright in a commissioned work of art would have vested in the person placing an order. However, having regard to the

---

[33] See § 20–8, *ante.*
[34] See *Ornamin (U.K.) Ltd.* v. *Bacsa Ltd.* [1964] R.P.C. 293.
[35] See para. 8 of Sched. 7 to the Copyright Act 1956.
[36] See § 20–34, *post.*
[37] See § 20–35, *post.*

amendment to section 6 of the Registered Designs Act 1949, by the 1956 Act,[38] it would probably not have been possible for the person who was to be proprietor of the design to obtain registration without the consent of the owner of the artistic copyright.

Effect of such registration. The purport of these provisions therefore seems clear, namely, that they applied whenever a design was registered under the Designs Act with the consent of the owner of the artistic copyright for articles, the reproduction of which would, under the Copyright Act, constitute an infringement of the artistic copyright. **20–15**

In these circumstances, it was provided that it should not be an infringement of the artistic copyright to do anything during the subsistence of the copyright in the registered design under the Registered Designs Act 1949, which was within the scope of the copyright in the design, or to do anything after the copyright in the design had come to an end which, if it had been done while the copyright in the design subsisted, would have been within the scope of that copyright as extended to all associated designs and articles.[39]

"Scope of the copyright." By section 10(6) of the 1956 Act the expression "scope of the copyright in a registered design" was defined as referring to the aggregate of the things, which, by virtue of section 7 of the Registered Designs Act 1949, the registered proprietor of the design had the exclusive right to do. "Scope of the copyright . . . in a registered design as extended to all associated designs and articles" was defined by the same subsection as referring to the aggregate of the things which, by virtue of section 7 aforesaid, the registered proprietor would have had the exclusive right to do if, (a) when the design was registered there had at the same time been registered every possible design consisting of that design with modifications or variations not sufficient to alter the character or substantially to affect the identity thereof, and the said proprietor had been registered as the proprietor of every such design, and (b), the design in question, and every other design such as is mentioned in paragraph (a), had been registered in respect of all the articles to which it was capable of being applied. **20–16**

Rights on registration. Section 7 of the Registered Designs Act 1949, prior to amendment by the 1988 Act, gave to the proprietor the exclusive right, in the United Kingdom and the Isle of Man, to make or import for sale or for use for the purposes of any trade or business, or to sell, hire or offer for sale or hire, any article in respect of which the design was registered, being an article to which the registered design or a design not substantially different from the registered design had been applied, and to make anything for enabling any such article to be made as aforesaid, whether in the United Kingdom, or the Isle of Man, or elsewhere. **20–17**

---

[38] § 20–27, *post.*
[39] Copyright Act 1956, s.10(1).

20-18 **Extent of artistic copyright during period of registration.** It should be noted, therefore, that, during the period of registration, artistic copyright continued to protect the owner thereof in respect of any infringement not concerned with the article in respect of which the design was registered, and even in respect of such an article against any infringement not concerned with purposes of trade. Moreover the words "as aforesaid" in the last sentence involve making "for sale or use for the purposes of a trade or business," so that the making of kits of parts to be sold to amateurs to enable them to make the article for their private use was not within the section.[40]

20-19 **Extent of artistic copyright after determination of designs copyright.** After the determination of the designs copyright, the artistic copyright only protected the owner of the artistic copyright in relation to infringements not capable of being protected under the Designs Act by any design registration, either of a design corresponding to the original artistic work, or of a design corresponding to the artistic work with modifications or variations. To some extent this reintroduced the problem of what was capable of registration under the Designs Act.[41]

(iii) Artistic copyright used for industrial purpose and no design
registered

20-20 The second set of circumstances envisaged by section 10 of the 1956 Act, before amendment by the 1968 Act, was where the artistic copyright was used for an industrial purpose and no design was registered.

These circumstances were described in the original section 10(2) of the 1956 Act and arose where:

(a) a design corresponding to an artistic work in which copyright subsisted was applied industrially by or with the licence of the owner of the copyright in the work and
(b) articles produced by so applying the design were sold, let for hire, or offered for sale or hire, and
(c) at the time when those articles were sold, let for hire, or offered for sale or hire, the design had not been registered under the Registered Designs Act 1949.

It is to be noted that these three conditions were cumulative. If, therefore, one condition was not satisfied it would seem that section 10(2) would not have applied. This could have occurred, it is suggested, if, for instance, the industrial application took place in America and the relevant articles were sold in America and this country. That is to say, neither the condition relating to industrial application, nor the condition relating to sale specified where that activity had to take place for the condition to be satisfied. It is suggested, therefore, that, in the circumstances, both were confined to this country since it would seem surprising if, by reason of industrial

---

[40] *Dorling* v. *Honnor Marine Ltd.* [1965] Ch. 1.
[41] See §§ 20-8 and 20-9, *ante* and Copyright Act 1956, s.10(6)(*b*).

application and sale in, for instance, America alone, there should be a limitation on the English artistic copyright. Some support for this suggestion is to be found in the Design Copyright Act 1968, which, in amending section 10, inserted the words "whether in the United Kingdom or elsewhere" at the end of the condition relating to sale, but made no similar provision in relation to the condition relating to industrial application.[42]

The meaning of "corresponding design" has already been discussed.[43] Here the expression used in relation thereto was "applied industrially" and thus "design" had its normal meaning of the idea of shape or form involved.

Use for industrial purpose. By section 10(5) of the 1956 Act the Board   **20–21**
of Trade was given power to make rules for the purpose of determining the circumstances in which a design was to be taken to be applied industrially. Under the rules, a design was to be taken to be applied industrially if it was applied by any process to, or was reproduced on or in, more than 50 articles not together constituting a single set, or to goods manufactured in lengths or pieces other than hand-made goods.[44] The word "industrially," therefore, merely had the signification of quantity and had no relation to the method of application.

Only designs which infringe. Again it is suggested that, if the design   **20–22**
was a design which, by virtue of section 9(8) of the 1956 Act would not have been an infringement of the artistic copyright, the provision would not have operated. It would not, for example, have imposed any restriction upon the artistic copyright in a plan or engineer's drawing for an industrial design, if the design would not have appeared to non-experts to be a reproduction of the plan or drawing.

Effect of industrial use. If the circumstances envisaged as aforesaid   **20–23**
occurred then, during the period of 15 years beginning with the date on which articles to which the design had been so applied were first sold or otherwise dealt with as aforesaid, it was not an infringement of the artistic copyright to do anything which would have been within the scope of the copyright in the design, if the design had been registered in respect of all such articles. After the expiration of the period of 15 years the copyright owner's artistic copyright was cut down in respect of all designs within the scope of such design as extended to all associated designs and articles.

Test of capacity for registration no longer applicable. It is, however,   **20–24**
to be observed that the test "applied industrially" was different in kind from the test "capable of registration" in the 1911 Act. A design might be applied industrially although not capable of registration.

---

[42] See Registered Designs Act 1949, s.6(4), before amendment by the 1988 Act; *Bissell A.G.'s Design* [1964] R.P.C. 125 and para. 148 of the 1962 Report of the Departmental Committee on Industrial Designs, Cmnd. 1808; see also § 20–32, *post*.
[43] See § 20–12, *ante*.
[44] Copyright (Industrial Designs) Rules 1957 (S.I. 1957 No. 867) (Copinger 12th ed. § 1742).

20–25 **Certain designs excluded.** The 1956 Act therefore provided some relief to meet such cases. In the first place, by virtue of section 1(4) of the Registered Designs Act 1949, before amendment by the 1988 Act, rules could be made excluding from registration certain designs for articles of a primarily literary or artistic character. Accordingly, section 10(4) of the 1956 Act provided that, for the purposes of section 10(2) and 10(3) thereof, no account was to be taken of articles in respect of which the design in question was excluded by rules made under section 1(4) of the Registered Designs Act 1949.[45] It was further provided that, for the purposes of proceedings for infringement of copyright, a design was to be conclusively presumed to have been so excluded if, before the commencement of the proceedings, an application for registration of the design in respect of those articles had been refused and one of the reasons for refusal was such rules, and no appeal from such refusal had been allowed or was pending.

20–26 **Certain designs not "designs."** But there were also cases where a design was not capable of registration because it was not a "design" within the meaning of section 1(3) of the Registered Designs Act 1949, before amendment by the 1988 Act, for instance where it constituted features of shape or configuration dictated solely by function.[46] Nevertheless, it could still have constituted a corresponding design and have been applied industrially for the purposes of section 10(2) of the 1956 Act. This problem arose in *Dorling* v. *Honnor Marine Ltd.*[47] where the plaintiffs alleged that the defendants had infringed the plaintiffs' copyright in plans for a boat, by the making of boats, by the making of kits or parts for the construction of boats, and by photographs of the parts. Cross J. and the Court of Appeal took the view that the design of the kits of parts was not registrable as purely functional and the Court of Appeal took the view that the design of the boat itself was functional. Consequently, as no design, at least for the kits of parts, could have been registered, even though section 10(2) applied, section 10(3) did not.

20–27 **Lack of "novelty" in copyright work not necessarily bar to registration.** But this does not meet the difficulty that an artistic work issued to the public would prima facie be incapable of registration for lack of novelty.

It was for this reason that it was necessary to amend the Registered Designs Act 1949, since, otherwise, the prior publication of the artistic work might have prevented registration under that Act but, an article to which a corresponding design was applied having been sold or disposed of, section 10(2) of the 1956 Act would have applied to defeat any claim of the owner of the artistic copyright to protection.

Section 44(1) of the 1956 Act accordingly provided for a new subsection

---

[45] *Ante*, § 20–8.
[46] *Amp Incorporated* v. *Utilux Proprietary Ltd.* [1972] R.P.C. 103 (H.L.); *Interlego A.G.* v. *Tyco Industries Inc.* [1988] R.P.C. 343 (P.C.); *British Leyland Motor Corp.* v. *Armstrong Patents Co. Ltd.* [1986] R.P.C. 279; *Interlego A.G.* v. *Alex Folley, etc., Ltd.* [1987] F.S.R. 283; *Gardex Ltd.* v. *Sorata Ltd.* [1986] R.P.C. 623.
[47] [1965] Ch. 1: compare *Bayliner Marine Corp.* v. *Doral Boats Ltd.* [1987] F.S.R. 497.

(4) to be inserted in section 6 of the Registered Designs Act 1949[48] as follows:

> "Where copyright under the Copyright Act 1956, subsists in an artistic work, and an application is made by, or with the consent of, the owner of that copyright for the registration of a corresponding design, that design shall not be treated for the purposes of this Act as being other than new or original[49] by reason only of any use previously made of the artistic work, unless—(*a*) the previous use consisted of or included the sale, letting for hire, or offer for sale or hire of articles to which the design in question (or a design differing from it only as mentioned in subsection (2) of section one of this Act) had been applied industrially, other than articles of a description specified in rules made under subsection (4) of section one of this Act, and (*b*) that previous use was made by, or with the consent of, the owner of the copyright in the artistic work."[50]

In relation to this provision, reference should be made to section 4 of the **20–28** Registered Designs Act 1949, before amendment by the 1988 Act, which provided, in effect, that where a design had been registered in respect of any article, it could have been subsequently registered in respect of other articles notwithstanding the previous registration, but the term of copyright under the 1949 Act for all such articles was not to exceed that in respect of the original registration. There was a further provision of the same section enabling an assignee of the original proprietor to obtain additional registrations under the section.

(iv) Limit on duration of designs copyright

Section 44(2) and (3) of the 1956 Act contained amendments of sections 8 **20–29** and 11 of the Registered Designs Act 1949, providing that, where a design corresponding to an artistic work had been registered and the period of copyright protection in the artistic work determines, the designs copyright shall also determine and may be cancelled. This only applied where there had been a previous use of the artistic work so that the design would not have been registrable but for the new section 6(4) previously mentioned.[51]

(v) Summary

The general effect of the foregoing provisions was as follows. Unless and **20–30** until an industrial design was either registered or used, full copyright protection was preserved for the artistic work. If the copyright owner of the artistic work decided to embark upon an industrial use for his work, he was at liberty to register under the Designs Act, notwithstanding the pre-

---

[48] Compare ss.6(4), (5) and 44 of the 1949 Act, as amended by C.D.P.A. 1988.
[49] See *Aspro-Nicholas Limited's Design Application* [1974] R.P.C. 645.
[50] See *Bissell A.G.'s Design* [1964] R.P.C. 125; *Bampal Materials Handling Limited's Design* [1981] R.P.C. 44.
[51] *Ante*, § 20–27. Compare ss.8 and 11 of the 1949 Act as amended by the 1988 Act.

vious copyright publication. If he registered in respect of one article, he continued to enjoy copyright protection in respect of use on other articles during the term of designs registration in the article which he had registered and during that period he could have obtained additional designs registrations for other articles, but only for the original period. The effect of the two branches of the section was therefore similar. If a corresponding design was registered, or if it was applied industrially without registration, artistic copyright during 15 years would not protect against infringements within the scope of the design and, after 15 years, would not protect against infringements within the scope of the design as extended. After 15 years copyright protection continued, but only in respect of use which was not use for industrial purposes.[52]

C. *Artistic works created on or after October 25, 1968 and before August 1, 1989*

20–31 **Design Copyright Act 1968.** The relationship between artistic copyright under the Copyright Acts, and designs copyright under the Designs Acts, was radically changed by the Design Copyright Act 1968[53] which came into force on October 25, 1968. As has been mentioned,[54] under the 1911 Act works were excluded altogether from artistic copyright, if capable of registration under the Designs Acts and if intended for use as a model or pattern for industrial production.[55] Under the 1956 Act, however, before amendment by the 1968 Act, full artistic copyright subsisted from the creation of the work, although the protection afforded by that Act was cut down if, either a corresponding design was registered under the Designs Acts, or a corresponding design was applied industrially without a design being so registered.[56]

20–32 **New approach under 1968 Act.** The 1968 Act adopted a completely new approach and permitted full artistic copyright to subsist without restriction for a limited period, whether or not a corresponding design was registered under the Designs Acts, and whether or not a corresponding design was applied industrially without a design being so registered. As a result, subject to the question of novelty[57] and registrability,[58] it was possible to have a duality of protection, that is under the Copyright Acts and, if a corresponding design had been registered, also under the Designs Acts.[59] This was a great advantage to many owners of artistic copyrights in works whose viable exploitation time was of short duration, such as toys.

---

[52] See *post*, § 20–31, *et seq.* as to effect of the Design Copyright Act 1968, and § 20–36, *post*, as to the repeal of the 1956 Act by the 1988 Act.

[53] c. 68.

[54] *Ante*, § 20–6.

[55] Copyright Act 1911, s.22(1).

[56] Copyright Act 1956, s.10.

[57] See Registered Designs Act 1949, before amendment by the 1988 Act, ss.1(2) and 6(4) and (5), and § 20–27, *ante*.

[58] See Registered Designs Act 1949, before amendment by the 1988 Act, s.1(3),(4), r. 26 Designs Rules 1949, 1984 and 1989 § 20–8 n. 19, *ante* and §§ 20–8, 20–25 and 20–26, *ante*.

[59] See *Merchant Adventurers Ltd.* v. *M. Grew & Co. Ltd.* [1972] Ch. 242. But see ss.8 and 11 of the Registered Designs Act 1949, before amendment by the 1988 Act, and § 20–29, *ante*.

The manner in which this was achieved was that the 1968 Act amended section 10 of the 1956 Act, which applied to works made after the commencement of the 1956 Act, first of all by deleting subsection (1), which contained the limiting provisions where a corresponding design had been registered under the Designs Acts and, secondly, by amending subsection (2), and substituting a new subsection (3) which, together, contained the limiting provisions where a corresponding design was applied industrially and no design had been so registered.

The amended subsection (2) then read as follows:

> "Where copyright subsists in an artistic work, and (*a*) a corresponding design is applied industrially by or with the licence of the owner of the copyright in the work, and (*b*) articles to which the design has been so applied are sold, let for hire, or offered for sale or hire whether in the United Kingdom or elsewhere, [and⁶⁰] the following provisions of this section shall apply."

The words "whether in the United Kingdom or elsewhere" were added to what was the original subsection (2)(*b*), but not to what was the original subsection (2)(*a*), which raised the question, since these conditions were cumulative, as to when the subsection applied. That is to say, if it was necessary to provide expressly that sale anywhere was relevant, presumably industrial application was only relevant if it took place in the United Kingdom. Therefore it would seem that, if industrial application took place, say, in America, but sale took place in this country and America, the subsection would not have applied.⁶¹

Extent of protection where corresponding design applied industrially.   **20–33** Where the amended section 10 applied, it permitted full artistic copyright to subsist without restriction for a limited term. Thus, the new subsection (3) provided that, after the end of "the relevant period of fifteen years," it was not to be an infringement of the copyright in the work to do anything, which, at the time when it was done would, if a corresponding design had been registered under the Registered Designs Act 1949 immediately before that time, have been within the scope of the copyright in the design as extended to all associated designs and articles. Such new subsection defined "the relevant period of fifteen years" as meaning the period of 15 years beginning with the date on which articles such as were mentioned in subsection (2)(*b*) were first sold, let for hire or offered for sale or hire, whether in the United Kingdom or elsewhere. Again, no account was to be taken of articles in respect of which the design in question was excluded by rules made under section 1(4) of the Registered Designs Act 1949.⁶² "Scope of the copyright in a registered design as extended to all associated designs and articles" was defined by subsection (6).⁶³ In the result, where the amended section 10 applied, there was

---

⁶⁰ Although deleting sub-para. (*c*), the 1968 Act did not, in fact, delete the word "and" which joined sub-para. (*c*) with sub-para. (*b*).

⁶¹ See *Bissell A.G.'s Design* [1964] R.P.C. 125 and para. 148 of the 1962 Report of the Departmental Committee on Industrial Designs, Cmnd. 1808; see also § 20–20, *ante*.

⁶² Copyright Act 1956, s.10(3) and (4), and see §§ 20–25 and 20–26, *ante*.

⁶³ See § 20–16 *ante*.

unrestricted artistic copyright for 15 years from first sale, etc., of articles to which the design had been applied industrially. After that period the position would have been the same as it was under the original subsection (3) at the end of the relevant period of 15 years there mentioned.[64]

But where the design was not registrable, being excluded by the rules,[65] or by the definition of "design",[66] then the amended section 10 did not apply and the design would have enjoyed the full Copyright Act term.

20–34   Corresponding design registered without the knowledge of the copyright owner. As has been mentioned,[67] a corresponding design would normally have been registered by the owner of the copyright in the artistic work and, to safeguard the copyright owner where this was not the case, provision was made in Schedule 1 to the 1956 Act. Reference was made, in paragraphs 2 and 3 of Schedule 1, to section 10(1) and, in view of the deletion of section 10(1) by the 1968 Act, that Act also amended Schedule 1 accordingly. However, the surprising fact is that section 10(1) contained the only reference in section 10 to Schedule 1 and the amended section contains no reference thereto. It is therefore difficult to see how Schedule 1 thereafter had any application to artistic works made after the commencement of section 10 since the 1968 Act had no transitional provisions.[68] Subject to this, where copyright subsisted in an artistic work, and proceedings were brought under the 1956 Act, and a corresponding design had been registered, but it was proved or admitted that the person registered was not the proprietor thereof for the purposes of the Registered Designs Act 1949, and was registered without the knowledge of the owner of the copyright in the artistic work, then, for the purposes of the copyright proceedings, the registration was to be treated as never having been effected; accordingly, in relation to that registration, nothing in section 7 of the 1949 Act was to provide any defence. If, however, the act of infringement alleged was done in pursuance of an assignment or licence from the registered proprietor in good faith in reliance upon the registration, and without notice of any proceedings for cancellation or rectification, then this would have been a good defence.[69]

20–35   No transitional provisions. The biggest problem created by the 1968 Act arose from the fact that such Act had no transitional provisions. In view of the important changes in the law effected by this Act, and the benefit it was no doubt intended to confer on a large section of the public, it is, perhaps, unfortunate that it was uncertain as to how that Act affected works created before it came into force on October 25, 1968.

That is to say, the 1968 Act clearly applied to works created after it came into force in respect of which any acts of infringement would have

---

[64] See § 20–23 *ante.*

[65] *Ibid.* n.62.

[66] *British Leyland Motor Corp.* v. *Armstrong Patents Co. Ltd.* [1984] F.S.R. 591 (C.A.) [1986] A.C. 577 (H.L.) overruling *Hoover plc* v. *George Hulme (Stockport) Ltd.* [1982] F.S.R. 565: and see *Weir Pumps Ltd.* v. *CML Pumps Ltd.* [1984] F.S.R. 33 at 38. See also *Silent Gliss International A.G.* v. *Module, etc. Ltd.* [1981] F.S.R. 423.

[67] § 20–13, *ante.*

[68] See para. 8, Sched. 7, Copyright Act 1956.

[69] Compare C.D.P.A. 1988, s.53.

had to take place after that date. But the position was not clear as to works created before that date, either in respect of acts of infringement which occurred before that date, or in respect of acts of infringement which occurred after that date. It therefore becomes necessary to examine the position under section 10 of the 1956 Act before amendment in respect of works made before the commencement of the 1956 Act,[70] and then to consider the effect of such amendment.

As has been mentioned,[71] the 1956 Act, unlike the 1911 Act, permitted full artistic copyright to subsist from the creation of the work. However, under section 10 before amendment, this protection was cut down if, either a corresponding design was registered under the Registered Designs Act 1949, or a corresponding design was applied industrially without a design being so registered. The manner in which section 10 cut down this protection was to provide that, in those circumstances, "it shall not be an infringement of the copyright in the work" to do certain things.[72] The effect of such provisions, it is submitted, was not to destroy part of the artistic copyright but, whilst leaving the whole of such copyright intact, to provide a defence to proceedings for infringement of such copyright in the circumstances mentioned.[73]

This view would appear to be supported by the judgment of Cross J., at first instance, in the case of *Dorling* v. *Honnor Marine Ltd.*,[74] who said,[75] "The general effect of section 10 is clear enough. If the owner of the copyright in an artistic work exploits it industrially, he does not lose his copyright under the 1956 Act, but, whether or not he actually registers the design which corresponds to the artistic work under the Registered Designs Act 1949, he ceases to be entitled to protection under the 1956 Act in respect of matters which are—or, if he had registered the design, would have been—infringements of the design copyright. When the period of design copyright expires, his copyright protection under the 1956 Act goes on, but only in respect of non-industrial use." The judgments in the Court of Appeal are not so clear, both Harman and Danckwerts L.JJ. saying, in effect, that section 10 was designed to prevent duality of protection.[76] However, Danckwerts L.J. also said,[77] "If the shape of the completed boat ought to have been registered as a design under the Registered Designs Act 1949, the plaintiff is deprived of his remedies under the Copyright Act 1956, by virtue of section 10 of that Act."

If this view of the effect of section 10 before amendment is correct, what is the effect of the amendment on works created after the commencement of the 1956 Act and before the 1968 Act came into force, bearing in mind

---

[70] Para. 8(1), Sched. 7, Copyright Act 1986.
[71] §§ 20–11, 20–31 and 20–32, *ante.*
[72] Copyright Act 1956, s.10(1) and (3), before amendment.
[73] This was the view taken by Whitford J. in *I.M.I. Developments Ltd.* v. *F. C. Harrison Ltd.* [1970] R.P.C. 299: *cf.* Copyright Act 1956, ss.6(1), 9(1), 7(1) and 8(1). And see *Hawkes & Son (London) Ltd.* v. *Paramount Film Service Ltd.* [1934] Ch. 593; *Johnstone* v. *Bernard Jones Publications Ltd.* [1938] Ch. 599.
[74] [1964] Ch. 560; and see *Sifam Electrical Instrument Co. Ltd.* v. *Sangamo Weston Ltd.* [1973] R.P.C. 899.
[75] *Ibid.* at 573.
[76] [1965] Ch. 1 at 15, 18, 19 and 20.
[77] *Ibid.* at 21.

that the amended section 10 gave unrestricted artistic copyright for the relevant period of 15 years, where there had been industrial application, by removing the provisions of section 10 which gave what, it is submitted, was a statutory defence during that period? It is suggested that the position as to such works is that they were entitled to the full unrestricted artistic copyright for the relevant period of 15 years. Further, that that being so, proceedings could have been brought (subject to the limitation period) for infringements of that copyright which occurred after October 25, 1968 (when the 1968 Act came into force) and before the expiry of that period, because no part of the copyright was ever destroyed and the statutory defences had been removed. But proceedings could not have been brought in respect of "infringements" which occurred before the 1968 Act came into force since they were not "infringements" when they occurred and, it is submitted they could not have become "infringements" by reason of the removal of the statutory defences.[78] This was the view taken by Graham J. in *Sifam Electrical Instrument Co. Ltd.* v. *Sangamo Weston Ltd..*[79]

A further difficulty, arising from the fact that the 1968 Act merely amended section 10 of, and Schedule 1 to, the 1956 Act, was the effect of paragraph 8 of Schedule 7 to the 1956 Act following such amendment. Thus, paragraph 8(1) provided that section 10 of, and Schedule 1 to, the 1956 Act were not to apply to artistic works made "before the commencement of that section." Clearly, before the 1968 Act came into force, this was a reference to the commencement of the original section 10 and Schedule 1 on June 1, 1957. It is submitted that, notwithstanding that the 1968 Act merely amended section 10 and Schedule 1, paragraph 8(1) of Schedule 7 does not mean, following such amendment, that the amended section 10 and Schedule 1 were not to apply to works created before the 1968 Act came into force, particularly in view of paragraphs 8(2) and (3) of Schedule 7 and section 50 of the 1956 Act.

D. *Position after August 1, 1989*

20–36   **Repeal.** The 1988 Act repealed the whole of the 1956 Act, including the amended section 10, and the whole of the 1968 Act, as of August 1, 1989, when the copyright provisions of the 1988 Act came into force. Further, the 1988 Act, in respect of new works, does not contain any provisions excluding them from copyright as under the 1911 Act,[80] or limiting their copyright as under the 1956 Act.[81] Therefore, all post August 1, 1989 designs are entitled to full artistic copyright under the 1988 Act, subject to certain particular exceptions from infringement contained in sections 51 to 53 of the 1988 Act.[82] However, as has been seen,[83] the 1988 Act has continued the 1911 Act position for artistic works created before June 1, 1957. Further, in relation to artistic works created after June 1, 1957 and

---

[78] See *Ex p. Todd* (1887) 19 Q.B.D. 186; *Lauri* v. *Renad* [1892] 3 Ch. 402; see also Interpretation Act 1889, s.38(2)(*b*) and Interpretation Act 1978 (c. 30) s.16(1)(*b*).
[79] [1973] R.P.C. 899; and see *I.M.I. Developments Ltd.* v. *F. C. Harrison Ltd.* [1970] R.P.C. 299.
[80] § 20–6 *et seq., ante.*
[81] § 20–11 *et seq., ante.*
[82] See § 20–41 *et seq., post* and C.D.P.A. 1988, Sched. 1, paras. 19 and 20.
[83] § 20–10, *ante.*

before August 1, 1989, the 1988 Act provides a more stringent version of section 52 of the 1988 Act.

Section 52 of the 1988 Act. This section, like sections 51 and 53 of the   **20–37**
1988 Act, is an exception to what would otherwise be an infringement,[84] as was section 10 of the 1956 Act in its unamended and amended forms. However, it is important to bear in mind that these exceptions do not apply to acts of infringement done before August 1, 1989 to which the 1956 Act exceptions, including section 10, still apply.[85] Section 52 of the 1988 Act only applies to acts of infringement done after August 1, 1989.[86]

Application of section 52. Section 52[87] of the 1988 Act applies where an   **20–38**
artistic work has been exploited, by or with the licence of the copyright owner, by making by an industrial process articles falling to be treated for the purposes of the copyright Part of the 1988 Act as copies of the work, and marketing such articles, in the United Kingdom or elsewhere. No doubt "copies" is to be construed in the context of what constitutes copying for the purposes of the 1988 Act.[88] The Secretary of State may by Order provide (a) as to what constitutes making by an industrial process and (b) for excluding from the operation of section 52 articles of a primarily literary or artistic character.[89] Such an Order has been made.[90] The former bears some resemblance to the Rules made under section 10(5) of the 1956 Act,[91] and the latter bears some resemblance to the Rules made under section 1(4) of the Registered Designs Act 1949.[92] "Articles" in section 52 do not include films.[93] "Marketing an article" means its sale, or letting for hire, or offering or exposing for sale or hire.[94]

Permitted acts. In cases where section 52 applies then, after the end of   **20–39**
the period of 25 years from the end of the calendar year in which such articles are first marketed, the work may be copied by making articles of any description, or doing anything for the purpose of making articles of any description, and anything may be done in relation to articles so made, without infringing copyright in the work.[95] Where only part of an artistic work is exploited as mentioned above,[96] this exception applies only in relation to that part.[97] Although, apparently, the first of the conditions to be satisfied to bring section 52 into operation, namely the making of the articles, can take place before or after August 1, 1989, the second con-

---

[84] C.D.P.A. 1988, s.28.
[85] *Ibid.* Sched. 1, para. 14(1).
[86] See n. 84, *supra.*
[87] See § 20–43, *post.*
[88] See C.D.P.A. 1988, ss.17 and 179: and see § 8–92 *et seq., ante.*
[89] *Ibid.* s.52(4), (5).
[90] The Copyright (Industrial Process and Excluded Articles) (No. 2) Order 1989 (1989 S.I. No. 1070) § B–37, *post.*
[91] § 20–20, *ante.*
[92] See s.10(4) Copyright Act 1956, and §§ 20–9, 20–12 and 20–25, *ante.*
[93] C.D.P.A. 1988, s.52(6), and see *ibid.* s.5(1): see also § 20–45, *post.*
[94] *Ibid.* s.52(6).
[95] *Ibid.* s.52(2).
[96] § 20–38, *ante.*
[97] C.D.P.A. 1988, s.52(3).

dition, namely marketing the articles, has to take place after August 1, 1989,[98] except where section 10 of the 1956 Act applied to the work.[99] Section 52 therefore reflects the situation under the amended section 10 of the 1956 Act,[1] although the period is 25, rather than 15 years. The effect of section 52 is that, for the 25-year period, full artistic copyright exists. After that period has expired such copyright is then limited in the way provided by such section, but otherwise is unaffected.

20–40   **Artistic works to which section 10 of the 1956 Act applied.** In respect of artistic works to which section 10 of the 1956 Act applied at any time before August 1, 1989, the relevant period of 15 years, as defined in section 10(3) of the 1956 Act,[2] is to be substituted for the period of 25 years mentioned in section 52(2) of the 1988 Act.[3]

E. Design documents and models

20–41   **Application of section 51.** In relation to acts of infringement committed on or after August 1, 1989, section 51 of the 1988 Act has partial application. The provisions of this section are discussed in more detail below.[4] In general, where a design was "recorded or embodied" in a design document or model before August 1, 1989, section 51 does not apply for a period of 10 years after that date.[5] During this period it will therefore prima facie be an infringement of copyright in such existing design documents or models to make articles to such designs, and no defence equivalent to that of section 9(8) of the 1956 Act will be available. The effect of this is modified by enabling a person to apply during the last five years of this 10-year period for a licence under the modified provisions of section 237 of the 1988 Act.[6] This section entitles a person to a licence as of right on terms to be settled by the Comptroller[7] in the absence of agreement.[8] Provision is also made enabling licences of right to be available following a report of the Monopolies and Mergers Commission under section 238 of the 1988 Act.[9] Such licences are not to extend further than permitting acts which would be permitted by section 51 in the case of a design document or model made on or after August 1, 1989.[10] If such a licence of right is available under either of these provisions, no injunction is to be granted, and no order for delivery up is to be made, against a defendant who undertakes to take such a licence, and the amount recoverable from him by way of damages or on an account of profits is to be limited to twice the amount which would have been payable under a licence of right.[11] In

---

[98] C.D.P.A. 1988, Sched. 1, para. 20(2).
[99] *Ibid.* Sched. 1, para. 20(1), (2): see § 20–40, *post.*
[1] See § 20–31 *et seq., ante.*
[2] § 20–32, *ante.*
[3] C.D.P.A. 1988, Sched. 1, para. 20(1).
[4] See § 20–50, *post.*
[5] C.D.P.A. 1988, Sched. 1, para. 19(1).
[6] *Ibid.* Sched. 1, para. 19(2).
[7] The Comptroller-General of Patents, Designs and Trade Marks: C.D.P.A. 1988, s.263(1).
[8] See § 20–152, *post.*
[9] See n. 5, *ante.*
[10] C.D.P.A. 1988, Sched. 1, para. 19(7).
[11] *Ibid.* Sched. 1, para. 19(4), s.239.

addition, in applying the new right of seizure provisions contained in section 100 of the 1988 Act, it must be assumed that during the 10-year period the design in question had been first recorded or embodied in the design document or model on or after August 1, 1989, so that, to the extent that on this assumption articles would not have been infringing copies, the right of seizure does not apply.[12] Also, where before August 1, 1989 a person had been granted a licence, then during the last five years of the 10-year period following August 1, 1989 he may apply to the Comptroller-General for an order adjusting the terms of that licence.[13] It is specifically provided that nothing in the transitional provisions shall affect the operation of any rule of law preventing or restricting the enforcement of copyright in relation to a design.[14] Presumably this will enable the defences of implied licence or non-derogation from grant to continue to be set up during the transitional period, although it is not clear why such defences should not have remained available without such statutory provision.

As has been seen, in relation to acts of infringement committed before **20–42** August 1, 1989, the provisions of the 1956 Act will continue to apply.[15] The making of articles to design documents or models before this date will therefore have been an infringement of copyright unless the consent of the copyright owner was obtained or some other defence was available. What is the position where such articles are dealt in after the commencement date? Such articles will be infringing copies for the purposes of section 27 of the 1988 Act since this question is to be determined by the law in force when the article was made, that is in relation to an article made between June 1, 1957 and August 1, 1989, by the provisions of the 1956 Act.[16] It will therefore be an infringement of copyright under the 1988 Act for anyone on or after August 1, 1989 to sell, distribute in the course of trade, etc., such articles knowing or having reason to believe them to be infringing copies.[17] The question then arises whether a person will be liable for infringement who, for example, not having such knowledge, issues copies of such articles to the public within the meaning of section 18 of the 1988 Act. As will be seen,[18] section 51(2) permits such dealings if the making of the article was not an infringement of copyright by virtue of section 51(1). As to this, the 1988 Act provides that, for the purposes of applying section 51(2) to such articles, it is to be assumed that Part I of the 1988 Act and the transitional provisions in Schedule 1 to that Act were in force at all material times.[19] However, as has also been seen,[20] section 51 will not apply for these purposes for 10 years after August 1, 1989. It follows that in this 10-year period the issue to the public of existing copies not previously in circulation could be infringement of copyright. The same

---

[12] C.D.P.A. 1988, Sched. 1, para. 19(8).
[13] *Ibid.* Sched. 1, para. 19(5).
[14] *Ibid.* Sched. 1, para. 19(9): and see §§ 8–159 and 8–160, *ante.*
[15] *Ibid.* Sched. 1, para. 14(1).
[16] *Ibid.* Sched. 1, para. 14(3).
[17] *Ibid.* s.23, § 9–3, *ante.*
[18] § 20–58, *post.*
[19] C.D.P.A. 1988, Sched. 1, para. 14(4).
[20] § 20–41, *ante.*

applies to the inclusion of such existing copies in a film, broadcast or cable programme service.

3. Position under Part I of Works Created on or after August 1, 1989

A. *Artistic Works*

20–43   **Introduction.** The 1988 Act operates to limit the rights of the copyright owner where a design derived from a copyright work has been commercially exploited. Thus, section 52 provides that, where an artistic work has been exploited by or with the copyright owner's licence by making by an industrial process articles to be treated as copies of the work, and by marketing such articles in the United Kingdom or elsewhere, then, after the end of the period of 25 years from the end of the calendar year in which such articles were first marketed, the artistic work may be copied by making articles of any description, or doing anything for the purpose of making articles of any description, without infringing copyright.[21] For this purpose, "marketing" means selling, letting for hire or offering or exposing for sale or hire, and the expression "articles" does not include films.[22] It is also provided that anything may be done in relation to articles so made without infringing copyright in the artistic work. Where only part of an artistic work has been exploited in this way, the right for others to exploit the work after a 25-year period only extends to that part.[23] The Secretary of State may by order exclude from the operation of this section such articles of a primarily literary or artistic character as he thinks fit.[24] The section therefore resembles section 10 of the 1956 Act in its broad effect.[25]

20–44   **Making by an industrial process.** It is provided that the Secretary of State may by order make provision as to the circumstances in which an article is to be regarded for these purposes as made by an industrial process.[26] This provision echoes the similar provision in the 1956 Act.[27] Such an order has been made which provides that an article is to be regarded as being made by an industrial process if more than 50 such articles are made which do not constitute a set of articles under the Registered Designs Act 1949, or if it consists of goods manufactured in lengths or pieces.[28]

---

[21] C.D.P.A. 1988, s.52(2).

[22] *Ibid.* s.52(6): and see § 20–45, *post.*

[23] *Ibid.* s.52(3).

[24] *Ibid.* s.52(4)(*b*). This echoes s.10(4) Copyright Act 1956.

[25] See § 20–11 *et seq., ante.*

[26] *Ibid.* s.52(4)(*a*).

[27] Copyright Act 1956, s.10(5), Copyright (Industrial Designs) Rules 1957 (1957 S.I. No. 867) (*Copinger* (12th ed.) § 1742).

[28] The Copyright (Industrial Process and Excluded Articles) (No. 2) Order 1989 (1989 S.I. No. 1070) clause 2: see § B–39, *post.*

Films excluded as articles. It is provided that, for the purpose of section 52, references to "articles" are not to include films.[29] Animated or cartoon films are invariably made from artistic works, and, were it not for this exclusion, the making of a quantity of prints of a cartoon film would mean that after 25 years it would be permissible to make copies of those artistic works on articles of any description. **20-45**

Exclusion of literary or artistic articles. The Secretary of State is empowered, by order to exclude from the operation of section 52 articles of a primarily literary or artistic character. Such an order has been made,[30] which excludes: **20-46**

(a) works of sculpture other than casts or models used as models or patterns to be multiplied by an industrial process;

(b) wall plaques and the like; and

(c) printed matter primarily of a literary or artistic character.

The making of copies. The principal question under section 52 will usually be to determine whether articles have previously been made and marketed which fall to be treated for the purposes of Part I of the 1988 Act as copies of an artistic work. No doubt the expression "copies of" a work is to be construed in the context of what, under section 17 of the 1988 Act, constitutes copying. This section provides that, in relation to an artistic work, copying means reproducing the work in any material form, and in the case of a two-dimensional work, includes making a copy of it in three dimensions, and, in the case of a three-dimensional work, includes making a copy in two dimensions. These provisions have already been considered.[31] Where the artistic work is reproduced on only part of the article, for example a pattern on only one side of a plate, or an aspect of shape which is only present in part of the article in question, presumably the article as a whole will be regarded as a "copy" of the artist's work, for otherwise the section would be of very limited application. Where the article does not reproduce the whole of the artistic work, but only a substantial part of it, the article is still apparently to be regarded as a copy of the whole work so that, after the 25-year period, it will be permissible to make articles, not only by copying the substantial part, but also by copying the whole of the artistic work.[32] **20-47**

The permitted acts. Where an artistic work has been exploited in this way it will be permissible, at the end of the 25-year period, to copy the work by making articles of any description.[33] Thus, where the artistic work has been exploited by the making, for example, of table mats, it will be permissible to copy the work in the form of wallpaper or material fabric. The only exception to this is that it will not be permissible to copy the work in the form of a film, a film being expressly excluded from the mean- **20-48**

---

[29] C.D.P.A. 1988, s.52(6)(*a*).
[30] Under C.D.P.A. 1988, s.52(4)(*b*): see clause 3, 1989 S.I. No. 1070 § B-40, *post.*
[31] See § 8-3 *et seq., ante.*
[32] C.D.P.A. 1988, s.16(3) and s.52(3).
[33] *Ibid.* s.52(2).

ing of "article".[34] It will also be permissible to copy the work in the form, for example, of a drawing or stencil, made either from the artistic work itself, or from some other source, provided that it is done for the purpose of making the articles on which the work is copied.[35] Where the making of articles is permitted by virtue of section 52, it will also be permissible to do any act in relation to those articles, for example, issue copies to the public, or include them in a film, broadcast or cable programme.[36]

20–49   **Acts done in reliance on registered design.** The 1988 Act makes new provision in the case of acts done in reliance on the registration of a design under the Registered Designs Act 1949. Thus section 53 provides that the copyright in an artistic work is not infringed by anything done:

> (a) in pursuance of an assignment or licence made or granted by a person registered under the Registered Designs Act 1949 as the proprietor of a corresponding design and
> (b) in good faith in reliance on the registration and without notice of any proceedings for the cancellation of the registration or for rectifying the relevant entry in the Register of Designs.[37]

This defence is to be available notwithstanding that the person registered as the proprietor was not in fact the proprietor of the design for the purposes of the 1949 Act.[38] The reference to a "corresponding design" is to a design within the meaning of the 1949 Act which, if applied to an article, would produce something which would be treated for the purposes of Part I of the 1988 Act as a copy of the artistic work.[39] This defence only applies in relation to acts committed on or after August 1, 1989.[40]

B. *Design documents and models other than for artistic works and typefaces*

20–50   **Introduction.** Under section 51 of the 1988 Act it is not:

> "an infringement of any copyright in a design document or model recording or embodying a design for anything other than an artistic work or a typeface to make an article to the design or to copy an article made to the design."

20–51   **Design document.** The section applies to restrict the copyright in "design documents" and also certain models. As to a "design document," this is defined as being any record of a design, whether in the form of a drawing, a written description, a photograph, data stored in a computer or otherwise.[41] The expression "record of a design" has not been used in

---

[34] C.D.P.A. 1988, s.52(6)(a).
[35] See n. 32, *ante.*
[36] See n. 32, *ante.*
[37] C.D.P.A. 1988, s.53(1).
[38] See n. 36, *ante.*
[39] C.D.P.A. 1988, s.53(2).
[40] *Ibid.* Sched. 1, para. 14(1).
[41] *Ibid.* s.51(3).

previous Copyright Acts.[42] Presumably, however, it refers to a document, such as a drawing which in some way represents a design. Thus a drawing which shows the shape of an article, such as a machine part, would clearly be a design document. So too would a photograph of the article itself. The section refers specifically to a "drawing" as being one example of a design document. A "drawing" is, however, only one example of a "graphic work" as defined in section 4(2) of the 1988 Act, others being a "diagram" and a "plan." It is not thought, however, that the reference in section 52 to a "drawing" is intended to exclude from the definition of a design document such works as diagrams or plans if they in fact can be described as drawings or otherwise record the design of articles. For reasons which will be mentioned below, the inclusion of a "written description" and "data stored in a computer" within the definition of design document appears curious. Nevertheless, it seems that a literary work which adequately describes the shape of an article will fall within the definition of a design document. So too, apparently, will the co-ordinates of an article's shape which are stored in the form of data within a computer. A photograph,[43] whether of an article itself or, presumably, in the form of a photographic copy of a drawing or written description, is also capable of being a design document.

Models. The section also applies to restrict the copyright in models.   **20–52**
Although the drafting of the section is not entirely clear, the section apparently applies to any model which records or embodies a design for anything other than an artistic work or a typeface.[44] As to such models, it must be remembered that the section only applies to prevent what would otherwise be an infringement of the copyright in a copyright work. Models in which copyright can subsist include a model for a building, a model which is itself a sculpture or a model which is a work of artistic craftsmanship.[45] It seems, however, that a model for a building and a model for a sculpture would be excluded from the operation of section 51, since such works would record or embody a design for an artistic work, namely the building (a work of architecture and thus an artistic work)[46] and a sculpture,[47] respectively. On the other hand, a sculpture representing the shape of a machine part would fall within the ambit of the section, assuming the machine part were not itself a work of artistic craftsmanship.[48] Models recording or embodying designs for typefaces, assuming copyright subsists in them, are excluded, such works being subject to the separate regime for typefaces considered elsewhere.[49]

---

[42] It is also used, however, in relation to the design right. See *ibid.* s.213, § 20–79, *post.*
[43] For the definition of a photograph, see C.D.P.A. 1988, s.4(2).
[44] C.D.P.A. 1988, s.51(1).
[45] *Ibid.* s.4, where "sculpture" is further defined.
[46] *Ibid.* s.4(1)(b).
[47] *Ibid.* s.4(1)(a).
[48] But as to such works being sculptures see *Wham-O Manufacturing Co.* v. *Lincoln Industries* [1985] R.P.C. 127, § 2–21, *ante.*
[49] § 2–23 *et seq., ante.*

20–53 **Design.** Design is defined as meaning the design of any aspect of the shape or configuration (whether internal or external) of the whole or part of an article, other than surface decoration.[50] It is clear, therefore, that all aspects of an article's shape or configuration are included within the expression "design," so the question whether such shape or configuration is dictated by functional or aesthetic considerations does not apply. It is clear that the shape or configuration referred to can be the shape or configuration of part only of an article.[51] The only matters excluded from the definition of "design" are aspects of shape or configuration which constitute "surface decoration."[52] In so far as an article may have applied to it decoration in, for example, the form of paint, it is thought that the exception of "surface decoration" is not directed to this, since such decoration would not constitute an aspect of the article's "shape or configuration." The exception is therefore thought to apply to an article's decoration which to some extent does affect its shape or configuration. Thus items of pottery or china often carry decoration in the form of bas-relief. In the same way features engraved on an article would, it is thought, amount to surface decoration. However, the dividing line between aspects of shape and configuration consisting of surface decoration and other such aspects may be difficult to draw. In the case of some articles, decoration often takes extravagant form and in part is an essential feature of an article's shape. In such cases, it is submitted that it will always be a matter of degree whether such aspects truly constitute (a) "decoration" and (b) are merely "surface" decoration.

20–54 **To make an article to the design.** Section 51 of the 1988 Act provides that it is not an infringement of any copyright in any such design document or model to make an article to the design or to copy an article made to the design.[53] The expression "to make an article to the design" is not an expression which has been used in previous Copyright Acts.[54] The section, however, sets up a defence and therefore can only be of relevance when it has already been established that the defendant has done an act restricted by the copyright in the design document or model, the relevant act for these purposes presumably being the reproduction of the design document or model, or a substantial part of it. The expression "to make an article to the design" is therefore to be understood in this context, so that it is the reproduction of a design document or model in the form of a three-dimensional article which will not be an infringement. Presumably, therefore, if the design of the article, meaning aspects of its shape or configuration other than surface decoration, is the same as that of the design document or model, there will be no infringement of copyright. Questions of substantiality will not, it is thought, arise in this context since section 51 can only be of application where it has already been established that a substantial part of a design document or model has been reproduced.

---

[50] C.D.P.A. 1988, s.51(3).
[51] *Ibid.* s.51(3).
[52] See n. 50, *ante.*
[53] C.D.P.A. 1988, s.51(1).
[54] Again, it is used in relation to the design right, see for example, *ibid.* s.226.

Copying "an article made to the design." The use of these words may **20–55**
be intended to show that the indirect copying of a design document or
model, by the copying of an article made from such a work, will amount to
infringement. It is not clear, however, why these words were required. As
has been seen,[55] the principal provision of the section is not framed in
terms of permitting the direct copying of a design document, but in terms
of permitting the making of an article to the design. Thus, if an article
made to the design is copied, it would appear that the copy itself will be
made "to the design" in the sense suggested above.

Where the design document consists of a written description recording **20–56**
the design[56] the section in terms provides that the making of an article to
that design will not infringe the copyright in that written description. The
provision is curious because, in accordance with usual principles, the
making of a three-dimensional artistic article would not in any event be
considered as amounting to reproducing a literary work.[57] The same
applies where the design document is in the form of data stored in a computer, where this amounts to a literary work.

Not all acts restricted by the copyright in a design document or model **20–57**
are permitted by section 51. Thus, the section only permits the making of
an article or the copying of an article made to the design. It appears,
therefore, that it will still be an infringement of the copyright in a design
document to make a direct copy of a design drawing, for example, by
photocopying it. On the other hand, it will not apparently be an infringement of copyright to make a drawing from an article itself, even if such a
drawing, when made, is identical to the underlying design document,
since the making of such drawing would be to copy an article made to the
design, and so would be permitted.[58]

In addition, section 51(2) provides that it is not an infringement of "the **20–58**
copyright" to issue to the public, or include in a film, broadcast or cable
programme service, anything the making of which was by virtue of section
51(1) not an infringement of copyright. Where the making of an article
was not an infringement of copyright by virtue of section 51(1), it will not
of course be an infringing copy, so that most dealings with such an article
could not amount to an infringement of copyright.[59] As has been seen,[60]
however, the issue to the public of copies of a work not previously in circulation can amount to an infringement of copyright, even though the
articles are not infringing copies.[61] These and the other acts referred to are
therefore expressly permitted by the 1988 Act.

---

[55] See § 20–54, *ante.*
[56] C.D.P.A. 1988, s.51(3).
[57] See § 8–11, *ante.*
[58] C.D.P.A. 1988, s.51(1).
[59] See Chap. 9, *ante.*
[60] § 8–92, *ante.*
[61] C.D.P.A. 1988, s.18.

20–59 **The 1956 Act.** The 1956 Act contained no equivalent provisions, and only provided a limited defence under section 9(8) which has already been discussed.[62] The 1988 Act does not contain any provisions equivalent to section 9(8) of the 1956 Act.

4. Design Right

A. *Introduction*

20–60 **1986 White Paper.** The White Paper on Intellectual Property and Innovation published in April 1986[63] addressed the question of protection of designs in the light of the discussion of the House of Lords in *British Leyland Motor Corporation* v. *Armstrong Patents Company Limited.*[64] The Government concluded that even in the case of functional designs having little or no aesthetic quality, the manufacturer who has spent money on a design should be given the opportunity to benefit from his investment.[65] A copyright registration system and some form of unfair copying law were considered but dismissed. The Government proposed a new form of protection which provided protection on copyright principles but without the more objectionable features of copyright protection and in particular the long term of protection available under full copyright.[66] The Government proposed a much shorter term of 10 years following first marketing of an article made to the design, with licences of right being available during the final five years of the term. It was proposed that the spare parts exception expounded by the House of Lords in the *British Leyland* case would not apply but there would be a more limited exception to enable the owner of the equipment to repair it or contract for someone else to repair it.

20–61 The Government also considered the interrelationship between the new unregistered design right, normal copyright, and registered design protection. For example, it was proposed that the new unregistered design right would not impinge on articles which are themselves artistic works and thus enjoy full copyright protection.

20–62 Since the White Paper, the House of Lords, in deciding the case of *Interlego A.G.* v. *Tyco Industries Inc.*[67] considered the need for a competitor's toy brick to be compatible with a Lego brick for there to be effective competition.

20–63 Many of the proposals in the White Paper have been adopted in Part III of the 1988 Act dealing with design right while others have been modified or even dropped altogether.

---

[62] § 8–70, *ante, et seq.*
[63] Cmnd. 9712
[64] [1986] R.P.C. 279.
[65] Cmnd. 9712, clause 3.21.
[66] *Ibid.* clause 3.30.
[67] [1988] R.P.C. 343.

In the United States a law relating to the protection of semiconductor **20–64** topographies was enacted.[68] This law only gave protection to non-United States citizens if the country concerned provided similar rights for United States citizens. Initially regulations were enacted in the United Kingdom under an EEC directive. These regulations have now been re-enacted under the design right provisions.[69]

B. *Nature of design right*

Design right. Design right is a property right which subsists in certain **20–65** original designs.[70] The owner of a design right is entitled to prevent copying of the design so that the right is similar to normal copyright.

Date of design. Design right does not subsist in a design which was **20–66** recorded in a design document or to which an article was made before August 1, 1989.[71]

C. *Conditions for subsistence*

Summary

The conditions which a design must satisfy for design right to subsist are **20–67** summarised below:

   (i) The design must fall within the definition of design in section 213(2) of the 1988 Act.[72]
  (ii) The design must not fall within one of those categories which are specifically excluded from enjoying design right protection.[73]
 (iii) The design must be original.[74]
 (iv) The design must have been recorded in a design document or an article made to the design on or after August 1, 1989.[75]
  (v) The design must qualify for design right protection under the provisions of section 213(5) of the 1988 Act (qualification by reference to the designer, commissioner, employer, or first marketer).

(i) Definition of "design"

Design means the design of any aspect of the shape or configuration **20–68** (whether internal or external) of the whole or part of an article.[76] It is to be noted that there is no requirement for the design to have any artistic

---

[68] See "Copyright," Jan. 1988, p. 29 and § 18–41, *ante*.
[69] For a more detailed discussion see § 20–208 *et seq.*, *post*.
[70] C.D.P.A. 1988, s.213(1).
[71] Copyright, Designs and Patents Act 1988 (Commencement No. 1) Order 1989 (1989 S.I. No. 816). See § B–5, *post*.
[72] § 20–68, *post*.
[73] C.D.P.A. 1988, s.213(3).
[74] *Ibid*. s.213(4).
[75] *Ibid*. s.213(6) and s.213(7).
[76] *Ibid*. s.213(2).

merit or aesthetic quality and consequently, subject to certain exclusions, design right will subsist in designs of certain functional articles. For example, designs of machine tools and designs of chairs having no artistic merit will fall within the definition of "design." It is significant that the definition includes the shape or configuration of part of an article, as will be discussed below.[77]

20–69 **Comparison with Part I definition.** The definition of "design" in connection with design right is identical with the corresponding definition in Part I of the 1988 Act, section 51(3), other than for a specific exclusion of surface decoration. Instead, the definition of "design" under Part III includes surface decoration providing this relates to some aspect of the shape or configuration of the whole or part of an article. However, as is discussed below[78] designs constituted by surface decoration aspects of shape or configuration are excluded from enjoying design right protection.

20–70 **Kits.** The design right provisions apply equally to parts of a kit as they apply to the assembled article. Of course design right can subsist in the individual components of the kit as well as the assembled article.[79]

(ii) Excluded designs

20–71 Certain designs are excluded from enjoying design right protection.

(a) *Method or principle of construction*

20–72 These words[80] are to be found in the Registered Designs Act 1949[81] and it is suggested have the same meaning under the 1988 Act as under the 1949 Act. As has always been the case, such concepts are not protectable under copyright law.

(b) *Must-fit exclusion*

20–73 Designs which consist of features of shape or configuration of an article which enable the article to be connected to, or placed in, around or against, another article so that either article may perform its function, are excluded.[82] This exclusion has arisen as a result of a consideration of the *British Leyland* case,[83] *supra*, and limits design right protection in, for example, spare parts. The exclusion must be considered in the light of the fact that design right can subsist in the design of part of an article. Thus, a spare part could have certain design features which are excluded from design right protection but have other design features in which design right subsists.

---

[77] § 20–73, *post.*
[78] § 20–75, *post.*
[79] C.D.P.A. 1988, s.260.
[80] *Ibid.* s.213(3)(a).
[81] Registered Designs Act 1949, s.1(1)(a).
[82] C.D.P.A. 1988, s.213(3)(b)(i).
[83] [1986] R.P.C. 279.

(c) *Must-match exclusion*

Designs which consist of features of shape or configuration of an article, **20–74** which are dependent on the appearance of another article of which the article is intended by the designer to form an integral part, are excluded.[84]

(d) *Surface decoration*

As has been noted above,[85] the definition of "design" does not exclude **20–75** features of shape and configuration which constitute surface decoration, in contrast to the definition in section 51(3) of the 1988 Act. However, section 213(3)(c) of the 1988 Act makes it clear that design right does not subsist in such features.[86]

(iii) Originality

The requirement for a design to be "original" is not further defined in a **20–76** positive sense. It must exclude a design created by direct copying. Further, additional circumstances are envisaged in which a design is not considered to be "original." These are where the design is commonplace in the design field in question at the time of its creation.[87] It should be noted, however, that this definition does not provide for the only circumstances in which a design is not original, but merely provides one set of circumstances in which there is no originality. In practice it may be difficult to determine whether a design is commonplace in the design field in question. Further, it is not clear, for example, whether "commonplace" refers to the territory to which the 1988 Act applies or whether the commonality of the design worldwide must be considered.

Further difficulties are introduced by the reference to the "design field." **20–77** It is suggested that this relates to the field of design in relation to the article of which the design is the shape or configuration. Thus, the design field of a design of an automobile body is the field of automobiles. On the other hand, the design of a spoon handle in the shape of a well-known automobile would not lack originality, due to the different design fields of spoons and automobiles.

It should also be noted that the effect of this section is to exclude certain **20–78** designs from enjoying design right protection which, nevertheless, have sufficient originality to enjoy copyright protection under Part I of the 1988 Act.

---

[84] C.D.P.A. 1988, s.213(3)(b)(ii).
[85] § 20–69 *ante.*
[86] Compare C.D.P.A. 1988, s.265.
[87] *Ibid.* s.213(4).

(iv) Subsistence of design right

(a) *Recording of design in design document*

20–79   Design right will subsist when the design has been recorded in a design document.[88] A "design document" is defined as any record of a design, whether in the form of a drawing, a written description, a photograph, data stored in a computer or otherwise.[89] The corresponding definition in section 51(3) of the 1988 Act is identical.

(b) *Making article to the design*

20–80   As an alternative to being recorded in a design document, design right can subsist in an article which has "been made to the design."[90] In other words, there need not be a previous design document such as a drawing to enable design right to subsist in an article made to the design. For example, if an article, such as a machine part having no artistic merit, is constructed without the assistance of a previously-made drawing, it will enjoy design right protection.

20–81   It will be noted that "making an article to the design" is mentioned, in relation to copyright, in section 51 of the 1988 Act, but it is defined for the purposes of design right in section 226(2) of such Act which deals primarily with infringement. Here it is stated that reproduction of a design by making articles to the design means copying the design so as to produce articles exactly or substantially to that design. It is suggested that the reference to producing articles substantially to the design is not relevant in the context of whether or not an article has been made to the design for the purposes of determining subsistence of design right. That is, design right subsists in the design to which an article has been made. The question of substantiality only arises in connection with infringement.

(v) Qualification for design right protection

20–82   Design right only subsists in a design if the design qualifies for design right protection by reference to:

(a) the designer, or

(b) the person by whom the design was commissioned or the designer employed, or

(c) the person by whom and country in which articles made to the design were first marketed, or

(d) in accordance with any Order which is made under section 221.[91]

20–83   **Qualifying individual.** A qualifying individual is defined as a citizen or subject of, or an individual habitually resident in, a qualifying country.[92] Where qualification is by citizenship then, in the case of the United King-

---

[88] C.D.P.A. 1988, s.213(6).
[89] *Ibid.* s.263(1).
[90] See n. 87, *ante.*
[91] C.D.P.A. 1988, s.213(5).
[92] *Ibid.* s.217(1).

dom, this means that the individual must be a British citizen, and in relation to a colony of the United Kingdom, means that the individual is a British Dependent Territories' citizen by connection with that colony.[93]

A qualifying individual also includes an individual habitually resident **20–84** in a qualifying country. The requirement for habitual residence should be contrasted with the requirement for simple residence under Part I of the 1988 Act.[94] This suggests a longer term of residence is necessary for qualification under Part III.

Qualifying person. Section 217(1) of the 1988 Act defines a qualifying **20–85** person as a qualifying individual or a body corporate or other body having legal personality which is formed under the law of a part of the United Kingdom or another qualifying country, and has in any qualifying country a place of business at which substantial business activity is carried on. "Business" includes a trade or profession[95] and in determining whether substantial business activity is carried on at a place of business in any country, no account shall be taken of dealings in goods which are at all material times outside that country.[96] It is interesting to compare the definition of a qualifying person under the design right provisions with the equivalent definition under Part I of the 1988 Act.[97] In the latter, there is no requirement for a body corporate to have a substantial business activity. It should be noted, however, that, under the design right provision, there is no requirement for that business activity to be in the field of the articles made to the design in question.

A qualifying person also includes the Crown and the government of any **20–86** other qualifying country.[98]

Qualifying country. The following are defined as qualifying countries. **20–87** The United Kingdom, that is England and Wales, Scotland and Northern Ireland[99]; another member State of the European Economic Community; a country to which the design right provisions have been extended by Order in Council under section 255 of the 1988 Act; or a country designated by an Order in Council under section 256 of the 1988 Act as enjoying reciprocal protection.[1]

Order in Council under section 255 of the 1988 Act. Orders in Coun- **20–88** cil may be made under this section to extend the design right provisions of Part III of the 1988 Act to the Channel Islands, the Isle of Man, or any colony. The legislature of a country to which the design right provisions have been extended by Order in Council may modify or add to the design right provisions, in their operation as part of the law of that country, as

---

[93] C.D.P.A. 1988, s.217(4).
[94] *Ibid.* s.154.
[95] C.D.P.A. 1988, s.263(1).
[96] *Ibid.* s.217(5).
[97] See n. 93, *ante.*
[98] C.D.P.A. 1988, s.217(2).
[99] See also *ibid.* s.257 which adds territorial waters and parts of the continental shelf.
[1] *Ibid.* s.217(3).

the legislature may consider necessary to adapt the provisions to the circumstances of that country; but not so as to deny design right protection in a case where it would otherwise exist.[2]

20–89   If a country ceases to be a colony of the United Kingdom, it shall continue to be treated as such a country until an Order in Council is made designating it as a country enjoying reciprocal protection, or an Order in Council is made declaring that it will cease to be so treated because the design right provisions as part of the law of that country have been amended or repealed.[3]

20–90   **Reciprocal protection countries.** An Order in Council under section 256 of the 1988 Act may designate that a country enjoys reciprocal protection under the design right provisions if the law of the country provides adequate protection for British designs. A British design is a design which qualifies for design right protection by reason of a connection with the United Kingdom of the designer or the person by whom the design is commissioned or the designer is employed.[4] An Order has been made under section 256 specifying *inter alia* the Channel Islands, the Isle of Man, Hong Kong, and New Zealand.[5]

20–91   If the law of such a country provides adequate protection only for certain classes of British design, or only for designs applied to certain classes of article, any Order designating that country shall contain provisions limiting, to a corresponding extent, the protection afforded by the design right provisions in relation to designs connected with that country.[6]

(a) *Qualification by reference to the designer*

20–92   If a design is created neither in pursuance of a commission nor in the course of employment, then the design qualifies for design right protection if the designer is a qualifying individual or, in the case of a computer-generated design, a qualifying person.[7] The designer is the person who creates the design.[8] It is suggested that, in most cases, the designer will be the person who records the design in a design document or makes an article to the design, and will not include any person or persons who simply provide a suggestion for the general concept of a design.

20–93   "Computer-generated" means that the design is generated by computer in circumstances such that there is no human designer[9] and in this case the "designer" is taken to be the person by whom the arrangements necessary for the creation of the design are undertaken. A similar defi-

---

[2] C.D.P.A. 1988, s.255(4).
[3] *Ibid.* s.255(5).
[4] C.D.P.A. 1988, s.263(1).
[5] The Design Right (Reciprocal Protection) (No. 2) Order 1989 (1989 S.I. No. 1294): see § D–36, *post.*
[6] C.D.P.A. 1988, s.256(2).
[7] *Ibid.* s.218(1) and 218(2).
[8] *Ibid.* s.214(1).
[9] *Ibid.* s.263(1).

nition can be found, in section 9(3) of the 1988 Act, in relation to the meaning of an author of a computer-generated literary, dramatic, musical or artistic work under Part I of the 1988 Act.[10]

Joint design. A design created by a number of designers, but not in pur- **20–94**
suance of a commission or in the course of employment, qualifies for design right protection if any of the designers is a qualifying individual or a qualifying person.[11] A joint design is a design produced by the collaboration of two or more designers in which the contribution of each is not distinct from that of the other or others.[12] It should be noted that in the case of a joint design qualifying for design right protection, only those designers who are qualifying individuals or qualifying persons are entitled to ownership of the design right.[13]

(b) *Qualification by reference to commissioning or employment*

A design may qualify for design right protection if it is created in pur- **20–95**
suance of a commission from, or in the course of employment with, a qualifying person.[14] Employment means that the designer must be employed under a contract of service or of apprenticeship.[15] It should be noted that the designer in these circumstances may not himself constitute a qualifying individual or qualifying person. It is necessary only that the commissioner or employer is a qualifying person.

Joint commission or joint employment. Where a design is created in **20–96**
pursuance of a commission from joint commissioners, or in the course of employment with joint employers, a design qualifies for design right protection if any of the commissioners or employers is a qualified person.[16]

Qualification at time design created not necessary. In contrast to the **20–97**
corresponding provisions under Part I of the 1988 Act,[17] it is not a requirement under Part III of that Act that the designer, employer or commissioner should be a qualifying person at the time the design was created. This suggests that a design could be created at a time when it does not qualify for design right protection but later, due for example to a change of citizenship by the designer, could then qualify for design right.

(c) *Qualification by reference to first marketing*

If a design does not qualify for design right protection by reference to **20–98**
the designer, commissioner or employer, it may still so qualify if the first marketing of articles made to the design is by a qualifying person who is exclusively authorised to put such articles on the market in the United

---

[10] C.D.P.A. 1988, s.9(3): see § 4–14, *ante*.
[11] *Ibid.* s.218(3).
[12] *Ibid.* s.259. Compare *ibid.* s.10(1) "work of joint authorship."
[13] See n. 11, *ante*.
[14] C.D.P.A. 1988, s.219(1).
[15] *Ibid.* s.263(1). "Commission" means a commission for money or money's worth.
[16] *Ibid.* s.219(2): see § 4–35 *et seq.*, *ante*.
[17] *Ibid.* s.154: and see § 3–4 *et seq.*, *ante*.

Kingdom, and that first marketing takes place in the United Kingdom, in another member State of the European Economic Community, or in a colony to which the design right provisions have been extended by Order under section 255 of the 1988 Act.[18] No such Order has yet been made. Marketing an article means the sale, letting for hire, offer or exposure for sale or hire of the article in the course of business. No account is taken, however, of marketing which is merely colourable and not intended to satisfy the reasonable requirements of the public.[19]

20–99 **Exclusively authorised.** A qualifying person is exclusively authorised if he is authorised by the person who would have been first owner of the design right as designer, commissioner of the design or employer of the designer if he had been a qualifying person or by a person lawfully claiming under such a person, and the exclusivity is capable of being enforced by legal proceedings in the United Kingdom.[20]

20–100 **Joint first marketing.** If the first marketing of articles made to the design is done jointly by two or more persons then the design qualifies for design right protection if any of those persons is a qualifying person who is exclusively authorised to put such articles on the market in the United Kingdom.[21]

(d) *Qualification by reason of Order in Council*

20–101 Further provision may be made by Order in Council as to requirements that a design must meet to qualify for design right protection.[22] No such Order has yet been made.

D. *First owner of design right*

20–102 The provisions for first ownership of design right are very similar to those relating to proprietorship of a registered design under the Registered Designs Act 1949.[23]

20–103 **Designer.** Where a design is created other than in pursuance of a commission or in the course of employment, then the designer is the first owner of any design right.[24] The meaning of designer is discussed above.[25]

20–104 **Commission.** If a design is created in pursuance of a commission, which means a commission for money or money's worth,[26] the person commissioning the design is the first owner of any design right in it.[27]

---

[18] C.D.P.A. 1988, s.220(1).
[19] *Ibid.* s.263(2): and see § 3–17, *ante.*
[20] C.D.P.A. 1988, s.220(4).
[21] *Ibid.* s.220(2).
[22] *Ibid.* s.221.
[23] Registered Designs Act 1949, s.2.
[24] C.D.P.A. 1988, s.215(1).
[25] § 20–92, *ante.*
[26] C.D.P.A. 1988, s.263(1).
[27] *Ibid.* s.215(2).

Employment. If, in a case which does not amount to a commission, a **20–105**
design is created by an employee in the course of his employment under a
contract of service or of apprenticeship, then his employer is the first
owner of any design right in the design.[28]

First marketing. As has been explained above,[29] in some circumstances a **20–106**
design may qualify for design right by virtue of the fact that the first marketing of articles made to the design took place under certain specified circumstances. In such a situation, the first owner of the design right is then
the person by whom the articles in question are marketed.[30]

Joint ownership. In some circumstances, design right may be owned **20–107**
jointly by a number of different persons (where a person includes a body
corporate or other body having legal personality). These circumstances
are where there are joint designers, joint commissioners, joint employers,
or joint first marketers. In these circumstances, only those designers, commissioners, employers or first marketers who are qualifying individuals or
persons, as the case may be, are entitled to first ownership of any design
right.[31]

Multiple ownership. The situation in which the same design right is **20–108**
jointly owned by a number of persons should be contrasted with the situation where different aspects of a design are owned by different persons.
Thus, it is possible for separate design rights to subsist in different parts of
a single design, with each design right being owned by a different person.
In these circumstances, the first owner of each design right is determined
by reference to the appropriate aspect of the design. It must be remembered, however, that when a design is broken down into different aspects,
then some of these aspects themselves may be excluded from design right
protection by virtue of the "must-match", "must-fit" exclusions. This
could happen, for example, in the case of an automobile body where
several designers will contribute to different aspects of the car body.

Interrelationship of design right with copyright and registered **20–109**
designs. There is clearly a degree of overlap between the three forms of
protection accorded by copyright, design right, and registered design.
Thus, it is quite possible for a design to enjoy copyright protection and
design right protection (not necessarily simultaneously) and to be entitled
to be registered in respect of the article of which it defines the shape or
configuration under the Registered Designs Act 1949. However, the
ownership and the rights which can be exercised in each case may differ
significantly.

The provisions for design right ownership are very similar to those for **20–110**
proprietorship of a registered design under the Registered Designs Act
1949.[32] It is suggested that there is no substantive difference between the

---

[28] C.D.P.A. 1988, ss.215(3) and 263(1): and see § 4–39 *et seq., ante.*
[29] § 20–98, *ante.*
[30] C.D.P.A. 1988, s.215(4).
[31] C.D.P.A. 1988, ss.218(4), 219(3), 220(3): and see § 7–1 *et seq., ante.*
[32] Registered Designs Act 1949, s.2.

"designer" of a design in which design right subsists, and the "author" of the design as defined under the Registered Designs Act. The ownership provisions in connection with both the commissioning of a design and the creation of a design by an employee are also substantially the same.

20–111   The first ownership provisions for design right under the 1988 Act diverge from those for registered design under the Registered Designs Act 1949 if a design qualifies for design right protection by virtue of the manner in which articles made to the design were first marketed. In those circumstances, design right is owned by the person by whom the articles in question are marketed. No similar provision is contained in the Registered Designs Act and it is quite possible, therefore, that the first owner of design right in a design will not be the same as the proprietor of any corresponding registered design.

20–112   In some circumstances, copyright under Part I of the 1988 Act may also subsist in a design which enjoys design right protection. In those circumstances it should be noted that, where the design is created in pursuance of a commission, the first owner of any copyright under Part I will not be the person commissioning the design, but the author of the design.[33] In the case where the design is created by an employee in the course of his employment under a contract of service or apprenticeship, however, then his employer will be the first owner of any copyright, subject to any agreement to the contrary.

20–113   It appears, therefore, that, although, in some circumstances, a given design may enjoy (not necessarily simultaneously) copyright, design right, and registered design protection, each right may belong to a different person. An example of such a situation is the case of a children's toy, designed under commission by a company, which does not satisfy the requirements for a qualifying person under the design right provisions (for example, a United States or Japanese company), that toy then being marketed in the United Kingdom by a qualifying person having exclusive marketing rights in the United Kingdom. In this case, the first owner of any copyright will be the author of the design. On the other hand, the first owner of any design right will be the person who exclusively markets the toy in the United Kingdom. This is because the commissioner is not a qualifying person since he does not have a substantial business activity in a qualifying country. The proprietor of any registered design, however, will be the commissioner.

E. *Transmission and dealings with design right*

20–114   The provisions for transmission and dealings in design right are very similar to those concerned with copyright under Part I of the 1988 Act.[34]

---

[33] C.D.P.A. 1988, s.11: and see § 4–16 *et seq.*, § 4–35 *et seq.* and § 4–67 *et seq., ante.*
[34] See Chap. 5, *ante.*

(i) Assignments

Design right is transmissible by assignment, by testamentary disposition **20–115** or by operation of law, as personal or movable property.[35] An assignment is not effective unless it is in writing signed by or on behalf of the assignor.[36] An assignment or other transmission of design right may be partial so as to apply to one or more, but not all, of the things the design right owner has the exclusive right to do; or to part, but not the whole, of the period for which the right is to subsist.[37] Any licence granted by the owner of the design right is binding on every successor in title to his interest in the right, except a purchaser in good faith for valuable consideration and without notice (actual or constructive) of the licence or a person deriving title from such a purchaser.[38]

Future design right. In contrast to the position under the Registered **20–116** Designs Act 1949, but in a similar way to copyright under Part I of the 1988 Act,[39] an agreement can be made for assignment of a future design right.[40] Thus, where by an agreement made in relation to future design right, and signed[41] by or on behalf of the prospective owner of the design right, the prospective owner purports to assign the future design right (wholly or partially) to another person, then if, on the right coming into existence, the assignee or another person claiming under him would be entitled to require the right to be vested in him, the right shall vest in him. Similar provisions to those in Part I of the 1988 Act[42] apply to a licence granted by a prospective owner of design right as to a licence granted by the actual owner of design right.[43]

(ii) Exclusive licences

An exclusive licence is a licence in writing and signed[44] by or on behalf of **20–117** the design right owner authorising the licensee to the exclusion of all other persons, including the person granting the licence, to exercise a right which would otherwise be exercisable exclusively by the design right owner.[45] An exclusive licensee has the same rights against any successor in title who is bound by the licence as he has against the person granting the licence.[46]

---

[35] C.D.P.A. 1988, s.222(1).

[36] *Ibid.* s.222(3). See also *ibid.* s.261 providing that in the case of a body corporate this requirement is satisfied by affixing its seal: and see Companies Act 1989 (c.40) s.130. See also as to deeds, Law of Property (Miscellaneous Provisions) Act 1989, c. 34.

[37] *Ibid.* s.222(2).

[38] *Ibid.* s.222(4).

[39] *Ibid.* s.91: and see § 5–40, *ante.*

[40] *Ibid.* s.223.

[41] See n. 36, *ante.*

[42] C.D.P.A. 1988, s.91(3): and see § 5–42, *ante.*

[43] *Ibid.* s.223(3).

[44] See n. 35, *ante.*

[45] C.D.P.A. 1988, s.225(1).

[46] *Ibid.* s.225(2): compare *ibid.* s.92.

(iii) Assignment of registered design also assignment of design right

20–118   Section 224 of the 1988 Act provides that where a design consisting of a design in which design right subsists is registered under the Registered Designs Act 1949 and the proprietor of the registered design is also the design right owner, an assignment of the right in the registered design shall be taken to be also an assignment of the design right, unless a contrary intention appears.

20–119   In most cases, the owner of design right will be the proprietor of the corresponding registered design. Nevertheless, there are circumstances where this may not be so. For example, separate design rights may subsist in different aspects or parts of the design of an article and be owned by different persons. A registered design, however, will in most cases protect the design of the whole article. Furthermore the proprietor of the registered design may not be the same as one or more of the design right owners. Consequently, if the registered design is assigned, not all the design rights may automatically be assigned at the same time by virtue of the provisions of section 224.

(iv) Licence under registered design

20–120   The provisions of section 224 of the 1988 Act concerning assignment of registered designs do not assist a licensee under a registered design who intends to market articles made to the design. Such a licensee will have to take steps to confirm that the licensor is the owner of all design rights subsisting in the design protected by the registered design or obtain additional licences from the other design right owners.

(v) Joint owners

20–121   Where design right (or any aspect of design right) is owned by more than one person jointly, then all the owners must licence the design right.[47]

F. *Duration*

20–122   **15-year rule.** Design right will ordinarily subsist for 15 years from the end of the calendar year in which the design was first recorded in a design document or an article was first made to the design, whichever first occurred.[48]

20–123   **10-year rule.** However, the design right term is cut short if articles made to the design are made available for sale or hire anywhere in the world by or with the licence of the design right owner within five years from the end of the calendar year in which the design was first recorded in a design document or an article was first made to the design. In that event, the

---

[47] C.D.P.A. 1988, s.258: and see § 7–4, *ante.*
[48] *Ibid.* s.216(1)(*a*).

design right expires 10 years from the end of the calendar year in which articles were first made available for sale or hire.[49]

G. *Infringement of design right*

(i) Primary infringement

Exclusive right of design right owner. The owner of design right has the exclusive right to reproduce the design for commercial purposes by making articles to that design, or by making a design document recording the design for the purpose of enabling such articles to be made.[50] It is made clear that this exclusive right is similar to normal copyright in that reproduction of a design by making articles to the design means copying the design so as to produce articles exactly or substantially to that design.[51] In other words, there has to be an act of copying for an infringement to be committed.

       20–124

Making a design document. As stated above, in addition to having the exclusive right to make articles to the design, the owner of design right also has the exclusive right to reproduce the design by making a design document recording the design for the purpose of enabling such articles to be made. A "design document" can include, not only a written record of the design, but also data stored on computer.[52] It should be noted, however, that the design right owner does not have the exclusive right to all forms of reproduction. The design document must be for the purpose of enabling articles to be made to the design, and it is suggested that, for example, a painting of the design would fall outside the design right owner's exclusive right.

       20–125

Commercial purposes. The exclusive right of the design right owner only extends to reproduction of the design for commercial purposes, which means that the act of reproduction is done with a view to the article in question being sold or hired in the course of a business.[53]

       20–126

Infringement. Design right is infringed by a person who, without the licence of the design right owner does, or authorises another to do, anything which by virtue of section 226 of the 1988 Act is the exclusive right of the design right owner.[54] Thus, the unauthorised reproduction of the design for commercial purposes by making articles to that design, or by making a design document recording the design for the purpose of enabling such articles to be made, is an infringement. There may be infringement by directly reproducing the design by copying a representation of the design from a design document or an article made to the

       20–127

---

[49] C.D.P.A. 1988, s.216(1)(*b*), s.216(2).
[50] *Ibid.* s.226(1).
[51] *Ibid.* s.226(2).
[52] *Ibid.* s.263(1).
[53] *Ibid.* s.263(3).
[54] *Ibid.* s.226(3).

design; or indirectly where there have been a number of intervening acts. Furthermore, it is immaterial whether any such intervening acts themselves infringe the design right.[55]

(ii) Secondary infringement

20–128 In addition to the primary infringing acts described above, design right is infringed by a person who, without the licence of the design right owner, imports into the United Kingdom for commercial purposes, or has in his possession for commercial purposes, or sells, lets for hire, or offers or exposes for sale or hire, in the course of a business, an article which is, and which he knows, or has reason to believe is, an infringing article.[56]

20–129 **Knowledge part of infringement.** Thus, as with secondary copyright infringement, it is a requirement for the person concerned to have knowledge or at least reasonable belief that the article which he is handling is an infringing article.

(iii) Infringing article

20–130 An article is an infringing article if its making to the design was an infringement of design right in the design.[57] An article is also an infringing article if it has been, or is proposed to be, imported into the United Kingdom, and its making to that design in the United Kingdom would have been an infringement of design right in the design or a breach of an exclusive licence agreement relating to the design.[58]

20–131 **Design document not an infringing article.** It should be noted that design documents are specifically excluded from constituting "infringing articles" even if the making of the document was or would have been an infringement of design right.[59]

20–132 **Presumption as to time of making an article.** If an article is shown to be made to a design in which design right subsists or has subsisted at any time, then it is to be presumed, until the contrary is proved, that the article was made at a time when design right subsisted.[60] The onus is therefore on the defendant in infringement proceedings to prove that design right did not subsist when the article was made.

20–133 **Importation from another European Community country.** If an article may be lawfully imported into the United Kingdom by virtue of any enforceable Community right within the meaning of section 2(1) of the European Communities Act 1972,[61] then that article is not an infringing article.[62]

---

[55] C.D.P.A. 1988, s.226(4).
[56] *Ibid.* s.227: and see § 9–3 *et seq., ante.*
[57] *Ibid.* s.228(2): and see § 9–4, *ante.*
[58] *Ibid.* s.228(3).
[59] *Ibid.* s.228(6).
[60] *Ibid.* s.228(4).
[61] c. 68.
[62] C.D.P.A. 1988, s.228(5): and see Chap. 14, *ante.*

Territory. When considering infringement, the provisions of section 257 **20–134**
of the 1988 Act should be noted. These treat the territorial waters of the
United Kingdom as part of the United Kingdom. The territory to which
the design right provisions apply also extends to the United Kingdom sector of the continental shelf in connection with things done on a structure
or vessel which is present there for the purposes of exploration of the sea
bed or exploration of their natural resources.

H. *Exceptions from infringement of design right*

Parallel copyright protection. If copyright subsists in a work which **20–135**
consists of or includes a design in which design right subsists, it is not an
infringement of design right in the design to do anything which is an
infringement of copyright in that work.[63] In other words, where dual protection exists, copyright overrides design right.

This dual protection is most likely to occur when considering infringe- **20–136**
ment of a design document or model recording or embodying a design for
an artistic work. It is possible, for example, to envisage a design for a vase
in which artistic copyright subsists and in which design right also subsists.
In such circumstances, copying of the design by making an article to the
design will not infringe the design right, but could infringe the artistic
copyright.

However, where copyright and design right both subsist, it may never- **20–137**
theless be wise to plead infringement of copyright and infringement of
design right. The owners both of the copyright and of the design right
would need to be named as plaintiffs.[64]

Special exceptions. Section 245 of the 1988 Act allows the Secretary of **20–138**
State by order to provide that acts of certain descriptions do not infringe
design right in order to comply with an international obligation of the
United Kingdom, or to secure or maintain reciprocal protection of British
designs in other countries. An order made for this purpose may make different provision for different descriptions of design or article.[65]

I. *Remedies for infringement of design right*

Damages, injunctions and accounts. An infringement of design right is **20–139**
actionable by the design right owner. In such an action the usual remedies
are available as in the case of infringement of any other property right
including damages, injunctions, and accounts. The court may award such
additional damages as the justice of the case may require having regard to
all the circumstances and in particular to the flagrancy of the infringement
and any benefit accruing to the defendant by reason of the infringement.[66]

---

[63] C.D.P.A. 1988, s.236. And see *ibid.* ss.51 and 52 and § 20–43 *et seq.* and § 20–50 *et seq., ante.*
[64] See Ord. 15, r. 4: and see § 20–200, *post.*
[65] See The Design Right (Semiconductor Topographies) Regulations 1989 (1989 S.I.
No. 1100). For a discussion of these regulations see § 20–208 *et seq., post* and § A–577A,
post.
[66] C.D.P.A. 1988, s.229: and see § 11–66, *ante.*

20–140 **Innocent infringement.** Some of the usual remedies are not available against innocent infringers. If an action for primary infringement is brought and it is shown that at the time of the infringement the defendant did not know, and had no reason to believe, that design right subsisted in the design to which the action relates, the plaintiff is not entitled to damages.[67]

20–141   In the case of an action for secondary infringement, if a defendant shows that the infringing article was innocently acquired by him or a predecessor in title of his, the only remedy available against him in respect of the infringement is damages not exceeding a reasonable royalty in respect of the act complained of. In this context, "innocently acquired" means that the person acquiring the article did not know and had no reason to believe that it was an infringing article.[68]

20–142 **Order for delivery up.** The plaintiff in an action for infringement of design right can apply for an order for delivery up in certain circumstances. These are (a) where a person has in his possession, custody or control for commercial purposes an infringing article, or (b) where a person has in his possession, custody or control anything specifically designed or adapted for the making of articles to a particular design, knowing or having reason to believe that it has been or is to be used to make an infringing article.[69]

20–143 **Limitations on delivery up order.** Firstly, an application for an order for delivery up may not be made after the end of the period of six years from the date on which the infringing article or means for making articles was made as the case may be.[70] However, provision is made if, during the whole or any part of the six-year period, the design right owner is under a disability or is prevented by fraud or concealment from discovering the facts entitling him to apply for an order.[71] In these latter circumstances, an application may be made at any time before the end of the period of six years from the date on which he ceased to be under a disability[72] or, as the case may be, could with reasonable diligence have discovered the facts entitling him to apply for an order. Secondly, the court can only make an order for delivery up if it also makes an order under section 231 of the 1988 Act (relating to disposal of infringing articles) or considers there are grounds for making such an order.[73]

---

[67] C.D.P.A. 1988, s.233(1): compare *ibid.* s.97(1) § 11–25 *ante.*
[68] *Ibid.* s.233(2) and (3).
[69] *Ibid.* s.230(1): and see § 11–17 *ante.*
[70] *Ibid.* s.230(2) and (3).
[71] *Ibid.* s.230(4).
[72] "Disability"is defined in *ibid.* s.230(5) as having the meanings ascribed under the Limitation Act 1980 (c. 58) for England and Wales, the Prescription and Limitation (Scotland) Act 1973 (c. 52), and the Statute of Limitations (Northern Ireland) 1958 (c. 10 (N.I.)) as the case may be.
[73] C.D.P.A. 1988, s.230(2).

A person to whom an infringing article or other thing is delivered up **20–144**
must retain it pending the making of an order for its disposal under section 231 of the 1988 Act or a decision not to make such an order.[74]

Order for disposal. An application can be made to the court under sec- **20–145**
tion 231 of the 1988 Act that an infringing article or other thing delivered
up shall be forfeited to the design right owner or destroyed or otherwise
dealt with, or for a decision that no such order should be made. In deciding what order (if any) should be made, the court will consider whether
other remedies would be adequate to compensate the design right owner
and to protect his interests.[75]

Notice[76] has to be served on persons having an interest in the article or **20–146**
other thing and any such person is entitled to appear in proceedings for an
order and to appeal against any order made, whether or not he appeared
in the proceedings. An order will not take effect until the end of the period
within which notice of appeal may be given or until the final determination or abandonment of the proceedings on the appeal as the case
may be.[77]

Where there is more than one person interested in an article or other **20–147**
thing, the court may direct that the thing be sold, or otherwise dealt with,
and the proceeds divided.[78] A person having an interest in an article or
other thing includes any person in whose favour an order could be made
in respect of it under the design right provisions or under the corresponding copyright provisions of Part I of the 1988 Act or under similar provisions of the Trade Marks Act 1938.[79]

If the court decides that no order shall be made, then the person from **20–148**
whom the article or other thing was delivered up or seized is entitled to its
return.[80]

Exclusive licensee. An exclusive licensee has, except against the design **20–149**
right owner, the same rights and remedies in respect of matters occurring
after the grant of a licence as if the licence had been an assignment.[81] The
rights and remedies of the exclusive licensee are concurrent with those of
the design right owner.[82] Correspondingly, in any action brought by the
exclusive licensee, a defendant may avail himself of any defence which

---

[74] C.D.P.A. 1988, s.230(6).
[75] *Ibid.* s.231(2): and see § 11–77 *ante.*
[76] Ord. 93, r. 24. For Scotland see 1990 S.I. No. 380, § B–214, *post.*
[77] C.D.P.A. 1988, s.231(3).
[78] *Ibid.* s.231(4): and see § 11–79, *ante.*
[79] *Ibid.* s.231(6). Trade Marks Act 1938 (1938 c. 22).
[80] *Ibid.* s.231(5).
[81] *Ibid.* s.234(1): and see § 11–09, *ante.*
[82] *Ibid.* s.234(2).

would have been available to him if the action had been brought by the design right owner.[83]

20–150 **Concurrent rights of the design right owner and exclusive licensee.** Where an action is brought for infringement in respect of which both the design right owner and the exclusive licensee have concurrent rights of action, each must be a party to the action unless the court otherwise orders.[84] Thus, in the case of an action brought by the design right owner, the exclusive licensee must be joined as a plaintiff or added as a defendant. Where either the design right owner or exclusive licensee is added as a defendant, he is not liable for any costs in the action unless he takes part in the proceedings.[85] This requirement to join the design right owner and exclusive licensee does not affect the granting of interlocutory relief on the application of the design right owner or an exclusive licensee.[86]

20–151 In the case where an action for infringement of design right is brought in respect of which the design right owner and an exclusive licensee have concurrent rights of action, the court shall take into account when assessing damages the terms of the licence, and any pecuniary remedy already awarded or available to either of them in respect of the infringement. In these circumstances, no account of profits shall be directed if an award of damages has been made, or an account of profits has been directed, in favour of the other of them in respect of the infringement. Furthermore, if an account of profits is directed, the court will apportion the profits between them in such a manner as the court considers just, subject to any agreement between the design right owner and exclusive licensee.[87]

20–152 These provisions apply whether or not the design right owner and the exclusive licensee are both parties to the action.[88]

20–153 **Notification to exclusive licensee.** If the design right owner wishes to apply for an order for delivery up under section 230 of the 1988 Act, he has to notify any exclusive licensee having concurrent rights before applying for that order. The court may then, on the application of the licensee, make such order as it thinks fit having regard to the terms of the licence.[89] There is no corresponding provision requiring an exclusive licensee to notify the design right owner.

20–154 **Criminal proceedings.** It should be noted that there are no criminal remedies under the design right provisions comparable to those in Part I of the 1988 Act dealing with copyright.[90]

---

[83] C.D.P.A. 1988, s.234(3).
[84] *Ibid.* s.235(1): and see § 11–09, *ante*.
[85] *Ibid.* s.235(2).
[86] *Ibid.* s.235(3).
[87] *Ibid.* s.235(4).
[88] *Supra*, n.87.
[89] *Ibid.* s.235(5).
[90] *Ibid.* s.107.

J. *Threat of infringement proceedings*

Section 253 provides that it is an offence to issue an unjustified threat of proceedings for infringement of design right. A similar provision is made under the Registered Designs Act 1949 and the Patents Act 1977,[91] but no equivalent provision exists under Part I of the 1988 Act.

20–155

Person aggrieved. Only an aggrieved person, can take action under this provision. Clearly, the person to whom the threats are issued is such an aggrieved person, but it is suggested that other persons could also take action. For example, if a retailer is threatened with infringement proceedings as a result of his sale of a particular article, then the person who supplies that article to the retailer may satisfy the requirement of an aggrieved person.[92]

20–156

Form of threat. This section does not state that an actionable threat has to be in writing and it would seem, therefore, that not only written threats, but also verbal threats are actionable. However, the plaintiff must prove that the threats were made, which would be more difficult in the latter case.

20–157

Available relief. A successful plaintiff may obtain a declaration to the effect that the threats are unjustifiable; an injunction against the continuance of the threats; and damages in respect of any loss which he has sustained by the threats.[93]

20–158

Defence to threats action. A defendant can succeed in a threats action if he can show that the threat was justifiable. That is, if he can show that the act in respect of which proceedings were threatened did constitute, or if done would have constituted, an infringement of the design right concerned.[94]

20–159

Exceptions to actionable threats. Simple notification that a design is protected by design right does not constitute a threat of proceedings.[95] In addition, a threats action may not be brought in respect of a threat to bring proceedings for an infringement alleged to consist of making or importing anything.[96]

20–160

Person issuing threats. It should be noted that action can be taken under these provisions against a person who threatens another person with infringement proceedings even though the person issuing the threats had no rights in the design right itself. It appears, further, that even though the defendant has no interest in the design right he could succeed in a threats action brought under these provisions by proving that the acts

20–161

---

[91] Registered Designs Act 1949 (c. 88), s.26 and Patents Act 1977 (c. 37), s.70.
[92] See § 21–52, *post*. See also *Terrell on the Law of Patents* (13th ed.), Chap. 13.
[93] C.D.P.A. 1988, s.253(1).
[94] *Ibid.* s.253(2).
[95] *Ibid.* s.253(4).
[96] *Ibid.* s.253(3); *cf.* Patents Act 1977 (c. 37) s.70(4) and *Neild* v. *Rockley* [1986] F.S.R. 3.

of the plaintiff did constitute, or would have constituted, an infringement of the design right.

K. *Licences of right*

20–162   Following a proposal in the White Paper on Intellectual Property,[97] the design right provisions introduce a new concept to the field of intellectual property relating to designs. That is, during the last five years of the term of a design right, or upon a determination that it would be in the public interest, any person is entitled, as of right, to a licence to do anything which would otherwise infringe the design right.[98] In practice, it is likely to be difficult to determine when licences begin to be available as of right under a design right. This is because the term of the design right is related to the times at which the design was created and at which articles made to the design were first marketed.[99] Similar licence provisions exist in connection with patents granted under the Patents Act 1949, but still in force at the time when the Patents Act 1977 came into force.[1] However, in this case, a reference to the Register of Patents enables the time at which licences are available as of right to be accurately determined. No such register exists for design rights.

20–163   **Settlement of terms.** The 1988 Act provides that the terms of a licence shall be settled by the Comptroller,[2] in default of agreement between the design right owner and the prospective licensee.[3] This indicates that the Comptroller will only entertain an application to settle the terms of a licence if there has been an attempt by the prospective licensee to settle terms with the design right owner.

20–164   **Time of application for licence.** Where licences are available as of right by virtue of the design right entering its last five years of subsistence, an application for settlement of the terms of such a licence may not be made earlier than one year before the earliest date on which the licence may take effect.[4]

20–165   **Terms of licence.** The terms of a licence settled by the Comptroller must give the licensee, in the case where the design right is in its last five years of subsistence, the right to do everything which would be an infringement of the design right in the absence of a licence.[5] This will include both primary and secondary infringements.

20–166   **Public interest.** The 1986 White Paper recommended that licences should be made available as of right under a design right if the Monopolies and Mergers Commission finds that a design right owner is acting

---

[97] Intellectual Property and Innovation, Cmnd. 9712 (1986) clause 3.27.
[98] C.D.P.A. s.237(1).
[99] See § 20–122 *et seq., ante.*
[1] Patents Act 1977 (c. 37), Sched. 1, para. 4(2)(*c*).
[2] Comptroller-General of Patents, Designs and Trade Marks, see C.D.P.A. 1988, s.263(1).
[3] C.D.P.A. 1988, ss.237(2) and 247(1)(*a*).
[4] *Ibid.* s.247(2).
[5] *Ibid.* s.247(3)(*a*).

against the public interest.[6] This has been implemented by section 238 of the 1988 Act which provides that, if the Monopolies and Mergers Commission reports that certain matters in connection with a design right have, will, or do operate against the public interest, then the powers set out under the Fair Trading Act 1973[7] are increased. The matters concerned include conditions in licences granted by a design right owner restricting the use of the design by a licensee or restricting the owner's right to grant other licences, or a refusal of a design right owner to grant licences on reasonable terms. The additional powers include the power to cancel or modify the conditions of a licence and/or to provide that licences are available as of right.

Once again, if licences are available as of right under these provisions, **20–167** the Comptroller may settle the terms of a licence in default of agreement between the parties.[8]

Terms of licence. Where a licence is available as of right in the public **20–168** interest by virtue of section 238 of the 1988 Act, a licensee is to be entitled to do everything in respect of which such a licence is available.[9] Such a licence may not, therefore, cover all otherwise infringing acts.

Date of commencement of licence. A licence settled by the Comptroller **20–169** is to take effect, either from the date on which the application to the Comptroller was made to settle the terms of the licence or, in the case of a licence available by virtue of the term of the design right entering its last five years and in which the application was made before the earliest date on which the licence could take effect, from that earliest date.[10]

Secretary of State. In some circumstances, the Secretary of State may by **20–170** order prohibit the granting of licences of right in respect of designs of certain descriptions in order to comply with any international obligations or to secure or maintain reciprocal protection of British designs in other countries.[11] The Secretary of State may also prescribe by order factors which the Comptroller must take into account when settling the terms of a licence.[12] No such orders have yet been made.

Limitations on licensee. A person who has a licence by virtue of the **20–171** licence of right provisions must not apply a trade description to goods marketed or to be marketed under the licence unless he has the design right owner's consent. He must also not use any such trade description in an advertisement for such goods. A breach of these requirements is actionable by the design right owner.[13]

---

[6] Intellectual Property and Innovation, Cmnd. 9712 (1986), clause 3.27.
[7] Fair Trading Act 1973 (c. 41), Sched. 8 (Part I).
[8] C.D.P.A. 1988, s.247(1)(*b*).
[9] *Ibid.* s.247(3)(*b*).
[10] *Ibid.* s.247(6): and see *ibid.* s.123(3) and § 15–174, *ante*.
[11] *Ibid.* s.237(3). Also see § 20–208 *et seq., post*.
[12] *Ibid.* s.247(4).
[13] *Ibid.* s.254. "Trade description" and "advertisement" have the same meaning as in the Trade Descriptions Act 1968 (c. 29).

20–172 **Design right owner unknown.** Since there is no provision of the 1988 Act requiring registration of a design right, it may well happen that the identity of the design right owner cannot be discovered despite reasonable inquiry. In these circumstances, the Comptroller may order that a licence under the design right shall be free of any obligation to pay royalties or other payments.[14]

20–173 **Subsequent appearance of design right owner.** Subsequent to the grant of a licence, the previously unknown design right owner may apply to the Comptroller to vary the terms of the licence with effect from the date on which his application is made. Furthermore, if it is subsequently established that a licence was not available as of right, the licensee is not to be liable in damages for, or for an account of profits in respect of, anything done before he was aware of any claim by the design right owner that a licence was not available. Such a licensee could, however, be subject to an injunction, order for delivery up, etc.[15]

20–174 **Infringement proceedings where licences of right available.** A defendant in proceedings for infringement of design right may take advantage of licences being available as of right under a design right to minimise the remedies available against him if he undertakes to take a licence. In these circumstances, if the defendant cannot agree terms with the design right owner, terms can be settled by the Comptroller.[16]

20–175 **Available remedies.** Where a suitable undertaking is given by the defendant during infringement proceedings, or at any time before a final order in the proceedings, no injunction may be granted against him, no order for delivery up may be made, and the amount recoverable by way of damages or an account of profits must not exceed double the amount which would have been payable by him as licensee if such a licence on the terms agreed, or settled by the Comptroller, had been granted before the earliest infringement.[17]

20–176 In giving an undertaking to take a licence, the defendant does not have to admit liability.[18]

20–177 **Infringement before licence of right available.** The reduction in severity of the remedies available to a design right owner where a defendant undertakes to take a licence does not apply in connection with infringing acts which occurred before licences of right were available.[19] For example, where articles embodying the design have been sold over a period of time and licences of right only became available during that period, then the normal, full remedies are available in respect of infringing articles made before licences of right were available, but only the reduced remedies are available in respect of infringing articles made thereafter.

---

[14] C.D.P.A. 1988, s.248.
[15] See n. 14, *ante.*
[16] C.D.P.A. 1988, s.239(1).
[17] See n. 14, *ante.*
[18] C.D.P.A. 1988, s.239(2).
[19] *Ibid.* s.239(3).

L. *Crown use*

(i) General

Crown use not infringement. Provision is made for a government **20–178**
department[20] or a person authorised in writing by a government department to do anything for the purpose of supplying articles for the services of
the Crown, or to dispose of articles no longer required for the service of the
Crown, without the licence of the design right owner and without infringing the design right.[21] Similar provisions exist under the Registered
Designs Act 1949 and under the Patents Act 1977.[22]

Services of the Crown. The references to services of the Crown relate to **20–179**
the defence of the realm, foreign defence purposes, and health service purposes.[23]

The supply of articles for "foreign defence purposes" relates to their **20–180**
supply for the defence of a country outside the realm but with which the
British Government has an agreement or arrangement; or for use by
armed forces in pursuance of a resolution of the United Nations.[24]

"Health Service purposes" includes pharmaceutical services, general **20–181**
medical services, or general dental services and is further defined as
including services of those kinds under Part 2 of the National Health Service Act 1977 and equivalent provisions in Scotland and Northern Ireland.[25]

A person does not have to be authorised by a government department **20–182**
before he commits what would otherwise be an infringing act on behalf of
that government department, since authorisation can be given both before
and after use and irrespective of whether or not the person is authorised
by the design right owner. Furthermore, any person acquiring anything
sold as a result of the exercise of the Crown use powers is entitled to deal
with it in the same manner as if the design right were held on behalf of the
Crown.[26]

Compensation for loss of profit. In addition to any terms which may be **20–183**
settled between the design right owner, exclusive licensee or other person
entitled to benefit and a government department, the government department will also have to pay to the design right owner or to an exclusive
licensee compensation for any loss resulting from his not being awarded a
contract to supply the articles made to the design.[27] The only relevant

---

[20] Including a Northern Ireland department: C.D.P.A. 1988, s.263(1).
[21] *Ibid.* s.240.
[22] Registered Designs Act 1949 (c. 88), s.12; Patents Act 1977 (c. 37), ss.55–59.
[23] C.D.P.A. 1988, s.240(2).
[24] *Ibid.* s.240(3).
[25] *Ibid.* s.240(4). See also National Health Service Act 1977 (c. 49), and Part II of the National Health Service (Scotland) Act 1978 (c. 29).
[26] *Ibid.* s.240(6) and 240(7).
[27] *Ibid.* s.243(1).

contracts, however, are contracts for the supply of articles made to the design for the services of the Crown.[28]

20–184   The degree of compensation is dependent upon the extent that such a contract could have been fulfilled from the design right owner's or exclusive licensee's existing manufacturing capacity and having regard to the actual profit which would have been made on such a contract and to the extent to which any manufacturing capacity was under-used.[29]

20–185   In some circumstances, the design right owner or exclusive licensee will be ineligible for the award of such a contract. Compensation is payable notwithstanding this ineligibility.[30]

20–186   If agreement cannot be reached between the design right owner or licensee and the government department concerned, then compensation for loss of profit shall be determined by the court.[31]

20–187   Crown use during emergency. Section 244 of the 1988 Act contains certain special provisions which apply during a period of emergency as determined by Order in Council. These provisions increase the Crown use powers and include the power to do any act which would otherwise be an infringement of design right for any purpose which appears to the government department concerned necessary or expedient:

> (a) for the efficient prosecution of any war in which the Government is engaged;
> (b) for the maintenance of supplies and services essential to the life of the community;
> (c) for securing a sufficiency of supplies and services essential to the well-being of the community;
> (d) for promoting the productivity of industry, commerce and agriculture;
> (e) for fostering and directing export and reducing imports and generally for redressing the balance of trade;
> (f) generally for ensuring that the whole resources of the community are available for use; or
> (g) for assisting the relief of suffering and the restoration and distribution of essential supplies and services in any country outside the United Kingdom which is in grave distress as a result of war.

(ii) Settlement of disputes

20–188   Notification to design right owner. Unless it is contrary to the public interest, or the identity of the design right owner cannot be ascertained, the design right owner must be notified as soon as practicable of the

---

[28] C.D.P.A. 1988, s.243(4).
[29] *Ibid.* s.243(2) and 243(3).
[30] *Ibid.* s.243(2).
[31] *Ibid.* s.243(5).

Crown use and must be given such information as to the extent of the use as he may from time to time require.[32]

Settlement. Terms may be agreed between the government department **20–189** and the design right owner with the approval of the Treasury before or after the Crown use has taken place. In default of an agreement application may be made to the court.[33]

Design right owner unknown. Where the identity of the design right **20–190** owner cannot be ascertained, application may be made to the court by the government department and the court may order that no royalty or other sum shall be payable until the design right owner agrees terms with the department or refers the matter to the court.[34]

Factors considered by court. In determining a dispute between a **20–191** government department and a person concerning the terms for Crown use, the court shall have regard to any remuneration which the person concerned has received or is entitled to receive, directly, or indirectly, from any government department in respect of the design; and the conduct of that person, in particular whether, in the court's opinion, that person has without reasonable cause failed to comply with a request of the department for the use of the design on reasonable terms.[35]

Joint owners. In the case where there are joint owners of the design right, **20–192** one such joint owner may refer a dispute to the court, but only if the others are made parties. None of the others are liable for costs, however, unless they take part in the proceedings.[36]

(iii) Effect of existing agreements

Rights of third parties. In some cases, an agreement, such as a licence or **20–193** assignment, may exist between the design right owner and a third party when Crown use is made of the design. In these circumstances, any restrictions in such a licence, assignment, or other agreement will in general have no effect in relation to the Crown use of the design. Relevant restrictions include those which restrict or regulate anything done in relation to the design, or the use of any model, document or other information relating to it, or provide for the making of payments in respect of such use. Furthermore, the copying or issuing to the public of copies of any such model or document, or any such use, is deemed not to be an infringement in any copyright in the model or document.[37] However, this is not to be construed as authorising the disclosure of any such model, document or information in contravention of the licence, assignment or other agreement.[38]

---

[32] C.D.P.A. 1988, s.241(1).
[33] *Ibid.* s.241(2).
[34] *Ibid.* s.241(3).
[35] *Ibid.* s.252(2).
[36] *Ibid.* s.252(3).
[37] *Ibid.* s.242(1).
[38] *Ibid.* s.242(2).

20–194 **Exclusive licence.** Special provisions exist where an exclusive licence has been granted under a design right. The provisions applicable depend on whether or not the exclusive licence was granted for royalties, which includes any benefit determined by reference to the use of the design.

(a) *Exclusive licence granted for royalties*

20–195   In these circumstances, any agreement reached between the design right owner and a government department to settle the terms for Crown use will require the consent of the licensee, as the licensee is entitled to recover from the design right owner a proportion of the payment for Crown use. The proportion recoverable is to be agreed between the licensee and the design right owner or, in default of agreement, by the court.[39]

20–196   The holder of an exclusive licence for royalties must be notified of any reference to the court by the design right owner for compensation and be given an opportunity to be heard, before the court determines the amount of any payment. If the licensee is not so notified the determination is of no effect.[40] Furthermore, if the court is asked to settle the proportion payable to the licensee, the court shall determine what is a just payment having regard to any expenditure incurred by the licensee in developing the design, or in making payments to the design right owner in consideration of the licence other than royalties or other payments determined by reference to the use of the design.[41]

(b) *Exclusive licence not granted for royalties*

20–197   In these circumstances, the exclusive licensee takes the place of the design right owner in settling the terms for Crown use. Further, section 241 of the 1988 Act, which deals with the settlement of terms for Crown use and notification of the design right owner, does not apply where the licensee has been authorised by a government department in respect of Crown use.[42]

20–198 **Assignment for royalties.** Special provisions[43] also exist where the design right has been assigned to the design right owner in consideration of royalties. In these circumstances, the settlement of terms for Crown use has to take into account both the design right owner and the assignor, and any payment for Crown use is to be divided between them. The division of payment shall be in such proportion as they can agree, or in default of agreement, as determined by the court. In these circumstances, there can be settlement of terms under section 241 in relation to any act done for the services of the Crown to the order of a government department by the design right owner in respect of a design.

---

[39] C.D.P.A. 1988, s.242(3)(a).
[40] *Ibid.* s.252(4).
[41] *Ibid.* s.252(5).
[42] *Ibid.* s.242(3)(b).
[43] *Ibid.* s.242(4).

Use of model, document or other information. As mentioned above, **20–199** the provisions of any licence, assignment or agreement between the design right owner and any person other than a government department are of no effect in relation to Crown use of a design so far as they restrict or regulate anything done in relation to the design, or the use of any model, document or other information relating to it. However, the person entitled to the benefit of any such provision which is rendered inoperative is placed in the position of the design right owner as regards settlement of terms for Crown use.[44]

M. *Jurisdiction*

Each of the Comptroller, county court, patents county court, and High **20–200** Court has jurisdiction to decide certain matters which can arise under the design right provisions. Not all matters can be considered by all jurisdictions, however.

(i) Comptroller

Subsistence, term and first owner of design right. The Comptroller- **20–201** General of Patents, Designs and Trade Marks has jurisdiction to determine any dispute relating to subsistence of design right, the term of design right, or the identity of the first owner of design right.[45] His decision is binding on the parties to the dispute. Also, the Comptroller can decide any incidental question of fact or law which arises during the proceedings.[46] Any decision of the Comptroller can be appealed to the High Court.[47]

No other court or tribunal may decide these issues except on a reference **20–202** or appeal from the Comptroller, in infringement or other proceedings in which the issue arises incidentally, or upon agreement of the parties or leave of the Comptroller.[48]

Licences of right. The Comptroller also has jurisdiction to settle the **20–203** terms of a licence which is available as of right under a design right.[49] In this case, the decision of the Comptroller can be appealed to the Appeal Tribunal constituted under the Registered Designs Act 1949.[50] Special rules may be made in connection with such appeals. No such rules have so far been made.

---

[44] C.D.P.A. 1988, s.242(5).
[45] *Ibid.* s.246(1).
[46] *Ibid.* s.246(3).
[47] *Ibid.* s.251(4).
[48] *Ibid.* s.246(2).
[49] See § 20–163, *ante.*
[50] C.D.P.A. 1988, s.249 and see Registered Designs Act 1949 (1949 c. 88), s.28.

20–204 **Rules of procedure before Comptroller.** Rules have been made under section 250 of the 1988 Act which empower the Comptroller to regulate the procedure for the conduct of disputes falling within his jurisdiction.[51] These include providing for the appointment of advisers to assist the Comptroller, providing the Comptroller with the power to compel the attendance of witnesses and the discovery and production of documents, and empowering the Comptroller to award costs.

(ii) Court

20–205 **Transfer to the court.** The High Court (or the Court of Session in Scotland) is entitled to determine any question or issue referred to it by the Comptroller in connection with subsistence, term, or first owner of design right. These questions or issues may relate to fact or law. Furthermore, the Comptroller shall effect such a transfer if the parties agree that he should do so. The court may exercise any power available to the Comptroller and, following its determination, may refer any matter back to the Comptroller.[52]

20–206 **Crown use.** Disputes relating to Crown use must be referred to the court which, in this case, includes the High Court or equivalents in Scotland and Northern Ireland or any patents county court. The court thus has jurisdiction to settle the terms for Crown use, to settle the rights of third parties in the case of Crown use, and to settle compensation for loss of profit in the case of Crown use.[53]

20–207 **Infringement.** Infringement of design right is, presumably, a tort[54] and actions for infringement of design right may be brought in the High Court,[55] or the county court if within county court limits,[56] or in any patents county court given jurisdiction.[57] A county court or sheriff court in Scotland can entertain proceedings relating to orders for delivery up or disposal of infringing articles, or to an application by an exclusive licensee under section 235(5), providing the value of infringing articles does not exceed the county court limit for actions in tort.[58]

---

[51] The Design Right (Proceedings before Comptroller) Rules 1989, (1989 S.I. No. 1130) as amended by The Design Right (Proceedings before Comptroller) (Amendment) Rules 1990, (1990 S.I. No. 1453) and The Design Right (Proceedings before Comptroller) (Amendment) (No. 2) Rules 1990, (1990 S.I. No. 1699): see § B–138, *post.*

[52] C.D.P.A. 1988, s.251(1) to (3).

[53] *Ibid.* s.252(1), (6). As to proceedings against the Crown, see Crown Proceedings Act 1947, s.3 (1947 c. 44) as amended by C.P.D.A. 1988, Sched. 7, para. 4.

[54] See C.D.P.A. 1988, s.235 and § 8–5, *ante.*

[55] See *ibid.* Sched. 7, para. 28(3).

[56] See *ibid.* s.287(5).

[57] See *ibid.* s.287. The Edmonton County Court was designated as a patents county court by the Patents County Court (Designation and Jurisdiction) Order 1990, (1990 S.I. No. 1496): see § B–233 *post.* The procedure for patents county courts is established by The County Court (Amendment No. 2) Rules 1990, (1990 S.I. No. 1495 (L.14)).

[58] *Ibid.* s.232.

N. *Semiconductor topographies*

(i) General

Historical context. Since November 7, 1987 regulations[59] have been in **20–208** force to protect semiconductor products. The original regulations were made as a result of an EEC Council Directive[60] and provided for protection similar to copyright for certain semiconductor topographies. These regulations have now been revoked and replaced by new regulations[61] which provide similar protection to design right under Part III of the 1988 Act. However, since the provisions of Part III are different in some respects from the protection which is to be afforded to semiconductor products under the original EEC Council Directive[62] and later Council Decisions,[63] the new regulations amend certain sections of Part III of the 1988 Act in respect of semiconductor topographies.[64] The new regulations have themselves been amended.[65]

Amendments to Part III. In summary, the regulations make the follow- **20–209** ing changes:

Section 228(6) (Definition of Infringing Article) and section 237 **20–210** (Licences of Right) do not apply.

The following sections are amended: 215 (First Ownership),[66] 216 **20–211** (Duration),[67] 213(5) (Qualifications for Design Right Protection),[68] 217 (General Requirements for Qualification),[69] 219 (Qualification by Reference to Commissioner or Employer),[70] 220 (Qualification by Reference to First Marketing),[71] 226(1) (Infringement),[72] and 263(2) (Definition of "marketing").[73]

---

[59] The Semiconductor Products (Protection of Topography) Regulations 1987 (1987 S.I. No. 1497): see § A–565, *post.*
[60] Council Directive 87/54/EEC (O.J. No. L24, 27.1.1987, p. 36).
[61] The Design Right (Semiconductor Topographies) Regulations 1989 (1989 S.I. No. 1100): see § A–577A, *post.*
[62] See n. 58, *ante.*
[63] Council Decisions 87/532/EEC (O.J. No. 313, 4.11.1987, p. 22) and 88/311/EEC (O.J. No. 140, 7.6.1988, p. 13).
[64] See § 20–60 *et seq., ante.*
[65] The Design Right (Semiconductor Topographies) (Amendment) Regulations 1989 (1989 S.I. No. 2147) and The Design Right (Semiconductor Topographies) (Amendment) Regulations 1990 (1990 S.I. No. 1003): see § A–577L, *post.*
[66] See § 20–102 *et seq., ante.*
[67] See § 20–122 *et seq., ante.*
[68] See § 20–82 *et seq., ante.*
[69] See n. 66, *ante.*
[70] See § 20–95 *et seq., ante.*
[71] See § 20–98 *et seq., ante.*
[72] See § 20–124 *et seq., ante.*
[73] See § 20–98, *ante.*

(ii) Semiconductor topography

20–212 In order to determine whether Part III of the 1988 Act applies in its unamended or amended form it is necessary to decide whether the design in question constitutes a "semiconductor topography." A "semiconductor topography" is defined by the regulations as meaning: "a design of any aspect of the shape or configuration (whether internal or external) of the whole or part of an article which is a design of either of the following:

(a) the pattern fixed, or intended to be fixed, in or upon
  (i) a layer of a semiconductor product, or
  (ii) a layer of material in the course of and for the purpose of the manufacture of a semiconductor product, or
(b) the arrangement of the patterns fixed, or intended to be fixed, in or upon the layers of a semiconductor product in relation to one another."

20–213 In this connection, a "semiconductor product" is an article the purpose, or one of the purposes, of which is the performance of an electronic function and which consists of two or more layers, at least one of which is composed of semiconductor material and in or upon one or more of which is fixed a pattern appertaining to that or another function.[74]

(iii) Qualification for design right protection

20–214 **Subsistence of design right.** Section 213(5) of the 1988 Act states that design right subsists in the design only if the design qualifies for design right protection by reference to the designer, the person by whom the design was commissioned or the designer employed, or the person by whom and country in which articles made to the design were first marketed. These qualifications are defined in more detail in sections 217–220 of the 1988 Act.

20–215 **Qualifying person.** In the case of semiconductor topographies, section 217 is amended.[75] The section after amendment provides that a "qualifying person" includes, not only the persons already defined under the unamended section, but also a body corporate or other body having legal personality which has a place of business in Gibraltar at which substantial business activity is carried on. In addition a qualifying person includes a person who falls within one of a number of additional classes set out in the Schedule to the regulations. These additional classes include British Dependent Territory citizens, citizens and subjects of any country specified in Parts II and III of the Schedule, habitual residents of any such country and also of the Isle of Man, the Channel Islands or any colony. Further, firms and bodies corporate formed under the law of, or of any part of, the United Kingdom, Gibraltar, another Member State of the

---

[74] The Design Right (Semiconductor Topographies) Regulations 1989 (1989 S.I. No. 1100), reg. 2: see § A–577A, *post.*
[75] 1989 S.I. No. 1100, reg. 4(2).

EEC or any country specified in Part II of the Schedule to the regulations with a place of business within any country at which substantial business activity is carried on also comprise qualified persons.

The countries in Part II of the Schedule to the regulations as amended **20–216** are Austria, Japan, Switzerland, Sweden and the United States; while in Part III the countries are Finland, French Overseas Territories, Iceland, and Norway.

It will be noted that the number of persons or corporate bodies falling **20–217** within the definition of a "qualifying person" is rather wider with designs of semiconductor topographies than is the case with other designs.

Semiconductor topography created under a commission or during **20–218** **employment.** Section 215 of the 1988 Act, which relates to the first owner of the design right, is modified by the regulations.[76] The modified section makes provision for the possibility of an agreement in writing to override the normal situation in which the person commissioning a design is the first owner of any design right or the employer is the first owner of any design right.

In the circumstances of such an agreement, the question of qualification **20–219** is determined by reference to the designer in accordance with section 218(2) to (4) of the 1988 Act as if the topography had not been created in pursuance of a commission or in the course of employment.[77]

First marketing. Section 220 of the 1988 Act is modified[78] to specify that **20–220** a semiconductor topography design may qualify for design right protection if the first marketing of articles made to the design is by a qualifying person who is exclusively authorised to put such articles on the market in every Member State of the EEC, and that first marketing takes place within the territory of any Member State. In other words, the requirement in the original, unamended section 220 for a qualifying person requiring only to be exclusively authorised to put articles on the market in the United Kingdom, is tightened to require a qualified person to be exclusively authorised for all Member States of the EEC.

Meaning of marketing. For this purpose marketing of an article made to **20–221** a design has the same meaning as under Part III of the 1988 Act for the purposes of section 220. However, no account is to be taken of any sale or hire, or any offer or exposure for sale or hire, which is subject to an obligation of confidence in respect of information about the semiconductor topography in question. There are, however, two exceptions to this in which a sale or hire and so on, despite being under an obligation of confidence, still amounts to marketing. These exceptions are:

(a) where the article or semiconductor topography has been sold or

---

[76] See § 20–222, *post.*
[77] 1989 S.I. No. 1100, reg. 4(3) § A–577E, *post.*
[78] *Ibid.* reg. 4(4).

hired on a previous occasion (whether or not subject to an obligation of confidence), or

(b) the obligation is imposed at the behest of the Crown, or of the government of any country outside the United Kingdom, for the protection of security in connection with the production of arms, munitions or war material.[79]

(iv) Ownership of design right

20–222   The first owner of any design right is determined in accordance with section 215 of the 1988 Act. This section is amended, however, by the regulations to provide that, where a design is created in pursuance of a commission or in the course of employment, although normally the person commissioning the design or the employer is the first owner of any design right, there may be an agreement in writing to the contrary.[80] In such circumstances, to determine whether a design qualifies for design right protection, reference must be made to the designer.[81]

(v) Duration

20–223   The rules concerning the duration of design right in a semiconductor topography are different from those set out under section 216 of the 1988 Act.[82]

20–224   **10-year rule.** Design right in a semiconductor topography will expire 10 years from the end of the calendar year in which the topography or articles made to the topography were first made available for sale or hire anywhere in the world by or with the licence of the design right owner. Marketing has the meaning set out in Part III of the 1988 Act but is subject to the exclusion of certain acts made under an obligation of confidence as described above in connection with section 220.[83]

20–225   **15-year rule.** If neither the topography nor articles made to the topography are made available for sale or hire as mentioned above within a period of 15 years commencing with the earlier of the time when the topography was first recorded in a design document or the time when an article was first made to the topography, then the design right will expire at the end of that 15-year period.

20–226   Unlike the rules for normal design right duration under Part III of the 1988 Act,[84] it is possible for the design right in a semiconductor topography to expire later than the period of 15 years from when the topography

---

[79] 1989 S.I. No. 1100, reg. 7. This also applies to amended sections 215(4) and 216 of the 1988 Act.

[80] *Ibid.* reg. 5.

[81] See § 20–218, *ante.*

[82] 1989 S.I. No. 1100, reg. 6 § A–577G, *post.*

[83] See § 20–221, *ante.*

[84] See § 20–122, *ante.*

was first recorded in a design document or an article first made to the topography. Thus, it would seem that up to 25 years' protection could be available if the first time at which the topography or articles made to the topography were made available for sale or hire was just before the end of the 15-year period.

(vi) Infringement

One of the major differences between the provisions for semiconductor **20–227** topographies and those for other designs lies in what does not constitute an infringement, by virtue of the amendments by the regulations to sections 226, 227 and 228(6) of the 1988 Act.[85]

Private reproduction. The first additional exclusion from infringement **20–228** is the reproduction of a design privately for non-commercial aims. No equivalent provisions exist under Part III of the 1988 Act.

Analysis or evaluation. The second exclusion is where the reproduction **20–229** of a design is for the purpose of analysing or evaluating the design or analysing, evaluating or teaching the concepts, processes, systems or techniques embodied in it.

Reverse engineering. Probably the most significant difference between **20–230** semiconductor topographies and other designs enjoying design right protection lies in the exclusion from infringement of design right in a semiconductor topography of the creation of another original semiconductor topography as a result of an analysis or evaluation of the first topography or of the concepts, processes, systems or techniques embodied in it, or the reproduction of that other topography. Thus, a person may obtain legitimately a semiconductor product embodying a semiconductor topography in which design right subsists. He may then analyse it to determine the structure of the different layers of the product and then create his own masks from which he can reproduce the topography commercially without infringement.

Previous sale or hire. Section 227 of Part III of the 1988 Act defines cer- **20–231** tain secondary infringements. In the case of semiconductor topographies, it is provided that this section does not apply if the article in question has previously been sold or hired within the United Kingdom by or with the licence of the owner of design right in the topography in question, or within the territory of any other member State of the European Economic Community or Gibraltar by or with the consent of a person for the time being entitled to import it into or sell or hire it within that territory.

Infringing article. The exclusion under section 228(6) of the 1988 Act of **20–232** a design document from what constitutes an "infringing article" is stated not to apply in connection with semiconductor topographies. Thus, the importation, possession and so on of an infringing article in the form of a

---

[85] 1989 S.I. No. 1100, reg. 8 § A–577I, *post.*

design document may constitute infringement. For this purpose, it is suggested that a "design document" would normally be a representation of a semiconductor mask.

(vii) Licences of right

20–233 The provisions relating to licences of right under a design right do not apply in connection with semiconductor topographies.[86]

(viii) Transitional provisions

20–234 The regulations[87] override the postponement of the effect of section 51 of the 1988 Act in connection with semiconductor topographies created between November 7, 1987 and July 31, 1989. For semiconductor topographies created before November 7, 1987 paragraph 19(2) of Schedule 1 to the 1988 Act is amended to exclude the reference to section 237 (licence of right in last five years) and accordingly paragraph 19(3) does not apply.

---

[86] 1989 S.I. No. 1100, reg. 9.
[87] *Ibid.* reg. 10.

CHAPTER 21

RELATED FORMS OF PROTECTION—2

BREACH OF CONFIDENCE, PASSING OFF AND MALICIOUS
FALSEHOOD

Contents   *Para.*

1. Breach of Confidence

A. Rule stated

21–1 The 1988 Act, repeating in substance section 46(4) of the 1956 Act, provides that nothing in Part I of that Act affects the operation of any rule of equity relating to breaches of trust or confidence.[1] This judge-made rule has been stated as follows.[2] There is a broad and developing equitable doctrine that he who has received information in confidence shall not take unfair advantage of it or profit from the wrongful use or publication of it.[3] He must not make any use of it to the prejudice of him who gave it, without obtaining his consent or, at any rate, without paying him for it.[4] It has for long been clear that the courts can restrain a breach of confidence arising out of a contract or any right to property.[5] For example, under the law of copyright prior to the 1911 Act, there were many cases in which publication of an unpublished literary work was restrained upon the ground of breach of confidence, but inasmuch as all unpublished works were entitled to common law copyright[6] it is often difficult to know how far the injunctions granted were based on a breach of the common law copyright and how far upon breach of confidence. In recent years, however, a number of cases have established that the action for breach of confidence is independent of any right of property or contract or right of law[7] and rests upon an equitable obligation of confidence which may be implied from the circum-

---

[1] C.D.P.A. 1988 s.171(1)(*e*). See generally "Restitution of benefits obtained in breach of another's confidence" 86 L.Q.R. 463. Goff & Jones, *Law of Restitution* (3rd ed.), Ch. 35; Law Commission Working Paper No. 58 Law Commission Report (1981) Cmnd 8388 Gurry, Breach of Confidence (1984).

[2] For examples of statutory protection for information and for access to it see Data Protection Act, 1984; Local Government (Access to Information) Act, 1985; Access to Personal Files 1987.

[3] *Att.-Gen.* v. *Jonathan Cape Ltd.* [1976] Q.B. 752 at 769.

[4] *Seager* v. *Copydex* [1967] 1 W.L.R. 923 at 931; *Potters-Ballotini Ltd.* v. *Weston-Baker & Ors.* [1977] R.P.C. 202 at 205; this passage was cited with approval in *Fraser* v. *Thames Television* [1984] Q.B. 44 at 58.

[5] *Argyll (Duchess)* v. *Argyll (Duke)* [1967] Ch. 302 at 318; *Seager* v. *Copydex* [1967] 1 W.L.R. 923; *Fraser* v. *Evans* [1969] 1 Q.B. 349; *Att.-Gen.* v. *Jonathan Cape Ltd.* [1976] Q.B. 752 at 769; *Morison* v. *Moat* [1851] 20 L.J.Ch.(N.S.) 513 at 522; *McNicol* v. *Sportsman's Book Stores* [1928–35] Mac.C.C. 116. (As to Scotland see *Chill Foods (Scotland) Ltd.* v. *Cool Foods Ltd.* [1977] R.P.C. 522 (Court of Session); *Grant* v. *Procurator Fiscal* [1988] R.P.C. 41 (High Court of Justiciary—dishonest use and exploitation of confidential information not a crime in Scotland); *Lord Advocate* v. *The Scotsman Publications Ltd.* [1990] A.C. 812) *Paezy* v. *Haendler & Natermann GmbH* [1979] F.S.R. 420; *Amway Corpn.* v. *Eurway International Ltd.* [1974] R.P.C. 82; *fac Minerals Ltd.* v. *International Corona Resources Ltd.* [1990] F.S.R. 441 (Supreme Court of Canada).

[6] *Ante*, §§ 1–2, 1–43.

[7] See. n. 5 *ante*.

stances of the case. The principles affecting breach of confidence were fully considered by the House of Lords for the first time in *Attorney-General v. Guardian Newspapers (No. 2)*.[8] The speeches in that case contain a full discussion of the basis of the duty, its impact on third parties, the effect of unauthorised publication of the information, the defences of public interest and the requirement of damage. The ground of equitable intervention is that it is unconscionable for a person who has received information on the basis that it is confidential subsequently to reveal that information. Acceptance of information on the basis that it will be kept secret affects the conscience of the recipient of the information.[9] In general it is in the public interest that confidences should be respected, even where the confider can point to no specific financial detriment to himself.[10] If a defendant is proved to have used confidential information, directly or indirectly obtained from a plaintiff, without his consent, express or implied, he will be guilty of an infringement of the plaintiff's rights.[11] So stated the rule may seem somewhat too wide. It is, therefore, necessary to elaborate upon that rule by expounding, with reference to the decided cases, what is meant by describing information as "confidential," in what circumstances the obligation not to disclose or use such information is implied or imposed, to what extent the courts will enforce such obligation and what remedies are available for that purpose. Particular reference will be made to those cases which concern literary and other copyright works.

B. Relation between copyright and confidence

The right to restrain the publication of a work upon the ground that to do **21–2** so would be a breach of trust or confidence is, it is submitted, a broader right than the proprietary right of copyright. There can be no copyright in ideas or information, and it is no infringement of copyright to adopt or appropriate the ideas of another or to publish information received from another, provided there is no substantial copying of the form in which those ideas have, or that information has, been previously embodied.[12] As Lord Denning remarked in *Fraser v. Evans*[13] *à propos* a written report, "copyright does not subsist in the information contained in the report. It exists only in the literary form in which the information is dressed." But if the ideas or information have been acquired by a person under such circumstances that it would be a breach of good faith to publish them and he has no just cause or excuse for doing so, the court may grant an injunction against him.[14] The distinction between copyright and confidence may be

---

[8] [1990] A.C. 109 See also *Lord Advocate v. The Scotsman Publications Ltd.* [1990] A.C. 812.
[9] *Stephens v. Avery* [1988] Ch. 449 at 456.
[10] See n. 8, *ante.*
[11] *Saltman Engineering Co. Ltd. v. Campbell Engineering Co. Ltd.* (1948) 65 R.P.C. 203 at 213 (C.A.); *Nichrotherm Electrical Co. Ltd. v. Percy* [1957] R.P.C. 207 (C.A.); *Brian D. Collins (Engineers) Ltd. v. Charles Roberts & Co. Ltd.* [1965] R.P.C. 429.
[12] *Ante,* § 1–1; *Hollinrake v. Truswell* [1894] 3 Ch. 420; *Walter v. Steinkopff* [1892] 3 Ch. 489; *Chilton v. Progress Printing, etc., Co.* [1895] 2 Ch. 29; *Rees v. Melville* [1911–16] Mac.C.C. 96 at 98; *Johnstone Safety Ltd. v. Peter Cook (Int.) plc* [1990] F.S.R. 161, at 165, but see *Corelli v. Gray* (1913) 30 T.L.R. 116.
[13] [1969] Q.B. 349 at 361, 362.
[14] See n. 13, *ante.*

of considerable importance with regard to unpublished manuscripts submitted, and not accepted, for publication or use. In general, it is thought that in such circumstances an obligation not to use or disclose would be implied, and this would extend to a plot or elaborated idea which would not, in general, be protected under the law of copyright.[15]

Whereas copyright protects material which has been reduced to a permanent form, the general law of confidence may protect either written or oral confidential communications. Copyright is good against the world generally, while confidence operates against those who receive information or ideas in confidence. Copyright has a fixed, statutory time limit which does not apply to confidential information, though in practice the obligation of confidence usually ceases when the information or idea becomes public knowledge.[16] There may also be differences as to the ownership of copyright in a work and the entitlement to restrain a breach of confidence in respect of it. Thus, it is no answer to a claim for breach of confidence in a suite of computer programs that the employee in breach of confidence owns the copyright in the programs.[17]

C. Elements of action for breach of confidence

21–3 In order to succeed in an action for breach of confidence, the plaintiff must establish, to the satisfaction of the court, three elements: first, that the information which he is seeking to protect is of a confidential nature; secondly, that the information in question was communicated in circumstances importing an obligation of confidence; and, thirdly, that the defendant is about to make, or has made, an unauthorised disclosure or use of that information.[18]

(i) Definition of information

21–4 Unlike copyright, it is not necessary that the information should be embodied in any document, though it may be easier in practice to identify and restrain the use and disclosure of information in documentary form.[19] The information must, however, be traced to a particular source or be identifiable in reasonably specific terms, and the Courts will not protect information which has become so completely merged in the mind of the

---

[15] *Moore* v. *Edwards* [1901–4] Mac.C.C. 44; *Fraser* v. *Edwards* [1905–10] Mac.C.C. 10.

[16] *Fraser* v. *Thames Television* [1984] Q.B. 44 at 60.

[17] *Northern Office Microcomputers (Pty) Ltd.* v. *Rosenstein* [1982] F.S.R. 124 (Supreme Court of South Africa).

[18] *Coco* v. *A.N. Clark (Engineers) Ltd.* [1969] R.P.C. 41; *Greer* v. *Sketchley* [1979] F.S.R. 197; *Thomas Marshall (Exports) Ltd.* v. *Guinle* [1979] F.S.R. 208; *Yates Circuit Foil & Anor.* v. *Electrofoils Ltd.* [1976] F.S.R. 345 at 385; *Interfirm Comparison (Australia) Pty Ltd.* v. *Law Society of New South Wales* [1977] R.P.C. 137 (Supreme Court of New South Wales); *Stephens* v. *Avery* [1988] Ch. 449 at 452; *Lac Minerals Ltd.* v. *International Corona Resources Ltd.* [1990] F.S.R. 441 (Supreme Court of Canada); *Smith Kline & French Laboaratories (Australia) Ltd.* v. *Secretary to the Department of Community Services and Health* [1990] F.S.R. 617 (Federal Court of Australia N.S.W. Division).

[19] *Terrapin Ltd.* v. *Builders' Supply Co. (Hayes) Ltd.* [1967] R.P.C. 375; *Ansell Rubber Co. Pty. Ltd.* v. *Allied Rubber Industries Pty. Ltd.* [1972] R.P.C. 811 (Supreme Court of Victoria); *G.D. Searle & Co. Ltd.* v. *Celltech Ltd.* [1982] F.S.R. 92 at 109.

person informed that it is impossible to say from what precise source or quarter he derived the information which led to the knowledge which he is found to possess.[20] This point is well illustrated in the cases in which employers have sought to restrain former employees from disclosing or using confidential information acquired by them in the course of their employment.[21] In the case of an employee occupying a responsible executive position, it may be particularly difficult to identify the confidential information which he has acquired about his employer's business.[22] It is, however, necessary for the court to investigate the degree of secrecy attaching to individual items of information. It is not enough for the employer to prove that the employee has a body of information of a general character or a particular size which a trade rival would consider worth purchasing.[23] It has been held that the granting of an injunction against an ex-employee is not prevented by the fact that the information is carried in his head rather than being embodied in a document. In appropriate circumstances a person can be restrained from using confidential information, even though he appears to have memorised it without making use of any written document,[24] but in the sphere of soliciting customers of a former employer or other classes of persons an injunction is always directed against the use of a written list.[25] The true test of protectability is whether the information in question can fairly be regard as a separate part of the employee's stock of knowledge which a man of ordinary honesty and intelligence would recognise to be the property of his old employer and not his own to do with as he likes.[26] Where there are trade secrets which an employee will inevitably carry away in his head, it is not generally the proper course to invoke the general equitable doctrine to prevent breaches of confidence, but to exact from the employee a contract of service restricting, in reasonable terms, the employee's field of activity after he has left his employment.[27]

(ii) *Requirement of confidentiality*

Having defined or identified the relevant information, the court must then **21–5** determine whether that information has the requisite quality of confentiality about it to merit protection. It is far from easy to state in general terms what is confidential information or a trade secret,[28] and it is difficult

---

[20] See n.19, *ante.*

[21] *Printers & Finishers Ltd.* v. *Holloway* [1965] 1 W.L.R. 1; *Coral Index Ltd.* v. *Regent Index Ltd.* [1970] R.P.C. 147; *Stevenson, Jordan & Harrison Ltd.* v. *MacDonald & Evans* [1952] 1 T.L.R. 101; *P.A. Thomas & Co.* v. *Mould* [1968] 2 Q.B. 913. See §21–17, *post.*

[22] *Potters-Ballotini Ltd.* v. *Weston-Baker & Ors.* [1977] R.P.C. 202; *Greer* v. *Sketchley Ltd.* [1979] F.S.R. 197 at 204; *Littlewoods Organisation* v. *Harris* [1977] 1 W.L.R. 1472.

[23] *Yates Circuit Foil Co. & Anor.* v. *Electrofoils Ltd.* [1976] F.S.R. 345; see also *Commercial Plastics Ltd.* v. *Vincent* [1965] 1 Q.B. 623.

[24] *Baker* v. *Gibbons* [1972] 1 W.L.R. 693.

[25] *Louis* v. *Smellie* (1895) 73 L.T. 226; *Baker* v. *Gibbons, supra,* at 701.

[26] *Printers & Finishers Ltd.* v. *Holloway, supra; United Sterling Corporation Ltd.* v. *Felton & Mannion* [1974] R.P.C. 162; *Thomas Marshall (Exports) Ltd.* v. *Guinle* [1979] Ch. 227; *Harvey Tiling Co. (Pty.) Ltd.* v. *Rodomac (Pty.) Ltd.* [1977] R.P.C. 399 (Supreme Court of South Africa).

[27] See n. 26, *ante.*

[28] *Thomas Marshall (Exports)* v. *Guinle* [1979] Ch. 227.

to enunciate any general test by which the Courts decide whether the information which is sought to be protected is of a confidential nature or not. In some cases, the Courts have paid attention to considerations which also arise in cases where they have to determine whether copyright subsists in a particular work; for example, the amount of time, skill and labour expended on its creation. Thus, it has been said that what makes a document confidential is the fact that the maker of the document has used his brain and has produced a result which can only be produced by somebody who goes through the same process; and a person breaches that confidence when he dispenses with the necessity of going through the process which has been gone through in compiling the document or collecting the information and avails himself of the fruits of the other's efforts, thereby saving himself a great deal of labour and calculation.[29] This consideration has been emphasised in the various cases in which news agencies have sought to protect the improper acquisition and use of information supplied by them to subscribers. Thus, in the case of *Exchange Telegraph Co. Ltd.* v. *Central News Ltd.*[30] Stirling J. said: "By the expenditure of labour and money the plaintiffs had acquired this information, and it was, in their hands, valuable property in this sense—that persons to whom it was not known were willing to pay, and did pay, money to acquire it." On the other hand: "Equity ought not to be invoked to protect trivial tittle-tattle, however confidential."[31] There must be brought into existence, by the application of the skill and ingenuity of the human brain, some novel or confidential information.

(iii) *Private or secret information*

21–6 It is submitted, however, that although the expenditure of time, skill and labour on the acquisition of information may often be relevant to determining whether information has a confidential quality, it is not of itself a necessary or sufficient condition of the confidentiality of that information. For example, there are cases where the courts have prevented publication of facts relating to a person's private life on the grounds of breach of confidence.[32] No time, labour or skill has in these cases been spent by the plaintiff on the acquisition of information: the facts themselves are protected from disclosure simply because they are private, because the knowledge of

---

[29] *Saltman Engineering Co. Ltd.* v. *Campbell Engineering Co. Ltd.* (1948) 65 R.P.C. 203 at 215 (C.A.); *Industrial Furnaces Ltd.* v. *Reaves* [1970] R.P.C. 605 at 617. *Ansell Rubber Co. Pty. Ltd.* v. *Allied Rubber Industries Pty. Ltd.* [1972] R.P.C. 811 (Supreme Court of Victoria); *Harvey Tiling Co. (Pty.) Ltd.* v. *Rodomac (Pty.) Ltd.* [1977] R.P.C. 399 (Supreme Court of South Africa); *Interfirm (Comparison) Australia Pty. Ltd.* v. *Law Society of New South Wales* [1977] R.P.C. 137 (Supreme Court of New South Wales); *Alfa Laval Cheese Systems Ltd.* v. *Wincanton Engineering Ltd.* [1990] F.S.R. 583.

[30] [1897] 2 Ch. 48.

[31] *Coco* v. *A.N. Clark (Engineers) Ltd.* [1969] R.P.C. 41 at 48; *Franchi* v. *Franchi* [1967] R.P.C. 149; *Church of Scientology of California* v. *Kaufman* [1973] R.P.C. 635; *Amway Corpn.* v. *Eurway International Ltd.* [1974] R.P.C. 82; *Thomas Marshall (Exports) Ltd.* v. *Guinle, supra; Lennon* v. *News Group Newspapers Ltd. & Twist* [1978] F.S.R. 573; *Ansell Rubber Co. Pty. Ltd.* v. *Allied Rubber Industries Pty. Ltd.* [1972] R.P.C. 811 (Supreme Court of Victoria); *Interfirm Comparison (Australia) Pty. Ltd.* v. *Law Society of New South Wales, supra.*

[32] See § 21–9, *post.*

them was acquired by the person seeking to publish them in the course of a confidential relationship and because the publication cannot be justified as being in the public interest. It is, therefore, submitted that the necessary condition of confidentiality is that the information in question is private or secret. Something which is public property or public knowledge at the date when it is imparted cannot *per se* provide any foundation for proceedings for breach of confidence.[33] Information may also lose its original confidential character if it subsequently enters the public domain. The secrecy may be imperfect, but nevertheless give rise to confidential obligation. There may, for example, be cases in which, even in the light of widespread publication of the information abroad, a person whom that information concerned could restrain publication by a third party in this country.[34] Partial or limited disclosure or publication will not destroy the confidentiality of the whole. For example, the fact that the information in question is available in the sense that it could be obtained by chemical analysis of a product, does not mean that it is public or common knowledge. The secrecy is not in what is produced but the way in which it is produced.[35] All the separate features of a product may have been published or be capable of ascertainment by actual inspection by any member of the public, but if the whole result has not been achieved, and could not be achieved, except by someone going through the same kind of process as the owner, the information will not fail to qualify as confidential by reason of such publication.[36] Ascertainment of features of a product or device by members of the public does not constitute publication of all the details of the whole plan or device so as to put it into the public domain.[37] The process as a whole may be secret, even though constituent parts are not. Something which has been constructed solely from materials in the public domain may possess the necessary quality of confidentiality, for something new and confidential may have been created by the effort of the human brain; novelty or confidentiality depend upon the thing or information itself rather than upon the quality of its constituent parts.[38]

Four elements may be discerned in the identification of confidential information in an industrial or trade secrets setting: first, the information must be information, the release of which the owner believes would be injurious to him or of advantage to his rivals or others; secondly, the owner must believe that the information is confidential or secret; thirdly, the owner's beliefs on the first two points must be reasonable; and fourthly, the information must be judged in the light of the usage and practices of the particular industry or trade concerned. Information which does not satisfy these four requirements may nevertheless be entitled to

---

[33] See n. 31, *ante*

[34] *Att.-Gen.* v. *Guardian Newspapers (No. 2)* [1990] A.C. 109 at 260F.

[35] *Yates Circuit Foil Co. & Anor.* v. *Electrofoils Ltd.* [1976] F.S.R. 345; *Deta Nominees* v. *Viscount Plastic Products* [1979] V.R. 167.

[36] *Ansell Rubber Co. Pty. Ltd.* v. *Allied Rubber Industries Pty. Ltd.* [1972] R.P.C. 811 (Supreme Court of Victoria); *Alfa Laval Cheese Systems Ltd.* v. *Wincanton Engineering Ltd.* [1990] F.S.R. 583 at 590.

[37] *Harvey Tiling Co. (Pty.) Ltd.* v. *Rodomac (Pty.) Ltd.* [1977] R.P.C. 399; *House of Spring Gardens Ltd.* v. *Point Blank Ltd.* [1983] F.S.R. 213 at 250.

[38] See n. 31, *ante*.

protection. Information which does satisfy them is of a type entitled to protection.[39]

(iv) *Mixed information*

21–7   The principle is clear enough when the whole of the information is private. Difficulties can arise when the information is in part public and in part private, as, for example, when some of the information is published in the form of a patent specification. "When the information is mixed, being partly public and partly private, then the recipient must take special care to use only the material which is in the public domain. He should go to the public source and get it, or, at any rate, not be in a better position than if he had gone to the public source. He should not get a start over others by using the information which he received in confidence. At any rate, he should not get a start without paying for it."[40] It has been said that this "springboard" principle extends so far as to prevent a person who has received information in confidence from using that information even after it has been published by or with the consent of the person from whom the information was originally acquired. Thus in *Terrapin Ltd.* v. *Builders' Supply Co. (Hayes) Ltd.* Roxburgh J. said[41]: "As I understand it, the essence of this branch of the law, whatever the origin of it may be, is that a person who has obtained information in confidence is not allowed to use it as a springboard for activities detrimental to the person who made the confidential communication, and springboard it remains even when all the features have been published or can be ascertained by actual inspection by any member of the public." Similarly in the *Saltman* case Lord Greene pointed out[42] that while the recipient of the confidential information could, like any one else, buy the article, measure it and make his own mould, he could not lawfully shorten his labours by resort to the confidential know-how he had learned. On this view the recipient of the confidential information is placed under a special and permanent disability in the field of competition in order to ensure that he does not get un unfair start. On the other hand, it was argued for the defendants in *Peter Pan Manufacturing Corporation* v. *Corsets Silhouette Ltd.*[43] that these views were inconsistent with the decision of the House of Lords in *Mustad (O.) & Son* v. *Dosen.*[44] The point was not decided as being a future question but, in *Cranleigh Precision Engineering Ltd.* v. *Bryant*[45] Roskill J. held that there was no conflict. The better view is that, although a man must not use information as a springboard to get a start over others, nevertheless the springboard

---

[39] *Thomas Marshall (Exports) Ltd.* v. *Guinle* [1979] Ch. 227; *Ansell Rubber Co. Pty. Ltd.* v. *Allied Rubber Industries Pty. Ltd.* [1972] R.P.C. 811 (Supreme Court of Victoria).

[40] *Seager* v. *Copydex* [1967] 1 W.L.R. 923 at 931.

[41] [1967] R.P.C. 375 at 391. Approved in *Seager* v. *Copydex, supra*; and see *Ackroyds (London) Ltd.* v. *Islington Plastics Ltd.* [1962] R.P.C. 97; *Ansell Rubber Co. Pty. Ltd.* v. *Allied Rubber Industries Pty. Ltd.* [1972] R.P.C. 811 (Supreme Court of Victoria); *Harvey Tiling Co. (Pty.) Ltd.* v. *Rodomac (Pty.) Ltd.* [1977] R.P.C. 399 (Supreme Court of South Africa); *Alfa Laval Cheese Systems Ltd.* v. *Wincanton Engineering Ltd.* [1990] F.S.R. 583 at 590, 591.

[42] (1948) 65 R.P.C. 203 at 215; *Underwater Welders & Repairers Ltd.* v. *Street* [1967] F.S.R. 194.

[43] [1963] R.P.C. 45.

[44] [1963] R.P.C. 41.

[45] [1964] 3 All E.R. 289 at 302.

does not last forever. If he does use it, a time may come when so much of the information has become public knowledge that he can no longer be restrained.[46] The confidential obligation may thus be of limited duration. An injunction is not an appropriate remedy where the information has in fact ceased to be confidential. "The widespread use of the information drives a hole into the blanket of confidence."[47] Where confidentiality exists, however, the obligation to preserve it is not necessarily terminated by publicity; re-publication of information published in breach of confidence may inflict further damage and may therefore be restrained.[48] If the information has been published by or with the consent of the person to whom the duty of confidence is owed, the person who owed the duty is released from it and has the same right to use it as every other member of the public. If, however, publication is by or with the consent of the person who owed the duty or by a stranger the duty of confidence is not necessarily discharged.[49] A person cannot free himself from his obligation of confidence by breaking it, but he may be released from it if a third party has put the confidential information in the public domain. Further, if the stipulation for confidence was unreasonable at the time of making it, or if it was reasonable at the beginning, but afterwards, in the course of subsequent events, it becomes unreasonable that it should be enforced, then the court will decline to enforce it.[50] There may thus be a limit in time after which the confidential character of the information and the duty of the court to restrain publication will lapse.[51]

(v) *Examples of confidential information*

Most of the cases in which the courts have laid down the principles on **21–8** which they decide what information should, or should not, be protected concern trade secrets and industrial designs, but the principles contained in these decisions have been applied in other areas. While, as has been seen, ideas or plots are not protected under copyright law,[52] they may be protected by an action for breach of confidence if they are private or confidential and knowledge of them has been acquired in confidence. So also may be information imparted in confidence during the course of researches for a book,[53] information contained in computer programs con-

---

[46] *Potters-Ballotini Ltd.* v. *Weston-Baker & Ors.* [1977] R.P.C. 202 at 206; *Harrison* v. *Project & Design Co. (Redcar) Ltd.* [1978] F.S.R. 81; *British Franco Electric pty.* v. *Dowling Plastics pty.* [1981] 1 N.S.W.L.R. 448 (Supreme Court of New South Wales.)

[47] *per* Lord Denning M.R. *Dunford & Elliott Ltd.* v. *Johnston & Firth Brown Ltd.* [1978] F.S.R. 143 at 148 *Cf. Interfirm Comparison (Australia) Pty. Ltd.* v. *Law Society of New South Wales* [1977] R.P.C. 137 (Supreme Court of New South Wales).

[48] *Schering Chemicals Ltd.* v. *Falkman Ltd.* [1982] Q.B. 1 at 29 and 37.

[49] *Speed Seal Products Ltd.* v. *Paddington* [1985] 1 W.L.R. 1327 at 1331; *Att.-Gen.* v. *Guardian Newspapers (No. 2)* [1990] A.C. 109 at 268D.

[50] See n. 47, *ante.*

[51] *Att.-Gen.* v. *Jonathan Cape Ltd.* [1976] Q.B. 752 at 771; *Roger Bullivant Ltd.* v. *Ellis* [1987] F.S.R. 172.

[52] See §§ 2–16 and 4–6, 8–50, 8–130, *ante.*

[53] *Fosters & Ors.* v. *Mountford and Rigby Ltd.* [1978] F.S.R. 582 (confidential communication to anthropologist of Aboriginal tribal secrets) (Supreme Court of the Northern Territory of Australia).

fidentially acquired[54] and information contained in a confidential report on the financial and technical prospects of a company[55] or in the form of a questionnaire prepared for a limited purpose.[56] Examples of this kind of protection in the general field of copyright works are given below.

21–9 **Private and personal facts.** In some cases a breach of confidence involves an invasion of personal privacy which the courts will protect even though there has been no financial detriment suffered by the plaintiff. In such cases an account of profits made by the revelation of the details of a person's private life may be ordered, as well as an injunction to restrain future breaches.[57] A leading case in this regard is *Prince Albert* v. *Strange*[58] in which Prince Albert successfully applied to the court for an injunction restraining the defendants from exhibiting, publishing copies of, and publishing a catalogue of, drawings and etchings made by Queen Victoria and Prince Albert of their children and other subjects of interest to the family for their private use and amusement. Impressions of these drawings and etchings had, by some means, come into the defendants' hands, without the consent of Queen Victoria or Prince Albert, as a result of a breach of confidence committed by an employee of a printer, who had been entrusted with plates for the purpose of printing off impressions of Queen Victoria and Prince Albert. The defendants contended that a man who acquired knowledge of another man's property without his consent was not forbidden from communicating or publishing that knowledge to the world, or from informing or describing to the public what the property was, even though the other man might have kept, or tried to keep, his property secret. It was further argued that as regards portraits there were three distinct and independent rights: first, the property in the physical canvas itself; secondly, the copyright on the portrait painted on the canvas and, thirdly, the knowledge of the existence of the portrait on the canvas. On this basis, it was conceded that a person might be restrained from reproducing the portrait on the canvas, but contended that there was no legal principle which could restrain a person from describing the attributes of the portrait as was sought, for example, to be done in the case of the catalogue. These arguments were rejected by both Knight-Bruce V.C., in the first instance, and by Lord Cottenham on appeal, and an injunction was granted both on the ground of infringement of the plaintiff's proprietary rights in the copyright of the pictures and upon the ground of breach of confidence. Lord Cottenham said that he was bound to assume that the possession of the impressions of the etchings by the defendants had its foundation in a breach of trust, confidence or contract. It could not be suggested by the defendants that the impressions had been properly obtained from the plaintiff. He said: "But this case by no means depends solely on the question of property, for a breach of trust, confidence or contract would entitle the plaintiff to an injunction . . . the matter or thing of which the party had obtained knowledge, being the

---

[54] See Colin Tapper, *Computer Law* (4th Ed.).
[55] See n. 47, *ante*.
[56] *Interfirm Comparison (Australia) Pty. Ltd.* v. *Law Society of New South Wales, supra.*
[57] *Att.-Gen.* v. *Guardian Newspapers (No. 2)* [1990] A.C. 109 at 255H–256A.
[58] (1849) 1 M. & G. 25; affirmed (1849) 2 De G. Sm.652.

exclusive property of the owner, he has a right to the interposition of this court to prevent any use being made of it, that is to say, he is entitled to be protected in the exclusive use and enjoyment of that which is exclusively his."

The same principle was applied in the case of *Argyll (Duchess)* v. *Argyll (Duke)*[59] in which the plaintiff obtained an injunction to restrain the publication by the defendant of the secrets of the plaintiff relating to her private life, personal affairs and private conduct communicated by her to the defendant during the subsistence of their marriage to each other. Ungoed-Thomas J. held that communications between husband and wife during their marriage were protected against breach of confidence and that the subsequent adultery of the plaintiff did not relieve the defendant from the obligation to preserve earlier confidences. If, however, both parties to the marriage have published details about their marriage secrets, their relationship has ceased to be their private affair and the facts of it are in the public domain, so that no action for breach of confidence can be maintained.[60]

The duty of confidence is not limited to a married relationship. Information relating to the sexual conduct of an individual may be the subject matter of a duty of confidence,[61] unless it is of "a grossly immoral tendency".[62] Cases of this kind raise fundamental conflicts between, on the one hand, the privacy which every individual is entitled to expect and, on the other hand, freedom of information.

Private letters. Confidential information in letters was recognised by **21-10** Kekewich J. in the case of *Philip* v. *Pennell*.[63] In that case the plaintiffs sought to restrain the defendants from publishing letters written by the artist, Whistler, or the information contained in them, in a biography of Whistler which the defendants proposed to publish. Inasmuch as the letters were in the lawful possession of the defendants, Kekewich J. refused to prohibit them from making use of the information they might derive from a perusal of the letters, although he indicated that he might have arrived at a different conclusion if there had been any circumstances which would have rendered it a breach of confidence on the part of the defendants to make use of that information.

Plots of plays and literary ideas and information. In the case of *Gilbert* **21-11** v. *The Star Newspaper Co. Ltd.*[64] Mr. W.S. Gilbert obtained an *ex parte* injunction restraining the publication of the plot of his play, *His Excellency,*

---

[59] [1967] Ch. 302.
[60] *Lennon* v. *News Group Newspapers Ltd. & Twist* [1978] F.S.R. 573; see also *Woodward* v. *Hutchins* [1977] 1 W.L.R. 760 (press relations employee publishing details of employers' personal lives).
[61] *Stephens* v. *Avery* [1988] Ch. 449 at 455.
[62] *Glyn* v. *Weston Feature Film Co.* [1916] 1 Ch. 261; *Stephens* v. *Avery (supra)* at p. 453.
[63] [1907] 2 Ch. 577; see also *Hopkinson* v. *Lord Burghley* (1866) 2 L.R. Ch.App. 447; *McNicol* v. *Sportsman's Book Stores* [1928–35] Mac.C.C. 116; *Tett Bros. Ltd.* v. *Drake & Gorham Ltd.* [1928–35] Mac.C.C. 492 (business letter not marked "confidential" held not to be confidential); *Cooksley* v. *Johnson & Sons* (1906) 25 N.Z.L.R. 834.
[64] (1894) 11 T.L.R. 4; *cf. Exchange Telegraph Co. Ltd.* v. *Central News Ltd.* [1897] 2 Ch. 48; *Ashmore* v. *Douglas-Home* [1987] F.S.R. 553.

then being rehearsed but not yet publicly performed, on the ground that the defendants had obtained the information with the knowledge that it was given to them in breach of confidence. Similarly, in *Macklin* v. *Richardson*[65] the defendant was restrained from publishing the text of a play *Love à la Mode* which a shorthand writer, employed by him, had taken down upon its performance at the theatre. In other cases injunctions have been granted to restrain the printing of conveyancing precedents stolen from the plaintiff's chambers,[66] though a pupil might make copies for his own use, as long as he did not publish them[67]; the printing of notes copied by a clerk of a gentleman to whom the plaintiff had lent them[68]; the selling or exhibiting of copies of a photograph without the sitter's consent[69] and the publishing of the text of private lectures on the part of persons attending them.[70] There have also been cases in which the plaintiff has recovered substantial damages against a defendant who has rejected a scenario for a play submitted to him by the plaintiff, but has then gone on to make considerable use of the dramatic ideas, characters and plot contained in the scenario.[71]

A developed idea or format for a proposed television programme, even though not a full synopsis or script, may be protected by an action for breach of confidence, if it is established that it was communicated in confidence, was clearly identifiable, sufficiently original, of potential commercial attractiveness and capable of being realised in practice.[72]

21–12   **News.** In a number of cases the courts have protected information in the form of news which has been collected by news agencies and has been surreptitiously obtained from a subscriber to the agency's news service, though it is difficult to say how far the decisions are based upon infringement of common law copyright, and how far upon the breach of confidence. For example, in *Exchange Telegraph Co. Ltd.* v. *Gregory & Co.*[73] the plaintiffs, under a contract with the committee of the London Stock Exchange, obtained valuable information as to the prices of stocks and shares from time to time during the day. This information the plaintiffs handed on to their subscribers by means of tape machines, the subscribers expressly agreeing not to sell or communicate to non-subscribers the information which had been supplied to them. The defendants had been at one

---

[65] (1770) 2 Amb. 694.

[66] *Webb* v. *Rose* (1732) cited (1766) 4 Burr. 2303 at 2330.

[67] *Abernethy* v. *Hutchinson* (1825) 3 L.J.(o.s.) Ch. 209; *Lamb* v. *Evans* [1893] 1 Ch. 218.

[68] *Forrester* v. *Waller* (1741) cited (1766) 4 Burr. 2303 at 2331; see also *Turner* v. *Robinson* (1860) 10 Ir.Ch. 121 at 510; *Southey* v. *Sherwood* (1817) 2 Mer. 435; *Gee (A.P.)* v. *Pritchard (W.)* (1818) 2 Sw. 402.

[69] *Pollard* v. *Photographic Co.* (1889) 40 Ch.D. 345; *cf. Ellis* v. *Marshall (H.) & Son* (1895) 64 L.J.Q.B. 757; and see § 4–21 et seq. *ante*. See also the statutory moral right to photographic privacy § 22–52 *et seq., post.*

[70] *Caird* v. *Sime* (1887) 12 App.Cas. 326.

[71] *Moore* v. *Edwards* [1901–4] Mac.C.C. 44; *Fraser* v. *Edwards* [1905–10] Mac.C.C. 10.

[72] *Fraser* v. *Thames Television* [1984] Q.B. 44; *Talbot* v. *General Television Corporation Pty. Ltd.* [1981] R.P.C. 1. (Supreme Court of Victoria); *Green* v. *Broadcasting Corpn. of New Zealand* [1989] 2 All E.R. 1056; *Promotivate International Inc.* v. *Toronto Star Newspapers* [1986] 23 D.L.R. (4th) 196 (Ontario High Court).

[73] [1896] 1 Q.B. 147; and see *Tillett* v. *The Cosmopolitan Press Ltd.* [1928–35] Mac.C.C. 331; *cf. Chilton* v. *Progress Printing, etc., Co.* [1895] 2 Ch. 29.

time subscribers of the plaintiffs, but the latter had recently refused to continue them as such, and they had succeeded in surreptitiously obtaining the information from another subscriber, and posted the information thus received in their offices. The court granted an injunction restraining the defendants from infringing the plaintiffs' copyright and from continuing to induce any subscriber of the plaintiffs to supply them with the information in breach of his contract with the plaintiffs. This case was followed in *Exchange Telegraph Co. Ltd.* v. *Central News Ltd.*,[74] where an injunction was sought to restrain the defendants from improperly copying information as to the results of horse-races at Manchester, collected by the plaintiffs' subscribers, and from communicating the information so copied to the defendants' subscribers. It was sought to distinguish this case from the case of *Exchange Telegraph Co. Ltd.* v. *Gregory & Co., supra*, on the ground that the result of a horse-race is public property, but Stirling J. refused to acknowledge the distinction. "The information," he said, "was not made known to the whole world; it was, no doubt, known to a large number of persons, but a great many more were ignorant of it. By the expenditure of labour and money the plaintiffs had acquired this information, and it was, in their hands, valuable property in this sense—that persons to whom it was not known were willing to pay, and did pay, money to acquire it. . . . I think that it is established as against the syndicate that they published for their own benefit information acquired from or through some subscribers to the plaintiffs, with knowledge or notice on the part of their manager, that it was acquired contrary to the terms imposed on the plaintiffs' subscribers." An injunction was accordingly granted.

State and government secrets. In recent years there have been a **21–13** number of important cases in which the Crown has invoked the law of confidence against former Crown servants and third parties, such as book and newspaper publishers, to prevent disclosure of confidential information concerning governmental activities. Public interest considerations, particularly the public interest in freedom of speech, play a more important part in such cases than in the more common case of information imparted in a private, industrial or commercial setting.[75] The courts have power, for example, to restrain the publication of State secrets which threaten national security and the improper publication of information received in confidence by a cabinet minister. It has been held that opinions expressed by individual members at cabinet meetings are confidential and remain so until such time as their disclosure would not undermine the doctrine of joint cabinet responsibility. The maintenance of that doctrine is in the public interest and the doctrine might be prejudiced by

---

[74] [1897] 2 Ch. 48; *The Exchange Telegraph Co. Ltd.* v. *Howard* (1906) 22 T.L.R. 375; *Press Association Ltd.* v. *Northern and Midland Reporting Agency* [1905–10] Mac.C.C. 306; *London & Provincial Sporting News Agency Ltd.* v. *Levy* [1923–28] Mac.C.C. 340.

[75] *Att.-Gen.* v. *Guardian Newspapers (No. 1)* [1987] 1 W.L.R. 1248; *Att.-Gen.* v. *Guardian Newspapers (No. 2)* [1990] A.C. 109; *Att.-Gen.* v. *Brandon Book Publishers Ltd.* [1989] F.S.R. 37 (High Court of Ireland) *cf. Att.-Gen.* v. *Turnaround Distribution Ltd.* [1989] F.S.R. 169; *Lord Advocate* v. *The Scotsman Publications Ltd.* [1990] A.C. 812.

the premature disclosure of views of individual ministers.[76] The obligation of confidence does not extend, however, to advice given by civil servants to ministers or to observations made by ministers on civil servants.[76]

A member of the Security Service is under a lifelong duty of confidence to the Crown enforceable at the instance of the Attorney-General. The purpose of the duty is to preserve the secrets of the service which it would be against the public interest to disclose[77] and it extends to all secret or confidential information which he acquired during his service, without discrimination between secrets of greater or lesser importance.[78] In order to prevent disclosure, however, or to obtain redress the Crown must be in a position to show that the disclosure is likely to damage, or has damaged, the public interest.

21-14 **Confidentiality and court proceedings.** The fact that information has been communicated by one person to another in confidence is not of itself a sufficient ground for protecting from disclosure in legal proceedings or in a court of law the nature of the information or the identity of the informant if either of these matters would assist the court to ascertain facts which are relevant to an issue upon which it is adjudicating. The private obligation of confidentiality must yield to the general public interest that in the administration of justice truth will out unless, by reason of the character of the information or the relationship of the recipient of the information to the informant, a more important public interest is served by protecting the information or the identity of the informant from disclosure in a court of law. Thus, the identity of police informers may not be disclosed, by discovery in a civil action or by oral evidence, nor need the identity of persons giving information about the neglect or ill-treatment of children be disclosed to the local authority or N.S.P.C.C.[79] On the other hand, the court may order a newspaper proprietor, television company or a journalist to disclose the name of its informant in cases where the public interest in securing justice outweighs the public interest in protecting a confidential source of information to such an extent that disclosure has become a necessity.[80] No court may require a person to disclose, nor is any person guilty of contempt of court for refusing to disclose, the source of information contained in a publication for which he is responsible, unless it is established to the satisfaction of the court that disclosure is necessary in

---

[76] *Att.-Gen.* v. *Jonathan Cape Ltd.* [1976] Q.B. 752.

[77] *Att.-Gen.* v. *Guardian Newspapers (No. 2)* [1990] A.C. 109 at 259, 265, 269 and 284; *Commonwealth of Australia* v. *John Fairfax & Sons Ltd.* (1980) 147 C.L.R. 39; *Smith Kline & French Laboratories (Australia) Ltd.* v. *Secretary to the Department of Community Services and Health* [1990] F.S.R. 617 (Federal Court of Australia: N.S.W. Division).

[78] See n. 77, *ante.*

[79] *D.* v. *N.S.P.C.C.* [1978] A.C. 171. See also *Alfred Crompton Amusement Machines Ltd.* v. *Customs and Excise Commissioners (No. 2)* [1974] A.C. 405; *Campbell* v. *Tameside Metropolitan B.C.* [1982] Q.B. 1065 at 1075. (Educational records of a child alleged to have assaulted the plaintiff teacher in class); *G.* v. *Day.* [1982] 1 N.S.W.R. 24. (Supreme Court of New South Wales); *D.*v. *Hall* [1984] 1 N.Z.L.R. 727.

[80] *British Steel Corp.* v. *Granada Television Ltd.,* [1981] A.C. 1096; *X. Ltd.* v. *Morgan Grampian (Publishers) Ltd.* [1990] 2 W.L.R. 1000.

the interests of justice or national security or for the prevention of disorder or crime.[81]

(vi) *Confidential relationships*

However secret and confidential the information may be, there can be no **21–15** binding obligation of confidence unless the information is communicated or acquired in circumstances importing an obligation of confidence.[82] The law has long recognised that an obligation of confidence can arise out of particular relationships, such as doctor and patient,[83] priest and penitent, solicitor and client, banker and customer.[84] It is difficult to deduce from the decided cases any precise, comprehensive test for determining whether the circumstances of a particular case import an obligation of confidence. One general test which has been suggested is that a confidential relationship exists if the circumstances are such that any reasonable man, standing in the shoes of the recipient of the information, would have realised that upon reasonable grounds the information was being given to him in confidence.[85] For example, it would be relatively easy for a plaintiff to establish a confidential relationship where information which is of commercial or industrial value is communicated during business negotiations with a view to a joint venture or to the commercial exploitation of the information by one party for, or with the co-operation of, the other party.[86] The plaintiffs in both *Seager* v. *Copydex*[87] and *Coco* v. *A.N. Clark (Engineers) Ltd.*[88] were inventors who alleged that they had disclosed to the defendants details of their invention during the course of negotiations with a view to the defendants using the information in the manufacture of articles under agreements with the plaintiffs. In both cases the court found that those circumstances gave rise to a confidential relationship.

Confidence in contracts. The initial obligation to keep the information **21–16** confidential often arises from an express or implied contract under which the information was originally communicated.[89] Such a case involves the determination of the nature and extent of the contract from its terms and surrounding circumstances. In the case of an express covenant questions of construction may arise. For example, it has been held that an express term in a contract of service not to "disclose" any confidential information

---

[81] s.10, Contempt of Court Act 1981; *Secretary of State for Defence* v. *Guardian Newspapers Ltd.* [1985] A.C. 339; *Re an Inquiry under the Company Securities (Insider Dealing) Act 1985* [1988] A.C. 660; *X. Ltd.* v. *Morgan Grampian (Publishers) Ltd.* [1990] 2 W.L.R. 1000.

[82] *Coco* v. *A.N. Clark (Engineers) Ltd.* [1969] R.P.C. 41.

[83] *W.* v. *Egdell* [1990] 2 W.L.R. 471; *Hunter* v. *Mann* [1974] Q.B. 767.

[84] *Att.-Gen.* v. *Guardian Newspapers (No. 2)* (*supra*) at p. 255; *F.O.C.C.Ltd.* v. *Chase Manhattan Bank* [1990] 1 H.K.L.R. 277.

[85] See n. 82, *ante*.

[86] *House of Spring Gardens Ltd.* v. *Point Blank Ltd.* [1983] F.S.R. 213 at 252; *A.B. Consolidated Ltd.* v. *Europe Strength Food Co. Pty Ltd.* [1978] 2 N.Z.L.R. 515; *Lac Minerals Ltd.* v. *International Corona Resources Ltd.* [1990] F.S.R. 441 (Supreme Court of Canada).

[87] [1967] 1 W.L.R. 923.

[88] See n. 82, *ante*.

[89] See *Fraser* v. *Evans* [1969] 1 Q.B. 349; *Yates Circuit Foil Co.* v. *Electrofoils Ltd.* [1976] F.S.R. 345 and *Thomas Marshall (Exports) Ltd.* v. *Guinle* [1979] Ch. 227 for examples of express covenants.

relating to the employer's affairs may not prevent "use" of the information by the former employee.[90] Questions relating to the doctrine of restraint of trade may also arise.[91] An express term as to confidence may, but does not necessarily, exclude any implication of terms or obligations in equity or as a matter of business efficacy, relating to ownership or use of information, invention or discoveries, even if the express term is unenforceable as being in restraint of trade.[92] The confidential obligation is not automatically terminated by a wrongful repudiation of the contract of service by the employee.[93] A common example of an implied term or obligation is when a contract, under which documents, drawings and technical information have been supplied for the purpose of assisting the manufacture of goods, has been terminated. In that case the court can restrain the use of the drawings and information for the purposes of continuing to manufacture the goods.[94]

A similar situation arose in the case of *Saltman Engineering Co. Ltd. & Ors.* v. *Campbell Engineering Co.*[95] where the defendants had been entrusted under a contract with certain engineering designs for the purpose of carrying out an order for the manufacture of a quantity of goods. The defendants thereafter used the designs for purposes outside the contract and it was held that such action was a breach of a confidential relationship which could be restrained by the court. Lord Greene said that if two persons make a contract under which one of them obtains, for the purposes of the contract or in connection with it, some confidential material, the law will imply an obligation to treat that confidential material in a confidential way as one of the terms of the contract. He added, however, that the obligation to respect confidence is not limited to cases where the parties are in a contractual relationship.

21–17 **Contracts of service.** Another common contractual situation which can import a confidential obligation is a contract of service between employer and employee. A servant may not, either during his employment or after the termination of his employment, disclose or use confidential information, knowledge of which he has acquired during his employment,[96]

---

[90] *Thomas Marshall (Exports) Ltd.* v. *Guinle (supra).*

[91] *Triplex Safety Glass Co. Ltd.* v. *Scorah* (1938) 55 R.P.C. 21 at 28; *Commercial Plastics Ltd.* v. *Vincent* [1965] 1 Q.B. 623, at 646; *Lupton* v. *Potts* [1969] 1 W.L.R. 1749 at 1753.

[92] See n. 90, *ante.*

[93] See n. 89, *ante.*

[94] *Brian D. Collins (Engineers) Ltd.* v. *Charles Roberts & Co. Ltd.* [1965] R.P.C. 429 but *cf. Regina Glass Fibre Ltd.* v. *Werner Schuller* [1972] F.S.R. 141 (if recipient given information under contract to establish business, right to the information does not necessarily terminate with the contract); *Alfa Laval Cheese Systems Ltd.* v. *Wincanton Engineering Ltd.* [1990] F.S.R. 583.

[95] (1948) 65 R.P.C. 203 (C.A.); *Interfirm Comparison (Australia) Pty. Ltd.* v. *Law Society of New South Wales* [1977] R.P.C. 137 (Supreme Court of New South Wales).

[96] *Lamb* v. *Evans* [1893] 1 Ch. 218; *Merryweather* v. *Moore* [1892] 2 Ch. 518; *Robb* v. *Green* [1895] 2 Q.B. 315; *Measures Bros. Ltd.* v. *Measures* [1910] 2 Ch. 248; *Amber Size, etc., Co. Ltd.* v. *Menzel* [1913] 2 Ch. 239; *Reid & Sigrist Ltd.* v. *Moss & Mechanism Ltd.* (1932) 49 R.P.C. 461; *Printers & Finishers Ltd.* v. *Holloway* [1965] 1 W.L.R. 1; *Coral Index Ltd.* v. *Regent Index Ltd.* [1970] R.P.C. 147; *British Industrial Plastics Ltd.* v. *Ferguson* (1941) 58 R.P.C. 1; *Lord Ashburton* v. *Pape* [1913] 2 Ch. 469; *Initial Services Ltd.* v. *Putterill* [1968] 1 Q.B. 396; *Litholite Ltd.* v. *Thomas Travis etc. Ltd.* (1913) 30 R.P.C. 266, 532; *Industrial Furnaces Ltd.* v. *Reaves* [1970] R.P.C. 605; *Greer* v. *Sketchley Ltd.* [1979] F.S.R. 197; *United Sterling Corporation Ltd.* v. *Felton & Mannion* [1974] R.P.C. 162. *Balston Ltd.* v. *Headline Filters Ltd.* [1990] F.S.R. 385.

nor make unauthorised copies of documents belonging to his master,[97] for to do so would be a breach of the confidence reposed in him. The rights and obligations of employees in the regard to the disclosure and use of confidential information have been re-stated by the Court of Appeal in *Faccenda Chicken Ltd.* v. *Fowler*.[98] The rights and obligations of the employer and employee are determined by the express or implied terms of the contract of employment. A distinction is drawn between the position of an employee during his period of employment and after his employment has ceased. While the employee remains in employment he owes to his employer a duty of good faith or fidelity, the extent of which will vary according to the nature of the contract. That duty will be broken if the employee makes or copies a list of customers of his employer for use after his employment ends or if he deliberately memorises a list.

The implied term in respect of confidential information after cesser of employment is more restricted than the duty of good faith. The obligation not to use or disclose information covers information which is of a sufficiently high degree of confidentiality to amount to a "trade secret," e.g. secret processes of manufacture, such as chemical formulae, and designs or special methods of construction. It is not enough that the employer claims that the information which the employee intends to use or disclose is confidential. Regard must be had to all the circumstances of the case; in particular, to the nature of the employment (e.g. if the employee habitually handles sensitive material), the nature of the information (*i.e.* whether it is a trade secret or of such a highly confidential nature as to require the same protection as a trade secret), restrictions imposed on the circulation of the information, whether the employer has impressed on the employee the confidentiality of the information and whether the information in question can be easily isolated from other information which the employee is free to use or disclose.

The overriding general principle is that, subject to the duty of confidence, every person has the right to use and exploit for the purpose of earning a living all the skill, experience and knowledge which he has at his disposal, including the skill, experience and knowledge which he has acquired in the course of previous periods of employment.[99] In the case of *Amber Size Co.* v. *Menzel*[1] the court granted an injunction against a dismissed servant of the plaintiff company, restraining him from making use of information as to a secret process of manufacture obtained in the course of his confidential employment with the plaintiffs, although the defendant had not abstracted anything tangible, such as a list of customers, and was not proposing to publish the information he had gained, but simply to use

---

[97] *Louis* v. *Smellie* [1895] W.N. 115; *Tuck & Sons* v. *Priester* (1887) 19 Q.B.D. 48; *British Steel Corp.* v. *Granada Television Ltd.* [1981] A.C. 1096.

[98] [1987] Ch. 117; *Roger Bullivant Ltd.* v. *Ellis* [1987] F.S.R. 172; *Manor Electronics Ltd.* v. *Dickson* [1988] R.P.C. 618; *Balston Ltd.* v. *Headline Filters Ltd.* [1987] F.S.R. 330 [1990] F.S.R. 385; *Johnson & Bloy (Holdings) Ltd.* v. *Wolstenholme Rink p.l.c.* [1989] F.S.R. 135; *Berkeley Administration Inc.* v. *McClelland* [1990] F.S.R. 505.

[99] *Balston Ltd.* v. *Headline Filters Ltd. (supra)* at 351.

[1] See n. 96, *ante.*

the same for the benefit of a rival firm into whose employment he had subsequently entered. Astbury J. granted an injunction in general terms restraining the defendant from using the whole or any material part of the plaintiffs' secret method or process of manufacture, the knowledge of which was acquired or obtained by him during his employment by the plaintiffs and from disclosing to any other person any information with respect thereto. The case of *Stevenson Jordan & Harrison Ltd.* v. *MacDonald & Evans*[2] illustrates the limits of the confidential obligations inherent in a contract of employment. The plaintiffs there contended that the defendant, who had written a textbook with regard to the subject-matter of his employment, had in so doing disclosed confidential information. Lord Evershed said that if an employee writes a book which discloses confidential information learnt by him in the course of his employment, the court would restrain the publication. He added, however, that this did not apply to "know-how" learned in the course of his employment. "Know-how" indicates the way in which a skilled man does a job and is an expression of his individual skill and experience. Denning L.J. said that a servant, when he leaves his employment, cannot be restrained from using knowledge he has acquired so long as he does not take away trade secrets or lists of customers.[3] Thus, not all information which is given to a servant in confidence, and which it would be a breach of his duty for him to disclose to another person during his employment, is a trade secret which he can be prevented from using for his own advantage or for the benefit of a future employer after the employment is over.[4]

For example, the employer's general organisation and method of business is not regarded as protectable,[5] but such matters as names and addresses of the employer's suppliers and contacts, negotiated prices paid by or to the employer, names of agents, information as to customer requirements, details of current negotiations and actual or future sales proposals are, if not generally known, capable of being confidential.[6]

A distinction is drawn between, on the one hand, general information inevitably acquired by an employee in the ordinary course of his employment as part of the sum total of his experience and stock of knowledge and, on the other hand, special information distinguished by a particular badge of confidence, such as chemical formulae, lists of customers and design features in drawings which a man of ordinary honesty and intelligence would recognise as the property of his employer and not his own to

---

[2] [1952] 1 T.L.R. 101; *Morris (B. O.) Ltd.* v. *F. Gilman (B.S.T.) Ltd.* (1943) 60 R.P.C. 20; *Canada Bonded Attorney and Legal Dictionary Ltd.* v. *Leonard-Parmeter Ltd.* (1918) 42 D.L.R. 342; *Nichrotherm Electrical Co. Ltd.* v. *Percy* [1957] R.P.C. 207.

[3] See *Baker* v. *Gibbons* [1972] 1 W.L.R. 693.

[4] *Printers & Finishers Ltd.* v. *Holloway* [1965] R.P.C. 239 at 253; *cf. Industrial Furnaces Ltd.* v. *Reaves* [1970] R.P.C. 605 at 618.

[5] *Herbert Morris Ltd.* v. *Saxelby* [1916] 1 A.C. 688; *Commercial Plastics Ltd.* v. *Vincent* [1965] 1 Q.B. 623 at 641; *Greer* v. *Sketchley Ltd.* [1979] F.S.R. 197 at 201; *Ixora Trading Inc.* v. *Jones* [1990] F.S.R. 251. *Berkeley Administration Inc.* v. *McClelland* [1990] F.S.R. 505 at 527. *cf. Littlewoods Organisation* v. *Harris* [1977] 1 W.L.R. 1472.

[6] *Thomas Marshall (Exports) Ltd.* v. *Guinle* [1979] Ch. 227; see *British Northrop Co.* v. *Texteam* [1974] R.P.C. 5; *cf. Faccenda Chicken Ltd.* v. *Fowler* [1987] Ch. 117.

deal with as he likes.[7] The latter is protected as binding on the employee's conscience, but use of the former cannot be restrained in the absence of a reasonable covenant restricting the employee's post-termination activities.

Other examples of confidential relationships. In *Argyll (Duchess)* v. **21–18**
Argyll (Duke)[8] it was held that the obligation of confidence was implied in the relationship of marriage. The confidential nature of the relationship was of its very essence and so obviously and necessarily implicit in it that there was no need for it to be expressed; it was the policy of the law to preserve the close confidence and trust between husband and wife and an injunction would therefore be granted to restrain the publication of communications made between spouses during the subsistence of that relationship.

The duty of confidence is not limited to the sexual or private conduct of married partners. Information relating sexual conduct, heterosexual or homosexual, may be the subject matter of a legally enforceable duty of confidentiality.[9]

If a person lends his manuscript to another, there will generally be implied an obligation that the latter shall not publish it.[10] Similarly, where a person sits for his portrait by a photographer, there will usually be implied on the part of the latter an obligation that he will not sell or exhibit copies without the sitter's consent,[11] and an obligation may be implied on the part of persons attending private lectures not to take them down and publish them.[12] An obligation of confidence may even arise where there is no "relationship" in the literal sense, as where a person has obtained the confidential information from another person without his consent and by reprehensible means, such as by theft[13] or by finding and keeping an obviously confidential document which has been lost or mislaid or by unauthorised telephone tapping[14] or by stealth or by a trick[15] or even by accident.[16] Those who disclose documents on discovery in the

---

[7] *United Sterling Corporation* v. *Felton & Mannion* [1974] R.P.C. 162; *Ansell Rubber Co. Pty. Ltd.* v. *Allied Rubber Industries Pty. Ltd.* [1972] R.P.C. 811 (Supreme Court of Victoria); *Standex International Ltd.* v. *C.B. Blades & Anor.* [1976] F.S.R. 114; *Yates Circuit Foil Co. & Anor.* v. *Electrofoils Ltd. & Anor.* [1976] F.S.R. 345; *Northern Office Microcomputers (Pty.) Ltd.* v. *Rosenstein* [1982] F.S.R. 124; *Fisher Karpark Industries Ltd.* v. *Nichols* [1982] F.S.R. 351.

[8] [1967] Ch. 302; *cf. Lennon* v. *News Group Newspapers Ltd.* [1978] F.S.R. 573.

[9] *Stephens* v. *Avery* [1988] Ch. 449 at 455.

[10] *Queensberry (Duke)* v. *Shebbeare* (1761) 2 Eden 32; and see as to letters, *ante*, §§ 4–71 *et seq.*, 21–10.

[11] *Pollard* v. *Photographic Co.* (1889) 40 Ch.D. 345; see § 22–57, *post*, as to statutory moral right to privacy.

[12] *Caird* v. *Sime* (1887) 12 App.Cas. 320.

[13] *Franklin* v. *Giddings* [1978] 1 Q.D.R. 72 (Supreme Court of Queensland); *Church of Scientology of California* v. *D.H.S.S.* [1979] 1 W.L.R. 723; *Union Carbide Corp.* v. *Naturin Ltd.* [1987] F.S.R. 538 at 547.

[14] *Francome* v. *Mirror Group Newspapers Ltd.* [1984] 1 W.L.R. 892; *Malone* v. *Metropolitan Police Commissioner* [1979] Ch. 344.

[15] See *ITC Film Distributors Ltd.* v. *Video Exchange Ltd.* [1982] Ch. 431 (Documents obtained by a trick excluded from evidence).

[16] *English & American Insurance Co. Ltd.* v. *Herbert Smith* [1988] F.S.R. 232. (Papers of plaintiff's counsel mistakenly sent to defendant's solicitors: injunction granted to restrain use of information derived from documents by defendant's solicitors).

course of legal proceedings are entitled to the protection of the court against any use of the documents, whether by the other person or a third person into whose hands the documents have come, otherwise than in the proceedings in which they were disclosed. This protection is independent of any obligation under the general law relating to confidentiality and is available as part of and in the interests of the proper administration of justice. There is an implied undertaking to the court on discovery, which is the result of a compulsory process of law, constituting a very serious invasion of the privacy of the litigant's affairs, that documents disclosed should not be used improperly for any collateral or ulterior purpose. Anyone who receives those documents is under the same duty.[17] The plaintiff has a private right to confidentiality in such documents and there is a public interest in the administration of justice involved in protecting documents disclosed in the action greater than the public interest to make public.[18] Any undertaking, whether express or implied, not to use a document for any purposes other than those of the proceedings in which it is disclosed, ceases to apply to such a document after it has been read to or by the court, or referred to, in open court, unless the Court for special reasons has otherwise ordered on the application of a party or of the person to whom the document belongs.[19]

(vii) *Wrongful use of confidential information*

21–19 Once a person has acquired confidential information in the course of a confidential relationship, he is generally under a duty not to disclose or use that information without the consent of the person who imparted that information. He is liable even if he uses the information unconsciously.[20] He is also liable, even though his use or disclosure of the information is not for reasons of financial gain or out of malice.[21] This is not, however, an absolute duty. It has been said that in some cases the duty is more accurately expressed in a qualified form as a duty not to use the information without paying a reasonable sum for it.[22] This might be the case in the fields of industry and commerce where there are difficulties involved in granting an injunction when a person has added information of his own to the information he has acquired in confidence and the two have become commercially inextricable. In such cases damages are a more appropriate remedy. But in other fields, such as the protection of privacy or the preservation of marital confidences, the duty probably exists in a more stringent form, and an injunction will be a more appropriate remedy, as the object of the plaintiff is to ensure the preservation of secrecy, rather than to

---

[17] *Distillers Co. (Biochemicals) Ltd.* v. *Times Newspapers Ltd.* [1975] Q.B. 613; *Riddick* v. *Thames Board Mills Ltd.* [1977] Q.B. 881 (document disclosed on discovery cannot be used as basis for subsequent defamation action); *Home Office* v. *Harman* [1983] 1 A.C. 280.

[18] See n. 17, *ante.*

[19] R.S.C., O. 24 r. 14A which came into force on October 1, 1987; *Bibby Bulk Carriers Ltd.* v. *Cansulex Ltd.* [1989] Q.B. 155; *cf. Home Office* v. *Harman (supra)*; *Sybron Corpn.* v. *Barclays Bank plc* [1985] Ch. 299.

[20] *Seager* v. *Copydex* [1967] 1 W.L.R. 923.

[21] *British Steel Corporation* v. *Granada Television Ltd.* [1981] A.C. 1096.

[22] *Coco* v. *A.N. Clark (Engineers) Ltd.* [1969] R.P.C. 41; *Bostitch Inc.* v. *McGarry & Cole Ltd.* [1964] R.P.C. 173.

obtain compensation for its ultimate exploitation. Actions for misuse of confidential information should not be brought unless there is a reasonable basis for the allegation that the defendants are making use of the information. There is a tendency to bring speculative actions, particularly against former employees, and actions of such a character are discouraged by the Courts as being thinly disguised attempts to restrain competition by employees and may be struck out, on failure to give particulars, as an abuse of the process of the Court.[23]

Justifiable use and public interest. The duty of confidence is subject to   **21–20** a limiting principle that the public interest in the preservation of confidences may be outweighed by a countervailing public interest in favour of disclosure. Although a person is not generally permitted to divulge to the world information which he has received in confidence, there are circumstances in which he has a just cause or excuse for doing so and, indeed, it may be his duty to reveal what he knows.[24] The Courts have always refused to uphold the right to confidence when to do so would be to cover up wrongdoing. If the information, which has been acquired in confidence, ought in the public interest to be disclosed to one who has a proper interest to receive it, the Courts will not restrain its disclosure.[25] The public, as well as the private, interest in the preservation of the right to keep secret confidential information may be overborne by the public interest in disclosure, provided that a sufficiently strong case for disclosure has been made out by the defendant. In order to rely on the defence of just cause or excuse it is not sufficient merely to make allegations of wrongdoing or show that such allegations have been made by others. There must be at least a prima facie case that the allegations have substance.[26] For example, in *Initial Services Ltd.* v. *Putterill*[27] the plaintiffs tried to restrain the defendant, a former employee, from disclosing to a newspaper information to the effect that the plaintiffs had entered into agreements which should have been registered under the Restrictive Trade Practices Act 1956. It was held that the law would not lend its assistance to anyone who was proposing to commit, and to continue to commit, a breach of statutory duty imposed in the public interest. It was also suggested that there may be cases where the misdeed is of such a character that the public interest may demand, or at least excuse, publication to a broader field, even to the press. In some cases the public interest would be served by more limited disclosure of the confidential information, such as to the

---

[23] *Reinforced Plastics Applications (Swansea) Ltd.* v. *Swansea Plastics & Engineering Co. Ltd.* [1979] F.S.R. 182; *J. Zinc Co. Ltd.* v. *Lloyds Bank Ltd.* [1973] R.P.C. 717 (C.A.) and [1975] R.P.C. 385; *Yates Circuit Foil Co. & Anor.* v. *Electrofoils Ltd. & Anor.* [1976] F.S.R. 345; *Ixora Trading Inc.* v. *Jones* [1990] F.S.R. 251; *Berkeley Administration Inc.* v. *McClelland* [1990] F.S.R. 505; see § 21–17, *ante*.

[24] *Schering Chemicals Ltd.* v. *Falkman Ltd.* [1982] Q.B. 1 at 27; *Lion Laboratories Ltd.* v. *Evans* [1985] Q.B. 527.

[25] *Fraser* v. *Evans* [1969] 1 Q.B. 349 at 361; *Church of Scientology of California & Ors.* v. *Kaufman* [1973] R.P.C. 635; *cf. British Steel Corporation* v. *Granada Television Ltd.*, *(supra)*.

[26] *Att.-Gen.* v. *Guardian Newspapers (No. 2)* [1990] A.C. 109 at 262A.

[27] [1968] 1 Q.B. 396; see *Distillers Co. (Biochemicals) Ltd.* v. *Times Newspapers Ltd.* [1975] Q.B. 613.

police or to a professional body, rather than to the media.[28] There is, therefore, no breach of confidence in the disclosure of iniquity and that principle is not confined to cases of fraud, or the contemplated commission of a crime or civil wrong or even to cases of general wrongdoing on the part of the plaintiff.

Public interest might justify disclosure of matters, carried out or contemplated, in breach of the country's security, or in breach of law, including statutory duty, fraud or otherwise destructive of the country or its people, including matters medically dangerous to the public[29] and other misdeeds of similar gravity.[30] It extends to cases where the subject-matter of the alleged confidence is dangerous or absurd and ought, in the public interest, to be disclosed.[31] This is especially so where the person claiming the benefit of the confidential information has used deplorable methods to suppress inquiry or criticism.[32] The Court may also decline to grant an injunction restraining breach of confidence where the public have been misled by publicity emanating from the plaintiff about the plaintiff's affairs and activities and there is a public interest in the truth being told, albeit in breach of confidence, to correct that position.[33] The Courts recognise, however, that there is a wide difference between what is interesting to the public and what it is in the public interest to make known. Not everything which the media wish to make public is in the public interest. The media have a private interest of their own in publishing what appeals to the public to boost their circulation or audience ratings.[34]

On the other hand, the plaintiff's private right to confidentialty in documents disclosed on discovery in legal proceedings and the public interest in the protection of such documents in the administration of justice, may only be overriden on by a competing and paramount public interest in the disclosure of crime, fraud or similar misdeeds. Such misdeeds would not include, it seems, an allegation of negligence against the person seeking to restrain disclosure.[35]

In many cases the court is faced with the problem of balancing two aspects of the public interest; on the one hand, it is usually in the public interest that when information is received in confidence for a limited and restricted purpose, it should not be used for other purposes; on the other hand, confidences will sometimes be overcome by a higher public interest,

---

[28] *Francome* v. *Mirror Group Newspapers Ltd.* [1984] 1 W.L.R. 892 at p. 897; *Lion Laboratories Ltd.* v. *Evans (supra)*; *cf. Cork* v. *McVicar, The Times,* October 31, 1984 (disclosure of alleged corruption in the police force).

[29] *X* v. *Y* [1988] 2 All E.R. 648 (Doctor believed to have AIDS); *W.* v. *Egdell* [1990] Ch. 359 (Psychiatrist's report).

[30] *Beloff* v. *Pressdram Ltd.* [1973] 1 All E.R. 241 at 260; *Schering Chemicals Ltd.* v. *Falkman Ltd.* [1982] Q.B. 1 at 27; *Francome* v. *Mirror Group Newspapers Ltd.* [1984] 1 W.L.R. 892.

[31] *Hubbard* v. *Vosper* [1972] 2 Q.B. 84; *Church of Scientology of California & Ors.* v. *Kaufman* [1973] R.P.C. 627 at 635; *Castrol* v. *Emtech* (1980–81) 33 A.L.R. 31 (Supreme Court of New South Wales).

[32] See n. 31, *ante.*

[33] *Woodward* v. *Hutchins* [1977] 1 W.L.R. 760.

[34] *Lion Laboratories Ltd.* v. *Evans* [1985] Q.B. 527 at 537; *British Steel* v. *Granada Television Ltd.* [1981] A.C. 1096 at 1168; *Express Newspapers plc* v. *News (U.K.) Ltd.* [1990] F.S.R. 359 at 367, 368.

[35] *Distillers Co. (Biochemicals) Ltd.* v. *Times Newspapers Ltd.* [1975] Q.B. 613.

such as the interest of justice itself, the prevention of wrongdoing or the security of the State.

For example, those who provide confidential information to employees of a local authority, such as social workers, are entitled to expect and can reasonably be assured that, save as may be necessary for the performance of the authority's statutory duties, the information will never be divulged to anyone outside the authority or even to anyone within the authority who has no need to know.[36] Even a councillor on the local authority would need to have a good reason for access to the files, e.g. if the files related to a committee on which he served.[37]

On grounds of public policy a man cannot be restrained, either by contract or confidence, from using, after his employment is terminated, the personal skill, aptitude and experience acquired by him during his employment.[38] The ex-employee is entitled to use his own expertise and his personal knowledge for his own benefit or for the benefit of his new employer.[39] The law has always looked with favour upon the efforts of employees to advance themselves, provided that they do not steal or use the secrets of their former employer. In the absence of a restrictive covenant or breach of confidence, there is nothing in the general law to prevent a number of employees in concert deciding to leave their employer and set themselves up in competition with him.[40] The courts will not allow new forms of "industrial slavery" to be created by use of actions for alleged breach of confidence.[41]

(viii) *Benefit of confidence*

Further, there may be cases in which, although it is established that information has been wrongfully disclosed or used in breach of confidence, the plaintiff has no right to relief. The person entitled to the benefit of confidential information is normally the person who creates it or the employer, if created by an employee. Such a case was *Fraser* v. *Evans*[42] where the plaintiff was a public relations consultant who had entered into a contract with the Greek Government, which contained an express term that he would not reveal any information about his work for the Government either during or after his contract. The defendant newspaper proposed to publish an article based on a report the plaintiff had made to the Greek Government in pursuance of the contract. An injunction was refused on the ground that the party complaining must be the person who is entitled to the confidence and to have it respected. In this case no duty of good

21–21

---

[36] *R.* v. *Birmingham City Council ex p. D.* [1983] 1 A.C. 578.

[37] See n. 36, *ante.*

[38] *Commercial Plastics Ltd.* v. *Vincent* [1965] 1 Q.B. 623 at 641; *Ansell Rubber Co. Pty.* v. *Allied Rubber Industries Pty. Ltd.* [1972] R.P.C. 811; *Triplex Safety Glass Co. Ltd.* v. *Scorah* (1938) 55 R.P.C. 21; *Stevenson, Jordan & Harrison Ltd.* v. *Macdonald & Evans* [1952] 1 T.L.R. 101; see § 21–17, *ante.*

[39] *Potters-Ballotini Ltd.* v. *Weston-Baker & Ors.* [1977] R.P.C. 202 at 205.

[40] *G.D. Searle & Co. Ltd.* v. *Celltech Ltd.* [1982] F.S.R. 92 at 99; *Berkeley Administration Inc.* McClelland [1990] F.S.R. 505 at 528.

[41] See n. 40, *ante.*

[42] [1969] 1 Q.B. 349 at 362; *Gartside* v. *Outram* (1858) 26 L.J.Ch. 113 at 114; *Weld Blundell* v. *Stephens* [1919] 1 K.B. 520. See also *Butler* v. *Board of Trade* [1971] Ch. 680.

faith was owed by the Greek Government or the defendants to the plaintiff. There was a duty of confidence owed to the Greek Government, but they were not the plaintiffs in the action. There was thus no duty, express or implied, owed to the plaintiff. It appears that the benefit of confidence can, in certain circumstances, be assigned.[43]

Where the confidential information concerns information disclosed and views expressed at cabinet meetings the Attorney-General is entitled to enforce the obligation of confidence on behalf of the Crown.[44] Similarly, the Attorney-General is entitled to enforce the duty of confidence owed to the Crown by civil servants and former Crown servants.[45]

(ix) *Liability of third parties*

21–22   As a general rule a third party who comes into possession of confidential information, which he knows to be such, may come under a duty not to pass it on to anyone else.[46] The third party to whom the information has been wrongfully revealed himself comes under a duty of confidence to the original confider,[47] though the extent to which that obligation is enforced will vary widely according to the circumstances of each case. As the liability arises from the breach of an equitable obligation and not from the infringement of a proprietary right, such as copyright where ignorance is generally no defence,[48] a purchaser for value without notice ought not to be liable to restraint. In several cases it has been held that, even if a person comes by the information innocently, nevertheless if he gets to know that it was originally given in confidence, he can be restrained from breaking that confidence.[49] In order to be fixed with an obligation of confidence the third party must know that the information was confidential; knowledge of a mere assertion that a breach of confidence has been committed in respect of information received by him is insufficient.[50] It is, however, sufficient if the third party was aware of the circumstances in which the person imparting information to him acquired that information.[51] Knowledge of the circumstances includes the case where the recipient of the information has deliberately closed his eyes to the obvious.[52]

---

[43] *Mustad & Son* v. *Dosen* [1963] R.P.C. 41.

[44] *Att.-Gen.* v. *Jonathan Cape Ltd.* [1976] Q.B. 752.

[45] *Att.-Gen.* v. *Guardian Newspapers Ltd. (No. 2)* [1990] A.C. 109.

[46] See n. 43, *ante.*

[47] See n. 43, *ante.*

[48] *Mansell* v. *Valley Printing Co.* [1908] 2 Ch. 441; see C.D.P.A. 1988, s.97(1).

[49] *Fraser* v. *Evans* [1969] 1 Q.B. 349; *Argyll (Duchess)* v. *Argyll (Duke)* [1967] Ch. 302; *Printers & Finishers Ltd.* v. *Holloway* [1965] 1 W.L.R. 1 at 7; *Distillers Co. (Biochemicals) Ltd.* v. *Times Newspapers Ltd.* [1975] Q.B. 613; *Butler* v. *Board of Trade* [1971] Ch. 680 at 690; *British Steel Corporation* v. *Granada Television Ltd.* [1981] A.C. 1069.

[50] *Fraser* v. *Thames Television* [1984] 44 at 58; *Union Carbide Corpn.* v. *Naturin Ltd.* [1987] F.S.R. 538.

[51] *Schering Chemicals Ltd.* v. *Falkman Ltd.* [1982] Q.B. 1; *Union Carbide Corpn.* v. *Naturin Ltd. (supra)* at 547.

[52] *Att.-Gen.* v. *Guardian Newspapers (No. 2)* [1990] A.C. 109 at 281C.

D. Remedies

(i) *Injunction*

Where the obligation of confidence is breached, damages for past breaches **21–23** and an injunction to prevent future breaches can be obtained. Interlocutory and permanent injunctions may be granted.[53] Damages are rarely an adequate remedy because of the difficulty of quantifying the loss caused by unauthorised publicity,[54] and the effect of an interlocutory injunction will be to postpone until trial the publication of the information, whereas publication before trial may prejudice the position of the plaintiff by destroying the subject matter of the action.[55] If an injunction is granted it must identify the particular items of information that the person restrained is not to use or disclose, since otherwise the person restrained would be placed in the difficult and embarrassing position of not knowing what he would have to avoid using or disclosing to keep clear of a contempt of court.[56] Injunctions are normally aimed at the prevention of some specific wrong, not at the prevention of wrongdoing in general. The court will not therefore normally grant a wide form of injunction restraining the disclosure or misuse of any information obtained by a person in confidence.[57] Further, the injunction granted may be of limited duration,[58] confined to the period during which the information retains its confidential character. Once the information is made public by the confider, he is not entitled to an injunction[59] or to damages for misuse occurring subsequent to publication of the information.[60] The court will not grant an interim injunction to restrain breach of confidence where there is also a claim for libel, to which the defendant pleads justification, and it is impossible to extricate the claim for breach of confidence from the claim for defamation.[61]

(ii) *Damages*

Damages are the main remedy for loss in cases where the information is of **21–24** a commercial character. The purpose of an award of damages is to put the plaintiff in the position which he would have been in if the defendant had

---

[53] See §§ 11–35 *et seq., ante.*

[54] *Schering Chemicals Ltd.* v. *Falkman Ltd.* [1982] Q.B. 1 at 37 and 39.

[55] *Francome* v. *Mirror Group Newspapers Ltd.* [1984] 1 W.L.R. 892; *Att.-Gen.* v. *Guardian Newspapers Ltd.* [1987] 1 W.L.R. 1248.

[56] *Amway Corpn.* v. *Eurway International Ltd.* [1974] R.P.C. 82; *Potters-Ballotini Ltd.* v. *Weston-Baker & Ors.* [1977] R.P.C. 202; *Woodward* v. *Hutchins* [1977] 1 W.L.R. 760 at 764; *John Zink Co. Ltd.* v. *Lloyds Bank Ltd* [1975] R.P.C. 385; *Ixora Trading Inc.* v. *Jones* [1990] F.S.R. 251; *O'Brien* v. *Kamesaroff* [1981–82] 150 C.L.R. 310.

[57] *Att.-Gen.* v. *Guardian Newspapers (No. 2)* [1990] A.C. 109.

[58] *Att.-Gen.* v. *Jonathan Cape Ltd.* [1976] Q.B. 752 at 771.

[59] *Mustad & Son* v. *Dosen* [1963] R.P.C. 41.

[60] *Franchi* v. *Franchi* [1967] R.P.C. 149.

[61] *Woodward* v. *Hutchins* [1977] 1 W.L.R. 760; see § 11–44 *ante* n. 74.

not wrongly obtained and used the confidential information in question.[62] The burden is on the plaintiff to prove that he has suffered loss. If the act complained of also involves infringement of copyright, the damages are alternative, and not cumulative, under these two heads.[63] There are circumstances in which a breach of an obligation of confidence may occur, though no contractual relationship exists between the parties and so there is no common law cause of action. In such a case it had been doubted whether damages as well as an injunction could be obtained.[64] It has now been held that compensation is recoverable and that the proper basis for assessing such compensation in a case where the person imparting the information would have licensed its use at a price, is to determine the market value of the confidential information on a sale between a willing seller and a willing buyer.[65] That value depends on a decision by a competent tribunal, such as a patent judge, of the question whether the information involved a true inventive step, or was such as could have been provided by any competent consultant. In the former case compensation would be the capitalised value of the royalty payable on a sale of the invention, while, in the latter case, its value would be the reasonable fee payable to such a consultant. Once the compensation, as assessed, has been paid, the right to exploit the information belongs to the defendant as on an outright purchase under an agreement for sale.[66]

The measure of damages is different, however, in the case of wrongful disclosure of information by an employee to his employer's competitors who would not have been licensed by the employer to use the information. In such a case the employer is exposed to damaging competition as a result of his employee's wrongdoing and he is entitled to damages for loss of manufacturing profits suffered as a result of the breach of confidence.[67] There is in fact no one method of assessing damages applicable to all cases of breach of confidence. Bearing in mind that the purpose of awarding damages is to compensate the plaintiff and not to punish the defendant, the Court selects the most appropriate method of assessment for the particular case.

Thus, in a case where the plaintiff claimed that, as a result of the breach of confidence, he had lost the chance of securing a contract for the use of the information which would have brought him profits, the Court held that a comparison had to be made between the value of his chance to exploit the information before the breach of confidence and the value of that chance afterwards. That chance had to be evaluated on the evidence if it was substantial and not slender, even though it was not certain that the plaintiff would ever have secured the contract.[68]

---

[62] *Dowson & Mason Ltd.* v. *Potter* [1986] 1 W.L.R. 1419 (distinguishing *Seager* v. *Copydex Ltd.* *(No. 2) (supra)*).

[63] *Nichrotherm Electrical Co. Ltd.* v. *Percy* [1957] R.P.C. 207; *Interfirm Comparison (Australia) Pty. Ltd.* v. *Law Society of New South Wales* [1977] R.P.C. 137 (Supreme Court of New South Wales).

[64] See n. 63, *ante.*

[65] *Seager* v. *Copydex Ltd. (No. 2)* [1969] 1 W.L.R. 809.

[66] See n. 65, *ante.*

[67] See n. 62, *ante.*

[68] *Talbot* v. *General Television Corporation Pty. Ltd.* [1981] R.P.C. 1 at 30, 31 (Supreme Court of Victoria).

(iii) *Account of profits*

An account of profits is based on the principle that no one should be per- **21–25**
mitted to gain from his own wrongdoing and, in particular, that recipients
of confidential information should be deterred from using it for financial
gain.[69] An account of profits can be ordered as an alternative to damages
at the option of the plaintiff.[70] In the taking of an account of profits, difficulties may be encountered in apportioning the profit attributable to the
different elements, some confidential and some not confidential, which
have contributed to the final product. The profits may, for example,
include the profits of contracts or property obtained by unauthorised use
of the confidential information,[71] and possibly the copyright in any work
created by use of the information in breach of trust or fiduciary duty.[72]
The account is ordered on the basis that there should be no unjust enrichment of a defendant. In calculating profits made by sales of goods manufactured by the use of confidential information, manufacturing and
transport costs are deducted from the sale price, but not any money paid
by the defendant for the acquisition of the information.[73] A plaintiff is not
entitled to be paid twice in respect of the same profit. The account can be
ordered against all persons involved in the wrongful act.[74]

It is doubtful whether exemplary damages can be awarded for breach of
confidence being a breach of an equitable obligation and not a tort.[75]

(iv) *Delivery up*

In addition to damages and an injunction the court can also make an **21–26**
order for delivery up of material containing confidential information.[76]
This may be ordered as an alternative to destruction of such material on
oath and is useful where a defendant has shown, by his past conduct, that
his oath is not to be relied upon. If the defendant has added material of his
own to the information which he has obtained from the plaintiff in breach
of confidence he can still be ordered to deliver up the material.[77] A person
to whom confidential documents and information have been disclosed in
breach of confidence may be ordered to disclose the identity of his informant to the person entitled to the benefit of the information,[78] and, subject

---

[69] See n. 57, *ante* See § 11–76, *ante*.
[70] *Peter Pan Manufacturing Corpn.* v. *Corsets Silhouette* [1963] R.P.C. 45 at 57 and see *Seager* v.
Copydex Ltd. [1967] 1 W.L.R. 923; and *General Tire & Rubber Co.* v. *Firestone Tyre & Rubber
Co. Ltd.* [1975] 1 W.L.R. 819 at 833; *Att.-Gen.* v. *Guardian Newspapers (No. 2)* [1990] A.C.
109 at 262.
[71] *Industrial Development Consultants Ltd.* v. *Cooley* [1972] 1 W.L.R. 443; *Lac Minerals Ltd* v. *International Corona Resources Ltd* [1990] F.S.R. 441 (Supreme Court of Canada). (Constructive
trust of property acquired in breach of confidence); *Pacifica Shipping Co.* v. *Anderson* [1986]
2 N.Z.L.R. 328.
[72] See n. 57, *ante*.
[73] See n. 57, *ante*.
[74] *House of Spring Gardens Ltd.* v. *Point Blank Ltd.* [1985] F.S.R. 327.
[75] But see (1972) 12 J.S.P.T.L. (P. M. North).
[76] *Franklin* v. *Gidding* [1978] 1 Q.D.R. 72 (Supreme Court of Queensland); See § 11–80, *ante*.
[77] *Industrial Furnaces Ltd.* v. *Reaves* [1970] R.P.C. 605 at 627, 628; see § 11–61, *ante*.
[78] *British Steel Corporation* v. *Granada Television Ltd.* [1981] A.C. 1096, applying *Norwich Pharmacal Co.* v. *Customs and Excise Commrs.* [1974] A.C. 133.

to the provisions of section 10 of the Contempt of Court Act 1981, to deliver up documents to enable the informant responsible for a breach of confidence to be identified.[79]

(v) *Procedure*

21–27 For the protection of the plaintiff claiming to be entitled to confidential information the Court may require the defendant to give an undertaking that he will make no use of information disclosed in particulars of pleadings or in documents disclosed on discovery, save such use as is necessary for the purpose of the proceedings.[80] In some cases, depending on the surrounding circumstances and the state of knowledge generally in the art, the plaintiff may have to disclose the essential features of his process in affidavits in support of his application for an interim injunction[81] though the court can protect the confidentiality of the information by a hearing *in camera*[82] Where there is a real risk that a party, exercising his right to inspect the other party's documents in legal proceedings, would use matters so disclosed for a collateral purpose, the court will exercise its inherent jurisdiction to restrict inspection, impose safeguards and prevent an abuse of the process of the court[83] or order the appointment of a court expert. A fair balance has to be struck between the natural wish of a plaintiff to have his trade secrets adequately protected and the natural wish of a defendant to see any document which may support his case.[84]

2. Passing Off

A. General

21–28 There are a number of torts which may be committed in relation to copyright works without infringing copyright but which are damaging to the interests of the author or owner of the copyright. For example, questions commonly arise in relation to copyright works as to the protection of titles of the works, the names of the authors and fictional characters, and the general goodwill and reputation attaching both to the copyright work and its author.

---

[79] *Secretary of State for Defence* v. *Guardian Newspapers* [1985] A.C. 339.
[80] *Zink (John) & Co. Ltd.* v. *Wilkinson* [1973] R.P.C. 717; *Centri-Spray Corpn.* v. *Cera International Ltd. & Ors.* [1979] F.S.R. 175.
[81] *Diamond Stylus Co. Ltd.* v. *Baudon Precision Diamonds Ltd.* [1973] R.P.C. 675.
[82] See *Yates Circuit Foil Co.* v. *Electrofoils Ltd.* [1976] F.S.R. 345; *General Motors-Holden's Ltd.* v. *D. Syme & Co. Ltd.* [1985] F.S.R. 413 (Supreme Court of New South Wales).
[83] *Church of Scientology* v. *D.H.S.S.* [1979] 1 W.L.R. 723; *Centri-Spray Corpn.* v. *Cera International Ltd. & Ors.* [1979] F.S.R. 175. See § 11–95, *ante.*
[84] *Format Communications Mfg. Ltd.* v. *ITT (U.K.) Ltd.* [1983] F.S.R. 473 at 481 and 485; *Rousel Uclaf* v. *I.C.I.* [1989] R.P.C. 59 at 62, 66.; *John Zinc Co. Ltd.* v. *Lloyds Bank Ltd.* (*supra*); *Ixora Trading Inc.* v. *Jones* (*supra*).

B. Titles

No copyright in titles. The titles of books, newspapers, periodicals and other copyright works are not generally in themselves the subject of copyright. It is difficult to say that there is any original literary work in the formation of several ordinary English words into a title. The words or phrases chosen may be original in their application to the subject-matter of the work. It may require much skill and judgment to produce an apt title, but that skill and judgment is generally employed in choosing and selecting from common words and phrases, and not in stringing together words in an original form or in affording to others information, instruction or pleasure.[85] **21–29**

In a number of early cases there appeared to be some support for the proposition that the title of, for example, a literary work was protected by copyright.[86] Those cases have been overruled by later cases so far as short titles of unoriginal character[87] are concerned. The question was, however, kept open as to whether there might be copyright in a whole page of title, or something of that kind requiring invention.[88] **21–30**

More recent authorities confirm the difficulty of establishing that the copyright in a work has been infringed simply by the taking of a title consisting of a few ordinary English words. **21–31**

In *Francis, Day and Hunter Ltd.* v. *Twentieth Century Fox Corporation Ltd.*[89] the Privy Council held that the copyright in the words of a song was not infringed by the use of its title as the title of a film which did not use any other part of the song. Lord Wright said: "The theme of the film is different from that of the song, and their Lordships see no ground in copyright law to justify the appellants' claim to prevent the use by the respondents of these few obvious words, which are too unsubstantial to constitute an infringement, especially when used in so different a connection."

In *Ladbroke (Football) Ltd.* v. *William Hill (Football) Ltd.*,[90] however, Lord Hodson stated that neither *Dicks* v. *Yates*[91] nor *Francis, Day and Hunter Ltd.* v. *Twentieth Century Fox Corporation Ltd.*[92] supported the proposition that, as a matter of law, copyright cannot subsist in titles. "No doubt," he said, "they will not as a rule be protected, since alone they would not be regarded as a sufficiently substantial part of the book or other copyright document to justify the preventing of copying by others. In any event, there is good authority for the protection of headings in a proper case in

---

[85] *Exxon Corp.* v. *Exxon Insurance Consultants International Ltd.* [1982] Ch. 119.
[86] *Weldon* v. *Dicks* (1878) 10 Ch.D. 247; *Mack* v. *Petter* (1872) L.R. 14 Eq. 431.
[87] *Dicks* v. *Yates* (1881) 18 Ch.D. 76; *per* Lindley L.J. in *Licensed Victuallers' Newspaper Co.* v. *Bingham* (1888) 38 Ch.D. 139; *Broemel* v. *Meyer* (1912) 29 T.L.R. 148; *Maxwell* v. *Hogg* (1867) L.R. 2 Ch. 307 at 318; *Miss World (Jersey) Ltd.* v. *James Street Productions Ltd.* [1981] F.S.R. 300; *Exxon Corp.* v. *Exxon Insurance Consultants International Ltd.* [1982] Ch. 119.
[88] *Dicks* v. *Yates, supra,* at 89.
[89] [1940] A.C. 112.
[90] [1964] 1 W.L.R. 273 at 286.
[91] See n. 87, *ante.*
[92] See n. 89, *ante.*

Lamb v. *Evans*[93] where the headings in question were elaborate and given in each case in English, French, German and Spanish."

It is submitted, therefore, that a title, unless it is sufficiently lengthy and original to have had labour in construction as well as in choice expended upon it, will not be protected as an original literary work, and that the copyright in a work will not be infringed in cases where only the title has been reproduced. The position might be different if the title is prominently repeated in the work itself (*e.g.* in a poem or song), or if the title takes the form of or incorporates an artistic work.

C. Actions for passing off

21–32   Titles of books and other copyright works are, in certain circumstances, protected from imitation by means of a passing-off action.

The action for passing off lies where the defendant has represented to the public that his goods or business are the goods or business of the plaintiff.[94] A defendant may make himself liable to this action by publishing a work under the same title as the plaintiff's,[95] or by publishing a work where title and "get up" so resemble that of the plaintiff as to deceive the public into the belief that it is the plaintiff's work,[96] or is associated or connected with the plaintiff. Examples are given below of a number of cases in which publishers of books or periodicals have obtained protection on this ground for the goodwill in the title.[97]

Thus, although an author probably has no copyright in his title, he has a valuable proprietary right, in that he may be able to prevent its use upon any similar publication on the grounds of passing off.[98] Further, if the title is distinctive of the publisher or is otherwise indicative of any connection in the course of trade, it may be registered as a trade mark.[99] The action for passing off is not limited to misappropriation of a title or name or get up. It applies to other *indicia* or material which has given a producer or business a distinctive character. Thus, it can encompass descriptive material, such as slogans or visual images which radio, television and

---

[93] [1893] 1 Ch. 218.

[94] See *Cellular Clothing Co.* v. *Maxton & Murray* [1890] A.C. 326 at 323; *Spalding (A.G.) & Bros.* v. *A.W. Gamage Ltd.* (1915) 32 R.P.C.; *Clock (The) Ltd.* v. *The Clock House Hotel Ltd.* (1936) 53 R.P.C. 269; *Brestian* v. *Try* [1958] R.P.C. 161 at 162, 171; *H.P. Bulmer Ltd. & Showerings Ltd.* v. *J. Bollinger* [1978] R.P.C. 79; *Erven Warnink, etc.* v. *J. Townend & Sons (Hull) Ltd.* [1979] A.C. 731.

[95] *Primrose Press Agency Co. (The)* v. *Knowles (M.)* (1885) 2 T.L.R. 404; *Clement* v. *Maddick* (1859) 1 Giff. 98; *Kelly* v. *Hutton* (1867) 3 Ch.App. 703; *Borthwick* v. *Evening Post* (1888) 37 Ch.D. 449.

[96] *Metzler* v. *Wood* (1878) 8 Ch.D. 606; *Spottiswoode* v. *Clark* (1846) 2 Phil. 154; *Reddaway (F.), etc.* v. *Banham (G.), etc.* [1896] A.C. 199; *Lord Byron* v. *Johnston* (1816) 2 Mer. 29; and see *Tavener Rutledge Ltd.* v. *Specters Ltd.* [1959] R.P.C. 83; A useful exposition of the legal propositions relevant to an action for "passing off" concerned with "get up" is to be found in a Scottish case, *John Haig and Co. Ltd.* v. *Forth Blending Co. Ltd.* (1953) 70 R.P.C. 259.

[97] See § 21–47, *post*.

[98] *Longman (T. N.)* v. *Tripp (J.)* (1805) 2 Bos. & P. 67; *Ex p. Foss* (1858) 2 De G. & J. 230; *Bradbury* v. *Dickens* (1859) 27 Beav. 53; *Wotherspoon* v. *Currie* (1872) L.R. 5 H.L. 508; *cf. Kelly* v. *Byles* (1880) 13 Ch.D. 682.

[99] Trade Marks Act 1938, ss.9, 10 and 68; *"Science and Health" Trade Mark* [1968] R.P.C. 402. For example, the title "Encyclopaedia Britannica" was allowed to proceed to registration. See also *John Lang & Co. Ltd.* v. *Gold Star Publications Ltd.* [1967] F.S.R. 75.

newspaper advertising campaigns can lead the market to associate with the plaintiff's product and which becomes part of the goodwill of the product. The test is whether the product has derived from the advertising a distinctive character which the market recognises.[1]

(i) Elements of passing off

The House of Lords has held that five characteristics must be present in order to create a valid cause of action for passing off: (1) a misrepresentation, (2) made by a trader in the course of trade, (3) to prospective customers of his or ultimate consumers of goods or services supplied by him, (4) which is calculated to injure the business or goodwill of another trader (in the sense that this is a reasonably foreseeable consequence), and (5) which causes actual damage to a business or goodwill of the trader by whom the action is brought or, in a *quia timet* action, will probably do so.[2] It is not, however, necessary for a plaintiff to establish that the defendant intends to gain, or is actually gaining, additional custom or business.[3] **21–33**

It does not follow that, because all passing-off actions can be shown to present these five characteristics, all factual situations which present these characteristics give rise to an action for passing off. Further, it must be remembered that any established trader is liable to have his goodwill damaged by fair competition, and it is not every falsehood told by a competitor that will give him a right of action. A trader has no monopoly of his trade or in the manner of carrying it on and cannot prevent a rival trader from merely copying his ideas.[4] Generally speaking, however, where the falsehood is a misrepresentation that the competitor's goods are goods of a definite class with a valuable reputation, and where the misrepresentation is likely to cause damage to established traders who own goodwill in relation to that class of goods, business morality will require that they should be entitled to protect their goodwill.[5] The law will not permit the plaintiff's legitimate business interests to be prejudiced by the exploitation of the plaintiff's goodwill by another person.[6]

---

[1] *Cadbury Schweppes Pty. Ltd.* v. *The Pub Squash Co. Ltd.* [1981] 1 W.L.R. 193 at 200; *My Kinda Town* v. *Soll* [1983] R.P.C. 407.

[2] *Erven Warnink, etc.* v. *J. Townend & Sons (Hull) Ltd.* [1979] A.C. 731 at 742; *H. P. Bulmer Ltd. & Showerings Ltd.* v. *J. Bollinger S.A.* [1978] R.P.C. 79 at 113; *Revlon Inc. & Ors.* v. *Cripps & Lee & Ors* [1980] F.S.R. 85; *A. G. Spalding Bros.* v. *A. W. Gamage Ltd.* (1915) 32 R.P.C. 273; *Draper* v. *Trist* (1939) 56 R.P.C. 429 at 442. *Lego System Aktieselkab* v. *Lego M. Lemelstrich* [1983] F.S.R. 155; *Associated Newspapers plc* v. *Insert Media Ltd.* [1990] 1 W.L.R. 900; *Reckitt & Colman Ltd.* v. *Borden Inc.* [1990] 1 W.L.R. 491. The law of Scotland does not differ from the English law of passing off: *Lang Brothers Ltd.* v. *Goldwell Ltd.* [1983] R.P.C. 289 at 294; see *James North & Sons Ltd.* v. *North Cape Textiles Ltd.* [1986] F.S.R. 28 for an instance of proceedings for passing off in England by a defendant resident in Scotland.

[3] *Stringfellow* v. *McCain Foods (G.B.) Ltd.* [1984] R.P.C. 501.

[4] *Compatibility Research Ltd.* v. *Computer Psyche Co. Ltd.* [1967] F.S.R. 63; *Cadbury Schweppes Pty. Ltd.* v. *The Pub Squash Co. Ltd.* [1981] 1 W.L.R. 193; *Reckitt & Colman Ltd.* v. *Borden Inc* [1990] 1 W.L.R. 491 at 509, 513.

[5] See n. 17, *ante*

[6] *Lyngstad* v. *Anabas Products Ltd.* [1977] F.S.R. 62 at 66.

(ii) Goodwill

21–34 It is well established at common law that there is no property in the nature of copyright or otherwise in a name or a word, whether invented or otherwise.[7] The proprietary right which is protected by the law of passing off is the incorporeal property in the business reputation or goodwill of which the name, mark or get up is the badge or vehicle.[8] Goodwill has no independent existence apart from the business to which it is attached.[9] Indeed, it has been defined as "the benefit and advantage of the good name, reputation and connection of a business. It is the attractive force which brings in custom."[10] In a passing-off action the plaintiff must, therefore, first establish that his activities consist of or include carrying on a business or selling goods to which a particular name or get up has been applied, so that the plaintiff is, in respect of that name or get up, the owner of a reputation and goodwill of substantial value.[11] In general, no goodwill attaches to the activities of a non-trader and the courts will be reluctant to interfere to prevent a person from adopting the name of a non-trader, even if annoyance and inconvenience result, *e.g.* an injunction was refused to protect the name of a political party from being adopted by the defendant.[12] Once a goodwill has been established it will continue to exist until it has been abandoned. A goodwill is not abandoned simply because the plaintiff ceases to carry on his business.[13] There may be cases in which both the plaintiff and the defendant concurrently acquire a goodwill in respect of the name or get up of particular goods in different geographical areas or different sections of the market. In those circumstances a situation may arise in which when they expand and clash neither is entitled to relief against the other in respect of the goodwill and reputation which he has acquired in his area.[14] In the case of a literary work, the plaintiff must prove that his publication has been in the market long enough to acquire a

---

[7] *Tavener Rutledge Ltd.* v. *Trexapalm Ltd.* [1977] R.P.C. 275 at 278; *Star Industrial Co. Ltd.* v. *Yap Kwee Kor* [1976] F.S.R. 256. See also *McCulloch* v. *May Ltd.* [1947] 2 All E.R. 845 at 849; *Exxon Corp.* v. *Exxon Insurance Consultants International Ltd.* [1982] R.P.C. 69; *McCain International Ltd.* v. *Country Fair Foods Ltd.* [1981] R.P.C. 69 at 77; *Kean* v. *McGivan* [1982] F.S.R. 119 at 120; *Century Electronics Ltd.* v. *CVS Enterprises Ltd.* [1983] F.S.R. 1; *My Kinda Bones Ltd.* v. *Dr. Pepper's Stove Co. Ltd.* [1984] F.S.R. 289 at 296.

[8] *H. P. Bulmer Ltd. & Showerings Ltd.* v. *J. Bollinger S.A.* [1978] R.P.C. 79; *Unicorn Products Ltd.* v. *Roban Jig & Tool Co. (U.K.) Ltd.* [1976] F.S.R. 169; *Anheuser-Busch Inc.* v. *Budejovicky Budvar NP* [1984] F.S.R. 413 at 476.

[9] See n. 7, *ante.*

[10] *Commissioners of Inland Revenue* v. *Muller & Co. Margarine Ltd.* [1901] A.C. 217 at 223.

[11] *Erven Warnink, etc.* v. *J. Townend & Sons (Hull) Ltd., supra;* difficulties may arise over ownership where, for instance, goods manufactured by A are distributed by B; see *Busmar (S.A.) Pty. Ltd.* v. *Hendon Enterprises Pty. Ltd.* (1975) 4 S.A.L.R. 626.

[12] *Kean* v. *McGivan* [1982] F.S.R. 119 ("Social Democratic Party").

[13] *Norman Kark Publications Ltd.* v. *Odhams Press* [1962] 1 W.L.R. 380; *Ad-Lib Club Ltd.* v. *Granville* [1971] F.S.R. 1; *Levey* v. *Henderson-Kenton (Holdings) Ltd.* [1974] R.P.C. 617; *Star Industrial Co. Ltd.* v. *Yap Kwee Kor, supra* at 269; *Polakow Brothers (Pty) Ltd.* v. *Gershlowitz* [1976] 1 S.A.L.R. 863; *Heller Financial Services* v. *Boire* [1988] A.L.M.D. § 2312.

[14] *Evans* v. *Eradicure Ltd.* [1972] R.P.C. 808, *cf. Levey* v. *Henderson Kenton (Holdings) Ltd., supra; Habib Bank Ltd.* v. *Habib Bank AG Zurich* [1982] R.P.C. 1; *Taylor Bros.* v. *Taylors Corp. Ltd.* [1988] 2 N.Z.L.R.1. *cf. Chelsea Man Menswear Ltd.* v. *Chelsea Girl Ltd.* [1987] R.P.C. 189.

public reputation.[15] A reputation or goodwill can be built up by substantial sales over a short period of time,[16] or by an intensive advertising campaign.[17] There must be some sort of entry into the market.[18] The relevant date for determining whether a plaintiff has established the necessary goodwill or reputation of his product or business is the date of the commencement of the conduct complained of, not the date of the commencement of the proceedings.[19]

Goodwill of foreign business or publication. The question has arisen **21–35** in many cases as to whether an action for passing off can be maintained in England by a person or company which does not carry on business in England either at all or to any appreciable extent,[20] *e.g.* the plaintiff makes no sales in England or has no customers or other persons in a business relationship with him in England. As it is established that a passing-off action exists for the protection of goodwill in England it logically follows that no passing-off action can be maintained where no such goodwill exists. In general, goodwill is local in character and divisible so that if a business is carried on in several different countries a separate goodwill will attach to that business in each of those countries.[21] The goodwill generated in the United Kingdom by the sale of goods may, however, extend to any goods of the same sort dealt in by other companies within the same

---

[15] *Licensed Victuallers' Newspaper Co.* v. *Bingham* (1888) 38 Ch.D. 139; *Oertli A.G.* v. *Bowman (London) Ltd.* [1957] R.P.C. 388; the plaintiff's intentions may be relevant; see *Dunlop Pneumatic Tyre Co. Ltd.* v. *Dunlop Lubricant Co.* (1899) 16 R.P.C. 12; *Hulton Press Ltd.* v. *White Eagle Youth Holiday Camp Ltd.* [1951] 68 R.P.C. 126; *L.R.C. International Ltd.* v. *Lilla Edets Sales Co. Ltd.* [1973] R.P.C. 560; *Brestian* v. *Try* [1958] R.P.C. 161; *D. C. Thomson Ltd.* v. *Kent Messenger Ltd.* [1975] R.P.C. 191; *B.B.C.* v. *Talbot Motor Co. Ltd.* [1981] F.S.R. 228; *Reckitt & Colman Ltd.* v. *Borden Inc.* (*supra*).

[16] *Stannard* v. *Reay* [1967] R.P.C. 589; but see as to pre-publication advertising: *Maxwell* v. *Hogg* (1866) L.R. 2 Ch.App. 307 and *Schove* v. *Schmincke* (1886) 33 Ch.D. 546; *Politechnika, etc.* v. *Dallas Print Transfers* [1982] F.S.R. 529; *Marcus Publishing plc* v. *Hutton-Wild Communications Ltd.* [1990] R.P.C. 576.

[17] *Elida Gibbs Ltd.* v. *Colgate-Palmolive Ltd.* [1983] F.S.R. 95.

[18] *My Kinda Bones Ltd.* v. *Dr. Pepper's Store Co. Ltd.* [1984] F.S.R. 289 at 296; *Marcus Publishing plc* v. *Hutton-Wild Communications Ltd.* [1990] R.P.C. 576.

[19] *Cadbury-Schweppes Pty. Ltd.* v. *The Pub Squash Co. Ltd.* [1981] 1 W.L.R. 193 at 204; *cf. My Kinda Bones Ltd.* v. *Dr. Pepper's Stove Co. Ltd.* [1984] F.S.R. 289; *Nationwide Building Society* v. *Nationwide Estate Agents Ltd.* [1987] F.S.R. 579 at 585, 592.

[20] *Panhard et Levassor S.A.* v. *Panhard-Levassor Motor Co. Ltd.* (1901) 18 R.P.C. 405; *Poiret* v. *J. Poiret Ltd.* (1920) 32 R.P.C. 177; *Sheraton Corpn. of America* v. *Sheraton Motels Ltd.* [1964] R.P.C. 202; *A. Bernardin et Cie* v. *Pavilion Properties Ltd.* [1967] R.P.C. 581; *Amway Corpn.* v. *Eurway International Ltd.* [1974] R.P.C. 82; *Globelegance B.V.* v. *Sarkissian* [1974] R.P.C. 603; *Baskin-Robbins Ice Cream Co.* v. *Gutman* [1976] F.S.R. 545; *Maxim's Ltd.* v. *Dye* [1977] F.S.R. 364; *C. & A. Modes* v. *C. & A. (Waterford) Ltd.* [1978] F.S.R. 126; *Star Industrial Co. Ltd.* v. *Yap Kwee Kor* [1976] F.S.R. 256; *Erven Warnink, etc.* v. *J. Townend & Sons (Hull) Ltd.*, *supra*; *Metric Resources Corpn.* v. *Lease Metrix Ltd.* [1979] F.S.R. 571; *Wienerwald Holding A.G.* v. *Kwan Wong Tan & Fong* [1979] F.S.R. 381 (Supreme Court of Hong Kong); *Lyngstad* v. *Anabas Products Ltd.* [1977] F.S.R. 62 at 66. For an unusual case see *Serville* v. *Constance* (1954) 71 R.P.C. 146 (Foreign boxing championship title). See also *Suhner & Co. A.G.* v. *Suhner Ltd.* [1967] R.P.C. 336; *The Athletes Foot Marketing Associates Inc.* v. *Cobra Sports Co. Ltd.* [1980] R.P.C. 343; *Anheuser-Busch Inc.* v. *Budejovicky Budvar NP* [1984] F.S.R. 413.; *Nishika Corp.* v. *Goodchild* [1990] F.S.R. 371; *Consorzio del Prosciutto di Parma* v. *Marks & Spencer plc* [1990] F.S.R. 530.

[21] *Star Industrial Co. Ltd.* v. *Yap Kwee Kor*, *supra* at 269; *Globelegance B.V.* v. *Sarkissian* [1974] R.P.C. 603.

multi-national group as the company which sells the goods in the United Kingdom. In such a case the United Kingdom company may be unable to prevent, on the grounds of passing off, the unauthorised sale of "parallel imports" of similar quality and character to those goods sold in the United Kingdom.[22] Further, it has to be recognised that, with the modern growth of travel and improved communications, some companies may claim to own a truly international goodwill, even though they do not carry on business or sell goods in the particular country in which proceedings are brought to protect that goodwill.[23] It may no longer be practical and realistic to draw dividing lines at national frontiers. It is a matter of evidence as to how far a plaintiff has established a goodwill in England. On the one hand, it has been held that simply advertising a business or goods in England is not sufficient to establish a goodwill[24]; nor is the fact of negotiation by an overseas business with prospective English franchisees[25]; while, on the other hand, it has been held sufficient that the plaintiff company has taken and carried out bookings or orders in relation to its goods or services[26]; but sporadic and occasional sales of goods in England are not sufficient to establish a business goodwill.[27] The mere existence of a trading reputation in England is insufficient in the absence of customers.[28] Once some goodwill is established in England, the plaintiff is entitled to supplement that goodwill by evidence of his reputation and activities in other countries.[29] In appropriate cases, it may be possible for a foreign company to establish that it has acquired some reputation and goodwill in England through the activities of a subsidiary company.[30]

(iii) Misrepresentation

21–36 The plaintiff must also establish that there has been a misrepresentation by the defendant, either express or implied, conscious or unconscious, but not necessarily fraudulent, calculated to lead to confusion between the goods or business of the plaintiff and those of the defendant.[31] Cases of

---

[22] *Revlon Inc. & Ors. v. Cripps & Lee Ltd. & Ors.* [1980] F.S.R. 85; *Winthrop Products Inc. v. Sun Ocean (M) SDN BHD* [1988] F.S.R. 430 at 437 (High Court of Malaya); *cf. Wilkinson Sword Ltd. v. Cripps & Lee* [1982] F.S.R. 16; *Colgate-Palmolive v. Markwell Finance Ltd.* [1988] R.P.C. 283.

[23] *J. C. Penny Co. Inc. v. Punjabi Nick* [1979] F.S.R. 26 (Supreme Court of Hong Kong); *Baskin-Robbins Ice Cream Co. v. Gutman* [1976] F.S.R. 545 at 548; *Fletcher Challenge Ltd. v. Fletcher Challenge Pty. Ltd.* [1982] F.S.R. 1 (Supreme Court of New South Wales); *Orkin Exterminating Co. Inc. v. Pestco Co. of Canada Ltd.* (1985) 11 D.L.R. (4th) 84 (Ontario High Court).

[24] *A. Bernardin et Cie v. Pavilion Properties Ltd.*, supra; *Wienerwald Holding A.G. v. Kwan Wong Tan & Fong, supra; Esanda Ltd. v. Esanda Finance Ltd.* [1984] F.S.R. 96 at 100.

[25] *The Athletes Foot Marketing Associates Ltd. v. Cobra Sports Ltd.* [1980] R.P.C. 343.

[26] *Poiret v. J. Poiret Ltd.*, supra; *Sheraton Corpn. of America v. Sheraton Motels Ltd.*, supra.

[27] *Anheuser-Busch Inc. v. Budejovicky Budvar NP* [1984] F.S.R. 413; *cf. Esanda Ltd. v. Esanda Finance Ltd.* [1984] F.S.R. 96 (High Court of New Zealand).

[28] See n. 24, ante.

[29] *Globelegance B.V. v. Sarkissian, supra* at 613; see also *Alfred Dunhill Ltd. v. Sunoptic S.A.* [1979] F.S.R. 337.

[30] See n. 23, ante.

[31] *H. P. Bulmer Ltd. & Showerings Ltd. v. J. Bollinger S.A.* [1978] R.P.C. 79 at 99; *Morning Star Co-operative Society Ltd. v. Express Newspapers Ltd.* [1979] F.S.R. 113 at 114; *Newsweek Inc. v. B.B.C.* [1979] R.P.C. 441 at 447; *Lyngstad v. Anabas Products Ltd.* [1977] F.S.R. 62.

express misrepresentation are unusual. It may, for example, be actionable for an author of a biography falsely to represent that the book written by him has been authorised or approved by the subject or his family.[32] It is more common for the misrepresentation to be implied from the fact that the defendant has selected as the name or get up for his business or goods a name or get up which is similar to that used by the plaintiff in relation to his business or goods. It is not necessary for the plaintiff to prove that the misrepresentation was intentionally made, though where a dishonest intention is established the courts will readily find that there is a likelihood of deception which is damaging to the plaintiff.[33] Where there is an intention to deceive it is not difficult to infer that the intention has been, or in all probability will be, effective.[34] In the absence of a satisfactory explanation by the defendant as to why he has chosen a particular name or get up for his goods, the court will often infer that that choice was made with the deliberate object of attracting to himself part of the plaintiff's established reputation and goodwill.[35] For example, where there is a close resemblance in general style and arrangement of the contents of a book,[36] particularly in the case of a new publication which is alleged to resemble an existing publication,[37] or a claim of certain attributes which are known to belong to the original work,[38] or a sudden change from an unobjectionable title, style of publication and arrangement of contents, to a title, style and arrangement more closely resembling the plaintiff's,[39] an intention to deceive may be established.

It has been said that it is neither possible nor desirable to define all the

---

[32] *Lord Brabourne* v. *Hough* [1981] F.S.R. 79 (interim injunction refused). See also *H. P. Bulmer Ltd. & Showerings Ltd.* v. *J. Bollinger S.A.*, *supra* at 113; *Bar's Leaks (N.Z.) Ltd.* v. *Motor Specialities Ltd.* [1973] R.P.C. 21 (Supreme Court of New Zealand); *Lowenbrau München* v. *Grünhalle Lager International Ltd.* [1974] R.P.C. 492; *C. & A. Modes* v. *C. & A. (Waterford) Ltd.* [1978] F.S.R. 126 at 138; *Chill Foods (Scotland) Ltd.* v. *Cool Foods Ltd.* [1977] R.P.C. 522 (Court of Session); *Hayter Motor Underwriting Agencies* v. *R.B.H.S. Agencies* [1977] F.S.R. 285 at 292.

[33] *Boswell-Wilkie Armis (Pty.) Ltd.* v. *Brian Boswell Circus (Pty.) Ltd.* [1986] F.S.R. 429 (Supreme Court of South Africa); *Harrods Ltd.* v. *Schwartz-Sackin Co. Ltd.* [1986] F.S.R. 490; *James Buchanan & Co Ltd.* v. *Chung Battery Factory* [1962] H.K.L.R. 535 (High Court of Hong Kong).

[34] *Cadbury-Schweppes Pty. ltd.* v. *The Pub Squash Co. Ltd.* [1981] 1 W.L.R. 193 at 203; *R.H.M. Foods Ltd.* v. *Bovril Ltd.* [1983] R.P.C. 275 at 278, 281; *Telmark Tele Products (Aus.) Pty Ltd.* v. *Coles* (1990) 89 A.L.R. 48 (Federal Court of Australia.)

[35] *F. Hoffmann-La Roche & Co. A.G.* v. *D.D.S.A. Pharmaceuticals Ltd.* [1972] R.P.C. 1 at 22; *Hymac* v. *Priestman Brothers Ltd.* [1978] R.P.C. 495; *Elan Digital Systems Ltd.* v. *Elan Computers Ltd.* [1984] F.S.R. 373 at 385.

[36] *Mack* v. *Petter* (1872) L.R. 14 Eq. 431; *Corns* v. *Griffiths* [1873] W.N. 93; *Norman Kark Publications Ltd.* v. *Odhams Press Ltd.* [1962] 1 W.L.R. 380 at 392; *Masson, Seeley & Co. Ltd.* v. *Embosotype Manufacturing Co.* (1924) 41 R.P.C. 160 (where the catalogue in question was an infringement of copyright); *Van Oppen & Co. Ltd.* v. *Leonard Van Oppen* (1903) 20 R.P.C. 617 (where the consignment note in question was an infringement of copyright), *cf. Crotch* v. *Arnold* [1905–10] Mac.C.C 227 (where the titles were identical—"Cottage Homes of England"—but the subject-matter and price were totally different).

[37] *Rubber & Technical Press Ltd.* v. *Maclaren & Sons Ltd.* [1961] R.P.C. 264 at 266.

[38] *Chappell* v. *Sheard* (1855) 2 K. & J. 117; *Chappell* v. *Davidson* (1855) 2 K. & J. 122.

[39] *Corns* v. *Griffiths*, *supra*; *Metzler* v. *Wood* (1878) 8 Ch.D. 606; see *Rubber & Technical Press Ltd.* v. *Maclaren & Sons Ltd.*, *supra*.

different forms that actionable misrepresentations may take.[40] In general, the defendant's conduct must be such as to mislead members of the public to believe that the goods or services offered by him are the goods or services of the plaintiff or are connected with or associated with the plaintiff's goods or services in a way which is likely to damage the plaintiff's goodwill.[41] Thus, the essence of the actionable misrepresentation is the false suggestion by the defendant, whether deliberate or unintentional, that his goods or services are connected with the plaintiff.[42] Where the different names of the plaintiff and the defendant are prominently displayed on the similarly named articles it may be difficult to establish that there is a misrepresentation, for there is a clear message conveyed by the dissimilar names that the two are not connected or associated.[43] If, however, there is only a disclaimer in small print which would not be noticed or read by the purchasing public, the mispresentation is not removed[44] and the risk of deception or confusion is not eliminated.

(iv) Common field of activity

21–37 Similarity between the fields of business activities of the plaintiff and the defendant enhances the likelihood of confusion or deception.[45] In order to establish an actionable misrepresentation it is generally necessary for the plaintiff to show that there is a common field of activity between the plaintiff and defendant in respect of the relevant goods or business, though it is not necessary that they should be in precisely the same line of business.[46] The goodwill of a plaintiff may extend well beyond the field of the particular products which he is engaged in manufacturing or selling. The action for passing off is not limited to competing traders in the same line of business.[47] As part of the ultimate decision as to whether there is likely to be confusion as a result of the misrepresentation the court will inquire whether there is some overlap in the fields of activity of the plaintiff and

---

[40] *H. P. Bulmer Ltd. & Showerings Ltd.* v. *Bollinger S.A.* [1978] R.P.C. 79 at 99, 100; *Granada Group Ltd.* v. *Ford Motor Co. Ltd.* [1973] R.P.C. 49; *Unitex Ltd.* v. *Union Texturing Co. Ltd.* [1974] F.S.R. 181.

[41] See n. 40, *ante*.

[42] *My Kinda Town* v. *Soll* [1983] R.P.C. 407.

[43] *Fison Ltd.* v. *E. J. Godwin (Peat Industries) Ltd.* [1976] R.P.C. 653 at 658; *Malaysia Dairy Industries Pte. Ltd.* v. *Yakult (Singapore) Pte. Ltd.* [1980] F.S.R. 43 (High Court of Singapore).

[44] *Children's Television Workshop Inc.* v. *Woolworths (NSW)* [1981] R.P.C. 187 at 196 (High Court of New South Wales) *cf. Sony ICL* v. *Saray Electronics (London) Ltd.* [1983] F.S.R. 302; *Associated Newspapers plc* v. *Insert Media Ltd.* [1990] 1 W.L.R. 900 at 911, 912.

[45] *Boswell-Wilkie Circus (Pty.) Ltd.* v. *Brian Boswell Circus (Pty.) Ltd.* [1985] F.S.R. 434; [1986] F.S.R. 429 (Supreme Court of South Africa); *Nationwide Building Society* v. *Nationwide Estate Agents Ltd.* [1987] F.S.R. 579 at 588.

[45] *McCulloch* v. *L. A. May (Produce Distributors) Ltd.* (1947) 65 R.P.C. 58; *Wombles Ltd.* v. *Wombles Skips Ltd.* [1977] R.P.C. 99; *Taverner Rutledge Ltd.* v. *Trexapalm Ltd.* [1977] R.P.C. 275 at 279; *Lyngstad* v. *Anabas Products Ltd.* [1977] F.S.R. 62; *cf. Walter* v. *Ashton* [1902] 2 Ch. 282; *Hulton Press Ltd.* v. *White Eagle Youth Holiday Camp Ltd.* (1951) 68 R.P.C. 126; *News Group Newspapers Ltd.* v. *The Rocket Record Co. Ltd.* [1981] F.S.R. 89.

[47] *Lego System* v. *Lego Lemelstritch Ltd.* [1983] F.S.R. 155; *Stringfellow* v. *McCain Foods (G.B.) Ltd.* [1984] R.P.C. 501; *Chelsea Man Menswear Ltd.* v. *Chelsea Girl Ltd.* [1987] R.P.C. 189.

the defendant.[48] The proximity of the relevant areas of activity both geographically and as to the kind of business is relevant to the question of misrepresentation, likelihood of confusion and probability of damage to the plaintiff's goodwill.[49] The areas of activity are not confined to those in which the plaintiff is actually engaged at the date when he brings his proceedings. His field of activity extends to potential trade in other allied areas to which his business might reasonably extend or, at least, be thought by the public to have extended. Those other fields must be so closely related and so much a part of the normal and natural expansion of his business that confusion is likely to be occasioned among members of the public particularly with modern commercial developments of licensing and franchising of business operations.[50] It has been said in some cases that this requirement of a common field of activity is not an essential ingredient of the law of passing off though, as far as the English authorities are concerned, it appears to be well established.[51]

(v) Descriptive names

The name or get up of the plaintiff must be one in respect of a defined class **21–38** of goods or business which distinguishes his business or goods from other similar goods or similar businesses.[52] The plaintiff must show that the name or mark is exclusively associated with his business and goods and has become so distinctive of them that it is a valuable asset in bringing his goods to the notice of the public.[53] He must show that the name or get up in question denotes his goods or business with members of the public, though it is not necessary for him to show that the public actually knows who is responsible for carrying on the business.[54] It follows from this requirement of distinctiveness that it is difficult to succeed in establishing a misrepresentation where the word or name used by the plaintiff is one in ordinary use and is descriptive of the business carried on by him or the goods marketed by him. A fancy name can only indicate that the product

---

[48] *Annabel's (Berkeley Square) Ltd.* v. *Schock* [1972] R.P.C. 838 at 844; *Granada Group Ltd.* v. *Ford Motor Co. Ltd.* [1973] R.P.C. 49; *Computer Vision Corpn.* v. *Computer Vision Ltd.* [1975] R.P.C. 171; *Newsweek Inc.* v. *B.B.C.* [1979] R.P.C. 441 at 449 (different media).

[49] See n. 47, *ante.*

[50] *Wombles Ltd.* v. *Wombles Skips Ltd., supra; L.R.C. International Ltd.* v. *Lilla Edets Sales Co. Ltd.* [1973] R.P.C. 560; *Ames Crosta Ltd.* v. *Pionex International* [1977] F.S.R. 46; *John Walker & Sons Ltd.* v. *Rothmans International* [1978] F.S.R. 357; *D. C. Thomson & Co. Ltd.* v. *Kent Messenger Ltd.* [1975] R.P.C. 191 at 199; *Sterwin A.G.* v. *Brocades (Great Britain) Ltd.* [1979] R.P.C. 481 at 490; *Television Broadcasts Ltd.* v. *Home Guide Publication Co.* [1982] F.S.R. 505 (Supreme Court of Hong Kong).

[51] *McCulloch* v. *L. A. May (Produce Distributors) Ltd.* [1947] 2 All E.R. 845; *Harrison & Starkey* v. *Polydor Ltd.* [1977] F.S.R. 1, *cf. Henderson* v. *Radio Corporation Pty. Ltd.* [1969] R.P.C. 218 (Supreme Court of New South Wales); *Totalizator Agency Board* v. *Turf News Pty. Ltd.* [1972] R.P.C. 579 (Supreme Court of Victoria); *Krouse* v. *Chrysler* (1974) 40 D.L.R. (3d) 15 (Can.); *Mountain Shadows Records Ltd.* v. *Peawall Enterprises Ltd.* (1974) 40 D.L.R. (3d) 231; *Capital Estate, etc., Ltd.* v. *Holiday Inns Inc.* [1977] 2 S.A.L.R. 916.; *Lego System* v. *Lego M. Lemelstrich Ltd.* [1983] F.S.R. 155.

[52] *Erven Warnink* v. *J. Townend & Sons (Hull) Ltd.,* [1979] A.C. 731 at 755.

[53] *H. P. Bulmer Ltd. and Showerings Ltd.* v. *J. Bollinger S.A.* [1978] R.P.C. 79 at 94.

[54] *F. Hoffmann-La Roche & Co. A.G.* v. *D.D.S.A. Pharmaceuticals Ltd.* [1972] R.P.C. 1; *Roche Products Ltd.* v. *Berk Pharmaceuticals* [1973] R.P.C. 473 at 482; *British American Glass Co. Ltd.* v. *Winton Products (Blackpool) Ltd.* [1962] R.P.C. 230.

bearing that name is, or is licensed by, or is derived from one and the same supplier. A descriptive name does not indicate the source of the goods or business, but the nature of the goods or business.[55] In such cases small differences are accepted by the court as sufficient to avert confusion and some risk of confusion is accepted as inevitable. For example, it has been held that in the case of newspapers the use of such words as "Star,"[56] "Advertiser"[57] and "Post"[58] are descriptive rather than distinctive so that small differences in the name, coupled with differences in the appearance of the newspapers, the price of them, the content and the manner of distribution are sufficient to avoid the confusion among members of the public which might otherwise arise from similarities in the names of the newspapers.

There are cases in which words in common use are used in a combination that is unusual and is distinctive or where the words, though descriptive initially, have acquired a secondary meaning.[59] Because the courts are reluctant to give a monopoly to a plaintiff in descriptive words the plaintiff is required to adduce sufficient evidence of distinctiveness in order to establish that the defendant's use of the same or similar words is in fact a misrepresentation.

Thus, where the title of a book is purely descriptive of the contents no passing off can arise by virtue of the use of the title alone, unless such title is shown by evidence to have acquired a secondary meaning and to be distinctive. On the other hand, if the title is an invented or fancy title it will be relatively easy to establish a claim. The difficult cases are where the titles, though descriptive, have an element of fancy.[60]

The publishers of a work entitled "My Life and Loves by Frank Harris" obtained an injunction against another firm of publishers who later published an abridged version of the same book, which had been previously published under the title "Frank Harris: My Life and Adventures," under an identical title to the plaintiffs' book. It was held the plaintiffs had acquired a distinctive reputation in the title although it was descriptive; that the defendants' publication under a similar title was calculated to

---

[55] *McCain International Ltd.* v. *Country Fair Foods Ltd.* [1981] R.P.C. 69 (Oven Chips); *My Kinda Town* v. *Soll* [1983] R.P.C. 407 (Chicago Pizza).

[56] *Morning Star Co-operative Society Ltd.* v. *Express Newspapers Ltd.* [1979] F.S.R. 113; *The Cricketer Ltd.* v. *Newspress Pty. Ltd.* [1974] V.R. 477 (Supreme Court of Victoria). For other newspaper cases see *Hogg* v. *Kirby* (1803) 8 Ves. 215; *Cowen* v. *Hulton* (1882) 46 L.T. 897; *Borthwick* v. *Evening Post* (1888) 37 Ch.D. 449; *Mail Newspapers plc* v. *Insert Media Ltd.* [1987] R.P.C. 521; [1990] 1 W.L.R. 900 (unauthorised inserts in newspapers).

[57] *Baylis & Co. (The Maidenhead Advertisers) Ltd.* v. *Darlenko Ltd.* [1974] F.S.R. 384.

[58] *D. C. Thomson & Co. Ltd.* v. *Kent Messenger Ltd.* [1975] R.P.C. 191; *World Athletics & Sporting Publications Ltd.* v. *A.C.M. Webb (Publishing) Ltd.* [1981] F.S.R. 27. ("*Athletics Weekly*" v. "*Athletics Monthly*": injunction refused).

[59] *Pickwick International Inc. (G.B.) Ltd.* v. *Multiple Sound Distributors Ltd.* [1972] R.P.C. 795 ("Top of the Pops"/"Pick of the Pops"); *Computer Vision Corpn.* v. *Computer Vision Ltd.* [1975] R.P.C. 171; *Alltransport International Group Ltd.* v. *Alltrans Express Ltd.* [1976] F.S.R. 13; *Style Patterns Ltd.* v. *K-Tel International (U.K.) Ltd.* [1974] F.S.R. 499 at 506; *Hymac* v. *Priestman Brothers Ltd.* [1978] R.P.C. 495 (number distinctive); *City Link Travel Holdings Ltd. & Others* v. *Lakin & Anor.* [1979] F.S.R. 653.

[60] *Mathieson* v. *Sir I. Pitman & Sons Ltd.* (1930) 47 R.P.C. 541; *International Press Ltd.* v. *Tunnell* [1938] 1 D.L.R. 393 (Can.); *Houghton* v. *Film Booking Offices Ltd.* (1931) 48 R.P.C. 329; *Legal & General Assurance Society Ltd.* v. *Daniel* [1968] R.P.C. 253.

deceive the public into buying copies of the defendants' book in the belief that they were copies of the plaintiffs' book; and that the plaintiffs had not lost their right to bring a passing-off action simply because they had granted rights in the book to some other person.[61] However, the fact that the title chosen consists of common words makes it more difficult for a plaintiff to succeed.[62] Thus the plaintiffs, who marketed a series of books called "The Pet Library," failed to restrain the defendants from displaying their books on a stand bearing the legend "Ellson's Pet Library," because in the case of common descriptive words comparatively small differences are accepted as sufficient to avert confusion. Megarry J. remarked that "the success of a claim to monopolise such words as the 'Pet Library' would be to fence off from commercial employment many phrases compounded of ordinary English words in general use; and I have heard nothing to persuade me of the justice of authorising such a literary enclosure."[63]

(vi) Get up

Goods of a particular get up just as much proclaim their origin as if they had a particular name attached to them.[64] When goods are sold with a particular get up for long enough, they may come to be recognised by the public as goods of a particular manufacturer, even if the public does not   **21–39**

---

[61] *W. H. Allen & Co.* v. *Brown Watson Ltd.* [1965] R.P.C. 191.
[62] *Ridgeway Co. (The)* v. *The Amalgamated Press Ltd.* (1911) 28 T.L.R. 149; *Ridgeway Co. (The)* v. *Hutchinson* (1923) 40 R.P.C. 335 at 344; *Pearl Cooper Ltd.* v. *Richmond Hill Press Ltd.* [1957] R.P.C. 363; *Technical Productions (London) Ltd.* v. *Contemporary Exhibitions & Whittaker (G.)* [1961] R.P.C. 242; and see *Brittain Publishing Co. (London) Ltd.* v. *Trade and Commercial Press Ltd. (No. 2)* [1957] R.P.C. 271.
[63] *The Pet Library (London) Ltd.* v. *Walter Ellson & Son Ltd.* [1968] F.S.R. 359 at 362. See also cases on similar descriptive trade names; *Reddaway* v. *Banham* [1896] A.C. 199; *Office Cleaning Services Ltd.* v. *Westminster Window and General Cleaners Ltd.* (1946) 68 R.P.C. 39; *Morecambe & Heysham* v. *Mecca Ltd.* [1962] R.P.C. 145 (titles for beauty contests); *Associated Booking Corporation* v. *Associated Booking Agency* [1964] R.P.C. 372; *Industrial Furnaces Ltd.* v. *Reaves* [1970] R.P.C. 605 at 625; *Park Court Hotel Ltd.* v. *Transworld Hotels Ltd.* [1972] R.P.C. 27; *Morning Star Co-operative Society Ltd.* v. *Express Newspapers Ltd.* [1979] F.S.R. 113; *Baylis & Co. (The Maidenhead Advertiser) Ltd.* v. *Darlenko Ltd.* [1974] F.S.R. 284; *D. C. Thomson & Co. Ltd.* v. *Kent Messenger Ltd.* [1975] R.P.C. 191 at 199; *Newsweek Inc.* v. *B.B.C.* [1979] R.P.C. 441; *World Athletics & Sporting Publications Ltd.* v. *A.C.M. Webb (Publishing) Ltd.* [1981] F.S.R. 27; *McCain International Ltd.* v. *Country Fair Foods Ltd.* [1981] R.P.C. 69; *Mothercare U.K. Ltd.* v. *Penguin Books Ltd.* [1988] R.P.C. 113; *Marcus Publishing plc* v. *Hutton-Wild Communications Ltd.* [1990] R.P.C. 576 (Leisure Week/Leisure News).
[64] *F. Hoffmann-La Roche & Co. A.G.* v. *D.D.S.A. Pharmaceuticals Ltd,* [1972] R.P.C. 1 at 20; *Roche Products Ltd.* v. *Berk Pharmaceuticals* [1973] R.P.C. 473; *Adidas Sports, etc.* v. *Harry Walt & Co. Pty. Ltd.* (1976) 1 S.A. 530; *Adcock-Ingram Products Ltd.* v. *Beecham (S.A.) Pty. Ltd.* [1978] R.P.C. 232; *cf. Tetrosyl Ltd.* v. *Silver Paint & Lacquer Co. Ltd.* [1980] F.S.R. 68; *Malaysia Dairy Industrial Pte. Ltd. & Anor.* v. *Yakult (Singapore) Pte. Ltd.* [1980] F.S.R. 43; *Sodastream Ltd.* v. *Thorn Cascade Co. Ltd.* [1982] R.P.C. 459; *Rizla Ltd.* v. *Bryant & May Ltd.* [1986] R.P.C. 389; *Adidas Sportschuhfabriken* v. *O'Neill & Co. Ltd.* [1983] F.S.R. 76; *Plix Products Ltd.* v. *F.M. Winston (Merchants) Ltd.* [1986] F.S.R. 608 (Court of Appeal of New Zealand); *Reckitt & Colman Products Inc.* v. *Borden Inc.* [1987] F.S.R. 228 at 407; [1988] F.S.R. 501; *Komesaroff* v. *Mickle* [1988] F.S.R. 204 (Supreme Court of Victoria); *The Boots Co. Ltd.* v. *Approved Prescription Services Ltd.* [1988] F.S.R. 45; *John Wyeth & Brothers Ltd.* v. *M. & A. Pharmachem Ltd.* [1988] F.S.R. 26.; *Reckitt & Colman Products Ltd.* v. *Borden Inc* [1990] 1 W.L.R. 491.

know who is in fact the particular manufacturer.[65] By adopting a similar get up for his goods the defendant may in fact be representing to the public that his goods are the goods of the plaintiff and thereby attract to himself some part of the goodwill and reputation enjoyed by the plaintiff in respect of his goods.

In order to establish goodwill in a particular get up, there must be something more than mere similarity between the goods themselves. Get up is mainly concerned with such matters as the design of the packaging and any associated labels which, over a period of time, the public come to associate with goods of a particular manufacturer. To copy is not to pass off. Merely copying the shape of that other person's goods or articles is not in itself a false representation. Subject to some such monopoly as registered design or statutory right of property, such as copyright, anyone is entitled to copy and sell an article on the market, provided that he does not make a false representation suggesting that the article which he is selling is in fact that of the plaintiff. A person does not, for example, hold himself out as a licensee of another simply by reproducing that other's work, whether in an altered or unaltered form.[66] There is thus a difference between imitating get up and reproducing the article. The plaintiff must show something more than mere similarity between the goods themselves to constitute a representation amounting to passing off. There may, indeed, be cases where an article itself is shaped in an unusual way, not primarily for the purpose of giving some benefit in use or for any other practical purpose but capriciously in order purely to give the article a distinctive appearance characteristic of that particular manufacturer's goods. In such a case the manufacturer might be able, in the course of time, to establish that he has a reputation and goodwill in the distinctive appearance of the article itself which will give him a cause of action in passing off if his goods were copied. In those circumstances, the putting of a copy on to the market with the distinctive feature or combination of features in question would amount to a misrepresentation that it emanated from the plaintiff.[67]

(vii) Deception of the public

21–40   The misrepresentation must be made to members of the public in such a way that it is likely to cause confusion amongst them between the plaintiff's and defendant's goods or business.[68] Confusion *per se* does not give rise to a cause of action for passing off. It is necessary to inquire not only

---

[65] See n. 64, *ante*.

[66] *Merchandising Corp. of America* v. *Harpbond Ltd.* [1983] F.S.R. 32.

[67] *Benchairs Ltd.* v. *Chair Centre Ltd.* [1974] R.P.C. 429 at 436; *Kemtron Properties Ltd.* v. *Jimmy's Co. Ltd.* [1979] F.S.R. 86 (Supreme Court of Hong Kong); *H. P. Bulmer Ltd. & Showerings Ltd.* v. *J. Bollinger S.A.* [1973] R.P.C. 439; *Adcock-Ingram Products Ltd.* v. *Beecham (S.A.) Pty. Ltd.* [1978] R.P.C. 232. See also *British American Glass Co. Ltd.* v. *Winton Products (Blackpool) Ltd.* [1962] R.P.C. 230; *George Hensher Ltd.* v. *Restawile Upholstery (Lancs) Ltd.* [1972] F.S.R. 557; *Cadbury Ltd.* v. *Ulmer GmbH* [1988] F.S.R. 385 (similar flake chocolate bars); *Komesaroff* v. *Mickle* [1988] R.P.C. 204 (Supreme Court of Victoria); *Reckitt & Colman Products Ltd.* v. *Borden Inc* [1990] 1 W.L.R. 491. (Plastic lemon container); *Charles Church Developments plc* v. *Cronin* [1990] F.S.R.1. (Appearance of a house not distinctive of plaintiff).

[68] *H. P. Bulmer Ltd. & Showerings Ltd.* v. *J. Bollinger S.A.*, *supra*.

whether there is or is likely to be confusion, but also why it has taken place, *i.e.* whether it is the result of a misrepresentation.[69] Mere intention to deceive the public is not sufficient; there must be grounds for apprehending actual deception or confusion.[70] It is not necessary to establish that anyone, as a result of passing off, is induced to deal with the defendant in the mistaken view that he was dealing with the plaintiff; it is sufficient to show probability of injury to the plaintiff's goodwill.[71] Evidence of mere postal confusion may not be sufficient to show a likelihood of confusion, being merely embarrassment and inconvenience rather than loss of trade.[72]

The judge has to decide whether the public at large or a particular relevant section of the public is likely to be deceived and what would be the effect of the misrepresentation made by the defendant upon reasonable prospective purchasers or clients.[73] The test is whether ordinary sensible members of the public would be confused and it is not sufficient to show the confusion would be confined to a small unobservant section of society.[74] The reaction of people to the defendant's misrepresentation must be a reasonable one.[75] In a case where the services or goods are used by bodies of specialised or professional people, it may be difficult to show that confusion is likely to occur.[76] In all cases the court must trust its own perception of the mind of a reasonable man.[77] The court may be assisted by instances of actual confusion, but they are not conclusive. Indeed, it is rare for a court to be faced with examples of actual confusion.

(viii) Evidence

In adducing evidence of goodwill and reputation it may be permissible for the plaintiff to put before the court not only evidence of his advertising and sales activities, but also the results of a scientifically conducted **21–41**

---

[69] *My Kinda Town* v. *Soll* [1983] R.P.C. 407 at 418; *Anheuser-Busch Inc.* v. *Budejovicky Budvar N.P.* [1984] F.S.R. 413 at 477.

[70] *Borthwick* v. *The Evening Post* (1888) Ch.D. 449; *Hall* v. *Barrows* (1863) 4 De G.J. & S. 150; *Chappell* v. *Davidson* (1855) 2 K. & J. 123, *cf. Warwick Tyre Co. Ltd.* [1973] F.S.R. 181; *John Hayter Motor Underwriting Agencies* v. *R.B.H.S. Agencies Ltd.* [1977] F.S.R. 285 at 292, 293; *Miss World (Jersey) Ltd.* v. *James Street Productions Ltd.* [1981] F.S.R. 309.

[71] *Illustrated Newspapers Ltd.* v. *Publicity Services (London) Ltd.* (1938) 55 R.P.C. 172; *Morcam Products Ltd.* v. *Heatherfresh (Foods) Ltd.* [1972] R.P.C. 799; *Unitex Ltd.* v. *Union Texturing Co. Ltd.* [1973] F.S.R. 181; *Bar's Leaks (N.Z.) Ltd.* v. *Motor Specialities Ltd.* [1973] R.P.C. 21 (Supreme Court of New Zealand); *Colgate Palmolive Ltd.* v. *Pattron* [1978] R.P.C. 635 at 665; *Associated Newspapers plc* v. *Insert Media Ltd* [1990] 1 W.L.R. 900.

[72] *Rubber & Technical Press Ltd.* v. *Maclaren & Sons Ltd.* [1961] R.P.C. 264; *George Outram & Co. Ltd.* v. *The London Evening Newspapers Co. Ltd.* (1910) 27 T.L.R. 231; *Street* v. *Union Bank of Spain and England* (1885) 30 Ch.D. 156; *Scottish Union and National Insurance Co.* v. *Scottish National Insurance Co. Ltd.* (1909) 26 R.P.C. 105 at 110.

[73] *Colgate Palmolive Ltd.* v. *Pattron* [1978] R.P.C. 635; *Berkeley Hotel Co. Ltd.* v. *Berkeley International (Mayfair) Ltd.* [1972] R.P.C. 237; *John Hayter Motor Underwriting Agencies Ltd.* v. *R.B.H.S. Agencies Ltd.* [1977] F.S.R. 285 at 293.

[74] *Newsweek Inc.* v. *B.B.C.* [1979] R.P.C. 441 at 447; *D. C. Thomson & Co. Ltd.* v. *Kent Messenger Ltd.* [1975] R.P.C. 191 at 199; *Morning Star Co-operative Society Ltd.* v. *Express Newspapers Ltd.* [1979] F.S.R. 113.

[75] *Stringfellow* v. *McCain Foods (G.B.) Ltd.* [1984] R.P.C. 501.

[76] *Glaxo Laboratories Ltd.* v. *Pharmax Ltd.* [1976] F.S.R. 278.

[77] See n. 73, *ante.*

research survey among members of the public.[78] It is important, however, that any such survey is conducted fairly and upon proper lines; that is, that the questions asked are formulated so as not to be leading questions and so as to preclude conditioned responses, that there is clear proof that the answers were faithfully and accurately recorded and that the survey was conducted among a statistically significant cross-section of society relevant to the matter in dispute. All surveys conducted must be disclosed to the other party, along with instructions to interviewers, coding instructions to computers and the records of the answers.[79] The objection often made to such evidence is that it is of a hearsay character, because it consists of a compilation of statements made by persons out of court who are not called as witnesses to any proceedings and are not therefore subject to cross-examination. The court is more reluctant to admit such evidence on the question of the likelihood of confusion. Market research surveys are in general an unsatisfactory way of trying to establish disputed questions of fact and are often of little value.[80] They create an artificial situation which never reproduces actual customer behaviour.[81] It is rare for the court to have direct evidence of actual examples of confusion. Very often the court is faced with a situation in which it has to make up its own mind on the probability of confusion without such evidence; or with a mass of evidence of what people not called as witnesses have said or been told by other people not called as witnesses and to which the court will give little weight.[82] It is not permissible for those giving oral evidence or swearing affidavits to state that, in their opinion, confusion is likely to arise.[83] That is a statement of opinion on the very question which the court has to answer. It is, however, competent for a witness, familiar with the goods or business, to state that he would be misled.[84] The courts will give little weight to affidavits in standard form.[85]

---

[78] *Customs Glass Boats Ltd.* v. *Salthouse Brothers Ltd.* [1976] R.P.C. 589 (Supreme Court of New Zealand); *Rusmar (S.A.) Pty. Ltd.* v. *Hendon Enterprises Pty. Ltd.* (1975) 4 S.A.L.R. 626; *Coca-Cola Co.* v. *W. Struthers & Sons Ltd.* [1968] R.P.C. 231; *D. C. Thomson & Co. Ltd.* v. *Kent Messenger Ltd.* [1976] R.P.C. 191; *Combe International Ltd.* v. *Scholl (U.K.) Ltd.* [1980] R.P.C. 1; *WEE MCGLEN Trade Mark* [1980] R.P.C. 115 at 118; *Mobil Oil Corpn* v. *Registrar of Trade Marks* [1984] V.R. 25.

[79] *Imperial Group plc* v. *Philip Morris Ltd.* [1984] R.P.C. 293 at 302. cf. *McDonald's Hamburgers Ltd.* v. *Burger King (U.K.) Ltd.* [1986] F.S.R. 45 at 59; *Reckitt & Coleman Products Inc.* v. *Borden Inc.* [1987] F.S.R. 407; *Mothercare U.K. Ltd.* v. *Penguin Books Ltd.* [1988] R.P.C. 113; *Scott Ltd.* v. *Nice-Pak Products Ltd.* [1988] F.S.R. 125.

[80] See n. 79, *ante*.

[81] *Klissen Farmhouse Bakeries Ltd.* v. *Harvest Bakeries Ltd.* [1989] R.P.C. 27 (Court of Appeal of New Zealand).

[82] *Annabel's (Berkeley Square) Ltd.* v. *G. Schock* [1972] R.P.C. 838 at 844; *John Hayter, etc. Ltd.* v. *R.B.H.S. Agencies Ltd.* [1977] F.S.R. 285; *G.E. Trade Mark* [1973] R.P.C. 297; *My Kinda Town* v. *Soll* [1983] R.P.C. 407 at 424; *Klissen Farmhouse Bakeries Ltd.* v. *Harvest Bakeries Ltd.* [1989] R.P.C. 27 at p. 34 (Court of Appeal of New Zealand); cf. *Chelsea Man Menswear Ltd.* v. *Chelsea Girl Ltd* [1985] F.S.R. 567 at 575.

[83] *Berkeley Hotel Co. Ltd.* v. *Berkeley International (Mayfair) Ltd.* [1972] R.P.C. 237; *A. Bailey & Co. Ltd.* v. *Clark Son and Morland* [1938] A.C. 557 at 565; *Mothercare U.K. Ltd.* v. *Penguin Books Ltd.* [1988] R.P.C. 113; *Associated Newspapers plc* v. *Insert Media Ltd.* [1990] 1 W.L.R. 900 at 903, 904

[84] *Claudius Ash, Sons & Co. Ltd.* v. *Invicta Manufacturing Co. Ltd.* (1912) 29 R.P.C. 465 at 476.

[85] *Park Court Hotel Ltd.* v. *Trans World Hotels Ltd.* [1972] R.P.C. 27 at 36; see also *OREAL Trade Mark* [1980] R.P.C. 107; *Tetrosyl Ltd.* v. *Silver Paint & Lacquer Co. Ltd.* [1980] F.S.R. 68.

(ix) Damage

Damage is the gist of the action. The damage suffered in passing off is nor- **21–42**
mally the result of confusion occurring between the plaintiff's and defendant's products and business by reason of the similarity of names or get up.
The damage suffered may take a number of forms. The most common is
that the plaintiff loses sales of his goods which he might otherwise have
made. In addition, the general reputation which the plaintiff's goods and
business enjoy for quality and other characteristics may be depreciated by
confusion so that the strength of his mark is eroded and his competitive
position in the market is weakened.[86] Damage is usually a matter of inference. The question for the court is whether there has been or is likely to be
damage to business or goodwill. If, however, the defendant has for a
number of years used a name or get up similar to that of the plaintiff and
the plaintiff is unable to produce instances of actual confusion or proof of
actual damage, the court is likely to conclude that there has been no passing off. If there is only a limited risk of confusion the court will not readily
infer the likelihood of resulting damage to the plaintiff, particularly if the
defendant is in a completely different line of business. There is a heavy
onus on the plaintiff to show that damage is likely in such a case.[87S1]

(x) Characters and character merchandising

The general principles of passing off which have been explained above are **21–43**
not limited to trading in goods in the strict sense. A goodwill and reputation may be established, for example, by an author or film company or
television company in the name and characteristics of a fictional character
depicted in the relevant work.[88] The goodwill in a character may be
acquired if the fictional character has become well known to the public by
reason of the plaintiff's activities and his capital investment in the creation
and exploitation of the character. The public may come to associate that
character with the plaintiff, so that if the defendant uses a fictional charac-

---

[86] *H.P. Bulmer Ltd. & Showerings Ltd.* v. *J. Bollinger S.A.* [1978] R.P.C. 79 at 94; *Alfred Dunhill Ltd.* v. *Sunoptic S.A. & C. Dunhill* [1979] F.S.R. 337 at 362, 365; *Lowenbrau München* v. *Grün-halle Lager International Ltd.* [1974] R.P.C. 492; *Annabel's (Berkeley Square) Ltd.* v. *Schock* [1972] R.P.C. 838 at 845; *Totalizator Agency Board* v. *Turf News Pty. Ltd.* [1972] R.P.C. 579 (Supreme Court of Victoria); *News Group Newspapers Ltd.* v. *The Rocket Record Co. Ltd.* [1981] F.S.R. 89.

[87] *Unitex Ltd.* v. *Union Texturing Co. Ltd* [1972] F.S.R. 181.; *Stringfellow* v. *McCain Foods (G.B.) Ltd.* [1984] R.P.C. 501 at 545, 546.

[88] *Shaw Brothers (Hong Kong) Ltd.* v. *Golden Harvest (H.K.) Ltd.* [1972] R.P.C. 559 (Supreme Court of Hong Kong); *Hexagon Pty. Ltd.* v. *Australian Broadcasting Commission* [1976] R.P.C. 628 (Supreme Court of New South Wales); *Conan Doyle* v. *London Mystery Magazine* (1949) 66 R.P.C. 312; *Chaplin* v. *Amador* (1928) 269 Pacific Reporter 544 (U.S.); *Patten* v. *Superior Talking Pictures Inc.* (1934) 8 Fed.Supp. 196 (U.S.); *Lone Ranger Inc.* v. *Cox* (1942) 124 Fed. Rep. (2d) 650 (U.S.); *Lone Ranger Inc.* v. *Currey* (1948) 79 Fed.Supp. 190 (U.S.); *Bulletin of Copyright Society of U.S.A.* (1965) Vol. 12, No. 4, p. 210; *Lorimar Productions Inc.* v. *Sterling Clothing Manufacturers Pty. Ltd.* [1982] R.P.C. 395 (character merchandising of "Dallas" T.V. Series: Supreme Court of South Africa); *Children's Television Workshop Inc.* v. *Wool-worths (N.S.W.)* [1981] R.P.C. 187 (Muppet characters: High Court of New South Wales); *Hogan* v. *Koala Dundee Pty Ltd.* (1989) 83 A.L.R 187 (Federal Court of Australia) ("Croco-dile Dundee"); *Pacific Dunlop Ltd.* v. *Hogan* (1989) 87 A.L.R. 14; *Shophanna* v. *10th Cantamac* (1988) 79 A.L.R. 279 (Federal Court of Australia).

ter of a similar name or characteristics there will be a likelihood of confusion. That confusion, however, is unlikely to occur if the name or representation of the fictional character is used in a different field of activity.[89] Passing off does not occur simply because a person attempts to take advantage of the publicity and public interest generated by another's activities, *e.g.* in a book or film or TV series.[90] A defendant does no wrong by entering a market created by another and competing with the creator. In order to succeed the plaintiff would have to establish that ordinary reasonable people would associate the use of the name of the character or a representation of the character by the defendant with the activities of the plaintiff so that there is implied some real association or connection between the plaintiff, as creator or promoter of the fictional character, and the defendant and his activities; in the form, for example, of a trading arrangement licensing, sponsoring, endorsing, recommending, authorising or otherwise exercising some kind of control over or responsibility for the defendant's activity and the quality of the defendant's goods or services.[91] There must be some relevant business nexus. The damage which the plaintiff is likely to suffer as a result of such representation and resulting deception is that it will be more difficult for him to grant other people exclusive licences or any licences for the use of the character's name and likeness.[92] Character merchandising is, however, a comparatively recent, though fast-growing, development and the application of familiar principles of passing off to such transactions is still far from clear.[93]

It may also be an infringement of the copyright in a literary, dramatic or artistic work to reproduce the distinctive and essential features of a fictional character depicted in the work.[94]

(xi) Other instances of passing off

21–44   There are many instances in the decided cases of the application of the action of passing off for the protection of the authors and publishers of literary, musical, dramatic and artistic works and other copyright works.

---

[89] *Henderson & Anor.* v. *Radio Corporation Pty. Ltd.* [1969] R.P.C. 218 (High Court of New South Wales); *Taverner Rutledge Ltd.* v. *Trexapalm Ltd.* [1977] R.P.C. 275; *Wombles Ltd.* v. *Wombles Skips Ltd.* [1977] R.P.C. 99; *H. P. Bulmer & Showerings Ltd.* v. *J. Bollinger S.A.* [1978] R.P.C. 79 at 117; *Lyngstad* v. *Anabas Products Ltd.* [1977] F.S.R. 62; *Lorimar Productions Inc.* v. *Sterling Clothing Manufacturing Pty. Ltd.* [1982] R.P.C. 395 (Supreme Court of South Africa) *cf. Children's Television Workshop Inc.* v. *Woolworths (N.S.W.)* [1981] R.P.C. 187 (High Court of New South Wales); *IPC Magazines Ltd.* v. *Black and White Music Corp.* [1983] F.S.R. 348; *Grundy Television Pty. Ltd.* v. *Startrain Ltd.* [1988] F.S.R. 581; and see *Noddy Subsidiary Rights Co. Ltd.* v. *I.R.C.* [1967] 1 W.L.R. 1 and *"Rawhide" Trade Mark* [1962] R.P.C. 133; *Re American Greetings Corporation Application* [1984] 1 W.L.R. 189 at 191, 192, 195, 197; *cf. Hogan* v. *Koala Dundee Pty Ltd.* (1988) ATPR 40–902 (Federal Court of Australia).

[90] See n. 89, *ante.*

[91] See n. 89, *ante.*

[92] See n. 89, *ante.*

[93] *IPC Magazines Ltd.* v. *Black and White Music Corp.* [1983] F.S.R. 348 ("Judge Dredd"); *Re American Greetings Corporation Application* [1984] 1 W.L.R. 189 at 191.

[94] See §§ 8–130, 8–48 *et seq.*, 8–131., *ante.* As to registration of the name of a fictional character as a trade mark with a view to licensing, see *"Pussy Galore" Trade Mark* [1967] R.P.C. 265. See also *"Tarzan" Trade Mark* [1970] R.P.C. 450 (registration refused);

They are, like all passing-off cases, examples of applying well-settled principles of law to particular sets of facts.[95] The court has restrained a publisher from advertising a new work in such a way as to be calculated to lead the public to believe that such work was the plaintiff's work.[96] In the case of *Samuelson* v. *Producers' Distributing Co. Ltd.*,[97] the owner of the copyright in a dramatic sketch, of which there existed no film version, was granted an injunction to restrain a producer of a film from representing to the public that the film was a film version of the sketch on the ground that such a representation was an injury to the plaintiff's sole right under the 1911 Act of producing the sketch in film form. But in *O'Gorman* v. *Paramount Film Service Ltd.*,[98] it was held, distinguishing the *Samuelson* case, that the plaintiff, as author of a play called "Irish and Proud of it" produced during the years 1914 to 1934, was not entitled to an injunction in respect of a film of the same title, since there was no evidence at the date of the action that the plaintiff contemplated producing a film version of his play. In the case of *Francis, Day and Hunter Ltd.* v. *Twentieth Century Fox Corporation Ltd.*,[99] the Privy Council decided that no case of passing off was made out where the title of a song was used as the title of a film, on the ground that the thing said to be passed off must resemble the thing for which it is passed off, and the song and the film were incapable of comparison in any reasonable sense. Again in *McCulloch* v. *L.A. May (Produce Distributors) Ltd.*,[1] it was held that the broadcaster "Uncle Mac" was not entitled to complain of the sale of Puffed Wheat under the name "Uncle Mac's Puffed Wheat" on the ground that there was no common field of activity in which, however remotely, both the plaintiff and the defendant were engaged. The decision in *McCulloch* v. *L.A. May (Produce Distributors) Ltd.* has, however, been criticised in *Henderson* v. *Radio Corporation Pty Ltd.*[2]

---

[95] *Habib Bank Ltd.* v. *Habib Bank AG Zurich* [1982] R.P.C. 1. at 23; *Cadbury-Schweppes Pty. Ltd.* v. *The Pub Squash Co. Ltd.* [1981] 1 W.L.R. 193 at 201.; *Reckitt & Colman Products Ltd.* v. *Borden Inc.* [1990] 1 W.L.R. 491 at 505; *Associated Newspapers plc* v. *Insert Media Ltd.* [1990] 1 W.L.R. 900 at 909.

[96] *Seeley* v. *Fisher* (1841) 11 Sim. 581; *Dr. Barnardo's Homes: National Incorporated Association* v. *Barnardo Amalgamated Industries Ltd.* (1949) 66 R.P.C. 103.

[97] [1932] 1 Ch. 201. See also *Cheyney* v. *Rialto Productions Ltd.* [1936–45] Mac.C.C. 386. In *Menchen* v. *Elite Sales Agency Ltd.* (*The Times*, December 18, 1912), both plaintiff and defendant had given the title of "The Miracle" to a cinematograph production, and upon an application for an interlocutory injunction the defendant, at the judge's suggestion, agreed to alter his title. In *Elkin & Co.* v. *Francis, Day and Hunter*, [1905–10] Mac.C.C. 294, the defendants were restrained from publishing the "Blue Bird Valse," as calculated to lead to the belief that it was the music of an opera of that name which was published by the plaintiffs; see also *Flamland* v. *Société Radio-Canada* (1967) 53 C.P.R. 217.

[98] [1937] 2 All E.R. 113; and see *Houghton* v. *Film Booking Offices Ltd.* (1931) 48 R.P.C. 329.

[99] [1940] A.C. 112; *cf. News Group Newspapers Ltd.* v. *The Rocket Record Co. Ltd.* [1981] F.S.R. 89 (where the plaintiffs, who were not in the record business, obtained an interim injunction against defendants' record of song entitled "Page Three").

[1] [1947] 2 All E.R. 845; *Marathon Oil Co.* v. *Marathon Shipping Co. Ltd.* [1968] R.P.C. 443; *Grundy Television Pty. Ltd.* v. *Startrain Ltd.* [1988] F.S.R. 581 at 583.

[2] [1969] R.P.C. 218; (High Court of New South Wales) *cf. Harrison & Starkey* v. *Polydor Ltd.* [1977] F.S.R. 1; *Lyngstad* v. *Anabas Products Ltd.* [1977] F.S.R. 62; *Television Broadcasts Ltd.* v. *Home Guide Publication Co.* [1982] F.S.R. 505 (Supreme Court of Hong Kong); *Corelli* v. *Wall* [1905–10] M.C.C. 55 where injunctions to restrain the unauthorised publication of a person's likeness were refused; see also *Totalizator Agency Board* v. *Turf News Pty. Ltd.* [1972] R.P.C. 579 (Supreme Court of Victoria), and cases in n. 51, *supra*. The case of *Corelli* v.

where it was held that it was not necessary, in order to establish passing off, that there should be an actual or potential area in which the activities of the plaintiff and the defendant conflicted. The plaintiffs in that case were well-known professional dancers and the defendants had, without their consent, published, on the sleeve of a gramophone record, a photograph of the plaintiffs dancing so as to represent that the plaintiffs had sponsored or recommended the record. It was held that the defendants had thereby wrongfully appropriated the plaintiffs' professional reputation: "In our view once it is proved that A is falsely representing his goods as the goods of B or his business to be the same as or connected with the business of B, the wrong of passing off has been established and B is entitled to relief."[3] The essence of the wrong lies in the fact that the plaintiffs had acquired a reputation which placed them in a position to earn a fee for any recommendation which they might be disposed to give and the defendants had for their own commercial advantage appropriated the benefit of that recommendation without payment for the value of it. The authority of the case is somewhat weakened by the finding that the activities of the parties were, in any event, competitive in a broad sense and that there was, therefore, a real possibility of confusion.

21–45   The limited nature of the protection afforded in this action has been well illustrated in the case of *Gordon Fraser Gallery Ltd.* v. *Tatt*[4] where the court refused to grant an injunction to the plaintiff, who published a distinctive style of greetings card, restraining the defendants from offering for sale cards bearing a distinct resemblance to the plaintiff's. The defendants' cards were not copies of, but were obviously derived from, the plaintiff's cards. The court held that merely imitating the style of an artist was a difficult ground on which to base a claim for passing off. Similarity of artistic style and content, not amounting to breach of copyright, were not sufficiently defined features on which to base an allegation that somebody would be persuaded to buy the defendants' goods in the belief that they were the plaintiff's goods. Similarly, an injunction was refused to restrain the deliberate adoption by a defendant of an advertising campaign based on themes and slogans closely related to those which the plaintiff had developed and made familiar in the market in radio and television advertisements for its products.[5] On the other hand, an actor may be able to establish that his distinctive voice is part of his stock in trade and goodwill, and that the unauthorised imitation of his voice for advertising purposes is actionable passing off.[6]

This area of the law is being expanded by judicial decision to adapt to

---

Wall, supra, was not followed in *Krouse* v. *Chrysler* (1970) 12 D.L.R. (3d) 463; (1974) 40 D.L.R. (3d) 15 (Can.), which concerned a claim for invasion of privacy. See also *Tolley* v. *J. S. Fry & Sons Ltd.* [1930] 1 K.B. 467 (charicature for advertising purposes not defamatory).

[3] *Henderson & Anor.* v. *Radio Corporation Pty Ltd.* [1969] R.P.C. 218 *per* Evatt J. at 234. *Fleetwood Mac Promotions Ltd.* v. *Clifford Davis Management Ltd.* [1975] F.S.R. 150 (injunction granted to restrain use of same name by different "pop group.")

[4] [1966] R.P.C. 505; and see *Weldons Ltd.* v. *United Press Ltd.* [1905–10] M.C.C. 293.

[5] *Cadbury-Schweppes Pty. Ltd.* v. *The Pub Squash Co. Ltd.* [1981] 1 W.L.R. 193.

[6] *Sim* v. *H. J. Heinz Co. Ltd.* [1959] 1 W.L.R. 313.

changing economic and social conditions,[7] though it has not developed into a general action of unfair trading or competition.[8] A flexible approach has, however, been maintained by the courts. For example, the law of passing off has been expanded to cover certain aspects of unfair trading which do not give rise to deception or confusion. It is a wrong, actionable at the suit of a person thereby injured, to sell goods under an unlawful trade description.[9] In this "new-fangled tort of unlawful competition" the concepts of confusion and deception are irrelevant. Thus, it is actionable for a person to call his alcoholic product "sherry" without further qualification if it does not come from the Jerez district of Spain.[10]

This new tort may cover cases where there was previously held to be no wrong. It has been held in the past that a representation that an old work of an author was a new work of that author did not give a cause of action,[11] and that a representation that the defendant's work had some quality possessed by the plaintiff's work would not give a cause of action unless the quality was unique.[12] Such cases might now be decided differently.

(xii) "Nom de plume"

Where a common field of activity is established, an author or artist who **21-46** has acquired a reputation under a *nom de plume* is entitled to protect it by a passing-off action.[13] In several cases, the point has arisen whether an employee, who has acquired a reputation under a *nom de plume* or in a fictional character under whose name he has written,[14] is entitled to use it

---

[7] *Hexagon Pty. Ltd.* v. *Australian Broadcasting Commission* [1976] R.P.C. 629; *Morny Ltd.* v. *Ball & Rogers* (1975) *Ltd.* [1978] F.S.R. 91 at 92.

[8] *Lorimar Productions Inc.* v. *Sterling Clothing Manufacturing Pty. Ltd.* [1982] R.P.C. 395 (Supreme Court of South Africa); *Cadbury-Sweppes Pty. Ltd.* v. *The Pub Squash Co. Ltd.* [1981] 1 W.L.R. 193 at 201; *Moorgate Tobacco Co. Ltd.* v. *Philip Morris Ltd.* [1985] R.P.C. 219 (High Court of Australia) at 237; *Harrods Ltd.* v. *Schwartz-Sackin & Co. Ltd.* [1986] F.S.R. 490 at 494; *Associated Newspapers Group plc* v. *Insert Media Ltd.* [1988] 1 W.L.R. 509: *Consumers Distributing Co. Ltd.* v. *Seikco Time Canada Ltd.* (1984) 10 DLR (4th) 161 (Supreme Court of Canada).

[9] *Bollinger* v. *Costa Brava Wine Co.* [1960] Ch. 262, [1961] R.P.C. 116; *Vine Products Ltd.* v. *Mackenzie & Co. Ltd.* [1969] R.P.C. 1; *John Walker & Sons Ltd.* v. *Henry Ost & Co. Ltd.* [1970] R.P.C. 489; *Shaw Bros. (Hong Kong) Ltd.* v. *Golden Harvest (H.K.) Ltd.* [1972] R.P.C. 559; *Lang Bros.* v. *Goldwill* [1977] F.S.R. 353 (Court of Session); *H. P. Bulmer Ltd. & Showerings Ltd.* v. *J. Bollinger S.A.* [1978] R.P.C. 79; *Erven Warnink, etc.* v. *J. Townend & Sons (Hull) Ltd.* [1979] A.C. 731 (Advocaat); *Testut Frères* v. *J. E. Lightbourne & Co. Ltd.* [1981] F.S.R. 458 (Chablis; Court of Appeal of Bermuda); *I.N.A.O.* v. *Andrez* (1988) 40 D.L.R. 239 (Ontario High Court). (Canadian Champagne); *Union Wine* v. *E.Snell & Co.* [1990] 2 S.A. 180.

[10] See. n. 9, *ante.*

[11] *Harris & Co.* v. *Warren and Phillips* (1918) 35 R.P.C. 217; *cf. Morris Motors Ltd.* v. *Lilley* [1959] 1 W.L.R. 1184.

[12] *Cambridge University Press* v. *University Tutorial Press Ltd.* (1928) 45 R.P.C. 335.

[13] *Marengo* v. *Daily Sketch, etc., Ltd.* [1948] 1 All E.R. 406; *Serville* v. *Constance* [1954] 1 W.L.R. 487; *Fleetwood Mac Promotions Ltd.* v. *Clifford Davis Management Ltd.* [1975] F.S.R. 150 ("pop group").

[14] *Sykes* v. *Fairfax and Sons Ltd.* [1978] F.S.R. 312 (New South Wales—Equity Division).

after the employment has been discontinued.[15] The effect of these decisions seems to be that, in the absence of some clear term to the contrary, the name is the property of the individual for whom the reputation has been acquired and that he alone is entitled to use it after the severance of his relationship with the employer.

(xiii) Examples where injunctions granted

21–47 "The Wonderful Magazine," "The Wonderful Magazine, New Series, Improved."[16] "Minnie," "Minnie Dale."[17] "Minnie," "Minnie, Dear Minnie."[18] "The John Bull and Britannia," "The True Britannia."[19] "London Journal," "Daily London Journal."[20] "Bell's Life," "Penny Bell's Life."[21] "Church and State," "Church and State."[22] "The Decorators and Painters Magazine," "The Decorator."[23] "My Life and Loves by Frank Harris,"[24] "Oxford Dictionary," "Oxford Dictionary of Perfect Spelling."[25]

(xiv) Examples where injunctions refused

21–48 "Magazine of Fiction," "Monthly Magazine of Fiction."[26] "Post Office Directory of the West Riding of Yorkshire," "The Post Office Bradford Directory."[27] "Punch," "Punch and Judy."[28] "Evening Times," "Evening Times."[29] "Morning Post," "Evening Post."[30] "Everybody's Magazine," "Everybody's Weekly."[31] "Adventure," "Hutchinson's Adventure Story Magazine."[32] "How to Appeal against your Rates in the Metropo-

---

[15] *Maitland-Davidson* v. *The Sphere and Tatler Ltd.* [1917–23] Mac.C.C. 128; *Hines* v. *Winnick* [1947] Ch. 708; *Modern Fiction Ltd.* v. *Fawcett* [1948–49] Mac.C.C. 22; *Forbes* v. *Kemsley Newspapers Ltd.* [1951] 2 T.L.R. 656; *Landa* v. *Greenberg* (1908) 24 T.L.R. 441, apparently decided on the ground that the defendants were using the name in a manner calculated to deceive the public.

[16] *Hogg* v. *Kirby* (1803) 8 Ves. 215. In *Hulton Press Ltd.* v. *White Eagle Youth Holiday Camp Ltd.* (1951) 68 R.P.C. 126, an injunction was granted to the proprietors of the "Eagle" magazine to prevent the use of the name "White Eagle Youth Holiday Camp" for a children's holiday camp.

[17] *Chappell* v. *Sheard* (1855) 2 K. & J. 117.

[18] *Chappell* v. *Davidson* (1855) 2 K. & H. 123.

[19] *Prowett* v. *Mortimer* (1856) 4 W.R. 519.

[20] *Ingram* v. *Stiff* (1859) 5 Jur. 947.

[21] *Clement* v. *Maddick* (1859) 1 Giff. 98.

[22] *Primrose Press Agency Co. (The)* v. *Knowles (M.)* (1885) 2 T.L.R. 404.

[23] *Dale Reynolds & Co.* v. *Trade Papers Publishing Co.* [1901–04] Mac.C.C. 32.

[24] *W. H. Allen & Co.* v. *Brown Watson Ltd.* [1965] R.P.C. 191.

[25] *Chancellor, Masters and Scholars of Oxford University* v. *Pergamon Press Ltd.* (1977) 121 S.J. 758: See *Cambridge Plan* v. *Moore* [1987] 4 S.A.L.R. 821 (Cambridge Diet not used geographically).

[26] *Stevens (W.) Ltd.* v. *Cassell & Co. Ltd.*, *The Times*, February 7, 1913.

[27] *Kelly* v. *Byles* (1879) 13 Ch.D. 682.

[28] *Bradbury* v. *Beeton* (1869) 18 W.R. 33.

[29] *George Outram and Co. Ltd.* v. *The London Evening Newspapers Co. Ltd.* (1910) 27 T.L.R. 231; the plaintiffs' was a Scottish paper and the defendants' a London paper.

[30] *Borthwick* v. *The Evening Post* (1888) 37 Ch.D. 449.

[31] *Ridgeway Co. (The)* v. *The Amalgamated Press Ltd.* (1911) 28 T.L.R. 149.

[32] *Ridgeway Co. (The)* v. *Hutchinson* (1923) 40 R.P.C. 335.

lis," "How to Appeal against your Rates within the Metropolis."[33] "London Weekly Advertiser" and "National Advertiser," "National Weekly."[34] "Sports Car and Lotus Owner," "Sports Cars Illustrated."[35] "Rubber and Plastics Age," "Rubber and Plastics Weekly."[36] "Courier" incorporating 'Today,'" "Today, The New John Bull."[37] "The Field," "The Field and Kennel."[38] "Mainly About People," "People Talked Of."[39] "The Evening Express," "The North Express."[40] "The Pet Library," "Ellson's Pet Library."[41] "Maidenhead Advertiser," "The New Advertiser."[42] "Morning Star," "Daily Star."[43] "The Sunday Post," "The South East Sunday Post."[44] "The Cricketer," "Cricketer."[45] "Athletics Weekly," "Athletics Monthly."[46] "Miss World," "Miss Alternative World."[47] "Complete Mothercare Manual," "Mother Care/Other Care."[48] "Neighbours," "Neighbours Who's Who."[49] "International Telex Directory Intercontex," "International Telex Directory."[50]

(xv) Remedies

As in a copyright action, a plaintiff may obtain an injunction, interlocutory or final, damages or, at his option, an account of profits.[51] The account may be limited to the period subsequent to the date on which the defendant became aware of the true facts, if the defendant initially acted innocently; similarly where the defendant acted innocently the plaintiff may only recover nominal damages.[52] The profits recoverable are limited to those which were made improperly by the acts of passing off, since the purpose of an account is not to inflict punishment on the defendant, but to prevent him from enjoying unjust enrichment.[53] The court has a discretion, even where it has granted an injunction, to refuse to order an

21–49

---

[33] *Mathieson* v. *Sir I. Pitman & Sons Ltd.* (1930) 47 R.P.C. 541.

[34] *Brittain Publishing Co. (London) Ltd.* v. *Trade & Commercial Press Ltd.* [1957] R.P.C. 134 and 271.

[35] *Pearl Cooper Ltd.* v. *Richmond Hill Press Ltd.* [1957] R.P.C. 363.

[36] *Rubber & Technical Press Ltd.* v. *Maclaren & Sons Ltd.* (1961) R.P.C. 264.

[37] *Norman Kark Publications Ltd.* v. *Odhams Press Ltd.* [1962] 1 W.L.R. 380.

[38] *Cox* v. *Sports Publishing Co.* [1901–04] Mac.C.C. 27.

[39] *C. Arthur Pearson Ltd.* v. *T. P. O'Connor* [1905–10] Mac.C.C. 43.

[40] *Dillon* v. *Pearson* [1901–04] Mac.C.C. 17.

[41] *The Pet Library (London) Ltd.* v. *Walter Ellson & Son Ltd.* [1968] F.S.R. 359.

[42] *Baylis & Co. (The Maidenhead Advertiser) Ltd.* v. *Darlenko Ltd.* [1974] F.S.R. 284.

[43] *Morning Star Co-operative Society Ltd.* v. *Express Newspapers Ltd.* [1979] F.S.R. 113.

[44] *D. C. Thomson & Co. Ltd.* v. *Kent Messenger Ltd.* [1975] R.P.C. 191.

[45] *The Cricketer Ltd.* v. *Newspapers Pty. Ltd.* [1974] V.R. 477 (Supreme Court of Victoria).

[46] *World Athletics & Sporting Publications Ltd.* v. *A.C.M. Webb (Publishing) Ltd.* [1981] F.S.R. 27.

[47] *Miss World (Jersey) Ltd.* v. *James Street Productions Ltd.* [1981] F.S.R. 309.

[48] *Mothercare U.K. Ltd.* v. *Penguin Books Ltd.* [1988] R.P.C. 113.

[49] *Grundy Television Pty. Ltd.* v. *Startrain Ltd.* [1988] F.S.R. 581.

[50] *Intercontex* v. *Schmidt* [1988] F.S.R. 575.

[51] See Chap. 11, *ante; Sterwin A.G.* v. *Brocades (Great Britain) Ltd.* [1979] R.P.C. 481 and *International Scientific Communications Inc.* v. *Pattison* [1979] F.S.R. 429 where no injunction ordered; *Combe International Ltd. & Ors.* v. *Scholl* [1980] R.P.C. 1; *Dormeuil Frères S.A.* v. *Feraglow Ltd.* [1990] R.P.C. 449 (no damages on a royalty basis).

[52] See *A.G. Spalding & Bros.* v. *A. W. Gamage Ltd.* (1915) 32 R.P.C. 273 at 283; *Draper* v. *Trist* (1939) 56 R.P.C. 429; *Procea Products Ltd.* v. *Evans* (1951) 68 R.P.C. 210.

[53] *My Kinda Town* v. *Soll* [1983] R.P.C. 15 at 55.

inquiry as to damages if satisfied that the inquiry would be fruitless.[54] In practice, many passing-off actions are effectively decided on motion or summons for an interlocutory injunction.[55] If a claim for passing off is coupled with a claim for defamation raising similar issues, the court will generally decline to grant an interlocutory injunction if it is intended to plead justification as a defence.[56]

3. Malicious Falsehood

A. Nature of action

21–50 Actions of this type have been known by different names at different times; for instance "slander of title," "slander of goods," "injurious falsehood." The description "malicious falsehood" is used in the Defamation Act 1952,[57] as a comprehensive definition for such actions.

An action will lie for malicious falsehood where there has been a malicious and false statement, written or oral, made to some third party about, for instance, a person's business or his goods.[58] In deciding whether a false statement has been made the court will not read the statements in question carefully considering every word as in the case of a will, contract or other legal document.[59] This action is distinct from the action for passing off which is essentially based on a misrepresentation by a defendant about his own goods or business, not about the plaintiff's goods or business.[60] A material omission from a statement which would create an erroneous impression may itself justify a finding of falsity.[61] Claims based upon malicious falsehood sometimes arise in the fields of literature or art and, when they do so, are often the reverse of the action for passing off. If a publisher publishes the work of an unknown writer A under the name of the well-known writer B, this could be the subject of a passing-off action at the suit of B. But if the publication is made with the approval of B and without the consent of A, because A has produced a clever book which the publisher thinks will sell better under B's name, the only action open for A, in the absence of express or implied contract or of retention of the relevant copyrights, is for malicious falsehood. His damage is loss of reputation. His difficulty is to prove malice unless, as suggested below, an intent to deceive

[54] *McDonald's Hamburgers Ltd.* v. *Burger King (U.K.) Ltd.* [1987] F.S.R. 112 at 118.

[55] *B.B.C.* v. *Talbot Motor Co. Ltd.* [1981] F.S.R. 228; *Rizla Ltd.* v. *Bryant & May Ltd.* [1986] R.P.C. 389 at p. 391; *The Athletes Foot Marketing Associates Inc.* v. *Cobra Sports Ltd.* [1980] R.P.C. 343 at p. 348; *C.P.C. (United Kingdom) Ltd.* v. *Keenan* [1986] F.S.R. 527 at 530; *cf.* *British Association of Aesthetic Plastic Surgeons* v. *Cambright Ltd.* [1987] R.P.C. 549.

[56] *Sim* v. *H. J. Heinz Co. Ltd.* [1959] 1 W.L.R. 313; see § 11–44, *ante.*

[57] (c. 66) s.3.

[58] *Ratcliffe* v. *Evans* [1892] 2 Q.B. 524 at 527 and 532; *Loudon* v. *Ryder (No. 2)* [1953] Ch. 423; *R. J. Reuter Co. Ltd.* v. *Muhlens* [1954] Ch. 50 at 74. And see *Eothen Films Ltd.* v. *Industrial & Commercial Education—Macmillan Ltd.* [1966] F.S.R. 356; *Bestobell Paints Ltd.* v. *Bigg* [1975] F.S.R. 421. Express malice and falsity must be pleaded and proved: *A. & M. Records Inc. & Ors.* v. *Audio Magnetics Incorporated (U.K.) Ltd.* [1979] F.S.R. 1 at 9.

[59] *McDonalds Hamburgers Ltd.* v. *Burger King (U.K.) Ltd.* [1986] F.S.R. 45 at 50.

[60] *Polydor Ltd. & Anor.* v. *Harlequin Record Shops Ltd. & Anor.* [1980] F.S.R. 26; see passing off §§ 21–28 *et seq., ante.*

[61] *Pfizer Corporation* v. *D.D.S.A. Pharmaceuticals Ltd.* [1965] R.P.C. 8 at 14.

the public is sufficient malice. In one unreported case a translator obtained damages against a publisher in an action so constituted for loss of reputation because the translation was attributed to someone else. The 1988 Act confers moral rights on authors, including the right to be identified as the author of a work in specified circumstances.[62]

B. *Whether necessary to prove damage*

Before the Defamation Act 1952, it was always necessary for a plaintiff to **21–51** show that his material interests had been damaged. If the statement was intended or reasonably likely to produce, and in the ordinary course of things did produce, a general loss of business as distinct from the loss of particular known customers, evidence of such general decline of business was admissible and sufficient to support the action.[63] However, the 1952 Act now provides that it is not necessary to allege, or prove, special damage in such actions in certain circumstances. These are where either the words upon which the action is founded are calculated to cause pecuniary damage to the plaintiff and are published in writing or other permanent form (including the broadcasting of words by means of wireless telegraphy), or where such words are calculated to cause pecuniary damage to the plaintiff in respect of any office, profession, calling, trade or business held or carried on by him at the time of the publication.[64] In this context "calculated" is equivalent to "likely to cause pecuniary damage."[65] Damages can only be recovered for actual or probable money loss, and not for injured feelings.[66] In appropriate cases the court may also grant relief by way of injunction, interim or final, and by way of declaration.[67]

C. *Examples*

A plaintiff succeeded where a statement had been published in a news- **21–52** paper by the defendant importing that the plaintiff had ceased to carry on his business[68]; where the defendants had falsely stated that they were selling the plaintiff's hairdriers at cost price[69]; where the plaintiff was tenant of certain premises for the purposes of his motor tyre business, the defendant being his landlord, and the defendant informed the tyre makers that the plaintiff's tenancy had ceased[70]; and where the plaintiff company's production of a play was falsely described by the defendants as a "disastrous flop."[71] It would also be actionable if a person wrongly alleged that

---

[62] See § 22–8 *et seq., post.*

[63] *Ratcliffe* v. *Evans, supra,* at 528 and 533.

[64] Defamation Act 1952, s.3(1).

[65] *Customglass Boats Ltd.* v. *Salthouse Brothers Ltd.* [1976] R.P.C. 589 (Supreme Court of New Zealand).

[66] *Fielding* v. *Variety Incorporated* [1967] 2 Q.B. 841.

[67] See n. 86, *post.*

[68] *Ratcliffe* v. *Evans, supra; Plant Location International A.S.B.L.* v. *Yaseen* [1964] R.P.C. 345.

[69] *Rima Electric Ltd.* v. *Rolls Razor Ltd.* [1964] F.S.R. 138.

[70] *Joyce* v. *Motor Surveys Ltd.* [1948] Ch. 252.

[71] *Fielding* v. *Variety Incorporated* [1967] 2 Q.B. 841.

the sale of copies of a work in any form would be an infringement of that person's copyright.[72] The court will also restrain a defendant from sending letters to important customers of the plaintiff implying that the plaintiff's products infringe the defendant's copyright. Such an injunction can be made either on the basis of malicious falsehood or interference with contractual relations or with the plaintiff's business. If a person in good faith asserts that his copyright would be infringed by the performance of a contract between two others, and the contract is as a result not performed, that person is not liable for unjustified interference with that contractual relationship.[73] A person is entitled to draw other people's attention to the existence of his copyright provided that he does it in such a way as to avoid an interference of an unjustifiable nature.[74] However, there is not under the 1988 Act a statutory remedy against any person threatening any other person with proceedings for infringement of copyright generally.[75] A remedy has been provided for groundless threats of proceedings for infringement of design right. The person aggrieved by the threats may bring an action for a declaration that the threats are unjustifiable, for an injunction against continuance of the threats and for damages for loss sustained.[76] Mere notification that a design is protected by design right does not constitute a threat of proceedings for this purpose.[77]

The court will not restrain, by interlocutory injunction, the publication of a statement where the defendant says that he is going to justify it at the trial of the action, except in cases where the statement is obviously untruthful and libellous.[78]

D. Meaning of "malice"

21–53 The most difficult aspect of this type of action is the question of malice. It is necessary to establish malice and the mere absence of a just cause for making a statement is insufficient to create liability.[79] Various interpretations have been given by the courts on different occasions. Thus, in one case[80] it was said to be "without just cause or excuse." But, in a later case,[81] it was said " 'Maliciously,' not in the sense of illegally, but in the sense of being made with some indirect or dishonest or improper motive. Honest belief in an unfounded claim is not malice; but the nature of the

---

[72] *Dicks* v. *Brooks* (1880) 15 Ch.D. 22 at 40. *cf. Mackay* v. *Edwardes* [1905–10] Mac.C.C.69.
[73] *Granby Marketing Services Ltd.* v. *Interlego A.G.* [1984] R.P.C. 209 at 212.; *S.W.Hart* v. *Edwards Hot Water Systems* (1979–80) 30 ALR 657.
[74] *Jaybeam Ltd.* v. *ABRU Aluminium Ltd.* [1976] R.P.C. 308; and see *Jacey (Printers)* v. *Norton, etc., Ltd.* [1977] F.S.R. 475; *Polydor Ltd. & Anor.* v. *Harlequin Record Shops Ltd. & Anor.* [1980] F.S.R. 26.
[75] *cf.* Patents Act 1977 (c. 37), s.70; see *Jacey (Printers)* v. *Norton & Wright Group Ltd.* [1977] F.S.R. 475.
[76] C.P.D.A 1988, s. 253(1). See § 20–155, *ante.*
[77] *Ibid* s.253(4).
[78] *Bestobell Paints Ltd.* v. *Bigg* [1975] F.S.R. 421; *Lord Brabourne* v. *Hough* [1981] F.S.R. 79; *Consorzio del Prosciutto di Parma* v. *Marks & Spencer plc* [1990] F.S.R. 530; see § 11–44, *ante.*
[79] *Anheuser-Busch Inc.* v. *Budejovicky Budvar NP* [1984] F.S.R. 413 at 479.
[80] *Royal Baking Powder Co. (The)* v. *Wright Crossley & Co.* (1901) 18 R.P.C. 95 at 99.
[81] *Greers Ltd.* v. *Pearman & Corder Ltd.* (1922) 39 R.P.C. 406 at 417; *Polydor Ltd. & Anor.* v. *Harlequin Record Shops Ltd. & Anor.* [1980] F.S.R. 26; *Anheuser-Busch Inc.* v. *Budejovicky Budvar NP* [1984] F.S.R. 413 at 479.

unfounded claim may be evidence that there was not an honest belief in it. It may be so unfounded that the particular fact that it is put forward may be evidence that it is not honestly believed." More recently it was said[82] that it meant the wilful and intentional doing of damage without just occasion or excuse. On the other hand, the making of careless statements, believing them to be true, and without any indirect motive, and without any intention of injuring the plaintiff, is not malicious.[83] Statements merely "puffing" a person's goods, that is, saying that they are better than another's, are not actionable even though they cause damage, unless, possibly, where done intentionally to injure the other and maliciously and falsely.[84] In a case where the defendants had circulated to their customers a pamphlet purporting to compare in great detail the respective performances of the plaintiff's and the defendant's product and reached a conclusion unfavourable to the plaintiff, the court refused to strike out as disclosing no reasonable cause of action a statement of claim alleging that the statements in the circular were false, misleading and actionable. While a mere puff by a trader about his own goods, property or services is not actionable, the position might well be different if a trader particularises precisely why his product is better than his competitor's or his competitor's is worse than his. In order to draw the line between those statements which are actionable and those which are not, the court will apply the test whether the reasonable man would take the claim by the defendant as being a serious claim or not. A possible alternative test is whether the defendant has in his statements pointed to some specific allegation of some defect or demerit in the plaintiff's goods.[85] Where malice is not established the court may make a declaration, even if not claimed in the writ.[86]

A useful summary of the position was given by Stable J. in the case of **21–54** *Wilts United Dairies Ltd.* v. *Thomas Robinson Sons & Co. Ltd.*,[87] a decision after the Defamation Act 1952. In that case it was alleged that the defendants, knowing what they were doing, purchased a large quantity of the plaintiffs' "British Maid" tinned condensed milk, which they knew was old stock and stale stock, and put that milk into circulation through various wholesalers and retailers as being the normal standard of "British Maid" milk. The plaintiffs complained that that was an injurious falsehood, or that it was a passing off, as being milk of the current production, milk that had, in the course of time, been relegated to a class of old or stale milk. It

---

[82] *Joyce* v. *Motor Surveys Ltd.* [1948] Ch. 252 at 254; *Plant Location International A.S.B.L.* v. *Yaseen* [1964] R.P.C. 345; *Customglass Boats Ltd.* v. *Salthouse Brothers Ltd.* [1976] R.P.C. 589 (Supreme Court of New Zealand).

[83] *Balden* v. *Shorter* [1933] Ch. 427 at 431; *Mackay* v. *Edwards* [1905–10] Mac.C.C. 69; *Ucan Products Ltd.* v. *Hilti (Great Britain) Ltd.* [1968] F.S.R. 248.

[84] *White* v. *Mellin* [1895] A.C. 154 at 164 and 165; and see *Hubbuck & Sons Ltd.* v. *Wilkinson, etc., Ltd.* [1899] 1 Q.B. 86 at 94; *Lyne* v. *Nicholls* (1906) 23 T.L.R. 86 and s.3 of the Defamation Act 1952; *Erven Warnink* v. *Townend (J.) & Sons (Hull) Ltd* [1979] A.C. 731 at 742G.

[85] *De Beers Ltd.* v. *International Co. Ltd.* [1975] 1 W.L.R. 972; See also *McDonald's Hamburgers Ltd.* v. *Burger King (U.K.) Ltd.* [1986] F.S.R. 45.

[86] *Loudon* v. *Ryder (No. 2)* [1953] Ch. 423; but see *R.J. Reuter Co. Ltd.* v. *Muhlens* [1954] Ch. 50.

[87] [1957] R.P.C. 220 at 237; affirmed on appeal [1958] R.P.C. 94, though the question of malicious falsehood was not specifically dealt with by the Court of Appeal. See also *London Ferro-Concrete Co. Ltd. (The)* v. *Justicz* (1951) 68 R.P.C. 261 at 265; *Horrocks* v. *Lowe* [1975] A.C. 135; *Redwood Music Ltd.* v. *Francis, Day & Hunter Ltd.* [1978] R.P.C. 429.

was held that there had been passing off and injurious falsehood. On the meaning of malice, Stable J. said "As I understand the law it is this, that if you publish a defamatory statement about a man's goods which is injurious to him, honestly believing that it is true, your object being your own advantage and no detriment to him, you obviously are not liable. If you publish a statement which turns out to be false but which you honestly believe to be true, but you publish that statement, not for the purpose of protecting your own interests and achieving some advantage to yourself, but for the purpose of doing him harm, and it transpires, contrary to your belief, that the statement that you believed to be true has turned out to be false, notwithstanding the bona fides of your belief because the object you had in mind was to injure him and not to advantage yourself, you would be liable for an injurious falsehood."

"The third proposition which I derive from the cases is this, that if you publish an injurious falsehood which you know to be false, albeit that your only object is your own advantage and with no intention or desire to injure the person in relation to whose goods the falsehood is published, then provided that it is clear from the nature of the falsehood that it is intrinsically injurious—I say 'intrinsically,' meaning not deliberately aimed with intent to injure but as being inherent in the statement itself, the defendant is responsible, the malice consisting in the fact that what he published he knew to be false."

21–55   It is thought that "knew to be false" may be too wide. If the defendant has made a false representation with intent to defraud a third party or the public, the plaintiff can rely upon such false representation so made as evidence of a dishonest motive. Applying this third proposition, it has been held that a claim made by a party to third persons asserting title to the plaintiff's copyright works was not made maliciously in circumstances where the person making the claim to title had invested a considerable sum of money in advancing the claim, in preparing documents and taking assignments of the rights claimed and in taking legal advice on the claim and had subsequently embarked on litigation with a view to establishing the correctness of the claim.[88]

---

[88] *Redwood Music Ltd.* v. *Francis, Day & Hunter Ltd.* [1978] R.P.C. 429.

RELATED FORMS OF PROTECTION—3

MORAL RIGHTS

1. Introduction

A. *Historical*

22–1 **Droit moral.** The term "Moral Rights," introduced into English law by Chapter IV of the 1988 Act, has its origins in the "droit moral" enjoyed by authors in various European countries, notably France, Germany and Italy. It refers collectively to a number of rights which are more of a personal than commercial character and are not normally included in the term "copyright."

22–2 **Convention provisions.** Moral rights first appeared in International Copyright in the Rome Convention in 1928. They were extended by Article 6 *bis* of the Brussels Convention and the Stockholm Convention. The essence of the rights contained in Article 6 *bis* is that, independently of his copyright or "economic rights," and even after the transfer of those rights, an author should have the right to claim authorship of his work and to object to any distortion, mutilation, modification of, or other derogatory action in relation to, his work which would be prejudicial to his honour or reputation. The means of safeguarding those rights were to be governed by the law of the country where protection was claimed.

22–3 **1956 Act.** The only provision in the 1956 Act which recognised any of the rights in Article 6 *bis* was section 43. That imposed restrictions on the false attribution of authorship of literary, dramatic, musical and artistic works. The restrictions were not limited to the protection of professional authors, artists or composers. Contravention of those restrictions was actionable as a breach of statutory duty by the person against whom the offence was committed. After his death contravention was actionable by his personal representatives for a period of up to 20 years.

Common law. In addition to the provisions of section 43 an author could **22–4** invoke the common law to protect his moral rights by bringing proceedings to establish liability for a breach of contract or for torts such as defamation, slander and passing off. Those common law rights are not abrogated or limited by the provisions of the 1988 Act.

B. *Chapter IV of the 1988 Act*

The United Kingdom has now taken steps to implement its obligations **22–5** under Article 6 *bis* by the enactment of sections 77 to 89 of the 1988 Act. Those sections are in Part I, which is entitled "Copyright", and are set out in Chapter IV.

Rights created. The following rights are created, namely, the right: **22–6**
(1) to be identified as author of a work or as director of a film[1] ("the paternity right");
(2) to object to derogatory treatment of a work[2] ("the integrity right");
(3) to restrain false attribution of a work[3]; and
(4) to preserve privacy of certain photographs and films.[4]

Nature of rights. Generally speaking, the first two rights are conferred on **22–7** the author of a work, apply to the whole or part of a work[5] and are non-assignable. The term "author" has the same meaning as in the context of copyright, namely the person who creates a work.[6] There is no statutory definition of the term "director" of a film. He is not necessarily the same person who is taken to be the "author" of a film for the purposes of determining who is the first owner of the copyright in it, *i.e.* the person who undertakes the arrangements necessary for the making of the film.[7]

2. Right to be Identified as Author or Director

A. *General*

The right. In general, the author of a copyright literary, dramatic, musi- **22–8** cal or artistic work has the right to be identified as the author of the work. A similar right is conferred on the director of a copyright film to be identified as the director of that work.[8]

---

[1] C.D.P.A. 1988, ss.77–79.
[2] *Ibid.* ss.80–83.
[3] *Ibid.* s.84.
[4] *Ibid.* s.85.
[5] *Ibid.* s.89(1)(2).
[6] *Ibid.* s.9(1), See § 4–5 *et seq., ante.*
[7] *Ibid.* s.9(2)(a), s.11(1), See § 4–55 *et seq., ante.*
[8] *Ibid.* s.77(1); s.1(2). For form of Statement of Claims see § G–10, *post.*

22–9 Infringement. This right is infringed by the doing of any of the acts specified in the relevant provisions[9] without consent of the person entitled to the right.[10] This general statement is, however, subject to three important qualifications:

(1) the circumstances in which the author has the right vary according to the character of the particular copyright work[11];

(2) the right is not infringed unless it has been asserted in a specified manner[12]; and

(3) the right is subject to numerous exceptions.[13]

B. *The Circumstances in which the right exists*

(i) Literary and dramatic works

22–10 The author of a literary or dramatic work has the right to be identified whenever certain events occur in relation to the work or a substantial part of it.[14] In this context words intended to be sung or spoken with music are not treated in the same way as a literary work, but in the same way as a musical work.

22–11 Events. The relevant events in which there is a right to be identified as the author of a literary or dramatic work are as follows:

(1) *Commercial publication*

A work is published commercially when copies of the work are issued to the public at a time when copies made in advance of the receipt of orders are generally available to the public.[15] A work is also published commercially when it is made available to the public by means of an electronic retrieval system.[16]

(2) *Performance in public*

Performance in general includes any mode of visual or acoustic presentation, including presentation by means of a sound recording, film, broadcast or cable programme of the work.[17] It also includes delivery in the case of lectures, addresses, speeches and sermons.[18]

---

[9] *Ibid.* s.77(2)–(8).
[10] *Ibid.* s.87(1).
[11] *Ibid.* s.77(2)–(8). See § 22–10 to 22–19, *post.*
[12] *Ibid.* s.78. See § 22–20 to 22–26, *post.*
[13] *Ibid.* s.79. See § 22–27 to 22–34, *post.*
[14] *Ibid.* s.77(2), s.89(1).
[15] *Ibid.* s.175(2)(*a*). See § 8–92 *et seq., ante.*
[16] *Ibid.* s.175(2)(*b*). See § 8–92 *et seq., ante.*
[17] *Ibid.* s.19(2)(*b*). See § 8–99 *et seq., ante.*
[18] *Ibid.* s.19(2)(*a*). See § 8–99 *et seq., ante.*

(3) *Broadcast*

Broadcast means a transmission by wireless telegraphy of visual images, sounds or other information which is capable of being lawfully received by members of the public or is transmitted for presentation to members of the public.[19]

(4) *Inclusion in a cable programme service*

This refers, with certain exceptions, to a service which consists wholly or mainly in sending visual images, sounds or other information by means of a telecommunications system, otherwise than by wireless telegraphy,[20] for reception either at two or more places (whether for simultaneous reception or at different times in response to requests by different users) or for presentation to members of the public.[21]

(5) *Inclusion in films and sound recordings issued to public*

The author of a literary or dramatic work also has the right to be identified whenever copies of a film or sound recording including the work are issued to the public.[22] This occurs when there are put into circulation copies of a work not previously put into circulation, in the United Kingdom or elsewhere. The issue of copies of films or sound recordings to the public also includes any rental of copies to the public.[23] Rental means any arrangement under which a copy of a work is made available for payment in money or money's worth or in the course of a business as part of services or amenities for which payment is made in either case on terms that it will or may be returned.[24]

(ii) Musical works

The circumstances in which the author of a musical work and of a literary **22–12** work consisting of words intended to be sung or spoken with music has such a right are more restricted.[25] That right is limited to whenever the work is published commercially or copies of a sound recording of the work are issued to the public or a film, of which the sound-track includes the work, is shown in public or copies of such a film are issued to the public.

Thus, there is no right to be identified as the author of a musical work where the work is performed in public or broadcast or included in a cable programme service.

---

[19] *Ibid.* s.6(1). See § 8–118 *et seq., ante.*
[20] *Ibid.* s.178 defines this term.
[21] *Ibid.* s.7(1). For the exceptions from the definition of "cable programme service" see *Ibid.*, s.7(2), (3). See § 2–34 *et seq ante*, § 8–121 *ante.*
[22] *Ibid.* s.77(2)(*b*).
[23] *Ibid.* s.18(2). See § 8–98,*ante.*
[24] *Ibid.* s.178.
[25] *Ibid.* s.77(3).

(iii) Adaptations of Literary Dramatic and Musical Works

22–13 The right to be identified also applies whenever any of the relevant events occur in relation to an adaptation of the work. The right is to be identified as the author of the work from which the particular adaptation was made.[26] In the case of a literary or dramatic work an adaptation means a translation of the work or a version of it in a different form, *e.g.* conversion from dramatic to non-dramatic and vice-versa and conversion into comic strip.[27] In relation to a musical work an adaptation means an arrangement or transcription of the work.[28]

(iv) Artistic works

22–14 The author of an artistic work has the right to be identified whenever the work is published commercially, or exhibited in public, or a visual image of it is broadcast or included in a cable programme service.[29] The right also exists whenever a film including a visual image of the artistic work is shown in public or copies of such a film are issued to the public.[30]

22–15 **Architecture and Sculpture.** There are special provisions relating to particular classes of artistic work. In the case of a work of architecture in the form of a building or a model for a building, a sculpture or a work of artistic craftsmanship, the author has the right to be identified whenever copies of a graphic work representing it, or a photograph of it, are issued to the public.[31] A building includes any fixed structure, and a part of a building or fixed structure.[32] A "sculpture" includes a cast or model made for purposes of sculpture.[33] A "graphic work" includes any painting, drawing, diagram, map, chart or plan, and any engraving, etching, lithograph, woodcut or similar work.[34]

22–16 The author of a work of architecture in the form of a building also has the right to be identified on the building as constructed. Where more than one building is constructed to the design (for example, on a housing estate), the right is to be identified on the first building to be constructed.[35]

(v) Films

22–17 The director of a film has the right to be identified whenever the film is shown in public, or is broadcast or is included in a cable programme service or copies of the film are issued to the public.[36] A "film" means a

---

[26] *Ibid.* s.77(2), (3).
[27] *Ibid.* s.21(3)(*a*). See § 8–122 *et seq., ante.*
[28] *Ibid.* s.21(3)(*b*). See § 8–133, *ante.*
[29] *Ibid.* s.77(4)(*a*).
[30] *Ibid.* s.77(4)(*b*).
[31] *Ibid.* s.77(4)(*c*).
[32] *Ibid.* s.4(2). See § 8–72 *et seq., ante.*
[33] See n. 32, *ante.*
[34] See n. 32, *ante.*
[35] *Ibid.* s.77(5).
[36] *Ibid.* s.77(6).

recording on any medium from which a moving image may by any means be produced.[37]

C. *Mode of identification*

The mode of identification which is required also varies according to the **22–18** character of the work and the manner of its exploitation. Thus, in the case of commercial exploitation of a work or the issue to the public of copies of a film or sound recording, the author or director, as the case may be, must be identified in or on each copy.[38] If, however, that is not appropriate, identification must be in some other manner which is likely to bring the identity of the author or director to the notice of a person acquiring a copy. In the case of identification on a building, the author has the right to be identified by appropriate means visible to persons entering or approaching the building.[39] In any other case, the right is to be identified in a manner likely to bring the identity of the author or director to the attention of a person seeing or hearing the performance, exhibition, showing, broadcast or cable programme in question.[40] In each case the identification must be clear and reasonably prominent.

D. *Form of identification*

Any reasonable form of identification may be used. This will usually take **22–19** the form of the name of the author or director. If the author or director in asserting his right to be identified specifies a pseudonym, initials or some other particular form of identification, that form must be used.[41] It may also be reasonable to employ such a form of identification in fact used by the author or director, even though it has not been specified on assertion of the right.

E. *Assertion of the right*

The 1988 Act imposes a requirement that the right to be identified must **22–20** be asserted as a prerequisite of liability for infringement of the right.[42]

(i) General

A person does not infringe the right to be identified by doing any of the **22–21** acts mentioned unless the right has been asserted in accordance with the relevant provisions so as to bind him in relation to that act. Thus, a person need not assert the right to be identified if he does not want to, but, if a

---

[37] *Ibid.* s.5(1). See § 2–30, *ante*.
[38] *Ibid.* s.77(7)(*a*).
[39] *Ibid.* s.77(7)(*b*).
[40] *Ibid.* s.77(7)(*c*).
[41] *Ibid.* s.77(8). As to assertion of the right see § 22–20 to 22–26 *post*.
[42] *Ibid.* s.78(1); See § G–5, *post*, for a precedent for assertion of right to be identified as author.

person wishes to enforce the right to be identified by infringement proceedings, he must first have asserted it both in the particular manner required and in such a way as to bind the person he wishes to hold liable for infringing the right. It is important that the assertion should be made as soon as possible as, in an action for infringement of the right, the Court, in considering remedies, must take into account any delay in asserting the right.[43]

(ii) Mode and effect of assertion of right

22–22   The right may be asserted generally, or in relation to any specified act or description of acts.[44] It may be asserted in one of two ways: either on an assignment of copyright or by an instrument in writing. No particular form of words is required. An assertion, in ordinary language, is simply an insistence or positive statement of a right or claim.

(a) Assignment of copyright

22–23   The first method of asserting the right is on an assignment of copyright in the work by including in the instrument effecting the assignment a statement that the author or director asserts, in relation to that work, his right to be identified. An assertion made in this manner is binding on the assignee.[45] It is also binding on anyone claiming through the assignee, whether or not he has notice of the assertion.[46] An assignment of copyright is not effective unless it is in writing signed by or on behalf of the assignor.[47] It may be partial, limited so as to apply to particular acts or part of the copyright period.[48]

(b) Instrument in writing

22–24   The right may also be asserted, either generally or in relation to a specified act or description of acts, by an instrument in writing signed by the author or director.[49] "Writing" includes any form of notation or code, whether by hand or otherwise, and regardless of the method by which, or the medium in or on which, it is recorded.[50] An "instrument", in its ordinary meaning, includes any formal or informal document.[51]

An assertion made in this manner is binding on any persons to whose notice the assertion is brought.[52]

---

[43] *Ibid.* s.78(5).
[44] *Ibid.* s.78(2).
[45] *Ibid.* s.78(4)(a).
[46] See n. 45, *ante.*
[47] *Ibid.* s.90(3). See § 5–7, *ante.*
[48] *Ibid.* s.90(2). See § 5–9, *ante.*
[49] *Ibid.* s.78(2)(b); For a precedent see § G–5, *post.*
[50] *Ibid.* s.178. See § 2–4, *ante.*
[51] *R. v. Registrar of Companies, ex p. Central Bank of India* [1986] Q.B. 1114 at 1174, 1179.
[52] C.D.P.A. 1988 s.78(4)(b).

(iii) Joint works

In the case of joint authorship the right must be asserted by each joint **22–25** author in relation to himself.[53] A work of joint authorship is produced by the collaboration of two or more authors in which the contribution of each author is not distinct from that of the other author or authors.[54]

(iv) Public exhibition of artistic works

Special additional provisions concern the assertion of the right to be iden- **22–26** tified in relation to the public exhibition of an artistic work.[55] In that case the assertion may be made in one of two ways. First, by securing that when the author or other first owner of copyright parts with possession of the original, or of a copy made by him or under his direction or control, the author is identified on the original or copy, or on a frame, mount or other thing to which it is attached. In this case the assertion is binding on any one into whose hands that original or copy comes. It remains binding whether or not the identification is still present or visible.[56]

Secondly, the right may be asserted by including in a licence by which the author or other first owner of copyright authorises the making of copies of the work, a statement signed by or on behalf of the person granting the licence. The statement must be that the author asserts his right to be identified in the event of the public exhibition of a copy made in pursuance of the licence.[57] In this case the assertion is binding on the licensee and on anyone into whose hands a copy made in pursuance of the licence comes. The assertion is binding whether or not that person has notice of it.[58]

F. *Exceptions*

The right to be identified is subject to exceptions of various kinds[59]: as to **22–27** the description of work, as to the acts done in relation to a work and as to the circumstances in which those acts are done.

(i) Excepted descriptions of work

The right does not apply at all in relation to a computer program, the **22–28** design of a typeface, or any computer-generated work.[60] The "design of a typeface" includes an ornamental motif used in printing.[61] A computer-generated work is one that is generated by computer in circumstances such that there is no human author of the work.[62]

---

[53] *Ibid.* s.88(1).
[54] *Ibid.* s.10(1). See Ch.7, *ante.*
[55] *Ibid.* s.78(3)(*a*).
[56] *Ibid.* s.78(4)(*c*).
[57] *Ibid.* s.78(3)(*b*).
[58] *Ibid.* s.78(4)(*d*).
[59] *Ibid.* s.79.
[60] *Ibid.* s.79(2).
[61] *Ibid.* s.178. See § 2–23, *ante.*
[62] See n.61, *ante.*

(ii) Qualified exception of works by reference to nature of copyright

22–29   The right to be identified does not apply in relation to a work in which Crown copyright or Parliamentary copyright subsists or a work in which copyright originally vested in an international organisation by virtue of section 168 of the 1988 Act, unless the author or director has previously been identified as such in or on published copies of the work.[63]

Crown copyright subsists where a work is made by Her Majesty or by an officer or servant of the Crown in the course of his duties.[64] Parliamentay copyright subsists when a work is made by or under the direction or control of the House of Commons or the House of Lords.[65] Parliamentary copyright extends to every Bill introduced into Parliament.[66]

An international organisation is the first owner of copyright in every original literary, dramatic, musical or artistic work made by an officer or employee of, or is published by, an international organisation as specified in an Order in Council.[67]

(iii) Authority of copyright-owning employer

22–30   The right does not apply to anything done by or with the authority of the copyright owner where the copyright in the work originally vested in the author's employer by virtue of section 11(2) of the 1988 Act or the director's employer by virtue of section 9(2)(a) of that Act.[68]

(iv) Non-infringing acts

22–31   The right is not infringed by an act which would not, by virtue of various provisions of the 1988 Act, infringe the copyright in the work.[69] In those cases, where there is or would be a good defence to a claim for infringement of copyright in the work, there will also be a valid defence to any claim for the infringement of the right to be identified.

22–32   Those provisions concern fair dealing[70] so far as it relates to the reporting of current events by means of a sound recording, film, broadcast or cable programme[71]; incidental inclusion of a work in an artistic work, sound recording, film, broadcast or cable programme[72]; anything done for the purposes of an examination[73] by way of setting the questions, communicating the questions to the candidates or answering the questions[74];

---

[63] *Ibid.* s.79(7).
[64] *Ibid.* s.163(1). See § 13–18 *et seq.*, *ante*.
[65] *Ibid.* s.165(1). See § 13–33 *et seq.*, *ante*.
[66] *Ibid.* s.166(1).
[67] *Ibid.* s.168(1), (2). See § 17–110, *ante*.
[68] *Ibid.* s.79(3). See § 4–28 *et seq.*, *ante*.
[69] *Ibid.* s.79(4).
[70] *Ibid.* s.30. See § 10–4 *et seq.*, *ante*.
[71] *Ibid.* s.79(4)(a).
[72] *Ibid.* s.79(4)(b); s.31. See § 10–16 *et seq.*, *ante*.
[73] *Ibid.* s.32(3). See § 10–19 *et seq.*, *ante*.
[74] *Ibid.* s.79(4)(c).

anything done for the purposes of parliamentary or judicial proceedings[75] or reporting the same[76]; anything done for the purposes of the proceedings of a Royal Commission or statutory inquiry or for the purpose of reporting any such proceedings held in public[77]; making an article to the design, or copying an article made to the design, in a design document or model recording or embodying a design for anything other than an artistic work or a typeface[78]; copying an artistic work by making articles of any description after the end of the period of 25 years after the end of the calendar year in which the artistic work has been exploited by or with the copyright owner's licence by making articles by industrial process and marketing such articles in the United Kingdom and elsewhere[79]; and those cases where acts are permitted in relation to the copyright in an anonymous or pseudonymous work on the assumption that the copyright has expired or the author has died 50 years or more before the act is done. Those are cases in which it is not possible by reasonable inquiry to ascertain the identity of the author.[80]

In addition, the right does not apply in relation to any work made for **22–33** the purpose of reporting current events.[81]

(v) Non-infringing publications

The right does not apply in relation to the publication in a newspaper, **22–34** magazine or similar periodical or in an encyclopedia, dictionary, yearbook or other collective work of reference, of a literary, dramatic, musical or artistic work made for the purposes of such publication or made available with the consent of the author for the purposes of such publication.[82] A collective work is a work of joint authorship or a work in which there are distinct contributions by different authors or in which works or parts of works of different authors are incorporated.[83]

3. Right to Object to Derogatory Treatment of a Work

A. *General*

In general, the author of a copyright literary, dramatic, musical or artistic **22–35** work, and the director of a copyright film, has the right not to have his work subjected to derogatory treatment.[84] The right applies in relation to the whole or any part of a work[85] and it is infringed by the doing of any of

---

[75] *Ibid.* s.45. See § 10–48 *et seq., ante.*
[76] *Ibid.* s.79(4)(*d*).
[77] *Ibid.* s.79(4)(*e*); s.46(1), (2). See § 10–50 *et seq., ante.*
[78] *Ibid.* s.79(4)(*f*); s.51. See § 20–50 *et seq., ante.*
[79] *Ibid.* s.79(4)(*g*); s.52. See § 20–43 *et seq., ante.*
[80] *Ibid.* s.79(4)(*h*); s.57. See § 10–69 *et seq., ante.*
[81] *Ibid.* s.79(5). See § 10–13, *ante.*
[82] *Ibid.* s.79(6).
[83] *Ibid.* s.178. See § 5–27, *ante; Chappell & Co Ltd.* v. *Redwood Music Ltd.* [1981] R.P.C. 337.
[84] *Ibid.* s.80(1); s.1(2). For a form of Statement of Claim see § G–11, *post.*
[85] *Ibid.* s.89(2).

the acts mentioned in section 80 of the 1988 Act without the consent of the person entitled to the right. As with the case of the right to be identified, the circumstances in which the right is infringed vary according to the character of the copyright work. The right is also subject to exceptions and qualifications. There is, however, no requirement that this right should have been asserted as a prerequisite to liability for infringement. In the case of a work of joint authorship, the right is a right of each joint author and his right is satisfied if he consents to the treatment in question.[86] A work of joint authorship is a work produced by the collaboration of two or more authors in which the contribution of each author is not distinct from that of the other author or authors.

B. *Derogatory treatment*

22–36   It is first necessary to define what is meant by the expression "derogatory treatment."

In order to establish infringement a person must prove that his work has been subject to "treatment." Then he must prove that the relevant treatment of his work is "derogatory."

22–37   "Treatment" of a work means, in general, any addition to, deletion from or alteration to or adaptation of the work. This definition does not, however, extend to a translation of a literary or dramatic work, or to an arrangement or transcription of a musical work involving no more than a change of key or register.[87] The definition does, however, include, by its use of "adaptation,"[88] the conversion of a dramatic work into a non-dramatic work and of a non-dramatic work into a dramatic work.[89] It also includes a version of a work in which the story or action is conveyed wholly or mainly by means of pictures in a form suitable for reproduction in a book or in a newspaper, magazine or similar periodical.[90]

The right extends to the treatment of parts of a work resulting from a previous treatment by a person other than the author or director, if those parts are attributed to, or are likely to be regarded as the work of, the author or director.[91]

22–38   The treatment of a work is "derogatory" if it amounts to a distortion or mutilation of the work or is otherwise prejudicial to the honour or reputation of the author or director.[92] Distortion of a work, as a matter of ordinary language, involves a misrepresentation of the work as created by the author. Mutilation of a work is a more specific act: it involves excisions from a work so as to render it imperfect. "Honour" and "reputation" have differing shades of meaning. Reputation has a more objective connotation, referring to what is generally said or believed about a person's character.

---

[86] *Ibid.* s.88(2); See s.10(1) for definitions of "work of joint authorship". See Ch. 7, *ante.*
[87] *Ibid.* s.80(2)(a).
[88] *Ibid.* s.21(3). See § 8–122 *et seq., ante.*
[89] *Ibid.* s.21(3) (a) (ii). See § 8–130, 131, *ante.*
[90] *Ibid.* s.21(3)(a) (iii). See § 8–132, *ante.*
[91] *Ibid.* s.80(7).
[92] *Ibid.* s.80(2)(b).

Honour, which is associated with reputation and good name, is more a matter of respect for a person and his position.

C. *Circumstances in which the right is infringed*

(i) Literary, dramatic and musical works

In the case of a literary, dramatic or musical work the right is infringed by **22–39** a person who publishes commercially, performs in public, broadcasts or includes in a cable programme service a derogatory treatment of the work. It is also infringed by a person who issues to the public copies of a film or sound recording of, or including, a derogatory treatment of the work.[93]

(ii) Artistic works

In the case of an artistic work the right is infringed by a person who pub- **22–40** lishes commercially or exhibits in public a derogatory treatment of the work or broadcasts or includes in a cable programme service a visual image of a derogatory treatment of the work.[94] The right is also infringed by a person who shows in public a film including a visual image of a derogatory treatment of a work or issues to the public copies of such a film.[95]

There are further special infringement provisions affecting the case of a **22–41** work of architecture in the form of a model for a building (but not in the form of a building), a sculpture and a work of artistic craftsmanship. In those cases a person infringes the right if he issues to the public copies of a graphic work representing, or of a photograph of, a derogatory treatment of the work.[96] Where the author of a work of architecture in the form of a building is identified on the building and it is the subject of derogatory treatment, he has the right to require the identification to be removed.[97] He does not have the right to have the derogatory treatment eradicated from the building. Where the architect is not identified on the building, he has no statutory rights in respect of derogatory treatment of the building.

(iii) Films

In the case of a film the right is infringed by a person who shows in public, **22–42** broadcasts or includes in a cable programme service a derogatory treatment of the film or issues to the public copies of a derogatory treatment of the film.[98] Infringement is also committed by a person who, along with the film, plays in public, broadcasts or includes in a cable programme service, or issues to the public copies of a derogatory treatment of the film sound-track.

---

[93] *Ibid.* s.80(3)(*a*), (*b*). See § 8–92 *et seq.*, *ante.*
[94] *Ibid.* s.80(4)(*a*).
[95] *Ibid.* s.80(4)(*b*).
[96] *Ibid.* s.80(4)(*c*).
[97] *Ibid.* s.80(5).
[98] *Ibid.* s.80(6).

D. *Other persons liable for infringement*

22–43   The right is also infringed by persons possessing or dealing with infringing articles. An infringing article is a work or a copy of a work which has been subjected to derogatory treatment within the meaning of section 80 of the 1988 Act and has been, or is likely to be, the subject of any of the acts mentioned in section 80 in circumstances infringing that right.[99] The right is infringed by a person who does certain acts in relation to the article which is and which he knows, or has reason to believe is, an infringing article.[1] He is liable if he does any of the following acts in relation to the infringing article:

(1) possesses it in the course of a business;

(2) sells it or lets it for hire, or offers it or exposes it for sale or hire; or

(3) in the course of a business exhibits it in public or distributes it; or

(4) distributes it otherwise than in the course of a business so as to affect prejudicially the honour or reputation of the author or director.

E. *Exceptions*

22–44   The right is subject to various exceptions depending upon the character of the work, the acts done in relation to it and the circumstances in which the various acts are done.

(i) Excepted works

22–45   The right does not apply to a computer program or to any computer-generated work.[2] A "computer-generated work" means one that is generated by computer in circumstances such that there is no human author of the work.[3]

(ii) Reporting current events

22–46   The right does not apply to any work made for the purpose of reporting current events.[4]

(iii) Publications

22–47   The right does not apply in relation to the publication in a newspaper, magazine or similar periodical,[5] or in an encyclopedia, dictionary, year-book or other collective work of reference,[6] of a literary, dramatic, musical or artistic work made for the purposes of such publication or made avail-

---

[99] *Ibid.* s.83(2).

[1] *Ibid.* s.83(1). See § 9–3 *et seq., ante.*

[2] *Ibid.* s.81(2). See § 2–9, *et seq.*

[3] *Ibid.* s.178.

[4] *Ibid.* s.81(3). See § 10–13, *ante.*

[5] *Ibid.* s.81(4)(*a*).

[6] *Ibid.* s.81(4)(*b*). "Collective work" is defined in *ibid* s.178. See n.83, *ante.*

able with the consent of the author for the purposes of such publication. The right does not apply in relation to any subsequent exploitation elsewhere of such a work without any modification of the published version.

(iv) Section 57 of the 1988 Act

The right is not infringed by an act which, by virtue of section 57, would **22–48** not infringe copyright in the work.[7] That section refers to anonymous or pseudonymous works and to acts permitted on assumptions as to the expiration of copyright or death of the author.[8]

(v) Purposes

The right is not infringed by anything done for certain specified purposes, **22–49** provided that, where the author or director is identified at the time of the relevant act or has previously been identified in or on published copies of the work, there is a "sufficient disclaimer".[9] Those purposes are:[10]
(1) avoiding the commission of an offence;
(2) complying with a duty imposed by or under an enactment; or
(3) in the case of the British Broadcasting Corporation, avoiding the inclusion in a programme broadcast by them of anything which offends against good taste or decency or which is likely to encourage or incite to crime or to lead to disorder or to be offensive to public feeling.
A "sufficient disclaimer" means a clear and reasonably prominent indication given at the time of the act, and if the author or director is then identified, appearing along with the identification, that the work has been subjected to treatment to which the author or director has not consented.[11]

F. *Qualification of the right*

In the case of certain works the right is qualified.[12] Those works are: **22–50**
(1) works in which copyright originally vested in the author's employer by virtue of section 11(2);
(2) works in which copyright originally vested in the director's employer by virtue of section 9(2)(a);
(3) works in which Crown copyright or Parliamentary copyright subsists; and
(4) works in which copyright originally vested in an international organisation by virtue of section 168.
In all these cases the right does not apply to anything done in relation to such work by or with the authority of the copyright owner, unless the

---

[7] *Ibid.* s.81(5).
[8] *Ibid.* s.57 See § 10–69, *ante*.
[9] *Ibid.* s.81(6).
[10] *Ibid.* s.81(6).
[11] *Ibid.* s.178.
[12] *Ibid.* s.82. See § 4–28 *et seq.*, *ante*.; Ch. 13 *ante*; § 17–110 *ante*.

author or director is identified at the time of the relevant act, or has previously been identified in or on published copies of the work. Where, in such cases, the right does apply, it is not infringed if there is a sufficient disclaimer.[13]

4. False Attribution of Authorship or Directorship

A. Summary of the position under the 1956 Act

22–51   Section 43 of the 1956 Act continues to apply in relation to acts done before commencement of the relevant provisions of the 1988 Act.[14] No act done before commencement is actionable by virtue of any of the provisions of Chapter IV of Part I of the 1988 Act.[15] It will, therefore, be necessary, in pre-1988 Act cases, to have regard to the provisions of section 43. Those provisions may be summarised as follows:

(1)   The primary provisions restricted any person, without licence, from inserting or affixing the name of another in or on a work of which that other was not the author, or on a reproduction of such a work, in such a way as to imply that that other person was the author of the work.[16] The right of action was not limited to professional authors or confined to cases where there was a common field of activity of the parties. The restriction was held to apply to a case where a newspaper published an article in the first person attributing to that person words which that person did not in fact use.[17]

(2)   The provisions applied to literary, dramatic, musical and artistic works.[18] They did not apply to sound recordings or films.

(3)   Similar restrictions were placed on persons selling, letting for hire, by way of trade offering or exposing for sale or hire or by way of trade exhibiting in public a work, or reproductions of a work, or the distribution of reproductions of a work on which the name was so inserted or affixed if, to the offender's knowledge, the person named was not the author of the work.[19]

(4)   An offence was also committed when a work was performed in public or broadcast as being the work of an author if, to the offender's knowledge, that person was not the author of the work.[20]

(5)   The provisions applied after the author's death for a period of 20 years.[21] Proceedings could be brought by the personal representatives of the deceased person and any damages recovered devolved as part of the author's estate as if the right of action had subsisted and been vested in the author immediately before his death.[22]

---

[13] *Ibid.* For definition of "sufficient disclaimer" see *ibid* s.178 and § 22–49 *ante*.
[14] *Ibid.* Sched. 1, para. 22(2).
[15] *Ibid.* Sched. 1, para. 22(1).
[16] *Ibid.* s.43(2) Copyright Act 1956.
[17] *Moore* v. *News of the World Ltd.* [1972] 1 Q.B. 441.
[18] s.43(1). Copyright Act 1956.
[19] *Ibid.* s.43(2)(*b*), (*c*).
[20] *Ibid.* s.43(2)(*d*).
[21] *Ibid.* s.43(5).
[22] *Ibid.* s.43(9).

(6) The provisions applied to a work represented, contrary to the fact, as being an adaptation of the work of another person.[23] Adaptation included dramatisations, translations, cartoon versions and arrangements of music.[24]

(7) They also applied to a substantial part of a work, as well as to the whole work,[25] and to acts done in relation to two or more persons in connection with the same work.[26]

(8) In the case of an artistic work, it was necessary for certain purposes that copyright should subsist in the work.[27]

(9) There were also special provisions making it a wrongful act if an artistic work had been altered after the author had parted with possession of it and another published, sold, let for hire, by way of trade offered or exposed for sale or hire, the work as so altered with a representation that it was the unaltered work or a reproduction of the unaltered work of the author, and the offender knew it was not the unaltered work or a reproduction of the unaltered work of the author.[28] An offence might be committed whether or not the author retained the copyright and up to 20 years from his death.[29]

(10) The restrictions were actionable as a breach of statutory duty.[30]

B. *The 1988 Act—general*

In general, a person has the right not to have a literary, dramatic, musical   **22–52**
or artistic work falsely attributed to him as author or a film falsely attributed to him as director.[31] The right is conferred on authors and non-authors alike. The right also applies in relation to the whole or any part of the work.[32]

"Attribution" in relation to the relevant work means a statement,   **22–53**
express or implied, as to who is the author or director of the work. The right extends to cases where, contrary to the fact, a literary, dramatic or musical work is falsely represented as being an adaptation of a work of a person or where a copy of an artistic work is falsely represented as being a copy made by the author of the artistic work.[33] The right extends to the case of altered artistic works. In the case of an artistic work that right is infringed by a person who, in the course of a business, deals with the work which has been altered after the author has parted with possession of it, as being the unaltered work of the author, or deals with a copy of such work as being a copy of the unaltered work of the author, knowing, or having reason to believe, that that is not the case.[34] The Courts are likely to hold

---

[23] *Ibid.* s.43(3).
[24] *Ibid.* s.2(6).
[25] *Ibid.* s.49(1).
[26] *Ibid.* s.43(7).
[27] *Ibid.* s.43(6).
[28] *Ibid.* s.43(4), derived from s.7 of the Fine Arts Copyright Act 1862 (25 & 26 Vict. c.68).
[29] *Ibid.* s.43(5).
[30] *Ibid.* s.43(8).
[31] C.D.P.A. 1988 s.84(1).
[32] *Ibid.* s.89(2).
[33] *Ibid.* s.84(8).
[34] *Ibid.* s.84(6).

that the provisions only apply to the case of a material alteration and that an alteration is material if it might affect adversely the honour or reputation of the artist.[35] The addition of colours to an uncoloured artistic work or a change in the colours of a coloured work would probably amount to an alteration within the meaning of the provisions.[36]

22–54 The right is also infringed by any false statement as to the authorship of a work of joint authorship or by the false attribution of joint authorship in relation to a work of sole authorship.[37] Such a false attribution infringes the right of every person to whom authorship of any description is, whether rightly or wrongly, attributed.

C. *Infringing acts*

22–55 Rights in relation to false attribution are infringed by a person who commits the following acts:

(1) *Publication*

This occurs if a person issues to the public copies of a literary, dramatic, musical or artistic work or a film, in or on which there is a false attribution.[38]

(2) *Public exhibition*

This occurs when a person exhibits in public an artistic work, or a copy of an artistic work, in or on which there is a false attribution.[39]

(3) *Public performance*

This occurs if a person in the case of a literary, dramatic or musical work, performs the work in public, broadcasts it or includes it in a cable programme service as being the work of a person or, in the case of a film, shows it in public, broadcasts it or includes it in a cable programme service as being directed by a person. Infringement only occurs, however, if that person knows or has reason to believe that the attribution is false.[40]

(4) *Associated material*

The right is infringed by the issue to the public or by the public display of material containing a false attribution in connection with any of the acts mentioned above.[41]

---

[35] *Carlton Illustrators* v. *Coleman & Co. Ltd.* [1911] 1 K.B. 771 at 780.
[36] See n.35, *ante.*
[37] *Ibid.* s.88(4).
[38] *ibid.* s.84(2)(*a*).
[39] *Ibid.* s.84(2)(*b*).
[40] *Ibid.* s.84(3)(*a*)(*b*).
[41] *Ibid.* s.84(4).

(5) *Indirect infringement*

The right is infringed by a person who, in the course of a business, possesses or deals with a copy of a literary, dramatic, musical or artistic work or a film in or on which there is a false attribution or, in the case of an artistic work, possesses or deals with the work itself when there is a false attribution in or on it. Liability is dependent on that person knowing or having reason to believe that there is such an attribution and that it is false.[42] The references to "dealing" are to selling or letting for hire, offering or exposing for sale or hire, exhibiting in public, or distributing.[43]

D. *Other causes of action*

In addition to a statutory claim for false attribution of authorship, an **22–56** author may, on the same facts, be entitled to maintain a claim for common law passing off,[44] for libel[45] and for breach of contract.

5. Right to Privacy of Certain Photographs and Films

A. *General*

There is no general right of privacy in English law. The provisions of the **22–57** 1988 Act contain piecemeal provisions in respect of photographs and films.

A person who, for private and domestic purposes, commissions the taking of a photograph or the making of a film has, where copyright subsists in the resulting work, certain rights to privacy, as well as possibly to copyright, in such works. In general, such a person has the right[46] not to have:
(1) copies of the work issued to the public;
(2) the work exhibited or shown in public; or
(3) the work broadcast or included in a cable programme service.
Those rights are infringed by a person who does, or authorises the doing of, any of those acts.

A photograph means a recording of light or other radiation on any medium on which an image is produced or from which an image may by any means be produced, and which is not part of a film.[47] A film means a recording on any medium from which a moving image may by any means be produced.[48]

---

[42] *Ibid.* s.84(3).

[43] *Ibid.* s.84(7).

[44] *Lord Byron* v. *Johnston* (1816) 2 Mer. 29; *Sim* v. *H.J. Heinz Co. Ltd.* [1959] 1 W.L.R. 313.: See Copinger (12th Ed) para. 1332 n.45 for cases on moral right in English cases on law. See § 22–4, *ante.*

[45] *Tolley* v. *J.S. Fry & Son Ltd.* [1930] 1 K.B. 467; *Moore* v. *News of the World Ltd.* [1972] 1 Q.B. 441.

[46] C.D.P.A. 1988 s.85(1).

[47] *Ibid.* s.4(2). See § 2–21, *ante.*

[48] *Ibid.* s.5(1). See § 2–30, *ante.*

B. *Exceptions*

22–58   The right is not infringed by an act which, by virtue of various provisions, would not infringe copyright in the work. The provisions are those which relate to the incidental inclusion of the work in an artistic work, film, broadcast or cable programme[49]; parliamentary and judicial proceedings[50]; Royal Commissions and statutory inquiries[51]; acts done under statutory authority[52]; and anonymous or pseudonymous works and acts permitted on assumptions as to the expiry of copyright or death of the author.[53]

C. *Joint commissions*

22–59   In the case of a work made in pursuance of a joint commission, the right is that of each person who commissions the making of the work.[54] Thus, the right of each is satisfied if he consents to the act in question[55] and a waiver by one of them under section 87 of the 1988 Act does not affect the rights of the others.[56]

D. *Substantial part*

22–60   The right applies in relation to the whole or any substantial part of the work.[57]

6. Duration of Moral Rights

22–61   The right to be identified as author or director, the right to object to derogatory treatment of a work and the right to privacy in certain photographs and films continue to subsist so long as copyright subsists in the work.[58]

22–62   The right of a person not to have works falsely attributed to him endures for a different period. It continues to subsist until 20 years after a person's death.[59] Any infringement of the right occurring after the person's death is actionable by his personal representatives.[60]

---

[49] *Ibid.* s.85(2)(*a*) s.31. See § 10–16 *et seq., ante.*
[50] *Ibid.* s.85(2)(*b*) s.45. See § 10–48 *et seq., ante.*
[51] *Ibid.* s.85(2)(*c*) s.46. See § 10–50 *et seq., ante.*
[52] *Ibid.* s.85(2)(*d*) s.50. See § 10–58, *ante.*
[53] *Ibid.* s.85(2)(*e*) s.57. See § 10–69, *ante.*
[54] *Ibid.* s.88(6).
[55] *Ibid.* s.88(6)(*a*).
[56] *Ibid.* s.88(6)(*b*); See § 22–71 *et seq, post.*
[57] *Ibid.* s.89(1). See § 8–20 *et seq., ante.*
[58] *Ibid.* s.86(1). See Ch. 6, *ante.*
[59] *Ibid.* s.86(2).
[60] *Ibid.* s.95(5).

7. Transmission of Moral Rights

A. *General*

Moral rights are not assignable.[61] They are personal, not proprietary, rights.   **22–63**

However, special provision is made for the transmission on death of the right to be identified as author or director, the right to object to derogatory treatment of the work and the right to privacy of photographs and films.[62]   **22–64**

On the death of a person entitled to any of those rights the right passes to such persons as he may by testamentary disposition specifically direct.[63] If there is no specific testamentary disposition of the right, but the copyright in the work in question forms part of that person's estate, then the right passes to the person to whom the copyright passes.[64] If and to the extent that the right does not pass as aforesaid, it is exercisable by that person's personal representative.[65]

B. *Split copyright*

Special provision is made for cases where a split in the copyright occurs.   **22–65**
Where copyright forming part of a person's estate passes in part to one person and in part to another, any right which passes with the copyright by virtue of section 95(1) of the 1988 Act is correspondingly divided.[66] This will occur, for example, where a bequest is limited so as to apply to one or more, but not all of the things the copyright owner has the exclusive right to do or authorise, or to part, but not the whole, of the period for which the copyright is to subsist.[67]

Where by virtue of section 95(1)(*a*) or (*b*) of the 1988 Act a right becomes   **22–66**
exercisable by more than one person, it may, in the case of the right to be identified, be asserted by any of them. In the case of the right to object to derogatory treatment or the privacy right, the right is exercisable by each of them and is satisfied in relation to any of them if he consents to the treatment or act in question. Any waiver of the right in accordance with section 87 of the 1988 Act by one of them does not affect the rights of the others.[68]

A consent or waiver previously given or made binds any person to whom   **22–67**
the right passes by virtue of section 95(1) of the 1988 Act.[69]

---

[61] *Ibid.* s.94. *cf.* copyright assignments in Ch. 5, *ante.*
[62] *Ibid.* s.95.
[63] *Ibid.* s.95(1)(*a*).
[64] *Ibid.* s.95(1)(*b*).
[65] *Ibid.* s.95(1)(*c*).
[66] *Ibid.* s.95(2).
[67] *Ibid.* s.95(2)(*a*), (*b*).
[68] *Ibid.* s.95(3); See § 22–71 *et seq., post.*
[69] *Ibid.* s.95(4). See § 22–70 *et seq, post.*

C. *Damages*

22–68 Any damages recovered by personal representatives by virtue of these provisions in respect of an infringement occurring after a person's death devolve as part of his estate as if the right of action had subsisted and been vested in that person immediately before his death.[70]

8. Remedies for Infringement of Moral Rights

22–69 An infringement of a moral right is actionable as a breach of statutory duty owed to the person entitled to the right.[71] An author would, in an appropriate case, be entitled to recover general and special damages and an injunction to restrain threatened future breaches of duty.

In proceedings for infringement of the right to object to derogatory treatment of a work the Court may, if it thinks it is an adequate remedy in the circumstances, grant an injunction on terms prohibiting the doing of any act unless a disclaimer is made, in such terms and in such manner as may be approved by the Court, dissociating the author or director from the treatment of the work.[72]

9. Supplementary Provisions

A. *Consent and waiver of rights*

22–70 **Consent.** It is not an infringement of any moral right to do any act to which the person entitled to the right has consented.[73] Consent may be given orally or in writing, formally or informally and it may be express or implied from words or conduct.

22–71 **Waiver.** Any of the rights may also be waived by an instrument in writing signed by the person giving up the right.[74] A waiver by one joint author does not affect the rights of the other joint authors.[75]

22–72 A waiver may relate to a specific work, to works of a specified description or to works generally, and may relate to existing or future works.[76] A waiver may also be conditional or unconditional and may be expressed to be subject to revocation.[77]

22–73 If a waiver is made in favour of the owner or prospective owner of the copyright in the work or works to which it relates, the waiver is presumed to extend to his licensees and successors in title, unless a contrary intention is expressed.[78]

---

[70] *Ibid.* s.95(6).
[71] *Ibid.* s.103(1). See Ch.11 on remedies generally. For forms of Statement of Claims see §§ G–10, G–11, *post.*
[72] *Ibid.* s.103(2). For definition of a "sufficient disclaimer" see *ibid* s.178. See § 22–49, *ante.*
[73] *Ibid.* s.87(1).
[74] *Ibid.* s.87(2); for a precedent for waiver of moral rights, see § G–6, *post.*
[75] *Ibid.* s.88(3).
[76] *Ibid.* s.87(3)(*a*).
[77] *Ibid.* s.87(3)(*b*).
[78] *Ibid.* s.87(3).

The provisions as to formal waiver by instrument in writing do not **22–74** exclude the operation of the general law of contract or estoppel in relation to an informal waiver or other transaction in relation to the right to be identified,[79] the right to object to derogatory treatment and the privacy right.[80]

B. *Joint directors*

The various provisions applicable in relation to joint authorship of a work **22–75** apply in relation to a film which was, or is alleged to have been, jointly directed.[81] A film is "jointly directed" if it is made by the collaboration of two or more directors and the contribution of each director is not distinct from that of the other director or directors.[82]

10. Transitional Provisions

A. *Pre-1988 Acts*

No act done before the commencement of the 1988 Act is actionable by **22–76** virtue of any provisions in Chapter IV of Part I thereof.[83] Section 43 of the 1956 Act continues to apply in relation to acts of false attribution of authorship done before commencement.[84]

B. *Existing works*

As to the right to be identified and the right to object to derogatory treat- **22–77** ment, they do not apply in relation to a literary, dramatic, musical or artistic work the author of which died before the commencement of the 1988 Act or in relation to a film made before the commencement of that Act.[85]

The rights in relation to an existing literary, dramatic, musical or artis- **22–78** tic work do not apply, where the copyright first vested in the author, to anything which by virtue of an assignment of copyright made or licence granted before commencement may be done without infringing copyright.[86] In cases where copyright first vested in a person other than the author, the rights in relation to existing works do not apply to anything done by or with the licence of the copyright owner.[87]

---

[79] *Ibid.* s.87(4). As to estoppel in relation to copyright see *British Leyland Motor Corpn.* v. *Armstrong Patents Co. Ltd.* [1986] A.C. 577. See § 8–159 *et seq., ante.*
[80] *Ibid.* s.87(4).
[81] *Ibid.* s.88(5). Works of joint authorship are defined in *ibid* s.10(1). See Ch.7, *ante.*
[82] See n. 81, *ante.*
[83] *Ibid.* Sched. 1, para. 22(1).
[84] *Ibid.* Sched. 1, para. 22(2).
[85] *Ibid.* Sched. 1, para. 23(1), (2).
[86] *Ibid.* Sched. 1, para. 23(3)(*a*).
[87] *Ibid.* Sched. 1, para. 23(3)(*b*).

22–79   The rights do not apply to anything done in relation to a record made in pursuance of section 8 of the 1956 Act,[88] which provided for a statutory recording licence.

22–80   The right to privacy of certain photographs and films does not apply to photographs taken or films made before the commencement of the 1988 Act.[89]

---

[88] *Ibid.* Sched. 1, para. 23(4).
[89] *Ibid.* Sched. 1, para. 24.

CHAPTER 23

RELATED FORMS OF PROTECTION—4

PERFORMERS' RIGHTS AND RECORDING RIGHTS

Contents   *Para.*

1. Introduction

A. *Historical*

Neither the 1911 Act nor the 1956 Act created any copyright in respect of   **23–1**
live performances. The extension of copyright or the grant of a similar
right in respect of performances had been considered, but was not thought
to be justified on the grounds that such a right would add to the number of
licences needed for the exploitation of certain copyright works.[1]

Performers had, however, enjoyed some form of statutory protection as   **23–2**
a result of the provisions of the Dramatic and Musical Performers' Protection Act 1925 which was modified by the 1956 Act and later repealed and
re-enacted by the Dramatic and Musical Performers' Protection Act 1958.
That Act was in turn amended by the Performers' Protection Acts 1963
and 1972.

All those Acts are now repealed in their entirety by the 1988 Act.[2]   **23–3**
Rights in performances are conferred by Part II of that Act. Those rights
apply even in relation to performances taking place before the commencement of Part II but no act done before commencement is to be regarded as
infringing those rights nor is any act done after commencement in pursuance of arrangements which were made before commencement.[3]

B. *Summary of law pre-1988 Act — Performers' Protection Acts 1958 to 1972*

Although these Acts have been repealed it is helpful to an understanding   **23–4**
of the new law to summarise the position before the commencement of the
1988 Act.

(i) Criminal offences

The main method adopted for the protection of performances was the cre-   **23–5**
ation of criminal offences, punishable summarily or on indictment, for
knowingly making and exploiting records, films and broadcasts of perfor-

---

[1] Report of the Committee on the Law of Copyright, Cmd. 8662 (1952) para. 172. See 1977
   Copyright Committee, Cmnd. 6732 para. 406 *et seq.*
[2] C.D.P.A. 1988, s.303(2); Sched. 8; See § A–624 *et seq.* for the text of the repealed Acts.
[3] *Ibid.* s.180(3).

mances which had been made without the written consent of the performers. The 1988 Act also creates criminal liability for making, dealing with and using "illicit recordings" of performances.[4]

(ii) Private rights

23–6 Although the 1958 to 1972 Acts provided on their face only for penalties in criminal proceedings against a person found guilty of committing a statutory offence, it was held that those Acts, on their true construction, disclosed an intention to create private rights of action for the benefit of performers. This conclusion was reached because it was apparent from the provisions that the obligations and prohibitions were imposed for the benefit or protection of performers as a particular class of individuals. A performer was, therefore, entitled to bring a civil action for breach of statutory duty claiming an injunction and damages.[5]

(iii) Duration of the private right

23–7 It was also held that the private rights thereby conferred did not cease on the death of the performer. The right to consent to the recording and exploitation of a performance vested in the performer's personal representatives when the performer died. The Acts were not limited to the protection of the reputation and future employment prospects of a performer. They were also passed for the protection of the performer's economic interests by ensuring that he was paid for the use of his performances.[5]

23–8   The consequence of this construction of the Acts was that a performer enjoyed more extensive rights in respect of his performances than an author in respect of his works. The performer enjoyed a quasi-proprietary right akin to copyright, but without any of the safeguards and provisions in the 1956 Act which limited the duration of the right and provided for compulsory licensing and other restrictions on enforcement.

(iv) Persons having exclusive recording rights

23–9 The protection of the Acts was, however, confined to performers. It did not extend to recording companies or other persons who had obtained exclusive recording contracts in respect of the artists' performances. They had no right of action under those Acts because they did not fall within the class for whose benefit the Acts were passed.[6] They had no cause of action at common law, even though the making and distribution of unauthorised "bootleg" records inflicted serious economic loss on the record companies. They could not claim relief for interference with contractual relations of

---

[4] *Ibid.* s.198. See § 19–22 *et seq., ante.*

[5] *Rickless* v. *United Artists Corpn.* [1988] Q.B. 40, applying *Lonrho Ltd.* v. *Shell Petroleum Ltd.* (No. 2) [1982] A.C. 173 at 185 *Grower* v. *B.B.C.* [1990] F.S.R. 595. *cf. Musical Performers' Protection Association Ltd.* v. *British International Pictures Ltd.* [1930] 46 T.L.R. 485; *Apple Corps Ltd.* v. *Lingasong Ltd.* [1977] F.S.R. 345.

[6] *R.C.A. Corporation* v. *Pollard* [1983] Ch. 135.

the performers, because the "bootlegger" who made and sold the recording of a live performance of the artist did not interfere with the performance or induce the artist to act in breach of any of his contractual obligations to the record companies.[7]

This position has now been remedied by the 1988 Act which creates recording rights in performances.[8]

C. *The international perspective*

On October 26, 1961, the International Convention for the Protection of **23–10** Performers, Producers of Phonograms and Broadcasting Organisations was entered into at Rome.[8a] By Article 7(1) of the Rome Convention, as it is known, the United Kingdom, as one of the parties, undertook to protect performers' rights. The performer himself was to have rights which would make it possible for him to prevent unauthorised reproduction of his performances. The 1963 Performers' Protection Act was passed to enable effect to be given to that Convention. Those obligations are now. further implemented in the 1988 Act.

2. Comparison between Copyright and Performers' Rights

The nature of the new performers' rights can be better understood by **23–11** comparing them with the long-established rights of copyright.

A. *Differences*

(i) Nature of right

Infringement of copyright is treated as an infringment of a property right **23–12** actionable by the copyright owner.[9] An infringement of performers' rights and of the rights of a person having recording rights is actionable by the person entitled to the right as a breach of statutory duty.[10]

(ii) Assignment and transmission

Copyright is treated as personal or moveable property transmissible by **23–13** assignment, by testamentary disposition or by operation of law.[11] The rights conferred by Part II of the 1988 Act (Part II rights) are not assignable.[12] Performers' rights are transmissible only to a limited extent[13] and the rights of a person having recording rights are not transmissible at all.[14]

---

[7] *R.C.A. Corporation* v. *Pollard* [1983] Ch.135. See § 23–42 *et seq., post.*
[8] See § 23–42 *et seq., post.*
[8a] See § C–121 *et seq., post.*
[9] C.D.P.A. 1988, s.96(1), (2). See § 11–1, *ante.*
[10] *Ibid.* s.194.
[11] *Ibid.* s.90(1). See Ch. 5, *ante.*
[12] *Ibid.* s.192(1).
[13] *Ibid.* s.192(2).
[14] *Ibid.* s.192(1).

(iii) Duration

23–14   The copyright in a literary, dramatic, musical or artistic work is limited to the life of the author and a period of 50 years from the end of the calendar year in which the author dies.[15] The duration of Part II rights is similar to that of copyright in sound recordings, films, broadcasts and cable programmes. The right continues to subsist in relation to a performers' rights until the end of a period of 50 years from the end of the calendar year in which the peformance takes place.[16]

(iv) The Copyright Tribunal

23–15   The jurisdiction of the Copyright Tribunal in relation to licensing is mainly concerned with copyright licensing.[17] The Tribunal only has a limited jurisdiction in the case of performers' rights[18] and no jurisdiction at all in the case of recording rights.

B. *Similarities*

23–16   In many respects, however, copyright and Part II rights are treated in similar ways.

(i) Subsistence

The conditions for subsistence of copyright and Part II rights employ the concepts of qualifying persons and qualifying countries.[19]

(ii) Infringement

23–17   Both copyright and Part II rights may be infringed by primary acts of infringement and secondary acts of infringement. The primary acts of infringement of copyright include copying the work, issuing copies to the public, performing, showing, playing in public and broadcasting the work.[20] Primary acts of infringement of Part II rights include the making of recordings and broadcasting performances live and including them live in cable programme services.[21]

23–18   Secondary infringements of copyright include importing, possessing and dealing with infringing copies.[22] Secondary infringements of Part II rights also include importing, possessing or dealing with illicit recordings.[23] In the case of secondary infringement liability depends on proof

---

[15] *Ibid.* s.12(1). See Ch. 6, *ante*.

[16] *Ibid.* s.191.

[17] *Ibid.* s.116–152. See § 15–50 *et seq.*, *ante*.

[18] *Ibid.* s.190; See § 23–57 *et seq.*, *post*.

[19] *Ibid.* ss.153–156; ss.181, 185(2) and s.206. See Ch. 3, *ante*.

[20] *Ibid.* s.16. See § 8–7 *et seq.*, *ante*.

[21] *Ibid.* ss.182, 183.

[22] *Ibid.* ss.22, 23. See § 9–3 *et seq.*, *ante*.

[23] *Ibid.* ss.184, 188.

that the alleged infringer knew or had reason to believe the illicit nature of the relevant article.

(iii) Defences

In many cases the acts permitted in relation to copyright works[24] are also permitted in relation to Part II rights.[25] **23–19**

(iv) Remedies

In both cases civil remedies are available, including special provisions for the delivery up, disposal and seizure of infringing copies and illicit recordings.[26] Criminal penalties are also imposed for offences involving making and dealing with infringing articles and illicit recordings.[27] **23–20**

3. Conditions for Subsistence

A. *General*

Part II of the 1988 Act (Part II) does three things. **23–21**
(1) It confers rights on a performer by requiring his consent to the exploitation of his performances.[28]
(2) It confers rights on a person having recording rights in relation to a performance, in relation to recordings made without his consent or that of the performer.[29]
(3) It creates criminal offences in relation to dealing with or using illicit recordings and certain other related acts.[30]

Part II extends to England and Wales, Scotland and Northern Ireland.[31] Other countries may be designated by Order in Council as enjoying reciprocal protection under Part II.[32] **23–22**

It should be noted that the rights conferred by Part II are independent of any copyright in, or moral rights relating to, any work performed or any film or sound recording of, or broadcast or programme including, the performance.[33] The rights are also independent of any other right or obligation arising otherwise than under Part II of the Act,[34] *e.g.* under another statutory provision or by reason of contractual provisions or as the result of a duty of confidence. **23–23**

---

[24] *Ibid.* ss.28–76. See § 10–4 *et seq., ante.*
[25] *Ibid* s.189; Sched. 2.
[26] *Ibid.* ss.99, 100, 114; ss.195, 196, 204. See Ch. 11, *ante.*
[27] *Ibid.* ss.107–110; ss.198–202. See Ch. 19, *ante.*
[28] *Ibid* ss.181–184.
[29] *Ibid* ss.185–188.
[30] *Ibid* s.198, s.202; See § 19–22 *et seq., ante.*
[31] *Ibid.* s.207.
[32] *Ibid.* s.208; See S.I. 1989 No. 1296, § D–40, *post.*
[33] *Ibid.* s.180(4)(*a*).
[34] *Ibid.* s.180(4)(*b*).

23–24   The rights conferred by Part II apply in relation to performances taking place before the commencement of Part II, but no act done before commencement, or in pursuance of arrangements made before commencement, is to be regarded as infringing those rights.[35] There are no other transitional provisions. It is probable that the rights and remedies under the Performers' Protection Acts are preserved by the operation of the Interpretation Act 1978 in respect of pre-commencement acts.

B. *Definition of performance*

23–25   There is no definition of a performer in the 1988 Act, but the meaning of that term can be gathered from the statutory definition of a performance. In Part II "performance" refers to live performances of various kinds given by one or more individuals. The relevant kinds of performance are a dramatic performance,[36] which includes dance and mime; a musical performance;[37] a reading or recitation of a literary work;[38] and a performance of a variety act or any similar presentation.[39] Part II applies to any such performance which is, or so far as it is, a live performance given by one or more individuals.[40] This definition thus excludes from protection under Part II the use of recorded material or material on film which might form part of, for example, a dramatic or musical presentation. If the performance is given by more than one individual each performer is entitled to the rights conferred. Although the performance may be given by more than one individual there is no express concept of a joint performance. In most, if not all cases, the performance of each performer is distinct from the performance of the other or others.[41] It might be argued, however, that as rights are conferred on performers in respect of a performance, if one qualifying individual takes part or if it takes place in a qualifying country, rights may be enjoyed jointly with him by other performers taking part.

C. *Definition of recording*

23–26   The definition of "recording" is important for the purposes of the persons having recording rights under Part II. Recording, in relation to a performance, means a film or sound recording of three kinds: firstly, one made directly from the live performance;[42] secondly, one made from a broadcast of, or cable programme including, the performance;[43] and, thirdly, one made, directly or indirectly, from another recording of the performance.[44]

---

[35] *Ibid.* s.180(3).
[36] *Ibid.* s.180(2)(*a*); see *ibid.* s.3(1).
[37] *Ibid.* s.180(2)(*b*); see *ibid.* s.3(1); s.211(1).
[38] *Ibid.* s.180(2)(*c*).
[39] *Ibid.* s.180(2)(*d*).
[40] *Ibid.* s.180(2).
[41] *cf.* s.10(1). See Ch. 7, *ante.*
[42] *Ibid* s.180(2)(*a*).
[43] *Ibid.* s.180(2)(*b*).
[44] *Ibid.* s.180(2)(*c*).

4. Performers' Rights

A. *Qualifying performances of performers*

(i) General

Performers' rights subsist only in relation to a qualifying performance. A **23–27**
performance is a qualifying performance for the purposes of Part II if it is
either,
(1) given by a qualifying individual; or
(2) takes place in a qualifying country.[45]

A qualifying individual means a citizen or subject of, or an individual **23–28**
resident in, a qualifying country.[46] A qualifying country means the United
Kingdom[47] or another member of the European Economic Community[48]
or, to the extent that any order under section 208 of the 1988 Act so provides, a country designated under that section as enjoying reciprocal protection.[49]

The reference in the definition of a qualifying individual to a person's **23–29**
being a citizen or subject of a qualifying country is to be construed, in
relation to the United Kingdom, as a reference to his being a British citizen[50] and, in relation to a colony of the United Kingdom, as a reference
to his being a British Dependant Territories' citizen by connection with
that colony.[51]

(ii) Reciprocal protection

Her Majesty may, by Order in Council, designate as enjoying reciprocal **23–30**
protection under Part II a Convention Country[52] or a country as to which
Her Majesty is satisfied that provision has been made or will be made
under the law giving adequate protection for British performances.[53] A
statutory instrument containing an Order in Council under section 208 of
the 1988 Act is subject to annulment in pursuance of a resolution of either
House of Parliament.[54]

(iii) Convention country

This expression means a country which is a party to a Convention relating **23–31**
to performers rights to which the United Kingdom is also a party.[55]

---

[45] *Ibid.* s.181. See Ch. 3, *ante.*
[46] *Ibid.* s.206(1).
[47] *Ibid.* s.206(1)(*a*).
[48] *Ibid.* s.206(1)(*b*).
[49] *Ibid.* s.206(1)(*c*).
[50] *Ibid.* s.206(2)(*a*).
[51] *Ibid.* s.206(2)(*b*).
[52] *Ibid.* s.208(1)(*a*); see S.I. 1989 No. 1296, § D–40, *post.*
[53] *Ibid.* s.208(1)(*b*).
[54] *Ibid.* s.208(6).
[55] *Ibid.* s.208(2).

(iv) British performances

23–32   A British performance means a performance given by an individual who is a British citizen or a resident in the United Kingdom, or taking place in the United Kingdom.[56]

23–33   The power conferred in relation to non-convention countries is exercisable in relation to any of the Channel Islands, the Isle of Man or any colony of the United Kingdom as in relation to a foreign country.[57] If the law of a non-convention country contains adequate protection only for certain descriptions of performance, an Order designating that country must contain provision limiting to a corresponding extent the protection afforded by Part II in relation to performances connected with that country.[58]

(v) Territorial waters and the continental shelf

23–34   For the purposes of Part II the territorial waters of the United Kingdom are treated as part of the United Kingdom.[59] Part II applies to things done in the United Kingdom sector of the continental shelf (being an area designated by order under section 7(1) of the Continental Shelf Act 1964),[60] on a structure or vessel which is present there for purposes directly connected with the exploration of the sea bed or subsoil or the exploitation of their national resources as it applies to things done in the United Kingdom.[61]

(vi) Ships, aircraft and hovercraft

23–35   Part II also applies to things done on a British ship, aircraft or hovercraft as it applies to things done in the United Kingdom.[62] A "British ship" means a ship which is a British ship for the purposes of the Merchant Shipping Acts (see section 2 of the Merchant Shipping Act 1988) otherwise than by virtue of registration in a country outside the United Kingdom.[63] "British aircraft" and "British hovercraft" mean an aircraft or hovercraft registered in the United Kingdom.

B. *Infringement of performers' rights*

23–36   Performers' rights in a qualifying performance are infringed by various acts done by a person without the consent of the performer. Those acts are the following:

---

[56] *Ibid.* s.208(3).
[57] *Ibid.* s.208(5).
[58] *Ibid.* s.208(4).
[59] *Ibid.* s.209(1).
[60] *Ibid.* s.209(3).
[61] *Ibid.* s.209(2).
[62] *Ibid.* s.210(1).
[63] *Ibid.* s.210(2).

(i) Recording

It is an infringement of the performers' rights for a person to make, other- **23–37**
wise than for his private and domestic use, a recording of the whole or any
substantial part of a qualifying performance.[64]

(ii) Live transmission

It is also an infringement to broadcast live or include live in a cable pro- **23–38**
gramme service, the whole or any substantial part of a qualifying performance.[65]

(iii) Use of recording made without consent

An infringement is committed by a person who shows or plays in public or **23–39**
broadcasts or includes in a cable programme service the whole or any substantial part of a qualifying performance by means of a recording which
was made without the consent of the performer.[66] It must also be shown
that the person knew or had reason to believe that the recording was made
without the performer's consent.[67]

(iv) Dealing with illicit recordings

An infringement is committed by a person who, without the performer's **23–40**
consent, imports into the United Kingdom, otherwise than for his private
and domestic use, or in the course of a business possesses, sells, lets for
hire, offers or exposes for sale or hire, or distributes a recording of a qualifying performance which is an illicit recording. It must also be shown that
that person knew or had reason to believe that it was an illicit recording.[68]

For the purposes of performers' rights a recording of the whole or any **23–41**
substantial part of a performance of his is an illicit recording if it is made,
otherwise than for private purposes, without his consent.[69] It is immaterial where the recording was made.[70] Illicit recordings also include certain recordings falling to be treated as illicit recordings by virtue of special
provisions. *viz.*,[71] recordings made for purposes of instruction or examination[72]; recordings made by educational establishments for educational
purposes[73]; recordings of performances in electronic form retained on
transfer of the principal recording[74]; and recordings made for the purposes
of broadcast or cable programme.[75]

---

[64] *Ibid.* s.182(1)(*a*).
[65] *Ibid.* s.182(1)(*b*).
[66] *Ibid.* s.183(*a*)(*b*).
[67] *Ibid.* s.183.
[68] *Ibid.* s.184(1).
[69] *Ibid.* s.197(2).
[70] *Ibid.* s.197(6).
[71] *Ibid.* s.197(5).
[72] *Ibid.* Sched. 2, para. 4(3). See § 10–21, *ante.*
[73] *Ibid.* Sched. 2, para. 6(2). See § 10–25, *et seq., ante.*
[74] *Ibid.* Sched. 2, para. 12(2). See § 10–65 *et seq., ante.*
[75] *Ibid.* Sched. 2, para. 16(3). See § 10–112 *et seq., ante.*

5. Recording Rights

A. *Persons entitled to recording rights*

(i) General

23–42 The 1988 Act also creates recording rights in relation to a performance. No right of this kind existed before the 1988 Act. The right is conferred on a person who is a party to and has the benefit of an exclusive recording contract to which the performance is subject[76] or to whom the benefit of the contract has been assigned[77] and who is a qualifying person. Such a person is referred to as a "person having recording rights." That person may be either an individual or a corporate entity.

23–43 If a performance is subject to an exclusive recording contract, but the person who is a party to or has the benefit of it is not a qualifying person, then the person having the recording rights is any person who is licensed by such a person to make recordings of the performance with a view to their commercial exploitation[78] or any person to whom the benefit of such a licence has been assigned[79] and who is a qualifying person.

(ii) Exclusive recording contract

23–44 An "exclusive recording contract" is defined as having certain characteristics[80]:
  (1) It must be a contract;
  (2) It must be between a performer and another person;
  (3) It must entitle that other person to make recordings of one or more of the performer's performances with a view to their commercial exploitation. The performances do not have to be qualifying performances within the meaning of the provisions.
  (4) It must so entitle him to the exclusion of all other persons, including the performer.

  The expression "with a view to commercial exploitation" means with a view to the recordings being sold or let for hire, or shown or played in public.[81]

(iii) Qualifying person

23–45 A "qualifying person" means a qualifying individual or a body corporate or other body having legal personality which is formed under the law of part of the United Kingdom or another qualifying country,[82] and has in

---

[76] *Ibid.* s.185(2)(*a*).
[77] *Ibid.* s.185(2)(*b*).
[78] *Ibid.* s.185(3)(*a*).
[79] *Ibid.* s.185(3)(*b*).
[80] *Ibid.* s.185(1).
[81] *Ibid.* s.185(4).
[82] *Ibid* s.206(1)(*a*). See § 23–28 *ante.* See also Ch. 3, *ante.*

any qualifying country a place of business at which substantial business activity is carried on.[83] In determining whether substantial business activity is carried on at a place of business in any country, no account is to be taken of dealings in goods which are at all material times outside that country.[84]

B. *Infringement of recording rights*

The rights of the persons having recording rights in relation to a perfor- **23–46** mance may be infringed by various acts done without consent. The provisions as to the relevant consent vary according to the different acts.

(i) Recording

A person infringes the rights of the person having recording rights if, with- **23–47** out the consent of the person having such rights or that of the performer, he makes a recording of the whole or any substantial part of the performance, otherwise than for his private and domestic use.[85] The performance does not have to be a qualifying performance.

(ii) Use of recording made without consent

The recording rights are also infringed by a person who, without the con- **23–48** sent of the person having the rights, or, in the case of a qualifying performance, that of the performer, shows or plays in public the whole or any substantial part of the performance, or broadcasts or includes in a cable programme service the whole or any substantial part of the performance, by means of a recording which was, and which the person knows or has reason to believe was, made without the appropriate consent.[86] The "appropriate consent" is that of the performer or the person who, at the time the consent was given, had recording rights in relation to the performance.[87] If there was more than one such person the consent of all of them is necessary.

(iii) Dealing with illicit recordings

The recording rights are also infringed by a person who, without the con- **23–49** sent of the person having the right or, in the case of a qualifying performance, that of the performer, imports into the United Kingdom, otherwise than for his private and domestic use, or in the course of business possesses, sells or lets for hire, offers or exposes for sale or hire, or distributes a recording of the performance which is, and which that person knows or has reason to belive is, an illicit recording.[88] For the purposes of

---

[83] C.D.P.A. 1988, s.206(1)(*b*).
[84] *Ibid.* s.206(3).
[85] *Ibid.* s.186(1).
[86] *Ibid.* s.187(1).
[87] *Ibid.* s.187(2).
[88] *Ibid.* s.188(1).

the rights of a person having recording rights, a recording of the whole or any substantial part of a performance subject to the exclusive recording contract is an "illicit recording" if it is made, otherwise than for private purposes, without his consent or that of the performer.[89]

6. Duration of Rights

23–50 The performers' rights and the recording rights continue to subsist in relation to a performance until the end of the period of 50 years from the end of the calendar year in which the performance takes place.[90]

7. Transmission of Rights

23–51 Neither performers' rights nor recording rights are assignable. Further, recording rights are not transmissible.[91]

23–52 Performers' rights are, however, transmissible to a limited extent in accordance with the statutory provisions. On the death of a person entitled to performers' rights, the rights pass to such person as he may by testamentary disposition specifically direct.[92] If, and to the extent that there is no such direction, the rights are exercisable by the person's personal representatives.[93] Thus the person having the performers' rights includes the persons for the time being entitled to exercise those rights.[94] If, by virtue of a testamentary disposition, a right becomes exercisable by more than one person, it is exercisable by each of them independently of the other or others.[95]

These provisions do not affect the rights conferred on a person to whom the benefit of a contract or licence is assigned.[96]

8. Consent

A. *General*

23–53 In general, the rights are not infringed if an act is done with the appropriate consent. Consent for the purposes of Part II may be given in relation to a specific performance, a specified description of performances or performances generally. Consent may relate to past or future performances.[96a]

---

[89] *Ibid.* s.197(3).
[90] *Ibid.* s.191.
[91] *Ibid.* s.192(1) c.f. copyright. See Ch. 5, *ante.*
[92] *Ibid.* s.192(2)(*a*).
[93] *Ibid.* s.192(2)(*b*).
[94] *Ibid.* s.192(2).
[95] *Ibid.* s.192(3).
[96] *Ibid* s.192(4); s.185(2)(*b*) and 3(*b*).
[96a] *Ibid.* s.193(1).

A person having recording rights in a performance is bound by any con- **23–54**
sent given by a person through whom he derives his rights under the
exclusive recording agreement or licence in question, in the same way as if
the consent had been given by him.[97]

Where a performers' right or recording right passes to another person, **23–55**
any consent binding on the person previously entitled binds the person to
whom the right passes in the same way as if the consent had been given by
him.[98]

Consent is not required to be in writing or to be express. It may be oral **23–56**
or inferred from all the circumstances.

B. *Power of the Copyright Tribunal*

(i) Jurisdiction

In certain cases the Copyright Tribunal may give consent on behalf of a **23–57**
performer.[99] The Tribunal does not, however, have power to give consent
on behalf of a person having recording rights.

Application for consent is made to a Tribunal by a person wishing to **23–58**
make a record from a previous recording of a performance.[1] The Tribunal
may give consent in a case where the identity or whereabouts of the performer cannot be ascertained by reasonable inquiry[2] or where a performer
unreasonably withholds his consent.[3]

(ii) Relevant factors

There are certain factors which the Tribunal must take into account in **23–59**
any case: firstly, whether the original recording was made with the performer's consent and is lawfully in the possession or control of the person
proposing to make the further recording; secondly, whether the making of
the further recording is consistent with the obligations of the parties to the
arrangements under which, or is otherwise consistent with the purposes
for which, the original recording was made.[4]

Although the 1988 Act does not expressly so provide, it is submitted **23–60**
that the Tribunal may take into account any other factors relevant to the
issue as to whether consent should be given.

---

[97] *Ibid.* s.193(2).
[98] *Ibid.* s.193(3) *et seq.*
[99] *Ibid.* s.190. As to Copyright Tribunal generally see § 15–55 *et seq.* especially § 15–93
[1] *Ibid.* s.190(1).
[2] *Ibid.* s.190(1)(a).
[3] *Ibid.* s.190(1)(b).
[4] *Ibid.* s.190(5).

(iii) Consent on conditions

23–61 Consent may be given by the Tribunal subject to any conditions specified in the Tribunal's order.[5] Such consent by the Tribunal has effect as consent of the performer for the purposes of Part II relating to performers' rights and as sufficient consent in relation to qualifying performances for the purposes of criminal liability.[6]

23–62 Where the Tribunal gives consent it must, in default of agreement between the applicant and the performer, make such order as it thinks fit as to the payment to be made to the performer in consideration of consent being given.[7]

(i) Restrictions on power

23–63 In certain cases the Tribunal must not give consent unless certain matters have been satisfied. Before it gives consent in a case where it is claimed that the identity or whereabouts of a performer cannot be ascertained by reasonable inquiry, notices must have been served or published as required by the general procedural rules[8] or as the Tribunal may in any particular case direct.[9] The Tribunal must not give consent in the case above where a performer is claimed to be unreasonably withholding his consent, unless satisfied that the performer's reasons for withholding consent do not include the protection of any legitimate interest of his. It is for the performer to show what his reasons are for withholding consent and, in default of evidence as to his reasons, the Tribunal may draw such inferences as it thinks fit.[10]

9. Permitted Acts

A. *General*

23–64 Various acts may be done notwithstanding the rights conferred by Part II.[11] Those acts correspond broadly to those acts which are permitted notwithstanding copyright.[12]

23–65 Permitted acts are dealt with in Schedule 2 to the 1988 Act. The provisions of the Schedule specify acts which may be done in relation to a performance or a recording. They relate only to the question of infringement of the rights conferred by Part II. They do not affect any right or obligation restricting the doing of any of the specified acts.[13]

---

[5] *Ibid.* s.190(2).
[6] *Ibid.* s.198(3)(a); s.190(2).
[7] *Ibid.* s.190(6).
[8] *Ibid.* s.190(3). Made under *ibid.* s.150. See S.I. 1989 No. 1129; See § B–49, *post*, § B–84 *et seq.*, *post*.
[9] *Ibid.* s.190(3).
[10] *Ibid.* s.190(4).
[11] *Ibid.* s.189; Sched. 2.
[12] *Ibid.* See Chap. III of Part II. See Ch. 10, *ante*.
[13] *Ibid.* Sched. 2, para. 1(1).

No inference is to be drawn as to the scope of Part II rights from the **23–66** description of any of the permitted acts.[14] The provisions of the Schedule are to be construed independently of each other. Thus, the fact that an act does not fall within one provision does not mean that it is not covered by another provision.[15]

B. *Particular acts*

(i) Criticism, reviews and news reporting

Rights in performances are not infringed by fair dealing with a perfor- **23–67** mance or recording

(a) for the purpose of criticism or review, of that or another perfor- mance or recording, or of a work; or

(b) for the purpose of reporting current events.[16]

(ii) Incidental inclusion of performance or recording

By virtue of paragraph 3(1) of Schedule 2 the rights are not infringed by **23–68** the incidental inclusion of a performance or recording in a sound record- ing, film, broadcast, or cable programme.[17] A performance or recording, so far as it consists of music or words spoken or sung with music, is not to be regarded as incidentally included in a sound recording, broadcast or cable programme if it is deliberately included.[18] The rights are not infringed by anything done in relation to copies of, or the playing, show- ing, broadcasting or inclusion in a cable programme service of anything which was, by virtue of paragraph 3(1), not an infringement of those rights.[19]

(iii) Things done for purposes of instruction or examination

By virtue of paragraph 4(1) of Schedule 2 the rights are not infringed by **23–69** the copying of a recording of a performance in the course of instruction, or of preparation for instruction, in the making of films or film sound tracks, provided the copying is done by a person giving or receiving instruction.[20] The rights are not infringed by the copying of a recording of a perfor- mance for the purposes of setting or answering the questions in an exam- ination or by anything done for the purposes of an examination by way of communicating the questions to the candidates.[21]

---

[14] *Ibid.* Sched. 2, para. 1(2).
[15] *Ibid.* Sched. 2, para. 1(3).
[16] *Ibid.* Sched. 2, para. 2. Expressions have the same meaning as in *ibid.* s.30; see § 10–8 *et seq., ante.*
[17] *Ibid.* Sched. 2, para. 3(1). Expressions have the same meaning as in *ibid.* s.31: see § 10–16 *et seq., ante.*
[18] *Ibid.* Sched. 2, para. 3(3).
[19] *Ibid.* Sched. 2, para. 3(2).
[20] *Ibid.* Sched. 2, para. 4(1); Expressions have the same meaning as in *ibid.* s.32; see § 10–19 *et seq., ante.*
[21] *Ibid.* Sched. 2, para. 4(2).

Where a recording, which would otherwise be an illicit recording, is made in accordance with paragraph 4, but is subsequently dealt with, it is to be treated as an illicit recording for the purposes of that dealing. If that dealing infringes any right conferred by Part II it is to be treated as an illicit recording for all subsequent purposes.[22] For this purpose, "dealing with" means sold, let for hire, or offered or exposed for sale or hire.

(iv) Playing or showing sound recording, film, broadcast or cable programme at educational establishments

23–70 The playing or showing of a sound recording, film, broadcast or cable programme at an educational establishment for the purposes of instruction before an audience consisting of teachers and pupils at the establishment and other persons directly connected with the activities of the establishment is not a playing or showing of a performance in public for the purposes of infringement of the Part II rights.[23] A person is not for this purpose directly connected with the activities of the educational establishment simply because he is a parent of a pupil at the establishment.[24]

(v) Recording of broadcasts and cable programmes by educational establishments

23–71 By virtue of paragraph 6(1) of Schedule 2 a recording of a broadcast or cable programme, or a copy of such a recording, may be made by or on behalf of an educational establishment for the educational purposes of that establishment without thereby infringing any of the rights conferred by Part II in relation to any performance or recording included in it.[25] Where a recording, which would otherwise be an illicit recording, is made in accordance with paragraph 6, but is subsequently dealt with, it is to be treated as an illicit recording for the purposes of that dealing. If that dealing infringes any rights conferred by Part II it is to be treated as an illicit recording for all subsequent purposes.[26] "Dealt with" means sold or let for hire or offered or exposed for sale or hire.

(vi) Copy of work required to be made as condition of export

23–72 If an article of cultural or historical importance or interest cannot lawfully be exported from the United Kingdom unless a copy of it is made and deposited in an appropriate library or archive, it is not an infringement of any right conferred by Part II to make that copy.[27]

---

[22] *Ibid.* Sched. 2, para. 4(3).
[23] *Ibid.* Sched. 2, para. 5(1); Expressions have the same meaning as in *ibid.* s.34; see § 10–25 *et seq., ante.*
[24] *Ibid.* Sched. 2, para. 5(2).
[25] *Ibid.* Sched. 2, para. 6(1); Expressions have the same meaning as in *ibid.* s.35; See § 10–27.
[26] *Ibid.* Sched. 2, para. 6(2).
[27] *Ibid.* Sched. 2, para. 7(1); Expressions have the same meaning as in *ibid.* s.44; see § 10–47, *ante.*

(vii) Parliamentary and judicial proceedings

The rights conferred by Part II are not infringed by anything done for the **23-73**
purposes of parliamentary or judicial proceedings or for the purposes of
reporting such proceedings.[28]

(viii) Royal Commissions and statutory inquiries

The rights conferred by Part II are not infringed by anything done for the **23-74**
purposes of the proceedings of a Royal Commission or statutory inquiry or
for the purposes of reporting any such proceedings held in public.[29]

(ix) Public records

Material which is comprised in public records[30] which are open to public **23-75**
inspection in pursuance of the relevant legislation may be copied and a
copy may be supplied to any person by or with the authority of any officer
appointed under the relevant legislation, without infringing Part II
rights.[31]

(x) Acts done under statutory authority

Where the doing of a particular act is specifically authorised by an Act **23-76**
(including an enactment contained in Northern Ireland legislation),[32]
whenever passed, then, unless the Act provides otherwise, the doing of
that act does not infringe the rights conferred by Part II.[33] This provision
is not to be construed as excluding any defence of statutory authority
otherwise available under or by virtue of any enactment.[34]

(xi) Transfer of copies of works in electronic form

Special provision is made for the case where a recording of a performance **23-77**
in electronic form has been purchased on terms which, expressly or
impliedly or by virtue of any rule of law, allow the purchaser to make
further recordings in connection with his use of the recording.[35]
  If there are no express terms prohibiting the transfer of the recording by

---

[28] *Ibid.* Sched. 2, para. 8(1); Expressions have the same meaning as in *ibid.* s.45; see § 10–48
et seq., ante.

[29] *Ibid.* Sched. 2, para. 9(1); Expressions have the same meaning as in *ibid.* s.46; see § 10–50
et seq., ante.,

[30] As defined in the Public Records Act 1958, (c. 51), the Public Records (Scotland) Act
1937 and the Public Records Act (Northern Ireland) 1923.

[31] C.D.P.A. 1988 Sched. 2, para. 10(1); Expressions have the same meaning as in *ibid.* s.49;
see § 10–56 *et seq., ante.*

[32] *Ibid.* Sched. 2, para. 11(2).

[33] *Ibid.* Sched. 2, para. 11(1); Expressions have the same meaning as in *ibid.* s.50; see
§ 10–58 *et seq., ante.*

[34] *Ibid.* Sched. 2, para. 11(3).

[35] *Ibid.* Shed. 2, para. 12(1); Expressions have the same meaning as in *ibid.* s.56; see § 10–65
et seq., ante.

the purchaser, imposing obligations which continue after a transfer, prohibiting the assignment of any consent or terminating any consent on a transfer or providing for the terms on which a transferee may do the things which the purchaser was permitted to do, anything which the purchaser was allowed to do may also be done by a transferee without infringing Part II rights. But any recording made by the purchaser which is not also transferred is to be treated as an illicit recording for all purposes after the transfer.[36] The same applies where the original purchased recording is no longer usable for all purposes after the transfer and what is transferred is a further copy used in its place.[37]

These provisions also apply on a subsequent transfer, but do not apply in relation to a recording purchased before the commencement of Part II.[38]

(xii) Use of recordings of spoken words in certain cases

23–78 Where a recording of the reading or the recitation of a literary work is made for the purpose of reporting current events, or of broadcasting or including in a cable programme service the whole or part of the reading or recitation, it is not an infringement of the Part II rights to use the recording or to copy the recording and use the copy for that purpose, provided that specified conditions are met.[39] Those conditions are that[40]:

(a) the recording is a direct recording of the reading or recitation and is not taken from a previous recording or from a broadcast or cable programme; and

(b) the making of the recording was not prohibited by or on behalf of the person giving the reading or recitation; and

(c) the use made of the recording is not of a kind prohibited by or on behalf of that person before the recording was made; and

(d) the use is by or with the authority of a person who is lawfully in possession of the recording.

(xiii) Recordings of folk songs

23–79 The recording of a performance of a song may be made for the purpose of including it in an archive maintained by a designated body without infringing any Part II rights. Certain conditions must, however, be met.[41] They are that,

(a) the words are unpublished and of unknown authorship at the time the recording is made,

---

[36] *Ibid.* Sched. 2, para. 12(2).
[37] *Ibid.* Sched. 2, para. 12(3).
[38] *Ibid.* Sched. 2, para. 12(5).
[39] *Ibid.* Sched. 2, para. 13(1); Expressions have the same meaning as in *ibid.* s.58; see § 10–71 *et seq., ante.*
[40] *Ibid.* Sched. 2, para. 13(2).
[41] *Ibid.* Sched. 2, para. 14(1); Expressions have the same meaning as in *ibid.* s.61; see § 10–84 *et seq., ante.*

(b) the making of the recording does not infringe any copyright,

(c) its making is not prohibited by the performer.[42]

Copies of a recording made in reliance on these provisions and included in an archive maintained by a designated body may, if the prescribed conditions are met, be made and supplied by the archivist without infringing Part II rights.[43] The "prescribed conditions" means the conditions prescribed for the purposes of section 61(3). A designated body means a body designated for the purposes of section 61.[44]

(xiv) Playing of sound recordings for the purposes of clubs and societies

23–80 It is not an infringement of Part II rights to play a sound recording as part of the activities of or for the benefit of, a club, society or other organisation provided that certain conditions are met.[45] Those conditions are that,

(a) the organisation is not established or conducted for profit and its main objects are charitable or are otherwise concerned with the advancement of religion, education or social welfare, and

(b) the proceeds of any charge for admission to the place where the recording is to be heard are applied solely for the purposes of the organisation.[46]

(xv) Incidental recording for purposes of broadcast or cable programme

23–81 A person who proposes to broadcast a recording of a performance, or include a recording of a performance in a cable programme service, in circumstances not infringing Part II rights is to be treated as having consent for the purpose of Part II for the making of a further recording for the purposes of a broadcast or cable programme.[47]

That consent is subject to certain conditions. They are that the further recording shall not be used for any other purpose and shall be destroyed within 28 days of being first used for broadcasting the performance or including it in a cable programme service.[48]

A recording made in accordance with these provisions is to be treated as an illicit recording for the purposes of any use in breach of the condition as to non-user for any other purpose and for all purposes after that condition or the condition as to destruction within 28 days is broken.[49]

---

[42] *Ibid.* Sched. 2, para. 14(2).
[43] *Ibid.* Sched. 2, para. 14(3).
[44] *Ibid.* Sched. 2, para. 14(4). See S.I. 1989 No. 1012; See § B–20 *post.*
[45] *Ibid.* Sched. 2, para. 15(1); Expressions have the same meaning as in *ibid.* s.67; see § 10–102 *et seq., ante.*
[46] *Ibid.* Sched. 2, para. 15(2).
[47] *Ibid.* Sched. 2, para. 16(1); Expressions have the same meaning as in *ibid.* s.68; see § 10–112 *et seq., ante.*
[48] *Ibid.* Sched. 2, para. 16(2).
[49] *Ibid.* Sched. 2, para. 16(3).

(xvi) Recordings for purposes of supervision and control of broadcasts
and cable programmes

23–82   The rights conferred by Part II are not infringed by the making or use by
the British Broadcasting Corporation, for the purpose of maintaining
supervision and control over programmes broadcast by them, of recordings of those programmes.[50] The rights conferred by Part II are not
infringed by anything done in pursuance of various provisions of the
Broadcasting Act 1990 or of a condition which, by virtue of section 11(2)
or 95(2) of that Act, is included in a licence granted under section 109(2)
of that Act or of a direction given under section 109(2) of that Act.[51]
   The rights conferred by Part II are not infringed by—[52]

(a) the use by the Independent Television Commission or the Radio
Authority, in connection with the performance of any of their functions under the Broadcasting Act 1990, of any recording, script or
transcript which is provided to them under or by virtue of any provision of that Act[53]: or

(b) the use by the British Broadcasting Complaints Commission or the
Broadcasting Standards Council,[54] in connection with any complaint made to them under that Act, of any recording or transcript
requested or required to be provided to them, and so provided,
under section 145(4) or (7) or section 155(3) of that Act.[55]

(xvii) Free public showing or playing of broadcast or cable programme

23–83   The showing or playing in public of a broadcast or cable programme to an
audience who have not paid for admission to the place where the broadcast or programme is to be seen or heard does not infringe any Part II
rights in relation to a performance or recording included in the broadcast
or cable programme, or any sound recording or film which is played or
shown in public by reception of the broadcast or cable programme.[56] The
audience is to be treated as having paid for admission to a place in two
sets of circumstances: firstly, if they have paid for admission to a place of
which that place forms part and, secondly, if goods or services are supplied at that place or a place of which it forms part, at prices which are
substantially attributable to the facilities afforded for seeing or hearing the
broadcast or programme, or at prices exceeding those usually charged
there and which are partly attributable to those facilities.[57]
   In two cases persons are not regard as having paid for admission to a
place: firstly, persons admitted as residents or inmates of the place:

---

[50] *Ibid.* Sched. 2, para. 17(1); See § 10–115 *et seq., ante.*
[51] *Ibid.* Sched. 2, para. 17(2), as amended by the Broadcasting Act 1990, Sched. 20 para.
50(2).
[52] *Ibid.* Sched. 2, para. 17(3), as amended by the Broadcasting Act 1990, Sched. 20, para.
50(2).
[53] See Broadcasting Act 1990 (C. 42).
[54] *Ibid.*
[55] *Ibid.*
[56] C.D.P.A. 1988 Sched. 2, para. 18(1); Expressions have the same meaning as in *ibid.* s.72;
see § 10–121 *et seq., ante.*
[57] *Ibid.* Sched. 2, para. 18(2).

secondly, persons admitted as members of a club or society where the payment is only for membership of the club or society and the provision of facilities for seeing or hearing broadcasts or programmes is only incidental to the main purposes of the club or society.[58]

(xviii) Reception and re-transmission of broadcast in cable programme service

Provision is made for the case where a broadcast made from a place in the United Kingdom is, by reception and immediate re-transmission, included in a cable programme service.[59] The rights conferred by Part II in relation to a performance or recording included in the broadcast are not infringed[60] if and to the extent that the broadcast is made for reception in the area in which the cable programme service is provided.[61]   **23–84**

(xix) Provision of sub-titled copies of broadcast or cable programme

Certain bodies designated for the purposes of section 74 of the 1988 Act may, for the purposes of providing people who are deaf or hard of hearing, or physically or mentally handicapped in other ways, with copies which are sub-titled or otherwise modified for their special needs, make recordings of television broadcasts or cable programmes without infringing Part II rights in relation to a performance or recording included in the broadcast or cable programme.[62]   **23–85**

(xx) Recording of broadcast or cable programme for archival purposes

The recording of a broadcast or cable programme of a designated class[63] or a copy of such a recording may be made for the purpose of being placed in an archive maintained by designated bodies without thereby infringing any right conferred by Part II in relation to a performance or recording included in the broadcast or cable programme.[64]   **23–86**

10. Remedies for Infringement of Rights

(i) General

An infringement of any of the rights conferred by Part II is actionable by the person entitled to the right as a breach of statutory duty.[65] This is similar to the case of infringement of moral rights[66] and is to be contrasted   **23–87**

---

[58] *Ibid.* Sched. 2, para. 18(3).
[59] *Ibid.* Sched. 2, para. 19(1); Expressions have the same meaning as in *ibid.* s.73. See § 10–123 *et seq., ante.*
[60] *Ibid.* Sched. 2, para. 19(2), as amended by Broadcasting Act 1990, Sched. 21.
[61] *Ibid.* Sched. 2, para. 19(2)(*b*).
[62] *Ibid.* Sched. 2, para. 20(1); Expressions have the same meaning as in *ibid.* s.74; see § 10–125 *et seq., ante.*
[63] *Ibid.* See s.75, § 10–126, *ante.*
[64] *Ibid.* Sched. 2, para. 21(1); Expressions have the same meaning as in *ibid* s.75; see § 10–126, *ante.* See S.I. 1989 S.I. No. 2510; See § B–208, *post.*
[65] *Ibid.* s.194.
[66] *Ibid.* s.103(1). See § 22–69, *ante.*

with infringement of copyright which is treated as an infringement of a proprietary right.[67]

(ii) Damages

23–88   Part II contains special provisions in relation to liability for damages for infringement of the rights thereby conferred. In certain cases damages are not recoverable at all. Thus, in an action for infringement of performers' rights by making the recording of a qualifying performance or broadcasting a qualifying performance live or including it live in a cable performance, damages are not recoverable against a defendant who shows that, at the time of the infringement, he believed on reasonable grounds that consent had been given.[68]

23–89   A similar defence to damages is available to a defendant in an action for infringement of the recording rights by the making of a recording of the performance.[69]

23–90   In the case of infringement of performer's rights by importing, possessing or dealing with illicit copies, the only remedy available in certain cases is damages not exceeding a reasonable payment in respect of the act complained of. That limitation on remedy applies in a case where a defendant shows that the illicit recording was innocently acquired by him or a predecessor in title of his.[70] A recording is "innocently acquired" if the person acquiring the recording did not know and had no reason to believe that it was an illicit recording.[71]

23–91   A similar limitation applies in the case of infringement of recording rights by importing, possessing or dealing with an illicit recording.[72]

23–92   Any damages recovered by a personal representative in respect of infringement of performer's rights in respect of an infringement after a person's death devolve as part of his estate as if the right of action had subsisted and been vested in him immediately before his death.[73]

23–93   In some cases the 1988 Act directs that certain facts are to be taken into account in assessing damages for infringement. Thus, where the making of a broadcast or inclusion of the programme in a cable programme service was an infringement of the rights conferred by Part II in relation to a performance or recording, the fact that it was heard or seen in public by the reception of the broadcast or programme is to be taken into account in assessing damages for that infringement.[74] Similarly, where the making of

---

[67] *Ibid.* s.96(2). See § 11–1, *ante*.
[68] *Ibid.* s.182(2).
[69] *Ibid.* s.186(2).
[70] *Ibid.* s.184(2).
[71] *Ibid.* s.184(3).
[72] *Ibid.* s.188(2)(3).
[73] *Ibid.* s.192(5).
[74] *Ibid.* Sched. 2, para. 18(4).

the broadcast was an infringement of the rights conferred by Part II in relation to a performance or recording included in a broadcast, the fact that the broadcast is re-transmitted as a programme in a cable programme service is to be taken into account in assessing the damages for that infringement.[75]

(iii) Delivery up

The Court also has jurisdiction to order delivery up of illicit recordings.   **23–94** The powers conferred by the Act do not affect the other powers of the Court, for example, under the Rules of the Supreme Court. The remedy of delivery up is available where a person has in his possession, custody or control in the course of a business an illicit recording of a performance.[76] A person having performer's rights or recording rights in relation to the performance may apply to the Court for an order that the recording be delivered up to him or to such other person as the Court may direct.[77]

There is a limitation period for the making of the application. An appli-   **23–95** cation may not be made after the end of the period of six years from the date on which the illicit recording in question was made.[78] In two cases that period may be extended. If, during the whole or any part of that period, a person entitled to apply for an order was under a disability or was prevented by fraud or concealment from discovering the facts entitling him to apply, an application may be made by him at any time before the end of the period of 6 years from the date on which he ceased to be under a disability or, as the case may be, could with reasonable diligence have discovered those facts.[79] "Disability" has the same meaning as in the relevant Limitation Act.[80]

There is a further restriction on the making of an order for delivery up.   **23–96** The Court must not make a delivery up order, unless it also makes, or it appears to the Court that there are grounds for making, an order as to the disposal of the illicit recording under section 204 of the 1988 Act.[81]

(iv) Disposal order

Such an order may be made on application to the Court by originating   **23–97** summons or by summons or motion in a pending action.[82] The application is for an order that an illicit recording of a performance delivered up in pursuance of an order or[83] seized and detained[84] should be forfeited

---

[75] *Ibid.* Sched. 2, para. 19(2).
[76] *Ibid.* s.195(1). See § 11–80, *ante.*
[77] *Ibid.* s.195(1).
[78] *Ibid.* s.195(2), s.203(1).
[79] *Ibid.* s.203(2).
[80] *Ibid.* s.203(3); Limitation Act 1980 (c. 58); Prescription and Limitations (Scotland) Act 1973; Statute of Limitation (Northern Ireland) 1958.
[81] C.D.P.A. 1988 s.195(2); See § 23–97 *et seq., post.*
[82] *Ibid.* s.204. See S.I. 1990 No. 380 as to proceedings in Scotland. See § B–214, *post.* R.S.C. Ord. 93 r. 24 for England. See also § 11–77 *et seq., ante.*
[83] Under *ibid.* s.195.
[84] Under *ibid.* s.196.

to such person having performer's rights or recording rights in relation to the performance as the Court may direct, or destroyed or otherwise dealt with as the Court might think fit. Alternatively, an application can be made for a decision that no such order should be made.[85]

23–98 In considering what order (if any) should be made, the Court must consider whether other remedies available in an action for infringement of the rights conferred by Part II would be adequate to compensate the person or persons entitled to the rights and to protect their interests.[86]

23–99 Provision is made by rules of court as to the service of notice on persons having an interest in the recording.[87] This includes any person in whose favour an order could be made in respect of the recording under section 204 or sections 114 or 231 of the 1988 Act or section 58C of the Trade Marks Act 1938 which make similar provisions in relation to infringement of copyright, design right and trade marks respectively. Any such person is entitled to appear in proceedings for an order as to the disposal of the illicit recording, whether or not he was served with notice and to appeal against any order made, whether or not he appeared.[88]

23–100 An order does not take effect until the end of the period in which notice of an appeal may be given or, if before the end of that period notice of appeal is duly given, until the final determination or abandonment of the proceedings on the appeal.[89]

23–101 Where there is more than one person interested in a recording, the Court shall make such order as it thinks just and may, in particular, direct that the recording be sold or otherwise dealt with, and the proceeds divided.[90]

23–102 If the Court decides that no disposal order should be made, the person in whose possession, custody or control the recording was before being delivered up or seized is entitled to its return.[91] A person to whom a recording is delivered up in pursuance of a delivery up order shall, if a disposal order is not made, retain it pending the making of a disposal order, or the decision not to make a disposal order.[92]

(v) Seizure of illicit recording

23–103 The 1988 Act also contains "self help" provisions in relation to illicit recordings. An illicit recording of a performance which is found exposed or otherwise immediately available for sale or hire and in respect of which

---

[85] *Ibid.* s.204(1).
[86] *Ibid.* s.204(2).
[87] *Ibid.* s.204(3): R.S.C. Ord. 93 r. 24.
[88] *Ibid.* s.204(3)(*a*), (*b*).
[89] *Ibid.* s.204(3).
[90] *Ibid.* s.204(4).
[91] *Ibid.* s.204(5).
[92] *Ibid.* s.195(3).

a person would be entitled to apply for a delivery up order, may be seized and detained by him or by a person authorised by him.[93] The right to seize and detain is exercisable subject to specified conditions. It is also subject to any decision of the Court as to the disposal of an illicit recording.[94]

Before anything is seized notice of the time and place of the proposed **23–104** seizure must be given to a local police station.[95] For the purposes of exercising the right of seizure a person may enter premises to which the public have access.[96] "Premises" includes land, buildings, fixed or moveable structures, vehicles, vessels, aircraft and hovercraft.[97] A person may not, however, seize anything in the possession, custody or control of a person at a permanent or regular place of business of his.[98] A person exercising the right may not use any force.[99]

At the time when anything is seized there must be left at the place **23–105** where it was seized a notice in the prescribed form. This should contain the prescribed particulars of the person by whom or on whose authority the seizure is made and the grounds on which it is made.[1] The form and particulars are such as may be prescribed by order of the Secretary of State made by statutory instrument subject to annulment in pursuance of a resolution of either House of Parliament.[2] As already noted, a disposal order may be made by the Court in respect of any illicit recording seized or detained under section 196 of the 1988 Act.

11. Transitional Provisions

The rights conferred by Part II apply in relation to performances taking **23–106** place before the commencement of Part II. However, no act done before commencement or in pursuance of arrangements made before commencement is to be regarded as infringing those rights.[3]

The whole of the Performers' Protection Acts 1958, 1963 and 1972 have been repealed by the 1988 Act.[4]

---

[93] *Ibid.* s.196. See § 11–18 *et seq., ante.*
[94] *Ibid. i.e.* s.204; s.196(1).
[95] *Ibid.* s.196(2).
[96] *Ibid.* s.196(3).
[97] *Ibid.* s.196(5).
[98] *Ibid.* s.196(3).
[99] See n. 98, *ante.*
[1] *Ibid.* s.196(4).
[2] *Ibid.* s.196(6). See S.I. 1989 No. 1006: See § B–16, *post.*
[3] *Ibid.* s.180(3): *Grower* v. *B.B.C.* [1990] F.S.R. 595 at 610, 611.
[4] *Ibid.* s.303(2); Sched. 8.

RELATED FORMS OF PROTECTION—5

DEVICES DESIGNED TO CIRCUMVENT COPY-PROTECTION
AND FRAUDULENT RECEPTION OF TRANSMISSIONS

Contents

1. Devices Designed to Circumvent Copy-Protection

A. *Position before the 1988 Act*

History. The prevalance, nowadays, of "home taping," in particular of **24–1** records, and the widespread infringement resulting therefrom, was referred to in the 1977 Report of the Whitford Committee, and that Committee recommended the introduction of a levy on the sale price of recording equipment.[1] Such Report also referred to the evidence received to the effect that policing was impracticable.[2] The inability, in practice, of enforcing copyright in relation to copying carried out in the home was mentioned in the 1985 Green Paper.[3] This referred to two possible solutions open to the copyright owners, one of which was that the recording industry might perfect a spoiler to prevent copying, but that such a solution had been explored and found wanting.[4] The Green Paper therefore proposed the imposition of a levy on blank tapes.[5] The 1986 White Paper,[6] when dealing with the problem, mentioned that attempts to prevent home taping by spoiler systems had not proved feasible and concluded that a compulsory levy on blank recording tape was the only way of dealing with the problem.[7] However, notwithstanding the proposals in the Green

---

[1] Cmnd. 6732 para. 292 *et seq.*
[2] *Ibid.* para. 305.
[3] Cmnd. 9445 para. 2.1 *et seq.*
[4] *Ibid.* para. 3.1.
[5] *Ibid.* para. 6.1.
[6] Cmnd. 9712.
[7] *Ibid.* Part II paras. 6.3 and 6.6.

Paper and in the White Paper, and the views expressed by the House of Lords,[8] the 1988 Act does not provide for such a levy.

B. *The 1988 Act*

24–2　**Section 296.** The use of spoilers to prevent copying, for instance of sound recordings and pre-recorded computer programs, has been undermined by the production of devices to circumvent such spoilers. Therefore, in an attempt, it would seem, to go some way to stopping this activity, section 296 has been included in the 1988 Act.[9] This section applies where copies of a copyright work are issued to the public, by or with the licence of the copyright owner,[10] in an electronic form which is copy-protected. Copy-protection includes any device or means intended to prevent or restrict copying of a work or to impair the quality of copies made.[11] "Copyright work" means all works protected by the 1988 Act,[12] and therefore includes sound recordings and computer programs.[13] "In electronic form" means in a form usable only by electronic means and "electronic" means actuated by electric, magnetic, electro-magnetic, electro-chemical or electro-mechanical energy.[14]

24–3　**Offences under section 296.** Offences under section 296 of the 1988 Act are committed by a person who, knowing or having reason to believe[15] that it will be used to make infringing copies,[16] either makes, imports, sells or lets for hire, offers or exposes for sale or hire, or advertises for sale or hire, any device or means specifically designed or adapted to circumvent the form of copy-protection employed, or publishes information intended to enable or assist persons to circumvent that form of copy-protection.[17] Strangely, the requirement of knowledge or belief governs both the offence of making, etc., a device, and the offence of publishing information. Such knowledge or belief is that it will be used to make infringing copies, presumably of a copyright work or works but not, it would seem, necessarily, infringing copies of the copyright work in question, but of any copyright work.[18] Again, such knowledge or belief is that it will be used to make infringing copies, so it would seem that the offences would not be committed if the knowledge or belief was only that it would be used to make one infringing copy.[19]

---

[8] In *C.B.S. Songs Ltd.* v. *Amstrad Consumer Electronics plc* [1988] A.C. 1013 at 1048 and 1062.
[9] Under C.D.P.A. 1988, s.296(5) expressions used in that section defined for the purposes of Part I of that Act have the same meanings as under that Part.
[10] *Ibid.* ss.101(2) and 173.
[11] *Ibid.* s.296(4).
[12] *Ibid.* s.1(2).
[13] *Ibid.* ss.1(1) and 3(1).
[14] *Ibid.* s.178.
[15] Compare *ibid.* s.22, Chap. 9 *ante.*
[16] See as to meaning of "infringing copies" *ibid.* s.27.
[17] *Ibid.* s.296(2).
[18] Compare *ibid.* s.24, and see *ibid.* s.296(1), (3).
[19] But see Interpretation Act 1978 (c. 30), s.6.

Relief where offence committed. If an offence under section 296 of the **24-4** 1988 Act is committed, then the person issuing the copies of the copyright work to the public is given the same rights against the offender as a copyright owner has in respect of an infringement of copyright.[20] Issuing to the public of copies of a work means the act of putting into circulation copies not previously put into circulation, in the United Kingdom or elsewhere, and not to any subsequent distribution, sale, hiring or loan of those copies, or, any subsequent importation of those copies into the United Kingdom.[21] It is clear, from section 296(1) of the 1988 Act, that the person having these rights will not necessarily be the copyright owner although given the rights of a copyright owner. Strangely, however, section 296 of the 1988 Act only refers to such person having the same "rights" as a copyright owner, not the same "rights and remedies,"[22] and rights without remedies would be pointless.[23] The rights and remedies of a copyright owner are dealt with in sections 96–100 of the 1988 Act.[24] It is not precisely clear how far proceedings under section 296 of the 1988 Act will parallel proceedings for infringement of copyright.[25]

Section 296 not retrospective? Since section 296 of the 1988 Act is new **24-5** and creates new offences, it is thought that such section will not apply to acts done before the commencement of the 1988 Act, although the position is not clear.[26]

2. Fraudulent Reception of Transmissions

A. *Position before the 1988 Act*

History. The advent of satellite broadcasting has brought with it the diffi- **24-6** culty of controlling where such broadcasts can be received and by whom, on the basis that reception is intended to be limited to certain countries and by certain persons in those countries only. In 1974 this difficulty was recognised by the Convention Relating to the Distribution of Programme-Carrying Signals Transmitted by Satellite[27] which provided, in Article 2, that each contracting state undertook to take adequate measures to prevent the distribution on or from its territory of any programme-carrying signal by any distributor for whom the signal emitted to or passing through the satellite is not intended. Although this Convention has entered into force, the United Kingdom is not a signatory. However, the

---

[20] C.D.P.A. 1988, s.296(2).
[21] *Ibid.* s.18(2) under which infringement by issuing copies to the public in relation to sound recordings, films and computer programs includes any rental of copies to the public: "rental" is defined *ibid.* s.178.
[22] Compare *ibid.* s.298(1), (2).
[23] Compare headings to *ibid.* Chaps. II and VI and sub-heading to Chap. VI, and see *ibid.* s.296(3) reference to "rights" under *ibid.* ss.99 and 100.
[24] And see *ibid.* ss.113–115 and s.296(3),(6).
[25] *Ibid.* s.296(6), and see *ibid.* s.56.
[26] See *ibid.* Sched. 1, para. 31; and see *Smith* v. *Callander* [1901] A.C. 297 at 305, *Sifam etc. Ltd.* v. *Sangamo Weston Ltd.* [1973] R.P.C. 899.
[27] § C–192 *et seq. post.*

possibility of United Kingdom accession to the Convention was alluded to in the Green Paper[28] and in the White Paper.[29] One way of meeting this difficulty has been to have coded transmissions, with the necessary decoding equipment being made available to those whom it is intended should receive the broadcast. But this can be defeated by persons not so intended improperly acquiring the necessary decoding equipment. A related difficulty occurs in relation to the dishonest reception of broadcasts with the intention of avoiding payment of charges applicable to such reception.[30] Some redress in respect of these matters was given by the Cable and Broadcasting Act 1984[31] sections 53 and 54. These sections were repealed by the 1988 Act,[32] and were replaced by sections 297–299 of the 1988 Act which provide for similar, but not identical, offences. An additional offence, relating to unauthorised decoders, was created by section 297A of the 1988 Act, inserted by the Broadcasting Act 1990.[33]

B. *Position under the 1988 Act*

(i) *Fraudulently receiving programmes*

24–7 **Offence under section 297.** This section of the 1988 Act makes it an offence dishonestly to receive a programme included in a broadcasting or cable programme service provided from a place in the United Kingdom with intent to avoid payment of any charge applicable to the reception of the programme. In section 297 of the 1988 Act "programme," "broadcasting" and "cable programme service," and related expressions have the same meaning as in Part I of the 1988 Act.[34] Section 299(4) of the 1988 Act provides that, where section 297 of that Act applies in relation to a broadcasting service or cable programme service, it also applies to any service run for the person providing that service, or a person providing programmes for that service, which consists wholly or mainly in the sending by means of a telecommunications system of sound or visual images, or both.

24–8 **Penalty for such offence.** A person who commits such an offence is liable on summary conviction to a fine not exceeding level 5 on the standard scale.[35] Further, if such an offence is committed by a body corporate and is proved to have been committed with the consent or connivance of a director, manager, secretary or other similar officer of the body, or a person purporting to act in any such capacity, he as well as the body corporate will be guilty of the offence and liable to be proceeded against and punished accordingly.[36] In relation to a body corporate whose affairs are

---

[28] Cmnd. 8302 para. 6.

[29] Cmnd. 9712 Part II, para. 12.

[30] See *ibid.* Part II, para. 10.11 *et seq.*

[31] c. 46.

[32] C.D.P.A. 1988, s.303(2) and Sched. 8. And see The Unlawful Decoding of Encrypted Television signals etc., *Copyright*, December 1990, p. 367.

[33] c. 42.

[34] *Ibid.* s.299(5). See *ibid.* ss.6 and 7, and *ibid.* s.178 "telecommunications system" and "electronic."

[35] *Ibid.* s.297(1).

[36] *Ibid.* s.297(2).

managed by its members, "director" means a member of the body corporate.[37]

Section 297 not retrospective? Although section 297 of the 1988 Act contains a similar offence to section 53 of the 1984 Act which it replaced, as the offence is not identical, it is assumed that section 297 of the 1988 Act will not apply to acts done before the commencement of that Act, although the position is not clear.[38]   **24–9**

(ii) *Unauthorised decoders*

Offence under section 297A. This section was inserted in the 1988 Act by the Broadcasting Act 1990[39] and makes it an offence to make, import, sell or let for hire any unauthorised decoder. "Decoder" means any apparatus which is designed or adapted to enable (whether on its own or with any other apparatus) an encrypted[40] transmission to be decoded. "Apparatus" includes any device, component or electronic data. "Transmission" means any programme included in a broadcasting or cable programme service which is provided from a place in the United Kingdom. "Programme" "broadcasting" and "cable programme service", and related expressions, have the same meanings as in Part I of the 1988 Act.[41] "Unauthorised", in relation to a decoder, means a decoder which will enable encrypted transmissions to be viewed in decoded form without payment of the fee (however imposed) which the person making the transmission, or on whose behalf it is made, charges for viewing those transmissions, or viewing any service of which they form part.   **24–10**

Penalty for such offence. A person who commits such an offence is liable on summary conviction to a fine not exceeding level 5 on the standard scale.[42] However, it is a defence to any prosecution for such an offence for the defendant to prove that he did not know, and had no reasonable ground for knowing, that the decoder was an unauthorised decoder.[43]   **24–11**

Section 297A not retrospective? Since section 297A of the 1988 Act is new and creates a new offence, it is thought that such section will not apply to acts done before the commencement of the Broadcasting Act 1990 which inserted this section in the 1988 Act, but the position is not clear.[44]   **24–12**

---

[37] See n. 36, *ante.*
[38] See n. 25 *ante* and s.16 Interpretation Act 1978, (c. 30) § A–645 *post.*
[39] c. 42 s.179(1) with effect from January 1, 1991: see The Broadcasting Act 1990 (Commencement No. 1 and Transitional Provisions) Order 1990 (S.I. 1990 No. 2347 (C. 61)), § B–254 *post.*
[40] See n. 47 *post.*
[41] C.D.P.A. 1988, s.299(5), as amended by s.179(2) Broadcasting Act 1990.
[42] C.D.P.A. 1988, s.297A(1).
[43] *Ibid.* s.297A(2): and see as to "unauthorised" and "decoder" § 24–10 *ante.*
[44] See n. 26 *ante.*

(iii) *Apparatus for unauthorised reception of transmissions*

24–13 **Offences under section 298.** Offences under section 298 of the 1988 Act are committed by a person who either makes, imports or sells or lets for hire any apparatus or device designed or adapted to enable or assist persons to receive programmes or other transmissions mentioned in section 298(1) of that Act[45] when they are not entitled to do so, or publishes any information which is calculated to enable or assist persons to receive the programmes or other transmissions when they are not entitled to do so.[46]

24–14 **Relief where offence is committed.** The person entitled to relief, where an offence is committed under section 298 of the 1988 Act, is the person who either makes charges for the reception of programmes included in a broadcasting or cable programme service provided from a place in the United Kingdom, or sends encrypted transmissions of any other description from a place in the United Kingdom.[47] If such an offence is committed, then that person is entitled to the same rights and remedies as a copyright owner has in respect of an infringement of copyright.[48] Again, "programme," "broadcasting" and "cable programme service," and related expressions have the same meaning as in Part I of the 1988 Act.[49] Section 299(4) of the 1988 Act provides that, where section 298 of that Act applies in relation to a broadcasting service or cable programme service, it also applies to any service run for the person providing that service, or a person providing programmes for that service, which consist wholly or mainly in the sending by means of a telecommunications system of sounds or visual images, or both. The use of the expression "as a copyright owner" indicates that the person entitled to relief will not necessarily be the copyright owner. The rights and remedies of a copyright owner are dealt with in sections 96–100 of the 1988 Act.[50] Again, it is not clear precisely how far proceedings under section 298 of the 1988 Act will parallel proceedings for infringement of copyright.[51]

24–15 **Section 298 not retrospective?** Although section 298 of the 1988 Act contains similar offences to section 54 of the 1984 Act which it replaced, it is assumed that section 298 of the 1988 Act will not apply to acts done before the commencement of that Act, although the position is not clear.[52]

---

[45] § 24–14 *post.*
[46] C.D.P.A. 1988, s.298(2); and see *ibid.* s.6(1) and (2). It was held, in *BBC Enterprises Ltd.* v. *Hi-Tech Xtravision Ltd.* [1990] Ch. 609 (C.A.), that s.298 itself created the right and the remedy. Leave to appeal has been given by the House of Lords [1990] Ch. at 623.
[47] *Ibid.* s.298(1). "Encrypted" is not defined in the 1988 Act, but, presumably, means "encoded": see *ibid.* s.6(2). And see *BBC Enterprises Ltd., supra.*
[48] *Ibid.* s.298(1), (2),(3).
[49] See n. 34, *ante.*
[50] And see C.D.P.A. 1988, ss.113–115 and *ibid.* s.298(6). See also R.S.C. Ord. 93, r. 24 and, as to Scotland, Act of Sederunt (Copyright, Designs and Patents) 1990 (S.I. 1990 No. 380 (S.37)).
[51] See *ibid.* s.298(3), (4),(5).
[52] See n. 38, *ante.*

(iv) *Extent and application of sections 297–299*

Extent. Sections 297–299 of the 1988 Act extend to England, Wales, Scot-　**24–16**
land and Northern Ireland.[53] However, sections 297–299 of the 1988 Act
may be extended to the Isle of Man by Order in Council with such exceptions and modifications as may be specified in the Order.[54] Similarly, sections 297–299 of the 1988 Act may be extended to any of the Channel
Islands by Order in Council with such exceptions and modifications as
may be specified in the Order.[55] An Order in Council has been made in
respect of Guernsey under section 304(5) of the 1988 Act.[56]

Application. Under section 299(1) of the 1988 Act, section 297 of that　**24–17**
Act[57] may be applied by Order in Council in relation to programmes
included in services provided from a country or territory outside the
United Kingdom.[58] Section 299(1) of the 1988 Act also provides that section 298 of that Act[59] may be applied by Order in Council in relation to
such programmes and to encrypted transmissions sent from such a
country or territory. A statutory instrument containing such an Order in
Council is subject to annulment in pursuance of a resolution of either
House of Parliament.[60] Under section 299(2) of the 1988 Act, no such
Order was to be made unless it appeared that provision had been or
would be made under the laws of that country or territory giving adequate
protection to persons making charges for programmes included in broadcasting or cable programme services provided from the United Kingdom
or, as the case may be, for encrypted transmissions sent from the United
Kingdom. However, section 299(2) of the 1988 Act was repealed by the
Broadcasting Act 1990.[61] An Order in Council has been made in respect
of Guernsey under section 299(1) of the 1988 Act relating to sections 297
and 298 of the 1988 Act.[62]

---

[53] C.D.P.A. 1988, s.304(2): see § 24–17 *post* as to *ibid.* s.299.

[54] *Ibid.* s.304(4).

[55] *Ibid.* s.304(5).

[56] The Copyright, Designs and Patents Act 1988 (Guernsey) Order 1989 (S.I. 1989
No. 1997): § B–201, *post*. Although referring to ss.297–299 of the 1988 Act, this Order was
made on November 1, 1989, before s.297A was inserted in the 1988 Act by the Broadcasting Act 1990.

[57] As to C.D.P.A. 1988, s.297, see § 24–7 *et seq. ante.*

[58] "Country" includes any territory: *ibid.* s.178. *Ibid.* s.299(5) provides that certain
expressions in *ibid.* s.299 are to have the same meaning as in Part I of the 1988 Act.

[59] As to *ibid.* s.298, see § 24–13 *et seq. ante.*

[60] *Ibid.* s.299(3).

[61] c. 42 s.179 (new s.297(A)(2)(*a*) C.D.P.A. 1988) and Sched. 21 with effect from January 1,
1991: see n. 39 *ante.*

[62] The Fraudulent Reception of Transmissions (Guernsey) Order 1989 (1989 S.I. No. 2003):
§ B–205, *post.*

Appendix A

UNITED KINGDOM STATUTES, SEMICONDUCTOR REGULATIONS, PUBLIC LENDING RIGHT SCHEME

PART I

COMPARATIVE TABLE—I   **A–1**

COPYRIGHT ACT 1956

COMPARED WITH

COPYRIGHT ETC. ACT 1988

1956	1988	1956	1988
s. 1 (1)	ss. 2 (1), 157 (1)	s. 9 (7)	s. 45
(2), (3), (4)	16 (1), (2)	(8)	—
(5)	153, 154	(9)	64
2 (1), (2)	1, 153, 154, 155	(10)	65
		(11)	—
(3), (4)	s. 12	10	ss. 51–53
(5) (a)	17	11 (1)	—
(b)	18	(2)	—
(c)	19	(3)	s. 10 (1), (2)
(d), (e)	20	12 (1), (2)	ss. 1, 153, 154, 155
(f), (g)	21		
(6)	21	(3)	s. 13
3 (1)	4 (1), (2)	(4)	11
(2), (3)	ss. 1, 153, 154, 155	(5) (a)	17
		(b)	19
(4)	s. 12	(c)	20
(5) (a)	17	(6)	—
(b)	18	(7)	67
(c), (d)	20	(8)	9 (1)–(3)
4	11	(9)	5 (1)
5 (1)	—	13 (1), (2)	ss. 1, 153, 154, 155
(2)	22		
(3), (4)	23	(3)	s. 13
(5), (6)	25	(4)	11
6 (1)	29	(5) (a)	17
(2)	30 (1), (3)	(b)	19
(3)	30 (2), (3)	(c), (d)	20
(4)	45	(6)	45
(5)	59	(7), (8), (9)	—
(6)	33	(10)	ss. 5(1), 9 (1)–(3)
(7)	68	(11)	—
(8)	76	14 (1)	1, 9 (1)–(3), 153, 156
(9)	—		
(10)	178	(2), (3)	11, 14
7 (1)–(5), (9)	ss. 37–42	(4) (a), (b)	s. 17
(6)–(8), (9)	s. 43	(c)	19
8	—	(d)	20
9 (1)	29	(5)	—
(2)	30 (1), (3)	(6)	17 (4)
(3), (4)	62	(7)	—
(5), (6)	31	(8)	72

1956	1988	1956	1988
s. 14 (8A)	s. 73	s. 21 (3), (4)	s. 107 (2)
(9)	45	(5)	(3)
(10)	6 (3), (4)	(6)	—
(11)	—	(7), (7A),	107 (4), (5)
14A (1), (2),	ss. 1, 153, 154,	(7B), (7C),	
(4)	156	(7D), (8)	
(3), (4)	9 (1)–(3), 11,	(9)	ss. 108,114
	14	(10)	s. 108
(5) (a),	s. 17	21 (A)	109
(b)		(B)	109
(c)	19	22	ss. 111, 112
(d)	20	ss. 23, 24	145–152
(6)	—	25–27A	116–128
(7)	17 (4)	27B, 28	129–135
(8)	—	s. 29	123, 128
(9)	72	30	s. 152
(10)	45	31	157 (2)–(5)
(11)	7	32	159
(12)	—	33	168
15 (1)	ss. 1, 8 (1), (2)	34	156
(1) (a)	153, 155	35	160
(b)	153, 154	36	ss. 90, 176 (1)
(2)	9 (1)–(3), 11,	37	91, 176 (1)
	15	38	s. 93
(3)	s. 17	39	163
(4)	ss. 37–42	40 (1), (2)	—
16 (1)	—	(3), (3A),	73
(2)	s. 22	(4), (5)	
(3), (4)	23	40A	—
(5), (6), (7)	—	41 (1), (5)	ss. 32, 76,
17 (1)	96		174 (5)
(2)	97 (1)	(2)	36, 76
(3)	(2)	(3), (4), (5)	34, 174
(4), (5)	—		(5)
(6)	177	(6)	—
18 (1)	99	(7)	s. 174
(2)	—	42	49
(3)	27	43	84
(4)	177	44	ss. 265–273,
19 (1)	—		Sched. 3
(2)	101	45	ss. 180–212
(3)	102 (1), (3)	46	s. 171
(4)	101	47	Individual
(5), (6), (7)	102 (4)		sections
(8)	(2)	48	s. 178
(9)	ss. 92, 176 (1)	(1)	Individual
20 (1)	—		sections
(2), (3)	s. 104 (1), (2),	(2)	s. 6 (1)
	(3)	(3), (3A),	
(4)	(4)	(3B)	7
(5), (6)	(5)	(4)	—
(7)	105 (1)	(5)	19 (4)
21 (1), (2),	107 (1)	(6)	26
(4), (4A)		(7)	—
		49 (1)	16 (3)

1956	1988	1956	1988
s. 49 (2), (3)	s. 175	paras. 20–24	paras. 31–33
(2) (d)	155 (3)	25, 26	para. 34
(4)	3 (2), (3)	para. 27	44
(5), (6)	173	28 (1), (2),	25 (1),
(7)–(10)	—	(4), (5)	(2)
50 (1)	170	(3), (4)	
(2)	303	(5) and	
51 (1)	306	Sched. 8	
(2)	305	paras. 6,	
(3)	ss. 157 (1), 304	9	27
Sched. 1	51–53	29	30
Scheds. 2, 3	9 (4), (5), 10 (3), 12, 153, 154	paras. 30, 31	paras. 40–42
		para. 32	22–24
Sched. 4	145–152	paras. 34–36	para. 17
Sched. 5	—	para. 37	18
Sched. 6	180–212	38	28
Sched. 7	Sched. 1	paras. 39, 40	—
paras. 1, 8, 10, 12, 13, 14–16, 17–18, 33 and Sched. 8, para. 2	paras. 5–9, 35	para. 41	36
		paras. 42, 43	—
		para. 44	4
		45 (1)	3
		(2)	1 (3)
para. 2	para. 12	paras. 46, 47	paras. 1, 2
3	11	Sched. 8	—
paras. 4–7	paras. 14–16	para. 2	Sched. 1, paras. 5–9, 35
para. 9	—	paras. 6, 9	para. 27
11	para. 12	Sched. 9	Sched. 8
19	—		

Comparative Table—II

Copyright etc. Act 1988

Compared with

Copyright Act 1956

1988	1956	1988	1956
s. 1	ss. 2 (1), (2), 3 (2), (3), 12 (1), (2), 13 (1), (2), 14 (1), 14A (1), (2), (4), 15 (1)	s. 17	ss. 2 (5) (a), 3 (5) (a), 12 (5) (a), 13 (5) (a), 14 (4) (a), (b), (6), 14A (5) (a), (b), (7), 15 (3)
2 (1)	s. 1 (1)	(3)	s. 48 (1)
(2)	—	18	ss. 2 (5) (b), 3 (5) (b)
3 (1)	48 (1)	19	2 (5) (c), 12 (5) (b), 13 (5), (6), 14 (4) (c), 14A (5) (c)
(2), (3)	49 (4)		
4 (1), (2)	ss. 3 (1), 48 (1)		
5 (1)	12 (9), 13 (10)		
(2)	—		
6 (1)	s. 48 (2)	(2)	s. 48 (1)
(2)	—	(4)	48 (5)
(3), (4)	14 (10)	20	ss. 2 (5) (d), (e), 3 (5) (c), (d), 12 (5) (c), 13 (5) (c), (d), 14 (4) (d), 14A (5) (d)
(5), (6)	—		
7	ss. 14A (11), 48 (3), (3A), (3B)		
8 (1), (2)	s. 15 (1)		
9 (1)–(3)	ss. 12 (8), 13 (10), 14 (1), 14A (3), 15 (2), 48 (1)	21	s. 2 (5) (f), (g), (6)
(4), (5)	Scheds. 2, 3		
10 (1), (2)	s. 11 (3)	22	ss. 5 (2), 16 (2)
(3)	Sched. 3	23	5 (3), (4), 16 (3), (4)
11	ss. 4, 12 (4), 13 (4), 14 (2), 14A (3), 15 (2)	24	—
12	2 (3), (4), 3 (4), Scheds. 2, 3	25	s. 5 (5), (6)
		26	48 (6)
		27	18 (3)
		28	—
		29	ss. 6 (1), 9 (1)
13	ss. 12 (3), 13 (3)	30 (1), (3)	6 (2), 9 (2)
14	14 (2), (3), 14A (3), (4)	(2), (3)	s. 6 (3)
		31	9 (5), (6)
		32	41 (1), (5)
15	s. 15 (2)	33	6 (6)
16 (1), (2)	1 (2), (3), (4)	34	41 (3), (4), (5)
(3)	49 (1)	35	—
(4)	—	36	41 (2)

1988	1956	1988	1956
ss. 37–42	ss. 7 (1)–(5), (9), 15 (4)	s. 102 (1), (3)	s. 19 (3)
s. 43	s. 7 (6)–(8), (9)	(2)	(8)
44	—	(4)	(5), (6), (7)
45	ss. 6 (4), 9 (7), 13 (6), 14 (9), 14A (10)	(5)	—
46	—	103	—
47	—	104 (1), (2), (3)	20 (2), (3)
48	—	(4)	(4)
49	42	(5)	(5), (6)
50	—	105 (1)	(7)
ss. 51–53	s. 10, Sched. 1	(2)–(5)	—
54, 55	—	106	—
s. 56	—	107 (1)	21 (1), (2), (4), (4A)
57	—	(2)	(3), (4)
58	—	(3)	(5)
59	s. 6 (5)	(4), (5)	(7), (7A), (7B), (7C), (7D), (8)
60	—		
61	—	(6)	—
62	9 (3), (4)	108	21 (9), (10)
63	—	109	ss. 21 (A), 21 (B)
64	9 (9)	110	—
65	9 (10)	ss. 111, 112	s. 22
66	—	s. 113	—
67	12 (7)	114	21 (9)
68	6 (7)	115	—
69	—	ss. 116–128	ss. 25–27A, 29
70	—	129–135	27 (B), 28
71	—	135A–135G	—
72	ss. 14 (8), 14A (9)	136–144	—
73	14 (8A), 40 (3), (3A), (4), (5)	145–152	ss. 23, 24, 30, Sched. 4
74	—	153, 154	ss. 1 (5), 2 (1), 3 (2), 12 (1), 13 (1), 14A (1), 15 (1) (b), Sched. 3
75	—		
76	6 (8), 41 (1), (2)		
ss. 77–83	—		
s. 84	s. 43	153, 155	ss. 2 (2), 3 (3), 12 (2), 13 (2), 15 (1) (a)
ss. 85–89	—		
s. 90	36		
91	37	s. 155 (3)	s. 49 (2) (d)
92	19 (9)	ss. 153, 156	ss. 14 (1), 14A (1), 34
93	38		
ss. 94, 95	—	s. 157 (1)	1 (1), 51 (3)
s. 96	17 (1)	157 (2)–(5)	s. 31
97 (1)	(2)	158	—
(2)	(3)	159	32
98	—	160	35
99	18 (1)	ss. 161, 162	—
100	—	s. 163	39
101	19 (2), (4)	ss. 164–167	—

1988	1956	1988	1956
s. 168	s. 33	para. 10	—
169	—	11	para. 3
170	50 (1)	12	paras. 2, 11
171	46	13	—
172	—	paras. 14–16	4–7
173	49 (5), (6)	para. 17	34–36
174	41 (7)	18	37
(5)	(1), (3), (4)	paras. 19, 20, 21	—
175	49 (2), (3)	paras. 22–24	32
176 (1)	ss. 19 (9), 36 (3), 37 (1)	para. 25 (1), (2)	28 (1), (2), (4), (5)
(2)	—	26	—
177	17 (6), 18 (4), 48 (1)	27	paras. 28 (3), (4), (5), paras. 6, 9,
178	s. 48 and individual		Sched. 8
	sections	28	para. 38
179	—	29	—
ss. 180–212	s. 45, Sched. 6	30	39
213–264	—	paras. 31–33	paras. 20–24
265–273	s. 44	para. 34	25, 26
274–286	—	35	paras. 1, 8, 10,
287–292	—		12, 13, 14–16,
293–295	—		17–18, 33,
296–297	—		para. 2,
297A–299	—		Sched. 8
s. 300	—	36	para. 41
301	—	37	—
302	—	paras. 38, 39	—
303	50 (2)	40–42	paras. 30, 31
304	51 (3)	43	—
305	(2)	44	para. 27
306	(1)	45	—
Sched. 1	Sched. 7	46	—
paras. 1, 2	paras. 45 (2), 46, 47	Sched. 2	—
		Sched. 3	s. 44
para. 3	para. 45 (1)	Sched. 4	—
4	44	Sched. 5	—
paras. 5–9	paras. 1, 8, 10, 12, 13, 14, 16, 17, 18, 33, para. 2, Sched. 8	Sched. 6	—
		Sched. 7	—
		Sched. 8	Sched. 9

Copyright, Designs and Patents Act 1988[1]　　　　　　**A–3**

(c.48)

ARRANGEMENT OF SECTIONS

PART I

COPYRIGHT

CHAPTER I

SUBSISTENCE, OWNERSHIP AND DURATION OF COPYRIGHT

Introductory

---

[1] (1) The 1988 Act contains provisions relating to Patent and Trade Mark Agents and to Patents and Trade Marks which are not printed in this book. These are sections 274–286, 293–295 and 300, and Schedule 5. The correction by HMSO in December 1988 to para. 14(5), Sched. 1 has been made, 'subsection (2)' instead of 'subsection (3)'.

(2) Some of the sections of and Schedules to the 1988 Act have been amended or repealed, new provisions substituted for original provisions and new ss. 135A to 135G and 297A added by the Broadcasting Act 1990 (c. 42). These matters are dealt with in the body of the 1988 Act, where relevant, with explanatory Notes. The 1990 Act also provided, in s. 176 of and Sched. 17 to that Act, provisions relating to the new statutory duty to provide information about programmes and to settling the terms of payment by the Copyright Tribunal. These provisions, which do not amend the 1988 Act, are printed as §§A–79A and A–79B *post* with an explanatory Note.

CHAPTER IV

MORAL RIGHTS

Right to be identified as author or director

CHAPTER VIII

THE COPYRIGHT TRIBUNAL

The tribunal

CHAPTER IX

QUALIFICATION FOR AND EXTENT OF COPYRIGHT PROTECTION

Qualification for copyright protection

Supplementary

PART III

DESIGN RIGHT

CHAPTER I

DESIGN RIGHT IN ORIGINAL DESIGNS

Introductory

849

Appendix A

Fraudulent reception of transmissions

An Act to restate the law of copyright, with amendments; to make fresh provision as to the rights of performers and others in performances; to confer a design right in original designs; to amend the Registered Designs Act 1949; to make provision with respect to patent agents and trade mark agents; to confer patents and designs jurisdiction on certain county courts; to amend the law of patents; to make provision with respect to devices designed to circumvent copy-protection of works in electronic form; to make fresh provision penalising the fraudulent reception of transmissions; to make the fraudulent application or use of a trade mark an offence; to make provision for the benefit of the Hospital for Sick Children, Great Ormond Street, London; to enable financial assistance to be given to certain international bodies; and for connected purposes. [15th November 1988]

852

PART I

COPYRIGHT

CHAPTER I

SUBSISTENCE, OWNERSHIP AND DURATION OF COPYRIGHT

Introductory

Copyright and copyright works

1.—(1) Copyright is a property right which subsists in accordance with this **A–4**
Part in the following descriptions of work—
  (*a*) original literary, dramatic, musical or artistic works,
  (*b*) sound recordings, films, broadcasts or cable programmes, and
  (*c*) the typographical arrangement of published editions.

(2) In this Part "copyright work" means a work of any of those descriptions in
which copyright subsists.
(3) Copyright does not subsist in a work unless the requirements of this Part
with respect to qualification for copyright protection are met (see section 153 and
the provisions referred to there).

Rights subsisting in copyright works

2.—(1) The owner of the copyright in a work of any description has the exclu- **A–5**
sive right to do the acts specified in Chapter II as the acts restricted by the copyright in a work of that description.
(2) In relation to certain descriptions of copyright work the following rights conferred by Chapter IV (moral rights) subsist in favour of the author, director or
commissioner of the work, whether or not he is the owner of the copyright—
  (*a*) section 77 (right to be identified as author or director),
  (*b*) section 80 (right to object to derogatory treatment of work), and
  (*c*) section 85 (right to privacy of certain photographs and films).

Descriptions of work and related provisions

Literary, dramatic and musical works

3.—(1) In this Part— **A–6**

"literary work" means any work, other than a dramatic or musical work, which is
  written, spoken or sung, and accordingly includes—
  (*a*) a table or compilation, and
  (*b*) a computer program;

"dramatic work" includes a work of dance or mime; and

"musical work" means a work consisting of music, exclusive of any words or
  action intended to be sung, spoken or performed with the music.

(2) Copyright does not subsist in a literary, dramatic or musical work unless
and until it is recorded, in writing or otherwise; and references in this Part to the
time at which such a work is made are to the time at which it is so recorded.
(3) It is immaterial for the purposes of subsection (2) whether the work is
recorded by or with the permission of the author; and where it is not recorded by

the author, nothing in that subsection affects the question whether copyright subsists in the record as distinct from the work recorded.

Artistic works

A–7 **4.**—(1) In this Part "artistic work" means—
  (*a*) a graphic work, photograph, sculpture or collage, irrespective of artistic quality,
  (*b*) a work of architecture being a building or a model for a building or
  (*c*) a work of artistic craftsmanship.

(2) In this Part—

"building" includes any fixed structure, and a part of a building or fixed structure;

"graphic work" includes—
  (*a*) any painting, drawing, diagram, map, chart or plan, and
  (*b*) any engraving, etching, lithograph, woodcut or similar work;

"photograph" means a recording of light or other radiation on any medium on which an image is produced or from which an image may by any means be produced, and which is not part of a film;

"sculpture" includes a cast or model made for purposes of sculpture.

Sound recordings and films

A–8 **5.**—(1) In this Part—

"sound recording" means—
  (*a*) a recording of sounds, from which the sounds may be reproduced, or
  (*b*) a recording of the whole or any part of a literary, dramatic or musical work, from which sounds reproducing the work or part may be produced, regardless of the medium on which the recording is made or the method by which the sounds are reproduced or produced; and

"film" means a recording on any medium from which a moving image may by any means be produced.

(2) Copyright does not subsist in a sound recording or film which is, or to the extent that it is, a copy taken from a previous sound recording or film.

Broadcasts

A–9 **6.**—(1) In this Part a "broadcast" means a transmission by wireless telegraphy of visual images, sounds or other information which—
  (*a*) is capable of being lawfully received by members of the public, or
  (*b*) is transmitted for presentation to members of the public;
and references to broadcasting shall be construed accordingly.

(2) An encrypted transmission shall be regarded as capable of being lawfully received by members of the public only if decoding equipment has been made available to members of the public by or with the authority of the person making the transmission or the person providing the contents of the transmission.

(3) References in this Part to the person making a broadcast, broadcasting a work, or including a work in a broadcast are—
  (*a*) to the person transmitting the programme, if he has responsibility to any extent for its contents, and
  (*b*) to any person providing the programme who makes with the person transmitting it the arrangements necessary for its transmission;
and references in this Part to a programme, in the context of broadcasting, are to any item included in a broadcast.

(4) For the purposes of this Part the place from which a broadcast is made is, in the case of a satellite transmission, the place from which the signals carrying the broadcast are transmitted to the satellite.

(5) References in this Part to the reception of a broadcast include reception of a broadcast relayed by means of a telecommunications system.

(6) Copyright does not subsist in a broadcast which infringes, or to the extent that it infringes, the copyright in another broadcast or in a cable programme.

Cable programmes

7.—(1) In this Part—

"cable programme" means any item included in a cable programme service; and

"cable programme service" means a service which consists wholly or mainly in sending visual images, sounds or other information by means of a telecommunications system, otherwise than by wireless telegraphy, for reception—
  (*a*) at two or more places (whether for simultaneous reception or at different times in response to requests by different users), or
  (*b*) for presentation to members of the public,
and which is not, or so far as it is not, excepted by or under the following provisions of this section.

(2) The following are excepted from the definition of "cable programme service"—
  (*a*) a service or part of a service of which it is an essential feature that while visual images, sounds or other information are being conveyed by the person providing the service there will or may be sent from each place of reception, by means of the same system or (as the case may be) the same part of it, information (other than signals sent for the operation or control of the service) for reception by the person providing the service or other persons receiving it;
  (*b*) a service run for the purposes of a business where—
    (i) no person except the person carrying on the business is concerned in the control of the apparatus comprised in the system,
    (ii) the visual images, sounds or other information are conveyed by the system solely for purposes internal to the running of the business and not by way of rendering a service or providing amenities for others, and
    (iii) the system is not connected to any other telecommunications system;
  (*c*) a service run by a single individual where—
    (i) all the apparatus comprised in the system is under his control,
    (ii) the visual images, sounds or other information conveyed by the system are conveyed solely for domestic purposes of his, and
    (iii) the system is not connected to any other telecommunications system;
  (*d*) services where—
    (i) all the apparatus comprised in the system is situated in, or connects, premises which are in single occupation, and
    (ii) the system is not connected to any other telecommunications system,
    other than services operated as part of the amenities provided for residents or inmates of premises run as a business;
  (*e*) services which are, or to the extent that they are, run for persons providing broadcasting or cable programme services or providing programmes for such services.

(3) The Secretary of State may by order amend subsection (2) so as to add or remove exceptions, subject to such transitional provision as appears to him to be appropriate.

(4) An order shall be made by statutory instrument; and no order shall be made unless a draft of it has been laid before and approved by resolution of each House of Parliament.

(5) References in this Part to the inclusion of a cable programme or work in a cable programme service are to its transmission as part of the service; and references to the person including it are to the person providing the service.

(6) Copyright does not subsist in a cable programme—

    (*a*) if it is included in a cable programme service by reception and immediate re-transmission of a broadcast, or

    (*b*) if it infringes, or to the extent that it infringes, the copyright in another cable programme or in a broadcast.

Published editions

A–11   **8.**—(1) In this Part "published edition," in the context of copyright in the typographical arrangement of a published edition, means a published edition of the whole or any part of one or more literary, dramatic or musical works.

(2) Copyright does not subsist in the typographical arrangement of a published edition if, or to the extent that, it reproduces the typographical arrangement of a previous edition.

Authorship and ownership of copyright

Authorship of work

A–12   **9.**—(1) In this Part "author," in relation to a work, means the person who creates it.

(2) That person shall be taken to be—

    (*a*) in the case of a sound recording or film, the person by whom the arrangements necessary for the making of the recording or film are undertaken;

    (*b*) in the case of a broadcast, the person making the broadcast (see section 6(3)) or, in the case of a broadcast which relays another broadcast by reception and immediate re-transmission, the person making that other broadcast;

    (*c*) in the case of a cable programme, the person providing the cable programme service in which the programme is included;

    (*d*) in the case of the typographical arrangement of a published edition, the publisher.

(3) In the case of a literary, dramatic, musical or artistic work which is computer-generated, the author shall be taken to be the person by whom the arrangements necessary for the creation of the work are undertaken.

(4) For the purposes of this Part a work is of "unknown authorship" if the identity of the author is unknown or, in the case of a work of joint authorship, if the identity of none of the authors is known.

(5) For the purposes of this Part the identity of an author shall be regarded as unknown if it is not possible for a person to ascertain his identity by reasonable inquiry; but if his identity is once known it shall not subsequently be regarded as unknown.

Works of joint authorship

A–13   **10.**—(1) In this Part a "work of joint authorship" means a work produced by the collaboration of two or more authors in which the contribution of each author is not distinct from that of the other author or authors.

(2) A broadcast shall be treated as a work of joint authorship in any case where more than one person is to be taken as making the broadcast (see section 6(3)).

(3) References in this Part to the author of a work shall, except as otherwise provided, be construed in relation to a work of joint authorship as references to all the authors of the work.

First ownership of copyright

11.—(1) The author of a work is the first owner of any copyright in it, subject to **A–14**
the following provisions.

(2) Where a literary, dramatic, musical or artistic work is made by an employee in the course of his employment, his employer is the first owner of any copyright in the work subject to any agreement to the contrary.

(3) This section does not apply to Crown copyright or Parliamentary copyright (see sections 163 and 165) or to copyright which subsists by virtue of section 168 (copyright of certain international organisations).

Duration of copyright

Duration of copyright in literary, dramatic, musical or artistic works

12.—(1) Copyright in a literary, dramatic, musical or artistic work expires at **A–15**
the end of the period of 50 years from the end of the calendar year in which the author dies, subject to the following provisions of this section.

(2) If the work is of unknown authorship, copyright expires at the end of the period of 50 years from the end of the calendar year in which it is first made available to the public; and subsection (1) does not apply if the identity of the author becomes known after the end of that period.

For this purpose making available to the public includes—
  (*a*) in the case of a literary, dramatic or musical work—
    (i) performance in public, or
    (ii) being broadcast or included in a cable programme service;
  (*b*) in the case of an artistic work—
    (i) exhibition in public,
    (ii) a film including the work being shown in public, or
    (iii) being included in a broadcast or cable programme service;
but in determining generally for the purposes of this subsection whether a work has been made available to the public no account shall be taken of any unauthorised act.

(3) If the work is computer-generated neither of the above provisions applies and copyright expires at the end of the period of 50 years from the end of the calendar year in which the work was made.

(4) In relation to a work of joint authorship—
  (*a*) the reference in subsection (1) to the death of the author shall be construed—
    (i) if the identity of all the authors is known, as a reference to the death of the last of them to die, and
    (ii) if the identity of one or more of the authors is known and the identity of one or more others is not, as a reference to the death of the last of the authors whose identity is known; and
  (*b*) the reference in subsection (2) to the identity of the author becoming known shall be construed as a reference to the identity of any of the authors becoming known.

(5) This section does not apply to Crown copyright or Parliamentary copyright (see sections 163 to 166) or to copyright which subsists by virtue of section 168 (copyright of certain international organisations).

Duration of copyright in sound recordings and films

A–16   **13.**—(1) Copyright in a sound recording or film expires—

    (*a*) at the end of the period of 50 years from the end of the calendar year in which it is made, or

    (*b*) if it is released before the end of that period, 50 years from the end of the calendar year in which it is released.

(2) A sound recording or film is "released" when—

    (*a*) it is first published, broadcast or included in a cable programme service, or

    (*b*) in the case of a film or film sound-track, the film is first shown in public;

but in determining whether a work has been released no account shall be taken of any unauthorised act.

Duration of copyright in broadcasts and cable programmes

A–17   **14.**—(1) Copyright in a broadcast or cable programme expires at the end of the period of 50 years from the end of the calendar year in which the broadcast was made or the programme was included in a cable programme service.

(2) Copyright in a repeat broadcast or cable programme expires at the same time as the copyright in the original broadcast or cable programme; and accordingly no copyright arises in respect of a repeat broadcast or cable programme which is broadcast or included in a cable programme service after the expiry of the copyright in the original broadcast or cable programme.

(3) A repeat broadcast or cable programme means one which is a repeat either of a broadcast previously made or of a cable programme previously included in a cable programme service.

Duration of copyright in typographical arrangement of published editions

A–18   **15.** Copyright in the typographical arrangement of a published edition expires at the end of the period of 25 years from the end of the calendar year in which the edition was first published.

CHAPTER II

RIGHTS OF COPYRIGHT OWNER

The acts restricted by copyright

The acts restricted by copyright in a work

A–19   **16.**—(1) The owner of the copyright in a work has, in accordance with the following provisions of this Chapter, the exclusive right to do the following acts in the United Kingdom—

    (*a*) to copy the work (see section 17);

    (*b*) to issue copies of the work to the public (see section 18);

    (*c*) to perform, show or play the work in public (see section 19);

    (*d*) to broadcast the work or include it in a cable programme service (see section 20);

    (*e*) to make an adaptation of the work or do any of the above in relation to an adaptation (see section 21);

and those acts are referred to in this Part as the "acts restricted by the copyright."

(2) Copyright in a work is infringed by a person who without the licence of the copyright owner does, or authorises another to do, any of the acts restricted by the copyright.

(3) References in this Part to the doing of an act restricted by the copyright in a work are to the doing of it—

(*a*) in relation to the work as a whole or any substantial part of it, and

(*b*) either directly or indirectly;

and it is immaterial whether any intervening acts themselves infringe copyright.

(4) This Chapter has effect subject to—

(*a*) the provisions of Chapter III (acts permitted in relation to copyright works), and

(*b*) the provisions of Chapter VII (provisions with respect to copyright licensing).

Infringement of copyright by copying

17.—(1) The copying of the work is an act restricted by the copyright in every description of copyright work; and references in this Part to copying and copies shall be construed as follows. **A–20**

(2) Copying in relation to a literary, dramatic, musical or artistic work means reproducing the work in any material form.

This includes storing the work in any medium by electronic means.

(3) In relation to an artistic work copying includes the making of a copy in three dimensions of two-dimensional work and the making of a copy in two dimensions of a three-dimensional work.

(4) Copying in relation to a film, television broadcast or cable programme includes making a photograph of the whole or any substantial part of any image forming part of the film, broadcast or cable programme.

(5) Copying in relation to the typographical arrangement of a published edition means making a facsimile copy of the arrangement.

(6) Copying in relation to any description of work includes the making of copies which are transient or are incidental to some other use of the work.

Infringement by issue of copies to the public

18.—(1) The issue to the public of copies of the work is an act restricted by the copyright in every description of copyright work. **A–21**

(2) References in this Part to the issue to the public of copies of a work are to the act of putting into circulation copies not previously put into circulation, in the United Kingdom or elsewhere, and not to—

(*a*) any subsequent distribution, sale, hiring or loan of those copies, or

(*b*) any subsequent importation of those copies into the United Kingdom;

except that in relation to sound recordings, films and computer programs the restricted act of issuing copies to the public includes any rental of copies to the public.

Infringement by performance, showing or playing of work in public

19.—(1) The performance of the work in public is an act restricted by the copyright in a literary, dramatic or musical work. **A–22**

(2) In this Part "performance," in relation to a work—

(*a*) includes delivery in the case of lectures, addresses, speeches and sermons, and

(*b*) in general, includes any mode of visual or acoustic presentation, including presentation by means of a sound recording, film, broadcast or cable programme of the work.

(3) The playing or showing of the work in public is an act restricted by the copyright in a sound recording, film, broadcast or cable programme.

(4) Where copyright in a work is infringed by its being performed, played or shown in public by means of apparatus for receiving visual images or sounds con-

veyed by electronic means, the person by whom the visual images or sounds are sent, and in the case of a performance the performers, shall not be regarded as responsible for the infringement.

Infringement by broadcasting or inclusion in a cable programme service

A–23   **20.** The broadcasting of the work or its inclusion in a cable programme service is an act restricted by the copyright in—

(*a*) a literary, dramatic, musical or artistic work,

(*b*) a sound recording or film, or

(*c*) a broadcast or cable programme.

Infringement by making adaptation or act done in relation to adaptation

A–24   **21.**—(1) The making of an adaptation of the work is an act restricted by the copyright in a literary, dramatic or musical work.

For this purpose an adaptation is made when it is recorded, in writing or otherwise.

(2) The doing of any of the acts specified in sections 17 to 20, or subsection (1) above, in relation to an adaptation of the work is also an act restricted by the copyright in a literary, dramatic or musical work.

For this purpose it is immaterial whether the adaptation has been recorded, in writing or otherwise, at the time the act is done.

(3) In this Part "adaptation"—

(*a*) in relation to a literary or dramatic work, means—

(i) a translation of the work;

(ii) a version of a dramatic work in which it is converted into a non-dramatic work or, as the case may be, of a non-dramatic work in which it is converted into a dramatic work;

(iii) a version of the work in which the story or action is conveyed wholly or mainly by means of pictures in a form suitable for reproduction in a book, or in a newspaper, magazine or similar periodical;

(*b*) in relation to a musical work, means an arrangement or transcription of the work.

(4) In relation to a computer program a "translation" includes a version of the program in which it is converted into or out of a computer language or code or into a different computer language or code, otherwise than incidentally in the course of running the program.

(5) No inference shall be drawn from this section as to what does or does not amount to copying a work.

Secondary infringement of copyright

Secondary infringement: importing infringing copy

A–25   **22.** The copyright in a work is infringed by a person who, without the licence of the copyright owner, imports into the United Kingdom, otherwise than for his private and domestic use, an article which is, and which he knows or has reason to believe is, an infringing copy of the work.

Secondary infringement: possessing or dealing with infringing copy

A–26   **23.** The copyright in a work is infringed by a person who, without the licence of the copyright owner—

(*a*) possesses in the course of a business,

(*b*) sells or lets for hire, or offers or exposes for sale or hire, (*c*) in the course of a business exhibits in public or distributes, or

(*d*) distributes otherwise than in the course of a business to such an extent as to affect prejudicially the owner of the copyright,

an article which is, and which he knows or has reason to believe is, an infringing copy of the work.

Secondary infringement: providing means for making infringing copies

24.—(1) Copyright in a work is infringed by a person who, without the licence   **A–27** of the copyright owner—

(*a*) makes,

(*b*) imports into the United Kingdom,

(*c*) possesses in the course of a business, or

(*d*) sells or lets for hire, or offers or exposes for sale or hire,

an article specifically designed or adapted for making copies of that work, knowing or having reason to believe that it is to be used to make infringing copies.

(2) Copyright in a work is infringed by a person who without the licence of the copyright owner transmits the work by means of a telecommunications system (otherwise than by broadcasting or inclusion in a cable programme service), knowing or having reason to believe that infringing copies of the work will be made by means of the reception of the transmission in the United Kingdom or elsewhere.

Secondary infringement: permitting use of premises for infringing performance

25.—(1) Where the copyright in a literary, dramatic or musical work is   **A–28** infringed by a performance at a place of public entertainment, any person who gave permission for that place to be used for the performance is also liable for the infringement unless when he gave permission he believed on reasonable grounds that the performance would not infringe copyright.

(2) In this section "place of public entertainment" includes premises which are occupied mainly for other purposes but are from time to time made available for hire for the purposes of public entertainment.

Secondary infringement: provision of apparatus for infringing performance, &c

26.—(1) Where copyright in a work is infringed by a public performance of the   **A–29** work, or by the playing or showing of the work in public, by means of apparatus for—

(*a*) playing sound recordings,

(*b*) showing films, or

(*c*) receiving visual images or sounds conveyed by electronic means,

the following persons are also liable for the infringement.

(2) A person who supplied the apparatus, or any substantial part of it, is liable for the infringement if when he supplied the apparatus or part—

(*a*) he knew or had reason to believe that the apparatus was likely to be so used as to infringe copyright, or

(*b*) in the case of apparatus whose normal use involves a public performance, playing or showing, he did not believe on reasonable grounds that it would not be so used as to infringe copyright.

(3) An occupier of premises who gave permission for the apparatus to be brought on to the premises is liable for the infringement if when he gave permission he knew or had reason to believe that the apparatus was likely to be so used as to infringe copyright.

(4) A person who supplied a copy of a sound recording or film used to infringe copyright is liable for the infringement if when he supplied it he knew or had reason to believe that what he supplied, or a copy made directly or indirectly from it, was likely to be so used as to infringe copyright.

Infringing copies

Meaning of "infringing copy"

A–30   **27.**—(1) In this Part "infringing copy," in relation to a copyright work, shall be construed in accordance with this section.

(2) An article is an infringing copy if its making constituted an infringement of the copyright in the work in question.

(3) An article is also an infringing copy if—

(*a*) it has been or is proposed to be imported into the United Kingdom, and

(*b*) its making in the United Kingdom would have constituted an infringement of the copyright in the work in question, or a breach of an exclusive licence agreement relating to that work.

(4) Where in any proceedings the question arises whether an article is an infringing copy and it is shown—

(*a*) that the article is a copy of the work, and

(*b*) that copyright subsists in the work or has subsisted at any time,

it shall be presumed until the contrary is proved that the article was made at a time when copyright subsisted in the work.

(5) Nothing in subsection (3) shall be construed as applying to an article which may lawfully be imported into the United Kingdom by virtue of any enforceable Community right within the meaning of section 2(1) of the European Communities Act 1972.

(6) In this Part "infringing copy" includes a copy falling to be treated as an infringing copy by virtue of any of the following provisions—

section 32(5) (copies made for purposes of instruction or examination),
section 35(3) (recordings made by educational establishments for educational purposes),
section 36(5) (reprographic copying by educational establishments for purposes of instruction),
section 37(3)(*b*) (copies made by librarian or archivist in reliance on false declaration),
section 56(2) (further copies, adaptations, &c. of work in electronic form retained on transfer of principal copy),
section 63(2) (copies made for purpose of advertising artistic work for sale),
section 68(4) (copies made for purpose of broadcast or cable programme), or
any provision of an order under section 141 (statutory licence for certain reprographic copying for educational establishments).

CHAPTER III

ACTS PERMITTED IN RELATION TO COPYRIGHT WORKS

Introductory

Introductory provisions

A–31   **28.**—(1) The provisions of this Chapter specify acts which may be done in relation to copyright works notwithstanding the subsistence of copyright; they relate only to the question of infringement of copyright and do not affect any other right or obligation restricting the doing of any of the specified acts.

(2) Where it is provided by this Chapter that an act does not infringe copyright, or may be done without infringing copyright, and no particular description of copyright work is mentioned, the act in question does not infringe the copyright in a work of any description.

(3) No inference shall be drawn from the description of any act which may by virtue of this Chapter be done without infringing copyright as to the scope of the acts restricted by the copyright in any description of work.

(4) The provisions of this Chapter are to be construed independently of each other, so that the fact that an act does not fall within one provision does not mean that it is not covered by another provision.

General

Research and private study

29.—(1) Fair dealing with a literary, dramatic, musical or artistic work for the purposes of research or private study does not infringe any copyright in the work or, in the case of a published edition, in the typographical arrangement.   **A–32**

(2) Fair dealing with the typographical arrangement of a published edition for the purposes mentioned in subsection (1) does not infringe any copyright in the arrangement.

(3) Copying by a person other than the researcher or student himself is not fair dealing if—

    (*a*) in the case of a librarian, or a person acting on behalf of a librarian, he does anything which regulations under section 40 would not permit to be done under section 38 or 39 (articles or parts of published works: restriction on multiple copies of same material), or

    (*b*) in any other case, the person doing the copying knows or has reason to believe that it will result in copies of substantially the same material being provided to more than one person at substantially the same time and for substantially the same purpose.

Criticism, review and news reporting

30.—(1) Fair dealing with a work for the purpose of criticism or review, of that or another work or of a performance of a work, does not infringe any copyright in the work provided that it is accompanied by a sufficient acknowledgement.   **A–33**

(2) Fair dealing with a work (other than a photograph) for the purpose of reporting current events does not infringe any copyright in the work provided that (subject to subsection (3)) it is accompanied by a sufficient acknowledgement.

(3) No acknowledgement is required in connection with the reporting of current events by means of a sound recording, film, broadcast or cable programme.

Incidental inclusion of copyright material

31.—(1) Copyright in a work is not infringed by its incidental inclusion in an artistic work, sound recording, film, broadcast or cable programme.   **A–34**

(2) Nor is the copyright infringed by the issue to the public of copies, or the playing, showing, broadcasting or inclusion in a cable programme service, of anything whose making was, by virtue of subsection (1), not an infringement of the copyright.

(3) A musical work, words spoken or sung with music, or so much of a sound recording, broadcast or cable programme as includes a musical work or such words, shall not be regarded as incidentally included in another work if it is deliberately included.

Education

Things done for purposes of instruction or examination

A–35　**32.**—(1) Copyright in a literary, dramatic, musical or artistic work is not infringed by its being copied in the course of instruction or of preparation for instruction, provided the copying—

(*a*) is done by a person giving or receiving instruction, and

(*b*) is not by means of a reprographic process.

(2) Copyright in a sound recording, film, broadcast or cable programme is not infringed by its being copied by making a film or film sound-track in the course of instruction, or of preparation for instruction, in the making of films or film sound-tracks, provided the copying is done by a person giving or receiving instruction.

(3) Copyright is not infringed by anything done for the purposes of an examination by way of setting the questions, communicating the questions to the candidates or answering the questions.

(4) Subsection (3) does not extend to the making of a reprographic copy of a musical work for use by an examination candidate in performing the work.

(5) Where a copy which would otherwise be an infringing copy is made in accordance with this section but is subsequently dealt with, it shall be treated as an infringing copy for the purpose of that dealing, and if that dealing infringes copyright for all subsequent purposes.

For this purpose "dealt with" means sold or let for hire or offered or exposed for sale or hire.

Anthologies for educational use

A–36　**33.**—(1) The inclusion of a short passage from a published literary or dramatic work in a collection which—

(*a*) is intended for use in educational establishments and is so described in its title, and in any advertisements issued by or on behalf of the publisher, and

(*b*) consists mainly of material in which no copyright subsists,

does not infringe the copyright in the work if the work itself is not intended for use in such establishments and the inclusion is accompanied by a sufficient acknowledgement.

(2) Subsection (1) does not authorise the inclusion of more than two excerpts from copyright works by the same author in collections published by the same publisher over any period of five years.

(3) In relation to any given passage the reference in subsection (2) to excerpts from works by the same author—

(*a*) shall be taken to include excerpts from works by him in collaboration with another, and

(*b*) if the passage in question is from such a work, shall be taken to include excerpts from works by any of the authors, whether alone or in collaboration with another.

(4) References in this section to the use of a work in an educational establishment are to any use for the educational purposes of such an establishment.

Performing, playing or showing work in course of activities of educational establishment

A–37　**34.**—(1) The performance of a literary, dramatic or musical work before an audience consisting of teachers and pupils at an educational establishment and other persons directly connected with the activities of the establishment—

(*a*) by a teacher or pupil in the course of the activities of the establishment, or

(*b*) at the establishment by any person for the purposes of instruction,

is not a public performance for the purposes of infringement of copyright.

(2) The playing or showing of a sound recording, film, broadcast or cable programme before such an audience at an educational establishment for the purposes of instruction is not a playing or showing of the work in public for the purposes of infringement of copyright.

(3) A person is not for this purpose directly connected with the activities of the educational establishment simply because he is the parent of a pupil at the establishment.

Recording by educational establishments of broadcasts and cable programmes

35.—(1) A recording of a broadcast or cable programme, or a copy of such a **A–38** recording, may be made by or on behalf of an educational establishment for the educational purposes of that establishment without thereby infringing the copyright in the broadcast or cable programme, or in any work included in it.

(2) This section does not apply if or to the extent that there is a licensing scheme certified for the purposes of this section under section 143 providing for the grant of licences.

(3) Where a copy which would otherwise be an infringing copy is made in accordance with this section but is subsequently dealt with, it shall be treated as an infringing copy for the purposes of that dealing, and if that dealing infringes copyright for all subsequent purposes.

For this purpose "dealt with" means sold or let for hire or offered or exposed for sale or hire.

Reprographic copying by educational establishments of passages from published works

36.—(1) Reprographic copies of passages from published literary, dramatic or **A–39** musical works may, to the extent permitted by this section, be made by or on behalf of an educational establishment for the purposes of instruction without infringing any copyright in the work, or in the typographical arrangement.

(2) Not more than one per cent. of any work may be copied by or on behalf of an establishment by virtue of this section in any quarter, that is, in any period 1st January to 31st March, 1st April to 30th June, 1st July to 30th September or 1st October to 31st December.

(3) Copying is not authorised by this section if, or to the extent that, licences are available authorising the copying in question and the person making the copies knew or ought to have been aware of that fact.

(4) The terms of a licence granted to an educational establishment authorising the reprographic copying for the purposes of instruction of passages from published literary, dramatic or musical works are of no effect so far as they purport to restrict the proportion of a work which may be copied (whether on payment or free of charge) to less than that which would be permitted under this section.

(5) Where a copy which would otherwise be an infringing copy is made in accordance with this section but is subsequently dealt with, it shall be treated as an infringing copy for the purposes of that dealing, and if that dealing infringes copyright for all subsequent purposes.

For this purpose "dealt with" means sold or let for hire or offered or exposed for sale or hire.

Libraries and archives

Libraries and archives: introductory

A–40   37.—(1) In sections 38 to 43 (copying by librarians and archivists)—

(*a*) references in any provision to a prescribed library or archive are to a library or archive of a description prescribed for the purposes of that provision by regulations made by the Secretary of State; and

(*b*) references in any provision to the prescribed conditions are to the conditions so prescribed.

(2) The regulations may provide that, where a librarian or archivist is required to be satisfied as to any matter before making or supplying a copy of a work—

(*a*) he may rely on a signed declaration as to that matter by the person requesting the copy, unless he is aware that it is false in a material particular, and

(*b*) in such cases as may be prescribed, he shall not make or supply a copy in the absence of a signed declaration in such form as may be prescribed.

(3) Where a person requesting a copy makes a declaration which is false in a material particular and is supplied with a copy which would have been an infringing copy if made by him—

(*a*) he is liable for infringement of copyright as if he had made the copy himself, and

(*b*) the copy shall be treated as an infringing copy.

(4) The regulations may make different provision for different descriptions of libraries or archives and for different purposes.

(5) Regulations shall be made by statutory instrument which shall be subject to annulment in pursuance of a resolution of either House of Parliament.

(6) References in this section, and in sections 38 to 43, to the librarian or archivist include a person acting on his behalf.

Copying by librarians: articles in periodicals

A–41   38.—(1) The librarian of a prescribed library may, if the prescribed conditions are complied with, make and supply a copy of an article in a periodical without infringing any copyright in the text, in any illustrations accompanying the text or in the typographical arrangement.

(2) The prescribed conditions shall include the following—

(*a*) that copies are supplied only to persons satisfying the librarian that they require them for purposes of research or private study, and will not use them for any other purpose;

(*b*) that no person is furnished with more than one copy of the same article or with copies of more than one article contained in the same issue of a periodical; and

(*c*) that persons to whom copies are supplied are required to pay for them a sum not less than the cost (including a contribution to the general expenses of the library) attributable to their production.

Copying by librarians: parts of published works

A–42   39.—(1) The librarian of a prescribed library may, if the prescribed conditions are complied with, make and supply from a published edition a copy of part of a literary, dramatic or musical work (other than an article in a periodical) without infringing any copyright in the work, in any illustrations accompanying the work or in the typographical arrangement.

(2) The prescribed conditions shall include the following—

(*a*) that copies are supplied only to persons satisfying the librarian that they require them for purposes of research or private study, and will not use them for any other purpose;

(*b*) that no person is furnished with more than one copy of the same material or with a copy of more than a reasonable proportion of any work; and

(*c*) that persons to whom copies are supplied are required to pay for them a sum not less than the cost (including a contribution to the general expenses of the library) attributable to their production.

Restriction on production of multiple copies of the same material

40.—(1) Regulations for the purposes of sections 38 and 39 (copying by librarian of article or part of published work) shall contain provision to the effect that a copy shall be supplied only to a person satisfying the librarian that his requirement is not related to any similar requirement of another person. **A–43**

(2) The regulations may provide—

(*a*) that requirements shall be regarded as similar if the requirements are for copies of substantially the same material at substantially the same time and for substantially the same purpose; and

(*b*) that requirements of persons shall be regarded as related if those persons receive instructions to which the material is relevant at the same time and place.

Copying by librarians: supply of copies to other libraries

41.—(1) The librarian of a prescribed library may, if the prescribed conditions are complied with, make and supply to another prescribed library a copy of— **A–44**

(*a*) an article in a periodical, or

(*b*) the whole or part of a published edition of a literary, dramatic or musical work,

without infringing any copyright in the text of the article or, as the case may be, in the work, in any illustrations accompanying it or in the typographical arrangement.

(2) Subsection (1)(*b*) does not apply if at the time the copy is made the librarian making it knows, or could by reasonable inquiry ascertain, the name and address of a person entitled to authorise the making of the copy.

Copying by librarians or archivists: replacement copies of works

42.—(1) The librarian or archivist of a prescribed library or archive may, if the prescribed conditions are complied with, make a copy from any item in the permanent collection of the library or archive— **A–45**

(*a*) in order to preserve or replace that item by placing the copy in its permanent collection in addition to or in place of it, or

(*b*) in order to replace in the permanent collection of another prescribed library or archive an item which has been lost, destroyed or damaged,

without infringing the copyright in any literary, dramatic or musical work, in any illustrations accompanying such a work or, in the case of a published edition, in the typographical arrangement.

(2) The prescribed conditions shall include provision for restricting the making of copies to cases where it is not reasonably practicable to purchase a copy of the item in question to fulfil that purpose.

Copying by librarians or archivists: certain unpublished works

43.—(1) The librarian or archivist of a prescribed library or archive may, if the prescribed conditions are complied with, make and supply a copy of the whole or part of a literary, dramatic or musical work from a document in the library or **A–46**

archive without infringing any copyright in the work or any illustrations accompanying it.

(2) This section does not apply if—

(a) the work had been published before the document was deposited in the library or archive, or

(b) the copyright owner has prohibited copying of the work,

and at the time the copy is made the librarian or archivist making it is, or ought to be, aware of that fact.

(3) The prescribed conditions shall include the following—

(a) that copies are supplied only to persons satisfying the librarian or archivist that they require them for purposes of research or private study and will not use them for any other purpose;

(b) that no person is furnished with more than one copy of the same material; and

(c) that persons to whom copies are supplied are required to pay for them a sum not less than the cost (including a contribution to the general expenses of the library or archive) attributable to their production.

Copy of work required to be made as condition of export

A–47   **44.** If an article of cultural or historical importance or interest cannot lawfully be exported from the United Kingdom unless a copy of it is made and deposited in an appropriate library or archive, it is not an infringement of copyright to make that copy.

Public administration

Parliamentary and judicial proceedings

A–48   **45.**—(1) Copyright is not infringed by anything done for the purposes of parliamentary or judicial proceedings.

(2) Copyright is not infringed by anything done for the purposes of reporting such proceedings; but this shall not be construed as authorising the copying of a work which is itself a published report of the proceedings.

Royal Commissions and statutory inquiries

A–49   **46.**—(1) Copyright is not infringed by anything done for the purposes of the proceedings of a Royal Commission or statutory inquiry.

(2) Copyright is not infringed by anything done for the purpose of reporting any such proceedings held in public; and this shall not be construed as authorising the copying of a work which is itself a published report of the proceedings.

(3) Copyright in a work is not infringed by the issue to the public of copies of the report of a Royal Commission or statutory inquiry containing the work or material from it.

(4) In this section—

"Royal Commission" includes a Commission appointed for Northern Ireland by the Secretary of State in pursuance of the prerogative powers of Her Majesty delegated to him under section 7(2) of the Northern Ireland Constitution Act 1973; and

"statutory inquiry" means an inquiry held or investigation conducted in pursuance of a duty imposed or power conferred by or under an enactment.

Material open to public inspection or on official register

47.—(1) Where material is open to public inspection pursuant to a statutory   **A–50**
requirement, or is on a statutory register, any copyright in the material as a literary work is not infringed by the copying of so much of the material as contains factual information of any description, by or with the authority of the appropriate
person, for a purpose which does not involve the issuing of copies to the public.

(2) Where material is open to public inspection pursuant to a statutory requirement, copyright is not infringed by the copying or issuing to the public of copies of
the material, by or with the authority of the appropriate person, for the purpose of
enabling the material to be inspected at a more convenient time or place or otherwise facilitating the exercise of any right for the purpose of which the requirement
is imposed.

(3) Where material which is open to public inspection pursuant to a statutory
requirement, or which is on a statutory register, contains information about
matters of general scientific, technical, commercial or economic interest, copyright
is not infringed by the copying or issuing to the public of copies of the material, by
or with the authority of the appropriate person, for the purpose of disseminating
that information.

(4) The Secretary of State may by order provide that subsection (1), (2) or (3)
shall, in such cases as may be specified in the order, apply only to copies marked in
such manner as may be so specified.

(5) The Secretary of State may by order provide that subsections (1) to (3)
apply, to such extent and with such modifications as may be specified in the
order—

    (*a*) to material made open to public inspection by—
        (i) an international organisation specified in the order, or
        (ii) a person so specified who has functions in the United Kingdom under
            an international agreement to which the United Kingdom is party, or
    (*b*) to a register maintained by an international organisation specified in the
        order,

as they apply in relation to material open to public inspection pursuant to a statutory requirement or to a statutory register.

(6) In this section—

"appropriate person" means the person required to make the material open to
    public inspection or, as the case may be, the person maintaining the register;

"statutory register" means a register maintained in pursuance of a statutory
    requirement; and

"statutory requirement" means a requirement imposed by provision made by or
    under an enactment.

(7) An order under this section shall be made by statutory instrument which
shall be subject to annulment in pursuance of a resolution of either House of Parliament.

Material communicated to the Crown in the course of public business

48.—(1) This section applies where a literary, dramatic, musical or artistic   **A–51**
work has in the course of public business been communicated to the Crown for any
purpose, by or with the licence of the copyright owner and a document or other
material thing recording or embodying the work is owned by or in the custody of
control of the Crown.

(2) The Crown may, for the purpose for which the work was communicated to
it, or any related purpose which could reasonably have been anticipated by the

copyright owner, copy the work and issue copies of the work to the public without infringing any copyright in the work.

(3) The Crown may not copy a work, or issue copies of a work to the public, by virtue of this section if the work has previously been published otherwise than by virtue of this section.

(4) In subsection (1) "public business" includes any activity carried on by the Crown.

(5) This section has effect subject to any agreement to the contrary between the Crown and the copyright owner.

Note: New subsection (b) added by 1990 (c.19) Schedule 8

Public records

A–52   **49.** Material which is comprised in public records within the meaning of the Public Records Act 1958, the Public Records (Scotland) Act 1937 or the Public Records Act (Northern Ireland) 1923 which are open to public inspection in pursuance of that Act, may be copied, and a copy may be supplied to any person, by or with the authority of any officer appointed under that Act, without infringement of copyright.

Acts done under statutory authority

A–53   **50.**—(1) Where the doing of a particular act is specifically authorised by an Act of Parliament, whenever passed, then, unless the Act provides otherwise, the doing of that act does not infringe copyright.

(2) Subsection (1) applies in relation to an enactment contained in Northern Ireland legislation as it applies in relation to an Act of Parliament.

(3) Nothing in this section shall be construed as excluding any defence of statutory authority otherwise available under or by virtue of any enactment.

Designs

Design documents and models

A–54   **51.**—(1) It is not an infringement of any copyright in a design document or model recording or embodying a design for anything other than an artistic work or a typeface to make an article to the design or to copy an article made to the design.

(2) Nor is it an infringement of the copyright to issue to the public, or include in a film, a broadcast or cable programme service, anything the making of which was, by virtue of subsection (1), not an infringement of that copyright.

(3) In this section—

"design" means the design of any aspect of the shape or configuration (whether internal or external) of the whole or part of an article, other than surface decoration; and

"design document" means any record of a design, whether in the form of a drawing, a written description, a photograph, data stored in a computer or otherwise.

Effect of exploitation of design derived from artistic work

A–55   **52.**—(1) This section applies where an artistic work has been exploited, by or with the licence of the copyright owner, by—

(*a*) making by an industrial process articles falling to be treated for the purposes of this Part as copies of the work, and

(*b*) marketing such articles, in the United Kingdom or elsewhere.

(2) After the end of the period of 25 years from the end of the calendar year in

which such articles are first marketed, the work may be copied by making articles of any description, or doing anything for the purpose of making articles of any description, and anything may be done in relation to articles so made, without infringing copyright in the work.

(3) Where only part of an artistic work is exploited as mentioned in subsection (1), subsection (2) applies only in relation to that part.

(4) The Secretary of State may by order make provision—

(*a*) as to the circumstances in which an article, or any description of article, is to be regarded for the purposes of this section as made by an industrial process;

(*b*) excluding from the operation of this section such articles of a primarily literary or artistic character as he thinks fit.

(5) An order shall be made by statutory instrument which shall be subject to annulment in pursuance of a resolution of either House of Parliament.

(6) In this section—

(*a*) references to articles do not include films; and

(*b*) references to the marketing of an article are to its being sold or let for hire or offered or exposed for sale or hire.

Things done in reliance on registration of design

53.—(1) The copyright in an artistic work is not infringed by anything done— **A–56**

(*a*) in pursuance of an assignment or licence made or granted by a person registered under the Registered Designs Act 1949 as the proprietor of a corresponding design, and

(*b*) in good faith in reliance on the registration and without notice of any proceedings for the cancellation of the registration or for rectifying the relevant entry in the register of designs;

and this is so notwithstanding that the person registered as the proprietor was not the proprietor of the design for the purposes of the 1949 Act.

(2) In subsection (1) a "corresponding design", in relation to an artistic work, means a design within the meaning of the 1949 Act which if applied to an article would produce something which would be treated for the purposes of this Part as a copy of the artistic work.

Typefaces

Use of typeface in ordinary course of printing

54.—(1) It is not an infringement of copyright in an artistic work consisting of **A–57** the design of a typeface—

(*a*) to use the typeface in the ordinary course of typing, composing text, typesetting or printing,

(*b*) to possess an article for the purpose of such use, or

(*c*) to do anything in relation to material produced by such use;

and this is so notwithstanding that an article is used which is an infringing copy of the work.

(2) However, the following provisions of this Part apply in relation to persons making, importing or dealing with articles specifically designed or adapted for producing material in a particular typeface, or possessing such articles for the purpose of dealing with them, as if the production of material as mentioned in subsection (1) did infringe copyright in the artistic work consisting of the design of the typeface—

section 24 (secondary infringement: making, importing, possessing or dealing with article for making infringing copy),

sections 99 and 100 (order for delivery up and right of seizure),
section 107(2) (offence of making or possessing such an article), and
section 108 (order for delivery up in criminal proceedings).

(3) The references in subsection (2) to "dealing with" an article are to selling, letting for hire, or offering or exposing for sale or hire, exhibiting in public, or distributing.

Articles for producing material in particular typeface

A–58   **55.**—(1) This section applies to the copyright in an artistic work consisting of the design of a typeface where articles specifically designed or adapted for producing material in that typeface have been marketed by or with the licence of the copyright owner.

(2) After the period of 25 years from the end of the calendar year in which the first such articles are marketed, the work may be copied by making further such articles, or doing anything for the purpose of making such articles, and anything may be done in relation to articles so made, without infringing copyright in the work.

(3) In subsection (1) "marketed" means sold, let for hire or offered or exposed for sale or hire, in the United Kingdom or elsewhere.

Works in electronic form

Transfers of copies of works in electronic form

A–59   **56.**—(1) This section applies where a copy of a work in electronic form has been purchased on terms which, expressly or impliedly or by virtue of any rule of law, allow the purchaser to copy the work, or to adapt it or make copies of an adaptation, in connection with his use of it.

(2) If there are no express terms—
  (*a*) prohibiting the transfer of the copy by the purchaser, imposing obligations which continue after a transfer, prohibiting the assignment of any licence or terminating any licence on a transfer, or
  (*b*) providing for the terms on which a transferee may do things which the purchaser was permitted to do,
anything which the purchaser was allowed to do may also be done without infringement of copyright by a transferee; but any copy, adaptation or copy of an adaptation made by the purchaser which is not also transferred shall be treated as an infringing copy for all purposes after the transfer.

(3) The same applies where the original purchased copy is no longer usable and what is transferred is a further copy used in its place.

(4) The above provisions also apply on a subsequent transfer, with the substitution for references in subsection (2) to the purchaser of references to the subsequent transferor.

Miscellaneous: literary, dramatic, musical and artistic works

Anonymous or pseudonymous works: acts permitted on assumptions as to expiry of copyright or death of author

A–60   **57.**—(1) Copyright in a literary, dramatic, musical or artistic work is not infringed by an act done at a time when, or in pursuance of arrangements made at a time when—
  (*a*) it is not possible by reasonable inquiry to ascertain the identity of the author, and

(*b*) it is reasonable to assume—
   (i) that copyright has expired, or
   (ii) that the author died 50 years or more before the beginning of the calendar year in which the act is done or the arrangements are made.

(2) Subsection (1)(*b*)(ii) does not apply in relation to—
(*a*) a work in which Crown copyright subsists, or
(*b*) a work in which copyright originally vested in an international organisation by virtue of section 168 and in respect of which an Order under that section specifies a copyright period longer than 50 years.

(3) In relation to a work of joint authorship—
(*a*) the reference in subsection (1) to its being possible to ascertain the identity of the author shall be construed as a reference to its being possible to ascertain the identity of any of the authors, and
(*b*) the reference in subsection (1)(b)(ii) to the author having died shall be construed as a reference to all the authors having died.

Use of notes or recordings of spoken words in certain cases

58.—(1) Where a record of spoken words is made, in writing or otherwise, for **A–61**
the purpose—
(*a*) of reporting current events, or
(*b*) of broadcasting or including in a cable programme service the whole or part of the work,
it is not an infringement of any copyright in the words as a literary work to use the record or material taken from it (or to copy the record, or any such material, and use the copy) for that purpose, provided the following conditions are met.

(2) The conditions are that—
(*a*) the record is a direct record of the spoken words and is not taken from a previous record or from a broadcast or cable programme;
(*b*) the making of the record was not prohibited by the speaker and, where copyright already subsisted in the work, did not infringe copyright;
(*c*) the use made of the record or material taken from it is not of a kind prohibited by or on behalf of the speaker or copyright owner before the record was made; and
(*d*) the use is by or with the authority of a person who is lawfully in possession of the record.

Public reading or recitation

59.—(1) The reading or recitation in public by one person of a reasonable **A–62**
extract from a published literary or dramatic work does not infringe any copyright in the work if it is accompanied by a sufficient acknowledgement.

(2) Copyright in a work is not infringed by the making of a sound recording, or the broadcasting or inclusion in a cable programme service, of a reading or recitation which by virtue of subsection (1) does not infringe copyright in the work, provided that the recording, broadcast or cable programme consists mainly of material in relation to which it is not necessary to rely on that subsection.

Abstracts of scientific or technical articles

60.—(1) Where an article on a scientific or technical subject is published in a **A–63**
periodical accompanied by an abstract indicating the contents of the article, it is not an infringement of copyright in the abstract, or in the article, to copy the abstract or issue copies of it to the public.

(2) This section does not apply if or to the extent that there is a licensing scheme

certified for the purposes of this section under section 143 providing for the grant of licences.

Recordings of folksongs

61.—(1) A sound recording of a performance of a song may be made for the purpose of including it in an archive maintained by a designated body without infringing any copyright in the words as a literary work or in the accompanying musical work, provided the conditions in subsection (2) below are met.

(2) The conditions are that—

(a) the words are unpublished and of unknown authorship at the time the recording is made,

(b) the making of the recording does not infringe any other copyright, and

(c) its making is not prohibited by any performer.

(3) Copies of a sound recording made in reliance on subsection (1) and included in an archive maintained by a designated body may, if the prescribed conditions are met, be made and supplied by the archivist without infringing copyright in the recording or the works included in it.

(4) The prescribed conditions shall include the following—

(a) that copies are only supplied to persons satisfying the archivist that they require them for purposes of research or private study and will not use them for any other purpose, and

(b) that no person is furnished with more than one copy of the same recording.

(5) In this section—

(a) "designated" means designated for the purposes of this section by order of the Secretary of State, who shall not designate a body unless satisfied that it is not established or conducted for profit,

(b) "prescribed" means prescribed for the purposes of this section by order of the Secretary of State, and

(c) references to the archivist include a person acting on his behalf.

(6) An order under this section shall be made by statutory instrument which shall be subject to annulment in pursuance of a resolution of either House of Parliament.

Representation of certain artistic works on public display

62.—(1) This section applies to—

(a) buildings, and

(b) sculptures, models for buildings and works of artistic craftsmanship, if permanently situated in a public place or in premises open to the public.

(2) The copyright in such a work is not infringed by—

(a) making a graphic work representing it,

(b) making a photograph or film of it, or

(c) broadcasting or including in a cable programme service a visual image of it.

(3) Nor is the copyright infringed by the issue to the public of copies, or the broadcasting or inclusion in a cable programme service, of anything whose making was, by virtue of this section, not an infringement of the copyright.

Advertisement of sale of artistic work

63.—(1) It is not an infringement of copyright in an artistic work to copy it, or to issue copies to the public, for the purpose of advertising the sale of the work.

(2) Where a copy which would otherwise be an infringing copy is made in

accordance with this section but is subsequently dealt with for any other purpose, it shall be treated as an infringing copy for the purposes of that dealing, and if that dealing infringes copyright for all subsequent purposes.

For this purpose "dealt with" means sold or let for hire, offered or exposed for sale or hire, exhibited in public or distributed.

Making of subsequent works by same artist

64. Where the author of an artistic work is not the copyright owner, he does not   **A–67** infringe the copyright by copying the work in making another artistic work, provided he does not repeat or imitate the main design of the earlier work.

Reconstruction of buildings

65. Anything done for the purposes of reconstructing a building does not   **A–68** infringe any copyright—
  (*a*) in the building, or
  (*b*) in any drawings or plans in accordance with which the building was, by or with the licence of the copyright owner, constructed.

Miscellaneous: sound recordings, films and computer programs

Rental of sound recordings, films and computer programs

66.—(1) The Secretary of State may by order provide that in such cases as may   **A–69** be specified in the order the rental to the public of copies of sound recordings, films or computer programs shall be treated as licensed by the copyright owner subject only to the payment of such reasonable royalty or other payment as may be agreed or determined in default of agreement by the Copyright Tribunal.

(2) No such order shall apply if, or the extent that, there is a licensing scheme certified for the purposes of this section under section 143 providing for the grant of licences.

(3) An order may make different provision for different cases and may specify cases by reference to any factor relating to the work, the copies rented, the renter or the circumstances of the rental.

(4) An order shall be made by statutory instrument; and no order shall be made unless a draft of it has been laid before and approved by a resolution of each House of Parliament.

(5) Copyright in a computer program is not infringed by the rental of copies to the public after the end of the period of 50 years from the end of the calendar year in which copies of it were first issued to the public in electronic form.

(6) Nothing in this section affects any liability under section 23 (secondary infringement) in respect of the rental of infringing copies.

Playing of sound recordings for purposes of club, society, &c

67.—(1) It is not an infringement of the copyright in a sound recording to play   **A–70** it as part of the activities of, or for the benefit of, a club, society or other organisation if the following conditions are met.

(2) The conditions are—
  (*a*) that the organisation is not established or conducted for profit and its main objects are charitable or are otherwise concerned with the advancement of religion, education or social welfare, and
  (*b*) that the proceeds of any charge for admission to the place where the recording is to be heard are applied solely for the purposes of the organisation.

Incidental recording for purposes of broadcast or cable programme

A–71   **68.**—(1) This section applies where by virtue of a licence or assignment of copyright a person is authorised to broadcast or include in a cable programme service—

   (*a*) a literary, dramatic or musical work, or an adaptation of such a work,

   (*b*) an artistic work, or

   (*c*) a sound recording or film.

   (2) He shall by virtue of this section be treated as licensed by the owner of the copyright in the work to do or authorise any of the following for the purposes of the broadcast or cable programme—

   (*a*) in the case of a literary, dramatic or musical work, or an adaptation of such a work, to make a sound recording or film of the work or adaptation;

   (*b*) in the case of an artistic work, to take a photograph or make a film of the work;

   (*c*) in the case of a sound recording or film, to make a copy of it.

   (3) That licence is subject to the condition that the recording, film, photograph or copy in question—

   (*a*) shall not be used for any other purpose, and

   (*b*) shall be destroyed within 28 days of being first used for broadcasting the work or, as the case may be, including it in a cable programme service.

   (4) A recording, film, photograph or copy made in accordance with this section shall be treated as an infringing copy—

   (*a*) for the purposes of any use in breach of the condition mentioned in subsection (3)(*a*), and

   (*b*) for all purposes after that condition or the condition mentioned in subsection (3)(*b*) is broken.

Recording for purposes of supervision and control of broadcasts and cable programmes

A–72   **69.**—(1) Copyright is not infringed by the making or use by the British Broadcasting Corporation, for the purpose of maintaining supervision and control over programmes broadcast by them, of recordings of those programmes.

   [(2) Copyright is not infringed by—

   (*a*) *the making or use of recordings by the Independent Broadcasting Authority for the purposes mentioned in section 4(7) of the Broadcasting Act 1981 (maintenance of supervision and control over programmes and advertisements); or*

   (*b*) *anything done under or in pursuance of provision included in a contract between a programme contractor and the Authority in accordance with section 21 of that Act.*

   (3) Copyright is not infringed by—

   (*a*) *the making by or with the authority of the Cable Authority, or the use by that Authority, for the purpose of maintaining supervision and control over programmes included in services licensed under Part I of the Cable and Broadcasting Act 1984, of recordings of those programmes; or*

   (*b*) *anything done under or in pursuance of—*

      (*i*) *a notice or direction given under section 16 of the Cable and Broadcasting Act 1984 (power of Cable Authority to require production of recordings); or*

      (*ii*) *a condition included in a licence by virtue of section 35 of that Act (duty of Authority to secure that recordings are available for certain purposes).]*

   [(2) Copyright is not infringed by anything done in pursuance of—

(a) section 11(1), 95(1), 145(4), (5) or (7), 155(3) or 167(1) of the Broadcasting Act 1990;

(b) a condition which, by virtue of section 11(2) or 95(2) of that Act, is included in a licence granted under Part I or III of that Act; or

(c) a direction given under section 109(2) of that Act (power of Radio Authority to require production of recordings etc.).

(3) Copyright is not infringed by—

(a) the use by the Independent Television Commission or the Radio Authority, in connection with the performance of any of their functions under the Broadcasting Act 1990, of any recording, script or transcript which is provided to them under or by virtue of any provision of that Act; or

(b) the use by the Broadcasting Complaints Commission or the Broadcasting Standards Council, in connection with any complaint made to them under that Act, of any recording or transcript requested or required to be provided to them, and so provided, under section 145(4) or (7) or section 155(3) of that Act.]

Note: New subsections (2) and (3) were substituted for the original subsections (2) and (3) in the 1988 Act, printed in italics, by section 203(1) of and para. 50(1) of Sched. 20 to the Broadcasting Act 1990 (c. 42) as provided by the Broadcasting Act 1990 (Commencement No. 1 and Transitional Provisions) Order 1990 (S.I. 1990 No. 2347 (c. 61)) § B–254 *post.*

Recording for purposes of time-shifting

70. The making for private and domestic use of a recording of a broadcast or cable programme solely for the purpose of enabling it to be viewed or listened to at more convenient time does not infringe any copyright in the broadcast or cable programme or in any work included in it.   **A–73**

Photographs of television broadcasts or cable programmes

71. The making for private and domestic use of a photograph of the whole or any part of an image forming part of a television broadcast or cable programme, or a copy of such a photograph, does not infringe any copyright in the broadcast or cable programme or in any film included in it.   **A–74**

Free public showing or playing of broadcast or cable programme

72.—(1) The showing or playing in public of a broadcast or cable programme to an audience who have not paid for admission to the place where the broadcast or programme is to be seen or heard does not infringe any copyright in—   **A–75**

(*a*) the broadcast or cable programme, or

(*b*) any sound recording or film included in it.

(2) The audience shall be treated as having paid for admission to a place—

(*a*) if they have paid for admission to a place of which that place forms part; or

(*b*) if goods or services are supplied at that place (or a place of which it forms part)—

　(i) at prices which are substantially attributable to the facilities afforded for seeing or hearing the broadcast or programme, or

　(ii) at prices exceeding those usually charged there and which are partly attributable to those facilities.

(3) The following shall not be regarded as having paid for admission to a place—

(*a*) persons admitted as residents or inmates of the place;

(*b*) persons admitted as members of a club or society where the payment is only for membership of the club or society and the provision of facilities for seeing or hearing broadcasts or programmes is only incidental to the main purposes of the club or society.

(4) Where the making of the broadcast or inclusion of the programme in a cable programme service was an infringement of the copyright in a sound recording or film, the fact that it was heard or seen in public by the reception of the broadcast or programme shall be taken into account in assessing the damages for that infringement.

Reception and re-transmission of broadcast in cable programme service

A–76   **73.**—(1) This section applies where a broadcast made from a place in the United Kingdom is, by reception and immediate re-transmission, included in a cable programme service.

(2) The copyright in the broadcast is not infringed—

[(a) if the inclusion is in pursuance of a requirement imposed under section 13(1) of the Cable and Broadcasting Act 1984 (duty of Cable Authority to secure inclusion in cable service of certain programmes), or]

(*b*) if and to the extent that the broadcast is made for reception in the area in which the cable programme service is provided and is not a satellite transmission or an encrypted transmission.

(3) The copyright in any work included in the broadcast is not infringed—

[(a) if the inclusion is in pursuance of a requirement imposed under section 13(1) of the Cable and Broadcasting Act 1984 (duty of Cable Authority to secure inclusion in cable service of certain programmes), or]

(*b*) if and to the extent that the broadcast is made for reception in the area in which the cable programme service is provided;

but where the making of the broadcast was an infringement of the copyright in the work, the fact that the broadcast was re-transmitted as a programme in a cable programme service shall be taken into account in assessing the damages for that infringement.

Note: The words in square brackets, printed in italics were repealed by section 203(3) of and Schedule 21 to the Broadcasting Act 1990 (c. 42) as provided by The Broadcasting Act 1990 (Commencement No. 1 and Transitional Provisions) Order 1990 (S.I. 1990 No. 2347 (c. 61)) § B–254 *post*.

Provision of sub-titled copies of broadcast or cable programme

A–77   **74.**—(1) A designated body may, for the purpose of providing people who are deaf or hard of hearing, or physically or mentally handicapped in other ways, with copies which are sub-titled or otherwise modified for their special needs, make copies of television broadcasts or cable programmes and issue copies to the public, without infringing any copyright in the broadcasts or cable programmes or works included in them.

(2) A "designated body" means a body designated for the purposes of this section by order of the Secretary of State, who shall not designate a body unless he is satisfied that it is not established or conducted for profit.

(3) An order under this section shall be made by statutory instrument which shall be subject to annulment in pursuance of a resolution of either House of Parliament.

(4) This section does not apply if, or to the extent that, there is a licensing scheme certified for the purposes of this section under section 143 providing for the grant of licences.

Recording for archival purposes

75.—(1) A recording of a brodcast or cable programme of a designated class, or **A–78** a copy of such a recording, may be made for the purpose of being placed in an archive maintained by a designated body without thereby infringing any copyright in the broadcast or cable programme or in any work included in it.

(2) In subsection (1) "designated" means designated for the purposes of this section by order of the Secretary of State, who shall not designate a body unless he is satisfied tht it is not established or conducted for profit.

(3) An order under this section shall be made by statutory instrument which shall be subject to annulment in pursuance of a resolution of either House of Parliament.

Adaptations

Adaptations

76. An act which by virtue of this Chapter may be done without infringing copy- **A–79** right in a literary, dramatic or musical work does not, where that work is an adaptation, infringe any copyright in the work from which the adaptation was made.

Broadcasting Act 1990
Section 176 and Schedule 17

Duty to provide advance information about programmes

176.—(1) A person providing a programme service to which this section applies **A–79A** must make available in accordance with this section information relating to the programmes to be included in the service to any person (referred to in this section and Schedule 17 to this Act as "the publisher") wishing to publish in the United Kingdom any such information.

(2) The duty imposed by subsection (1) is to make available information as to the titles of the programmes which are to be, or may be, included in the service on any date, and the time of their inclusion, to any publisher who has asked the person providing the programme service to make such information available to him and reasonably requires it.

(3) Information to be made available to a publisher under this section is to be made available as soon after it has been prepared as is reasonably practicable but, in any event—

(*a*) not later than when it is made available to any other publisher, and

(*b*) in the case of information in respect of all the programmes to be included in the service in any period of seven days, not later than the beginning of the preceding period of fourteen days, or such other number of days as may be prescribed by the Secretary of State by order.

(4) An order under subsection (3) shall be subject to annulment in pursuance of a resolution of either House of Parliament.

(5) The duty imposed by subsection (1) is not satisfied by providing the information on terms, other than terms as to copyright, prohibiting or restricting publication in the United Kingdom by the publisher.

(6) Schedule 17 applies to any information or future information which the person providing a programme service to which this section applies is or may be required to make available under this section.

(7) For the purposes of this section and that Schedule, the following table shows the programme services to which the section and Schedule apply and the persons who provide them or are to be treated as providing them.

Programme service	Provider of service
Services other than services under the Act	
Television and national radio services provided by the BBC for reception in the United Kingdom	The BBC
Services under the Act	
Television programme services subject to regulation by the Independent Television Commission	The person licensed to provide the service
The television broadcasting service provided by the Welsh Authority	The Authority
Any national service (see section 84(2)(a)(ii)) subject to regulation by the Radio Authority	The person licensed to provide the service
Services provided during interim period only	
Television broadcasting services provided by the Independent Commission in accordance with Schedule 11, other than Channel 4	The programme contractor
Channel 4, as so provided	The body corporate referred to in section 12(2) of the Broadcasting Act 1981

(8) This section does not require any information to be given about any advertisement.

SCHEDULE 17

INFORMATION ABOUT PROGRAMMES: COPYRIGHT

PART I

COPYRIGHT LICENSING

1.—(1) This paragraph applies where the person providing a progrmme service has assigned to another the copyright in works containing information to which this Schedule applies.

(2) The person providing the programme service, not the assignee, is to be treated as the owner of the copyright for the purposes of licensing any act restricted by the copyright on or after the day on which this paragraph comes into force.

(3) Where the assignment by the person providing the programme service occurred before 29th September 1989 then, in relation to any act restricted by the copyright so assigned—

(a) sub-paragraph (2) does not have effect, and

(b) references below in this Schedule to the person providing the programme service are to the assignee.

Part II

Use of Information as of Right

Circumstances in which right available

2.—(1) Paragraph 4 applies to any act restricted by the copyright in works containing information to which this Schedule applies done by the publisher if—

(a) a licence to do the act could be granted by the person providing the programme service but no such licence is held by the publisher.

(b) the person providing the programme service refuses to grant to the publisher a licence to do the act, being a licence of such duration, and of which the terms as to payment for doing the act are such, as would be acceptable to the publisher, and

(c) the publisher has complied with paragraph 3.

(2) The reference in sub-paragraph (1) to refusing to grant a licence includes failing to do so within a reasonable time of being asked.

(3) References below in this Schedule to the terms of payment are to the terms as to payment for doing any act restricted by the copyright in works containing information to which this Schedule applies.

Notice of intention to exercise right

3.—(1) A publisher intending to avail himself of the right conferred by paragraph 4 must—

(a) give notice of his intention to the person providing the programme service, asking that person to propose terms of payment, and

(b) after receiving the proposal or the expiry of a reasonable time, give reasonable notice to the person providing the programme service of the date on which he proposes to begin exercising the right and the terms of payment in accordance with which he intends to do so.

(2) Before exercising the right the publisher must—

(a) give reasonable notice to the Copyright Tribunal of his intention to exercise the right and of the date on which he proposes to begin to do so, and

(b) apply to the Tribunal under paragraph 5 to settle the terms of payment.

Conditions for exercise of right

4.—(1) Where the publisher, on or after the date specified in a notice under paragraph 3(1)(b), does any act in circumstances in which this paragraph applies, he shall, if he makes the payments required by this paragraph, be in the same position as regards infringement of copyright as if he had at all material times been the holder of a licence to do so granted by the person providing the programme service.

(2) Payments are to be made at not less than quarterly intervals in arrears.

(3) The amount of any payment is that determined in accordance with any order of the Copyright Tribunal under paragraph 5 or, if no such order has been made—

(a) in accordance with any proposal for terms of payment made by the person providing the programme service pursuant to a request under paragraph 3(1)(a), or

(b) where no proposal has been so made or the amount determined in accordance with the proposal so made appears to the publisher to be unreasonably high, in accordance with the terms of payment notified under paragraph 3(1)(b).

Applications to settle payments

5.—(1) On an application to settle the terms of payment, the Copyright Tribunal shall consider the matter and make such order as it may determine to be reasonable in the circumstances.

(2) An order under sub-paragraph (1) has effect from the date the applicant begins to exercise the right conferred by paragraph 4 and any necessary repayments, or further payments, shall be made in respect of amounts that have fallen due.

Application for review of order

6.—(1) A person exercising the right conferred by paragraph 4, or the person poviding the programme service, may apply to the Tribunal to review any order under paragraph 5.

(2) An application under sub-paragraph (1) shall not be made, except with the special leave of the Tribunal—

(a) within twelve months from the date of the order, or of the decision on a previous application under this paragraph, or

(b) if the order was made so as to be in force for fifteen months or less, or as a result of a decision on a previous application is due to expire within fifteen months of that decision, until the last three months before the expiry date.

(3) On the application the Tribunal shall consider the matter and make such order confirming or varying the original order as it may determine to be reasonable in the circumstances.

(4) An order under this paragraph has effect from the date on which it is made or such later date as may be specified by the Tribunal.

Part III

Supplementary

7.—(1) This Schedule and the Copyright, Designs and Patents Act 1988 shall have effect as if the Schedule were included in Chapter III of Part I of that Act, and that Act shall have effect as if proceedings under this Schedule were listed in section 149 of that Act (jurisdiction of the Copyright Tribunal).

(2) References in this Schedule to anything done by the publisher include anything done on his behalf.

(3) References in this Schedule to works include future works, and references to the copyright in works include future copyright.

Note: Section 176 of and Schedule 17 to the Broadcasting Act 1990 contain provisions relating to the new statutory duty to provide information about programmes and the settling of terms of payment by the Copyright Tribunal. The 1988 Act is not amended by these provisions but, in view of paragraph 7(1) of Schedule 17, these provisions are printed at the end of Chapter III of Part I of the 1988 Act. These provisions come into force as provided by The Broadcasting Act 1990 (Commencement No. 1 and Transitional Provisions) Order 1990 (S.I. 1990 No. 2347 (c. 61)) § B–254 *post*.

Chapter IV

Moral Rights

Right to be identified as author or director

Right to be identified as author or director

77.—(1) The author of a copyright literary, dramatic, musical or artistic work,   **A–80** and the director of a copyright film, has the right to be identified as the author or director of the work in the circumstances mentioned in this section; but the right is not infringed unless it has been asserted in accordance with section 78.

(2) The author of a literary work (other than words intended to be sung or spoken with music) or a dramatic work has the right to be identified whenever—

- (*a*) the work is published commercially, performed in public, broadcast or included in a cable programme service; or
- (*b*) copies of a film or sound recording including the work are issued to the public;

and that right includes the right to be identified whenever any of those events occur in relation to an adaptation of the work as the author of the work from which the adaptation was made.

(3) The author of a musical work, or a literary work consisting of words intended to be sung or spoken with music, has the right to be identified whenever—

- (*a*) the work is published commercially;
- (*b*) copies of a sound recording of the work are issued to the public; or
- (*c*) a film of which the sound-track includes the work is shown in public or copies of such a film are issued to the public;

and that right includes the right to be identified whenever any of those events occur in relation to an adaptation of the work as the author of the work from which the adaptation was made.

(4) The author of an artistic work has the right to be identified whenever—

- (*a*) the work is published commercially or exhibited in public, or a visual image of it is broadcast or included in a cable programme service;
- (*b*) a film including a visual image of the work is shown in public or copies of such a film are issued to the public; or
- (*c*) in the case of a work of architecture in the form of a building or a model for a building, a sculpture or a work of artistic craftsmanship, copies of a graphic work representing it, or of a photograph of it, are issued to the public.

(5) The author of a work of architecture in the form of a building also has the right to be identified on the building as constructed or, where more than one building is constructed to the design, on the first to be constructed.

(6) The director of a film has the right to be identified whenever the film is shown in public, broadcast or included in a cable programme service or copies of the film are issued to the public.

(7) The right of the author or director under this section is—

- (*a*) in the case of commercial publication or the issue to the public of copies of a film or sound recording, to be identified in or on each copy or, if that is not appropriate, in some other manner likely to bring his identity to the notice of a person acquiring a copy,
- (*b*) in the case of identification on a building, to be identified by appropriate means visible to persons entering or approaching the building, and

(*c*) in any other case, to be identified in a manner likely to bring his identity to the attention of a person seeing or hearing the performance, exhibition, showing, broadcast or cable programme in question;

and the identification must in each case be clear and reasonably prominent.

(8) If the author or director in asserting his right to be identified specifies a pseudonym, initials or some other particular form of identification, that form shall be used; otherwise any reasonable form of identification may be used.

(9) This section has effect subject to section 79 (exceptions to right).

Requirement that right be asserted

A–81   **78.**—(1) A person does not infringe the right conferred by section 77 (right to be identified as author or director) by doing any of the acts mentioned in that section unless the right has been asserted in accordance with the following provisions so as to bind him in relation to that act.

(2) The right may be asserted generally, or in relation to any specified act or description of acts—

(*a*) on an assignment of copyright in the work, by including in the instrument effecting the assignment a statement that the author or director asserts in relation to that work his right to be identified, or

(*b*) by instrument in writing signed by the author or director.

(3) The right may also be asserted in relation to the public exhibition of an artistic work—

(*a*) by securing that when the author or other first owner of copyright parts with possession of the original, or of a copy made by him or under his direction or control, the author is identified on the original or copy, or on a frame, mount or other thing to which it is attached, or

(*b*) by including in a licence by which the author or other first owner of copyright authorises the making of copies of the work a statement signed by or on behalf of the person granting the licence that the author asserts his right to be identified in the event of the public exhibition of a copy made in pursuance of the licence.

(4) The persons bound by an assertion of the right under subsection (2) or (3) are—

(*a*) in the case of an assertion under subsection (2)(a), the assignee and anyone claiming through him, whether or not he has notice of the assertion;

(*b*) in the case of an assertion under subsection (2)(b), anyone to whose notice the assertion is brought;

(*c*) in the case of an assertion under subsection (3)(a), anyone into whose hands that original or copy comes, whether or not the identification is still present or visible;

(*d*) in the case of an assertion under subsection (3)(b), the licensee and anyone into whose hands a copy made in pursuance of the licence comes, whether or not he has notice of the assertion.

(5) In an action for infringement of the right the court shall, in considering remedies, take into account any delay in asserting the right.

Exceptions to right

A–82   **79.**—(1) The right conferred by section 77 (right to be identified as author or director) is subject to the following exceptions.

(2) The right does not apply in relation to the following descriptions of work—

(*a*) a computer program;

(*b*) the design of a typeface;

(*c*) any computer-generated work.

(3) The right does not apply to anything done by or with the authority of the copyright owner where copyright in the work originally vested—

(*a*) in the author's employer by virtue of section 11(2) (works produced in course of employment), or

(*b*) in the director's employer by virtue of section 9(2)(*a*) (person to be treated as author of film).

(4) The right is not infringed by an act which by virtue of any of the following provisions would not infringe copyright in the work—

(*a*) section 30 (fair dealing for certain purposes), so far as it relates to the reporting of current events by means of a sound recording, film, broadcast or cable programme;

(*b*) section 31 (incidental inclusion of work in an artistic work, sound recording, film, broadcast or cable programme);

(*c*) section 32(3) (examination questions);

(*d*) section 45 (parliamentary and judicial proceedings);

(*e*) section 46(1) or (2) (Royal Commissions and statutory inquiries);

(*f*) section 51 (use of design documents and models);

(*g*) section 52 (effect of exploitation of design derived from artistic work);

(*h*) section 57 (anonymous or pseudonymous works: acts permitted on assumptions as to expiry of copyright or death of author).

(5) The right does not apply in relation to any work made for the purpose of reporting current events.

(6) The right does not apply in relation to the publication in—

(*a*) a newspaper, magazine or similar periodical, or

(*b*) an encyclopaedia, dictionary, yearbook or other collective work of reference,

of a literary, dramatic, musical or artistic work made for the purposes of such publication or made available with the consent of the author for the purposes of such publication.

(7) The right does not apply in relation to—

(*a*) a work in which Crown copyright or Parliamentary copyright subsists, or

(*b*) a work in which copyright originally vested in an international organisation by virtue of section 168,

unless the author or director has previously been identified as such in or on published copies of the work.

Right to object to derogatory treatment of work

Right to object to derogatory treatment of work

80.—(1) The author of a copyright literary, dramatic, musical or artistic work, **A–83** and the director of a copyright film, has the right in the circumstances mentioned in this section not to have his work subjected to derogatory treatment.

(2) For the purposes of this section—

(*a*) "treatment" of a work means any addition to, deletion from or alteration to or adaptation of the work, other than—

(i) a translation of a literary or dramatic work, or

(ii) an arrangement or transcription of a musical work involving no more than a change of key or register; and

(*b*) the treatment of a work is derogatory if it amounts to distorting or mutilation of the work or is otherwise prejudicial to the honour or reputation of the author or director;

and in the following provisions of this section references to a derogatory treatment of a work shall be construed accordingly.

(3) In the case of a literary, dramatic or musical work the right is infringed by a person who—
- (*a*) publishes commercially, performs in public, broadcasts or includes in a cable programme service a derogatory treatment of the work; or
- (*b*) issues to the public copies of a film or sound recording of, or including, a derogatory treatment of the work.

(4) In the case of an artistic work the right is infringed by a person who—
- (*a*) publishes commercially or exhibits in public a derogatory treatment of the work, or broadcasts or includes in a cable programme service a visual image of a derogatory treatment of the work,
- (*b*) shows in public a film including a visual image of a derogatory treatment of the work or issues to the public copies of such a film, or
- (*c*) in the case of—
  - (i) a work of architecture in the form of a model for a building,
  - (ii) a sculpture, or
  - (iii) a work of artistic craftsmanship,

  issues to the public copies of a graphic work representing, or of a photograph of, a derogatory treatment of the work.

(5) Subsection (4) does not apply to a work of architecture in the form of a building; but where the author of such a work is identified on the building and it is the subject of derogatory treatment he has the right to require the identification to be removed.

(6) In the case of a film, the right is infringed by a person who—
- (*a*) shows in public, broadcasts or includes in a cable programme service a derogatory treatment of the film; or
- (*b*) issues to the public copies of a derogatory treatment of the film,

or who, along with the film, plays in public, broadcasts or includes in a cable programme service, or issues to the public copies of, a derogatory treatment of the film sound-track.

(7) The right conferred by this section extends to the treatment of parts of a work resulting from a previous treatment by a person other than the author or director, if those parts are attributed to, or are likely to be regarded as the work of, the author or director.

(8) This section has effect subject to sections 81 and 82 (exceptions to and qualifications of right).

Exceptions to right

81.—(1) The right conferred by section 80 (right to object to derogatory treatment of work) is subject to the following exceptions.

(2) The right does not apply to a computer program or to any computer-generated work.

(3) The right does not apply in relation to any work made for the purpose of reporting current events.

(4) The right does not apply in relation to the publication in—
- (*a*) a newspaper, magazine or similar periodical, or
- (*b*) an encyclopaedia, dictionary, yearbook or other collective work of reference,

of a literary, dramatic, musical or artistic work made for the purposes of such publication or made available with the consent of the author for the purposes of such publication.

Nor does the right apply in relation to any subsequent exploitation elsewhere of such a work without any modification of the published version.

(5) The right is not infringed by an act which by virtue of section 57 (anony-

mous or pseudonymous works: acts permitted on assumptions as to expiry of copyright or death of author) would not infringe copyright.

(6) The right is not infringed by anything done for the purpose of—

(a) avoiding the commission of an offence,

(b) complying with a duty imposed by or under an enactment, or

(c) in the case of the British Broadcasting Corporation, avoiding the inclusion in a programme broadcast by them of anything which offends against good taste or decency or which is likely to encourage or incite to crime or to lead to disorder or to be offensive to public feeling,

provided, where the author or director is identified at the time of the relevant act or has previously been identified in or on published copies of the work, that there is a sufficient disclaimer.

Qualification of right in certain cases

82.—(1) This section applies to—   **A-85**

(a) works in which copyright originally vested in the author's employer by virtue of section 11(2) (works produced in course of employment) or in the director's employer by virtue of section 9(2)(a) (person to be treated as author of film),

(b) works in which Crown copyright or Parliamentary copyright subsists, and

(c) works in which copyright originally vested in an international organisation by virtue of section 168.

(2) The right conferred by section 80 (right to object to derogatory treatment of work) does not apply to anything done in relation to such a work by or with the authority of the copyright owner unless the author or director—

(a) is identified at the time of the relevant act, or

(b) has previously been identified in or on published copies of the work;

and where in such a case the right does apply, it is not infringed if there is a sufficient disclaimer.

Infringement of right by possessing or dealing with infringing article

83.—(1) The right conferred by section 80 (right to object to derogatory treat-   **A-86**
ment of work) is also infringed by a person who—

(a) possesses in the course of a business, or

(b) sells or lets for hire, or offers or exposes for sale or hire, or

(c) in the course of a business exhibits in public or distributes, or

(d) distributes otherwise than in the course of a business so as to affect prejudicially the honour or reputation of the author or director,

an article which is, and which he knows or has reason to believe is, an infringing article.

(2) An "infringing article" means a work or a copy of a work which—

(a) has been subjected to derogatory treatment within the meaning of section 80, and

(b) has been or is likely to be the subject of any of the acts mentioned in that section in circumstances infringing that right.

False attribution of work

False attribution of work

84.—(1) A person has the right in the circumstances mentioned in this sec-   **A-87**
tion—

(a) not to have a literary, dramatic, musical or artistic work falsely attributed to him as author, and (*b*) not to have a film falsely attributed to him as director;

and in this section an "attribution", in relation to such a work, means a statement (express or implied) as to who is the author or director.

(2) The right is infringed by a person who—

(*a*) issues to the public copies of a work of any of those descriptions in or on which there is a false attribution, or

(*b*) exhibits in public an artistic work, or a copy of an artistic work, in or which there is a false attribution.

(3) The right is also infringed by a person who—

(*a*) in the case of a literary, dramatic or musical work, performs the work in public, broadcasts it or includes it in a cable programme service as being the work of a person, or

(*b*) in the case of a film, shows it in public, broadcasts it or includes it in a cable programme service as being directed by a person,

knowing or having reason to believe that the attribution is false.

(4) The right is also infringed by the issue to the public or public display of material containing a false attribution in connection with any of the acts mentioned in subsection (2) or (3).

(5) The right is also infringed by a person who in the course of a business—

(*a*) possesses or deals with a copy of a work of any of the descriptions mentioned in subsection (1) in or on which there is a false attribution, or

(*b*) in the case of an artistic work, possesses or deals with the work itself when there is a false attribution in or on it,

knowing or having reason to believe that there is such an attribution and that it is false.

(6) In the case of an artistic work the right is also infringed by a person who in the course of a business—

(*a*) deals with a work which has been altered after the author parted with possession of it as being the unaltered work of the author, or

(*b*) deals with a copy of such a work as being a copy of the unaltered work of the author,

knowing or having reason to believe that that is not the case.

(7) References in this section to dealing are to selling or letting for hire, offering or exposing for sale or hire, exhibiting in public, or distributing.

(8) This section applies where, contrary to the fact—

(*a*) a literary, dramatic or musical work is falsely represented as being an adaptation of the work of a person, or

(*b*) a copy of an artistic work is falsely represented as being a copy made by the author of the artistic work,

as it applies where the work is falsely attributed to a person as author.

Right to privacy of certain photographs and films

Right to privacy of certain photographs and films

A–88   **85.**—(1) A person who for private and domestic purposes commissions the taking of a photograph or the making of a film has, where copyright subsists in the resulting work, the right not to have—

(*a*) copies of the work issued to the public,

(*b*) the work exhibited or shown in public, or

(*c*) the work broadcast or included in a cable programme service;

and, except as mentioned in subsection (2), a person who does or authorises the doing of any of those acts infringes that right.

(2) The right is not infringed by an act which by virtue of any of the following provisions would not infringe copyright in the work—

   (a) section 31 (incidental inclusion of work in an artistic work, film, broadcast or cable programme);
   (b) section 45 (parliamentary and judicial proceedings);
   (c) section 46 (Royal Commissions and statutory inquiries);
   (d) section 50 (acts done under statutory authority);
   (e) section 57 (anonymous or pseudonymous works: acts permitted on assumptions as to expiry of copyright or death of author).

Supplementary

Duration of rights

86.—(1) The rights conferred by section 77 (right to be identified as author or **A-89** director), section 80 (right to object to derogatory treatment of work) and section 85 (right to privacy of certain photographs and films) continue to subsist so long as copyright subsists in the work.

(2) The right conferred by section 84 (false attribution) continues to subsist until 20 years after a person's death.

Consent and waiver of rights

87.—(1) It is not an infringement of any of the rights conferred by this Chapter **A-90** to do any act to which the person entitled to the right has consented.

(2) Any of those rights may be waived by instrument in writing signed by the person giving up the right.

(3) A waiver—

   (a) may relate to a specific work, to works of a specified description or to works generally, and may relate to existing or future works, and
   (b) may be conditional or unconditional and may be expressed to be subject to revocation;

and if made in favour of the owner or prospective owner of the copyright in the work or works to which it relates, it shall be presumed to extend to his licensees and successors in title unless a contrary intention is expressed.

(4) Nothing in this Chapter shall be construed as excluding the operation of the general law of contract or estoppel in relation to an informal waiver or other transaction in relation to any of the rights mentioned in subsection (1).

Application of provisions to joint works

88.—(1) The right conferred by section 77 (right to be identified as author or **A-91** director) is, in the case of a work of joint authorship, a right of each joint author to be identified as a joint author and must be asserted in accordance with section 78 by each joint author in relation to himself.

(2) The right conferred by section 80 (right to object to derogatory treatment of work) is, in the case of a work of joint authorship, a right of each joint author and his right is satisfied if he consents to the treatment in question.

(3) A waiver under section 87 of those rights by one joint author does not affect the rights of the other joint authors.

(4) The right conferred by section 84 (false attribution) is infringed, in the circumstances mentioned in that section—

   (a) by any false statement as to the authorship of a work of joint authorship, and
   (b) by the false attribution of joint authorship in relation to a work of sole authorship;

and such a false attribution infringes the right of every person to whom authorship of any description is, whether rightly or wrongly, attributed.

(5) The above provisions also apply (with any necessary adaptations) in relation to a film which was, or is alleged to have been, jointly directed, as they apply to a work which is, or is alleged to be, a work of joint authorship.

A film is "jointly directed" if it is made by the collaboration of two or more directors and the contribution of each director is not distinct from that of the other director or directors.

(6) The right conferred by section 85 (right to privacy of certain photographs and films) is, in the case of a work made in pursuance of a joint commission, a right of each person who commissioned the making of the work, so that—

    (*a*) the right of each is satisfied if he consents to the act in question, and

    (*b*) a waiver under section 87 by one of them does not affect the rights of the others.

Application of provisions to parts of works

A–92   **89.**—(1) The rights conferred by section 77 (right to be identified as author or director) and section 85 (right to privacy of certain photographs and films) apply in relation to the whole or any substantial part of a work.

(2) The rights conferred by section 80 (right to object to derogatory treatment of work) and section 84 (false attribution) apply in relation to the whole or any part of a work.

CHAPTER V

DEALINGS WITH RIGHTS IN COPYRIGHT WORKS

Copyright

Assignment and licences

A–93   **90.**—(1) Copyright is transmissible by assignment, by testamentary disposition or by operation of law, as personal or moveable property.

(2) An assignment or other transmission of copyright may be partial, that is, limited so as to apply—

    (*a*) to one or more, but not all, of the things the copyright owner has the exclusive right to do;

    (*b*) to part, but not the whole, of the period for which the copyright is to subsist.

(3) An assignment of copyright is not effective unless it is in writing signed by or on behalf of the assignor.

(4) A licence granted by a copyright owner is binding on every successor in title to his interest in the copyright, except a purchaser in good faith for valuable consideration and without notice (actual or constructive) of the licence or a person deriving title from such a purchaser; and references in this Part to doing anything with, or without, the licence of the copyright owner shall be construed accordingly.

Prospective ownership of copyright

A–94   **91.**—(1) Where by an agreement made in relation to future copyright, and signed by or on behalf of the prospective owner of the copyright, the prospective owner purports to assign the future copyright (wholly or partially) to another person, then if, on the copyright coming into existence, the assignee or another person claiming under him would be entitled as against all other persons to require the copyright to be vested in him, the copyright shall vest in the assignee or his successor in title by virtue of this subsection.

(2) In this Part—

"future copyright" means copyright which will or may come into existence in respect of a future work or class of works or on the occurrence of a future event; and

"prospective owner" shall be construed accordingly, and includes a person who is prospectively entitled to copyright by virtue of such an agreement as is mentioned in subsection (1).

(3) A licence granted by a prospective owner of copyright is binding on every successor in title to his interest (or prospective interest) in the right, except a purchaser in good faith for valuable consideration and without notice (actual or constructive) of the licence or a person deriving title from such a purchaser; and references in this Part to doing anything with, or without, the licence of the copyright owner shall be construed accordingly.

Exclusive licences

92.—(1) In this Part an "exclusive licence" means a licence in writing signed by or on behalf of the copyright owner authorising the licensee to the exclusion of all other persons, including the person granting the licence, to exercise a right which would otherwise be exercisable exclusively by the copyright owner.   **A–95**

(2) The licensee under an exclusive licence has the same rights against a successor in title who is bound by the licence as he has against the person granting the licence.

Copyright to pass under will with unpublished work

93. Where under a bequest (whether specific or general) a person is entitled, beneficially or otherwise, to—   **A–96**

    (*a*) an original document or other material thing recording or embodying a literary, dramatic, musical or artistic work which was not published before the death of the testator, or

    (*b*) an original material thing containing a sound recording or film which was not published before the death of the testator,

the bequest shall, unless a contrary intention is indicated in the testator's will or a codicil to it, be construed as including the copyright in the work in so far as the testator was the owner of the copyright immediately before his death.

Moral rights

Moral rights not assignable

94. The rights conferred by Chapter IV (moral rights) are not assignable.   **A–97**

Transmission of moral rights on death

95.—(1) On the death of a person entitled to the right conferred by section 77 (right to identification of author or director), section 80 (right to object to derogatory treatment of work) or section 85 (right to privacy of certain photographs and films)—   **A–98**

    (*a*) the right passes to such person as he may by testamentary disposition specifically direct,

    (*b*) if there is no such direction but the copyright in the work in question forms part of his estate, the right passes to the person to whom the copyright passes, and (*c*) if or to the extent that the right does not pass under paragraph (*a*) or (*b*) it is exercisable by his personal representatives.

(2) Where copyright forming part of a person's estate passes in part to one person and in part to another, as for example where a bequest is limited so as to apply—

    (*a*) to one or more, but not all, of the things the copyright owner has the exclusive right to do or authorise, or

    (*b*) to part, but not the whole, of the period for which the copyright is to subsist,

any right which passes with the copyright by virtue of subsection (1) is correspondingly divided.

(3) Where by virtue of subsection (1)(a) or (b) a right becomes exercisable by more than one person—

    (*a*) it may, in the case of the right conferred by section 77 (right to identification of author or director), be asserted by any of them;

    (*b*) it is, in the case of the right conferred by section 80 (right to object to derogatory treatment of work) or section 85 (right to privacy of certain photographs and films), a right exercisable by each of them and is satisfied in relation to any of them if he consents to the treatment or act in question; and

    (*c*) any waiver of the right in accordance with section 87 by one of them does not affect the rights of the others.

(4) A consent or waiver previously given or made binds any person to whom a right passes by virtue of subsection (1).

(5) Any infringement after a person's death of the right conferred by section 84 (false attribution) is actionable by his personal representatives.

(6) Any damages recovered by personal representatives by virtue of this section in respect of an infringement after a person's death shall devolve as part of his estate as if the right of action had subsisted and been vested in him immediately before his death.

CHAPTER VI

REMEDIES FOR INFRINGEMENT

Rights and remedies of copyright owner

Infringement actionable by copyright owner

A–99   **96.**—(1) An infringement of copyright is actionable by the copyright owner.

(2) In an action for infringement of copyright all such relief by way of damages, injunctions, accounts or otherwise is available to the plaintiff as is available in respect of the infringement of any other property right.

(3) This section has effect subject to the following provisions of this Chapter.

Provisions as to damages in infringement action

A–100   **97.**—(1) Where in an action for infringement of copyright it is shown that at the time of the infringement the defendant did not know, and had no reason to believe, that copyright subsisted in the work to which the action relates, the plaintiff is not entitled to damages against him, but without prejudice to any other remedy.

(2) The court may in an action for infringement of copyright having regard to all the circumstances, and in particular to—

    (*a*) the flagrancy of the infringement, and

(*b*) any benefit accruing to the defendant by reason of the infringement,

award such additional damages as the justice of the case may require.

Undertaking to take licence of right in infringement proceedings

98.—(1) If in proceedings for infringement of copyright in respect of which a **A–101** licence is available as of right under section 144 (powers exercisable in consequence of report of Monopolies and Mergers Commission) the defendant undertakes to take a licence on such terms as may be agreed or, in default of agreement, settled by the Copyright Tribunal under that section—

(*a*) no injunction shall be granted against him,

(*b*) no order for delivery up shall be made under section 99, and

(*c*) the amount recoverable against him by way of damages or on an account of profits shall not exceed double the amount which would have been payable by him as licensee of such a licence on those terms had been granted before the earliest infringement.

(2) An undertaking may be given at any time before the final order in the proceedings, without any admission of liability.

(3) Nothing in this section affects the remedies available in respect of an infringement committed before licences of right were available.

Order for delivery up

99.—(1) Where a person— **A–102**

(*a*) has an infringing copy of a work in his possession, custody or control in the course of a business, or

(*b*) has in his possession, custody or control an article specifically designed or adapted for making copies of a particular copyright work, knowing or having reason to believe that it has been or is to be used to make infringing copies,

the owner of the copyright in the work may apply to the court for an order that the infringing copy or article be delivered up to him or to such other person as the court may direct.

(2) An application shall not be made after the end of the period specified in section 113 (period after which remedy of delivery up not available); and no order shall be made unless the court also makes, or it appears to the court that there are grounds for making, an order under section 114 (order as to disposal of infringing copy or other article).

(3) A person to whom an infringing copy or other article is delivered up in pursuance of an order under this section shall, if an order under section 114 is not made, retain it pending the making of an order, or the decision not to make an order, under that section.

(4) Nothing in this section affects any other power of the court.

Right to seize infringing copies and other articles

100.—(1) An infringing copy of a work which found exposed or otherwise **A–103** immediately available for sale or hire, and in respect of which the copyright owner would be entitled to apply for an order under section 99, may be seized and detained by him or a person authorised by him.

The right to seize and detain is exercisable subject to the following conditions and is subject to any decision of the court under section 114.

(2) Before anything is seized under this section notice of the time and place of the proposed seizure must be given to a local police station.

(3) A person may for the purpose of exercising the right conferred by this section

enter premises to which the public have access but may not seize anything in the possession, custody or control of a person at a permanent or regular place of business of his, and may not use any force.

(4) At the time when anything is seized under this section there shall be left at the place where it was seized a notice in the prescribed form containing the prescribed particulars as to the person by whom or on whose authority the seizure is made and the grounds on which it is made.

(5) In this section—

"premises" includes land, buildings, moveable structures, vehicles, vessels, aircraft and hovercraft; and

"prescribed" means prescribed by order of the Secretary of State.

(6) An order of the Secretary of State under this section shall be made by statutory instrument which shall be subject to annulment in pursuance of a resolution of either House of Parliament.

Rights and remedies of exclusive licensee

Rights and remedies of exclusive licensee

A–104   **101.**—(1) An exclusive licensee has, except against the copyright owner, the same rights and remedies in respect of matters occurring after the grant of the licence as if the licence had been an assignment.

(2) His rights and remedies are concurrent with those of the copyright owner; and references in the relevant provisions of this Part to the copyright owner shall be construed accordingly.

(3) In an action brought by an exclusive licensee by virtue of this section a defendant may avail himself of any defence which would have been available to him if the action had been brought by the copyright owner.

Exercise of concurrent rights

A–105   **102.**—(1) Where an action for infringement of copyright brought by the copyright owner or an exclusive licensee relates (wholly or partly) to an infringement in respect of which they have concurrent rights of action, the copyright owner or, as the case may be, the exclusive licensee may not, without the leave of the court, proceed with the action unless the other is either joined as a plaintiff or added as a defendant.

(2) A copyright owner or exclusive licensee who is added as a defendant in pursuance of subsection (1) is not liable for any costs in the action unless he takes part in the proceedings.

(3) The above provisions do not affect the granting of interlocutory relief on an application by a copyright owner or exclusive licensee alone.

(4) Where an action for infringement of copyright is brought which relates (wholly or partly) to an infringement in respect of which the copyright owner and an exclusive licensee have or had concurrent rights of action—

   (a) the court shall in assessing damages take into account—
      (i) the terms of the licence, and
      (ii) any pecuniary remedy already awarded or available to either of them in respect of the infringement;
   (b) no account of profits shall be directed if an award of damages has been made, or an account of profits has been directed, in favour of the other of them in respect of the infringement; and
   (c) the court shall if an account of profits is directed apportion the profits between them as the court considers just, subject to any agreement between them;

and these provisions apply whether or not the copyright owner and the exclusive licensee are both parties to the action.

(5) The copyright owner shall notify any exclusive licensee having concurrent rights before applying for an order under section 99 (order for delivery up) or exercising the right conferred by section 100 (right of seizure); and the court may on the application of the licensee make such order under section 99 or, as the case may be, prohibiting or permitting the exercise by the copyright owner of the right conferred by section 100, as it thinks fit having regard to the terms of the licence.

Remedies for infringement of moral rights

Remedies for infringement of moral rights

103.—(1) An infringement of a right conferred by Chapter IV (moral rights) is actionable as a breach of statutory duty owed to the person entitled to the right.   **A–106**

(2) In proceedings for infringement of the right conferred by section 80 (right to object to derogatory treatment of work) the court may, if it thinks it is an adequate remedy in the circumstances, grant an injunction on terms prohibiting the doing of any act unless a disclaimer is made, in such terms and in such manner as may be approved by the court, dissociating the author or director from the treatment of the work.

Presumptions

Presumptions relevant to literary, dramatic, musical and artistic works

104.—(1) The following presumptions apply in proceedings brought by virtue of this Chapter with respect to a literary, dramatic, musical or artistic work.   **A–107**

(2) Where a name purporting to be that of the author appeared on copies of the work as published or on the work when it was made, the person whose name appeared shall be presumed, until the contrary is proved—
   (*a*) to be the author of the work;
   (*b*) to have made it in circumstances not falling within section 11(2), 163, 165 or 168 (works produced in course of employment, Crown copyright, Parliamentary copyright or copyright of certain international organisations).

(3) In the case of a work alleged to be a work of joint authorship, subsection (2) applies in relation to each person alleged to be one of the authors.

(4) Where no name purporting to be that of the author appeared as mentioned in subsection (2) but—
   (*a*) the work qualifies for copyright protection by virtue of section 155 (qualification by reference to country of first publication), and
   (*b*) a name purporting to be that of the publisher appeared on copies of the work as first published,
the person whose name appeared shall be presumed, until the contrary is proved, to have been the owner of the copyright at the time of publication.

(5) If the author of the work is dead or the identity of the author cannot be ascertained by reasonable inquiry, it shall be presumed, in the absence of evidence to the contrary—
   (*a*) that the work is an original work, and
   (*b*) that the plaintiff's allegations as to what was the first publication of the work and as to the country of first publication are correct.

Presumptions relevant to sound recordings and films

105.—(1) In proceedings brought by virtue of this Chapter with respect to a sound recording, where copies of the recording as issued to the public bear a label or other mark stating—   **A–108**

(*a*) that a named person was the owner of copyright in the recording at the date of issue of the copies, or

(*b*) that the recording was first published in a specified year or in a specified country,

the label or mark shall be admissible as evidence of the facts stated and shall be presumed to be correct until the contrary is proved.

(2) In proceedings brought by virtue of this Chapter with respect to a film, where copies of the film as issued to the public bear a statement—

(*a*) that a named person was the author or director of the film,

(*b*) that a named person was the owner of copyright in the film at the date of issue of the copies, or

(*c*) that the film was first published in a specified year or in a specified country,

the statement shall be admissible as evidence of the facts stated and shall be presumed to be correct until the contrary is proved.

(3) In proceedings brought by virtue of this Chapter with respect to a computer program, where copies of the program are issued to the public in electronic form bearing a statement—

(*a*) that a named person was the owner of copyright in the program at the date of issue of the copies, or

(*b*) that the program was first published in a specified country or that copies of it were first issued to the public in electronic form in a specified year,

the statement shall be admissible as evidence of the facts stated and shall be presumed to be correct until the contrary is proved.

(4) The above presumptions apply equally in proceedings relating to an infringement alleged to have occurred before the date on which the copies were issued to the public.

(5) In proceedings brought by virtue of this Chapter with respect to a film, where the film as shown in public, broadcast or included in a cable programme service bears a statement—

(*a*) that a named person was the author or director of the film, or

(*b*) that a named person was the owner of copyright in the film immediately after it was made,

the statement shall be admissible as evidence of the facts stated and shall be presumed to be correct until the contrary is proved.

This presumption applies equally in proceedings relating to an infringement alleged to have occurred before the date on which the film was shown in public, broadcast or included in a cable programme service.

Presumptions relevant to works subject to Crown copyright

A–109 **106.** In proceedings brought by virtue of this Chapter with respect to a literary, dramatic or musical work in which Crown copyright subsists, where there appears on printed copies of the work a statement of the year in which the work was first published commercially, that statement shall be admissible as evidence of the fact stated and shall be presumed to be correct in the absence of evidence to the contrary.

Offences

Criminal liability for making or dealing with infringing articles, &c

A–110 **107.**—(1) A person commits an offence who, without the licence of the copyright owner—

(*a*) makes for sale or hire, or

(*b*) imports into the United Kingdom otherwise than for his private and domestic use, or

(*c*) possesses in the course of a business with a view to committing any act infringing the copyright, or

(*d*) in the course of a business—

(i) sells or lets for hire, or

(ii) offers or exposes for sale or hire, or

(iii) exhibits in public, or

(iv) distributes, or

(*e*) distributes otherwise than in the course of a business to such an extent as to affect prejudicially the owner of the copyright,

an article which is, and which he knows or has reason to believe is, an infringing copy of a copyright work.

(2) A person commits an offence who—

(*a*) makes an article specifically designed or adapted for making copies of a particular copyright work, or

(*b*) has such an article in his possession,

knowing or having reason to believe that it is to be used to make infringing copies for sale or hire or for use in the course of a business.

(3) Where copyright is infringed (otherwise than by reception of a broadcast or cable programme)—

(*a*) by the public performance of a literary, dramatic or musical work, or

(*b*) by the playing or showing in public of a sound recording or film,

any person who caused the work to be so performed, played or shown is guilty of an offence if he knew or had reason to believe that copyright would be infringed.

(4) A person guilty of an offence under subsection (1)(*a*), (*b*), (*d*)(iv) or (*e*) is liable—

(*a*) on summary conviction to imprisonment for a term not exceeding six months or a fine not exceeding the statutory maximum, or both;

(*b*) on conviction on indictment to a fine or imprisonment for a term not exceeding two years, or both.

(5) A person guilty of any other offence under this section is liable on summary conviction to imprisonment for a term not exceeding six months or a fine not exceeding level 5 on the standard scale, or both.

(6) Sections 104 to 106 (presumptions as to various matters connected with copyright) do not apply to proceedings for an offence under this section; but without prejudice to their application in proceedings for an order under section 108 below.

Order for delivery up in criminal proceedings

108.—(1) The court before which proceedings are brought against a person for **A–111** an offence under section 107 may, if satisfied that at the time of his arrest or charge—

(*a*) he had in his possession, custody or control in the course of a business an infringing copy of a copyright work, or

(*b*) he had in his possession, custody or control an article specifically designed or adapted for making copies of a particular copyright work, knowing or having reason to believe that it had been or was to be used to make infringing copies,

order that the infringing copy or article be delivered up to the copyright owner or to such other person as the court may direct.

(2) For this purpose a person shall be treated as charged with an offence—

(*a*) in England, Wales and Northern Ireland, when he is orally charged or is served with a summons or indictment;

(*b*) in Scotland, when he is cautioned, charged or served with a complaint or indictment.

(3) An order may be made by the court of its own motion or on the application of the prosecutor (or, in Scotland, the Lord Advocate or procurator-fiscal), and may be made whether or not the person is convicted of the offence, but shall not be made—

(*a*) after the end of the period specified in section 113 (period after which remedy of delivery up is not available), or

(*b*) if it appears to the court unlikely that any order will be made under section 114 (order as to disposal of infringing copy or other article).

(4) An appeal lies from an order made under this section by a magistrates' court—

(*a*) in England and Wales, to the Crown Court, and

(*b*) in Northern Ireland, to the county court;

and in Scotland, where an order has been made under this section, the person from whose possession, custody or control the infringing copy or article has been removed may, without prejudice to any other form of appeal under any rule of law, appeal against the order in the same manner as against sentence.

(5) A person to whom an infringing copy or other article is delivered up in pursuance of an order under this section shall retain it pending the making of an order, or the decision not to make an order, under section 114.

(6) Nothing in this section affects the powers of the court under section 43 of the Powers of Criminal Courts Act 1973, section 223 or 436 of the Criminal Procedure (Scotland) Act 1975 or Article 7 of the Criminal Justice (Northern Ireland) Order 1980 (general provisions as to forfeiture in criminal proceedings).

Search warrants

A-112   **109.**—(1) Where a justice of the peace (in Scotland, a sheriff or justice of the peace) is satisfied by information on oath given by a constable (in Scotland, by evidence on oath) that there are reasonable grounds for believing—

(*a*) that an offence under section 107(1)(*a*), (*b*), (*d*)(iv) or (*e*) has been or is about to be committed in any premises, and

(*b*) that evidence that such an offence has been or is about to be committed is in those premises,

he may issue a warrant authorising a constable to enter and search the premises, using such reasonable force as is necessary.

(2) The power conferred by subsection (1) does not, in England and Wales, extend to authorising a search for material of the kinds mentioned in section 9(2) of the Police and Criminal Evidence Act 1984 (certain classes of personal or confidential material).

(3) A warrant under this section—

(*a*) may authorise persons to accompany any constable executing the warrant, and

(*b*) remains in force for 28 days from the date of its issue.

(4) In executing a warrant issued under this section a constable may seize an article if he reasonably believes that it is evidence that any offence under section 107(1) has been or is about to be committed.

(5) In this section "premises" includes land, buildings, moveable structures, vehicles, vessels, aircraft and hovercraft.

Offence by body corporate: liability of officers

110.—(1) Where an offence under section 107 committed by a body corporate is   **A–113**
proved to have been committed with the consent or connivance of a director,
manager, secretary or other similar officer of the body, or a person purporting to
act in any such capacity, he as well as the body corporate is guilty of the offence
and liable to be proceeded against and punished accordingly.

(2) In relation to a body corporate whose affairs are managed by its members
"director" means a member of the body corporate.

Provision for preventing importation of infringing copies

Infringing copies may be treated as prohibited goods

111.—(1) The owner of the copyright in a published literary, dramatic or musi-   **A–114**
cal work may give notice in writing to the Commissioners of Customs and
Excise—
  (*a*) that he is the owner of the copyright in the work, and
  (*b*) that he requests the Commissioners, for a period specified in the notice, to
      treat as prohibited goods printed copies of the work which are infringing
      copies.

(2) The period specified in a notice under subsection (1) shall not exceed five
years and shall not extend beyond the period for which copyright is to subsist.

(3) The owner of the copyright in a sound recording or film may give notice in
writing to the Commissioners of Customs and Excise—
  (*a*) that he is the owner of the copyright in the work,
  (*b*) that infringing copies of the work are expected to arrive in the United
      Kingdom at a time and a place specified in the notice, and
  (*c*) that he requests the Commissioners to treat the copies as prohibited goods.

(4) When a notice is in force under this section the importation of goods to
which the notice relates, otherwise than by a person for his private and domestic
use, is prohibited; but a person is not by reason of the prohibition liable to any
penalty other than forfeiture of the goods.

Power of Commissioners of Customs and Excise to make regulations

112.—(1) The Commissioners of Customs and Excise may make regulations   **A–115**
prescribing the form in which notice is to be given under section 111 and requiring
a person giving notice—
  (*a*) to furnish the Commissioners with such evidence as may be specified in the
      regulations, either on giving notice or when the goods are imported, or at
      both those times, and
  (*b*) to comply with such other conditions as may be specified in the regula-
      tions.

(2) The regulations may, in particular, require a person giving such a notice—
  (*a*) to pay such fees in respect of the notice as may be specified by the regula-
      tions;
  (*b*) to give such security as may be so specified in respect of any liability or
      expense which the Commissioners may incur in consequence of the notice
      by reason of the detention of any article or anything done to an article
      detained;
  (*c*) to indemnify the Commissioners against any such liability or expense,
      whether security has been given or not.

(3) The regulations may make different provision as respects different classes of

899

case to which they apply and may include such incidental and supplementary provisions as the Commissioners consider expedient.

(4) Regulations under this section shall be made by statutory instrument which shall be subject to annulment in pursuance of a resolution of either House of Parliament.

(5) Section 17 of the Customs and Excise Management Act 1979 (general provisions as to Commissioners' receipts) applies to fees paid in pursuance of regulations under this section as to receipts under the enactments relating to customs and excise.

Supplementary

Period after which remedy of delivery up not available

A–116   **113.**—(1) An application for an order under section 99 (order for delivery up in civil proceedings) may not be made after the end of the period of six years from the date on which the infringing copy or article in question was made, subject to the following provisions.

(2) If during the whole or any part of that period the copyright owner—

(*a*) is under a disability, or

(*b*) is prevented by fraud or concealment from discovering the facts entitling him to apply for an order,

an application may be made at any time before the end of the period of six years from the date on which he ceased to be under a disability or, as the case may be, could with reasonable diligence have discovered those facts.

(3) In subsection (2) "disability"—

(*a*) in England and Wales, has the same meaning as in the Limitation Act 1980;

(*b*) in Scotland, means legal disability within the meaning of the Prescription and Limitation (Scotland) Act 1973;

(*c*) in Northern Ireland, has the same meaning as the Statute of Limitations (Northern Ireland) Act 1958.

(4) An order under section 108 (order for delivery up in criminal proceedings) shall not, in any case, be made after the end of the period of six years from the date on which the infringing copy or article in question was made.

Order as to disposal of infringing copy or other article

A–117   **114.**—(1) An application may be made to the court for an order that an infringing copy or other article delivered up in pursuance of an order under section 99 or 108, or seized and detained in pursuance of the right conferred by section 100, shall be—

(*a*) forfeited to the copyright owner, or

(*b*) destroyed or otherwise dealt with as the court may think fit,

or for a decision that no such order should be made.

(2) In considering what order (if any) should be made, the court shall consider whether other remedies available in an action for infringement of copyright would be adequate to compensate the copyright owner and to protect his interests.

(3) Provision shall be made by rules of court as to the service of notice on persons having an interest in the copy or other articles, and any such person is entitled—

(*a*) to appear in proceedings for an order under this section, whether or not he was served with notice, and

(*b*) to appeal against any order made, whether or not he appeared;

and an order shall not take effect until the end of the period within which notice of an appeal may be given or, if before the end of that period notice of appeal is duly given, until the final determination or abandonment of the proceedings on the appeal.

(4) Where there is more than one person interested in a copy or other article, the court shall make such order as it thinks just and may (in particular) direct that the article be sold, or otherwise dealt with, and the proceeds divided.

(5) If the court decides that no order should be made under this section, the person in whose possession, custody or control the copy or other article was before being delivered up or seized is entitled to its return.

(6) References in this section to a person having an interest in a copy or other article include any person in whose favour an order could be made in respect of it under this section or under section 204 or 231 of this Act or section 58C of the Trade Marks Act 1938 (which make similar provision in relation to infringement of rights in performances, design right and trade marks).

Jurisdiction of county court and sheriff court

115.—(1) In England, Wales and Northern Ireland a county court may enter- **A-118** tain proceedings under—

section 99 (order for delivery up of infringing copy or other article),
section 10(5) (order as to exercise of rights by copyright owner where exclusive licensee has concurrent rights) or
section 114 (order as to disposal of infringing copy or other article),
where the value of the infringing copies and other articles in question does not exceed the county court limit for actions in tort.

(2) In Scotland proceedings for an order under any of those provisions may be brought in the sheriff court.

(3) Nothing in this section shall be construed as affecting the jurisdiction of the High Court or, in Scotland, the Court of Session.

CHAPTER VII

COPYRIGHT LICENSING

Licensing schemes and licensing bodies

Licensing schemes and licensing bodies

116.—(1) In this Part a "licensing scheme" means a scheme setting out— **A-119**
  (*a*) the classes of case in which the operator of the scheme, or the person on whose behalf he acts, is willing to grant copyright licences, and
  (*b*) the terms on which licences would be granted in those classes of case;
and for this purpose a "scheme" includes anything in the nature of a scheme, whether described as a scheme or as a tariff or by any other name.

(2) In this Chapter a "licensing body" means a society or other organisation which has as its main object, or one of its main objects, the negotiation or granting, either as owner or prospective owner of copyright or as agent for him, of copyright licences, and whose objects include the granting of licences covering works of more than one author.

(3) In this section "copyright licences" means licences to do, or authorise the doing of, any of the acts restricted by copyright.

(4) References in this Chapter to licences or licensing schemes covering works of more than one author do not include licences or schemes covering only—

901

(*a*) a single collective work or collective works of which the authors are the same, or

(*b*) works made by, or by employees of or commissioned by, a single individual, firm, company or group of companies.

For this purpose a group of companies means a holding company and its subsidiaries, within the meaning of section 736 of the Companies Act 1985.

References and applications with respect to licensing schemes

Licensing schemes to which sections 118 to 123 apply

A–120 **117.** Sections 118 to 123 (references and applications with respect to licensing schemes) apply to—

(*a*) licensing schemes operated by licensing bodies in relation to the copyright in literary, dramatic, musical or artistic works or films (or film sound-tracks when accompanying a film) which cover works of more than one author, so far as they relate to licences for—

(i) copying the work,

(ii) performing, playing or showing the work in public, or

(iii) broadcasting the work or including it in a cable programme service;

(*b*) all licensing schemes in relation to the copyright in sound recordings (other than film sound-tracks when accompanying a film), broadcasts or cable programmes, or the typographical arrangement of published editions; and

(*c*) all licensing schemes in relation to the copyright in sound recordings, films or computer programs so far as they relate to licences for the rental of copies to the public;

and in those sections "licensing scheme" means a licensing scheme of any of those descriptions.

Reference of proposed licensing scheme to tribunal

A–121 **118.**—(1) The terms of a licensing scheme proposed to be operated by a licensing body may be referred to the Copyright Tribunal by an organisation claiming to be representative of persons claiming that they require licences in cases of a description to which the scheme would apply, either generally or in relation to any description of case.

(2) The Tribunal shall first decide whether to entertain the reference, and may decline to do so on the ground that the reference is premature.

(3) If the Tribunal decides to entertain the reference it shall consider the matter referred and made such order, either confirming or varying the proposed scheme, either generally or so far as it relates to cases of the description to which the reference relates, as the Tribunal may determine to be reasonable in the circumstances.

(4) The order may be made so as to be in force indefinitely or for such period as the Tribunal may determine.

Reference of licensing scheme to tribunal

A–122 **119.**—(1) If while a licensing scheme is in operation a dispute arises between the operator of the scheme and—

(*a*) a person claiming that he requires a licence in a case of a description to which the scheme applies, or

(*b*) an organisation claiming to be representative of such persons,

that person or organisation may refer the scheme to the Copyright Tribunal in so far as it relates to cases of that description.

(2) A scheme which has been referred to the Tribunal under this section shall remain in operation until proceedings on the reference are concluded.

(3) The Tribunal shall consider the matter in dispute and make such order, either confirming or varying the scheme so far as it relates to cases of the description to which the reference relates, as the Tribunal may determine to be reasonable in the circumstances.

(4) The order may be made so as to be in force indefinitely or for such period as the Tribunal may determine.

Further reference of scheme to tribunal

120.—(1) Where the Copyright Tribunal has on a previous reference of a licens- **A–123** ing scheme under section 118 or 119, or under this section, made an order with respect to the scheme, then, while the order remains in force—

  (*a*) the operator of the scheme,

  (*b*) a person claiming that he requires a licence in a case of the description to which the order applies, or

  (*c*) an organisation claiming to be representative of such persons,

may refer the scheme again to the Tribunal so far as it relates to cases of that description.

(2) A licensing scheme shall not, except with the special leave of the Tribunal, be referred again to the Tribunal in respect of the same description of cases—

  (*a*) within twelve months from the date of the order on the previous reference, or

  (*b*) if the order was made so as to be in force for 15 months or less, until the last three months before the expiry of the order.

(3) A scheme which has been referred to the Tribunal under this section shall remain in operation until proceedings on the reference are concluded.

(4) The Tribunal shall consider the matter in dispute and make such order, either confirming, varying or further varying the scheme so far as it relates to cases of the description to which the reference relates, as the Tribunal may determine to be reasonable in the circumstances.

(5) The order may be made so as to be in force indefinitely or for such period as the Tribunal may determine.

Application for grant of licence in connection with licensing scheme

121.—(1) A person who claims, in a case covered by a licensing scheme, that **A–124** the operator of the scheme has refused to grant him or procure the grant to him of a licence in accordance with the scheme, or has failed to do so within a reasonable time after being asked, may apply to the Copyright Tribunal.

(2) A person who claims, in a case excluded from a licensing scheme, that the operator of the scheme either—

  (*a*) has refused to grant him a licence or procure the grant to him of a licence, or has failed to do so within a reasonable time of being asked, and that in the circumstances it is unreasonable that a licence should not be granted, or

  (*b*) proposes terms for a licence which are unreasonable,

may apply to the Copyright Tribunal.

(3) A case shall be regarded as excluded from a licensing scheme for the purposes of subsection (2) if—

  (*a*) the scheme provides for the grant of licences subject to terms excepting matters from the licence and the case falls within such an exception, or

  (*b*) the case is so similar to those in which licences are granted under the scheme that it is unreasonable that it should not be dealt with in the same way.

(4) If the Tribunal is satisfied that the claim is well-founded, it shall make an

order declaring that, in respect of the matters specified in the order, the applicant is entitled to a licence on such terms as the Tribunal may determine to be applicable in accordance with the scheme or, as the case may be, to be reasonable in the circumstances.

(5) the order may be made so as to be in force indefinitely or for such period as the Tribunal may determine.

Application for review of order as to entitlement to licence

A–125 **122.**—(1) Where the Copyright Tribunal has made an order under section 121 that a person is entitled to a licence under a licensing scheme, the operator of the scheme or the original applicant may apply to the Tribunal to review its order.

(2) An application shall not be made, except with the special leave of the Tribunal—

(a) within twelve months from the date of the order, or of the decision on a previous application under this section, or

(b) if the order was made so as to be in force for 15 months or less, or as a result of the decision on a previous application under this section is due to expire within 15 months of that decision, until the last three months before the expiry date.

(3) The Tribunal shall on an application for review confirm or vary its order as the Tribunal may determine to be reasonable having regard to the terms applicable in accordance with the licensing scheme or, as the case may be, the circumstances of the case.

Effect of order of tribunal as to licensing scheme

A–126 **123.**—(1) A licensing scheme which has been confirmed or varied by the Copyright Tribunal—

(a) under section 118 (reference of terms of proposed scheme), or

(b) under section 119 or 120 (reference of existing scheme to Tribunal),

shall be in force or, as the case may be, remain in operation, so far as it relates to the description of case in respect of which the order was made, so long as the order remains in force.

(2) While the order is in force a person who in a case of a class to which the order applies—

(a) pays to the operator of the scheme any charges payable under the scheme in respect of a licence covering the case in question or, if the amount cannot be ascertained, gives an undertaking to the operator to pay them when ascertained, and

(b) complies with the other terms applicable to such a licence under the scheme,

shall be in the same position as regards infringement of copyright as if he had at all material times been the holder of a licence granted by the owner of the copyright in question in accordance with the scheme.

(3) The Tribunal may direct that the order, so far as it varies the amount of charges payable, has effect from a date before that on which it is made, but not earlier than the date on which the reference was made or, if later, on which the scheme came into operation.

If such a direction is made—

(a) any necessary repayments, or further payments, shall be made in respect of charges already paid, and

(b) the reference in subsection (2)(a) to the charges payable under the scheme shall be construed as a reference to the charges so payable by virtue of the order.

No such direction may be made where subsection (4) below applies.

(4) An order of the Tribunal under section 119 or 120 made with respect to a scheme which is certified for any purpose under section 143 has effect, so far as it varies the scheme by reducing the charges payable for licences, from the date on which the reference was made to the Tribunal.

(5) Where the Tribunal has made an order under section 121 (order as to entitlement to licence under licensing scheme) and the order remains in force, the person in whose favour the order is made shall if he—

(*a*) pays to the operator of the scheme any charges payable in accordance with the order or, if the amount cannot be ascertained, gives an undertaking to pay the charges when ascertained, and

(*b*) complies with the other terms specified in the order,

be in the same position as regards infringement of copyright as if he had at all material times been the holder of a licence granted by the owner of the copyright in question on the terms specified in the order.

References and applications with respect to licensing by licensing bodies

Licences to which ss. 125 to 128 apply

124. Sections 125 to 128 (references and applications with respect to licensing **A–127** by licensing bodies) apply to the following descriptions of licence granted by a licensing body otherwise than in pursuance of a licensing scheme—

(*a*) licences relating to the copyright in literary, dramatic, musical or artistic works or films (or film sound-tracks when accompanying a film) which cover works of more than one author, so far as they authorise—
 (i) copying the work,
 (ii) performing, playing or showing the work in public, or
 (iii) broadcasting the work or including it in a cable programme service;

(*b*) any licence relating to the copyright in a sound recording (other than a film sound-track when accompanying a film), broadcast or cable programme, or the typographical arrangement of a published edition; and

(*c*) all licences in relation to the copyright in sound recordings, films or computer programs so far as they relate to the rental of copies to the public;

and in those sections a "licence" means a licence of any of those descriptions.

Reference to tribunal of proposed licence

125.—(1) The terms on which a licensing body proposes to grant a licence may **A–128** be referred to the Copyright Tribunal by the prospective licensee.

(2) The Tribunal shall first decide whether to entertain the reference, and may decline to do so on the ground that the reference is premature.

(3) If the Tribunal decides to entertain the reference it shall consider the terms of the proposed licence and make such order, either confirming or varying the terms, as it may determine to be reasonable in the circumstances.

(4) The order may be made so as to be in force indefinitely or for such period as the Tribunal may determine.

Reference to tribunal of expiring licence

126.—(1) A licensee under a licence which is due to expire, by effluxion of time **A–129** or as a result of notice given by the licensing body, may apply to the Copyright Tribunal on the ground that it is unreasonable in the circumstances that the licence should cease to be in force.

(2) Such an application may not be made until the last three months before the licence is due to expire.

(3) A licence in respect of which a reference has been made to the Tribunal shall remain in operation until proceedings on the reference are concluded.

(4) If the Tribunal finds the application well-founded, it shall make an order declaring that the licensee shall continue to be entitled to the benefit of the licence on such terms as the Tribunal may determine to be reasonable in the circumstances.

(5) An order of the Tribunal under this section may be made so as to be in force indefinitely or for such period as the Tribunal may determine.

Application for review of order as to licence

A–130
127.—(1) Where the Copyright Tribunal has made an order under section 125 or 126, the licensing body or the person entitled to the benefit of the order may apply to the Tribunal to review its order.

(2) An application shall not be made, except with the special leave of the Tribunal—
  (*a*) within twelve months from the date of the order or of the decision on a previous application under this section, or
  (*b*) if the order was made so as to be in force for 15 months or less, or as a result of the decision on a previous application under this section is due to expire within 15 months of that decision, until the last three months before the expiry date.

(3) The Tribunal shall on an application for review confirm or vary its order as the Tribunal may determine to be reasonable in the circumstances.

Effect of order of tribunal as to licence

A–131
128.—(1) Where the Copyright Tribunal has made an order under section 125 or 126 and the order remains in force, the person entitled to the benefit of the order shall if he—
  (*a*) pays to the licensing body any charges payable in accordance with the order or, if the amount cannot be ascertained, gives an undertaking to pay the charges when ascertained, and
  (*b*) complies with the other terms specified in the order,
be in the same position as regards infringement of copyright as if he had at all material times been the holder of a licence granted by the owner of the copyright in question on the terms specified in the order.

(2) The benefit of the order may be assigned—
  (*a*) in the case of an order under section 125, if assignment is not prohibited under the terms of the Tribunal's order; and
  (*b*) in the case of an order under section 126, if assignment was not prohibited under the terms of the original licence.

(3) The Tribunal may direct that an order under section 125 or 126, or an order under section 127 varying such an order, so far as it varies the amount of charges payable, has effect from a date before that on which it is made, but not earlier than the date on which the reference or application was made or, if later, on which the licence was granted or, as the case may be, was due to expire.
If such a direction is made—
  (*a*) any necessary repayments, or further payments, shall be made in respect of charges already paid, and
  (*b*) the reference in subsection (1)(*a*) to the charges payable in accordance with the order shall be construed, where the order is varied by a later order, as a reference to the charges so payable by virtue of the later order.

Factors to be taken into account in certain classes of case

General considerations: unreasonable discrimination

129. In determining what is reasonable on a reference or application under this **A–132** Chapter relating to a licensing scheme or licence, the Copyright Tribunal shall have regard to—

(*a*) the availability of other schemes, or the granting of other licences, to other persons in similar circumstances, and

(*b*) the terms of those schemes or licences,

and shall exercise its powers so as to secure that there is no unreasonable discrimination between licensees, or prospective licensees, under the scheme or licence to which the reference or application relates and licensees under other schemes operated by, or other licences granted by, the same person.

Licences for reprographic copying

130. Where a reference or application is made to the Copyright Tribunal under **A–133** this Chapter relating to the licensing of reprographic copying of published literary, dramatic, musical or artistic works, or the typographical arrangement of published editions, the Tribunal shall have regard to—

(*a*) the extent to which published editions of the works in question are otherwise available,

(*b*) the proportion of the work to be copied, and

(*c*) the nature of the use to which the copies are likely to be put.

Licences for educational establishments in respect of works included in broadcasts or cable programmes

131.—(1) This section applies to references or applications under this Chapter **A–134** relating to licences for the recording by or on behalf of educational establishments of broadcasts or cable programmes which include copyright works, or the making of copies of such recordings, for educational purposes.

(2) The Copyright Tribunal shall, in considering what charges (if any) should be paid for a licence, have regard to the extent to which the owners of copyright in the works included in the broadcast or cable programme have already received, or are entitled to receive, payment in respect of their inclusion.

Licences to reflect conditions imposed by promoters of events

132.—(1) This section applies to references or applications under this Chapter **A–135** in respect of licences relating to sound recordings, films, broadcasts or cable programmes which include, or are to include, any entertainment or other event.

(2) The Copyright Tribunal shall have regard to any conditions imposed by the promoters of the entertainment or other event; and, in particular, the Tribunal shall not hold a refusal or failure to grant a licence to be unreasonable if it could not have been granted consistently with those conditions.

(3) Nothing in this section shall require the Tribunal to have regard to any such conditions in so far as they—

(*a*) purport to regulate the charges to be imposed in respect of the grant of licences, or

(*b*) relate to payments to be made to the promoters of any event in consideration of the grant of facilities for making the recording, film, broadcast or cable programme.

Licences to reflect payments in respect of underlying rights

A–136   **133.**—(1) In considering what charges should be paid for a licence—

    (*a*) on a reference or application under this Chapter relating to licences for the rental to the public of copies of sound recordings, films or computer programs, or

    (*b*) on an application under section 142 (settlement of royalty or other sum payable for deemed licence),

the Copyright Tribunal shall take into account any reasonable payments which the owner of the copyright in the sound recording, film or computer program is liable to make in consequence of the granting of the licence, or of the acts authorised by the licence, to owners of copyright in works included in that work.

(2) On any reference or application under this Chapter relating to licensing in respect of the copyright in sound recordings, films, broadcasts or cable programmes, the Copyright Tribunal shall take into account, in considering what charges should be paid for a licence, any reasonable payments which the copyright owner is liable to make in consequence of the granting of the licence, or of the acts authorised by the licence, in respect of any performance included in the recording, film, broadcast or cable programme.

Licences in respect of works included in re-transmissions

A–137   **134.**—(1) This section applies to references or applications under this Chapter relating to licences to include in a broadcast or cable programme service—

    (*a*) literary, dramatic, musical or artistic works, or,

    (*b*) sound recordings or films,

where one broadcast or cable programme ("the first transmission") is, by reception and immediate re-transmission, to be further broadcast or included in a cable programme service ("the further transmission").

(2) So far as the further transmission is to the same area as the first transmission, the Copyright Tribunal shall, in considering what charges (if any) should be paid for licences for either transmission, have regard to the extent to which the copyright owner has already received, or is entitled to receive, payment for the other transmission which adequately remunerates him in respect of transmissions to that area.

(3) So far as the further transmission is to an area outside that to which the first transmission was made, the Tribunal shall (except where subsection (4) applies) leave the further transmission out of account in considering what charges (if any) should be paid for licences for the first transmission.

[*(4) If the Tribunal is satisfied that requirements imposed under section 13(1) of the Cable and Broadcasting Act 1984 (duty of Cable Authority to secure inclusion of certain broadcasts in cable programme services) will result in the further transmission being to areas part of which fall outside the area to which the first transmission is made, the Tribunal shall exercise its powers so as to secure that the charges payable for licences for the first transmission adequately reflect that fact.*]

Note. The words in square brackets, printed in italics, were repealed by Section 203(3) of and Schedule 21 to the Broadcasting Act 1990 (c. 42) as provided by The Broadcasting Act 1990 (Commencement No. 1 and Transitional Provisions) Order 1990 (S.I. 1990 No. 2347 (c. 61) § B–254 *post*.

Mention of specific matters not to exclude other relevant considerations

A–138   **135.** The mention in sections 129 to 134 of specific matters to which the Copyright Tribunal is to have regard in certain classes of case does not affect the Tribunal's general obligation in any case to have regard to all relevant considerations.

[*Use as of right of sound recordings in broadcasts and cable programme services*

Circumstances in which right available

135A.—(1) Section 135C applies to the inclusion in a broadcast or cable pro- **A–138A**
gramme service of any sound recordings if—

 (*a*) a licence to include those recordings in the broadcast or cable programme
 service could be granted by a licensing body or such a body could procure
 the grant of a licence to do so,

 (*b*) the condition in subsection (2) or (3) applies, and

 (*c*) the person including those recordings in the broadcast or cable programme
 service has complied with section 135B.

(2) Where the person including the recordings in the broadcast or cable programme service does not hold a licence to do so, the condition is that the licensing
body refuses to grant, or procure the grant of, such a licence, being a licence—

 (*a*) whose terms as to payment for including the recordings in the broadcast or
 cable programme service would be acceptable to him or comply with an
 order of the Copyright Tribunal under section 135D relating to such a
 licence or any scheme under which it would be granted, and

 (*b*) allowing unlimited needletime or such needletime as he has demanded.

(3) Where he holds a licence to include the recordings in the broadcast or cable
programme service, the condition is that the terms of the licence limit needletime
and the licensing body refuses to substitute or procure the substitution of terms
allowing unlimited needletime or such needletime as he has demanded, or refuses
to do so on terms that fall within subsection (2)(*a*).

(4) The references in subsection (2) to refusing to grant, or procure the grant of,
a licence, and in subsection (3) to refusing to substitute or procure the substitution
of terms, include failing to do so within a reasonable time of being asked.

(5) In the group of sections from this section to section 135G—

 "needletime" means the time in any period (whether determined as a number
 of hours in the period or a proportion of the period, or otherwise) in which
 any recordings may be included in a broadcast or cable programme service;

 "sound recording" does not include a film sound track when accompanying a
 film.

(6) In sections 135B to 135G, "terms of payment" means terms as to payment
for including sound recordings in a broadcast or cable programme service.

Notice of intention to exercise right

135B.—(1) A person intending to avail himself of the right conferred by section **A–138B**
135C must—

 (*a*) give notice to the licensing body of his intention to exercise the right, asking
 the body to propose terms of payment, and

 (*b*) after receiving the proposal or the expiry of a reasonable period, give
 reasonable notice to the licensing body of the date on which he proposes to
 begin exercising that right, and the terms of payment in accordance with
 which he intends to do so.

(2) Where he has a licence to include the recordings in a broadcast or cable
programme service, the date specified in a notice under subsection (1)(*b*) must not
be sooner than the date of expiry of that licence except in a case falling within section 135A(3).

(3) Before the person intending to avail himself of the right begins to exercise it,
he must—

(*a*) give reasonable notice to the Copyright Tribunal of his intention to exercise the right, and of the date on which he proposes to begin to do so, and

(*b*) apply to the Tribunal under section 135D to settle the terms of payment.

Conditions for exercise of right

A–138C   **135C.**—(1) A person who, on or after the date specified in a notice under section 135B(1)(b), includes in a broadcast or cable programme service any sound recordings in circumstances in which this section applies, and who—

(*a*) complies with any reasonable condition, notice of which has been given to him by the licensing body, as to inclusion in the broadcast or cable programme service of those recordings,

(*b*) provides that body with such information about their inclusion in the broadcast or cable programme service as it may reasonably require, and

(*c*) makes the payments to the licensing body that are required by this section,

shall be in the same position as regards infringement of copyright as if he had at all material times been the holder of a licence granted by the owner of the copyright in question.

(2) Payments are to be made at not less than quarterly intervals in arrears.

(3) The amount of any payment is that determined in accordance with any order of the Copyright Tribunal under section 135D or, if no such order has been made—

(*a*) in accordance with any proposal for terms of payment made by the licensing body pursuant to a request under section 135B, or

(*b*) where no proposal has been so made or the amount determined in accordance with the proposal so made is unreasonably high, in accordance with the terms of payment notified to the licensing body under section 135B(1)(*b*).

(4) Where this section applies to the inclusion in a broadcast or cable programme service of any sound recordings, it does so in place of any licence.

Applications to settle payments

A–138D   **135D.**—(1) On an application to settle the terms of payment, the Copyright Tribunal shall consider the matter and make such order as it may determine to be reasonable in the circumstances.

(2) An order under subsection (1) has effect from the date the applicant begins to exercise the right conferred by section 135C and any necessary repayments, or further payments, shall be made in respect of amounts that have fallen due.

References etc. about conditions, information and other terms

A–138E   **135E.**—(1) A person exercising the right conferred by section 135C, or who has given notice to the Copyright Tribunal of his intention to do so, may refer to the Tribunal—

(*a*) any question whether any condition as to the inclusion in a broadcast or cable programme service of sound recordings, notice of which has been given to him by the licensing body in question, is a reasonable condition, or

(*b*) any question whether any information is information which the licensing body can reasonably require him to provide.

(2) On a reference under this section, the Tribunal shall consider the matter and make such order as it may determine to be reasonable in the circumstances.

Application for review of order

135F.—(1) A person exercising the right conferred by section 135C or the   **A–138F**
licensing body may apply to the Copyright Tribunal to review any order under
section 135D or 135E.

(2) An application shall not be made, except with the special leave of the Tribunal—

    (*a*) within twelve months from the date of the order, or of the decision on a pre-
        vious application under this section, or

    (*b*) if the order was made so as to be in force for fifteen months or less, or as a
        result of a decision on a previous application is due to expire within fifteen
        months of that decision, until the last three months before the expiry date.

(3) On the application the Tribunal shall consider the matter and make such
order confirming or varying the original order as it may determine to be reasonable in the circumstances.

(4) An order under this section has effect from the date on which it is made or
such later date as may be specified by the Tribunal.

Factors to be taken into account

135G.—(1) In determining what is reasonable on an application or reference   **A–138G**
under section 135D or 135E, or on reviewing any order under section 135F, the
Copyright Tribunal shall—

    (*a*) have regard to the terms of any orders which it has made in the case of per-
        sons in similar circumstances exercising the right conferred by section
        135C, and

    (*b*) exercise its powers so as to secure that there is no unreasonable discrimi-
        nation between persons exercising that right against the same licensing
        body.

(2) In settling the terms of payment under section 135D, the Tribunal shall not
be guided by any order it has made under any enactment other than that section.

(3) Section 134 (factors to be taken into account: retransmissions) applies on an
application or reference under sections 135D to 135F as it applies on an application or reference relating to a licence.]

Note: Sections 135A – G were inserted in the 1988 Act by section 175 of the
Broadcasting Act 1990 (c. 42) with effect from February 1, 1991 by virtue of The
Broadcasting Act 1990 (Commencement No. 1 and Transitional Provisions)
Order 1990 (S.I. 1990 No. 2347 (c. 61)) § B–254 *post*.

Implied indemnity in schemes or licences for reprographic copying

**Implied indemnity in certain schemes and licences for reprographic
copying**

136.—(1) This section applies to—   **A–139**

    (*a*) schemes for licensing reprographic copying of published literary, dramatic,
        musical or artistic works, or the typographical arrangement of published
        editions, and

    (*b*) licences granted by licensing bodies for such copying,
where the scheme or licence does not specify the works to which it applies with
such particularity as to enable licensees to determine whether a work falls within
the scheme or licence by inspection of the scheme or licence and the work.

(2) There is implied—

    (*a*) in every scheme to which this section applies an undertaking by the operator of the scheme to indemnify a person granted a licence under the scheme, and

(*b*) in every licence to which this section applies an undertaking by the licensing body to indemnify the licensee,

against any liability incurred by him by reason of his having infringed copyright by making or authorising the making of reprographic copies of a work in circumstances with the apparent scope of his licence.

(3) The circumstances of a case are within the apparent scope of a licence if—

(*a*) it is not apparent from inspection of the licence and the work that it does not fall within the description of works to which the licence applies; and

(*b*) the licence does not expressly provide that it does not extend to copyright of the description infringed.

(4) In this section "liability" includes liability to pay costs; and this section applies in relation to costs reasonably incurred by a licensee in connection with actual or contemplated proceedings against him for infringement of copyright as it applies to sums which he is liable to pay in respect of such infringement.

(5) A scheme or licence to which this section applies may contain reasonable provision—

(*a*) with respect to the manner in which, and time within which, claims under the undertaking implied by this section are to be made;

(*b*) enabling the operator of the scheme or, as the case may be, the licensing body to take over the conduct of any proceedings affecting the amount of his liability to indemnify.

Reprographic copying by educational establishments

Power to extend coverage of scheme or licence

A–140   **137.**—(1) This section applies to—

(*a*) a licensing scheme to which sections 118 to 123 apply (see section 117) and which is operated by a licensing body, or

(*b*) a licence to which sections 125 to 128 apply (see section 124),

so far as it provides for the grant of licences, or is a licence, authorising the making by or on behalf of educational establishments for the purposes of instruction of reprographic copies of published literary, dramatic, musical or artistic works, or of the typographical arrangement of published editions.

(2) If it appears to the Secretary of State with respect to a scheme or licence to which this section applies that—

(*a*) works of a description similar to those covered by the scheme or licence are unreasonably excluded from it, and

(*b*) making them subject to the scheme or licence would not conflict with the normal exploitation of the works or unreasonably prejudice the legitimate interests of the copyright owners,

he may by order provide that the scheme or licence shall extend to those works.

(3) Where he proposes to make such an order, the Secretary of State shall give notice of the proposal to—

(*a*) the copyright owners,

(*b*) the licensing body in question, and

(*c*) such persons or organisations representative of educational establishments, and such other persons or organisations, as the Secretary of State thinks fit.

(4) The notice shall inform those persons of their right to make written or oral representations to the Secretary of State about the proposal within six months from the date of the notice; and if any of them wishes to make oral representations,

the Secretary of State shall appoint a person to hear the representations and report to him.

(5) In considering whether to make an order the Secretary of State shall take into account any representations made to him in accordance with subsection (4), and such other matters as appear to him to be relevant.

Variation or discharge of order extending scheme or licence

138.—(1) The owner of the copyright in a work in respect of which an order is **A–141** in force under section 137 may apply to the Secretary of State for the variation or discharge of the order, stating his reasons for making the application.

(2) The Secretary of State shall not entertain an application made within two years of the making of the original order, or of the making of an order on a previous application under this section, unless it appears to him that the circumstances are exceptional.

(3) On considering the reasons for the application the Secretary of State may confirm the order forthwith; if he does not do so, he shall give notice of the application to—

(a) the licensing body in question, and

(b) such persons or organisations representative of educational establishments, and such other persons or organisations, as he thinks fit.

(4) The notice shall inform those persons of their right to make written or oral representations to the Secretary of State about the application within the period of two months from the date of the notice; and if any of them wishes to make oral representations, the Secretary of State shall appoint a person to hear the representations and report to him.

(5) In considering the application the Secretary of State shall take into account the reasons for the application, any representations made to him in accordance with subsection (4), and such other matters as appear to him to be relevant.

(6) The Secretary of State may make such order as he thinks fit confirming or discharging the order (or, as the case may be, the order as previously varied), or varying (or further varying) it so as to exclude works from it.

Appeals against orders

139.—(1) The owner of the copyright in a work which is the subject of an order **A–142** under section 137 (order extending coverage of scheme or licence) may appeal to the Copyright Tribunal which may confirm or discharge the order, or vary it so as to exclude works from it, as it thinks fit having regard to the considerations mentioned in subsection (2) of that section.

(2) Where the Secretary of State has made an order under section 138 (order confirming, varying or discharging order extending coverage of scheme or licence)—

(a) the person who applied for the order, or

(b) any person or organisation representative of educational establishments who was given notice of the application for the order and made representations in accordance with subsection (4) of that section,

may appeal to the Tribunal which may confirm or discharge the order or make any other order which the Secretary of State might have made.

(3) An appeal under this section shall be brought within six weeks of the making of the order or such further period as the Tribunal may allow.

(4) An order under section 137 or 138 shall not come into effect until the end of the period of six weeks from the making of the order or, if an appeal is brought before the end of that period, until the appeal proceedings are disposed of or withdrawn.

(5) If an appeal is brought after the end of that period, any decision of the Tribunal on the appeal does not affect the validity of anything done in reliance on the order appealed against before that decision takes effect.

Inquiry whether new scheme or general licence required

A–143   **140.**—(1) The Secretary of State may appoint a person to inquire into the question whether new provision is required (whether by way of a licensing scheme or general licence) to authorise the making by or on behalf of educational establishments for the purposes of instruction of reprographic copies of—

(*a*) published literary, dramatic, musical or artistic works, or

(*b*) the typographical arrangement of public editions,

of a description which appears to the Secretary of State not to be covered by an existing licensing scheme or general licence and not to fall within the power conferred by section 137 (power to extend existing schemes and licences to similar works).

(2) The procedure to be followed in relation to an inquiry shall be such as may be prescribed by regulations made by the Secretary of State.

(3) The regulations shall, in particular, provide for notice to be given to—

(*a*) persons or organisations appearing to the Secretary of State to represent the owners of copyright in works of that description, and

(*b*) persons or organisations appearing to the Secretary of State to represent educational establishments,

and for the making of written or oral representations by such persons; but without prejudice to the giving of notice to, and the making of representations by, other persons and organisations.

(4) The person appointed to hold the inquiry shall not recommend the making of new provision unless he is satisfied—

(*a*) that it would be of advantage to educational establishments to be authorised to make reprographic copies of the works in question, and

(*b*) that making those works subject to a licensing scheme or general licence would not conflict with the normal exploitation of the works or unreasonably prejudice the legitimate interests of the copyright owners.

(5) If he does recommend the making of new provision he shall specify any terms, other than terms as to charges payable, on which authorisation under the new provision should be available.

(6) Regulations under this section shall be made by statutory instrument which shall be subject to annulment in pursuance of a resolution of either House of Parliament.

(7) In this section (and section 141) a "general licence" means a licence granted by a licensing body which covers all works of the description to which it applies.

Statutory licence where recommendation not implemented

A–144   **141.**—(1) The Secretary of State may, within one year of the making of a recommendation under section 140 by order provide that if, or to the extent that, provision has not been made in accordance with the recommendation, the making by or on behalf of an educational establishment, for the purposes of instruction, of reprographic copies of the works to which the recommendation relates shall be treated as licensed by the owners of the copyright in the works.

(2) For that purpose provision shall be regarded as having been made in accordance with the recommendation if—

(*a*) a certified licensing scheme has been established under which a licence is available to the establishment in question, or

(*b*) a general licence has been—

(i) granted to or for the benefit of that establishment, or

(ii) referred by or on behalf of that establishment to the Copyright Tribunal under section 125 (reference in terms of proposed licence), or

(iii) offered to or for the benefit of that establishment and refused without such a reference,

and the terms of the scheme or licence accord with the recommendation.

(3) The order shall also provide that any existing licence authorising the making of such copies (not being a licence granted under a certified licensing scheme or a general licence) shall cease to have effect to the extent that it is more restricted or more onerous than the licence provided for by the order.

(4) The order shall provide for the licence to be free of royalty but, as respects other matters, subject to any terms specified in the recommendation and to such other terms as the Secretary of State may think fit.

(5) The order may provide that where a copy which would otherwise be an infringing copy is made in accordance with the licence provided by the order but is subsequently dealt with, it shall be treated as an infringing copy for the purposes of that dealing, and if that dealing infringes copyright for all subsequent purposes.

In this subsection "dealt with" means sold or let for hire, offered or exposed for sale or hire, or exhibited in public.

(6) The order shall not come into force until at least six months after it is made.

(7) An order may be varied from time to time, but not so as to include works other than those to which the recommendation relates or remove any terms specified in the recommendation, and may be revoked.

(8) An order under this section shall be made by statutory instrument which shall be subject to annulment in pursuance of a resolution of either House of Parliament.

(9) In this section a "certified licensing scheme" means a licensing scheme certified for the purposes of this section under section 143.

Royalty or other sum payable for rental of certain works

Royalty or other sum payable for rental of sound recording, film or computer program

142.—(1) An application to settle the royalty or other sum payable in pursuance of section 66 (rental of sound recordings, films and computer programs) may be made to the Copyright Tribunal by the copyright owner or the person claiming to be treated as licensed by him.   **A–145**

(2) The Tribunal shall consider the matter and make such order as it may determine to be reasonable in the circumstances.

(3) Either party may subsequently apply to the Tribunal to vary the order, and the Tribunal shall consider the matter and make such order confirming or varying the original order as it may determine to be reasonable in the circumstances.

(4) An application under subsection (3) shall not, except with the special leave of the Tribunal, be made within twelve months from the date of the original order or of the order on a previous application under that subsection.

(5) An order under subsection (3) has effect from the date on which it is made or such later date as may be specified by the Tribunal.

Certification of licensing schemes

Certification of licensing schemes

143.—(1) A person operating or proposing to operate a licensing scheme may apply to the Secretary of State to certify the scheme for the purposes of—   **A–146**

(a) section 35 (educational recording of broadcasts or cable programmes),

(b) section 60 (abstracts of scientific or technical articles),

(c) section 66 (rental of sound recordings, films and computer programs),

(d) section 74 (sub-titled copies of broadcasts or cable programmes for people who are deaf or hard of hearing), or

(e) section 141 (reprographic copying of published works by educational establishments).

(2) The Secretary of State shall by order made by statutory instrument certify the scheme if he is satisfied that it—

(a) enables the works to which it relates to be identified with sufficient certainty by persons likely to require licences, and

(b) sets out clearly the charges (if any) payable and the other terms on which licences will be granted.

(3) The scheme shall be scheduled to the order and the certification shall come into operation for the purposes of section 35, 60, 66, 74 or 141, as the case may be—

(a) on such date, not less than eight weeks after the order is made, as may be specified in the order, or

(b) if the scheme is the subject of a reference under section 118 (reference of proposed scheme), any later date on which the order of the Copyright Tribunal under that section comes into force or the reference is withdrawn.

(4) A variation of the scheme is not effective unless a corresponding amendment of the order is made; and the Secretary of State shall make such an amendment in the case of a variation ordered by the Copyright Tribunal on a reference under section 118, 119 or 120, and may do so in any other case if he thinks fit.

(5) The order shall be revoked if the scheme ceases to be operated and may be revoked if it appears to the Secretary of State that it is no longer being operated according to its terms.

Powers exercisable in consequence of competition report

Powers exercisable in consequence of report of Monopolies and Mergers Commission

A–147   144.—(1) Where the matters specified in a report of the Monopolies and Mergers Commission as being those which in the Commission's opinion operate, may be expected to operate or have operated against the public interest include—

(a) conditions in licences granted by the owner of copyright in a work restricting the use of the work by the licensee or the right of the copyright owner to grant other licences, or

(b) a refusal of a copyright owner to grant licences on reasonable terms, the powers conferred by Part I of Schedule 8 to the Fair Trading Act 1973 (powers exercisable for purpose of remedying or preventing adverse effects specified in report of Commission) include power to cancel or modify those conditions and, instead or in addition, to provide that licences in respect of the copyright shall be available as of right.

(2) The references in sections 56(2) and 73(2) of that Act, and sections 10(2)(b) and 12(5) of the Competition Act 1980, to the powers specified in that Part of that Schedule shall be construed accordingly.

(3) A Minister shall only exercise the powers available by virtue of this section if he is satisfied that to do so does not contravene any Convention relating to copyright to which the United Kingdom is a party.

(4) The terms of a licence available by virtue of this section shall, in default of agreement, be settled by the Copyright Tribunal on an application by the person

requiring the licence; and terms so settled shall authorise the licensee to do every-thing in respect of which a licence is so available.

(5) Where the terms of a licence are settled by the Tribunal, the licence has effect from the date on which the application to the Tribunal was made.

CHAPTER VIII

THE COPYRIGHT TRIBUNAL

The Tribunal

The Copyright Tribunal

145.—(1) The Tribunal established under section 23 of the Copyright Act 1956   **A–148** is renamed the Copyright Tribunal.

(2) The Tribunal shall consist of a chairman and two deputy chairmen appointed by the Lord Chancellor, after consultation with the Lord Advocate, and not less than two or more than eight ordinary members appointed by the Secretary of State.

(3) A person is not eligible for appointment as chairman or deputy chairman unless he is a barrister, advocate or solicitor of not less than seven years' standing or has held judicial office.

Membership of the Tribunal

146.—(1) The members of the Copyright Tribunal shall hold and vacate office   **A–149** in accordance with their terms of appointment, subject to the following provisions.

(2) A member of the Tribunal may resign office by notice in writing to the Secretary of State or, in the case of the chairman or a deputy chairman, to the Lord Chancellor.

(3) The Secretary of State or, in the case of the chairman or a deputy chairman, the Lord Chancellor may by notice in writing to the member concerned remove him from office if—

(a) he has become bankrupt or made an arrangement with his creditors or, in Scotland, his estate has been sequestrated or he has executed a trust deed for his creditors or entered into a composition contract, or

(b) he is incapacitated by physical or mental illness,

or if he is in the opinion of the Secretary of State or, as the case may be, the Lord Chancellor otherwise unable or unfit to perform his duties as member.

(4) If a member of the Tribunal is by reason of illness, absence or other reasonable cause for the time being unable to perform the duties of his office, either generally or in relation to particular proceedings, a person may be appointed to discharge his duties for a period not exceeding six months at one time or, as the case may be, in relation to those proceedings.

(5) The appointment shall be made—

(a) in the case of the chairman or deputy chairman, by the Lord Chancellor, who shall appoint a person who would be eligible for appointment to that office, and

(b) in the case of an ordinary member, by the Secretary of State;

and a person so appointed shall have during the period of his appointment, or in relation to the proceedings in question, the same powers as the person in whose place he is appointed.

(6) The Lord Chancellor shall consult the Lord Advocate before exercising his powers under this section.

Financial provisions

A–150   **147.**—(1) There shall be paid to the members of the Copyright Tribunal such remuneration (whether by way of salaries or fees), and such allowances, as the Secretary of State with the approval of the Treasury may determine.

(2) The Secretary of State may appoint such staff for the Tribunal as, with the approval of the Treasury as to members and remuneration, he may determine.

(3) The remuneration and allowances of members of the Tribunal, the remuneration of any staff and such other expenses of the Tribunal as the Secretary of State with the approval of the Treasury may determine shall be paid out of money provided by Parliament.

Constitution for purposes of proceedings

A–151   **148.**—(1) For the purposes of any proceedings the Copyright Tribunal shall consist of—

> (*a*) a chairman, who shall be either the chairman or a deputy chairman of the Tribunal, and
>
> (*b*) two or more ordinary members.

(2) If the members of the Tribunal dealing with any matter are not unanimous, the decision shall be taken by majority vote; and if, in such a case, the votes are equal the chairman shall have a further, casting vote.

(3) Where part of any proceedings before the Tribunal has been heard and one or more members of the Tribunal are unable to continue, the Tribunal shall remain duly constituted for the purpose of those proceedings so long as the number of members is not reduced to less than three.

(4) If the chairman is unable to continue, the chairman of the Tribunal shall—

> (*a*) appoint one of the remaining members to act as chairman, and
>
> (*b*) appoint a suitably qualified person to attend the proceedings and advise the members on any questions of law arising.

(5) A person is "suitably qualified" for the purposes of subsection (4)(b) if he is, or is eligible for appointment as, a deputy chairman of the Tribunal.

Jurisdiction and procedure

Jurisdiction of the Tribunal

A–152   **149.** The function of the Copyright Tribunal is to hear and determine proceedings under—

> (*a*) section 118, 119, or 120 (reference of licensing scheme);
>
> (*b*) section 121 or 122 (application with respect to entitlement to licence under licensing scheme);
>
> (*c*) section 125, 126 or 127 (reference or application with respect to licensing by licensing body);
>
> [(*cc*) section 135D or 135E (application or references with respect to use as of right of sound recordings in broadcasts or cable programme services);]
>
> (*d*) section 139 (appeal against order as to coverage of licensing scheme or licence);
>
> (*e*) section 142 (application to settle royalty or other sum payable for rental of sound recording, film or computer program);
>
> (*f*) section 144(4) (application to settle terms of copyright licence available as of right);
>
> (*g*) section 190 (application to give consent for purposes of Part II on behalf of performer);
>
> (*h*) paragraph 5 of Schedule 6 (determination of royalty or other remuneration to be paid to trustees for the Hospital for Sick Children).

Note: (1) Subsection (*cc*) was inserted in the 1988 Act by section 175 of the Broadcasting Act 1990 (c. 42) with effect from February 1, 1991 by virtue of the Broadcasting Act 1990 (Commencement No.1 and Transitional Provisions) Order 1990 (S.I. 1990 No. 2347 (c. 61)) § B-254 *post*.

(2) See §§ A-79A and A-79B *ante* as to proceedings under Schedule 17 to the 1990 Act.

General power to make rules

150.—(1) The Lord Chancellor may, after consultation with the Lord Advocate, make rules for regulating proceedings before the Copyright Tribunal and, subject to the approval of the Treasury, as to the fees chargeable in respect of such proceedings.   **A-153**

(2) The rules may apply in relation to the Tribunal—

(*a*) as respects proceedings in England and Wales, any of the provisions of the Arbitration Act 1950;

(*b*) as respects proceedings in Northern Ireland, and any of the provisions of the Arbitration Act (Northern Ireland) 1937;

and any provisions so applied shall be set out in or scheduled to the rules.

(3) Provision shall be made by the rules—

(*a*) prohibiting the Tribunal from entertaining a reference under section 118, 119 or 120 by a representative organisation unless the Tribunal is satisfied that the organisation is reasonably representative of the class of persons which it claims to represent;

(*b*) specifying the parties to any proceedings and enabling the Tribunal to make a party to the proceedings any person or organisation satisfying the Tribunal that they have a suitable interest in the matter; and

(*c*) requiring the Tribunal to give the parties to proceedings an opportunity to state their case, in writing or orally as the rules may provide.

(4) The rules may make provision for regulating or prescribing any matters incidental to or consequential upon any appeal from the Tribunal under section 152 (appeal to the court on point of law).

(5) Rules under this section shall be made by statutory instrument which shall be subject to annulment in pursuance of a resolution of either House of Parliament.

Costs, proof of orders, &c

151.—(1) The Copyright Tribunal may order that the costs of a party to proceedings before it shall be paid by such other party as the Tribunal may direct; and the Tribunal may tax or settle the amount of the costs, or direct in what manner they are to be taxed.   **A-154**

(2) A document purporting to be a copy of an order of the Tribunal and to be certified by the chairman to be a true copy shall, in any proceedings, be sufficient evidence of the order unless the contrary is proved.

(3) As respect proceedings in Scotland, the Tribunal has the like powers for securing the attendance of witnesses and the production of documents, and with regard to the examination of witnesses on oath, as an arbiter under a submission.

Appeals

Appeal to the court on point of law

152.—(1) An appeal lies on any point of law arising from a decision of the Copyright Tribunal to the High Court or, in the case of proceedings of the Tribunal in Scotland, to the Court of Session.   **A-155**

(2) Provision shall be made by rules under section 150 limiting the time within which an appeal may be brought.

(3) Provision may be made by rules under that section—

(*a*) for suspending, or authorising or requiring the Tribunal to suspend, the operation of orders of the Tribunal in cases where its decision is appealed against;

(*b*) for modifying in relation to an order of the Tribunal whose operation is suspended the operation of any provision of this Act as to the effect of the order;

(*c*) for the publication of notices or the taking of other steps for securing that persons affected by the suspension of an order of the Tribunal will be informed of its suspension.

CHAPTER IX

QUALIFICATION FOR AND EXTENT OF COPYRIGHT PROTECTION

Qualification for copyright protection

Qualification for copyright protection

A–156   **153.**—(1) Copyright does not subsist in a work unless the qualification requirements of this Chapter are satisfied as regards—

(*a*) the author (see section 154), or

(*b*) the country in which the work was first published (see section 155), or

(*c*) in the case of a broadcast or cable programme, the country from which the broadcast was made or the cable programme was sent (see section 156).

(2) Subsection (1) does not apply in relation to Crown copyright or Parliamentary copyright (see sections 163 to 166) or to copyright subsisting by virtue of section 168 (copyright of certain international organisations).

(3) If the qualification requirements of this Chapter, or section 163, 165 or 168, are once satisfied in respect of a work, copyright does not cease to subsist by reason of any subsequent event.

Qualification by reference to author

A–157   **154.**—(1) A work qualifies for copyright protection if the author was at the material time a qualifying person, that is—

(*a*) a British citizen, a British Dependent Territories citizen, a British National (Overseas), a British Overseas Citizen, a British subject or a British protected person within the meaning of the British Nationality Act 1981, or

(*b*) an individual domiciled or resident in the United Kingdom or another country to which the relevant provisions of this Part extend, or

(*c*) a body incorporated under the law of a part of the United Kingdom or of another country to which the relevant provisions of this Part extend.

(2) Where, or so far as, provision is made by Order under section 159 (application of this Part to countries to which it does not extend), a work also qualifies for copyright protection if at the material time the author was a citizen or subject of, an individual domiciled or resident in, or a body incorporated under the law of, a country to which the Order relates.

(3) A work of joint authorship qualifies for copyright protection if at the material time any of the authors satisfies the requirements of subsection (1) or (2);

but where a work qualifies for copyright protection only under this section, only those authors who satisfy those requirements shall be taken into account for the purposes of—

section 11(1) and (2) (first ownership of copyright; entitlement of author or author's employer),
section 12(1) and (2) (duration of copyright; dependent on life of author unless work of unknown authorship), and section 9(4) (meaning of "unknown authorship") so far as it applies for the purposes of section 12(2), and
section 57 (anonymous or pseudonymous works: acts permitted on assumptions as to expiry of copyright or death of author).

(4) The material time in relation to a literary, dramatic, musical or artistic work is—
    (*a*) in the case of an unpublished work, when the work was made or, if the making of the work extended over a period, a substantial part of that period;
    (*b*) in the case of a published work, when the work was first published or, if the author had died before that time, immediately before his death.

(5) The material time in relation to other descriptions of work is as follows—
    (*a*) in the case of a sound recording or film, when it was made;
    (*b*) in the case of a broadcast, when the broadcast was made;
    (*c*) in the case of a cable programme, when the programme was included in a cable programme service;
    (*d*) in the case of the typographical arrangement of a published edition, when the edition was first published.

Qualification by reference to country of first publication

155.—(1) A literary, dramatic, musical or artistic work, a sound recording or   **A–158** film, or the typographical arrangement of a published edition, qualifies for copyright protection if it is first published—
    (*a*) in the United Kingdom, or
    (*b*) in another country to which the relevant provisions of this Part extend.

(2) Where, or so far as, provision is made by Order under section 159 (application of this Part to countries to which it does not extend), such a work also qualifies for copyright protection if it is first published in a country to which the Order relates.

(3) For the purposes of this section, publication in one country shall not be regarded as other than the first publication by reason of simultaneous publication elsewhere; and for this purpose publication elsewhere within the previous 30 days shall be treated as simultaneous.

Qualification by reference to place of transmission

156.—(1) A broadcast qualifies for copyright protection if it is made from, and a   **A–159** cable programme qualifies for copyright protection if it is sent from, a place in—
    (*a*) the United Kingdom, or
    (*b*) another country to which the relevant provisions of this Part extend.

(2) Where, or so far as, provision is made by Order under section 159 (application of this Part to countries to which it does not extend), a broadcast or cable programme also qualifies for copyright protection if it is made from or, as the case may be, sent from a place in a country to which the Order relates.

Extent and application of this Part

Countries to which this Part extends

A–160   **157.**—(1) This Part extends to England and Wales, Scotland and Northern Ireland.

(2) Her Majesty may by Order in Council direct that this Part shall extend, subject to such exceptions and modifications as may be specified in the Order, to—

   (*a*) any of the Channel Islands,

   (*b*) the Isle of Man, or

   (*c*) any colony.

(3) That power includes power to extend, subject to such exceptions and modifications as may be specified in the Order, any Order in Council made under the following provisions of this Chapter.

(4) The legislature of a country to which this Part has been extended may modify or add to the provisions of this Part, in their operation as part of the law of that country, as the legislature may consider necessary to adapt the provisions to the circumstances of that country—

   (*a*) as regards procedure and remedies, or

   (*b*) as regards works qualifying for copyright protection by virtue of a connection with that country.

(5) Nothing in this section shall be construed as restricting the extent of paragraph 36 of Schedule 1 (transitional provisions: dependent territories where the Copyright Act 1956 or the Copyright Act 1911 remains in force) in relation to the law of a dependent territory to which this Part does not extend.

Countries ceasing to be colonies

A–161   **158.**—(1) The following provisions apply where a country to which this Part has been extended ceases to be a colony of the United Kingdom.

(2) As from the date on which it ceases to be a colony it shall cease to be regarded as a country to which this Part extends for the purposes of—

   (*a*) section 160(2)(*a*) (denial of copyright protection to citizens of countries not giving adequate protection to British works), and

   (*b*) sections 163 and 165 (Crown and Parliamentary copyright).

(3) But it shall continue to be treated as a country to which this Part extends for the purposes of sections 154 to 156 (qualification for copyright protection) until—

   (*a*) an Order in Council is made in respect of that country under section 159 (application of this Part to countries to which it does not extend), or

   (*b*) an Order in Council is made declaring that it shall cease to be so treated by reason of the fact that the provisions of this Part as part of the law of that country have been repealed or amended.

(4) A statutory instrument containing an Order in Council under subsection (3)(*b*) shall be subject to annulment in pursuance of a resolution of either House of Parliament.

Application of this Part to countries to which it does not extend

A–162   **159.**—(1) Her Majesty may by Order in Council make provision for applying in relation to a country to which this Part does not extend any of the provisions of this Part specified in the Order, so as to secure that those provisions—

   (*a*) apply in relation to persons who are citizens or subjects of that country or are domiciled or resident there, as they apply to persons who are British citizens or are domiciled or resident in the United Kingdom, or

(b) apply in relation to bodies incorporated under the law of that country as they apply in relation to bodies incorporated under the law of a part of the United Kingdom, or

(c) apply in relation to works first published in that country as they apply in relation to works first published in the United Kingdom, or

(d) apply in relation to broadcasts made from or cable programmes sent from that country as they apply in relation to broadcasts made from or cable programmes sent from the United Kingdom.

(2) An Order may make provision for all or any of the matters mentioned in subsection (1) and may—

(a) apply any provisions of this Part subject to such exceptions and modifications as are specified in the Order; and

(b) direct that any provisions of this Part apply either generally or in relation to such classes of works, or other classes of case, as are specified in the Order.

(3) Except in the case of a Convention country or another member State of the European Economic Community, Her Majesty shall not make an Order in Council under this section in relation to a country unless satisfied that provision has been or will be made under the law of that country, in respect of the class of works to which the Order relates, giving adequate protection to the owners of copyright under this Part.

(4) In subsection (3) "Convention country" means a country which is a party to a Convention relating to copyright to which the United Kingdom is also a party.

(5) A statutory instrument containing an Order in Council under this section shall be subject to annulment in pursuance of a resolution of either House of Parliament.

Denial of copyright protection to citizens of countries not giving adequate protection to British works

160.—(1) If it appears to Her Majesty that the law of a country fails to give **A–163** adequate protection to British works to which this section applies, or to one or more classes of such works, Her Majesty may make provision by Order in Council in accordance with this section restricting the rights conferred by this Part in relation to works of authors connected with that country.

(2) An Order in Council under this section shall designate the country concerned and provide that, for the purposes specified in the Order, works first published after a date specified in the Order shall not be treated as qualifying for copyright protection by virtue of such publication if at that time the authors are—

(a) citizens or subjects of that country (not domiciled or resident in the United Kingdom or another country to which the relevant provisions of this Part extend), or

(b) bodies incorporated under the law of that country;

and the Order may make such provision for all the purposes of this Part or for such purposes as are specified in the Order, and either generally or in relation to such class of cases as are specified in the Order, having regard to the nature and extent of that failure referred to in subsection (1).

(3) This section applies to literary, dramatic, musical and artistic works, sound recordings and films; and "British works" means works of which the author was a qualifying person at the material time within the meaning of section 154.

(4) A statutory instrument containing an Order in Council under this section shall be subject to annulment in pursuance of a resolution of either House of Parliament.

Supplementary

Territorial waters and the continental shelf

A–164   **161.**—(1) For the purposes of this Part the territorial waters of the United Kingdom shall be treated as part of the United Kingdom.

(2) This Part applies to things done in the United Kingdom sector of the continental shelf on a structure or vessel which is present there for purposes directly connected with the exploration of the sea bed or subsoil or the exploitation of their natural resources as it applies to things done in the United Kingdom.

(3) The United Kingdom sector of the continental shelf means the areas designated by order under section 1(7) of the Continental Shelf Act 1964.

British ships, aircraft and hovercraft

A–165   **162.**—(1) This Part applies to things done on a British ship, aircraft or hovercraft as it applies to things done in the United Kingdom.

(2) In this section—

"British ship" means a ship which is a British ship for the purposes of the Merchant Shipping Acts (see section 2 of the Merchant Shipping Act 1988) otherwise than by virtue of registration in a country outside the United Kingdom; and

"British aircraft" and "British hovercraft" mean an aircraft or hovercraft registered in the United Kingdom.

Chapter X

Miscellaneous and General

Crown and Parliamentary copyright

Crown copyright

A–166   **163.**—(1) Where a work is made by Her Majesty or by an officer or servant of the Crown in the course of his duties—

(a) the work qualifies for copyright protection notwithstanding section 153(1) (ordinary requirement as to qualification for copyright protection), and

(b) Her Majesty is the first owner of any copyright in the work.

(2) Copyright in such a work is referred to in this Part as "Crown copyright", notwithstanding that it may be, or have been, assigned to another person.

(3) Crown copyright in a literary, dramatic, musical or artistic work continues to subsist—

(a) until the end of the period of 125 years from the end of the calendar year in which the work was made, or

(b) if the work is published commercially before the end of the period of 75 years from the end of the calendar year in which it was made, until the end of the period of 50 years from the end of the calendar year in which it was first so published.

(4) In the case of a work of joint authorship where one or more but not all of the authors are persons falling within subsection (1), this section applies only in relation to those authors and the copyright subsisting by virtue of their contribution to the work.

(5) Except as mentioned above, and subject to any express exclusion elsewhere in this Part, the provisions of this Part apply in relation to Crown copyright as to other copyright.

(6) This section does not apply to a work if, or to the extent that, Parliamentary copyright subsists in the work (see sections 165 and 166).

Copyright in Acts and Measures

164.—(1) Her Majesty is entitled to copyright in every Act of Parliament or **A–167** Measure of the General Synod of the Church of England.

(2) The copyright subsists from Royal Assent until the end of the period of 50 years from the end of the calendar year in which Royal Assent was given.

(3) References in this Part to Crown copyright (except in section 163) include copyright under this section; and, except as mentioned above, the provisions of this Part apply in relation to copyright under this section as to other Crown copyright.

(4) No other copyright, or right in the nature of copyright, subsists in an Act or Measure.

Parliamentary copyright

165.—(1) Where a work is made by or under the direction or control of the **A–168** House of Commons or the House of Lords—

   (*a*) the work qualifies for copyright protection notwithstanding section 153(1) (ordinary requirement as to qualification for copyright protection), and

   (*b*) the House by whom, or under whose direction or control, the work is made is the first owner of any copyright in the work, and if the work is made by or under the direction or control of both Houses, the two Houses are joint first owners of copyright.

(2) Copyright in such a work is referred to in this Part as "Parliamentary copyright", notwithstanding that it may be, or have been, assigned to another person.

(3) Parliamentary copyright in a literary, dramatic, musical or artistic work continues to subsist until the end of the period of 50 years from the end of the calendar year in which the work was made.

(4) For the purposes of this section, works made by or under the direction or control of the House of Commons or the House of Lords include—

   (*a*) any work made by an officer or employee of that House in the course of his duties, and

   (*b*) any sound recording, film, live broadcast or live cable programme of the proceedings of that House;

but a work shall not be regarded as made by or under the direction or control of either House by reason only of its being commissioned by or on behalf of that House.

(5) In the case of a work of joint authorship where one or more but not all of the authors are acting on behalf of, or under the direction or control of, the House of Commons or the House of Lords, this section applies only in relation to those authors and the copyright subsisting by virtue of their contribution to the work.

(6) Except as mentioned above, and subject to any express exclusion elsewhere in this Part, the provisions of this Part apply in reltion to Parliamentary copyright as to other copyright.

(7) The provisions of this section also apply, subject to any exceptions or modifications specified by Order in Council, to works made by or under the direction or control of any other legislative body of a country to which this Part extends; and references in this Part to "Parliamentary copyright" shall be construed accordingly.

(8) A statutory instrument containing an Order in Council under subsection (7)

shall be subject to annulment in pursuance of a resolution of either House of Parliament.

Copyright in Parliamentary Bills

A–169   **166.**—(1) Copyright in every Bill introduced into Parliament belongs, in accordance with the following provisions, to one or both of the Houses of Parliament.

(2) Copyright in a public Bill belongs in the first instance to the House into which the Bill is introduced, and after the Bill has been carried to the second House to both Houses jointly, and subsists from the time when the text of the Bill is handed in to the House in which it is introduced.

(3) Copyright in a private Bill belongs to both Houses jointly and subsists from the time when a copy of the Bill is first deposited in either House.

(4) Copyright in a personal Bill belongs in the first instance to the House of Lords, and after the Bill has been carried to the House of Commons to both Houses jointly, and subsists from the time when it is given a First Reading in the House of Lords.

(5) Copyright under this section ceases—

   (*a*) on Royal Assent, or

   (*b*) if the Bill does not receive Royal Assent, on the withdrawal or rejection of the Bill or the end of the Session:

Provided that, copyright in a Bill continues to subsist notwithstanding its rejection in any Session by the House of Lords if, by virtue of the Parliament Acts 1911 and 1949, it remains possible for it to be presented for Royal Assent in that Session.

(6) References in this Part to Parliamentary copyright (except in section 165) include copyright under this section; and, except as mentioned above, the provisions of this Part apply in relation to copyright under this section as to other Parliamentary copyright.

(7) No other copyright, or right in the nature of copyright, subsists in a Bill after copyright has once subsisted under this section; but without prejudice to the subsequent operation of this section in relation to a Bill which, not having passed in one Session, is reintroduced in a subsequent Session.

Houses of Parliament: supplementary provisions with respect to copyright

A–170   **167.**—(1) For the purposes of holding, dealing with and enforcing copyright, and in connection with all legal proceedings relating to copyright, each House of Parliament shall be treated as having the legal capacities of a body corporate, which shall not be affected by a prorogation or dissolution.

(2) The functions of the House of Commons as owner of copyright shall be exercised by the Speaker on behalf of the House; and if so authorised by the Speaker, or in case of a vacancy in the office of Speaker, those functions may be discharged by the Chairman of Ways and Means or a Deputy Chairman.

(3) For this purpose a person who on the dissolution of Parliament was Speaker of the House of Commons, Chairman of Ways and Means or a Deputy Chairman may continue to act until the corresponding appointment is made in the next Session of Parliament.

(4) The functions of the House of Lords as owner of copyright shall be exercised by the Clerk of the Parliaments on behalf of the House; and if so authorised by him, or in case of a vacancy in the office of Clerk of the Parliaments, those functions may be discharged by the Clerk Assistant or the Reading Clerk.

(5) Legal proceedings relating to copyright—

   (*a*) shall be brought by or against the House of Commons in the name of "The Speaker of the House of Commons"; and (*b*) shall be brought by or against the House of Lords in the name of "The Clerk of the Parliaments".

Copyright vesting in certain international organisations

168.—(1) Where an original literary, dramatic, musical or artistic work— **A–171**

(*a*) is made by an officer or employee of, or is published by, an international organisation to which this section applies, and

(*b*) does not qualify for copyright protection under section 154 (qualification by reference to author) or section 155 (qualification by reference to country of first publication),

copyright nevertheless subsists in the work by virtue of this section and the organisation is first owner of that copyright.

(2) The international organisations to which this section applies are those as to which Her Majesty has by Order in Council declared that it is expedient that this section should apply.

(3) Copyright of which an international organisation is first owner by virtue of this section continues to subsist until the end of the period of 50 years from the end of the calendar year in which the work was made or such longer period as may be specified by Her Majesty by Order in Council for the purpose of complying with the international obligations of the United Kingdom.

(4) An international organisation to which this section applies shall be deemed to have, and to have had at all material times, the legal capacities of a body corporate for the purpose of holding, dealing with and enforcing copyright and in connection with all legal proceedings relating to copyright.

(5) A statutory instrument containing an Order in Council under this section shall be subject to annulment in pursuance of a resolution of either House of Parliament.

Folklore, &c.: anonymous unpublished works

169.—(1) Where in the case of an unpublished literary, dramatic, musical or **A–172** artistic work of unknown authorship there is evidence that the author (or, in the case of a joint work, any of the authors) was a qualifying individual by connection with a country outside the United Kingdom, it shall be presumed until the contrary is proved that he was such a qualifying individual and that copyright accordingly subsists in the work, subject to the provisions of this Part.

(2) If under the law of that country a body is appointed to protect and enforce copyright in such works, Her Majesty may by Order in Council designate that body for the purposes of this section.

(3) A body so designated shall be recognised in the United Kingdom as having authority to do in place of the copyright owner anything, other than assign copyright, which it is empowered to do under the law of that country; and it may, in particular, bring proceedings in its own name.

(4) A statutory instrument containing an Order in Council under this section shall be subject to annulment in pursuance of a resolution of either House of Parliament.

(5) In subsection (1) a "qualifying individual" means an individual who at the material time (within the meaning of section 154) was a person whose works qualified under that section for copyright protection.

(6) This section does not apply if there has been an assignment of copyright in the work by the author of which notice has been given to the designated body; and nothing in this section affects the validity of an assignment of copyright made, or licence granted, by the author or a person lawfully claiming under him.

Transitional provisions and savings

A–173   **170.** Schedule 1 contains transitional provisions and savings relating to works made, and acts or events occurring, before the commencement of this Part, and otherwise with respect to the operation of the provisions of this Part.

Rights and privileges under other enactments or the common law

A–174   **171.**—(1) Nothing in this Part affects—

(*a*) any right or privilege of any person under any enactment (except where the enactment is expressly repealed, amended or modified by this Act);

(*b*) any right or privilege of the Crown subsisting otherwise than under an enactment;

(*c*) any right or privilege of either House of Parliament;

(*d*) the right of the Crown or any person deriving title from the Crown to sell, use or otherwise deal with articles forfeited under the laws relating to customs and excise;

(*e*) the operation of any rule of equity relating to breaches of trust or confidence.

(2) Subject to those savings, no copyright or right in the nature of copyright shall subsist otherwise than by virtue of this Part or some other enactment in that behalf.

(3) Nothing in this Part affects any rule of law preventing or restricting the enforcement of copyright, on grounds of public interest or otherwise.

(4) Nothing in this Part affects any right of action or other remedy, whether civil or criminal, available otherwise than under this Part in respect of acts infringing any of the rights conferred by Chapter IV (moral rights).

(5) The savings in subsection (1) have effect subject to section 164(4) and section 166(7) (copyright in Acts, Measures and Bills: exclusion of other rights in the nature of copyright).

Interpretation

General provisions as to construction

A–175   **172.**—(1) This Part restates and amends the law of copyright, that is, the provisions of the Copyright Act 1956, as amended.

(2) A provision of this Part which corresponds to a provision of the previous law shall not be construed as departing from the previous law merely because of a change of expression.

(3) Decisions under the previous law may be referred to for the purpose of establishing whether a provision of this Part departs from the previous law, or otherwise for establishing the true construction of this Part.

Construction of references to copyright owner

A–176   **173.**—(1) Where different persons are (whether in consequence of a partial assignment or otherwise) entitled to different aspects of copyright in a work, the copyright owner for any purpose of this Part is the person who is entitled to the aspect of copyright relevant for that purpose.

(2) Where copyright (or any aspect of copyright) is owned by more than one person jointly, references in this Part to the copyright owner are to all the owners, so that, in particular, any requirement of the licence of the copyright owner requires the licence of all of them.

Meaning of "educational establishment" and related expressions

174.—(1) The expression "educational establishment" in a provision of this **A–177**
Part means—

(*a*) any school, and

(*b*) any other description of educational establishment specified for the purposes of this Part, or that provision, by order of the Secretary of State.

(2) The Secretary of State may by order provide that the provisions of this Part
relating to educational establishments shall apply, with such modifications and
adaptations as may be specified in the order, in relation to teachers who are
employed by a local education authority to give instruction elsewhere to pupils
who are unable to attend an educational establishment.

(3) In subsection (1)(*a*) "school"—

(*a*) in relation to England and Wales, has the same meaning as in the Education Act 1944;

(*b*) in relation to Scotland, has the same meaning as in the Education (Scotland) Act 1962, except that it includes an approved school within the
meaning of the Social Work (Scotland) Act 1968; and

(*c*) in relation to Northern Ireland, has the same meaning as in the Education
and Libraries (Northern Ireland) Order 1986.

(4) An order under subsection (1)(*b*) may specify a description of educational
establishment by reference to the instruments from time to time in force under any
enactment specified in the order.

(5) In relation to an educational establishment the expressions "teacher" and
"pupil" in this Part include, respectively, any person who gives and any person
who receives instruction.

(6) References in this Part to anything being done "on behalf of" an educational
establishment are to its being done for the purposes of that establishment by any
person.

(7) An order under this section shall be made by statutory instrument which
shall be subject to annulment in pursuance of a resolution of either House of Parliament.

Meaning of publication and commercial publication

175.—(1) In this Part "publication", in relation to a work— **A–178**

(*a*) means the issue of copies to the public, and

(*b*) includes, in the case of a literary, dramatic, musical or artistic work,
making it available to the public by means of an electronic retrieval system;
and related expressions shall be construed accordingly.

(2) In this Part "commercial publication", in relation to a literary, dramatic,
musical or artistic work means—

(*a*) issuing copies of the work to the public at a time when copies made in
advance of the receipt of orders are generally available to the public, or

(*b*) making the work available to the public by means of an electronic retrieval
system;
and related expressions shall be construed accordingly.

(3) In the case of a work of architecture in the form of a building, or an artistic
work incorporated in a building, construction of the building shall be treated as
equivalent to publication of the work.

(4) The following do not constitute publication for the purposes of this Part and
references to commercial publication shall be construed accordingly—

(*a*) in the case of a literary, dramatic or musical work—

(i) the performance of the work, or

    (ii) the broadcasting of the work or its inclusion in a cable programme service (otherwise than for the purposes of an electronic retrieval system);

  (*b*) in the case of an artistic work—

    (i) the exhibition of the work,

    (ii) the issue to the public of copies of a graphic work representing, or of photographs of, a work of architecture in the form of a building or a model for a building, a sculpture or a work of artistic craftsmanship,

    (iii) the issue to the public of copies of a film including the work, or

    (iv) the broadcasting of the work or its inclusion in a cable programme service (otherwise than for the purposes of an electronic retrieval system);

  (*c*) in the case of a sound recording or film—

    (i) the work being played or shown in public, or

    (ii) the broadcasting of the work or its inclusion in a cable programme service.

(5) References in this Part to publication or commercial publication do not include publication which is merely colourable and not intended to satisfy the reasonable requirements of the public.

(6) No account shall be taken for the purposes of this section of any unauthorised act.

Requirement of signature: application in relation to body corporate

A–179   **176.**—(1) The requirement in the following provisions that an instrument be signed by or on behalf of a person is also satisfied in the case of a body corporate by the affixing of its seal—

section 78(3)(*b*) (assertion by licensor of right to identification of author in case of public exhibition of copy made in pursuance of the licence),
section 90(3) (assignment of copyright),
section 91(1) (assignment of future copyright),
section 92(1) (grant of exclusive licence).

(2) The requirement in the following provisions that an instrument be signed by a person is satisfied in the case of a body corporate by signature on behalf of the body or by the affixing of its seal—

section 78(2)(*b*) (assertion by instrument in writing of right to have author identified),
section 87(2) (waiver of moral rights).

Adaptation of expressions for Scotland

A–180   **177.** In the application of this Part to Scotland—

"account of profits" means accounting and payment of profits;

"accounts" means count, reckoning and payment;

"assignment" means assignation;

"costs" means expenses;

"defendant" means defender;

"delivery up" means delivery;

"estoppel" means personal bar;

"injunction" means interdict;

"interlocutory relief" means interim remedy; and

"plaintiff" means pursuer.

Minor definitions

178. In this Part—

"article", in the context of an article in a periodical, includes an item of any description;

"business" includes a trade or profession;

"collective work" means—
   (a) a work of joint authorship, or
   (b) a work in which there are distinct contributions by different authors or in which works or part of works of different authors are incorporated;

"computer-generated", in relation to a work, means that the work is generated by computer in circumstances such that there is no human author of the work;

"country" includes any territory;

"the Crown" includes the Crown in right of Her Majesty's Government in Northern Ireland or in any country outside the United Kingdom to which this Part extends;

"electronic" means actuated by electric, magnetic, electro-magnetic, electrochemical or electro-mechanical energy, and "in electronic form" means in a form usable only by electronic means;

"employed", "employee", "employer" and "employment" refer to employment under a contract of service or of apprenticeship;

"facsimile copy" includes a copy which is reduced or enlarged in scale;

"international organisation" means an organisation the members of which include one or more states;

"judicial proceedings" includes proceedings before any court, tribunal or person having authority to decide any matter affecting a person's legal rights or liabilities;

"parliamentary proceedings" includes proceedings of the Northern Ireland Assembly or of the European Parliament;

"rental" means any arrangement under which a copy of a work is made available—
   (a) for payment (in money or money's worth), or
   (b) in the course of a business, as part of services or amenities for which payment is made,

on terms that it will or may be returned;

"reprographic copy" and "reprographic copying" refer to copying by means of a reprographic process;

"reprographic process" means a process—
   (a) for making facsimile copies, or
   (b) involving the use of an appliance for making multiple copies,

and includes, in relation to a work held in electronic form, any copying by electronic means, but does not include the making of a film or sound recording;

"sufficient acknowledgement" means an acknowledgement identifying the work in question by its title or other description, and identifying the author unless—
   (a) in the case of a published work, it is published anonymously;
   (b) in the case of an unpublished work, it is not possible for a person to ascertain the identity of the author by reasonable inquiry;

"sufficient disclaimer", in relation to an act capable of infringing the right conferred by section 80 (right to object to derogatory treatment of work), means a clear and reasonably prominent indication—

(a) given at the time of the act, and

(b) if the author or director is then identified, appearing along with the identification,

that the work has been subjected to treatment to which the author or director has not consented;

"telecommunications system" means a system for conveying visual images, sounds or other information by electronic means;

"typeface" includes an ornamental motif used in printing;

"unauthorised", as regards anything done in relation to a work, means done otherwise than—

(a) by or with the licence of the copyright owner, or

(b) if copyright does not subsist in the work, by or with the licence of the author or, in a case where section 11(2) would have applied, the author's employer or, in either case, persons lawfully claiming under him, or

(c) in pursuance of section 48 (copying, &c. of certain material by the Crown);

"wireless telegraphy" means the sending of electro-magnetic energy over paths not provided by a material substance constructed or arranged for that purpose;

"writing" includes any form of notation or code, whether by hand or otherwise and regardless of the method by which, or medium in or on which, it is recorded, and "written" shall be construed accordingly.

Index of defined expressions

A–182   **179.** The following Table shows provisions defining or otherwise explaining expressions used in this Part (other than provisions defining or explaining an expression used only in the same section)—

account of profits and accounts (in Scotland)	section 177
acts restricted by copyright	section 16(1)
adaptation	section 21(3)
archivist (in sections 37 to 43)	section 37(6)
article (in a periodical)	section 178
artistic work	section 4(1)
assignment (in Scotland)	section 177
author	sections 9 and 10(3)
broadcast (and related expressions)	section 6
building	section 4(2)
business	section 178
cable programme, cable programme service (and related expressions)	section 7
collective work	section 178
commencement (in Schedule 1)	paragraph 1(2) of that Schedule
commercial publication	section 175
computer-generated	section 178
copy and copying	section 17
copyright (generally)	section 1
copyright (in Schedule 1)	paragraph 2(2) of that Schedule

copyright owner	sections 101(2) and 173
Copyright Tribunal	section 145
copyright work	section 1(2)
costs (in Scotland)	section 177
country	section 178
the Crown	section 178
Crown copyright	sections 163(2) and 164(3)
defendant (in Scotland)	section 177
delivery up (in Scotland)	section 177
dramatic work	section 3(1)
educational establishment	sections 174(1) to (4)
electronic and electronic form	section 178
employed, employee, employer and employment	section 178
exclusive licence	section 92(1)
existing works (in Schedule 1)	paragraph 1(3) of that Schedule
facsimile copy	section 178
film	section 5
future copyright	section 91(2)
general licence (in sections 140 and 141)	section 140(7)
graphic work	section 4(2)
infringing copy	section 27
injunction (in Scotland)	section 177
interlocutory relief (in Scotland)	section 177
international organisation	section 178
issue of copies to the public	section 18(2)
joint authorship (work of)	sections 10(1) and (2)
judicial proceedings	section 178
librarian (in sections 37 to 43)	section 37(6)
licence (in sections 125 to 128)	section 124
licence of copyright owner	sections 90(4), 91(3) and 173
licensing body (in Chapter VII)	section 116(2)
licensing scheme (generally)	section 116(1)
licensing scheme (in sections 118 to 121)	section 117
literary work	section 3(1)
made (in relation to a literary, dramatic or musical work)	section 3(2)
musical work	section 3(1)
[needletime	section 135A]
the new copyright provisions (in Schedule 1)	paragraph 1(1) of that Schedule
the 1911 Act (in Schedule 1)	paragraph 1(1) of that Schedule
the 1956 Act (in Schedule 1)	paragraph 1(1) of that Schedule
on behalf of (in relation to an educational establishment)	section 174(5)
Parliamentary copyright	sections 165(2) and (7) and 166(6)
parliamentary proceedings	section 178
performance	section 19(2)
photograph	section 4(2)
plaintiff (in Scotland)	section 177

prescribed conditions (in sections 38 to 43)	section 37(1)(b)
prescribed library or archive (in sections 38 to 43)	section 37(1)(a)
programme (in the context of broadcasting)	section 6(3)
prospective owner (of copyright)	section 91(2)
publication and related expressions	section 175
published edition (in the context of copyright in the typographical arrangement)	section 8
pupil	section 174(5)
rental	section 178
reprographic copies and reprographic copying	section 178
reprographic process	section 178
sculpture	section 4(2)
signed	section 176
sound recording	section [5]5 [and 135A]
sufficient acknowledgement	section 178
sufficient disclaimer	section 178
teacher	section 174(5)
telecommunications system	section 178
[terms of payment	section 135A]
typeface	section 178
unauthorised (as regards things done in relation to a work)	section 178
unknown (in relation to the author of a work)	section 9(5)
unknown authorship (work of)	section 9(4)
wireless telegraphy	section 178
work (in Schedule 1)	paragraph 2(1) of that Schedule
work of more than one author (in Chapter VII)	section 116(4)
writing and written	section 178

Note: Section 179 of the 1988 Act was amended as indicated by square brackets by section 175 of the Broadcasting Act 1990 (c. 42) with effect from February 1, 1991 by virtue of The Broadcasting Act 1990 (Commencement No. 1 and Transitional Provisions) Order 1990 (S.I. 1990 No. 2347 (c. 61)) §B–254 *post*.

PART II

RIGHTS IN PERFORMANCES

Introductory

Rights conferred on performers and persons having recording rights

A–183   **180.**—(1) This Part confers rights—

(*a*) on a performer, by requiring his consent to the exploitation of his performances (see sections 181 to 184), and

(*b*) on a person having recording rights in relation to a performance, in relation to recordings made without his consent or that of the performer (see sections 185 to 188), and creates offences in relation to dealing with or using illicit recordings and certain other related acts (see sections 198 and 201).

(2) In this Part—

"performance" means—

(a) a dramatic performance (which includes dance and mime),

(b) a musical performance,

(c) a reading or recitation of a literary work, or

(d) a performance of a variety act or any similar presentation,

which is, or so far as it is, a live performance given by one or more individuals; and

"recording," in relation to a performance, means a film or sound recording—

(a) made directly from the live performance,

(b) made from a broadcast of, or cable programme including, the performance, or

(c) made, directly or indirectly, from another recording of the performance.

(3) The rights conferred by this Part apply in relation to performances taking place before the commencement of this Part; but no act done before commencement, or in pursuance of arrangements made before commencement, shall be regarded as infringing those rights.

(4) The rights conferred by this Part are independent of—

(a) any copyright in, or moral rights relating to, any work performed or any film or sound recording of, or broadcast or cable programme including, the performance, and

(b) any other right or obligation arising otherwise than under this Part.

Performers' rights

Qualifying performances

181. A performance is a qualifying performance for the purposes of the provisions of this Part relating to performers' rights if it is given by a qualifying individual (as defined in section 206) or takes place in a qualifying country (as so defined).　　**A–184**

Consent required for recording or live transmission of performance

182.—(1) A performer's rights are infringed by a person who, without his consent—　　**A–185**

(a) makes, otherwise than for his private and domestic use, a recording of the whole or any substantial part of a qualifying performance, or

(b) broadcasts live, or includes live in a cable programme service, the whole or any substantial part of a qualifying performance.

(2) In an action for infringement of a performer's rights brought by virtue of this section damages shall not be awarded against a defendant who shows that at the time of the infringement he believed on reasonable grounds that consent had been given.

Infringement of performer's rights by use of recording made without consent

183. A performer's rights are infringed by a person who, without his consent—　　**A–186**

(a) shows or plays in public the whole or any substantial part of a qualifying performance, or

(b) broadcasts or includes in a cable programme service the whole or any substantial part of a qualifying performance, by means of a recording which was, and which that person knows or has reason to believe was, made without the performer's consent.

Infringement of performer's rights by importing, possessing or dealing with illicit recording

184.—(1) A performer's rights are infringed by a person who, without his consent—

> (a) imports into the United Kingdom otherwise than for his private and domestic use, or
>
> (b) in the course of a business possesses, sells or lets for hire, offers or exposes for sale or hire, or distributes,

a recording of a qualifying performance which is, and which that person knows or has reason to believe is, an illicit recording.

(2) Where in an action for infringement of a performer's rights brought by virtue of this section a defendant shows that the illicit recording was innocently acquired by him or a predecessor in title of his, the only remedy available against him in respect of the infringement is damages not exceeding a reasonable payment in respect of the act complained of.

(3) In subsection (2) "innocently acquired" means that the person acquiring the recording did not know and had no reason to believe that it was an illicit recording.

Rights of person having recording rights

Exclusive recording contracts and persons having recording rights

185.—(1) In this Part an "exclusive recording contract" means a contract between a performer and another person under which that person is entitled to the exclusion of all other persons (including the performer) to make recordings of one or more of his performances with a view to their commercial exploitation.

(2) References in this Part to a "person having recording rights", in relation to a performance, are (subject to subsection (3)) to a person—

> (a) who is party to and has the benefit of an exclusive recording contract to which the performance is subject, or
>
> (b) to whom the benefit of such a contract has been assigned,

and who is a qualifying person.

(3) If a performance is subject to an exclusive recording contract but the person mentioned in subsection (2) is not a qualifying person, references in this Part to a "person having recording rights" in relation to the performance are to any person—

> (a) who is licensed by such a person to make recordings of the performance with a view to their commercial exploitation, or
>
> (b) to whom the benefit of such a licence has been assigned,

and who is a qualifying person.

(4) In this section "with a view to commercial exploitation" means with a view to the recordings being sold or let for hire, or shown or played in public.

Consent required for recording of performance subject to exclusive contract

186.—(1) A person infringes the rights of a person having recording rights in relation to a performance who, without his consent or that of the performer, makes a recording of the whole or any substantial part of the performance, otherwise than for his private and domestic use.

(2) In an action for infringement of those rights brought by virtue of this section damages shall not be awarded against a defendant who shows that at the time of the infringement he believed on reasonable grounds that consent had been given.

Infringement of recording rights by use of recording made without consent

187.—(1) A person infringes the rights of a person having recording rights in relation to a performance who, without his consent or, in the case of a qualifying performance, that of the performer— **A–190**

(a) shows or plays in public the whole or any substantial part of the performance, or

(b) broadcasts or includes in a cable programme service the whole or any substantial part of the performance,

by means of a recording which was, and which that person knows or has reason to believe was, made without the appropriate consent.

(2) The reference in subsection (1) to "the appropriate consent" is to the consent of—

(a) the performer, or

(b) the person who at the time the consent was given had recording rights to the performance (or, if there was more than one such person, of all of them).

Infringement of recording rights by importing, possessing or dealing with illicit recording

188.—(1) A person infringes the rights of a person having recording rights in relation to a performance who, without his consent or, in the case of a qualifying performance, that of the performer— **A–191**

(a) imports into the United Kingdom otherwise than for his private and domestic use, or

(b) in the course of a business possesses, sells or lets for hire, offers or exposes for sale or hire, or distributes,

a recording of the performance which is, and which that person knows or has reason to believe is, an illicit recording.

(2) Where in an action for infringement of those rights brought by virtue of this section a defendant shows that the illicit recording was innocently acquired by him or a predecessor in title of his, the only remedy available against him in respect of the infringement is damages not exceeding a reasonable payment in respect of the act complained of.

(3) In subsection (2) "innocently acquired" means that the person acquiring the recording did not know and had no reason to believe that it was an illicit recording.

Exceptions to rights conferred

Acts permitted notwithstanding rights conferred by this Part

189. The provisions of Schedule 2 specify acts which may be done notwithstanding the rights conferred by this Part, being acts which correspond broadly to certain of those specified in Chapter III of Part I (acts permitted notwithstanding copyright). **A–192**

Power of tribunal to give consent on behalf of performer in certain cases

190.—(1) The Copyright Tribunal may, on the application of a person wishing to make a recording from a previous recording of a performance, give consent in a case where— **A–193**

(a) the identity or whereabouts of a performer cannot be ascertained by reasonable inquiry, or

(b) a performer unreasonably withholds his consent.

(2) Consent given by the Tribunal has effect as consent of the performer for the purposes of—

(a) the provisions of this Part relating to performers' rights, and

(b) section 198(3)(a) (criminal liability: sufficient consent in relation to qualifying performances),

and may be given subject to any conditions specified in the Tribunal's order.

(3) The Tribunal shall not give consent under subsection (1)(a) except after the service or publication of such notices as may be required by rules made under section 150 (general procedural rules) or as the Tribunal may in any particular case direct.

(4) The Tribunal shall not give consent under subsection (1)(b) unless satisfied that the performer's reasons for withholding consent do not include the protection of any legitimate interest of his; but it shall be for the performer to show what his reasons are for withholding consent, and in default of evidence as to his reasons the Tribunal may draw such inferences as it thinks fit.

(5) In any case the Tribunal shall take into account the following factors—

(a) whether the original recording was made with the performer's consent and is lawfully in the possession or control of the person proposing to make the further recording;

(b) whether the making of the further recording is consistent with the obligations of the parties to the arrangements under which, or is otherwise consistent with the purposes for which, the original recording is made.

(6) Where the Tribunal gives consent under this section it shall, in default of agreement between the applicant and the performer, make such order as it thinks fit as to the payment to be made to the performer in consideration of consent being given.

Duration and transmission of rights; consent

Duration of rights

A–194   **191.** The rights conferred by this Part continue to subsist in relation to a performance until the end of the period of 50 years from the end of the calendar year in which the performance takes place.

Transmission of rights

A–195   **192.**—(1) The rights conferred by this Part are not assignable or transmissible, except to the extent that performers' rights are transmissible in accordance with the following provisions.

(2) On the death of a person entitled to performer's rights—

(a) the rights pass to such person as he may by testamentary disposition specifically direct, and

(b) if or to the extent that there is no such direction, the rights are exercisable by his personal representatives;

and references in this Part to the performer, in the context of the person having performers' rights, shall be construed as references to the person for the time being entitled to exercise those rights.

(3) Where by virtue of subsection (2)(a) a right becomes exercisable by more than one person, it is exercisable by each of them independently of the other or others.

(4) The above provisions do not affect section 185(2)(*b*) or (3)(*b*), so far as those provisions confer rights under this Part on a person to whom the benefit of a contract or licence is assigned.

(5) Any damages recovered by personal representatives by virtue of this section in respect of an infringement after a person's death shall devolve as part of his estate as if the right of action had subsisted and been vested in him immediately before his death.

Consent

193.—(1) Consent for the purposes of this Part may be given in relation to a **A–196** specific performance, a specified description of performances or performances generally, and may relate to past or future performances.

(2) A person having recording rights in a performance is bound by any consent given by a person through whom he derives his rights under the exclusive recording contract or licence in question, in the same way as if the consent had been given by him.

(3) Where a right conferred by this Part passes to another person, any consent binding on the person previously entitled binds the person to whom the right passes in the same way as if the consent had been given by him.

Remedies for infringement

Infringement actionable as breach of statutory duty

194. An infringement of any of the rights conferred by this Part is actionable by **A–197** the person entitled to the right as a breach of statutory duty.

Order for delivery up

195.—(1) Where a person has in his possession, custody or control in the course **A–198** of a business an illicit recording of a performance, a person having performer's rights or recording rights in relation to the performance under this Part may apply to the court for an order that the recording be delivered up to him or to such other person as the court may direct.

(2) An application shall not be made after the end of the period specified in section 203; and no order shall be made unless the court also makes, or it appears to the court that there are grounds for making, an order under section 204 (order as to disposal of illicit recording).

(3) A person to whom a recording is delivered up in pursuance of an order under this section shall, if an order under section 204 is not made, retain it pending the making of an order, or the decision not to make an order, under that section.

(4) Nothing in this section affects any other power of the court.

Right to seize illicit recordings

196.—(1) An illicit recording of a performance which is found exposed or other- **A–199** wise immediately available for sale or hire, and in respect of which a person would be entitled to apply for an order under section 195, may be seized and detained by him or a person authorised by him.

The right to seize and detain is exercisable subject to the following conditions and is subject to any decision of the court under section 204 (order as to disposal of illicit recording).

(2) Before anything is seized under this section notice of the time and place of the proposed seizure must be given to a local police station.

(3) A person may for the purpose of exercising the right conferred by this section enter premises to which the public have access but may not seize anything in the

possession, custody or control of a person at a permanent or regular place of business of his and may not use any force.

(4) At the time when anything is seized under this section there shall be left at the place where it was seized a notice in the prescribed form containing the prescribed particulars as to the person by whom or on whose authority the seizure is made and the grounds on which it is made.

(5) In this section—

"premises" includes land, buildings, fixed or moveable structures, vehicles, vessels, aircraft and hovercraft; and

"prescribed" means prescribed by order of the Secretary of State.

(6) An order of the Secretary of State under this section shall be made by statutory instrument which shall be subject to annulment in pursuance of a resolution of either House of Parliament.

Meaning of "illicit recording"

A–200   **197.**—(1) In this Part "illicit recording", in relation to a performance, shall be construed in accordance with this section.

(2) For the purposes of a performer's rights, a recording of the whole or any substantial part of a performance of his is an illicit recording if it is made, otherwise than for private purposes, without his consent.

(3) For the purposes of the rights of a person having recording rights, a recording of the whole or any substantial part of a performance subject to the exclusive recording contract is an illicit recording if it is made, otherwise than for private purposes, without his consent or that of the performer.

(4) For the purposes of sections 198 and 199 (offences and orders for delivery up in criminal proceedings), a recording is an illicit recording if it is an illicit recording for the purposes mentioned in subsection (2) or subsection (3).

(5) In this Part "illicit recording" includes a recording falling to be treated as an illicit recording by virtue of any of the following provisions of Schedule 2—

paragraph 4(3) (recordings made for purposes of instruction or examination),
paragraph 6(2) (recordings made by educational establishments for educational purposes),
paragraph 12(2) (recordings of performance in electronic form retained on transfer of principal recording), or
paragraph 16(3) (recordings made for purposes of broadcast or cable programme),

but otherwise did not include a recording made in accordance with any of the provisions of that Schedule.

(6) It is immaterial for the purposes of this section where the recording was made.

Offences

Criminal liability for making, dealing with or using illicit recordings

A–201   **198.**—(1) A person commits an offence who without sufficient consent—
  (a) makes for sale or hire, or
  (b) imports into the United Kingdom otherwise than for his private and domestic use, or
  (c) possesses in the course of a business with a view to committing any act infringing the rights conferred by this Part, or
  (d) in the course of a business—

(i) sells or lets for hire, or

(ii) offers or exposes for sale or hire, or

(iii) distributes,

a recording which is, and which he knows or has reason to believe is, an illicit recording.

(2) A person commits an offence who causes a recording of a performance made without sufficient consent to be—

(*a*) shown or played in public, or

(*b*) broadcast or included in a cable programme service,

thereby infringing any of the rights conferred by this Part, if he knows or has reason to believe that those rights are thereby infringed.

(3) In subsections (1) and (2) "sufficient consent" means—

(*a*) in the case of a qualifying performance, the consent of the performer, and

(*b*) in the of a non-qualifying performance subject to an exclusive recording contract—

(i) for the purposes of subsection (1)(*a*) (making of recording), the consent of the performer or the person having recording rights, and

(ii) for the purposes of subsection (1)(*b*), (*c*) and (*d*) and subsection (2) (dealing with or using recording), the consent of the person having recording rights.

The references in this subsection to the person having recording rights are to the person having those rights at the time the consent is given or, if there is more than one such person, to all of them.

(4) No offence is committed under subsection (1) or (2) by the commission of an act which by virtue of any provision of Schedule 2 may be done without infringing the rights conferred by this Part.

(5) A person guilty of an offence under subsection (1)(*a*), (*b*) or (*d*)(iii) is liable—

(*a*) on summary conviction to imprisonment for a term not exceeding six months or a fine not exceeding the statutory maximum, or both;

(*b*) on conviction on indictment to a fine or imprisonment for a term not exceeding two years, or both.

(6) A person guilty of any other offence under this section is liable on summary conviction to a fine not exceeding level 5 on the standard scale or imprisonment for a term not exceeding six months, or both.

Order for delivery up in criminal proceedings

199.—(1) The court before which proceedings are brought against a person for an offence under section 198 may, if satisfied that at the time of his arrest or charge he had in his possession, custody or control in the course of a business an illicit recording of a performance, order that it be delivered up to a person having performers' rights or recording rights in relation to the performance or to such other person as the court may direct.   **A–202**

(2) For this purpose a person shall be treated as charged with an offence—

(*a*) in England, Wales and Northern Ireland, when he is orally charged or is served with a summons or indictment;

(*b*) in Scotland, when he is cautioned, charged or served with a complaint or indictment.

(3) An order may be made by the court of its own motion or on the application of the prosecutor (or, in Scotland, the Lord Advocate or procurator-fiscal), and may be made whether or not the person is convicted of the offence, but shall not be made—

(a) after the end of the period specified in section 203 (period after which remedy of delivery up not available), or

(b) if it appears to the court unlikely that any order will be made under section 204 (order as to disposal of illicit recording).

(4) An appeal lies from an order made under this section by a magistrates' court—

(a) in England and Wales, to the Crown Court, and

(b) in Northern Ireland, to the county court;

and in Scotland, where an order has been made under this section, the person from whose possession, custody or control the illicit recording has been removed may, without prejudice to any other form of appeal under any rule of law, appeal against that order in the same manner as against sentence.

(5) A person to whom an illicit recording is delivered up in pursuance of an order under this section shall retain it pending the making of an order, or the decision not to make an order, under section 204.

(6) Nothing in in this section affects the powers of the court under section 43 of the Powers of Criminal Courts Act 1973, section 223 or 436 of the Criminal Procedure (Scotland) Act 1975 or Article 7 of the Criminal Justice (Northern Ireland) Order 1980 (general provisions as to forfeiture in criminal proceedings).

Note. Official version of this Act has the word "in" twice at start of subsection (6), presumably in error.

Search warrants

A–203 **200.**—(1) Where a justice of the peace (in Scotland, a sheriff or justice of the peace) is satisfied by information on oath given by a constable (in Scotland, by evidence on oath) that there are reasonable grounds for believing—

(a) that an offence under section 198(1)(a), (b) or (d)(iii) (offences of making, importing or distributing illicit recordings) has been or is about to be committed in any premises, and

(b) that evidence that such an offence has been or is about to be committed is in those premises,

he may issue a warrant authorising a constable to enter and search the premises, using such reasonable force as is necessary.

(2) The power conferred by subsection (1) does not, in England and Wales, extend to authorising a search for material of the kinds mentioned in section 9(2) of the Police and Criminal Evidence Act 1984 (certain classes of personal or confidential material).

(3) A warrant under subsection (1)—

(a) may authorise persons to accompany any constable executing the warrant, and

(b) remains in force for 28 days from the date of its issue.

(4) In this section "premises" includes land, buildings, fixed or moveable structures, vehicles, vessels, aircraft and hovercraft.

False representation of authority to give consent

A–204 **201.**—(1) It is an offence for a person to represent falsely that he is authorised by any person to give consent for the purposes of this Part in relation to a performance, unless he believes on reasonable grounds that he is so authorised.

(2) A person guilty of an offence under this section is liable on summary conviction to imprisonment for a term not exceeding six months or a fine not exceeding level 5 of the standard scale or both.

Offence by body corporate: liability of officers

202.—(1) Where an offence under this Part committed by a body corporate is proved to have been committed with the consent or connivance of a director, manager, secretary or other similar officer of the body, or a person purporting to act in any such capacity, he as well as the body corporate is guilty of the offence and liable to be proceeded against and punished accordingly.

    A–205

(2) In relation to a body corporate whose affairs are managed by its members "director" means a member of the body corporate.

Supplementary provisions with respect to delivery up and seizure

Period after which remedy of delivery up not available

203.—(1) An application for an order under section 195 (order for delivery up in civil proceedings) may not be made after the end of the period of six years from the date on which the illicit recording in question was made, subject to the following provisions.

    A–206

(2) If during the whole or any part of that period a person entitled to apply for an order—

(*a*) is under a disability, or

(*b*) is prevented by fraud or concealment from discovering the facts entitling him to apply,

an application may be made by him at any time before the end of the period of six years from the date on which he ceased to be under a disability or, as the case may be, could with reasonable diligence have discovered those facts.

(3) In subsection (2) "disability"—

(*a*) in England and Wales, has the same meaning as in the Limitation Act 1980;

(*b*) in Scotland, means legal disability within the meaning of the Prescription and Limitations (Scotland) Act 1973;

(*c*) in Northern Ireland, has the same meaning as in the Statute of Limitation (Northern Ireland) 1958.

(4) An order under section 199 (order for delivery up in criminal proceedings) shall not, in any case, be made after the end of the period of six years from the date on which the illicit recording in question was made.

Order as to disposal of illicit recording

204.—(1) An application may be made to the court for an order that an illicit recording of a performance delivered up in pursuance of an order under section 195 or 199, or seized and detained in pursuance of the right conferred by section 196, shall be—

    A–207

(*a*) forfeited to such person having performer's rights or recording rights in relation to the performance as the court may direct, or

(*b*) destroyed or otherwise dealt with as the court may think fit,

or for a decision that no such order should be made.

(2) In considering what order (if any) should be made, the court shall consider whether other remedies available in an action for infringement of the rights conferred by this Part would be adequate to compensate the person or persons entitled to the rights and to protect their interests.

(3) Provision shall be made by rules of court as to the service of notice on persons having an interest in the recording, and any such person is entitled—

(*a*) to appear in proceedings for an order under this section, whether or not he was served with notice, and

(*b*) to appeal against any order made, whether or not he appeared;
and an order shall not take effect until the end of the period within which notice of an appeal may be given or, if before the end of that period notice of appeal is duly given, until the final determination or abandonment of the proceedings on the appeal.

(4) Where there is more than one person interested in a recording, the court shall make such order as it thinks just and may (in particular) direct that the recording be sold, or otherwise dealt with, and the proceeds divided.

(5) If the court decides that no order should be made under this section, the person in whose possession, custody or control the recording was before being delivered up or seized is entitled to its return.

(6) References in this section to a person having an interest in a recording include any person in whose favour an order could be made in respect of the recording under this section or under section 114 or 231 of this Act or section 58C of the Trade Marks Act 1938 (which make similar provision in relation to infringement of copyright, design right and trade marks).

Jurisdiction of county court and sheriff court

A–208   **205.**—(1) In England, Wales and Northern Ireland a county court may entertain proceedings under—

section 195 (order for delivery up of illicit recording), or
section 204 (order as to disposal of illicit recording),

where the value of the illicit recordings in question does not exceed the county court limit for actions in tort.

(2) In Scotland proceedings for an order under either of those provisions may be brought in the sheriff court.

(3) Nothing in this section shall be construed as affecting the jurisdiction of the High Court or, in Scotland, the Court of Session.

Qualification for protection and extent

Qualifying countries, individuals and persons

A–209   **206.**—(1) In this Part—

"qualifying country" means—
    (*a*) the United Kingdom,
    (*b*) another member State of the European Economic Community, or
    (*c*) to the extent that an Order under section 208 so provides, a country designated under that section as enjoying reciprocal protection;

"qualifying individual" means a citizen or subject of, or an individual resident in, a qualifying country; and

"qualifying person" means a qualifying individual or a body corporate or other body having legal personality which—
    (*a*) is formed under the law of a part of the United Kingdom or another qualifying country, and
    (*b*) has in any qualifying country a place of business at which substantial business activity is carried on.

(2) The reference in the definition of "qualifying individual" to a person's being a citizen or subject of a qualifying country shall be construed—
    (*a*) in relation to the United Kingdom, as a reference to his being a British citizen, and

944

(*b*) in relation to a colony of the United Kingdom, as a reference to his being a British Dependent Territories' citizen by connection with that colony.

(3) In determining for the purpose of the definition of "qualifying person" whether substantial business activity is carried on at a place of business in any country, no account shall be taken of dealings in goods which are at all material times outside that country.

Countries to which this Part extends

207. This Part extends to England and Wales, Scotland and Northern Ireland.   **A–210**

Countries enjoying reciprocal protection

208.—(1) Her Majesty may by Order in Council designate as enjoying recipro-   **A–211**
cal protection under this Part—
(*a*) a Convention country, or
(*b*) a country as to which Her Majesty is satisfied that provision has been or will be made under its law giving adequate protection for British performances.

(2) A "Convention country" means a country which is a party to a Convention relating to performers' rights to which the United Kingdom is also a party.

(3) A "British performance" means a performance—
(*a*) given by an individual who is a British citizen or resident in the United Kingdom, or
(*b*) taking place in the United Kingdom.

(4) If the law of that country provides adequate protection only for certain descriptions of performance, an Order under subsection (1)(*b*) designating that country shall contain provision limiting to a corresponding extent the protection afforded by this Part in relation to performances connected with that country.

(5) The power conferred by subsection (1)(*b*) is exercisable in relation to any of the Channel Islands, the Isle of Man or any colony of the United Kingsdom, as in relation to a foreign country.

(6) A statutory instrument containing an Order in Council under this section shall be subject to annulment in pursuance of a resolution of either House of Parliament.

Territorial waters and the continental shelf

209.—(1) For the purposes of this Part the territorial waters of the United   **A–212**
Kingdom shall be treated as part of the United Kingdom.
(2) This Part applies to things done in the United Kingdom sector of the continental shelf on a structure or vessel which is present there for purposes directly connected with the exploration of the sea bed or subsoil or the exploitation of their natural resources as it applies to things done in the United Kingdom.
(3) The United Kingdom sector of the continental shelf means the areas designated by order under section 1(7) of the Continental Shelf Act 1964.

British ships, aircraft and hovercraft

210.—(1) This Part applies to things done on a British ship, aircraft or hover-   **A–213**
craft as it applies to things done in the United Kingdom.
(2) In this section—

"British ship" means a ship which is a British ship for the purposes of the Merchant Shipping Acts (see section 2 of the Merchant Shipping Act 1988) otherwise than by virtue of registration in a country outside the United Kingdom; and

"British aircraft" and "British hovercraft" mean an aircraft or hovercraft registered in the United Kingdom.

Interpretation

Expressions having same meaning as in copyright provisions

A-214   **211.**—(1) The following expressions have the same meaning in this Part as in Part I (copyright)—

> broadcast,
> business,
> cable programme,
> cable programme service,
> country,
> defendant (in Scotland),
> delivery up (in Scotland),
> film,
> literary work,
> published, and
> sound recording.

(2) The provisions of section 6(3) to (5), section 7(5) and 19(4) (supplementary provisions relating to broadcasting and cable programme services) apply for the purposes of this Part, and in relation to an infringement of the rights conferred by this Part, as they apply for the purposes of Part I and in relation to an infringement of copyright.

Index of defined expressions

A-215   **212.** The following Table shows provisions defining or otherwise explaining expressions used in this Part (other than provisions defining or explaining an expression used only in the same section)—

broadcast (and related expressions)	section 211 (and section 6)
business	section 211(1) (and section 178)
cable programme, cable programme service (and related expressions)	section 211 (and section 7)
country	section 211(1) (and section 178)
defendant (in Scotland)	section 211(1) (and section 177)
delivery up (in Scotland)	section 211(1)(and section 177)
exclusive recording contract	section 185(1)
film	section 211(1) (and section 5)
illicit recording	section 197
literary work	section 211(1) (and section 3(1))
performance	section 180(2)
published	section 211(1) (and section 175)

qualifying country	section 206(1)
qualifying individual	section 206(1) and (2)
qualifying performance	section 181
qualifying person	section 206(1) and (3)
recording (of a performance)	section 180(2)
recording rights (person having)	section 185(2) and (3)
sound recording	section 211(1) (and section 5).

Part *III*

Design Right

Chapter I

Design Right in Original Designs

Introductory

Design right

213.—(1) Design right is a property right which subsists in accordance with this Part in an original design.

(2) In this Part "design" means the design of any aspect of the shape or configuration (whether internal or external) of the whole or part of an article.

(3) Design right does not subsist in—

(*a*) a method or principle of construction,

(*b*) features of shape or configuration of an article which—

    (i) enable the article to be connected to, or placed in, around or against, another article so that either article may perform its function, or

    (ii) are dependent upon the appearance of another article of which the article is intended by the designer to form an integral part, or

(*c*) surface decoration.

(4) A design is not "original" for the purposes of this Part if it is commonplace in the design field in question at the time of its creation.

(5) Design right subsists in a design only if the design qualifies for design right protection by reference to—

(*a*) the designer or the person by whom the design was commissioned or the designer employed (see sections 218 and 219), or

(*b*) the person by whom and country in which articles made to the design were first marketed (see section 220),

or in accordance with any Order under section 221 (power to make further provision with respect to qualification).

(6) Design right does not subsist unless and until the design has been recorded in a design document or an article has been made to the design.

(7) Design right does not subsist in a design which was so recorded, or to which an article was made, before the commencement of this Part.

The designer

214.—(1) In this Part the "designer", in relation to a design, means the person who creates it.

(2) In the case of a computer-generated design the person by whom the arrange-

A–216

A–217

ments necessary for the creation of the design are undertaken shall be taken to be the designer.

Ownership of design right

A–218   **215.**—(1) The designer is the first owner of any design right in a design which is not created in pursuance of a commission or in the course of employment.

(2) Where a design is created in pursuance of a commission, the person commissioning the design is the first owner of any design right in it.

(3) Where, in a case not falling within subsection (2) a design is created by an employee in the course of his employment, his employer is the first owner of any design right in the design.

(4) If a design qualifies for design right protection by virtue of section 220 (qualification by references to first marketing of articles made to the design), the above rules do not apply and the person by whom the articles in question are marketed is the first owner of the design right.

Duration of design right

A–219   **216.**—(1) Design right expires—

(a) fifteen years from the end of the calendar year in which the design was first recorded in a design document or an article was first made to the design, whichever first occurred, or

(b) if articles made to the design are made available for sale or hire within five years from the end of that calendar year, ten years from the end of the calendar year in which that first occurred.

(2) The reference in subsection (1) to articles being made available for sale or hire is to their being made so available anywhere in the world by or with the licence of the design right owner.

Qualification for design right protection

Qualifying individuals and qualifying persons

A–220   **217.**—(1) In this Part—

"qualifying individual" means a citizen or subject of, or an individual habitually resident in, a qualifying country; and

"qualifying person" means a qualifying individual or a body corporate or other body having legal personality which—

(a) is formed under the law of a part of the United Kingdom or another qualifying country, and

(b) has in any qualifying country a place of business at which substantial business activity is carried on.

(2) References in this Part to a qualifying person include the Crown and the government of any other qualifying country.

(3) In this section "qualifying country" means—

(a) the United Kingdom,

(b) a country to which this Part extends by virtue of an Order under section 255,

(c) another member State of the European Economic Community, or

(d) to the extent that an Order under section 256 so provides, a country designated under that section as enjoying reciprocal protection.

(4) The reference in the definition of "qualifying individual" to a person's being a citizen or subject of a qualifying country shall be construed—

(*a*) in relation to the United Kingdom, as a reference to his being a British citizen, and

(*b*) in relation to a colony of the United Kingdom, as a reference to his being a British Dependent Territories' citizen by connection with that colony.

(5) In determining for the purpose of the definition of "qualifying person" whether substantial business activity is carried on at a place of business in any country, no account shall be taken of dealings in goods which are at all material times outside that country.

Qualification by reference to designer

218.—(1) This section applies to a design which is not created in pursuance of a commission or in the course of employment.　　　　　**A–221**

(2) A design to which this section applies qualifies for design right protection if the designer is a qualifying individual or, in the case of a computer-generated design, a qualifying person.

(3) A joint design to which this section applies qualifies for design right protection if any of the designers is a qualifying individual or, as the case may be, a qualifying person.

(4) Where a joint design qualifies for design right protection under this section, only those designers who are qualifying individuals or qualifying persons are entitled to design right under section 215(1) (first ownership of design right: entitlement of designer).

Qualification by reference to commissioner or employer

219.—(1) A design qualifies for design right protection if it is created in pursuance of a commission from, or in the course of employment with, a qualifying person.　　　　　**A–222**

(2) In the case of a joint commission or joint employment a design qualifies for design right protection if any of the commissioners or employers is a qualifying person.

(3) Where a design which is jointly commissioned or created in the course of joint employment qualifies for design right protection under this section, only those commissioners or employers who are qualifying persons are entitled to design right under section 215(2) or (3) (first ownership of design right: entitlement of commissioner or employer).

Qualification by reference to first marketing

220.—(1) A design which does not qualify for design right protection under section 218 or 219 (qualification by reference to designer, commissioner or employer) qualifies for design right protection if the first marketing of articles made to the design—　　　　　**A–223**

(*a*) is by a qualifying person who is exclusively authorised to put such articles on the market in the United Kingdom, and

(*b*) takes place in the United Kingdom, another country to which this Part extends by virtue of an Order under section 255, or another member State of the European Economic Community.

(2) If the first marketing of articles made to the design is done jointly by two or more persons, the design qualifies for design right protection if any of those persons meets the requirements specified in subsection (1)(*a*).

(3) In such a case only the persons who meet those requirements are entitled to design right under section 215(4) (first ownership of design right: entitlement of first marketer of articles made to the design).

(4) In subsection (1)(*a*) "exclusively authorised" refers—

    (*a*) to authorisation by the person who would have been first owner of design right as designer, commissioner of the design or employer of the designer if he had been a qualifying person, or by a person lawfully claiming under such a person, and

    (*b*) to exclusivity capable of being enforced by legal proceedings in the United Kingdom.

Power to make further provision as to qualification

A–224　　**221.**—(1) Her Majesty may, with a view to fulfilling an international obligation of the United Kingdom, by Order in Council provide that a design qualifies for design right protection if such requirements as are specified in the Order are met.

(2) An Order may make different provision for different descriptions of design or article; and may make such consequential modifications of the operation of sections 215 (ownership of design right) and sections 218 to 220 (other means of qualification) as appear to Her Majesty to be appropriate.

(3) A statutory instrument containing an Order in Council under this section shall be subject to annulment in pursuance of a resolution of either House of Parliament.

Dealings with design right

Assignment and licences

A–225　　**222.**—(1) Design right is transmissible by assignment, by testamentary disposition or by operation of law, as personal or moveable property.

(2) An assignment or other transmission of design right may be partial, that is, limited so as to apply—

    (*a*) to one or more, but not all, of the things the design right owner has the exclusive right to do;

    (*b*) to part, but not the whole, of the period for which the right is to subsist.

(3) An assignment of design right is not effective unless it is in writing signed by or on behalf of the assignor.

(4) A licence granted by the owner of design right is binding on every successor in title to his interest in the right, except a purchaser in good faith for valuable consideration and without notice (actual or constructive) of the licence or a person deriving title from such a purchaser; and references in this Part to doing anything with, or without, the licence of the design right owner shall be construed accordingly.

Prospective ownership of design right

A–226　　**223.**—(1) Where by an agreement made in relation to future design right, and signed by or on behalf of the prospective owner of the design right, the prospective owner purports to assign the future design right (wholly or partially) to another person, then if, on the right coming into existence, the assignee or another person claiming under him would be entitled as against all other persons to require the right to be vested in him, the right shall vest in him by virtue of this section.

(2) In this section—

"future design right" means design right which will or may come into existence in respect of a future design or class of designs or on the occurrence of a future event; and

"prospective owner" shall be construed accordingly, and includes a person who is prospectively entitled to design right by virtue of such an agreement as is mentioned in subsection (1).

(3) A licence granted by a prospective owner of design right is binding on every successor in title to his interest (or prospective interest) in the right, except a purchaser in good faith for valuable consideration and without notice (actual or constructive) of the licence or a person deriving title from such a purchaser; and references in this Part to doing anything with, or without, the licence of the design right owner shall be construed accordingly.

Assignment of right in registered design presumed to carry with it design right

224. Where a design consisting of a design in which design right subsists is registered under the Registered Designs Act 1949 and the proprietor of the registered design is also the design right owner, an assignment of the right in the registered design shall be taken to be also an assignment of the design right, unless a contrary intention appears.

A–227

Exclusive licences

225.—(1) In this Part an "exclusive licence" means a licence in writing signed by or on behalf of the design right owner authorising the licensee to the exclusion of all other persons, including the person granting the licence, to exercise a right which would otherwise be exercisable exclusively by the design right owner.

(2) The licensee under an exclusive licence has the same rights against any successor in title who is bound by the licence as he has against the person granting the licence.

A–228

CHAPTER II

RIGHTS OF DESIGN RIGHT OWNER AND REMEDIES

Infringement of design right

Primary infringement of design right

226.—(1) The owner of design right in a design has the exclusive right to reproduce the design for commercial purposes—
(*a*) by making articles to that design, or
(*b*) by making a design document recording the design for the purpose of enabling such articles to be made.

(2) Reproduction of a design by making articles to the design means copying the design so as to produce articles exactly or substantially to that design, and references in this Part to making articles to a design shall be construed accordingly.

(3) Design right is infringed by a person who without the licence of the design right owner does, or authorises another to do, anything which by virtue of this section is the exclusive right of the design right owner.

(4) For the purposes of this section reproduction may be direct or indirect, and it is immaterial whether any intervening acts themselves infringe the design right.

(5) This section has effect subject to the provisions of Chapter III (exceptions to rights of design right owner).

A–229

Secondary infringement: importing or dealing with infringing article

227.—(1) Design right is infringed by a person who, without the licence of the design right owner—
(*a*) imports into the United Kingdom for commercial purposes, or
(*b*) has in his possession for commercial purposes, or

A–230

(c) sells, lets for hire, or offers or exposes for sale or hire, in the course of a business,

an article which is, and which he knows or has reason to believe is, an infringing article.

(2) This section has effect subject to the provisions of Chapter III (exceptions to rights of design right owner).

Meaning of "infringing article"

A–231   **228.**—(1) In this Part "infringing article", in relation to a design, shall be construed in accordance with this section.

(2) An article is an infringing article if its making to that design was an infringement of design right in the design.

(3) An article is also an infringing article if—

(a) it has been or is proposed to be imported into the United Kingdom, and

(b) its making to that design in the United Kingdom would have been an infringement of design right in the design or a breach of an exclusive licence agreement relating to the design.

(4) Where it is shown that an article is made to a design in which design right subsists or has subsisted at any time, it shall be presumed until the contrary is proved that the article was made at a time when design right subsisted.

(5) Nothing in subsection (3) shall be construed as applying to an article which may lawfully be imported into the United Kingdom by virtue of any enforceable Community right within the meaning of section 2(1) of the European Communities Act 1972.

(6) The expression "infringing article" does not include a design document, notwithstanding that its making was or would have been an infringement of design right.

Remedies for infringement

Rights and remedies of design right owner

A–232   **229.**—(1) An infringement of design right is actionable by the design right owner.

(2) In an action for infringement of design right all such relief by way of damages, injunctions, accounts or otherwise is available to the plaintiff as is available in respect of the infringement of any other property right.

(3) The court may in an action for infringement of design right, having regard to all the circumstances and in particular to—

(a) the flagrancy of the infringement, and

(b) any benefit accruing to the defendant by reason of the infringement,

award such additional damages as the justice of the case may require.

(4) This section has effect subject to section 233 (innocent infringement).

Order for delivery up

A–233   **230.**—(1) Where a person—

(a) has in his possession, custody or control for commercial purposes an infringing article, or

(b) has in his possession, custody or control anything specifically designed or adapted for making articles to a particular design, knowing or having reason to believe that it has been or is to be used to make an infringing article,

the owner of the design right in the design in question may apply to the court for an order that the infringing article or other thing be delivered up to him or to such other person as the court may direct.

(2) An application shall not be made after the end of the period specified in the following provisions of this section; and no order shall be made unless the court also makes, or it appears to the court that there are grounds for making, an order under section 231 (order as to disposal of infringing article, &c.).

(3) An application for an order under this section may not be made after the end of the period of six years from the date on which the article or thing in question was made, subject to subsection (4).

(4) If during the whole or any part of that period the design right owner—

(*a*) is under a disability, or

(*b*) is prevented by fraud or concealment from discovering the facts entitling him to apply for an order,

an application may be made at any time before the end of the period of six years from the date on which he ceased to be under a disability or, as the case may be, could with reasonable diligence have discovered those facts.

(5) In subsection (4) "disability"—

(*a*) in England and Wales, has the same meaning as in the Limitation Act 1980;

(*b*) in Scotland, means legal disability within the meaning of the Prescription and Limitation (Scotland) Act 1973;

(*c*) in Northern Ireland, has the same meaning as in the Statute of Limitations (Northern Ireland) 1958.

(6) A person to whom an infringing article or other thing is delivered up in pursuance of an order under this section shall, if an order under section 231 is not made, retain it pending the making of an order, or the decision not to make an order, under that section.

(7) Nothing in this section affects any other power of the court.

Order as to disposal of infringing articles, &c

231.—(1) An application may be made to the court for an order that an infring- **A–234** ing articvle or other thing delivered up in pursuance of an order under section 230 shall be—

(*a*) forfeited to the design right owner, or

(*b*) destroyed or otherwise dealt with as the court may think fit,

or for a decision that no such order should be made.

(2) In considering what order (if any) should be made, the court shall consider whether other remedies available in an action for infringement of design right would be adequate to compensate the design right owner and to protect his interests.

(3) Provision shall be made by rules of court as to the service of notice on persons having an interest in the article or other thing, and any such person is entitled—

(*a*) to appear in proceedings for an order under this section, whether or not he was served with notice, and

(*b*) to appeal against any order made, whether or not he appeared;

and an order shall not take effect until the end of the period within which notice of an appeal may be given or, if before the end of that period notice of appeal is duly given, until the final determination or abandonment of the proceedings on the appeal.

(4) Where there is more than one person interested in an article or other thing, the court shall make such order as it thinks just and may (in particular) direct that the thing be sold, or otherwise dealt with, and the proceeds divided.

(5) If the court decides that no order should be made under this section, the person in whose possession, custody or control the article or other thing was before being delivered up or seized is entitled to its return.

(6) References in this section to a person having an interest in an article or other thing include any person in whose favour an order could be made in respect of it under this section or under section 114 or 204 of this Act or section 58C of the Trade Marks Act 1938 (which make similar provisions in relation to infringement of copyright, rights in performances and trade marks).

Jurisdiction of county court and sheriff court

A-235   **232.**—(1) In England, Wales and Northern Ireland a county court may entertain proceedings under—

section 230 (order for delivery up of infringing article, &c.),
section 231 (order as to disposal of infringing article, &c.), or
section 235(5) (application by exclusive licensee having concurrent rights),

where the value of the infringing articles and other things in question does not exceed the county court limit for actions in tort.

(2) In Scotland proceedings for an order under any of those provisions may be brought in the sheriff court.

(3) Nothing in this section shall be construed as affecting the jurisdiction of the High Court or, in Scotland, the Court of Session.

Innocent infringement

A-236   **233.**—(1) Where in an action for infringement of design right brought by virtue of section 226 (primary infringement) it is shown that at the time of the infringement the defendant did not know, and had no reason to believe, that design right subsisted in the design to which the action relates, the plaintiff is not entitled to damages against him, but without prejudice to any other remedy.

(2) Where in an action for infringement of design right brought by virtue of section 227 (secondary infringement) a defendant shows that the infringing article was innocently acquired by him or a predecessor in title of his, the only remedy available against him in respect of the infringement is damages not exceeding a reasonable royalty in respect of the act complained of.

(3) In subsection (2) "innocently acquired" means that the person acquiring the article did not know and had no reason to believe that it was an infringing article.

Rights and remedies of exclusive licensee

A-237   **234.**—(1) An exclusive licensee has, except against the design right owner, the same rights and remedies in respect of matters occurring after the grant of the licence as if the licence had been an assignment.

(2) His rights and remedies are concurrent with those of the design right owner; and references in the relevant provisions of this Part to the design right owner shall be construed accordingly.

(3) In an action brought by an exclusive licensee by virtue of this section a defendant may avail himself of any defence which would have been available to him if the action had been brought by the design right owner.

Exercise of concurrent rights

A-238   **235.**—(1) Where an action for infringement of design right brought by the design right owner or an exclusive licensee relates (wholly or partly) to an infringement in respect of which they have concurrent rights of action, the design right owner or, as the case may be, the exclusive licensee may not, without the leave of the court, proceed with the action unless the other is either joined as a plaintiff or added as a defendant.

(2) A design right owner or exclusive licensee who is added as a defendant in pursuance of subsection (1) is not liable for any costs in the action unless he takes part in the proceedings.

(3) The above provisions do not affect the granting of interlocutory relief on the application of the design right owner or an exclusive licensee.

(4) Where an action for infringement of design right is brought which relates (wholly or partly) to an infringement in respect of which the design right owner and an exclusive licensee have concurrent rights of action—

(a) the court shall, in assessing damages, take into account—
    (i) the terms of the licence, and
    (ii) any pecuniary remedy already awarded or available to either of them in respect of the infringement;

(b) no account of profits shall be directed if an award of damages has been made, or an account of profits has been directed, in favour of the other of them in respect of the infringement; and

(c) the court shall if an account of profits is directed apportion the profits between them as the court considers just, subject to any agreement between them;

and these provisions apply whether or not the design right owner and the exclusive licensee are both parties to the action.

(5) The design right owner shall notify any exclusive licensee having concurrent rights before applying for an order under section 230 (order for delivery up of infringing article, &c.); and the court may on the application of the licensee make such order under that section as it thinks fit having regard to the terms of the licence.

CHAPTER III

EXCEPTIONS TO RIGHTS OF DESIGN RIGHT OWNERS

Infringement of copyright

Infringement of copyright

236. Where copyright subsists in a work which consists of or includes a design   **A–239** in which design right subsists, it is not an infringement of design right in the design to do anything which is an infringement of the copyright in that work.

Availability of licences of right

Licences available in last five years of design right

237.—(1) Any person is entitled as of right to a licence to do in the last five   **A–240** years of the design right term anything which would otherwise infringe the design right.

(2) The terms of the licence shall, in default of agreement, be settled by the comptroller.

(3) The Secretary of State may if it appears to him necessary in order to—

(a) comply with an international obligation of the United Kingdom, or

(b) secure or maintain reciprocal protection for British designs in other countries,

by order exclude from the operation of subsection (1) designs of a description specified in the order or designs applied to articles of a description so specified.

(4) An order shall be made by statutory instrument; and no order shall be made unless a draft of it has been laid before and approved by a resolution of each House of Parliament.

Powers exercisable for protection of the public interest

A–241   **238.**—(1) Where the matters specified in a report of the Monopolies and Mergers Commission as being those which in the Commission's opinion operate, may be expected to operate or have operated against the public interest include—

(*a*) conditions in licences granted by a design right owner restricting the use of the design by the licensee or the right of the design right owner to grant other licences, or

(*b*) a refusal of a design right owner to grant licences on reasonable terms,

the powers conferred by Part I of Schedule 8 to the Fair Trading Act 1973 (powers exercisable for purpose of remedying or preventing adverse effects specified in report of Commission) include power to cancel or modify those conditions and, instead or in addition, to provide that licences in respect of the design right shall be available as of right.

(2) The references in sections 56(2) and 73(2) of that Act, and sections 10(2)(*b*) and 12(5) of the Competition Act 1980, to the powers specified in that Part of that Schedule shall be construed accordingly.

(3) The terms of a licence available by virtue of this section shall, in default of agreement, be settled by the comptroller.

Undertaking to take licence of right in infringement proceedings

A–242   **239.**—(1) If in proceedings for infringement of design right in a design in respect of which a licence is available as of right under section 237 or 238 the defendant undertakes to take a licence on such terms as may be agreed or, in default of agreement, settled by the comptroller under that section—

(*a*) no injunction shall be granted against him,

(*b*) no order for delivery up shall be made under section 230, and

(*c*) the amount recoverable against him by way of damages or on an account of profits shall not exceed double the amount which would have been payable by him as licensee if such a licence on those terms had been granted before the earliest infringement.

(2) An undertaking may be given at any time before final order in the proceedings, without any admission of liability.

(3) Nothing in this section affects the remedies available in respect of an infringement committed before licences of right were available.

Crown use of designs

Crown use of designs

A–243   **240.**—(1) A government department, or a person authorised in writing by a government department, may without the licence of the design right owner—

(*a*) do anything for the purpose of supplying articles for the services of the Crown, or

(*b*) dispose of articles no longer required for the services of the Crown;

and nothing done by virtue of this section infringes the design right.

(2) References in this Part to "the services of the Crown" are to—

(*a*) the defence of the realm,

(*b*) foreign defence purposes, and

(*c*) health service purposes.

(3) The reference to the supply of articles for "foreign defence purposes" is to their supply—

    (*a*) for the defence of a country outside the realm in pursuance of an agreement or arrangement to which the government of that country and Her Majesty's Government in the United Kingdom are parties; or

    (*b*) for use by armed forces operating in pursuance of a resolution of the United Nations or one of its organs.

(4) The reference to the supply of articles for "health service purposes" are to their supply for the purposes of providing—

    (*a*) pharmaceutical services,

    (*b*) general medical services, or

    (*c*) general dental services,

that is, services of those kinds under Part II of the National Health Service Act 1977, Part II of the National Health Service (Scotland) Act 1978 or the corresponding provisions of the law in force in Northern Ireland.

(5) In this Part—

"Crown use", in relation to a design, means the doing of anything by virtue of this section which would otherwise be an infringement of design right in the design; and

"the government department concerned", in relation to such use, means the government department by whom or on whose authority the act was done.

(6) The authority of a government department in respect of Crown use of a design may be given to a person either before or after the use and whether or not he is authorised, directly or indirectly, by the design right owner to do anything in relation to the design.

(7) A person acquiring anything sold in the exercise of powers conferred by this section, and any person claiming under him, may deal with it in the same manner as if the design right were held on behalf of the Crown.

Settlement of terms for Crown use

241.—(1) Where Crown use is made of a design, the government department **A–244** concerned shall—

    (*a*) notify the design right owner as soon as practicable, and

    (*b*) give him such information as to the extent of the use as he may from time to time require,

unless it appears to the department that it would be contrary to the public interest to do so or the identity of the design right owner cannot be ascertained on reasonable inquiry.

(2) Crown use of a design shall be on such terms as, either before or after the use, are agreed between the government department concerned and the design right owner with the approval of the Treasury or, in default of agreement, are determined by the court.

In the application of this subsection to Northern Ireland the reference to the Treasury shall, where the government department referred to in that subsection is a Northern Ireland department, be construed as a reference to the Department of Finance and Personnel.

(3) Where the identity of the design right owner cannot be ascertained on reasonable inquiry, the government department concerned may apply to the court who may order that no royalty or other sum shall be payable in respect of Crown use of the design until the owner agrees terms with the department or refers the matter to the court for determination.

Rights of third parties in case of Crown use

A–245   **242.**—(1) The provisions of any licence, assignment or agreement made between the design right owner (or anyone deriving title from him or from whom he derives title) and any person other than a government department are of no effect in relation to Crown use of a design, or any act incidental to Crown use, so far as they—

(*a*) restrict or regulate anything done in relation to the design, or the use of any model, document or other information relating to it, or

(*b*) provide for the making of payments in respect of, or calculated by reference to such use;

and the copying or issuing to the public of copies of any such model or document in connection with the thing done, or any such use, shall be deemed not to be an infringement of any copyright in the model or document.

(2) Subsection (1) shall not be construed as authorising the disclosure of any such model, document or information in contravention of the licence, assignment or agreement.

(3) Where an exclusive licence is in force in respect of the design—

(*a*) if the licence was granted for royalties—

(i) any agreement between the design right owner and a government department under section 241 (settlement of terms for Crown use) requires the consent of the licensee, and

(ii) the licensee is entitled to recover from the design right owner such part of the payment for Crown use as may be agreed between them or, in default of agreement, determined by the court;

(*b*) if the licence was granted otherwise than for royalties—

(i) section 241 applies in relation to anything done which but for section 240 (Crown use) and subsection (1) above would be an infringement of the rights of the licensee with the substitution for references to the design right owner of references to the licensee, and

(ii) section 241 does not apply in relation to anything done by the licensee by virtue of an authority given under section 240.

(4) Where the design right has been assigned to the design right owner in consideration of royalties—

(*a*) section 241 applies in relation to Crown use of the design as if the references to the design right owner included the assignor, and any payment for Crown use shall be divided between them in such proportion as may be agreed or, in default of agreement, determined by the court; and

(*b*) section 241 applies in relation to any act incidental to Crown use as it applies in relation to Crown use of the design.

(5) Where any model, document or other information relating to a design is used in connection with Crown use of the design, or any act incidental to Crown use, section 241 applies to the use of the model, document or other information with the substitution for the references to the design right owner of references to the person entitled to the benefit of any provision of an agreement rendered inoperative by subsection (1) above.

(6) In this section—

"act incidental to Crown use" means anything done for the services of the Crown to the order of a government department by the design right owner in respect of a design;

"payment for Crown use" means such amount as is payable by the government department concerned by virtue of section 241; and

"royalties" includes any benefit determined by reference to the use of the design.

Crown use: compensation for loss of profit

243.—(1) Where Crown use is made of a design, the government department   **A–246**
concerned shall pay—
  (*a*) to the design right owner, or
  (*b*) if there is an exclusive licence in force in respect of the design, to the exclu-
      sive licensee,
compensation for any loss resulting from his not being awarded a contract to
supply the articles made to the design.

  (2) Compensation is payable only to the extent that such a contract could have
been fulfilled from his existing manufacturing capacity; but is payable notwithstanding the existence of circumstances rendering him ineligible for the award of
such a contract.
  (3) In determining the loss, regard shall be had to the profit which would have
been made on such a contract and to the extent to which any manufacturing
capacity was under-used.
  (4) No compensation is payable in respect of any failure to secure contracts for
the supply of articles made to the design otherwise than for the services of the
Crown.
  (5) The amount payable shall, if not agreed between the design right owner or
licensee and the government department concerned with the approval of the
Treasury, be determined by the court on a reference under section 252; and it is in
addition to any amount payable under section 241 or 242.
  (6) In the application of this section to Northern Ireland, the reference in subsection (5) to the Treasury shall, where the government department concerned is a
Northern Ireland department, be construed as a reference to the Department of
Finance and Personnel.

Special provision for Crown use during emergency

244.—(1) During a period of emergency the powers exercisable in relation to a   **A–247**
design by virtue of section 240 (Crown use) include power to do any act which
would otherwise be an infringement of design right for any purpose which appears
to the government department concerned necessary or expedient—
  (*a*) for the efficient prosecution of any war in which Her Majesty may be
      engaged;
  (*b*) for the maintenance of supplies and services essential to the life of the com-
      munity;
  (*c*) for securing a sufficiency of supplies and services essential to the well-being
      of the community;
  (*d*) for promoting the productivity of industry, commerce and agriculture;
  (*e*) for fostering and directing exports and reducing imports, or imports of any
      classes, from all or any countries and for redressing the balance of trade;
  (*f*) generally for ensuring that the whole resources of the community are avail-
      able for use, and are used, in a manner best calculated to serve the interests
      of the community; or
  (*g*) for assisting the relief of suffering and the restoration and distribution of
      essential supplies and services in any country outside the United Kingdom
      which is in grave distress as the result of war.

  (2) References in this Part to the services of the Crown include, as respects a
period of emergency, those purposes; and references to "Crown use" include any
act which would apart from this section be an infringement of design right.
  (3) In this section "period of emergency" means a period beginning with such
date as may be declared by Order in Council to be the beginning, and ending with

such date as may be so declared to be the end, of a period of emergency for the purposes of this section.

(4) No Order in Council under this section shall be submitted to Her Majesty unless a draft of it has been laid before and approved by a resolution of each House of Parliament.

General

Power to provide for further exceptions

A–248   **245.**—(1) The Secretary of State may if it appears to him necessary in order to—

    (*a*) comply with an international obligation of the United Kingdom, or

    (*b*) secure or maintain reciprocal protection for British designs in other countries,

by order provide that acts of a description specified in the order do not infringe design right.

(2) An order may make different provision for different descriptions of design or article.

(3) An order shall be made by statutory instrument and no order shall be made unless a draft of it has been laid before and approved by a resolution of each House of Parliament.

CHAPTER IV

JURISDICTION OF THE COMPTROLLER AND THE COURT

Jurisdiction of the comptroller

Jurisdiction to decide matters relating to design right

A–249   **246.**—(1) A party to a dispute as to any of the following matters may refer the dispute to the comptroller for his decision—

    (*a*) the subsistence of design right,

    (*b*) the term of design right, or

    (*c*) the identity of the person in whom design right first vested;

and the comptroller's decision on the reference is binding on the parties to the dispute.

(2) No other court or tribunal shall decide any such matter except—

    (*a*) on a reference or appeal from the comptroller,

    (*b*) in infringement or other proceedings in which the issue arises incidentally, or

    (*c*) in proceedings brought with the agreement of the parties or the leave of the comptroller.

(3) The comptroller has jurisdiction to decide any incidental question of fact or law arising in the course of a reference under this section.

Application to settle terms of licence of right

A–250   **247.**—(1) A person requiring a licence which is available as of right by virtue of—

    (*a*) section 237 (licences available in the last five years of design right), or

    (*b*) an order under section 238 (licences made available in the public interest),

may apply to the comptroller to settle the terms of the licence.

(2) No application for the settlement of the terms of a licence available by virtue of section 237 may be made earlier than one year before the earliest date on which the licence may take effect under that section.

(3) The terms of a licence settled by the comptroller shall authorise the licensee to do—

(*a*) in the case of licence available by virtue of section 237, everything which would be an infringement of the design right in the absence of a licence;

(*b*) in the case of a licence available by virtue of section 238, everything in respect of which a licence is so available.

(4) In settling the terms of a licence the comptroller shall have regard to such factors as may be prescribed by the Secretary of State by order made by statutory instrument.

(5) No such order shall be made unless a draft of it has been laid before and approved by a resolution of each House of Parliament.

(6) Where the terms of a licence are settled by the comptroller, the licence has effect—

(*a*) in the case of an application in respect of a licence available by virtue of section 237 made before the earliest date on which the licence may take effect under that section, from that date;

(*b*) in any other case, from the date on which the application to the comptroller was made.

Settlement of terms where design right owner unknown

248.—(1) This section applies where a person making an application under section 247 (settlement of terms of licence of right) is unable on reasonable inquiry to discover the identity of the design right owner.   **A–251**

(2) The comptroller may in settling the terms of the licence order that the licence shall be free of any obligation as to royalties or other payments.

(3) If such an order is made the design right owner may apply to the comptroller to vary the terms of the licence with effect from the date on which his application is made.

(4) If the terms of a licence are settled by the comptroller and it is subsequently established that a licence was not available as of right, the licensee shall not be liable in damages for, or for an account of profits in respect of, anything done before he was aware of any claim by the design right owner that a licence was not available.

Appeals as to terms of licence of right

249.—(1) An appeal lies from any decision of the comptroller under section 247 or 248 (settlement of terms of licence of right) to the Appeal Tribunal constituted under section 28 of the Registered Designs Act 1949.   **A–252**

(2) Section 28 of that Act applies to appeals from the comptroller under this section as it applies to appeals from the registrar under that Act; but rules made under that section may make different provision for appeals under this section.

Rules

250.—(1) The Secretary of State may make rules for regulating the procedure to be followed in connection with any proceeding before the comptroller under this Part.   **A–253**

(2) Rules may, in particular, make provision—

(*a*) prescribing forms;

(*b*) requiring fees to be paid;

(*c*) authorising the rectification of irregularities of procedure;

(*d*) regulating the mode of giving evidence and empowering the comptroller to compel the attendance of witnesses and the discovery of and production of documents;

(*e*) providing for the appointment of advisers to assist the comptroller in proceedings before him;

(*f*) prescribing time limits for doing anything required to be done (and providing for the alteration of any such limit); and

(*g*) empowering the comptroller to award costs and to direct how, to what party and from what parties, costs are to be paid.

(3) Rules prescribing fees require the consent of the Treasury.

(4) The remuneration of an adviser appointed to assist the comptroller shall be determined by the Secretary of State with the consent of the Treasury and shall be defrayed out of money provided by Parliament.

(5) Rules shall be made by statutory instrument which shall be subject to annulment in pursuance of a resolution of either House of Parliament.

Jurisdiction of the court

References and appeals on design right matters

A–254   **251.**—(1) In any proceedings before him under section 246 (reference of matter relating to design right), the comptroller may at any time order the whole proceedings or any question or issue (whether of fact or law) to be referred, on such terms as he may direct, to the High Court or, in Scotland, the Court of Session.

(2) The comptroller shall make such an order if the parties to the proceedings agree that he should do so.

(3) On a reference under this section the court may exercise any power available to the comptroller by virtue of this Part as respects the matter referred to it and, following its determination, may refer any matter back to the comptroller.

(4) An appeal lies from any decision of the comptroller in proceedings before him under section 246 (decisions on matters relating to design right) to the High Court or, in Scotland, the Court of Session.

Reference of disputes relating to Crown use

A–255   **252.**—(1) A dispute as to any matter which falls to be determined by the court in default of agreement under—

(*a*) section 241 (settlement of terms for Crown use),

(*b*) section 242 (rights of third parties in case of Crown use), or

(*c*) section 243 (Crown use: compensation for loss of profit),

may be referred to the court by any party to the dispute.

(2) In determining a dispute between a government department and any person as to the terms for Crown use of a design the court shall have regard to—

(*a*) any sums which that person or a person from whom he derives title has received or is entitled to receive, directly or indirectly, from any government department in respect of the design; and

(*b*) whether that person or a person from whom he derives title has in the court's opinion without reasonable cause failed to comply with a request of the department for the use of the design on reasonable terms.

(3) One of two or more joint owners of design right may, without the concurrence of the others, refer a dispute to the court under this section, but shall not do so unless the others are made parties; and none of those others is liable for any costs unless he takes part in the proceedings.

(4) Where the consent of an exclusive licensee is required by section 242(3)(*a*)(i)

to the settlement by agreement of the terms for Crown use of a design, a determination by the court of the amount of any payment to be made for such use is of no effect unless the licensee has been notified of the reference and given an opportunity to be heard.

(5) On the reference of a dispute as to the amount recoverable as mentioned in section 242(3)(*a*)(ii) (right of exclusive licensee to recover part of amount payable to design right owner) the court shall determine what is just having regard to any expenditure incurred by the licensee—

  (*a*) in developing the design, or
  (*b*) in making payments to the design right owner in consideration of the licence (other than royalties or other payments determined by reference to the use of the design).

(6) In this section "the court" means—

  (*a*) in England and Wales, the High Court or any patents county court having jurisdiction by virtue of an order under section 287 of this Act,
  (*b*) in Scotland, the Court of Session, and
  (*c*) in Northern Ireland, the High Court.

CHAPTER V

MISCELLANEOUS AND GENERAL

Miscellaneous

Remedy for groundless threats of infringement proceedings

253.—(1) Where a person threatens another person with proceedings for **A–256** infringement of design right, a person aggrieved by the threats may bring an action against him claiming—

  (*a*) a declaration to the effect that the threats are unjustifiable;
  (*b*) an injunction against the continuance of the threats;
  (*c*) damages in respect of any loss which he has sustained by the threats.

(2) If the plaintiff proves that the threats were made and that he is a person aggrieved by them, he is entitled to the relief claimed unless the defendant shows that the acts in respect of which proceedings were threatened did constitute, or if done would have constituted, an infringement of the design right concerned.

(3) Proceedings may not be brought under this section in respect of a threat to bring proceedings for an infringement alleged to consist of making or importing anything.

(4) Mere notification that a design is protected by design right does not constitute a threat of proceedings for the purposes of this section.

Licensee under licence of right not to claim connection with design right owner

254.—(1) A person who has a licence in respect of a design by virtue of section **A–257** 237 or 238 (licences of right) shall not, without the consent of the design right owner—

  (*a*) apply to goods which he is marketing, or proposes to market, in reliance on that licence a trade description indicating that he is the licensee of the design right owner, or
  (*b*) use any such trade description in an advertisement in relation to such goods.

(2) A contravention of subsection (1) is actionable by the design right owner.

(3) In this section "trade description", the reference to applying a trade description to goods and "advertisement" have the same meaning as in the Trade Descriptions Act 1968.

Extent of operation of this Part

Countries to which this Part extends

A–258   **255.**—(1) This Part extends to England and Wales, Scotland and Northern Ireland.

(2) Her Majesty may by Order in Council direct that this Part shall extend, subject to such exceptions and modifications as may be specified in the Order to—

    (*a*)   any of the Channel Islands,

    (*b*)   the Isle of Man, or

    (*c*)   any colony.

(3) That power includes power to extend, subject to such exceptions and modifications as may be specified in the Order, any Order in Council made under section 221 (further provision as to qualification for design right protection) or section 256 (countries enjoying reciprocal protection).

(4) The legislature of a country to which this Part has been extended may modify or add to the provisions of this Part, in their operation as part of the law of that country, as the legislature may consider necessary to adapt the provisions to the circumstances of that country; but not so as to deny design right protection in a case where it would otherwise exist.

(5) Where a country to which this Part extends ceases to be a colony of the United Kingdom, it shall continue to be treated as such a country for the purposes of this Part until—

    (*a*)   an Order in Council is made under section 256 designating it as a country enjoying reciprocal protection, or

    (*b*)   an Order in Council is made declaring that it shall cease to be so treated by reason of the fact that the provisions of this Part as part of the law of that country have been amended or repealed.

(6) A statutory instrument containing an Order in Council under subsection (5)(*b*) shall be subject to annulment in pursuance of a resolution of either House of Parliament.

Countries enjoying reciprocal protection

A–259   **256.**—(1) Her Majesty may, if it appears to Her that the law of a country provides adequate protection for British designs, by Order in Council designate that country as one enjoying reciprocal protection under this Part.

(2) If the law of a country provides adequate protection only for certain classes of British design, or only for designs applied to certain classes of article, any Order designating that country shall contain provision limiting, to a corresponding extent, the protection afforded by this Part in relation to designs connected with that country.

(3) An Order under this section shall be subject to annulment in pursuance of a resolution of either House of Parliament.

Territorial waters and the continental shelf

A–260   **257.**—(1) For the purposes of this Part the territorial waters of the United Kingdom shall be treated as part of the United Kingdom.

(2) This Part applies to things done in the United Kingdom sector of the continental shelf on a structure or vessel which is present there for purposes directly

connected with the exploration of the sea bed or subsoil or the exploitation of their natural resources as it applies to things done in the United Kingdom.

(3) The United Kingdom sector of the continental shelf means the areas designated by order under section 1(7) of the Continental Shelf Act 1964.

Interpretation

Construction of references to design right owner

258.—(1) Where different persons are (whether in consequence of a partial assignment or otherwise) entitled to different aspects of design right in a work, the design right owner for any purpose of this Part is the person who is entitled to the right in the respect relevant for that purpose.

(2) Where design right (or any aspect of design right) is owned by more than one person jointly, references in this Part to the design right owner are to all the owners, so that, in particular, any requirement of the licence of the design right owner requires the licence of all of them.

Joint designs

259.—(1) In this Part a "joint design" means a design produced by the collaboration of two or more designers in which the contribution of each is not distinct from that of the other or others.

(2) References in this Part to the designer of a design shall, except as otherwise provided, be construed in relation to a joint design as references to all the designers of the design.

Application of provisions to articles in kit form

260.—(1) The provisions of this Part apply in relation to a kit, that is, a complete or substantially complete set of components intended to be assembled into an article, as they apply in relation to the assembled article.

(2) Subsection (1) does not affect the question whether design right subsists in any aspect of the design of the components of a kit as opposed to the design of the assembled article.

Requirement of signature: application in relation to body corporate

261. The requirement in the following provisions that an instrument be signed by or on behalf of a person is also satisfied in the case of a body corporate by the affixing of its seal—

section 222(3) (assignment of design right),
section 223(1) (assignment of future design right),
section 225(1) (grant of exclusive licence).

Adaptation of expressions in relation to Scotland

262. In the application of this Part to Scotland—

"account of profits" means accounting and payment of profits;

"accounts" means count, reckoning and payment;

"assignment" means assignation;

"costs" means expenses;

"defendant" means defender;

"delivery up" means delivery;

A–261

A–262

A–263

A–264

A–265

"injunction" means interdict;

"interlocutory relief" means interim remedy; and

"plaintiff" means pursuer.

Minor definitions

A–266   **263.**—(1) In this Part—

"British design" means a design which qualifies for design right protection by reason of a connection with the United Kingdom of the designer or the person by whom the design is commissioned or the designer is employed;

"business" includes a trade or profession;

"commission" means a commission for money or money's worth;

"the comptroller" means the Comptroller-General of Patents, Designs and Trade Marks;

"computer-generated", in relation to a design, means that the design is generated by computer in circumstances such that there is no human designer,

"country" includes any territory;

"the Crown" includes the Crown in right of Her Majesty's Government in Northern Ireland;

"design document" means any record of a design, whether in the form of a drawing, a written description, a photograph, data stored in a computer or otherwise;

"employee", "employment" and "employer" refer to employment under a contract of service or of apprenticeship;

"government department" includes a Northern Ireland department.

(2) References in this Part to "marketing", in relation to an article, are to its being sold or let for hire, or offered or exposed for sale or hire, in the course of a business, and related expressions shall be construed accordingly; but no account shall be taken for the purposes of this Part of marketing which is merely colourable and not intended to satisfy the reasonable requirements of the public.

(3) References in this Part to an act being done in relation to an article for "commercial purposes" are to its being done with a view to the article in question being sold or hired in the course of a business.

Index of defined expressions

A–267   **264.** The following Table shows provisions defining or otherwise explaining expressions used in this Part (other than provisions defining or explaining an expression used only in the same section)—

account of profits and accounts (in Scotland)	section 262
assignment (in Scotland)	section 262
British designs	section 263(1)
business	section 263(1)
commercial purposes	section 263(3)
commission	section 263(1)
the comptroller	section 263(1)
computer-generated	section 263(1)
costs (in Scotland)	section 262

country	section 263(1)
the Crown	section 263(1)
Crown use	sections 240(5) and 244(2)
defendant (in Scotland)	section 262
delivery up (in Scotland)	section 262
design	section 213(2)
design document	section 263(1)
designer	sections 214 and 259(2)
design right	section 213(1)
design right owner	sections 234(2) and 258
employee, employment and employer	section 263(1)
exclusive licence	section 225(1)
government department	section 263(1)
government department concerned (in relation to Crown use)	section 240(5)
infringing article	section 228
injunction (in Scotland)	section 262
interlocutory relief (in Scotland)	section 262
joint design	section 259(1)
licence (of the design right owner)	sections 222(4), 223(3) and 258
making articles to a design	section 226(2)
marketing (and related expressions)	section 263(2)
original	section 213(4)
plaintiff (in Scotland)	section 262
qualifying individual	section 217(1)
qualifying person	section 217(1) and (2)
signed	section 261

PART IV

REGISTERED DESIGNS

Amendments of the Registered Designs Act 1949

Registrable designs

265.—(1) For section 1 of the Registered Designs Act 1949 (designs registrable under that Act) substitute—   **A–268**

"Designs registrable under Act

1.—(1) In this Act 'design' means features of shape, configuration, pattern or ornament applied to an article by any industrial process, being features which in the finished article appeal to and are judged by the eye, but does not include—
(a) a method or principle of construction, or
(b) features of shape or configuration of an article which—
    (i) are dictated solely by the function which the article has to perform, or
    (ii) are dependent upon the appearance of another article of which the article is intended by the author of the design to form an integral part.
(2) A design which is new may, upon application by the person claiming to be the proprietor, be registered under this Act in respect of any article, or set of articles, specified in the application.
(3) A design shall not be registered in respect of an article if the appearance of the article is not material, that is, if aesthetic considerations are not normally taken into account to a material extent by persons acquiring or using articles of

that description, and would not be so taken into account if the design were to be applied to the article.

(4) A design shall not be regarded as new for the purposes of this Act if it is the same as a design—

(a) registered in respect of the same or any other article in pursuance of a prior application, or

(b) published in the United Kingdom in respect of the same or any other article before the date of the application,

or if it differs from such a design only in immaterial details or in features which are variants commonly used in the trade.

This subsection has effect subject to the provisions of sections 4, 6 and 16 of this Act.

(5) The Secretary of State may by rules provide for excluding from registration under this Act designs for such articles of a primarily literary or artistic character as the Secretary of State thinks fit.''.

(2) The above amendment does not apply in relation to applications for registration made before the commencement of this Part; but the provisions of section 266 apply with respect to the right in certain designs registered in pursuance of such an application.

Provisions with respect to certain designs registered in pursuance of application made before commencement

A–269   **266.**—(1) Where a design is registered under the Registered Designs Act 1949 in pursuance of an application made after 12th January 1988 and before the commencement of this Part which could not have been registered under section 1 of that Act as substituted by section 265 above—

(a) the right in the registered design expires ten years after the commencement of this Part, if it does not expire earlier in accordance with the 1949 Act, and

(b) any person is, after the commencement of this Part, entitled as of right to a licence to do anything which would otherwise infringe the right in the registered design.

(2) The terms of a licence available by virtue of this section shall, in default of agreement, be settled by the registrar on an application by the person requiring the licence; and the terms so settled shall authorise the licensee to do everything which would be an infringement of the right in the registered design in the absence of a licence.

(3) In settling the terms of a licence the registrar shall have regard to such factors as may be prescribed by the Secretary of State by order made by statutory instrument.

No such order shall be made unless a draft of it has been laid before and approved by a resolution of each House of Parliament.

(4) Where the terms of a licence are settled by the registrar, the licence has effect from the date on which the application to the registrar was made.

(5) Section 11B of the 1949 Act (undertaking to take licence of right in infringement proceedings), as inserted by section 270 below, applies where a licence is available as of right under this section, as it applies where a licence is available as of right under section 11A of that Act.

(6) Where a licence is available as of right under this section, a person to whom the licence was granted before the commencement of this Part may apply to the registrar for an order adjusting the terms of that licence.

(7) An appeal lies from any decision of the registrar under this section.

(8) This section shall be construed as one with the Registered Designs Act 1949.

Authorship and first ownership of designs

267.—(1) Section 2 of the Registered Designs Act 1949 (proprietorship of **A–270** designs) is amended as follows:

(2) For subsection (1) substitute—

"(1) The author of a design shall be treated for the purposes of this Act as the original proprietor of the design, subject to the following provisions.

(1A) Where a design is created in pursuance of a commission for money or money's worth, the person commissioning the design shall be treated as the original proprietor of the design.

(1B) Where, in a case not falling within subsection (1A), a design is created by an employee in the course of his employment, his employer shall be treated as the original proprietor of the design.".

(3) After subsection (2) insert—

"(3) In this Act the 'author' of a design means the person who creates it.

(4) In the case of a design generated by computer in circumstances such that there is no human author, the person by whom the arrangements necessary for the creation of the design are made shall be taken to be the author.".

(4) The amendments made by this section do not apply in relation to an application for registration made before the commencement of this Part.

Right given by registration of design

268.—(1) For section 7 of the Registered Designs Act 1949 (right given by regis- **A–271** tration) substitute—

"Right given by registration

7.—(1) The registration of a design under this Act gives the registered proprietor the exclusive right—
(a) to make or import—
    (i) for sale or hire, or
    (ii) for use for the purposes of a trade or business, or
(b) to sell, hire or offer or expose for sale or hire,
    an article in respect of which the design is registered and to which that design or a design not substantially different from it has been applied.

(2) The right in the registered design is infringed by a person who without the licence of the registered proprietor does anything which by virtue of subsection (1) is the exclusive right of the proprietor.

(3) The right in the registered design is also infringed by a person who without the licence of the registered proprietor makes anything for enabling any such article to be made, in the United Kingdom or elsewhere, as mentioned in subsection (1).

(4) The right in the registered design is also infringed by a person who without the licence of the registered proprietor—
(a) does anything in relation to a kit that would be an infringement if done in relation to the assembled article (see subsection (1)), or
(b) makes anything for enabling a kit to be made or assembled, in the United Kingdom or elsewhere, if the assembled article would be such an article as is mentioned in subsection (1);
    and for this purpose a 'kit' means a complete or substantially complete set of components intended to be assembled into an article.

(5) No proceedings shall be taken in respect of an infringement committed before the date on which the certificate of registration of the design under this Act is granted.

(6) The right in a registered design is not infringed by the reproduction of a feature of the design which, by virtue of section 1(1)(b), is left out of account in determining whether the design is registrable.".

(2) The above amendment does not apply in relation to a design registered in pursuance of an application made before the commencement of this Part.

Duration of right in registered design

269.—(1) For section 8 of the Registered Designs Act 1949 (period of right) substitute—

"Duration of right in registered design

8.—(1) The right in a registered design subsists in the first instance for a period of five years from the date of the registration of the design.

(2) The period for which the right subsists may be extended for a second, third, fourth and fifth period of five years, by applying to the registrar for an extension and paying the prescribed renewal fee.

(3) If the first, second, third or fourth period expires without such application and payment being made, the right shall cease to have effect; and the registrar shall, in accordance with rules made by the Secretary of State, notify the proprietor of that fact.

(4) If during the period of six months immediately following the end of that period an application for extension is made and the prescribed renewal fee and any prescribed additional fee is paid, the right shall be treated as if it had never expired, with the result that—

(a) anything done under or in relation to the right during that further period shall be treated as valid,

(b) an act which would have constituted an infringement of the right if it had not expired shall be treated as an infringement, and

(c) an act which would have constituted use of the design for the services of the Crown if the right had not expired shall be treated as such use.

(5) Where it is shown that a registered design—

(a) was at the time it was registered a corresponding design in relation to an artistic work in which copyright subsists, and

(b) by reason of a previous use of that work would not have been registrable but for section 6(4) of this Act (registration despite certain prior applications of design),

the right in the registered design expires when the copyright in that work expires, if that is earlier than the time at which it would otherwise expire, and it may not thereafter be renewed.

(6) The above provisions have effect subject to the proviso to section 4(1) (registration of same design in respect of other articles, &c.)

Restoration of lapsed right in design

8A.—(1) Where the right in a registered design has expired by reason of a failure to extend, in accordance with section 8(2) or (4), the period for which the right subsists, an application for the restoration of the right in the design may be made to the registrar within the prescribed period.

(2) The application may be made by the person who was the registered proprietor of the design or by any other person who would have been entitled to the right in the design if it had not expired; and where the design was held by two or more persons jointly, the application may, with the leave of the registrar, be made by one or more of them without joining the others.

(3) Notice of the application shall be published by the registrar in the prescribed manner.

(4) If the registrar is satisfied that the proprietor took reasonable care to see that the period for which the right subsisted was extended in accordance with section 8(2) or (4), he shall, on payment of any unpaid renewal fee and any prescribed additional fee, order the restoration of the right in the design.

(5) The order may be made subject to such conditions as the registrar thinks fit, and if the proprietor of the design does not comply with any condition the registrar may revoke the order and give such consequential directions as he thinks fit.

(6) Rules altering the period prescribed for the purposes of subsection (1) may contain such transitional provisions and savings as appear to the Secretary of State to be necessary or expedient.

Effect of order for restoration of right

8B.—(1) The effect of an order under section 8A for the restoration of the right in a registered design is as follows.

(2) Anything done under or in relation to the right during the period between expiry and restoration shall be treated as valid.

(3) Anything done during that period which would have constituted an infringement if the right had not expired shall be treated as an infringement—
(a) if done at a time when it was possible for an application for extension to be made under section 8(4); or
(b) if it was a continuation or repetition of an earlier infringing act.

(4) If, after it was no longer possible for such an application for extension to be made and before publication of notice of the application for restoration, a person—
(a) began in good faith to do an act which would have constituted an infringement of the right in the design if it had not expired, or
(b) made in good faith effective and serious preparations to do such an act,
he has the right to continue to do the act or, as the case may be, to do the act, notwithstanding the restoration of the right in the design; but this does not extend to granting a licence to another person to do the act.

(5) If the act was done, or the preparations were made, in the course of a business, the person entitled to the right conferred by subsection (4) may—
(a) authorise the doing of that act by any partners of his for the time being in that business, and
(b) assign that right, or transmit it on death (or in the case of a body corporate on its dissolution), to any person who acquires that part of the business in the course of which the act was done or the preparations were made.

(6) Where an article is disposed of to another in exercise of the rights conferred by subsection (4) or subsection (5), that other and any person claiming through him may deal with the article in the same way as if it had been disposed of by the registered proprietor of the design.

(7) The above provisions apply in relation to the use of a registered design for the services of the Crown as they apply in relation to infringment of the right in the design.".

(2) The above amendment does not apply in relation to the right in a design registered in pursuance of an application made before the commencement of this Part.

Powers exercisable for protection of the public interest

270. In the Registered Designs Act 1949 after section 11 insert— **A–273**

"Powers exercisable for protection of the public interest

11A.—(1) Where a report of the Monopolies and Mergers Commission has been laid before Parliament containing conclusions to the effect—

(a) on a monopoly reference, that a monopoly situation exists and facts found by the Commission operate or may be expected to operate against the public interest,

(b) on a merger reference, that a merger situation qualifying for investigation has been created and the creation of the situation, or particular elements in or consequences of it specified in the report, operate or may be expected to operate against the public interest,

(c) on a competition reference, that a person was engaged in an anti-competitive practice which operated or may be expected to operate against the public interest, or

(d) on a reference under section 11 of the Competition Act 1980 (reference of public bodies and certain other persons), that a person is pursuing a course of conduct which operates against the public interest,

the appropriate Minister or Ministers may apply to the registrar to take action under this section.

(2) Before making an application the appropriate Minister or Ministers shall publish, in such a manner as he or they think appropriate, a notice describing the nature of the proposed application and shall consider any representations which may be made within 30 days of such publication by persons whose interests appear to him or them to be affected.

(3) If on an application under this section it appears to the registrar that the matters specified in the Commission's report as being those which in the Commission's opinion operate or operated or may be expected to operate against the public interest include—

(a) conditions in licences granted in respect of a registered design by its proprietor restricting the use of the design by the licensee or the right of the proprietor to grant other licences, or

(b) a refusal by the proprietor of a registered design to grant licences on reasonable terms,

he may by order cancel or modify any such condition or may, instead or in addition, make an entry in the register to the effect that licences in respect of the design are to be available as of right.

(4) The terms of a licence available by virtue of this section shall, in default of agreement, be settled by the registrar on an application by the person requiring the licence; and terms so settled shall authorise the licensee to do everything which would be an infringement of the right in the registered design in the absence of a licence.

(5) Where the terms of a licence are settled by the registrar the licence has effect from the date on which the application to him was made.

(6) An appeal lies from any order of the registrar under this section.

(7) In this section 'the appropriate Minister or Ministers' means the Minister or Ministers to whom the report of the Monopolies and Mergers Commission was made.

Undertaking to take licence of right in infringement proceedings

11B.—(1) If in proceedings for infringement of the right in a registered design in respect of which a licence is available as of right under section 11A of this Act the defendant undertakes to take a licence on such terms as may be agreed or, in default of agreement, settled by the registrar under that section—

(a) no injunction shall be granted against him, and

(b) the amount recoverable against him by way of damages or on an account of profits shall not exceed double the amount which would have been payable by him as licensee if such a licence on those terms had been granted before the earliest infringement.

(2) An undertaking may be given at any time before final order in the proceedings, without any admission of liability.

(3) Nothing in this section affects the remedies available in respect of an infringement committed before licences of right were available.".

Crown use: compensation for loss of profit

271.—(1) In Schedule 1 to the Registered Designs Act 1949 (Crown use), after **A-274** paragraph 2 insert—

"Compensation for loss of profit

2A.—(1) Where Crown use is made of a registered design, the government department concerned shall pay—
(a) to the registered proprietor, or
(b) if there is an exclusive licence in force in respect of the design, to the exclusive licensee,
   compensation for any loss resulting from his not being awarded a contract to supply the articles to which the design is applied.

(2) Compensation is payable only to the extent that such a contract could have been fulfilled from his existing manufacturing capacity; but is payable notwithstanding the existence of circumstances rendering him ineligible for the award of such a contract.

(3) In determining the loss, regard shall be had to the profit which would have been made on such a contract and to the extent to which any manufacturing capacity was underused.

(4) No compensation is payable in respect of any failure to secure contracts for the supply of articles to which the design is applied otherwise than for the services of the Crown.

(5) The amount payable under this paragraph shall, if not agreed between the registered proprietor or licensee and the government department concerned with the approval of the Treasury, be determined by the court on a reference under paragraph 3; and it is in addition to any amount payable under paragraph 1 or 2 of this Schedule.

(6) In this paragraph—
'Crown use', in relation to a design, means the doing of anything by virtue of paragraph 1 which would otherwise be an infringement of the right in the design; and

'the government department concerned', in relation to such use, means the government department by whom or on whose authority the act was done.".

(2) In paragraph 3 of that Schedule (reference of disputes as to Crown use), for sub-paragraph (1) substitute—

"(1) Any dispute as to—
   (a) the exercise by a Government department, or a person authorised by a Government department, of the powers conferred by paragraph 1 of this Schedule,
   (b) terms of the use of a design for the services of the Crown under that paragraph,
   (c) the right of any person to receive any part of a payment made under paragraph 1(3), or
   (d) the right of any person to receive a payment under paragraph 2A,
   may be referred to the court by either party to the dispute.".

(3) The above amendments apply in relation to any Crown use of a registered

design after the commencement of this section, even if the terms for such use were settled before commencement.

Minor and consequential amendments

A–275   **272.** The Registered Design Act 1949 is further amended in accordance with Schedule 3 which contains minor amendments and amendments consequential upon the provisions of this Act.

Supplementary

Text of Registered Designs Act 1949 as amended

A–276   **273.** Schedule 4 contains the text of the Registered Designs Act 1949 as amended.

PART V

[SECTIONS 274—286 RELATE TO PATENT AGENTS AND TRADE MARK AGENTS]

PART VI

PATENTS

Patents county courts

Patents county courts: special jurisdiction

A–277   **287.**—(1) The Lord Chancellor may by order made by statutory instrument designate any county court as a patents county court and confer on it jurisdiction (its "special jurisdiction") to hear and determine such descriptions of proceedings—

    (*a*) relating to patents or designs, or

    (*b*) ancillary to, or arising out of the same subject-matter as, proceedings relating to patents or designs,

as may be specified in the order.

(2) The special jurisdiction of a patents county court is exercisable throughout England and Wales, but rules of court may provide for a matter pending in one such court to be heard and determined in another or partly in that and partly in another.

(3) A patents county court may entertain proceedings within its special jurisdiction notwithstanding that no pecuniary remedy is sought.

(4) An order under this section providing for the discontinuance of any of the special jurisdiction of a patents county court may make provision as to proceedings pending in the court when the order comes into operation.

(5) Nothing in this section shall be construed as affecting the ordinary jurisdiction of a county court.

Financial limits in relation to proceedings within special jurisdiction of patents county court

288.—(1) Her Majesty may by Order in Council provide for limits of amount or value in relation to any description of proceedings within the special jurisdiction of a patents county court.   **A–278**

(2) If a limit is imposed on the amount of a claim of any description and the plaintiff has a cause of action for more than that amount, he may abandon the excess; in which case a patents county court shall have jurisdiction to hear and determine the action, but the plaintiff may not recover more than that amount.

(3) Where the court has jurisdiction to hear and determine an action by virtue of subsection (2), the judgment of the court in the action is in full discharge of all demands in respect of the cause of action, and entry of the judgment shall be made accordingly.

(4) If the parties agree, by a memorandum signed by them or by their respective solicitors or other agents, that a patents county court shall have jurisdiction in any proceedings, that court shall have jurisdiction to hear and determine the proceedings notwithstanding any limit imposed under this section.

(5) No recommendation shall be made to Her Majesty to make an Order under this section unless a draft of the Order has been laid before and approved by a resolution of each House of Parliament.

Transfer of proceedings between High Court and patents county court

289.—(1) No order shall be made under section 41 of the County Courts Act 1984 (power of High Court to order proceedings to be transferred from the county court) in respect of proceedings within the special jurisdiction of a patents county court.   **A–279**

(2) In considering in relation to proceedings within the special jurisdiction of a patents county court whether an order should be made under section 40 or 42 of the County Courts Act 1984 (transfer of proceedings from or to the High Court), the court shall have regard to the financial position of the parties and may order the transfer of the proceedings to a patents county court or, as the case may be, refrain from ordering their transfer to the High Court notwithstanding that the proceedings are likely to raise an important question of fact or law.

Limitation of costs where pecuniary claim could have been brought in patents county court

290.—(1) Where an action is commenced in the High Court which could have been commenced in a patents county court and in which a claim for a pecuniary remedy is made, then, subject to the provisions of this section, if the plaintiff recovers less than the prescribed amount, he is not entitled to recover any more costs than those to which he would have been entitled if the action had been brought in the county court.   **A–280**

(2) For this purpose a plaintiff shall be treated as recovering the full amount recoverable in respect of his claim without regard to any deduction made in respect of matters not falling to be taken into account in determining whether the action could have been commenced in a patents county court.

(3) This section does not affect any question as to costs if it appears to the High Court that there was reasonable ground for supposing the amount recoverable in respect of the plaintiff's claim to be in excess of the prescribed amount.

(4) The High Court, if satisfied that there was sufficient reason for bringing the action in the High Court, may make an order allowing the costs or any part of the costs on the High Court scale or on such one of the county court scales as it may direct.

(5) This section does not apply to proceedings brought by the Crown.

(6) In this section "the prescribed amount" means such amount as may be prescribed by Her Majesty for the purposes of this section by Order in Council.

(7) No recommendation shall be made to Her Majesty to make an Order under this section unless a draft of the Order has been laid before and approved by a resolution of each House of Parliament.

Proceedings in patents county court

A–281   **291.**—(1) Where a county court is designated a patents county court, the Lord Chancellor shall nominate a person entitled to sit as a judge of that court as the patents judge.

(2) County court rules shall make provision for securing that, so far as is practicable and appropriate—

　　(*a*) proceedings within the special jurisdiction of a patents county court are dealt with by the patents judge, and

　　(*b*) the judge, rather than a registrar or other officer of the court, deals with interlocutory matters in the proceedings.

(3) County court rules shall make provision empowerng a patents county court in proceedings within its special jurisdiction, on or without the application of any party—

　　(*a*) to appoint scientific advisers or assessors to assist the court, or

　　(*b*) to order the Patent Office to inquire into and report on any question of fact or opinion.

(4) Where the court exercises either of those powers on the application of a party, the remuneration of fees payable to the Patent Office shall be at such rate as may be determined in accordance with county court rules and shall be costs of the proceedings unless otherwise ordered by the judge.

(5) Where the court exercises either of those powers of its own motion, the remuneration or fees payable to the Patent Office shall be at such rate as may be determined by the Lord Chancellor with the approval of the Treasury and shall be paid out of money provided by Parliament.

Rights and duties of registered patent agents in relation to proceedings in patents county court

A–282   **292.**—(1) A registered patent agent may do, in or in connection with proceedings in a patents county court which are within the special jurisdiction of that court, anything which a solicitor of the Supreme Court might do, other than prepare a deed.

(2) The Lord Chancellor may by regulations provide that the right conferred by subsection (1) shall be subject to such conditions and restrictions as appear to the Lord Chancellor to be necessary or expedient; and different provision may be made for different descriptions of proceedings.

(3) A patents county court has the same power to enforce an undertaking given by a registered patent agent acting in pursuance of this section as it has, by virtue of section 142 of the County Courts Act 1984, in relation to a solicitor.

(4) Nothing in section 143 of the County Courts Act 1984 (prohibition on persons other than solicitors receiving remuneration) applies to a registered patent agent acting in pursuance of this section.

(5) The provisions of county court rules prescribing scales of costs to be paid to solicitors apply in relation to registered patent agents acting in pursuance of this section.

(6) Regulations under this section shall be made by statutory instrument which shall be subject to annulment in pursuance of a resolution of either House of Parliament.

PART VII

MISCELLANEOUS AND GENERAL

Devices designed to circumvent copy-protection

Devices designed to circumvent copy-protection

296.—(1) This section applies where copies of a copyright work are issued to   **A–283**
the public, by or with the licence of the copyright owner, in an electronic form
which is copy-protected.

(2) The person issuing the copies to the public has the same rights against a person who, knowing or having reason to believe that it will be used to make infringing copies—

  (a) makes, imports, sells or lets for hire, offers or exposes for sale or hire, or
      advertises for sale or hire, any device or means specifically designed or
      adapted to circumvent the form of copy-protection employed, or

  (b) publishes information intended to enable or assist persons to circumvent
      that form of copy-protection,

as a copyright owner has in respect of an infringement of copyright.

(3) Further, he has the same rights under section 99 or 100 (delivery up or seizure of certain articles) in relation to any such device or means which a person has
in his possession, custody or control with the intention that it should be used to
make infringing copies of copyright works, as a copyright owner has in relation to
an infringing copy.

(4) References in this section to copy-protection include any device or means
intended to prevent or restrict copying of a work or to impair the quality of copies
made.

(5) Expressions used in this section which are defined for the purposes of Part I
of this Act (copyright) have the same meaning as in that Part.

(6) The following provisions apply in relation to proceedings under this section
as in relation to proceedings under Part I (copyright)—

  (a) sections 104 to 106 of this Act (presumptions as to certain matters relating
      to copyright), and

  (b) section 72 of the Supreme Court Act 1981, section 15 of the Law Reform
      (Miscellaneous Provisions) (Scotland) Act 1985 and section 94A of the
      Judicature (Northern Ireland) Act 1978 (withdrawal of privilege against
      self-incrimination in certain proceedings relating to intellectual property);

and section 114 of this Act applies, with the necessary modifications, in relation to
the disposal of anything delivered up or seized by virtue of subsection (3) above.

Fraudulent reception of transmissions

Offence of fraudulently receiving programmes

297.—(1) A person who dishonestly receives a programme included in a broad-   **A–284**
casting or cable programme service provided from a place in the United Kingdom
with intent to avoid payment of any charge applicable to the reception of the programme commits an offence and is liable on summary conviction to a fine not
exceeding level 5 on the standard scale.

(2) Where an offence under this section committed by a body corporate is

977

proved to have been committed with the consent or connivance of a director, manager, secretary or other similar officer of the body, or a person purporting to act in any such capacity, he as well as the body corporate is guilty of the offence and liable to be proceeded against and published accordingly.

In relation to a body corporate whose affairs are managed by its members "director" means a member of the body corporate.

[Unauthorised decoders

A–284A   **297A.**—(1) A person who makes, imports, sells or lets for hire any unauthorised decoder shall be guilty of an offence and liable on summary conviction to a fine not exceeding level 5 on the standard scale.

(2) It is a defence to any prosecution for an offence under this section for the defendant to prove that he did not know, and had no reasonable ground for knowing, that the decoder was an unauthorised decoder.

(3) In this section—

"apparatus" includes any device, component or electronic data;

"decoder" means any apparatus which is designed or adapted to enable (whether on its own or with any other apparatus) an encrypted transmission to be decoded;

"transmission" means any programme included in a broadcasting or cable programme service which is provided from a place in the United Kingdom; and

"unauthorised", in relation to a decoder, means a decoder which will enable encrypted transmissions to be viewed in decoded form without payment of the fee (however imposed) which the person making the transmission, or on whose behalf it is made, charges for viewing those transmissions, or viewing any service of which they form part.]

Note: Section 297A was inserted in the 1988 Act by section 179 of the Broadcasting Act 1990 (c.42) as provided by The Broadcasting Act 1990 (Commencement No. 1 and Transitional Provisions) Order 1990 (S.I. 1990 No. 2347 (c.61)) § B–254 *post*.

Rights and remedies in respect of apparatus, &c. for unauthorised reception of transmissions

A–285   **298.**—(1) A person who—
  (a) makes charges for the reception of programmes included in a broadcasting or cable programme service provided from a place in the United Kingdom, or
  (b) sends encrypted transmissions of any other description from a place in the United Kingdom,
is entitled to the following rights and remedies.

(2) He has the same rights and remedies against a person who—
  (a) makes, imports or sells or lets for hire any apparatus or device designed or adapted to enable or assist persons to receive the programmes or other transmissions when they are not entitled to do so, or
  (b) publishes any information which is calculated to enable or assist persons to receive the programmes or other transmissions when they are not entitled to do so,
as a copyright owner has in respect of an infringement of copyright.

(3) Further, he has the same rights under section 99 or 100 (delivery up or seizure of certain articles) in relation to any such apparatus or device as a copyright owner has in relation to an infringing copy.

(4) Section 72 of the Supreme Court Act 1981, section 15 of the Law Reform (Miscellaneous Provisions) (Scotland) Act 1985 and section 94A of the Judicature (Northern Ireland) Act 1978 (withdrawal of privilege against self-incrimination in certain proceedings relating to intellectual property) apply to proceedings under this section as to proceedings under Part I of this Act (copyright).

(5) In section 97(1) (innocent infringement of copyright) as it applies to proceedings for infringement of the rights conferred by this section, the reference to the defendant not knowing or having reason to believe that copyright subsisted in the work shall be construed as a reference to his not knowing or having reason to believe that his acts infringed the rights conferred by this section.

(6) Section 114 of this Act applies, with the necessary modifications, in relation to the disposal of anything delivered up or seized by virtue of subsection (3) above.

Supplementary provisions as to fraudulent reception

299.—(1) Her Majesty may by Order in Council—   **A–286**
  (*a*) provide that section 297 applies in relation to programmes included in services provided from a country or territory outside the United Kingdom, and
  (*b*) provide that section 298 applies in relation to such programmes and to encrypted transmissions sent from such a country or territory.

[*(2) No such Order shall be made unless it appears to Her Majesty that provision has been or will be made under the laws of that country or territory giving adequate protection to persons making charges for programmes included in broadcasting or cable programme services provided from the United Kingdom or, as the case may be, for encrypted transmissions sent from the United Kingdom.*]

(3) A statutory instrument containing an Order in Council under subsection (1) shall be subject to annulment in pursuance of a resolution of either House of Parliament.

(4) Where sections 297 and 298 apply in relation to a broadcasting service or cable programme service, they also apply to any service run for the person providing that service, or a person providing programmes for that service, which consists wholly or mainly in the sending by means of a telecommunications system of sounds or visual images, or both.

(5) In sections 297 [, 297A] and 298, and this section, "programme", "broadcasting" and "cable programme service", and related expressions, have the same meaning as in Part I (copyright).

Note: Subsection (2) was repealed by sections 179(2) and 203(3) of and Schedule 21 to the Broadcasting Act 1990 (c.42), and the words in square brackets subsection (5) were inserted by section 179(2) of that Act, as provided by The Broadcasting Act 1990 (Commencement No.1 and Transitional Provisions) Order 1990 (S.I. 1990 No. 2347 (c.61)) § B–254 *post*.

[Section 300 Relates to Fraudulent Application or use of Trade Mark]

Provisions for the benefit of the Hospital for Sick Children

Provisions for the benefit of the Hospital for Sick Children

301. The provisions of Schedule 6 have effect for conferring on trustees for the   **A–287**
benefit of the Hospital for Sick Children, Great Ormond Street, London, a right to a royalty in respect of the public performance, commercial publication, broadcasting or inclusion in a cable programme service of the play "Peter Pan" by Sir James Matthew Barrie, or of any adaptation of that work, notwithstanding that copyright in the work expired on December 31, 1987.

Financial assistance for certain international bodies

A–288   **302.**—(1) The Secretary of State may give financial assistance, in the form of grants, loans or guarantees to—

(a) any international organisation having functions relating to trade marks or other intellectual property, or

(b) any Community institution or other body established under any of the Community Treaties having any such functions,

with a view to the establishment or maintenance by that organisation, institution or body of premises in the United Kingdom.

(2) Any expenditure of the Secretary of State under this section shall be defrayed out of money provided by Parliament; and any sums received by the Secretary of State in consequence of this section shall be paid into the Consolidated Fund.

General

Consequential amendments and repeals

A–289   **303.**—(1) The enactments specified in Schedule 7 are amended in accordance with that Schedule, the amendments being consequential on the provisions of this Act.

(2) The enactments specified in Schedule 8 are repealed to the extent specified.

Extent

A–290   **304.**—(1) Provision as to the extent of Part I (copyright), Part II (rights in performances) and Part III (design right) is to be found in sections 157, 207 and 255 respectively; the extent of the other provisions of this Act is as follows.

(2) Parts IV to VII extend to England and Wales, Scotland and Northern Ireland, except that—

(a) sections 287 to 292 (patents county courts) extend to England and Wales only,

(b) the proper law of the trust created by Schedule 6 (provisions for the benefit of the Hospital for Sick Children) is the law of England and Wales, and

(c) the amendments and repeals in Schedules 7 and 8 have the same extent as the enactments amended or repealed.

(3) The following provisions extend to the Isle of Man subject to any modifications contained in an Order made by Her Majesty in Council—

(a) sections 293 and 294 (patents: licences of right), and

(b) paragraphs 24 and 29 of Schedule 5 (patents: effect of filing international application for patent and power to extend time limits).

(4) Her Majesty may by Order in Council direct that the following provisions extend to the Isle of Man, with such exceptions and modifications as may be specified in the Order—

(a) Part IV (registered designs),

(b) Part V (patent agents),

(c) the provisions of Schedule 5 (patents: miscellaneous amendments) not mentioned in subsection (3) above,

(d) sections 297 to 299 (fraudulent reception of transmissions), and

(e) section 300 (fraudulent application or use of trade mark).

(5) Her Majesty may by Order in Council direct that sections 297 to 299

(fraudulent reception of transmissions) extend to any of the Channel Islands, with such exceptions and modifications as may be specified in the Order.

(6) Any power conferred by this Act to make provision by Order in Council for or in connection with the extent of provisions of this Act to a country outside the United Kingdom includes power to extend to that country, subject to any modifications specified in the Order, any provision of this Act which amends or repeals an enactment extending to that country.

Commencement

305.—(1) The following provisions of this Act come into force on Royal **A–291** Assent—

paragraphs 24 and 29 of Schedule 5 (patents: effect of filing international application for patent and power to extend time limits);

section 301 and Schedule 6 (provisions for the benefit of the Hospital for Sick Children).

(2) Sections 293 and 294 (licences of right) come into force at the end of the period of two months beginning with the passing of this Act.

(3) The other provisions of this Act come into force on such day as the Secretary of State may appoint by order made by statutory instrument, and different days may be appointed for different provisions and different purposes.

Short title

306. This Act may be cited as the Copyright, Designs and Patents Act 1988. **A–292**

SCHEDULES

SCHEDULE 1

Section 170.

COPYRIGHT: TRANSITIONAL PROVISIONS AND SAVINGS

Introductory

1.—(1) In this Schedule— **A–293**

"the 1911 Act" means the Copyright Act 1911,

"the 1956 Act" means the Copyright Act 1956, and

"the new copyright provisions" means the provisions of this Act relating to copyright, that is, Part I (including this Schedule) and Schedules 3, 7 and 8 so far as they make amendments or repeals consequential on the provisions of Part I.

(2) References in this Schedule to "commencement", without more, are to the date on which the new copyright provisions come into force.

(3) References in this Schedule to "existing works" are to works made before commencement; and for this purpose a work of which the making extended over a period shall be taken to have been made when its making was completed.

2.—(1) In relation to the 1956 Act, references in this Schedule to a work include any work or other subject-matter within the meaning of that Act.

(2) In relation to the 1911 Act—

(*a*) references in this Schedule to copyright include the right conferred by section 24 of that Act in substitution for a right subsisting immediately before the commencement of that Act;

(*b*) references in this Schedule to copyright in a sound recording are to the copyright under that Act in records embodying the recording; and

(*c*) references in this Schedule to copyright in a film are to any copyright under that Act in the film (so far as it constituted a dramatic work for the purposes of that Act) or in photographs forming part of the film.

General principles: continuity of the law

A–294   3. The new copyright provisions apply in relation to things existing at commencement as they apply in relation to things coming into existence after commencement, subject to any express provision to the contrary.

4.—(1) The provisions of this paragraph have effect for securing the continuity of the law so far as the new copyright provisions re-enact (with or without modification) earlier provisions.

(2) A reference in an enactment, instrument or other document to copyright, or to a work or other subject-matter in which copyright subsists, which apart from this Act would be construed as referring to copyright under the 1956 Act shall be construed, so far as may be required for continuing its effect, as being, or as the case may require, including, a reference to copyright under this Act or to works in which copyright subsists under this Act.

(3) Anything done (including subordinate legislation made), or having effect as done, under or for the purposes of a provision repealed by this Act has effect as if done under or for the purposes of the corresponding provision of the new copyright provisions.

(4) References (expressed or implied) in this Act or any other enactment, instrument or document to any of the new copyright provisions shall, so far as the context permits, be construed as including, in relation to times, circumstances and purposes before commencement, a reference to corresponding earlier provisions.

(5) A reference (express or implied) in an enactment, instrument or other document to a provision repealed by this Act shall be construed, so far as may be required for continuing its effect, as a reference to the corresponding provision of this Act.

(6) The provisions of this paragraph have effect subject to any specific transitional provision or saving and to any express amendment made by this Act.

Subsistence of copyright

A–295   5.—(1) Copyright subsists in an existing work after commencement only if copyright subsisted in it immediately before commencement.

(2) Sub-paragraph (1) does not prevent an existing work qualifying for copyright protection after commencement—

(*a*) under section 155 (qualification by virtue of first publication), or

(*b*) by virtue of an Order under section 159 (application of Part I to countries to which it does not extend).

6.—(1) Copyright shall not subsist by virtue of this Act in an artistic work made before June 1, 1957 which at the time when the work was made constituted a design capable of registration under the Registered Designs Act 1949 or under the enactments repealed by that Act, and was used, or intended to be used, as a model or pattern to be multiplied by an industrial process.

(2) For this purpose a design shall be deemed to be used as a model or pattern to be multiplied by any industrial process—

(*a*) when the design is reproduced or is intended to be reproduced on more than 50 single articles, unless all the articles in which the design is reproduced or is intended to be reproduced together form only a single set of articles as defined in section 44(1) of the Registered Designs Act 1949, or

(*b*) when the design is to be applied to—
  (i) printed paper hangings,
  (ii) carpets, floor cloths or oil cloths, manufactured or sold in lengths or pieces,
  (iii) textile piece goods, or textile goods manufactured or sold in lengths or pieces, or
  (iv) lace, not made by hand.

7.—(1) No copyright subsists in a film, as such, made before June 1, 1957.

(2) Where a film made before that date was an original dramatic work within the meaning of the 1911 Act, the new copyright provisions have effect in relation to the film as if it was an original dramatic work within the meaning of Part I.

(3) The new copyright provisions have effect in relation to photographs forming part of a film made before June 1, 1957 as they have effect in relation to photographs not forming part of a film.

8.—(1) A film sound-track to which section 13(9) of the 1956 Act applied before commencement (film to be taken to include sounds in associated sound-track) shall be treated for the purposes of the new copyright provisions not as part of the film, but as a sound recording.

(2) However—
  (*a*) copyright subsists in the sound recording only if copyright subsisted in the film immediately before commencement, and it continues to subsist until copyright in the film expires;
  (*b*) the author and first owner of the copyright in the film shall be treated as having been author and first owner of the copyright in the sound recording; and
  (*c*) anything done before commencement under or in relation to the copyright in the film continues to have effect in relation to the sound recording as in relation to the film.

9. No copyright subsists in—
  (*a*) a broadcast made before 1st June 1957, or
  (*b*) a cable programme included in a cable programme service before 1st January 1985; and any such broadcast or cable programme shall be disregarded for the purposes of section 14(2) (duration of copyright in repeats).

Authorship of work

10. The question who was the author of an existing work shall be determined in accord- **A–296**
ance with the new copyright provisions for the purposes of the rights conferred by Chapter IV of Part I (moral rights), and for all other purposes shall be determined in accordance with the law in force at the time the work was made.

First ownership of copyright

11.—(1) The question who was first owner of copyright in an existing work shall be deter- **A–297**
mined in accordance with the law in force at the time the work was made.

(2) Where before commencement a person commissioned the making of a work in circumstances falling within—
  (*a*) section 4(3) of the 1956 Act or paragraph (*a*) of the proviso to section 5(1) of the 1911 Act (photographs, portraits and engravings), or
  (*b*) the proviso to section 12(4) of the 1956 Act (sound recordings),
those provisions apply to determine first ownership of copyright in any work made in pursuance of the commission after commencement.

Duration of copyright in existing works

12.—(1) The following provisions have effect with respect to the duration of copyright in **A–298**
existing works.

The question which provision applies to a work shall be determined by reference to the facts immediately before commencement; and expressions used in this paragraph which were defined for the purposes of the 1956 Act have the same meaning as in that Act.

(2) Copyright in the following descriptions of work continues to subsist until the date on which it would have expired under the 1956 Act—

   (*a*) literary, dramatic or musical works in relation to which the period of 50 years mentioned in the proviso to section 2(3) of the 1956 Act (duration of copyright in works made available to the public after the death of the author) has begun to run;

   (*b*) engravings in relation to which the period of 50 years mentioned in the proviso to section 3(4) of the 1956 Act (duration of copyright in works published after the death of the author) has begun to run;

   (*c*) published photographs and photographs taken before 1st June 1957;

   (*d*) published sound recordings and sound recordings made before 1st June 1957;

   (*e*) published films and films falling within section 13(3)(*a*) of the 1956 Act (films registered under former enactments relating to registration of films).

(3) Copyright in anonymous or pseudonymous literary, dramatic, musical or artistic works (other than photographs) continues to subsist—

   (*a*) if the work is published, until the date on which it would have expired in accordance with the 1956 Act, and

   (*b*) if the work is unpublished, until the end of the period of 50 years from the end of the calendar year in which the new copyright provisions come into force or, if during that period the work is first made available to the public within the meaning of section 12(2) (duration of copyright in works of unknown authorship), the date on which copyright expires in accordance with that provision;

unless, in any case, the identity of the author becomes known before that date, in which case section 12(1) applies (general rule: life of the author plus 50 years).

(4) Copyright in the following descriptions of work continues to subsist until the end of the period of 50 years from the end of the calendar year in which the new copyright provisions come into force—

   (*a*) literary, dramatic and musical works of which the author has died and in relation to which none of the acts mentioned in paragraphs (*a*) to (*e*) of the proviso to section 2(3) of the 1956 Act has been done;

   (*b*) unpublished engravings of which the author has died;

   (*c*) unpublished photographs taken on or after 1st June 1957.

(5) Copyright in the following descriptions of work continues to subsist until the end of the period of 50 years from the end of the calendar year in which the new copyright provisions come into force—

   (*a*) unpublished sound recordings made on or after 1st June 1957;

   (*b*) films not falling within sub-paragraph (2)(*e*) above,

unless the recording or film is published before the end of that period in which case copyright in it shall continue until the end of the period of 50 years from the end of the calendar year in which the recording or film is published.

(6) Copyright in any other description of existing work continues to subsist until the date on which copyright in that description of work expires in accordance with sections 12 to 15 of this Act.

(7) The above provisions do not apply to works subject to Crown or Parliamentary copyright (see paragraphs 41 to 43 below).

Perpetual copyright under the Copyright Act 1775

A–299   13.—(1) The rights conferred on universities and colleges by the Copyright Act 1775 shall continue to subsist until the end of the period of 50 years from the end of the calendar year in which the new copyright provisions come into force and shall then expire.

(2) The provisions of the following Chapters of Part I—

Chapter III (acts permitted in relation to copyright works),

984

Chapter VI (remedies for infringement),
Chapter VII (provisions with respect to copyright licensing), and
Chapter VIII (the Copyright Tribunal),
apply in relation to those rights as they apply in relation to copyright under this Act.

Acts infringing copyright

14.—(1) The provisions of Chapters II and III of Part I as to the acts constituting an **A–300** infringement of copyright apply only in relation to acts done after commencement; the provisions of the 1956 Act continue to apply in relation to acts done before commencement.

(2) So much of section 18(2) as extends the restricted act of issuing copies to the public to include the rental to the public of copies of sound recordings, films or computer programs does not apply in relation to a copy of a sound recording, film or computer program acquired by a person before commencement for the purpose of renting it to the public.

(3) For the purposes of section 27 (meaning of "infringing copy") the question whether the making of an article constituted an infringement of copyright, or would have done if the article had been made in the United Kingdom, shall be determined—

(*a*) in relation to an article made on or after 1st June 1957 and before commencement, by reference to the 1956 Act, and

(*b*) in relation to an article made before 1st June 1957, by reference to the 1911 Act.

(4) For the purposes of the application of sections 31(2), 51(2) and 62(3) (subsequent exploitation of things whose making was, by virtue of an earlier provision of the section, not an infringement of copyright) to things made before commencement, it shall be assumed that the new copyright provisions were in force at all material times.

(5) Section 55 (articles for producing material in a particular typeface) applies where articles have been marketed as mentioned in subsection (1) before commencement with the substitution for the period mentioned in subsection (2) of the period of 25 years from the end of the calendar year in which the new copyright provisions come into force.

(6) Section 56 (transfer of copies, adaptations, &c. of work in electronic form) does not apply in relation to a copy purchased before commencement.

(7) In section 65 (reconstruction of buildings) the reference to the owner of the copyright in the drawings or plans is, in relation to buildings constructed before commencement, to the person who at the time of the construction was the owner of the copyright in the drawings or plans under the 1956 Act, the 1911 Act or any enactment repealed by the 1911 Act.

15.—(1) Section 57 (anonymous or pseudonymous works: acts permitted on assumptions as to expiry of copyright or death of author) has effect in relation to existing works subject to the following provisions.

(2) Subsection (1)(*b*)(i) (assumption as to expiry of copyright) does not apply in relation to—

(*a*) photographs, or

(*b*) the rights mentioned in paragraph 13 above (rights conferred by the Copyright Act 1775).

(3) Subsection (1)(*b*)(ii) (assumption as to death of author) applies only—

(*a*) where paragraph 12(3)(*b*) above applies (unpublished anonymous or pseudonymous works), after the end of the period of 50 years from the end of the calendar year in which the new copyright provisions come into force, or

(*b*) where paragraph 12(6) above applies (cases in which the duration of copyright is the same under the new copyright provisions as under the previous law).

16. The following provisions of section 7 of the 1956 Act continue to apply in relation to existing works—

(*a*) subsection (6) (copying of unpublished works from manuscript or copy in library, museum or other institution);

(*b*) subsection (7) (publication of work containing material to which subsection (6) applies), except paragraph (*a*) (duty to give notice of intended publication);

(*c*) subsection (8) (subsequent broadcasting, performance, &c. of material published in accordance with subsection (7));

and subsection (9)(*d*) (illustrations) continues to apply for the purposes of those provisions.

17. Where in the case of a dramatic or musical work made before 1st July 1912, the right conferred by the 1911 Act did not include the sole right to perform the work in public, the acts restricted by the copyright shall be treated as not including—

(*a*) performing the work in public,

(*b*) broadcasting the work or including it in a cable programme service, or

(*c*) doing any of the above in relation to an adaptation of the work;

and where the right conferred by the 1911 Act consisted only of the sole right to perform the work in public, the acts restricted by the copyright shall be treated as consisting only of those acts.

18. Where a work made before 1st July 1912 consists of an essay, article or portion forming part of and first published in a review, magazine or other periodical or work of a like nature, the copyright is subject to any right of publishing the essay, article, or portion in a separate form to which the author was entitled at the commencement of the 1911 Act, or would if that Act had not been passed, have become entitled under section 18 of the Copyrght Act 1842.

Designs

A–301

19.—(1) Section 51 (exclusion of copyright protection in relation to works recorded or embodied in design document or models) does not apply for ten years after commencement in relation to a design recorded or embodied in a design document or model before commencement.

(2) During those ten years the following provisions of Part III (design right) apply to any relevant copyright as in relation to design right—

(*a*) sections 237 to 239 (availability of licences of right), and

(*b*) sections 247 and 248 (application to comptroller to settle terms of licence of right).

(3) In section 237 as it applies by virtue of this paragraph, for the reference in subsection (1) to the last five years of the design right term there shall be substituted a reference to the last five years of the period of ten years referred to in sub-paragraph (1) above, or to so much of those last five years during which copyright subsists.

(4) In section 239 as it applies by virtue of this paragraph, for the reference in subsection (1)(*b*) to section 230 there shall be substituted a reference to section 99.

(5) Where a licence of right is available by virtue of this paragraph, a person to whom a licence was granted before commencement may apply to the comptroller for an order adjusting the terms of that licence.

(6) The provisions of sections 249 and 250 (appeals and rules) apply in relation to proceedings brought under or by virtue of this paragraph as to proceedings under Part III.

(7) A licence granted by virtue of this paragraph shall relate only to acts which would be permitted by section 51 if the design document or model had been made after commencement.

(8) Section 100 (right to seize infringing copies, &c.) does not apply during the period of ten years referred to in sub-paragraph (1) in relation to anything to which it would not apply if the design in question had been first recorded or embodied in a design document or model after commencement.

(9) Nothing in this paragraph affects the operation of any rule of law preventing or restricting the enforcement of copyright in relation to a design.

20.—(1) Where section 10 of the 1956 Act (effect of industrial application of design corresponding to artistic work) applied in relation to an artistic work at any time before commencement, section 52(2) of this Act applies with the substitution for the period of 25 years mentioned there of the relevant period of 15 years as defined in section 10(3) of the 1956 Act.

(2) Except as provided in sub-paragraph (1), section 52 applies only where articles are marketed as mentioned in subsection (1)(*b*) after commencement.

Abolition of statutory recording licence

21. Section 8 of the 1956 Act (statutory licence to copy records sold by retail) continues to **A–302** apply where notice under subsection (1)(*b*) of that section was given before the repeal of that section by this Act, but only in respect of the making of records—

(*a*)　within one year of the repeal coming into force, and

(*b*)　up to the number stated in the notice as intended to be sold.

Moral rights

22.—(1) No act done before commencement is actionable by virtue of any provision of **A–303** Chapter IV of Part I (moral rights).

(2) Section 43 of the 1956 Act (false attribution of authorship) continues to apply in relation to acts done before commencement.

23.—(1) The following provisions have effect with respect to the rights conferred by—

(*a*)　section 77 (right to be identified as author or director), and

(*b*)　section 80 (right to object to derogatory treatment of work).

(2) The rights do not apply—

(*a*)　in relation to a literary, dramatic, musical and artistic work of which the author died before commencement; or

(*b*)　in relation to a film made before commencement.

(3) The rights in relation to an existing literary, dramatic, musical or artistic work do not apply—

(*a*)　where copyright first vested in the author, to anything which by virtue of an assignment of copyright made or licence granted before commencement may be done without infringing copyright;

(*b*)　where copyright first vested in a person other than the author, to anything done by or with the licence of the copyright owner.

(4) The rights do not apply to anything done in relation to a record made in pursuance of section 8 of the 1956 Act (statutory recording licence).

24. The right conferred by section 85 (right to privacy of certain photographs and films) does not apply to photographs taken or films made before commencement.

Assignments and licences

25.—(1) Any document made or event occurring before commencement which had any **A–304** operation—

(*a*)　affecting the ownership of the copyright in an existing work, or

(*b*)　creating, transferring or terminating an interest, right or licence in respect of the copyright in an existing work,

has the corresponding operation in relation to copyright in the work under this Act.

(2) Expressions used in such a document shall be construed in accordance with their effect immediately before commencement.

26.—(1) Section 91(1) of this Act (assignment of future copyright: statutory vesting of legal interest on copyright coming into existence) does not apply in relation to an agreement made before 1st June 1957.

(2) The repeal by this Act of section 37(2) of the 1956 Act (assignment of future copyright: devolution of right where assignee dies before copyright comes into existence) does not affect the operation of that provision in relation to an agreement made before commencement.

27.—(1) Where the author of a literary, dramatic, musical or artistic work was the first owner of the copyright in it, no assignment of the copyright and no grant of any interest in it, made by him (otherwise than by will) after the passing of the 1911 Act and before 1st June

1957, shall be operative to vest in the assignee or grantee any rights with respect to the copyright in the work beyond the expiration of 25 years from the death of the author.

(2) The reversionary interest in the copyright expectant on the termination of that period may after commencement be assigned by the author during his life but in the absence of any assignment shall, on his death, devolve on his legal personal representatives as part of his estate.

(3) Nothing in this paragraph affects—

(a) an assignment of the reversionary interest by a person to whom it has been assigned,

(b) an assignment of the reversionary interest after the death of the author by his personal representatives or any person becoming entitled to it, or

(c) any assignment of the copyright after the reversionary interest has fallen in.

(4) Nothing in this paragraph applies to the assignment of the copyright in a collective work or a licence to publish a work or part of a work as part of a collective work.

(5) In sub-paragraph (4) "collective work" means—

(a) any encyclopaedia, dictionary, yearbook, or similar work;

(b) a newspaper, review, magazine, or similar periodical; and

(c) any work written in distinct parts by different authors, or in which works or parts of works of different authors are incorporated.

28.—(1) This paragraph applies where copyright subsists in a literary, dramatic, musical or artistic work made before 1st July 1912 in relation to which the author, before the commencement of the 1911 Act, made such an assignment or grant as was mentioned in paragraph (a) of the proviso to section 24(1) of that Act (assignment or grant of copyright or performing right for full term of the right under the previous law).

(2) If before commencement any event has occurred or notice has been given which by virtue of paragraph 38 of Schedule 7 to the 1956 Act had any operation in relation to copyright in the work under that Act, the event or notice has the corresponding operation in relation to copyright under this Act.

(3) Any right which immediately before commencement would by virtue of paragraph 38(3) of that Schedule have been exercisable in relation to the work, or copyright in it, is exercisable in relation to the work or copyright in it under this Act.

(4) If in accordance with paragraph 38(4) of that Schedule copyright would, on a date after the commencement of the 1956 Act, have reverted to the author or his personal representatives and that date falls after the commencement of the new copyright provisions—

(a) the copyright in the work shall revert to the author or his personal representatives, as the case may be, and

(b) any interest of any other person in the copyright which subsists on that date by virtue of any document made before the commencement of the 1911 Act shall thereupon determine.

29. Section 92(2) of this Act (rights of exclusive licensee against successors in title of person granting licence) does not apply in relation to an exclusive licence granted before commencement.

Bequests

A–305   30.—(1) Section 93 of this Act (copyright to pass under will with original document or other material thing embodying unpublished work)—

(a) does not apply where the testator died before 1st June 1957, and

(b) where the testator died on or after that date and before commencement, applies only in relation to an original document embodying a work.

(2) In the case of an author who died before 1st June 1957, the ownership after his death of a manuscript of his, where such ownership has been acquired under a testamentary disposition made by him and the manuscript is of a work which has not been published or performed in public, is prima facie proof of the copyright being with the owner of the manuscript.

Remedies for infringement

31.—(1) Sections 96 and 97 of this Act (remedies for infringement) apply only in relation **A-306** to an infringement of copyright committed after commencement; section 17 of the 1956 Act continues to apply in relation to infringements committed before commencement.

(2) Sections 99 and 100 of this Act (delivery up or seizure of infringing copies, &c.) apply to infringing copies and other articles made before or after commencement; section 18 of the 1956 Act, and section 7 of the 1911 Act, (conversion damages, &c.), do not apply after commencement except for the purposes of proceedings begun before commencement.

(3) Sections 101 to 102 of this Act (rights and remedies of exclusive licensee) apply where sections 96 to 100 of this Act apply; section 19 of the 1956 Act continues to apply where section 17 or 18 of that Act applies.

(4) Sections 104 to 106 of this Act (presumptions) apply only in proceedings brought by virtue of this Act; section 20 of the 1956 Act continues to apply in proceedings brought by virtue of that Act.

32. Sections 101 and 102 of this Act (rights and remedies of exclusive licensee) do not apply to a licence granted before 1st June 1957.

33.—(1) The provisions of section 107 of this Act (criminal liability for making or dealing with infringing articles, &c.) apply only in relation to acts done after commencement; section 21 of the 1956 Act (penalties and summary proceedings in respect of dealings which infringe copyright) continues to apply in relation to acts done before commencement.

(2) Section 109 of this Act (search warrants) applies in relation to offences committed before commencement in relation to which section 21A or 21B of the 1956 Act applied; sections 21A and 21B continue to apply in relation to warrants issued before commencement.

Copyright Tribunal: proceedings pending on commencement

34.—(1) The Lord Chancellor may, after consultation with the Lord Advocate, by rules **A-307** make such provision as he considers necessary or expedient with respect to proceedings pending under Part IV of the 1956 Act immediately before commencement.

(2) Rules under this paragraph shall be made by statutory instrument which shall be subject to annulment in pursuance of a resolution of either House of Parliament.

Qualification for copyright protection

35. Every work in which copyright subsisted under the 1956 Act immediately before com- **A-308** mencement shall be deemed to satisfy the requirements of Part I of this Act as to qualification for copyright protection.

Dependent territories

36.—(1) The 1911 Act shall remain in force as part of the law of any dependent territory in **A-309** which it was in force immediately before commencement until—

   (a) the new copyright provisions come into force in that territory by virtue of an Order under section 157 of this Act (power to extend new copyright provisions), or

   (b) in the case of any of the Channel Islands, the Act is repealed by Order under sub-paragraph (3) below.

(2) An Order in Council in force immediately before commencement which extends to any dependent territory any provisions of the 1956 Act shall remain in force as part of the law of that territory until—

   (a) the new copyright provisions come into force in that territory by virtue of an Order under section 157 of this Act (power to extend new copyright provisions), or

   (b) in the case of the Isle of Man, the Order is revoked by Order under sub-paragraph (3) below;

and while it remains in force such an Order may be varied under the provisions of the 1956 Act under which it was made.

(3) If it appears to Her Majesty that provision with respect to copyright has been made in the law of any of the Channel Islands or the Isle of Man otherwise than by extending the provisions of Part I of this Act, Her Majesty may by Order in Council repeal the 1911 Act as it has effect as part of the law of that territory or, as the case may be, revoke the Order extending the 1956 Act there.

(4) A dependent territory in which the 1911 or 1956 Act remains in force shall be treated, in the law of the countries to which Part I extends, as a country to which that Part extends; and those countries shall be treated in the law of such a territory as countries to which the 1911 Act or, as the case may be, the 1956 Act extends.

(5) If a country in which the 1911 or 1956 Act is in force ceases to be a colony of the United Kingdom, section 158 of this Act (consequences of country ceasing to be colony) applies with the substitution for the reference in subsection (3)(b) to the provisions of Part I of this Act of a reference to the provisions of the 1911 or 1956 Act, as the case may be.

(6) In this paragraph "dependent territory" means any of the Channel Islands, the Isle of Man or any colony.

37.—(1) This paragraph applies to a country which immediately before commencement was not a dependent territory within the meaning of paragraph 36 above but—
> (a) was a country to which the 1956 Act extended, or
> (b) was treated as such a country by virtue of paragraph 39(2) of Schedule 7 to that Act (countries to which the 1911 Act extended or was treated as extending);

and Her Majesty may by Order in Council conclusively declare for the purposes of this paragraph whether a country was such a country or was so treated.

(2) A country to which this paragraph applies shall be treated as a country to which Part I extends for the purposes of sections 154 to 156 (qualification for copyright protection) until—
> (a) an Order in Council is made in respect of that country under section 159 (application of Part I to countries to which it does not extend), or
> (b) an Order in Council is made declaring that it shall cease to be so treated by reason of the fact that the provisions of the 1956 Act or, as the case may be, the 1911 Act, which extended there as part of the law of that country have been repealed or amended.

(3) A statutory instrument containing an Order in Council under this paragraph shall be subject to annulment in pursuance of a resolution of either House of Parliament.

Territorial waters and the continental shelf

A–310 38. Section 161 of this Act (application of Part I to things done in territorial waters or the United Kingdom sector of the continental shelf) does not apply in relation to anything done before commencement.

British ships, aircraft and hovercraft

A–311 39. Section 162 (British ships, aircraft and hovercraft) does not apply in relation to anything done before commencement.

Crown copyright

A–312 40.—(1) Section 163 of this Act (general provisions as to Crown copyright) applies to an existing work if—
> (a) section 39 of the 1956 Act applied to the work immediately before commencement, and

(*b*) the work is not one to which section 164, 165 or 166 applies (copyright in Acts, Measures and Bills and Parliamentary copyright: see paragraphs 42 and 43 below).

(2) Section 163 (1)(b) (first ownership of copyright) has effect subject to any agreement entered into before commencement under section 39(6) of the 1956 Act.

41.—(1) The following provisions have effect with respect to the duration of copyright in existing works to which section 163 (Crown copyright) applies.

The question which provision applies to a work shall be determined by reference to the facts immediately before commencement; and expressions used in this paragraph which were defined for the purposes of the 1956 Act have the same meaning as in that Act.

(2) Copyright in the following descriptions of work continues to subsist until the date on which it would have expired in accordance with the 1956 Act—

(*a*) published literary, dramatic or musical works;

(*b*) artistic works other than engravings or photographs;

(*c*) published engravings;

(*d*) published photographs and photographs taken before 1st June 1957;

(*e*) published sound recordings and sound recordings made before 1st June 1957;

(*f*) published films and films falling within section 13(3)(a) of the 1956 Act (films registered under former enactments relating to registration of films).

(3) Copyright in unpublished literary, dramatic or musical works continues to subsist until—

(*a*) the date on which copyright expires in accordance with section 163(3), or

(*b*) the end of the period of 50 years from the end of the calendar year in which the new copyright provisions come into force,

whichever is the later.

(4) Copyright in the following descriptions of work continues to subsist until the end of the period of 50 years from the end of the calendar year in which the new copyright provisions come into force—

(*a*) unpublished engravings;

(*b*) unpublished photographs taken on or after 1st June 1957.

(5) Copyright in a film or sound recording not falling within sub-paragraph (2) above continues to subsist until the end of the period of 50 years from the end of the calendar year in which the new copyright provisions come into force, unless the film or recording is published before the end of that period, in which case copyright expires 50 years from the end of the calendar year in which it is published.

42.—(1) Section 164 (copyright in Acts and Measures) applies to existing Acts of Parliament and Measures of the General Synod of the Church of England.

(2) References in that section to Measures of the General Synod of the Church of England include Church Assembly Measures.

Parliamentary copyright

43.—(1) Section 165 of this Act (general provisions as to Parliamentary copyright) applies **A–313** to existing unpublished literary, dramatic, musical or artistic works, but does not otherwise apply to existing works.

(2) Section 166 (copyright in Parliamentary Bills) does not apply—

(*a*) to a public Bill which was introduced into Parliament and published before commencement,

(*b*) to a private Bill of which a copy was deposited in either House before commencement, or

(*c*) to a personal Bill which was given a First Reading in the House of Lords before commencement.

Copyright vesting in certain international organisations

A–314   44.—(1) Any work in which immediately before commencement copyright subsisted by virtue of section 33 of the 1956 Act shall be deemed to satisfy the requirements of section 168(1); but otherwise section 168 does not apply to works made or, as the case may be, published before commencement.

(2) Copyright in any such work which is unpublished continues to subsist until the date on which it would have expired in accordance with the 1956 Act, or the end of the period of 50 years from the end of the calendar year in which the new copyright provisions come into force, whichever is the earlier.

Meaning of "publication"

A–315   45. Section 175(3) (construction of building treated as equivalent to publication) applies only where the construction of the building began after commencement.

Meaning of "unauthorised"

A–316   46. For the purposes of the application of the definition in section 178 (minor definitions) of the expression "unauthorised" in relation to things done before commencement—

(a) paragraph (a) applies in relation to things done before 1st June 1957 as if the reference to the licence of the copyright owner were a reference to his consent or acquiescence;

(b) paragraph (b) applies with the substitution for the words from "or, in a case" to the end of the words "or any person lawfully claiming under him"; and

(c) paragraph (c) shall be disregarded.

Section 189.   SCHEDULE 2

RIGHTS IN PERFORMANCES: PERMITTED ACTS

Introductory

A–317   1.—(1) The provisions of this Schedule specify acts which may be done in relation to a performance or recording notwithstanding the rights conferred by Part II; they relate only to the question of infringement of those rights and do not affect any other right or obligation restricting the doing of any of the specified acts.

(2) No inference shall be drawn from the description of any act which may by virtue of this Schedule be done without infringing the rights conferred by Part II as to the scope of those rights.

(3) The provisions of this Schedule are to be construed independently of each other, so that the fact that an act does not fall within one provision does not mean that it is not covered by another provision.

Criticism, reviews and news reporting

A–318   2.—(1) Fair dealing with a performance or recording—

(a) for the purpose of criticism or review, of that or another performance or recording, or of a work, or

(b) for the purpose of reporting current events,

does not infringe any of the rights conferred by Part II.

(2) Expressions used in this paragraph have the same meaning as in section 30.

Incidental inclusion of performance or recording

3.—(1) The rights conferred by Part II are not infringed by the incidental inclusion of a **A–319** performance or recording in a sound recording, film, broadcast or cable programme.

(2) Nor are those rights infringed by anything done in relation to copies of, or the playing, showing, broadcasting or inclusion in a cable programme service of, anything whose making was, by virtue of sub-paragraph (1), not an infringement of those rights.

(3) A performance or recording so far as it consists of music, or words spoken or sung with music, shall not be regarded as incidentally included in a sound recording, broadcast or cable programme if it is deliberately included.

(4) Expressions used in this paragraph have the same meaning as in section 31.

Things done for purposes of instruction or examination

4.—(1) The rights conferred by Part II are not infringed by the copying of a recording of a **A–320** performance in the course of instruction, or of preparation for instruction, in the making of films or film sound-tracks, provided the copying is done by a person giving or receiving instruction.

(2) The rights conferred by Part II are not infringed—
- (a) by the copying of a recording of a performance for the purposes of setting or answering the questions in an examination, or
- (b) by anything done for the purposes of an examination by way of communicating the questions to the candidates.

(3) Where a recording which would otherwise be an illicit recording is made in accordance with this paragraph but is subsequently dealt with, it shall be treated as an illicit recording for the purposes of that dealing, and if that dealing infringes any right conferred by Part II for all subsequent purposes.

For this purpose "dealt with" means sold or let for hire, or offered or exposed for sale or hire.

(4) Expressions used in this paragraph have the same meaning as in section 32.

Playing or showing sound recording, film, broadcast or cable programme at educational establishment

5.—(1) The playing or showing of a sound recording, film, broadcast or cable programme **A–321** at an educational establishment for the purposes of instruction before an audience consisting of teachers and pupils at the establishment and other persons directly connected with the activities of the establishment is not a playing or showing of a performance in public for the purposes of infringement of the rights conferred by Part II.

(2) A person is not for this purpose directly connected with the activities of the educational establishment simply because he is the parent of a pupil at the establishment.

(3) Expressions used in this paragraph have the same meaning as in section 34 and any provision made under section 174(2) with respect to the application of that section also applies for the purposes of this paragraph.

Recording of broadcasts and cable programmes by educational establishments

6.—(1) A recording of a broadcast or cable programme, or a copy of such a recording, may **A–322** be made by or on behalf of an educational establishment for the educational purposes of that establishment without thereby infringing any of the rights conferred by Part II in relation to any performance or recording included in it.

(2) Where a recording which would otherwise be an illicit recording is made in accordance with this paragraph but is subsequently dealt with, it shall be treated as an illicit recording for the purposes of that dealing, and if that dealing infringes any right conferred by Part II for all subsequent purposes.

For this purpose "dealt with" means sold or let for hire, or offered or exposed for sale or hire.

(3) Expressions used in this paragraph have the same meaning as in section 35 and any provision made under section 174(2) with respect to the application of that section also applies for the purposes of this paragraph.

Copy of work required to be made as condition of export

A–323   7.—(1) If an article of cultural or historical importance or interest cannot lawfully be exported from the United Kingdom unless a copy of it is made and deposited in an appropriate library or archive, it is not an infringement of any right conferred by Part II to make that copy.

(2) Expressions used in this paragraph have the same meaning as in section 44.

Parliamentary and judicial proceedings

A–324   8.—(1) The rights conferred by Part II are not infringed by anything done for the purposes of parliamentary or judicial proceedings or for the purpose of reporting such proceedings.

(2) Expressions used in this paragraph have the same meaning as in section 45.

Royal Commissions and statutory inquiries

A–325   9.—(1) The rights conferred by Part II are not infringed by anything done for the purposes of the proceedings of a Royal Commission or statutory inquiry or for the purpose of reporting any such proceedings held in public.

(2) Expressions used in this paragraph have the same meaning as in section 46.

Public records

A–326   10.—(1) Material which is comprised in public records within the meaning of the Public Records Act 1958, the Public Records (Scotland) Act 1937 or the Public Records Act (Northern Ireland) 1923 which are open to public inspection in pursuance of that Act, may be copied, and a copy may be supplied to any person, by or with the authority of any officer appointed under that Act, without infringing any right conferred by Part II.

(2) Expressions used in this paragraph have the same meaning as in section 49.

Acts done under statutory authority

A–327   11.—(1) Where the doing of a particular act is specifically authorised by an Act of Parliament, whenever passed, then, unless the Act provides otherwise, the doing of that act does not infringe the rights conferred by Part II.

(2) Sub-paragraph (1) applies in relation to an enactment contained in Northern Ireland legislation as it applies to an Act of Parliament.

(3) Nothing in this paragraph shall be construed as excluding any defence of statutory authority otherwise available under or by virtue of any enactment.

(4) Expressions used in this paragraph have the same meaning as in section 50.

Transfer of copies of works in electronic form

A–328   12.—(1) This paragraph applies where a recording of a performance in electronic form has been purchased on terms which, expressly or impliedly or by virtue of any rule of law, allow the purchaser to make further recordings in connection with his use of the recording.

(2) If there are no express terms—

(*a*) prohibiting the transfer of the recording by the purchaser, imposing obligations which continue after a transfer, prohibiting the assignment of any consent or terminating any consent on a transfer, or

(*b*) providing for the terms on which a transferee may do the things which the purchaser was permitted to do,

anything which the purchaser was allowed to do may also be done by a transferee without infringement of the rights conferred by this Part, but any recording made by the purchaser which is not also transferred shall be treated as an illicit recording for all purposes after the transfer.

(3) The same applies where the original purchased recording is no longer usable and what is transferred is a further copy used in its place.

(4) The above provisions also apply on a subsequent transfer, with the substitution for references in sub-paragraph (2) to the purchaser of references to the subsequent transferor.

(5) This paragraph does not apply in relation to a recording purchased before the commencement of Part II.

(6) Expressions used in this paragraph have the same meaning as in section 56.

Use of recordings of spoken works in certain cases

13.—(1) Where a recording of the reading or recitation of a literary work is made for the purpose— **A–329**

(*a*) of reporting current events, or

(*b*) of broadcasting or including in a cable programme service the whole or part of the reading or recitation,

it is not an infringement of the rights conferred by Part II to use the recording (or to copy the recording and use the copy) for that purpose, provided the following conditions are met.

(2) The conditions are that—

(*a*) the recording is a direct recording of the reading or recitation and is not taken from a previous recording or from a broadcast or cable programme;

(*b*) the making of the recording was not prohibited by or on behalf of the person giving the reading or recitation;

(*c*) the use made of the recording is not of a kind prohibited by or on behalf of that person before the recording was made; and

(*d*) the use is by or with the authority of a person who is lawfully in possession of the recording.

(3) Expressions used in this paragraph have the same meaning as in section 58.

Recordings of folksongs

14.—(1) A recording of a performance of a song may be made for the purpose of including it in an archive maintained by a designated body without infringing any of the rights conferred by Part II, provided the conditions in sub-paragraph (2) below are met. **A–330**

(2) The conditions are that—

(*a*) the words are unpublished and of unknown authorship at the time the recording is made,

(*b*) the making of the recording does not infringe any copyright, and

(*c*) its making is not prohibited by any performer.

(3) Copies of a recording made in reliance on sub-paragraph (1) and included in an archive maintained by a designated body may, if the prescribed conditions are met, be made and supplied by the archivist without infringing any of the rights conferred by Part II.

(4) In this paragraph—

"designated body" means a body designated for the purposes of section 61, and

"the prescribed conditions" means the conditions prescribed for the purposes of subsection
   (3) of that section;

and other expressions used in this paragraph have the same meaning as in that section.

Playing of sound recordings for purposes of club, society, &c.

A–331   15.—(1) It is not an infringement of any right conferred by Part II to play a sound recording as part of the activities of, or for the benefit of, a club, society or other organisation if the
following conditions are met.
   (2) The conditions are—
      (*a*) that the organisation is not established or conducted for profit and its main objects
            are charitable or are otherwise concerned with the advancement of religion, edu-
            cation or social welfare, and
      (*b*) that the proceeds of any charge for admission to the place where the recording is to
            be heard are applied solely for the purposes of the organisation.
   (3) Expressions used in this paragraph have the same meaning as in section 67.

Incidental recording for purposes of broadcast or cable programme

A–332   16.—(1) A person who proposes to broadcast a recording of a performance, or include a
recording of a performance in a cable programme service, in circumstances not infringing the
rights conferred by Part II shall be treated as having consent for the purposes of that Part for
the making of a further recording for the purposes of the broadcast or cable programme.
   (2) That consent is subject to the condition that the further recording—
      (*a*) shall not be used for any other purpose, and
      (*b*) shall be destroyed within 28 days of being first used for broadcasting the perfor-
            mance or including it in a cable programme service.
   (3) A recording made in accordance with this paragraph shall be treated as an illicit
recording—
      (*a*) for the purposes of any use in breach of the condition mentioned in sub-paragraph
            (2)(*a*), and
      (*b*) for all purposes after that condition or the condition mentioned in sub-paragraph
            (2)(*b*) is broken.
   (4) Expressions used in this paragraph have the same meaning as in section 68.

Recordings for purposes of supervision and control of broadcasts and cable programmes

A–333   17.—(1) The rights conferred by Part II are not infringed by the making or use by the
British Broadcasting Corporation, for the purpose of maintaining supervision and control
over programmes broadcast by them, of recordings of those programmes.
   [(2) The rights conferred by Part II are not infringed by—
      (a) *the making or use of recordings by the Independent Broadcasting Authority for the purposes men-*
           tioned in section 4(7) of the Broadcasting Act 1981 (maintenance of supervision and control over
           programmes and advertisements); or
      (b) *anything done under or in pursuance of provision included in a contract between a programme con-*
           tractor and the Authority in accordance with section 21 of that Act.
   (3) The rights conferred by Part II are not infringed by—
      (a) *the making by or with the authority of the Cable Authority, or the use by that Authority, for the*
           purpose of maintaining supervision and control over programmes included in services licensed under
           Part I of the Cable and Broadcasting Act 1984, of recordings of those programmes; or
      (b) *anything done under or in pursuance of—*
           (i) a notice or direction given under section 16 of the Cable and Broadcasting Act 1984 (power of
              Cable Authority to require production of recordings); or

(ii) a condition included in a licence by virtue of section 35 of that Act (duty of Authority to secure that recordings are available for certain purposes).

(4) Expressions used in this paragraph have the same meaning as in section 69.]

[(2) The rights conferred by Part II are not infringed by anything done in pursuance of—
  (a) section 11(1), 95(1), 145(4), (5) or (7), 155(3) or 167(1) of the Broadcasting Act 1990;
  (b) a condition which, by virtue of section 11(2) or 95(2) of that Act, is included in a licence granted under Part I or III of that Act; or
  (c) a direction given under section 109(2) of that Act (power of Radio Authority to require production of recordings etc.).

(3) The rights conferred by Part II are not infringed by—
  (a) the use by the Independent Television Commission or the Radio Authority, in connection with the performance of any of their functions under the Broadcasting Act 1990, of any recording, script or transcript which is provided to them under or by virtue of any provision of that Act; or
  (b) the use by the Broadcasting Complaints Commission or the Broadcasting Standards Council, in connection with any complaint made to them under that Act, of any recording or transcript requested or required to be provided to them, and so provided, under section 145(4) or (7) or section 155(3) of that Act.]

Note: New sub-paragraphs (2) and (3) were substituted for the original sub-paragraphs (2) to (4), printed in italics, by section 203(1) of and paragraph 50(2) Schedule 20 to the Broadcasting Act 1990 (c. 42) as provided by The Broadcasting Act 1990 (Commencement No. 1 and Transitional Provisions) Order 1990 (S.I. 1990 No. 2347 (c. 61)) § B–254 *post*.

Free public showing or playing of broadcast or cable programme

18.—(1) The showing or playing in public of a broadcast or cable programme to an   **A–334**
audience who have not paid for admission to the place where the broadcast or programme is to be seen or heard does not infringe any right conferred by Part II in relation to a performance or recording included in—
  (a) the broadcast or cable programme, or
  (b) any sound recording or film which is played or shown in public by reception of the broadcast or cable programme.

(2) The audience shall be treated as having paid for admission to a place—
  (a) if they have paid for admission to a place of which that place forms part; or
  (b) if goods or services are supplied at that place (or a place of which it forms part)—
    (i) at prices which are substantially attributable to the facilities afforded for seeing or hearing the broadcast or programme, or
    (ii) at prices exceeding those usually charged there and which are partly attributable to those facilities.

(3) The following shall not be regarded as having paid for admission to a place—
  (a) persons admitted as residents or inmates of the place;
  (b) persons admitted as members of a club or society where the payment is only for membership of the club or society and the provision of facilities for seeing or hearing broadcasts or programmes is only incidental to the main purposes of the club or society.

(4) Where the making of the broadcast or inclusion of the programme in a cable programme service was an infringement of the rights conferred by Part II in relation to a performance or recording, the fact that it was heard or seen in public by the reception of the broadcast or programme shall be taken into account in assessing the damages for that infringement.

(5) Expressions used in this paragraph have the same meaning as in section 72.

Reception and re-transmission of broadcast in cable programme service

A–335   19.—(1) This paragraph applies where a broadcast made from a place in the United King-dom is, by reception and immediate re-transmission, included in a cable programme service.

(2) The rights conferred by Part II in relation to a performance or recording included in the broadcast are not infringed—

[*(a) if the inclusion of the broadcast in the cable programme service is in pursuance of a requirement imposed under section 13(1) of the Cable and Broadcasting Act 1984 (duty of Cable Authority to secure inclusion in cable service of certain programmes), or*]

(*b*) if and to the extent that the broadcast is made for reception in the area in which the cable programme service is provided;

but where the making of the broadcast was an infringement of those rights, the fact that the broadcast was re-transmitted as a programme in a cable programme service shall be taken into account in assessing the damages for that infringement.

(3) Expressions used in this paragraph have the same meaning as in section 73.

Note: The words in square brackets, printed in italics, were repealed by section 203(3) of and Schedule 21 to the Broadcasting Act 1990 (c. 42) as provided by The Broadcasting Act 1990 (Commencement No. 1 and Transitional Provisions) Order 1990 (S.I. 1990 No. 2347 (c. 61)) § B–254 *post*.

Provision of sub-titled copies of broadcast or cable programme

A–336   20.—(1) A designated body may, for the purpose of providing people who are deaf or hard of hearing, or physically or mentally handicapped in other ways, with copies which are sub-titled or otherwise modified for their special needs, make recordings of television broadcasts or cable programmes without infringing any right conferred by Part II in relation to a perfor-mance or recording included in the broadcast or cable programme.

(2) In this paragraph "designated body" means a body designated for the purposes of sec-tion 74 and other expressions used in this paragraph have the same meaning as in that sec-tion.

Recording of broadcast or cable programme for archival purposes

A–337   21.—(1) A recording of a broadcast or cable programme of a designated class, or a copy of such a recording, may be made for the purpose of being placed in an archive maintained by a designated body without thereby infringing any right conferred by Part II in relation to a performance or recording included in the broadcast or cable programme.

(2) In this paragraph "designated class" and "designated body" means a class or body designated for the purposes of section 75 and other expressions used in this paragraph have the same meaning as in that section.

Section 272.   SCHEDULE 3

REGISTERED DESIGNS: MINOR AND CONSEQUENTIAL AMENDMENTS OF 1949 ACT

Section 3: proceedings for registration

A–338   1. In section 3 of the Registered Designs Act 1949 (proceedings for registration) for sub-sections (2) to (6) substitute—

"(2) An application for the registration of a design in which design right subsists shall not be entertained unless made by the person claiming to be the design right owner.

(3) For the purpose of deciding whether a design is new, the registrar may make such searches, if any, as he thinks fit.

(4) The registrar may, in such cases as may be prescribed, direct that for the purpose of deciding whether a design is new an application shall be treated as made on a date earlier or later than that on which it was in fact made.

(5) The registrar may refuse an application for the registration of a design or may register the design in pursuance of the application subject to such modifications, if any, as he things fit; and a design when registered shall be registered shall be registered as of the date on which the application was made or treated as having been made.

(6) An application which, owing to any default or neglect on the part of the applicant, has not been completed so as to enable registration to be effected within such time as may be prescribed shall be deemed to be abandoned.

(7) An appeal lies from any decision of the registrar under this section.".

Section 4: registration of same design in respect of other articles, etc.

2. In section 4 of the Registered Designs Act 1949 (registration of same design in respect of **A-339** other articles, etc.), in subsection (1), for the proviso substitute—

"Provided that the right in a design registered by virtue of this section shall not extend beyond the end of the period, and any extended period, for which the right subsists in the original registered design.".

Section 5: provisions for secrecy of certain designs

3.—(1) Section 5 of the Registered Designs Act 1949 is amended as follows. **A-340**
(2) For "a competent authority" or "the competent authority", wherever occurring, substitute "the Secretary of State"; and in subsection (3)(c) for "that authority" substitute "he".
(3) For subsection (2) substitute—

"(2) The Secretary of State shall by rules make provision for securing that where such directions are given—
 (a) any representation or specimen of the design, and
 (b) any evidence filed in support of the applicant's contention that the appearance of an article is material (for the purposes of section 1(3) of this Act),
shall not be open to public inspection at the Patent Office during the continuance in force of the directions."

(4) In subsection (3)(b) after "representation or specimen of the design" insert ", or any such evidence as is mentioned in subsection (2)(b) above,".
(5) Omit subsection (5).

Section 6: provisions as to confidential disclosure, etc.

4.—(1) Section 6 of the Registered Designs Act 1949 (provisions as to confidential dis- **A-341** closure, etc.) is amended as follows.
(2) In subsection (2) (display of design at certified exhibition), in paragraph (a) for "certified by the Board of Trade" substitute "certified by the Secretary of State".
(3) For subsections (4) and (5) (registration of designs corresponding to copyright artistic works) substitute—

"(4) Where an application is made by or with the consent of the owner of copyright in an artistic work for the registration of a corresponding design, the design shall not be treated for the purposes of this Act as being other than new by reason only of any use previously made of the artistic work, subject to subsection (5).
(5) Subsection (4) does not apply if the previous use consisted of or included the sale, letting for hire or offer or exposure for sale or hire of articles to which had been applied industrially—

(*a*) the design in question, or

(*b*) a design differing from it only in immaterial details or in features which are variants commonly used in the trade,

and that previous use was made by or with the consent of the copyright owner.

(6) The Secretary of State may make provision by rules as to the circumstances in which a design is to be regarded for the purposes of this section as 'applied industrially' to articles, or any description of articles.".

Section 9: exemption of innocent infringer from liability for damages

A–342 5. In section 9 of the Registered Designs Act 1949 (exemption of innocent infringer from liability for damages), in subsections (1) and (2) for "copyright in a registered design" substitute "the right in a registered design".

Section 11: cancellation of registration

A–343 6.—(1) Section 11 of the Registered Designs Act 1949 (cancellation of registration) is amended as follows.

(2) In subsection (2) omit "or original".

(3) For subsections (2A) and (3) substitute—

"(3) At any time after a design has been registered, any person interested may apply to the registrar for the cancellation of the registration on the ground that—

(*a*) the design was at the time it was registered a corresponding design in relation to an artistic work in which copyright subsisted, and

(*b*) the right in the registered design has expired in accordance with section 8(4) of this Act (expiry of right in registered design on expiry of copyright in artistic work);

and the registrar may make such order on the application as he thinks fit.

(4) A cancellation under this section takes effect—

(*a*) in the case of cancellation under subsection (1), from the date of the registrar's decision,

(*b*) in the case of cancellation under subsection (2), from the date of registration,

(*c*) in the case of cancellation under subsection (3), from the date on which the right in the registered design expired,

or, in any case, from such other date as the registrar may direct.

(5) An appeal lies from any order of the registrar under this section.".

Section 14: registration where application has been made in convention country

A–344 7. In section 14 of the Registered Designs Act 1949 (registration where application has been made in convention country), for subsections (2) and (3) substitute—

"(2) Where an application for registration of a design is made by virtue of this section, the application shall be treated, for the purpose of determining whether that or any other design is new, as made on the date of the application for protection in the convention country or, if more than one such application was made, on the date of the first such application.

(3) Subsection (2) shall not be construed as excluding the power to give directions under section 3(4) of this Act in relation to an application made by virtue of this section.".

Section 15: extension of time for application under s.14 in certain cases

A–345 8. In section 15(1) of the Registered Designs Act 1949 (power to make rules empowering registrar to extend time for applications under s.14) for "the Board of Trade are satisfied" substitute "the Secretary of State is satisfied" and for "they" substitute "he".

Section 16: protection of designs communicated under international agreements

9. In section 16 of the Registered Designs Act 1949 (protection of designs communicated under international agreements)— **A–346**
  (a) in subsection (1) for "the Board of Trade" substitute "the Secretary of State", and
  (b) in subsection (3) for "the Board of Trade" substitute "the Secretary of State" and for "the Board are satisfied" substitute "the Secretary of State is satisfied".

Section 19: registration of assignments, &c.

10. In section 19 of the Registered Designs Act 1949 (registration of assignments, &c.), after subsection (3) insert— **A–347**

"(3A) Where design right subsists in a registered design, the registrar shall not register an interest under subsection (3) unless he is satisfied that the person entitled to that interest is also entitled to a corresponding interest in the design right.

(3B) Where design right subsists in a registered design and the proprietor of the registered design is also the design right owner, an assignment of the design right shall be taken to be also an assignment of the right in the registered design, unless a contrary intention appears.".

Section 20: rectification of the register

11. In section 20 of the Registered Designs Act 1949 (rectification of the register), after subsection (4) add— **A–348**

"(5) A rectification of the register under this section has effect as follows—
(a) an entry made has effect from the date on which it should have been made,
(b) an entry varied has effect as if it had originally been made in its varied form, and
(c) an entry deleted shall be deemed never to have had effect,
unless, in any case, the court directs otherwise.".

Section 22: inspection of registered designs

12.—(1) Section 22 of the Registered Designs Act 1949 (inspection of registered designs) is amended as follows. **A–349**
  (2) For subsection (1) substitute—

"(1) Where a design has been registered under this Act, there shall be open to inspection at the Patent Office on and after the day on which the certificate of registration is issued—
  (a) the representation or specimen of the design, and
  (b) any evidence filed in support of the applicant's contention that the appearance of an article is material (for the purposes of section 1(3) of this Act).
This subsection has effect subject to the following provisions of this section and to any rules made under section 5(2) of this Act.".
  (3) In subsection (2), subsection (3) (twice) and subsection (4) for "representation or specimen of the design" substitute "representation, specimen or evidence".

Section 23: information as to existence of right in registered design

13. For section 23 of the Registered Designs Act 1949 (information as to existence of right in registered design) substitute— **A–350**

"Information as to existence of right in registered design

23. On the request of a person furnishing such information as may enable the registrar to identify the design, and on payment of the prescribed fee, the registrar shall inform him—

(a) whether the design is registered and, if so, in respect of what articles, and

(b) whether any extension of the period of the right in the registered design has been granted,

and shall state the date of registration and the name and address of the registered proprietor.".

Section 25: certificate of contested validity of registration

A–351 14. In section 25 of the Registered Design Act 1949 (certificate of contested validity of registration), in subsection (2) for "the copyright in the registered design" substitute "the right in the registered design".

Section 26: remedy for groundless threats of infringement proceedings

A–352 15.—(1) Section 26 of the Registered Designs Act 1949 (remedy for groundless threats of infringement proceedings) is amended as follows.

(2) In subsections (1) and (2) for "the copyright in a registered design" substitute "the right in a registered design".

(3) After subsection (2) insert—

"(2A) Proceedings may not be brought under this section in respect of a threat to bring proceedings for an infringement alleged to consist of the making or importing of anything.".

Section 27: the court

A–353 16. For section 27 of the Registered Designs Act 1949 (the court) substitute—

"The court

27.—(1) In this Act 'the court' means—

(a) in England and Wales the High Court or any patents county court having jurisdiction by virtue of an order under section 287 of the Copyright, Designs and Patents Act 1988,

(b) in Scotland, the Court of Session, and

(c) in Northern Ireland, the High Court.

(2) Provision may be made by rules of court with respect to proceedings in the High Court in England and Wales for references and applications under this Act to be dealt with by such judge of that court as the Lord Chancellor may select for the purpose.".

Section 28: the Appeal Tribunal

A–354 17.—(1) Section 28 of the Registered Designs Act 1949 (the Appeal Tribunal) is amended as follows.

(2) For subsection (2) (members of Tribunal) substitute—

"(2) The Appeal Tribunal shall consist of—

(a) one or more judges of the High Court nominated by the Lord Chancellor, and

(b) one judge of the Court of Session nominated by the Lord President of that Court."

(3) In subsection (5) (costs), after "costs" (twice) insert "or expenses", and for the words from "and any such order" to the end substitute—

"and any such order may be enforced—

(a) in England and Wales or Northern Ireland, in the same way as an order of the High Court;

(b) in Scotland, in the same way as a decree for expenses granted by the Court of Session.".

(4) For subsection (10) (seniority of judges) substitute—

"(10) In this section 'the High Court' means the High Court in England and Wales; and for the purposes of this section the seniority of judges shall be reckoned by reference to the dates on which they were appointed judges of that court or the Court of Session.".

(5) The amendments to section 28 made by section 10(5) of the Administration of Justice Act 1970 (power to make rules as to right of audience) shall be deemed always to have extended to Northern Ireland.

Section 29: exercise of discretionary powers of registrar

18. In section 29 of the Registered Designs Act 1949 (exercise of discretionary powers of registrar) for "the registrar shall give" substitute "rules made by the Secretary of State under this Act shall require the registrar to give".   **A–355**

Section 30: costs and security for costs

19. For section 30 of the Registered Designs Act 1949 (costs and security for costs) substitute—   **A–356**

"Costs and security for costs

30.—(1) Rules made by the Secretary of State under this Act may make provision empowering the registrar, in any proceedings before him under this Act—
(a) to award any party such costs as he may consider reasonable, and
(b) to direct how and by what parties they are to be paid.

(2) Any such order of the registrar may be enforced—
(a) in England and Wales or Northern Ireland, in the same way as an order of the High Court;
(b) in Scotland, in the same way as a decree for expenses granted by the Court of Session.

(3) Rules made by the Secretary of State under this Act may make provision empowering the registrar to require a person, in such cases as may be prescribed, to give security for the costs of—
(a) an application for cancellation of the registration of a design,
(b) an application for the grant of a licence in respect of a registered design, or
(c) an appeal from any decision of the registrar under this Act,
and enabling the application or appeal to be treated as abandoned in default of such security being given.".

Section 31: evidence before registrar

20. For section 31 of the Registered Designs Act 1949 (evidence before registrar) substitute—   **A–357**

"Evidence before registrar

31. Rules made by the Secretary of State under this Act may make provision—
(a) as to the giving of evidence in proceedings before the registrar under this Act by affidavit or statutory declaration;
(b) conferring on the registrar the powers of an official referee of the Supreme Court as regards the examination of witnesses on oath and the discovery and production of documents; and
(c) applying in relation to the attendance of witnesses in proceedings before the registrar the rules applicable to the attendance of witnesses in proceedings before such a referee.".

A–358   21. Section 32 of the Registered Designs Act 1949 (power of registrar to refuse to deal with certain agents) is repealed.

Section 33: offences under s.5 (secrecy of certain designs)

A–359   22.—(1) Section 33 of the Registered Designs Act 1949 (offences under s.5 (secrecy of certain designs)) is amended as follows.

(2) In subsection (1), for paragraphs (*a*) and (*b*) substitute—

"(*a*) on conviction on indictment to imprisonment for a term not exceeding two years or a fine, or both;

  (*b*) on summary conviction to imprisonment for a term not exceeding six months or a fine not exceeding the statutory maximum, or both.".

(3) Omit subsection (2).

(4) The above amendments do not apply in relation to offences committed before the commencement of Part IV.

Section 34: falsification of register, &c.

A–360   23.—(1) In section 34 of the Registered Designs Act 1949 (falsification of register, &c.) for "shall be guilty of a misdemeanour" substitute—

"shall be guilty of an offence and liable—

  (*a*) on conviction on indictment to imprisonment for a term not exceeding two years or a fine, or both;

  (*b*) on summary conviction to imprisonment for a term not exceeding six months or a fine not exceeding the statutory maximum, or both.".

(2) The above amendment does not apply in relation to offences committed before the commencement of Part IV.

Section 35: fine for falsely representing a design as registered

A–361   24.—(1) Section 35 of the Registered Designs Act 1949 (fine for falsely representing a design as registered) is amended as follows.

(2) In subsection (1) for the words from "a fine not exceeding £50" substitute "a fine not exceeding level 3 on the standard scale".

(3) In subsection (2)—

  (*a*) for "the copyright in a registered design" substitute "the right in a registered design";

  (*b*) for "subsisting copyright in the design" substitute "subsisting right in the design under this Act"; and

  (*c*) for the words from "a fine" to the end substitute "a fine not exceeding level 1 on the standard scale".

(4) The amendment in sub-paragraph (2) does not apply in relation to offences committed before the commencement of Part IV.

Section 35A: offence by body corporate—liability for officers

A–362   25.—(1) In the Registered Designs Act 1949 after section 35 insert—

"Offence by body corporate: liability of officers

35A.—(1) Where an offence under this Act committed by a body corporate is proved to have been committed with the consent or connivance of a director, manager, secretary or other similar officer of the body, or a person purporting to act in any such capacity, he as well as the body corporate is guilty of the offence and liable to be proceeded against and punished accordingly.

(2) In relation to a body corporate whose affairs are managed by its members "director" means a member of the body corporate.".

(2) The above amendment does not apply in relation to offences committed before the commencement of Part IV.

Section 36: general power to make rules, &c.

26.—(1) Section 36 of the Registered Designs Act 1949 (general power to make rules, &c.)   **A–363**
is amended as follows.

(2) In subsection (1) for "the Board of Trade" and "the Board" substitute "the Secretary of State", and for "as they think expedient" substitute "as he thinks expedient".

(3) For the words in subsection (1) from "and in particular" to the end substitute the following subsections—

"(1A) Rules may, in particular, make provision—
(a) prescribing the form of applications for registration of designs and of any representations or specimens of designs or other documents which may be filed at the Patent Office, and requiring copies to be furnished of any such representations, specimens or documents;
(b) regulating the procedure to be followed in connection with any application or request to the registrar or in connection with any proceeding before him, and authorising the rectification of irregularities of procedure;
(c) providing for the appointment of advisers to assist the registrar in proceedings before him;
(d) regulating the keeping of the register of designs;
(e) authorising the publication and sale of copies of representations of designs and other documents in the Patent Office;
(f) prescribing anything authorised or required by this Act to be prescribed by rules.
(1B) The remuneration of an adviser appointed to assist the registrar shall be determined by the Secretary of State with the consent of the Treasury and shall be defrayed out of money provided by Parliament.".

Section 37: provisions as to rules and Orders

27.—(1) Section 37 of the Registered Designs Act 1949 (provisions as to rules and orders)   **A–364**
is amended as follows.

(2) Omit subsection (1) (duty to advertise making of rules).

(3) In subsections (2), (3) and (4) for "the Board of Trade" substitute "the Secretary of State".

Section 38: proceedings of the Board of Trade

28. Section 38 of the Registered Designs Act 1949 (proceedings of the Board or Trade) is   **A–365**
repealed.

Section 39: hours of business and excluded days

29. In section 39 of the Registered Designs Act 1949 (hours of business and excluded   **A–366**
days), in subsection (1) for "the Board of Trade" substitute "the Secretary of State".

Section 40: fees

30. In section 40 of the Registered Designs Act 1949 (fees) for "the Board of Trade" substi-   **A–367**
tute "the Secretary of State".

A–368

Section 44: interpretation

31.—(1) In section 44 of the Registered Designs Act 1949 (interpretation), subsection (1) is amended as follows.

(2) In the definition of "artistic work" for "the Copyright Act 1956" substitute "Part I of the Copyright, Designs and Patents Act 1988".

(3) At the appropriate place insert—

" 'author' in relation to a design, has the meaning given by section 2(3) and (4);".

(4) Omit the definition of "copyright".

(5) In the definition of "corresponding design", for the words from "has the same meaning" to the end substitute ", in relation to an artistic work, means a design which if applied to an article would produce something which would be treated for the purposes of Part I of the Copyright, Designs and Patents Act 1988 as a copy of that work;".

(6) For the definition of "court" substitute—

" 'the court' shall be construed in accordance with section 27 of this Act;".

(7) In the definition of "design" for "subsection (3) of section one of this Act" substitute "section 1(1) of this Act".

(8) At the appropriate place insert—

" 'employee', 'employment' and 'employer' refer to employment under a contract of service or of apprenticeship,".

(9) Omit the definition of "Journal".

(10) In the definition of "prescribed" for "the Board of Trade" substitute "the Secretary of State".

Section 45: application to Scotland

A–369   32. In section 45 of the Registered Designs Act 1949 (application to Scotland) omit paragraphs (1) and (2).

Section 46: application to Northern Ireland

A–370   33.—(1) Section 46 of the Registered Designs Act 1949 (application to Northern Ireland) is amended as follows.

(2) Omit paragraphs (1) and (2).

(3) For paragraph (3) substitute—

"(3) References to enactments include enactments comprised in Northern Ireland legislation:".

(4) After paragraph (3) insert—

"(3A) References to the Crown include the Crown in right of Her Majesty's Government in Northern Ireland:".

(5) In paragraph (4) for "a department of the Government of Northern Ireland" substitute "a Northern Ireland department", and at the end add "and in relation to a Northern Ireland department references to the Treasury shall be construed as references to the Department of Finance and Personnel".

Section 47: application to Isle of Man

A–371   34. For section 47 of the Registered Designs Act 1949 (application to Isle of Man) substitute—

"Application to Isle of Man

47. This Act extends to the Isle of Man, subject to any modifications contained in an Order made by Her Majesty in Council, and accordingly, subject to any such Order,

references in this Act to the United Kingdom shall be construed as including the Isle of Man.".

Section 47A: territorial waters and the continental shelf

35. In the Registered Designs Act 1949, after section 47 insert—

"*Territorial waters and the continental shelf*

47A.—(1) For the purposes of this Act the territorial waters of the United Kingdom shall be treated as part of the United Kingdom.

(2) This Act applies to things done in the United Kingdom sector of the continental shelf on a structure or vessel which is present there for purposes directly connected with the exploration of the sea bed or subsoil or the exploitation of their natural resources as it applies to things done in the United Kingdom.

(3) The United Kingdom sector of the continental shelf means the areas designated by order under section 1(7) of the Continental Shelf Act 1964.".

Section 48: repeals, savings and transitional provisions

36. In section 48 of the Registered Designs Act 1949 (repeals, savings and transitional provisions), omit subsection (1) (repeals).

Schedule 1: provisions as to Crown use of registered designs

37.—(1) The First Schedule to the Registered Designs Act 1949 (provisions as to Crown use of registered designs) is amended as follows.

(2) In paragraph 2(1) after "copyright" insert "or design right."

(3) In paragraph 3(1) omit "in such manner as may be prescribed by rules of court."

(4) In paragraph 4(2) (definition of "period of emergency") for the words from "the period ending" to "any other period" substitute "a period."

(5) For paragraph 4(3) substitute—

"(3) No Order in Council under this paragraph shall be submitted to Her Majesty unless a draft of it has been laid before and approved by a resolution of each House of Parliament.".

Schedule 2: enactments repealed

38. Schedule 2 to the Registered Designs Act 1949 (enactments repealed) is repealed.

Section 273.   SCHEDULE 4

THE REGISTERED DESIGNS ACT 1949 AS AMENDED

ARRANGEMENT OF SECTIONS

Registrable designs and proceedings for registration

Section

Supplemental

An Act to consolidate certain enactments relating to registered designs.

[16th December 1949]

Registrable designs and proceedings for registration

Designs registrable under Act

1.—(1) In this Act "design" means features of shape, configuration, pattern or ornament applied to an article by any industrial process, being features which in the finished article appeal to and are judged by the eye, but does not include—   **A–376**

(*a*) a method or principle of construction, or

(*b*) features of shape or configuration of an article which—

   (i) are dictated solely by the function which the article has to perform, or

   (ii) are dependent upon the appearance of another article of which the article is intended by the author of the design to form an integral part.

(2) A design which is new may, upon application by the person claiming to be the proprietor, be registered under this Act in respect of any article, or set of articles, specified in the application.

(3) A design shall not be registered in respect of an article if the appearance of the article is not material, that is, if aesthetic considerations are not normally taken into account to a material extent by persons acquiring or using articles of that description, and would not be so taken into account if the design were to be applied to the article.

(4) A design shall not be regarded as new for the purposes of this Act if it is the same as a design—

(*a*) registered in respect of the same or any other article in pursuance of a prior application, or

(*b*) published in the United Kingdom in respect of the same or any other article before the date of the application,

or if it differs from such a design only in immaterial details or in features which are variants commonly used in the trade.

This subsection has effect subject to the provisions of section 4, 6 and 16 of this Act.

(5) The Secretary of State may by rules provide for excluding from registration under this Act designs for such articles of a primarily literary or artistic character as the Secretary of State thinks fit.

Proprietorship of designs

A-377   2.—(1) The author of a design shall be treated for the purposes of this Act as the original proprietor of the design, subject to the following provisions.

(1A) Where a design is created in pursuance of a commission for money or money's worth, the person commissioning the design shall be treated as the original proprietor of the design.

(1B) Where, in a case not falling within subsection (1A), a design is created by an employee in the course of his employment, his employer shall be treated as the original proprietor of the design.

(2) Where a design, or the right to apply a design to any article, becomes vested, whether by assignment, transmission or operation of law, in any person other than the original proprietor, either alone or jointly with the original proprietor, that other person, or as the case may be the original proprietor and that other person, shall be treated for the purposes of this Act as the proprietor of the design or as the proprietor of the design in relation to that article.

(3) In this Act the "author" of a design means the person who creates it.

(4) In the case of a design generated by computer in circumstances such that there is no human author, the person by whom the arrangements necessary for the creation of the design are made shall be taken to be the author.

Proceedings for registration

A-378   3.—(1) An application for the registration of a design shall be made in the prescribed form and shall be filed at te Patent Office in the prescribed manner.

(2) An application for the registration of a design in which design right subsists shall not be entertained unless made by the person claiming to be the design right owner.

(3) For the purpose of deciding whether a design is new, the registrar may make such searches, if any, as he thinks fit.

(4) The registrar may, in such cases as may be prescribed, direct that for the purpose of deciding whether a design is new an application shall be treated as made on a date earlier or later than that on which it was in fact made.

(5) The registrar may refuse an application for the registration of a design or may register the design in pursuance of the application subject to such modifications, if any, as he thinks fit; and a design when registered shall be registered as of the date on which the application was made or is treated as having been made.

(6) An application which, owing to any default or neglect on the part of the applicant, has not been completed so as to enable registration to be effected within such time as may be prescribed shall be deemed to be abandoned.

(7) An appeal lies from any decision of the registrar under this section.

Registration of same design in respect of other articles, etc.

A-379   4.—(1) Where the registered proprietor of a design registered in respect of any article makes an application—

    (a) for registration in respect of one or more other articles, of the registered design, or

    (b) for registration in respect of the same or one or more other articles, of a design consisting of the registered design with modifications or variations not sufficient to alter the character or substantially to affect the identity thereof,

the application shall not be refused and the registration made on that application shall not be invalidated by reason only of the previous registration or publication of the registered design:

Provided that the right in a design registered by virtue of this section shall not extend beyond the end of the period, and any extended period, for which the right subsists in the original registered design.

(2) Where any person makes an application for the registration of a design in respect of any article and either—

    (a) that design has been previously registered by another person in respect of some other article; or (*b*) the design to which the application relates consists of a design previously registered by another person in respect of the same or some other article with modifications or variations not sufficient to alter the character or substantially to affect the identity thereof,

then, if at any time while the application is pending the applicant becomes the registered proprietor of the design previously registered, the foregoing provisions of this section shall apply as if at the time of making the application the applicant had been the registered proprietor of that design.

Provisions for secrecy of certain designs

5.—(1) Where, either before or after the commencement of this Act, an application for the registration of a design has been made, and it appears to the registrar that the design is one of a class notified to him by the Secretary of State as relevant for defence purposes, he may give directions for prohibiting or restricting the publication of information with respect to the design, or the communication of such information to any person or class of persons specified in the directions.

(2) The Secretary of State shall by rules make provision for securing that where such directions are given—

(*a*) the representation or specimen of the design, and

(*b*) any evidence filed in support of the applicant's contention that the appearance of an article is material (for the purposes of section 1(3) of this Act),

shall not be open to public inspection at the Patent Office during the continuance in force of the directions.

(3) Where the registrar gives any such directions as aforesaid, he shall give notice of the application and of the directions to the Secretary of State, and thereupon the following provisions shall have effect, that is to say:

(*a*) the Secretary of State shall, upon receipt of such notice, consider whether the publication of the design would be prejudicial to the defence of the realm and unless a notice under paragraph (c) of this subsection has previously been given by that authority to the registrar, shall reconsider that question before the expiration of nine months from the date of filing of the application for registration of the design and at least one in every subsequent year;

(*b*) for the purpose aforesaid, the Secretary of State may, at any time after the design has been registered or, with the consent of the applicant, at any time before the design has been registered, inspect the representation or specimen of the design, or any such evidence as is mentioned in subsection (2)(b) above, filed in pursuance of the application;

(*c*) if upon consideration of the design at any time it appears to the Secretary of State that the publication of the design would not, or would no longer, be prejudicial to the defence of the realm, he shall give notice to the registrar to that effect;

(*d*) on the receipt of any such notice the registrar shall revoke the directions and may, subject to such conditions, if any, as he thinks fit, extend the time for doing anything required or authorised to be done by or under this Act in connection with the application or registration, whether or not that time has previously expired.

(4) No person resident in the United Kingdom shall, except under the authority of a written permit granted by or on behalf of the registrar, make or cause to be made any application outside the United Kingdom for the registration of a design of any class prescribed for the purposes of this section unless—

(*a*) an application for registration of the same design has been made in the United Kingdom not less than six weeks before the application outside the United Kingdom; and

(*b*) either no directions have been given under subsection (1) of this section in relation to the application in the United Kingdom or all such directions have been revoked:

Provided that this subsection shall not apply in relation to a design for which an application for protection has first been filed in a country outside the United Kingdom by a person resident outside the United Kingdom.

. . . .

Provisions as to confidential disclosure, etc.

A–381 6.—(1) An application for the registration of a design shall not be refused, and the registration of a design shall not be invalidated, by reason only of—

    (*a*) the disclosure of the design by the proprietor to any other person in such circumstances as would make it contrary to good faith for that other person to use or publish the design;

    (*b*) the disclosure of the design in breach of good faith by any person other than the proprietor of the design; or

    (*c*) in the case of a new or original textile design intended for registration, the acceptance of a first and confidential order for goods bearing the design.

(2) An application for the registration of a design shall not be refused and the registration of a design shall not be invalidated by reason only—

    (*a*) that a representation of the design, or any article to which the design has been applied, has been displayed, with the consent of the proprietor of the design, at an exhibition certified by the Secretary of State for the purposes of this subsection;

    (*b*) that after any such display as aforesaid, and during the period of the exhibition, a representation of the design or any such article as aforesaid has been displayed by any person without the consent of the proprietor; or

    (*c*) that a representation of the design has been published in consequence of any such display as is mentioned in paragraph (a) of this subsection,

if the application for registration of the design is made not later than six months after the opening of the exhibition.

(3) An application for the registration of a design shall not be refused, and the registration of a design shall not be invalidated, by reason only of the communication of the design by the proprietor thereof to a government department or to any person authorised by a government department to consider the merits of the design, or of anything done in consequence of such a communication.

(4) Where an application is made by or with the consent of the owner of copyright in an artistic work for the registration of a corresponding design, the design shall not be treated for the purposes of this Act as being other than new by reason only of any use previously made of the artistic work, subject to subsection (5).

(5) Subsection (4) does not apply if the previous use consisted of or included the sale, letting for hire or offer or exposure for sale or hire of articles to which had been applied industrially—

    (*a*) the design in question, or

    (*b*) a design differing from it only in immaterial details or in features which are variants commonly used in the trade,

and that previous use was made by or with the consent of the copyright owner.

(6) The Secretary of State may make provision by rules as to the circumstances in which a design is to be regarded for the purposes of this section as "applied industrially" to articles, or any description of articles.

Effect of registration, &c.

Right given by registration

A–382 7.—(1) The registration of a design under this Act gives the registered proprietor the exclusive right—

    (*a*) to make or import—

        (i) for sale or hire, or

(ii) for use for the purposes of a trade or business, or

(b) to sell, hire or offer or expose for sale or hire,

an article in respect of which the design is registered and to which that design or a design not substantially different from it has been applied.

(2) The right in the registered design is infringed by a person who without the licence of the registered proprietor does anything which by virtue of subsection (1) is the exclusive right of the proprietor.

(3) The right in the registered design is also infringed by a person who, without the licence of the registered proprietor makes anything for enabling any such article to be made, in the United Kingdom or elsewhere, as mentioned in subsection (1).

(4) The right in the registered design is also infringed by a person who without the licence of the registered proprietor—

(a) does anything in relation to a kit that would be an infringement if done in relation to the assembled article (see subsection (1)), or

(b) makes anything for enabling a kit to be made or assembled, in the United Kingdom or elsewhere, if the assembled article would be such an article as is mentioned in subsection (1);

and for this purpose a "kit" means a complete or substantially complete set of components intended to be assembled into an article.

(5) No proceedings shall be taken in respect of an infringement committed before the date on which the certificate of registration of the design under this Act is granted.

(6) The right in a registered design is not infringed by the reproduction of a feature of the design which, by virtue of section 1(1)(b), is left out of account in determining whether the design is registrable.

Duration of right in registered design

8.—(1) The right in a registered design subsists in the first instance for a period of five **A–383** years from the date of the registration of the design.

(2) The period for which the right subsists may be extended for a second, third, fourth and fifth period of five years, by applying to the registrar for an extension and paying the prescribed renewal fee.

(3) If the first, second, third or fourth period expires without such application and payment being made, the right shall cease to have effect; and the registrar shall, in accordance with rules made by the Secretary of State, notify the proprietor of that fact.

(4) If during the period of six months immediately following the end of that period an application for extension is made and the prescribed renewal fee and any prescribed additional fee is paid, the right shall be treated as if it had never expired, with the result that—

(a) anything done under or in relation to the right during that further period shall be treated as valid,

(b) an act which would have constituted an infringement of the right if it had not expired shall be treated as an infringement, and

(c) an act which would have constituted use of the design for the services of the Crown if the right had not expired shall be treated as such use.

(5) Where it is shown that a registered design—

(a) was at the time it was registered a corresponding design in relation to an artistic work in which copyright subsists, and

(b) by reason of a previous use of that work would not have been registrable but for section 6(4) of this Act (registration despite certain prior applications of design),

the right in the registered design expires when the copyright in that work expires, if that is earlier than the time at which it would otherwise expire, and it may not thereafter be renewed.

(6) The above provisions have effect subject to the proviso to section 4(1) (registration of same design in respect of other articles, &c.).

Restoration of lapsed right in design

A–384   8A.—(1) Where the right in a registered design has expired by reason of a failure to extend, in accordance with section 8(2) or (4), the period for which the right subsists, an application for the restoration of the right in the design may be made to the registrar within the prescribed period.

(2) The application may be made by the person who was the registered proprietor of the design or by any other person who would have been entitled to the right in the design if it had not expired; and where the design was held by two or more persons jointly, the application may, with the leave of the registrar, be made by one or more of them without joining the others.

(3) Notice of the application shall be published by the registrar in the prescribed manner.

(4) If the registrar is satisfied that the proprietor took reasonable care to see that the period for which the right subsisted was extended in accordance with section 8(2) or (4), he shall, on payment of any unpaid renewal fee and any prescribed additional fee, order the restoration of the right in the design.

(5) The order may be made subject to such conditions as the registrar thinks fit, and if the proprietor of the design does not comply with any condition the registrar may revoke the order and give such consequential directions as he thinks fit.

(6) Rules altering the period prescribed for the purposes of subsection (1) may contain such transitional provisions and savings as appear to the Secretary of State to be necessary or expedient.

Effect of order for restoration of right

A–385   8B.—(1) The effect of an order under section 8A for the restoration of the right in a registered design is as follows.

(2) Anything done under or in relation to the right during the period between expiry and restoration shall be treated as valid.

(3) Anything done during that period which would have constituted an infringement if the right had not expired shall be treated as an infringement—

    (*a*) if done at a time when it was possible for an application for extension to be made under section 8(4); or

    (*b*) if it was a continuation or repetition of an earlier infringing act.

(4) If after it was no longer possible for such an application for extension to be made, and before publication of notice of the application for restoration, a person—

    (*a*) began in good faith to do an act which would have constituted an infringement of the right in the design if it had not expired, or

    (*b*) made in good faith effective and serious preparations to do such an act,

he has the right to continue to do the act or, as the case may be, to do the act, notwithstanding the restoration of the right in the design; but this does not extend to granting a licence to another person to do the act.

(5) If the act was done, or the preparations were made, in the course of a business, the person entitled to the right conferred by subsection (4) may—

    (*a*) authorise the doing of that act by any partners of his for the time being in that business, and

    (*b*) assign that right, or transmit it on death (or in the case of a body corporate on its dissolution), to any person who acquires that part of the business in the course of which the act was done or the preparations were made.

(6) Where an article is disposed of to another in exercise of the rights conferred by subsection (4) or subsection (5), that other and any person claiming through him may deal with the article in the same way as if it had been disposed of by the registered proprietor of the design.

(7) The above provisions apply in relation to the use of a registered design for the services of the Crown as they apply in relation to infringement of the right in the design.

Exemption of innocent infringer from liability for damages

9.—(1) In proceedings for the infringement of the right in a registered design damages **A–386** shall not be awarded against a defendant who proves that at the date of the infringement he was not aware, and had no reasonable ground for supposing, that the design was registered; and a person shall not be deemed to have been aware or to have had reasonable grounds for supposing as aforesaid by reason only of the marking of an article with the word "registered" or any abbreviation thereof, or any word or words expressing or implying that the design applied to the article has been registered, unless the number of the design accompanied the word or words or the abbreviation in question.

(2) Nothing in this section shall affect the power of the court to grant an injunction in any proceedings for infringement of the right in a registered design.

Compulsory licence in respect of registered design

10.—(1) At any time after a design has been registered any person interested may apply to **A–387** the registrar for the grant of a compulsory licence in respect of the design on the ground that the design is not applied in the United Kingdom by any industrial process or means to the article in respect of which it is registered to such an extent as is reasonable in the circumstances of the case; and the registrar may make such order on the application as he thinks fit.

(2) An order for the grant of a licence shall, without prejudice to any other method of enforcement, have effect as if it were a deed executed by the registered proprietor and all other necessary parties, granting a licence in accordance with the order.

(3) No order shall be made under this section which would be at variance with any treaty, convention, arrangement or engagement applying to the United Kingdom and any convention country.

(4) An appeal shall lie from any order of the registrar under this section.

Cancellation of registration

11.—(1) The registrar may, upon a request made in the prescribed manner by the regis- **A–388** tered proprietor, cancel the registration of a design.

(2) At any time after a design has been registered any person interested may apply to the registrar for the cancellation of the registration of the design on the ground that the design was not, at the date of the registration thereof, new . . . , or on any other ground on which the registrar could have refused to register the design; and the registrar may make such order on the application as he thinks fit.

(3) At any time after a design has been registered, any person interested may apply to the registrar for the cancellation of the registration on the ground that—

(a) the design was at the time it was registered a corresponding design in relation to an artistic work in which copyright subsisted, and

(b) the right in the registered design has expired in accordance with section 8(4) of this Act (expiry of right in registered design on expiry of copyright in artistic work);

and the registrar may make such order on the application as he thinks fit.

(4) A cancellation under this section takes effect—

(a) in the case of cancellation under subsection (1), from the date of the registrar's decision,

(b) in the case of cancellation under subsection (2), from the date of registration,

(c) in the case of cancellation under subsection (3), from the date on which the right in the registered design expired, or, in any case, from such other date as the registrar may direct.

(5) An appeal lies from any order of the registrar under this section.

Powers exercisable for protection of the public interest

A–389   11A.—(1) Where a report of the Monopolies and Mergers Commission has been laid before Parliament containing conclusions to the effect—

    (*a*) on a monopoly reference, that a monopoly situation exists and facts found by the Commission operate or may be expected to operate against the public interest,

    (*b*) on a merger reference, that a merger situation qualifying for investigation has been created and the creation of the situation, or particular elements in or consequences of it specified in the report, operate or may be expected to operate against the public interest,

    (*c*) on a competition reference, that a person was engaged in an anti-competitive practice which operated or may be expected to operate against the public interest, or

    (*d*) on a reference under section 11 of the Competition Act 1980 (reference of public bodies and certain other persons), that a person is pursuing a course of conduct which operates against the public interest,

the appropriate Minister or Ministers may apply to the registrar to take action under this section.

(2) Before making an application the appropriate Minister or Ministers shall publish, in such manner as he or they think appropriate, a notice describing the nature of the proposed application and shall consider any representations which may be made within 30 days of such publication by persons whose interests appear to him or them to be affected.

(3) If on an application under this section it appears to the registrar that the matters specified in the Commission's report as being those which in the Commission's opinion operate, or operated or may be expected to operate, against the public interest include—

    (*a*) conditions in licences granted in respect of a registered design by its proprietor restricting the use of the design by the licensee or the right of the proprietor to grant other licences, or

    (*b*) a refusal by the proprietor of a registered design to grant licences on reasonable terms,

he may by order cancel or modify any such condition or may, instead or in addition, make an entry in the register to the effect that licences in respect of the design are to be available as of right.

(4) The terms of a licence available by virtue of this section shall, in default of agreement, be settled by the registrar on an application by the person requiring the licence; and terms so settled shall authorise the licensee to do everything which would be an infringement of the right in the registered design in the absence of a licence.

(5) Where the terms of a licence are settled by the registrar, the licence has effect from the date on which the application to him was made.

(6) An appeal lies from any order of the registrar under this section.

(7) In this section "the appropriate Minister or Ministers" means the Minister or Ministers to whom the report of the Monopolies and Mergers Commission was made.

Undertaking to take licence of right in infringement proceedings

A–390   11B.—(1) If in proceedings for infringement of the right in a registered design in respect of which a licence is available as of right under section 11A of this Act the defendant undertakes to take a licence on such terms as may be agreed or, in default of agreement, settled by the registrar under that section—

    (*a*) no injunction shall be granted against him, and

    (*b*) the amount recoverable against him by way of damages or on account of profits shall not exceed double the amount which would have been payable by him as licensee if such a licence on those terms had been granted before the earliest infringement.

(2) An undertaking may be given at any time before final order in the proceedings, without any admission of liability.

(3) Nothing in this section affects the remedies available in respect of an infringement committed before licences of right were available.

Use for services of the Crown

12. The provisions of the First Schedule to this Act shall have effect with respect to the use **A–391** of registered designs for the services of the Crown and the rights of third parties in respect of such use.

International Arrangements

Orders in Council as to convention countries

13.—(1) His Majesty may, with a view to the fulfilment of a treaty, convention, arrange- **A–392** ment or engagement, by Order in Council declare that any country specified in the Order is a convention country for the purposes of this Act:

Provided that a declaration may be made as aforesaid for the purposes either of all or of some only of the provisions of this Act, and a country in the case of which a declaration made for the purposes of some only of the provisions of this Act is in force shall be deemed to be a convention country for the purposes of those provisions only.

(2) His Majesty may by Order in Council direct that any of the Channel Islands, any col- ony, . . . shall be deemed to be a convention country for the purposes of all or any of the pro- visions of this Act; and an Order made under this subsection may direct that any such provisions shall have effect, in relation to the territory in question, subject to such conditions or limitations, if any, as may be specified in the Order.

(3) For the purposes of subsection (1) of this section, every colony, protectorate, territory subject to the authority or under the suzerainty of another country, and territory adminis- tered by another country . . . under the trusteeship system of the United Nations, shall be deemed to be a country in the case of which a declaration may be made under that sub- section.

Registration of design where application for protection in convention country has been made

14.—(1) An application for registration of a design in respect of which protection has been **A–393** applied for in a convention country may be made in accordance with the provisions of this Act by the person by whom the application for protection was made or his personal represen- tative or assignee:

Provided that no application shall be made by virtue of this section after the expiration of six months from the date of the application for protection in a convention country or, where more than one such application for protection has been made, from the date of the first appli- cation.

(2) Where an application for registration of a design is made by virtue of this section, the application shall be treated, for the purpose of determining whether that or any other design is new, as made on the date of the application for protection in the convention country or, if more than one such application was made, on the date of the first such application.

(3) Subsection (2) shall not be construed as excluding the power to give directions under section 3(4) of this Act in relation to an application made by virtue of this section.

(4) Where a person has applied for protection for a design by an application which—

(a) in accordance with the terms of a treaty subsisting between two or more convention countries, is equivalent to an application duly made in any one of those convention countries; or

(b) in accordance with the law of any convention country, is equivalent to an appli- cation duly made in that convention country, he shall be deemed for the purposes of this section to have applied in that convention country.

Extension of time for applications under s.14 in certain cases

A–394   15.—(1) If the Secretary of State is satisfied that provision substantially equivalent to the provision to be made by or under this section has been or will be made under the law of any convention country, he may make rules empowering the registrar to extend the time for making application under subsection (1) of section 14 of this Act for registration of a design in respect of which protection has been applied for in that country in any case where the period specified in the proviso to that subsection expires during a period prescribed by the rules.

(2) Rules made under this section—

(a) may, where any agreement or arrangement has been made between His Majesty's Government in the United Kingdom and the government of the convention country for the supply or mutual exchange of information or articles, provide, either generally or in any class of case specified in the rules, that an extension of time shall not be granted under this section unless the design has been communicated in accordance with the agreement or arrangement;

(b) may, either generally or in any class of case specified in the rules, fix the maximum extension which may be granted under this section;

(c) may prescribe or allow any special procedure in connection with applications made by virtue of this section;

(d) may empower the registrar to extend, in relation to an application made by virtue of this section, the time limited by or under the foregoing provisions of this Act for doing any act, subject to such conditions, if any, as may be imposed by or under the rules;

(e) may provide for securing that the rights conferred by registration on an application made by virtue of this section shall be subject to such restrictions or conditions as may be specified by or under the rules and in particular to restrictions and conditions for the protection of persons (including persons acting on behalf of His Majesty) who, otherwise than as the result of a communication made in accordance with such an agreement or arrangement as is mentioned in paragraph (a) of this subsection, and before the date of the application in question or such later date as may be allowed by the rules, may have imported or made articles to which the design is applied or may have made any application for registration of the design.

Protection of designs communicated under international agreements

A–395   16.—(1) Subject to the provisions of this section, the Secretary of State may make rules for securing that, where a design has been communicated in accordance with an agreement or arrangement made between His Majesty's Government in the United Kingdom and the government of any other country for the supply or mutual exchange of information or articles,—

(a) an application for the registration of the design made by the person from whom the design was communicated or his personal representative or assignee shall not be prejudiced, and the registration of the design in pursuance of such an application shall not be invalidated, by reason only that the design has been communicated as aforesaid or that in consequence thereof—

(i) the design has been published or applied, or

(ii) an application for registration of the design has been made by any other person, or the design has been registered on such an application;

(b) any application for the registration of a design made in consequence of such a communication as aforesaid may be refused and any registration of a design made on such an application may be cancelled.

(2) Rules made under subsection (1) of this section may provide that the publication or

application of a design, or the making of any application for registration thereof shall, in such circumstances and subject to such conditions or exceptions as may be prescribed by the rules, be presumed to have been in consequence of such a communication as is mentioned in that subsection.

(3) The powers of the Secretary of State under this section, so far as they are exercisable for the benefit of persons from whom designs have been communicated to His Majesty's Government in the United Kingdom by the government of any other country, shall only be exercised if and to the extent that the Secretary of State is satisfied that substantially equivalent provision has been or will be made under the law of that country for the benefit of persons from whom designs have been communicated by His Majesty's Government in the United Kingdom to the government of that country.

(4) References in the last foregoing subsection to the communication of a design to or by His Majesty's Government or the government of any other country shall be construed as including references to the communication of the design by or to any person authorised in that behalf by the government in question.

Register of designs, etc.

Register of designs

17.—(1) The registrar shall maintain the register of designs, in which shall be entered— **A–396**
   (*a*) the names and addresses of proprietors of registered designs;
   (*b*) notices of assignments and of transmissions of registered designs; and
   (*c*) such other matters as may be prescribed or as the registrar may think fit.

(2) No notice of any trust, whether express, implied or constructive, shall be entered in the register of designs, and the registrar shall not be affected by any such notice.

(3) The register need not be kept in documentary form.

(4) Subject to the provisions of this Act and to rules made by the Secretary of State under it, the public shall have a right to inspect the register at the Patent Office at all convenient times.

(5) Any person who applies for a certified copy of an entry in the register or a certified extract from the register shall be entitled to obtain such a copy or extract on payment of a fee prescribed in relation to certified copies and extracts; and rules made by the Secretary of State under this Act may provide that any person who applies for an uncertified copy or extract shall be entitled to such a copy or extract on payment of a fee prescribed in relation to uncertified copies and extracts.

(6) Applications under subsection (5) above or rules made by virtue of that subsection shall be made in such manner as may be prescribed.

(7) In relation to any portion of the register kept otherwise than in documentary form—
   (*a*) the right of inspection conferred by subsection (4) above is a right to inspect the material on the register; and
   (*b*) the right to a copy or extract conferred by subsection (5) above or rules is a right to a copy or extract in a form in which it can be taken away and in which it is visible and legible.

(8) Subject to subsection (11) below, the register shall be prima facie evidence of anything required or authorised to be entered in it and in Scotland shall be sufficient evidence of any such thing.

(9) A certificate purporting to be signed by the registrar and certifying that any entry which he is authorised by or under this Act to make has or has not been made, or that any other thing which he is so authorised to do has or has not been done, shall be prima facie evidence, and in Scotland shall be sufficient evidence, of the matters so certified.

(10) Each of the following—
   (*a*) a copy of an entry in the register or an extract from the register which is supplied under subsection (5) above;
   (*b*) a copy or any representation, specimen or document kept in the Patent Office or an extract from any such document,

which purports to be a certified copy or certified extract shall, subject to subsection (11) below, be admitted in evidence without further proof and without production of any original; and in Scotland such evidence shall be sufficient evidence.

(11) In the application of this section to England and Wales nothing in it shall be taken as detracting from section 69 or 70 of the Police and Criminal Evidence Act 1984 or any provision made by virtue of either of them.

(12) In this section "certified copy" and "certified extract" means a copy and extract certified by the registrar and sealed with the seal of the Patent Office.

Certificate of registration

A-397   18.—(1) The registrar shall grant a certificate of registration in the prescribed form to the registered proprietor of a design when the design is registered.

(2) The registrar may, in a case where he is satisfied that the certificate of registration has been lost or destroyed, or in any other case in which he thinks it expedient, furnish one or more copies of the certificate.

Registration of assignments, etc.

A-398   19.—(1) Where any person becomes entitled by assignment, transmission or operation of law to a registered design or to a share in a registered design, or becomes entitled as mortgagee, licensee or otherwise to any other interest in a registered design, he shall apply to the registrar in the prescribed manner for the registration of his title as proprietor or co-proprietor or, as the case may be, of notice of his interest, in the register of designs.

(2) Without prejudice to the provisions of the foregoing subsection, an application for the registration of the title of any person becoming entitled by assignment to a registered design or a share in a registered design, or becoming entitled by virtue of a mortgage, licence or other instrument to any other interest in a registered design, may be made in the prescribed manner by the assignor, mortgagor, licensor or other party to that instrument, as the case may be.

(3) Where application is made under this section for the registration of the title of any person, the registrar shall, upon proof of title to his satisfaction—

    (a) where that person is entitled to a registered design or a share in a registered design, register him in the register of designs as proprietor or co-proprietor of the design, and enter in that register particulars of the instrument or event by which he derives title; or

    (b) where that person is entitled to any other interest in the registered design, enter in that register notice of his interest, with particulars of the instrument (if any) creating it.

(3A) Where design right subsists in a registered design, the registrar shall not register an interest under subsection (3) unless he is satisfied that the person entitled to that interest is also entitled to a corresponding interest in the design right.

(3B) Where design right subsists in a registered design and the proprietor of the registered design is also the design right owner, an assignment of the design right shall be taken to be also an assignment of the right in the registered design, unless a contrary intention appears.

(4) Subject to any rights vested in any other person of which notice is entered in the register of designs, the person or persons registered as proprietor of a registered design shall have power to assign, grant licences under, or otherwise deal with the design, and to give effectual receipts for any consideration for any such assignment, licence or dealing.

Provided that any equities in respect of the design may be enforced in like manner as in respect of any other personal property.

(5) Except for the purposes of an application to rectify the register under the following provisions of this Act, a document in respect of which no entry has been made in the register of designs under subsection (3) of this section shall not be admitted in any court as evidence of the title of any person to a registered design or share of or interest in a registered design unless the court otherwise directs.

Rectification of register

20.—(1) The court may, on the application of any person aggrieved, order the register of designs to be rectified by the making of any entry therein or the variation or deletion of any entry therein.

(2) In proceedings under this section the court may determine any question which it may be necessary or expedient to decide in connection with the rectification of the register.

(3) Notice of any application to the court under this section shall be given in the prescribed manner to the registrar, who shall be entitled to appear and be heard on the application, and shall appear if so directed by the court.

(4) Any order made by the court under this section shall direct that notice of the order shall be served on the registrar in the prescribed manner; and the registrar shall, on receipt of the notice, rectify the register accordingly.

(5) A rectification of the register under this section has effect as follows—
   (a) an entry made has effect from the date on which it should have been made,
   (b) an entry varied has effect as if it had originally been made in its varied form, and
   (c) an entry deleted shall be deemed never to have had effect,
unless, in any case, the court directs otherwise.

Power to correct clerical errors

21.—(1) The registrar may, in accordance with the provisions of this section, correct any error in an application for the registration or in the representation of a design, or any error in the register of designs.

(2) A correction may be made in pursuance of this section either upon a request in writing made by any person interested and accompanied by the prescribed fee, or without such a request.

(3) Where the registrar proposes to make any such correction as aforesaid otherwise than in pursuance of a request made under this section, he shall give notice of the proposal to the registered proprietor or the applicant for registration of the design, as the case may be, and to any other person who appears to him to be concerned, and shall give them an opportunity to be heard before making the correction.

Inspection of registered designs

22.—(1) Where a design has been registered under this Act, there shall be open to inspection at the Patent Office on and after the day on which the certificate of registration is issued—
   (a) the representation or specimen of the design, and
   (b) any evidence filed in support of the applicant's contention that the appearance of an article is material (for the purposes of section 1(3) of this Act).

This subsection has effect subject to the following provisions of this section and to any rules made under section 5(2) of this Act.

(2) In the case of a design registered in respect of an article of any class prescribed for the purposes of this subsection, no representation, specimen or evidence filed in pursuance of the application shall, until the expiration of such period after the day on which the certificate of registration is issued as may be prescribed in relation to articles of that class, be open to inspection at the Patent Office except by the registered proprietor, a person authorised in writing by the registered proprietor, or a person authorised by the registrar or by the court:

Provided that where the registrar proposes to refuse an application for the registration of any other design on the ground that it is the same as the first-mentioned design or differs from that design only in immaterial details or in features which are variants commonly used in the trade, the applicant shall be entitled to inspect the representation or specimen of the first-mentioned design filed in pursuance of the application for registration of that design.

(3) In the case of a design registered in respect of an article of any class prescribed for the purposes of the last foregoing subsection, the representation, specimen or evidence shall not,

during the period prescribed as aforesaid, be inspected by any person by virtue of this section except in the presence of the registrar or of an officer acting under him; and except in the case of an inspection authorised by the proviso to that subsection, the person making the inspection shall not be entitled to take a copy of the representation, specimen or evidence or any part thereof.

(4) Where an application for the registration of a design has been abandoned or refused, neither the application for registration nor any representation, specimen or evidence filed in pursuance thereof shall at any time be open to inspection at the Patent Office or be published by the registrar.

Information as to existence of right in registered design

A–402 23. On the request of a person furnishing such information as may enable the registrar to identify the design, and on payment of the prescribed fee, the registrar shall inform him—

    (*a*) whether the design is registered and, if so, in respect of what articles, and

    (*b*) whether any extension of the period of the right in the registered design has been granted,

and shall state the date of registration and the name and address of the registered proprietor.

. . . .

Legal proceedings and appeals

Certificate of contested validity of registration

A–403 25.—(1) If in any proceedings before the court the validity of the registration of a design is contested, and it is found by the court that the design is validly registered, the court may certify that the validity of the registration of the design was contested in those proceedings.

(2) Where any such certificate has been granted, then if in any subsequent proceedings before the court for infringement of the right in the registered design or for cancellation of the registration of the design, a final order or judgment is made or given in favour of the registered proprietor, he shall, unless the court otherwise directs, be entitled to his costs as between solicitor and client:

Provided that this subsection shall not apply to the costs of any appeal in any such proceedings as aforesaid.

Remedy for groundless threats of infringement proceedings

A–404 26.—(1) Where any person (whether entitled to or interested in a registered design or an application for registration of a design or not) by circulars, advertisements or otherwise threatens any other person with proceedings for infringement of the right in a registered design, any person aggrieved thereby may bring an action against him for any such relief as is mentioned in the next following subsection.

(2) Unless in any action brought by virtue of this section the defendant proves that the acts in respect of which proceedings were threatened constitute or, if done, would constitute, an infringement of the right in a registered design the registration of which is not shown by the plaintiff to be invalid, the plaintiff shall be entitled to the following relief, that is to say:

    (*a*) a declaration to the effect that the threats are unjustifiable;

    (*b*) an injunction against the continuance of the threats; and

    (*c*) such damages, if any, as he has sustained thereby.

(2A) Proceedings may not be brought under this section in respect of a threat to bring proceedings for an infringement alleged to consist of the making or importing of anything.

(3) For the avoidance of doubt it is hereby declared that a mere notification that a design is registered does not constitute a threat of proceedings within the meaning of this section.

The court

27.—(1) In this Act "the court" means— **A–405**
- (*a*) in England and Wales, the High Court or any patents county court having jurisdiction by virtue of an order under section 287 of the Copyright, Designs and Patents Act 1988,
- (*b*) in Scotland, the Court of Session, and
- (*c*) in Northern Ireland, the High Court.

(2) Provision may be made by rules of court with respect to proceedings in the High Court in England and Wales for references and applications under this Act to be dealt with by such judge of that court as the Lord Chancellor may select for the purpose.

The Appeal Tribunal

28.—(1) Any appeal from the registrar under this Act shall lie to the Appeal Tribunal. **A–406**

(2) The Appeal Tribunal shall consist of—
- (*a*) one or more judges of the High Court nominated by the Lord Chancellor, and
- (*b*) one judge of the Court of Session nominated by the Lord President of that Court.

(2A) At any time when it consists of two or more judges, the jurisdiction of the Appeal Tribunal—
- (*a*) where in the case of any particular appeal the senior of those judges so directs, shall be exercised in relation to that appeal by both of the judges, or (if there are more than two) by two of them, sitting together, and
- (*b*) in relation to any appeal in respect of which no such direction is given, may be exercised by any one of the judges;

and, in the exercise of that jurisdiction, different appeals may be heard at the same time by different judges.

(3) The expenses of the Appeal Tribunal shall be defrayed and the fees to be taken therein may be fixed as if the Tribunal were a court of the High Court.

(4) The Appeal Tribunal may examine witnesses on oath and administer oaths for that purpose.

(5) Upon any appeal under this Act the Appeal Tribunal may by order award to any party such costs or expenses as the Tribunal may consider reasonable and direct how and by what parties the costs or expenses are to be paid; and any such order may be enforced—
- (*a*) in England and Wales or Northern Ireland, in the same way as an order of the High Court;
- (*b*) in Scotland, in the same way as a decree for expenses granted by the Court of Session.

. . . .

(7) Upon any appeal under this Act the Appeal Tribunal may exercise any power which could have been exercised by the registrar in the proceeding from which the appeal is brought.

(8) Subject to the foregoing provisions of this section the Appeal Tribunal may make rules for regulating all matters relating to proceedings before it under this Act, including right of audience.

(8A) At any time when the Appeal Tribunal consists of two or more judges, the power to make rules under subsection (8) of this section shall be exercisable by the senior of those judges:

Provided that another of those judges may exercise that power if it appears to him that it is necessary for rules to be made and that the judge (or, if more than one, each of the judges) senior to him is for the time being prevented by illness, absence or otherwise from making them.

(9) An appeal to the Appeal Tribunal under this Act shall not be deemed to be a proceeding in the High Court.

(10) In this section "the High Court" means the High Court in England and Wales; and for the purposes of this section the seniority of judges shall be reckoned by reference to the dates on which they were appointed judges of that court or the Court of Session.

Powers and duties of Registrar

Exercise of discretionary powers of registrar

A–407   29. Without prejudice to any provisions of this Act requiring the registrar to hear any party to proceedings thereunder, or to give to any such party an opportunity to be heard, rules made by the Secretary of State under this Act shall require the registrar to give to any applicant for registration of a design an opportunity to be heard before exercising adversely to the applicant any discretion vested in the registrar by or under this Act.

Costs and security for costs

A–408   30.—(1) Rules made by the Secretary of State under this Act may make provision empowering the registrar, in any proceedings before him under this Act—

    (*a*) to award any party such costs as he may consider reasonable, and

    (*b*) to direct how and by what parties they are to be paid.

(2) Any such order of the registrar may be enforced—

    (*a*) in England and Wales or Northern Ireland, in the same way as an order of the High Court,

    (*b*) in Scotland, in the same way as a decree for expenses granted by the Court of Session.

(3) Rules made by the Secretary of State under this Act may make provision empowering the registrar to require a person, in such cases as may be prescribed, to give security for the costs of—

    (*a*) an application for cancellation of the registration of a design,

    (*b*) an application for the grant of a licence in respect of a registered design, or

    (*c*) an appeal from any decision of the registrar under this Act,

and enabling the application or appeal to be treated as abandoned in default of such security being given.

Evidence before registrar

A–409   31. Rules made by the Secretary of State under this Act may make provision—

    (*a*) as to the giving of evidence in proceedings before the registrar under this Act by affidavit or statutory declaration;

    (*b*) conferring on the registrar the powers of an official referee of the Supreme Court as regards the examination of witnesses on oath and the discovery and production of documents; and

    (*c*) applying in relation to the attendance of witnesses in proceedings before the registrar the rules applicable to the attendance of witnesses in proceedings before such a referee.

. . . .

Offences

Offences under s.5

A–410   33.—(1) If any person fails to comply with any direction under section five of this Act or makes or causes to be made an application for the registration of a design in contravention of that section, he shall be guilty of an offence and liable—

    (*a*) on conviction on indictment to imprisonment for a term not exceeding two years or a fine, or both;

(*b*) on summary conviction to imprisonment for a term not exceeding six months or a fine not exceeding the statutory maximum, or both.

. . . .

Falsification of register, etc.

34. If any person makes or causes to be made a false entry in the register of designs, or a   **A–411** writing falsely purporting to be a copy of an entry in that register, or produces or tenders or causes to be produced or tendered in evidence any such writing, knowing the entry or writing to be false, he shall be guilty of an offence and liable—

    (*a*) on conviction on indictment to imprisonment for a term not exceeding two years or a fine, or both;

    (*b*) on summary conviction to imprisonment for a term not exceeding six months or a fine not exceeding the statutory maximum, or both.

Fine or falsely representing a design as registered

35.—(1) If any person falsely represents that a design applied to any article sold by him is   **A–412** registered in respect of that article, he shall be liable on summary conviction to a fine not exceeding level 3 on the standard scale; and for the purposes of this provision a person who sells an article having stamped, engraved or impressed thereon or otherwise applied thereto the word "registered", or any other word expressing or implying the design applied to the article is registered, shall be deemed to represent that the design applied to the article is registered in respect of that article.

(2) If any person, after the right in a registered design has expired, marks any article to which the design has been applied with the word "registered", or any word or words implying that there is a subsisting right in the design under this Act, or causes any such article to be so marked, he shall be liable on summary conviction to a fine not exceeding level 1 on the standard scale.

Offence by body corporate: liability of officers

35A.—(1) Where an offence under this Act committed by a body corporate is proved to   **A–413** have been committed with the consent or connivance of a director, manager, secretary or other similar officer of the body, or a person purporting to act in any such capacity, he as well as the body corporate is guilty of the offence and liable to be proceeded against and punished accordingly.

(2) In relation to a body corporate whose affairs are managed by its members "director" means a member of the body corporate.

Rules, etc.

General power of Secretary of State to make rules, etc.

36.—(1) Subject to the provisions of this Act, the Secretary of State may make such rules   **A–414** as he thinks expedient for regulating the business of the Patent Office in relation to designs and for regulating all matters by this Act placed under the direction or control of the registrar or the Secretary of State.

(1A) Rules may, in particular, make provision—

    (*a*) prescribing the form of applications for registration of designs and of any representations or specimens of designs or other documents which may be filed at the Patent Office, and requiring copies to be furnished of any such representations, specimens or documents;

    (*b*) regulating the procedure to be followed in connection with any application or request to the registrar or in connection with any proceeding before him, and authorising the rectification of irregularities of procedure;

(*c*) providing for the appointment of advisers to assist the registrar in proceedings before him;

(*d*) regulating the keeping of the register of designs;

(*e*) authorising the publication and sale of copies of representations of designs and other documents in the Patent Office;

(*f*) prescribing anything authorised or required by this Act to be prescribed by rules.

(1B) The remuneration of an adviser appointed to assist the registrar shall be determined by the Secretary of State with the consent of the Treasury and shall be defrayed out of money provided by Parliament.

(2) Rules made under this section may provide for the establishment of branch offices for designs and may authorise any document or thing required by or under this Act to be filed or done at the Patent Office to be filed or done at the branch office at Manchester or any other branch office established in pursuance of the rules.

Provisions as to rules and Orders

A–415   37.—(1) . . . .

(2) Any rules made by the Secretary of State in pursuance of section 15 or section 16 of this Act, and any order made, direction given, or other action taken under the rules by the registrar, may be made, given or taken so as to have effect as respects things done or omitted to be done on or after such date, whether before or after the coming into operation of the rules or of this Act, as may be specified in the rules.

(3) Any power to make rules conferred by this Act on the Secretary of State or on the Appeal Tribunal shall be exercisable by statutory instrument; and the Statutory Instruments Act 1946 shall apply to a statutory instrument containing rules made by the Appeal Tribunal in like manner as if the rules had been made by a Minister of the Crown.

(4) Any statutory instrument containing rules made by the Secretary of State under this Act shall be subject to annulment in pursuance of a resolution of either House of Parliament.

(5) Any Order in Council made under this Act may be revoked or varied by a subsequent Order in Council.

. . . .

Supplemental

Hours of business and excluded days

A–416   39.—(1) Rules made by the Secretary of State under this Act may specify the hour at which the Patent Office shall be deemed to be closed on any day for purposes of the transaction by the public of business under this Act or of any class of such business, and may specify days as excluded days for any such purposes.

(2) Any business done under this Act on any day after the hour specified as aforesaid in relation to business of that class, or on a day which is an excluded day in relation to business of that class, shall be deemed to have been done on the next following day not being an excluded day; and where the time for doing anything under this Act expires on an excluded day, that time shall be extended to the next following day not being an excluded day.

Fees

A–417   40. There shall be paid in respect of the registration of designs and applications therefor, and in respect of other matters relating to designs arising under this Act, such fees as may be prescribed by rules made by the Secretary of State with the consent of the Treasury.

Service of notices, &c., by post

A–418   41. Any notice required or authorised to be given by or under this Act, and any application or other document so authorised or required to be made or filed, may be given, made or filed by post.

Annual report of registrar

42. The Comptroller-General of Patents, Designs and Trade Marks shall, in his annual report with respect to the execution of the Patents Act 1977, include a report with respect to the execution of this Act as if it formed a part of or was included in that Act.

A–419

Savings

43.—(1) Nothing in this Act shall be construed as authorising or requiring the registrar to register a design the use of which would, in his opinion, be contrary to law or morality.

A–420

(2) Nothing in this Act shall affect the right of the Crown or of any person deriving title directly or indirectly from the Crown to sell or use articles forfeited under the laws relating to customs or excise.

Interpretation

44.—(1) In this Act, except where the context otherwise requires, the following expressions have the meanings hereby respectively assigned by them, that is to say—

A–421

"Appeal Tribunal" means the Appeal Tribunal constituted and acting in accordance with section 28 of this Act as amended by the Administration of Justice Act 1969;

"article" means any article of manufacture and includes any part of an article if that part is made and sold separately;

"artistic work" has the same meaning as in Part I of the Copyright, Designs and Patents Act 1988;

"assignee" includes the personal representative of a deceased assignee, and references to the assignee of any person include references to the assignee of the personal representative or assignee of that person;

"author", in relation to a design, has the meaning given by section 2(3) and (4);

. . . .

"corresponding design", in relation to an artistic work, means a design which if applied to an article would produce something which would be treated for the purposes of Part I of the Copyright, Designs and Patents Act 1988 as a copy of that work;

"the court" shall be construed in accordance with section 27 of this Act;

"design" has the meaning assigned to it by section 1(1) of this Act;

"employee", "employment" and "employer" refer to employment under a contract of service or of apprenticeship;

. . . .

"prescribed" means prescribed by rules made by the Secretary of State under this Act;

"proprietor" has the meaning assigned to it by section two of this Act;

"registered proprietor" means the person or persons for the time being entered in the register of designs as proprietor of the design;

"registrar" means the Comptroller-General of Patents Designs and Trade-Marks;

"set of articles" means a number of articles of the same general character ordinarily on sale or intended to be used together, to each of which the same design, or the same design with modifications or variations not sufficient to alter the character or substantially to affect the identity thereof, is applied.

(2) Any reference in this Act to an article in respect of which a design is registered shall, in

the case of a design registered in respect of a set of articles, be construed as a reference to any article of that set.

(3) Any question arising under this Act whether a number of articles constitute a set of articles shall be determined by the registrar; and notwithstanding anything in this Act any determination of the registrar under this subsection shall be final.

(4) For the purposes of subsection (1) of section 14 and of section 16 of this Act, the expression "personal representative," in relation to a deceased person, includes the legal representative of the deceased appointed in any country outside the United Kingdom.

Application to Scotland

A–422   45. In the application of this Act to Scotland—

. . . .

(3) The expression "injunction" means "interdict"; the expression "arbitrator" means "arbiter"; the expression "plaintiff" means "pursuer"; the expression "defendant" means "defender."

Application to Northern Ireland

A–423   46. In the application of this Act to Northern Ireland—

. . . .

(3) References to enactments include enactments comprised in Northern Ireland legislation:

(3A) References to the Crown include the Crown in right of Her Majesty's Government in Northern Ireland:

(4) References to a government department shall be construed as including references to a Northern Ireland department, and in relation to a Northern Ireland department references to the Treasury shall be construed as references to the Department of Finance and Personnel.

. . . .

Application to Isle of Man

A–424   47. This Act extends to the Isle of Man, subject to any modifications contained in an Order made by Her Majesty in Council, and accordingly, subject to any such Order, references in this Act to the United Kingdom shall be construed as including the Isle of Man.

Territorial waters and the continental shelf

A–425   47A.—(1) For the purposes of this Act the territorial waters of the United Kingdom shall be treated as part of the United Kingdom.

(2) This Act applies to things done in the United Kingdom sector of the continental shelf on a structure or vessel which is present there for purposes directly connected with the exploration of the sea bed or subsoil or the exploitation of their natural resources as it applies to things done in the United Kingdom.

(3) The United Kingdom sector of the continental shelf means the areas designated by order under section 1(7) of the Continental Shelf Act 1964.

Repeals, savings, and transitional provisions

A–426   48.—(1) . . . .

(2) Subject to the provisions of this section, any Order in Council, rule, order, requirement, certificate, notice, decision, direction, authorisation, consent, application, request or thing made, issued given or done under any enactment repealed by this Act shall, if in force at the commencement of this Act, and so far as it could have been made, issued, given or

done under this Act, continue in force and have effect as if made, issued, given or done under the corresponding enactment of this Act.

(3) Any register kept under the Patents and Designs Act 1907 shall be deemed to form part of the corresponding register under this Act.

(4) Any design registered before the commencement of this Act shall be deemed to be registered under this Act in respect of articles of the class in which it is registered.

(5) Where, in relation to any design, the time for giving notice to the registrar under section 59 of the Patents and Designs Act 1907 expired before the commencement of this Act and the notice was not given, subsection (2) of section 6 of this Act shall not apply in relation to that design or any registration of that design.

(6) Any document referring to any enactment repealed by this Act shall be construed as referring to the corresponding enactment of this Act.

(7) Nothing in the foregoing provisions of this section shall be taken as prejudicing the operation of section 38 of the Interpretation Act 1889 (which relates to the effect of repeals).

Short title and commencement

49.—(1) This Act may be cited as the Registered Designs Act 1949.   **A–427**

(2) This Act shall come into operation on the first day of January, nineteen hundred and fifty, immediately after the coming into operation of the Patents and Designs Act 1949.

FIRST SCHEDULE

Provisions as to the Use of Registered Designs for the Services of the Crown and as to the Rights of Third Parties in Respect of such Use

Use of registered designs for services of the Crown

1.—(1) Notwithstanding anything in this Act, any Government department, and any per-   **A–428**
son authorised in writing by a Government department, may use any registered design for the services of the Crown in accordance with the following provisions of this paragraph.

(2) If and so far as the design has before the date of registration thereof been duly recorded by or applied by or on behalf of a Government department otherwise than in consequence of the communication of the design directly or indirectly by the registered proprietor or any person from whom he derives title, any use of the design by virtue of this paragraph may be made free of any royalty or other payment to the registered proprietor.

(3) If and so far as the design has not been so recorded or applied as aforesaid, any use of the design made by virtue of this paragraph at any time after the date of registration thereof, or in consequence of any such communication as aforesaid, shall be made upon such terms as may be agreed upon, either before or after the use, between the Government department and the registered proprietor with the approval of the Treasury, or as may in default of agreement be determined by the court on a reference under paragraph 3 of this Schedule.

(4) The authority of a Government department in respect of a design may be given under this paragraph either before or after the design is registered and either before or after the acts in respect of which the authority is given are done, and may be given to any person whether or not he is authorised directly or indirectly by the registered proprietor to use the design.

(5) Where any use of a design is made by or with the authority of a Government department under this paragraph, then, unless it appears to the department that it would be contrary to the public interest so to do, the department shall notify the registered proprietor as soon as practicable after the use is begun and furnish him with such information as to the extent of the use as he may from time to time require.

(6) For the purposes of this and the next following paragraph "the services of the Crown" shall be deemed to include—

(a) the supply to the government of any country outside the United Kingdom, in pursuance of an agreement or arrangement between Her Majesty's Government in the United Kingdom and the government of that country, of articles required—
  (i) for the defence of that country; or
  (ii) for the defence of any other country whose government is party to any agreement or arrangement with Her Majesty's said Government in respect of defence matters;
(b) the supply to the United Nations, or the government of any country belonging to that organisation, in pursuance of an agreement or arrangement between Her Majesty's Government and that organisation or government, of articles required for any armed forces operating in pursuance of a resolution of that organisation or any organ of that organisation;

and the power of a Government department or a person authorised by a Government department under this paragraph to use a design shall include power to sell to any such government or to the said organisation any articles the supply of which is authorised by this sub-paragraph, and to sell to any person any articles made in the exercise of the powers conferred by this paragraph which are no longer required for the purpose for which they were made.

(7) The purchaser of any articles sold in the exercise of powers conferred by this paragraph, and any person claiming through him, shall have power to deal with them in the same manner as if the rights in the registered design were held on behalf of His Majesty.

Rights of third parties in respect of Crown use

A–429   2.—(1) In relation to any use of a registered design, or a design in respect of which an application for registration is pending, made for the services of the Crown—
  (a) by a Government department or a person authorised by a Government department under the last foregoing paragraph; or
  (b) by the registered proprietor or applicant for registration to the order of a Government department,
the provisions of any licence, assignment or agreement made, whether before or after the commencement of this Act, between the registered proprietor or applicant for registration or any person who derives title from him or from whom he derives title and any person other than a Government department shall be of no effect so far as those provisions restrict or regulate the use of the design, or any model, document or information relating thereto, or provide for the making of payments in respect of any such use, or calculated by reference thereto; and the reproduction or publication of any model or document in connection with the said use shall not be deemed to be an infringement of any copyright or design right subsisting in the model or document.

(2) Where an exclusive licence granted otherwise than for royalties or other benefits determined by reference to the use of the designs is in force under the registered design then—
  (a) in relation to any use of the design which, but for the provisions of this and the last foregoing paragraph, would constitute an infringement of the rights of the licensee, sub-paragraph (3) of the last foregoing paragraph shall have effect as if for the reference to the registered proprietor there were substituted a reference to the licensee; and
  (b) in relation to any use of the design by the licensee by virtue of an authority given under the last foregoing paragraph, that paragraph shall have effect as if the said sub-paragraph (3) were omitted.

(3) Subject to the provisions of the last foregoing sub-paragraph, where the registered design or the right to apply for or obtain registration of the design has been assigned to the registered proprietor in consideration of royalties or other benefits determined by reference to the use of the design, then—
  (a) in relation to any use of the design by virtue of paragraph 1 of this Schedule, sub-paragraph (3) of that paragraph shall have effect as if the reference to the registered

proprietor included a reference to the assignor, and any sum payable by virtue of that sub-paragraph shall be divided between the registered proprietor and the assignor in such proportion as may be agreed upon between them or as may in default or agreement be determined by the court on a reference under the next following paragraph; and

(b) in relation to any use of the design made for the services of the Crown by the registered proprietor to the order of a Government department, sub-paragraph (3) of paragraph 1 of this Schedule shall have effect as if that use were made by virtue of an authority given under that paragraph.

(4) Where, under sub-paragraph (3) of paragraph 1 of this Schedule, payments are required to be made by a Government department to a registered proprietor in respect of any use of a design, any person being the holder of an exclusive licence under the registered design (not being such a licence as is mentioned in sub-paragraph (2) of this paragraph) authorising him to make that use of the design shall be entitled to recover from the registered proprietor such part (if any) of those payments as may be agreed upon between that person and the registered proprietor, or as may in default of agreement be determined by the court under the next following paragraph to be just having regard to any expenditure incurred by that person—

(a) in developing the said design; or

(b) in making payments to the registered proprietor, other than royalties or other payments determined by reference to the use of the design, in consideration of the licence;

and if, at any time before the amount of any such payment has been agreed upon between the Government department and the registered proprietor, that person gives notice in writing of his interest to the department, any agreement as to the amount of that payment shall be of no effect unless it is made with his consent.

(5) In this paragraph "exclusive licence" means a licence from a registered proprietor which confers on the licensee, or on the licensee and persons authorised by him, to the exclusion of all other persons (including the registered proprietor), any right in respect of the registered design.

Compensation for loss of profit

2A.—(1) Where Crown use is made of a registered design, the government department **A—430** concerned shall pay—

(a) to the registered proprietor, or

(b) if there is an exclusive licence in force in respect of the design, to the exclusive licensee,

compensation for any loss resulting from his not being awarded a contract to supply the articles to which the design is applied.

(2) Compensation is payable only to the extent that such a contract could have been fulfilled from his existing manufacturing capacity; but is payable notwithstanding the existence of circumstances rendering him ineligible for the award of such a contract.

(3) In determining the loss, regard shall be had to the profit which would have been made on such a contract and to the extent to which any manufacturing capacity was under-used.

(4) No compensation is payable in respect of any failure to secure contracts for the supply of articles to which the design is applied otherwise than for the services of the Crown.

(5) The amount payable under this paragraph shall if not agreed between the registered proprietor or licensee and the government department concerned with the approval of the Treasury, be determined by the court on a reference under paragraph 3; and it is in addition to any amount payable under paragraph 1 or 2 of this schedule.

(6) In this paragraph—

"Crown use", in relation to a design, means the doing of anything by virtue of paragraph 1 which would otherwise be an infringement of the right in the design; and "the government department concerned", in relation to such use, means the government department by whom or on whose authority the act was done.

Reference of disputes as to Crown use

A–431   3.—(1) Any dispute as to—

    (*a*) the exercise by a Government department, or a person authorised by a Government department, of the powers conferred by paragraph 1 of this Schedule,

    (*b*) terms for the use of a design for the services of the Crown under that paragraph,

    (*c*) the right of any person to receive any part of a payment made under paragraph 1(3), or

    (*d*) the right of any person to receive a payment under paragraph 2A,

may be referred to the court by either party to the dispute.

(2) In any proceedings under this paragraph to which a Government department are a party, the department may—

    (*a*) if the registered proprietor is a party to the proceedings, apply for cancellation of the registration of the design upon any ground upon which the registration of a design may be cancelled on an application to the court under section twenty of this Act;

    (*b*) in any case, put in issue the validity of the registration of the design without applying for its cancellation.

(3) If in such proceedings as aforesaid any question arises whether a design has been recorded or applied as mentioned in paragraph 1 of this Schedule, and the disclosure of any document recording the design, or of any evidence of the application thereof, would in the opinion of the department be prejudicial to the public interest, the disclosure may be made confidentially to counsel for the other party or to an independent expert mutually agreed upon.

(4) In determining under this paragraph any dispute between a Government department and any person as to terms for the use of a design for the services of the Crown, the court shall have regard to any benefit or compensation which that person or any person from whom he derives title may have received or may be entitled to receive, directly or indirectly from any Government department in respect of the design in question.

(5) In any proceedings under this paragraph the court may at any time order the whole proceedings or any question or issue of fact arising therein to be referred to a special or official referee or an arbitrator on such terms as the court may direct; and references to the court in the foregoing provisions of this paragraph shall be construed accordingly.

Special provisions as to Crown use during emergency

A–432   4.—(1) During any period of emergency within the meaning of this paragraph, the powers exercisable in relation to a design by a Government department, or a person authorised by a Government department under paragraph 1 of this Schedule shall include power to use the design for any purpose which appears to the department necessary or expedient—

    (*a*) for the efficient prosecution of any war in which His Majesty may be engaged;

    (*b*) for the maintenance of supplies and services essential to the life of the community;

    (*c*) for securing a sufficiency of supplies and services essential to the well-being of the community;

    (*d*) for promoting the productivity of industry, commerce and agriculture;

    (*e*) for fostering and directing exports and reducing imports, or imports of any classes, from all or any countries and for redressing the balance of trade;

    (*f*) generally for ensuring that the whole resources of the community are available for use, and are used, in a manner best calculated to serve the interests of the community; or

    (*g*) for assessing the relief of suffering and the restoration and distribution of essential supplies and services in any part of His Majesty's dominions or any foreign countries that are in grave distress as the result of war;

and any reference in this Schedule to the services of the Crown and shall be construed as including a reference to the purposes aforesaid.

(2) In this paragraph the expression "period of emergency" means a period beginning on such date as may be declared by Order in Council to be the commencement, and ending on such date as may be so declared to be the termination, of a period of emergency for the purposes of this paragraph.

(3) No Order in Council under this paragraph shall be submitted to Her Majesty unless a draft of it has been laid before and approved by a resolution of each House of Parliament.

SCHEDULE 5

PATENTS: MISCELLANEOUS AMENDMENTS
[RELATES TO SECTION 295]

Section 301.   SCHEDULE 6

PROVISIONS FOR THE BENEFIT OF THE HOSPITAL FOR SICK CHILDREN

Interpretation

1.—(1) In this Schedule—   **A–433**

"the Hospital" means The Hospital for Sick Children, Great Ormond Street, London,

"the trustees" means the special trustees appointed for the Hospital under the National Health Service Act 1977; and

"the work" means the play "Peter Pan" by Sir James Matthew Barrie.

(2) Expressions used in this Schedule which are defined for the purposes of Part I of this Act (copyright) have the same meaning as in that Part.

Entitlement to royalty

2.—(1) The trustees are entitled, subject to the following provisions of this Schedule, to a   **A–434** royalty in respect of any public performance, commercial publication, broadcasting or inclusion in a cable programme service of the whole or any substantial part of the work or an adaptation of it.

(2) Where the trustees are or would be entitled to a royalty, another form of remuneration may be agreed.

Exceptions

3. No royalty is payable in respect of—   **A–435**
   (a) anything which immediately before copyright in the work expired on 31st December 1987 could lawfully have been done without the licence, or further licence, of the trustees as copyright owners; or
   (b) anything which if copyright still subsisted in the work could, by virtue of any provision of Chapter III of Part I of this Act (acts permitted notwithstanding copyright), be done without infringing copyright.

Saving

4. No royalty is payable in respect of anything done in pursuance of arrangements made   **A–436** before the passing of this Act.

Procedure for determining amount payable

A–437   5.—(1) In default of agreement application may be made to the Copyright Tribunal which shall consider the matter and make such order regarding the royalty or other remuneration to be paid as it may determine to be reasonable in the circumstances.

(2) Application may subsequently be made to the Tribunal to vary its order, and the Tribunal shall consider the matter and make such order confirming or varying the original order as it may determine to be reasonable in the circumstances.

(3) An application for variation shall not, except with the special leave of the Tribunal, be made within twelve months from the date of the original order or of the order on a previous application for variation.

(4) A variation order has effect from the date on which it is made or such later date as may be specified by the Tribunal.

Sums received to be held on trust

A–438   6. The sums received by the trustees by virtue of this Schedule, after deduction of any relevant expenses, shall be held by them on trust for the purposes of the Hospital.

Right only for the benefit of the Hospital

A–439   7.—(1) The right of the trustees under this Schedule may not be assigned and shall cease if the trustees purport to assign or charge it.

(2) The right may not be the subject of an order under section 92 of the National Health Service Act 1977 (transfers of trust property by order of the Secretary of State) and shall cease if the Hospital ceases to have a separate identity or ceases to have purposes which include the care of sick children.

(3) Any power of Her Majesty, the court (within the meaning of the Charities Act 1960) or any other person to alter the trusts of a charity is not exercisable in relation to the trust created by this Schedule.

Section 303(1).   SCHEDULE 7

Consequential amendments: general

British Mercantile Marine Uniform Act 1919 (c. 62)

A–440   1. For section 2 of the British Mercantile Marine Uniform Act 1919 (copyright in distinctive marks of uniform) substitute—

"Right in registered design of distinctive marks of uniform

2. The right of the Secretary of State in any design forming part of the British mercantile marine uniform which is registered under the Registered Designs Act 1949 is not limited to the period prescribed by section 8 of that Act but shall continue to subsist so long as the design remains on the register.".

Chartered Associations (Protection of Names and Uniforms) Act 1926 (c. 26)

A–441   2. In section 1(5) of the Chartered Associations (Protection of Names and Uniforms) Act 1926 for "the copyright in respect thereof" substitute "the right in the registered design".

Patents, Designs, Copyright and Trade Marks (Emergency) Act 1939 (c. 107)

A–442   3.—(1) The Patents, Designs, Copyright and Trade Marks (Emergency) Act 1939 is amended as follows.

(2) In section 1 (effect of licence where owner is enemy or enemy subject)—

(*a*) in subsection (1) after "a copyright" and "the copyright" insert "or design right";

(*b*) in subsection (2) after "the copyright" insert "or design right" and for "or copyright" substitute ", copyright or design right".

(3) In section 2 (power of comptroller to grant licences)—

(*a*) in subsection (1) after "a copyright", "the copyright" (twice) and "the said copyright" insert "or design right" and for "or copyright" (twice) substitute, ", copyright or design right";

(*b*) in subsections (2) and (3) for ", or copyright" substitute ", copyright or design right";

(*c*) in subsection (4) and in subsection (5) (twice), after "the copyright" insert "or design right";

(*d*) in subsection (8)(c) for "or work in which copyright subsists" substitute "work in which copyright subsists or design in which design right subsists".

(4) In section 5 (effect of war on international arrangements)—

(*a*) in subsection (1) for "section twenty-nine of the Copyright Act 1911" substitute "section 159 or 256 of the Copyright, Designs and Patents Act 1988 (countries enjoying reciprocal copyright or design right protection)";

(*b*) in subsection (2) after "copyright" (four times) insert "or design right" and for "the Copyright Act 1911" (twice) substitute "Part I or III of the Copyright, Designs and Patents Act 1988".

(5) In section 10(1) (interpretation) omit the definition of "copyright", and for the definitions of "design", "invention", "patent" and "patentee" substitute—

" 'design' has in reference to a registered design the same meaning as in the Registered Designs Act 1949, and in reference to design right the same meaning as in Part III of the Copyright, Designs and Patents Act 1988;

'invention' and 'patent' have the same meaning as in the Patents Act 1977.".

Crown Proceedings Act 1947 (c. 44)

4.—(1) In the Crown Proceedings Act 1947 for section 3 (provisions as to industrial property) substitute— **A–443**

"Infringement of intellectual property rights

3.—(1) Civil proceedings lie against the Crown for an infringement committed by a servant or agent of the Crown, with the authority of the Crown, of—

(a) a patent,

(b) a registered trade mark or registered service mark,

(c) the right in a registered design,

(d) design right, or

(e) copyright;

but save as provided by this subsection no proceedings lie against the Crown by virtue of this Act in respect of an infringement of any of those rights.

(2) Nothing in this section, or any other provision of this Act, shall be construed as affecting—

(a) the rights of a government department under section 55 of the Patents Act 1977, Schedule 1 to the Registered Designs Act 1949 or section 240 of the Copyright, Designs and Patents Act 1988 (Crown use of patents and designs), or

(b) the rights of the Secretary of State under section 22 of the Patents Act 1977 or section 5 of the Registered Designs Act 1949 (security of information prejudicial to defence or public safety).".

(2) In the application of sub-paragraph (1) to Northern Ireland—

(*a*) the reference to the Crown Proceedings Act 1947 is to that Act as it applies to the

Crown in right of Her Majesty's Government in Northern Ireland, as well as to the Crown in right of Her Majesty's Government in the United Kingdom, and
(*b*) in the substituted section 3 as it applies in relation to the Crown in right of Her Majesty's Government in Northern Ireland, subsection (2)(*b*) shall be omitted.

Patents Act 1949 (c. 87)

A–444   5. In section 47 of the Patents Act 1949 (rights of third parties in respect of Crown use of patent), in the closing words of subsection (1) (which relate to the use of models or documents), after "copyright" insert "or design right".

Public Libraries (Scotland) Act 1955 (c. 27)

A–445   6. In section 4 of the Public Libraries (Scotland) Act 1955 (extension of lending power of public libraries), make the existing provision subsection (1) and after it add—

"(2) The provisions of Part I of the Copyright, Designs and Patents Act 1988 (copyright) relating to the rental of copies of sound recordings, films and computer programs apply to any lending by a statutory library authority of copies of such works, whether or not a charge is made for that facility.".

London County Council (General Powers) Act 1958 (c. xxi)

A–446   7. In section 36 of the London County Council (General Powers) Act 1958 (power as to libraries: provision and repair of things other than books) for subsection (5) substitute—

"(5) Nothing in this section shall be construed as authorising an infringement of copyright.".

Public Libraries and Museums Act 1964 (c. 75)

A–447   8. In section 8 of the Public Libraries and Museums Act 1964 (restrictions on charges for library facilities), after section (5) add—

"(6) The provisions of Part I of the Copyright, Designs and Patents Act 1988 (copyright) relating to the rental of copies of sound recordings, films and computer programs apply to any lending by a library authority of copies of such works, whether or not a charge is made for that facility.".

Marine, &c., Broadcasting (Offences) Act 1967 (c. 41)

A–448   9. In section 5 of the Marine, &c., Broadcasting (Offences) Act 1967 (provision of material for broadcasting by pirate radio stations)—
(*a*) in subsection (3)(*a*) for the words from "cinematograph film" to "in the record" substitute "film or sound recording with intent that a broadcast of it"; and
(*b*) in subsection (6) for the words from "and references" to the end substitute "and "film", "sound recording", "literary, dramatic or musical work" and "artistic work" have the same meaning as in Part I of the Copyright, Designs and Patents Act 1988 (copyright)".

Medicines Act 1968 (c. 67)

A–449   10.—(1) Section 92 of the Medicines Act 1968 (scope of provisions restricting promotion of sales of medicinal products) is amended as follows.
(2) In subsection (1) (meaning of "advertisement") for the words from "or by the exhibi-

tion" to "service" substitute "or by means of a photograph, film, sound recording, broadcast or cable programme,".

(3) In subsection (2) (exception for the spoken word)—

(*a*) in paragraph (*a*) omit the words from "or embodied" to "film"; and

(*b*) in paragraph (*b*) for the words from "by way of" to the end substitute "or included in a cable programme service".

(4) For subsection (6) substitute—

"(6) In this section 'film', 'sound recording', 'broadcast', 'cable programme', 'cable programme service', and related expressions, have the same meaning as in Part I of the Copyright, Designs and Patents Act 1988 (copyright).".

Post Office Act 1969 (c. 48)

11. In Schedule 10 to the Post Office Act 1969 (special transitional provisions relating to   **A–450**
use of patents and registered designs), in the closing words of paragraphs 8(1) and 18(1) (which relate to the use of models and documents), after "copyright" insert "or design right".

Merchant Shipping Act 1970 (c. 36)

12. In section 87 of the Merchant Shipping Act 1970 (merchant navy uniform), for sub-   **A–451**
section (4) substitute—

"(4) Where any design forming part of the merchant navy uniform has been registered under the Registered Designs Act 1949 and the Secretary of State is the proprietor of the design, his right in the design is not limited to the period prescribed by section 8 of that Act but shall continue to subsist so long as the design remains registered.".

Taxes Management Act 1970 (c. 9)

13. In section 16 of the Taxes Management Act 1970 (returns to be made in respect of cer-   **A–452**
tain payments)—

(*a*) in subsection (1)(*c*), and

(*b*) in subsection (2)(*b*),

for "or public lending right" substitute ", public lending right, right in a registered design or design right".

Tribunals and Inquiries Act 1971 (c. 62)

14. In Part I of Schedule 1 to the Tribunals and Inquiries Act 1971 (tribunals under direct   **A–453**
supervision of Council on Tribunals) renumber the entry inserted by the Data Protection Act 1984 as "5B" and before it insert—

"Copyright.   5A. The Copyright Tribunal."

Fair Trading Act 1973 (c. 41)

15. In Schedule 4 to the Fair Trading Act 1973 (excluded services), for paragraph 10 (ser-   **A–454**
vices of patent agents) substitute—

"10. The services of registered patent agents (within the meaning of Part V of the Copyright, Designs and Patents Act 1988) in their capacity as such.";

and in paragraph 10A (services of European patent attorneys) for "section 84(7) of the Patents Act 1977" substitute "Part V of the Copyright, Designs and Patents Act 1988".

House of Commons Disqualification Act 1975 (c. 24)

A–455   16. In Part II of Schedule 1 to the House of Commons Disqualification Act 1975 (bodies of which all members are disqualified), at the appropriate place insert "The Copyright Tribunal".

Northern Ireland Assembly Disqualification Act 1975 (c. 25)

A–456   17. In Part II of Schedule 1 to the Northern Ireland Assembly Disqualification Act 1975 (bodies of which all members are disqualified), at the appropriate place insert "The Copyright Tribunal".

Restrictive Trade Practices Act 1976 (c. 34)

A–457   18.—(1) The Restrictive Trade Practices Act 1976 is amended as follows.

(2) In Schedule 1 (excluded services) for paragraph 10 (services of patent agents) substitute—

"10. The services of registered patent agents (within the meaning of Part V of the Copyright, Designs and Patents Act 1988) in their capacity as such.";

and in paragraph 10A (services of European patent attorneys) for "section 84(7) of the Patents Act 1977" substitute "Part V of the Copyright, Designs and Patents Act 1988".

(3) In Schedule 3 (excepted agreements), after paragraph 5A insert—

"Design right

5B.—(1) This Act does not apply to—

(a) a licence granted by the owner or a licensee of any design right,

(b) an assignment of design right, or

(c) an agreement for such a licence or assignment,

if the licence, assignment or agreement is one under which no such restrictions as are described in section 6(1) above are accepted, or no such information provisions as are described in section 7(1) above are made, except in respect of articles made to the design; but subject to the following provisions.

(2) Sub-paragraph (1) does not exclude a licence, assignment or agreement which is a design pooling agreement or is granted or made (directly or indirectly) in pursuance of a design pooling agreement.

(3) In this paragraph a 'design pooling agreement' means an agreement—

(a) to which the parties are or include at least three persons (the "principal parties") each of whom has an interest in one or more design rights, and

(b) by which each principal party agrees, in respect of design right in which he has, or may during the currency of the agreement acquire, an interest to grant an interest (directly or indirectly) to one or more of the other principal parties, or to one or more of those parties and to other persons.

(4) In this paragraph—

'assignment', in Scotland, means assignation; and

'interest' means an interest as owner or licensee of design right.

(5) This paragraph applies to an interest held by or granted to more than one person jointly as if they were one person.

(6) References in this paragraph to the granting of an interest to a person indirectly are to its being granted to a third person for the purpose of enabling him to make a grant to the person in question.".

Resale Prices Act 1976 (c. 53)

A–458   19. In section 10(4) of the Resale Prices Act 1976 (patented articles: articles to be treated in same way), in paragraph (a) after "protected" insert "by design right or".

Patents Act 1977 (c. 37)

20. In section 57 of the Patents Act 1977 (rights of third parties in respect of Crown use of **A–459**
patent), in the closing words of subsection (1) (which relate to the use of models or documents), after "copyright" insert "or design right".

21. In section 105 of the Patents Act 1977 (privilege in Scotland for communications relating to patent proceedings), omit "within the meaning of section 104 above", make the existing text subsection (1) and after it insert—

"(2) In this section—

"patent proceedings" means proceedings under this Act or any of the relevant conventions,
   before the court, the comptroller or the relevant convention court, whether contested or
   uncontested and including an application for a patent; and

"the relevant conventions" means the European Patent Convention, the Community Patent
   Convention and the Patent Co-operation Treaty.".

22. In section 123(7) of the Patents Act 1977 (publication of case reports by the comptroller)—
   (*a*) for "and registered designs" substitute "registered designs or design right",
   (*b*) for "and copyright" substitute ", copyright and design right".

23. In section 130(1) of the Patents Act 1977 (interpretation), in the definition of "court",
for paragraph (a) substitute—
   "(a) as respects England and Wales, the High Court or any patents county court having
   jurisdiction by virtue of an order under section 287 of the Copyright, Designs and Patents
   Act 1988;".

Unfair Contract Terms Act 1977 (c. 50)

24. In paragraph 1 of Schedule 1 to the Unfair Contract Terms Act 1977 (scope of main **A–460**
provisions: excluded contracts), in paragraph (c) (contracts relating to grant or transfer of
interest in intellectual property) after "copyright" insert "or design right".

Judicature (Northern Ireland) Act 1978 (c. 23)

25. In section 94A of the Judicature (Northern Ireland) Act 1978 (withdrawal of privilege **A–461**
against self-incrimination in certain proceedings relating to intellectual property), in subsection (5) (meaning of "intellectual property") after "copyright" insert "or design right".

Capital Gains Tax Act 1979 (c. 14)

26. In section 18(4) of the Capital Gains Tax 1979 (situation of certain assets for purposes **A–462**
of Act), for paragraph (h) (intellectual property) substitute—
   "(ha) patents, trade marks, service marks and registered designs are situated where they
      are registered, and if registered in more than one register, where each register is situ-
      ated, and rights or licences to use a patent, trade mark, service mark or registered
      design are situated in the United Kingdom if they or any right derived from them
      are exercisable in the United Kingdom,
   (hb) copyright, design right and franchises, and rights or licences to use any copyright
      work or design in which design right subsists, are situated in the United Kingdom if
      they or any right derived from them are exercisable in the United Kingdom,".

British Telecommunications Act 1981 (c. 38)

27. In Schedule 5 to the British Telecommunications Act 1981 (special transitional pro- **A–463**
visions relating to use of patents and registered designs), in the closing words of paragraphs .
9(1) and 19(1) (which relate to the use of models and documents), after "copyright" insert
"or design right".

Supreme Court Act 1981 (c. 54)

A–464   28.—(1) The Supreme Court Act 1981 is amended as follows.

(2) In section 72 (withdrawal of privilege against self-incrimination in certain proceedings relating to intellectual property), in subsection (5) (meaning of "intellectual property") after "copyright" insert ", design right".

(3) In Schedule 1 (distribution of business in the High Court), in paragraph 1(i) (business assigned to the Chancery Division: causes and matters relating to certain intellectual property) for "or copyright" substitute ", copyright or design right".

[Broadcasting Act 1981 (c. 68)

A–465   *29.—(1) The Broadcasting Act 1981 is amended as follows.*

(2) In section 4 (general duties of IBA as regards programmes) for subsection (7) substitute—

"(7) For the purpose of maintaining supervision and control over the programmes (including advertisements) broadcast by them the Authority may make and use recordings of those programmes or any part of them.".

(3) In section 20(9), omit paragraph (a).]

[Cable and Broadcasting Act 1984 (c. 46)

A–466   *30.—(1) The Cable and Broadcasting Act 1984 is amended as follows.*

(2) In section 8, omit subsection (8).

(3) In section 49 (power of Secretary of State to give directions in the public interest), for subsection (7) substitute—

"(7) For the purposes of this section the place from which a broadcast is made is, in the case of a satellite transmission, the place from which the signals carrying the broadcast are transmitted to the satellite.".

(4) In section 56(2) (interpretation) omit the definition of "the 1956 Act".]

Note: Paragraphs 29 and 30 were repealed by Section 203(3) of and Schedule 21 to the Broadcasting Act 1990 (c.42) as provided by The Broadcasting Act 1990 (Commencement No.1 and Transitional Provisions) Order 1990 (S.I. 1990 No. 2347 (c.61)) § B–254 post.

Companies Act 1985 (c. 6)

A–467   31.—(1) Part XII of the Companies Act 1985 (registration of charges) is amended as follows.

(2) In section 396 (registration of charges in England and Wales: charges which must be registered), in subsection (1)(j) for the words from "on a patent" to the end substitute "or on any intellectual property", and after subsection (3) insert—

"(3A) The following are 'intellectual property' for the purposes of this section—
  (a) any patent, trade mark, service mark, registered design, copyright or design right;
  (b) any licence under or in respect of any such right.".

(3) In section 410 (registration of charges in Scotland: charges which must be registered), in subsection (3)(c) (incorporeal moveable property) after subparagraph (vi) insert—

"(vii) a registered design or a licence in respect of such a design,
(viii) a design right or a licence under a design right,".

Law Reform (Miscellaneous Provisions) (Scotland) Act 1985 (c. 73)

A–468   32. In section 15 of the Law Reform (Miscellaneous Provisions) (Scotland) Act 1985 (withdrawal of privilege against self-incrimination in certain proceedings relating to intellectual property), in subsection (5) (meaning of "intellectual property") after "copyright" insert "or design right".

Atomic Energy Authority Act 1986 (c. 3)

33. In section 8(2) of the Atomic Energy Authority Act 1986 (powers of Authority as to   **A–469**
exploitation of research: meaning of "intellectual property"), after "copyrights" insert ",
design rights".

Education and Libraries (Northern Ireland) Order 1986 (S.I. 1986/594 (N.I.3))

34. In Article 77 of the Education and Libraries (Northern Ireland) Order 1986 (charges   **A–470**
for library services), after paragraph (2) add—

"(3) The provisions of Part I of the Copyright, Designs and Patents Act 1988 (copyright) relating to the rental of copies of sound recordings, films and computer programs
apply to any lending by a board of copies of such works, whether or not a charge is made
for that facility.".

Companies (Northern Ireland) Order 1986 (S.I. 1986/1032 (N.I.6))

35. In Article 403 of the Companies (Northern Ireland) Order 1986 (registration of   **A–471**
charges: charges which must be registered), in paragraph (1)(j) for the words from "on a
patent" to the end substitute "or on any intellectual property", and after paragraph (3)
insert—

"(3A) The following are "intellectual property" for the purposes of this Article—
(a) any patent, trade mark, service mark, registered design, copyright or design right;
(b) any licence under or in respect of any such right.".

Income and Corporation Taxes Act 1988 (c. 1)

36.—(1) The Income and Corporation Taxes Act 1988 is amended as follows.   **A–472**
(2) In section 83 (fees and expenses deductible in computing profits and gains of trade) for
"the extension of the period of copyright in a design" substitute "an extension of the period
for which the right in a registered design subsists".
(3) In section 103 (charge on receipts after discontinuance of trade, profession or vocation), in subsection (3) (sums to which the section does not apply), after paragraph (b)
insert—

"(bb) a lump sum paid to the personal representatives of the designer of a design in which
design right subsists as consideration for the assignment by them, wholly or partially, of that right,".

(4) In section 387 (carry forward as losses of certain payments made under deduction of
tax), in subsection (3) (payments to which the section does not apply), in paragraph (e)
(copyright royalties) after "applies" insert "or royalties in respect of a right in a design to
which section 537B applies".
(5) In section 536 (taxation of copyright royalties where owner abroad), for the definition
of "copyright" in subsection (2) substitute—
" 'copyright' does not include copyright in—
(i) a cinematograph film or video recording, or
(ii) the sound-track of such a film or recording, so far as it is not separately exploited;
and".
(6) In Chapter I of Part XIII (miscellaneous special provisions: intellectual property),
after section 537 insert—

"Designs

Relief for payments in respect of designs

537A.—(1) Where the designer of a design in which design right subsists assigns that right, or the author of a registered design assigns the right in the design, wholly or partially, or grants an interest in it by licence, and—

(*a*) the consideration for the assignment or grant consists, in whole or in part, of a payment to which this section applies, the whole amount of which would otherwise be included in computing the amount of his profits or gains for a single year of assessment, and

(*b*) he was engaged in the creation of the design for a period of more than 12 months,

he may, on making a claim require that effect shall be given to the following provisions in connection with that payment.

(2) If the period for which he was engaged in the creation of the design does not exceed 24 months, then, for all income tax purposes, one-half only of the amount of the payment shall be treated as having become receivable on the date on which it actually became receivable and the remaining half shall be treated as having become receivable 12 months before that date.

(3) If the period for which he was engaged in the creation of the design exceeds 24 months, then, for all income tax purposes, one-third only of the amount of the payment shall be treated as having become receivable on the date on which it actually became receivable, and one-third shall be treated as having become receivable 12 months, and one-third 24 months, before that date.

(4) This section applies to—

(*a*) a lump sum payment, including an advance on account of royalties which is not returnable, and

(*b*) any other payment of or on account of royalties or sums payable periodically which does not only become receivable more than two years after articles made to the design or, as the case may be, articles to which the design is applied are first made available for sale or hire.

(5) A claim under this section with respect to any payment to which it applies by virtue only of subsection (4)(b) above shall have effect as a claim with respect to all such payments in respect of rights in the design in question which are receivable by the claimant, whether before or after the claim; and such a claim may be made at any time not later than 5th April next following the expiration of eight years after articles made to the design or, as the case may be, articles to which the design is applied were first made available for sale or hire.

(6) In this section—

(*a*) "designer" includes a joint designer, and

(*b*) any reference to articles being made available for sale or hire is to their being so made available anywhere in the world by or with the licence of the design right owner or, as the case may be, the proprietor of the registered design.

Taxation of design royalties where owner abroad

537B.—(1) Where the usual place of abode of the owner of a right in a design is not within the United Kingdom, section 349(1) shall apply to any payment of or on account of any royalties or sums paid periodically for or in respect of that right as it applies to annual payments not payable out of profits or gains brought into charge to income tax.

(2) In subsection (1) above—

(*a*) "right in a design" means design right or the right in a registered design,

(*b*) the reference to the owner of a right includes a person who, notwithstanding that he has assigned the right to some other person, is entitled to receive periodical payments in respect of the right, and

(*c*) the reference to royalties or other sums paid periodically for or in respect of a right does not include royalties or sums paid in respect of articles which are shown on a claim to have been exported from the United Kingdom for distribution outside the United Kingdom.

(3) Where a payment to which subsection (1) above applies is made through an agent resident in the United Kingdom and that agent is entitled as against the owner of the right to deduct any sum by way of commission in respect of services rendered, the amount of the payment shall for the purposes of section 349(1) be taken to be diminished by the sum which the agent is entitled to deduct.

(4) Where the person by or through whom the payment is made does not know that any such commission is payable or does not know the amount of any such commission, any income tax deducted by or assessed and charged on him shall be computed in the first instance on, and the account to be delivered of the payment shall be an account of, the total amount of the payment without regard being had to any diminution thereof, and in that case, on proof of the facts on a claim, there shall be made to the agent on behalf of the owner of the right such repayment of income tax as is proper in respect of the sum deducted by way of commission.

(5) The time of the making of a payment to which subsection (1) above applies shall, for all tax purposes, be taken to be the time when it is made by the person by whom it is first made and not the time when it is made by or through any other person.

(6) Any agreement for the making of any payment to which subsection (1) above applies in full and without deduction of income tax shall be void.".

(7) In section 821 (payments made under deduction of tax before passing of Act imposing income tax for that year), in subsection (3) (payments subject to adjustment) after paragraph (*a*) insert—

"(*aa*) any payment for or in respect of a right in a design to which section 537B applies; and".

(8) In Schedule 19 (apportionment of income of close companies), in paragraph 10(4) (cessation or liquidation: debts taken into account although creditor is participator or associate), in paragraph (c) (payments for use of certain property) for the words from "tangible property" to "extend)" substitute—

"—

(i) tangible property,
(ii) copyright in a literary, dramatic, musical or artistic work within the meaning of Part I of the Copyright, Designs and Patents Act 1988 (or any similar right under the law of a country to which that Part does not extend), or
(iii) design right,".

(9) In Schedule 25 (taxation of UK-controlled foreign companies: exempt activities), in paragraph 9(1)(*a*) (investment business: holding of property) for "patents or copyrights" substitute "or intellectual property" and after that subparagraph insert—

"(1A) In sub-paragraph (1)(a) above 'intellectual property' means patents, registered designs, copyright and design right (or any similar rights under the law of a country outside the United Kingdom).".

Appendix A

SCHEDULE 8

Repeals

Chapter	Short title	Extent of repeal
1939 c. 107.	Patents, Designs, Copyright and Trade Marks (Emergency) Act 1939.	In section 10(1), the definition of "copyright".
1945 c. 16.	Limitation (Enemies and War Prisoners) Act 1945.	In sections 2(1) and 4(a), the reference to section 10 of the Copyright Act 1911.
1949 c. 88.	Registered Designs Act 1949.	In section 3(2), the words "or original". Section 5(5). In section 11(2), the words "or original". In section 14(3), the words "or the Isle of Man". Section 32. Section 33(2). Section 37(1). Section 38. In section 44(1), the definitions of "copyright" and "Journal". In section 45, paragraphs (1) and (2). In section 46, paragraphs (1) and (2). Section 48(1). In Schedule 1, in paragraph 3(1), the words "in such manner as may be prescribed by rules of court". Schedule 2.
1956 c. 74.	Copyright Act 1956.	The whole Act.
1957 c. 6.	Ghana Independence Act 1957.	In Schedule 2, paragraph 12.
1957 c. 60.	Federation of Malaya Independence Act 1957.	In Schedule 1, paragraphs 14 and 15.
1958 c. 44.	Dramatic and Musical Performers' Protection Act 1958.	The whole Act.
1958 c. 51.	Public Records Act 1958.	Section 11. Schedule 3.
1960 c. 52.	Cyprus Independence Act 1960.	In the Schedule, paragraph 13.
1960 c. 55.	Nigeria Independence Act 1960.	In Schedule 2, paragraphs 12 and 13.
1961 c. 1.	Tanganyika Independence Act 1961.	In Schedule 2, paragraphs 13 and 14.
1961 c. 16.	Sierra Leone Independence Act 1961.	In Schedule 3, paragraphs 13 and 14.

Chapter	Short title	Extent of repeal
1961 c. 25.	Patents and Designs (Renewals, Extensions and Fees) Act 1961.	The whole Act.
1962 c. 40.	Jamaica Independence Act 1962.	In Schedule 2, paragraph 13.
1962 c. 54.	Trinidad and Tobago Independence Act 1962.	In Schedule 2, paragraph 13.
1963 c. 53.	Performers' Protection Act 1963.	The whole Act.
1964 c. 46.	Malawi Independence Act 1964.	In Schedule 2, paragraph 13.
1964 c. 65.	Zambia Independence Act 1964.	In Schedule 1, paragraph 9.
1964 c. 86.	Malta Independence Act 1964.	In Schedule 1, paragraph 11.
1964 c. 93.	Gambia Independence Act 1964.	In Schedule 2, paragraph 12.
1966 c. 24.	Lesotho Independence Act 1966.	In the Schedule, paragraph 9.
1966 c. 37.	Barbados Independence Act 1966.	In Schedule 2, paragraph 12.
1967 c. 80.	Criminal Justice Act 1967.	In Parts I and IV of Schedule 3, the entries relating to the Registered Designs Act 1949.
1968 c. 56.	Swaziland Independence Act 1968.	In the Schedule, paragraph 9.
1968 c. 67.	Medicines Act 1968.	In section 92(2)(a), the words from "or embodied" to "film". Section 98.
1968 c. 68.	Design Copyright Act 1968.	The whole Act.
1971 c. 4.	Copyright (Amendment) Act 1971.	The whole Act.
1971 c. 23	Courts Act 1971.	In Schedule 9, the entry relating to the Copyright Act 1956.
1971 c. 62.	Tribunals and Inquiries Act 1971.	In Schedule 1, paragraph 24.
1972 c. 32.	Performers' Protection Act 1972.	The whole Act.
1975 c. 24.	House of Commons Disqualification Act 1975.	In Part II of Schedule 1, the entry relating to the Performing Right Tribunal.
1975 c. 25.	Northern Ireland Assembly Disqualification Act 1975.	In Part II of Schedule 1, the entry relating to the Performing Right Tribunal.
1977 c. 37.	Patents Act 1977.	Section 14(4) and (8). In section 28(3), paragraph (b) and the word "and" preceding it. Section 28(5) to (9). Section 49(3). Section 72(3). Sections 84 and 85. Section 88. Section 104. In section 105, the words "within the meaning of section 104 above".

Chapter	Short title	Extent of repeal
		Sections 114 and 115.
		Section 123(2)(k).
		In section 130(1), the definition of "patent agent".
		In section 130(7), the words "88(6) and (7),".
		In Schedule 5, paragraphs 1 and 2, in paragraph 3 the words "and 44(1)" and "in each case", and paragraphs 7 and 8.
1979 c. 2.	Customs and Excise Management Act 1979.	In Schedule 4, the entry relating to the Copyright Act 1956.
1980 c. 21.	Competition Act 1980.	Section 14.
1981 c. 68.	Broadcasting Act 1981.	Section 20(9)(a).
1982 c. 35.	Copyright Act 1956 (Amendment) Act 1982.	The whole Act.
1983 c. 42.	Copyright (Amendment) Act 1983.	The whole Act.
1984 c. 46.	Cable and Broadcasting Act 1984.	Section 8(8).
		Section 16(4) and (5).
		Sections 22 to 24.
		Section 35(2) and (3).
		Sections 53 and 54.
		In section 56(2), the definition of "the 1956 Act".
		In Schedule 5, paragraphs 6, 7, 13 and 23.
1985 c. 21.	Films Act 1985.	Section 7(2).
1985 c. 41.	Copyright (Computer Software) Amendment Act 1985.	The whole Act.
1985 c. 61.	Administration of Justice Act 1985.	Section 60.
1986 c. 39.	Patents, Designs and Marks Act 1986.	In Schedule 2, paragraphs 1(2)(a), in paragraph 1(2)(k) the words "subsection (1)(j) of section 396 and" and in paragraph 1(2)(l) the words "subsection (2)(i) of section 93".
1988 c. 1.	Income and Corporation Taxes Act 1988.	In Schedule 29, paragraph 5.

PART II

COMPARATIVE TABLE—III A–474

COPYRIGHT ACT, 1911

COMPARED WITH

COPYRIGHT ACT, 1956

1911	1956	1911	1956	1911	1956
s. 1 (1) (a)	ss. 2 (2), 3	s. 5 (1) (b)	s. 4 (2), (5)	s. 19 (6)	s. 8 (11)
	(3)	(2)	36 (1), (2),	(7)	(9)
(b)	1 (5), 2		(3)	(8)	omitted
	(1), 3 (2)	proviso	omitted	20	omitted
(2)	1 (1), 2	(3)	49 (5)	21	3 (4)
	(5), 3 (5)	6 (1)	17 (1)	22	ss. 10, 44
	46 (1),	(2)	omitted	23	s. 35
	48 (1),	(3)	20 (1)	24	omitted
	49 (1)	(a)	20 (2)	25	ss. 1 (1), 31
(a) (b) (c)	s. 2 (6)	(b)	20 (4)	26	omitted
(d)	ss. 2 (5), 3	7	18 (1)	27	s. 31 (3)
	(5), 48 (1)	8	ss. 17 (2), 18	28	(1)
(3)	s. 49 (2)		(2)	29	32
2 (1)	1 (2)	9 (1)	s. 17 (4)	30	omitted
(i)	6 (1), (2),	(2)	omitted	31	46 (4), (5)
	(3)	10	omitted	32	47
	9 (1), (2)	11	21	33	46 (1)
(ii)	9 (9)	12	21 (10)	34	not repealed
(iii)	9 (3),	13	21 (6)	35 (1)	ss. 3 (1), 13
	(4), (6)	14	22		(10)
(iv)	6 (6)	15	not repealed		18 (3), 48
(v) (vi)	omitted	16	11, Sch. 3		(1)
(2) (a)	5 (3)	(4)	16 (3)		s. 49 (2), (3)
(b)	(4)	17 (1)	ss. 2 (3), 3	(2)	49 (3)
(c)	(3)		(4)	(3)	(2)
(d)	(2)	(2)	s. 38	(4)	(9)
(3)	(5)	18	39	(5)	1 (5) (a)
3	ss. 2 (3), 3	19 (1)	12 (1)	36	omitted
	(4)	(2)	8 (1), (5),	37	not repealed
proviso	omitted		(6), (8)	Sch. 1	omitted
4	omitted	(3)	(2)	Sch. 2	omitted
5 (1)	s. 4 (1)	(3)	(3)		
(a)	(3), (5)	proviso			
		(4)	(4)		
		(5)	(7)		

COMPARATIVE TABLE—IV

COPYRIGHT ACT, 1956

COMPARED WITH

COPYRIGHT ACT, 1911

1956	1911	1956	1911	1956	1911
s. 1 (1)	s. 1 (2)	s. 9 (1), (2)	s. 2 (1) (i)	s. 31 (2)	——
(2)	2 (1)	(3), (4)	(iii)	(3)	s. 27
(3), (4)	——	(5)	——	32	29
(5)	1 (1) (b)	(6)	2 (1) (iii)	ss. 33, 34	——
2 (1)	(b)	(7), (8)	——	s. 35	23
(2)	(a)	(9)	2 (1) (ii)	36	5 (2)
(3)	ss. 3, 17	(10), (11)	——	37	——
(4)	——	10	——	38	17 (2)
(5)	s. 1 (2)	11 (1)	——	39	18
(6)	(2)	(2), (3)	16	ss. 40–45	——
3 (1)	35 (1)	12	19 (1)	s. 46 (1)	33
(2)	1 (1) (b)	ss. 13–16	——	(2)	18
(3)	(a)	s. 17 (1)	6 (1)	(3)	——
(4)	ss. 3, 17, 21	(2)	(8)	(4), (5)	31
(5)	s. 1 (2)	(3)	——	47	32
4 (1)	5 (1)	(4)	9 (1)	48 (1)	35 (1)
(2)	(b)	18 (1)	7	(2)–(7)	——
(3)	(a)	(2) (a)	8	49 (1)	1 (2)
(4)	(b)	(b) (c)	——	(2)	ss. 1 (3), 35
(5)	5 (1)	(3)	35 (1)		(3)
(6)	——	19	——	(3)	s. 35 (2)
5	2 (2), (3)	20 (1), (2)	6 (3)	(4)	(4)
6 (1), (2), (3)	(1) (i)	(3)	——	(5)	5 (3)
(4)	——	(4)	6 (3)	(6)–(10)	——
(5)	2 (1) (ii)	(5), (6)	——	50	24
(6)	(iv)	21	ss. 11, 12	51	——
(7)–(10)	——	22	s. 14	Schs. 1, 2	——
7	——	ss. 23–30	——	Sch. 3	16
8	19 (2)–(7)	s. 31 (1)	28	Schs. 4–9	——

Copyright Act, 1956[2]

(4 & 5 Eliz. 2, c. 74)

ARRANGEMENT OF SECTIONS

PART I

COPYRIGHT IN ORIGINAL WORKS

PART II

COPYRIGHT IN SOUND RECORDINGS, CINEMATOGRAPH FILMS, BROADCASTS, ETC.

PART III

REMEDIES FOR INFRINGEMENTS OF COPYRIGHT

---

[2] This Act (and the Copyright (Computer Software) Amendment Act 1985) were repealed by the C.O.P.A. 1988 *ante* as from August 1, 1989. Comparative Tables showing the correspondence of this Act to the 1988 Act, and of the 1988 Act to this Act are printed at §§ A–1 and A–2 *ante*.

Part IV

Performing Right Tribunal

Part V

Extension or Restriction of Operation of Act

Part VI

Miscellaneous and Supplementary Provisions

An Act to make new provision in respect of copyright and related matters, in substitution for the provisions of the Copyright Act, 1911, and other enactments relating thereto; to amend the Registered Designs Act, 1949, with respect to designs related to artistic works in which copyright subsists, and to amend the Dramatic and Musical Performers' Protection Act, 1925; and for purposes connected with the matters aforesaid. [5th November, 1956]

PART I

COPYRIGHT IN ORIGINAL WORKS

Nature of copyright under this Act

1.—(1) In this Act "copyright" in relation to a work (except where the context **A–477** otherwise requires) means the exclusive right, by virtue and subject to the provisions of this Act, to do, and to authorise other persons to do, certain acts in relation to that work in the United Kingdom or in any other country to which the relevant provision of this Act extends.

The said acts, in relation to a work of any description, are those acts which, in the relevant provision of this Act, are designated as the acts restricted by the copyright in a work of that description.

(2) In accordance with the preceding subsection, but subject to the following provisions of this Act, the copyright in a work is infringed by any person who, not being the owner of the copyright, and without the licence of the owner thereof, does, or authorises another person to do, any of the said acts in relation to the work in the United Kingdom or in any other country to which the relevant provision of this Act extends.

(3) In the preceding subsections references to the relevant provision of this Act, in relation to a work of any description, are references to the provision of this Act whereby it is provided that (subject to compliance with the conditions specified therein) copyright shall subsist in works of that description.

(4) The preceding provisions of this section shall apply, in relation to any sub-

---

[3] By virtue of the Sound Broadcasting Act 1972 (c.31), s.1 repealed and replaced by the Independent Broadcasting Authority Act 1973 (c.19), ss.1, 38 and 39, repealed and replaced by the Broadcasting Act 1981 (c.68), s.65 and Sched. 8, references to "Independent Broadcasting Authority" *inter alia* in the 1956 Act are to be substituted for "Independent Television Authority". This Act is therefore printed with the necessary substituted references. The Broadcasting Act 1981 was repealed by s. 203(3) of and Sched. 21 to the Broadcasting Act 1990 (c. 42) as provided by The Broadcasting Act 1990 (Commencement No. 1 and Transitional Provisions) Order 1990 (S.I. 1990 No. 2347) (c. 61) § B–254 *post.* See s. 127 of the 1990 Act and S.I. 1990 No. 2347 (c. 61) as to the dissolution of the IBA.

ject-matter (other than a work) of a description to which any provision of Part II of this Act relates, as they apply in relation to a work.

(5) For the purposes of any provision of this Act which specifies the conditions under which copyright may subsist in any description of work or other subject-matter, "qualified person"—

  (*a*) in the case of an individual, means a person who is a British subject or British protected person or a citizen of the Republic of Ireland or (not being a British subject or British protected person or a citizen of the Republic of Ireland) is domiciled or resident in the United Kingdom or in another country to which that provision extends, and

  (*b*) in the case of a body corporate, means a body incorporated under the laws of any part of the United Kingdom or of another country to which that provision extends.

In this subsection "British protected person" has the same meaning as in [the British Nationality Act, 1981.]

AMENDMENT

This section was amended by the British Nationality (Modification of Enactments) Order 1982 (1982 S.I. No. 1832) and is printed as amended. As to "British subject" see British Nationality Act 1981 (c. 61) s. 51(1) and *Milltronics Ltd. v. Hycontrol* Ltd. [1990] FSR 273.

Copyright in literary, dramatic and musical works

A–478   2.—(1) Copyright shall subsist, subject to the provisions of this Act, in every original literary, dramatic or musical work which is unpublished, and of which the author was a qualified person at the time when the work was made, or, if the making of the work extended over a period, was a qualified person for a substantial part of that period.

(2) Where an original literary, dramatic or musical work has been published, then, subject to the provisions of this Act, copyright shall subsist in the work (or, if copyright in the work subsisted immediately before its first publication, shall continue to subsist) if, but only if,—

  (*a*) the first publication of the work took place in the United Kingdom, or in another country to which this section extends, or

  (*b*) the author of the work was a qualified person at the time when the work was first published, or

  (*c*) the author had died before that time, but was a qualified person immediately before his death.

(3) Subject to the last preceding subsection, copyright subsisting in a work by virtue of this section shall continue to subsist until the end of the period of fifty years from the end of the calendar year in which the author died, and shall then expire:

Provided that if before the death of the author none of the following acts had been done, that is to say,—

  (*a*) the publication of the work,

  (*b*) the performance of the work in public,

  (*c*) the offer for sale to the public of records of the work,

  (*d*) the broadcasting of the work,

  [(*e*) the inclusion of the work in a cable programme.]

the copyright shall continue to subsist until the end of the period of fifty years from the end of the calendar year which includes the earliest occasion on which one of those acts is done.

(4) In the last preceding subsection references to the doing of any act in relation to a work include references to the doing of that act in relation to an adaptation of the work.

(5) The acts restricted by the copyright in a literary, dramatic or musical work are—

  (*a*) reproducing the work in any material form;

  (*b*) publishing the work;

  (*c*) performing the work in public;

  (*d*) broadcasting the work;

  [(*e*) including the work in a cable programme;]

  (*f*) making any adaptation of the work;

  (*g*) doing, in relation to an adaptation of the work, any of the acts specified in relation to the work in paragraphs (*a*) to (*e*) of this subsection.

(6) In this Act "adaptation"—

  (*a*) in relation to a literary or dramatic work, means any of the following, that is to say,—

    (i) in the case of a non-dramatic work, a version of the work (whether in its original language or a different language) in which it is converted into a dramatic work;

    (ii) in the case of a dramatic work, a version of the work (whether in its original language or a different language) in which it is converted into a non-dramatic work;

    (iii) a translation of the work;

    (iv) a version of the work in which the story or action is conveyed wholly or mainly by means of pictures in a form suitable for reproduction in a book, or in a newspaper, magazine or similar periodical; and

  (*b*) in relation to a musical work, means an arrangement or transcription of the work,

so however that the mention of any matter in this definition shall not affect the generality of paragraph (*a*) of the last preceding subsection.

AMENDMENT

This section was amended by the Cable and Broadcasting Act 1984 (c. 46) and is printed as amended.

Copyright in artistic works

3.—(1) In this Act "artistic work" means a work of any of the following descrip- **A–479**
tions, that is to say,—

  (*a*) the following, irrespective of artistic quality, namely paintings, sculptures, drawings, engravings and photographs;

  (*b*) works of architecture, being either buildings or models for buildings;

  (*c*) works of artistic craftsmanship, not falling within either of the preceding paragraphs.

(2) Copyright shall subsist, subject to the provisions of this Act, in every original artistic work which is unpublished, and of which the author was a qualified person at the time when the work was made, or, if the making of the work extended over a period, was a qualified person for a substantial part of that period.

(3) Where an original artistic work has been published, then, subject to the provisions of this Act, copyright shall subsist in the work (or, if copyright in the work subsisted immediately before its first publication, shall continue to subsist) if, but only if,—

  (*a*) the first publication of the work took place in the United Kingdom, or in another country to which this section extends, or

  (*b*) the author of the work was a qualified person at the time when the work was first published, or

  (*c*) the author had died before that time, but was a qualified person immediately before his death.

(4) Subject to the last preceding subsection, copyright subsisting in a work by

virtue of this section shall continue to subsist until the end of the period of fifty years from the end of the calendar year in which the author died, and shall then expire:

Provided that—

    (*a*) in the case of an engraving, if before the death of the author the engraving had not been published, the copyright shall continue to subsist until the end of the period of fifty years from the end of the calendar year in which it is first published;

    (*b*) the copyright in a photograph shall continue to subsist until the end of the period of fifty years from the end of the calendar year in which the photograph is first published, and shall then expire.

(5) The acts restricted by the copyright in an artistic work are—

    (*a*) reproducing the work in any material form;

    (*b*) publishing the work;

    (*c*) including the work in a television broadcast;

    [(*d*) including the work in a cable programme.]

AMENDMENT

This section was amended by the Cable and Broadcasting Act 1984 (c. 46) and is printed as amended.

Ownership of copyright in literary, dramatic, musical and artistic works

A–480   **4.**—(1) Subject to the provisions of this section, the author of a work shall be entitled to any copyright subsisting in the work by virtue of this Part of this Act.

(2) Where a literary, dramatic or artistic work is made by the author in the course of his employment by the proprietor of a newspaper, magazine or similar periodical under a contract of service or apprenticeship, and is so made for the purpose of publication in a newspaper, magazine or similar periodical, the said proprietor shall be entitled to the copyright in the work in so far as the copyright relates to publication of the work in any newspaper, magazine or similar periodical, or to reproduction of the work for the purpose of its being so published; but in all other respects the author shall be entitled to any copyright subsisting in the work by virtue of this Part of this Act.

(3) Subject to the last preceding subsection, where a person commissions the taking of a photograph, or the painting or drawing of a portrait, or the making of an engraving, and pays or agrees to pay for it in money or money's worth, and the work is made in pursuance of that commission, the person who so commissioned the work shall be entitled to any copyright subsisting therein by virtue of this Part of this Act.

(4) Where, in a case not falling within either of the two last preceding subsections, a work is made in the course of the author's employment by another person under a contract of service or apprenticeship, that other person shall be entitled to any copyright subsisting in the work by virtue of this Part of this Act.

(5) Each of the three last preceding subsections shall have effect subject, in any particular case, to any agreement excluding the operation thereof in that case.

(6) The preceding provisions of this section shall all have effect subject to the provisions of Part VI of this Act.

Infringements by importation, sale and other dealings

A–481   **5.**—(1) Without prejudice to the general provisions of section one of this Act as to infringements of copyright, the provisions of this section shall have effect in relation to copyright subsisting by virtue of this Part of this Act.

(2) The copyright in a literary, dramatic, musical or artistic work is infringed by any person who, without the licence of the owner of the copyright, imports an article (otherwise than for his private and domestic use) into the United Kingdom,

or into any other country to which this section extends, if to his knowledge the making of that article constituted an infringement of that copyright, or would have constituted such an infringement if the article had been made in the place into which it is so imported.

(3) The copyright in a literary, dramatic, musical or artistic work is infringed by any person who, in the United Kingdom, or in any other country to which this section extends, and without the licence of the owner of the copyright,—

(*a*) sells, lets for hire, or by way of trade offers or exposes for sale or hire any article, or

(*b*) by way of trade exhibits any article in public,

if to his knowledge the making of the article constituted an infringement of that copyright, or (in the case of an imported article) would have constituted an infringement of that copyright if the article had been made in the place into which it was imported.

(4) The last preceding subsection shall apply in relation to the distribution of any articles either—

(*a*) for purposes of trade, or

(*b*) for other purposes, but to such an extent as to affect prejudicially the owner of the copyright in question,

as it applies in relation to the sale of an article.

(5) The copyright in a literary, dramatic or musical work is also infringed by any person who permits a place of public entertainment to be used for a performance in public of the work, where the performance constitutes an infringement of the copyright in the work:

Provided that this subsection shall not apply in a case where the person permitting the place to be so used—

(*a*) was not aware, and had no reasonable grounds for suspecting, that the performance would be an infringement of the copyright, or

(*b*) gave the permission gratuitously, or for a consideration which was only nominal or (if more than nominal) did not exceed a reasonable estimate of the expenses to be incurred by him in consequence of the use of the place for the performance.

(6) In this section "place of public entertainment" includes any premises which are occupied mainly for other purposes, but are from time to time made available for hire to such persons as may desire to hire them for purposes of public entertainment.

General exceptions from protection of literary, dramatic and musical works

6.—(1) No fair dealing with a literary, dramatic or musical work for purposes of **A–482** research or private study shall constitute an infringement of the copyright in the work.

(2) No fair dealing with a literary, dramatic or musical work shall constitute an infringement of the copyright in the work if it is for purposes of criticism or review, whether of that work or of another work, and is accompanied by a sufficient acknowledgement.

(3) No fair dealing with a literary, dramatic or musical work shall constitute an infringement of the copyright in the work if it is for the purpose of reporting current events—

(*a*) in a newspaper, magazine or similar periodical, or

(*b*) by means of broadcasting, or in a cinematograph film,

and, in a case falling within paragraph (*a*) of this subsection, is accompanied by a sufficient acknowledgement.

(4) The copyright in a literary, dramatic or musical work is not infringed by

reproducing it for the purposes of a judicial proceeding, or for the purposes of a report of a judicial proceeding.

(5) The reading or recitation in public by one person of any reasonable extract from a published literary or dramatic work, if accompanied by a sufficient acknowledgement, shall not constitute an infringement of the copyright in the work:

Provided that this subsection shall not apply to anything done for the purposes of broadcasting.

(6) The copyright in a published literary or dramatic work is not infringed by the inclusion of a short passage therefrom in a collection intended for the use of schools, if—

(*a*) the collection is described in its title, and in any advertisements thereof issued by or on behalf of the publisher, as being so intended, and

(*b*) the work in question was not published for the use of schools, and

(*c*) the collection consists mainly of material in which no copyright subsists, and

(*d*) the inclusion of the passage is accompanied by a sufficient acknowledgment:

Provided that this subsection shall not apply in relation to the copyright in a work if, in addition to the passage in question, two or more other excerpts from works by the author thereof (being works in which copyright subsists at the time when the collection is published) are contained in that collection, or are contained in that collection taken together with every similar collection (if any) published by the same publisher within the period of five years immediately preceding the publication of that collection.

(7) Where by virtue of an assignment or licence a person is authorised to broadcast a literary, dramatic or musical work from a place in the United Kingdom, or in another country to which section two of this Act extends, but (apart from this subsection) would not be entitled to make reproductions of it in the form of a record or of a cinematograph film, the copyright in the work is not infringed by his making such a reproduction of the work solely for the purpose of broadcasting the work:

Provided that this subsection shall not apply if—

(*a*) the reproduction is used for making any further reproduction therefrom, or for any other purpose except that of broadcasting in accordance with the assignment or licence, or

(*b*) the reproduction is not destroyed before the end of the period of twenty-eight days beginning with the day on which it is first used for broadcasting the work in pursuance of the assignment or licence, or such extended period (if any) as may be agreed between the person who made the reproduction and the person who (in relation to the making of reproductions of the description in question) is the owner of the copyright.

(8) The preceding provisions of this section shall apply to the doing of any act in relation to an adaptation of a work as they apply in relation to the doing of that act in relation to the work itself.

(9) The provisions of this section shall apply where a work, or adaptation of a work, is [included in a cable programme] as they apply where a work or adaptation is broadcast.

(10) In this Act "sufficient acknowledgment" means an acknowledgment identifying the work in question by its title or other description and, unless the work is anonymous or the author has previously agreed or required that no acknowledgment of his name should be made, also identifying the author.

AMENDMENT

This section was amended by the Cable and Broadcasting Act 1984 (c. 46) and is printed as amended.

Special exceptions as respects libraries and archives

7.—(1) The copyright in an article contained in a periodical publication is not **A–483** infringed by the making or supplying of a copy of the article, if the copy is made or supplied by or on behalf of the librarian of a library of a class prescribed by regulations made under this subsection by the Board of Trade, and the conditions prescribed by those regulations are complied with.

(2) In making any regulations for the purposes of the preceding subsection the Board of Trade shall make such provision as the Board may consider appropriate for securing—

(*a*) that the libraries to which the regulations apply are not established or conducted for profit;

(*b*) that the copies in question are supplied only to persons satisfying the librarian, or a person acting on his behalf, that they require them for purposes of research or private study and will not use them for any other purpose;

(*c*) that no person is furnished under the regulations with two or more copies of the same article;

(*d*) that no copy extends to more than one article contained in any one publication; and

(*e*) that persons to whom copies are supplied under the regulations are required to pay for them a sum not less than the cost (including a contribution to the general expenses of the library) attributable to their production,

and may impose such other requirements (if any) as may appear to the Board to be expedient.

(3) The copyright in a published literary, dramatic or musical work, other than an article contained in a periodical publication, is not infringed by the making or supplying of a copy of part of the work, if the copy is made or supplied by or on behalf of the librarian of a library of a class prescribed by regulations made under this subsection by the Board of Trade, and the conditions prescribed by those regulations are complied with:

Provided that this subsection shall not apply if, at the time when the copy is made, the librarian knows the name and address of a person entitled to authorise the making of the copy, or could by reasonable inquiry ascertain the name and address of such a person.

(4) The provisions of subsection (2) of this section shall apply for the purposes of the last preceding subsection:

Provided that paragraph (*d*) of the said subsection (2) shall not apply for those purposes, but any regulations made under the last preceding subsection shall include such provision as the Board of Trade may consider appropriate for securing that no copy to which the regulations apply extends to more than a reasonable proportion of the work in question.

(5) The copyright in a published literary, dramatic or musical work is not infringed by the making or supplying of a copy of the work, or of part of it, by or on behalf of the librarian of a library of a class prescribed by regulations made under this subsection by the Board of Trade, if—

(*a*) the copy is supplied to the librarian of any library of a class so prescribed;

(*b*) at the time when the copy is made, the librarian by or on whose behalf it is supplied does not know the name and address of any person entitled to authorise the making of the copy, and could not by reasonable inquiry ascertain the name and address of such a person; and

(*c*) any other conditions prescribed by the regulations are complied with:

Provided that the condition specified in paragraph (*b*) of this subsection shall not apply in the case of an article contained in a periodical publication.

(6) Where, at a time more than fifty years from the end of the calendar year in

which the author of a literary, dramatic or musical work died, and more than one hundred years after the time, or the end of the period, at or during which the work was made,—

(*a*) copyright subsists in the work, but

(*b*) the work has not been published, and

(*c*) the manuscript or a copy of the work is kept in a library, museum or other institution where (subject to any provisions regulating the institution in question) it is open to public inspection,

the copyright in the work is not infringed by a person who reproduces the work for purposes of research or private study, or with a view to publication.

(7) Where a published literary, dramatic or musical work (in this subsection referred to as "the new work") incorporates the whole or part of a work (in this subsection referred to as "the old work") in the case of which the circumstances specified in the last preceding subsection existed immediately before the new work was published, and—

(*a*) before the new work was published, such notice of the intended publication as may be prescribed by regulations made under this subsection by the Board of Trade had been given, and

(*b*) immediately before the new work was published, the identity of the owner of the copyright in the old work was not known to the publisher of the new work,

then for the purposes of this Act—

(i) that publication of the new work, and

(ii) any subsequent publication of the new work, either in the same or in an altered form,

shall, in so far as it constitutes a publication of the old work, not be treated as an infringement of the copyright in the old work or as an unauthorised publication of the old work:

Provided that this subsection shall not apply to a subsequent publication incorporating a part of the old work which was not included in the new work as originally published, unless (apart from this subsection) the circumstances specified in the last preceding subsection, and in paragraphs (*a*) and (*b*) of this subsection, existed immediately before that subsequent publication.

(8) In so far as the publication of a work, or of part of a work, is, by virtue of the last preceding subsection, not to be treated as an infringement of the copyright in the work, a person who subsequently broadcasts the work, or that part thereof, as the case may be, or [includes it in a cable programme,] or performs it in public, or makes a record of it, does not thereby infringe the copyright in the work.

(9) In relation to an article or other work which is accompanied by one or more artistic works provided for explaining or illustrating it (in this subsection referred to as "illustrations"), the preceding provisions of this section shall apply as if—

(*a*) wherever they provide that the copyright in the article or work is not infringed, the reference to that copyright included a reference to any copyright in any of the illustrations;

(*b*) in subsections (1) and (2), references to a copy of the article included references to a copy of the article together with a copy of the illustrations or any of them;

(*c*) in subsections (3) to (5), references to a copy of the work included references to a copy of the work together with a copy of the illustrations or any of them, and references to a copy of part of the work included references to a copy of that part of the work together with a copy of any of the illustrations which were provided for explaining or illustrating that part; and

(*d*) in subsections (6) and (7), references to the doing of any act in relation to the work included references to the doing of that act in relation to the work together with any of the illustrations.

(10) In this section "article" includes an item of any description.

AMENDMENT
This section was amended by the Cable and Broadcasting Act 1984 (c. 46) and is printed as amended.

Special exception in respect of records of musical works

8.—(1) The copyright in a musical work is not infringed by a person (in this sec-   **A–484**
tion referred to as "the manufacturer") who makes a record of the work or of an adaptation thereof in the United Kingdom, if—

   (a) records of the work, or, as the case may be, of a similar adaptation of the work, have previously been made in, or imported into, the United Kingdom for the purposes of retail sale, and were so made or imported by, or with the licence of, the owner of the copyright in the work;
   (b) before making the record, the manufacturer gave to the owner of the copyright the prescribed notice of his intention to make it;
   (c) the manufacturer intends to sell the record by retail, or to supply it for the purpose of its being sold by retail by another person, or intends to use it for making other records which are to be so sold or supplied; and
   (d) in the case of a record which is sold by retail, the manufacturer pays to the owner of the copyright, in the prescribed manner and at the prescribed time, a royalty of an amount ascertained in accordance with the following provisions of this section.

(2) Subject to the following provisions of this section, the royalty mentioned in paragraph (d) of the preceding subsection shall be of an amount equal to six and one-quarter per cent. of the ordinary retail selling price of the record, calculated in the prescribed manner:

Provided that, if the amount so calculated includes a fraction of a farthing, that fraction shall be reckoned as one farthing, and if, apart from this proviso, the amount of the royalty would be less than three-farthings, the amount thereof shall be three-farthings.

(3) If, at any time after the end of the period of one year beginning with the coming into operation of this section, it appears to the Board of Trade that the ordinary rate of royalty, or the minimum amount thereof, in accordance with the provisions of the last preceding subsection, or in accordance with those provisions as last varied by an order under this subsection, has ceased to be equitable, either generally or in relation to any class of records, the Board may hold a public inquiry in the prescribed manner; and if, in consequence of such an inquiry, the Board are satisfied of the need to do so, the Board may make an order prescribing such different rate or amount, either generally or in relation to any one or more classes of records, as the Board may consider just:

Provided that—

   (a) no order shall be made under this subsection unless a draft of the order has been laid before Parliament and approved by a resolution of each House of Parliament; and
   (b) where an order comprising a class of records (that is to say, either a general order or an order relating specifically to that class, or to that class together with one or more other classes of records) has been made under this subsection, no further order comprising that class of records shall be made thereunder less than five years after the date on which the previous order comprising that class (or, if more than one, the last previous order comprising that class) was made thereunder.

(4) In the case of a record which comprises (with or without other material, and either in their original form or in the form of adaptations) two or more musical works in which copyright subsists—

(*a*) the minimum royalty shall be three-farthings in respect of each of those works, or, if a higher or lower amount is prescribed by an order under the last preceding subsection as the minimum royalty, shall be that amount in respect of each of those works; and

(*b*) if the owners of the copyright in the works are different persons, the royalty shall be apportioned among them in such manner as they may agree or as, in default of agreement, may be determined by arbitration.

(5) Where a record comprises (with or without other material) a performance of a musical work, or of an adaptation of a musical work, in which words are sung, or are spoken incidentally to or in association with the music, and either no copyright subsists in that work or, if such copyright subsists, the conditions specified in subsection (1) of this section are fulfilled in relation to that copyright, then if—

(*a*) the words consist or form part of a literary or dramatic work in which copyright subsists, and

(*b*) such previous records as are referred to in paragraph (*a*) of subsection (1) of this section were made or imported by, or with the licence of, the owner of the copyright in that literary or dramatic work, and

(*c*) the conditions specified in paragraphs (*b*) and (*d*) of subsection (1) of this section are fulfilled in relation to the owner of that copyright,

the making of the record shall not constitute an infringement of the copyright in the literary or dramatic work:

Provided that this subsection shall not be construed as requiring more than one royalty to be paid in respect of a record; and if copyright subsists both in the musical work and in the literary or dramatic work, and their owners are different persons, the royalty shall be apportioned among them (or among them and any other person entitled to a share thereof in accordance with the last preceding subsection) as they may agree or as, in default of agreement, may be determined by arbitration.

(6) For the purposes of this section an adaptation of a work shall be taken to be similar to an adaptation thereof contained in previous records if the two adaptations do not substantially differ in their treatment of the work, either in respect of style or (apart from any difference in numbers) in respect of the performers required for performing them.

(7) Where, for the purposes of paragraph (*a*) of subsection (1) of this section, the manufacturer requires to know whether such previous records as are mentioned in that paragraph were made or imported as therein mentioned, the manufacturer may make the prescribed inquiries; and if the owner of the copyright fails to reply to those inquiries within the prescribed period, the previous records shall be taken to have been made or imported, as the case may be, with the licence of the owner of the copyright.

(8) The preceding provisions of this section shall apply in relation to records of part of a work or adaptation as they apply in relation to records of the whole of it:

Provided that subsection (1) of this section—

(*a*) shall not apply to a record of the whole of a work or adaptation unless the previous records referred to in paragraph (*a*) of that subsection were records of the whole of the work or of a similar adaptation, and

(*b*) shall not apply to a record of part of a work or adaptation unless those previous records were records of, or comprising, that part of the work or of a similar adaptation.

(9) In relation to musical works published before the first day of July, nineteen hundred and twelve, the preceding provisions of this section shall apply as if para-

graph (*a*) of subsection (1), paragraph (*b*) of subsection (5), subsections (6) and (7), and the proviso to the last preceding subsection, were omitted:

Provided that this subsection shall not extend the operation of subsection (5) of this section to a record in respect of which the condition specified in paragraph (*b*) of that subsection is not fulfilled, unless the words comprised in the record (as well as the musical work) were published before the first day of July, nineteen hundred and twelve, and were so published as words to be sung to, or spoken incidentally to or in association with, the music.

(10) Nothing in this section shall be construed as authorising the importation of records which could not lawfully be imported apart from this section; and accordingly, for the purposes of any provision of this Act relating to imported articles, where the question arises whether the making of a record made outside the United Kingdom would have constituted an infringement of copyright if the record had been made in the United Kingdom, that question shall be determined as if subsection (1) of this section had not been enacted.

(11) In this section "prescribed" means prescribed by regulations made under this section by the Board of Trade; and any such regulations made for the purposes of paragraph (*d*) of subsection (1) of this section may provide that the taking of such steps as may be specified in the regulations (being such steps as the Board consider most convenient for ensuring the receipt of the royalties by the owner of the copyright) shall be treated as constituting payment of the royalties in accordance with that paragraph.

General exceptions from protection of artistic works

9.—(1) No fair dealing with an artistic work for purposes of research or private **A—485** study shall constitute an infringement of the copyright in the work.

(2) No fair dealing with an artistic work shall constitute an infringement of the copyright in the work if it is for purposes of criticism or review, whether of that work or of another work, and is accompanied by a sufficient acknowledgment.

(3) The copyright in a work to which this subsection applies which is permanently situated in a public place, or in premises open to the public, is not infringed by the making of a painting, drawing, engraving or photograph of the work, or the inclusion of the work in a cinematograph film or in a television broadcast.

This subsection applies to sculptures, and to such works of artistic craftsmanship as are mentioned in paragraph (*c*) of subsection (1) of section three of this Act.

(4) The copyright in a work of architecture is not infringed by the making of a painting, drawing, engraving or photograph of the work, or the inclusion of the work in a cinematograph film on in a television broadcast.

(5) Without prejudice to the two last preceding subsections, the copyright in an artistic work is not infringed by the inclusion of the work in a cinematograph film or in a television broadcast, if its inclusion therein is only by way of background or is otherwise only incidental to the principal matters represented in the film or broadcast.

(6) The copyright in an artistic work is not infringed by the publication of a painting, drawing, engraving, photograph or cinematograph film, if by virtue of any of the three last preceding subsections the making of that painting, drawing, engraving, photograph or film did not constitute an infringement of the copyright.

(7) The copyright in an artistic work is not infringed by reproducing it for the purposes of a judicial proceeding or for the purposes of a report of a judicial proceeding.

(8) The making of an object of any description which is in three dimensions shall not be taken to infringe the copyright in an artistic work in two dimensions, if

the object would not appear, to persons who are not experts in relation to objects of that description, to be a reproduction of the artistic work.

(9) The copyright in an artistic work is not infringed by the making of a subsequent artistic work by the same author, notwithstanding that part of the earlier work—

(a) is reproduced in the subsequent work, and

(b) is so reproduced by the use of a mould, cast, sketch, plan, model or study made for the purposes of the earlier work,

if in making the subsequent work the author does not repeat or imitate the main design of the earlier work.

(10) Where copyright subsists in a building as a work of architecture, the copyright is not infringed by any reconstruction of that building; and where a building has been constructed in accordance with architectural drawings or plans in which copyright subsists, and has been so constructed by, or with the licence of, the owner of that copyright, any subsequent reconstruction of the building by reference to those drawings or plans shall not constitute an infringement of that copyright.

(11) The provisions of this section shall apply in relation to a [cable programme] as they apply in relation to a television broadcast.

Amendment

This section was amended by the Cable and Broadcasting Act 1984 (c. 46) and is printed as amended.

Special exception in respect of industrial designs

A–486   **10.**—[(*1*) *Where copyright subsists in an artistic work, and a corresponding design is registered under the Registered Designs Act, 1949 (in this section referred to as "the Act of 1949"), it shall not be an infringement of the copyright in the work—*

(a) *to do anything, during the subsistence of the copyright in the registered design under the Act of 1949, which is within the scope of the copyright in the design, or*

(b) *to do anything, after the copyright in the registered design has come to an end, which, if it had been done while the copyright in the design subsisted, would have been within the scope of that copyright as extended to all associated designs and articles:*
        Provided that this subsection shall have effect subject to the provisions of the First Schedule to this Act in cases falling within that Schedule.

(*2*) *Where copyright subsists in an artistic work, and—*

(a) *a corresponding design is applied industrially by or with the licence of the owner of the copyright in the work, and*

(b) *articles to which the design has been so applied are sold, let for hire, or offered for sale or hire, and*

(c) *at the time when those articles are sold, let for hire, or offered for sale or hire, they are not articles in respect of which the design has been registered under the Act of 1949,*

the following provisions of this section shall apply.

(*3*) *Subject to the next following subsection,—*

(a) *during the relevant period of fifteen years, it shall not be an infringement of the copyright in the work to do anything which, at the time when it is done, would have been within the scope of the copyright in the design if the design had, immediately before that time, been registered in respect of all relevant articles; and*

(b) *after the end of the relevant period of fifteen years, it shall not be an infringement of the copyright in the work to do anything which, at the time when it is done, would, if the design had been registered immediately before that time, have been within the scope of the copyright in the design as extended to all associated designs and articles.*

In this subsection "the relevant period of fifteen years" means the period of fifteen years beginning with the date on which articles, such as are mentioned in paragraph (b) of the last preced-

ing subsection, were first sold, let for hire, or offered for sale or hire in the circumstances men-
tioned in paragraph (c) *of that subsection; and "all relevant articles", in relation to any time*
within that period, means all articles falling within the said paragraph (b) *which had before*
that time been sold, let for hire, or offered for sale or hire in those circumstances.]

[(2) Where copyright subsists in an artistic work, and—

(*a*) a corresponding design is applied industrially by or with the licence of the owner of the copyright in the work, and

(*b*) articles to which the design has been so applied are sold, let for hire, or offered for sale or hire whether in the United Kingdom or elsewhere, and

the following provisions of this section shall apply.

(3) Subject to the next following subsection, after the end of the relevant period of fifteen years it shall not be an infringement of the copyright in the work to do anything which at the time when it was done would, if a corresponding design had been registered under the Registered Designs Act 1949 (in this section referred to as "the Act of 1949") immediately before that time, have been within the scope of the copyright in the design as extended to all associated designs and articles.

In this subsection "the relevant period of fifteen years" means the period of fifteen years beginning with the date on which articles, such as are mentioned in paragraph (*b*) of the last preceding subsection, were first sold, let for hire or offered for sale or hire, whether in the United Kingdom or elsewhere.]

(4) For the purposes of subsections (2) and (3) of this section, no account shall be taken of any articles in respect of which, at the time when they were sold, let for hire, or offered for sale or hire, the design in question was excluded from registration under the Act of 1949 by rules made under subsection (4) of section one of that Act (which relates to the exclusion of designs for articles which are primarily literary or artistic in character); and for the purposes of any proceedings under this Act a design shall be conclusively presumed to have been so excluded if—

(*a*) before the commencement of those proceedings, an application for the registration of the design under the Act of 1949 in respect of those articles had been refused;

(*b*) the reason or one of the reasons stated for the refusal was that the design was excluded from such registration by rules made under the said subsection (4); and

(*c*) no appeal against that refusal had been allowed before the date of the commencement of the proceedings or was pending on that date.

(5) The power of the Board of Trade to make rules under section thirty-six of the Act of 1949 shall include power to make rules for the purposes of this section for determining the circumstances in which a design is to be taken to be applied industrially.

(6) In this section, references to the scope of the copyright in a registered design are references to the aggregate of the things, which, by virtue of section seven of the Act of 1949, the registered proprietor of the design has the exclusive right to do, and references to the scope of the copyright in a registered design as extended to all associated designs and articles are references to the aggregate of the things which, by virtue of that section, the registered proprietor would have had the exclusive right to do if—

(*a*) when that design was registered, there had at the same time been registered every possible design consisting of that design with modifications or variations not sufficient to alter the character or substantially to affect the identity thereof, and the said proprietor had been registered as the proprietor of every such design, and

(*b*) the design in question, and every other design such as is mentioned in the preceding paragraph, had been registered in respect of all the articles to which it was capable of being applied.

(7) In this section "corresponding design", in relation to an artistic work, means a design which, when applied to an article, results in a reproduction of that work.

AMENDMENT

This section and the First Schedule were amended by the Design Copyright Act, 1968 (1968 c. 68). The amendment consisted of deleting subs. (1), amending subs. (2) and substituting a new subs. (3). The original subss. (1), (2) and (3) are printed in italics. The word "and" at the end of subs. (2)(*b*) was not deleted by the 1968 Act.

Provisions as to anonymous and pseudonymous works, and works of joint authorship

A–487   **11.**—(1) The preceding provisions of this Part of this Act shall have effect subject to the modifications specified in the Second Schedule to this Act in the case of works published anonymously or pseudonymously.

(2) The provisions of the Third Schedule to this Act shall have effect with respect to works of joint authorship.

(3) In this Act "work of joint authorship" means a work produced by the collaboration of two or more authors in which the contribution of each author is not separate from the contribution of the other author or authors.

PART II

COPYRIGHT IN SOUND RECORDINGS, CINEMATOGRAPH FILMS, BROADCASTS, ETC.

Copyright in sound recordings

A–488   **12.**—(1) Copyright shall subsist, subject to the provisions of this Act, in every sound recording of which the maker was a qualified person at the time when the recording was made.

(2) Without prejudice to the preceding subsection, copyright shall subsist, subject to the provisions of this Act, in every sound recording which has been published, if the first publication of the recording took place in the United Kingdom or in another country to which this section extends.

(3) Copyright subsisting in a sound recording by virtue of this section shall continue to subsist until the end of the period of fifty years from the end of the calendar year in which the recording is first published, and shall then expire.

(4) Subject to the provisions of this Act, the maker of a sound recording shall be entitled to any copyright subsisting in the recording by virtue of this section:

Provided that where a person commissions the making of a sound recording, and pays or agrees to pay for it in money or money's worth, and the recording is made in pursuance of that commission, that person, in the absence of any agreement to the contrary, shall, subject to the provisions of Part VI of this Act, be entitled to any copyright subsisting in the recording by virtue of this section.

(5) The acts restricted by the copyright in a sound recording are the following, whether a record embodying the recording is utilised directly or indirectly in doing them, that is to say,—

(*a*) making a record embodying the recording;

(*b*) causing the recording to be heard in public;

(*c*) broadcasting the recording [or including it in a cable programme].

(6) The copyright in a sound recording is not infringed by a person who does any of those acts in the United Kingdom in relation to a sound recording, or part of a sound recording, if—

(*a*) records embodying that recording, or that part of the recording, as the case may be, have previously been issued to the public in the United Kingdom, and (*b*) at the time when those records were so issued, neither the records nor the containers in which they were so issued bore a label or other mark indicating the year in which the recording was first published:

Provided that this subsection shall not apply if it is shown that the records in question were not issued by or with the licence of the owner of the copyright, or that the owner of the copyright had taken all reasonable steps for securing that records embodying the recording or part thereof would not be issued to the public in the United Kingdom without such a label or mark either on the records themselves or on their containers.

(7) Where a sound recording is caused to be heard in public—

(*a*) at any premises where persons reside or sleep, as part of the amenities provided exclusively or mainly for residents or inmates therein, or

(*b*) as part of the activities of, or for the benefit of, a club, society or other organisation which is not established or conducted for profit and whose main objects are charitable or are otherwise concerned with the advancement of religion, education or social welfare,

the act of causing it to be so heard shall not constitute an infringement of the copyright in the recording:

Provided that this subsection shall not apply—

(i) in the case of such premises as are mentioned in paragraph (*a*) of this subsection, if a special charge is made for admission to the part of the premises where the recording is to be heard; or

(ii) in the case of such an organisation as is mentioned in paragraph (*b*) of this subsection, if a charge is made for admission to the place where the recording is to be heard, and any of the proceeds of the charge are applied otherwise than for the purposes of the organisation.

(8) For the purposes of this Act a sound recording shall be taken to be made at the time when the first record embodying the recording is produced, and the maker of a sound recording is the person who owns that record at the time when the recording is made.

(9) In this Act "sound recording" means the aggregate of the sounds embodied in, and capable of being reproduced by means of, a record of any description, other than a sound-track associated with a cinematograph film; and "publication", in relation to a sound recording, means the issue to the public of records embodying the recording or any part thereof.

AMENDMENT

This section was amended by the Cable and Broadcasting Act 1984 (c. 46) and is printed as amended.

Copyright in cinematograph films

13.—(1) Copyright shall subsist, subject to the provisions of this Act, in every **A—489** cinematograph film of which the maker was a qualified person for the whole or a substantial part of the period during which the film was made.

(2) Without prejudice to the preceding subsection, copyright shall subsist, subject to the provisions of this Act, in every cinematograph film which has been published, if the first publication of the film took place in the United Kingdom or in another country to which this section extends.

(3) Copyright subsisting in a cinematograph film by virtue of this section—

[(*a*) in the case of any film which was registered under a former enactment relating to the registration of films, shall continue until the end of the period of fifty years from the end of the calendar year in which it was so registered;]

(*b*) in the case [of any other film], shall continue until the film is published, and thereafter until the end of the period of fifty years from the end of the calendar year which includes the date of its first publication, or, if copyright in the film subsists by virtue only of the last preceding subsection, shall continue as from the date of first publication until the end of the period of fifty years from the end of the calendar year which includes that date,

and then shall expire:

[In this subsection "former enactment relating to the registration of films" means Part II of the Films Act 1960 or Part III of the Cinematograph Films Act 1938.]

(4) Subject to the provisions of Part VI of this Act, the maker of a cinematograph film shall be entitled to any copyright subsisting in the film by virtue of this section.

(5) The acts restricted by the copyright in a cinematograph film are—

(*a*) making a copy of the film;

(*b*) causing the film, in so far as it consists of visual images, to be seen in public, or, in so far as it consists of sounds, to be heard in public;

(*c*) broadcasting the film;

[(*d*) including the film in a cable programme.]

(6) The copyright in a cinematograph film is not infringed by making a copy of it for the purposes of a judicial proceeding, or by causing it to be seen or heard in public for the purposes of such a proceeding.

(7) Where by virtue of this section copyright has subsisted in a cinematograph film, a person who, after that copyright has expired, causes the film to be seen, or to be seen and heard, in public does not thereby infringe any copyright subsisting by virtue of Part I of this Act in any literary, dramatic, musical or artistic work.

(8) In the case of [any film consisting wholly or mainly of photographs which, at the time when they were taken, were means of communicating news,] the copyright in the film is not infringed by causing it to be seen or heard in public after the end of the period of fifty years from the end of the calendar year in which the principal events depicted in the film occurred.

(9) For the purposes of this Act a cinematograph film shall be taken to include the sounds embodied in any sound-track associated with the film, and references to a copy of a cinematograph film shall be construed accordingly:

Provided that where those sounds are also embodied in a record, other than such a sound-track or a record derived (directly or indirectly) from such a sound-track, the copyright in the film is not infringed by any use made of that record.

(10) In this Act—

"cinematograph film" means any sequence of visual images recorded on material of any description (whether translucent or not) so as to be capable, by the use of that material,—

(*a*) of being shown as a moving picture, or

(*b*) of being recorded on other material (whether translucent or not), by the use of which it can be so shown;

"the maker", in relation to a cinematograph film, means the person by whom the arrangements necessary for the making of the film are undertaken;

"publication", in relation to a cinematograph film, means the sale, letting on hire, or offer for sale or hire, of copies of the film to the public;

"copy", in relation to a cinematograph film, means any print, negative, tape or other article on which the film or part of it is recorded,

and references in this Act to a sound-track associated with a cinematograph film are references to any record of sounds which is incorporated in any print, negative, tape or other article on which the film or part of it, in so far as it consists of visual images, is recorded, or which is issued by the maker of the film for use in conjunction with such an article.

AMENDMENT

This section, as amended by the Films Act, 1960 (8 & 9 Eliz. 2, c. 57), was further amended to Films Act, 1985 (c. 21), which repealed the Films Act, 1960. A new subsection (5)(d) was substituted by the Cable and Broadcasting Act 1984 (c. 46). The section is printed as amended by the 1984 and 1985 Acts.

Copyright in television broadcasts and sound broadcasts

14.—(1) Copyright shall subsist, subject to the provisions of this Act,—   **A–490**

   (*a*) in every television broadcast made by the British Broadcasting Corporation (in this Act referred to as "the Corporation") or by the Independent [Broadcasting] Authority (in this Act referred to as "the Authority") from a place in the United Kingdom or in any other country to which this section extends, and

   (*b*) in every sound broadcast made by the Corporation or the Authority from such a place.

(2) Subject to the provisions of this Act, the Corporation or the Authority, as the case may be, shall be entitled to any copyright subsisting in a television broadcast or sound broadcast made by them; and any such copyright shall continue to subsist until the end of the period of fifty years from the end of the calendar year in which the broadcast is made, and shall then expire.

(3) In so far as a television broadcast or sound broadcast is a repetition (whether the first or any subsequent repetition) of a television broadcast or sound broadcast previously made as mentioned in subsection (1) of this section (whether by the Corporation or by the Authority), and is made by broadcasting material recorded on film, records or otherwise,—

   (*a*) copyright shall not subsist therein by virtue of this section if it is made after the end of the period of fifty years from the end of the calendar year in which the previous broadcast was made; and

   (*b*) if it is made before the end of that period, any copyright subsisting therein by virtue of this section shall expire at the end of that period.

(4) The acts restricted by the copyright in a television broadcast or sound broadcast are—

   (*a*) in the case of a television broadcast in so far as it consists of visual images, making, otherwise than for private purposes, a cinematograph film of it or a copy of such a film;

   (*b*) in the case of a sound broadcast, or of a television broadcast in so far as it consists of sounds, making, otherwise than for private purposes, a sound recording of it or a record embodying such a recording;

   (*c*) in the case of a television broadcast, causing it, in so far as it consists of visual images, to be seen in public, or, in so far as it consists of sounds, to be heard in public, if it is seen or heard by a paying audience;

   (*d*) in the case either of a television broadcast or of a sound broadcast, re-broadcasting it [or including it in a cable programme].

(5) The restrictions imposed by virtue of the last preceding subsection in relation to a television broadcast or sound broadcast made by the Corporation or by the Authority shall apply whether the act in question is done by the reception of the broadcast or by making use of any record, print, negative, tape or other article on which the broadcast has been recorded.

(6) In relation to copyright in television broadcasts, in so far as they consist of visual images, the restrictions imposed by virtue of subsection (4) of this section shall apply to any sequence of images sufficient to be seen as a moving picture; and

accordingly, for the purpose of establishing an infringement of such copyright, it shall not be necessary to prove that the act in question extended to more than such a sequence of images.

(7) For the purposes of subsection (4) of this section a cinematograph film or a copy thereof, or a sound recording or a record embodying a recording, shall be taken to be made otherwise than for private purposes if it is made for the purposes of the doing by any person of any of the following acts, that is to say,—

(a) the sale or letting for hire of any copy of the film, or, as the case may be, of any record embodying the recording;

(b) broadcasting the film or recording [or including it in a cable programme];

(c) causing the film or recording to be seen or heard in public.

(8) For the purposes of paragraph (c) of subsection (4) of this section, a television broadcast shall be taken to be seen or heard by a paying audience if it is seen or heard by persons who either—

(a) have been admitted for payment to the place where the broadcast is to be seen or heard, or have been admitted for payment to a place of which that place forms part, or

(b) have been admitted to the place where the broadcast is to be seen or heard in circumstances where goods or services are supplied there at prices which exceed the prices usually charged at that place and are partly attributable to the facilities afforded for seeing or hearing the broadcast:

Provided that for the purposes of paragraph (a) of this subsection no account shall be taken—

(i) of persons admitted to the place in question as residents or inmates therein, or

(ii) of persons admitted to that place as members of a club or society, where the payment is only for membership of the club or society and the provision of facilities for seeing or hearing television broadcasts is only incidental to the main purposes of the club or society.

[(8A) The copyright in a television broadcast or sound broadcast is not infringed by any person who, by the reception and immediate re-transmission of the broadcast, includes a programme in a cable programme service—

(a) if the programme is so included in pursuance of a requirement imposed under subsection (1) of section 13 of the Cable and Broadcasting Act 1984; or

(b) where the broadcast is made otherwise than in a DBS service (as defined in subsection (6) of that section) or an additional teletext service (as so defined), if and to the extent that it is made for reception in the area in which the cable programme service is provided.]

(9) The copyright in a television broadcast or sound broadcast is not infringed by anything done in relation to the broadcast for the purposes of a judicial proceeding.

(10) In this Act "television broadcast" means visual images broadcast by way of television, together with any sounds broadcast for reception along with those images, and "sound broadcast" means sounds broadcast otherwise than as part of a television broadcast; and for the purposes of this Act a television broadcast or sound broadcast shall be taken to be made by the body by whom, at the time when, and from the place from which,

[(a) the visual images or sounds in question, or both, as the case may be, are broadcast; or

(b) in the case of a television broadcast or sound broadcast made by the technique known as direct broadcasting by satellite, the visual images or sounds in question, or both, as the case may be, are transmitted to the satellite transponder.]

[(11) The foregoing provisions of this section shall have effect as if references in

1068

those provisions and in section 12(9) of this Act to sounds included references to signals serving for the impartation of matter otherwise than in the form of sounds or visual images.]

AMENDMENT
This section was amended by the Cable and Broadcasting Act 1984 (c. 46) and is printed as amended.

[Copyright in cable programmes

14A.—(1) Copyright shall subsist, subject to the provisions of this Act, in every cable programme which is included in a cable programme service provided by a qualified person in the United Kingdom or in any other country to which this section extends. **A–491**

(2) Copyright shall not subsist in a cable programme by virtue of this section if the programme is included in the cable programme service by the reception and immediate re-transmission of a television broadcast or a sound broadcast.

(3) Subject to the provisions of this Act, a person providing a cable programme service shall be entitled to any copyright subsisting in a cable programme included in that service and any such copyright shall continue to subsist until the end of the period of fifty years from the end of the calendar year in which the cable programme is so included, and shall then expire.

(4) In so far as a cable programme is a repetition (whether the first or any subsequent repetition) of a cable programme previously included as mentioned in subsection (1) of this section—

(a) copyright shall not subsist therein by virtue of this section if it is so included after the end of the period of fifty years from the end of the calendar year in which it was previously so included; and

(b) if it is so included before the end of that period any copyright subsisting therein by virtue of this section shall expire at the end of that period.

(5) The acts restricted by the copyright in a cable programme are—

(a) in so far as it consists of visual images, making, otherwise than for private purposes, a cinematograph film of it or a copy of such a film;

(b) in so far as it consists of sounds, making, otherwise than for private purposes, a sound recording of it or a record embodying such a recording;

(c) causing it, in so far as it consists of visual images, to be seen in public, or, in so far as it consists of sounds, to be heard in public, if it is seen or heard by a paying audience;

(d) broadcasting it or including it in a cable programme service.

(6) The restrictions imposed by virtue of the last preceding subsection in relation to a cable programme shall apply whether the act in question is done by the reception of the programme or by making use of any record, print, negative, tape or other article on which the programme has been recorded.

(7) In relation to copyright in cable programmes, in so far as they consist of visual images, the restrictions imposed by virtue of subsection (5) of this section shall apply to any sequence of images sufficient to be seen as a moving picture; and accordingly, for the purpose of establishing an infringement of such copyright, it shall not be necessary to prove that the act in question extended to more than such a sequence of images.

(8) For the purposes of subsection (5) of this section a cinematograph film or a copy thereof, or a sound recording or a record embodying a recording, shall be taken to be made otherwise than for private purposes if it is made for the purposes of the doing by any person of any of the following acts, that is to say,—

(a) the sale or letting for hire of any copy of the film, or, as the case may be, of any record embodying the recording;

(*b*) broadcasting the film or recording or including it in a cable programme service;

(*c*) causing the film or recording to be seen or heard in public.

(9) For the purposes of paragraph (*c*) of subsection (5) of this section, a cable programme shall be taken to be seen or heard by a paying audience if it is seen or heard by persons who either—

(*a*) have been admitted for payment to the place where the programme is to be seen or heard, or have been admitted for payment to a place of which that place forms part, or

(*b*) have been admitted to the place where the programme is to be seen or heard in circumstances where goods or services are supplied there at prices which exceed the prices usually charged at that place and are partly attributable to the facilities afforded for seeing or hearing the programme:

Provided that for the purposes of paragraph (*a*) of this subsection no account shall be taken—

(i) of persons admitted to the place in question as residents or inmates therein, or

(ii) of persons admitted to that place as members of a club or society, where payment is only for membership of the club or society and the provision of facilities for seeing or hearing cable programmes is only incidental to the main purposes of the club or society.

(10) The copyright in a cable programme is not infringed by anything done in relation to the programme for the purposes of a judicial proceeding.

(11) In this Act—

"cable programme" means a programme which is included, after the commencement of section 22 of the Cable and Broadcasting Act 1984, in a cable programme service;

"cable programme service" means a cable programme service within the meaning of the said Act of 1984 or a service provided outside the United Kingdom which would be such a service if subsection (7) of section 2 of that Act and references in subsection (1) of that section to the United Kingdom were omitted;

"programme", in relation to a cable programme service, includes any item included in that service.

(12) The foregoing provisions of this section shall have effect as if references in those provisions and in section 12(9) of this Act to sounds included references to signals serving for the impartation of matter otherwise than in the form of sounds or visual images.]

AMENDMENT

Section 14A was added by the Cable and Broadcasting Act 1984 (c. 46). The 1984 Act was repealed by section 203(3) of and Schedule 21 to the Broadcasting Act 1990 (c. 42) as provided by The Broadcasting Act 1990 (Commencement No. 1 and Transitional Provisions) Order 1990 (S.I. 1990 No. 2347 (c. 61)) § B–254 *post*.

Copyright in published editions of works

15.—(1) Copyright shall subsist, subject to the provisions of this Act, in every published edition of any one or more literary, dramatic or musical works in the case of which either—

(*a*) the first publication of the edition took place in the United Kingdom, or in another country to which this section extends, or

(*b*) the publisher of the edition was a qualified person at the date of the first publication thereof:

Provided that this subsection does not apply to an edition which reproduces the typographical arrangement of a previous edition of the same work or works.

(2) Subject to the provisions of this Act, the publisher of an edition shall be entitled to any copyright subsisting in the edition by virtue of this section; and any such copyright shall continue to subsist until the end of the period of twenty-five years from the end of the calendar year in which the edition was first published, and shall then expire.

(3) The act restricted by the copyright subsisting by virtue of this section in a published edition is the making, by any photographic or similar process, of a reproduction of the typographical arrangement of the edition.

(4) The copyright under this section in a published edition is not infringed by the making by or on behalf of a librarian of a reproduction of the typographical arrangement of the edition, if he is the librarian of a library of a class prescribed by regulations made under this subsection by the Board of Trade, and the conditions prescribed by those regulations are complied with.

Supplementary provisions for purposes of Part II

16.—(1) The provisions of this section shall have effect with respect to copyright   **A–493** subsisting by virtue of this Part of this Act in sound recordings, cinematograph films, television broadcasts, [sound broadcasts and cable programmes,] and in published editions of literary, dramatic and musical works; and in those provisions references to the relevant provision of this Part of this Act, in relation to copyright in a subject-matter of any of those descriptions, are references to the provision of this Part of this Act whereby it is provided that (subject to compliance with the conditions secified therein) copyright shall subsist in that description of subject-matter.

(2) Any copyright subsisting by virtue of this Part of this Act is infringed by any person who, without the licence of the owner of the copyright, imports an article (otherwise than for his private and domestic use) into the United Kingdom, or into any other country to which the relevant provision of this Part of this Act extends, if to his knowledge the making of that article constituted an infringement of that copyright, or would have constituted such an infringement if the article had been made in the place into which it is so imported.

(3) Any such copyright is also infringed by any person who, in the United Kingdom, or in any other country to which the relevant provision of this Part of this Act extends, and without the licence of the owner of the copyright,—

    (*a*) sells, lets for hire, or by way of trade offers or exposes for sale or hire any article, or

    (*b*) by way of trade exhibits any article in public,

if to his knowledge the making of the article constituted an infringement of that copyright, or (in the case of an imported article) would have constituted an infringement of that copyright if the article had been made in the place into which it was imported.

(4) The last preceding subsection shall apply in relation to the distribution of any articles either—

    (*a*) for purposes of trade, or

    (*b*) for other purposes, but to such an extent as to affect prejudicially the owner of the copyright in question,

as it applies in relation to the sale of an article.

(5) The three last preceding subsections shall have effect without prejudice to the general provisions of section one of this Act as to infringements of copyright.

(6) Where by virtue of this Part of this Act copyright subsists in a sound recording, cinematograph film, broadcast, [cable programme] or other subject-matter, nothing in this Part of this Act shall be construed as affecting the operation of Part

I of this Act in relation to any literary, dramatic, musical or artistic work from which that subject-matter is wholly or partly derived; and copyright subsisting by virtue of this Part of this Act shall be additional to, and independent of, any copyright subsisting by virtue of Part I of this Act:

Provided that this subsection shall have effect subject to the provisions of subsection (7) of section thirteen of this Act.

(7) The subsistence of copyright under any of the preceding sections of this Part of this Act shall not affect the operation of any other of those sections under which copyright can subsist.

AMENDMENT

This section was amended by the Cable and Broadcasting Act 1984 (c. 46) and is printed as amended.

PART III

REMEDIES FOR INFRINGEMENTS OF COPYRIGHT

Action by owner of copyright for infringement

A–494   17.—(1) Subject to the provisions of this Act, infringements of copyright shall be actionable at the suit of the owner of the copyright; and in any action for such an infringement all such relief, by way of damages, injunction, accounts or otherwise, shall be available to the plaintiff as is available in any corresponding proceedings in respect of infringements of other proprietary rights.

(2) Where in an action for infringement of copyright it is proved or admitted—

    (*a*) that an infringement was committed, but

    (*b*) that at the time of the infringement the defendant was not aware, and had no reasonable grounds for suspecting, that copyright subsisted in the work or other subject-matter to which the action relates,

the plaintiff shall not be entitled under this section to any damages against the defendant in respect of the infringement, but shall be entitled to an account of profits in respect of the infringement whether any other relief is granted under this section or not.

(3) Where in an action under this section an infringement of copyright is proved or admitted, and the court, having regard (in addition to all other material considerations) to—

    (*a*) the flagrancy of the infringement, and

    (*b*) any benefit shown to have accrued to the defendant by reason of the infringement,

is satisfied that effective relief would not otherwise be available to the plaintiff, the court, in assessing damages for the infringement, shall have power to award such additional damages by virtue of this subsection as the court may consider appropriate in the circumstances.

(4) In an action for infringement of copyright in respect of the construction of a building, no injunction or other order shall be made—

    (*a*) after the construction of the building has been begun, so as to prevent it from being completed, or

    (*b*) so as to require the building, in so far as it has been constructed, to be demolished.

(5) In this Part of this Act "action" includes a counterclaim, and references to the plaintiff and to the defendant in an action shall be construed accordingly.

(6) In the application of this Part of this Act to Scotland, "injunction" means an interdict and "interlocutory injunction" means an interim interdict, "accounts"

means count, reckoning and payment, "an account of profits" means an account-ing and payment of profits, "plaintiff" means pursuer, "defendant" means defender and "costs" means expenses.

Rights of owner of copyright in respect of infringing copies, etc.

18.—(1) Subject to the provisions of this Act, the owner of any copyright shall **A–495** be entitled to all such rights and remedies, in respect of the conversion or detention by any person of any infringing copy, or of any plate used or intended to be used for making infringing copies, as he would be entitled to if he were the owner of every such copy or plate and had been the owner thereof since the time when it was made:

Provided that if, by virtue of subsection (2) of section three of the Limitation Act, 1939 (which relates to successive conversions or detentions), or of any corre-sponding provision which may be enacted by the Parliament of Northern Ireland, the title of the owner of the copyright to such a copy or plate would (if he had then been the owner of the copy or plate) have been extinguished at the end of the period mentioned in that subsection or corresponding provision, he shall not be entitled to any rights or remedies under this subsection in respect of anything done in relation to that copy or plate after the end of that period.

(2) A plaintiff shall not be entitled by virtue of this section to any damages or to any other pecuniary remedy (except costs) if it is proved or admitted that, at the time of the conversion or detention in question,—

(a) the defendant was not aware, and had no reasonable grounds for suspect-ing, that copyright subsisted in the work or other subject-matter to which the action relates, or

(b) where the articles converted or detained were infringing copies, the defend-ant believed, and had reasonable grounds for believing, that they were not infringing copies, or

(c) where the article converted or detained was a plate used or intended to be used for making any articles, the defendant believed, and had reasonable grounds for believing, that the articles so made or intended to be made were not, or (as the case may be) would not be, infringing copies.

(3) In this Part of this Act "infringing copy"—

(a) in relation to a literary, dramatic, musical or artistic work, or to such a published edition as is mentioned in section fifteen of this Act, means a reproduction otherwise than in the form of a cinematograph film,

(b) in relation to a sound recording, means a record embodying that recording,

(c) in relation to a cinematograph film, means a copy of the film, and

(d) in relation to a television broadcast or [a sound broadcast or a cable pro-gramme], means a copy of a cinematograph film of it or a record embody-ing a sound recording of it,

being (in any such case) an article the making of which constituted an infringe-ment of the copyright in the work, edition, recording, film, [broadcast or pro-gramme,] or, in the case of an imported article, would have constituted an infringement of that copyright if the article had been made in the place into which it was imported; and "plate" includes any stereotype, stone, block, mould, matrix, transfer, negative or other appliance.

(4) In the application of this section to Scotland, for any reference to the conver-sion or detention by any person of an infringing copy there shall be substituted a reference to an intromission by any person with an infringing copy, and for any reference to articles converted or detained there shall be substituted a reference to articles intromitted with.

AMENDMENT

This section was amended by the Cable and Broadcasting Act 1984 (c. 46) and is printed as amended.

REPEAL

The Limitation Act 1939 was repealed by the Limitation Act 1980 (c. 58) s.40(3) and Schedule 4; see § A–653 *post.*

Proceedings in case of copyright subject to exclusive licence

A–496   **19.**—(1) The provisions of this section shall have effect as to proceedings in the case of any copyright in respect of which an exclusive licence has been granted and is in force at the time of the events to which the proceedings relate.

(2) Subject to the following provisions of this section—

  (*a*) the exclusive licensee shall (except against the owner of the copyright) have the same rights of action, and be entitled to the same remedies, under section seventeen of this Act as if the licence had been an assignment, and those rights and remedies shall be concurrent with the rights and remedies of the owner of the copyright under that section;

  (*b*) the exclusive licensee shall (except against the owner of the copyright) have the same rights of action, and be entitled to the same remedies, by virtue of the last preceding section as if the licence had been an assignment; and

  (*c*) the owner of the copyright shall not have any rights of action, or be entitled to any remedies, by virtue of the last preceding section which he would not have had or been entitled to if the licence had been an assignment.

(3) Where an action is brought either by the owner of the copyright or by the exclusive licensee, and the action, in so far as it is brought under section seventeen of this Act, relates (wholly or partly) to an infringement in respect of which they have concurrent rights of action under that section, the owner or licensee, as the case may be, shall not be entitled, except with the leave of the court, to proceed with the action, in so far as it is brought under that section and relates to that infringement, unless the other party is either joined as a plaintiff in the action or added as a defendant:

Provided that this subsection shall not affect the granting of an interlocutory injunction on the application of either of them.

(4) In any action brought by the exclusive licensee by virtue of this section, any defence which would have been available to a defendant in the action, if this section had not been enacted and the action had been brought by the owner of the copyright, shall be available to that defendant as against the exclusive licensee.

(5) Where an action is brought in the circumstances mentioned in subsection (3) of this section, and the owner of the copyright and the exclusive licensee are not both plaintiffs in the action, the court, in assessing damages in respect of any such infringement as is mentioned in that subsection,—

  (*a*) if the plaintiff is the exclusive licensee, shall take into account any liabilities (in respect of royalties or otherwise) to which the licence is subject, and

  (*b*) whether the plaintiff is the owner of the copyright or the exclusive licensee, shall take into account any pecuniary remedy already awarded to the other party under section seventeen of this Act in respect of that infringement, or, as the case may require, any right of action exercisable by the other party under that section in respect thereof.

(6) Where an action, in so far as it is brought under section seventeen of this Act, relates (wholly or partly) to an infringement in respect of which the owner of the copyright and the exclusive licensee have concurrent rights of action under that section, and in that action (whether they are both parties to it or not) an account of profits is directed to be taken in respect of that infringement, then, subject to any agreement of which the court is aware, whereby the application of those

profits is determined as between the owner of the copyright and the exclusive licensee, the court shall apportion the profits between them as the court may consider just, and shall give such directions as the court may consider appropriate for giving effect to that apportionment.

(7) In an action brought either by the owner of the copyright or by the exclusive licensee,—

(*a*) no judgment or order for the payment of damages in respect of an infringement of copyright shall be given or made under section seventeen of this Act, if a final judgment or order has been given or made awarding an account of profits to the other party under that section in respect of the same infringement; and

(*b*) no judgment or order for an account of profits in respect of an infringement of copyright shall be given or made under that section, if a final judgment or order has been given or made awarding either damages or an account of profits to the other party under that section in respect of the same infringement.

(8) Where, in an action brought in the circumstances mentioned in subsection (3) of this section, whether by the owner of the copyright or by the exclusive licensee, the other party is not joined as a plaintiff (either at the commencement of the action or subsequently), but is added as a defendant, he shall not be liable for any costs in the action unless he enters an appearance and takes part in the proceedings.

(9) In this section "exclusive licence" means a licence in writing, signed by or on behalf of an owner or prospective owner of copyright, authorising the licensee, to the exclusion of all other persons, including the grantor of the licence, to exercise a right which by virtue of this Act would (apart from the licence) be exercisable exclusively by the owner of the copyright, and "exclusive licensee" shall be construed accordingly; "the other party", in relation to the owner of the copyright, means the exclusive licensee, and, in relation to the exclusive licensee, means the owner of the copyright; and "if the licence had been an assignment" means if, instead of the licence, there had been granted (subject to terms and conditions corresponding as nearly as may be with those subject to which the licence was granted) an assignment of the copyright in respect of its application to the doing, at the places and times authorised by the licence, of the acts so authorised.

Proof of facts in copyright actions

20.—(1) In any action brought by virtue of this Part of this Act— **A–497**

(*a*) copyright shall be presumed to subsist in the work or other subject-matter to which the action relates, if the defendant does not put in issue the question whether copyright subsists therein, and

(*b*) where the subsistence of the copyright is proved or admitted, or is presumed in pursuance of the preceding paragraph, the plaintiff shall be presumed to be the owner of the copyright, if he claims to be the owner of the copyright and the defendant does not put in issue the question of his ownership thereof.

(2) Subject to the preceding subsection, where, in the case of a literary, dramatic, musical or artistic work, a name purporting to be that of the author appeared on copies of the work as published, or, in the case of an artistic work, appeared on the work when it was made, the person whose name so appeared (if it was his true name or a name by which he was commonly known) shall, in any action brought by virtue of this Part of this Act, be presumed, unless the contrary is proved,—

(*a*) to be the author of the work, and

(*b*) to have made the work in circumstances not falling within subsection (2), subsection (3) or subsection (4) of section four of this Act.

(3) In the case of a work alleged to be a work of joint authorship, the last preceding subsection shall apply in relation to each person alleged to be one of the authors of the work, as if references in that subsection to the author were references to one of the authors.

(4) Where, in an action brought by virtue of this Part of this Act, with respect to a literary, dramatic, musical or artistic work, subsection (2) of this section does not apply, but it is established—

(*a*) that the work was first published in the United Kingdom, or in another country to which section two, or, as the case may be, section three, of this Act extends, and was so published within the period of fifty years ending with the beginning of the calendar year in which the action was brought, and

(*b*) that a name purporting to be that of the publisher appeared on copies of the work as first published,

then, unless the contrary is shown, copyright shall be presumed to subsist in the work and the person whose name so appeared shall be presumed to have been the owner of that copyright at the time of the publication.

For the purposes of this subsection a fact shall be taken to be established if it is proved or admitted, or if it is presumed in pursuance of the following provisions of this section.

(5) Where in an action brought by virtue of this Part of this Act with respect to a literary, dramatic, musical or artistic work it is proved or admitted that the author of the work is dead,—

(*a*) the work shall be presumed to be an original work unless the contrary is proved, and

(*b*) if it is alleged by the plaintiff that a publication specified in the allegation was the first publication of the work, and that it took place in a country and on a date so specified, that publication shall be presumed, unless the contrary is proved, to have been the first publication of the work, and to have taken place in that country and on that date.

(6) Paragraphs (*a*) and (*b*) of the last preceding subsection shall apply where a work has been published, and—

(*a*) the publication was anonymous, or was under a name alleged by the plaintiff to have been a pseudonym, and

(*b*) it is not shown that the work has ever been published under the true name of the author, or under a name by which he was commonly known, or that it is possible for a person without previous knowledge of the facts to ascertain the identity of the author by reasonable inquiry,

as those paragraphs apply in a case where it is proved that the author is dead.

(7) In any action brought by virtue of this Part of this Act with respect to copyright in a sound recording, if records embodying that recording or part thereof have been issued to the public, and at the time when those records were so issued they bore a label or other mark comprising any one or more of the following statements, that is to say,—

(*a*) that a person named on the label or mark was the maker of the sound recording;

(*b*) that the recording was first published in a year specified on the label or mark;

(*c*) that the recording was first published in a country specified on the label or mark, that label or mark shall be sufficient evidence of the facts so stated except in so far as the contrary is proved.

Penalties and summary proceedings in respect of dealings which infringe copyright

21.—(1) Any person who, at a time when copyright subsists in a work,— **A–498**

(*a*)　makes for sale or hire, or

(*b*)　sells or lets for hire, or by way of trade offers or exposes for sale or hire, or

(*c*)　by way of trade exhibits in public, or

(*d*)　imports into the United Kingdom, otherwise than for his private and domestic use,

any article which he knows to be an infringing copy of the work, shall be guilty of an offence under this subsection.

(2) Any person who, at a time when copyright subsists in a work, distributes, either—

(*a*)　for purposes of trade, or

(*b*)　for other purposes, but to such an extent as to affect prejudicially the owner of the copyright,

articles which he knows to be infringing copies of the work, shall be guilty of an offence under this subsection.

(3) Any person who, at a time when copyright subsists in a work, makes or has in his possession a plate, knowing that it is to be used for making infringing copies of the work, shall be guilty of an offence under this subsection.

(4) The preceding subsections shall apply in relation to copyright subsisting in any subject-matter by virtue of Part II of this Act, as they apply in relation to copyright subsisting by virtue of Part I of this Act.

[(4A) Any person who, at a time when copyright subsists in a sound recording or in a cinematograph film, by way of trade has in his possession any article which he knows to be an infringing copy of the sound recording or cinematograph film, as the case may be, shall be guilty of an offence under this subsection.]

(5) Any person who causes a literary, dramatic or musical work to be performed in public, knowing that copyright subsists in the work and that the performance constitutes an infringement of the copyright, shall be guilty of an offence under this subsection.

(6) The preceding provisions of this section apply only in respect of acts done in the United Kingdom.

(7) A person guilty of an offence under subsection (1) [or subsection (2) of this section, other than an offence for which a penalty is provided by subsection (7A) or (7B) of this section,] shall on summary conviction—

(*a*)　if it is his first conviction of an offence under this section, be liable to a fine not exceeding forty shillings for each article to which the offence relates;

(*b*)　in any other case, be liable to such a fine, or to imprisonment for a term not exceeding two months:

Provided that a fine imposed by virtue of this subsection shall not exceed fifty pounds in respect of articles comprised in the same transaction.

[(7A) A person guilty of an offence under subsection (1)(*b*) or (*c*) or (4A) of this section relating to an infringing copy of a sound recording or cinematograph film shall be liable on summary conviction to a fine not exceeding level 5 on the standard scale or imprisonment for a term not exceeding two months or to both.

(7B) A person guilty of an offence under subsection (1)(*a*) or (*d*) or (2) of this section relating to an infringing copy of a sound recording or cinematograph film shall be liable—

(*a*)　on summary conviction, to a fine not exceeding the statutory maximum;

(*b*) on conviction on indictment, to a fine or to imprisonment for a term not exceeding two years or to both.

(7C) In subsection (7A) of this section "the standard scale" has the meaning given by section 75 of the Criminal Justice Act 1982 and for the purposes of that subsection—

(*a*) section 37 of that Act; and

(*b*) an order under section 143 of the Magistrates' Courts Act 1980 which alters the sums specified in subsection (2) of the said section 37,

shall extend to Northern Ireland and the said section 75 shall have effect as if after the words "England and Wales" there were inserted the words "or Northern Ireland".

(7D) In subsection (7B) of this section "statutory maximum" has the meaning given by section 74 of the Criminal Justice Act 1982 and for the purposes of that subsection—

(*a*) section 32 of the Magistrates' Courts Act 1980; and

(*b*) an order made under section 143 of that Act which alters the sum specified in the definition of "the prescribed sum" in subsection (9) of the said section 32,

shall extend to Northern Ireland and subsection (1) of the said section 74 shall have effect as if after the words "England and Wales" there were inserted the words "or Northern Ireland".]

(8) A person guilty of an offence under subsection (3) or subsection (5) of this section shall on summary conviction—

(*a*) if it is his first conviction of an offence under this section, be liable to a fine not exceeding fifty pounds;

(*b*) in any other case, be liable to such a fine, or to imprisonment for a term not exceeding two months.

(9) The court before which a person is charged with an offence under this section may, whether he is convicted of the offence or not, order that any article in his possession which appears to the court to be an infringing copy, or to be a plate used or intended to be used for making infringing copies, shall be destroyed or delivered up to the owner of the copyright in question or otherwise dealt with as the court may think fit.

(10) An appeal shall lie to a court of quarter sessions from any order made under the last preceding subsection by a court of summary jurisdiction; and where such an order is made by the sheriff there shall be a like right of appeal against the order as if it were a conviction.

AMENDMENT

This section was amended by the Copyright Act 1956 (Amendment) Act 1982 (c. 35) and again by the Copyright (Amendment) Act 1983 (c. 42) and is printed as amended by such Acts.

[Search warrants

A–499 **21A.**—(1) Where, on information on oath given by a constable, a justice of the peace is satisfied that there are reasonable grounds for believing—

(*a*) that an offence under subsection (1)(*a*) or (*d*) or (2) of section 21 of this Act relating to an infringing copy of a sound recording or a cinematograph film has been or is about to be committed in any premises, and

(*b*) that evidence that the offence has been or is about to be committed is in those premises,

he may issue a warrant authorising a constable to enter and search the premises, using such reasonable force as is necessary.

(2) A warrant under this section may authorise persons to accompany any con-

stable who is executing it and must be executed within twenty-eight days from the date of its issue.

(3) In executing a warrant issued under this section a constable may seize any article if he reasonably believes that it is evidence that an offence under subsection (1), (2) or (4A) of section 21 of this Act relating to an infringing copy of a sound recording or a cinematograph film has been or is about to be committed.

(4) In this section "premises" includes land, buildings, moveable structures, vehicles, vessels, aircraft and hovercraft.

(5) This section shall have effect in Northern Ireland as if in subsection (1)—

(*a*) for the reference to an information there were substituted a reference to a complaint, and

(*b*) for the reference to a justice of the peace there were substituted a reference to a resident magistrate.

(6) This section shall not extend to Scotland.

Persons accompanying constable under search warrant or order of court in Scotland

21B.—(1) Where in Scotland an application is made for a warrant or order of   **A–500**
court to authorise a constable to enter and search any premises where there are reasonable grounds for believing that an offence under subsection (1)(*a*) or (*d*) or (2) of section 21 of this Act relating to an infringing copy of a sound recording or a cinematograph film has been or is about to be committed, the court may in any such warrant or order of court authorise any person named in the warrant or order to accompany any constable who is executing the warrant or order.

(2) In this section "premises" includes land, buildings, moveable structures, vehicles, vessels, aircraft and hovercraft.

(3) This section applies to Scotland only.]

AMENDMENT

Sections 21A and 21B were added by the Copyright (Amendment) Act 1983 (c. 42).

Provision for restricting importation of printed copies

22.—(1) The owner of the copyright in any published literary, dramatic or   **A–501**
musical work may give notice in writing to the Commissioners of Customs and Excise (in this section referred to as "the Commissioners")—

(*a*) that he is the owner of the copyright in the work, and

(*b*) that he requests the Commissioners, during a period specified in the notice, to treat as prohibited goods copies of the work to which this section applies:

Provided that the period specified in a notice under this subsection shall not exceed five years and shall not extend beyond the end of the period for which the copyright is to subsist.

(2) This section applies, in the case of a work, to any printed copy made outside the United Kingdom which, if it had been made in the United Kingdom, would be an infringing copy of the work.

(3) Where a notice has been given under this section in respect of a work, and has not been withdrawn, the importation into the United Kingdom, at a time before the end of the period specified in the notice, of any copy of the work to which this section applies shall, subject to the following provisions of this section, be prohibited:

Provided that this subsection shall not apply to the importation of any article by a person for his private and domestic use.

(4) The Commissioners may make regulations prescribing the form in which notices are to be given under this section, and requiring a person giving such a notice, either at the time of giving the notice or at the time when the goods in ques-

tion are imported, or at both those times, to furnish the Commissioners with such evidence, and to comply with such other conditions (if any), as may be specified in the regulations; and any such regulations may include such incidental and supplementary provisions as the Commissioners consider expedient for the purposes of this section.

(5) Without prejudice to the generality of the last preceding subsection, regulations made under that subsection may include provision for requiring a person who has given a notice under subsection (1) of this section, or a notice purporting to be a notice under that subsection,—

(*a*) to pay such fees in respect of the notice as may be prescribed by the regulations;

(*b*) to give to the Commissioners such security as may be so prescribed, in respect of any liability or expense which they may incur in consequence of the detention, at any time within the period specified in the notice, of any copy of the work to which the notice relates, or in consequence of anything done in relation to a copy so detained;

(*c*) whether any such security is given or not, to keep the Commissioners indemnified against any such liability, or expense as is mentioned in the last preceding paragraph.

(6) For the purpose of [section 17 of the Customs and Excise Management Act 1979] (which relates to the disposal of duties), any fees paid in pursuance of regulations made under this section shall be treated as money collected on account of [duties (whether of customs or excise) charged on imported goods.]

(7) Notwithstanding anything in [the Customs and Excise Management Act 1979] a person shall not be liable to any penalty under that Act (other than forfeiture of the goods) by reason that any goods are treated as prohibited goods by virtue of this section.

AMENDMENT

Subsections (6) and (7) were amended by the Customs and Excise Management Act 1979 (c. 2) s.177(1) and Schedule 4 and are printed as amended.

PART IV

PERFORMING RIGHT TRIBUNAL

Establishment of tribunal

A–502
23.—(1) There shall be established a tribunal, to be called the Performing Right Tribunal (in this Act referred to as "the tribunal"), for the purpose of exercising the jurisdiction conferred by the provisions of this Part of this Act.

(2) The tribunal shall consist of a chairman appointed by the Lord Chancellor, who shall be a barrister, advocate or solicitor of not less than seven years' standing or a person who has held judicial office, and of not less than two nor more than four other members appointed by the Board of Trade.

[*(3) A person shall be disqualified for being appointed, or being, a member of the tribunal so long as he is a member of the Commons House of Parliament, or of the Senate or House of Commons of Northern Ireland.*]

(4) The provisions of the Fourth Schedule to this Act shall have effect with respect to the tribunal.

(5) There shall be paid to the members of the tribuanl such remuneration (whether by way of salaries or fees), and such allowances, as the Board of Trade, with the approval of the Treasury, may determine in the case of those members respectively.

(6) The Board of Trade may appoint such officers and servants of the tribunal

as the Board, with the approval of the Treasury as to numbers and remuneration, may determine.

(7) The remuneration and allowances of members of the tribunal, the remuneration of any officers and servants appointed under the last preceding subsection, and such other expenses of the tribunal as the Board of Trade with the approval of the Treasury may determine shall be paid out of moneys provided by Parliament.

AMENDMENT

Subsection (3) was repealed by the House of Commons Disqualification Act 1957 (5 & 6 Eliz. 2, c. 20) and was itself repealed by the House of Commons Disqualification Act 1975 (c. 24) and the Northern Ireland Assembly Disqualification Act 1975 (c. 25), which provide instead that a person is disqualified for membership of the House of Commons and the Northern Ireland Assembly, who for the time being is a member of the Performing Right Tribunal.

General provisions as to jurisdiction of tribunal

24.—(1) Subject to the provisions of this Part of this Act, the function of the tri-   **A–503**
bunal shall be to determine disputes arising between licensing bodies and persons requiring licences, or organisations claiming to be representative of such persons, either—

(a) on the reference of a licence scheme to the tribunal, or

(b) on the application of a person requiring a licence either in accordance with a licence scheme or in a case not covered by a licence scheme.

(2) In this Part of this Act "licence" means a licence granted by or on behalf of the owner, or prospective owner, of the copyright in a literary, dramatic or musical work, or in a sound recording or a television broadcast, being—

(a) in the case of a literary, dramatic or musical work, a licence to perform in public, or to broadcast, the work or an adaptation thereof, or to [include the work or an adaptation thereof in a cable programme];

(b) in the case of a sound recording, a licence to cause it to be heard in public, [to broadcast it or to include it in a cable programme];

(c) in the case of a television broadcast, a licence to cause it, in so far as it consists of visual images, to be seen in public and, in so far as it consists of sounds, to be heard in public.

(3) In this Part of this Act "licensing body"—

(a) in relation to such licences as are mentioned in paragraph (a) of the last preceding subsection, means a society or other organisation which has as its main object, or one of its main objects, the negotiation or granting of such licences, either as owner or prospective owner of copyright or as agent for the owners or prospective owners thereof;

(b) in relation to such licences as are mentioned in paragraph (b) of the last preceding subsection, means any owner or prospective owner of copyright in sound recordings, or any person or body of persons acting as agent for any owners or prospective owners of copyright in sound recordings in relation to the negotiation or granting of such licences; and

(c) in relation to such licences as are mentioned in paragraph (c) of the last preceding subsection, means the Corporation or the Authority or any organisation appointed by them, or either of them, in accordance with the provisions of the Fifth Schedule to this Act:

Provided that paragraph (a) of this subsection shall not apply to an organisation by reason that its objects include the negotiation or granting of individual licences, each relating to a single work or the works of a single author, if they do not include the negotiation or granting of general licences, each extending to the works of several authors.

(4) In this Part of this Act "licence scheme", in relation to licences of any des-

cription, means a scheme made by one or more licensing bodies, setting out the classes of cases in which they, or the persons on whose behalf they act, are willing to grant licences of that description, and the charges (if any), and terms and conditions, subject to which licences would be granted in those classes of cases; and in this subsection "scheme" includes anything in the nature of a scheme, whether described therein as a scheme or as a tariff or by any other name.

(5) References in this Part of this Act to terms and conditions are references to any terms and conditions other than those relating to the amount of a charge for a licence; and references to giving an opportunity to a person of presenting his case are references to giving him an opportunity, at his option, of submitting representations in writing, or of being heard, or of submitting representations in writing and being heard.

Amendment

This section was amended by the Cable and Broadcasting Act 1984 (c. 46) and is printed as amended.

Reference of licence schemes to tribunal

A–504   **25.**—(1) Where, at any time while a licence scheme is in operation, a dispute arises with respect to the scheme between the licensing body operating the scheme and—

(a) an organisation claiming to be representative of persons requiring licences in cases of a class to which the scheme applies, or

(b) any person claiming that he requires a licence in a case of a class to which the scheme applies,

the organisation or person in question may refer the scheme to the tribunal in so far as it relates to cases of that class.

(2) The parties to a reference under this section shall be—

(a) the organisation or person at whose instance the reference is made;

(b) the licensing body operating the scheme to which the reference relates; and

(c) such other organisations or persons (if any) as apply to the tribunal to be made parties to the reference and, in accordance with the next following subsection, are made parties thereto.

(3) Where an organisation (whether claiming to be representative of persons requiring licences or not) or a person (whether requiring a licence or not) applies to the tribunal to be made a party to a reference, and the tribunal is satisfied that the organisation or person has a substantial interest in the matter in dispute, the tribunal may, if it thinks fit, make that organisation or person a party to the reference.

(4) The tribunal shall not entertain a reference under this section by an organisation unless the tribunal is satisfied that the organisation is reasonably representative of the class of persons which it claims to represent.

(5) Subject to the last preceding subsection, the tribunal, on any reference under this section, shall consider the matter in dispute, and, after giving to the parties to the reference an opportunity of presenting their cases respectively, shall make such order, either confirming or varying the scheme, in so far as it relates to cases of the class to which the reference relates, as the tribunal may determine to be reasonable in the circumstances.

(6) An order of the tribunal under this section may, notwithstanding anything contained in the licence scheme to which it relates, be made so as to be in force either indefinitely or for such period as the tribunal may determine.

(7) Where a licence scheme has been referred to the tribunal under this section, then, notwithstanding anything contained in the scheme,—

(*a*) the scheme shall remain in operation until the tribunal has made an order in pursuance of the reference, and

(*b*) after such an order has been made, the scheme shall remain in operation, in so far as it relates to the class of cases in respect of which the order was made, so long as the order remains in force:

Provided that this subsection shall not apply in relation to a reference as respects any period after the reference has been withdrawn, or has been discharged by virtue of subsection (4) of this section.

Further reference of scheme to tribunal

26.—(1) Where the tribunal has made an order under the last preceding section **A–505** with respect to a licence scheme, then, subject to the next following subsection, at any time while the order remains in force,—

(*a*) the licensing body operating the scheme, or

(*b*) any organisation claiming to be representative of persons requiring licences in cases of the class to which the order applies, or

(*c*) any person claiming that he requires a licence in a case of that class,

may refer the scheme again to the tribunal in so far as it relates to cases of that class.

(2) A licence scheme shall not, except with the special leave of the tribunal, be referred again to the tribunal under the preceding subsection at a time earlier than—

(*a*) the end of the period of twelve months beginning with the date on which the order in question was made, in the case of an order made so as to be in force indefinitely or for a period exceeding fifteen months, or

(*b*) the beginning of the period of three months ending with the date of expiry of the order, in the case of an order made so as to be in force for fifteen months or less.

(3) The parties to a reference under this section shall be—

(*a*) the licensing body, organisation or person at whose instance the reference is made;

(*b*) the licensing body operating the scheme to which the reference relates, if the reference is not made at their instance; and

(*c*) such other organisations or persons (if any) as apply to the tribunal to be made parties to the reference and, in accordance with the provisions applicable in that behalf by virtue of subsection (5) of this section, are made parties thereto.

(4) Subject to the next following subsection, the tribunal, on any reference under this section, shall consider the matter in dispute, and, after giving to the parties to the reference an opportunity of presenting their cases respectively, shall make such order in relation to the scheme as previously confirmed or varied, in so far as it relates to cases of the class in question, either by way of confirming, varying or further varying the scheme, as the tribunal may determine to be reasonable in the circumstances.

(5) Subsections (3), (4), (6) and (7) of the last preceding section shall apply for the purposes of this section.

(6) The preceding provisions of this section shall have effect in relation to orders made under this section as they have effect in relation to orders made under the last preceding section.

(7) Nothing in this section shall be construed as preventing a licence scheme, in respect of which an order has been made under the last preceding section, from being again referred to the tribunal under that section, either—

(*a*) at any time, in so far as the scheme relates to cases of a class to which the order does not apply, or (*b*) after the expiration of the order, in so far as the scheme relates to cases of the class to which the order applied while it was in force.

Applications to tribunal

A–506   **27.**—(1) For the purposes of this Part of this Act a case shall be taken to be covered by a licence scheme if, in accordance with a licence scheme for the time being in operation, licences would be granted in cases of the class to which that case belongs:

Provided that where, in accordance with the provisions of a licence scheme,—

(*a*) the licences which would be so granted would be subject to terms and conditions whereby particular matters would be excepted from the licences, and

(*b*) the case in question relates to one or more matters falling within such an exception,

that case shall be taken not to be covered by the scheme.

(2) Any person who claims, in a case covered by a licence scheme, that the licensing body operating the scheme have refused or failed to grant him a licence in accordance with the provisions of the scheme, or to procure the grant to him of such a licence, may apply to the tribunal under this section.

(3) Any person who claims that he requires a licence in a case not covered by a licence scheme, and either—

(*a*) that a licensing body have refused or failed to grant the licence, or to procure the grant thereof, and that in the circumstances it is unreasonable that the licence should not be granted, or

(*b*) that any charges, terms or conditions subject to which a licensing body propose that the licence should be granted are unreasonable,

may apply to the tribunal under this section.

(4) Where an organisation (whether claiming to be representative of persons requiring licences or not) or a person (whether requiring a licence or not) applies to the tribunal to be made a party to an application under the preceding provisions of this section, and the tribunal is satisfied that the organisation or person has a substantial interest in the matter in dispute, the tribunal may, if it thinks fit, make that organisation or person a party to the application.

(5) On any application under subsection (2) or subsection (3) of this section the tribunal shall give to the applicant and to the licensing body in question and to every other party (if any) to the application an opportunity of presenting their cases respectively; and if the tribunal is satisfied that the claim of the applicant is well founded, the tribunal shall make an order declaring that, in respect of the matters specified in the order, the applicant is entitled to a licence on such terms and conditions, and subject to the payment of such charges (if any) as—

(*a*) in the case of an application under subsection (2) of this section, the tribunal may determine to be applicable in accordance with the licence scheme, or

(*b*) in the case of an application under subsection (3) of this section, the tribunal may determine to be reasonable in the circumstances.

(6) Any reference in this section to a failure to grant or procure the grant of a licence shall be construed as a reference to a failure to grant it, or to procure the grant thereof, within a reasonable time after being requested to do so.

[Applications for review by tribunal of orders

A–507   **27A.**—(1) Where the tribunal has made an order under subsection (5) of the last preceding section, then subject to the next following subsection, at any time while the order remains in force,—

(*a*) the licensing body in question, or

(*b*) the original applicant

may apply to the tribunal to review its original order.

(2) An application shall not be made pursuant to subsection (1) of this section, except with the special leave of the tribunal, at a time earlier than—

(*a*) the end of a period of twelve months beginning with the date on which the original order was made, in the case of an order made so as to be in force indefinitely or for a period exceeding fifteen months, or

(*b*) the beginning of the period of three months ending with the date of expiry of the order in the case of an order made so as to be in force for fifteen months or less.

(3) The parties to an application under this section shall be—

(*a*) the parties to the original application proceedings; and

(*b*) any organisation or person who is made party thereto pursuant to subsection (5) of this section.

(4) The tribunal, on any application under this section, after giving all the parties an opportunity of presenting their cases shall make such order in relation to the application either by way of confirming or varying the order in question as—

(*a*) in the case of an order made pursuant to an application under subsection (2) of the last preceding section, the tribunal may determine to be applicable in accordance with the licence scheme, or

(*b*) in the case of an order made pursuant to an application under subsection (3) of the last preceding section, the tribunal may determine to be reasonable in the circumstances.

(5) Subsection (4) of section 27 (applications by organisations and person to be made party to proceedings) shall apply in relation to proceedings under this section as it applies in relation to proceedings under that section.

(6) The preceding provisions of this section shall have effect in relation to orders made under this section as they have in relation to orders made under the last preceding section.]

AMENDMENT

This section was inserted by the Copyright (Amendment) Act, 1971 (c. 4). See Amendment to section 14A *ante.*

[Exercise of jurisdiction of tribunal in relation to inclusion of broadcasts in cable programmes

27B.—(1) On a reference to the tribunal under this Part of this Act relating to   **A–508**
licences to broadcast works or sound recordings for reception in any area, the tribunal shall exercise its powers under this Part of this Act so as to secure that the charges payable for the licences adequately reflect the extent to which the works or recordings will be included, in pursuance of requirements imposed under section 13(1) of the Cable and Broadcasting Act 1984, in cable programme services provided in areas parts of which fall outside that area.

(2) The preceding subsection shall have effect, with the necessary modifications, in relation to applications under this Part of this Act as it has effect in relation to references thereunder.]

AMENDMENT

This section was inserted by the Cable and Broadcasting Act 1984 (c. 46). See Amendments to section 14A *ante.*

Exercise of jurisdiction of tribunal in relation to diffusion of foreign broadcasts

28.—(1) Where, on a reference to the tribunal under this Part of this Act relating   **A–509**
ing to licences to [include works or sound recordings in a cable programme service provided] in the United Kingdom, the tribunal is satisfied—

(*a*) that the licences are required wholly or partly for the purpose of [including in such a service] programmes broadcast, from a place outside the United Kingdom, by an organisation other than the Corporation and the Authority, and

(*b*) that, under the arrangements in accordance with which the programmes are broadcast by that organisation, charges are payable by or on behalf of the organisation to another body, as being the body entitled under the relevant copyright law to authorise the broadcasting of those works [or recordings] from that place,

the tribunal shall, subject to the next following subsection, exercise its powers under this Part of this Act as the tribunal may consider appropriate for securing that the persons requiring the licences are exempted from the payment of any charges for them in so far as the licences are required for the purpose of [including those programmes in a cable programme service].

(2) If on such a reference as is mentioned in the last preceding subsection the tribunal is satisfied as to the matters mentioned in paragraphs (*a*) and (*b*) of that subsection, but it is shown to the satisfaction of the tribunal that the charges payable by or on behalf of the organisation, as mentioned in paragraph (*b*) of that subsection,—

(*a*) make no allowance for the fact that, in consequence of the broadcasting of the works [or recordings] in question by that organisation, the persons requiring the licences may be enabled to [include those works or recordings in cable programme services provided] in the United Kingdom, or

(*b*) do not adequately reflect the extent to which it is likely that those persons will [so include those works or recordings] in consequence of their being so broadcast,

the last preceding subsection shall not apply, but the tribunal shall exercise its powers under this Part of this Act so as to secure that the charges payable for the licences, in so far as the licences are required for the purpose mentioned in the last preceding subsection, are on a scale not exceeding that appearing to the tribunal to be requisite for making good the deficiency (as mentioned in paragraph (*a*) or paragraph (*b*) of this subsection, as the case may be) in the charges payable by or on behalf of the organisation broadcasting the works [or recordings].

(3) The preceding provisions of this section shall have effect, with the necessary modifications, in relation to applications under this Part of this Act as they have effect in relation to references thereunder.

(4) In this section "the relevant copyright law", in relation to works [or sound recordings] broadcast from a place outside the United Kingdom, means so much of the laws of the country in which that place is situated as confers rights similar to copyright under this Act or as otherwise relates to such rights; and any reference to works includes a reference to adaptations thereof.

AMENDMENT

This section was amended by the Cable and Broadcasting Act 1984 (c. 46) and is printed as amended.

Effect of orders of tribunal, and supplementary provisions relating thereto

A–510   **29.**—(1) Where an order made on a reference under this Part of this Act with respect to a licence scheme is for the time being in force, any person who, in a case covered by the scheme as confirmed or varied by the order, does anything which—

(*a*) apart from this subsection would be an infringement of copyright, but

(*b*) would not be such an infringement if he were the holder of a licence granted in accordance with the scheme, as confirmed or varied by the order, in so far as the scheme relates to cases comprised in the order, shall, if he has complied with the requirements specified in the next following sub-section, be in the like position, in any proceedings for infringement of that copy-right, as if he had at the material time been the holder of such a licence.

(2) The said requirements are—

(*a*) that, at all material times, the said person has complied with the terms and conditions which, in accordance with the licence scheme as confirmed or varied by the order, would be applicable to a licence covering the case in question, and

(*b*) if, in accordance with the scheme as so confirmed or varied, any charges are payable in respect of such a licence, that at the material time he had paid those charges to the licensing body operating the scheme, or, if at that time the amount payable could not be ascertained, he had given an under-taking to the licensing body to pay the charges when ascertained.

(3) Where the tribunal has made an order under section twenty-seven [or sec-tion twenty-seven A] of this Act declaring that a person is entitled to a licence in respect of any matters specified in the order, then if—

(*a*) that person has complied with the terms and conditions specified in the order, and

(*b*) in a case where the order requires the payment of charges, he has paid those charges to the licensing body in accordance with the order, or, if the order so provides, has given to the licensing body an undertaking to pay the charges when ascertained,

he shall be in the like position, in any proceedings for infringement of copyright relating to any of those matters, as if he had at all material times been the holder of a licence granted by the owner of the copyright in question on the terms and con-ditions specified in the order.

(4) In the exercise of its jurisdiction in respect of licences relating to television broadcasts, the tribunal shall have regard (among other matters) to any con-ditions imposed by the promoters of any entertainment or other event which is to be comprised in the broadcasts; and, in particular, the tribunal shall not hold a refusal or failure to grant a licence to be unreasonable if it could not have been granted consistently with those conditions:

Provided that nothing in this subsection shall require the tribunal to have regard to any such conditions in so far as they purport to regulate the charges to be imposed in respect of the grant of licences, or in so far as they relate to payments to be made to the promoters of any event in consideration of the grant of facilities for broadcasting.

(5) Where, on a reference to the tribunal under this Part of this Act,—

(*a*) the reference relates to licences in respect of copyright in sound recordings or in television broadcasts, and

(*b*) the tribunal is satisfied that any of the licences in question are required for the purposes of organisations such as are mentioned in paragraph (*b*) of subsection (7) of section twelve of this Act,

the tribunal may, if it thinks fit, exercise its powers under this Part of this Act so as to reduce, in the case of those organisations, to such extent as the tribunal thinks fit, the charges which it determines generally to be reasonable in relation to cases of the class to which the reference relates, or, if it thinks fit, so as to exempt those organisations from the payment of any such charges.

(6) The last preceding subsection shall have effect, with the necessary modifica-tions, in relation to applications under this Part of this Act as it has effect in rela-tion to references thereunder.

(7) In relation to copyright in a literary, dramatic or musical work, any refer-ence in this section to proceedings for infringement of copyright includes a refer-

ence to proceedings brought by virtue of subsection (5) of section twenty-one of this Act.

AMENDMENT

The words in square brackets in subsection (3) were inserted by the Copyright (Amendment) Act, 1971 (c. 4).

Reference of questions of law to the court

A–511   **30.**—(1) Any question of law arising in the course of proceedings before the tribunal may, at the request of any party to the proceedings, be referred by the tribunal to the court for decision, whether before or after the tribunal has given its decision in the proceedings:

Provided that a question shall not be referred to the court by virtue of this subsection in pursuance of a request made after the date on which the tribunal gave its decision, unless the request is made before the end of such period as may be prescribed by rules made under the Fourth Schedule to this Act.

(2) If the tribunal, after giving its decision in any proceedings, refuses any such request to refer a question to the court, the party by whom the request was made may, within such period as may be prescribed by rules of court, apply to the court for an order directing the tribunal to refer the question to the court.

(3) On any reference to the court under this section with respect to any proceedings before the tribunal, and on any application under the last preceding subsection with respect to any such proceedings, every party to the proceedings before the tribunal shall be entitled to appear and to be heard.

(4) Where, after the tribunal has given its decision in any proceedings, the tribunal refers to the court under this section a question of law which arose in the course of the proceedings, and the court decides that the question was erroneously determined by the tribunal,—

   (*a*) the tribunal, if it considers it requisite to do so for the purpose of giving effect to the decision of the court, shall give to the parties to the proceedings a further opportunity of presenting their cases respectively;

   (*b*) in any event, the tribunal shall reconsider the matter in dispute in conformity with the decision of the court;

   (*c*) if on such reconsideration it appears to the tribunal to be appropriate to do so, the tribunal shall make such order revoking or modifying any order previously made by it in the proceedings, or, in the case of proceedings under section twenty-seven of this Act where the tribunal refused to make an order, shall make such order under that section, as on such reconsideration the tribunal determines to be appropriate.

(5) Any reference of a question by the tribunal to the court under this section shall be by way of stating a case for the opinion of the court; and the decision of the court on any such reference shall be final.

(6) In this section "the court"—

   (*a*) in relation to any proceedings of the tribunal in England or Wales, or in Northern Ireland, means the High Court; and

   (*b*) in relation to any proceedings of the tribunal in Scotland, means the Court of Session.

AMENDMENT

By virtue of s.7 of and Sched. 1 to the Northern Ireland Act, 1962 (10 & 11 Eliz. 2, c. 30), s.30 of the Copyright Act, 1956, in its application to proceedings in Northern Ireland, was to have effect with the omission, from subs. (2), of the words "within such period as may be prescribed by rules of court." This section and Schedule were repealed by the Judicature (Northern Ireland) Act 1978 (c. 23).

See as to meaning of "High Court" the Interpretation Act 1978 (c. 30), s.5 and Sched. 1.

PART V

EXTENSION OR RESTRICTION OF OPERATION OF ACT

Extension of Act to Isle of Man, Channel Islands, colonies and dependencies

31.—(1) Her Majesty may by Order in Council direct that any of the provisions **A–512** of this Act specified in the Order (including any enactments for the time being in force amending or substituted for those provisions) shall extend, subject to such exceptions and modifications (if any) as may be specified in the Order, to—

(*a*) the Isle of Man;

(*b*) any of the Channel Islands;

(*c*) any colony;

(*d*) any country outside Her Majesty's dominions in which for the time being Her Majesty has jurisdiction;

(*e*) any country consisting partly of one or more colonies and partly of one or more such countries as are mentioned in the last preceding paragraph.

(2) The powers conferred by the preceding subsection shall be exercisable in relation to any Order in Council made under the following provisions of this Part of this Act, as those powers are exercisable by virtue of that subsection in relation to the provisions of this Act.

(3) The legislature of any country to which any provisions of this Act have been extended may modify or add to those provisions, in their operation as part of the law of that country, in such manner as that legislature may consider necessary to adapt the provisions to the circumstances of that country:

Provided that no such modifications or additions, except in so far as they relate to procedure and remedies, shall be made so as to apply to any work or other sub-ject-matter in which copyright can subsist unless—

(*a*) in the case of a literary, dramatic, musical or artistic work, the author of the work, or, in the case of a sound recording or a cinematograph film, the maker of the recording or film, was domiciled or resident in that country at the time when, or during the period while, the work, recording or film was made, or

(*b*) in the case of a published edition of a literary, dramatic or musical work, the publisher of the edition was domiciled or resident in that country at the date of its first publication, or

(*c*) in the case of a literary, dramatic, musical or artistic work, or of a sound recording or a cinematograph film or a published edition, it was first pub-lished in that country, or

(*d*) in the case of a television broadcast or sound broadcast, it was made from a place in that country, [or

(*e*) in the case of a cable programme, it was sent from a place in that country.]

(4) For the purposes of any proceedings under this Act in the United Kingdom, where the proceedings relate to an act done in a country to which any provisions of this Act extend subject to exceptions, modifications or additions,—

(*a*) the procedure applicable to the proceedings, including the time within which they may be brought, and the remedies available therein, shall be in accordance with this Act in its operation as part of the law of the United Kingdom; but

(*b*) if the act in question does not constitute an infringement of copyright under this Act in its operation as part of the law of the country where the act was

1089

done, it shall (notwithstanding anything in this Act) be treated as not constituting an infringement of copyright under this Act in its operation as part of the law of the United Kingdom.

AMENDMENT

This section was amended by the Cable and Broadcasting Act 1984 (c. 46) and is printed as amended.

Application of Act to countries to which it does not extend

A–513   **32.**—(1) Her Majesty may by Order in Council make provision for applying any of the provisions of this Act specified in the Order, in the case of a country to which those provisions do not extend, in any one or more of the following ways, that is to say, so as to secure that those provisions—

(a) apply in relation to literary, dramatic, musical or artistic works, sound recordings, cinematograph films or editions first published in that country as they apply in relation to literary, dramatic, musical or artistic works, sound recordings, cinematograph films or editions first published in the United Kingdom;

(b) apply in relation to persons who, at a material time, are citizens or subjects of that country as they apply in relation to persons who, at such a time, are British subjects;

(c) apply in relation to persons who, at a material time, are domiciled or resident in that country as they apply in relation to persons who, at such a time, are domiciled or resident in the United Kingdom;

(d) apply in relation to bodies incorporated under the laws of that country as they apply in relation to bodies incorporated under the laws of any part of the United Kingdom;

(e) apply in relation to television broadcasts and sound broadcasts made from places in that country, by one or more organisations constituted in, or under the laws of, that country, as they apply in relation to television broadcasts and sound broadcasts made from places in the United Kingdom by the Corporation or the Authority;

[(f) apply in relation to cable programmes sent from places in that country as they apply in relation to cable programmes sent from places in the United Kingdom.]

(2) An Order in Council under this section—

(a) may apply the provisions in question as mentioned in the preceding subsection, but subject to exceptions or modifications specified in the Order;

(b) may direct that the provisions in question shall so apply either generally or in relation to such classes of works, or other classes of cases, as may be specified in the Order.

(3) Her Majesty shall not make an Order in Council under this section applying any of the provisions of this Act in the case of a country, other than a country which is a party to a Convention relating to copyright to which the United Kingdom is also a party, unless Her Majesty is satisfied that, in respect of the class of works or other subject-matter to which those provisions relate, provision has been or will be made under the laws of that country whereby adequate protection will be given to owners of copyright under this Act.

AMENDMENT

This section was amended by the Cable and Broadcasting Act 1984 (c. 46) and is printed as amended.

Provisions as to international organisations

33.—(1) Where it appears to Her Majesty that one or more sovereign Powers, **A–514**
or the government or governments thereof, are members of an organisation, and
that it is expedient that the provisions of this section should apply to that organisation, Her Majesty may by Order in Council declare that the organisation is one
to which this section applies.

(2) Where an original literary, dramatic, musical or artistic work is made by or
under the direction or control of an organisation to which this section applies in
such circumstances that—

(*a*) copyright would not subsist in the work apart from this subsection, but

(*b*) if the author of the work had been a British subject at the time when it was
made, copyright would have subsisted in the work immediately after it was
made and would thereupon have vested in the organisation,

copyright shall subsist in the work as if the author had been a British subject when
it was made, that copyright shall continue to subsist so long as the work remains
unpublished, and the organisation shall, subject to the provisions of this Act, be
entitled to that copyright.

(3) Where an original literary, dramatic, musical or artistic work is first published by or under the direction or control of an organisation to which this section
applies, in such circumstances that, apart from this subsection, copyright does not
subsist in the work immediately after the first publication thereof, and either—

(*a*) the work is so published in pursuance of an agreement with the author
which does not reserve to the author the copyright (if any) in the work, or

(*b*) the work was made in such circumstances that, if it had been first published in the United Kingdom, the organisation would have been entitled
to the copyright in the work,

copyright shall subsist in the work (or, if copyright in the work subsisted immediately before its first publication, shall continue to subsist) as if it had been first
published in the United Kingdom, that copyright shall subsist until the end of the
period of fifty years from the end of the calendar year in which the work was first
published, and the organisation shall, subject to the provisions of Part VI of this
Act, be entitled to that copyright.

(4) The provisions of Part I of this Act, with the exception of provisions thereof
relating to the subsistence, duration or ownership of copyright, shall apply in relation to copyright subsisting by virtue of this section as they apply in relation to
copyright subsisting by virtue of the said Part I.

(5) An organisation to which this section applies which otherwise has not, or at
some material time otherwise had not, the legal capacities of a body corporate
shall have, and shall be deemed at all material times to have had, the legal capacities of a body corporate for the purpose of holding, dealing with and enforcing
copyright and in connection with all legal proceedings relating to copyright.

Extended application of provisions relating to broadcasts

34. Her Majesty may by Order in Council provide that, subject to such excep- **A–515**
tions and modifications (if any) as may be specified in the Order, such provisions
of this Act relating to television broadcasts or to sound broadcasts as may be so
specified shall apply in relation to the operation of wireless telegraphy apparatus
by way of the emission (as opposed to reception) of electro-magnetic energy—

(*a*) by such persons or classes of persons, other than the Corporation and the
Authority, as may be specified in the Order, and

(*b*) for such purposes (whether involving broadcasting or not) as may be so
specified,

as they apply in relation to television broadcasts, or, as the case may be, to sound
broadcasts, made by the Corporation and the Authority.

Denial of copyright to citizens of countries not giving adequate protection to British works

A–516   **35.**—(1) If it appears to Her Majesty that the laws of a country fail to give adequate protection to British works to which this section applies, or fail to give such protection in the case of one or more classes of such works (whether the lack of protection relates to the nature of the work or the country of its author or both), Her Majesty may make an Order in Council designating that country and making such provision in relation thereto as is mentioned in the following provisions of this section.

(2) An Order in Council under this section shall provide that, either generally or in such classes of cases as are specified in the Order, copyright under this Act shall not subsist in works to which this section applies which were first published after a date specified in the Order, if at the time of their first publication the authors thereof were—

(*a*) citizens or subjects of the country designated by the Order, not being at that time persons domiciled or resident in the United Kingdom or in another country to which the relevant provision of this Act extends, or

(*b*) bodies incorporated under the laws of the country designated by the Order.

(3) In making an Order in Council under this section Her Majesty shall have regard to the nature and extent of the lack of protection for British works in consequence of which the Order is made.

(4) This section applies to the following works, that is to say, literary, dramatic, musical and artistic works, sound recordings and cinematograph films.

(5) In this section—

"British work" means a work of which the author, at the time when the work was made, was a qualified person for the purposes of the relevant provision of this Act;

"author", in relation to a sound recording or a cinematograph film, means the maker of the recording or film;

"the relevant provision of this Act", in relation to literary, dramatic and musical works means section two, in relation to artistic works means section three, in relation to sound recordings means section twelve, and in relation to cinematograph films means section thirteen, of this Act.

PART VI

MISCELLANEOUS AND SUPPLEMENTARY PROVISIONS

Assignments and licences in respect of copyright

A–517   **36.**—(1) Subject to the provisions of this section, copyright shall be transmissible by assignment, by testamentary disposition, or by operation of law, as personal or moveable property.

(2) An assignment of copyright may be limited in any of the following ways, or in any combination of two or more of those ways, that is to say,—

(*a*) so as to apply to one or more, but not all, of the classes of acts which by virtue of this Act the owner of the copyright has the exclusive right to do (including any one or more classes of acts not separately designated in this Act as being restricted by the copyright, but falling within any of the classes of acts so designated);

(*b*) so as to apply to any one or more, but not all, of the countries in relation to which the owner of the copyright has by virtue of this Act that exclusive right;

(c) so as to apply to part, but not the whole, of the period for which the copyright is to subsist;

and references in this Act to a partial assignment are references to an assignment so limited.

(3) No assignment of copyright (whether total or partial) shall have effect unless it is in writing signed by or on behalf of the assignor.

(4) A licence granted in respect of any copyright by the person who, in relation to the matters to which the licence relates, is the owner of the copyright shall be binding upon every successor in title to his interest in the copyright, except a purchaser in good faith for valuable consideration and without notice (actual or constructive) of the licence or a person deriving title from such a purchaser; and references in this Act, in relation to any copyright, to the doing of anything with, or (as the case may be) without, the licence of the owner of the copyright shall be construed accordingly.

Prospective ownership of copyright

37.—(1) Where by an agreement made in relation to any future copyright, and **A–518** signed by or on behalf of the prospective owner of the copyright, the prospective owner purports to assign the future copyright (wholly or partially) to another person (in this subsection referred to as "the assignee"), then if, on the coming into existence of the copyright, the assignee or a person claiming under him would, apart from this subsection, be entitled as against all other persons to require the copyright to be vested in him (wholly or partially, as the case may be), the copyright shall, on its coming into existence, vest in the assignee or his successor in title accordingly by virtue of this subsection and without further assurance.

(2) Where, at the time when any copyright comes into existence, the person who, if he were then living, would be entitled to the copyright is dead, the copyright shall devolve as if it had subsisted immediately before his death and he had then been the owner of the copyright.

(3) Subsection (4) of the last preceding section shall apply in relation to a licence granted by a prospective owner of any copyright as it applies in relation to a licence granted by the owner of a subsisting copyright, as if any reference in that subsection to the owner's interest in the copyright included a reference to his prospective interest therein.

(4) The provisions of the Fifth Schedule to this Act shall have effect with respect to assignments and licences in respect of copyright (including future copyright) in television broadcasts.

(5) In this Act "future copyright" means copyright which will or may come into existence in respect of any future work or class of works or other subject-matter, or on the coming into operation of any provisions of this Act, or in any other future event, and "prospective owner" shall be construed accordingly and, in relation to any such copyright, includes a person prospectively entitled thereto by virtue of such an agreement as is mentioned in subsection (1) of this section.

Copyright to pass under will with unpublished work

38. Where under a bequest (whether specific or general) a person is entitled, **A–519** beneficially or otherwise, to the manuscript of a literary, dramatic or musical work, or to an artistic work, and the work was not published before the death of the testator, the bequest shall, unless a contrary intention is indicated in the testator's will or a codicil thereto, be construed as including the copyright in the work in so far as the testator was the owner of the copyright immediately before his death.

Provisions as to Crown and Government departments

39.—(1) In the case of every original literary, dramatic, musical or artistic work made by or under the direction or control of Her Majesty or a Government department,—

    (*a*) if apart from this section copyright would not subsist in the work, copyright shall subsist therein by virtue of this subsection, and

    (*b*) in any case, Her Majesty shall, subject to the provisions of this Part of this Act, be entitled to the copyright in the work.

(2) Her Majesty shall, subject to the provisions of this Part of this Act, be entitled—

    (*a*) to the copyright in every original literary, dramatic or musical work first published in the United Kingdom, or in another country to which section two of this Act extends, if first published by or under the direction or control of Her Majesty or a Government department;

    (*b*) to the copyright in every original artistic work first published in the United Kingdom, or in another country to which section three of this Act extends, if first published by or under such direction or control.

(3) Copyright in a literary, dramatic or musical work, to which Her Majesty is entitled in accordance with either of the preceding subsections,—

    (*a*) where the work is unpublished, shall continue to subsist so long as the work remains unpublished, and

    (*b*) where the work is published, shall subsist (or, if copyright in the work subsisted immediately before its first publication, shall continue to subsist) until the end of the period of fifty years from the end of the calendar year in which the work was first published, and shall then expire.

(4) Copyright in an artistic work to which Her Majesty is entitled in accordance with the preceding provisions of this section shall continue to subsist until the end of the period of fifty years from the end of the calendar year in which the work was made, and shall then expire:

Provided that where the work in question is an engraving or a photograph, the copyright shall continue to subsist until the end of the period of fifty years from the end of the calendar year in which the engraving or photograph is first published.

(5) In the case of every sound recording or cinematograph film made by or under the direction or control of Her Majesty or a Government department,—

    (*a*) if apart from this section copyright would not subsist in the recording or film, copyright shall subsist therein by virtue of this subsection, and

    (*b*) in any case, Her Majesty shall, subject to the provisions of this Part of this Act, be entitled to the copyright in the recording or film, and it shall subsist for the same period as if it were copyright subsisting by virtue of, and owned in accordance with, section twelve or, as the case may be, section thirteen of this Act.

(6) The preceding provisions of this section shall have effect subject to any agreement made by or on behalf of Her Majesty or a Government department with the author of the work, or the maker of the sound recording or cinematograph film, as the case may be, whereby it is agreed that the copyright in the work, recording or film shall vest in the author or maker, or in another person designated in the agreement in that behalf.

(7) In relation to copyright subsisting by virtue of this section—

    (*a*) in the case of a literary, dramatic, musical or artistic work, the provisions of Part I of this Act, with the exception of provisions thereof relating to the subsistence, duration or ownership of copyright, and

    (*b*) in the case of a sound recording or cinematograph film, the provisions of Part II of this Act, with the exception of provisions thereof relating to the subsistence or ownership of copyright, shall apply as those provisions apply in relation to copyright subsisting by virtue of Part I or, as the case may be, Part II of this Act.

(8) For the avoidance of doubt, it is hereby declared that the provisions of section three of the Crown Proceedings Act, 1947 (which relates to infringements of industrial property by servants or agents of the Crown) apply to copyright under this Act.

(9) In this section "Government department" means any department of Her Majesty's Government in the United Kingdom or of the Government of Northern Ireland, or any department or agency of the Government of any other country to which this section extends.

Broadcasts of sound recordings and cinematograph films, and diffusion of broadcast programmes

40.—(1) Where a sound broadcast or television broadcast is made by the Corporation or the Authority, and a person, by the reception of that broadcast, causes a sound recording to be heard in public, he does not thereby infringe the copyright (if any) in that recording under section twelve of this Act. **A–521**

(2) Where a television broadcast or sound broadcast is made by the Corporation or the Authority, and the broadcast is an authorised broadcast, any person who, by the reception of the broadcast, causes a cinematograph film to be seen or heard in public shall be in the like position, in any proceedings for infringement of the copyright (if any) in the film under section thirteen of this Act, as if he had been the holder of a licence granted by the owner of that copyright to cause the film to be seen or heard in public by the reception of the broadcast.

[(3) Where a television broadcast or sound broadcast is made by the Corporation or the Authority and the broadcast is an authorised broadcast, then, subject to subsection (3A) below, any person who, by the reception and immediate re-transmission of the broadcast, includes a programme in a cable programme service, being a programme comprising a literary, dramatic or musical work, or an adaptation of such a work, or an artistic work, or a sound recording or cinematograph film, shall be in the like position, in any proceedings for infringement of the copyright (if any) in the work, recording or film, as if he had been the holder of a licence granted by the owner of that copyright to include the work, adaptation, recording or film in any programme so included in that service.

(3A) Subsection (3) above applies only—

(a) if the programme is included in the service in pursuance of a requirement imposed under section 13(1) of the Cable and Broadcasting Act 1984; or

(b) if and to the extent that the broadcast is made for reception in the area in which the service is provided.]

(4) If, in the circumstances mentioned in either of the two last preceding subsections, the person causing the cinematograph film to be seen or heard, or [including the programme in a cable programme service,] as the case may be, infringed the copyright in question, by reason that the broadcast was not an authorised broadcast,—

(a) no proceedings shall be brought against that person under this Act in respect of his infringement of that copyright, but

(b) it shall be taken into account in assessing damages in any proceedings against the Corporation or the Authority, as the case may be, in respect of that copyright, in so far as that copyright was infringed by them in making the broadcast.

(5) For the purposes of this section, a broadcast shall be taken, in relation to a work [or sound recording] or cinematograph film, to be an authorised broadcast if, but only if, it is made by, or with the licence of, the owner of the copyright in the work [or recording] or film.

AMENDMENT
This section was amended by the Cable and Broadcasting Act 1984 (c. 46) and is printed as amended. See Amendment to section 14A *ante*.

[Inclusion of sound recordings and cinematograph films in cable programmes

A-522   **40A.**—(1) Where a cable programme is sent and a person, by the reception of that programme, causes a sound recording to be heard in public, he does not thereby infringe the copyright (if any) in that recording under section 12 of this Act.

(2) Where a cable programme is sent and the programme is an authorised programme, any person who, by the reception of the programme, causes a cinematograph film to be seen or heard in public shall be in the like position, in any proceedings for infringement of copyright (if any) in the film under section 13 of this Act, as if he had been the holder of a licence granted by the owner of that copyright to cause the film to be seen or heard in public by the reception of the programme.

(3) If, in the circumstances mentioned in the last preceding subsection, a person causing a cinematograph film to be seen or heard infringes the copyright in the film by reason that the cable programme was not an authorised programme—

(a) no proceedings shall be brought against that person under this Act in respect of his infringement of that copyright, but

(b) it shall be taken into account in assessing damages in any proceedings against the person sending the programme, in so far as that copyright was infringed by him in sending the programme.

(4) For the purposes of this section, a cable programme shall be taken, in relation to a cinematograph film, to be an authorised programme if, but only if, it is sent by, or with the licence of, the owner of the copyright in the film.]

AMENDMENT
This section was inserted by the Cable and Broadcasting Act 1984 (c. 46).

Use of copyright material for education

A-523   **41.**—(1) Where copyright subsists in a literary, dramatic, musical or artistic work, the copyright shall not be taken to be infringed by reason only that the work is reproduced, or an adaptation of the work is made or reproduced,—

(a) in the course of instruction, whether at a school or elsewhere, where the reproduction or adaptation is made by a teacher or pupil otherwise than by the use of a duplicating process, or

(b) as part of the questions to be answered in an examination, or in an answer to such a question.

(2) Nothing in the preceding subsection shall apply to the publication of a work or of an adaptation of a work; and, for the purposes of section five of this Act, the fact that to a person's knowledge the making of an article would have constituted an infringement of copyright but for the preceding subsection shall have the like effect as if, to his knowledge, the making of it had constituted such an infringement.

(3) For the avoidance of doubt it is hereby declared that, where a literary, dramatic or musical work—

(a) is performed in class, or otherwise in the presence of an audience, and

(b) is so performed in the course of the activities of a school, by a person who is a teacher in, or a pupil in attendance at, the school,

the performance shall not be taken for the purposes of this Act to be a performance in public if the audience is limited to persons who are teachers in, or pupils in attendance at, the school, or are otherwise directly connected with the activities of the school.

(4) For the purposes of the last preceding subsection a person shall not be taken to be directly connected with the activities of a school by reason only that he is a parent or guardian of a pupil in attendance at the school.

(5) The two last preceding subsections shall apply in relation to sound recordings, cinematograph films [television broadcasts and cable programmes] as they apply in relation to literary, dramatic and musical works, as if any reference to performance were a reference to the act of causing the sounds or visual images in question to be heard or seen.

(6) Nothing in this section shall be construed—

(*a*) as extending the operation of any provision of this Act as to the acts restricted by copyright of any description, or

(*b*) as derogating from the operation of any exemption conferred by any provision of this Act other than this section.

(7) In this section "school"—

(*a*) in relation to England and Wales, has the same meaning as in the Education Act, 1944;

(*b*) in relation to Scotland, has the same meaning as in the Education (Scotland) Act, 1946, except that it includes an approved school within the meaning of the Children and Young Persons (Scotland) Act, 1937; and

(*c*) in relation to Northern Ireland, has the same meaning as in the Education Act (Northern Ireland), 1947;

and "duplicating process" means any process involving the use of an appliance for producing multiple copies.

Amendment

This section was amended by the Cable and Broadcasting Act 1984 (c. 46) and is printed as amended.

Operation

The definition of "approved school" in sections 83 and 110 of the Children and Young Persons (Scotland) Act 1937 (1 Edw. 8 and 1 Geo. 6, c. 37) was repealed as to Scotland by the Social Work (Scotland) Act 1968 (c. 49). The Education (Scotland) Act 1946 (9 & 10 Geo. 6, c. 72) was repealed by the Education (Scotland) Act 1962 (10 & 11 Eliz. 2, c. 47). The Education Act (Northern Ireland) 1947 (c. 3) was repealed by the Education and Libraries (Northern Ireland) Order 1972 (No. 1263) (N.I. 12), which was itself repealed by the Education and Libraries (Northern Ireland) Order 1986 (No. 594) (N.I. 3).

Special provisions as to public records

42.—(1) Where any work in which copyright subsists, or a reproduction of any   **A–524** such work, is comprised in—

(*a*) any records belonging to Her Majesty which are under the charge and superintendence of the Master of the Rolls by virtue of an Order in Council under section two of the Public Record Office Act, 1838, and are open to public inspection in accordance with rules made under that Act, or

(*b*) any public records to which the Public Records Act (Northern Ireland), 1923, applies, being records which are open to public inspection in accordance with rules made under that Act,

the copyright in the work is not infringed by the making, or the supplying to any person, of any reproduction of the work by or under the direction of any officer appointed under the said Act of 1838 or the said Act of 1923, as the case may be.

(2) In the preceding subsection "records"—

(*a*) in paragraph (*a*) of that subsection has the same meaning as in the Public Record Office Act, 1838;

(*b*) in paragraph (*b*) of that subsection has the same meaning as in the Public Records Act (Northern Ireland), 1923.

(3) Any reference in this section to the Public Records Act (Northern Ireland), 1923, shall be construed as including a reference to that Act as for the time being amended or re-enacted (with or without modifications) by any enactment of the Parliament of Northern Ireland.

AMENDMENT

The Public Record Office Act, 1838, was repealed by s.13 of and Sched. 4 to the Public Records Act, 1958 (6 & 7 Eliz. 2, c. 51) and by virtue of s.11 of and Sched. 3 to that Act, as respects any reproduction made after the commencement of that Act, the reference in s.42(1)(*a*) of the Copyright Act, 1956, to records of the description there mentioned is to be taken as a reference to public records which are open to public inspection in pursuance of the provisions of the 1958 Act. See as to the Public Records Act (Northern Ireland) 1923, the Administration of Justice Act 1969 (c. 58), s.27 and the Statute Law (Repeals) Act 1978 (c. 45), s.1 and Scheds. 1 and 2.

False attribution of authorship

A–525   **43.**—(1) The restrictions imposed by this section shall have effect in relation to literary, dramatic, musical or artistic works; and any reference in this section to a work shall be construed as a reference to such a work.

(2) A person (in this subsection referred to as "the offender") contravenes those restrictions as respects another person if, without the licence of that other person, he does any of the following acts in the United Kingdom, that is to say, he—

(*a*) inserts or affixes that other person's name in or on a work of which that person is not the author, or in or on a reproduction of such a work, in such a way as to imply that the other person is the author of the work, or

(*b*) publishes, or sells or lets for hire, or by way of trade offers or exposes for sale or hire, or by way of trade exhibits in public, a work in or on which the other person's name has been so inserted or affixed, if to the offender's knowledge that person is not the author of the work, or

(*c*) does any of the acts mentioned in the last preceding paragraph in relation to, or distributes, reproductions of a work, being reproductions in or on which the other person's name has been so inserted or affixed, if to the offender's knowledge that person is not the author of the work, or

(*d*) performs in public, [broadcasts or includes in a cable programme] a work of which the other person is not the author, as being a work of which he is the author, if to the offender's knowledge that person is not the author of the work.

(3) The last preceding subsection shall apply where, contrary to the fact, a work is represented as being an adaptation of the work of another person as it applies where a work is so represented as being the work of another person.

(4) In the case of an artistic work which has been altered after the author parted with the possession of it, the said restrictions are contravened, in relation to the author, by a person who in the United Kingdom, without the licence of the author,—

(*a*) publishes, sells or lets for hire, or by way of trade offers or exposes for sale or hire the work as so altered, as being the unaltered work of the author, or

(*b*) publishes, sells or lets for hire, or by way of trade offers or exposes for sale or hire a reproduction of the work as so altered, as being a reproduction of the unaltered work of the author,

if to his knowledge it is not the unaltered work, or, as the case may be, a reproduction of the unaltered work, of the author.

(5) The three last preceding subsections shall apply with respect to anything

done in relation to another person after that person's death, as if any reference to that person's licence were a reference to a licence given by him or by his personal representatives:

Provided that nothing in those subsections shall apply to anything done in relation to a person more than twenty years after that person's death.

(6) In the case of an artistic work in which copyright subsists, the said restrictions are also contravened, in relation to the author of the work, by a person who in the United Kingdom—

> (a) publishes, or sells or lets for hire, or by way of trade offers or exposes for sale or hire, or by way of trade exhibits in public, a reproduction of the work, as being a reproduction made by the author of the work, or
>
> (b) distributes reproductions of the work as being reproductions made by the author of the work,

if (in any such case) the reproduction or reproductions was or were to his knowledge not made by the author.

(7) The preceding provisions of this section shall apply (with the necessary modifications) with respect to acts done in relation to two or more persons in connection with the same work.

(8) The restrictions imposed by this section shall not be enforceable by any criminal proceedings; but any contravention of those restrictions, in relation to a person, shall be actionable at his suit, or, if he is dead, at the suit of his personal representatives, as a breach of statutory duty.

(9) Any damages recovered under this section by personal representatives, in respect of a contravention committed in relation to a person after his death, shall devolve as part of his estate, as if the right of action had subsisted and had been vested in him immediately before his death.

(10) Nothing in this section shall derogate from any right of action or other remedy (whether civil or criminal) in proceedings instituted otherwise than by virtue of this section:

Provided that this subsection shall not be construed as requiring any damages recovered by virtue of this section to be disregarded in assessing damages in any proceedings instituted otherwise than by virtue of this section and arising out of the same transaction.

(11) In this section "name" includes initials or a monogram.

AMENDMENT

This section was amended by the Cable and Broadcasting Act 1984 (c. 46) and is printed as amended.

Amendments of Registered Designs Act, 1949

44.—(1) In section six of the Registered Designs Act, 1949, (under which the **A–526** disclosure of a design in certain circumstances is not to be a reason for refusing registration), the following subsections shall be inserted after subsection (3):

> "(4) Where copyright under the Copyright Act, 1956, subsists in an artistic work, and an application is made by, or with the consent of, the owner of that copyright for the registration of a corresponding design, that design shall not be treated for the purposes of this Act as being other than new or original by reason only of any use previously made of the artistic work, unless—
>
> > (a) the previous use consisted of or included the sale, letting for hire, or offer for sale or hire of articles to which the design in question (or a design differing from it only as mentioned in subsection (2) of section one of this Act) had been applied industrially, other than articles of a description specified in rules made under subsection (4) of section one of this Act, and

(*b*) that previous use was made by, or with the consent of, the owner of the copyright in the artistic work.

(5) Any rules made by virtue of subsection (5) of section ten of the Copyright Act, 1956 (which relates to rules for determining the circumstances in which a design is to be taken to be applied industrially) shall apply for the purposes of the last foregoing subsection."

(2) The following subsection shall be added at the end of section eight of the said Act of 1949 (which relates to the period of copyright in registered designs):

"(3) Where in the case of a registered design it is shown—

(*a*) that the design, at the time when it was registered, was a corresponding design in relation to an artistic work in which copyright subsisted under the Copyright Act, 1956;

(*b*) that, by reason of a previous use of that artistic work, the design would not have been registrable under this Act but for subsection (4) of section six of this Act; and

(*c*) that the copyright in that work under the Copyright Act, 1956, expired before the date of expiry of the copyright in the design,

the copyright in the design shall, notwithstanding anything in this section, be deemed to have expired at the same time as the copyright in the artistic work, and shall not be renewable after that time."

(3) In section eleven of the said Act of 1949 (which relates to cancellation of the registration of designs), the following subsection shall be inserted after subsection (2):

"(2A) At any time after a design has been registered, any person interested may apply to the registrar for the cancellation of the registration of the design on the grounds—

(*a*) that the design, at the time when it was registered, was a corresponding design in relation to an artistic work in which copyright subsisted under the Copyright Act, 1956;

(*b*) that, by reason of a previous use of that artistic work, the design would not have been registrable under this Act but for subsection (4) of section six of this Act; and

(*c*) that the copyright in that work under the Copyright Act, 1956, has expired;

and the registrar may make such order on the application as he thinks fit."

(4) In subsection (3) of the said section eleven, for the words "the last foregoing subsection" there shall be substituted the words "either of the two last foregoing subsections."

(5) In subsection (1) of section forty-four of the said Act of 1949 (which relates to the interpretation of that Act)—

(*a*) after the definition of "article" there shall be inserted the words " 'artistic work' has the same meaning as in the Copyright Act, 1956"; and

(*b*) after the definition of "copyright" there shall be inserted the words " 'corresponding design' has the same meaning as in section ten of the Copyright Act, 1956."

Amendment of Dramatic and Musical Performers' Protection Act, 1925

A–527   [**45.** *In the Dramatic and Musical Performers' Protection Act, 1925,—*

(a) *after section one there shall be inserted the two sections set out in Part I of the Sixth Schedule to this Act; and*

(b) *after section three there shall be inserted the two sections set out in Part II of that Schedule;*

and the provisions of that Act specified in Part III of that Schedule shall have effect subject to the amendments set out in relation thereto in the second column of the said Part III (being minor amendments of that Act and amendments consequential upon the insertion therein of the sections referred to in paragraphs (a) *and* (b) *of this section).]*

AMENDMENT

This provision and the Sixth Schedule were repealed by the Dramatic and Musical Performers' Protection Act, 1958 (6 & 7 Eliz. 2, c. 44), which also repealed the Dramatic and Musical Performers' Protection Act, 1925 (15 & 16 Geo. 5, c. 46).

Savings

46.—(1) Any rights conferred on universities and colleges by the Copyright Act, **A–528** 1775, which continued to subsist in accordance with section thirty-three of the Copyright Act, 1911, notwithstanding the repeal of the said Act of 1775, shall continue to subsist in accordance with the said Act of 1775 notwithstanding any repeal effected by this Act:

Provided that no proceedings shall be brought under the Copyright Act, 1775, but the provisions of Part III of this Act shall apply for the enforcement of those rights as if they were copyright subsisting by virtue of this Act.

(2) Nothing in this Act shall affect any right or privilege of the Crown subsisting otherwise than by virtue of an enactment; and nothing in this Act shall affect any right or privilege of the Crown or of any other person under any enactment (including any enactment of the Parliament of Northern Ireland), except in so far as that enactment is expressly repealed, amended or modified by this Act.

(3) Nothing in this Act shall affect the right of the Crown or of any person deriving title from the Crown to sell, use or otherwise deal with articles forfeited under the laws relating to customs or excise, including any articles so forfeited by virtue of this Act or of any enactment repealed by this Act.

(4) Nothing in this Act shall affect the operation of any rule of equity relating to breaches of trust or confidence.

(5) Subject to the preceding provisions of this section, no copyright, or right in the nature of copyright, shall subsist otherwise than by virtue of this Act or of some other enactment in that behalf.

General provisions as to Orders in Council, regulations, rules and orders, and as to Board of Trade

47.—(1) Any power to make regulations, rules or orders under this Act shall be **A–529** exercisable by statutory instrument.

(2) Any statutory instrument containing—

(*a*) any Order in Council or regulations made under this Act, or

(*b*) any rules made by the Lord Chancellor under the Fourth Schedule to this Act,

shall be subject to annulment in pursuance of a resolution of either House of Parliament.

(3) Any Order in Council, or other order, made under any of the preceding provisions of this Act may be varied or revoked by a subsequent Order in Council or order made thereunder.

(4) Where a power to make regulations or rules is conferred by any provision of this Act, regulations or rules under that power may be made either as respects all, or as respects any one or more, of the matters to which the provision relates; and different provision may be made by any such regulations or rules as respects different classes of cases to which the regulations or rules apply.

[(5) *Anything required or authorised by or under this Act to be done by, to or before the Board of Trade may be done by, to or before the President of the Board of Trade, any Minister of State with duties concerning the affairs of the Board, any secretary, under-secretary or assistant secretary of the Board, or any person authorised in that behalf by the President.*]

(6) In this section "order" does not include an order of a court or of the tribunal.

AMENDMENT

Subsection (5) was repealed by section 18 of and Schedule 4 to the Industrial Expansion Act, 1968, (1968, c. 32), s.14 of which provides that anything authorised or required by or under that Act or any other enactments (including an enactment of the Parliament of Northern Ireland), whether passed before or after that Act, to be done by, to or before the Board of Trade may be done by, to or before the President of the Board or any person acting with his authority. See as to concurrent exercise of functions by the Secretary of State, The Secretary of State for Trade and Industry Order, 1970 (1970 S.I. No. 1537), as amended.

Interpretation

A–530 **48.**—(1) In this Act, except in so far as the context otherwise requires, the following expressions have the meanings hereby assigned to them respectively, that is to say:

"adaptation", in relation to a literary, dramatic or musical work, has the meaning assigned to it by section two of this Act;

"artistic work" has the meaning assigned to it by section three of this Act;

"assignment", in relation to Scotland, means an assignation;

"building" includes any structure;

["cable programme", "cable programme service" and "programme" have the meanings assigned to them by section 14A of this Act;]

"cinematograph film" has the meaning assigned to it by section thirteen of this Act;

"construction" includes erection, and references to reconstruction shall be construed accordingly;

"the Corporation" and "the Authority" have the meanings assigned to them by section fourteen of this Act;

"country" includes any territory;

"dramatic work" includes a choreographic work or entertainment in dumb show if reduced to writing in the form in which the work or entertainment is to be presented, but does not include a cinematograph film, as distinct from a scenario or script for a cinematograph film;

"drawing" includes any diagram, map, chart or plan;

"engraving" includes any etching, lithograph, woodcut, print or similar work, not being a photograph;

"future copyright" and "prospective owner" have the meanings assigned to them by section thirty-seven of this Act;

"judicial proceeding" means a proceeding before any court, tribunal or person having by law power to hear, receive and examine evidence on oath;

"literary work" includes any written table or compilation;

"manuscript", in relation to a work, means the original document embodying the work, whether written by hand or not;

"performance" includes delivery, in relation to lectures, addresses, speeches and sermons, and in general, subject to the provisions of subsection (5) of this section, includes any mode of visual or acoustic presentation, including any such presentation by the operation of wireless telegraphy apparatus, or by the exhibition of a cinematograph film, or by the use of a record, or by any other means, and references to performing a work or an adaptation of a work shall be construed accordingly;

"photograph" means any product of photography or of any process akin to photography, other than a part of a cinematograph film, and "author", in relation to a photograph, means the person who, at the time when the photograph is taken, is the owner of the material on which it is taken;

"qualified person" has the meaning assigned to it by section one of this Act;

"record" means any disc, tape, perforated roll or other device in which sounds are embodied so as to be capable (with or without the aid of some other instrument) of being automatically reproduced therefrom, and references to a record of a work or other subject-matter are references to a record (as herein defined) by means of which it can be performed;

"reproduction", in the case of a literary, dramatic or musical work, includes a reproduction in the form of a record or of a cinematograph film, and, in the case of an artistic work, includes a version produced by converting the work into a three-dimensional form, or, if it is in three dimensions, by converting it into a two-dimensional form, and references to reproducing a work shall be construed accordingly;

"sculpture" includes any cast or model made for purposes of sculpture;

"sound recording" has the meaning assigned to it by section twelve of this Act;

"sufficient acknowledgment" has the meaning assigned to it by section six of this Act;

"television broadcast" and "sound broadcast" have the meanings assigned to them by section fourteen of this Act;

"wireless telegraphy apparatus" has the same meaning as in the Wireless Telegraphy Act, 1949;

"work of joint authorship" has the meaning assigned to it by section eleven of this Act;

"writing" includes any form of notation, whether by hand or by printing, typewriting or any similar process.

(2) References in this Act to broadcasting are references to broadcasting by wireless telegraphy (within the meaning of the Wireless Telegraphy Act, 1949), whether by way of sound broadcasting or of television.

[(3) References in this Act to the inclusion of a programme in a cable programme service are references to its inclusion in such a service by the person providing that service.

(3A) For the purposes of this Act no account shall be taken of a cable programme service if, and to the extent that, it is provided for—

(a) a person providing another such service;

(b) the Corporation; or

(c) the Authority;

and for the purposes of this subsection a cable programme service provided for the Welsh Fourth Channel Authority, the subsidiary mentioned in section 12(2) of the

Broadcasting Act 1981 or a programme contractor within the meaning of that Act shall be treated as provided for the Authority.

(3B) For the purposes of this Act no account shall be taken of a cable programme service which is only incidental to a business of keeping or letting premises where persons reside or sleep, and is operated as part of the amenities provided exclusively or mainly for residents or inmates therein.]

(4) References in this Act to the doing of any act by the reception of a television broadcast or sound broadcast made by the Corporation or the Authority are references to the doing of that act by means of receiving the broadcast either—

(a) from the transmission whereby the broadcast is made by the Corporation or the Authority, as the case may be, or

(b) from a transmission made by the Corporation or the Authority, as the case may be, otherwise than by way of broadcasting, but simultaneously with the transmission mentioned in the preceding paragraph,

whether (in either case) the reception of the broadcast is directly from the transmission in question or from a re-transmission thereof made by any person from any place, whether in the United Kingdom or elsewhere; and in this subsection "re-transmission" means any re-transmission, whether over paths provided by a material substance or not, including any re-transmission made by making use of any record, print, negative, tape or other article on which the broadcast in question has been recorded.

(5) For the purposes of this Act, broadcasting, or [including a work or other subject matter in a cable programme] shall not be taken to constitute performance, or to constitute causing visual images or sounds to be seen or heard; and where visual images or sounds are displayed or emitted by any receiving apparatus, to which they are conveyed by the transmission of electromagnetic signals (whether over paths provided by a material substance or not),—

(a) the operation of any apparatus whereby the signals are transmitted, directly or indirectly, to the receiving apparatus shall not be taken to constitute performance or to constitute causing the visual images or sounds to be seen or heard; but

(b) in so far as the display or emission of the images or sounds constitutes a performance, or causes them to be seen or heard, the performance, or the causing of the images or sounds to be seen or heard, as the case may be, shall be taken to be effected by the operation of the receiving appparatus.

(6) Without prejudice to the last preceding subsection, where a work or an adaptation of a work is performed, or visual images or sounds are caused to be seen or heard, by the operation of any apparatus to which this subsection applies, being apparatus provided by or with the consent of the occupier of the premises where the apparatus is situated, the occupier of those premises shall, for the purposes of this Act, be taken to be the person giving the performance, or causing the images or sounds to be seen or heard, whether he is the person operating the apparatus or not.

This subsection applies to any such receiving apparatus as is mentioned in the last preceding subsection, and to any apparatus for reproducing sounds by the use of a record.

(7) Except in so far as the context otherwise requires, any reference in this Act to an enactment shall be construed as a reference to that enactment as amended or extended by or under any other enactment.

AMENDMENT

This section was amended by the Cable and Broadcasting Act 1984 (c. 46) and is printed as amended.

Supplementary provisions as to interpretation

49.—(1) Except in so far as the context otherwise requires, any reference in this Act to the doing of an act in relation to a work or other subject-matter shall be taken to include a reference to the doing of that act in relation to a substantial part thereof, and any reference to a reproduction, adaptation or copy of a work, or a record embodying a sound recording, shall be taken to include a reference to a reproduction, adaptation or copy of a substantial part of the work, or a record embodying a substantial part of the sound recording, as the case may be:

Provided that, for the purposes of the following provisions of this Act, namely subsections (1) and (2) of section two, subsections (2) and (3) of section three, subsections (2) and (3) of section thirty-three, section thirty-eight, and subsections (2) to (4) of section thirty-nine, this subsection shall not affect the construction of any reference to the publication, or absence of publication, of a work.

(2) With regard to publication, the provisions of this subsection shall have effect for the purposes of this Act, that is to say,—

(a) the performance, or the issue of records, of a literary, dramatic or musical work, the exhibition of an artistic work, the construction of a work of architecture, and the issue of photographs or engravings of a work of architecture or of a sculpture, do not constitute publication of the work;

(b) except in so far as it may constitute an infringement of copyright, or a contravention of any restriction imposed by section forty-three of this Act, a publication which is merely colourable, and not intended to satisfy the reasonable requirements of the public, shall be disregarded;

(c) subject to the preceding paragraphs, a literary, dramatic or musical work, or an edition of such a work, or an artistic work, shall be taken to have been published if, but only if, reproductions of the work or edition have been issued to the public;

(d) a publication in the United Kingdom, or in any other country, shall not be treated as being other than the first publication by reason only of an earlier publication elsewhere, if the two publications took place within a period of not more than thirty days;

and in determining, for the purposes of paragraph (c) of this subsection, whether reproductions of a work or edition have been issued to the public, the preceding subsection shall not apply.

(3) In determining for the purposes of any provision of this Act—

(a) whether a work or other subject-matter has been published, or

(b) whether a publication of a work or other subject-matter was the first publication thereof, or

(c) whether a work or other subject-matter was published or otherwise dealt with in the lifetime of a person,

no account shall be taken of any unauthorised publication or of the doing of any other unauthorised act; and (subject to subsection (7) of section seven of this Act) a publication or other act shall for the purposes of this subsection be taken to have been unauthorised—

(i) if copyright subsisted in the work or other subject-matter and the act in question was done otherwise than by, or with the licence of, the owner of the copyright, or

(ii) if copyright did not subsist in the work or other subject-matter, and the act in question was done otherwise than by, or with the licence of, the author (or, in the case of a sound recording or a cinematograph film, or an edition of a literary, dramatic or musical work, the maker or publisher, as the case may be) or persons lawfully claiming under him:

Provided that nothing in this subsection shall affect any provisions of this Act as to the acts restricted by any copyright or as to acts constituting infringements of copyrights, or any provisions of section forty-three of this Act.

(4) References in this Act to the time at which, or the period during which, a literary, dramatic or musical work was made are references to the time or period at or during which it was first reduced to writing or some other material form.

(5) In the case of any copyright to which (whether in consequence of a partial assignment or otherwise) different persons are entitled in respect of the application of the copyright—

(*a*) to the doing of different acts or classes of acts, or

(*b*) to the doing of one or more acts or classes of acts in different countries or at different times,

the owner of the copyright, for any purpose of this Act, shall be taken to be the person who is entitled to the copyright in respect of its application to the doing of the particular act or class of acts, or, as the case may be, to the doing thereof in the particular country or at the particular time, which is relevant to the purpose in question; and, in relation to any future copyright to which different persons are prospectively entitled, references in this Act to the prospective owner of the copyright shall be construed accordingly.

(6) Without prejudice to the generality of the last preceding subsection, where under any provision of this Act a question arises whether an article of any description has been imported or sold, or otherwise dealt with, without the licence of the owner of any copyright, the owner of the copyright, for the purpose of determining that question, shall be taken to be the person entitled to the copyright in respect of its application to the making of articles of that description in the country into which the article was imported, or, as the case may be, in which it was sold or otherwise dealt with.

(7) Where the doing of anything is authorised by the grantee of a licence, or a person deriving title from the grantee, and it is within the terms (including any implied terms) of the licence for him to authorise it, it shall for the purposes of this Act be taken to be done with the licence of the grantor and of every other person (if any) upon whom the licence is binding.

(8) References in this Act to deriving title are references to deriving title either directly or indirectly.

(9) Where, in the case of copyright of any description,—

(*a*) provisions contained in this Act specify certain acts as being restricted by the copyright, or as constituting infringements thereof, and

(*b*) other provisions of this Act specify certain acts as not constituting infringements of the copyright,

the omission or exclusion of any matter from the latter provisions shall not be taken to extend the operation of the former provisions.

(10) Any reference in this Act to countries to which a provision of this Act extends includes a country to which that provision extends subject to exceptions, modifications or additions.

Transitional provisions, and repeals

A–532   **50.**—(1) The transitional provisions contained in the Seventh Schedule to this Act shall have effect for the purposes of this Act; and the provisions of the Eighth Schedule to this Act shall have effect in accordance with those transitional provisions.

[(2) Subject to the said transitional provisions, the enactments specified in the Ninth Schedule to this Act are hereby repealed to the extent specified in the third column of that Schedule.]

Subsection (2) of this section and Schedule 9 were repealed by the Statute Law (Repeals) Act 1974 (c. 22).

Short title, commencement and extent

51.—(1) This Act may be cited as the Copyright Act, 1956.   **A–533**

(2) This Act shall come into operation on such day as the Board of Trade may by order appoint; and different days may be appointed for the purposes of different provisions of this Act, and, for the purposes of any provision of this Act whereby enactments are repealed, different days may be appointed for the operation of the repeal in relation to different enactments, including different enactments contained in the same Act.

(3) It is hereby declared that this Act extends to Northern Ireland.

SCHEDULES

Section 10.   FIRST SCHEDULE   **A–534**

FALSE REGISTRATION OF INDUSTRIAL DESIGNS

1. The provisions of this Schedule shall have effect where—
  (a) copyright subsists in an artistic work, and proceedings are brought under this Act relating to that work;
  (b) a corresponding design has been registered under the Act of 1949, and the copyright in the design subsisting by virtue of that registration has not expired by effluxion of time before the commencement of those proceedings; and
  (c) it is proved or admitted in the proceedings that the person registered as the proprietor of the design was not the proprietor thereof for the purposes of the Act of 1949, and was so registered without the knowledge of the owner of the copyright in the artistic work.

2. For the purposes of those proceedings (but subject to the next following paragraph) the registration shall be treated as never having been effected, and accordingly, in relation to that registration, [*subsection (1) of section ten of this Act shall not apply, and*] nothing in section seven of the Act of 1949 shall be construed as affording any defence in those proceedings.

(3) Notwithstanding anything in the last preceding paragraph, if in the proceedings it is proved or admitted that any act to which the proceedings relate—
  (a) was done in pursuance of an assignment or licence made or granted by the person registered as proprietor of the design, and
  (b) was so done in good faith in reliance upon the registration, and without notice of any proceedings for the cancellation of the registration or for rectifying the entry in the register of designs relating thereto,
[*subsection (1) of section ten of this Act shall apply in relation to that act for the purposes of the first-mentioned proceedings*] [this shall be a good defence to such proceedings].

4. In this Schedule "the Act of 1949" means the Registered Designs Act, 1949, and "corresponding design" has the meaning assigned to it by subsection (7) of section ten of this Act.

AMENDMENT
Paragraphs 2 and 3 were amended by the Design Copyright Act, 1968 (1968, c. 68) by deleting the words in italics and by substituting new words at the end of para. 3 as shown in square brackets.

A–535   **Section 11.**   SECOND SCHEDULE

Duration of Copyright in Anonymous and Pseudonymous Works

1. Where the first publication of a literary, dramatic, or musical work, or of an artistic work other than a photograph, is anonymous or pseudonymous, then subject to the following provisions of this Schedule—

    (*a*) subsection (3) of section two of this Act, or, as the case may be, subsection (4) of section three of this Act, shall not apply, and

    (*b*) any copyright subsisting in the work by virtue of either of those sections shall continue to subsist until the end of the period of fifty years from the end of the calendar year in which the work was first published, and shall then expire.

2. The preceding paragraph shall not apply in the case of a work if, at any time before the end of the period mentioned in that paragraph, it is possible for a person without previous knowledge of the facts to ascertain the identity of the author by reasonable inquiry.

3. For the purposes of this Act a publication of a work under two or more names shall not be taken to be pseudonymous unless all those names are pseudonyms.

A–536   **Section 11.**   THIRD SCHEDULE

Works of Joint Authorship

1. In relation to a work of joint authorship, the references to the author in subsections (1) and (2) of section two of this Act, in subsections (2) and (3) of section three of this Act, and in paragraph 2 of the Second Schedule to this Act, shall be construed as references to any one or more of the authors.

2. In relation to a work of joint authorship, other than a work to which the next following paragraph applies, references to the author in subsection (3) of section two, in subsection (4) of section three, and in subsection (6) of section seven, of this Act, shall be construed as references to the author who died last.

3.—(1) This paragraph applies to any work of joint authorship which was first published under two or more names, of which one or more (but not all) were pseudonyms.

(2) This paragraph also applies to any work of joint authorship which was first published under two or more names all of which were pseudonyms, if, at any time within the period of fifty years from the end of the calendar year in which the work was first published, it is possible for a person without previous knowledge of the facts to ascertain the identity of any one or more (but not all) of the authors by reasonable inquiry.

(3) In relation to a work to which this paragraph applies, references to the author in subsection (3) of section two of this Act, and in subsection (4) of section three of this Act, shall be construed as references to the author whose identity was disclosed, or, if the identity of two or more of the authors was disclosed, as references to that one of those authors who died last.

(4) For the purposes of this paragraph the identity of an author shall be taken to have been disclosed if either—

    (*a*) in his case, the name under which the work was published was not a pseudonym, or

    (*b*) it is possible to ascertain his identity as mentioned in subparagraph (2) of this paragraph.

4.—(1) In relation to a work of joint authorship of which one or more of the authors are persons to whom this paragraph applies, subsection (1) of section four of this Act shall have effect as if the author or authors, other than persons to whom this paragraph applies, had been the sole author, or (as the case may be) sole joint authors, of the work.

(2) This paragraph applies, in the case of a work, to any person such that, if he had been the sole author of the work, copyright would not have subsisted in the work by virtue of Part I of this Act.

5. In the proviso to subsection (6) of section six of this Act, the reference to other excerpts from works by the author of the passage in question—

(*a*) shall be taken to include a reference to excerpts from works by the author of that passage in collaboration with any other person, or

(*b*) if the passage in question is from a work of joint authorship, shall be taken to include a reference to excerpts from works by any one or more of the authors of that passage, or by any one or more of those authors in collaboration with any other person.

6. Subject to the preceding provisions of this Schedule, any reference in this Act to the author of a work shall (unless it is otherwise expressly provided) be construed, in relation to a work of joint authorship, as a reference to all the authors of the work.

Sections 23, 30, 47. FOURTH SCHEDULE **A–537**

PROVISIONS AS TO PERFORMING RIGHT TRIBUNAL

1.—(1) Subject to the provisions of this paragraph, the members of the tribunal shall hold office for such period as may be determined at the time of their respective appointments; and a person who ceases to hold office as a member of the tribunal shall be eligible for re-appointment.

(2) Any member of the tribunal may at any time by notice in writing to the Board of Trade, or, in the case of the chairman of the tribunal, to the Lord Chancellor, resign his appointment.

(3) The Board of Trade, or, in the case of the chairman of the tribunal, the Lord Chancellor, may declare the office of any member of the tribunal vacant on the ground of his unfitness to continue in office or incapacity to perform the duties thereof.

2. If any member of the tribunal is, by reason of illness, absence or other reasonable cause, for the time being unable to perform the duties of his office, either generally or in relation to any particular proceedings, the Board of Trade, or, in the case of the chairman of the tribunal, the Lord Chancellor, may appoint some other duly qualified person to discharge the duties of that member for any period, not exceeding six months at one time, or, as the case may be, in relation to those proceedings; and a person so appointed shall, during that period or in relation to those proceedings, have the same powers as the person in whose place he is appointed.

3. If at any time there are more than two members of the tribunal, in addition to the chairman, then, for the purposes of any proceedings, the tribunal may consist of the chairman together with any two or more of those members.

4. If the members of the tribunal dealing with any reference or application are unable to agree as to the order to be made by the tribunal, a decision shall be taken by the votes of the majority; and, in the event of an equality of votes, the chairman shall be entitled to a second or casting vote.

5. The tribunal may order that the costs or expenses of any proceedings before it incurred by any party shall be paid by any other party, and may tax or settle the amount of any costs or expenses to be paid under any such order or direct in what manner they are to be taxed.

6.—(1) The Lord Chancellor may make rules as to the procedure in connection with the making of references and applications to the tribunal, and for regulating proceedings before the tribunal and, subject to the approval of the Treasury, as to the fees chargeable in respect of those proceedings.

(2) Any such rules may apply in relation to the tribunal—

(*a*) as respects proceedings in England and Wales, any of the provisions of the Arbitration Act, 1950, and

(*b*) as respects proceedings in Northern Ireland, any of the provisions of the Arbitration Act (Northern Ireland), 1937.

(3) Any such rules may include provision—

(a) for prescribing the period within which, after the tribunal has given its decision in any proceedings, a request may be made to the tribunal to refer a question of law to the court;

(b) for requiring notice of any intended application to the court under subsection (2) of section thirty of this Act to be given to the tribunal and to the other parties to the proceedings, and for limiting the time within which any such notice is to be given;

(c) for suspending, or authorising or requiring the tribunal to suspend, the operation of orders of the tribunal, in cases where, after giving its decision, the tribunal refers a question of law to the court;

(d) for modifying, in relation to orders of the tribunal whose operation is suspended, the operation of any provisions of Part IV of this Act as to the effect of orders made thereunder;

(e) for the publication of notices, or the taking of any other steps, for securing that persons affected by the suspension of an order of the tribunal will be informed of its suspension;

(f) for regulating or prescribing any other matters incidental to or consequential upon any request, application, order or decision under section thirty of this Act.

(4) Provision shall be made by rules of court for limiting the time for instituting proceedings under subsection (2) of section thirty of this Act, and for authorising or requiring the court, where it makes an order directing the tribunal to refer a question of law to the court, to provide in the order for suspending the operation of any order made by the tribunal in the proceedings in which the question of law arose.

(5) In this paragraph "the court" has the same meaning as in section thirty of this Act.

7. As respects proceedings in Scotland, the tribunal shall have the like powers for securing the attendance of witnesses and the production of documents, and with regard to the examination of witnesses on oath, as if the tribunal were an arbiter under a submission.

8. Without prejudice to any method available by law for the proof of orders of the tribunal, a document purporting to be a copy of any such order, and to be certified by the chairman of the tribunal to be a true copy thereof, shall, in any legal proceedings, be sufficient evidence of the order unless the contrary is proved.

A–538   **Sections 24, 37.**   FIFTH SCHEDULE

APPOINTMENT OF TELEVISION COPYRIGHT ORGANISATIONS BY BRITISH BROADCASTING CORPORATION AND INDEPENDENT [BROADCASTING] AUTHORITY

1. In this Schedule—

(a) references to a right to which this Schedule applies are references to the copyright (including any future copyright) in any television broadcast, in so far as the copyright relates, or when it comes into existence will relate, to the acts specified in paragraph (c) of subsection (4) of section fourteen of this Act;

(b) references to the purposes of this Schedule are references to the purposes of negotiating or granting licences in respect of rights to which this Schedule applies.

2. The Corporation and the Authority may jointly appoint an organisation for the purposes of this Schedule; and if they do so, no other organisation shall be appointed by them or either of them for those purposes until the appointment of that organisation has been duly terminated.

3. Subject to the last preceding paragraph, the Corporation or the Authority, or each of them, may appoint an organisation for the purposes of this Schedule; and if an organisation is so appointed by the Corporation or by the Authority, no other organisation shall be appointed for the purposes of this Schedule by the Corporation or the Authority, as the case may be, until the appointment of that organisation has been duly terminated.

4. A right to which this Schedule applies shall not be assignable by the Corporation or by the Authority except to an organisation duly appointed for the purposes of this Schedule; and where such a right has been assigned to such an organisation, it shall not be assignable by the organisation except to the Corporation or the Authority, as the case may be, or to another organisation subsequently appointed for the purposes of this Schedule.

5.—(1) Neither the Corporation nor the Authority shall authorise any organisation or person, other than any person in their employment under a contract of service, to negotiate or act for them with respect to the granting of licences in respect of rights to which this Schedule applies, except an organisation duly appointed for the purposes of this Schedule.

(2) An organisation appointed for the purposes of this Schedule shall not authorise any other organisation or person, other than any person in their employment under a contract of service, to negotiate or act for them, or for the Corporation or the Authority, with respect to the granting of licences in respect of rights to which this Schedule applies.

6. The appointment, or the termination of the appointment, of an organisation for the purposes of this Schedule shall not have effect unless, not less than fourteen days before the appointment or termination is to take effect, a notice is published in the London Gazette, the Edinburgh Gazette and the Belfast Gazette, specifying the name and address of the organisation, and the date on which the appointment or termination is to take effect, and stating whether the appointment, or termination of appointment, is made by the Corporation or the Authority or by both of them.

7. Where notice of the appointment of an organisation for the purposes of this Schedule has been given under the last preceding paragraph, the organisation shall be taken for the purposes of this Act to be authorised to act in accordance with the appointment until their appointment is duly terminated in pursuance of a notice published in accordance with that paragraph.

Section 45.   [*SIXTH SCHEDULE*   **A–539**

Amendment of Dramatic and Musical Performers' Protection Act, 1925

Part I

New Sections 1a and 1b

Penalties for making, etc., cinematograph films without consent of performers

1A. *Subject to the provisions of this Act, if any person knowingly—*

(a) *makes a cinematograph film, directly or indirectly, from or by means of the performance of any dramatic or musical work without the consent in writing of the performers, or*

(b) *sells or lets for hire, or distributes for the purposes of trade, or by way of trade exposes or offers for sale or hire, a cinematograph film made in contravention of this Act, or*

(c) *uses for the purposes of exhibition to the public a cinematograph film made in contravention of this Act,*

he shall be guilty of an offence under this Act, and shall be liable on summary conviction to a fine not exceeding fifty pounds:

Provided that, where a person is charged with an offence under paragraph (a) of this section, it shall be a defence to prove that the cinematograph film was made for his private and domestic use only.

Penalties for broadcasting without consent of performers

1B. *Subject to the provisions of this Act, any person who, otherwise than by the use of a record or a cinematograph film, knowingly broadcasts a performance of any dramatic or musical work, or any part of such a performance, without the consent in writing of the performers shall be guilty of an offence under this Act, and shall be liable on summary conviction to a fine not exceeding fifty pounds.*

Part II

New Sections 3A and 3B

Special defences

3A. *Notwithstanding anything in the preceding provisions of this Act, it shall be a defence to any proceedings under this Act to prove—*

    (a) *that the record, cinematograph film or broadcast to which the proceedings relate was made only for the purpose of reporting current events, or*

    (b) *that the inclusion of the performance in question in the record, cinematograph film or broadcast to which the proceedings relate was only by way of background or was otherwise only incidental to the principal matters comprised or represented in the record, film or broadcast.*

Consent on behalf of performers

3B. *Where in any proceedings under this Act it is proved—*

    (a) *that the record, cinematograph film or broadcast to which the proceedings relate was made with the consent in writing of a person who, at the time of giving the consent, represented that he was authorised by the performers to give it on their behalf, and*

    (b) *that the person making the record, film or broadcast had no reasonable grounds for believing that the person giving the consent was not so authorised,*

the provisions of this Act shall apply as if it had been proved that the performers had themselves consented in writing to the making of the record, film or broadcast.

Part III

Minor and Consequential Amendments

Provision amended	*Amendment*
Section one ...	*At the beginning of the section there shall be inserted the words "Subject to the provisions of this Act"; and at the end of the section, for the words "not made for purposes of trade" there shall be substituted the words "made for his private and domestic use only."*
Section three ...	*For the words "records or" there shall be substituted the words "records, cinematograph films."*
Section four ...	*At the end of the definition of the expression "record" there shall be inserted the words "including the soundtrack of a cinematograph film"; and at the end of the section there shall be inserted the following definitions:*
	"The expression 'cinematograph film' means any print, negative, tape or other article on which a performance of a dramatic or musical work or part thereof is recorded for the purposes of visual reproduction, and any reference to the making of a cinematograph film is a reference to the carrying out of any process whereby such a performance or part thereof is so recorded;
	The expression 'broadcast' means broadcast by wireless telegraphy (within the meaning of the Wireless Telegraphy Act, 1949), whether by way of sound broadcasting or of television."]

Amendment

The provisions of this Schedule and section 45 were repealed by the Dramatic and Musical Performers' Protection Act, 1958 (6 & 7 Eliz. 2, c. 44), which also repealed the Dramatic and Musical Performers' Protection Act, 1925 (15 & 16 Geo. 5, c. 46).

Section 50.   SEVENTH SCHEDULE

TRANSITIONAL PROVISIONS

PART I

PROVISIONS RELATING TO PART I OF ACT

Conditions for subsistence of copyright

1. In the application of sections two and three to works first published before the com-   **A–540**
mencement of those sections, subsection (2) of section two, and subsection (3) of section
three, shall apply as if paragraphs (*b*) and (*c*) of those subsections were omitted.

Duration of copyright

2. In relation to any photograph taken before the commencement of section three, sub-   **A–541**
section (4) of that section shall not apply, but, subject to subsection (3) of that section, copyright subsisting in the photograph by virtue of that section shall continue to subsist until the
end of the period of fifty years from the end of the calendar year in which the photograph was
taken, and shall then expire.

Ownership of copyright

3.—(1) Subsections (2) to (4) of section four shall not apply—   **A–542**
  (*a*) to any work made as mentioned in subsection (2) or subsection (4) of that section, if
       the work was so made before the commencement of that section, or
  (*b*) to any work made as mentioned in subsection (3) of that section, if the work was or is
       so made in pursuance of a contract made before the commencement of that section.
(2) In relation to any work to which the preceding sub-paragraph applies, subsection (1)
of section four shall have effect subject to the proviso set out in paragraph 1 of the Eighth
Schedule to this Act (being the proviso to subsection (1) of section five of the Act of 1911).

Infringements of copyright

4. For the purposes of section five, the fact that, to a person's knowledge, the making of an   **A–543**
article constituted an infringement of copyright under the Act of 1911, or would have constituted such an infringement if the article had been made in the place into which it is imported,
shall have the like effect as if, to that person's knowledge, the making of the article had constituted an infringement of copyright under this Act.

5. Subsection (7) of section six does not apply to assignments made or licences granted
before the commencement of that section.

6.—(1) References in section eight to records previously made by, or with the licence of,
the owner of the copyright in a work include references to records previously made by, or
with the consent of, the owner of the copyright in that work under the Act of 1911.
(2) The repeal by this Act of any provisions of section nineteen of the Act of 1911, or of the
provisions of the Copyright Order Confirmation (Mechanical Instruments: Royalties) Act,
1928, shall not affect the operation of those provisions, or of any regulations or order made
thereunder, in relation to a record made before the repeal.

7.—(1) In relation to a painting, drawing, engraving, photograph or cinematograph film
made before the commencement of section nine, subsection (6) of that section shall apply if,
by virtue of subsection (3) or subsection (4) of that section, the making of the painting, drawing, engraving, photograph or film would not have constituted an infringement of copyright
under this Act if this Act had been in operation at the time when it was made.
(2) In subsection (10) of section nine, the reference to construction by, or with the licence

1113

of, the owner of the copyright in any architectural drawings or plans includes a reference to construction by, or with the licence of, the person who, at the time of the construction, was the owner of the copyright in the drawings or plans under the Act of 1911, or under any enactment repealed by that Act.

8.—(1) Section ten and the First Schedule to this Act do not apply to artistic works made before the commencement of that section.

(2) Copyright shall not subsist by virtue of this Act in any artistic work made before the commencement of section ten which, at the time when the work was made, constituted a design capable of registration under the Registered Designs Act, 1949, or under the enactments repealed by that Act, and was used, or intended to be used, as a model or pattern to be multiplied by any industrial process.

(3) The provisions set out in paragraph 2 of the Eighth Schedule to this Act (being the relevant provisions of the Copyright (Industrial Designs) Rules, 1949) shall apply for the purposes of the last preceding sub-paragraph.

9.—(1) Where, before the repeal by this Act of section three of the Act of 1911, a person has, in the case of a work, given the notice requisite under the proviso set out in paragraph 3 of the Eighth Schedule to this Act (being the proviso to the said section three), then, as respects reproductions by that person of that work after the repeal of that section by this Act, that proviso shall have effect as if it had been re-enacted in this Act as a proviso to subsection (2) of section one:

Provided that the said proviso shall so have effect subject to the provisions set out in paragraphs 4 and 5 of the Eighth Schedule to this Act (being so much of subsection (1) of sections sixteen and seventeen respectively of the Act of 1911 as is applicable to the said proviso), as if those provisions had also been re-enacted in this Act.

(2) For the purposes of the operation of the said proviso in accordance with the preceding sub-paragraph, any regulations made by the Board of Trade thereunder before the repeal of section three of the Act of 1911 shall have effect as if they had been made under this Act, and the power of the Board of Trade to make further regulations thereunder shall apply as if the proviso had been re-enacted as mentioned in the preceding sub-paragraph.

Works of joint authorship

A–544   10.—(1) Notwithstanding anything in section eleven, or in the Third Schedule to this Act, copyright shall not subsist by virtue of Part I of this Act in any work of joint authorship first published before the commencement of section eleven, if the period of copyright had expired before the commencement of that section.

(2) In this paragraph "the period of copyright" means whichever is the longer of the following periods, that is to say,—

    (*a*)   the life of the author who died first and a term of fifty years after his death, and

    (*b*)   the life of the author who died last.

Part II

Provisions Relating to Part II of Act

Sound recordings

A–545   11. In the case of a sound recording made before the commencement of section twelve, subsection (3) of that section shall apply with the substitution, for the period mentioned in that subsection, of the period of fifty years from the end of the calendar year in which the recording was made.

12. Subsection (6) of section twelve shall not apply to a sound recording made before the commencement of that section.

13. Notwithstanding anything in section twelve, copyright shall not subsist by virtue of

that section in a sound recording made before the first day of July, nineteen hundred and twelve, unless, immediately before the commencement of that section, a corresponding copyright subsisted, in relation to that recording, by virtue of subsection (8) of section nineteen of the Act of 1911 (which relates to records made before the commencement of that Act).

Cinematograph films

14. Section thirteen shall not apply to cinematograph films made before the commencement of that section. **A–546**

15. Where a cinematograph film made before the commencement of section thirteen was an original dramatic work within the definition of "dramatic work" set out in paragraph 9 of the Eighth Schedule to this Act (being the definition thereof in the Act of 1911), the provisions of this Act, including the provisions of this Schedule other than this paragraph, shall have effect in relation to the film as if it had been an original dramatic work within the meaning of this Act; and the person who was the author of the work for the purposes of the Act of 1911 shall be taken to be the author thereof for the purposes of the said provisions as applied by this paragraph.

16. The provisions of this Act shall have effect in relation to photographs forming part of a cinematograph film made before the commencement of section thirteen as those provisions have effect in relation to photographs not forming part of a cinematograph film.

Television broadcasts and sound broadcasts

17. Copyright shall not subsist by virtue of section fourteen in any television broadcast or sound broadcast made before the commencement of that section. **A–547**

18. For the purposes of subsection (3) of section fourteen, a previous television broadcast or sound broadcast shall be disregarded if it was made before the commencement of that section.

Supplementary

19. For the purposes of subsections (2) to (4) of section sixteen, the fact that, to a person's knowledge, the making of an article constituted an infringement of copyright under the Act of 1911, or would have constituted such an infringement if the article had been made in the place into which it is imported, shall have the like effect as if, to that person's knowledge, the making of the article had constituted an infringement of copyright under this Act. **A–548**

PART III

PROVISIONS RELATING TO PART III OF ACT

20. Nothing in section seventeen shall apply to any infringement of copyright under the Act of 1911, or shall affect any proceedings under that Act, whether begun before or after the commencement of that section. **A–549**

21. Section eighteen shall not apply with respect to any article made, or, as the case may be, imported, before the commencement of that section; but, notwithstanding the repeal by this Act of section seven of the Act of 1911 (which contains provisions corresponding to subsection (1) of section eighteen), proceedings may (subject to the provisions of that Act) be brought or continued by virtue of the said section seven in respect of any article made or imported before the repeal, although the proceedings relate to the conversion or detention thereof after the repeal took effect.

22. Section nineteen shall not apply to any licence granted before the commencement of that section, and shall not affect any proceedings under the Act of 1911, whether begun before or after the commencement of that section.

23. For the purposes of section twenty-one the definition of "infringing copy" in section eighteen shall apply as if any reference to copyright in that definition included a reference to copyright under the Act of 1911.

24. Where before the commencement of section twenty-two a notice had been given in respect of a work under section fourteen of the Act of 1911 (which contains provisions corresponding to section twenty-two), and that notice had not been withdrawn and had not otherwise ceased to have effect before the commencement of section twenty-two, the notice shall have effect after the commencement of that section as if it had been duly given thereunder:

Provided that a notice shall not continue to have effect by virtue of this paragraph after the end of the period of six months beginning with the commencement of section twenty-two.

Part IV

Provisions Relating to Part IV of Act

A–550   25. The provisions of Part IV of this Act shall apply in relation to licence schemes made before the commencement of that Part as they apply in relation to licence schemes made thereafter, as if references in Part IV of this Act to copyright included references to copyright under the Act of 1911.

26. In section twenty-seven, references to a refusal or failure to grant or procure the grant of a licence, or to a proposal that a licence should be granted, do not include a refusal or failure which occurred, or a proposal made, before the commencement of that section.

Part V

Provisions Relating to Part V of Act

A–551   27. In section thirty-three, subsection (2) shall not apply to works made before the commencement of that section, and subsection (3) shall not apply to works first published before the commencement of that section.

Part VI

Provisions Relating to Part VI of Act

Assignments, licences and bequests

A–552   28.—(1) Where by virtue of any provision of this Act copyright subsists in a work, any document or event which—

(a) was made or occurred before the commencement of that provision, and

(b) had any operation affecting the title to copyright in the work under the Act of 1911, or would have had such an operation if the Act of 1911 had continued in force,

shall have the corresponding operation in relation to the copyright in the work under this Act:

Provided that, if the operation of any such document was or would have been limited to a period specified in the document, it shall not have any operation in relation to the copyright under this Act, except in so far as that period extends beyond the commencement of the provision of this Act by virtue of which copyright subsists in the work.

(2) For the purposes of the operation of a document in accordance with the preceding sub-paragraph,—

(a) expressions used in the document shall be construed in accordance with their effect immediately before the commencement of the provision in question, notwithstanding that a different meaning is assigned to them for the purposes of this Act; and

(b) subsection (1) of section thirty-seven shall not apply.

(3) Without prejudice to the generality of sub-paragraph (1) of this paragraph, the proviso set out in paragraph 6 of the Eighth Schedule to this Act (being the proviso to subsection (2)

of section five of the Act of 1911) shall apply to assignments and licences having effect in relation to copyright under this Act in accordance with that sub-paragraph, as if that proviso had been re-enacted in this Act.

(4) In relation to copyright under this Act in a sound recording or in a cinematograph film, the preceding provisions of this paragraph shall apply subject to the following modifications, that is to say,—

    (*a*) in the case of a sound recording, references to the copyright under the Act of 1911 shall be construed as references to the copyright under that Act in records embodying the recording, and

    (*b*) in the case of a cinematograph film, references to the copyright under the Act of 1911 shall be construed as references to any copyright under that Act in the film (in so far as it constituted a dramatic work for the purposes of the Act of 1911) or in photographs forming part of the film.

(5) In this paragraph "operation affecting the title", in relation to copyright under the Act of 1911, means any operation affecting the ownership of that copyright, or creating, transferring or terminating an interest, right or licence in respect of that copyright.

29.—(1) Section thirty-eight shall not apply to a bequest contained in the will, or a codicil to the will, of a testator who died before the commencement of that section.

(2) In the case of an author who died before the commencement of section thirty-eight, the provisions set out in paragraph 7 of the Eighth Schedule to this Act (being subsection (2) of section seventeen of the Act of 1911) shall have effect as if it had been re-enacted in this Act.

Crown and Government departments

30. Subsection (4) of section thirty-nine shall apply in relation to photographs taken before   **A–553** the commencement of that section as if the proviso to that subsection were omitted.

31.—(1) In the application of subsection (5) of section thirty-nine to a sound recording made before the commencement of that section, paragraph (*b*) of that subsection shall apply as if for the period mentioned in that paragraph there were substituted the period of fifty years from the end of the calendar year in which the recording was made.

(2) With respect to cinematograph films made before the commencement of section thirty-nine—

    (*a*) subsection (5) of that section shall not apply, but

    (*b*) in the case of a cinematograph film made as mentioned in that subsection, but before the commencement of section thirty-nine, if it was an original dramatic work as mentioned in paragraph 15 of this Schedule, the provisions of subsections (1) to (3) of section thirty-nine shall apply in accordance with that paragraph, and

    (*c*) in relation to photographs forming part of such a cinematograph film the provisions of subsections (1), (2) and (4) of section thirty-nine (as modified by the last preceding paragraph) shall apply as they apply in relation to photographs not forming part of a cinematograph film.

False attribution of authorship

32.—(1) Paragraphs (*b*) and (*c*) of subsection (2) of section forty-three shall apply to any   **A–554** such act as is therein mentioned, if done after the commencement of that section, notwithstanding that the name in question was inserted or affixed before the commencement of that section.

(2) Subject to the preceding sub-paragraph, no act done before the commencement of section forty-three shall be actionable by virtue of that section.

(3) In this paragraph "name" has the same meaning as in section forty-three.

Other provisions

33.—(1) In the application of subsection (2) of section forty-nine to a publication effected   **A–555** before the commencement of that section, the reference in paragraph (*d*) to thirty days shall be treated as a reference to fourteen days.

(2) For the purposes of the application of subsection (3) of section forty-nine to an act done before the commencement of a provision of this Act to which that subsection applies, references to copyright include references to copyright under the Act of 1911, and, in relation to copyright under that Act, references to the licence of the owner are references to the consent or acquiescence of the owner.

PART VII

WORKS MADE BEFORE 1ST JULY, 1912

A–556   34.—(1) This part of this Schedule applies to works made before the first day of July, nineteen hundred and twelve.

(2) In this Part of this Schedule "right conferred by the Act of 1911", in relation to a work, means such a substituted right as, by virtue of section twenty-four of the Act of 1911, was conferred in place of a right subsisting immediately before the commencement of that Act.

35. Notwithstanding anything in Part I of this Schedule, neither subsection (1) or subsection (2) of section two, nor subsection (2) or subsection (3) of section three, shall apply to a work to which this Part of this Schedule applies, unless a right conferred by the Act of 1911 subsisted in the work immediately before the commencement of section two or section three, as the case may be.

36.—(1) Where, in the case of a dramatic or musical work to which this Part of this Schedule applies, the right conferred by the Act of 1911 did not include the sole right to perform the work in public, then, in so far as copyright subsists in the work by virtue of this Act, the acts restricted by the copyright shall be treated as not including those specified in subparagraph (3) of this paragraph.

(2) Where, in the case of a dramatic or musical work to which this Part of this Schedule applies, the right conferred by the Act of 1911 consisted only of the sole right to perform the work in public, then, in so far as copyright subsists in the work by virtue of this Act, the acts restricted by the copyright shall be treated as consisting only of those specified in sub-paragraph (3) of this paragraph.

(3) The said acts are—

  (a) performing the work or an adaptation thereof in public;

  (b) broadcasting the work or an adaptation thereof;

  [(c) including the work or an adaptation thereof in a cable programme.]

37. Where a work to which this Part of this Schedule applies consists of an essay, article or portion forming part of and first published in a review, magazine or other periodical or work of a like nature, and immediately before the commencement of section two a right of publishing the work in a separate form subsisted by virtue of the provision set out in paragraph 8 of the Eighth Schedule to this Act (being the note appended to the First Schedule to the Act of 1911), that provision shall have effect, in relation to that work, as if it had been re-enacted in this Act with the substitution, for the word "right" where it first occurs, of the word "copyright".

38.—(1) Without prejudice to the generality of sub-paragraph (1) of paragraph 28 of this Schedule, the provisions of this paragraph shall have effect where—

  (a) the author of a work to which this Part of this Schedule applies had, before the commencement of the Act of 1911, made such an assignment or grant as is mentioned in paragraph (a) of the proviso to subsection (1) of section twenty-four of that Act (which relates to transactions whereby the author had assigned, or granted an interest in, the copyright or performing right in a work for the full term of that right under the law in force before the Act of 1911), and

  (b) copyright subsists in the work by virtue of any provision of this Act.

(2) If, before the commencement of that provision of this Act, any event occurred, or notice was given, which in accordance with paragraph (a) of the said proviso had any operation affecting the ownership of the right conferred by the Act of 1911 in relation to the work,

or creating, transferring or terminating an interest, right or licence in respect of that right, that event or notice shall have the corresponding operation in relation to the copyright in the work under this Act.

(3) Any right which, at a time after the commencement of that provision of this Act, would, by virtue of paragraph (*a*) of the said proviso, have been exercisable in relation to the work, or to the right conferred by the Act of 1911, if this Act had not been passed, shall be exercisable in relation to the work or to the copyright therein under this Act, as the case may be.

(4) If, in accordance with paragraph (*a*) of the said proviso, the right conferred by the Act of 1911 would have reverted to the author or his personal representatives on the date referred to in that paragraph, and the said date falls after the commencement of the provision of this Act whereby copyright subsists in the work, then on that date—

  (*a*) the copyright in the work under this Act shall revert to the author or his personal representatives, as the case may be, and

  (*b*) any interest of any other person in that copyright which subsists on that date by virtue of any document made before the commencement of the Act of 1911 shall thereupon determine.

Part VIII

General and Supplementary Provisions

39.—(1) The provisions of this paragraph shall have effect for the construction of any **A–557** reference in any provision of this Act—

  (*a*) to countries to which that provision extends, or

  (*b*) to qualified persons.

(2) Where, at any time after the commencement of any provisions of this Act, a provision which contains such a reference—

  (*a*) has not yet been extended by virtue of section thirty-one to a country to which the Act of 1911 extended (or which, by virtue of that Act, was to be treated as a country to which it extended), and

  (*b*) has not been applied in the case of that country by virtue of section thirty-two, then, with respect to any time before the provision is so extended or applied, the reference shall be construed as if the provision did extend to that country.

(3) For the purpose of determining whether copyright subsists in any work or other subject-matter at a time when a provision containing such a reference has been extended to a country other than the United Kingdom, the reference shall be construed, in relation to past events, as if that provision had always been in operation and had always extended to that country.

(4) In relation to photographs taken before the commencement of section three, and to sound recordings made before the commencement of section twelve, the definition of "qualified person" in subsection (5) of section one shall apply as if, in paragraph (*b*) of that subsection, for the words "body incorporated under the laws of" there were substituted the words "body corporate which has established a place of business in".

[40.—(1) The provisions of the two next following sub-paragraphs shall apply where—

  (*a*) immediately before the date on which any provisions of the Act of 1911 (in this paragraph referred to as "the repealed provisions") are repealed in the law of the United Kingdom by this Act, the repealed provisions have effect as applied by an Order in Council made in respect of a foreign country under section twenty-nine of the Act of 1911; and

  (*b*) no Order in Council under section thirty-two of this Act, applying any provisions of this Act in the case of that country, is made so as to come into force on or before that date.

(2) The repealed provisions, as applied by the Order in Council under section twenty-nine of the Act of 1911 (or by that Order as varied by any subsequent Order thereunder), shall

continue to have effect, notwithstanding the repeal, until the occurrence of whichever of the following events first occurs, that is to say—

(*a*) the revocation of the Order in Council under section twenty-nine of the Act of 1911;

(*b*) the coming into operation of an Order in Council under section thirty-two of this Act applying any of the provisions of this Act in the case of the foreign country in question;

(*c*) the expiration of the period of two years beginning with the date mentioned in the preceding sub-paragraph.

(3) For the purposes of continuing, varying or terminating the operation of the repealed provisions in accordance with the last preceding sub-paragraph, and for the purposes of any proceedings arising out of the operation of those provisions in accordance with that sub-paragraph, all the provisions of the Act of 1911 (including the power to revoke or vary Orders in Council under section twenty-nine of that Act) shall be treated as continuing in force as if none of those provisions had been repealed by this Act.

(4) In relation to a country in respect of which an Order in Council has been made under subsection (3) of section twenty-six of the Act of 1911 (which relates to countries therein referred to as self-governing dominions to which that Act does not extend), the preceding provisions of this paragraph shall apply as they apply in relation to a foreign country, with the substitution, for references to section twenty-nine of the Act of 1911, of references to the said subsection (3).]

41. In so far as the Act of 1911 or any Order in Council made thereunder forms part of the law of any country other than the United Kingdom, at a time after that Act has been wholly or partly repealed in the law of the United Kingdom, it shall, so long as it forms part of the law of that country, be construed and have effect as if that Act had not been so repealed.

42. The mention of any particular matter in the preceding provisions of this Schedule with regard to the repeal of any of the provisions of the Act of 1911 shall not affect the general application to this Act of section thirty-eight of the Interpretation Act, 1889[4] (which relates to the effect of repeals), either in relation to the Act of 1911 or to any other enactment repealed by this Act.

43. For the purposes of the application, by virtue of any of the preceding paragraphs of this Schedule, of any of the provisions set out in the Eighth Schedule to this Act,—

(*a*) the expressions of which definitions are set out in paragraph 9 of that Schedule (being the definitions of those expressions in the Act of 1911) shall, notwithstanding anything in this Act, be construed in accordance with those definitions; and

(*b*) where, for those purposes, any of those provisions is to be treated as if re-enacted in this Act, it shall be treated as if it had been so re-enacted with the substitution, for the words "this Act", wherever the reference is to the passing or the commencement of the Act of 1911, of the words "the Copyright Act, 1911".

44. Without prejudice to the operation of any of the preceding provisions of this Schedule—

(*a*) any enactment or other document referring to an enactment repealed by this Act shall be construed as referring (or as including a reference) to the corresponding enactment of this Act;

(*b*) any enactment or other document referring to copyright, or to works in which copyright subsists, if apart from this Act it would be construed as referring to copyright under the Act of 1911, or to works in which copyright subsists under that Act, shall be construed as referring (or as including a reference) to copyright under this Act, or, as the case may be, to works or any other subject-matter in which copyright subsists under this Act;

(*c*) any reference in an enactment or other document to the grant of an interest in copy-

---

[4] The Interpretation Act 1889 (52 & 53 Vict., c. 63) was repealed almost entirely by the Interpretation Act 1978 (c. 30); see ss.16, 17, 22, 26 and Sched. 2, Pt. I of the latter Act.

right by licence shall be construed, in relation to copyright under this Act, as a reference to the grant of a licence in respect of that copyright.

45.—(1) Except in so far as it is otherwise expressly provided in this Schedule, the provisions of this Act apply in relation to things existing at the commencement of those provisions as they apply in relation to things coming into existence thereafter.

(2) For the purposes of any reference in this Schedule to works, sound recordings or cinematograph films made before the commencement of a provision of this Act, a work, recording or film, the making of which extended over a period, shall not be taken to have been so made unless the making of it was completed before the commencement of that provision.

46.—(1) Any reference in this Schedule to a numbered section shall, unless the reference is to a section of a specified Act, be construed as a reference to the section bearing that number in this Act.

(2) Any reference in this Schedule to the commencement of a provision of this Act is a reference to the date on which that provision comes into operation as part of the law of the United Kingdom.

47.—(1) In this Schedule "photograph" has the meaning assigned to it in the definition set out in paragraph 9 of the Eighth Schedule to this Act, and not the meaning assigned to it by section forty-eight.

(2) In this Schedule "the Act of 1911" means the Copyright Act, 1911.

AMENDMENT

Paragraph 36(3) was amended by the Cable and Broadcasting Act 1984 (c. 46) and is printed as amended.

REPEAL

Paragraph 40 was repealed by the Statute Law (Repeals) Act 1986 (c. 12).

Section 50.   EIGHTH SCHEDULE   **A–558**

PROVISIONS OF COPYRIGHT ACT, 1911, AND RULES, REFERRED TO IN SEVENTH SCHEDULE

1. *Proviso to s.5(1) of the Copyright Act, 1911 (referred to in paragraph 3 of Seventh Schedule)*:
Provided that—

(a) where, in the case of an engraving, photograph, or portrait, the plate or other original was ordered by some other person and was made for valuable consideration in pursuance of that order, then, in the absence of any agreement to the contrary, the person by whom such plate or other original was ordered shall be the first owner of the copyright; and

(b) where the author was in the employment of some other person under a contract of service or apprenticeship and the work was made in the course of his employment by that person, the person by whom the author was employed shall, in the absence of any agreement to the contrary, be the first owner of the copyright, but where the work is an article or other contribution to a newspaper, magazine, or similar periodical, there shall, in the absence of any agreement to the contrary, be deemed to be reserved to the author a right to restrain the publication of the work, otherwise than as part of a newspaper, magazine, or similar periodical.

2. *Rule 2 of the Copyright (Industrial Designs) Rules, 1949 (referred to in paragraph 8 of Seventh Schedule)*:
A design shall be deemed to be used as a model or pattern to be multiplied by any industrial process—

(a) when the design is reproduced or is intended to be reproduced on more than fifty single articles, unless all the articles in which the design is reproduced or is intended to be reproduced together form only a single set of articles as defined in subsection (1) of section 44 of the Registered Designs Act, 1949, or

(*b*) when the design is to be applied to—

    (i) printed paper hangings,

    (ii) carpets, floor cloths or oil cloths, manufactured or sold in lengths or pieces,

    (iii) textile piece goods, or textile goods manufactured or sold in lengths or pieces, or

    (iv) lace, not made by hand.

3. *Proviso to s.3 of the Copyright Act,* 1911 (*referred to in paragraph 9 of Seventh Schedule*):

Provided that at any time after the expiration of twenty-five years, or in the case of a work in which copyright subsists at the passing of this Act thirty years, from the death of the author of a published work, copyright in the work shall not be deemed to be infringed by the reproduction of the work for sale if the person reproducing the work proves that he has given the prescribed notice in writing of his intention to reproduce the work, and that he has paid in the prescribed manner to, or for the benefit of, the owner of the copyright royalties in respect of all copies of the work sold by him calculated at the rate of ten per cent. on the price at which he publishes the work; and, for the purposes of this proviso, the Board of Trade may make regulations prescribing the mode in which notices are to be given, and the particulars to be given in such notices, and the mode, time, and frequency of the payment of royalties, including (if they think fit) regulations requiring payment in advance or otherwise securing the payment of royalties.

4. *S.16(1) of the Copyright Act,* 1911 (*referred to in paragraph 9 of Seventh Schedule*):

In the case of a work of joint authorship . . . references in this Act to the period after the expiration of any specified number of years from the death of the author shall be construed as references to the period after the expiration of the like number of years from the death of the author who dies first or after the death of the author who dies last, whichever period may be the shorter . . .

5. *S.17(1) of Copyright Act,* 1911 (*referred to in paragraph 9 of Seventh Schedule*):

In the case of a literary, dramatic or musical work, or an engraving, in which copyright subsists at the date of the death of the author or, in the case of a work of joint authorship, at or immediately before the date of the death of the author who dies last, but which has not been published, nor, in the case of a dramatic or musical work, been performed in public, nor, in the case of a lecture, been delivered in public, before that date, . . . the proviso to section three of this Act shall . . . apply as if the author had died at the date of such publication or performance or delivery in public as aforesaid.

6. *Proviso to s.5(2) of the Copyright Act,* 1911 (*referred to in paragraph 28 of Seventh Schedule*):

Provided that, where the author of a work is the first owner of the copyright therein, no assignment of the copyright, and no grant of any interest therein, made by him (otherwise than by will) after the passing of this Act, shall be operative to vest in the assignee or grantee any rights with respect to the copyright in the work beyond the expiration of twenty-five years from the death of the author, and the reversionary interest in the copyright expectant on the termination of that period shall, on the death of the author, notwithstanding any agreement to the contrary, devolve on his legal personal representatives as part of his estate, and any agreement entered into by him as to the disposition of such reversionary interest shall be null and void, but nothing in this proviso shall be construed as applying to the assignment of the copyright in a collective work or a licence to publish a work or part of a work as part of a collective work.

7. *S.17(2) of the Copyright Act,* 1911 (*referred to in paragraph 29 of Seventh Schedule*):

The ownership of an author's manuscript after his death, where such ownership has been acquired under a testamentary disposition made by the author and the manuscript is of a work which has not been published nor performed in public nor delivered in public, shall be prima facie proof of the copyright being with the owner of the manuscript.

8. *Note to First Schedule to the Copyright Act,* 1911 (*referred to in paragraph 37 of Seventh Schedule*):

In the case of an essay, article, or portion forming part of and first published in a review, magazine, or other periodical or work of a like nature, the right shall be subject to any right of publishing the essay, article, or portion in a separate form to which the author is entitled at the commencement of this Act, or would, if this Act had not been passed, have become entitled under section eighteen of the Copyright Act, 1842.

9. *Definitions in s.35(1) of the Copyright Act, 1911 (referred to in paragraphs 15, 43 and 47 of Seventh Schedule):*

"literary work" includes maps, charts, plans, tables, and compilations;

"dramatic work" includes any piece for recitation, choreographic work or entertainment in dumb show the scenic arrangement or acting form of which is fixed in writing or otherwise, and any cinematograph production where the arrangement or acting form or the combination of incidents represented give the work an original character;

"performance" means any acoustic representation of a work and any visual representation of any dramatic action in a work, including such a representation made by means of any mechanical instrument;

"photograph" includes photo-lithograph and any work produced by any process analogous to photography;

"collective work" means—

    (*a*) any encyclopaedia, dictionary, year book, or similar work;

    (*b*) a newspaper, review, magazine, or similar periodical; and

    (*c*) any work written in distinct parts by different authors, or in which works or parts of works of different authors are incorporated;

"delivery" in relation to a lecture, includes delivery by means of any mechanical instrument;

"lecture" includes address, speech and sermon.

Note—In this Schedule "this Act" means the Copyright Act, 1911.

Section 50.   NINTH SCHEDULE   **A–559**

ENACTMENTS REPEALED

Session and Chapter	Short Title	Extent of Repeal
25 & 26 Vict. c. 68.	The Fine Arts Copyright Act, 1862.	The whole Act.
2 Edw. 7. c. 15.	The Musical (Summary Proceedings) Copyright Act, 1902.	The whole Act.
6 Edw. 7. c. 36.	The Musical Copyright Act, 1906.	The whole Act.
1 & 2 Geo. 5. c. 46.	The Copyright Act, 1911.	The whole Act, except sections fifteen, thirty-four and thirty-seven thereof.
18 & 19 Geo. 5. c. lii.	The Copyright Order Confirmation (Mechanical Instruments: Royalties) Act, 1928.	The whole Act.
11 & 12 Geo. 6. c. 7.	The Ceylon Independence Act, 1947.	Paragraph 10 of the Second Schedule.

Table of Statutes referred to in this Act

Short Title	Session and Chapter
Copyright Act, 1775	15 Geo. 3. c. 53.
Public Record Office Act, 1838	1 & 2 Vict. c. 94.
Interpretation Act, 1889...	52 & 53 Vict. c. 63.
Copyright Act, 1911	1 & 2 Geo. 5. c. 46.
Dramatic and Musical Performers' Protection Act, 1925	15 & 16 Geo. 5. c. 46.
Children and Young Persons (Scotland) Act, 1937... ...	1 Edw. 8. & 1 Geo. 6. c. 37.
Cinematograph Films Act, 1938	1 & 2 Geo. 6. c. 17.
Limitation Act, 1939	2 & 3 Geo. 6. c. 21.
Education Act, 1944..	7 & 8 Geo. 6. c. 31.
Education (Scotland) Act, 1946	9 & 10 Geo. 6. c. 72.
Crown Proceedings Act, 1947	10 & 11 Geo. 6. c. 44.
British Nationality Act, 1948	11 & 12 Geo. 6. c. 56.
Wireless Telegraphy Act, 1949	12, 13 & 14 Geo. 6. c. 54.
Registered Designs Act, 1949..	12, 13 & 14 Geo. 6. c. 88.
Arbitration Act, 1950	14 Geo. 6. c. 27.
Customs and Excise Act, 1952	15 & 16 Geo. 6. & 1 Eliz. 2. c. 44.

REPEAL

Subsection (2) of section 50 and Schedule 9 were repealed by the Statute Law (Repeals) Act 1974 (c. 22).

A–560 ### Copyright (Computer Software) Amendment Act 1985

(c. 41)

An Act to amend the Copyright Act 1956 in its application to computer programs and computer storage. [16th July 1985]

BE IT ENACTED by the Queen's most Excellent Majesty, by and with the advice and consent of the Lords Spiritual and Temporal, and Commons, in this present Parliament assembled, and by the authority of the same, as follows:—

Copyright in computer programs

A–561 1.—(1) The Copyright Act 1956 shall apply in relation to a computer program (including one made before the commencement of this Act) as it applies in relation to a literary work and shall so apply whether or not copyright would subsist in that program apart from this Act.

(2) For the purposes of the application of the said Act of 1956 in relation to a computer program, a version of the program in which it is converted into or out of a computer language or code, or into a different computer language or code, is an adaptation of the program.

Computer storage

A–562 2. References in the Copyright Act 1956 to the reduction of any work to a material form, or to the reproduction of any work in a material form, shall include references to the storage of that work in a computer.

Offences and search warrants

A–563 3. Where an infringing copy of a computer program consists of a disc, tape or chip or of any other device which embodies signals serving for the impartation of the program or part of it, sections 21 to 21B of the Copyright Act 1956 (offences and search warrants) shall apply in relation to that copy as they apply in relation to an infringing copy of a sound recording or cinematograph film.

Short title, interpretation, commencement and extent

4.—(1) This Act may be cited as the Copyright (Computer Software) Amendment Act 1985.   **A–564**

(2) This Act shall be construed as one with the Copyright Act 1956 and Part V of that Act (extension and restriction of operation of Act) shall apply in relation to the provisions of this Act as it applies in relation to the provisions of that Act.

(3) This Act shall come into force at the end of the period of two months beginning with the day on which it is passed.

(4) Nothing in this Act shall affect—

(*a*) the determination of any question as to whether anything done before the commencement of this Act was an infringement of copyright or an offence under section 21 of the said Act of 1956; or

(*b*) the penalty which may be imposed for any offence under that section committed before the commencement of this Act.

(5) This Act extends to Northern Ireland.

The Semiconductor Products (Protection of Topography) Regulations 1987   **A–565**
(S.I. 1987 No. 1497)[4a]

Made - - - - - -	*20th August 1987*
Laid before Parliament	*1st September 1987*
Coming into force - - - -	*7th November 1987*

The Secretary of State, being designated[5] for the purposes of section 2(2) of the European Communities Act 1972[6] in relation to the conferment and protection of exclusive rights in the topographies of semiconductor products, in exercise of the powers conferred on him by the said section 2(2) hereby makes the following Regulations:

1. These Regulations may be cited as the Semiconductor Products (Protection   **A–566** of Topography) Regulations 1987 and shall come into force on 7th November, 1987.

2.—(1) In these Regulations—   **A–567**

"semiconductor product" means an article the purpose, or one of the purposes, of which is the performance of an electronic function and which consists of two or more layers, at least one of which is composed of semiconducting material and in or upon one or more of which is fixed a pattern appertaining to that or another function;

"topography" means the design, however expressed, of any of the following:

(*a*) the pattern fixed, or intended to be fixed, in or upon a layer of a semiconductor product;

(*b*) the pattern fixed, or intended to be fixed, in or upon a layer of material in

---

[4a] These Regulations were revoked and replaced by the Design Right (Semiconductor Topographies) Regulations 1989 (1989 S.I. No. 1100) §A–577A *post.*
[5] 1987 S.I. No. 448.
[6] c. 68.

the course of, and for the purpose of, the manufacture of a semiconductor product;

(*c*) the arrangement of the layers of a semiconductor product in relation to one another;

"topography right" has the meaning given in regulation 4(1) below and, unless the context otherwise requires, references to topography right are references to topography right subsisting in a topography.

(2) For the purposes of these Regulations, the creation of a topography occurs upon its first expression in a form from which it can be reproduced.

(3) For the purposes of these Regulations, and subject to paragraph (4) below, the commercial exploitation of a topography is the sale or hire, or the offer or exposure for sale or hire, of—

(*a*) a reproduction of the whole or a substantial part of the topography, or

(*b*) a semiconductor product incorporating such a reproduction,

being (except for the purposes of Regulation 3(2) below) lawful exploitation by or with the licence or consent of the owner of topography right in the topography or of any predecessor in title of the owner.

(4) No account shall be taken of any commercial exploitation which is subject to an obligation of confidence in respect of information about the topography exploited unless either—

(*a*) the topography has been commercially exploited on a previous occasion (whether or not subject to an obligation of confidence), or

(*b*) the obligation is imposed at the behest of the Crown, or of the government of any country outside the United Kingdom, for the protection of security in connection with the production of arms, munitions or war material.

(5) For the purposes of these Regulations, no account shall be taken of any offer for sale or hire the acceptance of which would lead to an agreement to sell or hire but not yet an actual sale or hire.

3.—(1) Where a topography is original and its creator is a qualified person or, in the case of a topography created in the course of employment or pursuant to commission, the employer or commissioner is a qualified person, topography right shall, subject to Regulation 8 below, subsist in the topography in favour of the creator, employer or commissioner, as the case may be.

(2) If paragraph (1) above does not apply, topography right shall subsist where—

(*a*) the topography is original;

(*b*) the first commercial exploitation of the topography in the world occurs within the territory of a member state;

(*c*) the person so exploiting the topography is a qualified person; and

(*d*) that person at the time of that exploitation has been exclusively authorised to exploit the topography commercially in every member state by, as the case may be, the creator, his employer or the commissioner of the topography or, as the case may be, by a person lawfully claiming through the creator, employer or commissioner;

and in such a case topography right shall, subject to regulation 8 below, subsist in the topography in favour of that person.

(3) A topography is original if it satisfies the requirements of being—

(*a*) the result of the creator's own intellectual effort (or of the combined intellectual efforts of the creators if there are more than one), and

(*b*) not commonplace among creators of topographies or manufacturers of semiconductor products,

or if it consists of a combination of elements in which the combination itself satisfies those requirements, irrespective of whether the several elements do.

(4) For the purposes of this regulation, a person is a qualified person if—

(a) being an individual he is a British citizen or a citizen or subject of another member state or has his habitual residence in the United Kingdom, Gibraltar or another member state, or

(b) being a firm or a body corporate it has a place of business within the United Kingdom, Gibraltar or another member state at which substantial business activity is carried on,

or if he falls within one of the additional classes of qualified persons set out in Part I of Schedule 1 to these Regulations.

(5) In determining whether, for the purposes of paragraph (4)(b) above or Schedule 1 below, a person has a place of business within any territory at which substantial business activity is carried on, no account shall be taken of dealings in goods which are at all material times outside that territory.

(6) For the purposes of this regulation, a topography is created in the course of employment or pursuant to commission if it is created in the course of the creator's employment under a contract of service or apprenticeship or pursuant to a contract (other than a contract of service or apprenticeship) under which a person other than the creator commissions the creation of the topography and pays or agrees to pay for it in money or money's worth, unless in either case the contract provides to the contrary; and "employer" and "commissioner" shall be construed accordingly.

4.—(1) Topography right is, subject to paragraph (2) below, the exclusive right **A–569** to make a reproduction of the whole or a substantial part of the topography or deal in such a reproduction or a semiconductor product incorporating such a reproduction; and a person deals in a reproduction or a semiconductor product if he sells or hires it, offers or exposes it for sale or hire or imports it into the United Kingdom for the purpose of selling or hiring it.

(2) Paragraph (1) above shall not apply in respect of—

(a) the making of any reproduction privately for non-commercial purposes;

(b) the making of any reproduction for the purpose of analysing or evaluating the topography or analysing, evaluating or teaching the concepts, processes, systems or techniques embodied in it;

(c) dealing in any reproduction or product after it has been sold or hired within—

(i) the United Kingdom by or with the licence of the owner of topography right in the topography, or

(ii) the territory of any other member state or of Gibraltar by or with the consent of the person, or one of the persons, for the time being entitled to import it into or sell or hire it within that territory;

(d) any act restricted by copyright in the topography as an artistic work within the meaning of the Copyright Act 1956.

5. Topography right shall commence upon the creation of the topography or, in **A–570** a case falling within regulation 3(2) above, upon its first commercial exploitation, and shall cease—

(a) at the end of the tenth year after the end of the year in which it was first commercially exploited anywhere in the world, or

(b) if it is not commercially exploited anywhere in the world within a period of fifteen years commencing with its creation, at the end of that period.

6.—(1) Topography right is infringed, subject to paragraphs (2) and (3) below, **A–571** by any person who, in the United Kingdom, during the subsistence of the right and without the licence of the owner of the right, does or authorises any other person to do any act within the exclusive right provided for in regulation 4(1) above.

(2) Topography right in one original topography is not infringed by creating

another original topography as a result of an analysis or evaluation falling within regulation 4(2)(*b*) above, making a reproduction of that other topography or dealing in such a reproduction or a semiconductor product incorporating such a reproduction.

(3) Topography right is not infringed by dealing in a reproduction or a semiconductor product if the person dealing in it does not know, and has no reasonable grounds to believe, that the dealing is an infringement.

7.—(1) Infringement of topography right shall be actionable at the suit of the owner of the right and, subject to paragraphs (2) and (3) below, in any action for such an infringement all such relief, by way of damages, injunction, accounts or otherwise, shall be available to the plaintiff as is available in any corresponding proceedings in respect of infringement of other proprietary rights.

(2) Where in an action for infringement of topography right it is proved or admitted that an infringement was committed (other than by dealing in a reproduction or a semiconductor product) but that at the time of the infringement the defendant did not know, and had no reasonable grounds to believe, that topography right subsisted in the topography, the plaintiff shall not be entitled to any damages against the defendant in respect of the infringement, but shall be entitled to an account of profits in respect of the infringement whether any other relief is granted or not.

(3) Where in an action for infringement of topography right it is proved or admitted that an infringement was committed by dealing in a reproduction or a semiconductor product but that the defendant's acquisition of the reproduction or product was innocent, the plaintiff shall not be entitled to any relief against the defendant in respect of the infringement other than damages, and any damages awarded shall be limited to an amount which, in the opinion of the court, would have been a reasonable royalty payment under a licence had one been granted by the plaintiff to the defendant in respect of the acts constituting the infringement.

(4) For the purposes of paragraph (3) above, the defendant's acquisition was innocent if at the time of acquiring the reproduction or product he did not know, and had no reasonable grounds to believe, that dealing in it in the United Kingdom would be an infringement, or if—

> (*a*) his title to the reproduction or product was derived, directly or indirectly, from a person who, at the time that he acquired it, did not know, and had no reasonable grounds to believe, that dealing in it in the United Kingdom would be an infringement, and
>
> (*b*) the disposal of the reproduction or product by that person either—
>> (i) would have been an infringement of topography right but for regulation 6(3) above, or
>> (ii) was an infringement in respect of which paragraph (3) above applied, or
>> (iii) occurred within the territory of a member state other than the United Kingdom or in Gibraltar and could not have been prevented because of Article 5(6) of Council Directive 87/54/EEC on the legal protection of topographies of semiconductor products.[7]

(5) In this regulation, "action" includes a counterclaim, and references to the plaintiff and to the defendant in an action shall be construed accordingly; and in the application of this regulation to Scotland, "injunction" means an interdict, "accounts" means count, reckoning and payment, "an account of profits" means an accounting and payment of profits, "plaintiff" means pursuer and "defendant" means defender.

---

[7] O.J. No. L 24, 27.1.1987, p. 36.

8.—(1) For the purposes of these Regulations, the owner of topography right is   **A–573**
the person who for the time being is actually entitled to it or will become entitled to
it upon the creation of the topography (where the topography has not yet been
created) or upon the subsistence of topography right in the topography (where the
right does not yet subsist in it).

(2) The owner of topography right may assign it (or his prospective entitlement
to it) by instrument in writing signed by him or on his behalf; and topography
right (and the prospective entitlement to it) is transmissible by testamentary disposition or operation of law as personal or moveable property.

(3) A licence granted by the owner in respect of topography right shall be binding upon all his successors in title in respect of it except for subsequent purchasers
in good faith for valuable consideration without actual or constructive notice of the
licence and persons deriving title from such purchasers; and where the owner of
topography right is not such a purchaser in good faith and does not derive title
from such a purchaser, references in these Regulations to the licence of the owner
include the licence of a predecessor in title of the owner.

9.—(1) The acts restricted by the copyright in an artistic work in accordance   **A–574**
with section 3(5) of the Copyright Act 1956 shall exclude—
   (*a*) the reproduction of a topography in three dimensions;
   (*b*) the reproduction of a topography in two dimensions—
      (i) in the course of, and for the purposes of, the manufacture of a semicon-
         ductor product, or
      (ii) where the making of the thing from which the reproduction is immedi-
         ately taken is, by virtue of this paragraph, not an act restricted by
         copyright; and
   (*c*) the publication of any such reproduction as is mentioned in subparagraph
      (*a*) or (*b*) above or its inclusion in a television broadcast or a cable pro-
      gramme.

(2) Schedule 2 to these Regulations shall have effect for the purpose of modifying other legislation.

10.—(1) These Regulations shall not apply in respect of any topography created   **A–575**
before 7th November 1987.

(2) Regulation 9(1) above shall not apply in respect of any artistic work made
before 7th November 1987.

SCHEDULE 1   Regulation 3(4)   **A–576**

ADDITIONAL CLASSES OF QUALIFIED PERSONS

PART I

DESCRIPTIONS OF ADDITIONAL CLASSES

1. British Dependent Territory citizens.

2. Citizens and subjects of any country specified in Part II below.

3. Habitual residents of any country specified in Part II below, the Isle of Man,
the Channel Islands or any colony.

4. Firms and bodies corporate formed under the law of, or of any part of, the
United Kingdom, Gibraltar, another member state or any country specified in
Part II below with a place of business within any country so specified at which
substantial business activity is carried on.

PART II

SPECIFIED COUNTRIES

United States of America.

SCHEDULE 2 Regulation 9(2)

CONSEQUENTIAL MODIFICATION OF LEGISLATION

1. The provisions specified in Table A below shall apply as if references therein to copyright, or to copyright in a work, extended to topography right, and as if references therein to a work in which copyright subsists extended to a topography in which topography right subsists.

Table A

Act	Section or Schedule
Patents, Designs, Copyright and Trade Marks (Emergency) Act 1939	Sections 1 and 2
Crown Proceedings Act 1947	Section 3
Defence Contracts Act 1958	Section 6(2)
Restrictive Trade Practices Act 1976	Schedule 3, paragraph 5A
Unfair Contract Terms Act 1977	Schedule 1, paragraph 1(c)
Judicature (Northern Ireland) Act 1978	Section 94A(5)
State Immunity Act 1978	Section 7(b)
Supreme Court Act 1981	Section 72(5) and Schedule 1, paragraph 1(i)
Companies Act 1985	Sections 396(1)(j) and 410(4)(c)(vi)
Law Reform (Miscellaneous Provisions) (Scotland) Act 1985	Section 15(5)

2. The provisions specified in Table B below shall apply as if there were inserted at the end of each thereof the words, "or of any topography right",

Table B

Act	Section or Schedule
Patents Act 1949	Sections 47(1)
Registered Designs Act 1949	Schedule 1, paragraph 2(1)
Post Office Act 1969	Schedule 10, paragraphs 8(1) and 18(1)
Patents Act 1977	Section 57(1)
British Telecommunications Act 1981	Schedule 5, paragraphs 9(1) and 19(1)

3. Subject to any Order made by virtue of subsection (1)(a) of section 3 of the Northern Ireland Constitution Act 1973[8] after the making of these Regulations, topography right shall not be a transferred matter for the purposes of that Act but shall for the purposes of subsection (2) of that section be treated as specified in Schedule 3 to that Act.

The Design Right (Semiconductor Topographies) Regulations 1989   A–577A
(S.I. 1989 No. 1100)

Made - - - - - - -	*29th June 1989*
Coming into force - - - -	*1st August 1989*

Whereas a draft of the following Regulations has been approved by resolution of each House of Parliament:

Now, therefore, the Secretary of State, being designated[8a] for the purposes of section 2(2) of the European Communities Act 1972[8b] in relation to the conferment and protection of exclusive rights in the topographies of semiconductor products, in exercise of the powers conferred on him by the said section 2(2) hereby makes the following Regulations:

Citation and commencement

1. These Regulations may be cited as the Design Right (Semiconductor Topographies) Regulations 1989 and shall come into force on 1st August 1989.   **A–577B**

Interpretation

2.—(1) In these Regulations—   **A–577C**

"the Act" means the Copyright, Designs and Patents Act 1988;

"semiconductor product" means an article the purpose, or one of the purposes, of which is the performance of an electronic function and which consists of two or more layers, at least one of which is composed of semiconducting material and in or upon one or more of which is fixed a pattern appertaining to that or another function; and

"semiconductor topography" means a design within the meaning of section 213(2) of the Act which is a design of either of the following:
  (*a*) the pattern fixed, or intended to be fixed, in or upon—
    (i) a layer of a semiconductor product, or
    (ii) a layer of material in the course of and for the purpose of the manufacture of a semiconductor product, or
  (*b*) the arrangement of the patterns fixed, or intended to be fixed, in or upon the layers of a semiconductor product in relation to one another.

(2) Except where the context otherwise requires, these Regulations shall be construed as one with Part III of the Act (design right).

Application of Copyright, Designs and Patents Act 1988, Part III

3. In its application to a design which is a semiconductor topography, Part III of the Act shall have effect subject to regulations 4 to 9 below.   **A–577D**

---

[8] c. 36.
[8a] S.I. 1987/448.
[8b] c. 68.

Qualification

4.—(1) Section 213(5) of the Act has effect subject to paragraphs (2) to (4) below.

(2) Part III of the Act has effect as if for section 217 of the Act there was substituted the following:

"217.—(1) In this Part—

"qualifying individual" means a citizen or subject of, or an individual habitually resident in, a qualifying country; and

"qualifying person" means—

(a) a qualifying individual,
(b) a body corporate or other body having legal personality which has in any qualifying country or in Gibraltar a place of business at which substantial business activity is carried on, or
(c) a person who falls within one of the additional classes set out in Part I of the Schedule to the Design Right (Semiconductor Topographies) Regulations 1989.

(2) References in this Part to a qualifying person include the Crown and the government of any other qualifying country.

(3) In this section "qualifying country" means—

(a) the United Kingdom, or
(b) another member State of the European Economic Community.

(4) The reference in the definition of "qualifying individual" to a person's being a citizen or subject of a qualifying country shall be construed in relation to the United Kingdom as a reference to his being a British citizen.

(5) In determining for the purpose of the definition of "qualifying person" whether substantial business activity is carried on at a place of business in any country, no account shall be taken of dealings in goods which are at all material times outside that country.".

(3) Where a semiconductor topography is created in pursuance of a commission or in the course of employment and the designer of the topography is, by virtue of section 215 of the Act (as substituted by regulation 5 above), the first owner of design right in that topography, section 219 of the Act does not apply and section 218(2) to (4) of the Act shall apply to the topography as if it had not been created in pursuance of a commission or in the course of employment.

(4) Section 220 of the Act has effect subject to regulation 7 below and as if for subsection (1) there was substituted the following:

"220.—(1) A design which does not qualify for design right protection under section 218 or 219 (as modified by regulation 4(3) of the Design Right (Semiconductor Topographies) Regulations 1989) or under the said regulation 4(3) qualifies for design right protection if the first marketing of articles made to the design—

(a) is by a qualifying person who is exclusively authorised to put such articles on the market in every member State of the European Economic Community, and
(b) takes place within the territory of any member State.";

and subsection (4) of section 220 accordingly has effect as if the words "in the United Kingdom" were omitted.

Ownership of design right

5. Part III of the Act has effect as if for section 215 of the Act there was substi-   **A-577F**
tuted the following:

"215.—(1) The designer is the first owner of any design right in a design which is
not created in pursuance of a commission or in the course of employment.

(2) Where a design is created in pursuance of a commission, the person commissioning the design is the first owner of any design right in it subject to any
agreement in writing to the contrary.

(3) Where, in a case not falling within subsection (2) a design is created by an
employee in the course of his employment, his employer is the first owner of any
design right in the design subject to any agreement in writing to the contrary.

(4) If a design qualifies for design right protection by virtue of section 220 (as
modified by regulation 4(4) of the Design Right (Semiconductor Topographies)
Regulations 1989), the above rules do not apply and, subject to regulation 7 of
the said Regulations, the person by whom the articles in question are marketed
is the first owner of the design right.".

Duration of design right

6.—(1) Part III of the Act has effect as if for section 216 of the Act there was   **A-577G**
substituted the following:

"216. The design right in a semiconductor topography expires—

(a) ten years from the end of the calendar year in which the topography or
articles made to the topography were first made available for sale or hire
anywhere in the world by or with the licence of the design right owner, or

(b) if neither the topography nor articles made to the topography are so made
available with a period of fifteen years commencing with the earlier of the
time when the topography was first recorded in a design document or the
time when an article was first made to the topography, at the end of that
period.".

(2) Subsection (2) of section 263 of the Act has effect as if the words "or a semiconductor topography" were inserted after the words "in relation to an article".

(3) The substitute provision set out in paragraph (1) above has effect subject to
regulation 7 below.

Confidential information

7. In determining, for the purposes of section 215(4), 216 or 220 of the Act (as   **A-577H**
modified by these Regulations), whether there has been any marketing, or anything has been made available for sale or hire, no account shall be taken of any sale
or hire, or any offer or exposure for sale or hire, which is subject to an obligation of
confidence in respect of information about the semiconductor topography in question unless either—

(a) the article or semiconductor topography sold or hired or offered or exposed
for sale or hire has been sold or hired on a previous occasion (whether or
not subject to an obligation of confidence), or

(b) the obligation is imposed at the behest of the Crown, or of the government
of any country outside the United Kingdom, for the protection of security
in connection with the production of arms, munitions or war material.

Infringement

A–577I   **8.**—(1) Section 226 of the Act has effect as if for subsection (1) there was substituted the following:

"226.—(1) Subject to subsection (1A), the owner of design right in a design has the exclusive right to reproduce the design—
   (*a*) by making articles to that design, or
   (*b*) by making a design document recording the design for the purpose of enabling such articles to be made.

(1A) Subsection (1) does not apply to—

   (*a*) the reproduction of a design privately for non-commerical aims; or
   (*b*) the reproduction of a design for the purpose of analysing or evaluating the design or analysing, evaluating or teaching the concepts, processes, systems or techniques embodied in it.".

   (2) Section 227 of the Act does not apply if the article in question has previously been sold or hired within—
   (*a*) the United Kingdom by or with the licence of the owner of design right in the semiconductor topography in question, or
   (*b*) the territory of any other member of State of the European Economic Community or the territory of Gibraltar by or with the consent of the person for the time being entitled to import it into or sell or hire it within that territory.

   (3) Section 228(6) of the Act does not apply.
   (4) It is not an infringement of design right in a semiconductor topography to—
   (*a*) create another original semiconductor topography as a result of an analysis or evaluation of the first topography or of the concepts, processes, systems or techniques embodied in it, or
   (*b*) reproduce that other topography.
   (5) Anything which would be an infringement of the design right in a semiconductor topography if done in relation to the topography as a whole is an infringement of the design right in the topography if done in relation to a substantial part of the topography.

Licences of right

A–577J   **9.** Section 237 of the Act does not apply.

Revocation and transitional provisions

A–577K   **10.**—(1) The Semiconductor Products (Protection of Topography) Regulations 1987 are hereby revoked.
   (2) Sub-paragraph (1) of paragraph 19 of Schedule 1 to the Act shall not apply in respect of a semiconductor topography created between 7th November 1987 and 31st July 1989.
   (3) In its application to copyright in a semiconductor topography created before 7th November 1987, sub-paragraph (2) of the said paragraph 19 shall have effect as if the reference to sections 237 to 239 were a reference to sections 238 and 239; and sub-paragraph (3) of that paragraph accordingly shall not apply to such copyright.

Additional Classes of Qualifying Persons

Part I

Descriptions of Additional Classes

1. British Dependent Territory citizens.

2. Citizens and subjects of any country specified in Part II or III below.

3. Habitual residents of any country specified in Part II or III below, the Isle of Man, the Channel Islands or any colony.

4. Firms and bodies corporate formed under the law of, or of any part of, the United Kingdom, Gibraltar, another member State of the European Economic Community or any country specified in Part II below with a place of business within any country so specified at which substantial business activity is carried on.

Part II

Specified Countries: Citizens, Subjects, Habitual Residents, Bodies Corporate and Other Bodies Having Legal Personality

Austria[8c]
Japan
Sweden[8d]
Switerland
United States of America

Part III

Specified Countries: Citizens, Subjects and Habitual Residents Only

Austria
Finland
French overseas territories (French Polynesia; French Southern and Antarctic Territories; Mayotte; New Caledonia and dependencies; Saint-Pierre and Miquelon; Wallis and Futuna Islands)
Iceland
Norway
Sweden

[8c] Austria was transferred from Part III to Part II of the Schedule by 1990 S.I. No. 1003.
[8d] Sweden was transferred from Part III to Part II of the Schedule by 1989 S.I. No. 2147.

PART III

Copyright Act, 1911[9]

(1 & 2 Geo. 5, c. 46)

An Act to amend and consolidate the Law relating to Copyright.

[16th December, 1911.]

PART I.—IMPERIAL COPYRIGHT

Rights

Copyright

A–578 **1.**—(1) Subject to the provisions of this Act, copyright shall subsist throughout the parts of His Majesty's dominions to which this Act extends for the term hereinafter mentioned in every original literary dramatic musical and artistic work, if—

(*a*) in the case of a published work, the work was first published within such parts of His Majesty's dominions as aforesaid; and

(*b*) in the case of an unpublished work, the author was at the date of the making of the work a British subject or resident within such parts of His Majesty's dominions as aforesaid;

but in no other works, except so far as the protection conferred by this Act is extended by Orders in Council thereunder relating to self-governing dominions to which this Act does not extend and to foreign countries.

(2) For the purposes of this Act, "copyright" means the sole right to produce or reproduce the work or any substantial part thereof in any material form whatsoever, to perform, or in the case of a lecture to deliver, the work or any substantial part thereof in public; if the work is unpublished, to publish the work or any substantial part thereof; and shall include the sole right,—

(*a*) to produce, reproduce, perform, or publish any translation of the work;

(*b*) in the case of a dramatic work, to convert it into a novel or other non-dramatic work;

(*c*) in the case of a novel or other non-dramatic work, or of an artistic work, to convert it into a dramatic work, by way of performance in public or otherwise;

(*d*) in the case of a literary, dramatic, or musical work, to make any record, perforated roll, cinematograph film, or other contrivance by means of which the work may be mechanically performed or delivered,

and to authorise any such acts as aforesaid.

(3) For the purposes of this Act, publication, in relation to any work, means the issue of copies of the work to the public, and does not include the performance in public of a dramatic or musical work, the delivery in public of a lecture, the exhibition in public of an artistic work, or the construction of an architectural work of art, but, for the purposes of this provision, the issue of photographs and engravings

---

[9] This Act was repealed by the Copyright Act, 1956, *ante*, as from June 1, 1957 H.C. with the exception of ss.15, 34, 37. ss.34 and 37(2) were repealed by the Statute Law (Repeals) Act 1986 (c. 12).

    Comparative Tables showing the correspondence of this Act to the 1956 Act, and of the 1956 Act to this Act, are printed at §§ A–474 and A–475 *ante*.

of works of sculpture and architectural works of art shall not be deemed to be publication of such works.

Infringement of copyright

2.—(1) Copyright in a work shall be deemed to be infringed by any person who, without the consent of the owner of the copyright, does anything the sole right to do which is by this Act conferred on the owner of the copyright: Provided that the following acts shall not constitute an infringement of copyright:

    (i) Any fair dealing with any work for the purposes of private study, research, criticism, review, or newspaper summary:

    (ii) Where the author of an artistic work is not the owner of the copyright therein, the use by the author of any mould, cast, sketch, plan, model, or study made by him for the purpose of the work, provided that he does not thereby repeat or imitate the main design of that work:

    (iii) The making or publishing of paintings, drawings, engravings, or photographs of a work of sculpture or artistic craftsmanship, if permanently situate in a public place or building, or the making or publishing of paintings, drawings, engravings, or photographs (which are not in the nature of architectural drawings or plans) of any architectural work of art:

    (iv) The publication in a collection, mainly composed of non-copyright matter, bona fide intended for the use of schools, and so described in the title and in any advertisements issued by the publisher, of short passages from published literary works not themselves published for the use of schools in which copyright subsists: provided that not more than two of such passages from works by the same author are published by the same publisher within five years, and that the source from which such passages are taken is acknowledged:

    (v) The publication in a newspaper of a report of a lecture delivered in public, unless the report is prohibited by conspicuous written or printed notice affixed before and maintained during the lecture at or about the main entrance of the building in which the lecture is given, and, except whilst the building is being used for public worship, in a position near the lecturer; but nothing in this paragraph shall affect the provisions in paragraph (i) as to newspaper summaries:

    (vi) The reading or recitation in public by one person of any reasonable extract from any published work.

(2) Copyright in a work shall also be deemed to be infringed by any person who—

    (*a*) sells or lets for hire, or by way of trade exposes or offers for sale or hire; or

    (*b*) distributes either for the purposes of trade or to such an extent as to affect prejudicially the owner of the copyright; or

    (*c*) by way of trade exhibits in public; or

    (*d*) imports for sale or hire into any part of His Majesty's dominions to which this Act extends,

any work which to his knowledge infringes copyright or would infringe copyright if it had been made within the part of His Majesty's dominions in or into which the sale or hiring, exposure, offering for sale or hire, distribution, exhibition, or importation took place.

(3) Copyright in a work shall also be deemed to be infringed by any person who for his private profit permits a theatre or other place of entertainment to be used for the performance in public of the work without the consent of the owner of the copyright, unless he was not aware, and had no reasonable ground for suspecting, that the performance would be an infringement of copyright.

Term of copyright

A–580   **3.** The term for which copyright shall subsist shall, except as otherwise expressly provided by this Act, be the life of the author and a period of fifty years after his death:

Provided that at any time after the expiration of twenty-five years, or in the case of a work in which copyright subsists at the passing of this Act thirty years, from the death of the author of a published work, copyright in the work shall not be deemed to be infringed by the reproduction of the work for sale if the person reproducing the work proves that he has given the prescribed notice in writing of his intention to reproduce the work, and that he has paid in the prescribed manner to, or for the benefit of, the owner of the copyright royalties in respect of all copies of the work sold by him calculated at the rate of ten per cent. on the price at which he publishes the work; and, for the purposes of this proviso, the Board of Trade may make regulations prescribing the mode in which notices are to be given, and the particulars to be given in such notices, and the mode, time, and frequency of the payment of royalties, including (if they think fit) regulations requiring payment in advance or otherwise securing the payment of royalties.

Compulsory licences

A–581   **4.** If at any time after the death of the author of a literary, dramatic, or musical work which has been published or performed in public a complaint is made to the Judicial Committee of the Privy Council that the owner of the copyright in the work has refused to republish or to allow the republication of the work or has refused to allow the performance in public of the work, and that by reason of such refusal the work is withheld from the public, the owner of the copyright may be ordered to grant a licence to reproduce the work or perform the work in public, as the case may be, on such terms and subject to such conditions as the Judicial Committee may think fit.

Ownership of copyright, etc.

A–582   **5.**—(1) Subject to the provisions of this Act, the author of a work shall be the first owner of the copyright therein:

Provided that—

    (*a*) where, in the case of an engraving, photograph, or portrait, the plate or other original was ordered by some other person and was made for valuable consideration in pursuance of that order, then, in the absence of any agreement to the contrary, the person by whom such plate or other original was ordered shall be the first owner of the copyright; and

    (*b*) where the author was in the employment of some other person under a contract of service or apprenticeship and the work was made in the course of his employment by that person, the person by whom the author was employed shall, in the absence of any agreement to the contrary, be the first owner of the copyright, but where the work is an article or other contribution to a newspaper, magazine, or similar periodical, there shall, in the absence of any agreement to the contrary, be deemed to be reserved to the author a right to restrain the publication of the work, otherwise than as part of a newspaper, magazine, or similar periodical.

(2) The owner of the copyright in any work may assign the right, either wholly or partially, and either generally or subject to limitations to the United Kingdom or any self-governing dominion or other part of His Majesty's dominions to which this Act extends, and either for the whole term of the copyright or for any part thereof, and may grant any interest in the right by licence, but no such assignment

or grant shall be valid unless it is in writing signed by the owner of the right in respect of which the assignment or grant is made, or by his duly authorised agent:

Provided that, where the author of a work is the first owner of the copyright therein, no assignment of the copyright, and no grant of any interest therein, made by him (otherwise than by will) after the passing of this Act, shall be operative to vest in the assignee or grantee any rights with respect to the copyright in the work beyond the expiration of twenty-five years from the death of the author, and the reversionary interest in the copyright expectant on the termination of that period shall, on the death of the author, notwithstanding any agreement to the contrary, devolve on his legal personal representatives as part of his estate, and any agreement entered into by him as to the disposition of such reversionary interest shall be null and void, but nothing in this proviso shall be construed as applying to the assignment of the copyright in a collective work or a licence to publish a work or part of a work as part of a collective work.

(3) Where, under any partial assignment of copyright, the assignee becomes entitled to any right comprised in copyright, the assignee as respects the right so assigned, and the assignor as respects the rights not assigned, shall be treated for the purposes of this Act as the owner of the copyright, and the provisions of this Act shall have effect accordingly.

Civil Remedies

Civil remedies for infringement of copyright

6.—(1) Where copyright in any work has been infringed, the owner of the copy-   **A–583**
right shall, except as otherwise provided by this Act, be entitled to all such remedies by way of injunction or interdict, damages, accounts, and otherwise, as are or may be conferred by law for the infringement of a right.

(2) The costs of all parties in any proceedings in respect of the infringement of copyright shall be in the absolute discretion of the court.

(3) In any action for infringement of copyright in any work, the work shall be presumed to be a work in which copyright subsists and the plaintiff shall be presumed to be the owner of the copyright, unless the defendant puts in issue the existence of the copyright, or, as the case may be, the title of the plaintiff, and where any such question is in issue, then—

   (a) if a name purporting to be that of the author of the work is printed or otherwise indicated thereon in the usual manner, the person whose name is so printed or indicated shall, unless the contrary is proved, be presumed to be the author of the work;

   (b) if no name is so printed or indicated, or if the name so printed or indicated is not the author's true name or the name by which he is commonly known, and a name purporting to be that of the publisher or proprietor of the work is printed or otherwise indicated thereon in the usual manner the person whose name is so printed or indicated shall, unless the contrary is proved, be presumed to be the owner of the copyright in the work for the purposes of proceedings in respect of the infringement of copyright therein.

Rights of owner against persons possessing or dealing with infringing copies, etc.

7. All infringing copies of any work in which copyright subsists, or of any sub-   **A–584**
stantial part thereof, and all plates used or intended to be used for the production of such infringing copies, shall be deemed to be the property of the owner of the copyright, who accordingly may take proceedings for the recovery of the possession thereof or in respect of the conversion thereof.

Exemption of innocent infringer from liability to pay damages, etc.

A–585   **8.** Where proceedings are taken in respect of the infringement of the copyright in any work and the defendant in his defence alleges that he was not aware of the existence of the copyright in the work, the plaintiff shall not be entitled to any remedy other than an injunction or interdict in respect of the infringement if the defendant proves that at the date of the infringement he was not aware and had no reasonable ground for suspecting that copyright subsisted in the work.

Restriction on remedies in the case of architecture

A–586   **9.**—(1) Where the construction of a building or other structure which infringes or which, if completed, would infringe the copyright in some other work has been commenced, the owner of the copyright shall not be entitled to obtain an injunction or interdict to restrain the construction of such building or structure or to order its demolition.

(2) Such of the other provisions of this Act as provide that an infringing copy of a work shall be deemed to be the property of the owner of the copyright, or as impose summary penalties, shall not apply in any case to which this section applies.

Limitation of actions

A–587   **10.** An action in respect of infringement of copyright shall not be commenced after the expiration of three years next after the infringement.

Summary Remedies

Penalties for dealing with infringing copies, etc.

A–588   **11.**—(1) If any person knowingly—

(*a*) makes for sale or hire any infringing copy of a work in which copyright subsists; or

(*b*) sells or lets for hire, or by way of trade exposes or offers for sale or hire any infringing copy of any such work; or

(*c*) distributes infringing copies of any such work either for the purposes of trade or to such an extent as to affect prejudicially the owner of the copyright; or

(*d*) by way of trade exhibits in public any infringing copy of any such work; or

(*e*) imports for sale or hire into the United Kingdom any infringing copy of any such work:

he shall be guilty of an offence under this Act and be liable on summary conviction to a fine not exceeding forty shillings for every copy dealt with in contravention of this section, but not exceeding fifty pounds in respect of the same transaction; or, in the case of a second or subsequent offence, either to such fine or to imprisonment with or without hard labour for a term not exceeding two months.

(2) If any person knowingly makes or has in his possession any plate for the purpose of making infringing copies of any work in which copyright subsists, or knowingly and for his private profit causes any such work to be performed in public without the consent of the owner of the copyright, he shall be guilty of an offence under this Act, and be liable on summary conviction to a fine not exceeding fifty pounds, or, in the case of a second or subsequent offence, either to such fine or to imprisonment with or without hard labour for a term not exceeding two months.

(3) The court before which any such proceedings are taken may, whether the alleged offender is convicted or not, order that all copies of the work or all plates in the possession of the alleged offender, which appear to it to be infringing copies or plates for the purpose of making infringing copies, be destroyed or delivered up to the owner of the copyright or otherwise dealt with as the court may think fit.

(4) Nothing in this section shall, as respects musical works, affect the provisions of the Musical (Summary Proceedings) Copyright Act, 1902, or the Musical Copyright Act, 1906.

Appeals to quarter sessions

12. Any person aggrieved by a summary conviction of an offence under the fore- **A–589** going provisions of this Act may in England and Ireland appeal to a court of quarter sessions and in Scotland under and in terms of the Summary Jurisdiction (Scotland) Acts.

Extent of provisions as to summary remedies

13. The provisions of this Act with respect to summary remedies shall extend **A–590** only to the United Kingdom.

Importation of Copies

Importation of copies

14.—(1) Copies made out of the United Kingdom of any work in which copy- **A–591** right subsists which if made in the United Kingdom would infringe copyright, and as to which the owner of the copyright gives notice in writing by himself or his agent to the Commissioners of Customs and Excise, that he is desirous that such copies should not be imported into the United Kingdom, shall not be so imported, and shall, subject to the provisions of this section, be deemed to be included in the table of prohibitions and restrictions contained in section forty-two of the Customs Consolidation Act, 1876, and that section shall apply accordingly.

(2) Before detaining any such copies or taking any further proceedings with a view to the forfeiture thereof under the law relating to the Customs, the Commissioners of Customs and Excise may require the regulations under this section, whether as to information, conditions, or other matters, to be complied with, and may satisfy themselves in accordance with those regulations that the copies are such as are prohibited by this section to be imported.

(3) The Commissioners of Customs and Excise may make regulations, either general or special, respecting the detention and forfeiture of copies the importation of which is prohibited by this section, and the conditions, if any, to be fulfilled before such detention and forfeiture, and may, by such regulations, determine the information, notices, and security to be given, and the evidence requisite for any of the purposes of this section, and the mode of verification of such evidence.

(4) The regulations may apply to copies of all works the importation of copies of which is prohibited by this section, or different regulations may be made respecting different classes of such works.

(5) The regulations may provide for the informant reimbursing the Commissioners of Customs and Excise all expenses and damages incurred in respect of any detention made on his information, and of any proceedings consequent on such detention; and may provide for notices under any enactment repealed by this Act being treated as notices given under this section.

(6) The foregoing provisions of this section shall have effect as if they were part of the Customs Consolidation Act, 1876: Provided that, notwithstanding anything in that Act, the Isle of Man shall not be treated as part of the United Kingdom for the purposes of this section.

(7) This section shall, with the necessary modifications, apply to the importation into a British possession to which this Act extends of copies of works made out of that possession.

AMENDMENT

In subsection (1) the words "and shall, subject to the provisions of this section" onwards were repealed by the Customs and Excise Act, 1952 (15 & 16 Geo. 6 and 1 Eliz. 2, c. 44), s.320, Sched. 12, Part I.

Delivery of Books to Libraries

Delivery of copies to British Museum and other libraries

A–592   **15.**—(1) The publisher of every book published in the United Kingdom shall, within one month after the publication, deliver, at his own expense, a copy of the book to the [British Library Board] who shall give a written receipt for it.

(2) He shall also, if written demand is made before the expiration of twelve months after publication, deliver within one month after receipt of that written demand or, if the demand was made before publication, within one month after publication, to some depôt in London named in the demand a copy of the book for, or in accordance with the directions of, the authority having the control of each of the following libraries, namely: the Bodleian Library, Oxford, the University Library, Cambridge, the [National Library of Scotland] and the Library of Trinity College, Dublin, and subject to the provisions of this section the National Library of Wales. In the case of an encyclopaedia, newspaper, review, magazine, or work published in a series of numbers or parts, the written demand may include all numbers or parts of the work which may be subsequently published.

(3) The copy delivered to the [British Library Board] shall be a copy of the whole book with all maps and illustrations belonging thereto, finished and coloured in the same manner as the best copies of the book are published, and shall be bound, sewed, or stitched together, and on the best paper on which the book is printed.

(4) The copy delivered for the other authorities mentioned in this section shall be on the paper on which the largest number of copies of the book is printed for sale, and shall be in the like condition as the books prepared for sale.

(5) The books of which copies are to be delivered to the National Library of Wales shall not include books of such classes as may be specified in regulations to be made by the [Lord President of the Council].

(6) If a publisher fails to comply with this section, he shall be liable on summary conviction to a fine not exceeding five pounds and the value of the book, and the fine shall be paid to the [British Library Board] or authority to whom the book ought to have been delivered.

(7) For the purposes of this section, the expression "book" includes every part or division of a book, pamphlet, sheet of letterpress, sheet of music, map, plan, chart or table separately published, but shall not include any second or subsequent edition of a book unless such edition contains additions or alterations either in the letterpress or in the maps, prints, or other engravings belonging thereto.

OPERATION AND AMENDMENT

This section was not repealed by the 1956 Act, nor by the 1988 Act, but was amended by the British Library Act, 1972 (c. 54), s.4 to substitute references to the British Library Board for the trustees of the British Museum.

A proviso added to subsection (1) by the Copyright (British Museum) Act, 1915 (5 & 6 Geo. 5, c. 38), was repealed by the British Museum Act, 1932 (22 & 23 Geo. 5, c. 34), s.2(2).

The National Library of Scotland was substituted in subsection (2) for the Library of the Faculty of Advocates at Edinburgh by the National Library of Scotland Act, 1925 (15 & 16 Geo. 5, c. 73), s.5.

The Lord President of the Council was substituted for the Board of Trade by The Transfer of Functions (Arts, Libraries and National Heritage) Order 1986 (S.I. 1986 No. 600).

Special Provisions as to certain Works

Works of joint authors

16.—(1) In the case of a work of joint authorship, copyright shall subsist during   **A–593**
the life of the author who first dies and for a term of fifty years after his death, or
during the life of the author who dies last, whichever period is the longer, and
references in this Act to the period after the expiration of any specified number of
years from the death of the author shall be construed as references to the period
after the expiration of the like number of years from the death of the author who
dies first or after the death of the author who dies last, whichever period may be
the shorter, and in the provisions of this Act with respect to the grant of compulsory licences a reference to the date of the death of the author who dies last shall be
subsituted for the reference to the date of the death of the author.

(2) Where, in the case of a work of joint authorship, some one or more of the
joint authors do not satisfy the conditions conferring copyright laid down by this
Act, the work shall be treated for the purposes of this Act as if the other author or
authors had been the sole author or authors thereof:

Provided that the term of the copyright shall be the same as it would have been
if all the authors had satisfied such conditions as aforesaid.

(3) For the purposes of this Act, "a work of a joint authorship" means a work
produced by the collaboration of two or more authors in which the contribution of
one author is not distinct from the contribution of the other author or authors.

(4) Where a married woman and her husband are joint authors of a work the
interest of such married woman therein shall be her separate property.

AMENDMENT

In subsection (4) the word "separate" was repealed by the Law Reform (Married Woman
and Tortfeasors) Act, 1935 (25 & 26 Geo. 5, c. 30), s.5, Sched. 2.

Posthumous works

17.—(1) In the case of a literary dramatic or musical work, or an engraving, in   **A–594**
which copyright subsists at the date of the death of the author or, in the case of a
work of joint authorship, at or immediately before the date of the death of the
author who dies last, but which has not been published, nor, in the case of a dramatic or musical work, been performed in public, nor, in the case of a lecture, been
delivered in public, before that date, copyright shall subsist till publication, or performance or delivery in public, whichever may first happen, and for a term of fifty
years thereafter, and the proviso to section three of this Act shall, in the case of
such a work, apply as if the author had died at the date of such publication or performance or delivery in public as aforesaid.

(2) The ownership of an author's manuscript after his death, where such ownership has been acquired under a testamentary disposition made by the author and
the manuscript is of a work which has not been published nor performed in public
nor delivered in public, shall be prima facie proof of the copyright being with the
owner of the manuscript.

Provisions as to Government publications

18. Without prejudice to any rights or privileges of the Crown, where any work   **A–595**
has, whether before or after the commencement of this Act, been prepared or published by or under the direction or control of His Majesty or any Government
department, the copyright in the work shall, subject to any agreement with the
author, belong to His Majesty, and in such case shall continue for a period of fifty
years from the date of the first publication of the work.

Provisions as to mechanical instruments

19.—(1) Copyright shall subsist in records, perforated rolls, and other contrivances by means of which sounds may be mechanically reproduced, in like manner as if such contrivances were musical works, but the term of copyright shall be fifty years from the making of the original plate from which the contrivance was directly or indirectly derived, and the person who was the owner of such original plate at the time when such plate was made shall be deemed to be the author of the work, and, where such owner is a body corporate, the body corporate shall be deemed for the purposes of this Act to reside within the parts of His Majesty's dominions to which this Act extends if it has established a place of business within such parts.

(2) It shall not be deemed to be an infringement of copyright in any musical work for any person to make within the parts of His Majesty's dominions to which this Act extends records, perforated rolls, or other contrivances by means of which the work may be mechanically performed, if such person proves—

(a) that such contrivances have previously been made by, or with the consent or acquiescence of, the owner of the copyright in the work; and

(b) that he has given the prescribed notice of his intention to make the contrivances, and has paid in the prescribed manner to, or for the benefit of, the owner of the copyright in the work royalties in respect of all such contrivances sold by him, calculated at the rate hereinafter mentioned:

Provided that—

(i) nothing in this provision shall authorise any alterations in, or omissions from, the work reproduced, unless contrivances reproducing the work subject to similar alterations and omissions have been previously made by, or with the consent or acquiescence of, the owner of the copyright, or unless such alterations or omissions are reasonably necessary for the adaptation of the work to the contrivances in question; and

(ii) for the purposes of this provision, a musical work shall be deemed to include any words so closely associated therewith as to form part of the same work, but shall not be deemed to include a contrivance by means of which sounds may be mechanically reproduced.

(3) The rate at which such royalties as aforesaid are to be calculated shall—

(a) in the case of contrivances sold within two years after the commencement of this Act by the person making the same, be two and one-half per cent.; and

(b) in the case of contrivances sold as aforesaid after the expiration of that period, five per cent.

on the ordinary retail selling price of the contrivance calculated in the prescribed manner, so however that the royalty payable in respect of a contrivance shall, in no case, be less than a halfpenny for each separate musical work in which copyright subsists reproduced thereon, and, where the royalty calculated as aforesaid includes a fraction of a farthing, such fraction shall be reckoned as a farthing:

Provided that, if, at any time after the expiration of seven years from the commencement of this Act, it appears to the Board of Trade that such rate as aforesaid is no longer equitable, the Board of Trade may, after holding a public inquiry, make an order either decreasing or increasing that rate to such extent as under the circumstances may seem just, but any order so made shall be provisional only and shall not have any effect unless and until confirmed by Parliament; but, where an order revising the rate has been so made and confirmed, no further revision shall be made before the expiration of fourteen years from the date of the last revision.

(4) If any such contrivance is made reproducing two or more different works in which copyright subsists and the owners of the copyright therein are different persons, the sums payable by way of royalties under this section shall be apportioned

amongst the several owners of the copyright in such proportions as, failing agreement, may be determined by arbitration.

(5) When any such contrivances by means of which a musical work may be mechanically performed have been made, then, for the purposes of this section, the owner of the copyright in the work shall, in relation to any person who makes the prescribed inquiries, be deemed to have given his consent to the making of such contrivances if he fails to reply to such inquiries within the prescribed time.

(6) For the purposes of this section, the Board of Trade may make regulations prescribing anything which under this section is to be prescribed, and prescribing the mode in which notices are to be given and the particulars to be given in such notices, and the mode, time, and frequency of the payment of royalties, and any such regulations may, if the Board think fit, include regulations requiring payment in advance or otherwise securing the payment of royalties.

(7) In the case of musical works published before the commencement of this Act, the foregoing provisions shall have effect, subject to the following modifications and additions:

(*a*) The conditions as to the previous making by, or with the consent or acquiescence of, the owner of the copyright in the work, and the restrictions as to alterations in or omissions from the work, shall not apply:

(*b*) The rate of two and one-half per cent. shall be substituted for the rate of five per cent. as the rate at which royalties are to be calculated, but no royalties shall be payable in respect of contrivances sold before the first day of July, nineteen hundred and thirteen, if contrivances reproducing the same work had been lawfully made, or placed on sale, within the parts of His Majesty's dominions to which this Act extends before the first day of July, nineteen hundred and ten:

(*c*) Notwithstanding any assignment made before the passing of this Act of the copyright in a musical work, any rights conferred by this Act in respect of the making, or authorising the making, of contrivances by means of which the work may be mechanically performed shall belong to the author or his legal personal representatives and not to the assignee, and the royalties aforesaid shall be payable to, and for the benefit of, the author of the work or his legal personal representatives:

(*d*) The saving contained in this Act of the rights and interests arising from, or in connexion with, action taken before the commencement of this Act shall not be construed as authorising any person who has made contrivances by means of which the work may be mechanically performed to sell any such contrivances, whether made before or after the passing of this Act, except on the terms and subject to the conditions laid down in this section:

(*e*) Where the work is a work on which copyright is conferred by an Order in Council relating to a foreign country, the copyright so conferred shall not, except to such extent as may be provided by the Order, include any rights with respect to the making of records, perforated rolls, or other contrivances by means of which the work may be mechanically performed.

(8) Notwithstanding anything in this Act, where a record, perforated roll, or other contrivance by means of which sounds may be mechanically reproduced has been made before the commencement of this Act, copyright shall, as from the commencement of this Act, subsist therein in like manner and for the like term as if this Act had been in force at the date of the making of the original plate from which the contrivance was directly or indirectly derived:

Provided that—

(i) the person who, at the commencement of this Act, is the owner of such original plate shall be the first owner of such copyright; and

(ii) nothing in this provision shall be construed as conferring copyright in any such contrivance if the making thereof would have infringed copyright in some other such contrivance, if this provision had been in force at the time of the making of the first-mentioned contrivance.

Provision as to political speeches

A–597   **20.** Notwithstanding anything in this Act, it shall not be an infringement of copyright in an address of a political nature delivered at a public meeting to publish a report thereof in a newspaper.

Provisions as to photographs

A–598   **21.** The term for which copyright shall subsist in photographs shall be fifty years from the making of the original negative from which the photograph was directly or indirectly derived, and the person who was the owner of such negative at the time when such negative was made shall be deemed to be the author of the work, and, where such owner is a body corporate, the body corporate shall be deemed for the purposes of this Act to reside within the parts of His Majesty's dominions to which this Act extends if it has established a place of business within such parts.

Provisions as to designs registrable under 7 Edw. 7, c. 29

A–599   **22.**—(1) This Act shall not apply to designs capable of being registered under the Patents and Designs Act, 1907, except designs which, though capable of being so registered, are not used or intended to be used as models or patterns to be multiplied by any industrial process.

(2) General rules under section eighty-six of the Patents and Designs Act, 1907, may be made for determining the conditions under which a design shall be deemed to be used for such purposes as aforesaid.

Works of foreign authors first published in parts of His Majesty's dominions to which Act extends

A–600   **23.** If it appears to His Majesty that a foreign country does not give, or has not undertaken to give, adequate protection to the works of British authors, it shall be lawful for His Majesty by Order in Council to direct that such of the provisions of this Act as confer copyright on works first published within the parts of His Majesty's dominions to which this Act extends, shall not apply to works published after the date specified in the Order, the authors whereof are subjects or citizens of such foreign country, and are not resident in His Majesty's dominions, and thereupon those provisions shall not apply to such works.

Existing works

A–601   **24.**—(1) Where any person is immediately before the commencement of this Act entitled to any such right in any work as is specified in the first column of the First Schedule to this Act, or to any interest in such a right, he shall, as from that date, be entitled to the substituted right set forth in the second column of that schedule, or to the same interest in such a substituted right, and to no other right or interest, and such substituted right shall subsist for the term for which it would have subsisted if this Act had been in force at the date when the work was made and the work had been one entitled to copyright thereunder:

Provided that—

    (*a*) if the author of any work in which any such right as is specified in the first column of the First Schedule to this Act subsists at the commencement of this Act has, before that date, assigned the right or granted any interest therein for the whole term of the right, then at the date when, but for the passing of this Act, the right would have expired the substituted right conferred by this section shall, in the absence of express agreement, pass to the author of the work, and any interest therein created before the commencement of this Act and then subsisting shall determine; but the person who immediately before the date at which the right would so have expired was the owner of the right or interest shall be entitled at his option either—

(i) on giving such notice as hereinafter mentioned, to an assignment of the right or the grant of a similar interest therein for the remainder of the term of the right for such consideration as, failing agreement, may be determined by arbitration; or

(ii) without any such assignment or grant, to continue to reproduce or perform the work in like manner as theretofore subject to the payment, if demanded by the author within three years after the date at which the right would have so expired, of such royalties to the author as, failing agreement, may be determined by arbitration, or, where the work is incorporated in a collective work and the owner of the right or interest is the proprietor of that collective work, without any such payment;

The notice above referred to must be given not more than one year nor less than six months before the date at which the right would have so expired, and must be sent by registered post to the author, or, if he cannot with reasonable diligence be found, advertised in the *London Gazette* and in two London newspapers:

(*b*) where any person has, before the twenty-sixth day of July nineteen hundred and ten, taken any action whereby he has incurred any expenditure or liability in connexion with the reproduction or performance of any work in a manner which at the time was lawful, or for the purpose of or with a view to the reproduction or performance of a work at a time when such reproduction or performance would, but for the passing of this Act, have been lawful, nothing in this section shall diminish or prejudice any rights or interest arising from or in connexion with such action which are subsisting and valuable at the said date, unless the person who by virtue of this section becomes entitled to restrain such reproduction or performance agrees to pay such compensation as, failing agreement, may be determined by arbitration.

(2) For the purposes of this section, the expression "author" includes the legal personal representatives of a deceased author.

(3) Subject to the provisions of section nineteen subsections (7) and (8) and of section thirty-three of this Act, copyright shall not subsist in any work made before the commencement of this Act, otherwise than under, and in accordance with, the provisions of this section.

Application to British Possessions

Application of Act to British dominions

25.—(1) This Act, except such of the provisions thereof as are expressly restricted to the United Kingdom, shall extend throughout His Majesty's dominions: Provided that it shall not extend to a self-governing dominion, unless declared by the Legislature of that dominion to be in force therein either without any modifications or additions, or with such modifications and additions relating exclusively to procedure and remedies, or necessary to adapt this Act to the circumstances of the dominion, as may be enacted by such Legislature. **A–602**

(2) If the Secretary of State certifies by notice published in the *London Gazette* that any self-governing dominion has passed legislation under which works, the authors whereof were at the date of the making of the works British subjects resi-

dent elsewhere than in the dominion or (not being British subjects) were resident in the parts of His Majesty's dominions to which this Act extends, enjoy within the dominion rights substantially identical with those conferred by this Act, then, whilst such legislation continues in force, the dominion shall, for the purposes of the rights conferred by this Act, be treated as if it were a dominion to which this Act extends; and it shall be lawful for the Secretary of State to give such a certificate as aforesaid, notwithstanding that the remedies for enforcing the rights, or the restrictions on the importation of copies of works, manufactured in a foreign country, under the law of the dominion, differ from those under this Act.

Legislative powers of self-governing dominions

A–603   **26.**—(1) The Legislature of any self-governing dominion may, at any time, repeal all or any of the enactments relating to copyright passed by Parliament (including this Act) so far as they are operative within that dominion: Provided that no such repeal shall prejudicially affect any legal rights existing at the time of the repeal, and that, on this Act or any part thereof being so repealed by the Legislature of a self-governing dominion, that dominion shall cease to be a dominion to which this Act extends.

(2) In any self-governing dominion to which this Act does not extend, the enactments repealed by this Act shall, so far as they are operative in that dominion, continue in force until repealed by the Legislature of that dominion.

(3) Where His Majesty in Council is satisfied that the law of a self-governing dominion to which this Act does not extend provides adequate protection within the dominion for the works (whether published or unpublished) of authors who at the time of the making of the work were British subjects resident elsewhere than in that dominion, His Majesty in Council may, for the purpose of giving reciprocal protection, direct that this Act, except such parts (if any) thereof as may be specified in the Order, and subject to any conditions contained therein, shall, within the parts of His Majesty's dominions to which this Act extends, apply to works the authors whereof were, at the time of the making of the work, resident within the first-mentioned dominion, and to works first published in that dominion; but, save as provided by such an Order, works the authors whereof were resident in a dominion to which this Act does not extend shall not, whether they are British subjects or not, be entitled to any protection under this Act except such protection as is by this Act conferred on works first published within the parts of His Majesty's dominions to which this Act extends:

Provided that no such Order shall confer any rights within a self-governing dominion, but the Governor in Council of any self-governing dominion to which this Act extends, may, by Order, confer within that dominion the like rights as His Majesty in Council is, under the foregoing provisions of this subsection, authorised to confer within other parts of His Majesty's dominions.

For the purposes of this subsection, the expression "a dominion to which this Act extends" includes a dominion which is for the purposes of this Act to be treated as if it were a dominion to which this Act extends.

Power of Legislatures of British possessions to pass supplemental legislation

A–604   **27.** The Legislature of any British possession to which this Act extends may modify or add to any of the provisions of this Act in its application to the possession, but, except so far as such modifications and additions relate to procedure and remedies, they shall apply only to works the authors whereof were, at the time of the making of the work, resident in the possession, and to works first published in the possession.

Application to protectorates

28. His Majesty may, by Order in Council, extend this Act to any territories **A–605** under his protection and to Cyprus, and, on the making of any such Order, this Act shall, subject to the provisions of the Order, have effect as if the territories to which it applies or Cyprus were part of His Majesty's dominions to which this Act extends.

PART II.—INTERNATIONAL COPYRIGHT

Power to extend Act to foreign works

29.—(1) His Majesty may, by Order in Council, direct that this Act (except **A–606** such parts, if any, thereof as may be specified in the Order) shall apply—

- (*a*) to works first published in a foreign country to which the Order relates, in like manner as if they were first published within the parts of His Majesty's dominions to which this Act extends;
- (*b*) to literary, dramatic, musical, and artistic works, or any class thereof, the authors whereof were at the time of the making of the work subjects or citizens of a foreign country to which the Order relates, in like manner as if the authors were British subjects;
- (*c*) in respect of residence in a foreign country to which the Order relates, in like manner as if such residence were residence in the parts of His Majesty's dominions to which this Act extends;

and thereupon, subject to the provisions of this Part of this Act and of the Order, this Act shall apply accordingly:

Provided that—

- (i) before making an Order in Council under this section in respect of any foreign country (other than a country with which His Majesty has entered into a convention relating to copyright), His Majesty shall be satisfied that that foreign country has made, or has undertaken to make, such provisions, if any, as it appears to His Majesty expedient to require for the protection of works entitled to copyright under the provisions of Part I of this Act;
- (ii) the Order in Council may provide that the term of copyright within such parts of His Majesty's dominions as aforesaid shall not exceed that conferred by the law of the country to which the Order relates;
- (iii) the provisions of this Act as to the delivery of copies of books shall not apply to works first published in such country, except so far as is provided by the Order;
- (iv) the Order in Council may provide that the enjoyment of the rights conferred by this Act shall be subject to the accomplishment of such conditions and formalities (if any) as may be prescribed by the Order;
- (v) in applying the provision of this Act as to ownership of copyright, the Order in Council may make such modifications as appear necessary having regard to the law of the foreign country;
- (vi) in applying the provisions of this Act as to existing works, the Order in Council may make such modifications as appear necessary, and may provide that nothing in those provisions as so applied shall be construed as reviving any right of preventing the production or importation of any translation in any case where the right has ceased by virtue of section five of the International Copyright Act, 1886.

(2) An Order in Council under this section may extend to all the several countries named or described therein.

Application of Part II to British possessions

A–607   **30.**—(1) An Order in Council under this Part of this Act shall apply to all His Majesty's dominions to which this Act extends except self-governing dominions and any other possession specified in the Order with respect to which it appears to His Majesty expedient that the Order should not apply.

(2) The Governor in Council of any self-governing dominion to which this Act extends may, as respects that dominion, make the like orders as under this Part of this Act His Majesty in Council is authorised to make with respect to His Majesty's dominions other than self-governing dominions, and the provisions of this Part of this Act shall, with the necessary modifications, apply accordingly.

(3) Where it appears to His Majesty expedient to except from the provisions of any Order any part of his dominions not being a self-governing dominion, it shall be lawful for His Majesty by the same or any other Order in Council to declare that such Order and this Part of this Act shall not, and the same shall not, apply to such part, except so far as is necessary for preventing any prejudice to any rights acquired previously to the date of such Order.

PART III.—SUPPLEMENTAL PROVISIONS

Abrogation of common law rights

A–608   **31.** No person shall be entitled to copyright or any similar right in any literary, dramatic, musical, or artistic work, whether published or unpublished, otherwise than under and in accordance with the provisions of this Act, or of any other statutory enactment for the time being in force, but nothing in this section shall be construed as abrogating any right or jurisdiction to restrain a breach of trust or confidence.

Provisions as to Orders in Council

A–609   **32.**—(1) His Majesty in Council may make Orders for altering, revoking, or varying any Order in Council made under this Act, or under any enactments repealed by this Act, but any Order made under this section shall not affect prejudicially any rights or interests acquired or accrued at the date when the Order comes into operation, and shall provide for the protection of such rights and interests.

(2) Every Order in Council made under this Act shall be published in the *London Gazette* and shall be laid before both Houses of Parliament as soon as may be after it is made, and shall have effect as if enacted in this Act.

Saving of university copyright

A–610   **33.** Nothing in this Act shall deprive any of the universities and colleges mentioned in the Copyright Act, 1775, of any copyright they already possess under the Act, but the remedies and penalties for infringement of any such copyright shall be under this Act and not under that Act.

Saving of compensation to certain libraries

A–611   **34.** There shall continue to be charged on, and paid out of, the Consolidated Fund of the United Kingdom such annual compensation as was immediately before the commencement of this Act payable in pursuance of any Act as compensation to a library for the loss of the right to receive gratuitous copies of books:

Provided that this compensation shall not be paid to a library in any year, unless the Treasury are satisfied that the compensation for the previous year has been applied in the purchase of books for the use of and to be preserved in the library.

OPERATION

This section was not repealed by the 1956 Act, but was repealed by the Statute Law (Repeals) Act 1986 (c. 12).

Interpretation

35.—(1) In this Act, unless the context otherwise requires— **A–612**

"Literary work" includes maps, charts, plans, tables, and compilations;

"Dramatic work" includes any piece for recitation, choreographic work or entertainment in dumb show, the scenic arrangement or acting form of which is fixed in writing or otherwise, and any cinemtatograph production where the arrangement or acting form or the combination of incidents represented give the work an original character;

"Artistic work" includes works of painting, drawing, sculpture and artistic craftsmanship, and architectural works of art and engravings and photographs;

"Work of sculpture" includes casts and models;

"Architectural work of art" means any building or structure having an artistic character or design, in respect of such character or design, or any model for such building or structure, provided that the protection afforded by this Act shall be confined to the artistic character and design, and shall not extend to processes or methods of construction;

"Engravings" include etchings, lithographs, wood-cuts, prints, and other similar works, not being photographs;

"Photograph" includes photo-lithograph and any work produced by any process analogous to photography;

"Cinematograph" includes any work produced by any process analogous to cinematography;

"Collective work" means—
    (a) an encyclopaedia, dictionary, year book, or similar work;
    (b) a newspaper, review, magazine, or similar periodical; and
    (c) any work written in distinct parts by different authors, or in which works or parts of works of different authors are incorporated;

"Infringing", when applied to a copy of a work in which copyright subsists, means any copy, including any colourable imitation, made, or imported in contravention of the provisions of this Act;

"Performance" means any acoustic representation of a work and any visual representation of any dramatic action in a work, including such a representation made by means of any mechanical instrument;

"Delivery", in relation to a lecture, includes delivery by means of any mechanical instrument;

"Plate" includes any stereotype or other plate, stone, block, mould, matrix, transfer, or negative used or intended to be used for printing or reproducing copies of any work, and any matrix or other appliance by which records, perforated rolls or other contrivances for the acoustic representation of the work are or are intended to be made;

"Lecture" includes address, speech, and sermon;

"Self-governing dominion" means the Dominion of Canada, the Commonwealth of Australia, the Dominion of New Zealand, the Union of South Africa, and Newfoundland.

(2) For the purposes of this Act (other than those relating to infringements of copyright), a work shall not be deemed to be published or performed in public, and a lecture shall not be deemed to be delivered in public, if published, performed in public, or delivered in public, without the consent or acquiescence of the author, his executors administrators or assigns.

(3) For the purposes of this Act, a work shall be deemed to be first published within the parts of His Majesty's dominions to which this Act extends, notwithstanding that it has been published simultaneously in some other place, unless the publication in such parts of His Majesty's dominions as aforesaid is colourable only and is not intended to satisfy the reasonable requirements of the public, and a work shall be deemed to be published simultaneously in two places if the time between the publication in one such place and the publication in the other place does not exceed fourteen days, or such longer period as may, for the time being, be fixed by Order in Council.

(4) Where, in the case of an unpublished work, the making of a work has extended over a considerable period, the conditions of this Act conferring copyright shall be deemed to have been complied with, if the author was, during any substantial part of that period, a British subject or a resident within the parts of His Majesty's dominions to which this Act extends.

(5) For the purposes of the provisions of this Act as to residence, an author of a work shall be deemed to be a resident in the parts of His Majesty's dominions to which this Act extends if he is domiciled within any such part.

Repeal

A–613 **36.** Subject to the provisions of this Act, the enactments mentioned in the Second Schedule to this Act are hereby repealed to the extent specified in the third column of that schedule:

Provided that this repeal shall not take effect in any part of His Majesty's dominions until this Act comes into operation in that part.

Short title and commencement

A–614 **37.**—(1) This Act may be cited as the Copyright Act, 1911.

(2) This Act shall come into operation—

   (*a*) in the United Kingdom, on the first day of July nineteen hundred and twelve or such earlier date as may be fixed by Order in Council;

   (*b*) in a self-governing dominion to which this Act extends, at such date as may be fixed by the Legislature of that dominion;

   (*c*) in the Channel Islands, at such date as may be fixed by the States of those islands respectively;

   (*d*) in any other British possession to which this Act extends, on the proclamation thereof within the possession by the Governor.

OPERATION

This section was not repealed by the 1956 Act, but subsection (2) thereof was repealed by the Statute Law (Repeals) Act 1986 (c. 12).

SCHEDULES

FIRST SCHEDULE

EXISTING RIGHTS

Existing Right	Substituted Right
(a) In the case of Works other than Dramatic and Musical Works.	
Copyright	Copyright as defined by this Act.*
(b) In the case of Musical and Dramatic Works.	
Both copyright and performing right	Copyright as defined by this Act.*
Copyright, but not performing right	Copyright as defined by this Act, except the sole right to perform the work or any substantial part thereof in public.
Performing right, but not copyright	The sole right to perform the work in public, but none of the other rights comprised in copyright as defined by this Act.

For the purposes of this Schedule, the following expressions, where used in the first column thereof, have the following meanings:

"Copyright", in the case of a work which according to the law in force immediately before the commencement of this Act has not been published before that date and statutory copyright wherein depends on publication, includes the right at common law (if any) to restrain publication or other dealing with the work;

*In the case of an essay, article, or portion forming part of and first published in a review, magazine, or other periodical or work of a like nature, the right shall be subject to any right of publishing the essay, article, or portion in a separate form to which the author is entitled at the commencement of this Act, or would, if this Act had not been passed, have become entitled under section eighteen of the Copyright Act, 1842.

"Performing right", in the case of a work which has not been performed in public before the commencement of this Act, includes the right at common law (if any) to restrain the performance thereof in public.

Section 36.   SECOND SCHEDULE   **A–616**

ENACTMENTS REPEALED

Session and Chapter	Short Title	Extent of Repeal
8 Geo. 2. c. 13.	The Engraving Copyright Act, 1734.	The whole Act.
7 Geo. 3. c. 38.	The Engraving Copyright Act, 1767.	The whole Act.
15 Geo. 3. c. 53.	The Copyright Act, 1775.	The whole Act.
17 Geo. 3. c. 57.	The Prints Copyright Act, 1777.	The whole Act.
54 Geo. 3. c. 56.	The Sculpture Copyright Act, 1814.	The whole Act.
3 & 4 Will. 4. c. 15.	The Dramatic Copyright Act, 1833.	The whole Act.

Session and Chapter	Short Title	Extent of Repeal
5 & 6 Will. 4. c. 65.	The Lectures Copyright Act, 1835.	The whole Act.
6 & 7 Will. 4. c. 59.	The Prints and Engravings Copyright (Ireland) Act, 1836.	The whole Act.
6 & 7 Will. 4. c. 110.	The Copyright Act, 1836.	The whole Act.
5 & 6 Vict. c. 45.	The Copyright Act, 1842	The whole Act.
7 & 8 Vict. c. 12.	The International Copyright Act, 1844.	The whole Act.
10 & 11 Vict. c. 95.	The Colonial Copyright Act, 1847.	The whole Act.
15 & 16 Vict. c. 12.	The International Copyright Act, 1852.	The whole Act.
25 & 26 Vict. c. 68.	The Fine Arts Copyright Act, 1862.	Sections one to six. In section eight the words "and pursuant to any Act for the protection of copyright engravings," and "and in any such Act as aforesaid." Sections nine to twelve.
38 & 39 Vict. c. 12.	The International Copyright Act, 1875.	The whole Act.
39 & 40 Vict. c. 36.	The Customs Consolidation Act, 1876.	Section forty-two, from "Books wherein" to "such copyright will expire." Sections forty-four, forty-five, and one hundred and fifty-two.
45 & 46 Vict. c. 40.	The Copyright (Musical Compositions) Act, 1882.	The whole Act.
49 & 50 Vict. c. 33.	The International Copyright Act, 1886.	The whole Act.
51 & 52 Vict. c. 17.	The Copyright (Musical Compositions) Act, 1888.	The whole Act.
52 & 53 Vict. c. 42.	The Revenue Act, 1889.	Section one, from "Books first published" to "as provided in that section."
6 Edw. 7. c. 36.	The Musical Copyright Act, 1906.	In section three the words "and which has been registered in accordance with the provisions of the Copyright Act, 1842, or of the International Copyright Act, 1844, which registration may be effected notwithstanding anything in the International Copyright Act, 1886."

PART IV

Interpretation Act, 1889

(52 & 53 Vict. c. 63)

Effect of repeal in future Acts

38.—(1) Where this Act or any Act passed after the commencement of this Act **A–617**
repeals and re-enacts, with or without modification, any provisions of a former
Act, references in any other Act to the provisions so repealed, shall, unless the contrary intention appears, be construed as references to the provisions so re-enacted.

(2) Where this Act or any Act passed after the commencement of this Act
repeals any other enactment, then, unless the contrary intention appears, the
repeal shall not—

  (*a*) revive anything not in force or existing at the time at which the repeal takes
    effect; or
  (*b*) affect the previous operation of any enactment so repealed or anything duly
    done or suffered under any enactment so repealed; or
  (*c*) affect any right, privilege, obligation, or liability acquired, accrued, or
    incurred under any enactment so repealed; or
  (*d*) affect any penalty, forfeiture, or punishment incurred in respect of any
    offence committed against any enactment so repealed; or
  (*e*) affect any investigation, legal proceeding, or remedy in respect of any such
    right, privilege, obligation, liability, penalty, forfeiture, or punishment as
    aforesaid;

and any such investigation, legal proceeding, or remedy may be instituted, continued, or enforced, and any such penalty, forfeiture, or punishment may be
imposed, as if the repealing Act had not been passed.

REPEAL

Virtually the whole of the Interpretation Act, 1889, was repealed by the Interpretation
Act, 1978 (c. 30), which came into force on January 1, 1979 (see s.25 and Sched. 3). See now
sections 16 and 17 of the 1978 Act *post* §§ A–645 and A–646.

* * *

British Museum Act, 1932

(22 & 23 Geo. 5, c. 34)

An Act to enable the Trustees of the British Museum to except certain publications from the provisions of subsection (1) of section 15 of the Copyright Act,
1911. [12th July, 1932.]

Power of Trustees to except certain publications from s.15(1) of 1 & 2 Geo. 5, c. 46

1.—(1) Notwithstanding anything in subsection (1) of section fifteen of the **A–618**
Copyright Act, 1911, the publisher of any publication of a class to which this Act
for the time being applies shall not be required to deliver a copy of the publication
to the Trustees of the British Museum (hereafter in this Act referred to as "the
Trustees") unless a written demand for the delivery thereof is made by the

Trustees; and the Trustees shall not be required to accept or give a receipt for a copy of any publication which is not required to be delivered to them.

(2) The Trustees may by regulations—

(*a*) apply this Act to publications of such classes as may be specified in the regulations, being publications of all or any of the descriptions set out in the Schedule to this Act;

(*b*) except any particular publication from any class of publication to which this Act is applied by the regulations, or to which this Act has been applied by previous regulations.

(3) All regulations made under this Act shall be laid before each House of Parliament as soon as may be after they are made, and if either House, within the next subsequent twenty-eight days on which that House has sat after the regulations are laid before it, resolves that the regulations be annulled, the regulations shall thenceforth be void, but without prejudice to anything previously done thereunder or to the making of any new regulations.

Short title and repeal

A–619   **2.**—(1) This Act may be cited as the British Museum Act, 1932.

(2) The Copyright (British Museum) Act, 1915 (which empowers the Board of Trade on the application of the Trustees to except publications wholly or mainly in the nature of trade advertisements from the provisions of subsection (1) of section fifteen of the Copyright Act, 1911), is hereby repealed:

Provided that, notwithstanding the repeal of that Act, any regulations made thereunder shall continue in force and shall have effect as if they had been made by the Trustees under this Act and as if this Act were thereby applied to publications of the descriptions therein specified.

SCHEDULE

Publications to which Act May Be Applied

A–620   Publications wholly or mainly in the nature of trade advertisements.

Registers of voters prepared under the Representation of the People Act, 1918, as amended by any subsequent enactment.

Specifications of inventions prepared for the purposes of the Patents and Designs Act, 1907, as amended by any subsequent enactment.

Publications wholly or mainly in the nature of time tables of passenger transport services, being publications prepared for local use.

Publications wholly or mainly in the nature of calendars.

Publications wholly or mainly in the nature of blank forms of accounts, or blank forms of receipts, or other blank forms of a similar character.

Wall sheets printed with alphabets, mottoes, religious texts or other matter for the purpose of elementary instruction.

Amendment

Section 4 of the British Library Act, 1972 (c. 54), provides that all references in section 1(1) of the 1932 Act to the Trustees of the British Museum are to be references to the British Library Board instead. Also that the power under section 1(2) of the 1932 Act to make regulations shall instead of being exercised by the Trustees, be exercisable by the Board.

*   *   *

Limitation Act, 1939

(2 & 3 Geo. 6, c. 21)

Actions of contract and tort and certain other actions

Limitation of actions of contract and tort, and certain other actions

2.—(1) The following actions shall not be brought after the expiration of six **A–621**
years from the date on which the cause of action accrued, that is to say:
 (*a*) actions founded on simple contract or on tort;

*   *   *

(2) An action for an account shall not be brought in respect of any matter which
arose more than six years before the commencement of the action.

*   *   *

(7) This section shall not apply to any claim for specific performance of a contract or for an injunction or for other equitable relief, except in so far as any provision thereof may be applied by the Court by analogy in like manner as the
corresponding enactment repealed by this Act has heretofore been applied.

Limitation in case of successive conversions and extinction of title of owner of converted goods

3.—(1) Where any cause of action in respect of the conversion or wrongful **A–622**
detention of a chattel has accrued to any person and, before he recovers possession
of the chattel, a further conversion or wrongful detention takes place, no action
shall be brought in respect of the further conversion or detention after the expiration of six years from the accrual of the cause of action in respect of the original
conversion or detention.

(2) Where any such cause of action has accrued to any person and the period
prescribed for bringing that action and for bringing any action in respect of such a
further conversion or wrongful detention as aforesaid has expired and he has not
during that period recovered possession of the chattel, the title of that person to the
chattel shall be extinguished.

REPEAL

 The Limitation Act 1939 was repealed by the Limitation Act 1980 (c. 58): see *post* § A–653
et seq.

*   *   *

Wireless Telegraphy Act, 1949

(12, 13 & 14 Geo. 6, c. 54)

Interpretation

19.—(1) In this Act, except where the context otherwise requires, the **A–623**
expression "wireless telegraphy" means the emitting or receiving, over paths
which are not provided by any material substance constructed or arranged for that
purpose, of electro-magnetic energy of a frequency not exceeding three million
megacycles a second, being energy which either—
 (*a*) serves for the conveying of messages, sound or visual images (whether the
    messages, sound or images are actually received by any person or not), or
    for the actuation or control of machinery or apparatus; or

(*b*) is used in connection with the determination of position, bearing or distance, or for the gaining of information as to the presence, absence, position or motion of any object or of any objects of any class,

and references to stations for wireless telegraphy and apparatus for wireless telegraphy or wireless telegraphy apparatus shall be construed as references to stations and apparatus for the emitting or receiving as aforesaid of such electromagnetic energy as aforesaid.

*   *   *

A–624   **Dramatic and Musical Performers' Protection Act, 1958**[10]

(6 & 7 Eliz. 2, c. 44)

An Act to consolidate the Dramatic and Musical Performers' Protection Act, 1925, and the provisions of the Copyright Act, 1956, amending it.

[23rd July 1958]

Penalization of making, etc., records without consent of performers

A–625   **1.** Subject to the provisions of this Act, if a person knowingly—

(*a*) makes a record, directly or indirectly from or by means of the performance of a dramatic or musical work without the consent in writing of the performers, or

(*b*) sells or lets for hire, or distributes for the purposes of trade, or by way of trade exposes or offers for sale or hire, a record made in contravention of this Act, or

(*c*) uses for the purposes of a public performance a record so made,

he shall be guilty of an offence under this Act, and shall be liable, on summary conviction, to a fine not exceeding forty shillings for each record in respect of which an offence is proved, but not exceeding fifty pounds in respect of any one transaction:

Provided that, where a person is charged with an offence under paragraph (*a*) of this section, it shall be a defence to prove that the record was made for his private and domestic use only.

Penalization of making, etc., cinematograph films without consent of performers

A–626   **2.** Subject to the provisions of this Act, if a person knowingly—

(*a*) makes a cinematograph film, directly or indirectly, from or by means of the performance of a dramatic or musical work without the consent in writing of the performers, or

(*b*) sells or lets for hire, or distributes for the purposes of trade, or by way of trade exposes or offers for sale or hire, a cinematograph film made in contravention of this Act, or

(*c*) uses for the purposes of exhibition to the public a cinematograph film so made;

he shall be guilty of an offence under this Act, and shall be liable, on summary conviction, to a fine not exceeding fifty pounds:

Provided that, where a person is charged with an offence under paragraph (*a*) of this section, it shall be a defence to prove that the cinematograph film was made for his private and domestic use only.

---

[10] This Act, and the Performers' Protection Act, 1963 and the Performers' Protection Act, 1972 were repealed by the 1988 Act, *ante* as from August 1, 1989.

Penalization of broadcasting without consent of performers

3. Subject to the provisions of this Act, a person who, otherwise than by the use **A–627** of a record or cinematograph film, knowingly broadcasts a performance of a dramatic or musical work, or any part of such a performance, without the consent in writing of the performers, shall be guilty of an offence under this Act, and shall be liable, on summary conviction, to a fine not exceeding fifty pounds.

Penalization of making or having plates, etc., for making records in contravention of Act

4. If a person makes, or has in his possession, a plate or similar contrivance for **A–628** the purpose of making records in contravention of this Act, he shall be guilty of an offence under this Act, and shall be liable, on summary conviction, to a fine not exceeding fifty pounds for each plate or similar contrivance in respect of which an offence is proved.

Power of court to order destruction of records, etc., contravening Act

5. The court before which any proceedings are taken under this Act may, on **A–629** conviction of the offender, order that all records, cinematograph films, plates or similar contrivances in the possession of the offender which appear to the court to have been made in contravention of this Act, or to be adapted for the making of records in contravention of this Act, and in respect of which the offender has been convicted, be destroyed, or otherwise dealt with as the court may think fit.

Special defences

6. Notwithstanding anything in the preceding provisions of this Act, it shall be a **A–630** defence to any proceedings under this Act to prove—
- (*a*) that the record, cinematograph film or broadcast to which the proceedings relate was made only for the purpose of reporting current events, or
- (*b*) that the inclusion of the performance in question in the record, cinematograph film or broadcast to which the proceedings relate was only by way of background or was otherwise only incidental to the principal matters comprised or represented in the record, film or broadcast.

Consent on behalf of performers

7. Where in any proceedings under this Act it is proved— **A–631**
- (*a*) that the record, cinematograph film or broadcast to which the proceedings relate was made with the consent in writing of a person who, at the time of giving the consent, represented that he was authorised by the performers to give it on their behalf, and
- (*b*) that the person making the record, film or broadcast had no reasonable grounds for believing that the person giving the consent was not so authorised,

the provisions of this Act shall apply as if it had been proved that the performers had themselves consented in writing to the making of the record, film or broadcast.

Interpretation

8.—(1) In this Act, unless the context otherwise requires, the following **A–632** expressions have the meanings hereby respectively assigned to them, that is to say,—

"broadcast" means broadcast by wireless telegraphy (within the meaning of the Wireless Telegraphy Act, 1949), whether by way of sound broadcasting or of television;

["cable programme" means a programme included in a cable programme service, and references to the inclusion of a cable programme shall be construed accordingly;

"cable programme service" means a cable programme service within the meaning of the Cable and Broadcasting Act 1984 or a service provided outside the United Kingdom which would be such a service if subsection (7) of section 2 of that Act and references in subsection (1) of that section to the United Kingdom were omitted;]

"cinematograph film" means any print, negative, tape or other article on which a performance of a dramatic or musical work or part thereof is recorded for the purposes of visual reproduction;

"performance of a dramatic or musical work" includes any performance, mechanical or otherwise, of any such work, being a performance rendered or intended to be rendered audible by mechanical or electrical means;

"performers", in the case of a mechanical performance, means the persons whose performance is mechanically reproduced;

["programme", in relation to a cable programme service, includes any item included in that service;]

"record" means any record or similar contrivance for reproducing sound, including the sound-track of a cinematograph film.

(2) Any reference in this Act to the making of a cinematograph film is a reference to the carrying out of any process whereby a performance of a dramatic or musical work or part thereof is recorded for the purposes of visual reproduction.

[(3) Section 48(3) of the Copyright Act 1956 (which explains the meaning of references in that Act to the inclusion of a programme in a cable programme service) shall apply for the purposes of this Act as it applies for the purposes of that Act.]

Short title, extent, repeal and commencement

A–633   **9.**—(1) This Act may be cited as the Dramatic and Musical Performers' Protection Act, 1958.

(2) It is hereby declared that this Act extends to Northern Ireland.

[(3) The Dramatic and Musical Performers' Protection Act, 1925, and section forty-five of, and the Sixth Schedule to, the Copyright Act, 1956, are hereby repealed.]

(4) This Act shall come into operation at the expiration of a period of one month beginning with the date of its passing.

AMENDMENT

The 1958 Act was amended by the Cable and Broadcasting Act, 1984 (c. 46). It is printed as amended save as to sections 6 and 7, as to which see Amendments § A–639 *post*.

REPEAL

Subsection (3) of section 9 was repealed by the Statute Law (Repeals) Act, 1974 c. 22.

* * *

A–634   ### Performer's Protection Act, 1963

(c. 53)

An Act to amend the law relating to the protection of performers so as to enable effect to be given to a Convention entered into at Rome on 26th October 1961.

[31st July 1963]

Performances to which principal Act[11] applies

1.—(1) The principal Act shall have effect as if for references therein to the per- **A–635**
formance of a dramatic or musical work there were substituted references to the
performance of any actors, singers, musicians, dancers or other persons who act,
sing, deliver, declaim, play in or otherwise perform literary, dramatic, musical or
artistic works, and the definition contained in section 8(1) of that Act of the
expression "performance of a dramatic or musical work" (by which that
expression is made to include a performance rendered or intended to be rendered
audible by mechanical or electrical means) shall be construed accordingly.

(2) For the avoidance of doubt it is hereby declared that the principal Act
applies as respects anything done in relation to a performance notwithstanding
that the performance took place out of the United Kingdom, but this shall not
cause anything done out of the United Kingdom to be treated as an offence.

Sales, etc., of records made abroad

2. For the purposes of paragraphs (*b*) and (*c*) of section 1 of the principal Act (by **A–636**
which sales of, and other dealings with, records made in contravention of the Act
are rendered punishable), a record made in a country outside the United Kingdom directly or indirectly from or by means of a performance to which the principal Act applies shall, where the civil or criminal law of that country contains a
provision for the protection of performers under which the consent of any person to
the making of the record was required, be deemed to have been made in contravention of the principal Act if, whether knowingly or not, it was made without the
consent so required and without the consent in writing of the performers.

Relaying of performances

3.—(1) A person who, otherwise than by the use of a record or cinematograph **A–637**
film or the reception [and immediate re-transmission] of a broadcast, knowingly
[includes a performance to which the principal Act applies, or any part of such
performance, in a cable programme without the consent in writing of the performers,] shall be guilty of an offence, and shall be liable, on summary conviction,
to a fine not exceeding fifty pounds.

* * *

(3) Section 6 of the principal Act (which provides for special defences) shall
have effect as if the preceding subsections were inserted immediately before that
section, and that section and section 7 of the principal Act (which provides for the
giving of consent on behalf of performers) shall have effect as if for the words "or
broadcast" in each place where they occur there were substituted the words
"broadcast or transmission".

Giving of consent without authority

4.—(1) Where— **A–638**
    (*a*) a record, cinematograph film, [or broadcast is made or a cable programme
        is included] with the consent in writing of a person who, at the time of giv-
        ing the consent, represented that he was authorised by the performers to
        give it on their behalf when to his knowledge he was not so authorised, and
    (*b*) if proceedings were brought against the person to whom the consent was
        given, the consent would by virtue of section 7 of the principal Act afford a
        defence to those proceedings,

---

[11] The Preamble to the 1963 Act defines the Dramatic and Musical Performers' Protection
Act, 1958 (6 & 7 Eliz. 2, c. 44), for the purposes of the 1963 Act, as "the principal Act".

the person giving the consent shall be guilty of an offence, and shall be liable, on summary conviction, to a fine not exceeding fifty pounds.

(2) The said section 7 shall not apply to proceedings under this section.

Citation, construction, commencement and extent

A–639   **5.**—(1) This Act may be cited as the Performers' Protection Act, 1963, and the principal Act and this Act may be cited together as the Performers' Protection Acts, 1958 and 1963.

(2) This Act shall be construed as one with the principal Act.

(3) This Act shall come into operation at the expiration of the period of one month beginning with the date of its passing, and shall apply only in relation to performances taking place after its commencement.

(4) It is hereby declared that this Act extends to Northern Ireland.

AMENDMENTS

(1) The 1963 Act was amended by the Cable and Broadcasting Act, 1984 (c. 46) and is printed as amended.

(2) The 1984 Act also amended sections 6 and 7 of the Dramatic and Musical Performers' Protection Act, 1958 para. A–624 *ante*: see s.3, 1963 Act *supra*. The amendments were as follows. In section 6, for the word "transmission," in each place where it occurs, the words "cable programme" substituted and after the word "made" the words "or included" inserted. In section 7, for the word "transmission", in each place where it occurs, the words "cable programme" substituted, after the word "made" the words "or included" inserted and after the word "making," in both places where it occurs, the words "or including" inserted.

* * *

Performers' Protection Act, 1972

(c. 32)

An Act to amend the Performers' Protection Acts 1958 and 1963.

[29th June, 1972]

Increase of fines under Performers' Protection Acts, 1958 and 1963

A–640   **1.** The enactments specified in column 1 of the Schedule to this Act (being enactments creating the offences under the Performers' Protection Acts 1958 and 1963 broadly described in column 2 of that Schedule) shall each have effect as if the maximum fine which may be imposed on summary conviction of any offence specified in that enactment were a fine not exceeding the amount specified in column 4 of that Schedule instead of a fine not exceeding the amount specified in column 3 of that Schedule.

Amendment of section 1 of Dramatic and Musical Performers' Protection Act, 1958

A–641   **2.** Section 1 of the Dramatic and Musical Performers' Protection Act 1958 (by which the making of records without the consent of the performers and sales of, and other dealings with, such records are rendered punishable) shall have effect as if after the word "transaction" there were inserted the words "or, on conviction on indictment, to imprisonment for a term not exceeding two years, or to a fine, or to both."

Amendment of Performers' Protection Act, 1963

3. In the Performers' Protection Act, 1963, there shall be inserted after section 4   **A–642** the following section:

"Offences by bodies corporate.

4A. Where an offence under the principal Act or this Act committed by a body corporate is proved to have been committed with the consent or connivance of, or to be attributable to any neglect on the part of, any director, manager, secretary or other similar officer of the body corporate or any person who was purporting to act in any such capacity, he, as well as the body corporate, shall be guilty of that offence and shall be liable to be proceeded against and punished accordingly."

Citation, construction, commencement and extent

4.—(1) This Act may be cited as the Performers' Protection Act, 1972, and the   **A–643** Performers' Protection Acts, 1958 and 1963 and this Act may be cited together as the Performers' Protection Acts, 1958 to 1972.

(2) This Act shall come into operation at the expiration of the period of one month beginning with the date of its passing, but nothing in this Act shall affect the punishment for an offence committed before the commencement of this Act.

(3) It is hereby declared that this Act extends to Northern Ireland.

Section 1.   SCHEDULE   **A–644**

INCREASE OF FINES

(1) Enactment	(2) Description of Offence	(3) Old Maximum Fine	(4) New Maximum Fine
The Dramatic and Musical Performers' Protection Act 1958— Section 1	Making, etc., records without consent of performers.	£2 for each record in respect of which an offence is proved subject to a limit of £50 in respect of any one transaction.	£20 for each record in respect of which an offence is proved subject to a limit of £400 in respect of any one transaction.
Section 2	Making, etc., cinematograph films without consent of performers.	£50	£400
Section 3	Broadcasting without consent of performers.	£50	£400

(1) Enactment	(2) Description of Offence	(3) Old Maximum Fine	(4) New Maximum Fine
Section 4	Making or having plates, etc., for making records in contravention of Act.	£50	£400
The Performers' Protection Act 1963—			
Section 3(1) ..	Relaying performances without consent of performers.	£50	£400
Section 4(1) ..	Giving consent without authority.	£50	£400

* * *

Interpretation Act 1978[12]

(c. 30)

General savings

16.—(1) Without prejudice to section 15, where an Act repeals an enactment, the repeal does not, unless the contrary intention appears—

- (a) revive anything not in force or existing at the time at which the repeal takes effect;
- (b) affect the previous operation of the enactment repealed or anything duly done or suffered under that enactment;
- (c) affect any right, privilege, obligation or liability acquired, accrued or incurred under that enactment;
- (d) affect any penalty, forfeiture or punishment incurred in respect of any offence committed against that enactment;
- (e) affect any investigation, legal proceeding or remedy in respect of any such right, privilege, obligation, liability, penalty, forfeiture or punishment;

and any such investigation, legal proceedings or remedy may be instituted, continued or enforced, and any such penalty, forfeiture or punishment may be imposed, as if the repealing Act had not been passed.

(2) This section applies to the expiry of a temporary enactment as if it were repealed by an Act.

Repeal and re-enactment

17.—(1) Where an Act repeals a previous enactment and substitutes provisions for the enactment repealed, the repealed enactment remains in force until the substituted provisions come into force.

---

[12] This Act applies to itself, to any Act passed after the commencement of that Act, and, to the extent specified in Pt. I of Sched. 2 thereto, to Acts passed before the commencement of that Act; s.22.

(2) Where an Act repeals and re-enacts, with or without modification, a previous enactment then, unless the contrary intention appears,—

(*a*) any reference in any other enactment to the enactment so repealed shall be construed as a reference to the provision re-enacted;

(*b*) in so far as any subordinate legislation made or other thing done under the enactment so repealed, or having effect as if so made or done, could have been made or done under the provision re-enacted, it shall have effect as if made or done under that provision.

* * *

Public Lending Right Act 1979

(c. 10)

An Act to provide public lending right for authors, and for connected purposes.
[22nd March, 1979]

Establishment of public lending right

1.—(1) In accordance with a scheme to be prepared and brought into force by the Secretary of State, there shall be conferred on authors a right, known as "public lending right", to receive from time to time out of a Central Fund payments in respect of such of their books as are lent out to the public by local library authorities in the United Kingdom. **A–647**

(2) The classes, descriptions and categories of books in respect of which public lending right subsists, and the scales of payments to be made from the Central Fund in respect of it, shall be determined by or in accordance with the scheme; and in preparing the scheme the Secretary of State shall consult with representatives of authors and library authorities and of others who appear to be likely to be affected by it.

(3) The Secretary of State shall appoint an officer to be known as the Registrar of Public Lending Right; and the Schedule to this Act has effect with respect to the Registrar.

(4) The Registrar shall be charged with the duty of establishing and maintaining in accordance with the scheme a register showing the books in respect of which public lending right subsists and the persons entitled to the right in respect of any registered book.

(5) The Registrar shall, in the case of any registered book determine in accordance with the scheme the sums (if any) due by way of public lending right; and any sum so determined to be due shall be recoverable from the Registrar as a debt due to the person for the time being entitled to that right in respect of the book.

(6) Subject to any provision made by the scheme, the duration of public lending right in respect of a book shall be from the date of the book's first publication (or, if later, the beginning of the year in which application is made for it to be registered) until 50 years have elapsed since the end of the year in which the author died.

(7) Provision shall be made by the scheme for the right—

(*a*) to be established by registration;

(*b*) to be transmissible by assignment or assignation, by testamentary disposition or by operation of law, as personal or moveable property;

(*c*) to be claimed by or on behalf of the person for the time being entitled;

(*d*) to be renounced (either in whole or in part, and either temporarily or for all time) on notice being given to the Registrar to that effect.

The Central Fund

A–648   2.—(1) The Central Fund shall be constituted by the Secretary of State and placed under the control and management of the Registrar.

(2) There shall be paid into the Fund from time to time such sums, out of money provided by Parliament, as the Secretary of State with Treasury approval determines to be required for the purpose of satisfying the liabilities of the Fund; but in respect of the liabilities of any one financial year of the Fund the total of those sums shall not exceed £2 million less the total of any sums paid in that year, out of money so provided, under paragraph 2 of the Schedule to this Act (pay, pension, etc. of Registrar).

(3) With the consent of the Treasury, the Secretary of State may from time to time by order in a statutory instrument increase the limit on the sums to be paid under subsection (2) above in respect of financial years beginning after that in which the order is made; but no such order shall be made unless a draft of it has been laid before the House of Commons and approved by a resolution of that House.

(4) There shall be paid out of the Central Fund—

(a) such sums as may in accordance with the scheme be due from time to time in respect of public lending right; and

(b) the administrative expenses of the Registrar and any other expenses and outgoings mentioned in this Act which are expressed to be payable from the Fund.

(5) Money received by the Registrar in respect of property disposed of, or otherwise in the course of his functions, or under this Act, shall be paid into the Central Fund, except in such cases as the Secretary of State otherwise directs with the approval of the Treasury; and in any such case the money shall be paid into the Consolidated Fund.

(6) The Registrar shall keep proper accounts and other records and shall prepare in respect of each financial year of the Fund statements of account in such form as the Secretary of State may direct with Treasury approval; and those statements shall, on or before 31st August next following the end of that year, be transmitted to the Comptroller and Auditor General, who shall examine and certify the statements and lay copies thereof, together with his report thereon, before each House of Parliament.

The scheme and its administration

A–649   3.—(1) As soon as may be after this Act comes into force, the Secretary of State shall prepare the draft of a scheme for its purposes and lay a copy of the draft before each House of Parliament.

(2) If the draft scheme is approved by a resolution of each House, the Secretary of State shall bring the scheme into force (in the form of the draft) by means of an order in a statutory instrument, to be laid before Parliament after it is made; and the order may provide for different provisions of the scheme to come into force on different dates.

(3) The scheme shall be so framed as to make entitlement to public lending right dependent on, and its extent ascertainable by reference to, the number of occasions on which books are lent out from particular libraries, to be specified by the scheme or identified in accordance with provision made by it.

(4) For this purpose, "library"—

(a) means any one of a local library authority's collections of books held by them for the purpose of being borrowed by the public; and

(b) includes any such collection which is taken about from place to place.

(5) The scheme may provide for requiring local library authorities—

(a) to give information as and when, and in the form in which, the Registrar may call for it or the Secretary of State may direct, as to loans made by them to the public of books in respect of which public lending right subsists, or of other books; and

(*b*) to arrange for books to be numbered, or otherwise marked or coded, with a view to facilitating the maintenance of the register and the ascertainment and administration of public lending right.

(6) The Registrar shall, by means of payments out of the Central Fund, reimburse to local library authorities any expenditure incurred by them in giving effect to the scheme, the amount of that expenditure being ascertained in accordance with such calculations as the scheme may prescribe.

(7) Subject to the provisions of this Act (and in particular to the foregoing provisions of this section), the scheme may be varied from time to time by the Secretary of State, after such consultation as is mentioned in section 1(2) above, and the variation brought into force by an order in a statutory instrument, subject to annulment in pursuance of a resolution of either House of Parliament; and the variation may comprise such incidental and transitional provisions as the Secretary of State thinks appropriate for the purposes of continuing the scheme as varied.

(8) The Secretary of State shall in each year prepare and lay before each House of Parliament a report on the working of the scheme.

The register

4.—(1) The register shall be kept in such form, and contain such particulars of **A–650** books and their authors, as may be prescribed.

(2) No application for an entry in the register is to be entertained in the case of any book unless it falls within a class, description or category of books prescribed as one in respect of which public lending right subsists.

(3) The scheme shall provide for the register to be conclusive both as to whether public lending right subsists in respect of a particular book and also as to the persons (if any) who are for the time being entitled to the right.

(4) Provision shall be included in the scheme for entries in the register to be made and amended, on application made in the prescribed manner and supported by prescribed particulars (verified as prescribed) so as to indicate, in the case of any book who (if any one) is for the time being entitled to public lending right in respect of it.

(5) The Registrar may direct the removal from the register of every entry relating to a book in whose case no sum has become due by way of public lending right for a period of at least 10 years, but without prejudice to a subsequent application for the entries to be restored to the register.

(6) The Registrar may require the payment of fees, according to prescribed scales and rates, for supplying copies of entries in the register; and a copy of an entry, certified under the hand of the Registrar or an officer of his with authority in that behalf (which authority it shall be unnecessary to prove) shall in all legal proceedings be admissible in evidence as of equal validity with the original.

(7) It shall be an offence for any person, in connection with the entry of any matter whatsoever in the register, to make any statement which he knows to be false in a material particular or recklessly to make any statement which is false in a material particular; and a person who commits an offence under this section shall be liable on summary conviction to a fine of not more than £1,000.

(8) Where an offence under subsection (7) above which has been committed by a body corporate is proved to have been committed with the consent or connivance of, or to be attributable to any neglect on the part of, a director, manager, secretary or other similar officer of the body corporate, or any person who was pur-

porting to act in any such capacity, he (as well as the body corporate) shall be guilty of that offence and be liable to be proceeded against accordingly.

Where the affairs of a body corporate are managed by its members, this subsection applies in relation to the acts and defaults of a member in connection with his functions of management as if he were a director of the body corporate.

Citation, etc.

5.—(1) This Act may be cited as the Public Lending Right Act, 1979.

(2) In this Act any reference to "the scheme" is to the scheme prepared and brought into force by the Secretary of State in accordance with sections 1 and 3 of this Act (including the scheme as varied from time to time under section 3(7); and—

"local library authority" means—

(a) a library authority under the Public Libraries and Museums Act, 1964,[13]

(b) a statutory library authority within the Public Libraries (Scotland) Act, 1955,[14] and

(c) an Education and Library Board within the Education and Libraries (Northern Ireland) Order 1972[15];

"prescribed" means prescribed by the scheme;

"the register" means the register required by section 1(4) to be established and maintained by the Registrar; and

"the Registrar" means the Registrar of Public Lending Right.

(3) This Act comes into force on a day to be appointed by an order made by the Secretary of State in a statutory instrument to be laid before Parliament after it has been made.

(4) This Act extends to Northern Ireland.

Section 1(3). SCHEDULE

THE REGISTRAR OF PUBLIC LENDING RIGHT

1. The Registrar shall hold and vacate office as such in accordance with the terms of his appointment; but he may at any time resign his office by notice in writing addressed to the Secretary of State; and the Secretary of State may at any time remove a person from the office of Registrar on the ground of incapacity or misbehaviour.

2.—(1) There shall be paid to the Registrar out of money provided by Parliament such remuneration and allowances as the Secretary of State may determine with the approval of the Minister for the Civil Service.

(2) In the case of any such holder of the office of Registrar as may be determined by the Secretary of State with that approval, there shall be paid out of money so provided such pension, allowance or gratuity to or in respect of him, or such contributions or payments towards provision of such a pension, allowance or gratuity, as may be so determined.

3. If, when a person ceases to hold office as Registrar, it appears to the Secretary of State that there are special circumstances which make it right that he should receive compensation, there may (with the approval of the Minister for the Civil Service) be paid to him out of the Central Fund a sum by way of compensation of such amount as may be so determined.

4. In House of Commons Disqualification Act 1975,[16] in Part III of Schedule 1 (other dis-

---

[13] c. 75.
[14] c. 27.
[15] S.I. 1972 No. 1263 (N.I. 12).
[16] c. 24.

qualifying offices), the following shall be inserted at the appropriate place in alphabetical order—

"Registrar of Public Lending Right";

and the like insertion shall be made in Part III of Schedule 1 to the Northern Ireland Assembly Disqualification Act 1975.[17]

5.—(1) The Registrar of Public Lending Right shall be by that name a corporation sole, with a corporate seal.

(2) He is not to be regarded as the servant or agent of the Crown.

6. The Documentary Evidence Act 1868[18] shall have effect as if the Registrar were included in the first column of the Schedule to that Act, as if the Registrar and any person authorised to act on his behalf were mentioned in the second column of that Schedule, and as if the regulations referred to in that Act included any documents issued by the Registrar or by any such person.

7.—(1) The Registrar may appoint such assistant registrars and staff as he thinks fit, subject to the approval of the Secretary of State as to their numbers; and their terms and conditions of service, and the remuneration and allowances payable to them, shall be such as the Registrar may determine.

(2) The Registrar may direct, in the case of persons appointed by him under this paragraph—

(*a*) that there be paid to and in respect of them such pensions, allowances and gratuities as he may determine;

(*b*) that payments be made towards the provision for them of such pensions, allowances and gratuities as he may determine; and

(*c*) that schemes be provided and maintained (whether contributory or not) for the payment to and in respect of them of such pensions, allowances and gratuities as he may determine.

(3) Any money required for the payment of remuneration and allowances under this paragraph, and of pensions, allowances and gratuities, and otherwise for the purpose of sub-paragraph (2) above, shall be paid from the Central Fund.

(4) The approval of the Secretary of State and the Minister for the Civil Service shall be required for any directions or determination by the Registrar under this paragraph.

8. Anything authorised or required under this Act (except paragraph 7 of this Schedule), or by or under the scheme, to be done by the Registrar may be done by any assistant registrar or member of the Registrar's staff who is authorised generally or specially in that behalf in writing by the Registrar.

* * *

Limitation Act, 1980

(c. 58)

Actions founded on tort

Time limit for actions founded on tort

2. An action founded on tort shall not be brought after the expiration of six years   **A–653**
from the date on which the cause of action accrued.

---

[17] c. 25.
[18] c. 37.

Time limit in case of successive conversions and extinction of title of owner of converted goods

A–654   **3.**—(1) Where any cause of action in respect of the conversion of a chattel has accrued to any person and, before he recovers possession of the chattel, a further conversion takes place, no action shall be brought in respect of the further conversion after the expiration of six years from the accrual of the cause of action in respect of the original conversion.

(2) Where any such cause of action has acrrued to any person and the period prescribed for bringing that action has expired and he has not during that period recovered possession of the chattel, the title of that person to the chattel shall be extinguished.

* * *

Actions for an account

Time limit in respect of actions for an account

A–655   **23.** An action for an account shall not be brought after the expiration of any time limit under this Act which is applicable to the claim which is the basis of the duty to account.

* * *

Equitable jurisdiction and remedies

A–656   **36.**—(1) The following time limits under this Act, that is to say—
  (*a*) the time limit under section 2 for actions founded on tort;
  (*b*) the time limit under section 5 for actions founded on simple contract;
  (*c*) the time limit under section 7 for actions to enforce awards where the submission is not by an instrument under seal;
  (*d*) the time limit under section 8 for actions on a specialty;
  (*e*) the time limit under section 9 for actions to recover a sum recoverable by virtue of any enactment; and
  (*f*) the time limit under section 24 for actions to enforce a judgment;
shall not apply to any claim for specific performance of a contract or for an injunction or for other equitable relief, except in so far as any such time limit may be applied by the court by analogy in like manner as the corresponding time limit under any enactment repealed by the Limitation Act 1939 was applied before 1st July 1940.

(2) Nothing in this Act shall affect any equitable jurisdiction to refuse relief on the ground of acquiescence or otherwise.

The Public Lending Right Scheme 1982 (Commencement of Variations)   **A–657**
Order 1990

(S.I. 1990 No. 2360)

(S.I. 1990 No. 2360)

Made - - - - - -	*26th November 1990*
Laid before Parliament	*6th December 1990*
Coming into force - - - -	*27th December 1990*

Whereas the Public Lending Right Scheme 1982[19] ("the Scheme") was brought into force on 14th June 1982;

Whereas the Scheme has been varied[20];

And whereas the Lord President of the Council has, after consultation with representatives of authors and library authorities and of others who appear likely to be affected, further varied the Scheme;

Now therefore, the Lord President of the Council, in exercise of the powers conferred by section 3(7) of the Public Lending Right Act 1979[21] and now vested in him, hereby makes the following Order:—

1. This Order may be cited as the Public Lending Right Scheme 1982 (Commencement of Variations) Order 1990.

2. The variations in the Public Lending Right Scheme 1982 which were made on the 26th November 1990 by the Lord President of the Council and are set out in Appendix 1 to this Order shall come into force on 27th December 1990; and accordingly on and after that date that Scheme has effect as set out in Appendix 2 to this Order.

Appendix 1   **A–658**

Variations in the Public Lending Right Scheme 1982 Made by the Lord President of the Council on 26th November 1990[22]

. . . . . .

---

[19] 1982 S.I. No. 719.

[20] By 1983 S.I. No. 480, 1983 S.I. No. 1688, 1984 S.I. No. 1847, 1985 S.I. No. 1581, 1986 S.I. No. 2103, 1987 S.I. No. 1908, 1988 S.I. No. 2070, 1989 S.I. No. 2188 and 1990 S.I. No. 2360. The Scheme as varied up to the 1990 Order was set out in Appendix 2 to the 1990 Order. Article 4(1)(*b*) of the Scheme in the 1990 Order still refers to the 1956 Act, rather than to the 1988 Act. Various printing errors arising on previous occasions have been corrected by the 1990 Order, but such Order itself contains fresh errors. Thus Article 38(2)(*c*) thereof refers to "with the County of Dyfed", "with" presumably in error for "within", and "an" in paragraph 6(*c*) of Part I of Schedule 1 thereof is presumably in error for "and". Also that "or" has been omitted before "of" in Article 14(*a*). All have been printed with the errors corrected.

[21] c. 10.

[22] This Appendix is not included in view of para. 2 of the Order.

A–659   **Public Lending Right Scheme 1982**

Arrangement of Scheme

Part I

Title and Interpretation

Part II

Books and Authors Eligible Under the Scheme

Part III

Registration of Public Lending Right

The Register

Procedure for Registration

First Registration

Subsequent dealings with Public Lending Right

Part IV

Ascertainment of the Number of Loans of Books

Part V

Calculation and Payment of Public Lending Right

SCHEDULES

A–660 ## Public Lending Right Scheme 1982

PART I

TITLE AND INTERPRETATION

Citation and extent

1. This Scheme may be cited as the Public Lending Right Scheme 1982, and shall extend to the whole of the United Kingdom.

General definitions

2.—(1) In this Scheme, except where the context otherwise requires, the following expressions have the meanings hereby respectively assigned to them, that is to say—

"the Act" means the Public Lending Right Act 1979;

"author", in relation to an eligible book, means a person who is, or one of a number of persons who are, treated as such by article 4;

"eligible author", in relation to an eligible book, means an author of that book who is an eligible person;

"eligible book" has the meaning assigned thereto by article 6;

"eligible person", in relation to an author, has the meaning assigned thereto by article 5;

"financial year" means a period of twelve months ending on the 31st March;

"identifying number" means the number entered in the Register in pursuance of article 8(1)(a)(iv);

"local library authority" has the meaning assigned thereto by section 5(2) of the Act;

"posthumously eligible book" has the meaning assigned thereto by article 6A;

"posthumously eligible person" has the meaning assigned thereto by article 5A;

"the Registrar" and "the Register" have the meanings assigned thereto by section 5(2) of the Act;

"registered interest" means the interest (being the whole or a share thereof), in the Public Lending Right in respect of a particular book, shown on the Register as belonging to a particular person, and "registered owner" means the person for the time being so registered;

"the registry" means the place at which the Register is for the time being maintained in pursuance of article 7;

"sampling year" has the meaning assigned thereto by article 36.

(2) In this Scheme, except where the context otherwise requires, any reference to an article or to a Part or to a Schedule shall be construed as a reference to an article contained in, or to a Part of or a Schedule to, this Scheme, as the case may be, and any reference in any article to a paragraph shall be construed as a reference to a paragraph in that article.

Delivery of documents and service of notice

3. Unless the context otherwise requires, any requirement in this Scheme for—

(*a*) a document or an application to be delivered at the registry or produced to the Registrar or for notice to be given to him, shall be satisfied if the same is either—

(i) delivered in person at the registry between the hours of 11 am and 3 pm on a working day; or

(ii) sent through the post by recorded delivery;

(*b*) a local library authority or a registered owner to be notified of any matter shall be satisfied if such notification is sent through the post.

Part II   **A–661**

Books and Authors Eligible Under the Scheme

Authors

4.—(1) Subject to paragraph (2), a person shall be treated as an author of a book for the purpose of this Scheme if he is either—

(*a*) a writer of the book, including without prejudice to the generality of that expression,

(i) a translator thereof, and

(ii) an editor or compiler thereof, who in either case has contributed more than ten per cent of the contents of the book or more than ten pages of the contents, whichever is the less; or

(*b*) an illustrator thereof, which for this purpose includes the author of a photograph (within the meaning of section 48 of the Copyright Act 1956).

(2) Notwithstanding paragraph (1), a person shall not be treated as an author of a book unless the fact that he is an author within the meaning of paragraph (1)—

(*a*) is evidenced by his being named on the title page of the book; or

(*b*) in the case of a person treated as an author by virtue of paragraph (1)(*a*)(i), is evidenced as aforesaid or, if the translated text amounts to at least half of the book's contents, by his being named on the cover or the title page verso of the book.

Eligible persons

5.—(1) For the purposes of the Scheme, and in relation to each application by a person relating to an eligible book, the applicant is an eligible person if he is an author (within the meaning of article 4) of that book who at the date of the application has his only or principal home in one of the countries specified in Schedule 5, or, if he has no home, has been present in one of those countries for not less than twelve months out of the preceding twenty-four months.

(2) In this Article "principal home", in the case of a person having more than one home means that one of those homes at which he has been for the longest aggregate period during the twenty-four months immediately preceding the application for registration.

Posthumously eligible persons

5A. For the purposes of the Scheme, and in relation to each application relating to a posthumously eligible book, an author who is dead is a posthumously eligible person if, had he been an applicant for first registration of Public Lending Right in relation to that book at the date of his death, he would have been an eligible person in accordance with article 5.

Eligible books

6.—(1) For the purposes of this Scheme, an eligible book is a book (as defined in paragraph (2)) the sole author, or at least one of the authors, of which is an eligible person; and there shall be treated as a separate book—

(*a*) each volume of a work published in two or more volumes, and

(*b*) each new edition of a book.

(2) In paragraph (1) "book" means a printed and bound publication (including a paper-back edition) but does not include—

(*a*) a book bearing, in lieu of the name of an author who is a natural person, the name of a body corporate or an unincorporated association;

(*b*) a book with four or more authors, but for the purpose of this sub-paragraph a translator, editor or compiler shall not be treated as an author of the book unless each of his co-authors is a translator, editor or compiler,

(*c*) a book which is wholly or mainly a musical score;

(*d*) a book the copyright of which is vested in the Crown;

(*e*) a book which has not been offered for sale to the public;

(*f*) a serial publication including, without prejudice to the generality of that expression, a newspaper, magazine, journal or periodical; or

(*g*) a book in respect of which an application for first registration of Public Lending Right has not been made before 30th June 1991 and which does not have an International Standard Book Number.

Posthumously eligible books

6A. For the purposes of the Scheme, a book is a posthumously eligible book if—

(*a*) it is a book within the meaning of article 6(2),

(*b*) the sole author, or at least one of the authors, of the book is a posthumously eligible person, and

(*c*) the book is either—

(i) published within one year before or ten years after the date of that person's death and that person had made a successful application during his lifetime for registration of Public Lending Right or of an eligible author's share of the Right in respect of at least one other book, or

(ii) a book which consists of or incorporates a work of that person which had previously been the constituent of or incorporated in a book in relation to which that person had made such an application as aforesaid.

PART III

REGISTRATION OF PUBLIC LENDING RIGHT

THE REGISTER

The Register

7. The Registrar shall establish and maintain a Public Lending Right Register at such place as the Secretary of State may from time to time determine, and upon each such determination notice shall be published in the London Gazette, the Edinburgh Gazette and the Belfast Gazette, of such place and the time of the commencement of registration thereat.

The content of the Register

8.—(1) The Register shall contain—
  (a) particulars of each book in respect of which Public Lending Right subsists, including—
    (i) the title of the book;
    (ii) the name or names of the persons appearing on the title page as the authors thereof;
    (iii) the true identity of an author if different from (ii) above;
    (iv) a number for that book, determined by, or in accordance with arrangements made by, the Registrar;
  (b) the name and address of each person entitled to the Right in respect of each such book and, if more than one, the share of each such person in such Right.

(2) The Registrar shall also keep at the registry an index whereby all entries in the Register can readily be traced, and for this purpose "index" includes any device or combination of devices serving the purpose of an index.

Registration

9.—(1) Public Lending Right in respect of a book may, and may only, be registered if—
  (a) the book is an eligible book and application in that behalf is made in accordance with articles 14 and 17, or
  (b) the book is a posthumously eligible book and application in that behalf is made in accordance with articles 14A and 17B.

(2) Subject to paragraph (3), an eligible author's share of the Public Lending Right in respect of an eligible book with two or more authors (including any who are not eligible persons) may, and may only, be registered on application in that behalf made in accordance with articles 14 and 17.

(3) The share of the Public Lending Right in such a book as is mentioned in paragraph (2) of an author who was not an eligible person at the time when application was first made for the registration of the share of the Right of any co-author may, and may only, be registered if—
  (a) he has become and remains an eligible person, and
  (b) application in that behalf is made in accordance with Articles 14 and 17.

(4) A posthumously eligible person's share of the Public Lending Right in respect of a posthumously eligible book with two or more authors (including any who are not eligible persons) may, and may only, be registered on application made in accordance with articles 14A and 17B.

Shares in Public Lending Right

9A.—(1) Subject to the following paragraphs an eligible person's registered share of Public Lending Right in respect of a book of which he is author shall be the whole of that Right or, where a book has two or more authors (including any who are not eligible persons), such share of the Public Lending Right as may be specified in accordance with article 17(1)(c) in the application for first registration of the Right.

(2) A translator's share of Public Lending Right in respect of a book shall be thirty per cent of that Right, or if there is more than one translator (including any who are not eligible persons), an equal share of thirty per cent, but this paragraph

shall not apply where a translator is an author of the book in another capacity unless he makes an application in accordance with article 17(1)(*c*)(ii).

(3) An editor's or compiler's share of Public Lending Right in respect of a book shall be

(*a*) twenty per cent of that Right, or

(*b*) if he satisfies the Registrar that he has contributed more than twenty per cent of the contents of the book, the percentage equal to that percentage contribution, or

(*c*) if there is more than one editor or compiler (including any who are not eligible persons), an equal share of twenty per cent or the higher percentage attributable to the editors or compilers in accordance with sub-para graph (*b*).

(4) An illustrator's share of Public Lending Right in respect of a book, and each eligible person's share of Public Lending Right in respect of a book with two or more authors (including any who are not eligible persons) none of whom is an illustrator, translator or editor or compiler, shall not exceed fifty per cent of that Right unless the Registrar is satisfied that any share exceeding fifty per cent which is specified in accordance with article 17(1)(*c*) in the application for first registration of the Right or in accordance with Article 17(2) in the application for first registration of an eligible author's share of the Right is reasonable in relation to that author's contribution.

(5) Where a book has two or more authors (including any who are not eligible persons) and the Registrar is satisfied that one or more of them is dead or cannot be traced at the date of application despite all reasonable steps having been taken to do so, the Public Lending Right shall be apportioned amongst all the authors (including any who are not eligible persons)

(*a*) by attributing to each author the same share of Public Lending Right as has been attributed to that author in respect of any other book by the same authors or, if there is more than one such other book, the most recent book by those authors in respect of which Public Lending Right has been registered, if the Registrar is satisfied that there has been no significant change in the respective contributions of the authors;

(*b*) where sub-paragraph (*a*) does not apply, equally, subject to

(i) the prior application of paragraphs (2), (3) and (7), and

(ii) where the book is illustrated,

(*aa*) the attribution of twenty per cent of the Public Lending Right to the illustrator, or

(*bb*) if he satisfies the Registrar that he has contributed more than twenty per cent of the contents of the book, the attribution of the percentage equal to that percentage contribution, or

(*cc*) if there is more than one illustrator (including any who are not eligible persons), the attribution of an equal share of twenty per cent or the higher percentage attributable to illustrators in accordance with sub-paragraph (*bb*).

(6) Where paragraph 5(*b*)(ii) applies an illustrator who is also an author of a book in another capacity shall, in addition to any share of Public Lending Right to which he is entitled under that paragraph, be entitled to any further share of the Right which is attributable to him as author in that other capacity.

(7) Where all the persons (including the personal representatives of a posthumously eligible person) amongst whom the Public Lending Right would otherwise be apportioned equally in accordance with paragraph (5)(*b*) jointly notify the Registrar in writing that they wish the Right to be apportioned in a manner other than equally, the apportionment specified by them shall apply if the Registrar is satisfied that it is reasonable in that case.

(8) Where all the authors who are party to an application under article 17(1)(c) and who are entitled under paragraphs (2), (3), and 5(b)(ii) to a share of a percentage of Public Lending Right in respect of the relevant book specify in accordance with article 17(1)(c) that the said percentage shall be apportioned in a manner other than that provided for by those paragraphs the specified apportionment shall apply if the Registrar is satisfied that it is reasonable in that case.

Dealings to be effected only on the Register

10. No Public Lending Right in respect of a particular book shall subsist and no transmission of a registered interest shall be effective until such Right or such transmission has been entered in the Register by the Registrar.

Register to be conclusive

11. The Register shall be conclusive as to whether Public Lending Right subsists in respect of a particular book and also as to the persons (if any) who are for the time being entitled to the Right.

Amendment of the Register

12. The Register may be amended pursuant to an Order of a Court of competent jurisdiction or by the decision of the Registrar in any of the following cases—
- (a) in any case and at any time with the consent of the registered owner or owners of the Right in respect of a particular book;
- (b) where a Court of competent jurisdiction or the Registrar is satisfied that an entry in the Register has been obtained by fraud;
- (c) where a decision of a Court of competent jurisdiction affects any interest in an eligible book and, in consequence thereof, the Registrar is of the opinion that amendment of the Register is required;
- (d) where two or more persons are erroneously registered as being entitled to the same interest in Public Lending Right in respect of a particular book;
- (e) where an entry erroneously relates to a book which is not an eligible book;
- (f) in any other case where by reason of any error or omission in the Register, or by reason of any entry made under a mistake, it appears to the Registrar just to amend the Register.

Payments consequent upon amendment

13. The person who, as a result of an amendment of the Register pursuant to article 12 or 17A, becomes the registered owner of a registered interest shall be entitled to the payment of Public Lending Right in respect of that interest from the date upon which the Register was amended.

PROCEDURE FOR REGISTRATION

Forms of application

14. Any application required under this Scheme other than an application required under article 14A—
- (a) for first registration of Public Lending Right or of an eligible author's share of the Right;
- (b) for the transfer of a registered interest, or
- (c) for renunciation of a registered interest,

shall be made in writing to the Registrar and provide the information specified in Part I, II or III of Schedule 1 (as the case may be) in such form as he may from time to time require.

Forms of application in respect of posthumously eligible books

14A. An application under article 17B for first registration of Public Lending Right, or of a posthumously eligible person's share of the Right, in relation to a posthumously eligible book shall be made in writing to the Registrar and shall provide in such form as he may from time to time require

(*a*) the information specified in paragraphs 1 to 4 of Part I of Schedule 1 other than the address specified in paragraph 4,

(*b*) a statement signed by the personal representatives of the posthumously eligible person that the conditions as to eligibility specified in articles 5A and 6A are satisfied, and

(*c*) in the case of a work by more than one author, a statement signed as aforesaid that the posthumously eligible person in relation to whom the application is being made was translator, editor or compiler or illustrator of the book and that the claim to Public Lending Right in respect thereof is limited to the percentage prescribed in article 9A(2), (3) or (5)(*b*)(ii) or that the other author, or one of the other authors, of the work is a translator and that the claim to Public Lending Right in respect thereof is limited to that share or to a share of that share to which the translator is not entitled,

and shall be accompanied, when the personal representatives have not previously made an application under article 17B in relation to that posthumously eligible person, by

(i) the probate, letters of administration or confirmation of executors of the posthumously eligible person in relation to whom the application is being made, and

(ii) a certificate signed by a Member of Parliament, Justice of the Peace, Minister of Religion, lawyer, bank officer, school teacher, police officer, doctor or other person accepted by the Registrar as being of similar standing and stating that he had known the posthumously eligible person in relation to whom the application is being made for at least two years before the date of his death, that he was not related to him and that to the best of his knowledge the contents of the statement referred to in paragraph (b) are true.

Recording of receipt of application

15. The Registrar shall record the date upon which each application for first registration is received by him.

Completion of registration

16.—(1) When the Registrar is satisfied as to the eligibility of a book for registration and as to the persons entitled to Public Lending Right in respect of that book and, if more than one, of their respective shares therein, the registration shall be completed and, as regards a first registration of the Right, each registration shall be effective as from the day the application was recorded by the Registrar as having been received by him.

(2) On completion of a registration the Registrar shall issue to any person so entered in the Register as having an interest in the Public Lending Right in respect of the book to which the entry relates, an acknowledgement of registration in the

form of a copy of the relevant entry, indicating therein the date from which the entry takes effect.

Application for first registration

17.—(1) An application for first registration of Public Lending Right in respect of an eligible book—

    (*a*) shall satisfy the requirements of article 14 and be made by delivery at the registry;

    (*b*) shall be made by an eligible author, and

    (*c*) where the book has two or more authors (including any who are not eligible persons), shall specify the proposed shares of each of them and for that purpose each of those authors who is alive at the date of application shall be a party to the application, unless

      (i) the Registrar is satisfied that he cannot be traced, despite all reasonable steps having been taken to do so, or

      (ii) the application is made by the translator or editor or compiler of the book and he specifies that he is making the application only in his capacity as such, or

      (iii) any author of the book who is not a party to the application is a translator and the application specifies that it relates only to that share of Public Lending Right in the book to which the translator is not entitled, or.

      (iv) the application is made by an author of the book and he specifies that he is making the application otherwise than wholly or partly in the capacity of translator, editor, or compiler of the book, and—

        (*aa*) there is at the date of the application an effective agreement or arrangement between each person who is an author of the book (including any author who is not an eligible person or who does not wish to register);

        (*bb*) each such person is a party to the agreement or arrangement otherwise than wholly or partly in the capacity of translator, editor or compiler of the book; and

        (*cc*) the agreement or arrangement relates to the apportionment of shares of Public Lending Right in the book or, where there is any eligible person who would be entitled to a share of the Right by virtue of being a translator, editor, or compiler, to the apportionment of shares in such proportion of the Right as would remain after taking account of any such entitlement.

(2) An application for first registration of an eligible author's share of Public Lending Right in respect of an eligible book with two or more authors (including any who are not eligible persons)—

    (*a*) shall satisfy the requirements of article 14 and be made by delivery at the registry,

    (*b*) shall be made by the author concerned, and

    (*c*) shall, when made by an author otherwise than wholly or partly in the capacity of translator, editor or compiler of the book, satisfy the requirements of paragraph (1)(*c*)(iv).

(3) Anything which falls to be done by an author under this article shall, if he is not of full age, be done by his parent or guardian and that parent or guardian shall be recorded in the Register as the person to whom are payable sums in respect of any registered interest of the author until such time as a transfer of the registration into the author's own name has been recorded in pursuance of article 25.

Transitional provisions for translators, editors and compilers

17A.—(1) Where an application for first registration of Public Lending Right in respect of a book was made before 28th December 1984 and a translator, editor or compiler thereof would have been party to the said application if it had been made on or after that date he may, if he is an eligible person, make an application for the registered shares of the Right to be revised.

(2) Subject to the following paragraphs, the provisions of this Scheme shall apply to an application under paragraph (1) as though it were an application for first registration of Public Lending Right.

(3) Where a successful application is made under paragraph (1)—

  (*a*) the applicant's share of the Public Lending Right shall be that prescribed in article 9A(2) or (3) as the case may be, and

  (*b*) the relevant shares of his co-authors, one to another, shall remain unaltered, unless all the authors who were party to the original application before 28th December 1984 are party to the application under paragraph (1) and specify an apportionment of their shares in a different manner and the Registrar is satisfied that such apportionment is reasonable.

(4) Where a successful application is made in accordance with paragraph (1) the Registrar shall amend the Register accordingly.

Application for first registration in respect of posthumously eligible books

17B. An application for first registration of Public Lending Right in respect of a posthumously eligible book and an application for first registration of a posthumously eligible person's share of Public Lending Right in respect of such a book with two or more authors (including any who are not eligible persons)—

  (*a*) shall satisfy the requirements of article 14A and be made by delivery at the registry, and

  (*b*) shall be made by the personal representatives of the posthumously eligible person concerned.

Evidence required in connection with the applications

18. The Registrar may require the submission of evidence to satisfy him that—

  (*a*) a book is an eligible book,

  (*b*) a person applying as author for the first registration of Public Lending Right, or the registration of a share of the Right, is in fact the author of that book and is an eligible person,

  (*c*) any co-author who is not a party to an application for first registration of Public Lending Right is dead or cannot be traced despite all reasonable steps having been taken to do so, and

  (*d*) where such an application as is mentioned in article 17(1)(*c*)(iv) has been made in accordance with paragraph (1) or (2) of that article—

    (i) there is such an agreement or arrangement as is mentioned in article 17(1)(*c*)(iv), and

    (ii) the share of Public Lending Right of the person making the application is as specified in that agreement or arrangement.

and may for the purpose of obtaining any such evidence require a statutory declaration to be made by any person.

SUBSEQUENT DEALINGS WITH PUBLIC LENDING RIGHT

Public Lending Right to be transmissible

19. A registered interest shall be transmissible by assignment or assignation, by testamentary disposition or by operation of law, as personal or movable property, so long, as regards a particular book, as the Right in respect of that book is capable of subsisting.

Period during which the Right may be transferred

20. The duration of Public Lending Right in respect of any book and the period during which there may be dealings therein shall be from the date of the book's first publication (or, if later, the beginning of the sampling year in which application is made for it to be registered) until fifty years have elapsed since the end of the sampling year in which the author died or, if the book is registered as the work of more than one author, as regards dealings in the share of the Right attributable to that author, the end of the year in which that author died.

Whole interest to be assigned

21.—(1) The disposition of Public Lending Right, after the first registration thereof, shall, as respects each registered interest in any book, be for the whole of that interest.

(2) On such disposition the interest may be registered in the name of joint owners, being not more than four in number and all being of full age, but in such case the senior only shall be deemed, for the purposes of the Scheme, to be the registered owner; seniority shall be determined by the order in which names stand in the Register.

(3) Subject to articles 29 and 30, no notice of any trusts, expressed, implied or constructive, shall be entered on the Register or be receivable by the Registrar.

Applications for transfer

22. Every application for registration of a transfer of Public Lending Right shall satisfy the requirements of article 14 and be made by delivery at the registry.

Stamp duty

23.—(1) An application for transfer shall bear the proper Inland Revenue stamp impressed thereon to show that all duty payable (if any) in respect of the transaction has been paid.

(2) Where an application for transfer is submitted for the purpose of giving effect to a transaction under a deed or other instrument on which the Inland Revenue stamp has already been impressed, such stamped instrument shall, before completion of the registration, be produced to the Registrar to show that all duty payable (if any) in respect of the transaction has been paid.

Proof of author's existence

24. It shall be a condition of registration of every transfer that the transferee provides, and gives an undertaking to the Registrar in future to provide at such intervals and in such form as the Registar may require, evidence that the author is still alive, or, as the case may be, evidence of the author's death.

Registration by an author on attainment of full age

25. An author whose interest is, pursuant to article 17(3), registered in the name of his parent or guardian may, on attaining full age, make application to the Registrar in accordance with articles 21 to 23, so far as they are applicable, for the transfer of the registration of the Right into his own name, and until such transfer has been recorded the Registrar shall be entitled to remit any sums due in respect of the Right to such parent or guardian.

TRANSMISSION ON DEATH

Registration of personal representatives

26. On production of the probate, letters of administration, or confirmation of executors of a registered owner, the personal representatives named in such probate, letters of confirmation shall, on production of the same to the Registrar, be registered as owner in place of the deceased owner with the addition of the words "executor *or* executrix (*or* administrator *or* administratrix) of *[name]* deceased".

Transfer by personal representatives

27. The personal representatives registered under the preceding article may transfer the interest of the deceased owner, such transfer being in accordance with articles 21 to 24 or such provisions thereof as are applicable in the circumstances of the case.

TRANSFER ON BANKRUPTCY, LIQUIDATION OR SEQUESTRATION

Registration of Official Receiver, Official Assignees or Judicial Factor

28.—(1) On the production to the Registrar of an office copy of an Order of a Court having jurisdiction in bankruptcy adjudging a registered owner bankrupt or directing the estate of a deceased registered owner to be administered in accordance with an order under section 421 of the Insolvency Act 1986[23] or section 21 of the Bankruptcy Amendment Act (Northern Ireland) 1929,[24] together with a certificate signed by the Official Receiver or Official Assignee, as the case may be, that any registered interest in the name of the bankrupt registered owner, or deceased registered owner, is part of his property divisible amongst his creditors, the Official Receiver or the Official Assignee may be registered as the registered owner in place of the bankrupt or deceased registered owner.

(2) Where there is produced to the Registrar a certified copy of an Order of a Court having competent jurisdiction in Scotland awarding sequestration of the estate of a registered owner (including a deceased registered owner) and appointing a judicial factor the Registrar shall on receipt of such a copy enter in the Register the name of the judicial factor as registered owner with the addition of the words "judicial factor in the estate of *[name]*".

Registration of Trustee in Bankruptcy in place of Official Receiver, Assignees in Bankruptcy or Judicial Factor

29.—(1) Where the Official Receiver or the Official Assignee has been registered as registered owner and some other person is subsequently appointed trustee, or, in Northern Ireland, a creditor's assignee is appointed, the trustee or the assignee may be registered as registered owner in place of the Official Receiver, or the Official Assignee, on production of an office copy of the certificate by the Department of Trade of his appointment as trustee, or in Northern Ireland an office copy of the certificate under section 90 of the Bankruptcy (Ireland) Amendment Act 1872[25] or of the certificate of the vesting of the estate and effects of the registered owner in the assignee.

(2) Where a judicial factor has been registered as an owner in terms of article 28(2) and some other person is subsequently elected as a trustee for behoof of the creditors of the former registered owner, the Registrar, on receipt of the notifi-

---

[23] c. 45.
[24] c. 1 (N.I.).
[25] c. 58.

cation of such election and of sufficient evidence to demonstrate that that person has been so elected, shall enter in the Register the name of the trustee as registered owner with the addition of the words "trustee in the estate of *[name]*".

(3) If the Official Receiver or the Official Assignee has not been entered on the Register under article 28(1) the trustee or the assignee may be registered as registered owner on production of office copies of the Order adjudging the registered owner bankrupt and the appropriate certificate referred to in paragraph (1) with a certificate signed by the trustee or the assignee that the registered interest is part of the property of the bankrupt divisible amongst his creditors.

(4) If a judicial factor has not been entered in the Register as owner under article 28(2) the Registrar shall, on receipt of the certified copy of an Order of a Court under article 28(2) together with the notification and evidence referred to in paragraph (2), enter in the Register as registered owner the name of the duly elected trustee with the addition of the words "trustee in the estate of *[name]*".

Registration of a trust under a Scheme of Arrangement or an Arrangement under the control of the Court

30.—(1) If any registered interest is vested in a trustee under the provisions of a Scheme of Arrangement approved by a Court having jurisdiction in bankruptcy, the Official Receiver or other trustee may be registered as owner in like manner as a trustee in bankruptcy upon production of an office copy of the Scheme of Arrangement, a certificate signed by the Official Receiver, or such other trustee, that the registered interest was part of the property vested in him under the provisions of the Scheme, and in the case of a trustee other than the Official Receiver, an office copy of the certificate by the Department of Trade of his appointment as trustee.

(2) If any registered interest of an arranging debtor who is a registered owner is vested in the Official Assignee alone or jointly with other persons under section 349 of the Irish Bankrupt and Insolvent Act 1857,[26] the Official Assignee and such other persons (if any) may be registered as owner in his place on production of an office copy of the Order of the Court approving and confirming the resolution or agreement referred to in the said section with a certificate by the Official Assignee identifying the arranging debtor named in the Order of the Court with the registered owner endorsed thereon and a certificate signed by the Official Assignee and other such person (if any) that the registered interest was part of the property vested under the resolution or agreement.

(3) If, as regards Scotland, a registered owner—

   (*a*) has entered into a deed of arrangement for behoof of his creditors, the Registrar shall, on receiving a certified copy of the Order of the Court approving such arrangement, enter on the Register as owner the name of the person who is under the said deed of arrangement to receive any payments due to the owner (where that person is not the registered owner at the date of approval of the arrangement);

   (*b*) has entered into a private trust deed or composition contract for behoof of his creditors, the trustee under such deed or contract may make an application, accompanied by such evidence as the Registrar may require, for transmission of the registered interest into his name as such trustee; and on receipt of such an application the Registrar shall make the appropriate entry in the Register.

Liquidation of a company

31. In the liquidation of a company in which an interest in Public Lending Right is vested, any resolution or order appointing a liquidator may be filed and

---

[26] c. 60.

referred to on the Register, and, when so registered, shall be deemed to be in force until it is cancelled or superseded on the Register.

Renunciation

32.—(1) On making application in that behalf which satisfies the requirements of article 14, the registered owner of a registered interest may absolutely and unconditionally renounce that interest as provided in paragraph (2).

(2) Such renunciation may, as to extent, be in respect of either the whole or a half share of the registered interest and may be effective for all time, or in respect of such financial years as shall be specified by the registered owner.

(3) An application for renunciation shall bear the proper Inland Revenue stamp impressed thereon.

(4) The Registrar shall as at the date from which the renunciation is to have effect amend the Register—

    (*a*) in the case of a renunciation for all time of the whole of the registered interest by removing from the Register the entry relating to the registered owner and, if that interest represents the whole of the Public Lending Right in a book, the entry relating to that book; or

    (*b*) in all other cases, by noting against the relevant entry in the Register the extent of the renunciation and the period during which it is effective.

(5) Immediately upon the amendment of the Register as provided in paragraph (4), any sum due by way of Public Lending Right which, apart from the renunciation would become payable to the registered owner by 31st March in any year falling within the period to which the renunciation applies, shall cease to be so payable.

GENERAL

Neglected applications for registration

33. Where in the case of any application for first or any subsequent registration an applicant has failed to provide within three months information requested by the Registrar, notice may be given to the applicant that the application will be treated as abandoned unless the information is duly furnished within a time (not being less than one month) determined by the Registrar and specified in the notice; and if, at the expiration of that time, the information so requested is not furnished, the application may be treated as abandoned.

Removal of entries from the Register

34. Where the Registrar, pursuant to section 4(5) of the Act, directs the removal from the Register of any entry relating to a book in whose case no sum has become due by way of Public Lending Right for a period of at least ten years, any subsequent application for the entry to be restored to the Register may be made only by the person who, at the date of the removal of the entry, was the registered owner, or by his legal personal representatives.

Copies of entries in the Register

35.—(1) The Registrar shall not supply a copy of any entry in the Register otherwise than to—

    (*a*) a registered owner, as regards any entry which relates to his registered interest; or

    (*b*) such other person as the registered owner may direct, but if the entry in question also relates to other registered owners, only with the consent of all such owners.

(2) The Registrar may require a payment of a fee for supplying a copy of an entry in the Register, not exceeding £5 in respect of each such entry.

PART IV

ASCERTAINMENT OF THE NUMBER OF LOANS OF BOOKS

Special definitions

36. In this Part, unless the context otherwise requires—

"copy" means an individual copy of a particular book, and "copy number" means a number which distinguishes the copy to which it is applied from other copies of the same book in the same library;

"group", in relation to service points, means a group specified in Schedule 2;

"library" has the meaning assigned to it by section 3(4) of the Act;

"loans" means loans whereby books are lent out from a service point to individual borrowers, and includes loans of books not normally held at that service point;

"mobile library service point" means a service point which is taken about from place to place;

"month" means one of the twelve months in the calendar year;

"operative sampling point" means a sampling point at which loans are for the time being required to be recorded in pursuance of article 40(1);

"ordinary service point" means a service point for which fewer than 500,000 loans were made during the preceding period of twelve months;

"participating period", in relation to a sampling point, means the period commencing on the date on which the local library authority having responsibility for it receives from the Registrar notice of designation pursuant to article 38(6) and ending on the date specified in a notice given thereunder as the date upon which it is to cease to act as a sampling point;

"principal service point", in relation to a library authority, means any of the following—
  (a) whichever of the service points for which that authority is responsible is the service point from which the greatest number of loans were made during the preceding period of twelve months;
  (b) any service point for which that authority is responsible, the number of loans from which during the preceding period of twelve months was not less than three-quarters of the number of loans made from the service point referred to in paragraph (a) during the same period;
  (c) any other such service point from which 500,000 or more loans were made during the aforesaid period;
  and "principal service points" means every service point, or any number of such points in relation to any local library authority, which is a principal service point, in relation to any library authority;

"sampling point" means any principal service point, ordinary service point or mobile library service point or any number of such points in relation to any local library authority, which has been designated, for the time being, by the Registrar under article 38;

"sampling year" means the period of twelve months ending on 30th June;

"service point" means a place from which books comprised in a library are lent out to the public at large.

Number of loans to be ascertained by means of a sample

37. The number of occasions on which a book is lent out shall be determined by means of a sample of the lendings of that book from particular service points, designated in accordance with the provisions of this Part; and for the purpose of the sample, service points shall be classified into the groups, according to local library authority areas, specified in Schedule 2.

Designation of sampling points

38.—(1) Such local library authorities as the Registrar may require shall, not later than 30th September in each year, furnish to the Registrar lists, as at 31st March of that year, of all their principal, ordinary and mobile service points. The Registrar shall, not later than 31st December of that year, designate in accordance with paragraph (5) those service points which are to be operative sampling points or which are to be included in operative sampling points as from the beginning of the ensuing sampling year.

(1A) The Registrar may, at any time after he has designated a sampling point in accordance with paragraph (1), discontinue the designation of that point and designate a new sampling point, such discontinuance and new point to take effect from 1st January in the ensuing sampling year. Notice of discontinuance and designation pursuant to this paragraph shall be given in accordance with paragraph (5).

(2) The Registrar shall so exercise his powers under this article as to secure, subject to paragraph (4), that—

(*a*) at all times there shall be not less than 30 operative sampling points comprising—

    (i) 5 points falling within not less than 3 local library authority areas in Group A and 5 points falling within not less than 4 local library authority areas in Group D in Schedule 2,

    (ii) 4 points falling within not less than 3 local library authority areas in each of Groups B, C and E in Schedule 2,

    (iii) 3 points falling within not less than 3 local library authority areas in each of Groups F and G in Schedule 2, and

    (iv) 2 points falling within not less than 2 local library authority areas in Group H in Schedule 2;

(*b*) at all times the operative sampling points falling within each Group in Schedule 2 shall include, subject to paragraph (3), a principal service point and an ordinary service point;

(*c*) at all times one of the 3 operative sampling points falling within Group F in Schedule 2 shall be within the County of Dyfed or that of Gwynedd or the Districts of Colwyn or Glyndwr in the County of Clwyd;

(*d*) at all times one of the 3 operative sampling points falling within Group G in Schedule 2 shall be outside the Metropolitan Districts of Edinburgh and Glasgow;

(*e*) no operative sampling point shall consist only of a mobile library service point other than an operative sampling point falling within the County of Dyfed, or that of Gwynedd or the Districts of Colwyn or Glyndwr in the County of Clwyd;

(*f*) during each sampling year at least 8 operative sampling points shall be replaced by new such points; and

(*g*) no operative sampling point shall remain as such for a continuous period of more than 4 years.

(3) The relevant local library authority shall notify the Registrar of any change

in the categorisation of a sampling point which consists of a single principal, ordinary or mobile service point but the Registrar shall not be required by paragraph (2)(*a*) to discontinue the designation of the point as a sampling point before the expiry of the sampling year in which he receives such notice or, if that year has less than six months to run, before the expiry of the next following sampling year.

For the purposes of this paragraph and of paragraph (2)(*a*), a change in the categorisation of a sampling point shall be disregarded if it is occasioned by an increase or decrease of less than 10 per cent in the number of loans made therefrom.

(4) The local library authority shall notify the Registrar of any decision to close a service point which is or is included in a sampling point and the date on which the closure takes effect but, if it is not reasonably practicable for the Registrar to satisfy the requirements of paragraph (2) before the closure takes effect, those requirements shall be treated as satisfied if satisfied as soon as is reasonably practicable thereafter.

(5) The Registrar shall give to the local library authority responsible for a sampling point—

(*a*) for the purposes of designating that point under paragraphs (1) or (1A), notice in writing of such designation specifying the period ending on 31st December or 30th June, in any sampling year for which he intends the point to be an operative sampling point;

(*b*) for the purpose of discontinuing that point as a sampling point, not less than six months notice in writing of such discontinuance.

Provisions by libraries of recording facilities

39. Upon receipt of a notice under article 38(6)(*a*) a local library authority shall—

(*a*) arrange for every book which may be lent out from the sampling point to which the designation refers to be marked, in such form as the Registrar may require, with its identifying number and (where more than one copy may be lent out) copy number, and shall notify the Registrar at such time and in such manner as he may direct of the number of books so marked; and

(*b*) acquire, in accordance with arrangements approved by the Registrar, such equipment (including computer programs) as may be necessary to enable the authority to comply with the provision of article 40 regarding the furnishing of information to the Registrar.

Duty to record lendings

40.—(1) A local library authority which has received a notice under article 38(6)(*a*) shall, for such period as is specified in the notice, record every occasion on which a copy of a book is lent out to the public from the sampling point to which the notice refers and shall furnish to the Registrar, in such form and at such intervals as he may direct, details of such lendings, including the identifying number and any copy number of the copy in question.

(2) For the purpose of this article each volume of a work published in two or more volumes shall be treated as a separate book.

Provision of book loan data

41. Each local library authority shall submit to the Registrar, in such form, at such intervals and in respect of such periods as he may direct, a return of the total number of occasions on which the books comprised in all its collections were the subject of loans.

Method of determining the number of notional loans

42.—(1) The Registrar shall, from the details of loans furnished to him by local library authorities pursuant to the provisions of this Part (upon the accuracy of which the Registrar shall be entitled to rely), calculate, in accordance with paragraph (2), the number of notional loans of each book in respect of which Public Lending Right subsists in each sampling year.

(2) The number of notional loans of each book made during a sampling year shall be the aggregate of the number of notional loans of that book made in all groups; and the number of notional loans for a group shall be determined in accordance with the following formula:—

$$\text{Total notional loans in the group} = \frac{A}{B} \times C$$

Where—

A represents the number of loans of that book recorded during the sampling year at the operative sampling points in that group;

B represents the total number of loans of books made to the public during the sampling year from the operative sampling point in that group; and

C represents the aggregate of the loans of all books made to the public from all libraries (within the meaning of section 3(4) of the Act) in the area of the group during the financial year ending in the sampling year in question, or, as regards any particular library for which loan data relating to that financial year is not available to the Registrar, the most recent financial year for which he has such data.

(3) For the purposes of paragraph (2)—

(*a*) Groups A, B and C in Schedule 2 shall be treated as one group;

(*b*) if on any occasion on which any details of lendings at a particular sampling point which consists of a single service point are furnished to the Registrar in accordance with article 40 and record loans of a copy of a book in excess of an average of one loan for each period of five days covered by the details, the loans in excess of that average shall be disregarded; and

(*c*) the Registrar may disregard any loan of a book made after 30th June 1991 from a sampling point if a local library authority, on the first occasion after 30th June 1991 on which it reports, in accordance with article 40, a loan of that book from that sampling point, does not specify an International Standard Book Number in respect of the book, and the book is not registered at the time of such report.

Reimbursement of local library authorities

43.—(1) The Registrar shall, subject to the provisions of this article and article 44, reimburse to local library authorities the net expenditure incurred by them in giving effect to this Scheme.

(2) It shall be the duty of local library authorities to keep proper accounts and records in respect of the expenditure (including overhead expenses) incurred by them in giving effect to this Scheme and the Registrar may withhold payment to a local library authority, in whole or in part, until such time as such authority has

furnished to him sufficient evidence as to the amount of the expenditure so incurred.

Expense incurred in respect of sampling points

44.—(1) Without prejudice to the generality of article 43(2) each local library authority to which a notice has been given under article 38(6)(a) shall submit to the Registrar at such time and in such form as he may require estimates of the net expenditure to be incurred in giving effect to this Scheme at the sampling point or points specified in such notice.

(2) Such local library authority may from time to time during the participating period submit to the Registrar claims in respect of the expenditure incurred, or estimated to have been incurred by it, and the Registrar shall be entitled to rely upon the accuracy of such claims and to make payments on account of the expenditure incurred by that authority in giving effect to the Scheme.

(3) The total amount payable by way of reimbursement to such local library authority shall be finally determined by the Registrar after examination of such audited financial statements and such books, records, documents, and accounts relating thereto as he may require; and any balance found after such final determination to be due by or to the Registrar in account with the local library authority in question shall be paid to or recovered from such local library authority.

(4) In reckoning the net expenditure for the purposes of this article and of article 43, the following shall be deducted from the gross expenditure incurred by a local library authority in connection with a sampling point—

(*a*) any sum received in connection with the disposal (by sale, lease or otherwise) of any property or equipment purchased pursuant to paragraph (b) of article 39;

(*b*) any sum which it might reasonably be expected would have been received on such a disposal (whether or not there has been a disposal of the property or equipment in question);

(*c*) any insurance monies received in respect of the loss or destruction of or damage to any such property or equipment;

(*d*) an amount representing the appropriate proportion of the net cost (whether by way of purchase, lease, or otherwise) of any property or equipment which is used by a local library authority partly in connection with this Scheme and partly for other purposes not connected therewith:

Provided that where deductions are made under both sub-paragraphs (a) and (b) in respect of the same property or equipment, the aggregate deductions thereunder shall not exceed whichever is the greater of the sums mentioned in those sub-paragraphs.

(5) In determining the amount finally to be paid to or recovered from a local library authority pursuant to paragraph (3), account shall be taken of any expenditure reasonably incurred by that authority in discontinuing the sampling point.

PART V   **A–664**

CALCULATION AND PAYMENT OF PUBLIC LENDING RIGHT

Determination of the sum due in respect of Public Lending Right

46.—(1) For any financial year, the sum due by way of Public Lending Right in respect of a registered interest to the registered owner thereof shall be ascertained by reference to—

(*a*) the product of the number of notional loans attributable to that interest (calculated in accordance with paragraph (4)) and 1.37p, and

(*b*) the aggregate amount of that product and the like products in the case of all other registered interests which initially were registered interests of the same author or were interests registered by the personal representatives of the same author.

(2) Subject to paragraph (3) the sum so due for the financial year shall be—

(*a*) except where the following sub-paragraph applies, the product mentioned in paragraph (1)(*a*);

(*b*) if the aggregate amount mentioned in paragraph (1)(*b*) exceeds £6,000, the product of

$$\frac{x}{y} \text{ and £6,000 where}—$$

x is the number of notional loans attributable to the interest in question, and

y is the aggregate of that number and the number of notional loans attributable to all other registered interests which initially were registered interests of the same author or were interests registered by the personal representatives of the same author.

(3) If the aggregate of the amounts determined in accordance with paragraph (2) in respect of each registered interest of the registered owner thereof is less than £1, the sum due in respect of the registered interest shall be nil.

(4) For the purposes of paragraphs (1) and (2)(*b*), the number of notional loans attributable to any registered interest in any financial year shall be calculated by ascertaining, in accordance with article 42(2), the number of notional loans of the book to which it relates which were made during the sampling year ending in that financial year, and shall be—

(*a*) if the registered interest represents the whole of the Public Lending Right in respect of that book, the total notional loans of the book in question;

(*b*) if the registered interest relates only to a share of the Public Lending Right in respect of that book, such proportion of the total notional loans of the book as the registered interest bears to the whole of the Public Lending Right in that book, fractions of a loan being disregarded;

(*c*) if the Right in respect of that registered interest has been renounced in part, such proportion of the notional loans attributable to the registered interest under sub-paragraph (*a*) or (*b*), as the case may be, which the unrenounced share bears to the whole of the registered interest, fractions of a loan being disregarded;

(*d*) nil, if the Right in respect of the registered interest has been wholly renounced for the financial year in question.

(5) For the purposes of paragraphs (1) and (2)(*b*), the references to interests which were initially registered interests of the same author include interests which, in pursuance of article 17(3), were registered in the name of his parent or guardian.

Persons to whom the payment is due

47. The person entitled to the Public Lending Right in respect of any registered book in any financial year shall be the registered owner thereof as at 30th June of that year.

Right to be claimed

48.—(1) No payment shall be made in respect of Public Lending Right unless that Right has been claimed by or on behalf of the person for the time being entitled.

(2) A claim in respect of the Right may be made for—

(*a*) a specified period;

(*b*) an unspecified period determinable by not less than three months written notice of termination given to the Registrar by or on behalf of the person for the time being entitled to the Right.

(3) A claim shall automatically lapse in the event of any change of ownership recorded on the Register, subsequent to first registration thereof, in respect of the Right to which the claim relates.

Notification of entitlement and payment of sums due under the Scheme

49.—(1) Any sum payable by way of Public Lending Right in respect of a registered interest, for any financial year, shall (unless sooner paid) fall due for payment on the last day of that year.

(2) Any such sum may be paid by cheque or warrant sent through the post directed to the registered address of the registered owner or, in the case of joint owners, to the registered address of the senior owner (as defined in article 21(2)), or to such person and to such address as the owner or joint owners may direct by a written payment mandate to the Registrar, delivered at the registry, in the form set out in Schedule 4 or a form to the like effect; every such cheque or warrant shall be made payable to the order of the person to whom it is sent and any one of two or more joint owners may give a good receipt for any money due to them under this Scheme.

(3) The Registrar shall at the end of each financial year, or as soon as is reasonably practicable thereafter, inform each registered owner to whom a sum is payable by way of Public Lending Right in respect of that year, by notice posted to his registered address of—

(*a*) the notional number of lendings for that year of each book in respect of which he is a registered owner; and

(*b*) the amount of such sum.

(4) If, after the Registrar has notified the registered owner as provided in paragraph (3), the cheque or warrant for the sum referred to therein is not presented for payment and thereby lapses—

(*a*) there shall be no further duty on the part of the Registrar to take steps to trace the registered owner and it shall be the responsibility of such owner to make application to the Registrar for payment; and

(*b*) if at the end of six years from the date upon which a payment in respect of Public Lending Right becomes due no such application has been made by the person entitled thereto, the entitlement to such payment shall lapse.

(5) At the request of a registered owner to whom no notice is required to be given under paragraph (3) in respect of any financial year, the Registrar shall supply to him particulars (calculated in accordance with article 42) of the number of notional loans during the sampling year ending in that financial year of any book in respect of which he is the registered owner, provided the request is made no later than six months after the end of that financial year.

Power to call for information

50. The Registrar may at any time require a statutory declaration or other sufficient evidence that an author or any registered owner is alive and is the person to whom money is payable under this Scheme, and may withhold payment until such declaration or evidence as he may require is produced.

Interest

51. No sum determined to be due under this Scheme shall carry interest.

SCHEDULE 1 Article 14

Information to be Provided in Connection with Applications

Part I

Application for First Registration

Each application shall provide the Registrar, in such form as he may from time to time require, with the following—

1. The title of the book to which the application relates.

2. The name of every person named on the title page as author (within the meaning of article 4).

3. The true identity (if different from 2 above) of each such person, and his address.

4. The International Standard Book Number (if any) of the book.

5. A statement signed by each applicant that in each case the conditions as to eligibility specified in Part II of the Scheme are satisfied at the date of application, accompanied, when the applicant has not previously made an application under article 17 of this Scheme, by a certificate signed by a Member of Parliament, Justice of the Peace, Minister of Religion, lawyer, bank officer, school teacher, police officer, doctor or other person accepted by the Registrar as being of similar standing and stating that he has known the applicant for at least two years, that he is not related to the applicant and that to the best of his knowledge the contents of the statement by the applicant are true.

6. In the case of a work by more than one author—

(*a*) a statement signed by all the authors who are alive and can be traced at the date of application specifying—

(i) the agreed share in the Public Lending Right of each author, and

(ii) whether any author is translator, editor, compiler or, if any author is dead or untraced at the date of application, illustrator of the book and, if so, whether he is also an author of the book in another capacity, or

(*b*) a statement by the applicant that he is translator, editor or compiler of the book and that his claim to the Public Lending Right in respect thereof is limited to the percentage prescribed in article 9A(2) or (3) as the case may be, or

(*c*) where one of the authors of the work is a translator, a statement signed by the other author or, if more than one, all the other authors who are alive and can be traced at the date of application specifying—

(i) that another author of the book who is not a party to the application is a translator,

(ii) that the claim to Public Lending Right in respect thereof is limited to that share to which the translator is not entitled, and

(iii) where there is more than one author other than the translator

(*aa*) the agreed share of each such author in that share of the Public Lending Right to which the translator is not entitled, and

(*bb*) whether any such author is editor or compiler or, if any such author is dead or untraced at the date of application, illustrator of the book and, if so, whether he is also an author of the book in another capacity, or

(*d*) where such an application as is mentioned in paragraph (1)(*c*)(iv) of article 17 is made in accordance with paragraph (1) or (2) of that article, a statement specifying the names of all the other persons whether or not party to such agreement or arrangement as is mentioned in paragraph (1)(*c*)(iv) of article 17, who are eligible for a share of Public Lending Right in respect of the book.

7. Where an editor or compiler of a book wishes to claim, or claim an equal share of more than twenty per cent of the Public Lending Right in accordance with article 9A(3), particulars indicating evidence of the percentage that he has, or where there are two or more editors or compilers that they have jointly, contributed to the contents of the book.

8. In the case of an author not of full age, a declaration by the applicant that he is the parent or guardian, as the case may be, of the author, and a copy of the author's birth certificate.

PART II

APPLICATION FOR TRANSFER OF REGISTERED INTEREST

Each application shall provide the Registrar, in such form as he may from time to time require, with the following—

1. The title of the book.

2. The International Standard Book Number (if any) of the book.

3. The name and address of the transferor.

4. The name and address of the transferee.

5. An undertaking by the transferee to furnish to the Registrar, whenever so required, proof that the author is still alive.

PART III

APPLICATION FOR RENUNCIATION OF REGISTERED INTEREST

Each application shall provide the Registrar, in such form as he may from time to time require, with the following—

1. The name and address of the person renouncing.

2. The title of the book to which the renunciation relates.

3. The International Standard Book Number (if any) of the book.

4. The extent of the Right being renounced.

5. The period in respect of which the Right is renounced.

SCHEDULE 2   Articles 36–38   **A–666**

GROUPING SERVICE POINTS

Service points shall be grouped according to local library authority areas as follows—

GROUP A
Those within the areas of the following non-metropolitan counties—

Bedfordshire	Essex	Oxfordshire
Berkshire	Hertfordshire	Suffolk
Buckinghamshire	Kent	Surrey
Cambridgeshire	Norfolk	West Sussex
East Sussex	Northamptonshire	

GROUP B
Those within the areas of the following non-metropolitan counties—

Avon	Hampshire	Somerset
Cornwall	Hereford & Worcester	Staffordshire
Devon	The Isle of Wight	Warwickshire
Dorset	The Isles of Scilly	Wiltshire
Gloucestershire	Shropshire	

1195

A–666 *Appendix A*

GROUP C
Those within the areas of the following non-metropolitan counties—

Cheshire	Humberside	North Yorkshire
Cleveland	Lancashire	Nottinghamshire
Cumbria	Leicestershire	
Derbyshire	Lincolnshire	
Durham	Northumberland	

GROUP D
Those within the areas of the metropolitan districts of England.

GROUP E
Those within the area of Greater London.

GROUP F
Those in Wales.

GROUP G
Those in Scotland.

GROUP H
Those in Northern Ireland.

A–667 SCHEDULE 4 Article 49

PAYMENT MANDATE

"Please forward, until further notice, all sums that may from time to time become due to me/us or the survivor(s) of us by way of Public Lending Right to *[here state full name and address of the bank, firm or person to whom payments are to be sent]* or *[where payment is to be made to a Bank]* to such other Branch of that Bank as the Bank may from time to time request. Your compliance with this request shall discharge the Registrar's liability in respect of such sums."

Date .... Signature ....

Name ....
(Block Capitals)

Address ....

....

....

A–668 SCHEDULE 5 Article 5

SPECIFIED COUNTRIES

Federal Republic of Germany
United Kingdom

Appendix B

UNITED KINGDOM ORDERS

PRACTICE DIRECTION
GENERAL NOTICE

Appendix B

PART I

British Museum (Delivery of Books) Regulation[1]   **B–1**

(S.R. & O. 1915 No. 773)

DATED AUGUST 9, 1915

The Board of Trade on the application of the Trustees of the British Museum, and by virtue of the powers given them by section 1 of the Copyright (British Museum) Act, 1915, hereby make the following Regulation, to come into operation as from the date hereof:

There shall be excepted from the provisions of section 15(1) of the Copyright Act, 1911, whereby the publisher of any book published in the United Kingdom is required within one month after the publication to deliver, at his own expense, a copy of the book to the Trustees of the British Museum, the following publications, *viz.*:

Trade Advertisements,	Trade Labels,
Trade Cards,	Trade Leaflets,
Trade Catalogues,	Trade Plans,
Trade Circulars,	Trade Posters,
Trade Coupons,	Trade Price Lists,
Trade Designs,	Trade Prospectuses,
Trade Forms,	Trade Show Cards,

Trade Wrappers.

British Museum (Publications Not Required) Regulation[2]   **B–2**

(S.R. & O. 1935 No. 278)

DATED OCTOBER 12, 1932

The Trustees of the British Museum, being empowered under the British Museum Act, 1932, by regulations to apply the said Act to publications of such classes as may be specified in such regulations being publications of the descriptions set out in the Schedule to the said Act and thereby to except certain publications from subsection (1) of section 15 of the Copyright Act, 1911, hereby make the following regulation within their said powers. The delivery by publishers of publications falling under the following categories is no longer required, unless a written demand for delivery of them or any of them is made by the Trustees:

Publications wholly or mainly in the nature of trade advertisements.

Registers of voters prepared under the Representation of the People Act, 1918, as amended by any subsequent enactment.

Specifications of inventions prepared for the purposes of the Patents and Designs Act, 1907, as amended by any subsequent enactment.

---

[1] References to the British Library Board are to be substituted for references to the Trustees by virtue of s.4 of the British Library Act 1972 (c. 54).
[2] References to the British Library Board are to be substituted for references to the Trustees by virtue of s.4 of the British Library Act 1972 (c. 54).

Publications wholly or mainly in the nature of time tables of passenger transport services, being publications prepared for local use.

Publications wholly or mainly in the nature of calendars.

Publications wholly or mainly in the nature of blank forms of accounts, or blank forms of receipts, or other blank forms of a similar character.

Wall sheets printed with alphabets, mottoes, religious texts or other matter for the purpose of elementary instruction.

B–3   ## The Designs Rules 1984[3]

(S.I. 1984 No. 1989)

Made - - - - - -	*18th December 1984*
Laid before Parliament	*20th December 1984*
Coming into Operation	*4th March 1985*

Citation and Commencement

1. These Rules may be cited as the Designs Rules 1984 and shall come into operation on 4th March 1985.

* * *

DESIGNS EXCLUDED FROM REGISTRATION UNDER SECTION 1(4)

Exclusion of designs to be applied to certain articles

26. There shall be excluded from registration under the Act designs to be applied to any of the following articles, namely—

(1) works of sculpture other than casts or models used or intended to be used as models or patterns to be multiplied by any industrial process;

(2) wall plaques, medals and medallions;

(3) printed matter primarily of a literary or artistic character, including book-jackets, calendars, certificates, coupons, dressmaking patterns, greetings cards, leaflets, maps, plans, postcards, stamps, trade advertisements, trade forms and cards, transfers, playing cards, labels and the like.

B–4   ## The Registered Designs Rules 1989[4]

(S.I. 1989 No. 1105)

Made - - - - - -	*29th June 1989*
Laid before Parliament	*10th July 1989*
Coming into force	*1st August 1989*

Citation and Commencement

1. These Rules may be cited as the Registered Designs Rules 1989 and shall come into force on 1st August 1989.

* * *

---

[3] These Rules revoked and replaced the Designs Rules 1949 (S.I. 1949 No. 2368) (*Copinger*, 12th ed. § 1734).

[4] These Rules revoked and replaced the Design Rules 1984 (S.I. 1984 No. 1989) § B–3 *ante*.

DESIGNS EXCLUDED FROM REGISTRATION UNDER SECTION 1(5)

Exclusion of designs to be applied to certain articles

26. There shall be excluded from registration under the Act designs to be applied to any of the following articles, namely—

(1) works of sculpture, other than casts or models used or intended to be used as models or patterns to be multiplied by any industrial process;

(2) wall plaques, medals and medallions;·

(3) printed matter primarily of a literary or artistic character, including book jackets, calendars, certificates, coupons, dress-making patterns, greetings cards, labels, leaflets, maps, plans, playing cards, postcards, stamps, trade advertisements, trade forms and cards, transfers and similar articles.

PART II

B–5   **The Copyright, Designs and Patents Act 1988 (Commencement No. 1)
Order 1989**

(S.I. 1989 No. 816 (c. 21))[5]

Made - - - - - - -   *9th May 1989*

The Secretary of State, in exercise of the powers conferred upon him by section
305(3) of the Copyright, Designs and Patents Act 1988, hereby makes the following Order:

B–6   **1.** This Order may be cited as the Copyright, Designs and Patents Act 1988
(Commencement No. 1) Order 1989.

B–7   **2.** The following provisions of the Copyright, Designs and Patents Act 1988
shall come into force on 1st August 1989:
    Part I (copyright);
    Part II (rights in performances);
    Part III (design right);
    Part IV (registered designs), except—
        section 272 in so far as it relates to paragraph 21 of Schedule 3, and
        section 273;
    Part VI (patents), except—
        sections 293 and 294, and
        section 295 in so far as it relates to paragraphs 1 to 11 and 17 to 30 of
        Schedule 5;
    Part VII (miscellaneous and general), except—
        section 301,
        section 303(1) in so far as it relates to paragraphs 15, 18(2) and 21 of
        Schedule 7, and
        section 303(2) in so far as it relates to the references in Schedule 8 to section
        32 of the Registered Designs Act 1949 and to the provisions of the
        Patents Act 1977, other than section 49(3) of, and paragraphs 1 and 3 of
        Schedule 5 to, that Act;
    Schedule 1 (copyright: transitional provisions and savings);
    Schedule 2 (rights in performances: permitted acts);
    Schedule 3 (minor and consequential amendments to the Registered Designs
    Act 1949), other than paragraph 21;
    Schedule 5 (patents: miscellaneous amendments), other than paragraphs 1 to
    11 and 17 to 30;
    Schedule 7 (consequential amendments), other than paragraphs 15, 18(2)
    and 21;
    Schedule 8 (repeals), except in so far as it relates to—
        section 32 of the Registered Designs Act 1949, and
        the provisions of the Patents Act 1977, other than section 49(3) of, and
        paragraphs 1 and 3 of Schedule 5 to, that Act.

---

[5] This Order was amended by S.I. 1989 No. 1303 (c. 45) § B–12 *post.*

**The Copyright, Designs and Patents Act 1988 (Commencement No. 2)   B–8
Order 1989**[6]

(S.I. 1989 No. 955 (c. 25))

Made - - - - - - -   *9th June 1989*

The Secretary of State, in exercise of the powers conferred upon him by section 305(3) of the Copyright, Designs and Patents Act 1988 ("the Act"), hereby makes the following Order:

1. This Order may be cited as the Copyright, Designs and Patents Act 1988   **B–9**
(Commencement No. 2) Order 1989.

2. The provisions of the Act specified in the Schedule to this Order (which,   **B–10**
apart from this Order, come into force on 1st August 1989[7]) shall come into force forthwith for the purpose only of enabling the making of subordinate legislation thereunder, by the authority shown in relation to those provisions, expressed to come into force on 1st August 1989.

SCHEDULE   **B–11**

PROVISIONS OF THE ACT COMING INTO FORCE FORTHWITH

Provision and Authority	Subject matter
Regulations by the Secretary of State under sections 37 and 38 to 43	Copying by librarians and archivists of prescribed libraries and archives.
Orders by the Secretary of State under—	
section 47	Specification of material to be marked in relation to public inspection and copying of the same, and application of provisions relating to public inspection of material to material or registers maintained by international organisations.
section 52	Articles to be regarded as made by industrial process and excluded articles.
section 61	Recordings of folksongs for archival purposes for designated bodies.
section 74	Provision of subtitled copies of broadcasts and cable programmes by designated bodies.

[6] This Order was amended by The Copyright, Designs and Patents Act 1988 (Commencement No. 3) Order 1989 (S.I. 1989 No. 1032 (c.27)), made on June 20, 1989, by substituting for the Schedule to this Order the Schedule in the Schedule to the amending Order. This Order is, therefore, printed with the substituted Schedule.

[7] S.I. 1989 No. 816 (c. 21) § B–5 *ante.*

Provision and Authority	Subject matter
section 75	Recordings for archives of designated class of broadcasts and cable programmes.
sections 100 and 196	Prescribing the form of notice of seizure when infringing articles or illicit recordings are seized and detained.
Regulations by Commissioners of Customs and Excise under section 112	Prescribing the form of notices required under section 111 in respect of goods to be treated as prohibited goods.
Rules by the Lord Chancellor under sections 150, 152 and paragraph 34 of Schedule 1	Proceedings before the Copyright Tribunal.
Order in Council by Her Majesty under—	
section 159	Application of Part I of the Act to other countries.
section 168	Vesting of copyright in certain international organisations.
Order by Secretary of State under—	
section 174	Descriptions of educational establishments for the purposes of Part I of the Act, and application of provisions relating to educational establishments to certain teachers.
Order in Council by Her Majesty under section 208	Designation of Convention countries enjoying reciprocal protection under Part II of the Act (performances).
Rules by Secretary of State under section 250	Proceedings before Comptroller under Part III of the Act (design right).
Order in Council by Her Majesty under section 256	Designation of countries enjoying reciprocal protection under Part III of the Act (design right).]

B–12   **The Copyright, Designs and Patents Act 1988 (Commencement No. 4) Order 1989**

(S.I. 1989 No. 1303 (c. 45))

Made - - - - - - -   *27th July 1989*

The Secretary of State, in exercise of the powers conferred upon him by section 305(3) of the Copyright, Designs and Patents Act 1988, hereby makes the following Order:

B–13   **1.** This Order may be cited as the Copyright, Designs and Patents Act 1988 (Commencement No. 4) Order 1989.

2. Section 304(4) and (6) of the Copyright, Designs and Patents Act 1988 ("the **B–14**
1988 Act") shall come into force on 28th July 1989.

3. In article 2 of the Copyright, Designs and Patents Act 1988 (Commencement **B–15**
No. 1) Order 1989 there shall be added to the list of the provisions of Part VII of
the 1988 Act which do not come into force on 1st August 1989 a reference to section 304(4) and (6).

The Copyright and Rights in Performances (Notice of Seizure) Order 1989 **B–16**

(S.I. 1989 No. 1006)

Made - - - - - - -	*13th June 1989*
Laid before Parliament	*26th June 1989*
Coming into force	*1st August 1989*

The Secretary of State, in exercise of the powers conferred upon him by section
100(4) and (5) and section 196(4) and (5) of the Copyright, Designs and Patents
Act 1988 ("the Act"), hereby makes the following Order:—

1. This Order may be cited as the Copyright and Rights in Performances **B–17**
(Notice of Seizure) Order 1989 and shall come into force on 1st August 1989.

2. The form set out in the Schedule to this Order is hereby prescribed for the **B–18**
notice required under section 100(4) and section 196(4), respectively, of the Act.

SCHEDULE   Article 2 **B–19**

THE COPYRIGHT AND RIGHTS IN PERFORMANCES (NOTICE OF
SEIZURE) ORDER 1989

NOTICE OF SEIZURE

To Whom it May Concern

1. Goods in which you were trading have been seized. This notice tells you who
carried out the seizure, the legal grounds on which this has been done and the
goods which have been seized and detained. As required by the Copyright,
Designs and Patents Act 1988, notice of the proposed seizure was given to the
police station at (state address).

Person carrying out seizure

2. (State name and address)
*acting on the authority of (state name and address).

Legal grounds for seizure and detention

3. This action has been taken under *section 100/section 196 of the Act which
(subject to certain conditions) permits a copyright owner, or a person having per-

forming rights or recording rights, to seize and detain infringing copies or illicit recordings found exposed or immediately available for sale or hire, or to authorise such seizure. The right to seize and detain is subject to a decision of the court under *section 114/section 204 of the Act (order as to disposal of goods seized and detained).

Nature of the goods seized and detained

*4. Infringing copies of works (within the meaning of section 27 of the Act)— (specify all articles seized)

      Illicit recordings (within the meaning of section 197 of the Act)—(specify all articles seized)

Signed ....   Date ....

*Delete as necessary

B–20   **The Copyright (Recordings of Folksongs for Archives) (Designated Bodies) Order 1989**

(S.I. 1989 No. 1012)

Made - - - - - - -	*13th June 1989*
Laid before Parliament	*26th June 1989*
Coming into force	*1st August 1989*

The Secretary of State, in exercise of the powers conferred upon him by section 61 of the Copyright, Designs and Patents Act 1988 ("the Act"), and upon being satisfied that the bodies designated by this Order are not established or conducted for profit, hereby makes the following Order:—

B–21   **1.** This Order may be cited as the Copyright (Recordings of Folksongs for Archives) (Designated Bodies) Order 1989 and shall come into force on 1st August 1989.

B–22   **2.** Each of the bodies specified in the Schedule to this Order is designated as a body for the purposes of section 61 of the Act.

B–23   **3.**—(1) For the purposes of section 61(3) of the Act the conditions specified in paragraph (2) of this article are prescribed as the conditions which must be met for the making and supply, by the archivist of an archive maintained by a body designated by this Order, of a copy of a sound recording made in reliance on section 61(1) of the Act and included in such archive.

    (2) The prescribed conditions are—
        (*a*) that the person requiring a copy satisfies the archivist that he requires it for purposes of research or private study and will not use it for any other purpose, and
        (*b*) that no person is furnished with more than one copy of the same recording.

B–24   SCHEDULE   Article 2

1.   The Archive of Traditional Welsh Music, University College of North Wales.

2.   The Centre for English Cultural Tradition and Language.

3. The Charles Parker Archive Trust (1982).

4. The European Centre for Traditional and Regional Cultures.

5. The Folklore Society.

6. The Institute of Folklore Studies in Britain and Canada.

7. The National Museum of Wales, Welsh Folk Museum.

8. The National Sound Archive, the British Library.

9. The North West Sound Archive.

10. The Sound Archives, British Broadcasting Corporation.

11. Ulster Folk and Transport Museum.

12. The Vaughan Williams Memorial Library, English Folk Dance and Song Society.

The Copyright (Sub-titling of Broadcasts and Cable Programmes)   **B–25**
(Designated Body) Order 1989

(S.I. 1989 No. 1013)

Made - - - - - - -	*13th June 1989*
Laid before Parliament	*26th June 1989*
Coming into force	*1st August 1989*

The Secretary of State, in exercise of the powers conferred upon him by section 74 of the Copyright, Designs and Patents Act 1988 ("the Act"), and upon being satisfied that the body designated by this Order is not established or conducted for profit, hereby makes the following Order:—

1. This Order may be cited as the Copyright (Sub-titling of Broadcasts and   **B–26** Cable Programmes) (Designated Body) Order 1989 and shall come into force on 1st August 1989.

2. The National Subtitling Library for Deaf People is designated as a body for   **B–27** the purposes of section 74 of the Act.

The Copyright (Application of Provisions relating to Educational   **B–28**
Establishments to Teachers) (No. 2) Order 1989

(S.I. 1989 No. 1067)

Made - - - - - - -	*26th June 1989*
Laid before Parliament	*4th July 1989*
Coming into force	*1st August 1989*

The Secretary of State, in exercise of the powers conferred upon him by section 174(2) of the Copyright, Designs and Patents Act 1988 ("the Act"), hereby makes the following Order:

B–29 **1.** This Order may be cited as the Copyright (Application of Provisions relating to Educational Establishments to Teachers) (No. 2) Order 1989 and shall come into force on 1st August 1989.

B–30 **2.** Sections 35 and 36 of the Act (which provide for educational use of recordings of broadcasts and cable programmes and copying of passages from published works in which copyright subsists) and sections 137 to 141 of the Act (which provide for reprographic copying of works under licence) shall apply in relation to teachers who are employed by a local education authority to give instruction elsewhere to pupils who are unable to attend an educational establishment.

B–31 **3.** The Copyright (Application of Provisions relating to Educational Establishments to Teachers) Order 1989[8] is hereby revoked.

B–32 **The Copyright (Educational Establishments) (No. 2) Order 1989**

(S.I. 1989 No. 1068)

Made - - - - - - -	*26th June 1989*
Laid before Parliament	*4th July 1989*
Coming into force	*1st August 1989*

The Secretary of State, in exercise of the powers conferred upon him by section 174(1)(*b*) of the Copyright, Designs and Patents Act 1988 ("the Act"), hereby makes the following Order:—

B–33 **1.** This Order may be cited as the Copyright (Educational Establishments) (No. 2) Order 1989 and shall come into force on 1st August 1989.

B–34 **2.** The descriptions of educational establishments mentioned in the Schedule to this Order are specified for the purposes of Part I of the Act.

B–35 **3.** The Copyright (Educational Establishments) Order 1989[9] is hereby revoked.

B–36 SCHEDULE

1. Any university empowered by Royal Charter or Act of Parliament to award degrees and any college, or institution in the nature of a college, in such a university.

2. Any institution providing further education within the meaning of section 1(5)(*b*) of the Education (Scotland) Act 1980[10] and any educational establishment (other than a school) within the meaning of section 135(1) of that Act.

3. Any institution providing further education within the meaning of article 5(c)

---

[8] S.I. 1989 No. 1007: made but not laid before Parliament.
[9] S.I. 1989 No. 1008: made but not laid before Parliament.
[10] c. 44.

of the Education and Libraries (Northern Ireland) Order 1986[11] and any college of education within the meaning of that Order.

4. Any institution the sole or main purpose of which is to provide further education within the meaning of section 41 of the Education Act 1944[12] or higher education within the meaning of section 120 of the Education Reform Act 1988,[13] or both.

5. Any theological college.

The Copyright (Industrial Process and Excluded Articles) (No. 2) Order 1989   B–37

(S.I. 1989 No. 1070)

Made - - - - - - -	*26th June 1989*
Laid before Parliament	*4th July 1989*
Coming into force	*1st August 1989*

The Secretary of State, in exercise of the powers conferred upon him by section 52(4) of the Copyright, Designs and Patents Act 1988 ("the Act"), hereby makes the following Order:—

1. This Order may be cited as the Copyright (Industrial Process and Excluded   **B–38** Articles) (No. 2) Order 1989 and shall come into force on 1st August 1989.

2. An article is to be regarded for the purposes of section 52 of the Act (limi-   **B–39** tation of copyright protection for design derived from artistic work) as made by an industrial process if—
> (*a*) it is one of more than fifty articles which—
>> (i) all fall to be treated for the purposes of Part I of the Act as copies of a particular artistic work, but
>> (ii) do not all together constitute a single set of articles as defined in section 44(1) of the Registered Designs Act 1949; or
> (*b*) it consists of goods manufactured in lengths or pieces, not being hand-made goods.

3.—(1) There are excluded from the operation of section 52 of the Act—   **B–40**
> (*a*) works of sculpture, other than casts or models used or intended to be used as models or patterns to be multiplied by any industrial process;
> (*b*) wall plaques, medals and medallions; and
> (*c*) printed matter primarily of a literary or artistic character, including book jackets, calendars, certificates, coupons, dress-making patterns, greetings cards, labels, leaflets, maps, plans, playing cards, postards, stamps, trade advertisements, trade forms and cards, transfers and similar articles.

(2) Nothing in article 2 of this Order shall be taken to limit the meaning of "industrial process" in paragraph (1)(*a*) of this article.

---

[11] S.I. 1986 No. 594 (N.I. 3).
[12] c. 31.
[13] c. 40.

B–41   4. The Copyright (Industrial Designs) Rules 1957[14] and the Copyright (Industrial Process and Excluded Articles) Order 1989[15] are hereby revoked.

B–42   ### The Copyright (Material Open to Public Inspection) (International Organisations) Order 1989

(S.I. 1989 No. 1098)

Made - - - - - - -	*29th June 1989*
Laid before Parliament	*10th July 1989*
Coming into force	*1st August 1989*

The Secretary of State, in exercise of the powers conferred upon him by section 47(5) of the Copyright, Designs and Patents Act 1988, hereby makes the following Order:

B–43   1. This Order may be cited as the Copyright (Material Open to Public Inspection) (International Organisations) Order 1989 and shall come into force on 1st August 1989.

B–44   2. Subsections (1) to (3) of section 47 of the Copyright, Designs and Patents Act 1988 apply, subject to the modifications set out in article 3 below, to material made open to public inspection by—
   (a) the European Patent Office under the Convention on the Grant of European Patents[16]; and
   (b) the World Intellectual Property Organisation under the Patent Co-operation Treaty[17];
as they apply in relation to material open to public inspection pursuant to a statutory requirement or to a statutory register.

B–45   3. Subsections (1) to (3) of the said section 47 shall be modified by the substitution for the words "the appropriate person", in each place where they occur, of the words "the Comptroller-General of Patents, Designs and Trade Marks".

B–46   ### The Copyright (Material Open to Public Inspection) (Marking of Copies of Maps) Order 1989

(S.I. 1989 No. 1099)

Made - - - - - - -	*29th June 1989*
Laid before Parliament	*10th July 1989*
Coming into force	*1st August 1989*

The Secretary of State, in exercise of the powers conferred upon him by section 47(4) of the Copyright, Designs and Patents Act 1988, hereby makes the following Order:

---

[14] S.I. 1957 No. 867 (*Copinger*, 12th ed. § 1742).
[15] S.I. 1989 No. 1010: made but not laid before Parliament.
[16] Cmnd. 8510.
[17] Cmnd. 7340.

1. This Order may be cited as the Copyright (Material Open to Public Inspec- **B–47**
tion) (Marking of Copies of Maps) Order 1989 and shall come into force on 1st
August 1989.

2. Subsections (2) and (3) of section 47 of the Copyright, Designs and Patents **B–48**
Act 1988 shall, in the case of a map which is open to public inspection pursuant to
a statutory requirement, or is on a statutory register, apply only to copies of the
map marked in the following manner—

> "This copy has been made by or with the authority of [insert the name of the
> person required to make the map open to public inspection or the person
> maintaining the register] pursuant to section 47 of the Copyright, Designs
> and Patents Act 1988 ("the Act"). Unless the Act provides a relevant excep-
> tion to copyright, the copy must not be copied without the prior permission of
> the copyright owner.".

The Copyright Tribunal Rules 1989[17A]   B–49

(S.I. 1989 No. 1129)

Made - - - - - - -	*4th July 1989*
Laid before Parliament	*10th July 1989*
Coming into force	*1st August 1989*

ARRANGEMENT OF RULES   B–50

Preliminary

[17A] Because of the extension of the jurisdiction of the Copyright Tribunal by the Broadcasting Act 1990 (c. 42), these Rules were amended by The Copyright Tribunal (Amendment) Rules 1991 (S.I. 1991 No. 201) § B–265 *et seq., post.*

The Lord Chancellor in exercise of the powers conferred upon him by sections 150 and 152(2) and (3) of, and paragraph 34 of Schedule 1 to, the Copyright, Designs and Patents Act 1988, after consultation with the Lord Advocate, with the approval of the Treasury as to the fees chargeable under these Rules in respect of proceedings before the Copyright Tribunal, and after consultation with the Council on Tribunals in accordance with section 10(1) of the Tribunals and Inquiries Act 1971, hereby makes the following Rules:—

Preliminary

Citation and commencement

1. These Rules may be cited as the Copyright Tribunal Rules 1989 and shall come into force on 1st August 1989.   **B–51**

Interpretation

2.—(1) In these Rules, unless the context otherwise requires—   **B–52**
   "the Act" means the Copyright, Designs and Patents Act 1988;
   "applicant" means a person or organisation who has made a reference or application to the Tribunal;

"the Chairman" means the Chairman of the Tribunal or a deputy chairman or any other member of the Tribunal appointed to act as chairman;
"costs", in relation to proceedings in Scotland, means "expenses";
"credentials" means—
>(a) the validity of an organisation's claim to be representative of a class of persons, or
>(b) the possession by an intervener of a substantial interest in the matter in dispute;

"intervener" means a person or organisation who has applied under rule 7, 23, 26, 30, 33, 37, 41 or 44 to be made a party to proceedings;
"the office" means the office for the time being of the Tribunal;
"proceedings" means proceedings in respect of a reference or an application before the Tribunal;
"the Secretary" means the Secretary for the time being of the Tribunal; and
"the Tribunal" means the Copyright Tribunal.

(2) A rule or schedule referred to by number means the rule or schedule so numbered in these Rules; a form referred to by number means a form in Schedule 3 so numbered, and a requirement in these Rules for the service of a notice in a specified form shall be taken to have been complied with if the service of the notice is in a form which is substantially in accordance with the form so specified.

References and applications with respect to licensing schemes

Commencement of proceedings (Forms 1 & 2)

B–53   3.—(1) Proceedings in relation to a reference or an application with respect to a licensing scheme shall be commenced by the service on the Secretary by the applicant of a notice—
>(a) in Form 1 in the case of a reference under section 118, 119 or 120 of the Act,
>(b) in Form 2 in the case of an application for the grant of a licence or a review of the Tribunal's order under section 121 or 122 of the Act,

together with a statement of the applicant's case.

(2) A soon as practicable after receipt of the notice, the Secretary shall serve a copy of the same (with a copy of the applicant's statement) on the operator of the licensing scheme named in the notice and, in the case of a further reference under section 120 of the Act or an application for a review of an order under section 122 of the Act, as the case may be, on every person who was a party to the proceedings when the order of the Tribunal was made.

(3) In the case of a reference under section 118 of the Act the Tribunal shall, as soon as practicable after the receipt of the applicant's notice, decide whether to entertain the reference and may for that purpose, at its discretion, allow representations in writing to be made by the applicant or the operator of the scheme or both and if, after considering the reference and representations (if any), the Tribunal—
>(a) decides to entertain the reference, it shall give such directions as to the taking of any steps required or authorised under these Rules, or as to any further matter (including any order as to costs) as the Tribunal thinks fit, and
>(b) declines to entertain the reference, it shall direct that no further proceedings shall be taken by any party in connection with the reference, otherwise than in relation to any order for costs which the Tribunal may make under rule 48.

(4) The decision of the Tribunal shall be in writing and shall include a state-

ment of its reasons, and the Secretary shall serve a copy thereof on the applicant and the operator of the licensing scheme.

Application for special leave (Form 3)

4.—(1) An application under section 120 of the Act for the special leave of the **B–54** Tribunal on a further reference under that section or an application under section 122 of the Act for the special leave of the Tribunal to review its order under that section shall be made by the service on the Secretary by the applicant of a notice in Form 3, together with a statement of the grounds for the application. The applicant shall serve a copy of the notice and statement on every person who was a party to the reference or application on which the Tribunal made the last previous order with respect to the licensing scheme.

(2) Within 14 days of the service upon him of such notice, any such party may make representations in writing to the Tribunal regarding the application for special leave, and he shall serve a copy of any such representations on the applicant and inform the Secretary of the date of such service.

(3) The Tribunal, after considering the application and any representations and, if it considers necessary, after having given the applicant and any such party who has made such representations an opportunity of being heard, shall grant or dismiss the application (with such order as to costs) as it may think fit, and if it grants the application it may give such directions as to the taking of any steps required or authorised under these Rules, or as to any further matter as the Tribunal thinks fit.

(4) The decision of the Tribunal shall be in writing and shall include a statement of its reasons, and the Secretary shall serve a copy thereof on the applicant and any party who made representations.

Advertisement of reference or application

5.—(1) Except where the Tribunal has declined to entertain a reference under **B–55** section 118 of the Act, or the Chairman in any other case otherwise directs, the Secretary shall give notice by advertisement in such manner as the Chairman may think fit of every reference or application under section 118, 119, 120, 121 or 122 of the Act.

(2) An advertisement shall state—
   (*a*) the names and addresses of the applicant and any organisation or person on whom a copy of the notice of reference or application has been served in accordance with rule 3;
   (*b*) the nature of the reference or application;
   (*c*) the time, not being less than 21 days from the date of publication of the advertisement, within which—
      (i) an objection to the applicant's credentials may be made in accordance with rule 6, and
      (ii) any other organisation or person may apply to the Tribunal to be made a party to the proceedings in accordance with rule 7.

Objections to applicant's credentials (Form 4)

6.—(1) Any organisation or person intending to object to the applicant's cre- **B–56** dentials shall, within the time specified under rule 5(2)(*c*), serve on the Secretary a notice of objection in Form 4:

Provided that the Tribunal or the Chairman may give leave, subject to such conditions as the Tribunal or Chairman may think fit, to serve such notice notwithstanding the expiration of the time specified under that rule.

(2) If notice of objection to the applicant's credentials has been served on the

Secretary in accordance with this rule or if the Tribunal intends to make such objection of its own motion, the Secretary shall, on the expiration of the time specified in the advertisement under rule 5(2)(c), serve upon every party to the proceedings a notice of the same, and the proceedings shall (unless the Tribunal or the Chairman shall otherwise direct on the grounds that no reasonable cause of objection has been disclosed) be stayed from the date of such notice until further order.

(3) As soon as practicable after service of the notice under paragraph (2) above, the Chairman shall give directions for the making of representations in writing for the purpose of the consideration by the Tribunal of the objection. After consideration of the representations by the Tribunal the Chairman may, if he thinks fit, give the applicant, any objector and any other party an opportunity of being heard at a hearing to be appointed by the Chairman.

(4) If, after considering the objection and any written or oral representations, the Tribunal is not satisfied of the applicant's credentials, it shall direct that no further proceedings shall be taken by any party in connection with the reference or application, otherwise than in relation to any order for costs which the Tribunal may make under rule 48.

(5) If, after considering the objection and any written or oral representations, the Tribunal is satisfied of the applicant's credentials it shall direct that the reference or application shall proceed and the Tribunal or the Chairman may give such consequential directions as to the taking of any steps required or authorised under these Rules, or as to any further matter as the Tribunal or Chairman may think fit.

(6) When the Tribunal has arrived at its decision on the objection, or where the objection has been withdrawn or is not proceeded with, the Secretary shall serve notice of the same on every party to the proceedings.

Intervener's application (Form 5)

B–57 **7.**—(1) An application to the Tribunal by a person or organisation to be made a party to a reference or an application referred to in rule 3 may be made by serving on the Secretary, within the time specified under rule 5(2)(c), a notice of intervention in Form 5, together with a statement of his interest:

Provided that the Tribunal or the Chairman may give leave, subject to such conditions as the Tribunal or Chairman may think fit, to serve such notice notwithstanding the expiration of the time specified under that rule.

(2) As soon as practicable after receipt of a notice served under this rule the Secretary shall—

(a) serve a copy of the notice on every other party to the proceedings, and

(b) serve on the intervener a copy of the applicant's reference or application and statement of case, together with any other notice of intervention which has been served upon him.

Objections to intervener's credentials (Form 6)

B–58 **8.**—(1) Any party intending to object to an intervener's credentials shall, within 14 days of being served with a copy of the notice of intervention under rule 7, serve on the Secretary a notice of objection in Form 6.

(2) The Secretary shall, as soon as practicable after receipt of any notice of objection, serve on every other party to the proceedings a copy of the same.

(3) If the Tribunal intends of its own motion to object to an intervener's credentials, the Secretary shall, on the expiration of the time specified under rule 5(2)(c), serve on the intervener and every other party notice of that intention with a statement of the Tribunal's reasons for the objection.

(4) An objection to an intervener's credentials shall not, subject to any direction to the contrary that the Chairman may give under rule 11(2)(vii), operate as a stay

of the proceedings and shall be considered by the Tribunal at the same time as the reference or application in question.

Written response by operator of scheme or intervener

9.—(1) Except where otherwise directed under rule 3(3)(a), the operator of the licensing scheme shall, within 28 days of the service on him of a copy of the applicant's statement of case in accordance with rule 3(2), serve on the Secretary a written answer to the applicant's statement setting out his case. **B–59**

(2) Within 21 days of the expiration of the time specified under rule 5(2)(c), an intervener shall serve on the Secretary a statement of the case he intends to make.

(3) The Secretary shall serve a copy of such case or answer on every other party to the proceedings within 10 days of the receipt thereof.

Amendment of statement of case and answer

10.—(1) Subject to paragraph (3) of this rule, a party may at any time amend his statement of case or answer by serving on the Secretary the amended statement or answer. **B–60**

(2) On being served with an amended statement of case or answer, the Secretary shall as soon as practicable serve a copy thereof on every other party.

(3) No amended statement of case or answer shall, without the leave of the Chairman, be served after such date as the Chairman may direct under rule 11(2)(iii).

Chairman's directions[18]

11.—(1) Upon the expiration of the time specified by rule 9(2) for the service on the Secretary of a statement of case or answer, the Chairman shall appoint a date and place for the attendance of the parties for the purpose of his giving directions as to the further conduct of the proceedings, and the Secretary shall serve on every party and every person whose application under rule 7(1) has not been determined not less than 21 days' notice of such date and place. **B–61**

(2) On the appointed day, the Chairman shall afford every party attending the appointment an opportunity of being heard and, after considering any representations made orally or in writing, give such directions as he thinks fit with a view to the just, expeditious and economical disposal of the proceedings and, without prejudice to the generality of the foregoing, may give directions as to—

   (i) the date and place of any oral hearing requested by any party or which the Chairman for any reason considers necessary, and the procedure (including the number of representatives each party may appoint for the purpose of such hearing) and the timetable (including the allocation of time for the making of representations by each party) to be followed at such a hearing;

  (ii) the procedure to be followed with regard to the submission and exchange of written arguments;

 (iii) the date after which no amended statement of case or answer may be served without leave;

 (iv) the preparation and service by each party, or any one party if all other parties agree, of a schedule setting out the issues to be determined by the Tribunal and brief particulars of the contentions of each party in relation thereto;

  (v) the admission of any facts or documents, and the discovery and inspection of documents;

---

[18] See Practice Direction § B–127 *post.*

(vi) the giving of evidence on affidavit; and

(vii) the consideration by the Tribunal of whether any objection made to an intervener's credentials under rule 8 shall operate as a stay of the proceedings.

(3) The Chairman may postpone or adjourn to a later date to be appointed by him the giving of any directions under this rule and, at any time after directions have been given under this rule the Chairman may, whether or not any application on that behalf has been made under rule 12, give such further directions as he may think fit.

(4) If any party fails to comply with any direction given or order made under this rule or rule 12, the Chairman may, without prejudice to the making of any order under rule 53, give such consequential directions as may be necessary and may order such a party to pay any costs occasioned by his default.

Application for directions

B–62   **12.**—(1) A party may, at any stage of the proceedings, apply to the Tribunal for directions with respect to any issue or other matter in the proceedings and, except where the Tribunal (whether generally or in any particular case) otherwise directs or these Rules otherwise provide, every such application shall be disposed of by the Chairman.

(2) The application shall be made by the service of a notice on the Secretary (stating the grounds upon which it is made) and, unless the notice is accompanied by the written consent of all parties to the proceedings, the party making the application shall serve a copy of the application on every other party to the proceedings and inform the Secretary of the date of such service.

(3) Any party who objects to the application may, within 7 days after being served with the copy thereof, serve a notice of objection (stating the grounds of objection) on the Secretary and he shall serve a copy of the same on the applicant and any other party to the proceedings and inform the Secretary of the date of such service.

(4) After considering the application and any objection thereto and, if he considers necessary, after having given all parties concerned an opportunity of being heard, the Chairman may make such order in the matter as he thinks fit and give such consequential directions as may be necessary.

Consolidation of proceedings

B–63   **13.** Where there is pending before the Tribunal more than one reference under section 118, 119, or 120 of the Act, or more than one application under section 121 or 122 of the Act relating to the same licensing scheme, the Chairman may if he thinks fit, either of his own motion or on an application made under rule 12, order that some or all of the references or applications, as the case may be, shall be considered together, and may give such consequential directions as may be necessary:

Provided that the Chairman shall not make an order under this rule of his own motion without giving all parties concerned a reasonable opportunity of objecting to the proposed order.

Procedure and evidence at hearing

B–64   **14.**—(1) Every party to a reference or application which is considered at an oral hearing before the Tribunal shall be entitled to attend the hearing, to address the Tribunal, to give evidence and call witnesses.

(2) Except where the Tribunal or the Chairman otherwise orders in the case of an application for directions under rule 12, the hearing shall be in public.

(3) Evidence before the Tribunal shall be given orally or, if the parties so agree or the Tribunal or the Chairman so orders, by affidavit, but the Tribunal may at

any stage of the proceedings require the personal attendance of any deponent for examination and cross-examination.

Representation and rights of audience

15.—(1) Subject to paragraph (5) of this rule, a party may at any stage of the **B–65** proceedings appoint some other person to act as agent for him in the proceedings.

(2) The appointment of an agent shall be made in writing and shall not be effective until notice thereof has been served on the Secretary, and a copy of the same has been served on every other party and the Secretary informed of the date of such service.

(3) Only one agent shall be appointed to act for a party at any one time.

(4) For the purpose of service on a party of any document, or the taking of any step required or authorised by these Rules, an agent appointed by a party shall be deemed to continue to have authority to act for such a party until the Secretary and every other party has received notice of the termination of his appointment.

(5) A party or an agent appointed by him under paragraph (1) of this rule may be represented at any hearing, whether before the Tribunal or the Chairman, by a barrister, or in Scotland an advocate, or a solicitor, or by any other person allowed by the Tribunal or the Chairman to appear on his behalf or may, save in the case of a corporation or unincorporated body, appear in person.

Withdrawal of reference or application

16.—(1) The applicant may withdraw his reference or application made under **B–66** rule 3 at any time before it has been finally disposed of by serving a notice thereof on the Secretary, but such withdrawal shall be without prejudice to the Tribunal's power to make an order as to the payment of costs incurred up to the time of service of the notice. The applicant shall serve a copy of the notice on every other party to the proceedings and inform the Secretary of the date of such service.

(2) Any party to the proceedings upon whom a copy of the notice of withdrawal is served under this rule may, within 14 days of such service, apply to the Tribunal for an order that, notwithstanding such withdrawal, such reference or application should proceed to be determined by the Tribunal, and if the Tribunal decides, at its discretion, to proceed with such reference or application it may for that purpose substitute such party as the applicant to the proceedings and give such consequential directions as may be necessary.

Decision of Tribunal

17. The final decision of the Tribunal on a reference or an application made **B–67** under rule 3 shall be given in writing and shall include a statement of the Tribunal's reasons and, where on any further reference or application for review of the Tribunal's order under section 120 or 122 of the Act the Tribunal has varied the licensing scheme, there shall be annexed to the decision a copy of the scheme as so varied, and the Secretary shall as soon as practicable serve on every party to the proceedings a copy of the Tribunal's decision.

Publication of decision

18. The Secretary shall cause a copy of the Tribunal's decision to be made avail- **B–68** able at the office for public inspection during office hours and, if the Chairman so directs, shall cause to be advertised, in such manner as the Chairman thinks fit, short particulars of the decision.

Effective date of order

B–69   **19.** Except where the operation of the order is suspended under rule 42 or 43, the order of the Tribunal shall take effect from such date, and shall remain in force for such period, as shall be specified in the order.

References and applications with respect to licensing by licensing bodies

Commencement of proceedings (Forms 7 & 8)

B–70   **20.**—(1) Proceedings with respect to licensing by licensing bodies shall be commenced by the service on the Secretary by the applicant of a notice—
  (*a*) in Form 7 in the case of a reference under section 125 or 126 of the Act,
  (*b*) in Form 8 in the case of an application for a review of an order under section 127 of the Act,
together with a statement of the applicant's case.

(2) As soon as practicable after receipt of the notice, the Secretary shall serve a copy of the same (with a copy of the applicant's statement) on the licensing body named in the notice under paragraph (1)(a) above, and in the case of an application for review of an order under section 127, on any person named in the notice under paragraph (1)(b) above.

(3) In the case of a reference under section 125 of the Act the Tribunal shall, as soon as practicable after the receipt of the applicant's notice, decide whether to entertain the reference and may for that purpose, at its discretion, allow representations in writing to be made by the applicant or the licensing body or both and if, after considering the reference and representations (if any) the Tribunal—
  (*a*) decides to entertain the reference, it shall give such directions as to the taking of any steps required or authorised under these Rules, or as to any further matter (including any order as to costs) as the Tribunal thinks fit, and
  (*b*) declines to entertain the reference, it shall direct that no further proceedings shall be taken by any party in connection with the reference, otherwise than in relation to any order for costs which the Tribunal may make under rule 48.

(4) The decision of the Tribunal shall be in writing and shall include a statement of its reasons, and the Secretary shall serve a copy thereof on the applicant and the licensing body.

Application for special leave (Form 3)

B–71   **21.**—(1) An application under section 127(2) of the Act for the special leave of the Tribunal for the review of its order under that section shall be made by the service on the Secretary by the applicant of a notice in Form 3 together with a statement of the grounds for the application. The applicant shall serve a copy of the notice and statement on every person who was a party to the reference on which the Tribunal made the last previous order with respect to the licence.

(2) Within 14 days of the service upon him of such notice, any such party may make representations in writing to the Tribunal regarding the application for special leave, and he shall serve a copy of any such representations on the applicant and inform the Secretary of the date of such service.

(3) The Tribunal, after considering the application and any representations and, if it considers necessary, after having given the applicant and any such party who has made such representations an opportunity of being heard, shall grant or

dismiss the application (with such order as to costs) as it may think fit, and if it grants the application it may give such directions as to the taking of any steps required or authorised under these Rules or as to any further matter as the Tribunal thinks fit.

(4) The decision of the Tribunal shall be in writing and shall include a statement of its reasons, and the Secretary shall serve a copy thereof on the applicant and on any party who made representations.

Procedure, and decision of Tribunal

22.—(1) Except where otherwise directed under rule 20(3), the licensing body **B–72** or other person shall, within 21 days of the service of the notice under rule 20(2), serve on the Secretary his written answer to the applicant's statement, and shall serve a copy of the same on the applicant and inform the Secretary of the date of such service.

(2) Rules 10 to 16 shall apply to proceedings in respect of a reference or application under rules 20 and 21 as they apply to proceedings in respect of a reference or an application under rule 3.

(3) The final decision of the Tribunal on a reference or an application under rule 20 shall be given in writing and shall include a statement of the Tribunal's reasons and there shall be annexed to the decision a copy of the order and, where the Tribunal has varied a previous order, a copy of that order as varied.

(4) The Secretary shall as soon as practicable serve on every party to the proceedings a copy of the Tribunal's decision. Rules 18 and 19 shall apply with regard to the publication and the effective date of the decision.

Intervener's application (Forms 5 & 6)

23.—(1) A person or organisation who claims to have a substantial interest in **B–73** proceedings in respect of a reference or an application under rule 20 may apply to the Tribunal to be made a party to that reference or application by serving on the Secretary a notice of intervention in Form 5, together with a statement of his interest.

(2) As soon as practicable after receipt of a notice under this rule the Secretary shall—

(*a*) serve a copy of the notice on every other party to the proceedings, and

(*b*) serve on the intervener a copy of the applicant's reference or application and statement of case, together with any other notice of intervention which has been served on him.

(3) Within 14 days of the service upon him of the notice, a party intending to object to an intervener's credentials shall serve on the Secretary a notice of objection in Form 6 and shall serve a copy of the same on the intervener and inform the Secretary of the date of such service.

(4) The Tribunal, after considering the intervener's application and any objection to his credentials and, if it considers necessary, after having given the intervener and any party who has served a notice of objection an opportunity of being heard, shall, if satisfied of the substantial interest of the intervener, grant the application and may thereupon give such directions or further directions as to the taking of any steps required or authorised under these Rules or as to any further matter as may be necessary to enable the intervener to participate in the proceedings as a party.

(5) Subject to any direction to the contrary that the Chairman may give under rule 11(2)(vii) an objection to an intervener's credentials shall not operate as a stay of proceedings and shall be considered by the Tribunal at the same time as the reference or application in question.

Commencement of appeal proceedings (Forms 9 & 10)

B–74   **24.** An appeal to the Tribunal under section 139 of the Act against an order made by the Secretary of State may be made within 6 weeks of the making of the order or such further period as the Tribunal may allow—

    (*a*) in the case of an order under section 137 of the Act, by the service by the copyright owner on the Secretary of a notice in Form 9, together with a statement of his case, and by serving a copy thereof on the licensing body and any person or organisation who was given notice under that section; and

    (*b*) in the case of an order under section 138, by the copyright owner or any person or organisation who was given notice under that section and who made representations, by the service on the Secretary of a notice in Form 10, together with a statement of his case, and by serving a copy thereof on any other person or organisation who made representations under that section.

Procedure, and decision of Tribunal

B–75   **25.**—(1) Within 21 days of the service of the notice upon him under this rule a person or organisation shall serve on the Secretary a written answer to the appellant's statement setting out his case, and shall serve a copy thereof on the appellant and any other person served with notice under this rule and inform the Secretary of the date of such service.

    (2) Rules 10 to 16 shall apply to proceedings in respect of an appeal under rule 24 as they apply to proceedings in respect of an application under rule 3.

    (3) The final decision of the Tribunal on an appeal under rule 24 shall be given in writing and shall include a statement of the Tribunal's reasons and, where the Tribunal varies any previous order or makes any other order, there shall be annexed to the decision a copy of that order as varied or, as the case may be, that other order; and the Secretary shall as soon as practicable serve on every party to the appeal a copy of the Tribunal's decision. Rules 18 and 19 shall apply with regard to the publication and the effective date of the decision.

Intervener's application (Forms 5 & 6)

B–76   **26.** A person or organisation who claims to have a substantial interest in proceedings in respect of an appeal under rule 24 may, in accordance with rule 23, apply to the Tribunal to be made a party and that rule shall apply to proceedings in respect of such an application as it applies to proceedings in respect of an application under rule 20.

Application to settle the royalty or other sum payable

Commencement of proceedings (Forms 11 & 12)

B–77   **27.** Proceedings in relation to an application under section 142 of the Act shall be commenced by the service on the Secretary by the copyright owner or the person claiming to be treated as licensed by him—

    (*a*) of a notice in Form 11, in the case of an application under subsection (1) of that section to settle the royalty or other sum payable in pursuance of section 66 of the Act, and

    (*b*) of a notice in Form 12, in the case of an application under subsection (3) of that section for a variation of an order of the Tribunal made under subsection (2) of that section, together with a statement of the applicant's case, and by serving a copy thereof on the other party.

Application for special leave (Form 3)

28.—(1) An application under section 142(4) of the Act for the special leave of **B–78** the Tribunal for a variation of an order under that section shall be made by the service on the Secretary by the applicant of a notice in Form 3, together with a statement of the grounds for the application, and by serving a copy thereof on the other party.

(2) Within 14 days of the service upon him of a copy of the notice under this rule, the other party may make representations in writing to the Tribunal regarding the application for special leave, and he shall serve a copy of any such representations on the applicant and inform the Secretary of the date of such service.

(3) The Tribunal, after considering the application and any representations and, if it considers necessary, after having given the applicant and any such party who has made such representations an opportunity of being heard, shall grant or dismiss the application (with such order as to costs) as it may think fit, and if it grants the application it may give such directions as to the taking of any steps required or authorised under these Rules or as to any further matter as the Tribunal thinks fit.

(4) The decision of the Tribunal shall be in writing and shall include a statement of its reasons, and the Secretary shall serve a copy thereof on the applicant and on every party who made representations.

Procedure, and decision of Tribunal

29.—(1) Within 21 days of the service of the notice under rule 27 the other party **B–79** shall serve on the Secretary his written answer to the applicant's statement, and shall serve a copy of the same on the applicant and inform the Secretary of the date of such service.

(2) Rules 10 to 16 shall apply to proceedings in respect of an application under rules 27 and 28 as they apply to proceedings in respect of an application under rule 3.

(3) The final decision of the Tribunal on an application under rule 27 shall be given in writing and shall include a statement of the Tribunal's reasons, and there shall be annexed to the decision a copy of the order and where the Tribunal has varied a previous order, a copy of that order as varied; and the Secretary shall as soon as practicable serve on every party to the proceedings a copy of the Tribunal's decision. Rules 18 and 19 shall apply with regard to the publication and the effective date of the decision.

Intervener's application (Forms 5 & 6)

30. A person or organisation who claims to have a substantial interest in pro- **B–80** ceedings in respect of an application under rule 27 may, in accordance with rule 23, apply to the Tribunal to be made a party and that rule shall apply to proceedings in respect of such an application as it applies to proceedings in respect of an application under rule 20.

Application to settle terms of licence as of right

Commencement of proceedings (Form 13)

31. Proceedings in relation to an application by a person requiring a licence in **B–81** the circumstances described in section 144(4) of the Act shall be commenced by the service on the Secretary by the applicant of a notice in Form 13 with a statement of the terms required and the reasons for the same, and he shall serve a copy of the same on the copyright owner.

Procedure, and decision of Tribunal

B–82   **32.**—(1) Within 21 days of the service of the notice under rule 31, the copyright owner may serve on the Secretary his written answer setting out the grounds of his objection and the terms of the licence which he considers the Tribunal should settle, and shall serve a copy of the same on the applicant and inform the Secretary of the date of such service.

(2) Rules 10 to 16 shall apply to proceedings in respect of an application under rule 31 as they apply to proceedings in respect of an application under rule 3.

(3) The final decision of the Tribunal on an application under rule 31 shall be given in writing and shall include a statement of the Tribunal's reasons, and the Secretary shall as soon as practicable serve on every party to the proceedings a copy of the Tribunal's decision. Rule 18 shall apply with regard to the publication of the decision.

Intervener's application (Forms 5 & 6)

B–83   **33.** A person or organisation who claims to have a substantial interest in proceedings in respect of an application under rule 31 may, in accordance with rule 23, apply to the Tribunal to be made a party and that rule shall apply to proceedings in respect of such an application as it applies to proceedings in respect of an application under rule 20.

Application for Tribunal's consent on behalf of performer

Commencement of proceedings (Form 14)

B–84   **34.** Proceedings under section 190 of the Act for the Tribunal's consent on behalf of the performer to the making of a recording from a previous recording of a performance shall be commenced by the service by the applicant on the Secretary of a notice in Form 14 together with a statement—

(*a*) where the identity or whereabouts of the performer cannot be ascertained, of the inquiries made by him in that respect and the result of those inquiries, or

(*b*) where the identity or whereabouts of the performer are known, of the grounds on which the applicant considers that the performer's withholding of consent is unreasonable, and by serving a copy thereof on the performer.

Inquiries by Tribunal

B–85   **35.**—(1) Where a notice has been served in accordance with rule 34(a), the Tribunal shall, after requiring of the applicant such further particulars as it may consider necessary, cause to be served on such persons as it considers are likely to have relevant information with regard to the identity or the whereabouts of the performer a notice seeking such information, and at the same time cause to be published, in such publications as it considers appropriate and at such intervals as it may determine, a notice setting out brief particulars of the application and requesting information on the identity or whereabouts of the performer.

(2) On the expiration of 28 days from the date of the publication of the notice, or the date of publication of the last such notice, the Tribunal may, on being satisfied that the identity or whereabouts of the performer cannot be ascertained, make an order giving its consent on such terms as it thinks fit.

Procedure, and decision of Tribunal

36.—(1) Within 21 days of the service of the notice under rule 34(b), the per- **B–86**
former may serve on the Secretary his answer setting out his case and of the
grounds for his withholding of consent, and shall serve a copy of the same on the
applicant and inform the Secretary of the date of such service.

(2) Rules 10 to 16 shall apply to proceedings in respect of an application under
rule 34(*b*) as they apply to proceedings in respect of an application under rule 3.

(3) The final decision of the Tribunal on an application under rule 34 shall be
given in writing and shall include a statement of the Tribunal's reasons and where
the Tribunal has, in default of an agreement between the applicant and the performer, made an order as to the payment to be made to the performer in consideration of the consent given on his behalf by the Tribunal, there shall be annexed to
the decision a copy of that order; and the Secretary shall as soon as practicable
serve on every party to the proceedings a copy of the Tribunal's decision. Rules 18
and 19 shall apply with regard to the publication and the effective date of the
decision.

Intervener's application (Forms 5 & 6)

37. A person or organisation who claims to have a substantial interest in pro- **B–87**
ceedings in respect of an application under rule 34 may, in accordance with rule
23, apply to the Tribunal to be made a party, and that rule shall apply to proceedings in respect of such an application as it applies to proceedings in respect of an
application under rule 20.

Application for Tribunal's determination of royalty payable to the Hospital for Sick Children

Commencement of proceedings (Forms 15 & 16)

38. Proceedings under paragraph 5 of Schedule 6 to the Act for the determi- **B–88**
nation of the royalty or other remuneration to be paid to the Hospital for Sick
Children shall be commenced by the service on the Secretary by the applicant of a
notice—
   (*a*) in Form 15, in the case of an application under paragraph 5(1) of Sched-
      ule 6 to the Act, and
   (*b*) in Form 16, in the case of an application for a review of an order under
      paragraph 5(2) of that Schedule,
together with a statement of the applicant's case, and by serving a copy thereof on
the other party.

Application for special leave (Form 3)

39.—(1) An application for the special leave of the Tribunal for the review of an **B–89**
order under paragraph 5(3) of Schedule 6 to the Act shall be made by serving on
the Secretary a notice in Form 3 together with a statement of the grounds for the
application, and by serving a copy thereof on the person who was a party to the
proceedings when the order of the Tribunal was made.

(2) Within 14 days of the service upon him of a copy of the notice under this
rule, the other party may make representations in writing to the Tribunal regarding the application for special leave, and he shall serve a copy of any such representations on every other party to the proceedings and inform the Secretary of
the date of such service.

(3) The Tribunal, after considering the application and any representations
and, if it considers necessary, after having given the applicant and any such party
who has made such representations an opportunity of being heard, shall grant or
dismiss the application (with such order as to costs) as it may think fit, and if it

grants the application it may give such directions as to the taking of any steps required or authorised under these Rules or as to any further matter as the Tribunal thinks fit.

(4) The decision of the Tribunal shall be in writing and shall include a statement of its reasons, and the Secretary shall serve a copy thereof on the applicant and on any party who made representations.

Procedure, and decision of Tribunal

B–90   **40.**—(1) Within 21 days of the service of the notice under rule 38, the other party shall serve on the Secretary a written answer to the applicant's statement, and shall serve a copy of the same on the applicant and inform the Secretary of the date of such service.

(2) Rules 10 to 16 shall apply to proceedings in respect of an application under rules 38 and 39 as they apply to proceedings in respect of an application under rule 3.

(3) The final decision of the Tribunal on an application under rule 38 shall be given in writing and shall include a statement of the Tribunal's reasons and where the Tribunal has varied a previous order there shall be annexed to the decision a copy of that order as varied; and the Secretary shall as soon as practicable serve on every party to the proceedings a copy of the Tribunal's decision. Rule 18 shall apply with regard to the publication of the decision.

Intervener's application (Forms 5 & 6)

B–91   **41.** A person or organisation who claims to have a substantial interest in proceedings in respect of an application under rule 38 may, in accordance with rule 23, apply to the Tribunal to be made a party and that rule shall apply to proceedings in respect of such an application as it applies to proceedings in respect of an application under rule 20.

Appeal to the Court from decision of Tribunal and suspension of Tribunal's orders

Notice of appeal (Form 17)

B–92   **42.**—(1) An appeal to the High Court or, in the case of proceedings of the Tribunal in Scotland, to the Court of Session under section 152 of the Act on a point of law arising from a decision of the Tribunal shall be brought within 28 days of the date of the decision of the Tribunal or within such further period as the court may, on an application to it, allow.

(2) A party so appealing to the court on a point of law shall as soon as may be practicable serve on the Secretary a notice in Form 17 of such an appeal, and shall serve a copy thereof on every person who was a party to the proceedings giving rise to that decision.

(3) Where an appeal has been lodged with the court, the Tribunal shall not make any further order on the reference or application which is the subject of the appeal until the court has given its decision thereon.

(4) On receipt of the notice of appeal by the Secretary the Tribunal may of its own motion suspend the operation of any order contained in its decision, and shall, if an order is so suspended, cause notice of the same to be served on every person affected by the suspension and may, if it thinks fit, cause notice of the suspension to be published in such manner as it may direct.

Application for suspension of order (Form 18)

B–93   **43.**—(1) A party to the proceedings may, pending the determination of an appeal under rule 42, apply to the Tribunal to suspend the operation of an order made by it by serving on the Secretary a notice in Form 18 within 7 days of the receipt of the decision of the Tribunal together with a statement of the grounds for suspension, and he shall serve a copy of the same on every person who was a party to the proceedings giving rise to that decision and inform the Secretary of the date of such service.

(2) Within 14 days of the service of the notice under paragraph (1) above a party may serve on the Secretary a statement setting out the grounds of his objection to the applicant's case, and shall serve a copy of the same on every person who was a party to the proceedings giving rise to the decision and inform the Secretary of the date of such service.

(3) Rules 10 to 16 shall apply to proceedings in respect of an application under this rule as they apply to proceedings in respect of an application under rule 3.

(4) Where the Tribunal, after consideration of the application and any representations, refuses an application to suspend the operation of its order, the Secretary shall as soon as practicable serve on every party to the proceedings a copy of the Tribunal's decision together with a statement of the Tribunal's reasons for refusal.

(5) Where any order of the Tribunal has been suspended upon the application of a party to the proceedings or by the court the Secretary shall serve notice of the suspension on all parties to the proceedings, and if particulars of the order have been advertised shall cause notice of the suspension to be advertised in the same manner, and rule 18 shall apply with regard to the publication of the decision.

Intervener's application (Forms 5 & 6)

44. A person or organisation who claims to have a substantial interest in proceedings in respect of an application under rule 43 may, in accordance with rule 23, apply to the Tribunal to be made a party, and that rule shall apply to proceedings in respect of such an application as it applies to proceedings in respect of an application under rule 20.   **B–94**

Effect of suspension of order

45. If the operation of any order is suspended under rule 42 or 43, then, while the order remains suspended, sections 123 and 128 of the Act shall not have effect in relation to the order.   **B–95**

Miscellaneous and general

Application of Arbitration Acts

46. The provisions of sections 12, 14, 17 and 26 of the Arbitration Act 1950[19] (which are set out in Part 1 of Schedule 2), shall apply in the case of proceedings before the Tribunal in England and Wales, and the provisions of sections 13, 14, 16, 21 and 24 of, and paragraphs 4, 5 and 8 of Schedule 1 to, the Arbitration Act (Northern Ireland) 1937[20] (which are set out in Part 2 of Schedule 2), shall apply in the case of proceedings before the Tribunal in Northern Ireland, as those provisions respectively apply to an arbitration where no contrary intention is expressed in the arbitration agreement.   **B–96**

Enforcement of Tribunal's orders in Scotland

47. Any decision of the Tribunal may be enforced in Scotland in like manner as a recorded decree arbitral.   **B–97**

---

[19] c. 27.
[20] c. 8 (N.I.).

Costs

B–98   **48.**—(1) The Tribunal may, at its discretion, at any stage of the proceedings make any order it thinks fit in relation to the payment of costs by one party to another in respect of the whole or part of the proceedings.

(2) Any party against whom an order for costs is made shall, if the Tribunal so directs, pay to any other party a lump sum by way of costs, or such proportion of the costs as may be just, and in the last mentioned case the Tribunal may assess the sum to be paid or may direct that it be assessed by the Chairman, or taxed by a taxing officer of the Supreme Court or the Supreme Court of Northern Ireland or by the Auditor of the Court of Session.

Fees

B–99   **49.** The fees specified in Schedule 1 shall be payable in respect of the matters therein mentioned.

Service of documents

B–100   **50.**—(1) Any notice or other document required by these Rules to be served on any person may be sent to him by pre-paid post at his address for service, or, where no address for service has been given, at his registered office, principal place of business or last known address, and every notice or other document required to be served on the Secretary may be sent by pre-paid post to the Secretary at the office.

(2) Service of any notice or document on a successor in title or successor in interest of a party to any proceedings shall be effective if served or sent to him in accordance with this rule.

(3) Any notice or other document required to be served on a licensing body or organisation which is not a body corporate may be sent to the secretary, manager or other similar officer.

(4) The Tribunal or the Chairman may direct that service of any notice or other document be dispensed with or effected otherwise than in the manner provided by these Rules.

(5) Service of any notice or document on a party's solicitor or agent shall be deemed to be service on such party, and service on a solicitor or agent acting for more than one party shall be deemed to be service on every party for whom such a solicitor or agent acts.

Time

B–101   **51.**—(1) Except in the case of the time limit imposed under rule 42(1), the time for doing any act may (whether it has already expired or not) be extended—
   (a) with the leave of the Tribunal or the Chairman, or
   (b) by the consent in writing of all parties, except where the Tribunal or Chairman has fixed the time by order or, if the time is prescribed by these Rules, has directed that it may not be extended or further extended without leave.

(2) A party in whose favour time is extended by consent under paragrraph (1)(b) above shall, as soon as may be practicable after the necessary consents have been obtained, serve notice thereof on the Secretary.

(3) Where the last day for the doing of any act falls on a day on which the office is closed and by reason thereof the act cannot be done on that day, it may be done on the next day on which the office is open.

Office hours

52. The office shall be open between 10.00am and 4.00pm Monday to Friday, **B–102** excluding Good Friday, Christmas Day and any day specified or proclaimed to be a bank holiday under section 1 of the Banking and Financial Dealings Act 1971.

Failure to comply with directions

53. If any party fails to comply with any direction given, in accordance with **B–103** these Rules, by the Tribunal or the Chairman, the Tribunal may, if it considers that the justice of the case so requires, order that such party be debarred from taking any further part in the proceedings without leave of the Tribunal.

Power of Tribunal to regulate procedure

54. Subject to the provisions of the Act and these Rules, the Tribunal shall have **B–104** power to regulate its own procedure.

Transitional provisions and revocation of previous Rules

55.—(1) In relation to any proceedings which are pending under Part IV of the **B–105** Copyright Act 1956 when these Rules come into force, these Rules shall apply subject to such modifications as the Tribunal or the Chairman may, in the circumstances, consider appropriate.

(2) The Performing Right Tribunal Rules 1965, and the Performing Right Tribunal (Amendment) Rules 1971[21] are hereby revoked, but without prejudice to anything done thereunder.

SCHEDULE 1   Rule 49   **B–106**

TABLE OF FEES

(1) On serving notice in Forms 1, 2, 7, 8, 12, 14, 15 or 16	£30
(2) On serving notice in Forms 3, 4, 5, 6, 9, 10, 11, 13, 17 or 18	£15
(3) On every application for directions under rule 12	£10

SCHEDULE 2   Rule 46

PROVISIONS OF ARBITRATION ACTS

Part 1

Provisions of the Arbitration Act 1950 which apply in the case of procedings **B–107** before the Tribunal in England and Wales.
Sections 12, 14, 17 and 26 shown below—

---

[21] S.I. 1965 No. 1506, S.I. 1971 No. 636 (*Copinger*, 12th ed. § 1758).

Conduct of proceedings, witnesses, &c.

12.—(1) Unless a contrary intention is expressed therein, every arbitration agreement shall, where such a provision is applicable to the reference, be deemed to contain a provision that the parties to the reference, and all persons claiming through them respectively, shall, subject to any legal objection, submit to be examined by the arbitrator or umpire, on oath or affirmation, in relation to the matters in dispute, and shall, subject as aforesaid, produce before the arbitrator or umpire all documents within their possession or power respectively which may be required or called for, and do all other things which during the proceedings on the reference the arbitrator or umpire may require.

(2) Unless a contrary intention is expressed therein, every arbitration agreement shall, where such a provision is applicable to the reference, be deemed to contain a provision that the witnesses on the reference shall, if the arbitrator or umpire thinks fit, be examined on oath or affirmation.

(3) An arbitrator or umpire shall, unless a contrary intention is expressed in the arbitration agreement, have power to administer oaths to, or take the affirmations of, the parties to and witnesses on a reference under the agreement.

(4) Any party to a reference under an arbitration agreement may sue out a writ of subpoena ad testificandum or a writ of subpoena duces tecum, but no person shall be compelled under any such writ to produce any document which he could not be compelled to produce on the trial of an action, and the High Court or a judge thereof may order that a writ of subpoena ad testificandum or of subpoena duces tecum shall issue to compel the attendance before an arbitrator or umpire of a witness wherever he may be within the United Kingdom.

(5) The High Court or a judge thereof may also order that a writ of habeas corpus ad testificandum shall issue to bring up a prisoner for examination before an arbitrator or umpire.

(6) The High Court shall have, for the purpose of and in relation to a reference, the same power of making orders in respect of—

    (*a*) security for costs;

    (*b*) discovery of documents and interrogatories;

    (*c*) the giving of evidence by affidavit;

    (*d*) examination on oath of any witness before an officer of the High Court or any other person, and the issue of a commission or request for the examination of a witness out of the jurisdiction;

    (*e*) the preservation, interim custody or sale of any goods which are the subject matter of the reference;

    (*f*) securing the amount in dispute in the reference;

    (*g*) the detention, preservation or inspection of any property or thing which is the subject of the reference or as to which any question may arise therein, and authorising for any of the purposes aforesaid any persons to enter upon or into any land or building in the possession of any party to the reference, or authorising any samples to be taken or any observation to be made or experiment to be tried which may be necessary or expedient for the purpose of obtaining full information or evidence; and

    (*h*) interim injunctions or the appointment of a receiver;

as it has for the purpose of an in relation to an action or matter in the High Court:

Provided that nothing in this subsection shall be taken to prejudice any power which may be vested in an arbitrator or umpire of making orders with respect to any of the matters aforesaid.

Interim awards

14. Unless a contrary intention is expressed therein, every arbitration agreement shall, where such a provision is applicable to the reference, be deemed to contain a provision that the arbitrator or umpire may, if he thinks fit, make an interim award, and any reference in this Part of this Act to an award includes a reference to an interim award.

Power to correct slips

17. Unless a contrary intention is expressed in the arbitration agreement, the arbitrator or umpire shall have power to correct in an award any clerical mistake or error arising from any accidental slip or omission.

Enforcement of award

26.[22]—(1) An award on an arbitration agreement may, by leave of the High Court or a judge thereof, be enforced in the same manner as a judgment or order to the same effect, and where leave is so given, judgment may be entered in terms of the award.

(2) If—

    (*a*) the amount sought to be recovered does not exceed the county court limit, and

    (*b*) a county court so orders,

it shall be recoverable (by execution issued from the county court or otherwise) as if payable under an order of that court and shall not be enforceable under subsection (1) above.

(3) An application to the High Court under this section shall preclude an application to a county court and an application to a county court under this section shall preclude an application to the High Court.

(4) In subsection (2)(*a*) above "the county court limit" means the amount which for the time being is the county court limit for the purposes of section 16 of the County Courts Act 1984 (money recoverable by statute).

Part 2

Provisions of the Arbitration Act (Northern Ireland) 1937 which apply in the **B–108** case of proceedings before the Tribunal in Northern Ireland.

A. Sections 13, 14, 16, 21 and 24 shown below—

Powers of arbitrators

13. The arbitrators or umpire acting under a reference in an arbitration agreement shall, unless the arbitration agreement or the reference thereunder expresses a contrary intention, have power to administer oaths to or take the affirmations of the parties and witnesses appearing, and to correct in an award any clerical mistake or error arising from any accidental slip or omission.

Attendance of witnesses

14. Any party to a reference under an arbitration agreement may sue out a writ of subpoena ad testificandum, or a writ of subpoena duces tecum, but no person shall be compelled under any such writ to produce any document which he could not be compelled to produce on the trial of an action:

Provided that no writ shall issue under this section unless the arbitrator has entered on the reference or has been called on to act by notice in writing from a party to the reference and has agreed to do so.

---

[22] s.26 was amended by s.17(2) Administration of Justice Act 1977 (c. 38) and s.148(1) and para. 22, Sched. 2 County Courts Act 1984 (c. 28).

Entry of judgment in terms of award

16. An award on a reference under an arbitration agreement may, by leave of the court, be entered as a judgment in terms of the award, and shall thereupon have the same force and effect as a judgment or order of the court.

Additional powers of court

21.—(1) The court shall have, for the purpose of and in relation to a reference, the same power of making orders in respect of any of the matters set out in the Second Schedule to this Act as it has for the purpose of and in relation to an action or matter in the court:

Provided that nothing in the foregoing provision shall be taken to prejudice any power which may be vested in an arbitrator or umpire of making orders with respect to any of the matters aforesaid.

(2) Where relief by way of interpleader is granted and it appears to the court that the claims in question are matters to which an arbitration agreement, to which the claimants are parties, applies, the court may direct the issue between the claimants to be determined in accordance with the agreement.

(3) Where an application is made to set aside an award the court may order that any money made payable by the award shall be brought into court or otherwise secured pending the determination of the application.

Additional powers to compel attendance of witnesses

24.—(1) The court may order that a writ of subpoena ad testificandum or of subpoena duces tecum shall issue to compel the attendance of a witness before any referee, arbitrator or umpire.

(2) The court may also order that a writ of habeas corpus ad testificandum shall issue to bring up a prisoner for examination before any referee, arbitrator or umpire.

B. First Schedule (provisions to be implied in arbitration agreements), paragraphs 4, 5 and 8 shown below—

4. The parties to the reference and all persons claiming through them respectively shall, subject to any legal objection, submit to be examined by the arbitrators or umpire on oath or affirmation in relation to the matters in dispute and shall, subject as aforesaid, produce before the arbitrators or umpire all books, deeds, papers, accounts, writings and documents within their possession or power respectively which may be required or called for, and do all other things which during the proceedings on the reference the arbitrators or umpire may require.

5. The witnesses on the reference shall, if the arbitrators or umpire think fit, be examined on oath or affirmation.

8. The arbitrators or umpire may, if they think fit, make an interim award.

C. Second Schedule (matters in respect of which court may make orders) referred to in section 21(1), shown below—

1. Security for costs.

2. Discovery of documents and interrogatories.

3. The giving of evidence by affidavit.

4. Examination on oath of any witnesses before an officer of the court or any other person, and the issue of a commission or request for the examination of a witness out of the jurisdiction.

5. The preservation, interim custody, or sale, of any goods which are the subject matter of the reference.

6. Securing the amount in dispute in the reference.

7. The detention, preservation or inspection of any property or thing which is the subject of the reference or as to which any question may arise therein, and

authorising for any of the purposes aforesaid any persons to enter upon or into any land or building in the possession of any party to the reference, or authorising any samples to be taken or any observation to be made or experiment to be tried which may be necessary or expedient for the purpose of obtaining full information or evidence.

8. Interim injunctions or the appointment of a receiver.

SCHEDULE 3   Rule 2(2)

FORM 1   Rule 3(1)(a)

COPYRIGHT, DESIGNS AND PATENTS ACT 1988
COPYRIGHT TRIBUNAL

Notice of Reference under Section 118, 119 or 120

To,
   The Secretary to the Tribunal

   1. TAKE NOTICE that

Reference under s.118

*Whereas

[state name and address of *organisation*] ("the Applicant"), being representative of persons claiming that they require licences [describe case(s) for which licence is required] to which the licensing scheme proposed (specified below) would apply;

Reference under s.119

*Whereas

*[state name and address of *person*] ("the Applicant") claims that a licence [describe case for which licence is required] is required

*[state name and address of *organisation*] ("the Applicant"), being representative of persons claiming that they require licences [describe case(s) for which licence is required]

to which the licensing scheme (specified below) applies;

Further reference under s.120

*Whereas

*[state name and address of *operator of scheme*] ("the Applicant"), is the operator of the scheme (specified below)

*[state name and address of *person*] ("the Applicant") claims that a licence [describe case for which licence is required] is required to which the licensing scheme (specified below) applies

*[state name and address of *organisation*] ("the Applicant"), being representative of persons claiming that they require licences [describe case(s) for which licence is required] to which the licensing scheme (specified below) applies;

the Applicant hereby refers to the Tribunal the licensing scheme, particulars of which are—

[state name and address of operator of scheme and the scheme] ....

*as confirmed/varied by the Tribunal by an Order dated ....
and bearing the reference number ....

2. The Applicant is an organisation representing [here give particulars of the persons whom the Applicant claims to represent and the grounds on which it claims to represent them].

3. There is delivered herewith a statement of the Applicant's case.

4. All communications about this reference should be addressed to

*[the Applicant at the address shown above]

*[name and address of Applicant's solicitor/agent].

Signed ....

Status of signatory .... [Applicant,
an officer of Applicant, solicitor or agent]

Date ....
*Delete whichever is inappropriate

COPYRIGHT, DESIGNS AND PATENTS ACT 1988
COPYRIGHT TRIBUNAL

Notice of Application under Section 121 or 122

To,
The Secretary to the Tribunal

1. TAKE NOTICE that

*[name and address of person]

*[name and address of operator of licensing scheme]

("the Applicant") hereby applies to the Tribunal in connection with the licensing scheme (specified below)—

Application under s.121(1) or (2)

*being in a case covered by the scheme, for the grant of a licence in connection with the scheme which the operator of the scheme has *refused/failed to grant or procure the gant within a reasonable time

*being a case excluded from the scheme, the operator of the scheme has *refused/failed to grant or procure the grant within a reasonable time/has proposed terms for a licence which are unreasonable

Application for review under s.122

*for a review of its Order dated .... and bearing the reference number ....

2. The particulars of the licensing scheme are [name and address of operator of scheme and the case covered or excluded by the scheme].

3. Description of the case for which a licence is required ....

4. There is delivered herewith a statement of the Applicant's case.

5. All communications about this reference should be addressed to

*[the Applicant at the address shown above]

*[name and address of Applicant's solicitor/agent].

Signed ....

Status of signatory .... [Applicant, an officer of Applicant, solicitor or agent]

Date ....
*Delete whichever is inappropriate

COPYRIGHT, DESIGNS AND PATENTS ACT 1988
COPYRIGHT TRIBUNAL

Application for Special Leave under Section 120, 122, 127 or 142 or Schedule 6, paragraph 5

To,

The Secretary to the Tribunal

1. TAKE NOTICE that [name and address of person, organisation or operator of licensing scheme] ("the Applicant") hereby applies for the special leave of the Tribunal—

Application unders s.120(2)

*to refer again to the Tribunal the licensing scheme which was *confirmed/ varied by the Tribunal by an Order

Application under s.122(2)

*to review its Order as to entitlement to licence

Application under s.127(2)

*to review its Order as to licence

Application under s.142(4) or Sch. 6, para 5(3)

*to review its Order as to royalty or other sum/remuneration payable

dated .... and bearing reference number ....

2. There is delivered herewith a statement of the grounds for the application.

3. A copy of this Notice, together with the statement, *has been/will be served on [date of service] on every person who was a party to the proceedings to which the above Order of the Tribunal relates, namely [specify names and addresses of parties].

4. All communications about this application should be addressed to

*[the Applicant at the address shown above]

*[name and address of Applicant's solicitor/agent].

Signed ....

Status of signatory .... [Applicant,
an officer of Applicant, solicitor or agent]

Date ....
*Delete whichever is inappropriate

COPYRIGHT, DESIGNS AND PATENTS ACT 1988
COPYRIGHT TRIBUNAL

Notice of Objection to Applicant's Credentials

To,
    The Secretary to the Tribunal

1. TAKE NOTICE that in connection with the proceedings commenced by notice of *reference/application dated ....
served by [name of Applicant] [name and address of party making objection] ("the Objector"), being

*[*a person/an organisation on whom a copy of the aforementioned notice was served on [date of service]]

*[an intervener by virtue of a notice of intervention served on [date of service]]

objects to the Applicant's credentials.

2. The Objector's grounds for the objection are as follows [state grounds].

4. All communications about this objection should be addressed to

*[the Objector at the address shown above]

*[name and address of Objector's solicitor/agent].

Signed ....

Status of signatory .... [Objector,
                                    an officer of Objector, solicitor or agent]

Date ....
*Delete whichever is inappropriate

FORM 5   Rules 7(1), 23(1), 26, 30,   **B–113**
                                            33, 37, 41 and 44

COPYRIGHT, DESIGNS AND PATENTS ACT 1988
COPYRIGHT TRIBUNAL

Notice of Intervention

To,

    The Secretary to the Tribunal

1. TAKE NOTICE that [name and address of intervener] ("the Intervener") wishes to be made a party to the proceedings commenced by notice of *reference/ application/appeal dated ....

    *[which was advertised in [name of publication and date of issue]].

2. The Intervener has a substantial interest in the matter for the following reasons [state reasons].

3. All communications about this reference should be addressed to

    *[the Intervener at the address shown above]

    *[name and address of Intervener's solicitor/agent].

Signed ....

Status of signatory .... [Intervener,
                                    an officer of Intervener, solicitor or agent]

Date ....
*Delete whichever is inappropriate

FORM 6   Rules 8(1), 23(3), 26, 30,
                              33, 37, 41 and 44

COPYRIGHT, DESIGNS AND PATENTS ACT 1988
COPYRIGHT TRIBUNAL

Notice of Objection to Intervener's Credentials

To,
    The Secretary to the Tribunal

1. TAKE NOTICE that in connection with *proceedings commenced by notice of *reference/application dated ....
served by [name of Applicant], and with the notice of intervention given by [name of Intervener] dated ....
[name and address of party making objection] ("the Objector"), being

*[the Applicant]

*[the licensing body named in the notice of *reference/application]

*[*a person/an organisation on whom the notice of *reference/application was served]

*[an intervener in the proceedings by virtue of a notice of intervention served on [date of service]]

objects to the Intervener's credentials.

2. The Objector's grounds for the objection are as follows [state grounds].

3. All communications about this reference should be addressed to

*[the Objector at the address shown above]

*[name and address of Objector's solicitor/agent].

Signed ....

Status of signatory .... [Objector,
                              an officer of Objector, solicitor or agent]

Date ....
*Delete whichever is inappropriate

COPYRIGHT, DESIGNS AND PATENTS ACT 1988
COPYRIGHT TRIBUNAL

Notice of Reference under Section 125 or 126

To,

The Secretary to the Tribunal

1. TAKE NOTICE that [name and address of prospective licensee or licensee] ("the Applicant"),

Reference under s.125

*[being the prospective licensee under the terms of a licence to be granted by [name and address of licensing body]]

Reference under s.126

*[being a licensee under a licence granted by [name and address of licensing body], which licence is due to expire *by effluxion of time/as a result of a notice given by the licensing body on ....]

hereby—

*[refer to the Tribunal the terms on which the licensing body proposes to grant the licence]

*[apply to the Tribunal on the ground that it is unreasonable that the licence should cease to be in force].

2. There is delivered herewith a statement of the Applicant's case.

3. All communications about this reference should be addressed to

*[the Applicant at the address shown above]

*[name and address of Applicant's solicitor/agent].

Signed ....

Status of signatory .... [Applicant, an officer of Applicant, solicitor or agent]

Date ....
*Delete whichever is inappropriate

COPYRIGHT, DESIGNS AND PATENTS ACT 1988
COPYRIGHT TRIBUNAL

Notice of Application for Review of Order under Section 127

To,
    The Secretary to the Tribunal

1. TAKE NOTICE that [name and address of licensing body or person seeking review] ("the Applicant") hereby applies to the Tribunal for a review of its Order dated .... and bearing the reference number .... relating to the licence granted *to/by [name and address of licensee or licensing body].

2. There is delivered herewith a statement of the Applicant's case.

3. All communications about this application should be addressed to

   *[the Applicant at the address shown above]

   *[name and address of Applicant's solicitor/agent].

Signed ....

Status of signatory .... [Applicant, an officer of Applicant, solicitor or agent]

Date ....
*Delete whichever is inappropriate

COPYRIGHT, DESIGNS AND PATENTS ACT 1988
COPYRIGHT TRIBUNAL

Notice of Appeal under Section 139 against Order under Section 137

To,
The Secretary to the Tribunal

1. TAKE NOTICE that [name and address of appellant] ("the Appellent"), being the owner of the copyright in [describe the work] which is the subject of an Order by the Secretary of State under section 137 of the Act dated .... and bearing the reference number .... (a copy of which is attached) hereby appeals to the Tribunal against that Order.

2. There is delivered herewith a statement of the Appellant's case.

3. A copy of this Notice, together with the statement, *has been/will be served on [date of service] on the licensing body and any person or organisation who was given notice under section 137(3), namely [specify names and addresses of parties].

4. All communications about this appeal should be addressed to

*[the Appellant at the address shown above]

*[name and address of Appellant's solicitor/agent].

Signed ....

Status of signatory .... [Appellant, an officer of Appellant, solicitor or agent]

Date ....
*Delete whichever is inappropriate

COPYRIGHT, DESIGNS AND PATENTS ACT 1988
COPYRIGHT TRIBUNAL

Notice of Appeal under Section 139 against Order under Section 138

To,
  The Secretary to the Tribunal

1. TAKE NOTICE that [name and address of appellant] ("the Appellent"), being

*[the owner of the copyright in [describe the work]]

*[*a person/an organisation who was given notice under section 138(3) and made representations in accordance with section 138(4)]

hereby appeals to the Tribunal against the Order by the Secretary of State dated .... and bearing the reference number .... (a copy of which is attached).

2. There is delivered herewith a statement of the Appellant's case.

3. A copy of this Notice, together with the statement, *has been/will be served on [date of service] on every person or organisation who made representations under section 138, namely [specify names and addresses of parties].

4. All communications about this appeal should be addressed to

*[the Appellant at the address shown above]

*[name and address of Appellant's solicitor/agent].

Signed ....

Status of signatory .... [Appellant,
                    an officer of Appellant, solicitor or agent]

Date ....
*Delete whichever is inappropriate

COPYRIGHT, DESIGNS AND PATENTS ACT 1988
COPYRIGHT TRIBUNAL

Notice of Application to Settle Royalty or Other Sum Payable under Section 142

To,
　The Secretary to the Tribunal

　1. TAKE NOTICE that [name and address of applicant] ("the Applicant"), being

　　*[the owner of the copyright in [describe the works]]

　　*[The person claiming to be treated as licensed by the owner of the copyright in [describe the works]]

hereby applies to the Tribunal to settle the royalty or other sum payable in pursuance of section 66 of the Act.

　2. There is delivered herewith a statement of the Applicant's case with respect to the royalty or other sum payable.

　3. A copy of this Notice, together with the statement, *has been/will be served on [date of service] on [state name and address of other party].

　4. All communications about this application should be addressed to

　　*[the Applicant at the address shown above]

　　*[name and address of Applicant's solicitor/agent].

Signed ....

Status of signatory .... [Applicant,
an officer of Applicant, solicitor or agent]

Date ....
*Delete whichever is inappropriate

COPYRIGHT, DESIGNS AND PATENTS ACT 1988
COPYRIGHT TRIBUNAL

Notice of Application for Review of Order under Section 142(3)

To,

The Secretary to the Tribunal

1. TAKE NOTICE that

*[state name and address of owner of copyright]

*[state name and address of person claiming to be treated as licensed by the owner of copyright]

("the Applicant") hereby applies to the Tribunal for a review of its Order dated .... and bearing the reference number .... in respect of the settlement of the royalty or other sum payable to [name and address of owner of copyright in respect of the work].

2. There is delivered herewith a statement of the Applicant's case.

3. A copy of this Notice, together with the statement, *has been/will be served on [date of service] on the other party [state name and address of other party].

4. All communications about this application should be addressed to

*[the Applicant at the address shown above]

*[name and address of Applicant's solicitor/agent].

Signed ....

Status of signatory .... [Applicant,
an officer of Applicant, solicitor or agent]

Date ....
*Delete whichever is inappropriate

COPYRIGHT, DESIGNS AND PATENTS ACT 1988
COPYRIGHT TRIBUNAL

Notice of Application to Settle Terms of Licence of Right under Section 144

To,
     The Secretary to the Tribunal

1. TAKE NOTICE that [name and address of applicant] ("the Applicant") hereby applies to the Tribunal to settle the terms of a licence available by virtue of section 144 of the Act in respect of [describe the works].

2. There is delivered herewith a statement setting out the terms required by the Applicant and the reasons for the same.

3. A copy of this Notice, together with the statement, *has been/will be served on [date of service] on the copyright owner, namely [state name and address of owner of copyright in the work].

4. All communications about this reference should be addressed to

     *[the Applicant at the address shown above]

     *[name and address of Applicant's solicitor/agent].

Signed ....

Status of signatory .... [Applicant,
                              an officer of Applicant, solicitor or agent]

Date ....
*Delete whichever is inappropriate

COPYRIGHT, DESIGNS AND PATENTS ACT 1988
COPYRIGHT TRIBUNAL

Notice of Application for Tribunal's Consent on behalf of Performer
under Section 190

To,
The Secretary to the Tribunal

1. TAKE NOTICE that [name and address of applicant] ("the Applicant")
wishes to make a recording from a previous recording of [specify performance]

*[the identity or whereabouts of the performer(s) of which cannot be ascertained by reasonable inquiry]

*[the performer(s) of which unreasonably withhold his/their consent]

hereby applies to the Tribunal for its consent to the recording.

2. There is delivered herewith a statement setting out—

*[the inquiries made by the Applicant as to the identity or whereabouts of the performer(s) and the result of those inquiries]

*[the grounds on which the Applicant considers that the withholding of consent is unreasonable].

*3. [A copy of the Applicant's statement *has been/will be served on [date of service] on the performer(s) [state name(s) and address(es) of performer(s)]].

4. All communications about this reference should be addressed to

*[the Applicant at the address shown above]

*[name and address of Applicant's solicitor/agent].

Signed ....

Status of signatory .... [Applicant,
an officer of Applicant, solicitor or agent]

Date ....
*Delete whichever is inappropriate

COPYRIGHT, DESIGNS AND PATENTS ACT 1988
COPYRIGHT TRIBUNAL

Notice of Application for Tribunal's Determination of Royalty Payable under
Paragraph 5(1) of Schedule 6

To,

The Secretary to the Tribunal

1. TAKE NOTICE that

*[the Trustees of The Hospital for Sick Children]

*[state name and address of person]

("the Applicant") hereby applies to the Tribunal to settle the royalty or other remuneration payable in respect of the *public performance/commercial publication/broadcasting/inclusion in a cable programme service of the *whole/part of "Peter Pan" or its adaptation.

2. There is delivered herewith a statement of the Applicant's case.

3. A copy of this Notice, together with the statement, *has been/will be served on [date of service] on *the other party [state name and address of other party]/ the Trustees of The Hospital for Sick Children.

4. All communications about this application should be addressed to

*[the Applicant at the address shown above]

*[name and address of Applicant's solicitor/agent].

Signed ....

Status of signatory .... [Applicant,
an officer of Applicant, solicitor or agent]

Date ....
*Delete whichever is inappropriate

COPYRIGHT, DESIGNS AND PATENTS ACT 1988
COPYRIGHT TRIBUNAL

Notice of Application for Review of Order under Paragraph 5(2) of Schedule 6

To,
   The Secretary to the Tribunal

   1. TAKE NOTICE that

   *[the Trustees of The Hospital for Sick Children]

   *[state name and address of person]

("the Applicant") hereby applies to the Tribunal for a review of its Order dated
.... and bearing the reference number .... in respect of the determination of the royalty or other remuneration payable to the Trustees of The Hospital for Sick Children.

   2. There is delivered herewith a statement of the Applicant's case.

   3. A copy of this Notice, together with the statement, *has been/will be served on [date of service] on *the other party [state name and address of other party]/ the Trustees of The Hospital for Sick Children.

   4. All communications about this application should be addressed to

   *[the Applicant at the address shown above]

   *[name and address of Applicant's solicitor/agent].

Signed ....

Status of signatory .... [Applicant,
                                 an officer of Applicant, solicitor or agent]

Date ....
*Delete whichever is inappropriate

COPYRIGHT, DESIGNS AND PATENTS ACT 1988
COPYRIGHT TRIBUNAL

Notice of Appeal on Point of Law under Section 152

To,
    The Secretary to the Tribunal

1. TAKE NOTICE that [name and address of appellant] ("the Appellant"), being a party to the proceedings on the *reference/application/appeal intends to appeal to the *High Court/Court of Session against the decision of the Tribunal dated .... and bearing the reference number .... on the following point(s) of law—

    [state point(s) of law].

2. A copy of this Notice *has been/will be served on [date of service] on every person or organisation who was a party to the proceedings, namely [specify names and addresses of parties].

3. All communications about this appeal should be addressed to

    *[the Appellant at the address shown above]

    *[name and address of Appellant's solicitor/agent].

Signed ....

Status of signatory .... [Appellant,
                                        an officer of Appellant, solicitor or agent]

Date ....
*Delete whichever is inappropriate

COPYRIGHT, DESIGNS AND PATENTS ACT 1988
COPYRIGHT TRIBUNAL

Notice of Application to Suspend Order of Tribunal

To,
The Secretary to the Tribunal

1. TAKE NOTICE that [name and address of applicant] ("the Applicant"), being a party to the proceedings on the *reference/application/appeal [specify the proceedings] hereby applies to the Tribunal for the suspension of the operation of the Order of the Tribunal dated .... and bearing the reference number ....

2. There is delivered herewith a statement setting out the grounds for suspension—

[state grounds for suspension].

3. A copy of this Notice, together with the statement, *has been/will be served on [date of service] on every person or organisation who was a party to the proceedings, namely [specify names and addresses of parties].

4. All communications about this application should be addressed to

*[the Applicant at the address shown above]

*[name and address of Applicant's solicitor/agent].

Signed ....

Status of signatory .... [Applicant, an officer of Applicant, solicitor or agent]

Date ....
*Delete whichever is inappropriate

COPYRIGHT TRIBUNAL

PRACTICE DIRECTION[23]

1. Procedure before the Copyright Tribunal is governed overall by the Copyright Tribunal Rules 1989. This Direction is given for the guidance of parties with a view to achieving a just, expeditious and economical disposal of proceedings. The procedure which follows will be compulsory except in cases where the Tribunal otherwise directs, but this Direction may be altered from time to time.

2. In this Direction, reference is made to service of copies of a variety of documents. Wherever service on the Secretary is referred to the Secretary will inform the party concerned of the number of copies he requires for himself and for the members of the Tribunal who are to hear the case, or the relevant stage of the case. Substantive hearings will be taken by a Tribunal consisting of the Chairman or a Deputy Chairman and at least two and ordinarily not more than four other members.

Pre-Hearing Procedure

3. In cases of proposed licensing schemes and proposed licences the Tribunal will, pursuant to s.118(2) and s.125(2) of the Act, consider whether the reference is premature. The respondent will be invited to comment on this point before the Tribunal makes its decision. It will normally consider the matter on the basis of written submissions only.

4. Chairman's Directions (Rule 11)

(a) The Schedule contains the draft of the kind of order likely to be made by way of directions as to the further conduct of the proceedings in a case where there are only two parties. This draft is non-binding and the parties are free to propose alternative directions. Cases where there are more than two parties may require a more complicated form of order.

(b) In a two-party case the following procedure before the hearing for directions is desirable. Not less than 14 days before the day appointed for the giving of directions the applicant should send to the respondent and the Secretary his written proposals for directions. Not less than 7 days before such day the respondent should send to the applicant a written statement stating whether or not he agrees with such proposals, and if not, containing his counter-proposals.

(c) In cases with three or more parties, each party should, not less than 10 days before the appointed day, send to the other parties and the Secretary its written proposals for directions.

(d) If any party wishes the Order for Directions to specify a date for the substantive hearing, it should, well in advance of the hearing for directions, make inquiries of all other parties and of the Secretary to the Tribunal as to a suitable date or dates. The parties should also make an estimate or estimates as to the likely length of the hearing. The Chairman will normally set a date but if no party wishes for a date to be set at this time, normally the Chairman will not do so.

(e) If the parties agree a proposed Order for Directions before the appointed day and submit a written proposal therefor signed on behalf of all parties, the Chairman may make an order accordingly. If however the Chairman considers that the

---

[23] This Practice Direction was issued by the Chairman of the Copyright Tribunal in early 1990. It may be varied or additional directions issued later.

attendance of the parties before him will result in a more expeditious and economical disposal of the proceedings consistent with reaching a just result he will require the attendance of the parties.

B–129 **Preparation of Written Evidence**

5. To facilitate the reading and handling of written evidence the Tribunal desires that the following procedure should normally be followed.

(a) Where a witness statement is particularly lengthy, consideration should be given to shortening the main part thereof by putting matters of a background or peripheral nature into exhibits referred to in the body of the main part. The use of headings in lengthy witness statements is helpful, and individual paragraphs should not normally be longer than a page.

(b) Originals of witness statements and exhibits should be retained by the party concerned and brought to the substantive hearing for reference if necessary.

(c) The hearing will normally be conducted using copy witness statements and exhibits.

(d) Copies of witness statements should be served in a file or files indexed and tabbed (by witness statement) with the pages of the file or files numbered consecutively. Copies of exhibits should be served in a similar fashion but in a file or files separate from the witness statements so that a reader can look at the witness statement and exhibit side by side.

(e) Where an exhibit is particularly bulky consideration should be given to the need to copy the whole document as opposed to only the relevant parts thereof. If parts are omitted a sheet so indicating should be included in the file with the copy of the relevant parts of the exhibit.

(f) Backsheets are unnecessary in copy files.

B–130 **Agreement of Facts and Skeleton Arguments**

6. It is desirable following the close of the written evidence stage of the proceedings that the parties should, so far as possible, agree such matters of fact as they consider are not in dispute. If any such agreement can be reached a written memorandum thereof should be prepared and sent to the Secretary as soon as practicable before the date appointed for the substantive hearing.

7. Not less than 14 days before the date appointed for the hearing each party should send to the other and to the Secretary a skeleton argument setting out briefly that party's arguments, including references to all portions of evidence particularly relied upon and any authorities relied upon. The skeleton argument should also have annexed to it a concise summary of the written evidence of each of that party's witnesses.

8. An important purpose of the skeleton argument is to assist the members of the Tribunal to read in advance the evidence and pleadings. The skeleton argument will not be taken as binding a party but failure to comply with this direction or substantial departure therefrom may well result in an adverse costs order.

B–131 **Core Bundle**

9. Parties are encouraged to co-operate in preparing a single file containing copies of only the key portions of all parties' evidence and exhibits. If copies of such a bundle can be supplied to the Secretary 7 days in advance of the hearing, time at the hearing should be saved.

B–132 **10. Bundle of Authorities**

The parties should co-operate to lodge at least 7 days before the date appointed for the hearing copies of a bundle containing tabbed copies of all authorities upon which they intend to rely.

Procedure at the Hearing

Opening Speeches

11. The Tribunal will have read in advance the pleadings, the parties' written evidence and the skeleton arguments. Accordingly, where there is a hearing attended by both parties with cross-examination of witnesses, substantial opening speeches by or on behalf of the parties are not necessary. Unless the Tribunal is persuaded otherwise in any particular case, it would want to hear, before the first witness is called, an opening speech by or on behalf of the applicant for a period of not more than $1\frac{1}{2}$ hours and then or at a later stage an opening speech from the respondent of not more than $1\frac{1}{2}$ hours. The purpose of these speeches should be to focus attention on the matters in dispute rather than introduce the Tribunal to the case. The Tribunal particularly wishes to have a good grasp of both parties' contentions so that it can follow the relevance of any cross-examination more readily.

Cross-examination

12. Cross-examination should be limited to matters in dispute. Lengthy cross-examination, most of which is directed to matters of peripheral relevance, is to be deprecated. Attention is particularly drawn to paragraph 9 of the Schedule indicating that a witness's evidence need not be cross-examined to be challenged.

Speeches following Close of Oral Evidence

13. Normally the closing order of speeches will be the respondent and finally the applicant in reply. Lengthy speeches are not called for and each party is encouraged to provide at the beginning of its closing speech a written summary of the main points being made on its behalf in that speech.

Power to Award Costs

14. Parties are reminded that under Rule 48(1) the Tribunal has power to award costs. The Tribunal will consider exercising this power against any party which it considers is guilty of undue prolixity in its evidence or at the hearing. Further, though it is not the Tribunal's practice that in all cases costs will follow the event, the fact that a party's case may have been unreasonably maintained will weigh heavily with the Tribunal.

15. The parties are also reminded that in considering any application for costs following determination of a dispute the Tribunal will consider any offer which has been made by any party "without prejudice save as to costs."

SCHEDULE

Draft Chairman's Order for Directions

(In a Case Involving only Two Parties)

1. The evidence of all parties shall be by signed statements in typescript, paginated and with numbered paragraphs.

2. Reference herein to service of documents means, in the case of service on the Secretary, service of a number of copies sufficient for all the members of the Tribunal who are to hear the case plus the Secretary (this number being obtainable by inquiry from the Secretary) and in the case of service on another party service of at least one copy.

3. The evidence of the applicant is to be served on the respondent and Secretary on or before............. ....

4. The evidence of the respondent is to be served on the applicant and Secretary within . . . . weeks after service of the evidence of the applicant in chief.

5. The evidence of the applicant in reply (and strictly limited to reply) shall be served on the respondent and Secretary within . . . . weeks after service of the evidence of the respondent.

6. There shall be a hearing, but any party shall be at liberty to make any or all of its submissions in writing.

7. The hearing shall commence on..

8. If any party desires to cross-examine any witness for another party it shall on or before . . . . give notice in writing to the Secretary and the other party to that effect.

9. It shall not be necessary for a witness to be cross-examined in order to challenge his evidence. This provision applies also to parts of the statement of a witness who is cross-examined but not on those parts.

10. The parties have liberty to apply for further or other directions.

B–138

The Design Right (Proceedings before Comptroller) Rules 1989

(S.I. 1989 No. 1130)

Made - - - - - - -	*4th July 1989*
Laid before Parliament	*10th July 1989*
Coming into force	*1st August 1989*

The Secretary of State, in exercise of the powers conferred upon him by section 250[24] of the Copyright, Designs and Patents Act 1988, with the consent of the Treasury pursuant to subsection (3) of that section as to the fees prescribed under these Rules, and after consultation with the Council on Tribunals in accordance with section 10(1) of the Tribunal and Inquiries Act 1971, hereby makes the following Rules:—

Citation and commencement

B–139 1. These Rules may be cited as the Design Right (Proceedings before Comptroller) Rules 1989 and shall come into force on 1st August 1989.

Interpretation

B–140 2.—(1) In these Rules, unless the context otherwise requires—
"the Act" means the Copyright, Designs and Patents Act 1988;
"applicant" means a person who has referred a dispute or made an application to the Comptroller;
"application" means an application to the Comptroller to settle or vary the terms of a licence of right or to adjust the terms of a licence;
"dispute" means a dispute as to any of the matters referred to in rule 3(1); and

---

[24] See para. 19(6), Sched. 1, C.D.P.A. 1988. These Rules were amended, as to Rule 6(4)(*a*) and (*b*), by the Design Right (Proceedings before Comptroller) (Amendment) Rules 1990 (S.I. 1990 No. 1453) and, as to Sched. 2, by The Design Right (Proceedings before Comptroller) (Amendment) (No. 2) Rules 1990 (S.I. 1990 No. 1699), and are printed as amended in square brackets.

"proceedings" means proceedings before the Comptroller in respect of a dispute or application.

(2) A rule or schedule referred to by number means the rule or schedule so numbered in these Rules; and a requirement under these Rules to use a form set out in Schedule 1 is satisfied by the use either of a replica of that form or of a form which contains the information required by the form set out in the said Schedule and which is acceptable the Comptroller.

Proceedings in respect of a dispute

Commencement of proceedings

3.—(1) Proceedings under section 246 of the Act in respect of a dispute as to— **B-141**
(a) the subsistence of design right,
(b) the term of design right, or
(c) the identity of the person in whom design right first vested,
shall be commenced by the service by the applicant on the Comptroller of a notice in Form 1 in Schedule 1. There shall be served with that notice a statement in duplicate setting out the name and address of the other party to the dispute (hereinafter in this rule referred to as the respondent), the issues in dispute, the applicant's case and the documents relevant to his case.

(2) Within 14 days of the receipt of the notice the Comptroller shall send a copy of the notice, together with a copy of the applicant's statement, to the respondent.

(3) Within 28 days of the receipt by him of the documents referred to in paragraph (2) above, the respondent shall serve on the Comptroller a counter-statement and shall at the same time serve a copy of it on the applicant. Such counter-statement shall set out full particulars of the grounds on which he contests the applicant's case, any issues on which he and the applicant are in agreement and the documents relevant to his case.

(4) Within 21 days of the service on him of the counter-statement, the applicant may serve a further statement on the Comptroller setting out the grounds on which he contests the respondent's case, and shall at the same time serve a copy of it on the respondent.

(5) No amended statement or further statement shall be served by either party except by leave or direction of the Comptroller.

Comptroller's directions

4.—(1) The Comptroller shall give such directions as to the further conduct of **B-142**
proceedings as he considers appropriate.

(2) If a party fails to comply with any direction given under this rule, the Comptroller may in awarding costs take account of such default.

Procedure and evidence at hearing

5.—(1) Unless the Comptroller otherwise directs, all evidence in the proceed- **B-143**
ings shall be by statutory declaration or affidavit.

(2) Where the Comptroller thinks fit in any particular case to take oral evidence in lieu of or in addition to evidence by statutory declaration or affidavit he may so direct and, unless he directs otherwise, shall allow any witness to be cross-examined on his evidence.

(3) A party to the proceedings who desires to make oral representations shall so notify the Comptroller and the Comptroller shall, unless he and the parties agree to a shorter period, give at least 14 days' notice of the time and place of the hearing to the parties.

(4) If a party intends to refer at a hearing to any document not already referred

to in the proceedings, he shall, unless the Comptroller and the other party agree to a shorter period, give 14 days' notice of his intention, together with particulars of every document to which he intends to refer, to the Comptroller and the other party.

(5) At any stage of the proceedings the Comptroller may direct that such documents, information or evidence as he may require shall be filed within such time as he may specify.

(6) The hearing of any proceedings, or part of proceedings, under this rule shall be in public, unless the Comptroller, after consultation with the parties, otherwise directs.

Representation and rights of audience

B-144 **6.**—(1) Any party to the proceedings may appear in person or be represented by counsel or a solicitor (of any part of the United Kingdom) or, subject to paragraph (4) below, a patent agent or any other person whom he desires to represent him.

(2) Anything required or authorised by these Rules to be done by or in relation to any person may be done by or in relation to his agent.

(3) Where after a person has become a party to the proceedings he appoints an agent for the first time or appoints an agent in substitution for another, the newly appointed agent shall give written notice of his appointment to the Comptroller and to every other party to the proceedings.

(4) The Comptroller may refuse to recognise as such an agent in respect of any proceedings before him—

(a) a person who has been convicted of an offence under section 88 of the Patents Act 1949 or section 114 of the Patents Act 1977 [or section 276 of the Act];

(b) any individual whose name has been erased from and not restored to, or who is suspended from, the register of patent agents (kept in pursuance of rules made under [section 275 of the Act]) on the ground of misconduct;

(c) a person who is found by the Secretary of State to have been guilty of such conduct as would, in the case of an individual registered in the register of patent agents, render him liable to have his name erased from the register on the ground of misconduct;

(d) a partnership or body corporate of which one of the partners or directors is a person whom the Comptroller could refuse to recognise under sub-paragraphs (a), (b) or (c) above.

Application to be made a party to proceedings

B-145 **7.**—(1) A person who claims to have a substantial interest in a dispute in respect of which proceedings have been commenced may apply to the Comptroller to be made a party to the dispute in Form 2 in Schedule 1, supported by a statement of his interest. He shall serve a copy of his application, together with his statement, on every party to the proceedings.

(2) The Comptroller shall, upon being satisfied of the substantial interest of that person in the dispute, grant the application and shall give such directions or further directions under rule 4(1) as may be necessary to enable that person to participate in the proceedings as a party to the dispute.

Withdrawal of reference

B-146 **8.** A party (including a person made a party to the proceedings under rule 7) may at any time before the Comptroller's decision withdraw from the proceedings by serving a notice to that effect on the Comptroller and every other party to the proceedings, but such withdrawal shall be without prejudice to the Comptroller's power to make an order as to the payment of costs incurred up to the time of service of the notice.

Decision of the Comptroller

9. After hearing the party or parties desiring to be heard, or if none of the parties so desires, then without a hearing, the Comptroller shall decide the dispute and notify his decision to the parties, giving written reasons for his decision if so required by any party.   **B–147**

Proceedings in respect of application to settle terms of licence of right or adjust terms of licence

Commencement of proceedings

10.—(1) Proceedings in respect of an application to the Comptroller—   **B–148**

    (*a*) under section 247 of the Act, to settle the terms of a licence available as of right by virtue of section 237 or under an order under section 238 of the Act, or

    (*b*) under paragraph 19(2) of Schedule 1 to the Act, to settle the terms of a licence available as of right in respect of a design recorded or embodied in a design document or model before 1st August 1989, or

    (*c*) brought by virtue of paragraph 19(5) of Schedule 1 to the Act, to adjust the terms of a licence granted before 1st August 1989 in respect of a design referred to in sub-paragraph (*b*) above,

shall be commenced by the service by the applicant on the Comptroller of a notice in Form 3 in Schedule 1.

(2) There shall be served with the notice a statement in duplicate setting out—

    (*a*) in the case of an application referred to in paragraph (1)(*a*) or (*b*) above, the terms of the licence which the applicant requires the Comptroller to settle and, unless the application is one to which rule 13 relates, the name and address of the owner of the design right or, as the case may be, the copyright owner of the design;

    (*b*) in the case of an application referred to in paragraph (1)(*c*) above, the date and terms of the licence and the grounds on which the applicant requires the Comptroller to adjust those terms and the name and address of the grantor of the licence.

(3) Within 14 days of the receipt of the notice the Comptroller shall send a copy of it, together with a copy of the applicant's statement, to the person (hereinafter in this rule referred to as the respondent) shown in the application as the design right owner, copyright owner or grantor of the licence, as appropriate.

(4) Within 6 weeks of the receipt by him of the notice sent under paragraph (3) above the respondent shall, if he does not agree to the terms of the licence required by the applicant to be settled or, as the case may be, adjusted, serve a notice of objection on the Comptroller with a statement setting out the grounds of his objection and at the same time shall serve a copy of the same on the applicant.

(5) Within 4 weeks of the receipt of the notice of objection the applicant may serve on the Comptroller a counter-statement and at the same time serve a copy of it on the respondent.

(6) No amended statement or further statement shall be served by either party except by leave or direction of the Comptroller.

Directions, procedure and evidence

11. Rules 4, 5, 6 and 8 shall apply in respect of proceedings under rule 10 as they apply in respect of proceedings under rule 3.   **B–149**

Decision of the Comptroller

B–150   12. After hearing the party or parties desiring to be heard, or if none of the parties so desires, then without a hearing, the Comptroller shall decide the application and notify his decision to the parties, giving written reasons for his decision if so required by any party.

Settlement of terms where design right owner unknown

Commencement of proceedings

B–151   **13.**—(1) Where a person making an application under rule 10(1)(a) or (b) is unable (after making such inquiries as he considers reasonable) to discover the identity of the design right owner or, as the case may be, the copyright owner, he shall serve with his notice under that rule a statement to that effect, setting out particulars of the inquiries made by him as to the identity of the owner of the right and the result of those inquiries.

(2) The Comptroller may require the applicant to make such further inquiries into the identity of the owner of the right as he thinks fit and, may for that purpose, require him to publish in such a manner as the Comptroller considers appropriate particulars of the application.

(3) The Comptroller shall, upon being satisfied from the applicant's statement or the further inquiries made under paragraph (2) above that the identity of the owner of the right cannot be discovered, consider the application and settle the terms of the licence.

Proceedings in respect of application by design right owner to vary terms of licence

Commencement of proceedings

B–152   **14.**—(1) Where the Comptroller has, in settling the terms of the licence under rule 13, ordered that the licence shall be free of any obligation as to royalties or other payments, the design right owner or copyright owner (as the case may be) may serve on the Comptroller a notice in Form 4 in Schedule 1 applying for the terms of the licence to be varied from the date of his application. There shall be served with the notice a statement in duplicate setting out the particulars of the grounds for variation and the terms required to be varied.

(2) Within 14 days of the receipt of the notice the Comptroller shall send a copy of the notice, together with the design right or copyright owner's statement, to the applicant under rule 10 (hereinafter in this rule referred to as the licensee).

(3) The licensee shall, if he does not agree to the terms as required to be varied by the design right or copyright owner, within 6 weeks of the receipt of the notice serve notice of objection on the Comptroller with a statement setting out the grounds of his objection and at the same time shall serve a copy of the same on the design right or copyright owner, as the case may be.

(4) Within 4 weeks of the receipt of the notice of objection the design right or copyright owner may serve on the Comptroller a counter-statement, and at the same time shall serve a copy of it on the licensee.

(5) No amended statement or further statement shall be served by either party except by leave or direction of the Comptroller.

Directions, procedure and evidence

B–153   15. Rules 4, 5, 6 and 8 shall apply in respect of proceedings under rule 14 as they apply in respect of proceedings under rule 3.

Decision of the Comptroller

16. After hearing the party or parties desiring to be heard, or if none of the parties so desires, then without a hearing, the Comptroller shall decide the application and notify his decision to the parties, giving written reasons for his decision if so required by any party. **B–154**

General

Rectification of irregularities

17. Any document filed in any proceedings may, if the Comptroller thinks fit, be amended, and any irregularity in procedure may be rectified by the Comptroller on such terms as he may direct. **B–155**

Evidence

18.—(1) Any statutory declaration or affidavit filed in any proceedings shall be made and subscribed as follows— **B–156**

(*a*) in the United Kingdom, before any justice of the peace or any commissioner or other officer authorised by law in any part of the United Kingdom to administer an oath for the purpose of any legal proceedings;

(*b*) in any other part of Her Majesty's dominions or in the Republic of Ireland, before any court, judge, justice of the peace or any officer authorised by law to administer an oath there for the purpose of any legal proceedings; and

(*c*) elsewhere, before a British Minister, or person exercising the functions of a British Minister, or a Consul, Vice-Consul or other person exercising the functions of a British Consul or before a notary public, judge or magistrate.

(2) Any document purporting to have fixed, impressed or subscribed thereto or thereon the seal or signature of any person authorised by paragraph (1) above to take a declaration may be admitted by the Comptroller without proof of the genuineness of the seal or signature or of the official character of the person or his authority to take the declaration.

(3) In England and Wales, the Comptroller shall, in relation to the giving of evidence (including evidence on oath), the attendance of witnesses and the discovery and production of documents, have all the powers of a judge of the High Court, other than the power to punish summarily for contempt of court.

(4) In Scotland, the Comptroller shall, in relation to the giving of evidence (including evidence on oath), have all the powers which a Lord Ordinary of the Court of Session has in an action before him, other than the power to punish summarily for contempt of court, and, in relation to the attendance of witnesses and the recovery and production of documents, have all the powers of the Court of Session.

Appointment of advisers

19. The Comptroller may appoint an adviser to assist him in any proceedings and shall settle the question or instructions to be submitted or given to such an adviser. **B–157**

Time

20.—(1) The times or periods prescribed by these Rules for doing any act or taking any proceedings thereunder may be extended by the Comptroller if he thinks fit, upon such notice and upon such terms as he may direct, and such exten- **B–158**

tion may be granted although the time for doing such act or taking such proceedings has already expired.

(2) Where the last day for the doing of any act falls on a day on which the Patent Office is closed and by reason thereof the act cannot be done on that day, it may be done on the next day on which the Office is open.

Hours of business

B–159 **21.** For the purposes of these Rules the Patent Office shall be open Monday to Friday—

(*a*) between 10.00 a.m. and midnight, for the filing of applications, forms and other documents, and

(*b*) between 10.00 a.m. and 4.00 p.m. for all other purposes,

excluding Good Friday, Christmas Day and any day specified or proclaimed to be a bank holiday under section 1 of the Banking and Financial Dealings Act 1971.

Costs

B–160 **22.**—(1) The Comptroller may, in respect of any proceedings, by order award such costs or, in Scotland, such expenses as he considers reasonable and direct how, to what party and from what parties they are to be paid.

(2) Where any applicant or a person making an application under rule 7 neither resides nor carries on business in the United Kingdom or another member State of the European Economic Community the Comptroller may require him to give security for the costs or expenses of the proceedings and in default of such security being given may treat the reference or application as abandoned.

Service and translation of documents

B–161 **23.**—(1) Every person concerned in any proceedings to which these Rules relate shall furnish to the Comptroller an address for service in the United Kingdom, and that address may be treated for all purposes connected with such proceedings as the address of the person concerned.

(2) Where any document or part of a document which is in a language other than English is served on the Comptroller or any party to proceedings or filed with the Comptroller in pursuance of these Rules, it shall be accompanied by a translation into English of the document or part, verified to the satisfaction of the Comptroller as corresponding to the original text.

Fees

B–162 **24.** The fees specified in Schedule 2 shall be payable in respect of the matters there mentioned.

SCHEDULE 1   Rules 3(1), 7(1), 10(1) and 14(1)   **B—163**

FORMS

Design Right Form 1

Reference of dispute to Comptroller

For Official Use

Copyright, Designs & Patents Act 1988

Notes

Please type or write in dark ink using BLOCK LETTERS. For details of prescribed fees please contact the Patent Office.

Rule 3 of the Design Right (Proceedings before Comptroller) Rules 1989 is the main rule governing the completion and filing of this form.

This form must be filed together with a statement in duplicate setting out the matters referred to in Rule 3(1).

❹ Identification may be made by providing drawings, photographs or other identifying material.

Please mark correct box (es)

Please sign here ➤

dti
the department for Enterprise

1. Your reference

2. Please give full name and address of person making the reference.
Name

Address

Postcode

ADP number (if known)

3. Please give an address for service in the United Kingdom to which all correspondence will be sent.
Name

Address

Postcode

ADP number (if known)

4. Please identify the design which is the subject of the proceedings.

5. The dispute to be settled is in respect of :-

the subsistence of the design right ☐

the term of the design right ☐

the identity of the person in whom design right first vested ☐

6. Please give the name and address of the other party to the dispute.
Name

Address

Postcode

ADP number (if known)

Signed _____ Date _____
day   month   year

Reminder
Have you attached   the statement of case in duplicate? ☐

the prescribed fee? ☐

Issued   1989

The Patent Office

Design Right Form 2

Application to be made a party to proceedings.

Copyright, Designs
& Patents Act 1988

For Official Use

Notes

Please type or write in dark ink using
BLOCK LETTERS. For details of
prescribed fees please contact the
Patent Office.

Rule 7 of the Design Right
(Proceedings before Comptroller)
Rules 1989 is the main rule governing
the completion and filing of this form.

A statement to show your substantial
interest in the dispute in respect of
which proceedings have been
commenced must accompany this
form. You must also serve a copy of
the form and statement on every party
to the proceedings.

1. Your reference

2. Please give full name and address of person applying to be made a
party to dispute.
Name

Address

          Postcode

ADP number (if known)

3. Please give an address for service in the United Kingdom to which all
correspondence will be sent.
Name

Address

          Postcode

ADP number (if known)

4. Please identify the proceedings relating to the dispute in which you
claim to have a substantial interest.

Please sign here ➤   Signed _____ Date _____

                                                  day   month   year

Reminder
Have you attached   a statement of your interest? ☐

                                        the prescribed fee? ☐

dti
the department for Enterprise

Issued   1989

The Patent Office

Copyright, Designs
& Patents Act 1988

Design Right Form 3

Application to settle terms of Licence of Right or to adjust terms of Licence granted before 1st August 1989

For Official Use	**B—165**

Notes

Please type or write in dark ink using BLOCK LETTERS. For details of prescribed fees please contact the Patent Office.

Rules 10 and 13 of the Design Right (Proceedings before Comptroller) Rules 1989 are the main rules governing the completion and filing of this form.

This form must be filed, by the person requiring the settlement or adjustment of the licence, together with a statement in duplicate setting out the terms required. Where the applicant has been unable to discover the identity of the design right or copyright owner a statement must also be filed setting out the particulars of and result of the inquiries made to try to identify the owner.

❶ Identification may be made by providing drawings, photographs or other identifying material.

❷ If part 6(a) of this form applies, give the name and address of the design right or copyright owner (if known). If part 6(b) applies give the name and address of the grantor of the licence in question.

Please mark correct box

Please sign here ➤

Important note
This form is **not** for use by the design right or copyright owner.

dti
the department for Enterprise

1. Your reference

2. Please give full name and address of applicant.
Name

Address

Postcode
ADP number (if known)

3. Please give an address for service in the United Kingdom to which all correspondence will be sent.
Name

Address

Postcode
ADP number (if known)

4. Please identify the design which is the subject of these proceedings.

5. Please give the name and address of the respondent (see note 5).
Name

Address

Postcode
ADP number (if known)

6. Application is made to the Comptroller:
(a) to settle the terms of a licence for the design which is available as of right by virtue of: Section 237 ☐

an order under Section 238 ☐

paragraph 19(2) of Schedule 1 ☐

(b) to adjust terms of a licence under paragraph 19(5) of Schedule 1 ☐

Signed _____ Date _____
day month year

Reminder
Have you attached the prescribed fee? ☐

the statement in duplicate of the terms required ? ☐

a statement of inquiries made to identify the design right or copyright owner (if inquiries unsuccessful)? ☐

Issued 1989

B–166

The
**Patent
Office**

Copyright, Designs
& Patents Act 1988

Design Right Form 4

**Application by
Design Right or
Copyright owner to
vary terms of
licence of right.**

For Official Use

Notes

Please type or write in dark ink using
BLOCK LETTERS. For details of
prescribed fees please contact the
Patent Office.

Rule 14 of the Design Right
(Proceedings before Comptroller)
Rules 1989 is the main rule governing
the completion and filing of this form.

This form must be filed together with a
statement in duplicate setting out the
particulars of the grounds for
variation and the terms required to be
varied.

1. Your reference

2. Please give full name and address of applicant.
Name

Address

Postcode

ADP number (if known)

3. Please give an address for service in the United Kingdom to which all
correspondence will be sent.
Name

Address

Postcode

ADP number (if known)

4. Please identify the licence which is the subject of the application.

5. Please give the name and address of the licence holder.
Name

Address

Postcode

ADP number (if known)

Please sign here ➤

Signed _____ Date _____
day month year

Reminder

Have you attached

a statement in duplicate of the grounds for ☐
variation and the terms required?

the prescribed fee? ☐

dti
the department for Enterprise

Issued 1989

[SCHEDULE 2

FEES

Rule 24 **B–167**

1. On reference of dispute (Form 1) under rule 3(1)..£54
2. On application (Form 2) under rule 7(1) £30
3. On application (Form 3) under rule 10(1) £54
4. On application (Form 4) under rule 14(1) ....£54]

The Copyright (Customs) Regulations 1989

B–168

(S.I. 1989 No. 1178)

Made - - - - - - -	*10th July 1989*
Laid before Parliament	*11th July 1989*
Coming into force	*1st August 1989*

The Commissioners of Customs and Excise, in exercise of the powers conferred on them by section 112(1), (2) and (3) of the Copyright, Designs and Patents Act 1988 and of all other powers enabling them in that behalf, hereby make the following Regulations:

1. These Regulations may be cited as the Copyright (Customs) Regulations 1989 and shall come into force on 1st August 1989.

B–169

2.—(1) Notice given under section 111(1) of the Copyright, Designs and Patents Act 1988 shall be in the form set out in Schedule 1 or a form to the like effect approved by the Commissioners; and a separate notice shall be given in respect of each work.

B–170

(2) Notice given under section 111(3) of that Act shall be in the form set out in Schedule 2 or a form to the like effect approved by the Commissioners; and a separate notice shall be given in respect of each work and in respect of each expected importation into the United Kingdom.

(3) In regulations 3 to 9 "notice" means a notice given under either of those subsections.

3. The notice shall contain full particulars of the matters specified therein and shall contain a declaration by the signatory that the information given by him in the notice is true.

B–171

4. A fee of £30 (plus value added tax) in respect of the notice shall be paid to the Commissioners at the time it is given.

B–172

5. The person giving the notice shall furnish to the Commissioners a copy of the work specified in the notice at the time the notice is given and at that time or at the time the goods to which the notice relates are imported shall furnish to them such evidence as they may reasonably require to establish—

B–173

(*a*) his ownership of the copyright in such work;
(*b*) that goods detained are infringing copies; or
(*c*) that a person who has signed the notice as agent is duly authorised.

6. The person giving the notice shall give security or further security within such time and in such manner, whether by bond or by deposit of a sum of money, as the Commissioners may require, in respect of any liability or expense which they may

B–174

incur in consequence of the notice by reason of the detention of any article or anything done to an article detained.

B–175   **7.** In every case, whether any security or further security is given or not, the person who has given the notice shall keep the Commissioners indemnified against all such liability and expense as it mentioned in regulation 6.

Note: The word "it" in the official version would appear to be an error for "is".

B–176   **8.** The person giving the notice shall notify the Commissioners in writing of any change in the ownership of the copyright in the work specified in the notice or other change affecting the notice within fourteen days of such change.

B–177   **9.** The notice shall be deemed to have been withdrawn—
  (*a*) as from the expiry of fourteen days from any change in ownership of the copyright specified in the notice, whether notified to the Commissioners in accordance with regulation 8 or not; or
  (*b*) if the person giving the notice has failed to comply with any requirement of these Regulations.

B–178   **10.** The Copyright (Customs) Regulations 1957[25] and the Copyright (Customs) (Amendment) Regulations 1982 are revoked.

---

[25] S.I. 1957 No. 875 (*Copinger*, 12th ed § 1754).

SCHEDULE 1

Regulation 2(1)
C&E 996

HM Customs
and Excise

Notice under the Copyright, Designs & Patents Act 1988 Requesting Infringing Copies of a Literary , Dramatic or Musical Work to be treated as Prohibited Goods.

Please read these notes before completing this notice.

1. This notice may only be given by the owner of the copyright in a published literary, dramatic or musical work or a person acting on his behalf. A separate notice must be given for each work.

2. The period specified in part 1 shall not exceed 5 years and shall not extend beyond the period for which copyright is to subsist.

3. A fee of £30(plus VAT) is payable. Please enclose a cheque for the required amount made payable to "Commissioners of Customs and Excise".

4. A copy of the work specified in part 2 should be enclosed.

5. The person who has given the notice shall keep the Commissioners of Customs and Excise indemnified against any liability or expense which they may incur as a result of detaining any article or anything done to an article detained because of this notice.
   You may need to provide the Commissioners with security to cover this indemnity.
   You will be informed when this is required.

6. **Part 3 is not obligatory, but please give as many details as possible.**

Part 1.

I, ...give notice that

Full name of signatory in BLOCK LETTERS

....

Name and address of Owner of Copyright

....

....

is the owner of the copyright in the work specified below which subsists under the Copyright, Designs and Patents Act 1988 and I request that any infringing copies of the said work be treated as prohibited goods for a period starting

on...and ending on...

Part 2.

Particulars of Work

Title: ....

....

Full name of author/authors: ....

....

Date copyright expires: ....

C&E 996   CD 1632/N1(7.89)   F 8118(

Part 3.
Details of expected importation

a) Date of importation ....

b) Place of customs declaration ....

c) Place of unloading ....

d) Country of origin ....

e) Country from which goods consigned ....

f) Bill of lading / airway bill / consignment reference number ....

g) Name of ship / aircraft flight number / vehicle registration number ....

h) Name and address of importer / consignee ....

....

i) Tariff classification and commodity code ....

Part 4.
Declaration

I declare that the information given by me in this notice is true.

Signature .... Date ....

             (*Owner of copyright / Authorised agent)

* Delete as necessary

Part 5.

Please send the completed notice,
enclosing fee and a copy of the work, to:-   HM Customs and Excise
                                          CDB3(B)
                                          Dorset House
                                          Stamford Street
                                          LONDON SE1 9PS

CD 1632/P/N1(7 89)

SCHEDULE 2   **Regulation 2(2)**   **B–180**
                                      C&E 997

Notice under the Copyright, Designs & Patents Act 1988
Requesting Infringing Copies of a Sound Recording or Film
to be treated as Prohibited Goods.

HM Customs
and Excise

Please read these notes before completing this notice.

1. This notice may only be given by the owner of the copyright in a sound recording or film or a person acting on his behalf. A separate notice must be given in respect of each work and each expected importation of infringing copies of the work.

2. A fee of £30(plus VAT) is payable. Please enclose a cheque for the required amount made payable to "Commissioners of Customs and Excise".

3. A copy of the work specified in part 2 should be enclosed.

4. The person who has given the notice shall keep the Commissioners of Customs and Excise indemnified against any liability or expense which they may incur as a result of detaining any article or anything done to an article detained because of this notice.
You may need to provide the Commissioners with security to cover this indemnity.
You will be informed when this is required.

5. **Part 4 is not obligatory, but please give as many details as possible.**

Part 1.

I, ...give notice that
Full name of signatory in BLOCK LETTERS

....
Name and address of Owner of Copyright

....

....

is the owner of the copyright in the work specified below which subsists under the Copyright, Designs and Patents Act 1988 and that infringing copies of the work are expected to be imported into the United Kingdom and I request that these copies be treated as prohibited goods.

Part 2.
Particulars of Work

Title: ....

....

Label, marking or statement borne by work: ....

....

Date copyright expires: ....

C&E 997   CD 1633/N1(7.89)   F 8119(

Part 3.
Expected arrival in United Kingdom

Date ....

Place..

Part 4.
Details of expected importation

a) Place of customs declaration ....

b) Place of unloading ....

c) Country of origin ....

d) Country from which goods consigned ....

e) Bill of lading / airway bill / consignment reference number ....

f) Name of ship / aircraft flight number / vehicle registration number ....

g) Name and address of importer / consignee ....

....

h) Tariff classification and commodity code ....

Part 5.
Declaration

I declare that the information given by me in this notice is true.

Signature .... Date ....

(*Owner of copyright / Authorised agent)

* *Delete as necessary*

Part 6.

Please send the completed notice,
enclosing fee and a copy of the work, to:-   HM Customs and Excise
                                                 CDB3(B)
                                                 Dorset House
                                                 Stamford Street
                                                 LONDON SE1 9PS

CD 1635/R/N1(7 89)

The Copyright (Librarians and Archivists) (Copying of Copyright Material) Regulations 1989 — B–181

(S.I. 1989 No. 1212)

Made - - - - - - -	*14th July 1989*
Laid before Parliament	*18th July 1989*
Coming into force	*1st August 1989*

The Secretary of State, in exercise of the powers conferred upon him by sections 37(1), (2) and (4) and 38 to 43 of the Copyright, Designs and Patents Act 1988, hereby makes the following Regulations:—

Citation and commencement

1. These Regulations may be cited as the Copyright (Librarians and Archivists) **B–182** (Copying of Copyright Material) Regulations 1989 and shall come into force on 1st August 1989.

Interpretation

2. In these Regulations— **B–183**
"the Act" means the Copyright, Designs and Patents Act 1988;
"the archivist" means the archivist of a prescribed archive;
"the librarian" means the librarian of a prescribed library;
"prescribed archive" means an archive of the descriptions specified in paragraph (4) of regulation 3 below;
"prescribed library" means a library of the descriptions specified in paragraphs (1), (2) and (3) of regulation 3 below.

Descriptions of libraries and archives

3.—(1) The descriptions of libraries specified in Part A of Schedule 1 to these **B–184** Regulations are prescribed for the purposes of section 38 and 39 of the Act:
Provided that any library conducted for profit shall not be a prescribed library for the purposes of those sections.

(2) All libraries in the United Kingdom are prescribed for the purposes of sections 41, 42 and 43 of the Act as libraries the librarians of which may make and supply copies of any material to which those sections relate.

(3) Any library of a description specified in Part A of Schedule 1 to these Regulations which is not conducted for profit and any library of the description specified in Part B of that Schedule which is not conducted for profit are prescribed for the purposes of sections 41 and 42 of the Act as libraries for which copies of any material to which those sections relate may be made and supplied by the librarian of a prescribed library.

(4) All archives in the United Kingdom are prescribed for the purposes of sections 42 and 43 of the Act as archives which may make and supply copies of any material to which those sections relate and any archive within the United Kingdom which is not conducted for profit is prescribed for the purposes of section 42 of the Act as an archive for which copies of any material to which that section relates may be made and supplied by the archivist of a prescribed archive.

(5) In this regulation "conducted for profit", in relation to a library or archive, means a library or archive which is established or conducted for profit or which forms part of, or is administered by, a body established or conducted for profit.

Copying by librarian of article or part of published work

B–185   **4.**—(1) For the purposes of sections 38 and 39 of the Act the conditions specified in paragraph (2) of this regulation are prescribed as the conditions which must be complied with when the librarian of a prescribed library makes and supplies a copy of any article in a periodical or, as the case may be, of a part of a literary, dramatic or musical work from a published edition to a person requiring the copy.

(2) The prescribed conditions are—

(*a*) that no copy of any article or any part of a work shall be supplied to the person requiring the same unless—

(i) he satisfies the librarian that he requires the copy for purposes of research or private study and will not use it for any other purpose; and

(ii) he has delivered to the librarian a declaration in writing, in relation to that article or part of a work, substantially in accordance with Form A in Schedule 2 to these Regulations and signed in the manner therein indicated;

(*b*) that the librarian is satisfied that the requirement of such person and that of any other person—

(i) are not similar, that is to say, the requirements are not for copies of substantially the same article or part of a work at substantially the same time and for substantially the same purpose; and

(ii) are not related, that is to say, he and that person do not receive instruction to which the article or part of the work is relevant at the same time and place;

(*c*) that such person is not furnished—

(i) in the case of an article, with more than one copy of the article or more than one article contained in the same issue of a periodical; or

(ii) in the case of a part of a published work, with more than one copy of the same material or with a copy of more than a reasonable proportion of any work; and

(*d*) that such person is required to pay for the copy a sum not less than the cost (including a contribution to the general expenses of the library) attributable to its production.

(3) Unless the librarian is aware that the signed declaration delivered to him pursuant to paragraph (2)(*a*)(ii) above is false in a material particular, he may rely on it as to the matter he is required to be satisfied on under paragraph (2)(*a*)(i) above before making or supplying the copy.

Copying by librarian to supply other libraries

B–186   **5.**—(1) For the purposes of section 41 of the Act the conditions specified in paragraph (2) of this regulation are prescribed as the conditions which must be complied with when the librarian of a prescribed library makes and supplies to another prescribed library a copy of any article in a periodical or, as the case may be, of the whole or part of a published edition of a literary, dramatic or musical work required by that other prescribed library.

(2) The prescribed conditions are—

(*a*) that the other prescribed library is not furnished with more than one copy of the article or of the whole or part of the published edition; or

(*b*) that, where the requirement is for a copy of more than one article in the same issue of a periodical, or for a copy of the whole or part of a published edition, the other prescribed library furnishes a written statement to the effect that it is a prescribed library and that it does not know, and could not by reasonable inquiry ascertain, the name and address of a person entitled to authorise the making of the copy; and (*c*) that the other prescribed library shall be required to pay for the copy a sum not less than the cost (including a contribution to the general expenses of the library) attributable to its production.

Copying by librarian or archivist for the purposes of replacing items in a permanent collection

6.—(1) For the purposes of section 42 of the Act the conditions specified in para-   **B-187** graph (2) of this regulation are prescribed as the conditions which must be complied with before the librarian or, as the case may be, the archivist makes a copy from any item in the permanent collection of the library or archive in order to preserve or replace that item in the permanent collection of that library or archive or in the permanent collection of another prescribed library or archive.

   (2) The prescribed conditions are—

     (*a*) that the item in question is an item in the part of the permanent collection maintained by the library or archive wholly or mainly for the purposes of reference on the premises of the library or archive, or is an item in the permanent collection of the library or archive which is available on loan only to other libraries or archives;

     (*b*) that it is not reasonably practicable for the librarian or archivist to purchase a copy of that item to fulfil the purpose under section 42(1)(*a*) or (b) of the Act;

     (*c*) that the other prescribed library or archive furnishes a written statement to the effect that the item has been lost, destroyed or damaged and that it is not reasonably practicable for it to purchase a copy of that item, and that if a copy is supplied it will only be used to fulfil the purpose under section 42(1)(*b*) of the Act; and

     (*d*) that the other prescribed library or archive shall be required to pay for the copy a sum not less than the cost (including a contribution to the general expenses of the library or archive) attributable to its production.

Copying by librarian or archivist of certain unpublished works

7.—(1) For the purposes of section 43 of the Act the conditions specified in para-   **B-188** graph (2) of this regulation are prescribed as the conditions which must be complied with in the circumstances in which that section applies when the librarian or, as the case may be, the archivist makes and supplies a copy of the whole or part of a literary, dramatic or musical work from a document in the library or archive to a person requiring the copy.

   (2) The prescribed conditions are—

     (*a*) that no copy of the whole or part of the work shall be supplied to the person requiring the same unless—

       (i) he satisfies the librarian or archivist that he requires the copy for purposes of research or private study and will not use it for any other purpose; and

       (ii) he has delivered to the librarian or, as the case may be, the archivist a declaration in writing, in relation to that work, substantially in accordance with Form B in Schedule 2 to these Regulations and signed in the manner therein indicated;

     (*b*) that such person is not furnished with more than one copy of the same material; and

     (*c*) that such person is required to pay for the copy a sum not less than the cost (including a contribution to the general expenses of the library or archive) attributable to its production.

   (3) Unless the librarian or archivist is aware that the signed declaration delivered to him pursuant to paragraph (2)(*a*)(ii) above is false in a material par-

ticular, he may rely on it as to the matter he is required to be satisfied on under paragraph (2)(*a*)(i) above before making or supplying the copy.

Revocations

B–189   **8.** The Regulations mentioned in Schedule 3 to these Regulations are hereby revoked.

SCHEDULE 1   Regulation 3

B–190   PART A   Regulation 3(1) and (3)

1. Any library administered by—
    (*a*) a library authority within the meaning of the Public Libraries and Museums Act 1964[26] in relation to England and Wales;
    (*b*) a statutory library authority within the meaning of the Public Libraries (Scotland) Act 1955,[27] in relation to Scotland;
    (*c*) an Education and Library Board within the meaning of the Education and Libraries (Northern Ireland) Order 1986,[28] in relation to Northern Ireland.

2. The British Library, the National Library of Wales, the National Library of Scotland, the Bodleian Library, Oxford and the University Library, Cambridge.

3. Any library of a school within the meaning of section 174 of the Act and any library of a description of educational establishment specified under that section in the Copyright (Educational Establishments) (No. 2) Order 1989.[29]

4. Any parliamentary library or library administered as part of a government department, including a Northern Ireland department, or any library conducted for or administered by an agency which is administered by a Minister of the Crown.

5. Any library administered by—
    (*a*) in England and Wales, a local authority within the meaning of the Local Government Act 1972,[30] the Common Council of the City of London or the Council of the Isles of Scilly;
    (*b*) in Scotland, a local authority within the meaning of the Local Government (Scotland) Act 1973[31];
    (*c*) in Northern Ireland, a district council established under the Local Government Act (Northern Ireland) 1972.[32]

6. Any other library conducted for the purpose of facilitating or encouraging the study of bibliography, education, fine arts, history, languages, law, literature, medicine, music, philosophy, religion, science (including natural and social science) or technology, or administered by any establishment or organisation which is conducted wholly or mainly for such a purpose.

---

[26] c. 75.
[27] c. 27.
[28] S.I. 1986 No. 594 (N.I. 3).
[29] S.I. 1989 No. 1068 § B–32 *ante*.
[30] c. 70.
[31] c. 65.
[32] c. 9 (N.I.).

PART B   Regulation 3(3)   **B–191**

Any library outside the United Kingdom which is conducted wholly or mainly for the purpose of facilitating or encouraging the study of bibliography, education, fine arts, history, languages, law, literature, medicine, music, philosophy, religion, science (including natural and social science) or technology.

SCHEDULE 2   Regulations 4 and 7

FORM A   **B–192**

DECLARATION: COPY OF ARTICLE OR PART OF PUBLISHED WORK

To:

The Librarian of .... Library
[Address of Library]

Please supply me with a copy of:
   *the article in the periodical, the particulars of which are [

                                                                                        ]

   *the part of the published work, the particulars of which are [

                                                                                        ]

required by me for the purposes of research or private study.

   2. I declare that —
      (a) I have not previously been supplied with a copy of the same material by you or any other librarian;
      (b) I will not use the copy except for research or private study and will not supply a copy of it to any other person; and
      (c) to the best of my knowledge no other person with whom I work or study has made or intends to make, at or about the same time as this request, a request for substantially the same material for substantially the same purpose.

   3. I understand that if the declaration is false in a material particular the copy supplied to me by you will be an infringing copy and that I shall be liable for infringement of copyright as if I had made the copy myself.

                          †Signature ....

                          Date ....

Name ....

Address ....

          ....

          ....

---

*Delete whichever is inappropriate.
†This must be the personal signature of the person making the request. A stamped or type-written signature, or the signature of an agent, is NOT acceptable.

Note: The official version of FORM A has no paragraph numbered "1". It may be that the paragraph starting "Please supply" was intended to be so numbered.

DECLARATION: COPY OF WHOLE OR PART OF UNPUBLISHED WORK

To:

    The *Librarian/Archivist of .... *Library/Archive
    [Address of Library/Archive]

Please supply me with a copy of:

    the *whole/following part [particulars of part] of the [particulars of the unpublished work] required by me for the purposes of research or private study.

    2. I declare that —

        (a) I have not previously been supplied with a copy of the same material by you or any other librarian or archivist;

        (b) I will not use the copy except for research or private study and will not supply a copy of it to any other person; and

        (c) to the best of my knowledge the work had not been published before the document was deposited in your *library/archive and the copyright owner has not prohibited copying of the work.

    3. I understand that if the declaration is false in a material particular the copy supplied to me by you will be an infringing copy and that I shall be liable for infringement of copyright as if I had made the copy myself.

                †Signature ....

                Date ....

Name ....

Address ....

        ....

        ....

---

*Delete whichever is inappropriate.
†This must be the personal signature of the person making the request. A stamped or type-written signature, or the signature of an agent, is NOT acceptable.

Note: The official version of FORM B has no paragraph numbered "1". It may be that the paragraph starting "Please supply" was intended to be so numbered.

SCHEDULE 3[33]   Regulation 8 **B–194**

REVOCATIONS

Number	Title
S.I. 1957/868	The Copyright (Libraries) Regulations 1957
S.I. 1989/1009	The Copyright (Copying by Librarians and Archivists) Regulations 1989
S.I. 1989/1069	The Copyright (Copying by Librarians and Archivists) (Amendment) Regulations 1989

The Copyright, Designs and Patents Act 1988 (Isle of Man) (No. 2) Order   **B–195**
1989

(S.I. 1989 No. 1292)

Made - - - - - - -   *28th July 1989*

Coming into force   *1st August 1989*

At the Court at Windsor Castle, the 28th day of July 1989

Present,

The Queen's Most Excellent Majesty in Council

Her Majesty, in pursuance of section 304(4) and (6) of the Copyright, Designs and Patents Act 1988, is pleased, by and with the advice of Her Privy Council, to order, and it is hereby ordered, as follows:

1. This Order may be cited as the Copyright, Designs and Patents Act 1988   **B–196**
(Isle of Man) (No. 2) Order 1989 and shall come into force on 1st August 1989.

2.—(1) The following provisions of the Copyright, Designs and Patents Act   **B–197**
1988 shall extend to the Isle of Man subject to the exceptions and modifications specified in paragraphs (2) and (3) below—
  (a) Part IV (*registered designs*), except section 272 (so far as that section relates to paragraph 21 of Schedule 3) and section 273;
  (b) section 300 (*fraudulent application or use of trade marks an offence*);
  (c) Schedule 3 (*registered designs: minor and consequential amendments*), except paragraph 21, and
  (d) paragraphs 12 to 16 of Schedule 5 (*patents: miscellaneous amendments*).
  (2) Any reference in any of those provisions to an Act of Parliament or to a provision of such an Act shall be construed, unless the contrary intention appears, as a reference to that Act or provision as it has effect in the Isle of Man.
  (3) Without prejudice to paragraph (2) above, sections 58A to 58D of the Trade Marks Act 1938 inserted by section 300 shall have effect subject to the exceptions and modifications specified in the Schedule to this Order.

3. The following provisions of the Copyright, Designs and Patents Act 1988   **B–198**
shall extend to the Isle of Man—
  (a) section 303 (*consequential amendments and repeals*), so far as it relates to the provisions specified in paragraphs (b) and (c) below;

---

[33] As to first Order, see *Copinger*, 12th ed. § 1743. The last two Orders were defective and were revoked before they came into force.

(*b*) paragraphs 5, 20, 22 and 23 of Schedule 7, and
(*c*) Schedule 8, so far as it relates to—
    (i) the Registered Designs Act 1949 (except section 32 of that Act), and
    (ii) section 49(3) of, and paragraphs 1 and 3 of Schedule 5 to, the Patents Act 1977.

B–199   **4.** The Copyright, Designs and Patents Act 1988 (Isle of Man) Order 1989[34] is hereby revoked.

B–200 SCHEDULE Article 2(3)

EXCEPTIONS AND MODIFICATIONS SUBJECT TO WHICH
PROVISIONS OF THE TRADE MARKS ACT 1938 HAVE EFFECT IN
THE ISLE OF MAN

1. In section 58A(4)(b), for "indictment" substitute "information".

2.—(1) In section 58B(2), for paragraphs (a) and (b) substitute "when he is orally charged or is served with a summons or information".

(2) In section 58B(3), omit "(or, in Scotland, the Lord Advocate or procurator-fiscal)".

(3) For section 58B(4) substitute—

    "(4) An appeal lies from an order made under this section by a court of summary jurisdiction to Her Majesty's High Court of Justice of the Isle of Man.".

(4) Omit section 58B(6).

3.—(1) In section 58C(4), for the words from "or under" onwards substitute "or an order for delivery up could be made under section 21(9) of the Copyright Act 1956.[35]".

(2) Omit section 58C(5).

4. Omit section 58D.

B–201   **The Copyright, Designs and Patents Act 1988 (Guernsey) Order 1989**

(S.I. 1989 No. 1997)

Made - - - - - - -	*1st November 1989*
Coming into force	*1st December 1989*

At the Court at Buckingham Palace, the 1st day of November 1989

Present,

The Queen's Most Excellent Majesty in Council

Her Majesty, in pursuance of section 304(5) of the Copyright, Designs and Patents Act 1988, is pleased, by and with the advice of Her Privy Council, to order, and it is hereby ordered, as follows:

---

[34] S.I. 1989 No. 981.
[35] See S.I. 1986 No. 1299 and para. 36(2), Sched. 1, C.D.P.A. 1988.

1. This Order may be cited as the Copyright, Designs and Patents Act 1988   **B–202**
(Guernsey) Order 1989 and shall come into force on 1st December 1989.

2. Sections 297 to 299 of the Copyright, Designs and Patents Act 1988 (fraudu-   **B–203**
lent reception of transmissions) shall extend to the Bailiwick of Guernsey with the
exceptions and modifications specified in the Schedule to this Order.

SCHEDULE   Article 2 **B–204**

EXCEPTIONS AND MODIFICATIONS IN THE EXTENSION OF
SECTIONS 297 TO 299 OF THE COPYRIGHT, DESIGNS AND PATENTS
ACT 1988 TO THE BAILIWICK OF GUERNSEY

1. Any reference to an enactment shall be construed, unless the contrary intention appears, as a reference to it as it has effect in the Bailiwick of Guernsey.

2. In section 297(1), after "United Kingdom" there shall be inserted "or Bailiwick of Guernsey".

3. In section 298—
  (*a*) in subsection (1)(*a*) and (*b*), after "United Kingdom" there shall be
       inserted "or Bailiwick of Guernsey";
  (*b*) in subsection (3), for "99 or 100 (delivery up or seizure of certain
       articles)" there shall be substituted "7 of the Copyright Act 1911 (rights
       of owner against persons possessing or dealing with infringing copies
       etc.)", and
  (*c*) for subsections (4) to (6) there shall be substituted the following sub-
       section:
         "(4) In section 8 of the Copyright Act 1911 (exemption of innocent
         infringer from liability to pay damages etc.) as it applies to pro-
         ceedings for infringement of the rights conferred by this section, the
         references to the defendant not being aware of the existence of the
         copyright in the work, and to his not being aware and having no
         reasonable ground for suspecting that copyright subsisted in the
         work, shall be construed respectively as references to his not being
         aware, and to his not being aware and having no reasonable
         ground for suspecting, that his acts infringed the rights conferred
         by this section.".

4. In section 299—
  (*a*) in subsection (1)(*a*), after "United Kingdom" there shall be inserted
       "and Bailiwick of Guernsey";
  (*b*) in subsection (2), for "United Kingdom" whenever occurring there shall
       be substituted "Bailiwick of Guernsey";
  (*c*) subsection (3) shall be omitted, and
  (*d*) in subsection (5), for "(copyright)" there shall be substituted "of this Act
       as it has effect in England and Wales.".

1281

B–205 **The Fraudulent Reception of Transmissions (Guernsey) Order 1989**

(S.I. 1989 No. 2003)

Made - - - - - - -	*1st November 1989*
Laid before Parliament	*8th November 1989*
Coming into force	*1st December 1989*

At the Court at Buckingham Palace, the 1st day of November 1989

Present,

The Queen's Most Excellent Majesty in Council

Whereas it appears to Her Majesty that provision will be made under the laws of the Bailiwick of Guernsey giving adequate protection to persons making charges for programmes included in broadcasting or cable programme services provided from the United Kingdom and for encrypted transmissions sent from the United Kingdom:

Now, therefore, Her Majesty, by virtue of the authority conferred upon Her by section 299(1) of the Copyright, Designs and Patents Act 1988, is pleased, by and with the advice of Her Privy Council, to order, and it is hereby ordered, as follows:

B–206 **1.** This Order may be cited as the Fraudulent Reception of Transmissions (Guernsey) Order 1989 and shall come into force on 1st December 1989.

B–207 **2.** Section 297 of the Copyright, Designs and Patents Act 1988 applies in relation to programmes included in broadcasting or cable programme services provided from a place in the Bailiwick of Guernsey, and section 298 of the said Act applies in relation to such programmes and to encrypted transmissions of any other description provided or sent from a place in the Bailiwick of Guernsey.

B–208 **The Copyright (Recording for Archives of Designated Class of Broadcasts and Cable Programmes) (Designated Bodies) (No. 2) Order 1989**

(S.I. 1989 No. 2510)

Made - - - - - - -	*28th December 1989*
Laid before Parliament	*22nd January 1990*
Coming into force	*12th February 1990*

The Secretary of State, in exercise of the powers conferred upon him by section 75 of the Copyright, Designs and Patents Act 1988 ("the Act"), and upon being satisfied that the bodies designated by this Order are not established or conducted for profit, hereby makes the following Order:—

B–209 **1.** This Order may be cited as the Copyright (Recording for Archives of Designated Class of Broadcasts and Cable Programmes) (Designated Bodies) (No. 2) Order 1989 and shall come into force on 12th February 1990.

B–210 **2.** Each of the bodies specified in the Schedule to this Order is designated as a body for which a recording of a broadcast or cable programme of the class designated under article 3 below, or a copy thereof, may be made for the purpose of placing the same in any archive maintained by it.

3. All broadcasts other than encrypted transmissions and all cable programmes   **B–211**
are designated as a class for the purposes of section 75 of the Act.

4. The Copyright (Recording for Archives of Designated Class of Broadcasts   **B–212**
and Cable Programmes) (Designated Bodies) Order 1989[36] is hereby revoked.

SCHEDULE   Article 2   **B–213**

DESIGNATED BODIES

The British Film Institute
The British Library
The Music Performance Research Centre
The Scottish Film Council

Act of Sederunt (Copyright, Designs and Patents) 1990   **B–214**

(S.I. 1990 No. 380 (s.37))

Made - - - - - -   *27th February 1990*

Coming into force   *26th March 1990*

The Lords of Council and Session, under and by virtue of the powers conferred on
them by section 32 of the Sheriff Courts (Scotland) Act 1971, section 58C of the
Trade Marks Act 1938 and sections 114, 204 and 231 of the Copyright, Designs
and Patents Act 1988, and of all other powers enabling them in that behalf, do
hereby enact the following Act of Sederunt which embodies, with modifications,
draft rules submitted by the Sheriff Court Rules Council under section 39 of the
said Act of 1971:

Citation and commencement

1.—(1) This Act of Sederunt may be cited as the Act of Sederunt (Copyright,   **B–215**
Designs and Patents) 1990 and shall come into force on 26th March 1990.
   (2) This Act of Sederunt shall be inserted in the Books of Sederunt.
   (3) In this Act of Sederunt—
   "the 1938 Act" means the Trade Marks Act 1938; and
   "the 1988 Act" means the Copyright, Designs and Patents Act 1988.

Orders for delivery up, forfeiture, destruction or other disposal

2.—(1) An application to the sheriff made under section 58C of the 1938 Act   **B–216**
shall be made by summary application.
   (2) An application to the sheriff made under section 99, 114, 195, 204, 230, 231
or 298 of the 1988 Act shall be made—
      (*a*) by motion or incidental application, as the case may be, where proceed-
         ings have been commenced; or
      (*b*) by summary application where no proceedings have been commenced.

---

[36] S.I. 1989 No. 1011.

Service of notice on interested persons

B–217   **3.**—(1) Where an application has been made to the sheriff under section 58C of the 1938 Act or section 114, 204 or 231 of the 1988 Act, the sheriff shall order that there be intimated to any person who has an interest in the goods, material, copy, recording, article or other thing which forms the subject matter of the application—

      (*a*) a copy of the pleadings in the principal proceedings and a copy of the motion or incidental application; or

      (*b*) the summary application,

as the case may be.

  (2) In any such application the applicant shall—

      (a) specify the name and address of any person known or believed by him to have such an interest; or

      (b) state that to the best of his knowledge and belief no other person has any such interest.

Leave of the court for certain actions to proceed

B–218   **4.**—(1) Where, in an action for infringement of copyright or for infringement of design right, leave of the sheriff is required before the action may proceed the pursuer shall lodge along with the initial writ or summons a written motion or incidental application, as the case may be, seeking such leave and stating the grounds upon which it is sought.

  (2) The sheriff may hear the pursuer on the motion or incidental application and may grant or refuse it or may make such other order in relation to it as he considers appropriate prior to such determination.

  (3) Where such a motion or application is granted, a copy of the sheriff's interlocutor shall be served upon the defender along with the warrant of citation.

B–219   GENERAL NOTICE GEN 90/23[37]

                    CROWN AND PARLIAMENTARY COPYRIGHT

                              (June 25, 1990)

B–220 **Scope and purpose**

  1. This Notice states the practice to be followed with regard to Crown and Parliamentary copyright, as defined by the Copyright, Designs and Patents Act 1988 (published by HMSO, ISBN 0 10 544888 5).

B–221 **References**

  2. This Notice supersedes General Notice GEN 75/76.[38] General Notice GEN 75/10 (Transfer of Government Rights in Inventions: Crown Copyright) also refers.

  3. The Copyright, Designs and Patents Act 1988 came into effect on 1 August 1989 and replaced the Copyright Act 1956 and the Copyright (Computer Software) Amendment Act 1985.

---

[37] This General Notice is Crown Copyright and is published with the permission of the Controller of HMSO.
[38] *Copinger*, 12th ed. § 1813.

Summary of points

4. A summary of the advice contained in this notice is as follows:
- (i) All applications received by Departments for permission to reproduce Crown copyright material not covered by a specific delegated authority should be referred to HMSO's Copyright Section (see paragraph 8).
- (ii) Conditions relating to the reproduction of Parliamentary copyright items published by HMSO are similar to those for Crown copyright material. All applications to reproduce this material should be referred to HMSO's Copyright Section (see paragraph 9).
- (iii) For copyright purposes, official material is divided into six categories (see paragraph 11).
- (iv) Considerable freedom is allowed in the reproduction of material in the first three categories listed in paragraph 11 within guidelines issued by HMSO (see paragraphs 12–13).
- (v) Any Department wishing to reproduce Parliamentary material not published by HMSO should apply to the officials of the relevant House (see paragraph 14).
- (vi) Fees should be levied for the reproduction for commercial purposes of non Parliamentary material (see paragraph 15).
- (vii) The administration of Crown copyright relating to charts and Ordnance Survey maps is subject to special delegation arrangements (see paragraph 16).
- (viii) If a work is commissioned, first copyright normally rests with the author or his employer (see paragraph 18).
- (ix) The Central Computer and Telecommunications Agency provides advice in cases where computer software is commissioned (see paragraph 19).
- (x) Advice on the levying of fees is set out in paragraphs 21–23.
- (xi) Any apparent infringement of Crown or Parliamentary copyright should be reported to HMSO (see paragraph 24).

Background

5. The 1988 Act revises the definition in the 1956 Act of Crown copyright and, in addition, introduces a new category of Parliamentary copyright. In the Act, copyright is defined as a "property right", which means that it should be dealt with like any other property, which could include licensing or outright sale to a third party, or prohibition of use by a third party, for breach of which the owner can seek legal damages.

6. Copyright covers a wide variety of material, published and unpublished, including books, reports, photographs, drawings and computer programs. In general, the first owner of copyright is the creator or author of the work or his employer, although there are some exceptions to this. The most notable exceptions are in the fields of Crown and Parliamentary copyright.

7. Under the 1956 Act, the copyright in works commissioned by a Government Department was generally claimed for the Crown on the grounds that:
- (i) the work in question was "made by or under the direction or control of Her Majesty or a Government department"; or
- (ii) because the work was first published by the Crown.

Under the 1988 Act, however, Crown copyright only covers those works "made by Her Majesty or by an officer or servant of the Crown in the course of his duties". Consequently, if an author or consultant is hired by a Department to produce a work, the copyright in that work would normally rest with the author (or his employer) and not with the commissioner. If, therefore, it is necessary for the Crown to hold the copyright in a particular commissioned work, then this should be made a specific condition of contract with the author or consultant. The 1988 Act also covers computer works which are defined by the Act as "literary works" and are accorded, with some exceptions, the same status as, for example, a novel or a textbook.

B–224 Reproduction of official material

8. The rights in respect of all Crown copyright and other copyrights belonging to the Crown are administered by HMSO. The unique authority to do so is granted by Her Majesty to the Controller of HMSO by means of Royal Letters Patent. All applications received by Departments for permission to reproduce official material not known to be covered by a specific delegated authority to a Department should be referred to HMSO's Copyright Section, who will normally take account of the views of the Department of origin of the material before authorising its use.

9. Under the 1988 Act, authority for Parliamentary copyright lies with the Clerk of the Parliaments for House of Lords material and with the Speaker of the House of Commons for Commons material. For those Parliamentary items which HMSO publishes, the Controller of HMSO administers Parliamentary copyright. The conditions relating to the reproduction of this Parliamentary copyright material will be similar to those for Crown copyright.

10. In cases where a published version of a Crown or Parliamentary copyright work is available, Departments should obtain the required number of official copies rather than engage in multiple or extensive photocopying.

B–225 Classes of official material for copyright purposes

11. For copyright purposes, official material may be divided into the following categories:—

    i. Statutory material, including Bills and Acts of Parliament, Statutory Rules and Orders, and Statutory Instruments;

    ii. The Official Report of the House of Lords and House of Commons Debates (Hansard), Lords' Minutes, the Vote Bundle, Commons Order-books and Commons Statutory Instrument Lists;

    iii. Other Parliamentary papers published by HMSO, including Reports of Select Committees of both Houses;

    iv. Other Parliamentary material not published by HMSO;

    v. Non-Parliamentary material comprising all papers of Government Departments and Crown bodies—both published and unpublished—not contained in other classes;

    vi. Charts and Navigational material published by the Ministry of Defence (Hydrographic Department) and maps and other items in all media published by Ordnance Survey.

12. Considerable freedom is allowed in the reproduction of material in the first three categories, within guidelines issued by HMSO through the Publishers Association, the Library Association and other outlets (copies are available from HMSO's Copyright Section on request). Nevertheless, all Crown rights in respect of this material are reserved and will be asserted in cases such as those where the material would be reproduced in an undesirable context or where the reproduction of the whole or part of the material falls outside the conditions specified in HMSO's guidelines, or where its reproduction could result in a significant loss of sales of official publications. All Departments have a responsibility to ensure that Crown (and Parliamentary) copyright is not being used illegally. However, any

action to enforce the Crown's rights in copyright matters would be taken in consultation with HMSO.

13. Copies of Acts of Parliament, Statutory Rules and Orders and Statutory Instruments, other than those reproduced by the order of HMSO, do not have the legal standing of officially published versions produced by HMSO. Any organisation or individual wishing to reproduce the Official Report of Parliamentary Debates (Hansard) should be warned that, even though these may be verbatim reports of speeches as reported in the Official Report, it will not have the same rights of privilege in proceedings for defamation as those enjoyed by the Official Report. Reproducing all or part of the Official Report for advertising purposes is not permitted.

14. All applications for reproduction of material falling in the fourth category should be referred to the officials of the relevant House (see addresses at paragraph 26).

15. The fifth category comprises a wide range of Government material, including many items which explain the operation of Acts of Parliament, or make available the results of research, and other activities of Departments. It is desirable that this information should be widely known, but official publication is the usual channel for this purpose and, subject to the exercise of the discretions described in paragraph 22 below, there is no reason why free reproduction should be allowed of this kind of material for commercial purposes. The exercise of the Crown's copyrights is also necessary to protect official material from misuse by unfair or misleading selection, undignified association, or undesirable use for advertising purposes. The rights of the Crown will therefore normally be enforced for material in this category. Acknowledgment of source and of the permission of the Controller of HMSO should be given, and suitable fees levied for reproduction.

16. The administration of Crown copyright relating to material in the sixth category, charts and Ordnance Survey maps, is subject to appropriate arrangements for delegation between the Controller of HMSO and the Ministry of Defence (Hydrographic Department) and Ordnance Survey.

17. In the reproduction of copyright material not belonging to the Crown, Departments should ensure that they abide by the terms of the Copyright, Designs and Patents Act 1988.

18. If a work is commissioned by a Department or other Crown body, first copyright, in the normal course of events, would rest with the author, artist, photographer, composer or creator of the work or with his employer and not with the commissioner. If, therefore, it is considered necessary for the Crown to hold copyright in a particular commissioned or similar work, this must be negotiated as a specific condition within the commissioning agreement. For practical purposes, the decision as to whether or not copyright should be claimed for the Crown on commissioned work will rest with the commissioning body, but the general benefit to the Crown of securing rights in commissioned works should always be borne in mind. Rights thus acquired in commissioned works, however, should not be referred to as "Crown copyright", since that specific status only exists as defined in Section 163 of the 1988 Act. They are nevertheless copyrights held by the Crown and, as such, are administered by the Controller of HMSO. Care should be taken in acquiring such rights for the Crown rather than for a named individual or postholder. In the latter case, the copyright may not be the Crown's and therefore the Crown would be unable to assert or defend its rights with regard to the material in question.

19. In cases where computer software is commissioned (specifically defined by the 1988 Act as "literary work"), the copyright should remain the property of the software developer where the Crown intention is generally to acquire use of the software rather than to buy the software outright for further exploitation. This is the normal policy advocated by the Central Computer and Telecommunications

Agency (CCTA). CCTA provide guidance on how Crown requirements are best met in this situation and also offer appropriate contract terms to use where it is seen as essential to acquire rights for the Crown.

20. Departments (or other Crown bodies) should consult HMSO's Copyright Section before concluding any agreement to publish through a private publisher material whose copyright is held by the Crown or is the responsibility of the Controller of HMSO. An exception is the material specified at paragraph 23. Departments or other Crown bodies should also take into account the Tradeable Information guidelines issued by the Department of Trade and Industry.

B–226 Fees

21. In assessing fees payable to the Crown in respect of all categories of official material, the Controller will consider the value of the material to the applicant and the extent to which commercial or private reproduction will affect the revenue from sales of official publications. The Controller can use his discretion to waive or reduce fees in appropriate circumstances.

22. The Controller will waive or reduce fees in respect of applications for use of material for professional, technical or scientific purposes where profit is not a primary purpose of reproduction. Consideration of reduction or remission of fees will also be given to reproduction in works of scholarship, in the journals of learned societies and similar non-profit making bodies, for educational purposes and in other cases where the need for the fullest dissemination of official information is paramount and the commercial or other aspects are relatively unimportant.

23. In this connection all Departments and other Crown bodies are now hereby given the right to authorise the publication of papers in learned journals and in the Proceedings of Conferences and Seminars, provided that the source is acknowledged and that the copyright in the work is not assigned to the publisher concerned. In these particular cases, fees may be waived or reduced at the discretion of the authorising Department or other Crown body in line with paragraph 22 above. In the case of any doubts, reference should be made to HMSO's Copyright Section.

B–227 Infringement of Crown and Parliamentary copyright

24. Any apparent infringement of Crown or Parliamentary copyright or other copyright held by the Crown which comes to the notice of a Department or other Crown body should be reported to HMSO's Copyright Section or in the case of Ordnance Survey maps etc., to the Ordnance Survey. Consideration will then be given to further action, including the possibility of legal proceedings.

B–228 Action

25. Departments are asked to ensure that the arrangements set out in this Notice are brought to the attention of all staff concerned. Departments should also be aware that HMSO issue other guidance material on Crown and Parliamentary copyright and copies can be readily obtained on application to HMSO's Copyright Section at the address given below.

B–229 Contacts

26. Any enquiries or problems arising should be addressed to the Copyright Section, HMSO, St Crispins, Duke Street, Norwich NR3 1PD. Telephone 0603 695513 or via GTN 3014 5513. Other useful contacts are:

Chief Clerk	or	Clerk of the Journals
Journal Office		Journal Office
House of Lords		House of Commons
London, SW1A 0PW		London, SW1A 0AA

Tel: 071 219 3187/3327   Tel: 071 219 3315/3320

Copyright Branch		Hydrographic Department
Ordnance Survey		Finance Section
Romsey Road		Ministry of Defence
Maybush		Taunton
Southampton SO9 4DH		Somerset TA1 2DN

Tel: 0703 792302   Tel: 0823 337900 Ext 337

Authorised by: A J HOWIE

File reference: 2MGD 10/062

Date of issue: 25 June 1990

Machinery of Government Division
CABINET OFFICE (OMCS)
Horse Guards Road
LONDON SW1P 3AL

Valid until superseded

The Copyright (Material Open to Public Inspection) (Marking of Copies of **B–230**
Plans and Drawings) Order 1990

(S.I. 1990 No. 1427)

Made - - - - - - -	*16th July 1990*
Laid before Parliament	*23rd July 1990*
Coming into force	*15th August 1990*

The Secretary of State, in exercise of the powers conferred upon him by section 47(4) of the Copyright, Designs and Patents Act 1988, hereby makes the following Order:—

1. This Order may be cited as the Copyright (Material Open to Public Inspec- **B–231**
tion) (Marking of Copies of Plans and Drawings) Order 1990 and shall come into force on 15th August 1990.

2. Subsection (2) of section 47 of the Copyright, Designs and Patents Act 1988 **B–232**
shall, in the case of a plan or drawing which is open to public inspection pursuant to a statutory requirement, apply only to copies of the plan or drawing marked in the following manner—

"This copy has been made by or with the authority of [insert the name of the person required to make the plan or drawing open to public inspection] pursuant to section 47 of the Copyright, Designs and Patents Act 1988. Unless that Act provides a relevant exception to copyright, the copy must not be copied without the prior permission of the copyright owner.".

B–233   **Patents County Court (Designation and Jurisdiction) Order 1990**

(S.I. 1990 No. 1496)

Made   -   -   -   -   -   -   -   *19th July 1990*

Coming into force   *3rd September 1990*

The Lord Chancellor, in exercise of the powers conferred upon him by section 287(1) of the Copyright, Designs and Patents Act 1988, hereby makes the following Order:

Title and Commencement

B–234   **1.** This Order may be cited as the Patents County Court (Designation and Jurisdiction) Order 1990 and shall come into force on 3rd September 1990.

Designation as Patents County Court

B–235   **2.** The Edmonton County Court is hereby designated as a patents county court.

B–236   **3.** As a patents county court, the Edmonton County Court shall have jurisdiction, subject to article 4 below, to hear and determine any action or matter relating to patents or designs over which the High Court would have jurisdiction, together with any claims or matters ancillary thereto or arising therefrom.

B–237   **4.** The jurisdiction conferred by article 3 above shall not include jurisdiction to hear appeals from the comptroller.

B–238   **The Copyright, Designs and Patents Act 1988 (Isle of Man) Order 1990**

(S.I. 1990 No. 1505)

Made   -   -   -   -   -   -   -   *24th July 1990*

Coming into force   *13th August 1990*

At the Court at Buckingham Palace, the 24th day of July 1990

Present,

The Queen's Most Excellent Majesty in Council

Her Majesty, in pursuance of section 304(4) and (6) of the Copyright, Designs and Patents Act 1988, is pleased, by and with the advice of Her Privy Council, to order, and it is hereby ordered, as follows:

1. This Order may be cited as the Copyright, Designs and Patents Act 1988   **B–239**
(Isle of Man) Order 1990 and shall come into force on 13th August 1990.

2. The following provisions of the Copyright, Designs and Patents Act 1988   **B–240**
shall extend to the Isle of Man subject to the exceptions and modifications specified in the Schedule to this Order—

    (*a*) section 272, so far as it relates to paragraph 21 of Schedule 3, and that
        paragraph (*registered designs : minor and consequential amendments*);
    (*b*) section 273 and Schedule 4 (*text of Registered Designs Act 1949 as amended*);
    (*c*) Part V (*patent agents and trade mark agents*);
    (*d*) paragraph 27 of Schedule 5 (*patents: miscellaneous amendments*).

3. Section 303(2) of and Schedule 8 to the Copyright, Designs and Patents Act   **B–241**
1988 shall extend to the Isle of Man so far as they relate to the repeal of—

    (*a*) section 32 of the Registered Designs Act 1949, and
    (*b*) the following provisions of the Patents Act 1977—
        (i) sections 84 and 85;
        (ii) section 104;
        (iii) in section 105, the words "within the meaning of section 104 above";
        (iv) sections 114 and 115;
        (v) section 123(2)(k), and
        (vi) in section 130(1), the definition of "patent agent".

SCHEDULE   Article 2 **B–242**

EXCEPTIONS AND MODIFICATIONS IN THE EXTENSION OF
PROVISIONS OF THE COPYRIGHT, DESIGNS AND PATENTS ACT 1988
TO THE ISLE OF MAN

1. Any reference to an Act of Parliament or to a provision of such an Act shall be
construed, unless the contrary intention appears, as a reference to that Act or provision as it has effect in the Isle of Man.

2. Schedule 4 shall have effect as if the text of the Registered Designs Act 1949
contained therein were the text of that Act as modified by the Registered Designs
Act 1949 (Isle of Man) Order 1989[39].

3.—(1) Part V shall have effect subject to the following provisions of this paragraph.

    (2) In section 278—
    (*a*) in subsection (1), for "solicitor" and "solicitors" there shall be substituted
        respectively "advocate" and "advocates";
    (*b*) in subsection (2), for the words from "the enactments" to the end there
        shall be substituted "section 1 of the Legal Practitioners Registration Act
        1986 (an Act of Tynwald) (which restricts the use of certain expressions in
        reference to persons not qualified to act as advocates)", and
    (*c*) subsection (3) shall be omitted.

---

[39] S.I. 1989 No. 982.

(3) In section 280—

    (*a*) in subsection (2), for "England, Wales or Northern Ireland" and "solicitor" there shall be substituted respectively "the Isle of Man" and "advocate", and

    (*b*) subsection (4) shall be omitted.

(4) In section 284—

    (*a*) in subsection (2), for "England, Wales or Northern Ireland" and "solicitor" there shall be substituted respectively "the Isle of Man" and "advocate", and

    (*b*) subsection (4) shall be omitted.

(5) Section 285(2)(*b*) shall be omitted.

B–243   **The Copyright, Designs and Patents Act 1988 (Commencement No. 5) Order 1990**

(S.I. 1990 No. 1400 (c.42))

Made - - - - - - -   *10th July 1990*

The Secretary of State, in exercise of the powers conferred upon him by section 305(3) of the Copyright, Designs and Patents Act 1988, hereby makes the following Order:

B–244   **1.** This Order may be cited as the Copyright, Designs and Patents Act 1988 (Commencement No. 5) Order 1990.

B–245   **2.** The following provisions of the Copyright, Designs and Patents Act 1988 shall come into force on 13th August 1990—

    (*a*) in Part IV (registered designs)—

        section 272 in so far as it relates to paragraph 21 of Schedule 3, and section 273;

    (*b*) Part V (patent agents and trade mark agents) save in so far as article 3 below otherwise provides;

    (*c*) in Part VI (patents)—

        section 295 in so far as it relates to paragraph 27 of Schedule 5;

    (*d*) in Part VII (miscellaneous and general)—

        section 303(1) in so far as it relates to paragraphs 15, 18(2) and 21 of Schedule 7, and

        section 303(2) in so far as it relates to the references in Schedule 8 to—

            section 32 of the Registered Designs Act 1949, and sections 84, 85, 104, the words "within the meaning of section 104 above" in section 105, sections 114 and 115, section 123(2)(*k*), and the definition of "patent agent" in section 130(1), of the Patents Act 1977;

    (*e*) in Schedule 3 (minor and consequential amendments to the Registered Designs Act 1949) paragraph 21;

    (*f*) Schedule 4;

    (*g*) in Schedule 5 (patents: miscellaneous amendments), paragraph 27;

    (*h*) in Schedule 7 (consequential amendments), paragraphs 15, 18(2) and 21;

(*i*) in Schedule 8 (repeals) the references to—
> section 32 of the Registered Designs Act 1949, and sections 84, 85, 104, the words "within the meaning of section 104 above" in section 105, sections 114 and 115, section 123(2)(k), and the definition of "patent agent" in section 130(1), of the Patents Act 1977.

3. For the purpose only of making rules expressed to come into force on or after **B–246**
13th August 1990, any provision of Part V of the Copyright, Designs and Patents Act 1988 conferring power to make rules shall come into force forthwith.

The Copyright, Designs and Patents Act 1988 (Commencement No. 6) **B–247**
Order 1990

(S.I. 1990 No. 2168 (c. 53))

Made - - - - - - - *1st November 1990*

The Secretary of State, in exercise of the powers conferred upon him by section 305(3) of the Copyright, Designs and Patents Act 1988, hereby makes the following Order:—

1. This Order may be cited as the Copyright, Designs and Patents Act 1988 **B–248**
(Commencement No. 6) Order 1990.

2. The following provisions of the Copyright, Designs and Patents Act 1988 **B–249**
shall come into force on 7th January 1990—
> (*a*) in Part VI (patents), save in so far as article 3 below otherwise provides—
> section 295 in so far as it relates to paragraphs 1 to 11, 17 to 23, 25, 26, 28 and 30 of Schedule 5;
> (*b*) in Part VII (miscellaneous and general), section 303(2) in so far as it relates to the references in Schedule 8 to—
> section 14(4) and (8), paragraph (b) and the word "and" preceding it in section 28(3), section 28(5) to (9), sections 72(3) and 88, the words "88(6) and (7)" in section 130(7) of, and paragraphs 2, 7 and 8 of Schedule 5 to, the Patents Act 1977;
> (*c*) in Schedule 5 (patents: miscellaneous amendments), save in so far as article 3 below otherwise provides—
> paragraphs 1 to 11, 17 to 23, 25, 26, 28 and 30;
> (*d*) in Schedule 8 (repeals) the references to—
> section 14(4) and (8), paragraph (b) and the word "and" preceding it in section 28(3), section 28(5) to (9), sections 72(3) and 88, the words "88(6) and (7)" in section 130(7) of, and paragraphs 2, 7 and 8 of Schedule 5 to, the Patents Act 1977.

3. For the purposes only of making rules expressed to come into force on or after **B–250**
7th January 1991, any amendment to the Patents Act 1977 effected by a provision referred to in article 2(a) and (c) above which confers power to make rules or prescribe anything shall come into force forthwith.

B–251   **The Copyright, Designs and Patents Act 1988 (Isle of Man) (No. 2) Order 1990**

(S.I. 1990 No. 2293)

Made   -   -   -   -   -   -   *20th November 1990*

Coming into force   *7th January 1991*

At the Court at Buckingham Palace, the 20th day of November 1990

Present,

The Queen's Most Excellent Majesty in Council

Her Majesty, in pursuance of section 304(4) and (6) of the Copyright, Designs and Patents Act 1988, is pleased, by and with the advice of Her Privy Council, to order, and it is hereby ordered, as follows:

B–252   **1.** This Order may be cited as the Copyright, Designs and Patents Act 1988 (Isle of Man) (No. 2) Order 1990 and shall come into force on 7th January 1991.

B–253   **2.**—(1) Paragraphs 1 to 11, 17 to 23, 25, 26, 28 and 30 of Schedule 5 to the Copyright, Designs and Patents Act 1988 shall extend to the Isle of Man subject to the modification specified in paragraph (3) below.

(2) Section 303(2) of and Schedule 8 to the Copyright, Designs and Patents Act 1988 shall extend to the Isle of Man so far as they relate to the repeal of the following provisions of the Patents Act 1977—

> (*a*) sections 14(4) and (8);
> (*b*) in section 28(3), paragraph (b) and the word "and" preceding it;
> (*c*) section 28(5) to (9);
> (*d*) sections 72(3) and 88;
> (*e*) in section 130(7), the words "88(6) and (7)", and
> (*f*) in Schedule 5, paragraphs 2, 7 and 8.

(3) The modification referred to in paragraph (1) above is that any reference to an Act of Parliament or to a provision of such an Act shall be construed, unless the contrary intention appears, as a reference to that Act or provision as it has effect in the Isle of Man.

B–254   **The Broadcasting Act 1990 (Commencement No. 1 and Transitional Provisions) Order 1990**

(S.I. 1990 No. 2347 (c. 61))

Made   -   -   -   -   -   -   *27th November 1990*

Note: This Order was made by David Waddington, one of Her Majesty's Principal Secretaries of State, Home Office.

In exercise of the powers conferred upon me by sections 200 and 204(2) of the Broadcasting Act 1990, I hereby make the following Order:

B–255   **1.**—(1) This Order may be cited as the Broadcasting Act 1990 (Commencement No. 1 and Transitional Provisions) Order 1990.

(2) In this Order "the 1990 Act" means the Broadcasting Act 1990.

2. The provisions of the 1990 Act which are specified in Schedule 1 to this Order   **B-256**
shall come into force on 1st December 1990.

3.—(1) Subject to paragraphs (2) and (3) below, the provisions of the 1990 Act   **B-257**
which are specified in Schedule 2 to this Order shall come into force on 1st January 1991.

(2) Paragraph (1) above and Schedule 2 to this Order shall not apply so as to bring into force the replacement of the reference to the Independent Broadcasting Authority by the amendment made by paragraph 36 of Schedule 20 to the 1990 Act until such time as that Authority is dissolved by order under section 127(3) of the 1990 Act.

(3) Paragraph (1) above and Schedule 2 to this Order shall not apply so as to bring into force the repeal by Schedule 21 to the 1990 Act of those provisions of the Broadcasting Act 1981[40] and the Cable and Broadcasting Act 1984[41], together with the entries in the said Schedule 21 in respect of paragraph 81 of Schedule 4 to and paragraphs 8(1) and (3) and 30 of Schedule 5 to the Telecommunications Act 1984[42], the Companies Consolidation (Consequential Provisions) Act 1985[43], the Finance Act 1986[44], the Broadcasting Act 1987[45], the Education Reform Act 1988[46], sections 73 and 134(4) of, paragraph 19 of Schedule 2 to, and paragraph 29 of Schedule 7 to the Copyright, Designs and Patents Act 1988 and the Finance Act 1989[47], which continue to have effect under or by virtue of sections 127 to 129 and 134 of, and Schedules 9 to 12 to, the 1990 Act.

4. Section 175 of the 1990 Act shall come into force on 1st February 1991.   **B-258**

5. Section 176 of, and Schedule 17 to, the 1990 Act shall come into force on 1st   **B-259**
March 1991 except that for the purpose of enabling publication of information about programmes to be included in a programme service on or after that date, those provisions shall come into force on 1st January 1991.

6. The following provisions shall come into force on 1st April 1991; those pro-   **B-260**
visions are:
   (*a*) section 180 of, and Schedule 18 to, the 1990 Act; and
   (*b*) the entries in Schedule 21 to the 1990 Act relating to the appeal of–
       (i) the Wireless Telegraphy (Blind Persons) Act 1955[48]; and
       (ii) the Wireless Telegraphy Act 1967[49].

7.—(1) Subject to paragraph (2) below, the provisions of the 1990 Act which are   **B-261**
specified in Schedule 3 to this Order shall come into force on 1st January 1993.

(2) For the purposes of enabling conditions of the type specified in sections 34(2), 35(1) and 185(3) of the 1990 Act to be included in a Channel 3 or Channel 5 licence or licence to provide Channel 4, sections 34, 35 and 185 of that Act shall come into force on 1st January 1991.

---

[40] c. 68.
[41] c. 46.
[42] c. 12.
[43] c. 9.
[44] c. 41.
[45] c. 10.
[46] c. 40.
[47] c. 26.
[48] c. 7.
[49] c. 72.

SCHEDULE 1   Article 2

PROVISIONS OF THE 1990 ACT COMING INTO FORCE ON 1ST DECEMBER 1990

Section 1
Section 2, except subsection (1)
Sections 3 to 9
Section 11
Section 43
Sections 45 to 47
Section 71
Section 83
Sections 126 and 127
Sections 130 to 133
Section 141
Sections 198 to 202
In section 203, subsections (3) and (4)
Section 204

Schedules 1 and 2
Schedules 8 and 9
In Schedule 21, the entry relating to the repeal of the Cable and Broadcasting Act 1984 to the extent that the repeal concerns paragraphs (a) and (b) of section 8(1) of that Act.

Paragraphs 1 to 3 of Schedule 22

B–263   SCHEDULE 2   Article 3

PROVISIONS OF THE 1990 ACT COMING INTO FORCE ON 1ST JANUARY 1991, SUBJECT TO THE PROVISIONS OF ARTICLE 3 OF THIS ORDER

Section 2(1)
Section 10
Sections 12 to 22
Section 26
Sections 28 to 33
Sections 36 to 42
Section 44
Sections 48 to 70
Sections 72 to 82
Sections 84 to 125
Sections 128 and 129
Sections 134 to 140
Sections 142 to 174
Sections 177 to 179

Sections 181 to 184
Section 186
Sections 188 to 197
In section 203, subsections (1) and (2)

Schedules 4 to 7, 10 to 16 and 19
In Schedule 20, paragraphs 1 to 36 and 38 to 54
In Schedule 21, all of the entries except those relating to:
  (*a*) the Wireless Telegraphy (Blind Persons) Act 1955;
  (*b*) the Wireless Telegraphy Act 1967;
  (*c*) the entries in Part II of Schedule 1 to the House of Commons Disquali-
      fication Act 1975[50] relating to the Cable Authority and the Independent
      Broadcasting Authority; and
  (*d*) the Northern Ireland Assembly Disqualification Act 1975[51];

In Schedule 22, paragraphs 4 to 7

SCHEDULE 3   Article 7 **B-264**

PROVISIONS OF THE 1990 ACT COMING INTO FORCE ON 1ST
JANUARY 1993, SUBJECT TO THE PROVISIONS OF ARTICLE 7 OF
THIS ORDER

Sections 23 to 25
Section 27
Sections 34 and 35
Section 185
Section 187

Schedule 3
In Schedule 20, paragraph 37

The Copyright Tribunal (Amendment) Rules 1991   **B-265**
(S.I. 1991 No. 201)

Made - - - - - -   *5th February 1991*

Laid before Parliament   *8th February 1991*

Coming into force   *1st March 1991*

The Lord Chancellor in exercise of the powers conferred upon him by sections 150
and 152(2) and (3) of, and paragraph 34 of Schedule 1 to, the Copyright, Designs
and Patents Act 1988, after consultation with the Lord Advocate, with the approval of the Treasury as to the fees chargeable under these Rules in respect of

---

[50] c. 24.
[51] c. 25.

proceedings before the Copyright Tribunal, and after consultation with the Council on Tribunals in accordance with section 10(1) of the Tribunals and Inquiries Act 1971, hereby makes the following Rules:—

Citation and commencement

B–266   **1.** These Rules, which amend the Copyright Tribunal Rules 1989[52] ("the Principal Rules"), may be cited as the Copyright Tribunal (Amendment) Rules 1991 and shall come into force on 1st March 1991.

B–267   **2.** The Principal Rules are amended as follows:—
(*a*) there shall be inserted in rule 2(1)—
    (i) after the definition of "the Act" and before the definition of "applicant", " "the 1990 Act" means the Broadcasting Act 1990;";
    (ii) in the definition of "intervener", in place of the numbered rules there mentioned, a reference to rule 7, 23, 26, 26D, 30, 33, 37, 41, 41D or 44;
    (iii) after the definition of "proceedings" and before the definition of "the Secretary",
      " "programme service" has the meaning given to it by section 201 of the 1990 Act;".
(*b*) there shall be inserted after rule 26—

"Applications and references with respect to use as of right of sound recordings in broadcasts and cable programme services

Commencement of proceedings (Forms 10A, 10B & 10C)

26A.—(1) Proceedings with respect to use as of right of sound recordings in broadcasts or cable programme services shall be commenced by the service on the Secretary by the applicant of a notice—
(*a*) in Form 10A in the case of an application to settle terms of payment under section 135D of the Act,
(*b*) in Form 10B in the case of a reference under section 135E of the Act,
(*c*) in Form 10C in the case of an application for a review of an order under section 135F of the Act,
together with a statement of the applicant's case.

(2) As soon as practicable after receipt of the notice, the Secretary shall serve a copy of the same (with a copy of the applicant's statement) on the licensing body named in the notice and, in the case of an application for review of an order under section 135F, on every person who was a party to the proceedings when the original order of the Tribunal was made.

(3) Except where the Chairman otherwise directs, the Secretary shall give notice by advertisement in such manner as the Chairman may think fit of every reference or application under section 135D, 135E or 135F of the Act.

Application for special leave (Form 3)

26B.—(1) An application under section 135F(2) of the Act for the special leave of the Tribunal for the review of its order under that section shall be made by the service on the Secretary by the applicant of a notice in Form 3 together with a statement of the grounds for the application. The applicant shall serve a copy of the notice and statement on every person who was a party to the application or

---

[52] See § B–49 *et seq. ante.*

reference on which the Tribunal made the last previous order with respect to the licence.

(2) Within 14 days of the service upon him of such notice, any such party may make representations in writing to the Tribunal regarding the application for special leave, and he shall serve a copy of any such representations on the applicant and inform the Secretary of the date of such service.

(3) The Tribunal, after considering the application and any representations and, if it considers necessary, after having given the applicant and any such party who has made such representations an opportunity of being heard, shall grant or dismiss the application (with such order as to costs) as it may think fit, and if it grants the application it may give such directions as to the taking of any steps required or authorised under these Rules or as to any further matter as the Tribunal thinks fit.

(4) The decision of the Tribunal shall be in writing and shall include a statement of its reasons, and the Secretary shall serve a copy thereof on the applicant and on any party who made representations.

Procedure, and decision of Tribunal

26C.—(1) Within 21 days of the service of the notice under rule 26A, the licensing body or other person shall serve on the Secretary his written answer to the applicant's statement, and shall serve a copy of the same on the applicant and inform the Secretary of the date of such service.

(2) Rules 10 to 16 shall apply to proceedings in respect of a reference or application under rules 26A and 26B as they apply to proceedings in respect of a reference or an application under rule 3.

(3) The final decision of the Tribunal on a reference or an application under rule 26A shall be given in writing and shall include a statement of the Tribunal's reasons and there shall be annexed to the decision a copy of the order and, where the Tribunal has varied a previous order, a copy of that order as varied.

(4) The Secretary shall as soon as practicable serve on every party to the proceedings a copy of the Tribunal's decision. Rule 18 shall apply with regard to the publication of the decision.

Intervener's application (Forms 5 & 6)

26D. A person or organisation who claims to have a substantial interest in proceedings in respect of a reference or an application under rule 26A may, in accordance with rule 23, apply to the Tribunal to be made a party to that reference or application and that rule shall apply to proceedings in respect of such an application as it applies to proceedings in respect of an application under rule 20.".

(*c*) there shall be inserted after rule 41—

"Use of information as of right: application to settle terms of payment

Commencement of proceedings (Forms 16A & 16B)

41A.—(1) Proceedings under Schedule 17 to the 1990 Act for the settlement of terms of payment to be made by a publisher to a person providing a programme service shall be commenced by the service on the Secretary by the applicant of a notice—

(*a*) in Form 16A, in the case of an application under paragraph 5(1) of Schedule 17 to the 1990 Act,

(*b*) in Form 16B, in the case of an application for a review of an order under paragraph 6(1) of that Schedule,

together with a statement of the applicant's case.

(2) As soon as practicable after receipt of the notice, the Secretary shall serve a copy of the same (with a copy of the applicant's statement) on the person providing the programme service named in the notice and, in the case of an application for review of an order under paragraph 6(1) of Schedule 17 to the 1990 Act, on every person who was a party to the proceedings when the original order of the Tribunal was made.

(3) Except where the Chairman otherwise directs, the Secretary shall give notice by advertisement in such manner as the Chairman may think fit of every reference or application under paragraph 5(1) or 6(1) of Schedule 17 to the 1990 Act.

Application for special leave (Form 3)

41B.—(1) An application for the special leave of the Tribunal for the review of an order under paragraph 6(2) of Schedule 17 to the 1990 Act shall be made by serving on the Secretary a notice in Form 3, together with a statement of the grounds for the application. The applicant shall serve a copy of the notice and statement on every person who was a party to the application when the order of the Tribunal was made.

(2) Within 14 days of the service upon him of a copy of the notice under that rule, the other party may make representations in writing to the Tribunal regarding the application for special leave, and he shall serve a copy of any such representations on every other party to the proceedings and inform the Secretary of the date of such service.

(3) The Tribunal, after considering the application and any representations and, if it considers necessary, after having given the applicant and any such party who has made representations an opportunity of being heard, shall grant or dismiss the application for special leave (with such order as to costs) as it may think fit, and if it grants the application it may give such directions as to the taking of any steps required or authorised under these Rules or as to any further matter as the Tribunal thinks fit.

(4) The decision of the Tribunal shall be in writing and shall include a statement of its reasons, and the Secretary shall serve a copy thereof on the applicant and on any party who made representations.

Procedure, and decision of Tribunal

41C.—(1) Within 21 days of the service of the notice under rule 41A, the other party shall serve on the Secretary a written answer to the applicant's statement, and shall serve a copy of the same on the applicant and inform the Secretary of the date of service.

(2) Rules 10 to 16 shall apply in respect of an application under rules 41A and 41B as they apply to proceedings in respect of an application under rule 3.

(3) The final decision of the Tribunal on an application under rule 41A shall be given in writing and shall include a statement of the Tribunal's reasons, and there shall be annexed to the decision a copy of the order and where the Tribunal has varied a previous order, a copy of that order as varied, and the Secretary shall as soon as practicable serve on every party to the proceedings a copy of the Tribunal's decision. Rule 18 shall apply with regard to the publication of the decision.

Intervener's application (Forms 5 & 6)

41D. A person or organisation who claims to have a substantial interest in the proceedings in respect of any application under rule 41A may, in accordance with rule 23, apply to the Tribunal to be made a party to that application and that rule shall apply to proceedings in respect of such an application as it applies to proceedings in respect of an application under rule 20.".

(*d*) there shall be inserted after rule 50—

"Notice of intention to exercise right

50A. Notice of an intention to exercise rights conferred by section 135C of the Act or paragraph 4 of Schedule 17 to the 1990 Act to be given to the Tribunal under section 135B(3)(*a*) of the Act and paragraph 3(2)(*a*) of Schedule 17 to the 1990 Act may be effected by service on the Secretary of such notice and rule 50(1) shall apply to such service as it applies to any notice required to be served on the Secretary by these Rules.".

3. Schedule 1 to the Principal Rules shall be replaced by the following:— **B–268**

"SCHEDULE 1   Rule 49

TABLE OF FEES

(1) On serving notice in Forms 1, 2, 7, 8, 10A, 10B, 12, 14, 15, 16 or 16A.   £30

(2) On serving notice in Forms 3, 4, 5, 6, 9, 10, 10C, 11, 13, 16B, 17 or 18.   £15

(3) On every application for directions under rule 12.   £10".

4. Schedule 3 to the Principal Rules shall be amended as follows:— **B–269**
  (*a*) the forms numbered 3, 5 and 6 in that Schedule shall be replaced by the forms so numbered and set out in Part I of the Schedule to these Rules;
  (*b*) there shall be inserted in that Schedule in the appropriate numerical order those forms referred to in these Rules numbered 10A, 10B, 10C, 16A and 16B as so numbered and set out in Part II of the Schedule to these Rules.

SCHEDULE   Article 4(a)

PART I

FORM 3   Rules 4(1), 21(1),   **B–270**
                          26B(1), 28, 39(1) and 41B

BROADCASTING ACT 1990
COPYRIGHT, DESIGNS AND PATENTS ACT 1988
COPYRIGHT TRIBUNAL

Application for special leave under section 120, 122, 127, 135F or 142 or Schedule 6, paragraph 5 of the Act or Schedule 17, paragraph 6 of the 1990 Act

To,
    The Secretary to the Tribunal

1. TAKE NOTICE that [name and address of person, organisation, operator of licensing scheme, licensing body, publisher or person providing a programme service] ("the Applicant") hereby applies for the special leave of the Tribunal

Application unders s.120(2)

*to refer again to the Tribunal the licensing scheme which was *confirmed/ varied by the Tribunal by an Order

Application under s.122(2)

*to review its Order as to entitlement to licence

Application under s.127(2)

*to review its Order as to licence

Application under s.142(4) or Sch. 6, para 5(3)

*to review its Order as to royalty or other sum/remuneration payable

Application under s.135F(2)

*to review its Order as to terms of payment

Application under s.135F(2)

*to review its Order as to reasonableness of a *condition/requirement for information

Application under Sch. 17, para 6(2) of 1990 Act

*to review its Order as to terms of payment

dated .... and bearing reference number ....

2. There is delivered herewith a statement of the grounds for the application.

3. A copy of this Notice, together with the statement, *has been/will be served on [date of service] on every person who was a party to the proceedings to which the above Order of the Tribunal relates, namely [specify names and addresses of parties].

4. All communications about this application should be addressed to

*[the Applicant at the address shown above]

*[name and address of Applicant's solicitor/agent].

Signed ....

Status of signatory .... [Applicant, an officer of Applicant, solicitor or agent]

Date ....
*Delete whichever is inappropriate

FORM 5   Rules 7(1), 23(1), 26,
                                                                                                                   26D, 30, 33, 37,
                                                                                                                   41, 41D and 44

BROADCASTING ACT 1990
COPYRIGHT, DESIGNS AND PATENTS ACT 1988
COPYRIGHT TRIBUNAL

Notice of intervention

To,
    The Secretary to the Tribunal

1. TAKE NOTICE that [name and address of intervener] ("the Intervener") wishes to be made a party to the proceedings commenced by notice of *reference/ application/appeal dated ....

*[which was advertised in [name of publication and date of issue]].

2. The Intervener has a substantial interest in the matter for the following reasons [state reasons].

3. All communications about this reference should be addressed to

*[the Intervener at the address shown above]

*[name and address of Intervener's solicitor/agent].

Signed ....

Status of signatory .... [Intervener,
an officer of Intervener, solicitor or agent]

Date ....
*Delete whichever is inappropriate

FORM 6 Rules 8(1), 23(3), 26, **B–272**
26D, 30, 33, 37,
41, 41D and 44

BROADCASTING ACT 1990
COPYRIGHT, DESIGNS AND PATENTS ACT 1988
COPYRIGHT TRIBUNAL

Notice of objection to Intervener's credentials

To,
The Secretary to the Tribunal

1. TAKE NOTICE that in connection with *proceedings commenced by notice of *reference/application dated .... served by [name of Applicant], and with the notice of intervention given by [name of Intervener] dated .... [name and address of party making objection] ("the Objector"), being

*[the Applicant]

*[the licensing body named in the notice of *reference/application]

*[person providing a programme service named in the notice of *reference/application]

*[*a person/an organisation on whom the notice of *reference/application was served]

*[an intervener in the proceedings by virtue of a notice of intervention served on [date of service]]

objects to the Intervener's credentials.

2. The Objector's grounds for the objection are as follows [state grounds].

3. All communications about this reference should be addressed to

*[the Objector at the address shown above]

*[name and address of Objector's solicitor/agent].

Signed ....

Status of signatory .... [Objector,
an officer of Objector, solicitor or agent]

Date ....
*Delete whichever is inappropriate

PART II

FORM 10A

Rule 26A(1)(a)

COPYRIGHT, DESIGNS AND PATENTS ACT 1988
COPYRIGHT TRIBUNAL

Notice of application under section 135D

To,
    The Secretary to the Tribunal

1. TAKE NOTICE that [name and address of prospective licensee or licensee] ("the Applicant") being a person intending to avail himself of the right to include sound recordings in a *broadcast/and/cable programme service for which [name and address of licensing body] could *grant/procure the grant of a licence.

    *having given notice to the Tribunal on [date on which notice was given] of the intention to exercise that right: and the date on which it was proposed to begin to do so. namely [   ].

    *who herewith gives notice to the Tribunal of the intention to exercise that right: and of the date on which it is proposed to begin to do so, namely [   ].

hereby applies to the Tribunal to settle the terms as to payment for including sound recordings in a *broadcast/and/cable programme service.

2. There is delivered herewith a statement of the Applicant's case.

3. All communications about this application should be addressed to

    *[the Applicant at the address shown above]

    *[name and address of Applicant's solicitor/agent].

Signed ....

Status of signatory .... [Applicant,
an officer of Applicant, solicitor or agent]

Date ....
*Delete whichever is inappropriate

FORM 10B

Rule 26A(1)(b)

COPYRIGHT, DESIGNS AND PATENTS ACT 1988
COPYRIGHT TRIBUNAL

Notice of reference under section 135E

To,
    The Secretary to the Tribunal

1. TAKE NOTICE that [name and address of person making reference] ("the Applicant") being a person who

    *has given notice to the Copyright Tribunal on [date on which notice was given] of his intention to exercise

    *has exercised

the right to include sound recordings in a *broadcast/and/cable programme service.

> *having been given notice of [a] condition[s] as to the inclusion in a *broadcast/and/cable programme service by:

> *having been required to provide information to:

[name and address of licensing body]. hereby refers to the Tribunal the question whether

> *the condition[s] [setting out condition objected to] is a reasonable condition

> *the information [setting out item objected to] can reasonably be required to be provided.

2. There is delivered herewith a statement of the Applicant's case.

3. All communications about this reference should be addressed to

> *[the Applicant at the address shown above]

> *[name and address of Applicant's solicitor/agent].

Signed ....

Status of signatory .... [Applicant, an officer of Applicant, solicitor or agent]

Date ....
*Delete whichever is inappropriate

FORM 10C   Rule 26A(1)(c)   **B–275**

COPYRIGHT, DESIGNS AND PATENTS ACT 1988
COPYRIGHT TRIBUNAL

Notice of application for review of Order under section 135F

To,
    The Secretary to the Tribunal

1. TAKE NOTICE that [name and address of licensing body or person seeking review] ("the Applicant") hereby applies to the Tribunal for a review of its Order dated .... and bearing the reference number ....

> *in respect of the settlement of the terms as to payment for including sound recordings in a *broadcast/and/cable programme service payable to [name and address of licensing body]

> *in respect of the reasonableness of *a/condition[s]/requirement to provide information to [name and address of licensing body].

2. There is delivered herewith a statement of the Applicant's case.

3. All communications about this application should be addressed to

*[the Applicant at the address shown above]

*[name and address of Applicant's solicitor/agent].

Signed ....

Status of signatory .... [Applicant,
an officer of Applicant, solicitor or agent]

Date ....
*Delete whichever is inappropriate

FORM 16A Rule 41A(1)(a)

BROADCASTING ACT 1990
COPYRIGHT, DESIGNS AND PATENTS ACT 1988
COPYRIGHT TRIBUNAL

Notice of application under section 176 of, and paragraph 5 of Schedule 17 to, the
Broadcasting Act 1990

To,

The Secretary to the Tribunal

1. TAKE NOTICE that [name and address of publisher] ("the Applicant")
being a person intending to exercise the right to be treated as if he had at all
material times been the holder of a licence granted by [name and address of per-
son] *providing/treated as providing [name of programme service] authorising
him to publish copyright information relating to the titles of the programmes
which are to be, or may be, included in the service and the times of their inclusion
("the act restricted by copyright").

*having given notice to the Tribunal on [   ] of the intention to exercise
that right and the date on which it was proposed to begin to do so, namely
[   ].

*who herewith gives notice to the Tribunal of the intention to exercise that
right and of the date on which it is proposed to begin to do so, namely
[   ].

hereby applies to the Tribunal to settle the terms of payment for doing the act
restricted by copyright.

2. There is delivered herewith a statement of the Applicant's case.

3. All communications about this application should be addressed to

*[the Applicant at the address shown above]

*[name and address of Applicant's solicitor/agent].

Signed ....

Status of signatory .... [Applicant,
an officer of Applicant, solicitor or agent]

Date ....
*Delete whichever is inappropriate

FORM 16B   Rule 41A(1)(b) **B–277**

BROADCASTING ACT 1990
COPYRIGHT, DESIGNS AND PATENTS ACT 1988
COPYRIGHT TRIBUNAL

Notice of application for review of Order under section 176 of, and paragraph 6(1) of Schedule 17 to, the Broadcasting Act 1990

To,
    The Secretary to the Tribunal

    1. TAKE NOTICE that

        *[name and address of person] providing [name of programme service]

        *[name and address of publisher]

seeking review ("the Applicant") hereby applies to the Tribunal for a review of its Order dated .... and bearing the reference number .... in respect of the settlement of the terms of payment for exercising the right to publish copyright information relating to titles of programmes which are to be or may be included in the programme service and the times of their inclusion.

    2. There is delivered herewith a statement of the Applicant's case.

    3. All communications about this application should be addressed to

        *[the Applicant at the address shown above]

        *[name and address of Applicant's solicitor/agent].

Signed ....

Status of signatory .... [Applicant,
                        an officer of Applicant, solicitor or agent]

Date ....
*Delete whichever is inappropriate

Appendix C

COPYRIGHT CONVENTIONS AND AGREEMENTS

BERNE COPYRIGHT CONVENTION (PARIS REVISION, 1971)[1]

THE International Convention for the Protection of Literary and Artistic Works **C–1** signed at Berne on 9th September, 1886, revised at Berlin in 1908, at Rome in 1928, at Brussels in 1948 and Stockholm in 1967, was further revised in Paris in 1971 and amended in 1979.

It has been the custom, in previous editions of this book, to print, in parallel columns, the text of the current revision and the previous revision of the Berne Convention. However, because the Paris revision largely follows the Stockholm revision,[2] this course has not been adopted in this edition. The main differences from the Stockholm revision occur in Articles 21, 28, 29, 29 *bis*, 30, 31, 32, 34, 37, 38 and the Appendix. The 1979 amendments occur in Articles 22 and 23 which are printed as amended.

ARTICLE 1

The countries to which this Convention applies constitute a Union for the pro- **C–2** tection of the rights of authors in their literary and artistic works.

ARTICLE 2

(1) The expression "literary and artistic works" shall include every production **C–3** in the literary, scientific and artistic domain, whatever may be the mode or form of its expression, such as books, pamphlets and other writings; lectures, addresses, sermons and other works of the same nature; dramatic or dramatico-musical works; choreographic works and entertainments in dumb show; musical compositions with or without words; cinematographic works to which are assimilated works expressed by a process analogous to cinematography; works of drawing, painting, architecture, sculpture, engraving and lithography; photographic works to which are assimilated works expressed by a process analogous to photography; works of applied art; illustrations, maps, plans, sketches and three-dimensional works relative to geography, topography, architecture or science.

(2) It shall, however, be a matter for legislation in the countries of the Union to prescribe that works in general or any specified categories of works shall not be protected unless they have been fixed in some material form.

(3) Translations, adaptations, arrangements of music and other alterations of a literary or artistic work shall be protected as original works without prejudice to the copyright in the original work.

(4) It shall be a matter for legislation in the countries of the Union to determine the protection to be granted to official texts of a legislative administrative and legal nature, and to official translations of such texts.

(5) Collections of literary or artistic works such as encyclopaedias and anthologies which, by reason of the selection and arrangement of their contents, constitute intellectual creations shall be protected as such, without prejudice to the copyright in each of the works forming part of such collections.

(6) The works mentioned in this Article shall enjoy protection in all countries of the Union. This protection shall operate for the benefit of the author and his successors in title.

(7) Subject to the provisions of Article 7(4) of this Convention, it shall be a

---

[1] Cmnd. 5002. See comparison between the Stockholm revision and the Brussels revision, *Copinger* (11th ed.) § 1681 *et seq.* As to the position of the United Kingdom see § 17–9 *ante.*
[2] Cmnd. 4412.

matter for legislation in the countries of the Union to determine the extent of the application of their laws to works of applied art and industrial designs and models, as well as the conditions under which such works, designs and models shall be protected. Works protected in the country of origin solely as designs and models shall be entitled in another country of the Union only to such special protection as is granted in that country to designs and models; however, if no such special protection is granted in that country, such works shall be protected as artistic works.

(8) The protection of this Convention shall not apply to news of the day or to miscellaneous facts having the character of mere items of press information.

Article 2bis

C–4   (1) It shall be a matter for legislation in the countries of the Union to exclude, wholly or in part, from the protection provided by the preceding Article political speeches and speeches delivered in the course of legal proceedings.

(2) It shall also be a matter for legislation in the countries of the Union to determine the conditions under which lectures, addresses and other works of the same nature which are delivered in public may be reproduced by the press, broadcast, communicated to the public by wire and made the subject of public communication as envisaged in Article 11bis (1) of this Convention, when such use is justified by the informatory purpose.

(3) Nevertheless, the author shall enjoy the exclusive right of making a collection of his works mentioned in the preceding paragraphs.

Article 3

C–5   (1) The protection of this Convention shall apply to:
  (*a*) authors who are nationals of one of the countries of the Union, for their works, whether published or not;
  (*b*) authors who are not nationals of one of the countries of the Union, for their works first published in one of those countries, or simultaneously in a country outside the Union and in a country of the Union.

(2) Authors who are not nationals of one of the countries of the Union but who have their habitual residence in one of them shall, for the purposes of this Convention, be assimilated to nationals of that country.

(3) The expression "published works" means works published with the consent of their authors, whatever may be the means of manufacture of the copies, provided that the availability of such copies has been such as to satisfy the reasonable requirements of the public, having regard to the nature of the work. The performance of a dramatic, dramatico-musical, cinematographic or musical work, the public recitation of a literary work, the communication by wire or the broadcasting of literary or artistic works, the exhibition of a work of art and the construction of a work of architecture shall not constitute publication.

(4) A work shall be considered as having been published simultaneously in several countries if it has been published in two or more countries within thirty days of its first publication.

Article 4

C–6   The protection of this Convention shall apply, even if the conditions of Article 3 are not fulfilled, to:
  (*a*) authors of cinematographic works the maker of which has his headquarters or habitual residence in one of the countries of the Union;
  (*b*) authors of works of architecture erected in a country of the Union or of other artistic works incorporated in a building or other structure located in a country of the Union.

ARTICLE 5

(1) Authors shall enjoy, in respect of works for which they are protected under **C–7** this Convention, in countries of the Union other than the country of origin, the rights which their respective laws do now or may hereafter grant to their nationals, as well as the rights specially granted by this Convention.

(2) The enjoyment and the exercise of these rights shall not be subject to any formality; such enjoyment and such exercise shall be independent of the existence of protection in the country of origin of the work. Consequently, apart from the provisions of this Convention the extent of protection, as well as the means of redress afforded to the author to protect his rights, shall be governed exclusively by the laws of the country where protection is claimed.

(3) Protection in the country of origin is governed by domestic law. However, when the author is not a national of the country of origin of the work for which he is protected under this Convention, he shall enjoy in that country the same rights as national authors.

(4) The country of origin shall be considered to be:

(*a*) in the case of works first published in a country of the Union, that country; in the case of works published simultaneously in several countries of the Union which grant different terms of protection, the country whose legislation grants the shortest term of protection;

(*b*) in the case of works published simultaneously in a country outside the Union and in a country of the Union, the latter country;

(*c*) in the case of unpublished works or of works first published in a country outside the Union, without simultaneous publication in a country of the Union, the country of the Union of which the author is a national, provided that:

 (i) when these are cinematographic works the maker of which has his headquarters or his habitual residence in a country of the Union, the country of origin shall be that country, and

 (ii) when these are works of architecture erected in a country of the Union or other artistic works incorporated in a building or other structure located in a country of the Union, the country of origin shall be that country.

ARTICLE 6

(1) Where any country outside the Union fails to protect in an adequate manner **C–8** the works of authors who are nationals of one of the countries of the Union, the latter country may restrict the protection given to the works of authors who are, at the date of the first publication thereof, nationals of the other country and are not habitually resident in one of the countries of the Union. If the country of first publication avails itself of this right, the other countries of the Union shall not be required to grant to works thus subjected to special treatment a wider protection than that granted to them in the country of first publication.

(2) No restrictions introduced by virtue of the preceding paragraph shall affect the rights which an author may have acquired in respect of a work published in a country of the Union before such restrictions were put into force.

(3) The countries of the Union which restrict the grant of copyright in accordance with this Article shall give notice thereof to the Director General of the World Intellectual Property Organization (hereinafter designated as "the Director General") by a written declaration specifying the countries in regard to which protection is restricted, and the restrictions to which rights of authors who are nationals of those countries are subjected. The Director General shall immediately communicate this declaration to all the countries of the Union.

ARTICLE 6bis

C–9 (1) Independently of the author's economic rights, and even after the transfer of the said rights, the author shall have the right to claim authorship of the work and to object to any distortion, mutilation or other modification of, or other derogatory action in relation to, the said work, which would be prejudicial to his honour or reputation.

(2) The rights granted to the author in accordance with the preceding paragraph shall, after his death, be maintained, at least until the expiry of the economic rights, and shall be exercisable by the persons or institutions authorised by the legislation of the country where protection is claimed. However, those countries whose legislation, at the moment of their ratification of or accession to this Act, does not provide for the protection after the death of the author of all the rights set out in the preceding paragraph may provide that some of these rights may, after his death, cease to be maintained.

(3) The means of redress for safeguarding the rights granted by this Article shall be governed by the legislation of the country where protection is claimed.

ARTICLE 7

C–10 (1) The term of protection granted by this Convention shall be the life of the author and fifty years after his death.

(2) However, in the case of cinematographic works, the countries of the Union may provide that the term of protection shall expire fifty years after the work has been made available to the public with the consent of the author, or, failing such an event within fifty years from the making of such a work, fifty years after the making.

(3) In the case of anonymous or pseudonymous works, the term of protection granted by this Convention shall expire fifty years after the work has been lawfully made available to the public. However, when the pseudonym adopted by the author leaves no doubt as to his identity, the term of protection shall be that provided in paragraph (1). If the author of an anonymous or pseudonymous work discloses his identity during the above-mentioned period, the term of protection applicable shall be that provided in paragraph (1). The countries of the Union shall not be required to protect anonymous or pseudonymous works in respect of which it is reasonable to presume that their author has been dead for fifty years.

(4) It shall be a matter for legislation in the countries of the Union to determine the term of protection of photographic works and that of works of applied art in so far as they are protected as artistic works; however, this term shall last at least until the end of a period of twenty-five years from the making of such a work.

(5) The term of protection subsequent to the death of the author and the terms provided by paragraphs (2), (3) and (4) shall run from the date of death or of the event referred to in those paragraphs, but such terms shall always be deemed to begin on the first of January of the year following the death or such event.

(6) The countries of the Union may grant a term of protection in excess of those provided by the preceding paragraphs.

(7) Those countries of the Union bound by the Rome Act of this Convention which grant, in their national legislation in force at the time of signature of the present Act, shorter terms of protection than those provided for in the preceding paragraphs shall have the right to maintain such terms when ratifying or acceding to the present Act.

(8) In any case, the term shall be governed by the legislation of the country where protection is claimed; however, unless the legislation of that country otherwise provides, the term shall not exceed the term fixed in the country of origin of the work.

ARTICLE 7bis

The provisions of the preceding Article shall also apply in the case of a work of **C–11** joint authorship, provided that the terms measured from the death of the author shall be calculated from the death of the last surviving author.

ARTICLE 8

Authors of literary and artistic works protected by this Convention shall enjoy **C–12** the exclusive right of making and of authorising the translation of their works throughout the term of protection of their rights in the original works.

ARTICLE 9

(1) Authors of literary and artistic works protected by this Convention shall **C–13** have the exclusive right of authorising the reproduction of these works, in any manner or form.

(2) It shall be a matter for legislation in the countries of the Union to permit the reproduction of such works in certain special cases, provided that such reproduction does not conflict with a normal exploitation of the work and does not unreasonably prejudice the legitimate interests of the author.

(3) Any sound or visual recording shall be considered as a reproduction for the purposes of this Convention.

ARTICLE 10

(1) It shall be permissible to make quotations from a work which has already **C–14** been lawfully made available to the public, provided that their making is compatible with fair practice, and their extent does not exceed that justified by the purpose, including quotations from newspaper articles and periodicals in the form of press summaries.

(2) It shall be a matter for legislation in the countries of the Union, and for special agreements existing or to be concluded between them, to permit the utilisation, to the extent justified by the purpose, of literary or artistic works by way of illustration in publications, broadcasts or sound or visual recordings for teaching, provided such utilisation is compatible with fair practice.

(3) Where use is made of works in accordance with the preceding paragraphs of this Article, mention shall be made of the source, and of the name of the author if it appears thereon.

ARTICLE 10bis

(1) It shall be a matter for legislation in the countries of the Union to permit the **C–15** reproduction by the press, the broadcasting or the communication to the public by wire of articles published in newspapers or periodicals on current economic, political or religious topics, and of broadcast works of the same character, in cases in which the reproduction, broadcasting or such communication thereof is not expressly reserved. Nevertheless, the source must always be clearly indicated; the legal consequences of a breach of this obligation shall be determined by the legislation of the country where protection is claimed.

(2) It shall also be a matter for legislation in the countries of the Union to determine the conditions under which, for the purpose of reporting current events by means of photography, cinematography, broadcasting or communication to the public by wire, literary or artistic works seen or heard in the course of the event may, to the extent justified by the informatory purpose, be reproduced and made available to the public.

ARTICLE 11

C–16   (1) Authors of dramatic, dramatico-musical and musical works shall enjoy the exclusive right of authorising:
>   (i) the public performance of their works, including such public performance by any means or process;
>   (ii) any communication to the public of the performance of their works.

(2) Authors of dramatic or dramatico-musical works shall enjoy, during the full term of their rights in the original works, the same rights with respect to translations thereof.

ARTICLE 11bis

C–17   (1) Authors of literary and artistic works shall enjoy the exclusive right of authorising:
>   (i) the broadcasting of their works or the communication thereof to the public by any other means of wireless diffusion of signs, sounds or images;
>   (ii) any communication to the public by wire or by rebroadcasting of the broadcast of the work, when this communication is made by an organization other than the original one;
>   (iii) the public communication by loudspeaker or any other analogous instrument transmitting, by signs, sounds or images, the broadcast of the work.

(2) It shall be a matter for legislation in the countries of the Union to determine the conditions under which the rights mentioned in the preceding paragraph may be exercised, but these conditions shall apply only in the countries where they have been prescribed. They shall not in any circumstances be prejudicial to the moral rights of the author, nor to his right to obtain equitable remuneration which, in the absence of agreement, shall be fixed by competent authority.

(3) In the absence of any contrary stipulation, permission granted in accordance with paragraph (1) of this Article shall not imply permission to record, by means of instruments recording sounds or images, the work broadcast. It shall, however, be a matter for legislation in the countries of the Union to determine the regulations for ephemeral recordings made by a broadcasting organization by means of its own facilities and used for its own broadcasts. The preservation of these recordings in official archives may, on the ground of their exceptional documentary character, be authorised by such legislation.

ARTICLE 11ter

C–18   (1) Authors of literary works shall enjoy the exclusive right of authorising:
>   (i) the public recitation of their works, including such public recitation by any means or process;
>   (ii) any communication to the public of the recitation of their works.

(2) Authors of literary works shall enjoy, during the full term of their rights in the original works, the same rights with respect to translations thereof.

ARTICLE 12

C–19   Authors of literary or artistic works shall enjoy the exclusive right of authorising adaptations, arrangements and other alterations of their works.

ARTICLE 13

C–20   (1) Each country of the Union may impose for itself reservations and conditions on the exclusive right granted to the author of a musical work and to the author of any words, the recording of which together with the musical work has already been authorised by the latter, to authorise the sound recording of that musical work, together with such words, if any; but all such reservations and conditions shall apply only in the countries which have imposed them and shall not, in any circumstances, be prejudicial to the rights of these authors to obtain equitable remuneration which, in the absence of agreement, shall be fixed by competent authority.

(2) Recordings of musical works made in a country of the Union in accordance with Article 13(3) of the Conventions signed at Rome on June 2, 1928, and at Brussels on June 26, 1948, may be reproduced in that country without the permission of the author of the musical work until a date two years after that country becomes bound by this Act.

(3) Recordings made in accordance with paragraphs (1) and (2) of this Article and imported without permission from the parties concerned into a country where they are treated as infringing recordings shall be liable to seizure.

ARTICLE 14

(1) Authors of literary or artistic works shall have the exclusive right of authoris-   **C–21**
ing:

    (i) the cinematographic adaptation and reproduction of these works, and the distribution of the works thus adapted or reproduced;

    (ii) the public performance and communication to the public by wire of the works thus adapted or reproduced.

(2) The adaptation into any other artistic form of a cinematographic production derived from literary or artistic works shall, without prejudice to the authorization of the author of the cinematographic production, remain subject to the authorization of the authors of the original works.

(3) The provisions of Article 13(1) shall not apply.

ARTICLE 14bis

(1) Without prejudice to the copyright in any work which may have been   **C–22**
adapted or reproduced, a cinematographic work shall be protected as an original work. The owner of copyright in a cinematographic work shall enjoy the same rights as the author of an original work, including the rights referred to in the preceding Article.

(2) (*a*) Ownership of copyright in a cinematographic work shall be a matter for legislation in the country where protection is claimed.

    (*b*) However, in the countries of the Union which, by legislation, include among the owners of copyright in a cinematographic work authors who have brought contributions to the making of the work, such authors, if they have undertaken to bring such contributions, may not, in the absence of any contrary or special stipulation, object to the reproduction, distribution, public performance, communication to the public by wire, broadcasting or any other communication to the public, or to the subtitling or dubbing of texts, of the work.

    (*c*) The question whether or not the form of the undertaking referred to above should, for the application of the preceding subparagraph (*b*), be in a written agreement or a written act of the same effect shall be a matter for the legislation of the country where the maker of the cinematographic work has his headquarters or habitual residence. However, it shall be a matter for the legislation of the country of the Union where protection is claimed to provide that the said undertaking shall be in a written agreement or a written act of the same effect. The countries whose legislation so provides shall notify the Director General by means of a written declaration, which will be immediately communicated by him to all the other countries of the Union.

(*d*) By "contrary or special stipulation" is meant any restrictive condition which is relevant to the aforesaid undertaking.

(3) Unless the national legislation provides to the contrary, the provisions of paragraph (2)(*b*) above shall not be applicable to authors of scenarios, dialogues and musical works created for the making of the cinematographic work, or to the principal director thereof. However, those countries of the Union whose legislation does not contain rules providing for the application of the said paragraph (2)(*b*) to such director shall notify the Director General by means of a written declaration, which will be immediately communicated by him to all other countries of the Union.

Article 14ter

C–23 (1) The author, or after his death the persons or institutions authorized by national legislation, shall, with respect to original works of art and original manuscripts of writers and composers, enjoy the inalienable right to an interest in any sale of the work subsequent to the first transfer by the author of the work.

(2) The protection provided by the preceding paragraph may be claimed in a country of the Union only if the legislation in the country to which the author belongs so permits, and to the extent permitted by the country where this protection is claimed.

(3) The procedure for collection and the amounts shall be matters for determination by national legislation.

Article 15

C–24 (1) In order that the author of a literary or artistic work protected by this Convention shall, in the absence of proof to the contrary, be regarded as such, and consequently be entitled to institute infringement proceedings in the countries of the Union, it shall be sufficient for his name to appear on the work in the usual manner. This paragraph shall be applicable even if this name is a pseudonym, where the pseudonym adopted by the author leaves no doubt as to his identity.

(2) The person or body corporate whose name appears on a cinematographic work in the usual manner shall, in the absence of proof to the contrary, be presumed to be the maker of the said work.

(3) In the case of anonymous and pseudonymous works, other than those referred to in paragraph (1) above, the publisher whose name appears on the work shall, in the absence of proof to the contrary, be deemed to represent the author, and in this capacity he shall be entitled to protect and enforce the author's rights. The provisions of this paragraph shall cease to apply when the author reveals his identity and establishes his claim to authorship of the work.

(4) (*a*) In the case of unpublished works where the identity of the author is unknown, but where there is every ground to presume that he is a national of a country of the Union, it shall be a matter for legislation in that country to designate the competent authority which shall represent the author and shall be entitled to protect and enforce his rights in the countries of the Union.

(*b*) Countries of the Union which make such designation under the terms of this provision shall notify the Director General by means of a written declaration giving full information concerning the authority thus designated. The Director General shall at once communicate this declaration to all other countries of the Union.

ARTICLE 16

(1) Infringing copies of a work shall be liable to seizure in any country of the **C–25**
Union where the work enjoys legal protection.

(2) The provisions of the preceding paragraph shall also apply to reproductions
coming from a country where the work is not protected, or has ceased to be protected.

(3) The seizure shall take place in accordance with the legislation of each
country.

ARTICLE 17

The provisions of this Convention cannot in any way affect the right of the **C–26**
Government of each country of the Union to permit, to control, or to prohibit, by
legislation or regulation, the circulation, presentation, or exhibition of any work or
production in regard to which the competent authority may find it necessary to
exercise that right.

ARTICLE 18

(1) This Convention shall apply to all works which, at the moment of its coming **C–27**
into force, have not yet fallen into the public domain in the country of origin
through the expiry of the term of protection.

(2) If, however, through the expiry of the term of protection which was previously granted, a work has fallen into the public domain of the country where protection is claimed, that work shall not be protected anew.

(3) The application of this principle shall be subject to any provisions contained
in special conventions to that effect existing or to be concluded between countries
of the Union. In the absence of such provisions, the respective countries shall
determine, each in so far as it is concerned, the conditions of application of this
principle.

(4) The preceding provisions shall also apply in the case of new accessions to the
Union and to cases in which protection is extended by the application of Article 7
or by the abandonment of reservations.

ARTICLE 19

The provisions of this Convention shall not preclude the making of a claim to **C–28**
the benefit of any greater protection which may be granted by legislation in a
country of the Union.

ARTICLE 20

The Governments of the countries of the Union reserve the right to enter into **C–29**
special agreements among themselves, in so far as such agreements grant to
authors more extensive rights than those granted by the Convention, or contain
other provisions not contrary to this Convention. The provisions of existing agreements which satisfy these conditions shall remain applicable.

ARTICLE 21

(1) Special provisions regarding developing countries are included in the **C–30**
Appendix.

(2) Subject to the provisions of Article 28(1)(*b*), the Appendix forms an integral
part of this Act.

ARTICLE 22

ARTICLE 22

C–31   (1) (*a*) The Union shall have an Assembly consisting of those countries of the Union which are bound by Articles 22 to 26.

   (*b*) The Government of each country shall be represented by one delegate, who may be assisted by alternate delegates, advisors, and experts.

   (*c*) The expenses of each delegation shall be borne by the Government which has appointed it.

   (2) (*a*) The Assembly shall:

      (i) deal with all matters concerning the maintenance and development of the Union and the implementation of this Convention;

      (ii) give directions concerning the preparation for conferences of revision to the International Bureau of Intellectual Property (hereinafter designated as "the International Bureau") referred to in the Convention Establishing the World Intellectual Property Organization (hereinafter designated as "the Organization"), due account being taken of any comments made by those countries of the Union which are not bound by Articles 22 to 26;

      (iii) review and approve the reports and activities of the Director General of the Organization concerning the Union, and give all necessary instructions concerning matters within the competence of the Union;

      (iv) elect the members of the Executive Committee of the Assembly;

      (v) review and approve the reports and activities of its Executive Committee, and give instructions to such Committee;

      (vi) determine the programme and adopt the triennial budget of the Union and approve its final accounts;

      (vii) adopt the financial regulations of the Union;

      (viii) establish such committees of experts and working groups as may be necessary for the work of the Union;

      (ix) determine which countries not members of the Union and which intergovernmental and international non-governmental organizations shall be admitted to its meetings as observers;

      (x) adopt amendments to Articles 22 to 26;

      (xi) take any other appropriate action designed to further the objectives of the Union;

      (xii) exercise such other functions as are appropriate under this Convention;

      (xiii) subject to its acceptance, exercise such rights as are given to it in the Convention establishing the Organization.

   (*b*) With respect to matters which are of interest also to other Unions administered by the Organization, the Assembly shall make its decisions after having heard the advice of the Co-ordination Committee of the Organization.

   (3) (*a*) Each country member of the Assembly shall have one vote.

   (*b*) One-half of the countries members of the Assembly shall constitute a quorum.

   (*c*) Notwithstanding the provisions of subparagraph (*b*), if, in any session, the number of countries represented is less than one-half but equal to or more than one-third of the countries members of the Assembly, the Assembly may make decisions but, with the exception of decisions concerning its own procedure, all such decisions shall take effect only if the following conditions are fulfilled. The International Bureau shall communicate the said decisions to the countries members of the Assembly which were not represented and shall invite them to express in writing their vote or abstention within a period of three months from the date of the communication. If, at the expiration of this period, the number of countries having thus expressed their vote or abstention attains the number of countries which was lacking for attaining the quorum in the session itself, such decisions shall take effect provided that at the same time the required majority still obtains.

(*d*) Subject to the provisions of Article 26(2), the decisions of the Assembly shall require two-thirds of the votes cast.

(*e*) Abstentions shall not be considered as votes.

(*f*) A delegate may represent, and vote in the name of, one country only.

(*g*) Countries of the Union not members of the Assembly shall be admitted to its meetings as observers.

(4) (*a*) The Assembly shall meet once in every second calendar year in ordinary session upon convocation by the Director General and, in the absence of exceptional circumstances, during the same period and at the same place as the General Assembly of the Organization.

(*b*) The Assembly shall meet in extraordinary session upon convocation by the Director General, at the request of the Executive Committee or at the request of one-fourth of the countries members of the Assembly.

(5) The Assembly shall adopt its own rules of procedure.

Article 23

(1) The Assembly shall have an Executive Committee.   **C–32**

(2) (*a*) The Executive Committee shall consist of countries elected by the Assembly from among countries members of the Assembly. Furthermore, the country on whose territory the Organisation has its headquarters shall, subject to the provisions of Article 25(7)(*b*), have an *ex-officio* seat on the Committee.

(*b*) The Government of each country member of the Executive Committee shall be represented by one delegate, who may be assisted by alternate delegates, advisors and experts.

(*c*) The expenses of each delegation shall be borne by the Government which has appointed it.

(3) The number of countries members of the Executive Committee shall correspond to one-fourth of the number of countries members of the Assembly. In establishing the number of seats to be filled, remainders after division by four shall be disregarded.

(4) In electing the members of the Executive Committee, the Assembly shall have due regard to an equitable geographical distribution and to the need for countries party to the Special Agreements which might be established in relation with the Union to be among the countries constituting the Executive Committee.

(5) (*a*) Each member of the Executive Committee shall serve from the close of the session of the Assembly which elected it to close of the next ordinary session of the Assembly.

(*b*) Members of the Executive Committee may be re-elected, but not more than two-thirds of them.

(*c*) The Assembly shall establish the details of the rules governing the election and possible re-election of the members of the Executive Committee.

(6) (*a*) The Executive Committee shall:

(i) prepare the draft agenda of the Assembly;

1321

(ii) submit proposals to the Assembly respecting the draft programme and triennial budget of the Union prepared by the Director General;

[. . . . .]

(iv) submit, with appropriate comments, to the Assembly the periodical reports of the Director General and the yearly audit reports on the accounts;

(v) in accordance with the decisions of the Assembly and having regard to circumstances arising between two ordinary sessions of the Assembly, take all necessary measures to ensure the execution of the programme of the Union by the Director General;

(vi) perform such other functions as are allocated to it under this Convention.

(*b*) With respect to matters which are of interest also to other Unions administered by the Organization, the Executive Committee shall make its decisions after having heard the advice of the Co-ordination Committee of the Organization.

(7) (*a*) The Executive Committee shall meet once a year in ordinary session upon convocation by the Director General, preferably during the same period and at the same place as the Co-ordination Committee of the Organization.

(*b*) The Executive Comittee shall meet in extraordinary session upon convocation by the Director General, either on his own initiative, or at the request of its Chairman or one-fourth of its members.

(8) (*a*) Each country member of the Executive Committee shall have one vote.

(*b*) One-half of the members of the Executive Committee shall constitute a quorum.

(*c*) Decisions shall be made by a simple majority of the votes cast.

(*d*) Abstentions shall not be considered as votes.

(*e*) A delegate may represent, and vote in the name of, one country only.

(9) Countries of the Union not members of the Executive Committee shall be admitted to its meetings as observers.

(10) The Executive Committee shall adopt its own rules of procedure.

ARTICLE 24

C–33

(1) (*a*) The administrative tasks with respect to the Union shall be performed by the International Bureau, which is a continuation of the Bureau of the Union united with the Bureau of the Union established by the International Convention for the Protection of Industrial Property.

(*b*) In particular, the International Bureau shall provide the secretariat of the various organs of the Union.

(*c*) The Director General of the Organization shall be the chief executive of the Union and he shall represent the Union.

(2) The International Bureau shall assemble and publish information concerning the protection of copyright. Each country of the Union shall promptly communicate to the International Bureau all new laws and official texts concerning the protection of copyright.

(3) The International Bureau shall publish a monthly periodical.

(4) The International Bureau shall, on request, furnish information to any country of the Union on matters concerning the protection of copyright.

(5) The International Bureau shall conduct studies, and shall provide services, designed to facilitate the protection of copyright.

(6) The Director General and any staff member designated by him shall participate, without the right to vote, in all meetings of the Assembly, the Executive Committee and any other committee of experts or working group. The Director General, or a staff member designated by him, shall be *ex officio* secretary of these bodies.

(7) (*a*) The International Bureau shall, in accordance with the directions of the Assembly and in cooperation with the Executive Committee, make the preparations for the conferences of revision of the provisions of the Convention other than Articles 22 to 26.

    (*b*) The International Bureau may consult with inter-governmental and international non-governmental organizations concerning preparations for conferences of revision.

    (*c*) The Director General and persons designated by him shall take part, without the right to vote, in the discussions at these conferences.

(8) The International Bureau shall carry out any other tasks assigned to it.

ARTICLE 25

(1) (*a*) The Union shall have a budget.   **C–34**

    (*b*) The budget of the Union shall include the income and expense proper to the Union, its contribution to the budget of expenses common to the Unions, and, where applicable, the sum made available to the budget of the Conference of the Organization.

    (*c*) Expenses not attributable exclusively to the Union but also to one or more other Unions administered by the Organization shall be considered as expenses common to the Unions. The share of the Union in such common expenses shall be in proportion to the interest the Union has in them.

(2) The budget of the Union shall be established with due regard to the requirements of co-ordination with the budgets of the other Unions administered by the Organization.

(3) The budget of the Union shall be financed from the following sources:

    (i) contributions of the countries of the Union;

    (ii) fees and charges due for services performed by the International Bureau in relation to the Union;

    (iii) sale of, or royalties on, the publications of the International Bureau concerning the Union;

    (iv) gifts, bequests, and subventions;

    (v) rent, interests, and other miscellaneous income.

(4) (*a*) For the purpose of establishing its contribution towards the budget, each country of the Union shall belong to a class, and shall pay its annual contributions on the basis of a number of units fixed as follows:

Class	I	25
Class	II	20
Class	III	15
Class	IV	10
Class	V	5
Class	VI	3
Class	VII	1

    (*b*) Unless it has already done so, each country shall indicate, concurrently with depositing its instrument of ratification or accession, the class to which it wishes to belong. Any country may change class. If it chooses a lower class, the country must announce it to the Assembly at one of its ordinary sessions. Any such change shall take effect at the beginning of the calendar year following the session.

(c) The annual contribution of each country shall be an amount in the same proportion to the total sum to be contributed to the annual budget of the Union by all countries as the number of units is to the total of the units of all contributing countries.

(d) Contributions shall become due on the first of January of each year.

(e) A country which is in arrears in the payment of its contributions shall have no vote in any of the organs of the Union of which it is a member if the amount of its arrears equals or exceeds the amount of the contributions due from it for the preceding two full years. However, any organ of the Union may allow such a country to continue to exercise its vote in that organ if, and as long as, it is satisfied that the delay in payment is due to exceptional and unavoidable circumstances.

(f) If the budget is not adopted before the beginning of a new financial period, it shall be at the same level as the budget of the previous year, in accordance with the financial regulations.

(5) The amount of the fees and charges due for services rendered by the International Bureau in relation to the Union shall be established, and shall be reported to the Assembly and the Executive Committee, by the Director General.

(6) (a) The Union shall have a working capital fund which shall be constituted by a single payment made by each country of the Union. If the fund becomes insufficient, an increase shall be decided by the Assembly.

(b) The amount of the initial payment of each country to the said fund or of its participation in the increase thereof shall be a proportion of the contribution of that country for the year in which the fund is established or the increase decided.

(c) The proportion and the terms of payment shall be fixed by the Assembly on the proposal of the Director General and after it has heard the advice of the Co-ordination Committee of the Organization.

(7) (a) In the headquarters agreement concluded with the country on the territory of which the Organization has its headquarters, it shall be provided that, whenever the working capital fund is insufficient, such country shall grant advances. The amount of these advances and the conditions on which they are granted shall be the subject of separate agreements, in each case, between such country and the Organization. As long as it remains under the obligation to grant advances, such country shall have an *ex officio* seat on the Executive Committee.

(b) The country referred to in subparagraph (a) and the Organization shall each have the right to denounce the obligation to grant advances, by written notification. Denunciation shall take effect three years after the end of the year in which it has been notified.

(8) The auditing of the accounts shall be effected by one or more of the countries of the Union or by external auditors, as provided in the financial regulations. They shall be designated, with their agreement, by the Assembly.

ARTICLE 26

C–35   (1) Proposals for the amendment of Articles 22, 23, 24, 25 and the present Article, may be initiated by any country member of the Assembly, by the Executive Committee, or by the Director General. Such proposals shall be communicated by the Director General to the member countries of the Assembly at least six months in advance of their consideration by the Assembly.

(2) Amendment to the Articles referred to in paragraph (1) shall be adopted by the Assembly. Adoption shall require three-fourths of the votes cast, provided that any amendments of Article 22, and of the present paragraph, shall require four-fifths of the votes cast.

(3) Any amendment to the Articles referred to in paragraph (1) shall enter into force one month after written notifications of acceptance, effected in accordance with their respective constitutional processes, have been received by the Director General from three-fourths of the countries members of the Assembly at the time it adopted the amendment. Any amendment to the said Articles thus accepted shall bind all the countries which are members of the Assembly at the time the amendment enters into force, or which become members thereof at a subsequent date, provided that any amendment increasing the financial obligations of countries of the Union shall bind only those countries which have notified their acceptance of such amendment.

ARTICLE 27

(1) This Convention shall be submitted to revision with a view to the introduc- **C–36**
tion of amendments designed to improve the system of the Union.

(2) For this purpose, conferences shall be held successively in one of the countries of the Union among the delegates of the said countries.

(3) Subject to the provisions of Article 26 which apply to the amendment of Articles 22 to 26, any revision of this Act, including the Appendix, shall require the unanimity of the votes cast.

ARTICLE 28

(1) (a) Any country of the Union which has signed this Act may ratify it, and, if **C–37**
it has not signed it, may accede to it. Instruments of ratification or accession shall be deposited with the Director General.

(b) Any country of the Union may declare in its instrument of ratification or accession that its ratification or accession shall not apply to Articles 1 to 21 and the Appendix, provided that, if such country has previously made a declaration under Article VI (1) of the Appendix, then it may declare in the said instrument only that its ratification or accession shall not apply to Articles 1 to 20.

(c) Any country of the Union, which in accordance with subparagraph (b), has excluded provisions therein referred to from the effects of its ratification or accession may at any later time declare that it extends the effects of its ratification or accession to those provisions. Such declaration shall be deposited with the Director General.

(2) (a) Articles 1 to 21 and the Appendix shall enter into force three months after both of the following two conditions are fulfilled:

    (i) at least five countries of the Union have ratified or acceded to this Act without making a declaration under paragraph (1) (b),

    (ii) France, Spain, the United Kingdom of Great Britain and Northern Ireland, and the United States of America, have become bound by the Universal Copyright Convention as revised at Paris on July 24, 1971.

(b) The entry into force referred to in subparagraph (a) shall apply to those countries of the Union which, at least three months before the said entry into force, have deposited instruments of ratification or accession not containing a declaration under paragraph (1) (b).

(*c*) With respect to any country of the Union not covered by subparagraph (*b*) and which ratifies or accedes to this Act without making a declaration under paragraph (1) (*b*), Articles 1 to 21 and the Appendix shall enter into force three months after the date on which the Director General has notified the deposit of the relevant instrument of ratification or accession, unless a subsequent date has been indicated in the instrument deposited. In the latter case, Articles 1 to 21 and the Appendix shall enter into force with respect to that country on the date thus indicated.

(*d*) The provisions of subparagraphs (*a*) to (*c*) do not affect the application of Article VI of the Appendix.

(3) With respect to any country of the Union which ratifies or accedes to this Act with or without a declaration made under paragraph (1) (*b*), Articles 22 to 38 shall enter into force three months after the date on which the Director General has notified the deposit of the relevant instrument of ratification or accession, unless a subsequent date has been indicated in the instrument deposited. In the latter case, Articles 22 to 38 shall enter into force with respect to that country on the date thus indicated.

ARTICLE 29

C–38   (1) Any country outside the Union may accede to this Act and thereby become party to this Convention and a member of the Union. Instruments of accession shall be deposited with the Director General.

(2) (*a*) Subject to subparagraph (*b*), this Convention shall enter into force with respect to any country outside the Union three months after the date on which the Director General has notified the deposit of its instrument of accession, unless a subsequent date has been indicated in the instrument deposited. In the latter case, this Convention shall enter into force with respect to that country on the date thus indicated.

(*b*) If the entry into force according to subparagraph (*a*) precedes the entry into force of Articles 1 to 21 and the Appendix according to Article 28 (2) (*a*), the said country shall, in the meantime, be bound, instead of by Articles 1 to 21 and the Appendix, by Articles 1 to 20 of the Brussels Act of this Convention.

ARTICLE 29bis

C–39   Ratification of or accession to this Act by any country not bound by Articles 22 to 38 of the Stockholm Act of this Convention shall, for the sole purposes of Article 14 (2) of the Convention establishing the Organization, amount to ratification of or accession to the said Stockholm Act with the limitation set forth in Article 28 (1) (*b*) (i) thereof.

ARTICLE 30

C–40   (1) Subject to the exceptions permitted by paragraph (2) of this Article, by Article 28 (1) (*b*), by Article 33 (2), and by the Appendix, ratification or accession shall automatically entail acceptance of all the provisions and admission to all the advantages of this Convention.

(2) (*a*) Any country of the Union ratifying or acceding to this Act may, subject to Article V (2) of the Appendix, retain the benefit of the reservations it has previously formulated on condition that it makes a declaration to that effect at the time of the deposit of its instrument of ratification or accession.

(*b*) Any country outside the Union may declare, in acceding to this Convention and subject to Article V (2) of the Appendix, that it intends to substitute, temporarily at least, for Article 8 of this Act concerning the right of translation, the provisions of Article 5 of the Union Convention of 1886, as completed at Paris in 1896, on the clear understanding that the said provisions are applicable only to translations into a language in general use in the said country. Subject to Article I (6) (*b*) of the Appendix, any country has the right to apply, in relation to the right of translation of works whose country of origin is a country availing itself of such a reservation, a protection which is equivalent to the protection granted by the latter country.

(*c*) Any country may withdraw such reservations at any time by notification addressed to the Director General.

ARTICLE 31

(1) Any country may declare in its instrument of ratification or accession, or **C–41** may inform the Director General by written notification at any time thereafter, that this Convention shall be applicable to all or part of those territories, designated in the declaration or notification, for the external relations of which it is responsible.

(2) Any country which has made such a declaration or given such a notification may, at any time, notify the Director General that this Convention shall cease to be applicable to all or part of such territories.

(3) (*a*) Any declaration made under paragraph (1) shall take effect on the same date as the ratification or accession in which it was included, and any notification given under that paragraph shall take effect three months after its notification by the Director General.

(*b*) Any notification given under paragraph (2) shall take effect twelve months after its receipt by the Director General.

(4) This Article shall in no way be understood as implying the recognition of tacit acceptance by a country of the Union of the factual situation concerning a territory to which this Convention is made applicable by another country of the Union by virtue of a declaration under paragraph (1).

ARTICLE 32

(1) This Act shall, as regards relations between the countries of the Union, and **C–42** to the extent that it applies, replace the Berne Convention of September 9, 1886, and the subsequent Acts of revision. The Acts previously in force shall continue to be applicable, in their entirety or to the extent that this Act does not replace them by virtue of the preceding sentence, in relations with countries of the Union which do not ratify or accede to this Act.

(2) Countries outside the Union which become party to this Act shall, subject to paragraph (3), apply it with respect to any country of the Union not bound by this Act or which, although bound by this Act, has made a declaration pursuant to Article 28 (1) (*b*). Such countries recognize that the said country of the Union, in its relations with them:

(i) may apply the provisions of the most recent Act by which it is bound, and

(ii) subject to Article 1 (6) of the Appendix, has the right to adapt the protection to the level provided for by this Act.

(3) Any country which has availed itself of any of the faculties provided for in the Appendix may apply the provisions of the Appendix relating to the faculty or faculties of which it has availed itself in its relations with any other country of the Union which is not bound by this Act, provided that the latter country has accepted the application of the said provisions.

Article 33

C–43   (1) Any dispute between two or more countries of the Union concerning the interpretation or application of this Convention, not settled by negotiation, may, by any one of the countries concerned, be brought before the International Court of Justice by application in conformity with the Statute of the Court, unless the countries concerned agree on some other method of settlement. The country bringing the dispute before the Court shall inform the International Bureau; the International Bureau shall bring the matter to the attention of the other countries of the Union.

(2) Each country may, at the time it signs this Act or deposits its instrument of ratification or accession, declare that it does not consider itself bound by the provisions of paragraph (1). With regard to any dispute between such country and any other country of the Union, the provisions of paragraph (1) shall not apply.

(3) Any country having made a declaration in accordance with the provisions of paragraph (2) may, at any time, withdraw its declaration by notification addressed to the Director General.

Article 34

C–44   (1) Subject to Article 29bis, no country may ratify or accede to earlier Acts of this Convention once Articles 1 to 21 and the Appendix have entered into force.

(2) Once Articles 1 to 21 and the Appendix have entered into force, no country may make a declaration under Article 5 of the Protocol Regarding Developing Countries attached to the Stockholm Act.

Article 35

C–45   (1) This Convention shall remain in force without limitation as to time.

(2) Any country may denounce this Act by notification addressed to the Director General. Such denunciation shall constitute also denunciation of all earlier Acts and shall affect only the country making it, the Convention remaining in full force and effect as regards the other countries of the Union.

(3) Denunciation shall take effect one year after the day on which the Director General has received the notification.

(4) The right of denunciation provided by this Article shall not be exercised by any country before the expiration of five years from the date upon which it becomes a member of the Union.

Article 36

C–46   (1) Any country party to this Convention undertakes to adopt, in accordance with its constitution, the measures necessary to ensure the application of this Convention.

(2) It is understood that, at the time a country becomes bound by this Convention, it will be in a position under its domestic law to give effect to the provisions of this Convention.

Article 37

C–47   (1) (*a*) This Act shall be signed in a single copy in the French and English languages and, subject to paragraph (2), shall be deposited with the Director General.

      (*b*) Official texts shall be established by the Director General, after consultation with the interested Governments, in the Arabic, German, Italian, Portuguese and Spanish languages, and such other languages as the Assembly may designate.

(*c*) In the case of differences of opinion on the interpretation of the various texts, the French text shall prevail.

(2) This Act shall remain open for signature until January 31, 1972. Until that date, the copy referred to in paragraph (1) (*a*) shall be deposited with the Government of the French Republic.

(3) The Director General shall certify and transmit two copies of the signed text of this Act to the Governments of all countries of the Union and, on request, to the Government of any other country.

(4) The Director General shall register this Act with the Secretariat of the United Nations.

(5) The Director General shall notify the Governments of all countries of the Union of signatures, deposits of instruments of ratification or accession and any declarations included in such instruments or made pursuant to Articles 28 (1) (*c*), 30 (2) (*a*) and (*b*), and 33 (2), entry into force of any provisions of this Act, notifications of denunciation, and notifications pursuant to Articles 30 (2) (*c*), 31 (1) and (2), 33 (3), and 38 (1), as well as the Appendix.

ARTICLE 38

(1) Countries of the Union which have not ratified or acceded to this Act and **C–48** which are not bound by Articles 22 to 26 of the Stockholm Act of this Convention may, until April 26, 1975, exercise, if they so desire, the rights provided under the said Articles as if they were bound by them. Any country desiring to exercise such rights shall give written notification to this effect to the Director General; this notification shall be effective on the date of its receipt. Such countries shall be deemed to be members of the Assembly until the said date.

(2) As long as all the countries of the Union have not become Members of the Organization, the International Bureau of the Organization shall also function as the Bureau of the Union, and the Director General as Director of the said Bureau.

(3) Once all the countries of the Union have become Members of the Organization, the rights, obligations, and property, of the Bureau of the Union shall devolve on the International Bureau of the Organization.

APPENDIX

ARTICLE I

(1) Any country regarded as a developing country in conformity with the estab- **C–49** lished practice of the General Assembly of the United Nations which ratifies or accedes to this Act, of which this Appendix forms an integral part, and which, having regard to its economic situation and its social or cultural needs, does not consider itself immediately in a position to make provision for the protection of all the rights as provided for in this Act, may, by a notification deposited with the Director General at the time of depositing its instrument of ratification or accession or, subject to Article V (1) (*c*), at any time thereafter, declare that it will avail itself of the faculty provided for in Article II, or of the faculty provided for in Article III, or of both of those faculties. It may, instead of availing itself of the faculty provided for in Article II, make a declaration according to Article V (1) (*a*).

(2) (*a*) Any declaration under paragraph (1) notified before the expiration of the period of ten years from the entry into force of Articles 1 to 21 and this Appendix according to Article 28 (2) shall be effective until the expiration of the said period. Any such declaration may be renewed in whole or in part for periods of ten years each by a notification deposited with the Director General not more than fifteen months and not less than three months before the expiration of the ten-year period then running.

(*b*) Any declaration under paragraph (1) notified after the expiration of the period of ten years from the entry into force of Articles 1 to 21 and this Appendix according to Article 28 (2) shall be effective until the expiration of the ten-year period then running. Any such declaration may be renewed as provided for in the second sentence of subparagraph (*a*).

(3) Any country of the Union which has ceased to be regarded as a developing country as referred to in paragraph (1) shall no longer be entitled to renew its declaration as provided in paragraph (2), and, whether or not it formally withdraws its declaration, such country shall be precluded from availing itself of the faculties referred to in paragraph (1) from the expiration of the ten-year period then running or from the expiration of a period of three years after it has ceased to be regarded as a developing country, whichever period expires later.

(4) Where, at the time when the declaration made under paragraph (1) or (2) ceases to be effective, there are copies in stock which were made under a licence granted by virtue of this Appendix, such copies may continue to be distributed until their stock is exhausted.

(5) Any country which is bound by the provisions of this Act and which has deposited a declaration or a notification in accordance with Article 31 (1) with respect to the application of this Act to a particular territory, the situation of which can be regarded as analogous to that of the countries referred to in paragraph (1), may, in respect of such territory, make the declaration referred to in paragraph (1) and the notification of renewal referred to in paragraph (2). As long as such declaration or notification remains in effect, the provisions of this Appendix shall be applicable to the territory in respect of which it was made.

(6) (*a*) The fact that a country avails itself of any of the faculties referred to in paragraph (1) does not permit another country to give less protection to works of which the country of origin is the former country than it is obliged to grant under Articles 1 to 20.

(*b*) The right to apply reciprocal treatment provided for in Article 30 (2) (*b*), second sentence, shall not, until the date on which the period applicable under Article I (3) expires, be exercised in respect of works the country of origin of which is a country which has made a declaration according to Article V (1) (*a*).

ARTICLE II

(1) Any country which has declared that it will avail itself of the faculty provided for in this Article shall be entitled, so far as works published in printed or analogous forms of reproduction are concerned, to substitute for the exclusive right of translation provided for in Article 8 a system of non-exclusive and non-transferable licences, granted by the competent authority under the following conditions and subject to Article IV.

(2) (*a*) Subject to paragraph (3), if, after the expiration of a period of three years, or of any longer period determined by the national legislation of the said country, commencing on the date of the first publication of the work, a translation of such work has not been published in a language in general use in that country by the owner of the right of translation, or with his authorization, any national of such country may obtain a licence to make a translation of the work in the said language and publish the translation in printed or analogous forms of reproduction.

(*b*) A licence under the conditions provided for in this Article may also be granted if all the editions of the translation published in the language concerned are out of print.

(3) (*a*) In the case of translations into a language which is not in general use in one or more developed countries which are members of the Union, a

period of one year shall be substituted for the period of three years referred to in paragraph (2) (*a*).

(*b*) Any country referred to in paragraph (1) may, with the unanimous agreement of the developed countries which are members of the Union and in which the same language is in general use, substitute, in the case of translations into that language, for the period of three years referred to in paragraph (2) (*a*) a shorter period as determined by such agreement but not less than one year. However, the provisions of the foregoing sentence shall not apply where the language in question is English, French or Spanish. The Director General shall be notified of any such agreement by the Governments which have concluded it.

(4) (*a*) No licence obtainable after three years shall be granted under this Article until a further period of six months has elapsed, and no licence obtainable after one year shall be granted under this Article until a further period of nine months has elapsed

    (i) from the date on which the applicant complies with the requirements mentioned in Article IV (1), or

    (ii) where the identity or the address of the owner of the right of translation is unknown, from the date on which the applicant sends, as provided for in Article IV (2), copies of his application submitted to the authority competent to grant the licence.

(*b*) If, during the said period of six or nine months, a translation in the language in respect of which the application was made is published by the owner of the right of translation or with his authorization, no licence under this Article shall be granted.

(5) Any licence under this Article shall be granted only for the purpose of teaching, scholarship or research.

(6) If a translation of a work is published by the owner of the right of translation or with his authorization at a price reasonably related to that normally charged in the country for comparable works, any licence granted under this Article shall terminate if such translation is in the same language and with substantially the same content as the translation published under the licence. Any copies already made before the licence terminates may continue to be distributed until their stock is exhausted.

(7) For works which are composed mainly of illustrations, a licence to make and publish a translation of the text and to reproduce and publish the illustrations may be granted only if the conditions of Article III are also fulfilled.

(8) No licence shall be granted under this Article when the author has withdrawn from circulation all copies of his work.

(9) (*a*) A licence to make a translation of a work which has been published in printed or analogous forms of reproduction may also be granted to any broadcasting organization having its headquarters in a country referred to in paragraph (1), upon an application made to the competent authority of that country by the said organization, provided that all of the following conditions are met:

    (i) the translation is made from a copy made and acquired in accordance with the laws of the said country;

    (ii) the translation is only for use in broadcasts intended exclusively for teaching or for the dissemination of the results of a specialized technical or scientific research to experts in a particular profession;

    (iii) the translation is used exclusively for the purposes referred to in condition (ii) through broadcasts made lawfully and intended for recipients on the territory of the said country, including broadcasts made through the medium of sound or visual recordings lawfully and exclusively made for the purpose of such broadcasts;

(iv) all uses made of the translation are without any commercial purpose.

(*b*) Sound or visual recordings of a translation which was made by a broadcasting organization under a licence granted by virtue of this paragraph may, for the purposes and subject to the conditions referred to in subparagraph (*a*) and with the agreement of that organization, also be used by any other broadcasting organization having its headquarters in the country whose competent authority granted the licence in question.

(*c*) Provided that all of the criteria and conditions set out in subparagraph (*a*) are met, a licence may also be granted to a broadcasting organization to translate any text incorporated in an audio-visual fixation where such fixation was itself prepared and published for the sole purpose of being used in connection with systematic instructional activities.

(*d*) Subject to subparagraphs (*a*) to (*c*), the provisions of the preceding paragraphs shall apply to the grant and exercise of any licence granted under this paragraph.

ARTICLE III

(1) Any country which has declared that it will avail itself of the faculty provided for in this Article shall be entitled to substitute for the exclusive right of reproduction provided for in Article 9 a system of non-exclusive and non-transferable licences, granted by the competent authority under the following conditions and subject to Article IV.

(2) (*a*) If, in relation to a work to which this Article applies by virtue of paragraph (7), after the expiration of

(i) the relevant period specified in paragraph (3), commencing on the date of first publication of a particular edition of the work, or

(ii) any longer period determined by national legislation of the country referred to in paragraph (1), commencing on the same date,

copies of such edition have not been distributed in that country to the general public or in connection with systematic instructional activities, by the owner of the right of reproduction or with his authorization, at a price reasonably related to that normally charged in the country for comparable works, any national of such country may obtain a licence to reproduce and publish such edition at that or a lower price for use in connection with systematic instructional activities.

(*b*) A licence to reproduce and publish an edition which has been distributed as described in subparagraph (*a*) may also be granted under the conditions provided for in this Article if, after the expiration of the applicable period, no authorised copies of that edition have been on sale for a period of six months in the country concerned to the general public or in connection with systematic instructional activities at a price reasonably related to that normally charged in the country for comparable works.

(3) The period referred to in paragraph (2) (*a*) (i) shall be five years, except that

(i) for works of the natural and physical sciences, including mathematics, and of technology, the period shall be three years;

(ii) for works of fiction, poetry, drama and music, and for art books, the period shall be seven years.

(4) (*a*) No licence obtainable after three years shall be granted under this Article until a period of six months has elapsed

  (i) from the date on which the applicant complies with the requirements mentioned in Article IV (1), or

  (ii) where the identity or the address of the owner of the right of reproduction is unknown, from the date on which the applicant sends, as provided for in Article IV (2), copies of his application submitted to the authority competent to grant the licence.

(*b*) Where licences are obtainable after other periods and Article IV (2) is applicable, no licence shall be granted until a period of three months has elapsed from the date of the dispatch of the copies of the application.

(*c*) If, during the period of six or three months referred to in subparagraphs (*a*) and (*b*), a distribution as described in paragraph (2) (*a*) has taken place, no licence shall be granted under this Article.

(*d*) No licence shall be granted if the author has withdrawn from circulation all copies of the edition for the reproduction and publication of which the licence has been applied for.

(5) A licence to reproduce and publish a translation of a work shall not be granted under this Article in the following cases:

  (i) where the translation was not published by the owner of the right of translation or with his authorization, or

  (ii) where the translation is not in a language in general use in the country in which the licence is applied for.

(6) If copies of an edition of a work are distributed in the country referred to in paragraph (1) to the general public or in connection with systematic instructional activities, by the owner of the right of reproduction or with his authorization, at a price reasonably related to that normally charged in the country for comparable works, any licence granted under this Article shall terminate if such edition is in the same language and with substantially the same content as the edition which was published under the said licence. Any copies already made before the licence terminates may continue to be distributed until their stock is exhausted.

(7) (*a*) Subject to subparagraph (*b*), the works to which this Article applies shall be limited to works published in printed or analogous forms of reproduction.

(*b*) This Article shall also apply to the reproduction in audio-visual form of lawfully made audio-visual fixations including any protected works incorporated therein and to the translation of any incorporated text into a language in general use in the country in which the licence is applied for, always provided that the audio-visual fixations in question were prepared and published for the sole purpose of being used in connection with systematic instructional activities.

Article IV

(1) A licence under Article II or Article III may be granted only if the applicant, in accordance with the procedure of the country concerned, establishes either that he has requested, and has been denied, authorization by the owner of the right to make and publish the translation or to reproduce and publish the edition, as the case may be, or that, after due diligence on his part, he was unable to find the owner of the right. At the same time as making the request, the applicant shall inform any national or international information centre referred to in paragraph (2).

(2) If the owner of the right cannot be found, the applicant for a licence shall send, by registered airmail, copies of his application, submitted to the authority competent to grant the licence, to the publisher whose name appears on the work and to any national or international information centre which may have been designated, in a notification to that effect deposited with the Director General, by the Government of the country in which the publisher is believed to have his principal place of business.

(3) The name of the author shall be indicated on all copies of the translation or reproduction published under a licence granted under Article II or Article III. The title of the work shall appear on all such copies. In the case of a translation, the original title of the work shall appear in any case on all the said copies.

(4) (a) No licence granted under Article II or Article III shall extend to the export of copies, and any such licence shall be valid only for publication of the translation or of the reproduction, as the case may be, in the territory of the country in which it has been applied for.

(b) For the purposes of subparagraph (a), the notion of export shall include the sending of copies from any territory to the country which, in respect of that territory, has made a declaration under Article I (5).

(c) Where a governmental or other public entity of a country which has granted a licence to make a translation under Article II into a language other than English, French or Spanish sends copies of a translation published under such licence to another country, such sending of copies shall not, for the purposes of subparagraph (a), be considered to constitute export if all of the following conditions are met:

(i) the recipients are individuals who are nationals of the country whose competent authority has granted the licence, or organizations grouping such individuals;

(ii) the copies are to be used only for the purpose of teaching, scholarship or research;

(iii) the sending of the copies and their subsequent distribution to recipients is without any commercial purpose; and

(iv) the country to which the copies have been sent has agreed with the country whose competent authority has granted the licence to allow the receipt, or distribution, or both, and the Director General has been notified of the agreement by the Government of the country in which the licence has been granted.

(5) All copies published under a licence granted by virtue of Article II or Article III shall bear a notice in the appropriate language stating that the copies are available for distribution only in the country or territory to which the said licence applies.

(6) (a) Due provision shall be made at the national level to ensure

(i) that the licence provides, in favour of the owner of the right of translation or of reproduction, as the case may be, for just compensation that is consistent with standards of royalties normally operating on licences freely negotiated between persons in the two countries concerned, and

(ii) payment and transmittal of the compensation: should national currency regulations intervene, the competent authority shall make all efforts, by the use of international machinery, to ensure transmittal in internationally convertible currency or its equivalent.

(b) Due provision shall be made by national legislation to ensure a correct translation of the work, or an accurate reproduction of the particular edition, as the case may be.

Article V

(1) (*a*) Any country entitled to make a declaration that it will avail itself of the faculty provided for in Article II may, instead, at the time of ratifying or acceding to this Act:

  (i) if it is a country to which Article 30 (2) (*a*) applies, make a declaration under that provision as far as the right of translation is concerned;

  (ii) if it is a country to which Article 30 (2) (*a*) does not apply, and even if it is not a country outside the Union, make a declaration as provided for in Article 30 (2) (*b*), first sentence.

(*b*) In the case of a country which ceases to be regarded as a developing country as referred to in Article I (1), a declaration made according to this paragraph shall be effective until the date on which the period applicable under Article I (3) expires.

(*c*) Any country which has made a declaration according to this paragraph may not subsequently avail itself of the faculty provided for in Article II even if it withdraws the said declaration.

(2) Subject to paragraph (3), any country which has availed itself of the faculty provided for in Article II may not subsequently make a declaration according to paragraph (1).

(3) Any country which has ceased to be regarded as a developing country as referred to in Article I (1) may, not later than two years prior to the expiration of the period applicable under Article I (3), make a declaration to the effect provided for in Article 30 (2) (*b*), first sentence, notwithstanding the fact that it is not a country outside the Union. Such declaration shall take effect at the date on which the period applicable under Article I (3) expires.

Article VI

(1) Any country of the Union may declare, as from the date of this Act, and at any time before becoming bound by Articles 1 to 21 and this Appendix:

  (i) if it is a country which, were it bound by Articles 1 to 21 and this Appendix, would be entitled to avail itself of the faculties referred to in Article I (1), that it will apply the provisions of Article II or of Article III or of both to works whose country of origin is a country which, pursuant to (ii) below, admits the application of those Articles to such works, or which is bound by Articles 1 to 21 and this Appendix; such declaration may, instead of referring to Article II, refer to Article V;

  (ii) that it admits the application of this Appendix to works of which it is the country of origin by countries which have made a declaration under (i) above or a notification under Article I.

(2) Any declaration made under paragraph (1) shall be in writing and shall be deposited with the Director General. The declaration shall become effective from the date of its deposit.

DECLARATION BY THE UNITED KINGDOM UNDER ARTICLE VI (1) (ii) OF THE APPENDIX

In a communication deposited with the Director General of the World Intellectual Property Organisation on 27 September, 1971, the Government of the United Kingdom declared that the United Kingdom admits the application of the Appendix to works of which it is the country of origin by countries which have made a declaration under Article VI (1) (i) of the Appendix or a notification under Article I of the Appendix.

* * *

C–50   Universal Copyright Convention (Paris Revision, 1971)[3]

The Universal Copyright Convention signed at Geneva on September 6, 1952[4] was revised in Paris in 1971. Because there are differences in the texts both texts are printed so that a comparison may be made. The omissions from the 1952 text and the changes in the 1971 text are printed in italics.

ARTICLE I

ARTICLE I

C–51   Each Contracting State undertakes to provide for the adequate and effective protection of the rights of authors and other copyright proprietors in literary, scientific and artistic works, including writings, musical, dramatic and cinematographic works, and paintings, engravings and sculpture.

Each Contracting State undertakes to provide for the adequate and effective protection of the rights of authors and other copyright proprietors in literary, scientific and artistic works, including writings, musical, dramatic and cinematographic works, and paintings, engravings and sculpture.

ARTICLE II

ARTICLE II

C–52   1. Published works of nationals of any Contracting State and works first published in that State shall enjoy in each other Contracting State the same protection as that other State accords to works of its nationals first published in its own territory.

1. Published works of nationals of any Contracting State and works first published in that State shall enjoy in each other Contracting State the same protection as that other State accords to works of its nationals first published in its own territory, *as well as the protection specially granted by this Convention.*

2. Unpublished works of nationals of each Contracting State shall enjoy in each other Contracting State the same protection as that other State accords to unpublished works of its own nationals.

2. Unpublished works of nationals of each Contracting State shall enjoy in each other Contracting State the same protection as that other State accords to unpublished works of its own nationals, *as well as the protection specially granted by this Convention.*

3. For the purpose of this Convention any Contracting State may, by domestic legislation, assimilate to its own nationals any person domiciled in that State.

3. For the purpose of this Convention any Contracting State may, by domestic legislation, assimilate to its own nationals any person domiciled in that State.

ARTICLE III

ARTICLE III

C–53   1. Any Contracting State which, under its domestic law, requires as a condition of copyright, compliance with formalities such as deposit, registration, notice, notarial certificates,

1. Any Contracting State which, under its domestic law, requires as a condition of copyright, compliance with formalities such as deposit, registration, notice, notarial certificates,

---

[3] Cmnd. 4905. As to the position of the United Kingdom see § 17–67 *ante.*
[4] Cmnd. 8912.

<table>
<tr><td>*Geneva*</td><td>*Paris*</td></tr>
</table>

payment of fees or manufacture or publication in that Contracting State, shall regard these requirements as satisfied with respect to all works protected in accordance with this Convention and first published outside its territory and the author of which is not one of its nationals, if from the time of the first publication all the copies of the work published with the authority of the author or other copyright proprietor bear the symbol © accompanied by the name of the copyright proprietor and the year of first publication placed in such manner and location as to give reasonable notice of claim of copyright.	payment of fees or manufacture or publication in that Contracting State, shall regard these requirements as satisfied with respect to all works protected in accordance with this Convention and first published outside its territory and the author of which is not one of its nationals, if from the time of the first publication all the copies of the work published with the authority of the author or other copyright proprietor bear the symbol © accompanied by the name of the copyright proprietor and the year of first publication placed in such manner and location as to give reasonable notice of claim of copyright.
2. The provisions of paragraph 1 *of this Article* shall not preclude any Contracting State from requiring formalities or other conditions for the acquisition and enjoyment of copyright in respect of works first published in its territory or works of its nationals wherever published.	2. The provisions of paragraph 1 shall not preclude any Contracting State from requiring formalities or other conditions for the acquisition and enjoyment of copyright in respect of works first published in its territory or works of its nationals wherever published.
3. The provisions of paragraph 1 *of this Article* shall not preclude any Contracting State from providing that a person seeking judicial relief must, in bringing the action, comply with procedural requirements, such as that the complainant must appear through domestic counsel or that the complainant must deposit with the court or an administrative office, or both, a copy of the work involved in the litigation; provided that failure to comply with such requirements shall not affect the validity of the copyright, nor shall any such requirement be imposed upon a national of another Contracting State if such requirement is not imposed on nationals of the State in which protection is claimed.	3. The provisions of paragraph 1 shall not preclude any Contracting State from providing that a person seeking judicial relief must, in bringing the action, comply with procedural requirements, such as that the complainant must appear through domestic counsel or that the complainant must deposit with the court or an administrative office, or both, a copy of the work involved in the litigation; provided that failure to comply with such requirements shall not affect the validity of the copyright, nor shall any such requirement be imposed upon a national of another Contracting State if such requirement is not imposed on nationals of the State in which protection is claimed.
4. In each Contracting State there shall be legal means of protecting without formalities the unpublished works of nationals of other Contracting States.	4. In each Contracting State there shall be legal means of protecting without formalities the unpublished works of nationals of other Contracting States.
5. If a Contracting State grants protection for more than one term of copyright and the first term is for a period longer than one of the minimum periods prescribed in Article IV, such State shall not be required to comply with the provisions of paragraph 1 of	5. If a Contracting State grants protection for more than one term of copyright and the first term is for a period longer than one of the minimum periods prescribed in Article IV, such State shall not be required to comply with the provisions of paragraph 1 of

Geneva	Paris
this Article III in respect of the second or any subsequent term of copyright.	this Article in respect of the second or any subsequent term of copyright.

ARTICLE IV

ARTICLE IV

C–54 1. The duration of protection of a work shall be governed, in accordance with the provisions of Article II and this Article, by the law of the Contracting State in which protection is claimed.

2. The term of protection for works protected under this Convention shall not be less than the life of the author and 25 years after his death.

However, any Contracting State which, on the effective date of this Convention in that State has limited this term for certain classes of works to a period computed from the first publication of the work, shall be entitled to maintain these exceptions and to extend them to other classes of works. For all these classes the term of protection shall not be less than twenty-five years from the date of first publication.

Any Contracting State which, upon the effective date of this Convention in that State, does not compute the term of protection upon the basis of the life of the author, shall be entitled to compute the term of protection from the date of the first publication of the work or from its registration prior to publication, as the case may be, provided the term of protection shall not be less that twenty-five years from the date of first publication or from its registration prior to publication, as the case may be.

If the legislation of a Contracting State grants two or more successive terms of protection, the duration of the first term shall not be less than one of the minimum periods specified above.

3. The provisions of paragraph 2 *of this Article* shall not apply to photographic works or to works of applied

---

1. The duration of protection of a work shall be governed, in accordance with the provisions of Article II and this Article, by the law of the Contracting State in which protection is claimed.

2. (*a*) The term of protection for works protected under this Convention shall not be less than the life of the author and twenty-five years after his death. However, any Contracting State which, on the effective date of this Convention in that State, has limited this term for certain classes of works to a period computed from the first publication of the work, shall be entitled to maintain these exceptions and to extend them to other classes of works. For all these classes the term of protection shall not be less than twenty-five years from the date of first publication.

(*b*) Any Contracting State which, upon the effective date of this Convention in that State, does not compute the term of protection upon the basis of the life of the author, shall be entitled to compute the term of protection from the date of the first publication of the work or from its registration prior to publication, as the case may be, provided the term of protection shall not be less than twenty-five years from the date of first publication or from its registration prior to publication, as the case may be.

(*c*) If the legislation of a Contracting State grants two or more successive terms of protection, the duration of the first term shall not be less than one of the minimum periods specified *in subparagraphs* (a) *and* (b).

3. The provisions of paragraph 2 shall not apply to photographic works or to works of applied art; provided,

art; provided however, that the term of protection in those Contracting States which protect photographic works, or works of applied art in so far as they are protected as artistic works, shall not be less than ten years for each of said classes of works.

4. No Contracting State shall be obliged to grant protection to a work for a period longer than that fixed for the classes of works to which the work in question belongs, in the case of unpublished works by the law of the Contracting State of which the author is a national, and in the case of published works by the law of the Contracting State in which the work has been first published.

For the purposes of the application of the preceding provision, if the law of any Contracting State grants two or more successive terms of protection, the period of protection of that State shall be considered to be the aggregate of those terms. However, if a specified work is not protected by such State during the second or any subsequent term for any reason, the other Contracting State shall not be obliged to protect it during the second or any subsequent term.

5. For the purposes of the application of paragraph 4 *of this Article*, the work of a national of a Contracting State, first published in a non-Contracting State, shall be treated as though first published in the Contracting State of which the author is a national.

6. For the purposes of the application of paragraph 4 *of this Article*, in case of simultaneous publication in two or more Contracting States, the work shall be treated as though first published in the State which affords the shortest term; any work published in two or more Contracting States within thirty days of its first publication shall be considered as having been published simultaneously in said Contracting States.

however, that the term of protection in those Contracting States which protect photographic works, or works of applied art in so far as they are protected as artistic works, shall not be less than ten years for each of said classes of works.

4. (*a*) No Contracting State shall be obliged to grant protection to a work for a period longer than that fixed for the classes of works to which the work in question belongs, in the case of unpublished works by the law of the Contracting State of which the author is a national, and in the case of published works by the law of the Contracting State in which the work has been first published.

(*b*) For the purposes of the application of *sub-paragraph (a)*, if the law of any Contracting State grants two or more successive terms of protection, the period of protection of that State shall be considered to be the aggregate of those terms. However, if a specified work is not protected by such State during the second or any subsequent term for any reason, the other Contracting States shall not be obliged to protect it during the second or any subsequent term.

5. For the purposes of the application of paragraph 4, the work of a national of a Contracting State, first published in a non-Contracting State, shall be treated as though first published in the Contracting State of which the author is a national.

6. For the purposes of the application of paragraph 4, in case of simultaneous publication in two or more Contracting States, the work shall be treated as though first published in the State which affords the shortest term; any work published in two or more Contracting States within thirty days of its first publication shall be considered as having been published simultaneously in said Contracting States.

C–55

ARTICLE IVbis

1. The rights referred to in Article I shall include the basic rights ensuring the author's economic interests, including the exclusive right to authorize reproduction by any means, public performance and broadcasting. The provisions of this Article shall extend to works protected under this Convention either in their original form or in any form recognizably derived from the original.

2. However, any Contracting State may, by its domestic legislation, make exceptions that do not conflict with the spirit and provisions of this Convention, to the rights mentioned in paragraph 1 of this Article. Any State whose legislation so provides, shall nevertheless accord a reasonable degree of effective protection to each of the rights to which exception has been made.

ARTICLE V   ARTICLE V

C–56   1. Copyright shall include the exclusive right of the author to make, publish, and authorise the making and publication of translations of works protected under this Convention.

1. *The rights referred to in Article I* shall include the exclusive right of the author to make, publish and authorize the making and publication of translations of works protected under this Convention.

2. However, any Contracting State may, by its domestic legislation, restrict the right of translation of writings, but only subject to the following provisions:

If, after the expiration of a period of seven years from the date of the first publication of a writing, a translation of such writing has not been published in the national language or languages, as the case may be, of the Contracting State, by the owner of the right of translation or with his authorisation, any national of such Contracting State may obtain a non-exclusive licence from the competent authority thereof to translate the work and publish the work so translated *in any of the national languages in which it has not been published; provided that* such national, in accordance with the procedure of the State concerned, establishes either that he has requested, and been denied, authorisation by the proprietor of the right to make and publish the translation, or that, after due diligence on his part, he was

2. However, any Contracting State may, by its domestic legislation restrict the right of translation of writings, but only subject to the following provisions:

(*a*) If, after the expiration of a period of seven years from the date of the first publication of a writing, a translation of such writing has not been published *in a language in general use in the Contracting State*, by the owner of the right of translation or with his authorization, any national of such Contracting State may obtain a non-exclusive licence from the competent authority thereof to translate the work into that language and publish the work so translated.

(*b*) Such national shall in accordance with the procedure of the State concerned, establish either that he has requested, and been denied, authorization by the proprietor of the right to make

Geneva	*Paris*

unable to find the owner of the right. A licence may also be granted on the same conditions if all previous editions of a translation in such language are out of print.

If the owner of the right of translation cannot be found, then the applicant for a licence shall send copies of his application to the publisher whose name appears on the work and, if the nationality of the owner of the right of translation is known, to the diplomatic or consular representative of the State of which such owner is a national, or to the organisation which may have been designated by the government of that State. The licence shall not be granted before the expiration of a period of two months from the date of the despatch of the copies of the application.

Due provision shall be made by domestic legislation to assure to the owner of the right of translation a compensation which is just and conforms to international standards to assure payment and transmittal of such compensation, and to assure a correct translation of the work.

The original title and the name of the author of the work shall be printed on all copies of the published translation. The licence shall be valid only for publication of the translation in the territory of the Contracting State where it has been applied for. Copies so published may be imported and sold in another Contracting State if one of the national languages of such other State is the same language as that into which the work has been so translated, and if the domestic law in such other State makes provision for such licences and does not prohibit such importation and sale. Where the foregoing conditions do

and publish the translation, or that, after due diligence on his part, he was unable to find the owner of the right. A licence may also be granted on the same conditions if all previous editions of a translation in *a language in general use in the Contracting State* are out of print.

(c) If the owner of the right of translation cannot be found, then the applicant for a licence shall send copies of his application to the publisher whose name appears on the work and, if the nationality of the owner of the right of translation is known, to the diplomatic or consular representative of the State of which such owner is a national, or to the organization which may have been designated by the government of that State. The licence shall not be granted before the expiration of a period of two months from the date of the dispatch of the copies of the application.

(d) Due provision shall be made by domestic legislation *to ensure* to the owner of the right of translation a compensation which is just and conforms to international standards, *to ensure* payment and transmittal of such compensation, and *to ensure* a correct translation of the work.

(e) The original title and the name of the author of the work shall be printed on all copies of the published translation. The licence shall be valid only for publication of the translation in the territory of the Contracting State where it has been applied for. Copies so published may be imported and sold in another Contracting State if *a language in general use in such other State* is the same language as that into which the work has been so translated, and if the domestic law in such other State makes

not exist, the importation and sale of such copies in a Contracting State shall be governed by its domestic law and its agreements. The licence shall not be transferred by the licensee. The licence shall not be granted when the author has withdrawn from circulation all copies of the work.

provision for such licences and does not prohibit such importation and sale. Where the foregoing conditions do not exist, the importation and sale of such copies in a Contracting State shall be governed by its domestic law and its agreements. The licence shall not be transferred by the licensee.

(*f*) The licence shall not be granted when the author has withdrawn from circulation all copies of the work.

ARTICLE V*bis*

C–57

1. *Any Contracting State regarded as a developing country in conformity with the established practice of the General Assembly of the United Nations may, by a notification deposited with the Director-General of the United Nations Educational, Scientific and Cultural Organization (hereinafter called "the Director-General") at the time of its ratification, acceptance or accession or thereafter, avail itself of any or all of the exceptions provided for in Articles V^{ter} and V^{quater}.*

2. *Any such notification shall be effective for ten years from the date of coming into force of this Convention, or for such part of that ten-year period as remains at the date of deposit of the notification, and may be renewed in whole or in part for further periods of ten years each if, not more than fifteen or less than three months before the expiration of the relevant ten-year period, the Contracting State deposits a further notification with the Director-General. Initial notifications may also be made during these further periods of ten years in accordance with the provisions of this Article.*

3. *Notwithstanding the provisions of paragraph 2, a Contracting State that has ceased to be regarded as a developing country as referred to in paragraph 1 shall no longer be entitled to renew its notification made under the provisions of paragraph 1 or 2, and whether or not it formally withdraws the notification such State shall be precluded from availing itself of the exceptions provided for in Articles V^{ter} and V^{quater} at the end of the current ten-year period, or at the end of three*

years after it has ceased to be regarded as a developing country, whichever period expires later.

4. Any copies of a work already made under the exceptions provided for in Articles V^{ter} and V^{quater} may continue to be distributed after the expiration of the period for which notifications under this Article were effective until their stock is exhausted.

5. Any Contracting State that has deposited a notification in accordance with Article XIII with respect to the application of this Convention to a particular country or territory, the situation of which can be regarded as analogous to that of the States referred to in paragraph 1 of this Article, may also deposit notifications and renew them in accordance with the provisions of this Article with respect to any such country or territory. During the effective period of such notifications, the provisions of Articles V^{ter} and V^{quater} may be applied with respect to such country or territory. The sending of copies from the country or territory to the Contracting State shall be considered as export within the meaning of Articles V^{ter} and V^{quater}.

ARTICLE V^{ter}

1. (a) Any Contracting State to which Article V^{bis} (1) applies may substitute for the period of seven years provided for in Article V (2) a period of three years or any longer period prescribed by its legislation. However, in the case of a translation into a language not in general use in one or more developed countries that are party to this Convention or only the 1952 Convention, the period shall be one year instead of three.

(b) A Contracting State to which Article V^{bis} (1) applies may, with the unanimous agreement of the developed countries party to this Convention or only the 1952 Convention and in which the same language is in general use, substitute, in the case of translation into that language, for the period of three years provided for in sub-paragraph (a) another period as determined by such agreement but not shorter than one year. However, this sub-paragraph shall not apply where the

C–58

Geneva   *Paris*

language in question is English, French or Spanish. Notification of any such agreement shall be made to the Director-General.

(c) The licence may only be granted if the applicant, in accordance with the procedure of the State concerned, establishes either that he has requested, and been denied, authorization by the owner of the right of translation, or that, after due diligence on his part, he was unable to find the owner of the right. At the same time as he makes his request he shall inform either the International Copyright Information Centre established by the United Nations Educational, Scientific and Cultural Organization or any national or regional information centre which may have been designated in a notification to that effect deposited with the Director-General by the government of the State in which the publisher is believed to have his principal place of business.

(d) If the owner of the right of translation cannot be found, the applicant for a licence shall send, by registered airmail, copies of his application to the publisher whose name appears on the work and to any national or regional information centre as mentioned in sub-paragraph (c). If no such centre is notified he shall also send a copy to the International Copyright Information Centre established by the United Nations Educational, Scientific and Cultural Organization.

2. (a) Licences obtainable after three years shall not be granted under this Article until a further period of six months has elapsed and licences obtainable after one year until a further period of nine months has elapsed. The further period shall begin either from the date of the request for permission to translate mentioned in paragraph 1(c) or, if the identity or address of the owner of the right of translation is not known, from the date of dispatch of the copies of the application for a licence mentioned in paragraph 1(d).

(b) Licences shall not be granted if a

translation has been published by the owner of the right of translation or with his authorization during the said period of six or nine months.

3. Any licence under this Article shall be granted only for the purpose of teaching, scholarship or research.

4. (a) Any licence granted under this Article shall not extend to the export of copies and shall be valid only for publication in the territory of the Contracting State where it has been applied for.

(b) Any copy published in accordance with a licence granted under this Article shall bear a notice in the appropriate language stating that the copy is available for distribution only in the Contracting State granting the licence. If the writing bears the notice specified in Article III (1) the copies shall bear the same notice.

(c) The prohibition of export provided for in sub-paragraph (a) shall not apply where a governmental or other public entity of a State which has granted a licence under this Article to translate a work into a language other than English, French or Spanish sends copies of a translation prepared under such licence to another country if:

(i) the recipients are individuals who are nationals of the Contracting State granting the licence, or organizations grouping such individuals;

(ii) the copies are to be used only for the purpose of teaching, scholarship or research;

(iii) the sending of the copies and their subsequent distribution to recipients is without the object of commercial purpose; and

(iv) the country to which the copies have been sent has agreed with the Contracting State to allow the receipt, distribution or both and the Director-General has been notified of such agreement by any one of the governments which have concluded it.

5. Due provision shall be made at the national level to ensure:

(a) that the licence provides for just compensation that is consistent with stan-

dards of royalties normally operating
in the case of licences freely negotiated
between persons in the two countries
concerned; and

(b) payment and transmittal of the compensation; however, should national
currency regulations intervene, the
competent authority shall make all
efforts, by the use of international
machinery, to ensure transmittal in
internationally convertible currency or
its equivalent.

6. Any licence granted by a Contracting
State under this Article shall terminate if a
translation of the work in the same language
with substantially the same content as the edition in respect of which the licence was
granted is published in the said State by the
owner of the right of translation or with his
authorization, at a price reasonably related to
that normally charged in the same State for
comparable works. Any copies already made
before the licence is terminated may continue to
be distributed until their stock is exhausted.

7. For works which are composed mainly of
illustrations a licence to translate the text and
to reproduce the illustrations may be granted
only if the conditions of Article V^{quater} are also
fulfilled.

8. (a) A licence to translate a work protected under this Convention, published in printed or analogous forms
of reproduction, may also be granted
to a broadcasting organization having
its headquarters in a Contracting
State to which Article V^{bis} (1)
applies, upon an application made in
that State by the said organization
under the following conditions:

(i) the translation is made from a
copy made and acquired in accordance
with the laws of the Contracting
State;

(ii) the translation is for use only
in broadcasts intended exclusively for
teaching or for the dissemination of
the results of specialized technical or
scientific research to experts in a particular profession;

(iii) the translation is used exclusively for the purposes set out in condition (ii), through broadcasts
lawfuly made which are intended for

recipients on the territory of the Contracting State, including broadcasts
made through the medium of sound or
visual recordings lawfully and exclusively made for the purpose of such
broadcasts;

　　(iv) sound or visual recordings of
the translation may be exchanged only
between broadcasting organizations
having their headquarters in the Contracting State granting the licence;
and

　　　(v) all uses made of the translation
are without any commercial purpose.

(b) Provided all of the criteria and conditions set out in sub-paragraph (a)
are met, a licence may also be granted
to a broadcasting organisation to
translate any text incorporated in an
audio-visual fixation which was itself
prepared and published for the sole
purpose of being used in connection
with systematic instructional activities.

(c) Subject to sub-paragraphs (a) and
(b), the other provisions of this
Article shall apply to the grant and
exercise of the licence.

9. Subject to the provisions of this Article,
any licence granted under this Article shall be
governed by the provisions of Article V, and
shall continue to be governed by the provisions
of Article V and of this Article, even after the
seven-year period provided for in Article V (2)
has expired. However, after the said period
has expired, the licensee shall be free to request
that the said licence be replaced by a new
licence governed exclusively by the provisions
of Article V.

ARTICLE V*quater*

1. Any Contracting State to which Article   **C–59**
V*bis* (1) applies may adopt the following provisions:

(a) If, after the expiration of (i) the relevant period specified in sub-paragraph (c) commencing from the date
of first publication of a particular edition of a literary, scientific or artistic
work referred to in paragraph 3, or
(ii) any longer period determined by
national legislation of the State,
copies of such edition have not been

distributed in that State to the general public or in connexion with systematic instructional activities at a price reasonably related to that normally charged in the State for comparable works, by the owner of the right of reproduction or with his authorisation, any national of such State may obtain a non-exclusive licence from the competent authority to publish such edition at that or a lower price for use in connexion with systematic instructional activities. The licence may only be granted if such national, in accordance with the procedure of the State concerned, establishes either that he has requested, and been denied, authorization by the proprietor of the right to publish such work, or that, after due diligence on his part, he was unable to find the owner of the right. At the same time as he makes his request he shall inform either the International Copyright Information Centre established by the United Nations Educational, Scientific and Cultural Organization or any national or regional information centre referred to in sub-paragraph (*d*).

(*b*) A licence may also be granted on the same conditions if, for a period of six months, no authorized copies of the edition in question have been on sale in the State concerned to the general public or in connexion with systematic instructional activities at a price reasonably related to that normally charged in the State for comparable works.

(*c*) The period referred to in sub-paragraph (*a*) shall be five years except that:

(*i*) for works of the natural and physical sciences, including mathematics, and of technology, the period shall be three years;

(*ii*) for works of fiction, poetry, drama and music, and for art books, the period shall be seven years.

(*d*) If the owner of the right of reproduction cannot be found, the applicant for a licence shall send, by registered air *mail, copies of his application to the publisher whose name appears on the work and to any national or regional information centre identified as such in a notification deposited with the Director-General by the State in which the publisher is believed to have his principal place of business. In the absence of any such notification, he shall also send a copy to the International Copyright Information Centre established by the United Nations Educational, Scientific and Cultural Organization. The licence shall not be granted before the expiration of a period of three months from the date of dispatch of the copies of the application.*

(e) *Licences obtainable after three years shall not be granted under this Article:*

(i) *until a period of six months has elapsed from the date of the request for permission referred to in sub-paragraph (a) or, if the identity or address of the owner of the right of reproduction is unknown, from the date of the dispatch of the copies of the application for a licence referred to in sub-paragraph (d);*

(ii) *if any such distribution of copies of the edition as is mentioned in sub-paragraph (a) has taken place during that period.*

(f) *The name of the author and the title of the particular edition of the work shall be printed on all copies of the published reproduction. The licence shall not extend to the export of copies and shall be valid only for publication in the territory of the Contracting State where it has been applied for. The licence shall not be transferable by the licensee.*

(g) *Due provision shall be made by domestic legislation to ensure an accurate reproduction of the particular edition in question.*

(h) *A licence to reproduce and publish a translation of a work shall not be granted under this Article in the following cases:*

(i) *where the translation was not*

published by the owner of the right of
translation or with his authorization;

(ii) where the translation is not in
a language in general use in the State
with power to grant the licence.

2. The exceptions provided for in paragraph 1 are subject to the following additional
provisions:

(a) Any copy published in accordance
with a licence granted under this
Article shall bear a notice in the
appropriate language stating that the
copy is available for distribution only
in the Contracting State to which the
said licence applies. If the edition
bears the notice specified in Article III
(1), the copies shall bear the same
notice.

(b) Due provision shall be made at the
national level to ensure:

(i) that the licence provides for just
compensation that is consistent with
standards of royalties normally operating in the case of licences freely
negotiated between persons in the two
countries concerned; and

(ii) payment and transmittal of
the compensation; however, should
national currency regulations intervene, the competent authority shall
make all efforts, by the use of international machinery, to ensure transmittal in internationally convertible
currency or its equivalent.

(c) Whenever copies of an edition of a
work are distributed in the Contracting State to the general public or in
connexion with systematic instructional activities by the owner of the
right of reproduction or with his authorization, at a price reasonably
related to that normally charged in the
State for comparable works, any
licence granted under this Article shall
terminate if such edition is in the same
language and is substantially the
same in content as the edition published under the licence. Any copies
already made before the licence is terminated may continue to be distributed
until their stock is exhausted.

(d) No licence shall be granted when the
author has withdrawn from circula-

Geneva	Paris

tion all copies of the edition in question.

3. (a) Subject to sub-paragraph (b), the literary, scientific or artistic works to which this Article applies shall be limited to works published in printed or analogous forms of reproduction.

(b) The provisions of this Article shall also apply to reproduction in audio-visual form of lawfully made audio-visual fixations including any protected works incorporated therein and to the translation of any incorporated text into a language in general use in the State with power to grant the licence; always provided that the audio-visual fixations in question were prepared and published for the sole purpose of being used in connexion with systematic instructional activities.

ARTICLE VI

"Publication," as used in this Convention, means the reproduction in tangible form and the general distribution to the public of copies of a work from which it can be read or otherwise visually perceived.

ARTICLE VI

"Publication," as used in this Convention, means the reproduction in tangible form and the general distribution to the public of copies of a work from which it can be read or otherwise visually perceived. **C–60**

ARTICLE VII

This Convention shall not apply to works or rights in works which, at the effective date of the Convention in a Contracting State where protection is claimed, are permanently in the public domain in the said Contracting State.

ARTICLE VII

This Convention shall not apply to works or rights in works which, at the effective date of the Convention in a Contracting State where protection is claimed, are permanently in the public domain in the said Contracting State. **C–61**

ARTICLE VIII

1. This Convention, which shall bear the date of September 6, 1952, shall be deposited with the Director-General *of the United Nations Educational, Scientific and Cultural Organisation* and shall remain open for signatures by all States for a period of 120 days after that date. It shall be subject to ratification or acceptance by the signatory States.

2. Any State which has not signed this Convention may accede thereto.

3. Ratification, acceptance or accession shall be effected by the

ARTICLE VIII

1. This Convention, which shall bear the date of *24 July 1971*, shall be deposited with the Director-General and shall remain open for signature by all States *party to the 1952 Convention* for a period of 120 days after *the date of this Convention*. It shall be subject to ratification or acceptance by the signatory States. **C–62**

2. Any State which has not signed this Convention may accede thereto.

3. Ratification, acceptance or accession shall be effected by the

Geneva	*Paris*
deposit of an instrument to that effect with the Director-General *of the United Nations Educational, Scientific and Cultural Organisation.*	deposit of an instrument to that effect with the Director-General.

<table>
<tr><td>

ARTICLE IX

</td><td>

ARTICLE IX

</td></tr>
</table>

C–63

1. This Convention shall come into force three months after the deposit of twelve instruments of ratification, acceptance or accession, *among which there shall be those of four States which are not members of the International Union for the Protection of Literary and Artistic Works.*

2. Subsequently, this Convention shall come into force in respect of each State three months after that State has deposited its instrument of ratification, acceptance or accession.

1. This Convention shall come into force three months after the deposit of twelve instruments of ratification, acceptance or accession.

2. Subsequently, this Convention shall come into force in respect of each State three months after that State has deposited its instrument of ratification, acceptance or accession.

3. *Accession to this Convention by a State not party to the 1952 Convention shall also constitute accession to that Convention; however, if its instrument of accession is deposited before this Convention comes into force, such State may make its accession to the 1952 Convention conditional upon the coming into force of this Convention. After the coming into force of this Convention, no State may accede solely to the 1952 Convention.*

4. *Relations between States party to this Convention and States that are party only to the 1952 Convention, shall be governed by the 1952 Convention. However, any State party only to the 1952 Convention may, by a notification deposited with the Director-General, declare that it will admit the application of the 1971 Convention to works of its nationals or works first published in its territory by all States party to this Convention.*

ARTICLE X

ARTICLE X

C–64

1. Each State party to this Convention undertakes to adopt, in accordance with its Constitution, such measures as are necessary to ensure the application of this Convention.

2. It is understood, *however,* that at the time an instrument of ratification, acceptance or accession is deposited on behalf of any State, such State must be in a position under its domestic law to give effect to the terms of this Convention.

1. Each Contracting State undertakes to adopt, in accordance with its Constitution, such measures as are necessary to ensure the application of this Convention.

2. It is understood that at the *date this Convention comes into force in respect of any State, that* State must be in a position under its domestic law to give effect to the terms of this Convention.

Geneva	*Paris*

ARTICLE XI

1. An Intergovernmental Committee is hereby established with the following duties:

   (*a*) to study the problems concerning the application and operation of this Convention;

   (*b*) to make preparation for periodic revision of this Convention;

   (*c*) to study any other problems concerning the international protection of copyright, in co-operation with the various interested international organisations, such as the United Nations Educational, Scientific and Cultural Organisation, the International Union for the Protection of Literary and Artistic Works, and the Organisation of American States;

   (*d*) to inform the Contracting States as to its activities.

2. The Committee shall consist of the representatives of twelve Contracting States to be selected with due consideration to fair geographical representation and in conformity with the Resolution relating to this article, annexed to this Convention.

The Director-General of the United Nations Educational, Scientific and Cultural Organisation, the Director of the Bureau of the International Union for the Protection of Literary and Artistic Works and the Secretary-General of the Organisation of American States, or their representatives, may attend meetings of the Committee in an advisory capacity.

ARTICLE XII

The Intergovernmental Committee shall convene a conference for revision *of this Convention* whenever it deems necessary, or at the request of at least ten Contracting States, or a majority of Contracting States if there are less than twenty Contracting States.

ARTICLE XI   **C–65**

1. An Intergovernmental Committee is hereby established with the following duties:

   (*a*) to study the problems concerning the application and operation of *the Universal Copyright Convention*;

   (*b*) to make preparation for periodic revisions of this Convention;

   (*c*) to study any other problems concerning the international protection of copyright, in co-operation with the various interested international organizations, such as the United Nations Educational, Scientific and Cultural Organization, the International Union for the Protection of Literary and Artistic Works, and the Organization of American States;

   (*d*) to inform *States party to the Universal Copyright Convention* as to its activities.

2. The Committee shall consist of the representatives of *eighteen States party to this Convention or only to the 1952 Convention.*

3. *The Committee shall be selected with due consideration to a fair balance of national interests on the basis of geographical location, population, languages and stages of development.*

4. The Director-General of the United Nations Educational, Scientific and Cultural Organization, the *Director-General of the World Intellectual Property Organization*, and the Secretary-General of the Organization of American States, or their representatives, may attend meetings of the Committee in an advisory capacity.

ARTICLE XII

The Intergovernmental Committee shall convene a conference for revision *whenever it deems necessary, or at the request of at least ten States party to this Convention.*   **C–66**

Article XIII

C–67   Any Contracting State may, at the time of deposit of its instrument of ratification, acceptance or accession, or at any time thereafter, declare by notification addressed to the Director-General *of the United Nations Educational, Scientific and Cultural Organisation* that this Convention shall apply to all or any of the countries or territories for the international relations of which it is responsible and this Convention shall thereupon apply to the countries or territories named in such notification after the expiration of the term of three months provided for in Article IX. In the absence of such notification, this Convention shall not apply to any such country or territory.

Article XIII

1. Any Contracting State may, at the time of deposit of its instrument of ratification, acceptance or accession, or at any time thereafter, declare by notification addressed to the Director-General that this Convention shall apply to all or any of the countries or territories for the international relations of which it is responsible and this Convention shall thereupon apply to the countries or territories named in such notification after the expiration of the term of three months provided for in Article IX. In the absence of such notification, this Convention shall not apply to any such country or territory.

2. *However, nothing in this Article should be understood as implying the recognition or tacit acceptance by a Contracting State of the factual situation concerning a country or territory to which this Convention is made applicable by another Contracting State in accordance with the provisions of this Article.*

Article XIV

C–68   1. Any Contracting State may denounce this Convention in its own name or on behalf of all or any of the countries or territories as to which a notification has been given under Article XIII. The denunciation shall be made by notification addressed to the Director-General *of the United Nations Educational, Scientific and Cultural Organisation.*

2. Such denunciation shall operate only in respect of the State or of the country or territory on whose behalf it was made and shall not take effect until twelve months after the date of receipt of the notification.

Article XIV

1. Any Contracting State may denounce this Convention in its own name or on behalf of all or any of the countries or territories *with respect to* which a notification has been given under Article XIII. The denunciation shall be made by notification addressed to the Director-General. *Such denunciation shall also constitute denunciation of the 1952 Convention.*

2. Such denunciation shall operate only in respect of the State or of the country or territory on whose behalf it was made and shall not take effect until twelve months after the date of receipt of the notification.

Article XV

C–69   A dispute between two or more Contracting States concerning the interpretation   or   application   of   this

Article XV

A dispute between two or more Contracting States concerning the interpretation   or   application   of   this

Convention, not settled by negotiation, shall unless the States concerned agree on some other method of settlement be brought before the International Court of Justice for determination by it.

A dispute between two or more Contracting States concerning the interpretation or application of this Convention, not settled by negotiation, shall, unless the States concerned agree on some other method of settlement, be brought before the International Court of Justice for determination by it.

ARTICLE XVI

1. This Convention shall be established in English, French and Spanish. The three texts shall be signed and shall be equally authoritative.

2. Official texts of this Convention shall be established in German, Italian and Portuguese.

Any Contracting State or group of Contracting States shall be entitled to have established by the Director-General *of the United Nations Educational, Scientific and Cultural Organisation* other texts in the language of its choice by arrangement with the Director-General.

All such texts shall be annexed to the signed texts of this Convention.

ARTICLE XVI **C–70**

1. This Convention shall be established in English, French and Spanish. The three texts shall be signed and shall be equally authoritative.

2. Official texts of this Convention shall be established *by the Director-General, after consultation with the governments concerned, in Arabic, German, Italian and Portuguese.*

3. Any Contracting State or group of Contracting States shall be entitled to have established by the Director-General other texts in the language of its choice by arrangement with the Director-General.

4. All such texts shall be annexed to the signed texts of this Convention.

ARTICLE XVII

1. This Convention shall not in any way affect the provisions of the Berne Convention for the Protection of Literary and Artistic Works or membership in the Union created by that Convention.

2. In application of the foregoing paragraph, a Declaration has been annexed to the present article. This Declaration is an integral part of this Convention for the States bound by the Berne Convention on January 1, 1951, or which have or may become bound to it at a later date. The signature of this Convention by such States shall also constitute signature of the said Declaration, and ratification, acceptance or accession by such States shall include the Declaration as well as the Convention.

ARTICLE XVII **C–71**

1. This Convention shall not in any way affect the provisions of the Berne Convention for the Protection of Literary and Artistic Works or membership in the Union created by that Convention.

2. In application of the foregoing paragraph, a Declaration has been annexed to the present Article. This Declaration is an integral part of this Convention for the States bound by the Berne Convention on 1 January 1951, or which have or may become bound to it at a later date. The signature of this Convention by such States shall also constitute signature of the said Declaration, and ratification, acceptance or accession by such States shall include the Declaration, as well as *this* Convention.

ARTICLE XVIII

This Convention shall not abrogate multilateral or bilateral copyright con-

ARTICLE XVIII

This Convention shall not abrogate **C–72** multilateral or bilateral copyright con

ventions or arrangements that are or may be in effect exclusively between two or more American Republics. In the event of any difference either between the provisions of such existing conventions or arrangements and the provisions of this Convention, or between the provisions of this Convention and those of any new convention or arrangement which may be formulated between two or more American Republics after this Convention comes into force, the convention or arrangement most recently formulated shall prevail between the parties thereto. Rights in works acquired in any Contracting State under existing conventions or arrangements before the date this Convention comes into force in such State shall not be affected.

ventions or arrangements that are or may be in effect exclusively between two or more American Republics. In the event of any difference either between the provisions of such existing conventions or arrangements and the provisions of this Convention, or between the provisions of this Convention and those of any new convention or arrangement which may be formulated between two or more American Republics after this Convention comes into force, the convention or arrangement most recently formulated shall prevail between the parties thereto. Rights in works acquired in any Contracting State under existing conventions or arrangements before the date this Convention comes into force in such State shall not be affected.

ARTICLE XIX

C–73   This Convention shall not abrogate multilateral or bilateral conventions or arrangements in effect between two or more Contracting States. In the event of any difference between the provisions of such existing conventions or arrangements and the provisions of this Convention, the provisions of this Convention shall prevail. Rights in works acquired in any Contracting State under existing conventions or arrangements before the date on which this Convention comes into force in such State shall not be affected. Nothing in this Article shall affect the provisions of Articles XVII and XVIII *of this Convention.*

ARTICLE XIX

This Convention shall not abrogate multilateral or bilateral conventions or arrangements in effect between two or more Contracting States. In the event of any difference between the provisions of such existing conventions or arrangements and the provisions of this Convention, the provisions of this Convention shall prevail. Rights in works acquired in any Contracting State under existing conventions or arrangements before the date on which this Convention comes into force in such State shall not be affected. Nothing in this Article shall affect the provisions of Articles XVII and XVIII.

ARTICLE XX

C–74   Reservations to this Convention shall not be permitted.

ARTICLE XX

Reservations to this Convention shall not be permitted.

ARTICLE XXI

C–75   The Director-General *of the United Nations Educational, Scientific and Cultural Organisation* shall send duly certified copies of this Convention to the States interested, *to the Swiss Federal Council* and to the Secretary-General of the United Nations for registration by him.
He shall also inform all interested

ARTICLE XXI

1. The Director-General shall send duly certified copies of this Convention to the States interested and to the Secretary-General of the United Nations for registration by him.

2. He shall also inform all interested

Geneva	Paris

States of the ratifications, acceptances and accessions which have been deposited, the date on which this Convention comes into force, the notifications under *Article XIII of* this Convention, and denunciations under Article XIV.

States of the ratifications, acceptances and accessions which have been deposited, the date on which this Convention comes into force, the notifications under this Convention and denunciations under Article XIV.

Appendix Declaration *relating to Article* XVII

Appendix Declaration Relating to Article XVII   **C–76**

The States which are members of the International Union for the Protection of Literary and Artistic Works, and which are signatories to the Universal Copyright Convention.

The States which are members of the International Union for the Protection of Literary and Artistic Works (*hereinafter called "the Berne Union"*) and which are signatories to this Convention.

Desiring to reinforce their mutual relations on the basis of the said Union and to avoid any conflict which might result from the co-existence of the Convention of Berne and the Universal Convention,

Desiring to reinforce their mutual relations on the basis of the said Union and to avoid any conflict which might result from the co-existence of the Berne Convention and the Universal Copyright Convention,

Recognizing the temporary need of some States to adjust their level of copyright protection in accordance with their stage of cultural, social and economic development,

Have, by common agreement, accepted the terms of the following declaration:

Have, by common agreement, accepted the terms of the following declaration:

(*a*) Works which, according to the Berne Convention, have as their country of origin a country which has withdrawn from the International Union created by the said Convention, after January 1, 1951, shall not be protected by the Universal Copyright Convention in the countries of the Berne Union;

(*a*) *Except as provided by paragraph (b),* works which, according to the Berne Convention, have as their country of origin a country which has withdrawn from the *Berne Union* after 1 January 1951, shall not be protected by the Universal Copyright Convention in the countries of the Berne Union;

(*b*) *Where a Contracting State is regarded as a developing country in conformity with the established practice of the General Assembly of the United Nations, and has deposited with the Director-General of the United Nations Educational, Scientific and Cultural Organization, at the time of its withdrawal from the Berne Union, a notification to the effect that it regards itself as a developing country, the provisions of paragraph (a) shall not be applicable as long as such State may avail itself of the exceptions provided for by this Convention in accordance with Article V^{bis};*

1357

| Geneva | Paris |

(*b*) The Universal Copyright Convention shall not be applicable to the relationships among countries of the Berne Union in so far as it relates to the protection of works having as their country of origin, within the meaning of the Berne Convention, a country of the International Union created by the said Convention.

(*c*) The Universal Copyright Convention shall not be applicable to the relationships among countries of the Berne Union in so far as it relates to the protection of works having as their country of origin, within the meaning of the Berne Convention, a country of the *Berne Union.*

RESOLUTION CONCERNING
ARTICLE XI

RESOLUTION CONCERNING
ARTICLE XI

C–77   The Intergovernmental Copyright Conference,

Having considered the problems relating to the Intergovernmental Committee provided for in Article XI of the Universal Copyright Convention,
    resolves:

1. The first members of the Committee shall be representatives of the following twelve States, each of those States designating one representative and an alternate: Argentina, Brazil, France, Germany, India, Italy, Japan, Mexico, Spain, Switzerland, United Kingdom and United States of America.

2. The Committee shall be constituted as soon as the Convention comes into force in accordance with Article XI of this Convention.

The Conference for Revision of the Universal Copyright Convention,

Having considered the problems relating to the Intergovernmental Committee provided for in Article XI of *this Convention, to which this resolution is annexed,*
    Resolves *that*:

1. At its inception, the Committee shall include representatives of the twelve States members of the Intergovernmental Committee established under Article XI of the 1952 Convention and the resolution annexed to it, and, in addition, representatives of the following States: Algeria, Australia, Japan, Mexico, Senegal and Yugoslavia.

2. Any States that are not party to the 1952 Convention and have not acceded to this Convention before the first ordinary session of the Committee following the entry into force of this Convention shall be replaced by other States to be selected by the Committee at its first ordinary session in conformity with the provisions of Article XI (2) and (3).

3. As soon as this Convention comes into force the Committee as provided for in paragraph 1 shall be deemed to be constituted in accordance with Article XI of this Convention.

4. A session of the Committee shall take place within one year after the coming into force of this Convention; thereafter the Committee shall meet in ordinary session at intervals of not more than two years.

3. The Committee shall elect its Chairman and one Vice-Chairman. It shall establish its rules of procedure having regard to the following principles:

5. The Committee shall elect its Chairman and *two* Vice-Chairmen. It shall establish its Rules of Procedure having regard to the following principles:

Geneva	*Paris*

(a) the normal duration of the term of office of the representatives shall be six years; with one-third retiring every two years;

(b) before the expiration of the term of office of any members, the Committee shall decide which States shall cease to be represented on it and which States shall be called upon to designate representatives; the representatives of those States which have not ratified, accepted or acceded shall be the first to retire;

(c) the different parts of the world shall be fairly represented;

(a) The normal duration of the term of office of the *members represented on the Committee* shall be six years with one-third retiring every two years, *it being however understood that, of the original terms of office, one-third shall expire at the end of the Committee's second ordinary session which will follow the entry into force of this Convention, a further third at the end of its third ordinary session, and the remaining third at the end of its fourth ordinary session.*

(b) *The rules governing the procedure whereby the Committee shall fill vacancies, the order in which terms of membership expire, eligibility for re-election, and election procedures, shall be based upon a balancing of the needs for continuity of membership and rotation of representation, as well as the considerations set out in Article XI (3).*

and expresses the wish that the United Nations Educational, Scientific and Cultural Organisation provide its Secretariat.

Expresses the wish that the United Nations Educational, Scientific and Cultural Organization provide its Secretariat.

* * *

Protocol 1 annexed to the Universal Copyright Convention concerning the application of that Convention to the works of Stateless Persons and Refugees

The States parties hereto, being also parties to the Universal Copyright Convention (hereinafter referred to as the "Convention") have accepted the following provisions:

1. Stateless persons and refugees who have their habitual residence in a State party to this Protocol shall, for the purposes of the Convention, be assimilated to the nationals of that State.

2.—(a) This Protocol shall be signed and shall be subject to ratifica-

Protocol 1 annexed to the Universal C–78 Copyright Convention as Revised at Paris on 24 July 1971 concerning the Application of that Convention to works of Stateless Persons and Refugees

The States party hereto, being also party to the Universal Copyright Convention *as revised at Paris on 24 July 1971* (hereinafter *called* "the *1971* Convention"),

Have accepted the following provisions:

1. Stateless persons and refugees who have their habitual residence in a State party to this Protocol shall, for the purposes of the *1971* Convention, be assimilated to the nationals of that State.

2. (a) This Protocol shall be signed and be subject to ratification or

Geneva

Paris

tion or acceptance, or may be acceded to, as if the provisions of Article VIII of the Convention applied hereto.

(b) This Protocol shall enter into force in respect of each State on the date of deposit of the instrument of ratification, acceptance or accession of the State concerned or on the date of entry into force of the Convention with respect to such State, whichever is the later.

acceptance, or may be acceded to, as if the provisions of Article VIII of the *1971* Convention applied hereto.

(b) This Protocol shall enter into force in respect of each State, on the date of deposit of the instrument of ratification, acceptance or accession of the State concerned or on the date of entry into force of the *1971* Convention with respect to such State, whichever is the later.

(c) *On the entry into force of this Protocol in respect of a State not party to Protocol 1 annexed to the 1952 Convention, the latter Protocol shall be deemed to enter into force in respect of such State.*

*   *   *

C–79 **Protocol 2 annexed to the Universal Copyright Convention, concerning the application of that Convention to the works of certain International Organisations**

The State parties hereto, being also parties to the Universal Copyright Convention (hereinafter referred to as the "Convention"),

Have accepted the following provisions:

1.—(a) The protection provided for in Article II (1) of the Convention shall apply to works published for the first time by the United Nations, by the Specialised Agencies in relationship therewith, or by the Organisation of American States;

(b) Similarly, Article II (2) of the Convention shall apply to the said organisation or agencies.

2.—(a) This Protocol shall be signed and shall be subject to ratification or acceptance, or may be acceded to, as if the provisions of Article VIII of the Convention applied hereto.

Protocol 2 annexed to the Universal Copyright Convention as revised at Paris on 24 July 1971 concerning the application of that Convention to the works of certain International Organizations

The State party hereto, being also party to the Universal Copyright Convention *as revised at Paris on 24 July 1971* (hereinafter *called* "the *1971* Convention"),

Have accepted the following provisions:

1. (a) The protection provided for in Article II (1) of the *1971* Convention shall apply to works published for the first time by the United Nations, by the Specialized Agencies in relationship therewith, or by the Organization of American States;

(b) Similarly, Article II (2) of the *1971* Convention shall apply to the said organization or agencies.

2. (a) This Protocol shall be signed and shall be subject to ratification or acceptance, or may be acceded to, as if the provisions of Article VIII of the *1971* Convention applied hereto.

Geneva	Paris

(*b*) This Protocol shall enter into force for each State on the date of deposit of the instrument of ratification, acceptance or accession of the State concerned or on the date of entry into force of the Convention with respect to such State, whichever is the later.

(*b*) This Protocol shall enter into force for each State on the date of deposit of the instrument of ratification, acceptance or accession of the State concerned or on the date of entry into force of the *1971* Convention with respect to such State, whichever is the later.

*   *   *

Protocol 3 annexed to the Universal Copyright Convention concerning the effective date of Instruments of Ratification or Acceptance of or Accession to that Convention

States parties hereto,

Recognising that the application of the Universal Copyright Convention (hereinafter referred to as the "Convention") to States participating in all the international copyright systems already in force will contribute greatly to the value of the Convention.

Have agreed as follows:

1. Any State party hereto may, on depositing its instrument of ratification or acceptance of or accession to the Convention, notify the Director-General of the United Nations Educational, Scientific and Cultural Organisation (hereinafter referred to as "Director-General") that that instrument shall not take effect for the purposes of Article IX of the Convention until any other State named in such notification shall have deposited its instrument.

2. The notification referred to in paragraph 1 above shall accompany the instrument to which it relates.

3. The Director-General shall inform all States signatory or which have then acceded to the Convention of any notifications received in accordance with this Protocol.

4. This Protocol shall bear the same date and shall remain open for signature for the same period as the Convention.

5. It shall be subject to ratification or acceptance by the signatory States. Any

State which has not signed this Protocol may accede thereto.

6.—(a) *Ratification or acceptance or accession shall be effected by the deposit of an instrument to that effect with the Director-General.*

(b) *This Protocol shall enter into force on the date of deposit of not less than four instruments of ratification or acceptance or accession. The Director-General shall inform all interested States of this date. Instruments deposited after such date shall take effect on the date of their deposit.*

*   *   *

C–81 **EUROPEAN AGREEMENT ON THE PROTECTION OF TELEVISION BROADCASTS[5]**

Strasbourg, June 22, 1960

The Governments signatory hereto, being Members of the Council of Europe,

Considering that the object of the Council is to achieve a greater unity between its Members;

Considering that exchanges of television programmes between the countries of Europe are calculated to further the achievement of that object;

Considering that these exchanges are hampered by the fact that the majority of television organisations are at present powerless to restrain the re-broadcasting, fixation or public performance of their broadcasts, whereas the organisers of musical or dramatic performances or the like, and the promoters of sports meetings, make their consent to broadcasting to other countries conditional upon an undertaking that the relays will not be used for purposes other than private viewing;

Considering that the international protection of television broadcasts will in no way affect any rights of third parties in these broadcasts;

Considering that the problem is one of some urgency, in view of the installations and links now being brought into service throughout Europe, which are such as to make it easy from the technical point of view for European television organisations to exchange their programmes;

Considering that, pending the conclusion of a potentially universal Convention on "neighbouring rights" at present in contemplation, it is fitting to conclude a regional Agreement restricted in scope to television broadcasts and of limited duration.

Have agreed as follows:

ARTICLE 1

C–82 Broadcasting organisations constituted in the territory and under the laws of a Party to this Agreement or transmitting from such territory shall enjoy, in respect of all their television broadcasts:

1. in the territory of all Parties to this Agreement, the right to authorise or prohibit:

---

[5] Cmnd. 1508. Ratified by the United Kingdom on March 9, 1961, and came into force on July 1, 1961.

(a) the re-broadcasting of such broadcasts;

(b) the diffusion of such broadcasts to the public by wire;

(c) the communication of such broadcasts to the public by means of any instrument for the transmission of signs, sounds or images;

(d) any fixation of such broadcasts or still photographs thereof, and any reproduction of such a fixation; and

(e) re-broadcasting, wire diffusion or public performance with the aid of the fixations or reproductions referred to in sub-paragraph (d) of this paragraph, except where the organisation in which the right vests has authorised the sale of the said fixations or reproductions to the public;

2. in the territory of any other Party to this Agreement, the same protection as that other Party may extend to organisations constituted in its territory and under its laws or transmitting from its territory, where such protection is greater than that provided for in paragraph 1 above.

ARTICLE 2

1. Subject to paragraph 2 of Article 1, and Articles 13 and 14, the protection **C–83** provided for in paragraph 1 of Article 1 shall continue until the end of the tenth calendar year following the year in which the first broadcast was made from the territory of a Party to this Agreement.

2. No Party to this Agreement shall be required, in pursuance of paragraph 2 of Article 1, to accord to the broadcasts of any broadcasting organisations constituted in the territory and under the laws of another Party to this Agreement or transmitting from the territory of another Party longer protection than that granted by the said other Party.

ARTICLE 3

1. Parties to this Agreement, by making a declaration as provided in Article 10, **C–84** and in respect of their own territory, may:

(a) withhold the protection provided for in sub-paragraph 1(b) of Article 1;

(b) withhold the protection provided for in sub-paragraph 1(c) of Article 1, where the communication is not to a paying audience within the meaning of their domestic law;

(c) withhold the protection provided for in sub-paragraph 1(d) of Article 1, where the fixation or reproduction of the fixation is made for private use, or solely for educational purposes;

(d) withhold the protection provided for in sub-paragraphs 1(d) and (e) of Article 1, in respect of still photographs or reproductions of such photographs;

(e) withhold the protection provided for in this Agreement from television broadcasts by broadcasting organisations constituted in their territory and under their laws or transmitting from such territory, where such broadcasts enjoy protection under their domestic law;

(f) restrict the operation of this Agreement to broadcasting organisations constituted in the territory and under the laws of a Party to this Agreement and also transmitting from the territory of such party.

2. It shall be open to the aforesaid Parties, in respect of their own territory, to provide exceptions to the protection of television broadcasts:

(a) for the purpose of reporting current events, in respect of the re-broadcasting, fixation or reproduction of the fixation, wire diffusion or public performance of short extracts from a broadcast which itself constitutes the whole or part of the event in question;

(b) in respect of the making of ephemeral fixations of television broadcasts by a broadcasting organisation by means of its own facilities and for its own broadcasts.

3. The aforesaid Parties may, in respect of their own territory, provide for a body with jurisdiction over cases where the right of communication to the public referred to in sub-paragraph 1(*c*) of Article 1 has been unreasonably refused, or granted on unreasonable terms, by the broadcasting organisation in which the said right vests.

ARTICLE 4

C–85   1. Fixations of a broadcast in which protection under this Agreement subsists, or still photographs thereof, as well as reproductions of such photographs, made in a territory to which this Agreement does not apply and imported into the territory of a Party to this Agreement where they would be unlawful without the consent of the broadcasting organisation in which the right vests, shall be liable to seizure in the latter territory.

2. The provisions of the last preceding paragraph shall apply to the importation into the territory of a Party to this Agreement of still photographs of a broadcast in which protection under this Agreement subsists and of reproductions of such photographs, where such photographs or reproductions are made in the territory of another Party to this Agreement by virtue of sub-paragraph 1(*d*) of Article 3.

3. Seizure shall be effected in accordance with the domestic law of each Party to this Agreement.

4. No Party to this Agreement shall be required to provide protection in respect of still photographs, or the reproduction of such photographs, of broadcasts made by a broadcasting organisation constituted in the territory and under the laws of another Party to this Agreement or transmitting from such territory, if the said other Party has availed itself of the reservation provided for in sub-paragraph 1(*d*) of Article 3.

ARTICLE 5

C–86   The protection afforded by this Agreement shall apply both in relation to the visual element and in relation to the sound element of a television broadcast. It shall not affect the sound element when broadcast separately.

ARTICLE 6

C–87   1. The protection provided for in Article 1 shall not affect any rights in respect of a television broadcast that may accrue to third parties, such as authors, performers, film makers, manufacturers of phonographic records or organisers of entertainments.

2. It shall likewise be without prejudice to any protection of television broadcasts that may be accorded apart from this Agreement.

ARTICLE 7

C–88   1. This Agreement shall be open to signature by the Members of the Council of Europe, who may become Parties to it either by
(*a*) signature without reservation in respect of ratification; or
(*b*) signature with reservation in respect of ratification, followed by the deposit of an instrument of ratification.

2. Instruments of ratification shall be deposited with the Secretary-General of the Council of Europe.

ARTICLE 8

C–89   1. This Agreement shall enter into force one month after the date on which three Members of the Council of Europe shall, in accordance with Article 7 thereof, have signed it without reservation in respect of ratification or shall have ratified it.

2. In the case of any Member of the Council of Europe who shall subsequently sign the Agreement without reservation in respect of ratification or who shall ratify it, the Agreement shall enter into force one month after the date of such signature or deposit of the instrument of ratification.

ARTICLE 9

1. After this Agreement has come into force, any European Government which **C–90** is not a Member of the Council of Europe or any non-European Government having political ties with a Member of the Council of Europe may accede to it, subject to the prior approval of the Committee of Ministers of the Council of Europe.

2. Such accession shall be effected by the deposit of an instrument of accession with the Secretary-General of the Council of Europe and shall take effect one month after the date of deposit.

ARTICLE 10

Signature, ratification or accession shall imply full acceptance of all the pro- **C–91** visions of this Agreement; provided always that any country may declare,[6] at the time of signature or of deposit of its instrument of ratification or accession, that it intends to avail itself of one or more of the options in paragraph 1 of Article 3 above.

ARTICLE 11

The Secretary-General of the Council of Europe shall notify Members of the **C–92** Council, the Governments of any countries which may have acceded to this Agreement and the Director of the Bureau of the International Union for the Protection of Literary and Artistic Works:

(a) of any signatures, together with any reservations as to ratification, of the deposit of instruments of ratification and of the date of entry into force of this Agreement;

(b) of the deposit of any instruments of accession in accordance with Article 9;

---

[6] The instrument of ratification deposited with the Secretary-General of the Council of Europe by the Permanent Representative of the United Kingdom contains the following reservations:

"(1) The Government of the United Kingdom of Great Britain and Northern Ireland withhold the protection provided for in sub-paragraph (b) of paragraph 1 of Article 1 of the said Agreement;

"(2) The Government of the United Kingdom of Great Britain and Northern Ireland withhold the protection provided for in sub-paragraph (c) of paragraph 1 of Article 1 of the said Agreement, where the communication is not to a paying audience within the meaning of the domestic law of the United Kingdom of Great Britain and Northern Ireland;

"(3) The Government of the United Kingdom of Great Britain and Northern Ireland withhold the protection provided for in sub-paragraph (d) of paragraph 1 of Article 1 of the said Agreement, where the fixation or reproduction of the fixation is made for private use or solely for educational purposes;

"(4) The Government of the United Kingdom of Great Britain and Northern Ireland withhold the protection provided for in sub-paragraphs (d) and (e) of paragraph 1 of Article 1 of the said Agreement, in respect of still photographs or reproductions of such photographs;

"(5) The Government of the United Kingdom of Great Britain and Northern Ireland restrict the operation of the said Agreement to broadcasting organisations constituted in the territory and under the laws of a Party to the said Agreement and also transmitting from the territory of such Party."

    (c) of any declaration or notification received in accordance with Articles 12, 13 or 14;

    (d) of any decision of the Committee of Ministers taken in pursuance of paragraph 2 of Article 12.

ARTICLE 12

C–93   1. This Agreement shall apply to the metropolitan territories of the Parties.

    2. Any Party may, at the time of signature, of the deposit of its instrument of ratification or accession, or at any later date, declare by notice addressed to the Secretary-General of the Council of Europe that this Agreement shall extend to any or all of the territories for whose international relations it is responsible.

    3. Any Government which has made a declaration under paragraph 2 of this Article extending this Agreement to any territory for whose international relations it is responsible may denounce the Agreement separately in respect of that territory in accordance with Article 14 thereof.

ARTICLE 13

C–94   1. This Agreement shall cease to be effective, except in regard to fixations already made, at such time as a Convention on "neighbouring rights", including the protection of television broadcasts and open to European countries, amongst others, shall have entered into force for at least a majority of the Members of the Council of Europe that are themselves Parties to the Agreement.

    2. The Committee of Ministers of the Council of Europe shall at the appropriate time declare that the conditions laid down in the preceding paragraph have been fulfilled, thereby entailing the termination of this Agreement.

ARTICLE 14

C–95   Any Contracting Party may denounce this Agreement by giving one year's notice to that effect to the Secretary-General of the Council of Europe.

    In witness whereof, the undersigned,[7] being duly authorised thereto, have signed this Agreement.

    Done at Strasbourg, this 22nd day of June, 1960, in English and French, both texts being equally authoritative, in a single copy, which shall remain in the archives of the Council of Europe and of which the Secretary-General shall send certified copies to each of the signatory and acceding Governments and to the Director of the Bureau of the International Union for the Protection of Literary and Artistic Works.

* * *

C–96 **PROTOCOL TO THE EUROPEAN AGREEMENT ON THE PROTECTION OF TELEVISION BROADCASTS**[8]

Strasbourg, January 22, 1965

The member States of the Council of Europe, signatory hereto.

Considering the desirability of amending the European Agreement on the Pro-

---

[7] At the time of signature by the United Kingdom, the following declaration was made: "Her Majesty's Government understand the word 'signature' in the first line of Article 10 to refer only to signature without reservation as to ratification."

[8] Cmnd. 2744. Signed without reservation in respect of ratification by the United Kingdom on February 23, 1965, and entered into force on March 24, 1965.

tection of Television Broadcasts, signed at Strasbourg on 22nd June 1960,[9] hereinafter referred to as "the Agreement";

Considering that the International Convention for the Protection of Performers, Producers of Phonograms and Broadcasting Organisations, signed in Rome on 26th October 1961, entered into force on 18th May 1964,[10]

Have agreed as follows:

ARTICLE 1

1. Paragraph 1 of Article 2 of the Agreement shall be amended as follows: **C–97**

"Subject to paragraph 2 of Article 1, and Articles 13 and 14, the protection provided for in paragraph 1 of Article 1 shall last not less than a period of twenty years from the end of the year in which the broadcast took place."

2. Paragraph 2 of Article 2 of the Agreement shall be deleted.

ARTICLE 2

1. Sub-paragraph 1(*a*) of Article 3 of the Agreement shall be amended as fol- **C–98** lows:

"(*a*) withhold the protection provided for in sub-paragraph 1(*b*) of Article 1 as regards broadcasting organisations constituted in their territory or transmitting from such territory, and restrict the exercise of such protection, as regards broadcasts by broadcasting organisations constituted in the territory of another Party to this Agreement or transmitting from such territory, to a percentage of the transmissions by such organisations, which shall not be less than 50% of the average weekly duration of the broadcasts of each of these organisations."

2. Sub-paragraph 1(*e*) of Article 3 of the Agreement shall be amended as follows:

"(*e*) without prejudice to sub-paragraph 1(*a*) of this Article, withhold all protection provided for in this Agreement from television broadcasts by broadcasting organisations constituted in their territory and under their laws or transmitting from such territory, where such broadcasts enjoy protection under their domestic law."

3. Paragraph 3 of Article 3 of the Agreement shall be amended as follows:

"3. The aforesaid Parties may, in respect of their own territory, provide for a body with jurisdiction over cases where the right of diffusion to the public by wire referred to in sub-paragraph 1(*b*) of Article 1, or the right of communication to the public referred to in sub-paragraph 1(*c*) of Article 1, has been unreasonably refused or granted on unreasonable terms by the broadcasting organisation in which the said right vests."

4. Any State which in accordance with Article 10 of the Agreement has, before the entry into force of this Protocol, availed itself of the option in sub-paragraph 1(*a*) of Article 3 of the Agreement may, notwithstanding anything in paragraph 1 of the present Article, maintain the application of such option.

---

[9] § C–81, *ante.*
[10] § C–121, *post.*

ARTICLE 3

C–99   Article 13 of the Agreement shall be deleted and replaced by the following:

"1. This Agreement shall remain in force indefinitely.

2. Nevertheless, as from 1st January 1975, no State may remain or become a Party to this Agreement unless it is also a Party to the International Convention for the Protection of Performers, Producers of Phonograms and Broadcasting Organisations signed in Rome on 26th October 1961."

ARTICLE 4

C–100   1. The Governments signatory to the Agreement and the Governments having acceded thereto may become Parties to this Protocol by the procedure laid down in Article 7 or Article 9 of the Agreement, according to whether they are member States of the Council of Europe or not.

2. This Protocol shall enter into force one month after the date on which all the Parties to the Agreement have signed this Protocol without reservation in respect of ratification, or deposited their instrument of ratification or accession in accordance with the provisions of the preceding paragraph.

3. As from the date on which this Protocol enters into force, no State may become a Party to the Agreement without becoming also a Party to this Protocol.

ARTICLE 5

C–101   The Secretary-General of the Council of Europe shall notify member States of the Council, other States Parties to the Agreement, and the Director of the Bureau of the International Union for the Protection of Literary and Artistic Works of any signature of this Protocol, together with any reservations as to ratification, and of the deposit of any instrument of ratification of the Protocol or of accession to it, and of the date referred to in paragraph 2 of Article 4 of this Protocol.

In witness whereof the undersigned, being duly authorised thereto have signed this Protocol.

Done at Strasbourg, this 22nd day of January 1965 in English and in French, both texts being equally authoritative, in a single copy which shall remain deposited in the archives of the Council of Europe. The Secretary-General of the Council of Europe shall transmit certified copies to each of the signatory and acceding states.

* * *

C–102   **ADDITIONAL PROTOCOL TO THE PROTOCOL TO THE EUROPEAN AGREEMENT ON THE PROTECTION OF TELEVISION BROADCASTS**[11]

Strasbourg, January 14, 1974

The member States of the Council of Europe, signatory hereto,

Considering the desirability of extending the duration of the European Agreement on the Protection of Television Broadcasts and the Protocol to this Agreement for the benefit of States which are not yet Parties to the International Convention for the Protection of Performers, Producers of Phonograms and Broadcasting Organisations, signed in Rome on 26 October 1961,[10]

Have agreed as follows:

---

[11] Cmnd. 5954. Signed by the United Kingdom without reservation in respect of ratification on March 15, 1974, and entered into force on December 31, 1974.

ARTICLE 1

Paragraph 2 of Article 3 of the Protocol to the Agreement is substituted by the **C–103** following:

"2. Nevertheless, as from 1 January 1985, no State may remain or become a Party to this Agreement unless it is also a Party to the International Convention for the Protection of Performers, Producers of Phonograms and Broadcasting Organisations, signed in Rome on 26 October 1961."

ARTICLE 2

1. The States signatory to the Agreement and the Protocol thereto may become **C–104** Parties to this Additional Protocol in accordance with the procedure laid down in Article 7 of the Agreement.

2. The States having acceded to the Agreement and to the Protocol may become Parties to this Additional Protocol by the deposit of an instrument of accession with the Secretary General of the Council of Europe.

ARTICLE 3

1. This Additional Protocol shall enter into force one month after the date on **C–105** which all the Parties to the Agreement and the Protocol have signed this Additional Protocol without reservation in respect of ratification, or have deposited their instrument of ratification or accession in conformity with the provisions of Article 2.

2. After the date of entry into force of this Additional Protocol, no State may become a Party to the Agreement and the Protocol without becoming also a Party to this Additional Protocol.

ARTICLE 4

The Secretary General of the Council of Europe shall notify member States of **C–106** the Council, other Contracting Parties to the Agreement and the Director General of the World Intellectual Property Organisation of any signature of this Additional Protocol, together with any reservations as to ratification, and of the deposit of any instrument of ratification of the Additional Protocol or of accession to it, and of the date referred to in paragraph 1 of Article 3 of this Additional Protocol.

In witness whereof the undersigned, being duly authorised thereto, have signed this Additional Protocol.

Done at Strasbourg, this 14th day of January 1974, in the English and French languages, both texts being equally authoritative, in a single copy which shall remain deposited in the archives of the Council of Europe. The Secretary General of the Council of Europe shall transmit certified copies to each of the signatory and acceding States.

* * *

ADDITIONAL PROTOCOL TO THE PROTOCOL TO THE EUROPEAN **C–107** AGREEMENT ON THE PROTECTION OF TELEVISION BROADCASTS[12]

Strasbourg, March 21, 1983

The member States of the Council of Europe, signatory hereto,
Having regard to the European Agreement on the protection of television

---

[12] Cmnd. 9459. Signed by the United Kingdom on July 4, 1983 and entered into force on January 1, 1985.

broadcasts of 22 June 1960, hereinafter called "the Agreement", as modified by the Protocol of 22 January 1965 and the Additional Protocol of 14 January 1974;

Having regard to the fact that the date given in Article 13, paragraph 2, of the Agreement was extended by the said Additional Protocol of 14 January 1974;

Considering the desirability of further extending this date for the benefit of States which are not yet Parties to the International Convention for the Protection of Performers, Producers of Phonograms and Broadcasting Organisations, signed in Rome on 26 October 1961,

Have agreed as follows:

ARTICLE 1

Paragraph 2 of Article 13 of the Agreement, as last modified by Article 1 of the Additional Protocol of 14 January 1974, is replaced by the following text:

"2. Nevertheless, as from 1 January 1990, no State may remain or become a Party to this Agreement unless it is also a Party to the International Convention for the Protection of Performers, Producers of Phonograms and Broadcasting Organisations signed in Rome on 26 October 1961."

ARTICLE 2

1. This Additional Protocol shall be open for signature by member States of the Council of Europe which have signed or acceded to the Agreement, which may become Parties to this Additional Protocol by:

(*a*) signature without reservation as to ratification, acceptance or approval, or
(*b*) signature subject to ratification, acceptance or approval, followed by ratification, acceptance or approval.

2. Any State not a member of the Council which has acceded to the Agreement may also accede to this Additional Protocol.

3. Instruments of ratification, acceptance, approval or accession shall be deposited with the Secretary General of the Council of Europe.

ARTICLE 3

This Additional Protocol shall enter into force on the first day of the month following the date on which all the Parties to the Agreement have become Parties to this Additional Protocol in accordance with provisions of Article 2.

ARTICLE 4

From the date of entry into force of this Additional Protocol, no State may become a Party to the Agreement without at the same time becoming a Party to this Additional Protocol.

ARTICLE 5

The Secretary General of the Council of Europe shall notify the member States of the Council of Europe, any State which has acceded to the Agreement and the Director General of the World Intellectual Property Organisation of:

(*a*) any signature of this Additional Protocol;
(*b*) the deposit of any instrument of ratification, acceptance, approval or accession;
(*c*) the date of entry into force of this Additional Protocol, in accordance with Article 3.

In witness whereof the undersigned, being duly authorised thereto, have signed this Additional Protocol.

Done at Strasbourg, this 21st day of March 1983, in English and French, both texts being equally authentic, in a single copy which shall be deposited in the archives of the Council of Europe. The Secretary General of the Council of Europe shall transmit certified copies to each member State of the Council of Europe, to any State invited to accede to the Agreement and to the Director General of the World Intellectual Property Organisation.

*   *   *

EUROPEAN AGREEMENT CONCERNING PROGRAMME EXCHANGES BY MEANS OF TELEVISION FILMS[13]   C–108

Paris, December 15, 1958

The Governments signatory hereto, being Members of the Council of Europe.

Considering that the aim of the Council of Europe is to achieve a greater unity between its Members;

Considering that it is important in the interests of European cultural and economic unity that programmes may be exchanged by means of television films between the member countries of the Council of Europe as freely as possible; .

Considering that national legislations allow different conclusions as regards the legal nature of television films and as regards the rights which they grant in respect of such films;

Considering that it is necessary to resolve the difficulties arising from this situation;

Having regard to Article 20 of the Berne Convention for the Protection of Literary and Artistic Works, by the terms of which the Governments of the countries of the Union reserve to themselves the right to enter into special arrangements which do not embody stipulations contrary to that Convention.

Have agreed as follows:

ARTICLE 1

In the absence of any contrary or special stipulation within the meaning of **C–109** Article 4 of the present Agreement, a broadcasting organisation under the jurisdiction of a country which is a Party to this Agreement has the right to authorise in the other countries which are Parties thereto the exploitation for television of television films of which it is the maker.

ARTICLE 2

1. All visual or sound and visual recordings intended for television shall be **C–110** deemed to be television films within the meaning of the present Agreement.

2. A broadcasting organisation shall be deemed to be the maker if it has taken the initiative in, and responsibility for, the making of a television film.

ARTICLE 3

1. If the television film has been made by a maker other than the one defined in **C–111** Article 2, paragraph 2, the latter is entitled, in the absence of contrary or special stipulations within the meaning of Article 4, to transfer to a broadcasting organisation the right provided in Article 1.

---

[13] Cmnd. 1509. Signed by the United Kingdom without reservation in respect of ratification on December 15, 1958, and entered into force on July 1, 1961.

2. The provision contained in the preceding paragraph applies only if the maker and the broadcasting organisation are under the jurisdiction of countries which are Parties to the present Agreement.

ARTICLE 4

C–112 By "contrary or special stipulation" is meant any restrictive condition agreed between the maker and persons who contribute to the making of the television film.

ARTICLE 5

C–113 This Agreement shall not affect the following rights, which shall be entirely reserved:

(*a*) any moral right recognised in relation to films;
(*b*) the copyright in literary, dramatic or artistic works from which the television film is derived;
(*c*) the copyright in a musical work, with or without words, accompanying a television film;
(*d*) the copyright in films other than television films;
(*e*) the copyright in the exploitation of television films otherwise than on television.

ARTICLE 6

C–114 1. This Agreement shall be open to signature by the Members of the Council of Europe, who may accede to it either by:

(*a*) signature without reservation in respect of ratification; or
(*b*) signature with reservation in respect of ratification, followed by the deposit of an instrument of ratification.

2. Instruments of ratification shall be deposited with the Secretary-General of the Council of Europe.

ARTICLE 7

C–115 1. This Agreement shall enter into force thirty days after the date on which three Members of the Council shall, in accordance with Article 6 thereof, have signed it without reservation in respect of ratification or shall have ratified it.

2. In the case of any Member of the Council who shall subsequently sign the Agreement without reservation in respect of ratification or who shall ratify it, the Agreement shall enter into force thirty days after the date of such signature or deposit of the instrument of ratification.

ARTICLE 8

C–116 1. After this Agreement has come into force, any country which is not a Member of the Council of Europe may accede to it, subject to the prior approval of the Committee of Ministers of the Council of Europe.

2. Such accession shall be effected by the deposit of an instrument of accession with the Secretary-General of the Council of Europe, and shall take effect thirty days after the date of deposit.

ARTICLE 9

C–117 Signature without reservation in respect of ratification, ratification or accession shall imply full acceptance of all the provisions of this Agreement.

ARTICLE 10

The Secretary-General of the Council of Europe shall notify Members of the **C–118** Council, the Governments of any countries which may have acceded to this Agreement and the Director of the Bureau of the International Union for the protection of literary and artistic works:

(a) of the date of entry into force of this Agreement and the names of any Members of the Council which have become Parties thereto;

(b) of the deposit of any instruments of accession in accordance with Article 8 of the present Agreement;

(c) of any declaration or notification received in accordance with Articles 11 and 12 thereof.

ARTICLE 11

1. This Agreement shall apply to the metropolitan territories of the Contracting **C–119** Parties.

2. Any Contracting Party may, at the time of signature, ratification or accession, or at any later date, declare by notice addressed to the Secretary-General of the Council of Europe that this Agreement shall apply to any territory or territories mentioned in the said declaration and for whose international relations it is responsible.

3. Any declaration made in accordance with the preceding paragraph may, in respect of any territory mentioned in such a declaration, be withdrawn under the conditions laid down in Article 12 of this Agreement.

ARTICLE 12

1. This Agreement shall remain in force for an unlimited period. **C–120**

2. Any Contracting Party may denounce this Agreement at one year's notice by notification to this effect to the Secretary-General of the Council of Europe.

In witness whereof, the undersigned, being duly authorised thereto, have signed this Agreement.

Done at Paris, this 15th day of December 1958, in English and French, both texts being equally authoritative, in a single copy, which shall remain in the archives of the Council of Europe and of which the Secretary-General shall send certified copies to each of the signatory and acceding Governments and to the Director of the International Bureau for the Protection of Literary and Artistic Works.

* * *

INTERNATIONAL CONVENTION FOR THE PROTECTION OF **C–121** PERFORMERS, PRODUCERS OF PHONOGRAMS AND BROADCASTING ORGANISATIONS[14]

Rome, October 26, 1961

The Contracting States, moved by the desire to protect the rights of performers, producers of phonograms, and broadcasting organisations,

Have agreed as follows:

---

[14] Cmnd. 2425. Ratified by the United Kingdom on October 30, 1963, and entered into force on May 18, 1964.

ARTICLE 1

C–122 Protection granted under this Convention shall leave intact and shall in no way affect the protection of copyright in literary and artistic works. Consequently, no provision of this Convention may be interpreted as prejudicing such protection.

ARTICLE 2

C–123 1. For the purposes of this Convention, national treatment shall mean the treatment accorded by the domestic law of the Contracting State in which protection is claimed:

(a) to performers who are its nationals, as regards performances taking place, broadcast, or first fixed, on its territory;

(b) to producers of phonograms who are its nationals, as regards phonograms first fixed or first published on its territory;

(c) to broadcasting organisations which have their headquarters on its territory, as regards broadcasts transmitted from transmitters situated on its territory.

2. National treatment shall be subject to the protection specifically guaranteed, and the limitations specifically provided for, in this Convention.

ARTICLE 3

C–124 For the purposes of this Convention:

(a) "Performers" means actors, singers, musicians, dancers, and other persons who act, sing, deliver, declaim, play in, or otherwise perform literary or artistic works;

(b) "Phonogram" means any exclusively aural fixation of sounds of a performance or of other sounds;

(c) "Producer of phonograms" means the person who, or the legal entity which, first fixes the sounds of a performance or other sounds;

(d) "Publication" means the offering of copies of a phonogram to the public in reasonable quantity;

(e) "Reproduction" means the making of a copy or copies of a fixation;

(f) "Broadcasting" means the transmission by wireless means for public reception of sounds or of images and sounds;

(g) "Rebroadcasting" means the simultaneous broadcasting by one broadcasting organisation of the broadcast of another broadcasting organisation.

ARTICLE 4

C–125 Each Contracting State shall grant national treatment to performers if any of the following conditions is met:

(a) the performance takes place in another Contracting State;

(b) the performance is incorporated in a phonogram which is protected under Article 5 of this Convention;

(c) the performance, not being fixed on a phonogram, is carried by a broadcast which is protected by Article 6 of this Convention.

ARTICLE 5

C–126 1. Each Contracting State shall grant national treatment to producers of phonograms if any of the following conditions is met:

(a) the producer of the phonogram is a national of another Contracting State (criterion of nationality);

(b) the first fixation of the sound was made in another Contracting State (criterion of fixation);

(*c*) the phonogram was first published in another Contracting State (criterion of publication).

2. If a phonogram was first published in a non-contracting State but if it was also published, within thirty days of its first publication, in a Contracting State (simultaneous publication), it shall be considered as first published in the Contracting State.

3. By means of a notification deposited with the Secretary-General of the United Nations, any Contracting State may declare that it will not apply the criterion of publication or, alternatively, the criterion of fixation. Such notification may be deposited at the time of ratification, acceptance or accession, or at any time thereafter; in the last case, it shall become effective six months after it has been deposited.

ARTICLE 6

1. Each Contracting State shall grant national treatment to broadcasting organ-   **C–127**
isations if either of the following conditions is met:
(*a*) the headquarters of the broadcasting organisation is situated in another Contracting State;
(*b*) the broadcast was transmitted from a transmitter situated in another Contracting State.

2. By means of a notification deposited with the Secretary-General of the United Nations, any Contracting State may declare that it will protect broadcasts only if the headquarters of the broadcasting organisation is situated in another Contracting State and the broadcast was transmitted from a transmitter situated in the same Contracting State. Such notification may be deposited at the time of ratification, acceptance or accession, or at any time thereafter; in the last case, it shall become effective six months after it has been deposited.

ARTICLE 7

1. The protection provided for performers by this Convention shall include the   **C–128**
possibility of preventing:
(*a*) the broadcasting and the communication to the public, without their consent, of their performance, except where the performance used in the broadcasting or the public communication is itself already a broadcast performance or is made from a fixation;
(*b*) the fixation, without their consent, of their unfixed performance;
(*c*) the reproduction, without their consent, of a fixation of their performance:
  (i) if the original fixation itself was made without their consent;
  (ii) if the reproduction is made for purposes different from those for which the performers gave their consent;
  (iii) if the original fixation was made in accordance with the provisions of Article 15, and the reproduction is made for purposes different from those referred to in those provisions.

2.—(1) If broadcasting was consented to by the performers, it shall be a matter for the domestic law of the Contracting State where protection is claimed to regulate the protection against rebroadcasting, fixation for broadcasting purposes, and the reproduction of such fixation for broadcasting purposes.

(2) The terms and conditions governing the use by broadcasting organisations of fixations made for broadcasting purposes shall be determined in accordance with the domestic law of the Contracting State where protection is claimed.

(3) However, the domestic law referred to in sub-paragraphs (1) and (2) of this paragraph shall not operate to deprive performers of the ability to control, by contract, their relations with broadcasting organisations.

ARTICLE 8

C–129   Any Contracting State may, by its domestic laws and regulations, specify the manner in which performers will be represented in connexion with the exercise of their rights if several of them participate in the same performance.

ARTICLE 9

C–130   Any Contracting State may, by its domestic laws and regulations, extend the protection provided for in this Convention to artistes who do not perform literary or artistic works.

ARTICLE 10

C–131   Producers of phonograms shall enjoy the right to authorise or prohibit the direct or indirect reproduction of their phonograms.

ARTICLE 11

C–132   If, as a condition of protecting the rights of producers of phonograms, or of performers, or both, in relation to phonograms, a Contracting State, under its domestic law, requires compliance with formalities, these shall be considered as fulfilled if all the copies in commerce of the published phonogram or their containers bear a notice consisting of the symbol Ⓟ, accompanied by the year date of the first publication, placed in such a manner as to give reasonable notice of claim of protection; and if the copies or their containers do not identify the producer or the licensee of the producer (by carrying his name, trade mark or other appropriate designation), the notice shall also include the name of the owner of the rights of the producer; and, furthermore, if the copies or their containers do not identify the principal performers, the notice shall also include the name of the person who, in the country in which the fixation was effected, owns the rights of such performers.

ARTICLE 12

C–133   If a phonogram published for commercial purposes, or a reproduction of such phonogram, is used directly for broadcasting or for any communication to the public, a single equitable remuneration shall be paid by the user to the performers, or to the producers of the phonograms, or to both. Domestic law may, in the absence of agreement between these parties, lay down the conditions as to the sharing of this remuneration.

ARTICLE 13

C–134   Broadcasting organisations shall enjoy the right to authorise or prohibit:
(*a*) the rebroadcasting of their broadcasts;
(*b*) the fixation of their broadcasts;
(*c*) the reproduction:
(i) of fixations, made without their consent, of their broadcasts;
(ii) of fixations, made in accordance with the provisions of Article 15, of their broadcasts, if the reproduction is made for purposes different from those referred to in those provisions;
(*d*) the communication to the public of their television broadcasts if such communication is made in places accessible to the public against payment of an entrance fee; it shall be a matter for the domestic law of the State where protection of this right is claimed to determine the conditions under which it may be exercised.

ARTICLE 14

The term of protection to be granted under this Convention shall last at least   **C–135**
until the end of a period of twenty years computed from the end of the year in
which:

(*a*) the fixation was made—for phonograms and for performances incorporated
therein;

(*b*) the performance took place—for performances not incorporated in phonograms;

(*c*) the broadcast took place—for broadcasts.

ARTICLE 15

1. Any Contracting State may, in its domestic laws and regulations, provide for   **C–136**
exceptions to the protection guaranteed by this Convention as regards:

(*a*) private use;

(*b*) use of short excerpts in connexion with the reporting of current events;

(*c*) ephemeral fixation by a broadcasting organisation by means of its own facilities and for its own broadcasts;

(*d*) use solely for the purposes of teaching or scientific research.

2. Irrespective of paragraph 1 of this Article, any Contracting State may, in its
domestic laws and regulations, provide for the same kinds of limitations with
regard to the protection of performers, producers and phonograms and broadcasting organisations, as it provides for, in its domestic laws and regulations, in connexion with the protection of copyright in literary and artistic works. However,
compulsory licences may be provided for only to the extent to which they are compatible with this Convention.

ARTICLE 16

1. Any State, upon becoming party to this Convention, shall be bound by all the   **C–137**
obligations and shall enjoy all the benefits thereof. However a State may at any
time, in a notification deposited with the Secretary-General of the United Nations,
declare that:

(*a*) as regards Article 12:

(i) it will not apply the provisions of that Article;

(ii) it will not apply the provisions of that Article in respect of certain uses;

(iii) as regards phonograms the producer of which is not a national of another
Contracting State, it will not apply that Article;

(iv) as regards phonograms the producer of which is a national of another
Contracting State, it will limit the protection provided for by that Article
to the extent to which, and to the term for which, the latter State grants
protection to phonograms first fixed by a national of the State making the
declaration; however, the fact that the Contracting State of which the
producer is a national does not grant the protection to the same beneficiary or beneficiaries as the State making the declaration shall not be considered as a difference in the extent of the protection;

(*b*) as regards Article 13, it will not apply item (*d*) of that Article; if a Contracting
State makes such a declaration, the other Contracting States shall not be
obliged to grant the right referred to in Article 13, item (*d*), to broadcasting
organisations whose headquarters are in that State.

2. If the notification referred to in paragraph 1 of this Article is made after the
date of the deposit of the instrument of ratification, acceptance or accession, the
declaration will become effective six months after it has been deposited.

ARTICLE 17

C–138 Any State which, on October 26, 1961, grants protection to producers of phonograms solely on the basis of the criterion of fixation may, by a notification deposited with the Secretary-General of the United Nations at the time of ratification, acceptance or accession, declare that it will apply, for the purposes of Article 5, the criterion of fixation alone and, for the purposes of paragraph 1(*a*)(iii) and (iv) of Article 16, the criterion of fixation instead of the criterion of nationality.

ARTICLE 18

C–139 Any State which has deposited a notification under paragraph 3 of Article 5, paragraph 2 of Article 6, paragraph 1 of Article 16 or Article 17, may, by a further notification deposited with the Secretary-General of the United Nations, reduce its scope or withdraw it.

ARTICLE 19

C–140 Notwithstanding anything in this Convention, once a performer has consented to the incorporation of his performance in a visual or audio-visual fixation, Article 7 shall have no further application.

ARTICLE 20

C–141 1. This Convention shall not prejudice rights acquired in any Contracting State before the date of coming into force of this Convention for that State.

2. No Contracting State shall be bound to apply the provisions of this Convention to performances or broadcasts which took place, or to phonograms which were fixed, before the date of coming into force of this Convention for that State.

ARTICLE 21

C–142 The protection provided for in this Convention shall not prejudice any protection otherwise secured to performers, producers of phonograms and broadcasting organisations.

ARTICLE 22

C–143 Contracting States reserve the right to enter into special agreements among themselves in so far as such agreements grant to performers, producers of phonograms or broadcasting organisations more extensive rights than those granted by this Convention or contain other provisions not contrary to this Convention.

ARTICLE 23

C–144 This Convention shall be deposited with the Secretary-General of the United Nations. It shall be open until June 30, 1962 for signature by any State invited to the Diplomatic Conference on the International Protection of Performers, Producers of Phonograms and Broadcasting Organisations which is a party to the Universal Copyright Convention or a member of the International Union for the Protection of Literary and Artistic Works.

ARTICLE 24

C–145 1. This Convention shall be subject to ratification or acceptance by the signatory States.

2. This Convention shall be open for accession by any State invited to the Conference referred to in Article 23, and by any State Member of the United Nations, provided that in either case such State is a party to the Universal Copyright Convention or a member of the International Union for the Protection of Literary and Artistic Works.

3. Ratification, acceptance or accession shall be effected by the deposit of an instrument to that effect with the Secretary-General of the United Nations.

ARTICLE 25

1. This Convention shall come into force three months after the date of deposit of the sixth instrument of ratification, acceptance or accession.   **C–146**

2. Subsequently, this Convention shall come into force in respect of each State three months after the date of deposit of its instrument of ratification, acceptance or accession.

ARTICLE 26

1. Each Contracting State undertakes to adopt, in accordance with its Constitution, the measures necessary to ensure the application of this Convention.   **C–147**

2. At the time of deposit of its instrument of ratification, acceptance or accession, each State must be in a position under its domestic law to give effect to the terms of this Convention.

ARTICLE 27

1. Any State may, at the time of ratification, acceptance or accession, or at any time thereafter, declare by notification addressed to the Secretary-General of the United Nations that this Convention shall extend to all or any of the territories for whose international relations it is responsible, provided that the Universal Copyright Convention or the International Convention for the Protection of Literary and Artistic Works applies to the territory or territories concerned. This notification shall take effect three months after the date of its receipt.   **C–148**

2. The notifications referred to in paragraph 3 of Article 5, paragraph 2 of Article 6, paragraph 2 of Article 16 and Articles 17 and 18, may be extended to cover all or any of the territories referred to in paragraph 1 of this Article.

ARTICLE 28

1. Any Contracting State may denounce this Convention, on its own behalf, or on behalf of all or any of the territories referred to in Article 27.   **C–149**

2. The denunciation shall be effected by a notification addressed to the Secretary-General of the United Nations and shall take effect twelve months after the date of receipt of the notification.

3. The right of denunciation shall not be exercised by a Contracting State before the expiry of a period of five years from the date on which the Convention came into force with respect to that State.

4. A Contracting State shall cease to be a party to this Convention from that time when it is neither a party to the Universal Copyright Convention nor a member of the International Union for the Protection of Literary and Artistic Works.

5. This Convention shall cease to apply to any territory referred to in Article 27 from that time when neither the Universal Copyright Convention nor the International Convention for the Protection of Literary and Artistic Works applies to that territory.

ARTICLE 29

1. After this Convention has been in force for five years, any Contracting State may, by notification addressed to the Secretary-General of the United Nations, request that a conference be convened for the purpose of revising the Convention. The Secretary-General shall notify all Contracting States of this request. If, within a period of six months following the date of notification by the Secretary-General of the United Nations, not less than one half of the Contracting States notify him of   **C–150**

their concurrence with the request, the Secretary-General shall inform the Director-General of the International Labour Office, the Director-General of the United Nations Educational, Scientific and Cultural Organization and the Director of the Bureau of the International Union for the Protection of Literary and Artistic Works, who shall convene a revision conference in co-operation with the Intergovernmental Committee provided for in Article 32.

2. The adoption of any revision of this Convention shall require an affirmative vote by two-thirds of the States attending the revision conference, provided that this majority includes two-thirds of the States which, at the time of the revision conference, are parties to the Convention.

3. In the event of adoption of a Convention revising this Convention in whole or in part, and unless the revising Convention provides otherwise:

(a) this Convention shall cease to be open to ratification, acceptance or accession as from the date of entry into force of the revising Convention;

(b) this Convention shall remain in force as regards relations between or with Contracting States which have not become parties to the revising Convention.

ARTICLE 30

C–151 Any dispute which may arise between two or more Contracting States concerning the interpretation or application of this Convention and which is not settled by negotiation shall, at the request of any one of the parties to the dispute, be referred to the International Court of Justice for decision, unless they agree to another mode of settlement.

ARTICLE 31

C–152 Without prejudice to the provisions of paragraph 3 of Article 5, paragraph 2 of Article 6, paragraph 1 of Article 16 and Article 17, no reservation may be made to this Convention.

ARTICLE 32

C–153 1. An Intergovernmental Committee is hereby established with the following duties:

(a) to study questions concerning the application and operation of this Convention; and

(b) to collect proposals and to prepare documentation for possible revision of this Convention.

2. The Committee shall consist of representatives of the Contracting States, chosen with due regard to equitable geographical distribution. The number of members shall be six if there are twelve Contracting States or less, nine if there are thirteen to eighteen Contracting States and twelve if there are more than eighteen Contracting States.

3. The Committee shall be constituted twelve months after the Convention comes into force by an election organised among the Contracting States, each of which shall have one vote, by the Director-General of the International Labour Office, the Director-General of the United Nations Educational, Scientific and Cultural Organization and the Director of the Bureau of the International Union for the Protection of Literary and Artistic Works, in accordance with rules previously approved by a majority of all Contracting States.

4. The Committee shall elect its Chairman and officers. It shall establish its own rules of procedure. These rules shall in particular provide for the future operation of the Committee and for a method of selecting its members for the future in such a way as to ensure rotation among the various Contracting States.

5. Officials of the International Labour Office, the United Nations Educational,

Scientific and Cultural Organization and the Bureau of the International Union for the Protection of Literary and Artistic Works, designated by the Directors-General and the Director thereof, shall constitute the Secretariat of the Committee.

6. Meetings of the Committee, which shall be convened whenever a majority of its members deems it necessary, shall be held successively at the headquarters of the International Labour Office, the United Nations Educational, Scientific and Cultural Organization and the Bureau of the International Union for the Protection of Literary and Artistic Works.

7. Expenses of members of the Committee shall be borne by their respective Governments.

ARTICLE 33

1. The present Convention is drawn up in English, French and Spanish, the **C–154** three texts being equally authentic.

2. In addition, official texts of the present Convention shall be drawn up in German, Italian and Portuguese.

ARTICLE 34

1. The Secretary-General of the United Nations shall notify the States invited to **C–155** the Conference referred to in Article 23 and every State Member of the United Nations, as well as the Director-General of the International Labour Office, the Director-General of the United Nations Educational, Scientific and Cultural Organization and the Director of the Bureau of the International Union for the Protection of Literary and Artistic Works:

(*a*) of the deposit of each instrument of ratification, acceptance or accession;
(*b*) of the date of entry into force of the Convention;
(*c*) of all notifications, declarations[15] or communications provided for in this Convention;
(*d*) if any of the situations referred to in paragraphs 4 and 5 of Article 28 arise.

---

[15] The United Kingdom ratification was accompanied by the following declaration:
    (1) in respect of Article 5(1)(*b*) and in accordance with Article 5(3) of the Convention, the United Kingdom will not apply, in respect of phonograms, the criterion of fixation;
    (2) in respect of Article 6(1) and in accordance with Article 6(2) of the Convention, the United Kingdom will protect broadcasts only if the headquarters of the broadcasting organisation is situated in another Contracting State and the broadcast was transmitted from a transmitter situated in the same Contracting State;
    (3) in respect of Article 12 and in accordance with Article 16(1) of the Convention,
      (*a*) the United Kingdom will not apply the provisions of Article 12 in respect of the following uses:
        (i) the causing of a phonogram to be heard in public at any premises where persons reside or sleep, as part of the amenities provided exclusively or mainly for residents or inmates therein except where a special charge is made for admission to the part of the premises where the phonogram is to be heard,
        (ii) the causing of a phonogram to be heard in public as part of the activities of, or for the benefit of, a club, society or other organisation which is not established or conducted for profit and whose main objects are charitable or are otherwise concerned with the advancement of religion, education or social welfare, except where a charge is made for admission to the place where the phonogram is to be heard, and any of the proceeds of the charge are applied otherwise than for the purpose of the organisation;
      (*b*) as regards phonograms the producer of which is not a national of another Contracting State or as regards phonograms the producer of which is a national of a Contracting State which has made a declaration under Article 16(1)(*a*)(i) stating that it will not apply the provisions of Article 12, the United Kingdom will not grant the protection provided for by Article 12, unless, in either event, the phonogram has been first published in a Contracting State which has made no such declaration.

2. The Secretary-General of the United Nations shall also notify the Director-General of the International Labour Office, the Director-General of the United Nations Educational, Scientific and Cultural Organization and the Director of the Bureau of the International Union for the Protection of Literary and Artistic Works of the requests communicated to him in accordance with Article 29, as well as of any communication received from the Contracting States concerning the revision of the Convention.

IN FAITH WHEREOF, the undersigned, being duly authorised thereto, have signed this Convention.

DONE at Rome, this twenty-sixth day of October 1961, in a single copy in the English, French and Spanish languages. Certified true copies shall be delivered by the Secretary-General of the United Nations to all the States invited to the Conference referred to in Article 23 and to every State Member of the United Nations, as well as to the Director-General of the International Labour Office, the Director-General of the United Nations Educational, Scientific and Cultural Organization and the Director of the Bureau of the International Union for the Protection of Literary and Artistic Works.

* * *

C–156 **CONVENTION ESTABLISHING THE WORLD INTELLECTUAL PROPERTY ORGANIZATION**[16]

Stockholm, July 14, 1967 to January 13, 1968

THE CONTRACTING PARTIES,

Desiring to contribute to better understanding and co-operation among States for their mutual benefit on the basis of respect for their sovereignty and equality,

Desiring, in order to encourage creative activity, to promote the protection of intellectual property throughout the world,

Desiring to modernize and render more efficient the administration of the Unions established in the fields of the protection of industrial property and the protection of literary and artistic works, while fully respecting the independence of each of the Unions,

AGREE AS FOLLOWS:

ARTICLE 1

Establishment of the Organization

C–157   The World Intellectual Property Organization is hereby established.

ARTICLE 2

Definitions

C–158   For the purposes of this Convention:

(i) "Organization" shall mean the World Intellectual Property Organization (WIPO);

---

[16] Cmnd. 4408. Ratified by the United Kingdom on February 26, 1969, and entered into force on April 26, 1970.

(ii) "International Bureau" shall mean the International Bureau of Intellectual Property;

(iii) "Paris Convention" shall mean the Convention for the Protection of Industrial Property signed on March 20, 1883, including any of its revisions;

(iv) "Berne Convention" shall mean the Convention for the Protection of Literary and Artistic Works signed on September 9, 1886, including any of its revisions;

(v) "Paris Union" shall mean the International Union established by the Paris Convention;

(vi) "Berne Union" shall mean the International Union established by the Berne Convention;

(vii) "Unions" shall mean the Paris Union, the Special Unions and Agreements established in relation with that Union, the Berne Union, and any other international agreement designed to promote the protection of intellectual property whose administration is assumed by the Organization according to Article 4(iii);

(viii) "intellectual property" shall include the rights relating to:
— literary, artistic and scientific works,
— performances of performing artists, phonograms, and broadcasts,
— inventions in all fields of human endeavour,
— scientific discoveries,
— industrial designs,
— trademarks, service marks, and commercial names and designations,
— protection against unfair competition,

and all other rights resulting from intellectual activity in the industrial, scientific, literary or artistic fields.

ARTICLE 3

Objectives of the Organization

The objectives of the Organization are: **C–159**

(i) to promote the protection of intellectual property throughout the world through co-operation among States and, where appropriate, in collaboration with any other international organization,

(ii) to ensure administrative co-operation among the Unions.

ARTICLE 4

Functions

In order to attain the objectives described in Article 3, the Organization, **C–160** through its appropriate organs, and subject to the competence of each of the Unions:

(i) shall promote the development of measures designed to facilitate the efficient protection of intellectual property throughout the world and to harmonize national legislations in this field;

(ii) shall perform the administrative tasks of the Paris Union, the Special Unions established in relation with that Union, and the Berne Union;

(iii) may agree to assume, or participate in, the administration of any other international agreement designed to promote the protection of intellectual property;

(iv) shall encourage the conclusion of international agreements designed to promote the protection of intellectual property;

(v) shall offer its co-operation to States requesting legal-technical assistance in the field of intellectual property;

(vi) shall assemble and disseminate information concerning the protection of intellectual property, carry out and promote studies in this field, and publish the results of such studies;

(vii) shall maintain services facilitating the international protection of intellectual property and, where appropriate, provide for registration in this field and the publication of the data concerning the registrations;

(viii) shall take all other appropriate action.

ARTICLE 5

Membership

C–161   (1) Membership in the Organization shall be open to any State which is a member of any of the Unions as defined in Article 2(vii).

(2) Membership in the Organization shall be equally open to any State not a member of any of the Unions, provided that:

(i) it is a member of the United Nations, any of the Specialized Agencies brought into relationship with the United Nations, or the International Atomic Energy Agency, or is a party to the Statute of the International Court of Justice, or

(ii) it is invited by the General Assembly to become a party to this Convention.

ARTICLE 6

General Assembly

C–162   (1)(*a*) There shall be a General Assembly consisting of the States party to this Convention which are members of any of the Unions.

(*b*) The Government of each State shall be represented by one delegate, who may be assisted by alternate delegates, advisors, and experts.

(*c*) The expenses of each delegation shall be borne by the Government which has appointed it.

(2) The General Assembly shall:

(i) appoint the Director-General upon nomination by the Co-ordination Committee;

(ii) review and approve reports of the Director-General concerning the Organization and give him all necessary instructions;

(iii) review and approve the reports and activities of the Co-ordination Committee and give instructions to such Committee;

(iv) adopt the triennial budget of expenses common to the Unions;

(v) approve the measures proposed by the Director-General concerning the administration of the international agreements referred to in Article 4(iii);

(vi) adopt the financial regulations of the Organization;

(vii) determine the working languages of the Secretariat, taking into consideration the practice of the United Nations;

(viii) invite States referred to under Article 5(2)(ii) to become party to this Convention;

(ix) determine which States not Members of the Organization and which intergovernmental and international non-governmental organizations shall be admitted to its meetings as observers;

(x) exercise such other functions as are appropriate under this Convention.

(3)(*a*) Each State, whether member of one or more Unions, shall have one vote in the General Assembly.

(*b*) One-half of the States members of the General Assembly shall constitute a quorum.

(*c*) Notwithstanding the provisions of sub-paragraph (*b*), if, in any session, the number of States represented is less than one-half but equal to or more than one-third of the States members of the General Assembly, the General Assembly may make decisions but, with the exception of decisions concerning its own procedure, all such decisions shall take effect only if the following conditions are fulfilled. The International Bureau shall communicate the said decisions to the States members of the General Assembly which were not represented and shall invite them to express in writing their vote or abstention within a period of three months from the date of the communication. If, at the expiration of this period, the number of States having thus expressed their vote or abstention attains the number of States which was lacking for attaining the quorum in the session itself, such decisions shall take effect provided that at the same time the required majority still obtains.

(*d*) Subject to the provisions of sub-paragraphs (*e*) and (*f*), the General Assembly shall make its decisions by a majority of two-thirds of the votes cast.

(*e*) The approval of measures concerning the administration of international agreements referred to in Article 4(iii) shall require a majority of three-fourths of the votes cast.

(*f*) The approval of an agreement with the United Nations under Articles 57 and 63 of the Charter of the United Nations shall require a majority of nine-tenths of the votes cast.[17]

(*g*) For the appointment of the Director-General (paragraph (2)(i)), the approval of measures proposed by the Director-General concerning the administration of international agreements (paragraph (2)(v)), and the transfer of headquarters (Article 10), the required majority must be attained not only in the General Assembly but also in the Assembly of the Paris Union and the Assembly of the Berne Union.

(*h*) Abstentions shall not be considered as votes.

(*i*) A delegate may represent, and vote in the name of, one State only.

(4)(*a*) The General Assembly shall meet once in every third calendar year in ordinary session, upon convocation by the Director-General.

(*b*) The General Assembly shall meet in extraordinary session upon convocation by the Director-General either at the request of the Co-ordination Committee or at the request of one-fourth of the States members of the General Assembly.

(*c*) Meetings shall be held at the headquarters of the Organization.

(5) States party to this Convention which are not members of any of the Unions shall be admitted to the meetings of the General Assembly as observers.

(6) The General Assembly shall adopt its own rules of procedure.

ARTICLE 7

Conference

(1)(*a*) There shall be a Conference consisting of the States party to this Convention whether or not they are members of any of the Unions. **C–163**

(*b*) The Government of each State shall be represented by one delegate, who may be assisted by alternate delegates, advisors, and experts.

---

[17] See the 1974 Agreement between the United Nations and the World Intellectual Property Organisation and the 1975 Protocol thereto *"Copyright,"* January and February 1975.

(*c*) The expenses of each delegation shall be borne by the Government which has appointed it.

(2) The Conference shall:

    (i) discuss matters of general interest in the field of intellectual property and may adopt recommendations relating to such matters, having regard for the competence and autonomy of the Unions;

    (ii) adopt the triennial budget of the Conference;

    (iii) within the limits of the budget of the Conference, establish the triennial programme of legal-technical assistance;

    (iv) adopt amendments to this Convention as provided in Article 17;

    (v) determine which States not Members of the Organization and which intergovernmental and international non-governmental organizations shall be admitted to its meetings as observers;

    (vi) exercise such other functions as are appropriate under this Convention.

(3)(*a*) Each Member State shall have one vote in the Conference.

(*b*) One-third of the Member States shall constitute a quorum.

(*c*) Subject to the provisions of Article 17, the Conference shall make its decisions by a majority of two-thirds of the votes cast.

(*d*) The amounts of the contributions of States party to this Convention not members of any of the Unions shall be fixed by a vote in which only the delegates of such States shall have the right to vote.

(*e*) Abstentions shall not be considered as votes.

(*f*) A delegate may represent, and vote in the name of, one State only.

(4)(*a*) The Conference shall meet in ordinary session, upon convocation by the Director-General, during the same period and at the same place as the General Assembly.

(*b*) The Conference shall meet in extraordinary session, upon convocation by the Director-General, at the request of the majority of the Member States.

(5) The Conference shall adopt its own rules of procedure.

ARTICLE 8

Co-ordination Committee

C–164 (1)(*a*) There shall be a Co-ordination Committee consisting of the States party to this Convention which are members of the Executive Committee of the Paris Union, or the Executive Committee of the Berne Union, or both. However, if either of these Executive Committees is composed of more than one-fourth of the number of the countries members of the Assembly which elected it, then such Executive Committee shall designate from among its members the States which will be members of the Co-ordination Committee, in such a way that their number shall not exceed the one-fourth referred to above, it being understood that the country on the territory of which the Organization has its headquarters shall not be included in the computation of the said one-fourth.

(*b*) The Government of each State member of the Co-ordination Committee shall be represented by one delegate, who may be assisted by alternate delegates, advisors, and experts.

(*c*) Whenever the Co-ordination Committee considers either matters of direct interest to the programme or budget of the Conference and its agenda, or proposals for the amendment of this Convention which would affect the rights or obligations of States party to this Convention not members of any of the Unions, one-fourth of such States shall participate in the meetings of the Co-ordination Committee with the same rights as members of that Committee. The Conference shall, at each of its ordinary sessions, designate these States.

(*d*) The expenses of each delegation shall be borne by the Government which has appointed it.

(2) If the other Unions administered by the Organization wish to be represented as such in the Co-ordination Committee, their representatives must be appointed from among the States members of the Co-ordination Committee.

(3) The Co-ordination Committee shall:

   (i) give advice to the organs of the Unions, the General Assembly, the Conference, and the Director-General, on all administrative, financial and other matters of common interest either to two or more of the Unions, or to one or more of the Unions and the Organization, and in particular on the budget of expenses common to the Unions;

   (ii) prepare the draft agenda of the General Assembly;

   (iii) prepare the draft agenda and the draft programme and budget of the Conference;

   (iv) on the basis of the triennial budget of expenses common to the Unions and the triennial budget of the Conference, as well as on the basis of the triennial programme of legal-technical assistance, establish the corresponding annual budgets and programmes;

   (v) when the term of office of the Director-General is about to expire, or when there is a vacancy in the post of the Director-General, nominate a candidate for appointment to such position by the General Assembly; if the General Assembly does not appoint its nominee, the Co-ordination Committee shall nominate another candidate; this procedure shall be repeated until the latest nominee is appointed by the General Assembly;

   (vi) if the post of the Director-General becomes vacant between two sessions of the General Assembly, appoint an Acting Director-General for the term preceding the assuming of office by the new Director-General;

   (vii) perform such other functions as are allocated to it under this Convention.

(4)(*a*) The Co-ordination Committee shall meet once every year in ordinary session, upon convocation by the Director-General. It shall normally meet at the headquarters of the Organization.

(*b*) The Co-ordination Committee shall meet in extraordinary session, upon convocation by the Director-General, either on his own initiative, or at the request of its Chairman or one-fourth of its members.

(5)(*a*) Each State, whether a member of one or both of the Executive Committees referred to in paragraph (1)(*a*), shall have one vote in the Co-ordination Committee.

(*b*) One-half of the members of the Co-ordination Committee shall constitute a quorum.

(*c*) A delegate may represent, and vote in the name, of one State only.

(6)(*a*) The Co-ordination Committee shall express its opinions and make its decisions by a simple majority of the votes cast. Abstentions shall not be considered as votes.

(*b*) Even if a simple majority is obtained, any member of the Co-ordination Committee may, immediately after the vote, request that the votes be the subject of a special recount in the following manner: two separate lists shall be prepared, one containing the names of the States members of the Executive Committee of the Paris Union and the other the names of the States members of the Executive Committee of the Berne Union; the vote of each State shall be inscribed opposite its name in each list in which it appears. Should this special recount indicate that a simple majority has not been obtained in each of those lists, the proposal shall not be considered as carried.

(7) Any State Member of the Organization which is not a member of the Co-ordination Committee may be represented at the meetings of the Committee by observers having the right to take part in the debates but without the right to vote.

(8) The Co-ordination Committee shall establish its own rules of procedure.

ARTICLE 9

International Bureau

C–165   (1) The International Bureau shall be the Secretariat of the Organization.

(2) The International Bureau shall be directed by the Director-General, assisted by two or more Deputy Directors-General.

(3) The Director-General shall be appointed for a fixed term, which shall be not less than six years. He shall be eligible for reappointment for fixed terms. The periods of the initial appointment and possible subsequent appointments, as well as all other conditions of the appointment, shall be fixed by the General Assembly.

(4)(*a*) The Director-General shall be the chief executive of the Organization.

(*b*) He shall represent the Organization.

(*c*) He shall report to, and conform to the instructions of, the General Assembly as to the internal and external affairs of the Organization.

(5) The Director-General shall prepare the draft programmes and budgets and periodical reports on activities. He shall transmit them to the Governments of the interested States and to the competent organs of the Unions and the Organization.

(6) The Director-General and any staff member designated by him shall participate, without the right to vote, in all meetings of the General Assembly, the Conference, the Co-ordination Committee, and any other committee or working group. The Director-General or a staff member designated by him shall be *ex officio* secretary of these bodies.

(7) The Director-General shall appoint the staff necessary for the efficient performance of the tasks of the International Bureau. He shall appoint the Deputy Directors-General after approval by the Co-ordination Committee. The conditions of employment shall be fixed by the staff regulations to be approved by the Co-ordination Committee on the proposal of the Director-General. The paramount consideration in the employment of the staff and in the determination of the conditions of service shall be the necessity of securing the highest standards of efficiency, competence, and integrity. Due regard shall be paid to the importance of recruiting the staff on as wide a geographical basis as possible.

(8) The nature of the responsibilities of the Director-General and of the staff shall be exclusively international. In the discharge of their duties they shall not seek or receive instructions from any Government or from any authority external to the Organization. They shall refrain from any action which might prejudice their position as international officials. Each Member State undertakes to respect the exclusively international character of the responsibilities of the Director-General and the staff, and not to seek to influence them in the discharge of their duties.

ARTICLE 10

Headquarters

C–166   (1) The headquarters of the Organization shall be at Geneva.

(2) Its transfer may be decided as provided for in Article 6(3)(*d*) and (*g*).

ARTICLE 11

Finances

(1) The Organization shall have two separate budgets: the budget of expenses **C–167** common to the Unions, and the budget of the Conference.

(2)(*a*) The budget of expenses common to the Unions shall include provision for expenses of interest to several Unions.

(*b*) This budget shall be financed from the following sources:

    (i) contributions of the Unions, provided that the amount of the contribution of each Union shall be fixed by the Assembly of that Union, having regard to the interest the Union has in the common expenses;

    (ii) charges due for services performed by the International Bureau not in direct relation with any of the Unions or not received for services rendered by the International Bureau in the field of legal-technical assistance;

    (iii) sale of, or royalties on, the publications of the International Bureau not directly concerning any of the Unions;

    (iv) gifts, bequests, and subventions, given to the Organization, except those referred to in paragraph (3)(*b*)(iv);

    (v) rents, interests, and other miscellaneous income, of the Organization.

(3)(*a*) The budget of the Conference shall include provision for the expenses of holding sessions of the Conference and for the cost of the legal-technical assistance programme.

(*b*) This budget shall be financed from the following sources:

    (i) contributions of States party to this Convention not members of any of the Unions;

    (ii) any sums made available to this budget by the Unions, provided that the amount of the sum made available by each Union shall be fixed by the Assembly of that Union and that each Union shall be free to abstain from contributing to the said budget;

    (iii) sums received for services rendered by the International Bureau in the field of legal-technical assistance;

    (iv) gifts, bequests and subventions, given to the Organization for the purposes referred to in sub-paragraph (*a*).

(4)(*a*) For the purpose of establishing its contribution towards the budget of the Conference, each State party to this Convention not member of any of the Unions shall belong to a class, and shall pay its annual contributions on the basis of a number of units fixed as follows:

Class A	10
Class B	3
Class C	1

(*b*) Each such State shall, concurrently with taking action as provided in Article 14(1), indicate the class to which it wishes to belong. Any such State may change class. If it chooses a lower class, the State must announce it to the Conference at one of its ordinary sessions. Any such change shall take effect at the beginning of the calendar year following the session.

(*c*) The annual contribution of each such State shall be an amount in the same proportion to the total sum to be contributed to the budget of the Conference by all such States as the number of its units is to the total of the units of all the said States.

(*d*) Contributions shall become due on the first of January of each year.

(*e*) If the budget is not adopted before the beginning of a new financial period, the budget shall be at the same level as the budget of the previous year, in accordance with the financial regulations.

(5) Any State party to this Convention not member of any of the Unions which is in arrears in the payment of its financial contributions under the present Article, and any State party to this Convention member of any of the Unions which is in arrears in the payment of its contributions to any of the Unions, shall have no vote in any of the bodies of the Organization of which it is a member, if the amount of its arrears equals or exceeds the amount of the contributions due from it for the preceding two full years. However, any of these bodies may allow such a State to continue to exercise its vote in that body if, and as long as, it is satisfied that the delay in payment arises from exceptional and unavoidable circumstances.

(6) The amount of the fees and charges due for services rendered by the International Bureau in the field of legal-technical assistance shall be established, and shall be reported to the Co-ordination Committee, by the Director-General.

(7) The Organization, with the approval of the Co-ordination Committee, may receive gifts, bequests, and subventions, directly from Governments, public or private institutions, associations or private persons.

(8)(*a*) The Organizations shall have a working capital fund which shall be constituted by a single payment made by the Unions and by each State party to this Convention not member of any Union. If the fund becomes insufficient, it shall be increased.

(*b*) The amount of the single payment of each Union and its possible participation in any increase shall be decided by its Assembly.

(*c*) The amount of the single payment of each State party to this Convention not member of any Union and its part in any increase shall be a proportion of the contribution of that State for the year in which the fund is established or the increase decided. The proportion and the terms of payment shall be fixed by the Conference on the proposal of the Director-General and after it has heard the advice of the Co-ordination Committee.

(9)(*a*) In the headquarters agreement concluded with the State on the territory of which the Organization has its headquarters, it shall be provided that, whenever the working capital fund is insufficient, such State shall grant advances. The amount of these advances and the conditions on which they are granted shall be the subject of separate agreements, in each case, between such State and the Organization. As long as it remains under the obligation to grant advances, such State shall have an *ex officio* seat on the Co-ordination Committee.

(*b*) The State referred to in sub-paragraph (*a*) and the Organization shall each have the right to denounce the obligation to grant advances, by written notification. Denunciation shall take effect three years after the end of the year in which it has been notified.

(10) The auditing of the accounts shall be effected by one or more Member States, or by external auditors, as provided in the financial regulations. They shall be designated, with their agreement, by the General Assembly.

Article 12

Legal Capacity; Privileges and Immunities

C–168   (1) The Organization shall enjoy on the territory of each Member State, in conformity with the laws of that State, such legal capacity as may be necessary for the fulfilment of the Organization's objectives and for the exercise of its functions.

(2) The Organization shall conclude a headquarters agreement with the Swiss Confederation and with any other State in which the headquarters may subsequently be located.

(3) The Organization may conclude bilateral or multilateral agreements with the other Member States with a view to the enjoyment by the Organization, its officials, and representatives of all Member States, of such privileges and immunities as may be necessary for the fulfilment of its objectives and for the exercise of its functions.

(4) The Director-General may negotiate and, after approval by the Co-ordination Committee, shall conclude and sign on behalf of the Organization the agreements referred to in paragraphs (2) and (3).

ARTICLE 13

Relations with other Organizations

(1) The Organization shall, where appropriate, establish working relations and **C–169** co-operate with other intergovernmental organizations. Any general agreement to such effect entered into with such organizations shall be concluded by the Director-General after approval by the Co-ordination Committee.

(2) The Organization may, on matters within its competence, make suitable arrangements for consultation and co-operation with international non-governmental organizations and, with the consent of the Governments concerned, with national organizations, governmental or non-governmental. Such arrangements shall be made by the Director-General after approval by the Co-ordination Committee.

ARTICLE 14

Becoming Party to the Convention

(1) States referred to in Article 5 may become party to this Convention and **C–170** Member of the Organization by:
    (i) signature without reservation as to ratification, or
    (ii) signature subject to ratification followed by the deposit of an instrument of ratification, or
    (iii) deposit of an instrument of accession.

(2) Notwithstanding any other provision of this Convention, a State party to the Paris Convention, the Berne Convention, or both Conventions, may become party to this Convention only if it concurrently ratifies or accedes to, or only after it has ratified or acceded to:

either the Stockholm Act of the Paris Convention in its entirety or with only the limitations set forth in Article 20(1)(*b*)(i) thereof, or the Stockholm Act of the Berne Convention in its entirety or with only the limitation set forth in Article 28(1)(*b*)(i) thereof.

(3) Instruments of ratification or accession shall be deposited with the Director-General.

ARTICLE 15

Entry into Force of the Convention

(1) This Convention shall enter into force three months after ten States mem- **C–171** bers of the Paris Union and seven States members of the Berne Union have taken action as provided in Article 14(1), it being understood that, if a State is a member of both Unions, it will be counted in both groups. On that date, this Convention shall enter into force also in respect of States which, not being members of either of

the two Unions, have taken action as provided in Article 14(1) three months or more prior to that date.

(2) In respect to any other State, this Convention shall enter into force three months after the date on which such State takes action as provided in Article 14(1).

ARTICLE 16

Reservations

C–172   No reservations to this Convention are permitted.

ARTICLE 17

Amendments

C–173   (1) Proposals for the amendment of this Convention may be initiated by any Member State, by the Co-ordination Committee, or by the Director-General. Such proposals shall be communicated by the Director-General to the Member States at least six months in advance of their consideration by the Conference.

(2) Amendments shall be adopted by the Conference. Whenever amendments would affect the rights and obligations of States party to this Convention not members of any of the Unions, such States shall also vote. On all other amendments proposed, only States party to this Convention members of any Union shall vote. Amendments shall be adopted by a simple majority of the votes cast, provided that the Conference shall vote only on such proposals for amendments as have previously been adopted by the Assembly of the Paris Union and the Assembly of the Berne Union according to the rules applicable in each of them regarding the adoption of amendments to the administrative provisions of their respective Conventions.

(3) Any amendment shall enter into force one month after written notifications of acceptance, effected in accordance with their respective constitutional processes, have been received by the Director-General from three-fourths of the States members of the Organization, entitled to vote on the proposal for amendment pursuant to paragraph (2), at the time the Conference adopted the amendment. Any amendments thus accepted shall bind all the States which are Members of the Organization at the time the amendment enters into force or which become Members at a subsequent date, provided that any amendment increasing the financial obligations of Member States shall bind only those States which have notified their acceptance of such amendment.

ARTICLE 18

Denunciation

C–174   (1) Any Member State may denounce this Convention by notification addressed to the Director-General.

(2) Denunciation shall take effect six months after the day on which the Director-General has received the notification.

ARTICLE 19

Notifications

C–175   The Director-General shall notify the Governments of all Member States of:
  (i) the date of entry into force of the Convention,
  (ii) signatures and deposits of instruments of ratification or accession,

(iii) acceptances of an amendment to this Convention, and the date upon which the amendment enters into force,

(iv) denunciations of this Convention.

ARTICLE 20

Final Provisions

(1)(*a*) This Convention shall be signed in a single copy in English, French, Russian and Spanish, all texts being equally authentic, and shall be deposited with the Government of Sweden. **C–176**

(*b*) This Convention shall remain open for signature at Stockholm until January 13, 1968.

(2) Official texts shall be established by the Director-General, after consultation with the interested Governments, in German, Italian and Portuguese, and such other languages as the Conference may designate.

(3) The Director-General shall transmit two duly certified copies of this Convention and of each amendment adopted by the Conference to the Governments of the States members of the Paris or Berne Unions, to the Government of any other State when it accedes to this Convention, and, on request, to the Government of any other State. The copies of the signed text of the Convention transmitted to the Governments shall be certified by the Government of Sweden.

(4) The Director-General shall register this Convention with the Secretariat of the United Nations.

ARTICLE 21

Transitional Provisions

(1) Until the first Director-General assumes office, references in this Convention to the International Bureau or to the Director-General shall be deemed to be references to the United International Bureaux for the Protection of Industrial, Literary and Artistic Property (also called the United International Bureaux for the Protection of Intellectual Property (BIRPI)), or its Director, respectively. **C–177**

(2)(*a*) States which are members of any of the Unions but which have not become party to this Convention may, for five years from the date of entry into force of this Convention, exercise, if they so desire, the same rights as if they had become party to this Convention. Any State desiring to exercise such rights shall give written notification to this effect to the Director-General; this notification shall be effective on the date of its receipt. Such States shall be deemed to be members of the General Assembly and the Conference until the expiration of the said period.

(*b*) Upon expiration of this five-year period, such States shall have no right to vote in the General Assembly, the Conference, and the Co-ordination Committee.

(*c*) Upon becoming party to this Convention, such States shall regain such right to vote.

(3)(*a*) As long as there are States members of the Paris or Berne Unions which have not become party to this Convention, the International Bureau and the Director-General shall also function as the United International Bureaux for the Protection of Industrial, Literary and Artistic Property, and its Director, respectively.

(*b*) The staff in the employment of the said Bureaux on the date of entry into force of this Convention shall, during the transitional period referred to in subparagraph (*a*), be considered as also employed by the International Bureau.

(4)(*a*) Once all the States members of the Paris Union have become Members of the Organization, the rights, obligations, and property, of the Bureau of that Union shall devolve on the International Bureau of the Organization.

(*b*) Once all the States members of the Berne Union have become Members of the Organization, the rights, obligations, and property, of the Bureau of that Union shall devolve on the International Bureau of the Organization.

* * *

CONVENTION FOR THE PROTECTION OF PRODUCERS OF PHONOGRAMS AGAINST UNAUTHORISED DUPLICATION OF THEIR PHONOGRAMS[18]

Geneva, October 29, 1971

C–178   The Contracting States,

concerned at the widespread and increasing unauthorized duplication of phonograms and the damage this is occasioning to the interests of authors, performers and producers of phonograms;

convinced that the protection of producers of phonograms against such acts will also benefit the performers whose performances, and the authors whose works, are recorded on the said phonograms;

recognizing the value of the work undertaken in this field by the United Nations Educational, Scientific and Cultural Organization and the World Intellectual Property Organization;

anxious not to impair in any way international agreements already in force and in particular in no way to prejudice wider acceptance of the Rome Convention of October 26, 1961, which affords protection to performers and to broadcasting organizations as well as to producers of phonograms;

have agreed as follows:

ARTICLE 1

C–179   For the purposes of this Convention:
- (*a*) "phonogram" means any exclusively aural fixation of sounds of a performance or of other sounds;
- (*b*) "producer of phonograms" means the person who, or the legal entity which, first fixes the sounds of a performance or other sounds;
- (*c*) "duplicate" means an article which contains sounds taken directly or indirectly from a phonogram and which embodies all or a substantial part of the sounds fixed in that phonogram;
- (*d*) "distribution to the public" means any act by which duplicates of a phonogram are offered, directly or indirectly, to the general public or any section thereof.

ARTICLE 2

C–180   Each Contracting State shall protect producers of phonograms who are nationals of other Contracting States against the making of duplicates without the consent of the producer and against the importation of such duplicates, provided that any such making or importation is for the purpose of distribution to the public, and against the distribution of such duplicates to the public.

---

[18] Cmnd. 5275. Ratified by the United Kingdom on December 5, 1972, and entered into force on April 18, 1973.

ARTICLE 3

The means by which this Convention is implemented shall be a matter for the **C–181**
domestic law of each Contracting State and shall include one or more of the following: protection by means of the grant of a copyright or other specific right; protection by means of the law relating to unfair competition; protection by means of
penal sanctions.

ARTICLE 4

The duration of the protection given shall be a matter for the domestic law of **C–182**
each Contracting State. However, if the domestic law prescribes a specific
duration for the protection, that duration shall not be less than twenty years from
the end either of the year in which the sounds embodied in the phonogram were
first fixed or of the year in which the phonogram was first published.

ARTICLE 5

If, as a condition of protecting the producers of phonograms, a Contracting **C–183**
State, under its domestic law, requires compliance with formalities, these shall be
considered as fulfilled if all the authorized duplicates of the phonogram distributed
to the public or their containers bear a notice consisting of the symbol ℗, accompanied by the year date of the first publication, placed in such manner as to give
reasonable notice of claim of protection; and, if the duplicates or their containers
do not identify the producer, his successor in title or the exclusive licensee (by
carrying his name, trademark or other appropriate designation), the notice shall
also include the name of the producer, his successor in title or the exclusive licensee.

ARTICLE 6

Any contracting State which affords protection by means of copyright or other **C–184**
specific right, or protection by means of penal sanctions, may in its domestic law
provide, with regard to the protection of producers of phonograms, the same kinds
of limitations as are permitted with respect to the protection of authors of literary
and artistic works. However, no compulsory licences may be permitted unless all
of the following conditions are met:
  (a) the duplication is for use solely for the purpose of teaching or scientific
      research;
  (b) the licence shall be valid for duplication only within the territory of the Con-
      tracting State whose competent authority has granted the licence and shall
      not extend to the export of duplicates;
  (c) the duplication made under the licence gives rise to an equitable remuner-
      ation fixed by the said authority taking into account, *inter alia*, the number of
      duplicates which will be made.

ARTICLE 7

(1) This Convention shall in no way be interpreted to limit or prejudice the pro- **C–185**
tection otherwise secured to authors, to performers, to producers of phonograms or
to broadcasting organizations under any domestic law or international agreement.

(2) It shall be a matter for the domestic law of each Contracting State to determine the extent, if any, to which performers whose performances are fixed in a
phonogram are entitled to enjoy protection and the conditions for enjoying any
such protection.

(3) No Contracting State shall be required to apply the provisions of this Convention to any phonogram fixed before this Convention entered into force with
respect to that State.

(4) Any Contracting State which, on October 29, 1971, affords protection to producers of phonograms solely on the basis of the place of first fixation may, by a notification deposited with the Director General of the World Intellectual Property Organization, declare that it will apply this criterion instead of the criterion of the nationality of the producer.

ARTICLE 8

C–186   (1) The International Bureau of the World Intellectual Property Organization shall assemble and publish information concerning the protection of phonograms. Each Contracting State shall promptly communicate to the International Bureau all new laws and official texts on this subject.

(2) The International Bureau shall, on request, furnish information to any Contracting State on matters concerning this Convention, and shall conduct studies and provide services designed to facilitate the protection provided for therein.

(3) The International Bureau shall exercise the functions enumerated in paragraphs (1) and (2) above in co-operation, for matters within their respective competence, with the United Nations Educational, Scientific and Cultural Organization and the International Labour Organization.

ARTICLE 9

C–187   (1) This Convention shall be deposited with the Secretary-General of the United Nations. It shall be open until April 30, 1972, for signature by any State that is a member of the United Nations, any of the Specialized Agencies brought into relationship with the United Nations, or the International Atomic Energy Agency, or is a party to the Statute of the International Court of Justice.

(2) This Convention shall be subject to ratification or acceptance by the signatory States. It shall be open for accession by any State referred to in paragraph (1) of this Article.

(3) Instruments of ratification, acceptance or accession shall be deposited with the Secretary-General of the United Nations.

(4) It is understood that, at the time a State becomes bound by this Convention, it will be in a position in accordance with its domestic law to give effect to the provisions of the Convention.

ARTICLE 10

C–188   No reservations to this Convention are permitted.

ARTICLE 11

C–189   (1) This Convention shall enter into force three months after deposit of the fifth instrument of ratification, acceptance or accession.

(2) For each State ratifying, accepting or acceding to this Convention after the deposit of the fifth instrument of ratification, acceptance or accession, the Convention shall enter into force three months after the date on which the Director General of the World Intellectual Property Organization informs the States, in accordance with Article 13, paragraph (4), of the deposit of its instrument.

(3) Any State may, at the time of ratification, acceptance or accession or at any later date, declare by notification addressed to the Secretary-General of the United Nations that this Convention shall apply to all or any one of the territories for whose international affairs it is responsible. This notification will take effect three months after the date on which it is received.

(4) However, the preceding paragraph may in no way be understood as implying the recognition or tacit acceptance by a Contracting State of the factual situation concerning a territory to which this Convention is made applicable by another Contracting State by virtue of the said paragraph.

ARTICLE 12

(1) Any Contracting State may denounce this Convention, on its own behalf or **C–190** on behalf of any of the territories referred to in Article 11, paragraph (3), by written notification addressed to the Secretary-General of the United Nations.

(2) Denunciation shall take effect twelve months after the date on which the Secretary-General of the United Nations has received the notification.

ARTICLE 13

(1) This Convention shall be signed in a single copy in English, French, Russian **C–191** and Spanish, the four texts being equally authentic.

(2) Official texts shall be established by the Director General of the World Intellectual Property Organization, after consultation with the interested Governments, in the Arabic, Dutch, German, Italian and Portuguese languages.

(3) The Secretary-General of the United Nations shall notify the Director General of the World Intellectual Property Organization, the Director-General of the United Nations Educational, Scientific and Cultural Organization and the Director-General of the International Labour Office of:

(*a*) signatures to this Convention;

(*b*) the deposit of instruments of ratification, acceptance or accession;

(*c*) the date of entry into force of this Convention;

(*d*) any declaration notified pursuant to Article 11, paragraph (3);

(*e*) the receipt of notifications of denunciation.

(4) The Director General of the World Intellectual Property Organization shall inform the States referred to in Article 9, paragraph (1), of the notifications received pursuant to the preceding paragraph and of any declarations made under Article 7, paragraph (4). He shall also notify the Director-General of the United Nations Educational, Scientific and Cultural Organization and the Director-General of the International Labour Office of such declarations.

(5) The Secretary-General of the United Nations shall transmit two certified copies of this Convention to the States referred to in Article 9, paragraph (1).

* * *

CONVENTION RELATING TO THE DISTRIBUTION OF PROGRAMME-CARRYING SIGNALS TRANSMITTED BY SATELLITE[19]

Brussels, May 21, 1974

The Contracting States, **C–192**

Aware that the use of satellites for the distribution of programme-carrying signals is rapidly growing both in volume and geographical coverage;

Concerned that there is no world-wide system to prevent distributors from distributing programme-carrying signals transmitted by satellite which were not intended for those distributors, and that this lack is likely to hamper the use of satellite communications;

Recognizing, in this respect, the importance of the interests of authors, performers, producers of phonograms and broadcasting organizations;

Convinced that an international system should be established under which measures would be provided to prevent distributors from distributing programme-

---

[19] The United Kingdom is not a signatory. This Convention has entered into force.

carrying signals transmitted by satellite which were not intended for those distributors;

Conscious of the need not to impair in any way international agreements already in force, including the International Telecommunication Convention and the Radio Regulations annexed to that Convention, and in particular in no way to prejudice wider acceptance of the Rome Convention of October 26, 1961, which affords protection to performers, producers of phonograms and broadcasting organizations,

Have agreed as follows:

ARTICLE 1

C–193   For the purposes of this Convention:

    (i) "signal" is an electronically-generated carrier capable of transmitting programmes;

    (ii) "programme" is a body of live or recorded material consisting of images, sounds or both, embodied in signals emitted for the purpose of ultimate distribution;

    (iii) "satellite" is any device in extraterrestrial space capable of transmitting signals;

    (iv) "emitted signal" or "signal emitted" is any programme-carrying signal that goes to or passes through a satellite;

    (v) "derived signal" is a signal obtained by modifying the technical characteristics of the emitted signal, whether or not there have been one or more intervening fixations;

    (vi) "originating organization" is the person or legal entity that decides what programme the emitted signals will carry;

    (vii) "distributor" is the person or legal entity that decides that the transmission of the derived signals to the general public or any section thereof should take place;

    (viii) "distribution" is the operation by which a distributor transmits derived signals to the general public or any section thereof.

ARTICLE 2

C–194   (1) Each Contracting State undertakes to take adequate measures to prevent the distribution on or from its territory of any programme-carrying signal by any distributor for whom the signal emitted to or passing through the satellite is not intended. This obligation shall apply where the originating organization is a national of another Contracting State and where the signal distributed is a derived signal.

(2) In any Contracting State in which the application of the measures referred to in paragraph (1) is limited in time, the duration thereof shall be fixed by its domestic law. The Secretary-General of the United Nations shall be notified in writing of such duration at the time of ratification, acceptance or accession, or if the domestic law comes into force or is changed thereafter, within six months of the coming into force of that law or of its modification.

(3) The obligation provided for in paragraph (1) shall not apply to the distribution of derived signals taken from signals which have already been distributed by a distributor for whom the emitted signals were intended.

ARTICLE 3

C–195   This Convention shall not apply where the signals emitted by or on behalf of the originating organization are intended for direct reception from the satellite by the general public.

ARTICLE 4

No Contracting State shall be required to apply the measures referred to in **C–196**
Article 2(1) where the signal distributed on its territory by a distributor for whom
the emitted signal is not intended

(i) carries short excerpts of the programme carried by the emitted signal,
consisting of reports of current events, but only to the extent justified by
the informatory purpose of such excerpts, or

(ii) carries, as quotations, short excerpts of the programme carried by the
emitted signal, provided that such quotations are compatible with fair
practice and are justified by the informatory purpose of such quotations,
or

(iii) carries, where the said territory is that of a Contracting State regarded as
a developing country in conformity with the established practice of the
General Assembly of the United Nations, a programme carried by the
emitted signal, provided that the distribution is solely for the purpose of
teaching, including teaching in the framework of adult education, or
scientific research.

ARTICLE 5

No Contracting State shall be required to apply this Convention with respect to **C–197**
any signal emitted before this Convention entered into force for that State.

ARTICLE 6

This Convention shall in no way be interpreted to limit or prejudice the protec- **C–198**
tion secured to authors, performers, producers of phonograms, or broadcasting
organizations, under any domestic law or international agreement.

ARTICLE 7

This Convention shall in no way be interpreted as limiting the right of any Con- **C–199**
tracting State to apply its domestic law in order to prevent abuses of monopoly.

ARTICLE 8

(1) Subject to paragraphs (2) and (3), no reservation to this Convention shall be **C–200**
permitted.

(2) Any Contracting State whose domestic law, on May 21, 1974, so provides
may, by a written notification deposited with the Secretary-General of the United
Nations, declare that, for its purposes, the words "where the originating organization is a national of another Contracting State" appearing in Article 2(1) shall be
considered as if they were replaced by the words "where the signal is emitted from
the territory of another Contracting State."

(3)(a) Any Contracting State which, on May 21, 1974, limits or denies protection with respect to the distribution of programme-carrying signals by
means of wires, cable or other similar communications channels to
subscribing members of the public may, by a written notification
deposited with the Secretary-General of the United Nations, declare
that, to the extent that and as long as its domestic law limits or denies
protection, it will not apply this Convention to such distributions.

(b) Any State that has deposited a notification in accordance with subparagraph (a) shall notify the Secretary-General of the United Nations in
writing, within six months of their coming into force, of any changes in
its domestic law whereby the reservation under that subparagraph
becomes inapplicable or more limited in scope.

ARTICLE 9

C–201   (1) This Convention shall be deposited with the Secretary-General of the United Nations. It shall be open until March 31, 1975, for signature by any State that is a member of the United Nations, any of the Specialized Agencies brought into relationship with the United Nations, or the International Atomic Energy Agency, or is a party to the Statute of the International Court of Justice.

(2) This Convention shall be subject to ratification or acceptance by the signatory States. It shall be open for accession by any State referred to in paragraph (1).

(3) Instruments of ratification, acceptance or accession shall be deposited with the Secretary-General of the United Nations.

(4) It is understood that, at the time a State becomes bound by this Convention, it will be in a position in accordance with its domestic law to give effect to the provisions of the Convention.

ARTICLE 10

C–202   (1) This Convention shall enter into force three months after the deposit of the fifth instrument of ratification, acceptance or accession.

(2) For each State ratifying, accepting or acceding to this Convention after the deposit of the fifth instrument of ratification, acceptance or accession, this Convention shall enter into force three months after the deposit of its instrument.

ARTICLE 11

C–203   (1) Any Contracting State may denounce this Convention by written notification deposited with the Secretary-General of the United Nations.

(2) Denunciation shall take effect twelve months after the date on which the notification referred to in paragraph (1) is received.

ARTICLE 12

C–204   (1) This Convention shall be signed in a single copy in English, French, Russian and Spanish, the four texts being equally authentic.

(2) Official texts shall be established by the Director-General of the United Nations Educational, Scientific and Cultural Organization and the Director General of the World Intellectual Property Organization, after consultation with the interested Governments, in the Arabic, Dutch, German, Italian and Portuguese languages.

(3) The Secretary-General of the United Nations shall notify the States referred to in Article 9(1), as well as the Director-General of the United Nations Educational, Scientific and Cultural Organization, the Director General of the World Intellectual Property Organization, the Director-General of the International Labour Office and the Secretary-General of the International Telecommunication Union, of

    (i) signatures to this Convention;

    (ii) the deposit of instruments of ratification, acceptance or accession;

    (iii) the date of entry into force of this Convention under Article 10(1);

    (iv) the deposit of any notification relating to Article 2(2) or Article 8(2) or (3), together with its text;

    (v) the receipt of notifications of denunciation.

(4) The Secretary-General of the United Nations shall transmit two certified copies of this Convention to all States referred to in Article 9(1).

Appendix D

UNITED KINGDOM ORDERS IN COUNCIL

PART I

Order in Council dated June 24, 1912   D–1

EXTENDING THE COPYRIGHT ACT 1911, TO CERTAIN BRITISH PROTECTORATES[1]

(S.R. & O. 1912 No. 912)

At the Court at Buckingham Palace, the 24th day of June, 1912.

PRESENT,

The King's Most Excellent Majesty

Lord President.	Sir Henry W. Primrose.
Earl Beauchamp.	Mr. C. F. G. Masterman.
Lord Richard Cavendish.	Sir David Brynmor Jones.
Viscount Allendale.	Sir James Henry Dalziel.
Lord Chamberlain.	Sir Albert Spicer, Bart.

Whereas it is, among other things, provided by the Copyright Act, 1911, that His Majesty may, by Order in Council, extend the said Act to any territories under His Protection and to Cyprus, and that on the making of any such Order the said Act shall, subject to the provisions of the Order, have effect as if the territories to which it applies or Cyprus were part of His Majesty's dominions to which the said Act extends:

Now, therefore, His Majesty, by and with the advice of His Privy Council, is pleased to order, and it is hereby ordered, as follows:

1. The Copyright Act, 1911, shall apply to Cyprus[2] and to the following territories under His Majesty's protection, namely the Bechuanaland Protectorate,[3]

---

[1] Similar Orders were made as to the Cameroons under British Mandate by an Order in Council dated March 16, 1933 (S.R. & O. 1933 No. 254), and as to Tanganyika by an Order in Council dated April 16, 1924 (S.R. & O. 1924 No. 521). See as to Tanganyika, Tanganyika Independence Act, 1961 (10 Eliz. 2, c. 1), Sched. II, paras. 13 and 14 repealed by the C.D.P.A. 1988 s.303 (2) and Sched. 8: and see Tanzania Act, 1969 (1969, c. 29) and § 17–152, *ante*. See as to Jamaica, Jamaica Independence Act, 1962 (10 & 11 Eliz. 2, c. 40), Sched. II, para. 13 repealed by the C.D.P.A. 1988 s.303 (2) and Sched. 8; as to Trinidad and Tobago, Trinidad and Tobago Independence Act, 1962 (10 & 11 Eliz. 2, c. 54), Sched. II, para. 13 repealed by the C.D.P.A. 1988 s.303 (2) and Sched. 8, and Trinidad and Tobago Copyright Act 1985; as to Malta, Malta Independence Act, 1964 (1964, c. 86), Sched. II, para. 13 (the C.D.P.A., 1988 s.303 (2) and Sched. 8 purported to repeal Sched. I para. 11) and Malta Republic Act, 1975 (c. 31), and § 17–152, *ante*; as to Basutoland, Lesotho Independence Act, 1966 (1966, c. 24), Sched., para. 9 repealed by the C.D.P.A. 1988 s.303 (2) and Sched. 8; as to Barbados, Barbados Independence Act, 1966 (1966, c. 37), Sched. II, para. 12 repealed by the C.D.P.A. 1988 s.303 (2) and Sched. 8.

[2] As to Cyprus, see Cyprus Act, 1960 (8 & 9 Eliz. 2, c. 52), Sched., para. 13 repealed by the C.D.P.A. 1988 s.303(2) and Sched. 8.

[3] As to Bechuanaland Protectorate, see Botswana Independence Act, 1966 (1966, c. 23).

East Africa Protectorate,[4] Gambia Protectorate,[5] Gilbert[6] and Ellice[7] Islands Protectorate, Northern Nigeria Protectorate,[8] Northern Territories of the Gold Coast,[9] Nyasaland Protectorate,[10] Northern Rhodesia,[11] Southern Rhodesia,[12] Sierra Leone Protectorate,[13] Somaliland Protectorate, Southern Nigeria Protectorate, Solomon Islands Protectorate,[14] Swaziland,[15] Uganda Protectorate,[16] and Weihaiwei.[17]

2. In Article 12 of "The Somaliland Order in Council, 1899,"[18] the word "Copyright" is hereby revoked and shall be deleted.

D–2   **Order in Council dated February 9, 1920**

UNDER THE COPYRIGHT ACT, 1911 (1 & 2 GEO. 5, C. 46), FURTHER REGULATING
COPYRIGHT REGULATIONS WITH THE UNITED STATES OF AMERICA AS REGARDS
WORKS FIRST PUBLISHED BETWEEN AUGUST 1, 1914, AND THE TERMINATION OF THE
WAR[19]

(S.R. & O. 1920 No. 257)

At the Court at Buckingham Palace, the 9th day of February, 1920.

---

[4] Kenya. Repealed as to Kenya by an Order in Council dated June 26, 1963 (S.I. 1963 No. 1147). See Kenya Independence Act, 1963 (1963, c. 54); and see § 17–152, *ante* and § D–7, *post*.

[5] As to Gambia Protectorate, see Gambia Independence Act, 1964 (1964, c. 93), Sched. II, para. 12 repealed by the C.D.P.A. 1988 s.303 (2) and Sched. 8.

[6] As to Gilbert Islands, see Kiribati Act, 1979 (c. 27).

[7] As to Ellice Islands, see Tuvalu Act, 1978 (c. 20).

[8] As to Nigeria, see Nigeria Independence Act, 1960 (8 & 9 Eliz. 2, c. 55), Sched. II, paras. 12 and 13 repealed by the C.D.P.A. 1988 s.303 (2) and Sched. 8: and see § D–7, *post*.

[9] As to the territories of the Gold Coast, see Ghana Independence Act, 1957 (5 & 6 Eliz. 2, c. 6), Sched. II, para. 12 repealed by the C.D.P.A. 1988 s.303 (2) and Sched. 8: and see § 17–152, *ante* and § D–7, *post*.

[10] As to Nyasaland Protectorate, see Malawi Independence Act, 1964 (1964, c. 46), Sched. II; para. 13 repealed by the C.D.P.A. 1988 s. 303 (2) and Sched. 8; and see § 17–152, *ante* and § D–7, *post*.

[11] As to Northern Rhodesia, see Zambia Independence Act, 1964 (1964, c. 65), Sched. I, para. 9 repealed by the C.D.P.A. 1988 s.303 (2) and Sched. 8; and see § 17–152, *ante* and § D–7, *post*.

[12] As to Southern Rhodesia, see Southern Rhodesia Act 1979 (c. 52) and Zimbabwe Act 1979 (c. 60).

[13] As to Sierra Leone, see Sierra Leone Independence Act, 1961 (9 & 10 Eliz. 2, c. 16), Sched. III, para. 13 and 14 repealed by the C.D.P.A. 1988 s.303 (2) and Sched. 8; and § 17–152, *ante*.

[14] As to Solomon Islands Protectorate see Solomon Islands Act, 1978 (c. 15).

[15] As to Swaziland, see Swaziland Independence Act, 1968 (1968, c. 56), Sched., para. 9 repealed by the C.D.P.A. 1988 s.303 (2) and Sched. 8.

[16] Repealed as to Uganda by an Order in Council dated December 21, 1961 (S.I. 1961 No. 2462). See Uganda Independence Act, 1962 (10 & 11 Eliz. 2, c. 57) and § 17–152, *ante*.

[17] Repealed as to Weihaiwei by Order in Council dated November 27, 1930 (S.R. & O. 1930 No. 1144).

[18] Revoked by S.R. & O. 1930 No. 222.

[19] Revoked by S.I. 1957 No. 1523, but see § 17–115, *ante*.

PRESENT,

The King's Most Excellent Majesty

Lord President.   Lord Colebrooke.
Earl Curzon of Kedleston.   Sir Frederick Ponsonby.

Whereas by reason of conditions arising out of the war difficulties have been experienced by citizens of the United States of America in complying with the requirements of the Copyright Act, 1911, as to first publication within the parts of His Majesty's dominions to which the Act extends of their works first published in the United States of America during the war:

And whereas His Majesty is advised that the Government of the United States of America has undertaken, upon issue of this Order, to extend the protection afforded by the United States Law of December 18, 1919, entitled "An Act to amend sections 8 and 21 of the Copyright Act, approved March 4, 1909," to British subjects:

And whereas by reason of the said undertaking of the Government of the United States of America His Majesty is satisfied that the said Government has made, or has undertaken to make, such provision as it is expedient to require for the protection of works first made or published between the 1st August, 1914, and the termination of the war in the parts of His Majesty's dominions to which this Order applies, and entitled to copyright under Part I of the Copyright Act, 1911:

And whereas by the Copyright Act, 1911, authority is conferred upon His Majesty to extend, by Order in Council, the protection of the said Act to certain classes of foreign works within any part of His Majesty's dominions, other than self-governing dominions, to which the said Act extends:

And whereas by reason of these premises it is desirable to provide protection within the said dominions for literary or artistic works first published in the United States of America between August 1, 1914, and the termination of the war which have failed to accomplish the formalities prescribed by the Copyright Act, 1911, by reason of conditions arising out of the war:

Now, therefore, His Majesty, by and with the advice of His Privy Council, and by virtue of the authority conferred upon him by the Copyright Act, 1911, is pleased to order, and it is hereby ordered, as follows:

1. The Copyright Act, 1911, shall, subject to the provisions of the said Act and of this Order, apply to works first published in the United States of America between the 1st August, 1914, and the termination of the war, which have not been republished prior to the commencement of this Order in the parts of His Majesty's dominions to which this Order applies, in like manner as if they had been first published within the parts of His Majesty's dominions to which the said Act extends:

Provided that the enjoyment by any work of the rights conferred by the Copyright Act, 1911, shall be conditional upon publication of the work in the dominion to which this Order relates not later than six months after the termination of the war, and shall commence from and after such publication, which shall not be colourable only, but shall be intended to satisfy the reasonable requirements of the public.

2. The provisions of section 15 of the Copyright Act, 1911, as to the delivery of books to libraries, shall apply to works to which this Order relates upon their publication in the United Kingdom.

3. In the case of musical works to which this Order relates and provided that no contrivances by means of which the work may be mechanically performed have before the commencement of this Order been lawfully made, or placed on sale, within the parts of His Majesty's dominions to which this Order applies, copyright

in the work shall include all rights conferred by the said Act with respect to the making of records, perforated rolls and other contrivances by means of which the work may be mechanically performed.

4. This Order shall apply to all His Majesty's dominions, colonies and possessions with the exception of those hereinafter named, that is to say:

> The Dominion of Canada;
> The Commonwealth of Australia;
> The Dominion of New Zealand;
> The Union of South Africa;
> Newfoundland.

5. Nothing in this Order shall be construed as depriving any work of any rights which have been lawfully acquired under the provisions of the Copyright Act, 1911, or any Order in Council thereunder.

6. This Order shall take effect as from the 2nd day of February, 1920, which day is in this Order referred to as the commencement of this Order.

And the Lords Commissioners of His Majesty's Treasury are to give the necessary orders accordingly.

D–3   **Copyright (Federated Malay States) Order, 1931**[20]

(1931 No. 105)

At the Court at Buckingham Palace, the 12th day of February, 1931

PRESENT,

The King's Most Excellent Majesty

Earl of Desart.	Sir Dinshah Mulla.
Mr. Secretary Henderson.	Mr. Kennedy.
Sir Charles Trevelyan.	Mr. Morrison.

Whereas by the Copyright Act, 1911, authority is conferred upon His Majesty to extend by Order in Council the protection of the said Act to certain classes of foreign works within any part of His Majesty's dominions, other than self-governing dominions, to which the said Act extends:

And whereas His Majesty is satisfied that the Rulers of the Federated Malay States have made, or have undertaken to make, such provisions as it appears to His Majesty expedient to require for the protection of works entitled to copyright under the provisions of Part I of the said Act:

Now, therefore, His Majesty, by and with the advice of His Privy Council, and by virtue of the authority conferred upon Him by the Copyright Act, 1911, is pleased to order and it is hereby ordered as follows:

---

[20] Extended to Southern Rhodesia by Order in Council dated April 9, 1932 (S.R & O. 1932 No. 255) and see n. 12, *ante*. As to Malaya, see Federation of Malaya Independence Act, 1957 (5 & 6 Eliz. 2, c. 60), Sched. I, paras. 14, 15 repealed by the C.D.P.A. 1988 s.303 (2) and Sched. 8; see § 17–152, *ante* and Malaysia Copyright Act 1987. As to the federation of North Borneo, Sarawak and Singapore with Malaya, see Malaysia Act, 1963 (c. 35), Sched. II, para. 1 (*a*); as to Singapore becoming an independent sovereign state separate from and independent of Malaysia, see Singapore Act, 1966 (1966, c. 29). See § 17–152, *ante* and § D–19 *post*, and Singapore Copyright Act, 1987.

1. The Copyright Act, 1911, including the provisions as to existing works, shall subject to the provisions of the said Act and of this Order apply—

(*a*) to works first published in the Federated Malay States, in like manner as if they had been first published within parts of His Majesty's dominions to which the said Act extends:

(*b*) to literary, dramatic, musical and artistic works the authors whereof were at the time of the making of the work subjects of the Rulers of the Federated Malay States, in like manner as if the authors had been British subjects;

(*c*) in respect of residence in the Federated Malay States, in like manner as if such residence had been residence in the parts of His Majesty's dominions to which the said Act extends.

2. Where any musical work to which this Order applies has been published before the date of this Order but no contrivances by means of which the work may be mechanically performed have before the said date been lawfully made or placed on sale within the parts of His Majesty's dominions to which this Order applies, copyright in the work shall include all rights conferred by the said Act with respect to the making of records, perforated rolls and other contrivances by means of which the work may be mechanically performed.

3. In the application to works to which this Order applies of sections 1 (2) (*d*) and 19 of the Copyright Act, 1911, the date of this Order shall be substituted for the commencement of the Act and for the passing of the Act in section 19 (7) and 19 (8) wherever those expressions occur.

4. Where any person has, before the date of this Order, taken any action whereby he has incurred any expenditure or liability in connection with the reproduction or performance of any work in a manner which at the time was lawful, or for the purpose of or with a view to the reproduction or performance of a work at a time when such reproduction or performance would, but for the making of this Order, have been lawful, nothing in this Order shall diminish or prejudice any rights or interest arising from or in connection with such action which are subsisting and valuable at the said date unless the person who, by virtue of this Order, becomes entitled to restrain such reproduction or performance agrees to pay such compensation as failing agreement may be determined in accordance with the provisions of the Copyright Act, 1911.

5. This Order shall apply to all parts of His Majesty's dominions, including any territories under His Majesty's protection, to which the Copyright Act, 1911, extends, except to the self-governing dominions and to Southern Rhodesia.

6. This Order shall be construed as if it formed part of the Copyright Act, 1911.

7. This Order may be cited as the Copyright (Federated Malay States) Order, 1931.

Copyright (United States of America) Order, 1942   **D–4**

(1942 No. 1579 as amended in square brackets by S.I. 1950 No. 1641)[21]
At the Court at Buckingham Palace, the 6th day of August, 1942.

Present,

The King's Most Excellent Majesty

Lord President.	Secretary Sir Archibald Sinclair.
Lord Macmillan.	Mr. Williams.

---

[21] Revoked by S.I. 1957 No. 1523, but see § 17–115, *ante*.

Whereas by reason of conditions arising out of the war difficulties have been experienced by citizens of the United States of America in complying with the requirements of the Copyright Act, 1911, as to first publication within the parts of His Majesty's dominions to which the Act extends of their works first published in the United States of America during the war:

And whereas His Majesty is advised that the Government of the United States of America has undertaken to grant such extension of time as may be deemed appropriate for the fulfilment of the conditions and formalities prescribed by the laws of the United States with respect to the works of British subjects first produced or published outside the United States and subject to copyright or to renewal of copyright under the laws of the United States including works subject to ad interim copyright:

And whereas by reason of the said undertaking of the Government of the United States of America His Majesty is satisfied that the said Government has made, or has undertaken to make, such provision as is expedient to require for the protection of works first made or published during the period commencing on the 3rd day of September, 1939, and ending one year after the termination of the present war within the parts of His Majesty's dominions to which this Order applies and entitled to copyright under Part I of the Copyright Act, 1911:

And whereas by the Copyright Act, 1911, authority is conferred upon His Majesty to extend, by Order in Council, the protection of the said Act to certain classes of foreign works within any part of His Majesty's dominions, other than the self-governing dominions, to which the Act extends:

And whereas by reason of these premises it is desirable to provide protection within the parts of His Majesty's dominions to which this Order applies for literary or artistic works first published in the United States of America during the period commencing on the 3rd day of September, 1939, and ending one year after the termination of the present war which have failed to accomplish the formalities prescribed by the Copyright Act, 1911, by reason of conditions arising out of the war:

Now, therefore, His Majesty, by and with the advice of His Privy Council, and by virtue of the authority conferred upon Him by the Copyright Act, 1911, and of all other powers enabling Him in that behalf, is pleased to direct and doth hereby direct as follows:

1. The Copyright Act, 1911, shall, subject to the provisions of the said Act and of this Order, apply to works first published in the United States of America during the period commencing on the 3rd day of September, 1939 [and ending on the 29th day of December 1950], which have not been republished in the parts of His Majesty's dominions to which this Order applies within fourteen days of the publication in the United States of America, in like manner as if they had been first published within the parts of His Majesty's dominions to which the said Act extends:

Provided that the enjoyment by any such work of the rights conferred by the Copyright Act, 1911, shall be conditional upon publication of the work within the parts of His Majesty's dominions to which this Order relates [not later than the 28th day of December, 1950], and shall commence from and after such publication, which shall not be colourable only, but shall be intended to satisfy the reasonable requirements of the public.

2. The provisions of section 15 of the Copyright Act, 1911, as to the delivery of books to libraries, shall apply to works to which this Order relates upon their publication in the United Kingdom.

3. Nothing in this Order shall be construed as depriving any work of any rights which have been lawfully acquired under the provisions of the Copyright Act, 1911, or any Order in Council thereunder.

4. Where any person has, before the commencement of this Order, taken any

action whereby he has incurred any expenditure or liability in connection with the reproduction or performance of any work which at the time was lawful, or for the purpose of or with a view to the reproduction or performance of a work at a time when such reproduction or performance would, but for the making of this Order, have been lawful, nothing in this Order shall diminish or prejudice any rights or interest arising from or in connection with such action which were subsisting and valuable at the said date, unless the person who by virtue of this Order becomes entitled to restrain such reproduction or performance agrees to pay such compensation as, failing agreement, may be determined by arbitration.

5. The Interpretation Act, 1889, shall apply to the interpretation of this Order as if it were an Act of Parliament.[22]

6. This Order may be cited as the Copyright (United States of America) Order, 1942.

7. This Order shall come into operation on the date of its publication in the London Gazette, which day is in this Order referred to a the commencement of this Order. [The date of publication was March 10, 1944.]

---

[22] See §§ A–645 and A–646, *ante.*

PART II

D–5   **The Copyright (International Conventions) Order, 1979**

(S.I. 1979 No. 1715)

Made - - - - - - -	*19th December 1979*
Laid before Parliament	*3rd January 1980*
Coming into Operation - - -	*24th January 1980*

At the Court at Buckingham Palace, the 19th day of December 1979

Present,

The Queen's Most Excellent Majesty in Council

Her Majesty, by and with the advice of Her Privy Council, and by virtue of the authority conferred upon Her by sections 31, 32 and 47 of the Copyright Act 1956 and of all other powers enabling Her in that behalf, is pleased to order, and it is hereby ordered, as follows:—

PART I

Citation, commencement and interpretation

D–6   1. This Order may be cited as the Copyright (International Conventions) Order 1979, and shall come into operation on 24th January 1980.
    2. In this Order—

"the Act" means the Copyright Act 1956; and

"material time" means—
>   (i) in relation to an unpublished work or subject-matter, the time at which such work or subject-matter was made, or, if the making thereof extended over a period, a substantial part of that period;
>   (ii) in relation to a published work or subject-matter, the time of first publication.

PART II

Protection for literary, dramatic, musical and artistic works, sound recordings, cinematograph films and published editions

D–7   3. Subject to the following provisions of this Order, the provisions of Parts I and II of the Act (except section 14) and all the other provisions of the Act relevant to those Parts shall in the case of any country mentioned in Schedules 1 or 2 hereto apply—
>   (*a*) in relation to literary, dramatic, musical or artistic works, sound recordings, cinematograph films or published editions first published in that country, as they apply to such works, recordings, films or editions first published in the United Kingdom;
>   (*b*) in relation to persons who at any material time are citizens or subjects of,

or domiciled or resident in, that country, as they apply to persons who at such time are British subjects or domiciled or resident in the United Kingdom; and

(c) in relation to bodies incorporated under the laws of that country, as they apply to bodies incorporated under the laws of any part of the United Kingdom.

4.—(1) Subject to the following provisions of this Article, the relevant provisions of Schedule 7 to the Act shall have effect in relation to any work or other subject-matter in which copyright subsists by virtue of this Part of this Order as if for any references therein to the commencement of the Act or any of its provisions or to the date of the repeal of any provision of the Copyright Act 1911 or of any other enactment there were substituted references to 27th September 1957 (being the date on which the Copyright (International Conventions) Order 1957[23] came into operation).

(2) Subject to the following provisions of this Article, in the case of any country mentioned in Schedule 2 hereto in relation to which a date is specified in that Schedule—

(a) paragraph (1) of this Article shall have effect as if for the reference to 27th September 1957 there were substituted that date (if different); and

(b) copyright shall not subsist by virtue of this Part of this Order in any work or other subject-matter by reason only of its publication in such a country before the date so specified.

(3) This Article shall not apply—

(a) in the case of Bahamas, Barbados, Belize, Cyprus, Fiji, Ghana, Kenya, Malawi, Malta, Mauritius, Nigeria, Trinidad and Tobago, St. Vincent and the Grenadines, Zambia or Zimbabwe[24]; or

(b) to any work or subject-matter first published in the United States of America if immediately before 27th September 1957 copyright under the Copyright Act 1911 subsisted in such work or subject-matter by virtue of either an Order in Council dated 9th February 1920[25] regulating copyright relations with the United States of America or the Copyright (United States of America) Order 1942.[26]

5. The acts restricted by section 12 of the Act as applied by this Part of this Order shall not include—

(a) causing the recording to be heard in public; or

(b) broadcasting the recording;

except in the case of the countries mentioned in Schedule 3 to this Order.

6. Where any person has before the commencement of this Order incurred any expenditure or liability in connection with the reproduction or performance of any work or other subject-matter in a manner which at the time was lawful, or for the purpose of or with a view to the reproduction or performance of a work at a time when such reproduction or performance would, but for the making of this Order, have been lawful, nothing in this Part of this Order shall diminish or prejudice any right or interest arising from or in connection with such action which is subsisting and valuable immediately before the commencement of this Order unless the person who by virtue of this Part of this Order becomes entitled to restrain such

---

[23] See § 2105 *Copinger* (12th ed.).
[24] Belize was added by S.I. 1986 No. 2235. Bahamas, Barbados, Cyprus, Fiji, Malta and Zimbabwe were added by S.I. 1987 No. 2060. Trinidad and Tobago was added by S.I. 1988 No. 1307. St. Vincent and the Grenadines was added by S.I. 1988 No. 1855.
[25] *Ante*, § D–2.
[26] *Ante*, § D–4.

reproduction or performance agrees to pay such compensation as, failing agreement, may be determined by arbitration.

7. Nothing in the provisions of the Act as applied by this Part of this Order shall be construed as reviving any right to make, or restrain the making of, or any right in respect of, translations, if such right has ceased before the commencement of this Order.

PART III

Protection in respect of broadcasts

D–8   8. The provisions of section 14 of the Act, so far as they relate to sound broadcasts and all the other provisions of the Act relevant thereto other than section 40(3), shall apply, in the case of the countries mentioned in Schedule 4 to this Order, in relation to sound broadcasts made from places in any such country by an organisation constituted in, or under the laws of, the country in which the broadcast is made as they apply in relation to sound broadcasts made from places in the United Kingdom by the British Broadcasting Corporation: so, however, that paragraphs 17 and 18 of Schedule 7 to the Act shall have effect as if for the references therein to the commencement of section 14 there were substituted references to the relevant date set out in the said Schedule 4 (being the date on which the provisions of section 14 of the Act so far as they relate to sound broadcasts were first applied in the case of that country).

9. The provisions of section 14 of the Act, so far as they relate to television broadcasts and all the other provisions of the Act relevant thereto, other than section 37 (4), section 40 (3) and Schedule 5, shall apply, in the case of each of the countries mentioned in Schedule 5 to this Order, in relation to television broadcasts made from places in any such country by an organisation constituted in, or under the laws of, the country in which the broadcast was made as they apply in relation to television broadcasts made from places in the United Kingdom by the British Broadcasting Corporation or the Independent Broadcasting Authority; so, however, that—

    (*a*) section 24 (3) (*c*) of the Act shall have effect as if for the reference to the Corporation or the Authority or any organisation appointed by them there were substituted a reference to any owner or prospective owner of copyright in television broadcasts; and

    (*b*) paragraphs 17 and 18 of Schedule 7 to the Act shall have effect as if for the references therein to the commencement of section 14 there were substituted references to the relevant date set out in Schedule 5 to this Order (being the date on which the provisions of section 14 of the Act so far as they relate to television broadcasts were first applied in the case of that country).

PART IV

Extensions and revocations

D–9   10. Parts I and II of this Order shall extend to the countries mentioned in Schedule 6 to this Order subject to the modifications mentioned in that Schedule and Part III shall extend to Gibraltar and Bermuda subject to the modifications mentioned in Schedule 7 to this Order.

11. The Orders mentioned in Schedule 8 to this Order are hereby revoked insofar as they form any part of the law of the United Kingdom or any country mentioned in Schedule 6 to this Order.

SCHEDULE 1

Countries of the Berne Copyright Union   **D–10**

(The countries indicated with an asterisk are also party to the Universal Copyright Convention.)

Arab Republic of Egypt
Argentina*
Australia* (and Norfolk Island)
Austria*
Bahamas*
Barbados*[27]
Belgium*
Benin
Brazil*
Bulgaria*
Cameroon*
Canada*
Central African Empire
Chad
Chile*
Colombia*[28]
Congo (People's Republic)
Costa Rica*
Cyprus
Czechoslovakia*
Denmark*
Fiji*
Finland*
France (and French territories overseas)*
Gabon
German Democratic Republic (and Berlin (East))*
Federal Republic of Germany (and Berlin (West))*
Greece*
Hungary*
Iceland*
India*
Republic of Ireland*
Israel*
Italy*
Ivory Coast
Japan*
Lebanon*
Liberia*[29]
Libya
Liechtenstein*
Luxembourg*
Madagascar
Mali

---

[27] Added by S.I. 1983 No. 1708. Asterisk added by S.I. 1984 No. 549.
[28] Added by S.I. 1988 No. 250. By the same Order Colombia was deleted from Schedule 2.
[29] Added by S.I. 1989 No. 157. By the some Order Liberia and the United States of America etc. were deleted from Schedule 2.

Malta*
Mauritania
Mexico*
Monacco*
Morocco*
Netherlands* (and Netherlands Antilles)
New Zealand*
Niger
Norway*
Pakistan*
Peru*[30]
Philippines*
Poland*
Portugal* (including Portuguese provinces overseas)
Republic of Guinea*[31]
Romania
Rwanda[32]
Senegal
South Africa (and South West Africa)
Spain* (and its Colonies)
Sri Lanka*[33]
Surinam
Sweden*
Switzerland*
Thailand
Togo
Trinidad and Tobago[34]
Tunisia*
Turkey
United States of America (including Guam, Panama Canal Zone, Puerto Rico and the
    Virgin Islands of the United States of America)*[35]
Upper Volta
Uruguay
Vatican City*
Venezuela*[36]
Yugoslavia*
Zaire
Zimbabwe[37]

---

[30] Added by S.I. 1988 No. 1307. By the same Order Peru was deleted from Schedule 2.
[31] Added by S.I. 1980 No. 1723. Asterisk added by S.I. 1984 No. 549.
[32] Added by S.I. 1984 No. 549.
[33] Asterisk added by S.I. 1984 No. 549.
[34] Added by S.I. 1988 No. 1307.
[35] See n. 29 *ante*.
[36] Added by S.I. 1983 No. 1708. By the same Order Venezuela was deleted from Schedule 2.
[37] Added by S.I. 1983 No. 1708.

SCHEDULE 2

COUNTRIES PARTY TO THE UNIVERSAL COPYRIGHT CONVENTION BUT NOT   **D–11**
MEMBERS OF THE BERNE UNION

Algeria	28th August, 1973[38]
Andorra	27th September, 1957
Bangladesh	5th August, 1975
Belize[39]	—
Cuba	27th September, 1957
Dominican Republic[40]	8th May, 1983
Ecuador	27th September, 1957
El Salvador	29th March, 1979[41]
Ghana	—
Guatemala	28th October, 1964
Haiti	27th September, 1957
Kampuchea	27th September, 1957
Kenya	—
Laos	27th September, 1957
Malawi	—
Mauritius	—
Nicaragua	16th August, 1961
Nigeria	—
Panama	17th October, 1962
Paraguay	11th March, 1962
Republic of Korea[42]	1st October, 1987
St. Vincent and the Grenadines[43]	—
Union of Soviet Socialist Republics	27th May, 1973
Zambia	—

SCHEDULE 3

COUNTRIES IN WHOSE CASE COPYRIGHT IN SOUND RECORDINGS INCLUDES   **D–12**
EXCLUSIVE RIGHT TO PERFORM IN PUBLIC AND TO BROADCAST

Australia
Austria
Barbados[44]
Brazil
Burkina[45]
Chile
Colombia
Congo (People's Republic)[46]

---

[38] Date amended by S.I. 1988 No. 1855.
[39] Added by S.I. 1984 No. 549. The date 1st December, 1982 mistakenly included by that Order was deleted by S.I. 1986 No. 2235.
[40] Added by S.I. 1984 No. 549.
[41] See n. 38 *ante.*
[42] Added by S.I. 1987 No. 2060.
[43] Added by S.I. 1988 No. 1855.
[44] Added by S.I. 1984 No. 549.
[45] See n. 43 *ante.*
[46] See n. 43 *ante.*

Costa Rica
Cyprus
Czechoslovakia
Denmark
Dominican Republic[47]
Ecuador
El Salvador
Federal Republic of Germany (and Berlin (West))
Fiji
Finland[48]
France[49]
Guatemala
India
Republic of Ireland
Italy
Israel
Luxembourg[50]
Mexico
Monaco[51]
New Zealand
Niger[52]
Nigeria
Norway
Pakistan
Panama[53]
Paraguay
Peru[54]
Philippines[55]
Spain
Sri Lanka
Sweden
Switzerland
Uruguay

---

[47] See n. 43 *ante.*
[48] Added by S.I. 1984 No. 549.
[49] Added by S.I. 1987 No. 2060.
[50] See n. 43 *ante.*
[51] See n. 43 *ante.*
[52] See n. 43 *ante.*
[53] Added by S.I. 1984 No. 549.
[54] See n. 43 *ante.*
[55] Added by S.I. 1984 No. 1987.

SCHEDULE 4[56]

Austria	9th June, 1973[0]
Barbados[57]	18th September, 1983
Brazil	29th September, 1965[0]
Burkina[58]	14th February, 1988
Chile	5th September, 1974
Colombia	17th September, 1976
Congo (People's Republic)	18th May, 1964[0]
Costa Rica	9th September, 1971[0]
Czechoslovakia	14th August, 1964
Denmark	1st July, 1965
Dominican Republic[59]	27th January, 1987
Ecuador	18th May, 1964[0]
El Salvador	29th June, 1979[0]
Federal Republic of Germany (and Berlin (West))	21st October, 1966[0]
Fiji	11th April, 1972[0]
Finland[60]	21st October, 1983
France[61]	3rd July, 1987
Guatemala	14th January, 1977
Republic of Ireland	19th September, 1979[0]
Italy	8th April, 1975
Luxembourg	25th February, 1976[0]
Mexico	18th May, 1964[0]
Monaco[62]	6th December, 1985
Niger	18th May, 1964[0]
Norway	10th July, 1978[0]
Panama[63]	2nd September, 1983
Peru[64]	7th August, 1985
Paraguay	26th February, 1970
Philippines[65]	25th September, 1984
Sweden	18th May, 1964[0]
Uruguay	4th July, 1977[0]

[56] The dates in Schedule 4 marked° are those substituted for the original dates by S.I. 1988 No. 1855.
[57] Added by S.I. 1984 No. 549.
[58] Added by S.I. 1988 No. 1855.
[59] See n. 58 *ante*.
[60] Added by S.I. 1984 No. 549.
[61] Added by S.I. 1987 No. 2060.
[62] See n. 58 *ante*.
[63] Added by S.I. 1984 No. 549.
[64] See n. 58 *ante*.
[65] Added by S.I. 1984 No. 1987.

SCHEDULE 5

D–14 Countries Whose Organisations are Protected in Relation to Television Broadcasts[66]

Austria	9th June, 1973[0]
Barbados[67]	18th September, 1983
Belgium	8th March, 1968
Brazil	29th September, 1965[0]
Burkina[68]	14th January, 1988
Chile	5th September, 1974
Colombia	17th September, 1976
Congo (People's Republic)	18th May, 1964[0]
Costa Rica	9th September, 1971[0]
Cyprus	5th May, 1970
Czechoslovakia	14th August, 1964
Denmark	1st February, 1962
Dominican Republic[69]	14th January, 1988
Ecuador	18th May, 1964[0]
El Salvador	29th June, 1979[0]
Federal Republic of Germany (and Berlin (West))	21st October, 1966[0]
Fiji	11th April, 1972[0]
Finland[70]	21st October, 1983
France	1st July, 1961
Guatemala	19th September, 1979[0]
Republic of Ireland	24th January, 1980
Italy	8th April, 1975
Luxembourg	25th February, 1976[0]
Mexico	18th May, 1964[0]
Monaco[71]	6th December, 1985
Niger	18th May, 1964[0]
Norway	10th August, 1968
Panama[72]	2nd September, 1983
Paraguay	26th February, 1970
Peru[73]	7th August, 1985
Philippines[74]	25th September, 1984
Spain	19th November, 1971
Sweden	1st July, 1961
Uruguay	4th July, 1977[0]

[66] The dates in Schedule 5 marked° are those substituted for the original dates by S.I. 1988 No. 1855.
[67] Added by S.I. 1984 No. 549.
[68] See n. 58 *ante*.
[69] See n. 58 *ante*.
[70] Added by S.I. 1984 No. 549.
[71] See n. 58 *ante*.
[72] Added by S.I. 1984 No. 549.
[73] See n. 58 *ante*.
[74] Added by S.I. 1984 No. 1987.

SCHEDULE 6

COUNTRIES TO WHICH PARTS I AND II OF THIS ORDER EXTEND[75]   **D—15**

Bermuda	6th December, 1962
British Indian Ocean Territory[76]	21st November, 1964
British Virgin Islands	11th February, 1963
Cayman Islands	4th June, 1966
Falkland Islands and its Dependencies ...	10th October, 1963
Gibraltar	1st October, 1960
Hong Kong	12th December, 1972
Isle of Man	31st May, 1959
Montserrat	5th March, 1966
St. Helena and it Dependencies	10th October, 1963

Modifications to this Order as extended

1. Article 3 shall have effect as part of the law of any country to which it extends as if for references to the United Kingdom there were substituted references to the country in question.

2. Article 4 shall have effect as part of the law of any country to which it extends as if in paragraphs (1) and (3) there were substituted for "27th September 1957" the date indicated in relation to that country in the preceding provisions of this Schedule (being the date when the Act was first extended to that country).

3. Schedule 2 to this Order shall have effect as part of the law of any such country as if for any date in that Schedule which is earlier than the date mentioned in this Schedule in relation to the relevant country there were substituted that later date.

SCHEDULE 7

MODIFICATIONS OF PART III OF, AND SCHEDULES 4 AND 5 TO, THE ORDER IN ITS EXTENSION TO   **D—16**
BERMUDA AND GIBRALTAR

1. (*a*) In Article 8 the words "other than section 40 (3)" shall be omitted;
   (*b*) in Article 9 the words "other than section 37 (4), section 40 (3) and Schedule 5" shall be omitted.

2. Insofar as Part III is part of the law of Bermuda—
   (*a*) in Schedule 4 to this Order the date mentioned in the second column shall be altered to 23rd August 1969 in relation to Brazil, Congo (People's Republic), Czechoslovakia, Denmark, Ecuador, Federal Republic of Germany (and Berlin (West)), Mexico, Niger and Sweden;
   [(*b*) in Schedule 5, the names of Belgium, Cyprus and Spain shall be omitted; and
   (*c*) the date mentioned in the second column in the said Schedule 5 shall be altered to:-
      (i) 23rd August 1969, in relation to Brazil, Congo (People's Republic), Czechoslovakia, Denmark, Ecuador, Federal Republic of Germany (and Berlin (West)), Mexico, Niger and Sweden;
      (ii) 23rd August 1978, in relation to Norway;
      (iii) 3rd July 1987, in relation to France.[77]]

3. Insofar as Part III is part of the law of Gibraltar—
   (*a*) in Schedule 4 to this Order the date mentioned in the second column shall be altered

---

[75] Reference to Belize was deleted by S.I. 1984 No. 549.
[76] Added by S.I. 1984 No. 549.
[77] New subparagraphs (b) and (c) were substituted by S.I. 1988 No. 1855.

to 28th October 1966 in relation to Brazil, Congo (People's Republic), Czechoslovakia, Denmark, Ecuador, Federal Republic of Germany (and Berlin (West)),[78] Mexico, Niger and Sweden.

(*b*) in Schedule 5 the date mentioned in the second column shall be altered to 28th October 1966 in relation to Brazil, Congo (People's Republic), Czechoslovakia, Denmark, Ecuador, Federal Republic of Germany (and Berlin (West)),[79] France, Mexico, Niger and Sweden.

SCHEDULE 8

D–17

ORDERS REVOKED

Order	S.I. Number
The Copyright (International Conventions) Order 1972	1972/673
The Copyright (International Conventions) (Amendment) Order 1973	1973/72
The Copyright (International Conventions) (Amendment No. 2) Order 1973	1973/772
The Copyright (International Conventions) (Amendment No. 3) Order 1973	1973/963
The Copyright (International Conventions) (Amendment No. 4) Order 1973	1973/1089
The Copyright (International Conventions) (Amendment No. 5) Order 1973	1973/1751
The Copyright (International Conventions) (Amendment) Order 1974	1974/1276
The Copyright (International Conventions) (Amendment) Order 1975	1975/431
The Copyright (International Conventions) (Amendment No. 2) Order 1975	1975/1837
The Copyright (International Conventions) (Amendment No. 3) Order 1975	1975/2193
The Copyright (International Conventions) (Amendment) Order 1976	1976/227
The Copyright (International Conventions) (Amendment No. 2) Order 1976	1976/1784
The Copyright (International Conventions) (Amendment No. 3) Order 1976	1976/2153
The Copyright (International Conventions) (Amendment) Order 1977	1977/56
The Copyright (International Conventions) (Amendment No. 2) Order 1977	1977/830
The Copyright (International Conventions) (Amendment No. 3) Order 1977	1977/1256
The Copyright (International Conventions) (Amendment No. 4) Order 1977	1977/1632
The Copyright (International Conventions) (Amendment) Order 1978	1978/1060
The Copyright (International Conventions) (Amendment) Order 1979	1979/577

---

[78] Added by S.I. 1988 No. 1855.
[79] See n. 78 *ante*.

The Copyright (Taiwan) Order 1985[80]

(S.I. 1985 No. 1777)

Made - - - - - - -	*18th November 1985*
Laid before Parliament	*26th November 1985*
Coming into Operation - - -	*17th December 1985*

At the Court at Buckingham Palace, the 18th day of November 1985.

Present,

The Queen's Most Excellent Majesty in Council.

Whereas Her Majesty is satisfied that, in respect of the matters provided for in this Order, provision has been made under the laws of the territory of Taiwan whereby adequate protection will be given to owners of copyright under the Copyright Act 1956:

Now, therefore, Her Majesty, by and with the advice of Her Privy Council, and by virtue of the authority conferred on Her by sections 32 and 47 of the said Act, is pleased to order, and it is hereby ordered, as follows:

1.—(1) This Order may be cited as the Copyright (Taiwan) Order 1985 and shall come into operation on 17th December 1985.

(2) In this Order—

"the Act" means the Copyright Act 1956; and

"material time" means—

    (i) in relation to an unpublished work or subject matter, the time at which such work or subject matter was made, or, if the making thereof extended over a period, a substantial part of that period: and

    (ii) in relation to a published work or subject matter, the time of first publication.

2. Subject to the following provisions of this Order, the provisions of Parts I and II of the Act (except sections 14 and 14A) and all other provisions of the Act relevant to those Parts shall in the case of the territory of Taiwan apply—

    (*a*) in relation to literary, dramatic, musical or artistic works, sound recordings, cinematograph films or published editions first published in that territory as they apply to such works, recordings, films or editions first published in the United Kingdom;

    (*b*) in relation to persons who at any material time are citizens or subjects of China, being citizens or subjects who at the same material time are resident or domiciled in the territory of Taiwan, as they apply to persons who at such time are British subjects within the meaning of the Act; and

    (*c*) in relation to bodies incorporated under the laws of that territory, as they apply to bodies incorporated under the laws of any part of the United Kingdom.

---

[80] Extended to Bermuda, British Indian Ocean Territory, British Virgin Islands, Cayman Islands, Falkland Islands, Gibraltar, Montserrat, St. Helena and Dependencies, South Georgia and The South Sandwich Islands by The Copyright (Taiwan) (Extension to Territories) Order 1987 (S.I. 1987 No. 1826). Extended to the Isle of Man by The Copyright (Taiwan Order) (Isle of Man Extension) Order 1987 (S.I. 1987 No. 1833).

3. The relevant provisions of Schedule 7 to the Act shall have effect in relation to any work or other subject matter in which copyright subsists by virtue of this Order as if for any references therein to the commencement of the Act or any of its provisions there were substituted references to 10th July 1985; and copyright shall not subsist by virtue of this Order in any work or other subject matter by reason only of its publication in the territory of Taiwan before that date.

4. The acts restricted by section 2(5)(*f*) of the Act as applied by this Order shall not include making a translation of the work.

5. Where any person has before the commencement of this Order incurred any expenditure or liability in connection with the reproduction or performance of any work or other subject matter in a manner which at the time was lawful, or for the purpose of or with a view to the reproduction or performance of a work at a time when such reproduction or performance would, but for the making of this Order, have been lawful, nothing in this Order shall diminish or prejudice any right or interest arising from or in connection with such action which is subsisting and valuable immediately before the commencement of this Order unless the person who by virtue of this Order becomes entitled to restrain such reproduction or performance agrees to pay such compensation as, failing agreement, may be determined by arbitration.

D–19
The Copyright (Singapore) Order 1987
(S.I. 1987 No. 940)

Made - - - - - - -	*18th May 1987*
Laid before Parliament	*17th June 1987*
Coming into force - - - -	*18th June 1987*

At the Court at Buckingham Palace, the 18th day of May 1987

Present,

The Queen's Most Excellent Majesty in Council

Whereas Her Majesty is satisfied that, in respect of the matters provided for in this Order, provision has been made under the laws of Singapore whereby adequate protection will be given to owners of copyright under the Copyright Act 1956:

Now, therefore, Her Majesty, by and with the advice of Her Privy Council, and by virtue of the authority conferred on Her by sections 31, 32 and 47 of the said Act, is pleased to order, and it is hereby ordered, as follows:

1.—(1) This Order may be cited as the Copyright (Singapore) Order 1987 and shall come into force on 18th June 1987.

(2) In this Order—

"the Act" means the Copyright Act 1956; and

"material time" means—
 (i) in relation to an unpublished work or subject-matter, the time at which such work or subject-matter was made or, if the making thereof extended over a period, a substantial part of that period; and
 (ii) in relation to a published work or subject-matter, the time of first publication.

2. Subject to the following provisions of this Order, the provisions of Parts I and II of the Act and all the other provisions of the Act relevant to those Parts shall apply—

   (a) in relation to literary, dramatic, musical or artistic works, sound recordings, cinematograph films or published editions first published in Singapore as they apply to such works, recordings, films or editions first published in the United Kingdom;

   (b) in relation to persons who at any material time are resident in Singapore as they apply to persons who at such time are resident in the United Kingdom; and

   (c) in relation to bodies incorporated under the laws of Singapore as they apply to bodies incorporated under the laws of any part of the United Kingdom.

3. The acts restricted by section 12 of the Act as applied by this Order shall not include causing the recording to be heard in public, broadcasting the recording or including it in a cable programme.

4. Where any person has before the commencement of this Order incurred any expenditure or liability in connection with the reproduction or performance of any work or other subject matter in a manner which at the time was lawful, or for the purpose of or with a view to the reproduction or performance of a work at a time when such reproduction or performance would, but for the making of this Order, have been lawful, nothing in this Order shall diminish or prejudice any right or interest arising from or in connection with such action which is subsisting and valuable immediately before the commencement of this Order unless the person who by virtue of this Order becomes entitled to restrain such reproduction or performance agrees to pay such compensation as, failing agreement, may be determined by arbitration.

5. This Order shall extend to the countries mentioned in the Schedule hereto, subject to the modification that article 2 above shall have effect as part of the law of any of those countries as if for references to the United Kingdom there were substituted references to the country in question.[81]

---

[81] Extended to Gibraltar by The Copyright (Singapore) (Amendment) Order 1987 (S.I. 1987 No. 1030). Extended to Bermuda by The Copyright (Singapore) (Amendment) Order 1988 (S.I. 1988 No. 1297).

SCHEDULE

Article 5

COUNTRIES TO WHICH THIS ORDER EXTENDS

British Indian Ocean Territory
British Virgin Islands
Cayman Islands
Falkland Islands
Falkland Islands Dependencies
Hong Kong
Isle of Man
Montserrat
St Helena
St Helena Dependencies (Ascension, Tristan da Cunha)

D–20 **The Copyright (Sound Recordings) (Indonesia) Order 1988**

(S.I. 1988 No. 797)

Made - - - - - - -	*27th April 1988*
Laid before Parliament	*5th May 1988*
Coming into force - - - -	*26th May 1988*

At the court of Saint James, the 27th day of April 1988

Present,

The Counsellors of State in Council

Whereas Her Majesty in pursuance of the Regency Acts 1937 to 1953 was pleased, by Letters Patent dated the 28th day of March 1988, to delegate to the six Counsellors of State therein named or any two or more of them full power and authority during the period of Her Majesty's absence from the United Kingdom to summon and hold on Her Majesty's behalf Her Privy Council and to signify thereat Her Majesty's approval for anything for which Her Majesty's approval in Council is required:

And whereas Her Majesty Queen Elizabeth The Queen Mother and His Royal Highness The Prince Charles, Prince of Wales, being authorised thereto by the said Letters Patent, are satisfied that, in respect of the matters provided for in this Order, provision will be made under the laws of Indonesia whereby adequate protection will be given to owners of copyright under the Copyright Act 1956:

Now, therefore, Her Majesty Queen Elizabeth The Queen Mother and His Royal Highness The Prince Charles, Prince of Wales, being authorised as aforesaid, and in pursuance of the powers conferred by sections 32 and 47 of the said Act of 1956, and by and with the advice of Her Majesty's Privy Council, do on Her Majesty's behalf order, and it is hereby ordered, as follows:

1. This Order may be cited as the Copyright (Sound Recordings) (Indonesia) Order 1988 and shall come into force on 26th May 1988.

2. Subject to Article 3 below, the provisions of section 12 of the Copyright Act 1956 and all the other provisions of that Act relevant to that section shall apply—

(*a*) in relation to sound recordings first published in Indonesia as they apply in relation to sound recordings first published in the United Kingdom; and

(*b*) in relation to every maker of a sound recording who—

    (i) being an individual was, at the time when the recording was made, a citizen or subject of, or resident in, Indonesia, or

    (ii) being a body corporate was, at the time when the recording was made, incorporated under the laws of Indonesia,

as they apply in relation to individuals who at such a time were British subjects within the meaning of the said Act or resident in the United Kingdom and in relation to bodies incorporated under the laws of any part of the United Kingdom.

3. Where any person has before the commencement of this Order incurred any expenditure or liability in connection with—

(*a*) the making of a record embodying a sound recording, or

(*b*) causing a sound recording to be heard in public, or

(*c*) the broadcasting of a sound recording or its inclusion in a cable programme,

in a manner which at the time was lawful, or for the purpose of or with a view to the doing of any such act at a time when that act would, but for the making of this Order, have been lawful, nothing in this Order shall diminish or prejudice any right or interest arising from or in connection with the incurring of that expenditure or liability which is subsisting and valuable immediately before the commencement of this Order unless the person who by virtue of this Order becomes entitled to restrain any such act as aforesaid agrees to pay such compensation as, failing agreement, may be determined by arbitration.

PART III

D–21   **The Copyright (International Organisations) Order 1989**

(S.I. 1989 No. 989)

Made - - - - - -	*13th June 1989*
Laid before Parliament	*21st June 1989*
Coming into force - - - -	*1st August 1989*

At the Court at Buckingham Palace, the 13th day of June 1989

Present,

The Queen's Most Excellent Majesty in Council

Her Majesty, by virtue of the authority conferred upon Her by section 168(2) of the Copyright, Designs and Patents Act 1988, is pleased, by and with the advice of Her Privy Council, to order, and it is hereby ordered, as follows:

1. This Order may be cited as the Copyright (International Organisations) Order 1989 and shall come into force on 1st August 1989.

2. It is hereby declared to be expedient that section 168 of the Copyright, Designs and Patents Act 1988 (copyright vesting in certain international organisations) should apply to the United Nations, the Specialised Agencies of the United Nations and the Organisation of American States.

D–22   **The Copyright (Application to Other Countries) (No. 2) Order 1989**

(S.I. 1989 No. 1293)

Made - - - - - -	*28th July 1989*
Laid before Parliament	*31st July 1989*
Coming into force - - - -	*1st August 1989*

At the Court at Windsor Castle, the 28th day of July 1989

Present,

The Queen's Most Excellent Majesty in Council

Whereas Her Majesty is satisfied that, in respect of the classes of works to which this Order relates, provision has been made under the laws of Singapore and the territory of Taiwan and (in the case of sound recordings only) under the laws of Australia, Indonesia, New Zealand and Pakistan, giving adequate protection to the owners of copyright under Part I of the Copyright, Designs and Patents Act 1988:

Now, therefore, Her Majesty, by and with the advice of Her Privy Council, and by virtue of the authority conferred upon Her by section 159 of the said Act, is pleased to order, and it is hereby ordered, as follows:–

1.—(1) This Order may be cited as the Copyright (Application to Other Coun- **D–23** tries) (No. 2) Order 1989 and shall come into force on 1st August 1989.

(2) In this Order—

"the Act" means the Copyright, Designs and Patents Act 1988, and

"first published" shall be construed in accordance with section 155(3) of the Act

2.—(1) In relation to literary, dramatic, musical and artistic works, films and **D–24** the typographical arrangements of published editions, sections 153, 154 and 155 of the Act (qualification for copyright protection) apply in relation to—

(a) persons who are citizens or subjects of a country specified in Schedule 1 to this Order or are domiciled or resident there as they apply to persons who are British citizens or are domiciled or resident in the United Kingdom;

(b) bodies incorporated under the law of such a country as they apply in relation to bodies incorporated under the law of a part of the United Kingdom; and

(c) works first published in such a country as they apply in relation to works first published in the United Kingdom;

but subject to paragraph (2) and article 5 below.

(2) Copyright does not subsist—

(a) in a literary, dramatic, musical or artistic work by virtue of section 154 of the Act as applied by paragraph (1) above (qualification by reference to author) if it was first published—

(i) before 1st June 1957 (commencement of Copyright Act 1956), or

(ii) before 1st August 1989 (commencement of Part I of the Act) and at the material time (as defined in section 154(4)(b) of the Act) the author was not a relevant person; or

(b) in any work by virtue of paragraph (1) above if—

(i) a date is, or dates are, specified in Schedule 1 to this Order in respect of the only country or countries relevant to the work for the purposes of paragraph (1) above, and

(ii) the work was first published before that date or (as the case may be) the earliest of those dates;

and for the purposes of sub-paragraph (a)(ii) of this paragraph, a "relevant person" is a Commonwealth citizen, a British protected person, a citizen or subject of any country specified in Schedule 1 to this Order, or a person resident or domiciled in the United Kingdom, another country to which the relevant provisions of Part I of the Act extend or (subject to article 5 below) a country specified in Schedule 1 to this Order.

(3) Where copyright subsists in a work by virtue of paragraph (1) above, the whole of Part I of the Act (including Schedule 1 to the Act) applies in relation to the work, save that in relation to an artistic work consisting of the design of a typeface—

(a) section 54(2) (articles for producing material in particular typeface) does not apply,

(b) section 55 (making such articles not an infringement) applies as if the words in subsection (2) from the beginning to "marketed" were omitted, and

(c) paragraph 14(5) of Schedule 1 (transitional provision) does not apply,

and subject also to articles 5 and 7 below.

D–25   **3.** In relation to sound recordings, article 2 above shall apply as it applies in relation to films, subject to the following modifications:

>   (*a*) sections 19, 20, 26 and 107(3) of the Act (infringement by playing in public, broadcasting or inclusion in a cable programme service and related provisions) apply only if—
>
>>   (i) at least one of the countries relevant to the work for the purposes of article 2(1) above is specified in Schedule 2 to this Order, or
>>
>>   (ii) the sound recording in question is a film sound-track accompanying a film; and
>
>   (*b*) paragraph (1) of article 2 shall (subject to article 5 below) apply as if Indonesia were specified in Schedule 1 to this Order.

D–26   **4.**—(1) In relation to broadcasts, sections 153, 154 and 156 of the Act (qualification for copyright protection) apply in relation to—

>   (*a*) persons who are citizens or subjects of a country specified in Schedule 3 to this Order or are domiciled or resident there as they apply to persons who are British citizens or are domiciled or resident in the United Kingdom;
>
>   (*b*) bodies incorporated under the law of such a country as they apply in relation to bodies incorporated under the law of a part of the United Kingdom; and
>
>   (*c*) broadcasts made from such a country as they apply to broadcasts made from the United Kingdom;

but subject to paragraphs (2) and (3) and article 5 below.

(2) If the only country or countries relevant to a broadcast for the purposes of paragraph (1) above are identified in Schedule 3 to this Order by the words "TV only", copyright subsists in the broadcast only if it is a television broadcast.

(3) Copyright does not subsist in a broadcast by virtue of paragraph (1) above if it was made before the relevant date.

(4) Where copyright subsists in a broadcast by virtue of paragraph (1) above, the whole of Part I of the Act (including Schedule 1 to the Act) applies in relation to the broadcast, save that for the purposes of section 14(2) (duration of copyright in repeats)—

>   (*a*) a broadcast shall be disregarded if it was made before the relevant date, and
>
>   (*b*) a cable programme shall be disregarded if it was included in a cable programme service before the later of the relevant date and 1st January 1985;

and subject also to article 7 below.

(5) For the purposes of paragraphs (3) and (4) above, the "relevant date" is the date or (as the case may be) the earliest of the dates specified in Schedule 3 to this Order in respect of the country or countries relevant to the broadcast for the purposes of paragraph (1) above, being (where different dates are specified for television and non-television broadcasts) the date appropriate to the type of broadcast in question.

(6) In respect of Singapore, this article applies in relation to cable programmes as it applies in relation to broadcasts, subject to article 5 below.

D–27   **5.** Schedule 4 to this Order shall have effect so as to modify the application of this Order in respect of certain countries.

D–28   **6.** Nothing in this Order shall be taken to derogate from the effect of paragraph 35 of Schedule 1 to the Act (continuation of existing qualification for copyright protection).

D–29   **7.**—(1) This article applies in any case in which—

>   (*a*) a work was made before 1st August 1989 (commencement of Part I of the

Act) and copyright under the Copyright Act 1956 did not subsist in it when it was made, or

(*b*) a work is made on or after 1st August 1989 and copyright under the Act does not subsist in it when it is made,

but copyright subsequently subsists in it by virtue of article 2(1), 3 or 4(1) above.

(2) Where in any such case a person incurs or has incurred any expenditure or liability in connection with, for the purpose of or with a view to the doing of an act which at the time is not or was not an act restricted by any copyright in the work, the doing, or continued doing, of that act after copyright subsequently subsists in the work by virtue of article 2(1), 3 or 4(1) above shall not be an act restricted by the copyright unless the owner of the copyright or his exclusive licensee (if any) pays such compensation as, failing agreement, may be determined by arbitration.

8. The Orders listed in Schedule 5 to this Order are hereby revoked insofar as   **D-30** they form part of the law of the United Kingdom.

SCHEDULE 1   Article 2(1) and (2)

COUNTRIES ENJOYING PROTECTION IN RESPECT OF ALL WORKS   **D-31** EXCEPT BROADCASTS AND CABLE PROGRAMMES

(The countries specified in this Schedule either are parties to the Berne Copyright Convention and/or the Universal Copyright Convention or otherwise give adequate protection under their law.)

Algeria (28th August 1973)
Andorra (27th September 1957)
Argentina
Australia (including Norfolk Island)
Austria
Bahamas
Bangladesh
Barbados
Belgium
Belize
Benin
Brazil
Bulgaria
Burkina
Cameroon
Canada
Central African Republic
Chad
Chile
Colombia
Congo, People's Republic of
Costa Rica
Côte d'Ivoire
Cuba (27th September 1957)
Cyprus, Republic of

1429

Czechoslovakia
Denmark (including the Faeroe Islands)
Dominican Republic (8th May 1983)
Ecuador (27th September 1957)
Egypt
El Salvador (29th March 1979)
Fiji
Finland
France (including all Overseas Departments and Territories)
Gabon
German Democratic Republic (and Berlin (East))
Germany, Federal Republic of (and Berlin (West))
Ghana
Greece
Guatemala (28th October 1964)
Guinea, Republic of
Haiti (27th September 1957)
Holy See
Hungary
Iceland
India
Ireland, Republic of
Israel
Italy
Japan
Kampuchea (27th September 1957)
Kenya
Korea, Republic of (1st October 1987)
Laos (27th September 1957)
Lebanon
Liberia
Libya
Liechtenstein
Luxembourg
Madagascar
Malawi
Malaysia[82]
Mali
Malta
Mauritania
Mauritius
Mexico
Monaco
Morocco
Netherlands (including Aruba and the Netherlands Antilles)
New Zealand
Nicaragua (16th August 1961)
Niger
Nigeria
Norway
Pakistan
Panama (17th October 1962)

---

[82] Added by S.I. 1990 No. 2153.

Paraguay (11th March 1962)
Peru
Philippines
Poland
Portugal
Romania
Rwanda
St. Vincent and the Grenadines
Senegal
Singapore
South Africa
Soviet Union (27th May 1973)
Spain
Sri Lanka
Suriname
Sweden
Switzerland
Taiwan, territory of (10th July 1985)
Thailand
Togo
Trinidad and Tobago
Tunisia
Turkey
United States of America (including Puerto Rico and all territories and possessions)
Uruguay
Venezuela
Yugoslavia
Zaire
Zambia
Zimbabwe

SCHEDULE 2   Article (3)(a)(i)

COUNTRIES ENJOYING FULL PROTECTION FOR SOUND **D–32** RECORDINGS

(The countries specified in this Schedule either are parties to the Rome Convention for the Protection of Performers, Producers of Phonograms and Broadcasting Organisations or otherwise give adequate protection under their law.)

Australia (including Norfolk Island)
Austria
Barbados
Brazil
Burkina
Chile
Colombia
Congo, People's Republic of
Costa Rica
Czechoslovakia
Denmark (including the Faeroe Islands)
Dominican Republic

Ecuador
El Salvador
Fiji
Finland
France (including all Overseas Departments and Territories)
Germany, Federal Republic of (and Berlin (West))
Guatemala
India[83]
Indonesia
Ireland, Republic of
Italy
Luxembourg
Malaysia[84]
Mexico
Monaco
New Zealand
Niger
Norway
Pakistan
Panama
Paraguay
Peru
Philippines
Sweden
Taiwan, territory of
Uruguay

SCHEDULE 3   Article 4(1), (2) and (5)

D–33   COUNTRIES ENJOYING PROTECTION IN RESPECT OF BROADCASTS

(The countries specified in this Schedule either are parties to the Rome Convention for the Protection of Performers, Producers of Phonograms and Broadcasting Organisations and/or the European Agreement on the Protection of Television Broadcasts or otherwise give adequate protection under their law.)

Austria (9th June 1973)
Barbados (18th September 1983)
Belgium—TV only (8th March 1968)
Brazil (29th September 1965)
Burkina (14th January 1988)
Chile (5th September 1974)
Colombia (17th September 1976)
Congo, People's Republic of (18th May 1964)
Costa Rica (9th September 1971)
Cyprus, Republic of—TV only (5th May 1970)
Czechoslovakia (14th August 1964)
Denmark (including the Faeroe Islands)
       (1st February 1962—television;
       1st July 1965—non-television)

---

[83] Added by S.I. 1989 No. 2415.
[84] See n. 82 *ante.*

Dominican Republic (27th January 1987)
Ecuador (18th May 1964)
El Salvador (29th June 1979)
Fiji (11th April 1972)
Finland (21st October 1983)
France (including all Overseas Departments and Territories)
          (1st July 1961—television; 3rd July 1987—non-television)
Germany, Federal Republic of (and Berlin (West))
          (21st October 1966)
Guatemala (14th January 1977)
Ireland, Republic of (19th September 1979)
Italy (8th April 1975)
Luxembourg (25th February 1976)
Malaysia[85]
Mexico (18th May 1964)
Monaco (6th December 1985)
Niger (18th May 1964)
Norway (10th August 1968—television; 10th July 1978—non-television)
Panama (2nd September 1983)
Paraguay (26th February 1970)
Peru (7th August 1985)
Philippines (25th September 1984)
Singapore (1st June 1957)
Spain—TV only (19th November 1971)
Sweden (1st July 1961—television; 18th May 1964—non-television)
Uruguay (4th July 1977)

SCHEDULE 4   Article 5

MODIFICATIONS   **D–34**

1. In respect of Indonesia, article 2(1)(a) above as applied by article 3(b) above shall apply as if the reference to persons domiciled in Indonesia were omitted.

2. In respect of Singapore—
(a) articles 2(1)(a) and (2) and 4(1)(a) above shall apply as if the references to persons domiciled in Singapore were omitted, and
(b) in the application of article 4(3) above in relation to cable programmes by virtue of article 4(6), the relevant date is 1st January 1985.

3. In respect of the territory of Taiwan—
(a) article 2(1)(a) and (2) above shall apply as if the references to persons domiciled or resident in the territory of Taiwan were limited to such persons who are also citizens or subjects of China, and
(b) in the application of Part I of the Act by virtue of article 2(3) above, subsection (1) of section 21 (infringement by making adaptation) applies as if subsection (3)(a)(i) of that section (translation of literary or dramatic work) were omitted.

---

[85] Added, without a date, by S.I. 1990 No. 2153 which came into force on November 29, 1990.

SCHEDULE 5

Article 8

ORDERS IN COUNCIL REVOKED

Number	Title
S.I. 1979/1715	The Copyright (International Conventions) Order 1979
S.I. 1980/1723	The Copyright (International Conventions) (Amendment) Order 1980
S.I. 1983/1708	The Copyright (International Conventions) (Amendment) Order 1983
S.I. 1984/549	The Copyright (International Conventions) (Amendment) Order 1984
S.I. 1984/1987	The Copyright (International Conventions) (Amendment No. 2) Order 1984
S.I. 1985/1777	The Copyright (Taiwan) Order 1985
S.I. 1986/2235	The Copyright (International Conventions) (Amendment) Order 1986
S.I. 1987/940	The Copyright (Singapore) Order 1987
S.I. 1987/2060	The Copyright (International Conventions) (Amendment) Order 1987
S.I. 1988/250	The Copyright (International Conventions) (Amendment) Order 1988
S.I. 1988/797	The Copyright (Sound Recordings) (Indonesia) Order 1988
S.I. 1988/1307	The Copyright (International Conventions) (Amendment No. 2) Order 1988
S.I. 1988/1855	The Copyright (International Conventions) (Amendment No. 3) Order 1988
S.I. 1989/157	The Copyright (International Conventions) (Amendment) Order 1989
S.I. 1989/988	The Copyright (Application to Other Countries) Order 1989

The Design Right (Reciprocal Protection) (No. 2) Order 1989

(S.I. 1989 No. 1294)

Made - - - - - - -	*28th July 1989*
Laid before Parliament	*31st July 1989*
Coming into force - - - -	*1st August 1989*

At the Court at Windsor Castle, the 28th day of July 1989

Present,

The Queen's Most Excellent Majesty in Council

Whereas, it appears to Her Majesty that the laws of the countries mentioned in article 2 of this Order provide adequate protection for British designs:

Now, therefore, Her Majesty, by virtue of the authority conferred upon Her by section 256(1) of the Copyright, Designs and Patents Act 1988, is pleased, by and with the advice of Her Privy Council, to order, and it is hereby ordered, as follows:

1. This Order may be cited as the Design Right (Reciprocal Protection) (No. 2)   **D–37**
Order 1989 and shall come into force on 1st August 1989.

2. The following countries are hereby designated as enjoying reciprocal protec-   **D–38**
tion under Part III of the Copyright, Designs and Patents Act 1988 (design
right)—

Anguilla
Bermuda
British Indian Ocean Territory
British Virgin Islands
Cayman Islands
Channel Islands
Falklands Islands
Gibraltar
Hong Kong
Isle of Man
Montserrat
New Zealand
Pitcairn, Henderson, Ducie and Oeno Islands
St Helena and Dependencies
South Georgia and the South Sandwich Islands
Turks and Caicos Islands.

3. The Design Right (Reciprocal Protection) Order 1989[86] is hereby revoked.   **D–39**

The Performances (Reciprocal Protection) (Convention Countries) (No. 2)   **D–40**
Order 1989

(S.I. 1989 No. 1296)

Made - - - - - - -	*28th July 1989*
Laid before Parliament	*31st July 1989*
Coming into force - - - -	*1st August 1989*

At the Court at Windsor Castle, the 28th day of July 1989

Present,

The Queen's Most Excellent Majesty in Council

Her Majesty, by virtue of the authority conferred upon Her by section 208(1)(*a*) of
the Copyright, Designs and Patents Act 1988, is pleased, by and with the advice of
Her Privy Council, to order, and it is hereby ordered, as follows:

1. This Order may be cited as the Performances (Reciprocal Protection) (Con-   **D–41**
vention Countries) (No. 2) Order 1989 and shall come into force on 1st August
1989.

---

[86] S.I. 1989 No. 990.

D–42   **2.** The following countries are hereby designated as enjoying reciprocal protection under Part II of the Copyright, Designs and Patents Act 1988 (rights in performances):

Austria
Barbados
Brazil
Burkina
Chile
Colombia
Congo, People's Republic of
Costa Rica
Czechoslovakia
Denmark (including the Faeroe Islands)
Dominican Republic
Ecuador
El Salvador
Fiji
Finland
France (including all Overseas Departments and Territories)
Germany, Federal Republic of (and Berlin (West))
Guatemala
Ireland, Republic of
Italy
Luxembourg
Mexico
Monaco
Niger
Norway
Panama
Paraguay
Peru
Philippines
Sweden
Uruguay.

D–43   **3.** The Performances (Reciprocal Protection) (Convention Countries) Order 1989[87] is hereby revoked.

---

[87] S.I. 1989 No. 991.

The Copyright (Status of Former Dependent Territories) Order 1990 **D–44**

(S.I. 1990 No. 1512)

Made - - - - - - -	*24th July 1990*
Laid before Parliament	*1st August 1990*
Coming into force - - - -	*22nd August 1990*

At the Court at Buckingham Palace, the 24th day of July 1990

Present,

The Queen's Most Excellent Majesty in Council

Her Majesty, by virtue of the authority conferred on Her by paragraph 37(1) and (2)(b) of Schedule 1 to the Copyright, Designs and Patents Act 1988 ("the Act"), is pleased, by and with the advice of Her Privy Council, to order, and it is hereby ordered, as follows:—

1. This Order may be cited as the Copyright (Status of Former Dependent **D–45** Territories) Order 1990 and shall come into force on 22nd August 1990.

2. It is hereby declared for the purposes of paragraph 37(1) of Schedule 1 to **D–46** the Act (copyright status of former dependent territories) that immediately before the commencement of Part I of the Act on 1st August 1989 each of the countries specified in Schedule 1 to this Order was a country to which the Copyright Act 1956 extended or was treated as such a country by virtue of paragraph 39(2) of Schedule 7 to that Act (countries to which the Copyright Act 1911 extended or was treated as extending).

3. It is hereby declared that each of the countries specified in Schedule 2 to this **D–47** Order shall cease to be treated as a country to which Part I of the Act extends for the purposes of sections 154 to 156 of the Act (qualification for copyright protection) by reason of the fact that the provisions of the Copyright Act 1956 or, as the case may be, the Copyright Act 1911, which extended there as part of the law of that country have been repealed or amended.

SCHEDULE 1 Article 2 **D–48**

Countries to which the Copyright Act 1956 extended or was treated as extending immediately before 1st August 1989:

Antigua
Botswana
Dominica
Gambia
Grenada

Guyana
Jamaica
Kiribati
Lesotho
St. Christopher-Nevis
St. Lucia
Seychelles
Solomon Islands
Swaziland
Tuvalu
Uganda

D–49   SCHEDULE 2   Article 3

Countries ceasing to be treated as countries to which Part I of the Copyright, Designs and Patents Act 1988 extends;

Botswana
Seychelles
Solomon Islands
Uganda

Appendix E

UNITED STATES OF AMERICA CODE

United States Code 1976. Title 17—Copyrights[1]

GENERAL REVISION OF COPYRIGHT LAW

SEC. 101. Title 17 of the United States Code, entitled "Copyrights," is hereby amended in its entirety to read as follows:

COPYRIGHTS

SUBJECT MATTER AND SCOPE OF COPYRIGHT

---

[1] The Act of October 19, 1976, Public Law 94–553, 90 Stat. 2598, effective January 1, 1978.
Chronology of Amendments
Public Law 95–598, 92 Stat. 2676 (Nov. 6, 1978) amended s.201.
Public Law 96–517, 94 Stat. 3028 (Dec. 12, 1980) amended ss.101 and 117.
Public Law 97–180, 96 Stat. 93 (May 24, 1982) amended s.506.
Public Law 97–215, 96 Stat. 178 (July 13, 1982) amended s.601.
Public Law 97–366, 96 Stat. 1759 (Oct. 15, 1982) amended s.110, 708.
Public Law 98–450, 98 Stat. 1727 (Oct. 4, 1984) amended ss.109 and 115.
Public Law 98–620, 98 Stat. 3347 (Nov. 8, 1984) added Chap. 9 (§§ 901 *et seq.*).
Public Law 99–397, 100 Stat. 848 (Aug. 27, 1986) amended ss.111 and 801.
Public Law 100–159, 101 Stat. 900 (Nov. 9, 1987) amended ss.902 and 914.
Public Law 100–568, 102 Stat. 2853 (Oct. 31, 1988) amended ss.101, 116, 205, 301, 401, 402, 403, 404, 405, 406, 407, 408, 411, 501, 504, 801, 804, and added s.116A.
Public Law 100–617, 102 Stat. 3935 (Nov. 16, 1988) amended s.109 and 17 U.S.C. § 109 note.
Public Law 100–677, 102 Stat. 3935 (Nov. 16, 1988) amended ss.111, 501, 801, and 804 and added Section 119.
See the Transitional and Saving Provisions at the end of this Appendix for important information regarding the effective dates and construction of the Act and amendments.

109. Limitations on exclusive rights: Effect of transfer of particular copy or pho-
     norecord.
110. Limitations on exclusive rights: Exemption of certain performances and
     displays.
111. Limitations on exclusive rights: Secondary transmissions.
112. Limitations on exclusive rights: Ephemeral recordings.
113. Scope of exclusive rights in pictorial, graphic, and sculptural works.
114. Scope of exclusive rights in sound recordings.
115. Scope of exclusive rights in nondramatic musical works: Compulsory
     license for making and distributing phonorecords.
116. Scope of exclusive rights in nondramatic musical works: Compulsory
     licenses for public performances by means of coin-operated phonorecord
     players.
116A. Negotiated licenses for public performances by means of coin-operated
     phonorecord players.
117. Limitations on exclusive rights: Computers programs.
118. Scope of exclusive rights: Use of certain works in connection with non-com-
     mercial broadcasting.
119. Limitations on exclusive rights: Secondary transmissions of superstations
     and network stations for private home viewing.

E–4   101. Definitions[2]

As used in this title, the following terms and their variant forms mean the following:

An "anonymous work" is a work on the copies or phonorecords of which no natural person is identified as author.

"Audiovisual works" are works that consist of a series of related images which are
intrinsically intended to be shown by the use of machines or devices such as pro-
jectors, viewers, or electronic equipment, together with accompanying sounds, if
any, regardless of the nature of the material objects, such as films or tapes, in
which the works are embodied.

The "Berne Convention" is the Convention for the Protection of Literary and
Artistic Works, signed at Berne, Switzerland, on September 9, 1886, and all acts,
protocols, and revisions thereto.[3]

A work is a "Berne Convention work" if:

(1) in the case of an unpublished work, one or more of the authors is a national of a

---

[2] As amended Dec. 12, 1980, P.L. 96–517, § 10(*a*), 94 Stat. 3028; Oct. 31, 1988, P.L.
100–568, § 4(*a*)(1), 102 Stat. 2854–55.
[3] Section 2 of the Berne Convention Implementation Act of 1988, Pub. L. 100–568, 102
Stat. 2853 (Oct. 31, 1988), provides the following declarations:
The Congress makes the following declarations:
(1) The Convention for the Protection of Literary and Artistic Works, signed at Berne,
Switzerland, on September 9, 1886, and all acts, protocols, and revisions thereto (hereafter in this Act referred to as the "Berne Convention") are not self-executing under the
Constitution and laws of the United States.
(2) The obligations of the United States under the Berne Convention may be performed
only pursuant to appropriate domestic law.
(3) The amendments made by this Act, together with the law as it exists on the date of the
enactment of this Act, satisfy the obligations of the United States in adhering to the Berne
Convention and no further rights or interests shall be recognized or created for that purpose.

nation adhering to the Berne Convention, or in the case of a published work, one or more of the authors is a first publication;

(2) the work was first published in a nation adhering to the Berne Convention, or was simultaneously first published in a nation adhering to the Berne Convention and in a foreign nation that does not adhere to the Berne Convention;

(3) in the case of an audiovisual work:

    (A) if one or more of the authors is a legal entity, that author has its head-quarters in a nation adhering to the Berne Convention; or

    (B) if one or more of the authors is an individual, that author is domiciled, or has his or her habitual residence in, a nation adhering to the Berne Convention; or

(4) in the case of a pictorial, graphic, or sculptural work that is incorporated in a building or other structure, the building or structure is located in a nation adhering to the Berne Convention. For purposes of paragraph (1), an author who is domiciled in or has his or her habitual residence in, a nation adhering to the Berne Convention is considered to be a national of that nation. For purposes of paragraph (2), a work is considered to have been simultaneously published in two or more nations if its dates of publication are within 30 days of one another.

The "best edition" of a work is the edition, published in the United States at any time before the date of deposit, that the Library of Congress determines to be most suitable for its purposes.

A person's "children" are that person's immediate offspring, whether legitimate or not, and any children legally adopted by that person.

A "collective work" is a work, such as a periodical issue, anthology, or encyclopedia, in which a number of contributions, constituting separate and independent works in themselves, are assembled into a collective whole.

A "compilation" is a work formed by the collection and assembling of preexisting materials or of data that are selected, coordinated, or arranged in such a way that the resulting work as a whole constitutes an original work of authorship. The term "compilation" includes collective works.

A "computer program" is a set of statements or instructions to be used directly or indirectly in a computer in order to bring about a certain result.

"Copies" are material objects, other than phonorecords, in which a work is fixed by any method now known or later developed, and from which the work can be perceived, reproduced, or otherwise communicated, either directly or with the aid of a machine or device. The term "copies" includes the material object, other than a phonorecord, in which the work is first fixed.

"Copyright owner," with respect to any one of the exclusive rights comprised in a copyright, refers to the owner of that particular right.

The "country of origin" of a Berne Convention work, for purposes of section 411, is the United States if

(1) in the case of a published work, the work is first published
(A) in the United States;
(B) simultaneously in the United States and another nation or nations adhering to the Berne Convention, whose law grants a term of copyright protection that is the same as or longer than the term provided in the United States;

(C) simultaneously in the United States and a foreign nation that does not adhere to the Berne Convention; or

(D) in a foreign nation that does not adhere to the Berne Convention, and all of the authors of the work are nationals, domiciliaries, or habitual residents of, or in the case of an audiovisual work legal entities with headquarters in, the United States;

(2) in the case of an unpublished work, all the authors of the work are nationals, domiciliaries, or habitual residents of the United States, or, in the case of an unpublished audiovisual work, all the authors are legal entities with headquarters in the United States; or

(3) in the case of a pictorial, graphic, or sculptural work incorporated in a building or structure, the building or structure is located in the United States.

For the purposes of section 411, the "country of origin" of any other Berne Convention work is not the United States.

A work is "created" when it is fixed in a copy or phonorecord for the first time; where a work is prepared over a period of time, the portion of it that has been fixed at any particular time constitutes the work as of that time, and where the work has been prepared in different versions, each version constitutes a separate work.

A "derivative work" is a work based upon one or more preexisting works, such as a translation, musical arrangement, dramatization, fictionalization, motion picture version, sound recording, art reproduction, abridgment, condensation, or any other form in which a work may be recast, transformed, or adapted. A work consisting of editorial revisions, annotations, elaborations, or other modifications which, as a whole, represent an original work of authorship, is a "derivative work."

A "device," "machine," or "process" is one now known or later developed.

To "display" a work means to show a copy of it, either directly or by means of a film, slide, television image, or any other device or process or, in the case of a motion picture or other audiovisual work, to show individual images nonsequentially.

A work is "fixed" in a tangible medium of expression when its embodiment in a copy or phonorecord, by or under the authority of the author, is sufficiently permanent or stable to permit it to be perceived, reproduced, or otherwise communicated for a period of more than transitory duration. A work consisting of sounds, images, or both, that are being transmitted, is "fixed" for purposes of this title if a fixation of the work is being made simultaneously with its transmission.

The terms "including" and "such as" are illustrative and not limitative.

A "joint work" is a work prepared by two or more authors with the intention that their contributions be merged into inseparable or interdependent parts of a unitary whole.

"Literary works" are works, other than audiovisual works, expressed in words, numbers, or other verbal or numerical symbols or indicia, regardless of the nature of the material objects, such as books, periodicals, manuscripts, phonorecords, film, tapes, disks, or cards, in which they are embodied.

"Motion pictures" are audiovisual works consisting of a series of related images which, when shown in succession, impart an impression of motion, together with accompanying sounds, if any.

To "perform" a work means to recite, render, play, dance, or act it, either directly or by means of any device or process or, in the case of a motion picture or other audiovisual work, to show its images in any sequence or to make the sounds accompanying it audible.

"Phonorecords" are material objects in which sounds, other than those accompanying a motion picture or other audiovisual work, are fixed by any method now known or later developed, and from which the sounds can be perceived, reproduced, or otherwise communicated, either directly or with the aid of a machine or device. The term "phonorecords" includes the material object in which the sounds are first fixed.

"Pictorial, graphic, and sculptural works" include two-dimensional and three-dimensional works of fine, graphic, and applied art, photographs, prints and art reproductions, maps, globes, charts, diagrams, models, and technical drawings, including architectural plans. Such works shall include works of artistic craftsmanship insofar as their form but not their mechanical or utilitarian aspects are concerned; the design of a useful article, as defined in this section, shall be considered a pictorial, graphic, or sculptural work only if, and only to the extent that, such design incorporates pictorial, graphic, or sculptural features that can be identified separately from, and are capable of existing independently of, the utilitarian aspects of the article.

A "pseudonymous work" is a work on the copies or phonorecords of which the author is identified under a fictitious name.

"Publication" is the distribution of copies or phonorecords of a work to the public by sale or other transfer of ownership, or by rental, lease, or lending. The offering to distribute copies or phonorecords to a group of persons for purposes of further distribution, public performance, or public display, constitutes publication. A public performance or display of a work does not of itself constitute publication.

To perform or display a work "publicly" means

(1) to perform or display it at a place open to the public or at any place where a substantial number of persons outside of a normal circle of a family and its social acquaintances is gathered; or
(2) to transmit or otherwise communicate a performance or display of the work to a place specified by clause (1) or to the public, by means of any device or process, whether the members of the public capable of receiving the performance or display receive it in the same place or in separate places and at the same time or at different times.

"Sound recordings" are works that result from the fixation of a series of musical, spoken, or other sounds, but not including the sounds accompanying a motion picture or other audiovisual work, regardless of the nature of the material objects, such as disks, tapes, or other phonorecords, in which they are embodied.

"State" includes the District of Columbia and the Commonwealth of Puerto Rico, and any territories to which this title is made applicable by an Act of Congress.

A "transfer of copyright ownership" is an assignment, mortgage, exclusive license, or any other conveyance, alienation, or hypothecation of a copyright or of any of the exclusive rights comprised in a copyright, whether or not it is limited in time or place of effect, but not including a nonexclusive license.

A "transmission program" is a body of material that, as an aggregate, has been produced for the sole purpose of transmission to the public in sequence and as a unit.

To "transmit" a performance or display is to communicate it by any device or process whereby images or sounds are received beyond the place from which they are sent.

The "United States," when used in a geographical sense, comprises the several States, the District of Columbia and the Commonwealth of Puerto Rico, and the organized territories under the jurisdiction of the United States Government.

A "useful article" is an article having an intrinsic utilitarian function that is not merely to portray the appearance of the article or to convey information. An article that is normally a part of a useful article is considered a "useful article."

The author's "widow" or "widower" is the author's surviving spouse under the law of the author's domicile at the time of his or her death, whether or not the spouse has later remarried.

A "work of the United States Government" is a work prepared by an officer or employee of the United States Government as part of that person's official duties.

A "work made for hire" is

(1) a work prepared by an employee within the scope of his or her employment; or

(2) a work specially ordered or commissioned for use as a contribution to a collective work, as a part of a motion picture or other audiovisual work, as a translation, as a supplementary work, as a compilation, as an instructional text, as a test, as answer material for a test, or as an atlas, if the parties expressly agree in a written instrument signed by them that the work shall be considered a work made for hire. For the purpose of the foregoing sentence, a "supplementary work" is a work prepared for publication as a secondary adjunct to a work by another author for the purpose of introducing, concluding, illustrating, explaining, revising, commenting upon, or assisting in the use of the other work, such as forewords, afterwords, pictorial illustrations, maps, charts, tables, editorial notes, musical arrangements, answer material for tests, bibliographies, appendixes, and indexes, and an "instructional text" is a literary, pictorial, or graphic work prepared for publication and with the purpose of use in systematic instructional activities.

E-5   102. Subject matter of copyright: In general

(a) Copyright protection subsists, in accordance with this title, in original works of authorship fixed in any tangible medium of expression, now known or later developed, from which they can be perceived, reproduced, or otherwise communicated, either directly or with the aid of a machine or device. Works of authorship include the following categories:

(1) literary works;
(2) musical works, including any accompanying words;

(3) dramatic works, including any accompanying music;
(4) pantomimes and choreographic works;
(5) pictorial, graphic, and sculptural works;
(6) motion pictures and other audiovisual works; and
(7) sound recordings.

(b) In no case does copyright protection for an original work of authorship extend to any idea, procedure, process, system, method of operation, concept, principle, or discovery, regardless of the form in which it is described, explained, illustrated, or embodied in such work.

103. Subject matter of copyright: Compilations and derivative works   E–6

(a) The subject matter of copyright as specified by section 102 includes compilations and derivative works, but protection for a work employing preexisting material in which copyright subsists does not extend to any part of the work in which such material has been used unlawfully.

(b) The copyright in a compilation or derivative work extends only to the material contributed by the author of such work, as distinguished from the preexisting material employed in the work, and does not imply an exclusive right in the preexisting material. The copyright in such work is independent of, and does not affect or enlarge the scope, duration, ownership, or subsistence of, any copyright protection in the preexisting material.

104. Subject matter of copyright: National origin[4]   E–7

(*a*) UNPUBLISHED WORKS.

The works specified by sections 102 and 103, while unpublished, are subject to protection under this title without regard to the nationality or domicile of the author.

(*b*) PUBLISHED WORKS.

The works specified by sections 102 and 103, when published, are subject to protection under this title if:

(1) on the date of first publication, one or more of the authors is a national or domiciliary of the United States, or is a national, domiciliary, or sovereign authority of a foreign nation that is a party to a copyright treaty to which the United States is also a party, or is a stateless person, wherever that person may be domiciled; or
(2) the work is first published in the United States or in a foreign nation that, on the date of first publication, is a party to the Universal Copyright Convention; or
(3) the work is first published by the United Nations or any of its specialized agencies, or by the Organization of American States; or
(4) the work is a Berne Convention work; or
(5) the work comes within the scope of a Presidential proclamation. Whenever the President finds that a particular foreign nation extends, to works by authors who are nationals or domiciliaries of the United States or to works that are first published in the United States, copyright protection on substantially the same basis as that on which the foreign nation extends protection to works of its own nationals and domiciliaries and works first published in that nation, the President may by proclamation extend protection under this title

---

[4] Amended Oct. 31, 1988, Pub. L. 100–568, § 4(*a*)(2)–(3), 102 Stat. 2855.

to works of which one or more of the authors is, on the date of first publication, a national, domiciliary, or sovereign authority of that nation, or which was first published in that nation. The President may revise, suspend, or revoke any such proclamation or impose any conditions or limitations on protection under a proclamation.

(*c*) EFFECT OF BERNE CONVENTION.

No right or interest in a work eligible for protection under this title may be claimed by virtue of, or in reliance upon, the provisions of the Berne Convention, or the adherence of the United States thereto. Any rights in a work eligible for protection under this title that derive from this title, other Federal or State statutes, or the common law, shall not be expanded or reduced by virtue of, or in reliance upon, the provisions of the Berne Convention, or the adherence of the United States thereto.

E–8   105. Subject matter of copyright: United States Government works

Copyright protection under this title is not available for any work of the United States Government, but the United States Government is not precluded from receiving and holding copyrights transferred to it by assignment, bequest, or otherwise.

E–9   106. Exclusive rights in copyrighted works

Subject to sections 107 through 118, the owner of copyright under this title has the exclusive rights to do and to authorize any of the following:

(1) to reproduce the copyrighted work in copies or phonorecords;
(2) to prepare derivative works based upon the copyrighted work;
(3) to distribute copies or phonorecords of the copyrighted work to the public by sale or other transfer of ownership, or by rental, lease, or lending;
(4) in the case of literary, musical, dramatic, and choreographic works, pantomimes, and motion pictures and other audiovisual works, to perform the copyrighted work publicly; and
(5) in the case of literary, musical, dramatic, and choreographic works, pantomimes, and pictorial, graphic, or sculptural works, including the individual images of a motion picture or other audiovisual work, to display the copyrighted work publicly.

E–10   107. Limitations on exclusive rights: Fair use

Notwithstanding the provisions of section 106, the fair use of a copyrighted work, including such use by reproduction in copies or phonorecords or by any other means specified by that section, for purposes such as criticism, comment, news reporting, teaching (including multiple copies for classroom use), scholarship, or research, is not an infringement of copyright. In determining whether the use made of a work in any particular case is a fair use the factors to be considered shall include:

(1) the purpose and character of the use, including whether such use is of a commercial nature or is for nonprofit educational purposes;
(2) the nature of the copyrighted work;
(3) the amount and substantiality of the portion used in relation to the copyrighted work as a whole; and
(4) the effect of the use upon the potential market for or value of the copyrighted work.

108. Limitations on exclusive rights: Reproduction by libraries and archives

(*a*) Notwithstanding the provisions of section 106, it is not an infringement of copyright for a library or archives, or any of its employees acting within the scope of their employment, to reproduce no more than one copy or phonorecord of a work, or to distribute such copy of phonorecord, under the conditions specified by this section if:

(1) the reproduction or distribution is made without any purpose of direct or indirect commercial advantage;
(2) the collections of the library or archives are:
   (i) open to the public, or
   (ii) available not only to researchers affiliated with the library or archives or with the institution of which it is a part, but also to other persons doing research in a specialized field; and
(3) the reproduction or distribution of the work includes a notice of copyright.

(*b*) The rights of reproduction and distribution under this section apply to a copy or phonorecord of an unpublished work duplicated in facsimile form solely for purposes of preservation and security or for deposit for research use in another library or archives of the type described by clause (2) of subsection (*a*), if the copy or phonorecord reproduced is currently in the collections of the library or archives.

(*c*) The right of reproduction under this section applies to a copy or phonorecord of a published work duplicated in facsimile form solely for the purpose of replacement of a copy or phonorecord that is damaged, deteriorating, lost, or stolen, if the library or archives has, after a reasonable effort, determined that an unused replacement cannot be obtained at a fair price.

(*d*) The rights of reproduction and distribution under this section apply to a copy, made from the collection of a library or archives where the user makes his or her request or from that of another library or archives, of no more than one article or other contribution to a copyrighted collection or periodical issue, or to a copy or phonorecord of a small part of any other copyrighted work, if—

(1) the copy or phonorecord becomes the property of the user, and the library or archives has had no notice that the copy or phonorecord would be used for any purpose other than private study, scholarship, or research; and
(2) the library or archives displays prominently, at the place where orders are accepted, and includes on its order form, a warning of copyright in accordance with requirements that the Register of Copyrights shall prescribe by regulation.

(*e*) The rights of reproduction and distribution under this section apply to the entire work, or to a substantial part of it, made from the collection of a library or archives where the user makes his or her request or from that of another library or archives, if the library or archives has first determined, on the basis of a reasonable investigation, that a copy or phonorecord of the copyrighted work cannot be obtained at a fair price, if—

(1) the copy or phonorecord becomes the property of the user, and the library or archives has had no notice that the copy or phonorecord would be used for any purpose other than private study, scholarship, or research; and
(2) the library or archives displays prominently, at the place where orders are accepted, and includes on its order form, a warning of copyright in accordance with requirements that the Register of Copyrights shall prescribe by regulation.

(*f*) Nothing in this section—
(1) shall be construed to impose liability for copyright infringement upon a

library or archives or its employees for the unsupervised use of reproducing equipment located on its premises: *Provided*, That such equipment displays a notice that the making of a copy may be subject to the copyright law;

(2) excuses a person who uses such reproducing equipment or who requests a copy or phonorecord under subsection (*d*) from liability for copyright infringement for any such act, or for any later use of such copy or phono-record, if it exceeds fair use as provided by section 107;

(3) shall be construed to limit the reproduction and distribution by lending of a limited number of copies and excerpts by a library or archives of an audiovi-sual news program, subject to clauses (1), (2), and (3) of subsection (*a*); or

(4) in any way affects the right of fair use as provided by section 107, or any con-tractual obligations assumed at any time by the library or archives when it obtained a copy or phonorecord of a work in its collections.

(*g*) The rights of reproduction and distribution under this section extend to the isolated and unrelated reproduction or distribution of a single copy or phonore-cord of the same material on separate occasions, but do not extend to cases where the library or archives, or its employee—

(1) is aware or has substantial reason to believe that it is engaging in the related or concerted reproduction or distribution of multiple copies or phonorecords of the same material, whether made on one occasion or over a period of time, and whether intended for aggregate use by one or more individuals or for sep-arate use by the individual members of a group; or

(2) engages in the systematic reproduction or distribution of single or multiple copies or phonorecords of material described in subsection (*d*): *Provided*, That nothing in this clause prevents a library or archives from participating in interlibrary arrangements that do not have, as their purpose or effect, that the library or archives receiving such copies or phonorecords for distribution does so in such aggregate quantities as to substitute for a subscription to or purchase of such work.

(*h*) The rights of reproduction and distribution under this section do not apply to a musical work, a pictorial, graphic or sculptural work, or a motion picture or other audiovisual work other than an audiovisual work dealing with news, except that no such limitation shall apply with respect to rights granted by subsections (*b*) and (*c*), or with respect to pictorial or graphic works published as illustrations, diagrams, or similar adjuncts to works of which copies are reproduced or distri-buted in accordance with subsections (*d*) and (*e*).

(i) Five years from the effective date of this Act, and at five-year intervals there-after, the Register of Copyrights, after consulting with representatives of authors, book and periodical publishers, and other owners of copyrighted materials, and with representatives of library users and librarians, shall submit to the Congress a report setting forth the extent to which this section has achieved the intended statutory balancing of the rights of creators, and the needs of users. The report should also describe any problems that may have arisen, and present legislative or other recommendations, if warranted.

E–12   **109. Limitations on exclusive rights: Effect of transfer of particular copy or phonorecord**[5]

(*a*) Notwithstanding the provisions of section 106(3), the owner of a particular copy or phonorecord lawfully made under this title, or any person authorized by

---

[5] This text is Section 109 as amended by the Act of October 4, 1984, Pub. L. 98–450 (98 Stat. 1727), and further amended by the Act of November 5, 1988. Pub. L. 100–617 (102 Stat. 3194) (extending the effect of the Act from five to 13 years). Section 4 of the 1984 Act, as amended by the 1988 Act, provides that:

(a) The amendments made by this Act shall take effect on the date of the enactment of this

such owner, is entitled, without the authority of the copyright owner, to sell or otherwise dispose of the possession of that copy or phonorecord.

(*b*)(1) Notwithstanding the provisions of subsection (a), unless authorized by the owners of copyright in the sound recording and in the musical works embodied therein, the owner of a particular phonorecord may not, for purposes of direct or indirect commercial advantage, dispose of, or authorize the disposal of, the possession of that phonorecord by rental, lease, or lending, or by any other act or practice in the nature of rental, lease, or lending. Nothing in the preceding sentence shall apply to the rental, lease, or lending of a phonorecord for nonprofit purposes of a nonprofit library or nonprofit educational institution.

(2) Nothing in this subsection shall affect any provision of the antitrust laws. For purposes of the preceding sentence, "antitrust laws" has the meaning given that term in the first section of the Clayton Act and includes section 5 of the Federal Trade Commission Act to the extent that section relates to unfair methods of competition.

(3) Any person who distributes a phonorecord in violation of clause (1) is an infringer of copyright under section 501 of this title and is subject to the remedies set forth in sections 502, 503, 504, 505, and 509. Such violation shall not be a criminal offense under section 506 or cause such person to be subject to the criminal penalties set forth in section 2319 of title 18.

(*c*) Notwithstanding the provisions of section 106(5), the owner of a particular copy lawfully made under this title, or any person authorized by such owner, is entitled, without the authority of the copyright owner, to display that copy publicly, either directly or by the projection of no more than one image at a time, to viewers present at the place where the copy is located.

(*d*) The privileges prescribed by subsections (*a*) and (*c*) do not, unless authorized by the copyright owner, extend to any person who has acquired possession of the copy or phonorecord from the copyright owner by rental, lease, loan, or otherwise, without acquiring ownership of it.

110. Limitations on exclusive rights: Exemption of certain performances E–13 and displays[6]

Notwithstanding the provisions of section 106, the following are not infringements of copyright:

(1) performance or display of a work by instructors or pupils in the course of face-to-face teaching activities of a nonprofit educational institution, in a classroom or similar place devoted to instruction, unless, in the case of a motion picture or other audiovisual work, the performance, or the display of individual images, is given by means of a copy that was not lawfully made under this title, and that the person responsible for the performance knew or had reason to believe was not lawfully made;

(2) performance of a nondramatic literary or musical work or display of a work, by or in the course of a transmission, if—

Act [October 4, 1984].

(b) The provisions of section 109(*b*) of title 17, United States Code, as added by section 2 of this Act, shall not effect the right of an owner of a particular phonorecord of a sound recording, who acquired such ownership before the date of the enactment of this Act, to dispose of the possession of that particular phonorecord on or after such date of enactment in any manner permitted by section 109 of title 17, United States Code, as in effect on the day before the date of the enactment of this Act.

(c) The amendments made by this Act shall not apply to rentals, leasings, lendings (or acts or practices in the nature of rentals, leasings, or lendings) occurring after the date which is 13 years after the date of the enactment of this Act.

[6] As amended Oct. 15, 1982, Pub. L. 97–366, § 3, 96 Stat. 1759.

(A) the performance or display is a regular part of the systematic instructional activities of a governmental body or a nonprofit educational institution; and

(B) the performance or display is directly related and of material assistance to the teaching content of the transmission; and

(C) the transmission is made primarily for—

(i) reception in classrooms or similar places normally devoted to instruction, or

(ii) reception by persons to whom the transmission is directed because their disabilities or other special circumstances prevent their attendance in classrooms or similar places normally devoted to instruction, or

(iii) reception by officers or employees of governmental bodies as a part of their official duties or employment;

(3) performance of a nondramatic literary or musical work or of a dramatico-musical work of a relgious nature, or display of a work, in the course of services at a place of worship or other religious assembly;

(4) performance of a nondramatic literary or musical work otherwise than in a transmission to the public, without any purpose of direct or indirect commercial advantage and without payment of any fee or other compensation for the performance to any of its performers, promoters, or organizers, if—

(A) there is no direct or indirect admission charge; or

(B) the proceeds, after deducting the reasonable costs of producing the performance, are used exclusively for educational, religious, or charitable purposes and not for private financial gain, except where the copyright owner has served notice of objection to the performance under the following conditions;

(i) the notice shall be in writing and signed by the copyright owner or such owner's duly authorized agent; and

(ii) the notice shall be served on the person responsible for the performance at least seven days before the date of the performance, and shall state the reasons for the objection; and

(iii) the notice shall comply, in form, content, and manner of service, with requirements that the Register of Copyrights shall prescribe by regulation;

(5) communication of a transmission embodying a performance or display of a work by the public reception of the transmission on a single receiving apparatus of a kind commonly used in private homes, unless—

(A) a direct charge is made to see or hear the transmission; or

(B) the transmission thus received is further transmitted to the public;

(6) performance of a nondramatic musical work by a governmental body or a nonprofit agricultural or horticultural organization, in the course of an annual agricultural or horticultural fair or exhibition conducted by such body or organization; the exemption provided by this clause shall extend to any liability for copyright infringement that would otherwise be imposed on such body or organization, under doctrines of vicarious liability or related infringement, for a performance by a concessionnaire, business establishment, or other person at such fair or exhibition, but shall not excuse any such person from liability for the performance;

(7) performance of a nondramatic musical work by a vending establishment open to the public at large without any direct or indirect admission charge, where the sole purpose of the performance is to promote the retail sale of copies or phonorecords of the work, and the performance is not transmitted beyond the place

where the establishment is located and is within the immediate area where the sale is occurring;

(8) performance of a nondramatic literary work, by or in the course of a transmission specifically designed for and primarily directed to blind or other handicapped persons who are unable to read normal printed material as a result of their handicap, or deaf or other handicapped persons who are unable to hear the aural signals accompanying a transmission of visual signals, if the performance is made without any purpose of direct or indirect commercial advantage and its transmission is made through the facilities of: (i) a governmental body; or (ii) a noncommercial educational broadcast station (as defined in section 397 of title 47), or (iii) a radio subcarrier authorization (as defined in 47 CFR 73.293–73.295 and 73.593–73.595); or (iv) a cable system (as defined in section 111(f)).

(9) performance on a single occasion of a dramatic literary work published at least ten years before the date of the performance, by or in the course of a transmission specifically designed for and primarily directed to blind or other handicapped persons who are unable to read normal printed material as a result of their handicap, if the performance is made without any purpose of direct or indirect commercial advantage and its transmission is made though the facilities of a radio subcarrier authorization referred to in clause (8)(iii), *Provided,* That the provisions of this clause shall not be applicable to more than one performance of the same work by the same performers or under the auspices of the same organization.

(10) notwithstanding paragraph 4 above, the following is not an infringement of copyright: performance of a nondramatic literary or musical work in the course of a social function which is organized and promoted by a nonprofit veterans' organization or a nonprofit fraternal organization to which the general public is not invited, but not including the invitees of the organizations, if the proceeds from the performance, after deducting the reasonable costs of producing the performance, are used exclusively for charitable purposes and not for financial gain. For purposes of this section the social functions of any college or university fraternity or sorority shall not be included unless the social function is held solely to raise funds for a specific charitable purpose.[7]

111. Limitations on exclusive rights: Secondary transmissions[8]   E–14

(*a*) CERTAIN SECONDARY TRANSMISSIONS EXEMPTED.

The secondary transmission of a primary transmission embodying a performance or display of a work is not an infringement of copyright if—

(1) the secondary transmission is not made by a cable system, and consists entirely of the relaying, by the management of a hotel, apartment house, or similar establishment, of signals transmitted by a broadcast station licensed by the Federal Communications Commission, within the local service area of such station, to the private lodgings of guests or residents of such establishment, and no direct charge is made to see or hear the secondary transmission; or

(2) the secondary transmission is made solely for the purpose and under the conditions specified by clause (2) of section 110;

(3) the secondary transmission is made by any carrier who has no direct or

---

[7] Section 110(10) only was added by Pub. L. 97–366, 96 Stat. 1759.

[8] Amended Aug. 27, 1986, Pub. L. 99–397, §§ 1, 2(*a*), (*b*), 100 Stat. 848, Nov. 16, 1988, 1988, Pub. L. 100–667, § 202(2), 102 Stat. 3935.

indirect control over the content or selection of the primary transmission or over the particular recipients of the secondary transmission, and whose activities with respect to the secondary transmission consist solely of providing wire, cables, or other communications channels for the use of others: Provided, that the provisions of this clause extend only to the activities of said carrier with respect to secondary transmission and do not exempt from liability the activities of others with respect to their own primary or secondary transmissions; or

(4) the secondary transmission is made by a satellite carrier for private home viewing pursuant to a statutory license under section 119; or

(5) the secondary transmission is not made by a cable system but is made by a governmental body, or other nonprofit organization, without any purpose of direct or indirect commercial advantage, and without charge to the recipients of the secondary transmission other than assessments necessary to defray the actual and reasonable costs of maintaining and operating the secondary transmission service.

(*b*) SECONDARY TRANSMISSION OF PRIMARY TRANSMISSION TO CONTROLLED GROUP.

Notwithstanding the provisions of subsections (*a*) and (*c*), the secondary transmission to the public of a primary transmission embodying a performance or display of a work is actionable as an act of infringement under section 501, and is fully subject to the remedies provided by sections 502 through 506 and 509, if the primary transmission is not made for reception by the public at large but is controlled and limited to reception by particular members of the public: Provided, however, that such secondary transmission is not actionable as an act of infringement if—

(1) the primary transmission is made by a broadcast station licensed by the Federal Communications Commission; and

(2) the carriage of the signals comprising the secondary transmission is required under the rules, regulations, or authorizations of the Federal Communications Commission; and

(3) the signal of the primary transmitter is not altered or changed in any way by the secondary transmitter.

(*c*) SECONDARY TRANSMISSIONS BY CABLE SYSTEMS.

(1) Subject to the provisions of clauses (2), (3), and (4) of this subsection, secondary transmissions to the public by a cable system of a primary transmission made by a broadcast station licensed by the Federal Communications Commission or by an appropriate governmental authority of Canada or Mexico and embodying a performance or display of a work shall be subject to compulsory licensing upon compliance with the requirements of subsection (*d*) where the carriage of the signals comprising the secondary transmission is permissible under the rules, regulations, or authorizations of the Federal Communications Commission.

(2) Notwithstanding the provisions of clause (1) of this subsection, the willful or repeated secondary transmission to the public by a cable system of a primary transmission made by a broadcast station licensed by the Federal Communications Commission or by an appropriate governmental authority of Canada or Mexico and embodying a performance or display of a work is actionable as an act of infringement under section 501, and is fully subject to the remedies provided by sections 502 through 506 and 509, in the following cases:

(A) where the carriage of the signals comprising the secondary transmission is not permissible under the rules, regulations, or authorizations of the Federal Communications Commission; or

(B) where the cable system has not recorded the notice specified by subsection (*d*) and deposited the statement of account and royalty fee
required by subsection (*d*).

(3) Notwithstanding the provisions of clause (1) of this subsection and subject
to the provisions of subsection (*e*) of this section, the secondary transmission to the public by a cable system of a primary transmission made by
a broadcast station licensed by the Federal Communications Commission
or by an appropriate governmental authority of Canada or Mexico and
embodying a performance or display of a work is actionable as an act of
infringement under section 501, and is fully subject to the remedies provided by sections 502 through 506 and sections 509 and 510, if the content
of the particular program in which the performance or display is embodied,
or any commercial advertising or station announcements transmitted by
the primary transmitter during, or immediately before or after, the transmission of such program, is in any way willfully altered by the cable system
through changes, deletions, or additions, except for the alteration, deletion,
or substitution of commercial advertisements performed by those engaged
in television commercial advertising market research: Provided, that the
research company has obtained the prior consent of the advertiser who has
purchased the original commercial advertisement, the television station
broadcasting that commercial advertisement, and the cable system performing the secondary transmission: And provided further, that such commercial alteration, deletion, or substitution is not performed for the
purpose of deriving income from the sale of that commercial time.

(4) Notwithstanding the provisions of clause (1) of this subsection, the secondary transmission to the public by a cable system of a primary transmission
made by a broadcast station licensed by an appropriate governmental
authority of Canada or Mexico and embodying a performance or display of
a work is actionable as an act of infringement under section 501, and is
fully subject to the remedies provided by sections 502 through 506 and section 509, if (A) with respect to Canadian signals, the community of the
cable system is located more than 150 miles from the United States-Can-
adian border and is also located south of the forty-second parallel of lati-
tude, or (B) with respect to Mexican signals, the secondary transmission is
made by a cable system which received the primary transmission by means
other than direct interception of a free space radio wave emitted by such
broadcast television station, unless prior to April 15, 1976, such cable system was actually carrying, or was specifically authorized to carry, the signal of such foreign station on the system pursuant to the rules, regulations,
or authorizations of the Federal Communications Commission.

(*d*) COMPULSORY LICENSE FOR SECONDARY TRANSMISSIONS BY CABLE SYSTEMS.

(1) A cable system whose secondary transmissions have been subject to compulsory licensing under subsection (c) shall, on a semiannual basis, deposit
with the Register of Copyrights, in accordance with requirements that the
Register shall, after consultation with the Copyright Royalty Tribunal (if
and when the Tribunal has been constituted), prescribe by regulation—

(A) a statement of account, covering the six months next preceding, specifying the number of channels on which the cable system made secondary transmissions to its subscribers, the names and locations of all
primary transmitters whose transmissions were further transmitted by

1455

the cable system, the total number of subscribers, the gross amounts paid to the cable system for the basic service of providing secondary transmissions of primary broadcast transmitters, and such other data as the Register of Copyrights may, after consultation with the Copyright Royalty Tribunal (if and when the Tribunal has been constituted), from time to time prescribe by regulation. In determining the total number of subscribers and the gross amounts paid to the cable system for the basic service of providing secondary transmissions of primary broadcast transmitters, the system shall not include subscribers an amounts collected from subscribers receiving transmissions for private home viewing pursuant to section 119. Such statement shall also include a special statement of account covering any nonnetwork television programming that was carried by the cable system in whole or in part beyond the local service area of the primary transmitter, under rules, regulations, or authorizations of the Federal Communications Commission permitting the substitution or addition of signals under certain circumstances, together with logs showing the times, dates, stations, and programs involved in such substituted or added carriage; and

(B) except in the case of a cable system whose royalty is specified in subclause (C) or (D), a total royalty fee for the period covered by the statement, computed on the basis of specified percentages of the gross receipts from subscribers to the cable service during said period for the basic service of providing secondary transmissions of primary broadcast transmitters, as follows:

    (i) 0.675 of 1 per centum of such gross receipts for the privilege of further transmitting any nonnetwork programming of a primary transmitter in whole or in part beyond the local service area of such primary transmitter, such amount to be applied against the fee, if any, payable pursuant to paragraphs (ii) through (iv);

    (ii) 0.675 of 1 per centum of such gross receipts for the first distant signal equivalent;

    (iii) 0.425 of 1 per centum of such gross receipts for each of the second, third, and fourth distant signal equivalents;

    (iv) 0.2 of 1 per centum of such gross receipts for the fifth distant signal equivalent and each additional distant signal equivalent thereafter; and

    in computing the amounts payable under paragraph (ii) through (iv), above, any fraction of a distant signal equivalent shall be computed at its fractional value and, in the case of any cable system located partly within and partly without the local service area of a primary transmitter, gross receipts shall be limited to those gross receipts derived from subscribers located without the local service area of such primary transmitter; and

(C) if the actual gross receipts paid by subscribers to a cable system for the period covered by the statement for the basic service of providing secondary transmissions of primary broadcast transmitters total $80,000 or less, gross receipts of the cable system for the purpose of this subclause shall be computed by subtracting from such actual gross receipts the amount by which $80,000 exceeds such actual gross receipts, except that in no case shall a cable system's gross receipts be reduced to less than $3,000. The royalty fee payable under this subclause shall be 0.5 of 1 per centum, regardless of the number of distant signal equivalents, if any; and

(D) if the actual gross receipts paid by subscribers to a cable system for the period covered by the statement, for the basic service of providing secondary transmissions of primary broadcast transmitters, are more than $80,000 but less than $160,000, the royalty fee payable under this subclause shall be:

    (i) 0.5 of 1 per centum of any gross receipts up to $80,000; and

    (ii) 1 per centum of any gross receipts in excess of $80,000 but less than $160,000, regardless of the number of distant signal equivalents, if any.

(2) The Register of Copyrights shall receive all fees deposited under this section and, after deducting the reasonable costs incurred by the Copyright Office under this section, shall deposit the balance in the Treasury of the United States, in such manner as the Secretary of the Treasury directs. All funds held by the Secretary of the Treasury shall be invested in interest-bearing United States securities for later distribution with interest by the Copyright Royalty Tribunal as provided by this title. The Register shall submit to the Copyright Royalty Tribunal, on a semiannual basis, a compilation of all statements of account covering the relevant six-month period provided by paragraph (1) of this subsection.

(3) The royalty fees thus deposited shall, in accordance with the procedures provided by clause (4), be distributed to those among the following copyright owners who claim that their works were the subject of secondary transmissions by cable systems during the relevant semiannual period:

    (A) any such owner whose work was included in a secondary transmission made by a cable system of a nonnetwork television program in whole or in part beyond the local service area of the primary transmitter; and

    (B) any such owner whose work was included in a secondary transmission identified in a special statement of account deposited under paragraph (1)(A); and

    (C) any such owner whose work was included in nonnetwork programing consisting exclusively of aural signals carried by a cable system in whole or in part beyond the local service area of the primary transmitter of such programs.

(4) The royalty fees thus deposited shall be distributed in accordance with the following procedures:

    (A) During the month of July in each year, every person claiming to be entitled to compulsory license fees for secondary transmissions shall file a claim with the Copyright Royalty Tribunal, in accordance with requirements that the Tribunal shall prescribe by regulation. Notwithstanding any provisions of the antitrust laws, for purposes of this clause any claimants may agree among themselves as to the proportionate division of compulsory licensing fees among them, may lump their claims together and file them jointly or as a single claim, or may designate a common agent to receive payments on their behalf.

    (B) After the first day of August of each year, the Copyright Royalty Tribunal shall determine whether there exists a controversy concerning the distribution of royalty fees. If the Tribunal determines that no such controversy exists, it shall, after deducting its reasonable administrative costs under this section, distribute such fees to the copyright owners entitled, or to their designated agents. If the Tribunal finds the existence of a controversy, it shall, pursuant to chapter 8 of this title, conduct a proceeding to determine the distribution of royalty fees.

    (C) During the pendency of any proceeding under this subsection, the Copyright Royalty Tribunal shall withhold from distribution an amount sufficient to satisfy all claims with respect to which a controversy exists, but shall have discretion to proceed to distribute any amounts that are not in controversy.

(*e*) NONSIMULTANEOUS SECONDARY TRANSMISSIONS BY CABLE SYSTEMS.

(1) Notwithstanding those provisions of the second paragraph of subsection (*f*) relating to nonsimultaneous secondary transmissions by a cable system, any such transmissions are actionable as an act of infringement under section 501, and are fully subject to the remedies provided by sections 502 through 506 and sections 509 and 510, unless—

(A) the program on the videotape is transmitted no more than one time to the cable system's subscribers; and

(B) the copyrighted program, episode, or motion picture videotape, including the commercials contained within such program, episode, or picture, is transmitted without deletion or editing; and

(C) an owner or officer of the cable system (i) prevents the duplication of the videotape while in the possession of the system, (ii) prevents unauthorized duplication while in the possession of the facility making the videotape for the system if the system owns or controls the facility, or take reasonable precautions to prevent such duplication if it does not own or control the facility, (iii) takes adequate precautions to prevent duplication while the tape is being transported, and (iv) subject to clause (2), erases or destroys, or causes the erasure or destruction of, the videotape; and

(D) within forty-five days after the end of each calendar quarter, an owner or officer of the cable system executes an affidavit attesting (i) to the steps and precautions taken to prevent duplication of the videotape, and (ii) subject to clause (2), to the erasure or destruction of all videotapes made or used during such quarter; and

(E) such owner or officer places or causes each such affidavit, and affidavits received pursuant to clause (2)(C), to be placed in a file, open to public inspection, at such system's main office in the community where the transmission is made or in the nearest community where such system maintains an office; and

(F) the nonsimultaneous transmission is one that the cable system would be authorized to transmit under the rules, regulations, and authorizations of the Federal Communications Commission in effect at the time of the nonsimultaneous transmission if the transmission had been made simultaneously, except that this subclause shall not apply to inadvertent or accidental transmissions.

(2) If a cable system transfers to any person a videotape of a program nonsimultaneously transmitted by it, such transfer is actionable as an act of infringement under section 501, and is fully subject to the remedies provided by sections 502 through 506 and 509, except that, pursuant to a written, nonprofit contract providing for the equitable sharing of the costs of such videotape and its transfer, a videotape nonsimultaneously transmitted by it, in accordance with clause (1), may be transferred by one cable system in Alaska to another system in Alaska, by one cable system in Hawaii permitted to make such nonsimultaneous transmissions to another such cable system in Hawaii, or by one cable system in Guam, the Northern Mariana Islands, or the Trust Territory of the Pacific Islands, to another cable system in any of those three territories, if—

(A) each such contract is available for public inspection in the offices of the cable systems involved, and a copy of such contract is filed, within thirty days after such contract is entered into, with the Copyright Office (which

Office shall make each such contract available for public inspection); and

(B) the cable system to which the videotape is transferred complies with clause (1)(A), (B), (C)(i), (iii), and (iv), and (D) through (F); and (C) such system provides a copy of the affidavit required to be made in accordance with clause (1)(D) to each cable system making a previous nonsimultaneous transmission of the same videotape.

(3) This subsection shall not be construed to supersede the exclusivity protection provisions of any existing agreement, or any such agreement hereafter entered into, between a cable system and a television broadcast station in the area in which the cable system is located, or a network with which such station is affiliated.

(4) As used in this subsection, the term "videotape," and each of its variant forms, means the reproduction of the images and sounds of a program or programs broadcast by a television broadcast station licensed by the Federal Communications Commission, regardless of the nature of the material objects, such as tapes or films, in which the reproduction is embodied.

(*f*) DEFINITIONS.

As used in this section, the following terms and their variant forms mean the following:

A "primary transmission" is a transmission made to the public by the transmitting facility whose signals are being received and further transmitted by the secondary transmission service, regardless of where or when the performance or display was first transmitted. In the case of a low power television station, as defined by the rules and regulations of the Federal Communication Commission, the "local service area of a primary transmitter" comprises the area within 35 miles of the transmitter site, except that in the case of such a station located in a standard metropolitan statistical area which has one of the 50 largest populations of all standard metropolitan statistical areas (based on the 1980 decennial census of population taken by the Secretary of Commerce), the number of miles shall be 20 miles.

A "secondary transmission" is the further transmitting of a primary transmission simultaneously with the primary transmission, or nonsimultaneously with the primary transmission if by a "cable system" not located in whole or in part within the boundary of the forty-eight contiguous States, Hawaii, or Puerto Rico: Provided, however, That a nonsimultaneous further transmission by a cable system located in Hawaii of a primary transmission shall be deemed to be a secondary transmission if the carriage of the television broadcast signal comprising such further transmission is permissible under the rules, regulations, or authorizations of the Federal Communications Commission.

A "cable system" is a facility, located in any State, Territory, Trust Territory, or Posession, that in whole or in part receives signals transmitted or programs broadcast by one or more television broadcast stations licensed by the Federal Communications Commission, and makes secondary transmissions of such signals or programs by wires, cables, or other communications channels to subscribing members of the public who pay for such service. For purposes of determining the royalty fee under subsection (*d*)(1), two or more cable systems in contiguous communities under common ownership or control or operating from one headend shall be considered as one system.

The "local service area of a primary transmitter," in the case of a television broadcast station, comprises the area in which such station is entitled to insist upon its signal being retransmitted by a cable system pursuant to the rules, regulations, and authorizations of the Federal Communications Commission in effect on April 15, 1976, or in the case of a television broadcast station licensed by an appropriate governmental authority of Canada or Mexico, the area in which it would be entitled to insist upon its signal being retransmitted if it were a television broadcast station subject to such rules, regulations, and authorizations. In the case of a low power television station, as defined by the rules and regulations of the Federal Communications Commission, the "local service area of a primary transmitter" comprises the area within 35 miles of the transmitter site, except that in the case of such a station located in a standard metropolitan statistical area which has one of the 50 largest populations of all standard metropolitan statistical areas (based on the 1980 decennial census of population taken by the Secretary of Commerce), the number of miles shall be 20 miles. The "local service area of a primary transmitter," in the case of a radio broadcast station, comprises the primary service area of such station, pursuant to the rules and regulations of the Federal Communications Commission. Pursuant to the rules, regulations, and authorizations of the Federal Communications Commission in effect on April 15, 1976, or in the case of a television broadcast station licensed by an appropriate governmental authority of Canada or Mexico, the area in which it would be entitled to insist upon its signal being retransmitted if it were a television broadcast station subject to such rules, regulations, and authorizations. The "local service area of a primary transmitter," in the case of a radio broadcast station, comprises the primary service area of such station, pursuant to the rules and regulations of the Federal Communications Commission.

A "distant signal equivalent" is the value assigned to the secondary transmission of any nonnetwork television programming carried by a cable system in whole or in part beyond the local service area of the primary transmitter of such programming. It is computed by assigning a value of one to each independent station and a value of one-quarter to each network station and noncommercial educational station for the nonnetwork programming so carried pursuant to the rules, regulations, and authorizations of the Federal Communications Commission. The foregoing values for independent, network, and noncommercial educational stations are subject, however, to the following exceptions and limitations. Where the rules and regulations of the Federal Communications Commission require a cable system to omit the further transmission of a particular program and such rules and regulations also permit the substitution of another program embodying a performance or display of a work in place of the omitted transmission, or where such rules and regulations in effect on the date of enactment of this Act permit a cable system, at its election, to effect such deletion and substitution of a nonlive program or to carry additional programs not transmitted by primary transmitters within whose local service area the cable system is located, no value shall be assigned for the substituted or additional program; where the rules, regulations, or authorizations of the Federal Communications Commission in effect on the date of enactment of this Act permit a cable system, at its election, to omit the further transmission of a particular program and such rules, regulations, or authorizations also permit the substitution of another program embodying a performance or display of a work in place of the omitted transmission, the value assigned for the substituted or additional program shall be, in the case of a live program, the value of one full distant signal equivalent multiplied by a fraction that has as its numerator the number of days in the year in which such substitution occurs and as its denominator the number of days in the year. In the case of a station carried pursuant to the late-night or specialty programming rules of the

Federal Communications Commission, or a station carried on a part-time basis where full-time carriage is not possible because the cable system lacks the activated channel capacity to retransmit on a full-time basis all signals which it is authorized to carry, the values for independent, network, and noncommercial educational stations set forth above, as the case may be, shall be multiplied by a fraction which is equal to the ratio of the broadcast hours of such station carried by the cable system to the total broadcast hours of the station.

A "network station" is a television broadcast station that is owned or operated by, or affiliated with, one or more of the television networks in the United States providing nationwide transmissions, and that transmits a substantial part of the programming supplied by such networks for a substantial part of that station's typical broadcast day.

An "independent station" is a commercial television broadcast station other than a network station.

A "noncommercial educational station" is a television station that is a noncommercial educational broadcast station as defined in section 397 of title 47.

112. Limitations on exclusive rights: Ephemeral recordings E–15

(*a*) Notwithstanding the provisions of section 106, and except in the case of a motion picture or other audiovisual work, it is not an infringement of copyright for a transmitting organization entitled to transmit to the public a performance or display of a work, under a license or transfer of the copyright or under the limitations on exclusive rights in sound recordings specified by section 114(a), to make no more than one copy or phonorecord of a particular transmission program embodying the performance or display, if—

(1) the copy or phonorecord is retained and used solely by the transmitting organization that made it, and no further copies or phonorecords are reproduced from it; and

(2) the copy or phonorecord is used solely for the transmitting organization's own transmissions within its local service area, or for purposes of archival preservation or security; and

(3) unless preserved exclusively for archival purposes, the copy or phonorecord is destroyed within six months from the date the transmission program was first transmitted to the public.

(*b*) Notwithstanding the provisions of section 106, it is not an infringement of copyright for a governmental body or other nonprofit organization entitled to transmit a performance or display of a work, under section 110(2) or under the limitations on exclusive rights in sound recordings specified by section 114(a), to make no more than thirty copies or phonorecords of a particular transmission program embodying the performance or display, if—

(1) no further copies or phonorecords are reproduced from the copies or phonorecords made under this clause; and

(2) except for one copy or phonorecord that may be preserved exclusively for archival purposes, the copies or phonorecords are destroyed within seven years from the date the transmission program was first transmitted to the public.

(*c*) Notwithstanding the provisions of section 106, it is not an infringement of copyright for a governmental body or other nonprofit organization to make for distribution no more than one copy or phonorecord, for each transmitting organization specified in clause (2) of this subsection, of a particular transmission program embodying a performance of a nondramatic musical work of a religious nature, or of a sound recording of such a musical work, if—

    (1) there is no direct or indirect charge for making or distributing any such copies or phonorecords; and

    (2) none of such copies or phonorecords is used for any performance other than a single transmission to the public by a transmitting organization entitled to transmit to the public a performance of the work under a license or transfer of the copyright; and

    (3) except for one copy or phonorecord that may be preserved exclusively for archival purposes, the copies or phonorecords are all destroyed within one year from the date the transmission program was first transmitted to the public.

(*d*) Notwithstanding the provisions of section 106, it is not an infringement of copyright for a governmental body or other nonprofit organization entitled to transmit a performance of a work under section 110(8) to make no more than ten copies or phonorecords embodying the performance, or to permit the use of any such copy or phonorecord by any governmental body or nonprofit organization entitled to transmit a performance of a work under section 110(8), if

    (1) any such copy or phonorecord is retained and used solely by the organization that made it, or by a governmental body or nonprofit organization entitled to transmit a performance of a work under section 110(8), and no further copies or phonorecords are reproduced from it; and

    (2) any such copy or phonorecord is used solely for transmissions authorized under section 110(8), or for purposes of archival preservation or security; and

    (3) the governmental body or nonprofit organization permitting any use of any such copy or phonorecord by any governmental body or nonprofit organization under this subsection does not make any charge for such use.

(*e*) The transmission program embodied in a copy or phonorecord made under this section is not subject to protection as a derivative work under this title except with the express consent of the owners of copyright in the preexisting works employed in the program.

E–16   **113. Scope of exclusive rights in pictorial, graphic, and sculptural works**

(*a*) Subject to the provisions of subsections (*b*) and (*c*) of this section, the exclusive right to reproduce a copyrighted pictorial, graphic, or sculptural work in copies under section 106 includes the right to reproduce the work in or on any kind of article, whether useful or otherwise.

(*b*) This title does not afford, to the owner of copyright in a work that portrays a useful article as such, any greater or lesser rights with respect to the making, distribution, or display of the useful article so portrayed than those afforded to such works under the law, whether title 17 or the common law or statutes of a State, in effect on December 31, 1977, as held applicable and construed by a court in an action brought under this title.

(*c*) In the case of a work lawfully reproduced in useful articles that have been offered for sale or other distribution to the public, copyright does not include any right to prevent the making, distribution, or display of pictures or photographs of such articles in connection with advertisements or commentaries related to the distribution or display of such articles, or in connection with news reports.

E–17   **114. Scope of exclusive rights in sound recordings**

(*a*) The exclusive rights of the owner of copyright in a sound recording are limited to the rights specified by clauses (1), (2), and (3) of section 106, and do not include any right of performance under section 106(4).

(*b*) The exclusive right of the owner of copyright in a sound recording under clause (1) of section 106 is limited to the right to duplicate the sound recording in the form of phonorecords, or of copies of motion pictures and other audiovisual works, that directly or indirectly recapture the actual sounds fixed in the recording. The exclusive right of the owner of copyright in a sound recording under clause (2) of section 106 is limited to the right to prepare a derivative work in which the actual sounds fixed in the sound recording are rearranged, remixed, or otherwise altered in sequence or quality. The exclusive rights of the owner of copyright in a sound recording under clauses (1) and (2) of section 106 do not extend to the making or duplication of another sound recording that consists entirely of an independent fixation of other sounds, even though such sounds imitate or simulate those in the copyrighted sound recording. The exclusive rights of the owner of copyright in a sound recording under clauses (1), (2), and (3) of section 106 do not apply to sound recordings included in educational television and radio programs (as defined in section 397 of title 47) distributed or transmitted by or through public broadcasting entities (as defined by section 118(*g*)); *Provided*, That copies or phonorecords of said programs are not commercially distributed by or through public broadcasting entities to the general public.

(*c*) This section does not limit or impair the exclusive right to perform publicly, by means of a phonorecord, any of the works specified by section 106(4).

(*d*) On January 3, 1978, the Register of Copyrights, after consulting with representatives of owners of copyrighted materials, representatives of the broadcasting, recording, motion picture, entertainment industries, and arts organizations, representatives of organized labor and performers of copyrighted materials, shall submit to the Congress a report setting forth recommendations as to whether this section should be amended to provide for performers and copyright owners of copyrighted material any performance rights in such material. The report should describe the status of such rights in foreign countries, the views of major interested parties, and specific legislative or other recommendations, if any.

115. Scope of exclusive rights in nondramatic musical works: Compulsory license for making and distributing phonorecords[9]

In the case of nondramatic musical works, the exclusive rights provided by clauses (1) and (3) of section 106, to make and to distribute phonorecords of such works, are subject to compulsory licensing under the conditions specified by this section.

(*a*) Availability and Scope of Compulsory License.

(1) When phonorecords of a nondramatic musical work have been distributed to the public in the United States under the authority of the copyright owner, any other person may, by complying with the provisions of this section, obtain a compulsory license to make and distribute phonorecords of the work. A person may obtain a compulsory license only if his or her primary purpose in making phonorecords is to distribute them to the public for private use. A person may not obtain a compulsory license for use of the work in the making of phonorecords duplicating a sound recording fixed by another, unless: (i) such sound recording was fixed lawfully; and (ii) the making of the phonorecords was authorized by the owner of copyright in the sound recording or, if the sound recording was fixed before February 15, 1972, by any person who fixed the sound recording pursuant to an express license from the owner of the copyright in the musical work or pursuant to a valid compulsory license for use of such work in a sound recording.

---

[9] As amended Oct. 4, 1984, Pub. L. 98–450, § 3, 98 Stat. 1727.

(2) A compulsory license includes the privilege of making a musical arrangement of the work to the extent necessary to conform it to the style or manner of interpretation of the performance involved, but the arrangement shall not change the basic melody or fundamental character of the work, and shall not be subject to protection as a derivative work under this title, except with the express consent of the copyright owner.

(*b*) Notice of Intention to Obtain Compulsory License.

(1) Any person who wishes to obtain a compulsory license under this section shall, before or within thirty days after making, and before distributing any phonorecords of the work, serve notice of intention to do so on the copyright owner. If the registration or other public records of the Copyright Office do not identify the copyright owner and include an address at which notice can be served, it shall be sufficient to file the notice of intention in the Copyright Office. The notice shall comply, in form, content, and manner of service, with requirements that the Register of Copyrights shall prescribe by regulation.

(2) Failure to serve or file the notice required by clause (1) forecloses the possibility of a compulsory license and, in the absence of a negotiated license, renders the making and distribution of phonorecords actionable as acts of infringement under section 501 and fully subject to the remedies provided by sections 502 through 506 and 509.

(*c*) Royalty Payable under Compulsory License.[10]

(1) To be entitled to receive royalties under a compulsory license, the copyright owner must be identified in the registration or other public records of the Copyright Office. The owner is entitled to royalties for phonorecords made and distributed after being so identified, but is not entitled to recover for any phonorecords previously made and distributed.

(2) Except as provided by clause (1), the royalty under a compulsory license shall be payable for every phonorecord made and distributed in accordance with the license. For this purpose, a phonorecord is considered "distributed" if the person exercising the compulsory license has voluntarily and permanently parted with its possession. With respect to each work embodied in the phonorecord, the royalty shall be either two and three-fourths cents, or one-half of one cent per minute of playing time or fraction thereof, whichever amount is larger.

(3) A compulsory license under this section includes the right of the maker of a phonorecord of a nondramatic musical work under subsection (a)(1) to distribute or authorize distribution of such phonorecord by rental, lease, or lending (or by acts or practices in the nature of rental, lease, or lending). In addition to any royalty payable under clause (2) and chapter 8 of this title, a royalty shall be payable by the compulsory licensee for every act of distribution of a phonorecord by or in the nature of rental, lease, or lending, by or under the authority of the compulsory licensee. With respect to each nondramatic musical work embodied in the phonorecord, the royalty shall be a proportion of the revenue received by the compulsory licensee from every such act of distribution of the phonorecord under this clause equal to the proportion of the revenue received by the compulsory licensee from distribution of the phonorecord under clause (2) that is payable by a compul-

---

[10] Section 115(*c*) as amended by the Act of October 4, 1984, Pub. L. 98–450 (98 Stat. 1727). For Section 4 of that Act see § E–12 n. 5 *ante*.

sory licensee under that clause and under chapter 8. The Register of Copyright shall issue regulations to carry out the purpose of this clause.

(4) Royalty payments shall be made on or before the twentieth day of each month and shall include all royalties for the month next preceding. Each monthly payment shall be made under oath and shall comply with requirements that the Register of Copyrights shall prescribe by regulation. The Register shall also prescribe regulations under which detailed cumulative annual statements of account, certified by a certified public accountant, shall be filed for every compulsory license under this section. The regulations covering both the monthly and the annual statements of account shall prescribe the form, content and manner of certification with respect to the number of records made and the number of records distributed.

(5) If the copyright owner does not receive the monthly payment and the monthly and annual statements of account when due, the owner may give written notice to the licensee that, unless the default is remedied within thirty days from the date of the notice, the compulsory license will be automatically terminated. Such termination renders either the making or the distribution, or both, of all phonorecords for which the royalty has not been paid, actionable as acts of infringement under section 501 and fully subject to the remedies provided by sections 502 through 506 and 509.

116. Scope of exclusive rights in nondramatic musical works: Compulsory licenses for public performances by means of coin-operated phonorecord players[11]   **E–19**

(*a*) Limitation on Exclusive Right.

In the case of a nondramatic musical work embodied in a phonorecord the performance of which is subject to this section as provided in section 116A, the exclusive right under clause (4) of section 106 to perform the work publicly by means of a coin-operated phonorecord player is limited as follows:

(1) The proprietor of the establishment in which the public performance takes place is not liable for infringement with respect to such public performance unless—
  (A) such proprietor is the operator of the phonorecord player; or
  (B) such proprietor refuses or fails, within one month after receipt by registered or certified mail of a request, at a time during which the certificate required by clause (1)(C) of subsection (*b*) is not affixed to the phonorecord player, by the copyright owner, to make full disclosure, by registered or certified mail, of the identity of the operator of the phonorecord player.

(2) The operator of the coin-operated phonorecord player may obtain a compulsory license to perform the work publicly on that phonorecord player by filing the application, affixing the certificate, and paying the royalties provided by subsection (*b*).

(*b*) Recordation of Coin-operated Phonorecord Player, Affixation of Certificate, and Royalty Payable under Compulsory License.

(1) Any operator who wishes to obtain a compulsory license for the public performance of works on a coin-operated phonorecord player shall fulfill the following requirements:
  (A) Before or within one month after such performances are made avail-

---

[11] Amended Oct. 31, 1988, Pub. L. 100–569, § 4(*b*)(1), 102 Stat. 2857. The 1988 amendments to this Section were technical, reflecting the concurrent addition of Section 116A § E–20 *post.*

able on a particular phonorecord player, and during the month of January in each succeeding year that such performances are made available on that particular phonorecord player, the operator shall file in the Copyright Office, in accordance with requirements that the Register of Copyrights, after consultation with the Copyright Royalty Tribunal (if and when the Tribunal has been constituted), shall prescribe by regulation, an application containing the name and address of the operator of the phonorecord player and the manufacturer and serial number or other explicit identification of the phonorecord player, and deposit with the Register of Copyrights a royalty fee for the current calendar year of $8 for that particular phonorecord player. If such performances are made available on a particular phonorecord player for the first time after July 1 of any year, the royalty fee to be deposited for the remainder of that year shall be $4.

(B) Within twenty days of receipt of an application and a royalty fee pursuant to subclause (A), the Register of Copyrights shall issue to the applicant a certificate for the phonorecord player.

(C) On or before March 1 of the year in which the certificate prescribed by subclause (B) of this clause is issued, or within ten days after the date of issue of the certificate, the operator shall affix to the particular phonorecord player, in a position where it can be readily examined by the public, the certificate, issued by the Register of Copyrights under subclause (B), of the latest application made by such operator under subclause (A) of this clause with respect to that phonorecord player.

(2) Failure to file the application, to affix the certificate, or to pay the royalty required by clause (1) of this subsection renders the public performance actionable as an act of infringement under section 501 and fully subject to the remedies provided by sections 502 through 506 and 509.

(*c*) DISTRIBUTION OF ROYALTIES.

(1) The Register of Copyrights shall receive all fees deposited under this section and, after deducting the reasonable costs incurred by the Copyright Office under this section, shall deposit the balance in the Treasury of the United States, in such manner as the Secretary of the Treasury directs. All funds held by the Secretary of the Treasury shall be invested in interest-bearing United States securities for later distribution with interest by the Copyright Royalty Tribunal as provided by this title. The Register shall submit to the Copyright Royalty Tribunal, on an annual basis, a detailed statement of account covering all fees received for the relevant period provided by subsection (*b*).

(2) During the month of January in each year, every person claiming to be entitled to compulsory license fees under this section for performances during the preceding twelve-month period shall file a claim with the Copyright Royalty Tribunal, in accordance with requirements that the Tribunal shall prescribe by regulation. Such claim shall include an agreement to accept as final, except as provided in section 810 of this title, the determination of the Copyright Royalty Tribunal in any controversy concerning the distribution of royalty fees deposited under subclause (A) of subsection (*b*)(1) of this section to which the claimant is a party. Notwithstanding any provisions of the antitrust laws, for purposes of this subsection any claimants may agree among themselves as to the proportionate division of compulsory licensing fees among them, may lump their claims together and file them jointly or as a single claim, or may designate a common agent to receive payment on their behalf.

(3) After the first day of October of each year, the Copyright Royalty Tribunal shall determine whether there exists a controversy concerning the distribution of royalty fees deposited under subclause (A) of subsection (*b*)(1). If the Tribunal determines that no such controversy exists, it shall, after deducting its reasonable administrative costs under this section, distribute such fees to the copyright owners entitled, or to their designated agents. If it finds that such a controversy exists, it shall, pursuant to chapter 8 of this title, conduct a proceeding to determine the distribution of royalty fees.

(4) The fees to be distributed shall be divided as follows:

(A) to every copyright owner not affiliated with a performing rights society, the pro rata share of the fees to be distributed to which such copyright owner proves entitlement.

(B) to the performing rights societies, the remainder of the fees to be distributed in such pro rata shares as they shall by agreement stipulate among themselves, or, if they fail to agree, the pro rata share to which such performing rights societies prove entitlement.

(C) during the pendency of any proceeding under this section, the Copyright Royalty Tribunal shall withhold from distribution an amount sufficient to satisfy all claims with respect to which a controversy exists, but shall have discretion to proceed to distribute any amounts that are not in controversy.

(5) The Copyright Royalty Tribunal shall promulgate regulations under which persons who can reasonably be expected to have claims may, during the year in which performances take place, without expense to or harassment of operators or proprietors of establishments in which phonorecord players are located, have such access to such establishments and to the phonorecord players located therein and such opportunity to obtain information with respect thereto as may be reasonably necessary to determine, by sampling procedures or otherwise, the proportion of contribution of the musical works of each such person to the earnings of the phonorecord players for which fees shall have been deposited. Any person who alleges that he or she has been denied the access permitted under the regulations prescribed by the Copyright Royalty Tribunal may bring an action in the United States District Court for the District of Columbia for the cancellation of the compulsory license of the phonorecord player to which such access has been denied, and the court shall have the power to declare the compulsory license thereof invalid from the date of issue thereof.

(*d*) CRIMINAL PENALTIES.

Any person who knowingly makes a false representation of a material fact in an application filed under clause (1)(A) of subsection (*b*), or who knowingly alters a certificate issued under clause (1)(B) of subsection (*b*) or knowingly affixes such a certificate to a phonorecord player other than the one it covers, shall be fined not more than $2,500.

(*e*) DEFINITIONS.

As used in this section and section 116A, the following terms and their variant forms mean the following:

(1) A "coin-operated phonorecord player" is a machine or device that—

(A) is employed solely for the performance of nondramatic musical works by means of phonorecords upon being activated by insertion of coins, currency, tokens, or other monetary units or their equivalent;

(B) is located in an establishment making no direct or indirect charge for admission;

(C) is accompanied by a list of the titles of all the musical works available for performance on it, which list is affixed to the phonorecord player or posted in the establishment in a prominent position where it can be readily examined by the public; and

(D) affords a choice of works available for performance and permits the choice to be made by the patrons of the establishment in which it is located.

(2) An "operator" is any person who, alone or jointly with others:

(A) owns a coin-operated phonorecord player; or

(B) has the power to make a coin-operated phonorecord player available for placement in an establishment for purposes of public performance; or

(C) has the power to exercise primary control over the selection of the musical works made available for public performance on a coin-operated phonorecord player.

(3) A "performing right society" is an association or corporation that licenses the public performance of nondramatic musical works on behalf of the copyright owners, such as the American Society of Composers, Authors and Publishers, Broadcast Music, Inc., and SESAC, Inc.

E–20   116A. Negotiated licenses for public performances by means of coin-operated phonorecord players[12]

(*a*) APPLICABILITY OF SECTION.

This section applies to any nondramatic musical work embodied in a phonorecord.

(*b*) LIMITATION ON EXCLUSIVE RIGHT IF LICENSES NOT NEGOTIATED.

(1) Applicability. In the case of a work to which this section applies, the exclusive right under clause (4) of section 106 to perform the work publicly by means of a coin-operated phonorecord player is limited by section 116 to the extent provided in this section.

(2) Determination by Copyright Royalty Tribunal. The Copyright Tribunal, at the end of the 1 year period beginning on the effective date of the Berne Convention Implementation Act of 1988, and periodically thereafter to the extent necessary to carry out subsection (*f*), shall determine whether or not negotiated licenses authorized by subsection (c) are in effect so as to provide permission to use a quantity of musical works not substantially smaller than the quantity of such works performed on coin-operated phonorecord players during the 1 year period ending on the effective date of that Act. If the Copyright Royalty Tribunal determines that such negotiated licenses are not so in effect, the Tribunal shall, upon making th determination, publish the determination in the Federal Register. Upon such publication, section 116 shall apply with respect to musical works that are not the subject of such negotiated licenses.

(*c*) NEGOTIATED LICENSES.

(1) Authority for negotiations. Any owners of copyright in works to which this section applies and any operators of coin-operated phonorecord players may negotiate and agree upon the terms and rates of royalty payments for the performance of such works and the proportionate division of fees paid

---

[12] Added October 31, 1988, Pub. L. 100–568, § 4(A)(4), 102 Stat. 2855–57.

among copyright owners, and may designate common agents to negotiate, agree to, pay, or receive such royalty payments.

(2) Arbitration.—Parties to such a negotiation, within such time as may be specified by the Copyright Royalty Tribunal by regulation, may determine the result of the negotiation by arbitration. Such arbitration shall be governed by the provisions of title 9, to the extent such title is not inconsistent with this section. The parties shall give notice to the Copyright Royalty Tribunal of any determination reached by arbitration and any such determination shall, as between the parties to the arbitration, be dispositive of the issues to which it relates.

(*d*) License Agreements Superior to Copyright Royalty Tribunal Determinations.

License agreements between one or more copyright owners and one or more operators of coin-operated phonorecord players, which are negotiated in accordance with subsection (*c*), shall be given effect in lieu of any otherwise applicable determination by the Copyright Royalty Tribunal.

(*e*) Negotiation Schedule.

Not later than 60 days after the effective date of the Berne Convention Implementation Act of 1988, if the Chairman of the Copyright Royalty Tribunal has not received notice, from copyright owners and operators of coin-operated phonorecord players referred to in subsection (*c*)(1), of the date and location of the first meeting between such copyright owners and such operators to commence negotiations authorized by subsection (*c*), the Chairman shall announce the date and location of such meeting. Such meeting may not be held more than 90 days after the effective date of such Act.

(*f*) Copyright Royalty Tribunal to Suspend Various Activities.

The Copyright Royalty Tribunal shall not conduct any ratemaking activity with respect to coin-operated phonorecord players unless, at any time more than one year after the effective date of the Berne Convention Implementation Act of 1988, the negotiated licenses adopted by the parties under this section do not provide permission to use a quantity of musical works not substantially smaller than the quantity of such works performed on coin-operated phonorecord players during the one-year period ending on the effective date of such Act.

(*g*) Transition Provisions; Retention of Copyright Royalty Tribunal Jurisdiction.

Until such time as licensing provisions are determined by the parties under this section, the terms of the compulsory license under section 116, with respect to the public performance of nondramatic musical works by means of coin-operated phonorecord players, which is in effect on the day before the effective date of the Berne Convention Implementation Act of 1988, shall remain in force. If a negotiated license authorized by this section comes into force so as to supersede previous determinations of the Copyright Royalty Tribunal, as provided in subsection (*d*), but thereafter is terminated or expires and is not replaced by another licensing agreement, then section 116 shall be effective with respect to musical works that were the subject of such terminated or expired licenses.

E–21   117. Limitations on exclusive rights: Computer programs[13]

Notwithstanding the provisions of section 106, is not an infringement for the owner of a copy of a computer program to make or authorize the making of another copy or adaptation of that computer program provided:

(1) that such a new copy or adaptation is created as an essential step in the utilization of the computer program in conjunction with a machine and that it is used in no other manner, or

(2) that such new copy or adaptation is for archival purposes only and that all archival copies are destroyed in the event that continued possession of the computer program should cease to be rightful.

Any exact copies prepared in accordance with the provisions of this section may be leased, sold, or otherwise transferred, along with the copy from which such copies were prepared, only as part of the lease, sale, or other transfer of all rights in the program. Adaptations so prepared may be transferred only with the authorization of the copyright owner.

E–22   118. Scope of exclusive rights: Use of certain works in connection with noncommercial broadcasting

(*a*) The exclusive rights provided by section 106 shall, with respect to the works specified by subsection (*b*) and the activities specified by subsection (*d*), be subject to the conditions and limitations prescribed by this section.

(*b*) Not later than thirty days after the Copyright Royalty Tribunal has been constituted in accordance with section 802, the Chairman of the Tribunal shall cause notice to be published in the Federal Register of the initiation of proceedings for the purpose of determining reasonable terms and rates of royalty payments for the activities specified by subsection (*d*) with respect to published nondramatic musical works and published pictorial, graphic, and sculptural works during a period beginning as provided in clause (3) of the subsection and ending on December 31, 1982. Copyright owners and public broadcasting entities shall negotiate in good faith and cooperate fully with the Tribunal in an effort to reach reasonable and expeditious results. Notwithstanding any provision of the antitrust laws, any owners of copyright in works specified by this subsection and any public broadcasting entities, respectively, may negotiate and agree upon the terms and rates of royalty payments and the proportionate division of fees paid among various copyright owners, and may designate common agents to negotiate, agree to, pay, or receive payments.

(1) Any owner of copyright in a work specified in this subsection or any public broadcasting entity may, within one hundred and twenty days after publication of the notice specified in this subsection, submit to the Copyright Royalty Tribunal proposed licenses covering such activities with respect to such works. The Copyright Royalty Tribunal shall proceed on the basis of the proposals submitted to it as well as any other relevant information. The

---

[13] s.117 as amended by the Act of December 12, 1980, Pub. L. 96–517 (94 Stat. 3028). Prior to this amendment. s.117 read as follows:

117. Scope of exclusive rights: Use in conjunction with computers and similar information systems

Notwithstanding the provisions of ss.106 through 116 and 118, this title does not afford to the owner of copyright in a work any greater or lesser rights with respect to the use of the work in conjunction with automatic systems capable of storing, processing, retrieving, or transferring information, or in conjunction with any similar device, machine, or process, than those afforded to works under the law, whether title 17 or the common law or statutes of a State, in effect on December 31, 1977, as held applicable and construed by a court in an action brought under this title.

Copyright Royalty Tribunal shall permit any interested party to submit information relevant to such proceedings.

(2) License agreements voluntarily negotiated at any time between one or more copyright owners and one or more public broadcasting entities shall be given effect in lieu of any determination by the Tribunal: *Provided*, That copies of such agreements are filed in the Copyright Office within thirty days of execution in accordance with regulations that the Register of Copyrights shall prescribe.

(3) Within six months, but not earlier than one hundred and twenty days, from the date of publication of the notice specified in this subsection the Copyright Royalty Tribunal shall make a determination and publish in the Federal Register a schedule of rates and terms which, subject to clause (2) of this subsection, shall be binding on all owners of copyright in works specified by this subsection and public broadcasting entities, regardless of whether or not such copyright owners and public broadcasting entities have submitted proposals to the Tribunal. In establishing such rates and terms the Copyright Royalty Tribunal may consider the rates for comparable circumstances under voluntary license agreements negotiated as provided in clause (2) of this subsection. The Copyright Royalty Tribunal shall also establish requirements by which copyright owners may receive reasonable notice of the use of their works under this section, and under which records of such use shall be kept by public broadcasting entities.

(4) With respect to the period beginning on the effective date of this title and ending on the date of publication of such rates and terms, this title shall not afford to owners of copyright or public broadcasting entities any greater or lesser rights with respect to the activities specified in subsection (*d*) as applied to works specified in this subsection than those afforded under the law in effect on December 31, 1977, as held applicable and construed by a court in an action brought under this title.

(*c*) The initial procedure specified in subsection (*b*) shall be repeated and concluded between June 30 and December 31, 1982, and at five-year intervals thereafter, in accordance with regulations that the Copyright Royalty Tribunal shall prescribe.

(*d*) Subject to the transitional provisions of subsection (*b*)(4), and to the terms of any voluntary license agreements that have been negotiated as provided by subsection (*b*)(2), a public broadcasting entity may, upon compliance with the provisions of this section, including the rates and terms established by the Copyright Royalty Tribunal under subsection (*b*)(3), engage in the following activities with respect to published nondramatic musical works and published pictorial, graphic and sculptural works:

(1) performance or display of work by or in the course of a transmission made by a noncommercial educational broadcast station referred to in subsection (*g*); and

(2) production of a transmission program, reproduction of copies or phonorecords of such a transmission program, and distribution of such copies or phonorecords, where such production, reproduction, or distribution is made by a nonprofit institution or organization solely for the purpose of transmissions specified in clause (1); and

(3) the making of reproductions by a governmental body or a nonprofit institution of a transmission program simultaneously with its transmission as specified in clause (1), and the performance or display of the contents of such program under the conditions specified by clause (1) of section 110, but only if the reproductions are used for performances or displays for a period of no more than seven days from the date of the transmission speci-

fied in clause (1), and are destroyed before or at the end of such period. No person supplying, in accordance with clause (2), a reproduction of a transmission program to governmental bodies or nonprofit institutions under this clause shall have any liability as a result of failure of such body or institution to destroy such reproduction: *Provided,* That it shall have notified such body or institution of the requirement for such destruction pursuant to this clause: *And provided further,* That if such body or institution itself fails to destroy such reproduction it shall be deemed to have infringed.

(*e*) Except as expressly provided in this subsection, this section shall have no applicability to works other than those specified in subsection (*b*).

(1) Owners of copyright in nondramatic literary works and public broadcasting entitities may, during the course of voluntary negotiations, agree among themselves, respectively, as to the terms and rates of royalty payments without liability under the antitrust laws. Any such terms and rates of royalty payments shall be effective upon filing in the Copyright Office, in accordance with regulations that the Register of Copyrights shall prescribe.

(2) On January 3, 1980, the Register of Copyrights, after consulting with authors and other owners of copyright in nondramatic literary works and their representatives, and with public broadcasting entities and their representatives, shall submit to the Congress a report setting forth the extent to which voluntary licensing arrangements have been reached with respect to the use of nondramatic literary works by such broadcast stations. The report should also describe any problems that may have arisen, and present legislative or other recommendations, if warranted.

(*f*) Nothing in this section shall be construed to permit, beyond the limits of fair use as provided by section 107, the unauthorized dramatization of a nondramatic musical work, the production of a transmission program drawn to any substantial extent from a published compilation of pictorial, graphic, or sculptural works, or the unauthorized use of any portion of an audiovisual work.

(*g*) As used in this section, the term "public broadcasting entity" means a noncommercial educational broadcast station as defined in section 397 of title 47 and any nonprofit institution or organization engaged in the activities described in clause (2) of subsection (*d*).

E–23   **119. Limitations on exclusive rights: Secondary transmissions of superstations and network stations for private home viewing**[14]

(*a*) SECONDARY TRANSMISSIONS BY SATELLITE CARRIERS.

(1) Superstations. Subject to provisions of paragraphs (3), (4), and (6) of this subsection, transmissions of a primary transmission made by a superstation and embodying a performance or display of a work shall be subject to statutory licensing under this section if the secondary transmission is made by a satellite carrier to the public for private home viewing, and the carrier makes a direct or indirect charge for each retransmission service to each household receiving the secondary transmission or to a distributor that has contracted with the carrier for direct or indirect delivery of the secondary transmission to the public for private home viewing.

(2) Network stations.

(A) In general.—Subject to the provisions of subparagraphs (B) and (C) of this paragraph and paragraphs (3), (4), (5), and (6) of this subsection,

---

[14] Added Nov. 16, 1988, Pub. L. 100–667, § 202(2), 102 Stat. 3935.

secondary transmissions of programming contained in a primary transmission made by a network station and embodying a performance or display of a work shall be subject to statutory licensing under this section if the secondary transmission is made by a satellite carrier to the public for private home viewing, and the carrier makes a direct or indirect charge for such retransmission service to each subscriber receiving the secondary transmission.

(B) Secondary transmissions to unserved households.—The statutory license provided for in subparagraph (A) shall be limited to secondary transmissions to persons who reside in unserved households.

(C) Submission of subscriber lists to networks.—A satellite carrier that makes secondary transmissions of a primary transmission made by a network station pursuant to subparagraph (A) shall, 90 days after the effective date of the Satellite Home Viewer Act of 1988, or 90 days after commencing such secondary transmissions, whichever is later, submit to the network that owns or is affiliated with the network station a list identifying (by street address, including county and zip code) all subscribers to which the satellite carrier currently makes secondary transmissions of that primary transmission. Thereafter, on the 15th of each month, the satellite carrier shall submit to the network a list identifying (by street address, including county and zip code) any persons who have been added or dropped as such subscribers since the last submission under this subparagraph. Such subscriber information submitted by a satellite carrier may be used only for purposes of monitoring compliance by the satellite carrier with this subsection. The submission requirements of this subparagraph shall apply to a satellite carrier only if the network to whom the submissions are to be made places on file with the Register of Copyrights, on or after the effective date of the Satellite Home Viewer Act of 1988, a document identifying the name and address of the person to whom such submissions are to be made. The Register shall maintain for public inspection a file of all such documents.

(3) Noncompliance with reporting and payment requirements. Notwithstanding the provisions of paragraphs (1) and (2), the willful or repeated secondary transmission to the public by a satellite carrier of a primary transmission made by a superstation or a network station and embodying a performance or display of a work is actionable as an act of infringement under section 501, and is fully subject to the remedies provided by sections 502 through 506 and 509, where the satellite carrier has not deposited the statement of account and royalty fee required by subsection (*b*), or has failed to make the submissions to networks required by paragraph (2)(C).

(4) Willful alterations.—Notwithstanding the provisions of paragraphs (1) and (2), the secondary transmission to the public by a satellite carrier of a primary transmission made by a superstation or a network station and embodying a performance or display of a work is actionable as an act of infringement under section 501, and is fully subject to the remedies provided by sections 502 through 506 and sections 509 and 510, if the content of the particular program in which the performance or display is embodied, or any commercial advertising or station announcement transmitted by the primary transmitter during, or immediately before or after, the transmission of such program, is in any way willfully altered by the satellite carrier through changes, deletions, or additions, or is combined with programming from any other broadcast signal.

(5) Violation of Territorial Restrictions on Statutory License for Network Stations.

(A) Individual violations.—The willful or repeated secondary transmission by a satellite carrier of a primary transmission made by a network station and embodying a performance or display or a work to a subscriber who does not reside in an unserved household is actionable as an act of infringement under section 501 and is fully subject to the remedies provided by sections 502 through 506 and 509, except that—

    (i) no damages shall be awarded for such act of infringement if the satellite carrier took corrective action by promptly withdrawing service from the ineligible subscriber, and

    (ii) any statutory damages shall not exceed $5 for such subscriber for each month during which the violation occurred.

(B) Pattern of violations.—If a satellite carrier engages in a willful or repeated pattern or practice of delivering a primary transmission made by a network station and embodying a performance or display of a work to subscribers who do not reside in unserved households, then in addition to the remedies set forth in subparagraph (A)—

    (i) If the pattern or practice has been carried out on a substantially nationwide basis, the court shall order a permanent injunction barring the secondary transmission by the satellite carrier, for private home viewing, of the primary transmissions of any primary network station affiliated with the same network, and the court may order statutory damages of not to exceed $250,000 for each 6 month period during which the pattern of practice was carried out; and

    (ii) if the pattern or practice has been carried out on a local or regional basis, the court shall order a permanent injunction barring the secondary transmission, for private home viewing in that locality or region, by the satellite carrier of the primary transmissions of any primary network station affiliated with the same network, and the court may order statutory damages of not to exceed $250,000 for each 6 month period during which the pattern of practice was carried out.

(C) Previous subscribers excluded.—Subparagraphs (A) and (B) do not apply to secondary transmissions by a satellite carrier to persons who subscribed to receive such secondary transmissions from the satellite carrier or a distributor before the date of the enactment of the Satellite Home Viewer Act of 1988.

(6) Discrimination by a satellite carrier.—Notwithstanding the provisions of paragraph (1), the willful or repeated secondary transmission to the public by a satellite carrier of a primary transmission made by a superstation or a network station and embodying a performance or display of a work is actionable as an act of infringement under section 501, and is fully subject to the remedies provided by sections 502 through 506 and 509, if the satellite carrier unlawfully discriminates against distributor.

(7) Geographic limitation on secondary transmissions.—The statutory license created by this section shall apply only to secondary transmissions to households located in the United States.

(*b*) STATUTORY LICENSE FOR SECONDARY TRANSMISSIONS FOR PRIVATE HOME VIEWING.

(1) Deposits with the Register of Copyrights.—A satellite carrier whose secondary transmissions are subject to statutory licensing under subsection (a) shall, on a semiannual basis, deposit with the Register of Copyrights, in accordance with requirements that the Register shall, after consultation with the Copyright Royalty Tribunal, prescribe by regulation—

(A) a statement of account, covering the preceding 6 month period, specifying the names and locations of all superstations and network stations whose signals were transmitted, at any time during that period, to subscribers for private home viewing as described in subsections $(a)(1)$ and $(a)(2)$, the total number of subscribers that received such transmissions, and such other data as the Register of Copyrights may, after consultation with the Copyright Royalty Tribunal, from time to time prescribe by regulation; and

(B) a royalty fee for that 6 month period, computed by—

(i) mutiplying the total number of subscribers receiving each secondary transmission of a superstation during each calendar month by 12 cents;

(ii) multiplying the number of subscribers receiving each secondary transmission of a network station during each calendar month by 3 cents; and

(iii) adding together the totals computed under clauses (i) and (ii).

(2) Investment of fees.—The Register of Copyrights shall receive all fees deposited under this section and, after deducting the reasonable costs incurred by the Copyright Office under this section (other than the costs deducted under paragraph (4), shall deposit the balance in the Treasury of the United States, in such manner as the Secretary of the Treasury directs. All funds held by the Secretary of the Treasury shall be invested in interest-bearing securities of the United States for later distribution with interest by the Copyright Royalty Tribunal as provided by this title.

(3) Persons to whom fees are distributed.—The royalty fees deposited under paragraph (2) shall, in accordance with the procedures provided by paragraph (4), be distributed to those copyright owners whose works were included in a secondary transmission for private home viewing made by a satellite carrier during the applicable 6 month accounting period and who file a claim with the Copyright Royalty Tribunal under paragraph (4).

(4) Procedures for distribution.—The royalty fees deposited under paragraph (2) shall be distributed in accordance with the following procedures:

(A) Filing of claims for fees.—During the month of July in each year, each person claiming to be entitled to statutory license fees for secondary transmissions for private home viewing shall file a claim with the Copyright Royalty Tribunal, in accordance with requirements that the Tribunal shall prescribe by regulation. For purposes of this paragraph, any claimants may agree among themselves as to the proportionate division of statutory license fees among them, may lump their claims together and file them jointly or as a single claim, or may designate a common agent to receive payment on their behalf.

(B) Determination of controversy; distributions.—After the first day of August of each year, the Copyright Royalty Tribunal shall determine whether there exists a controversy concerning the distribution of royalty fees. If the Tribunal determines that no such controversy exists, the Tribunal shall, after deducting reasonable administrative costs under this paragraph, distribute such fees to the copyright owners entitled to receive them, or to their designated agents. If the Tribunal finds the existence of a controversy, the Tribunal shall, pursuant to chapter 8 of this title, conduct a proceeding to determine the distribution of royalty fees.

(C) Withholding of fees during controversy.—During the pendency of any proceeding under this subsection, the Copyright Royalty Tribunal shall withhold from distribution an amount sufficient to satisfy all claims with respect to which a controversy exists, but shall have discretion to proceed to distribute any amounts that are not in controversy.

(c) Determination of Royalty Fees.

(1) Applicability and determination of royalty fees.—The rate of the royalty fee payable under subsection (*b*)(1)(B) shall be effective until December 31, 1992, unless a royalty fee is established under paragraph (2), (3), or (4) of this subsection. After that date, the fee shall be determined either in accordance with the voluntary negotiation procedure specified in paragraph (2) or in accordance with the compulsory arbitration procedure specified in paragraphs (3) and (4).

(2) Fee set by voluntary negotiation.

(A) Notice of initiation of proceedings.—On or before July 1, 1991, the Copyright Royalty Tribunal shall cause notice to be published in the Federal Register of the initiation of voluntary negotiation proceedings for the purpose of determining the royalty fee to be paid by satellite carriers under subsection (*b*)(1)(B).

(B) Negotiations.—Satellite carriers, distributors, and copyright owners entitled to royalty fees under this section shall negotiate in good faith in an effort to reach a voluntary agreement or voluntary agreements for the payment of royalty fees. Any such satellite carriers, distributors, and copyright owners may at any time negotiate and agree to the royalty fee, and may designate common agents to negotiate, agree to, or pay such fees. If the parties fail to identify common agents, the Copyright Royalty Tribunal shall do so, after requesting recommendations from the parties to the negotiation proceeding. The parties to each negotiation proceeding shall bear the entire cost thereof.

(C) Agreements binding on parties; filing of agreements.—Voluntary agreements negotiated at any time in accordance with this paragraph shall be binding upon all satellite carriers, distributors, and copyright owners that are parties thereto. Copies of such agreements shall be filed with the Copyright Office within 30 days after execution in accordance with regulations that the Register of Copyrights shall prescribe.

(D) Period agreement is in effect.—The obligation to pay the royalty fees established under a voluntary agreement which has been filed with the Copyright Office in accordance with this paragraph shall become effective on the date specified in the agreement, and shall remain in effect until December 31, 1994.

(3) Fee set by compulsory arbitration.

(A) Notice of initiation of proceedings.—On or before December 31, 1991, the Copyright Royalty Tribunal shall cause notice to be published in the Federal Register of the initiation of arbitration proceedings for the purpose of determining a reasonable royalty fee to be paid under subsection (*b*)(1)(B) by satellite carriers who are not parties to a voluntary agreement filed with the Copyright Office in accordance with paragraph (2). Such notice shall include the names and qualifications of potential arbitrators chosen by the Tribunal from a list of available arbitrators obtained from the American Arbitration Association or such similar organization as the Tribunal shall select.

(B) Selection of Arbitration Panel.—Not later than 10 days after publication of the notice initiating an arbitration proceeding, and in accordance with procedures to be specified by the Copyright Royalty Tribunal, one arbitrator shall be selected from the published list by copyright owners who claim to be entitled to royalty fees under subsection (*b*)(4) and who are not party to a voluntary agreement filed with the Copyright Office in accordance with paragraph (2), and one arbitrator shall be selected from the published list by satellite carriers and distributors who are not parties to such a voluntary agreement. The two arbitrators so selected shall, within 10 days after their selection, choose a third arbitrator from the same list, who shall serve as chairperson of the arbitrators. If either group fail to agree upon the selection of an arbitrator, or if the arbitrators selected by such groups fail to agree upon the selection of a chairperson, the Copyright Royalty Tribunal shall promptly select the arbitrator or chairperson, respectively. The arbitrators selected under this subparagraph shall constitute an Arbitration Panel.

(C) Arbitration proceeding.—The Arbitration Panel shall conduct an arbitration proceeding in accordance with such procedures as it may adopt. The Panel shall act on the basis of a fully documented written record. Any copyright owner who claims to be entitled to royalty fees under subsection $(b)(4)$, any satellite carrier, and any distributor, who is not party to a voluntary agreement filed with the Copyright Office in accordance with paragraph (2), may submit relevant information and proposals to the Panel. The parties to the proceeding shall bear the entire cost thereof in such manner and proportion as the Panel shall direct.

(D) Factors for determining royalty fees.—In determining royalty fees under this paragraph, the Arbitration Panel shall consider the approximate average cost to a cable system for the right to secondarily transmit to the public a primary transmission made by a broadcast station, the fee established under any voluntary agreement filed with the Copyright Office in accordance with paragraph (2), and the last fee proposed by the parties, before proceedings under this paragraph, for the secondary transmission of superstations or network stations for private home viewing. The fee shall also be calculated to achieve the following objectives:

(i) To maximize the availability of creative works to the public.

(ii) To afford the copyright owner a fair return for his or her creative work and the copyright user a fair income under existing economic conditions.

(iii) to reflect the relative roles of the copyright owner and the copyright user in the product made available to the public with respect to relative creative contribution, technological contribution, capital investment, cost, risk, and contribution to the opening of new markets for creative expression and media for their communication.

(iv) to minimize any disruptive impact on the structure of the industries involved and on generally prevailing industry practices.

(E) Report to Copyright Royalty Tribunal.—Not later than 60 days after publication of the notice initiating an arbitration proceeding, the Arbitration Panel shall report to the Copyright Royalty Tribunal its determination concerning the royalty fee. Such report shall be accompanied by the written record, and shall set forth the facts that the Panel found relevant to its determination and the reasons why its determination is consistent with the criteria set forth in subparagraph (D).

(F) Action by Copyright Royalty Tribunal.—Within 60 days after receiving the report of the Arbitration Panel under subparagraph (E), the Copyright Royalty Tribunal shall adopt or reject the determination of the Panel. The Tribunal shall adopt the determination of the Panel unless the Tribunal finds tht the determination is clearly inconsistent with the criteria set forth in subparagraph (D). If the Tribunal rejects the determination of the Panel, the Tribunal shall, before the end of that 60 day period, and after full examination of the record created in the arbitration proceeding, issue an order, consistent with the criteria set forth in subparagraph (D), setting the royalty fee under this paragraph. The Tribunal shall cause to be published in the Federal Register the

1477

determination of the Panel, and the decision of the Tribunal with respect to the determination (including any order issued under the preceding sentence). The Tribunal shall also publicize such determination and decision in such other manner as the Tribunal considers appropriate. The Tribunal shall also make the report of the Arbitration Panel and the accompanying record available for public inspection and copying.

(G) Period during which decision of Panel or order of the Tribunal effective.—The obligation to pay the royalty fee established under a determination of the Arbitration Panel which is confirmed by the Copyright Royalty Tribunal in accordance with this paragraph, or established by any order issued under subparagraph (F), shall become effective on the date when the decision of the Tribunal is published in the Federal Register under subparagraph (F), and shall remain in effect until modified in accordance with paragraph (4), or until December 31, 1994.

(H) Persons subject to royalty fee.—The royalty fee adopted or ordered under subparagraph (F) shall be binding of all satellite carriers, distributors, and copyright owners, who are not party to a voluntary agreement filed with the Copyright Office under paragraph (2).

(4) Judicial review.—Any decision of the Copyright Royalty Tribunal under paragraph (3) with respect to a determination of the Arbitration Panel may be appealed, by any aggrieved party who would be bound by the determination, to the United States Court of Appeals for the District of Columbia Circuit, within 30 days after the publication of the decision in the Federal Register. The pendency of an appeal under this paragraph shall not relieve satellite carriers of the obligation under subsection (*b*)(1) to deposit the statement of account and royalty fees specified in that subsection. The court shall have jurisdiction to modify or vacate a decision of the Tribunal only if it finds, on the basis of the record before the Tribunal and the statutory criteria set forth in paragraph (3)(D), that the Arbitration Panel or the Tribunal acted in an arbitrary manner. If the court modifies the decision of the Tribunal, the court shall have jurisdiction to enter its own determination with respect to royalty fees, to order the repayment of any excess fees deposited under subsection (*b*)(1)(B), and to order the payment of any unpaid fees, and the interest pertaining respectively thereto, in accordance with its final judgment. The court may further vacate the decision of the Tribunal and remand the case for arbitration proceedings in accordance with paragraph (3).

(*d*) DEFINITIONS. AS USED IN THIS SECTION—

(1) Distributor.—The term "distributor" means an entity which contracts to distribute secondary transmissions from a satellite carrier and, either as a single channel or in a package with other programming, provides the secondary transmission either directly to individual subscribers for private home viewing or indirectly through other program distribution entities.

(2) Network station.—The term "network station" has the meaning given that term in section 111(*f*) of this title, and includes any translator station or terrestrial satellite station that rebroadcasts all or substantially of the programming broadcast by a network station.

(3) Primary network station.—The term "primary network station" means a network station that broadcasts or rebroadcasts the basic programming service of a particular national network.

(4) Primary transmission.—The term "primary transmission" has the meaning given that term in section 111(*f*) of this title.

(5) Private home viewing.—The term "private home viewing" means the

viewing, for private use in a household by means of satellite reception equipment which is operated by an individual in that household and which serves only such household, of a secondary transmission delivered by a satellite carrier of a primary transmission of a television station licensed by the Federal Communications Commission.

(6) Satellite carrier.—The term "satellite carrier" means an entity that uses the facilities of a satellite or satellite service licensed by the Federal Communications Commission, to establish and operate a channel of communications for point-to-multipoint distribution of television station signals, and that owns or leases a capacity or service on a satellite in order to provide such point-to-multipoint distribution, except to the extent that such entity provides such distribution pursuant to tariff under the Communications Act of 1934, other than for private home viewing.

(7) Secondary transmission.—The term "secondary transmission" has the meaning given that term in section 111(f) of this title.

(8) Subscriber.—The term "subscriber" means an individual who receives a secondary transmission service for private home viewing by means of a secondary transmission from a satellite carrier and pays a fee for the service, directly or indirectly, to the satellite carrier or to a distributor.

(9) Superstation.—The term "superstation" means a television broadcast station, other than a network station, licensed by the Federal Communications Commission that is secondarily transmitted by a satellite carrier.

(10) Unserved household.—The term "unserved household," with respect to a particular television network, means a household that—

(A) cannot receive, through the use of a conventional outdoor rooftop receiving antenna, an over-the-air signal of grade B intensity (as defined by the Federal Communications Commission) of a primary network station affiliated with that network, and

(B) has not, within 90 days before the date on which that household subscribes, either initially or on renewal, to receive secondary transmissions by a satellite carrier of a network station affiliated with that network subscribed to a cable system that provides the signal of a primary network station affiliated with that network.

(e) EXCLUSIVITY OF THIS SECTION WITH RESPECT TO SECONDARY TRANSMISSIONS OF BROADCAST STATIONS BY SATELLITE TO MEMBERS OF THE PUBLIC.

No provision of section 111 of this title or any other law (other than this section) shall be construed to contain any authorization, exemption, or license through which secondary transmissions by satellite carrier for private home viewing of programming contained in a primary transmission made by a superstation or a network station may be made without obtaining the consent of the copyright owner.

CHAPTER 2 E–24

COPYRIGHT OWNERSHIP AND TRANSFER

E–25   201. Ownership of copyright[15]

(*a*) INITIAL OWNERSHIP.

Copyright in a work protected under this title vests initially in the authors of the work. The authors of a joint work are co-owners of copyright in the work.

(*b*) WORKS MADE FOR HIRE.

In the case of a work made for hire, the employer or other person for whom the work was prepared is considered the author for purposes of this title, and, unless the parties have expressly agreed otherwise in a written instrument signed by them, owns all of the rights comprised in the copyright.

(*c*) CONTRIBUTIONS TO COLLECTIVE WORKS.

Copyright in each separate contribution to a collective work is distinct from copyright in the collective work as a whole, and vests initially in the author of the contribution. In the absence of an express transfer of the copyright or of any rights under it, the owner of copyright in the collective work is presumed to have acquired only the privilege of reproducing and distributing the contribution as part of that particular collective work, any revision of that collective work, and any later collective work in the same series.

(*d*) TRANSFER OF OWNERSHIP.

(1)   The ownership of a copyright may be transferred in whole or in part by any means of conveyance or by operation of law, and may be bequeathed by will or pass as personal property by the applicable laws of intestate succession.

(2)   Any of the exclusive rights comprised in a copyright, including any subdivision of any of the rights specified by section 106, may be transferred as provided by clause (1) and owned separately. The owner of any particular exclusive right is entitled, to the extent of that right, to all of the protection and remedies accorded to the copyright owner by this title.

(*e*) INVOLUNTARY TRANSFER.

When an individual author's ownership of a copyright, or of any of the exclusive rights under a copyright, has not previously been transferred voluntarily by that individual author, no action by any governmental body or other official or organization purporting to seize, expropriate, transfer, or exercise rights of ownership with respect to the copyright, or any of the exclusive rights under a copyright, shall be given effect under this title, except as provided under title 11.

E–26   202. Ownership of copyright as distinct from ownership of material object

Ownership of a copyright, or of any of the exclusive rights under a copyright, is distinct from ownership of any material object in which the work is embodied. Transfer of ownership of any material object, including the copy or phonorecord in which the work is first fixed, does not of itself convey any rights in the copyrighted work embodied in the object; nor, in the absence of an agreement, does transfer of ownership of a copyright or of any exclusive rights under a copyright convey property rights in any material object.

---

[15] As amended Nov. 6, 1978, Pub. L. 95–598, Title III, § 313, 92 Stat. 2676.

203. Termination of transfers and licenses granted by the author

(*a*) Conditions for Termination.

In the case of any work other than a work made for hire, the exclusive or nonexclusive grant of a transfer or license of copyright or of any right under a copyright, executed by the author on or after January 1, 1978, otherwise than by will, is subject to termination under the following conditions:

(1) In the case of a grant executed by one author, termination of the grant may be effected by that author or, if the author is dead, by the person or persons who, under clause (2) of this subsection, own and are entitled to exercise a total of more than one-half of that author's termination interest. In the case of a grant executed by two or more authors of a joint work, termination of the grant may be effected by a majority of the authors who executed it; if any of such authors is dead, the termination interest of any such author may be exercised as a unit by the person or persons who, under clause (2) of this subsection, own and are entitled to exercise a total of more than one-half of that author's interest.

(2) Where an author is dead, his or her termination interest is owned, and may be exercised, by his widow or her widower and his or her children or grandchildren as follows:

   (A) the widow or widower owns the author's entire termination interest unless there are any surviving children or grandchildren of the author, in which case the widow or widower owns one-half of the author's interest;

   (B) the author's surviving children, and the surviving children of any dead child of the author, own the author's entire termination interest unless there is a widow or widower, in which case the ownership of one-half of the author's interest is divided among them;

   (C) the rights of the author's children and grandchildren are in all cases divided among them and exercised on a per stirpes basis according to the number of such author's children represented; the share of the children of a dead child in a termination interest can be exercised only by the action of a majority of them.

(3) Termination of the grant may be effected at any time during a period of five years beginning at the end of thirty-five years from the date of execution of the grant; or, if the grant covers the right of publication of the work, the period begins at the end of thirty-five years from the date of publication of the work under the grant or at the end of forty years from the date of execution of the grant, whichever term ends earlier.

(4) The termination shall be effected by serving an advance notice in writing, signed by the number and proportion of owners of termination interests required under clauses (1) and (2) of this subsection, or by their duly authorized agents, upon the grantee or the grantee's successor in title.

   (A) The notice shall state the effective date of the termination which shall fall within the five-year period specified by clause (3) of this subsection, and the notice shall be served not less than two or more than ten years before that date. A copy of the notice shall be recorded in the Copyright Office before the effective date of termination, as a condition to its taking effect.

   (B) The notice shall comply, in form, content, and manner of service, with requirements that the Register of Copyrights shall prescribe by regulation.

(5) Termination of the grant may be effected notwithstanding any agreement to the contrary, including an agreement to make a will or to make any future grant.

(*b*) Effect of Termination.

Upon the effective date of termination, all rights under this title that were covered by the terminated grants revert to the author, authors, and other persons owning termination interests under clauses (1) and (2) of subsection (*a*), including those owners who did not join in signing the notice of termination under clause (4) of subsection (*a*), but with the following limitations:

(1) A derivative work prepared under authority of the grant before its termination may continue to be utilized under the terms of the grant after its termination, but this privilege does not extend to the preparation after the termination of other derivative works based upon the copyrighted work covered by the terminated grant.

(2) The future rights that will revert upon termination of the grant become vested on the date the notice of termination has been served as provided by clause (4) of subsection (*a*). The rights vest in the author, authors, and other persons named in, and in the proportionate shares provided by, clauses (1) and (2) of subsection (*a*).

(3) Subject to the provisions of clause (4) of this subsection, a further grant, or agreement to make a further grant, of any right covered by a terminated grant is valid only if it is signed by the same number and proportion of the owners, in whom the right has vested under clause (2) of this subsection, as are required to terminate the grant under clauses (1) and (2) of subsection (*a*). Such further grant or agreement is effective with respect to all of the persons in whom the right it covers has vested under clause (2) of this subsection, including those who did not join in signing it. If any person dies after rights under a terminated grant have vested in him or her, that person's legal representatives, legatees, or heirs at law represent him or her for purposes of this clause.

(4) A further grant, or agreement to make a further grant, of any right covered by a terminated grant is valid only if it is made after the effective date of the termination. As an exception, however, an agreement for such a further grant may be made between the persons provided by clause (3) of this subsection and the original grantee or such grantee's successor in title, after the notice of termination has been served as provided by clause (4) of subsection (*a*).

(5) Termination of a grant under this section affects only those rights covered by the grants that arise under this title, and in no way affects rights under any other Federal, State, or foreign laws.

(6) Unless and until termination is effected under this section, the grant, if it does not provide otherwise, continues in effect for the term of copyright provided by this title.

E–28   204. Execution of transfers of copyright ownership

(*a*) A transfer of copyright ownership, other than by operation of law, is not valid unless an instrument of conveyance, or a note or memorandum of the transfer, is in writing and signed by the owner of the rights conveyed or such owner's duly authorized agent.

(*b*) A certificate of acknowledgement is not required for the validity of a transfer, but is prima facie evidence of the execution of the transfer if—

(1) in the case of a transfer executed in the United States, the certificate is issued by a person authorized to administer oaths within the United States; or

(2) in the case of a transfer executed in a foreign country, the certificate is issued by a diplomatic or consular officer of the United States, or by a person, authorized to administer oaths, whose authority is proved by a certificate of such an officer.

205. Recordation of transfers and other documents[16]

(*a*) CONDITIONS FOR RECORDATION.

Any transfer of copyright ownership or other document pertaining to a copyright may be recorded in the Copyright Office if the document filed for recordation bears the actual signature of the person who executed it, or if it is accompanied by a sworn or official certification that it is a true copy of the original, signed document.

(*b*) CERTIFICATE OF RECORDATION.

The Register of Copyrights shall, upon receipt of a document as provided by subsection (*a*) and of the fee provided by section 708, record the document and return it with a certificate of recordation.

(*c*) RECORDATION AS CONSTRUCTIVE NOTICE.

Recordation of a document in the Copyright Office gives all persons constructive notice of the facts stated in the recorded document, but only if—
  (1) the document, or material attached to it, specifically identifies the work to which it pertains so that, after the document is indexed by the Register of Copyrights, it would be revealed by a reasonable search under the title or registration number of the work; and
  (2) registration has been made for the work.

(*d*) PRIORITY BETWEEN CONFLICTING TRANSFERS.

As between two conflicting transfers, the one executed first prevails if it is recorded, in the manner required to give constructive notice under subsection (*c*), within one month after its execution in the United States or within two months after its execution outside the United States, or at any time before recordation in such manner of the later transfer. Otherwise the later transfer prevails if recorded first in such manner, and if taken in good faith, for valuable consideration or on the basis of a binding promise to pay royalties, and without notice of the earlier transfer.
  (*e*) PRIORITY BETWEEN CONFLICTING TRANSFER OF OWNERSHIP AND NONEXCLUSIVE LICENSE. A nonexclusive license, whether recorded or not, prevails over a conflicting transfer of copyright ownership if the license is evidenced by a written instrument signed by the owner of the rights licensed or such owner's duly authorized agent, and if—
  (1) the license was taken before execution of the transfer; or
  (2) the license was taken in good faith before recordation of the transfer and without notice of it.

(*d*) RECORDATION AS PREREQUISITE TO INFRINGEMENT SUIT.

No person claiming by virtue of a transfer to be the owner of copyright or of any exclusive right under a copyright is entitled to institute an infringement action under this title until the instrument of transfer under which such person claims has been recorded in the Copyright Office, but suit may be instituted after such recordation on a cause of action that arose before recordation.

(*e*) PRIORITY BETWEEN CONFLICTING TRANSFERS.

As between two conflicting transfers, the one executed first prevails if it is recorded, in the manner required to give constructive notice under subsection (c),

---

[16] Amended October 31, 1988, Pub. L. 100–568, § 4, 102 Stat. 2857.

within one month after its execution in the United States or within two months after its execution outside the United States, or at any time before recordation in such manner of the later transfer. Otherwise the later transfer prevails if recorded first in such manner, and if taken in good faith, for valuable consideration or on the basis of a binding promise to pay royalties, and without notice of the earlier transfer.

(*f*) PRIORITY BETWEEN CONFLICTING TRANSFER OF OWNERSHIP AND NONEXCLUSIVE LICENSE.

A nonexclusive license, whether recorded or not, prevails over a conflicting transfer of copyright ownership if the license is evidenced by a written instrument signed by the owner of the rights licensed or such owner's duly authorized agent, and if—

(1) the license was taken before execution of the transfer; or
(2) the license was taken in good faith before recordation of the transfer and without notice of it.

E-30

CHAPTER 3

DURATION OF COPYRIGHT

Sec.

301. Preemption with respect to other laws.
302. Duration of copyright: Works created on or after January 1, 1978.
303. Duration of copyright: Works created but not published or copyrighted before January 1, 1978.
304. Duration of copyright: Subsisting copyrights.
305. Duration of copyright: Terminal date.

E-31 **301. Preemption with respect to other laws**[17]

(*a*) On and after January 1, 1978, all legal or equitable rights that are equivalent to any of the exclusive rights within the general scope of copyright as specified by section 106 in works of authorship that are fixed in a tangible medium of expression and come within the subject matter of copyright as specified by sections 102 and 103, whether created before or after that date and whether published or unpublished, are governed exclusively by this title. Thereafter, no person is entitled to any such right or equivalent right in any such work under the common law or statutes of any State.

(*b*) Nothing in this title annuls or limits any rights or remedies under the common law or statutes of any State with respect to—

(1) subject matter that does not come within the subject matter of copyright as specified by sections 102 and 103, including works of authorship not fixed in any tangible medium of expression; or
(2) any cause of action arising from undertakings commenced before January 1, 1978; or
(3) activities violating legal or equitable rights that are not equivalent to any of the exclusive rights within the general scope of copyright as specified by section 106.

(*c*) With respect to sound recordings fixed before February 15, 1972, any rights or remedies under the common law or statutes of any State shall not be annulled or

---

[17] Amended Oct. 31, 1988, Pub. L. 100–568, § 6, 102 Stat. 2857. The 1988 Amendment added subsection (*e*).

limited by this title until February 15, 2047. The preemptive provisions of subsection (a) shall apply to any such rights and remedies pertaining to any cause of action arising from undertakings commenced on and after February 15, 2047. Notwithstanding the provision of section 303, no sound recording fixed before February 15, 1972, shall be subject to copyright under this title before, on, or after February 15, 2047.

(*d*) Nothing in this title annuls or limits any rights or remedies under any other Federal statute.

(*e*) The scope of Federal preemption under this section is not affected by the adherence of the United States to the Berne Convention or the satisfaction of obligations of the United States thereunder.

302. Duration of copyright: Works created on or after January 1, 1978   E–32

(*a*) In General.

Copyright in a work created on or after January 1, 1978, subsists from its creation and, except as provided by the following subsections, endures for a term consisting of the life of the author and fifty years after the author's death.

(*b*) Joint Works.

In the case of a joint work prepared by two or more authors who did not work for hire, the copyright endures for a term consisting of the life of the last surviving author and fifty years after such last surviving author's death.

(*c*) Anonymous Works, Pseudonymous Works, and Works Made for Hire.

In the case of an anonymous work, a pseudonymous work, or a work made for hire, the copyright endures for a term of seventy-five years from the year of its first publication, or a term of one hundred years from the year of its creation, whichever expires first. If, before the end of such term, the identity of one or more of the authors of an anonymous or pseudonymous work is revealed in the records of a registration made for that work under subsections (*a*) or (*d*) of section 408, or in the records provided by this subsection, the copyright in the work endures for the term specified by subsection (*a*) or (*b*), based on the life of the author or authors whose identity has been revealed. Any person having an interest in the copyright in an anonymous or pseudonymous work may at any time record, in records to be maintained by the Copyright Office for that purpose, a statement identifying one or more authors of the work; the statement shall also identify the person filing it, the nature of that person's interest, the source of the information recorded, and the particular work affected, and shall comply in form and content with requirements that the Register of Copyrights shall prescribe by regulation.

(*d*) Records Relating to Death of Authors.

Any person having an interest in a copyright may at any time record in the Copyright Office a statement of the date of death of the author of the copyrighted work, or a statement that the author is still living on a particular date. The statement shall identify the person filing it, the nature of that person's interest, and the source of the information recorded, and shall comply in form and content with requirements that the Register of Copyrights shall prescribe by regulation. The Register shall maintain current records of information relating to the death of authors of copyrighted works, based on such recorded statements and, to the extent the Register considers practicable, on data contained in any of the records of the Copyright Office or in other reference sources.

(*e*) Presumption as to Author's Death.

After a period of seventy-five years from the year of first publication of a work, or a period of one hundred years from the year of its creation, whichever expires first, any person who obtains from the Copyright Office a certified report that the records provided by subsection (*d*) disclose nothing to indicate that the author of the work is living, or died less than fifty years before, is entitled to the benefit of a presumption that the author has been dead for at least fifty years. Reliance in good faith upon this presumption shall be a complete defense to any action for infringement under this title.

E–33 **303. Duration of copyright: Works created but not published or copyrighted before January 1, 1978**

Copyright in a work created before January 1, 1978, but not theretofore in the public domain or copyrighted, subsists from January 1, 1978, and endures for the term provided by section 302. In no case, however, shall the term of copyright in such a work expire before December 31, 2002; and, if the work is published on or before December 31, 2002, the term of copyright shall not expire before December 31, 2027.

E–34 **304. Duration of copyright: Subsisting copyrights**

(*a*) Copyrights in Their First Term on January 1, 1978.

Any copyright, the first term of which is subsisting on January 1, 1978, shall endure for twenty-eight years from the date it was originally secured: *Provided*, That in the case of any posthumous work or of any periodical, cyclopedic, or other composite work upon which the copyright was originally secured by the proprietor thereof, or of any work copyrighted by a corporate body (otherwise than as assignee or licensee of the individual author) or by an employer for whom such work is made for hire, the proprietor of such copyright shall be entitled to a renewal and extension of the copyright in such work for the further term of forty-seven years when application for such renewal and extension shall have been made to the Copyright Office and duly registered therein within one year prior to the expiration of the original term of copyright: *And provided further*, That in the case of any other copyrighted work, including a contribution by an individual author to a periodical or to a cyclopedic or other composite work, the author of such work, if still living, or the widow, widower, or children of the author, if the author be not living, or if such author, widow, widower, or children be not living, then the author's executors, or in the absence of a will, his or her next of kin shall be entitled to a renewal and extension of the copyright in such work for a further term of forty-seven years when application for such renewal and extension shall have been made to the Copyright Office and duly registered therein within one year prior to the expiration of the original term of copyright: *And provided further*, That in default of the registration of such application for renewal and extension, the copyright in any work shall terminate at the expiration of twenty-eight years from the date copyright was originally secured.

(*b*) Copyrights in their Renewal Term or Registered for Renewal before January 1, 1978.

The duration of any copyright, the renewal term of which is subsisting at any time between December 31, 1976, and December 31, 1977, inclusive, or for which renewal registration is made between December 31, 1976, and December 31, 1977, inclusive, is extended to endure for a term of seventy-five years from the date copyright was originally secured.

(*c*) Termination of Transfers and Licenses Covering Extended Renewal Term.

In the case of any copyright subsisting in either its first or renewal term on January 1, 1978, other than a copyright in a work made for hire, the exclusive or nonexclusive grant of a transfer or license of the renewal copyright or any right under it, executed before January 1, 1978, by any of the persons designated by the second proviso of subsection (*a*) of this section, otherwise than by will, is subject to termination under the following conditions:

(1) In the case of a grant executed by a person or persons other than the author, termination of the grant may be effected by the surviving person or persons who executed it. In the case of a grant executed by one or more of the authors of the work, termination of the grant may be effected, to the extent of a particular author's share in the ownership of the renewal copyright, by the author who executed it or, if such author is dead, by the person or persons who, under clause (2) of this subsection, own and are entitled to exercise a total of more than one-half of that author's termination interest.

(2) Where an author is dead, his or her termination interest is owned, and may be exercised by his widow or her widower and his or her children or grandchildren as follows:

(A) the widow or widower owns the author's entire termination interest unless there are any surviving children or grandchildren of the author, in which case the widow or widower owns one-half of the author's interest;

(B) the author's surviving children, and the surviving children of any dead child of the author, own the author's entire termination interest unless there is a widow or widower in which case the ownership of one-half of the author's interest is divided among them;

(C) the rights of the author's children and grandchildren are in all cases divided among them and exercised on a per stirpes basis according to the number of such author's children represented; the share of the children of a dead child in a termination interest can be exercised only by the action of a majority of them.

(3) Termination of the grant may be effected at any time during a period of five years beginning at the end of fifty-six years from the date copyright was originally secured, or beginning on January 1, 1978, whichever is later.

(4) The termination shall be effected by serving an advance notice in writing upon the grantee or the grantee's successor in title. In the case of a grant executed by a person or persons other than the author, the notice shall be signed by all of those entitled to terminate the grant under clause (1) of this subsection, or by their duly authorized agents. In the case of a grant executed by one or more of the authors of the work, the notice as to any one author's share shall be signed by that author or his or her duly authorized agent or, if that author is dead, by the number and proportion of the owners of his or her termination interest required under clauses (1) and (2) of this subsection, or by their duly authorized agents.

(A) The notice shall state the effective date of the termination, which shall fall within the five-year period specified by clause (3) of this subsection, and the notice shall be served not less than two or more than ten years

1487

before that date. A copy of the notice shall be recorded in the Copyright Office before the effective date of termination, as a condition to its taking effect.

(B) The notice shall comply, in form, content, and manner of service, with requirements that the Register of Copyrights shall prescribe by regulation.

(5) Termination of the grant may be effected notwithstanding any agreement to the contrary, including an agreement to make a will or to make any future grant.

(6) In the case of a grant executed by a person or persons other than the author, all rights under this title that were covered by the terminated grant revert, upon the effective date of termination, to all of those entitled to terminate the grant under clause (1) of this subsection. In the case of a grant executed by one or more of the authors of the work, all of a particular author's rights under this title that were covered by the terminated grant revert, upon the effective date of termination, to that author or, if that author is dead, to the persons owning his or her termination interest under clause (2) of this subsection, including those owners who did not join in signing the notice of termination under clause (4) of this subsection. In all cases the reversion of rights is subject to the following limitations:

(A) A derivative work prepared under authority of the grant before its termination may continue to be utilized under the terms of the grant after its termination, but this privilege does not extend to the preparation after the termination of other derivative works based upon the copyrighted work covered by the terminated grant.

(B) The future rights that will revert upon termination of the grant become vested on the date the notice of termination has been served as provided by clause (4) of this subsection.

(C) Where the author's rights revert to two or more persons under clause (2) of this subsection, they shall vest in those persons in the proportionate shares provided by that clause. In such a case, and subject to the provisions of subclause (D) of this clause, a further grant, or agreement to make a further grant, of a particular author's share with respect to any right covered by a terminated grant is valid only if it is signed by the same number and proportion of the owners, in whom the right has vested under this clause, as are required to terminate the grant under clause (2) of this subsection. Such further grant or agreement is effective with respect to all the persons in whom the right it covers has vested under this subclause, including whose who did not join in signing it. If any person dies after rights under a terminated grant have vested in him or her, that person's legal representatives, legatees, or heirs at law represent him or her for purposes of this subclause.

(D) A further grant, or agreement to make a further grant, of any right covered by a terminated grant is valid only if it is made after the effective date of the termination. As an exception, however, an agreement for such a further grant may be made between the author or any of the persons provided by the first sentence of clause (6) of this subsection, or between the persons provided by subclause (C) of this clause, and the original grantee or such grantee's successor in title, after the notice of termination has been served as provided by clause (4) of this subsection.

(E) Termination of a grant under this subsection affects only those rights covered by the grant that arise under this title, and in no way affects rights arising under any other Federal, State, or foreign laws.

(F) Unless and until termination is effected under this subsection, the grant, if it does not provide otherwise, continues in effect for the remainder of the extended renewal term.

305. Duration of copyright: Terminal date   E–35

All terms of copyright provided by sections 302 through 304 run to the end of the calendar year in which they would otherwise expire.

CHAPTER 4   E–36

COPYRIGHT NOTICE, DEPOSIT, AND REGISTRATION

Sec.

401. Notice of copyright: Visually perceptible copies[18]   E–37

(*a*) GENERAL PROVISIONS.

Whenever a work protected under this title is published in the United States or elsewhere by authority of the copyright owner, a notice of copyright as provided by this section may be placed on publicly distributed copies from which the work can be visually perceived, either directly or with the aid of a machine or device.

(*b*) FORM OF NOTICE.

If a notice appears on the copies, it shall consist of the following three elements:
(1) the symbol © (the letter C in a circle), or the word "Copyright," or the abbreviation "Copr."; and
(2) the year of first publication of the work; in the case of compilations or derivative works incorporating previously published material, the year date of first publication of the compilation or derivative work is sufficient. The year date may be omitted where a pictorial, graphic, or sculptural work, with accompanying text matter, if any, is reproduced in or on greeting cards, postcards, stationery, jewelry, dolls, toys, or any useful articles; and
(3) the name of the owner of copyright in the work, or an abbreviation by which the name can be recognized, or a generally known alternative designation of the owner.

(*c*) POSITION OF NOTICE.

---

[18] Amended Oct. 31, 1988, Pub. L. 100–568, § 7(a), 102 Stat. 2857.

The notice shall be affixed to the copies in such manner and location as to give reasonable notice of the claim of copyright. The Register of Copyrights shall prescribe by regulation, as examples, specific methods of affixation and positions of the notice on various types of works that will satisfy this requirement, but these specifications shall not be considered exhaustive.

(*d*) EVIDENTIARY WEIGHT OF NOTICE.

If a notice of copyright in the form and position specified by this section appears on the published copy or copies to which a defendant in a copyright infringement suit had access, then no weight shall be given to such a defendant's interposition of a defense based on innocent infringement in mitigation of actual or statutory damages, except as provided in the last sentence of section 504(*c*)(2).

E–38   **402. Notice of copyright: Phonorecords of sound recordings**[19]

(*a*) GENERAL PROVISIONS.

Whenever a sound recording protected under this title is published in the United States or elsewhere by authority of the copyright owner, a notice of copyright as provided by this section may be placed on publicly distributed phonorecords of the sound recording.

(*b*) FORM OF NOTICE.

If a notice appears on the phonorecords, it shall consist of the following three elements:

(1) the symbol ℗ (the letter P in a circle); and
(2) the year of first publication of the sound recording; and
(3) the name of the owner of copyright in the sound recording, or an abbreviation by which the name can be recognized, or a generally known alternative designation of the owner; if the producer of the sound recording is named on the phonorecord labels or containers, and if no other name appears in conjunction with the notice, the producer's name shall be considered a part of the notice.

(*c*) POSITION OF NOTICE.

The notice shall be placed on the surface of the phonorecord, or on the phonorecord label or container, in such manner and location as to give reasonable notice of the claim of copyright.

(*d*) EVIDENTIARY WEIGHT OF NOTICE.

If a notice of copyright in the form and position specified by this section appears on the published phonorecord or phonorecords to which a defendant in a copyright infringement suit had access, then no weight shall be given to such a defendant's interposition of a defense based on innocent infringement in mitigation of actual or statutory damages, except as provided in the last sentence of section 504(*c*)(2).

E–39   **403. Notice of copyright: Publications incorporating United States Government works**[20]

Sections 401(*d*) and 402(*d*) shall not apply to a work published in copies or phonorecords consisting predominantly of one or more works of the United States

---

[19] Amended Oct. 31, 1988, Pub. L. 100–568, § 7(*b*), 102 Stat. 2857–58.
[20] Amended Oct. 31, 1988, Pub. L. 100–568, § 7(*c*), 102 Stat. 2858.

Government unless the notice of copyright appearing on the published copies or phonorecords to which a defendant in the copyright infringement suit had access includes a statement identifying, either affirmatively or negatively, those portions of the copies or phonorecords embodying any work or works protected under this title.

404. Notice of copyright: Contributions to collective works[21]

(*a*) A separate contribution to a collective work may bear its own notice of copyright, as provided by sections 401 through 403. However, a single notice applicable to the collective work as a whole is sufficient to invoke the provisions of section 401(*d*) or 402(*d*), as applicable with respect to the separate contributions it contains (not including advertisements inserted on behalf of persons other than the owner of copyright in the collective work), regardless of the ownership of copyright in the contributions and whether or not they have been previously published.

(*b*) With respect to copies and phonorecords publicly distributed by authority of the copyright owner before the effective date of the Berne Convention Implementation Act of 1988, where the person named in a single notice applicable to a collective work as a whole is not the owner of copyright in a separate contribution that does not bear its own notice, the case is governed by the provisions of section 406(*a*).

405. Notice of copyright: Omission of notice on certain copies and
phonorecords[22]

(*a*) EFFECT OF OMISSION ON COPYRIGHT.

With respect to copies and phonorecords publicly distributed by authority of the copyright owner before the effective date of the Berne Convention Implementation Act of 1988, the omission of the copyright notice described in sections 401 through 403 from copies or phonorecords publicly distributed by authority of the copyright owner does not invalidate the copyright in a work if—

  (1) the notice has been omitted from no more than a relatively small number of copies or phonorecords distributed to the public; or
  (2) registration for the work has been made before or is made within five years after the publication without notice, and a reasonable effort is made to add notice to all copies or phonorecords that are distributed to the public in the United States after the omission has been discovered; or
  (3) the notice has been omitted in violation of an express requirement in writing that, as a condition of the copyright owner's authorization of the public distribution of copies or phonorecords, they bear the prescribed notice.

(*b*) EFFECT OF OMISSION ON INNOCENT INFRINGERS.

Any person who innocently infringes a copyright, in reliance upon an authorized copy or phonorecord from which the copyright notice has been omitted and which was publicly distributed by authority of the copyright owner before the effective date of the Berne Convention Implementation Act of 1988, incurs no liability for actual or statutory damages under section 504 for any infringing acts committed before receiving actual notice that registration for the work has been made under section 408, if such person proves that he or she was misled by the omission of notice. In a suit for infringement in such a case the court may allow or disallow recovery of any of the infringer's profits attributable to the infringement, and may

---

[21] Amended Oct. 31, 1988, Pub. L. 100–568, § 7(*d*), 102 Stat. 2858.
[22] Amended Oct. 31, 1988, Pub. L. 100–568, § 7(*e*), 102 Stat. 2858.

enjoin the continuation of the infringing undertaking or may require, as a condition of permitting the continuation of the infringing undertaking, that the infringer pay the copyright owner a reasonable license fee in an amount and on terms fixed by the court.

(c) REMOVAL OF NOTICE.

Protection under this title is not affected by the removal, destruction, or obliteration of the notice, without the authorization of the copyright owner, from any publicly distributed copies or phonorecords.

406. Notice of copyright: Omission of notice on certain copies and phonorecords[23]

(a) ERROR IN NAME.

With respect to copies and phonorecords publicly distributed by authority of the copyright owner before the effective date of the Berne Convention Implementation Act of 1988, where the person named in the copyright notice on copies or phonorecords publicly distributed by authority of the copyright owner is not the owner of copyright, the validity and ownership of the copyright are not affected. In such a case, however, any person who innocently begins an undertaking that infringes the copyright has a complete defense to any action for such infringement if such person proves that he or she was misled by the notice and began the undertaking in good faith under a purported transfer or license from the person named therein, unless before the undertaking was begun—

(1) registration for the work had been made in the name of the owner of copyright; or

(2) a document executed by the person named in the notice and showing the ownership of the copyright has been recorded.

The person named in the notice is liable to account to the copyright owner for all receipts from transfers or licenses purportedly made under the copyright by the person named in the notice.

(b) ERROR IN DATE.

When the year date in the notice on copies or phonorecords distributed before the effective date of the Berne Convention Implementation Act of 1988 by authority of the copyright owner is earlier than the year in which publication first occurred, any period computed from the year of first publication under section 302 is to be computed from the year in the notice. Where the year date is more than one year later than the year in which publication first occurred, the work is considered to have been published without any notice and is governed by the provisions of section 405.

(c) OMISSION OF NAME OR DATE.

Where copies or phonorecords publicly distributed before the effective date of the Berne Convention Implementation Act of 1988 by authority of the copyright owner contain no name or no date that could reasonably be considered a part of the notice, the work is considered to have been published without any notice and is

---

[23] Amended Oct. 31, 1988, Pub. L. 100–568, § 7(f), 102 Stat. 2858–59.

governed by the provisions of section 405 as in effect on the day before the effective date of the Berne Convention Implementation Act of 1988.

407. Deposit of copies or phonorecords for Library of Congress[24] **E–43**

(a) Except as provided by subsection (c), and subject to the provisions of subsection (e), the owner of copyright or of the exclusive right of publication in a work published in the United States shall deposit, within three months after the date of such publication—

    (1) two complete copies of the best edition; or

    (2) if the work is a sound recording, two complete phonorecords of the best edition, together with any printed or other visually perceptible material published with such phonorecords.

Neither the deposit requirements of this subsection nor the acquisition provisions of subsection (e) are conditions of copyright protection.

(b) The required copies or phonorecords shall be deposited in the Copyright Office for the use or disposition of the Library of Congress. The Register of Copyrights shall, when requested by the depositor and upon payment of the fee prescribed by section 708, issue a receipt of the deposit.

(c) The Register of Copyrights may by regulation exempt any categories of material from the deposit requirements of this section, or require deposit of only one copy or phonorecord with respect to any categories. Such regulations shall provide either for complete exemption from the deposit requirements of this section, or for alternative forms of deposit aimed at providing a satisfactory archival record of a work without imposing practical or financial hardships on the depositor, where the individual author is the owner of copyright in a pictorial, graphic, or sculptural work and (i) less than five copies of the work have been published, or (ii) the work has been published in a limited edition consisting of numbered copies, the monetary value of which would make the mandatory deposit of two copies of the best edition of the work burdensome, unfair, or unreasonable.

(d) At any time after publication of a work as provided by subsection (a), the Register of Copyright may make written demand for the required deposit on any of the persons obligated to make the deposit under subsection (a). Unless deposit is made within three months after the demand is received, the person or persons on whom the demand was made are liable—

    (1) to a fine of not more than $250 for each work; and

    (2) to pay into a specially designated fund in the Library of Congress the total retail price of the copies or phonorecords demanded, or, if no retail price has been fixed, the reasonable cost of the Library of Congress of acquiring them; and

    (3) to pay a fine of $2,500, in addition to any fine or liability imposed under clauses (1) and (2), if such person willfully or repeatedly fails or refuses to comply with such a demand.

(e) With respect to transmission programs that have been fixed and transmitted to the public in the United States but have not been published, the Register of Copyrights shall, after consulting with the Librarian of Congress and other interested organizations and officials, establish regulations governing the acquisition, through deposit or otherwise, of copies or phonorecords of such programs for the collections of the Library of Congress.

    (1) The Librarian of Congress shall be permitted, under the standards and conditions set forth in such regulations, to make a fixation of a transmission

---

[24] Amended Oct. 31, 1988, Pub. L. 100–568, § 8, 102 Stat. 2859.

program directly from a transmission to the public, and to reproduce one copy or phonorecord from such fixation for archival purposes.

(2) Such regulations shall also provide standards and procedures by which the Register of Copyrights may make written demand, upon the owner of the right of transmission in the United States, for the deposit of a copy or phonorecord of a specific transmission program. Such deposit may, at the option of the owner of the right of transmission in the United States, be accomplished by gift, by loan for purposes of reproduction, or by sale at a price not to exceed the cost of reproducing and supplying the copy or phonorecord. The regulations established under this clause shall provide reasonable periods of not less than three months for compliance with a demand, and shall allow for extensions of such periods and adjustments in the scope of the demand or the methods for fulfilling it, as reasonably warranted by the circumstances. Willful failure or refusal to comply with the conditions prescribed by such regulations shall subject the owner of the right of transmission in the United States to liability for an amount, not to exceed the cost of reproducing and supplying the copy or phonorecord in question, to be paid into a specially designated fund in the Library of Congress.

(3) Nothing in this subsection shall be construed to require the making or retention, for purposes of deposit, of any copy or phonorecord of an unpublished transmission program, the transmission of which occurs before the receipt of a specific written demand as provided by clause (2).

(4) No activity undertaken in compliance with regulations prescribed under clauses (1) or (2) of this subsection shall result in liability if intended solely to assist in the acquisition of copies or phonorecords under this subsection.

E-44   408. Copyright registration in general[25]

(*a*) REGISTRATION PERMISSIVE.

At any time during the subsistence of copyright in any published or unpublished work, the owner of copyright or of any exclusive right in the work may obtain registration of the copyright claim by delivering to the Copyright Office the deposit specified by this section, together with the application and fee specified by sections 409 and 708. Such registration is not a condition of copyright protection.

(*b*) DEPOSIT FOR COPYRIGHT REGISTRATION.

Except as provided by subsection (*c*), the material deposited for registration shall include—

(1) in the case of an unpublished work, one complete copy or phonorecord;
(2) in the case of a published work, two complete copies or phonorecords of the best edition;
(3) in the case of a work first published outside the United States, one complete copy or phonorecord as so published;
(4) in the case of a contribution to a collective work, one complete copy or phonorecord of the best edition of the collective work.

---

[25] Amended Oct. 31, 1988, Pub. L. 100–568, § 9(*a*), 102 Stat. 2859.

Copies or phonorecords deposited for the Library of Congress under section 407 may be used to satisfy the deposit provisions of this section, if they are accompanied by the prescribed application and fee, and by any additional identifying material that the Register may, by regulation, require. The Register shall also prescribe regulations establishing requirements under which copies or phonorecords acquired for the Library of Congress under subsection (*e*) of section 407, otherwise than by deposit, may be used to satisfy the deposit provisions of this section.

5(*c*) ADMINISTRATIVE CLASSIFICATION AND OPTIONAL DEPOSIT.

(1) The Register of Copyrights is authorized to specify by regulation the administrative classes into which works are to be placed for purposes of deposit and registration, and the nature of the copies or phonorecords to be deposited in the various classes specified. The regulations may require or permit, for particular classes, the deposit of identifying material instead of copies or phonorecords, the deposit of only one copy or phonorecord where two would normally be required, or a single registration for a group of related works. This administrative classification of works has no significance with respect to the subject matter of copyright or the exclusive rights provided by this title.

(2) Without prejudice to the general authority provided under clause (1), the Register of Copyrights shall establish regulations specifically permitting a single registration for a group of works by the same individual author, all first published as contributions to periodicals, including newspapers, within a twelve-month period, on the basis of a single deposit, application, and registration fee, under the following conditions:

(A) if the deposit consists of one copy of the entire issue of the periodical, or of the entire section in the case of a newspaper, in which each contribution was first published; and

(B) if the application identifies each work separately, including the periodical containing it and its date of first publication.

(3) As an alternative to separate renewal registrations under subsection (*a*) of section 304, a single renewal registration may be made for a group of works by the same individual author, all first published as contributions to periodicals, including newspapers, upon the filing of a single application.

(A) the renewal claimant or claimants, and the basis of claim or claims under section 304(*a*), is the same for each of the works; and

(B) the works were all copyrighted upon their first publication, either through separate copyright notice and registration or by virtue of a general copyright notice in the periodical issue as a whole; and

(C) the renewal application and fee are received not more than twenty-eight or less than twenty-seven years after the thirty-first day of December of the calendar year in which all of the works were first published; and

(D) the renewal application identifies each work separately, including the periodical containing it and its date of first publication.

(*d*) CORRECTIONS AND AMPLIFICATIONS.

The Register may also establish, by regulation, formal procedures for the filing of an application for supplementary registration, to correct an error in a copyright registration or to amplify the information given in a registration. Such application shall be accompanied by the fee provided by section 708, and shall clearly identify the registration to be corrected or amplified. The information contained in a supplementary registration augments but does not supersede that contained in the earlier registration.

(*e*) Published Edition of a Previously Registered Work.

Registration for the first published edition of a work previously registered in unpublished form may be made even though the work as published is substantially the same as the unpublished version.

409. Application for copyright registration

The application for copyright registration shall be made on a form prescribed by the Register of Copyrights and shall include—
  (1) the name and address of the copyright claimant;
  (2) in the case of a work other than an anonymous or pseudonymous work, the name and nationality or domicile of the author or authors, and, if one or more of the authors is dead, the dates of their deaths;
  (3) if the work is anonymous or pseudonymous, the nationality or domicile of the author or authors;
  (4) in the case of a work made for hire, a statement to this effect;
  (5) if the copyright claimant is not the author, a brief statement of how the claimant obtained ownership of the copyright;
  (6) the title of the work, together with any previous or alternative titles under which the work can be identified;
  (7) the year in which creation of the work was completed;
  (8) if the work has been published, the date and nation of its first publication;
  (9) in the case of a compilation or derivative work, an identification of any preexisting work or works that it is based on or incorporates, and a brief, general statement of the additional material covered by the copyright claim being registered;
  (10) in the case of a published work containing material of which copies are required by section 601 to be manufactured in the United States, the names of the persons or organizations who performed the processes specified by subsection (*c*) of section 601 with respect to that material, and the places where those processes were performed; and
  (11) any other information regarded by the Register of Coprights as bearing upon the preparation or identification of the work or the existence, ownership, or duration of the copyright.

410. Registration of claim and issuance of certificate

(*a*) When, after examination, the Register of Copyrights determines that, in accordance with the provisions of this title, the material deposited constitutes copyrightable subject matter and that the other legal and formal requirements of this title have been met, the Register shall register the claim and issue to the applicant a certificate of registration under the seal of the Copyright Office. The certificate shall contain the information given in the application, together with the number and effective date of the registration.

(*b*) In any case in which the Register of Copyrights determines that, in accordance with the provisions of this title, the material deposited does not constitute copyrightable subject matter or that the claim is invalid for any other reason, the Register shall refuse registration and shall notify the applicant in writing of the reasons for such refusal.

(*c*) In any judicial proceedings the certificate of a registration made before or within five years after first publication of the work shall constitute prima facie evidence of the validity of the copyright and of the facts stated in the certificate. The evidentiary weight to be accorded the certificate of a registration made thereafter shall be within the discretion of the court.

(*d*) The effective date of a copyright registration is the day on which an application, deposit, and fee, which are later determined by the Register of Copyrights or by a court of competent jurisdiction to be acceptable for registration, have all been received in the Copyright Office.

411. Registration and infringement actions[26]   **E–47**

(a) Except for actions for infringement of copyright in Berne Convention works whose country of origin is not the United States, and subject to the provisions of subsection (b), no action for infringement of the copyright in any work shall be instituted until registration of the copyright claim has been made in accordance with this title. In any case, however, where the deposit, application, and fee required for registration have been delivered to the Copyright Office in proper form and registration has been refused, the applicant is entitled to institute an action for infringement if notice thereof, with a copy of the complaint, is served on the Register of Copyrights. The Register may, at his or her option, become a party to the action with respect to the issue of registrability of the copyright claim by entering an appearance within sixty days after such service, but the Register's failure to become a party shall not deprive the court of jurisdiction to determine that issue.

(b) In the case of a work consisting of sounds, images, or both, the first fixation of which is made simultaneously with its transmission, the copyright owner may, either before or after such fixation takes place, institute an action for infringement under section 501, fully subject to the remedies provided by sections 502 through 506 and sections 509 and 510, if, in accordance with requirements that the Register of Copyrights shall prescribe by regulation, the copyright owner—

    (1) serves notice upon the infringer, not less than ten or more than thirty days before such fixation, identifying the work and the specific time and source of its first transmission, and declaring an intention to secure copyright in the work; and

    (2) makes registration for the work, if required by subsection (a), within three months after its first transmission.

412. Registration as prerequisite to certain remedies for infringement   **E–48**

In any action under this title, other than an action instituted under section 411(b), no award of statutory damages or of attorney's fees, as provided by sections 504 and 505, shall be made for—

    (1) any infringement of copyright in an unpublished work commenced before the effective date of its registration; or

    (2) any infringement of copyright commenced after first publication of the work and before the effective date of its registration, unless such registration is made within three months after the first publication of the work.

CHAPTER 5   **E–49**

COPYRIGHT INFRINGEMENT AND REMEDIES

Sec.

501. Infringement of copyright.
502. Remedies for infringement: Injunctions.
503. Remedies for infringement: Impounding and disposition of infringing articles.
504. Remedies for infringement: Damage and profits.
505. Remedies for infringement: Costs and attorney's fees.
506. Criminal offenses.

---

[26] Amended Oct. 31, 1988, Pub. L. 100–568, § 9(b), 102 Stat. 2859.

E–50   **501. Infringement of copyright**[27]

(*a*) Anyone who violates any of the exclusive rights of the copyright owner as provided by sections 106 through 118, or who imports copies or phonorecords into the United States in violation of section 602, in an infringer of the copyright.

(*b*) The legal or beneficial owner of an exclusive right under a copyright is entitled, subject to the requirements of section 411, to institute an action for any infringement of that particular right committed while he or she is the owner of it. The court may require such owner to serve written notice of the action with a copy of the complaint upon any person shown, by the records of the Copyright Office or otherwise, to have or claim an interest in the copyright, and shall require that such notice be served upon any person whose interest is likely to be affected by a decision in the case. The court may require the joinder, and shall permit the intervention, of any person having or claiming an interest in the copyright.

(*c*) For any secondary transmission by a cable system that embodies a performance or a display of a work which is actionable as an act of infringement under subsection (*c*) of section 111, a television broadcast station holding a copyright or other license to transmit or perform the same version of that work shall, for purposes of subsection (*b*) of this section, be treated as a legal or beneficial owner if such secondary transmission occurs within the local service area of that television station.

(*d*) For any secondary transmission by a cable system that is actionable as an act of infringement pursuant to section 111(*c*)(3), the following shall also have standing to sue: (i) the primary transmitter whose transmission has been altered by the cable system; and (ii) any broadcast station within whose local service area the secondary transmission occurs.

(*e*) With respect to any secondary transmission that is made by a satellite carrier of a primary transmission embodying the performance or display of a work and is actionable as an act of infringement under section 119(*a*)(5), a network station holding a copyright or other license to transmit or perform the same version of that work shall, for purposes of subsection (*b*) of this section, be treated as a legal or beneficial owner if such secondary transmission occurs within the local service area of that section.

E–51   **502. Remedies for infringement: Injunctions**

(*a*) Any court having jurisdiction of a civil action arising under this title may, subject to the provisions of section 1498 of title 28, grant temporary and final injunctions on such terms as it may deem reasonable to prevent or restrain infringement of a copyright.

(*b*) Any such injunction may be served anywhere in the United States on the person enjoined; it shall be operative throughout the United States and shall be enforceable, by proceedings in contempt or otherwise, by any United States court having jurisdiction of that person. The clerk of the court granting the injunction shall, when requested by any other court in which enforcement of the injunction is sought, transmit promptly to the other court a certified copy of all the papers in the case on file in such clerk's office.

---

[27] Amended Oct. 31, 1988, Pub. L. 100–568, § 10(*a*), 102 Stat. 2860, Nov. 16, 1988, Pub. L. 100–667, § 202(2), 102 Stat. 3935. Public Law 100–667 added subsection (*e*).

503. Remedies for infringement: Impounding and disposition of infringing articles

(*a*) At any time while an action under this title is pending, the court may order the impounding, on such terms as it may deem reasonable, of all copies or phonorecords claimed to have been made or used in violation of the copyright owner's exclusive rights, and of all plates, molds, matrices, masters, tapes, film negatives, or other articles by means of which such copies or phonorecords may be reproduced.

(*b*) As part of a final judgment or decree, the court may order the destruction or other reasonable disposition of all copies or phonorecords found to have been made or used in violation of the copyright owner's exclusive rights, and of all plates, molds, matrices, masters, tapes, film negatives, or other articles by means of which such copies or phonorecords may be reproduced.

504. Remedies for infringement: Damages and profits[28]

(*a*) In General.

Except as otherwise provided by this title, an infringer of copyright is liable for either—
(1) the copyright owner's actual damages and any additional profits of the infringer, as provided by subsection (*b*); or
(2) statutory damages, as provided by subsection (*c*).

(*b*) Actual Damages and Profits.

The copyright owner is entitled to recover the actual damages suffered by him or her as a result of the infringement, and any profits of the infringer that are attributable to the infringement and are not taken into account in computing the actual damages. In establishing the infringer's profits, the copyright owner is required to present proof only of the infringer's gross revenue, and the infringer is required to prove his or her deductible expenses and the elements of profit attributable to factors other than the copyrighted work.

(*c*) Statutory Damages.

(1) Except as provided by clause (2) of this subsection, the copyright owner may elect, at any time before final judgment is rendered, to recover, instead of actual damages and profits, an award of statutory damages for all infringements involved in the action, with respect to any one work, for which any one infringer is liable individually, or for which any two or more infringers are liable jointly and severally, in a sum of not less than $500 or more than $10,000 as the court considers just. For the purposes of this subsection, all the parts of a compilation or derivative work constitute one work.
(2) In the case where a copyright owner sustains the burden of proving, and the court finds, that infringement was committed willfully, the court in its discretion may increase the award of statutory damages to a sum of not more than $100,000. In a case where the infringer sustains the burden of proving, and the court finds, that such infringer was not aware and had no reason to believe that his or her acts constituted an infringement of copyright, the court in its discretion may reduce the award of statutory damages

---

[28] Amended Oct. 31, 1988, Pub. L. 100–568, § 10(*b*), 102 Stat. 2860.

to a sum of not less than $200. The court shall remit statutory damages in any case where an infringer believed and had reasonable grounds for believing that his or her use of the copyright work was a fair use under section 197, if the infringer was: (i) an employee or agent of a nonprofit educational institution, library, or archives acting within the scope of his or her employment who, or such institution, library, or archives itself, which infringed by reproducing the work in copies or phonorecords; or (ii) a public broadcasting entity which or a person who, as a regular part of the nonprofit activities of a public broadcasting entity (as defined in subsection (g) of section 118) infringed by performing a published nondramatic literary work or by reproducing a transmission program embodying a performance of such a work.

E–54   505. Remedies for infringement: Costs and attorney's fees

In any civil action under this title, the court in its discretion may allow the recovery of full costs by or against any party other than the United States or an officer thereof. Except as otherwise provided in this title, the court may also award a reasonable attorney's fee to the prevailing party as part of the costs.

E–55   506. Criminal offenses[29]

(a) CRIMINAL INFRINGEMENT.

Any person who infringes a copyright willfully and for purposes of commercial advantage or private financial gain shall be punished as provided in section 2319 of title 18.[30]

---

[29] Section 506(a) as amended by the Act of May 24, 1982 (Pub. L. 97–180, 96 Stat. 93.) Prior to this amendment, subsection (a) was as follows:

(a) Criminal Infringement.—Any person who infringes a copyright willfully and for purposes of commercial advantage or private financial gain shall be fined not more than $10,000 or imprisoned for not more than one year, or both: *Provided, however,* That any person who infringes willfully and for purposes of commercial advantage or private financial gain the copyright in a sound recording afforded by subsections (1), (2), or (3) of section 106 or the copyright in a motion picture afforded by subsections (1), (3), or (4) of section 106 shall be fined not more than $25,000 or imprisoned for not more than one year, or both, for the first such offense and shall be fined not more than $50,000 or imprisoned for not more than two years, or both, for any subsequent offense.

[30] 18 U.S.C. Section 2319 (Act of May 24, 1982—Pub. L. 97—180) reads as follows:

2319. Criminal infringement of a copyright

(a) Whoever violates section 506(a) (relating to criminal offenses) of title 17 shall be punished as provided in subsection (b) of this section and such penalties shall be in addition to any other provisions of title 17 or any other law.

(b) Any person who commits an offense under subsection (a) of this section—

(1) shall be fined not more than $250,000 or imprisoned for not more than five years, or both, if the offense—

(A) involves the reproduction or distribution, during any one-hundred-and-eighty-day period, of at least one thousand phonorecords or copies infringing the copyright in one or more sound recordings;

(B) involves the reproduction or distribution, during any one-hundred-and-eighty-day period, of at least sixty-five copies infringing the copyright in one or more motion pictures or other audiovisual works; or

(C) is a second or subsequent offense under either of subsection (b)(1) or (b)(2) of this section, where a prior offense involved a sound recording, or a motion picture or other audiovisual work;

(2) shall be fined not more than $250,000 or imprisoned for not more than two years, or both, if the offense—

(A) involves the reproduction or distribution, during any one-hundred-and-eighty-day period, of more than one hundred but less than one thousand phonorecords or copies infringing the copyright in one or more sound recordings; or

(*b*) Forfeiture and Destruction.

When any person is convicted of any violation of subsection (*a*), the court in its judgment of conviction shall, in addition to the penalty therein prescribed, order the forfeiture and destruction or other disposition of all infringing copies or phonorecords and all implements, devices, or equipment used in the manufacture of such infringing copies or phonorecords.

(*c*) Fraudulent Copyright Notice.

Any person who, with fraudulent intent, places on any article a notice of copyright or words of the same purport that such person knows to be false, or who, with fraudulent intent, publicly distributes or imports for public distribution any article bearing such notice or words that such person knows to be false, shall be fined not more than $2,500.

(*d*) Fraudulent Removal of Copyright Notice.

Any person who, with fraudulent intent, removes or alters any notice of copyright appearing on a copy of a copyrighted work shall be fined not more than $2,500.

(*e*) False Representation.

Any person who knowingly makes a false representation of a material fact in the application for copyright registration provided for by section 409, or in any written statement filed in connection with the application, shall be fined not more than $2,500.

507. Limitations on actions

(*a*) Criminal Proceedings.

1No criminal proceeding shall be maintained under the provisions of this title unless it is commenced within three years after the cause of action arose.

(*b*) Civil Actions.

No civil action shall be maintained under the provisions of this title unless it is commenced within three years after the claim accrued.

508. Notification of filing and determination of actions

(*a*) Within one month after the filing of any action under this title, the clerks of the courts of the United States shall send written notification to the Register of Copyrights setting forth, as far as is shown by the papers filed in the court, the names and addresses of the parties and the title, author, and registration number of each work involved in the action. If any other copyrighted work is later included in the action by amendment, answer, or other pleading, the clerk shall also send a

---

(B) involves the reproduction or distribution, during any one-hundred-and-eighty-day period, of more than seven but less than sixty-five copies infringing the copyright in one or more motion pictures or other audiovisual works; and
(3) shall be fined not more than $25,000 or imprisoned for not more than one year, or both, in any other case.
(*c*) As used in this section—
(1) the terms "sound recording," "motion picture," "audiovisual work," "phonorecord," and "copies" have, respectively, the meanings set forth in section 101 (relating to definitions) of title 17; and
(2) the terms "reproduction" and "distribution" refer to the exclusive rights of a copyright owner under clauses (1) and (3) respectively of section 106 (relating to exclusive rights in copyrighted works), as limited by sections 107 through 118, of title 17.

notification concerning it to the Register within one month after the pleading is filed.

(*b*) Within one month after any final order or judgment is issued in the case, the clerk of the court shall notify the Register of it, sending with the notification a copy of the order or judgment together with the written opinion, if any, of the court.

(*c*) Upon receiving the notifications specified in this section, the Register shall make them a part of the public records of the Copyright Office.

E–58   **509. Seizure and forfeiture**

(*a*) All copies or phonorecords manufactured, reproduced, distributed, sold, or otherwise used, intended for use, or possessed with intent to use in violation of section 506(*a*), and all plates, molds, matrices, masters, tapes, film negatives, or other articles by means of which such copies or phonorecords may be reproduced, and all electronic, mechanical, or other devices for manufacturing, reproducing, or assembling such copies or phonorecords may be seized and forfeited to the United States.

(*b*) The applicable procedures relating to (i) the seizure, summary and judicial forfeiture, and condemnation of vessels, vehicles, merchandise, and baggage for violations of the customs laws contained in title 19, (ii) the disposition of such vessels, vehicles, merchandise, and baggage or the proceeds from the sale thereof, (iii) the remission or mitigation of such forfeiture, (iv) the compromise of claims, and (v) the award of compensation to informers in respect of such forfeitures, shall apply to seizures and forfeitures incurred, or alleged to have been incurred, under the provisions of this section, insofar as applicable and not inconsistent with the provisions of this section; except that such duties as are imposed upon any officer or employee of the Treasury Department or any other person with respect to the seizure and forfeiture of vessels, vehicles, merchandise; and baggage under the provisions of the customs laws contained in title 19 shall be performed with respect to seizure and forfeiture of all articles described in subsection (*a*) by such officers, agents, or other persons as may be authorized or designated for that purpose by the Attorney General.

E–59   **510. Remedies for alteration of programing by cable systems**

(*a*) In any action filed pursuant to section 111(*c*)(3), the following remedies shall be available:

(1) Where an action is brought by a party identified in subsections (*b*) or (*c*) of section 501, the remedies provided by sections 502 through 505, and the remedy provided by subsection (*b*) of this section; and

(2) When an action is brought by a party identified in subsection (*d*) of section 501, the remedies provided by sections 502 and 505, together with any actual damages suffered by such party as a result of the infringement, and the remedy provided by subsection (*b*) of this section.

(*b*) In any action filed pursuant to section 111(*c*)(3), the court may decree that, for a period not to exceed thirty days, the cable system shall be deprived of the benefit of a compulsory license for one or more distant signals carried by such cable system.

E–60   CHAPTER 6

MANUFACTURING REQUIREMENTS AND IMPORTATION

Sec.

601. Manufacture, importation, and public distribution of certain copies.
602. Infringing importation of copies or phonorecords.
603. Importation prohibitions: Enforcement and disposition of excluded articles.

601. Manufacture, importation and public distribution of certain copies   **E–61**

(*a*) Prior to July 1, 1986,[31] and except as provided by subsection (*b*), the importation into or public distribution in the United States of copies of a work consisting preponderantly of nondramatic literary material that is in the English language and is protected under this title is prohibited unless the portions consisting of such material have been manufactured in the United States or Canada.

(*b*) The provisions of subsection (*a*) do not apply—

(1) where, on the date when importation is sought or public distribution in the United States is made, the author of any substantial part of such material is neither a national nor a domiciliary of the United States or, if such author is a national of the United States, he or she has been domiciled outside the United States for a continuous period of at least one year immediately preceding that date; in the case of a work made for hire, the exemption provided by this clause does not apply unless a substantial part of the work was prepared for an employer or other person who is not a national or domiciliary of the United States or a domestic corporation or enterprise;

(2) where the United States Customs Service is presented with an important statement issued under the seal of the Copyright Office, in which case a total of no more than two thousand copies of any one such work shall be allowed entry; the import statement shall be issued upon request to the copyright owner or to a person designated by such owner at the time of registration for the work under section 408 or at any time thereafter;

(3) where importation is sought under the authority or for the use, other than in schools, of the Government of the United States or of any State or political subdivision of a State;

(4) where importation, for use and not for sale, is sought—

(A) by any person with respect to no more than one copy of any work at any one time;

(B) by any person arriving from outside the United States, with respect to copies forming part of such person's personal baggage; or

(C) by an organization operated for scholarly, educational, or religious purposes and not for private gain, with respect to copies intended to form a part of its library;

(5) where the copies are reproduced in raised characters for the use of the blind; or

(6) where, in addition to copies imported under clauses (3) and (4) of this subsection, no more than two thousand copies of any one such work, which have not been manufactured in the United States or Canada, are publicly distributed in the United States; or

(7) where, on the date when importation is sought or public distribution in the United States is made—

(A) the author of any substantial part of such material is an individual and receives compensation for the transfer or license of the right to distribute the work in the United States; and

(B) the first publication of the work has previously taken place outside the United States under a transfer or license granted by such author to a transferee or licensee who was not a national or domiciliary of the United States or a domestic corporation or enterprise; and

(C) there has been no publication of an authorized edition of the work of which the copies were manufactured in the United States; and

---

[31] S.601(*a*) as amended by the Act of July 13, 1982 (Pub. L. 97–215, 96 Stat. 178). The amendment struck "1982" and inserted "1986" in lieu thereof.

(D) the copies were reproduced under a transfer or license granted by such author or by the transferee or licensee of the right of first publication as mentioned by subclause (B), and the transferee or the licensee of the right of reproduction was not a national or domiciliary of the United States or a domestic corporation or enterprise.

(*c*) The requirement of this section that copies be manufactured in the United States or Canada is satisfied if—

(1) in the case where the copies are printed directly from type that has been set, or directly from plates made from such type, the setting of the type and the making of the plates have been performed in the United States or Canada; or

(2) in the case where the making of plates by a lithographic or photoengraving process is a final or intermediate step preceding the printing of the copies, the making of the plates has been performed in the United States or Canada; and

(3) in any case, the printing or other final process of producing multiple copies and any binding of the copies have been performed in the United States or Canada.

(*d*) Importation or public distribution of copies in violation of this section does not invalidate protection for a work under this title. However, in any civil action or criminal proceeding for infringement of the exclusive rights to reproduce and distribute copies of the work, the infringer has a complete defense with respect to all of the nondramatic literary material comprised in the work and any other parts of the work in which the exclusive rights to reproduce and distribute copies are owned by the same person who owns such exclusive rights in the nondramatic literary material, if the infringer proves

(1) that copies of the work have been imported into or publicly distributed in the United States in violation of this section by or with the authority of the owner of such exclusive rights; and

(2) that the infringing copies were manufactured in the United States or Canada in accordance with the provisions of subsection (*c*); and

(3) that the infringement was commenced before the effective date of registration for an authorized edition of the work, the copies of which have been manufactured in the United States or Canada in accordance with the provisions of subsection (*c*).

(*e*) In any action for infringement of the exclusive rights to reproduce and distribute copies of a work containing material required by this section to be manufactured in the United States or Canada, the copyright owner shall set forth in the complaint the names of the persons or organizations who performed the processes specified by subsection (*c*) with respect to that material, and the places where those processes were performed.

E-62   **602. Infringing importation of copies or phonorecords**

(*a*) Importation into the United States, without the authority of the owner of copyright under this title, of copies or phonorecords of a work that have been acquired outside the United States in an infringement of the exclusive right to distribute copies or phonorecords under section 106, actionable under section 501. This subsection does not apply to—

(1) importation of copies or phonorecords under the authority or for the use of the Government of the United States or of any State or political subdivision of a State, but not including copies or phonorecords for use in schools, or copies of any audiovisual work imported for purposes other than archival use;

(2) importation, for the private use of the importer and not for distribution, by any person with respect to no more than one copy or phonorecord of any one work at any one time, or by any person arriving from outside the United States with respect to copies or phonorecords forming part of such person's personal baggage; or

(3) importation by or for an organization operated for scholarly, educational, or religious purposes and not for private gain, with respect to no more than one copy of an audiovisual work solely for its archival purposes, and no more than five copies or phonorecords of any other work for its library lending or archival purposes, unless the importation of such copies or phonorecords is part of an activity consisting of systematic reproduction or distribution, engaged in by such organization in violation of the provisions of section 108(g)(2).

(*b*) In a case where the making of the copies or phonorecords would have constituted an infringement of copyright if this title had been applicable, their importation is prohibited. In a case where the copies or phonorecords were lawfully made, the United States Customs Service has no authority to prevent their importation unless the provisions of section 601 are applicable. In either case, the Secretary of the Treasury is authorized to prescribe, by regulation, a procedure under which any person claiming an interest in the copyright in a particular work may, upon payment of a specified fee, be entitled to notification by the Customs Service of the importation of articles that appear to be copies or phonorecords of the work.

603. Importation prohibitions: Enforcement and disposition of excluded articles   **E–63**

(*a*) The Secretary of the Treasury and the United States Postal Service shall separately or jointly make regulations for the enforcement of the provisions of this title prohibiting importation.

(*b*) These regulations may require, as a condition for the exclusion of articles under section 602—

(1) that the person seeking exclusion obtain a court order enjoining importation of the articles; or

(2) that the person seeking exclusion furnish proof, of a specified nature and in accordance with prescribed procedures, that the copyright in which such person claims an interest is valid and that the importation would violate the prohibition in section 602; the person seeking exclusion may also be required to post a surety bond for any injury that may result if the detention or exclusion of the articles proves to be unjustified.

(*c*) Articles imported in violation of the importation prohibitions of this title are subject to seizure and forfeiture in the same manner as property imported in violation of the customs revenue laws. Forfeited articles shall be destroyed as directed by the Secretary of the Treasury or the court, as the case may be; however, the articles may be returned to the country of export whenever it is shown to the satisfaction of the Secretary of the Treasury that the importer had no reasonable grounds for believing that his or her acts constituted a violation of law.

CHAPTER 7   **E–64**

COPYRIGHT OFFICE

Sec.

E–65   **701. The Copyright Office: General responsibilities and organization**

(*a*) All administrative functions and duties under this title, except as otherwise specified, are the responsibility of the Register of Copyrights as director of the Copyright Office of the Library of Congress. The Register of Copyrights, together with the subordinate officers and employees of the Copyright Office, shall be appointed by the Librarian of Congress, and shall act under the Librarian's general direction and supervision.

(*b*) The Register of Copyrights shall adopt a seal to be used on and after January 1, 1978, to authenticate all certified documents issued by the Copyright Office.

(*c*) The Register of Copyrights shall make an annual report to the Librarian of Congress of the work and accomplishments of the Copyright Office during the previous fiscal year. The annual report of the Register of Copyrights shall be published separately and as a part of the annual report of the Librarian of Congress.

(*d*) Except as provided by section 706(*b*) and the regulations issued thereunder, all actions taken by the Register of Copyrights under this title are subject to the provisions of the Administrative Procedure Act of June 11, 1946, as amended (c. 324, 60 Stat. 237, Title 5, United States Code, Chapter 5, Subchapter II and Chapter 7).

E–66   **702. Copyright Office regulations**

The Register of Copyrights is authorized to establish regulations not inconsistent with law for the administration of the functions and duties made the responsibility of the Register under this title. All regulations established by the Register under this title are subject to the approval of the Librarian of Congress.

E–67   **703. Effective date of actions in Copyright Office**

In any case in which time limits are prescribed under this title for the performance of an action in the Copyright Office, and in which the last day of the prescribed period falls on a Saturday, Sunday, holiday, or other nonbusiness day within the District of Columbia or the Federal Government, the action may be taken on the next succeeding business day, and is effective as of the date when the period expired.

E–68   **704. Retention and disposition of articles deposited in Copyright Office**

(*a*) Upon their deposit in the Copyright Office under sections 407 and 408, all copies, phonorecords, and identifying material, including those deposited in connection with claims that have been refused registration, are the property of the United States Government.

(*b*) In the case of published works, all copies, phonorecords, and identifying material deposited are available to the Library of Congress for its collections, or for exchange or transfer to any other library. In the case of unpublished works, the Library is entitled, under regulations that the Register of Copyrights shall prescribe, to select any deposits for its collections or for transfer to the National Archives of the United States or to a Federal records center, as defined in section 2901 of title 44.

(c) The Register of Copyrights is authorized, for specific or general categories of works, to make a facsimile reproduction of all or any part of the material deposited under section 408, and to make such reproduction a part of the Copyright Office records of the registration, before transferring such material to the Library of Congress as provided by subsection (b), or before destroying or otherwise disposing of such material as provided by subsection (d).

(d) Deposits not selected by the Library under subsection (b), or identifying portions or reproductions of them, shall be retained under the control of the Copyright Office, including retention in Government storage facilities, for the longest period considered practicable and desirable by the Register of Copyrights and the Librarian of Congress. After that period it is within the joint discretion of the Register and the Librarian to order their destruction or other disposition; but, in the case of unpublished works, no deposit shall be knowingly or intentionally destroyed or otherwise disposed of during its term of copyright unless a facsimile reproduction of the entire deposit has been made a part of the Copyright Office records as provided by subsection (c).

(e) The depositor of copies, phonorecords, or identifying material under section 408, or the copyright owner of record, may request retention, under the control of the Copyright Office, of one or more of such articles for the full term of copyright in the work. The Register of Copyrights shall prescribe, by regulation, the conditions under which such requests are to be made and granted, and shall fix the fee to be charged under section 708(a)(11) if the request is granted.

705. Copyright Office records: Preparation, maintenance, public inspection, and searching   E–69

(a) The Register of Copyrights shall provide and keep in the Copyright Office records of all deposits, registrations, recordations, and other actions taken under this title, and shall prepare indexes of all such records.

(b) Such records and indexes, as well as the articles deposited in connection with completed copyright registrations and retained under the control of the Copyright Office, shall be open to public inspection.

(c) Upon request and payment of the fee specified by section 708, the Copyright Office shall make a search of its public records, indexes, and deposits, and shall furnish a report of the information they disclose with respect to any particular deposits, registrations, or recorded documents.

706. Copies of Copyright Office records   E–70

(a) Copies may be made of any public records or indexes of the Copyright Office; additional certificates of copyright registration and copies of any public records or indexes may be furnished upon request and payment of the fees specified by section 708.

(b) Copies or reproductions of deposited articles retained under the control of the Copyright Office shall be authorized or furnished only under the conditions specified by the Copyright Office regulations.

707. Copyright Office forms and publications   E–71

(a) CATALOG OF COPYRIGHT ENTRIES.

The Register of Copyrights shall compile and publish at periodic intervals catalogs of all copyright registrations. These catalogs shall be divided into parts in accordance with the various classes of works, and the Register has discretion to determine, on the basis of practicability and usefulness, the form and frequency of publication of each particular part.

(*b*) OTHER PUBLICATIONS.

The Register shall furnish, free of charge upon request, application forms for copyright registration and general informational material in connection with the functions of the Copyright Office. The Register also has the authority to publish compilations of information, bibliographies, and other material he or she considers to be of value to the public.

(*c*) DISTRIBUTION OF PUBLICATIONS.

All publications of the Copyright Office shall be furnished to depository libraries as specified under section 1905 of title 44, and, aside from those furnished free of charge, shall be offered for sale to the public at prices based on the cost of reproduction and distribution.

E–72   **708. Copyright Office fees**

(*a*) The following fees shall be paid to the Register of Copyrights:
  (1) on filing each application for registration of a copyright claim for a supplementary registration under section 408, including the issuance of a certificate of registration if registration is made, $10;
  (2) on filing each application for registration of a claim to renewal of a subsisting copyright in its first term under section 304(*a*), including the issuance of a certificate or registration if registration is made, $6;
  (3) for the issuance of a receipt for a deposit under section 407, $2;
  (4) for the recordation, as provided by section 205, of a transfer of copyright ownership or other document of six pages or less, covering no more than one title, $10; for each page over six and each title over one, 50 cents additional;
  (5) for the filing, under section 115(*b*), of a notice of intention to make phonorecords, $6;
  (6) for the recordation, under section 302(*c*), of a statement revealing the identity of an author of an anonymous or pseudonymous work, or for the recordation, under section 302(*d*), of a statement relating to the death of an author, $10 for a document of six pages or less, covering no more than one title; for each page over six and for each title over one, $1 additional;
  (7) for the issuance, under section 601, of an import statement $3;
  (8) for the issuance, under section 706, of an additional certificate of registration, $4;
  (9) for the issuance of any other certification, $4; the Register of Copyrights has discretion, on the basis of their cost, to fix the fees for preparing copies of Copyright Office records, whether they are to be certified or not;
  (10) for the making and reporting of a search as provided by section 705, and for any related services, $10 for each hour or fraction of an hour consumed;
  (11) for any other special services requiring a substantial amount of time or expense, such fees as the Register of Copyrights may fix on the basis of the cost of providing the service.[32]

---

[32] S.708(*a*) as amended by the Act of October 25, 1982, Pub. L. 97–366, 96 Stat. 1759, effective November 24, 1982. (The amendments prospectively modified the method of charging fees.)

(*b*) The fees prescribed by or under this section are applicable to the United States Government and any of its agencies, employees, or officers, but the Register of Copyrights has discretion to waive the requirement of this subsection in occasional or isolated cases involving relatively small amounts.

(*c*) All fees received under this section shall be deposited by the Register of Copyrights in the Treasury of the United States and shall be credited to the appropriation for necessary expenses of the Copyright Office. The Register may, in accordance with regulations that he or she shall prescribe, refund any sum paid by mistake or in excess of the fee required by this section.[33]

709. Delay in delivery caused by disruption of postal or other services   E–73

In any case in which the Register of Copyrights determines, on the basis of such evidence as the Register may by regulation require, that a deposit, application, fee, or any other material to be delivered to the Copyright Office by a particular date, would have been received in the Copyright Office in due time except for a general disruption or suspension of postal or other transportation or communications services, the actual receipt of such material in the Copyright Office within one month after the date on which the Register determines that the disruption or suspension of such services has terminated, shall be considered timely.

710. Reproduction for use of the blind and physically handicapped: E–74
Voluntary licensing forms and procedures

The Register of Copyrights shall, after consultation with the Chief of the Division for the Blind and Physically Handicapped and other appropriate officials of the Library of Congress, established by regulation standardized forms and procedures by which, at the time applications covering certain specified categories of nondramatic literary works are submitted for registration under section 408 of this title, the copyright owner may voluntarily grant to the Library of Congress a license to reproduce the copyrighted work by means of Braille or similar tactile symbols, or by fixation of a reading of the work in a phonorecord, or both, and to distribute the resulting copies of phonorecords solely for the use of the blind and physically handicapped and under limited conditions to be specified in the standardized forms.

CHAPTER 8   E–75

COPYRIGHT ROYALTY TRIBUNAL

---

[33] S.708(*c*) as amended by the Act of August 5, 1977, Pub. L. No. 95–94, (91 Stat. 682) and as further amended by the Act of October 25, 1982, Pub. L. 97–366. (Before the 1982 amendment, the registrar could "in any case involving a refusal to register a claim under section 410(*b*) . . . deduct all or any part of the prescribed registration fee to cover the reasonable administrative costs of processing the claim.")

801. Copyright Royalty Tribunal: Establishment and purpose[34]

(*a*) There is hereby created an independent Copyright Royalty Tribunal in the legislative branch.

(*b*) Subject to the provisions of this chapter, the purposes of the Tribunal shall be—

(1) to make determinations concerning the adjustment of reasonable copyright royalty rates as provided in sections 115 and 116, and to make determinations as to reasonable terms and rates of royalty payments as provided in section 118. The rates applicable under sections 115 and 116 shall be calculated to achieve the following objectives:

(A) To maximize the availability of creative works to the public;

(B) To afford the copyright owner a fair return for his creative work and the copyright user a fair income under existing economic conditions;

(C) To reflect the relative roles of the copyright owner and the copyright user in the product made available to the public with respect to relative creative contribution, technological contribution, capital investment, cost, risk, and contribution to the opening of new markets for creative expression and media for their communication;

(D) To minimize any disruptive impact on the structure of the industries involved and on generally prevailing industry practices.

(2) to make determinations concerning the adjustment of the copyright royalty rates in section 111 solsely in accordance with the following provisions:

(A) The rates established by section 111(*d*)(1)(B) may be adjusted to reflect (i) national monetary inflation or deflation or (ii) changes in the average rates charged cable subscribers for the basic service of providing secondary transmissions to maintain the real constant dollar level of the royalty fee per subscriber which existed as of the date of enactment of this Act; *Provided*, That if the average rates charged cable system subscribers for the basic service of providing secondary transmissions are changed so that the average rates exceed national monetary inflation, no change in the rates established by section 111(*d*)(1)(B) shall be permitted: And provided further, That no increase in royalty fee shall be permitted based on any reduction in the average number of distant signal equivalents per subscriber. The Commission may consider all factors relating to the maintenance of such level of payments including, as an extenuating factor, whether the cable industry has been restrained by subscriber rate regulating authorities from increasing the rates for the basic service of providing secondary transmissions.

(B) In the event that the rules and regulations of the Federal Communications Commission are amended at any time after April 15, 1976, to permit the carriage by cable systems of additional television broadcast signals beyond the local service area of the primary transmitters of such signals, the royalty rates established by section 111(*d*)(1)(B) may be adjusted to insure that the rates for the additional distant signal equivalents resulting from such carriage are reasonable in the light of the changes effected by the amendment to such rules and regulations. In determining the reasonableness of rates proposed following an amendment of Federal Communications Commission rules and regulations, the Copyright Royalty Tribunal shall consider, among other factors, the economic impact on copyright owners and users: *Provided*, That no adjustment in royalty rates shall be made under this subclause with

---

[34] As amended Aug. 27, 1986, Pub. L. 99–397, § 2(*c*), (*d*), 100 Stat. 848, Oct. 31, 1988, Pub. L. 100–568, § 11, 102 Stat. 2860, Nov. 16, 1988, Pub. L. 100–667, § 202(4), 102 Stat. 3935.

respect to any distant signal equivalent or fraction thereof represented by (i) carriage of any signal permitted under the rules and regulations of the Federal Communications Commission in effect on April 15, 1976, or the carriage of a signal of the same type (that is, independent, network, or noncommercial educational) substituted for such permitted signal, or (ii) a television broadcast signal first carried after April 15, 1976, pursuant to an individual waiver of the rules and regulations of the Federal Communications Commission, as such rules and regulations were in effect on April 15, 1976.

(C) In the event of any change in the rules and regulations of the Federal Communications Commission with respect of syndicated and sports program exclusivity after April 15, 1976, the rates established by section 111(*d*)(1)(B) may be adjusted to assure that such rates are reasonable in light of the changes of such rules and regulations, but any such adjustment shall apply only to the affected television broadcast signals carried on those systems affected by the change.

(D) The gross receipts limitations established by section 111(*d*)(1)(C) and (D) shall be adjusted to reflect national monetary inflation or deflation or changes in the average rates charged cable system subscribers for the basic service of providing secondary transmissions to maintain the real constant dollar value of the exemption provided by such section; and the royalty rate specified therein shall not be subject to adjustment; and

(3) to distribute royalty fees deposited with the Register of Copyrights under sections 111, 116 and 119(*b*) and to determine, in cases where controversy exists, the distribution of such fees. In determining whether a return to a copyright owner under section 116 is fair, appropriate weight shall be given to—

(i) the rates previously determined by the Tribunal to provide a fair return to the copyright owner, and

(ii) the rates contained in any license negotiated pursuant to section 116A of this title.

(*c*) As soon as possible after the date of enactment of this Act, and no later than six months following such date, the President shall publish a notice announcing the initial appointments provided in section 802, and shall designate an order of seniority among the initially-appointed commissioners for purposes of section 802(*b*).

802. Membership of the Tribunal   E–77

(*a*) The Tribunal shall be composed of five commissioners appointed by the President with the advice and consent of the Senate for a term of seven years each; of the first five members appointed, three shall be designated to serve for seven years from the date of the notice specified in section 801(*c*), and two shall be designated to serve for five years from such date, respectively. Commissioners shall be compensated at the highest rate now or hereafter prescribe [sic] for grade 18 of the General Schedule pay rates (5 U.S.C. 5332).

(*b*) Upon convening the commissioners shall elect a chairman from among the commissioners appointed for a full seven-year term. Such chairman shall serve for a term of one year. Thereafter, the most senior commissioner who has not previously served as chairman shall serve as chairman for a period of one year, except that, if all commissioners have served a full term as chairman, the most senior commissioner who has served the least number of terms as chairman shall be designated as chairman.

(*c*) Any vacancy in the Tribunal shall not affect its powers and shall be filled, for the unexpired term of the appointment, in the same manner as the original appointment was made.

803. Procedures of the Tribunal

(a) The Tribunal shall adopt regulations, not inconsistent with law, governing its procedure and methods of operation. Except as otherwise provided in this chapter, the Tribunal shall be subject to the provisions of the Administrative Procedure Act of June 11, 1946, as amended (c. 324, 60 Stat. 237, Title 5, United States Code, Chapter 5, Subchapter II and Chapter 7).

(b) Every final determination of the Tribunal shall be published in the Federal Register. It shall state in detail the criteria that the Tribunal determined to be applicable to the particular proceeding, the various facts that it found relevant to its determination in that proceeding, and the specific reasons for its determination.

804. Institution and conclusion of proceedings[35]

(a) With respect to proceedings under section 801(b)(1) concerning the adjustment of royalty rates as provided in sections 115 and 116, and with respect to proceedings under section 801(b)(2)(A) and (D)—

(1) on January 1, 1980, the Chairman of the Tribunal shall cause to be published in the Federal Register notice of commencement of proceedings under this chapter; and

(2) during the calendar years specified in the following schedule, any owner or user of a copyrighted work whose royalty rates are specified by this title, or by a rate established by the Tribunal, may file a petition with the Tribunal declaring that the petitioner requests an adjustment of the rate. The Tribunal shall make a determination as to whether the applicant has a significant interest in the royalty rate in which an adjustment is requested. If the Tribunal determines that the petitioner has a significant interest, the Chairman shall cause notice of this determination, with the reasons therefor, to be published in the Federal Register, together with notice of commencement of proceedings under this chapter.

(A) In proceedings under section 801(b)(2)(A) and (D), such petition may be filed during 1985 and in each subsequent fifth calendar year.

(B) In proceedings under section 801(b)(1) concerning the adjustment of royalty rates as provided in section 115, such petition may be filed in 1987 and in each subsequent tenth calendar year.

(C)(i) In proceedings under section 801(b)(1) concerning the adjustment of royalty rates as provided in section 115, such petition may be filed in 1990 and in each subsequent tenth calendar year, and at any time within 1 year after negotiated licenses authorized by section 116A are terminated or expire and are not replaced by subsequent agreements.

(ii) If negotiated licenses authorized by section 116A come into force so as to supersede previous determinations of the Tribunal, as provided in section 116A(d), but thereafter are terminated or expire and are not replaced by subsequent agreements, the Tribunal shall, upon petition of any party to such terminated or expired negotiated license agreement, promptly establish and interim royalty rate or rates for the public performance by means of coin-operated phonorecord player of nondramatic musical works embodied in phonorecords which had been subject to the terminated or expired negotiated license agreement. Such interim

---

[35] Amended Oct. 31, 1988, Pub. L. 100–568, § 11, 102 Stat, 2860, Nov. 16, 1988, Pub. L. 100–667, § 202(5), 102 Stat. 3935.

royalty rate or rates shall be the same as the last such rate or rates and shall remain in force until the conclusion of proceedings to adjust the royalty rates applicable to such works, or until superseded by a new negotiated license agreement, as provided in section 116A(*d*).

(*b*) With respect to proceedings under subclause (B) or (C) of section 801(*b*)(2), following an event described in either of those subsections, any owner or user of a copyrighted work whose royalty rates are specified by section 111, or by a rate established by the Tribunal, may, within twelve months, file a petition with the Tribunal declaring that the petitioner requests an adjustment of the rate. In this event the Tribunal shall proceed as in subsection (*a*)(2), above. Any change in royalty rates made by the Tribunal pursuant to this subsection may be reconsidered in 1980, 1985, and each fifth calendar year thereafter, in accordance with the provisions in section 801(*b*)(2)(B) or (C), as the case may be.

(*c*) With respect to proceedings under section 801(*b*)(1), concerning the determination of reasonable terms and rates of royalty payments as provided in section 118, the Tribunal shall proceed when and as provided by that section.

(*d*) With respect to proceedings under section 801(*b*)(3), concerning the distribution of royalty fees in certain circumstances under sections 111 or 116, the Chairman of the Tribunal shall, upon determination by the Tribunal that a controversy exists concerning such distribution, cause to be published in the Federal Register notice of commencement of proceedings under this chapter.

(*e*) All proceedings under this chapter shall be initiated without delay following publication of the notice specified in this section, and the Tribunal shall render its final decision in any such proceeding within one year from the date of such publication.

805. Staff of the Tribunal   E–80

(*a*) The Tribunal is authorized to appoint and fix the compensation of such employees as may be necessary to carry out the provisions of this chapter, and to prescribe their functions and duties.

(*b*) The Tribunal may procure temporary and intermittent services to the same extent as is authorized by section 3109 of title 5.

806. Administrative support of the Tribunal   E–81

(*a*) The Library of Congress shall provide the Tribunal with necessary administrative services, including those related to budgeting, accounting, financial reporting, travel, personnel, and procurement. The Tribunal shall pay the Library for such services, either in advance or by reimbursement from the funds of the Tribunal, at amounts to be agreed upon between the Librarian and the Tribunal.

(*b*) The Library of Congress is authorized to disburse funds for the Tribunal, under regulations prescribed jointly by the Librarian of Congress and the Tribunal and approved by the Comptroller General. Such regulations shall establish requirements and procedures under which every voucher certified for payment by the Library of Congress under this chapter shall be supported with a certification by a duly authorized officer or employee of the Tribunal, and shall prescribe the responsibilities and accountability of said officers and employees of the Tribunal with respect to such certifications.

807. Deduction of costs of proceedings   E–82

Before any funds are distributed pursuant to a final decision in a proceeding involving distribution of royalty fees, the Tribunal shall assess the reasonable costs of such proceeding.

E–83   808. Reports

In addition to its publication of the reports of all final determinations as provided in section 803(*b*), the Tribunal shall make an annual report to the President and the Congress concerning the Tribunal's work during the preceding fiscal year, including a detailed fiscal statement of account.

E–84   809. Effective date of final determinations

Any final determination by the Tribunal under this chapter shall become effective thirty days following publication in the Federal Register as provided in section 803(*b*), unless prior to that time an appeal has been filed pursuant to section 810, to vacate, modify, or correct such determination, and notice of such appeal has been served on all parties who appear before the Tribunal in the proceeding in question. Where the proceeding involves the distribution of royalty fees under sections 111 or 116, the Tribunal shall, upon the expiration of such thirty-day period, distribute any royalty fees not subject to an appeal filed pursuant to section 810.

E–85   810. Judicial review

Any final decision of the Tribunal in a proceeding under section 801(*b*) may be appealed to the United States Court of Appeals, within thirty days after its publication in the Federal Register by an aggrieved party. The judicial review of the decision shall be had, in accordance with chapter 7 of title 5, on the basis of the record before the Tribunal. No court shall have jurisdiction to review a final decision of the Tribunal except as provided in this section.

E–86

CHAPTER 9

PROTECTION OF SEMICONDUCTOR CHIP PRODUCTS[36]

Sec.

901. Definitions.
902. Subject matter of protection.
903. Ownership and transfer.
904. Duration of protection.
905. Exclusion rights in mask works.
906. Limitation on exclusive rights: reverse engineering; first sale.
907. Limitation on exclusive rights: innocent infringement.
908. Registration of claims of protection.
909. Mask work notice.
910. Enforcement of exclusive rights.
911. Civil actions.
912. Relation to other laws.
913. Transitional provisions.
914. International transitional provisions.

E–87   901. Definitions

(*a*) AS USED IN THIS CHAPTER—

(1) a "semiconductor chip product" is the final or intermediate form of any product—

---

[36] Chap. added by Pub. L. 98–620, Title III, Sec. 302, Nov. 8, 1984, 98 Stat. 3348.

(A) having two or more layers of metallic, insulating, or semiconductor material, deposited or otherwise placed on, or etched away or otherwise removed from, a piece of semiconductor material in accordance with a predetermined pattern; and

(B) intended to perform electronic circuitry functions;

(2) a "mask work" is a series of related images, however, fixed or encoded—

(A) having or representing the predetermined, three-dimensional pattern of metallic, insulating, or semiconductor material present or removed from the layers of a semiconductor chip product; and

(B) in which series the relation of the images to one another is that each image has the pattern of the surface of one form of the semiconductor chip product;

(3) a mask work is "fixed" in a semiconductor chip product when its embodiment in the product is sufficiently permanent or stable to permit the mask work to be perceived or reproduced from the product for a period of more than transitory duration;

(4) "distribute" means to sell, or to lease, bail, or otherwise transfer, or to offer to sell, lease, bail, or otherwise transfer.

(5) to "commercially exploit" a mask work is to distribute to the public for commercial purposes a semiconductor chip product embodying the mask work; except that such term includes an offer to sell or transfer a semiconductor chip product only when the offer is in writing and occurs after the mask work is fixed in the semiconductor chip product;

(6) to "owner" of a mask work is the person who created the mask work, the legal representative of that person if that person is deceased or under a legal incapacity, or a party to whom all the rights under this chapter of such person or representative are transferred in accordance with section 903(*b*); except that, in the case of a work made within the scope of a person's employment, the owner is the employer for whom the person created the mask work or a party to whom all the rights under this chapter of the employer are transferred in accordance with section 903(*b*);

(7) an "innocent purchaser" is a person who purchases a semiconductor chip product in good faith and without having notice of protection with respect to the semiconductor chip product;

(8) having "notice of protection" means having actual knowledge that, or reasonable grounds to believe that, a mask work is protected under this chapter; and

(9) an "infringing semiconductor chip product" is a semiconductor chip product which is made, imported, or distributed in violation of the exclusive rights of the owner of a mask work under this chapter.

(*b*) For purposes of this chapter, the distribution or importation of a product incorporating a semiconductor chip product as a part thereof is a distribution or importation of that semiconductor chip product.

902. Subject matter of protection[37]   **E–88**

(*a*)(1) Subject to the provisions of subsection (*b*), a mask work fixed in a semiconductor chip product, by or under the authority of the owner of the mask work, is eligible for protection under this chapter if—

(A) on the date on which the mask work is registered under section 908, or is first commercially exploited anywhere in the world, whichever occurs first, the owner of the mask work is (i) a national or domiciliary of the

---

[37] As amended Nov. 9, 1987, Pub. L. 100–159, §§ 3, 101 Stat. 900.

United States, (ii) a national, domiciliary, or sovereign authority of a foreign nation that is a party to a treaty affording protection to mask works to which the United States is also a party, or (iii) a stateless person, wherever that person may be domiciled;

(B) the mask work is first commercially exploited in the United States; or

(C) the mask work comes within the scope of a Presidential proclamation issued under paragraph (2).

(2) Whenever the President finds that a foreign nation extends, to mask works of owners who are nationals or domiciliaries of the United States protection (A) on substantially the same basis as that on which the foreign nation extends protection to mask works of its own nationals and domiciliaries and mask works first commercially exploited in that nation, or (B) on substantially the same basis as provided in this chapter, the President may by proclamation extend protection under this chapter to mask works (i) of owners who are, on the date on which the mask works are registered under section 908, or the date on which the mask works are first commercially exploited anywhere in the world, whichever occurs first, nationals, domiciliaries, or sovereign authorities of that nation, or (ii) which are first commercially exploited in that nation. The President may revise, suspend, or revoke any such proclamation or impose any conditions or limitations on protection extended under any such proclamation.

(*b*) Protection under this chapter shall not be available for a mask work that—

(1) is not original; or

(2) consists of designs that are staple, commonplace, or familiar in the semiconductor industry, or variations of such designs, combined in a way that, considered as a whole, is not original.

(*c*) In no case does protection under this chapter for a mask work extend to any idea, procedure, process, system, method of operation, concept, principle, or discovery, regardless of the form in which it is described, explained, illustrated, or embodies in such work.

E–89   903. Ownership, transfer, licensing, and recordation

(*a*) The exclusive rights in a mask work subject to protection under this chapter belong the owner of the mask work.

(*b*) The owner of the exclusive rights in a mask work may transfer all of those rights, or license all or less than all of those rights, by any written instrument signed by such owner or a duly authorized agent of the owner. Such rights may be transferred or licensed by operation of law, may be bequeathed by will, and may pass as personal property by the applicable laws of intestate succession.

(*c*)(1) Any document pertaining to a mask work may be recorded in the Copyright Office if the document filed for recordation bears the actual signature of the person who executed it, or if it is accompanied by a sworn or official certification that it is a true copy of the original, signed document. The Register of Copyrights shall, upon receipt of the document and the fee specified pursuant to section 908(*d*), record the document and return it with a certificate of recordation. The recordation of any transfer or license under this paragraph gives all persons constructive notice of the facts stated in the recorded document concerning the transfer or license.

(2) In any case in which conflicting transfers of the exclusive rights in a mask work are made, the transfer first executed shall be void as against a subsequent transfer which is made for a valuable consideration and without notice of the first transfer, unless the first transfer is recorded in accordance with paragraph (1) within three months after the date on which it is

executed, but in no case later than the day before the date of such subsequent transfer.

(*d*) Mask works prepared by an officer or employee of the United States Government as part of that person's official duties are not protected under this chapter, but the United States Government is not precluded from receiving and holding exclusive rights in mask works transferred to the Government under subsection (*b*).

904. Duration of protection E–90

(*a*) The protection provided for a mask work under this chapter shall commence on the date on which the work is registered under section 908, or the date on which the mask work is first commercially exploited anywhere in the world, whichever comes first.

(*b*) Subject to subsection (*c*) and the provisions of this chapter, the protection provided under this chapter to mask work shall end ten years after the date on which such protection commences under subsection (*a*).

(C) All terms of protection provided in this section shall run to the end of the calendar year in which they would otherwise expire.

905. Exclusive rights in mask works E–91

The owner of a mask work provided protection under this chapter has the exclusive rights to do and to authorize any of the following:
(1) to reproduce the mask work by optical, electronic, or any other means;
(2) to import or distribute a semiconductor chip product in which the mask work is embodied; and
(3) to induce or knowingly to cause another person to do any of the acts described in paragraphs (1) and (2).

906. Limitation on exclusive rights: reverse engineering; first sale E–92

(*a*) Notwithstanding the provisions of section 905, it is not an infringement of the exclusive rights of the owner of a mask work for—
(1) a person to reproduce the mask work solely for the purpose of teaching, analyzing, or evaluating the concepts or techniques embodied in the mask work or the circuitry, logic flow, or organization of components used in the mask work; or
(2) a person who performs the analysis or evaluation described in paragraph (1) to incorporate the results of such conduct in an original mask work which is made to be distributed.

(*b*) Notwithstanding the provisions of section 905(2), the owner of a particular semiconductor chip product made by the owner of the mask work, or by any person authorized by the owner of the mask work, may import, distribute, or otherwise dispose of or use, but not reproduce, that particular semiconductor chip product without the authority of the owner of the mask work.

907. Limitation on exclusive rights: innocent infringement E–93

(*a*) Notwithstanding any other provision of this chapter, an innocent purchaser or an infringing semiconductor chip product—
(1) shall incur no liability under this chapter with respect to the importation or distribution of units of the infringing semiconductor chip product that occurs before the innocent purchaser has notice of protection with respect to the mask work embodied in the semiconductor chip product; and
(2) shall be liable only for a reasonable royalty on each unit of the infringing

semiconductor chip product that the innocent purchaser imports or distributes after having notice of protection with respect to the mask work embodied in the semiconductor chip product.

(*b*) The amount of the royalty deferred to in subsection (*a*)(2) shall be determined by the court in a civil action for infringement unless the parties resolve the issue by voluntary negotiation, mediation, or binding arbitration.

(*c*) The immunity of an innocent purchaser from liability referred to in subsection (*a*)(1) and the limitation of remedies with respect to an innocent purchaser referred to in subsection (*a*)(2) shall extend to any person who directly or indirectly purchases an infringing semiconductor chip product from an innocent purchaser.

(*d*) The provisions of subsections (*a*), (*b*), and (*c*) apply only with respect to those units of an infringing semiconductor chip product that an innocent purchaser purchased before having notice of protection with respect to the mask work embodied in the semiconductor chip product.

E–94   908. Registration of claims of protection

(*a*) The owner of a mask work may apply to the Register of Copyrights for registration of a claim of protection in a mask work. Protection of a mask work under this chapter shall terminate if application for registration of a claim of protection in the mask work is not made as provided in this chapter within two years after the date on which the mask work is first commercially exploited anywhere in the world.

(*b*) The Register of Copyrights shall be responsible for all administrative functions and duties under this chapter. Except for section 708, the provisions of chapter 7 of this title relating to the general responsibilities, organization, regulatory authority, actions, records, and publications of the Copyright Office shall apply to this chapter, except that the Register of Copyrights may make such changes as may be necessary in applying those provisions to this chapter.

(*c*) The application for registration of a mask work shall be made on a form prescribed by the Register of Copyrights. Such form may require any information regarded by the Register as bearing upon the preparation or identification of the mask work, the existence or duration of protection of the mask work under this chapter, or ownership of the mask work. The application shall be accompanied by the fee set pursuant to subsection (*d*) and the identifying material specified pursuant to such subsection.

(*d*) The Register of Copyrights shall by regulation set reasonable fees for the filing of applications to register claims of protection in mask works under this chapter, and for other services relating to the administration of this chapter or the rights under this chapter, taking into consideration the cost of providing those services, the benefits of a public record, and statutory fee schedules under this title. The Register shall also specify the identifying material to be deposited in connection with the claim for registration.

(*e*) If the Register of Copyrights, after examining an application for registration, determines, in accordance with the provisions of this chapter, that the application relates to a mask work which is entitled to protection under this chapter, then the Register shall register the claim of protection and issue to the applicant a certificate of registration of the claim of protection under the seal of the Copyright Office, the effective date of registration of a claim of protection shall be the date on which an application, deposit of identifying material, and fee, which are determined by the Register of Copyrights or by a court of competent jurisdiction to be acceptable for registration of the claim, have all been received in the Copyright Office.

(*f*) In any action for infringement under this chapter, the certificate of registration of a mask work shall constitute prima facie evidence (1) of the facts stated in the certificate, and (2) that the applicant issued the certificate has met, the requirements of this chapter, and the regulations issued under this chapter, with respect to the registration of claims.

(*g*) Any applicant for registration under this section who is dissatisfied with the refusal of the Register of Copyrights to issue a certificate of registration under this section may seek judicial review of that refusal by bringing an action for such review in an appropriate United States district court not later than sixty days after the refusal. The provisions of chapter 7 of title 5 shall apply to such judicial review. The failure of the Register of Copyrights to issue a certificate of registration within four months after an application for registration is filed shall be deemed to be a refusal to issue a certificate of registration for purposes of this subsection and section 910(*b*)(2), except that, upon a showing of good cause, the district court may shorten such four-month period.

909. Mask work notice E–95

(*a*) The owner of a mask work provided protection under this chapter may affix notice to the mask work, and to masks and semiconductor chip products embodying the mask work, in such manner and location as to give reasonable notice of such protection. The Register of Copyrights shall prescribe by regulation, as examples, specific methods of affixation and positions of notice for purposes of this section, but these specifications shall not be considered exhaustive. The affixation of such notice is not a condition of protection under this chapter, but shall constitute prima facie evidence of notice of protection.

(*b*) The notice referred to in subsection (*a*) shall consist of—

(1) the words "mask work," the symbol *M*, or the symbol Ⓜ (the letter M in a circle); and

(2) the name of the owner or owners of the mask work or an abbreviation by which the name is recognized or is generally known.

910. Enforcement of exclusive rights E–96

(*a*) Except as otherwise provided in this chapter, any person who violates any of the exclusive rights of the owner of a mask work under this chapter, by conduct in or affecting commerce, shall be liable as an infringer of such rights.

(*b*) (1) The owner of a mask work protected under this chapter, or the exclusive licensee of all rights under this chapter with respect to the mask work, shall, after a certificate of registration of a claim of protection in that mask work has been issued under section 908, be entitled to institute a civil action for any infringement with respect to the mask work which is committed after the commencement of protection of the mask work under section 904(*a*).

(2) In any case in which an application for registration of a claim of protection in a mask work and the required deposit of identifying material and fee have been received in the Copyright Office in proper form and registration of the mask work has been refused, the applicant is entitled to institute a civil action for infringement under this chapter with respect to the mask work if notice of the action, together with a copy of the complaint, is served on the Register of Copyrights, in accordance with the Federal Rules of Civil Procedure. The Register may, at his or her option, become a party to the action with respect to the issue of whether the claim of protection is eligible for registration by entering an appearance within sixty days after such service, but the failure of

the Register to become a party to the action shall not deprive the court of jurisdiction to determine that issue.

(*c*)　(1)　The Secretary of the Treasury and the United States Postal Service shall separately or jointly issue regulations for the enforcement of the rights set forth in section 905 with respect to importation. These regulations may require; as a condition for the exclusion of articles from the United States, that the person seeking exclusion take any one or more of the following actions:

(A)　Obtain a court order enjoining, or an order of the International Trade Commission under section 337 of the Tariff Act of 1930 excluding, importation of the articles.

(B)　Furnish proof that the mask work involved is protected under this chapter and that the importation of the articles would infringe the rights in the mask work under this chapter.

(C)　Post a surety bond for any injury that may result if the detention or exclusion of the articles proves to be unjustified.

(2)　Articles imported in violation of the rights set forth in section 905 are subject to seizure and forfeiture in the same manner as property imported in violation of the customs laws. Any such forfeited articles shall be destroyed as directed by the Secretary of the Treasury or the court, as the case may be, except that the articles may be returned to the country of export whenever it is shown to the satisfaction of the Secretary of the Treasury that the importer had no reasonable grounds for believing that his or her acts constituted a violation of the law.

　　911. Civil actions

(*a*) Any court having jurisdiction of a civil action arising under this chapter may grant temporary restraining orders, preliminary injunctions, and permanent injunctions on such terms as the court may deem reasonable to prevent or restrain infringement of the exclusive rights in a mask work under this chapter.

(*b*) Upon finding an infringer liable, to a person entitled under section 910(*b*)(1) to institute a civil action, for an infringement of any exclusive right under this chapter, the court shall award such person actual damages suffered by the person as a result of the infringement. The court shall also award such person the infringer's profits that are attributable to the infringement and are not taken into account in computing the award of actual damages. In establishing the infringer's profits, such person is required to present proof only if the infringer is required to prove his or her deductible expenses and the elements of profit attributable to factors other than the mask work.

(*c*) At any time before final judgment is rendered, a person entitled to institute a civil action for infringement may elect, instead of actual damages and profits as provided by subsection (*b*), an award of statutory damages for all infringements involved in the action, with respect to any one mask work for which any two or more infringers are liable jointly and severally, in an amount not more than $250,000 as the court considers just.

(*d*) An action for infringement under this chapter shall be barred unless the action is commenced within three years after the claim accrues.

(*e*)　(1)　At any time while an action for infringement of the exclusive rights in a mask work under this chapter is pending, the court may order the impounding, on such terms as it may deem reasonable, of all semiconductor chip products, and any drawings, tapes, masks, or other products by means of which such products may be reproduced, that are claimed to have been made, imported, or used in violation of those exclusive rights. Insofar as practicable, applications for orders under this paragraph shall be heard and determined in the same manner as an application for a termporary restraining order or preliminary injunction.

(2) As part of a final judgment or decree, the court may order the destruction or other disposition of any infringing semiconductor chips products, and any masks, tapes, or other articles by means of which such products may be reproduced.

(*f*) In any civil action arising under this chapter, the court in its discretion may allow the recovery of full costs, including reasonable attorney's fees, to the prevailing party.

912. Relation to other laws

(*a*) Nothing in this chapter shall affect any right or remedy held by any person under chapters 1 through 8 of this title, or under title 35.

(*b*) Except as provided in section 908(*b*) of this title, references to "this title" or "title 17" in chapters 1 through 8 of this title shall be deemed not to apply to this chapter.

(*c*) The provisions of this chapter shall preempt the laws of any State to the extent those laws provide any rights or remedies with respect to a mask work which are equivalent to those rights or remedies provided by this chapter, except that such preemption shall be effective only with respect to actions filed on or after January 1, 1986.

(*d*) The provisions of sections 1338, 1400(*a*) and 1498(*b*) and (*c*) of title 28 shall apply with respect to exclusive rights in mask works under this chapter.

(*e*) Notwithstanding subsection (*c*), nothing in this chapter shall detract from any rights of a mask work owner, whether under Federal law (exclusive of this chapter) or under the common law or the statutes of a State, heretofore or hereafter declared or enacted, with respect to any mask work first commercially exploited before July 1, 1983.

913. Transitional provisions

(*a*) No application for registration under section 908 may be filed, and no civil action under section 910 or other enforcement proceeding under this chapter may be instituted, until sixty days after the date of the enactment of this chapter.

(*b*) No monetary relief under section 911 may be granted with respect to any conduct that occurred before the date of the enactment of this chapter, except as provided in subsection (*d*).

(*c*) Subject to subsection (*a*), the provisions of this chapter apply to all mask works that are first commercially exploited or are registered under this chapter, or both, on or after the date of the enactment of this chapter.

(*d*) (1) Subject to subsection (*a*), protection is available under this chapter to any mask work that was first commercially exploited on or after July 1, 1983, and before the date of the enactment of this chapter, if a claim of protection in the mask work is registered in the Copyright Office before July 1, 1985, under section 908.

(2) In the case of any mask work described in paragraph (1) that is provided protection under this chapter, infringing semiconductor chip product units manufactured before the date of the enactment of this chapter may, without liability under sections 910 and 911, be imported into or distributed in the United States, or both, until two years after the date of registration of the mask work under section 908, but only if the importer or distributor, as the case may be, first pays or offers to pay the reasonable royalty referred to in section 907(*a*)(2) to the mask work

owner, on all such units imported or distributed, or both, after the date of the enactment of this chapter.

(3) In the event that a person imports or distributes infringing semiconductor chip product units described in paragraph (2) of this subsection without first paying or offering to pay the reasonable royalty specified in such paragraph, or if the person refuses or fails to make such payment, the mask work owner shall be entitled to the relief provided in sections 910 and 911.

E–100   ## 914. International transitional provisions[38]

(*a*) Notwithstanding the conditions set forth in subparagraphs (A) and (C) of section 902(*a*)(1) with respect to the availability of protection under this chapter to nationals, domiciliaries, and sovereign authorities of a foreign nation, the Secretary of Commerce may, upon the petition of any person, or upon the Secretary's own motion, issue an order extending protection under this chapter to such foreign nationals, domiciliaries, and sovereign authorities if the Secretary finds—

(1) that the foreign nation is making good faith efforts and reasonable progress toward—

(A) entering into a treaty described in section 902(*a*)(1)(A); or

(B) enacting legislation that would be in compliance with subparagraphs (A) or (B) of section 902(*a*)(2); and

(2) that the nationals, domiciliaries, and sovereign authorities of the foreign nation, and persons controlled by them, are not engaged in the misappropriation, or unauthorized distribution or commercial exploitation, of mask works; and

(3) that issuing the order would promote the purposes of this chapter and international comity with respect to the protection of mask works.

(*b*) While an order under subsection (*a*) is in effect with respect to a foreign

---

[38] As amended Nov. 9, 1987, Pub. L. 100–159, §§ 2, 4, 101 Stat. 899–900. Section 1 of Public Law 100–159, 101 Stat. 899 (Nov. 9, 1987), is as follows:

(*a*) FINDINGS.—The Congress finds that—

(1) section 914 of title 17, United States Code, which authorizes the Secretary of Commerce to issue orders extending interim protection under chapter 9 of title 17, United States Code, to mask works fixed in semiconductor chip products and originating in foreign countries that are making good faith efforts and reasonable progress toward providing protection, by treaty or legislation, to mask works of United States nationals, has resulted in substantial and positive legislative developments in foreign countries regarding protection of mask works;

(2) the Secretary of Commerce has determined that most of the industrialized countries of the world are eligible for orders affording interim protection under section 914 of title 17, United States Code;

(3) the World Intellectual Property Organization has commenced meetings to draft an international convention regarding the protection of integrated electronic circuits;

(4) these bilateral and multilateral developments are encouraging steps toward improving international protection of mask works in a consistent and harmonious manner; and

(5) it is inherent in section 902 of title 17, United States Code, that the President has the authority to revise, suspend, or revoke, as well as issue, proclamations extending mask work protection to nationals, domiciliaries, and sovereign authorities of other countries if conditions warrant.

(b) PURPOSES.—The purposes of this Act are—

(1) to extend the period within which the Secretary of Commerce may grant interim protective orders under section 914 of title 17, United States Code, to continue this incentive for the bilateral and multilateral protection of mask works; and

(2) to codify the President's existing authority to revoke, suspend, or limit the protection extended to mask works of foreign entities in nations that extend mask work protection to United States nationals.

nation, no application for registration of a claim for protection in a mask work under this chapter may be denied solely because the owner of the mask work is a national, domiciliary, or sovereign authority of that foreign nation, or solely because the mask work was first commercially exploited in that foreign nation.

(*c*) Any order issued by the Secretary of Commerce under subsection (*a*) shall be effective for such period as the Secretary designates in the order, except that no such order may be effective after the date on which the authority of the Secretary of Commerce terminates under subsection (*e*). The effective date of any such order shall also be designated in the order. In the case of an order issued upon the petition of a person, such effective date may be no earlier than the date on which the Secretary receives such petition.

(*d*) (1) Any order issued under this section shall terminate if—
  (A) the Secretary of Commerce finds that any of the conditions set forth in paragraphs (1), (2), and (3) of subsection (*a*) no longer exist; or
  (B) mask works of nationals, domiciliaries, and sovereign authorities of that foreign nation or mask works first commercially exploited in that foreign nation become eligible for protection under subparagraphs (A) or (C) of section 902(*a*)(1).

  (2) Upon the termination or expiration of an order issued under this section, registrations of claims of protection in mask works made pursuant to that order shall remain valid for the period specified in section 904.

(*e*) The authority of the Secretary of Commerce under this section shall commence on the date of the enactment of this chapter, and shall terminate on July 1, 1991.

(*f*) (1) The Secretary of Commerce shall promptly notify the Register of Copyrights and the Committees on the Judiciary of the Senate and the House of Representatives of the issuance or termination of any order under this section, together with a statement of the reasons for such action. The Secretary shall also publish such notification and statement of reasons in the Federal Register.

  (2) Two years after the date of the enactment of this chapter, the Secretary of Commerce, in consultation with the Register of Copyrights, shall transmit to the Committees on the Judiciary of the Senate and the House of Representatives a report on the actions taken under this section and on the current status of international recognition of mask work protection. The report shall include such recommendations for modifications of the protection accorded under this chapter to mask works owned by nationals, domiciliaries, or sovereign authorities of foreign nations as the Secretary, in consultation with the Register of Copyrights, considers would promote the purposes of this chapter and international comity with respect to mask work protection. Not later than July 1, 1990, the Secetary of Commerce, in consultation with the Register of Copyrights, shall transmit to the Committees on the Judiciary of the Senate and the House of Representatives a report updating the matters contained in the report transmitted under the preceding sentence.

TRANSITIONAL AND SUPPLEMENTARY PROVISIONS **E–101**

SEC. 102. This Act becomes effective on January 1, 1978, except as otherwise **E–102** expressly provided by this Act, including provisions of the first section of this Act. The provisions of sections 118.304(*b*), and chapter 8 of title 17, as amended by the first section of this Act, take effect upon enactment of this Act.

E–103   Sec. 103. This Act does not provide copyright protection for any work that goes into the public domain before January 1, 1978. The exclusive rights, as provided by section 106 of title 17 as amended by the first section of this Act, to reproduce a work in phonorecords and to distribute phonorecords of the work, does not extend to any nondramatic musical work copyrighted before July 1, 1909.

E–104   Sec. 104. All proclamations issued by the President under section 1(*e*) or 9(*b*) of title 17 as it existed on December 31, 1977, or under previous copyright statutes of the United States, shall continue in force until terminated, suspended, or revised by the President.

E–105   Sec. 105. (*a*)(1) Section 505 of title 44 is amended to read as follows:

"505. Sale of duplicate plates

"The Public Printer shall sell, under regulations of the Joint Committee on Printing to persons who may apply, additional or duplicate stereotype or electrotype plates from which a Government publication is printed, at a price not to exceed the cost of composition, the metal, and making to the Government, plus 10 per centum, and the full amount of the price shall be paid when the order is filed.".

(2)   The item relating to section 505 in the sectional analysis at the beginning of chapter 5 of title 44, is amended to read as follows: "505. Sale of duplicate plates.".

(*b*) Section 2113 of title 44 is amended to read as follows:

"2113. Limitation on liability

" 'When letters and other intellectual productions (exclusive of patented material, published works under copyright protection, and unpublished works for which copyright registration has been made) come into the custody or possession of the Administrator of General Services, the United States or its agents are not liable for infringement of copyright or analogous rights arising out of use of the materials for display, inspection, research, reproduction, or other purposes.".

(*c*) In section 1498(*b*) of title 28, the phrase "section 101(*b*) of title 17" is amended to read "section 504(*c*) of title 17." '.

(*d*) Section 543(*a*)(4) of the Internal Revenue Code of 1954, as amended, is amended by striking out "(other than by reason of section 2 or 6 thereof)."

(*e*) Section 3202(*a*) of title 39 is amended by striking out clause (5). Section 3206 of title 39 is amended by deleting the words "subsections (*b*) and (*c*)" and inserting "subsection (*b*)" in subsection (*a*), and by deleting subsection (*c*). Section 3206(*d*) is renumbered (*c*).

(*f*) Subsection (*a*) of section 290(*e*) of title 15 is amended by deleting the phrase "section 8" and inserting in lieu thereof the phrase "section 105."

(*g*) Section 131 of title 2 is amended by deleting the phrase "deposit to secure copyright," and inserting in lieu thereof the phrase "acquisition of material under the copyright law."

E–106   Sec. 106. In any case where, before January 1, 1978, a person has lawfully made parts of instruments serving to reproduce mechanically a copyrighted work under the compulsory license provisions of section 1(*e*) of title 17 as it existed on

December 31, 1977, such person may continue to make and distribute such parts embodying the same mechanical reproduction without obtaining a new compulsory license under the terms of section 115 of title 17 as amended by the first section of this Act. However, such parts made on or after January 1, 1978, constitute phonorecords and are otherwise subject to the provisions of said section 115.

SEC. 107. In the case of any work in which an ad interim copyright is subsisting or is capable of being secured on December 31, 1977, under section 22 of title 17 as it existed on that date, copyright protection is hereby extended to endure for the term or terms provided by section 304 of title 17 as amended by the first section of this Act. **E–107**

SEC. 108. The notice provisions of sections 401 through 403 of title 17 as amended by the first section of this Act apply to all copies or phonorecords publicly distributed on or after January 1, 1978. However, in the case of a work published before January 1, 1978, compliance with the notice provisions of title 17 either as it existed on December 31, 1977, or as amended by the first section of this Act, is adequate with respect to copies publicly distributed after December 31, 1977. **E–108**

SEC. 109. The registration of claims to copyright for which the required deposit, application, and fee were received in the Copyright Office before January 1, 1978, and the recordation of assignments of copyright or other instruments received in the Copyright Office before January 1, 1978, shall be made in accordance with title 17 as it existed on December 31, 1977. **E–109**

SEC. 110. The demand and penalty provisions of section 14 of title 17 as it existed on December 31, 1977, apply to any work in which copyright has been secured by publication with notice of copyright on or before that date, but any deposit and registration made after that date in response to a demand under that section shall be made in accordance with the provisions of title 17 as amended by the first section of this Act. **E–110**

SEC. 111. Section 2318 of title 18 of the United States Code is amended to read as follows: **E–111**

"2318. Transportation, sale or receipt of phonograph records bearing forged or counterfeit labels

"(a) Whoever knowingly and with fraudulent intent transports, causes to be transported, receives, sells, or offers for sale in interstate or foreign commerce any phonograph record, disk, wire, tape, film, or other article on which sounds are recorded, to which or upon which is stamped, pasted, or affixed any forged or counterfeited label, knowing the label to have been falsely made, forged, or counterfeited shall be fined not more than $10,000 or imprisoned for not more than one year, or both, for the first such offense and shall be fined not more than $25,000 or imprisoned for not more than two years, or both, for any subsequent offense.

"(b) When any person is convicted of any violation of subsection (a), the court in its judgment of conviction shall, in addition to the penalty therein prescribed, order the forfeiture and destruction or other disposition of all counterfeit labels and all articles to which counterfeit labels have been affixed or which were intended to have had such labels affixed.".

"(c) Except to the extent they are inconsistent with the provisions of this title, all provisions of section 509, title 17, United States Code, are applicable to violations of subsection (a).".

E–112 SEC. 112. All causes of action that arose under title 17 before January 1, 1978, shall be governed by title 17 as it existed when the cause of action arose.

E–113 SEC. 113. (*a*) The Librarian of Congress (hereinafter referred to as the "Librarian") shall establish and maintain in the Library of Congress a library to be known as the American Television and Radio Archives (hereinafter referred to as the "Archives"). The purpose of the Archives shall be to preserve a permanent record of the television and radio programs which are the heritage of the people of the United States and to provide access to such programs to historians and scholars without encouraging or causing copyright infringement.

    (1) The Librarian, after consultation with interested organizations and individuals, shall determine and place in the Archives such copies and phonorecords of television and radio programs transmitted to the public in the United States and in other countries which are of present or potential public or cultural interest, historical significance, cognitive value, or otherwise worthy of preservation, including copies and phonorecords of published and unpublished transmission programs—

      (A) acquired in accordance with sections 407 and 408 of title 17 as amended by the first section of this Act, and

      (B) transferred from the existing collections of the Library of Congress; and

      (C) given to or exchanged with the Archives by other libraries, archives, organizations, and individuals; and

      (D) purchased from the owner thereof.

    (2) The Librarian shall maintain and publish appropriate catalogs and indexes of the collections of the Archives, and shall make such collections available for study and research under the conditions prescribed under this section.

(*b*) Notwithstanding the provisions of section 106 of title 17 as amended by the first section of this Act, the Librarian is authorized with respect to a transmission program which consists of a regularly scheduled newscast or on-the-spot coverage of news events and, under standards and conditions that the Librarian shall prescribe by regulation—

    (1) to reproduce a fixation of such a program, in the same or another tangible form, for the purposes of preservation or security or for distribution under the conditions of clause (3) of this subsection; and

    (2) to compile, without abridgment or any other editing, portions of such fixations, according to subject matter, and to reproduce such compilations for the purpose of clause (1) of this subsection; and

    (3) to distribute a reproduction made under clause (1) or (2) of this subsection—

      (A) by loan to a person engaged in research; and

      (B) for deposit in a library or archives which meets the requirements of section 108(*a*) of title 17 as amended by the first section of this Act, in either case for use only in research and not for further reproduction or performance.

(*c*) The Librarian or any employee of the Library who is acting under the authority of this section shall not be liable in any action for copyright infringement committed by any other person unless the Librarian or such employee knowingly participated in the act of infringement committed by such person. Nothing in this section shall be construed to excuse or limit liability under title 17 as amended by the first section of this Act for any act not authorized by that tithe or this section, or for any act performed by a person not authorized to act under that title or this section.

(*d*) This section may be cited as the "American Television and Radio Archives Act."

SEC. 114. There are hereby authorized to be appropriated such funds as may be **E–114** necessary to carry out the purposes of this Act.

SEC. 115. If any provision of title 17, as amended by the first section of this Act, is **E–115** declared unconstitutional, the validity of the remainder of this title is not affected.

Berne Implementation Act 1988 Provisions   E–116

Section 3 of the Berne Convention Implementation Act of 1988, Pub. L. 100–568, 102 Stat. 2853–54 (Oct. 31, 1988) provides the following rules of construction:

3. CONSTRUCTION OF THE BERNE CONVENTION

(*a*) RELATIONSHIP WITH DOMESTIC LAW.

The provisions of the Berne Convention—
  (1) shall be given effect under title 17, as amended by this Act, and any other relevant provision of Federal or State law, including the common law; and
  (2) shall not be enforceable in any action brought pursuant to the provisions of the Berne Convention itself.

(*b*) CERTAIN RIGHTS NOT AFFECTED.

The provisions of the Berne Convention, the adherence of the United States thereto, and satisfaction of United States obligations thereunder, do not expand or reduce any right of any author of a work, whether claimed under Federal, State, or the common law—
  (1) to claim authorship of the work; or
  (2) to object to any distortion, mutilation, or other modification of, or other derogatory action in relation to, the work, that would prejudice the author's honor or reputation.

Section 12(*d*) of that Act (102 Stat. 2860) provides:

12. WORKS IN THE PUBLIC DOMAIN

Title 17, United States Code, as amended by this Act, does not provide copyright protection for any work that is in the public domain in the United States.

Section 13 of that Act (102 Stat. 2861) provides the following declarations:

13. EFFECTIVE DATE; EEFFECT ON PENDING CASES

(*a*) EFFECTIVE DATE.

This Act and the amendments made by this Act take effect on the date on which the Berne Convention (as defined in section 101 of title 17, United States Code) enters into force with respect to the United States.

(*b*) EFFECT ON PENDING CASES.

Any cause of action arising under title 17, United States Code, before the effective date of this Act shall be governed by the provisions of such title as in effect when the cause of action arose.

E–117 **Satellite Home Viewer Act 1988 Amendments**

Section 207 of The Satellite Home Viewer Act of 1988, Pub. L. 100–617, Title II, 102 Stat. 3935 (Nov. 16, 1988) provides, among other things, that the amendments made by that Act to the Copyright Act (creation of Section 119 and amendments to Sections 111, 501, 801 and 804) shall "cease to be effective" on December 31, 1994.

Appendix F

TREATY OF ROME

Treaty of Rome

March 25, 1957

(As amended by the Single European Act of February, 1986)

ARTICLE 2

The Community shall have as its task, by establishing a common market and **F–1** progressively approximating the economic policies of Member States, to promote throughout the Community a harmonious development of economic activities, a continuous and balanced expansion, an increase in stability, an accelerated raising of the standard of living and closer relations between the States belonging to it.

ARTICLE 3

For the purposes set out in Article 2, the activities of the Community shall **F–2** include, as provided in this Treaty and in accordance with the timetable set out therein:

(a) the elimination, as between Member States, of customs duties and of quantitative restrictions on the import and export of goods, and of all other measures having equivalent effect;

(b) the establishment of a common customs tariff and of a common commercial policy towards third countries;

(c) the abolition, as between Member States, of obstacles to freedom of movement for persons, services and capital;

(d) the adoption of a common policy in the sphere of agriculture;

(e) the adoption of a common policy in the sphere of transport;

(f) the institution of a system ensuring that competition in the common market is not distorted;

(g) the application of procedures by which the economic policies of Member States can be coordinated and disequilibria in their balances of payments remedied;

(h) the approximation of the laws of Member States to the extent required for the proper functioning of the common market;

(i) the creation of a European Social Fund in order to improve employment opportunities for workers and to contribute to the raising of their standard of living;

(j) the establishment of a European Investment Bank to facilitate the economic expansion of the Community by opening up fresh resources;

(k) the association of the overseas countries and territories in order to increase trade and to promote jointly economic and social development.

ARTICLE 5

Member States shall take all appropriate measures, whether general or particu- **F–3** lar, to ensure fulfilment of the obligations arising out of this Treaty or resulting from action taken by the institutions of the Community. They shall facilitate the achievement of the Community's tasks.

They shall abstain from any measure which could jeopardise the attainment of the objectives of this Treaty.

ARTICLE 8A

F–4   The Community shall adopt measures with the aim of progressively establishing the internal market over a period expiring on 31 December 1992, in accordance with the provisions of this Article and of Articles 8B, 8C, 28, 57(2), 59, 70(1), 84, 99, 100A and 100B and without prejudice to the other provisions of this Treaty.

The internal market shall comprise an area without internal frontiers in which the free movement of goods, persons, services and capital is ensured in accordance with the provisions of this Treaty.

ARTICLE 36

F–5   The provisions of Articles 30 to 34 shall not preclude prohibitions or restrictions on imports, exports or goods in transit justified on grounds of public morality, public policy or public security; the protection of health and life of humans, animals or plants; the protection of national treasures possessing artistic, historic or archaeological value; or the protection of industrial and commercial property. Such prohibitions or restrictions shall not, however, constitute a means of arbitrary discrimination or a disguised restriction on trade between Member States.

ARTICLE 59

F–6   Within the framework of the provisions set out below, restrictions on freedom to provide services within the Community shall be progressively abolished during the transitional period in respect of nationals of Member States who are established in a State of the Community other than that of the person for whom the services are intended.

The Council may, acting by a qualified majority on a proposal from the Commission, extend the provisions of this Chapter to nationals of a third country who provide services and who are established within the Community.

ARTICLE 60

F–7   Services shall be considered to be "services" within the meaning of this Treaty where they are normally provided for remuneration, in so far as they are not governed by the provisions relating to freedom of movement for goods, capital and persons.

"Services" shall in particular include:
(*a*) activities of an industrial character;
(*b*) activities of a commercial character;
(*c*) activities of craftsmen;
(*d*) activities of the professions.

Without prejudice to the provisions of the Chapter relating to the right of establishment, the person providing a service may, in order to do so, temporarily pursue his activity in the State where the service is provided, under the same conditions as are imposed by that State on its own nationals.

ARTICLE 85

F–8   1. The following shall be prohibited as incompatible with the common market: all agreements between undertakings, decisions by associations of undertakings and concerted practices which may affect trade between Member States and

which have as their object or effect the prevention, restriction or distortion of competition within the common market, and in particular those which:
- (*a*) directly or indirectly fix purchase or selling prices or any other trading conditions;
- (*b*) limit or control production, markets, technical development, or investment;
- (*c*) share markets or sources of supply;
- (*d*) apply dissimilar conditions to equivalent transactions with other trading parties, thereby placing them at a competitive disadvantage;
- (*e*) make the conclusion of contracts subject to acceptance by the other parties of supplementary obligations which, by their nature or according to commercial usage, have no connection with the subject of such contracts.

2. Any agreements or decisions prohibited pursuant to this Article shall be automatically void.

3. The provisions of paragraph 1 may, however, be declared inapplicable in the case of:
- — any agreement or category of agreements between undertakings;
- — any decision or category of decisions by associations of undertakings;
- — any concerted practice or category of concerted practices;

which contributes to improving the production or distribution of goods or to promoting technical or economic progress, while allowing consumers a fair share of the resulting benefit, and which does not:
- (*a*) impose on the undertakings concerned restrictions which are not indispensable to the attainment of these objectives;
- (*b*) afford such undertakings the possibility of eliminating competition in respect of a substantial part of the products in question.

ARTICLE 86

Any abuse by one or more undertakings of a dominant position within the common market or in a substantial part of it shall be prohibited as incompatible with the common market in so far as it may affect trade between Member States. Such abuse may, in particular, consist in: **F–9**
- (*a*) directly or indirectly imposing unfair purchase or selling prices or other unfair trading conditions;
- (*b*) limiting production, markets or technical development to the prejudice of consumers;
- (*c*) applying dissimilar conditions to equivalent transactions with other trading parties, thereby placing them at a competitive disadvantage;
- (*d*) making the conclusion of contracts subject to acceptance by the other parties of supplementary obligations which, by their nature or according to commercial usage, have no connection with the subject of such contracts.

ARTICLE 177

The Court of Justice shall have jurisdiction to give preliminary rulings concerning: **F–10**
- (*a*) the interpretation of this Treaty;
- (*b*) the validity and interpretation of acts of the institutions of the Community;
- (*c*) the interpretation of the statutes of bodies established by an act of the Council, where those statutes so provide.

Where such a question is raised before any court or tribunal of a Member State, that court or tribunal may, if it considers that a decision on the question is necessary to enable it to give judgment, request the Court of Justice to give a ruling thereon.

Where any such question is raised in a case pending before a court or tribunal of a Member State, against whose decisions there is no judicial remedy under national law, that court or tribunal shall bring the matter before the Court of Justice.

ARTICLE 222

F–11   This Treaty shall in no way prejudice the rules in Member States governing the system of property ownership.

Appendix G

PRECEDENTS AND COURT FORMS

1. Precedents[1]

(A) Assignment of Copyright[2]

THIS ASSIGNMENT is made the   day of   19   between A.B. **G–1**
of [*state address*] of the one part and C.D. of [*state address*] of the other part

Now this Assignment Witnesses as Follows:

1. [In consideration of the sum of £   now paid by C.D. to A.B. (the receipt of which A.B. hereby acknowledges)] A.B. [as beneficial owner[3]] hereby assigns to C.D. the copyright[4] and all rights in the nature of copyright throughout the world[5] in [*insert description of work*[6]] for all the residue of the term of copyright and such rights therein[7] and all renewals or extensions thereof[8] and together with all accrued causes of action in respect thereof.[9]

[2. *Assertion of right to be identified as author (See Precedent (E)), alternatively waiver of moral rights (See Precedent (F)).*]

3. A.B. shall at any time and from time to time hereafter at the request and expense of C.D. execute all such documents and do all such further acts as C.D. may require in order to vest the said rights in C.D.

---

[1] Precedents are provided of only the very basic forms of assignments and other instruments. It is beyond the scope of this work to provide more detailed precedents.

[2] See C.D.P.A. 1988, s.90 and § 5–7, *et seq., ante.* An assignment must be in writing, signed by or on behalf of the assignor, but need not be under seal. It should be born in mind that rights may also be granted by way of licence, and care should be taken to make it clear what is intended. Thus a grant of a licence should use some such words as "by way of licence only." As with an assignment, a licence should make clear the extent of the rights granted, the term and territory.

[3] If the assignment is for valuable consideration the qualified covenants set out in Part I of the Second Schedule to the Law of Property Act 1925 will be implied. See s.76 of that Act. As to their effect, see, for example, Emmett on Title, 19th ed., Chap. 14.

[4] A simple assignment of "the copyright" will assign all the things which the copyright owner has the exclusive right to do. See § 5–22, *ante.* Alternatively, the assignment may be limited, so as to transfer some only of the copyright owner's exclusive rights. See C.D.P.A. 1988 Act, s.90(2)(*a*) and § 5–9, *ante.*

[5] The assignment may of course be limited in its geographical extent, *e.g.* to "the copyright conferred by the law in force in the United Kingdom."

[6] Care should be taken to identify the work or works precisely, perhaps by reference to a Schedule, bearing in mind that a number of different copyright works may make up the "work" which is to be the subject-matter of the assignment.

[7] The assignment may be limited to part only of the period for which the copyright subsists, *e.g.* "for the period of ten years from the date hereof."

[8] This provision is directed to certain foreign systems of law, such as those of the United States of America, which provide for copyright to be periodically renewed or extended.

[9] This provision will ensure that the assignee can recover damages in respect of any infringement which may have taken place before the date of the assignment. Notice of the assignment should be given to the proposed Defendant. See Law of Property Act 1925, s. 136.

1537

[4. It is hereby certified that the transaction hereby effected does not form part of a larger transaction or of a series of transactions in respect of which the amount or value of the aggregate amount or value of the consideration exceeds £ .[10]]

As WITNESS ETC.

[Signature of both parties][11]

(B) ASSIGNMENT OF FUTURE COPYRIGHT[12]

G–2 THIS AGREEMENT is made the   day of   19   between A.B. of [*state address*] of the one part and C.D. of [*state address*] of the other part

1. [In consideration of the sum of £   paid by C.D. to A.B. (the receipt of which A.B. hereby acknowledges)] A.B. hereby assigns to C.D. the copyright and all rights in the nature of copyright in [*insert description of work*] about to be created by A.B. for the full term of copyright and such rights therein and all renewals or extensions thereof to the intent that the said rights therein shall forthwith upon the completion of the work vest in C.D.

[2. *Assertion of right to be identified as author (see Precedent (E)), alternatively waiver of moral rights (See Precedent (F)).*]

3. [*Covenant for further assurances (see Precedent (A), Clause 3).*]

[4. It is hereby certified that the transaction hereby effected does not form part of a larger transaction or of a series of transactions in respect of which the amount or value of the aggregate amount or value of the consideration exceeds £   .]

As WITNESS ETC.

[Signature of both parties][13]

(C) ASSIGNMENT OF DESIGN RIGHT[14]

G–3 THIS ASSIGNMENT is made the   day of   19   between A.B. of [*state address*] of the one part and C.D. of [*state address*] of the other part

NOW THIS ASSIGNMENT WITNESSES AS FOLLOWS:

1. [In consideration of the sum of £   now paid by C.D. to A.B. (the receipt of which A.B. hereby acknowledges)] A.B. [as beneficial owner[15]] hereby assigns to

---

[10] An assignment must be stamped in the same way as an assignment of any other property.

[11] In the case of a body corporate, the requirement that the assignment be signed will be satisfied by affixing the company's seal. See C.D.P.A. 1988, s.176(1). See also the amendments made to the Companies Act 1985 by the Companies Act 1989, s.130.

[12] By s.91 of the C.D.P.A. 1988, an agreement made in relation to future copyright, and signed by or on behalf of the prospective owner of the copyright, whereby the owner purports to assign the future copyright, shall as provided by the section (see § 5–40, *ante*) cause the copyright, when it comes into existence, to vest in the assignee or his successor in title. It should be noted that an agreement in this form will not necessarily have the same effect outside the United Kingdom, which is why a covenant for further assurances is desirable. The agreement should always be supported by valuable consideration (see § 5–40, *ante*), not least to make the covenant for further assurances specifically enforceable. See also the notes to Precedent (A) in relation to the present form generally.

[13] See n. 11, *ante*.

[14] See C.D.P.A. 1988, s.222. The assignment must be in writing, signed by or on behalf of the assignor, but need not be under seal. As with copyright, the design right may also be licensed. See n. 2, *ante*.

[15] See n. 3, *ante*.

C.D. the design right as conferred by Part III of the Copyright, Designs and Patents Act 1988 or any statutory modification or re-enactment thereof in [*insert description of design*] for all the residue of the term of design right therein together with all accrued causes of action in respect thereof.

2. [*Covenant for further assurances (see Precedent (A), Clause 3).*]

[3. It is hereby certified that the transaction hereby effected does not form part of a larger transaction or of a series of transactions in respect of which the amount or value of the aggregate amount or value of the consideration exceeds £   .]

As WITNESS ETC.

[Signature of both parties][16]

(D) ASSIGNMENT OF FUTURE DESIGN RIGHT[17]

THIS AGREEMENT is made the   day of   19   between A.B. **G–4** of [*state address*] of the one part and C.D. of [*state address*] of the other part

1. [In consideration of the sum of £   now paid by C.D. to A.B. (the receipt of which A.B. hereby acknowledges)] A.B. hereby assigns to C.D. the design right as conferred by Part III of the Copyright, Designs and Patents Act 1988 or any statutory modification or re-enactment thereof in [*insert description of design*] about to be created by A.B. for the full term of design right therein to the intent that the design right therein shall forthwith upon the completion of the work vest in C.D.

2. A.B. shall at any time and from time to time hereafter at the request and expense of C.D. execute all such documents and do all such further acts as C.D. may require in order to vest the said design right in C.D.

[3. It is hereby certified that the transaction hereby effected does not form part of a larger transaction or of a series of transactions in respect of which the amount or value of the aggregate amount or value of the consideration exceeds £   .]

As WITNESS ETC.

[Signature of both parties][18]

(E) ASSERTION OF RIGHT TO BE IDENTIFIED AS AUTHOR[19]

THIS INSTRUMENT is made the   day of   19   by A.B. of **G–5** [*state address*].

1. A.B. is the author of [*insert description of work*].

---

[16] In the case of a body corporate, the requirement that the assignment be signed will be satisfied by affixing the company's seal. See C.D.P.A. 1988, s.261. See also the amendments made to the Companies Act 1985 by the Companies Act 1989, s. 130.

[17] See C.D.P.A. 1988, s.223, and n. 12, *ante*. The provisions dealing with assignments of future copyright and future design right are in identical terms.

[18] See n. 16, *ante*.

[19] See C.D.P.A. 1988, s.78 and § 22–20 *et seq.*, *ante*. The form included here is intended to be a simple instrument in writing signed by the author, so as to satisfy s.78(2)(b) of the 1988 Act. It may be adapted to be included in an assignment of copyright (see Precedents (A) and (B)) so as to satisfy s.78(2)(*a*), or to be applicable to a director of a film.

2. Notice is hereby given that A.B. hereby asserts his right generally[20] to be identified as the author of the said work.

Signed,

(F) Waiver of Moral Rights[21]

G–6 THIS WAIVER is made this   day of   19   by A.B. of [*state address*].

1. I, A.B., hereby unconditionally and irrevocably[22] waive my rights [to be identified as the author[23] of [*insert description of work*[24]]]/[to be identified as the director of [*insert description of film*]] and not to have the said [work]/[film] subjected to derogatory treatment.[25]

[2. This waiver is made expressly in favour of C.D.[26] and for the avoidance of doubt shall extend to licensees and successors in title to the copyright in the said [work]/[film].[27]]

Signed,

2. Court Forms

G–7   (A) Infringement of Copyright: Generally Indorsed Writ[28]

In the High Court of Justice   CH 19   B No.

Chancery Division

Between:

A.B.

Plaintiff

and

C.D.

Defendant

---

[20] The right may be asserted generally or in relation to any specified act or description of acts. See C.D.P.A. 1988, s.78(2).

[21] The C.D.P.A. 1988, s.87 provides that any of the moral rights may be waived by an instrument in writing signed by or on behalf of the person giving up the right. See § 22–71, *et seq., ante*. The present form contains a waiver in respect of the right to be identified as the author of a literary, dramatic, musical or artistic work, or the director of a film, and the right not to have such works subjected to derogatory treatment.

[22] The waiver may be conditional or unconditional, and may be expressed to be subject to revocation. See C.D.P.A. 1988, s.87(3)(*b*).

[23] See C.D.P.A. 1988, s.77; § 22–8 *et seq., ante*.

[24] The waiver may relate to a specific work, to works of a specified description or to works generally, and may relate to existing or future works. See the 1988 Act, s.87(3)(*a*).

[25] See C.D.P.A. 1988, s.80 and § 22–35 *et seq., ante*.

[26] *I.e.*, the owner or the prospective owner of the copyright in the work.

[27] If the waiver is made in favour of the owner or the prospective owner of the copyright in the work, it shall be presumed, unless the contrary intention is expressed, to extend to his licensees and successors in title. See C.D.P.A. 1988, s.87(2).

[28] The form given here is suitable for a case of infringement of copyright in a literary, dramatic, musical or artistic work, and which has taken place since the commencement of the C.D.P.A. 1988, *i.e.* August 1, 1989. See generally, Chap. 8, *ante*. In suitable cases there may be added a claim relating to the Plaintiff's moral rights (see Court Forms (D) and (E), *post*).

THE PLAINTIFF'S CLAIM IS FOR:

1. An injunction restraining the Defendant (whether acting by himself his servants or agents or any of them or otherwise howsoever) from doing the following acts or any of them that is to say infringing the Plaintiff's copyright in [*insert description of the copyright work*] by without the Plaintiff's licence reproducing or issuing to the public copies of the said work or any substantial part thereof or authorising any of the acts aforesaid[29] or selling offering or exposing for sale exhibiting in public or distributing copies of the said work made without the Plaintiff's licence[30] or otherwise howsoever.

2. An inquiry as to damages for infringement of copyright (including damages under section 97(2) of the Copyright, Designs and Patents Act 1988[31]) alternatively and at the Plaintiff's option an account of profits together with an order for the payment to the Plaintiff of all sums found due upon the making of the said inquiry or the taking of the said account.

3. Interest pursuant to s.35A of the Supreme Court Act 1981.

4. Delivery up[32] of:
   (a) all infringing copies of the said work in the Defendant's possession custody or control[33];
   (b) any article in the Defendant's possession custody or control specifically designed or adapted for making copies of the said work.[34]

5. An Order that all infringing copies or articles delivered up pursuant to paragraph 4 of this prayer for relief be forfeited to the Plaintiff alternatively be destroyed or otherwise dealt with as this Honourable Court shall think fit.[35]

6. Further or other relief.

7. Costs.

This Writ, etc.

(B) INFRINGEMENT OF COPYRIGHT: STATEMENT OF CLAIM[36]   **G–8**

[Heading—See Court Form (A)]

STATEMENT OF CLAIM

1. The Plaintiff is the owner of the copyright in the [*insert description of copyright work*] ("the Work").

---

[29] As to these acts of primary infringement, see Chap. 8, *ante*.

[30] As to these acts of secondary infringement, see Chap. 9, *ante*.

[31] As to these damages, see § 11–66, *ante*.

[32] See n. 35, *post*.

[33] See C.D.P.A. 1988, s.99(1)(*a*), and §§ 11–17, 11–80, *ante*.

[34] See C.D.P.A. 1988, s.99(1)(*b*), and § 11–17, *ante*.

[35] See C.D.P.A. 1988, s.114(1) and § 11–77, *ante*. Until a decision is made as to whether to make an Order under this section, the Plaintiff must retain any item ordered to be delivered up pursuant to the previous paragraph of this prayer for relief. See C.D.P.A. 1988, s.99(3).

[36] The precedent given here follows on from the previous precedent, and is suitable to the case of infringement of copyright in a literary work.

PARTICULARS OF SUBSISTENCE[37]

[Insert details of how it is said that copyright subsists in the work, e.g.:

(1) The Work is an original[38] literary work and was made on [1st January 1990]/[between [1st January 1990] and [date when work was completed]].
(2) The Work was made by E.F., who, when the work was made was [a British citizen]/[British subject]/[domiciled/resident in the United Kingdom].
(3) The Work was first published on [30th June 1990] in [the United Kingdom.] At that time E.F. remained [a British citizen]/[a British subject]/ [domiciled/resident in the United Kingdom.]

PARTICULARS OF OWNERSHIP[39]

[Insert details of how it is said that the Plaintiff owns the copyright, e.g.:

(1) The Work was created by E.F.
(2) By an assignment in writing dated [*insert date*], E.F. assigned the copyright in the Work to the Plaintiff together with all accrued causes of action in respect thereof.]

2. Prior to the issue of the Writ herein, the Defendant has infringed the Plaintiff's copyright in the Work by (without the licence of the Plaintiff) reproducing a substantial part of the Work in a material form, putting into circulation copies of a substantial part of the Work not previously put into circulation, and/or authorising the said acts,[40] and possessing in the course of his business, selling, offering and exposing for sale, exhibiting in public and distributing in the course of his business articles which were, and which the Defendant knew or had reason to believe were, infringing copies of the Work.[41]

PARTICULARS OF INFRINGEMENT

[Give details of infringement, e.g.:

The Plaintiff will seek to recover in respect of all acts of infringement but prior to discovery and/or interrogatories herein relies on the printing by or for the Defendant, and the sale by the Defendant, of copies of a work entitled [*insert title*], which reproduces a substantial part of the Work. A Schedule of the passages of the Work which are reproduced in the Defendant's said work is served separately.]

PARTICULARS OF KNOWLEDGE[42]

Prior to discovery and/or interrogatories herein the Plaintiff relies on his Solicitors' letter to the Defendant dated [*insert date*].

---

[37] As to the qualification requirements for copyright subsistence, see C.D.P.A. 1988, ss.153–156 and Chap. 3, *ante*. It is in fact common practice not to give Particulars of Subsistence at this stage, but to await any Request for Further and Better Particulars which the Defendant may make.
[38] As to originality, see § 3–25 *et seq.*, *ante*.
[39] As to the considerations affecting authorship and ownership, see C.D.P.A. 1988, ss.9–11 and 90–93, and Chaps. 4 and 5, *ante*. Again, it is common practice not to give Particulars of Ownership at this stage.
[40] See n. 29, *ante*.
[41] See n. 30, *ante*.
[42] Particulars of knowledge should always be given. See R.S.C. Order 18, Rule 12(1).

3. All copies of the Defendant's said work are infringing copies of the Work and the Plaintiff is entitled to delivery up of the same.

4. Unless restrained by this Honourable Court the Defendant threatens and intends to continue the said acts complained of.

5. By reason of the matters aforesaid the Plaintiff has suffered and will suffer loss and damage.

6. The Plaintiff claims interest pursuant to section 35A of the Supreme Court Act 1981 for such period and at such rate as this Honourable Court thinks just.

AND THE PLAINTIFF CLAIMS:

[*Insert prayer for relief—see Court Form (A).*]
Served, *etc.*

(C) INFRINGEMENT OF DESIGN RIGHT: STATEMENT OF CLAIM[43]   **G–9**

[Heading—See Court Form (A)]

STATEMENT OF CLAIM

1. The Plaintiff is the owner of the design right ("the Plaintiff's Design Right") in the design ("the Plaintiff's Design") of the external and internal shape and configuration of [*insert description of the article*].

PARTICULARS OF QUALIFICATIONS FOR PROTECTION[44]

[*Insert details of how it is said that the design right qualifies for protection, e.g.:*

(1) The Plaintiff's Design was recorded in a design document consisting of [*insert description of design document*] on [*state date*] and an article was first made to the Plaintiff's Design on [*state date*].
(2) When it was created, the Plaintiff's Design was original.
(3) The designer of the Plaintiff's Design was E.F., who did not create the design in pursuance of a commission or in the course of employment and who, when the Plaintiff's Design was made, was [a British citizen]/[British subject]/[habitually resident in the United Kingdom.]

PARTICULARS OF OWNERSHIP[45]

[*Insert details of how it is said that the Plaintiff owns the Plaintiff's Design Right, e.g.:*

(1) E.F. was in the premises, the first owner of the Plaintiff's Design Right.
(2) By an assignment in writing dated [*insert date*], E.F. assigned the Plaintiff's Design Right to the Plaintiff together with all accrued causes of action in respect thereof.]

---

[43] As to the design right, see Chap. 20, *ante*, and, in particular, as to jurisdication, see § 20–202 *et seq.*, *ante*.
[44] As to the qualification requirements for design right protection, see C.D.P.A. 1988, ss.217–221 and § 20–82 *et seq.*, *ante*.
[45] As to the considerations affecting ownership, see C.D.P.A. 1988, ss.215, 222–224, and § 20–102 *et seq.*, *ante*.

2. Prior to the issue of the Writ herein, the Defendant has infringed the Plaintiff's Design Right by (without the Plaintiff's licence) reproducing the Plaintiff's Design for commercial purposes, making articles to the Plaintiff's Design, making design documents recording the Plaintiff's Design for the purpose of enabling such articles to be made, and/or authorising the said acts,[46] and possessing for commercial purposes, selling, offering and exposing for sale in the course of his business articles which were, and which the Defendant knew or had reason to believe were, articles whose making was an infringement of the Plaintiff's Design Right.[47]

Particulars of Infringement

The Plaintiff will seek to recover in respect of all acts of infringement but prior to discovery and/or interrogatories herein relies on the manufacture by or for the Defendant, and the sale by the Defendant of [*insert description of articles*], which are copies of the Plaintiff's Design such as to be exactly or substantially to the Plaintiff's Design.]

Particulars of Knowledge[48]

Prior to discovery and/or interrogatories herein the Plaintiff relies on his Solicitors' letter to the Defendant dated [*insert date*].

3. All copies of the Defendant's said articles are infringing articles and the Plaintiff is entitled to delivery up of the same.

[*Continue as in Court Form (B), paragraphs 4–6*]

And the Plaintiff Claims:

1. An injunction restraining the Defendant (whether acting by himself his servants or agents or any of them or otherwise howsoever) from doing the following acts or any of them that is to say infringing the Plaintiff's Design Right [in the internal and external shape and configuration of [*insert description of article*]] by (without the licence of the Plaintiff) making articles to the Plaintiff's Design or making any design document recording that design for the purpose of enabling such articles to be made or authorising any such act or selling offering or exposing for sale in the course of a business any article which was without the Plaintiff's licence made to the Plaintiff's Design or otherwise howsoever.

2. An inquiry as to damages for infringement of the Plaintiff's Design Right (including damages under section 229(3) of the Copyright, Designs and Patents Act 1988) alternatively and at the Plaintiff's option an account of profits together with an order for the payment to the Plaintiff of all sums found due upon the making of the said inquiry or the taking of the said account.

3. Interest pursuant to s.35A of the Supreme Court Act 1981.

4. Delivery up[49] of:
(a) all articles in the Defendant's possession custody or control whose making infringed the Plaintiff's Design Right;
(b) anything in the Defendant's possession custody or control specifically designed or adapted for making articles to the Plaintiff's Design.

---

[46] As to the acts of primary infringement of the design right, see C.D.P.A. 1988, s.226 and § 20–124 *et seq., ante.*

[47] As to the acts of secondary infringement of the design right, see C.D.P.A. 1988, s.227 and § 20–128 *et seq., ante.*

[48] Particulars of knowledge should always be given. See R.S.C. Order 18, Rule 12(1).

[49] See n. 50, *post.*

5. An Order that all articles and things delivered up pursuant to paragraph 4 of this prayer for relief be forfeited to the Plaintiff alternatively be destroyed or otherwise dealt with as this Honourable Court shall think fit.[50]

6. Further or other relief.

7. Costs.

Served, *etc.*

(D) INFRINGEMENT OF RIGHT TO BE IDENTIFIED AS AUTHOR[51]: STATEMENT OF CLAIM **G–10**

[Heading—See Court Form (A)]

STATEMENT OF CLAIM

1. The Plaintiff is the author of the copyright literary work [*insert description of work*] ("the Work").

2. By an assignment in writing dated [*insert date*], the Plaintiff assigned the copyright in the Work to E.F. Included in the assignment was a statement that the Plaintiff asserted his right to be identified as the author of the Work.[52]

3. Prior to the issue of the Writ herein, the Defendant has published the Work commercially[53] in the form of [*insert form of publication*].

4. The Defendant claims to be entitled to publish the Work as aforesaid by virtue of a licence from E.F. In the premises, the Defendant is bound by the Plaintiff's said assertion of his right to be identified as the author of the Work.[54]

5. When the Work was published as aforesaid the Plaintiff was not identified as the author of the Work. Further, the Plaintiff did not consent to such publication. In the premises, the Plaintiff's said right was thereby infringed.

[*Continue as in Court Form (B), paragraphs 4–6*]

AND THE PLAINTIFF CLAIMS[55]:

1. An injunction restraining the Defendant (whether acting by himself his servants or agents or any of them or otherwise howsoever) from doing the following acts or any of them that is to say infringing the Plaintiff's right to be identified as the author of the Work by without the Plaintiff's consent commercially publishing the Work without identifying the Plaintiff as the author thereof or otherwise howsoever.

---

[50] See C.D.P.A. 1988, s.231(1). Until a decision is made on whether to make an Order under this section, the Plaintiff must retain any item ordered to be delivered up pursuant to the previous paragraph of this prayer for relief. See C.D.P.A. 1988, s.230(6).

[51] As to infringement of the right to be identified as the author of a literary, dramatic, musical or artistic work, see C.D.P.A. 1988, ss.77–79 and § 22–8 *et seq., ante.*

[52] The right is not infringed unless (a) it has been asserted and (b) the Defendant is bound by that assertion. One of the ways in which the right may be asserted is on an assignment of the copyright, when the assignee and anyone claiming through him will be bound. See C.D.P.A. 1988, ss.77(1) and 78, and § 22–20 *et seq., ante.*

[53] As to the acts of infringement, see C.D.P.A. 1988, s.77 and § 22–10 *et seq., ante.*

[54] See n. 52, *ante.*

[55] An infringement of the right is actionable as a breach of statutory duty. See C.D.P.A. 1988, s.103(1) and § 22–69, *ante.*

2. An inquiry as to damages for infringement of the Plaintiff's right to be identified as the author of the Work alternatively and at the Plaintiff's option an account of profits together with an Order for the payment to the Plaintiff of all sums found due upon the making of the said inquiry or the taking of the said account.

3. Interest pursuant to section 35A of the Supreme Court Act 1981.

4. Further or other relief.

5. Costs.

Served, *etc.*

G–11   (E) Infringement of Right not to have Work Subjected to Derogatory Treatment[56]: Statement of Claim

[Heading —See Court Form (A)]

Statement of Claim

1. The Plaintiff is the author of the copyright literary work [*insert description of work*] ("the Work"). [The Defendant is the owner of the copyright in the Work.][57]

2. Prior to the issue of the Writ herein, the Defendant has published commercially a derogatory treatment of the Work.

Particulars

[*State form of derogatory publication, e.g.*:
The Plaintiff will rely on the version of the Work entitled [*insert title*] published by the Defendant in which passages were variously added to and deleted from the Work as set out in the Schedule served herewith, with the result that the Work was distorted and mutilated.[58]]

3. The Plaintiff did not consent to such publication. [Further, the Plaintiff was identified in the said version as the author thereof yet such publication took place without any clear or reasonably prominent indication being given at the time of publication that the Work had been subjected to treatment to which the Plaintiff had not consented.[59]] In the premises, the Plaintiff's right not to have the Work subjected to derogatory treatment was thereby infringed by the Defendant.

4. The Defendant has further infringed the Plaintiff's said right by without the Plaintiff's consent possessing in the course of his business, selling, offering and exposing for sale and distributing in the course of his business copies of the said work entitled [*insert title*] which he knew or had reason to believe had been distorted or mutilated as aforesaid.[60]

---

[56] As to such right, see C.D.P.A. 1988, ss.80–83 and § 22–35 *et seq., ante.*
[57] In the Precedent given here it is assumed that the Defendant is the owner of the copyright in the Work, in which case the right will not be infringed unless matters of the kind pleaded in the second sentence of paragraph 3 of this Precedent can be established. See C.D.P.A. 1988, s.82(2).
[58] As to the acts of infringement, see C.D.P.A. 1988, s.80 and § 22–39 *et seq., ante.*
[59] See n. 57, *ante.*
[60] As to such acts of infringement, see C.D.P.A. 1988, s.83 and § 22–43 *et seq., ante.*

PARTICULARS OF KNOWLEDGE[61]

Prior to discovery and/or interrogatories herein the Plaintiff relies on his Solicitors' letter to the Defendant dated [*insert date*].

[*Continue as in Court Form (B), paragraphs 4–6*]

AND THE PLAINTIFF CLAIMS[62]:

1. An injunction restraining the Defendant (whether acting by himself his servants or agents or any of them or otherwise howsoever) from doing the following acts or any of them that is to say infringing the Plaintiff's right not to have the Work subjected to derogatory treatment by (without the Plaintiff's consent) publishing commercially the Work in the form of the version referred to in paragraph 2 above or selling offering or exposing for sale or distributing in the course of his business copies of the said version of the Work [unless in every such case a disclaimer is made on such terms and in such manner as may be approved by this Honourable Court dissociating the Plaintiff from the said version[63]] or otherwise howsoever.

2. An inquiry as to damages for infringement of the Plaintiff's said right alternatively and at the Plaintiff's option an account of profits together with an Order for the payment to the Plaintiff of all sums found due upon the making of the said inquiry or the taking of the said account.

3. Delivery up for destruction of all copies of the said version in the Defendant's possession custody or control.[64]

4. Interest pursuant to section 35A of the Supreme Court Act 1981.

5. Further or other relief.

6. Costs.

Served, *etc.*

(F) NOTICE OF MOTION[65]   **G–12**

[Heading—See Court Form (A)]

TAKE NOTICE that this Honourable Court will be moved before the Honourable Mr Justice [*insert name*] sitting at the Royal Courts of Justice, Strand, London WC2A 2LL on   the   day of   19   at 10.30 a.m. or so soon thereafter as Counsel can be heard, by Counsel on behalf of the above named Plaintiff for relief in the following terms, namely:

1. An Order restraining the Defendant until after judgment or further Order in the meantime (whether acting by himself his servants or agents or any of them or otherwise howsoever) from doing the following acts or any of them that is to say [*insert appropriate relief, e.g.:*

---

[61] Particulars of knowledge should always be given. See R.S.C. Order 18, Rule 12(1).

[62] An infringement of the right is actionable as a breach of statutory duty. See C.D.P.A. 1988, s.103(1) and § 22–69, *ante.*

[63] See C.D.P.A. 1988, s.103(2) and § 22–69, *ante.*

[64] *I.e.* under the Court's inherent jurisdiction. See *Hole* v. *Bradbury* (1879) 12 Ch.D. 886 and § 11–80, *ante.*

[65] As to the practice on motion, see § 11–35 *et seq., ante.*

Manufacturing or authorising the manufacture of selling offering advertising or exposing for sale distributing destroying or otherwise disposing of any product an example of which forms exhibit "AB1" to the first Affidavit of A.B. sworn in this action on [*insert date*].[66]]

2. Such further or other relief as this Honourable Court shall think fit.

3. An order providing for the costs of this application.

Dated, *etc.*

G–13   (G) Ex parte Injunction[67]

In the High Court of Justice   CH 19   B No.

Chancery Division

Mr Justice

    DAY THE   DAY OF   19

IN THE MATTER OF AN INTENDED ACTION

Between:

A.B.

Intended Plaintiff

and

C.D.

Intended Defendant

UPON MOTION made by Counsel for the Intended Plaintiff (hereinafter called the Plaintiff) *ex parte*

AND UPON READING the draft Writ of Summons and the draft Affidavit of [*insert deponent's name*] together with the intended exhibits thereto

AND UPON the Plaintiff by his Counsel undertaking

(1) Forthwith to issue a Writ of Summons claiming relief similar to or connected with that hereinafter granted

(2) Forthwith to procure that an Affidavit substantially in the form of the said draft Affidavit of [*insert deponent's name*] be sworn and filed[68]

(3) To serve upon the Intended Defendant (hereinafter called the Defendant) a copy of this Order together with a copy of the said Affidavit and the photocopiable Exhibits thereto and Notice of Motion for [*insert return date for Motion*]

---

[66] Interlocutory relief should generally not be framed in such terms as, for example, to restrain the Defendant "from infringing the Plaintiff's copyright." On a committal motion, this may raise the very issues which must be resolved at trial. See *The Staver Company Inc.* v. *Digitext Display Ltd.* [1985] F.S.R. 512 and *Video Arts Ltd.* v. *Paget Industries Ltd.* [1986] F.S.R. 623.

[67] The form given here assumes that there has been no time to issue the writ before making the application. Where possible, however, the writ should be issued beforehand.

[68] If there has not been time even to prepare a draft affidavit, an undertaking should be given to swear an affidavit "verifying what was alleged by counsel."

(4) To obey any Order this Court may make as to damages if it shall consider that the Defendant shall have sustained any damages by reason of this Order which the Plaintiff ought to pay

IT IS ORDERED THAT the Defendant be restrained until after [*insert return date for motion*] or until further Order in the meantime from doing (whether acting by himself his servants agents or otherwise howsoever) the following acts or any of them that is to say: [*insert appropriate relief, see, e.g. Court Form (F), ante*]

[AND the Plaintiff is at liberty to serve short notice of Motion for [insert return date]]

AND the Defendant is to be at liberty to move to discharge or vary this Order upon giving to the Plaintiff 24 hours written notice of his intention so to do

(H) Anton Piller Order[69]   **G–14**
[Heading—see Court Form (G)]

UPON MOTION made by Counsel for the Intended Plaintiff (hereinafter called the Plaintiff) *ex parte*

AND UPON READING the draft Writ of Summons and the draft Affidavit of [*insert deponent's name*] together with the intended Exhibits thereto

AND UPON the Plaintiff by his Counsel undertaking
    (1) Forthwith to issue a Writ of Summons claiming relief similar to or connected with that hereinafter granted
    (2) Forthwith to procure that an Affidavit substantially in the form of the said draft Affidavit of [*insert deponent's name*] be sworn and filed
    (3) To serve this Order upon the Intended Defendant (hereinafter called the Defendant) by a Solicitor of the Supreme Court together with the said Writ of Summons the said draft Affidavit and photocopiable Exhibits thereto together with a Notice of Motion returnable on the [*insert return date*]
    (4) To refrain from executing this Order until after the Defendant has had the opportunity of seeking and obtaining professional legal advice provided that the Defendant seeks and obtains such advice forthwith upon service on him of this Order
    (5) To obey any Order this Court may make as to damages if it shall consider that the Defendant shall have sustained any damages by reason of this Order which the Plaintiff ought to pay

AND UPON the Solicitors for the Plaintiff by Counsel for the Plaintiff being their counsel for this purpose undertaking
    (1) To offer to explain to the person or persons served with this Order its meaning and effect fairly and in everyday language
    (2) To inform any person served with this Order at the time this Order is served upon him of his right to seek and obtain professional legal advice before complying with this Order provided that such advice is sought and obtained forthwith after such service
    (3) To inform the Defendant or the person served with this Order that if he fails to comply with this Order proceedings may be instituted by the Plaintiff for contempt of Court
    (4) To answer forthwith any query made by the Defendant as to whether any particular document or article is within the scope of this Order

---

[69] For a discussion of the practice relating to Anton Piller Orders generally, see § 11–48 *et seq., ante.*

(5) To make a detailed list of all documents and articles obtained as a result of this Order prior to their removal into their custody and to provide to the Defendant or the person served with this Order a copy of the said list

(6) To return within two working days of their removal the originals of any documents obtained as a result of this Order having taken photocopies of the same

(7) To retain in their safe custody until further Order all other articles obtained as a result of this Order

(8) Where ownership of any article obtained as a result of this Order is disputed to deliver up any such article to the custody of Solicitors acting on behalf of the Defendant within two working days of receipt of an undertaking in writing from the Defendant's Solicitors to retain the same in safe custody and produce them if required to the Court

IT IS ORDERED THAT

(1) the Defendant be restrained until after [*insert return date*] or until further Order in the meantime from doing (whether acting by himself his servants or agents or any of them or otherwise howsoever) the following acts or any of them that is to say

(a) save in compliance with this Order [*insert appropriate relief, see, e.g. Court Form (F), ante*]

(b) parting with possession of (save in compliance with this Order) or destroying any articles specifically designed or adapted for making copies of [such products]

(c) parting with possession of (save in compliance with this Order) or destroying any invoices records or other documents (including those in computer readable form) which relate to the manufacture supply or other dealing in [such products]

(d) directly or indirectly informing or notifying any person company or firm (otherwise than for the purpose of seeking legal advice from properly qualified professional lawyers) of the existence of this Order or of the provisions of this Order or of the Plaintiff's interest in these proceedings or otherwise warning any person company or firm that proceedings may be brought against them by the Plaintiff

(2) the Defendant do disclose forthwith to the person serving this Order upon him

(a) the whereabouts of all such articles and documents (including those in computer readable form) as are referred to in paragraphs (1)(a) (b) and (c) above which are in the possession power custody or control of the Defendant

(b) to the best of the Defendant's knowledge and belief

(i) the names and addresses of the persons companies or firms who have supplied or offered to supply the Defendant with [such products]

(ii) the names and addresses of the persons companies or firms to whom the Defendant has supplied or offered to supply [such products]

(iii) full details of the dates and quantities of each offer to supply and supply referred to in paragraphs (2)(b)(i) and (ii) above

(3) the Defendant do deliver forthwith to the Plaintiff's Solicitors all such articles and documents (including those in computer readable form) as are referred to in paragraphs (1)(a) (b) and (c) above which are in the possession power or custody of the Defendant and if any such item exists in computer readable form only the Defendant shall cause it forthwith to be printed out and deliver the print out to the Plaintiff's Solicitors or (failing a printer) to be displayed in a readable form

(4) the Defendant (whether by himself or by any person appearing to be in con-

trol of the premises as hereinafter specified) do permit the person serving this Order upon him and such other persons as may be authorised by the Plaintiff (such persons not to exceed [four] in number altogether) to enter forthwith

(1) the premises at [*insert address of premises*]

(2) and any other premises disclosed pursuant to this Order

(3) any outhouse or other building which forms part of the said premises and/ or any motor vehicles thereon or owned or used by the Defendant

on any weekday between 8 a.m. and 6 p.m. for the purpose of searching for photographing and removing into the custody of the Plaintiff's Solicitors all such articles and documents (including those in computer readable form) as are referred to in paragraphs (1)(a) (b) and (c) above or which appear to the Plaintiff's Solicitors to be such articles or documents

(5) within 7 days after the service of this Order the Defendant do make and serve on the Plaintiff's Solicitors an Affidavit setting forth and verifying the information ordered to be disclosed pursuant to this Order exhibiting thereto any documents in his possession power custody or control relating thereto and verifying that he has complied with the provisions of this Order

AND the Defendant is to be at liberty to move this Court to vary or discharge this Order upon giving 24 hours written notice to the Plaintiff's Solicitors of his intention so to do

(I) Mareva Order[70]   **G–15**

[Heading—see Court Form (G)]

UPON MOTION made by Counsel for the Intended Plaintiff (hereinafter called the Plaintiff) *ex parte*

AND UPON READING the draft Writ of Summons and the draft Affidavit of [*insert deponent's name*] together with the intended Exhibits thereto

AND UPON the Plaintiff by his Counsel undertaking

(1) Forthwith to issue a Writ of Summons claiming relief similar to or connected with that hereinafter granted

(2) Forthwith to procure that an Affidavit substantially in the form of the said draft Affidavit of [*insert deponent's name*] be sworn and filed

(3) To serve this Order upon the Intended Defendant (hereinafter called the Defendant) together with the said Writ of Summons the said draft Affidavit and photocopiable Exhibits thereto together with a Notice of Motion returnable on the [*insert return date*]

(4) To pay the reasonable costs incurred by any person other than the Defendant to whom notice of this Order may be given in ascertaining whether any assets to which this Order applies are within his possession power custody or control and in complying with this Order and to indemnify any such person against all liabilities which may flow from such compliance

(5) To obey any order this Court may make as to damages if it shall consider that the Defendant shall have sustained any damages by reason of this Order which the Plaintiff ought to pay

IT IS ORDERED THAT

(1) the Defendant be restrained until after [*insert return date*] or until further Order in the meantime from doing (whether acting by himself his servants or

---

[70] In appropriate circumstances, this Form may be combined with that for an Anton Piller Order, Court Form (H), *ante.*

agents or any of them or otherwise howsoever) the following acts or any of them that is to say removing from the jurisdiction of this Court or disposing of mortgaging assigning charging or otherwise dealing with howsoever any of his assets within [or without]⁷¹ the jurisdiction including but not limited to the following: *[insert description of specific assets known to the Plaintiff, e.g.:*

(a) the freehold property known as *[insert description]* or (if the same has been sold) the net proceeds of sale thereof after discharge of any subsisting mortgage or charge

(b) the property and assets of the business known as *[insert description]* carried on by the Defendant

(c) any monies standing to the credit of any account with *[state name and address of bank]*.

SAVE and in so far as the value of the said assets exceeds £

AND PROVIDED THAT

(i) The Defendant shall be at liberty (upon informing the Plaintiff's Solicitors of the source or accounts from which such sums are to be drawn) to

(a) withdraw and expend a sum not exceeding [£100] per week in respect of his ordinary and proper living expenses

(b) expend all necessary and reasonable sums for the purpose of obtaining legal advice and representation

(ii) The Defendant shall be at liberty to deal in the assets referred to in paragraph (1)(b) above for full value and in the ordinary course of the Defendant's said business and no third party shall be required to inquire whether full value is being given or such dealing is in the ordinary course of such business

(iii) Nothing in this Order shall prevent the exercise by any bank having notice of this Order of any right of set off which such bank may have in respect of facilities afforded by it to the Defendant prior to the date of this Order or the date on which such bank is notified of this Order (whichever is the later)

[(iv) In so far as this Order purports to have any extraterritorial effect no person shall be affected thereby or concerned with the terms thereof until it shall be declared enforceable or be enforced by a foreign Court and then it shall only affect them to the extent of such declaration or enforcement UNLESS they are (a) a person to whom this Order is addressed or an agent appointed by such a person or (b) persons who are subject to the jurisdiction of this Court and (i) have been given written notice of this Order at their residence or place of business within the jurisdiction and (ii) are able to prevent acts or omissions outside the jurisdiction of this Court which assist in the breach of the terms of this Order]⁷²

(2) the Defendant do forthwith disclose to the Plaintiff's Solicitors the full value of his assets within [and without]⁷³ the jurisdiction of this Court identifying with full particularity the nature of all such assets and their whereabouts and whether the same be held in his own name or by nominees or otherwise on his behalf and the sums standing in such accounts such disclosure to be verified by affidavit to be made by the Defendant and to be served on the Plaintiff's Solicitors within [7] days of the service of this Order or notice thereof being given

---

⁷¹ See n. 72, *post.*

⁷² As to the jurisdiction to grant an order affecting foreign assets, and the appropriate form of Order, see *Babanaft International Co. S.A.* v. *Bassatne* [1990] Ch. 13, *Republic of Haiti* v. *Duvalier* [1990] Q.B. 202 and *Derby & Co. Ltd.* v. *Weldon* [1990] Ch. 48.

⁷³ See n. 72, *ante.*

AND the Defendant is to be at liberty to move this Court to vary or discharge this Order upon giving 24 hours written notice to the Plaintiff of his intention so to do

(J) INFRINGEMENT OF COPYRIGHT: FINAL JUDGMENT **G–16**

[Heading—See Court Form (A)]

UPON THE TRIAL of this action
AND UPON HEARING oral evidence
AND UPON HEARING Counsel for the Plaintiff and for the Defendant
AND UPON READING the documents recorded on the Court file as having been read

IT IS ORDERED THAT

(1) The Defendant be restrained (whether acting by himself his servants or agents or any of them or otherwise howsoever) from doing the following acts or any of them that is to say

> Infringing the Plaintiff's copyright in [*insert description of work*] ("the Work") by (without the licence of the Plaintiff) reproducing or issuing to the public copies of the Work or any substantial part thereof or authorising any of the acts aforesaid or selling offering or exposing for sale or exhibiting in public or distributing copies of the Work made without the Plaintiff's licence or otherwise howsoever

(2) The following inquiries be made[74]
  (i) An inquiry as to what damages the Plaintiff has suffered by reason of the infringement of the Plaintiff's copyright in the Work committed by the Defendant by
    (a) (without the licence of the Plaintiff) reproducing or issuing to the public copies of the Work or any substantial part thereof or authorising any of the acts aforesaid or
    (b) (without the licence of the Plaintiff) selling offering or exposing for sale or exhibiting in public or distributing after [*insert date when sale, etc., with knowledge first took place*] copies of the Work made without the Plaintiff's licence
  (ii) An inquiry as to what damages (if any) the Plaintiff is entitled to under section 97(2) of the Copyright Designs and Patents Act 1988
  (iii) An inquiry as what interest (if any) the Plaintiff is entitled to on the said damages pursuant to section 35A of the Supreme Court Act 1981

(3) The Defendant do pay the Plaintiff the sums (if any) found due to the Plaintiff upon the making of the said inquiries

(4) The Defendant do within 14 days after service of this Order upon him deliver or cause to be delivered up to the Plaintiff
  (i) all copies of the Work made without the Plaintiff's licence in the Defendant's possession custody or control
  (ii) all articles specifically designed or adapted for making copies of the Work in the Defendant's possession custody or control
and do within 7 days thereafter make and serve upon the Plaintiff's Solicitors an Affidavit verifying that he no longer has in his possession custody or control any such copies or articles

---

[74] This assumes the Plaintiff has opted for damages rather than an account of profits.

(5) All such copies or articles as are delivered up by the Defendant as aforesaid be forfeited to the Plaintiff.[75]

(6) The Defendant do pay the Plaintiff his costs of this action down to and including this judgment such costs to be taxed if not agreed

AND the costs of the said inquiries are reserved

---

[75] See n. 35, *ante.*

INDEX

1557